The NFL's Official Encyclopedic History of Professional Football

Edited, Written, and Compiled by
Tom Bennett,
David Boss,
Jim Campbell,
Seymour Siwoff,
Rick Smith,
and John Wiebusch

Designed by
David Johnston

Prepared by the Creative Services Division,
National Football League Properties, Inc.
Produced by Rutledge Books

A National Football League Book

Macmillan Publishing Co., Inc.
New York
Collier Macmillan Publishers
London

The NFL's Official Encyclopedic History of Professional Football

A National Football League Book

Prepared by National Football League Properties, Inc.
Produced by Rutledge Books, a division of Arcata Consumer Products Corp.

"A Diagram History of Football"
From the book, *The Pro Style* by Tom Bennett.
© 1976 by National Football League Properties, Inc. Published by Prentice-Hall, Inc., Englewood Cliffs, New Jersey.

Library of Congress Cataloging in Publication Data
National Football League Properties, Inc. Creative Services.
   The NFL's Official Encyclopedic History of Professional Football.
   "A National Football League book."
   1. Football—United States. I. Rutledge Books, Inc. II. Title.
GV954.N37 1977   796.33'2'0973   76-30547

ISBN 0-02-589010-7

Published by
Macmillan Publishing Co., Inc.
866 Third Avenue, New York, N.Y. 10022
Collier Macmillan Canada, Ltd.
Printed in the United States of America

CONTENTS

John Madden, coach of the Oakland Raiders, after winning Super Bowl XI, 32–14 over the Minnesota Vikings.

INTRODUCTION

A dedicated, modest, and rather mysterious researcher in Pittsburgh walked into the office of Daniel M. Rooney of the Pittsburgh Steelers "about 15 years ago" and handed him a 49-page paper on early pro football in Pennsylvania. Rooney greeted him and studied the paper briefly. The two of them talked for a few moments and then the visitor departed. Rooney read further in the report and began to see that it had great value. The manuscript was, however, unsigned. Rooney frantically searched his memory; what was the visitor's name? It was, as best he could recall, Nelson Ross. He tried to track down Ross, even enlisting the help of the Pittsburgh newspapers. Finally he turned the manuscript over to the NFL office in New York City. After the construction of the Pro Football Hall of Fame in Canton, Ohio in 1963, the Ross paper was sent there and filed away.

Accompanying the paper was a yellowing expense sheet prepared by O.D. Thompson, manager of the Allegheny Athletic Association in Pittsburgh in 1892. The expenses included the following: "Game performance bonus to W. Heffelfinger for playing (cash) $500.00." This expense sheet was put on display in the Hall of Fame. Inexplicably, it was displayed for years immediately next to a cubicle of photos of John Brallier of the Latrobe, Pennsylvania Y.M.C.A. team of 1895. The display hailed Brallier as the first professional football player in history. William (Pudge) Heffelfinger, however, antedated Brallier by four years.

Ross's paper was "rediscovered." A determined effort was made to study its findings and put them in perspective. At the same time, a second researcher, Thomas Jable of William Paterson College in New Jersey, presented a paper to the annual convention of the American Association of Health, Physical Education, and Recreation in 1976 corroborating Ross's findings, largely through the study of old newspapers in Pittsburgh. Jable's report added new details to the account of Heffelfinger and the Allegheny Athletic Association.

The works of Ross, Jable, and an expert on early pro football in Ohio, Milton Roberts, are collected here for the first time in any pro football work of history, in the chapter entitled "Roots of Pro Football." Disciplined, determined to get to the heart of this subject, possessed of a wit that can be seen around the rough edges of his writing, and yet so modest that he did not even type his name on his manuscript, the mysterious Nelson Ross has left pro football an important document.

The presentation of Ross's research is one bit of evidence that *The NFL's Official Encyclopedic History of Professional Football* is a major effort to produce the most comprehensive and entertaining history of pro football ever done. Admittedly, this book has had an advantage—the source, subject, and creator are the same. This is the NFL's book about itself. It has been produced, however, with objectivity and with an eye for what is enjoyable to the reader and useful to the researcher.

Pro football is the greatest success story in American sport. Because of its stability and its relative youth, therefore, it may be assumed that producing a history of it is an easy thing to do. It is not. Ross's material and additional research into the early Pennsylvania and Ohio period opens up a whole new era, and uncovers numerous teams to study and classify.

Practically every pro football fan is familiar with the American Football League that began in 1960. How many are informed, however, about the AFLs of 1926, 1936–37, and 1940–41? Each of them failed and added to the profusion of franchises, teams, coaches, and players. So did the All-America Football Conference in 1946–49 and the World Football League of 1974–75.

Twelve current NFL teams played in another city, had another name, or started in the AAFC. The Decatur Staleys became the Chicago Staleys in 1921 and the Chicago Bears in 1922. The Boston Braves became the Boston Redskins in 1933 and the Washington Redskins in 1937. The Pittsburgh Pirates became the Pittsburgh Steelers in 1941. The Portsmouth Spartans became the Detroit Lions in 1934. The Cleveland Rams became the Los Angeles Rams in 1946. The Baltimore Colts, Cleveland Browns, and San Francisco 49ers moved from the AAFC to the NFL in 1950, but the Colts folded in one year's time; an entirely different Colts' team reappeared in 1953.

The Chicago Cardinals became the St. Louis Cardinals in 1960. The Los Angeles Chargers became the San Diego Chargers in 1961. The Dallas Texans became the Kansas City Chiefs and the New York Titans became the New York Jets in 1963. The Boston Patriots became the New England Patriots in 1971.

The appropriate nickname appears in this book anytime a New York team is mentioned because of the many teams that have played in that city—the Crescents, Knickerbockers, Giants, Yankees, Americans, Bulldogs, Yanks, Titans, Jets, and Stars.

There has been a tendency for cities to reinstate the nicknames of failed franchises. Even though a team may not succeed, it was the pioneer of pro football in a city and the citizens seemingly want to perpetuate that name. Examples are the nicknames "Baltimore Colts," "Buffalo Bills," and "Cincinnati Bengals." In each case, there was a team in the city by that name before the advent of the present team. Nelson Ross also proved there was a team called the "Pittsburgh Steelers" in 1902.

Philadelphia and Pittsburgh merged in 1943, when World War II made the going rough for pro football teams, and became a club named the "Steagles." When Pittsburgh and the Chicago Cardinals merged a year later, they became the less outlandish but functional "Card-Pitt." The wins, losses, and ties of these aberrations have gone into the record of each of their member teams.

In the contemporary method of figuring pro football percentages, ties count as a half-game won and a half game lost; that has been the rule since 1972. Every compilation done since then has been done by that rule. Thus, the all-time totals for teams in this history are figured that way, whereas, year-by-year percentages before 1972 are not.

"Modern" is the most relative of terms. Periodic references in football histories to "modern-day football" may only define the period of the writer's consciousness of the sport. So-called "firsts" may not be firsts at all. The Chicago Bears did not "invent" the T formation and man-in-motion in 1940; both were part of the game of football at the turn of the century. Marion Motley, Bill Willis, and Kenny Washington did not "break the color line" in football in 1946; there were black players in the sport as early as 1904. Dan Reeves and Tony Morabito did not "open the west coast to professional sports"; a football team called the Los Angeles Bulldogs made a transcontinental road trip in 1937, had an unbeaten record, and won the American Football League championship. The careless delineation of "firsts" and the setting up of a period of "modern-day football" in which all those "firsts" took place are two mistakes this encyclopedia has avoided.

Similarly, the Pro Bowl did not begin with Otto Graham's great performance for the American Conference in 1951. It began 12 years earlier, in the same city and with the same partners in sponsorship, the NFL and the *Los Angeles Times*. Five games were played before World War II. This book is the first ever to publish lineups, line scores, and scoring summaries of every Pro

Bowl game; Pro Bowl records covering the entire history of the event; and a table of all-time selections for the game.

Another famous football event, the Chicago All-Star Game, which is the subject of an entire chapter, was canceled while this book was being completed. It is now an extinct species but a complete history of it is preserved in this *Encyclopedic History.*

The all-pro teams listed in the book are the teams considered to have been official each year. All-pros were named between 1931 and 1942 by coaches of the National Football League. The selections were discontinued in 1942 but resumed in 1946 and made thereafter by news services—United Press from 1946 to 1949 and both United Press and Associated Press from 1950–1969. The all-star team of the American Football League was named by sportswriters from 1961 through 1966, and by wire services through 1968. In 1969 the official team was named by the Hall of Fame Selection Committee. The recognized all-pro team since 1970 has been the team named by the Professional Football Writers of America.

Only one other league ever suceeded in merging fully with the NFL and having its statistical feats entered for consideration along with those of the NFL as all-time professional records. That was the 1960–69 American Football League. Another league, the All-America Football Conference of 1946-49, had famous players who later became stars in the NFL after the limited merger of 1950, but AAFC achievements were not accepted for the all-time records. This has created a confusing situation in which lists distributed by the NFL of the top 10 or top 20 performers in each statistic omit the AAFC records of such performers as Otto Graham, Marion Motley, and Joe Perry, while the same lists distributed by the Hall of Fame include the AAFC marks. In NFL lists, Otto Graham is the sixth best passer in history; in Hall of Fame lists, he is first in history.

A variety of categories were used in the past to determine the passing leader each season. Since 1973, however, quarterbacks have been "rated." The ratings are based on performance standards established for completion percentage, interception percentage, touchdown percentage, and average gain. Passers are allocated points according to how their marks compare with those standards, and the points are then converted to a scale roughly approximating 100.0.

Another point to remember about the pro records is that the present AFC records include the 10 years of the AFL, 1960–69, and the present NFC records include all the years of the NFL before the start of the regular season interleague play in 1970.

Punting statistics began in 1939, interceptions in 1940, and punt returns and kickoff returns in 1941.

There are four position designations in pro football that are only about a decade old. They were first used in the American Football League and gained acceptance in the NFL, belatedly, about 1966. they are "running back" instead of "halfback" and "fullback"; "wide receiver" and "tight end" instead of "end"; and "corner-back" instead of "defensive halfback."

The first edition of *The NFL's Official Encyclopedic History of Professional Football,* published in 1973, was an outstanding effort.

As good as that book was, however, it pales in comparison to the 1977 edition. NFL history is a rich and lively subject that is captured and chronicled here as you have never seen it before.

This marvelous reference book is destined to aid the serious football student and settle countless arguments between fans. We recommend it to you highly.

Lamar Hunt
President, American Football Conference

George Halas, Sr.
President, National Football Conference

Roots of
Pro Football

The game we call "football" is indigenous to North America. It is about 100 years old. It did not have one inventor; rather, it developed gradually from soccer to rugby to "rugby football" to football. Why? Because these games were fun and people kept tinkering with them and improving them so they would be even more fun. At last football emerged, but then another quarter-century or more passed before it began to look anything like what we would recognize as the game today. Many rules changes were made and football became the biggest college sport. Athletic clubs and imitative town teams took it up. At the end of this long chain of events, professional football arrived, perhaps in 1892. It was centered in Pennsylvania and then it spread to Ohio. There the league that eventually became known as the "National Football League" was formed in 1920. It was a curious and novel little organization then but it went on to great success. How that happened cannot be fully understood without returning to the tumultuous years of the growth of this American game, to trace the roots of pro football.

I. GROWTH OF COLLEGE FOOTBALL

American football comes from English soccer and rugby. Soccer is called football on other continents; it is the most popular game in the world. Rugby is also played practically everywhere, the byproduct of British imperialism. American football is the cousin of these games and they all involve, in one way or another, the kicking of some object up and down a field. This has been a natural thing for humans to make a game of as long as the species has had feet. The kicking games of primitive tribes, *harpaston* in the Greek city-state of Sparta, *calcio* in ancient Rome, and the varieties of soccer that have been played for perhaps 2,000 years, according to Allison Danzig, can be considered ancestors of football. The ball used in those games might have been leather filled with sawdust, the bladder of some slaughtered animal, or the skull of an adversary slain in battle.

Soccer football was played in the American colonies, according to John Allen Krout in *Annals of American Sport*. "Here and there in the records of colonial days," he wrote, "one catches glimpses of boys and young men, occasionally young women, playing a game known as football. It might more accurately have been called handball, for throwing and passing the inflated bladder or sawdust-filled leather seems to have been more important than kicking it. In the latter part of the eighteenth century this haphazard game assumed a place with fisticuffs, wrestling matches, and drinking bouts, enjoyed by undergraduates, as a means of relief from the severe mental discipline of college life."

Two important steps in the evolution of football then occurred in the mother country of England. First, rugby was invented. A student at the Rugby School named William Webb Ellis picked up the ball and ran with it during a soccer football game in 1823. The rules forbade advancing the ball any way except kicking it, and the other players in the game were outraged at Ellis for breaking the rules. His innovation, however, became the basis for a new game, one that would influence American football greatly because the runner could carry the ball and not just kick it. Ellis also became the subject of countless stirring juvenile stories about bold young men unafraid to go against the mainstream of opinion, be nonconformists. A photograph of the plaque at Rugby College commemorating Ellis's achievement is virtually a requisite in any football history. Of Ellis's later life, Krout wrote that the inventor of rugby "became a London clergyman and rector of St. Clement Dane's in the Strand."

The second thing that happened in England was the formation of the London Football Association in

1862. It was organized by the proponents of the kicking game. They drew up rules forbidding the carrying of the ball. From then on their game was called association football or soccer. But that was not their largest contribution to American football. More importantly, they wrote rules that independent-minded Americans would overhaul and rewrite to create their own rules. And by having a rules convention the British established a rite of the sport, a tradition as much a part of it as bringing the uniforms out of storage for the first practice each year and blowing up the footballs.

There was high school soccer football before there was college soccer football. Boston secondary schools were playing games against each other on the Common as early as 1860, according to Allison Danzig in *The History of American Football*. Gerritt Smith Miller, a student at the Dixwell School from Peterboro, New York, organized the Oneida Football Club of Boston, "the first definite and formal football organization in the United States," in 1862.

College football began November 6, 1869. Rutgers and Princeton both had soccer football teams and they were close to each other, so they played a game. It vaguely resembled what we know as football today. Each team had 25 players, the ball was advanced by kicking it or butting it with the head, and there were goal posts that were 25 yards apart. These were modified London Football Association rules. The first team to make six goals won, and Rutgers triumphed six goals to four.

Yale and Columbia also had soccer football teams. Princeton and Yale formed football associations for games between classes. Harvard, however, played a different game, one more like rugby, called the "Boston Game." Canada then made the next and one of the most important contributions of all to the evolution of football. McGill University in Montreal played rugby; the sport had probably been brought to Canada by the British army. McGill played three games against Harvard in 1874, two at Cambridge and one at Montreal. As a result of these games Harvard took up rugby completely instead of soccer. The rugby principles of running with the ball and tackling had a foot in the door of American football.

It seemed as if everyone had different rules, and the sport was in a state of confusion. Then came the Massasoit convention of 1876 at which the first rules for American football were written. That same year the imposing figure of the man who would become the father of the game as we know it today, Walter Camp of Yale, appeared on the stage of football.

In a football game today, the ball does not pass back and forth at random but instead is held by each team for at least four downs. Each has to make a given number of yards, 10, in those four downs or lose the ball. Each has 11 players on the field. The principal handler of the ball is the "quarterback." The center snaps the ball to him. Walter Camp is responsible for all these innovations. Parke Davis, the Plutarch of early college football, wrote that, "What Washington was to his country, Camp was to American football — the friend, the founder, and the father."

A Yale athlete and coach, Camp was so heroic and romantic a figure, so chivalrous, so simon-pure of motive and deed, that he was said to have been the model for the fictional character "Frank Merriwell of Yale" on which a whole generation of American boys were weaned.

Camp was so respected as a football authority that, while he wore the hat of magazine writer, he alone was archbishop at the annual coronation in *Collier's Weekly* of the knights of the gridiron, the All-Americas.

He ruled over the first college football juggernaut, Yale, before 1910. And he created the Daily Dozen exercise program for a feeble and flabby American

public. He was aristocratic, a *bon vivant* and raconteur who was a celebrity and living legend everywhere he went.

When Walter Camp entered Yale in 1876, he was the product of one of the correct New Haven families and of the exclusive Hopkins Grammar School. He learned the variety of football then being played at Yale from Gene Baker, the captain of the team. Baker was Yale's delegate to the convention at the Massasoit House, a hotel, in Springfield, Massachusetts. Playing rules were adopted there and an intercollegiate association was formed; it was the forerunner of the National Collegiate Athletic Association. The rules it adopted resembled those of rugby and it was called rugby football.

Camp played halfback in rugby football. He was a brilliant runner and kicker, a dashing figure with a flowing mustache and long hair held in place by a headband; in actuality he looked very much like many young men a century later. With Camp making drop-kicks or picking up the ball and darting through the entire opposing team, Yale won 25, lost 1, and tied 6 in six years of intercollegiate play. At last, in a move aimed directly at him, the annual rules convention limited eligibility to five years. By then, Camp was in the Yale Medical School, and captain of the football team for the third time. He left medical school just one year short of his degree. He gave as his reason the fact that he could not stand the sight of blood, but it really may have been because he could no longer captain the Yale team and also compete, as he had, in baseball, track (he is credited by some with having been the first to run the hurdles and not jump each of them), tennis, and gymnastics.

The most remarkable fact of Camp's student days, however, is that he represented his university at the annual rules convention as a sophomore, in 1877. At that point, the game was one in which the ball was put down on the field with both teams clustering around it and all of them kicking at the ball and trying to drive it free. Someone finally would succeed in picking it up and starting off on a run. Then he probably would meet opposition and kick the ball away or make a lateral or backward pass. But he also may have been knocked to the turf before doing any of these things.

In 1880, Camp had an idea to give one side undisputed possession of the ball until that side, of its own volition, gave the ball up. This was passed by the rules convention, and Camp had invented scrimmage. In the same year, he convinced his colleagues that a team should number 11, not 15, players. Further, the person receiving the ball from a "snapback," later called a center, should be called the "quarterback." Snaps were first made with the foot. Later, players were allowed to guide the ball with a hand. Finally they came to center entirely with the hands.

Having created the position of quarterback, Camp, as Yale captain, then became the first to have his quarterback call signals. For example, the quarterback would say, "Play up sharp, Charlie!" if a kick was about to be made.

But Camp's conviction that the chivalrous Ivy Leaguers would gladly give up the ball when they could not gain ground during scrimmage was ill-founded. The "block game" resulted; one team kept the ball the whole first half and the other the whole second half. This led Camp to suggest — and the convention pass — a rule requiring a team to make five yards in three downs; it was increased later to 10 yards in four downs.

There always are ready opportunities for the well-born and the former football star; Camp was both. After leaving medical school he took a position with his uncle's business, the New Haven Clock Company. He also kept his affiliation with Yale; indeed, he would soon dominate its athletic department. And he would continue to be a member of one committee of football rulesmakers or another until the day he died.

Camp never was a paid coach nor did he ever assume the title. Instead, a series of coaches drew their authority from him. And he held the purse strings of the fund made from Yale Field gate receipts.

Tad Jones, who had been a Camp player and was later Yale's coach, explained that, "Camp coached through the coaches. He seldom took an active part on the field. ... He had no more authoritative position than treasurer of the Yale Field Association, but his advice had authority because it was good advice. The practice then was to have the former year's captain return as head coach, and Camp, by serving every year as adviser, gave unity and continuity to these shifting assistants."

Coach, captain, and quarterback met with Camp on Sunday afternoons in the library of his home on Gill Street in New Haven to discuss the mistakes of the previous day's game and plan the tactics of the coming game. Yale prospered, regularly beating the other members of the Big Three, Harvard and Princeton.

In 1888 Camp proposed—and the convention passed—a rule permitting tackling as low as the knees. Its effect on football was stupefying. Runners who were tackled that way went down to stay. The savage mass play era dawned. Offenses contracted and bunched themselves around the runner. The dangerous "wedge" appeared. Lorin Deland of Harvard created the even more dangerous flying wedge. Camp and Yale fostered the shoving wedge. Play became brutal, fights proliferated, and there were deaths on the gridiron.

A public outcry arose. The mass play era split intercollegiate football, led to the White House conference of 1905 and the subsequent formation of the NCAA.

President Theodore Roosevelt called representatives of Yale, Harvard, and Princeton to the White House, according to Allison Danzig, and told them to clean up football. "Brutality and foul play should receive the same summary punishment given to a man who cheats at cards."

The President could provide moral leadership but the real reform of football occurred in the nuts-and-bolts work of the rules committees. There were two meetings in December, 1905 and as a result of them an old and new committee combined themselves and the Intercollegiate Athletic Association was formed. The name was changed to National Collegiate Athletic Association later.

Camp headed the old committee, Captain Palmer Pierce of West Point the new, and they sat down together for the first time in January, 1906. They legalized the forward pass. More reforms were made in succeeding years. But the game of football had been defined by Camp and his associates and it was this game that the National Football League adopted in 1920 and did not change for more than a decade.

II. PREHISTORIC PRO FOOTBALL

Sports took root in America after the Civil War. People fled the factories and went outdoors to ride bicycles and play golf and other sports. One of the most important aspects of this movement was the advent of the athletic club. The first was the New York Athletic Club in 1868, according to sports historian John R. Betts. Virtually every other city acquired one after that. These clubs sponsored teams in a great variety of sports. They gave tremendous impetus to competition in all of them. And they probably started pro football.

The photographs are still with us today, legions of them in seemingly endless supply, with players reclining somber-faced in their uniforms in front of pastoral studio backdrops, a melon-shaped football at

their feet with lettering such as "Johnstown A.C. 1891" on them. It is astonishing how many team pictures remain. Clearly, club football teams were everywhere. Were they all, every club and every player, amateurs? Probably not.

One of their number, William (Pudge) Heffelfinger of the Allegheny Athletic Association of Pittsburgh, received what history records as the first payment to play football in 1892. But he was the most famous player of his day; others more obscure than Heffelfinger may have received payments earlier than he did. And it is known that some athletic clubs bent the rules and awarded their players in ways that carried the clubs to the brink of professionalism—and perhaps beyond.

Baseball had gone professional with the formation of the American Association in 1871 and the new Amateur Athletic Union was determined to stop this "evil" from spreading to other sports, and rid them all of the "tramp athlete," the opportunist who moved about and sold his services to college or athletic club. He was the bane of the athletic world and the AAU gained much support. It grew into an organization with great power. Each year it held a sports carnival in New York City where athletes could compete for national championships in their respective sports.

But the AAU inadvertently helped bring about the rise of pro football. In 1889, six athletic clubs in the East decided to copy the parent AAU and form their own union, or league. They were the Baltimore Athletic Club, the Boston Athletic Association, the New York Athletic Club, the New York Crescents Athletic Club, the New York Manhattans, and the Orange, New Jersey, Athletic Club. They played for the "amateur title of America" each year for over a decade. There was now a league of amateur teams. The next step was to begin talking about going professional.

The AAU moved against what it believed to be professionalism on two fronts in 1890. The San Francisco Olympic Athletic Club was accused by a rival of obtaining jobs for its players in order to get them to jump to the Olympic Club. The AAU decreed, however, that while San Francisco's action was not to be commended, it was not actually professionalism, only a "semi" form of it; the Olympic Club got off with a reprimand and the term "semipro" was born.

In New Jersey, the Orange Athletic Club awarded trophies or watches to its best players at the end of each season. Accusations were made against Orange but apparently this was the practice of several clubs in the New York City area. According to Dr. Harry March, the recipient of the gift could then be seen "threading his way to some well-known pawnbroker where the watch was placed in hock, the usual sum received thereby being a sawbuck—twenty smackers. Then the player, still strictly amateur, somehow ran across the man who managed those amateur games and sold him the pawn ticket for another twenty dollars. By some special sense of divination, second sightedness or mental telepathy, the promoter found himself urged towards the same pawn shop and under an irresistible impulse, retrieved the pawned watch, paying a small interest and twenty dollars. Then, after the next game, the player received as his trophy the same gold watch, which then went through the same identical loaning experience."

The AAU ruled that clubs could no longer award trophies; they had to limit their gifts to banners costing 25 cents apiece. But the big athletic clubs continued to find ways to get around the rules. One way was to hand out travel expenses equal to double the amount of the fare. There obviously were "professional" players on athletic clubs in other cities before a celebrated "ringer" named Pudge Heffelfinger was paid $500 under the table by a club in Pittsburgh and started the recorded history of pro football.

III. THE PENNSYLVANIA PERIOD

Pennsylvania is an historic state. It was one of the 13 original colonies. The Articles of Confederation, Declaration of Independence, and Constitution were signed there. General George Washington and his troops encamped there at Valley Forge in 1777. Later, the Civil War reached its turning point when a Confederate army led by General Robert E. Lee advanced as far north as Gettysburg—and met defeat.

Much westward expansion moved across Pennsylvania's breadth. In the west, the Allegheny and Monongahela rivers meet in Pittsburgh and form the mighty Ohio River. This great waterway was the gateway to the West for American settlers for 200 years.

Similarly, the game of football moved toward becoming a professional game westward from colleges such as Yale, Princeton, Rutgers, and Harvard, across Pennsylvania to Pittsburgh where, through the phenomenon of the athletic club, the first known pro football was played. Pro football then moved directly westward into Ohio, into towns such as Akron, Canton, and Massillon. And they and others formed what became the NFL.

Pittsburgh's first athletic clubs were the Allegheny Athletic Association and the Pittsburgh Athletic Club. Such clubs emerged after the Civil War, according to researcher Thomas Jable, as an antidote to Victorianism. American men could through competitive athletics at their clubs "countermand the Victorian principles of delicacy and refinement." Football, aggressive and sometimes violent, served this need especially well; it "represented a significant triumph of robust manliness over tender and fragile femininity." Membership in an athletic club also meant prestige and an opportunity to identify vicariously with the big names in college football.

Anyone who has ever arrived at a city park all set for a good, hard-fought touch football game, only to see that the opposition has brought along a few surprise players all of whom are better and more experienced than anyone else there, is familiar with the term "ringer." And ringers hired by the Allegheny Athletic Association of Pittsburgh in 1892 were the first pro football players.

In Jable's words, "As competition increased in intensity and winning became important, the athletic club turned to the established athlete from the outside ... In hiring the gifted player or professional, the athletic club shattered the amateur ideal upon which it was founded, that is, participation for the sheer love of the game. Victory meant fame, glory, and increased income for the athletic club. Big money was made by individual members who wagered heavily on their club's eleven. From this atmosphere at the athletic club, professionalism crept into football as the Allegheny Athletic Association and the Pittsburgh Athletic Club vied for notoriety, prestige, and profits."

The Allegheny Athletic Association was organized by two Pittsburgh businessmen, John Moorehead and O.D. Thompson, who were graduates of Yale and who had played football there. The club was called "A.A.A.," the "A.A.A.'s," "Three A's," and as it edged nearer professionalism, sometimes "Four A's" with a tongue-in-cheek extra "A" for "amateur." It had the first club football team in Pittsburgh in about 1890.

The Pittsburgh Athletic Club was located in the city's East End. Its gym was the largest and best in western Pennsylvania; for that reason the team was sometimes called the "Gyms." The Pittsburgh Athletic Club was older than the A.A.A. It formed a football team in 1891 because it felt the A.A.A. team was getting more than its share of publicity in the Pittsburgh newspapers.

Professor William Kirschner was the physical director of the P.A.C. and became its star football player. Researcher Nelson Ross writes that Kirschner "had little football experience, but he possessed tremendous strength and size and learned quickly." And he was probably a semi-professional.

"Professor Kirschner received a regular salary for teaching his gym classes," Ross writes. "It was noted, however, that during the football season his 'teaching' salary went up considerably. It was denied that this had any connection with his playing on the P.A.C. football team, but rivals noted that while his salary doubled his classes were only half their normal size during the football season. Pittsburgh papers were at times critical of Kirschner's status but no one accused him outright."

P.A.C. challenged A.A.A. to a game. A.A.A. ignored the challenge. The feud grew hotter when A.A.A. lured away four of P.A.C.'s best players. At last a game was scheduled for Columbus Day, October 21, 1892 at the P.A.C. field in Pittsburgh's East Liberty section. More than 3,000 spectators flocked to the grounds, Jable wrote, "in drags, tallyhos, dog carts, street cars, and railroad cars. They filled the seating accommodations at P.A.C. Park to more than capacity. Hundreds more packed the surrounding buildings from the first floor to the roof, viewing the game at no expense. More spectators would have been in attendance had not the lengthy Columbus Day parade prevented a number of street cars and other public conveyances from reaching East Liberty. The fashionable crowd was evenly split between the two teams, though each faction was easily distinguishable by the colors it wore. P.A.C. rooters wore red and white ribbons, while the A.A.A. followers donned blue and white colors."

The game ended in a 6–6 tie. Dr. George Proctor, a physician, scored the only goal for P.A.C. and Norman McClintock of Yale, playing for A.A.A., scored its goal. The same players also kicked their teams' goals; a touchdown counted four points and a successful place kick counted two. The teams divided $1,200 in gate receipts and as a result of the great interest in the game each club processed about 100 new members during the weeks that followed.

The news that P.A.C. had played a ringer, however, stirred new hostilities. A.C. Read, captain of the Pennsylvania State College team and a shotputter, had played for P.A.C. under the name of "Stayer." The P.A.C. captain had misled A.A.A., saying "Stayer" was an old friend he had met him on the street and invited him to play in the game. A.A.A. was incensed to learn that "Stayer" was actually the Penn State captain, and as A.A.A. plotted how to get even, a famous Yale All-America who was then in faraway Chicago loomed in the future of Pittsburgh football.

William Walter (Pudge) Heffelfinger played guard for Yale in 1888–1891. Walter Camp was his mentor and Amos Alonzo Stagg his teammate. Heffelfinger made the first All-America team ever selected, in 1889. He also made the team for two more years and has been one of the guards on virtually every all-time All-America team selected anywhere since. In 1892, his Yale days behind him, he was working in a nondescript railroad office job in Omaha, Nebraska, when he grew bored and asked for a leave of absence in order to join a Chicago amateur club called the Chicago A.A. on an Eastern tour in which it would play teams in Cleveland, Rochester, Princeton, Philadelphia, Cambridge, and Brooklyn. The Chicago A.A. was a controversial member of the AAU. Its playing manager, Billy Crawford, was paying ample expenses to players and enraging the AAU with talk of a "professional football league" in cities such as Chicago, Detroit, Cleveland, Pittsburgh, and New York; he was a man 28 years ahead of his time.

The Chicago A.A.'s tour was not scheduled to stop in Pittsburgh, but it was the talk of the athletic clubs there, and when the tour reached Cleveland two members of the Pittsburgh Athletic Club were in the stands to watch the game. "Both cheered wildly," wrote Ross, "when the magnificent Heffelfinger hit the Cleveland fullback so hard that he fumbled the ball, with William grabbing it and streaking with incredible speed for a man so large, over the Cleveland goal line."

The big rematch in Pittsburgh between the P.A.C. and A.A.A. was a few weeks away. The people of Pittsburgh were shocked to read in the *Press* of October 30 that P.A.C. was rumored to be offering $250 each to Heffelfinger and another Chicago A.A. player, Knowlton (Snake) Ames, to play against A.A.A. The rumors persisted as the game drew nearer.

Many years have gone by since that fateful game, and as time has passed football teams have learned to squash rumors that they are close to signing a player to a contract. Negotiations can always go sour at the last minute and the team is left with nothing except an unsigned contract and a credibility gap. This postulate of present-day football was not there for the Pittsburgh Athletic Club to follow in 1892. And when the arch-rivals of club football lined up against each other at Recreation Park on Pittsburgh's North Side November 13, Heffelfinger was there all right, but not with P.A.C. He was in the colors of the hated A.A.A. So were his former Chicago A.A. teammates Ed Malley, a shotputter from Detroit, and Ben (Sport) Donnelly, former Princeton star; Snake Ames had decided to forego the game rather than risk his amateur status.

It was a cold day and there was snow on the ground. A crowd of about 3,000 watched as the Pittsburgh Athletic Club angrily protested the presence of A.A.A. ringers. All bets were off, P.A.C. declared. It offered to play a scrub game. While the crowd grew restive, the substitutes of each team began to play while the regulars argued. O.D. Thompson, the manager of A.A.A., pointed out that P.A.C. planned to play A.C. Read, "Stayer" in the first game, this time under his real name, and P.A.C. also had Clarence Lomax of Cornell and Simon Martin of the Steelton, Pennsylvania Athletic Club in its lineup. The arguments continued until the two teams at last agreed to play an "exhibition" game with all bets canceled. They settled on two 30-minute halves. A.A.A. won 4–0. Heffelfinger picked up a fumble by one of his teammates, ran around end, and went 25 yards for a touchdown. Ed Malley missed the place-kick for goal. The bickering before the game had delayed it and darkness now ended it 18 minutes into the second half.

Heffelfinger demonstrated a vicious method for breaking P.A.C.'s wedge. "...When P.A.C. wedged down the field, he ran and jumped at it with full speed, bringing his knees against the mass. The wedge didn't last long."

The P.A.C. captain, Charley Aull, left the game with a badly injured back. His brother, Burt, retired after receiving "a fierce blow to the head." Sport Donnelly received "a terrific smash in the eye."

After the game Heffelfinger was paid $500 for playing and $25 for expenses, Malley and Donnelly $25 for travel. Heffelfinger was thus the first professional football player on record. Gross receipts totaled $1,683. After Heffelfinger's fee, a visitors' guarantee of $428, and miscellaneous expenses, the A.A.A. made a profit of $621.

A furor over professionalism raged for weeks in Pittsburgh's newspapers. O.D. Thompson, A.A.A. manager, a skillful lawyer, and the man primarily responsible for making Heffelfinger a professional, left town. He went to New York to defend A.A.A. track stars named E.V. Pant and J.B. McKennan

against AAU charges that *they* were professionals.

A guard and assistant manager on the football team named Billy Kountz was left to fend off the questions the press was asking about pros on the A.A.A. Thompson returned too late for a rubber match to be played against P.A.C. Heffelfinger and Malley left Pittsburgh but Sport Donnelly stayed and one week after the P.A.C. game played for A.A.A. against Washington and Jefferson College; he was paid $250 and thus became the second known pro football player in history. The next year three players named Rafferty, Van Cleve, and Wright (their first names are not known) became the third, fourth, and fifth when they received contracts to play for A.A.A. for $50 a game—the first pro football contracts in history. The athletic clubs threw caution and their AAU affiliation to the wind and ended forever the pretense that they were "amateur." Allegheny Athletic Association was barred permanently from the AAU in 1895. Many of its members resigned. The others, who openly admitted their professionalism, imported Heffelfinger, Donnelly, and other members of the touring Chicago A.A. and other well-known football players such as Tom (Doggie) Trenchard and Langdon (Biffy) Lea of Princeton. They played back-to-back games in 1896 against P.A.C. and the new Pittsburgh Duquesnes, November 10 and 11, and won both games, 18–0 and 12–0. Heffelfinger and the other imports apparently were paid a staggering $100 a game. The players who had been together in 1892 enjoyed their reunion and held marathon beer drinking sessions talking over old times. A.A.A. finished the season playing a barnstorming tour against amateur teams in western Pennsylvania, West Virginia, and Ohio. But the payroll for the back-to-back games in November had bankrupted the club. By 1897, "for all practical purposes, it ceased to exist as a functioning year-round club," Ross wrote. "Professionalism and its opponents had dealt it a death blow." There was one more uneventful season before the club broke up when its most patriotic members left to fight in the Spanish-American War. When they returned there were high-priced bidding contests as they sold their services to the Duquesnes or P.A.C. What was left of A.A.A. sponsored an amateur team made up of Western Pennsylvania Theological Seminary students, a team that must have been quite different in character from the rollicking Alleghenies of earlier years.

America's first known pro football team had come and gone. It was, however, just the beginning for Pittsburgh's early adventures in the sport. There followed a calamitous period in which a wealthy Pittsburgh man named W.C. Temple became the first known club owner in pro football history; he was joined in that capacity by two of the city's foremost steel tycoons, one of whom later became the president of U.S. Steel; open football professionalism spread to the clubs of the small towns in the surrounding coal region; pro football appeared in other states; and a "World Series" was played indoors at Madison Square Garden in New York City in both 1902 and 1903, antedating—and giving rise to—the same event in the game of professional baseball.

Wealthy men who donate their means to help others can count on never being forgotten. William Chase Temple was an industrialist who donated the "Temple Cup," a portentous silver trophy, to the winner of a playoff between the first-place and second-place finishers in the National League of Professional Baseball Clubs between 1894 and 1897 (there was no American League in baseball until 1901). Temple also gave a cup to the winner of the football "Challenge Cup" competition among Pittsburgh's three athletic club football teams. The newest of them was the Duquesne Country and Athletic Club, or Pittsburgh Duquesnes. This team ran up a

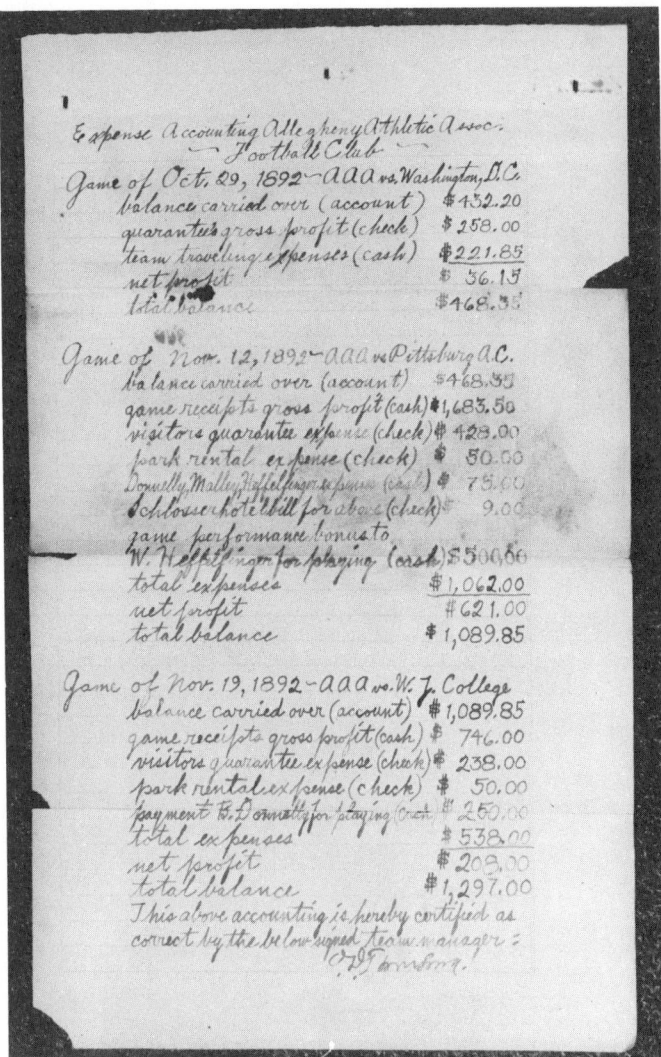

William (Pudge) Heffelfinger (left) and the Allegheny Athletic Association expense sheet proving he was a professional football player in 1892.

huge payroll in signing players returning from the Spanish-American War. In 1899, it found itself in the unique position, according to Ross, of having every player on the team salaried and its payroll considerable. It looked to the wealthy Temple for help. He bought the football team from the athletic club and thus became pro football's first individual owner.

William E. Corey and A. C. Dinkey were next. They were Pittsburgh steel barons and friends of Temple. They formed teams to play his Duquesnes. But while he had a big-city team theirs were located in the grimy steel mill towns of Braddock and Homestead east of the city. Interest in club football ran high there among the miners and mill laborers who dug the ore and worked the blast furnaces. Corey's team was the Braddock Carnegies, the original club team having been named earlier for steel magnate Andrew Carnegie; Dinkey's was the Homestead Library and Athletic Club, or Athletics, or, later, Homestead Steelers.

Corey was a generous, kindly man whose team was made up mostly of steelworkers; it had only a few token college products. The steelworkers got a football bonus in addition to their regular salaries and were excused from work in the mills during football season.

Dinkey, in contrast, went after the big college All-Americas. He also raided Temple's Duquesnes for players. With such high-priced talent, Dinkey won the "world's championship," which actually meant the championship of the athletic clubs in and around Pittsburgh, in 1900 and 1901.

Friendships among wealthy men often are tested by sports competition. Temple was outraged by Dinkey's actions. Temple and owner Barney Dreyfuss of the baseball Pittsburgh Pirates—a name gained through pirating the players of other teams—formed a new football club called the Pittsburgh Professionals, or Pros. For the first time a team openly admitted it was professional. It immediately began raiding back the players Dinkey had stolen. And to stir interest and support, Temple and Dreyfuss decided to use their contacts in baseball and get an intra-state rivalry going with Philadelphia.

There is still one team in American sports whose name goes all the way back to the era of athletic clubs and their preeminence. It is the Oakland Athletics. This baseball team, which a famous manager named Connie Mack led for a half-century, played in Philadelphia until 1954, in Kansas City until 1968, and is now in Oakland.

In 1902, Mack's team was American League champion. He and Ben Shibe, the owner, then decided to field a football team, too. So did the rival Philadelphia Nationals or Phillies of the National League. During the 1902 season, the Athletics, Phillies, and the Pittsburgh team that was known that year either as the Pros or the Stars played games against each other. Mack's team was 11–2–1 in all games for the season, according to researcher Milt

Roberts; 2–1 against the Phillies and 1–1–1 against Pittsburgh.

Pitcher Rube Waddell played on Mack's football team some of the time. In one of the three games against Pittsburgh, pitcher Christy Mathewson played fullback for Pittsburgh. Because of the presence of these famous baseball personages, the one-year foray of Mack into football is given perhaps more importance than it deserves in some histories. Nevertheless, he could rightfully claim the pro football championship of 1902.

Philadelphia defeated Pittsburgh 11–0 in midseason. They met again Thanksgiving Day, November 27, at Exposition Park in Pittsburgh. The crowd was not as large as expected because there was also a college game between Pittsburgh and Washington and Jefferson being played that day. Mack, the Athletics' manager, was concerned that the gate receipts were going to be too small and refused to put his team on the field unless he was paid his $3,000 guarantee in advance. Arguments followed and the crowd grew restive. William Corey, owner of the Homestead Steelers, was sitting in the stands; his enlightened methods of operation as a club owner, in which he employed his steelworkers as players instead of big-name stars, no doubt explained why he was merely a spectator at this championship game. He, too, was anxious for the game to begin.

"He went down to the cluster of debators on the field," Ross wrote. " 'What's the delay?' he asked.

When told by Mr. Mack that the Athletics wanted their $3,000 guarantee in advance, he snorted, wrote out a check for $3,000 and said, 'Let's get the game started.' Handing the check to Mack, he turned and walked away. Mack wasn't so sure about taking checks from strangers, but when he was informed Mr. Corey carried almost as much weight as Andrew Carnegie himself, his mouth dropped open and the game commenced."

It ended in a 0–0 tie but it was such a hard-fought, exhausting game that spectator Corey got his money's worth, according to Ross. Pittsburgh won a third game the following Saturday by the score of 11–0, which must have pleased Corey. Apparently that was Connie Mack's last trip to Pittsburgh with his football team.

The first "world series" was played in football, not baseball. Furthermore, football was played indoors more than half a century before the Astrodome, Louisiana Superdome, Silverdome, Kingdome and every other arena in which pro football was later played under a roof. Pro football was growing in popularity not only in Pennsylvania in 1902, but in other states as well. The New York Knickerbockers, a football team about which little else is known, was impressed with the interest shown in the Philadelphia-Pittsburgh games and conceived the idea of a world series. It was actually to be a four-team tournament, and a promoter named Tom O'Rourke arranged for it to be held in Madison Square Garden, the original Garden at Madison Avenue and Twenty-Sixth Street in New York City.

There was one world series in 1902 and another in 1903. The first was played between the Knickerbockers, the Philadelphia Athletics, the Watertown, New York, Red and Blacks, and the Syracuse, New York, Athletic Club. Syracuse won. Glenn (Pop) Warner, later a famous coach of the Carlisle Indian School, Stanford, and other college teams, played center for Syracuse in the first World Series.

The second was in 1903 and included Philadelphia, Watertown, the Orange, New Jersey, Athletic Club, and the Franklin, Pennsylvania, Athletic Club, which had lured away many of the best players from Pittsburgh with high salaries. Franklin defeated every other team and won the tournament.

World series were important events and, according to Dr. Harry March in *Pro Football's Ups and Downs,* "Frank Hinkey, former Yale end, and Big Bill Edwards officiated the night football games at Madison Square Garden in evening dress—tuxedos, top hats, white gloves, and patent leather shoes.

"In the very last play of the Franklin-Watertown game, with the contest safely in the bag, the Franklin backfield huddled and agreed to run over Frank Hinkey, dress suit and all. They did, soiling him effectively and emphatically. He took it good-naturedly and the Franklin management paid his cleaning and pressing bill."

Football's world series did not become a lasting event but baseball adopted the idea and, in its first series, Boston of the American League defeated Dreyfuss's Pittsburgh team of the National League in 1903, five games to three. There was no series in 1904 but it was resumed in 1905 and there has been one ever since.

There was professional football in other Pennsylvania cities. Lawson Fiscus, celebrated Princeton player, apparently got $20 a game in 1894 to play for the Greensburg, Pennsylvania, Athletic Association. John Brallier, quarterback at Indiana, Pennsylvania, State College in 1895, accepted $10 and "cakes"—expenses—to play for the Latrobe, Pennsylvania, Athletic Club.

Brallier later became a dentist in Latrobe. He corresponded with Dr. Henry March, the New York Giants' doctor and a dabbler in pro football. Brallier

wrote that he had been the first professional football player in history in 1895 with Latrobe. March published Brallier's claim in his 1934 book, the rambling, often misinformed *Pro Football's Ups and Downs.* Brallier became a figure of history. The game in which he had played for the first time for Latrobe was called the first pro game in history. The myth grew; the Pro Football Hall of Fame was almost located in Latrobe instead of the city of the founding of the NFL, Canton, Ohio. It was not until 1971 that Nelson Ross's research and an actual expense sheet of the Allegheny Athletic Association showing it paid Pudge Heffelfinger $500 in 1892 proved that Heffelfinger, not Brallier, was the first known pro.

Other pro football teams not in Pittsburgh included the Olympic Athletic Club of McKeesport, Jeanette Athletic Association, Pitcairn Quakers, Conshohocken Pros, Coaldale Big Green, and Pottsville All-Service.

Pro football declined in Pittsburgh after 1903. The Alleghenies had faded from view. The Duquesne Country and Athletic Club had been absorbed by the Pros or Stars and they in turn by the Franklin team that won the second world series. The Mill teams at Braddock and Homestead disappeared when their owners, Corey and Dinkey, lost interest; Corey, one of the first three club owners in pro football, became president of United States Steel in August, 1903 and held that position until 1911.

Several players from the Pittsburgh Athletic Club were hired by the Massillon, Ohio, Tigers. That made Massillon a professional team. More Ohio towns followed suit and hired pro players from Pennsylvania. The Pennsylvania period of early pro football history ended and the Ohio period began.

Pennsylvania had both the big-city athletic clubs and the small town teams. Arguments continue today over which contributed the most to the game. The sport is young enough that octogenarians who remember club or town football in Pennsylvania still totter into the Hall of Fame occasionally and argue long and hard for the contributions of one or the other. The stories they tell of pro football in Pennsylvania at the turn of the century are rich and colorful.

IV. THE OHIO PERIOD

Athletic clubs and their "ringers" ushered in pro football. It "came out of the closet" in Pennsylvania when teams there openly declared themselves pros. And it grew into a league in Ohio. This was one of the most important steps in American sports history.

That it happened where it did was no accident. Ohio is steeped in history and its strategic location between Lake Erie and the Ohio River in the path of westward expansion has made it the setting for countless historical events.

George Rogers Clark defeated the Indians in the French and Indian War in Ohio in 1780. Commodore Oliver H. Perry defeated the British in the War of 1812 off Put-in-Bay, Ohio, and sent his famous message, "We have met the enemy and he is ours." Settlers moved west along Ohio's National Road or went by water along the Ohio on barges, flatboats, or steamers. Some of the settlers rooted themselves in Ohio and became its farmers or its steel, coal, oil, and rubber barons and made the state one of the industrial centers of America. Army notables Ulysses S. Grant, William Tecumseh Sherman, and George Armstrong Custer were born in Ohio.

Ohio had seven presidents between 1876 and 1920: Grant, Rutherford B. Hayes, James A. Garfield, Benjamin Harrison, William McKinley, William Howard Taft, and Warren G. Harding. Both candidates in the presidential election of 1920 were Ohioans, Harding and Governor James M. Cox.

John D. Rockefeller and his associates formed the Standard Oil Company and cornered the oil markets

of the U.S. from their base in Cleveland. Wilbur and Orville Wright, Dayton bicycle repair shop mechanics, were the first to achieve flight in 1903 at Kitty Hawk, North Carolina. Annie Oakley of Darke County, Ohio, was traveling with Buffalo Bill's Wild West Show.

The purpose of this exterior history is an obvious one; it is to show that the advent of professional football in Ohio was not an isolated event in a remote place. The game grew up in prosperous, growing cities; the population of rubber capital Akron was 69,067 in 1910 and Canton's was 50,217. And these cities were in the eye of the press and public. McKinley and Harding both ran their presidential campaigns from their front porches, McKinley in Canton and Harding in Marion, and they kept their homes in those Ohio cities while they were president.

In this setting, pro football arrived. Predictably, it had its roots in athletic club teams. According to Nelson Ross, there were club teams in Dayton in 1889, Cleveland in 1890, Cincinnati in 1891, Akron in 1894, and Canton and Youngstown in 1895. Other club teams appeared in Alliance, Byesville, Columbus, Lorain, Marion, Newark, Sandusky, Salem, Shelby, and Toledo. There was a state champion proclaimed every year after 1896, according to Ross.

"But in 1903 a new team appeared on the horizon named the Massillon Tigers. That town had never had an independent football team before, but organized one for the '03 season, defeated amateur Canton in the first of many blood battles between them, and then promptly challenged defending and unscored-on state champion East Akron A.A. in a game for the amateur title of Ohio."

Massillon imported professionals from the Pittsburgh Athletic Club, won the game 12–0, and professionalism had invaded Ohio football.

Within one year, the state had at least eight pro teams and in 1904 there was an abortive attempt to form a league and end cutthroat bidding for players. It

Herman Kerchoffe, stolen from Massillon in 1906.

The Nesser family of Columbus, Ohio, which gave six sons to pro football.

became the second known discussion of a pro league, the first having been by Billy Crawford of the Chicago Athletic Association in 1892. Ohio's attempts to form a league in 1904 never amounted to anything, either, and the all-out scrambling for players continued.

There were three periods of pre-1920 pro football in Ohio. The first extended from the importation of the first pros by Massillon in 1903 until 1906, when scandal in a game between Canton and Massillon rocked the sport, shamed the participants, and caused interest in the sport to decline; the 1907-1914 era, which historian Roberts calls "the unglamorous years" of early Ohio pro football; and the period of 1915-19, when Canton signed Jim Thorpe, former Carlisle Indian Industrial School star and the hero of the 1912 Olympics. Thorpe had his greatest years in that period.

Canton also was the site of the organizational meeting of the league in 1920. But the other cities and teams of Ohio pro football had their appeal, too.

Eddie Stewart, the city editor of the *Massillon Independent,* and Charles (Cy) Rigler were prominent managers of the football team in Massillon. It got the name "Tigers" when Stewart bought a supply of jerseys with striped sleeves, in the style of Princeton University, at a cut rate from a sporting goods store. Massillon was state champion in 1904, 1905, and 1906. It suffered a stinging defeat at the hands of Canton in 1911, dropped out of football for a while, and returned in 1916.

A.A. (Buzz) Wesbacker, who was a high school coach in Greensburg, Pennsylvania in 1917, also played for the Massillon Tigers. "The pro games were always on Sunday," he recalled, "and each team would get together Sunday morning with the coach, who would map out the plays and signals. We would practice for an hour, and that was it. If the coach liked the way you played in the actual game, you were signed up for the following week.

"I got fifty dollars a game and expenses. The crowds were mostly rubber, steel, and factory workers. The games were played on baseball fields with stands on one side and a rope stretched on the other; that was standing room only, where most of the betting took place. The bets were placed on the ground, just inside the rope, anchored with a rock, never to be touched until the game ended. At times some young punk would try his luck at getting the loot, only to be warned with a big juicy spit of tobacco near his feet. It certainly was effective."

Akron was such a hotbed of football that in the days of amateur teams it had not one but two of them. When East Akron lost the 12-0 game to Massillon in 1903, the first known game west of Pennsylvania to have involved professionalism, Akron pretended to disdain the hiring of pros for a while. By the end of 1904, however, according to Ross, it was one of the cities pushing the hardest in the ill-fated attempt to organize a pro league that year.

The Akron Indians, state champions in 1909, were a team of players from Southeast Akron who had played football together since they were boys. They lost the championship in 1910, however, to the Shelby Blues, who were led by George (Peggy) Parrott, a former star player for Case Western College in Cleveland. By 1913, however, Parrott had switched his allegiance to Akron; he led that team to a victory over Shelby. Parrott became a celebrated player-manager who was a lively promoter of the game and recruiter of talent. He enjoyed beating the rival Canton Bulldogs. In 1914, he imported the entire left side of Norte Dame's 1913 line, including end Knute Rockne, later the Notre Dame coach, and Akron beat Canton 21-0 and was named the state champion.

The players for the Columbus Panhandles were, in their regular jobs, mechanics for the Panhandle Division of the Pennsylvania Railroad. "They had free transportation and so they were an inexpensive team to play," Dr. Harry March wrote. "The boys worked in the shop until four o'clock Saturday afternoon, got their suppers at home, grabbed the rattlers [trains] to any point within twelve hours' ride of Columbus, played the Sunday game, took another train to Columbus, and punched the time clock at seven Monday morning."

Joe Carr organized the Panhandles in 1904 when he was assistant sports editor of the *Ohio State Journal* in Columbus. Carr's sports involvement grew and he became the manager of the minor league baseball team in Columbus and a professional basketball team. He later became president of the National Football League from 1921 until his death in 1939.

Katherine and Theodore Nesser, German immigrants who lived in Columbus, had six sons and all of them became professional football players for the Columbus Panhandles. They were Al, Frank, Fred, John, Phil, and Ted. It was the only time in history that six members of the same family played pro football.

The Dover Canals got their name because Dover was a port on the Ohio and Erie Canals. The Elyria Athletics represented Elyria, named for the Ely family that founded the town. Elyria came out of nowhere and shocked Canton to win the Ohio championship in 1912. The Shelby Blues had the first known black professional football player, Charles Follis, in 1904.

No other Ohio team, however, made as much history or contributed as much to professional football before 1920 as the Canton Bulldogs. They turned pro in 1905. Outsiders were imported with the express purpose of beating the arch-rival Massillon Tigers, seven miles to the west, and taking the Stark County and Ohio professional championships. The ringers didn't help, however; Massillon went undefeated, beat Canton 14-4, and won the state championship again. More Canton-Massillon battles, and an eventful 1906 football season, loomed ahead.

In 1906, Peggy Parrott joined Massillon. Canton's playing coach, Bill Laub, was injured and did not return. He was replaced by Blondy Wallace, who would become a figure of notoriety almost unparalleled among all pro football coaches. Wallace, according to Dr. Harry March, "knew where to get the right men, how to condition them, and how to build up an attack and defense, but he never won their confidence in his integrity and honesty."

Wallace raided Massillon's team and landed four of its players—Clark Schrontz, Jack Lang, Jack Hayden, and Herman Kerchoffe. It was the year that the rules committee of Walter Camp and his associates legalized the forward pass, and Wallace took the Canton Bulldogs to Pennsylvania State College to learn the new maneuver from the coach there.

Canton and Massillon played a two-game series in 1906. The games were eagerly awaited in the neighboring cities and even far outside their realm of Stark County and Ohio. Grantland Rice, the most eminent of sportswriters, wrote grandly before the first game: "There have been a few football games before. Yale has faced Princeton, Harvard has tackled Penn, and Michigan and Chicago have met in one or two steamy affairs. But these were not the Real Product when measured by the football standard set by the warring factions of Stark County, Ohio, now posing in the football limelight."

He even penned these lines of verse about the game:

In days of old when Knights were bold,
And barons held their sway—
The atmosphere was rife, I hear,
With war cries day by day.
From morn to night, they'd scrap and fight
With battle ax and mace—
While seas of blood poured like a flood
About the market place.
But no fight ever fought beneath the shining sun
Will be like that when Canton's team lines up
   with Massillon.

The two titans of pro football squared off for the first time at the Tigers' field on the grounds of the Ohio state asylum in Massillon. A big crowd watched. Some stood atop a trolley car stopped on the tracks nearby, others along the top of the rickety wooden fence that surrounded the field. Massillon won 10–5. The second game was at Canton two weeks later and the Tigers won again 13–6.

Controversy swelled around both games. "Canton players had been drawing very little money from Wallace," March wrote, "letting him keep their funds for fear a big poker game or other luxuries would lead them to extravagance. They had asked him to bet the money on the first game with Massillon.

"When the game resulted in a Massillon victory he told the fellows he had bet it on the second game."

Wallace's troubles had just begun. The *Massillon Independent* accused him of having tried to throw the second game by influencing the Massillon players and, failing that, persuaded a Canton player to throw it. "When accused by his teammates," March wrote, "this player said he had simply obeyed orders as he was accustomed to do. At any rate he left town hurriedly, on the first train, in his playing togs—his belongings following later—maybe."

A Canton fan who lost heavily on the second game confronted the Bulldogs' players at the Courtland Hotel bar in Canton. Angry words were exchanged. Punches were thrown, and soon a brawl was in progress. The crowd surged through a plate glass window and out into Court Street, where police arrived and broke it up with their night sticks.

Blondy Wallace sued the *Massillon Independent* for libel. The suit was thrown out of court.

Shamed, Canton quit pro football. Its "big team" (there were neighborhood teams that sprang up periodically) apparently did not return for five years, until 1911. In 1912, a 21-year-old clerk at the Canton gas company named Jack Cusack became the secretary-treasurer of the team. Cusack had good business sense, organized well, and was a hard worker. During the next few years he would bring about one organizational triumph after another in behalf of the Canton Bulldogs, climaxed by signing Jim Thorpe. Then Cusack would leave the city forever, and perhaps also leave behind a chance at ever gaining a niche in the Hall of Fame for his contributions to early pro football.

Cusack accepted the job of secretary-treasurer in 1912 as a favor to Roscoe Oberlin, who owned the team. H.H. Halter was manager and resented the intrusion of a man as young as Cusack. Halter was having trouble negotiating a contract for games with Peggy Parrott and the Akron Indians; Parrott felt Akron was a bigger drawing card than Canton and therefore did not have to divide the gate receipts evenly with the Bulldogs. Cusack entered the negotiations and, after five hours of dealing with Parrott, came away with the half-and-half arrangement. Halter was ousted as manager.

The team took the name "Professionals," to make fans forget the tainted past of the Bulldogs. It moved out to lease a new field, League Park. Cusack was made a full partner with Oberlin. They added 1,500 seats to the park in 1913 and sold season tickets for the first time in 1914. Cusack quit his job at the gas company to work full-time for the team. There were hard times as Cusack struggled to make a profit. He found a financial angel in J. J. Frey of the Home Brewing Company, who opened a $10,000 line of credit for the team at the Canton Bank. But Cusack's troubles continued. Center Harry Turner died of injuries he received in a game in 1914; Canton played out the season amid protests and before small crowds.

Jim Thorpe came to Canton in November, 1915. Cusack signed him for $250 a game just before the first game of the season against Massillon. Thorpe

was the world's most celebrated athlete. A Sac and Fox Indian from Oklahoma, he had been a sensational halfback and All-America for the Carlisle Indian Industrial School in Carlisle, Pennsylvania, coached by Glenn (Pop) Warner. In 1912, he won the decathlon and pentathlon for the United States in the fifth modern Olympiad at Stockholm, Sweden. "Sir, you are the greatest athlete in the world," King Gustav V of Sweden told Thorpe as he presented him his medals. But heartbreaking sadness followed for Thorpe; his Olympic medals were taken from him when it was learned that he had played semipro baseball in Rocky Mount, North Carolina, for $25 a game in 1911 during the summer months while a student at Carlisle; unlike countless other college athletes who did the same thing, he had not played the professional sport under an assumed name. He was disgraced. When Jack Cusack signed him for Canton, Thorpe was the veteran of one season of pro football with Pine Village, Indiana, in 1913, was a reserve outfielder with the New York Giants during the summer months, and was employed in the fall months as backfield coach for the University of Indiana.

His one season with Pine Village had been insignificant; he now found in the Canton Bulldogs the right supporting cast to become a sensational professional player. Cusack also signed other notables from college football that year such as Hube Wagner of Pittsburgh, Bill Gardner of Carlisle, Earle (Greasy) Neale, the coach at West Virginia Wesleyan, and his line coach, John Kellison. Neale and Kellison played as pros under aliases.

Cusack's friends warned him he had made a terrible mistake in signing Thorpe for so much money. The Bulldogs, however, played before 6,000 fans at Massillon, losing 16–0. Thorpe is supposed to have slipped on the wet field on the way to two touchdowns. There were 8,000 fans for the second game at League Park in Canton. So many fans clamored to get into the park for the second meeting of the two teams that the Bulldogs sold standing-room-only tickets in the end zones and the two teams agreed on the ground rule that any player crossing the goal line into the crowd must be in possession of the ball when he emerged from it.

Thorpe dropkicked two field goals and Canton led 6–0. Three quarters went by and the Bulldogs were on the verge of a great victory. Massillon's passing attack began working, however, and an end named Briggs caught a pass on the 15-yard line and raced across the end zone, disappearing into the surging crowd. Gideon (Charley) Smith, the first black player on the Canton team, followed Briggs in mad pursuit into the crowd. There, out of sight, a Canton trolley-car conductor kicked the ball out of Briggs's hands and into the arms of Smith, who emerged from the sea of humanity onto the playing field, the ball in his hands. It was a touchback and Canton's victory was preserved.

Massillon fans streamed onto the field in protest. The officials called the game. Massillon demanded that the officials settle the matter by making a statement about the referee's decision awarding the touchback. The officials agreed but only if it could be placed in a sealed envelope and opened by the manager of the Massillon team at 30 minutes after midnight at the Courtland Hotel that night. A tense crowd divided equally among Canton and Massillon supporters was on hand at 12:30 A.M. as the envelope with the statement was opened. It was read aloud and Canton's victory was upheld. Years later, the conductor whose kicking game equaled Thorpe's that day confessed to his crime while riding a streetcar through Canton with Jack Cusack.

The next season, 1916, was the best of all for Canton and Thorpe. "The 1916 Bulldogs," Cusack wrote in the 1960s, "were one of the greatest teams

ever assembled, one I would match against any team in professional football today if they played under the rules and with the same ball in vogue at that time."

Thorpe missed the first two games because he was playing baseball for the Giants; Canton defeated Altoona, Pennsylvania, 23–0 and Pitcairn, Pa., 7–0. In his first game with the team, the Bulldogs swamped a team called the Buffalo All-Stars 77–0. The New York All-Stars fell 67–0. Canton then won a tough game against the Columbus Panhandles, who had five Nesser brothers in the lineup, by the score of 12–0; Cusack says in his memoirs that Thorpe made an 85-yard punt that day.

Canton defeated Peggy Parrott and the Cleveland Indians twice, 27–0 and 14–7. Thorpe made a 71-yard punt return in the first game and won the second on a touchdown run around end. Youngstown fell to Canton 13–0. The first game of the year against Massillon ended in a 0–0 tie when Thorpe left the game after the first quarter with a foot injury. For the second, Cusack signed Carlisle star Pete Calac and he and Thorpe led Canton to a 24–0 shutout of the Tigers. The season ended with Canton the professional champion of the world, winner of 10 straight games; its defense had allowed only seven points all season.

Early pro football in Pittsburgh had suffered when some of its players left the game to fight in the Spanish-American War in 1897. In 1917, 10 years later, Cusack and other pro managers in Ohio lost some of their best players to World War I. The Bulldogs still fielded another strong team, however, and played two stirring games against Massillon. Charlie Brickley, former Harvard All-America and a dropkicker of renown, now led Massillon. He imported "an entire Army Ambulance Corps team from Allentown, Pennsylvania" to play against Canton but the Bulldogs won the first game of the year between the two teams 14–3. In the second game, Thorpe and Stan Cofall, a former Notre Dame star now with Massillon, waged a dropkicking duel that Thorpe lost; Cofall's two field goals won the game for Massillon 6–0. Thorpe was later named the first president and Cofall the vice-president of the American Professional Football Association, forerunner of the NFL.

Cusack's strange and ill-timed departure from the Bulldogs followed. Apparently because of the war and the difficulties football managers were having in signing players, Cusack left the Bulldogs and went to Oklahoma to become an oil-field wildcatter. He caught malaria in Arkansas in 1921.

He eventually returned to Canton to recover from his illness and soon thereafter went to Cleveland where he became Jim Thorpe's personal business manager; Thorpe now played for the Cleveland Indians. Cusack visited Canton often but he never lived there again.

It remained for an automobile dealer named Ralph Hay to take over Cusack's Canton Bulldogs interests. It was Hay who was the owner of record when Canton was the site of the organizational meeting of the league that would become the NFL, in 1920. Every history of the sport, definitive or superficial, identifies Hay's Hupmobile agency showroom in Canton as the meeting site. He captured this permanent place in pro football history.

Cusack, in contrast, lived out his days in the oil business in Texas and Oklahoma. He was well off but he did not become a rich man. He enjoyed coming back to Canton and was prominent there even in the years after the completion of the Hall of Fame shrine in 1963. An old man, he could be seen at a gathering of one kind or another, standing quietly off to himself, alone in his thoughts of Jim Thorpe and the Bulldogs and the years when pro football grew up in Ohio. He died at 84 in 1974.

Six Decades of the NFL

1920 There had been professional football in the United States for at least 28 years, since Pudge Heffelfinger played for Allegheny Athletic Association in Pittsburgh for $500 in 1892. The sport, however, was in a state of confusion. Teams were loosely organized and players moved freely from one to another. There was no control of the competitive bidding among teams for the best college football players. Pro football was operated poorly and governed hardly at all. A league in which all the member teams would follow the same rules of operation clearly seemed the answer and there had been talk of forming such a league as early as 1892, when the era of athletic clubs and their semi-professional teams were at their peak. A serious attempt at organization failed in Ohio in 1904.

A second attempt to form a league was now under way. A meeting was held among interested teams in August. A second meeting was held September 17, 1920 in Canton, Ohio. This city was prominent in professional football because of the rivalry that had gone on for many years between the Canton Bulldogs, for whom the famous athlete Jim Thorpe played, and the Massillon, Ohio, Tigers, whose home city was located seven miles west of Canton.

The teams that were represented at the meeting were from five states. A. F. Ranney, coowner of the Akron, Ohio, Professionals, was elected the secretary of the group. He was faithful in recording in the minutes of the meeting the full names of the Ohio teams with which he was familiar. He was not as careful in recording for posterity the names of the other teams that were represented.

Attending were the Akron Pros; Canton Bulldogs; Cleveland, Ohio, Indians; Dayton, Ohio, Triangles; Decatur, Illinois, Staleys Athletic Club, or Staleys; Hammond, Indiana, Pros; Massillon Tigers; Muncie, Indiana, Flyers; Racine (a Chicago Street) Cardinals; Rochester, New York, Jeffersons; Rock Island, Illinois, Independents; and "Wisconsin."

It was named the American Professional Football Association. Capitalizing on his fame, Thorpe was named league president. Stan Cofall of Massillon was elected vice-president and Ranney secretary-treasurer. A membership fee of $100 per team was arrived at to give an appearance of respectability; no team ever paid it. Each team agreed to print the words, "Member of American Professional Football Association" on its stationery.

"Mr. Marshall of the Brunswick-Balke Connender Company, Tire Division, presented a silver loving cup to be given the team awarded the championship by the Association. Any team winning the cup three times should be adjudged the owner.

"It was moved and seconded that a vote of thanks be extended by the Secretary to Mr. Marshall.

"The meeting was adjourned."

The owner-manager of the Canton Bulldogs was named Ralph Hay. He operated a Hupmobile automobile dealership and the meeting was held in his showroom. There were not enough chairs in the room and some of the persons present had to sit on the running boards and fenders of the automobiles.

The Buffalo, New York, All-Americans; Chicago Tigers; Columbus, Ohio, Panhandles; and Detroit Heralds joined the league later.

Professional teams had good years and bad. When they were winning, they could draw crowds and prosper; when they were losing, they suffered through hard times and dropped out of the competition. The Massillon Tigers were going through losing seasons at the time of the formation of the league, and so were the Muncie Flyers, and they did not field teams in 1920.

There were professional teams that attended APFA and, later, NFL meetings held at Atlantic City each

Jim Thorpe of the Canton Bulldogs; he also played for seven other NFL teams.

season, keeping their membership and paying dues but staying out of the competition until their chances for success improved.

The league was loosely organized. Teams played as many non-members as they did member teams. There were either no standings kept by anyone in the league or they were kept and have since been lost.

The typical stadium of the league was a minor league baseball park or an open field with circus bleachers seating some fans and others standing along the side lines, separated from the action by a rope.

Akron, Buffalo, and Canton all claimed the championship and a hastily arranged series of games failed to decide the issue. One of the special games between the Canton Bulldogs and Buffalo All-Americans was played at the Polo Grounds in New York City. It "was the first real game between representative teams ever played in the metropolis and attracted over 15,000 paid admissions," Dr. Harry March wrote in *Pro Football's Ups and Downs.* "Buffalo won, 7 to 3, with Youngstrom blocking one of Thorpe's punts and falling on the ball for a touchdown. Thorpe kicked one field goal in three attempts. The New York newspapers said he was slowing down greatly."

The first recorded player deal occurred when Bob Nash, a tackle and end for Akron, was sold to Buffalo for $300 and five percent of the gate receipts.

1921 Professional football operators decided they needed more experienced leadership. Joe Carr, a

Columbus, Ohio, sportswriter, manager of the Columbus Panhandles, minor league baseball executive, and pioneer in professional basketball, was named president of the American Professional Football Association at a meeting in Akron April 30. Carr established the league office in Columbus. Carl Storck of the Dayton Triangles was named secretary-treasurer of the league.

The Chicago Tigers, beaten by the Cardinals in a 1920 game for the "rights" to Chicago, dropped out and so did Hammond. Green Bay, which was sponsored by the Acme Packing Company and coached by Earl (Curly) Lambeau, and the Cincinnati Celts joined to leave the membership at 13 franchises.

Jim Thorpe left the Canton Bulldogs and he and Joe Guyon, another famous Indian player who had attended the Carlisle Indian Industrial School, joined Cleveland.

Five teams who dropped out of the league early in the season had their records stricken, unfairly or not, from the league standings. They were Evansville, Indiana; Hammond, Indiana; Louisville, Kentucky; Minneapolis, Minnesota; and Muncie, Indiana.

A. E. Staley was the owner of the starch company in Decatur, Illinois that sponsored the Staleys Athletic Club. His business was not doing very well so he turned the football team over to its player-coach, George Halas. Halas was permitted to move the team to Chicago and Cubs' Park (renamed Wrigley Field when it was enlarged in 1926) if he would keep the name "Staleys" one more year. Dutch Sternaman, one of the Staleys' players, became Halas's partner in the ownership of the team. The two of them, along with Guy Chamberlin and George Trafton, were the nucleus of the relocated team.

The Staleys claimed the league championship with a 10–1–1 record, followed by Buffalo's 9–1–2. Buffalo objected, saying Chicago included nonleague games in its record, but president Joe Carr ruled in favor of the Staleys.

1921 STANDINGS	W	L	T	Pct.
Chicago Staleys	10	1	1	.909
Buffalo All-Americans	9	1	2	.900
Akron, Ohio, Pros	7	2	1	.778
Green Bay Packers	6	2	2	.750
Canton, Ohio, Bulldogs	4	3	3	.571
Dayton Triangles	4	3	1	.571
Rock Island, Ill., Independents	5	4	1	.556
Chicago Cardinals	2	3	2	.400
Cleveland Indians	2	6	0	.250
Rochester Jeffersons	2	6	0	.250
Detroit Heralds	1	7	1	.125
Columbus Panhandles	0	6	0	.000
Cincinnati Celts	0	8	0	.000

1922 The name of the league was changed to "National Football League." The Chicago Staleys became the Chicago Bears. The league grew to 18 teams. It disciplined the Green Bay Packers, who had been using college players under assumed names, and dismissed them from the league, but the Packers returned, bought back their franchise, and were restored to the good graces of the league.

The league's first powerhouse team, the Canton Bulldogs coached by Guy Chamberlin, emerged. Chamberlin left the Staleys/Bears and became coach in Canton. He was in the lineup and so were two great tackles, Wilbur (Pete) Henry and Link Lyman. The Bulldogs had a 10–0–2 record, starting a string of games in which they would win 21, lose 0, and tie 3 and capture three consecutive NFL championships.

Thorpe, once Canton's greatest star, moved to another team. He and other Indian players formed a team called the Oorang Indians, who were sponsored by a man named Walter Lingo who owned the Oorang Kennels; Oorang is a strain of Airedale. The kennel was in LaRue, Ohio, but the games were played in Marion, the hometown of Warren Harding, then President of the United States. Guyon was one of Thorpe's teammates.

Halas's Chicago team took the name "Bears" because he was a fan of the Cubs baseball team with which he shared the stadium. The Bears paid the Rock Island, Illinois, Independents $100 for Ed Healey, a great tackle. Chicago had a 9–3 record, finished second in the league to Canton, and coowners Halas and Sternaman made a profit of $1,476.92.

Carr, the president of the league, decided to make an example of the Packers and prevent other teams from using college players under assumed names. Green Bay's franchise was revoked and a $50 fee returned to the Acme Packing Company. Curly Lambeau, player-coach of the team, used $50 of his own money to buy back the franchise. A friend named Don Murphy sold his car so Lambeau would have train fare to the league meeting. There, Lambeau promised to obey the rules and the Green Bay franchise was awarded to him. Murphy, Lambeau's friend, was allowed to start the opening game of the season for Green Bay and play one minute of pro football in exchange for his financial help.

The Packers were plagued by bad weather and low attendance. Merchants of Green Bay raised $2,500 and loaned it to the team, and a public non-profit corporation was set up to operate it, with Lambeau as manager and coach.

Cincinnati, Cleveland, and Detroit left the league.

The 1920 Decatur Staleys; George Halas is in the center, front row.

1-GRIGGS, 2-BUCK, 3-O'CONNOR, 4-COCORAN, 5-MARTIN, 6-DADUM, 7-EDWARDS, 8-THORPE, 9-GUYON, 10-CALAC, 11-HENRY, 12-GREEN, 13-WAHLEN, 14-GILROY, 15-SPECK, 16-FEENY, 17-HALEY, 18-HENDREN

The 1920 Bulldogs; Thorpe is fourth from right, second row.

The 1921 Acme Packers, Green Bay; Earl (Curly) Lambeau stands in center, front row.

The 1925 Chicago Cardinals.

Within the image, text includes:
SQUAD MEMBERS NOT PICTURED:
WILFRID SMITH, WILLIS BRENNAN, JOHN HURLBURT,
ART FOLZ, MORRIS BLUMENTHAL, FRED DeSTAFANO,
"MICKEY" McDONNELL, PAUL McNULTY, "IKE" MAHONEY,
EVAR SWANSON.

Hagemeister Brewery Park, Green Bay, Wisconsin.

Evansville, Indiana; Hammond, Indiana; Louisville, Kentucky; Milwaukee; Minneapolis; Racine, Wisconsin; and Toledo, Ohio were new or returning franchises.

1922 STANDINGS	W	L	T	Pct.
Canton, Ohio, Bulldogs	10	0	2	1.000
Chicago Bears	9	3	0	.750
Chicago Cardinals	8	3	0	.727
Toledo Maroons	5	2	2	.714
Rock Island, Ill., Independents	4	2	1	.667
Dayton Triangles	4	3	1	.571
Green Bay Packers	4	3	3	.571
Racine, Wis., Legion	5	4	1	.556
Akron, Ohio, Pros	3	4	2	.429
Buffalo All-Americans	3	4	1	.429
Milwaukee Badgers	2	4	3	.333
Oorang Indians, Marion, Ohio	2	6	0	.250
Minneapolis Marines	1	3	0	.250
Evansville Crimson Giants	0	2	0	.000
Louisville Brecks	0	3	0	.000
Rochester Jeffersons	0	3	1	.000
Hammond, Ind., Pros	0	4	1	.000
Columbus Panhandles	0	7	0	.000

1923 Canton went undefeated again—it was tied once—and the Chicago Bears were runners-up again. The league grew to 20 teams but it did not regulate the schedule of each member team; some played as many as 12 games against member teams, others as few as 2. The Cleveland Indians returned to the league, the Duluth, Minnesota, Kelleys appeared for the first time, and Evansville, Indiana, left the league for good.

Jim Thorpe began the season as player-coach of the Oorang Indians but they folded with a 1–10 record and Thorpe joined the Toledo Maroons.

Player-coach George Halas of Chicago recovered a fumble by Thorpe in a game against Oorang and ran 98 yards for a touchdown. "I could feel Thorpe breathing down my neck all the way," Halas said.

John (Paddy) Driscoll was the star player of the rival Cardinals in Chicago. He scored four touchdowns and the Cardinals had nine in all against the Rochester Jeffersons October 7. These statistics were left to history but the score of the game was not.

1923 STANDINGS	W	L	T	Pct.
Canton, Ohio, Bulldogs	11	0	1	1.000
Chicago Bears	9	2	1	.818
Green Bay Packers	7	2	1	.778
Milwaukee Badgers	7	2	3	.778
Cleveland Indians	3	1	3	.750
Chicago Cardinals	8	4	0	.667
Duluth Kelleys	4	3	0	.571
Buffalo All-Americans	5	4	3	.556
Columbus Tigers	5	4	1	.556
Racine, Wis., Legion	4	4	2	.500
Toledo Maroons	2	3	2	.400
Rock Island, Ill., Independents	2	3	3	.400
Minneapolis Marines	2	5	2	.286
St. Louis All-Stars	1	4	2	.200
Hammond, Ind., Pros	1	5	1	.167
Dayton Triangles	1	6	1	.143
Akron, Ohio, Indians	1	6	0	.143
Oorang Indians, Marion, Ohio	1	10	0	.091
Rochester Jeffersons	0	2	0	.000
Louisville Brecks	0	3	0	.000

1924 At the height of their success, the Canton Bulldogs moved their francise to another city. Their payroll was rising and needed larger crowds and more income. Player-coach Guy Chamberlin and most of the players that had starred for Canton moved 55 miles north to the larger city of Cleveland, where they became the Cleveland Bulldogs. Star tackle Pete Henry did not make the move with his teammates; instead, he joined the Pottsville, Pennsylvania, Maroons, a pro team not then in the NFL.

Philadelphia was represented in the league for the first time by the Frankford Yellowjackets; Frankford is a suburb of Philadelphia. The Yellowjackets had been playing pro football for five or six years when they applied for and gained membership in the league. Blue laws in Pennsylvania prevented them from playing their home games on Sunday but it was common for them to play a home game on Saturday and a road game somewhere else the very next day.

The Kansas City Cowboys were another new team that played all its games on the road. The Cowboys had Steve Owen at tackle.

Cleveland and Frankford scheduled weak opponents late in the season so they could fatten their won-lost records. President Joe Carr, however, later ruled all games played after November 30 invalid. Cleveland and player-coach Chamberlin won its third straight league championship with a 7–1–1 record and an .875 percentage. The Chicago Bears lost their first game of the season but then came back to finish in second place. Frankford had 11 victories, a large number due to its frequent practice of playing back-to-back games on Saturday and Sunday, but its .846 percentage was only good for third place.

1924 STANDINGS	W	L	T	Pct.
Cleveland Bulldogs	7	1	1	.875
Chicago Bears	6	1	4	.857
Frankford Yellowjackets	11	2	1	.846
Duluth Kelleys	5	1	0	.833
Rock Island, Ill., Independents ...	6	2	2	.750
Green Bay Packers	8	4	0	.667
Buffalo Bisons	6	4	0	.600
Racine, Wis., Legion	4	3	3	.571
Chicago Cardinals	5	4	1	.556
Columbus Tigers	4	4	0	.500
Hammond, Ind., Pros	2	2	1	.500
Milwaukee Badgers	5	8	0	.385
Dayton Triangles	2	7	0	.222
Kansas City Cowboys	2	7	0	.222
Akron, Ohio, Indians	1	6	0	.143
Kenosha, Wis., Maroons	0	5	1	.000
Minneapolis Marines	0	6	0	.000
Rochester Jeffersons	0	7	0	.000

1925 The most momentous season in the NFL's brief history proceeded through a series of tumultuous events ending in a dispute between two teams for the league championship.

Red Grange of Illinois, "the Galloping Ghost," the most celebrated player in the history of college football, entered pro football and immeasurably changed it for the better. C. C. (Cash and Carry) Pyle, a promotion-minded individual who operated a movie theater in Champaign, Illinois, became Grange's manager. The University of Illinois season ended in mid-November, 1925. Grange signed a contract to play for the Chicago Bears immediately; there was no rule at the time preventing college players from doing so.

The Bears played their traditional Thanksgiving Day game against the rival Chicago Cardinals and, with Grange in the lineup, drew a crowd of 38,000 fans. Grange was spectacular on punt returns but Paddy Driscoll, the Cardinals' star, punted the ball away from Grange for the entire game and as a result was booed by the fans who wanted to see Grange make a long runback.

An unprecedented barnstorming tour then began in which the Bears played seven games in 11 days in St. Louis, Philadelphia, New York City, and then cities in the South and on the West Coast. Large crowds turned out everywhere to see Grange play. Newspapers followed the tour with great interest. College football had been popular for years while the "professionalism" of the sport had been looked on with disfavor. The Grange Tour, as it was called, helped dispel these prejudices and gained countless new fans for pro football.

New York City entered the NFL. Tim Mara, a bookmaker, and Billy Gibson, the manager of boxer Gene Tunney, were awarded a franchise for either $500 or $2,500; histories differ on the amount. Their team was named the football Giants and played at the Polo Grounds. They were losing money until the Grange Tour arrived. A crowd of over 70,000 people watched Grange and the Bears play against the Giants. This game ensured the future of the Giants

John (Paddy) Driscoll.

Red Grange, left, and C.C. (Cash and Carry) Pyle.

Joe F. Carr, NFL president.

and an all-important NFL franchise in the city.

Three more important franchises joined the league. They were the Detroit Panthers, who were coached by Jimmy Conzelman; the Pottsville, Pennsylvania, Maroons; and the Providence, Rhode Island, Steamroller. There was a new team in Canton, Ohio, again called the Bulldogs.

Guy Chamberlin, winner of three consecutive league championships, became the player-coach of the Frankford Yellowjackets.

The Pottsville Maroons had great success their first year in the league. They defeated the Chicago Cardinals 21–7 for what they thought was the championship of the NFL. One week later, however, the Maroons played the "Notre Dame All-Stars," a team of former players for the university, including the famous Four Horsemen backfield of Jim Crowley, Elmer Layden, Don Miller, and Harry Stuhldreher. The game was played in Philadelphia. Player-coach Chamberlin of the Frankford Yellowjackets protested, saying his team's "territorial rights" had been impinged upon.

President Joe Carr upheld the protest, canceled the Pottsville franchise, and ordered the Cardinals to play two more games. They did, defeating Hammond, Indiana and Milwaukee. Hammond had an 1–4 and Milwaukee an 0–6 record. The Cardinals now had a better record than Pottsville and were proclaimed NFL champions.

It was then learned that the Milwaukee team had used four high school players in its game against the Cardinals. Carr suspended Milwaukee's manager, Arthur Folz, "for life."

The Green Bay Packers left a ramshackle structure called Hegemeister Brewery Park and moved into City Stadium, a 6,000-seat park with wooden stands and fences that may have been the first stadium in the NFL built expressly for football.

1925 STANDINGS	W	L	T	Pct.
Chicago Cardinals	11	2	1	.846
Pottsville, Pa., Maroons	10	2	0	.833
Detroit Panthers	8	2	2	.800
New York Giants	8	4	0	.667
Akron, Ohio, Indians	4	2	2	.667
Frankford Yellowjackets	13	7	0	.650
Chicago Bears	9	5	3	.643
Rock Island, Ill., Independents ...	5	3	3	.625
Green Bay Packers	8	5	0	.615
Providence Steamroller	6	5	1	.545
Canton, Ohio, Bulldogs	4	4	0	.500
Cleveland Bulldogs	5	8	1	.385
Kansas City Cowboys	2	5	1	.286
Hammond, Ind., Pros	1	3	0	.250
Buffalo Bisons	1	6	2	.143
Duluth Kelleys	0	3	0	.000
Rochester Jeffersons	0	6	1	.000
Milwaukee Badgers	0	6	0	.000
Dayton Triangles	0	7	1	.000
Columbus Tigers	0	9	0	.000

1926 Red Grange's manager, C. C. (Cash and Carry) Pyle, told the Chicago Bears Grange would not play for them in 1926 unless he was paid a five-figure salary and was given one-third ownership of the team. The Bears refused and lost the services of Grange. Pyle leased Yankee Stadium in New York City, petitioned for an NFL franchise and was refused, and therefore decided to start his own league. It was named the American Football League.

Grange was the figure around which this league was built. He played for Pyle's team, the New York Yankees. The other teams in the league were the Boston Bulldogs, Brooklyn Horsemen, Chicago Bulls, Cleveland Panthers, Newark Bears, Philadelphia Quakers, and a road team called the Los Angeles Wildcats. The Rock Island, Illinois, Independents left the NFL and joined the AFL. These teams played before small crowds and the league folded up after one season. Its champion, the Philadelphia Quakers, played a postseason game against the New York Giants of the NFL and lost 31–0.

Red Grange of the New York Yankees against the Los Angeles Wildcats at Yankee Stadium, 1926, the first AFL.

The NFL allowed its membership to grow to 22 teams to frustrate the AFL. The league was in a confused state in which the names of teams and their true identities differed. The Los Angeles Buccaneers and the Louisville Colonels actually were road teams based in Chicago. Los Angeles was a growing center of pro football interest because of the enthusiastic crowd that had watched Red Grange play there on his tour in 1925, but the 1926 Buccaneers of the NFL and the Wildcats of the AFL never actually played a game in the city which they supposedly represented.

Paddy Driscoll of the Cardinals was sold to the rival Bears and they gave him a good contract, ensuring that he did not sign with the AFL. Ole Haugsrud, the operator of a team in Duluth, Minnesota, gained an NFL franchise and signed Ernie Nevers, the star fullback of Glenn (Pop) Warner's team at Stanford University. The NFL thus acquired a gate attraction to rival Grange of the AFL.

Haugsrud's team was called the Duluth Eskimos. They played two games at home while the weather in their city still permitted it, and then completed the season on the road. They played 28 league or exhibition games. There were only 13 players and sportswriter Grantland Rice named them "the Iron Men of the North."

Jim Thorpe rejoined Canton and played another season for the Bulldogs. Steve Owen moved from the Kansas City Cowboys to the New York Giants.

The Frankford Yellowjackets, led by player-coach Guy Chamberlin, won the championship. They defeated Chicago in a game that broke a 10-game winning streak for the Bears. Chamberlin broke through and blocked a field goal attempt by Driscoll.

Chicago finished second in the league and Pottsville third.

The NFL had been severely criticized for signing Grange immediately after his last college game. Coexistence with college football was assured when Halas of the Bears pushed through an NFL rule prohibiting any team from having in its lineup a player whose college class had not graduated.

Al Nesser, seated at left; Steve Owen, seated at right, and other 1926 New York Giants.

1926 STANDINGS	W	L	T	Pct.
Frankford Yellowjackets	14	1	1	.933
Chicago Bears	12	1	3	.923
Pottsville, Pa., Maroons	10	2	1	.833
Kansas City Cowboys	8	3	1	.727
Green Bay Packers	7	3	3	.700
Los Angeles Buccaneers	6	3	1	.667
New York Giants	8	4	1	.667
Duluth Eskimos	6	5	2	.545
Buffalo Rangers	4	4	2	.500
Chicago Cardinals	5	6	1	.455
Providence Steamroller	5	7	0	.417
Detroit Panthers	4	6	2	.400
Hartford Blues	3	7	0	.300
Brooklyn Lions	3	8	0	.273
Milwaukee Badgers	2	7	0	.222
Akron, Ohio, Indians	1	4	3	.200
Dayton Triangles	1	4	1	.200
Racine, Wis., Legion	1	4	0	.200
Columbus Tigers	1	6	0	.143
Canton, Ohio, Bulldogs	1	9	3	.100
Hammond, Ind., Pros	0	4	0	.000
Louisville Colonels	0	4	0	.000

1927 Professional football entered a depression. It went from 31 teams and two leagues to 12 teams and one league. Pyle's New York Yankees moved to the NFL; no other AFL team survived. The traveling Los Angeles Buccaneers and Kansas City Cowboys went out of business. And three midwest franchises that had been the foundation for the league in its earlier years—the Akron Indians, Canton Bulldogs, and Columbus Panhandles—vanished. They never appeared in the league membership again.

Grange was still with the Yankees but he suffered a knee injury in the third game of the season. His days as a feared runner were over. George (Wildcat) Wilson of the defunct Los Angeles Wildcats, joined the Providence Steamroller. Jimmy Conzelman left

Ernie Nevers.

Guy Chamberlin.

Jimmy Conzelman.

the defunct Detroit Heralds to become player-coach of the Steamroller. Guy Chamberlin, a player only and no longer a coach, moved to the Chicago Cardinals and ended his career with them.

The New York Giants won their first NFL championship. Earl Potteiger was their coach. The Giants had Steve Owen, rookie sensation Cal Hubbard, and Al Nesser of the famous Nesser brothers of Columbus, Ohio, in their lineup. The Giants scored 197 points and allowed only 20 in 13 games, and played five consecutive shutouts in midseason. They defeated the Chicago Bears 13–7 in what Owen called "the toughest, roughest game I ever played."

1927 STANDINGS	W	L	T	Pct.
New York Giants	11	1	1	.917
Green Bay Packers	7	2	1	.778
Chicago Bears	9	3	2	.750
Cleveland Bulldogs	8	4	1	.667
Providence Steamroller	8	5	1	.615
New York Yankees	7	8	1	.467
Frankford Yellowjackets	6	9	3	.400
Pottsville, Pa., Maroons	5	8	0	.385
Chicago Cardinals	3	7	1	.300
Dayton Triangles	1	6	1	.143
Duluth Eskimos	1	8	0	.111
Buffalo Bisons	0	5	0	.000

1928 The two most famous players in pro football left the game two years after the interleague war of 1926. Red Grange's knee still hurt him and so he spent the football season appearing on the vaudeville circuit and making a movie. The Duluth Eskimos disbanded and their great star, Ernie Nevers, quit pro football and returned to Stanford University as an assistant coach for Pop Warner; Nevers was also a professional baseball player.

Philadelphia's Frankford Yellowjackets were one of the strongest teams in the league. They played some of their games at Shibe Park and others in their own 10,000-seat Frankford Stadium. "It is worth the time of anyone to wander out to Frankford on a Saturday afternoon in the autumn," Bill Roper wrote in *Football Today and Tomorrow* in 1927. "A steady stream of men and women flow toward the football field. On the arms of girls are the colors of the Yellowjackets, in their hands, pennants. They cheer for the players because they know them, because it is their team. They have a clannishness that is refreshing, that would put most colleges to shame, and very few of them ever saw a college."

The Providence Steamroller had its greatest season, winning the championship. Conzelman was their player-coach and Wildcat Wilson their star player. The owners of the team were Charles Coppen, sports columnist and former sports editor of the *Providence Journal;* James (Judge) Dooley, an attorney; and Peter Laudati, a native Italian and sports promoter who built the Cycledrome on North Main Street in Providence for bicycle racing, a popular sport in the twenties. Laudati, researcher John Hogrogian wrote, always carried the pole of the first down marker at every home game.

The Steamroller played its home games at the Cycledrome. The wooden track, "steeply banked around the turns and flatter on the straightaways, enclosed just enough around to fit a football field, with some slight problems. The track, equipped with seats and a bench for the players on each straight-away, ran so close to the sidelines that players tackled near the boundary line frequently caromed into the front row of seats. One end zone extended the regulation 10 yards but the other went only five before the banked track cut across it." The 18-man Steamroller team found the Cycledrome dressing room, which had been built to accommodate two bicycle racers, somewhat cramped.

When the Steamroller went to New York to play the Yankees, "the Arcadia Ballroom in downtown

Benny Friedman, Detroit Wolverines, against the New York Yankees, NFL, 1928.

Providence was equipped with a Western Union wire to receive the play-by-play account from Yankee Stadium. Fans could pay 50 cents to hear the game announced there or at the Empire Theater."

The Steamroller clinched the NFL championship by tying the Green Bay Packers 7–7 in a climactic game before 10,500 fans at the Cycledrome. The Steamroller's touchdown came on a pass from Wildcat Wilson to Curly Oden, and Gus Sonnenberg kicked the extra point.

Frankford won more games but had a poorer percentage. The Detroit Wolverines, who had a brief but notable existence, were third. The Wolverines had Benny Friedman, All-America from the University of Michigan. He probably pioneered the use of the forward pass as a real weapon on offense. Big crowds came to see Friedman and the Wolverines. They played in the NFL for only one year at a time when it was shrinking in size and a financial depression was approaching. But the Wolverines won 7, lost 2, and tied 1 for the best lifetime percentage (.778), however brief, of any NFL team in history.

1928 STANDINGS	W	L	T	Pct.
Providence Steamroller	8	1	2	.889
Frankford Yellowjackets	11	3	2	.786
Detroit Wolverines	7	2	1	.778
Green Bay Packers	6	4	3	.600
Chicago Bears	7	5	1	.583
New York Giants	4	7	2	.364
New York Yankees	4	8	1	.333
Pottsville, Pa., Maroons	2	8	0	.200
Chicago Cardinals	1	5	0	.167
Dayton Triangles	0	7	0	.000

1929 The Green Bay Packers won their first NFL championship. Earl (Curly) Lambeau, manager and coach of the Packers, put together a sensational trio of "misfits" in Green Bay and had an undefeated season; the Packers were tied once. Lambeau acquired back Johnny Blood (McNally) from the defunct Pottsville Maroons franchise, tackle Cal Hubbard in a trade with the New York Giants, and guard Mike Michalske from the defunct New York Yankees.

Blood was colorful, enigmatic, and unconven-

tional. Hubbard had enjoyed Green Bay when the Giants played there and asked them to trade him to the Wisconsin team. Michalske was a star who had signed with the rival AFL rather than the NFL in 1926 after his college career.

Red Grange and Ernie Nevers returned to the NFL. Grange became an average back for the Chicago Bears. Nevers joined the Cardinals as a player-coach. He scored an incredible 40 points against the Bears Thanksgiving Day, November 28, on six touchdowns rushing and four extra points. Benny Friedman of the defunct Detroit Wolverines moved to the New York Giants.

Part of the Pottstown franchise became the Boston Bulldogs. Part of the Yankees' franchise became the Stapleton Stapes on Staten Island in the New York harbor. Stapleton had rookie back and kicker Ken Strong. The Dayton Triangles died, the last of the original Ohio NFL teams to leave the league.

Pro football games had been played for eight years with only three officials—referee, umpire, and head linesman—while college football had four. The NFL now added the fourth official, the field judge, for its games.

The Chicago Bears had their poorest season, losing nine games.

1929 STANDINGS	W	L	T	Pct.
Green Bay Packers	12	0	1	1.000
New York Giants	13	1	1	.929
Frankford Yellowjackets	9	4	5	.692
Chicago Cardinals	6	6	1	.500
Boston Bulldogs	4	4	0	.500
Orange, N.J. Tornadoes	3	4	4	.429
Stapleton Stapes	3	4	3	.429
Providence Steamroller	4	6	2	.400
Chicago Bears	4	9	2	.308
Buffalo Bisons	1	7	1	.125
Minneapolis Red Jackets	1	9	0	.100
Dayton Triangles	0	6	0	.000

1930 Arnie Herber, a rookie single wing tailback from tiny Regis College in Denver, Colorado, took command of the Green Bay Packers and they won their second straight NFL championship, the first time a team had achieved that feat since the Canton

Bulldogs of 1922–23.

Two franchises began. The Portsmouth Spartans were born in Portsmouth, an Ohio city on the Ohio river and at the mouth of the Ohio Canal. The defunct Dayton Triangles franchise was purchased by John Dwyer and became the Brooklyn Dodgers.

Pro football was played indoors for the first time since the football World Series of 1902 and 1903. The nation was in a depression and the Chicago Bears and Cardinals played an exhibition for unemployment relief funds at Chicago Stadium. A layer of dirt covered the floor of the arena.

A sellout crowd of 55,000 watched a charity game at the Polo Grounds in New York between the Giants and the "Notre Dame All-Stars." This all-star team also had the Four Horsemen backfield in its lineup and it was coached by Knute Rockne.

George Halas and Dutch Sternaman, coowners of the Chicago Bears, feuded. The team had a poor offense and each owner had a solution for it; neither worked and the team steadily declined. Halas resigned as player and coach; Paddy Driscoll also retired as a player. Halas and Sternaman hired Ralph Jones, coach of Lake Forest Academy outside Chicago, as the Bears' coach.

Jones radically changed the Bears T formation. He moved the ends wide, spaced the halfbacks wider, and made one of the halfbacks a man-in-motion. He had split ends and men-in-motion and by moving one of the backs out wide devised the professional "three-end offense." The team made a dramatic turn-around and won nine games.

1930 STANDINGS	W	L	T	Pct.
Green Bay Packers	10	3	1	.769
New York Giants	13	4	0	.765
Chicago Bears	9	4	1	.692
Brooklyn Dodgers	7	4	1	.636
Providence Steamroller	6	4	1	.600
Stapleton Stapes	5	5	2	.500
Chicago Cardinals	5	6	2	.455
Portsmouth, Ohio, Spartans	5	6	3	.455
Frankford Yellowjackets	4	14	1	.222
Minneapolis Red Jackets	1	7	1	.125
Newark Tornadoes	1	10	1	.091

Mike Michalske.

Cal Hubbard.

Earl (Dutch) Clark at Colorado College.

Cliff Battles.

Clarke Hinkle.

1931 Professional football shrank to 10 teams. Green Bay won its third consecutive NFL championship with Arnie Herber passing to Johnny Blood (McNally) and Verne Lewellen. The Portsmouth Spartans became a big winner behind rookie tailback Earl (Dutch) Clark of Colorado College. George (Potsy) Clark (who was not related to Dutch Clark) coached the Spartans. Green Bay was 12–2–0 and Portsmouth 11–3–0; there was apparently supposed to be a game between them for the championship but it was never played.

The player limit for NFL teams was 20 but the Packers would sometimes play an entire game with only 12 or 13 men.

The playing career of Al Nesser, last of the Nesser brothers in the NFL, ended when his team, the Cleveland Indians, disbanded.

Steve Owen and Benny Friedman became co-coaches of the New York Giants after LeRoy Andrews quit in midseason.

Joe Carr, president of the NFL, fined the Chicago Bears, Green Bay Packers, and Portsmouth Spartans $1,000 each for using players whose college classes had not graduated.

1931 STANDINGS	W	L	T	Pct.
Green Bay Packers	12	2	0	.857
Portsmouth, Ohio, Spartans	11	3	0	.786
Chicago Bears	8	5	0	.615
Chicago Cardinals	5	4	0	.556
New York Giants	7	6	1	.538
Providence Steamroller	4	4	3	.500
Stapleton Stapes	4	6	1	.400
Cleveland Indians	2	8	0	.200
Brooklyn Dodgers	2	12	0	.143
Frankford Yellowjackets	1	6	1	.143

1932 In the depths of the depression, the National Football League's membership fell to eight teams, the smallest in its history, and it hung on gamely, hoping things would improve.

This was the miniature league of 1932: Chicago's teams, the Bears and Cardinals; the New York Giants, Brooklyn Dodgers, and Stapleton Stapes in New York; the Boston Braves; the Green Bay Packers; and the Portsmouth Spartans. The Braves, the only new team, played at Braves Field, and were owned by George Preston Marshall, owner of a chain of laundries in Washington, D.C. Cliff Battles, a Braves' rookie, led the league in rushing with 576 yards. Glen (Turk) Edwards, a tackle, was another impressive rookie for Boston.

Battles's rushing figure is known because the league kept rudimentary individual statistics for the first time. Joe Carr, the league president, maintained his offices in Columbus, Ohio, even though most of the NFL's teams were in Chicago and New York. Carr was also the operator of the minor league baseball team in Columbus. Carl Storck, secretary-treasurer of the league, had a full-time job as the supervisor of shock absorbers production for General Motors in Dayton, Ohio.

The shortcomings of the style of pro football in 1932 cost the Green Bay Packers a fourth consecutive NFL championship and led to a playoff game that changed the sport as profoundly as any in its history.

Green Bay added rookie fullback Clarke Hinkle to its array of stars and ran up a 10–1–1 record with two weeks left to play in the season. However, the Packers then lost back-to-back games to Portsmouth and the Chicago Bears. Green Bay's 10–3–1 record

gave it a percentage of .769. The Bears' offense sputtered and the team compiled the outlandish total of six ties; its record was 6–1–6 for a percentage of .857. Portsmouth, 6–1–4, also had an .857 percentage. Both were better than Green Bay's; the tie games did not count in the winning percentage at all. The Packers were shunted to third place and a postseason playoff was arranged between the Bears and Spartans.

The Bears' victory over Green Bay in the last game of the season was played in the snow at Wrigley Field. The playoff game was scheduled for the same site but Chicago's weather grew worse. George Halas, owner of the Bears' team, decided to move the game indoors to Chicago Stadium.

There was a layer of dirt on the arena floor, left over from a circus. There was room for only an 80-yard field. It came right up to the walls, so each team agreed to move the goal posts from the end line to the goal line and create inbounds lines; each time the ball was carried outside them it would, for safety's sake, be returned to those lines for the start of the next play.

A crowd of 11,198 saw the game. Portsmouth was without its star, Earl (Dutch) Clark, who had already left the team for his off-season job as basketball coach at Colorado College.

The two teams played for three quarters without a score until Dick Nesbitt of the Bears intercepted a pass by Leroy (Ace) Gutowsky of Portsmouth at the Spartans' 7-yard line. Chicago fullback Bronko Nagurski made six yards, then was stopped for no gain twice. On fourth down and goal, quarterback Carl Brumbaugh handed off to Nagurski, who faked a plunge into the line, backed up two steps, and passed

Chicago Stadium, 1932 indoor playoff, Chicago Bears vs. Portsmouth Spartans.

to Red Grange in the end zone for a touchdown.

The rules of football stated that passes had to be thrown from at least five yards behind the line of scrimmage. Angry coach George (Potsy) Clark of Portsmouth screamed that Nagurski's pass to George broke this rule. His words fell on deaf ears. Chicago added a safety and won 9-0.

1932 STANDINGS

	W	L	T	Pct.
Chicago Bears	7	1	6	.875
Green Bay Packers	10	3	1	.769
Portsmouth, Ohio, Spartans	6	2	4	.750
Boston Braves	4	4	2	.500
New York Giants	4	6	2	.400
Brooklyn Dodgers	3	9	0	.250
Chicago Cardinals	2	6	2	.250
Stapleton Stapes	2	7	3	.222

1933 The NFL made a significant change in the rules of football for the first time and began to independently develop rules serving its needs and the style of play it preferred. As a result of the successful use of inbounds lines or hashmarks in the Chicago Stadium indoor playoff of 1932, the NFL passed a rule that the ball would be moved in 10 yards to inbounds lines whenever it was in play within five yards of the side lines. The goal posts were moved from the end lines to the goal lines to help field goal kickers, increase scoring, and reduce the number of tie games.

The league had 10 members and at the suggestion of George Preston Marshall of Boston it was divided into two five-team divisions, the winners of each to meet at the end of the season in a championship game, a parallel to baseball's World Series. Thus division play in football and the NFL championship were born.

Philadelphia returned to the NFL, and Pittsburgh, site of the first known pro football in the United States in 1892, joined the league. The Frankford Yellowjackets' franchise that had been inactive for a year was declared forfeited and the Philadelphia territory was awarded to Bert Bell and Lud Wray, who named their team the "Eagles" and adopted the symbol, an eagle, of the National Recovery Administration of the "New Deal" of President Franklin D. Roosevelt for the nation's recovery from the depression. A franchise for Pittsburgh was awarded to Art Rooney and he named it "Pirates"; that was also the name of the baseball team that played at Forbes Field.

Boston changed its name from Braves to "Redskins."

George Halas bought out his partner, Ed (Dutch) Sternaman, and became sole owner of the Chicago Bears.

The Stapleton Stapes disbanded. The Cincinnati Reds joined the league.

Harry Newman, New York Giants' rookie from Michigan, completed 11 touchdown passes. John (Shipwreck) Kelly, co owner of the Brooklyn Dodgers, led the league in pass receiving with 22 catches, the last time a back led the league in that statistic for 41 years. Ken Strong left the defunct Stapes, joined the New York Giants, and tied for the league scoring championship with Portsmouth's Glenn Presnell; each made 64 points.

Earl (Dutch) Clark decided to remain at his job as coach at Colorado College and did not play for the Portsmouth Spartans.

The New York Giants became the first Eastern Division champion and the Chicago Bears the first Western Division champion. They played the first NFL championship game in history at Wrigley Field in Chicago December 17. The Bears won 23-21 on a touchdown in the fourth quarter when Bronko Nagurski threw a pass to Bill Hewitt, who lateraled the ball to Bill Karr, who scored.

1933 STANDINGS

Eastern Division	W	L	T	Pct.	Pts.	OP
N.Y. Giants	11	3	0	.786	244	101
Brooklyn Dodgers	5	4	1	.556	93	54
Boston Redskins	5	5	2	.500	103	97
Philadelphia	3	5	1	.375	77	158
Pittsburgh	3	6	2	.333	67	208
Western Division	W	L	T	Pct.	Pts.	OP
Chi. Bears	10	2	1	.833	133	82
Portsmouth Spartans . . .	6	5	0	.545	128	87
Green Bay	5	7	1	.417	170	107
Cincinnati Reds	3	6	1	.333	38	110
Chi. Cardinals	1	9	1	.100	52	101

NFL championship: Chi. Bears 23, N.Y. Giants 21

LEADING RUSHERS

	Att.	Yards	Avg.	TD
Jim Musick, Boston	173	809	4.7	5
Cliff Battles, Boston	136	737	5.4	3
Bronko Nagurski, Chi. Bears	128	533	4.2	1
Glenn Presnell, Portsmouth	118	522	4.5	6
Tom Hanson, Philadelphia	133	475	3.6	3

LEADING PASSERS

	Att.	Comp.	Yards	TD	Int.
Harry Newman, N.Y. Giants	136	53	973	11	17
Glenn Presnell, Portsmouth	125	50	774	6	12
Arnie Herber, Green Bay	124	50	656	3	12
Benny Friedman, Brooklyn	80	42	594	5	7
Chris Cagle, Brooklyn	74	31	457	2	10

LEADING RECEIVERS

	No.	Yards	Avg.	TD
John (Shipwreck) Kelly, Brooklyn	22	246	11.2	3
Roger Grove, Green Bay	17	215	12.6	0
Ray Tesser, Pittsburgh	14	282	20.1	0
Bill Hewitt, Chi. Bears	14	273	19.5	2
Lavern Dilweg, Green Bay	13	225	17.3	0
Paul Moss, Pittsburgh	13	283	21.8	2
Les Peterson, Brooklyn	13	170	13.1	0

Mel Hein (7) and Ray Flaherty of the New York Giants tackling Bronko Nagurski of the Chicago Bears, 1934 championship, the "Sneakers Game."

1934 Professional football gained new prestige and there was more press and fan interest in it when the Chicago Bears, NFL champions, were matched against the best, most famous college players in the first Chicago All-Star Game. The *Chicago Tribune* sponsored the game and the college all-stars were selected in a poll of 105 newspapers throughout the country. Noble Kizer of Purdue accepted the job of coaching the all-stars despite the fact that some of his associates urged him not to coach a game against professionals. The game was a scoreless tie and there were only nine first downs but there was a huge crowd of 79,432 fans to see the game at Soldier Field on the lakefront in Chicago.

The NFL committed itself to a more wide-open game with more forward passes when it passed a rule permitting them to be thrown anywhere behind the line of scrimmage, a decision growing out of the controversial pass by Bronko Nagurski in the 1932 indoor playoff game.

G. A. (Dick) Richards bought the Portsmouth Spartans and moved them to Detroit, to play their games at University of Detroit Stadium and take the name "Lions." Dutch Clark ended his one-year retirement and rejoined the team.

The Cincinnati Reds lost eight straight games and the franchise and some of the players moved to St. Louis. The team played three games, losing two of them, as the St. Louis Gunners.

Beattie Feathers, rookie halfback for the Chicago

Bears, followed the blocking of fullback Bronko Nagurski and became the first professional runner in history to gain 1,000 yards in a season when he gained 1,004. "Did you ever see a fellow run so fast and so low as that Feathers?" Jack McEwan of Brooklyn asked after the Bears defeated the Dodgers 21–7 at Ebbets Field. "He's a sweetheart of a football player and he certainly beat us today."

Chicago won 13 straight games, and the new Detroit Lions' team, which had a tremendous defensive record, scoring seven consecutive shutouts, had to settle for second place in the Western Division behind Chicago. The two division rivals met in the first Thanksgiving Day game in Detroit, starting a pro football tradition there, and Chicago won 19–16. It was the first NFL game broadcast nationally; Graham McNamee was the announcer for NBC Radio.

The Bears had played in the first Chicago All-Star Game, given the league its first 1,000-yard rusher, won 13 straight games, and had one of their games broadcast nationally on radio. They appeared to be an unbeatable team as they faced the Eastern Division champion New York Giants for the NFL championship. It was an extremely cold day at the Polo Grounds in New York City and the field was icy and slick. Some of the Giants' players put on basketball shoes or sneakers at halftime to gain better footing and defeated the Bears 30-13 for the championship. The game was dubbed the "Sneakers Game." The winning share for the Giants' players was $621.

Red Grange retired from professional football.

1934 STANDINGS

Eastern Division

	W	L	T	Pct.	Pts.	OP
N.Y. Giants	8	5	0	.615	147	107
Boston Redskins	6	6	0	.500	107	94
Brooklyn Dodgers	4	7	0	.364	61	153
Philadelphia	4	7	0	.364	127	85
Pittsburgh	2	10	0	.167	51	206

Western Division

	W	L	T	Pct.	Pts.	OP
Chi. Bears	13	0	0	1.000	286	86
Detroit	10	3	0	.769	238	59
Green Bay	7	6	0	.538	156	112
Chi. Cardinals	5	6	0	.455	80	84
St. Louis Gunners	1	2	0	.333	27	61
Cincinnati Reds	0	8	0	.000	10	243

NFL championship: N.Y. Giants 30, Chi. Bears 13

LEADING RUSHERS

	Att.	Yards	Avg.	TD
Beattie Feathers, Chi. Bears	101	1,004	9.9	8
Tom Hanson, Philadelphia	146	805	5.5	7
Earl (Dutch) Clark, Detroit	123	763	6.2	8
Bronko Nagurski, Chi. Bears	123	586	4.8	7
Etnie Caddel, Detroit	105	528	5.0	4
Warren Heller, Pittsburgh	132	528	4.0	1

LEADING PASSERS

	Att.	Comp.	Yards	TD	Int.
Arnie Herber, Green Bay	115	42	799	8	12
Harry Newman, N.Y. Giants	93	35	391	1	12
Warren Heller, Pittsburgh	112	31	511	2	15
Earl (Dutch) Clark, Detroit	50	23	383	0	3
Ed Matesic, Philadelphia	60	20	278	2	5

LEADING RECEIVERS

	No.	Yards	Avg.	TD
Joe Carter, Philadelphia	16	238	14.9	4
Morris (Red) Badgro, N.Y. Giants	16	206	12.9	1
Ben Smith, Pittsburgh	14	218	15.6	0
John Grossman, Brooklyn	11	161	14.6	1
Charley Malone, Boston	11	131	11.9	2
Clarke Hinkle, Green Bay	11	113	10.3	1

1935 The Reds-Gunners franchise that had played in two cities did not return and professional football was reduced to nine teams again.

Alarmed by the domination of the league by the Chicago Bears and New York Giants, Bert Bell of Philadelphia proposed in May that the NFL teams draft college players, with the team that finished last in the standings having the first choice in each round of the draft. The proposal was accepted and the first draft was scheduled for 1936.

End Don Hutson of the University of Alabama joined the Green Bay Packers and made a feared passing combination with tailback Arnie Herber.

The inbounds lines or hashmarks established at 10 yards in 1933 were moved nearer the center of the field, 15 yards from each side line.

Detroit ousted the Chicago Bears as Western Division champions and, led by Earl (Dutch) Clark and Leroy (Ace) Gutowsky, defeated the New York Giants 26-7 in the NFL championship game on a raw, snowy day at the University of Detroit Stadium before a sparse crowd of 15,000 fans. Raymond (Buddy) Parker, a rookie back for the Lions, scored his team's final touchdown. The victory gave Detroit the football and baseball championships of 1935; the baseball Tigers had won their first World Series earlier.

1935 STANDINGS

Eastern Division	W	L	T	Pct.	Pts.	OP
N. Y. Giants	9	3	0	.750	180	96
Brooklyn Dodgers	5	6	1	.455	90	141
Pittsburgh	4	8	0	.333	100	209
Boston Redskins	2	8	1	.200	65	123
Philadelphia	2	9	0	.182	60	179
Western Division	**W**	**L**	**T**	**Pct.**	**Pts.**	**OP**
Detroit	7	3	2	.700	191	111
Green Bay	8	4	0	.667	181	96
Chi. Bears	6	4	2	.600	192	106
Chi. Cardinals	6	4	2	.600	99	97

NFL championship: Detroit 26, N.Y. Giants 7
One game between Boston and Philadelphia was canceled.

LEADING RUSHERS	Att.	Yards	Avg.	TD
Doug Russell, Chi. Cardinals	140	499	3.6	0
Ernie Caddel, Detroit	87	450	5.2	6
Elvin (Kink) Richards, N.Y. Giants	153	449	2.9	4
Earl (Dutch) Clark, Detroit	120	427	3.6	4
Bill Shepherd, Boston–Detroit	143	425	3.0	4

LEADING PASSERS	Att.	Comp.	Yards	TD	Int.
Ed Danowski, N.Y. Giants	113	57	794	10	9
Arnie Herber, Green Bay	109	40	729	8	14
Bob Monnett, Green Bay	65	31	354	2	5
Phil Sarboe, Chi. Cardinals	67	31	368	0	10
Bill Shepherd, Boston–Detroit	64	28	417	2	14
John Gildea, Pittsburgh	105	28	529	2	20

LEADING RECEIVERS	No.	Yards	Avg.	TD
Tod Goodwin, N.Y. Giants	26	432	16.6	4
J. Blood (McNally), Green Bay	25	404	16.2	3
Bill Smith, Chi. Cardinals	24	318	13.3	2
Charley Malone, Boston	22	433	19.7	2
Luke Johnsos, Chi. Bears	19	298	15.7	4

1936 There were no franchise shifts for the first time since the formation of the NFL. It also was the first year in which all member teams played the same number of games.

The player limit was increased to 25.

The Philadelphia Eagles of Bert Bell finished last with a 2–9 record, so the man who had proposed the draft now made the first choice in the first draft. Philadelphia chose Jay Berwanger, All-America halfback of the University of Chicago. The Eagles, however, traded the negotiation rights to him to the Chicago Bears in exchange for tackle Art Buss. Berwanger never agreed to terms with the Bears and never played pro football. The Bears, however, made exceptional choices when they took tackle Joe Stydahar of West Virginia and guard Danny Fortmann of Colgate.

A rival league was formed and it became the second organization to call itself the American Football League. The Boston Shamrocks was its champion and the other teams were the Brooklyn Tigers, Cleveland Rams, New York Yankees, Pittsburgh Ameri-

Five members of the 1934 St. Louis Gunners, one of whom disdained a helmet.

Jay Berwanger of the University of Chicago, first draft choice, 1936.

Sammy Baugh of Washington passing against the Chicago Bears, 1937 championship.

Johnny Blood (McNally), Byron (Whizzer) White, and Art Rooney, left to right, 1938 Pittsburgh Pirates.

cans, and Rochester Tigers. It was the "second AFL".

Green Bay had Arnie Herber and Clarke Hinkle in its backfield and Don Hutson at end. Hutson scored eight touchdowns and the Packers easily won the Western Division. The Boston Redskins emerged as a strong team and captured the Eastern Division championship.

There were only 5,000 fans at Fenway Park in Boston when the Redskins defeated Pittsburgh to win the division title. An angry George Preston Marshall, owner of the Boston team, moved the championship game with Green Bay to the Polo Grounds in New York. A crowd of 29,545 attended as Herber and Hutson led Green Bay to a 21–6 victory over Marshall's Redskins.

1936 STANDINGS

Eastern Division	W	L	T	Pct.	Pts.	OP
Boston Redskins	7	5	0	.583	149	110
Pittsburgh	6	6	0	.500	98	187
N.Y. Giants	5	6	1	.455	115	163
Brooklyn Dodgers	3	8	1	.273	92	161
Philadelphia	1	11	0	.083	51	206
Western Division	W	L	T	Pct.	Pts.	OP
Green Bay	10	1	1	.909	248	118
Chi. Bears	9	3	0	.750	222	94
Detroit	8	4	0	.667	235	102
Chi. Cardinals	3	8	1	.273	74	143

NFL championship: Green Bay 21, Boston 6

LEADING RUSHERS	Att.	Yards	Avg.	TD
A. (Tuffy) Leemans, N.Y. Giants	206	830	4.0	2
Leroy (Ace) Gutowsky, Detroit	191	827	4.3	5
Earl (Dutch) Clark, Detroit	123	628	5.1	7
Cliff Battles, Boston	176	614	3.5	5
G.Grosvenor, Chi. Bears–Cardinals	170	612	3.6	4

LEADING PASSERS	Att.	Comp.	Yards	TD	Int.
Arnie Herber, Green Bay	173	77	1,239	11	13
Ed Matesic, Pittsburgh	138	64	850	4	16
Phil Sarboe, Chi. Card.–Brooklyn	114	47	680	3	13
Ed Danowski, N.Y. Giants	104	47	515	5	10
Earl (Dutch) Clark, Detroit	71	38	.467	4	6

LEADING RECEIVERS	No.	Yards	Avg.	TD
Don Hutson, Green Bay	34	536	15.8	8
Bill Smith, Chi. Cardinals	20	414	20.7	1
Ernie Caddel, Detroit	19	150	7.9	1
Wayne Millner, Boston	18	211	11.7	0
E. (Eggs) Manske, Philadelphia	17	325	19.1	0

1937 George Preston Marshall moved the Redskins from Boston to his hometown of Washington, D.C. Griffith Stadium was leased for the Redskins' games. Washington signed All-America quarterback (tailback) Sammy Baugh of Texas Christian University to a contract for $8,000.

The nation's capital embraced the exciting Redskins. A Friday night game against the New York Giants was moved up to Thursday night so it would not conflict with one of President Franklin D. Roosevelt's "fireside chats" on the radio. The Redskins played the Giants in another game in New York and 12,000 fans accompanied them on the trip.

There had been a Cleveland Rams team in the 1936 season of the second American Football League. A new team called the Cleveland Rams, which had no relationship to the former team other than it had the same name, was formed by Homer Marshman and joined the NFL. The league once more had 10 teams.

Dutch Clark became the coach of the Detroit Lions and Johnny Blood (McNally) the coach of the Pittsburgh Pirates.

Philadelphia made the first draft choice again, selecting back Sam Francis of Nebraska but trading the rights to him to the Chicago Bears.

Tailback Clarence (Ace) Parker was a rookie star for the Brooklyn Dodgers. Rookies Pat Coffee and Gaynell Tinsley of Louisiana State University combined on a 97-yard touchdown pass while playing for the Chicago Cardinals against the Bears.

The Los Angeles Bulldogs had an 8–0 record in the American Football League, which then folded. The other 1937 teams were the Boston Shamrocks, Cincinnati Bengals, New York Yankees, Pittsburgh Americans, and Rochester Tigers.

Baugh was the NFL's leading passer and the Redskins won six of their last seven games enroute to the Eastern Division championship. They met the Western champions, the Chicago Bears, on a frigid day at Griffith Stadium in Washington. Despite the bitter cold, Baugh had a sensational passing game in which he completed 18 of 33 for an unprecedented 335 yards. The Redskins were the NFL champions, 28–21.

Bronko Nagurski of the Chicago Bears retired from football.

1937 STANDINGS

Eastern Division	W	L	T	Pct.	Pts.	OP
Washington	8	3	0	.727	195	120
N.Y. Giants	6	3	2	.667	128	109
Pittsburgh	4	7	0	.364	122	145
Brooklyn Dodgers	3	7	1	.300	82	174
Philadelphia	2	8	1	.200	86	177
Western Division	W	L	T	Pct.	Pts.	OP
Chi. Bears	9	1	1	.900	201	100
Green Bay	7	4	0	.636	220	122
Detroit	7	4	0	.636	180	105
Chi. Cardinals	5	5	1	.500	135	165
Cleveland Rams	1	10	0	.091	75	207

NFL championship: Washington 28, Chi. Bears 21

LEADING RUSHERS	Att.	Yards	Avg.	TD
Cliff Battles, Washington	216	874	4.0	5
Clarke Hinkle, Green Bay	129	552	4.3	5
John Karcis, Pittsburgh	127	513	4.0	3
Earl (Dutch) Clark, Detroit	96	468	4.9	5
George Grosvenor, Chi. Cardinals	143	461	3.2	2

LEADING PASSERS	Att.	Comp.	Yards	TD	Int.
Sammy Baugh, Washington	171	81	1,127	8	14
Ed Danowski, N.Y. Giants	134	66	814	8	5
J. (Pat) Coffee, Chi. Cardinals	119	52	824	4	11
Arnie Herber, Green Bay	104	47	684	7	10
Dave Smukler, Philadelphia	118	42	432	5	14

LEADING RECEIVERS	No.	Yards	Avg.	TD
Don Hutson, Green Bay	41	552	13.5	7
Gaynell Tinsley, Chi. Cardinals	36	675	18.8	5
Charley Malone, Washington	28	419	15.0	4
Jeff Barrett, Brooklyn	20	461	23.1	3
Bill Hewitt, Philadelphia	16	197	12.3	5

1938 Baugh of the Redskins had gotten rough treatment at times during his rookie season and, as a result, the rules were changed. A new rule called for a 15-yard penalty for roughing the passer after the ball had left his hand. The player limit increased to 30.

Hugh (Shorty) Ray, a Chicago school teacher, coach, and supervisor of football officials, became a technical advisor to the NFL on rules, at the suggestion of owner George Halas of the Chicago Bears.

Corbett Davis, back from Indiana, was the first choice in the NFL draft. He was the selection of the Cleveland Rams, who had finished 1–10. Sid Luckman was a rookie with the Chicago Bears, Ward Cuff with the New York Giants, Frank (Bruiser) Kinard with the Brooklyn Dodgers, and Alex Wojciechowicz with the Detroit Lions. Pittsburgh shocked the other teams when owner Art Rooney gave a $15,800 contract to All-America Byron (Whizzer) White of Colorado to play for the Pirates. White had a storied career in college, scoring 34 points in his last game at Colorado. He became the NFL's leading rusher with 567 yards as a rookie, but the Pirates won only two games and finished last in the Eastern Division.

The New York Giants captured the East, defeating the Redskins 36–0 on the last day of the season. Green Bay won the Western Division; Detroit was second. The Giants defeated Green Bay 23–17 in the NFL championship before a record crowd of 48,120 at the Polo Grounds.

George Preston Marshall of the Redskins had met in Los Angeles during the summer with two notable sports figures to discuss a pet idea of his. He wanted an annual all-star game between the league champions and a team of all-stars. He sold the idea to sports editor Bill Henry of the *Los Angeles Times* and promoter Tom Gallery. The game was to be called the "Pro Bowl."

Don Hutson, left, and Arnie Herber, Green Bay Packers.

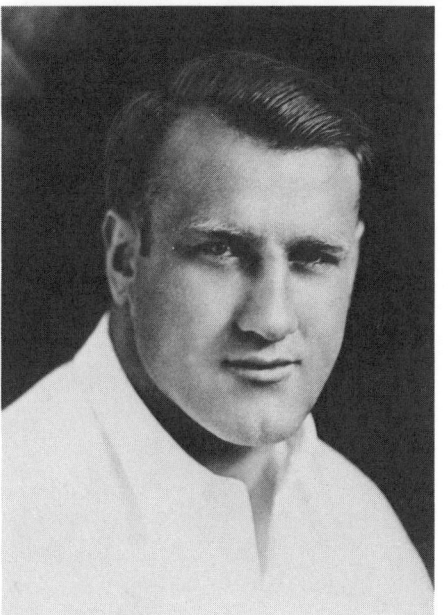

Bronko Nagurski.

A Chicago Bears' poster.

1938 STANDINGS

Eastern Division	W	L	T	Pct.	Pts.	OP
N.Y. Giants	8	2	1	.800	194	79
Washington	6	3	2	.667	148	154
Brooklyn Dodgers	4	4	3	.500	131	161
Philadelphia	5	6	0	.455	154	164
Pittsburgh	2	9	0	.182	79	169
Western Division	W	L	T	Pct.	Pts.	OP
Green Bay	8	3	0	.727	223	118
Detroit	7	4	0	.636	119	108
Chi. Bears	6	5	0	.545	194	148
Cleveland Rams	4	7	0	.364	131	215
Chi. Cardinals	2	9	0	.182	111	168

NFL championship: N.Y. Giants 23, Green Bay 17

LEADING RUSHERS	Att.	Yards	Avg.	TD
Byron (Whizzer) White, Pittsburgh	152	567	3.7	4
A. (Tuffy) Leemans, N.Y. Giants	121	463	3.8	4
Bill Shepherd, Detroit	100	455	4.6	3
Cecil Isbell, Green Bay	85	445	5.2	2
Leroy (Ace) Gutowsky, Detroit	131	444	3.4	2

LEADING PASSERS	Att.	Comp.	Yards	TD	Int.
Ed Danowski, N.Y. Giants	129	70	848	7	8
Clarence (Ace) Parker, Brooklyn	148	63	865	5	7
Sammy Baugh, Washington	128	63	853	5	11
John Robbins, Chi. Cardinals	97	52	577	2	9
Bernie Masterson, Chi. Bears	112	46	848	5	9

LEADING RECEIVERS	No.	Yards	Avg.	TD
Gaynell Tinsley, Chi. Cardinals	41	516	12.6	1
Don Hutson, Green Bay	32	548	17.1	9
Joe Carter, Philadelphia	27	386	14.3	7
Charley Malone, Washington	24	257	10.7	1
Jim Benton, Cleveland	21	418	19.9	5

1939 The first Pro Bowl game was played at Wrigley Field in Los Angeles January 15. The champion New York Giants defeated the "Pro All-Stars" 13–10 before a crowd of 20,000.

Joe F. Carr, president of the National Football League since 1921, died May 20. Secretary-treasurer Carl Storck was named to succeed Carr as acting president.

An NFL game was televised for the first time when the National Broadcasting Company took a camera to Ebbets Field in Brooklyn October 22 and beamed the game between the Dodgers and the Pittsburgh Pirates back to the studios of the network and to the handful of sets then in New York.

Sid Luckman replaced Bernie Masterson as the starting quarterback for the Chicago Bears. They played the T formation with man-in-motion while other clubs played long-snap formations such as the so-called "A" formation and double and single wing. Clark Shaughnessy of the University of Chicago was assisting George Halas and his Bears' coaching staff in developing new plays. Luckman became the smart leader and good ball-handler Halas needed to run the system, which was becoming more and more complex and radical. Bill Osmanski, the Bears' rookie fullback from Holy Cross, led the league in rushing with 699 yards.

New York and Washington were strong again and owner Marshall of the Redskins led both a parade of some 12,000 fans from Washington and the Redskins' Band up Broadway on the way to the Polo Grounds at 151st Street for the final game of the regular season. Sportswriter Bill Corum wrote later that, "At the head of a 150-piece brass band and 12,000 fans, George Preston Marshall slipped unobtrusively into New York today."

New York won the game, however, 9–7 and Marshall was angry afterwards, yelling "foul" over a call by referee Bill Halloran that a Redskins' field goal attempt by Torrance (Bo) Russell was no good.

The Giants were Eastern champions. They went to Wisconsin to meet the Western Division champion Green Bay Packers. There was limited seating in City Stadium in Green Bay, so the game was moved to the Wisconsin State Fair Park in Milwaukee and the ticket price increased to $4.40. A crowd of 32,279 watched as coach Earl (Curly) Lambeau gained revenge for the previous year's defeat with a 27–0 triumph for the NFL championship.

League attendance set a record. It was 1,071,200.

Davey O'Brien, Philadelphia Eagles.

Elmer Layden, NFL commissioner.

Art Rooney, left, and Bert Bell, Pittsburgh Pirates.

1939 STANDINGS

Eastern Division	W	L	T	Pct.	Pts.	OP
N.Y. Giants	9	1	1	.900	168	85
Washington	8	2	1	.800	242	94
Brooklyn Dodgers	4	6	1	.400	108	219
Philadelphia	1	9	1	.100	105	200
Pittsburgh	1	9	1	.100	114	216
Western Division	W	L	T	Pct.	Pts.	OP
Green Bay	9	2	0	.818	233	153
Chi. Bears	8	3	0	.727	298	157
Detroit	6	5	0	.545	145	150
Cleveland Rams	5	5	1	.500	195	164
Chi. Cardinals	1	10	0	.091	84	254

NFL championship: Green Bay 27, N.Y. Giants 0

LEADING RUSHERS	Att.	Yards	Avg.	TD
Bill Osmanski, Chi. Bears	121	699	5.8	7
Andy Farkas, Washington	139	547	3.9	5
Joe Maniaci, Chi. Bears	77	544	7.1	4
Clarence (Pug) Manders, Brooklyn	114	482	4.2	2
Parker Hall, Cleveland	120	458	3.8	2

LEADING PASSERS	Att.	Comp.	Yards	TD	Int.
Parker Hall, Cleveland	208	106	1,227	9	13
Davey O'Brien, Philadelphia	201	99	1,324	6	17
Clarence (Ace) Parker, Brooklyn	157	72	977	4	13
Arnie Herber, Green Bay	139	57	1,107	8	9
Frank Filchock, Washington	89	55	1,094	11	7

LEADING RECEIVERS	No.	Yards	Avg.	TD
Don Hutson, Green Bay	34	846	24.9	6
Perry Schwartz, Brooklyn	33	550	16.7	3
Vic Spadaccini, Cleveland	32	292	9.1	1
Herschel Ramsey, Philadelphia	31	359	11.6	1
Jim Benton, Cleveland	27	288	14.4	7

1940 Art Rooney left professional football, selling the Pittsburgh Pirates to Alexis Thompson. George Richards sold the Detroit Lions to Fred Mandel after the Lions were fined $5,000 by NFL president Carl Storck; the Lions had tampered with Clyde (Bulldog) Turner of Hardin-Simmons College after he had been drafted by the Chicago Bears.

Dr. John Bain (Jock) Sutherland, the former coach of national championship teams at the University of Pittsburgh, moved into pro football as coach of the Brooklyn Dodgers. Jimmy Conzelman took over as coach of the Chicago Cardinals.

Turner, back George McAfee, end Ken Kavanaugh, and linemen Ed Kolman and Lee Artoe joined the powerful Chicago Bears.

For the third time, a rival league appeared to challenge the NFL. Just as the earlier rival leagues had done, this one took the name "American Football League." The Columbus Bullies won its championship with an 8–1–1 record and the other teams were the Boston Bears, Buffalo Indians, Cincinnati Bengals, Milwaukee Chiefs, and New York Yankees.

Byron (Whizzer) White had been in England for studies as a Rhodes scholar. He returned to pro football, this time with the Detroit Lions, and again led the league in rushing, gaining 514 yards. Quarterback Davey O'Brien of the Philadelphia Eagles threw 60 passes in one game. End Don Looney of the Eagles caught 58 passes for the season.

The Chicago Bears won the Western Division, the Washington Redskins the Eastern Division. Chicago lost only three games, one of them to the Redskins by the score of 7–3; there was a disputed play late in the game in which the Bears demanded a pass interference call and were denied. George Preston Marshall of the Redskins later called the Bears "crybabies." The NFL championship game between the two teams was to be in Washington.

Clark Shaughnessy, who had become coach of Stanford University in Palo Alto, California, and won 10 straight games using the T formation with man-in-motion, rejoined the Bears for their preparations. He studied film of the 7–3 game and saw that the Redskins had a predictable defense. They stayed in a five-three and always shifted their linebackers toward the man-in-motion. He and the Bears' coaches saw that it was an easy defense to exploit. Counter plays were put in the game plan to send Bears' runners away from the movement of the linebackers. The Bears would control the ball, it was decided, and keep it away from Washington's great passer, Sammy Baugh. Shaughnessy also wrote new terminology for Bears' play-calling that made the team's blocking more efficient.

Fullback Bill Osmanski ran 68 yards for a touchdown on the second play of the game. It was not a counter play. Rather, it was to the same side as the man-in-motion, George McAfee, and Osmanski started off left guard but then cut outside. End George Wilson made a great block clearing the last Redskins' defender out of the way downfield.

Chicago's offense continued to work efficiently and mow down the Redskins. Baugh and other Washington tailbacks threw careless passes that the Bears returned for touchdowns. When it was over, the Bears had won the NFL championship by the astounding score of 73–0, the most one-sided of all title games and one of the most celebrated victories in football history.

The championship game was the first ever carried on network radio. Red Barber broadcast it to 120 stations of the Mutual Broadcasting System, which paid $2,500 for the rights to the game.

1940 STANDINGS

Eastern Division	W	L	T	Pct.	Pts.	OP
Washington	9	2	0	.818	245	142
Brooklyn Dodgers	8	3	0	.727	186	120
N.Y. Giants	6	4	1	.600	131	133
Pittsburgh	2	7	2	.222	60	178
Philadelphia	1	10	0	.091	111	211
Western Division	W	L	T	Pct.	Pts.	OP
Chi. Bears	8	3	0	.727	238	152
Green Bay	6	4	1	.600	238	155
Detroit	5	5	1	.500	138	153
Cleveland Rams	4	6	1	.400	171	191
Chi. Cardinals	2	7	2	.222	139	222

NFL championship: Chi. Bears 73, Washington 0

LEADING RUSHERS	Att.	Yards	Avg.	TD
Byron (Whizzer) White, Detroit	146	514	3.5	5
Johnny Drake, Cleveland	134	480	3.6	9
A. (Tuffy) Leemans, N.Y. Giants	132	474	3.6	1
Banks McFadden, Brooklyn	65	411	6.3	1
Dick Todd, Washington	76	408	5.4	4

LEADING PASSERS	Att.	Comp.	Yards	TD	Int.
Sammy Baugh, Washington	177	111	1,367	12	10
Davey O'Brien, Philadelphia	277	124	1,290	5	17
Cecil Isbell, Green Bay	150	68	1,037	9	12
Sid Luckman, Chi. Bears	105	48	941	4	9
Clarence (Ace) Parker, Brooklyn	111	49	817	10	7

LEADING RECEIVERS	No.	Yards	Avg.	TD
Don Looney, Philadelphia	58	707	12.1	4
Don Hutson, Green Bay	45	664	14.7	7
Jimmy Johnston, Washington	29	350	12.1	3
Jim Benton, Cleveland Rams	22	351	15.9	3
Vic Spadaccini, Cleveland Rams	22	276	12.5	2

1941 Elmer Layden, head coach and athletic director at the University of Notre Dame, and one of that university's famous "Four Horsemen" backfield of the 1920s, was named the first commissioner of the National Football League March 1. The title of "president" was discarded. Layden established the NFL office in Chicago. Carl Storck, acting president of the league since the death of Joe Carr in 1939, resigned.

Art Rooney returned to pro football, buying half-interest in the Philadelphia Eagles. He and Bert Bell were co-owners of the Eagles. They swapped them to Alexis Thompson in exchange for the Pittsburgh Steelers.

Homer Marshman sold the Cleveland Rams to Dan Reeves and Fred Levy, Jr.

The league by-laws were revised to provide for playoffs in case there were ties in division races, and sudden death overtime in case a playoff game was tied after four quarters.

An official *Record Manual* was published by the NFL for the first time. It replaced the pro football guides that had been published by the Spalding sporting goods company in the 1930s.

The third American Football League folded.

Earle (Greasy) Neale became the head coach and Tommy Thompson the quarterback of the Philadel-

Sid Luckman, hooded, and George Halas during the 1940 championship game.

Perry Schwartz gaining a first down for the Brooklyn Dodgers vs. Washington, 1941.

Tom Harmon of N.Y. Americans vs. Chicago Bulls, his first pro touchdown, 1941, the second AFL.

crushed the New York Giants 37–9 for the title.

1941 STANDINGS

Eastern Division	W	L	T	Pct.	Pts.	OP
N.Y. Giants	8	3	0	.727	238	114
Brooklyn Dodgers	7	4	0	.636	158	127
Washington	6	5	0	.545	176	174
Philadelphia	2	8	1	.200	119	218
Pittsburgh	1	9	1	.100	103	276

Western Division	W	L	T	Pct.	Pts.	OP
Chi. Bears	10	1	0	.909	396	147
Green Bay	10	1	0	.909	258	120
Detroit	4	6	1	.400	121	195
Chi. Cardinals	3	7	1	.300	127	197
Cleveland Rams	2	9	0	.182	116	244

Western Division playoff: Chi. Bears 33, Green Bay 14
NFL championship: Chi. Bears 37, N.Y. Giants 9

LEADING RUSHERS	Att.	Yards	Avg.	Long	TD
Clarence (Pug) Manders, Brooklyn	111	486	4.4	46	7
George McAfee, Chi. Bears	65	474	7.3	70	9
Marshall Goldberg, Chi. Cardinals	117	427	3.6	25	3
Norm Standlee, Chi. Bears	81	414	5.1	46	5
Clarke Hinkle, Green Bay	129	393	3.0	20	5

LEADING PASSERS	Att.	Comp.	Yards	TD	Int.
Cecil Isbell, Green Bay	206	117	1,479	15	11
Sammy Baugh, Washington	193	106	1,236	10	19
Sid Luckman, Chi. Bears	119	68	1,181	9	6
Tommy Thompson, Philadelphia	162	86	974	8	14
Clarence (Ace) Parker, Brooklyn	102	51	642	2	8

LEADING RECEIVERS	No.	Yards	Avg.	Long	TD
Don Hutson, Green Bay	58	738	12.7	45	10
Dick Humbert, Philadelphia	29	332	11.4	33	3
Bill Dewell, Chi. Cardinals	28	262	9.4	30	1
Perry Schwartz, Brooklyn	25	362	14.5	36	2
Lou Brock, Green Bay	22	307	14.0	36	2

1942 World War II ravaged the rosters and staffs of NFL teams. Numerous players, coaches, and team owners departed to serve in the armed forces. Teams became filled with men who had failed the draft physical examination and were classified "4-F," or older players who were beyond military age.

Don Hutson of the Green Bay Packers had a spectacular year, catching 74 passes for 1,211 yards and 17 touchdowns and scoring 138 points. Bill Dudley, star tailback in the Pittsburgh Steelers' single wing, gained 696 yards rushing.

Washington was still strong with Ray Flaherty as coach and Sammy Baugh was the team's star tailback. The Chicago Bears still had Sid Luckman as quarterback of their T formation but owner and coach George Halas left the team to join the armed forces. Assistant coaches Heartley (Hunk) Anderson and Luke Johnsos became co-coaches of the Bears.

The Redskins gained revenge for the 73–0 defeat in 1940 when they defeated the Bears 14–6 for the NFL championship.

1942 STANDINGS

Eastern Division	W	L	T	Pct.	Pts.	OP
Washington	10	1	0	.909	227	102
Pittsburgh	7	4	0	.636	167	119
N.Y. Giants	5	5	1	.500	155	139
Brooklyn Dodgers	3	8	0	.273	100	168
Philadelphia	2	9	0	.182	134	239

Western Division	W	L	T	Pct.	Pts.	OP
Chi. Bears	11	0	0	1.000	376	84
Green Bay	8	2	1	.800	300	215
Cleveland Rams	5	6	0	.455	150	207
Chi. Cardinals	3	8	0	.273	98	209
Detroit	0	11	0	.000	38	263

NFL championship: Washington 14, Chi. Bears 6

LEADING RUSHERS	Att.	Yards	Avg.	Long	TD
Bill Dudley, Pittsburgh	162	696	4.3	66	6
Merlyn Condit, Brooklyn	129	647	5.0	63	3
Gary Famiglietti, Chi. Bears	118	503	4.2	21	8
Andy Farkas, Washington	125	468	3.7	22	4
Dick Riffle, Pittsburgh	115	467	4.0	46	4

LEADING PASSERS	Att.	Comp.	Yards	TD	Int.
Cecil Isbell, Green Bay	268	146	2,021	24	14
Sammy Baugh, Washington	225	132	1,524	16	11
Sid Luckman, Chi. Bears	105	47	1,023	10	13
Tommy Thompson, Philadelphia	203	94	1,410	8	16
Wilson Schwenk, Chi. Cardinals	295	126	1,350	6	27

LEADING RECEIVERS	No.	Yards	Avg.	Long	TD
Don Hutson, Green Bay	74	1,211	16.4	73	17
Frank (Pop) Ivy, Chi. Cardinals	24	259	10.8	18	0
Dante Magnani, Cleveland	24	276	11.5	67	4
Jim Benton, Cleveland	23	345	15.0	45	1
Dick Todd, Washington	23	328	14.3	54	4

phia Eagles, and they became the second team after the Chicago Bears to change from a long-snap formation to the T formation.

Co-owner Bert Bell began the season as coach of the Pittsburgh Steelers but stepped down after losing two games and was succeeded by Aldo (Buff) Donelli. Donelli had been coach of Duquesne University and did not resign from that job; he continued to coach Duquesne in the afternoons and the Steelers in the mornings. The situation came to a head when Duquesne was scheduled to play a game at St. Mary's, California, on a Saturday and the Steelers were scheduled to play the Eagles in Philadelphia on Sunday. Donelli chose to attend the college instead of the professional game and was dismissed from his duties with the Steelers. Walt Kiesling coached the team for the rest of the season.

Fullback Norm Standlee of the Chicago Bears and halfback Tony Canadeo of the Green Bay Packers were outstanding rookies for their teams. Tom Harmon of Michigan, the number one draft choice of the league, played for the New York Americans of the AFL and did not sign an NFL contract.

The New York Giants had already clinched the Eastern Division championship and were playing the final game of the season against the Brooklyn Dodgers, December 7. News of the Japanese attack on Pearl Harbor was announced on the public address system and servicemen were instructed to report to their bases.

The Chicago Bears and Green Bay Packers finished in a tie for the Western Division championship, luckily the same year the league had provided for playoffs in case of ties. Chicago defeated Green Bay 33–14 in the first playoff in NFL history the Sunday following the attack on Pearl Harbor. The Bears then

Bill Osmanski (9) and other Chicago Bears tackle Clarke Hinkle of Green Bay, 1941 NFL playoff; 66 is Clyde (Bulldog) Turner.

Sid Luckman of the Bears the day he threw seven touchdown passes vs. New York Giants, 1943.

Don Hutson, Green Bay Packers.

1943 War reduced the NFL to eight teams. The Cleveland Rams' co-owner, Dan Reeves, was in the armed forces and the team asked for and was given permission to suspend its operation for the season. Another team was lost when the Philadelphia Eagles and Pittsburgh Steelers merged themselves, forming a single team called the "Steagles."

Playing talent was scarce. Some worked at defense plants during the day and practiced with their teams at night. Fathers were now being drafted for the war and the NFL, concerned about the effect that would have on its roster, increased the player limit from 25 to 28.

One of the most profound rules changes in NFL history was made when the league voted to permit free substitution. "Platoonery" was one of the disputed elements of football in the game's history and was widely opposed by those who believed the "iron man" who played both ways was more consistent with the rugged nature of the game. Abbreviated NFL rosters during World War II prevented its effects from taking place immediately, but free substitution made possible the development of separate platoons for offense and defense and the appearance of specialists at all positions in pro football.

Bronko Nagurski rejoined the Chicago Bears. He was 34 years old and had not played pro football since his first retirement from the game in 1937. He played tackle and fullback and while at fullback gained 84 yards on 16 carries with a long gain of 11 yards.

Sid Luckman of the Bears threw seven touchdown passes against the New York Giants November 14.

Bill Hewitt, 34, was another retired player who returned to the game. He played for the Steagles. Their games were divided between Philadelphia and Pittsburgh and Earle (Greasy) Neale and Walt Kiesling were co-coaches of the team.

Sammy Baugh, Washington's great player, led the league's quarterbacks with 23 touchdown passes and, playing safety on defense, led the league with 11 interceptions.

Washington tied for the Eastern title with the New York Giants and a playoff was necessary for the second consecutive year. Baugh led the Redskins to an easy 28–0 victory.

The Redskins and Bears played for the championship for the third time in four years and Luckman threw five touchdown passes as Chicago won 41–21. Luckman's touchdown passes set a championship game record. The winning share in the championship game exceeded $1,000 for the first time. Each Bears' player earned $1,146, each Giants' player $765.

1943 STANDINGS

Eastern Division	W	L	T	Pct.	Pts.	OP
Washington	6	3	1	.667	229	137
N.Y. Giants	6	3	1	.667	197	170
Phil–Pitt	5	4	1	.556	225	230
Brooklyn Dodgers	2	8	0	.200	65	234
Western Division	**W**	**L**	**T**	**Pct.**	**Pts.**	**OP**
Chi. Bears	8	1	1	.889	303	157
Green Bay	7	2	1	.778	264	172
Detroit	3	6	1	.333	178	218
Chi. Cardinals	0	10	0	.000	95	238

Eastern Division playoff: Washington 28, N.Y. Giants 0
NFL championship: Chi. Bears 41, Washington 21

LEADING RUSHERS	Att.	Yards	Avg.	Long	TD
Bill Paschal, N.Y. Giants	147	572	3.9	54	10
Clarke Hinkle, Phil–Pitt	116	571	4.9	56	4
Harry Clark, Chi. Bears	120	556	4.6	20	3
Ward Cuff, N. Y. Giants	80	523	6.5	65	3
Tony Canadeo, Green Bay	94	489	5.2	35	3

LEADING PASSERS	Att.	Comp.	Yards	TD	Int.
Sammy Baugh, Washington	329	133	1,754	23	19
Sid Luckman, Chi. Bears	202	110	2.194	28	12
Irv Comp, Green Bay	92	46	662	7	4
Ron Cahill, Chi. Cardinals	109	50	608	3	21
Dean McAdams, Brooklyn	75	37	315	0	7

LEADING RECEIVERS	No.	Yards	Avg.	Long	TD
Don Hutson, Green Bay	47	776	16.5	79	11
Joe Aguirre, Washington	37	420	11.3	44	7
Wilbur Moore, Washington	30	537	17.0	72	7
Ed Rucinski, Chi. Cardinals	26	398	15.3	47	3
Jarry Jacunski, Green Bay	24	528	22.0	86	3

1944 The league's shortage of teams and players remained an acute problem. The Philadelphia-Pittsburgh merger was dissolved and the Eagles began to operate on their own once more. The Steelers, however, merged themselves with the Chicago Cardinals, forming a team called Card-Pitt that had a 0–10 season.

The Cleveland Rams reappeared. The Brooklyn Dodgers changed their name to Brooklyn "Tigers." A tenth team was needed and Ted Collins, who had been trying to get an NFL franchise for years, was granted one to operate in Boston. His preference had been Yankee Stadium in New York. Failing that, he nevertheless named his team the Boston "Yanks."

The manpower shortage was so great that only 12 of the 330 players selected in the NFL draft actually played for their teams in 1944. Center Mel Hein and kicker Ken Strong were brought back to pro football by the New York Giants. The Giants also signed tailback Arnie Herber, who had retired from the Green Bay Packers' team in 1940. Sammy Baugh of the Washington Redskins spent part of the season operating his ranch in Rotan, Texas, and alternated in the Redskins' backfield with Frank Filchock. Clark Shaughnessy, coach of the University of Maryland, was an advisor to coach Dudley DeGroot of the Redskins as they adopted the T formation.

The Philadelphia Eagles grew stronger with rookie Steve Van Buren at halfback. They finished second to the New York Giants in the East. The Green Bay Packers won the Western Division again and defeated the Giants 14–7 in the championship game.

Tackle Al Blozis played for the Giants in the championship game while on leave from the U.S. Army; he was an infantry lieutenant. He was killed one month later while fighting in France.

1944 STANDINGS

Eastern Division	W	L	T	Pct.	Pts.	OP
N.Y. Giants	8	1	1	.889	206	75
Philadelphia	7	1	2	.875	267	131
Washington	6	3	1	.667	169	180
Boston Yanks	2	8	0	.200	82	233
Brooklyn Dodgers	0	10	0	.000	69	166
Western Division	W	L	T	Pct.	Pts.	OP
Green Bay	8	2	0	.800	238	141
Chi. Bears	6	3	1	.667	258	172
Detroit	6	3	1	.667	216	151
Cleveland Rams	4	6	0	.400	188	224
Card-Pitt	0	10	0	.000	108	328

NFL championship: Green Bay 14, N.Y. Giants 7

LEADING RUSHERS	Att.	Yards	Avg.	Long	TD
Bill Paschal, N.Y. Giants	196	737	3.8	68	9
John Grigas, Card-Pitt	185	610	3.2	29	3
Frank Sinkwich, Detroit	150	563	3.8	72	6
Henry Margarita, Chi. Bears	88	463	5.3	47	4
Steve Van Buren, Philadelphia	80	444	5.5	70	5

LEADING PASSERS	Att.	Comp.	Yards	TD	Int.
Frank Filchock, Washington	147	84	1,139	13	9
Sammy Baugh, Washington	146	82	849	4	8
Sid Luckman, Chi. Bears	143	71	1,018	11	11
Irv Comp, Green Bay	177	80	1,159	12	21
Al Reisz, Cleveland	113	49	777	8	10

LEADING RECEIVERS	No.	Yards	Avg.	Long	TD
Don Hutson, Green Bay	58	866	14.6	55	9
Jim Benton, Cleveland	39	505	12.9	36	4
Joe Aguirre, Washington	34	410	12.0	58	4
Wilbur Moore, Washington	33	424	12.5	59	5
Les Dye, Washington	24	281	11.7	61	2

1945 German armies surrendered between May 4 and May 8. American planes dropped the first atomic bombs used in war on Japanese cities August 6 and 9. The Japanese surrendered aboard the U.S.S. Missouri in the Tokyo harbor September 2. The war had taken a heavy toll among all Americans and among National Football League players: 638 had served in the war and 21 of them had died.

The NFL restored the pre-war player limit of 33. The hashmarks or inbounds lines were moved from 15 yards to 20 yards in from each side line. In a move that Commissioner Elmer Layden considered one of the most important of his years in the position, the league passed a rule requiring all players to wear long stockings because, he said, he thought some of the players' bare legs were unattractive.

Don Hutson of Green Bay led the NFL in receiving for the fifth consecutive year and scored a record 29 points in one quarter—four touchdowns and five extra points, in the second quarter of a 57–21 Green Bay victory over Detroit.

Bob Waterfield was a sensational rookie quarterback for the Cleveland Rams. His favorite receiver, Jim Benton, caught 10 passes for 303 yards in one game against Detroit. The Rams won the Western Division championship and Waterfield was awarded the Joe F. Carr trophy given to the most valuable player in the league.

The Chicago Bears fell to 3–7 and finished fourth in the West. Owner and coach George Halas rejoined them late in the season after his service with the U.S. Navy in the Pacific.

Steve Van Buren won the rushing title for the first time but the Philadelphia Eagles were runners-up to the Washington Redskins in the Eastern Division.

Sammy Baugh.

Bob Waterfield.

Quarterback Baugh of the Redskins was now accustomed to the team's new T formation.

Washington met the Cleveland Rams in the title game at Municipal Stadium in Cleveland on a frigid day when the temperature was six degrees. Baugh threw a pass from his own end zone in the first quarter. The pass hit the goal post and it was ruled a safety and two points for Cleveland. Waterfield threw a touchdown pass to Benton and the extra point was good, giving the Rams a 9–7 lead. Cleveland went on to win 15–14.

1945 STANDINGS

Eastern Division	W	L	T	Pct.	Pts.	OP
Washington	8	2	0	.800	209	121
Philadelphia	7	3	0	.700	272	133
N.Y. Giants	3	6	1	.333	179	198
Boston Yanks	3	6	1	.333	123	211
Pittsburgh	2	8	0	.200	79	220
Western Division	**W**	**L**	**T**	**Pct.**	**Pts.**	**OP**
Cleveland Rams	9	1	0	.900	244	136
Detroit	7	3	0	.700	195	194
Green Bay	6	4	0	.600	258	173
Chi. Bears	3	7	0	.300	192	235
Chi. Cardinals	1	9	0	.100	98	228

NFL championship: Cleveland Rams 15, Washington 14

LEADING RUSHERS	Att.	Yards	Avg.	Long	TD
Steve Van Buren, Philadelphia	143	832	5.8	69	15
Frank Akins, Washington	147	797	5.4	45	6
Henry Margarita, Chi. Bears	112	497	4.4	38	3
Fred Gehrke, Cleveland Rams	74	467	6.3	72	7
Fred Gillette, Cleveland Rams	63	390	6.1	52	1

LEADING PASSERS	Att.	Comp.	Yards	TD	Int.
Sammy Baugh, Washington	182	128	1,669	11	4
Sid Luckman, Chi. Bears	217	117	1,725	14	10
Bob Waterfield, Cleveland Rams	171	88	1,609	14	10
Leroy Zimmerman, Philadelphia	132	67	991	9	8
Paul Christman, Chi. Cardinals	219	89	1,147	5	12

LEADING RECEIVERS	No.	Yards	Avg.	Long	TD
Don Hutson, Green Bay	47	834	17.7	75	9
Jim Benton, Cleveland Rams	45	1,067	23.7	84	8
Steve Bagarus, Washington	35	623	17.8	70	5
George Wilson, Chi. Bears	28	259	9.2	18	3
John Greene, Detroit	26	550	21.1	63	4

1946 The NFL had waited for years for the return of peace and prosperity. It arrived at last, but when it did it had to be shared with a rival organization called the All-America Football Conference. Founded by sports editor Arch Ward of the *Chicago Tribune,* it began play in Brooklyn, Buffalo, Chicago, Cleveland, Los Angeles, Miami, New York, and San Francisco.

The NFL champion Cleveland Rams had been trying to gain league approval to move to Los Angeles. It was refused at first, and then the league relented and the team made its move. The NFL became a coast-to-coast league for the first time.

There was direct competition between NFL and AAFC teams in three cities. The New York Giants were in competition with the Brooklyn Dodgers and New York Yankees of the AAFC. The Chicago Bears and Cardinals had competition from the Chicago Rockets of the AAFC. And the new Los Angeles Rams were in competition with the Los Angeles Dons of the AAFC.

The contract of NFL Commissioner Elmer Layden was not renewed, and Bert Bell, co-owner of the Pittsburgh Steelers, was named to replace him. Bell won a three-year contract and accepted the job of leading the league against its rival, the AAFC. He moved the NFL headquarters from Chicago to Philadelphia.

The rule that cost the Washington Redskins a safety in the 1945 championship game was changed so that a forward pass hitting the goal posts was now an incomplete pass. Free substitution was being debated hotly, especially in college football, and the NFL restricted its rule, limiting substitutions to three men at a time.

The Los Angeles Rams averaged 38,700 fans in Memorial Coliseum. They added backs Tom Harmon and Kenny Washington to their lineup but failed to repeat as champions. The Chicago Bears won the Western Division, recapturing the glory they had

Bert Bell.

Dan Reeves.

Bill Dudley.

known before World War II. They had a backfield of Sid Luckman at quarterback, Hugh Gallarneau and Dante Magnani at halfbacks, and Bill Osmanski at fullback.

Frank Filchock, acquired from Washington, led the New York Giants to the Eastern championship. Philadelphia finished third for the third consecutive year. The Chicago Cardinals, coached by Jimmy Conzelman, were growing stronger and had Paul Christman, Marshall Goldberg, and Pat Harder in their backfield.

Dr. John Bain (Jock) Sutherland, who had coached great college teams at the University of Pittsburgh, returned from military service and became coach of the Pittsburgh Steelers. Tailback Bill Dudley of the Steelers had a great season, leading the league in scoring and winning the most valuable player award. But Dudley and Sutherland feuded and the Steelers remained unsuccessful.

There were reports of a betting scandal on the eve of the championship game in New York between the Giants and the Chicago Bears. The Giants' Filchock and Merle Hapes were questioned about an attempt by a New York man to fix the game. Hapes was suspended for failing to report the contact, but Filchock was permitted to play the game. He played well but Chicago won 24–14. Luckman ran 19 yards on a keeper play for the decisive touchdown. A title game record crowd of 58,346 watched.

The league was in competition with a rival organization and a number of its players had jumped to the other league. The NFL nevertheless set an attendance record of 1,732,135, an average of 31,494 a game.

Don Hutson of the Green Bay Packers retired from pro football.

1946 STANDINGS

Eastern Division	W	L	T	Pct.	Pts.	OP
N.Y. Giants	7	3	1	.700	236	162
Philadelphia	6	5	0	.545	231	220
Washington	5	5	1	.500	171	191
Pittsburgh	5	5	1	.500	136	117
Boston Yanks	2	8	1	.200	189	273
Western Division	**W**	**L**	**T**	**Pct.**	**Pts.**	**OP**
Chi. Bears	8	2	1	.800	289	193
Los Angeles	6	4	1	.600	277	257
Green Bay	6	5	0	.545	148	158
Chi. Cardinals	6	5	0	.545	260	198
Detroit	1	10	0	.091	142	310

NFL championship: Chi. Bears 24, N.Y. Giants 14

LEADING RUSHERS	Att.	Yards	Avg.	Long	TD
Bill Dudley, Pittsburgh	146	604	4.1	41	3
Pat Harder, Chi. Cardinals	106	545	5.1	55	4
Steve Van Buren, Philadelphia	116	529	4.6	58	5
Hugh Gallarneau, Chi. Bears	112	476	4.2	52	7
Tony Canadeo, Green Bay	122	476	3.9	27	0

LEADING PASSERS	Att.	Comp.	Yards	TD	Int.
Bob Waterfield, Los Angeles	251	127	1,747	18	17
Sid Luckman, Chi. Bears	229	110	1,826	17	16
Paul Governali, Boston	192	83	1,293	13	10
Paul Christman, Chi. Cardinals	229	100	1,656	13	18
Sammy Baugh, Washington	161	87	1,163	8	17

LEADING RECEIVERS	No.	Yards	Avg.	Long	TD
Jim Benton, Los Angeles	63	981	15.5	57	6
Harold Crisler, Boston Yanks	32	385	12.0	62	5
Steve Bagarus, Washington	31	438	14.1	51	3
Jack Ferrante, Philadelphia	28	451	16.1	48	4
Bill Dewell, Chi. Cardinals	27	643	23.8	82	7
Mal Kutner, Chi. Cardinals	27	634	23.5	63	5

1947 Charles W. Bidwill, owner of the Chicago Cardinals, won a bidding war with the New York Yankees of the All-America Football Conference and signed star halfback Charley Trippi of the University of Georgia. It gave the NFL a decisive victory over the AAFC.

A "bonus" draft choice was made for the first time. One team a year would get a special bonus choice before the first round began. The Chicago Bears won rights to the first "bonus" and chose back Bob Fenimore of Oklahoma A&M but he lasted only one season with them.

Sudden death was adopted for championship games. A fifth official, the back judge, was added.

The player limit was increased to 35 for the first three games and 34 for the rest of the season.

Jock Sutherland, coach of the Pittsburgh Steelers, traded star tailback Bill Dudley to the Detroit Lions and installed Johnny Clement as the Steelers' tailback.

Halfback Fred Gehrke of the Los Angeles Rams, who had studied art in college at Utah, painted horns on the leather helmets of the Rams, the first helmet emblems in pro football.

Illness took the life of Charles Bidwill, owner of the Chicago Cardinals. Bidwill's wife and sons retained ownership of the team that became the strongest in the league. The Cardinals had what was called a "dream backfield" made up of Trippi, Elmer Angsman, Paul Christman, and Pat Harder. They defeated the Bears 30–21 in a climactic game that gave the Cardinals the division championship. Harder scored 102 points to lead the league.

The Cardinals had won a title at last after years as an also-ran. The same thing happened in the Eastern Division, where the Philadelphia Eagles of coach Earle (Greasy) Neale were developing into a powerful team. Left halfback Steve Van Buren gained 1,008 yards rushing, becoming the first 1,000-yard rusher in the NFL since 1934.

A "day" was held for Redskins' star Sammy Baugh at Griffith Stadium in Washington and he responded by throwing six touchdown passes as the Redskins beat the New York Giants.

Philadelphia had a feared offense in which Van Buren went off the right side time after time on power plays from the T formation. The Eagles tied for the division championship with a Pittsburgh Steelers' team coached by Sutherland and still playing the single wing formation. They met in a playoff and Philadelphia won 21–0.

The Western champions, the Cardinals, changed from their usual passing attack to a running game and made 282 yards on the ground in the championship game against the Eagles. The running of Chicago's Trippi and Angsman offset the passing of Philadelphia's Tommy Thompson and the Cardinals won the NFL championship 28–21.

Sid Luckman, George McAfee, Ray (Scooter) McLean of the Bears, left to right, after 1946 title game.

1947 STANDINGS

Eastern Division	W	L	T	Pct.	Pts.	OP
Philadelphia	8	4	0	.667	308	242
Pittsburgh	8	4	0	.667	240	259
Boston Yanks	4	7	1	.364	168	256
Washington	4	8	0	.333	295	367
N.Y. Giants	2	8	2	.200	190	309

Western Division	W	L	T	Pct.	Pts.	OP
Chi. Cardinals	9	3	0	.750	306	231
Chi. Bears	8	4	0	.667	363	241
Green Bay	6	5	1	.545	274	210
Los Angeles	6	6	0	.500	259	214
Detroit	3	9	0	.250	231	305

Eastern Division playoff: Philadelphia 21, Pittsburgh 0
NFL championship: Chi. Cardinals 28, Philadelphia 21

LEADING RUSHERS	Att.	Yards	Avg.	Long	TD
Steve Van Buren, Philadelphia	217	1,008	4.6	45	14
J. (Zero) Clement, Pittsburgh	129	670	5.2	43	4
Tony Canadeo, Green Bay	103	464	4.5	35	2
Kenny Washington, Los Angeles	70	444	7.4	92	5
Walt Schlinkman, Green Bay	115	439	3.8	20	2

LEADING PASSERS	Att.	Comp.	Yards	TD	Int.
Sammy Baugh, Washington	354	210	2,938	25	15
Tommy Thompson, Philadelphia	201	106	1,680	16	15
Sid Luckman, Chi. Bears	323	176	2,712	24	31
Jack Jacobs, Green Bay	242	108	1,615	16	17
Paul Christman, Chi. Cardinals	301	138	2,191	17	22

LEADING RECEIVERS	No.	Yards	Avg.	Long	TD
Jim Keane, Chi. Bears	64	910	14.2	50	10
Bob Nussbaumer, Washington	47	597	12.7	55	4
Mal Kutner, Chi. Cardinals	43	944	21.9	70	7
Nolan Luhn, Green Bay	42	696	16.5	44	7
Bill Dewell, Chi. Cardinals	42	576	13.7	46	4

1948 The National Football League and All-America Football Conference were at war for players. Their clubs were strained to their financial limits as they vied to sign stars. Washington had the "bonus" choice in the NFL and used it to draft tailback Harry Gilmer

Bill, left, and Charles Bidwill, right, with Chicago Cardinals' coach Jimmy Conzelman, about 1947.

Pat Harder, Chicago Cardinals, vs. Los Angeles Rams, 1949.

Steve Van Buren, Philadelphia Eagles, vs. Washington Redskins, about 1949.

of Alabama, who was supposed to be the eventual successor to Sammy Baugh as quarterback of the Redskins. George Preston Marshall, owner of the Redskins, now had both Baugh and Gilmer and so he sold the rights to Charlie Conerly of Mississippi to the New York Giants. The Giants finally signed Conerly after a fight with the Brooklyn Dodgers of the AAFC and Dodgers' owner Branch Rickey.

The Detroit Lions drafted Y. A. Tittle of Louisiana State but he signed with the Baltimore Colts of the AAFC.

Baugh was nearing the end of his Redskins' career, and so was another NFL quarterbacking great, Sid Luckman of the Chicago Bears. Owner George Halas of the Bears signed both Bobby Layne of Texas and Johnny Lujack of Notre Dame. Layne had been drafted by Pittsburgh but didn't want to play the single wing formation of John Michelosen, who had taken over the Steelers after the death of Jock Sutherland. Layne asked to be traded to Chicago.

Prominent rookies included tackle George Connor with the Chicago Bears, safety Emlen Tunnell with the New York Giants, and end Tom Fears with the Los Angeles Rams. Fears caught 51 passes to lead the league.

Fred Mandel sold the Detroit Lions to a syndicate headed by D. Lyle Fife.

Each division champion repeated. Tommy Thompson threw 25 touchdown passes and Steve Van Buren gained 945 yards as the Philadelphia Eagles had a 9–2–1 record in the East. Pat Harder scored 110 points and the Chicago Cardinals ran up an 11–1 record.

A blizzard blanketed the field at Shibe Park in Philadelphia before the Eagles and Cardinals met in the championship game. The yard lines were obliterated, making the job of referee Ron Gibbs and his crew extremely difficult. The teams struggled for three quarters without any points until tackle Frank (Bucko) Kilroy of the Eagles recovered a Cardinals' fumble at the Chicago 17-yard line. Van Buren later scored from the 5 and the Eagles won 7–0.

1948 STANDINGS

Eastern Division	W	L	T	Pct.	Pts.	OP
Philadelphia	9	2	1	.818	376	156
Washington	7	5	0	.583	291	287
N.Y. Giants	4	8	0	.333	297	388
Pittsburgh	4	8	0	.333	200	243
Boston Yanks	3	9	0	.250	174	372

Western Division	W	L	T	Pct.	Pts.	OP
Chi. Cardinals	11	1	0	.917	395	226
Chi. Bears	10	2	0	.833	375	151
Los Angeles	6	5	1	.545	327	269
Green Bay	3	9	0	.250	154	290
Detroit	2	10	0	.167	200	407

NFL championship: Philadelphia 7, Chi. Cardinals 0

LEADING RUSHERS	Att.	Yards	Avg.	Long	TD
Steve Van Buren, Philadelphia	201	945	4.7	29	10
Charley Trippi, Chi. Cardinals	128	690	5.4	50	6
Elmer Angsman, Chi. Cardinals	131	638	4.9	72	8
Warren Wilson, Detroit	157	612	3.9	38	2
Tony Canadeo, Green Bay	123	589	4.8	49	4

LEADING PASSERS	Att.	Comp.	Yards	TD	Int.
Tommy Thompson, Philadelphia	246	141	1,965	25	11
Jim Hardy, Los Angeles	211	112	1,390	14	7
Charlie Conerly, N.Y. Giants	299	162	2.175	22	13
Sammy Baugh, Washington	315	185	2,599	22	23
Ray Mallouf, Chi. Cardinals	143	73	1,160	13	6

LEADING RECEIVERS	No.	Yards	Avg.	Long	TD
Tom Fears, Los Angeles	51	698	13.7	80	4
Pete Pihos, Philadelphia	46	766	16.7	48	11
Mal Kutner, Chi. Cardinals	41	943	23.0	71	14
Val Jansante, Pittsburgh	39	623	16.0	66	3
Bill Swiacki, N.Y. Giants	39	550	14.1	65	10

1949 The attrition of the NFL-AAFC war was felt by every team. The champion Philadelphia Eagles, at the peak of their greatness, lost money and were sold by Alexis Thompson to a syndicate headed by James P. Clark. The Green Bay Packers were in financial straits, having been hit the hardest of any NFL team in the bidding war with the AAFC to sign players. The Boston Yanks quit that city and moved to New York,

Tony Canadeo, Green Bay Packers.

Joe Golding, New York Bulldogs, vs. Washington, 1949.

became the "Bulldogs," and played home games at the Polo Grounds when the Giants were on the road.

The Chicago Rockets of the All-American Football Conference had new ownership and changed their name to "Hornets." The AAFC Brooklyn Dodgers merged with the New York Yankees. There had been talks between the two leagues about a possible merger ending the pro football war and these discussions continued.

Elroy (Crazylegs) Hirsch joined the Los Angeles Rams from the AAFC Chicago Rockets and he and ends Tom Fears and Bob Shaw became a great passing combination with quarterbacks Bob Waterfield and Norm Van Brocklin, a rookie from Oregon. George Blanda was a rookie with the Chicago Bears and Chuck Bednarik with the Philadelphia Eagles.

The league had two 1,000-yard rushers for the first time. Steve Van Buren gained 1,146 for Philadelphia and Tony Canadeo 1,052 for Green Bay.

In addition to Van Buren, Philadelphia also had Bosh Pritchard at halfback and quarterback Tommy Thompson passing to ends Pete Pihos and Jack Ferrante. The Eagles raced to an 11–1 record.

Los Angeles, coached by Clark Shaughnessy, won the Western Division. Fears caught 77 passes.

Peace came to pro football December 9. Bert Bell, the NFL commissioner, announced a merger agreement in which three teams of the AAFC—the Cleveland Browns, San Francisco 49ers, and Baltimore Colts—would join the NFL in 1950.

Los Angeles Memorial Coliseum was the site for the championship game between the Rams and the Philadelphia Eagles. Heavy rain drenched the field

and there were only 22,945 fans in attendance as Van Buren gained 196 yards on 31 carries, leading the Eagles to a 14–0 victory and their second straight NFL championship.

Earl (Curly) Lambeau, Green Bay's head coach since 1921, left the Packers.

1949 STANDINGS

Eastern Division	W	L	T	Pct.	Pts.	OP
Philadelphia	11	1	0	.917	364	134
Pittsburgh	6	5	1	.545	224	214
N.Y. Giants	6	6	0	.500	287	298
Washington	4	7	1	.364	268	339
N.Y. Bulldogs	1	10	1	.091	153	368
Western Division	W	L	T	Pct.	Pts.	OP
Los Angeles	8	2	2	.800	360	239
Chi. Bears	9	3	0	.750	332	218
Chi. Cardinals	6	5	1	.545	360	301
Detroit	4	8	0	.333	237	259
Green Bay	2	10	0	.167	114	329

NFL championship: Philadelphia 14, Los Angeles 0

LEADING RUSHERS

	Att.	Yards	Avg.	Long	TD
Steve Van Buren, Philadelphia	263	1,146	4.4	41	11
Tony Canadeo, Green Bay	208	1,052	5.1	54	4
Elmer Angsman, Chi. Cardinals	125	675	5.4	82	6
Gene Roberts, N.Y. Giants	152	634	4.2	63	9
Jerry Nuzum, Pittsburgh	139	611	4.4	64	5

LEADING PASSERS

	Att.	Comp.	Yards	TD	Int.
Sammy Baugh, Washington	255	145	1,903	18	14
Tommy Thompson, Philadelphia	214	116	1,727	16	11
Charlie Conerly, N.Y. Giants	305	152	2,138	17	20
Bobby Layne, N.Y. Bulldogs	299	155	1,796	9	18
Joe Geri, Pittsburgh	77	31	554	5	5

LEADING RECEIVERS

	No.	Yards	Avg.	Long	TD
Tom Fears, Los Angeles	77	1,013	13.2	51	9
Bob Mann, Detroit	66	1,014	15.4	64	4
Bill Chipley, N.Y. Bulldogs	57	631	11.1	69	2
Jim Keane, Chi. Bears	47	696	14.8	39	6
Bill Swiacki, N.Y. Giants	47	652	13.0	42	4

1950 The complicated terms were worked out for the assimilation of three new teams into the league. "Divisions" were scrapped and replaced by the "American Conference" and "National Conference." The Cleveland Browns entered the American and the Baltimore Colts and San Francisco 49ers went into the National. The team that had been the New York Bulldogs became the New York Yanks and it divided the players of the former AAFC Yankees with the New York Giants. A special allocation draft was held allowing the 13 teams to draft the remaining AAFC players, with Baltimore being granted special consideration with 15 choices compared to 10 for the other teams.

For the first time in history, an NFL team, the Los Angeles Rams, contracted to have all its games televised. The arrangement covered both home and away games and the sponsor agreed to make up the difference in home game income if it was lower than it had been the season before. Attendance fell and the cost to the sponsor was $307,000. The Washington Redskins followed the Rams in arranging to televise their games; other teams made deals to put selected games on television.

Unlimited free substitution was restored in the NFL and the way opened for the era of two platoons and specialization in pro football.

An exceptional number of talented players entered the league. Defensive tackle Arnie Weinmeister and defensive backs Tom Landry, Otto Schnellbacher, and Harmon Rowe joined the New York Giants from the defunct AAFC Yankees. The Cleveland Browns' array of stars such as quarterback Otto Graham, backs

Norm Van Brocklin of Los Angeles passes against Detroit in 1953; Jim Cain, 88, and Thurman McGraw, 73 rush for the Lions.

Marion Motley and Dub Jones, ends Dante Lavelli and Mac Speedie, and linemen Lou Groza and Bill Willis moved into the NFL, and so did San Francisco stars such as quarterback Frankie Albert and halfback Joe Perry, and quarterback Y.A. Tittle of the Baltimore Colts.

The NFL draft yielded tackle Art Donovan for Baltimore; end Leon Hart and back Doak Walker for Detroit (Walker had actually been drafted in 1949 but did not join Detroit until 1950); quarterback Tobin Rote for Green Bay; tackle Ernie Stautner for Pittsburgh; tackle Leo Nomellini and end Gordy Soltau for San Francisco; and halfback Charlie (Choo Choo) Justice and quarterback Eddie LeBaron for Washington.

Commissioner Bert Bell set up a first-weekend test of strength between the old NFL and AAFC when he scheduled the champion Philadelphia Eagles against the four-time champion AAFC champion Cleveland Browns at Philadelphia on Saturday night before the regular opening day of the season. Cleveland won 35–10 before 71,237 fans. The Browns, coached by Paul Brown, went on to compile a 10–2 regular season record. The New York Giants beat them 6–0 and 17–13, throwing an Umbrella defense over the Browns' passing attack of Graham to Lavelli, Speedie, and Jones.

Motley of the Browns won the league rushing championship with 810 yards. Tom Fears of the Los Angeles Rams had a great season, catching 84 passes. Rookie Walker of the Lions—who also placekicked—scored 128 points in the 12-game season.

For the first time ever, there were deadlocks in each conference, or division, and playoffs were necessary in each. Cleveland gained revenge against the New York Giants, winning their American Conference playoff 8–3 on two field goals by Groza and a safety. Los Angeles defeated the Chicago Bears 24–14 in the National Conference playoff.

The Browns edged the Rams 30–28 on a 16-yard field goal by Groza with 28 seconds to play at Cleveland Municipal Stadium in one of the most exciting title games ever played.

other. The game would be played in Los Angeles at the Memorial Coliseum each year after the championship game, and would be sponsored by the *Los Angeles Times*. Otto Graham, quarterback of the 1950 champion Cleveland Browns, completed 19 of 27 passes for 252 yards and a touchdown, and ran for two touchdowns, to lead the American Conference to a 28–27 victory over the National Conference in the first Pro Bowl game with this new format. It was one of the most exciting of all-star games, with Graham's quarterback rivals, teammates Bob Waterfield and Norm Van Brocklin of Los Angeles, combining for 21 completions in 44 pass attempts for 294 yards and three touchdowns.

The Baltimore Colts' franchise that had come into the NFL from the All-America Football Conference died after one season. Abraham Watner, its owner, turned the franchise and player contracts back to the NFL for $50,000. Baltimore's former pro players were made available for drafting at the same time as college players January 18. Four former Colts were among the 13 players selected in the first round—quarterback Y. A. Tittle by San Francisco, back Billy Stone by the Chicago Bears, back Jim Spavital by the New York Giants, and back Chet Mutryn by Philadelphia.

Tailback Kyle Rote of Southern Methodist was the "bonus" choice in the draft. He was selected by the New York Giants, who converted him into a halfback or flanker back.

The Los Angeles Rams had their greatest season. They had two fine quarterbacks in Bob Waterfield and Norm Van Brocklin, who shared the position, and

ends Tom Fears and Bob Boyd and flanker back Elroy (Crazylegs) Hirsch as pass targets. The starting backfield of big, fast Dan Towler, Dick Hoerner, and Paul (Tank) Younger was nicknamed the "Bull Elephant Backfield." The "pony backs" were in reserve. They were Glenn Davis, Volney (Skeet) Quinlan, and Verda (Vitamin T.) Smith.

Van Brocklin had an NFL record 554 yards passing in a game against the New York Yanks. Waterfield, however, ended the season as the NFL's leading passer. Waterfield also was the Rams' placekicker and Van Brocklin the punter. Hirsch caught 66 passes for a record 1,495 yards and 17 touchdowns.

The Rams' attendance went up as they reversed their television policy and aired only road games.

They were a high-scoring team but the Rams had to fight to win their conference championship. The Detroit Lions had Raymond (Buddy) Parker as coach and players such as quarterback Bobby Layne, fullback Pat Harder, and halfbacks Bob Hoernschemeyer and Doak Walker. Detroit beat Los Angeles in a key game one week before the end of the season and took over first place. The Lions then lost their final game to San Francisco while the Rams defeated Green Bay and captured the National Conference title.

The Cleveland Browns were the strongest team in the American Conference. Dub Jones, the Browns' all-around halfback, scored six touchdowns in one game against the Chicago Bears, tying an NFL record set by Ernie Nevers in 1929. Cleveland lost its opening game to San Francisco and then roared back, winning 11 straight.

The championship game was televised coast-to-

Otto Graham goes over for a one-yard touchdown in the 1951 Pro Bowl Game.

1950 STANDINGS

American Conference	W	L	T	Pct.	Pts.	OP
Cleveland	10	2	0	.833	310	144
N.Y. Giants	10	2	0	.833	268	150
Philadelphia	6	6	0	.500	254	141
Pittsburgh	6	6	0	.500	180	195
Chi. Cardinals	5	7	0	.417	233	287
Washington	3	9	0	.250	232	326
National Conference	**W**	**L**	**T**	**Pct.**	**Pts.**	**OP**
Los Angeles	9	3	0	.750	466	309
Chi. Bears	9	3	0	.750	279	207
N.Y. Yanks	7	5	0	.583	366	367
Detroit	6	6	0	.500	321	285
Green Bay	3	9	0	.250	244	406
San Francisco	3	9	0	.250	213	300
Baltimore	1	11	0	.083	213	462

American Conference playoff: Cleveland 8, N.Y. Giants 3
National Conference playoff: Los Angeles 24, Chi. Bears 14
NFL championship: Cleveland 30, Los Angeles 28

LEADING RUSHERS	Att.	Yards	Avg.	Long	TD
Marion Motley, Cleveland	140	810	5.8	69	3
Frank Ziegler, Philadelphia	172	733	4.3	52	1
Joe Geri, Pittsburgh	188	705	3.8	47	2
Eddie Price, N.Y. Giants	126	703	5.6	74	4
Joe Perry, San Francisco	124	647	5.2	78	5

LEADING PASSERS	Att.	Comp.	Yards	TD	Int.
Norm Van Brocklin, Los Angeles	233	127	2,061	18	14
Otto Graham, Cleveland	253	137	1,943	14	20
Joe Geri, Pittsburgh	113	41	866	6	15
George Ratterman, N.Y. Yanks	294	140	2,251	22	24
Charlie Conerly, N.Y. Giants	132	56	1,000	8	7

LEADING RECEIVERS	No.	Yards	Avg.	Long	TD
Tom Fears, Los Angeles	84	1,116	13.3	53	7
Dan Edwards, N.Y. Yanks	52	775	14.9	82	6
Cloyce Box, Detroit	50	1,009	20.2	82	11
Paul Salata, Baltimore	50	618	12.4	57	4
Bob Shaw, Chi. Cardinals	48	971	20.2	65	12

1951 The Pro Bowl game, dormant since 1942, was revived under a new format in which the all-stars of each conference would be matched against each

Jerry Williams returns a punt as a teammate leg-whips Pat Canamella of the Dallas Texans, 1952.

Autograph seekers surround Sammy Baugh after his last game for Washington, 1952.

Chick Jagade scores Cleveland's only touchdown in its 17–7 loss to Detroit in 1952 title game.

coast for the first time. It was on the DuMont network, which paid $75,000 for the rights to it. The Rams defeated the Browns 24–17 in an exciting game before 57,522 at Los Angeles Memorial Coliseum. Alternate quarterback Van Brocklin and Fears combined for a 73-yard touchdown pass in the final quarter to win the game. The winning and losing shares set records, $2,108 for each member of the Rams' team and $1,483 for each member of the Browns.

1951 STANDINGS

American Conference	W	L	T	Pct.	Pts.	OP
Cleveland	11	1	0	.917	331	152
N.Y. Giants	9	2	1	.818	254	161
Washington	5	7	0	.417	183	296
Pittsburgh	4	7	1	.364	183	235
Philadelphia	4	8	0	.333	234	264
Chi. Cardinals	3	9	0	.250	210	287
National Conference	**W**	**L**	**T**	**Pct.**	**Pts.**	**OP**
Los Angeles	8	4	0	.667	392	261
Detroit	7	4	1	.636	336	259
San Francisco	7	4	1	.636	255	205
Chi. Bears	7	5	0	.583	286	282
Green Bay	3	9	0	.250	254	375
N.Y. Yanks	1	9	2	.100	241	382

NFL championship: Los Angeles 24, Cleveland 17

LEADING RUSHERS	Att.	Yards	Avg.	Long	TD
Eddie Price, N.Y. Giants	271	971	3.6	80t	7
Rob Goode, Washington	208	951	4.6	33	9
Dan Towler, Los Angeles	126	854	6.8	79t	6
Bob Hoernschemeyer, Detroit	132	678	5.1	85t	2
Joe Perry, San Francisco	136	677	5.0	58t	3
LEADING PASSERS	**Att.**	**Comp.**	**Yards**	**TD**	**Int.**
Bob Waterfield, Los Angeles	176	88	1,566	13	10
Norm Van Brocklin, Los Angeles	194	100	1,725	13	11
Otto Graham, Cleveland	265	147	2,205	17	16
Steve Romanik, Chi. Bears	101	43	791	3	9
Bob Celeri, N.Y. Yanks	238	102	1,797	12	15
LEADING RECEIVERS	**No.**	**Yards**	**Avg.**	**Long**	**TD**
Elroy (Crazylegs) Hirsch, Los Angeles	66	1,495	22.7	91t	17
Gordy Soltau, San Francisco	59	826	14.0	48t	7
Fran Polsfoot, Chi. Cardinals	57	796	14.0	80t	4
Bob Mann, Green Bay	50	696	13.9	52	8
Dante Lavelli, Cleveland	43	586	13.6	47	6

1952 Ted Collins, owner of the New York Yanks' franchise, decided to give up trying to field a successful NFL team after eight years. He sold the Yanks to the NFL who in turn sold it to a Texas group. It moved to Dallas as the "Texans," the first NFL franchise in that state.

Collins had operated the team since 1944 as the Boston Yanks, New York Bulldogs, and New York Yanks during eight futile seasons.

One of the best groups of rookie players in history entered the NFL. It included the "bonus" draft choice, quarterback Bill Wade of Los Angeles, halfback Frank Gifford of the New York Giants, linebacker Bill George of the Chicago Bears, defensive end Gino Marchetti of the Dallas Texans, back Ollie Matson of the Chicago Cardinals, back Hugh McElhenny of San Francisco, and back Ed Modzelewski of Pittsburgh. Marchetti and Matson were from the same college, San Francisco.

Joe Bach replaced John Michelosen as coach at Pittsburgh and the Steelers abandoned the single wing for the T formation, the last professional team to do so.

The Dallas franchise drew small crowds and midway through the season became a traveling road team based at Hershey, Pennsylvania. It won a game Thanksgiving Day against the Chicago Bears at Akron, Ohio before 3,000 fans. The "Texans" lost 11 other games and went out of business. It was the last time an NFL team failed.

Bob Waterfield of the Los Angeles Rams led one of the most spectacular comebacks in the history of the league when he rallied the Rams from a 28–6 deficit with 12 minutes to play and they beat the Green Bay Packers 30–28.

Detroit lost two of its first three games but then stormed back to finish in a tie with Los Angeles for the National Conference championship. They met in a playoff and Pat Harder scored 19 points to lead Detroit to a 31–21 victory.

Cleveland lost four games but still won the American Conference title and the first NFL championship game between two growing rivals, the Lions and Browns, followed. Detroit won 17–7 and claimed its first NFL championship in 17 years. Raymond (Buddy) Parker, coach of the Lions, had been their quarterback when they won the championship the last time in 1935.

Two of the greatest NFL players in history, Sammy Baugh of the Washington Redskins and Steve Van Buren of the Philadelphia Eagles, retired.

1952 STANDINGS

American Conference	W	L	T	Pct.	Pts.	OP
Cleveland	8	4	0	.667	310	213
N.Y. Giants	7	5	0	.583	234	231
Philadelphia	7	5	0	.583	252	271
Pittsburgh	5	7	0	.417	300	273
Chi. Cardinals	4	8	0	.333	172	221
Washington	4	8	0	.333	240	287

National Conference	W	L	T	Pct.	Pts.	OP
Detroit	9	3	0	.750	344	192
Los Angeles	9	3	0	.750	349	234
San Francisco	7	5	0	.583	285	221
Green Bay	6	6	0	.500	295	312
Chi. Bears	5	7	0	.417	245	326
Dallas Texans	1	11	0	.083	182	427

National Conference playoff: Detroit 31, Los Angeles 21
NFL championship: Detroit 17, Cleveland 7

LEADING RUSHERS	Att.	Yards	Avg.	Long	TD
Dan Towler, Los Angeles	156	894	5.7	44t	10
Eddie Price, N.Y. Giants	183	748	4.1	75t	5
Joe Perry, San Francisco	158	725	4.6	78t	8
Hugh McElhenny, San Francisco	98	684	7.0	89t	6
Bob Hoernschemeyer, Detroit	106	457	4.3	41	4

LEADING PASSERS	Att.	Comp.	Yards	TD	Int.
Norm Van Brocklin, Los Angeles	205	113	1,736	14	17
Tobin Rote, Green Bay	157	82	1,268	13	8
Babe Parilli, Green Bay	177	77	1,416	13	17
Otto Graham, Cleveland	364	181	2,816	20	24
Frankie Albert, San Francisco	129	71	964	8	10

LEADING RECEIVERS	No.	Yards	Avg.	Long	TD
Mac Speedie, Cleveland	62	911	14.7	50	5
Harry (Bud) Grant, Philadelphia	56	997	17.8	84t	7
Elbie Nickel, Pittsburgh	55	884	16.1	54t	9
Gordie Soltau, San Francisco	55	774	14.1	49t	7
Don Stonesifer, Chi. Cardinals	54	617	11.4	26	0

1953 Baltimore rejoined the NFL. Commissioner Bert Bell awarded the holdings of the defunct Dallas Texans' franchise to a group headed by Carroll Rosenbloom, which formed a new team called the "Colts"; that was also the name of the former team in Baltimore that had died after the 1950 season.

The NFL won an important court victory when Bell's policy of blacking out television of home games was upheld by Judge Allan K. Grim of the United States District Court for the Eastern District of Philadelphia.

The names of the American and National Conferences were changed to "Eastern Conference" and "Western Conference."

Mickey McBride, founder of the Cleveland Browns, sold them to a group headed by Dave R. Jones.

The league had another fine collection of rookies. Roosevelt Brown, Jack Stroud, and Ray Wietecha joined the New York Giants; Joe Schmidt joined the Detroit Lions, Jim Ringo the Green Bay Packers, Doug Atkins the Chicago Bears, Bob St. Clair the San Francisco 49ers, and Gene (Big Daddy) Lipscomb, who had not played college football, was in his first year with the Los Angeles Rams.

Lou Groza of the Cleveland Browns kicked a record 23 field goals. Joe Perry of San Francisco gained 1,018 yards rushing and won a bonus of $5,090, $5 for every yard he gained. Harry (Bud) Grant, an end for the Philadelphia Eagles, left them to sign a contract with the Canadian Football League and his successor at his position, Pete Pihos, led the NFL with 63 pass receptions.

The Detroit Lions won the Western Conference.

J. R. Boone makes a catch for Green Bay; Bert Rechichar and Don Shula defend for Baltimore.

Joe Perry of the 49ers wearing the face mask that protected his broken jaw in 1953.

Otto Graham scores one of six touchdowns he accounted for in 56–10 victory, in 1954 championship.

Alan Ameche, leading rusher as a rookie in 1955, carries the ball against San Francisco.

Their Great Lakes rival, the Cleveland Browns, appeared on their way to a perfect season but lost their last game and finished 11-1. The Browns still won the Eastern Division easily. In the championship game, quarterback Bobby Layne of the Lions brought them from behind in the closing minutes and threw the winning touchdown pass to end Jim Doran for a 17–16 victory.

Steve Owen of the New York Giants suffered through a long season and one of his losses was a 62–14 drubbing at the hands of the Browns. He departed the Giants after 23 years as their head coach. Bob Waterfield of the Los Angeles Rams and Clyde (Bulldog) Turner of the Chicago Bears retired.

Jim Thorpe, former great player and president of the American Professional Football Association, forerunner of the NFL, died at Lomita, California, March 28.

1953 STANDINGS

Eastern Conference	W	L	T	Pct.	Pts.	OP
Cleveland	11	1	0	.917	348	162
Philadelphia	7	4	1	.636	352	215
Washington	6	5	1	.545	208	215
Pittsburgh	6	6	0	.500	211	263
N.Y. Giants	3	9	0	.250	179	277
Chi. Cardinals	1	10	1	.091	190	337

Western Conference	W	L	T	Pct.	Pts.	OP
Detroit	10	2	0	.833	271	205
San Francisco	9	3	0	.750	372	237
Los Angeles	8	3	1	.727	366	236
Chi. Bears	3	8	1	.273	218	262
Baltimore	3	9	0	.250	182	350
Green Bay	2	9	1	.182	200	338

NFL championship: Detroit 17, Cleveland 16

LEADING RUSHERS	Att.	Yards	Avg.	Long	TD
Joe Perry, San Francisco	192	1,018	5.3	51t	10
Dan Towler, Los Angeles	152	879	5.8	73t	7
Volney (Skeet) Quinlan, Los Angeles	97	705	7.3	74t	4
Charley (Choo Choo) Justice, Washington	115	616	5.4	43	2
Fran Rogel, Pittsburgh	137	527	3.8	58	2

LEADING PASSERS	Att.	Comp.	Yards	TD	Int.
Otto Graham, Cleveland	258	167	2,722	11	9
Norm Van Brocklin, Los Angeles	286	156	2,393	19	14
Y.A. Tittle, San Francisco	259	149	2,121	20	16
Bobby Thomason, Philadelphia	304	162	2,462	21	20
Bobby Layne, Detroit	273	125	2,088	16	21

LEADING RECEIVERS	No.	Yards	Avg.	Long	TD
Pete Pihos, Philadelphia	63	1,049	16.7	59	10
Elbie Nickel, Pittsburgh	62	743	12.0	40	4
Elroy (Crazylegs) Hirsch, Los Angeles	61	941	15.4	70	4
Don Stonesifer, Chi. Cardinals	56	684	12.2	46	2
Jim Dooley, Chi. Bears	53	841	15.9	72	4

1954 Commissioner Bert Bell was given a new 12-year contract by the NFL and two of its teams made significant coaching moves. The New York Giants named Jim Lee Howell head coach. He hired Vince Lombardi as offensive coach and had Tom Landry as player-coach of his defensive team. The Baltimore Colts hired Weeb Ewbank, an assistant to Paul Brown at Cleveland, as head coach.

Brown of the Browns was concerned that his quarterback, Otto Graham, was near retirement and drafted Bobby Garrett of Stanford as the NFL "bonus" choice. Garrett's availability became uncertain because of military commitments, however, and Brown traded him to Green Bay for Babe Parilli. Parilli himself was in the army but was due to return to pro football in two years.

Canadian Football League teams were raiding NFL teams and signed quarterback Eddie LeBaron and defensive end Gene Brito of the Washington Redskins.

Quarterback Adrian Burk of the Philadelphia Eagles threw seven touchdown passes in one game against Washington, tying the record set by Sid Luckman in 1943.

Joe Perry of the San Francisco 49ers became the first back in league history to gain 1,000 yards rushing in consecutive seasons. He led the league with 1,049.

Cleveland and Detroit were headed for their third straight meeting in the championship game. The

Browns again started slowly, losing two of their first three games before winning eight in a row. A game with the Lions, postponed because of a conflict with the Cleveland Indians' baseball World Series against the New York Giants, was rescheduled for December 19, a week after the other clubs finished their season. Detroit won 14–10 in a blizzard.

Raymond (Buddy) Parker of Detroit was gaining a reputation as one who held a jinx over his coaching rival, Brown of Cleveland. Parker had his alter ego, Bobby Layne, at quarterback. Giant tackle Les Bingaman anchored Detroit's five-man line on defense. Safety Jack Christiansen led a superb secondary nicknamed "Chris's Crew."

It was an exceptional team but it was not the equal of the Browns in the 1954 title game. Graham, playing what he said was his last game at quarterback for Cleveland, made it one of his greatest ever when he threw three touchdown passes and scored three times himself as the Browns routed the Lions 56–10.

1954 STANDINGS

Eastern Conference	W	L	T	Pct.	Pts.	OP
Cleveland	9	3	0	.750	336	162
Philadelphia	7	4	1	.636	284	230
N.Y. Giants	7	5	0	.583	293	184
Pittsburgh	5	7	0	.417	219	263
Washington	3	9	0	.250	207	432
Chi. Cardinals	2	10	0	.167	183	347
Western Conference	W	L	T	Pct.	Pts.	OP
Detroit	9	2	1	.818	337	189
Chi. Bears	8	4	0	.667	301	279
San Francisco	7	4	1	.636	313	251
Los Angeles	6	5	1	.545	314	285
Green Bay	4	8	0	.333	234	251
Baltimore	3	9	0	.250	131	279

NFL championship: Cleveland 56, Detroit 10

LEADING RUSHERS	Att.	Yards	Avg.	Long	TD
Joe Perry, San Francisco	173	1,049	6.1	58	8
John Henry Johnson, San Francisco	129	681	5.3	38t	9
Paul (Tank) Younger, Los Angeles	91	610	6.7	75t	8
Dan Towler, Los Angeles	149	599	4.0	24	11
Maurice Bassett, Cleveland	144	588	4.1	22	6

LEADING PASSERS	Att.	Comp.	Yards	TD	Int.
Norm Van Brocklin, Los Angeles	260	139	2,637	13	21
Otto Graham, Cleveland	240	142	2,092	11	17
Zeke Bratkowski, Chi. Bears	130	67	1,087	8	17
Tom Dublinski, Detroit	138	77	1,073	8	7
Bob Clatterbuck, N.Y. Giants	101	50	781	6	7

LEADING RECEIVERS	No.	Yards	Avg.	Long	TD
Pete Pihos, Philadelphia	60	872	14.5	34	10
Billy Wilson, San Francisco	60	830	13.8	43	5
Bob Boyd, Los Angeles	53	1,212	22.9	80t	6
Bill Howton, Green Bay	52	768	14.8	59	2
Dante Lavelli, Cleveland	47	802	17.1	64	7

1955 The Washington expatriates, LeBaron and Brito, returned from the Canadian Football League and rejoined the Redskins. Paul Brown, the Cleveland Browns' coach, talked his quarterback, Otto Graham, out of retirement. Semipro quarterback John Unitas tried out with the Pittsburgh Steelers but was rejected; Walt Kiesling, the Steelers' coach, chose quarterbacks Jim Finks and Ted Marchibroda over Unitas. The Baltimore Colts made an 80-cent telephone call to the rejected quarterback, and signed him as a free agent.

George Halas announced he was coaching his last season for the Chicago Bears. And Sid Gillman, a little-known college coach at Cincinnati, took over as head coach of the Los Angeles Rams.

Ball carriers in pro football could continue to advance the ball, even by crawling along the ground, until they were stopped. In contrast, runners in college and high school football were downed and the play blown dead as soon as anything other than their feet touched the ground. The professional rule led to a brand of rough-and-tumble football. There were charges of "dirty play." As a result, the rules were changed so that the ball would be declared dead immediately if a player touched the ground with any part of his body, except his hands or feet, while in the grasp of an opponent "and irrespective of the grasp

Jim Thorpe in his later years.

Adrian Burk.

Rookie coach Sid Gillman of Los Angeles, 1955.

being broken." It was called the NFL's "dead ball rule."

The league's sudden death overtime rule was used for the first time in a preseason game at Portland, Oregon. The promoter of the game there between the Los Angeles Rams and New York Giants convinced them to play under the rule of sudden death, and also an oddball system of numbering the field yard lines from 1 to 100. To the dismay of both coaches, Sid Gillman of the Rams and Jim Lee Howell of the Giants, the game was tied 17–17 after four quarters and an overtime period was necessary. The Rams scored three minutes later on a two-yard run by Paul (Tank) Younger and won 23–17.

Graham started slowly for Cleveland but hit his stride and led the league in passing. The Browns were strengthened by the acquisition of Ed Modzelewski from Pittsburgh and Fred (Curly) Morrison from the Chicago Bears to carry the ball, and Darrell (Pete) Brewster and Ray Renfro joined Dante Lavelli as targets for Graham's accurate passes. Cleveland won its sixth straight NFL division championship and tenth title in a row counting its four years in the All-America Football Conference.

Detroit did not do as well. It went into a tailspin after middle guard Les Bingaman retired and quarterback Bobby Layne strained his shoulder while lassoing a calf in the off-season in Texas. The Lions struggled to a 3-9 record and finished last in the Western Conference.

Rookie coach Gillman of Los Angeles lost twice to the Chicago Bears but still won the West in his first season. The Bears' attempts to win a title for Halas in his last season failed when the crosstown Chicago Cardinals crushed them 53–14.

The Los Angeles Memorial Coliseum, where the Rams and Browns had played their classic 1951 championship, was the scene once more for the title game. Graham of Cleveland, as he had the year before against Detroit, was once more playing what he said was his last game of professional football. He dominated the Rams, running for two touchdowns and passing for two others to swamp Los Angeles 38–14 before a championship game record crowd of 85,693.

The National Broadcasting Company replaced the DuMont network as the network carrying the title game, for which it paid a rights fee of $100,000.

1955 STANDINGS

Eastern Conference	W	L	T	Pct.	Pts.	OP
Cleveland	9	2	1	.818	349	218
Washington	8	4	0	.667	246	222
N.Y. Giants	6	5	1	.545	267	223
Chi. Cardinals	4	7	1	.364	224	252
Philadelphia	4	7	1	.364	248	231
Pittsburgh	4	8	0	.333	195	285
Western Conference	W	L	T	Pct.	Pts.	OP
Los Angeles	8	3	1	.727	260	231
Chi. Bears	8	4	0	.667	294	251
Green Bay	6	6	0	.500	258	276
Baltimore	5	6	1	.455	214	239
San Francisco	4	8	0	.333	216	298
Detroit	3	9	0	.250	230	275

NFL championship: Cleveland 38, Los Angeles 14

LEADING RUSHERS	Att.	Yards	Avg.	Long	TD
Alan Ameche, Baltimore	213	961	4.5	79t	9
Howie Ferguson, Green Bay	192	859	4.5	57	4
F. (Curley) Morrison, Cleveland	156	824	5.3	56	3
Ron Waller, Los Angeles	151	716	4.7	55t	7
Joe Perry, San Francisco	156	701	4.5	42	2

LEADING PASSERS	Att.	Comp.	Yards	TD	Int.
Otto Graham, Cleveland	185	98	1,721	15	8
Ed Brown, Chi. Bears	164	85	1,307	9	10
Bobby Thomason, Philadelphia	171	88	1,337	10	7
Y.A. Tittle, San Francisco	287	147	2,185	17	28
Eddie Le Baron, Washington	178	79	1,270	9	15

LEADING RECEIVERS	No.	Yards	Avg.	Long	TD
Pete Pihos, Philadelphia	62	864	13.9	40t	7
Billy Wilson, San Francisco	53	831	15.7	72t	7
Billy Howton, Green Bay	44	697	15.8	60	5
Dave Middleton, Detroit	44	663	15.1	77t	3
Tom Fears, Los Angeles	44	569	12.9	31	2
Lew Carpenter, Detroit	44	312	7.1	34t	2

Ollie Matson, Chicago Cardinals, 1955.

Bill Wade, Los Angeles Rams.

1956 The year began with Jack Christensen of Detroit and the Western Conference returning the opening kickoff of the Pro Bowl game 103 yards for a touchdown, and Ollie Matson of the Chicago Cardinals and the Eastern Conference returning the second half kickoff 91 yards for a touchdown. There were two more exciting returns when the 1956 season began. Al Carmichael of the Green Bay Packers went 106 yards with a kickoff against the Chicago Bears October 7, the longest play in pro football history, and the very next week the brilliant Matson raced 105 yards with a kickoff return against the Washington Redskins. In the same game, Frank Bernardi of the Cardinals returned a punt 95 yards.

The CBS television network became the first to broadcast some NFL regular season games to selected television markets across the nation.

The rules were changed so that it was illegal to grab an opponent's face mask. "Loudspeaker coaching" from the side line was prohibited. A brown ball with white stripes, not a white ball with black stripes, was ordered for use in night games. And the language of the "dead ball rule" was improved; the ball was now dead immediately when the runner was contacted by a defensive player and touched the ground with any part of his body except his hands or feet.

Frankie Albert, former quarterback of the San Francisco 49ers, took over as their head coach. There were several notable rookies such as back J. C.

Caroline of the Chicago Bears, back Howard (Hopalong) Cassady of the Detroit Lions, tackles Forrest Gregg and Bob Skoronski of the Green Bay Packers, quarterback Earl Morrall of San Francisco, and back Lenny Moore of the Baltimore Colts.

The championship teams of 1955, the Cleveland Browns and Los Angeles Rams, went from greatness to mediocrity. Otto Graham made good his retirement from pro football and the Browns tried unsuccessfully to replace him with Tommy O'Connell, Babe Parilli, and George Ratterman, finishing with their first losing season and failing to capture a divisional championship for the first time in club history.

Los Angeles plunged to last place in the Western Conference. Sid Gillman, the Rams' coach, vacillated between Norm Van Brocklin and Bill Wade at quarterback and had trouble replacing defensive linemen Andy Robustelli, who had been traded to the New York Giants, and Gene (Big Daddy) Lipscomb, who had been waived to the Baltimore Colts.

The season belonged, instead, to the New York Giants and Chicago Bears. The Giants moved from the Polo Grounds to Yankee Stadium. Trades brought them Robustelli and defensive back Ed Hughes from the Rams and defensive tackle Dick Modzelewski from the Pittsburgh Steelers. Kicker Don Chandler, linebacker Sam Huff, and defensive end Jim Katcavage were Giants' rookies. Frank Gifford, Kyle Rote, Mel Triplett, and Alex Webster were in the Giants'

backfield to run the ball and catch passes. And Jim Lee Howell had a novel system in which he would start Don Heinrich at quarterback to probe the defense and determine how it was playing, and then send in Charlie Conerly to play the rest of the game.

Paddy Driscoll, a former teammate and a longtime friend and coaching associate of George Halas, replaced him as coach of the Bears. They were humiliated 42–10 early in the season by the revived Detroit Lions, but came back to capture the conference championship by beating Detroit 38–21 in the final week of the season. The second game was marred by controversy when defensive end Ed Meadows hit Lions' quarterback Bobby Layne and put him out of action.

Ed Brown established himself as Chicago's quarterback and led the league in passing. His exciting receiver, Harlon Hill, caught 47 passes. Fullback Rick Casares gained 1,126 yards rushing.

John Unitas took over as quarterback of the Baltimore Colts after George Shaw suffered a broken leg.

The Giants and Bears met for the championship at Yankee Stadium. Clark Shaughnessy, the Bears' offensive coach, changed to an entirely different game plan the day of the game. New York got a quick touchdown when Gene Filipski returned the opening kickoff 58 yards and Triplett scored on a 17-yard run moments later. The Giants went on to rout the Bears 47–7.

1956 STANDINGS

Eastern Conference	W	L	T	Pct.	Pts.	OP
N.Y. Giants	8	3	1	.727	264	197
Chi. Cardinals	7	5	0	.583	240	182
Washington	6	6	0	.500	183	225
Cleveland	5	7	0	.417	167	177
Pittsburgh	5	7	0	.417	217	250
Philadelphia	3	8	1	.273	143	215

Western Conference	W	L	T	Pct.	Pts.	OP
Chi. Bears	9	2	1	.818	363	246
Detroit	9	3	0	.750	300	188
San Francisco	5	6	1	.455	233	284
Baltimore	5	7	0	.417	270	322
Green Bay	4	8	0	.333	264	342
Los Angeles	4	8	0	.333	291	307

NFL championship: N.Y. Giants 47, Chi. Bears 7

LEADING RUSHERS	Att.	Yards	Avg.	Long	TD
Rick Casares, Chi. Bears	234	1,126	4.8	68t	12
Ollie Matson, Chi. Cardinals	192	924	4.8	79t	5
Hugh McElhenny, San Francisco	185	916	5.0	86t	8
Alan Ameche, Baltimore	178	858	4.8	43	8
Frank Gifford, N.Y. Giants	159	819	5.2	69	5

LEADING PASSERS	Att.	Comp.	Yards	TD	Int.
Ed Brown, Chi. Bears	168	96	1,667	11	12
Bill Wade, Los Angeles	178	91	1,461	10	13
Bobby Layne, Detroit	244	129	1,909	9	17
Norm Van Brocklin, Los Angeles	124	68	966	7	12
Lamar McHan, Chi. Cardinals	152	72	1,159	10	8

LEADING RECEIVERS	No.	Yards	Avg.	Long	TD
Billy Wilson, San Francisco	60	889	14.8	77t	5
Billy Howton, Green Bay	55	1,188	21.6	66t	12
Frank Gifford, N.Y. Giants	51	603	11.8	48	4
Harlon Hill, Chi. Bears	47	1,128	24.0	79t	11
Jim Mutscheller, Baltimore	44	715	16.3	53t	6

Yankee Stadium, the Giants' new home in 1956.

1957 Raymond (Buddy) Parker, coach of the Detroit Lions, shocked the team, the city, and all pro football when he resigned while at the podium addressing a "Meet the Lions" banquet at a Detroit hotel before the season. He moved to the Pittsburgh Steelers as head coach and was replaced in Detroit by his former assistant, George Wilson.

Pete Rozelle was named general manager of the Los Angeles Rams.

The Pittsburgh Steelers and Cleveland Browns each had had 5–7 records and were tied for the fourth draft pick. A coin flip was held to break the tie and Pittsburgh won. It selected quarterback Len Dawson of Purdue and Cleveland took fullback Jim Brown of Syracuse. Dawson became a substitute with the Steelers; they traded with the San Francisco 49ers to get Earl Morrall as their starting quarterback. Brown, however, became a sensation with Cleveland.

Other notable first-year players included halfback Jon Arnett of Los Angeles, quarterback John Brodie of San Francisco, "bonus" draft choice halfback Paul Hornung and end Ron Kramer of Green Bay, quarterback Sonny Jurgensen and flanker Tommy McDonald of Philadelphia, and guard-tackle Jim Parker of Baltimore.

Cleveland ascended to the championship of the Eastern Conference again with Tommy O'Connell playing quarterback and Brown leading the league with 942 yards rushing and setting an NFL record with 237 yards in one game against the Los Angeles Rams.

The coaching change in Detroit did not affect the Lions adversely. They battled with the San Francisco 49ers for the Western Conference title. George Wilson, Detroit's new coach, used Bobby Layne and Tobin Rote in a two-quarterback system. Fullback John Henry Johnson was the major offensive weapon for the Lions. Layne suffered a broken ankle late in the season and Rote had the quarterback job to himself.

San Francisco went through one of the most momentous seasons any NFL team ever had. The 49ers had Hugh McElhenny and Joe Perry in the backfield with quarterback Y. A. Tittle, who had a sensational new passing target in end R. C. Owens. Owens stood 6 foot 5 inches. Tittle threw "alley-oop" passes high in the air and Owens leaped above smaller defensive backs to make the catch.

Tony Morabito, founder and coowner of the 49ers,

Anthony J. (Tony) Morabito.

Raymond (Buddy) Parker.

Rookie Paul Hornung of Green Bay, 1957; 45 is New York's Emlen Tunnell.

Tobin Rote during Detroit's amazing playoff game comeback against San Francisco in 1957.

suffered a heart attack and died during their game at Kezar Stadium against the Chicago Bears, October 28.

The 49ers were a big gate attraction everywhere they played and an NFL record crowd of 102,368 watched them play the Rams at Los Angeles Memorial Coliseum, November 10.

Detroit and San Francisco tied for the Western Conference lead and the Lions won an amazing playoff victory, coming from behind for a 31–27 victory after trailing 27–7 in the third quarter.

Detroit then met Cleveland for the NFL title and, with quarterback Tobin Rote throwing four touchdown passes and running for another, smashed the Browns 59–14. It was the worst defeat Cleveland ever suffered and avenged the Lions' one-sided loss to the Browns in the 1954 title game.

1957 STANDINGS

Eastern Conference	W	L	T	Pct.	Pts.	OP
Cleveland	9	2	1	.818	269	172
N.Y. Giants	7	5	0	.583	254	211
Pittsburgh	6	6	0	.500	161	178
Washington	5	6	1	.455	251	230
Philadelphia	4	8	0	.333	173	230
Chi. Cardinals	3	9	0	.250	200	299
Western Conference	**W**	**L**	**T**	**Pct.**	**Pts.**	**OP**
Detroit	8	4	0	.667	251	231
San Francisco	8	4	0	.667	260	264
Baltimore	7	5	0	.583	303	235
Los Angeles	6	6	0	.500	307	278
Chi. Bears	5	7	0	.417	203	211
Green Bay	3	9	0	.250	218	311

Western Conference playoff: Detroit 31, San Francisco 27
NFL championship: Detroit 59, Cleveland 14

LEADING RUSHERS	Att.	Yards	Avg.	Long	TD
Jim Brown, Cleveland	202	942	4.7	69t	9
Rick Casares, Chi. Bears	204	700	3.4	25t	6
Don Bosseler, Washington	167	673	4.0	28	7
John Henry Johnson, Detroit	129	621	4.8	62	5
Tommy Wilson, Los Angeles	127	616	4.9	46	3

LEADING PASSERS	Att.	Comp.	Yards	TD	Int.
Tommy O'Connell, Cleveland	110	63	1,229	9	8
Eddie LeBaron, Washington	167	99	1,508	11	10
Johnny Unitas, Baltimore	301	172	2,550	24	17
Norm Van Brocklin, Los Angeles	265	132	2,105	20	21
Lamar McHan, Chi. Cardinals	200	87	1,568	10	15

LEADING RECEIVERS	No.	Yards	Avg.	Long	TD
Billy Wilson, San Francisco	52	757	14.6	40	6
Raymond Berry, Baltimore	47	800	17.0	67t	6
Jack McClairen, Pittsburgh	46	630	13.7	48t	2
Frank Gifford, N.Y. Giants	41	588	14.3	63	4
Lenny Moore, Baltimore	40	687	17.2	82t	7

1958 George Halas reinstated himself as head coach of the Chicago Bears. It was the third time he had come back to coach, the others having been in 1933 and 1946.

Raymond (Buddy) Parker, coach of the Pittsburgh Steelers, traded quarterback Earl Morrall to the Detroit Lions in exchange for Bobby Layne, the quarterback of the Lions' great team when Parker was their coach.

Lawrence (Buck) Shaw was named coach of the Philadelphia Eagles and they made a trade with the Los Angeles Rams, landing quarterback Norm Van Brocklin.

Quarterback King Hill was selected by the Chicago Cardinals and became the last "bonus" draft choice. The practice was then abolished.

Quarterbacks were in the news but none more than John Unitas of the Baltimore Colts. A collapsed lung and three broken ribs kept him out of two games but when he returned he threw a 58-yard touchdown pass to halfback Lenny Moore on the first play against the Green Bay Packers. Baltimore beat the Chicago Bears 17–0 in an important game in November; it was the first time the Bears had been shut out since 1946. Halas had to settle for a tie with Los Angeles for second place behind Baltimore in his first year back as Bears' coach.

The Green Bay Packers lost 10 games and finished last in the Western Conference despite having players such as linebackers Dan Currie and Ray Nitschke,

Lawrence (Buck) Shaw.

Johnny Unitas.

center Jim Ringo, and backs Paul Hornung and Jim Taylor.

The New York Giants captured the Eastern Conference after a bitter fight with the Cleveland Browns. Jim Brown of the Browns broke Steve Van Buren's NFL rushing record with 1,527 yards and led the league in scoring with 18 touchdowns and 108 points. He also had a good running mate when Bobby Mitchell joined him in the Browns' backfield.

The Giants got into a playoff against Cleveland by beating the Browns 13-10 in the last week of the season. Pat Summerall of New York kicked a 49-yard field goal in the snow for the victory. In the playoff game, the Giants held Jim Brown to eight yards and the entire Browns' offense to 86 and won 10–0.

Baltimore and New York met for the championship at Yankee Stadium. The Giants rallied from a 14–3 halftime deficit for a 17–14 lead only to have Unitas of the Colts complete pass after pass to end Raymond Berry, setting up a tying 20-yard field goal by Steve Myhra with 10 seconds to play. They entered sudden death, the first time in history a title game had gone into overtime. New York had the ball first but had to punt and the Colts went all the way. A second down pass from Unitas to end Jim Mutscheller set up a one-yard plunge by fullback Alan Ameche, winning it for Baltimore 23–17.

A dramatic sudden death championship game on national television captured the imagination of millions. Tex Maule's story on the game for *Sports Illustrated* in its January 5, 1959 issue was headlined, "The Best Football Game Ever Played."

NBC's live telecast of the game, with Chuck Thompson of Baltimore doing the play-by-play, reached an estimated 10,820,000 homes in America. It was not shown in the largest market, however; New York City was blacked out. New Yorkers also could not read about it because the city was in the midst of a newspaper strike.

1958 STANDINGS

Eastern Conference	W	L	T	Pct.	Pts.	OP
N.Y. Giants	9	3	0	.750	246	183
Cleveland	9	3	0	.750	302	217
Pittsburgh	7	4	1	.636	261	230
Washington	4	7	1	.364	214	268
Chi. Cardinals	2	9	1	.182	261	356
Philadelphia	2	9	1	.182	235	306
Western Conference	W	L	T	Pct.	Pts.	OP
Baltimore	9	3	0	.750	381	203
Chi. Bears	8	4	0	.667	298	230
Los Angeles	8	4	0	.667	344	278
San Francisco	6	6	0	.500	257	324
Detroit	4	7	1	.364	261	276
Green Bay	1	10	1	.091	193	382

Eastern Conference playoff: N.Y. Giants 10, Cleveland 0
NFL championship: Baltimore 23, N.Y. Giants 17, sudden death overtime

LEADING RUSHERS	Att.	Yards	Avg.	Long	TD
Jim Brown, Cleveland	257	1,527	5.9	65t	17
Alan Ameche, Baltimore	171	791	4.6	28	8
Joe Perry, San Francisco	125	758	6.1	73t	4
Tom Tracy, Pittsburgh	169	714	4.2	64	5
Jon Arnett, Los Angeles	133	683	5.1	57	6

LEADING PASSERS	Att.	Comp.	Yards	TD	Int.
Eddie LeBaron, Washington	145	79	1,365	11	10
Milt Plum, Cleveland	189	102	1,619	11	11
Bobby Layne, Pittsburgh	294	145	2,510	14	12
Bill Wade, Los Angeles	341	181	2,875	18	22
John Unitas, Baltimore	263	136	2,007	19	7

LEADING RECEIVERS	No.	Yards	Avg.	Long	TD
Raymond Berry, Baltimore	56	794	14.2	54	9
Pete Retzlaff, Philadelphia	56	766	13.7	49	2
Del Shofner, Los Angeles	51	1,097	21.5	92t	8
Lenny Moore, Baltimore	50	938	18.5	77t	7
Clyde Conner, San Francisco	49	512	10.4	26	5

1959 Vince Lombardi, offensive coach of the New York Giants, was named head coach of the Green Bay Packers.

Tim Mara, cofounder of the Giants, died at the age of 71, February 17.

Randy Duncan, number one draft choice of Green Bay and the entire NFL, did not sign with the Packers and joined the Canadian Football League.

General manager Pete Rozelle of the Los Angeles Rams traded eight players and a draft choice—the rights to nine players—to the Chicago Cardinals in exchange for running back Ollie Matson.

Lamar Hunt, a Dallas, Texas businessman who had been unsuccessful in attempts to buy the Chicago Cardinals' franchise, announced his intentions to form a second professional football league. He found interested parties for franchises and the first meeting of the league was held at the Conrad Hilton Hotel in Chicago, August 14. The representatives and their cities were: Hunt, Dallas; Bob Howsam, Denver; K. S. (Bud) Adams, Houston; Barron Hilton, Los Angeles; Max Winter and William Boyer, Minneapolis-St. Paul; and Harry Wismer, New York City. They made plans to begin league play in 1960. Eight days later at another meeting in Dallas, they announced that the league would be called the "American Football League."

Buffalo became the seventh AFL team, October 28, and Boston the eighth, November 22. Buffalo was represented by Ralph C. Wilson and Boston by a syndicate headed by William H. Sullivan.

The AFL held a draft rivaling that of the NFL and named former flying ace and South Dakota governor Joe Foss its commissioner.

NFL commissioner Bert Bell died of a heart attack while attending a Philadelphia Eagles' game at Franklin Field, October 11. Austin Gunsel, the league treasurer, was named interim president.

Baltimore's passing combination of John Unitas and Raymond Berry had a great year as the Colts won the Western Conference championship again. Unitas

A fan exults as Pat Summerall's kick gives the Giants a playoff victory over Cleveland, 1958.

Jim Brown.

Lamar Hunt.

Paul Hornung looking for a pass receiver, 1959; number 64 is guard Jerry Kramer.

Joe Foss, seated at right, and the American Football League's "Foolish Club" of charter owners.

Dan Reeves, left, and Fred Levy congratulate Pete Rozelle on being elected NFL commissioner.

threw 32 touchdown passes and Berry had 66 receptions.

Green Bay was the West's most improved team. New coach Lombardi established Bart Starr as his quarterback and Paul Hornung as his left halfback. Hornung led the NFL in scoring with 94 points as a runner and kicker.

Quarterback Charlie Conerly led the New York Giants to another Eastern Conference championship. They beat the Cleveland Browns 10–6 and 48–7. Cleveland's Jim Brown had another season over 1,000 yards with 1,329.

Baltimore again defeated the Giants in the NFL title game. New York led 9–7 going into the last quarter but Unitas and Lenny Moore were the principal figures as the Colts put together a 24-point fourth period and Baltimore won 31–16, claiming its second straight championship.

1959 STANDINGS

Eastern Conference	W	L	T	Pct.	Pts.	OP
N.Y. Giants	10	2	0	.833	284	170
Cleveland	7	5	0	.583	270	214
Philadelphia	7	5	0	.583	268	278
Pittsburgh	6	5	1	.545	257	216
Washington	3	9	0	.250	185	350
Chi. Cardinals	2	10	0	.167	234	324

Western Conference	W	L	T	Pct.	Pts.	OP
Baltimore	9	3	0	.750	374	251
Chi. Bears	8	4	0	.667	252	196
Green Bay	7	5	0	.583	248	246
San Francisco	7	5	0	.583	255	237
Detroit	3	8	1	.273	203	275
Los Angeles	2	10	0	.167	242	315

NFL championship: Baltimore 31, N.Y. Giants 16

LEADING RUSHERS	Att.	Yards	Avg.	Long	TD
Jim Brown, Cleveland	290	1,329	4.6	70t	14
J.D. Smith, San Francisco	207	1,036	5.0	73t	10
Ollie Matson, Los Angeles	161	863	5.4	50	6
Tom Tracy, Pittsburgh	199	794	4.0	51	3
Bobby Mitchell, Cleveland	131	743	5.7	90t	5

LEADING PASSERS	Att.	Comp.	Yards	TD	Int.
Charlie Conerly, N.Y. Giants	194	113	1,706	14	4
Earl Morrall, Detroit	137	65	1,102	5	5
John Unitas, Baltimore	367	193	2,899	32	14
Norm Van Brocklin, Philadelphia	340	191	2,617	16	14
Bill Wade, Los Angeles	261	153	2,001	12	17

LEADING RECEIVERS	No.	Yards	Avg.	Long	TD
Raymond Berry, Baltimore	66	959	14.5	55t	14
Del Shofner, Los Angeles	47	936	19.9	72t	7
Lenny Moore, Baltimore	47	846	18.0	71	6
Tommy McDonald, Philadelphia	47	846	18.0	71	10
Jim Mutscheller, Baltimore	44	699	15.9	40t	8
Billy Wilson, San Francisco	44	540	12.3	57t	4

1960 Pete Rozelle was elected commissioner of the NFL. The Chicago Cardinals, one of the most eminent and longstanding NFL teams, left their original city and moved to St. Louis. Two new teams were born. The Dallas Cowboys were formed to begin play in the NFL in 1960 and would be in direct competition in the Texas city with the Dallas Texans of the American Football League. Tex Schramm was named the Cowboys' general manager and Tom Landry their head coach. The Minnesota Vikings became the second new team; they were to begin competition in 1961.

Lamar Hunt, founder of the AFL, was elected its president for 1960. The league's Minneapolis-St. Paul franchise withdrew and Oakland became the eighth AFL team. They were owned by an eight-man syndicate headed by Y. C. (Chet) Soda and acquired their first players by drafting from the rosters of the seven other clubs. The league signed a contract with ABC for its games to be televised. It split into divisions with Boston, Buffalo, Houston, and New York in the East and Dallas, Denver, Los Angeles, and Oakland in the West. Rules were adopted allowing for a one- or two-point conversion attempt after touchdowns; one point could be made by kicking and two points by running or passing successfully for the extra point. The players' names were added to the backs of their jerseys.

The first player dispute between the leagues ended

Charlie Conerly of the New York Giants, the NFL's leading passer for the 1959 season.

Billy Cannon.

Chuck Bednarik.

Art Modell.

with a Los Angeles court declaring invalid the contract halfback Billy Cannon had with the Rams and freed him to play for Houston of the AFL. Quarterback Don Meredith of Southern Methodist, sought by both Dallas teams, settled on the Cowboys.

The Boston Patriots defeated the Buffalo Bills 28–7 at Buffalo in the first AFL preseason game before 16,000, July 30, and the Denver Broncos defeated Boston 13–10 at Boston in the first AFL regular season game before 21,597, September 9.

The Houston Oilers, coached by Lou Rymkus and quarterbacked by George Blanda, compiled a 10–4 record and won the Eastern Division. The Los Angeles Chargers, coached by the former boss of the NFL Rams, Sid Gillman, also had a 10–4 record and captured the Western championship. Blanda threw three touchdown passes as Houston defeated Los Angeles 24–16 in the first AFL championship game.

Vince Lombardi won his first division championship as coach of the Green Bay Packers. They won a title for the first time since 1944. Halfback Paul Hornung had a sensational season, scoring 176 points on 15 touchdowns, 15 field goals, and 41 extra points in a 12-game regular season.

The Philadelphia Eagles, coached by Lawrence (Buck) Shaw and led by quarterback Norm Van Brocklin and center and linebacker Chuck Bednarik, took over from their rivals, the New York Giants, as Eastern champions.

Three NFL runners had over 1,000 yards. They were Jim Brown of Cleveland, Jim Taylor of Green Bay, and John David Crow of St. Louis.

The new Dallas Cowboys finished with an 0–11–1 record.

The San Francisco 49ers adopted a shotgun offense for their last five games and won four of them.

Bednarik went both ways, playing 60 minutes of offense and defense, during five games for Philadelphia. He accomplished the same feat in the Eagles' championship game against Green Bay. It was one of the most hard-fought title games ever and Philadelphia won 17–13. Time ran out after Bednarik tackled the Packers' Taylor at the Eagles' 9-yard line. Shaw, the coach, and Van Brocklin, the quarterback, announced their retirements.

The Detroit Lions won the first "Bert Bell Benefit Bowl" or "Playoff Bowl," defeating the Cleveland Browns 17–16.

The NFL attendance for the 1960 season was 3,128,296 for 78 games and the AFL's was 926,156 for 56 games.

1960 AFL STANDINGS

Eastern Division	W	L	T	Pct.	Pts.	OP
Houston	10	4	0	.714	379	285
N.Y. Titans	7	7	0	.500	382	399
Buffalo	5	8	1	.385	296	303
Boston Patriots	5	9	0	.357	286	349
Western Division	**W**	**L**	**T**	**Pct.**	**Pts.**	**OP**
Los Angeles Chargers	10	4	0	.714	373	336
Dallas Texans	8	6	0	.571	362	253
Oakland	6	8	0	.429	319	388
Denver	4	9	1	.308	309	393

AFL championship: Houston 24, Los Angeles Chargers 16

LEADING RUSHERS	Att.	Yards	Avg.	Long	TD
Abner Haynes, Dallas Texans	156	875	5.6	67	9
Paul Lowe, Los Angeles Chargers	136	855	6.3	69	9
Billy Cannon, Houston	152	644	4.2	60	1
Dave Smith, Houston	154	643	4.2	65	5
Tony Teresa, Oakland	139	608	4.4	83	6

LEADING PASSERS	Att.	Comp.	Yards	TD	Int.
Jack Kemp, Los Angeles Chargers	406	211	3,018	20	25
Al Dorow, N.Y. Titans	396	201	2,748	26	26
Frank Tripucka, Denver	478	248	3,038	22	34
E. (Butch) Songin, Boston	392	187	2,476	22	15
Cotton Davidson, Dallas Texans	379	179	2,474	15	16

LEADING RECEIVERS	No.	Yards	Avg.	Long	TD
Lionel Taylor, Denver	92	1,235	13.4	80	12
Bill Groman, Houston	72	1,473	20.5	92	12
Don Maynard, N.Y. Titans	72	1,265	17.6	65	6
Art Powell, N.Y. Titans	69	1,167	16.9	76	14
Abner Haynes, Dallas Texans	55	576	10.5	34	3

1960 NFL STANDINGS

Eastern Conference	W	L	T	Pct.	Pts.	OP
Philadelphia	10	2	0	.833	321	246
Cleveland	8	3	1	.727	362	217
N.Y. Giants	6	4	2	.600	271	261
St. Louis	6	5	1	.545	288	230
Pittsburgh	5	6	1	.455	240	275
Washington	1	9	2	.100	178	309
Western Conference	**W**	**L**	**T**	**Pct.**	**Pts.**	**OP**
Green Bay	8	4	0	.667	332	209
Detroit	7	5	0	.583	239	212
San Francisco	7	5	0	.583	208	205
Baltimore	6	6	0	.500	288	234
Chi. Bears	5	6	1	.455	194	299
Los Angeles	4	7	1	.364	265	297
Dallas	0	11	1	.000	177	369

NFL championship: Philadelphia 17, Green Bay 13

LEADING RUSHERS	Att.	Yards	Avg.	Long	TD
Jim Brown, Cleveland	215	1,257	5.8	71t	9
Jim Taylor, Green Bay	230	1,101	4.8	32	11
John David Crow, St. Louis	183	1,071	5.9	57	6
Nick Pietrosante, Detroit	161	872	5.4	57	8
J.D. Smith, San Francisco	174	780	4.5	41	5

LEADING PASSERS	Att.	Comp.	Yards	TD	Int.
Milt Plum, Cleveland	250	151	2,297	21	5
Norm Van Brocklin, Philadelphia	284	153	2,471	24	17
John Unitas, Baltimore	378	190	3,099	25	24
Bill Wade, Los Angeles	182	106	1,294	12	11
Bobby Layne, Pittsburgh	209	103	1,814	13	17

LEADING RECEIVERS	No.	Yards	Avg.	Long	TD
Raymond Berry, Baltimore	74	1,298	17.5	70t	10
Sonny Randle, St. Louis	62	893	14.4	57t	9
Jim (Red) Phillips, Los Angeles	52	883	17.0	61t	8
Jim Gibbons, Detroit	51	604	11.8	65t	2
Pete Retzlaff, Philadelphia	46	826	18.0	57t	5

1961 Commissioner Rozelle signed a two-year contract awarding NBC radio and television rights to the NFL championship game for $615,000 annually. Congress then passed a bill legalizing single network television contracts by professional sports leagues.

Norm Van Brocklin, quarterback of the champion Philadelphia Eagles, was named head coach of the new Minnesota Vikings. His former understudy, Sonny Jurgensen, took over at quarterback for the Eagles. Y. A. Tittle, one of four capable quarterbacks on the roster of the San Francisco 49ers, was traded to the New York Giants because rookie Billy Kilmer and veterans John Brodie and Bobby Waters were better suited for the needs of the 49ers' new shotgun offense. The Tittle trade was just one of several made by New York. It also acquired defensive back Erich Barnes from the Chicago Bears, end Del Shofner from the Los Angeles Rams, and end Joe Walton from the Washington Redskins.

The Redskins moved from Griffith Stadium to the new District of Columbia Stadium.

The first American Football League franchise shift occurred when the Los Angeles Chargers were moved and became the San Diego Chargers. Ed McGah, Wayne Valley, and Robert Osborne bought out their partners in the ownership of the Oakland Raiders; McGah was named Raiders' president. Bob and Lee Howsam sold the Denver Broncos to a group headed by Calvin Kunz.

Art Modell bought controlling interest in the Cleveland Browns.

Three original AFL coaches departed during the season. Wally Lemm replaced Lou Rymkus at Houston, Mike Holovak replaced Lou Saban at Boston, and Marty Feldman replaced Eddie Erdelatz at Oakland.

End Willard Dewveall of the Chicago Bears played out his option and joined Houston of the AFL, the first player to voluntarily move from one league to the other.

The Chargers, playing in a new city, won the Western Division title again and the Oilers repeated as Eastern champions. San Diego had two giant rookie linemen in Earl Faison and Ernie Ladd, and won its first 11 games in a row. Houston's Blanda completed seven touchdown passes in one game.

Lionel Taylor of the Denver Broncos caught a pro football record 100 passes.

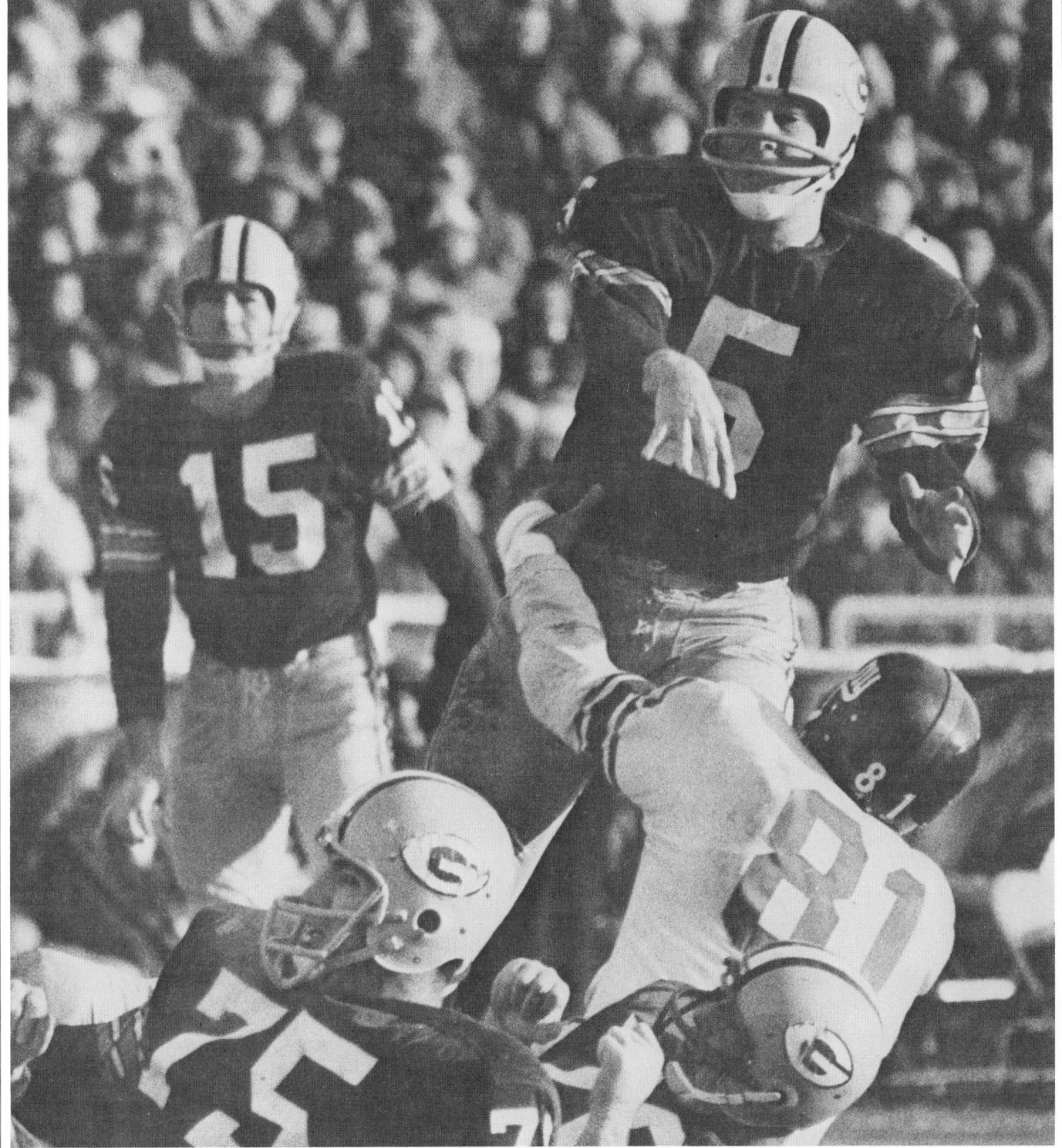

Paul Hornung passing for Green Bay in the 1961 title game; Andy Robustelli of the New York Giants tries to tackle him.

Houston defeated San Diego 10–3 for its second straight AFL title.

The Green Bay Packers of Vince Lombardi ruled the NFL. Halfback Paul Hornung led the league in scoring for the third year in a row despite the fact that it was the time of the Berlin crisis and he was on active duty in the army reserve and stationed at Fort Riley, Kansas; he had to travel back and forth each weekend from Fort Riley to the Packers' games. He scored 33 points in one game against Baltimore.

San Francisco's shotgun offense was the talk of the league. Coach Red Hickey alternated Brodie, Kilmer, and Waters at quarterback in the unusual formation in which they took the snap from center seven to nine yards back and then ran, passed, or handed off. The 49ers ran up a 4–1 record until the Chicago Bears stopped them 31–0, playing middle linebacker Bill George at middle guard, where he befuddled the 49ers' center and put pressure on their passers. San Francisco went back to an ordinary pro formation after that.

Detroit won six games on the road but only two at home. The new Minnesota Vikings had a respectable 3–11 record and their rookie quarterback, Fran Tar-kenton, starred as they won the first regular season game 37–13 over the Chicago Bears. Tarkenton passed for four touchdowns and ran for a fifth.

Tittle, the new leader of the New York Giants, had 17 touchdown passes as they won the Eastern Conference. Sonny Jurgensen of Philadelphia set an NFL record by passing for 3,723 yards but the Eagles lost both their games against New York. Jim Brown of Cleveland led the NFL in rushing for the fifth straight time and tied his own single game mark with 237 yards against Philadelphia.

Hornung set a championship record when he

Jim Taylor.

scored 19 points to lead the Green Bay Packers to their first NFL championship since 1944 and first under Lombardi, 37–0 over the New York Giants in the title game, December 31.

1961 AFL STANDINGS

Eastern Division	W	L	T	Pct.	Pts.	OP
Houston	10	3	1	.769	513	242
Boston Patriots	9	4	1	.692	413	313
N.Y. Titans	7	7	0	.500	301	390
Buffalo	6	8	0	.429	294	342
Western Division	W	L	T	Pct.	Pts.	OP
San Diego	12	2	0	.857	396	219
Dallas Texans	6	8	0	.429	334	343
Denver	3	11	0	.214	251	432
Oakland	2	12	0	.143	237	458

AFL championship: Houston 10, San Diego 3

LEADING RUSHERS	Att.	Yards	Avg.	Long	TD
Billy Cannon, Houston	200	948	4.7	61	6
Bill Mathis, N.Y. Titans	202	846	4.2	30	7
Abner Haynes, Dallas Texans	179	841	4.7	59	9
Paul Lowe, San Diego	175	767	4.4	87	9
Charlie Tolar, Houston	157	577	3.7	28	4
LEADING PASSERS	Att.	Comp.	Yards	TD	Int.
George Blanda, Houston	362	187	3,330	36	22
Tom Flores, Oakland	366	190	2,176	15	19
Jack Kemp, San Diego	364	165	2,686	15	22
Al Dorow, N.Y. Titans	438	197	2,651	19	30
Babe Parilli, Boston	198	104	1,314	13	9
LEADING RECEIVERS	No.	Yards	Avg.	Long	TD
Charley Hennigan, Houston	82	1,756	21.3	80	12
Art Powell, N.Y. Titans	71	881	12.4	48	5
Bill Groman, Houston	50	1,175	23.5	80	17
Glenn Bass, Buffalo	50	765	15.3	76	3
Gino Cappelletti, Boston	45	768	17.1	53	8

1961 NFL STANDINGS

Eastern Conference	W	L	T	Pct.	Pts.	OP
N.Y. Giants	10	3	1	.769	368	220
Philadelphia	10	4	0	.714	361	297
Cleveland	8	5	1	.615	319	270
St. Louis	7	7	0	.500	279	267
Pittsburgh	6	8	0	.429	295	287
Dallas	4	9	1	.308	236	380
Washington	1	12	1	.077	174	392
Western Conference	W	L	T	Pct.	Pts.	OP
Green Bay	11	3	0	.786	391	223
Detroit	8	5	1	.615	270	258
Baltimore	8	6	0	.571	302	307
Chi. Bears	8	6	0	.571	326	302
San Francisco	7	6	1	.538	346	272
Los Angeles	4	10	0	.286	263	333
Minnesota	3	11	0	.214	285	407

NFL championship: Green Bay 37, N.Y. Giants 0

LEADING RUSHERS	Att.	Yards	Avg.	Long	TD
Jim Brown, Cleveland	305	1,408	4.6	38	8
Jim Taylor, Green Bay	243	1,307	5.4	53	15
Alex Webster, N.Y. Giants	196	928	4.7	59	2
Nick Pietrosante, Detroit	201	841	4.2	42	5
J.D. Smith, San Francisco	167	823	4.9	33	8
LEADING PASSERS	Att.	Comp.	Yards	TD	Int.
Milt Plum, Cleveland	302	177	2,416	18	10
Sonny Jurgensen, Philadelphia	416	235	3,723	32	24
Bart Starr, Green Bay	295	172	2,418	16	16
John Brodie, San Francisco	283	155	2,588	14	12
Bill Wade, Chi. Bears	250	139	2,258	22	13
LEADING RECEIVERS	No.	Yards	Avg.	Long	TD
Jim (Red) Phillips, Los Angeles	78	1,092	14.0	69t	5
Raymond Berry, Baltimore	75	873	11.6	44	0
Del Shofner, N.Y. Giants	68	1,125	16.5	46t	11
Tommy McDonald, Phil.	64	1,144	17.9	66	13
Mike Ditka, Chicago	56	1,076	19.2	76t	12
Billy Howton, Dallas	56	785	14.0	53	4

1962 Pete Rozelle of the NFL and Joe Foss of the AFL each were given new five-year contracts.

Dan Reeves bought out his partners and took complete control of the Los Angeles Rams. There was an unusual coaching change when Wally Lemm left the Houston Oilers of the AFL after winning a championship and moved to the St. Louis Cardinals. Frank (Pop) Ivy, coach of the Cardinals, moved to the Oilers. Jack Kemp, a quarterback for the San Diego Chargers, was put on waivers and picked up by the Buffalo Bills. A strong contingent of NFL rookies included quarterback Roman Gabriel and defensive tackle Merlin Olsen of Los Angeles and end Gary Collins of Cleveland. Two old pros, quarterback Bobby Layne of Pittsburgh and linebacker Chuck Bednarik of Philadelphia, retired.

There was intense competition between the two

leagues for college players. The NFL signed most of the big-name players and also won a court victory after a two-and-a-half-year battle when a U.S. District judge ruled against the AFL's charges of monopoly and conspiracy in expansion, television, and signings.

Len Dawson requested and was granted his release from the Cleveland Browns. He signed with the Dallas Texans and was reunited with his former Purdue coach, Hank Stram.

The NFL entered into a single network agreement with CBS for telecasting of all regular season games for $4,650,000 annually.

The rules were changed, making it illegal to grab another player's face mask.

The AFL voted to make the scoreboard clock the official timer of the game.

Ivy, the new Oilers' coach, became the third to guide them to a division championship and had an 11–3 record. The Dallas Texans captured the West behind coach Hank Stram.

Cookie Gilchrist, who had been playing in the Canadian Football league, came into the AFL as a rookie with Buffalo and led its rushers with 1,096 yards.

The Texans defeated the Oilers 20–17 for the AFL championship in the longest pro game ever played up to that point. It went into a second quarter of sudden death overtime, 77 minutes and 54 seconds, before Tommy Brooker of Dallas kicked a 25-yard field goal to win it.

Green Bay withstood a challenge from Detroit to once again win the NFL's Western Conference. The Packers prevailed even though the Lions upset them 26–14 on Thanksgiving Day, sacking quarterback Bart Starr for 110 yards in losses. Starr survived and led the NFL in passing. Fullback Jim Taylor had his greatest season, gaining 1,474 yards to oust Jim Brown of Cleveland as the league champion. Taylor also led the league with 19 touchdowns.

Quarterback Y.A. Tittle of the New York Giants passed for seven touchdowns and 505 yards against Washington October 28.

Sam Huff, the Giants' middle linebacker, waged a fierce personal duel with the Packers' Taylor as the two teams played for the NFL championship. It was bitter cold and the wind was blowing 40 miles an hour at Yankee Stadium in New York. Taylor gained 85 yards and his teammate Jerry Kramer kicked three field goals as the Packers won their second consecutive NFL title, 16–7.

Len Dawson handing off to Curtis McClinton and faking to Jack Spikes, 1962 AFL title game.

1962 AFL STANDINGS

Eastern Division	W	L	T	Pct.	Pts.	OP
Houston	11	3	0	.786	387	270
Boston Patriots	9	4	1	.692	346	295
Buffalo	7	6	1	.538	309	272
N.Y. Titans	5	9	0	.357	278	423
Western Division	W	L	T	Pct.	Pts.	OP
Dallas Texans	11	3	0	.786	389	233
Denver	7	7	0	.500	353	334
San Diego	4	10	0	.286	314	392
Oakland	1	13	0	.071	213	370

AFL championship: Dallas Texans 20, Houston 17, sudden death overtime

LEADING RUSHERS

	Att.	Yards	Avg.	Long	TD
Cookie Gilchrist, Buffalo	214	1,096	5.1	44	13
Abner Haynes, Dallas Texans	221	1,049	4.7	71	13
Charlie Tolar, Houston	244	1,012	4.1	25	7
Clemon Daniels, Oakland	161	766	4.7	72	7
Curtis McClinton, Dallas Texans	111	604	5.4	69	2

LEADING PASSERS

	Att.	Comp.	Yards	TD	Int.
Len Dawson, Dallas Texans	310	189	2,759	29	17
Babe Parilli, Boston	253	140	1,988	18	8
Frank Tripucka, Denver	440	240	2,917	17	25
George Blanda, Houston	418	197	2,810	27	42
Johnny Green, N.Y. Titans	258	128	1,741	10	18

LEADING RECEIVERS

	No.	Yards	Avg.	Long	TD
Lionel Taylor, Denver	77	908	11.7	45	4
Art Powell, N.Y. Titans	64	1,130	17.6	80	8
Dick Christy, N.Y. Titans	62	538	8.6	41	3
Richard (Bo) Dickinson, Denver	60	554	9.2	33	4
Don Maynard, N.Y. Titans	56	1,041	18.5	86	8

Y. A. Tittle of the New York Giants passing to Joe Morrison against Cleveland, 1962.

A wintry Wrigley Field is the scene as George Halas of Chicago Bears wins his last NFL championship, 1963.

1962 NFL STANDINGS

Eastern Conference	W	L	T	Pct.	Pts.	OP
N.Y. Giants	12	2	0	.857	398	283
Pittsburgh	9	5	0	.643	312	363
Cleveland	7	6	1	.538	291	257
Washington	5	7	2	.417	305	376
Dallas	5	8	1	.385	398	402
St. Louis	4	9	1	.308	287	361
Philadelphia	3	10	1	.231	282	356

Western Conference	W	L	T	Pct.	Pts.	OP
Green Bay	13	1	0	.929	415	148
Detroit	11	3	0	.786	315	177
Chicago	9	5	0	.643	321	287
Baltimore	7	7	0	.500	293	288
San Francisco	6	8	0	.429	282	331
Minnesota	2	11	1	.154	254	410
Los Angeles	1	12	1	.077	220	334

NFL championship: Green Bay 16, N.Y. Giants 7

LEADING RUSHERS	Att.	Yards	Avg.	Long	TD
Jim Taylor, Green Bay	272	1,474	5.4	51	19
John Henry Johnson, Pittsburgh	251	1,141	4.5	40	7
Dick Bass, Los Angeles	196	1,033	5.3	57	6
Jim Brown, Cleveland	230	996	4.3	31	13
Don Perkins, Dalls	222	945	4.3	35	7

LEADING PASSERS	Att.	Comp.	Yards	TD	Int.
Bart Starr, Green Bay	285	178	2,438	12	9
Y.A. Tittle, N.Y. Giants	375	200	3,224	33	20
Eddie LeBaron, Dallas	166	95	1,436	16	9
Frank Ryan, Cleveland	194	112	1,541	10	7
Sonny Jurgensen, Philadelphia	366	196	3,261	22	26

LEADING RECEIVERS	No.	Yards	Avg.	Long	TD
Bobby Mitchell, Washington	72	1,385	19.2	81t	11
Sonny Randle, St. Louis	63	1,158	18.4	86t	7
Bobby Joe Conrad, St. Louis	62	954	15.4	72t	4
Jim (Red) Phillips, Los Angeles	60	875	14.6	65t	5
Tommy McDonald, Philadelphia	58	1,146	19.8	60t	10
Mike Ditka, Chicago	58	904	15.6	69t	5
Johnny Morris, Chicago	58	889	15.3	73t	5

1963 Commissioner Pete Rozelle indefinitely suspended Paul Hornung of Green Bay and Alex Karras of Detroit for placing bets on their own teams and also fined five other Detroit players $2,000 each for betting on games in which they did not participate. The Detroit Lions Football Company was fined $2,000 on each of two counts for failure to report information promptly and for lack of proper sideline supervision.

The competition between the NFL Cowboys and AFL Texans for Dallas football fans ended with the Texans moving to Kansas City and becoming the Chiefs. The struggling New York franchise of the AFL, the Titans, was taken over by the league from owner Harry Wismer and then passed to the control of a group headed by W.A. (Sonny) Werblin, who changed their name to the Jets. The Boston Patriots moved their games from Boston University Field to larger Fenway Park. The Jets and Oakland Raiders, losers of 19 straight games at one point, were allowed to select players from other franchises in hopes of giving the league more competitive balance.

Paul Brown, coach of the Cleveland Browns since their inception, was fired. Don Shula became coach of the Baltimore Colts and Weeb Ewbank coach of the New York Jets. Linebackers Lee Roy Jordan of Dallas and Dave Robinson of Green Bay were notable rookies in the NFL and defensive tackle Buck Buchanan and guard Ed Budde started their careers with the Kansas City Chiefs.

The Pro Football Hall of Fame was dedicated at Canton, Ohio, the city in which the league that became the NFL was organized in 1920. Seventeen charter members were inducted.

San Diego won the AFL Western Division title again, but only after a struggle with Oakland. The Raiders, coached by former Chargers' assistant Al Davis, won their last eight games and finished second with a 10–4 record.

Clemon Daniels of Oakland led the league with 1,099 yards rushing and Cookie Gilchrist of Buffalo set a professional record with 243 yards rushing in a game against the New York Jets.

The Boston Patriots and Buffalo Bills finished in a tie for the Eastern Division title and the Patriots won a playoff 26–8 on a snow-covered field at Buffalo.

San Diego crushed Boston 51–10 in the championship game behind 206 yards rushing and 329 combined net yards by halfback Keith Lincoln.

The Chicago Bears, coached by George Halas, denied the Green Bay Packers another NFL championship. The Bears had a solid defense led by linebackers Joe Fortunato, Bill George, and Larry Morris and won the Western Conference. Green Bay stayed close behind despite losing quarterback Bart Starr with a broken hand. Los Angeles had a massive defensive line called the "Fearsome Foursome," made up of ends David (Deacon) Jones and Lamar Lundy and tackles Roosevelt Grier and Merlin Olsen.

Y. A. Tittle of the New York Giants had another brilliant season, throwing 36 touchdown passes, and the Giants won their third straight Eastern Conference championship. Jim Brown, the Cleveland Browns' great fullback, thrived under a new coach, Blanton Collier, and had his most productive season with 1,863 yards and games of 232 against Dallas and 223 against Philadelphia on the way to his sixth title in seven years.

The domination of the Western Conference in the title game continued. The Chicago Bears stopped the Giants 14–10, intercepting five passes by Tittle, who twisted a knee in the second quarter but nevertheless played the second half in a losing effort.

1963 AFL STANDINGS

Eastern Division	W	L	T	Pct.	Pts.	OP
Boston Patriots	7	6	1	.538	317	257
Buffalo	7	6	1	.538	304	291
Houston	6	8	0	.429	302	372
N.Y. Jets	5	8	1	.385	249	399
Western Division	**W**	**L**	**T**	**Pct.**	**Pts.**	**OP**
San Diego	11	3	0	.786	399	255
Oakland	10	4	0	.714	363	282
Kansas City	5	7	2	.417	347	263
Denver	2	11	0	.154	301	473

Eastern Division playoff: Boston 26, Buffalo 8
AFL championship: San Diego 51, Boston 10

LEADING RUSHERS	Att.	Yards	Avg.	Long	TD
Clemon Daniels, Oakland	215	1,099	5.1	74	3
Paul Lowe, San Diego	177	1,010	5.7	66	8
Cookie Gilchrist, Buffalo	232	979	4.2	32	12
Keith Lincoln, San Diego	128	826	6.4	76	5
Larry Garron, Boston	179	750	4.1	47	2

LEADING PASSERS	Att.	Comp.	Yards	TD	Int.
Tobin Rote, San Diego	286	170	2,510	20	17
Tom Flores, Oakland	247	113	2,101	20	13
Jack Kemp, Buffalo	384	194	2,914	13	20
Len Dawson, Kansas City	352	190	2,389	26	19
George Blanda, Houston	423	224	3,003	24	25

LEADING RECEIVERS	No.	Yards	Avg.	Long	TD
Lionel Taylor, Denver	78	1,101	14.1	72	10
Art Powell, Oakland	73	1,304	17.8	85	16
Robert (Bake) Turner, N.Y. Jets	71	1,007	14.1	53	6
Bill Miller, Buffalo	69	860	12.4	36	3
Chris Burford, Kansas City	68	824	12.1	69	9

1963 NFL STANDINGS

Eastern Conference	W	L	T	Pct.	Pts.	OP
N.Y. Giants	11	3	0	.786	448	280
Cleveland	10	4	0	.714	343	262
St. Louis	9	5	0	.643	341	283
Pittsburgh	7	4	3	.636	321	295
Dallas	4	10	0	.286	305	378
Washington	3	11	0	.214	279	398
Philadelphia	2	10	2	.167	242	381
Western Conference	**W**	**L**	**T**	**Pct.**	**Pts.**	**OP**
Chicago	11	1	2	.917	301	144
Green Bay	11	2	1	.846	369	206
Baltimore	8	6	0	.571	316	285
Detroit	5	8	1	.385	326	265
Minnesota	5	8	1	.385	309	390
Los Angeles	5	9	0	.357	210	350
San Francisco	2	12	0	.143	198	391

NFL championship: Chicago 14, N.Y. Giants 10

LEADING RUSHERS	Att.	Yards	Avg.	Long	TD
Jim Brown, Cleveland	291	1,863	6.4	80t	12
Jim Taylor, Green Bay	248	1,018	4.1	40t	9
Timmy Brown, Philadelphia	192	841	4.4	34	6
John Henry Johnson, Pittsburgh	186	773	4.2	48	4
Tommy Mason, Minnesota	166	763	4.6	70t	7

LEADING PASSERS	Att.	Comp.	Yards	TD	Int.
Y.A. Tittle, N.Y. Giants	367	221	3,145	36	14
John Unitas, Baltimore	410	237	3,481	20	12
Earl Morrall, Detroit	328	174	2,621	24	14
Charley Johnson, St. Louis	423	222	3,280	28	21
Fran Tarkenton, Minnesota	297	170	2,311	15	15

LEADING RECEIVERS	No.	Yards	Avg.	Long	TD
Bobby Joe Conrad, St. Louis	73	967	13.2	48	10
Bobby Mitchell, Washington	69	1,436	20.8	99t	7
Terry Barr, Detroit	66	1,086	16.5	75t	13
Del Shofner, N.Y. Giants	64	1,181	18.5	70t	9
Buddy Dial, Pittsburgh	60	1,295	21.6	83t	9

1964 The NFL signed a new contract with CBS television for a total of $14.1 million for the rights to regular season games for the next two years. Each NFL club would receive more than $1 million a year. In addition, CBS acquired the rights to the 1964 and 1965 NFL championship games for $1.8 million each.

The AFL signed a new five year, $36 million television contract with NBC. The deal assured each team approximately $900,000 a year from television rights.

Jerry Wolman, the new owner of the Philadelphia

San Diego's Keith Lincoln in the 1963 AFL championship game in which he made 334 net yards.

The Pro Football Hall of Fame, which opened in 1963.

Fran Tarkenton of Minnesota passes as David (Deacon) Jones and Merlin Olsen rush for Los Angeles, 1965.

Joe Namath, a New York Jets' rookie in 1965.

Eagles, hired Joe Kuharich as head coach. Kuharich shook up the Eagles, trading quarterback Sonny Jurgensen to Washington for quarterback Norm Snead and also dealing with Green Bay for center Jim Ringo and with Detroit for halfback Ollie Matson.

The New York Giants traded linebacker Sam Huff to Washington and defensive tackle Ed Modzelewski to Cleveland.

In addition to Jurgensen and Huff, the Redskins also acquired rookie halfback sensation Charley Taylor.

The Chicago Bears suffered a stunning loss when halfback Willie Galimore and end John Farrington were killed in an auto crash near the Bears' training camp at Rensselaer, Indiana.

Soccer player Pete Gogolak of Cornell University became the first soccer-style kicker in pro football, signing a contract with the Buffalo Bills of the AFL.

The New York Jets moved from the shabby Polo Grounds to new Shea Stadium in Flushing Meadows.

Gogolak, the Bills' kicker, had 19 field goals but was overshadowed by Gino Cappelletti of Boston, who had 25, along with 38 extra points and seven touchdowns as a pass receiver to lead the league in scoring with 155 points. New York managed no better than third in the Eastern Division but set a club attendance record of 298,972 in its new stadium, despite having to play some home games on Saturday nights to avoid conflict with the baseball Mets. Buffalo captured the Eastern title by beating Boston 24–14 on the last day of the season at snow-covered Fenway Park in a near-blizzard.

The AFL's reputation for wide-open football grew as San Diego's Lance Alworth became perhaps the best wide receiver in the game and as Houston quarterback George Blanda attempted 505 passes for the season, including 68 in one game against Buffalo that the Oilers lost 24–10. Charley Hennigan caught 101 of Blanda's passes, breaking the one-season record set by Lionel Taylor of Denver in 1961.

San Diego won the West behind the pass catching of Alworth, the passing of John Hadl, the running of Keith Lincoln and Paul Lowe, and a solid defense. Kansas City embarrassed the Chargers late in the season, however, beating them 49–6.

In the title game, Cookie Gilchrist of Buffalo gained 144 yards on a foggy day at War Memorial Stadium in Buffalo and the Bills defeated the Chargers 20–7.

Blanton Collier, the successor to Paul Brown at Cleveland, continued to build a powerful team. Fullback Jim Brown led the league in rushing for the seventh time in eight years and boosted his career touchdown total to 105. Frank Ryan was the Browns' quarterback and he had Gary Collins at flanker and first-round draft choice Paul Warfield at split end. Warfield caught 52 passes and the Browns held off a challenge from the St. Louis Cardinals to win the Eastern Conference. The Giants, perennial powers in the East, fell to last place.

The same fate befell the Chicago Bears, defending Western champions. Shaken by the tragic accident during their training camp period, they dropped to sixth place despite end Johnny Morris's 93 pass receptions.

Paul Hornung of Green Bay, suspended the previous season, rejoined the Packers. Quarterback Bart Starr led the league's passers and fullback Jim Taylor had his fifth season with over 1,000 yards. Minnesota became a contending team in only its fourth season, tying the Packers for second place in the West behind 22 touchdown passes by Fran Tarkenton. Alex Karras, who like Hornung had been suspended, rejoined Detroit.

The Baltimore Colts were the Western champions and had the best record in the NFL, 12–2. Quarterback John Unitas guided the Colts' attack that included halfback–flanker Lenny Moore, who scored an NFL record 20 touchdowns.

Baltimore was favored in the title game against the surprising Eastern champions, the Cleveland Browns. Cleveland, however, pulled off one of the biggest upsets in the game's history. Ryan threw three touchdown passes to Collins and Cleveland won 27–0 before 79,544 at Cleveland Stadium. The winning and losing shares were records, $8,052 for each member of the Browns and $5,571 for each member of the Colts.

Y.A. Tittle and Andy Robustelli, two of the greatest players in New York Giants' history, retired from pro football.

1964 AFL STANDINGS

Eastern Division	W	L	T	Pct.	Pts.	OP
Buffalo	12	2	0	.857	400	242
Boston Patriots	10	3	1	.769	365	297
N.Y. Jets	5	8	1	.385	278	315
Houston	4	10	0	.286	310	355

Western Division	W	L	T	Pct.	Pts.	OP
San Diego	8	5	1	.615	341	300
Kansas City	7	7	0	.500	366	306
Oakland	5	7	2	.417	303	350
Denver	2	11	1	.154	240	438

AFL championship: Buffalo 20, San Diego 7

LEADING RUSHERS	Att.	Yards	Avg.	Long	TD
Cookie Gilchrist, Buffalo	230	981	4.3	67	6
Matt Snell, N.Y. Jets	215	948	4.4	42	5
Clemon Daniels, Oakland	173	824	4.8	42	2
Sid Blanks, Houston	145	756	5.2	91	6
Abner Haynes, Kansas City	139	697	5.0	80	4

LEADING PASSERS	Att.	Comp.	Yards	TD	Int.
Len Dawson, Kansas City	354	199	2,879	30	18
Babe Parilli, Boston	473	228	3,465	31	27
George Blanda, Houston	505	262	3,287	17	27
John Hadl, San Diego	274	147	2,157	18	15
Cotton Davidson, Oakland	320	155	2,497	21	19

LEADING RECEIVERS	No.	Yards	Avg.	Long	TD
Charley Hennigan, Houston	101	1,546	15.3	53	8
Art Powell, Oakland	76	1,361	17.9	77	11
Lionel Taylor, Denver	76	873	11.5	57	7
Frank Jackson, Kansas City	62	943	15.2	72	9
Lance Alworth, San Diego	61	1,235	20.2	82	13

1964 NFL STANDINGS

Eastern Conference	W	L	T	Pct.	Pts.	OP
Cleveland	10	3	1	.769	415	293
St. Louis	9	3	2	.750	357	331
Philadelphia	6	8	0	.429	312	313
Washington	6	8	0	.429	307	305
Dallas	5	8	1	.385	250	289
Pittsburgh	5	9	0	.357	253	315
N.Y. Giants	2	10	2	.167	241	399

Western Conference	W	L	T	Pct.	Pts.	OP
Baltimore	12	2	0	.857	428	225
Green Bay	8	5	1	.615	342	245
Minnesota	8	5	1	.615	355	296
Detroit	7	5	2	.583	280	260
Los Angeles	5	7	2	.417	283	339
Chicago	5	9	0	.357	260	379
San Francisco	4	10	0	.286	236	330

NFL championship: Cleveland 27, Baltimore 0

LEADING RUSHERS	Att.	Yards	Avg.	Long	TD
Jim Brown, Cleveland	280	1,446	5.2	71	7
Jim Taylor, Green Bay	235	1,169	5.0	84t	12
John Henry Johnson, Pittsburgh	235	1,048	4.5	45t	7
Don Perkins, Dallas	174	768	4.4	59	6
Charley Taylor, Washington	199	755	3.8	50	5

LEADING PASSERS	Att.	Comp.	Yards	TD	Int.
Bart Starr, Green Bay	272	163	2,144	15	4
Fran Tarkenton, Minnesota	306	171	2,506	22	11
Sonny Jurgensen, Washington	385	207	2,934	24	13
John Unitas, Baltimore	305	158	2,824	19	6
Milt Plum, Detroit	287	154	2,241	18	15

LEADING RECEIVERS	No.	Yards	Avg.	Long	TD
Johnny Morris, Chicago	93	1,200	12.9	63t	10
Mike Ditka, Chicago	75	897	12.0	34	5
Frank Clarke, Dallas	65	893	15.0	49	5
Bobby Joe Conrad, St. Louis	61	780	12.8	53	6
Bobby Mitchell, Washington	60	904	15.1	60	10

1965 Sonny Werblin signed quarterback Joe Namath of Alabama to a record contract reported to be $400,000 a year. He was the most talked-about member of an exceptional class of rookies that also included halfback Gale Sayers and linebacker Dick Butkus of the Chicago Bears, end Bob Hayes of the Dallas Cowboys, end Fred Biletnikoff of the Oakland

Y.A. Tittle.

Bob Hayes.

Tom Matte wearing plays on his wrist, 1965.

Raiders, and fullback Ken Willard of the San Francisco 49ers.

Cookie Gilchrist was traded from the Buffalo Bills to the Denver Broncos.

Raymond (Buddy) Parker quit as coach of the Pittsburgh Steelers.

CBS signed a new television contract with the NFL calling for $18.8 million a year, plus $2 milion for the championship game. The network also received permission to telecast three night games in prime time and also to modify the blackout so that one game could be seen in a city when the club was home.

Each league decided to expand. The NFL added Atlanta and the AFL added Miami, both for 1966.

NFL rules were changed increasing the number of officials for each game from five to six; the sixth official was called the "line judge." Officials' penalty flags were changed in color from white to bright gold.

The Houston Oilers, who had been playing their home games at Jeppesen Stadium, a 38,000-seat high school facility, announced they would not play in the new Astrodome because of "an unrealistic lease agreement." and signed a five-year lease for the use of 70,000-seat Rice Stadium.

Buffalo and San Diego repeated as champions of their divisions in the AFL. Namath, New York's new quarterback, took over as starter and threw 18 touchdown passes, 14 of them to wide receiver Don Maynard.

Buffalo won the title game for the second year in a row, shutting out San Diego 23–0.

Jim Brown's ninth season for Cleveland was another great one but the Browns got a challenge from the Dallas Cowboys in the Eastern Conference for the first time. Dallas reached .500 with a 7–7 record. Quarterback Don Meredith threw 22 touchdown passes and brilliant rookie split end Bob Hayes caught 46 for 1,003 yards, a sensational 21.8-yard average per catch, and 12 touchdowns.

Chicago finished third in the Western Conference but halfback Gale Sayers was almost unstoppable. He scored six touchdowns in one game against San Francisco and had a record 22 for the year.

Norm Van Brocklin quit as coach of the Vikings in midseason, then changed his mind and returned a few days later.

Green Bay and Baltimore were the conference's best teams but wound up deadlocked. The Packers missed a chance to clinch the title when they were tied by the 49ers on the last day of the season. The Colts went through a difficult season, losing quarterback John Unitas with a knee injury and his replacement, Gary Cuozzo, with a shoulder separation. Halfback Tom Matte, who had played quarterback in college at Ohio State, took over the position for Baltimore and, reading his plays off a band around his wrist, led the Colts to a victory over Los Angeles. That set up a playoff against the Packers at Green Bay. Matte was the makeshift quarterback for the Colts and the Packers' starter, Bart Starr, was injured early in the game and replaced by Zeke Bratkowski. The Colts argued unsuccessfully that a field goal by Chandler that tied the game 10–10 in the fourth quarter was wide of the goal posts. The teams played 13 minutes and 39 seconds of sudden death overtime before a field goal by Don Chandler won the game 13–10 for Green Bay.

Wintry Green Bay was the site of the title game between the Packers and Browns. A morning storm made roads nearly impassable, delayed the arrival of the Browns, and sent a work crew using shovels and snow plows into action. Playing on the muddy turf, the Packers used their ball-control game, with Paul Hornung gaining 105 yards and Jim Taylor 96, while Brown was held to 50 in a 23–12 Green Bay victory, its third NFL championship under coach Vince Lombardi.

Guard Gene Hickerson escorts Jim Brown of Cleveland, 1965; number 13 is quarterback Frank Ryan.

Except for the Pro Bowl it was the last game for Cleveland's Brown. He left behind a career total of 12,312 yards rushing, seven 1,000-yard seasons, 58 100-yard games, four 200-yard games, a career average of 5.2 yards per rush, and 126 touchdowns, 106 of them by rushing.

Brown ended his career appropriately in the Pro Bowl, scoring three touchdowns and winning the outstanding back award in the East's 36–7 victory.

After the season, the AFL all-star game ran into trouble in New Orleans when some players charged they were racially discriminated against. The game was shifted to Houston.

Two men who played important roles in NFL history died. They were Earl (Curly) Lambeau, founder and former coach of the Green Bay Packers, and Jack Mara, coowner of the New York Giants.

1965 AFL STANDINGS

Eastern Division

	W	L	T	Pct.	Pts.	OP
Buffalo	10	3	1	.769	313	226
N.Y. Jets	5	8	1	.385	285	303
Boston Patriots	4	8	2	.333	244	302
Houston	4	10	0	.286	298	429

Western Division

	W	L	T	Pct.	Pts.	OP
San Diego	9	2	3	.818	340	227
Oakland	8	5	1	.615	298	239
Kansas City	7	5	2	.583	322	285
Denver	4	10	0	.286	303	392

AFL championship: Buffalo 23, San Diego 0

LEADING RUSHERS

	Att.	Yards	Avg.	Long	TD
Paul Lowe, San Diego	222	1,121	5.1	59	7
Cookie Gilchrist, Denver	252	954	3.8	44	6
Clemon Daniels, Oakland	219	884	4.0	57	5
Matt Snell, N.Y. Jets	169	763	4.5	44	4
Curtis McClinton, Kansas City	175	661	3.8	48	6

LEADING PASSERS

	Att.	Comp.	Yards	TD	Int.
John Hadl, San Diego	348	174	2,798	20	21
Len Dawson, Kansas City	305	163	2,262	21	14
Joe Namath, N.Y. Jets	340	164	2,220	18	15
Jack Kemp, Buffalo	391	179	2,368	10	18
George Blanda, Houston	442	186	2,542	20	30

LEADING RECEIVERS

	No.	Yards	Avg.	Long	TD
Lionel Taylor, Denver	85	1,131	13.3	63	6
Lance Alworth, San Diego	69	1,602	23.2	85	14
Don Maynard, N.Y. Jets	68	1,218	17.9	56	14
Ode Burrell, Houston	55	650	11.8	52	4
Art Powell, Oakland	52	800	15.4	66	12

1965 NFL STANDINGS

Eastern Conference

	W	L	T	Pct.	Pts.	OP
Cleveland	11	3	0	.786	363	325
Dallas	7	7	0	.500	325	280
N.Y. Giants	7	7	0	.500	270	338
Washington	6	8	0	.429	257	301
Philadelphia	5	9	0	.357	363	359
St. Louis	5	9	0	.357	296	309
Pittsburgh	2	12	0	.143	202	397

Western Conference

	W	L	T	Pct.	Pts.	OP
Baltimore	10	3	1	.769	389	284
Green Bay	10	3	1	.769	316	224
Chicago	9	5	0	.643	409	275
San Francisco	7	6	1	.538	421	402
Minnesota	7	7	0	.500	383	403
Detroit	6	7	1	.462	257	295
Los Angeles	4	10	0	.286	269	328

Western Conference playoff: Green Bay 13, Baltimore 10, sudden death overtime
NFL championship: Green Bay 23, Cleveland 12

LEADING RUSHERS

	Att.	Yards	Avg.	Long	TD
Jim Brown, Cleveland	289	1,544	5.3	67	17
Gale Sayers, Chicago	166	867	5.2	61t	14
Timmy Brown, Philadelphia	158	861	5.4	54t	6
Ken Willard, San Francisco	189	778	4.1	32	5
Jim Taylor, Green Bay	207	734	3.5	35	4

LEADING PASSERS

	Att.	Comp.	Yards	TD	Int.
Rudy Bukich, Chicago	312	176	2,641	20	9
John Unitas, Baltimore	282	164	2,530	23	12
John Brodie, San Francisco	391	242	3,112	30	16
Bart Starr, Green Bay	251	140	2,055	16	9
Earl Morrall, N.Y. Giants	302	155	2,446	22	12

LEADING RECEIVERS

	No.	Yards	Avg.	Long	TD
Dave Parks, San Francisco	80	1,344	16.8	53t	12
Tommy McDonald, Los Angeles	67	1,036	15.5	51	9
Pete Retzlaff, Philadelphia	66	1,190	18.0	78	10
Bobby Mitchell, Washington	60	867	14.5	80t	6
Sonny Randle, St. Louis	51	845	16.6	72	9

1966 The war between the leagues reached a peak. They spent a combined total of $7 million to sign 1966 draft choices. The Green Bay Packers spent $1 million for running backs Donny Anderson of Texas Tech and Jim Grabowski of Illinois.

The NFL signed 75 percent of its 232 draftees, and the AFL 46 percent of its 181. Of 111 common draft choices, 79 went with the NFL, 28 with the AFL, and four went unsigned.

Joe Foss, commissioner of the AFL since its inception, resigned in April and was replaced by Al Davis,

coach of the Oakland Raiders. Lamar Hunt of the Kansas City Chiefs and Tex Schramm of the Dallas Cowboys held secret talks about a possible merger of the two leagues. Kicker Pete Gogolak, who had played out his option with the Buffalo Bills and became a free agent, was signed by the New York Giants. As a result, new Commissioner Davis of the AFL launched a drive in retaliation in which the AFL teams went all-out to sign such established NFL stars as John Brodie, Mike Ditka, and Roman Gabriel.

It came as a complete surprise when NFL Commissioner Pete Rozelle announced a merger of the NFL and AFL June 8. The leagues agreed that their champions would meet in a world championship game starting after the 1966 season. There would be a common draft of players and preseason games between the teams of each league starting in 1967. The new league would expand to 26 teams by 1968 and would continue to play separate schedules until 1970, when they would combine in one league with Rozelle as commissioner.

Congress approved the pro football merger, October 21.

The Atlanta Falcons became the fifteenth NFL team and were placed in the Eastern Conference for purposes of the standings but were given a round-robin schedule in which they would meet every other league team in 1966.

Another southern city, New Orleans, was accepted as the sixteenth NFL team, to begin play in 1967. A four-team reorganization plan was made in which the league would be split into four divisions starting in 1967.

Assistant coach George Allen left the Bears and became head coach of the Los Angeles Rams after a bitter court fight with Bears' owner George Halas, who finally withdrew his suit in opposition to Los Angeles's hiring of Allen.

The Raiders moved into the new Oakland-Alameda County Stadium.

Goal posts offset from the goal line were installed in NFL stadiums, and their uprights were raised to a minimum 20 feet above the crossbar.

The Kansas City Chiefs were coached by Hank Stram and quarterbacked by Len Dawson. They beat the Buffalo Bills 31–7 in the AFL championship game.

The Dallas Cowboys, who had been rivals in their city in the early sixties with the Texans, who moved to Kansas City and became the Chiefs, narrowly missed winning the NFL championship and joining them in the first world championship game. Dallas captured the Eastern Conference championship in its seventh season, becoming the first expansion team in history to win a division or conference title. The Cowboys, however, lost a thrilling NFL championship game to Green Bay. Dallas rallied in the final minutes and had the ball on the Packers' 2-yard line when quarterback Don Meredith rolled out and was hit by linebacker Dave Robinson. He got off the pass but it was intercepted in the end zone by safety Tom Brown. The Packers of Vince Lombardi had won 34–27 and gained the right to represent their league in its first confrontation with the AFL.

The Los Angeles Memorial Coliseum was the site for the first world championship game; the name "Super Bowl" was not yet official for the event. Both the CBS and NBC television networks broadcast the game and it was not a sellout; a crowd of 61,946 attended. Green Bay held a 14–10 lead at the half and broke the game open in the second half when Willie Wood ran 50 yards with an interception to set up a touchdown by Elijah Pitts. Quarterback Bart Starr threw two touchdown passes to Max McGee and the Packers won 35–10.

Gino Marchetti of the Baltimore Colts and Ollie Matson of the Philadelphia Eagles retired.

Tex Schramm.

Al Davis.

George Allen.

Pete Rozelle awarding Vince Lombardi of Green Bay the trophy for winning the first world championship game, later renamed "Super Bowl."

Charlie Mitchell (27) and Broncos beat Lions as an AFL team defeats an NFL team first time, 1967.

Jim Taylor ends his career playing for the New Orleans Saints, 1967.

Bud Grant.

George Blanda.

Eastern Division	W	L	T	Pct.	Pts.	OP
Buffalo	9	4	1	.692	358	255
Boston Patriots	8	4	2	.667	315	283
N.Y. Jets	6	6	2	.500	322	312
Houston	3	11	0	.214	335	396
Miami	3	11	0	.214	213	362
Western Division	**W**	**L**	**T**	**Pct.**	**Pts.**	**OP**
Kansas City	11	2	1	.846	448	276
Oakland	8	5	1	.615	315	288
San Diego	7	6	1	.538	335	284
Denver	4	10	0	.286	196	381

AFL championship: Kansas City 31, Buffalo 7

LEADING RUSHERS	Att.	Yards	Avg.	Long	TD
Jim Nance, Boston	299	1,458	4.9	65	11
Mike Garrett, Kansas City	147	801	5.5	77	6
Clemon Daniels, Oakland	204	801	3.9	64	7
Bobby Burnett, Buffalo	187	766	4.1	32	4
Wray Carlton, Buffalo	156	696	4.5	23	6

LEADING PASSERS	Att.	Comp.	Yards	TD	Int.
Len Dawson, Kansas City	284	159	2,527	26	10
John Hadl, San Diego	375	200	2,846	23	14
Tom Flores, Oakland	306	151	2,638	24	14
Joe Namath, N.Y. Jets	471	232	3,379	19	27
Babe Parilli, Boston	382	181	2,721	20	20

LEADING RECEIVERS	No.	Yards	Avg.	Long	TD
Lance Alworth, San Diego	73	1,383	18.0	78	13
George Sauer, N.Y. Jets	63	1,079	17.0	77	5
Otis Taylor, Kansas City	58	1,297	22.4	89	8
Chris Burford, Kansas City	58	758	13.1	38	8
Willie Frazier, Houston	57	1,129	19.8	79	5

1966 NFL STANDINGS

Eastern Conference	W	L	T	Pct.	Pts.	OP
Dallas	10	3	1	.769	445	239
Cleveland	9	5	0	.643	403	259
Philadelphia	9	5	0	.643	326	340
St. Louis	8	5	1	.615	264	265
Washington	7	7	0	.500	351	355
Pittsburgh	5	8	1	.385	316	347
Atlanta	3	11	0	.214	204	437
N.Y. Giants	1	12	1	.077	263	501
Western Conference	**W**	**L**	**T**	**Pct.**	**Pts.**	**OP**
Green Bay	12	2	0	.857	335	163
Baltimore	9	5	0	.643	314	226
Los Angeles	8	6	0	.571	289	212
San Francisco	6	6	2	.500	320	325
Chicago	5	7	2	.417	234	272
Detroit	4	9	1	.308	206	317
Minnesota	4	9	1	.308	292	304

NFL championship: Green Bay 34, Dallas 27
Super Bowl I: Green Bay (NFL) 35, Kansas City (AFL) 10

LEADING RUSHERS	Att.	Yards	Avg.	Long	TD
Gale Sayers, Chicago	229	1,231	5.4	58t	8
Leroy Kelly, Cleveland	209	1,141	5.5	70t	15
Dick Bass, Los Angeles	248	1,090	4.4	50	8
Bill Brown, Minnesota	251	829	3.3	33t	6
Ken Willard, San Francisco	191	763	4.0	49	5

LEADING PASSERS	Att.	Comp.	Yards	TD	Int.
Bart Starr, Green Bay	251	156	2,257	14	3
Sonny Jurgensen, Washington	436	252	3,209	28	19
Frank Ryan, Cleveland	382	200	2,974	29	14
Don Meredith, Dallas	344	177	2,805	24	12
John Unitas, Baltimore	348	195	2,748	22	24

LEADING RECEIVERS	No.	Yards	Avg.	Long	TD
Charley Taylor, Washington	72	1,119	15.5	86t	12
Pat Studstill, Detroit	67	1,266	18.9	99t	5
Dave Parks, San Francisco	66	974	14.8	65t	5
Bob Hayes, Dallas	64	1,232	19.3	95t	13
Tom Moore, Los Angeles	60	433	7.2	30t	3

1967 The NFL had four divisions for the first time. Its 16 teams were divided into the Century and Capitol divisions of the Eastern Conference and the Central and Coastal divisions of the Western Conference. New Orleans began play with Tom Fears as its head coach. Cincinnati came into pro football as the tenth AFL team, to begin competition in 1968.

The first combined AFL-NFL draft was held March 14. The Baltimore Colts traded with New Orleans for the first pick and chose defensive end Charles (Bubba) Smith of Michigan State. Bob Griese of the Miami Dolphins, and Gene Upshaw of the Oakland Raiders were other notable rookies.

Coach Norm Van Brocklin and quarterback Fran Tarkenton of the Minnesota Vikings had an estrangement. Van Brocklin quit as coach and was replaced by Bud Grant, and Tarkenton was traded to the New York Giants.

The San Diego Chargers moved into the new San Diego Stadium.

An NFL team lost to an AFL team for the first time when the Denver Broncos beat the Detroit Lions 13–7 August 5 in a preseason game.

Quarterback Daryle Lamonica led the Oakland Raiders to a 13–1 record and the AFL West title. George Blanda, 39 years old, signed as a free agent after being released by Houston, became the Raiders' kicker and Lamonica's backup at quarterback. Houston took the Eastern title despite a great year by quarterback Joe Namath for the New York Jets. He had 4,007 yards and 26 touchdowns passing.

Oakland whipped Houston 40–7 in the championship game.

Green Bay won the NFL Central Division with rookie Travis Williams setting a record by running back four kickoffs for touchdowns. The Packers beat Coastal Division winner Los Angeles 28–7 for the Western Conference title.

Jim Taylor, former Packers' star, ended his career playing part-time for the New Orleans Saints.

Dallas won the Capitol and Cleveland the Century Division. Sonny Jurgensen of Washington completed 288 passes for 3,747 yards passing, and Jim Bakken of St. Louis kicked seven field goals in one game against Pittsburgh. In the Eastern Conference title game, the Cowboys won a one-sided 52–14 victory over Cleveland.

Lambeau Field in Green Bay was the site for the title game. The weather in Green Bay was Arctic. The day before the game, Vince Lombardi showed the press the electric wiring under the turf which, he said, would guarantee an unfrozen field when the Packers and Cowboys played the next day.

The field did freeze, however. The temperature was 13 degrees below zero and the wind chill 40 below. Green Bay and Dallas played what many consider the most dramatic title game in league history. The Packers won 21-17. Trailing 17-14 with 13 seconds to play, they scored when quarterback Bart Starr went over on a one-yard sneak behind a tremendous block by guard Jerry Kramer on Dallas defensive tackle Jethro Pugh. Later, Lombardi said he had passed up an almost sure field goal in favor of the sneak for the touchdown because, he said, "I couldn't see going for a tie and making all those people in the stands suffer through sudden death in this weather."

The temperature was 78 degrees higher at 65 two weeks later when Green Bay beat Oakland 33–14 at the Orange Bowl in Miami in the second world championship game. Don Chandler kicked four field goals for the Packers and Starr directed an offensive attack that ran up 325 yards against the Raiders.

It was Lombardi's second consecutive world championship coming on the heels of his third straight NFL championship. He stunned the football world by announcing his retirement as Packers' head coach. Assistant coach Phil Bengtson would replace him and he would remain as general manager.

George Halas, 73, retired for the fourth and last time as head coach of the team he owned, the Chicago Bears.

End Raymond Berry and guard Jim Parker of the Baltimore Colts, kicker Lou Groza of the Cleveland Browns (for the second time), and center Jim Ringo of Philadelphia were notable players who retired from football.

Chuck Mercein of Green Bay runs to the 3-yard line, setting up the winning touchdown against Dallas, 1967 championship game.

Paul Brown.

Earl Morrall.

1967 AFL STANDINGS

Eastern Division	W	L	T	Pct.	Pts.	OP
Houston	9	4	1	.692	258	199
N.Y. Jets	8	5	1	.615	371	329
Buffalo	4	10	0	.286	237	285
Miami	4	10	0	.286	219	407
Boston Patriots	3	10	1	.231	280	389
Western Division	**W**	**L**	**T**	**Pct.**	**Pts.**	**OP**
Oakland	13	1	0	.929	468	233
Kansas City	9	5	0	.643	408	254
San Diego	8	5	1	.615	360	352
Denver	3	11	0	.214	256	409

AFL championship: Oakland 40, Houston 7

LEADING RUSHERS	Att.	Yards	Avg.	Long	TD
Jim Nance, Boston	269	1,216	4.5	53	7
Hoyle Granger, Houston	238	1,197	5.1	67	6
Mike Garrett, Kansas City	236	1,087	4.6	58	9
Dickie Post, San Diego	161	663	4.1	67t	7
Brad Hubbert, San Diego	116	643	5.5	80t	2
LEADING PASSERS	**Att.**	**Comp.**	**Yards**	**TD**	**Int.**
Daryle Lamonica, Oakland	425	220	3,228	30	20
Len Dawson, Kansas City	357	206	2,651	24	17
Joe Namath, N.Y. Jets	491	258	4,007	26	28
John Hadl, San Diego	427	217	3,365	24	22
Bob Griese, Miami	331	166	2,005	15	18
LEADING RECEIVERS	**No.**	**Yards**	**Avg.**	**Long**	**TD**
George Sauer, N.Y. Jets	75	1,189	15.9	61t	6
Don Maynard, N.Y. Jets	71	1,434	20.2	75t	10
Jack Clancy, Miami	67	868	13.0	44t	2
Otis Taylor, Kansas City	59	958	16.2	71t	11
Hewritt Dixon, Oakland	59	563	9.5	48	2

1967 NFL STANDINGS
EASTERN CONFERENCE

Capitol Division	W	L	T	Pct.	Pts.	OP
Dallas	9	5	0	.643	342	268
Philadelphia	6	7	1	.462	351	409
Washington	5	6	3	.455	347	353
New Orleans	3	11	0	.214	233	379

Century Division	W	L	T	Pct.	Pts.	OP
Cleveland	9	5	0	.643	334	297
N.Y. Giants	7	7	0	.500	369	379
St. Louis	6	7	1	.462	333	356
Pittsburgh	4	9	1	.308	281	320

WESTERN CONFERENCE

Coastal Division	W	L	T	Pct.	Pts.	OP
Los Angeles	11	1	2	.917	398	196
Baltimore	11	1	2	.917	394	198
San Francisco	7	7	0	.500	273	337
Atlanta	1	12	1	.077	175	422

Central Division	W	L	T	Pct.	Pts.	OP
Green Bay	9	4	1	.692	332	209
Chicago	7	6	1	.538	239	218
Detroit	5	7	2	.417	260	259
Minnesota	3	8	3	.273	233	294

Conference championships: Dallas 52, Cleveland 14;
Green Bay 28, Los Angeles 7
NFL championship: Green Bay 21, Dallas 17
Super Bowl II: Green Bay (NFL) 33, Oakland (AFL) 14

LEADING RUSHERS	Att.	Yards	Avg.	Long	TD
Leroy Kelly, Cleveland	235	1,205	5.1	42t	11
Dave Osborn, Minnesota	215	972	4.5	73	2
Gale Sayers, Chicago	186	880	4.7	70	7
Johnny Roland, St. Louis	234	876	3.7	70	10
Miller Farr, Detroit	206	860	4.2	57	3
LEADING PASSERS	**Att.**	**Comp.**	**Yards**	**TD**	**Int.**
Sonny Jurgensen, Washington	508	288	3,747	31	16
John Unitas, Baltimore	436	255	3,428	20	16
Fran Tarkenton, N.Y. Giants	377	204	3,088	29	19
Roman Gabriel, Los Angeles	371	196	2,779	25	13
Norm Snead, Philadelphia	434	240	3,399	29	24
LEADING RECEIVERS	**No.**	**Yards**	**Avg.**	**Long**	**TD**
Charley Taylor, Washington	70	990	14.1	86t	9
Jackie Smith, Washington	67	849	12.7	43	12
Willie Richardson, Baltimore	63	860	13.7	31t	8
Bobby Mitchell, Washington	60	866	14.4	65t	6
Ben Hawkins, Philadelphia	59	1,265	21.4	87t	10

1968 Sonny Werblin sold his interest in the New York Jets to four partners and one of them, Don Lillis, became the acting head of the corporation. Lillis died two months later and Phil Iselin was named Jets' president.

The Houston Oilers left Rice Stadium and began playing their games in the Astrodome.

The AFL reached an agreement with its players association for a pension increase but a prolonged dispute between NFL owners and the NFL Players Association turned into a strike in July. It was settled a few days before training camps opened.

Daryle Lamonica of Oakland, who threw 30 touchdown passes in 1967 and 34 in 1969.

Joe Namath passing for the New York Jets in their 16–7 victory over the Baltimore Colts in Super Bowl III.

Paul Brown returned to pro football as part-owner and head coach of the expansion team in Cincinnati, the Bengals.

The New York Jets easily won the AFL East behind a strong passing attack, Joe Namath throwing to George Sauer and Don Maynard. New York also had strong running with Matt Snell, Emerson Boozer, and Bill Mathis.

The Jets were in a tense game with the Oakland Raiders at Oakland. New York led 32–29 with one minute, five seconds to play when NBC television switched from the game to begin the movie, *Heidi*. The network's switchboard lit up with angry protests while the Raiders came back with two late touchdowns to win what was dubbed the "Heidi Game" 43–32.

Oakland and Kansas City tied for first place in the Western Division with 12–2 records. The Raiders won an overwhelming playoff victory 41–6 as Daryle Lamonica bombed the Chiefs with five touchdown passes.

The Jets won the East and met the surging Raiders for the AFL championship. Namath outpassed Lamonica, throwing for three touchdowns, and the Jets won 27–23.

Earl Morrall, acquired from the New York Giants, took over as quarterback of the Baltimore Colts when John Unitas went out with an elbow injury. Morrall had a sensational 26-touchdown season and the Colts,

coached by Don Shula, lost only to Cleveland 30–20 while compiling a 13–1 record, one of the best in NFL history. Baltimore won the Coastal Division easily. Minnesota had an excellent front four in ends Carl Eller and Jim Marshall and tackles Alan Page and Gary Larsen and won the Central, its first division title. The Colts won a playoff from the Vikings 24–14 for the Western Conference championship.

There was an important quarterback switch in the Eastern Conference, too. Bill Nelsen replaced Frank Ryan as leader of the Cleveland Browns and led them to the Century Division title and then a 31–20 victory over Capitol Division winner Dallas for the Eastern title. Leroy Kelly scored two touchdowns for Cleveland in its victory over Dallas.

The Browns met their match in the NFL title game, however. Baltimore swamped them 34–0 with an offensive barrage that included three touchdowns by Tom Matte.

"Super Bowl" was now the official name for what had been called the world championship game, and the Colts, 15–1 in regular and postseason games, were solid favorites as they faced the AFL champion Jets at Miami. Three days before the game, however, Namath of the Jets was attending a sports dinner at Miami Springs Villa where he predicted, "We are going to win on Sunday, I guarantee you."

Namath made his boast reality when he completed 17 of 28 passes, sent Matt Snell rushing for 121 yards,

and the Jets won 16–7 and became the first AFL team to win a Super Bowl.

1968 AFL STANDINGS

Eastern Division	W	L	T	Pct.	Pts.	OP
N.Y. Jets	11	3	0	.786	419	280
Houston	7	7	0	.500	303	248
Miami	5	8	1	.385	276	355
Boston Patriots	4	10	0	.286	229	406
Buffalo	1	12	1	.077	199	367
Western Division	W	L	T	Pct.	Pts.	OP
Kansas City	12	2	0	.857	371	170
Oakland	12	2	0	.857	453	233
San Diego	9	5	0	.643	382	310
Denver	5	9	0	.357	255	404
Cincinnati	3	11	0	.214	215	329

Western Division playoff: Oakland 41, Kansas City 6
AFL championship: N.Y. Jets 27, Oakland 23

LEADING RUSHERS	Att.	Yards	Avg.	Long	TD
Paul Robinson, Cincinnati	238	1,023	4.3	87t	8
Robert Holmes, Kansas City	174	866	5.0	76t	7
Hewritt Dixon, Oakland	206	865	4.2	28	2
Hoyle Granger, Houston	202	848	4.2	47t	7
Dickie Post, San Diego	151	758	5.0	62t	3

LEADING PASSERS	Att.	Comp.	Yards	TD	Int.
Len Dawson, Kansas City	224	131	2,019	17	9
Daryle Lamonica, Oakland	416	206	3.245	25	15
Joe Namath, N.Y. Jets	380	187	3,147	15	17
Bob Griese, Miami	355	186	2,473	21	16
John Hadl, San Diego	440	208	3,473	27	32

LEADING RECEIVERS	No.	Yards	Avg.	Long	TD
Lance Alworth, San Diego	68	1,312	19.3	80t	10
George Sauer, N.Y. Jets	66	1,141	17.3	43	3
Fred Biletnikoff, Oakland	61	1,037	17.0	82	6
Karl Noonan, Miami	58	760	13.1	50t	11
Don Maynard, N.Y. Jets	57	1,297	22.8	87t	10

Alworth congratulated by Don Hutson, breaking record for consec. games with at least one reception, 1969.

1969 George Allen, fired as coach of the Los Angeles Rams by owner Dan Reeves, was rehired after his players protested the firing. Vince Lombardi left the general managership of the Green Bay Packers and became part-owner, executive vice–president, and head coach of the Washington Redskins. John Madden became head coach of the Oakland Raiders and Chuck Noll head coach of the Pittsburgh Steelers.

O. J. Simpson of USC, winner of the Heisman trophy, was the first choice in the draft, by the Buffalo Bills.

Commissioner Pete Rozelle announced a new television contract with the ABC network for 13 regular season Monday night games in prime time during 1970, 1971, and 1972.

It was necessary to thrash out the format under which the 26 teams would compete once they were all one league starting in 1970. The owners alternately argued, dozed, agreed, ate, and eventually compromised in a marathon 35-hour, 45-minute realignment meeting in May. As a result of the meeting, the Baltimore Colts, Cleveland Browns, and Pittsburgh Steelers joined the 10 AFL teams in a new 13-team American Football Conference and the remaining 13 teams from the 16-club NFL became the National Football Conference. There would also be a "wild card" or best second-place team in each conference going into the playoffs each year. All this was to become effective the next year.

For 1969 only, the AFL played under a format in which the second-place team in each division would play the champion of the other division.

New York and Houston in the East and Oakland and Kansas City in the West were the best teams in the AFL again as it went through its last season with the identity it had had since 1960.

Quarterback Daryle Lamonica threw 34 touchdown passes. Kicker Jan Stenerud of Kansas City had

Bill Brown carries for Minnesota, pursued by Jim Purnell of Los Angeles in 1969 playoff.

Jack Concannon hands off to Gale Sayers, Chicago Bears, 1969.

Jan Stenerud kicking a 32-yard field goal in Super Bowl IV.

16 consecutive field goals. Wide receiver Lance Alworth of San Diego completed a string in which he caught at least one pass in 96 consecutive games.

Sid Gillman, coach of the Chargers since their inception, was forced to step down after nine games because of ulcers and was succeeded by assistant coach Charlie Waller.

Kansas City, second place in the West, unseated the defending champion Jets 13–6 in one hard-fought AFL playoff, while Oakland had no trouble in the other, routing Houston 56–7 behind six touchdown passes by the prolific Lamonica.

Kansas City won the AFL title game, stopping Oakland 17–7. Lamonica was injured and 42-year-old George Blanda took over in a losing effort. The Chiefs and their coach, Hank Stram, advanced to the Super Bowl and a chance to avenge their loss in the first world championship game four seasons before.

Los Angeles, behind Allen, ousted Baltimore as Coastal Division winner in the NFL. Minnesota again won the Central, Dallas the Capitol, and Cleveland the Century.

Washington came in second in the Capitol and had its best record, 7–5–2, since 1955 under its new coach, Lombardi.

Quarterback Bill Nelsen led Cleveland to a rousing victory over Dallas, 38–14, for the Eastern Conference title. Joe Kapp, unorthodox leader of the Vikings, led them from a 17–7 deficit to a 23–20 victory over Los Angeles to claim the Western Conference championship.

In the NFL title game, Kapp threw a touchdown pass and scored once as Minnesota defeated Cleveland 27–7.

Minnesota met Kansas City in Super Bowl IV at New Orleans. The Vikings were favored but Mike Garrett and Otis Taylor scored touchdowns and Jan Stenerud kicked three field goals, giving the Chiefs a 23–7 victory. Losers in the first Super Bowl, Kansas City won the last such game played between the champions of the two leagues before their reorganization and new format for 1970.

Owner George Preston Marshall of the Washington Redskins died at 72.

1969 AFL STANDINGS

Eastern Division	W	L	T	Pct.	Pts.	OP
N.Y. Jets	10	4	0	.714	353	269
Houston	6	6	2	.500	278	279
Boston Patriots	4	10	0	.286	266	316
Buffalo	4	10	0	.286	230	359
Miami	3	10	1	.231	233	332
Western Division	W	L	T	Pct.	Pts.	OP
Oakland	12	1	1	.923	377	242
Kansas City	11	3	0	.786	359	177
San Diego	8	6	0	.571	288	276
Denver	5	8	1	.385	297	344
Cincinnati	4	9	1	.308	280	367

Divisional Playoffs: Kansas City 13, N.Y. Jets 6; Oakland 56, Houston 7
AFL championship: Kansas City 17, Oakland 7

LEADING RUSHERS	Att.	Yards	Avg.	Long	TD
Dickie Post, San Diego	182	873	4.8	60	6
Jim Nance, Boston	193	750	3.9	43	6
Hoyle Granger, Houston	186	740	4.0	23	3
Mike Garrett, Kansas City	168	732	4.4	34t	6
Floyd Little, Denver	146	729	5.0	48t	6

LEADING PASSERS	Att.	Comp.	Yards	TD	Int.
Greg Cook, Cincinnati	197	106	1,854	15	11
Joe Namath, N.Y. Jets	361	185	2,734	19	17
Daryle Lamonica, Oakland	426	221	3,302	34	25
Mike Livingston, Kansas City	161	84	1,123	4	6
John Hadl, San Diego	324	158	2,253	10	11

LEADING RECEIVERS	No.	Yards	Avg.	Long	TD
Lance Alworth, San Diego	64	1,003	15.7	76t	4
Fred Biletnikoff, Oakland	54	837	15.5	53t	12
Moses Denson, Denver	53	809	15.3	62t	10
Alvin Reed, Houston	51	644	13.0	43t	4
Warren Wells, Oakland	47	1,260	26.8	80t	14

1969 NFL STANDINGS

EASTERN CONFERENCE						
Capitol Division	W	L	T	Pct.	Pts.	OP
Dallas	11	2	1	.846	369	223
Washington	7	5	2	.583	307	319
New Orleans	5	9	0	.357	311	393
Philadelphia	4	9	1	.308	279	377
Century Division	W	L	T	Pct.	Pts.	OP
Cleveland	10	3	1	.769	351	300
N.Y. Giants	6	8	0	.429	264	298
St. Louis	4	9	1	.308	314	389
Pittsburgh	1	13	0	.071	218	404
WESTERN CONFERENCE						
Coastal Division	W	L	T	Pct.	Pts.	OP
Los Angeles	11	3	0	.786	320	243
Baltimore	8	5	1	.615	279	268
Atlanta	6	8	0	.429	276	268
San Francisco	4	8	2	.333	277	319
Central Division	W	L	T	Pct.	Pts.	OP
Minnesota	12	2	0	.857	379	133
Detroit	9	4	1	.692	259	188
Green Bay	8	6	0	.571	269	221
Chicago	1	13	0	.071	210	339

Conference championships: Cleveland 38, Dallas 14; Minnesota 23, Los Angeles 20
NFL championship: Minnesota 27, Cleveland 7
Super Bowl IV: Kansas City (AFL) 23, Minnesota (NFL) 7

LEADING RUSHERS	Att.	Yards	Avg.	Long	TD
Gale Sayers, Chicago	236	1,032	4.4	28	8
Calvin Hill, Dallas	204	942	4.6	55	8
Tom Matte, Baltimore	235	909	3.9	26	11
Larry Brown, Washington	202	888	4.4	57	4
Tom Woodeshick, Philadelphia	186	831	4.5	21	4

LEADING PASSERS	Att.	Comp.	Yards	TD	Int.
Sonny Jurgensen, Washington	442	274	3,102	22	15
Bart Starr, Green Bay	148	92	1,161	9	6
Fran Tarkenton, N.Y. Giants	409	220	2,918	23	8
Roman Gabriel, Los Angeles	399	217	2,549	24	7
Craig Morton, Dallas	302	162	2,619	21	15

LEADING RECEIVERS	No.	Yards	Avg.	Long	TD
Dan Abramowicz, New Orleans	73	1,015	13.9	49t	7
Charley Taylor, Washington	71	883	12.4	88t	8
Roy Jefferson, Pittsburgh	67	1,079	16.1	63	9
Harold Jackson, Philadelphia	65	1,116	17.2	65t	9
Dave Williams, St. Louis	56	702	12.5	61	7

Vince Lombardi's funeral, St. Patrick's Cathedral, New York City, 1970.

Don Shula.

The late Brian Piccolo.

1970 The merger agreement of 1966 was implemented, and the 26 teams of pro football were realigned into the American and National Football Conferences and began playing interleague regular season games.

The AFC was made up of the Baltimore Colts, Boston Patriots, Buffalo Bills, Miami Dolphins, and New York Jets in the Eastern Division; the Cincinnati Bengals, Cleveland Browns, Houston Oilers, and Pittsburgh Steelers in the Central Division; and the Denver Broncos, Kansas City Chiefs, Oakland Raiders, and San Diego Chargers in the Western Division.

The NFC realignment was not arrived at until months of discussion and, finally, one of the five plans submitted by Commissioner Pete Rozelle was drawn in a lottery. The new NFC was made up of the Dallas Cowboys, New York Giants, Philadelphia Eagles, St. Louis Cardinals, and Washington Redskins in the Eastern Division; the Chicago Bears, Detroit Lions, Green Bay Packers, and Minnesota Vikings in the Central Division; and the Atlanta Falcons, Los Angeles Rams, New Orleans Saints, and San Francisco 49ers in the Western Division.

Each team was to play home-and-home with each other team in its division, three or five games with other teams of its own conference, and three interconference games. Because of the odd number of clubs, one would play four intersectional games.

Rozelle had to settle charges of tampering by the Miami Dolphins in their efforts to lure coach Don Shula from Baltimore. Shula was permitted to make the move but Miami was assessed a number one draft choice in 1971. Don McCafferty replaced Shula as coach of the Colts.

Vince Lombardi, former coach of the Green Bay Packers and Washington Redskins, and Brian Piccolo, former running back for the Chicago Bears, died of cancer.

Jimmy Conzelman, who had been a prominent figure in the early days of pro football and who is a member of the Hall of Fame, died.

The Cincinnati Bengals moved into new 56,200-seat Riverfront Stadium and the Pittsburgh Steelers into new 50,350-seat Three Rivers Stadium.

Monday night football became a TV success as ABC began the first year of a three-year contract.

There was the possibility of a strike by NFL players until early August. A new four-year agreement was signed between the owners and players' association.

The rules were changed requiring players' names on the backs of their jerseys, as they had been in the 1960–69 AFL, and making the stadium clock the official timer of the game, as had been the case in the AFL.

George Blanda, playing his twenty-first year of pro ball at the age of 43, engineered a series of dramatic finishes for Oakland. Blanda, backup to Daryle Lamonica as well as the Raiders' kicker, did this in a five-week span: threw two touchdown passes against Pittsburgh; kicked a 48-yard field goal with three seconds to go, tying Kansas City 17–17; kicked a 52-yard field goal with three seconds to play to beat Cleveland 23–20, drove the Raiders to a winning touchdown against Denver 24–19, and beat San Diego 20–17 on another field goal with four seconds left.

Tom Dempsey of New Orleans set an NFL field goal distance record of 63 yards on the game's last play to defeat Detroit 19–17, November 8.

Gale Sayers of the Chicago Bears underwent surgery for a knee injury in midseason and never again regained his form. The New York Jets were handicapped by Joe Namath's broken wrist and Matt Snell's injured Achilles tendon. Minnesota quarterback Joe Kapp went to Boston, where he reported late and threw only three touchdown passes and was intercepted 17 times.

McCafferty's Colts won the AFC east at 11–2–1 and runnerup Miami's 10–4 record put the Dolphins into the playoffs as the "wild card" team. Paul Brown's expansion team in Cincinnati won the AFC Central in its third season with an 8–6 record. Oakland's 8–4–2 beat Kansas City's 7–5–2 in the AFC West.

Dallas (10–4) beat out the New York Giants (9–5) in the NFC East with the help of rookie running back Duane Thomas. Quarterback John Brodie led the San Francisco 49ers to the Western title at 10–3–1. Defense and Fred Cox's field goals were major factors in Minnesota's 12–2 winning record in the NFC Central, where runnerup Detroit (10–4) was the "wild card" qualifier.

In the AFC playoffs, Baltimore blanked Cincinnati 17–0 and Oakland defeated Miami 21–14 in the first round. Dallas beat Detroit 5–0 on a field goal and safety and the 49ers surprised the Vikings at Minnesota 17–14 in the other NFC playoff.

Baltimore defeated Oakland 27–17 in the AFC title game. Duane Thomas gained 143 yards and Walt Garrison 71 in Dallas's 17–10 NFC championship game win over San Francisco.

The NFC won the competition with the AFC in the first season they played inter-conference games. There were 40 such games and the NFC won 27, the AFC 12, and there was one tie.

George Blanda tying Kansas City during five-week span of miracle finishes for Oakland, 1970.

1970 AFC STANDINGS

Eastern Division	W	L	T	Pct.	Pts.	OP
Baltimore	11	2	1	.846	321	234
Miami*	10	4	0	.714	297	228
N.Y. Jets	4	10	0	.286	255	286
Buffalo	3	10	1	.231	204	337
Boston Patriots	2	12	0	.143	149	361
Central Division	**W**	**L**	**T**	**Pct.**	**Pts.**	**OP**
Cincinnati	8	6	0	.571	312	255
Cleveland	7	7	0	.500	286	265
Pittsburgh	5	9	0	.357	210	272
Houston	3	10	1	.231	217	352
Western Division	**W**	**L**	**T**	**Pct.**	**Pts.**	**OP**
Oakland	8	4	2	.667	300	293
Kansas City	7	5	2	.583	272	244
San Diego	5	6	3	.455	282	278
Denver	5	8	1	.385	253	264

*Wild Card qualifier for playoffs
Divisional playoffs: Baltimore 17, Cincinnati 0;
　　　　Oakland 21, Miami 14
AFC championship: Baltimore 27, Oakland 17

LEADING RUSHERS	Att.	Yards	Avg.	Long	TD
Floyd Little, Denver	209	901	4.3	80t	3
Larry Csonka, Miami	193	874	4.5	53	6
Hewritt Dixon, Oakland	197	861	4.4	39t	1
Ed Podolak, Kansas City	168	749	4.5	65t	3
John (Frenchy) Fuqua, Pittsburgh	138	691	5.0	85t	7

LEADING PASSERS	Att.	Comp.	Yards	TD	Int.
Daryle Lamonica, Oakland	356	179	2,516	22	15
John Hadl, San Diego	327	162	2,388	22	15
Len Dawson, Kansas City	262	141	1,876	13	14
Bob Griese, Miami	245	142	2,019	12	17
Dennis Shaw, Buffalo	321	178	2,507	10	20

LEADING RECEIVERS	No.	Yards	Avg.	Long	TD
Marlin Briscoe, Buffalo	57	1,036	18.2	48	8
Eddie Hinton, Baltimore	47	733	15.6	40	5
Al Denson, Denver	47	646	13.7	42	2
Alvin Reed, Houston	47	604	12.9	34	2
Fred Biletnikoff, Oakland	45	768	17.1	51	7

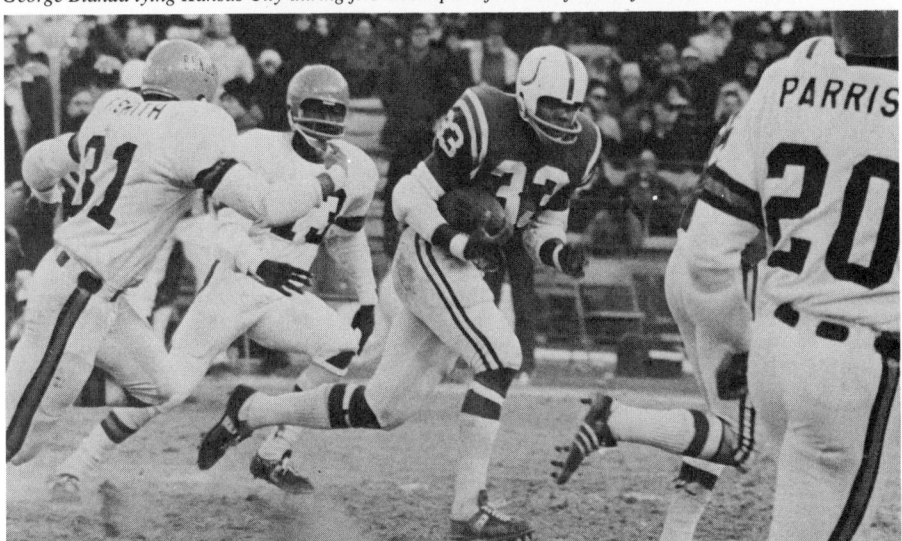

Bengals' defense chases Colts' Tony Lorick; Cincinnati makes playoffs its third year, 1970.

1970 NFC STANDINGS

Eastern Division	W	L	T	Pct.	Pts.	OP
Dallas	10	4	0	.714	299	221
N.Y. Giants	9	5	0	.643	301	270
St. Louis	8	5	1	.615	325	228
Washington	6	8	0	.429	297	314
Philadelphia	3	10	1	.231	241	332
Central Division	**W**	**L**	**T**	**Pct.**	**Pts.**	**OP**
Minnesota	12	2	0	.857	335	143
Detroit*	10	4	0	.714	347	202
Chicago	6	8	0	.429	256	261
Green Bay	6	8	0	.429	196	293
Western Division	**W**	**L**	**T**	**Pct.**	**Pts.**	**OP**
San Francisco	10	3	1	.769	352	267
Los Angeles	9	4	1	.692	325	202
Atlanta	4	8	2	.333	206	261
New Orleans	2	11	1	.154	172	347

*Wild Card qualifier for playoffs
Divisional playoffs: Dallas 5, Detroit 0;
　　　　San Francisco 17, Minnesota 14
NFC championship: Dallas 17, San Francisco 10
Super Bowl V: Baltimore (AFC) 16, Dallas (NFC) 13

Rookie Duane Thomas gains 143 yards as Cowboys defeat 49ers for NFC championship, 1970.

LEADING RUSHERS	Att.	Yards	Avg.	Long	TD
Larry Brown, Washington	237	1,125	4.7	75t	5
Ron Johnson, N.Y. Giants	263	1,027	3.9	68t	8
MacArthur Lane, St. Louis	206	977	4.7	75	11
Donny Anderson, Green Bay	222	853	3.8	54	5
Duane Thomas, Dallas	151	803	5.3	47t	5

LEADING PASSERS	Att.	Comp.	Yards	TD	Int.
John Brodie, San Francisco	387	223	2,941	24	10
Sonny Jurgensen, Washington	337	202	2,354	23	10
Fran Tarkenton, N.Y. Giants	389	219	2,777	19	12
Bob Berry, Atlanta	269	156	1,806	16	13
Craig Morton, Dallas	267	102	1,819	15	7

LEADING RECEIVERS	No.	Yards	Avg.	Long	TD
Dick Gordon, Chicago	71	1,026	14.5	69t	13
Dan Abramowicz, New Orleans	55	906	16.5	48	5
Gene Washington, San Francisco	53	1,100	20.8	79t	12
Jack Snow, Los Angeles	51	859	16.8	71	7
Clifton McNeil, N.Y. Giants	50	764	15.3	59	4
Lee Bougess, Philadelphia	50	401	8.0	34	2

1971 Super Bowl V was a battle of turnovers at the Orange Bowl. The Colts gave up three interceptions and three fumbles and the Cowboys had three passes intercepted and lost a fumble. Jim O'Brien's 32-yard field goal with five seconds to play won it for the Colts 16–13. Earl Morrall led Baltimore to victory after John Unitas suffered damaged ribs in the first half.

The NFC won the first AFC–NFC Pro Bowl 27–6 as Mel Renfro of the Dallas Cowboys returned punts 82 and 56 yards for touchdowns. The game was played at Los Angeles.

Five teams switched to new stadiums. The Dallas Cowboys left the Cotton Bowl, their home since 1960, to open a new 65,101-seat Texas Stadium at Irving, Texas, another suburban location. The Philadelphia Eagles occupied 66,052-seat Veterans Stadium and the San Francisco 49ers switched from Kezar Stadium to 61,246-seat Candlestick Park. The Chicago Bears, who had played at Wrigley Field (originally Cubs' Park) since they had moved from Decatur, Illinois, in 1921, moved into Soldier Field. The huge stadium's seating capacity was reduced to 55,049.

The Boston Patriots had wandered from Boston University, to Fenway Park, to Boston College, and Harvard Stadium. They finally got their own stadium in Foxboro, Massachusetts, when 61,275-seat Schaefer Stadium was opened. The team changed its name first to Bay State Patriots and then to New England Patriots.

George Allen, insisting "the future is now," took over the Washington Redskins and made a series of trades that brought defensive tackle Diron Talbert, linebacker Myron Pottios, lineman Jack Pardee, and a host of other former Los Angeles Rams to Washington in return mainly for future draft choices.

The San Diego Chargers brought back Sid Gillman, who lasted until midseason, when general manager Harland Svare took over as coach. Lou Saban quit as coach of the Denver Broncos after nine games and assistant Jerry Smith took over.

Three college quarterbacks were selected one, two, three in the draft. All of them became starters. Stanford's Jim Plunkett was number one for the Patriots, throwing 19 touchdown passes. Santa Clara's Dan Pastorini took over at Houston. Mississippi's Archie Manning started strong with the Saints but injuries made him a part-time performer.

The number one draft choice the Baltimore Colts had been awarded in exchange for coach Don Shula was used to draft running back Don McCauley of North Carolina.

Five players rushed for 1,000 yards or more. John Brockington of Green Bay led the NFC as a rookie with 1,105 and Denver's Floyd Little topped the AFC with 1,133. Steve Owens of Detroit had 1,035, Larry Csonka 1,051, and Willie Ellison of the Rams 1,000, including an NFL record 247-yard day against New Orleans.

George Blanda, Oakland's veteran kicker, moved into first place in the all-time scoring list with 1,647

Willie Ellison sets a then NFL record, gaining 247 yards against New Orleans, 1971.

points, topping Lou Groza, and Bob Tucker of the New York Giants became the first tight end to lead a conference in receiving with 59 in the NFC.

Allen coached the Redskins into the NFC playoffs as the "wild card" team with a 9–4–1 record. It was the first time Washington reached the playoffs since 1945. Dallas won the Eastern Division.

San Francisco won the Western Division championship again.

Cleveland overcame a midseason slump and won the AFC Central with a 9–5 record in Nick Skorich's first years as coach and Kansas City's 10–3–1 topped Oakland's 8–4–2.

Miami won 10 games and captured the AFC Eastern Division. Baltimore was the runner-up and "wild card" team.

In a first-round divisional playoff, the Dolphins edged Kansas City 27–24 in the longest game ever played when Yepremian kicked a 37-yard field goal after 22 minutes and 40 seconds of overtime play on Christmas afternoon. Jan Stenerud of the Chiefs missed a 31-yard field goal try with 35 seconds left in regulation time. Baltimore beat Cleveland 20–3 in the other playoff.

San Francisco defeated Washington 24–20 in a first-round divisional playoff. Dallas won the other first-round playoff 20–12 over Minnesota.

In the AFC championship, safety Dick Anderson of Miami intercepted three passes by John Unitas and Miami defeated Baltimore 21–0.

Dallas went ahead quickly and outlasted San Francisco 14–3 in the NFC championship game.

1971 AFC STANDINGS

Eastern Division	W	L	T	Pct.	Pts.	OP
Miami	10	3	1	.769	315	174
Baltimore*	10	4	0	.714	313	140
New England	6	8	0	.429	238	325
N.Y. Jets	6	8	0	.429	212	299
Buffalo	1	13	0	.071	184	394
Central Division	W	L	T	Pct.	Pts.	OP
Cleveland	9	5	0	.643	285	273
Pittsburgh	6	8	0	.429	246	292
Houston	4	9	1	.308	251	330
Cincinnati	4	10	0	.286	284	265
Western Division	W	L	T	Pct.	Pts.	OP
Kansas City	10	3	1	.769	302	208
Oakland	8	4	2	.667	344	278
San Diego	6	8	0	.429	311	341
Denver	4	9	1	.308	203	275

Wild Card qualifier for playoffs

Divisional playoffs: Miami 27, Kansas City 24, sudden death overtime
Baltimore 20, Cleveland 3
AFC championship: Miami 21, Baltimore 0

LEADING RUSHERS	Att.	Yards	Avg.	Long	TD
Floyd Litte, Denver	284	1,133	4.0	40	6
Larry Csonka, Miami	195	1,051	5.4	28	7
Marv Hubbard, Oakland	181	867	4.8	20	5
Leroy Kelly, Cleveland	234	865	3.7	35	10
Carl Garrett, New England	181	785	4.3	38	1

LEADING PASSERS	Att.	Comp.	Yards	TD	Int.
Bob Griese, Miami	263	145	2,089	19	9
Len Dawson, Kansas City	301	167	2,504	15	13
Virgil Carter, Cincinnati	222	138	1,624	10	7
John Hadl, San Diego	431	233	3,075	21	25
Bill Nelsen, Cleveland	325	174	2,319	13	23

LEADING RECEIVERS	No.	Yards	Avg.	Long	TD
Fred Biletnikoff, Oakland	61	929	15.2	49	9
Otis Taylor, Kansas City	57	1,110	19.5	82	7
Randy Vataha, New England	51	872	17.1	88t	9
Ron Shanklin, Pittsburgh	49	652	13.3	42	6
John (Frenchy) Fuqua, Pittsburgh	49	427	8.7	40t	1

Eastern Division	W	L	T	Pct.	Pts.	OP
Dallas	11	3	0	.786	406	222
Washington*	9	4	1	.692	276	190
Philadelphia	6	7	1	.462	221	302
St. Louis	4	9	1	.308	231	279
N.Y. Giants	4	10	0	.286	228	362
Central Division	W	L	T	Pct.	Pts.	OP
Minnesota	11	3	0	.786	245	139
Detroit	7	6	1	.538	341	286
Chicago	6	8	0	.429	185	276
Green Bay	4	8	2	.333	274	298
Western Division	W	L	T	Pct.	Pts.	OP
San Francisco	9	5	0	.643	300	216
Los Angeles	8	5	1	.615	313	260
Atlanta	7	6	1	.538	274	277
New Orleans	4	8	2	.333	266	347

Wild Card qualifier for playoffs
Divisional playoffs: Dallas 20, Minnesota 12;
                  San Francisco 24, Washington 20
NFC championship: Dallas 14, San Francisco 3
Super Bowl VI: Dallas (NFC) 24, Miami (AFC) 3

LEADING RUSHERS	Att.	Yards	Avg.	Long	TD
John Brockington, Green Bay	216	1,105	5.1	52t	4
Steve Owens, Detroit	246	1,035	4.2	23	8
Willie Ellison, Los Angeles	211	1,000	4.7	80t	4
Larry Brown, Washington	253	948	3.7	34	4
Ken Willard, San Francisco	216	855	4.0	49	4

LEADING PASSERS	Att.	Comp.	Yards	TD	Int.
Roger Staubach, Dallas	211	126	1,882	15	4
Greg Landry, Detroit	261	136	2,237	16	13
Billy Kilmer, Washington	306	166	2,221	13	13
Bob Berry, Atlanta	226	136	2,005	11	16
Roman Gabriel, Los Angeles	352	180	2,238	17	10

LEADING RECEIVERS	No.	Yards	Avg.	Long	TD
Bob Tucker, N.Y. Giants	59	971	13.4	63t	4
Ted Kwalick, San Francisco	52	664	12.8	42t	5
Harold Jackson, Philadelphia	47	716	15.2	69t	3
Roy Jefferson, Washington	47	701	14.9	70t	4
Gene Washington, San Francisco	46	884	19.2	71t	4
George Farmer, Chicago	46	737	16.0	64	5

1972 The NFC won the Super Bowl when Dallas beat Miami 24–3.

Three teams had management changes. Robert Irsay bought the Los Angeles Rams from the estate of the late Dan Reeves, and traded the franchise with Carroll Rosenbloom, owner of the Baltimore Colts. Isray wound up as owner of the Colts and Rosenbloom took control of the Rams. William Bidwill became the sole owner of the St. Louis Cardinals, buying out his brother, Charles (Stormy) Bidwill. Kansas City moved into 78,907-seat Arrowhead stadium.

In hopes of increasing scoring and countering the zone defense, the owners adopted a new rule to move in the hashmarks or inbound lines from 20 yards to 23 yards, 1 foot, 9 inches, leaving out 18 feet, 6 inches, the width of the goal post crossbar, in the middle.

A series of trades involved "big name" players in the league. Quarterback Fran Tarkenton, traded to the Giants by the Vikings in early 1967, went back to Minnesota in a swap that sent receiver Bob Grim and draft choices to New York. Running back Duane Thomas was shipped to San Diego by Dallas, and defensive end Fred Dryer went from the Giants to the Rams via the Patriots. Denver dealt with Houston to get quarterback Charley Johnson.

Jack Tatum of Oakland erased a 49-year-old record when he ran 104 yards with a recovered fumble, beating the old mark of 98 by George Halas of the Bears against the Oorang Indians of Marion, Ohio, in 1923.

The running backs responded to the rules changes with a record 10 players rushing for 1,000 yards or more. O.J. Simpson found the offensive style of the Buffalo Bills' new coach Lou Saban just what he wanted and led the league with 1,251 yards for Buffalo. Larry Brown of Washington led the NFC with 1,216. Ron Johnson of the Giants had 1,182, Calvin Hill of Dallas 1,036, John Brockington of Green Bay 1,027 in the NFC, and Larry Csonka of Miami 1,117, Marv Hubbard of Oakland 1,100, rookie Franco Harris of Pittsburgh 1,055, Mike Garrett of San Diego 1,031, and Eugene (Mercury) Morris of Miami 1,000 in the AFC. Morris made it when the league found an error in scoring in which Morris had been charged

Paul Warfield of Miami making a 75-yard touchdown catch against Baltimore in 1971 AFC championship.

Bill Bidwill.

Carroll Rosenbloom.

Jack Tatum of Oakland going 104 yards with a fumble recovery vs. Green Bay, 1972.

Don Maynard.

John Brockington.

Chuck Foreman.

with a nine-yard loss that should have been listed as a fumble by Earl Morrall. Dave Hampton of Atlanta made it to 1,001 yards in the last game but was thrown for a six-yard loss and finished at 995 yards.

Don Maynard of the New York Jets topped the all-time pass receivers with 632 receptions, one more than the retired Raymond Berry. Bobby Douglass of the Bears ran for 968 yards, a record for a quarterback, and led the Bears in rushing. Chester Marcol's 33 field goals for Green Bay were the most since Jim Turner kicked a record 34 for the Jets in 1968.

Coach Don Shula's Dolphins breezed to a 14–0 record, seven full games ahead of the runner-up Jets (7–7) in the AFC East. Oakland regained control of the AFC West at 10–3–1 after a one-year lapse. Chuck Noll brought Pittsburgh its first division title with 11–3 in the AFC Central and runner-up Cleveland (10–4) qualified as the "wild card" team.

Washington shaded Dallas in the NFC East with both qualifying for the playoffs. Green Bay won the NFC Central and San Francisco made it three in a row in the NFC West at 8–5–1.

Miami had to come from behind to beat Cleveland 20–14 in its first playoff game and Pittsburgh had to come up with a near-miraculous play to defeat Oakland 13–7. Terry Bradshaw threw a desperation pass on fourth and 10 with 22 seconds to play and the Raiders winning 7–6. The ball, intended for John (Frenchy) Fuqua, bounced off Oakland safety Jack Tatum and was caught by Franco Harris just off his shoe tops. Harris ran 60 yards for the winning touchdown.

In the NFC divisional playoffs, Roger Staubach threw two touchdown passes in 38 seconds as Dallas rallied to beat the 49ers 30–28 and Washington defeated Green Bay 16–3.

Miami beat Pittsburgh 21–17 for the AFC championship and Washington advanced to the Super Bowl with a 26–3 victory over the Cowboys on four field goals by Curt Knight and two touchdown passes by Billy Kilmer playing for the injured Sonny Jurgensen.

1972 AFC STANDINGS

Eastern Division	W	L	T	Pct.	Pts.	OP
Miami	14	0	0	1.000	385	171
N.Y. Jets	7	7	0	.500	367	324
Baltimore	5	9	0	.357	235	252
Buffalo	4	9	1	.321	257	377
New England	3	11	0	.214	192	446
Central Division	W	L	T	Pct.	Pts.	OP
Pittsburgh	11	3	0	.786	343	175
Cleveland*	10	4	0	.714	268	249
Cincinnati	8	6	0	.571	299	229
Houston	1	13	0	.071	164	380
Western Division	W	L	T	Pct.	Pts.	OP
Oakland	10	3	1	.750	365	248
Kansas City	8	6	0	.571	287	254
Denver	5	9	0	.357	325	350
San Diego	4	9	1	.321	264	344

*Wild Card qualifier for playoffs
Divisional playoffs: Pittsburgh 13, Oakland 7; Miami 20, Cleveland 14
AFC championship: Miami 21, Pittsburgh 17

LEADING RUSHERS	Att.	Yards	Avg.	Long	TD
O. J. Simpson, Buffalo	292	1,251	4.3	94t	6
Larry Csonka, Miami	213	1,117	5.2	45	6
Marv Hubbard, Oakland	219	1,100	5.0	39	4
Franco Harris, Pittsburgh	188	1,055	5.6	75t	10
Mike Garrett, San Diego	272	1,031	3.8	41t	6

LEADING PASSERS	Att.	Comp.	Yards	TD	Int.
Earl Morrall, Miami	150	83	1,360	11	7
Daryle Lamonica, Oakland	281	149	1,998	18	12
Charley Johnson, Denver	283	132	1,783	14	14
John Unitas, Baltimore	157	88	1,111	4	6
Ken Anderson, Cincinnati	301	171	1,918	7	7

LEADING RECEIVERS	No.	Yards	Avg.	Long	TD
Fred Biletnikoff, Oakland	58	803	13.8	39t	7
Otis Taylor, Kansas City	57	821	14.4	44	6
Philip (Chip) Myers, Cincinnati	57	792	13.9	42	3
J. D. Hill, Buffalo	52	754	14.5	58t	5
Gary Garrison, San Diego	52	744	14.3	52t	7

1972 NFC STANDINGS

Eastern Division	W	L	T	Pct.	Pts.	OP
Washington	11	3	0	.786	336	218
Dallas*	10	4	0	.714	319	240
N.Y. Giants	8	6	0	.571	331	247
St. Louis	4	9	1	.321	193	303
Philadelphia	2	11	1	.179	145	352
Central Division	W	L	T	Pct.	Pts.	OP
Green Bay	10	4	0	.714	304	226
Detroit	8	5	1	.607	339	290
Minnesota	7	7	0	.500	301	252
Chicago	4	9	1	.321	225	275
Western Division	W	L	T	Pct.	Pts.	OP
San Francisco	8	5	1	.607	353	249
Atlanta	7	7	0	.500	269	274
Los Angeles	6	7	1	.464	291	286
New Orleans	2	11	1	.179	215	361

*Wild Card qualifier for playoffs
Divisional playoffs: Dallas 30, San Francisco 28; Washington 16, Green Bay 3
NFC championship: Washington 26, Dallas 3
Super Bowl VII: Miami (AFC) 14, Washington (NFC) 7

LEADING RUSHERS	Att.	Yards	Avg.	Long	TD
Larry Brown, Washington	285	1,216	4.3	38t	8
Ron Johnson, N.Y. Giants	298	1,182	4.0	35t	9
Calvin Hill, Dallas	245	1,036	4.2	26	6
John Brockington, Green Bay	274	1,027	3.7	30t	8
Dave Hampton, Atlanta	230	995	4.3	56t	6

LEADING PASSERS	Att.	Comp.	Yards	TD	Int.
Norm Snead, N.Y. Giants	325	196	2,307	17	12
Bob Berry, Atlanta	277	154	2,158	13	12
Fran Tarkenton, Minnesota	378	215	2,651	18	13
Bill Kilmer, Washington	225	120	1,648	19	11
Steve Spurrier, San Francisco	269	147	1,983	18	16

LEADING RECEIVERS	No.	Yards	Avg.	Long	TD
Harold Jackson, Philadelphia	62	1,048	16.9	77t	4
Bob Tucker, N.Y. Giants	55	764	13.9	39	4
Art Malone, Atlanta	50	585	11.7	57t	2
Charley Taylor, Washington	49	673	13.7	70t	7
John Gilliam, Minnesota	47	1,035	22.0	66t	7
Bob Newland, New Orleans	47	579	12.3	42t	2

1973 The Miami Dolphins made NFL history when they went through an entire season without defeat, climaxing their 17–0 season with a 14–7 victory over Washington in Super Bowl VII before a record crowd of 90,182 at the Los Angeles Coliseum. No team ever had gone all the way to the championship without a defeat or a tie.

The Dolphins ended their perfect season by shutting out the Redskins until Garo Yepremian, trying to salvage something from an abortive field goal try,

attempted to pass and fumbled. Mike Bass grabbed the ball and ran 49 yards for the lone Washington score with 2:07 to play.

Running back Gale Sayers of the Chicago Bears, quarterback Bart Starr of the Green Bay Packers, and safety Larry Wilson of the St. Louis Cardinals retired.

Congress passed a three-year bill that lifted the hometown TV blackouts on games sold out 72 hours before kickoff. The NFL opposed the legislation as a threat to the sale of season tickets and the first step toward a television studio-type game with empty seats at the stadiums.

The league formed NFL Charities, a nonprofit foundation that would receive its revenue from licensing league and club trademarks, to meet educational and charitable needs and provide economic support for former players.

Chuck Knox became coach of the Los Angeles Rams. General manager Sid Gillman took over as head coach of the Houston Oilers during the season.

The Rams traded for quarterback John Hadl and wide receiver Harold Jackson and sent quarterback Roman Gabriel off to Philadelphia.

The New York Giants moved out of Yankee Stadium, their home since 1956, during the season and played their last five games at Yale Bowl in New Haven, Connecticut. Buffalo opened 80,020-seat Rich Stadium at suburban Orchard Park, New York.

An expansion committee, headed by Dan Rooney of Pittsburgh, was formed to explore future expansion.

The World Football League was formed in a meeting in Los Angeles in October and announced its plans to begin play in 1974.

Miami's bid for a second straight perfect season ended early. The Dolphins won their opener 21–13 over San Francisco for 18 straight, tying the record set by the 1933–34 Chicago Bears and equaled by the 1941–42 Bears. However, the Dolphins were tripped up by the Oakland Raiders 12–7 in their second game at Oakland, September 23.

O.J. Simpson of the Buffalo Bills broke the one-season rushing record with 2,003 yards. He had a record 250 yards against New England opening day. He passed midseason with 1,000 yards, the goal of most outstanding runners for a full season. At the end he set records with most rushing attempts (332), most 100-yard games in a season (11), and most 200-yard games in a season (3).

John Brockington of Green Bay also put his name in the record book as the only man to gain over 1,000 yards in each of his first three pro seasons. He gained 1,144 yards. Other 1,000-yard runners that season were Calvin Hill of Dallas with 1,142, rookie Lawrence McCutcheon of Los Angeles with 1,097, and Larry Csonka of Miami with 1,003.

The Dolphins lost only one more game on the way to a 12–2 record and a third straight title in the AFC East with Bob Griese doing the passing, a three-pronged running game of Csonka, Mercury Morris, and Jim Kiick, and the "No Name Defense," so-called because of its lack of individual recognition.

Ken Anderson and Essex Johnson, aided by rookies Charles (Boobie) Clark and Isaac Curtis, brought Cincinnati home first in the AFC Central at 10–4, winning the division despite Pittsburgh's matching 10–4 because the Bengals had a better record in intraconference games. The Steelers qualified for the playoffs as the "wild card" team. Oakland took the West at 9–4–1 by beating runner-up Denver (7–5–2) in the final game 21–7.

Dallas (10–4) and George Allen's "Over the Hill Gang" at Washington (10–4) ruled the NFC East, with Dallas winning the division on an edge in total points for the two games the clubs split. Washington got the NFC "wild card" spot.

Rookie Chuck Foreman teamed with Fran Tarkenton to help the Vikings to the NFC West title with a 12–2 record. The Los Angeles Rams' 12–2 mark under new coach Chuck Knox ended three years of domination by the 49ers in the NFC West.

In the AFC playoffs Miami disposed of Cincinnati 34–16 and Oakland got even with Pittsburgh 33–14. Minnesota ousted Washington 27–20 and Roger Staubach's 83-yard pass to Drew Pearson helped Dallas beat Los Angeles 27–16 in the NFC playoffs.

The Dolphins won the AFC championship by defeating Oakland 27–10 on 117 yards and three touchdowns by Larry Csonka. The Vikings ran over the Cowboys 27–10 for the NFC title.

A study group was assigned to consider proposals for rule changes that might increase scoring.

1973 AFC STANDINGS

Eastern Division	W	L	T	Pct.	Pts.	OP
Miami	12	2	0	.857	343	150
Buffalo	9	5	0	.643	259	230
New England	5	9	0	.357	258	300
Baltimore	4	10	0	.286	226	341
N.Y. Jets	4	10	0	.286	240	306

Central Division	W	L	T	Pct.	Pts.	OP
Cincinnati	10	4	0	.714	286	231
Pittsburgh*	10	4	0	.714	347	210
Cleveland	7	5	2	.571	234	255
Houston	1	13	0	.071	199	447

Western Division	W	L	T	Pct.	Pts.	OP
Oakland	9	4	1	.679	292	175
Denver	7	5	2	.571	354	296
Kansas City	7	5	2	.571	231	192
San Diego	2	11	1	.179	188	386

*Wild Card qualifier for playoffs
Divisional playoffs: Oakland 33, Pittsburgh 14;
Miami 34, Cincinnati 16
AFC championship: Miami 27, Oakland 10

LEADING RUSHERS
	Att.	Yards	Avg.	Long	TD
O. J. Simpson, Buffalo,	332	2,003	6.0	80t	12
Larry Csonka, Miami	219	1,003	4.6	25	5
Essex Johnson, Cincinnati	195	997	5.1	46	4
Charles (Boobie) Clark, Cincinnati	254	988	3.9	26	8
Floyd Little, Denver	256	979	3.8	47	12

LEADING PASSERS
	Att.	Comp.	Yards	TD	Int.
Ken Stabler, Oakland	260	163	1,997	14	10
Bob Griese, Miami	218	116	1,422	17	8
Ken Anderson, Cincinnati	329	179	2,428	18	12
Charley Johnson, Denver	346	184	2,465	20	17
Al Woodall, N.Y. Jets	201	101	1,228	9	8

LEADING RECEIVERS
	No.	Yards	Avg.	Long	TD
Fred Willis, Houston	57	371	6.5	50	1
Ed Podolak, Kansas City	55	445	8.1	25	0
Reggie Rucker, New England	53	743	14.0	64	3
Fred Biletnikoff, Oakland	48	660	13.8	32	4
Isaac Curtis, Cincinnati	45	843	18.7	77t	9
Mike Siani, Oakland	45	742	16.5	80t	3
Charles (Boobie) Clark, Cincinnati	45	347	7.7	39	0

1973 NFC STANDINGS

Eastern Division	W	L	T	Pct.	Pts.	OP
Dallas	10	4	0	.714	382	203
Washington*	10	4	0	.714	325	198
Philadelphia	5	8	1	.393	310	393
St. Louis	4	9	1	.321	286	365
N.Y. Giants	2	11	1	.179	226	362

Central Division	W	L	T	Pct.	Pts.	OP
Minnesota	12	2	0	.857	296	168
Detroit	6	7	1	.464	271	247
Green Bay	5	7	2	.429	202	259
Chicago	3	11	0	.214	195	334

Western Division	W	L	T	Pct.	Pts.	OP
Los Angeles	12	2	0	.857	388	178
Atlanta	9	5	0	.643	318	224
New Orleans	5	9	0	.357	163	312
San Francisco	5	9	0	.357	262	319

*Wild Card qualifier for playoffs
Divisional playoffs: Minnesota 27, Washington 20;
Dallas 27, Los Angeles 16
NFC championship: Minnesota 27, Dallas 10
Super Bowl VIII: Miami (AFC) 24, Minnesota (NFC) 7

LEADING RUSHERS
	Att.	Yards	Avg.	Long	TD
John Brockington, Green Bay	265	1,144	4.3	53	3
Calvin Hill, Dallas	273	1,142	4.2	21	6
Lawrence McCutcheon, Los Angeles	210	1,097	5.2	37	2
Dave Hampton, Atlanta	263	997	3.8	25	4
Tom Sullivan, Philadelphia	217	968	4.5	37	4

LEADING PASSERS
	Att.	Comp.	Yards	TD	Int.
Roger Staubach, Dallas	286	179	2,428	23	15
Fran Tarkenton, Minnesota	274	169	2,113	15	7
John Hadl, Los Angeles	258	135	2,008	22	11
Roman Gabriel, Philadelphia	460	270	3,219	23	12
Bill Kilmer, Washington	227	122	1,656	14	9

LEADING RECEIVERS
	No.	Yards	Avg.	Long	TD
Harold Carmichael, Philadelphia	67	1,116	16.7	73	9
Charley Taylor, Washington	59	801	13.6	53	7
Charles Young, Philadelphia	55	854	15.5	80t	6
Bob Tucker, N.Y. Giants	50	681	13.6	33	5
Tom Sullivan, Philadelphia	50	322	6.4	29	1

O. J. Simpson gaining 200 yards vs. New York Jets in the last game of his 2,003-yard season, 1973.

Weeb Ewbank of the Jets, retiring from coaching, is honored at Baltimore in 1974.

1974 The Dolphins joined the Green Bay Packers as two-time Super Bowl winners by beating the Vikings 24–7 with Csonka rushing for a record 145 yards at Rice Stadium in Houston.

Significant rules changes were made. Sudden death overtime was adopted for all preseason and regular season games. The goal posts were moved back to the end line and kickoffs were to be made from the 35, not the 40. Missed field goals outside the 20 were to go back to the line of scrimmage instead of being called touchbacks. Only two outside men of the kicking team were allowed downfield before the ball was punted. Defensive players were allowed to "chuck"—or bump—a pass reciever only once, and rolling blocks on wide receivers were made illegal. The holding penalty was reduced to 10 yards and receivers were prohibited from making "crackback" blocks below the waist.

The Toronto Northmen of the World Football League made news in March when they announced that Larry Csonka, Paul Warfield, and Jim Kiick of the NFL champion Miami Dolphins would play out their options in 1974 and join the Northmen in 1975 in a reported three-year $3 million deal.

The NFL decided to expand to 28 clubs by adding Tampa Bay and Seattle to begin play in 1976. Commissioner Rozelle was voted a new 10-year contract and a 47-man player limit was adopted.

Weeb Ewbank, coach of the New York Jets, retired and was replaced by his son-in-law, assistant Charley Winner.

Coach Don McCafferty of the Detroit Lions died of a heart attack during the preseason and was replaced by Rick Forzano.

Los Angeles traded quarterback John Hadl to Green Bay for draft choices. Dallas shipped quarterback Craig Morton to the New York Giants, who sent Norm Snead to San Francisco. John Unitas retired after 18 years. Defensive tackle Curley Culp moved from Kansas City to Houston, where he became the key as the middle guard in a three-man defensive line.

Owners and players were unable to agree on a new collective bargaining agreement as the old four-year pact expired. Rookies came to training camp but the veterans stayed out, many of them carrying picket signs. The annual Chicago All-Star game was canceled. The veterans reported under provisions of a 14-day cooling off period and the strike ended August 28 in time for the final preseason games, most of which were played with rookie teams.

The results of the rules changes were a considerable increase in touchdowns, fewer field goals, fewer fair catch signals, and longer punt and kickoff returns.

The Pittsburgh Steelers won the AFC Central Division. Miami won the Eastern and Oakland the Western Division.

Coach Don Coryell put the St. Louis Cardinals in the playoffs for the first time since they left Chicago in 1960 by winning the NFC East. St. Louis and Washington finished 10–4 but the Cardinals beat the Redskins twice to win the division while the Redskins became the "wild card" entry. The Minnesota Vikings and Los Angeles Rams easily won the Central and Western Divisions in the NFC.

Otis Armstrong of Denver led the league's rushers with 1,407 yards and rookie Don Woods of San Diego set a record for a first-year man with 1,162. Other 1,000-yard rushers were O.J. Simpson of Buffalo with 1,125, Lawrence McCutcheon of Los Angeles with 1,109, and Franco Harris of Pittsburgh with 1,006.

Cincinnati quarterback Ken Anderson set a record when he completed 16 consecutive passes against Baltimore, but Bert Jones of Baltimore broke it a month later with 17 straight against the New York Jets.

Otis Armstrong of Denver, who gained 1,407 yards, hugged by Mike Current after scoring, 1974.

Quarterback Bert Jones of Baltimore turning to hand off against Miami, 1974; he completed 17 straight passes in one game.

Lydell Mitchell of Baltimore set a record for a running back with a league-leading 72 pass receptions.

The WFL staggered through its first year, starting with eight teams and ending with five. Padded attendance figures, missed payrolls, and shifting franchises left the league's future in doubt. The Toronto Northmen were forced from Canada, moved to Memphis, and became the Southmen. The New York Stars moved to Charlotte, North Carolina, in midseason. The Chicago, Detroit, and Jacksonville franchises folded.

The Miami Dolphins' reign in the NFL ended when they were beaten by Oakland 28–26 on a sensational catch by Clarence Davis of Ken Stabler's pass with 26 seconds to play in the AFC divisional playoff. Pittsburgh beat Buffalo in the other AFC playoff. In the NFC, Minnesota defeated St. Louis 30–14 and Los Angeles won over Washington 19–10.

Pittsburgh reached the Super Bowl for the first time by defeating Oakland 24–13 in the AFC championship and Minnesota returned to the game by handing Los Angeles a 14–10 defeat for the NFC title.

1974 AFC STANDINGS

Eastern Division
	W	L	T	Pct.	Pts.	OP
Miami	11	3	0	.786	327	216
Buffalo*	9	5	0	.643	264	244
New England	7	7	0	.500	348	289
N.Y. Jets	7	7	0	.500	279	300
Baltimore	2	12	0	.143	190	329

Central Division
	W	L	T	Pct.	Pts.	OP
Pittsburgh	10	3	1	.750	305	189
Cincinnati	7	7	0	.500	283	259
Houston	7	7	0	.500	236	282
Cleveland	4	10	0	.286	251	344

Western Division
	W	L	T	Pct.	Pts.	OP
Oakland	12	2	0	.857	355	228
Denver	7	6	1	.536	302	294
Kansas City	5	9	0	.357	233	293
San Diego	5	9	0	.357	212	285

*Wild Card qualifier for playoffs

Divisional playoffs: Oakland 28, Miami 26; Pittsburgh 32, Buffalo 14
AFC championship: Pittsburgh 24, Oakland 13

LEADING RUSHERS
	Att.	Yards	Avg.	Long	TD
Otis Armstrong, Denver	263	1,407	5.3	43	9
Don Woods, San Diego	227	1,162	5.1	56t	7
O. J. Simpson, Buffalo	270	1,125	4.2	41t	3
Franco Harris, Pittsburgh	208	1,006	4.8	54	5
Marv Hubbard, Oakland	188	865	4.6	32	4

LEADING PASSERS
	Att.	Comp.	Yards	TD	Int.
Ken Anderson, Cincinnati	328	213	2,667	18	10
Ken Stabler, Oakland	310	178	2,469	26	12
Charley Johnson, Denver	244	136	1,969	13	9
Bob Griese, Miami	253	152	1,968	16	15
Dan Pastorini, Houston	247	140	1,571	10	10

LEADING RECEIVERS
	No.	Yards	Avg.	Long	TD
Lydell Mitchell, Baltimore	72	544	7.6	24	2
Cliff Branch, Oakland	60	1,092	18.2	67t	13
Ed Podolak, Kansas City	43	306	7.1	26	1
Riley Odoms, Denver	42	639	15.2	41	6
Fred Biletnikoff, Oakland	42	.593	14.1	46	7

1974 NFC STANDINGS

Eastern Division
	W	L	T	Pct.	Pts.	OP
St. Louis	10	4	0	.714	285	218
Washington*	10	4	0	.714	320	196
Dallas	8	6	0	.571	297	235
Philadelphia	7	7	0	.500	242	217
N.Y. Giants	2	12	0	.143	195	299

Central Division
	W	L	T	Pct.	Pts.	OP
Minnesota	10	4	0	.714	310	195
Detroit	7	7	0	.500	256	270
Green Bay	6	8	0	.429	210	206
Chicago	4	10	0	.286	152	279

Western Division
	W	L	T	Pct.	Pts.	OP
Los Angeles	10	4	0	.714	263	181
San Francisco	6	8	0	.429	226	236
New Orleans	5	9	0	.357	166	263
Atlanta	3	11	0	.214	111	271

*Wild Card qualifier for playoffs

Divisional playoffs: Minnesota 30, St. Louis 14; Los Angeles 19, Washington 10
NFC championship: Minnesota 14, Los Angeles 10
Super Bowl IX: Pittsburgh (AFC) 16, Minnesota (NFC) 6

LEADING RUSHERS
	Att.	Yards	Avg.	Long	TD
Lawrence McCutcheon, Los Angeles	236	1,109	4.7	23t	3
John Brockington, Green Bay	266	883	3.3	33	5
Calvin Hill, Dallas	185	844	4.6	27	7
Chuck Foreman, Minnesota	199	777	3.9	32	9
Tom Sullivan, Philadelphia	244	670	3.1	28t	11

LEADING PASSERS
	Att.	Comp.	Yards	TD	Int.
Sonny Jurgensen, Washington	167	107	1,185	11	5
James Harris, Los Angeles	198	106	1,544	11	6
Billy Kilmer, Washington	234	137	1,632	10	6
Fran Tarkenton, Minnesota	351	199	2,598	17	12
Jim Hart, St. Louis	388	200	2,411	20	8

LEADING RECEIVERS
	No.	Yards	Avg.	Long	TD
Charles Young, Philadelphia	63	696	11.0	29	3
Drew Pearson, Dallas	62	1,087	17.5	50t	2
Harold Carmichael, Philadelphia	56	649	11.6	39	8
Ron Jessie, Detroit	54	761	14.1	46	3
Charley Taylor, Washington	54	738	13.7	51	5

1975 Owner Art Rooney finally came up with a winner in Pittsburgh after 42 years. Chuck Noll's Steelers went all the way to a Super Bowl championship. Running back Franco Harris broke the record with 158 yards rushing in the Steelers' 16–6 victory over the Vikings in Super Bowl IX at Tulane Stadium in New Orleans.

Sonny Jurgensen of the Washington Redskins and Jim Otto of the Oakland Raiders retired.

An interpretation of the rules made oversized huddles and "lingering on the field" illegal. The owners established a 43-man player limit and did away with "taxi" squads.

The playoff format was changed to reward the teams with the highest won-lost percentages by making them the hosts for the divisional playoffs. The ultimate survivors with the best records would host the championship games.

Legal problems plagued the owners. A court decision declaring the compensation rule, commonly known as the "Rozelle Rule," illegal, was appealed. Several matters concerning the control of players were in court.

A one-game strike during the preseason schedule preceded another year without an agreement between the NFL and the Players Association. The New England Patriots refused to play a preseason game with the Jets but all five striking teams agreed to open the regular season despite rejection of a contract offer by the NFL Management Council.

The New Orleans Saints left Tulane Stadium, their home since 1967, and moved into the 72,000-seat Louisiana Superdome. The Detroit Lions left Tiger Stadium, where they had played since 1937, and moved to the new Pontiac Metropolitan Stadium in Pontiac, Michigan.

The Superdome was built on a 53-acre tract in downtown New Orleans and its huge dome rose 273 feet above the ground. It was equipped with five giant television screens to add to the fans' enjoyment of the games.

An unusual feature of the Pontiac stadium was its roof, a tent of Teflon-coated fiberglass fabric fitting over the top, held up by steel cables, and inflated by compressed air.

The reorganized World Football League under new president Chris Hemmeter ended its operation in the twelfth week of its second season, putting 380 players out of work.

Last in the Eastern Division at 2–12 in 1974, Baltimore started with a 1–4 record under new coach Ted Marchibroda, then ran off nine straight victories. The Colts beat Miami twice, 33–17 and 10–7 on a 31-yard field goal by Toni Linhart after 12:44 of sudden death overtime. Their success in those two games was the difference in the AFC East because Miami also was 10–4.

Chuck Noll's Steelers lost their second game of the season to Buffalo, then went on an 11-game win streak before bowing to the Rams in the finale for a 12–2 season. Until the Rams' game, the Steelers had won 10 in a row on the road and were 9–0 against the NFC since 1972. Despite the streaks, the Steelers had tough competition in the AFC Central with runner-up and "wild card" Cincinnati 11–3 and Houston 10–4. The Oilers lost two each to the Steelers and Bengals.

Oakland ran away with the AFC West for its fourth straight division title and eighth in nine years.

St. Louis, Minnesota, and Los Angeles won the NFC division races.

Quarterback Fran Tarkenton of the Minnesota Vikings finished the season with all time records for most touchdown passes in a career (291), most completions (2,931), and most attempts (5,225), all

Clarence Davis's catch stuns Miami in playoffs, 1974.

Charley Taylor after scoring against Philadelphia, 1974.

held previously by the retired John Unitas.

George Blanda, 49, played his final season for Oakland and left a list of records including most active seasons (26), most games played (340), most consecutive games played (224), most points scored (2,002), most field goals (335), and most points after touchdown (943). Charley Taylor, Washington's wide receiver, bested Don Maynard's record with a lifetime total of 635 receptions, an all-time high for pro football.

The NFL had eight 1,000-yard runners, led by O.J. Simpson of Buffalo with 1,817, third best in league history.

Simpson and Chuck Foreman engaged in a tight battle for the 1975 scoring title. Simpson won with 23 touchdowns, a record, and 138 points to Foreman's 132 on 22 touchdowns, tying the previous record set by Gale Sayers as a rookie in 1965.

The Colts' string was snapped by Pittsburgh 28–10 in the first playoff game, one in which quarterback Bert Jones was injured. Oakland held on against a Cincinnati closing rush for a 31–28 victory in the other divisional playoff.

Despite Tarkenton's 25 touchdown passes and Foreman's 22 touchdowns and 1,070 yards, Minnesota couldn't make it to Super Bowl X. The Vikings were eliminated in the first round by Dallas, the "wild card" team whose 10–4 was second to St. Louis' 11–3 in the NFC East. A last-minute 50-yard pass from Roger Staubach to Drew Pearson that was disputed by the Vikings gave Dallas a 17–14 playoff win. Los Angeles romped in the NFC West at 12–2 and defeated St. Louis 35–23 behind reserve quarterback Ron Jaworski.

Pittsburgh outlasted the Raiders 16–10 on an icy field at Pittsburgh for the AFC championship when Jack Lambert recovered three fumbles. The Raiders had reached the Steelers' 15 when time ran out.

Dallas became the first "wild card" team to reach the Super Bowl (although second-place Kansas City of the AFC West in 1969 had won Super Bowl IV before the "wild card" system) when the Cowboys shocked the Rams 37–7 on four touchdown passes by Roger Staubach, three to Preston Pearson, to win the NFC title.

1975 AFC STANDINGS

Eastern Division	W	L	T	Pct.	Pts.	OP
Baltimore	10	4	0	.714	395	269
Miami	10	4	0	.714	357	222
Buffalo	8	6	0	.571	420	355
New England	3	11	0	.214	258	358
N.Y. Jets	3	11	0	.214	258	433
Central Division	**W**	**L**	**T**	**Pct.**	**Pts.**	**OP**
Pittsburgh	12	2	0	.857	373	162
Cincinnati*	11	3	0	.786	340	246
Houston	10	4	0	.714	293	226
Cleveland	3	11	0	.214	218	372
Western Division	**W**	**L**	**T**	**Pct.**	**Pts.**	**OP**
Oakland	11	3	0	.786	375	255
Denver	6	8	0	.429	254	307
Kansas City	5	9	0	.357	282	341
San Diego	2	12	0	.143	189	345

*Wild Card qualifier for playoffs
Divisional playoffs: Pittsburgh 28, Baltimore 10; Oakland 31, Cincinnati 28
AFC championship: Pittsburgh 16, Oakland 10

LEADING RUSHERS	Att.	Yards	Avg.	Long	TD
O. J. Simpson, Buffalo	329	1,817	5.5	88t	16
Franco Harris, Pittsburgh	262	1,246	4.8	36	10
Lydell Mitchell, Baltimore	289	1,193	4.1	70t	11
Greg Pruitt, Cleveland	217	1,067	4.9	50	8
John Riggins, N.Y. Jets	238	1,005	4.2	42	8

LEADING PASSERS	Att.	Comp.	Yards	TD	Int.
Ken Anderson, Cincinnati	377	228	3,169	21	11
Len Dawson, Kansas City	140	93	1,095	5	4
Bert Jones, Baltimore	344	203	2,483	18	8
Terry Bradshaw, Pittsburgh	286	165	2,055	18	9
Bob Griese, Miami	191	118	1,693	14	13

LEADING RECEIVERS	No.	Yards	Avg.	Long	TD
Reggie Rucker, Cleveland	60	770	12.8	40t	3
Lydell Mitchell, Baltimore	60	544	9.1	35t	4
Bob Chandler, Buffalo	55	746	13.6	35	6
Ken Burrough, Houston	53	1,063	20.1	77t	8
Clifford Branch, Oakland	51	983	17.5	53	9

Quarterback Fran Tarkenton of Minnesota drops back to pass against Los Angeles, 1974.

Quarterback Ken Stabler swings a pass out to wide receiver Cliff Branch vs. San Diego, 1975.

*Wild Card qualifier for playoffs
Divisional playoffs: Los Angeles 35, St. Louis 23; Dallas 17, Minnesota 14
NFC championship: Dallas 37, Los Angeles 7
Super Bowl X: Pittsburgh (AFC) 21, Dallas (NFC) 17

LEADING RUSHERS	Att.	Yards	Avg.	Long	TD
Jim Otis, St. Louis	269	1,076	4.0	30	5
Chuck Foreman, Minnesota	280	1,070	3.8	31t	13
Dave Hampton, Atlanta	250	1,002	4.0	22	5
Robert Newhouse, Dallas	209	930	4.4	29	2
Mike Thomas, Washington	235	919	3.9	34	4

LEADING PASSERS	Att.	Comp.	Yards	TD	Int.
Fran Tarkenton, Minnesota	425	273	2,994	25	13
Roger Staubach, Dallas	348	198	2,666	17	16
Billy Kilmer, Washington	346	178	2,440	23	16
James Harris, Los Angeles	285	157	2,148	14	15
Norm Snead, San Francisco	189	108	1,337	9	10

LEADING RECEIVERS	No.	Yards	Avg.	Long	TD
Chuck Foreman, Minnesota	73	791	9.5	33	9
Ken Payne, Green Bay	58	766	13.2	54	0
Ed Marinaro, Minnesota	54	462	8.6	25	3
Charley Taylor, Washington	53	744	14.0	64	3
John Gilliam, Minnesota	50	777	15.5	46	7

1976 Terry Bradshaw's 64-yard pass to Lynn Swann helped the Steelers win their second straight Super Bowl at Miami 21–17 over the Cowboys who rallied and threatened again until Glen Edwards made an interception in the end zone on the final play.

The NFL expanded to 28 teams with the addition of the Seattle Seahawks and the Tampa Bay Buccaneers for the 1976 season. The Seahawks moved into the new 65,000-seat Kingdome and the Buccaneers took over Tampa Stadium, expanded to a capacity of 71,400. The New York Giants, who had wandered between New York and New Haven since 1973, settled into their new Giants Stadium with its 76,500 seats in East Rutherford, New Jersey.

Legal complicatons involving the process of allocating veteran players to Seattle and Tampa Bay delayed the process until March 30–31 with a resultant delay of the college draft until April 8–9.

Tampa Bay had the first draft pick after winning a coin toss with Seattle and selected Oklahoma's Lee Roy Selmon, a defensive lineman.

There were several trades. New England sent Jim Plunkett to San Francisco and decided to rely on young Steve Grogan, a second-year quarterback. Green Bay shipped veteran quarterback John Hadl to Houston for quarterback Lynn Dickey, who had been a reserve behind Dan Pastorini. San Francisco traded Steve Spurrier to Tampa Bay for Willie McGee, Bruce Elia, and a draft choice.

The NFL operated without an agreement with the Players Association for the third consecutive year although there were several meetings between the two groups. A court decision found the present draft system in violation of the law.

Thirty-second clocks were installed to make everyone aware of the time remaining between the ready-to-play signal and the snap of the ball. The 43-man player limit was continued.

Paul Brown stepped down at Cincinnati after coaching high school, college, military, and professional teams for 41 years. He picked a long-time assistant, Bill Johnson, as his successor and remained as general manager of the Bengals.

O. J. Simpson of Buffalo in 1975; he gained 1,817 yards.

O.J. Simpson sought a trade to the Los Angeles Rams, and did not re-sign with the Buffalo Bills until just before their opening game.

Free agents Calvin Hill, Jean Fugett and John Riggins wound up with Washington, Larry Csonka with the Giants, Paul Warfield with Cleveland, and John Gilliam with Atlanta.

A record 12 backs rushed for 1,000 or more yards, topped by O.J. Simpson, who wound up with 1,503, including an NFL single-game record of 273 yards against Detroit Thanksgiving Day. Walter Payton of the Bears had a sensational year, losing the league title to O.J. on the final day as he wound up with 1,390.

Tarkenton moved past John Unitas in career total passing yardage with 41,801 yards while increasing his other records to 308 touchdown passes, 5,637 attempts, and 3,186 completions. Jim Marshall of the Vikings extended his streak of consecutive games to 236, passing the retired George Blanda. Ken Stabler's .667 completion percentage was the best since Sammy Baugh in 1945. Ken Anderson of Cincinnati became the top active passer in the point rating system, but he lost the 1976 AFC title to Stabler after winning two in a row.

Baltimore repeated in the AFC East, although New England also matched the 11–3 record. The Colts took the division on a better intradivision record, 7–1 to 6–2. The Patriots made the playoffs for the first time since the merger as the "wild card" entry.

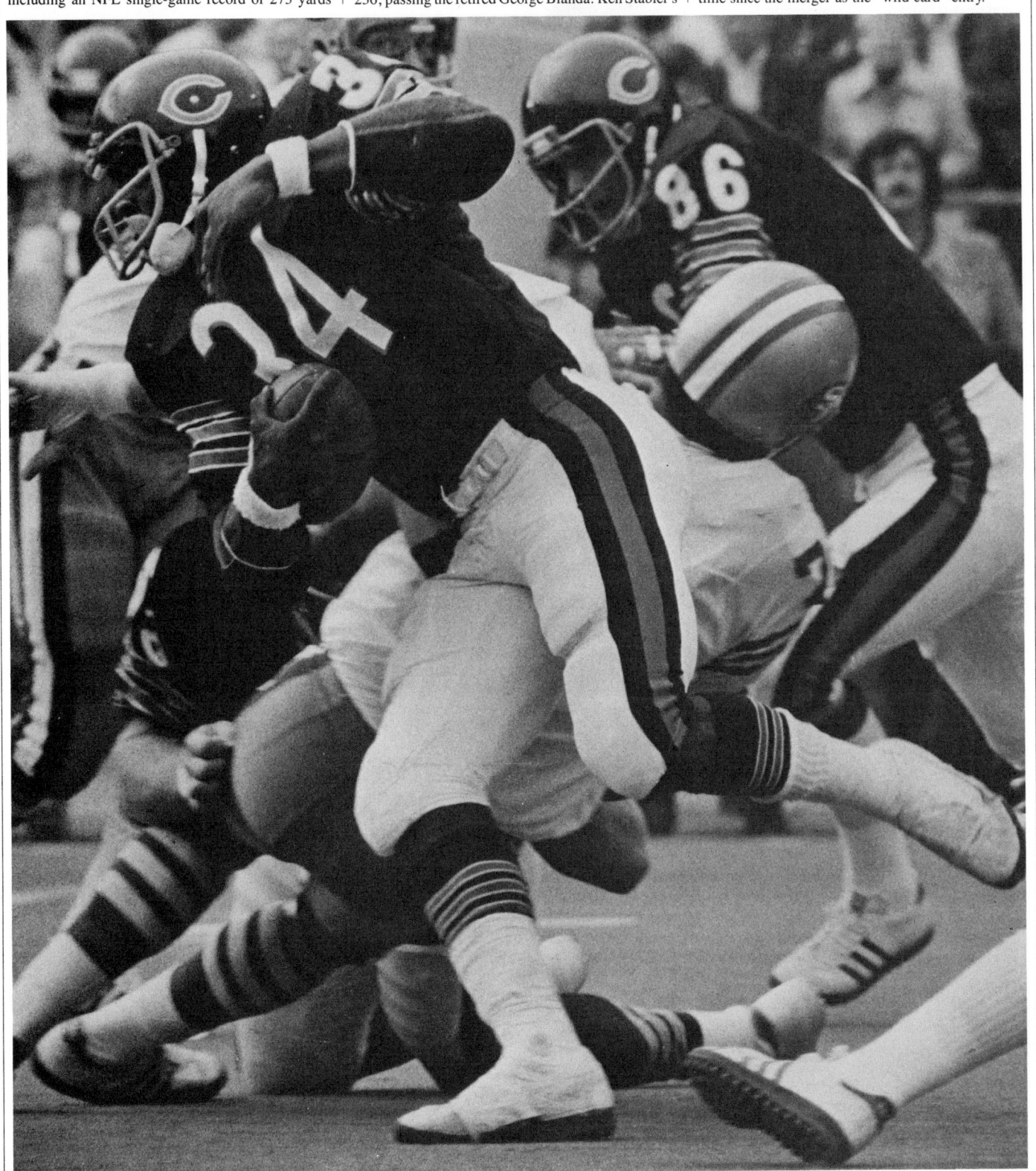

Walter Payton of Chicago running against San Francisco during his 1,390-yard season of 1976.

There is a melee at the goal line as Clarence Davis of Oakland scores against Pittsburgh in the 1976 AFC championship game.

Pittsburgh came back after losing four of its first five, including blowing a 28–14 lead at Oakland in the final three minutes of the season's first game. The Steelers swept their last nine, five by shutouts, matching front-running Cincinnati's 10–4 record in the AFC Central. The Steelers advanced to the playoffs since they had beaten the Bengals twice.

Oakland won the AFC West with a 10-game win streak despite injuries to the defensive unit that forced coach John Madden to use a three-man line.

In the NFC, Dallas won the Eastern Division, Minnesota the Central, and Los Angeles the Western. Washington, counted out several times, made the playoffs as the "wild card" team at 10–4 by beating Dallas in the final game.

Pittsburgh rolled over Baltimore 40–14 in the AFC divisional playoffs while Oakland won a 24–21 vic-

tory over New England, which suffered a costly roughing-the-passer call on the Raiders' game-winning drive in the final minute.

Brent McClanahan and Foreman each rushed for more than 100 yards in Minnesota's first-round win over Washington 35–20, while Los Angeles edged Dallas 14–12 in the AFC divisional playoffs.

Pittsburgh's hopes for a possible third Super Bowl ended in the AFC title game at Oakland. The Steelers lost 24–7 as both regular running backs, Franco Harris and Rocky Bleier, were out with injuries.

Minnesota shocked Los Angeles for the NFC championship as Bobby Bryant scooped up a blocked field-goal try and ran 90 yards for a touchdown that started them on the way to a 24–13 win.

Defensive tackle Merlin Olsen of the Los Angeles Rams retired.

1976 AFC STANDINGS

Eastern Division	W	L	T	Pct.	Pts.	OP
Baltimore	11	3	0	.786	417	246
New England*	11	3	0	.786	376	236
Miami	6	8	0	.429	263	264
N.Y. Jets	3	11	0	.214	169	383
Buffalo	2	12	0	.143	245	363
Central Division	W	L	T	Pct.	Pts.	OP
Pittsburgh	10	4	0	.714	342	138
Cincinnati	10	4	0	.714	335	210
Cleveland	9	5	0	.643	267	287
Houston	5	9	0	.357	222	273
Western Division	W	L	T	Pct.	Pts.	OP
Oakland	13	1	0	.929	350	237
Denver	9	5	0	.643	315	206
San Diego	6	8	0	.429	248	285
Kansas City	5	9	0	.357	290	376
Tampa Bay	0	14	0	.000	125	412

*Wild Card qualifier for playoffs
Divisional playoffs: Oakland 24, New England 21;
Pittsburgh 40, Baltimore 14
AFC championship: Oakland 24, Pittsburgh 7

LEADING RUSHERS

	Att.	Yards	Avg.	Long	TD
O. J Simpson, Buffalo	290	1,503	5.2	75	8
Lydell Mitchell, Baltimore	289	1,200	4.2	43	5
Franco Harris, Pittsburgh	289	1,128	3.9	30	14
Rocky Bleier, Pittsburgh	220	1,036	4.7	28	5
Mark van Eeghen, Oakland	233	1,012	4.3	21	3

LEADING PASSERS

	Att.	Comp.	Yards	TD	Int.
Ken Stabler, Oakland	291	194	2,737	27	17
Bert Jones, Baltimore	343	207	3,014	24	9
Joe Ferguson, Buffalo	151	74	1,086	9	1
Bob Griese, Miami	272	162	2,097	11	12
Mike Livingston, Kansas City	338	189	2,682	12	13

LEADING RECEIVERS

	No.	Yards	Avg.	Long	TD
MacArthur Lane, Kansas City	66	686	10.4	44	1
Bob Chandler, Buffalo	61	824	13.5	58	10
Lydell Mitchell, Baltimore	60	555	9.3	40	3
Dave Casper, Oakland	53	691	13.0	30	10
Ken Burrough, Houston	51	932	18.3	69	7

1976 NFC STANDINGS

Eastern Division	W	L	T	Pct.	Pts.	OP
Dallas	11	3	0	.786	296	194
Washington*	10	4	0	.714	291	217
St. Louis	10	4	0	.714	309	267
Philadelphia	4	10	0	.286	165	286
N.Y. Giants	3	11	0	.214	170	250
Central Division	**W**	**L**	**T**	**Pct.**	**Pts.**	**OP**
Minnesota	11	2	1	.821	305	176
Chicago	7	7	0	.500	253	216
Detroit	6	8	0	.429	262	220
Green Bay	5	9	0	.357	218	299
Western Division	**W**	**L**	**T**	**Pct.**	**Pts.**	**OP**
Los Angeles	10	3	1	.750	351	190
San Francisco	8	6	0	.571	270	190
Atlanta	4	10	0	.286	172	312
New Orleans	4	10	0	.286	253	346
Seattle	2	12	0	.143	229	429

*Wild Card qualifiers for playoffs
Divisional playoffs: Minnesota 35, Washington 20;
Los Angeles 14, Dallas 12
NFC championship: Minnesota 24, Los Angeles 13
Super Bowl XI: Oakland (AFC) 32, Minnesota (NFC) 14

LEADING RUSHERS

	Att.	Yards	Avg.	Long	TD
Walter Payton, Chicago	311	1,390	4.5	60	13
Delvin Williams, San Francisco	248	1,203	4.9	80t	7
Lawrence McCutcheon, Los Angeles	291	1,168	4.0	40	9
Chuck Foreman, Minnesota	276	1,155	4.2	46	13
Mike Thomas, Washington	254	1,101	4.3	28	5

LEADING PASSERS

	Att.	Comp.	Yards	TD	Int.
James Harris, Los Angeles	158	91	1,460	8	6
Greg Landry, Detroit	291	168	2,191	17	8
Fran Tarkenton, Minnesota	412	255	2,961	17	8
Jim Hart, St. Louis	388	218	2,946	18	13
Roger Staubach, Dallas	369	208	2,715	14	11

LEADING RECEIVERS

	No.	Yards	Avg.	Long	TD
Drew Pearson, Dallas	58	806	13.9	40t	6
Chuck Foreman, Minnesota	55	567	10.3	41t	1
Steve Largent, Seattle	54	705	13.1	45	4
Tony Galbreath, New Orleans	54	420	7.8	35	1
Ahmad Rashad, Minnesota	53	671	12.7	47	3

1977 The Raiders, who had lost to Green Bay in Super Bowl II, had undergone a series of other frustrating playoff and title game defeats in the intervening years. Coach John Madden finally cracked Oakland's championship jinx by taking the Raiders to victory in Super Bowl XI. Oakland routed Minnesota 32–14 before a record crowd of 103,424 at the Rose Bowl in Pasadena.

The National Football League Players Association and the National Football League Management Council ratified a collective bargaining agreement extending until July 15, 1982, covering five football seasons while continuing the pension plan—including the years 1974, 1975, and 1976—with contributions totaling more than $55 million. Total cost of the agreement was estimated at $107 million. The agreement called for a college draft at least through 1986, contained a no-strike, no-suit clause, established a 43-man player limit, reduced pension vesting to four years, and provided for increases in minimum salaries and preseason and postseason play, improved insurance, medical and dental benefits, and modified previous practices in player movement and control. The agreement reaffirmed the NFL commissioner's disciplinary authority. Additionally, the agreement called for the NFL member clubs to make payments totaling $16 million over the next 10 years to settle various legal disputes.

1976 NFC championship: Dempsey's kick is blocked, rolls toward Bryant; he went 90 yards to score.

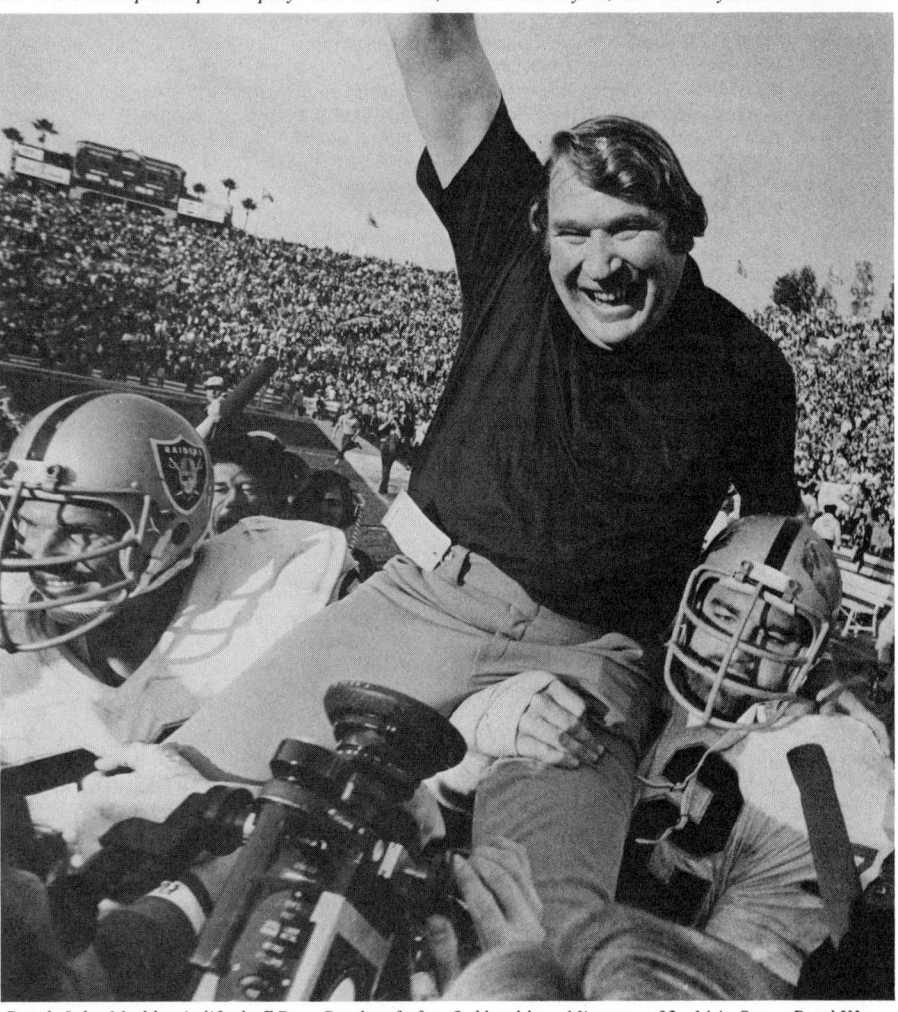

Coach John Madden is lifted off Rose Bowl turf after Oakland beat Minnesota 32–14 in Super Bowl XI.

Sargent Karch of NFL Management Council, right, and Ed Garvey of Players Association after reaching collective bargaining agreement, 1977.

The Growth
of Pro Football

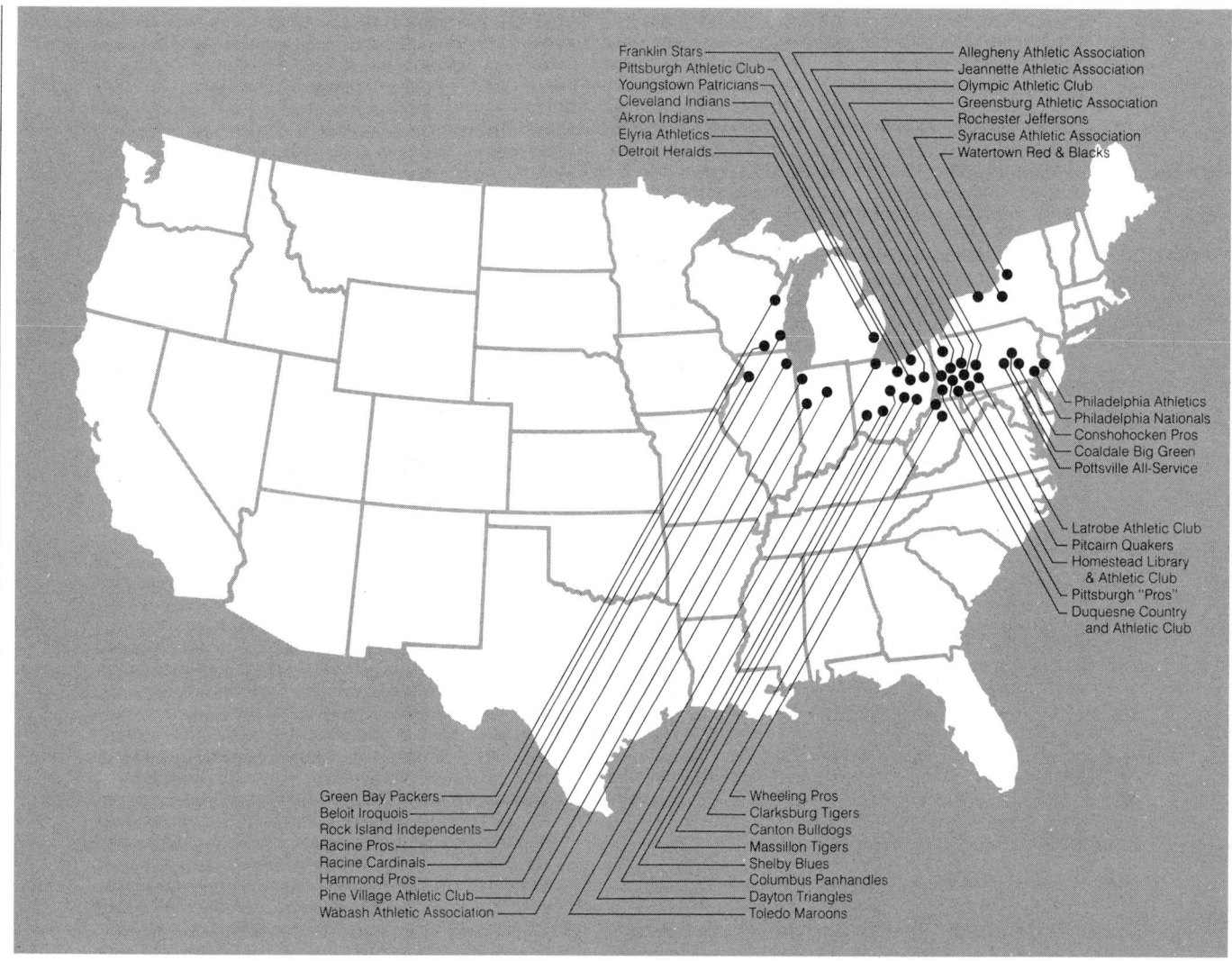

Franklin Stars
Pittsburgh Athletic Club
Youngstown Patricians
Cleveland Indians
Akron Indians
Elyria Athletics
Detroit Heralds

Allegheny Athletic Association
Jeannette Athletic Association
Olympic Athletic Club
Greensburg Athletic Association
Rochester Jeffersons
Syracuse Athletic Association
Watertown Red & Blacks

Philadelphia Athletics
Philadelphia Nationals
Conshohocken Pros
Coaldale Big Green
Pottsville All-Service

Latrobe Athletic Club
Pitcairn Quakers
Homestead Library
& Athletic Club
Pittsburgh "Pros"
Duquesne Country
and Athletic Club

Green Bay Packers
Beloit Iroquois
Rock Island Independents
Racine Pros
Racine Cardinals
Hammond Pros
Pine Village Athletic Club
Wabash Athletic Association

Wheeling Pros
Clarksburg Tigers
Canton Bulldogs
Massillon Tigers
Shelby Blues
Columbus Panhandles
Dayton Triangles
Toledo Maroons

1892-1919

PENNSYLVANIA
Allegheny Athletic Association, Pittsburgh
Pittsburgh Athletic Club
Greensburg Athletic Association
Latrobe Athletic Club
Duquesne Country & Athletic Club, Pittsburgh
Olympic Athletic Club, McKeesport
Jeanette Athletic Association
Homestead Library & Athletic Club
Pittsburgh "Pros"
Philadelphia Nationals
Philadelphia Athletics
Franklin Stars
Pitcairn Quakers
Conshohocken Pros
Coaldale Big Green
Pottsville All-Service

OHIO
Massillon Tigers
Shelby Blues
Akron Indians
Canton Bulldogs
Toledo Maroons
Columbus Panhandles
Youngstown Patricians
Dayton Triangles
Elyria Athletics
Cleveland Indians

INDIANA
Pine Village Athletic Club
Wabash Athletic Association
Hammond Pros

NEW YORK STATE
Syracuse Athletic Association
Watertown Red & Blacks
Rochester Jeffersons

WISCONSIN
Racine Pros
Beloit Iroquois
Green Bay Packers

ILLINOIS
Racine Cardinals, Chicago
Rock Island Independents

WEST VIRGINIA
Clarksburg Tigers
Wheeling Pros

MICHIGAN
Detroit Heralds

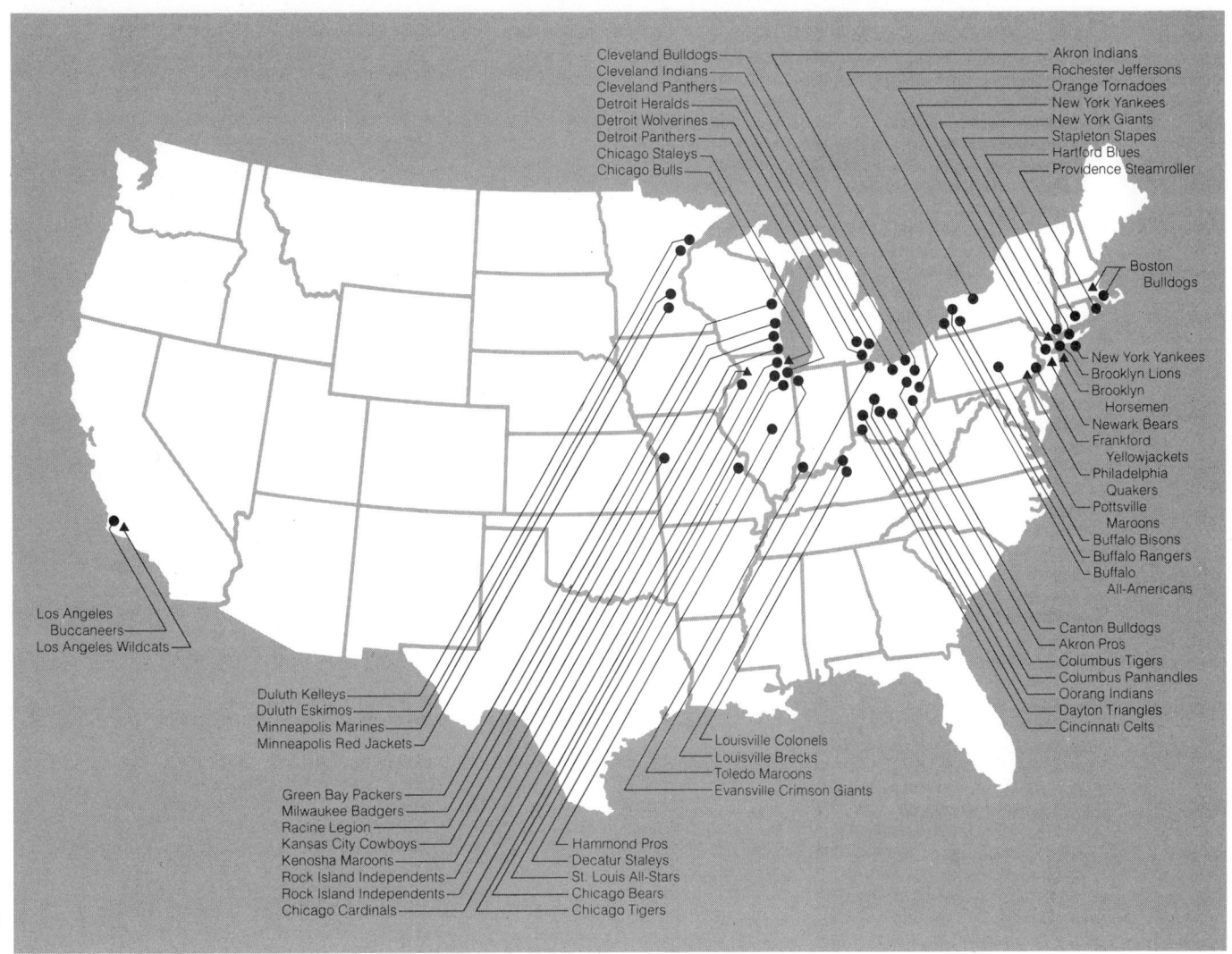

Cleveland Bulldogs
Cleveland Indians
Cleveland Panthers
Detroit Heralds
Detroit Wolverines
Detroit Panthers
Chicago Staleys
Chicago Bulls

Akron Indians
Rochester Jeffersons
Orange Tornadoes
New York Yankees
New York Giants
Stapleton Stapes
Hartford Blues
Providence Steamroller

Boston
Bulldogs

New York Yankees
Brooklyn Lions
Brooklyn
Horsemen
Newark Bears
Frankford
Yellowjackets
Philadelphia
Quakers
Pottsville
Maroons
Buffalo Bisons
Buffalo Rangers
Buffalo
All-Americans

Canton Bulldogs
Akron Pros
Columbus Tigers
Columbus Panhandles
Oorang Indians
Dayton Triangles
Cincinnati Celts

Los Angeles
Buccaneers
Los Angeles Wildcats

Duluth Kelleys
Duluth Eskimos
Minneapolis Marines
Minneapolis Red Jackets

Green Bay Packers
Milwaukee Badgers
Racine Legion
Kansas City Cowboys
Kenosha Maroons
Rock Island Independents
Rock Island Independents
Chicago Cardinals

Hammond Pros
Decatur Staleys
St. Louis All-Stars
Chicago Bears
Chicago Tigers

Louisville Colonels
Louisville Brecks
Toledo Maroons
Evansville Crimson Giants

1920s

● NATIONAL FOOTBALL LEAGUE

Akron Pros
Buffalo All-Americans
Canton Bulldogs
Chicago Cardinals
Chicago Tigers
Columbus Panhandles
Decatur Staleys
Dayton Triangles
Detroit Heralds
Hammond Pros
Rochester Jeffersons
Rock Island Independents
Akron Indians
Chicago Staleys
Chicago Bears
Cincinnati Celts
Cleveland Indians
Detroit Panthers
Evansville Crimson Giants
Green Bay Packers
Louisville Brecks
Minneapolis Marines
Milwaukee Badgers
Oorang Indians, Marion, Ohio
Racine Legion
Toledo Maroons

Columbus Tigers
Duluth Kelleys
St. Louis All-Stars
Buffalo Bisons
Cleveland Bulldogs
Frankford Yellowjackets
Kansas City Cowboys
Kenosha Maroons
New York Giants
Pottsville Maroons
Providence Steamroller
Brooklyn Lions
Louisville Colonels
Buffalo Rangers
Duluth Eskimos
Hartford Blues
Los Angeles Buccaneers*
Boston Bulldogs
New York Yankees
Detroit Wolverines
Minneapolis Red Jackets
Orange Tornadoes
Stapleton Stapes

▲ AMERICAN FOOTBALL LEAGUE, 1926

Boston Bulldogs
Brooklyn Horsemen
Chicago Bulls
Cleveland Panthers
Los Angeles Wildcats*
New York Yankees
Newark Bears
Philadelphia Quakers
Rock Island Independents

*Road teams that played no games in Los Angeles.

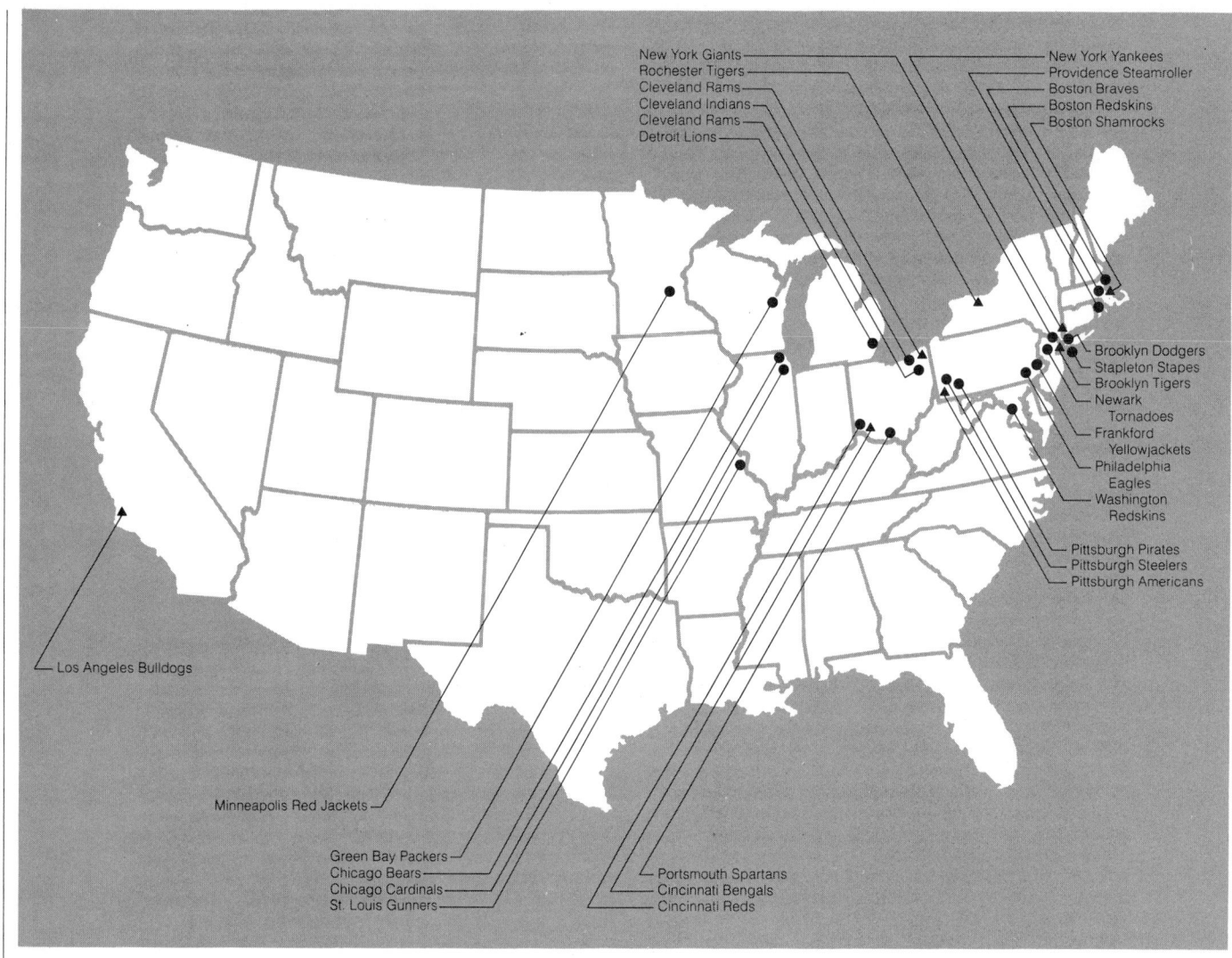

New York Giants
Rochester Tigers
Cleveland Rams
Cleveland Indians
Cleveland Rams
Detroit Lions

New York Yankees
Providence Steamroller
Boston Braves
Boston Redskins
Boston Shamrocks

Brooklyn Dodgers
Stapleton Stapes
Brooklyn Tigers
Newark Tornadoes
Frankford Yellowjackets
Philadelphia Eagles
Washington Redskins

Pittsburgh Pirates
Pittsburgh Steelers
Pittsburgh Americans

Los Angeles Bulldogs

Minneapolis Red Jackets

Green Bay Packers
Chicago Bears
Chicago Cardinals
St. Louis Gunners

Portsmouth Spartans
Cincinnati Bengals
Cincinnati Reds

1930s

● NATIONAL FOOTBALL LEAGUE
Brooklyn Dodgers
Chicago Bears
Chicago Cardinals
Frankford Yellowjackets
Green Bay Packers
Minneapolis Red Jackets
New York Giants
Newark Tornadoes
Portsmouth Spartans
Providence Steamroller
Stapleton Stapes
Cleveland Indians
Boston Braves
Boston Redskins
Cincinnati Reds
Philadelphia Eagles
Pittsburgh Pirates
Detroit Lions
St. Louis Gunners
Cleveland Rams
Washington Redskins
Pittsburgh Steelers

▲ AMERICAN FOOTBALL LEAGUE, 1936-37
Boston Shamrocks
Brooklyn Tigers
Cleveland Rams
New York Yankees
Pittsburgh Americans
Rochester Tigers
Cincinnati Bengals
Los Angeles Bulldogs

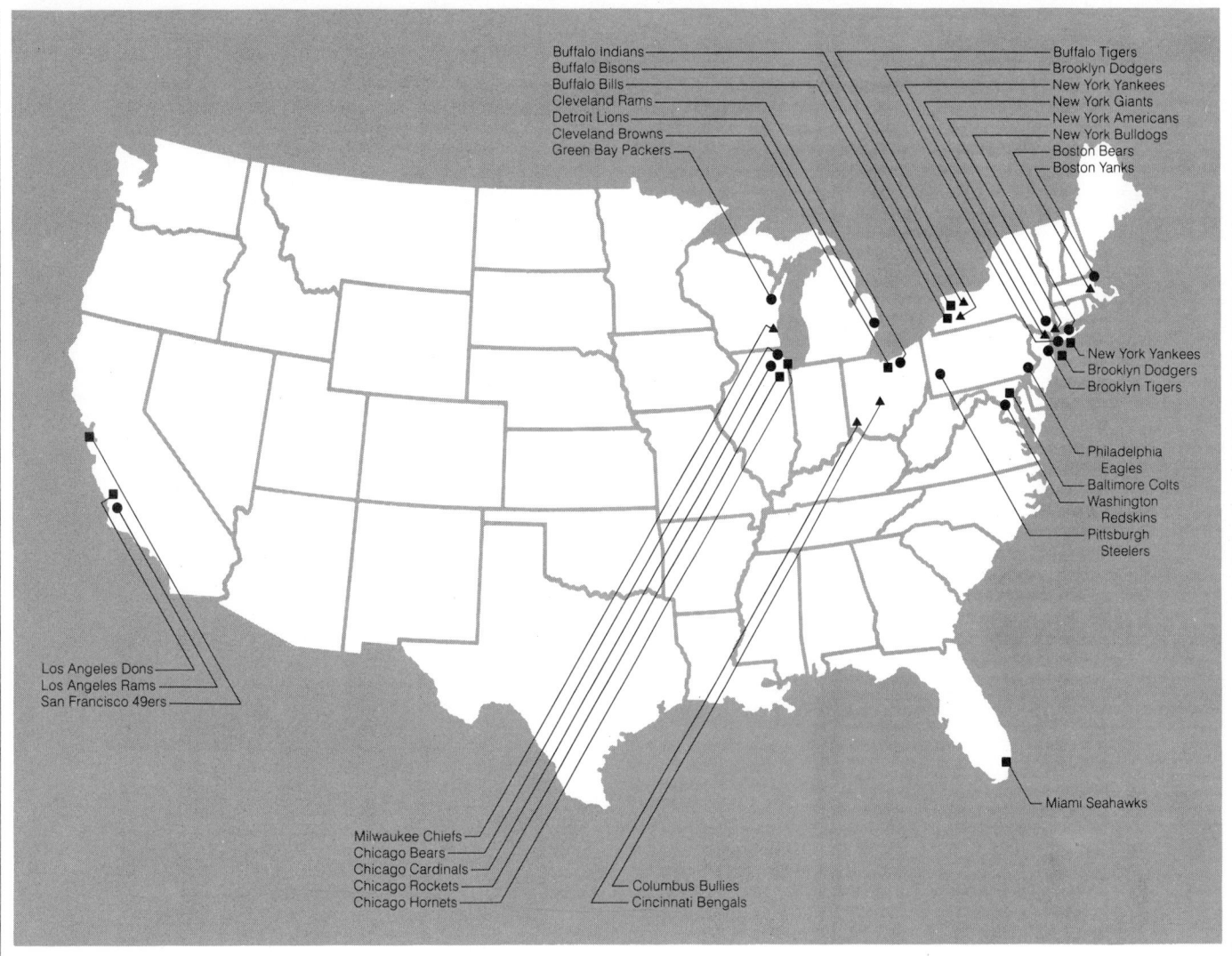

Buffalo Indians
Buffalo Bisons
Buffalo Bills
Cleveland Rams
Detroit Lions
Cleveland Browns
Green Bay Packers

Buffalo Tigers
Brooklyn Dodgers
New York Yankees
New York Giants
New York Americans
New York Bulldogs
Boston Bears
Boston Yanks

New York Yankees
Brooklyn Dodgers
Brooklyn Tigers

Philadelphia Eagles
Baltimore Colts
Washington Redskins
Pittsburgh Steelers

Miami Seahawks

Los Angeles Dons
Los Angeles Rams
San Francisco 49ers

Milwaukee Chiefs
Chicago Bears
Chicago Cardinals
Chicago Rockets
Chicago Hornets

Columbus Bullies
Cincinnati Bengals

1940s

● NATIONAL FOOTBALL LEAGUE

Brooklyn Dodgers
Chicago Bears
Chicago Cardinals
Cleveland Rams
Detroit Lions
Green Bay Packers
New York Giants
Philadelphia Eagles
Pittsburgh Steelers
Washington Redskins
Boston Yanks
Brooklyn Tigers
Los Angeles Rams
New York Bulldogs
Philadelphia-Pittsburgh merger, 1943
Chi. Cardinals-Pittsburgh merger, 1944

▲ AMERICAN FOOTBALL LEAGUE, 1940-41

Boston Bears
Buffalo Indians 1940
Cincinnati Bengals
Columbus Bullies
Milwaukee Chiefs
New York Yankees
Buffalo Tigers 1941
New York Americans 1941

■ ALL-AMERICA FOOTBALL CONFERENCE, 1946-49

Brooklyn Dodgers 1946-48
Buffalo Bisons 1946
Chicago Rockets 1946-48
Cleveland Browns
Los Angeles Dons
Miami Seahawks 1946
New York Yankees 1946-48
San Francisco 49ers
Baltimore Colts 1947-49
Buffalo Bills 1947-49
Chicago Hornets 1949
Brooklyn-New York Yankees merger, 1949

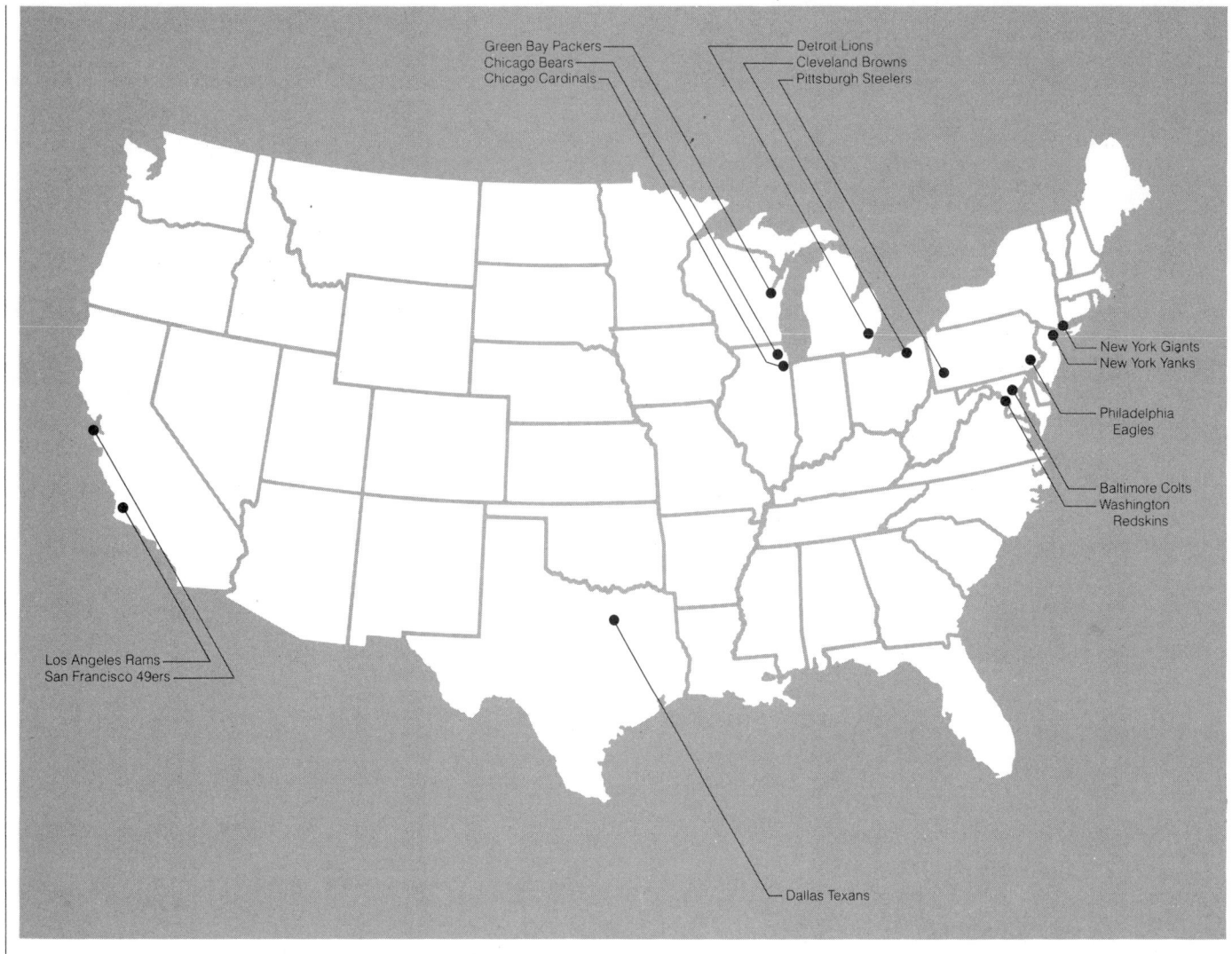

Green Bay Packers
Chicago Bears
Chicago Cardinals

Detroit Lions
Cleveland Browns
Pittsburgh Steelers

New York Giants
New York Yanks

Philadelphia
Eagles

Baltimore Colts
Washington
Redskins

Los Angeles Rams
San Francisco 49ers

Dallas Texans

1950s

● NATIONAL FOOTBALL LEAGUE
Baltimore Colts
Chicago Bears
Chicago Cardinals
Cleveland Browns
Detroit Lions
Green Bay Packers
Los Angeles Rams
New York Giants
New York Yanks
Philadelphia Eagles
Pittsburgh Steelers
Washington Redskins
Dallas Texans
San Francisco 49ers

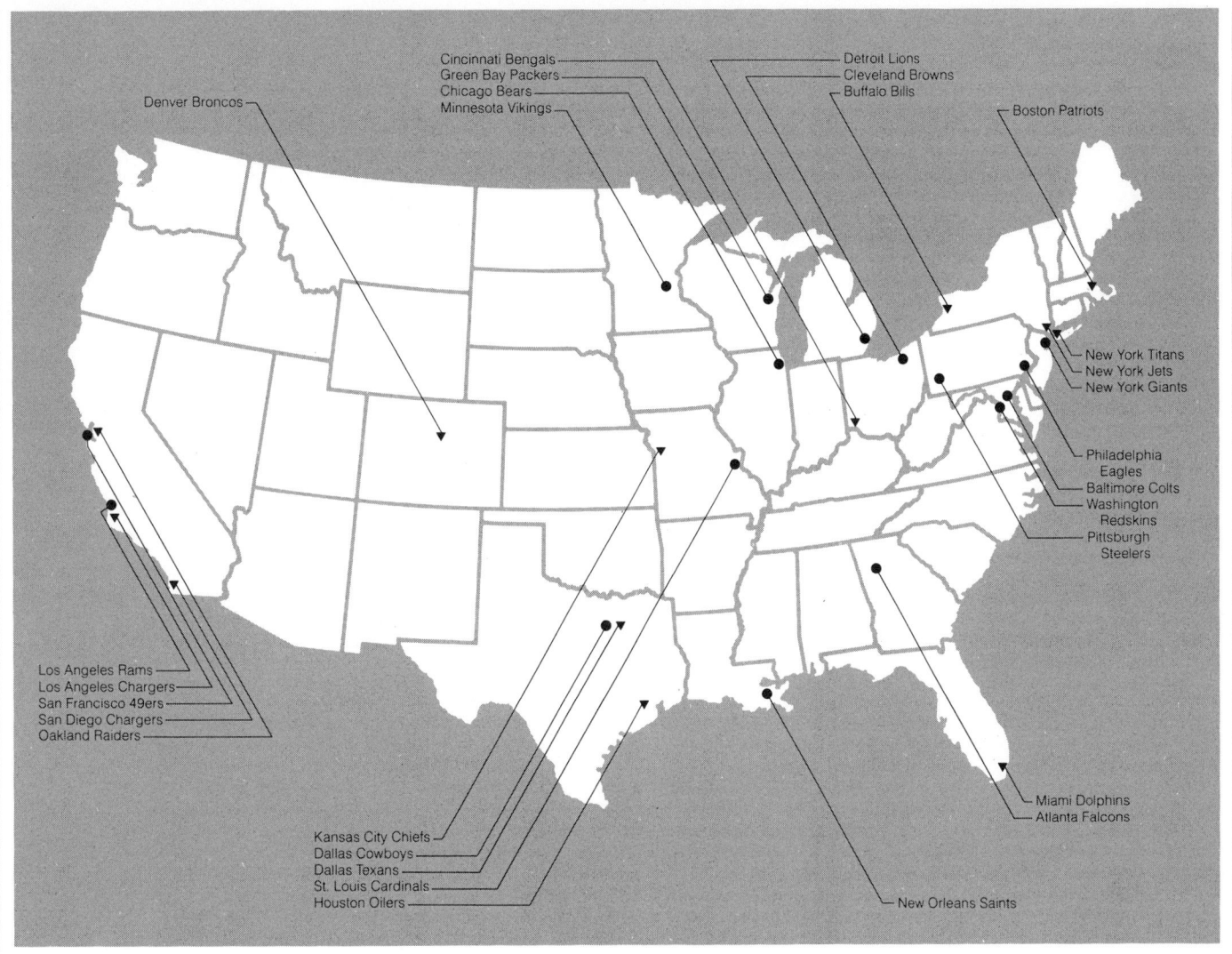

Denver Broncos

Cincinnati Bengals
Green Bay Packers
Chicago Bears
Minnesota Vikings

Detroit Lions
Cleveland Browns
Buffalo Bills

Boston Patriots

New York Titans
New York Jets
New York Giants

Philadelphia
Eagles
Baltimore Colts
Washington
Redskins
Pittsburgh
Steelers

Miami Dolphins
Atlanta Falcons

Los Angeles Rams
Los Angeles Chargers
San Francisco 49ers
San Diego Chargers
Oakland Raiders

Kansas City Chiefs
Dallas Cowboys
Dallas Texans
St. Louis Cardinals
Houston Oilers

New Orleans Saints

1960s

● NATIONAL FOOTBALL LEAGUE

Baltimore Colts
Chicago Bears
Cleveland Browns
Dallas Cowboys
Detroit Lions
Green Bay Packers
Los Angeles Rams
New York Giants
Philadelphia Eagles
Pittsburgh Steelers
St. Louis Cardinals
San Francisco 49ers
Washington Redskins
Minnesota Vikings
Atlanta Falcons
New Orleans Saints

▼ AMERICAN FOOTBALL LEAGUE

Boston Patriots
Buffalo Bills
Denver Broncos
Houston Oilers
Dallas Texans 1960-62
New York Titans 1960-62
Oakland Raiders
Los Angeles Chargers 1960
San Diego Chargers
Kansas City Chiefs
New York Jets
Miami Dolphins
Cincinnati Bengals

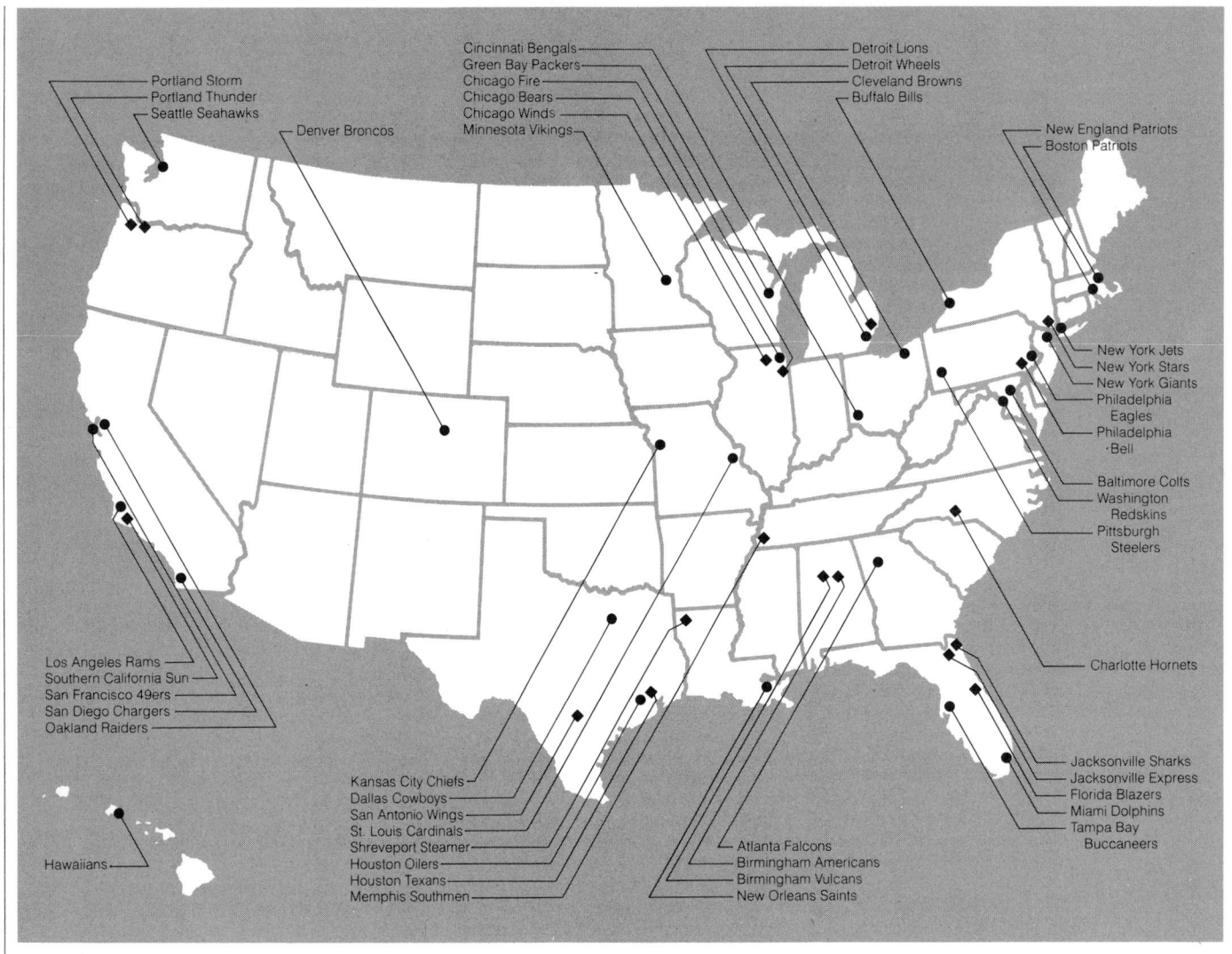

Portland Storm
Portland Thunder
Seattle Seahawks

Denver Broncos

Cincinnati Bengals
Green Bay Packers
Chicago Fire
Chicago Bears
Chicago Winds
Minnesota Vikings

Detroit Lions
Detroit Wheels
Cleveland Browns
Buffalo Bills

New England Patriots
Boston Patriots

New York Jets
New York Stars
New York Giants
Philadelphia Eagles
Philadelphia Bell

Baltimore Colts
Washington Redskins
Pittsburgh Steelers

Charlotte Hornets

Los Angeles Rams
Southern California Sun
San Francisco 49ers
San Diego Chargers
Oakland Raiders

Hawaiians

Kansas City Chiefs
Dallas Cowboys
San Antonio Wings
St. Louis Cardinals
Shreveport Steamer
Houston Oilers
Houston Texans
Memphis Southmen

Atlanta Falcons
Birmingham Americans
Birmingham Vulcans
New Orleans Saints

Jacksonville Sharks
Jacksonville Express
Florida Blazers
Miami Dolphins
Tampa Bay Buccaneers

1970s

● **NATIONAL FOOTBALL LEAGUE**

Atlanta Falcons
Baltimore Colts
Boston Patriots
Buffalo Bills
Chicago Bears
Cincinnati Bengals
Cleveland Browns
Dallas Cowboys
Denver Broncos
Detroit Lions
Green Bay Packers
Houston Oilers
Kansas City Chiefs
Los Angeles Rams
Miami Dolphins
Minnesota Vikings
New England Patriots
New Orleans Saints
New York Giants
New York Jets
Oakland Raiders
Philadelphia Eagles
Pittsburgh Steelers
St. Louis Cardinals
San Diego Chargers
San Francisco 49ers

Washington Redskins
Tampa Bay Buccaneers
Seattle Seahawks

◆ **WORLD FOOTBALL LEAGUE, 1974-75**

Birmingham Americans 1974
Birmingham Vulcans 1975
New York Stars 1974
Charlotte Hornets
Chicago Fire 1974
Chicago Winds 1975
Detroit Wheels 1974
Florida Blazers 1974
Hawaiians
Jacksonville Sharks 1974
Memphis Southmen (Grizzlies)
Philadelphia Bell
Portland Storm 1974
Portland Thunder 1975
Houston Texans 1974
Shreveport Steamer
Southern California Sun
Jacksonville Express
San Antonio Wings

Teams of the NFL

ATLANTA FALCONS

1964 Atlanta was being discussed by both the National and American Football Leagues as the possible location for a new pro football team. Baseball's Milwaukee Braves announced they intended to move and become the Atlanta Braves. Funding was being worked out for a new stadium. Mayor Ivan Allen, Jr. broke ground for the $18 million Atlanta Stadium, "with money we didn't have, for teams that didn't exist," April 15.

1965 Rivalry began in earnest between the NFL and AFL to locate an expansion team in Atlanta. The AFL awarded a franchise for Atlanta to J. Leonard Reinsch of the Cox Broadcasting Corporation, June 8. NFL commissioner Pete Rozelle, who earlier had said his league's next expansion was planned for 1967, two years hence, moved up the timetable. He sent public opinion pollster Louis Harris to Atlanta, and Harris conducted a poll showing that the citizens overwhelmingly favored an NFL team over an AFL team. Atlanta thus became the first city to be in a position to choose openly between the two leagues. "We're in the catbird seat," said Arthur Montgomery of the Atlanta-Fulton County Stadium Authority. The choice clearly was the NFL; Harris's poll had dealt the AFL a bitter defeat. Rankin M. Smith, 41-year-old executive vice-president of the Life Insurance Company of Georgia, was awarded an NFL franchise for approximately $8.5 million, June 30. Smith's franchise was awarded a lease for the stadium then under construction and Reinsch's AFL franchise ceased to exist. Smith was asked why he bought the team and he said, "Doesn't every adult male in America want to own his own football team?" "Five Smiths, Inc.," for his five children, was registered as the corporate name for the team. Julia Elliott, a Griffin, Georgia, schoolteacher, won a radio station's contest to name the team; she suggested "Falcons," August 29. Wayland Moore Studios of Atlanta designed the team's striking emblem. Tommy Nobis, Texas guard and linebacker, was the first draft choice of Atlanta and of the entire NFL; the Falcons, who got an extra choice on each of the first five rounds, also selected quarterback Randy Johnson of Texas A&I on the first round, November 27. Season ticket sales set a then NFL record when they reached 26,000 in November and were stopped when they reached 45,000, December 24.

1966 Norb Hecker, defensive backfield coach for Vince Lombardi of the Green Bay Packers, was named Falcons' head coach, January 26. Forty-two veteran players, three from each of the 14 established teams, were selected in an expansion draft stocking the Falcons, February 15. The Blue Ridge Assembly, a YMCA camp at Black Mountain, North Carolina, near Asheville, was selected to be the Falcons' training camp. The NFL and AFL merged, June 8. Smith's accountant Frank E. Wall, was named vice-president and treasurer of the Falcons, June 14. The Falcons lost four preseason games before defeating San Francisco 24–17 at Columbia, South Carolina, August 27. Atlanta lost its first regular season game, to Los Angeles 19–14 at Atlanta Stadium, September 11. Atlanta's first touchdown was a 53-yard pass from Randy Johnson to Gary Barnes. Nine more losses in a row followed before Atlanta defeated the New York Giants 27–16 at Yankee Stadium for its first regular season victory, November 20. Three weeks later, the Falcons won their first Atlanta Stadium victory by defeating St. Louis 16–10, December 11.

1967 Frank E. Wall was named general manager, January 31. Atlanta traded its number one draft choice for 1967 to San Francisco for wide receiver Bernie Casey, tackle Jim Wilson, and defensive end

Ken Reaves (36), John Mallory (22), and Tommy Nobis (60) stop Los Angeles's Larry Smith, 1969.

Tight end Jim Mitchell vs. Los Angeles, 1975.

Jim Norton, March 14. Training camp was moved to East Tennessee State University in Johnson City, Tennessee. The Falcons won a preseason game at Miami 27–17 and owner Smith left the city dry; he had promised to jump into the Miami River if the Falcons lost to their southern rivals, the AFL Dolphins. Linebacker Nobis returned an interception 41 yards to lead Atlanta over Minnesota 21–20 for the team's only victory in its second season, October 30. Nobis was named Atlanta's first all-pro by the Associated Press.

1968 The uniform was changed when the black Falcon bird emblem was removed from the sleeves of the jersey, and stripes were added to the sleeves. Norb Hecker was dismissed as coach and replaced by Norm Van Brocklin, former head coach of the Minnesota Vikings, October 1. The Falcons lost to Green Bay 38–7 in Van Brocklin's first game as coach, October 6. Atlanta ended an 11-game losing streak by defeating the New York Giants 24–21 the following week, October 13. Van Brocklin placed five starting players on waivers, November 14. He dismissed five assistant coaches the day after the last game of the season, a 14–12 loss to San Francisco, December 15.

1969 Van Brocklin assembled a new staff to replace the assistants he had dismissed. Atlanta had its best season yet with six victories. It defeated San Francisco 21–7 in the season opener, September 21. Atlanta set a club record for most points by defeating Chicago 48–31, November 16. And the Falcons ended Minnesota's 12-game winning streak with a 10–7 victory over the Vikings in the last game of the season, December 21. The last remaining Falcons' player from the expansion draft of 1966 left the team in the middle of the fourth season; running back Junior Coffey was traded to the New York Giants, October 29.

1970 Van Brocklin assumed the role of general manager in addition to being the head coach, and Frank E. Wall became president and Rankin M. Smith chairman of the board of the Falcons, January 6. The Falcons had their best preseason yet, a 4–1 record, but they won only four regular season games.

1971 The uniform was changed again; the team switched from black to red jerseys. The training camp site also was changed again, this time moving to Furman University in Greenville, South Carolina. Atlanta defeated San Francisco in its home opener for the third straight year, this time winning 20–17, September 19. The Falcons went on to record their first winning season ever, 7–6–1. The stadium authority decided not to install artificial turf. Linebacker Nobis and coach Van Brocklin signed new multi-year contracts.

1972 Van Brocklin made four trades during the NFL draft, sending six veterans to other teams for draft choices. He used one of the choices to draft Heisman trophy winner Pat Sullivan, quarterback from Auburn, on the second round, February 1. Running back Dave Hampton gained a club record 161 yards in a 31–3 victory over Los Angeles, the team's first victory over the Rams in 11 meetings, October 1. Atlanta lost 17–14 to Kansas City in the final game of the season, missing a chance to finish above .500, and Hampton went over 1,000 yards rushing to 1,001 but then lost six yards to complete the year with 995, December 17. Atlanta's record ended at 7–7.

1973 Atlanta traded quarterback Bob Berry and a number one draft choice to Minnesota for quarterback Bob Lee and linebacker Lonnie Warwick, May 14. An eventful season began when Atlanta, quarterbacked by Dick Shiner, set 35 team records while overwhelming New Orleans 62–7 in the opening game, September 16. Three defeats followed, then the Falcons defeated Chicago 46–6. Atlanta stopped the unbeaten Minnesota Vikings 20–14 on Monday night television; Shiner had since been put on waivers

and Lee was now the quarterback, November 11. A 28–20 triumph over the New York Jets was Atlanta's seventh victory in a row, December 9. The Falcons missed the playoffs, however, when they lost two of their last three games.

1974 Atlanta lost three of its first five games. Van Brocklin was fired as head coach and general manager and replaced by former defensive coordinator Marion Campbell, November 6. The team continued to lose often and there were an NFL record 40,202 "no-shows"—ticket buyers who did not attend the game—as Atlanta lost to Los Angeles 30–7, December 1. Rookie quarterback Kim McQuilken led Atlanta to a 10–3 victory over Green Bay in the final game of the season but there were 48,830 "no-shows" at rain-swept Atlanta Stadium.

1975 Atlanta traded tackle George Kunz to the Baltimore Colts for the Colts' first and sixth round draft choices, January 27. The Falcons made California quarterback Steve Bartkowski the first choice of the entire NFL draft by selecting him number one, January 28. Pat Peppler was named general manager, February 26. Running back Dave Hampton became the first Falcons' player to gain 1,000 yards in a season, getting 61 in the final game against Green Bay for a season's total of 1,002, December 21.

1976 Former Minnesota wide receiver John Gilliam, who had played out his option and was a free agent, signed with the Falcons, May 5. Atlanta lost four of its five games and Campbell was replaced as coach by general manager Peppler, October 12. A 17–10 upset of the defending NFC champion Dallas Cowboys was the Falcons' second straight victory and third in four games; quarterback Scott Hunter sneaked for the winning touchdown and linebacker Tommy Nobis made a key interception, November 21. Two weeks later, the Falcons were humiliated 59–0 at Los Angeles as the Rams made 30 first downs, 569 net yards, and a record eight touchdowns rushing, December 4.

1977 Eddie LeBaron, an attorney and a former quarterback for the Washington Redskins and Dallas Cowboys, was named Falcons' general manager replacing Peppler, February 1. Los Angeles Rams as-

sistant coach Leeman Bennett was named Falcons' head coach, February 3.

MEMBERS OF HALL OF FAME:
none

FALCONS RECORD, 1966-76

Year	Won	Lost	Tied	Pct.	Pts.	OP
1966	3	11	0	.214	204	437
1967	1	12	1	.077	175	422
1968	2	12	0	.143	170	389
1969	6	8	0	.429	276	268
1970	4	8	2	.333	206	261
1971	7	6	1	.538	274	277
1972	7	7	0	.500	269	274
1973	9	5	0	.643	318	224
1974	3	11	0	.214	111	271
1975	4	10	0	.286	240	289
1976	4	10	0	.286	172	312
11 Years	50	100	4	.338	2,415	3,424

RECORD HOLDERS

Rushing (Yards)	Dave Hampton, 1975	1,002
Passing (Pct.)	Bob Berry, 1971	60.2
Passing (Yards)	Bob Berry, 1972	2,158
Passing (TDs)	Bob Berry, 1970	16
Receiving (No.)	Art Malone, 1972	50
Receiving (Yards)	Paul Flatley, 1969	834
Interceptions (No.)	Rolland Lawrence, 1975	9
Punting (Avg.)	Billy Lothridge, 1968	44.3
Punt Ret. (Avg.)	Gerald Tinker, 1974	13.9
Kickoff Ret. (Avg.)	Willie Belton, 1971	25.2
Touchdowns (Total)	Eddie Ray, 1973	11
Field Goals Made	Nick Mike-Mayer, 1973	26
Points (No.)	Nick Mike-Mayer, 1973	112

COACHING HISTORY

1966–68	Norb Hecker*	4–26–1
1968–74	Norm Van Brocklin**	37–49–3
1974–76	Marion Campbell***	6–19–0
1976	Pat Peppler	3– 6–0

*Replaced after three games in 1968
**Replaced after eight games in 1974
***Replaced after five games in 1976

FIRST PLAYER SELECTED

1966	Tommy Nobis, LB, Texas
1967	Leo Carroll, DE (2), San Diego State
1968	Claude Humphrey, DE, Tennessee State
1969	George Kunz, T, Notre Dame
1970	John Small, LB, The Citadel
1971	Joe Profit, RB, Northeast Louisiana
1972	Clarence Ellis, DB, Notre Dame
1973	Greg Marx, DT (2), Notre Dame
1974	Gerald Tinker, WR (2), Kent State
1975	Steve Bartkowski, QB, California
1976	Bubba Bean, RB, Texas A&M

A number in parenthesis indicates a draft round other than first.

Junior Coffey makes a long gain vs. Dick Butkus (51) and Chicago Bears, 1967.

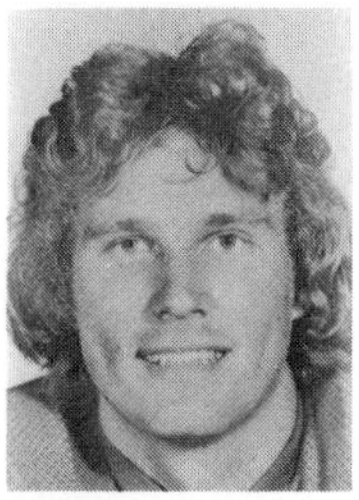
Steve Bartkowski

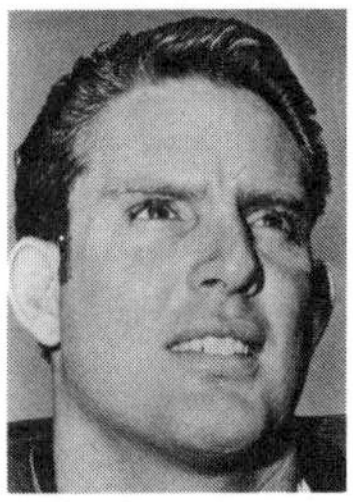
Bob Berry

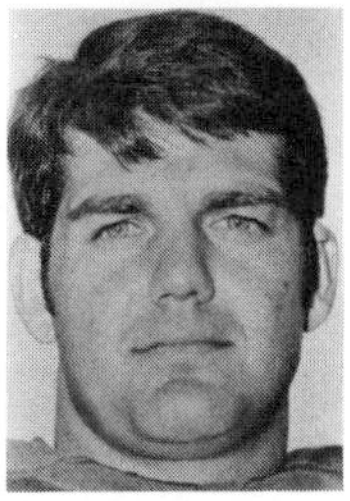
Greg Brezina

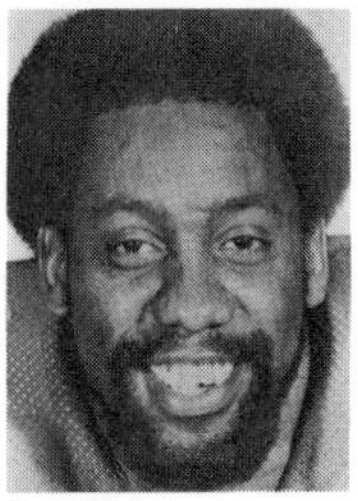
Ray Brown

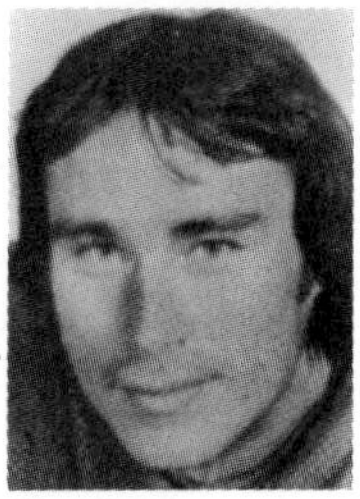
Ken Burrow

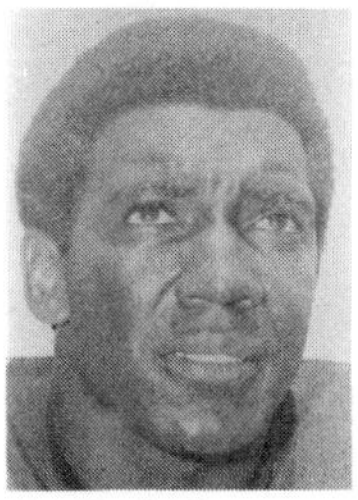
Jim Butler

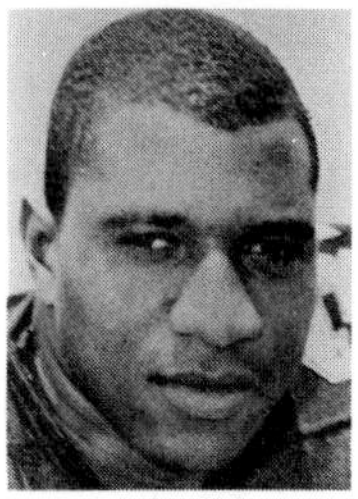
Junior Coffey

ATLANTA FALCONS, 1966–76

Absher, Dick, LB, Maryland ... 1967–68
Acks, Ron, LB, Illinois ... 1968–71
Adams, Brent, T, Tenn-Chattanooga ... 1975–76
Adams, Bob, TE, Pacific ... 1976
Allen, Grady, LB, Texas A&M ... 1969–72
Anderson, Taz, TE, Georgia Tech ... 1966–67
Auer, Joe, RB, Georgia Tech ... 1968

B

Bailey, Jim, DE, Kansas ... 1976
Bailey, Larry, DT, Pacific ... 1974
Barnes, Gary, WR, Clemson ... 1966–67
Bartkowski, Steve, QB, California ... 1975–76
Bean, Bubba, RB, Texas A&M ... 1976
Bebout, Nick, T, Wyoming ... 1973–75
Bell, Bill, PK, Kansas ... 1971–72
Belton, Willie, RB, Maryland State ... 1971–72
Benson, Duane, LB, Hamline ... 1972–73
Berry, Bob, QB, Oregon ... 1968–72
Bleick, Tom, S, Georgia Tech ... 1967
Bosley, Bruce, C, West Virginia ... 1969
Bowling, Andy, LB, Virginia Tech ... 1967
Bramlett, John, LB, Memphis State ... 1971
Breitenstein, Bob, G-T, Tulsa ... 1969–70
Brezina, Greg, LB, Houston ... 1968–69, 1971–76
Brown, Ray, S, W. Texas State ... 1971–76
Brunson, Mike, WR-RB, Arizona State ... 1970
Bryant, Charlie, RB, Allen ... 1969
Burke, Vern, WR, Oregon State ... 1966
Burrow, Ken, WR, San Diego State ... 1971–75
Burson, Jimmy, CB-S, Auburn ... 1968
Butler, Jim, RB, Edward Waters ... 1968–71
Byas, Rick, DB, Wayne State ... 1974–76

C

Cahill, Dave, DT, Northern Arizona ... 1969
Calland, Lee, CB, Louisville ... 1966–68
Campbell, Sonny, RB, No. Arizona ... 1970–71
Cash, Rick, DE, N.E. Missouri ... 1968
Cavness, Grady, CB, Texas-El Paso ... 1970
Cerne, Joe, C, Northwestern ... 1968
Chesson, Wes, WR, Duke ... 1971–73
Childs, Henry, TE, Kansas State ... 1974
Claridge, Dennis, QB, Nebraska ... 1966
Coffey, Junior, RB, Washington ... 1966–67, 1969
Cogdill, Gail, WR, Washington State ... 1969–70
Coia, Angie, WR, USC ... 1966
Collins, Sonny, RB, Kentucky ... 1976
Condren, Glen, DT, Oklahoma ... 1969–72
Cook, Ed, G, Notre Dame ... 1966–72
Cope, Jim, LB, Ohio State ... 1976
Cordill, Olie, WR, Memphis State ... 1968
Cottrell, Ted, LB, Delaware Valley ... 1969–70
Crowe, Larry, DB, Texas Southern ... 1975

D

Dabney, Carlton, DT, Morgan State ... 1968
Davis, Brad, RB, Louisiana State ... 1975–76
Donohoe, Mike, TE, SF ... 1968, 1970–71
Dodd, Al, WR, N.W. Louisiana St. ... 1973–74
Duich, Steve, G, San Diego State ... 1968
Dunaway, Dave, WR, Duke ... 1968
Dunn, Perry Lee, RB, Mississippi ... 1966–68

E

East, Ron, DE, Montana State ... 1976
Easterling, Ray, S, Richmond ... 1972–76
Eber, Rich, WR, Tulsa ... 1968
Eley, Monroe, RB, Arizona State ... 1975
Ellis, Clarence, CB, Notre Dame ... 1972–74
Enderle, Dick, G, Minnesota ... 1969–71
Esposito, Mike, RB, Boston College ... 1976
Etter, Bob, K, Georgia ... 1968–69

F

Farmer, Karl, WR, Pittsburgh ... 1976
Ferguson, Jim, C, USC ... 1969
Fitzgerald, Mike, CB-S, Iowa State ... 1967
Flatley, Paul, WR, Northwestern ... 1968–69
Francis, Wallace, WR, Ark. AM&N ... 1975–76
Freeman, Mike, CB-S, Fresno State ... 1968–70
Fritsch, Ted, C, St. Norbert ... 1972–74

G

Gallagher, Frank, G, North Carolina ... 1973
Garcia, Jim, DE, Purdue ... 1968
Geredine, Tom, WR, N.E. Missouri St. ... 1973–74
Germany, Willie, S, Morgan State ... 1972
Gilliam, John, WR, S. Carolina State ... 1976
Gipson, Paul, RB, Houston ... 1969–70
Glass, Glenn, WR, Tennessee ... 1966
Goodwin, Doug, RB, Maryland State ... 1968
Gotshalk, Len, T, Humboldt State ... 1972–76
Grimm, Dan, G-C, Colorado ... 1966–68

H

Halverson, Dean, LB, Washington ... 1970
Hampton, Dave, RB, Wyoming ... 1972–76
Hansen, Don, LB, Illinois ... 1969–75
Harmon, Tom, G, Gustavus Adolphus ... 1967
Harris, Bill, RB, Colorado ... 1968
Hart, Leo, QB, Duke ... 1971
Havig, Dennis, G, Colorado ... 1972–75
Hawkins, Alex, WR, South Carolina ... 1966–67
Hayes, Tom, CB, San Diego State ... 1971–75
Heck, Ralph, LB, Colorado ... 1966–68
Herron, Mack, RB, Kansas State ... 1975
Hettema, Dave, T, New Mexico ... 1970
Hilton, Roy, DE, Jackson State ... 1975
Holmes, Rudy, DB, Drake ... 1974
Hudlow, Floyd, CB-S, Arizona ... 1967–68
Hughes, Bob, DE, Jackson State ... 1967, 1969
Hunter, Scott, QB, Alabama ... 1976
Humphrey, Claude, DE, Tenn. State ... 1968–74, 1976
Hutchinson, Tom, WR, Kentucky ... 1966

J

Jackson, Larron, G, Missouri ... 1975–76
James, John, P, Florida ... 1972–76
Jarvis, Ray, WR, Norfolk State ... 1971–72
Jenke, Noel, LB, Minnesota ... 1972
Jenkins, Al, WR, Morris Brown ... 1975–76
Jobko, Bill, LB, Ohio State ... 1966
Johnson, Randy, QB, Texas A&M ... 1966–70
Johnson, Rudy, RB, Nebraska ... 1966
Jones, Bob, WR, San Diego State ... 1969
Jones, Bob, DB, Virginia Union ... 1975–76
Jones, Jerry, DT, Bowling Green ... 1966

K

Kendrick, Vince, RB, Florida ... 1974
Kindle, Gregg, G, Tennessee State ... 1976
Kirouac, Lou, G-K, Boston College ... 1966–67
Koeper, Rich, T, Oregon State ... 1966
Kuechenberg, Rudy, LB, Indiana ... 1971
Kunz, George, T, Notre Dame ... 1969–74
Kupp, Jake, G, Washington ... 1967
Kuykendall, Fulton, LB, UCLA ... 1975–76

L

Lamb, Ron, RB, South Carolina ... 1972
Lavan, Al, S, Colorado State ... 1969–70
Lawrence, Kent, WR, Georgia ... 1970
Lawrence, Rolland, DB, Tabor ... 1973–76
Ledbetter, Monte, WR, N.W. Louisiana ... 1969
Lee, Bob, WR, Minnesota ... 1969
Lee, Bob, QB, Pacific ... 1973–74
Lee, Dwight, RB, Michigan State ... 1968
Lemmerman, Bruce, QB, Cal St.-Northridge ... 1968–69
Lens, Greg, DT, Trinity, Texas ... 1970–71
Lewis, Mike, DE, Arkansas AM&N ... 1971–76
Linden, Errol, T, Houston ... 1966–68
Long, Bob, WR, Wichita State ... 1968
Lothridge, Billy, P-S, Georgia Tech ... 1966–71

M

Mabra, Ron, DB, Howard ... 1975–76
Mack, Red, WR, Notre Dame ... 1966
Mallory, John, S, West Virginia ... 1969–71
Malone, Art, RB, Arizona State ... 1970–74
Mankins, Jim, RB, Florida State ... 1967
Manning, Rosie, T, N.E. Oklahoma ... 1972
Marchlewski, Frank, C, Minnesota ... 1966–68
Marderian, Greg, DT, USC ... 1976
Marshall, Randy, DE, Linfield ... 1970–71
Marshall, Rich, DT, Stephen F. Austin ... 1966
Martin, Billy, TE, Georgia Tech ... 1966–67
Marx, Greg, DT, Notre Dame ... 1973
Matlock, John, C, Miami ... 1970–71
Matthews, Henry, RB, Michigan State ... 1973
Maurer, Andy, G, Oregon ... 1970–73
McCarthy, Brendan, RB, Boston College ... 1968
McCauley, Tom, S-WR, Wisconsin ... 1969–71
McClain, Dewey, TE, East Central ... 1976
McCrary, Greg, TE, Clark ... 1975
McDermott, Gary, RB, Tulsa ... 1969
McDonald, Tommy, WR, Oklahoma ... 1967
McGee, Molly, RB, Rhode Island ... 1974
McInnis, Hugh, TE, So. Mississippi ... 1966
McKinnely, Phil, T, UCLA ... 1976
McQuilken, Kim, QB, Lehigh ... 1974–76
Merrow, Jeff, DE West Virginia ... 1975–76
Mialik, Larry, TE, Wisconsin ... 1972–74
Mike-Mayer, Nick, K, Temple ... 1973–76
Miller, Jim, G, Iowa ... 1971–72, 1974
Mitchell, Ken, LB, Nevada-Las Vegas ... 1973–74
Mitchell, Jim, TE, Prairie View ... 1969–76
Moore, Tom, RB, Vanderbilt ... 1967
Morris, Larry, LB, Georgia Tech ... 1966

N

Neal, Louis, WR, Prairie View ... 1973–74
Nobis, Tommy, LB, Texas ... 1966–76
Nofsinger, Terry, QB, Utah ... 1967
Norton, Jim, DT-DE, Washington ... 1967–68

O

Ogden, Ray, TE, Alabama ... 1967–68
Ortega, Ralph, LB, Florida ... 1975–76

P

Palmer, Dick, LB, Kentucky ... 1974
Pesuit, Wally, T, Kentucky ... 1976
Piper, Scott, WR, Arizona ... 1976
Plummer, Tony, S, Pacific ... 1971–73
Poage, Ray, TE, Texas ... 1971
Pritchett, Billy, RB, West Texas State ... 1976
Profit, Joe, RB, N.E. Louisiana ... 1971–73

R

Rassas, Nick, S, Notre Dame ... 1966–68
Ray, Eddie, RB, Louisiana State ... 1972–74
Reaves, Ken, CB, Norfolk State ... 1966–73
Rector, Ron, RB, Northwestern ... 1966–67
Redmond, Rudy, CB, Pacific ... 1969–71
Reed, Frank, DB, Washington ... 1976
Reed, Oscar, RB, Colorado State ... 1975
Reese, Guy, DT, SMU ... 1976
Richards, Bobby, DE, Louisiana State ... 1966–67
Richardson, Jerry, CB-S, W. Texas St. ... 1966–67
Ridlehuber, Preston, RB, Georgia ... 1966
Riggle, Bob, S, Penn State ... 1966–67
Roberts, Gary, G, Purdue ... 1970
Roberts, Guy, LB, Maryland ... 1976
Rubke, Karl, DT, USC ... 1966–67
Rushing, Marion, LB, So. Illinois ... 1966–68
Russ, Carl, LB, Michigan ... 1975
Ryczek, Paul, C, Virginia ... 1974–76

S

Sabatino, Bill, DT, Colorado ... 1969
Sandeman, Bill, T, Pacific ... 1967–73
Sanders, Bob, LB, N. Texas State ... 1967
Scales, Charlie, RB, Indiana ... 1966
Schmidt, Roy, G-T, Long Beach State ... 1969
Scott, Dave, T, Kansas ... 1976
Shay, Jerry, DT, Purdue ... 1968–69
Shears, Larry, CB, Lincoln, Mo. ... 1971
Sherlag, Bob, WR, Memphis State ... 1966
Shiner, Dick, QB, Maryland ... 1971, 1973
Sidle, Jimmy, TE-RB, Auburn ... 1966
Sieminski, Chuck, DT, Penn State ... 1966–67
Silvestri, Carl, CB-S, Wisconsin ... 1966
Simmons, Jerry, WR, Bethune-Cookman ... 1967–69
Simon, Jim, G-T, Miami ... 1966–68
Sloan, Steve, QB, Alabama ... 1966–67
Small, John, DT, Citadel ... 1970–72
Smith, Ralph, TE, Mississippi ... 1969

Dave Hampton

Don Hansen

Claude Humphrey

Billy Lothridge

Ken Reaves

Harmon Wages

John Zook

Smith, Ron, CB-WR, Wisconsin	1966–67
Smith, Royce, G, Georgia	1974–76
Snider, Malcolm, G, Stanford	1969–71
Snyder, Todd, WR, Ohio U	1970–72
Sobocinski, Phil, C, Wisconsin	1968
Spiller, Phil, S, Cal. State-L.A.	1968
Stanback, Haskel, RB, Tennessee	1974–76
Stanciel, Jeff, RB, Mississippi Valley	1969
Strahan, Art, DT, Texas Southern	1968
Suchy, Larry, CB, Mississippi College	1968
Sullivan, Jim, DE, Lincoln, Mo.	1970
Sullivan, Pat, QB, Auburn	1972–75
Szczecko, Joe, DT, Northwestern	1966–68

T

Talbert, Don, T, Texas	1966–68
Thompson, Woody, RB, Miami	1975–76

Tilleman, Mike, DT, Montana	1973–76
Tinker, Gerald, WR, Kent State	1974–75
Tolleson, Tommy, WR, Alabama	1966
Traynham, Wade, K, Frederick	1966–67

V

Van Note, Jeff, C, Kentucky	1969–76
Vinyard, Kenny, K, Texas Tech	1970

W

Wages, Harmon, RB, Florida	1968–71, 1973
Walker, Chuck, DT, Duke	1972–75
Walker, Cleo, LB, Louisville	1971
Warwick, Lonnie, DB, Tennessee Tech	1973–74
Washington, Joe, RB, Illinois State	1973
Waskiewicz, Jim, C, Wichita State	1969
Weatherford, Jim, S, Tennessee	1969

Weatherly, Jim, C, None	1976
Wheelwright, Ernie, RB, So. Illinois	1966–67
Whitlow, Bob, C, Arizona	1966
Williams, Sam, DE, Michigan State	1966–67
Wilson, Jim, C, Georgia	1967
Windauer, Bill, DT, Iowa	1976
Winkler, Randy, G, Tarleton State	1968
Wolski, Bill, RB, Notre Dame	1966
Wood, Bo, DE, North Carolina	1967
Wright, John, WR, Illinois	1968
Wright, Nate, S, San Diego State	1969

Y

Yeates, Jeff, DT, Boston College	1976

Z

Zook, John, DE, Kansas	1969–75

Head coach Norm Van Brocklin and quarterback Bob Berry, 1971.

Defensive end Claude Humphrey, 1972.

BALTIMORE COLTS

1952 A team called the Baltimore Colts had played in the All-America Football Conference from 1946-49 and in the National Football League in 1950, but that franchise folded. NFL Commissioner Bert Bell, facing a suit by Baltimore stockholders for reinstatement of a franchise in the city, turned over the defunct Dallas Texans team, which had won just one game that season, December 3. But Bell insisted that Baltimore sell 15,000 season tickets before he would grant the franchise. That goal was met by the end of December. There was no club ownership or organization.

1953 By the time the campaign ended, $300,000 was in the bank and Bell found an owner, Carroll D. Rosenbloom, a business executive who had played in the backfield for Bell when Bell was coaching at the University of Pennsylvania in 1927. At Bell's suggestion, Rosenbloom hired Donald S. Kellett, a television executive who had been a coach and star athlete at Penn, as general manager, January 23. Keith Molesworth was named coach at the same time. Rosenbloom took 51 percent of the stock and distributed the rest among William F. Hilgenberg, Zanvyl Krieger, Tom Mullan, Sr., and R. Bruce Livie. The team set up training facilities at Western Maryland College in Westminister. The team nickname, "Colts," was taken from the extinct Baltimore team. The Colts were placed in the NFL's Western Conference. The team colors were blue, silver, and white. It had notable players it inherited from the Texans such as tackle Art Donovan, defensive end Gino Marchetti, and back Claude (Buddy) Young. The Colts stunned the Chicago Bears 13–9 in their first game, September 27. The team won three of its first five games, but then lost its last seven. Home crowds averaged 28,000.

1954 Molesworth was shifted to chief talent scout as the Colts prepared to start play in Baltimore's new Memorial Stadium. Rosenbloom and Kellett tried to get Cleveland assistant Blanton Collier as their head coach but settled instead on Browns' aide Wilbur C. (Weeb) Ewbank, May, 1954. The Colts won only three games under Ewbank, but he told Rosenbloom he would produce a champion within five years.

1955 Molesworth's scouting system began to pay off. Twelve rookies made the team, including quarterback George Shaw, fullback Alan Ameche, halfback L. G. Dupre, tackles Jack Patera and George Preas, and center Dick Szymanski. All became regulars. The team won five games and was fourth in the Western Conference.

1956 Four more important additions were made. Gene (Big Daddy) Lipscomb was picked up on waivers from Los Angeles. Lenny Moore was a first-round draft choice from Penn State. Billy Vessels, drafted first in 1953, joined the club after playing three seasons in Canada. And a lanky, bony-faced young man who had had a tryout with the Pittsburgh Steelers in 1955 responded to an 80-cent phone call from Kellett and joined the team to understudy Shaw. His name was Johnny Unitas. Shaw injured his knee during the season. The Colts tried to pry Gary Kerkorian away from law school to replace him. Kerkorian finally came but by that time the quarterback was Unitas. The season was erratic. Late in the year the team lost three games in a row and Ewbank's job was reported to be in jeopardy. But in the last game, Unitas threw a 53-yard scoring pass to beat Washington 19–17, December 23. Ewbank kept his job.

1957 Rosenbloom was named the team's president, February 4. Most of the personnel who would carry the Colts to the heights were assembled. Ends Raymond Berry and Jim Mutscheller joined Unitas,

Quarterback John Unitas throws a flare pass to Lenny Moore at Los Angeles, 1966.

Ameche, Moore, and Dupre. The linemen included Art Donovan, Lipscomb, Marchetti, Don Joyce, and rookie Jim Parker. Patera, Don Shinnick, and Doug Eggers were capable linebackers. Rookies Milt Davis and Andy Nelson joined veterans Carl Taseff and Bert Rechichar in the secondary. An injury to Taseff seriously weakened the pass defense, but with two games to play the Colts were tied with San Francisco and Detroit for the Western Conference lead. Then they lost to the 49ers (17–13), December 8, and the Rams (37–21), December 15.

1958 Linebacker Leo Sanford and tackle Ray Krouse joined the team in trades and three rookies—halfback Lenny Lyles and defensive backs Ray Brown, and Johnny Sample—made the team. The Colts won their first six games. The sixth was a 56–0 rout of the Packers but Unitas suffered fractured ribs and a punctured lung, November 2. Although Shaw played well in relief, Baltimore lost to New York 24–21. The defense was instrumental in a 17–0 win over the Bears, November 16. Unitas wore a special harness to protect his ribs and came back the next week. He threw a 58-yard pass to Moore on the first play from scrimmage and Baltimore romped over the Rams 34–7, November 23. By the end of the tenth game, and before they had to make what had become a "jinx" trip to the West Coast, the Colts had clinched their first division championship. New York won an Eastern Division playoff from Cleveland to advance

to the championship game. Baltimore led the Giants 14–3 at halftime. In the third quarter, the Colts threatened to break the game open, marching to the Giants' 1-yard line. But the New York defense held. It was the Giants' turn—for two touchdowns and a 17–14 lead with two minutes to play. Baltimore was on its own 14. Unitas hit Berry on three short passes and, with seven seconds left, Steve Myhra kicked a 20-yard field goal that sent the game into sudden death overtime, the first ever in league play. The Giants got the ball first but had to punt. Baltimore took over on its 21. Unitas put together a brilliant drive. Finally, from the Giants' 8, he threw to Mutscheller for seven yards. Then Ameche ran through a gaping hole for the winning touchdown and a 23–17 victory, December 28. The Colts were greeted by 30,000 people at the airport.

1959 The Colts had a 4–3 record after losing to Washington 27–24, November 8. Baltimore regrouped in the last five games, however, scoring 28, 45, 35, 34, and 45 points in consecutive victories. In the final game, the Colts scored 21 points in the fourth quarter to erase a 3-point deficit and defeat Los Angeles 45–26 in the Los Angeles Coliseum, December 12. In the championship game, played before 57,545 in Baltimore, Unitas combined with Moore on a first-half touchdown but New York led 9–7 in the third quarter. After that it was all Colts, however. Unitas ran for a touchdown. Two interceptions by Sample and one by Andy Nelson set up three more scores as Baltimore won 31–16, December 27.

1960 Some of the championship edge was gone. The superb defensive unit was growing slower with age. Unitas suffered a fractured vertebra high in his back early in the season, and, while he could still throw well enough, he was forbidden to run. So teams mounted an all-out rush against him. Ameche was benched. And the team's three top receivers—Berry, Moore, and Mutscheller—all were hurt. Baltimore came into the stretch with a 6–2 record, but lost four in a row and finished fourth. Unitas's 47-game touchdown passing streak was stopped by Los Angeles, December 11. But he set an NFL record with 3,099 yards passing.

1961 Running back Joe Perry was acquired in a trade with San Francisco. A jammed finger on his throwing hand slowed Unitas for much of the season. The highlight of a sporadic Colts' year was a 45–21 victory over eventual NFL champion Green Bay in Baltimore, November 5. The Colts finished with four victories in five games to tie for third place. Perry rushed for 675 yards.

1962 The Colts lost two close games to the Packers, 17–6, October 28, and 17–13, November 18, and had to win their last two games to finish 7–7. Unitas had an injury-free season, but his pass protection was suspect. Moore missed six games with a cracked kneecap. Perry gained only 359 yards.

1963 Rosenbloom changed coaches, signing a former Colts' defensive back, Don Shula, to replace Weeb Ewbank, January 8. Shula, who had been a defensive coach with the Detroit Lions, was only 33, but Rosenbloom said, "Football is a young man's game." Two Baltimore playing greats, defensive end Gino Marchetti and linebacker Bill Pellington, became player-coaches. Three other men who had helped the Colts to their 1958 and 1959 titles—Charley Winner, Don McCafferty, and John Sandusky—were retained on the coaching staff. A good nucleus was back in Unitas, Berry, Parker, Moore, Marchetti, and leading receiver Jimmy Orr, and the Colts looked more to youth than they had in years, with such rookies as tight end John Mackey, fullback Jerry Hill, tackles Bob Vogel and Fred Miller, and safety Jerry Logan. The team got off to a stumbling, injury-marred start but finished with five victories in its last six games and placed third.

1964 Rosenbloom purchased all remaining stock to gain full ownership, January 20. After an opening loss, the Colts won 11 games in a row, clinching their third Western Conference title by beating the Rams 24–7 in Los Angeles behind a strong defense, November 22. Baltimore scored a team high 428 points. Moore scored a then NFL record 20 touchdowns. Berry increased his then NFL career receiving total to 506. The defense forced opponents into 41 turnovers. The season was a huge success except for the NFL championship game with Cleveland, December 27. Neither team scored in the first half, but the Browns got 17 points in the third quarter behind Frank Ryan and Jim Brown and went on to win 27–0.

1965 Marchetti and Pellington retired as players. But the Colts still were a young team and players such as Dennis Gaubatz and Steve Stonebreaker filled in well. The Colts raced to a 9–1–1 record, and held first place in the Western Division. Then Unitas injured his back and number-two quarterback Gary Cuozzo suffered a shoulder separation. Shula had to make running back Tom Matte his quarterback. Matte responded with a dramatic performance that led the Colts past the Rams 20–17. He led the game's ball carriers with 99 yards, set up the deciding field goal, and handled the ball flawlessly. That victory got Baltimore into a Western Conference playoff with Green Bay. The undermanned Colts played courageously,

taking the Packers into sudden death, but they were beaten 13–10 by a Don Chandler field goal, December 26.

1966 The Colts defeated the Cowboys 35–3 in the Playoff Bowl, January 9. Baltimore won seven of its first nine games. Unitas injured his shoulder and the team collapsed in the stretch run. The Colts continued to have trouble with the Packers—Vince Lombardi maintaining a seeming jinx over Shula—and two more losses to Green Bay (in five seasons Baltimore's record against the Packers was 2–9) helped consign the Colts to second place, three games behind Green Bay.

1967 The Colts won 20–14 over Philadelphia in the Playoff Bowl, January 8. Shula and newly named general manager Joe Campanella were made vice presidents, January 23. Campanella died, February 15. Publicity director Harry Hulmes was selected to become general manager. The top draft choices were defensive lineman Bubba Smith and safetyman Rick Volk. Under an NFL realignment, the Colts were moved into the Coastal Division. In a match of unbeaten Coastal Division teams, the Colts and Rams battled to a 24–24 tie in Baltimore, October 15. It all came down to a rematch in Los Angeles in the final game of the season, December 17. Baltimore had an 11–0–2 record; Los Angeles was 10–1–2. The winner would advance to the playoffs. Rams quarterback Roman Gabriel threw touchdown passes to Jack Snow, Bernie Casey, and Billy Truax, hitting 18 of 22 passes for 257 yards as the Rams won 34–10. Baltimore finished with an 11–1–2 record and its defense allowed a club record of 198 points, but the Colts did not make the playoffs because of the loss to the Rams who were also 11–1–2. Shula was named NFL cocoach of the year with Los Angeles's George Allen.

1968 Art Donovan became the first Colt to be enshrined in the Pro Football Hall of Fame, August 3. The Colts began the season by winning five games, before losing 30–20 to Cleveland, October 20. The Colts then put together an eight-game winning streak, highlighted by two victories over Los Angeles and one over Green Bay. Baltimore ran its winning streak to nine by trouncing Minnesota 24–14 in the first round of the playoffs, December 22. The streak became 10 in the NFL championship game as Matte rushed for three touchdowns and Baltimore routed Cleveland 34–0, December 27. Some observers were comparing Baltimore with the finest NFL teams of all time. Earl Morrall, the Colts' quarterback most of the season with Unitas sidelined by injury, was named the most valuable player in the NFL.

1969 The Colts were heavily favored over the New York Jets, champions of the American Football League, in Super Bowl III in Miami, January 12. But the Jets posted a shocking 16–7 victory. New York's Joe Namath completed 17 of 28 passes for 206 yards. Matt Snell rushed for 121 yards. Jim Turner kicked three field goals. The Jets' defense intercepted four passes. The Colts, along with Cleveland and Pittsburgh, moved to the American Conference of the realigned NFL. Szymanski, Ordell Braase, and Bobby Boyd all retired, but Unitas was around along with veterans such as Morrall and Billy Ray Smith. Curtis was switched from outside linebacker to middle linebacker in the seventh game and Ted Hendricks and Bob Grant started outside. The Colts had an erratic season, struggling to a 8–5–1 record and finishing two and one half games behind Los Angeles.

1970 Don Klosterman was named general manager, January 6. Amid protests by Rosenbloom that started a long-standing feud, Shula moved to Miami to coach the Dolphins, February 18. Don McCafferty, an 11-year Colts' assistant, was named head coach, April 3. The Colts lost only two games—one to Shula and Miami—in the regular season, then beat Cincinnati 17–0 in the AFC divisional playoffs, December 26.

Behind Unitas's passing and rookie Norm Bulaich's running, the Colts powered past the Oakland Raiders 27–17 for their first AFC championship, January 3. Eddie Hinton caught five of Unitas's passes but the key completion was a 68-yard touchdown to Ray Perkins in the fourth quarter after Oakland had fought back to within 20–17 on the passing of George Blanda.

1971 The Colts were matched against the Dallas Cowboys in Super Bowl V at the Orange Bowl in Miami, January 17. There were 11 turnovers in a

MEMBERS OF HALL OF FAME:
Art Donovan, Gino Marchetti, Jim Parker

COLTS RECORD, 1950–76

Year	Won	Lost	Tied	Pct.	Pts.	OP
1953	3	9	0	.250	182	350
1954	3	9	0	.250	131	279
1955	5	6	1	.455	214	239
1956	5	7	0	.417	270	322
1957	7	5	0	.583	303	235
1958‡	9	3	0	.750	381	203
1959‡	9	3	0	.750	374	251
1960	6	6	0	.500	288	234
1961	8	6	0	.571	302	307
1962	7	7	0	.500	293	288
1963	8	6	0	.571	316	285
1964†	12	2	0	.857	428	225
1965	10	3	1	.769	389	284
1966	9	5	0	.643	314	226
1967	11	1	2	.917	398	196
1968‡	13	1	0	.929	402	144
1969	8	5	1	.615	279	268
1970**	11	2	1	.846	321	234
1971	10	4	0	.714	313	140
1972	5	9	0	.357	235	252
1973	4	10	0	.286	226	341
1974	2	12	0	.143	190	329
1975§	10	4	0	.714	395	269
1976§	11	3	0	.786	417	246
25 Years	186	128	6	.591	7,361	6,147

‡*NFL Champion*
†*Western Conference Champion*
***Super Bowl Champion*
§*AFC Eastern Division Champion*

RECORD HOLDERS

Rushing (Yards)	Lydell Mitchell, 1976	1,200
Passing (Pct.)	Bert Jones, 1976	60.4
Passing (Yards)	John Unitas, 1963	3,481
Passing (TDs)	John Unitas, 1959	32
Receiving (No.)	Raymond Berry, 1961	75
Receiving (Yards)	Raymond Berry, 1960	1,298
Interceptions (No.)	Tom Keane, 1953	11
Punting (Avg.)	David Lee, 1966	45.6
Punt Ret. (Avg.)	Wendell Harris, 1964	12.6
Kickoff Ret. (Avg.)	Jim Duncan, 1970	35.4
Touchdowns (Total)	Lenny Moore, 1964	20
Field Goals Made	Jim Martin, 1963	24
Points (No.)	Lenny Moore, 1964	120

COACHING HISTORY

1953	Keith Molesworth	3– 9–0
1954–62	Weeb Ewbank	59–52–1
1963–69	Don Shula	71–23–4
1970–72	Don McCafferty*	22–10–1
1972	John Sandusky	4– 5–0
1973–74	Howard Schnellenberger**	4–13–0
1974	Joe Thomas	2– 9–0
1975–76	Ted Marchibroda	21– 7–0

*Replaced after five games in 1972
**Replaced after three games in 1974

FIRST PLAYER SELECTED

1953	Billy Vessels, B, Oklahoma
1954	Cotton Davidson, B, Baylor
1955	George Shaw, B, Oregon
1956	Lenny Moore, B, Penn State
1957	Jim Parker, G, Ohio State
1958	Lenny Lyles, B, Louisville
1959	Jackie Burkett, C, Auburn
1960	Ron Mix, T, USC
1961	Tom Matte, RB, Ohio State
1962	Wendell Harris, S, Louisiana State
1963	Bob Vogel, T, Ohio State
1964	Marv Woodson, CB, Indiana
1965	Mike Curtis, LB, Duke
1966	Sam Ball, T, Kentucky
1967	Charles (Bubba) Smith, DT, Michigan State
1968	John Williams, G, Minnesota
1969	Eddie Hinton, WR, Oklahoma
1970	Norm Bulaich, RB, Texas Christian
1971	Leonard Dunlap, DB, North Texas State
1972	Tom Drougas, T, Oregon
1973	Bert Jones, QB, Louisiana State
1974	John Dutton, DE, Nebraska
1975	Ken Huff, G, North Carolina
1976	Ken Novak, DT, Purdue

Alan Ameche   *Bobby Boyd*   *Joe Campanella*   *Roger Carr*   *Mike Curtis*   *John Dutton*   *Ted Hendricks*

brutal defensive struggle. Baltimore, behind 13–6, tied the game midway through the fourth quarter. Volk intercepted a pass on the Dallas 33 and returned it to the 3, before Tom Nowatzke plunged into the end zone. Jim O'Brien, a rookie, converted. After Mike Curtis intercepted a Craig Morton pass in the final minute and returned it to the Dallas 28, O'Brien kicked a field goal with five seconds left for a 16–13 victory. Carroll Rosenbloom was elevated to chairman of the board, March 18. His son, Steve, took over as president. The Colts finished half a game behind Miami in the AFC East but qualified for the playoffs as the AFC wild card team. The Colts began with a 20–3 victory over Cleveland as Don Nottingham rushed for 92 yards and two touchdowns and the defense intercepted three passes, December 26.

1972 Rosenbloom and the Colts were matched against Shula and the Dolphins in the AFC championship game, at the Orange Bowl, January 2. The Colts, playing without injured backs Bulaich and Matte, outgained the Dolphins 302 yards to 286 but were burned on big plays by Bob Griese, Paul Warfield, and Dick Anderson and lost 21–0, even though Unitas completed 20 of 36 passes for 224 yards. It was the Colts' first shutout defeat since 1965. Running back Lydell Mitchell was chosen in the second round of the draft. Robert Irsay, a 49-year-old businessman from Winnetka, Illinois, took control of the Colts in one of the most unique transactions ever in pro sports, July 13. Irsay first purchased the Los Angeles Rams from the estate of the late Dan Reeves, then "traded" the Rams to Rosenbloom for the Colts. Joe Thomas, 49, who had helped turn the Minnesota Vikings and Miami Dolphins into Super Bowl teams, was named vice president and general manager. Gino Marchetti was inducted into the Pro Football Hall of Fame, July 29. The Colts moved their major training facilities to the University of South Florida in Tampa. After five games, four of them losses, McCafferty was replaced as head coach by long-time assistant John Sandusky, October 16. The Colts were just 4–5 the rest of the way, losing their last two and missing the playoffs.

1973 An era ended when Johnny Unitas was traded to San Diego "for future considerations," January 22. The Colts chose quarterback Bert Jones in the first round of the draft. Howard Schnellenberger, who had been Shula's top offensive coach for three years in Miami, was named head coach, February 14. The team again switched training sites, to McDonogh School in suburban Baltimore County. The Colts won their fewest games since 1954, finishing in a tie for last in the division.

1974 Thomas set about to rebuild the Colts through the draft. Thirteen players lasted the season, and another 10 from 1973 were around. Included were players such as Roger Carr, Fred Cook, John Dutton, and Freddie Scott. After the team lost its first three games, Thomas assumed the coaching duties from Schnellenberger, September 29. The Colts won just two games and placed last in their division. But they were competitive toward the end, never losing by more than 11 points in their last eight games. Mitchell set a one-game record of 40 rushes, October 20. Jones set an NFL record of 17 straight pass completions,

December 15. Mitchell won the league pass-catching title with 72 receptions, the most ever by a running back.

1975 Ted Marchibroda, a former NFL quarterback and long-time assistant to Allen at Los Angeles and Washington, was named head coach, January 15. "I'm a low-key coach who believes in the basics of football—execution, balance, and consistency," he said. Lenny Moore was inducted into the Pro Football Hall of Fame, August 2. The team switched training sites again, to Goucher College in suburban Baltimore. After losing four of their first five games, the Colts made one of the most startling turnarounds in NFL history, winning nine straight. The Colts lost to the Pittsburgh Steelers 28–10 in the first round of the playoffs, December 22. Marchibroda was named NFL coach of the year by numerous groups. Mitchell became the Colts' first back to rush for more than 1,000 yards in a season, gaining 1,193.

1976 After the team lost four of its six preseason games, Irsay stormed into the locker room and said, "I've got to make some changes," September 2. He lashed out at Colts players and Marchibroda. Marchibroda resigned, September 5. "I can't tolerate this kind of interference," he said. The Colts' players offered a statement, read by Bert Jones, that charged Irsay and Thomas "have completely destroyed this team," September 6. Marchibroda agreed to return, with increased responsibilities, September 7. "I will have complete control over football matters," he said. The team had a brilliant season, finishing 11–3 and winning the Eastern Division championship before losing to Pittsburgh in the AFL semifinal 40–14, December 19.

1977 Thomas resigned from the Colts' front office. Dick Szymanski was named general manager and Ernie Accorsi was named assistant general manager.

BALTIMORE COLTS, 1953–76 ·

Agase, Alex, G, Illinois	1953
Allen Gerald, B, Omaha	1966
Alley, Don, WR, Adams State	1967
Ameche, Alan, B, Wisconsin	1955–60
Amman, Richard, DE, Florida State	1972–73
Andrews, John, TE, Indiana	1973–74
Austin, Ocie, DB, Utah State	1968–69
Averno, Sisto, G, Muhlenberg	1953–54

B

Bailey, Jim, DT, Kansas	1970–74
Baldwin, Bob, B, Clemson	1966–67
Ball, Sam, T, Kentucky	1966–70
Barnes, Mike, DB, Miami	1973–76
Barwegen, Dick G, Purdue	1953–54
Baylor, Tim, DB, Morgan State	1976
Berra, Tim, WR, Massachusetts	1974
Bertuca, Tony, LB, Ohio State	1974
Berry, Raymond, WR, Southern Methodist	1955–67
Beutler, Tom, LB, Toledo	1970
Bielski, Dick, E, Maryland	1962–63
Bighead, Jack, E, Pepperdine	1954
Blandin, Ernie, T, Tulane	1953
Bleick, Tom, B, Georgia	1956
Blue, Forrest, C, Auburn	1975–76
Boyd, Bob, DB, Oklahoma	1960–68
Braase, Ordell, DE, South Dakota	1957–68
Brethauer, Monte, E, Oregon	1953, 1955
Brown, Barry, E, Florida	1966–67
Brown, Ed, QB, San Francisco	1965
Brown, Hardy, B, Tulsa	1950
Brown, Ray, DB, Mississippi	1958–60
Brown, Timmy, RB, Ball State	1968
Bryan, Walter, B, Texas Tech	1955

Buksar, George, B, San Francisco	1950
Bulaich, Norm, RB, Texas Christian	1970–72
Burkett, Jackie, LB, Auburn	1961–66

C

Call, Jack, B, Colgate	1957–58
Campanella, Joe, T, Ohio State	1953–57
Campbell, John, LB, Minnesota	1969
Carr, Roger, WR, Louisiana Tech	1974–76
Cheatham, Ernie, T, Loyola, L.A.	1954
Cherry, Stan, LB, Morgan State	1973
Chester, Raymond, TE, Morgan State	1973–76
Cheyunski, Jim, LB, Syracuse	1975–76
Chrovich, Dick, T, Miami, Ohio	1955–56
Clemens, Bob, B, Pittsburgh	1962
Cogdill, Gail, E, Washington State	1968
Cole, Terry, RB, Indiana	1968–69
Collett, Elmer, G, San Francisco St.	1973–76
Colteryahn, Lloyd, E, Maryland	1954–56
Colvin, Jim, T, Houston	1960–63
Conjar, Larry, RB, Notre Dame	1969–70
Cook, Fred, DE, So. Mississippi	1974–76
Cooke, Ed, E, Maryland	1959
Coutre, Larry, B, Notre Dame	1953
Craddock, Nate, RB, Parsons	1963
Cuozzo, Gary, QB, Virginia	1963–66
Curry, Bill, C, Georgia Tech	1967–72
Curtis, Mike, LB, Duke	1965–72
Curtis, Tom, DB, Michigan	1970–71

D

Davidson, Cotton, QB, Baylor	1954, 1957
Davis, Milt, B, UCLA	1957–60
Davis, Norman, G, Grambling	1967
Davis, Ted, LB, Georgia Tech	1964–66
DeCarlo, Art, E, Georgia	1957–60
DelBello, Jack, B, Miami	1953
Dickel, Dan, LB, Iowa	1974–76
Diekl, John, T, Virginia	1961–64
Domres, Marty, QB, Columbia	1972–75
Donovan, Art, DT, Boston College	1953–61
Doughty, Glenn, WR, Michigan	1972–76
Drougas, Tom, T, Oregon	1972–73
Duncan, James, DB, Maryland State	1969–71
Dunlap, Len, CB, N. Texas State	1971
Dunn, Perry Lee, RB, Mississippi	1969
Dupre, L.G., RB, Baylor	1955–59
Dutton, John, DE, Nebraska	1974–76

E

Ecklund, Brad, C, Oregon	1953
Edmunds, Randy, LB, Georgia Tech	1972
Edwards, Dan, E, Georgia	1953–54
Eggers, Doug, LB, S. Dakota State	1954–57
Ehrmann, Joe, DT, Syracuse	1973–76
Embree, Mel, E, Pepperdine	1953
Enke, Fred, QB, Arizona	1953–54

F

Feagin, Wiley, G, Houston	1961–62
Feamster, Tom, T, Florida State	1956
Felts, Bob, B, Florida A&M	1965
Fernandez, Ron, DE, Eastern Michigan	1976
Finnin, Tom, DT, Detroit	1953–56
Flowers, Bernie, E, Purdue	1956
Flowers, Dick, B, Northwestern	1953
Franklin, Willie, WR, Oklahoma	1972

G

Ganas, Rusty, DT, South Carolina	1971
Gardin, Ron, DB, Arizona	1970
Gaubatz, Dennis, LB, Louisiana State	1965–69
George, Ed, T, Wake Forest	1975
Gilburg, Tom, T, Syracuse	1961–65
Ginn, Hubert, RB, Florida A&M	1973
Glick, Gary, B, Colorado A&M	1961
Goode, Tom C, Mississippi State	1970
Grant, Bob, LB, Wake Forest	1968–70
Gregory, Ken, E, Whittier	1961
Grimm, Dan, G, Colorado	1969

H

Hall, Randy, CB, Idaho	1974, 1976

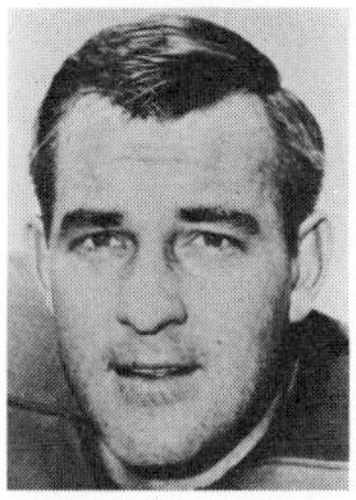
Jerry Hill

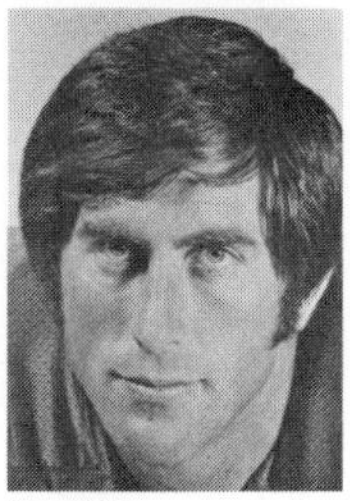
David Lee

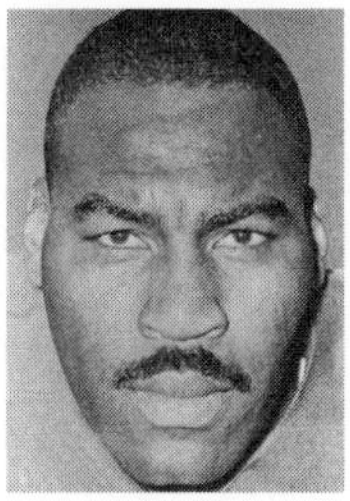
G. Lipscomb

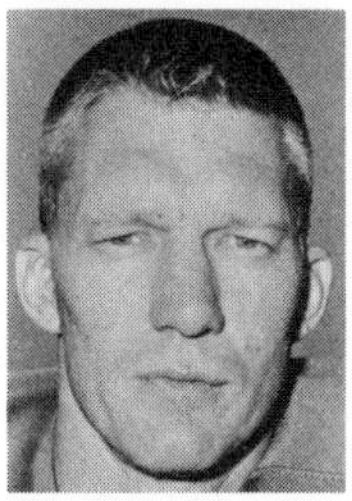
Jim Mutscheller

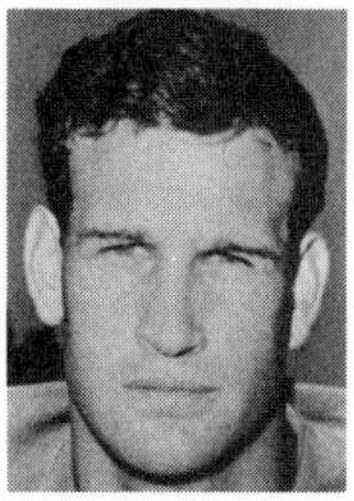
Andy Nelson

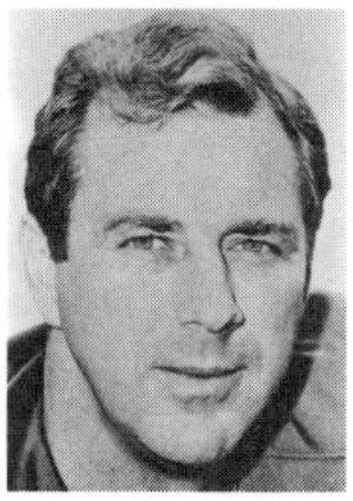
Jimmy Orr

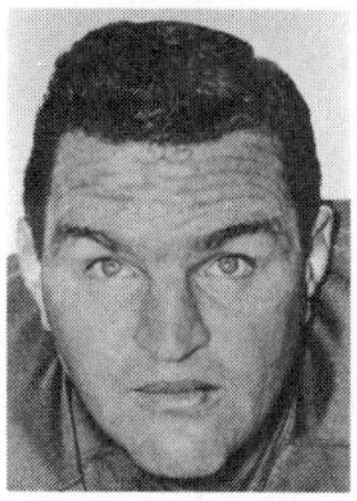
Bill Pellington

Harness, Jim, B, Mississippi State 1956
Harold, George, B, Allen 1966–67
Harris, Wendell, DB, Louisiana State 1962–65
Harrison, Bob, B, Ohio 1961
Havrilak, Sam, B, Bucknell 1969–72
Hawkins, Alex, B, S. Carolina 1955–65, 1967–68
Haymond, Alvin, DB-KR, Southern 1964–67
Hendricks, Ted, LB, Miami 1969–72
Hepburn, Lonnie, CB, Texas Southern 1971–72
Hermann, John, B, UCLA 1956
Herousian, Brian, S, Connecticut 1973
Hill, Jerry, B, Wyoming 1961, 1963–70
Hilton, Roy, DE, Jackson State 1965–73
Hinton, Chuck, DT, N. Carolina Coll. 1972
Hinton, Ed, WR, Oklahoma 1969–72
Hoaglin, Fred, C, Pittsburgh 1973
Horn, Dick, B, Stanford 1958
Huff, Ken, G, North Carolina 1975–76
Hugasian, Harry, B, Stanford 1955
Hunt, George, K, Tennessee 1973
Huzvar, John, RB, Pittsburgh 1953–54

J

Jackson, Ken, G, Texas 1953–57
James, Tommy, B, Ohio State 1956
Jefferson, Roy, WR, Utah 1970
Johnson, Cornelius, G, Virginia Union 1968–72
Johnson, Marshall, WR, Houston 1975
Jones, Bert, QB, Louisiana State 1973–76
Joyce, Don, DE, Tulane 1954–60

K

Kaczmarek, Mike, LB, So. Illinois 1973
Kalmanir, Tom, RB, Nevada 1953
Keane, Tom, E-DB, West Virginia 1953–54
Kennedy, Jimmie, TE, Colorado St. 1975–76
Kerkorian, Gary, QB, Stanford 1954–56, 1958
Kern, Rex, DB, Ohio State 1971–73
Kirchiro, Bill, G, Maryland 1962
Kirkland, Mike, QB, Arkansas, ... 1976
Kirouac, Lou, T, Boston College 1964
Koman, Bill, G, North Carolina 1956
Kostelnik, Ron, T, Cincinnati 1969
Kovac, Ed, B, Cincinnati 1960
Krouse, Ray, DE, Maryland 1958
Kunz, George, T, Notre Dame 1975–76

L

Laird, Bruce, S, Amer. International 1972–76
Langas, Bob, E, Wayne 1954
Lange, Bill, G, Dayton 1953
Larson, Lynn, T, Kansas State 1971–72
Laskey, Bill, LB, Michigan 1971–72
Leaks, Roosevelt, RB, Texas 1975–76
Leberman, Bob, B, Syracuse 1954
Lee, David, P, Louisiana Tech 1966–76
Lee, Monte, C, Texas 1965
Lee, Ron, RB, West Virginia 1976
Lesane, Jimmy, B, Virginia 1954
Lewis, Harold, B, Houston 1959
Lewis, Joe, T, Compton 1961
Linhart, Toni, K, Austria Tech 1974–75
Linne, Aubrey, E, Texas Christian 1961
Lipscomb, Gene (Big Daddy), T, None 1956–60
Little, Jack, T, Texas A&M 1953–54
Lockett, J.W., B, Oklahoma Central 1963
Logan, Jerry, S, W. Texas State 1963–72
Looney, Joe Don, RB, Oklahoma 1964
Lorick, Tony, RB, Arizona State 1964–67
Luce, Derrel, LB, Baylor 1975–76
Lyles, Lenny, DB, Louisville 1958, 1961–69

M

Mackey, Dee, E, E. Texas State 1961–62
Mackey, John, TE, Syracuse 1963–72
MacLeod, Tom, LB, Minnesota 1974–75
Maitland, Jack, RB, Williams 1970
Maples, Butch, C, Baylor 1963
Marchetti, Gino, DE, San Francisco 1953–64, 1966
Martin, Jim, K, Notre Dame 1963
Matte, Tom, RB, Ohio State 1961–72
Matuszak, Marv, B, Tulsa 1959–61
Mauck, Carl, LB, So. Illinois 1969
Maxwell, Tom, B, Texas A&M 1969–70
May, Ray, LB, USC 1970–72
Mayo, Ron, TE, Morgan State 1974
McCauley, Don, RB, North Carolina 1971–76
McHan, Lamar, QB, Arkansas 1961–63
McMillan, Chuck, B, John Carroll 1954
McPhail, Buck, RB, Oklahoma 1953
Memmelaar, Dale, G, Wyoming 1966–67
Mendenhall, Ken, C, Oklahoma 1971–76
Michaels, Lou, DE-K, Kentucky 1964–69
Mildren, Jack, S, Oklahoma 1972–73
Miller, Fred, DT, Louisiana State 1963–73
Mioduszewski, Ed, B, William & Mary 1953
Mitchell, Lydell, RB, Penn State 1972–76
Mitchell, Tom, TE, Bucknell 1968–73
Mooney, Ed, LB, Texas Tech 1972–73
Moore, Henry, B, Arkansas 1957
Moore, Lenny, RB, Penn State 1956–67
Morrall, Earl, QB, Michigan State 1968–71
Mosier, John, TE, Kansas 1972
Moss, Roland, TE, Toledo 1969
Mumphord, Lloyd, CB, Texas Southern 1975–76
Munsey, Nelson, CB, Wyoming 1972–76
Mutscheller, Jim, TE, Notre Dame 1954–61
Myers, Bob, T, Ohio State 1955
Myhra, Steve, G-LB-K, North Dakota 1957–61

N

Neal, Dan, C, Kentucky 1973–74
Nelson, Andy, DB, Memphis State 1957–63
Nelson, Dennis, T, Illinois State 1970–74
Nettles, Doug, CB, Vanderbilt 1974–75
Newsome, Billy, DE, Grambling 1970–72
Nichols, Robbie, LB, Tulsa 1970–71
Nottingham, Don, RB, Kent State 1971–73
Novak, Ken, DT, Purdue 1976
Nowatzke, Tom, RB, Indiana 1970–72
Nutter, Buzz, C, VPI 1954–60, 1965
Nyers, Dick, B, Indiana Central 1956–57

O

O'Brien, Jim, K-WR, Cincinnati 1970–72
Oldham, Ray, S, Mid. Tenn. St. 1973–76
Olds, Bill, RB, Nebraska 1973–75
Orduna, Joe, RB, Nebraska 1974
Orr, Jimmy, WR, Georgia 1961–70
Owens, Luke, T, Kent State 1957
Owens, R.C., WR, College of Idaho 1962

P

Parker, Jim, T-G, Ohio State 1957–67
Patera, Jack, LB, Oregon 1955–57
Pear, Dave, DT, Washington 1975
Pearson, Preston, RB, Illinois 1967–68
Pellington, Bill, LB, Rutgers 1953–64
Pepper, Gene, G, Mississippi 1954
Perkins, Ray, WR, Alabama 1967–71
Perry, Joe, RB, Compton 1961–62
Peterson, Gerald, T, Texas 1956
Petties, Neal, E. San Diego State 1964–66
Pittman, Charlie, RB, Penn State 1971
Plunkett, Sherm, T, Maryland State 1958–60
Poole, Barney, E, Mississippi 1953
Porter, Ron, LB, Idaho 1967–69
Pratt, Robert, G, North Carolina 1974–76
Preas, George, T, VPI 1955–65
Pricer, Billy, RB, Oklahoma 1957–60
Pyle, Palmer, G, Michigan State 1960–63

R

Radosevich, George, C, Pittsburgh 1954–56
Raiff, Jim, G, Dayton 1954
Rechichar, Bert, DB-K, Tennessee 1953–59
Reese, Guy, T, Southern Methodist 1964–65
Renfro, Dean, B, N. Texas State 1955
Ressler, Glenn, G, Penn State 1965–74
Rhodes, Danny, LB, Arkansas 1974
Richardson, Jerry, E, Wofford 1959–60
Richardson, Willie, WR, Jackson State 1963–69, 1971
Riley, Butch, LB, Texas A&I 1969
Robinson, Charles, G, Morgan State 1954
Robinson, Glenn, DE, Oklahoma St. 1975
Rudnick, Tim, DB, Notre Dame 1974

S

Salter, Bryant, DB, Pittsburgh 1976
Sample, John, DB, Maryland State 1958–60
Sandusky, Alex, G, Clarion 1954–66
Sanford, Leo, C, Louisiana Tech 1958
Saul, Bill, LB, Penn State 1962–63
Schmiesing, Joe, DT-DE, New Mexico St. 1973
Scott, Freddie, WR, Amherst, ... 1974–76
Sharkey, Ed, G, Nevada 1953
Shaw, George, QB, Oregon 1955–58
Sherer, Dave, WR, Southern Methodist 1959
Shields, Burrell, B, John Carroll 1955
Shields, Lebron, G, Tennessee 1960
Shinners, John, G, Xavier 1972
Shinnick, Don, LB, UCLA 1957–68
Shiver, Sanders, LB, Carson-Newman 1976
Shlapak, Boris, K, Michigan State 1972
Shula, Don, DB, John Carroll 1953–56
Simonini, Ed, LB, Texas A&M 1976
Simonson, David, T, Minnesota 1974
Simpson, Jack, B, Florida 1958–60
Smith, Billy Ray, T, Arkansas 1961–70
Smith, Bubba, DE, Michigan State 1967–71
Smith, Ollie, WR, Tennessee State 1973–74
Smith, Zeke, LB, Auburn 1960
Smolinski, Mark, RB, Wyoming 1961–62
Sommers, Mike, RB, George Washington 1959–61
Speyrer, Cotton, WR, Texas 1972–74
Spinney, Art, G, Boston College 1953–60
Stevens, Howard, RB, Louisville 1975–76
Stone, Avatus, B, Syracuse 1958
Stone, Billy, B, Bradley 1950
Stonebreaker, Steve, LB, Detroit 1964–66
Strofolino, Mike, LB, Villanova 1965
Stukes, Charlie, B, Maryland State 1967–72
Stynchula, Andy, T, Penn State 1966–67
Sullivan, Dan, G-T, Boston College 1962–72
Szymanski, Dick, C-LB, Notre Dame 1955, 1957–68

T

Taliaferro, George, B, Indiana 1953–54
Taseff, Carl, B, John Carroll 1953–61
Taylor, David T, Catawba 1973–76
Thomas, Jesse, B, Michigan State 1955–57
Thomas, Spencer, CB, Washburn 1976
Thompson, Don, DE, Richmond 1962–63
Thompson, Ricky, WR, Baylor 1976
Thurston, Fred (Fuzzy), G, Valparaiso 1958
Toth, Zollie, RB, Louisiana State 1953–54
Troup, Bill, QB, South Carolina 1974, 1976
Turner, Bake, B, Texas Tech 1962

U

Unitas, John, QB, Louisville 1956–72

V

Van Duyne, Bob, G, Idaho 1974–76
Varty, Mike, LB, Northwestern 1975
Vessels, Billy, RB, Oklahoma 1956
Vogel, Bob, T, Ohio State 1963–72
Volk, Rick, DB, Michigan 1967–72

W

Wallace, Jackie, S, Arizona 1975–76
Ward, Jim, QB, Gettysburg 1967–69
Welch, Jim, B, Southern Methodist 1960–67
White, Bob, B, Stanford 1955
White, Stan, LB, Ohio State 1972–76
Williams, John, G, Minnesota 1969–71
Williams, Steve, DT, Western Carolina 1974
Wilson, Butch, E, Alabama 1963–67
Windauer, Bill, DT, Iowa 1973–74
Wingate, Elmer, E, Maryland 1953
Winkler, Jim T, Texas A&M 1953
Womble, Royce, RB, N. Texas State 1954–57
Wright, George, DT, Houston 1970–71

Y

Yohn, Dave, C, Gettysburg 1962
Young, Claude (Buddy), RB, Illinois 1953–55
Young, Dick, B, Chattanooga 1955–56

BUFFALO BILLS

1959 Ralph C. Wilson, a minority stockholder of the Detroit Lions who long had sought a team of his own, was granted an American Football League franchise for Buffalo. Wilson put up a $100,000 performance bond and signed a lease on War Memorial Stadium. The city voted to increase the seating capacity in the stadium by 14,000, from 22,500 to 36,500. Wilson named the team the "Bills." Richie Lucas, an All-America quarterback from Penn State, was the team's first draft choice. Garrard (Buster) Ramsey was named head coach. Dick Gallagher, an assistant coach and director of player personnel with the Cleveland Browns, was selected as general manager.

1960 Richie Lucas, the top draft choice, signed with the Bills. The club opened its first training camp in East Aurora, New York. On the day before the first preseason game with Boston more than 100,000 Buffalo residents turned out on Main Street to greet the team in a welcome home parade. The Bills were beaten 28–7 by Lou Saban's Patriots in the AFL's first game at War Memorial Stadium. In the first league game, the New York Titans defeated Buffalo 27–3. The Bills recorded their first victory, shutting out Boston 13–0, September 23. The team averaged just 16,000 people at home the first year.

1961 Denver ruined the Bills' home opener at War Memorial Stadium with a 22–10 victory. Lou Saban was replaced by Mike Holovak in Boston, and immediately was hired as Buffalo's new director of player personnel, amid rumors he would be the Bills' next head coach. A 28–10 loss to San Diego concluded a disappointing Buffalo season with a 6–8 record.

1962 The rumors proved true. Ramsey was fired and Saban hired as head coach. The Bills signed a 6-foot 2-inch, 243-pound former Canadian Football League running back, Cookie Gilchrist. Quarterback Jack Kemp was claimed for the $100 waiver price from San Diego in a surprising deal. Houston ruined Saban's debut, beating the Bills 28–23. But Buffalo finished with seven wins and a tie in the last nine games. Gilchrist gained 1,099 yards, becoming the AFL's first 1,000-yard runner.

1963 The Bills signed their first two "name" players, Dave Behrman, a center from Michigan State, and Jim Dunaway, a tackle from Mississippi. They also signed quarterback Daryle Lamonica of Notre Dame. The club moved its training camp to suburban Blasdell, New York. Gilchrist set an all-time pro rushing record, gaining 243 yards and scoring five touchdowns in a 45–14 victory over the New York Jets. Buffalo lost 26–8 to Boston in an Eastern Division playoff game in 24-degree weather.

1964 The home opener proved a sign of things to come. The Bills defeated Kansas City 34–17. Before a crowd of 61,929, Buffalo won its ninth in a row, defeating the Jets 20–7 at Shea Stadium. The Eastern Division title was secured with a 24–14 victory over Boston in snow at Fenway Park, December 20. Before a standing-room-only crowd of 40,242 at War Memorial Stadium, the Bills won the AFL championship 20–7 over San Diego, December 27. Jack Kemp, the Chargers' former quarterback, completed 10 passes in the game and scored the Bills' final touchdown.

1965 Gilchrist, who had demanded extra money after the team won the championship in December, was traded to Denver for fullback Billy Joe in a deal that created controversy. In his three years with the Bills, Gilchrist had run for 3,058 yards and scored 35 touchdowns. Before a capacity crowd of 45,502, the defending AFL champions beat Boston 24–7 in the season opener. A 29–18 victory over Houston in Rice Stadium clinched the Bills' second straight Eastern

Cookie Gilchrist gains 144 yards in the fog vs. Chargers in 1964 AFL title game.

Division title, December 5. Buffalo's brilliant defense shut down the Chargers in San Diego and the Bills won their second consecutive AFL championship 23–0, December 26.

1966 In a shocking move, Saban announced he was resigning to accept a position as the head coach at the University of Maryland. He cited big bonuses and the fact they were ruining pro football as his main reason for leaving, although rumors persisted he was not able to get the security of a long-term contract he wanted from Wilson. Joe Collier, an assistant coach, was named head coach. The AFL all-stars defeated the Bills 30–19 in the league all-star game, January 15. Fullback Billy Joe was among four players claimed by Miami in the league's expansion draft. Collier's regular season head coaching debut was unsuccessful. San Diego beat the Bills 27–7, Sep-

tember 4. Buffalo rallied to have another good season and defeated Denver in the last game of the year to win a third straight Eastern Division championship. Bobby Burnett, running back from Arkansas, was named rookie of the year

1967 Kansas City ended the Bills' hold on the AFL championship, winning 31–7 in Buffalo before 42,080 at War Memorial Stadium, January 1. In what Ralph Wilson later called "the worst trade of all time," Daryle Lamonica was sent to Oakland for quarterback Tom Flores and wide receiver Art Powell. Playing a National Football League opponent for the first time in the preseason, the Bills lost to Detroit 19–17 before 43,503 in Buffalo.

1968 In what coach Joe Collier described as "a punishment scrimmage," quarterback Kemp was injured and lost for the season. Former Bill Daryle

Lamonica came to town and helped Oakland beat Buffalo 48–6. Collier was fired and replaced by Harvey Johnson, the team's director of player personnel. Bob Celeri and Marvin Bass were added to the coaching staff and Jerry Smith resigned. Flanker Elbert Dubenion, the last of the original Bills, retired as a player and joined the team's scouting department.

1969 John Rauch resigned as Oakland head coach and agreed to a four-year contract to coach the Bills. In the most significant draft in the history of the franchise, O.J. Simpson was selected as the first choice. Four months of intense negotiations followed with the Heisman trophy winner from USC and his agent. A month after training camp opened, O.J. signed a long-term contract with the Bills and reported for duty, August 9. Rauch got his first victory as a Buffalo coach, beating Denver 41–28, September 28 after losing two.

1970 In the first season of interleague play, the Bills began to show promise for the future. Dennis Shaw completed 178 of 321 passes for 2,507 yards and 10 touchdowns and was NFL rookie of the year in all polls. Marlin Briscoe was the AFL's top receiver with 57 catches. The roster contained several other highly regarded players, such as cornerback Robert James and Haven Moses, another speedy pass catcher. But through it all, there was concern about O.J. Simpson, who had been something of a disappointment in his first two years. Some felt he simply wasn't as good as advertised. Others contended it was impossible to run on a team that couldn't block. Still more wondered why Rauch didn't find ways to get him the ball more often.

1971 J.D. Hill, a receiver from Arizona State, was the club's first draft choice. Early in training camp, Rauch resigned. Harvey Johnson once again was named interim coach. The Bills defeated New England 27–20, November 28. It was significant because it was their first—and only—regular season victory of the year. Lou Saban returned from his six-year exile to become "vice president in charge of football" and head coach, December 23.

1972 Convinced the Bills had to be built from the bottom up, Saban began by fortifying the trenches. His first pick—and the number one choice in the NFL draft—was Walt Patulski, 6-foot 6-inch, 259-pound Notre Dame defensive end. His second pick was guard Reggie McKenzie, the All-America blocker from Michigan. Just before the season opened, he obtained tackle Dave Foley on waivers from the Jets.

Two other defensive linemen, Don Croft from Baltimore and Jerry Patton from Minnesota, were added. All were starters almost immediately. In April, ground was broken for the club's new 80,000-seat stadium in Orchard Park, New York. Saban won his first regular season game since returning, beating San Francisco 27–20, September 24. Getting the ball much more often, O.J. Simpson started to live up to his reputation. He had his first 1,000-yard season and was named the AFC's player of the year by United Press International.

1973 Simpson was named the most valuable player in the Pro Bowl. Teammates Robert James and J.D. Hill joined him in the game. Continuing his search for capable linemen, Saban made Michigan tackle Paul Seymour and Michigan State guard Joe DeLamielleure his first two selections in the draft. The Bills' season ticket sale for their first year in Orchard Park passed 46,206, the listed capacity of old War Memorial Stadium. A sellout crowd of 80,020 watched the first game in Orchard Park, a preseason game won by the Washington Redskins 37–21. O.J. Simpson set a single-game NFL record of 250 yards in Buffalo's 31–13 opening game over New England in Foxboro. The Bills made their Monday night television debut, beating Kansas City 23–14 with O.J. going over 1,000 yards for the season, October 29. In a dramatic final game at Shea Stadium, Simpson ran for 200 yards and finished with 2,003 for the season, breaking Jim Brown's 10-year-old rushing record. The Bills became the first team in league history to run for more than 3,000 yards.

1974 The Bills participated in the Hall of Fame game in Canton, Ohio, losing to St. Louis 21–13. In the season opener, Buffalo edged Oakland 21–20 in the final minute. A 29–28 victory over New England was the Bills' sixth consecutive victory and gave them possession of first place in the AFC Eastern Division, November 3. A 6–0 shutout of Baltimore was their ninth win of the season and first shutout since 1965. O.J. Simpson went over 1,000 yards for the season in that game, the third consecutive year he surpassed that mark. Miami defeated Cincinnati, assuring the Bills their first appearance in a postseason playoff since 1966, December 12. Pittsburgh beat the Bills 32–14 in the first round in Pittsburgh, December 22.

1975 In the season opener, Buffalo warmed up its potent offense to bombard the New York Jets 42–14. In their first Monday night television loss, the Bills dropped a 17–14 decision to the New York Giants.

O.J. Simpson went over 1,000 yards for the season, this time clearing that figure in a 24–23 win over the New York Jets, November 2. In the final game of the season, Simpson scored his twenty-third touchdown, setting another NFL record.

1976 The lingering story of the summer was O.J. Simpson's insistence on a trade to Los Angeles. On the day before the season opened, Simpson traveled to New York and signed a three-year contract estimated at $2 million-plus to play in Buffalo. After three losses in the first five games, Lou Saban resigned "in the best interests of the team," he said. Jim Ringo, the offensive line coach and former all-pro center with Vince Lombardi's Green Bay Packers, was signed as the new coach. Wilson insisted Ringo "was not just an interim coach," intimating he had signed a long-term contract. Two games later, the new coach lost his quarterback. Joe Ferguson suffered some broken bones in his back and was out for the season. The Bills never recovered and did not win a game under Ringo. Simpson started slowly, gaining only 105 yards in the first three games, but he finished with 1,503 to lead the league.

MEMBERS OF HALL OF FAME:
None

BILLS RECORD, 1960–76

Year	Won	Lost	Tied	Pct.	Pts.	OP
1960	5	8	1	.385	296	303
1961	6	8	0	.429	294	342
1962	7	6	1	.538	309	272
1963	7	6	1	.538	304	291
1964‡	12	2	0	.857	400	242
1965‡	10	3	1	.769	313	226
1966§	9	4	1	.692	358	255
1967	4	10	0	.286	237	285
1968	1	12	1	.077	199	367
1969	4	10	0	.286	230	359
1970	3	10	1	.231	204	337
1971	1	13	0	.071	184	394
1972	4	9	1	.321	257	377
1973	9	5	0	.643	259	230
1974	9	5	0	.643	264	244
1975	8	6	0	.571	420	355
1976	2	12	0	.143	245	363
17 Years	101	129	8	.441	4,773	5,242

‡AFL Champion
§AFL Eastern Division Champion

RECORD HOLDERS

Rushing (Yards)	O. J. Simpson, 1973,	2,003
Passing (Pct.)	Dennis Shaw, 1970	55.5
Passing (Yards)	Jack Kemp, 1963	2,910
Passing (TDs)	Joe Ferguson, 1975	25
Receiving (No.)	Bill Miller, 1963	69
Receiving (Yards)	Elbert Dubenion, 1964	1,139
Interceptions (No.)	Billy Atkins, 1961, and	
	Tom Janik, 1967	10
Punting (Avg.)	Billy Atkins, 1961	45.1
Punt Ret. (Avg.)	Ed Rutkowski, 1966	11.6
Kickoff Ret. (Avg.)	Ed Rutkowski, 1963	30.2
Touchdowns (Total)	O. J. Simpson, 1975	23
Field Goals Made	Pete Gogolak, 1964	28
Points (No.)	O. J. Simpson, 1975	138

COACHING HISTORY

1960–61	Garrard (Buster) Ramsey	11–16–1
1962–65	Lou Saban	36–17–3
1966–68	Joel Collier*	13–16–1
1968	Harvey Johnson	1–10–1
1969–70	John Rauch	7–20–1
1971	Harvey Johnson	1–13–0
1972–76	Lou Saban**	32–28–1
1976	Jim Ringo	0– 9–0

*Replaced after two games in 1968
**Resigned after five games in 1976

FIRST PLAYER SELECTED

1960	Richie Lucas, QB, Penn State
1961	Ken Rice, T, Auburn
1962	Ernie Davis, RB, Syracuse
1963	Dave Behrman, C, Michigan State
1964	Carl Eller, DE, Minnesota
1965	Jim Davidson, T, Ohio State
1966	Mike Dennis, RB, Mississippi
1967	John Pitts, S, Arizona State
1968	Haven Moses, WR, San Diego State
1969	O. J. Simpson, RB, USC
1970	Al Cowlings, DE, USC
1971	J. D. Hill, WR, Arizona State
1972	Walt Patulski, DE, Notre Dame
1973	Paul Seymour, T, Michigan
1974	Reuben Gant, TE, Oklahoma State
1975	Tom Ruud, LB, Nebraska
1976	Mario Clark, DB, Oregon

O.J. Simpson gains 200 vs. Jets, record 2,003 for season, 1973.

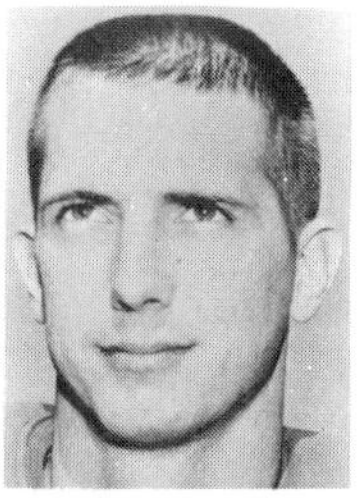
Bobby Burnett

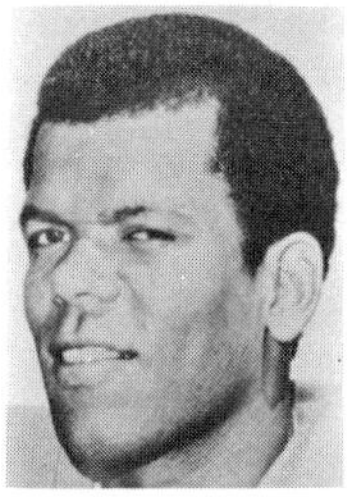
Butch Byrd

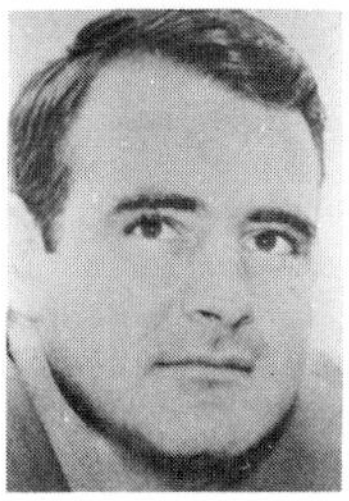
Wray Carlton

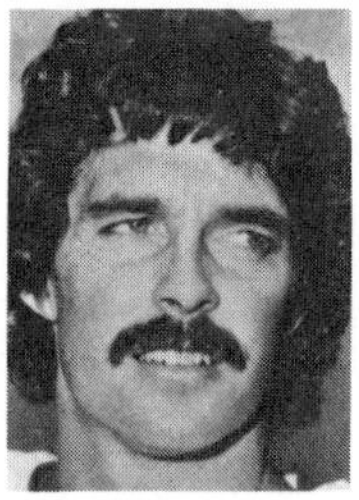
Bob Chandler

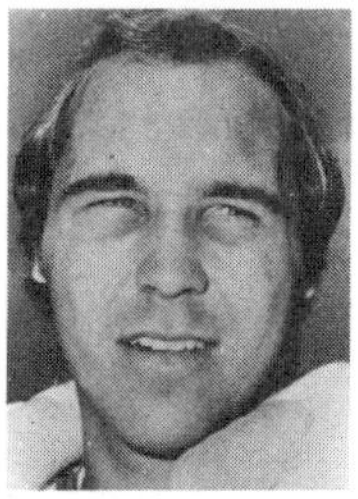
Joe DeLamielleure

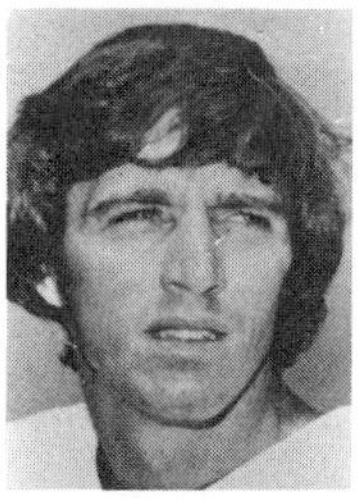
Joe Ferguson

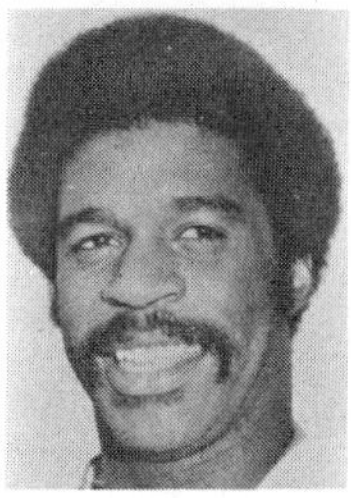
Tony Greene

BUFFALO BILLS, 1960–76

Abramowicz, Dan, WR, Xavier 1975
Abruzzese, Ray, DB, Alabama 1962–64
Adams, Bill, G, Holy Cross 1972–76
Alexander, Glenn, WR, Grambling 1970
Alford, Bruce, K, Texas Christian 1968–69
Allen, Doug, LB, Penn State 1974–75
Allen, Jackie, DB, Baylor 1970–71
Anderson, Max, RB, Arizona State 1968–70
Anderson, Tim, DB, Ohio State 1976
Andrews, Al, LB, New Mexico 1970–71
Atkins, Bill, DB, Auburn 1960–63
Auer, Joe, HB, Georgia Tech 1964–65

B

Bailey, Bill, RB, Cincinnati 1967
Baker, Art, RB, Syracuse 1961
Barber, Stew, T, Penn State 1961–69
Barrett, Robert, E, Baldwin 1960
Bass, Glenn, E, East Carolina 1961–66
Bateman, Marv, P, Utah 1974–76
Beamer, Tim, S, Johnson C. Smith 1971
Beard, Tom, C, Michigan State 1972
Behrman, Dave, C, Michigan State 1963–65
Bemiller, Al, C, Syracuse 1961–69
Bivins, Charley, HB, Morris Brown 1967
Blazer, Phil, G, North Carolina 1960
Bohling, Dewey, RB, Hardin-Simmons 1961
Borden, Nate, E, Indiana 1962
Braxton, Hezekiah, HB, Virginia Union 1963
Braxton, Jim, RB, West Virginia 1971–76
Briscoe, Marlin, WR, Omaha 1969–71
Brodhead, Bob, QB, Duke 1960
Brooks, Cliff, DB, Tennessee State 1976
Brown, Charley, S, Syracuse 1968
Brown, Fred, HB, Georgia 1961–63
Brubaker, Richard, E, Ohio State 1960
Bugenhagen, Gary, T, Syracuse 1967
Burnett, Bobby, HB, Arkansas 1966–67
Buziniski, Bernie, LB, Holy Cross 1960
Byrd, George, CB, Boston U 1964–70

C

Cahill, Bill, S, Washington 1973–74
Calhoun, Don, RB, Kansas State 1974–75
Cannavino, Joe, DB, Ohio State 1962
Cappadonna, Bob, RB, Northeastern 1968
Carlton, Wray, RB, Duke 1960–67
Carr, Levert, T, N. Central Illinois 1970–71
Carwell, Larry, S, Iowa State 1973
Chamberlain, Dan, E, Sacramento State 1960–61
Chandler, Bob, WR, USC 1971–76
Chandler, Edgar, LB, Georgia 1968–72
Chapple, Dave, P, Cal.-Santa Barbara 1971
Charon, Carl, DB, Michigan State 1962–63
Cheek, Richard, G, Auburn 1970–71
Chelf, Don, G, Iowa 1960–61
Cheyunski, Jim, LB, Syracuse 1973–74
Christiansen, Bob, TE, UCLA 1972
Clark, Mario, DB, Oregon 1976
Clark, Mike, K, Texas A&M 1972
Clarke, Hagood, DB, Florida 1964–68
Cole, Linzy, WR, Texas Christian 1972
Coleman, Fred, TE, Northeast Louisiana 1976
Colins, Jerald, LB, Western Michigan 1969–71
Cornell, Robert (Bo), LB, Washington 1973–76
Cornish, Frank, DT, Alcorn A&M 1972
Costa, Dave, DT, Utah 1966–74
Costa, Paul, TE-T, Notre Dame 1965–72
Cowlings, Al, DE, USC 1970–72
Craig, Neal, S, Fisk 1974
Carwford, Hilton, S, Grambling 1969
Crockett, Bobby, WR, Arkansas 1966–69
Crockett, Monte, E, New Mex. Highlands 1960–62
Croft, Don, DT, Texas-El Paso 1972–75
Crotty, Jim, DB, Notre Dame 1961–62
Crow, Wayne, RB, California 1962–63
Croyle, Phil. LB, California 1973
Cudzik, Walt, C, Purdue 1964
Cunningham, Dick, T, Arkansas 1967–72
Curchin, Jeff, G, Florida State 1972

D

Darragh, Dan, QB, William & Mary 1968–70
Day, Tom, DE, No. Carolina A&I 1961–66, 1968
DeLamielleure, Joe, G, Michigan State 1973–76
DeLucca, Gerry, T, Middle Tenn. St. 1962–63
Denney, Austin, TE, Tennessee 1970–71
Desutter, Wayne, T, Western Illinois 1966
Devleiger, Chuck, DT, Memphis State 1969
Devlin, Joe, T, Iowa 1976
Discenzo, Tony, T, Michigan State 1960
Dittrich, John, G, Wisconsin 1961
Dobbins, Oliver, DB, Morgan State 1964
Donaldson, Gene, RB, Purdue 1967
Dorow, Al, QB, Michigan State 1962
Dubenion, Elbert, WR, Bluffton 1960–68
Dunaway, Jim, DT, Mississippi 1963–71

E

Edgerson, Booker, CB, Western Illinois 1962–69
Edwards, Earl, DE, Wichita 1973–75
Edwards, Emmett, WR, Kansas 1976
Enyart, Bill, RB, Oregon State 1969–70

F

Farley, Dale, LB, West Virginia 1972–73
Felton, Ralph, LB, Maryland 1961–62
Ferguson, Charley, TE, Tennessee State 1963–69
Ferguson, Joe, QB, Arkansas 1973–76
Flint, George, G, Arizona State 1962–65, 1968
Flores, Tom, QB, Pacific 1967–69
Foley, Dave, T, Ohio State 1972–76
Ford, Charley, DB, Houston 1975
Ford, Fred, RB, Caltech 1960
Forsberg, Fred, LB, Washington 1973
Fowler, Wayne, C, Georgia 1970
Fowler, Willmer, RB, Northwestern 1960–61
Francis, Wallace, WR, Arkansas AM&N 1973–74
Frantz, Jack, C, California 1968
Frazier, Wayne, C, Auburn 1967
Freeman, Steve, DB, Mississippi 1975–76

G

Gaddis, Bob, WR, Mississippi Valley 1976
Gant, Reuben, TE, Oklahoma State 1974–76
Gantt, Jerome, T, N. Carolina Central 1970
Garror, Leon, S, Alcorn A&M 1972–73
Gilchrist, Cookie, RB, None 1962–64
Gladieux, Bob, RB, Notre Dame 1970
Glosson, Clyde, WR, Texas-El Paso 1970
Gogolak, Pete, K, Cornell 1964–65
Goode, Irv, G, Kentucky 1972
Goodwin, Doug, RB, Maryland State 1966
Grabosky, Gene, T, Syracuse 1960
Grant, Wes, DE, UCLA 1971
Grate, Willie, TE, S. Carolina State 1969–70
Green, Donnie, T, Purdue 1971–76
Green, John, QB, Chattanooga 1960–61
Green, Van, S, Shaw 1976
Greene, Tony, CB, Maryland 1971–76
Gregory, Ben, RB, Nebraska 1968–69
Groman, Bill, E, Heidelberg 1964–65
Guidry, Paul, LB, McNeese State 1966–72
Guthrie, Grant, K, Florida State 1970–71

H

Hagen, Halvor, T, Weber State 1973–75
Harper, Darrell, B, Michigan 1960
Harris, James, QB, Grambling 1969–72
Harrison, Dwight, WR, Texas A&I 1972–76
Hart, Dick, G, None 1972
Hart, Leo, QB, Duke 1972–73
Harvey, Waddey, DT, Virginia Tech 1969–70
Haselrig, Clint, RB, Michigan 1974–75
Hayman, Gary, RB, Penn State 1974–75
Healy, Don, T, Maryland 1962
Heath, Clayton, RB, Wake Forest 1976
Henley, Carey, B, Chattanooga 1962
Hergert, Joe, B, Florida 1960–61
Hews, Bob, T, Princeton 1971
Hill, Ike, CB, Catawba 1970–71
Hill, J.D., WR, Arizona State 1971–75
Hoisington, Al, WR, Pasadena 1960
Holland, John, WR, Tennessee State 1975–76
Holmes, Mike, WR, Texas Southern 1976
Hudlow, Floyd, DB, Arizona 1965
Hudson, Dick, T, Memphis States 1963–68
Hooks, Roland, RB, North Carolina State 1976
Hunter, Scott, QB, Alabama 1974
Hurston, Chuck, DE, Auburn 1971

J

Jackson, Randy, RB, Wichita State 1972
Jackunas, Frank, C, Detroit 1962
Jacobs, Harry, LB, Bradley 1963–69
Jakowenko, George, K, Syracuse 1976
James, Bob, CB, Fisk 1969–75
Janik, Tom, S, Texas A&I 1965–68
Jarvis, Bruce, C, Washington 1971–74
Jarvis, Ray, WR, Norfolk State 1973
Jenkins, Ed, RB, Holy Cross 1974
Jilek, Dan, LB, Michigan 1976
Joe, Billy, RB, Villanova 1965
Johnson, Jack, B, Miami 1960–61
Johnson, Mark, LB, Missouri 1975–76
Jones, Doug, DB, Cal State–Northridge 1975–76
Jones, Ed, DB, Rutgers 1975
Jones, Greg, RB, UCLA 1970–71
Jones, Ken, DE, Arkansas State 1976
Jones, Spike, P, Georgia 1971–74
Jones, Steve, RB, Duke 1973–74
Jones, Willie, B, Purdue 1962

K

Kadish, Mike, DT, Notre Dame 1973–76
Kalsu, Bob, G, Oklahoma 1968
Kampa, Bob, DT, California 1973–74
Keating, Tom, DT, Michigan 1964–65
Kellerman, Ernie, S, Miami, Ohio 1973
Kemp, Jack, QB, Occidental 1962–69
Kern, Rex, S, Ohio State 1974
Kinard, Bill, DB, Mississippi 1960
Kindig, Howard, C-DE, Cal State–L.A. 1967–71
King, Charley, DB, Purdue 1966–67
King, Tony, DB, Findlay 1967
Kingrea, Rick, LB, Tulane 1973
Kinney, Jeff, RB, Nebraska 1976
Kochman, Roger, B, Penn State 1963
Koy, Ted, TE-LB, Texas 1971–74
Krakau, Merv, LB, Iowa State 1973–76
Kruse, Bob, G, Wayne State 1969
Kulbacki, Joe, B, Purdue 1960

L

Lamonica, Daryle, QB, Notre Dame 1963–66
Laraway, Jack. LB, Purdue 1960
Laskey, Bill, LB, Michigan 1965
Laster, Art, T, Maryland State 1970
Lawson, Jerome, CB, Utah 1968
Ledbetter, Monte, WR, N.W. Louisiana 1967–69
Lee, Ken, LB, Washington 1972
LeMoine, Jim, G, Utah State 1967
Leo, Chuck, G, Indiana 1963
Lettner, Bob, LB, Tennessee 1961
Lewis, Harold, B, Houston 1960
Lewis, Richard, LB, Portland State 1973–74
Leypoldt, John, K, None 1971–76
Lincoln, Keith, RB, Washington State 1967–68
Lloyd, Jeff, DT, West Texas State 1976
Louderback, Tom, LB, San Jose State 1962
Loukas, Angelo, G, Northwestern 1969
Lucas, Richie, QB-HB, Penn State 1960–61
Lusteg, Booth, K, Connecticut 1966
Lyman, Jeff, LB, Brigham Young 1972

M

Maguire, Paul, LB-K, Citadel 1964–70
Majors, Bill, DB, Tennessee 1961
Marangi, Gary, QB, Boston College 1974–76
Marchlewski, Frank, C, Minnesota 1970
Masters, Billy, TE, Louisiana State 1967–69
Matlock, John, C, Miami 1972
Matsos, Archie, LB, Michigan State 1960–62
Matuszak, Marv, LB, Tulsa 1962–63
McBath, Mike, DE, Penn State 1968–72
McCabe, Richie, DB, Pittsburgh 1960–61
McCaffrey, Mike, LB, California 1970
McConnell, Brian, LB, Michigan State 1973
McCrumbly, John, LB, Texas A&M 1975

Tom Janik   *Paul Maguire*   *Reggie McKenzie*   *George Saimes*   *Tom Sestak*   *Billy Shaw*   *John Tracey*

McDermott, Gary, RB, Tulsa 1968
McDole, Ron, DE, Nebraska 1963–70
McDonald, Don, DB, Houston 1961
McFarland, Jim, TE, Nebraska 1970
McGrew, Dan, C, Purdue 1960
McKenzie, Reggie, G, Michigan 1972–76
McKinley, Bill, LB, Arizona 1971
McKinney, Royce, DB, Kentucky State 1975
McMurty, Chuck, DT, Whittier 1960–61
Means, Dave, DE, Southeast Missouri St. 1974
Mercer, Mike, K, No. Arizona 1967–68
Meredith, Dudley, DE, Lamar Tech 1964–68
Meyer, Ed, T, W. Texas State 1960
Miller, Bill, E, Miami 1963
Mills, Sullivan, E-DB, Wichita 1965–66
Minter, Tom, B, Baylor 1962
Mitchell, Charley, RB, Washington 1968
Montler, Mike, C, Colorado 1973–76
Moody, Keith, DB, Syracuse 1976
Moore, Leroy, DE, Ft. Valley State 1960, 1962–63
Moses, Haven, WR, San Diego State 1968–72
Mosley, Wayne, RB, Alabama A&M 1974
Moss, Roland, RB, Toledo 1970
Muelhaupt, Ed, G, Iowa State 1960–61
Murdock, Jessie, FB, California Western 1963

N

Nelson, Bob, LB, Nebraska 1975–76
Nighswander, Nick, C, Morehead St. 1974
Nunamaker, Julian, DE, Tenn-Martin 1969–71

O

O'Connell, Tom, QB, Illinois 1960–61
O'Donnell, Joe, G, Michigan 1964–71
Ogas, Dave, LB, San Diego State 1969
Okoniewski, Steve, DT, Montana 1972–73
Oliver, Frank, DB, Kentucky State 1975
Olson, Harold, T, Clemson 1960–62

P

Palmer, Dick, LB, Kentucky 1972
Palumbo, Sam, C, Notre Dame 1960

Parker, Willie, C, North Texas State 1973–76
Pate, Lloyd, RB, Cincinnati 1970
Paterra, Herb, LB, Michigan State 1963
Patrick, Wayne, RB, Louisville 1968–72
Patton, Bob, C, Delaware 1976
Patton, Jerry, DT, Nebraska 1972–73
Patulski, Walt, DE, Notre Dame 1972–75
Penchion, Robert, G, Alcorn A&M 1972–73
Petrich, Bob, DE, W, Texas State 1967
Pharr, Tommy, S, Mississippi State 1970
Pitts, John, S, Arizona State 1967–73
Ply, Bobby, DB, Baylor 1967
Powell, Art, TE, San Jose State 1967
Powell, Darnell, RB, Chattanooga 1976
Prudhomme, Remi, C, Louisiana State 1966–67, 1972

R

Rabb, Warren, QB, Louisiana State 1961–62
Randolph, Al, S, Iowa 1974
Rashad, Ahmad, WR, Oregon 1974–75
Ray, Eddie, RB, Louisiana State 1976
Reeves, Roy, WR, South Carolina 1969
Reid, Andy, RB, Georgia 1976
Reilly, Jim, G, Notre Dame 1970–71
Remmett, Dennis, T, Iowa State 1960
Reynolds, M.C., QB, Louisiana State 1961
Ricardo, Benny, K, San Diego State 1976
Rice, Ken, T, Auburn 1961–63
Richards, Perry, E, Detroit 1961
Richardson, Pete, CB, Dayton 1969–71
Richey, Mike, T, North Carolina 1969
Ridlehuber, Preston, RB, Georgia 1969
Rissmiller, Ray, T, Georgia 1968
Rivera, Hank, DB, Oregon State 1963
Roberson, Bo, E, Cornell 1965
Rosdahl, Harrison, DE, Penn State 1964
Ross, Louis, DE, So. Carolina State 1971–72
Ross, Willie, RB, Nebraska 1964
Russell, Ben, QB, Louisville 1968
Rutkowski, Charles, E, Ripon 1960
Rutkowski, Ed, QB-WR, Notre Dame 1963–68
Ruud, Tom, LB, Nebraska 1975–76

Rychlec, Tom, E, American International 1960–62

S

Saidock, Tom, DT, Michigan State 1962
Saimes, George, S, Michigan State 1963–69
Saunders, John, S, Toledo 1972
Schaffer, Joe, B, Tennessee 1960
Schmidt, Bob, C, Minnesota 1966–67
Schmidt, Henry, DT, USC 1965
Schnarr, Steve, RB, Otterbein 1975
Schottenheimer, Marty, LB, Pittsburgh 1965–68
Scott, John, T, Ohio State 1960–61
Sedlock, Bob, DT, Georgia 1960
Selfridge, Andy, LB, Virginia 1972
Sestak, Tom, DT, McNeese State 1962–68
Seymour, Paul, TE, Michigan State 1973–76
Shaw, Billy, G, Georgia Tech 1961–69
Shaw, Dennis, QB, San Diego State 1970–73
Sherman, Tom, QB, Penn State 1969
Shockley, Bill, B, West Chester State 1961
Simpson, O.J., RB, USC 1969–76
Skorupan, John, LB, Penn State 1973–76
Smith, Allen, HB, Ft. Valley State 1966–67
Smith, Bobby, RB, N. Texas State 1964–65
Smith, Carl, RB, Tennessee 1960
Smith, Marty, DT, Louisville 1976
Smith, Tody, DE, USC 1976
Snowden, Cal, DE, Indiana 1971
Sorey, Jim, DT, Texas Southern 1960–62
Spikes, Jack, RB, Texas Christian 1966–67
Stephenson, Kay, QB, Florida 1968
Stone, Don, RB, Arkansas 1965
Stone, Ken, S, Vanderbilt 1973
Stratton, Mike, LB, Tennessee 1962–73
Sykes, Gene, DB, Louisiana State 1963–65

T

Taliaferro, Mike, LB, Illinois 1972
Taseff, Carl, DB, John Carrol 1962
Tatarek, Bob, DT, Miami 1968–72
Thomas, Ike, DB, Bishop 1975
Thornton, Bubba, WR, Texas Christian 1969
Toomay, Pat, DE, Vanderbilt 1975
Torczon, Laverne, DE, Nebraska 1960–62
Tracey, John, LB, Texas A&M 1962–67
Trapp, Richard, WR, Florida 1968
Tyler, Maurice, S, Morgan State 1972–73

V

Valdez, Vernon, DB, San Diego State 1961
VanValkenburg, Pete, RB, BYU 1973

W

Wagstaff, Jim, DB, Idaho State 1960–61
Walker, Donnie, DB, Central St., Ohio 1973–74
Warlick, Ernie, E, N. Carolina Central 1962–65
Warner, Charley, DB, Prairie View 1964–66
Washington, Dave, LB, Alcorn A&M 1972–74
Washington, Vic, RB, Wyoming 1975–76
Watkins, Larry, RB, Alcorn A&M 1973–74
Wegert, Ted, B, None 1960
West, Willie, DB, Oregon 1962–63
Wheeler, Manch, QB, Maine 1962
White, Jan, TE, Ohio State 1971–72
White, Sherman, DE, California 1976
Williams, Ben, DT, Mississippi 1976
Wilson, Mike, G, Dayton 1971
Winans, Jeff, DT, USC 1973–75
Wolff, Wayne, G, Wake Forest 1961
Word, Roscoe, DB, Jackson State 1976
Wyatt, Alvin, DB, Bethune-Cookman 1971–72
Wyche, Sam, QB, Furman 1976

Y

Yaccino, John, DB, Pittsburgh 1962
Yeates, Jeff, DT, Boston College 1974–76
Yoho, Mack, DE, Miami, Ohio 1961–63
Young, Willie, T, Alcorn A&M 1971
Youngelman, Sid, T, Alabama 1962–63

Z

Zecher, Rich, DT, Utah State 1967

Quarterback Joe Ferguson and head coach Lou Saban, 1975.

CHICAGO BEARS

1920 A. E. Staley, who owned the Staley Starch Company in Decatur, Illinois, hired 25-year-old George Halas to work in his plant, play on his semipro baseball team, and organize a company football team. Staley promised Halas enough of a budget to attract top ballplayers, and he also agreed to let them practice on company time. Halas signed end Guy Chamberlin, halfback Jimmy Conzelman, halfback Ed (Dutch) Sternaman, center George Trafton, and quarterback Charley Dressen. Halas himself played end. Halas contacted Ralph Hay about playing the Canton Bulldogs, whom Hay managed. Hay told Halas of a plan to organize professional football. Representatives of the Staleys, Bulldogs, and nine other teams met in a preliminary meeting, August 20. The group formally organized itself as the American Professional Football Association, September 17. The league was loosely organized. There were either no standings kept, or they have been lost. The Staleys finished with a 10–1–2 record. They claimed a share of the championship on the grounds that they had held the other claimant, the undefeated Akron, Ohio, Pros to a scoreless tie in their only meeting. The Staleys had many odd formations in their small notebook of plays, but Halas's favorite was the T formation. He had played it under coach Bob Zuppke at Illinois. Decatur was one of the few teams to show a profit in the first year of operation. Each member of the squad received $1,900 for his season's work.

1921 A business recession after the 1920 season cut into Staley's starch profits, and he was forced to withdraw sponsorship of his football team. He suggested to George Halas that Halas take over the team. Halas agreed and decided to move the team to Chicago. For $5,000, he further agreed to call the team the "Chicago Staleys" for one year. Halas secured permission for the move from Chris O'Brien, owner of the Racine Cardinals, who held the territorial rights to the city of Chicago. Halas made his former Illinois classmate Dutch Sternaman half-owner of the team instead of paying him a salary. Halas and Sternaman signed a lease with William Veeck Sr., owner of the Chicago Cubs, to play at Cub Park in exchange for 15 percent of each game's gross. They signed Guy Chamberlin and George Trafton from the old Staleys team. The Staleys won the AFPA championship with a 10–1–1 record. Second-place Buffalo (9–1–2) protested that Chicago's record included nonleague games, but league president Joe Carr ruled in favor of Chicago.

1922 At Halas's suggestion the league rechristened itself the National Football League. Halas renamed his team the Chicago Bears, January 28. His agreement with Staley had expired, and he thought some nickname association with the Cubs would be appropriate. Halas engineered Chicago's first trade, November 27. Impressed after he was unable to block Rock Island's great end Ed Healey, Halas paid the Independents $100 for Healey's contract. The Bears lost two games to the Chicago Cardinals, 6–0 and 9–0, in which all the scoring came on John (Paddy) Driscoll's field goals. The Bears finished second behind Canton with a 9–3 record. Halas and Sternaman turned a profit; they made $1,476.92 for the season.

1923 Halas scooped up a fumble by Jim Thorpe of the Oorang Indians at the Bears' 2-yard line and raced a record 98 yards to a touchdown, November 4. The Bears finished second behind Canton once again. Chicago went 9–2–1, while Canton was undefeated at 11–0–1.

1924 The Bears lost to Green Bay in the opening game of the season, but did not lose again. They finished with a 6–1–4 record, which was good

Halfback Gale Sayers being tackled by safety Larry Wilson of the St. Louis Cardinals, 1967.

enough for second place behind the Cleveland Bulldogs. Halas and Sternaman split $20,000 profit at the end of the season.

1925 Halas signed Red Grange, who had finished his collegiate career with the University of Illinois one day earlier, November 22. In return for a significant share of the gate, Grange, through his agent, C.C. Pyle, agreed to play the rest of the season with the Bears, including a 19-game postseason barnstorming tour. On November 26, 36,000 people showed up for Grange's first game, but he gained only 36 yards in a 0–0 tie with the Cardinals. Nonetheless, Grange

proved he was the first strong gate attraction in the NFL. Over 73,000 New Yorkers watched as Grange and the Bears defeated the Giants at the Polo Grounds 19–7, December 6. The Bears played the Los Angeles Tigers before 75,000 at the Los Angeles Coliseum, January 16. The Bears beat the Washington All-Stars in Seattle 34–0, to end the tour, January 31. The tour netted Pyle and Grange $100,000 each. The Bears had a 13–5–1 record on the tour.

1926 Cubs Park was renamed Wrigley Field. Pyle asked the Bears for a five-figure salary and one-third ownership of the Bears for Grange. Halas refused, and Pyle started the American Football League, putting Grange with the New York Yankees. That left Chicago without a running star or a drawing card. The problem was solved when Halas acquired Paddy Driscoll from the financially depressed Cardinals for $3,500. The Bears, the Pottsville, Pennsylvania, Maroons, and the Frankford Yellowjackets all fought for the league championship. Chicago was in contention until late in the season, when it played Frankford. Former Bear Guy Chamberlin was the Yellowjackets' player-coach, and he blocked a Paddy Driscoll extra point attempt to give his team a 7–6 win. Frankford ended the season with a 14–1–1 record. The Bears were second at 12–1–3.

1927 The champion Giants beat Chicago in a key game. Joe Guyon sent George Halas out of the game with broken ribs on a play on which Halas also was called for clipping. The Bears dropped to third place with a 9–3–2 record.

1928 Friction between the owners caused some problems on the Bears. Both Halas and Sternaman wanted to run the offense. Chicago finished fifth with a 7–5–1 record.

1929 Red Grange came out of retirement to play for the Bears. A knee injury affected his once peerless maneuverability, but he was still a sound, all-purpose back. They were 4–1–1 in their first six games, but lost seven of their last eight, to finish with their first losing season.

1930 George Halas stepped down as coach and retired as a player. He and Sternaman compromised their disagreements by hiring former Illinois assistant Ralph Jones, who was the head coach at Lake Forest Academy, Illinois. Jones promised Halas and Sternaman a championship in three years. He changed the Bears' T formation. He moved the ends wide, spaced the halfbacks wider, and made one of the halfbacks a man-in-motion. He could become a third end and run downfield for a pass; turn and crackback block the defensive end; or cross up the defense by going in motion in one direction several plays and then begin going in the opposite direction. This spiced up the ancient, plodding T formation. Paddy Driscoll retired and George Trafton was not invited back. Trafton ignored the message, however. He reported and won back the center's job with outstanding preseason play. The Bears signed 6-foot 2-inch, 230-pound fullback Bronko Nagurski from the University of Minnesota. Carl Brumbaugh, a rookie from the University of Florida, became the Bears' quarterback. Right after the completion of the college season, Halas signed Notre Dame fullback Joe Savoldi. NFL President Carr fined the Bears $1,000 for signing a collegian before his class had graduated. Ironically, Savoldi lasted only four games; the competition with Nagurski was too great. The Bears moved into third place with a 9–4–1 record.

1931 The Bears gained a top halfback when they signed Keith Molesworth, who could run, pass, return kicks, and back up Brumbaugh. The Bears finished in third place again. The league announced its first official all-pro team. Red Grange was the only Bears' player to make it.

1932 The Bears signed end Bill Hewitt from Michigan. A veteran from the 1929 club, Joe Kopcha, returned from retirement to play guard. In the last game of the season, the Bears beat the Green Bay Packers 9–0 on a 14-yard field goal by Paul (Tiny) Engebretsen and a 56-yard run by Bronko Nagurski. That gave Chicago a 7–1–6 record and forced a playoff between the Bears and the Portsmouth, Ohio, Spartans which was held in Chicago, December 18. Below-zero temperatures forced Halas to move the game indoors to Chicago Stadium. The field was only 80 yards long, and it was surrounded by a solid fence only a few feet from the side and end lines. The Bears won 9–0 when Nagurski took a fourth down handoff near

the goal line but stopped suddenly, backed up, and lobbed a pass to Grange, who was all alone in the end zone. Ralph Jones had kept his promise to deliver a championship within three years. The Bears' Nagurski, end Luke Johnsos, and guard Jules Carlson were named to the all-pro team. The Bears, however, lost $18,000 for the year. As a result, Sternaman wanted out; he sold his half of the team to Halas for $38,000. Halas had to borrow the money, $5,000 of which came from Chicago businessman Charles Bidwill.

1933 The league aligned itself into Eastern and Western divisions; the Bears were named one of the five Western teams. Ralph Jones resigned as coach. Halas returned to the side lines as his replacement. The Bears had their first out-of-town training camp, at Notre Dame. Tackle Link Lyman ended a one-year retirement. Three promising rookies joined the club—fullback-kicker Jack Manders from Minnesota, 260-pound tackle George Musso from Millikin College, and end Bill Karr from West Virginia. The Bears won the Western Division title with a 10–2–1 record. In the NFL's first championship game, 26,000 people watched at Wrigley Field as Jack Manders kicked three field goals and two extra points and the Bears defeated the New York Giants 23–21. The winning points were scored when Nagurski lobbed a short pass to Hewitt, who lateraled to Karr, who scored a 36-yard touchdown.

1934 The Bears held training camp at Lane Tech High School in Chicago. They played the best college players in the first Chicago All-Star game, before 79,432 at Soldier Field, August 31. The game ended in a scoreless tie. Chicago signed rookie halfback Beattie Feathers of Tennessee. The Bears won all 13 league contests. Feathers became the first pro back to gain 1,000 yards, totaling 1,004 yards. He also set an NFL record by averaging 9.94 yards per carry. Nagurski's blocks helped clear the way for him. The Bears met the Giants in the Polo Grounds for the NFL championship, December 9. The day was cold, and the field was frozen. The Bears led 13–3 after three quarters. But some of the Giants' players switched to tennis shoes and gained better traction. New York scored 27 points in the final period and won 30–13. The Bears dominated the all-pro selections. Feathers, Nagurski, Hewitt, and Kopcha made first-team; Lyman and center Eddie Kawal made the second team. Red Grange, who had been a reserve during the season, retired.

1935 The Bears switched their training camp to St. Johns Military Academy in Delafield, Wisconsin. Brumbaugh and Lyman retired before the season. Nagurski was out most of the year with a hip injury. Feathers was hurt off and on all season. The Bears struggled to a 6–4–2 record. Karr, Musso, and Kopcha made the all-pro team.

1936 The NFL held its first draft of college seniors. On the advice of West Virginians Karr and Brumbaugh, Halas took lineman Joe Stydahar from that school in the first round. He also picked halfback Ray Nolting in a later round. On the thirtieth round he chose guard Danny Fortmann. The Bears obtained the rights from Philadelphia for the NFL's very first draft pick, Jay Berwanger, but the University of Chicago star chose not to play professional football. Stydahar became an immediate starter; so did Fortmann, who took over when Kopcha retired to pursue medical studies. Nagurski came back strong from his injuries. Manders led the league in field goals for the third year. Bill Hewitt, who refused to wear a helmet when he played, was named all-pro for the third time. The Bears finished third with a 9–3–0 record.

1937 Two outstanding newcomers, tackle George Wilson, and former Eagles' end Edgar (Eggs) Manske made the squad. Stydahar, Musso, Fortmann, and

Frank Bausch were named to the all-pro team. The Bears coasted to the Western Division title. In the NFL championship before 15,870 people at Wrigley Field, the Bears lost 28–21 to the Washington Redskins as Sammy Baugh completed 17 of 34 passes for 347 yards in near zero weather. Each Chicago player received $127.78 as his share of the championship purse.

1938 Nagurski retired, Beattie Feathers was traded to Brooklyn, and Keith Molesworth quit to coach at the U.S. Naval Academy. At mid-year, Halas purchased fullback Joe Maniaci from the Brooklyn Dodgers. The Bears finished with their poorest record since 1929, 6–5–0.

1939 The Bears' T formation was growing more complex each year. New plays were drawn for it constantly by Halas and his assistants and voluntary assistant Clark Shaughnessy, head coach of the University of Chicago. The offense acquired a complicated play-calling system. It also put emphasis on a quarterback who was a good ball-handler. The Bears drafted tailback Sid Luckman of Columbia on the first round, intending to develop him into a T quarterback who could absorb the system and run the plays. They also drafted fullback Bill Osmanski of Holy Cross. Luckman spent his rookie season playing left halfback and Osmanski led the league in rushing with 699 yards. Chicago moved up to second in the Western Division with an 8–3 record.

1940 The Bears obtained Duke halfback George McAfee, who had been drafted by the Philadelphia Eagles in the first round, in exchange for three players. The Bears also drafted center Clyde (Bulldog) Turner from Hardin-Simmons; Lee Artoe, a tackle from California; Ed Kolman, a tackle from Temple, end Ken Kavanaugh from Louisiana State; and halfback Ray (Scooter) McLean from St. Anselms in New Hampshire. Bernie Masterson retired and Luckman became the starting quarterback. McAfee ran 93 yards for a touchdown against the Green Bay Packers on the first kickoff he fielded in league competition. The Bears won the Western Division title with an 8–3 record. They faced the Redskins in Washington, D.C., for the NFL championship, December 8. Ten different Bears scored touchdowns as Chicago smashed Washington 73–0. Chicago's defense intercepted eight passes and allowed only 22 yards rushing. The Bears got $873 per man as their championship share.

1941 The Bears drafted backs Norm Standlee and Hugh Gallarneau from Stanford's 1940 Rose Bowl team. They alternated with Osmanski and McAfee in a backfield that rushed for more than 1,500 yards. McAfee led the league in average yards per carry at 7.3. The Bears averaged over 36 points a game on their way to tying Green Bay for the Western Division title. Both teams had 10–1–0 records, and they met in a playoff at Wrigley Field, before 43,425, December 14. Gallarneau returned a punt 81 yards for a touchdown in the first quarter, and the Bears went on to win 33–14. A crowd of 13,341 showed up at Wrigley Field to watch the Bears play the Giants for the NFL championship, December 21. Standlee scored two touchdowns and McAfee and Kavanaugh one each as the Bears won 37–9.

1942 McAfee and Standlee went into the service. Halas was down to his fourth-string fullback, Gary Famiglietti. Stydahar was inducted into the army toward the end of the year. Halas himself joined the navy, December 13. He was replaced by assistants Hunk Anderson and Luke Johnsos. The Bears posted an 11–0–0 season record. They faced the Redskins in Washington for the NFL title. Artoe picked up a fumble and ran 50 yards for a Chicago score in the second period. But a touchdown pass by Baugh and some fine running by Andy Farkas gave Washington a 14–6 victory.

1943 Bronko Nagurski, 35, came out of retirement to play tackle for the Bears. Luckman became the first professional quarterback to pass for over 400 yards in a game as he threw for 433 yards and seven touchdowns in a 56–7 win over the New York Giants, November 14. The Bears had 702 yards in total offense against New York. Chicago won the division with an 8–1–1 record and hosted the championship game against the Washington Redskins before 34,320 in Wrigley Field. Luckman threw five touchdown passes, and Nagurski scored his last NFL touchdown as the Bears won 41–21.

1944 Chicago set up training facilities at St. Joseph's College in Rensselaer, Indiana. Luckman was called into the merchant marine service and was available to the team only on weekends. His understudy was 38-year-old Gene Ronzani. The Bears lost their first two games, to Green Bay and Cleveland, and never caught the Packers. They finished second with a 6–3–1 record.

1945 The war-depleted Bears lost seven of their first eight games. Halas came back from the navy, November 22. Kavanaugh, Stydahar, McAfee, and Gallarneau all came back before the season ended. McAfee returned for the next-to-the-last game of the season. He made Halas promise to use him sparingly. Halas put him in for only 12 minutes, and in that time McAfee scored three touchdowns. The Bears won their last two games and finished fourth with a 3–7–0 record.

1946 Prewar stars McAfee, Osmanski, Gallarneau, Luckman, Turner, and Wilson were back. The Bears had an 8–2–1 record and won the Western Division title. In the championship game in New York, the Bears defeated the New York Giants 24–14. Luckman ran a quarterback keeper 19 yards for a fourth-quarter touchdown that broke a 14–14 tie.

1947 Chicago lost its first two games, including one to the crosstown rival Cardinals 31–7. But they won eight of their next nine contests and went into a game against the Cardinals in the final week of the season tied with the Cardinals at 8–3. The Cardinals scored on the first play of the game and went on to win 30–21. Luckman, Ken Kavanaugh, and tackle Fred Davis were named to the all-pro team.

1948 The Bears drafted Texas quarterback Bobby Layne in the first round. Halas outbid the All-America Football Conference to sign Layne with a $22,500 contract, including a $10,000 bonus for signing. Other promising rookies also came high. Notre Dame quarterback Johnny Lujack signed for $18,000, and Notre Dame tackle George Connor got a no-cut contract. Connor became an immediate starter. Lujack started on defense. Layne was a reserve. The Bears ended with a 10–2–0 record, but lost the Western Division title to the Cardinals on the last day of the season when the Cardinals beat them 24–21.

1949 Just before the season started, Halas sold Layne to the New York Bulldogs. Luckman contracted a thyroid condition which kept him out most of the season, and Johnny Lujack became the starting quarterback. Lujack set an NFL passing record by throwing for 468 yards against the Cardinals, December 11. Lujack threw six touchdown passes in the 52–21 victory over the Cardinals. The Bears finished at 9–3, a half game behind the Rams, who were 8–2–2. Guard Ray Bray was named to the all-pro team.

1950 The All-America Football Conference folded, and the NFL absorbed three of its teams and restructured into two conferences, the National and the American. The Bears became one of seven teams in the National Conference. The Bears had a 9–3 record, tying the Rams for the National Conference lead. The two teams played off in the Los Angeles Coliseum with the Rams' Tom Fears catching three touchdown passes in Los Angeles's 24–14 victory over Chicago, December 17.

1951 Quarterback Sid Luckman, halfback George McAfee, and end Ken Kavanaugh all retired. Going into the final week of the season, the Lions led the Bears and Rams by a half game. When Detroit lost to San Francisco, the Bears had a chance to tie the Rams for the championship. But they were surprised by the Chicago Cardinals 24–14 while the Rams were routing Green Bay.

1952 The Bears drafted end-defensive back Jim Dooley from Georgia in the first round. In later rounds, they got end Bill McColl from Stanford and linebacker Bill George from Wake Forest. Johnny Lujack retired to assist Frank Leahy at Notre Dame. Three young quarterbacks competed for his job: George Blanda, Steve Romanik, and Bob Williams. The Bears dropped to fifth place at 5–7–0, the first time since 1945 that they fell below .500.

1953 Bulldog Turner, the last of the 1940-41 championship players, retired. In the tenth week of the season, the Bears beat Los Angeles 24–21, a victory that knocked the Rams out of title contention. Still, the Bears struggled to a 3–8–1 season.

1954 Chicago drafted quarterback Zeke Bratkowski from Georgia in the first round. In a low round, the Bears also got end Harlon Hill from Florence State Teachers College in Alabama. Halas traded for fullback Harry (Chick) Jagade, formerly of Cleveland. Bratkowski alternated with Blanda at quarterback, and between them they threw for over 3,000 yards. Hill gained over 1,000 yards on 45 receptions. Two rookies, Stan Jones and Larry Strickland, became starters in the offensive line. George Connor was lost for the year with an injury. The Bears won their last four games, ending the season with a 28–24 victory over the National Conference champion Lions. Chicago had an 8–4 record for the year.

1955 George Halas announced he would retire in favor of a younger coach after the 1955 season. Rookie running backs Rick Casares and Bobby Watkins became starters. Both averaged over five yards a carry. Zeke Bratkowski went into the service, and second-year quarterback Ed Brown took over the position. Harlon Hill caught 42 passes. The Bears lost their first three games, then they won six in a row before suffering a 53–14 upset by the Cardinals. The loss knocked the Bears (8–4–1) out of a title, as the Rams (8–3–1) finished a half game in front.

1956 True to his promise, Halas gave way to a younger man. Long-time assistant Paddy Driscoll, who was two years younger than Halas, became the new head coach. George Connor retired. The Bears lost their first game to Baltimore 28–21, then won or tied the next eight. In a rematch with the Colts, Chicago won 58–27. In the tenth game, the Bears lost 42–10 to Detroit. Going into the final game, again against Detroit, the Bears were 8–2–1, while the Lions were 9–2. Chicago won the rematch 38–21 and with it the National Conference title. Harlon Hill ended the year with 47 catches. Rick Casares rushed 234 times for 1,126 yards. Ed Brown completed 57 percent of his passes. The NFL championship game was played against the Giants on an icy field in Yankee Stadium. The Giants wore tennis shoes for improved traction, and won 47–7.

1957 Zeke Bratkowski returned from the service. The Bears drafted running back Willie Galimore. They lost to Green Bay, Baltimore, and San Francisco in their first three starts. The defense actually allowed fewer points than it had in the 1956 championship season, but the Bears finished at 5–7–0.

1958 George Halas returned as head coach. The Bears were in a title race most of the year. Eventual winner Baltimore beat them twice, and their only other losses were to Los Angeles and Pittsburgh. The Bears and Rams drew 90,833 to a game in the Los Angeles Coliseum. Chicago finished second, one game behind the Colts at 8–4.

1959 Chicago lost four of its first five games, then won seven in a row. On the last Sunday of the season, the Bears were tied with San Francisco for second place at 7–4. Baltimore was on top with an 8–3 record. San Francisco lost to Green Bay 36–14, and Chicago beat Detroit 25–14. But Baltimore outscored Los Angeles 45–26 to clinch the National Conference title.

1960 The Bears were one-half game out of first place in mid-November with a 5–3–1 record. But then they lost to the Packers 41–13, the Browns 42–0, and the Lions 36–0. They finished fifth with a 5–6–1 record. It was only the sixth time the Bears were under .500 since 1920.

1961 Fire destroyed the Bears' offices, and they moved to new ones at 173 West Madison Street. In the first round of the draft, Chicago picked Mike Ditka from Purdue. Halas obtained veteran quarterback Billy Wade from the Rams. The Bears dismantled the 49ers' "shotgun" offense 31–0, October 22. Chicago yielded only six first downs and 132 yards to the previously unstoppable offense. Green Bay jumped off to a 28–7 lead over the Bears, then held off a Chicago comeback for a 31–28 victory, November 12. The Bears ended the season tied for third place at 8–6. Ditka caught 56 passes for 1,076 yards on the season. Wade passed for 2,258 yards and 22 touchdowns.

1962 Injuries sidelined running backs Rick Casares and Willie Galimore. Rookie Ronnie Bull from Baylor won rookie of the year honors at halfback. Wade set two team records by passing for 3,172 yards and by completing 225 passes. Both marks were previously held by Sid Luckman. Ditka and fifth-year receiver Johnny Morris caught 58 passes each. Chicago had a 9–5 record, third best in the Western Conference behind Green Bay (13–1) and Detroit (11–3).

1963 Assistant coach George Allen installed a zone defense, and suddenly the Bears had the strongest defense in the NFL. Chicago won its first five games before losing to San Francisco. The Bears defeated Green Bay twice, 10–3 and 26–7. Chicago won the Western Conference with an 11–1–2 record, one-half game ahead of the Packers, 11–2–1. The Bears' defense allowed an average of only 10.1 points a game. Ditka caught 59 passes, Morris 47. The NFL championship game was played in eight-degree weather before 45,801 at Wrigley Field against the New York Giants, December 29. Chicago intercepted five Y. A. Tittle passes, Wade scored two touchdowns, and the Bears won 14–10. The winning share was $5,899 a player. It was Chicago's first NFL championship since 1946.

1964 Running backs Willie Galimore and Bo Farrington were killed in an automobile accident during training camp. Injuries handicapped the Bears' defense, and one of the early season embarrassments was a 52–0 loss to Baltimore. Ends Doug Atkins and Ed O'Bradovich missed most of the season with injuries. Linebacker Bill George played the early season with a hamstring injury and missed the last six games with a bad knee. Halas switched from Wade to Rudy Bukich at quarterback. Johnny Morris set a league record by catching 93 passes for 1,200 yards. Ditka added 75 for 897 yards. Chicago finished sixth with a 5–9 record.

1965 Linebacker Dick Butkus from Illinois and running back Gale Sayers from Kansas both were drafted on the first round. Sayers scored six touchdowns against the 49ers in a 61–20 Chicago win that avenged an earlier 52–24 loss to San Francisco. The Bears finished third in the Western Conference with a 9–5 record. Sayers set an NFL record by scoring 22 touchdowns. He and Butkus both were all-pro after their first seasons.

1966 Assistant coach George Allen resigned to become head coach of the Rams. Johnny Morris was out for most of the year with an injured knee and caught only five passes. Gale Sayers had another record-setting year, gaining a combined 2,440 yards. He led the NFL in rushing with 1,231 yards, caught 34 passes, and led the league in kickoff returns. Chicago finished fifth with a 5-7-2 record.

1967 The NFL expanded to 16 teams. The Eastern and Western Conferences were subdivided into two four-team divisions each. Chicago was put into the Central Division of the Western Conference, with Detroit, Green Bay, and Minnesota. Halas traded Ditka to Philadelphia for quarterback Jack Concannon. After a slow start, the Bears finished with a 5-1-1 record in their last seven games, to place second behind the Packers at 7-6-1. Sayers had over 1,600 combined yards.

1968 George Halas, 73, retired as head coach of the Bears, May 27. After 40 seasons of pro coaching his record was 320 wins, 147 defeats, and 30 ties. Jim Dooley, a player or coach with the Bears since 1952, was named head coach, May 28. The Bears lost their first two games before beating the Vikings. In the Minnesota game, Concannon fractured a collarbone, and his backup, Rudy Bukich, separated a shoulder. Virgil Carter, third-string quarterback, led the Bears to four straight wins at midyear. The last game of that four was against San Francisco. In it, 49ers defensive back Kermit Alexander tackled Sayers low, and the impact tore ligaments and cartilage in Sayers's right knee, putting him out for the year. Carter broke his ankle a week later, against Atlanta. The Bears lost three of their last five games and finished second behind the Vikings at 7-7.

1969 Gale Sayers came back from knee surgery to lead the league in rushing with 1,032 yards. Concannon, Carter, and rookie Bobby Douglass alternated at quarterback. The defense allowed an average of 24.2 points a game. Chicago dropped into last place with a 1-13 record, their poorest in 50 years of play in the NFL.

1970 George Halas, 75, was elected president of the National Football Conference, March 19. Halfback Brian Piccolo, 26, died of cancer, June 16. Gale Sayers hurt his right knee in preseason. Bobby Douglass was made the starting quarterback in late season. In his first start, he threw four touchdown passes as the Bears beat Buffalo. But late in that game Douglass broke his wrist, sidelining him for the year. Sayers had to undergo knee surgery again in October. Rookie Cecil Turner returned four kickoffs for touchdowns tying the single-season NFL record. The Bears whipped Green Bay 35-17 in their last game in Wrigley Field, December 13. They finished third with a 6-8-0 record.

1971 The Bears moved into Soldier Field. Chicago won five out of its first seven games. Then both the first- and second-string quarterbacks, Kent Nix and Jack Concannon, got hurt. Bobby Douglass took over, but the Bears lost six of the last seven games. Gale Sayers's bad knee kept him immobilized most of the year; he carried the ball only 13 times for 38 yards. Butkus was a unanimous all-pro. Jim Dooley, whose four-year record was 20-36, was dismissed as coach.

1972 Abe Gibron, former Bears player and assistant coach since 1965, was named head coach, January 27. Gale Sayers retired before the season began. Bobby Douglass was given the starting quarterback spot again. Douglass completed only 38 percent of his passes, last in the NFL in that category, but he gained a quarterback rushing record of 968 yards. The Bears led the NFC in rushing yardage. Chicago played .500 football the first half of the season, then dropped six of its last seven games to finish last in the NFC Central with a 4-9-1 record.

1973 The Bears drafted tackle Wally Chambers from Eastern Kentucky on the first round. Gibron kept Bobby Douglass at quarterback until midseason;

rookie Gary Huff from Florida State was given the job, November 18. Huff threw four interceptions in his debut as the Lions beat the Bears 30-7. The Bears finished last again in the NFC Central at 3-11-0.

1974 The Bears drafted linebacker Waymond Bryant from Tennessee State in the first round. Chicago named a non-Bear, Jim Finks, to run their operation. Finks was named executive vice president, general manager, and chief operating officer. The Bears finished last for the third year in a row with a 4-10 record. After the last game, Abe Gibron, who compiled a three-year record of 11-30-1, was fired, December 17. Jack Pardee, former NFL linebacker, was named head coach December 31.

1975 Chicago took Walter Payton, a running back from Jackson State, on the first round of the draft. The Bears opened their new training facility at Lake Forest Academy in Lake Forest, Illinois, May 1. A 26-yard field goal by Bob Thomas gave Pardee his first NFL coaching win, 15-13 over Philadelphia, September 28. Bob Avellini, a rookie from Maryland, became the starting quarterback. Walter Payton gained a combined total of 300 yards in a 42-17 victory over the Saints, December 21. For the season, the Bears defense allowed 379 points, most in the NFC. Chicago waived, traded, or released 76 players under contract to them in 1975. Chicago ended the season with a 4-10 record, its seventh consecutive losing year.

1976 The Bears moved their executive offices to 55 East Jackson Street. Walter Payton rushed for 148 yards in Chicago's 19-12 surprise of San Francisco, September 19. Chicago upset eventual NFL champion Minnesota 14-13, October 31. Payton became the NFL's first rusher of the year to go over 1,000 yards, November 14. His 109 yards in 18 carries in a 24-13 victory over Green Bay gave him 1,008 yards, along with 12 touchdowns. Payton set a Bears' rushing record and led the NFC with 1,390 yards, finishing second only to O.J. Simpson's 1,503 yards in the NFL. The Bears had a 7-7 record, their best since 1968 and good for a second-place finish behind Minnesota.

MEMBERS OF HALL OF FAME:
Guy Chamberlin, George Connor, John (Paddy) Driscoll, Danny Fortmann, Bill George, Red Grange, George Halas, Ed Healey, Bill Hewitt, Walt Kiesling, Bobby Layne, Sid Luckman, Roy (Link) Lyman, George McAfee, Bronko Nagurski, Gale Sayers, Joe Stydahar, George Trafton, Clyde (Bulldog) Turner

BEARS RECORD, 1920-76

Year	Won	Lost	Tied	Pct.	Pts.	OP
Decatur Staleys						
1920	10	1	1	.909		
Chicago Staleys						
1921‡	10	1	1	.909		
Chicago Bears						
1922	9	3	0	.750		
1923	9	2	1	.818		
1924	6	1	4	.857		
1925	9	5	3	.643		
1926	12	1	3	.923		
1927	9	3	2	.750		
1928	7	5	1	.583		
1929	4	8	2	.333		
1930	9	4	1	.692		
1931	8	4	0	.667		
1932‡	7	1	6	.875		
1933‡	10	2	1	.833	133	82
1934§	13	0	0	1.000	286	86
1935	6	4	2	.600	192	106
1936	9	3	0	.750	222	94
1937§	9	1	1	.900	201	100
1938	6	5	0	.545	194	148
1939	8	3	0	.727	298	157
1940‡	8	3	0	.727	238	152
1941‡	10	1	0	.909	396	147
1942§	11	0	0	1.000	376	84
1943‡	8	1	1	.889	303	157
1944	6	3	1	.667	258	172
1945	3	7	0	.300	192	235
1946‡	8	2	1	.800	289	193
1947	8	4	0	.667	363	241
1948	10	2	0	.833	375	151
1949	9	3	0	.750	332	218
1950	9	3	0	.750	279	207
1951	7	5	0	.583	286	282
1952	5	7	0	.417	245	326

Year	Won	Lost	Tied	Pct.	Pts.	OP
1953	3	8	1	.273	218	262
1954	8	4	0	.667	301	279
1955	8	4	0	.667	294	251
1956†	9	2	1	.818	363	246
1957	5	7	0	.417	203	211
1958	8	4	0	.667	298	230
1959	8	4	0	.667	252	196
1960	5	6	1	.455	194	299
1961	8	6	0	.571	326	302
1962	9	5	0	.643	321	287
1963‡	11	1	2	.917	301	144
1964	5	9	0	.357	260	379
1965	9	5	0	.643	409	275
1966	5	7	2	.417	234	272
1967	7	6	1	.538	239	218
1968	7	7	0	.500	250	333
1969	1	13	0	.071	210	339
1970	6	8	0	.429	256	261
1971	6	8	0	.429	274	298
1972	4	9	1	.321	225	275
1973	3	11	0	.214	195	334
1974	4	10	0	.286	152	279
1975	4	10	0	.286	191	379
1976	7	7	0	.500	253	216
57 Years	**422**	**259**	**41**	**.613**		

‡*NFL Champion*
§*NFL Western Division Champion*
†*NFL Western Conference Champion*

RECORD HOLDERS

Rushing (Yards)	Walter Payton, 1976	1,390
Passing (Pct.)	Rudy Bukich, 1964	61.9
Passing (Yards)	Bill Wade, 1962	3,172
Passing (TDs)	Sid Luckman, 1943	28
Receiving (No.)	Johnny Morris, 1964	93
Receiving (Yards)	Johnny Morris, 1964	1,200
Interceptions (No.)	Roosevelt Taylor, 1963	9
Punting (Avg.)	George Gulyanics, 1949	47.2
Punt Ret. (Avg.)	Gale Sayers, 1966	14.9
Kickoff Ret. (Avg.)	Gale Sayers, 1967	37.7
Touchdowns (Total)	Gale Sayers, 1965	22
Field Goals Made	Mac Percival, 1968	25
Points (No.)	Gale Sayers, 1965	132

COACHING HISTORY

1920-29	George Halas	85-30-18
1930-32	Ralph Jones	24- 9- 7
1933-42	George Halas*	85-22- 4
1942-45	Hunk Anderson, Luke Johnsos**	22-11- 2
1946-55	George Halas	75-42- 2
1956-57	John (Paddy) Driscoll	14- 9- 1
1958-67	George Halas	75-53- 6
1968-71	Jim Dooley	20-36- 0
1972-74	Abe Gibron	11-30- 1
1975-76	Jack Pardee	11-17- 0

*Resigned after six games in 1942 to enter U.S. Navy
**Co-coaches

FIRST PLAYER SELECTED

1936	Joe Stydahar, T, West Virginia
1937	Les McDonald, E, Nebraska
1938	Joe Gray, B, Oregon State
1939	Bill Osmanski, B, Holy Cross
1940	Clyde (Bulldog) Turner, C, Hardin-Simmons
1941	Tom Harmon, B, Michigan
1942	Frankie Albert, B, Stanford
1943	Bob Steuber, B, Missouri
1944	Ray Evans, B, Kansas
1945	Don Lund, B, Michigan
1946	Johnny Lujack, B, Notre Dame
1947	Bob Fenimore, B, Oklahoma A&M
1948	Bobby Layne, B, Texas
1949	Dick Harris, C, Texas
1950	Chuck Hunsinger, B, Florida
1951	Billy Stone, B, Bradley
1952	Jim Dooley, B, Miami
1953	Billy Anderson, B, Compton (Calif.) JC
1954	Stan Wallace, B, Illinois
1955	Ron Drzewiecki, B, Marquette
1956	Menan (Tex) Schriewer, E, Texas
1957	Earl Leggett, T, Louisiana State
1958	Chuck Howley, G, West Virginia
1959	Don Clark, B, Ohio State
1960	Roger Davis, G, Syracuse
1961	Mike Ditka, E, Pittsburgh
1962	Ron Bull, RB, Baylor
1963	Dave Behrman, C, Michigan State
1964	Dick Evey, DT, Tennessee
1965	Dick Butkus, LB, Illinois
1966	George Rice, DT, Louisiana State
1967	Loyd Phillips, DE, Arkansas
1968	Mike Hull, RB, USC
1969	Rufus Mayes, T, Ohio State
1970	George Farmer, WR (3), UCLA
1971	Joe Moore, RB, Missouri
1972	Lionel Antoine, T, Southern Illinois
1973	Wally Chambers, DE, Eastern Kentucky
1974	Waymond Bryant, LB, Tennessee State
1975	Walter Payton, RB, Jackson State
1976	Dennis Lick, T, Wisconsin

H. (Hunk) Anderson　　*Doug Atkins*　　*Ray Bray*　　*Ed Brown*　　*Doug Buffone*　　*Ron Bull*　　*Jim Cadile*

DECATUR STALEYS, 1920; CHICAGO STALEYS, 1921; CHICAGO BEARS, 1922–76

Abbey, Joe, E, N. Texas State 1948–49
Adamle, Mike, RB, Northwestern 1975–76
Adams, John, B, Cal. State-L.A. 1959–62
Adkins, Roy, G, Millikin 1920–21
Akin, Len, G, Baylor 1942
Allen, Duane, TE, Santa Ana 1966–67
Allen, Ed, B, Pennsylvania 1947
Allman, Bob, E, Michigan State 1936
Amsler, Marty, DE, Evansville 1967
Andersen, Art, T, Idaho 1961–62
Anderson, Bill, B, Compton J.C. 1953–54
Anderson, Ed, E, Notre Dame 1923
Anderson, Henry, G, Northwestern 1931
Anderson, Hunk, G, Notre Dame 1922–25
Anderson, Ralph, E, Cal. State-L.A. 1958
Anderson, William, HB, Compton J.C. 1953
Antoine, Lionel, T, Southern Illinois 1972–76
Apolskis, Chuck, E, DePaul 1938–39
Arnett, Jon, RB, USC 1964–66
Artoe, Lee, T, California 1940–42, 1945
Ashburn, Cliff, T, Nebraska 1930
Asher, Bob, T, Vanderbilt 1972–75
Ashmore, Marion T, Gonzaga 1927
Aspatore, Ed. T, Marquette 1934
Atkins, Doug, DE, Tennesse 1955–66
Autrey, Bill, C, Stephen F. Austin 1953
Avellini, Bob, QB, Maryland 1975–76
Aveni, John, E, Indiana 1959–60

B

Babartsky, Al, T, Fordham 1943–45
Babinecz, John, LB, Villanova 1975
Badaczewski, John, G, Western Reserve 1953
Baisi, Al, G, West Virginia 1940–41, 1946
Barker, Dick, G, Iowa State 1921
Barnes, Erich, DB, Purdue 1958–60
Barnes, Gary, WR, Clemson 1964
Barnes, Joe, QB, Texas Tech 1974
Barnett, Steve, T, Oregon 1963
Barwegan, Dick, G, Purdue 1950–52
Baschnagel, Brian, S, Ohio State 1976
Bassi, Dick, G, Santa Clara 1938–39
Battles, Bill, E, Brown 1939
Bauman, Alf, T, Northwestern 1948–50
Bausch, Frank, C, Kansas 1937–40
Baynham, Craig, RB, Georgia Tech 1970
Becker, Wayland, E, Marquette 1934
Bell, Kay, T, Washington State 1937
Benton, Jim, E, Arkansas 1943
Bergerson, Gil, G, Oregon State 1932–33
Berry, Connie Mack, E, N. Carolina State .. 1942–46
Berry, Royce, DE, Houston 1976
Bettis, Tom, G, Purdue 1963
Bettridge, John B, Ohio State 1937
Bingham, Don, B, Sul Ross State 1956
Bishop, Bill, T, N. Texas State 1952–60
Bishop, Don, E, Cal. State-L.A. 1959
Bivins, Charley, RB, Morris Brown 1960–66
Bjork, Del, T, Oregon 1937–38
Blackburn, J.A., T, None 1923
Blacklock, Hugh T, Michigan State 1922–25
Blackman, Lennon, B, Tulsa 1930
Blanda, George, QB, Kentucky 1949–58
Bolan, George, B, Purdue 1921–24
Bonderant, J. Bourbon, G, Depauw 1922
Boone, J.R., B, Tulsa 1948–51
Brackett, Martin, T, Auburn 1956–57
Bradley, Ed. G. Wake Forest 1950, 1952
Braidwood, Charles, E, Chattanooga 1932
Bramhall, Art, B, Purdue 1931
Bratkowski, Zeke, QB, Georgia 1954, 57–60
Bray, Ray, G, West. Michigan 1939–42, 1946–51
Brink, Larry, E, No. Illinois 1954
Britton, Earl, B, Illinois 1925
Brockman, Ed, B, Oklahoma 1930
Brown, Bill, RB, Illinois 1961
Brown, Charley, DB, Syracuse 1966–67
Brown, Ed, QB, San Francisco 1954–61
Bruer, Bob, TE, Mankato State 1976
Brumbaugh, Carl, QB, Florida ... 1930–34, 1936, 1938

Brupbacher, Ross, LB, Texas A&M 1970, 1972
Bryan, Johnny, B, Chicago 1923–26
Bryant, Waymond, LB, Tennessee State 1974–76
Buck, Art, HB, Carroll 1941
Buckler, Bill, G, Alabama 1926–28, 1931–33
Buivid, Ray, B, Marquette 1937–38
Bukich, Rudy, QB, USC 1953–59, 1962–68
Bull, Ronnie, RB, Baylor 1962–70
Burdick, Lloyd, T, Illinois 1931–32
Burgeis, Glen, T, Tulsa 1945
Burks, Randy, WR, S.E. Oklahoma St. 1976
Burman, George, T, Northwestern 1964
Burnell, Max, B, Notre Dame 1944
Buss, Art, T, Michigan 1934
Bussey, Young, B, Louisiana State 1940–41
Butkus, Dick, LB, Illinois 1965–73
Butler, Gary, TE, Rice 1975
Buzin, Rich, T, Penn State 1972

C

Cadile, Jim T, San Jose State 1962–72
Caffey, Lee Roy, LB, Texas A&M 1970
Calland, Lee, CB, Louisville 1969
Campana, Al, B, Youngstown 1950–53
Campbell, Leon, B, Arkansas 1952–54
Canady, Jim B, Texas 1948
Carey, Bob, E, Michigan State 1958
Carl, Harland, B, Wisconsin 1956
Carlson, Jules, G, Oregon State 1929–36
Carlson, Roy, E, Bradley 1928
Caroline, J.C., RB, Illinois 1956–65

Carter, Virgil, QB, Brigham Young 1968–69, 1976
Casares, Rick, RB, Florida 1955–64
Casey, Tom, LB, Oregon 1969
Castete, Jesse, RB, McNeese State 1956
Chamberlain, Guy, E, Nebraska 1920–21
Chambers, Wally, DE, Eastern Kentucky 1973–76
Chesney, Chet, C, DePaul 1939–40
Childs, Clarence, DB, Florida A&M 1958
Cifers, Ed, E, Tennessee 1947–48
Clark, Bill, G 1920
Clark, Gail, LB, Michigan State 1973
Clark, Harry, B, West Virginia 1940–43
Clark, Herman, G, Oregon State ... 1952, 1954–57
Clark, Phil, S, Northwestern 1970
Clarkson, Stu, G, Texas A&I 1942, 1946–51
Clemons, Craig, CB, Iowa 1972–76
Coady, Rich, C, Memphis State 1970–74
Cody, Ed, B, Purdue 1949–50
Coia, Angelo, WR, USC 1960–63
Cole, Emerson, B, Toledo 1952
Cole, Linzy, WR, TCU 1970
Concannon, Jack, QB, Boston College 1967–71
Conkright, Red, C, Oklahoma 1937–38
Connor, George, T, Notre Dame 1948–55
Conzelman, Jim, B, Washington 1920
Cooke, Ed, E, Maryland 1958
Copeland, Ron, WR, UCLA 1969
Corbett, George, B, Millikin 1932–38
Cornish, Frank, DT, Grambling 1966–70
Corzine, Les, B, Davis & Elkins 1938
Cotton, Craig, TE, Youngstown 1973
Cowan, Les, T, McMurry 1951

Tight end Mike Ditka making a catch against the Green Bay Packers, 1964.

     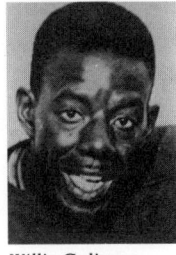 

J.C. Caroline　　*Rick Casares*　　*Wally Chambers*　　*Fred Davis*　　*Joe Fortunato*　　*Willie Galimore*　　*Hugh Gallarneau*

Abe Gibron

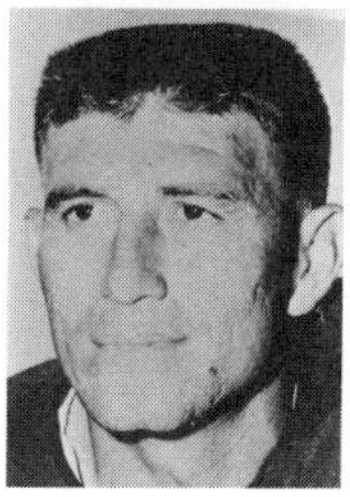
Harlon Hill

Luke Johnsos

Stan Jones

Bill McColl

Johnny Morris

Larry Morris

Klein, Dick, T, Iowa 1958–59
Knop, Oscar, B, Illinois 1923–28
Knox, Bill, DB, Purdue 1974–76
Knox, Ronnie, QB, UCLA 1957
Koehler, Bob, B, Northwestern 1920
Kolman, Ed, T, Temple 1940–42, 1946–47
Konovsky, Bob, G, Wisconsin 1960
Kopcha, Joe, G, Chattanooga 1929, 1932–35
Kortas, Ken, T, Louisville 1969
Kosins, Gary, RB, Dayton 1972–74
Kreamcheck, John, T, William & Mary 1953–55
Kreitling, Rich, E, Illinois 1964
Kreiwald, Doug, G, W. Texas State 1967–68
Kuechenberg, Rudy, LB, Indiana 1967–69
Kurek, Ralph, RB, Wisconsin 1967–70

L

LaFleur, Joe, B, Marquette 1922–24
LaForest, Bill, B 1920
Lahar, Hal, G, Oklahoma 1941
Lamb, Walt, E, Oklahoma 1946
Lanum, R. (Jake), B, Illinois 1920–24
Larson, Fred, C, Notre Dame 1922
Latta, Greg, TE, Morgan State 1975–76
Lawler, Al, B, Texas 1948
Lawson, Roger, RB, Western Michigan 1972–73
Layne, Bobby, QB, Texas 1948
Leahy, Bernie, B, Notre Dame 1932
Leclerc, Roger, C, Trinity, Conn. 1960–66
Lee, Herman, T, Florida A&M 1958–66
Leeuwehburg, Rich, T, Stanford 1965
Leggett, Earl, T, Louisiana State 1957–60, 1962–65
Lemon, Cliff, T, Centre 1926
Leonard, Jim T, Colgate 1924
Lesane, Jim, B, Virginia 1952, 1954
Lick, Dennis, T, Wisconsin 1976
Line, Bill, DT, Southern Methodist 1972
Lintzenich, Joe, B, St. Louis 1930–31
Lipscomb, Paul, T, Tennessee 1954
Livers, Virgil, CB, Western Kentucky 1975–76
Livingston, Andy, B, Phoenix J.C. 1964–65, 1967–68
Logan, Jim, G, Indiana 1943
Long, Harvey, T, Detroit 1929
Long, Johnny, QB, Colgate 1944–45
Lowe, Lloyd, B, N. Texas State 1953–54
Luckman, Sid, QB, Columbia 1939–50
Lujack, Johnny, QB, Notre Dame 1948–51
Lyle, Garry, RB, George Washington 1968–74
Lyman, Roy (Link), T, Nebraska 1933–34
Lyon, George, T, Kansas State 1929

M

MacLeod, Bob, B, Dartmouth 1939
MacWherter, Kyle, B, Bethany 1920
Macon, Ed, B, Pacific 1952–53
Magnani, Dante, B, St. Mary's, Calif. 1943, 1946, 1949
Maillard, Ralph, T, Creighton 1929
Malone, Charles, E, Texas A&M 1933
Manders, Jack, B, Minnesota 1933–40
Maniaci, Joe, B, Fordham 1938–41
Manning, Pete, E, Wake Forest 1960–61
Manske, Edgar (Eggs), E, Northwestern 1937–40
Marconi, Joe, RB, West Virginia 1962–66
Margarita, Bob, B, Brown 1944–46
Martin, Bill, RB, Minnesota 1962–64
Martin, Billy, TE, Georgia Tech 1964
Martin, Dave, LB, Notre Dame 1969
Martin, Frank, B, Alabama 1941
Martinovich, Phil, G, Pacific 1940
Maslowski, Matt, WR, San Diego 1972
Mass, Wayne, T, Clemson 1938–70
Masters, Bob, B, Baylor 1943–44
Masterson, Bernie, QB, Nebraska 1934–40
Masterson, Forest, C, Iowa 1945
Mastrogany, Gus, E, Iowa 1931
Matheson, Jack, E, Western Michigan 1947
Mattson, Riley, T, Oregon 1965
Matuza, Al, C, Georgetown 1941
May, Chester, G 1920
May, Walter, G 1920
Mayes, Rufus, T, Ohio State 1969
Maznicki, Frank, B, Boston College 1942–46
McAfee, George, B, Duke 1940–41, 1945–50
McColl, Bill, E, Stanford 1952–59
McDonald, Les, E, Nebraska 1937–39
McElwain, Bill, B, Northwestern 1925
McEnulty, Doug, B, Wichita 1943–44
McGee, Tony, DE, Bishop, Tex 1971
McKinney, Bill, LB, W. Texas State 1972
McLean, Ray, B, St. Anselms 1940–47
McMillen, Jim, G, Illinois 1924–28
McMullen, Dan, G, Nebraska 1930–31
McPherson, Forrest, G, Nebraska 1935
McRae, Bennie, DB, Michigan 1962–70
McRae, Franklin, DT, Tennessee State 1967
Meadows, Ed, E, Duke 1954, 1956–57
Mellekas, John, T, Arizona 1956, 1958–61
Merkel, Monte, G, Kansas 1943
Meyers, Jerry, DT, Northern Illinois 1976
Michaels, Ed, G, Villanova 1935
Mihal, Joe, T, Purdue 1940–41
Miller, Charles, C, Purdue 1932–36
Miller, Milford, T, Chadron State 1935
Milner, Bill, G, Duke 1947–49
Minini, Frank, B, San Jose State 1947–48
Mintun, John, C 1920–24
Mitchell, Charley, B, Tulsa 1945
Mohardt, John, B, Notre Dame 1925
Molesworth, Keith, B, Monmouth 1931
Montgomery, Randy, CB, Weber State 1974
Montgomery, Ross, RB, Texas Christian 1969–70
Mooney, Jim, E, Georgetown 1935
Mooney, Bow Tipp, B, Abilene Christian 1944–45
Moore, Allen, B, Northwestern 1932
Moore, Jerry, S, Arkansas 1971–27
Moore, Joe, RB, Missouri 1971
Moore, McNeil, B, Sam Houston 1954, 1956–57
Morris, Frank, B, Boston U 1942
Morris, Johnny, WR, California-Santa Barbara 1958–66
Morris, Larry, LB, Georgia Tech 1959–65
Morrison, Fred, B, Ohio State 1950–53
Morton, John, E, Purdue 1945
Moser, Bob, C, Pacific 1951–53
Mosley, Henry, RB, Morris Brown 1955
Mucha, Charles, G, Washington 1935
Mucha, Rudy, G, Washington 1945–46
Muckensturm, Jerry, LB, Arkansas State 1976
Mudd, Howard, G, Hillsdale 1969–70
Mullen, Verne, E, Illinois 1924–26
Mullins, Don, RB, Houston 1961–62
Mullins, Noah, B, Kentucky 1946–48
Mundee, Fred, C, Notre Dame 1943–45
Murray, Dick, T, Marquette 1924
Murry, Don T, Wisconsin 1925–32
Musso, George, G, Millikin 1933–44
Musso, Johnny, RB, Alabama 1975–76
Myers, Denny, T, Iowa 1931

N

Nagurski, Bronko, B, Minnesota 1930–37, 1943
Neacy, Clem, E, Colgate 1927
Neal, Dan, C, Kentucky 1975–76
Neal, Ed, G, Louisiana State 1951
Neck, Tommy, RB, Louisiana State 1962
Negus, Fred, C, Wisconsin 1950
Neidert, John, LB, Louisville 1970
Nelson, Ev, T, Illinois 1929
Nesbitt, Dick, B, Drake 1930–33
Newton, Bob, G, Nebraska 1971–72
Nickle, Ed, G, Maryland 1959
Nix, Kent, QB, Texas Christian 1970–71
Nolting, Ray, B, Cincinnati 1936–43
Norberg, Hank, E, Stanford 1948
Nordquist, Mark, G-C, Pacific 1975–76
Nori, Reino, B, Dekalb 1938
Norman, Dick, QB, Stanford 1961
Nowaskey, Bob, E, George Washington 1940–42

O

O'Bradovich, Ed, DE, Illinois 1962–71
O'Connell, Harry, C, Penn State 1924
O'Connell, Tom, QB, Illinois 1953
Oech, Verne, G, Minnesota 1936
Oelerich, John, B, St. Ambrose 1938
Ogden, Ray, TE, Alabama 1969–71
O'Quinn, John, E, Wake Forest 1950–51
O'Rourke, Charles, QB, Boston College 1942
Osborne, James, DT, Southern U. 1972–76
Osmanski, Bill, B, Holy Cross 1939–43, 1946–47
Osmanski, Joe, B, Holy Cross 1946–49

P

Pagac, Fred, TE, Ohio State 1975
Parsons, Bob, TE, Penn State 1972–76
Patterson, Bill, B, Baylor 1939
Pauley, Frank, T, Washington & Jefferson 1930
Payton, Walter, RB, Jackson State 1975–76
Pearce, Walter, B, Pennsylvania 1920–22
Pearson, Madison, C, Kansas 1929–34
Pederson, Jim, B, Augsburgh 1932
Peiffer, Dan, C, Southeast Missouri St. 1975–76
Percival, Mac, K, Texas Tech 1967–73
Perez, Pete, G, Illinois 1945
Perina, Bob, B, Princeton 1949
Perini, Pete, B, Ohio State 1954–55
Perkins, Don, B, Plattesville State 1945–46
Petitbon, Richie, S, Tulane 1959–68
Petty, John, B, Purdue 1942
Petty, Ross, G, Illinois 1920
Phillips, Loyd, DE, Arkansas 1967–69
Piccolo, Brian, RB, Wake Forest 1966–69
Pickens, Bob, T, Nebraska 1967–69
Pifferini, Bob, LB, UCLA 1972–75
Pinder, Cyril, RB, Illinois 1971–72
Plank, Doug, S, Ohio State 1975–76
Plasman, Dick, E, Vanderbilt 1937–41, 1944
Podmajersky, Paul, G, Illinois 1944
Polisky, John, G, Notre Dame 1929
Pollock, Bill, B, Penn. Military 1935
Pool, Hamp, E, Stanford 1940–43
Preston, Pat, G, Wake Forest 1946–49
Pride, Dan, LB, Jackson State 1968–69
Proctor, Rex, B, Rice 1953
Purnell, Jim, LB, Wisconsin 1964, 1966–68
Pyle, Mike, C, Yale 1961–69

R

Rabold, Mike, G, Indiana 1964–67
Rakestraw, Larry, QB, Georgia 1964, 1966–68
Ramsey, Frank, G, Oregon State 1945
Rather, Bo, WR, Michigan 1974–76
Reader, Russ, B, Michigan State 1947
Reese, Lloyd, B, Tennessee 1946
Reid, Floyd, B, Georgia 1950
Reilly, Mike, LB, Iowa 1964–68
Rentner, Pug, B, Northwestern 1937
Reppond, Mike, WR, Arkansas 1973
Rice, Andy, DT, Texas Southern 1972–73
Richards, Ray, T, Nebraska 1933, 1935
Richman, Harry, G, Illinois 1929
Rives, Don, LB, Texas Tech 1973–76
Roberts, Tom, G, DePaul 1944–45
Roberts, Willie, CB, Houston 1973
Roder, Mirro, K, None 1973–74
Roehnelt, Bill, LB, Bradley 1958–59
Roggeman, Tom, G, Purdue 1956–57
Romanik, Steve, QB, Villanova 1950–53
Romney, Milt, B, Chicago 1924–28
Ronzani, Gene, B, Marquette 1933–38
Rosequist, Ted, T, Ohio State 1934–36
Rowden, Larry, LB, Houston 1971
Rowland, Brad, B, McMurry 1951
Rowland, Justin, RB, Texas Christian 1960
Rupp, Nelson, B, Denison 1921
Russell, Reg, E, Northwestern 1928
Ryan, John, T, Detroit 1929
Ryan, Rocky, E, Illinois 1958
Rydalch, Ron, DT, Utah 1975–76
Rydzewski, Frank, C, Notre Dame 1923
Rykovich, Julie, B, Illinois 1949–51

S

Sacrinty, Nick, QB, Wake Forest 1947
Sanderson, Reggie, RB, Stanford 1973
Savoldi, Joe, B, Notre Dame 1930
Sayers, Gale, RB, Kansas 1965–71
Schiechl, John, C, Santa Clara 1945–46
Schmidt, Terry, CB, Ball State 1976
Schreiber, Larry, RB, Tennessee Tech 1976

Ed O'Bradovich

Bill Osmanski

Walter Payton

Brian Piccolo

Joe Sternaman

Billy Wade

George Wilson

Schroeder, Gene, E, Virginia 1951–52, 1954–57
Schubert, Steve, WR, Massachusetts 1975–76
Schuette, Paul, G, Wisconsin 1930–32
Schweda, Brian, DE, Kansas 1966
Schweidler, Dick, B, St. Louis 1938–39, 1946
Scott, James, WR, Henderson J.C. 1976
Scott, Ralph, T, Wisconsin 1921–25
Seals, George, G, Missouri 1965–71
Seiberling, Gerald, B, Drake 1932
Senn, Bill, B, Knox College 1926–31
Serini, Wash, G, Kentucky 1958–51
Sevy, Jeff, T, California 1975–76
Seymour, Jim, WR, Notre Dame 1970–72
Shank, Henry, B 1920
Shanklin, Ron, WR, North Texas State 1975–76
Shann, RB, Kentucky 1960
Shellog, Alec, T, Notre Dame 1939
Sherman, Saul, QB, Chicago 1939–40
Shipkey, Jerry, B, UCLA 1953
Shoemake, Hub, G, Illinois 1920
Shy, Don, RB, San Diego State 1970–72
Siegal, John, E, Columbia 1939–43
Sigillo, Dom, T, Xavier, Ohio 1943–44
Sigmund, Art, G 1923
Simmons, Jerry, WR, Bethune-Cookman 1969
Sisk, John, HB, Marquette 1932–36
Sisk, John, RB, Miami 1964
Smeja, Rudy, E, Michigan 1944–45
Smith, Clarence, E, Georgia 1942

Smith, Eugene, G, Georgia Tech 1930
Smith, H. Allen, E, Mississippi 1947–48
Smith, J.D., RB, North Carolina A&T 1956
Smith, Jim, B, Compton J.C. 1961
Smith, Ray Gene, B, Midwestern 1954–57
Smith, Ron, DB, Wisconsin 1965, 1970–72
Smith, Russ, T, Illinois 1921–22, 1925
Snyder, Bob, QB, Ohio U. 1939–43, 1945
Sorey, Rivie, G, Illinois 1975–76
Sprinkle, Ed, DE, Hardin-Simmons 1944–55
Stahlman, Dick, T, DePaul 1933
Standlee, Norm, B, Stanford 1941
Stautberg, Gerry, G, Cincinnati 1951
Staley, Bill, DT, Utah State 1970–71
Steinbach, Larry, G, St. Thomas 1930–31
Steinkemper, Bill T, Notre Dame 1943
Stenn, Paul, G, Villanova 1948–51
Sternaman, Ed, B, Illinois 1920–27
Sternaman, Joe, B, Illinois 1922–25, 1927–30
Steuber, Bob, B, Missouri 1942–43
Stickel, Walt, T, Pennsylvania 1946–49
Stillwell, Roger, DT, Stanford 1975–76
Stinchcomb, Pete, B, Ohio State 1921–22
Stoepel, Terry, G, Tulsa 1967
Stolfa, Anton, B, Luther 1939
Stone, Billy, B, Bradley 1951–54
Strickland, Larry, C, N. Texas State 1954–59
Sturtridge, Dick, B, DePauw 1928–29
Stydahar, Joe, T, West Virginia 1936–42, 1945–46

Sullivan, Frank, C, Loyola, La. 1935–39
Sumner, Charley, B, William & Mary 1955, 1958–60
Sweeney, Jake, T, Cincinnati 1944
Swisher, Bob, B, Northwestern 1938–41, 1945
Syzmanski, Frank, C, Notre Dame 1949

T

Tackwell, Cookie, E, Kansas State 1931–33
Taft, Merrill, RB, Wisconsin 1924
Taylor, Clifton, RB, Memphis State 1974
Taylor, Joe, DB, N. Carolina A&T 1967–72
Taylor, John, G, Ohio State 1920–21
Taylor, Lionel, E, New Mexico Highlands 1959
Taylor, Roosevelt, DB, Grambling 1961–69
Thomas, Bob, K, Notre Dame 1975–76
Thomas, Earl, TE, Houston 1971–73
Thompson, Russ, T, Nebraska 1936–39
Thrower, Willie, QB, Michigan State 1953
Tom, Mel, DE, San Jose State 1973–75
Torrance, Jack, T, Louisiana State 1939–40
Trafton, George, C, Notre Dame 1920–32
Trost, Milt, T, Marquette 1935–39
Tucker, Bill, RB, Tennessee State 1971
Turner, Cecil, WR, Cal. Poly 1968–73
Turner, Clyde (Bulldog), C, Hardin-Simmons 1940–52

U

Usher, Lou, T, Syracuse 1920

V

Vactor, Ted, CB, Nebraska 1975
Vallez, Emilo, TE, New Mexico 1968
Van Valkenburg, Pete, RB, BYU 1974
Veach, Walter, B 1920
Venturelli, Fred, K 1948
Vick, Ernie, C, Michigan 1927–28
Vick, Richard, QB, Washington & Jefferson 1925
Vodicka, Joe, B, None 1943, 1945
Voss, Walter (Tillie), E, Detroit 1927–28
Vucinich, Milt, G, Stanford 1945

W

Wade, Billy, QB, Vanderbilt 1961–66
Wade, Charles, WR, Tennessee State 1974
Wager, Clint, E, St. Mary's, Minn. 1942
Wallace, Bob, TE, Texas-El Paso 1968–72
Wallace, Stan, B, Illinois 1954, 1956–58
Walquist, Laurie, B, Illinois 1922–31
Ward, John, C-G, Oklahoma State 1976
Watkins, Bobby, RB, Ohio State 1955–57
Weatherly, Gerry, C, Rice 1950, 1952–54
Wetoska, Bob, T, Notre Dame 1960–69
Wetzel, Damon, B, Ohio State 1935
Wheeler, Ted, G, W. Texas State 1970
Wheeler, Wayne, WR, Alabama 1974
White, Roy, B, Valparaiso 1924–25, 1927–29
White, Wilford, B, Arizona State 1951–52
Whitman, Laverne, B, Tulsa 1953–54
Whitsell, Dave, DB, Indiana 1961–66
Whittenton, Jesse, HB, West Texas 1958
Wightkin, Bill, E, Notre Dame 1950–57
Williams, Bob, B, Notre Dame 1951–52, 1955
Williams, Broughton, T, Florida 1947
Williams, Fred, T, Arkansas 1952–63
Williams, Perry, RB, Purdue 1974
Wilson, George, E, Northwestern 1937–46
Wilson, Nemiah, CB, Grambling 1975
Wright, Steve, T, Alabama 1971
Wynne, Elmer, FB, Notre Dame 1928

Y

Youmans, Maury, E, Syracuse 1960–62
Young, Adrian, LB, USC 1973
Young, Randy, T, Millikin 1920
Youngblood, George, S, Cal. State-L.A. 1969
Yourist, Abe, E 1923

Z

Zarnas, Gus, G, Ohio State 1938
Zeller, Joe, G, Indiana 1933–38
Zizak, Vince, G, Villanova 1934
Zorich, George, G, Northwestern 1944–45
Zucco, Vic, RB, Michigan State 1957–60

Two Green Bay Packers' defenders stop safety Roosevelt Taylor, 1966.

CINCINNATI BENGALS

1965 Paul Brown was living comfortably in La Jolla, California, reflecting on his 13 seasons as head coach of the Cleveland Browns. He had left the Browns following the 1962 season with a record of 115 victories, 49 losses, and 6 ties, seven conference titles, and three NFL championships. Brown had the urge to get back into football but he wasn't sure where he wanted to be. His son, Mike, did a study on pro football expansion and recommended Cincinnati as a potential site. Brown met with Governor James Rhodes and the two agreed the state could accommodate a second pro football team.

1966 Fearful the Reds' baseball team would leave town and feeling pressure from local businessmen pushing for a pro football franchise, Cincinnati's City Council approved the construction of Riverfront Stadium, December 15. The stadium was granted a 48-acre downtown site, bounded by Second Street and the Ohio River.

1967 Brown's group was awarded an AFL expansion franchise, September 27. "I feel as if I'm breathing again," Brown said. Brown hired Al LoCasale as director of player personnel. Brown called the team the Bengals, the name of the previous Cincinnati AFL franchises in 1927, 1930, and 1931. The Bengals acquired their first player, trading two draft choices to Miami for quarterback John Stofa, December 26.

1968 The Bengals were awarded 40 veteran players in the allocation draft. Brown's AFL rivals were not particularly generous. As UPI reported: "The owners made sure that Brown doesn't start another dynasty too soon." Cincinnati fared better in the college draft, selecting Tennessee center Bob Johnson on its first pick. Other quality draftees included runners Jess Phillips and Essex Johnson, tight end Bob Trumpy, linebacker Al Beauchamp, and tackle Howard Fest. The Bengals lost their first preseason game 38–14 to Kansas City before 21,682 fans at Nippert Stadium. They went the entire first half without a first down. The Bengals played respectably during the regular season, upsetting Denver 24–10 and Buffalo 34–23 in their first two home games. Paul Robinson won the AFL rushing title with 1,023 yards and was named AFL rookie of the year.

1969 Brown selected quarterback Greg Cook of the University of Cincinnati in the first round of the draft, January 28. The same draft produced middle linebacker Bill Bergey, defensive end Royce Berry, cornerback Ken Riley, and wide receiver Speedy Thomas. Other AFL teams stopped referring to them as "the Baby Bengals" when they beat Miami 27–21 in the opener, September 14. It was Brown's three-hundredth coaching victory and an impressive debut for German-born Horst Muhlmann, who kicked two field goals out of Nippert Stadium. The following week, Cook passed for three touchdowns and ran for another as Cincinnati surprised San Diego 34–20. Then the Bengals defeated Kansas City 24–19 to stretch their record to 3–0. However, Cook suffered a serious arm injury when he was hit by Willie Lanier and sat out the next four games. The Bengals lost all four games. Cook returned to spark a 31–17 win over Oakland and a 31–31 tie with Houston. Against the Oilers, Cook passed for four touchdowns. Brown was named AFL coach of the year. Bergey was honored as AFL defensive rookie of the year. Cook won the AFL passing championship.

1970 The season opened gloomily as Cook's arm went dead at the Wilmington College training camp. Brown put Cook on the injured list and enlisted Virgil Carter, a Chicago Bears' and Buffalo Bills' castoff, to play quarterback. The Bengals beat Oakland in the opener 31–21 but lost the next six, falling to last place

Quarterback Ken Anderson, 1975.

Head coach Paul Brown, 1968.

in the Central Division. Carter ended the skid, throwing three touchdown passes in a 43–14 rout of Buffalo, November 8. The following week, the biggest sports crowd in Cincinnati history (60,007) jammed the new Riverfront Stadium to watch Brown upset his old Cleveland team 14–10. Key players in the win were rookie defensive tackles Mike Reid and Ron Carpenter. The Bengals staged a remarkable comeback, sweeping their last seven games to win the Central Division with an 8–6 record. They clinched their first division title with a 45–7 win over Boston before 60,157 fans at Riverfront Stadium, December 20. The inexperienced Bengals were no match for Baltimore in their AFC playoff game as the Colts dominated 17–0.

1971 The Bengals fared well in the draft, adding quarterback Ken Anderson and tackle Vernon Holland. The Bengals looked invincible as they rolled through a 5–0–1 preseason and manhandled Philadelphia 37–14 in the league opener. Carter passed for 273 yards and three touchdowns against the Eagles. Reid sacked Philadelphia passer Pete Liske five times. The season disintegrated rapidly, however, as the Bengals lost their next seven games. The most damaging setback was a 20–17 loss in Green Bay in which Carter and safety Ken Dyer were injured. Dyer snapped a vertebra in his neck and it was a year before he regained the use of his arms and legs. His football career was over. A 10–6 loss in Houston was the most humiliating game in Cincinnati's brief history. The Oilers scored on a 48-yard interception return on which no Bengals player gave chase. "I am embarrassed," an angry Brown said. "I just hope we never go through another season like this."

1972 Brown went for defensive help in the college draft, February 1. In order, Brown selected end Sherman White, safety Tommy Casanova, linebacker Jim LeClair, and cornerback Bernard Jackson. Anderson, rapidly gaining maturity, unseated Carter as Cincinnati's number-one quarterback. The season unfolded in three separate stages: the start—four wins in five games; the midseason slump—four losses in five games; and the finish—winning three of their last four. But they couldn't catch Cleveland for the AFC wild card berth. Chip Myers set a club record with 57 pass receptions.

1973 Brown went shopping for offense in the draft and came away with another splendid haul. Brown selected wide receiver Isaac Curtis (first round) and runners Charles (Boobie) Clark (thirteenth) and Lenvil Elliott (tenth). Those additions, combined with the rapid development of Anderson at quarterback, gave Cincinnati game-breaking potential. It took a while for the new players to blend as the Bengals went 4–4. They swept their last six games and won their second Central Division championship. Cincinnati lost to Miami 34–16 in the AFC playoffs at Miami, December 23. The Dolphins rushed for 241 yards and opened a 21–3 lead early in the second quarter. Neal Craig's interception return and two Muhlmann field goals cut it to 21–16 at halftime but the Bengals wilted in the third quarter. Clark, who finished the year with 988 yards rushing and 45 pass receptions, was named AFC rookie of the year. Veteran Essex Johnson led Cincinnati with a career-high 997 yards rushing. Curtis caught 45 passes.

1974 Cincinnati traded Bergey to Philadelphia for two first-round draft choices and a third-round pick in 1977. LeClair, an aggressive three-year veteran from North Dakota, replaced Bergey at middle linebacker. The Bengals won four of their first five games to lead the Central Division but couldn't keep pace with Super Bowl-bound Pittsburgh. Brown derived some consolation from his first season series sweep of Cleveland. Curtis caught five passes for 117 yards and a touchdown in the Bengals' 33–7 win over the

Bob Trumpy (84) and Archie Griffin (45) block for Charles (Boobie) Clark vs. Oakland, 1976.

Browns in the opener, September 15. Four weeks later, Anderson threw three more scoring passes as Cincinnati beat the Browns 34–24. Anderson threw four touchdown passes in a 33–6 rout of Kansas City, November 24. Anderson won the NFL passing championship, completing a club record 64.9 percent of his attempts. Cornerback Lemar Parrish led the NFL in punt returns, including a 90-yard touchdown against Washington, October 6.

1975 The Bengals launched their season by winning the first six games. LeClair preserved a 21–19 victory over Houston, making all four tackles in a goal-line stand. Anderson handled the scoring, throwing three touchdown passes. Rookie Marvin Cobb raced 52 yards with his first pro interception to give Cincinnati a 14–10 win over Oakland. The Bengals won their eighth game in nine starts against Buffalo, 33–24, as Anderson completed 30 of 46 passes for 447 yards and two touchdowns, November 17. The yardage was the tenth highest one-game total in NFL history. Anderson missed a game with an injury, but reserve quarterback John Reaves led the Bengals to a 23–19 win over Houston, November 30. Cincinnati scored 27 points in the first quarter to crush San Diego 47–14 and finish with its best regular season record, 11–3. The Bengals qualified as the wild card team for the AFC playoffs but their losing postseason record continued with a 31–28 loss to Oakland, December 28. They fell behind 31–14, then stormed back on Anderson's two fourth-quarter touchdown passes. Anderson won his second NFL passing championship. A serious blow was the loss of defensive tackle Mike Reid, who retired at 26 to pursue a career in music.

1976 Paul Brown announced his retirement after 41 seasons of coaching, January 1. Brown named Bill Johnson, his long-time line coach, to succeed him. Brown continued to serve as the club's general manager, vice president, and owner. The Bengals upgraded their roster, acquiring defensive end Coy Bacon in a trade with San Diego and drafting several top rookies, including halfback Archie Griffin, the two-time Heisman trophy winner from Ohio State. Other standout rookies included wide receiver Billy Brooks of Oklahoma and kicker Chris Bahr of Penn State. As always, the Bengals set a fast pace in the Central Division, winning 9 of their first 11 games.

Anderson had his best game in a 45–21 win over Cleveland, throwing for four touchdowns. Griffin, who became a starter as a rookie, rushed for 139 yards and scored on a 77-yard run as Cincinnati rallied to beat Kansas City 27–24. The season came down to two games against Pittsburgh and Oakland and the Bengals lost both—7–3 to the Steelers, November 28, and 35–20 to Oakland, December 6. Those defeats not only cost Cincinnati the Central Division title but the AFC wild card spot as well. Cornerback Ken Riley led the AFC with nine interceptions.

MEMBERS OF HALL OF FAME:
Paul Brown

BENGALS RECORD, 1968–76

Year	Won	Lost	Tied	Pct.	Pts.	OP
1968	3	11	0	.214	215	329
1969	4	9	1	.308	280	367
1970§	8	6	0	.571	312	255
1971	4	10	0	.286	284	265
1972	8	6	0	.571	299	229
1973§	10	4	0	.714	286	231
1974	7	7	0	.500	283	259
1975	11	3	0	.786	340	246
1976	10	4	0	.714	335	138
9 Years	65	60	1	.520	2,634	2,319

§*AFC Central Division Champion*

RECORD HOLDERS

Rushing (Yards)	Paul Robinson, 1968	1,023
Passing (Pct.)	Ken Anderson, 1974	64.9
Passing (Yards)	Ken Anderson, 1975	3,169
Passing (TDs)	Ken Anderson, 1975	21
Receiving (No.)	Philip (Chip) Meyers, 1972	57
Receiving (Yards)	Isaac Curtis, 1975	934
Interceptions (No.)	Ken Riley, 1976	9
Punting (Avg.)	Dave Lewis, 1970	46.2
Punt Ret. (Avg.)	Lemar Parrish, 1975	18.8
Kickoff Ret. (Avg.)	Lemar Parrish, 1970	30.1
Touchdowns (Total)	Isaac Curtis, 1974 and Stan Fritts, 1975	10
Field Goals Made	Horst Muhlmann, 1972	27
Points (No.)	Horst Muhlmann, 1972	111

COACHING HISTORY

1968–75	Paul Brown	55–56–1
1976	Bill Johnson	10– 4–0

FIRST PLAYER SELECTED

1968	Bob Johnson, C, Tennessee
1969	Greg Cook, QB, Cincinnati
1970	Mike Reid, DT, Penn State
1971	Vernon Holland, T, Tennessee State
1972	Sherman White, DE, California
1973	Isaac Curtis, WR, San Diego State
1974	Bill Kollar, DT, Montana State
1975	Glenn Cameron, LB, Florida
1976	Billy Brooks, WR, Oklahoma

Bill Bergey

Ron Carpenter

Virgil Carter

C. (Boobie) Clark

Archie Griffin

Vernon Holland

Bob Johnson

CINCINNATI BENGALS, 1968–76

Adams, Doug, LB, Ohio State 1971–74
Amsler, Martin, DE, Evansville 1970
Anderson, Ken, QB, Augustana 1971–76
Archer, Dan, T, Oregon 1968
Avery, Ken, LB, So. Mississippi 1969–74

B

Baccaglio, Martin, DT-DE, San Jose St. 1968–70
Bacon, Coy, DE, Jackson State 1976
Bahr, Chris, K, Penn State 1976
Banks, Estes, RB, Colorado 1968
Beauchamp, Al, LB, Southern U. 1968–75
Bergey, Bill, LB, Arkansas State 1969–75
Berry, Royce, DE, Houston 1969–75
Blackwood, Lyle, S, Texas Christian 1973–75
Brabham, Dan, LB, Arkansas 1968
Brooks, Billy, WR, Oklahoma 1976
Brown, Bob, DT, Arkansas AM&N 1975–76
Buchanan, Tim, LB, Hawaii 1969
Buie, Drew, WR, Catawba 1972
Bujnoch, Glenn, G, Texas A&M 1976
Buncom, Frank, LB, USC 1968
Burley, Gary, G, Pittsburgh 1976

C

Cameron, Glenn, LB, Florida 1975–76
Canale, Justin, G, Mississippi State 1969
Carpenter, Ron, DE, N. Carolina State 1969–76
Carter, Virgil, QB, Brigham Young 1970–73
Casanova, Tommy, S, Louisiana State 1972–76
Chandler, Al, TE, Oklahoma 1973–74
Chomyszak, Steve, DT, Syracuse 1968–73
Clark, Charles (Boobie), RB, Bethune-Cookman ... 1973–76

Clark, Wayne, QB, U.S. International 1974
Cobb, Marvin, CB-S, USC 1975–76
Coleman, Al, DB, Tennessee State 1969–71
Conley, Steve, LB, Kansas 1972
Cook, Greg, QB, Cincinnati 1969–74
Cornish, Frank, DT, Grambling 1970
Coslet, Bruce, TE, Pacific 1969–76
Cousino, Brad, LB, Miami, Ohio 1975
Crabtree, Eric, WR, Pittsburgh 1969–71
Craig, Neil, S, Fisk 1971–73
Curtis, Isaac, WR, San Diego State 1973–76

D

Davis, Charles, RB, Colorado 1974–75
Davis, Ricky, S, Alabama 1975
Davis, Tony, RB, Nebraska 1976
DeLeone, Tom, C-G, Ohio State 1972–73
Dennis, Guy, G, Florida 1969–72
Devlin, Chris, LB, Penn State 1975–76
Dressler, Doug, RB, Chico State 1970–74
Dunn, Paul, RB-WR, U.S. International 1970
Durko, Sandy, DB, USC 1970–71
Dyer, Ken, DB, Arizona State 1969–71

E

Elliott, Lenvil, RB, Northeast Missouri St. 1973–76
Ely, Larry, LB, Iowa 1970–71
Elzey, Paul, LB, Toledo 1968
Erickson, Bernard, LB, Abilene Christian 1968
Ernst, Mike, QB, Cal. St.-Fullerton 1973–74

F

Fairchild, Greg, G, Tulsa 1976
Fest, Howard, T, Texas 1968–75

Frazier, Curt, DB, Fresno State 1968
Fritts, Stan, RB, N. Carolina State 1975–76

G

Gehrke, Jack, WR, Utah 1969–70
George, Tim, WR, Carson-Newman 1973
Graham, Ken, DB, Washington State 1970
Graves, White, DB, Louisiana State 1968
Green, Dave, PK, Ohio 1974–75
Griffin, Archie, RB, Ohio State 1976
Griffin, Jim, DE, Grambling 1968–69
Guillory, John, DB, Stanford 1969–70
Gunner, Harry, DE, Oregon 1968–69

H

Haffner, Mike, WR, UCLA 1971
Harmon, Ed, LB, Louisville 1969
Harris, Bo, LB, Louisiana State 1975–76
Headrick, Sherrill, LB, Texas Christian 1968
Henson, Champ, RB, Ohio State 1975
Herock, Ken, TE, West Virginia 1968
Hibler, Mike, LB, Stanford 1968
Holland, Vernon, T, Tennessee State 1971–76
Hunt, Bobby, S, Auburn 1968–69
Hunt, Ron, T, Oregon 1976

J

Jackson, Bernard, S-CB, Washington St. 1972–76
Johnson, Bob, C, Tennessee 1968–76
Johnson, Essex, RB, Grambling 1968–75
Johnson, Jim, CB, S. Carolina State 1968–69
Johnson, Ken, DT, Indiana 1971–76
Joiner, Charlie, WR, Grambling 1972–75
Jolitz, Evan, LB, Cincinnati 1974

Wide receiver Isaac Curtis, 1976.

Cornerback Lemar Parrish, 1974.

Essex Johnson

Jim LeClair

Chip Myers

Mike Reid

Ken Riley

Paul Robinson

Bob Trumpy

Jones, Willie Lee, DT-DE, Kansas 1968–71

K

Kearney, Tim, LB, No. Michigan 1972–74
Keeling, Rex, P, Sanford 1968
Kellerman, Ernie, S, Miami, Ohio 1973
Kelly, Bob, T, New Mexico State 1968
Kelly, Mike, TE, Davidson 1970–72
Kindricks, Bill, DT, Alabama A&M 1968
King, Charley, S, Purdue 1968–69
Koegel, Vic, LB, Ohio State 1974
Kollar, Bill, DT, Montana State 1974–76
Krevis, Al, T, Boston College 1975

L

Lamb, Ron, RB, South Carolina 1968–71
Lapham, Dave, G, Syracuse 1974–76
Lawson, Steve, G, Kansas 1971–72
LeClair, Jim, LB, North Dakota 1972–76
Lewis, Dave, P-QB, Stanford 1970–73
Livingston, Dale, P, Western Michigan 1968–69

M

Maddox, Bob, DE, Frostburgh State 1974
Marshall, Ed, WR, Cameron 1971
Matlock, John, C, Miami 1968
Matson, Pat, G, Oregon 1968–74
Mayes, Rufus, G, Ohio State 1970–76
McClure, Wayne, LB, Mississippi 1968–70
McDaniel, John, WR, Lincoln 1974–76
McInally, Pat, WR-P, Harvard 1976
McVea, Warren, WR, Houston 1968
Middendorf, Dave, G, Washington State 1968–70
Moore, Maulty, DT, Bethune-Cookman 1975

Morgan, Melvin, DB, Mississippi Valley 1976
Morrison, Reece, RB, S.W. Texas State 1972–73
Muhlmann, Horst, PK, None 1969–74
Myers, Chip, WR, Northwest Oklahoma 1969–76

N

Neidert, John, LB, Louisville 1968
Novak, Jack, TE, Wisconsin 1975

P

Park, Ernie, T, McMurry 1969
Parrish, Lemar, DB, Lincoln 1970–76
Perreault, Pete, G, Boston U. 1968
Perry, Scott, DB, Williams 1976
Peterson, Bill, LB, San Jose State 1968–72
Phillips, Jess, RB, Michigan State 1968–72
Powers, Warren, DB, Nebraska 1968
Pritchard, Ron, LB, Arizona State 1972–76

R

Randall, Dennis, DE, Oklahoma State 1968
Randolph, Al, CB, Iowa 1972
Reaves, John, QB, Florida 1975–76
Reid, Mike, DT, Penn State 1970–75
Rice, Andy, DT, Texas Southern 1968–69
Riley, Ken, CB, Florida A&M 1969–76
Robinson, Paul, RB, Arizona 1968–72
Roman, Nick, DE, Ohio State 1970–71

S

Saffold, St., WR, San Jose State 1968
Sawyer, Ken, S, Syracuse 1974
Scott, Bill, DB, Idaho 1968
Shelby, Willie, RB, Alabama 1976

Sherman, Rod, WR, USC 1968
Shinners, John, G, Xavier 1972–76
Smiley, Tom, RB, Lamar Tech 1968
Smith, Fletcher, CB, Tennessee State 1968–71
Smith, Tommie, WR, San Jose State 1969
Spiller, Phil, S, Cal. State-L.A. 1968–69
Staley, Bill, DT, Utah 1968–69
Stofa, John, QB, Buffalo 1968–69
Swanson, Terry, P, Massachusetts 1968

T

Thomas, Lee, DE, Jackson State 1973
Thomas, Speedy, WR, Utah 1969–72
Trumpy, Bob, TE, Utah 1968–76
Turner, Clem, RB, Cincinnati 1969

W

Walters, Stan, T, Syracuse 1972–74
Warren, Dewey, QB, Tennessee 1968
Washington, Ted, TB, San Diego State 1968
Watson, Pete, CB, Tufts 1972
White, Andre, TE, Florida A&M 1968
White, Sherman, DE, California 1972–75
Willis, Fred, RB, Boston College 1971–72
Williams, Ed, RB, Langston 1974–75
Williams, Monk, WR, Arkansas A&M 1968
Williams, Jim, CB, Alcorn A&M 1968
Williams, Reggie, LB, Dartmouth 1976
Wilson, Joe, RB, Holy Cross 1973
Wilson, Mike, G-T, Dayton 1969–70
Wright, Ernie, T, Ohio State 1968–71
Wyche, Sam, QB, Furman 1968–70

Safety Tom Casanova returns a punt 74 yards during a 17–10 victory over Pittsburgh, 1974.

CLEVELAND BROWNS

1946 Arthur (Mickey) McBride was one of six prospective owners who met with Arch Ward, *Chicago Tribune* sports editor, at a St. Louis hotel to thrash out plans for the All-America Football Conference, June 4, 1944. Taking the advice of Ward and another newspaperman, John Dietrich of the *Cleveland Plain Dealer*, McBride—who owned taxicab companies, a radio station, a printing company and a race wire syndicate, and had real estate holdings—named Paul Brown as coach of the new Cleveland team. Brown had been a highly successful coach at Massillon, Ohio, High School, at Ohio State University, and at Great Lakes Naval Training Station during World War II. McBride offered a $1,000 war bond to the fan coming up with a nickname for the team. The winner was a navy man, John J. Harnett of Lawrence, Massachusetts, who was one of 36 entrants choosing "Panthers." But there had been an NFL team called the Cleveland Panthers in the 1920s. Brown vetoed the nickname. "I won't start out with anything associated with our enterprise that smacks of failure," he said. "That old Panther team failed. I want no part of that name." A large majority of the contest entrants had suggested the team be called the "Browns," in recognition of its head coach. Paul Brown had turned down the suggestion but he relented, and became the only man in pro football ever to have a team named after him. William E. Thompson got a $1,000 war bond for the Browns' nickname. Brown personally selected the style and colors—brown, orange, and white—of the uniforms. The other professional team in Cleveland, the Rams of the National Football League, had drawn just 73,000 fans in 1945, despite winning the league championship, and owner Dan Reeves announced in January, 1946, he was moving the team to Los Angeles. Brown was also general manager and the first player he signed was Otto Graham, a single wing tailback from Northwestern, whom he would convert into one of the finest T formation quarterbacks of all time. Brown filled out most of the rest of his roster with men who had played for him at Ohio State or Great Lakes—Lou Groza, Dante Lavelli, Marion Motley, Bill Willis—or against him—Mac Speedie, Ed (Special Delivery) Jones. The Browns' training camp was held at Bowling Green State University in northwestern Ohio. The Browns played their first AAFC regular season game, beating the Miami Seahawks 44–0 at Cleveland Stadium, September 6. They won seven in a row before losing to the San Francisco 49ers. They wrapped up the Western Division title with a 42–17 win over the Buffalo Bills, then defeated the New York Yankees in the championship game 14–9 as Graham and Motley—who, with Willis, helped break the post-World War II color line in pro football—starred.

1947 Tony Adamle, whom Brown had coached at Ohio State, and Horace Gillom, whom Brown had coached against at Massillon, joined the team. Enroute to a second straight championship, Graham and Speedie combined on a screen pass that went for a 99-yard touchdown. The 49ers posed the big Western Division threat again, but Cleveland beat them 37–14, then defeated the Yankees in the AAFC championship game 14–3 as Motley ripped apart New York's defense.

1948 Brown sent the draft rights to Michigan All-America Bob Chappius to the Brooklyn Dodgers for halfback Dub Jones, who combined with Speedie and Lavelli to give the Browns three brilliant receivers. Brown also traded for linemen Alex Agase and Forrest (Chubby) Grigg, and drafted defensive backs Tommy James and Warren Lahr. Lavelli was out until midseason with a broken leg, but the Browns rolled

on, this time to an unbeaten season. In the 31–28 division title-clinching win over San Francisco, Graham played all the way on a bad knee. The Browns buried Buffalo 49–7 in the AAFC title game. **1949** Brown brought in quite a bit of new talent and the team sputtered a little, losing to the 49ers 56–28. Brown exploded in anger at his players after that loss and they responded with a 61–14 victory over the Los Angeles Dons. Graham threw six touchdown passes, four to Lavelli. In a playoff game, the Browns stopped the Bills 31–21. Then they won the AAFC's last title game 21–7 over the 49ers, before just 22,550 fans. Two days before, a merger with the National Football League had been announced. The AAFC's last order of business was a game between the Browns and a league all-star team. Led by quarterback George Ratterman, who would join Cleveland two years later, the all-stars scored a 12–7 win. The Browns, ironically, helped kill the AAFC. "We were too good, if that sounds possible," Brown said. "Even in Cleveland, the fans stopped coming because they just assumed we'd go out and dominate the opposition so strongly, there would be no contest."

1950 Before starting play in the NFL, Brown picked up Abe Gibron, Rex Bumgardner, and John Kissell from the AAFC Bills and Len Ford from the Dons, and drafted tackle John Sandusky and halfback Ken Carpenter. Brown concentrated on defense; he had an excellent offensive nucleus. The rest of the NFL concentrated on the Browns, determined to make them prove how good they were. The Browns played the Philadelphia Eagles, the defending NFL champions, in the season opener. Eagles coach Earle (Greasy) Neale had said his team was better, that all Cleveland did was "throw the ball." The Browns won 35–10 as Graham threw three touchdown passes. But in the third game of the season, Steve Owen and the New York Giants used their "umbrella" defense to shut out Cleveland 6–0. It was the first time the Browns had ever been shut out. The Giants beat the Browns again that season and Cleveland needed a win over the Eagles to tie the Giants for first place in the American Conference. They got it 13–7 without Graham throwing a single pass. Lahr returned an interception for a touchdown, and Groza kicked two field goals. The Browns and Giants finished with 10–2 regular season records. They played it off in 10-degree cold at Cleveland, Groza kicked two field goals in an 8–3 win over the Giants. Willis saved the game when he tackled New York's Eugene (Choo Choo) Roberts from behind at the Brown's 4-yard line in the fourth quarter. In the NFL championship game, the Browns got a field goal from Groza with 28 seconds to play to beat the Los Angeles Rams 30–28.

1951 There were some rumors Brown would leave pro football and take over again as Ohio State coach. But he stayed and the Browns had another good season. This time, however, they failed to win a championship. In a title game rematch, the Rams beat them 24–17 on a 73-yard pass-and-run play from Norm Van Brocklin to Tom Fears.

1952 The Browns, after a battle with Philadelphia and New York, won their third straight Eastern Conference title but three players, Mac Speedie, Dub Jones, and John Kissell, were lost with injuries in a victory over the Giants. None was ready for the NFL championship game two weeks later against the Detroit Lions. Detroit had turned its fortunes around under coach Buddy Parker, quarterback Bobby Layne, halfback Doak Walker, and middle guard Les Bingaman. Graham, who had his poorest passing season as a pro, was working with two rookie receivers—Ray Renfro and Darrell (Pete) Brewster—and the Browns scored only on Harry (Chick) Jagade's run in a 17–7 loss.

1953 The Browns drafted Doug Atkins, the giant lineman from Tennessee, halfback Bill Reynolds, and

guard Chuck Noll (on the twenty-third round), and Brown swung a 15-player trade with Baltimore that brought tackles Mike McCormack and Don Colo, linebacker Tom Catlin, defensive back John Petitbon, and guard Herschel Forester. Defensive backs Ken Konz and Ken Gorgal came back from the service but the Browns lost Speedie and Kissell in a bidding war with the Canadian Football League. McBride sold the team to a group headed by David Jones, a Cleveland industrialist, for $600,000, the highest price ever paid for a pro football franchise at the time. The syndicate that owned the Browns took out a large life insurance policy on Paul Brown, figuring he was their primary asset. On the field, the Browns won every regular season game until the last one, a 42–27 loss to Philadelphia. In the championship game, Cleveland took a 16–10 lead over Detroit on Groza's two fourth quarter field goals. But a Bobby Layne pass to Jim Doran, a converted defensive end, denied Cleveland the NFL title again, 17–16. A depressed Graham announced he'd retire after the 1954 season.

1954 Willis, Lin Houston, and George Young, all from the original 1946 team, retired, and eight other players departed. McCormack took over at middle guard, Forester replaced Houston at guard, and Kissell returned from Canada. Brown made several important additions, including running back Fred (Curly) Morrison and defensive back Don Paul through trades; and running backs Maurice Bassett (who was billed as "the new Marion Motley") and Chet Hanulak through the draft. The team started poorly, going 1–2 and losing 55–27 to Pittsburgh, then won eight straight. They met the Lions again in the last regular season game, and Detroit won 14–10. But the game meant nothing, since both teams had already won division titles. The title game did, since Graham figured it would be his last. He threw three touchdown passes and scored three times himself as the Browns overwhelmed the Lions 56–10. Reynolds set up three scores with two kickoff returns and a punt return and Cleveland intercepted six passes and recovered a fumble.

1955 Four games into the preseason, it was obvious the old Browns magic was not there without Graham. Brown called Graham and asked if he would change his mind. "He came back without too much coaxing," Brown said. Graham suffered physically and mentally upon his return but he led the Browns into the NFL championship game again. Hanulak and Reynolds both were called into the air force, so Brown made a trade with Pittsburgh that brought in Ed Modzelewski to help Bassett. The team scored its highest NFL total in the regular season, 349 points. Graham and other veterans told Brown they felt a spread, wide-open offense would work best in the title game against the Rams and they were right. Cleveland rolled to a 38–14 victory. Graham passed for two touchdowns and ran for two and when he came out of the game the 85,000 fans in Los Angeles Coliseum gave him a long ovation. This time Graham retired for good. And Dub Jones retired, too.

1956 Dante Lavelli joined Otto Graham and Dub Jones in retirement. Missing three vital ingredients, the offense didn't respond. Brown vacillated between quarterbacks Babe Parilli and George Ratterman, who had sat on the bench as Graham's substitute for four years. Ratterman injured his knee in the fourth regular season game and his Browns' career was over. Parilli then hurt a shoulder and Tommy O'Connell, who had been cut by the Bears, was the quarterback. The team had its first losing season, 5–7.

1957 Brown wanted to draft a quarterback but two coin tosses went against him and Cleveland was dropped to sixth in drafting order. It turned out to be an incredible stroke of luck. The Browns chose Jim Brown, who was to become the most productive runner in NFL history. "There was no doubt," said chief talent scout Dick Gallagher, "he could do a lot of work for us—that he was the man to make our system go." Brown drafted a quarterback, Milt Plum, on the second round. John Bayuk, a running back from Colorado, was assigned uniform number 32 in training camp. Jim Brown, reporting from the Chicago All-Star game, wore number 45—for one game. Then Bayuk was released and Brown got the number 32. Parilli was traded to Green Bay for Bob Garrett, but Garrett was released and O'Connell and Plum were named to run the offense. The Browns started four rookies, including Jim Brown. Four games into the season, Brown ran for an NFL-record 237 yards against the Rams, breaking Motley's team record of 188 set in 1950. The Browns won the Eastern Division title, but came up against the Lions again in the championship game. This time they were buried 59–14. Brown was named rookie of the year.

1958 Quarterback Jim Ninowski and running backs Bobby Mitchell (eighth round) and Leroy Bolden were among the club's draft choices. O'Connell retired, even though he had been the league's leading passer. Jim Brown and Mitchell led the team to a 5–0 start, then Mitchell was benched in favor of Bolden after fumbling three times against the Giants. It was the start of a deteriorating relationship between Paul Brown and several of his players—notably Jim Brown, Mitchell, and Plum. Cleveland had only to beat New York in the final regular season game to win the Eastern Division title but it lost 13–10 on Pat Summerall's field goal with two minutes to play. It also lost a playoff game to the Giants 10–0 as Giants defensive coach Tom Landry devised a means to stop Paul and Jim Brown. Cleveland gained just 24 yards rushing and had only 86 yards total offense.

1959 The Browns had another good draft. Paul Brown picked end Rich Kreitling to team with Renfro and brought in two excellent offensive linemen, John Wooten and Dick Schafrath. And he acquired receiver Billy Howton from Green Bay. Plum emerged as the number-one quarterback and, after eight games, the Browns were tied with the Giants for first place in the East. But the team fell out of contention. Jim Brown, however, gained 1,329 yards on a record 290 carries and won his third NFL rushing title.

1960 Quarterback Len Dawson was acquired in a trade with the Steelers and Jim Houston, Prentice Gautt, and Jim Marshall were among draftees. But Groza, Konz, and Lahr retired and, eventually, only 19 players remained from the 1959 team. There were several problems starting the season—lack of a long passing game; defenses keying too much on Jim Brown; Paul Brown's relationship with his players. The team improved its record a bit but again lost to the Giants in a key game and finished a game and one-half behind Philadelphia in the East.

1961 Arthur Modell, a former New York City advertising executive with much experience in television, bought the Browns for $3,925,000, January 25. The price was more than six times what the Jones syndicate had paid original owner McBride eight years before. Modell didn't claim to know a lot about football. "My expertise was in one area, television," he said. There was suspicion about Modell's role at first but he told Paul Brown he wanted him to run the football end of the business while he would handle administration and details. "We were entertainment," Modell said. "The first thing I wanted to be sure we did was put on a good show." It was innovative thinking for the time. Lou Groza returned to the team after a one-year retirement. But the team slipped to third place in the Eastern Conference.

1962 Mitchell was traded to Washington for the first choice of the NFL draft. Paul Brown then used it to select Ernie Davis of Syracuse, the big back the coach wanted to team with Jim Brown. Plum was traded to Detroit in a deal that brought back Ninowski. Quarterback Frank Ryan joined the team in a trade with Los Angeles. Davis wore his jersey only for publicity pictures. Tragically, he was dying of leukemia. The Browns won all their preseason games and their league opener, then Mitchell and the Redskins beat them and they began to slump. They finished third in the Eastern Division. Jim Brown lost the rushing title for the only time in his nine-year career, and threatened to retire unless he could play for a new coach.

1963 Modell called Paul Brown into his office and told him he was through as coach and general manager—after 17 years—even though he had six years remaining on his contract, January 5. Brown's record was 158–48–8. Blanton Collier, 56, a Browns' assistant who had been the architect of the club's superb defenses and Paul Brown's most trusted associate, was named head coach. Collier signed a three-year contract. He was almost the antithesis of Brown—soft-spoken, openly warm, a man who didn't call plays from the side line via "messenger" guards. Under Collier the team won six straight with Ryan firmly in control at quarterback, and receiver Gary Collins beginning to hit his stride. Jim Brown was having his finest season as a pro, helped by Ernie Green's blocking. But the momentum collapsed in a 33–6 loss to the Giants and the Browns finished one game behind New York in the Eastern Conference.

1964 The offense was there, with Brown, Ryan, Collins, and Paul Warfield. Collier had to knit together a defense. In the 1963 postseason Playoff Bowl, he gave Jim Kanicki the starting job at defensive tackle in the second half against Green Bay and put Walter Beach in the defensive secondary. Collier traded with the Giants for tackle Dick Modzelewski, whose presence revitalized veterans such as Vince Costello and Galen Fiss. The team played well but still had to fight until the last day of the season to clinch a divisional title, smashing the Giants 52–20 on a muddy field as Ryan completed 12 of 13 passes for 202 yards and five touchdowns. Cleveland dominated the Baltimore Colts 27–0 in a major upset for the NFL championship as Ryan threw three touchdown passes to Collins.

1965 Ryan suffered a severe shoulder injury in the Pro Bowl and had his arm in a cast much of the winter. Warfield broke his shoulder in the College All-Star game and was ruled out for 10 weeks. Walter (the Flea) Roberts replaced Warfield. The team had nagging injuries to several players but didn't miss a step thanks mostly to Brown, who was named the NFL's most valuable player. The Browns clinched the Eastern Conference title three games before the season's end with a 42–21 win over Pittsburgh. But there was a major hurdle for the league title—the Green Bay Packers of Vince Lombardi. On a wet, snowy day on Lambeau Field in Green Bay, the Packers led only 13–12 at the half, but then dominated the second half and won 23–12. The Packers limited Jim Brown to 50 yards. After 12,312 yards rushing and 126 touchdowns, this was Jimmy Brown's last game.

1966 Leroy Kelly, an eighth-round draft choice in 1964 replaced Brown. With Ryan, Kelly, and Green performing well, the team made a run at a third straight Eastern title but lost to Dallas, the rising power in the conference. Still, Kelly gained 1,141 yards and scored 15 touchdowns.

1967 The NFL was realigned and the Browns were placed in the NFL's Century Division. They won it, then met the Cowboys, Capitol Division winners, for a spot in the NFL championship game. Devastated by Bob Hayes's pass catching and punt returning, the Browns lost 52–14.

1968 Ryan had begun to slip, so Collier obtained quarterback Bill Nelsen from Pittsburgh. He also got tackle Ron Snidow from Washington after Paul Wiggin and John Brewer retired. Bill Glass went out with an injury in training camp; Brewer was replaced by Jack Gregory, giving the Browns two new faces on the defense. Modzelewski took over as defensive coach. Groza, who was in a preseason kicking battle with Don Cockroft, decided to retire again. This time he meant it and "the Toe's" jersey, number 76, was

MEMBERS OF HALL OF FAME:
Jim Brown, Paul Brown, Dante Lavelli, Len Ford, Otto Graham, Lou Groza, Marion Motley, Bill Willis

BROWNS RECORD, 1946–76

Year	Won	Lost	Tied	Pct.	Pts.	OP
1946*	12	2	0	.857	423	137
1947*	12	1	1	.923	410	185
1948*	14	0	0	1.000	389	190
1949*	9	1	2	.900	339	171
1950‡	10	2	0	.833	310	144
1951§	11	1	0	.917	331	152
1952§	8	4	0	.667	310	213
1953§	11	1	0	.917	348	162
1954‡	9	3	0	.750	336	162
1955‡	9	2	1	.818	349	218
1956	5	7	0	.417	167	177
1957†	9	2	1	.818	269	172
1958	9	3	0	.750	302	217
1959	7	5	0	.583	270	214
1960	8	3	1	.727	362	217
1961	8	5	1	.615	319	270
1962	7	6	1	.538	291	257
1963	10	4	0	.714	343	262
1964‡	10	3	1	.769	415	293
1965§	11	3	0	.786	363	325
1966	9	5	0	.643	403	259
1967†	9	5	0	.643	334	297
1968§	10	4	0	.714	394	273
1969§	10	3	1	.769	351	300
1970	7	7	0	.500	286	265
1971§	9	5	0	.643	285	273
1972	10	4	0	.714	268	249
1973	7	5	2	.571	234	255
1974	4	10	0	.286	251	344
1975	3	11	0	.214	218	372
1976	9	5	0	.643	267	287
27 NFL Years	229	118	9	.656	8,376	6,629

*AAFC Champion
‡NFL Champion
§NFL Eastern Conference Champion
§AFC Central Division Champion
†NFL Eastern Division Champion

RECORD HOLDERS

Rushing (Yards)	Jim Brown, 1963	1,863
Passing (Pct.)	Otto Graham, 1953	64.7
Passing (Yards)	Frank Ryan, 1966	2,974
Passing (TDs)	Frank Ryan, 1966	29
Receiving (No.)	Mac Speedie, 1952	62
Receiving (Yards)	Paul Warfield, 1968	1,067
Interceptions (No.)	Tom James, 1950	9
Punting (Avg.)	Gary Collins, 1965	46.7
Punt Ret. (Avg.)	Leroy Kelly, 1965	15.6
Kickoff Ret. (Avg.)	Robert (Bo) Scott, 1969	28.9
Touchdowns (Total)	Jim Brown, 1965	21
Field Goals Made	Lou Groza, 1953	23
Points (No.)	Jim Brown, 1965	126

COACHING HISTORY

1946–62	Paul Brown	158–48–8
	NFL only	111–44–5
1963–70	Blanton Collier	76–34–2
1971–74	Nick Skorich	30–24–2
1975–76	Forrest Gregg	12–16–0

FIRST PLAYER SELECTED

1950	Ken Carpenter, B, Oregon State
1951	Ken Konz, B, Louisiana State
1952	Bert Rechichar, B, Tennessee
1953	Doug Atkins, T, Tennessee
1954	Bobby Garrett, B, Stanford
1955	Kent Burris, C, Oklahoma
1956	Preston Carpenter, B, Arkansas
1957	Jim Brown, B, Syracuse
1958	Jim Shofner, B, Texas Christian
1959	Rick Kreitling, E, Illinois
1960	Jim Houston, DE, Ohio State
1961	Bob Crespino, E, Mississippi
1962	Ernie Davis, RB, Syracuse
1963	Tom Hutchinson, WR, Kentucky
1964	Paul Warfield, WR, Ohio State
1965	Walter Johnson, DT (2), Cal. State–L.A.
1966	Milt Morin, TE, Massachusetts
1967	Bob Matheson, LB, Duke
1968	Marvin Upshaw, DT-DE, Trinity, Texas
1969	Ron Johnson, RB, Michigan
1970	Mike Phipps, QB, Purdue
1971	Clarence Scott, CB, Kansas State
1972	Thom Darden, DB, Michigan
1973	Pete Adams, T, USC
1974	Billy Corbett, T (2), Johnson C. Smith
1975	Mack Mitchell, T, Houston
1976	Mike Pruitt, RB, Purdue

Tom Catlin   Bob Gain   Gene Hickerson   Jim Houston   Walter Johnson   Mike McCormack   Walt Michaels

retired. Collins was out most of the year with a shoulder injury but Nelsen ignited the team and it won the Century Division again. Kelly led the NFL in rushing with 1,239 yards and scoring with 20 touchdowns. Cleveland beat Dallas 31–20 in the playoffs. But it was different against Baltimore in the NFL championship game. Tom Matte ran for three touchdowns and the Colts held the Browns to 56 yards rushing and won 34–0.

1969 The Browns won their third straight Century Division title, led again by Nelsen. He completed 18 passes for 219 yards, throwing eight of them to Warfield. Kelly and Bo Scott ran well as Cleveland beat Dallas 38–14 in the first round of the playoffs. Then the Browns lost to the Vikings 27–7 in eight-degree weather in Minnesota.

1970 The Browns became members of the American Football Conference Central Division as three old-line NFL teams joined American Football League teams in alignment. Collier announced at midseason that he planned to retire. The team couldn't beat Paul Brown's Cincinnati Bengals in its division.

1971 Nick Skorich, an aide to Collier, took over as the Browns' third head coach. The Browns traded Paul Warfield to Miami to get the first draft choice that enabled them to get a promising young quarterback, Mike Phipps of Purdue. But management believed the move was necessary because Nelsen was playing on two bad ankles. Skorich blended Nelsen and Phipps well and Cleveland won its first American Football Conference divisional title. But the Browns lost to Baltimore in the first round of the playoffs 20–3.

1972 Phipps was maturing and the team played well again, giving Miami its stiffest test of the season on the way to the Super Bowl. After finishing second in the AFC Central, the Browns were beaten 20–14 by the Dolphins in the playoffs.

1973 Gene Hickerson retired. Injuries hurt the Browns offensively. The Browns faced a tough schedule and didn't make the playoffs. Phipps didn't progress as hoped but there was a youngster of the future around, Oklahoma running back Greg Pruitt. The defense played well considering it spent so much time on the field. Cornerback Clarence Scott had an outstanding season. Scott, Pruitt, and Sherk were named to the Pro Bowl team.

1974 The Browns team lost five of their first six before they could put anything together, then lost its last two games. For the second time in their history, the Browns had a losing record, 4–10. For the first time, they finished in last place.

1975 Forrest Gregg, former star offensive tackle at Green Bay and a Skorich assistant for one season, was named the Browns' fourth head coach. Blanton Collier returned as quarterback coach. The team moved its training quarters from Hiram College to Kent State University. The team won just three games. "There was a definite turnaround in attitude and performance the last seven games," Gregg said. Pruitt had a good season, emerging as one of the NFL's finest runners.

1976 Paul Warfield was back after a six-year absence to lead a receiving corps that also included Reggie Rucker and Oscar Roan. Gregg found a quarterback

of the future in third-year man Brian Sipe. Sipe took over in the second half of the season opener with the Jets after Mike Phipps suffered a slight shoulder separation. Sipe completed 10 passes for 83 yards and a pair of touchdowns. The Browns won five of their last six to compile their finest record since 1972. They were in playoff contention until the final week. The Browns finished four games over .500 and just one game behind Pittsburgh and Cincinnati in the AFC Central Division. Greg Pruitt was handicapped by a badly sprained ankle for the last half of the season but he still managed to rush for 1,000 yards, seventh best in the AFC. The other running back, Cleo Miller, was one of the Browns' most pleasant surprises. Miller, who was signed as a free agent in the middle of 1975, earned a starting job with a great preseason effort and, despite a series of on and off the field injuries, gained 613 yards.

CLEVELAND BROWNS (AAFC), 1946–49, CLEVELAND BROWNS, 1950–76

Adamle, Tony, B, Ohio State	1950–51, 1954
Adams, Pete, G, USC	1974–76
Agase, Alex, G, Illinois	1950–51
Aldridge, Allen, DE, Prairie View	1974
Ambrose, Dick, LB, Virginia	1975–76
Amstutz, Joe, C, Indiana	1957
Anderson, Preston, S, Rice	1974
Andrews, Billy, LB, S. E. Louisiana	1967–72
Athas, Pete, S, Tennessee	1975
Atkins, Doug, DE, Tennessee	1953–54

B

Babich, Bob, LB, Miami, Ohio	1973–76
Baker, Sam, K, Oregon State	1960–61
Barisich, Carl, DT, Princeton	1973–75
Barnes, Erich, DB, Purdue	1965–71
Barney, Eppie, WR, Iowa State	1967–68
Bassett, Maurice, B, Langston, Okla.	1954–56
Battle, Jim, G, Southern U	1966
Beach, Walter, DB, Central Michigan	1963–66
Benz, Larry, DB, Northwestern	1963–65
Bettridge, Ed, LB, Bowling Green	1964
Beutler, Tom, LB, Toledo	1970
Bolden, Leroy, B, Michigan State	1958–59
Bolton, Ron, CB, Norfolk State	1976
Borton, John, QB, Ohio State	1957
Bradley, Harold, G, Iowa	1954–57
Brewer, Johnny, LB-TE, Mississippi	1961–67
Brewster, Darrell (Pete), E, Purdue	1952–58
Briggs, Bob, DE, Heidelberg	1971–73
Brinkman, Charles, WR, Louisville	1972
Brooks, Clifford, CB, Tennessee State	1972
Brown, Dean, RB, Ft. Valley State	1969
Brown, Eddie, S, Tennessee	1974–75
Brown, Jim, RB, Syracuse	1957–65
Brown, John, T, Syracuse	1961–66
Brown, Ken, B, None	1970–75
Brown, Stan, E, Purdue	1971
Brown, Terry, S, Oklahoma State	1976
Bumgardner, Rex, B, West Virginia	1950–52
Bundra, Mike, T, USC	1964

C

Caleb, Jamie, HB, Grambling	1960, 1965
Campbell, Milt, B, Indiana	1957
Carollo, Joe, T, Notre Dame	1972–73
Carpenter, Ken, B, Oregon State	1950–53
Carpenter, Lew, B, Arkansas	1957–58
Carpenter, Preston, B, Arkansas	1956–59
Cassady, Howard, B, Ohio State	1962
Catlin, Tom, LB, Oklahoma	1953–54, 1957–58
Caylor, Lowell, DB, Miami, Ohio	1964
Clark, Monte, T, USC	1963–69
Clarke, Frank, E, Colorado	1957–59
Clarke, Leon, E, USC	1960–62
Cockroft, Don, PK, Adams State	1968–76

Cole, Emerson, B, Toledo	1950–52
Collins, Gary, E, Maryland	1962–71
Colo, Don, T, Brown	1953–58
Conjar, Larry, RB, Notre Dame	1967
Connolly, Ted, G, Tulsa	1967
Copeland, Jim, G-C, Virginia	1967–71
Cornell, Bo, RB, Washington	1971–72
Costello, Vince, LB, Ohio U	1957–66
Cotton, Fest, DT, Dayton	1972
Craig, Neal, S, Fisk	1975–76
Craven, Billy, S, Harvard	1976
Crespino, Bob, E, Mississippi	1961–63
Cureton, Will, QB, East Texas State	1975
Cverko, Andy, G, Northwestern	1963

D

Darden, Thom, CB, Michigan	1972–74, 1976
Darrow, Barry, T, Montana	1974–76
Davis, Ben, DB, Defiance	1967–72
Davis, Dick, B, Nebraska	1969
Davis, Willie, DE, Grambling	1958–59
Dawson, Len, QB, Purdue	1960–61
DeLeone, Tom, C, Ohio State	1974–76
DeMarco, Bob, C, Dayton	1972–74
Demarie, John, G, Louisiana State	1967–75
Dennis, Al, G, Grambling	1976
Denton, Bob, T, Pacific	1960
Deschaine, Dick, E, None	1958
Devrow, Billy, B, So. Mississippi	1967
Dieken, Doug, T, Illinois	1971–76
Donaldson, Gene, G, Kentucky	1953
Dunbar, Jubilee, WR, Southern U.	1974
Duncan, Brian, G, Grambling	1976
Duncan, Ron, E, Wittenberg	1967

E

East, Ron, DE, Montana State	1975
Edwards, Earl, DT, Wichita State	1976
Engel, Steve, B, Colorado	1970

F

Feacher, Ricky, WR-KR, Mississippi Valley	1976
Ferguson, Charley, E, Tennessee A&I	1961
Fichtner, Ross, DB, Purdue	1960–67
Fiss, Galen, LB, Kansas	1956–66
Fleming, Don, B, Florida	1960–62
Ford, Len, G, Michigan	1950–57
Forester, Herschel, DB, Southern Methodist	1954–57
Franklin, Bobby, DB, Mississippi	1960–66
Freeman, Bob, B, Auburn	1957–58
Furman, John, QB, Texas Western	1962

G

Gain, Bob, T, Kentucky	1952, 1954–64
Garcia, Jim, DT, Purdue	1965
Garlington, John, LB, Louisiana State	1968–76
Gatski, Frank, C, Marshall	1950–56
Gaudio, Bob, G, Ohio State	1951
Gault, Don, QB, Hofstra	1970
Gautt, Prentice, RB, Oklahoma	1960
George, Tim, WR, Carson-Newman	1974
Gibron, Abe, G, Purdue	1950–56
Gillom, Horace, E, Nevada	1950–56
Glass, Bill, DE, Baylor	1962–68
Glass, Chip, TE, Florida State	1969–73
Goosby, Tom, LB, Baldwin-Wallace	1963
Gorgal, Ken, B, Purdue	1950, 1953–54
Goss, Don, T, Southern Methodist	1956
Graf, Dave, LB, Penn State	1975–76
Graham, Otto, QB, Northwestern	1950–55
Grant, Wes, DE, UCLA	1972
Green, Ernie, HB, Louisville	1962–68
Green, Ron, B, North Dakota	1967–68
Green, Van, S, Shaw	1973–76
Greenwood, Don, B, Illinois	1950–57
Gregg, Forrest, T, Tulsa	1950–51
Gregory, Jack, DE, Delta State	1967–71
Groza, Lou, T-K, Ohio State	1950–59, 1961–67

H

Hall, Charlie, LB, Houston	1971–76
Hanulak, Chet, B, Maryland	1954, 1957
Harraway, Charley, RB, San Jose State	1966–68

Bill Nelsen

Greg Pruitt

Ray Renfro

Jim Ray Smith

Tommy Thompson

Paul Wiggin

John Wooten

- Herring, Hal, C, Auburn ... 1950–52
- Helluin, Jerry, T, Tulane ... 1952–53
- Hickerson, Gene, G, Mississippi ... 1958–60, 1962–73
- Hill, Jim, S, Texas A&I ... 1975
- Hoaglin, Fred, C, Pittsburgh ... 1966–72
- Holden, Steve, WR, Arizona State ... 1973–76
- Holloway, Glen, G, North Texas State ... 1974
- Hooker, Fair, WR, Arizona State ... 1969–74
- Horn, Don, QB, San Diego State ... 1973
- Houston, Jim, LB, Ohio State ... 1960–72
- Houston, Lin, G, Ohio State ... 1950–53
- Howard, Sherman, B, Nevada ... 1952–53
- Howell, Mike, DB, Grambling ... 1965–72
- Howton, Bill, E, Rice ... 1959
- Humble, Weldon, G, Rice ... 1950
- Hunt, Bob, RB, Heidelberg ... 1974
- Hunter, Art, C, Notre Dame ... 1956–59
- Hutchinson, Tom, E, Kentucky ... 1963–65
- Hutchinson, Chuck, G, Ohio State ... 1973–75
- Hyonski, Henry, RB, Temple ... 1975

I

- Ilgenfritz, Mark, DE, Vanderbilt ... 1974
- Irons, Gerald, LB, Maryland State-E.S. ... 1975
- Isbell, Joe Bob, G, Houston ... 1966

J

- Jackson, Rich, DE, Southern U. ... 1972
- Jackson, Bob, G, Duke ... 1975–76
- Jagade, Harry (Chick), B, Indiana ... 1951–53
- James, Nathaniel, CB, Florida A&M ... 1968
- James, Tommy, B, Ohio State ... 1950–55
- Jenkins, Al, G, Tulsa ... 1969–70
- Johnson, Mitch, G-T, UCLA ... 1971
- Johnson, Ron, RB, Michigan ... 1969
- Johnson, Walter, DT, Cal. State-LA ... 1965–76
- Jones, Dave, WR, Kansas State ... 1969–71
- Jones, Dub, B, Tulane ... 1950–55
- Jones, Homer, WR, Texas Southern ... 1970
- Jones, Joe, DE, Tennessee State ... 1970–71, 1973, 1975–76
- Jordan, Henry, DT, Virginia ... 1957–58

K

- Kanicki, Jim, DT, Michigan State ... 1963–69
- Kellermann, Ernie, DB, Miami, Ohio ... 1966–71
- Kelly, Leroy, RB, Morgan State ... 1964–73
- Kinard, Billy, B, Mississippi ... 1956
- King, Don, T, Kentucky ... 1954
- Kingrea, Rick, LB, Tulane ... 1971–72
- Kissell, John, T, Boston Coll. ... 1950–52, 1954–56
- Konz, Ken, B, Louisiana State ... 1953–59
- Kreitling, Rich, E, Illinois ... 1959–63
- Kuechenberg, Rudy, LB, Purdue ... 1970

L

- Lahr, Warren, B, Western Reserve ... 1950–59
- Lane, Gary, QB, Missouri ... 1966–67
- Lavelli, Dante, E, Ohio State ... 1950–56
- Lefear, Billy, RB, Henderson, Ark. ... 1972–75
- Leigh, Charles, RB, No college ... 1968–69
- LeVeck, Jack, LB, Ohio ... 1975
- Lewis, Cliff, QB, Duke ... 1950–51
- Lewis, Stan, DE, Wayne State, Neb. ... 1975
- Linden, Errol, T, Houston ... 1961
- Lindsey, Dale, LB, Western Kentucky ... 1965–72
- Lloyd, Dave, LB, Georgia ... 1959–61
- Logan, Dave, WR, Colorado ... 1976
- Long, Mel, LB, Toledo ... 1972
- Lucci, Mike, LB, Tennessee ... 1962–64

M

- Macerelli, John, G, St. Vincent ... 1956
- Majors, Bobby, S, Tennessee ... 1972
- Marshall, Jim, DE, Ohio State ... 1960
- Martin, Jim, LB-K, Notre Dame ... 1950
- Massey, Carlton, E, Texas ... 1954–56
- Matheson, Bob, LB, Duke ... 1967–70
- Mays, Dave, QB-K, Texas Southern ... 1976
- McClung, Willie, T, Florida A&M ... 1958–59
- McCormack, Mike, T, Kansas ... 1954–62
- McCusker, Jim, T, Pittsburgh ... 1963
- McDonald, Tommy, E, Oklahoma ... 1968
- McKay, Bob, T, Texas ... 1970–75
- McKinnis, Hugh, RB, Arizona State ... 1973–75
- McNeil, Clifton, WR, Grambling ... 1964–67
- Memmelaar, Dale, G, Wyoming ... 1964–65
- Meylan, Wayne, LB, Nebraska ... 1968–69
- Michaels, Walt, G, Washington & Lee ... 1952–61
- Miller, Cleo, RB, Arkansas AM&N ... 1975–76
- Miller, Willie, WR, Colorado State ... 1975–76
- Minniear, Randy, B, Purdue ... 1970
- Mitchell, Alvin, CB, Morgan State ... 1968–69
- Mitchell, Bob, B, Illinois ... 1958–61
- Mitchell, Mack, DE, Houston ... 1975–76
- Modzelewski, Dick, DT, Maryland ... 1964–66
- Modzelewski, Ed, B, Maryland ... 1955–69
- Morin, Milt, TE, Massachusetts ... 1966–75
- Morris, Chris, T, Indiana ... 1972–73
- Morrison, Fred, B, Ohio State ... 1954–56
- Morrison, Reece, RB, S.W. Texas State ... 1968–72
- Morrow, John, C, Michigan ... 1960–66
- Morze, Frank, C, Boston College ... 1962–63
- Mosselle, Dom, B, Superior Teachers ... 1950
- Mostardo, Richard, B, Kent State ... 1960
- Motley, Marion, B, Nevada ... 1950–53
- Murphy, Fred, E, Georgia Tech ... 1960

N

- Nagler, Gern, E, Santa Clara ... 1960–61
- Nelsen, Bill, QB, USC ... 1968–72
- Ninowski, Jim, QB, Mich. St. ... 1958–59, 1962–66
- Noll, Chuck, G, Dayton ... 1953–59
- Nutting, Ed, T, Georgia Tech ... 1961

O

- O'Brien, Francis, T, Michigan State ... 1959
- O'Connell, Tom, QB, Illinois ... 1956–57
- O'Connor, Bill, E, Notre Dame ... 1949
- Oliver, Bob, DE, Abilene Christian ... 1969
- Oristaglio, Bob, E, Pennsylvania ... 1951

P

- Palmer, Darrell, T, Texas Christian ... 1950–53
- Palumbo, Sam, C, Notre Dame ... 1955–56
- Parilli, Babe, QB, Kentucky ... 1956
- Parker, Frank, DT, Oklahoma St. ... 1962–64, 1966–67
- Parris, Gary, TE, Florida State ... 1975–76
- Parrish, Bernie, DB, Florida ... 1959–66
- Paul, Don, LB, Washington State ... 1954–58
- Pena, Robet, G, Massachusetts ... 1972
- Perini, Pete, B, Ohio State ... 1955
- Peters, Floyd, T, San Francisco State ... 1959–62
- Peters, Tony, CB, Oklahoma ... 1975–76
- Petitbon, John, B, Notre Dame ... 1955–56
- Phelps, Don, B, Kentucky ... 1950–51
- Phipps, Mike, QB, Purdue ... 1970–76
- Pietrosante, Nick, RB, Notre Dame ... 1966–67
- Pitts, Frank, WR, Southern U ... 1971–73
- Pitts, John, S, Arizona State ... 1975
- Plum, Milt, QB, Penn State ... 1957–61
- Poole, Larry, RB, Kent State ... 1975–76
- Powell, Preston, B, Grambling ... 1961
- Prestel, Jim, T, Idaho ... 1960
- Pritchett, Billy, RB, West Texas State ... 1975
- Pruitt, Greg, RB, Oklahoma ... 1973–76
- Pruitt, Mike, RB, Purdue ... 1976
- Ptacek, Bob, QB, Michigan ... 1959
- Putnam, Duane, G, Pacific ... 1961

Q

- Quintan, Bill, E, Michigan State ... 1957–58
- Quinlan, Volney, B, San Diego State ... 1956

R

- Raimey, Dave, B, Michigan ... 1964
- Ratterman, George, QB, Notre Dame ... 1952–56
- Rechichar, Bert, LB-K, Tennessee ... 1952
- Renfro, Ray, B, No. Texas State ... 1952–63
- Reynolds, Billy, B, Pittsburgh ... 1953–54, 1957
- Reynolds, Chuck, C-G, Tulsa ... 1969–70
- Rhome, Jerry, QB, Tulsa ... 1969
- Richardson, Gloster, WR, Jackson State ... 1972–74
- Righetti, Joe, T, Waynesburg ... 1969–70
- Roan, Oscar, TE, Southern Methodist ... 1975–76
- Roberts, Walter, WR, San Jose State ... 1964–66
- Robinson, Fred, G, Washington ... 1957
- Roman, Nick, DE, Ohio State ... 192–74
- Romaniszyn, Jim, LB, Edinboro State ... 1973–74
- Rucker, Reggie, WR, Boston ... 1975–76
- Ryan, Frank, QB, Rice ... 1962–68
- Rymkus, Lou, T, Notre Dame ... 1950–51

S

- Sabatino, Bill, DT, Colorado ... 1968
- Sandusky, John, T, Villanova ... 1950–55
- Scales, Charley, FB, Indiana ... 1962–65
- Schafrath, Dick, T, Ohio State ... 1959–71
- Schoen, Tom, DB, Notre Dame ... 1970
- Schultz, Randy, RB, Iowa State Teachers ... 1966
- Scott, Bo, RB, Ohio State ... 1969–74
- Scott, Clarence, CB, Kansas State ... 1971–76
- Sczurek, Stan, LB, Purdue ... 1963–65
- Seifert, Mike, DE, Wisconsin ... 1974
- Selawski, Gene, T, Purdue ... 1960
- Sharkey, Ed, G, Duke ... 1952
- Sheppard, Henry, T, Southern Methodist ... 1976
- Sheriff, Stan, LB, Cal. Poly ... 1957
- Sherk, Jerry, DT, Oklahoma State ... 1970–76
- Shiner, Dick, QB, Maryland ... 1967
- Shoals, Roger, T-G, Maryland ... 1963–64
- Shofner, Jim, CB, Texas Christian ... 1958–63
- Shorter, Jim, CB, Detroit ... 1962–63
- Shula, Don, CB, John Carroll ... 1951–52
- Sikich, Mike, G, Northwestern ... 1971
- Sipe, Brian, QB, San Diego State ... 1974–76
- Skibinski, Joe, G, Purdue ... 1952
- Smith, Bob, B, Nebraska ... 1955–56
- Smith, Jim Ray, G, Baylor ... 1956–62
- Smith, Ken, TE, New Mexico ... 1973
- Smith, Ralph, E, Mississippi ... 1965–68
- Snidow, Ron, DE, Oregon ... 1968–72
- Speedie, Mac, E, Utah ... 1950–52
- Staroba, Paul, WR, Michigan ... 1972
- St. Clair, Mike, DE, Grambling ... 1976
- Steinbrunner, Don, E. Washington State ... 1953
- Stephens, Larry, T, Texas ... 1960–61
- Stevenson, Rickey, B, Arizona ... 1970
- Stienke, Jim, CB, Southwest Texas State ... 1973
- Sullivan, Dave, WR, Virginia ... 1973–74
- Sullivan, Gerry, T, Illinois ... 1974–76
- Summers, Fred, DB, Wake Forest ... 1969–71
- Sumner, Walt, S, Florida State ... 1969–74

T

- Taffoni, Joe, T, Tennessee-Martin ... 1967–70
- Taseff, Carl, B, John Carroll ... 1951
- Thaxton, Jim, TE, Tennessee State ... 1974
- Thompson, Tommy, C, William & Mary ... 1950–53
- Tidmore, Sam, LB, Ohio State ... 1962–63

U

- Upshaw, Marvin, DT, Trinity ... 1968–69

W

- Ward, Carl, S, Michigan ... 1967–68
- Warfield, Paul, WR, Ohio State ... 1964–69, 1976
- Watkins, Tom, B, Iowa State ... 1961
- Webb, Ken, B, Presbyterian ... 1963
- Weber, Chuck, LB, West Chester State ... 1955–56
- White, Bob, B, Stanford ... 1955
- Whitlow, Bob, C, Arizona ... 1968
- Wiggin, Paul, DE, Stanford ... 1957–67
- Williams, A. D., E, Pacific ... 1960
- Williams, Sidney, LB, Southern U. ... 1964–66
- Willis, Bill, G, Ohio State ... 1950–53
- Wilson, Tom, B, None ... 1962
- Wooten, John, G, Colorado ... 1959–67
- Wren, Junior, B, Missouri ... 1956–59
- Wright, George, DT, Sam Houston State ... 1972
- Wycinsky, Craig, S, Michigan State ... 1972

Y

- Yanchar, Bill, T, Purdue ... 1970
- Young, George, E, Georgia ... 1950–53
- Youngblood, George, B, Cal. State-L.A. ... 1967
- Youngelman, Sid, G, Alabama ... 1959

DALLAS COWBOYS

Wide receiver Bob Hayes after making a catch vs. the Saints, 1969.

1960 Clint Murchison, Jr. and Bedford Wynne were awarded an NFL expansion franchise for Dallas at the annual league meeting in Miami Beach, January 28. AFL Commissioner Joe Foss threatened an antitrust suit, claiming the NFL was trying to ruin his Dallas Texans franchise. Since the college draft was already completed, the Cowboys had to settle for 36 veterans selected from the 12 NFL teams. Tex Schramm, who had spent 10 years in the Los Angeles Rams' front office and worked for CBS Television as assistant director of sports, was named general manager. Tom Landry, a former University of Texas star and New York Giants assistant, was named head coach. Hoping to win the Dallas fans, Landry made his team offense–conscious. Dallas traded its first draft choice to Washington for Eddie LeBaron, the 5–foot 8–inch quarterback who led the NFL in passing in 1958. They also signed Don Meredith, a highly regarded rookie quarterback from Southern Methodist. The Cowboys played their home games in the Cotton Bowl. Attendance averaged 20,000. Dallas lost its first 10 league games before tying the New York Giants 31–31, December 4.

1961 Schramm hired Gil Brandt as talent scout and Brandt took charge of the Cowboys' college draft. His first pick was Bob Lilly, a superb defensive tackle from Texas Christian. Brandt also uncovered Amos Marsh, a fullback from Oregon State who was ignored by the other clubs. The Cowboys opened with two victories. They scored 10 points in the last 56 seconds to upset Pittsburgh 27-24 in the opener before 23,500 at the Cotton Bowl, September 17. The following week, Dallas knocked off Minnesota's expansion Vikings 21-7 before 20,500 at the Cotton Bowl. Don Perkins, a slashing halfback from New Mexico, rushed for 108 yards. The Cowboys scored their first shutout, 28-0 over the Vikings and were tied for first place in the Eastern Conference with a 3-1 record, October 1. The euphoria died quickly as the Cowboys won just one of their last 10 games.

1962 Landry introduced the shuttling quarterback offense. Rather than send in plays by alternating the guards, Paul Brown style, Landry let LeBaron and Meredith play alternate downs. The idea was an immediate success as the Cowboys bolted to a 4–3–1 start and stayed within a half-game of first place through midseason. A crowd of 45,668 fans was at the Cotton Bowl for the showdown between Dallas and the front-running New York Giants, November 15. The Giants routed the Cowboys 41–10 and LeBaron was injured, crippling the Dallas offense. The Cowboys won just one of their last six games but their wide-open offense (398 points) had captured the imagination of the Dallas fans.

1963 The rival AFL Texans announced that they were moving to Kansas City, February 8. The season started dismally as the Cowboys dropped six of their first seven games. The only bright spot came in a 21–17 loss to Washington when 33–year–old Billy Howton broke Don Hutson's all-time career record for pass receiving yardage, surpassing the 8,000-yard mark, September 29. Injuries took their toll on the diminutive LeBaron and he gave way to Meredith for the second half of the schedule. Following the season, LeBaron announced his retirement.

1964 With one year to go on his original contract, Landry was signed to a 10-year extension, giving him the longest coaching pact in the history of pro sports to that time. Howton joined LeBaron in retirement, and the Cowboys traded for two receivers, Buddy Dial of Pittsburgh and Tommy McDonald of Philadelphia. McDonald came through with 46 catches, but the price Dallas paid for his services—

kicker Sam Baker—was steep. Landry turned the kicking duties over to Dick Van Raaphorst, a rookie from Ohio State. The Cowboys lost several close games due to Van Raaphorst's erratic kicks. Second-round draft pick Mel Renfro of Oregon had a brilliant year, intercepting seven passes and leading the NFL in kick returns. Frank Clarke, an original Cowboy, set a club record with 65 pass receptions.

1965 Dallas had an extraordinary crop of rookies, including wide receiver Bob Hayes, tackle Ralph Neely, running back Dan Reeves, defensive tackle Jethro Pugh, and number one draft pick quarterback Craig Morton. Hayes, the Olympic champion sprinter, had the most immediate impact, catching 46 passes, returning punts and kickoffs, and scoring 13 touchdowns. Hayes's blazing speed forced defensive secondaries to abandon man-to-man coverage and adopt the zone. With receivers such as Hayes and Clarke at his disposal, Meredith had a great year, throwing 22 touchdown passes. The Cowboys were unpredictable and exciting. Following impressive victories over San Francisco and Pittsburgh, they attracted their first home sellout (76,251) to the Cotton Bowl for a game against Cleveland, September 21. The Browns won 24-17 but the Cowboys rallied to win three of their last four games to finish second and qualify for the Playoff Bowl. Dallas lost its first postseason game to Baltimore 35-3 in Miami's Orange Bowl.

1966 Schramm was named president of the club by owner Clint Murchison, who retained the title of chairman of the board. On the field, the pieces finally fell into place. The already abundant talent was enhanced by rookies John Niland, a guard, and Walt Garrison, a running back. Dallas opened with four straight victories, including romps over the New York Giants (52–7), Atlanta (47–14), and Philadelphia (56–7). Meredith threw five touchdown passes in the opener against New York and five more against the Eagles. In the first seven weeks, the Cowboys averaged 39 points a game. In a 31-30 win over Washington, Hayes gained 246 yards on pass receptions, including a 95-yard touchdown. Dallas practically clinched its first Eastern Conference championship with a dramatic 26–14 win over the second-place Cleveland Browns before an overflow crowd of 80,259 at the Cotton Bowl, November 24.

1967 The Cowboys and the Green Bay Packers played one of the most thrilling championship games in NFL history, January 1. Green Bay won 34–27 as

Bart Starr threw four touchdown passes. The Packers led throughout but had to withstand a furious Dallas comeback that came within two yards of forcing overtime. Meredith's try for the tying touchdown was a pass intercepted by Green Bay's Tom Brown. Early in the season, Meredith suffered severe rib injuries, a broken nose, and subsequent pneumonia. Morton, a rapidly maturing quarterback, filled in for Meredith in several key games. Reeves, a quarterback-turned-halfback from South Carolina, added versatility to the offense, totaling over 1,100 yards and 11 touchdowns rushing and receiving. Hayes and Lance Rentzel, who was obtained from the Vikings, combined for 18 touchdown receptions. In the Eastern conference title game against Cleveland, Meredith completed 10 of 12 passes for two scores as Dallas roared to a 24–0 lead. Dallas won 52–14. "It was our greatest game ever," said Landry. The Cowboys and Packers played for the NFL championship on the coldest December 31 in Green Bay history—13 degrees below zero. Dallas overcame a 14–0 deficit for a 17–14 fourth quarter lead on Reeves's 50-yard scoring pass to Rentzel. Starr's last-second quarterback sneak won the game for Green Bay 21–17. "You can tell the real Cowboys," Landry said afterward. "They're the ones with the frost-bitten fingers and the broken hearts."

1968 Late in the sluggish preseason, Landry held a closed-door meeting in which he blasted his players for a lack of pride and a poor attitude. The Cowboys responded by going unbeaten through their first six league games, including victories over Detroit (59–13) and Philadelphia (45–13). The Cowboys suffered a key loss in a 27–10 win over St. Louis when Dan Reeves went down with torn knee ligaments. He was replaced by second-year back Craig Baynham. The Cowboys finished strong with five straight wins and many forecasters said it was their year to go all the way. Dallas was upset by Cleveland in the Eastern Conference championship game 31–20, December 21. Meredith threw back-to-back interceptions early in the second half that led to Cleveland touchdowns and snapped a 10–10 tie. "This is my most disappointing day," Landry said. The dejected Cowboys regrouped to beat Minnesota in the Playoff Bowl 17–13.

1969 Ground was broken for Texas Stadium, a lavish $30 million structure in suburban Irving with a seating capacity of 65,000, January 25. That set the tone for a season of change. Meredith, the last of the original Cowboys, announced his retirement, July 5. Less than two weeks later, Perkins, the team's leading rusher the previous eight seasons, announced his retirement. Garrison replaced Perkins; Morton took over for Meredith. Roger Staubach, 27, joined the Cowboys as a rookie quarterback following four years of naval service. Calvin Hill, a rookie halfback from Yale, replaced Reeves at halfback and rushed for 942 yards. The Cowboys rolled to another Capitol Division title with an 11-2-1 record. Renfro set a club record with 10 interceptions. The season closed on a low note, however, as the Cowboys lost to Cleveland 38-14 in the Eastern Conference title game at the Cotton Bowl. Morton completed 8 of 24 passes and threw two damaging interceptions. In the Playoff Bowl, Los Angeles compounded the grief by defeating the Cowboys 31-0.

1970 The Cowboys finished the preseason 1-5 and Landry named Staubach to start the league opener against Philadelphia. Dallas won 17-7 but Staubach was unimpressive. After a 54-13 rout at the hands of Minnesota, Landry went back to Morton. The low point came in a 38-0 loss to division-leading St. Louis. The defeat dropped Dallas to third place with a 5-4 record. The free-and-easy Cowboys swept their last five games and shot past the Cardinals and New York Giants who faded in December. Duane Thomas, a rookie halfback from West Texas State, led the offense replacing the injured Hill. The defense did not allow a touchdown in the last 17 quarters. Dallas clinched the division title by burying Houston 52-10 on Morton's five touchdown passes, December 20. The Cowboys edged Detroit 5-0 in the NFL divisional playoff as Thomas rushed for 135 yards.

1971 Thomas gained 143 yards to lead the Cowboys past San Francisco 17-10 in the NFC championship game at Kezar Stadium, January 3. The Cowboys committed five costly turnovers and lost Super Bowl V to Baltimore 16-13 on Jim O'Brien's last-second 32-yard field goal, January 17. The Cowboys remained haunted by their inability to "win the big one." They moved into their new home, Texas Stadium, October 24. Through the first half of the season, Landry alternated Morton and Staubach at quarterback with poor results (4-3). When the Cowboys lost to the Chicago Bears with Morton and Staubach alternating plays and throwing four interceptions, Landry made a decision. He picked Staubach as his number-one man because of Staubach's scrambling ability and flair for leadership. Staubach quickly established himself as the NFL's most accurate passer (60 percent completions) and a skillful runner (averaging 8.4 yards a carry). With Thomas, Hill, and Garrison rotating in the backfield, Dallas had the best ground game in football. Under Staubach, the Cowboys won their last seven games and retained their Eastern Division title. The Dallas defense forced five turnovers to beat Minnesota 20-12 in the NFL playoff, December 25 at Bloomington.

1972 The Cowboys defeated San Francisco 14-3 in the NFC championship game as defensive end George Andrie returned an interception to the 1-yard line, January 2. With Staubach hitting 12 of 19 passes and Thomas rushing for 95 yards, Dallas rolled over Miami 24-3 in Super Bowl VI at New Orleans, January 16. Staubach suffered a shoulder separation in the final preseason game at Los Angeles and was sidelined for three months. The uncommunicative Thomas alienated Dallas management and was traded to San Diego. Andrie and Lilly were hampered much of the year with back injuries. With all these woes, the Cowboys struggled through an erratic season, slipping to second place in the Eastern Division behind Washington. They had a chance to tie for first the final week but lost 23-3 to the New York Giants. The one steady performer was Calvin Hill, who became the first Cowboys' player ever to rush for more than 1,000

yards, totaling 1,036. Hill also led Dallas receivers with 43 catches. Staubach came off the bench in the second half and sparked Dallas to a dramatic 30-28 win over San Francisco in the NFC playoff. Staubach threw two touchdown passes in the final 1:48 to reverse an almost-certain defeat. Appearing in their third straight NFC championship game, the Cowboys were thrashed 26-3 by the Redskins.

1973 The Cowboys and Landry recorded their one-hundredth NFL victory with a 40-3 win over New Orleans at Texas Stadium, September 24. After a 3-0 start, the Cowboys lost three of their next four games including a 14-7 affair in Washington in which Garrison was stopped on the goal line as the gun sounded. Lee Roy Jordan, the veteran middle linebacker, turned the season around, intercepting three Ken Anderson passes in the first quarter to inspire a 38-10 win over Cincinnati, November 4. Drew Pearson, a free-agent wide receiver, made his first NFL start replacing injured Mike Montgomery in a 31-10 win over Philadelphia. Dallas gained revenge on the Redskins with a 27-7 win at Texas Stadium, December 9. Hill rushed for 110 yards and two touchdowns as Dallas regained the Eastern Division crown. Staubach won his second NFL passing championship, hitting 63 percent of his attempts, 23 for touchdowns. Hill rushed for a club record 1,142 yards. Dallas held off Los Angeles 27-16 in an NFC divisional playoff game at Texas Stadium. The win, highlighted by Staubach's 83-yard touchdown pass to Pearson, was achieved without Hill, who suffered a dislocated elbow during the game after gaining 97 yards. Without the injured Hill and Lilly, the Cowboys were no match for Minnesota in the NFC championship game, losing 27-10 at Texas Stadium, December 30.

1974 For the first time, Dallas had the first pick overall in the NFL college draft. Using a choice they acquired from Houston in exchange for Tody Smith and Billy Parks, Dallas selected Ed (Too Tall) Jones, a massive defensive end from Tennessee State. The Cowboys got off to their poorest start since 1963, losing four of their first five games and slipping into last place. Hill ended the slump, rushing for 140 yards and scoring three touchdowns in a 31-24 win over Philadelphia, October 20. The Cowboys surged back into contention, winning seven of their next eight, highlighted by a 24-23 win over Washington, November 28. Rookie quarterback Clint Longley, subbing for the injured Staubach, threw two touchdown passes including a 50-yarder to Pearson with 28 seconds left to win it. The strong finish fell short, however, as Dallas missed the playoffs for the first time in eight years.

1975 With Hill signed by Hawaii of the World Football League and Garrison retired, Landry revamped his offense, installing the shotgun formation with Staubach taking the snap eight yards behind center. The new look surprised Los Angeles and the Cowboys upset the favored Rams 18-7 in the league opener, September 21. The following week, rookie linebacker Thomas Henderson returned a kickoff 97 yards for a touchdown as Dallas beat St. Louis in overtime 37-31. After a 4-0 start, the Cowboys hit the skids, slipping to third place at 5-3 before catching fire again. Bob Lilly was honored at a game against Philadelphia as his uniform number 74 was retired, November 23. The Cowboys won five of their last six to finish second to St. Louis in the Eastern Division and secure the NFC wild card berth. Dallas pulled off a stunner in the playoff opener, upending Minnesota 17-14 on Staubach's 50-yard touchdown pass to Drew Pearson with 24 seconds left, December 27.

1976 Staubach was magnificent in the NFC championship game, throwing four touchdown passes, three to free agent halfback Preston Pearson, as the underdog Cowboys embarrassed Los Angeles 37-7,

January 4. The Rams did not cross midfield until the final play of the third quarter. In Super Bowl X in Miami, Dallas led most of the way but lost to Pittsburgh 21-17, January 18. Staubach threw two touchdown passes and was still heaving the ball into the end zone hoping for another miracle as the game ended. When the 1976 season started, Scott Laidlaw, a second-year fullback from Stanford, gained 104 yards in his first NFL start as Dallas beat Philadelphia 27-7 in the opening game. Staubach had the best game of his career, passing for 339 yards and two touchdowns as Dallas outlasted Baltimore 30-27, September 26. The Cowboys won their first five games as Staubach completed a remarkable 73.5 percent of his passes. Dallas beat Chicago 31-21, but Staubach broke a finger on his passing hand, an injury that bothered him the remainder of the season, October 24. Drew Pearson caught nine passes for 135 yards and a touchdown in Dallas's 17-10 win over Buffalo, November 15. The Cowboys clinched their first Eastern Division title since 1973 by beating Philadelphia 26-7 December 5 at Philadelphia. The Cowboys' sputtering offense proved their undoing in the NFC playoffs as they lost to Los Angeles in the first round 14-12, December 19. Lee Roy Jordan announced his retirement after 14 seasons with the Cowboys. Don Meredith and Don Perkins joined Bob Lilly in the Cowboys' Hall of Fame.

MEMBERS OF HALL OF FAME:
None

COWBOYS RECORD, 1960-76

Year	Won	Lost	Tied	Pct.	Pts.	OP
1960	0	11	1	.000	177	369
1961	4	9	1	.308	236	380
1962	5	8	1	.385	398	402
1963	4	10	0	.286	305	378
1964	5	8	1	.385	250	289
1965	7	7	0	.500	325	280
1966§	10	3	1	.769	445	239
1967§	9	5	0	.643	342	268
1968†	12	2	0	.857	431	186
1969†	11	2	1	.846	369	223
1970‡	10	4	0	.714	299	221
1971**	11	3	0	.786	406	222
1972	10	4	0	.714	319	240
1973§	10	4	0	.714	382	203
1974	8	6	0	.571	297	235
1975‡	10	4	0	.714	350	266
1976*	11	3	0	.786	296	194
17 Years	137	93	6	.593	5,627	4,595

§*NFL Eastern Conference Champion*
†*NFL Capitol Division Champion*
‡*NFC Champion*
***Super Bowl Champion*
**NFC Eastern Division Champion*

RECORD HOLDERS

Rushing (Yards)	Calvin Hill, 1973	1,142
Passing (Pct.)	Roger Staubach, 1973	62.6
Passing (Yards)	Don Meredith, 1966	2,805
Passing (TDs)	Don Meredith, 1966	24
Receiving (No.)	Frank Clarke, 1964	65
Receiving (Yards)	Bob Hayes, 1966	1,232
Interceptions (No.)	Mel Renfro, 1969	10
Punting (Avg.)	Ron Widby, 1969	43.3
Punt Ret. (Avg.)	Bob Hayes, 1968	20.8
Kickoff Ret. (Avg.)	Mel Renfro, 1965	30.0
Touchdowns (Total)	Dan Reeves, 1966	16
Field Goals Made	Toni Fritsch, 1975	22
Points (No.)	Danny Villanueva, 1966	107

COACHING HISTORY

1960-76	Tom Landry	137-93-6

FIRST PLAYER SELECTED

1960	None
1961	Bob Lilly, DT, Texas Christian
1962	Guy (Sonny) Gibbs, QB (2 future),Texas Christian
1963	Lee Roy Jordan, LB, Alabama
1964	Scott Appleton, DT, Texas
1965	Craig Morton, QB, California
1966	John Niland, G, Iowa
1967	Phil Clark, DB (3), Northwestern
1968	Dennis Homan, WR, Alabama
1969	Calvin Hill, RB, Yale
1970	Duane Thomas, RB, West Texas State
1971	Tody Smith, DE, So. California
1972	Bill Thomas, RB, Boston College
1973	Billy Joe DuPree, TE, Michigan State
1974	Ed (Too Tall) Jones, DE, Tennessee State
1975	Randy White, LB, Maryland
1976	Aaron Kyle, DB, Wyoming

Frank Clarke

Dave Edwards

Mike Gaechter

Walt Garrison

Cliff Harris

Lee Roy Jordan

Harvey Martin

DALLAS COWBOYS, 1960–76

Adderley, Herb, CB, Michigan State ... 1970–72
Adkins, Margene, WR, Henderson J.C. ... 1970–71
Alworth, Lance, WR, Arkansas ... 1971–72
Andrie, George, DE, Marquette ... 1962–72
Arneson, Jim, G-C, Arizona ... 1973
Asher, Bob, T, Vanderbilt ... 1970

B

Babb, Gene, LB-RB, Austin ... 1960–61
Babinecz, John, LB, Villanova ... 1972–73
Baker, Sam, P-K, Oregon State ... 1962–63
Barnes, Benny, CB, Stanford ... 1972–76
Barnes, Gary, WR, Clemson ... 1963
Barnes, Rodrigo, LB, Rice ... 1973–74
Bateman, Marv, P, Utah ... 1972–74
Baynham, Craig, RB, Georgia Tech ... 1967–69
Belden, Bob, QB, Notre Dame ... 1969–70
Bercich, Bob, S, Michigan State ... 1960–61
Bielski, Dick, TE, Maryland ... 1960–61
Bishop, Don, CB, CC Los Angeles ... 1960–61
Boeke, Jim, T, Heidelberg ... 1964–67
Borden, Nate, DE, Indiana ... 1960–61
Braatz, Tom, LB, Marquette ... 1960
Bradfute, Byron, T, So. Mississippi ... 1960–61
Breunig, Bob, LB, Arizona State ... 1975–76
Brock, Clyde, DT, Utah State ... 1962–63
Brown, Otto, CB-S, Prairie View ... 1969
Bullocks, Amos, RB, So. Illinois ... 1962–64
Burkett, Jackie, LB, Auburn ... 1968–69
Butler, Bill, S, Chattanooga ... 1960

C

Caffey, Lee Roy, LB, Texas A&M ... 1971
Capone, Warren, LB, Louisiana State ... 1975
Carrell, Duane, P, Florida State ... 1974
Clark, Mike, K, Texas A&M ... 1968–71, 1973
Clark, Monte, T, USC ... 1962
Clark, Phil, CB-S, Northwestern ... 1967–69
Clarke, Frank, WR, Colorado ... 1960–67
Cole, Larry, DE, Hawaii ... 1968–76
Coleman, Ralph, LB, North Carolina A&T ... 1972
Colvin, Jim, DT, Houston ... 1964–66
Cone, Fred, K, Clemson ... 1960
Connelly, Mike, C, Utah State ... 1960–67
Conrad, Bobby Joe, WR, Texas A&M ... 1969
Cronin, Gene, DE, Pacific ... 1960
Cvercko, Andy, G, Northwestern ... 1961–62

D

Daniels, Dick, S, Pacific, Ore. ... 1966–68
Davis, Donnie, WR, Southern U. ... 1962
Davis, Kyle, C, Oklahoma ... 1975
Davis, Sonny, LB, Baylor ... 1961
Dennison, Doug, RB, Kutztown State ... 1974–76
Deters, Harold, K, N. Carolina State ... 1967
Dial, Buddy, WR, Rice ... 1964–66
Dickson, Paul, T, Baylor ... 1960
Diehl, John, DT, Virginia ... 1965
Ditka, Mike, TE, Pittsburgh ... 1969–72
Doelling, Fred, S, Pennsylvania ... 1960
Donohue, Leon, G, San Jose State ... 1965–67
Donovan, Pat, T, Stanford ... 1975–76
Doran, Jim, WR, Iowa State ... 1960–61
Douglas, Merrill, RB, Utah ... 1961
Dowdle, Mike, RB-LB, Texas ... 1960–62
Dugan, Fred, WR, Dayton ... 1960
Dunn, Perry Lee, RB, Mississippi ... 1964–65
Dupre, L.G., RB, Baylor ... 1960–61
DuPree, Billy Joe, TE, Michigan State ... 1973–76

E

East, Ron, DT, Montana State ... 1967–70
Edwards, Dave, LB, Auburn ... 1963–75
Eidson, Jim, C, Mississippi State ... 1976

F

Falls, Mike, G, Minnesota ... 1960–61
Fisher, Ray, TE, Illinois ... 1960
Fitzgerald, John, G-C, Boston College ... 1971–76
Folkins, Lee, TE, Washington ... 1962–64
Flowers, Richmond, S, Tennessee ... 1969–71
Franckhauser, Tom, CB, Purdue ... 1960–61
Frank, Bill, T, Colorado ... 1964
Fritsch, Toni, K, Austria Tech ... 1971–73, 75
Frost, Ken, DT, Tennessee ... 1961–62
Fry, Bob, T, Kentucky ... 1960–64
Fugett, Jean, TE, Amherst ... 1972–75

G

Gaechter, Mike, S, Oregon ... 1962–69
Garrison, Walt, RB, Oklahoma State ... 1966–74
Gent, Pete, WR-TE, Michigan State ... 1964–68
Gibbs, Sonny, QB, Texas Christian ... 1963
Gonzaga, John, DE, None ... 1960
Granger, Charlie, T, Southern U. ... 1961
Green, Allen, PK, Mississippi ... 1961
Green, Cornell, CB-S, Utah State ... 1962–74
Gregg, Forrest, G-T, Southern Methodist ... 1971
Gregory, Bill, DT, Wisconsin ... 1971–76
Gregory, Glynn, WR-CB-S, Southern Methodist ... 1961–62
Grottkau, Bob, G, Oregon ... 1961
Guy, Buzz, G, Duke ... 1960

H

Hagen, Halvor, C-G, Weber State ... 1969–70
Hansen, Wayne, LB, Texas-El Paso ... 1960
Harris, Cliff, S, Ouachita ... 1970–76
Harris, Jim, S, Oklahoma ... 1961
Hayes, Bob, WR, Florida A&M ... 1965–74
Hayes, Wendell, RB, Humboldt State ... 1963
Hays, Harold, LB, So. Mississippi ... 1963–67
Healy, Don, DT, Maryland ... 1960–61
Hegeman, Mike, LB, Tennessee State ... 1976
Heinrich, Don, QB, Washington ... 1960
Henderson, Tom, LB, Langston ... 1975–76
Herchman, Bill, DT, Texas Tech ... 1960–61
Herrera, Efren, K, UCLA ... 1974, 76
Hill, Calvin, RB, Yale ... 1969–74
Homan, Dennis, WR, Alabama ... 1968–70
Hoopes, Mitch, K, Arizona ... 1975
Houser, John, C-G, Redlands ... 1960–61
Houston, Bill, WR, Jackson State ... 1974
Howard, Percy, WR, Austin Peay ... 1975
Howard, Ron, TE, Seattle ... 1974–75
Howley, Chuck, LB, West Virginia ... 1961–75
Howton, Bill, WR, Rice ... 1960–63
Hoyem, Lynn, C-G, Cal St.-Long Beach ... 1962–63
Hughes, Randy, S, Oklahoma ... 1975–76
Humphrey, Buddy, QB, Baylor ... 1961
Husmann, Ed, DT, Nebraska ... 1960
Hutcherson, Ken, LB, Livingston State ... 1974

I

Isbell, Joe Bob, G, Houston ... 1962–65

J

Jensen, Jim, RB, Iowa ... 1976
Johnson, Butch, WR, California-Riverside ... 1976
Johnson, Mike, CB, Kansas ... 1966–69
Johnson, Mitch, G, UCLA ... 1965
Jones, Ed (Too Tall), DE, Tennessee State ... 1974–75
Jordan, Lee Roy, LB, Alabama ... 1963–76

K

Keller, Mike, LB, Michigan ... 1972
Killian, Gene, G, Tennessee ... 1974
Kiner, Steve, LB, Tennessee ... 1970
Kowalczyk, Walt, RB, Michigan State ... 1960
Kupp, Jake, G, Washington ... 1964–65
Kyle, Aaron, DB, Wyoming ... 1976

L

Laidlaw, Scott, RB, Stanford ... 1975–76
Lawless, Burton, G, Florida ... 1975–76
LeBaron, Eddie, QB, Pacific ... 1960–63
Lewis, D.D., LB, Mississippi State ... 1968–76
Lewis, Woodley, WR, Oregon ... 1960
Lilly, Bob, DT, Texas Christian ... 1961–74
Liscio, Tony, T, Tulsa ... 1963–64, 1966–71
Livingston, Warren, CB, Arizona ... 1961–66
Lockett, J.W., RB, Oklahoma Central ... 1961–72
Logan, Obert, S, Trinity, Tex. ... 1965–66
Long, Bob, LB, UCLA ... 1962
Longley, Clint, QB, Abilene Christian ... 1974–75
Lothridge, Billy, P-QB, Georgia Tech ... 1962

M

Moegle, Dick, S, Rice ... 1961
Manders, Dave, C, Mich. St. ... 1964–66, 1968–74
Marsh, Amos, RB, Oregon State ... 1961–64
Martin, Harvey, DE, East Texas State ... 1973–76
Mathews, Ray, WR, Clemson ... 1960
McCreary, Bob, T, Wake Forest ... 1961
McDaniels, David, WR, Miss. Valley ... 1968
McDonald, Tommy, WR, Oklahoma ... 1964
McIlhenny, Don, RB, Southern Methodist ... 1960–61
Memmelaar, Dale, G, Wyoming ... 1962–63
Meredith, Don, QB, Southern Methodist ... 1960–68
Meyers, John, DT, Washington ... 1962–63
Montgomery, Mike, RB, Kansas State ... 1972–73
Mooty, Jim, CB, Arkansas ... 1960
Morgan, Dennis, RB, Western Illinois ... 1974
Morton, Craig, QB, California ... 1965–74
Murchison, Ola Lee, WR, Pacific ... 1961

N

Neely, Ralph, G-T, Oklahoma ... 1965–76
Newhouse, Robert, RB, Houston ... 1972–76
Niland, John, G, Iowa ... 1966–74
Nolan, Dick, S, Maryland ... 1962
Norman, Pettis, TE, J.C. Smith ... 1962–70
Norton, Jerry, S, Southern Methodist ... 1962
Nutting, Ed, T, Georgia Tech ... 1963
Nye, Blaine, G, Stanford ... 1968–76

O

Overton, Jerry, S, Utah ... 1963

P

Parks, Billy, WR, Cal State-Long Beach ... 1972
Patera, Jack, LB, Oregon ... 1960–61
Pearson, Drew, WR, Tulsa ... 1973–76
Pearson, Preston, RB, Illinois ... 1975–76
Percival, Mac, K, Texas Tech ... 1974
Perkins, Don, RB, New Mexico ... 1961–68
Peterson, Calvin, LB, UCLA ... 1974–75
Pinder, Cyril, RB, Illinois ... 1973
Poimboeuf, Lance, K, S.W. Louisiana ... 1963
Porterfield, Garry, DE, Tulsa ... 1965
Pugh, Jethro, DT, Elizabeth City St. ... 1965–76
Putnam, Duane, G, Pacific ... 1960

R

Rafferty, Tom, G, Penn State ... 1976
Randle, Sonny, WR, Virginia ... 1968
Reece, Beasley, WR, North Texas State ... 1976
Reese, Guy, DT, Southern Methodist ... 1962–63
Reeves, Dan, RB, South Carolina ... 1965–72
Renfro, Mel, CB-S, Oregon ... 1964–76
Rentzel, Lance, WR, Oklahoma ... 1967–70
Rhome, Jerry, QB, Tulsa ... 1965–68
Richards, Golden, WR, Hawaii ... 1973–76
Richardson, Gloster, WR, Jackson State ... 1971
Ridgway, Colin, P-K, Lamar Tech ... 1965
Ridlon, Jim, S, Syracuse ... 1963–64
Roach, John, QB, Southern Methodist ... 1964
Robinson, Larry, RB, Tennessee ... 1973
Rucker, Reggie, WR, Boston U. ... 1970–71

S

Saldi, Jay, TE, South Carolina ... 1976
Sandeman, Bill, DT, Pacific ... 1966
Schaum, Greg, Michigan State ... 1976
Schoenke, Ray, T, Southern Methodist ... 1963–64
Scott, Herbert, G, Virginia Union ... 1975–76
Sellers, Ron, WR, Florida State ... 1972
Sherer, Dave, P, Southern Methodist ... 1960
Shy, Les, RB, Cal State-Long Beach ... 1966–69
Simmons, Dave, LB, Georgia Tech ... 1968
Smith, J.D., RB, N. Carolina A&T ... 1965–66
Smith, Jim Ray, G-T, Baylor ... 1963–64
Smith, John, WR, UCLA ... 1973
Smith, Tody, DE, USC ... 1971–72
Staubach, Roger, QB, Navy ... 1969–76
Stephens, Larry, DE, Texas ... 1963–67
Stiger, Jim, RB, Washington ... 1963–65
Stincic, Tom, LB, Michigan ... 1969–71

Ralph Neely   *Blaine Nye*   *Drew Pearson*   *Jethro Pugh*   *Dan Reeves*   *Jerry Tubbs*   *Rayfield Wright*

Stokes, Sims, WR, No. Arizona 1967
Stowe, Otto, WR, Iowa State 1973
Strayhorn, Les, RB, East Carolina 1973–74
Stynchula, Andy, DE, Penn State 1968

T

Talbert, Don, DE-T, Texas 1962, 1965, 1971
Thomas, Bill, RB, Boston College 1972
Thomas, Duane, RB, W. Texas State 1970–71
Thomas, Ike, CB, Bishop, Texas 1971
Toomay, Pat, DE, Vanderbilt 1970–74
Townes, Willie, DE, Tulsa 1966–68
Truax, Billy, TE, Louisiana State 1971–73
Tubbs, Jerry, LB, Oklahoma 1960–67

V

Van Raaphorst, Dick, K, Ohio State 1964
Villanueva, Danny, P-K, New Mexico State 1965–67

W

Walker, Louie, LB, Colorado State 1974
Walker, Malcolm, C, Rice 1966–69
Wallace, Rodney, G, New Mexico 1971–73
Walton, Bruce, G-C, UCLA 1973–75
Washington, Mark, CB, Morgan State 1970–76
Waters, Charlie, S-CB, Clemson 1970–76
Wayt, Russell, LB, Rice 1965
Welch, Claxton, RB, Oregon 1969–71

White, Danny, QB, Arizona State 1976
White, Randy, LB-DE, Maryland 1975–76
Whitfield, A.D., RB, N. Texas State 1965
Whittingham, Fred, LB, Cal. Poly 1969
Widby, Ron, P, Tennessee 1968–71
Wilbur, John, T, Stanford 1966–69
Williams, Joe, RB, Wyoming 1971
Wisener, Gary, WR, Baylor 1960
Woolsey, Rolly, CB-S, Boise State 1975
Wright, Rayfield, TE-T, Ft. Valley State 1967–76

Y

Youmans, Maury, DE, Syracuse 1964–65
Young, Charles, RB, North Carolina St. 1974–76

Defensive tackle Bob Lilly vs. Pittsburgh, 1972.

Running back Calvin Hill vs. Cardinals, 1969.

DENVER BRONCOS

1959 The Denver Broncos, with Bob Howsam as their principal owner, were named a charter member of the American Football League, August 14. Dean Griffing was named the team's first general manager. The Broncos' first selection in the AFL player draft was Roger Leclerc, a center from Trinity, Connecticut.

1960 Frank Filchock was named the first head coach of the Broncos, January 1. The team was placed in the AFL's Western Division with the Dallas Texans, Los Angeles Chargers, and Oakland Raiders. The Broncos' first training camp opened in July at Colorado School of Mines. The team played its games in Bears Stadium, primarily a baseball facility with limited seating capacity. In their first home game, 18,372 watched the Broncos beat Oakland 31–24. Attendance grew worse, dropping to 5,861 for the final home game.

1961 Bob Howsam and his brother Lee sold their stock to a new syndicate headed by Cal Kunz and Gerry Phipps. Kunz was named president. With an offense built around the passing of quarterback Frank Tripucka, end Lionel Taylor, who had been cut from the Chicago Bears, developed into one of the AFL's premier receivers. He set a pro record with his one-hundredth pass reception for the season. The team's record was only 3–11, and at the end of the year Filchock was released as head coach.

1962 Jack Faulkner, who had coached under Sid Gillman at the University of Cincinnati and with the Los Angeles and San Diego Chargers, was named head coach. He was also given the added assignment of general manager after Dean Griffing was dismissed. Faulkner changed the team's colors from brown and gold to orange, blue, and white. The team's vertically striped socks, objects of some ridicule, were burned at a public ceremony. In Faulkner's first regular season game, the Broncos stunned San Diego, a team they had never beaten, 30–21 before a crowd estimated at 28,000. When Denver defeated Houston 20–10 before a record crowd of 34,496 at Bears Stadium, it ran its record for the year to 6–1. Broncos' weaknesses became apparent, however, particularly in the defensive secondary, and the team slumped badly the second half of the season, finishing with a 7–7 record. Faulkner was named AFL coach of the year by both wire services and home attendance was up more than 100 percent over the previous year.

1963 Faulkner initiated a youth movement, managing to sign some top draft choices for the first time in the history of the franchise. Veteran Frank Tripucka retired, leaving Denver with a critical problem at quarterback. Mickey Slaughter, a rookie from Louisiana Tech, got the first crack at the job but was soon sidelined with a concussion. John McCormick, a rookie from Massachusetts, was next. He injured a knee and went out for the year, October 13. Don Breaux, formerly a taxi squad player at San Diego, shared the job with Slaughter. Fourteen rookies played regularly on a team that finished the year 2–11–1.

1964 Faulkner, desperate for a quarterback, completed a trade with Houston for Jacky Lee, who came to the team on a two-year, lend-lease arrangement. To get him, the Broncos had to give up Bud McFadin, their all-league tackle, and a high draft choice. A nine-player trade with the New York Jets, designed to bolster Denver's sagging defense, didn't work out and pressure began to build. Speaking before a game against Boston, Faulkner, whose team was winless, said the game was "the most important of my career." He proved prophetic. Denver lost and Faulkner was

fired. Mac Speedie, the team's receiver coach, was appointed to take over on an interim basis. The Broncos reacted by outscoring Kansas City 33–27 in a wild first game for Speedie. The Broncos then reverted to the losing ways. Speedie was signed to a two-year contract as head coach.

1965 A serious split occurred at the ownership-management level as attendance began to drop. Kunz and his bloc of majority stockholders became convinced the Broncos were a losing proposition and attempted to sell. Cox Broadcasting Company tendered a reported $4 million offer and announced it planned to move the franchise to Atlanta. Gerald and Allan Phipps, owners of 42 percent of the club, made what turned out to be the most important decision in the history of the franchise. They decided they wanted the team to remain in Denver. They bought out the holdings of the others for $1.5 million. The brief threat of the team moving out of town triggered a tremendous response from the citizens of the city. Ticket sales boomed at an unprecedented rate. Two major trades—for Kansas City running back Abner Haynes and Buffalo fullback Cookie Gilchrist—generated even more interest, and by May 1, the season ticket figure reached 22,000, an all-time high. Allan Phipps was named president of Empire Sports, Inc. Gerry Phipps was redesignated chairman of the board. Jim Burris, general manager of the baseball franchise also held by Empire Sports, Inc. was named executive vice-president of the Phipps corporation and assumed duties as the Broncos' new general manager. Although Gilchrist and Haynes both helped, the team finished with just four wins. Attendance, however, increased to an average of 31,398, a record for an AFL Western Division team. Six of the seven home crowds topped 30,000.

1966 Legislation was passed creating a Metropolitan Stadium district in Denver. Voters were informed a four-county metropolitan region would vote on building a multimillion dollar all-purpose stadium before March, 1967. One of the major provisions of the bill was that the tenants—the football Broncos and baseball Bears—sign a 10-year lease. Internal problems, which seemed to follow Gilchrist as stubbornly as opposing linebackers, surfaced again, with Speedie and his top offensive player finally reaching a point of no return. Gilchrist, a holdout, was traded to Miami. The Broncos felt the effects of his absence in

Defensive tackle Paul Smith lunges for the 49ers' Larry Schreiber, 1975.

Running back Floyd Little vs. the Eagles, 1975.

the first game of the season. Houston beat them 45–7 and they failed to generate even one first down. A week later, after a 24–10 loss to Boston, Speedie was released. Ray Malavasi, the line coach, was named the interim head coach. Late in December Phipps announced the signing of Lou Saban to a 10-year contract as coach and general manager of the Broncos.

1967 The team moved to new executive offices with adjacent practice field and locker room facilities for both training camp and regular season activity in suburban Denver. Voters turned down the stadium bond issue, but Broncos fans immediately organized a fund-raising drive to improve Bears Stadium and keep the team in Denver. Floyd Little, the Syracuse All-America running back, became the first number one draft choice ever to sign with the Broncos. Denver beat Detroit 13–7 in a preseason game; it was the first time an AFL team won a game over an NFL team. The Broncos gave up two number one draft choices to San Diego for quarterback Steve Tensi. The season ticket count reached a record 24,650. A single game attendance record was set when 35,565 watched Denver lose to the New York Jets 38–24.

1968 The civic drive to raise $1.8 million ended successfully and the city of Denver received the stadium as a gift after the purchase of the facility from Empire Sports, Inc. by a non-profit group. Construction began on a 16,000-seat upper deck that would raise capacity to 50,000. Another new season ticket record of 27,348 was reached. The Broncos drew more than 50,000 for the first time when 50,002 watched Denver and Oakland play, November 10. Bears Stadium was officially renamed Denver Mile High Stadium.

1969 The Broncos started the season with victories over Boston and the New York Jets. Little had a 166-yard rushing day, the top single game yardage figure for an AFL back, October 19. But injuries slowed the Broncos. Tensi was bothered by a bad knee. Little missed five games with shoulder and knee problems. A 13–0 win over San Diego at Mile High Stadium was the Broncos' first shutout in history.

1970 Bobby Anderson, the number one draft choice from the University of Colorado, signed with the Broncos. Season ticket sales reached 43,584, another new record. Quarterback problems again limited Denver's progress. Tensi was hurt again. Pete Liske and Al Pastrana were quarterback replacements. In the first season in which he managed to play in all 14 games, Little won the AFC rushing title with 901 yards.

1971 Defensive end Rich Jackson and Floyd Little were starters in the first AFC-NFC Pro Bowl game. Veteran quarterback Steve Tensi announced his re-

tirement. Quarterback Don Horn was acquired from Green Bay for defensive end Alden Roche and an exchange of first round draft positions. Season ticket sales reached 47,500. In the first of seven sellouts at Mile High Stadium, the Broncos tied Miami 10–10. After an inconspicuous first half of the season, Horn went out with an injury and was replaced by inexperienced Steve Ramsey at quarterback. After nine games, Saban resigned as head coach. A month later, he quit as general manager, too. Jerry Smith, one of his assistants, worked the final five games as interim head coach. Little became Denver's first 1,000-yard rusher and finished as pro football's top ground-gainer with a 1,133-yard season.

1972 John Ralston, successful head coach at Stanford University, was named new head coach and general manager. The team's number one draft pick, tight end Riley Odoms, signed a long-term contract. For the first time in the history of the franchise, there was no public sale of season tickets. Over 46,500 renewed their season tickets, however. Cal Poly-Pomona was chosen as the new Denver training camp site. Charley Johnson was acquired from Houston for a third draft choice, giving Ralston the experienced quarterback he was seeking. Veteran defensive linemen Rich Jackson and Dave Costa were traded, but Ralston's new front four, featuring Paul Smith and Lyle Alzado, performed well and Johnson and Little helped the team score enough points to propel the Broncos to five victories.

1973 Otis Armstrong, the record-breaking Big 10 running back from Purdue and Denver's number one draft choice, signed with the Broncos. In a game some Denver sports followers called the most significant in the club's history, the Broncos came back to tie Oakland 23–23 on Monday night television. Ralston had his team fighting for first place all season. In the last game of the year, the Broncos faced Oakland in a dramatic battle for the Western Division championship. Trailing 14–10 in the fourth quarter, Denver gambled on a fake punt that didn't work. The Raiders took over and scored to wrap up the win and the title 21–17.

1974 In a draft in which the plan was to fortify the team's defense, Ohio State linebacker Randy Gradishar became the top selection. Gradishar signed a long-term contract. Denver voters passed a $25 million bond issue to expand Mile High Stadium to more than 75,000 seats. The Broncos and Pittsburgh Steelers played the first regular season overtime game. It finished in a 35–35 tie after neither team scored in the sudden death period. Otis Armstrong ran for 1,407 yards and won the NFL rushing title.

1975 The expansion of Mile High Stadium officially

began. The projection called for 63,500 capacity for 1976 and 75,000 in 1977. The Broncos defeated Green Bay 23–13 for their first victory ever on Monday night television. Playing before the largest crowd ever to witness a Denver game, the Broncos lost to Buffalo 38–14 before 79,864 in Buffalo. In his final home game as a Bronco, Little scored two touchdowns, one on a 66-yard pass play in the 25–10 win over Philadelphia. He wound up his memorable career as the NFL's seventh all-time rusher with 6,323 yards.

1976 Quarterback Charley Johnson announced his retirement, although he remained with the team as a scout and quarterback coach on a part-time basis. Season ticket sales were cut off at 62,215, giving the team its seventh straight sellout season. With one of the most effective defensive teams in the league, the Broncos stayed in the fight for the playoffs all the way, just missing out at the end finishing at 9–5, the best record in Denver history.

1977 Fred Gehrke, assistant general manager, was promoted to general manager. Ralston resigned as coach. Robert (Red) Miller, New England Patriots' assistant, was named Broncos' head coach.

MEMBERS OF HALL OF FAME:
None

BRONCOS RECORD, 1960–76

Year	Won	Lost	Tied	Pct.	Pts.	OP
1960	4	9	1	.308	309	393
1961	3	11	0	.214	251	432
1962	7	7	0	.500	353	334
1963	2	11	1	.154	301	473
1964	2	11	1	.154	240	438
1965	4	10	0	.286	303	392
1966	4	10	0	.286	196	381
1967	3	11	0	.214	256	409
1968	5	9	0	.357	255	404
1969	5	8	1	.385	297	344
1970	5	8	1	.385	253	264
1971	4	9	1	.308	203	275
1972	5	9	0	.429	325	350
1973	7	5	2	.571	354	296
1974	7	6	1	.536	302	294
1975	6	8	0	.429	254	307
1976	9	5	0	.643	315	206
17 Years	82	147	9	.363	4,767	5,992

RECORD HOLDERS

Rushing (Yards)	Otis Armstrong, 1974	1,407
Passing (Pct.)	Charley Johnson, 1972	55.7
Passing (Yards)	Frank Tripucka, 1960	3,038
Passing (TDs)	Frank Tripucka, 1960	24
Receiving (No.)	Lionel Taylor, 1961	100
Receiving (Yards)	Lionel Tayor, 1960	1,235
Interceptions (No.)	Austin (Goose) Gonsoulin, 1960	11
Punting (Avg.)	Jim Fraser, 1963	46.1
Punt Ret. (Avg.)	Floyd Little, 1967	16.9
Kickoff Ret. (Avg.)	Billy Thompson, 1966, and Goldie Sellers, 1969	28.5
Touchdowns (Total)	Floyd Little, 1972	13
Field Goals Made	Gene Mingo, 1962	27
Points (No.)	Gene Mingo, 1962	137

COACHING HISTORY

1960–61	Frank Filchock	7–20–1
1962–64	Jack Faulkner*	9–22–1
1964–66	Mac Speedie**	6–19–1
1966	Ray Malavasi	4– 8–0
1967–71	Lou Saban***	20–42–3
1971	Jerry Smith	2– 3–0
1972–76	John Ralston	34–33–3

*Replaced after four games in 1964
**Resigned after two games in 1966
***Resigned after nine games in 1971

FIRST PLAYER SELECTED

1960	Roger Leclerc, C, Trinity, Connecticut
1961	Bob Gaiters, RB, New Mexico State
1962	Merlin Olsen, DT, Utah State
1963	Kermit Alexander, CB, UCLA
1964	Bob Brown, T, Nebraska
1965	Dick Butkus, LB (2), Illinois
1966	Jerry Shay, DT, Purdue
1967	Floyd Little, RB, Syracuse
1968	Curley Culp, DE (2), Arizona State
1969	Grady Cavness, DB (2), Texas-El Paso
1970	Bob Anderson, RB, Colorado
1971	Marvin Montgomery, T, USC
1972	Riley Odoms, TE, Houston
1973	Otis Armstrong, RB, Purdue
1974	Randy Gradishar, LB, Ohio State
1975	Louie Wright, DB, San Jose State
1976	Tom Glassic, G, Virginia

  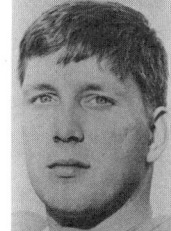  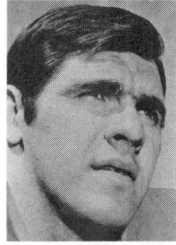  

Lyle Alzado *Otis Armstrong* *Tom Beer* *Dave Costa* *Pete Duranko* *Randy Gradishar* *Rich Jackson*

DENVER BRONCOS, 1960–76

Adams, Bob, TE, Pacific 1975
Adamson, Ken, G, Notre Dame 1960–62
Alexakos, Steve, G, San Jose State 1970
Alflen, Ted, RB, Springfield, Mass 1969
Allen Buddy, HB, Utah State 1961
Allen, Don, FB, Texas 1960
Alliston, Buddy, LB, Mississippi 1960
Alzado, Lyle, DE, Yankton, S.D. 1971–76
Ames, David, HB, Richmond 1961
Anderson, Bob HB, Colorado 1970–73
Andrus, Lou, LB, Brigham Young 1967
Armstrong, Otis, RB, Purdue 1973–75
Arnold, LeFrancis, G-C, Oregon 1974
Askea, Mike, T, Stanford 1973
Atkins, Billy, DB, Auburn 1964
Atkinson, Frank, DE, Stanford 1964

B

Bachman, Jay, C, Cincinnati 1968–71
Bain, Bill, T, USC 1976
Barnes, Ernie, G, North Carolina College 1963–64
Barnes, Walter, DE, Nebraska 1969–71
Barry, Odell, HB, Findlay 1964–65
Barton, James, C, Marshall 1961–62
Baska, Rich, LB, UCLA 1976
Bass, Norman, DB, Pacific 1964
Beer, Tom, TE, Houston 1967–69
Behrman, Dave, C, Michigan State 1967
Bell, Henry, HB, none 1960
Bernardi, Frank, HB, Colorado 1960
Bernet, Lee, T, Wisconsin 1965–66
Bowdell, Gordon, WR, Michigan State 1971
Brady, Phil, S, Brigham Young 1969
Bramlett, John, LB, Memphis State 1965–66
Breaux, Don, QB, McNeese State 1963
Breitenstein, Bob, T, Tulsa 1965–67
Briscoe, Marlin, QB, Omaha 1968
Brodnax, Red, FB, Louisiana State 1960
Brown, Boyd, TE, Alcorn A&M 1974–76
Brown, Hardy, LB, Tulsa 1960
Brown, Willie, DB, Grambling 1963–66
Brunelli, Sam, G, Colorado State College 1966–71
Buckman, Tom, TE, Texas A&M 1969
Bukaty, Fred, FB, Kansas 1961
Burnett, Bobby, RB, Arkansas 1969
Burrell, George, S, Pennsylvania 1969
Bussell, Gerry, DB, Georgia Tech 1965
Butler, Bill, LB, San Fernando Valley 1970
Byrd, George (Butch), DB, Boston 1971

C

Campbell, Carter, DE, Weber State 1971
Carmichael, Al, HB, USC 1960–61
Carmichael, Paul, HB, El Camino 1965
Carothers, Don, E, Bradley 1960
Carpenter, Ken, E, Oregon State 1960
Carter, Rubin, DT, Miami, ... 1975–76
Casey, Tim, LB, Oregon 1969
Cash, John, E, Allen 1961–62
Cassese, Tom, DB, C.W. Post 1967
Cavness, Grady, CB, Texas-El Paso 1969
Chavous, Barney, DE, South Carolina St. 1973–76
Choboian, Max, QB, San Fernando State 1966
Cichowski, Tom, T, Maryland 1967–68
Cindrich, Ralph, LB, Pittsburgh 1974
Coffey, Don, E, Memphis State 1963
Coleman, Steve, DE, Delaware State 1974
Cooke, Ed, E, Maryland 1964–65
Costa, Dave, DT, Utah 1967–71
Cottrell, Bill, G, Delaware 1972
Cox, Larry, DT, Abilene Christian 1966–68
Crabtree, Eric, FL, Pittsburgh 1966–68
Crane, Gary, LB, Arkansas State 1969
Crenshaw, Willis, FB, Kansas State 1970
Criter, Ken, LB, Wisconsin 1969–74
Cummings, Ed, LB, Stanford 1965
Cunningham, Carl, LB, Houston 1967–70
Current, Mike, T, Ohio State 1967–75

D

Danenhauer, Eldon, T, Emporia State 1960–65
Danenhauer, Bill, E, Emporia State 1960

Davis, Dick, RB, Nebraska 1970
Davis, Jack, T, Arizona 1960
Davis, Marvin, DT, Wichita State 1970
Dawkins, Joe, RB, Wisconsin 1971–73
Day, Albert E-T, E. Michigan 1960
Denson, Al, FL, Florida A&M 1964–70
Denvir, John, G, Colorado 1962
Dickey, Wallace, T, S.W. Texas State 1968–69
Dickinson, Bo, FB, So. Mississippi 1962–63
Dixon, Hewritt, HB-E, Florida A&M 1963–65
DiVito, Joe, QB, Boston College 1968
Dolbin, Jack, WR, Wake Forest 1975–76
Domres, Tom, DT, Wisconsin 1971–72
Doyle, Richard, HB, Ohio State 1960
Drougas, Tom T, Oregon 1974
Duncan, Rick, K, E. Montana State 1967
Duranko, Pete, DE, Notre Dame 1967–74

E

Edgerson, Booker, CB, Western Illinois 1970
Elfrid, Jim, LB, Colorado State 1961
Embree, John, WR, Compton J.C. 1969–70
Enis, Hunter, QB, Texas Christian 1962
Epperson, John, E, Adams State 1960
Erlandson, Tom, LB, Washington State 1962–65
Ernst, Mike, QB, Cal State-Fullerton 1972
Erwin, Terry, HB, Boston College 1968
Evans, Jay Dale, HB, Kansas 1961
Evans, Larry, LB, Mississippi College 1976

F

Fanning, Stan, E, Idaho 1964
Farr, Miller, DB, Wichita 1965
Fletcher, Billy Ray, OE, Memphis State 1966
Foley, Steve, DB, Tulane 1976
Ford, Garrett, FB, West Virginia 1968
Forsberg, Fred, LB, Washington 1968–73
Franci, Jason, E, Cal-Santa Barbara 1972
Franckowiak, Mike, RB, Central Michigan 1975–76
Fraser, James, LB-K, Wisconsin 1962–64
Frazier, Al, HB, Florida A&M 1961–63

G

Gaiser, George, T, Southern Methodist 1968
Gaiters, Bob, HB, New Mexico State 1963
Garrett, Drake, DB, Michigan State 1968–70
Gavin, Charles, E, Tennessee State 1960–63
Geddes, Bob, LB, UCLA 191972
Gehrke, Jack, WR, Utah 1971
Gilchrist, Cookie, FB, None 1965, 1967
Glacken, Scotty, QB, Duke 1966–67
Glass, Glenn, DB, Tennessee 1966
Glassic, Tom, G, Virginia 1976
Goeddeke, George, G, Notre Dame 1967–72
Gonsoulin, Austin (Goose), DB, Baylor 1960–66
Gonzaga, John, G, None 1966
Goodman, Brian, G, UCLA 1975

Goodman, Harvey, G, Colorado 1976
Gordon, Cornell, CB, North Carolina A&T 1970–72
Gradishar, Randy, LB, Ohio State 1974–76
Graham, Tom, LB, Oregon 1972–74
Grant, John, DE, USC 1973–76
Greer, Charles, DB, Colorado 1968–74
Greer, James, E, N. Carolina State 1960
Griffin, John, HB, Memphis State 1964–66
Groman, Bill, HB-E, Heidelberg 1963
Guesman, Dick, T, West Virginia 1964
Gulseth, Donald, LB, North Dakota 1966
Guy, Buzz, G, Duke 1961–62

H

Hackbart, Dale, S, Wisconsin 1973
Haffner, Mike, E, UCLA 1968–70
Haggerty, Steve, DB, Colorado 1975
Hammond, Wayne, DT, Montana State 1976
Hardee, Billy, CB, Virginia Tech 1976
Harris, Tony, WR, Toledo 1972
Harrison, Dwight, WR, Texas A&I 1971–72
Hatley, Johnny Ray, T, Sul Ross State 1960
Hauser, Arthur, T, Xavier 1961
Hayes, Wendell, HB, Humboldt State 1965–67
Haynes, Abner, HB, N. Texas State 1965–66
Haywood, Al, RB, Bethune-Cookman 1975
Hendren, Jerry, WR, Idaho 1970
Henson, Gary, E, Colorado 1964
Hepburn, Lonnie, CB, Texas Southern 1974
Herring, George, QB, So, Mississippi 1960–61
Hickey, Bo, FB, Maryland 1967
Highsmith, Walter, C, Florida A&M 1968–69
Hill, Jack, HB, Utah State 1961
Hoey, George, DB, Michigan 1975
Hoffman, John, DE, Hawaii 1972
Hohman, Jon, G, Wisconsin 1965–66
Holloman, Gus, DB, Houston 1968–69
Holz, Gordon, T, Minnesota 1960–63
Hopkins, Jerry, LB, Texas A&M 1963–66
Horn, Don, QB, San Diego State 1971–72
Howard, Paul, G, Brigham Young 1973–75
Howfield, Bobby, K, None 1968–70
Huard, John, LB, Maine 1967–69
Hudson, Robert, LB, Clemson 1960–61
Hufnagel, John, QB, Penn State 1974–75
Humphreys, Bob, K, Wichita State 1967–68
Hyde, Glenn, T, Pittsburgh 1976

I

Imhof, Martin, DE, San Diego State 1976
Inman, Jerry, DT, Oregon 1966–73

J

Jackson, Larron, G, Missourie 1971–74
Jackson, Richard, DE, Southern U. 1967–72
Jackson, Tom, LB, Louisville 1974–76
Jackunas, Frank, C, Detroit 1963

Rick Upchurch on one of his four punt returns for touchdowns, 1976.

Jon Keyworth

Bud McFadin

Bobby Maples

Gene Mingo

Bill Thompson

Frank Tripucka

Bill Van Heusen

Jacobs, Ray, T, Howard Payne ... 1963–66
Janerette, Charlie, T, Penn State ... 1964–65
Janik, Tom, HB, Texas A&I ... 1963–64
Jaquess, Pete, DB, E. New Mexico ... 1967–70
Jessup, William, E, USC ... 1960
Jeter, Eugene, LB, Arkansas AM&N ... 1965–67
Joe, Billy, FB, Villanova ... 1963–64
Johnson, Charley, QB, New Mexico State ... 1972
Jones, Calvin, CB, Washington ... 1973–76
Jones, Henry, RB, Grambling ... 1969
Jones, Jimmy, E, Wisconsin ... 1968
Jordan, Larry, E-LB, Youngstown ... 1962–64
Joyce, Don, E, Tulane ... 1962

K

Kaminski, Larry, C, Purdue ... 1966–73
Kampa, Bob, DT, California ... 1974
Keating, Bill, DT, Michigan ... 1966–67
Kellogg, Mike, FB, Santa Clara ... 1966–67
Keyworth, Jon, RB, Colorado ... 1974–76
Kiick, Jim, RB, Wyoming ... 1976
King, Donald, E, Kentucky ... 1960
Konovsky, Robert, E, Wisconsin ... 1961
Krieg, Jim, WR, Washington ... 1972
Kroner, Gary, K, Wisconsin ... 1965–67
Kubala, Ray, C, Texas A&M ... 1964–67
Kuchta, Frank, C, Notre Dame ... 1960

L

Lamb, Ron, FB, South Carolina ... 1968
Lambert, Gordon, LB, Tennessee-Martin ... 1968–69
Lamberti, Patsy, LB, Richmond ... 1961
LaRose, Dan, DE, Missouri ... 1966
Larpenter, Carl James, G, Texas ... 1960–61
Laskey, Bill, LB, Michigan ... 1973–74
Lassiter, Ike, E, St, Augustine ... 1962–64
Leclair, Jim, QB, C.W. Post ... 1967–68
Leclerc, Roger, C, Trinity, Conn. ... 1967
Lee, Jacky, QB, Cincinnati ... 1964–65
Leetzow, Max, DE, Idaho ... 1965–66
Lemon, Mike, LB, Kansas ... 1975
Lentz, Jack, DB, Holy Cross ... 1967–68
Lester, Darrell, FB, McNeese State ... 1965–66
Lewis, Herman, DE, Virginia Union ... 1968
Lindsey, Hub, HG, Wyoming ... 1968
Liske, Pete, QB, Penn State ... 1969–70
Little, Floyd, HB, Syracuse ... 1967–75
Luke, Tommy, LB, Mississippi ... 1968
Lynch, Fran, HB, Hofstra ... 1967–75
Lyons, Tom, G, Georgia ... 1971–76

M

Mangum, Pete, LB, Mississippi ... 1960
Maples, Bobby, C, Baylor ... 1972–76
Marshall, Charles, HB, Oregon State ... 1962
Martha, Paul, S, Pittsburgh ... 1970
Masters, Billy, TE, Louisiana State ... 1970–74
Matson, Pat, G, Oregon ... 1966–67
Matsos, Archie, LB Michigan State ... 1966
Mattox, Jack, T, Fresno State ... 1961–62
Matuszak, Marv, LB, Tulsa ... 1964
May, Ray, LB, USC ... 1973–75
McCarthy, Brendan, FB, Boston College ... 1968–69
McCormick, John, QB, Massachusetts .. 1963, 1965–66, 1968
McCullough, Bob, G, Colorado ... 1962–65
McDaniel, Wahoo, LB, Oklahoma ... 1961–63
McFadin, Bud, T, Texas ... 1960–63
McGeever, John, HB, Auburn ... 1962–65
McKoy, Bill, LB, Purdue ... 1970–72
McMillin, James R., HB, Colorado State ... 1960–62, 1964–65
McNamara, Robert, HB, Minnesota ... 1960–61
Mingo, Eugene, K, None ... 1960–64
Minor, Claudie, T, San Diego State ... 1974–76
Minter, Tommy Earl, HB, Baylor ... 1962
Mirich, Rex, DE, No. Arizona ... 1967–69
Mitchell, Alvin, S-WR, Morgan State ... 1970
Mitchell, Charlie, HB, Washington ... 1963–67
Mitchell, Leroy, CB, Texas Southern ... 1971–73
Montgomery, Marv, T, USC ... 1971–76
Montgomery, Randy, CB, Weber State ... 1971–75
Moore, Alex, HB, Norfolk State ... 1968
Moore, Leroy, E, Ft. Valley State ... 1964–65
Moore, Randy, DT, Arizona State ... 1976
Moses, Haven, WR, San Diego State ... 1972–76
Mosier, John, TE, Kansas ... 1971
Moten, Bobby, E, Bishop, Tex. ... 1968
Myrtle, Chip, LB, Maryland ... 1971–72

N

Nery, Ron, E, Wisconsin ... 1963
Nichols, Mike, C, Arkansas A&M ... 1960–61
Nocera, John, LB, Iowa ... 1963
Nomina, Tom, G, Miami, Ohio ... 1963–65
Nugent, Phil, HB, Tulane ... 1961

O

Oberg, Tom, DB, Portland State ... 1968–69
Odoms, Riley, TE, Houston ... 1972–76
Olsen, Phil, DT, Utah State ... 1975–76
Olson, Harold T, Clemson ... 1963–64
Olszewski, John, FB, California ... 1962
O'Malley, Jim, LB, Notre Dame ... 1973–75

P

Pane, Chris, S, Chico State ... 1976
Parish, Don, LB, Stanford ... 1972
Park, Ernie, G, McMurry ... 1967
Parker, Charlie, G, So. Mississippi ... 1965
Parrish, Scott, T, Utah State ... 1976
Pastrana, Al, QB, Maryland ... 1969–70
Penrose, Craig, QB, San Diego State ... 1976
Perkins, James, T, Colorado ... 1962–64
Perrin, Lonnie, RB, Illinois ... 1976
Pete, Dennis, CB-S, San Francisco St. ... 1972
Peters, Anton, T, Florida ... 1963
Pitts, John, S, Arizona State ... 1973–75
Pivec, Dave, TE, Notre Dame ... 1969
Ply, Bobby, DB, Baylor ... 1967
Poltl, Randy, DB, Stanford ... 1975–76
Post, Dickie, RB, Houston ... 1971
Prebola, Eugene, E, Boston U ... 1961–63
Preece, Steve, S, Oregon State ... 1972
Price, James, LB, Auburn ... 1964
Prisby, Errol, DB, Cincinnati ... 1967
Pyeatt, John, HB, None ... 1960

Q

Quayle, Frank, RB, Virginia ... 1969

R

Ramsey, Steve, QB, N. Texas State ... 1971–76
Reed, Leo, T, Colorado State ... 1961
Richardson, Bob, DB, UCLA ... 1966
Richter, Frank, LB, Georgia ... 1967–69
Rizzo, Joe, LB, Merchant Marine Academy ... 1974–76
Roche, Alden, DE, So. Illinois ... 1970
Roehnelt, Bill, LB, Bradley ... 1961–62
Rogers, Stan, T, Maryland ... 1975
Rolle, David, FB, Oklahoma ... 1960–61
Romine, Albert, HB, Florence State ... 1960
Ross, Oliver, RB, Alabama A&M ... 1973–75
Rote, Tobin, QB, Rice ... 1966
Rowland, Justin, HB, Texas Christian ... 1962
Rowser, John, CB, Michigan ... 1974–76
Rychlec, Tom, E, American Int'l ... 1963

S

Saimes, George, S, Michigan State ... 1970–72
Sbranti, Ron, LB, Utah State ... 1966
Scarpitto, Robert, FL, Notre Dame ... 1962–67
Schaukowitch, Carl, C, Penn State ... 1975
Schnitker, Mike, G, Colorado ... 1969–74
Schultz, John, WR, Maryland ... 1976
Scott, Lew, DB, Oregon State ... 1966
Sears, James, HB, USC ... 1960–61
Sellers, Goldie, DB, Grambling ... 1966–67
Severson, Jeff, DB, Cal St.-Long Beach ... 1975
Shackelford, Don, G, Pacific ... 1964
Sharp, Rick, T, Washington ... 1972
Shaw, George, QB, Oregon ... 1962
Sherman, Rod, WR, USC ... 1972
Shoals, Roger, T, Maryland ... 1971
Simmons, Jerry, WR, Bethune-Cookman ... 1971–72
Simmons, Leon, LB, Grambling ... 1963
Simone, Mike, LB, Stanford ... 1972
Simpson, Jack, LB, Mississippi ... 1961
Sklopan, John, HB, So. Mississippi ... 1963
Slaughter, Mickey, QB, Louisiana Tech ... 1963–66
Smiley, Tom, RB, Lamar Tech ... 1969
Smith, Dan, HB, N.E. Oklahoma ... 1961
Smith, Don, G, Florida A&M ... 1967
Smith, Ed, DE, Colorado College ... 1973–75
Smith, Harold, T, UCLA ... 1960
Smith, Hugh, E, Kansas ... 1962
Smith, James, S, Utah State ... 1969
Smith, Paul, DE, New Mexico ... 1968–76
Smith, Willie, G, Western Michigan ... 1960
Snorton, Matt, E, Michigan State ... 1964
Sorrell, Henry, LB, Chattanooga ... 1967
Stalcup, Jerry, LB, Wisconsin ... 1961–62
Starling, Bruce, HB, Florida ... 1963
Stinnette, James, FB-LB, Oregon State ... 1961–62
Stokes, Jesse, DB, Corpus Christi ... 1968
Stone, Don, FB, Arkansas ... 1961–64
Stowe, Otto, WR, Iowa State ... 1974
Stransky, Robert, HB, Colorado ... 1960
Strickland, David, T-G, Memphis State ... 1960
Sturm, Jerry, C-T-G, Illinois ... 1961–66
Summers, Jim, DB, Michigan State ... 1967
Sweeney, Neal, E, Tulsa ... 1967
Swenson, Bob, LB, California ... 1975–76
Sykes, Gene, DB, Louisiana State ... 1967

T

Tarasovic, George, DE, Louisiana State ... 1967
Tarr, Jerry L., E, Oregon ... 1962
Taylor, Lionel, E, New Mex. Highlands ... 1960–66
Tensi, Steve, QB, Florida State ... 1967–70
Thibert, Jim, LB, Toledo ... 1965
Thomas, Earlie, DB, Colorado State ... 1975
Thompson, Bill, CB, Maryland State ... 1969–76
Thompson, Jim, DT, So. Illinois ... 1965
Tobey, Dave, LB, Oregon ... 1968
Traynham, Jerry, HB, USC ... 1961
Tripucka, Frank, QB, Notre Dame ... 1960–63
Turk, Godwin, LB, Southern U. ... 1976
Turner, Clem, RB, Cincinnati ... 1970–72
Turner, Jim, K, Utah State ... 1971–76
Tyler, Maurice, S, Morgan State ... 1973–74
Tyson, Richard, G, Tulsa ... 1967

U

Upchurch, Rick, WR, Minnesota ... 1975–76
Underwood, Olen, LB, Texas ... 1971

V

Van Heusen, Bill, WR-P, Maryland ... 1968–76
Vaughan, Bob, G, Mississippi ... 1968
Voss, Lloyd, DT-DE, Nebraska ... 1972

W

Wade, Bob, CB, Morgan State ... 1970
Walker, Clarence, HB, So. Illinois ... 1963
Washington, Dave, LB, Alcorn A&M ... 1971
Washington, Dave, E, USC ... 1968
Weese, Norris, QB, Mississippi ... 1976
Wegert, Ted, FB, None ... 1961
West, Bill, CB, Tennessee State ... 1972
West, Willie, HB, Oregon ... 1964
Wettstein, Max, E, Florida State ... 1966
Whalen, Jim, TE, Boston College ... 1970–71
White, Andre, E, Florida A&M ... 1967
White, Jim, DE, Colorado State ... 1976
Williams, Harold, HB, Miami, Ohio ... 1961
Williams, Randy, RB, Hofstra ... 1969–70
Wilson, Nemiah, DB, Grambling ... 1965–67
Wood, Richard, QB, Auburn ... 1962
Wright, James Earl, HB, Memphis State ... 1964
Wright, Lonnie, DB, Colorado State ... 1966–67
Wright, Louis, DB, San Jose State ... 1975–76

Y

Yelverton, Bill, E, Mississippi ... 1960
Young, Joe, E, Arizona ... 1960–61
Young, Robert, G, Howard Payne ... 1966–70

Z

Zeman, Robert, HB, Wisconsin ... 1962–63

DETROIT LIONS

1930 The Portsmouth, Ohio, Spartans entered the National Football League. They played in Portsmouth, a city on the Ohio River and at the mouth of the Ohio Canal. The population of Portsmouth was 42,560. Harold Griffen, former player-coach of an independent professional team in Portsmouth, was one of the team's owners along with Harry Doerr, Homer C. Selby, and Harry Snyder. George (Potsy) Clark, coach of Butler University in Indianapolis, Indiana, and the former coach of five other colleges, was named Spartans' head coach. Roy (Father) Lumpkin of George Tech became the Spartans' quarterback in their single wing offense. They had a 5–6–3 record and finished eighth their first year in the NFL.

1931 Earl (Dutch) Clark, sensational all-around tailback from Colorado College, joined the Spartans. So did another excellent back, Glenn Presnell of Nebraska, and linemen George Christiansen, a tackle from Oregon, and Grover (Ox) Emerson, a guard from Texas. The Spartans became one of the best teams in an NFL that admittedly was a small one; it had only 10 teams. The Spartans won 11 games, second only to Green Bay, and there apparently was supposed to have been a playoff between the two of them for the championship but it was never played. The Spartans, Packers, and Chicago Bears were each fined $1,000 by the NFL for having players on their roster whose college classes had not graduated.

1932 Portsmouth won six games and lost only one, but it was tied four times. The Chicago Bears had an equally unusual 7–1–6 record. Ties did not count in the standings and because the Spartans and Bears had high percentages, and each of them won games late in the season against the Green Bay Packers, they qualified to meet in a postseason playoff, the first in NFL history. Green Bay was denied what would have been a fourth consecutive league championship. Earl (Dutch) Clark, star player for Portsmouth, left the team and started working at his off-season job, basketball coach at Colorado College, so he missed the playoff. It was held indoors at Chicago Stadium. Chicago fullback Bronko Nagurski made a pass which apparently was not thrown from a point at least five yards behind the line of scrimmage, breaking the NFL rules, and Portsmouth coach George (Potsy) Clark complained bitterly, to no avail. The Bears won the playoff 9–0.

1933 Earl (Dutch) Clark remained at his job at Colorado College and retired from pro football. Glenn Presnell replaced him at tailback and led the league in scoring, but the Spartans finished in third place in the league behind the Chicago Bears and Green Bay.

1934 George Richards, a radio station owner, purchased the Spartans for $15,000, plus $6,500 to pay off the team's debts. He moved the club to Detroit March 24. Richards used his own radio station to conduct a contest to name the team; the winner was "Lions." They were placed in the Western Division, with the Chicago Bears and Cardinals, Cincinnati Reds, and Green Bay Packers. They signed an agreement to play their home games at the 25,000-seat University of Detroit Stadium. Earl (Dutch) Clark rejoined the team. In their first game, the Lions beat the New York Giants 9–0 before 12,000 fans, September 23. They won their next nine games, including six more shutouts. Glenn Presnell kicked an NFL record 54-yard field goal in a 3–0 victory over Green Bay. The Lions won 10 straight games. Green Bay snapped the streak 3–0 on Clarke Hinkle's 47-yard field goal. The Lions began a Thanksgiving Day series against the Chicago Bears. Richards decided a coast-to-coast radio broadcast of the game was a good

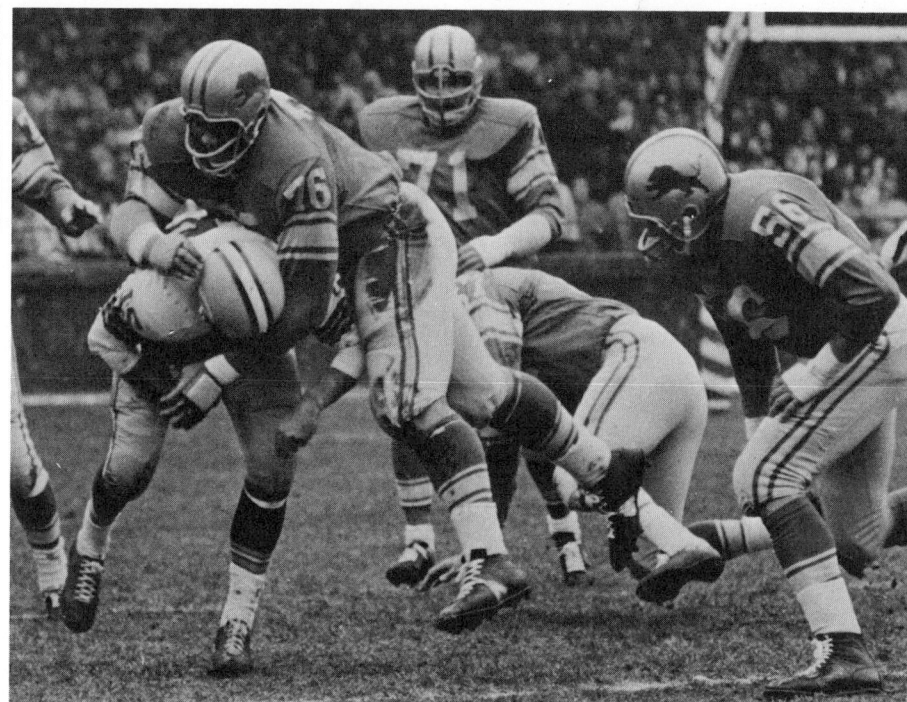

Roger Brown sacks Bart Starr during Lions' 1962 Thanksgiving Day victory over Packers.

Fullback Steve Owens running against the New Orleans Saints, 1972.

idea, so he solicited 94 interested stations and hired Graham McNamee to handle the play-by-play. Don Wilson was the color announcer. In Detroit the game attracted unusual interest. All 26,000 tickets, including standing room, were sold out early. The Bears won a close, exciting game 19–16. The Lions completed their season with a 10–3 record.

1935 The Lions won the Western Division championship with a 7–3–2 record, then beat the New York Giants in University of Detroit Stadium 26–7. Dutch Clark was the star of the title game, rushing for 80 yards, including a 42-yard touchdown, and gaining much more on kick returns. Other stars for Detroit were Raymond (Buddy) Parker, a rookie from Centenary who gained 70 yards and scored the Lions' final touchdown, and Ernie Caddel, who ran for 62 yards, mostly on wingback reverses. The Lions sliced the covering off the ball and cut it into 26 pieces. Then those peices were mounted on scrolls for team members.

1936 The Lions slipped to third place in the West, despite Fullback Leroy (Ace) Gutowsky's 827 yards rushing, just three short of the league ground-gaining title. At the end of the season, Potsy Clark quit as coach and moved to Brooklyn to coach the Dodgers. Richards hired Dutch Clark as head coach. The first draft of college players produced Sid Wagner, a guard from Michigan State.

1937 The highlight of the season was a 30–0 victory over Potsy Clark's Dodgers, October 17. Vern Huffman intercepted a pass and ran 100 yards to score in that game. Dutch Clark's team finished with a 7–4 record to tie for second in the West. The number one draft choice was Lloyd Cardwell, a back from Nebraska.

1938 The Lions moved their games to Briggs Stadium. They defeated Pittsburgh 16–7 in their first game there, September 9. Another 7–4 record secured undisputed second place. Dutch Clark accused Richards of "meddling." The two disagreed over Byron (Whizzer) White of the Pittsburgh Steelers. Richards wanted White; Clark didn't. So White stayed in Pittsburgh. At the end of the season, Clark became coach of the Cleveland Rams. Richards appointed Elmer (Gus) Henderson the new coach of the Lions. Detroit drafted Alex Wojciechowicz, a center from Fordham's famed Seven Blocks of Granite, number one.

1939 The club won its first four games, but lost its final four to wind up 6–5 and third in Henderson's first—and last—year. The coach got into a hassle with Richards over Clyde (Bulldog) Turner, the center from Hardin-Simmons. Since Richards reportedly had paid Turner money while he still was in college, Henderson figured he was all set with the Lions, so he bypassed him on the first round of the draft, choosing Doyle Nave, a back from USC, instead. That move wound up costing him his job as the Chicago Bears grabbed Turner. Richards was fined $5,000 by NFL President Joe Carr for having tampered with Turner while he was in school. Doyle Nave never played a game for Detroit. Richards sold the Lions to Fred Mandel, a Chicago department store magnate. The sale price was reported at $225,000, a profit of more than $200,000 for Richards.

1940 Mandel's first action as owner was to bring back Potsy Clark as coach. Whizzer White, returning from his Rhodes scholar studies at Oxford, England, was lured to Detroit after Mandel paid Pittsburgh $15,000 for his rights. White led the NFL in rushing with 514 yards in 12 games, but not even his play could turn the Lions into contenders. The Lions' record was 5–5–1 and Potsy Clark left for the second time.

1941 Bill Edwards from Western Reserve College was hired as the Lions' fourth head coach in four years. Bill Jefferson returned a kickoff 101 yards for a touchdown, a club record, against the Bears,

November 23. For the first time, Detroit suffered a losing season, going 4–6–1.

1942 Bob Westfall, a back from Michigan, was the top draft choice. World War II robbed the Lions of Whizzer White and most of their top players, but they continued to field a team. After two straight shutouts and a loss to Brooklyn, Mandel fired Edwards and hired John Karcis, an assistant, to replace him. The Lions became the first winless NFL team in nine years—since the Dayton Triangles of 1929—finishing the season with an 0–11 record. At the end of the season Karcis was fired.

1943 After a successful coaching career at the University of Detroit, Charles (Gus) Dorais was signed to a five-year contract as the Lions' head coach. The club received a lift from the signing of number one draft pick Frank Sinkwich, the Heisman trophy winning quarterback from Georgia, and finished in third place at 3–6–1.

1944 The Lions drafted Otto Graham of Northwestern number one, but he was called into military service before he could sign. He later said Detroit never even contacted him. Sinkwich, who had tried to join the service but had been rejected because of flat feet, wound up back with the Lions and enjoyed a brilliant season, running for 563 yards and throwing 12 touchdown passes in 10 games. Alex Wojciechowicz became a star on defense at linebacker, intercepting seven passes. The Lions became winners again, finishing 6–3–1 and tied for second place in the Western Division. Sinkwich was voted the NFL's most valuable player, narrowly winning the award over Green Bay's Don Hutson.

1945 The Army Air Corps finally accepted Sinkwich and kept him on for service football after the war ended. The Lions had some other weapons by then, however, including Westfall, Andy Farkas and Chuck Fenenbock in the backfield, and built a five-game winning streak early and an overall record of 7–3, good for second place. It was the Lions' best record in 10 years.

1946 Sinkwich was discharged from the service but promptly jumped leagues and signed with the New York Yankees of the new All-America Football Conference. He never played for Detroit again. Otto Graham, the top draft choice in 1943, also chose the Cleveland Browns of the AAFC. Preseason injuries hurt the Lions' chances and their record plummeted to 1–10, poorest in the league.

1947 Convinced something drastic was needed, Mandel signed Bill Dudley, after giving up Bob Cifers and Paul White to the Pittsburgh Steelers for the rights to Dudley. Mandel paid Dudley $20,000, the largest sum the Lions had ever given a player. The Lions also drafted Glenn Davis, Army's famed "Mr. Outside" in the Davis-Blanchard years. They installed the T formation. Davis didn't sign, the T formation didn't work well, and Dudley couldn't do it alone as Detroit suffered through a 3–9 season.

1948 Mandel asked Dorais to resign. Dorais refused until a settlement paid him $100,000 on the remaining years of his contract. A week later, Mandel, who had become discouraged and disenchanted, sold the club for $185,000 to a syndicate of Detroit socialites and sportsmen headed by D. Lyle Fife, an electrical contractor, and Edwin J. Anderson, a brewery executive. Fife was elected president and Anderson vice president of the Lions. Their choice for a coach was Alvin (Bo) McMillin, coach at the University of Indiana. They signed McMillin to a five-year contract as coach and general manager. McMillin had Fred Enke as his quarterback, Camp Wilson and Dudley as running backs, and Bob Mann, the Lions' first black player, Joe Margucci, and Johnny Greene as receivers. The number one draft choice was Y. A. Tittle, a quarterback from Louisiana State, but he never signed, choosing to go with the Baltimore Colts of the AAFC. The Lions

finished last for the third year in a row.

1949 McMillin shook up the club, bringing in key new players such as Cloyce Box, an end from West Texas State, and Don Doll, a back from USC, among others. The top draft choice was Johnny Rauch, a quarterback from Georgia, who never played for Detroit, but was traded to the New York Bulldogs. Fife and Anderson were having some problems in the front office. Anderson succeeded Fife as president. Nick Kerbawy, the club's publicity director, was appointed assistant to the general manager. For the first time since 1945, the Lions climbed out of last place. They were fourth with a 4–8 record.

1950 The Lions acquired Bobby Layne from the New York Bulldogs for end Bob Mann, who had caught 66 passes the year before. To go with their new passer, they also signed two of the most publicized college players of the decade, Southern Methodist halfback Doak Walker, and Notre Dame end Leon Hart, the Heisman trophy winner and top draft choice. The Lions also drafted Thurman McGraw, a tackle from Colorado A&M, and Lou Creekmur, a tackle from William and Mary. Bob (Hunchy) Hoernschemeyer, a strong runner, also was obtained from the allocation draft of players left without teams by the demise of the AAFC. Another key addition was made to the coaching staff. Raymond (Buddy) Parker, the star of Detroit's championship team in 1935, became an assistant coach. The improved Lions finished 6–6 and Doak Walker became the NFL scoring champion as a rookie with 128 points. Cloyce Box caught 12 passes in a game against Baltimore, four for touchdowns. He gained 302 yards for the day, one short of the Rams' Jim Benton's all-time record for one game. But a player revolt resulted in the dismissal of McMillin. Two years remained on his contract, and the owners had to give McMillin $60,000. They vowed never again to give a coach a contract of more than one year. Buddy Parker was named head coach, December 20. Nick Kerbawy became general manager.

1951 In training camp at Ypsilanti, Michigan, Parker brought in some new players such as defensive end-kicker Jim Martin, who was obtained in a trade with Cleveland for the number one draft pick in 1952; center Vince Banonis, a former all-pro, from the Chicago Cardinals, and end Bill Swiacki, the former Columbia star, from the Giants. Layne, Hart, and Walker were just three new stars. Others included running back Hoernschemeyer, blocker Creekmur, and 349-pound defensive middle guard Les Bingaman, a member of the team since 1948 but an important player in Parker's defense. The draft produced Jack Christiansen, a defensive back from Colorado A&M; Dorne Dibble, an end from Michigan State, and Lavern Torgeson, a center from Washington State. Just three weeks before the season opened, Parker got Pat Harder, the rugged Chicago Cardinals' fullback in their championship seasons, in exchange for John Panelli and the club's number two draft choice in 1952. Attendance doubled at Briggs Stadium and the largest crowd in history, 50,567, saw the Lions lose to the Los Angeles Rams 27–21, October 14. They battled the Rams all the way, beating the Rams 24–22 in Los Angeles before narrowly losing out when San Francisco, behind Y. A. Tittle, defeated Detroit 21–17 in the final game of the season. The Lions finished 7–4–1 to the Rams' 8–4.

1952 Parker signed a second one-year contract for a raise in pay. Despite no first- or second-round draft picks, Parker picked up Yale Lary, a back from Texas A&M, on the third round, and Jim David, a defensive back from Colorado A&M, on the twenty-second round. He also got Earl (Jug) Girard from the Packers to fill in for Doak Walker, who missed most of the preseason because of a severely cut arm suffered in a freak accident. Despite a poor start, Layne got his team moving again, beating Los Angeles twice in the first four games. He drove the Lions to five straight victories and into a tie with Los Angeles for the National Conference championship at 9–3, the Lions' best season since their first season in Detroit. In a playoff in Detroit, the Lions won the conference title 31–21. In the NFL championship game at Cleveland, Doak Walker broke open a tight defensive battle with a 67-yard touchdown run and the Lions defeated the Browns 17–7 for their first NFL championship in 17 years.

1953 Parker signed another one-year contract. The Lions drafted Harley Sewell, a guard from Texas, on the first round. They also signed linebacker Joe Schmidt from the University of Pittsburgh, tackle Charlie Ane from USC, and halfback Gene Gedman from Indiana. Layne continued to run the team in his raucous, but effective way, and the club marched to another conference title with a 10–2 record, including six straight victories at the end of the regular season. In the league championship game at Detroit, 54,577 watched Layne drive the Lions to a late touchdown. Then Doak Walker kicked the extra point to give Detroit its second consecutive NFL championship, 17–16 over Cleveland.

1954 Parker signed another one-year contract. Pat Harder, Vince Banonis, and Bill Swiacki all retired. Walker scored 106 points, second highest total in the league. The Lions' defense, led by Jack Christiansen and his teammates in a secondary that became known as Chris's Crew, was outstanding. The Lions won the Western Conference at 9–2–1, but their mastery over Cleveland ended in the league championship game in Ohio. Otto Graham put on a spectacular show passing for three touchdowns and running for three more, as the Browns whipped Detroit 56–10.

1955 Some off-season events started a disastrous slide in Detroit. Bingaman, Box, and McGraw all retired. Layne's shoulder was separated in an accident in Texas. Layne played, but much of the zip was missing from his arm. The defense was hurting, and the Lions fell from first place to last in the Western Conference, winning only three while losing nine. Walker, Hoernschemeyer, and Girard announced their retirements after the final game.

1956 The club drafted Heisman trophy winning halfback Howard (Hopalong) Cassady, from Ohio State, number one. His addition, plus Layne's recovery from his shoulder injury, and the emergence of Joe Schmidt as one of football's best middle linebackers, turned Detroit back into a contender again. A 42–10 win over Chicago gave the Lions a half-game lead late in the year, but on the last Sunday of the season Layne was knocked out of the game with a concussion and the Bears won 38–21 to take the Western Conference title.

1957 The Lions' draft choice included Terry Barr, a back from Michigan, and John Gordy, a guard from Tennessee. Parker finally won his battle for a longer contract, getting the directors to give him two years at $30,000 per season. Then, two days before the first preseason game, Parker made a dramatic and surprising announcement, August 12. He said he was resigning as head coach. "I am quitting," he told an audience at a "Meet the Lions" preseason banquet. "I can no longer control this team, and when I cannot control it, I can't coach it." Parker was depressed about the team's performance in training camp. "I don't want to get involved in another losing season, so I'm leaving Detroit," he said. But perhaps a more reasonable explanation for his sudden resignation was a scene just prior to the banquet at a cocktail party. Parker had walked in to see some of his star players socializing with the owners, a practice Parker deplored. Assistant coach George Wilson took over the team. Wilson picked up another proven quarterback in Tobin Rote from Green Bay, and got fullback John Henry Johnson from San Francisco. The Lions battled into a tie with the 49ers for the Western Conference title. In the playoff game with the 49ers in San Francisco, the Lions trailed 27–7 in the third quarter, then roared back behind Rote to win 31–27, scoring 24 points in 21 minutes. Then, with Layne out because of a broken leg, Rote led a 59–14 rout of Cleveland for the National Football League championship. Rote, who completed 12 of 19 passes for 280 yards, threw four touchdown passes and scored once himself on a one-yard sneak. The defense intercepted five passes and recovered two fumbles as the Lions avenged the 56–10 humiliation by the Browns in the 1954 championship game.

1958 The Champions picked up a prize rookie in number one draft choice Alex Karras, a myopic defensive tackle from Iowa. The Lions lost to the College All-Stars in Chicago 35–19, then split their four preseason games. Two games into the regular season, Bobby Layne was traded to Pittsburgh. The team, deeply tied to the colorful quarterback emotionally, never seemed to recover from that loss. A slow start—the Lions were 0–3–1 after four games—and a stumbling finished—1–3—helped the defending champion Lions finish fifth in the Western Conference. Off the field, Edwin J. Anderson took over as general manager of the club, replacing Nick Kerbawy. Jack Christiansen retired, breaking up Chris's Crew.

1959 While age crept into vital positions, the Lions were trying to rebuild with an outstanding rookie fullback, Nick Pietrosante, the top draft choice from Notre Dame, and a defense that featured Schmidt, defensive back Yale Lary, and the aggressive second-year tackle, Karras. The Lions beat only the two last-place teams in the divisions—Los Angeles twice and the Chicago Cardinals—and finished 3–8–1.

1960 Rote played out his option and defected to the Canadian Football League. Morrall took over at quarterback. The Lions lost their top draft choice, Johnny Robinson of Louisiana State, to Kansas City of the new American Football League. A 300-pound rookie defensive tackle from Maryland State, Roger Brown, and a wily, old defensive back, Dick (Night Train) Lane, arrived to further solidify a defense that was becoming one of the best in the league. Lane came in a trade with the St. Louis Cardinals. The new quarterback was Jim Ninowski, the ex-Cleveland Browns' passer, who had an exciting new target in Gail Cogdill, an end from Washington State. Jim David and Lou Creekmur retired and Jim Doran and Charlie Ane were lost in the draft to stock the new Dallas Cowboys' franchise. Coming fast the second half of the season, the Lions won six of their last seven games, including a 20–15 comeback victory over the world champion Colts, to finish second behind Green Bay in the Western Conference. Pietrosante broke Ace Gutkowsky's club rushing record with 872 yards. Wilson was rewarded with a new two-year contract and the Lions beat the Browns 17–16 in the Playoff Bowl.

1961 A bitter proxy fight for control of the club erupted, with D. Lyle Fife, the club's former president, trying to take over from the Edwin J. Anderson faction. The effort was unsuccessful. Anderson resigned as president, however, and was succeeded by William Clay Ford of the automotive family. Anderson remained as general manager. In a strange 8–5–1 season, the Lions lost five times at home, including a 49–0 embarrassment by San Francisco. But the Lions went undefeated on the road to once again finish second to the Packers in their division. The Lions beat the Eagles 38–10 in the Playoff Bowl. Because of the war with the AFL for talent, the NFL drafted early and the Lions picked John Hadl, a back from Kansas, number one; Eddie Wilson, a quarterback from Arizona, number two; and Bobby Thompson, a defensive back from Arizona State, number three. Hadl and Wilson signed with the AFL and Thompson went to the Canadian Football League.

1962 Trying to quell open bitterness among the veterans for the failure in the draft, the Lions acquired quarterback Milt Plum, runner Tom Watkins, and linebacker Dave Lloyd from the Browns, sending Ninowski back to Cleveland along with Cassady and Bill Glass. Detroit won the most games in the franchise's history, 11 but it still wasn't good enough to beat out Vince Lombardi's powerful Green Bay champions. They had the Packers virtually beaten 7–6 in their first meeting, October 7. Then Plum inexplicably threw a third down pass that was intercepted and a Green Bay field goal with 27 seconds left to play beat the Lions 9–7. On Thanksgiving Day, however, the Lions pulled an upset, beating the Packers 26–14 in one of the most memorable displays of aggressive defensive football ever witnessed on national television. The Lions sacked Bart Starr 11 times and deprived the Packers of a perfect season.

1963 Appearing in their third consecutive Playoff Bowl, the Lions made it three straight by beating Pittsburgh 17–10. The day following the game, Commissioner Pete Rozelle announced the Lions, among others, were being investigated for alleged gambling on games. Alex Karras and Green Bay's Paul Hornung were suspended a minimum of one year for betting on football games, April 17. The Lions' management was fined $4,000. Five Detroit players—Joe Schmidt, Wayne Walker, John Gordy, Gary Low, and Sam Williams—were fined $2,000 each. The Lions finally signed a number one draft choice, Daryl Sanders, a tackle from Ohio State, but without Karras, and bothered by an abundance of injuries, the Lions plummeted to the middle of the division standings. Plum was replaced by Morrall. The Lions struggled to a 5–8–1 record.

1964 William Clay Ford completed the transaction to consolidate ownership of the team. He bought all stock from the 140 shareholders for $6.5 million. One of Ford's first moves was the restructure the front office. The key new figure was Russ Thomas, who was given the job of signing players and overseeing the draft. He was assigned the title of director of player personnel. Wilson was retained as coach, but some of his authority was removed. Again, the three top draft choices signed with AFL teams. Karras was reinstated, March 16. Detroit's brilliant defense was growing old, and the offense, torn by the controversy between Plum and Morrall at quarterback, couldn't get untracked in a 7–5–2 season. Ford fired all of Wilson's assistants, in a clear warning to the head coach. Wilson resigned, December 23.

1965 Harry Gilmer, assistant coach for the Minnesota Vikings, was named the Lions' head coach. The draft produced fullback Tom Nowatzke from Indiana, center Ed Flanagan from Purdue, defensive end Larry Hand from Appalachian State, and defensive back Tom Vaughn from Iowa State. The Lions traded linebacker Dennis Gaubatz to Baltimore for Joe Don Looney, a powerful running back with a reputation as incorrigible. Gilmer's first decision was to go with one quarterback, so he traded Morrall to New York in a three-way deal that brought linebacker Mike Lucci to the Lions from Cleveland. Gilmer gave Plum the quarterback job. But Plum had a poor year, as did most of the Lions, and the club regressed. Looney played little, complaining of chronic headaches. Schmidt, one of the best linebackers in football for 13 seasons, and Barr retired after his final game.

1966 Resentment among the players surfaced over Gilmer and the team continued to have problems. But Ford tried to soothe matters by adding Schmidt to the coaching staff and naming Karras captain. Just before the season, Pietrosante, the Lions' career rushing leader with 3,933 yards, was cut from the team. Plum started at quarterback again, but went down with a knee injury at midseason. Karl Sweetan, who was signed off a semipro team, was given the quarterback job. In the third game of the season, Looney refused a Gilmer order during a game and was suspended indefinitely, then traded to Washington. Garo Yepremian, a soccer-style placekicker from Cyprus, arrived at midseason and kicked an NFL record six field goals in a game against Minnesota. The Lions and Vikings finished tied for last in the Western Conference.

1967 Gilmer was fired and paid off the final three years of his contract, January 5. Joe Schmidt signed a five-year contract as the new head coach. The NFL realigned and the Lions were placed in the Central Division of the Western Conference. The top draft choices included running back Mel Farr from UCLA and defensive back Lem Barney from Jackson State. Russ Thomas was named general manager and Carl Brettschneider was the new director of player personnel. The Lions became the first NFL team to be beaten by an AFL team when Denver beat the Lions 13–7 in the first interleague preseason game. Roger Brown was traded to Los Angeles for the Rams' first, second, and third draft choices in 1968. Farr and Barney were chosen rookie offensive and defensive players of the year, but the Lions finished 5–7–2.

1968 Another good draft produced quarterback Greg Landry from Massachusetts, tight end Charlie Sanders from Minnesota, and wide receiver Earl McCullouch from USC. Bill Munson was obtained from the Rams for a number one draft choice, Plum, Tom Watkins, and Pat Studstill. But Munson damaged his shoulder early, making Landry the starter in the season opener. Landry threw one touchdown pass and four interceptions in his first game. The offense never jelled and in one span the Lions went 16 successive quarters without producing a touchdown. In their last nine games, the Lions won only once.

1969 Brettschneider was dismissed, amid complaints that Thomas would not allow anyone else to have a voice in running the club. Thomas and Schmidt denied the charge publicly and vowed new unity. The Lions' defense finally started coming back to form, with the linebacking of Paul Naumoff, Mike Lucci, and Wayne Walker as its foundation. The quarterback situation still remained unsettled.

1970 Steve Owens, the Heisman trophy winner from Oklahoma, was the number one draft pick. Owens won the starting fullback job, then injured a shoulder in the final preseason game and was out for most of the season. Although Munson played more at the beginning and Landry more at the end, the quarterback confusion continued. The rest of the offense improved, with Farr and Altie Taylor enjoying good years running. Charlie Sanders developed into an all-pro tight end and the Lions made the playoffs as the "wild card" team with a stirring finish. They won five straight to finish with a 10–4 record. In the first round of the playoffs, the Dallas defense silenced the Lions 5–0, scoring their points on a safety and a field goal.

1971 Charlie Weaver, a linebacker from USC, was chosen in the draft. The week before the season opened, Alex Karras was released. Chuck Hughes, one of the Lions' wide receivers, died of a heart attack during the game against Chicago, collapsing on the field, October 24. Owens and Landry came into their own as full-fledged stars. Owens became the Lions' first 1,000-yard rusher with 1,035 yards. Landry set an NFL rushing record for his position with 530 yards. The Lions were in contention early in the season after a 4–1 start. But they lost their last three for a 7–6–1 record and placed second again.

1972 Herb Orvis, a defensive tackle from Colorado, and Ken Sanders, defensive end from Howard Payne, were the top two draft choices. Landry, Owens,

Taylor, Sanders and a strong offensive line provided plenty of points (339). But the defense gave little support (Lions' opponents scored 290) and the result was only frustration and a fourth straight second-place finish. The citizens of Pontiac, Michigan, passed a bond issue for a domed stadium.

1973 After six seasons, Joe Schmidt announced his resignation as head coach, January 12. Don McCafferty, who had won a Super Bowl with Baltimore in 1971, was named to replace him. The draft produced defensive end Ernie Price, from Texas A&I, and linebacker Jim Laslavic, from Penn State. Again, high hopes resulted in more disappointment, even though the club finished second behind Minnesota in the NFC Central with a 6–7–1 record. "I don't think they want to win—at least it doesn't look like it," said owner Ford. Construction began on a $55.7 million stadium in Pontiac, Michigan in December.

1974 Coach Don McCafferty died of a heart attack, July 28. Assistant coach Rick Forzano, a former head coach at the Naval Academy, was named the new head coach. The Lions lost their first four games, but came back to win seven of their last ten to finish second behind Minnesota's division champions. Forzano was given a three-year contract.

1975 The draft produced Lynn Boden, a 6-foot 5-inch, 270-pound guard from South Dakota State; Craig Hertwig, a 6-foot 8-inch, 270-pound tackle from Georgia; and Dennis Franklin, a wide receiver from Michigan. The team opened 80,638-seat Pontiac Metropolitan Stadium, or Ponmet, which featured a inflatable roof, with a 36–10 loss to Dallas before a record home crowd of 79,784. Detroit again won seven games and finished as the runner-up to Minnesota in the NFC Central. Both Munson and Landry went down with knee injuries. Joe Reed wound up getting considerable playing time at quarterback, completing 86 of 191 passes for 1,181 yards.

1976 The stadium's name was changed to the Pontiac Silverdome. The Lions won only one of their first four games. Forzano was fired and Tommy Hudspeth, coordinator of personnel and scouting, was named coach. The Lions responded with a 30–10 victory over New England. Detroit won five of its last nine games under Hudspeth and placed third in the NFC Central, behind Minnesota and the Chicago Bears. The finish ended a seven-year streak for the Lions as a second-place team.

MEMBERS OF HALL OF FAME:
Jack Christiansen, Earl (Dutch) Clark, Bill Dudley, Dick (Night Train) Lane, Bobby Layne, Ollie Matson, Hugh McElhenny, Joe Schmidt, Alex Wojciechowicz.

LIONS RECORD, 1930–76

Year	Won	Lost	Tied	Pct.	Pts.	OP
Portsmouth Spartans						
1930	5	6	3	.455		
1931	11	3	0	.786		
1932	6	2	4	.750		
1933	6	5	0	.545	128	87
Detroit Lions						
1934	10	3	1	.769	238	59
1935‡	7	3	2	.700	191	111
1936	8	4	0	.667	235	102
1937	7	4	0	.636	180	105
1938	7	4	0	.636	119	108
1939	6	5	0	.545	145	150
1940	5	5	1	.500	138	153
1941	4	6	1	.400	121	195
1942	0	11	0	.000	38	263
1943	3	6	1	.333	178	218
1944	6	3	1	.667	216	151
1945	7	3	0	.700	195	194
1946	1	10	0	.091	142	310
1947	3	9	0	.250	231	305
1948	2	10	0	.167	200	407
1949	4	8	0	.333	237	259
1950	6	6	0	.500	321	285
1951	7	4	1	.636	336	259
1952‡	9	3	0	.750	344	192
1953‡	10	2	0	.833	271	205
1954§	9	2	1	.818	337	189
1955	3	9	0	.250	230	275
1956	9	3	0	.750	300	188
1957‡	8	4	0	.667	251	231
1958	4	7	1	.364	261	276
1959	3	8	1	.273	203	275
1960	7	5	0	.583	239	212
1961	8	5	1	.615	270	258
1962	11	3	0	.786	315	177
1963	5	8	1	.385	326	265
1964	7	5	2	.583	280	260
1965	6	7	1	.462	257	295
1966	4	9	1	.308	206	317
1967	5	7	2	.417	260	259
1968	4	8	2	.333	207	241
1969	9	4	1	.692	259	188
1970	10	4	0	.714	347	202
1971	7	6	1	.538	341	286
1972	8	5	1	.607	339	290
1973	6	7	1	.464	271	247
1974	7	7	0	.500	256	270
1975	7	7	0	.500	245	262
1976	6	8	0	.429	262	220
47 Years	**293**	**258**	**32**	**.530**		

‡*NFL Championship*
§*NFL Western Conference Champion*

RECORD HOLDERS

Rushing (Yards)	Steve Owens, 1971	1,035
Passing (Pct.)	Greg Landry, 1976	57.7
Passing (Yards)	Earl Morrall, 1963	2,621
Passing (TDs)	Bobby Layne, 1951	26
Receiving (No.)	Pat Studstill, 1966	67
Receiving (Yards)	Pat Studstill, 1966	1,266
Interceptions (No.)	Don Doll, 1950, and Paul Christiansen, 1953	12
Punting (Avg.)	Yale Lary, 1963	48.9
Punt Ret. (Avg.)	Jack Christiansen, 1952	21.5
Kickoff Ret. (Avg.)	Tom Watkins, 1965	34.4
Touchdowns (Total)	Cloyce Box, 1952	15
Field Goals Made	Errol Mann, 1969	25
Points (Total)	Doak Walker, 1950	128

COACHING HISTORY

1930–36	George (Potsy) Clark	53–26–10
1937–38	Earl (Dutch) Clark	14– 8– 0
1939	Elmer (Gus) Henderson	6– 5– 0
1940	George (Potsy) Clark	5– 5– 1
1941–42	Bill Edwards*	4– 9– 1
1942	John Karcis	0– 8– 0
1943–47	Gus Dorais	20–31– 2
1948–50	Alvin (Bo) McMillin	12–24– 0
1951–56	Raymond (Buddy) Parker	47–23– 2
1957–64	George Wilson	53–45– 6
1965–66	Harry Gilmer	10–16– 2
1967–72	Joe Schmidt	43–34– 7
1973	Don McCafferty	6– 7– 1
1974–76	Rick Forzano**	15–17– 0
1976	Tommy Hudspeth	5– 5– 0

Replaced after three games in 1942
**Resigned after four games in 1976*

FIRST PLAYER SELECTED

1936	Sid Wagner, G, Michigan State
1937	Lloyd Cardwell, B, Nebraska
1938	Alex Wojciechowicz, C, Fordham
1939	John Pingel, B, Michigan State
1940	Doyle Nave, B, USC
1941	Jim Thomason, B, Texas A&M
1942	Bob Westfall, B, Michigan
1943	Frank Sinkwich, B, Georgia
1944	Otto Graham, B, Northwestern
1945	Frank Szymanski, C, Notre Dame
1946	Bill Dellastatious, B, Missouri
1947	Glenn Davis, B, Army
1948	Y.A. Tittle, B, Louisiana State
1949	John Rauch, B, Georgia
1950	Leon Hart, E, Notre Dame
1951	Dick Stanfel, G (2), San Francisco
1952	Yale Lary, B (3), Texas A&M
1953	Harley Sewell, G, Texas
1954	Dick Chapman, T, Rice
1955	Dave Middleton, B, Auburn
1956	Howard (Hopalong) Cassady, B, Ohio State
1957	Bill Glass, G, Baylor
1958	Alex Karras, T, Iowa
1959	Nick Pietrosante, B, Notre Dame
1960	John Robinson, S, Louisiana State
1961	Danny LaRose, T, Missouri
1962	John Hadl, QB, Kansas
1963	Daryl Sanders, T, Ohio State
1964	Pete Beathard, QB, USC
1965	Tom Nowatzke, RB, Indiana
1966	Nick Eddy, RB (2 future), Notre Dame
1967	Mel Farr, RB, UCLA
1968	Greg Landry, QB, Massachusetts
1969	Altie Taylor, RB (2), Utah State
1970	Steve Owens, RB, Oklahoma
1971	Bob Bell, DT, Cincinnati
1972	Herb Orvis, DE, Colorado
1973	Ernie Price, DE, Texas A&I
1974	Ed O'Neil, LB, Penn State
1975	Lynn Boden, G, South Dakota State
1976	James Hunter, DB, Grambling

Charley Ane

Terry Barr

Les Bingaman

Cloyce Box

G. (Ox) Emerson

Mel Farr

Jim Gibbons

PORTSMOUTH SPARTANS, 1930–33;
DETROIT LIONS, 1934–76

Addams, Abraham, E, Indiana 1949
Aiello, Anthony, B, Youngstown 1944
Alderman, Grady, G, Detroit 1960
Alford, Gene, B, Texas Tech 1931–33
Alford, Mike, C, Auburn 1966
Ambrose, Walt, G, John Carroll 1930
Andersen, Stanley, E, Stanford 1941
Ane, Charley, T, USC 1953–59
Arena, Anthony, C, Michigan State 1942–46
Armstrong, Bob, T, Missouri 1931–32
Ashcom, Richard, T, Oregon 1943
Atkins, George, G, Auburn 1955
Atty, Alexander, G, West Virginia 1941
Austin, James, E, St. Mary's, Calif. 1939

B

Bailey, Byron, B, Washington State 1953–54
Baker, John, DE, N. Carolina Coll. 1968
Ball, Larry, LB, Louisville 1975
Banas, Stephen, B, Notre Dame 1935
Banjavic, Emil, B, Arizona 1942
Banonis, Vincent, C, Detroit 1951–53
Barle, Louis, B, Duluth 1938
Barnes, Al, WR, New Mexico State 1971–73
Barney, Lem, DB, Jackson State 1967–76
Barr, Terry, B, Michigan 1957–65
Barton, Greg, QB, Tulsa 1969
Bass, Mike, DB, Michigan 1967
Batinski, Stanley, G, Temple 1941–47
Batten, Pat, FB, Hardin-Simmons 1964
Baumgartner, Maxie, E, Texas 1948
Behan, Charles, E, DeKalb 1942
Belichick, Stephen, B, Western Reserve 1941
Bell, Bob, DT, Cincinnati 1971–73
Bennett, Charles, B, Indiana 1930
Bernard, Charles, C, Michigan 1934
Berrang, Ed, E, Villanova 1951
Berry, Connie Mack, E, N. Carolina State 1939
Bingaman, Les, G, Illinois 1948–54
Blair, T.C., TE, Tulsa 1974
Blessing, Paul, E, Nebraska State Teachers 1944
Boden, Lynn, G, South Dakota State 1975–76
Bodenger, Morris, G, Tulane 1931–34
Bolinger, Russ, T, Long Beach State 1976
Bolton, Andrew, RB, Fisk 1976
Booth, Richard, B, Western Reserve 1941, 1945
Boswell, Ben, T, Texas Christian 1933
Bowdoin, Jim, G, Alabama 1933
Bowman, Bill, B, William & Mary 1954, 1956
Box, Cloyce, E, W. Texas State 1949–50, 1952–54
Bradshaw, Charlie, T, Baylor 1967–68
Braidwood, Charles, E, Chattanooga 1930
Brettschneider, Carl, LB, Iowa State 1960–63
Briggs, Paul, T, Colorado 1948
Brill, Harold, B, Wichita 1939
Briscoe, Marlin, WR, Omaha 1975
Britt, Maurice, E, Arkansas 1941
Brown, Charlie, WR, Northern Arizona 1970
Brown, Dick, C, Iowa 1930
Brown, Howard, G, Indiana 1948–50
Brown, Marvin, E, E. Texas State 1957
Brown, Roger, T, Maryland State 1960–66
Brumley, Robert, B, Rice 1945
Bulger, Chet, T, Auburn 1950
Bundra, Mike, T, USC 1962–63
Burleson, John, G, Southern Methodist 1933
Busich, Samuel, E, Ohio State 1943
Bussey, Dexter, RB, Texas-Arlington 1974–76

C

Caddel, Ernie, B, Stanford 1933–36
Cain, James, E, Alabama 1950–55
Callahan, J.R., B, Texas 1946
Callihan, William, B, Nebraska 1940–45
Calvelli, Anthony, C, Stanford 1939–40
Campbell, Mike, RB, Lenoir Rhyne 1968
Campbell, Stanley, G, Iowa State 1952, 1955–58
Cappleman, Bill, QB, Florida State 1973
Capria, Carl, DB, Purdue 1974
Cardwell, Lloyd, B, Nebraska 1937–43
Carpenter, Lew, B, Arkansas 1953–55
Cassady, Howard (Hopalong), B, Ohio State 1956–61, 1963
Cavosie, John B, Butler 1931–33
Chantiles, Thomas, T, USC 1942
Chase, Benjamin, G, Navy 1947
Christensen, Frank, B, Utah 1934–37
Christensen, George, T, Oregon 1931–38
Christensen, Koester, E, Michigan State 1930
Christiansen, Jack, DB, Colorado A&M 1951–58
Cifelli, Gus, T, Notre Dame 1951–53
Cifers, Robert, B, Tennessee 1944–46
Clark, Al, DB, Eastern Michigan 1971–72
Clark, Earl (Dutch), B, Colorado 1931–32, 1934–38
Clark, Ernie, LB, Michigan State 1963–67
Clark, Wayne, E, Utah 1944–45
Clemons, Raymond, G, Central Okla. St. 1939
Cline, Ollie, B, Ohio State 1950–53
Clowes, John, T, William & Mary 1951
Cody, Bill, LB, Auburn 1966
Cogdill, Gail, E, Washington State 1960–68
Colella, Thomas, B, Canisius 1941–43
Conlee, Gerald, C, St. Mary's, Calif. 1943
Compton, Dick, B, McMurry 1962–64
Concannon, Jack, QB, Boston College 1975
Cook, Gene, E, Toledo 1959
Cook, Ted, E, Alabama 1947
Cooper, Harold, G, Detroit 1937
Corgan, Michael, B, Notre Dame 1943
Cotton, Craig, TE, Youngstown State 1969–71
Cottrell, Bill, T, Delaware Valley 1967
Crabtree, Clement, T, Wake Forest 1940–41
Creekmur, Lou, T, William & Mary 1950–59
Cremer, Theodore, E, Auburn 1946–48
Croft, Don, DT, Texas-El Paso 1976
Cronin, Gene, G, Pacific 1956–59
Crosswhite, Leon, RB, Oklahoma 1973–74
Cunningham, Leon, C, South Carolina 1955

D

D'Alonzo, Peter, B, Villanova 1951–52
David, Jim, B, Colorado A&M 1952–59
Davis, Ben, DB, Defiance 1974–76
Davis, Glenn, E, Ohio State 1960–61
Davis, Milt, HB, UCLA 1956
Davis, Ray, G, Howard, Ala. 1932–33
Davis, Syl, B, Geneva 1933
Dawley, Frederick, B, Michigan 1944
DeCorrevont, Bill, B, Northwestern 1946
DeFruiter, Robert, B, Nebraska 1947
DeMarco, Mario, G, Miami 1949
Dennis, Guy, G, Florida 1973
DePoyster, Jerry, K, Wyoming 1968
DeShane, Charles, B, Alabama 1945–49
DeWeese, Everett (Abe), G, None 1930
Dibble, Dorne, E, Michigan State 1951, 1953–57
Diehl, David, E, Michigan St. 1939–40, 1944–45
Doll, Donald, DB, USC 1949–52
Doran, James, E, Iowa State 1951–59
D'Orazio, Joseph, T, Ithaca 1944
Douds, Forrest (Jap), T, Washington & Jefferson 1930–41
Dove, Robert, E-G, Notre Dame 1953–54
Dublinski, Tom, QB, Utah 1952–54
Dubzinski, Walter, G, Boston College 1941
Dudish, Andrew, C, Georgia 1948
Dudley, Bill, B, Virginia 1947–49
Dugger, John, E, Ohio State 1947–48
Duncan, James, E, Wake Forest 1950
Duncan, Rick, P, E, Montana State 1969
Dunlap, Leonard, DB, North Texas State 1975

E

Earon, Blaine, E, Duke 1952–53
Ebding, Harry, E. St. Mary's, Calif 1931–73
Eby, Byron, B, Ohio State 1930
Eddy, Nick, RB, Notre Dame 1968–72
Edien, Edmund, B, Scranton 1944
Ellis, Lawrence, B, Syracuse 1948
Elser, Earl, T, Butler 1933
Emerick, Robert, T, Miami, Ohio 1934
Emerson, Grover (Ox), G, Texas 1931–37
Engebretson, Paul, T, Northwestern 1934
English, Doug, DT, Texas 1975–76
Enke, Fren, QB, Arizona 1948–51
Evans, Murray, B, Hardin-Simmons 1942–43
Evey, Dick, DT, Tennessee 1971

F

Farkas, Andrew, B, Detroit 1945
Farmer, George, WR, UCLA 1975
Farr, Mel, RB, UCLA 1967–72
Farr, Miller, DB, Wichita 1973
Feldhaus, William T, Cincinnati 1937–40
Felts, Bob, HB, Florida A&M 1965–67
Fena, Thomas, G, Colorado 1937
Fenenbock, Charles, B, UCLA 1943–45
Fenner, Lee, E, St. Mary's, Ohio 1930
Ferguson, Leon, HB, Iowa 1963
Fichman, Leon, T, Alabama 1946–47
Fisk, William, E, USC 1940–43
Flanagan, Ed, C, Purdue 1965–72
Flanagan, Richard, LB, Ohio State 1950–52
Fleckenstein, Bill, G, Iowa 1930
Forte, Aldo, G, Montana 1946
Franklin, Dennis, WR, Michigan 1975–76
Freitas, Rockne, T, Oregon State 1968–76
French, Barry, G, Purdue 1951
Frohbose, Bill, DB, Miami 1974
Frutig, Edward, E, Michigan 1945–46
Fucci, Dominic, B, Kentucky 1955
Furst, Anthony, T, Dayton 1940–41, 1944

G

Gagnon, Roy, G, Oregon 1935
Gaines, Lawrence, RB, Wyoming 1976
Gallagher, Frank, G, North Carolina 1967–72
Gambrell, Bill, E, South Carolina 1968
Gandee, Sherwin, E, Ohio State 1952–57
Gatski, Frank, C, Marshall 1957
Gaubatz, Dennis, LB, Louisiana State 1963–64
Gedman, Gene, B, Indiana 1953, 1956–68
George, Ray, T, USC 1939
Geremsky, Thad, E, Pittsburgh 1951
Germany, Willie, DB, Morgan State 1973
Gibbons, Jim, E, Iowa 1958–68
Gibbs, Sonny, QB, Texas Christian 1964
Gill, Sloko, G, Youngstown 1942
Gillette, Jim, B, Virginia 1948
Gilmer, Harry, QB, Alabama 1955–56
Gipson, Paul, RB, Houston 1971
Girard, Earl, B, Wisconsin 1952–56
Glass, William, G, Baylor 1958–61
Glassgow, Will, B, Iowa 1930
Goich, Dan, DE, California 1969–71
Goldman, Samuel, E, Howard 1949
Gonzaga, John, T, None 1961–65
Goodman, Henry, T, West Virginia 1942
Goovert, Ron, LB, Michigan State 1967
Gordon, John, DT, Hawaii 1972
Gordy, John, G, Tennessee 1957, 1959–67
Gore, Gordon, B, Oklahoma S.W. Teachers 1939
Graham, Al, G, Dayton 1930
Graham, Lester, G, Tulsa 1938
Grant, Aaron, C, Chattanooga 1930
Greene, John, E, Michigan 1944–50
Greer, Albert, E, Jackson State 1963
Grefe, Theodore, E, Notre Dame 1945
Griffen, Hal, C, Iowa 1930, 1932
Grigonis, Frank, B, Chattanooga 1942
Grimes, George, B, Virginia 1948
Groomes, Melvin, B, Indiana 1948–49
Grossman, Rex, B, Indiana 1950
Grottkau, Robert, G, Oregon 1959–60
Gutowsky, Leroy (Ace), B, Oklahoma City U. 1932–38

H

Hackenbruck, John, T, Oregon State 1940
Hackney, Elmer, B, Kansas State 1942–46
Hafen, Bernard, E, Utah 1949–50
Haggerty, Mike T, Miami 1973
Hall, John, B, Texas Christian 1942
Hall, Tom, E, Minnesota 1962–63
Hamilton, Raymond, Eastern Arkansas 1939
Hamlin, Gene, C, Western Michigan 1972
Hand, Larry, DE, Appalachian State 1965–76
Hanneman, Chuck, E, Michigan Normal 1937–41
Hanny, Frank (Duke), E, Indiana 1930
Hansen, Dale, T, Michigan State 1944, 1948–49

John Gordy

L. (Ace) Gutowsky

Leon Hart

Alex Karras

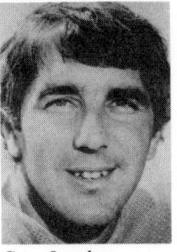
Greg Landry

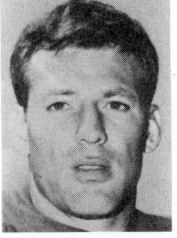
Dick LeBeau

Dan Lewis

Harder, Pat, B, Wisconsin 1951–53
Harding, Roger, C, California 1948
Hardy, James, QB, USC 1952
Harris, Tom (Dud), T, Marietta 1930
Harrison, Granville, E, Mississippi State 1942
Hart, Leon, E, Notre Dame 1950–57
Hastings, George (Bill), T, Ohio U 1930–31
Haverdick, Dave, DE, Morehead State 1970
Hekkers, George, T, Wisconsin 1947–49
Held, Paul, B, San Jose State 1955
Helms, John, E, Georgia Tech 1946
Henderson, John, E, Michigan 1965–67
Hennigan, Mike, LB, Tennessee Tech 1973
Hertwig, Craig T, Georgia 1975–76
Heywood, Ralph, E, USC 1947
Hicks, R.W., C, Humboldt State 1975
Hightower, John, E, Sam Houston 1943
Hilgenberg, Wally, LB, Iowa 1964–66
Hill, David, TE, Texas A&I 1976
Hill, Harlon, E, Florence State 1962
Hill, J.D., WR, Arizona State 1976
Hill, James, B, Tennessee 1951–52
Hill, Jimmy, DB, Sam Houston 1965
Hillman, Bill, B, Tennessee 1947
Hilton, John, TE, Richmond 1972–73
Hinchman, Hubert, B, Butler 1934
Hoernschemeyer, Bob, B, Indiana 1950–55

Hogland, Doug, G, Oregon State 1958
Hollar, John, B, Appalachian State 1949
Holm, Tony, B, Alabama 1931
Hooks, Jim, RB, Central State, Okla. 1973–76
Hopp, Harry, B, Nebraska 1940–43
Howard, Billy, DT, Alcorn A&M 1974–76
Howard, William, B, USC 1939
Huffman, Vernon, B, Indiana 1937–38
Hughes, Chuck, WR, Texas-El Paso 1970–71
Hunter, James, DB, Grambling 1976
Hunter, Romney, E, Marshall 1933
Hupke, Thomas, G, Alabama 1934–37
Hutchinson, Elvin, B, Whittier 1939

I

Isselhardt, Ralph, G, Franklin 1937
Ivory, Bob, G, Detroit 1947
Izo, George, QB, Notre Dame 1965

J

Jarvis, Ray, WR, Norfolk State 1974–76
Jaszewski, Floyd, T, Minnesota 1950–51
Jauron, Dick, DB, Yale 1973–76
Jefferson, William, B, Mississippi State 1941
Jenkins, Leon, DB, West Virginia 1972
Jenkins, Walter, E, Wayne State 1955
Jennings, Lou, E, Haskell 1930

Jessie, Ron, WR, Kansas 1971–72
Jett, John, E, Wake Forest 1941
Johnson, Bob, T, Chattanooga 1930
Johnson, John (Jack), T, Utah 1934–40
Johnson, John Henry, B, Arizona State 1957–59
Johnson, Levi, DB, Texas A&I 1973–76
Jolley, Gordon, T, Utah 1972–75
Jones, Elmer, G, Wake Forest 1947–48
Jones, James, B, Union Tennessee 1946
Jones, Jimmie, RB, UCLA 1974
Jones, Ralph, E, Alabama 1946
Joseph, Chalmers (Red), E, Miami, Ohio 1930
Junker, Steve, E, Xavier 1957, 1959–61
Jurkiewicz, Walter, C, Indiana 1946

K

Kahl, Cy, B, North Dakota 1930–31
Kamanu, Lew, DE, Weber State 1967–68
Kaporch, Albert, T, St. Bonaventure 1943–45
Karilivacz, Carl, B, Syracuse 1953–57
Karras, Alex, DT, Iowa 1958–62, 1964–70
Karras, Ted, G, Indiana 1965
Karstens, George, C, Indiana 1949
Kaska, Anton, B, Ill. Wesleyan 1935
Kearney, Jim, DB, Prairie View 1965–66
Keene, Robert, B, Detroit 1943–45
Kennedy, William, E, Michigan State 1942, 1944
Kent, Greg, DT, Utah 1968
Kercher, Richard, B, Tulsa 1954
Ketzko, Alexander, T, Michigan State 1943
King, Horace, RB, Georgia 1975–76
Kipp, James, T, Montana State 1942
Kizzire, Lee, B, Wyoming 1937
Klewicki, Edward, E, Michigan State 1935–38
Kmetovic, Peter, B, Stanford 1947
Knorr, Lawrence, C, Dayton 1942, 1945
Knox, Sam, G, New Hampshire 1934–36
Kopay, Dave, RB, Washington 1968
Kopcha, Joseph, G, Chattanooga 1936
Kostiuk, Michael, T, Detroit 1945
Kowalkowski Bob, G, Virginia 1966–76
Kramer, Ron, TE, Michigan 1965–67
Kring, Frank, B, Texas Christian 1945
Krol, Joseph, B, Western Ontario 1945
Krouse, Raymond, T, Maryland 1956–57
Kuczinski, Bert, E, Pennsylvania 1943

L

LaLonde, Roger, DT, Muskingum 1964
Landry, Greg, QB, Massachusetts 1968–76
Lane, Dick (Night Train), DB, Scottsbluff J.C. 1960–65
LaRose, Dan, T, Missouri 1961–63
Lary, Yale, DB, Texas A&M 1952–53, 1956–64
Laslavic, Jim, LB, Penn State 1973–76
Lay, Russell, G, Michigan State 1934
Layne, Robert, QB, Texas 1950–58
Lear, Leslie, G, Manitoba 1947
LeBeau, Dick, DB, Ohio State 1959–72
Lee, Hilary (Biff), E, Oklahoma 1931
Lee, Ken, LB, Washington 1971
Lee, Monte, LB, Texas 1963–64
LeForce, Clyde, QB, Tulsa 1947–49
Lewis, Dan, HB, Wisconsin 1958–64
Lewis, Leland, B, Northwestern 1930
Liles, Elvin, G, Oklahoma A&M 1943–45
Lindon, Luther, T, Kentucky 1944–45
Lininger, Jack, C, Ohio State 1950–51
Lio, Augie, G, Georgetown 1941–43
Lloyd, Dave, C, Georgia 1962
Lomakoski, John, T, Western Michigan 1962
Long, Ken, G, Purdue 1976
Long, Lou, E, Southern Methodist 1931
Long, Robert, E, UCLA 1955–59
Looney, Joe Don, HB, Oklahoma 1965–66
Lowe, Gary, B, Michigan State 1956–64
Lowther, Jackie, B, Detroit 1944
Lucci, Mike, LB, Tennessee 1965–73
Lumpkin, Roy (Father), B, Georgia Tech 1930–34
Lusk, Bob, C, William & Mary 1956
Lyons, George (Babe), T, Kansas State 1930

M

Mackenroth, John, C, North Dakota 1938

Tackle Rockne Freitas squares to block David (Deacon) Jones of San Diego, 1973.

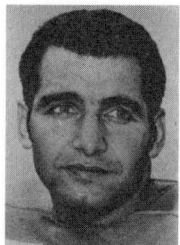 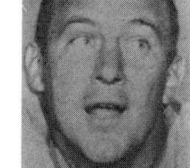     

Mike Lucci *Darris McCord* *Errol Mann* *Paul Naumoff* *Nick Pietrosante* *Bill Radovich* *Charlie Sanders*

Madarik, Elmer, B, Detroit 1945–47
Maggiolo, Chick, B, Illinois 1949
Magnani, Dante, B, St. Mary's, Calif. 1950
Maher, Bruce, DB, Detroit 1960–67
Mains, Gilbert, T, Murray State 1954–61
Malinchak, Bill, E, Indiana 1966–69
Mann, Errol, K, North Dakota 1969–76
Mann, Robert, E, Michigan 1948–49
Manzo, Joseph, T, Boston College 1945
Margucci, Joseph, B, USC 1946–48
Markovich, Mark, C, Penn State 1976
Maronic, Stephen, T, North Carolina 1939–40
Marsh, Amos, FB, Oregon State 1965–67
Martin, Jim, G, Notre Dame 1951–61
Martinovich, Philip, G, Pacific 1939
Matheson, Jack, E. Western Michigan 1943–46
Matheson, Riley, G, Texas Mines 1943
Mathews, Ned, B, UCLA 1940–43
Mathewson, Morley, E, California 1941
Matisi, Tony, T, Pittsburgh 1938–39
Matson, Ollie, FB, San Francisco 1963
Mattiford, John, G, Marshall 1941
Maves, Earl, B, Wisconsin 1948
Maxwell, Bruce, RB, Arkansas 1970–71
Mayer, Emil, E. Catholic U. 1930
Mazza, Vincent, E, None 1945–46
Mazzanti, Jerry, DE, Arkansas 1966
McCambridge, John, DE, Northwestern 1967
McClain, Mayes (Chief), B, Iowa 1930–31
McClung, Willie, T, Florida A&M 1960–61
McCord, Darris, DE, Tennessee 1955–67
McCoy, Joel, B, Alabama 1946
McCullouch, Earl, E, USC 1968–73
McDermott, Lloyd, T, Kentucky 1950
McDoland, James, B, Ohio State 1938–40
McElhenny, Hugh, HB, Washington 1964
McGraw, Thurman, T, Colorado A&M 1950–54
McIlhenny, Donald, B, Southern Methodist 1956
McInnis, Hugh, C, So. Mississippi 1964
McKalp, Bill, E, Oregon State 1931–32, 1934, 1936
McLain, Mayes, B, Iowa 1930–31
McLenna, Bruce, HB, Hillsdale 1966
McMakin, John, TE, Clemson 1975
McMullin, Dan, G, Nebraska 1932
McWilliams, William, B, Jordan 1934
Melinkovich, Mike, DE, Gray Harbour J.C. 1967
Mello, Jim, B, Notre Dame 1949
Mesak, Richard, T, St. Mary's 1945
Messner, Max, LB, Cincinnati 1960–63
Meyer, Ernie, G, Geneva 1930
Middleton, David, E, Auburn 1955–60
Miketa, Andrew, C, North Carolina 1954–55
Miklich, William, B, Idaho 1948
Milano, Arch, E, St. Francis 1945
Miller, Robert (Dutch), C, Wittenberg 1931
Miller, Robert, T, Virginia 1952–58
Miller, Terry, LB, Illinois 1970
Mills, Dick, G, Pittsburgh 1961–62
Mitchell, Granville (Buster), E-T, Davis-Elkins ... 1931–34
Mitchell, Jim, DE, Virginia State 1970–76
Mitrick, Frank, T. Oglethorpe 1945
Molesworth, Keith, B, Monmouth 1930
Momsen, Robert, G, Ohio State 1951
Monahan, Regis, G, Ohio State 1935–38
Montgomery, James, T, Texas A&M 1946
Mooney, Ed, LB, Texas Tech 1968–71
Moore, Denis, T, USC 1967–69
Moore, Paul, B, Presbyterian 1940–41
Moore, William, B, Loyola 1939
Morlock, John, B, Marshall 1940
Morrall, Earl, QB, Michigan State 1958–64
Morris, Glen, E, Colorado A&M 1940
Morris, Jon, C, Holy Cross 1975–76
Morse, Raymond, E, Oregon 1935–38, 1940
Moscrip, James, E, Stanford 1938–39
Mote, Kelly, E, Duke 1947–49
Mugg, Garvin, T, N. Texas State 1945
Munson, Bill, QB, Utah State 1968–72
Murakowski, Art, B, Northwestern 1951
Myers, Tom, QB, Northwestern 1965–66

N

Nardi, Richard, B, Ohio State 1938

Naumoff, Paul, LB, Tennessee 1967–76
Nelson, Reed, C, Brigham Young 1947
Nelson, Robert, C, Baylor 1941, 1945
Ninowski, Jim, QB, Michigan State 1960–61
Noppenberg, John, B, Miami 1941
Nori, Reino, B, No. Illinois State 1937
Nott, Douglas, B, Detroit 1935
Novotny, Ray, B, Ashland 1930
Nowatzke, Tom, FB, Indiana 1965–69

O

Obee, Duncan, C, Dayton 1941
O'Brien, Jim, WR, Cincinnati 1973
O'Brien, William, B, None 1947
Odle, Phil, E, Brigham Young 1968–70
Ogle, Rich, LB, Colorado 1972
Olenski, Mitchell, T, Alabama 1947
Olszewski, John, FB, California 1961
O'Neil, Ed, LB, Penn State 1974–76
O'Neill, William, B, Detroit 1935
Opalewski, Edward, T, Michigan Normal 1943–44
Orvis, Herb, DE, Colorado 1972–76
Owens, Steve, RB, Oklahoma 1970–75

P

Panciera, Donald, B, San Francisco 1950
Panelli, John, B, Notre Dame 1949–50

Paolucci, Ben, T, Wayne State 1959
Parker, Buddy, B, Centenary 1935–36
Parson, Ray, T, Minnesota 1971
Parsons, Lloyd, B, Gustavus Adolphus 1941
Patt, Maurice, E, Carnegie Tech 1938
Pavelec, Theodore, G, Detroit 1941–43
Pearson, Lindell, B, Oklahoma 1950
Perry, Gerald, T, California 1954, 1956–59
Peters, Floyd, T, San Francisco State 1963
Peters, Forest, B, Illinois 1930
Peterson, Ken, B, Gonzaga 1936
Peterson, Les, E, Texas 1930–31
Pickard, Bob, WR, Xavier 1974
Pierson, Reggie, DB, Oklahoma State 1976
Pietrosante, Nick, B, Notre Dame 1959–65
Pifferini, Robert, C, San Jose State 1949
Pingel, John, B, Michigan State 1939
Plum, Milt, QB, Penn State 1962–67
Polanski, John, B, Wake Forest 1942
Poole, Oliver, E, Mississippi 1949
Potts, Charlie, S, Purdue 1972
Prchlik, John, T, Yale 1949–53
Pregulman, Mervin, G, Michigan 1947–48
Prescott, Harold, E, Hardin-Simmons 1949
Presnell, Glenn, B, Nebraska 1931–36
Price, Charles, B, Texas A&M 1940–41, 1945

Guard Bob Kowalkowski leads Dexter Bussey on a sweep, 1975.

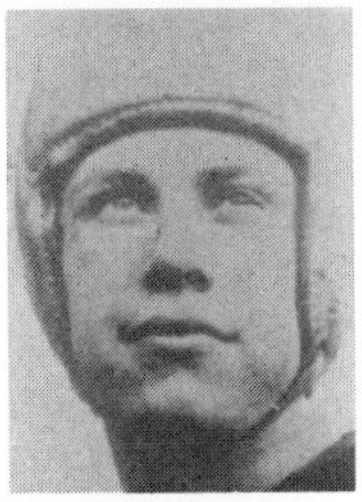
Frank Sinkwich

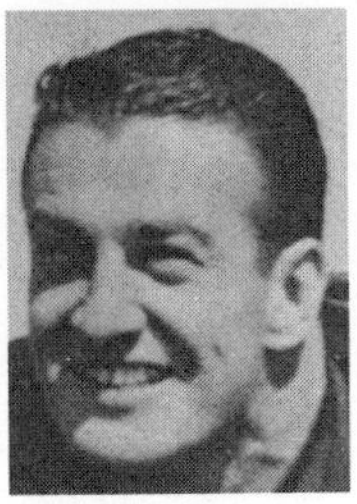
Dick Stanfel

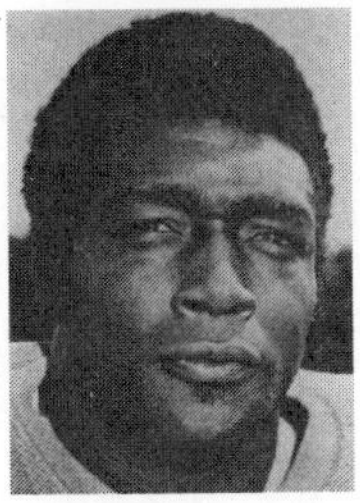
Altie Taylor

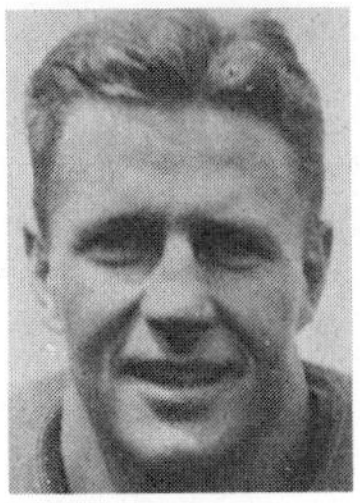
Doak Walker

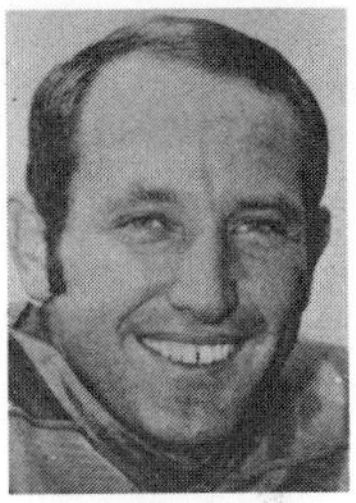
Wayne Walker

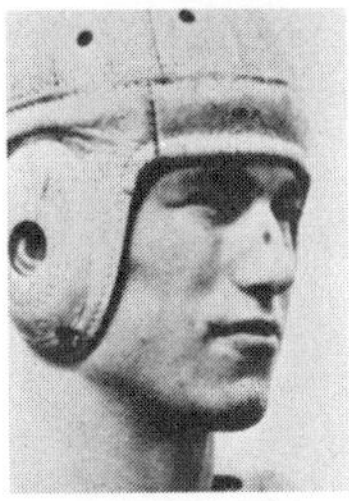
B. (Whizzer) White

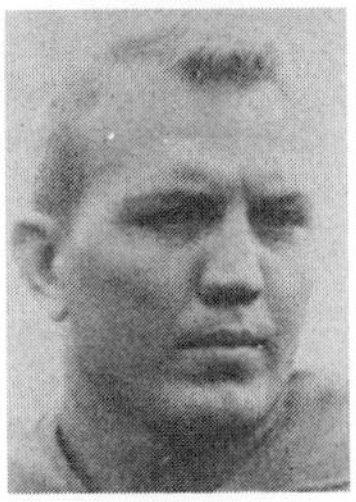
Sam Williams

Price, Ernie, DT, Texas A&I 1973–76
Pringle, Alan, K, Rice 1975

Q

Quinlan, Bill, DE, Michigan State 1964

R

Rabb, Warren, QB, Louisiana State 1960
Rabold, Mike, G, Indiana 1959
Radovich, William, G, USC 1938–41, 1945
Randolph, Al, DB, Iowa 1972
Randolph, Clare, C, Indiana 1931–36
Ranspot, Keith, E, Southern Methodist 1941
Rascher, Ambrose, T, Indiana 1932
Rasley, Rocky, G, Oregon State 1969–72
Rasmussen, Wayne, DB, So. Dakota State 1964–73
Reckmack, Raymond, B, Syracuse 1937
Redmond, Rudy, CB, Pacific 1972
Reeberg, Lucien, T, Hampton 1963
Reed, Joe, QB, Mississippi State 1975–76
Reese, Lloyd, B, Tennessee 1947
Reichow, Gerry, QB, Iowa 1956–59
Rexer, Freeman, E, Tulane 1944
Reynolds, Robert, T, Stanford 1937–38
Ribble, Loran, G, Hardin-Simmons 1932
Ricardo, Benny, K, San Diego State 1976
Ricca, James, T, Georgetown 1955
Richards, Perry, E, Detroit 1958
Richards, Ray, G, Nebraska 1934
Richins, Aldo, B, Utah 1935
Rifenburg, Richard, E, Michigan 1950
Riley, Lee, B, Detroit 1955
Ringwalt, Carroll, C-G, Indiana 1930
Ritchhart, Delbert, C, Colorado 1936–37
Robb, Joe, DE, Texas Christian 1968–71
Roberts, Fred, T, Iowa 1930–32
Robinson, John, DB, Tennessee State 1966–67
Rockenbach, Lyle, G, Michigan State 1943
Rogas, Daniel, G, Tulane 1951
Rogers, William T, Villanova 1938–40
Roskie, Kenneth, B, South Carolina 1948
Rosteck, Ernest, C, None 1944
Rote, Tobin, QB, Rice 1957–59
Rothwell, Fred, C, Kansas State 1974
Rouse, Stillman, E, Missouri 1940
Roussos, Michael, T, Pittsburgh 1949
Rowe, Robert, B, Colgate 1934
Rubino, Anthony, G, Wake Forest 1943, 1946
Rush, Jerry, DT, Michigan State 1965–71
Russas, Albert, T, Tennessee 1949
Russell, Kenneth, T, Bowling Green 1957–59
Ryan, David, B, Hardin-Simmons 1945–46
Ryan, John, T, Detroit 1930
Ryan, Kent, B, Utah State 1938–40
Rychlec, Tom, E. American International 1958
Ryder, Nick, FB, Miami 1963–64

S

Salsbury, James, G, UCLA 1955–56
Sanchez, John T, San Francisco 1947
Sanders, Charlie, TE, Minnesota 1968–76
Sanders, Daryl, T, Ohio State 1963–66
Sanders, Ken, DE, Howard Payne 1972–76
Sandifer, Daniel, B, Louisiana State 1950
Sanzotta, Dominic, B, West. Reserve 1942, 1946
Sarratt, Charles, B, Oklahoma 1948
Sarringhaus, Paul, B, Ohio State 1948
Sartori, Lawrence, G, Fordham 1942, 1945
Saul, Bill, LB, Penn State 1970
Schaake, Elmer, B, Kansas 1933
Schibanoff, Alexander, T, Franklin-Marshall 1942
Schiechl, John, C, Santa Clara 1942
Schleusner, Vin, T, Iowa 1930–31
Schmidt, Joseph, LB, Pittsburgh 1953–65
Schmiesing, Joe, DT, New Mexico State 1972
Schneller, John, E, Wisconsin 1933–36
Scholtz, Bob, C, Notre Dame 1960–64
Schottel, Ivan, B, N.W. Missouri State 1946, 1948
Schroll, Charles, B, Louisiana State 1950
Schwartz, Elmer, B, Washington State 1931
Scott, Clyde, B, Arkansas 1952
Scott, Perry, E, Muhlenberg 1942
Self, Clarence, B, Wisconsin 1950–51
Seltzer, Harry, B, Morris-Harvey 1942
Sewell, Harley, G, Texas 1953–62
Shearer, Ron, T, Drake 1930
Shelly, Dexter, B, Texas 1931
Shepherd, William, B, Western Maryland 1935–40
Shoals, Roger, T, Maryland 1965–70
Siegert, Wayne, T, Illinois 1951
Sieminski, Chuck, DT, Penn State 1968
Sigillo, Dominic, T, Xavier 1945
Simmons, John, C, Detroit 1949–50
Simon, Jim, G-T, Miami 1963–65
Sinkwich, Frank, B, Georgia 1943–44
Sirochman, George, G, Duquesne 1944
Slaby, Lou, LB, Pittsburgh 1966
Sloan, Dwight, B, Arkansas 1939–40
Small, John, DT, Citadel 1973–74
Smith, Bobby, DB, UCLA 1965–66
Smith, Gene, G, Georgia 1930
Smith, Harry, T, USC 1940
Smith, J.D., T, Rice 1964, 1966
Smith, J. Robert, HB, Iowa 1949–54
Smith, Ray, C, Missouri 1930
Smith, Robert, B, Texas A&M 1953–54
Sneddon, Robert, B, St. Mary's 1945
Soboleski, Joseph, T, Michigan 1950
Souders, Cecil, E, Ohio State 1947–49
Speelman, Harry, T, Michigan State 1940
Spencer, Oliver, T, Kansas 1953, 1956, 1959–61
Spangler, Eugene, B, Tulsa 1946
Speth, George, T, Murray State 1942
Stacco, Edward, T, Colgate 1947
Stacy, James, T, Oklahoma 1935–37
Staggers, Jon, WR, Missouri 1975
Stanfel, Richard, G, San Francisco 1952–55
Steen, James, T, Syracuse 1935–36
Steffen, Jim, DB, UCLA 1959–60
Stennett, Fred (Stud), B, St. Mary's, Calif. 1931
Stits, William, B, UCLA 1954–56
Stokes, Lee, C, Centenary 1937–39
Stovall, Richard, C, Abilene Christian 1947–48
Stringfellow, Joseph, E, So. Mississippi 1942
Stuart, Roy, T, Tulsa 1943
Studstill, Pat, FL, Houston 1961–67
Sucic, Stephen, B, Illinois 1947–48
Sugar, Leo, E, Purdue 1962
Summerall, Pat, E, Arkansas 1952
Sunter, Ian, K, None 1976
Swain, Bill, LB, Oregon 1968–69
Sweetan, Karl, QB, Wake Forest 1966–67
Swiacki, William, E, Columbia 1951–52
Szakash, Paul, B, Montana 1938–42
Szymanski, Frank, C, Notre Dame 1945–47

T

Tassos, Damon, G, Texas A&M 1945–46
Tatarek, Bob, DT, Miami 1972
Taylor, Altie, RB, Utah State 1969–76
Teal, Jim, LB, Purdue 1973
Ten Napel, Garth, LB, Texas A&M 1976
Thayer, Harry, T, Tennessee 1933
Thomas, Calvin, G, Tulsa 1939–40
Thomas, Russell, T, Ohio State 1946–49
Thomason, James, B, Texas A&M 1945
Thompson, Bobby, RB, Oklahoma 1975–76
Thompson, Bobby, DB, Arizona 1964–68
Thompson, Dave, C, Clemson 1971–73
Thompson, Leonard, RB, Oklahoma State 1975–76
Thrower, Jim, DB, East Texas State 1973–76
Thuerk, Owen, E, St. Joseph, Ind. 1941
Todd, Jim, HB, Ball State 1966
Tomasetti, Louis, B, Bucknell 1941
Tonelli, Anthony, C, USC 1939
Topor, Ted, LB, Michigan 1955
Torgeson, LaVern, C, Washington State 1951–54
Tracy, Tom, B, Tennessee 1956–57
Treadway, John, T, Hardin-Simmons 1949
Trebotich, Ivan. B, St. Mary's 1944–45
Tressa, Thomas, G, Davis-Elkins 1942
Triplett, Bill, RB, Miami, Ohio 1968–72
Triplett, Wallace, B, Penn State 1949–50
Tripson, John T, Mississippi State 1941
Tripucka, Frank, QB, Notre Dame 1949
Tsoutsouvas, John, C, Stanford 1940
Tully, Darrell, B, E. Texas Teachers 1939
Turner, Harold, E, Tennssee State 1954
Tyler, Maurice, DB, Morgan State 1976

U

Uremovich, Emil, T, Indiana 1940–42, 1945–46

V

Van Horn, Doug, G, Ohio State 1966
Van Tone, Arthur, B, Mississippi 1943–45
Vanzo, Frederick, B, Northwestern 1938–41
Vargo, Larry, E, Detroit 1963
Vaughn, Charles, B, Tennessee 1935
Vaughn, Tom, DB, Iowa State 1965–71
Vezmar, Walter, T, Michigan State 1946–47

W

Wager, John (Red), C, Carthage 1931–33
Wagner, Sidney, G, Michigan State 1936–38
Walker, Doak, B, Southern Methodist 1950–55
Walker, Wayne, LB, Idaho 1958–72
Walker, Willie, FL, Tennessee State 1966
Walton, Chuck, G, Iowa State 1967–74
Walton, Larry, WR, Arizona State 1969–76
Ward, Elmer, C, Utah State 1935–36
Ward, Paul, T, Whitworth 1961–62
Ward, William, G, Washington State 1947–49
Waters, Dale (Muddy), E, Florida 1931
Watkins, Larry, RB, Alcorn A&M 1969
Watkins, Tom, HB, Iowa State 1962–67
Watson, Joseph, C, Rice 1950
Watt, Joseph, B, Syracuse 1947–48
Weatherall, Jim, T, Oklahoma 1959–60
Weaver, Buck, C, Centre 1930
Weaver, Charlie, LB, USC 1971–76
Weaver, Herman, P, Tennessee 1970–76
Webb, Ken, HB, Presbyterian 1958–62
Weber, Richard, B, St. Louis 1945
Weger, Mike, DB, Bowling Green 1967–76
Weiss, Howard, B, Wisconsin 1939–40
Welch, Jim, RB, Southern Methodist 1968
Wells, Warren, E, Texas Southern 1964
Wesley, Lecil (Bull), C, Alabama 1930
West, Charlie, DB, Texas El Paso 1974–76
Westfall, Robert, B, Michigan 1944–47
Wetterlund, Chet, B, Illinois Wesleyan 1942
White, Byron (Whizzer), B, Colorado 1940–41
White, Daryl, G, Nebraska 1974
White, Wilbur, HB, Colorado A&M 1936
Whitlow, Bob, G-C, Arizona 1961–65
Whitsell, Dave, DB, Indiana 1958–60
Wiatrak, John, C, Washington 1939
Wickett, Lloyd, T, Oregon State 1943, 1946
Wiese, Robert, B, Michigan 1947–48
Wiethe, John, G, Xavier 1939–42
Williams, Bobby, DB, Central State 1969–71
Williams, Rex, C, Texas Tech 1945
Williams, Sam, DE, Michigan State 1960–65
Wilson, Camp, B, Tulsa 1946–49
Wilson, Fay (Mule), B, Texas A&M 1932–33
Winkler, Randy, T, Tarleton State 1967
Winslow, Robert, E, USC 1940
Wojciechowicz, Alex, C, Fordham 1938–46
Woit, Richard, B, Arkansas State 1955
Womack, Bruce, G, W, Texas State 1951
Woodcock, John, DT, Hawaii 1976
Woods, Larry, DT, Tennessee State 1971–72
Wright, John, WR, Illinois 1969
Wyatt, Doug, DB, Tulsa 1973–74
Wyche, Sam, QB, Furman 1974

Y

Yarbrough, Jim, T, Florida 1969–76
Yepremian, Garo, K, None 1966–67
Young, Adrian, LB, USC 1972
Yowarsky, Walt, E, Kentucky 1955

Z

Zatkoff, Roger, G, Michigan 1957–58
Zawadzkas, Jerry, E, Columbia 1967
Zimmerman, Leroy, B, San Jose State 1947
Zofko, Mickey, RB, Auburn 1971–74
Zuzzio, Anthony, G, Muhlenberg 1942

GREEN BAY PACKERS

1919 Earl (Curly) Lambeau, home from school at Notre Dame, went to work for the Indian Packing Company in Green Bay and talked his employer into spending $500 on equipment to back a football team.

1921 After two years of successful operation as an independent team playing clubs from Wisconsin and Upper Michigan, the team joined the American Professional Football Association, predecessor to the National Football League. The franchise was awarded to John Clair of the Acme Packing Company, successor to the Indian Packing Company, August 27, 1921. Green Bay played its home games at Hagemeister Brewery Park with bleachers on one side to seat about 200 people and a portable canvas fence to discourage nonpaying customers. Lambeau was coach, star halfback, passer, general manager, and publicity man. Howard (Cub) Buck, a 287-pound tackle from Wisconsin who had spent 1920 with the Canton Bulldogs, joined the new team; Buck also did the punting and extra point and field goal kicking. Lambeau surrounded himself with Wisconsin players and signed a couple of his old Notre Dame buddies, Norm Barry and Grover Malone, to work with him in the backfield. Playing a rather fluid schedule that included teams such as the Evansville, Indiana, Crimson Giants, Rock Island, Illinois, Independents, Chicago Staleys, and Chicago Cardinals, the Packers finished fourth in the 13-team league with a 6-2-2 record.

1922 John Clair was ordered to surrender the Packers' franchise to the league on charges of playing collegians who were still enrolled in college, January 28. A $1,000 bond was required from all clubs thereafter to guard against such violations. When Lambeau learned the NFL planned a midsummer meeting, he made plans to rescue the Packers' franchise. With the $50 franchise fee in his pocket but lacking the means of traveling to the NFL meeting at Canton, Ohio, Lambeau asked a friend for help. The friend, Don Murphy, sold his Marmon Roadster automobile for $1,500 and accompanied Lambeau to Canton on the promise that Murphy would open the season in the Packers' lineup. Lambeau was awarded the franchise. Murphy played one minute of the opening game with Duluth. The Packers signed Francis (Jug) Earp and Howard (Whitey) Woodin and quarterback Charlie Mathys, who had played for the Hammond, Indiana, Pros. The weather turned against the Packers and it rained at almost every home game. The club bought "rain insurance" for an early season game, calling for .10 of an inch of rain to meet the visiting guarantee. It rained only .09 and the insurance company wouldn't pay off. When it poured on a late November Sunday before a game with the Columbus, Ohio, Panhandles, the insurance had expired and Lambeau was ready to give up. Only the intervention of Andrew Turnbull, publisher of the Green Bay *Press-Gazette*, saved the franchise. Turnbull told Lambeau to play the game and he'd help work out the problems. The Packers finished the season $2,500 in the red.

1923 Civic pride in the community of about 30,000, combined with a love of football, brought solid financial backing to the Packers in 1923. Publisher Turnbull organized a group known as the "Hungry Five" who canceled the debt and started a campaign for civic support. The members were Turnbull; Lambeau; Lee Joannes, a grocery man; Dr. W. Webber Kelly, a physician; and Gerald Clifford, an attorney. At a meeting of 400 citizens at the local Elks club, the team was reorganized as the Green Bay Football Corporation. Stock was sold at $5 a share and every person who bought five shares was assured a season ticket. Fifty leading citizens pledged to put up $100 each if the club needed additional money. Hagemeister Park was to be the site of a new high school, so the Packers moved to the outskirts of town to play in the new baseball park known as Bellevue Park. The Chicago Bears came to town for the first time and 5,000 people stormed the park to see the visitors from the big city score a 3-0 won. The Packers split a pair of games with the Racine, Wisconsin, Legion for the championship of Wisconsin but never did play the Canton Bulldogs, who went unbeaten at 11-0-1. Green Bay improved its record to 7-2-1 and finished third in the 20-team expanded NFL.

1924 Vern Lewellen of Nebraska, one of the greatest punters of the era, joined the Packers and fit into the regular backfield with Oscar Hendrian, Charlie Mathys, and Lambeau. Green Bay beat the Bears for the first time in a bitterly fought opening game, 5-0. The Packers shut out the Kansas City Cowboys, the Milwaukee Badgers, and the Minneapolis Marines in succession and followed with a 6-3 victory over Racine on a sensational catch of a 45-yard pass by Lambeau to Walter (Tillie) Voss. However, the Packers lost a rematch with the Bears 3-0 in Chicago in a game in which Voss and the Bears' Frank Hanny were ejected for fighting, and also bowed to Racine 7-0 in their second game. The club was doing well at the gate and showed promise with an 8-4 record, good for sixth place among the 18 NFL teams.

1925 Green Bay opened City Stadium barely in time to start the season. The stadium, with stands on each side of the field between the 30-yard lines, had a capacity of 6,000. The bright promise of opening day, when a crowd of 6,000 packed into new City Stadium to watch the Packers beat the Bears 14-10, faded as the Packers ran into trouble in late season and dropped three in a row to the Bears, Pottsville, Pennsylvania, Maroons, and Frankford, Pennsylvania, Yellowjackets. Green Bay and the rest of the 20-team NFL were overshadowed by a college player in 1925, the final year of Red Grange's career at the University of Illinois. Unfortunately for the Packers' treasury, they had already finished their season series with the Bears before Grange turned professional and started off on his whirlwind tour with the Bears that attracted record crowds at nearly every stop. Green Bay finished with an 8-5 record.

1926 Red Grange organized a rival American Football League after his bid for an NFL franchise was turned down. The NFL countered by expanding into an unwieldy 22-team circuit, and getting Ernie Nevers of Stanford for the Duluth Eskimos. Nevers came to Green Bay with the Duluth Eskimos and the Packers played them to a scoreless tie. The Packers finished fifth at 7-3-3, but the three defeats were by a total of only 17 points.

1927 Lambeau was putting in less time as a halfback and more time as a coach and general manager. Joe (Red) Dunn, the former Marquette quarterback who had been playing with Milwaukee and the Chicago Cardinals, arrived to take over at quarterback. Another top acquisition was Lavern Dilweg, a talented end from Marquette who also played with Milwaukee while finishing law school. Another 1927 addition was center Bernard (Boob) Darling. With the help of this new talent the Packers finished second with a 7-2-1 record behind the 11-1-1 of the New York Giants, a team they never played.

1928 Although Green Bay tied the champion Providence, Rhode Island, Steamroller 7-7 in late season, two defeats by the Frankford Yellowjackets doomed their title hopes. The Packers played the New York Giants for the first time, losing 6-0 at Milwaukee but winning 7-0 at the Polo Grounds. During the season Lambeau picked up fullback John (Bo) Molenda from the New York Yankees. The Packers won their final game from the Bears 6-0 at Cub Park in Chicago on a 48-yard pass from Dunn to end Dick O'Donnell. Green Bay finished fourth. There was an unusual off-the-field competition when two players ran for the office of district attorney of Brown County. Lewellen won in the Republican primary and Dilweg lost in the Democratic primary. Lewellen won the general election and served until 1930.

1929 Lambeau made three master strokes during the offseason after discovering that three players—Johnny Blood (McNally), Cal Hubbard, and Mike Michalske—were unhappy with their teams. Blood, a free spirit, had sliced a wide path through Milwaukee, Duluth, and Pottsville and was anxious to move on. Hubbard had seen enough of New York in two years with the Giants. Michalske had played a year with the AFL New York Yankees and two with the NFL Yankees. With a backfield made up of quarterback Dunn, halfbacks Blood and Lewellen or Ed Kotal, and fullback Molenda, and a line that included Dilweg and Dick O'Donnell or Tom Nash at ends, Hubbard and Bill Kern at tackles, Michalske and Jim Bowdoin at the guards and Earp or Darling at center, the Packers went unbeaten 12-0-1, beating the Giants' 13-1-1. It was the first unbeaten team in the NFL since the Canton Bulldogs of 1922 (10-0-2) and 1923 (11-0-1). Many of the players on the 18-man squad played 60 minutes in all games. When injury forced a substitution in a game with the Giants, center Earp said, "Oh, how we hated to see a sub come in." When the Packers returned home after defeating the Bears 25-0 in the final game, a crowd of 20,000 surged onto the tracks and forced the train to halt. The Packers' allowed only 24 points in 13 games.

1930 Lambeau retired as a player to devote all his time to coaching. Determined to improve the team, Lambeau brought in a new quarterback, Arnie Herber, a hometown boy who had played at Wisconsin and tiny Regis College in Denver, Colorado. After beating Oshkosh, Wisconsin in an exhibition opener, the Packers ran their three-year string to 22 games without defeat, beating the Bears and Minneapolis twice and the Cardinals, Giants, Frankford, and Portsmouth once each. Their record string finally was broken by the Cardinals 13-6 in a rematch at Comiskey Park. Ernie Nevers, who had moved to the Cardinals, scored one touchdown, passed for another, and outkicked both Lewellen and Blood. A 13-6 loss to the Giants in the Polo Grounds threatened the Packers' plans for a second straight title but they rallied to beat Frankford and the Stapleton Stapes. Despite a 21-0 defeat by the Bears, a 6-6 tie in the last game at Portsmouth, Ohio, enabled Green Bay at 10-3-1 to edge the Giants' 13-4-0 by .004 percentage points, .769 to .765 (ties were disregarded in the standings). The two championships in a row touched off another rousing welcome home after a riotous trip by bus and train during which Blood crawled atop the train and rode home with the engineer and fireman.

1931 Lambeau picked up another excellent runner in Henry (Hank) Bruder of Northwestern. Starting with a 26-0 victory over the new Cleveland Indians, the Packers burst out of the starting gate and raced to nine straight wins. The streak ended against the Chicago Cardinals when Ernie Nevers staged another spectacular performance in a 21-13 win, November 15. Green Bay headed east and defeated the Giants, the Providence Steamroller, and the Brooklyn Dodgers, and won an unprecedented third straight championship despite a 7-6 defeat by the Bears in the final game. The Packers' 12-2 record was one game better than the Portsmouth Spartans' 11-3. Although the Spartans, who never met the Packers, complained bitterly that a game had been tentatively scheduled, the game was never played. Four Green Bay players—end Dilweg, tackle Hubbard, guard Michalske, and halfback Blood—were named to the first all-pro team. Tackle Dick Stahlman, quarterback

Dunn, and fullback Molenda were on the second team.

1932 The best rookie to join the team was Clarke Hinkle, a fullback and leading scorer in the nation at Bucknell. The game that killed Green Bay's hopes for a fourth consecutive title was a 19–0 defeat by the Spartans at Portsmouth, Ohio, December 5. Then the Packers lost 9–0 to the Bears the following Sunday. The Packers won 10 games, more than any other club in the eight-team league. Because ties did not count, the Bears' 7–1–6 record gave them an .875 percentage to the Packers 10–3–1 for .769. Actually the Bears and Portsmouth tied, and Chicago won an indoor playoff game at the Chicago Stadium. Quarterback Herber made the all-pro team along with Hubbard and Barrager. The first official league statistics showed Herber led the passers by completing 37 of 101 for 639 yards and nine touchdowns. At the end of the 1932 season the Packers were invited to play two games in Honolulu where they scored victories before sellout crowds. On the way home they stopped off in San Francisco to play Ernie Nevers's Pacific Coast All-Americans at Kezar Stadium, a charity game for the Knights of Columbus.

1933 A fan fell out of the temporary wooden bleachers at City Stadium and sued for $5,000 and the two firms carrying the Packers' insurance failed. The team went into receivership and once again the "Hungry Five" had to be called on to save the franchise, cutting front office expenses and player personnel. Top rookie was Charles (Buckets) Goldenberg, a blocking back-linebacker from Wisconsin. Hinkle teamed with Bob Monnett, a rookie halfback from Michigan State, behind Herber. Competing in the five-club Western Division of the newly-divided NFL, the Packers dropped four of their last five and finished third at 5–7–1. After the season Lee Joannes, president of the club from 1930 to 1947, invited 25 businessmen to a special meeting to start a fundraising campaign. Housewives, high school students, firemen, policemen, and other citizens chipped in for a $15,000 "save the Packers" fund. The club was incorporated by Dilweg, nearing the end of his career as an end, with 600 shares of common stock having no par value and a requirement that any profits be donated to the local American Legion post or other veterans' organization with no dividend or profit for the stockholders.

1934 With a new, sound financial base, the Packers were able to return their attention to the playing field where new opportunities for a passer like Herber had been opened up by the rules changes permitting forward passes anywhere behind the line of scrimmage. Fullback Hinkle was beginning to show the form of his college days. Herber led the league's passers for the second time in three seasons and the Packers started on the way back with a third-place 7–6 record in a division dominated by the 13–0 Bears. Seating capacity at City Stadium was increased to 15,000.

1935 Don Hutson signed with Green Bay after having been pursued by both the Packers and Brooklyn Dodgers following a brilliant career at Alabama. The nimble sprinter played with the College All-Stars in the Chicago All-Star game against the Bears and saw brief action as a sub in the Packers' opener. By the time the club was ready for its second game, Hutson was ready to start. On the first play Herber sent Blood down the right side line and threw to Hutson up the middle for a stunning 83-yard touchdown play. Blood, returning after a year in Pittsburgh, was used primarily as a receiver. Although Hutson's catches beat the Bears twice, 7–0 and 17–14, the Packers lost three to the Cardinals and split with Detroit, the Western Division champion, at 7–3 to the Packers 8–4. The arrival of Hutson, who led the league with seven touchdowns while catching 18 passes for 420 yards, an average of 23.3. yards, and the second-place finish

filled the stands with paying customers. After the season the Packers made another trip to San Francisco for a charity game with the Pacific All-Stars.

1936 The first college draft produced guard Russ Letlow. Green Bay picked seventh, or third-from-last, because its 1935 won-lost record was third best in the league. The Packers absorbed their worst beating, 30–3 at the hands of the Bears in the second game of the season, but didn't lose again, squaring matters with the Bears later 21–10. Defeats by the Lions and Cardinals in their last two games cost the Bears their chance of catching Green Bay. For the first time since the NFL split into two divisions in 1933 the Packers won the championship, taking the Western Division with a 10–1–1 record and then defeating the Boston Redskins 21–6 in a game played at New York's Polo Grounds because of poor attendance for the Redskins in Boston. Hutson led the league with a record 34 pass receptions and Herber topped the passers for the third time by throwing for 1,239 yards and 11 touchdowns. In addition, other main components in the offense were backs Hinkle, George Sauer, Bob Monnett, and Milt Gantenbein.

1937 The success of 1936 was short-lived. The Packers not only lost the Chicago All-Star game 6–0 to the collegians, who were led by Sammy Baugh, but also dropped their first two regular season games, bowing to both the Cardinals and Bears at City Stadium. They recovered in a seven-game winning streak, only to lose their last two games to the Giants and Redskins on the road, finishing at 7–4, one game behind the Bears. Herber was slowed by a hip injury and extra weight but he still could throw and Hutson broke his own record with 41 receptions and seven touchdowns. The bulk of the running was done by Hinkle and rookie Eddie Jankowski, a first-round draft pick from Wisconsin. It was the last year for Michalske and Lon Evans. Green Bay probably made its best first-round draft pick when Lambeau selected quarterback Cecil Isbell of Purdue, December 11. The Packers also picked up back Andy Uram of Minnesota on the fourth round.

1938 Lambeau played Herber and Isbell in the same backfield and both took turns throwing to Hutson. Hinkle scored enough points on runs, pass receptions, conversions, and field goals to lead the league with 58 points. After clinching the Western Division title November 21, the Packers had to wait until December 12 to play the Giants for the league championship. Green Bay lost 23–17 in the title game with a limping Hutson seeing only part-time action because of a knee injury.

1939 Green Bay played a unique doubleheader with the Pittsburgh Steelers with 10-minute exhibition quarters. The Packers tied the first game and won the second 17–0 in a program that lasted from 7:30 P.M. to 11 P.M. Then the Packers went south to Dallas for an exhibition game with the Southwest College All-Stars at the Cotton Bowl, beating a team led by Davey O'Brien and Ki Aldrich 31–20. The busy preseason didn't seem to bother the Packers, although they lost their third game in an upset by the Cleveland Rams. Andy Uram set a record with a 97-yard touchdown run against the Cardinals, October 8. The Packers straightened out and won seven of their last eight, beating out the Bears to win the Western Division for the second year in a row. Coach Lambeau gave Hutson some relief on defense, switching him to safety while moving Larry Craig, a rookie from South Carolina, to defensive end and blocking back. The championship game with the Giants was shifted to State Fair Park in Milwaukee, where 32,279 watched Herber, Isbell, and Hutson take the Giants apart 27–0 for their fifth NFL title.

1940 Charley Brock, drafted out of Nebraska in 1939, took over at center and also played in the defensive backfield. Green Bay barely hung on 27–20 when

passer Davey O'Brien of the Eagles threw 40 passes in the opening game at City Stadium. Then the Bears came in and won 41–10. "People are beginning to talk," warned Lambeau as he drove his Packers through heavy practice sessions. They responded by beating the Cardinals, but lost to Detroit, the New York Giants, and the Chicago Bears again for a second-place 6–4–1 finish. Although Isbell still kept his left arm taped to his side because of a shoulder separation in a college game, he did most of the passing. Hutson led the league in scoring with 57 points and also was first with six interceptions from his new defensive safety position. Hinkle's nine field goals were only one short of the record.

1941 Tony Canadeo, a rookie from Gonzaga, joined Hinkle and Uram in the backfield and Isbell did all the passing because Herber retired as the result of a leg injury. The formidable Bears, now known as the "Monsters of the Midway" and featuring Sid Luckman, George McAfee, and Bill Osmanski, held on to beat the Packers 25–17 in their first meeting at Green Bay, but the second game at Wrigley Field resulted in a 16–14 victory for the Packers. Green Bay swept its last eight games, including a rematch with the Bears, and wound up tied with Chicago (10–1) for the Western Division title. The Bears struck for 24 points in the second quarter of the playoff game at Chicago to go into a title game with the Giants. Hutson set records with 95 points and 58 pass receptions, Hinkle led with six field goals and Isbell was the NFL's top passer with 1,479 yards and 15 touchdowns.

1942 There was no stopping Hutson as he won his fifth pass-catching championship. There had been few more spectacular seasons by an individual in the history of the league. Huston scored 138 points by catching 17 touchdown passes from Isbell and Canadeo, kicking a field goal and 33 extra points. His 74 receptions for 1,211 yards set additional marks and Isbell's totals of 2,021 yards passing and 24 touchdowns were records. Ted Fritsch, a rookie from little Stevens Point College in Wisconsin, found a job in the backfield, helping to fill the gap left by the retirement of Hinkle. The Packers once again finished behind the unbeaten Bears (11–0) with an 8–2–1 record. Both defeats were to the Chicago Bears, 44–28 and 38–7. Cecil Isbell surprised Packers' fans by retiring after the season to return to his alma mater, Purdue, as an assistant coach. He explained, "I hadn't been up long when I saw Lambeau tell players like Herber, Gantenbein, and Bruder they were all done. I vowed I'd quit before they came around to tell me."

1943 Canadeo became the regular passer, backed by Irv Comp and Lou Brock. The Packers played a 21–21 tie with the Bears on opening day but a 33–7 loss to Washington and a 21–7 defeat by the Bears cost them any chance at first place and they finished fourth. Hutson led again in scoring and receiving and tied for the field goal leadership with three. Hutson even threw a touchdown pass.

1944 Green Bay, playing with veterans, servicemen on leave, and untried youngsters, opened with a six-game win streak before running into a 21–0 shutout by the Bears. They were blanked again 24–0 in New York but finished 8–2 to 6–3–1 for Chicago and Detroit in the west. The Packers went to New York and won their sixth league title, and first since 1939, by beating the Giants 14–7 in the Polo Grounds on two scores by Fritsch. Each Packer player took home $1,149, a record winning share, thanks to a crowd of 46,016. Herber, who had been with the Packers from 1930 to 1940, was the Giants' passer. Hutson still was available to catch 58 passes and 9 of the 12 touchdown passes thrown by Comp, and also to kick extra points for a leading total of 85 points.

1945 Hutson had been talking of retiring for years but Lambeau talked him into staying on as a player-coach for 1945. Hutson caught four touchdown passes and kicked five extra points for 29 points in the second quarter of a game against Detroit in which the Packers also set a record with 41 points in the same quarter en route to a 57–21 victory, October 7. Despite a strong start, the Packers' defense yielded 180 points and they lost four games, dropping to third place in the Western Division behind both the winning Cleveland Rams and the Lions. After winning his ninth pass receiving title, a league record, with 47 receptions, Hutson retired after 11 seasons. He had caught at least one pass in 95 consecutive games.

1946 World War II was over and talent began flowing back to NFL clubs, but the retirement of Hutson left a void in the Packers' offense. The Bears and the newly located Los Angeles Rams each beat Green Bay twice and the Packers also lost to the Chicago Cardinals for a 6–5 finish and third place. Without Hutson the passing game was hurt and the Packers tried to get by on the running of Canadeo, Fritsch, and Walt Schlinkman, a first-round draft choice from Texas Tech. The offense was sluggish, scoring only 148 points in 11 games. Fritsch accounted for most of the scoring. He led the league with 100 points on 10 touchdowns, 9 field goals, and 13 extra points. Roy McKay's 42.7-yard average enabled him to top the punters for the second straight year.

1947 Coach-general manager Lambeau was running into trouble from the front office. Some executive committee members criticized his decision to buy Rockwood Lodge, a training base 15 miles north of Green Bay, for $25,000. The club also bought land and cottages for the coaching staff and their wives to live in during preseason training. An organization of sub-committees on different aspects of club operation was put into operation. Jack Jacobs of Oklahoma became the new quarterback and led the league in punting. The Packers finished third at 6–5 but four of the five defeats were by a total of only nine points.

1948 The war with the rival All-America Football Conference was beginning to hurt the NFL, particularly teams such as the Packers that had limited resources to engage in bidding contests for players. Green Bay had lost first-round draft choices Johnny (Strike) Strzykalski and Ernie Case to the AAFC in 1946 and 1947 but signed Earl (Jug) Girard when he came out of Wisconsin in 1948. Coach Lambeau fined the entire squad a half week's salary after a 17–7 loss to the Chicago Cardinals and didn't relent after a 16–0 win over the Rams the following Sunday. For the first time since 1933 the team finished under .500, losing seven in a row for a 3–9 record. The running of Canadeo and Schlinkman provided the only bright spots.

1949 The Bears shut out the Packers on opening day 17–0 and the Rams bombed them 48–7 the following week. Green Bay beat only the New York Bulldogs and the Lions en route to a last-place 2–10 season, their poorest in history. Attendance dropped with a last-place club and financial problems mounted. Matters became so desperate in late season that an intrasquad game was played and oldtimers such as Verne Lewellen, Arnie Herber, and Johnny Blood (McNally) gave demonstrations to raise $50,000. Canadeo became the first Packer and the third player in NFL history to gain 1,000 yards with 1,052. But Girard and rookie Stan Heath, the number-one draft choice, threw more interceptions than touchdown passes.

1950 Lambeau, founder of the franchise, resigned under fire after a dispute with the citizen organization that ran the club, February 1. Lambeau criticized the system of operation by committee and was rebuffed in an effort to add Don Hutson to the executive committee. Adding to the problems, the Rockwood Lodge burned, January 24. New stock certificates were sold and more than $125,000 was raised. The committee

hired Gene Ronzani, a former halfback with the Bears, to become the new head coach. Clayton Tonnemaker, a center, was the number-one draft pick and the Packers got halfback Billy Grimes from the old Los Angeles Dons' roster in the special draft of former AAFC players. Tobin Rote, a draft choice from Rice, shared the quarterback job with Paul Christman, who was released by the Chicago Cardinals. Green Bay improved to 3–9, enough to get out of the cellar but still far out of contention.

1951 The Packers continued a modest improvement under Ronzani, winning three of their first five games before going into a seven-game tailspin that left them at 3–9 in fifth place in the newly named National Conference. Green Bay lost to the New York Yankees 31–28, the only game the Yanks won. Rote passed for 15 touchdowns and led the Packers with 523 yards rushing. Running back Fred Cone, drafted out of Clemson, proved to be an excellent kicker but only a fair runner. Rote was backed up by Bobby Thomason. The defense gave up 375 points, an average of over 31 a game.

1952 The draft brought in such players as Babe Parilli, quarterback from Kentucky, Billy Howton, an end from Rice, and Dave Hanner, a tackle from Arkansas, and the Packers' fortunes turned upward. Ronzani had the Packers in the thick of the race most of the way and was 6–3 with three games to go. One of the early season successes was a 35–20 win over Washington, coached by Earl (Curly) Lambeau. However, they lost the last three to Detroit, Los Angeles, and San Francisco and finished fourth behind those three teams. Parilli shared the quarterback job with Rote. Howton set a record of 13 touchdown passes in his rookie season while catching 53 for 1,231 yards, another NFL record.

1953 Among the rookies was Syracuse center Jim Ringo and linebacker Bill Forester of Southern Methodist. The Ronzani regime ended in late season when the coach "resigned" with two games to play at the request of the executive committee. Hugh Devore and Ray (Scooter) McLean, two assistants, finished up. The Packers' only victories in a 2–9–1 season were over the league's new entry in Baltimore.

1954 The 13-man executive committee realized a major change was in order, so they made Verne Lewellen, the punter and halfback of the 1924–1932 period, general manager, and hired Lisle Blackbourn, coach at Marquette University, to succeed Ronzani. The Packers were competitive for the first half at 3–3. But they lost five of their last six, including two tight games against the eventual-champion Lions, 21–17 and 28–24, and finished 4–8, barely ahead of the last-place Colts. The offense consisted largely of Rote's 14 touchdown passes and his eight scores by rushing. Veryl Switzer, a rookie from Kansas State, led the league in punt returns with a 12.8-yard average and another rookie, Max McGee of Tulane, caught 36 passes and averaged 41.7 yards punting.

1955 The Packers won five of six home games, but lost five of six road games and settled for 6–6 and third place in the Western Conference, their best season since 1947. Howard Ferguson became a solid fullback threat and Rote threw 17 touchdown passes, most of them to Howton and rookie Gary Knafelc of Colorado. Cone kicked 17 field goals. Parilli, McGee, and Art Hunter were in the military service. Attendance increased to 153,241 with City Stadium now at a capacity of more than 20,000. A home game at Milwaukee County Stadium drew a Wisconsin pro record of 40,199.

1956 The Packers were unbeaten in the preseason, including a win over the defending champion Browns. The Packers had an odd schedule that gave the team a bye on opening day. They lost their first two and were 2–5 before they staged a mild rally in midseason by beating the Lions and Cardinals. De-

feats by the Rams and 49ers on the road left them in fifth place at 4–8. Tackles Forrest Gregg and Bob Skoronski were rookies. Injuries slowed Ferguson, and Rote's talk of retirement gave rookie quarterback Bart Starr a chance to see limited action. Al Carmichael set an NFL record by returning a Bears' kickoff 106 yards for a touchdown, October 7. It was the Packers last season in City Stadium.

1957 Paul Hornung, Notre Dame's "golden boy," was the Packers' special bonus pick in the draft and quickly became the center of controversy. Coach Blackbourn tried him at quarterback, decided he didn't have the arm for the job, and then shifted him to fullback, where he gained only 319 yards. Tight end Ron Kramer of Michigan and safety John Symank of Florida also were chosen in the draft. Rote was traded to Detroit for four players, including halfback Don McIlhenny and tackle Norm Masters. The new City Stadium, a $1 million structure seating 32,150, was dedicated, September 29. The Packers beat the Bears 21–17. Unfortunately for Blackbourn, the club won only two more games the rest of the year. Blackbourn was fired with one more year to go on his contract.

1958 The executive committee named assistant coach Ray (Scooter) McLean head coach. McLean had a "nice guy" image and the players quickly took advantage of it. The result was a 1–10–0 record, the poorest in Green Bay history. The lone victory, 38–35 over Philadelphia, almost got away when the Packers frittered away most of a 38–7 lead. Starr and Parilli shared the quarterback job and the backfield included Hornung and rookie Jim Taylor from Lousiana State. Rookie guard Jerry Kramer from Idaho was in the offensive line and Ray Nitschke of Illinois at linebacker.

1959 Green Bay's executive committee hired Vince Lombardi, an assistant coach with the New York Giants, as head coach and general manager, January 28. "Let's get one thing straight," said Lombardi his first day on the job. "I'm in complete command here." Lombardi spent the winter looking at the films of the 1958 Packers and was convinced he had the basis of a contender. He selected Colorado quarterback Boyd Dowler in the draft, traded with Cleveland for defensive end Bill Quinlan and defensive tackle Henry Jordan, acquired safety Emlen Tunnell from the Giants to help the defensive backfield, and picked up guard Fred (Fuzzy) Thurston from Baltimore. One of Lombardi's first decisions was to shift Hornung to halfback. Lamar McHan, acquired from the Chicago Cardinals, started at quarterback. When the Packers beat the Bears opening day the players carried Lombardi off the field on their shoulders. Two more victories followed. Then came five straight defeats—two to the world champion Colts and one to the Giants. Lombardi switched to Bart Starr at quarterback when McHan was injured and the Packers swept their last four for a 7–5 record, their best since 1945, and a third-place tie with the 49ers. Hornung scored 94 points kicking and running and led the NFL.

1960 Lombardi drafted Tom Moore from Vanderbilt, traded with Cleveland for defensive end Willie Davis and signed free agent Willie Wood as a safety. The Packers had a tough fight in the Western Conference. They wrapped it up by winning their last three on the road, clinching the Western title with a 35–21 victory at Los Angeles where Starr threw a 91-yard touchdown pass to Dowler, who had been converted to flanker. The Packers came up short in the championship game at Philadelphia's Franklin Field, where Norm Van Brocklin led the Eagles to a 17–13 victory. Chuck Bednarik tackled Taylor on the Eagles' 9-yard line at the final gun. Starr again took over from McHan, Taylor rushed for 1,101 yards, and Hornung scored a record 176 points.

1961 Hornung, Dowler, and Nitschke fitted in as many games as possible on weekend leaves from military camps and 42-year-old Ben Agajanian was hired to do the kicking when Hornung was away. Herb Adderley of Michigan State worked as a rookie cornerback. In a regular season game against Baltimore, Hornung had four touchdowns, a field goal, and six extra points for 33 points. The Packers clinched the Western Conference by defeating the Giants at Milwaukee 20–17 and became the league champions by again beating the Giants 37–0 as Hornung scored 19 points, December 31. Hornung led the NFL in scoring again, with 146 points and Taylor gained 1,307 yards, second to Cleveland's Jim Brown. Starr hit Dowler, McGee, and Kramer with most of his 16 touchdown passes.

1962 Lombardi made very few changes. Earl Gros, the top draft choice from Louisiana State, was a part-time performer behind Taylor, Hornung, Moore, and Elijah Pitts in the backfield that had perfected the "run to daylight" formula of its coach. The Packers' 10-game win streak was broken on Thanksgiving Day in Detroit when Alex Karras led an assault on Starr for a 26–14 Lions' victory. The Packers won the rest and finished at 13–1 before adding a second straight league championship. When Hornung was injured in midseason, Jerry Kramer took over the kicking duties and booted three field goals in a 16–7 victory over the Giants in the title game played in 20-degree weather with 40-mile-per-hour wind gusts at Yankee Stadium. Taylor's 1,474 yards led the league, the only time in Jim Brown's career at Cleveland that he failed to win the rushing championship. The Packers' fullback scored a record 19 touchdowns by rushing. Starr showed the way in passing with 2,440 yards and Willie Wood was first with nine interceptions. Four former Packers—Lambeau, Hutson, Blood, and Hubbard—were among the 17 charter members of the new Pro Football Hall of Fame at Canton, Ohio.

1963 NFL Commissioner Pete Rozelle suspended Hornung indefinitely for betting on his own team and other NFL teams, April 17. Alex Karras of Detroit also was suspended for the same violations. Moore and Pitts filled in for Hornung. Kramer took over the place-kicking job again. The Packers lost their opener to the Bears 10–3, then were battered by the Bears in a 26–7 rematch after winning eight straight. By the time of the second game against the Bears, Starr was out of action with a broken hand and Zeke Bratkowski filled in. Another Thanksgiving Day visit to Detroit resulted in a 13–13 tie and the loss of Ray Nitschke with a broken arm. Although Taylor ran for 1,018 yards, the Packers finished a half game behind the Bears, 11–1–2 to 11–2–1, and had to settle for a 40–23 Playoff Bowl victory over Cleveland in a match of runner-up teams.

1964 Hornung came back to play when his suspension was lifted after one season, but he seemed to have lost his ability to kick under pressure. A missed extra point cost the Packers their first game with Baltimore, and another missed point and five missed field goals by Hornung accounted for a second 24–21 loss to the Colts. Jerry Kramer missed most of the season due to abdominal surgery and Jim Ringo was traded to Philadelphia. Taylor gained more than 1,000 yards for the fifth straight year with 1,169. Hornung contributed 415. Starr led the league in passing and the defense allowed only 227 yards a game. An 8–5–1 finish left the Packers far behind the champion Colts' 12–2 and they suffered another jolt by losing the Playoff Bowl game to St. Louis 24–17.

1965 After the kicking failures of 1964, Lombardi brought in Don Chandler from the Giants to handle both the punting and field goal work. He also acquired Carroll Dale, a receiver, from the Rams for Dan Currie and traded tight end Ron Kramer to Detroit. Dave Robinson had fit into the linebacking corps and Marv Fleming was the new tight end. The Packers trailed the Steelers 9–7 at halftime of their

opening game but scored 34 in the second half for a 41–9 victory and started a six-game winning streak that included a 20–17 win over the Colts in which Hornung, Taylor, and Starr were hurt. They beat the Colts again 42–27 on a foggy December day, with Hornung scoring five touchdowns, and appeared to have the title wrapped up. However, a tie with San Francisco in the final game set up a playoff with Baltimore. Starr was injured early in the playoff game which Chandler's disputed field goal sent into overtime, December 19. Another Chandler field goal won for Green Bay in 13:39 of sudden death. During the 1964 and 1965 seasons Starr had a string of 294 consecutive passes without an interception.

1966 The injury-ridden Packers pulled themselves together to ruin Jim Brown's last game by beating the Browns for the championship in the snow at newly-renamed Lambeau Field in Green Bay, January 2. The champion Packers signed running backs Donny Anderson of Texas Tech and Jim Grabowski of Illinois, reportedly for $750,000 and $250,000, respectively. The "Gold Dust Twins" were given back-up roles behind Taylor, Pitts, and Hornung. The Packers lost only to the 49ers and Vikings by a total of four points en route to a second Western Conference title at 12–2.

1967 Dallas had won the Eastern Conference for the first time and 74,152 turned out in the Cotton Bowl to watch the Cowboys and Packers play for the title, January 2. Green Bay opened with a 34–20 lead but barely survived a Dallas comeback. With the score 34–27, Dave Robinson pressured Don Meredith into a pass that was intercepted by the Packers' Tom Brown in the end zone. The first Super Bowl, pitting the champions of the NFL and AFL, was played at the Los Angeles Memorial Coliseum as a result of the merger agreement of June 8, 1966. Green Bay beat Kansas City 35–10 on two touchdown passes from Starr to Max McGee and a key interception by Willie Wood, although the Chiefs trailed only 14–10 at the half. Jim Taylor, who had played out his option, signed with the new New Orleans team, where he was joined by Hornung who went to the Saints in the expansion draft. No club had won three NFL championships in a row since the Packers of 1929-1931. Injuries sidelined Pitts and Grabowski, and Lombardi seldom had the same backfield combination. He used Anderson and Travis Williams, the sensational kickoff returner, with Ben Wilson and Chuck Mercein,

MEMBERS OF HALL OF FAME:
Johnny Blood (McNally), Tony Canadeo, Forrest Gregg, Arnie Herber, Clarke Hinkle, Cal Hubbard, Don Hutson, Walter Kiesling, Earl (Curly) Lambeau, Vince Lombardi, Mike Micalske, Bart Starr, Jim Taylor, Emlen Tunnell.

PACKERS RECORD, 1921–76

Year	Won	Lost	Tied	Pct.	Pts.	OP
1921	6	2	2	.750		
1922	4	3	3	.571		
1923	7	2	1	.778		
1924	8	4	0	.667		
1925	8	5	0	.615		
1926	7	3	3	.700		
1927	7	2	1	.778		
1928	6	4	3	.600		
1929‡	12	0	1	1.000		
1930‡	10	3	1	.769		
1931‡	12	2	0	.857		
1932	10	3	1	.769		
1933	5	7	1	.417	170	107
1934	7	6	0	.538	156	112
1935	8	4	0	.667	181	96
1936‡	10	1	1	.909	248	118
1937	7	4	0	.636	220	122
1938§	8	3	0	.727	223	118
1939†	9	2	0	.818	233	153
1940	6	4	1	.600	238	155
1941	10	1	0	.909	258	120
1942	8	2	1	.800	300	215
1943	7	2	1	.778	264	172
1944‡	8	2	0	.800	238	141
1945	6	4	0	.600	258	173
1946	6	5	0	.545	148	158
1947	6	5	1	.545	274	210
1948	3	9	0	.250	154	290
1949	2	10	0	.167	114	329
1950	3	9	0	.250	244	406
1951	3	9	0	.250	254	375
1952	6	6	0	.500	295	312
1953	2	9	1	.182	200	338
1954	4	8	0	.333	234	251
1955	6	6	0	.500	258	276
1956	4	8	0	.333	264	342
1957	3	9	0	.250	218	311
1958	1	10	1	.091	193	382
1959	7	5	0	.583	248	246
1960§	8	4	0	.667	332	209
1961‡	11	3	0	.786	391	223
1962‡	13	1	0	.929	415	148
1963	11	2	1	.846	369	206
1964	8	5	1	.615	342	245
1965‡	10	3	1	.769	316	224
1966**	12	2	0	.857	335	163
1967**	9	4	1	.692	332	209
1968	6	7	1	.462	281	227
1969	8	6	0	.571	269	221
1970	6	8	0	.429	196	293
1971	4	8	2	.333	274	298
1972†	10	4	0	.714	304	226
1973	5	7	2	.429	202	259
1974	6	8	0	.429	210	206
1975§	4	10	0	.286	226	285
1976	5	9	0	.357	218	299
56 Years	388	274	33	.582		

‡*NFL Champion*
§*NFL Western Conference Champion*
**Super Bowl Champion*
†*NFC Central Division Champion*

RECORD HOLDERS

Rushing (Yards)	Jim Taylor, 1962	1,474
Passing (Pct.)	Bart Starr, 1968	63.7
Passing (Yards)	Bart Starr, 1962	2,438
Passing (TDs)	Cecil Isbell, 1942	24
Receiving (No.)	Don Hutson, 1942	74
Receiving (Yards)	Billy Howton, 1952	1,231
Interceptions (No.)	Irv Comp, 1942	10
Punting (Avg.)	Jerry Norton, 1963	44.7
Punt Ret. (Avg.)	Bill Grimes, 1950	19.1
Kickoff Ret. (Avg.)	Travis Williams, 1967	41.1
Touchdowns (Total)	Jim Taylor, 1962	19
Field Goals Made	Chester Marcol, 1972	33
Points (No.)	Paul Hornung, 1960	176

COACHING HISTORY

1921–49	Earl (Curly) Lambeau	213-104-22
1950-53	Gene Ronzani	14-33- 1
1954-57	Lisle Blackbourn	17-31- 0
1958	Ray (Scooter) McLean	1-10- 1
1959-67	Vince Lombardi	89-29- 4
1968-70	Phil Bengtson	20-21- 1
1971-74	Dan Devine	25-27- 4
1975-76	Bart Starr	9-19- 0

FIRST PLAYER SELECTED

1936	Russ Letlow, G, San Francisco
1937	Ed Jankowski, B, Wisconsin
1938	Cecil Isbell, B, Purdue
1939	Larry Buhler, B, Minnesota
1940	Hal VanEvery, B, Marquette
1941	George Paskvan, B, Wisconsin
1942	Urban Odson, T, Minnesota
1943	Dick Wildung, T, Minnesota
1944	Merv Pregulman, G, Michigan
1945	Walt Schlinkman, G, Texas Tech
1946	Johnny (Strike) Strzykalski, B, Marquette
1947	Ernie Case, B, UCLA
1948	Earl (Jug) Girard, B, Wisconsin
1949	Stan Heath, B, Nevada
1950	Clayton Tonnemaker, C, Minnesota
1951	Bob Gain, T, Kentucky
1952	Babe Parilli, QB, Kentucky
1953	Al Carmichael, B, USC
1954	Art Hunter, T, Notre Dame
1955	Tom Bettis, G, Purdue
1956	Jack Losch, B, Miami
1957	Paul Hornung, B, Notre Dame
1958	Dan Currie, C, Michigan State
1959	Randy Duncan, B, Iowa
1960	Tom Moore, RB, Vanderbilt
1961	Herb Adderley, CB, Michigan State
1962	Earl Gros, RB, Louisiana State
1963	Dave Robinson, LB, Penn State
1964	Lloyd Voss, DT, Nebraska
1965	Donny Anderson, RB, Texas Tech
1966	Gale Gillingham, G, Minnesota
1967	Bob Hyland, C, Boston College
1968	Fred Carr, LB, Texas-El Paso
1969	Rich Moore, DT, Villanova
1970	Mike McCoy, DT, Notre Dame
1971	John Brockington, RB, Ohio State
1972	Willie Buchanon, CB, San Diego State
1973	Barry Smith, WR, Florida State
1974	Barty Smith, RB, Richmond
1975	Bill Bain, G (2), USC
1976	Mark Koncar, T, Colorado

| *Lionel Aldridge* | *Donny Anderson* | *Tom Bettis* | *Charley Brock* | *John Brockington* | *Lee Roy Caffey* | *Fred Cone* |

who had been cut by the Giants. Starr missed three games, so Bratkowski and rookie Don Horn saw action. In a game against Cleveland, Green Bay scored a record 35 points in the first quarter, November 12. It was the first year of the new four-division setup in the NFL. After winning the four-team Central Division at 9–4–1, the Packers defeated the Rams 28–7 to win the Western Conference. Then came the NFL championship game with Dallas in 13-degree below zero arctic climate at Green Bay, December 31. The Packers won the "Ice Game" 21–17 on Starr's third down, one-yard quarterback sneak behind Jerry Kramer's block on Jethro Pugh with 13 seconds to play.

1968 Super Bowl II was almost an anticlimax in the 68-degree heat of Miami's Orange Bowl. The Packers whipped Oakland of the AFL 33–14. Two weeks after his second Super Bowl triumph, Lombardi shocked the football world by announcing his retirement as coach. He remained at Green Bay as general manager and named Phil Bengtson, his long-time assistant, as his successor. Thurston, McGee, and Chandler retired. Starr's arm bothered him and he spent half the year on the bench watching Bratowski play. The Packers desperately tried Mike Mercer, Errol Mann, Kramer, and Mercein as kickers. Fuzzy Thurston's job at guard was taken by Gale Gillingham. Minnesota, on the way to its first of four straight divisional titles, beat the Packers twice. Green Bay finished with a 6–7–1 record.

1969 Lombardi left the Packers to become a part owner, vice president, general manager, and coach of the Washington Redskins, February 5. Bengtson was given the additional job of Packers' general manager. It was a time of change at Green Bay. Jerry Kramer and Skoronski retired, tackle Ron Kostelnik went to Baltimore, and defensive back Tom Brown to Washington. Travis Williams became the top rusher and rookie Dave Hampton outgained Anderson and Grabowski. Shoulder trouble forced Starr out of the last four games and Horn threw 11 touchdown passes. Both Mercer and Booth Lusteg were inconsistent kickers. The Packers (5–2) were in the race at the halfway mark, but lost four of their next five.

1970 Tackle Henry Jordan, defensive end Willie Davis, and flanker Boyd Dowler retired. The Packers traded Herb Adderley to Dallas, Marv Fleming to Miami, and Elijah Pitts, Bob Hyland, and Lee Roy Caffey to Chicago. Vince Lombardi died of cancer, September 3. The Packers were shut out by the Lions on opening day, their first blank since 1958, and their first at home since 1949. Starr was ailing and Dave Robinson tore an Achilles tendon. Anderson led the team in both rushing yardage and pass receptions. When the club lost six of its last eight, finishing with another 20–0 shutout by the Lions, Bengtson resigned. The 6–8 record tied for last in the NFC Central Division in the first year of the realigned NFL.

1971 Determined to make a complete break with the past, the Packers went into the college ranks to get a successor to Bengtson and signed Dan Devine of Missouri as head coach and general manager. Forrest Gregg moved to Dallas to wind up his career and linebacker Ray Nitschke, one of the last holdovers from the Lombardi days, was benched. On opening day, coach Devine was run over on the side lines by the New York Giants' Bob Hyland and suffered a broken leg while his team was losing to the Giants in a wild 42–40 game. One of the highlights of the year was a 100-yard run by Ken Ellis with a missed field goal against the Giants, September 19. Devine coached the rest of the year on crutches, watching a porous defense nullify the outstanding play of John Brockington, the top draft choice, who gained 1,105 yards. Starr threw only 45 passes and Scott Hunter, a rookie from Alabama, had 17 passes intercepted. The Packers finished last again with a 4–8–2 record.

1972 Coach Devine traded running back Donny Anderson to the St. Louis Cardinals for MacArthur Lane. The pairing of Lane and Brockington proved effective, with Brockington gaining 1,027 yards and Lane 821. Starr retired as a player but remained as an assistant coach to call the plays for Hunter, whose favorite targets were Brockington and Lane. Willie Wood also retired, but the new deep combination of Ken Ellis, Jim Hill, Al Matthews, and Willie Buchanon, the number-one draft choice, was a strong one. Kicker Chester Marcol, the team's third draft choice, led the league in scoring by hitting 33 of 48 field goal attempts and 29 straight extra points for 128 points. The Packers won six of their last seven games and took their first division title since 1967 but lost 16–3 to Washington in the first round of the playoffs.

1973 The club was 2–1–1 after four games but won only one of the next seven and settled into third place at 5–7–2. Brockington had his third straight year of more than 1,000 yards as he gained 1,144 and led the NFC. Lane gained 528 yards but the passing game was not productive. Jerry Tagge, Hunter, and Jim Del Gaizo all were erratic and the bumper stickers proclaiming "The Pack is Back" were out of style.

1974 Devine definitely was on the spot in his fourth year on the job. When Jerry Tagge floundered, Devine made a midseason deal with the Rams for 34-year-old quarterback John Hadl. The Packers gave up their first three draft choices for 1975 and their first two for 1976 in the deal. Marcol kicked four field goals in a 21–19 win over Detroit and four more in a 19–7 win at Minnesota. Steve Odom raced 95 yards with a punt return against the Bears, November 10. The club was in the division race until it nosedived into a three-game losing streak to end the year at 6–8 in third place. Marcol led the league with 94 points on 25 field goals in 39 attempts and 18 consecutive extra points. Devine resigned and moved back to the college game at Notre Dame.

1975 Bart Starr was given the job of trying to lead the Packers back to their former status. His only coaching experience had been one year as an assistant coach to Devine in 1972. Hadl didn't fit into Starr's style of play. The veteran put the ball in the air 353 times and completed 191 for 54.1 percent but only six went for touchdowns and 21 were intercepted. Brockington had his poorest season, dropping to 434 yards. Willard Harrell contributed 359 yards and caught 34 passes. Ken Payne had 12 receptions against Denver, September 29, and led the club with 58 for 766 yards, second best in the NFC. Marcol missed the entire season with a torn leg muscle and was replaced by Joe Danelo of Washington State. Green Bay lost its first four and eight of its first nine, but won three of the last five for a 4–10 record.

1976 Starr traded Hadl to Houston for quarterback Lynn Dickey in a deal that also cost Green Bay cornerback Ken Ellis and a fourth-round draft choice. It took Dickey time to get started after a long wait on the Houston bench but he was coming on when he suffered a shoulder separation in the first Chicago game, November 14. He was lost for the year. Carlos Brown and Randy Johnson finished up and the club lost four of its last five en route to a 5–9 finish and last place.

GREEN BAY PACKERS, 1921–76

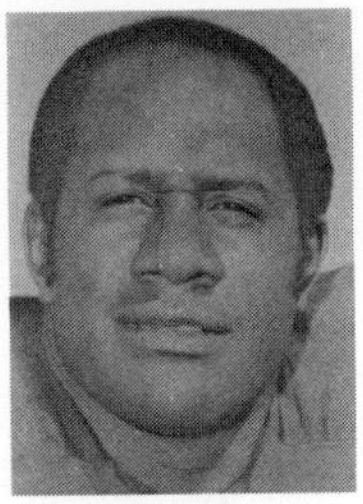
Willie Davis

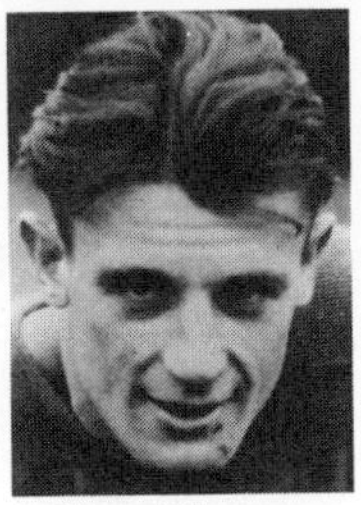
LaVern Dilweg

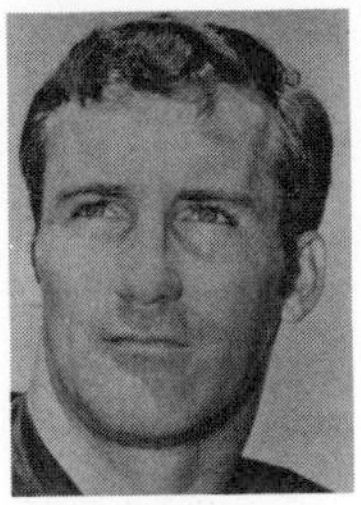
Boyd Dowler

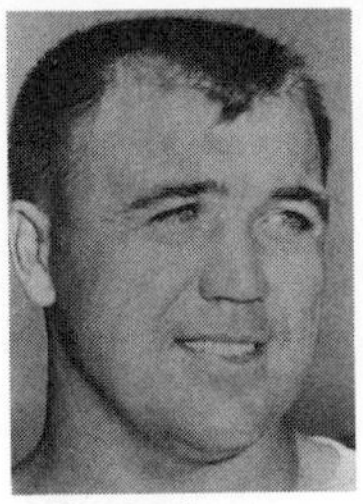
Ted Fritsch

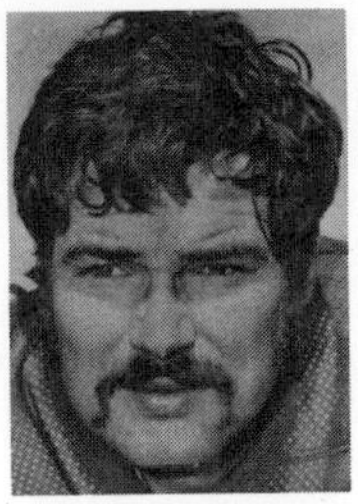
Gale Gillingham

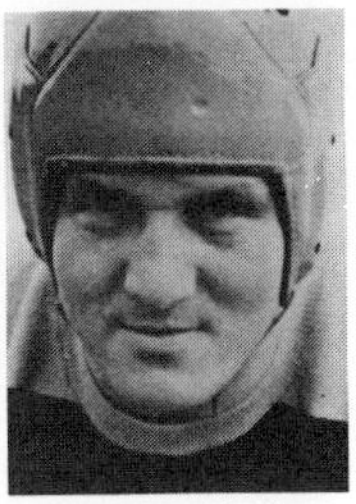
Buckets Goldenberg

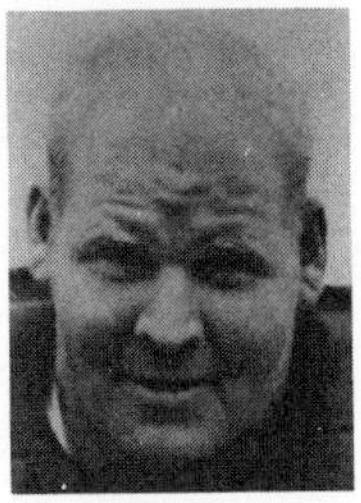
Dave Hanner

Bratkowski, Zeke, QB, Georgia 1963–68, 1971
Bray, Ray, G, W, Michigan 1952
Breen, Gene, LB, Virginia Tech 1964
Brennan, John, G. Michigan 1939–47
Brock, Charley, C, Nebraska 1939–47
Brock, Lou, B, Purdue 1940–45
Brockington, John, RB, Ohio State 1971–76
Broussard, Steve, P, Southern Mississippi 1975
Brown, Aaron, DE, Minnesota 1973–74
Brown, Allen, E, Mississippi 1966–67
Brown, Bill, G, Arkansas 1953–56
Brown, Bob, DT, Arkansas AM&N 1966–73
Brown, Carlos, QB, Pacific 1975–76
Brown, Tim, DB, Ball State 1959
Brown. Tom, HB, Maryland 1964–68
Bruder, Hank, B, Northwestern 1931–39
Bucchianeri, Mike, G, Indiana 1941, 1944–45
Buchanon, Willie, CB, San Diego State 1972–76
Buck, Cub, T, Wisconsin 1921–25
Buhler, Larry, B, Minnesota 1939–41
Buland, Walt, T, None 1924
Bullough, Hank, G, Michigan State 1955, 1958
Bultman, Art, C, Marquette 1932–34
Burris, Paul, G, Oklahoma 1949–51
Burrow, Jim, S, Nebraska 1976
Butler, Frank, C, Michigan State 1934–36, 1938
Butler, Bill, B, Chattanooga 1959

C

Caffey, Lee Roy, LB, Texas A&M 1964–69
Cahoon, Ivan, T, Gonzaga 1926–29
Canadeo, Tony, B, Gonzaga 1941–43, 1946–52
Cannava, Al, B, Boston College 1950
Capp, Dick, LB, Boston College 1967
Capuzzi, Jim, B, Cincinnati 1955–56
Carey, Joe, G, None 1921
Carlson, Dean, QB, Iowa State 1974
Carlson, Irv, G,St. John 1926
Carmichael, Al, B, USC 1953–58
Carpenter, Lew, B, Arkansas 1959–63
Carr, Fred, LB, Texas-El Paso 1968–76
Carroll, Leo, DE, San Diego 1968
Carter, Jim, LB, Minnesota 1970–75
Carter, Joe, E, Southern Methodist 1942
Carter, Mike, WR, Sacramento State 1970–71
Casper, Charley, B, Texas Christian 1934
Chandler, Don, K, Florida 1965–67
Christman, Paul, QB, Missouri 1950
Cifelli, Gus, T, Notre Dame 1953
Cifers, Bob, B. Tennessee 1949
Clancy, Jack, WR, Michigan 1970
Claridge, Dennis, QB, Nebraska 1964–65
Clemens, Bob, B, Georgia 1955
Clemens, Cal, B, USC 1936
Clemens, Ray, G, St. Mary's 1947
Cloud, Jack, B, William & Mary 1950–51
Cody, Ed, B, Purdue 1947–48
Coffey, Junior, RB, Washington 1965
Collins, Al, B, Louisiana State 1951
Comp, Irv, B, St. Benedict 1943–49
Comstock, Rudy, G, Georgetown 1931–33
Concannon, Jack, QB, Boston College 1974
Conway, Dave, K, Texas 1971
Cone, Fred, B, Clemson 1951–57
Cook, Jim, G, Wisconsin 1921
Cook, Ted, E. Alabama 1948–50
Cooke, Bill, DE, Massachusetts 1975
Cooney, Mark, DE, Colorado 1974
Coughlin, Frank, B, Notre Dame 1921
Coutre, Larry, B, Notre Dame 1950, 1953
Craig, Larry, B, South Carolina 1939–49
Cremer, Ted, E, Auburn 1948
Crenshaw, Leon, DT, Tuskegee 1968
Crimmins, Bernie, G, Notre Dame 1945
Croft, Milburn, T, Ripon 1942–47
Cronin, Tom, B, Marquette 1922
Crowley, Jim, B, Notre Dame 1925
Crutcher, Tommy, LB, Texas Christian 1964–67, 1971–72
Cuff, Ward, B, Marquette 1947
Culver, Al, T, Notre Dame 1932
Currie, Dan, LB, Michigan State 1958–64
Curry, Bill, LB, Georgia Tech 1965–60
Cvercko, Andy, G, Northwestern 1960
Cyre, Hector, T, Gonzaga 1926–28

D

Dahms, Tom, T, San Diego State 1955
Dale, Carroll, E, Virginia Tech 1965–72
Danelo, Joe, K, Washington State 1975
Daniell, Averell, T, Pittsburgh 1937
Danjean, Ernie, G, Auburn 1957
Darling, Bernard, C, Beloit 1927–31
Davenport, Bill, B, Hardin-Simmons 1931
Davidson, Ben, T, Washington 1961
Davis, Dave, WR, Tennessee A&I 1971–72
Davis, Harper, B, Mississippi State 1951
Davis, Paul, G, Marquette 1922
Davis, Ralph, G, Wisconsin 1947–48
Davis, Willie, DE, Grambling 1960–69
Dawson, Gib, B, Texas 1953
Deeks, Don, B, Texas 1948
Dees, Bob, T, Southwest Missouri 1952
DelGaizo, Jim, QB, Tampa 1973
DeLisle, Jim, DT, Wisconsin 1971
Deschaine, Dick, E, None 1955–57
Dickey, Lynn, QB, Kansas State 1976
Dillon, Bobby, B, Texas 1952–59
Dilweg, Lavvie, E, Marquette 1927–34
DiPierro, Ray, G, Ohio State 1950–51
Disend, Leo, T, Albright 1940
Dittrich, John, G, Wisconsin 1959
Doncarlos, J., C, Drake 1931
Donohoe, Mike, TE, San Francisco 1973–74
Douglas, George, C, Marquette 1921
Dowden, Steve, T, Baylor 1952
Dowler, Boyd, E, Colorado 1959–69
Dreyer, Wally, B, Wisconsin 1950–51
Drulis, Chuck, G, Temple 1950
Duford, Wilfred, B, Marquette 1924
Duhart, Paul, B, Florida 1944
Dumoe, Bill, E, Beloit 1921
Dunaway, Dave, E, Duke 1968
Duncan, Ken, P-WR, Tulsa 1971
Dunn, Red, B, Marquette 1927–31
Dunnigan, Walt, E, Minnesota 1922

E

Earhart, Ralph, B, Texas Tech 1948–49
Earpe, Jug, C, Monmouth 1922–32
Eason, Roger, T, Oklahoma 1949
Ecker, Ed, T, John Carroll 1950–51
Elliott, Burton, B, Marquette 1921
Elliott, Carleton, E, Virginia 1951–54
Ellis, Ken, CB, Southern U. 1970–75
Enderle, Dick, G, Minnesota 1976
Engebretsen, Tiny, G, Northwestern 1934–41
Engelmann, W., B, S. Dakota State 1930–33
Enright, Rex, B, Notre Dame 1926–27
Erickson, Harry, B, Washington & Jefferson 1923
Estes, Roy, B, Georgia 1928
Ethridge, Joe, T, Southern Methodist 1949
Evans, Dick, E, Iowa 1940, 1943
Evans, John, B, California 1929
Evans, Lon, G, Texas Christian 1933–37

F

Falkenstein, Tony, B, St. Mary's 1943
Fanucci, Mike, QB, Arizona State 1974
Faverty, Hal, C, Wisconsin 1952
Faye, Allen, E, Marquette 1922
Feathers, Beattie, B, Tennessee 1940
Felker, Art, E, Marquette 1951
Ferguson, Howie, B, None 1953–58
Ferry, Lou, T, Villanova 1949
Finley, Jim, G, Michigan State 1942
Finnin, Tom, T, Detroit 1957
Fitzgibbons, Paul, B, Creighton 1930–32
Flaherty, Dick, E, Marquette 1926–27
Flanigan, Jim, LB, Pittsburgh 1967–70
Fleming, Marv, TE, Utah 1963–69
Flowers, Bob, C, Texas Tech 1942–48
Floyd, Bobby, J., B, Texas Christian 1952, 1954
Folkins, Lee, E, Washington 1961
Ford, Len, E, Michigan 1958
Forester, Bill, LB, Southern Methodist 1953–63
Forte, Aldo, G, Montana 1947
Forte, Bob, B, Arkansas 1946–53
Francis, Joe, QB, Oregon State 1958–59
Frankowski, Bob, G, Washington 1945
Franta, Herb, T, St. Thomas 1930
Freeman, Bob, B, Auburn 1959
Fries, Sherwood, G, Colorado State 1943
Fritsch, Ted, B, Stevens Point 1942–50
Frutig, Ed, E, Michigan 1941–45

G

Gantenbein, Milt, B, Wisconsin 1931–40
Gardella, August, B, Holy Cross 1922
Gardner, Milt, G, Wisconsin 1922–26
Garrett, Bob, B, Stanford 1954
Garrett, Len, TE, New Mex. Highlands 1972–72
Gassert, Ron, T, Virginia 1962
Gatewood, Lester, B, Baylor 1946–47
Gavin, Fritz, E, Marquette 1921, 1923
Gaydos, Kent, WR, Florida State 1975
Gibson, Paul, S, Texas-El Paso 1972
Gilletee, Jim, B, Virginia 1947
Gillingham, Gale, G, Minnesota 1966–76
Girard, Jug, B, Wisconsin 1948–51
Glass, Leland, WR, Oregon 1972–73
Glick, Eddie, B, Marquette 1921–22
Goldenberg, Charles (Buckets), G, Wisconsin 1933–45
Goodman, Les, RB, Yankton 1973–74
Goodnight, Clyde, E, Tulsa 1945–49
Gordon, Lou, T, Illinois 1936–37
Gorgal, Ken, B, Purdue 1956
Grabowski, Jim, B, Illinois 1966–70
Gray, D, E, None 1923
Gray, Johnnie, DB, Cal. State-Fullerton 1975–76
Green, Jesse, WR, Doane 1976
Greeney, Norm, G, Notre Dame 1933
Greenfield, Tom, C, Arizona 1939–41
Gregg, Forrest, T, Southern Methodist 1956, 1958–70
Gremminger, Hank, B, Baylor 1956–65
Griffen, Harold, C, Iowa 1928
Grimes, Billy, B, Oklahoma A&M 1950–52
Grimm, Dan, G, Colorado 1963–65
Gros, Earl, B, Louisiana State 1962–63
Grove, Roger, B, Michigan State 1931–35
Gudauskas, Pete, G, Murray State 1942, 1945
Gude, Walter, G, Wisconsin 1943–44
Gueno, Jim, LB, Tulane 1976

H

Hackbart, Dale, B, Wisconsin 1960
Hadl, John, QB, Kansas 1974–75
Hall, Charles, DB, Pittsburgh 1971–76
Hampton, Dave, RB, Wyoming 1970–71
Hanner, Dave, T, Arkansas 1952–64
Hanny, Frank, T, Indiana 1930
Hansen, Don, LB, Illinois 1976
Hanson, Roy, B, Marquette 1923
Harden, Leon, DS, Texas-El Paso 1970
Harding, Roger, C, California 1949
Hardy, Kevin, DT, Notre Dame 1970
Harrell, Willard, RB, Pacific 1975–76
Hart, Doug, DB, Texas-Arlington 1964–71
Harris, John, B, Minnesota 1930
Hathcock, Dave, B, Memphis State 1966
Haycraft, Ken, E, Wisconsin 1964–66
Hayes, Norb, E, Marquette 1923
Hayhoe, Bill T, USC 1969–74
Hays, Dave, E, Notre Dame 1921–22
Hays, George, E, St. Bonaventure 1953
Hearden, Len, B, Ripon 1924
Hearden, Tom, B, Notre Dame 1927–28
Heath, Stan, B, Nevada 1949
Hefner, Larry, LB, Clemson 1972–75
Held, Paul, B, San Diego State 1955
Hellvin, Jerry, T,Tulane 1954–57
Hendrian, Warren, B, Pittsburgh 1924
Hendricks, Ted, LB, Miami 1974
Henry, Urban, T, Georgia Tech 1963
Herber, Arnie, B, Regis 1931–41
Hickman, Larry, B, Baylor 1960
Hill, Don, B, Stanford 1929
Hill, Jim, S, Texas A&I 1972–74
Hilton, John, TE, Richmond 1970
Himes, Dick, T, Ohio State 1968–76
Hinkle, Clarke, B, Bucknell 1932–41

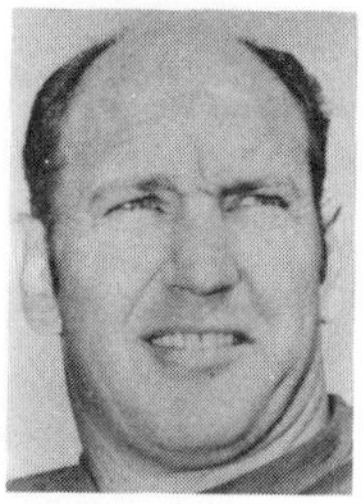
Henry Jordan

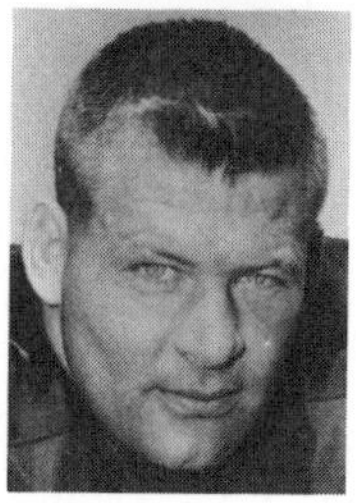
Jerry Kramer

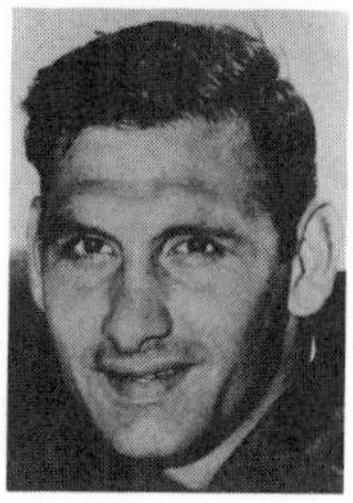
Ron Kramer

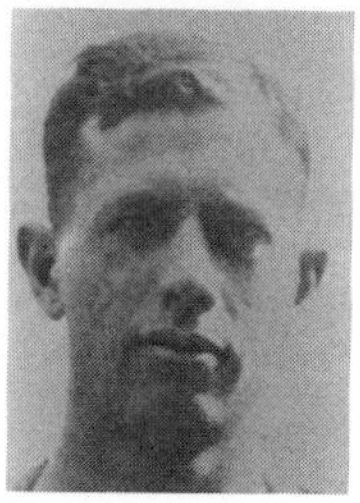
Vern Lewellen

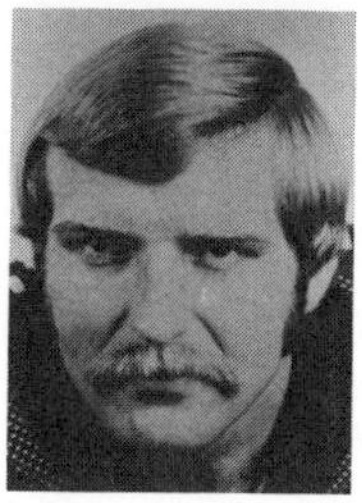
Mike P. McCoy

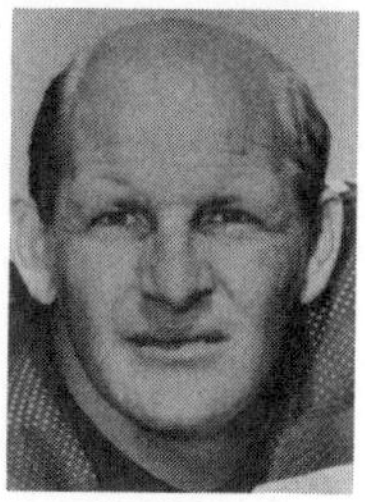
Ray Nitschke

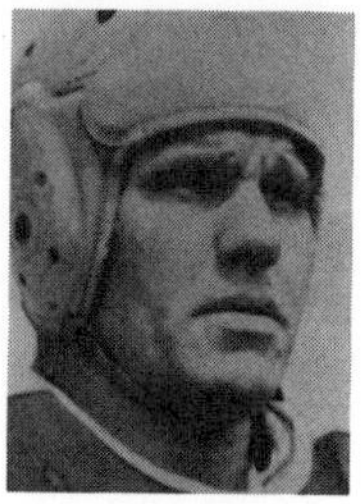
Buford (Baby) Ray

Hinte, Tex, E, Pittsburgh ... 1941
Holler, LB, South Carolina ... 1963
Horn, Don, QB, San Diego State ... 1967–70
Hornung, Paul, B, Notre Dame ... 1957–62, 1964–66
Howard, Lynn, B, Indiana ... 1921–22
Howell, John, B, Nebraska ... 1938
Howton, Bill, E, Rice ... 1952–58
Hubbard, Cal, T, Geneva ... 1929–35
Hudson, Bob, RB, Northeast Oklahoma ... 1972
Hull, Tom, LB, Penn State ... 1975
Hunt, Ervin, DB, Fresno State ... 1970
Hunt, Kevin, T, Doane ... 1972
Hunter, Art, C, Notre Dame ... 1954
Hunter, Scott, QB, Alabama ... 1971–72
Hutson, Don, E, Alabama ... 1935–45
Hyland, Bob, C, Boston College ... 1967–69, 1976

I

Iman, Ken, C, S.E. Missouri State ... 1960–63
Ingalls, Bob, C, Michigan ... 1942
Isbell, Cecil, B, Purdue ... 1938–42

J

Jacobs, Allen B, Utah ... 1965
Jacobs, Jack, B, Oklahoma ... 1947–49
Jackson, Melvin, G, USC ... 1976
Jacunski, Harry, E, Fordham ... 1939–44
James, Claudis, FL, Jackson State ... 1967–69
Jankowski, Eddie, B, Wisconsin ... 1937–41
Jansante, Val, E, Duquesne ... 1951
Jean, Walter, G, Missouri ... 1925–26
Jenison, Ray, T, S. Dakota State ... 1931
Jenke, Noel, LB, Minnesota ... 1973–74
Jennings, Jim, E, Missouri ... 1955
Jeter, Bob, DB, Iowa ... 1963–70
Johnson, Glen, T, Arizona State ... 1949
Johnson, Howard, G, Georgia ... 1940–41
Johnson, Joe, B, Boston College ... 1954–58
Johnson, Marv, B, San Jose State ... 1952–53
Johnson, Tom, T, Michigan ... 1952
Johnson, Bill, E, Minnesota ... 1941
Johnson, Chester, B, Marquette ... 1934–39
Johnson, Randy, QB, Texas A&I ... 1976
Johnstone, Art, B, Lawrence ... 1931
Jones, Bruce, G, Alabama ... 1927–28
Jones, Bob, G, Indiana ... 1934
Jones, Ron, TE, Texas-El Paso ... 1969
Jones, Tom, G, Bucknell ... 1938
Jordan, Henry, T, Virginia ... 1959–69
Jorgenson, Carl, T, St. Mary's ... 1934

K

Kahler, Bob, B, Nebraska ... 1941–44
Kahler, Royal, T, Nebraska ... 1942
Katalinas, Leo, T, Catholic U. ... 1938
Keane, Jim, E, Iowa ... 1952
Keefe, Emmett, T, Notre Dame ... 1921
Kekeris, Jim, T, Missouri ... 1948
Kell, Paul, T, Notre Dame ... 1939–40
Kelley, Bill, E, Texas Tech ... 1949
Kenyon, Crowell, G, Ripon ... 1923
Kercher, Bob, E, Georgetown ... 1944
Kern, Bill, T, Pittsburgh ... 1929–30
Keuper, Bill, T, Pittsburgh ... 1945–47
Kiesling, Walt, T, St. Thomas ... 1935–36
Kilbourn, Warren T, Michigan ... 1939
Kimmel, J.D., T, Houston ... 1958
Kinard, Bill, B, Mississippi ... 1957–58
King, Don, T, Kentucky ... 1956
Kirby, John, B, USC ... 1949
Klaus, Fee, C, None ... 1921
Kliebhan, Adolph, B, Milwaukee Teachers ... 1921
Knafelc, Gary, E, Colorado ... 1954–62
Knutson, Gene, E, Michigan ... 1954–56
Knutson, Steve, G, USC ... 1976
Koncar, Mark, T, Colorado ... 1976
Kopay, Dave, RB, Washington ... 1972
Kostelnik, Ron, T, Cincinnati ... 1961–68
Kotal, Eddie, B, Lawrence ... 1925–29
Kovatch, John, E, Notre Dame ... 1947
Kramer, Jerry, G, Idaho ... 1958–68
Kramer, Ron, TE, Michigan ... 1957, 1959–64
Kranz, Ken, B, Milwaukee Teachers ... 1949
Krause, Larry, RB, St. Norbert ... 1970–74
Kresky, Joe, G, Wisconsin ... 1930
Kroll, Bob, S, No. Michigan ... 1972–73
Kuechenberg, Rudy, LB, Indiana ... 1970
Kuick, Stan, G, Beloit ... 1926
Kurth, Joe, T, Notre Dame ... 1933–34
Kuusisto, Bill, G, Minnesota ... 1941–46

L

Laabs, Kermit, B, Beloit ... 1929
Ladrow, Wally, B, None ... 1921
Lally, Bob, LB, Cornell ... 1976
Lambeau, Earl (Curly), B, Notre Dame ... 1921–30
Lammons, Pete, TE, Texas ... 1972
Lande, Cliff, E, Carroll ... 1921
Lane, MacArthur, RB, Utah State ... 1972–75
Lankas, Jim, B, St. Mary's ... 1943
Larson, Fred, C, Notre Dame ... 1925
Lauer, John, B, Detroit ... 1922
Lauer, Larry, C, Alabama ... 1956–57
Lawrence, Jim, B, Texas Christian ... 1939
Laws, Joe, B, Iowa ... 1934–35
Leaper, Wesley, E, Wisconsin ... 1921, 1923
Lee, Bill T, Alabama ... 1937–42, 1946
Leigh, Charlie, RB, None ... 1974
Lester, Darrell, C, Texas Christian ... 1937–38
Letlow, Russ, G, San Francisco ... 1936–42, 1946
Lewellen, Verne, B, Nebraska ... 1924–32
Lidberg, Carl, B, Minnesota ... 1926–30
Lipscomb, Paul, T, Tennessee ... 1945–59
Livingston, Dale, K, Western Michigan ... 1970
Logan, Dick, T, Ohio State ... 1952–53
Lollar, George, B, Howard ... 1928
Long, Bob, E, Wichita ... 1964–67
Loomis, Ace, B, Lacrosse, Wisconsin ... 1951–53
Losch, John, B, Miami ... 1956
Lucky, Bill, T, Baylor ... 1955
Ludtke, Norm, G, John Carroll ... 1924
Lueck, Bill, G, Arizona ... 1968–74
Luhn, Nolan, E, Tulsa ... 1945–49
Luke, Steve, DB, Ohio State ... 1975–76
Lusteg, Booth, K, Connecticut ... 1969–70
Lyle, Dewey, E, Minnesota ... 1922–23
Lyman, Del, T, UCLA ... 1941

M

MacAuliffe, John, B, Beloit ... 1926
MacLeod, Tom, LB, Minnesota ... 1973
Mack, Red, E, Notre Dame ... 1966
Maddox, George, T, Kansas State ... 1935
Malone, B, Notre Dame ... 1921
Manely, Leon, G, Oklahoma ... 1950–51
Mann, Bob, E, Michigan ... 1950–54
Mann, Erroll, K, North Dakota ... 1958, 1976
Marcol, Chester, K, Hillsdale ... 1972–76
Marks, Larry, B, Indiana ... 1928
Marshall, Rich, T, Stephen F. Austin ... 1965
Martell, Herman, E, None ... 1921
Martinkovic, John, E, Xavier ... 1951–56
Mason, Dave, QB, Nebraska ... 1974
Mason, Joel, E, Western Michigan ... 1941–45
Massey, Carlton, E, Texas ... 1957–58
Masters, Norm, T, Michigan State ... 1957–64
Mathys, Charley, B, Indiana ... 1922–26
Matson, Pat, G, Colorado ... 1975
Matthews, Al, DB, Texas A&I ... 1970–75
Mattos, Harry, B, St. Mary's ... 1936
Matuszak, Marv, LB, Tulsa ... 1958
Mayer, Frank, G, Notre Dame ... 1927
McBride, Ron, RB, Missouri ... 1973
McCaffrey, Bob, C, USC ... 1975
McCarren, Larry, C, Illinois ... 1973–76
McCoy, Mike C., DB, Colorado ... 1976
McCoy, Mike P., DT, Notre Dame ... 1970–76
McCrary, Hurdis, B, Georgia ... 1929–33
McDougal, Bob, B, Miami ... 1947
McDowell, John, G, St. John's ... 1964
McGaw, Walter, G, Beloit ... 1926
McGeary, Clink, T, North Dakota ... 1950
McGee, Max, E, Tulane ... 1954, 1957–67
McGeorge, Rich, TE, Elon ... 1970–76
McHan, Lamar, B, Arkansas ... 1959–60
McIlhenny, Don, B, Southern Methodist ... 1957–59
McKay, Roy, B, Texas ... 1944–47
Mclaughlin, Lee, G, Virginia ... 1941
McLean, Ray, B, None ... 1921
McMillan, Ernie, T, Illinois ... 1975
McNally (Blood), Johnny, B, St. John's Minn. ... 1928–36
McPartland, Bill T, Texas ... 1947
McPherson, Forrest, T, Nebraska ... 1943–45
Meilinger, Steve, E, Kentucky ... 1958–60
Mendenhall, Ken, C, Oklahoma ... 1970
Mercein, Chuck, B, Yale ... 1967–69
Mercer, Mike, K, No. Arizona ... 1968–69
Mestnik, Frank, B, Marquette ... 1963
Michaels, Lou, K, Kentucky ... 1971
Michaels, Walt, G, Washington & Lee ... 1951
Michalske, Mike, G, Penn State ... 1929–37
Midler, Lou, G, Northwestern ... 1941
Mihajlovich, Lou, B, Indiana ... 1954
Miketanic, Nick, G, St. Norbert ... 1937
Milan, Don, QB, California Poly San Luis Obispo ... 1975
Miller, Charles, C, Purdue ... 1938
Miller, Don, B, Southern Methodist ... 1954
Miller, Don, B, Wisconsin ... 1941–42
Miller, John, T, Boston College ... 1960
Miller, Paul, B, South Dakota ... 1936–38
Miller, Tom, E, Hampden-Sydney ... 1946
Mills, Tom, B, Penn State ... 1922–23
Milton, Tom, E, Lake Forest ... 1924
Minick, Paul, G, Iowa ... 1928–29
Mitchell, Charles, B, Tulsa ... 1946
Moje, Dick, E, Loyola, Calif. ... 1951
Molenda, Bo, B, Michigan ... 1929–32
Monnett, Bobby, B, Michigan State ... 1933–38
Moore, Allen, E, Texas A&M ... 1939
Moore, Rich, DT, Villanova ... 1969–70
Moore, Tom, B, Vanderbilt ... 1960–65
Moselle, Dom, B, Superior ... 1951–52
Mosley, Russ, B, Alabama ... 1945–46
Moss, Perry, B, Illinois ... 1948
Mott, Norm, B, Georgia ... 1933
Mulleneaux, Carl, E, Utah State ... 1938–41, 1945–46
Mulleneaux, Lee, T, Arizona State ... 1938
Murray, Dick T, Marquette ... 1921–24

N

Nadolney, Romanus, G, Notre Dame ... 1922
Nash, Tom, E, Georgia ... 1928–32
Neal, Ed, G, Tulane ... 1945–51
Nichols, Ham, G, Rice ... 1951
Niemann, Walt, C, Michigan ... 1922–24
Nitschke, Ray, LB, Illinois ... 1958–72
Nix, Doyle, B, Southern Methodist ... 1955
Norgard, Al, E, Stanford ... 1934
Norton, Jerry, DB, Southern Methodist ... 1963–64
Norton, Martin, B, Carleton ... 1925–28
Nussbaumer, Bob, B, Michigan ... 1946
Nystrom, Lee, T, Macalester ... 1973–74

O

Oakes, Bill, T, Haskell ... 1921
Oats, Carleton, DT, Florida A&M ... 1973
O'Boyle, Harry, B, Notre Dame ... 1928–29, 1932
O'Connor, Bob, T, Stanford ... 1935
Odom, Steve, WR, Utah ... 1974–76
O'Donahue, Pat, E, Wisconsin ... 1955
O'Donnell, Dick, E, Minnesota ... 1924–30
Odson, Urban, T, Minnesota ... 1946–49
Ohlgren, Earl, E, Minnesota ... 1942
Okoniewski, Steve, DT, Montana ... 1974–75
Olsen, Ralph, E, Utah ... 1949
Olsonoski, Larry, G, Minnesota ... 1948–49
O'Malley, Bob, B, Cincinnati ... 1950
O'Malley, Jack T, USC ... 1970
Orllich, Dan, E, Nevada ... 1949–51
Osborn, Dave, RB, North Dakota ... 1976
Owens, Henry, G, Lake Forest ... 1922

P

Palumbo, Sam, G, Notre Dame ... 1957
Pannell, Ernie, T, Texas A&M ... 1941–42, 1945
Pape, Orrin, B, Iowa ... 1930
Papit, John, B, Virginia ... 1953
Parilli, Babe, B, Kentucky ... 1952–53, 1956–58
Paskvan, George, B, Wisconsin ... 1941

Dave Robinson *Tobin Rote* *Bob Skoronski* *F. (Fuzzy) Thurston* *Jesse Whittenton* *Dick Wildung* *Roger Zatkoff*

HOUSTON OILERS

1959 K.S. (Bud) Adams, Jr., an oilman, announced Houston's entry into the American Football League, joining five other franchises—Dallas, Denver, Los Angeles, Minneapolis-St. Paul, and New York. The AFL was to begin play in 1960. The name "Oilers" was selected for the team by Adams "for sentimental and social reasons." John Breen was hired as Oilers' player personnel director. Rice University refused to allow professional football the use of its 70,000-seat stadium; it had been Adams's first choice. In the first AFL player draft, the Oilers made Billy Cannon, All-America halfback and Heisman Trophy winner from Louisiana State University their first choice.

1960 The Oilers signed Cannon. A week later, however, they had to file suit to establish the validity of the contract because Cannon also signed with the Los Angeles Rams of the National Football League. Cannon then announced he wanted to play in Texas and the court eventually ruled he was free to join Houston. Lou Rymkus was named the Oilers' head coach and hired Wally Lemm to handle his defensive backfield. John Breen, searching for an experienced quarterback, decided on George Blanda, formerly of the Chicago Bears, and lured him out of a one-year retirement. "While he is not the greatest quarterback in the world in some departments, he really knows how to take a defense apart," said Breen. Adams leased Jeppesen Stadium, a high school facility, and spent $200,000 renovating it and increasing the seating capacity from 22,000 to 36,000. The team opened its first training camp at the University of Houston. The Oilers lost their first preseason game 27–10 to Dallas, but came back to beat Denver 42–3 before 18,500 in the home opener at Jeppesen. The Oilers went 10–4, scored 379 points, and clinched the AFL's Eastern Division title by beating Buffalo 31–23 in Houston.

1961 The Oilers won the first AFL championship 24–16 over the Los Angeles Chargers before 32,000 at Jeppesen Stadium, January 1. Cannon was named the game's most valuable player and Blanda completed 16 of 32 passes for 301 yards and three touchdowns. The winning players' share in the game was $1,016.42. Tight end Willard Dewveall, a former Southern Methodist University star, became the first player to jump leagues, playing out his option with the Chicago Bears and signing with Houston. Harris County voters passed a $22 million bond issue to finance a new domed stadium designated to be the home of the Oilers. Adams announced the team would train in Honolulu. Don Suman was named the club's new vice president and general manager. Lemm resigned as an assistant and entered private business. Six months later, after just one victory in the Oilers' first five starts, Lemm was re-hired to replace Rymkus as head coach. The Oilers ran off 10 victories in a row, became the first pro team in history to score more than 500 points in a season, and won the AFL title for the second year in a row 10–3 over the new San Diego Chargers in California.

1962 Lemm resigned to become head coach of the St. Louis Cardinals, of the NFL. Frank (Pop) Ivy was signed by Adams as his third head coach in three years. The owner also moved the training camp to Ellington Air Force Base, Texas. Blanda and running back Charlie Tolar both enjoyed big seasons, Blanda completing six touchdown passes in a 56–17 victory over the New York Titans, and Tolar finishing with 1,012 yards. The Oilers went 11–3 and won their third consecutive Eastern Division title, crushing the Titans 44–10. But in the AFL title game, Houston lost for the first time, although it took an historic six-quarter, double-overtime 20–17 win by the Dallas Texans to do it.

Defensive tackle Curley Culp goes 38 yards with a fumble recovery for a score vs. Chargers, 1975.

1963 Pop Ivy signed a new two-year contract as head coach and general manager. The Oilers also outbid the NFL competition for their top draft choice, Danny Brabham, a linebacker from Arkansas. The Oilers trained at Colorado Springs, Colorado. The season started with a 24–13 loss to Oakland and got worse. The club suffered its first losing record, finishing 6-8, then tried to make up for it by drafting Texas All-America tackle Scott Appleton number one and signing Baylor quarterback Don Trull, the top future pick in a previous draft.

1964 The Oilers signed another number one draft choice, Scott Appleton. The club began construction of a new training facility in Houston. Sammy Baugh was named backfield coach. Less than a month later, June 2, Adams relieved Ivy as head coach, replacing him with Baugh and naming Carroll Martin the new general manager. Billy Cannon, once the club's most distinguished player, was traded to Oakland for three little-known players, Bob Jackson, Sonny Bishop, and Dobie Craig. A 4-10 season ended with the final pro game in Jeppesen Stadium, a 34–15 Oilers' victory over Denver. Charley Hennigan, all-AFL wide receiver, established a professional record in that game, catching his one hundred and first pass. In still another coaching change, Baugh was relieved as head coach but stayed on to assist his successor, Hugh (Bones) Taylor. Lou Rymkus also rejoined the staff as offensive line coach.

1965 The club announced it would not play in the Astrodome, Houston's new domed stadium, because of "an unrealistic lease agreement." A five-year lease was completed with Rice University for its 70,000-seat stadium. The Houston contract of tackle Ralph Neely was declared invalid by an Oklahoma City Federal Court after the University of Oklahoma All-America had signed with both the Oilers and the NFL Dallas Cowboys. The club made Tommy Nobis of Texas, All-America linebacker, its number one draft choice, but eventually lost him to Atlanta. The Oilers finished their second straight 4-10 season with a 42–14 loss to Boston.

1966 Bud Adams appointed Don Klosterman the club's new executive vice president and general manager. Shortly afterward, it was announced the Hugh Taylor's contract was not renewed and that Wally Lemm was back as head coach again. Ernie Ladd, the Chargers' giant tackle, was signed by the Oilers. The league ruled that Willie Frazier and Pete Jaquess be awarded to San Diego as compensation. The Oilers finished 3–11, worst record in their history.

1967 In the first common draft involving the two leagues, the Oilers chose George Webster, the Michigan State All-America linebacker, number one. A month later, they signed him. Two of the stars of the early years in Houston, George Blanda and Charley Hennigan, were let go. Blanda was released, while Hennigan was traded to San Diego. The club announced still another new training camp site, this time at Schreiner Institute in Kerrville, Texas. The Oilers became the first team to go from the cellar to the division championship in one season, going 9-4-1 with 15 rookies on the squad to qualify for the AFL championship game.

1968 The Oakland Raiders ruined the New Year's celebrations in Texas, routing the Oilers 40-7 in the AFL championship game, January 1. Adams announced the team would move into the new Astrodome, after all, beginning with the 1968 season. The contract with Rice would be settled. After the players and owners settled their own controversial strike, the Oilers opened in the Astrodome by defeating Washington 9–3 in a preseason game. The regular season started in the dome, too, with Houston losing to Kansas City 26–21. Although 11 Oilers were named to various all-star teams, the club finished the season with a 7–7 record.

1969 George Webster was one of four AFL players named to the first combined all-pro team. Jim Norton, last of the original Oilers, retired and the club retired his jersey, number 43. Despite an up-and-down, 6-6-2 record, the team squeezed into the playoffs under the new system as runner up club, but lost to Oakland 56–7 as quarterback Daryle Lamonica threw six touchdown passes.

1970 Don Klosterman resigned as general manager to accept the same position with the Baltimore Colts. Quarterback Pete Beathard and cornerback Miller Farr were traded to St. Louis for quarterback Charley Johnson and cornerback Bob Atkins. Club veterans joined the NFL Players Association strike and were barred from training camp, June 30. The strike ended and the veterans reported August 3. In one of the most emotional games in the history of the franchise, the Oilers defeated the Dallas Cowboys for the first time, 37–21 in a preseason game. Wally Lemm announced late in the season he would retire when it was over. The Oilers finished with a 3-10-1 record, losing 52–10 to Dallas in the final game. Doug Wilkerson, the club's top draft pick, was traded to San Diego for tight end Willie Frazier.

1971 Ed Hughes, backfield coach for the San Francisco 49ers, was named the sixth coach in Oilers' history. He was signed to a five-year contract. In a draft known for its quality quarterbacks, Houston selected Dan Pastorini of Santa Clara on the first round and Kansas State's Lynn Dickey on round three. Bob Brodhead was announced as the team's new general manager. He resigned after only one month on the job. John Breen, the first pro football employee ever hired by Bud Adams, was given back his old job as general manager. Before the season was over, offensive line coach Ernie Zwahlen and offensive backfield coach Walt Schlinkman were fired. Shortly thereafter, Bud Adams reported Hughes's five-year contract had been terminated by "mutual

settlement." Rice University coach Bill Peterson was signed to replace him.

1972 Bud Adams campaigned for and won the 1974 Super Bowl VIII game for the city of Houston. Quarterback Charley Johnson was traded to Denver for an undisclosed draft choice. Second-year quarterback Lynn Dickey injured his hip in an exhibition game and was out for the season. In October, linebacker Ron Pritchard and wide receiver Charlie Joiner were traded to Cincinnati for running backs Paul Robinson and Fred Willis. In still another deal, former all-pro linebacker George Webster was traded to Pittsburgh for wide receiver Dave Smith. Houston finished 1-13.

1973 The Oilers made John Matuszak, a 6-foot 7-inch, 282-pound defensive end from Tampa, the first selection in the entire NFL draft. Veteran coach and front office executive Sid Gillman was announced as the new executive vice president and general manager, replacing John Breen, who retired. All-pro safety Ken Houston and a draft choice were shipped to Washington in return for five Redskins players. After Peterson's two-year record reached 1-18, he was fired October 16 and Gillman assumed a dual role of coach and general manager. The Oilers finished their second straight 1-13 season with a 27-14 loss to Cincinnati.

1974 Sid Gillman announced his decision to stay at least one more season as coach and general manager. O.A. (Bum) Phillips was hired as the club's new defensive coordinator. The Oilers moved their training camp to Sam Houston State College in Huntsville, Texas, their seventh camp in 15 years. Running back Vic Washington was acquired from San Francisco for a first-round draft choice in 1976 and a third-round pick in 1977. John Matuszak attempted to jump his contract to sign with Houston of the World Football League. He eventually was put on the Oilers' inactive list and was traded, along with a number-three draft choice, to Kansas City for defensive tackle Curley Culp and a number-one draft pick. Culp became an immediate force in Houston's new three-four defensive alignment and the Oilers won four in a row and six of their last eight to finish 7–7, their best record since 1969.

1975 O.A. (Bum) Phillips was named head coach by Gillman, January 25, who said he would remain as general manager. A few weeks later, Gillman had to

give up that job, too. The decision was announced by "mutual consent" of Gillman and owner Bud Adams. Phillips was given the added duties of general manager. The Oilers started fast with six wins in their first seven starts, including their first ever over an NFC team, 13–10 against Washington. Pittsburgh stopped the streak 24–17 on November 10, but the Oilers came back to beat Miami 20–19 as Billy (White Shoes) Johnson tied an NFL record for touchdowns in one season on kick returns. He had three on punts and one on a kickoff, including 83 yards with a punt in the Dolphins' win. The club finished the season with a 10-4 record in Phillips's first year as coach, setting a new Houston home attendance record (48,000 average) in seven home games, but missed the NFL playoffs.

1976 Billy Johnson was named the most valuable player in the Pro Bowl game in New Orleans after setting a record for kick returns and sprinting 90 years for one touchdown. After four wins in the first five games, the Oilers suffered a series of injuries and lost six in a row. They staggered home with a 5-9 record.

MEMBERS OF HALL OF FAME:
None

OILERS RECORD, 1960–76

Year	Won	Lost	Tied	Pct.	Pts.	OP
1960‡	10	4	0	.714	379	285
1961‡	10	3	1	.769	513	242
1962§	11	3	0	.786	387	270
1963	6	8	0	.429	302	372
1964	4	10	0	.286	310	355
1965	4	10	0	.286	298	429
1966	3	11	0	.214	335	396
1967§	9	4	1	.692	258	199
1968	7	7	0	.500	303	248
1969	6	6	2	.500	278	279
1970	3	10	1	.231	217	352
1971	4	9	1	.308	251	330
1972	1	13	0	.071	164	380
1973	1	13	0	.071	199	447
1974	7	7	0	.500	236	282
1975	10	4	0	.714	293	226
1976	5	9	0	.357	222	273
17 Years	101	131	6	.437	4,945	5,365

‡AFL Champion
§AFL Eastern Division Champion

RECORD HOLDERS

Rushing (Yards)	Hoyle Granger, 1967	1,194
Passing (Pct.)	Dan Pastorini, 1974	56.7
Passing (Yards)	George Blanda, 1961	3,330
Passing (TDs)	George Blanda, 1961	36
Receiving (No.)	Charley Hennigan, 1964	101
Receiving (Yards)	Charley Hennigan, 1961	1,746
Interceptions (No.)	Fred Glick, 1963	12
Punting (Avg.)	Jim Norton, 1965	44.2
Punt Ret. (Avg.)	Larry Carwell, 1967	17.1
Kickoff Ret. (Avg.)	Billy Cannon, 1960	33.2
Touchdowns (Total)	Bill Groman, 1961	17
Field Goals Made	Roy Gerela, 1969	19
Points (No.)	George Blanda, 1960	115

COACHING HISTORY

1960–61	Lou Rymkus*	11– 7-1
1961	Wally Lemm	9– 0-0
1962–63	Frank (Pop) Ivy	17–11-0
1964	Sammy Baugh	4–10-0
1965	Hugh (Bones) Taylor	4–10-0
1966–70	Wally Lemm	28–38-4
1971	Ed Hughes	4– 9-1
1972–73	Bill Peterson**	1–18-0
1973–74	Sid Gillman	8–15-0
1975–76	O.A. (Bum) Phillips	15–13-0

*Replaced after five games in 1961
**Replaced after five games in 1973

FIRST PLAYER SELECTED

1960	Billy Cannon, RB, Louisiana State
1961	Mike Ditka, E, Pittsburgh
1962	Ray Jacobs, DT, Howard Payne
1963	Danny Brabham, LB, Arkansas
1964	Scott Appleton, DT, Texas
1965	Lawrence Elkins, WR, Baylor
1966	Tommy Nobis, LB, Texas
1967	George Webster, LB, Michigan State
1968	Mac Haik, WR (2), Mississippi
1969	Ron Pritchard, LB, Arizona State
1970	Doug Wilkerson, G, North Carolina Central
1971	Dan Pastorini, QB, Santa Clara
1972	Greg Sampson, DE, Stanford
1973	John Matuszak, DE, Tampa
1974	Steve Manstedt, LB (4), Nebraska
1975	Robert Brazile, LB, Jackson State
1976	Mike Barber, TE (2), Louisiana Tech

Back Billy Cannon vs. Dallas Texans, 1962 AFL championship; 55 is Texans' E.J. Holub.

Pete Beathard

Garland Boyette

Robert Brazile

Ken Burrough

Don Floyd

Fred Glick

Hoyle Granger

HOUSTON OILERS, 1960–76

Aldridge, Allen, DE, Prairie View 1971–72
Alexander, Willie, CB, Alcorn A&M 1971–76
Allen, Dalva, DE, Houston 1960–61
Allen, George, DT, West Texas State 1966–67
Alston, Mack, TE, Maryland State 1973–76
Amundson, George, RB, Iowa State 1973–74
Anderson, Billy, QB, Tulsa 1967
Appleton, Scott, DT, Texas 1964–66
Atchason, Jack, E, Western Illinois 1960
Atkins, Bob, CB, Grambling 1970–76
Autry, Hank, C, So. Mississippi 1969–70

B

Babb, Gene, LB, Stephen F. Austin 1962–63
Baker, Ed, QB, Lafayette 1972
Baker, Johnny, LB, Mississippi State 1963–66
Baker, Melvin, WR, Texas Southern 1976
Banfield, Tony, CB, Oklahoma State 1960–65
Barber, Mike, TE, Louisiana Tech 1976
Barnes, Pete, LB, Southern U. 1967–68
Bass, Glenn, WR, E. Carolina 1967–68
Beathard, Pete, QB, USC 1967–69
Beams, Bryon, DT, Notre Dame 1961
Beck, Braden, K, Stanford 1971
Beirne, Jim, WR, Purdue 1968–73, 1976
Belotti, George, C, USC 1960–61
Benson, Duane, LB, Hamline 1974–76
Bergey, Bruce, DT, UCLA 1971
Bethea, Elvin, DE, N. Carolina A&T 1968–76
Beverly, David, P, Auburn 1974
Billingsley, Ron, DT, Wyoming 1971–72
Bingham, Gregg, LB, Purdue 1973–76
Bishop, Sonny, G, Fresno State 1964–69
Blahak, Joe, S, Nebraska 1973
Blanda, George, QB, Kentucky 1960–66
Blanks, Sid, RB, Texas A&I 1964–68
Botchan, Ron, LB, Occidental 1961
Boyette, Garland, LB, Grambling 1966–72
Brabham, Danny, LB, Arkansas 1963–67
Brazile, Robert, LB, Jackson State 1975–76
Brezina, Bobby, RB, Houston 1960
Broadnax, Jerry, TE, Southern U. 1974
Brooks, Leo, DT, Texas 1970–72
Brown, Don, RB, Houston 1960
Burke, Ed, G, Notre Dame 1964
Burrell, Ode, RB, Mississippi State 1964–69
Burrough, Ken, WR, Texas Southern 1971–76
Burton, Al, DE, Bethune-Cookman 1976
Butler, Jim, RB, Tulsa 1972
Butler, Skip, K, Texas-Arlington 1972–76

C

Campbell, Woody, RB, Northwestern 1967–71
Cannon, Billy, RB, Louisiana State 1960–63
Carr, Levert, T, N. Central State 1972
Carrell, John, LB, Texas Tech 1966
Carrington, Ed, TE, Virginia 1969
Carroll, Ronnie, G, Sam Houston State 1974–75
Carson, John, TE, Georgia 1960
Carwell, Larry, CB, Iowa State 1967–68
Caveness, Ron, LB, Arkansas 1966–68
Chancelor, Ken, C, Houston 1964
Charles, John, S, Purdue 1971–74
Cheek, Richard, G, Auburn 1972
Cheeks, B.W., RB, Texas Southern 1965
Cindrich, Ralph, LB, Pittsburgh 1973–75
Cline, Doug, LB, Clemson 1960–66
Cochrane, Kelly, QB, Miami, Fla. 1972
Cole, Linzy, WR, Texas Christian 1971–72
Coleman, Ronny, RB, Alabama A&M 1974–76
Compton, Dick, WR, McMurry 1965
Cotney, Mark, S, Cameron State 1975
Cowlings, Al, LB, USC 1973–74
Craig, Dobie, WR, Howard Payne 1964
Croyle, Phil, LB, California 1971–73
Culp, Curley, DT, Arizona State 1974–76
Culpepper, Ed, DT, Alabama 1962–63
Cunningham, Dick, LB, Arkansas 1973
Curry, Bill, C, Georgia Tech 1973
Cutsinger, Gary, DE, Oklahoma State 1962–68

D

Darby, Al, WR, Florida 1976

Davidson, Pete, WR, Citadel 1960
Davis, Bob, QB, Virginia 1967–69
Davis, Donnie, TE, Southern U. 1970
Davis, Marvin, LB, Southern U. 1974
Dawkins, Joe, RB, Wisconsin 1970, 1976
Dawson, Rhett, WR, Florida State 1972
Dewveall, Willard, TE, Southern Methodist 1961–64
Dickey, Lynn, QB, Kansas State 1971–75
Dickinson, Bo, RB, Mississippi Southern 1963
Domres, Tom, DT, Wisconsin 1968–71
Douglas, John, CB, Texas Southern 1969–70
Drungo, Elbert, G-T, Tennessee State 1969–76
Dukes, Mike, LB, Clemson 1960–63

E

Eaglin, Larry, CB, Stephen F. Austin 1973
Edwards, Emmett, WR, Kansas 1975–76
Elkins, Lawrence, WR, Baylor 1965–68
Ellis, Ken CB, Southern U. 1976
Evans, Norman, T, Texas Christian 1965

F

Fairley, Leonard, S, Alcorn A&M 1974
Fanning, Stan, DE, Idaho 1964
Fanucci, Mike, DE, Arizona State 1973
Farr, Miller, CB, Wichita State 1967–69
Faulkner, Staley, T, Texas 1964
Ferguson, Gene, T, Norfolk State 1971–72
Fisher, Ed, G, Arizona State 1974–76
Floyd, Don, DE, Texas Christian 1960–68
Foote, James, QB, Delaware Valley 1974–76
Fowler, Jerry, G, N.W. Louisiana 1964

Frazier, Charles, WR, Texas Southern 1962–68
Frazier, Wayne, C, Auburn 1965
Frazier, Willie, TE, Arkansas AM&N 1964–65, 1971, 1975
Freelon, Solomon, G, Grambling 1972–74
Frey, Dick G, Texas A&M 1961
Frongillo, John, C, Baylor 1962–66
Funchess, Tom, G, Jackson State 1972–73

G

Gerela, Roy, K, New Mexico State 1969–70
Germany, Willie, S, Morgan State 1975
Glick, Freddy, S, Colorado State 1961–66
Goode, Tom, G, Mississippi State 1962–65
Goodman, Brian, G, UCLA 1973–74
Gordon, Bobby, S, Tennessee 1960
Granger, Hoyle, RB, Mississippi State 1966–70, 1972
Grant, Wes, DT, UCLA 1973
Gray, Ken, G, Howard Payne 1970
Greaves, Gary, DE, Miami 1960
Green, Dave, P, Ohio 1973
Gresham, Bob, RB, West Virginia 1973–74
Groman, Bill, WR, Heidelberg 1961–62
Gruneisen, Sam, C, Villanova 1973
Guidry, Paul, LB, McNeese State 1973
Guy, Buzz, G, Duke 1961
Guzik, John, LB, Pittsburgh 1961

H

Hadl, John, QB, Kansas 1976
Haik, Mac, WR, Mississippi 1968–71
Hall, Ken, RB, Texas A&M 1960–61
Hardeman, Don, RB, Texas A&I 1975–76

Billy (White Shoes) Johnson returning a punt vs. San Francisco, 1975.

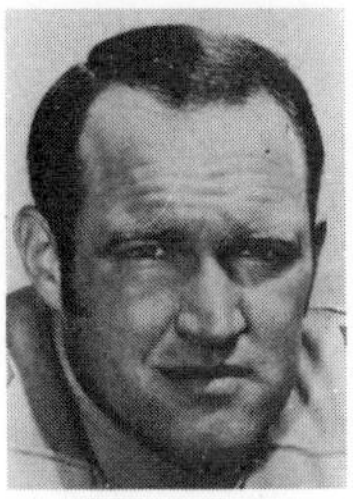

Glen Ray Hines

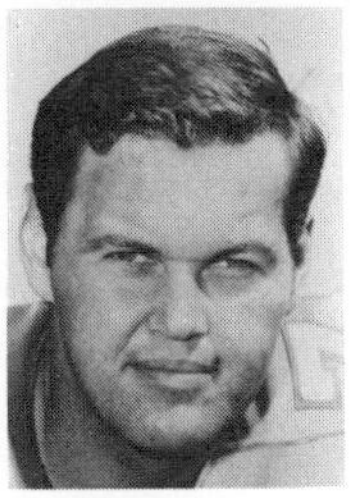

Pat Holmes

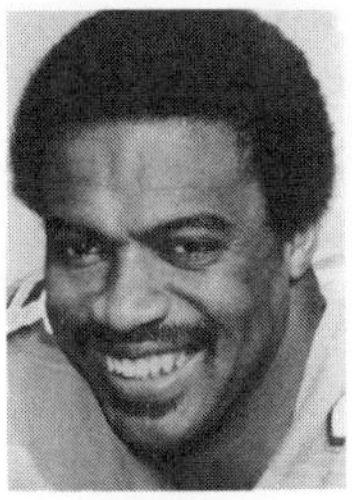

Jerry LeVias

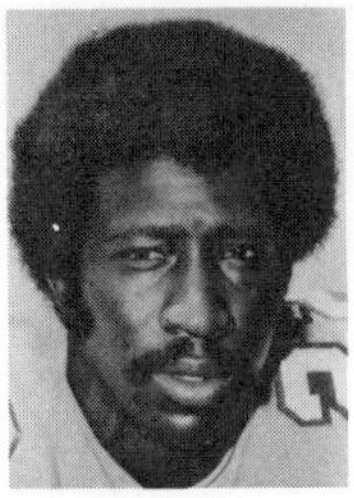

Zeke Moore

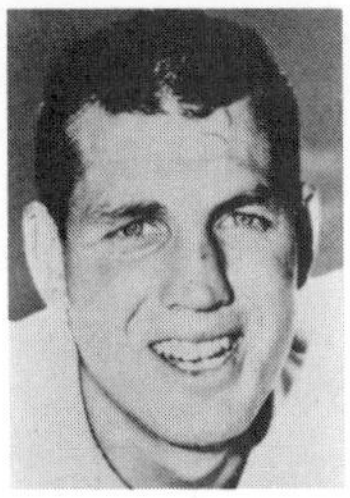

Jim Norton

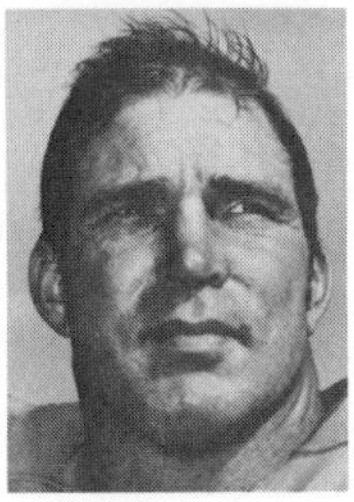

Walt Suggs

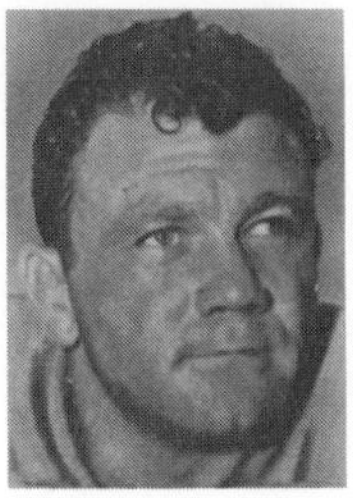

Charley Tolar

Hargett, Edd, QB, Texas A&M ... 1973
Harvey, Claude, LB, Prairie View ... 1970–71
Harvey, Jim, G, Mississippi ... 1972
Hawkins, Nat, WR, Nevada-Las Vegas ... 1975
Havig, Dennis, G, Colorado ... 1976
Hayes, Jim, DT, Jackson State ... 1965–66
Hayman, Conway, G, Delaware ... 1975–76
Helluin, Jerry, DT, Tulane ... 1960
Hennigan, Charley, WR, N.W. Louisiana ... 1960–66
Herchman, Bill, DT, Texas Tech ... 1962
Hicks, W. K., CB, Texas Southern ... 1964–69
Highsmith, Walter, T-C, Florida A&M ... 1972
Hines, Glen Ray, T, Arkansas ... 1966–70
Hinton, Eddie, WR, Oklahoma ... 1973
Hoaglin, Fred, C, Pittsburgh ... 1974–75
Hoffman, Dalton, RB, Baylor ... 1964
Holigan, Henry, RB, Bishop, Tex. ... 1965
Holmes, Pat, DE, Texas Tech ... 1966–72
Holmes, Robert, RB, Southern U. ... 1971–75
Hoopes, Mitch, P, Arizona ... 1976
Hopkins, Andy, RB, Stephen F. Austin ... 1971
Hopkins, Roy, RB, Texas Southern ... 1967–71
Houston, Ken, S, Prairie View ... 1967–72
Humphrey, Buddy, QB, Baylor ... 1966
Hunt, Calvin, C, Baylor ... 1972
Hunt, Kevin, T, Doane, Neb. ... 1973–76
Husmann, Ed, DT, Nebraska ... 1961–65

J

Jackson, Bob, New Mexico State ... 1964
Jacobs, Ray, DT, Howard Payne ... 1963
Jamison, Al, T, Colgate ... 1960–62
Jancik, Bobby, S, Lamar Tech ... 1962–67
Jaquess, Pete, CB, Eastern New Mexico ... 1964–65
Jenkins, Al, G, Morris Brown ... 1973
Johns, Pete, S, Tulane ... 1967–69
Johnson, Al, RB, Cincinnati ... 1972–74, 1976
Johnson, Benny, CB, J.C. Smith ... 1970, 1972–73
Johnson, Billy (White Shoes), WR, Widener ... 1974–76
Johnson, Charley, QB, New Mexico State ... 1970–71
Johnson, John Henry, RB, Arizona State ... 1966
Johnson, Rich, RB, Illinois ... 1969
Johnston, Mark, CB, Northwestern ... 1960–63
Joiner, Charlie, WR, Grambling ... 1969–72
Jolley, Lewis, RB, North Carolina ... 1972–73
Jones, Gene, CB, Rice ... 1961
Jones, Spike, P, Georgia ... 1970
Jones, Willie, DE, Kansas State ... 1967

K

Kelly, Bob, DT, New Mexico State ... 1961–63
Kendall, Chuck, S, UCLA ... 1960
Kerbow, Randy, WR, Rice ... 1963–64
Kinderman, Keith, RB, Florida State ... 1963–64
Kiner, Steve, LB, Tennessee ... 1974–76
King, Claude, RB, Houston ... 1961
Kinney, George, DE, Wylie ... 1965
Klotz, Jack, T, Penn Military ... 1964

L

Ladd, Ernie, DT, Grambling ... 1966–67
Lanphear, Dan, DE, Wisconsin ... 1960, 1962
Laraway, Jack, LB, Purdue ... 1961
Ledbetter, Monte, WR, N.W. Louisiana ... 1967
Lee, Jacky, QB, Cincinnati ... 1960–63, 1966–67
LeMoine, Jim, G, Utah State ... 1968–69
LeVias, Jerry, WR, Southern Methodist ... 1969–70
Lewis, Jess, LB, Oregon State ... 1970
Little, John, DT, Oklahoma State ... 1975–76
Lou, Ron, C, Arizona State ... 1972–73, 1976
Lumpkin, Ron, CB, Arizona State ... 1975

M

Majors, Joe, DB, Florida State ... 1960
Maples, Bobby, C, Baylor ... 1965–70
Marcontell, Ed, G, Lamar Tech ... 1967
Marshall, Rich, DT, Stephen F. Austin ... 1967–68
Matuszak, John, DT, Tampa ... 1973
Mauck, Carl, C, Southern Illinois ... 1975–76
Maxwell, Tommy, S, Texas A&M ... 1974
Mayes, Ben, DT, Drake ... 1969
Mayo, Ron, TE, Morgan State ... 1973
McCanless, Jim, G, Clemson ... 1960
McCollum, Bubba, DT, Kentucky ... 1974
McConnell, Brian, LB, Michigan ... 1973
McDaniel, Ed (Wahoo), LB, Oklahoma ... 1960
McDole, Ron, DE, Nebraska ... 1962
McFadin, Bud, DT, Texas ... 1964–65
McLeod, Bob, TE, Abilene Christian ... 1961–66
McNeil, Clifton, WR, Grambling ... 1973
Meredith, Dudley, DT, Lamar Tech ... 1963, 1968
Meyer, John, LB, Notre Dame ... 1966–67
Michael, Rich, T, Ohio State ... 1960–66
Miller, Bill, DT, New Mex. Highlands ... 1962
Miller, Ralph, G, Alabama State ... 1972–73
Milstead, Charlie, QB, Texas A&M ... 1960–61
Mitchell, Leroy, CB, Texas Southern ... 1969–70
Montgomery, Mike, WR, Kansas State ... 1974
Moore, Zeke, CB, Lincoln ... 1967–76
Morris, Dennit, LB, Oklahoma ... 1960–61
Morrison, Ron, T, New Mexico ... 1960
Moseley, Mark, K, Stephen F. Austin ... 1971–72
Murdock, Guy, C, Michigan ... 1972
Musgrove, Spain, T, Utah State ... 1970

N

Naponic, Bob, QB, Illinois ... 1970
Nelson, Benny, S, Alabama ... 1964
Nery, Ron, DE, Kansas State ... 1963
Nicholson, Oliver, LB, Texas Southern ... 1975
Nix, Kent, QB, Texas Christian ... 1972
Norton, Jim, S, Idaho ... 1960–68

O

Odom, Sammy, LB, N.W. Louisiana ... 1964
Olerich, Dave, LB, San Francisco ... 1971
Onesti, Larry, DB, Northwestern ... 1962–65
Owens, Joe, DE, Alcorn A&M ... 1976

P

Parker, Willie, DT, Arkansas AM&N ... 1967–70
Parks, Billy, WR, Cal State-Long Beach ... 1973–75
Parks, Dave, WR, Texas Tech ... 1973
Parrish, Bernie, CB, Florida ... 1966
Pastorini, Dan, QB, Santa Clara ... 1971–76
Peacock, Johnny, S, Houston ... 1969–70
Perkins, Willis, G, Texas Southern ... 1961, 1963
Perlo, Phil, LB, Maryland ... 1960
Pitts, Hugh, C, Texas Christian ... 1960
Pritchard, Ron, LB, Arizona State ... 1969–72
Poole, Bob, TE, Clemson ... 1966–67
Post, Dickie, RB, Houston ... 1971

Q

Queen, Jeff, TE, Morgan State ... 1974
Quinn, Steve, C, Notre Dame ... 1968

R

Reed, Alvin, TE, Prairie View ... 1967–72
Reed, Leo, G, Colorado State ... 1961
Regner, Tom, G, Notre Dame ... 1967–72
Reinfeldt, Mike, S, Wisconsin-Milwaukee ... 1976
Rhome, Jerry, QB, Tulsa ... 1970
Rice, Andy, DT, Texas Southern ... 1967
Rice, Floyd, LB, Alcorn A&M ... 1971–73
Rice, George, DT, Louisiana State ... 1966–69
Richardson, Mike, RB, Southern Methodist ... 1969–71
Rieves, Charles, LB, Houston ... 1964
Roberts, Guy, LB, Maryland ... 1972–75
Robertson, Bob, T, Illinois ... 1968
Robinson, Paul, RB, Arizona ... 1972–73
Rodgers, Willie, RB, Kentucky State ... 1972–75
Rossovich, Tim, LB, USC ... 1976
Rudolph, Council, DE, Kentucky State ... 1972
Rushing, Marion, LB, So. Illinois ... 1968

S

Sampson, Greg, DT, Stanford ... 1972–76
Saul, Ron, G, Michigan State ... 1970–75
Sawyer, John, TE, Southern Mississippi ... 1975–76
Schmidt, Bob, C, Minnesota ... 1961–63
Severson, Jeff, S, Cal State-Long Beach ... 1973–74
Shirkey, George, DT, Stephen F. Austin ... 1960–61
Simerson, John, G, Purdue ... 1960
Simon, Bobby, G, Grambling ... 1976
Simonson, Dave, T, Minnesota ... 1971
Sledge, Leroy, RB, Bakersfield J.C. ... 1971
Smiley, Tom, RB, Lamar Tech ... 1970
Smith, Bob, DB, Miami, Ohio ... 1968
Smith, Charles (Bubba), DE, Michigan State ... 1975–76
Smith, Dave, RB, Ripon ... 1960–64
Smith, Dave, WR, Indiana, Pa. ... 1972
Smith, Sid, C, USC ... 1974
Smith, Tody, DE, USC ... 1973–76
Spence, Julian, S, Houston-Tillotson ... 1960–61
Spikes, Jack, RB, Texas Christian ... 1965
Stemrick, Greg, CB, Colorado State ... 1975–76
Stith, Carel, DT, Nebraska ... 1967–69
Stoepel, Terry, T, Tulsa ... 1970
Stone, Donnie, RB, Arkansas ... 1966
Stotter, Rich, LB, Houston ... 1968
Strahan, Arthur, DE, Texas Southern ... 1965
Sturm, Jerry, C, Illinois ... 1971
Suci, Bob, S, Michigan State ... 1962
Suggs, Walt, T, Mississippi State ... 1962–71
Sutton, Mickey, S, Auburn ... 1966
Swatland, Dick, G, Notre Dame ... 1968

T

Talamini, Bob, G, Kentucky ... 1960–67
Taylor, Altie, RB, Utah State ... 1976
Taylor, Lionel, WR, New Mex. Highlands ... 1967–68
Thomas, Bill, RB, Boston College ... 1973
Thomas, Earl, WR, Houston ... 1976
Thomas, Lee, DE, Jackson State ... 1975
Thompson, Ted, LB, Southern Methodist ... 1975–76
Tilleman, Mike, DT, Montana ... 1971–72
Tobin, Bill, RB, Missouri ... 1963
Tolar, Charley, RB, N. W. Louisiana ... 1960–66
Tolbert, Jim, CB, Lincoln, Mo. ... 1972
Trammell, Allen, S, Florida ... 1966
Trask, Orville, DT, Rice ... 1960–61
Trull, Don, QB, Baylor ... 1964–69

U

Underwood, Olen, LB, Texas ... 1966–70

V

Vanoy, Vernon, DT, Kansas ... 1973
Viltz, Theo, CB, USC ... 1966

W

Wainscott, Loyd, LB, Texas ... 1969–70
Walker, Wayne, K, N.W. Louisiana ... 1968
Wallner, Fred, G, Notre Dame ... 1960
Walsh, Ward, RB, Colorado ... 1971–72
Walton, Sam T, E. Texas State ... 1971
Washington, Ted, LB, Mississippi Valley ... 1973–76
Washington, Vic, RB, Wyoming ... 1974
Watson, Ed, LB, Grambling ... 1969
Webster, George, LB, Michigan State ... 1967–72
Wegener, Bucky, DT, Missouri ... 1962–63
Weger, Mike, S, Bowling Green ... 1976
Weir, Sammy, WR, Arkansas State ... 1965
Wells, Robert, T, J.C. Smith ... 1972
Wells, Terence, RB, Southern Mississippi ... 1974
Wharton, Hogan, G, Houston ... 1960–63
White, Bob, RB, Ohio State ... 1960
White, Jim, DE, Colorado State ... 1974–76
White, John, TE, Texas Southern ... 1960–61
Whittington, C.L., S, Prairie View ... 1974–76
Wilkerson, Doug, G, N. Carolina Central ... 1970
Williams, Maxie, G, Southeastern Louisiana ... 1965
Williams, Sam, CB, New Mexico Highlands ... 1976
Willis, Fred, RB, Boston College ... 1972–76
Wisener, Gary, DB, Baylor ... 1961
Witcher, Albert, DB, Baylor ... 1960
Wittenborn, John, G-K, S.E. Missouri State ... 1964–68
Woods, Glenn, DT, Prairie View ... 1969
Wright, Elmo, WR, Houston ... 1975
Wyatt, Alvin, CB, Southern U. ... 1973

Y

Yeats, James, E, Florida ... 1960
Young, Bob, G, Howard Payne ... 1971

Z

Zaeske, Paul, WR, North Park, Ill. ... 1969–70

KANSAS CITY CHIEFS

1959 Unsuccessful in his attempts to acquire a National Football League franchise for Dallas, millionaire Lamar Hunt founded and organized the American Football League with six original cities—New York, Houston, Denver, Los Angeles, Minneapolis, and Hunt's home, Dallas. Buffalo and Boston were added and Oakland replaced Minneapolis. "Before there was a player, coach, or general manager in the league, there was Lamar Hunt," was the way Boston's Billy Sullivan put it. "Hunt was the cornerstone, the integrity of the league. Without him, there would have been no AFL." Not long after the Dallas Texans went into business, the National Football League announced it would establish a club in Dallas, to compete with the new league. The other Dallas franchise was awarded to Clint Murchison, Jr., and Bedford Wynne, both oil millionaires. Hunt hired an unknown assistant at the University of Miami named Hank Stram as his head coach. A self-styled disciplinarian, Stram was a short barrel-chested man who said, "Show me a good loser, and I'll show you a loser—period."

1960 For their inaugural season in the Cotton Bowl, the Texans had a strong home-state identity. The quarterback was Frank (Cotton) Davidson, an All-America from Baylor. Fullback Jack Spikes had been an outstanding player at Texas Christian, and Abner Haynes had developed his game at North Texas State. After winning five straight preseason games, the Texans drew 51,000 people for the final preseason game against Houston, a 42–3 victory. Haynes led the new league in rushing with 875 yards and touchdowns with nine. The Texans had a flashy, high-scoring club, and only three close losses kept them from challenging for the division championship. A variety of promotional ploys helped the Texans average 24,500 for their home games, highest in the new league.

1961 E.J. Holub, the Texas Tech All-America center described as "the best football player in America" by many scouts, was drafted first by both Dallas teams. Hunt, the Texans' owner, considered it a major victory when Holub decided to play for his club. Hunt also signed three more quality rookies, Southern Methodist's Jerry Mays, Michigan State's Fred Arbanas, and Ohio State's Jim Tyrer. The revitalized Texans won four of their five preseason games and three of their first four in the regular season. But during that period, Spikes was injured, and his absence from the running attack put even more pressure on Davidson's already erratic passing. The team fell into a six-game losing streak, then rallied to win three of its last four and finished second in the Western Division at 6–8.

1962 Don Klosterman was named the club's player personnel director. Stram made his most important acquisition when he invited Len Dawson, a quarterback he once coached at Purdue, to join Dallas. Dawson had been cut by the Cleveland Browns of the NFL, but he moved in to star for the Texans. Another key addition was Curtis McClinton, a 6-foot 3-inch, 227-pound running back who had enough speed to run the high hurdles at Kansas. With Dawson directing Haynes and McClinton, the Texans clinched the Western Division championship in November. They finished with an 11–3 record. Arbanas, fully recovered from the back injury that had kept him out of the 1961 season, was instrumental in the Texans' turnabout both as a receiver and an excellent blocker. His contribution to the ground game helped Haynes to his greatest year, which included 1,049 yards and a record 13 touchdowns by rushing. AFL writers voted Dawson, who threw 29 touchdown passes, player of the year, McClinton rookie of the year, and Stram

Ed Podolak returns a kickoff in the Chiefs' double-overtime playoff game against Miami, 1971.

coach of the year. Dallas won the AFL championship in the second overtime period when Tommy Brooker kicked a 25-yard field goal to make the final score 20–17 over Houston, December 23.

1963 Despite the artistic success, 1962 was a failure at the box office. The club had lost an estimated $400,000 in 1960, and probably just as much in the ensuing two years. H. Roe Bartle, mayor of Kansas City, invited Hunt to move his team to Missouri. Bartle promised Hunt he could deliver three times as many season tickets as the Texans had sold in Dallas. He said he would enlarge Kansas City's Municipal Stadium and rent it to the Texans for $1 a year the first two seasons. Impressed with the inducements and the fact the nearest pro football rival was 250 miles away, Hunt announced he was shifting the franchise to Kansas City and renaming it the Chiefs, May 14. Rookie Stone Johnson suffered a fatal injury in a preseason game. Kansas City opened the regular season with a 59–7 victory over Denver, but the new-look Chiefs managed only one win and two ties in their next nine games. Guard Ed Budde, defensive tackle Buck Buchanan, and linebacker Bobby Bell were rookies who became starters for the Chiefs.

1964 Ten regulars were hurt at one time or another during the season. Curtis McClinton broke a hand in training camp. It bothered him all year. E.J. Holub tore a knee and missed the last five games. Johnny Robinson, the outstanding defensive back, suffered a rib injury in November and was out for the season. Fred Arbanas, the tight end, was mugged on a Kansas City street and blinded in his left eye. Burdened with such ill fortune, the Chiefs played erratically. They beat the Chargers 49–6 and the Jets 24–7, but they lost to Denver 33–27. Attendance was as disappointing as the final 7–7 record. Seven home games at

Municipal Stadium drew only 126,881, and when AFL owners' meetings were held, there was discussion about the Chiefs' future in Kansas City.

1965 Gale Sayers, the spectacular breakaway runner from Kansas, was the club's number one draft choice. But the Chicago Bears also made him their first selection and finally won him in a bidding duel. Otis Taylor, a wide receiver from Prairie View A&M, joined the team. Abner Haynes was traded to Denver for linebacker Jim Fraser and cash. Mack Lee Hill, a virtually unknown free agent running back signed in 1964 muscled his way into the regular lineup. In a relatively routine knee surgery late in the season, Hill died on the operating table. The Chiefs finished 7–5–2; three of the losses were by three points or less.

1966 Running back Mike Garrett, the Heisman trophy winner from USC, was drafted in the twentieth round. Garrett also was drafted by his home town Los Angeles Rams, but the Chiefs signed the swift runner the team needed for $400,000. "In the past we ground out yardage inch by inch. We moved by bus; now we travel by jet," said Stram. A crowd of 43,885, largest ever to see a sports event in Kansas City, turned out for the home opener against Buffalo. The Chiefs lost 29–14, but after the game, in the middle of the field, Stram and Bills' coach Joe Collier negotiated a trade. Kansas City got field goal kicker Mike Mercer for a fifth-round draft pick. The deal solidified the one weak link in the Chiefs' attack. Mercer proved his worth in a title-clinching 32–24 win over New York in late November, hitting from 32, 15, 47, and 33 yards. Garrett's lateral swiftness gave the Chiefs a genuine outside threat. Garrett was second in AFL rushing with 801 yards and his 5.45 yards per carry was the league's top average. Dawson led the league in passing, and Chris Burford tied for third in pass receiving. The Chiefs finished three games ahead of Oakland in the Western Division.

1967 Using a flashy I formation offense and an assortment of defenses, the Chiefs confused and outplayed Buffalo to win the AFL championship 31–7 and gain a berth in the first Super Bowl. Kansas City went wild, with Chiefs' boosters mobbing the airport to greet the team upon its return. More than 6,300 fans purchased tickets for the trip to Los Angeles and the AFL-NFL World Championship Game, later renamed the Super Bowl. The Chiefs played Vince Lombardi's Green Bay Packers close for a half, trailing 14–10. But the Packers took charge in the final two periods for a 35–10 victory, January 15. The loss to Green Bay prompted an emphasis on defense in the Chiefs' 1967 draft. They got linebacking strength in Maxwell trophy winner Jim Lynch from Notre Dame and little All-America Willie Lanier from Morgan State. Specialists Jan Stenerud and Noland (Super Gnat) Smith also were selected. Interest in the team skyrocketed. Season ticket sales reached 22,000 in 1966. The figure went over 30,000 for 1967, and seating capacity for Municipal Stadium was increased from 40,000 to 47,000. In June, the voters in Jackson County approved a $43 million general obligation bond issue for construction of a sports complex that would feature both a football and baseball stadium. A two-thirds approval was required, and the bond carried with 67 percent of the vote. The Chiefs started well, but injuries to center Jon Gilliam and linebackers Holub and Lanier weakened the middle of the offensive and defensive lines. The team had to scramble for three consecutive wins at the end of the year, finishing second with a 9–5 mark. Stenerud, from Norway via Montana State, led the league in field goals with 21. Smith, a 5-foot 6-inch, 154-pound sprinter from Tennessee State, topped the AFL in kickoff yardage.

1968 The Chiefs' offensive firepower was depleted early in the season by injuries to backs Garrett and Bert Coan, and receivers Taylor and Gloster Richardson. Kansas City's offense scored no touchdowns, all were by the defense, in a 20–19 loss to the Jets. Stram improvised, bringing quarterback Jacky Lee and running back Robert Holmes off the bench, and both were outstanding in a 34–2 win over Denver in the third game. Dawson returned the next week to direct a 48–3 bombing of Miami. The Chiefs ran the winning streak to six, en route to a 12–2 finish and a tie with Oakland for the Western Division championship. But in the playoff game, the Raiders built a 21–0 lead in the first quarter and advanced to the championship with a 41–6 victory. All the Chiefs' scoring came in the second quarter, when they ran 10 plays inside the Raiders' 10-yard line and netted just two field goals.

1969 The Chiefs posted a 6–0 preseason mark and kept the string going with comfortable victories over San Diego and Boston at the outset of the regular schedule. But in the 31–0 drubbing of the Patriots, Dawson injured a knee and was replaced by Jacky Lee for game three against Cincinnati. The Chiefs lost the game 24–19, and lost Lee with a cracked bone in his ankle. Mike Livingston became the third quarterback in as many weeks, and helped turn things around in a 26–13 victory over Denver that began a seven-game winning streak. Two months into the season, Dawson returned to action. The Chiefs finished with an 11–3 record, second to Oakland's 12–1–1. But this was the first year of the new playoff system that pitted first- and second-place finishers in the opposite divisions against each other in the opening round. Kansas City relied on the strong defensive play, which had been the key to its season-long success, to turn back the defending Super Bowl champion New York Jets 13–6, while Oakland crushed Houston 56–7 in round one.

1970 The Chiefs, who had lost to Oakland twice in the regular season, rallied from an early 7–0 deficit to win 17–7 over the Raiders in the AFC championship game. Their opponents in Super Bowl IV in New Orleans were the Minnesota Vikings, and the Chiefs used the game as a crusade for the American Football League. They wore patches on their jerseys saying "AFL-10," which referred to the 10-year existence of the AFL, the league that would become extinct in the new NFL setup. Oddsmakers had established the Vikings two-touchdown favorites, but the Chiefs came out with three Stenerud field goals and a second quarter fumble recovery on the Minnesota 19-yard line that led to Mike Garrett's five-yard touchdown and a 16–0 halftime lead. A 46-yard pass from Dawson to Otis Taylor in the third quarter sealed Kansas City's first Super Bowl championship, 23–7. During the 1970 regular season, relations soured between Stram and Garrett, and Garrett was traded to San Diego. Despite key injuries, the Chiefs' record after 12 games was 7–3–2. They traveled to Oakland and lost 20–6, then dropped the final game to San Diego 31–13, as Garrett haunted them with his best day of the year, 95 yards.

1971 Stram opened up the offense again with the help of receivers such as rookie Elmo Wright and Morris Stroud. Taylor emerged as one of the best pass catchers in football, leading the NFL in yards gained on receptions. Ed Podolak became the new running star, and the linebacking trio of Lanier, Bell, and Lynch was among the league's best. After an opening loss to San Diego, the Chiefs won five straight. In the next-to-last game with Oakland, a late field goal by Stenerud gave the Chiefs a 16–14 victory and the Western Division title. Stram awarded game balls to all 40 squad members. The team finished with a 10–3–1 record, one-and-a-half games ahead of Oakland in the Western Division. But in the AFC playoff against Eastern Division champion Miami, Kansas City dropped a 27–24 double-overtime decision to the Dolphins, December 25.

1972 All-star safety Johnny Robinson retired, but Dawson ended speculation that he would do the same by signing a two-year contract in April. Kansas City fans were introduced to their new, modernistic Arrowhead stadium, one of the most impressive facilities in pro football. With a seating capacity of 78,097, it was formally opened in a preseason game with the St. Louis Cardinals, August 12. The Chiefs opened the regular season with a loss to Miami but eventually rose to 5–3 with a 27–14 win over Oakland in the eighth week. Consecutive losses to Pittsburgh, San Diego, and Oakland put them out of contention, however, and they finished 8–6, second in the West. The future no longer looked bright—except in the stands.

1973 The defense continued to play with its customary vigor, but new holes began appearing in the Chiefs' offense. Dawson was hurt much of the time and had to give way to backup quarterback Pete Beathard, who had returned for his second tour of duty under Stram. Beathard could not get the club moving, so Mike Livingston got the next chance and generated some excitement by leading the club into first place in late November. But a 14–10 loss to Denver and a 37–7 loss to the division-leading Raiders took the Chiefs out of title contention.

1974 The Chiefs were 3–4 at the midway point of the season, but then lost consecutive games to the New York Giants and San Diego. The Chiefs' age was beginning to show. Dawson was 39. The offensive linemen were older, slower, and ready to be replaced. The defensive front four had to be overhauled. The result was the first losing record in Kansas City in 11 years. The Chiefs finished 5–9 and Hank Stram, the only coach in the history of the franchise, was dismissed at the end of the season. Jack Steadman, the

club's general manager, was appointed by Lamar Hunt to revamp the organization. Statistically, the highlight of the year was Emmitt Thomas's 12 interceptions, best in the NFL.

1975 Paul Wiggin, an assistant coach with the San Francisco 49ers, was named Chiefs' head coach. Wiggin directed his young, inexperienced club to four victories in five games at one point early in the season, including a 34–31 upset of Dallas on Monday night television. Injuries handicapped the Chiefs, and by the end of the year, they barely had enough able bodies. A 24–21 victory over the Detroit Lions was the only bright spot in the final six games, and Kansas City again finished 5–9 and third in the Western Division. After 19 memorable seasons, 14 with the Texans-Chiefs, quarterback Len Dawson announced his retirement.

1976 Continuing what he hoped was a rebuilding program, Wiggin suffered through four straight losses at the start of the season, before getting his club turned around. Mike Livingston, who had seemed on the verge of becoming the regular quarterback several times in previous seasons, finally took over the position and improved noticeably as the season progressed. The team finished with two victories in its last three games, including an impressive 39–14 victory over Cleveland.

MEMBER OF HALL OF FAME:
Lamar Hunt

CHIEFS RECORD, 1960–72

Year	Won	Lost	Tied	Pct.	Pts.	OP
Dallas Texans						
1960	8	6	0	.571	362	253
1961	6	8	0	.429	334	343
1962‡	11	3	0	.786	389	233
Kansas City Chiefs						
1963	5	7	2	.417	347	263
1964	7	7	0	.500	366	306
1965	7	5	2	.583	322	285
1966‡	11	2	1	.846	448	276
1967	9	5	0	.643	408	254
1968	12	2	0	.857	371	170
1969**	11	3	0	.786	359	177
1970	7	5	2	.583	272	244
1971§	10	3	1	.769	302	208
1972	8	6	0	.571	287	254
1973	7	5	2	.571	231	192
1974	5	9	0	.357	212	285
1975	5	9	0	.357	282	341
1976	5	9	0	.357	290	376
17 Years	134	94	10	.584	5,582	4,460

‡AFL Champion
**Super Bowl Champion
§AFC Western Division Champion

RECORD HOLDERS

Rushing (Yards)	Mike Garrett, 1967	1,087
Passing (Pct.)	Len Dawson, 1975	66.4
Passing (Yards)	Len Dawson, 1964	2,879
Passing (TDs)	Len Dawson, 1964	30
Receiving (No.)	Chris Burford, 1962	68
Receiving (Yards)	Otis Taylor, 1966	1,297
Interceptions (No.)	Emmitt Thomas, 1974	12
Punting (Avg.)	Jerrel Wilson, 1965	46.1
Punt Ret. (Avg.)	Abner Haynes, 1960	15.4
Kickoff Ret. (Avg.)	Dave Grayson, 1962	29.7
Touchdowns (Total)	Abner Haynes, 1962	19
Field Goals Made	Jan Stenerud, 1968, 1970	30
Points (No.)	Jan Stenerud, 1968	129

COACHING HISTORY

1960–74	Hank Stram	124-76-10
1975–76	Paul Wiggin	10-18- 0

FIRST PLAYER SELECTED

1960	Don Meredith, QB, SMU
1961	E.J. Holub, C, Texas Tech
1962	Ronnie Bull, RB, Baylor
1963	Buck Buchanan, DT, Grambling
1964	Pete Beathard, QB, USC
1965	Gale Sayers, RB, Kansas
1966	Aaron Brown, DE, Minnesota
1967	Gene Trosch, DE-DT, Miami
1968	Mo Moorman, G, Texas A&M
1969	Jim Marsalis, CB, Tennessee State
1970	Sid Smith, T, USC
1971	Elmo Wright, WR, Houston
1972	Jeff Kinney, RB, Nebraska
1973	Gary Butler, TE (2), Rice
1974.	Woody Green, RB, Arizona State
1975	Elmore Stephens, TE (2), Kentucky
1976	Rod Walters, G, Iowa

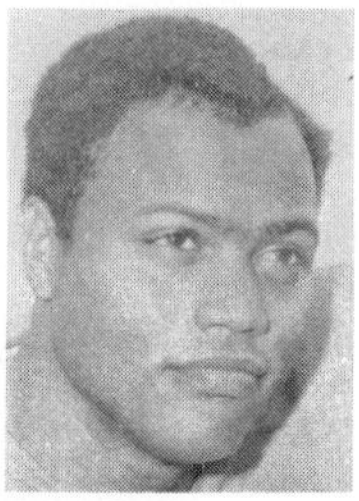

Aaron Brown

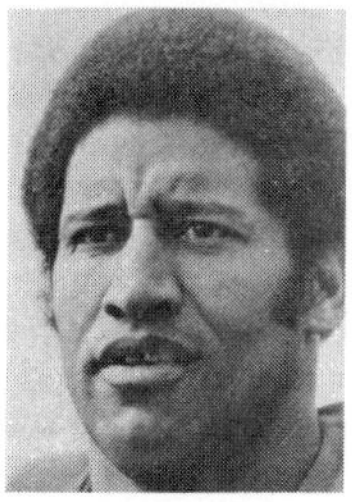

Buck Buchanan

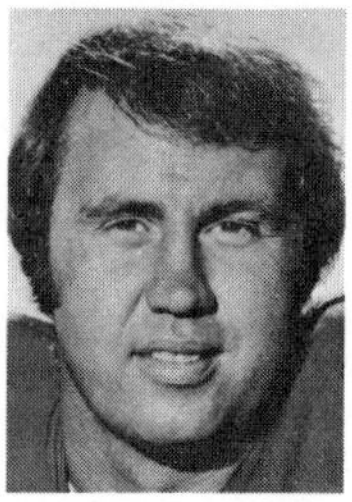

Ed Budde

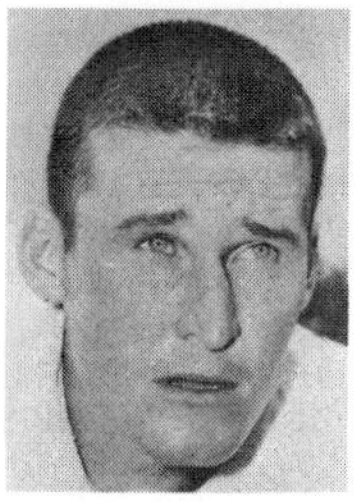

Chris Burford

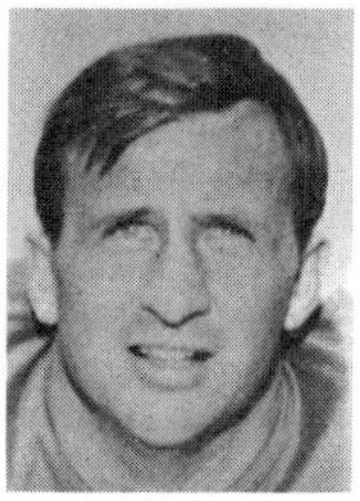

Bert Coan

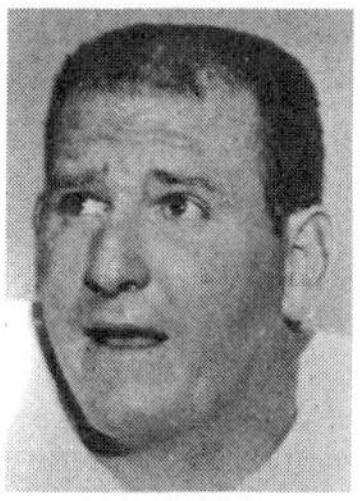

Sherrill Headrick

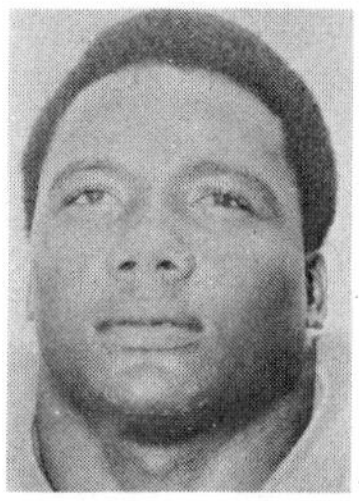

Robert Holmes

DALLAS TEXANS, 1960–62;
KANSAS CITY CHIEFS, 1963–76

Abell, Bud, LB, Missouri 1966–68
Adamle, Mike, RB, Northwestern 1971–72
Adams, Tony, QB, Utah State 1975–76
Agajanian, Ben, K, New Mexico 1961
Allen, Nate, CB, Texas Southern 1971–73
Andrews, Billy, LB, Southeastern Louisiana 1976
Ane, Charlie, C, Michigan State 1975–76
Arbanas, Fred, TE, Michigan State 1962–70
Austin, Hise, CB, Prairie View 1975
Avery, Ken, LB, Southern Mississippi 1975

B

Barbaro, Gary, S, Nicholls State 1976
Barnes, Charley, E, N.E. Louisiana 1961
Barton, Jim, C, Marshall 1960
Beathard, Pete, QB, USC 1964–67, 1973
Beisler, Randy, G, Indiana 1975
Bell, Bobby, LB, Minnesota 1963–74
Belser, Ceasar, DB, Arkansas AM&N 1968–71
Bergey, Bruce, TE, UCLA 1971
Bernet, Ed, E, Southern Methodist 1960
Bernhardt, Roger, G, Kansas 1975
Best, Keith, LB, Kansas State 1972–73
Biodrowski, Dennis, G, Memphis State 1963–67
Bishop, Sonny, G, Fresno State 1962
Bookman, John, DB, Miami 1960
Boydston, Max, E, Oklahoma 1960–61
Branch, Mel, DE, Louisiana State 1960–65
Brannon, Solomon, DB, Morris Brown 1965–66
Briggs, Bob, DE, Heidelberg 1974
Brooker, Tommy, TE–K, Alabama 1962–66
Brown, Aaron, DE, Minnesota 1966–72
Brunson, Larry, WR, Colorado 1974–76
Bryant, Bob, E, Texas 1960
Buchanan, Buck, DT, Grambling 1963–75
Budde, Ed, G, Michigan State 1963–76
Burford, Chris, E, Stanford 1960–67
Butler, Gary, TE, Rice 1973

C

Cadwell, John, G, Oregon State 1961
Cannon, Billy, TE, Louisiana State 1970
Carlson, Dean, QB, Iowa State 1972–74
Carolan, Reg, E, Idaho 1964–68
Clark, Wayne, QB, U.S. International 1975
Coan, Bert, RB, Kansas 1963–68
Collier, Tim, CB, East Texas State 1976
Collins, Ray, DT, Louisiana State 1960–61
Condon, Tom, G, Boston College 1974–76
Corey, Walt, LB, Miami 1960–66
Cornelison, Jerry, T, Southern Methodist 1960–65
Craig, Reggie, WR, Arkansas 1975–76
Culp, Curley, DT, Arizona State 1968–74

D

Daney, George, G, Texas-El Paso 1968–74
Daniels, Clemon, DB, Prairie View 1960
Davidson, Cotton, QB, Baylor 1960–61
Davis, Dick, DE, Kansas 1962
Dawson, Len, QB, Purdue 1962–75
DeBernardi, Fred, DE, Texas-El Paso 1974
Diamond, Charlie, T, Miami 1960–63
Dickinson, Bo, RB, So. Mississippi 1960–61
DiMidio, Tony, T, West Chester State 1966–67
Dimmick, Tom, C, Houston 1960
Dressler, Doug, RB, Chico State 1975
Drougas, Tom, T, Oregon 1974
Duncan, Randy, QB, Iowa 1961

E

Ellison, Willie, RB, Texas Southern 1973
Elrod, Jimbo, LB, Oklahoma 1976
Enis, Hunter, QB, Texas Christian 1960
Estes, Lawrence, DE, Alcorn A&M 1975–76

F

Farrier, Curt, DT, Montana State 1963–65
Flores, Tom, QB, Pacific 1969
Flynn, Don, DB, Houston 1960–61
Fournet, Sid, G, Louisiana State 1960–61
Fraser, Jim, LB, Wisconsin 1965
Frazier, Wayne, C, Auburn 1966–67
Frazier, Willie, TE, Arkansas AM&N 1972
Frey, Dick, DE, Texas A&M 1960

G

Gagner, Larry, G, Florida 1972
Garrett, Mike, RB, USC 1966–70
Gehrke, Jack, WR, Utah 1968
Getty, Charlie, T, Penn State 1974–76
Gilliam, Jon, C, E. Texas State 1961–67
Graham, Tom, LB, Oregon 1974
Granderson, Rufus, T, Prairie View 1960
Gray, Tim, S, Texas A&M 1976
Grayson, Dave, DB, Oregon 1961–64
Green, Woody, RB, Arizona State 1974–76
Greene, Ted, LB, Tampa 1960–62
Greene, Tom, QB, Holy Cross 1961

H

Hadley, David, CB, Alcorn A&M 1970–72
Hamilton, Andy, WR, Louisiana State 1973–74
Harris, Jimmy, DB, Oklahoma 1960
Harrison, Glynn, RB, Georgia 1976
Hayes, Wendell, RB, Humboldt State 1968–74
Haynes, Abner, RB, N. Texas State 1960–65
Headrick, Sherrill, LB, Texas Christian 1960–67
Herkenhoff, Matt, T, Minnesota 1976
Hill, Dave, T, Auburn 1963–74
Hill, Jim, DB, Sam Houston State 1966
Hill, Mack Lee, RB, Southern U. 1964–65
Himes, Jimmy, E, Texas Southern 1970
Holmes, Pat, DE, Texas Tech 1973
Holmes, Robert, RB, Southern U 1968–71
Holub, E.J., C-LB, Texas Tech 1961–70
Homan, Dennis, WR, Alabama 1971–72
Huarte, John, QB, Notre Dame 1969–71
Hudock, Mike, C, Miami 1967
Hudson, Bob, LB, Clemson 1960
Hull, Bill, DE, Wake Forest 1962
Humphrey, Tom, C, Abilene Christian 1974
Hunt, Bobby, DB, Auburn 1962–67
Hurston, Chuck, DE, Auburn 1965–70

J

Jackson, Charlie, DB, Southern Methodist 1960
Jackson, Frank, E, Southern Methodist 1961–65
Jankowski, Bruce, WR, Ohio State 1971–72
Jaynes, David, QB, Kansas 1974
Jeralds, Luther, DE, N. Carolina Coll. 1961
Johnson, Curley, RB, Houston 1961–62
Johnson, Dick, E, Minnesota 1963
Johnson, Jack, DB, Miami 1961
Jones, Doug, DB, Cal State-Northridge 1973

K

Kearney, Jim, DB, Prairie View 1967–75
Kearney, Tim, LB, Northern Michigan 1975
Keating, Tom, DT, Michigan 1974–75
Kelly, Bobby, T, New Mexico State 1967
Kelley, Ed, DB, Texas 1961
Keyes, Leroy, S, Purdue 1973
Kinney, Jeff, RB, Nebraska 1972–76
Kratzer, Dan, WR, Missouri Valley 1973
Krisher, Bill, G, Oklahoma 1960–61

L

Ladd, Ernie, DT, Grambling 1967–73
LaGrand, Morris, RB, Tampa 1975
Lane, MacArthur, RB, Utah State 1975–76
Lanier, Willie, LB, Morgan State 1967–76
Larpenter, Carl, G, Texas 1962
Lee, Jacky, QB, Cincinnati 1967–69
Lee, Willie, DT, Bethune-Cookman 1976
Liggett, Bob, DT, Nebraska 1970
Livingston, Mike, QB, Southern Methodist 1968–76
Lohmeyer, John, DE, Emporia State 1973, 1975–76
Longmire, Sam, DB, Purdue 1967–68
Lothamer, Ed, DT, Michigan State 1964–69, 1971–72
Lowe, Paul, RB, Oregon State 1968–69
Lynch, Jim, LB, Notre Dame 1967–76

M

Maczuzak, John, DT, Pittsburgh 1964
Maddox, Bob, DE, Frostburg State 1975–76
Marsalis, Jim, CB, Tennessee State 1969–75
Marshall, Henry, WR, Missouri 1976
Marshall, Larry, DB, Maryland 1972–73
Martin, Dave, LB, Notre Dame 1968
Martin, Don, CB, Yale 1975
Masters, Billy, TE, Louisiana State 1975–76
Matuszak, John, DT, Tampa 1974–75
Mays, Jerry, DT, Southern Methodist 1961–70
McCann, Jim, P, Arizona State 1975
McCarty, Mickey, E, Texas Christian 1969
McClinton, Curtis, RB, Kansas 1962–69
McNeil, Pat, RB, Baylor 1976
McVea, Warren, RB, Houston 1969–73
Mercer, Mike, K, Arizona State 1966
Merz, Curt, G, Iowa 1962–68
Miller, Bill, E, Miami 1962
Miller, Cleophus, RB, Arkansas AM&N 1974–75
Miller, Paul, DE, Louisiana State 1960–61
Mitchell, Willie, DB, Tennessee State 1964–71
Moorman, Mo, G, Texas A&M 1968–73
Morris, Donnie Joe, RB, North Texas State 1974

N

Napier, Buffalo, DT, Paul Quinn 1960–61
Nicholson, Jim, T, Michigan State 1974–76
Nix, Doyle, DB, Southern Methodist 1961
Nott, Mike, QB, Santa Clara 1976
Nunnery, RB, DT, Louisiana State 1960

O

Olsen, Orrin, C, Brigham Young 1976
Oriard, Mike, C, Notre Dame 1970–73
Osley, Willie, DB, Illinois 1974
Otis, Jim, RB, Ohio State 1971–72

P

Palewicz, Al, LB, Miami 1973
Palmer, Gary, G, Kansas 1975
Paul, Whitney, DE, Colorado 1976
Pearson, Barry, WR, Northwestern 1974–76
Peay, Francis, T, Missouri 1973–74
Pennington, Durwood, K, Georgia 1962
Peterson, Bill, LB, San Jose State 1975
Pitts, Frank, WR, Southern U. 1965–71
Ply, Bobby, DB, Baylor 1962–67
Podolak, Ed, RB, Iowa 1969–76
Porter, Lewis, E, Southern U. 1970
Pricer, Bill, RB, Oklahoma 1961
Prudhomme, Remi, G, Louisiana State 1968–69

R

Rasley, Rocky, G, Oregon State 1975
Reamon, Tommy, RB, Missouri 1976
Reardon, Kerry, CB, Iowa 1971–76
Reynolds, Al, G, Tarkio 1960–67
Rice, Andrew, DT, Texas Southern 1966
Richardson, Gloster, E, Jackson St. 1967–70
Robinson, Johnny, DB, Louisiana State 1960–71
Rochester, Paul, DT, Michigan State 1960–63
Romeo, Tony, E, Florida State 1961
Rosdahl, Hatch, DE, Penn State 1964–66
Ross, Louis, DE, South Carolina State 1975
Rozumek, Dave, LB, New Hampshire 1976
Rudnay, Jack, C, Northwestern 1970–76

S

Saxton, James, RB, Texas 1962
Seals, George, DT, Missouri 1972–73
Sellers, Goldie, DB, Grambling 1968–69
Sensibaugh, Mike, S, Ohio State 1971–75
Simons, Keith, DT, Minnesota 1976
Smith, Dave, WR, Indiana, Pa. 1973
Smith, Fletcher, DB, Tennessee State 1966–67
Smith, Noland, WR, Tennessee State 1967–69
Smith, Sid, T, USC 1970–72
Spikes, Jack, RB, Texas Christian 1960–64
Stein, Bob, LB, Minnesota 1969–72
Stenerud, Jan, K, Montana State 1967–76
Stone, Jack, T, Oregon 1960
Story, Bill, G, Southern Illinois 1975
Stover, Smokey, LB, N.E. Louisiana 1960–66
Strada, John, TE, William Jewell 1974

E.J. Holub

Willie Lanier

Mike Livingston

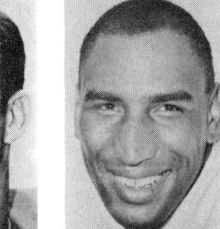
Jerry Mays

Curtis McClinton

Frank Pitts

Jim Tyrer

Stroud, Morris, TE, Clark 1969–74
Swink, Jim, RB, Texas Christian 1960

T

Taylor, Otis, WR, Prairie View 1965–75
Taylor, Steve, CB, Kansas 1976
Terrell, Marvin, G, Mississippi 1960–63
Thomas, Bill, RB, Boston College 1974
Thomas, Charlie, KR, Tennessee St. 1975
Thomas, Emmitt, CB, Bishop 1966–76
Thomas, Gene, RB, Florida A&M 1966–67
Thornbladh, Bob, LB, Michigan 1974
Trosch, Gene, DE, Miami 1967–69
Tyrer, Jim, T, Ohio State 1961–73

U

Upshaw, Marvin, DE, Trinity 1970–75

W

Walker, Wayne, K, N.W. Louisiana 1967
Walters, Rod, G, Iowa 1976
Walton, Wayne, G, Abilene Christian 1973
Warner, Charley, DB, Prairie View 1963–64
Webster, David, DB, Prairie View 1960–61
Werner, Clyde, LB, Washington 1970, 1972–74, 1976
West, Robert, WR, San Diego State 1972–73
White, Walter, TE, Maryland 1975–76
Williams, Lawrence, WR, Texas Tech 1976

Williamson, Fred, DB, Northwestern 1965–67
Wilson, Eddie, QB, Arizona 1962–64
Wilson, Jerrel, P, So. Mississippi 1963–76
Wilson, Mike, G, Dayton 1975
Wolf, James, DE, Prairie View 1976
Wood, Duane, DB, Oklahoma State 1960–64
Wright, Elmo, WR, Houston 1971–74

Y

Young, Wilbur, DE, William Penn 1971–76

Z

Zaruba, Carroll, DB, Nebraska 1960

Linebacker Bobby Bell, 1969.

Wide receiver Otis Taylor, 1972.

LOS ANGELES RAMS

1937 The National Football League granted a Cleveland franchise to a syndicate headed by Homer Marshman, February 13. Hugo Bezdek was named the first head coach. The Rams had a 1–10 record.
1938 After losing four games in a row, Marshman fired Bezdek and hired assistant Art Lewis. The Rams won three of their remaining seven games, led by quarterback Bob Snyder and a sure-handed end from Arkansas, Jim Benton.
1939 Earl (Dutch) Clark, former star player for Portsmouth and Detroit replaced Lewis as head coach, but Lewis remained with the Rams as an assistant. The club made it to .500 for the first time, finishing 5–5–1. Parker Hall, a rookie tailback who was the team's first draft choice, won the Joe Carr trophy awarded to the NFL's official most valuable player, although he was not named to the official all-league team.
1940 The Rams got off to a fast start, winning their first game. But despite the emergence of Johnny Drake, a powerful new all-pro fullback from Purdue, the team slumped to a 4–6–1 record.
1941 Marshman and his associates sold the Rams to Daniel F. Reeves and Fred Levy, Jr., in June, 1941. The price was $100,000. Reeves, 29, whose older brother, Ed, had owned a part of the Washington Redskins, became the youngest owner in pro football.
1942 Billy Evans, general manager, resigned. Charles (Chile) Walsh replaced Art Lewis as an assistant coach under Clark. Lt. Reeves and Maj. Levy departed for the armed forces. The team climbed to a 5–6–0 record. Johnny Drake retired.
1943 Levy sold out to Reeves, who obtained league permission to suspend operations in 1943. Clark resigned and Chile Walsh was named head coach. The team did not play because of World War II.
1944 Walsh became general manager and appointed Aldo (Buff) Donelli, the former Pittsburgh Steelers and Duquesne University coach, as new head coach. The team, comprised mostly of pickup players, finished with a 4–6 record. UCLA quarterback Bob Waterfield was drafted as a "future."
1945 Donelli entered the service and was replaced by Chile Walsh's brother, Adam, who had been the center on the Notre Dame teams that featured the Four Horsemen. Adam Walsh inherited a team bursting with talent. Waterfield joined the club and immediately demonstrated he was a brilliant all-around player and consummate leader. He led the Rams to a 9–1–0 season to win the team's first division title. Then, on an icy field, Waterfield led the Rams to a 15–14 victory over the Washington Redskins for the NFL championship. Despite the championship, Reeves lost $50,000. Reeves, who long had been dreaming of a shift to the West Coast, had to get a place to play. He coveted the Los Angeles Memorial Coliseum, an amateur stronghold since the 1932 Olympic Games were held there. By making a deal with George Preston Marshall to play a preseason game with Marshall's Redskins for *Los Angeles Times* Charities, Reeves secured the 101,296-seat Coliseum for his home field.
1946 Reeves petitioned the other owners at the league meeting to move his franchise from Cleveland to Los Angeles. He was refused, and he vowed he would sell the club and get out of football. The other owners reconsidered. The All-America Football Conference began operation the same year, meaning the new Los Angeles Rams had to compete with the Los Angeles Dons. The Rams drafted Notre Dame's All-America runner, Emil Sitko, number one, but he signed with the AAFC. However, in their first year in Los Angeles, the Rams had Tom Harmon, the former

Heisman trophy winner from Michigan who had returned from the armed forces, Kenny Washington, the former UCLA All-America, and Woody Strode. Washington and Strode were the first black players in the NFL since 1933. They also had Fred Gehrke at halfback, Jim Hardy as a backup quarterback, and Fred Naumetz, a center and linebacker. Waterfield led the NFL passers with 127 completions in 251 attempts for 1,747 yards and 18 touchdowns. Jim Benton led the league receivers with 63 catches for 981 yards. The Rams finished 6–4–1 but still lost money. Chile Walsh fired his brother, Adam, as head coach. Then Reeves fired Chile.
1947 Reeves assumed the duties of the general manager and hired Bob Snyder as head coach, with Joe Stydahar as an assistant. Financial losses mounted and Reeves decided he needed some partners. His former partner, Fred Levy; Ed Pauley and his brother Harold; and Hal Seley agreed to shoulder a proportionate share of the losses. In the process, they got one of the best bargains in sports history. For literally one dollar, Ed Pauley bought 30 percent of the stock.
1948 Snyder was fired and Clark Shaughnessy was named head coach, September 3. In the second game of the season, trailing the Eagles 28–0 with 16 minutes to play, Waterfield threw four touchdown passes and kicked four extra points for a 28–28 tie. The Rams lost four of their next five games before rebounding to win four of their last five. With Waterfield injured, Jim Hardy gained a club record 406 yards passing against the Chicago Cardinals in a 27–24 loss. Hardy completed 28 of 53 attempts. The team finished 6–5–1. Benton retired. Rookie receiver Tom Fears led the league receivers with 51 catches for 698 yards. Linebacker Don Paul of UCLA was another prominent rookie. The Rams lost approximately $250,000. Only the new partners kept the franchise alive by helping to absorb the losses. The AAFC Dons were the top pro team in Los Angeles, averaging 41,096 spectators to less than 34,000 for the Rams in the Coliseum.
1949 Reeves's scouting system, one of the most innovative in pro sports, began to produce some of its best results, and players started turning up with degrees from tiny, little-known colleges. The rookie crop included quarterback Norm Van Brocklin from Oregon; Elroy (Crazylegs) Hirsch, an end and back from Wisconsin who had played three seasons for the Chicago Rockets of the AAFC; runners Verda (Vitamin T.) Smith of Abilene Christian, and Paul (Tank) Younger from then little-known Grambling; and defensive back Jerry Williams from Washington State. Shaughnessy molded them into an exciting, wide-open, winning team and they began with six straight victories. The acquisition of Van Brocklin, while it provided depth at quarterback, was to begin a great controversy—one which has raged in Los Angeles down through the years even though many different players have been involved—of which man should be number one. This first controversy involved Waterfield and Van Brocklin. Although the Rams slumped near season's end, winning two and losing two with two ties, they hung on to win their first Western Division title since moving from Cleveland. Fears repeated as the top pass catcher in the NFL with 77 for 1,013 yards and nine touchdowns. Philadelphia, long a jinx team for the Rams, beat Los Angeles again, 14–0 in a mud-covered championship game in Los Angeles. A heavy rainstorm which had ruined the field kept the crowd down to 27,980.
1950 The National Football League absorbed three members of the All-America Football Conference, and the Rams were left as the only pro team in Los Angeles. Shaughnessy was fired because of "internal friction" within the organization. Joe Stydahar, 39, became the new head coach. Stydahar appointed Hampton Pool, Mel Hein, and Howard (Red) Hickey

as assistants. Another good group of rookies joined the Rams, players such as Bob Boyd, an end from Loyola of Los Angeles; Glenn Davis, half of the famed Army backfield combination of Davis and Blanchard; Woodley Lewis, a defensive back from Oregon; Dan Towler, a halfback from Washington & Jefferson, and Stan West, a middle guard from Oklahoma. In one game, the Rams ran up 70 points against Baltimore and 65 in another against Detroit. Against Green Bay, Fears caught 18 passes, an NFL single-game record. With a magnificent passing attack, the Rams ran up six straight victories and finished with a 9–3 record to tie the Chicago Bears for first place in the National Conference. They set 22 league records, scoring 466 points and 64 touchdowns. They gained 3,709 yards passing and 1,711 rushing. The Rams beat the Bears 24–14 in a playoff. In a classic league championship game, Cleveland used a field goal in the closing seconds to win 30–28 over Los Angeles in Cleveland. Glenn Davis, the former Heisman trophy winner at Army, raced 82 yards to a touchdown on a pass from Waterfield on the Rams' first play from scrimmage. Dick Hoerner scored on three- and one-yard runs and defensive end Larry Brink rumbled six yards to score with a recovered fumble. Otto Graham threw four touchdown passes to lead Cleveland. Fears led NFL receivers for the third straight year with 84 catches for 1,116 yards and seven touchdowns. Van Brocklin led NFL passers with 127 completions on 223 attempts for a club record 2,061 yards and 18 touchdowns.
1951 Stydahar was given a three-year contract. With Stydahar keeping the players happy and Pool devising ways to tap the great offensive resources, the Rams continued to win. The team drafted Bud McFadin, a 245-pound tackle from Texas, number one, and also picked up Dick Daugherty, a linebacker from Oregon; Norb Hecker, a defensive back from Baldwin-Wallace; Andy Robustelli, a defensive end from Arnold College, and Charley Toogood, a tackle from Nebraska. A preseason game with the Redskins drew 95,985 to the Coliseum. Towler and Younger, two big, fast backs, joined Hoerner in what was known as the "bull elephant backfield." Towler weighed 225 and Younger and Hoerner 220 each. Waterfield and Van Brocklin were still throwing passes to Hirsch and Fears. Van Brocklin passed for an NFL record 554 yards in a 54–14 win over the New York Yanks, September 28. Hirsch caught four from Van Brocklin against the Yanks for 41, 47, 26, and 1 yards. Later, against the Packers, he caught three scoring passes from Waterfield for 72, 37, and 19 yards. He led the NFL receivers with 66 catches for 1,495 yards. Waterfield took over the NFL leadership from Van Brocklin with 88 completions in 176 attempts for 1,566 yards and 13 touchdowns. The Rams amassed more total yards, 5,506, than any club in NFL history. The Rams won the division with an 8–4 record, finishing a half-game ahead of Detroit and San Francisco. In the NFL championship game, Los Angeles defeated Cleveland 24–17 on a pass from Van Brocklin to the double-teamed Fears which covered 73 yards. Hoerner and Towler also scored on one-yard bursts, and Waterfield kicked a 17-yard field goal. It was the Rams' first NFL championship in Los Angeles.
1952 Billy Wade, a quarterback from Vanderbilt, was the bonus draft choice. Guard Duane Putnam from College of the Pacific was another draft selection. Dick (Night Train) Lane was signed as a free agent. Skeet Quinlan, a back from San Diego State, was another promising rookie. The Rams traded 11 players to the Dallas Texans, including Hoerner, for linebacker Les Richter, who then entered the army for two years. A serious rift began to develop between Stydahar and his top assistant, Pool. After a season-opening loss to Cleveland, 37–7, Stydahar

brought his problems with Pool to Reeves and when the dust had settled, Stydahar was gone and Pool, 37, was named new head coach. The Rams lost three of their first four games, but their lone victory in that stretch was a 30–28 win over Green Bay in the third game of the season. Trailing 28–6 in the last quarter, Waterfield rallied the Rams to 24 points for the victory, climaxing with a 92-yard drive in the last two minutes that took seven plays, including three Waterfield pass completions for gains of 20, 30, and 26 yards. Then the Rams won eight straight to tie the Detroit Lions for first place in the National Conference. The Rams lost 31–21 to Detroit in the playoff game. Van Brocklin took over the NFL passing leadership from Waterfield by completing 113 of 205 attempts for 1,736 yards and 14 touchdowns. Towler became the first Ram to lead the NFL in rushing when he gained 894 yards. Waterfield announced his retirement. He had led the team to four division titles and two NFL championships. Pete Rozelle, the Sports Information Director at the University of San Francisco, was hired as a member of the Rams' public relations staff.

1953 Club coowner Harold Pauley died. The number one draft choice was Donn Moomaw, an All-America linebacker from UCLA, but he chose to go into the ministry instead of playing pro football. Rookies included Rudy Bukich, a quarterback from USC; Gene (Big Daddy) Lipscomb, a defensive tackle who had not attended college; and Harland Svare, a linebacker from Washington State. Los Angeles defeated Detroit twice, 31–19 and 37–24. The Rams finished 8–3–1, losing three games by a total of eight points. They placed third in the Western Conference.

1954 The Rams' bonus choice in the 1952 draft, Billy Wade, joined the team following military service. Richter also joined the club from the army and moved in to start at linebacker. Amid rumors of dissension, the Rams were no longer as consistent on offense and the defense began to deteriorate. They skidded to fourth place at 6–5–1 and all of Pool's assistant coaches resigned. Van Brocklin won the NFL passing title for the third time in five years, by completing 139 of 260 passes for 2,637 yards, third best yardage figure in NFL history. Elroy Hirsch announced his retirement at the end of the season.

1955 Pool resigned. "Hamp had too many strikes against him," said Reeves. Then began a long, well-publicized search from a new Rams' coach. When the announcement finally came, January 26, many people were disappointed. Sid Gillman was the selection. Although he was well respected by football people and had been highly successful at the University of Cincinnati, the general Los Angeles public reaction was skeptical. Ron Waller from Maryland was drafted as a defensive back. Other outstanding rookies were Don Burroughs, a defensive back from Colorado State University, and Larry Morris, a linebacker and the number one draft choice from Georgia Tech. Hirsch was talked out of his retirement just before the start of the regular season. Linebacker Don Paul was traded to Cleveland. Gillman switched Waller to offense and the rookie had an outstanding season, rushing for 716 yards and was named to the all-pro team. The Rams lost two games to the Chicago Bears, but still finished a half game in front of Chicago in the Western Conference. In the league championship game before a record crowd of 85,693 in Los Angeles, the Rams were no match for the Cleveland Browns, losing 38–14. Cleveland intercepted seven Los Angeles passes—six by Van Brocklin. Some problems developed among the feuding Rams' owners. Reeves's old friend, Fred Levy, switched his vote and Reeves was relieved of the directorship of the team. Deacon Dan Towler retired with a club record 3,493 yards rushing, a career average of 5.2 yards per carry.

1956 Leon Clarke, an end from USC, and Tom Wilson, a running back with no college experience, were among the new additions to the club. The championship game loss to Cleveland convinced Gillman to make major changes. Veterans such as Robustelli and Hughes were traded. Lipscomb was picked up by Baltimore for the $100 waiver price. Gillman soon found he was not compatible with Van Brocklin. Wade began to get more playing time. Many veterans on the club were angered over Van Brocklin's bench-sitting. The fans split into Van Brocklin and Wade factions. Fears, Quinlan, and Toogood retired.

1957 McFadin, who was seriously wounded in an off-season shooting incident, retired. The Rams' owners signed a five-year operational contract and named Rozelle general manager. The club itself still was in the midst of a major rebuilding program. New faces included John Arnett, who was the number one draft choice from USC; George Strugar, a hulking defensive tackle from Washington State; Jesse Witenton, a defensive back from Texas Western; and Del Shofner, a defensive back and end from Baylor. The Rams made Shofner a first round draft choice, obtained from the New York Giants in return for two players, Harland Svare and Andy Robustelli. In a game in the Coliseum, the Rams drew 102,368—a pro football record—to see a 37–24 victory over San Francisco. Hirsch retired again. A disgruntled Van Brocklin also announced his retirement.

1958 The top draft choice was Lou Michaels, a linebacker from Kentucky who was obtained in a trade with Washington. The Rams' other first-round pick was Jim (Red) Phillips, an end from Auburn. Van Brocklin was traded to Philadelphia in the preseason for guard Buck Lansford and defensive back Jimmy Harris and a first round draft pick that the Rams used to pick Dick Bass. That move made Wade the number one quarterback for Los Angeles, but as a backup for Wade the Rams drafted Frank Ryan, the Rice University science major. Gillman made other moves to improve the Rams' offense. He put Jon Arnett in the starting backfield and shifted Del Shofner from defensive back to wide receiver. A crowd of 100,470 saw the Rams defeat the Chicago Bears 41–35 on Arnett's biggest day as a Ram. In 60 minutes, he ran a screen pass from Wade for 72 yards to the Chicago 3 to set up a touchdown; returned punts for 36 and 58 yards to set up touchdowns, and ran 52 yards from scrimmage to the Bears' 4 to set up another score. He finished the day with 298 total yards, yet never scored. A crowd of 100,202 showed up as the Rams defeated Baltimore's championship-bound Colts 30–28. Wade hit Shofner on a pass play covering 92 yards against the Bears, October 19. Wade and Red Phillips combined on a 93-yard pass play against Green Bay, November 16. Wade set several team passing records, including most yardage in a season—2,875 yards, just 63 yards short of the all-time NFL single-season record for yards gained passing, set by Sammy Baugh. Wade hit 181 of 341 passes for 18 touchdowns, and the Rams improved to an 8–4 record. Shofner caught 51 passes and averaged 21 yards a catch. Daugherty retired.

1959 Rozelle traded the rights to nine players to the Chicago Cardinals for running back Ollie Matson. Included in the Rams' package to the Cardinals were Frank Fuller, a defensive tackle, and Ken Panfil, another starting tackle. Later, Rozelle acquired defensive end Gene Brito from Washington. Halfback Dick Bass of College of the Pacific was drafted as a "future." Joe Marconi, a running back from West Virginia, was another draft choice, and another was tough defensive back Ed Meador, who had been a running back at little Arkansas Tech. The New York Giants defeated the Rams 23–21 in the opening game. San Francisco shut the Rams out the next week 34–0. The Rams lost their last eight games to finish

last in the Western Conference with a 2–10 record. Matson gained 837 yards in his first season. Reeves reportedly still had confidence in his head coach, but some of the other owners didn't. Gillman and his entire staff resigned on the last day of the season. Clarke retired. Burroughs was traded to Philadelphia.

1960 The Rams drafted Billy Cannon, the Heisman trophy winning halfback from Louisiana State, number one. He also was picked number one by Houston of the new American Football League. His case went to court, which ruled he was property of the Houston club. Following the death of Commissioner Bert Bell in November, 1959 a search for a successor began—and Rozelle was the compromise selection of the owners. Reeves hired one of his all-time favorites, Hirsch, as the new general manager. Another all-time Ram, Waterfield, was named head coach; Waterfield chose his old coach, Pool, and former teammates Fears and Paul to be among his assistants. Bass, having graduated, joined the club and showed great promise as a rookie. He averaged nearly five yards per carry and gained 505 yards on rushing, pass receiving and kick returning. The club improved on its 1959 record, going 4–7–1.

1961 The top draft choice was Marlin McKeever, an end from USC. The Rams also picked up Joe Scibelli, an offensive guard from Notre Dame, and Charlie Cowan, an offensive tackle from New Mexico Highlands. The Ram quarterback controversy combined with the rebuilding drive in a series of complicated trades on March 2. The Rams traded Wade to Chicago's Bears for defensive back Erich Barnes and quarterback Zeke Bratkowski. Then the Rams traded Barnes and linebacker John Guzick to the New York Giants for defensive back Lindon Crow plus a first draft choice—which turned out to be North Carolina State's prized quarterback Roman Gabriel. Bass teamed with Arnett to give Los Angeles a dynamic, if little, running combination. But the defense, which boasted a promising rookie defensive end named David (Deacon) Jones, Meador, Lamar Lundy and others, had its problems and the Rams wound up only 4–10, ahead of only Minnesota, the expansion team.

1962 In a sealed-bid auction among Reeves, Pauley, Levy, Seley, and comedian Bob Hope, Reeves came up with the high bid of $7.1 million and reacquired control of the franchise. It cost Reeves $4.8 million to purchase the shares his partners had got for one dollar and a share of the liabilities just a few years earlier. A new corporation, the Los Angeles Rams Football Company, was headed by Reeves (51 percent), with 11 other minority partners. The Rams continued rebuilding through the draft. Besides Gabriel, Los Angeles also drafted defensive tackle Merlin Olsen from Utah State and Joe Carollo, a tackle from Notre Dame. Svare, 32, replaced Paul as defensive line coach. The new, promising rookies were unable to get the job done, however, and eight games into the season, Svare took over from Waterfield as head coach, and the Rams finished a dismal 1–12–1, the only victory a 28–14 victory over San Francisco. Bass became the first Ram to gain 1,000 yards rushing in a season, picking up 1,033 on 196 carries.

1963 Richter retired before the season. Defensive tackle Roosevelt Grier was obtained in a trade with the New York Giants. Torn by another quarterback controversy involving Bratkowski, Gabriel, and Terry Baker, the Heisman trophy winner and number one draft choice from Oregon State, the team lost its first five games. Svare installed Gabriel at quarterback and the team won five of its last nine games. A new defensive front four of Jones, Olsen, Lamar Lundy, and Grier began to make its presence felt. They became known as the Fearsome Foursome.

1964 The Rams signed a 10-year contract to play in the Coliseum's new, cut-down stadium—65,000 seats. Fourteen rookies made the team—including tight end Billy Truax from Louisiana State—but the team produced the same total of wins, five. And another quarterback Bill Munson from Utah State, entered the picture as the number one draft choice. Muson took over when Gabriel was injured early.

1965 After the Coliseum installed theater-type seats, Reeves cracked, "We want to be sure our fans suffer in comfort." In a trade with Minnesota, the Rams picked up Notre Dame receiver Jack Snow, the Vikings' number one choice, for Phillips and defensive tackle Gary Larsen. The Rams won only four games, but three came in the last four games—against Green Bay's NFL champions, St. Louis, and Cleveland—with Gabriel at quarterback after Munson injured his knee. Svare was fired as coach.

1966 The merger of the NFL and AFL was consummated, but no peace came to the Rams. It took a court battle to get Chicago Bears' assistant coach George Allen released from a contract with George Halas to become the Rams' new head coach. Allen had coached with the Rams as an assistant on Gillman's staff in 1957. The team's practice and coaching facilities were moved to Long Beach. The top draft choice was Tom Mack, a guard from Michigan. Bob Kelley, the radio voice of the Rams since 1937 and a vital force in their success in California, died. Allen made Gabriel the number one quarterback. The team had a chance to finish second in the Western Conference until the final game, a 27–23 loss to champion Green Bay, and finished 8–6.

1967 After five years at Chapman College in Orange County, the club moved its training camp to California State-Fullerton. Allen, who put little faith in draft picks, traded Los Angeles's number one choice to Minnesota. Allen picked up Willie Ellison, a running back from Texas Southern, on the second round. With the defense now operating at optimum efficiency and the offense exhibiting a new ball-control style, Los Angeles won eight in a row at season's end, including a 27–24 victory over Green Bay. Los Angeles was leading the Packers 17–10 when Green Bay's Travis Williams sprinted 104 yards with a kickoff to tie it. The Rams regained the lead on a Bruce Gossett field goal and seemed in control. Then Bass fumbled. Green Bay recovered and marched in for the go-ahead touchdown. With just 54 second left in the game, Tony Guillory blocked a Packers' punt and Claude Crabb picked up the ball and ran it to Green Bay's 5-yard line with 44 second to play. Ten seconds later, Gabriel threw a game-winning touchdown pass to Bernie Casey. The next week, the Rams beat Baltimore 34–10 to give Los Angeles an 11–1–2 record and its first division title since 1955. The year ended with a 28–7 loss to Green Bay in the Western Conference title game. Gabriel finished the year with a club record 25 touchdown passes, gaining 2,779 yards on 196 completions in 371 attempts.

1968 The Rams defeated Cleveland 30–6 in the Playoff Bowl, a game between conference runners-up, January 7. Los Angeles drafted Gary Beban, the All-America quarterback and Heisman Trophy winner from UCLA. Beban was traded to Washington for a number one pick before the preseason games began. Los Angeles had another outstanding season (10–3–1), and Baltimore won 13 of 14 games to finish first in the Coastal Division. The Rams' defense set a 14-game record for fewest yards allowed, 3,118. A strong personality difference surfaced between Reeves and Allen, and Reeves fired the head coach, December 26. Rams players immediately raised an outcry in defense of Allen. A dozen players appeared with Allen in a televised press conference.

1969 Reeves called Allen and asked him to come back as coach, January 1. Allen did not give an answer immediately. Then, at a press conference, Reeves announced that Allen had been retained as coach, January 6. Hirsch left his job as assistant to

Reeves to become athletic director at his alma mater, the University of Wisconsin. He was replaced by Jack Teele. John Sanders became assistant general manager. Los Angeles had three draft choices on the first round and they used them to pick running back Larry Smith from Florida, wide receiver Jim Seymour from Notre Dame, and tight end Bob Klein from USC. The Rams traded wide receiver Harold Jackson and defensive end John Zook for running back Izzy Lang. The team won its first 11 games. The streak ended at the Coliseum when Minnesota scored a 20–13 victory. Detroit shut out Los Angeles 28–0. Baltimore handed the Rams a 13–7 loss. Minnesota defeated the Rams 23–20 in the Western Conference title game in Bloomington, overcoming the Rams' 17–7 lead. Again, the Rams set new attendance records, drawing 1,307,989 to 22 games. Gabriel was named as the league's most valuable player. He completed 217 of 399 passes for 2,549 yards and 24 touchdowns. He set Rams' records for both attempts and completions. Bass retired with a career rushing record of 5,417 yards, tops in Rams' history.

1970 The Rams began their twenty-fifth anniversary year in Los Angeles with a 31–0 victory over Dallas in the Playoff Bowl in Miami. Los Angeles picked a linebacker, Jack Reynolds from Tennessee, number one in the draft. They also got center Rich Saul of Michigan State. The Rams compiled a 9–4–1 record, good for second place in the Western Division. The team drew a record 904,979 for 14 regular season games. At the end of the season, it was announced that George Allen's contract would not be renewed. Allen had lasted five years, tying him with Sid Gillman for the Rams' longevity record. Allen's teams had won 49, lost 17, and tied 4.

1971 Tommy Prothro, head coach of UCLA, was named the new Rams' coach. Dan Reeves died of Hodgkin's disease in New York, April 15. William A. Barnes, Reeves's long-time friend and business associate, became president and general manager. Prothro made a trade with George Allen, who had taken the job coaching the Washington Redskins. Prothro sent linebackers Jack Pardee, Myron Pottios, and Maxie Baughan, and defensive tackle Diron Talbert for linebacker Marlin McKeever and a host of draft choices. The Rams used one of the draft choices to choose Isiah Robertson, a linebacker from Southern University. The Rams also drafted Jack Youngblood, a defensive end from Florida; and Dave Elmendorf, a defensive back from Texas A&M. The Rams traded for Lance Rentzel, a controversial wide receiver from Dallas, and Travis Williams, a running back-kick returner from Green Bay. Faced with one of the toughest schedules in the league, the Rams went 8–5–1 and finished second to San Francisco in the NFC West. The Rams lost to George Allen and the Redskins 38–24 in a Monday night game.

1972 Robert Irsay, a Chicago-based industrialist, purchased the Rams from the Reeves estate for $19 million. Irsay then traded the franchise to Carroll Rosenbloom in exchange for the Baltimore Colts and $3 to $4 million. Rosenbloom named Don Klosterman as executive vice president and general manager and moved the training camp from Fullerton to California State-Long Beach. The Rams drafted Jim Bertelsen, a running back from Texas, on the second round, and Lawrence McCutcheon, a running back from Colorado State University, on the third. Larry Brooks, a defensive tackle from Virginia State, came on the fourteenth round. Fred Dryer, a defensive end, was obtained in a trade with New England. The season was marred by injuries, particularly a mysterious ailment in Gabriel's right arm. The Rams were in contention in the first half of the season, then lost five of their last six and finished 6–7–1. Prothro and his coaching staff were dismissed.

1973 Chuck Knox, a Detroit Lions' assistant, was

named head coach. The team returned to the colorful blue and gold uniforms of the 1950s after years of playing in blue and white. Klosterman traded defensive tackle Coy Bacon and running back Bob Thomas to San Diego for quarterback John Hadl. Ron Jaworski, a quick, strong-armed quarterback from Youngstown State, was drafted on the second round. Hadl moved in as the Rams' offensive leader and Gabriel asked to be traded. Gabriel was traded to Philadelphia for wide receiver Harold Jackson, plus first-round draft picks in 1974 and 1975 and a third-round choice in 1975. After a year in Long Beach, the team switched back to California State-Fullerton for training. The Rams won 12 of 14 games, the most victories in the team's history. Dallas upset the Rams 27–16 in the divisional playoffs. Hadl was named the NFC's most valuable player, and Knox was chosen coach of the year. McCutcheon gained 1,097 yards, becoming the third Ram in history to top 1,000 yards.

1974 Rosebloom's son, Steve, was named assistant to the president. John Cappelletti, the Heisman trophy winning running back from Penn State, was selected number one in the college draft. Hadl was traded to Green Bay after the Rams began the year with a 3–2 record and Los Angeles got five draft choices in return. Backup quarterback James Harris helped the Rams to a 10–4 record and another division title. Harris was the first black to quarterback a pro team to a championship. But the Rams were ousted once again in the playoffs. They beat Washington 19–10 in the divisional playoff, the Rams' first playoff victory since the 1951 championship. Then they lost 14–10 to Minnesota in the NFC title game at Minnesota. McCutcheon set a Rams' single-season rushing record by running for 1,109 yards on 236 carries. He added another 408 yards on 39 pass receptions and scored five touchdowns.

1975 The Rams had three first-round choices in the draft and they used them to select Mike Fanning, a defensive tackle from Notre Dame; Dennis Harrah, a guard from Miami; and Doug France, a tackle from Ohio State. The Rams lost 18–7 to Dallas in the opener. Los Angeles scored a 13–10 overtime victory over San Diego in the fourth week of the season. After a 24–23 loss to San Francisco, the Rams won six straight to close the regular season. Harris injured his shoulder in the third-to-last game against New Orleans and Ron Jaworski took over to lead victories over Green Bay and defending Super Bowl champion Pittsburgh. Led by the front four of Olsen, Youngblood, Larry Brooks (who was forced out with a knee injury the last six games), and Dryer, the Rams allowed the second fewest number of points, 135, in NFL history over a 14-game season. The Rams defeated St. Louis 35–23 in the divisional playoff game with Jaworski again filling in for Harris. McCutcheon broke an NFC playoff record with 202 yards on 37 carries. Dallas hammered the Rams 37–7 in the NFC championship game. Scibelli, Cowan, and Snow retired.

1976 Knox was given a new five-year contract by Rosenbloom, with a five-year mutual option. Then Knox was presented with that age-old problem for Rams head coaches: a quarterback controversy. Harris produced the Rams' best single-game passing performance in 25 years, completing 17 of 29 passes for 436 yards and two touchdowns in a 31–28 win over Miami. Shifting from Harris to Jaworski to first-year player Pat Haden, Knox finally settled on Haden for the last five games of the season. Haden, a poised, young Rhodes Scholar from USC who had played in the World Football League before coming to the Rams when the WFL folded, led the Rams to another Western Division championship. Los Angeles edged Dallas 14–12 in the first round of the playoffs. But there was frustration again in Minnesota. On their first drive in the NFC championship game, the Rams

Dick Bass   *Bob Boyd*   *Willie Ellison*   *Dick Huffman*   *Harold Jackson*   *Monte Jackson*   *D. (Deacon) Jones*

stalled inside the Vikings' 1-yard line on fourth down and elected to allow Tom Dempsey to try a field goal. It was blocked and returned for a 90-yard touchdown by the Vikings' Bobby Bryant. The Vikings went on to score a 24–13 victory. Olsen retired.

1977 Knox ended prolonged rumors that he would become the new head coach of the Detroit Lions by announcing that he intended to honor his Rams' contract and remain in Los Angeles. Jaworski played out his option and the rights to him were traded to Philadelphia for tight end Charles Young, who also had played out his option.

MEMBERS OF HALL OF FAME:
Tom Fears, Bill George, Elroy Hirsch, Dick (Night Train) Lane, Ollie Matson, Dan Reeves, Andy Robustelli, Norm Van Brocklin, Bob Waterfield.

RAMS RECORD 1937–76

Year	Won	Lost	Tied	Pct.	Pts.	OP
Cleveland Rams						
1937	1	10	0	.091	75	207
1938	4	7	0	.363	131	215
1939	5	5	1	.500	195	164
1940	4	6	1	.400	171	191
1941	2	9	0	.182	116	244
1942	5	6	0	.455	150	207
1943		The Rams suspended operations				
1944	4	6	0	.400	188	224
1945‡	9	1	0	.900	244	136
Los Angeles Rams						
1946	6	4	1	.600	277	257
1947	6	6	0	.500	259	214
1948	6	5	1	.545	327	269
1949§	8	2	2	.800	360	239
1950§	9	3	0	.750	466	309
1951‡	8	4	0	.667	392	261
1952	9	3	0	.750	349	234
1953§	8	3	1	.727	366	236
1954	6	5	1	.545	314	285
1955‡	8	3	1	.727	260	231
1956	4	8	0	.333	291	307
1957	6	6	0	.500	307	278
1958	8	4	0	.667	344	278
1959	2	10	0	.167	242	315
1960	4	7	1	.364	265	297
1961	4	10	0	.286	263	333
1962	1	12	1	.077	220	334
1963	5	9	0	.357	210	350
1964	5	7	2	.417	283	339
1965	4	10	0	.286	269	328
1966	8	6	0	.571	289	212
1967†	11	1	2	.917	398	196
1968	10	3	1	.769	312	200
1969†	11	3	0	.786	320	243
1970	9	4	1	.692	325	202
1971	8	5	1	.615	313	260
1972	6	7	1	.464	291	286
1973§	12	2	0	.857	388	178
1974§	10	4	0	.714	263	181
1975§	12	2	0	.857	312	135
1976§	10	3	1	.750	351	190
39 Years	**258**	**211**	**20**	**.548**	**10,622**	**9,226**

‡*NFL Champion*
§*NFC Western Division Champion*
†*NFL Coastal Division Champion*

RECORD HOLDERS

Rushing (Yards)	Lawrence McCutcheon, 1976	1,168
Passing (Pct.)	Bill Wade, 1959	58.6
Passing (Yards)	Bill Wade, 1958	2,875
Passing (TDs)	Roman Gabriel, 1967	25
Receiving (No.)	Tom Fears, 1950	84
Receiving (Yards)	Elroy (Crazylegs) Hirsch, 1951	1,495
Interceptions (No.)	Dick (Night Train) Lane, 1952	14
Punting (Avg.)	Danny Villanueva, 1962	45.5
Punt Ret. (Avg.)	Woodley Lewis, 1952	18.5
Kickoff Ret. (Avg.)	Verda (Vitamin T.) Smith, 1950	33.7
Touchdowns (Total)	Elroy (Crazylegs) Hirsch, 1951	17
Field Goals Made	David Ray, 1970	29
Points (No.)	David Ray, 1970	121

COACHING HISTORY

1937–39	Hugo Bezdek*	1–13–0
1938	Art Lewis	4– 4–0
1939–42	Earl (Dutch) Clark	16–26–2
1943	The Rams suspended operations	
1944	Aldo (Buff) Donelli	4– 6–0
1945–46	Adam Walsh	15– 5–1
1947	Bob Snyder	6– 6–0
1948–49	Clark Shaughnessy	14– 7–3
1950–51	Joe Stydahar	17– 7–0
1952–54	Hampton Pool	23–11–2
1955–59	Sid Gillman	28–31–1
1960–62	Bob Waterfield**	9–24–1
1962–65	Harland Svare	14–31–3
1966–70	George Allen	49–17–4
1971–72	Tommy Prothro	14–12–2
1973–76	Chuck Knox	44–11–1

*Replaced after three games in 1938
**Resigned after eight games in 1962

FIRST PLAYER SELECTED

1937	Johnny Drake, B, Purdue	
1938	Corbett Davis, B, Indiana	
1939	Parker Hall, B, Mississippi	
1940	Ollie Cordill, B, Rice	
1941	Rudy Mucha, C, Washington	
1942	Jack Wilson, B, Baylor	
1943	Mike Holovak, B, Boston College	
1944	Tony Butkovich, B, Illinois	
1945	Elroy (Crazylegs) Hirsch, B, Wisconsin	
1946	Emil Sitko, B, Notre Dame	
1947	Herman Wedemeyer, B, St. Mary's	
1948	Tom Keane, B (2), West Virginia	
1949	Bobby Thomason, B, VMI	
1950	Ralph Pasquariello, B, Villanova	
1951	Bud McFadin, G, Texas	
1952	Bill Wade, B, Vanderbilt	
1953	Donn Moomaw, C, UCLA	
1954	Ed Beatty, C, Cincinnati	
1955	Larry Morris, C, Georgia Tech	
1956	Joe Marconi, B, West Virginia	
1957	Jon Arnett, B, USC	
1958	Lou Michaels, T, Kentucky	
1959	Dick Bass, B, Pacific	
1960	Billy Cannon, RB, Louisiana State	
1961	Marlin McKeever, E-LB, USC	
1962	Roman Gabriel, QB, North Carolina	
1963	Terry Baker, QB, Oregon State	
1964	Bill Munson, QB, Utah State	
1965	Clarence Williams, CB, Washington State	
1966	Tom Mack, G, Michigan	
1967	Willie Ellison, RB (2), Texas Southern	
1968	Gary Beban, QB (2), UCLA	
1969	Larry Smith, RB, Florida	
1970	Jack Reynolds, LB, Tennessee	
1971	Isiah Robertson, LB, Southern U.	
1972	Jim Bertelsen, RB (2), Texas	
1973	Cullen Bryant, DB (2), Colorado	
1974	John Cappelletti, RB, Penn State	
1975	Mike Fanning, DT, Notre Dame	
1976	Kevin McLain, LB, Colorado State	

CLEVELAND RAMS, 1937–45;
LOS ANGELES RAMS, 1946–76

Adams, Chester, T, Ohio U.	1939–42
Adams, John, TE, Cal State-L.A.	1963
Agajanian, Ben, K, New Mexico	1953
Agler, Bob, RB, Otterbein	1948–49
Alexander, Kermit, DB, UCLA	1970–71
Alfonse, Jules, B, Minnesota	1937–38
Allen, Duane, E, Santa Ana J.C.	1961–64
Anderson, Bruce, DE, Williamette	1966
Anderson, Stanley, E, Stanford	1941
Andrako, Stephen, C, Ohio State	1941
Armstrong, Graham, T, John Carroll,	1941, 1945
Arnett, Jon, RB, USC	1957–63
Atkins, Pervis, RB, New Mexico State	1961–63
Atty, Alexander, G, West Virginia	1939

B

Bacon, Coy, DT, Jackson State	1968–72
Bagarus, Steve, RB, Notre Dame	1947
Baker, John, DT, N. Carolina Coll.	1968–61
Baker, Terry, QB-RB, Oregon State	1963–65
Baker, Tony, RB, Iowa State	1973–74

Banta, Jack, RB, USC	1946–48
Barber, Mark, B, S. Dakota State	1937
Barle, Louis, T, None	1939
Barry, Paul, RB, Tulsa	1960–69
Bass, Dick, RB, Pacific	1960–69
Baughan, Maxie, LB, Georgia Tech	1966–70
Beathard, Pete, QB, USC	1972
Benton, Jim, E, Arkansas	1938–42, 1944–47
Bernard, David, B, Mississippi	1944–45
Berry, Cornelius, E, N. Carolina State	1940
Bertelsen, Jim, RB, Texas	1972–76
Bettridge, John, B, Ohio State	1937
Bighead, Jack, E, Pepperdine	1955
Bleeker, Mel, RB, USC	1947
Boone, Robert, B, Elon	1942
Bostick, Lewis, G, Alabama	1939–42
Bouley, Gil, T, Boston College	1945–50
Bowers, Bill, DB, USC	1954
Boyd, Bob, E, Loyola, Calif.	1950–57
Boeke, Jim, T, Heidelberg	1960–63
Braatz, Tom, E, Marquette	1958
Bradshaw, Charles, T, Baylor	1958–60
Brahm, Lawrence, G, Temple	1942
Bratkowski, Zeke, QB, Georgia	1961–63
Bravo, Alex, DB, Cal Poly-San Luis Obispo	1957–58
Brazell, Carl, B, Baylor	1938
Breen, Gene, LB, Virginia Tech	1967–68
Brink, Larry, DE, No. Illinois	1948–53
Brito, Gene, DE, Loyola, Calif.	1959–60
Britt, Charley, DB, Georgia	1960–63
Brooks, Larry, DT, Virginia State	1972–76
Brown, Bob, T, Nebraska	1969–70
Brown, Fred, LB, Miami	1965
Brown, Roger, DT, Maryland State	1967–69
Brown, Willie, E-RB, USC	1964–65
Brumbaugh, Carl, B, Florida	1937
Bruney, Fred, DB, Ohio State	1948
Bryant, Cullen, RB, Colorado	1973–76
Buckley, Philip, E, Xavier	1937
Budka, Frank, DB, Notre Dame	1964
Bukich, Rudy, QB, USC	1953–56
Burke, Mike, P, Miami	1974
Burman, George, C-G, Northwestern	1967–70
Burmeister, Forrest, B, Purdue	1937
Burroughs, Don, DB, Colorado A&M	1955–59
Busich, Samuel, E, Ohio State	1937
Buzin, Rich, T, Penn State	1971
Byrd, Mac, LB, USC	1965

C

Cahill, Dave, DT, Northern Arizona	1967
Cappelletti, John, RB, Penn State	1974–76
Carrell, Duane, P, Florida State	1975
Carey, Bob, E, Michigan State	1952, 1954, 1956
Carollo, Joe T, Notre Dame	1962–68, 1971
Casey, Bernie, FL, Bowling Green	1967–68
Cash, Rick, DE, N.E. Missouri	1969–70
Casner, Ken, T, Baylor	1952
Cason, Jim, DB, Louisiana State	1955–56
Castete, Jesse, DB, McNeese State	1956–57
Champagne, Ed, T, Louisiana State	1947–50
Chapple, Dave, P, Cal-Santa Barbara	1972–74
Cherundolo, Chuck, C, Penn State	1937–39
Chesbro, Marcel, G, Colgate	1938
Chuy, Don, G, Clemson	1963–68
Clark, Al, CB-S, E. Michigan	1972–75
Clarke, Leon, E, USC	1956–59
Clay, Boyd, T, Tennessee	1940–42, 1944
Colella, Thomas, B, Canisius	1944–45
Collier, Bob, T, Southern Methodist	1951
Conkright, William, C, Oklahoma	1939–45
Conlee, Gerald, C, St. Mary's	1938
Cooper, William, T, Oberlin	1937
Corbo, Thomas, G, Duquesne	1944
Cordileone, Lou, G, Clemson	1962
Cordill, Oliver, B, Rice	1940
Corn, Joe, RB, None	
Cothren, Paige, PK, Mississippi	1957–58
Cowan, Charlie, T, New Mex. Highlands	1961–75
Cowhig, Jerry, RB, Notre Dame	1947–49
Cowlings, Al, DE, USC	1975
Coyle, Ross, DB, Oklahoma	1961
Crabb, Claude, DB, Colorado	1966–68

Les Josephson

Lamar Lundy

Tom Mack

Leon McLaughlin

Eddie Meador

Jack Pardee

Jim (Red) Phillips

Cross, Bobby, T, Kilgore J.C. 1954–55
Cross, Irv, DB, Northwestern 1966–68
Crow, Lindon, DB, USC 1961–64
Crowder, Earl, B, Oklahoma 1940
Curran, Pat, TE-RB, Lakeland 1969–74
Currie, Dan, LB, Michigan State 1965–66
Curry, Bill, C, Georgia Tech 1974
Currivan, Don, DE, Boston College 1948–49

D

Dahms, Tom, T, San Diego State 1951–54
Dale, Carroll, E, Virginia Tech 1960–64
Dalsasso, Christopher, T, Indiana 1937
Daniel, Willie, DB, Mississippi State 1967–69
Daugherty, Dick, LB, Oregon 1951–58
David, Bob, G, Villanova 1947–48
Davis, Corbett, QB, Indiana 1938–42
Davis, Glenn, RB, Army 1950–51
Davis, Roger, G, Syracuse 1964
Dean, Hal, G, Ohio State 1947–49
DeFruiter, Bob, DB, Nebraska 1948
deLauer, Robert, C, USC 1945–46
DeMarco, Bob, C, Dayton 1975
Dempsey, Tom, K, Palomar J.C. 1975–76
Dennis, Mike, RB, Mississippi 1968–69
Dickson, Paul, T, Baylor 1959
Doll, Don, DB, USC 1964
Dougherty, Bob, LB, Kentucky 1947
Dowd, Gerald, C, St. Mary's 1939
Drake, Bill, DB, Oregon 1973–74
Drake, John, B, Purdue 1937–41
Dryer, Fred, DE, San Diego State 1972–76
Dunstan, Elwyn, T, Portland 1939–41
Dwyer, Jack, DB, Loyola, Calif. 1952–54
Dyer, Henry, RB, Grambling 1966–68

E

Eason, Roger, G, Oklahoma 1945–48
Ekern, Carl, LB, San Jose State 1976
Ellena, Jack, MG, UCLA 1955–56
Ellersick, Don, DB, Washington State 1960
Ellison, Willie, RB, Texas Southern 1967–72
Elmendorf, Dave, S, Texas A&M 1971–76
Elston, Arthur, C, USC 1942
Emerick, Robert, T, Miami, Ohio 1937
Evey, Dick, DT, Tennessee 1970
Ezerins, Vilnis, RB, Whitewater State 1968

F

Fanning, Mike, DT, Notre Dame 1975–76
Fanning, Stan, DE, Idaho 1963
Farmer, Tom, RB, Iowa 1946
Fawcett, Jake, T, Southern Methodist 1942, 1944, 1946
Fears, Tom, E, UCLA 1948–54
Ferris, Neil, DB, Loyola, Calif. 1953
Finch, Karl, E, Cal. Poly-Pomona 1962
Finlay, Jack, G, UCLA 1947–51
Fournet, Sid, DT, Louisiana State 1955–56
France, Doug, T, Ohio State 1975–76
Franckhauser, Tom, DB, Purdue 1959
Friend, Benjamin, T, Louisiana State 1939
Fry, Bob, T, Kentucky 1953–59
Fuller, Frank, DT, Kentucky 1953–58

G

Gabriel, Roman, QB, N. Carolina State 1962–72
Gallovich, Anthony, B, Wake Forest 1941
Geddes, Ken, LB, Nebraska 1971–75
Gerhke, Fred, B, Utah 1940, 1945–49
George, Bill, LB, Wake Forest 1966
Geredine, Tom, WR, Northeast Missouri 1976
Giannoni, John, E, St. Mary's 1938
Gibson, Billy Joe, C, Tulsa 1942, 1944
Gift, Wayne, B, Purdue 1937
Goddard, Ed, B, Washington State 1937–38
Godfrey, Herb, E, Washington State 1942
Goodnight, Owen, B, Hardin-Simmons 1941
Goolsby, James, C, Mississippi State 1940
Gordon, Dick, WR, Michigan State 1972–73
Gossett, Bruce, PK, Richmond 1964–68
Greenwood, Don, B, Missouri 1945
Gregory, John, G, Chattanooga 1941–42
Gremminger, Hank, DB, Baylor 1966
Grier, Roosevelt, DT, Penn State 1963–66
Griffin, Bob, C, Arkansas 1953–57
Griffin, John, DB, Memphis State 1963
Gudauskas, Peter, G, Murray State 1940
Guillory, Tony, LB, Lamar Tech 1965, 1967–68
Guzik, John, LB, Pittsburgh 1959–60

H

Haden Pat, QB, USC 1976
Hadl, John, QB, Kansas 1973–74
Hall, Alvin, DB, None 1961–63
Hall, Parker, QB, Mississippi 1939–42
Halleck, Paul, B, Ohio 1937
Halliday, Jack, DT, Southern Methodist 1951
Halverson, Dean, LB, Washington 1968, 1971–72
Haman, John, C, Northwestern 1940–41
Hamilton, Ray, E, Arkansas 1938, 1944–47
Harding, Roger, C, California 1946
Hardy, Jim, QB, USC 1946–48
Harmon, Tom, RB, Michigan 1946–47
Harrah, Dennis, G, Miami, Ohio 1975–76
Harris, James, QB, Grambling 1973–76
Harris, Jim, DB, Oklahoma 1958
Harris, Marv, LB, Stanford 1964
Hauser, Art, DT, Xavier 1954–57
Hayes, Larry, C, Vanderbilt 1962–63
Haymond, Alvin, DB, Southern U. 1969–71
Haynes, Hall, DB, Santa Clara 1954–55
Heckard, Steve, E, Davidson 1965–66
Hecker, Bob, DB, Baldwin-Wallace 1952
Hecker, Norb, DB, Baldwin-Wallace 1951–53
Hector, Willie, T, Pacific 1961
Heineman, Ken, B, Texas Mines 1940–41
Henry, Mike, LB, USC 1962–64
Henry, Urban, DT, Georgia Tech 1961
Hershey, Kirk, E, Cornell 1941
Hickey, Howard, E, Arkansas 1941, 1945–48
Hightower, John, E, Sam Houston State 1942
Hirsch, Elroy (Crazylegs), E-RB, Wisconsin 1949–57
Hock, John, G, Santa Clara 1953–57
Hoerner, Dick, RB, Iowa 1947–51
Hoffman, Bob, RB, USC 1946–48
Holladay, Bob, RB, Tulsa 1956
Holovak, Mike, RB, Boston College 1946
Holtzman, Glenn, T, N. Texas State 1955–58
Hord, Roy, G, Duke 1960–62
Horton, Greg, G, Colorado 1976
Horvath, Les, RB, Ohio State 1947–48
Houser, John, C-G, Redlands 1957–59
Howard, Gene, DB, Langston, Okla. 1971–72
Hubbell, Frank, DE-TE, Tennessee 1947–49
Huffman, Dick, T, Tennessee 1947–50
Huggins, Roy, B, Vanderbilt 1944
Hughes, Ed, DB, Tulsa 1954–55
Humphrey, Buddy, QB, Baylor 1959–60
Hunter, Art, C, Notre Dame 1960–64
Hupke, Thomas, G, Alabama 1938–39

I

Iglehart, Floyd, DB, Wiley 1958
Iman, Ken, C, S.E. Missouri State 1965–74
Isselhardt, Ralph, G, Franklin 1937

J

Jackson, Harold, FL, Jackson State 1968, 1973–76
Jackson, Monte, CB, San Diego State 1975–76
Jackson, Rusty, P, Louisiana State 1976
Jacobs, Jack, QB, Oklahoma 1942, 1945
Janerette, Charlie, G, Penn State 1960
Janiak, Leonard, B, Ohio 1940–42
Jaworski, Ron, QB, Youngstown 1974–76
Jessie, Ron, WR, Kansas 1975–76
Jobko, Bill, LB, Ohio State 1958–62
Johns, Freeman, WR, Southern Methodist 1976
Johnson, Clyde, T, Kentucky 1946–47
Johnson, Donald, C, Northwestern 1942
Johnson, Marvin, DB, San Jose State 1951–52
Johnson, Mitch, T, UCLA 1969–70
Jones, Cody, DT, San Jose State 1974–76
Jones, David (Deacon), DE, S. Carolina State 1961–71
Jones, Harvey, B, Baylor 1944–45
Jones, Jimmy, RB, Washington 1958
Jordan, Jeff, RB, Washington 1970
Josephson, Les, RB, Augustana 1964–67, 1969–74

K

Kablealo, Michael, B, Ohio State 1944
Kalmanir, Tom, RB, Nevada 1949–51
Karilivacz, Carl, DB, Syracuse 1959–60
Karras, Ted, G, Indiana 1966
Karrs, John, B, Duquesne 1944
Kay, Rick, LB, Colorado 1973, 1975–76
Keane, Tom, DB, West Virginia 1948–51
Keeble, Joe, B, UCLA 1937
Kenerson, John, T, Kentucky State 1960
Kigore, Jon, P, Auburn 1965–67
Kimbrough, Elbert, DB, Northwestern 1961
Kinek, Michael, E, Michigan State 1940
Kirk, Ken, C, Mississippi 1963
Klein, Bob, TE, USC 1969–76
Klosterman, Don, QB, Loyola, Calif. 1952
Koch, George, B, Baylor 1945
Konetsky, Floyd, E, Florida 1944–45
Kovatch, John, E, Northwestern 1938
Krause, Paul, G, DePaul 1938
Ksionyak, John, QB, St. Bonaventure 1947

L

LaHood, Mike, G, Wyoming 1969, 1971–72
Lamson, Chuck, DB, Wyoming 1965–67
Lane, Dick, DB, Scottsbluff J.C. 1952–53
Lang, Israel, RB, Tennessee State 1969
Lange, Bill, G, Dayton 1951–52
Lansford, Buck, G, Texas 1958–60
Larsen, Gary, DT, Concordia 1964
Lazetich, Milan, G, Michigan 1945–50
Lazetich, William, B, Montana 1939, 1941–42
Lear, Les, G, Manitoba 1944–46
Leggett, Earl, DT, Louisiana State 1966
Levy, Len, G, Minnesota 1945–46
Lewis, Arthur, T, Ohio 1938–39
Lewis, Woodley, DB-E, Oregon 1950–55
Liles, Elvin, G, Oklahoma A&M 1945
Lipscomb, Gene (Big Daddy), DT, None 1953–55
Littlefield, Carl, B, Washington State 1938
Livingston, Cliff, LB, UCLA 1963–65
Livingston, Ted, T, Indiana 1937–40
Long, Bob, LB, UCLA 1960–61
Long. Bob, WR, Wichita State 1970
Lothridge, Billy, P, Georgia Tech 1965
Love, John, WR, N. Texas State 1972
LoVetere, John, DT, Compton J.C. 1959–62
Lundy, Lamar, DE-TE, Purdue 1957–69

M

Mack, Tom, G, Michigan 1966–76
Magnani, Dante, B, St. Mary's, Calif. 1940–42, 1947–48
Maher, Francis, B, Toledo 1941
Marchlewski, Frank, C, Minnesota 1965, 1968–69
Marconi, Joe, RB, West Virginia 1959–61
Markov, Victor, T, Washington 1938
Martin, Aaron, DB, N. Carolina Coll. 1964–65
Martin, John, C, Navy 1947–49
Maslowski, Matt, WR, San Diego State 1971
Mason, Tommy, RB, Tulane 1967–70
Matheson, Riley, G, Texas Mines 1939–42, 1944–47
Matson, Ollie, RB-E, San Francisco 1959–62
Mattos, Harry, B, St. Mary's 1937
Mayes, Carl, RB, Texas 1952
McCormick, Tom, RB, Pacific 1953–55
McCutcheon, Lawrence, RB, Colorado State 1972–76
McDonald, Tommy, FL, Oklahoma 1965–66
McDonough, Paul, E, Utah 1938
McFadin, Bud, DT-T, Texas 1952–56
McGarry, Bernard, G, Utah 1939–42
McGee, Willie, WR, Alcorn A&M 1974–75
McIlhany, Dan, DB, Texas A&M 1965
McKeever, Marlin, LB-TE, USC 1961–66, 1971–72
McLain, Kevin, LB, Colorado State 1976
McLaughlin, Leon, C, UCLA 1951–55
McMillan, Eddie, CB, Florida State 1973–75
Meador, Ed, DB, Arkansas Tech 1959–70
Mello, Jim, RB, Notre Dame 1948
Mergenthal, Art, G, Notre Dame 1945–46
Michaels, Lou, DE, Kentucky 1958–60
Miller, Charles, C, Purdue 1937

Duane Putnam

Les Richter

Isiah Robertson

Joe Scibelli

Dan Towler

Stan West

P. (Tank) Younger

Miller, Clark, DE, Utah State . . . 1970
Miller, Paul, DE, Louisiana State . . . 1954–57
Miller, Ralph, T, Rice . . . 1937–38
Miller, Ron, E, USC . . . 1956
Miller, Ron, QB, Wisconsin . . . 1962
Moan, Emmett, B, West Virginia . . . 1937
Molden, Frank, DT, Jackson State . . . 1965
Monaco, Raymond, G, Holy Cross . . . 1945
Moore, Tom, RB, Vanderbilt . . . 1966
Morris, George, B, Baldwin-Wallace . . . 1941–42
Morris, Jack, DB, Oregon . . . 1958–60
Morris, Larry, LB, Georgia Tech . . . 1955–57
Morrow, John, C, Michigan . . . 1956–59
Mucha, Rudolph, QB, Washington . . . 1941, 1945
Munson, Bill, QB, Utah State . . . 1964–67
Myers, Brad, RB, Bucknell . . . 1953–56
Myers, Jack, RB-DB, UCLA . . . 1952

N

Naumetz, Fred, LB-C, Boston College . . . 1946–50
Neihaus, Ralph, T, Cincinnati . . . 1939
Nelson, Bill, DT, Oregon State . . . 1971–75
Nelson, Terry, TE, Arkansas AM&N . . . 1973–76
Nemeth, Steve, B, Notre Dame . . . 1945
Nettles, Jim, DB, Wisconsin . . . 1969–72
Nichols, Bob, T, Stanford . . . 1966–67

O

Olsen, Merlin, DT, Utah State . . . 1962–76
Olsen, Norman, T, None . . . 1944
Olsen, Phil, DT, Utah State . . . 1971–74
O'Neill, William, B, Detroit . . . 1937

P

Panfil, Ken T, Purdue . . . 1956–58
Pardee, Jack, LB, Texas A&M . . . 1957–64, 1966–70
Parish, Don, LB, Stanford . . . 1971
Pasquariello, Ralph, RB, Villanova . . . 1950
Pasque, Joe, T, Southern Methodist . . . 1942, 1946
Patt, Maurice, E, Carnegie Tech . . . 1939–42
Paul, Don, LB, UCLA . . . 1948–55
Pergine, John, LB, Notre Dame . . . 1969–72
Perkins, Art, RB, N. Texas State . . . 1962–63
Perry, Rod, CB, Colorado . . . 1975–76
Petchell, John, B, Duquesne . . . 1942, 1944
Peterson, Jim, LB, San Diego State . . . 1974–75
Peterson, Nelson, B, West Virginia Wesleyan . . . 1938
Petitbon, Richie, DB, Tulane . . . 1969–70
Phillips, George, B, UCLA . . . 1945
Phillips, Jim, E, Auburn . . . 1958–64
Phillips, Rod, RB, Jackson State . . . 1975–76
Pillath, Roger, T, Wisconsin . . . 1965
Pincura, Stanley, B, Ohio State . . . 1937–38
Pitts, Elijah, RB, Philander Smith . . . 1970
Pitts, Hugh, LB, Texas Christian . . . 1956
Pivec, Dave, TE, Notre Dame . . . 1966–68
Platukas, George, E, Duquesne . . . 1941–42
Plum, Milt, QB, Penn State . . . 1968
Plummer, Tony, DB, Pacific . . . 1974
Plunkett, Warren, B, Minnesota . . . 1942
Pope, Bucky, FL, Catawba . . . 1964, 1966–67
Pottios, Myron, LB, Notre Dame . . . 1966–70
Powell, Tim, DE, Northwestern . . . 1965
Prather, Dale, E, George Washington . . . 1938–39
Preece, Steve, S, Oregon State . . . 1973–76
Pritchard, Abisha, B, VMI . . . 1942
Pritko, Steve, DE, Villanova . . . 1946–47
Prochaska, Ray, E, Nebraska . . . 1941
Pudloski, Chester, T, Villanova . . . 1944
Purnell, Jim, LB, Wisconsin . . . 1969–72
Putnam, Duane, G, Pacific . . . 1952–59, 1962

Q

Quinlan, Volney (Skeet), RB, San Diego State . . . 1952–56

R

Ragazzo, Philip, T, Western Reserve . . . 1938–39
Rapp, Manuel, B, St. Louis . . . 1941–42
Ray, David, PK-WR, Alabama . . . 1969–74
Ream, Charles, T, Ohio State . . . 1938
Reece, Geoff, C, Washington State . . . 1976
Reisz, Albert, B, S.E. Louisiana . . . 1944–46
Reinhard, Bob, T-DT, California . . . 1950
Reid, Joe, LB, Louisiana State . . . 1941
Rentzel, Lance, WR, Oklahoma . . . 1971–72, 1974
Repko, Joe, DT, Boston College . . . 1948–49
Reynolds, Jack, LB, Tennessee . . . 1970–76
Rhome, Jerry, QB, Tulsa . . . 1971
Rich, Herb, DB, Vanderbilt . . . 1951–53
Richardson, Jerry, DB, W. Texas State . . . 1964–65
Richter, Les, LB, California . . . 1954–62
Rickards, Paul, QB, Pittsburgh . . . 1948
Rieth, William, G, Carnegie Tech . . . 1941–42, 1944–45
Riffle, Charles, G, Notre Dame . . . 1944
Robertson, Isiah, LB, Southern U. . . . 1971–76
Robinson, John, T, N.E. Missouri . . . 1938
Robustelli, Andy, DE, Arnold . . . 1951–55
Rockwell, Henry, C, Arizona State . . . 1940–42
Rodak, Michael, G, Western Reserve . . . 1939–40
Rogers, Melvin, LB, Florida A&M . . . 1976
Rosequist, Ted, T, Ohio State . . . 1937
Russell, Douglas, B, Kansas . . . 1939
Russell, Lloyd, B, Baylor . . . 1939
Ruthstrom, Ralph, RB, Southern Methodist . . . 1945–46
Ryan, Frank, QB, Rice . . . 1958–61

S

Saul, Rich, C-G, Michigan State . . . 1971–76
Savatsky, Oliver, E, Miami, Ohio . . . 1937
Scales, Dwight, WR, Grambling . . . 1976
Scarry, Michael, C, Waynesburg . . . 1944–45
Schenken, Nathan, T, Howard . . . 1939
Schuh, Harry, T, Memphis State . . . 1971–72
Schultz, Eberle, T, Oregon State . . . 1946–47
Schumacher, Gregg, DE, Illinois . . . 1967–68
Schupbach, O.T., T, W. Texas State . . . 1941–42
Scibelli, Joe, G, Notre Dame . . . 1961–75
Scribner, Rob, RB, UCLA . . . 1973–76
Seabright, Charles, QB, West Virginia . . . 1941
Sebastian, Michael, B, Pittsburgh . . . 1937
Selawski, Gene, T, Purdue . . . 1959
Sewell, Harley, G, Texas . . . 1963
Shannon, Carver, DB-RB, So. Illinois . . . 1962–64
Shaw, Bob, E, Ohio State . . . 1945–49
Shaw, Glenn, RB, Kentucky . . . 1962
Shaw, Nate, DB, USC . . . 1969–70
Sherman, Rod, WR, USC . . . 1973
Sherman, Will, DB, St. Mary's . . . 1954–60
Shirey, Fred, T, Nebraska . . . 1940–41
Shiver, Ray, DB, Miami . . . 1956
Shofner, Del, E, Baylor . . . 1957–60
Sikich, Rudy, T, Minnesota . . . 1945
Simensen, Don, T, St. Thomas . . . 1951–52
Simington, Milton, G, Arkansas . . . 1941
Simpson, Bill, DB, Michigan State . . . 1974–76
Sims, George, DB, Baylor . . . 1949–50
Skoczen, Stanley, B, Western Reserve . . . 1944
Skoronski, Ed, C, Purdue . . . 1937
Slater, Jackie, G, Jackson State . . . 1976
Slovak, Martin, B, Toledo . . . 1939–41
Smith, Billy Ray, DE, Arkansas . . . 1957
Smith, Bobby, DB, UCLA . . . 1962–65
Smith, Bruce, RB, Minnesota . . . 1948
Smith, Gaylon, B, Southwestern . . . 1939–42
Smith, Larry, RB, Florida . . . 1969–73
Smith, Ron, DB, Richmond . . . 1965
Smith, Ron, QB, Wisconsin . . . 1968–69
Smith, Verda (Vitamin T.), RB, Abilene Christian . . . 1949–53
Smyth, Bill, T-TE, Cincinnati . . . 1947–50
Snow, Jack, WR, Notre Dame . . . 1965–75
Snyder, Robert, B, Ohio U . . . 1937–38
Spadaccini, Vic, DT, Minnesota . . . 1938–40
Sparkman, Alan, DT, Texas A&M . . . 1948–49
Stalcup, Jerry, LB, Wisconsin . . . 1960
Statuto, Art, C, Notre Dame . . . 1950
Stein, Bob, LB, Minnesota . . . 1973–74
Stephens, John, E, Marshall . . . 1938
Stephens, Larry, DT, Texas . . . 1962
Stephenson, Dave, G, West Virginia . . . 1950
Stevenson, Ralph, G, Oklahoma . . . 1940
Stiger, Jim, RB, Washington . . . 1965–67
Stokes, Tim, T, Oregon . . . 1974
Strode, Woody, E, UCLA . . . 1946
Strofolino, Mike, LB, Villanova . . . 1965
Strugar, George, DT, Washington . . . 1957–61
Studstill, Pat, WR-P, Houston . . . 1968–71
Stuart, Roy, B, Tulsa . . . 1942
Stukes, Charlie, CB, Maryland-E.S. . . . 1973–74
Sucic, Steve, RB, Illinois . . . 1946
Svare, Harland, LB, Washington State . . . 1953–54
Swain, Bill, LB, Oregon . . . 1963
Sweet, Joe, WR, Tennessee State . . . 1972–73
Sweetan, Karl, QB, Wake Forest . . . 1969–70

T

Talbert, Diron, DT, Texas . . . 1967–70
Tarbox, Bruce, G, Syracuse . . . 1961
Taylor, Corky, RB, Kansas State . . . 1955–57
Teeuws, Len, T, Tulane . . . 1952–53
Thomas, Bob, RB, Arizona State . . . 1971–72
Thomas, Clendon, RB, Oklahoma . . . 1958–61
Thomas, Pat, CB, Texas A&M . . . 1976
Thomason, Bob, QB, VMI . . . 1949
Thompson, Harry, G, UCLA . . . 1950–54
Toogood, Charley, DT-T, Nebraska . . . 1951–56
Towler, Dan, RB, Washington & Jefferson . . . 1950–55
Truax, Billy, TE, Louisiana State . . . 1964–70
Tucker, Wendell, FL, S. Carolina State . . . 1967–70
Tuckey, Richard, B, Manhattan . . . 1938
Turner, James, B. Oklahoma A&M . . . 1937

U

Underwood, Forrest, T, Davis-Elkins . . . 1937
Uzdavinis, Walter, E, Fordham . . . 1937

V

Valdez, Vernon, DB, San Diego State . . . 1960
Van Brocklin, Norm, QB, Oregon . . . 1949–57
Varrichione, Frank, T, Notre Dame . . . 1961–65
Vasicek, Vic, LB, Texas . . . 1950
Villanueva, Danny, K, New Mexico State . . . 1960–64
Von Sonn, Andy, LB, UCLA . . . 1964

W

Wade, Bill, QB, Vanderbilt . . . 1954–60
Waller, Ron, RB, Maryland . . . 1955–58
Wardlow, Duane, DE, Washington . . . 1954–56
Washington, Ken, RB-DB, UCLA . . . 1946–48
Waterfield, Bob, QB-DB, K, UCLA . . . 1945–52
Weisgerber, Richard, B, Willamette . . . 1938
Wendryhoski, Joe, C, Illinois . . . 1964–66
West, Pat, RB, USC . . . 1944–48
West, Stan, MG, Oklahoma . . . 1950–54
White, Lee, RB, Weber State . . . 1971
Whitmyer, Nat, DB, Washington . . . 1963
Whittenton, Jess, DB, Texas Western . . . 1956–57
Whittingham, Fred, LB, Cal. Poly-Obispo . . . 1964
Wilbur, John, G, Stanford . . . 1970
Wilkins, Roy, LB, Georgia . . . 1958–59
Williams, Charlie, WR, Prairie View . . . 1970
Williams, Clarence, DB, Washington State . . . 1965–72
Williams, Frank, RB, Pepperdine . . . 1961–64
Williams, Jerry, DB, Washington State . . . 1949–52
Williams, John, G-T, Minnesota . . . 1972–76
Williams, Roger, DB, Grambling . . . 1971–72
Williams, Sam, DE, Michigan State . . . 1959
Williams, Travis, RB, Arizona State . . . 1971
Wilson, Ben, RB, USC . . . 1963–65
Wilson, Jack, RB, Baylor . . . 1946–47
Wilson, Jim, T, Georgia . . . 1968
Wilson, John, E, Western Reserve . . . 1939–42
Wilson, Tom, RB, None . . . 1956–61
Winkler, Jim, DB, Texas A&M . . . 1951–52
Winkler, Joe, C, Purdue . . . 1945
Winston, Kelton, DB, Wiley . . . 1967–68
Wojcik, Greg, DT, USC . . . 1971
Woodlief, Doug, LB, Memphis State . . . 1965–69
Worden, James, B, Waynesburg . . . 1945

Y

Yagiello, Ray, G, Catawba . . . 1948–49
Youngblood, Jack, DE, Florida . . . 1971–76
Youngblood, Jim, LB, Tennessee Tech . . . 1973–76
Younger, Paul (Tank), RB-LB, Grambling . . . 1949–57

Z

Zilly, Jack, TE-DT, Notre Dame . . . 1947–51
Zirinsky, Walt, B, Lafayette . . . 1945
Zoll, Richard, G, Indiana . . . 1937–38

MIAMI DOLPHINS

1965 Joseph Robbie, a Minneapolis lawyer who owned a house in Miami, met AFL Commissioner Joe Foss in Washington, March 3. Robbie, a former classmate of Foss at the University of South Dakota, was representing a friend who sought an AFL expansion franchise for Philadelphia. Foss rejected Philadelphia as a site, noting the Eagles had exclusive rights to Franklin Field. Foss suggested Robbie apply for the franchise in Miami. "With the population growth and climate, it'll be the best franchise in the league," Foss said. Seeking financial backing, Robbie went to entertainer Danny Thomas, a coworker on the board of St. Jude's Hospital. Thomas, who earlier sought to buy the Chicago White Sox, agreed to become a partner. Thanks to the influence of then Vice President Hubert Humphrey, Robbie's friend from Minnesota, Miami Mayor Robert King agreed to invite the AFL to Miami, with the assurance that the team could play in the Orange Bowl, May 6. The AFL awarded its first expansion franchise to Robbie and Thomas for $7.5 million, August 16. Joe Thomas of the Minnesota Vikings was named director of player personnel, September 21. Mrs. Robert Swanson of West Miami won two lifetime passes in a contest to pick a team nickname. Her suggestion, "Dolphins," was chosen from over 20,000 entries. In the first round of the AFL college draft, the Dolphins selected Kentucky quarterback Rick Norton and Illinois fullback Jim Grabowski, November 27.

1966 In the expansion draft, Miami picked 31 players from the eight AFL teams, 19 of them starters. The player selected fourteenth, offensive tackle Norm Evans of the Houston Oilers, was destined to be a 10-year regular with the Dolphins. George Wilson was hired as head coach, January 29. Wilson had coached the Detroit Lions for eight seasons and had spent one year as an assistant in Washington. The Dolphins opened their first training camp with 83 players in St. Petersburg, Florida, July 5. Grumbling began immediately as the players complained about the gravel practice field and the dormitory that was next to Seaworld. "We couldn't sleep," Evans said. "The seals kept barking all night." The Dolphins left for their first game, a preseason test in San Diego, August 4. The flight, aboard an aged, propellor-driven aircraft, lasted 10 hours. Miami lost the game 30–10 and Wilson accused San Diego coach Sid Gillman of rolling up the score. Training camp was moved to Boca Raton, August 7. A crowd of 36,366 fans came to the Orange Bowl to see the Dolphins lose to Kansas City 33–0. The Dophins opened the regular season at the Orange Bowl against Oakland, September 2. Joe Auer, a Buffalo castoff who owned a pet lion, thrilled the 26,776 fans by returning the opening kickoff 95 yards for a touchdown. The Raiders rallied to win 23–14. When injuries sidelined Norton and Dick Wood, Wilson installed his son, George, Jr., at quarterback. Wilson led the Dolphins to their first AFL victory, passing 67 yards to Billy Joe for a touchdown in a 24–7 win over Denver, October 16. The following week, Wilson injured his shoulder in a 20–13 win at Houston and his father signed John Stofa from a semipro league in Lakeland, Florida, to finish the season at quarterback. Stofa threw four touchdown passes, one to Auer with 38 seconds left, to give the Miami team its third win, a 29–28 surprise over Houston, December 18.

1967 It was a year of reorganization—on the field and in the front office. W.H. Keland of Racine, Wisconsin, purchased the interests of Martin Decker, George Hamid, Sr., and George Hamid, Jr., March 23. Robbie and Keland bought out Danny Thomas, June 1. In the first round of the first AFL-NFL draft,

Head coach Don Shula and quarterback Bob Griese, 1973.

Miami drafted Purdue quarterback Bob Griese. Joe Thomas completed a seven-man trade, acquiring halfback Abner Haynes from Denver. In the regular season opener against Denver, Stofa broke his ankle, leaving Griese to run the offense. Griese played well and Haynes rushed for 151 yards in the 35–21 Miami win. Hard times followed as the Dolphins lost their next eight, scoring just seven touchdowns. They ended the losing streak by beating Buffalo 17–14 on a fourth down, 31-yard touchdown pass from Griese to

Howard Twilley, November 26. The Dolphins defeated San Diego 41-24 and the Boston Patriots 41-32 to close out their home schedule. Cornerback Dick Westmoreland intercepted his tenth pass of the season against the Patriots. Griese finished the season fifth among NFL passers, so Thomas traded Stofa.

1968 The draft brought a fresh supply of talent to Miami. In the first five rounds, Thomas selected running backs Larry Csonka and Jim Kiick, offensive tackle Doug Crusan, and safety Dick Anderson. All were starters in 1968. The Dolphins won their first interleague victory, beating the Eagles 23–7 in a pre-season game, August 17. Two weeks later, Griese's favorite receiver, Jack Clancy, suffered a broken leg in a 22–13 loss to Baltimore. In the regular season, Miami recovered from a 0-3 start to win five games. Griese set club passing records of 2,473 yards, 186 completions, and 21 touchdowns.

1969 Thomas continued to upgrade Miami's personnel, drafting defensive linemen Bill Stanfill and Bob Heinz, halfback Eugene (Mercury) Morris, and cornerback Lloyd Mumphord and trading for linebacker Nick Buoniconti and guard Larry Little. Griese passed for four touchdowns in a 34–31 loss to the New York Jets, November 2. One week later, Griese injured his right knee in a Boston downpour and missed the final five games. In all 20 players missed seven games or more due to injury. Robbie purchased the interest of W.H. Keland to become the club's majority owner. Racked by injuries, the Dolphins slipped back into last place (3-10-1) and Wilson was relieved of his coaching duties after the 1969 season.

1970 A new era began for the Dolphins when 40-year-old Don Shula left Baltimore to become head coach and vice-president in Miami, February 18. Commissioner Pete Rozelle ordered Miami to give Baltimore its first-round draft pick in 1971 as compensation. "I'm not a miracle worker," Shula said. "I have no magic formulas. The only way I know is hard work." Shula put the Dolphins through a grueling training camp at Biscayne College in North Miami, starting every day with a 7 A.M. two-mile run followed by two 90-minute practices, followed by an evening "walk-through." The regimen paid off as the Dolphins won four straight preseason games and four of their first five league games. On October 3, Miami beat Oakland for the first time, 20–13, as newly acquired receiver Paul Warfield caught two touchdown passes. One week later, the Dolphins scored their first victory over the New York Jets, 20–6. The Dolphins went into a brief tailspin, losing three in a row, before closing the season with six consecutive wins. They avenged a 35–0 loss to Baltimore 34–17 as rookie safety Jake Scott scored on a 77-yard punt return, November 22. The Dolphins beat Buffalo 45–7 to clinch the AFC wild card spot, December 20. In Oakland's muddy Coliseum, the Dolphins lost their first playoff game to the Raiders 21–14.

1971 Miami got off to a slow start, tying Denver and losing to the New York Jets. Angered, Shula cracked down on his players and they responded. The Dolphins won eight in a row, including Miami's first shutout ever, a 34–0 romp over Buffalo, November 7. Griese matured into a poised pro quarterback. In a 41–3 win over New England, Griese set a record by throwing three consecutive passes for touchdowns. He rallied Miami from a 21–3 deficit to a 24–21 victory over Pittsburgh, November 14. The Dolphins clinched first place in the AFC Eastern Division on the final day of the season, beating Green Bay 27–6 before a record crowd of 74,215 at the Orange Bowl, December 19. Csonka became the club's first 1,000-yard rusher with 1,051 yards and placekicker Garo Yepremian led the NFL with 117 points. The Dolphins won the longest game in NFL history (82 minutes, 40 seconds) as Yepremian kicked a 37-yard field goal in the second overtime to beat Kansas City 27–24 in an AFC divisional playoff game, December 25. Miami dethroned the Baltimore Colts, the defending world champions, in the AFC title game 21–0, January 2. It was the first shutout against the Colts in 97 games.

1972 The Dolphins fell to Dallas 24–3 in Super Bowl VI, January 16. "We'll be back," Robbie vowed. Joe Thomas left the Dolphins' front office. The Dolphins became the first team in NFL history to go through an entire season including postseason games, unbeaten and untied. They opened the year with a

20–10 win over Kansas City, September 17. Griese hit Jim Mandich with a last-minute touchdown pass to upset the Vikings in Minnesota 16–14, October 1. Two weeks later, Griese suffered a broken right leg and dislocated ankle when he was hit by San Diego's Ron East. He was replaced by Earl Morrall, a 38-year-old backup quarterback who had been claimed on waivers from Baltimore in the spring. Yepremian kicked the longest field goal of his career (54 yards) to beat Buffalo 24–23 in the Orange Bowl, October 22. Shula became the first NFL coach to win 100 games in 10 seasons as Miami crushed New England with 501 yards 52-0, November 12. The Dolphins achieved the NFL's first 14-0 record by closing the regular season with a 16–0 win over Baltimore. Csonka and Morris both finished over 1,000 yards as Miami set a league rushing record, 2,960 yards. Miami slipped past Cleveland 20–14 in an AFC divisional playoff, December 23. Griese came off the bench in the second half to spark the Dolphins to a 21–17 win over Pittsburgh in the AFC championship game, December 31.

1973 Miami capped its perfect season in Super Bowl VII at Los Angeles, defeating Washington for the world championship, 14–7, January 14. As the 1973 season began, hopes for another perfect season were dashed the second week when they fell to Oakland 12–7, September 23. The Dolphins bounced back the following week to crush New England 44–23 as Morris scored three touchdowns and set a team record with 197 yards rushing. Miami shut out Baltimore for the fourth consecutive time 44–0 as cornerback Tim Foley returned two blocked punts for touchdowns, an NFL first, November 11. The next week, the Dolphins recorded their second consecutive shutout, beating Buffalo 17–0 to clinch their third successive AFC Eastern Division championship. Warfield caught four touchdown passes from Griese in the first half to pace a 34–7 rout of Detroit, December 15. The win concluded the regular season, giving Miami the best two year record in NFL history, 26–2. Three days later, Shula signed a contract to coach the Dolphins through 1977. Miami defeated Cincinnati 34–16 in the AFC playoff, December 23. The Dolphins rushed for 266 yard to dominate Oakland 27–10 and win an unprecedented third straight AFC championship, December 30.

1974 Miami defeated Minnesota 24–7 in Super Bowl VIII at Houston's Rice Stadium, January 13. Csonka set Super Bowl records with 145 yards on 33 carries. He scored two touchdowns and Kiick one as the Dolphins became only the second team to win back-to-back Super Bowls. The organization was jolted by an announcement that Csonka, Kiick, and Warfield had signed a $3.3 million package deal to play for the Toronto Northmen in the World Football League a season away in 1975, March 31. The season began dismally as the Dolphins lost the opener in New England 34–24, September 15; Miami had not lost to the Patriots since 1971. The Dolphins struggled through the next six weeks, winning five lackluster games and losing to Washington 20–17. The offense finally exploded in a 42–7 rout of Atlanta, November 3. Two weeks later, Don Nottingham scored on a 23-yard run with 19 seconds left to beat Buffalo 35–28, the third time the Dolphins scored the winning points in the final minute. Csonka gained 123 yards in a 24–3 win over Cincinnati, the fifteenth time in his career he surpassed the 100-yard mark, December 2. Miami rallied from a 24-point deficit behind Morrall to beat New England 34–27 in the regular season finale, December 15. It was the Dolphins' thirty-first consecutive win at the Orange Bowl. A last-second desperation pass from Ken Stabler to Clarence Davis provided the winning touchdown as Oakland ended Miami's two-year domination of pro football with a dramatic 28–26 win in the playoffs, December 21.

1975 The departure of Csonka, Kiick, and Warfield weakened Miami. The Orange Bowl winning streak ended in the regular season opener as Oakland beat the Dolphins 31–21, despite three interceptions by safety Charlie Babb. The following week, the Dolphins rallied from a 14–0 halftime deficit to beat New England 22–14 and begin a seven-game winning streak. The Dolphins scored two touchdowns in the final two minutes to beat Buffalo 35–30 and reclaim first place in the AFC Eastern Division, October 26. Jake Scott became the club's all-time interception leader with 34 when he picked off a Joe Namath pass, November 9. In a showdown for the division lead, Baltimore beat Miami 33–17 at the Orange Bowl, November 23. Griese tore tendons in his toe and was sidelined for the rest of the season. Morrall was lost with torn knee ligaments the following week, but Don Strock guided Miami to two straight wins. Baltimore beat the Dolphins 10–7 in overtime to knock the Dolphins out of the playoffs for the first time since 1970, December 14.

1976 Shula's contract was extended for five more years, July 9. Jake Scott was suspended in a dispute with Shula, then traded to Washington, August 27. Miami was hampered by injuries that sidelined 18 players during the season. Bill Arnsparger, former assistant coach, rejoined the Dolphins at midseason after being released as head coach by the New York Giants; his return inspired the Dolphins' defense to its finest effort of the year, a 10–3 win over New England, October 31. Wide receiver Freddie Solomon had an electrifying game against Buffalo, scoring on a 79-yard punt return, a 59-yard run, and a 53-yard pass play, December 5. Shula suffered his first losing season in 14 years as an NFL head coach as the Dolphins fell to 6-8.

MEMBERS OF HALL OF FAME:
None

DOLPHINS RECORD, 1966–76

Year	Won	Lost	Tied	Pct.	Pts.	OP
1966	3	11	0	.214	213	362
1967	4	10	0	.286	219	407
1968	5	8	1	.385	276	355
1969	3	10	1	.231	233	332
1970	10	4	0	.714	297	228
1971‡	10	3	1	.769	315	174
1972**	14	0	0	1,000	385	171
1973**	12	2	0	.857	343	150
1974§	11	3	0	.786	327	216
1975	10	4	0	.714	357	222
1976	6	8	0	.429	263	264
11 Years	88	63	3	.581	3,228	2,881

‡AFC Champion
**Super Bowl Champion
§AFC Eastern Division Champion

RECORD HOLDERS

Rushing (Yards)	Larry Csonka, 1972	1,117
Passing (Pct.)	Bob Griese, 1975	61.8
Passing (Yards)	Bob Griese, 1968	2,473
Passing (TDs)	Bob Griese, 1968	21
Receiving (No.)	Jack Clancy, 1967	67
Receiving (Yards)	Paul Warfield, 1971	996
Interceptions (No.)	Dick Westmoreland, 1967	10
Punting (Avg.)	George Wilson Jr., 1966	42.1
Punt Ret. (Avg.)	Fred Solomon, 1976	15.8
Kickoff Ret. (Avg.)	Duriel Harris, 1976	32.9
Touchdowns (Total)	Eugene (Mercury) Morris, 1972, and Don Nottingham, 1975	12
Field Goals Made	Garo Yepremian, 1971	28
Points (No.)	Garo Yepremian, 1971	117

COACHING HISTORY

1966–69	George Wilson	15–39–2
1970–76	Don Shula	73–24–1

FIRST PLAYER SELECTED

1966	Rick Norton, QB, Kentucky
1967	Bob Griese, QB, Purdue
1968	Larry Csonka, RB, Syracuse
1969	Bill Stanfill, DE, Georgia
1970	Jim Mandich, TE (2), Michigan
1971	Otto Stowe, WR, Iowa State
1972	Mike Kadish, DT, Notre Dame
1973	Chuck Bradley, T (2), Oregon
1974	Don Reese, DE, Jackson State
1975	Darryl Carlton, T, Tampa
1976	Larry Gordon, LB, Arizona State

Jack Clancy *Vern Den Herder* *Manny Fernandez* *Tim Foley* *Mike Kolen* *Bob Kuechenberg* *Jim Langer*

MIAMI DOLPHINS, 1966–76

Anderson, Dick, S, Colorado 1968–76
Andrews, John, DE, Morgan State 1975–76
Auer, Joe, HB, Georgia Tech 1966–67

B

Babb, Charles, S, Memphis State 1972–76
Bachman, Ted, CB, New Mexico State 1976
Baker, Mel, WR, Texas Southern 1974
Ball, Larry, LB, Louisville 1972–74
Bannon, Bruce, LB, Penn State 1973–74
Barber, Rudy, LB, Bethune-Cookman 1968
Barnes, Rodrigo, LB, Rice 1975
Beier, Tom, S, Miami 1967, 1969
Berger, Ron, DE, Wayne State 1973
Boutwell, Tom, WR-QB, So. Mississippi 1969
Boynton, John, T, Tennessee 1969
Bramlett, John, LB, Memphis State 1967–68
Branch, Mel, DE, Louisiana State 1966–68
Briscoe, Marlin, WR, Omaha 1972–74
Brown, Dean, S, Ft. Valley State 1970
Brownlee, Claude, DE, Benedict 1967
Bruggers, Bob, LB, Minnesota 1966–68
Bulaich, Norm, RB, Texas Christian 1975–76
Buoniconti, Nick, LB, Notre Dame 1969–76

C

Canale, Whit, DE, Tennessee 1966
Carlton, Darryl, T, Tampa 1975–76
Carpenter, Preston, TE, Arkansas 1966
Casares, Rick, FB, Florida 1966
Chambers, Rusty, LB, Tulane 1976
Chesser, George, FB, Delta State 1966–67
Clancy, Jack, WR, Michigan 1967–69
Cole, Terry, RB, Indiana 1971
Cooke, Ed, DE, Maryland 1966–67
Cornish, Frank, DT, Grambling 1970–71
Cox, Jim, TE, Miami 1968
Cronin, Bill, TE, Boston College 1966
Crowder, Randy, DT, Penn State 1974–76
Crusan, Doug, T, Indiana 1968–74

Csonka, Larry, RB, Syracuse 1968–74
Current, Mike, T, Ohio State 1967

D

Darnall, Bill, WR, North Carolina 1968–69
Davis, Gary, RB, Cal Poly-SLO 1976
Davis, Ted, LB, Georgia Tech 1970
DelGaizo, Jim, QB, Tampa 1972–75
DeMarco, Bob, C, Dayton 1970–71
Den Herder, Vern, DE, Iowa Central 1971–76
Dennery, Mike, LB, Southern Mississippi 1976
Dotson, Alphonse, DT, Grambling 1966
Drougas, Tom, T-G, Oregon 1975–76
Dunaway, Jim, DT, Mississippi 1972

E

Edmunds, Randall, LB, Georgia Tech 1968–69
Elia, Bruce, LB, Ohio State 1975
Ellis, Ken, CB, Southern U 1976
Emanuel, Frank, LB, Tennessee 1966–69
Erlandson, Tom, LB, Washington State 1966–67
Evans, Norm, T, Texas Christian 1966–75

F

Faison, Earl, DE, Indiana 1966
Farley, Dale, LB, West Virginia 1971
Fernandez, Manny, DE, Utah 1968–75
Fleming, Marv, TE, Utah 1970–74
Foley, Tim, DB, Purdue 1970–76
Fowler, Charlie, G, Houston 1967–68
Funchess, Tom, T, Jackson State 1974

G

Gilchrist, Cookie, FB, None 1966
Ginn, Hubert, RB, Florida A&M 1970–75
Goode, Irv, C-G, Kentucky 1973–74
Goode, Tom, C, Mississippi State 1966–69
Gordon, Larry, LB, Arizona State 1976
Grady, Garry, DB, E. Michigan 1969
Griese, Bob, QB, Purdue 1967–76

H

Hammond, Kim, QB, Florida State 1968
Harper, Jack, HB, Florida 1967–68
Harris, Duriel, WR, New Mexico State 1976
Haynes, Abner, HB, N. Texas State 1967
Heath, Clayton, RB, Wake Forest 1976
Heinz, Bob, DT, Pacific 1969–76
Higgins, Jim, G, Xavier 1966
Hill, Barry, S, Iowa State 1975–76
Hill, Ike, WR, Catawba 1976
Hines, Jimmy, WR, Texas Southern 1969
Holmes, Johnny, DE, Florida A&M 1966
Holmes, Mike, WR, Texas Southern 1976
Hopkins, Jerry, LB, Texas A&M 1967–68
Howell, Mike, S, Grambling 1972
Hudock, Mike, C, Miami 1966
Hunter, Billy, HB, Syracuse 1966

J

Jackson, Frank, FL, Southern Methodist 1966–67
Jacobs, Ray, DT, Howard Payne 1967–68
Jaquess, Pete, DB, E. New Mexico 1966–67
Jenkins, Al, G-T, Tulsa 1972
Jenkins, Ed, RB, Holy Cross 1972
Joe, Billy, FB, Villanova 1966
Johnson, Curtis, DB, Toledo 1970–76
Joswick, Bob, DE, Tulsa 1968–69

K

Keating, Bill, DT, Michigan 1967
Keyes, Jimmy, LB-K, Mississippi 1968–69
Kiick, Jim, RB, Wyoming 1968–74
Kindig, Howard, T-C, Cal State-L.A. 1972–75
Kocourek, Dave, TE, Wisconsin 1966
Kolen, Mike, LB, Auburn 1970–75
Kremser, Karl, K, Tennessee 1969–70
Kuechenberg, Bob, G, Notre Dame 1970–76

L

Lamb, Mack, DB, Tennessee A&I 1967–68
Langer, Jim, G, S. Dakota State 1971–76
Leigh, Charles, RB, None 1971–73

Joe Auer, 95-yard touchdown, first game, 1966.

Jim Kiick, winning touchdown, 1972 playoff vs. Browns.

Stan Mitchell *Billy Neighbors* *Larry Seiple* *Freddie Solomon* *Bill Stanfill* *Steve Towle* *Howard Twilley*

Little, Larry, G, Bethune-Cookman 1969–76
Lothridge, Billy, P, Georgia Tech 1972
Lusteg, Booth, K, Connecticut 1967

M

Malone, Benny, P, Arizona State 1975–76
Mandich, Jim, TE, Michigan 1970–76
Mass, Wayne, T, Clemson 1971
Matheson, Bob, LB, Duke 1971–76
Matthews, Wes, FL, N.E. Oklahoma 1966
Mauck, Carl, C, So. Illinois 1970
McBride, Norm, DE, Utah 1969–70
McCreary, Loaird, TE, Tennessee State 1976
McCullers, Dale, LB, Florida State 1969
McDaniel, Ed (Wahoo), LB, Oklahoma 1966–68
McFarland, Jim, TE, Nebraska 1975
McGeever, John, DB, Auburn 1966
Mertens, Jim, TE, Fairmont State 1969
Milton, Gene, WR, Florida A&M 1968–69
Mingo, Gene, K, None 1966–67
Mira, George, QB, Miami 1971
Mitchell, Melvin, G, Tennessee State 1976
Mitchell, Stan, RB, Tennessee 1966–70
Moore, Maulty, DT, Bethune-Cookman 1972–74
Moore, Nat, WR, Florida 1974–76
Moore, Wayne, T, Lamar Tech 1970–76
Moreau, Doug, TE, Louisiana State 1966–69
Morrall, Earl, QB, Michigan State 1972–76
Morris, Eugene (Mercury), RB, W. Texas State 1969–75
Mumphord, Lloyd, CB, Texas Southern 1969–74

N

Neff, Bob, DB, Stephen F. Austin 1966–68
Neighbors, Billy, G, Alabama 1966–69
Newman, Ed, G, Duke 1973–76
Nomina, Tom, DT, Miami, Ohio 1966–68
Noonan, Karl, WR, Iowa 1966–71
Norton, Rick, QB, Kentucky 1966–69
Nottingham, Don, RB, Kent State 1973–76

O

Owens, Morris, WR, Arizona State 1975–76

P

Palmer, Dick, LB, Kentucky 1970
Park, Ernie, G, McMurry 1966
Pearson, Willie, CB, N. Carolina A&T 1969
Pesuit, Wally, T, Kentucky 1976
Petrella, Bob, DB, Tennessee 1966–71
Powell, Jesse, LB, W. Texas State 1969–73
Price, Sam, FB, Illinois 1966–68
Pryor, Barry, RB, Boston U 1969–70
Pyburn, Jack, T, Texas A&M 1967–68

R

Rather, Bo, WR, Michigan 1973
Reese, Don, DT, Jackson State 1974–76
Rhone, Earnest, LB, Henderson 1975
Rice, Ken, G, Auburn 1966–67
Richardson, Jeff, T, Michigan State 1969
Richardson, John, DT, UCLA 1967–71
Richardson, Willie, WR, Jackson State 1970
Riley, Jim, DE, Oklahoma 1967–71
Roberson, Bo, WR, Cornell 1966
Roberts, Archie, QB, Columbia 1967
Roderick, John, WR, Southern Methodist 1966–67
Rudolph, Jack, LB, Georgia Tech 1966

S

Salter, Bryant, S, Pittsburgh 1976
Selfridge, Andy, LB, Virginia 1976
Scott, Jake, S, Georgia 1970–75
Seiple, Larry, TE-P, Kentucky 1967–76
Sellers, Ron, WR, Florida State 1973
Smith, Tom, RB, Miami 1975
Solomon, Freddie, WR, Tampa 1975–76
Speyrer, Cotton, WR, Texas 1975
Stanfill, Bill, DE, Georgia 1969–76
Stofa, John, QB, Buffalo 1966–67, 1969–70
Stowe, Otto, WR, Iowa State 1971–72
Strock, Don, QB, Virginia Tech 1973–76
Stuckey, Henry, CB, Missouri 1972–74

T

Swift, Doug, LB, Amherst 1970–75

T

Thornton, Jack, LB, Auburn 1966
Tillman, Andre, TE, Texas Tech 1974–76
Torczon, Laverne, DE, Nebraska 1966
Towle, Steve, LB, Kansas 1975–76
Tucker, Gary, RB, Chattanooga 1968
Twilley, Howard, WR, Tulsa 1966–76

U

Urbanek, Jim, DT, Mississippi 1968

W

Wade, Charley, WR, Tennessee State 1973
Warfield, Paul, WR, Ohio State 1970–74
Warren, Jimmy, DB, Illinois 1966–69
Washington, Dick DB, Bethune-Cookman 1968
Weisacosky, Ed, LB, Miami 1968–70
West, Willie, DB, Oregon 1966–68
Westmoreland, Dick, DB, N. Carolina A&T 1966–69
White, Jeris, CB, Hawaii 1974–76
Wickert, Tom, T, Washington State 1974
Williams, Maxie, G-T, S.E. Louisiana 1966–70
Wilson, George, Jr., QB, Xavier 1966
Windauer, Bill, DT, Iowa 1975
Winfrey, Stan, RB, Arkansas State 1975–76
Wood, Dick, QB, Auburn 1966
Woods, Larry, DT, Tennessee State 1973
Woodson, Freddie, G, Florida A&M 1967–69

Y

Yepremian, Garo, K, None 1970–76
Young, Willie, T, Alcorn A&M 1973

Z

Zecher, DT, Utah State 1966–67

Safeties Dick Anderson (40) and Jake Scott (13) stop Pittsburgh's Al Young, 1972 AFC championship game.

MINNESOTA VIKINGS

1960 The Twin Cities of Minneapolis and St. Paul had a new stadium in suburban Bloomington, but no pro fooball team. A sports committee, headed by local auto dealer Bill Boyer, began shopping around for a franchise. After failing to lure the Cardinals from Chicago, the group was prepared to accept an AFL team. A telegram from George Halas, head of the NFL expansion committee, revealing the NFL would accept a request for an expansion franchise by a Minneapolis-St. Paul group, changed their plans. The NFL granted Minnesota a franchise to begin play the following season, January 28. Max Winter, former owner of the Minneapolis Lakers basketball team, was named team president. Bert Rose was named general manager. Joe Thomas was hired as talent scout.

1961 Rose came up with a nickname, "Vikings," and a head coach, Norm Van Brocklin. Van Brocklin had quarterbacked the Philadelphia Eagles to the world championship in 1960. The Vikings were stocked with 36 veteran players in the expansion draft. Most were castoffs and retreads, but Van Brocklin acquired Hugh McElhenny, the all-pro halfback, from San Francisco. The Vikings traded a first draft choice to New York for quarterback George Shaw. The draft yielded Tommy Mason, a talented halfback from Tulane; Francis Tarkenton, a daring quarterback from Georgia; and Ed Sharockman, a cornerback from Pitt. Defensive end Jim Marshall, who was to start in every game through 1976, was acquired in a trade with Cleveland. The Vikings had some talent but it was spread thin. "They're not big," line coach Stan West said of the Vikings, "but they sure are slow." Most observers predicted Minnesota, like Dallas in 1960, would go winless in its first season. The Vikings pulled a stunning upset in their first league game, embarrassing the Chicago Bears 37–13 at Metropolitan Stadium. Tarkenton replaced Shaw in the second quarter, threw four touchdown passes, and ran for the final score himself. The Vikings lost their next seven games but finished with a respectable 3–11 record.

1962 Van Brocklin made significant progress improving his personnel. With Tarkenton entrenched as the regular quarterback, Van Brocklin traded off Shaw. He phased out the aging McElhenny in favor of Mason, who had back-to-back 100-yard games against Detroit and Baltimore. He added free-agent center Mick Tingelhoff. The highlight of a 2–11–1 season was a 31–21 win over Philadelphia, sweet revenge for Van Brocklin, who had resented not being named Eagles' head coach following his retirement as a player.

1963 The Vikings began outgrowing their expansion image by beating San Francisco twice in the first three weeks as Bill Brown, a Chicago Bears' reject, established himself at fullback. The Vikings won three more games and just barely missed upsets of Green Bay and Baltimore. Minnesota played the Bears, the eventual world champions, to a 17–17 tie at Wrigley Field late in the season. Paul Flatley, a sure-handed receiver from Northwestern, led the team with 51 catches, and was voted the NFL rookie of the year.

1964 Prior to the season, Rose was dismissed as general manager and replaced by former Pittsburgh quarterback Jim Finks. The top draft choice was Carl Eller, a towering defensive end from Minnesota. The Vikings won all five preseason games and beat Baltimore in the league opener. Minnesota beat Green Bay for the first time 24–23 as Tarkenton completed a 44-yard pass to Gordie Smith on fourth-and-22 to set up Fred Cox's winning field goal. Marshall gained fame by picking up a San Francisco fumble and returning it 66 yards the wrong way for a 49ers' safety,

Fran Tarkenton hands off to Chuck Foreman and the Vikings sweep right vs. Green Bay, 1974.

October 26. The Vikings won the game 27–22. Minnesota went unbeaten in the final four weeks of the season, tying Detroit and beating Los Angeles, the New York Gaints, and Chicago by lopsided scores. Their strong stretch run enabled the Vikings to tie Green Bay for second place in the Western Conference at 8–5–1.

1965 With his strong veteran nucleus, plus additions such as defensive tackle Gary Larsen, linebacker Lonnie Warwick, running back Dave Osborn, and wide receiver Lance Rentzel, Van Brocklin expected to win the Western Conference. The Vikings staggered to a 2–3 start, with the defense allowing an average of 35 points a game. They rallied from a 35–14 deficit to beat San Francisco 42–41 and ignite a three-game win streak. Their title hopes were buried the following week when Baltimore beat them 41–21 on substitute Gary Cuozzo's five touchdown passes. The next morning Van Brocklin told reporters he was resigning as head coach. By late afternoon he changed his mind. Not surprisingly, the disillusioned Vikings lost their next three games and faded to a disappointing 7–7 finish.

1966 The unhealthy climate between Van Brocklin and his players was never more apparent than during the 1966 season. Van Brocklin and Tarkenton were hardly on speaking terms most of the year. After several seasons of contention, the Vikings were never a factor in the Western Conference, managing just one win in their first six games. Mason, the once-brilliant runner, was limping toward the end of his career on shattered knees. Bill Brown was Minnesota's only offensive threat, rushing for 829 yards and catching 37 passes. Late in the season, Van Brocklin started Bob Berry ahead of Tarkenton, "I think he's trying to tell me something," Tarkenton said.

1967 Tarktenton issued a statement suggesting that either he or Van Brocklin be sent to another NFL team, February 9. A few days later, Van Brocklin resigned. In March, Tarkenton was traded to the New York Giants for two first- and two second-round draft choices. The trade ensured a bountiful rookie crop, which included Alan Page, Gene Washington, Clint Jones, John Beasley, and Bob Grim. Finks signed Harry (Bud) Grant to a three-year contract as head

coach. Grant had been a candidate for the original Vikings job in 1961 but chose to remain with Winnipeg of the Canadian Football League. Finks also imported a quarterback from Canada, Joe Kapp, a brawling, charismatic figure who quickly became Minnesota's team leader. The 3–8–3 season was highlighted by 10–7 upset of Green Bay, the eventual Super Bowl champion.

1968 With the addition of top draft pick Ron Yary at offensive tackle and trade acquisition Paul Krause at free safety, Minnesota finally had the makings of a champion. The front four—Eller, Page, Larsen, and Marshall—emerged as the NFL's premier defensive line. The offense, led by the reckless, free-wheeling Kapp, was explosive and unpredictable. The Vikings pulled out of a midseason slump to win their last two games and move past Chicago and Green Bay for their first NFL Central Division championship. Brown rushed for 805 yards and scored 14 touchdowns. Minnesota lost its first playoff game to Baltimore 24–14, December 22.

1969 The Vikings opened the season with a stunning 24–23 loss to the lowly New York Giants and Fran Tarkenton. Tarkenton rallied the Giants from a two-touchdown deficit in the fourth quarter to beat his former teammates. The following week, Joe Kapp replaced Gary Cuozzo as Minnesota's quarterback and tied an NFL record by throwing seven touchdown passes in a 52–14 rout of NFL champion Baltimore, September 28. The Vikings won their next 11 games. They clinched the Central Division title with a 27–0 win over Detroit on Thanksgiving Day. Gene Washington was the leading receiver with 39 catches, nine for touchdowns. Dave Osborn led in rushing with 643 yards. The Vikings trailed Los Angeles by 10 points at the half but came back to win their Western Conference playoff game 23–20, December 27. Carl Eller sacked Roman Gabriel in the end zone for a safety to clinch it.

1970 Minnesota had little trouble with Cleveland in the NFC championship game, burying the Browns in 8-degree cold 27–7, January 4. The Vikings played their poorest game of the season in Super Bowl IV, losing to Kansas City 23–7 in New Orleans, January 11. The Vikings were favored by 13 points but they fell behind 16–0 in the first half. Kapp was forced from the game in the fourth quarter with a dislocated shoulder. As the 1970 season began, the Vikings lost their leader when Kapp sat out the early games over a contract dispute and was sold to the Boston Patriots. Cuozzo took over at quarterback and did a capable, if unspectacular, job. Minnesota continued to win on the strength of its outstanding defense, which allowed just 14 touchdowns in 14 regular season games. The Vikings opened the season with a 27–10 win over Kansas City in a rematch of Super Bowl IV teams. Following a 13–10 loss to Green Bay, the Vikings won 10 of their last 11 games to run away with the Central Division for the third straight year. Clint Jones emerged as a runner of promise, scoring nine touchdowns. Cornerback Ed Sharockman intercepted seven passes, and scored three touchdowns. Minnesota was shocked in the first round of the NFC playoffs, losing to San Francisco 17–14 at Metropolitan Stadium, December 27. The Vikings gave the game away on two interceptions and two fumbles, one of which the 49ers converted into the decisive field goal.

1971 Feeling they needed a more experienced quarterback, the Vikings traded offensive tackle Steve Smith and two high draft choices to Philadelphia for 31-year-old Norm Snead, January 22. Snead was a preseason disappointment and fell to third-string behind Cuozzo and Bob Lee. Injuries hampered Minnesota, sidelining receivers Gene Washington and John Beasley and middle linebacker Lonnie Warwick. Defense again carried the Vikings as they allowed just 12 touchdowns (2 rushing, 10 passing) during the regular season. Upset by Chicago in their second game 20–17, the Vikings allowed only two touchdowns in the next five weeks, shutting out Buffalo and Philadelphia. The season was typified by a 3–0 win over Green Bay in which the Vikings' defense stopped the Packers on the 1-yard line. Minnesota won its fourth consecutive Central Division title despite the quarterback problems. Lee, a three-year veteran, was given the starting assignment in the NFC playoff against Dallas, December 25. He threw two interceptions and was replaced by Cuozzo who threw two more. With the Vikings providing five turnovers, Dallas needed just 10 first downs and 183 net yards to win the game 20–12. Alan Page was named the NFC's most valuable player, the first time a lineman ever received the honor.

1972 Minnesota solidified its quarterback situation by trading Snead, Bob Grim, Vince Clements, a first- and a second-round draft pick to the New York Giants for Fran Tarkenton, whose return to the Vikings generated great hope for the 1972 season. The hope turned to frustration as the Vikings stumbled to a 7–7 finish. The defense, weakened by injuries to Page and Eller, was generally ineffective, allowing 252 points. The Vikings lost five games by four points or less. Tarkenton had an outstanding year, however, leading the NFC in most passing categories.

1973 A strong draft heralded a return to power for the Vikings. In the first round, Minnesota selected Chuck Foreman, a big, slashing runner from the University of Miami. In the fifth round, they added Brent McClanahan, a halfback from Arizona State. Foreman gave the offense the game-breaking backfield punch it had lacked since the decline of Tommy Mason. In his second regular season game, Foreman carried the ball 16 times for 116 yards in a 22–13 win over Chicago, September 23. Two weeks later, Foreman rushed for 114 yards in a 23–9 win over Detroit. Tarkenton's favorite receiver was John Gilliam, who was acquired in a trade with St. Louis in 1972. Gilliam caught 42 passes, and scored nine touchdowns. The defense, healthy once again, returned to form, permitting just 15 touchdowns and 168 points, both NFC lows. The Vikings (12–2) were the only Central

Division team to finish with a winning record. Tarkenton hit Gilliam with two second-half touchdown passes to beat Washington in an NFC playoff game 27–20, December 22. Oscar Reed rushed for 95 yards and caught five passes. The Vikings won their second NFC championship by defeating Dallas 27–10 in Texas Stadium, December 30. Tarkenton hit Gilliam with a 54-yard touchdown pass to put Minnesota ahead 17–7 in the third quarter. Bobby Bryant clinched it by returning an interception 63 yards for a score.

1974 The Vikings were crushed by Miami 24–7 in Super Bowl VIII at Rice Stadium in Houston, January 13. The Dolphins drove for touchdowns on their first two possessions and opened a 24–0 third-quarter lead. Miami limited Minnesota to just 72 yards rushing and pressured Tarkenton constantly. Jim Finks resigned in May. Mike Lynn was hired as assistant to president Max Winter, August 15. Six rookies made the team from another productive draft. Foreman tied a club record by rushing for three touchdowns in 32–17 win over Green Bay in the opener, September 15. Cox kicked a 27-yard field goal at the gun to beat Dallas 23–21, October 6. The Vikings won their fifth in a row as Tarkenton passed for 274 yards to rout Houston 51–10, October 13. Minnesota lost four of its next six and the Central Division lead dwindled to one game over Detroit and Green Bay. Tarkenton ended the slump, passing for 319 yards and three touchdowns in a 29–9 win over New Orleans. Foreman set a club record with his fifty-third pass reception of the season in a 23–10 win over Atlanta, December 7. In the NFC playoffs, the Vikings turned two St. Louis turnovers into touchdowns and a 30–14 victory, December 21. Tarkenton hit Gilliam for two scores. Minnesota's defense provided the key to a 14–10 win over Los Angeles in the NFC championship game at Metropolitan Stadium, December 29. Wally Hilgenberg's end zone interception ended one threat and two sacks by Page in the fourth quarter preserved the scant lead.

1975 Once again, the Vikings lost in the Super Bowl, this time to Pittsburgh 16–6 in New Orleans, January 12. A magnificent Pittsburgh defense limited the Vikings to just nine first downs and 17 yards rushing. Tarkenton threw three interceptions and fumbled once for a safety. Minnesota's only touchdown came on Terry Brown's recovery of a blocked punt. The Vikings got off to their fastest start ever, winning their first 10 games. Joe Blahak, a reserve cornerback, blocked a punt for a safety in a 29–21 win over the New York Jets, October 12. The following week, Marshall set an NFL record with his twenty-fifth career fumble recovery in a 25–19 win over Detroit. Safety Paul Krause intercepted two passes in a 28–17 win over Green Bay to move into second place among the NFL's all-time pass interceptors with 69. Tarkenton threw for 300 yards and two touchdowns to Gilliam in a 20–7 win over New Orleans, November 16. Foreman rushed for more than 100 yards for the third straight game and the fifth in six weeks as the Vikings pounded San Diego 28–13, November 23. Foreman finished the season with 1,070 yards rushing, 73 pass receptions (a record for a running back), and an NFC-high 22 touchdowns. Tarkenton surpassed three of John Unitas's career passing records: most attempts (5,225), most completions (2,931), and most touchdowns (291). The Vikings were eliminated in their NFC divisional playoffs 17–14 by Dallas at Metropolitan Stadium, December 28. Minnesota had the game won until Roger Staubach hit Drew Pearson with a dramatic 50-yard touchdown pass with just 24 seconds left. Tarkenton was named the NFL's most valuable player.

1976 Minnesota won its eighth Central Division title in nine years. The defense stopped Los Angeles twice at the 1-yard line to preserve a 10–10 overtime tie,

September 19. Cornerback Nate Allen, acquired in a trade with the 49ers, intercepted a pass and recovered a fumble to set up two Foreman touchdowns in a 17–6 upset of Pittsburgh, October 4. Tarkenton continued to make history, becoming the first man to reach 3,000 career completions in a 24–7 win over the New York Giants, October 17. He surpassed 40,000 yards passing in a 31–12 win over Philadelphia as Minnesota ran its unbeaten string to seven, October 24. And he threw his three hundredth touchdown pass in a 27–21 win over Seattle, November 14. Foreman set a Vikings' record with 200 yards rushing against the Eagles. Sammy White, a rookie receiver from Grambling, caught nine passes, three for touchdowns, in a 29–7 win over Miami, December 11. Tarkenton passed to White for two scores and Foreman and Brent McClanahan combined for 215 yards rushing as Minnesota defeated Washington 35–20 in the NFC divisional playoffs, December 18. In the NFC championship game, Allen blocked a field goal attempt by Los Angeles's Tom Dempsey and Bryant returned the loose ball 90 yards for a touchdown. Bryant also intercepted two passes to thwart a Rams' comeback and preserve Minnesota's 24–13 triumph. White was named NFC rookie of the year.

1977 Minnesota's third NFC championship in four seasons was tainted by another Super Bowl loss. "We're gonna keep coming back until we find an AFC team we can beat," Tarkenton said after the Vikings lost to Oakland 32–14 in Super Bowl XI at Pasadena, January 9.

MEMBER OF HALL OF FAME:
Hugh McElhenny

VIKINGS RECORD, 1961–76

Year	Won	Lost	Tied	Pct.	Pts.	OP
1961	3	11	0	.214	285	407
1962	2	11	1	.154	254	410
1963	5	8	1	.385	309	390
1964	8	5	1	.615	355	296
1965	7	7	0	.500	383	403
1966	4	9	1	.308	292	304
1967	3	8	3	.273	233	294
1968§	8	6	0	.571	282	242
1969‡	12	2	0	.857	379	133
1970§	12	2	0	.857	335	143
1971§	11	3	0	.786	245	139
1972	7	7	0	.500	301	252
1973‡	12	2	0	.857	296	168
1974‡	10	4	0	.714	310	195
1975§	12	2	0	.857	377	180
1976‡	11	2	1	.821	305	176
16 Years	127	89	8	.585	4,941	4,132

§ – NFC Central Division Champion
‡ – NFC Champion

RECORD HOLDERS

Rushing (Yards)	Chuck Foreman, 1976	1,155
Passing (Pct.)	Fran Tarkenton, 1975	64.2
Passing (Yards)	Fran Tarkenton, 1975	2,994
Passing (TDs)	Fran Tarkenton, 1975	25
Receiving (No.)	Chuck Foreman, 1975	73
Receiving (Yards)	John Gilliam, 1972	1,035
Interceptions (No.)	Paul Krause, 1975	10
Punting (Avg.)	Bobby Walden, 1964	46.4
Punt Ret. (Avg.)	Bill Butler, 1963	10.5
Kickoff Ret. (Avg.)	John Gilliam, 1972	26.4
Touchdowns (Total)	Chuck Foreman, 1975	22
Field Goals Made	Fred Cox, 1970	30
Points (No.)	Chuck Foreman, 1975	132

COACHING HISTORY

1961–66	Norm Van Brocklin	29–51–4
1967–76	Harry (Bud) Grant	98–38–4

FIRST PLAYER SELECTED

1961	Tommy Mason, RB, Tulane
1962	Bill Miller, WR (3), Miami
1963	Jim Dunaway, T, Mississippi
1964	Carl Eller, DE, Minnesota
1965	Jack Snow, WR, Notre Dame
1966	Jerry Shay, DT, Purdue
1967	Clint Jones, RB, Michigan State
1968	Ron Yary, T, USC
1969	Ed White, G (2), California
1970	John Ward, DT, Oklahoma State
1971	Leo Hayden, RB, Ohio State
1972	Jeff Siemon, LB, Stanford
1973	Chuck Foreman, RB, Miami
1974	Fred McNeill, LB, UCLA
1975	Mark Mullaney, DE, Colorado State
1976	James White, DT, Oklahoma State

Bill Brown

Carl Eller

Paul Flatley

Rip Hawkins

Wally Hilgenberg

Tommy Mason

Dave Osborn

MINNESOTA VIKINGS, 1961–76

Adams, Tom, C, Minnesota-Duluth 1962
Alderman, Grady, T, Detroit 1961–74
Allen, Nate, CB, Texas Southern 1976
Anderson, Scott, C, Missouri 1975–76
Arrobio, Chuck, T, USC 1966

B

Ballman, Gary, TE, Michigan State 1973
Barnes, Billy, RB, Wake Forest 1965–66
Battle, Jim, G, So. Illinois 1963
Beasley, John, TE, California 1967–73
Beamon, Autry, S, East Texas State 1975–76
Bedsole, Hal, TE, USC 1964–66
Berry, Bob, QB, Oregon 1965–67, 1973–76
Bishop, Bill, DT, N. Texas State 1961
Blahak, Joe, CB, Oklahoma 1974–75
Blair, Matt, LB, Iowa State 1974–76
Bolin, Bookie, G, Mississippi 1968–69
Boone, David, DE, Michigan State 1974
Bowie, Larry, G, Purdue 1962–68
Boylan, Jim, C, Washington State 1963–64
Breitenstein, Bob, T, Tulsa 1967
Britt, Charlie, DB, Georgia 1964
Brown, Bill, RB, Illinois 1962–74
Brown, Robert, TE, Alcorn A&M 1971
Brown, Terry, S, Oklahoma 1972

Bryant, Bob, DB, South Carolina 1968–76
Buetow, Bart, T, Minnesota 1976
Bundra, Mike, DT, USC 1964
Butler, Billy, TB, Chattanooga 1962–64
Byers, Ken, G, Cincinnati 1964–66

C

Caleb, Jamie, DB, Grambling 1961
Calland, Lee, DB, Louisville 1963–65
Campbell, John, LB, Minnesota 1963–64
Cappleman, Bill, QB, Florida State 1970
Carpenter, Preston, C, Arkansas 1966
Charles, John, DB, Purdue 1970
Christopherson, Jim, K, Concordia 1962
Clabo, Neil, P, Tennessee 1975–76
Clarke, Leon, E, USC 1963
Coleman, Al, DB, Tennessee State 1967
Cox, Fred, K, Pittsburgh 1963–76
Craig, Steve, TE, Northwestern 1974–76
Culpepper, Ed, DT, Alabama 1961
Cuozzo, Gary, QB, Virginia 1968–71

D

Dale, Carroll, WR, Virginia Tech 1973
Davis, Doug, T, Kentucky 1966–72
Dawson, Rhett, WR, Florida State 1973
Dean, Ted, RB, Wichita 1964

Demery, Calvin, WR, Arizona State 1972
Denny, Earl, RB, Missouri 1967–68
Denson, Al, WR, Florida A&M 1971
Denton, Bob, DE, Pacific 1961–64
Derby, Dean, DB, Washington 1961–62
Dickson, Paul, DT, Baylor 1961–70
Dillon, Terry, DB, Montana 1963
Donahue, Oscar, E, San Jose State 1962
Dumler, Doug, C, Nebraska 1975–76

E

Eischeid, Mike, P, Upper Iowa 1972–74
Eller, Carl, DE, Minnesota 1964–76

F

Farber, Hap, LB, Mississippi 1970
Faust, Paul, LB, Minnesota 1967
Ferguson, Bob, RB, Ohio State 1963
Ferguson, Charley, E, Tennessee State 1963
Fitzgerald, Mike, Louisiana State 1966
Flatley, Paul, E, Northwestern 1963–67
Foreman, Chuck, RB, Miami 1973–76
Franckhauser, Tom, DB, Purdue 1962–63

G

Gallagher, Frank, G, North Carolina 1973
Gault, Billy, DB, Texas Christian 1961
Gersbach, Carl, LB, West Chester State 1971
Gilliam, John, WR, South Carolina 1972–75
Goodrich, Bob, C, Vanderbilt 1968
Goodrum, Charles, T, Florida A&M 1973–76
Grecni, Dick, LB, Ohio U. 1961
Grim, Bob, WR, Oregon State 1967–71, 1976
Groce, Ron, RB, Macalester 1976
Guilford, Larry, DB, Pacific 1962

H

Hackbart, Dale, DB, Wisconsin 1966–70
Haley, Dick, DB, Pittsburgh 1961
Hall, Tom, WR, Minnesota 1964–66, 1968–70
Hall, Windlan, S, Arizona State 1976
Hamilton, Wes, G, Tulsa 1976
Hansen, Don, LB, Illinois 1966–67
Hargrove, Jim, LB, Howard Payne 1967–70
Harris, Bill, RB, Colorado 1969–70
Hawkins, Rip, LB, North Carolina 1961–65
Hayden, Leo, RB, Ohio State 1971
Hayes, Ray, RB, Central State, Okla. 1961
Henderson, John, E, Michigan 1968–72
Hilgenberg, Wally, LB, Iowa 1968–76
Hill, Gary, DB, USC 1965
Hill, King, P-QB, Rice 1968
Hilton, John, TE, Richmond 1970
Holland, John, WR, Tennessee State 1974
Hultz, Don, DE, So. Mississippi 1963
Huth, Gary, G, Wake Forest 1961–63

J

Jenke, Noel, LB, Minnesota 1971
Jobko, Bill, LB, Ohio State 1963–65
Johnson, Gene, DB, Cincinnati 1961
Johnson, Sammy, RB, North Carolina 1976
Jones, Clint, RB, Michigan State 1967–72
Jordan, Jeff, DB, Tulsa 1965–67
Joyce, Don, DE, Tulane 1961

K

Kapp, Joe, QB, California 1967–69
Kassulke, Karl, DB, Drake 1963–72
Kellar, Mark, RB, Northern Illinois 1976
Keys, Brady, DB, Colorado State 1967
King, Phil, RB, Vanderbilt 1965–66
Kirby, John, LB, Nebraska 1964–68
Kosens, Terry, DB, Hofstra 1963
Kramer, Kent, TE, Minnesota 1969–70
Krause, Paul, DB, Iowa 1968–76

L

Lacey, Bob, E, North Carolina 1964
Lamson, Chuck, DB, Wyoming 1962–63
Lapham, Bill, C, Iowa 1961
Larsen, Gary, DT, Concordia 1965–74
Lash, Jim, WR, Northwestern 1973–76

Grady Alderman, a member of the Vikings from their start until 1974.

Ed Sharockman

Jeff Siemon

Mick Tingelhoff

Gene Washington

Sammy White

Roy Winston

Ron Yary

Lee, Bob, QB-P, Pacific 1969–72, 1975–76
Leo, Jim, DE, Cincinnati 1961–62
Lester, Darrell, RB, McNeese State 1964
Linden, Errol, T, Houston 1962–65
Lindsey, Jim, RB, Arkansas 1966–71
Livingston, Cliff, LB, UCLA 1962
Lurtsema, Bob, DT, Western Michigan 1972–76

M

Mackbee, Earsell, DB, Utah State 1965–69
Marinaro, Ed, RB, Cornell 1972–76
Marshall, Jim, DE, Ohio State 1961–76
Marshall, Larry, S, Maryland 1974
Martin, Amos, LB, Louisville 1972–76
Martin, Billy, TE, Georgia Tech 1968
Mason, Tommy, RB, Tulane 1961–66
Mayberry, Doug, RB, Utah State 1961–62
McClanahan, Brent, RB, Arizona State 1973–76
McCormick, John, QB, Massachusetts 1962
McCullum, Sam, WR, Montana State 1974–75
McElhenny, Hugh, RB, Washington 1961–62
McGill, Mike, LB, Notre Dame 1968–70
McKeever, Marlin, TE, USC 1967
McNeill, Fred, LB, UCLA 1974–76
McNeill, Tom, P, Stephen F. Austin 1970
McWatters, Bill, RB, N. Texas State 1964
Mercer, Mike, K, Arizona State 1961
Meylan, Wayne, LB, Nebraska 1970
Michel, Tom, RB, East Carolina 1964
Middleton, Dave, E, Auburn 1961
Miller, Robert, RB, Kansas 1975–76
Morris, Jack DB, Oregon 1961
Mostardt, Rich, DB, Kent State 1961
Mullaney, Mark, DE, Colorado State 1975–76
Murphy, Fred, E, Georgia Tech 1961

O

O'Brien, Dave, G, Boston College 1963–64
Osborn, Dave, RB, North Dakota 1965–75
Osborne, Clancy, LB, Arizona State 1961–62

P

Page, Alan, DT, Notre Dame 1967–76
Patton, Jerry, DT, Nebraska 1971
Perreault, Pete, G, Cal. State-Long Beach 1971
Pesonen, Dick, DB, Minnesota-Duluth 1961
Peterson, Ken, E, Utah 1961
Phillips, Jim, E, Auburn 1965–67
Poage, Ray, C, Texas 1963
Poltl, Randy, S, Stanford 1974
Porter, Ron, LB, Idaho 1973
Powers, John, TC, Notre Dame 1966
Prestel, Jim, DT, Idaho 1961–65
Provost, Ted, DB, Ohio State 1970
Pyle, Palmer, G, Michigan State 1964

R

Rabold, Mike, G, Indiana 1961–62
Randolph, Al, DB, Iowa 1973
Rashad, Ahmad, WR, Oregon 1976
Reed, Bob, RB, Pacific 1962–63
Reed, Oscar, RB, Colorado State 1968–74
Reichow, Jerry, QB, Iowa 1961–64
Reilly, Mike, LB, Iowa 1969
Rentzel, Lance, E, Oklahoma 1965–66
Riley, Steve, T, USC 1974–76
Rose, George, DB, Auburn 1964–66
Rowland, Justin, DB, Texas Christian 1961
Rubke, Karl, LB, USC 1961
Russ, Pat, DT, Purdue 1963

S

Schmidt, Roy, G, Cal. State-Long Beach 1970
Schmitz, Bob, LB, Montana 1966
Schnelker, Bob, E, Bowling Green 1961
Sharockman, Ed, DB, Pittsburgh 1962–72
Shaw, George, QB, Oregon 1961
Shaw, Glenn, RB, Kentucky 1961
Shay, Jerry, DT, Purdue 1966–67
Sherman, Will, E, St. Mary's 1961
Shields, Lebron, DE, Tennessee 1961
Siemon, Jeff, LB, Stanford 1972–76
Simkus, Arnold, DT, Michigan 1966

Simpson, Howard, T, Auburn 1964
Smith, Gordon, C, Missouri 1961–65
Smith, Steve, DE, Michigan 1968–70
Snead, Norm, QB, Wake Forest 1971
Spencer, Willie, RB, None 1976
Stein, Bob, DB, Minnesota 1975
Stonebreaker, Steve, LB, Detroit 1962–63
Sumner, Charley, DB, William & Mary 1961–62
Sunde, Milt, G, Minnesota 1964–74
Sutherland, Doug, LB, Wisconsin State 1971–76
Sutton, Archie, T, Illinois 1965–67
Swain, Bill, LB, Oregon 1964

T

Tarkenton, Francis, QB, Georgia 1961–66, 1972–76
Tatman, Pete, RB, Nebraska 1967
Tillemann, Mike, DT, Montana 1966
Tingelhoff, Mick, C, Nebraska 1962–76
Tobey, Dave, LB, Oregon 1966
Triplett, Mel, RB, Toledo 1961–62

V

VanderKelen, Ron, QB, Wisconsin 1963–67
Vargo, Larry, DB, Detroit 1964–65
Vellone, Jim, G, USC 1966–70
Voigt, Stu, TE, Wisconsin 1971–76

W

Walden, Bobby, K, Georgia 1964–67
Wallace, Jackie, CB, Arizona 1973–74
Ward, John, DT, Oklahoma State 1970–74
Warwick, Lonnie, LB, Tennessee State 1965–72
Washington, Gene, E, Michigan State 1967–72
Wells, Mike, QB, Illinois 1973–74
West, Charlie, DB, Texas-El Paso 1968–73
White, Ed, G, California 1969–76
White, James, DT, Oklahoma State 1976
White, Sammy, WR, Grambling 1976
Williams, A.D., DB-RB, Pacific 1961
Williams, Jeff, TE, Oklahoma State 1966
Willis, Leonard, WR, Ohio State 1976
Wilson, Tom, RB, None 1963
Winfrey, Carl, LB, Wisconsin 1971
Winston, Roy, LB, Louisiana State 1962–76
Wright, Jeff, DB, Minnesota 1971–76
Wright, Nate, DB, San Diego State 1971–76

Y

Yary, Ron, T, USC 1968–76
Young, Jim, RB, Queens, Ontario 1965–66
Youso, Frank, T, Minnesota 1961–62

Z

Zaunbrecher, Godfrey, C, Louisiana State 1971

Tommy Mason, the Vikings' first all-pro, in 1963.

NEW ENGLAND PATRIOTS

1959 The American Football League's eighth franchise was awarded to Boston and William H. Sullivan, Jr. Mike Holovak, head coach at Boston College, was named director of player personnel. Ed McKeever was the club's first general manager. The team selected Northwestern running back Ron Burton as its first draft choice and Syracuse running back Gerhardt Schwedes as its "territorial" pick.

1960 Lou Saban, little-known coach at Western Illinois University, was signed as the team's first head coach. "He's a Paul Brown with heart," said McKeever. A local newspaper held a contest to name the team. "Patriots," suggested by 74 people, was the winner. Sullivan's biggest problem was finding a facility where his team could play. Fenway Park was unavailable. So were the stadiums of Boston College and Harvard Stadium. Boston University Field was chosen. Sullivan signed to play Patriots' games there for two years, with an option for a third. The Patriots became the first major league pro sports team in history to issue public stock, April 2. The club opened its first training camp at the University of Massachusetts in Amherst. Some 350 players showed up. One was Ed (Butch) Songin, a former Boston College star who had quit Canadian football and was working as a probation officer near Boston. It became evident early in camp that Songin would be the club's best passer. In the first pro sports event ever staged in Harvard Stadium, the Patriots lost a preseason game to the Dallas Texans 24–14 August 14. More importantly, the game had been played in one of the town's more influential settings. A crowd of 21,597 was present for the regular season opener at Boston University Field and welcomed pro football back to Boston after an 11-year absence, dating back to the 1949 Boston Yanks. But the Patriots lost the game to Denver 13–10. A week later, the Patriots defeated the New York Titans 28–24 for their first AFL victory. Financially, it was a rocky season for Sullivan. The team lost approximately $350,000, although the average home attendance of 16,500 provided some hope.

1961 In a five-player trade with Oakland, Boston acquired Babe Parilli, the experienced quarterback it felt it needed to build a winning team. A couple of second year men, wide receiver Gino Cappelletti and sprinter Larry Garron looked as if they would be of considerable help in the preseason. But Sullivan, who was hoping for 10,000 season ticket sales, sold barely a third that amount, and the team was not on solid footing as it began its second year. When the record fell to 2-3 and fan interest waned, Sullivan fired Saban and named Mike Holovak head coach, October 19. Holovak stressed defense and the turnaround was almost immediate. The Patriots were 7-1-1 with Holovak as coach, leading the division for awhile. Attendance improved, averaging more than 19,000. The club still lost money, but less than half the amount lost the previous year.

1962 Holovak was signed to a new two-year contract and made two acquisitions through the draft. Nick Buoniconti became the new middle linebacker and the key to the defense, and Billy Neighbors, an All-America blocker from Alabama, turned into the stabilizing force on the Patriots' offensive line. A victory over Houston 34–21 in the second game of the season stamped Boston as a strong contender. But in their next meeting later in the year, Parilli, now solidly entrenched as the quarterback, was hit just after throwing a second quarter pass. He broke his collarbone and was lost for the season. The Patriots lost the game and their chance at the championship, although finishing with a 9-4-1 record.

1963 The Patriots announced their new playing site of Fenway Park, home of the baseball Red Sox, with 38,000 seats. A severe spinal injury sidelined Burton and a pinched nerve inhibited Parilli. The team played erratically. In the highlight of what was probably Holovak's best coaching performance, Boston defeated Buffalo 26–8 in a snow-plagued playoff game dominated by Cappelletti's clutch field goal kicking. The collapse of Houston, the regrouping in New York, and a poor start by Buffalo kept the Patriots in the race, eventually allowing them to tie for first place in their division with a 7-6-1 record.

1964 In the AFL championship game with San Diego, the patched-up Patriots were no match for the Chargers. Keith Lincoln ran for 206 yards and San Diego scored an easy 51–10 victory. "They left nothing untouched," Holovak said afterward. The Patriots drafted Jack Concannon, the All-America quarterback from Boston College, number one. But after a wild bidding war, Concannon decided to sign with the Philadelphia Eagles. Although there was some criticism of Holovak's "old folks" roster, he managed to get a lot out of it, closing with a rush that fell just short of a repeat division championship. After setting a new attendance record of 199,707, the Patriots announced they had finished their first season in the black.

1965 Jim Nance, a powerful fullback from Syracuse, was drafted number 19 and signed. Joe Bellino, the former Heisman trophy winner from Navy who spent four years in the service, also joined the team. Already weakened by age, the Patriots were further crippled by a series of injuries. Burton, Garron, and Cappelletti were a few of the top players who were injured. Parilli threw 26 interceptions.

1966 John Huarte, who originally signed with New York for a $200,000 bonus, was acquired from the Jets in a trade for Jim Colclough. Plans for a mammoth year-round sports complex, complete with a stadium that would feature a retractable roof, were revealed for downtown Boston. The price tag, how-

Jim Nance during his 1,458-yard season for Boston, 1966.

ever, was estimated at $80 million, and the method of financing such a project remained a major stumbling block. The key to the Patriots' season turned out to be Jim Nance, who finished with 1,458 yards rushing, an AFL record. Nance's presence helped Parilli enjoy an excellent season. The Patriots battled Buffalo for first place all season, and a late 14–3 victory over the Bills had Boston fans thinking Super Bowl. But in the final game of the year, Joe Namath and the Jets knocked them out of the lead and cost them the title 38–28. Holovak was presented a new five-year contract with a substantial pay raise.

1967 Although Nance continued to gain big yardage, the Patriots slipped badly. Parilli showed signs of age, there was little outside speed, and the defense couldn't carry the team. The Patriots fell to last place in the Eastern Division. Nance still gained with 1,216 yards, tops in the league.

1968 In an attempt to trade some of the age for youth and enthusiasm, Holovak dealt Parilli to the New York Jets for quarterback Mike Taliaferro. But Taliaferro had his problems in Boston, eventually losing his job to rookie Tom Sherman. Few of the other Patriots responded with good seasons. Nance injured an ankle that limited his effectiveness. Bad knees knocked defensive end Larry Eisenhauer and middle linebacker Nick Buoniconti out of the lineup for a considerable time.

1969 Mike Holovak was replaced as head coach by Clive Rush, who lost the first seven games of the season. Linebacker Buoniconti was traded to Miami. The Patriots rallied to win four of seven games. Key new contributors included running back Carl Garrett, wide receiver Ron Sellers, and tackle Mike Montler, all rookies. All homes games were played at Boston College Alumni Stadium.

1970 A large sum of money was spent to pick up Joe Kapp from Minnesota. But the quarterback who had taken the Vikings to the Super Bowl wasn't the same one who showed up in Boston. He was out of shape and unfamiliar with the Patriots' system. He finished the season with a total of three touchdown passes and 17 interceptions. His year was indicative of the entire team's performance. By midseason, Clive Rush was fired and John Mazur was named head coach. Foxboro, Massachusetts, was officially selected as the new site for the team's home, and ground was broken for Schaefer Stadium. In the meantime, the Patriots played their home games at Harvard Stadium.

1971 Since it had moved out of Boston and would now represent a wider population area, the team's name was changed to New England Patriots. Schaefer Stadium was dedicated with a 20–14 preseason win over the Giants, before 60,423 fans. But the biggest new name in town was rookie Jim Plunkett, Heisman Trophy-winning quarterback from Stanford. In his regular season debut, Plunkett threw two touchdown passes to lead the Patriots to a 20–6 surprise of Oakland. His former Stanford teammate, Randy Vataha, cut by Los Angeles, was picked up and became Plunkett's favorite target. Other newcomers such as defensive lineman Julius Adams and linebacker Steve Kiner, made significant contributions in a year that made the Patriots' future seem brighter.

1972 A major difference of opinion erupted between general manager Upton Bell and head coach John Mazur on how the club should be built. The Patriots managed only three victories. Plunkett, with an inexperienced offensive line, was exposed to severe physical punishment. The defense was young and ineffective and several veterans, including Nance, Sellers and Houston Antwine, were dealt off as part of the rebuilding program. Both Bell and Mazur became victims of their own debates. Mazur quit before the season was over and Bell was dispatched soon thereafter. Phil Bengtson, who was scouting for the San

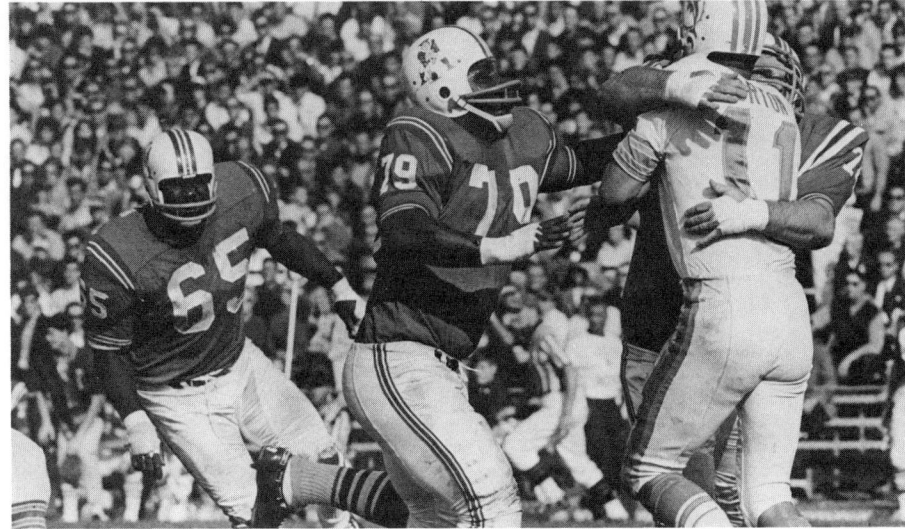

Sam Hunt (79) and Larry Eisenhauer stop Miami's Jim Norton in 1968; 65 is Houston Antwine.

Diego Chargers, was lent to the Patriots as interim coach after Mazur's departure.

1973 Chuck Fairbanks, the successful coach at the University of Oklahoma, was signed to a long-term contract as head coach and general manager. He immediately implemented a youth program. Rookies such as guard John Hannah, fullback Sam Cunningham, and wide receiver Darryl Stingley and running back Mack Herron, from the Canadian Football League, all enjoyed outstanding seasons.

1974 Fairbanks put in a three-four defense and it became an immediate boost for the Patriots, with Ray (Sugar Bear) Hamilton playing the key noseman position. New England opened the season by shocking defending Super Bowl champion Miami 34–24. The Patriots used that win as impetus to run off four more in a row before Buffalo beat them 30–28, October 20. An unusual siege of injuries ruined what might have been a great season for the Patriots. A 6-1 start deteriorated into a 1-6 finish and a 7-7 overall record. Herron, a 5-foot 5-inch, 170-pounder, set a league record for combined offensive yardage (2,444). Cunningham gained 811 yards before he broke his leg. Plunkett passed for 2,457 yards and 19 touchdowns.

1975 Plunkett's recurring injuries kept both the quarterback situation and the team unstable. Plunkett separated his shoulder in a preseason game, then reseparated it against San Francisco, October 26. Neil Graff was Plunkett's first replacement, but Fairbanks eventually settled on Steve Grogan, a big, fifth-round draft choice from Kansas State, as his new passer. By the time Plunkett returned a full-fledged quarterback controversy was underway. The team and the town were debating Plunkett versus Grogan. The fact that the club finished with a 3-11 record didn't help. William Sullivan became the majority owner as well as the president of the team, purchasing additional voting stock to give him 88 percent of the franchise.

1976 In the biggest trade in Patriots' history, Plunkett was sent to San Francisco for backup quarterback Tom Owen and four draft choices — two firsts in 1976 and a first and a second in 1977. With Grogan as the new quarterback, the young Patriots took off after an opening loss to Baltimore and won three games in a row, including a 48–17 victory over Oakland. The Patriots stayed in the AFC Eastern Division race all year, won their last six, and eventually landed the wild card spot in the AFC playoffs, meeting Oakland in the first round. Though leading 21–10 going into the fourth quarter, the Patriots lost 24–21 when the eventual Super Bowl champion Raiders scored with 39 seconds remaining.

MEMBERS OF HALL OF FAME:
None

PATRIOTS RECORD, 1960–76

Year	Won	Lost	Tied	Pct.	Pts.	OP
Boston Patriots						
1960	5	9	0	.357	286	349
1961	9	4	1	.692	413	313
1962	9	4	1	.692	346	295
1963§	7	6	1	.538	317	257
1964	10	3	1	.769	365	297
1965	4	8	2	.333	244	302
1966	8	4	2	.667	315	283
1967	3	10	1	.231	280	389
1968	4	10	0	.286	229	406
1969	4	10	0	.286	266	316
1970	2	12	0	.143	149	361
New England Patriots						
1971	6	8	0	.429	238	325
1972	3	11	0	.214	192	446
1973	5	9	0	.357	258	300
1974	7	7	0	.500	348	289
1975	3	11	0	.214	258	358
1976	11	3	0	.786	376	236
17 Years	100	129	9	.439	4,880	5,522

§AFL Eastern Division Champion

RECORD HOLDERS

Rushing (Yards)	Jim Nance, 1966	1,458
Passing (Pct.)	Babe Parilli, 1962	55.3
Passing (Yards)	Babe Parilli, 1964	3,465
Passing (TDs)	Babe Parilli, 1964	31
Receiving (No.)	Reggie Rucker, 1973	53
Receiving (Yards)	Jim Colclough, 1962	868
Interceptions (No.)	Ron Hall, 1964	11
Punting (Avg.)	Tom Yewcic, 1965	42.8
Punt Ret. (Avg.)	Carl Garrett, 1971	15.5
Kickoff Ret. (Avg.)	Larry Garron, 1962	28.6
Touchdowns (Total)	Steve Grogan, 1976	13
Field Goals Made	Gino Cappelletti, 1964	25
Points (No.)	Gino Cappelletti, 1964	155

COACHING HISTORY

1960–61	Lou Saban*	7–12–0
1961–68	Mike Holovak	52–46–9
1969–70	Clive Rush**	5–18–0
1970–72	John Mazur***	9–19–0
1972	Phil Bengtson	1– 4–0
1973–76	Chuck Fairbanks	26–30–0

*Replaced after five games in 1961
**Replaced after nine games in 1970
***Replaced after nine games in 1972

FIRST PLAYER SELECTED

1960	Gerhardt Schwedes, RB, Syracuse
1961	Tom Mason, RB, Tulane
1962	Gary Collins, WR, Maryland
1963	Art Graham, WR, Boston College
1964	Jack Concannon, QB, Boston College
1965	Jerry Rush, DE, Michigan State
1966	Karl Singer, T, Purdue
1967	John Charles, S, Purdue
1968	Dennis Byrd, DE, North Carolina State
1969	Ron Sellers, WR, Florida State
1970	Phil Olsen, DE, Utah State
1971	Jim Plunkett, QB, Stanford
1972	Tom Reynolds, WR (2), San Diego State
1973	John Hannah, G, Alabama
1974	Steve Corbett, G (2), Boston College
1975	Russ Francis, TE, Oregon
1976	Mike Haynes, DB, Arizona State

Julius Adams

Justin Canale

Jimmy Colclough

Sam Cunningham

Russ Francis

Larry Garron

Steve Grogan

BOSTON PATRIOTS, 1960–70;
NEW ENGLAND PATRIOTS, 1971–76

Acks, Ron, LB, Illinois 1972–73
Adams, Bob, TE, Pacific 1973–74
Adams, Julius, DT-DE, Texas Southern 1971–76
Adams, Sam, G, Prairie View 1972–76
Addison, Tom, LB, South Carolina 1960–67
Allard, Don, QB, Boston College 1962
Anderson, Bob, RB, Colorado 1975
Anderson, Ralph, S, West Texas St. 1973
Antwine, Houston, DT, So. Illinois 1961–71
Ashton, Josh, RB, Tulsa 1972–74
Atchason, Jack, E, Western Illinois 1960
Atessis, Bill, DE, Texas 1971
Avezzano, Joe, C, Florida State 1963

B

Bailey, Bill, RB, Cincinnati 1969
Baker, Melvin, WR, Texas Southern 1975
Ballou, Mike, LB, UCLA 1970
Banks, Willie, G, Alcorn A&M 1973
Barnes, Bruce, P, UCLA 1973–74
Barnes, Pete, LB, Southern U. 1976
Barnes, Rodrigo, LB, Rice 1974–75
Beach, Walter, DB, Central Michigan 1960–61
Beaudoin, Doug, S, Minnesota 1976
Beer, Tom, TE, Houston 1970–72
Bell, Bill, K, Kansas 1973
Bellino, Joe, RB, Navy 1965–67
Bennett, Phil, LB, Miami 1960
Berger, Ron, DE, Wayne State 1969–72
Beverly, Randy, DB, Colorado State 1970–71
Biscaha, Joe, E, Richmond 1960
Bishop, Richard, DT, Louisville 1976
Blahak, Joe, CB, Nebraska 1976
Blanchard, Dick, LB, Tulsa 1972
Blanks, Sid, RB, Texas A&I 1968–70
Bolton, Ron, CB, Norfolk State 1972–75
Boudreaux, Jim, DE, Louisiana Tech 1966–68
Boyd, Greg, S, Arizona 1973
Bramlett, John, LB, Memphis State 1968–70
Briscoe, Marlin, WR, Omaha 1976
Brock, Pete, C, Colorado 1976
Brown, Barry, TE-LB, Florida 1969–70
Brown, Bill, E, LB, Syracuse 1960
Bruney, Fred, DB, Ohio State 1960–62
Bryant, Hubie, WR, Minnesota 1971–72
Bugenhagen, Gary, T-G, Syracuse 1969–70
Buoniconti, Nick, LB, Notre Dame 1962–68
Burks, Steve, WR, Arkansas State 1975–76
Burton, Ron, RB, Northwestern 1960–65
Byrd, Dennis, DT, N. Carolina State 1968

C

Cagle, John, DT-LB-G, Clemson 1969
Calhoun, Don, RB, Kansas State 1975–76
Canale, Justin, G, Mississippi State 1965–68
Canale, Whit, DE, Tennessee 1968
Cappadona, Bob, RB, Northeastern 1966–67
Cappelletti, Gino, WR-K, Minnesota 1960–70
Carter, Allen, RB, USC 1975–76
Carter, Kent, LB, USC 1974
Carwell, Larry, DB, Iowa State 1968–72
Cash, Rick, DT, N.E. Missouri 1972–73
Caveness, Ron, LB, Arkansas 1968–69
Chandler, Al, TE, Oklahoma 1974–76
Chandler, Edgar, LB, Georgia 1973
Chapple, Dave, P, California-Santa Barbara 1974
Charles, John, DB, Purdue 1967–69
Cheyunski, Jim, LB, Syracuse 1968–72
Christy, Richard, RB, North Carolina 1960
Cindrich, Ralph, LB, Pittsburgh 1972
Clark, Gail, LB, Michigan State 1974
Clark, Phil, S, Northwestern 1971
Cloutier, Dave, DB, Maine 1964
Cohen, Abe, G, Chattanooga 1960
Colclough, Jim, WR, Boston College 1960–68
Coleman, Dennis, LB, Mississippi 1971
Conn, Dick, S, Georgia 1975–76
Corbett, Steve, G, Boston College 1975
Corcoran, Jim, QB, Maryland 1968
Crabtree, Eric, WR, Pittsburgh 1971
Crawford, Jim, RB, Wyoming 1960–64
Cross, Bob, T, Kilgore J.C. 1960
Crouthamel, Jake, RB, Dartmouth 1960
Crow, Albert, DT, William & Mary 1960
Crump, Harry, RB, Boston College 1963
Cudzik, Walt, C, Purdue 1960–63
Cunningham, Jay, DB, Bowling Green 1965–67
Cunningham, Sam, RB, USC 1973–76
Cusick, Pete, DT, Ohio State 1975

D

Damkroger, Maury, LB, Nebraska 1974
Danenhauer, Bill, DE, Emporia State 1960
Davis, Jack, G, Maryland 1960
Dawson, Bill, TE, Florida State 1965
Dee, Bob, DE, Holy Cross 1960–67
Delucca, Gerry, T, Mid. Tennessee St. 1960–64
Dimitroff, Tom, QB, Miami, Ohio 1960
Discenzo, Tony, T, Michigan State 1960
Dorsey, Nate, DE, Mississippi Valley 1973
Dowling, Brian, QB, Yale 1972–73
Dressler, Doug, RB, Chico State 1975
Dukes, Mike, LB, Clemson 1964–65
Du Lac, Bill, G, Eastern Michigan 1974–75
Dumler, Doug, C, Nebraska 1973–75
Durko, Sandy, S, USC 1973–74

E

Edmonds, Randy, LB, Georgia Tech 1971
Eisenhauer, Larry, DE, Boston College 1962–69

F

Farley, Dick, S, Boston U. 1970
Farmer, Lonnie, LB, Chattanooga 1964–66
Feacher, Ricky, WR, Mississippi Valley State 1976
Feldhausen, Paul, T, Northland 1968–69
Felt, Dick, DB, Brigham Young 1962–66
Forte, Ike, RB, Arkansas 1976
Foster, Will, LB, Eastern Michigan 1973–74
Fox, Tim, S, Ohio State 1976
Francis, Russ, TE, Oregon 1975–76
Fraser, Jim, LB-P, Wisconsin 1966
Frazier, Charley, WR, Texas Southern 1968–70
Funchess, Tommy, T, Jackson State 1968–70
Fussell, Tom, DE, Louisiana State 1967

G

Gallaher, Allen, T, USC 1974
Gamble, R.C., RB, S. Carolina State 1968–69
Gardin, Ron, WR, Arizona 1971
Garrett, Carl, RB, New Mex. Highlands 1969–72
Garrett, J.D., RB, Grambling 1964–67
Garron, Larry, RB, Western Illinois 1960–68
Geddes, Bob, LB, UCLA 1973–75
Germany, Willie, S, Morgan State 1976
Gipson, Paul, RB, Houston 1973
Glaudieux, Bob, RB, Notre Dame 1969–72
Gogolak, Charlie, K, Princeton 1970–72
Gonzalez, Noe, RB, S.W. Texas State 1974
Graff, Neil, QB, Wisconsin 1974–75
Graham, Art, WR, Boston College 1963–68
Graham, Milt, T, Colgate 1961–63
Graves, White, DB, Louisiana State 1965–67
Gray, Leon, T, Jackson State 1973–76
Green, Jerry, RB, Georgia Tech 1960
Greene, Tom, QB, Holy Cross 1960
Grogan, Steve, QB, Kansas State 1975–76

H

Hagen, Halvor, G, Weber State 1971–72
Haggerty, Mike, T, Miami 1971
Hall, Ron, DB, Missouri Valley 1961–67
Hamilton, Ray, DE, Oklahoma 1973–76
Hammond, Kim, QB, Florida State 1968–70
Hannah, John, G, Alabama 1973–76
Hanneman, Craig, DE, Oregon State 1974–75
Harris, Rickie, S, Arizona 1971–72
Hauser, Art, DT, Xavier 1960
Hayman, Conway, G, Delaware 1972
Haynes, Mike, CB, Arizona Sate 1976
Henke, Karl, T, Tulsa 1969
Hennessey, Tom, DB, Holy Cross 1965–66
Herock, Ken, LB, West Virginia 1969
Herron, Mack, RB, Kansas State 1973–75
Hinton, Eddie, WR, Oklahoma 1974
Hoey, George, CB, Michigan 1972
Howard, Bob, CB, San Diego State 1975–76
Huarte, John, QB, Notre Dame 1966–67
Hudson, Bill, DT, Clemson 1965
Hunt, Jim Lee, DT, Prairie View 1961–70
Hunt, Kevin, T, Doane 1973
Hunt, Sam, LB, Stephen F. Austin 1974–76

I

Ilg, Ray, LB, Colgate 1967–68
Imhof, Martin, DE, San Diego State 1975

J

Jackson, Honor, S, Pacific 1972
Jacobs, Harry, LB, Bradley 1960–62
Jacobs, Ray, DT, Howard Payne 1969
Jagielski, Harry, DT, Indiana 1960–61
Janik, Tom, P-S, Texas A&I 1969–71
Jenkins, Ed, RB, Holy Cross 1974
Johnson, Andy, RB, Georgia 1974–76
Johnson, Billy, DB, Nebraska 1966–69
Johnson, Daryl, DB, Morgan State 1967–71
Johnson, Ellis, RB, S.E. Louisiana 1965–66
Johnson, Joe, E, Boston College 1960–61
Johnson, Preston, RB, Florida A&M 1968
Jones, Ezell, T, Minnesota 1969–70
Jordan, Shelby, T, Washington, Mo. 1975

K

Kadziel, Ron, LB, Stanford 1972
Kapp, Joe, QB, California 1970
Kecman, Dan, LB, Maryland 1970
Keeton, Durwood, S, Oklahoma 1975
Khayat, Ed, DT, Mississippi 1966
Kimber, Bill, E, Florida State 1961
Kiner, Steve, LB, Tennessee 1971, 1973
King, Claude, RB, Houston 1962
King, Steve, LB, Tulsa 1973–76
Klein, Dick, T, Iowa State 1961–62
Knief, Gayle, WR, Morningside 1970
Koontz, Ed, LB, Catawba 1968

L

Larson, William, RB, Western Illinois 1960
Lassiter, Ike, DE, St. Augustine's, N.C. 1970–71
Lawson, Odell, RB, Langston 1970–71
Lee, Robert, G, Missouri 1960
Lenkaitis, Bill, G-C, Penn State 1971–76
Leo, Bobby, WR, Harvard 1967–68
Leo, Charlie, G, Indiana 1960–62
Lindquist, Paul, DT, New Hampshire 1961
Livingston, Walt, RB, Heidelberg 1960
Lofton, Oscar, E, S.E. Louisiana 1960
Long, Charlie, T, Chattanooga 1961–69
Long, Mike, E, Brandeis 1960
Lott, Billy, RB, Mississippi 1961–63
Loudd, Rommie, LB, UCLA 1961–62
Loukas, Angelo, G, Northwestern 1970
Lunsford, Mel, DT, Central St., Ohio 1973–76

M

Maitland, Jack, RB, Williams 1971–72
Mallory, Irvin, DB, Virginia Union 1971
Mangum, John, DT, So. Mississippi 1966–67
Marsh, Aaron, DE, E. Kentucky 1968–69
Marshall, Al, WR, Boise State 1974
Martin, Donald, CB, Yale 1973
Mason, Dave, S, Nebraska 1973
Mass, Wayne, T, Bowling Green 1972
Massey, Jim, CB, Linfield 1974–75
Matthews, Henry, RB, Michigan State 1972
May, Art, DE, Tuskegee 1971
McCall, Bob, RB, Arizona 1973
McComb, Don, DE, Bradley 1960
McCray, Prentice, S, Arizona State 1974–76
McCurry, Dave, S, Iowa State 1974
McGee, George, T, Southern U. 1960
McGee, Tony, DE, Bishop, Texas 1974–76
McKay, Bob, T, Texas 1976
McKinnon, Don, LB, Dartmouth 1963–64
McMahon, Art, S, N. Carolina State 1968–72
McQuay, Leon, RB, Tampa 1975

Sam Hunt

Bill Lenkaitis

Jon Morris

Babe Parilli

Jim Plunkett

Len St. Jean

Ron Sellers

Meixler, Ed, LB, Boston U. 1965
Mildren, Jack, S, Oklahoma 1974
Miller, Al, RB, Boston College 1960
Mirich, Rex, DT, No. Arizona 1970
Mitchell, Leroy, DB, Texas Southern 1967
Mix, Ron, G, USC 1972
Montler, Mike, T, Colorado 1969–72
Moore, Arthur, DT, Tulsa 1973–74, 1976
Moore, Leroy, DE, Ft. Valley State 1961–62
Morris, Jon, C, Holy Cross 1964–74
Mosier, John, TE, Kansas 1973
Moss, Roland, TE, Toledo 1971
Murphy, Bill, WR, Cornell 1968

N

Nance, Jim, RB, Syracuse 1965–71
Neighbors, Billy, G, Alabama 1962–65
Nelson, Steve, LB, N. Dakota State 1974–76
Neumann, Tom, RB, No. Michigan 1963
Neville, Tommy, T, Mississippi State 1965–74, 1976
Nichols, Bob, TE, Boston U. 1967–68

O

Oakes, Don, T, Virginia Tech 1963–68
O'Hanley, Ross, DB, Boston College 1960–65
Osley, Willie, CB, Illinois 1974
Outlaw, John, DB, Jackson State 1969–72
Owen, Tom, QB, Wichita State 1976

P

Parilli, Babe, QB, Kentucky 1961–67
Patrick, Mike, P, Mississippi State 1975–76

Patton, Jerry, DE, Nebraska 1975
Perkins, Willis, G, Texas Southern 1961
Phillips, Jess, RB, Michigan State 1976
Philpott, Ed, LB, Miami, Ohio 1967–71
Plunkett, Jim, QB, Stanford 1971–75
Pope, Ken, CB, Oklahoma 1974
Porter, Willie, DB, Texas Southern 1968
Price, Kenny, LB, Iowa 1971
Pruett, Perry, DB, N. Texas State 1971
Purvis, Vic, WR, So. Mississippi 1966–67
Pyne, George, T, Olivet 1965

R

Rademacher, Bill, WR, No. Michigan 1969–70
Ratkowski, Ray, RB, Notre Dame 1961
Ray, Eddie, RB-P, Louisiana State 1970
Reilly, Kevin, LB, Villanova 1975
Reynolds, Bob, T, Bowling Green 1972–73
Reynolds, Tom, WR, San Diego State 1972
Richardson, Al, DE, Grambling 1960
Richardson, Jesse, DT, Alabama 1962–64
Richardson, Tom, WR, Jackson State 1969–70
Robotti, Frank, LB-RB, Boston College 1961
Romanyiszyn, Jim, LB, Edinboro State 1976
Romeo, Tony, TE, Florida State 1962–67
Romine, Al, DB, Florence State 1961
Rowe, Dave, DT, Penn State 1971–73
Rucker, Reggie, WR, Boston U. 1971–74
Rudolph, Jack, LB, Georgia Tech 1960–65

S

Sanders, John, S, South Dakota 1974–76

Sardisco, Tony, G, Tulane 1960–62
Satcher, Doug, LB, So. Mississippi 1966–68
Scarpitto, Bob, WR, Notre Dame 1968
Schmidt, Bob, T, Minnesota 1964
Schottenheimer, Marty, LB, Pittsburgh 1969–70
Schubert, Steve, WR, Massachusetts 1974
Schwedes, Gerhardt, RB, Syracuse 1960–61
Scott, Clarence, S, Morgan State 1969–72
Sellers, Ron, WR, Florida State 1969–71
Sherman, Tom, QB-DB, Penn State 1968–69
Shiner, Dick, QB, Maryland 1973–74
Shoate, Rod, LB, Oklahoma 1975
Shonta, Chuck, DB, E. Michigan 1960–67
Simerson, John, T, Purdue 1961
Singer, Carl, T, Purdue 1966–68
Smith, Donnell, DE, Southern U. 1973–74
Smith, Hal, DT, UCLA 1960
Smith, John, K, None 1974–76
Snyder, Al, WR, Holy Cross 1964
Soltis, Bob, DB, Minnesota 1960–61
Songin, Ed (Butch), QB, Boston College 1960–61
St. Jean, Lennie, G, No. Michigan 1964–73
Stenger, Brian, LB, Notre Dame 1973
Stephens, Tom, DE-TE, Syracuse 1960–64
Stingley, Darryl, WR, Purdue 1973–76
Stolberg, Eric, WR, Indiana 1971
Streigal, Bill, LB, Pacific 1960
Studstill, Pat, P-WR, Houston 1972
Sturt, Fred, G, Bowling Green 1976
Suci, Bob, DB, Michigan State 1963
Swanson, Terry, K, Massachusetts 1967–68
Sweet, Joe, WR, Tennessee State 1974
Sykes, Alfred, WR, Florida A&M 1971

T

Taliaferro, Mike, QB, Illinois 1968–71
Tanner, John, LB-DE, Tennessee Tech 1973–74
Tarver, John, RB, Colorado 1972–74
Thomas, Donnie, LB, Indiana 1976
Thomas, Gene, RB, Florida A&M 1968
Tipton, Dave, DT, Western Illinois 1975–76
Toner, Ed, DT, Massachusetts 1967–70
Towns, Don, DB, Georgia 1961
Trull, Don, QB, Baylor 1967
Turner, Robert (Bake), WR, Texas Tech 1970

V

Vataha, Randy, WR, Stanford 1971–76

W

Walker, Mike, K, None 1972
Washington, Clyde, DB, Purdue 1960–61
Watson, Dave, G, Georgia Tech 1963–64
Webb, Don, S, Iowa State 1961–71
Webster, George, LB, Michigan State 1974–76
Weisacosky, Ed, LB, Miami 1971–72
Welch, Claxton, RB, Oregon 1973
Wells, Billy, RB, Michigan State 1960
West, Mel, DB, Missouri 1961
Whalen, Jim, TE, Boston College 1965–68
White, Harvey, QB, Clemson 1960
White, Jeff, K-P, Texas-El Paso 1973
White, Jim, DE, Colorado State 1972
Whittingham, Fred, LB, Cal. Poly 1970
Williamson, John, LB-C, Louisiana Tech 1968–70
Wilson, Ed, QB, Arizona State 1965
Wilson, Joe, RB, Holy Cross 1974
Windsor, Bob, TE, Kentucky 1972–75
Wirgowski, Dennis, DE, Purdue 1970–72
Witt, Mel, DT, Texas-Arlington 1967–70
Wright, Elmo, WR, Houston 1975

Y

Yates, Bob, T-G-C, Syracuse 1960–65
Yewcic, Tom, P-QB, Michigan State 1961–66

Z

Zabel, Steve, LB, Oklahoma 1975–76

Don Calhoun about to score for Patriots, 1976 playoff at Oakland.

NEW ORLEANS SAINTS

1966 The National Football League, long impressed by the support New Orleans fans displayed for pre-season games at Tulane Stadium, awarded an expansion franchise to the Crescent City, November 1. John W. Mecom, Jr., a millionaire sportsman, was designated majority stockholder and president of the franchise, December 15. Among his limited partners was Al Hirt, the Bourbon Street trumpet player. Until he was granted an NFL team, Mecom's passion was auto racing and his family's entry, driven by the late Graham Hill, won the Indianapolis 500 in 1966.

1967 The team was named the "Saints," in honor of the Dixieland classic "When the Saints Go Marchin'

In," which became the team's fight song. Mecom hired Tom Fears, former Hall of Fame end for Los Angeles and assistant coach for Green Bay under Vince Lombardi, as head coach, January 27. Fears chose to go with veteran players and assembled a cast of former NFL stars: Jim Taylor, Paul Hornung, Doug Atkins, Earl Leggett, and Lou Cordileone. The Saints traded their first draft choice to Baltimore for reserve quarterback Gary Cuozzo. New Orleans fans responded frantically to the Saints' arrival, purchasing 20,000 season tickets the day the box office opened. Fears played the preseason games to win and the Saints finished the preseason with a 5-1 record, best ever for a first-year team. When rookie John Gilliam returned the opening kickoff 94 yards for a touchdown in their regular season debut against Los Angeles, the 80,789 fans in Tulane Stadium nearly went berserk. The

Rams rallied to win 27–13 but the Saints made a strong first impression September 17. New Orleans went winless through the first seven games before beating Philadelphia 31–24 at Tulane Stadium, November 5. Walter Roberts scored three touchdowns. The Saints' leading receiver was rookie Danny Abramowicz, who caught 50 passes. Jim Taylor was the team's leading rusher with 390 yards.

1968 Vic Schwenk was promoted from head of player personnel to general manager, March 29. Fears improved his offense by signing end Dave Parks, who had played out his option in San Francisco, July 17. He had to pay a steep price, however, as Commissioner Pete Rozelle made New Orleans part with its top draft choice, defensive tackle Kevin Hardy of Notre Dame, and its number one pick in the 1969 draft as compensation. Following a painful preseason, Jim

Tom Dempsey kicks NFL record 63-yard field goal vs. Detroit, November 8, 1970; holder is Joe Scarpati, Alex Karras rushes for Lions.

Taylor announced his retirement as a player, September 10. New Orleans played competitive football in every league game, beating Pittsburgh 24–14 in its final game to finish third in the Century Division. The Saints' two-year record of 7-20-1 was the best to date for an expansion team.

1969 Fears added several exciting offensive players, including running backs Andy Livingston and Tony Baker and placekicker Tom Dempsey. He also got surprising mileage out of quarterback Billy Kilmer, the quarterback San Francisco considered finished two years earlier. After an 0-6 start, the Saints rebounded. The turning point was a wild 51–42 win over St. Louis, November 2. Kilmer passed for 354 yards and six touchdowns in the victory. Dempsey set a club record with four field goals including one with 11 seconds left to pull out a 25–24 win over the New York Giants, November 16. The Saints closed the season with a 27–24 win over Pittsburgh and finished in third place at 5-9 in the Capitol Division. Abramowicz led the NFL with 73 pass receptions for 1,015 yards and seven touchdowns. Atkins, 39, retired after 17 seasons in the NFL.

1970 The Saints won only one of their first seven games. Mecom fired Fears and hired J.D. Roberts, formerly of the Richmond, Virginia, team of the Atlantic Coast Football League, as head coach, November 3. In Roberts's first game, the Saints scored a memorable 19–17 upset of Detroit at Tulane Stadium, November 8. The winning points came on a record-setting, 63-yard field goal by Dempsey, the free-agent kicker who was born without a right hand and without toes on his right foot.

1971 In the first round of the draft, the Saints selected Archie Manning, the All-America quarterback from the University of Mississippi, January 28. Manning, a long-time favorite with football fans in the South, received a hero's welcome in New Orleans. In his pro debut, Manning scored the winning touchdown on the last play of the game to upset Los Angeles 24–20 at Tulane Stadium. It was the Saints' first win ever over the Rams. Manning's fourth-quarter heroics also led to a 24–14 victory over Dallas. Foot and leg injuries sidelined Manning late in the season and New Orleans slipped to last place in the Western Division of the NFC. Jim Strong, acquired from the 49ers, led the Saints with 404 yards rushing.

1972 The Saints appointed former astronaut Richard F. Gordon, Jr., executive vice president, January 7. Gordon, who had piloted the Apollo XII moon mission in 1969, took over the club's front-office operation. Gordon found exploring the galaxy easier than reversing the sinking fortunes of the Saints, who equalled their 1970 poorest season, 2-11-1. Manning netted more than 3,000 yards running and passing and accounted for 20 of the team's 26 touchdowns but took a terrible beating behind the Saints' porous offensive line.

1973 Mecom fired J.D. Roberts and appointed John North head coach, August 26. North, an ex-Marine, learned his football as an assistant under Blanton Collier at the University of Kentucky. After a scoreless first quarter, Atlanta erupted to embarrass New Orleans in the league opener 62–7 at Tulane Stadium, September 16. The following week, the Saints were humiliated 40–3 by Dallas at Texas Stadium. But the Saints won four of their next six games, including a 19–3 surprise of Washington, October 28. Bill McClard, acquired on waivers earlier in the week, kicked four field goals to beat the Redskins.

1974 The Saints snapped a 19-game winless streak on the road with a 13–3 decision over Atlanta, October 20. The Saints rushed for a club record 232 yards in the game and reserve quarterback Bobby Scott threw the first touchdown pass of his NFL career. New Orleans upset Philadelphia 14–10 the following week at Tulane Stadium. The Saints won their fifth game,

Wide receiver Dan Abramowicz vs. St. Louis at Tulane Stadium, 1968.

equaling their best record, as rookie quarterback Larry Cipa, a fifteenth-round draft choice, defeated St. Louis 14–10, December 8.

1975 The Saints selected Larry Burton, a wide receiver from Purdue, as their first round pick in the college draft. They traded defensive end Billy Newsome to New York for the Jets' first round pick and selected Kurt Schumacher, an offensive tackle from Ohio State. The Saints moved into the world's largest indoor stadium, the Louisiana Superdome, to open the preseason against Houston, August 9. The move culminated years of controversy surrounding the construction of the gigantic arena, which had a football seating capacity of 72,000. Rich Szaro, a free agent from Harvard, kicked a 20-yard field goal to give the Saints a last-second, 20–19 victory over Green Bay, October 12. Following a 38–14 loss to Los Angeles, North was fired as head coach and replaced by Ernie Hefferle, the Saints' director of pro personnel, October 25. The Saints won their first game under Hefferle, 23–7 over Atlanta, but lost the last seven to finish 2-12.

1976 The Saints hired Hank Stram, the man who coached Kansas City to the Super Bowl IV championship, as their fourth head coach, January 20. Stram traded linebacker Rick Middleton to San Diego for quarterback Bobby Douglass and a third-round draft choice, April 2. The Saints first two draft choices were Chuck Muncie, All-America running back from California, and Tony Galbreath, running back from Missouri. The offense missed Manning, who sat out the entire season following surgery on his right arm. Stram's first victory was sweet revenge as his Saints defeated the Chiefs in Kansas City 27–17, September 26. In that game, Galbreath rushed for 146 and two touchdowns, Muncie for 126 yards. The Saints scored the most one-sided win in their history, a 30–0 rout of Atlanta, October 10. The Saints also beat Seattle 51–27, November 21.

MEMBERS OF HALL OF FAME:
Jim Taylor

SAINTS RECORD, 1967-76

Year	Won	Lost	Tied	Pct.	Pts.	OP
1967	3	11	0	.214	233	379
1968	4	9	1	.308	246	327
1969	5	9	0	.357	311	393
1970	2	11	1	.154	172	347
1971	4	8	2	.333	266	347
1972	2	11	1	.179	215	361
1973	5	9	0	.357	163	312
1974	5	9	0	.357	166	263
1975	2	12	0	.143	165	360
1976	4	10	0	.286	253	346
10 Years	36	99	5	.275	2,190	3,435

RECORD HOLDERS

Rushing (Yards)	Andy Livingston, 1969	761
Passing (Pct.)	Billy Kilmer, 1970	57.0
Passing (Yards)	Archie Manning, 1972	2,781
Passing (TDs)	Billy Kilmer, 1969	20
Receiving (No.)	Dan Abramowicz, 1969	73
Receiving (Yards)	Dan Abramowicz, 1969	1,015
Interceptions (No.)	Dave Whitsell, 1967	10
Punting (Avg.)	Tom NcNeill, 1967	42.9
Punt Ret. (Avg.)	Gil Chapman, 1975	12.2
Kickoff Ret. (Avg.)	John Gilliam, 1967	30.1
Touchdowns (Total)	Andy Livingston, 1969, and	
	Tony Galbreath, 1976	8
Field Goals Made	Tom Dempsey, 1969	22
Points (No.)	Tom Dempsey, 1969	99

COACHING HISTORY

1967-70	Tom Fears*	13–34–2
1970-72	J.D. Roberts	7–25–3
1973-75	John North**	11–23–0
1975	Ernie Hefferle	1– 7–0
1976	Hank Stram	4–10–0

*Replaced after seven games in 1970
**Replaced after six games in 1975

FIRST PLAYER SELECTED

1967	Les Kelley, RB, Alabama
1968	Kevin Hardy, DE, Notre Dame
1969	John Shinners, G, Xavier
1970	Ken Burrough, WR, Texas Southern
1971	Archie Manning, QB, Mississippi
1972	Royce Smith, G, Georgia
1973	Derland Moore, DE (2), Oklahoma
1974	Rick Middleton, LB, Ohio State
1975	Larry Burton, WR, Purdue
1976	Chuck Muncie, RB, California

Tony Baker *Bo Burris* *Joe Federspiel* *John Gilliam* *Ernie Jackson* *Billy Kilmer* *Earl Leggett*

NEW ORLEANS SAINTS, 1967–76

Abramowicz, Dan, WR, Xavier 1967–73
Absher, Dick, LB, Maryland 1969–71
Adkins, Margene, WR, Henderson J.C. 1972
Anderson, Dick, T, Ohio State 1967
Askson, Bert, TE, Texas Southern 1973
Athas, Pete, CB, Tennessee 1976
Atkins, Doug, DE, Tennessee 1967–69

B

Baker, Melvin, WR, Michigan 1975
Baker, Tony, RB, Iowa State 1968–71
Barrington, Tom, RB, Ohio State 1967–70
Baumgartner, Steve, DE, Purdue 1973–76
Beasley, John, TE, California 1973–74
Bell, Carlos, TE, Houston 1971
Blanchard, Tom, P, Oregon 1974–76
Boeke, Jim, T, Heidelberg 1968
Bordelon, Ken, LB, Louisiana State 1976
Boyd, Greg, S, Arizona 1974
Brewer, Johnny, LB, Mississippi 1968–70

Brown, Bob, TE, Alcorn A&M 1972–73
Brown, Charlie, RB, Missouri 1967–68
Burchfield, Don, TE, Ball State 1971
Burke, Vern, TE, Oregon State 1967
Burkett, Jackie, LB, Auburn 1967, 1970
Burris, Bo, S, Houston 1967–69
Burrough, Ken, WR, Texas Southern 1970
Burton, Larry, WR, Purdue 1975–76
Butler, Bill, RB, Kansas State 1972–74
Butler, Skip, K, Texas-Arlington 1971

C

Capone, Warren, LB, Louisiana State 1976
Carr, Tom, DE, Morgan State 1968
Chambers, Rusty, LB, Tulane 1975–76
Chapman, Gil, WR, Michigan 1975–76
Childs, Henry, TE, Kansas State 1974–76
Cipa, Larry, QB, Michigan 1974–75
Cody, Bill, LB, Auburn 1967–70
Colchico, Dan, DE, San Jose State 1969
Coleman, Don, LB, Michigan 1974–75

Colman, Wayne, LB, Temple 1969–74, 1976
Cordileone, Lou, DT, Clemson 1967–68
Cordill, Olie, P, Memphis State 1969
Cortez, Bruce, CB, Parsons, Iowa 1967
Crangle, Mike, DE, Tennessee-Martin 1972
Creech, Bob, LB, Texas Christian 1973
Crist, Chuck, DB, Penn State 1975–76
Croom, Sylvester, C, Alabama 1975
Cunningham, Carl, LB, Houston 1971
Cuozzo, Gary, QB, Virginia 1967

D

Davis, Bob, QB, Virginia 1973
Davis, Dave, WR, Tennessee State 1974
Davis, Dick, RB, Nebraska 1970
Davis, Norman, G, Grambling 1969
Davis, Ted, LB, Georgia Tech 1967–69
DeGrenier, Jack, RB, Texas-Arlington 1974
Dempsey, Tom, K, Palomar J.C. 1969–70
Didion, John, LB-C, Oregon State 1971–74
Dodd, Al, WR, N.W. Louisiana 1969–71

Safety Dave Whitsell pursues the Cardinals' Johnny Roland, 1968.

Nine-year guard Jake Kupp vs. 49ers, 1971.

Archie Manning

Chuck Muncie

Bob Pollard

Elex Price

Paul Seal

Steve Stonebreaker

Del Williams

Dorris, Andy, DE, New Mexico State 1973–76
Douglas, John, CB, Texas Southern 1967–68
Douglass, Bobby, QB, Kansas 1976
Dunbar, Jubilee, WR, Southern U. 1973
Durkee, Charlie, K, Oklahoma State 1967–68, 1971–72
Dusenberry, Bill, RB, Johnson C. Smith 1970

E

Emanuel, Frank, LB, Tennessee 1970
Estes, Lawrence, DE, Alcorn A&M 1970–71

F

Fagan, Julian, P, Mississippi 1970–72
Farasopolous, Chris, S, Brigham Young 1974
Farber, Hap, LB, Mississippi 1970
Federspiel, Joe, LB, Kentucky 1972–76
Feller, Happy, K, Texas 1972–75
Ferguson, Jim, LB, USC 1968
Ferson, Paul, T, Georgia 1973–74
Fichtner, Ross, S, Purdue 1968
Fink, Mike, CB, Missouri 1973
Ford, James, RB, Texas Southern 1971–72
Fraser, Jim, P, Wisconsin 1968
Fuller, Johnny, S, Lamar 1973–75

G

Galbreath, Tony, RB, Missouri 1976
Garcia, Jim, DE, Purdue 1967
Garrett, Len, TE, New Mexico Highlands 1973–75
Gibbs, Donnie, P, Texas Christian 1974
Gilliam, John, WR, S. Carolina State 1967–68
Granger, Hoyle, RB, Mississippi State 1971
Green, Arthur, RB, Albany State 1972
Gresham, Bob, RB, West Virginia 1971–72
Grooms, Elois, DE, Tennessee Tech 1975–76
Gros, Earl, RB, Louisiana State 1970
Gross, Lee, C, Auburn 1975–76
Gwinn, Ross, G, N.W. Louisiana 1968

H

Hall, Tom, WR, Minnesota 1967
Hall, Willie, LB, S. Carolina 1972
Hamilton, Andy, WR, Louisiana State 1975
Hargett, Edd, QB, Texas A&M 1969–72
Harris, Bill, RB, Colorado 1971
Hart, Ben, S, Oklahoma 1967
Hart, Jeff, T, Oregon State 1976
Harvey, George, G, Kansas 1967
Havrilak, Sam, WR, Bucknell 1974
Hayes, Billie, CB, San Diego State 1972
Hazelton, Major, DB, Florida A&M 1970
Heidel, Jimmy, S, Mississippi 1967
Herrmann, Don, WR, Waynesburg 1975–76
Hester, Jim, TE, North Dakota 1967–69
Hester, Ray, LB, Tulane 1971–73
Hill, John, C, Lehigh 1975–76
Hines, Glen Ray, T, Arkansas 1971–72
Hobbs, Bill, LB, Texas A&M 1972
Holden, Sam, T, Grambling 1971
Hollas, Hugo, DB, Rice 1970–72
Howard, Gene, CB, Langston, Okla. 1968–70
Howell, Delles, DB, Grambling 1970–72
Huard, John, LB, Maine 1971
Hyatt, Fred, WR, Auburn 1973

J

Jackson, Ernie, CB, Duke 1972–76
Jacobs, Harry, LB, Bradley 1970
Johnson, Benny, CB, J.C. Smith 1976
Johnson, Carl, T, Nebraska 1972–73
Jones, Andy, RB, Washington 1975–76
Jones, Jerry, T, Bowling Green 1967–69
Jones, Kim, RB, Colorado State 1976
Jordan, Jimmy, RB, Florida 1967

K

Kearney, Jim, S, Prairie View 1976
Kelley, Les, LB, Alabama 1967–69
Kelly, Mike, TE, Davidson 1973
Kilmer, Bill, QB, UCLA 1967–70
Kimbrough, Elbert, S, Northwestern 1968
Kingrea, Rick, LB, Tulane 1973–76
Kopay, Dave, RB, Washington 1971
Kramer, Kent, TE, Minnesota 1967
Kupp, Jake, G, Washington 1967–75
Kuziel, Bob, C, Pittsburgh 1972

L

LaGrande, Morris, RB, Tampa 1975
La Porte, Phil, T, Penn State 1974–75
Lawson, Odell, RB, Langston 1973–74
Lee, Bivian, CB, Prairie View 1971–75
Leggett, Earl, DT, Louisiana State 1967–75
Lemon, Mike, LB, Kansas 1975
Lewis, Gary, RB, Arizona State 1970
Linden, Errol, T, Houston 1969–70
Linhart, Toni, K, Austria Tech 1972
Livingston, Andy, RB, Phoenix J.C. 1969–70
Logan, Obert, S, Trinity, Tex. 1967
Long, Dave, DE, Iowa 1969–72
Looney, Joe Don, RB, Oklahoma 1969
Lorick, Tony, RB, Arizona State 1968–69
Lyons, Dick, DB, Kentucky 1970

M

Manning, Archie, QB, Mississippi 1971–76
Martin, D'Artagnan, CB, Kentucky State 1971–72
Maurer, Andy, G, Oregon 1974
Maxson, Alvin, RB, Southern Methodist 1974–76
McCall, Don, RB, USC 1967–68, 1970
McClard, Bill, K, Arkansas 1973–75
McCormick, Dave, T, Louisiana State 1967–68
McCullouch, Earl, WR, USC 1974
McNeill, Tom, P, Stephen F. Austin 1967–69
McNeill, Rod, RB, USC 1974–76
McQuay, Leon, RB, Tampa 1976
Merlo, Jim, LB, Stanford 1973–76
Middleton, Rick, LB, Ohio State 1974–75
Minor, Lincoln, RB, New Mexico State 1973
Montgomery, Marv, T, USC 1976
Mooers, Doug, DE, Whittier 1971–72
Moore, Derland, DE, Oklahoma 1973–76
Moore, Jerry, S, Arkansas 1973–74
Moore, Reynaud, CB, UCLA 1971
Mooring, John, T, Tampa 1974
Morgan, Mike, LB, Louisiana State 1969–70
Morrison, Don, T, Texas-Arlington 1971–76
Muncie, Chuck, RB, California 1976
Myers, Tom, S, Syracuse 1972–75

N

Neal, Richard, DE, Southern U. 1969–72
Nevett, Elijah, CB, Clark 1967–70
Newland, Bob, WR, Oregon 1971–74
Newsome, Billy, DE, Grambling 1973–74
Ninowski, Jim, QB, Michigan State 1969
Nyvall, Vic, RB, N.W. Louisiana 1970

O

Ogden, Ray, WR, Alabama 1967
O'Neal, Steve, P, Texas A&M 1973
Otis, Jim, RB, Ohio State 1970
Owens, Joe, DE, Alcorn A&M 1971–75
Owens, Tinker, WR, Oklahoma 1976

P

Palmer, Dick, LB, Kentucky 1973
Parker, Joel, WR, Florida 1974–75
Parks, Dave, TE, Texas Tech 1968–72
Phillips, Jess, RB, Michigan State 1973–74
Pitts, Elijah, RB, Philander Smith 1970
Poage, Ray, TE, Texas 1967–70
Pollard, Bob, DT, Weber State 1971–76
Preece, Steve, S, Oregon State 1969
Price, Elex, DT, Alcorn A&M 1973–76
Profit, Joe, RB, Indiana 1973
Prudhomme, Remi, G-C, Louisiana State 1971–72

R

Ramsey, Nate, S, Indiana 1973
Ramsey, Steve, QB, N. Texas State 1970
Rasley, Rocky, G, Oregon State 1974
Reaves, Ken, CB, Norfolk State 1974
Rengel, Mike, DT, Hawaii 1969
Richey, Mike, T, North Carolina 1970
Riley, Preston, WR, Memphis State 1973
Rissmiller, Ray, T, Georgia 1967
Roberts, Walt, WR, San Jose State 1967
Robinson, Craig, T, Houston 1972–73
Robinson, Virgil, RB, Grambling 1971–72
Rogers, Steve, RB, Louisiana State 1975
Rose, George, CB, Auburn 1967
Roussel, Tom, LB, So. Mississippi 1971–72
Rowe, Dave, DT, Penn State 1967–70

S

Sandeman, Bill, T, Pacific 1967
Saul, Bill, LB, Penn State 1969
Scarpati, Joe, DB, N. Carolina State 1970
Schmidt, Roy, G, Long Beach State 1967–68
Schmidt, Terry, CB, Ball State 1974–75
Schultz, Randy, RB, Iowa State 1967–68
Schumacher, Kurt, G, Ohio State 1975–76
Schweda, Brian, DE, Kansas 1967–68
Scott, Bobby, QB, Tennessee 1972–76
Seal, Paul, TE, Michigan 1974–76
Shaw, Bob, WR, Winston-Salem 1970
Shinners, John, G, Miami, Ohio 1969–70
Shy, Don, RB, San Diego State 1969
Simmons, Dave, LB, Georgia Tech 1967
Simmons, Jerry, WR, Bethune-Cookman 1967
Smith, Royce, G, Georgia 1972–73
South, Ronny, QB, Arkansas 1968
Spencer, Maurice, CB, North Carolina Central 1974–76
Stevens, Howard, RB, Louisville 1973–74
Stickles, Monty, TE, Notre Dame 1968
Stieve, Terry, G, Wisconsin 1976
Stincic, Tom, LB, Michigan 1972
Stonebreaker, Steve, LB, Detroit 1967–68
Strachan, Mike, RB, Iowa State 1975–76
Strand, Eli, G, Iowa State 1967
Strong, Jim, RB, Houston 1971–72
Sturm, Jerry, T-C, Illinois 1967–70
Sutherland, Doug, G, Wisconsin State 1970
Sweetan, Karl, QB, Wake Forest 1968
Swinney, Clovis, DT, Arkansas State 1970
Szaro, Rich, K, Harvard 1975–76
Szymakowski, Dave, WR, W. Texas State 1968

T

Talbert, Don, T, Texas 1969–70
Taylor, Jim, RB, Louisiana State 1967
Taylor, Mike, T, USC 1969–70
Thaxton, James, TE, Tennessee State 1976
Thompson, Bobby, S, Arizona 1969
Thompson, Dave, T, Clemson 1974–75
Tilleman, Mike, DT, Montana 1967–70
Tillman, Faddie, DT, Boise State 1972
Townes, Willie, DE, Tulsa 1970

V

Vandersea, Phil, LB, Massachusetts 1967

W

Walker, Mike, DE, Tulane 1971
Ward, Carl, S, Michigan 1969
Welch, Claxton, RB, Oregon 1970
Weatherspoon, Cephus, WR, Fort Lewis, Col. 1972
Wendryhoski, Joe, C, Illinois 1967–68
Westbrooks, Greg, LB, Colorado 1975–76
Wheelwright, Ernie, RB, So. Illinois 1967–70
Whitaker, Creston, WR, N. Texas State 1972
Whitsell, Dave, S, Indiana 1967–69
Whittingham, Fred, LB, Cal. Poly 1967–68
Wickert, Tom, T, Washington State 1975–76
Wicks, Bob, WR, Utah State 1974
Williams, Del, G, Florida State 1967–73
Williams, Joe, RB, Wyoming 1972
Williams, Richard, WR, Abilene Christian 1974
Winans, Jeff, DT, USC 1976
Winslow, Doug, WR, Drake 1973
Winther, Wimpy, C, Mississippi 1972
Wood, Gary, QB, Cornell, ... 1967
Woodson, Marv, S, Indiana 1969
Wyatt, Doug, DB, Tulsa 1970–72

Y

Youngblood, George, S, Cal. State-L.A. 1967–68

Z

Zanders, Emanuel, G, Jackson State 1974–76

NEW YORK GIANTS

1925 Tim Mara went to see Billy Gibson in hopes of buying an interest in heavyweight boxer Gene Tunney and wound up becoming the owner of an NFL franchise for New York for $500, August 1. Mara named the team "Giants," after the baseball team with which it would share the Polo Grounds. He hired Bob Folwell, formerly of Navy, as coach and Dr. Harry March to recruit talent. Among the first Giants were old pros such as Jim Thorpe and Bob Nash and collegians such as Jack McBride and Paul Jappe of Syracuse, Hinkey Haines of Penn State, Century Milstead of Yale, Lynn Bomar of Vanderbilt, and Ed McGinley of Penn. The Giants won their first exhibition over Ducky Pond's All-Stars at New Britain, Connecticut. New York lost its first two regular season games, both on the road. With the help of at least 5,000 free tickets, they drew about 25,000 to watch the home opener, a 14–0 loss to the Frankford Yellowjackets, October 18. The Giants regrouped to win seven in a row, but Mara was $40,000 in the red when the Chicago Bears signed Red Grange and brought him to New York, December 6. A record crowd of over 70,000 jammed in the Polo Grounds, turning a dreary season into a financial bonanza. New York finished fourth at 8–4 in the 20-team league.

1926 Grange's business manager, C. C. Pyle, tried to force his way into the NFL with a franchise at Yankee Stadium, but Mara objected. Pyle organized a rival American Football League and Folwell left the Giants to coach the Philadelphia entry in the AFL. Milstead also quit the team to go to the AFL. Dr. Joe Alexander was named the Giants' new coach, in a league that expanded to 22 clubs. The Giants had a bitter war with the Yankees and Grange. Alexander signed first year players such as Jack Haggerty of Georgetown, Glenn Killinger of Penn State, and Walter Koppisch of Columbia, while Mara bought tackle Steve Owen of Phillips University from the Kansas City Cowboys. The Giants trained at Lake Ariel, Pennsylvania. The Giants beat Hartford and Providence to begin the season but then were shut out three games in a row. The Giants won five of their last six, but finished seventh at 8–4–1. After the season the Giants thumped coach Folwell's Philadelphia Quakers of the AFL 31–0. Despite free tickets, preliminary high school doubleheaders, and special entertainment, attendance was low. Mara lost $40,000. Pyle's Yankees lost $100,000, however, and the AFL folded.

1927 When the AFL folded the NFL let Pyle operate his Yankees in the stadium on a schedule that did not conflict with the Giants. Mara made a coaching change, promoting Earl Potteiger from assistant to succeed Alexander who was too busy with his medical chores. The Giants signed Cal Hubbard, a 250-pound tackle from Geneva, re-signed Milstead, and added Faye (Mule) Wilson and Joe Guyon. The new players helped make the Giants the strongest team in the NFL. New York had its problems with Cleveland—in two games, the Giants battled Cleveland to a scoreless tie and lost 6–0—but not with the rest of the league. The team's 11–1–1 record was their first NFL championship. They scored 197 points and gave up only 20.

1928 Overconfidence led to bickering and there was unrest in the club, despite its 4–2–2 record in mid-season. The Giants lost their last five, including two to Pyle's Yankees. Instead of an expected second straight title, Mara lost $40,000.

1929 Mara wanted quarterback Benny Friedman, a graduate of Manhattan's Columbia University, as a drawing card in the Polo Grounds, so he hired LeRoy Andrews, Benny's coach with the Detroit Wolverines. Andrews brought along Friedman and five other former Wolverines, with Detroit dropping out of the league. After a 0–0 tie with Orange, New Jersey, the Giants won eight in a row, including two each over the 1928 champion Steamroller and the Bears. Unbeaten Green Bay challenged the unbeaten Giants in a showdown game in the Polo Grounds in November and the Packers emerged with a 20–6 victory. The Giants won their last five for a 13–1–1 record, but the Packers were champions at 12–0–1. Attendance averaged 25,000 and the Giants made a small profit.

1930 Ownership of the club was turned over to Jack and Wellington Mara, the two sons of the founder. Andrews remained as coach, with Friedman commuting between his pro job and his part-time work with the Yale coaching staff. The arrival of Chris (Red) Cable, former All-America back at Army, brought huge crowds to the Polo Grounds when the Giants and Packers met in another important game late in the season. The Giants won 13–6 and moved into a first-place tie. New York lost its next two games, to the Stapleton Stapes and Brooklyn Dodgers. Two weeks before the season ended Andrews was fired and Friedman and Steve Owen coached the club. Green Bay finished on top with 10–3–1 and a .769 percentage to the Giants' 13–4 and .765. After the season the Giants played Knute Rockne's Notre Dame All-Stars in a charity game and raised $115,153 for the New York Unemployment Fund as 55,000 saw the Giants win 21–0.

1931 Center Mel Hein was signed by the Giants. Steve Owen was named head coach. Friedman decided to quit pro ball and take a full-time job at Yale until the Giants rescheduled practice for a morning hour to ease their quarterback's commuting problems. The Giants were 3–3 when Friedman returned to the team. With Friedman in the lineup the team scored four straight shutout victories. They collapsed in the final four weeks, however, and finished fifth with a 7–6–1 record.

1932 The NFL was down to eight teams in the midst of the depression and the Giants were beginning to show their age. Friedman left to join Brooklyn as a player-coach and Owen signed ex-Giant Jack McBride, who had been released by the Dodgers, to do the passing. McBride helped Owen score a 6–0 upset of Green Bay, winner of three straight NFL titles and unbeaten in nine games. The Giants wound up fifth at 4–6–2, losing the final game to the Bears, who clinched the championship. Ray Flaherty was the league's first official pass reception champion with 21 catches.

1933 New rules that opened up the game prompted the Giants to sign Harry Newman, a talented quarterback from Michigan, and Ken Strong, a versatile back who was available because the Stapleton Stapes went out of business. Training camp was at Pompton Lakes, New Jersey. Coach Steve Owen was back on the active list as a player for the last time as the Giants easily won the Eastern Division of the newly divided NFL with an 11–3 record. Philadelphia and Pittsburgh, new to the league, were in the same division, and the Giants ran up an NFL record point total against the Eagles 56–0. In the NFL's first championship game, the Giants lost to the Bears 23–21 at Wrigley Field in a thriller in which the lead changed hands six times. Newman led the league in passing and Strong tied for the scoring lead with 64 points.

1934 Ed Danowski and John Dell Isola, both of Fordham, were the most important newcomers. Newman set a league record with 34 carries in a game with Green Bay, November 11. Newman suffered two broken bones in his back in a late-season game against the Bears. Danowski took over in a backfield that also included Strong, Bo Molenda, and Dale Burnett. The Giants won the Eastern Division again and moved into a title game with the Bears at the Polo Grounds, December 9. That game came to be known as the "Sneakers Game" when the New York equipment manager made a hurried trip to Manhattan College and returned with basketball shoes for some of the Giants to wear in the second half on the icy turf. The Giants scored 27 points in the last quarter for a 30–13 victory and their first championship since 1927. Morris (Red) Badgro had 16 pass receptions to share the league lead with Joe Carter of Philadelphia.

1935 Newman quit the team after a contract dispute and Danowski took over as the starting quarterback. The Giants put together three straight shutouts in late season, beating the Bears 3–0, the Eagles 10–0, and the Dodgers 21–0. The new 24-man player limit helped Owen alternate a second team with his regulars who outclassed the opposition in the Eastern Division with a 9–3 record. In the NFC championship game, Detroit ground out a 26–7 victory over New York in the rain and snow at the University of Detroit Stadium. Danowski led the league's passers and helped his rookie receiver, Tod Goodwin, lead with 26 receptions. Elvin (Kink) Richards was second in rushing with 449 yards.

1936 Another rival AFL was organized and both Newman and Strong left the Giants after a salary dispute. Tackle Art Lewis of Ohio University and running back Alphonse (Tuffy) Leeman of George Washington University were the Giants' top choices in the first draft. The Giants even talked Cal Hubbard, an American League baseball umpire, out of retirement for a few games. A promising 4–2–1 start deteriorated into a 5–6–1 finish and third place. Leeman led the NFL in rushing with 830 yards.

1937 It was a year of change for the Giants, with 17 rookies on the 25-man squad, new uniforms with blue jerseys and silver pants, and a new Owen formation, the A formation. In the new offense the line was unbalanced to one side and the backs overbalanced on the other side. Among the newcomers were tackle Ed Widseth of Minnesota, backs Hank Soar of Providence and Ward Cuff of Marquette, and ends Jim Lee Howell of Arkansas and Jim Poole of Mississippi. The "A" was unveiled in Washington, first home game for the newly relocated Redskins, and the Giants lost 13–3. New York was 6–1–2 in its next nine games. The Giants had a chance at the Eastern Division title in a rematch with the Redskins. Over 10,000 Redskins fans made the trip, marched up Broadway behind their band, and stormed the Polo Grounds to see Washington blast the Giants 49–14.

1938 Only five members of the 1934 championship team still were around—Danowski, Hein, Richards, Burnett, and Dell Isola. Owen alternated complete units by quarters in a most successful season climaxed by the Giants' third NFL title. After losing two of their first three games, the Giants won six and tied one in their next seven games for a 7–2–1 record. The Redskins (6–2–2) had kept pace and it all came down to a final game at the Polo Grounds with another big delegation of fans following the Redskins' band up Broadway. The Giants won 36–0 this time, then went on to defeat Green Bay 23–17 in the NFL championship game. Danowski led the league's passers and Cuff had the most field goals, five. Hein was voted NFL most valuable player. The Giants wound up the year with a $200,000 profit.

1939 The Giants strayed far from home in preseason for the first time, switching their training camp to Superior, Wisconsin, to prepare for the Chicago All-Star game. The Giants beat the All-Stars 9–0 on two field goals by Strong and one by Cuff. The Giants were unbeaten until they ventured into Detroit's new home at Briggs Stadium for the first time and lost 18–14, November 5. For the third year in a row, it came down to a final game with Washington at the Polo Grounds. Both teams had 8–1–1 records. The Giants won 9–7 despite a hotly disputed field goal attempt by the Redskins' Torrance (Bo) Russell. The Giants intercepted 35 passes during the season but in the championship game at the State Fair Grounds in Milwaukee, Green Bay picked off six Giants' passes and got revenge for 1938 with a 27–0 victory.

1940 Danowski and John (Bull) Karcis retired. Leemans was injured in a midseason game with Pittsburgh and Eddie Miller, the quarterback, was sidelined in a 13–0 loss to Cleveland. Center Hein called the plays as the Giants beat Green Bay and Washington. However, they lost to the Dodgers 14–6 on Mel Hein Day, the last game of a 6–4–1 season.

1941 The draft produced backs Len Eshmont of Fordham, George Franck of Minnesota, Andy Marefos of St. Mary's, and Frank Reagan of Pennsylvania. The Giants came out of their Superior, Wisconsin, camp with 15 rookies on the squad. New York won its first five games. The Giants clinched their third Eastern Division title in four years by beating Washington 20–13 a week before they were beaten by the Dodgers for the second time, December 7, Pearl Harbor Day. With war declared, few people were interested in the league championship game with the Bears at Chicago, and only 13,341 saw Chicago capture a second consecutive title, 37–9, December 21.

1942 The military draft was beginning to cut into the pro rosters and the Giants had 20 rookies on the squad. Eshmont, Reagan, and Jim Poole were among those in military service. The top rookies were fullback Merle Hapes of Mississippi and tackle Al Blozis of Georgetown. The Giants lost two games to Pittsburgh, a team they had dominated 14–2–1 since it joined the league in 1933. Owen tried a bit of everything, including some T formation, but the Giants sagged to 5–5–1 and third place in the Eastern Division.

1943 Steve Filipowicz was drafted first, but wasn't able to report until 1945. Wartime football produced a patchwork Giants' team. Leemans in his last year saw limited action as a player-coach. After a 56–7 rout by the Bears in which Sid Luckman threw seven touchdown passes, November 14, the Giants rallied and gained a tie for first place in the Eastern Division by beating the Redskins in back-to-back games on the last two Sundays. Led by Sammy Baugh, Washington won 28–0 over New York in a playoff game at the Polo Grounds, December 19. Bill Paschal, a rookie back from Georgia Tech, led the league by rushing for 572 yards.

1944 The Giants lured 34-year-old Arnie Herber, retired since 1940, and kicker Ken Strong, retired since 1939, to take another try at pro ball. Paschal and Blozis played on weekend passes from the army. The Giants scored five shutouts en route to the Eastern title. The Giants whipped the Packers 24–0 as Herber had a big day against his old teammates. Paschal led the league in rushing with 737 yards and Strong's six field goals topped the league. Green Bay won the championship game with a 14-7 victory over the Giants at the Polo Grounds, December 17.

1945 Six weeks after he had played tackle in the 1944 title game, Blozis was killed in his first military action in France, January 31. World War II ended in late summer and the Giants' players began coming back. Paschal returned for half a year and gained 247 yards. Filipowicz, the top draft choice in 1943, reported. Herber threw four touchdown passes against the Eagles. After the Giants lost 17–0 to the Redskins, Herber retired. The 3–6–1 season was the Giants' poorest.

1946 The Giants got a competitor for New York's football attention when Dan Topping put the New York Yankees in Yankee Stadium in the newly organized All-America Football Conference. Frank Filchock's days as an understudy to Sammy Baugh at Washington ended when he signed with the Giants for a reported $35,000 salary. The Giants defeated the

Bears 14–0 before 62,539 at the Polo Grounds. The Giants won the Eastern Division with a 7–3–1 record. On the eve of the championship game against the Bears at the Polo Grounds, Filchock and Hapes were questioned about an attempt by a New York gambler to fix the game. Hapes was suspended for not reporting the contact but Filchock played the game and played well in a 23–14 defeat. Both Filchock and Hapes were suspended indefinitely.

1947 The loss of Filchock left the Giants without a quarterback until they acquired Paul Governali, a Columbia All-America, from the Boston Yanks in a trade for Paschal and the draft rights to Notre Dame tackle George Connor. The Giants gained the rights to tackle Dewitt (Tex) Coulter of Army in an unusual transaction. Coulter quit Army in 1946 and was permitted to play with the Giants with the stipulation he had to go into the 1947 draft because his original class had not graduated. The Chicago Cardinals drafted Coulter in the first round and then traded him to the Giants for the rights to Vic Schwall, New York's first-round draft pick. The Giants were 0–7–2 after nine games and finished last for the first time with a 2–8–2 record. Rookies Gene (Choo Choo) Roberts and Ray Poole were bright spots. One victory was 35–31 over the Chicago Cardinals who won the championship.

1948 Charlie Conerly, a rangy, angular passer who reminded Owen and Mara of Sammy Baugh, arrived on the scene from Mississippi. Washington had drafted Conerly in 1945 but he chose to return to college after serving in the marines. The Giants obtained the rights to Conerly in a trade with the Redskins. Emlen Tunnell, Bill Swiacki, and Tony (Skippy) Minisi were among the 20 rookies on the 35-man roster. The Giants' leaky defense allowed 388 points, losing to the Redskins 41–10, the Eagles 45–0, and the Cardinals 63-35. Conerly set an NFL record with 36 completions in 53 attempts in a losing game against Pittsburgh, December 5. Conerly threw 22 touchdown passes in the 4–8 season.

1949 Ted Collins moved his Boston Yanks' franchise to New York and changed the name to New York Bulldogs. The Bulldogs shared the Polo Grounds with the Giants. Owen brought in Allie Sherman to help teach Conerly, who had always played the single wing, the T formation. Rookies Bill Austin and Al DeRogatis made the squad. Consecutive losses to Philadelphia in the final two games dropped the Giants to 6–6 and third place in the East. Gene Roberts tied for the scoring lead with 102 points on 17 touchdowns, nine while rushing for 634 yards and eight while catching 35 passes for 711 yards. Swiacki caught 47 passes and Ray Poole 25. Conerly completed 152 passes, 17 for touchdowns. Tunnell intercepted 10 passes.

1950 The realigned NFL admitted Cleveland, Baltimore, and San Francisco from the AAFC and the Giants were placed in the American Conference with the Browns, four-time champions of the AAFC. Coach Owen devised a new "Umbrella" defense. Tom Landry, Otto Schnellbacher, and Harmon Rowe, three of five men assigned the Giants from the defunct Yankees, teamed with Tunnell in the four-man secondary. Ends Jim Duncan and Ray Poole sometimes dropped back, making it a four-three defense. Arnie Weinmeister, another former Yankees' player, anchored the defensive line at tackle. Roberts set a Giants' record with 218 yards rushing against the Cardinals, November 12. Conerly played with a shoulder separation and quarterback Travis Tidwell, the number one draft choice from Auburn, saw a lot of action. The Giants defeated Cleveland twice, 6–0 and 17–13, and tied the Browns for the conference title at 10–2. The Giants lost the playoff 8–3 to Cleveland on two field goals and a safety by Lou Groza. Rookie Eddie Price of Tulane led the rushers with 703 yards.

1951 Kyle Rote of Southern Methodist was the Giants' bonus pick in the draft. Rote was injured in preseason and saw limited action. The draft also brought tackle Ray Krouse from Maryland and end Bill Stribling from Mississippi. Coulter was lured out of a one-year retirement. After an opening day tie with Pittsburgh, the Giants won all the rest except for two losses to Cleveland. The Browns beat the Giants 14–13 and 10–0 and repeated as conference champions (11–1), with the Giants in second place at 9–2–1. Eddie Price, a second-year man, led the league in rushing with 971 yards and set an NFL record with 271 carries. Schnellbacher led the league with 11 interceptions and Tunnell had a record four touchdowns on kick returns.

1952 Frank Gifford, a back from USC, was the team's first draft choice. Owen still was using much of the old A formation, mixed occasionally with the T formation, and Polo Grounds crowds vented their frustration on the coach throughout the season. The booing reached a zenith after the Giants returned home from a 63–7 drubbing by Pittsburgh. Conerly's shoulder was injured again and Owen had to use rookie Fred Benners at quarterback. Rote ran for 421 yards and caught 21 passes for 240 yards. Gifford was used mostly at defensive back, carrying the ball only 38 times for 116 yards. Tunnell gained more yardage on kick returns and interceptions (a total of 924 yards) than the league's rushing leader (Dan Towler of Los Angeles with 894 yards).

1953 Offensive linemen Rosey Brown, Ray Wietecha, and Jack Stroud joined the team. Injuries to Conerly and Price contributed to another season of frustration, climaxed by a 62–14 loss to Cleveland. Owen's coaching career ended uncharacteristically—with a 27–16 defeat by Detroit. The Giants' head coach for 23 years, he retired with a career record of 151–100–17. Owen's teams won two NFL championships and finished first in their division six times.

1954 Jim Lee Howell, an end with the Giants from 1937 to 1948 with time out for service as a marine captain during World War II, was promoted from end coach to head coach. Allie Sherman left his assistant coaching position to become a head coach in Canada. Howell hired Vince Lombardi from Army to become his offensive coach, and made Tom Landry a player-coach with defensive responsibilities. Conerly announced his retirement, but Howell traveled to Conerly's home in Mississippi and talked him out of the decision. The Giants obtained end Bob Schnelker from Philadelphia and another end, Ken MacAfee joined the team after duty in the service. Other new faces on the team included Dick Nolan, a defensive back from Maryland, Don Heinrich, quarterback from Washington, and Bobby Clatterbuck, another quarterback from Houston. The Giants lost two games to the conference champion Browns but improved to a 7–5 record. Gifford became an offensive halfback and gained 368 yards. Schnelker caught 30 passes, MacAfee 24; each man scored eight touchdowns. Conerly missed considerable playing time with injuries but still threw 17 touchdown passes.

1955 Mel Triplett, a fullback from Toledo; Jim Patton, a defensive back from Mississippi; and Rosey Grier, a defensive tackle from Penn State, were among the draft choices signed. The Giants also signed Alex Webster, a running back who had been the Canadian Football League's most valuable player in 1954. The Giants started slowly, losing five of their first seven games but they were 4–0–1 in their last five games to finish third in the Eastern Conference. Webster rushed for 634 yards, while Gifford gained 351 yards and caught 33 passes.

1956 The Giants signed a contract to play in Yankee Stadium. Sam Huff, a linebacker from West Virginia, Don Chandler, a kicker from Florida, and Jim Katcavage, a defensive end from Dayton, were obtained in the draft; defensive end Andy Robustelli, defensive tackle Dick Mozelewski, and defensive back Ed Hughes were obtained in trades. Landry retired as a player to become the full-time defensive coordinator. The Giants proved their fast finish of 1955 was not a fluke with an impressive season. Their 8–3–1 record unseated the Browns as conference champions for the first time in Cleveland's six seasons in the NFL. The Giants routed the Chicago Bears 47–7 in Yankee Stadium to win the NFL title game, their first league championship since 1938. Gifford caught 51 passes and rushed for 819 yards for the season. Middle linebacker Huff was the rookie of the year.

1957 Grier joined the army. The Giants and the Browns were the primary contenders for the Eastern Conference title and Cleveland gained a big edge by winning both games between the two teams, 6–3 and 34–28. A three-game losing streak at the end of the season dropped the Giants to 7–5. Gifford and Webster were the one-two punch again, with Gifford rushing for 528 yards and catching 41 passes, while Webster rushed for 478 yards and caught 30 passes. Chandler led the league with a 44.6-yard punting average.

1958 The club got Phil King, a running back from Vanderbilt, through the draft and end and kicker Pat Summerall and back Lindon Crow through a trade with the Chicago Cardinals. The Giants edged the Baltimore Colts 24–21 before a record Yankee Stadium crowd of 71,163, November 9. A 49-yard field goal by Summerall in the snow gave the Giants a 13–10 victory over Cleveland in the final game of the regular season, enabling New York to tie the Browns for first place in the Eastern Conference. In a playoff game between the two teams, the Giants played a dazzling defensive game, holding Cleveland's Jim Brown to 18 yards and gaining a 10–0 victory, December 21. The Giants met Baltimore for the NFL championship in Yankee Stadium, December 28. The Colts tied the game 17–17 in the final seconds on a field goal by Steve Myrha. The Giants started with the ball in sudden-death overtime, but a drive fell inches short of a first down at midfield and Baltimore took over after a punt. Led by quarterback John Unitas, the Colts moved to the winning touchdown on a one-yard run by Alan Ameche after 8:15 of overtime. The 23–17 victory was seen by millions of people on NBC television and generally was credited with pushing interest in pro football to new heights.

1959 Tim Mara, founder of the Giants, died, February 16. Lombardi left the Giants to become head coach at Green Bay. Allie Sherman returned from Canada to succeed Lombardi. Lee Grosscup, a quarterback from Utah, was the number one draft choice. The Giants obtained a number of players by trade, among them guard Darrell Dess from Pittsburgh, cornerbacks Dick Lynch from Washington and Dick Nolan from the Chicago Cardinals, and quarterback George Shaw from Baltimore. Grosscup was cut in training camp at Bear Mountain, New York. Gifford failed in a brief preseason try at quarterback and returned to running back. The Giants eliminated their long-time nemesis, the Cleveland Browns, with a 48–7 romp, December 6. New York's 10–2 record was the best in the NFL. The Giants and the Colts were matched in the title game for the second consecutive year. New York led 9–7 after three quarters but Baltimore exploded for 24 points in the final 15 minutes in a 31–16 victory.

1960 Howell announced he would retire as coach after the 1960 season. Landry left the Giants to become head coach of the expansion Dallas Cowboys. The Giants had a new rival for New York's football attentions, the New York Titans, who played at the Polo Grounds. Webster suffered a serious knee injury in a preseason game. Conerly labored much of the

season with a sore arm. Gifford suffered a concussion from a blindside tackle by Philadelphia's Chuck Bednarik, November 20. The injuries severely damaged the Giants' hopes in the Eastern Conference and they finished third, behind the Eagles and Browns.

1961 The Giants' first offer for a coach to succeed Howell was to Lombardi, who had coached two years in Green Bay after leaving New York. When that bid failed, the Giants signed Sherman as the new head coach. Gifford announced his retirement, the result of his concussion the season before. The Giants obtained running back Bobby Gaiters of New Mexico State in the draft. The Giants made a number of significant trades, getting quarterback Y. A. Tittle from San Francisco, receiver Del Shofner from Los Angeles, and cornerback Erich Barnes from the Chicago Bears. Sherman began the season with Conerly at quarterback, but he shifted to Tittle in the second game and Tittle played the position the rest of the way. Barnes intercepted a Dallas pass and ran 102 yards for a touchdown, October 22. The Giants tied Philadelphia for first place in the Eastern Conference with a 38–21 victory in New York. The Giants won the rematch 28–24 in December and claimed undisputed first place. The Giants needed a tie in their final game against Cleveland to clinch the title and that's just what they got, 7–7. The Giants were no match for Lombardi's Green Bay team in the title game in Green Bay, December 31. The Packers won 37–0. Shofner caught 68 passes for 1,125 yards and 11 touchdowns. Webster rushed for 928 yards, while Gaiters added 460. Lynch led the league with nine interceptions.

1962 Conerly, Rote, and Summerall retired. Tight end Aaron Thomas was obtained in a trade with San Francisco. Gifford made a comeback after a one-year retirement. Sherman moved Gifford to flanker in training camp. Tittle threw seven touchdown passes and totaled 505 yards in a 49–34 victory over Washington, October 28. Shofner's 11 receptions totaled 269 yards in that game. The Giants won 12 of 14 games and finished three games ahead of Pittsburgh in the Eastern Conference. Tittle, 35, finished the season with 200 pass completions for 3,225 yards and 33 touchdowns. Shofner had 53 catches for 1,133 yards and 12 scores, while Gifford added 39 for 796 yards and seven touchdowns. Webster led the team in rushing with 743 yards. Chandler, who added the placekicking job to his punting duties, kicked 19 field goals. The Giants met the Packers in the NFL title game for the second consecutive year, this time in Yankee Stadium. The Packers won 16–7 on a day in which the temperature was 20 degrees and 40-mile-an-hour winds whipped the turf. Huff and Packers' running back Jim Taylor had a spectacular individual duel in the Green Bay victory.

1963 The Giants had 10 starters who were age 30 or over. New York had an unimpressive 3–2 record after five weeks, but the team rebounded to win eight of its final nine games. A 33–17 victory over Pittsburgh in the final game of the season enabled the Giants to win their third consecutive Eastern Conference title. Tittle finished with his best year: 36 touchdown passes and 3,145 yards. Shofner caught 64 passes for nine touchdowns and Gifford added 42 and seven scores. Chandler led the league with 106 points on 18 field goals and 52 conversions. The Giants had to play in another championship game on a cold winter day, this time in Chicago with the temperature at 8 degrees, December 29. Tittle was injured in the second quarter. He later returned to play but the Giants' offense never got going and Chicago won 14–10.

1964 Among the players drafted and signed by the Giants were running back Joe Don Looney from Oklahoma, quarterback Gary Wood from Cornell, and running backs Ernie Wheelright from Southern Illinois and Clarence Childs from Florida A&M. Sherman traded away two of the Giants' most notable

players—Huff to Washington and Modzelewski to Cleveland. Looney was traded to Baltimore during training camp. Tittle was injured in a 27–24 loss to Pittsburgh and was ineffective after he returned. Wood was given the quarterback's spot but the rookie could not reverse the Giants' slide. New York closed with a 2–10–2 record and finished in last place for the first time since 1947. Wheelright led the club in rushing with 402 yards. Childs led the league in kickoff returns with a 29-yard average. Webster and Gifford retired after the end of the season.

1965 The draft brought the Giants' running backs Tucker Fredrickson from Auburn (the number one selection in the entire draft) and Ernie Koy from Texas and cornerbacks Spider Lockhart from North Texas State and Willie Williams from Grambling. Tittle, Robustelli, and Stroud retired. Chandler was traded to Green Bay. Quarterback Earl Morrall was acquired from Detroit. Jack Mara, the club president for 31 years, died in June and his brother, Wellington, assumed the club president's duties. Fredrickson was teamed with Steve Thurlow and Koy in what was called the "Baby Bull" backfield. Morrall's passing helped the Giants to a 7–7 record.

1966 The Giants chose cornerback Henry Carr of Arizona State in the draft. New York signed soccer-style kicker Pete Gogolak after he played out his option with Buffalo of the American Football League, May 17. Less than a month later, the NFL and AFL agreed to merge, June 8. Morrall and wide receiver Homer Jones collaborated on a 98-yard touchdown pass play on opening day, September 11. Carr returned a kickoff 101 yards against Los Angeles, November 13. The Redskins bombarded the Giants 72–41 in a game that set league highs for most points scored by one team (72) and by both teams (113), November 27. Morrall was injured late in the season in a practice accident and Sherman had to make do with quarterbacks Wood and Tom Kennedy. Jones caught 48 passes and scored eight touchdowns. The Giants' defense gave up a league record 501 points and the team plunged to last place with a 1–12–1 record.

1967 The Giants obtained quarterback Fran Tarkenton from Minnesota in exchange for four high draft choices. New York also acquired middle linebacker Vince Costello from Cleveland. The Giants rebounded from their poor 1966 season by posting a 7–7 record. Tarkenton passed for 3,088 yards and 29 touchdowns. Aaron Thomas caught 51 passes for nine scores, while Homer Jones added 49 catches.

1968 The Tarkenton trade of 1967 virtually depleted the Giants of draft opportunities and they fared poorly in the draft. New York won its first four games. After 10 games, the team was 7–3 and only one game behind Dallas in the NFL's Capitol Division. The Giants lost their last four games to finish second again. Tarkenton passed for 2,555 yards and 21 touchdowns. Jones averaged 23.5 yards on 46 receptions for 1,057 yards. Fredrickson rushed for 486 yards; Koy added 394. Willie Williams led the league with 10 interceptions.

1969 The Giants obtained running back Junior Coffey in a trade with Atlanta. In their first game ever against an AFL team, the Giants lost 37–14 to the New York Jets in a preseason game at the Yale Bowl, August 17. When the Giants dropped a preseason game to Pittsburgh the following week, Sherman was fired. Webster, an assistant coach and former star running back, was named head coach a week before the regular season began. The Giants won three of their first four games but a seven-game losing streak dropped the team out of contention. New York won its last three outings for a 6–8 record. Jones caught 42 passes for 744 yards. Tarkenton passed for 2,918 yards and 23 touchdowns.

1970 Wide receiver Clifton McNeil was obtained

Del Shofner, left, and Y. A. Tittle, 1963.

from San Francisco. The Giants traded wide receiver Homer Jones to Cleveland for running back Ron Johnson and defensive tackle Jim Kanicki. New York lost its first three games, then won six of its next ten to tie Dallas for first place with one week left in the season. On the season's final Sunday, the Giants lost 31–3 to Los Angeles while Dallas defeated Houston. Johnson became the Giants' first 1,000-yard rusher, totaling 1,027 yards. He also caught 48 passes and totaled 1,654 yards in total offense. McNeil caught 50 passes. Tarkenton passed for 2,777 yards and 19 touchdowns.

1971 Running back Rocky Thompson was the club's first draft choice. The Giants announced that they planned to move to a new stadium in East Rutherford, New Jersey, hopefully by 1975. Tarkenton left the team for a few days in training camp, then returned. The team lost all six preseason games, including a 27–14 loss to the Jets. The Giants defeated Green Bay 42–40 in the opening game. Ron Johnson missed most of the season with a thigh injury; Fredrickson suffered an injured knee. The Giants had losing streaks of four and five games. Tarkenton, who had thrown only 11 touchdown passes, was benched in favor of Randy Johnson in the final game. Bob Tucker became the first tight end to lead the NFL in pass receiving with 59 receptions for 791 yards.

1972 The Giants traded Tarkenton back to Minnesota in exchange for quarterback Norm Snead, wide receiver Bob Grim, running back Vince Clements, and two draft choices. Defensive end Jack Gregory was obtained from Cleveland. The draft produced defensive tackle John Mendenhall. The Giants lost their first two games, then won four in a row. New York concluded the season with two victories—62–10 over Philadelphia (a club record for most points) and 23–3 over Dallas—to finish 8–6 and gain second place in the Eastern Division. Snead led the league in passing, completing 60.3 percent of his passes. Tucker had 55 receptions. Johnson rushed for 1,182 yards and led the league with 14 touchdowns, 9 by rushing and 5 by receiving. Pete Gogolak kicked 21 field goals in 31 attempts.

1973 The Giants had a 6–0 record in the preseason. The Giants won their opening game against Houston at Yankee Stadium 34–14. A week later New York tied Philadelphia 23–23 in the final game played at old Yankee Stadium, September 23. The Giants played the rest of their home schedule at the Yale Bowl in New Haven, Connecticut, and practiced in New Jersey. The team won only one of its last 12 games. Webster announced his resignation as coach before the final game, a 31–7 loss to Minnesota in New Haven. Johnson rushed for 902 yards. Tucker caught 50 passes. The defense surrendered 362 points in the 2–11–1 season.

1974 Bill Arnsparger, the assistant coach who helped guide Miami to two Super Bowl championships, was

named the Giants' ninth head coach. Andy Robustelli was named director of operations. New York obtained guards John Hicks from Ohio State and Tom Mullen from Southwest Missouri State in the draft. Running backs Joe Dawkins and Doug Kotar were obtained in trades with Denver and Pittsburgh, respectively. The team continued to play its games at the Yale Bowl. New York scored a 14–6 upset victory in Dallas, September 29. In a pair of midseason transactions, Arnsparger traded quarterback Norm Snead to San Francisco and obtained quarterback Craig Morton from Dallas. The Giants posted a 33–27 victory over Kansas City, November 3. New York lost all seven home games and ended with a 2–12 record.

1975 The new stadium in New Jersey wasn't ready yet, so the Giants shared Shea Stadium with the Jets. Two Giants' home games had to be scheduled on Saturday afternoons to avoid conflict with the Jets' schedule. The Giants won their first four preseason games and began the regular season with a 23–14 victory over Philadelphia. A series of close defeats followed, including 13–7 and 14–3 losses to Dallas and a 13–10 loss to Philadelphia. The Giants surprised Buffalo 17–14 in a Monday night game, October 20. The team finished 5–9.

1976 The draft produced defensive end Troy Archer from Colorado, running back Gordon Bell from Michigan, and linebacker Harry Carson from South Carolina State. Larry Csonka, the former Miami running back who had played in the World Football League, signed as a free agent for a reported $1 million. Quarterback Norm Snead was re-acquired from San Francisco, September 1. After three seasons without a permanent home, the Giants moved into the new 76,000-seat Giants stadium in East Rutherford, New Jersey, October 10. In the stadium's inaugural game, the Giants lost 24–14 to Dallas, their fifth consecutive loss. When the losing streak reached six the following week, Arnsparger was fired and an assistant coach, John McVay, was given the job. The losing streak reached nine before the Giants defeated Washington 12–9, November 14. The victory ended a 14-game winless streak against George Allen-coached teams. The Giants won two of their final three games for a 3–11 record. Csonka was injured much of the year and gained 569 yards; he underwent knee surgery after the season. Kotar led the club in rushing with 731 yards. Tucker caught 42 passes. McVay was signed to a long-term coaching contract.

1977 Morton was traded to Denver for quarterback Steve Ramsay.

MEMBERS OF HALL OF FAME:
Roosevelt Brown, Ray Flaherty, Frank Gifford, Joe Guyon, Mel Hein, Wilbur (Pete) Henry, Arnie Herber, Cal Hubbard, Vince Lombardi, Tim Mara, Hugh McElhenny, Steve Owen, Andy Robustelli, Ken Strong, Jim Thorpe, Y.A. Tittle, Emlen Tunnell.

GIANTS RECORD, 1925–76

Year	Won	Lost	Tied	Pct.	Pts.	OP
1925	8	4	0	.667	122	67
1926	8	4	1	.667	147	51
1927‡	11	1	1	.917	197	20
1928	4	7	2	.364	79	136
1929	13	1	1	.929	312	86
1930	13	4	0	.765	308	98
1931	7	6	1	.538	154	100
1932	4	6	2	.400	93	113
1933§	11	3	0	.786	244	101
1934‡	8	5	0	.615	147	107
1935§	9	3	0	.750	180	96
1936	5	6	1	.455	115	163
1937	6	3	2	.667	128	109
1938‡	8	2	1	.800	194	79
1939§	9	1	1	.900	168	85
1940	6	4	1	.600	131	133
1941§	8	3	0	.727	238	114
1942	5	5	1	.500	155	139
1943	6	3	1	.667	197	170
1944§	8	1	1	.889	206	75
1945	3	6	1	.333	179	198
1946§	7	3	1	.700	236	162
1947	2	8	2	.200	190	309
1948	4	8	0	.333	297	388
1949	6	6	0	.500	287	298
1950	10	2	0	.833	268	150
1951	9	2	1	.818	254	161
1952	7	5	0	.583	234	231
1953	3	9	0	.250	179	277
1954	7	5	0	.583	293	184
1955	6	5	1	.545	267	223
1956‡	8	3	1	.727	264	197
1957	7	5	0	.583	254	211
1958†	9	3	0	.750	246	183
1959†	10	2	0	.833	284	170
1960	6	4	2	.600	271	261
1961†	10	3	1	.769	368	220
1962†	12	2	0	.857	398	283
1963†	11	3	0	.786	448	280
1964	2	10	2	.167	241	399
1965	7	7	0	.500	270	338
1966	1	12	1	.077	263	501
1967	7	7	0	.500	369	379
1968	7	7	0	.500	294	325
1969	6	8	0	.429	264	298
1970	9	5	0	.643	301	270
1971	4	10	0	.286	228	362
1972	8	6	0	.571	331	247
1973	2	11	1	.179	226	362
1974	2	12	0	.143	195	299
1975	5	9	0	.357	216	306
1976	3	11	0	.214	170	250
52 Years	357	271	31	.565	12,100	10,764

‡*NFL Champion*
§*NFL Eastern Division Champion*
†*NFL Eastern Conference Champion*

RECORD HOLDERS

Rushing (Yards)	Ron Johnson, 1972	1,182
Passing (Pct.)	Norm Snead, 1972	60.3
Passing (Yards)	Y.A. Tittle, 1962	3,224
Passing (TDs)	Y.A. Tittle, 1963	36
Receiving (No.)	Del Shofner, 1961	68
Receiving (Yards)	Homer Jones, 1967	1,209
Interceptions (No.)	Otto Schnellbacher, 1951, and Jim Patton, 1958	11
Punting (Avg.)	Kay Eakin, 1941	47.4
Punt Ret. (Avg.)	Emlen Tunnell, 1951	14.4
Kickoff Ret. (Avg.)	Jack Salscheider, 1949	31.6
Touchdowns (Total)	Gene Roberts, 1949	17
Field Goals Made	Pete Gogolak, 1970	25
Points (No.)	Pete Gogolak, 1970	107

COACHING HISTORY

1925	Robert Folwell	8– 4– 0
1926	Joe Alexander	8– 4– 1
1927–28	Earl Potteiger	15– 8– 3
1929–30	LeRoy Andrews	26– 5– 1
1931–53	Steve Owen	151–100–17
1954–60	Jim Lee Howell	53– 27– 4
1961–68	Allie Sherman	57– 51– 4
1969–73	Alex Webster	29– 40– 1
1974–76	Bill Arnsparger*	7– 28– 0
1976	John McVay	3– 4– 0

Replaced after seven games in 1976

FIRST PLAYER SELECTED

1936	Art Lewis, T, Ohio U.
1937	Ed Widseth, T, Minnesota
1938	George Karamatic, B, Gonzaga
1939	Walt Nielson, B, Arizona
1940	Grenville Lansdell, B, USC
1941	George Franck, B, Minnesota
1942	Merle Hapes, B, Mississippi
1943	Steve Filipowicz, B, Fordham
1944	Billy Hillenbrand, B, Indiana
1945	Elmer Barbour, B, Wake Forest
1946	George Connor, T, Notre Dame
1947	Vic Schwall, B, Northwestern
1948	Tony Minisi, B, Pennsylvania
1949	Paul Page, B, SMU
1950	Travis Tidwell, B, Auburn
1951	Kyle Rote, B, SMU
1952	Frank Gifford, B, USC
1953	Bobby Marlow, B, Alabama
1954	Ken Buck, C, Pacific
1955	Joe Heap, B, Notre Dame
1956	Henry Moore, B, Arkansas
1957	Sam DeLuca, T (2), South Carolina
1958	Phil King, B, Vanderbilt
1959	Lee Grosscup, B, Utah
1960	Lou Cordileone, G, Clemson
1961	Bruce Tarbox, G (2), Syracuse
1962	Jerry Hillebrand, LB, Colorado
1963	Frank Lasky, T (2 future), Florida
1964	Joe Don Looney, B, Oklahoma
1965	Tucker Frederickson, RB, Auburn
1966	Francis Peay, T, Missouri
1967	Louis Thompson, DT (4), Alabama
1968	Dick Buzin, T (2), Penn State
1969	Fred Dryer, DE, San Diego State
1970	Jim Files, LB, Oklahoma
1971	Rocky Thompson, WR, West Texas State
1972	Eldridge Small, DB, Texas A&I
1973	Brad Van Pelt, LB, Michigan State
1974	John Hicks, G, Ohio State
1975	Al Simpson, T (2), Colorado State
1976	Troy Archer, DE, Colorado

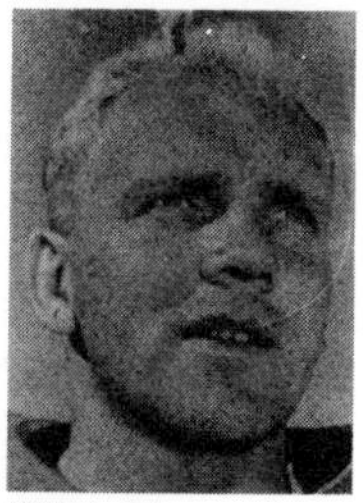

Bill Austin

Don Chandler

Charlie Conerly

DeWitt (Tex) Coulter

Darrell Dess

Pete Gogolak

Jack Gregory

NEW YORK GIANTS, 1925–76

Adamchik, Ed, C, Pittsburgh	1965
Adams, O'Neal, E, Arkansas	1941–45
Adams, Verlin, T, Morris Harvey	1942–45
Agajanian, Ben, K, New Mexico	1949, 1954–57
Albright, Bill, G, Wisconsin	1951–54
Alexander, Joe, G, Syracuse	1925–27
Alexander, John, T, Rutgers	1926
Alexakos, Steve, G, San Jose State	1971
Allison, Jim, E, Texas A&M	1928
Amberg, John, B, Kansas	1951–52
Anderson, Bob, B, Army	1963
Anderson, Bruce, DE, Williamette	1967–69
Anderson, Cliff, E, Indiana	1953
Anderson, Roger, DT, Virginia Union	1965–68
Anderson, Winston, E, Colgate	1936
Archer, Troy, DE, Colorado	1976
Artman, Corwan, T, Stanford	1931
Ashburn, Cliff, G, Nebraska	1929
Athas, Pete, DB, Tennessee	1971–74
Atwood, John, B, Wisconsin	1948
Austin, Bill, G, Oregon State	1949–50, 1953–57
Avedisian, Charles, G, Providence	1942–44
Averno, Sisto, G, Muhlenberg	1951
Avery, Ken, LB, So. Mississippi	1967–68
Avinger, Clarence, B, Alabama	1953

B

Badgro, Morris (Red), E, USC	1927–35
Baker, John, DE, Norfolk State	1970
Baker, Jon, G, California	1949–52
Ballman, Gary, TE, Michigan State	1973
Banks, Willie, G, Alcorn A&M	1970
Barber, Ernie, C, San Francisco	1945
Barbour, Wes, QB, Wake Forest	1945
Barker, Hubert, B, Arkansas	1942–45
Barnard, Charles, E, Edmond State	1938
Barnes, Erich, DB, Purdue	1961–64
Barnum, Len, QB, West Virginia Wesleyan	1938–40
Barrett, Emmet, C, Portland	1942–44
Barry, Al, G, USC	1958–59
Barzilauskas, Fritz, G, Yale	1951
Bauer, John, G, Illinois	1954
Beck, Ray, G, Georgia Tech	1952, 1955–57
Bednar, Al, G, Lafayette	1925–26
Beeble, Keith, B, Occidental	1944
Beil, Lawrence, T, Portland	1948
Bell, Gordon, RB, Michigan	1976
Bell, Kay, T, Washington State	1942
Bellinger, Bob, T, Gonzaga	1934–35
Benkert, Harry, B, Rutgers	1925
Benners, Fred, QB, Southern Methodist	1952
Berry, Wayne, B, Washington State	1954
Biggs, Riley, C, Baylor	1926–27
Biscaha, Joe, E, Richmond	1959
Blanchard, Tom, P-QB, Oregon	1971–73
Blazine, Anthony, T, Illinois Wesleyan	1940–41
Bloodgood, Elbert, B, Nebraska	1928
Blozis, Al, T, Georgetown	1942–44
Blumenstock, Jim, B, Fordham	1947
Blye, Ron, B, Notre Dame	1968
Boggan, Rex, T, Mississippi	1955
Bohovich, Reed, T, Lehigh	1962–63
Bolin, Bookie, G, Mississippi	1962–67
Boll, Don, T, Nebraska	1960
Bomer, Lynn, E, Vanderbilt	1925–26
Bookman, John, DB, Miami	1957
Borden, Les, E, Fordham	1935
Boston, McKinley, DE, Minnesota	1968–69
Bowdoin, Jim, G, Alabama	1932
Bowman, Steve, B, Alabama	1966
Boyle, Bill, T, None	1934
Brackett, Marty, G, Auburn	1958
Brahm, Larry, G, Temple	1943
Brennan, Matt, B, Lafayette	1925
Brenner, Al, DB, Michigan State	1969–70
Broadstone, Marion, T, Nebraska	1931
Brooks, Bobby, DB, Boston College	1974–76
Broussard, Fred, C, N.W. Louisiana	1955
Brovarney, Casimir, T, Detroit	1941
Brown, Barry, LB, Florida	1968
Brown, Dave, B, Alabama	1943, 1946–47
Brown, Otto, DB, Prairie View	1970–73
Brown, Rosie, T, Morgan State	1953–65
Browning, Greg, E, Denver	1947
Bryant, Bill, DB, Grambling	1976
Bucklin, Tom, B, Idaho	1931
Buetow, Bart, G, Minnesota	1973
Buffington, Harry, G, Oklahoma A&M	1942
Buggs, Danny, WR, West Virginia	1975–76
Bundra, Mike, DT, USC	1965
Burkhardt, Art, G, Rutgers	1928
Burnett, Dale, B, Kansas Teachers	1930–39
Burnine, Hal, E, Missouri	1956
Bushong, John, DE, Western Kentucky	1976
Butkus, Carl, T, George Washington	1949
Butler, Skip, K, Texas-Arlington	1971
Buzin, Dick, T, Penn State	1968–70
Byers, Ken, G, Cincinnati	1962–64
Byler, Joe, T, Nebraska	1946

C

Cagle, Chris, B, Army	1930–32
Caldwell, Bruce, B, Yale	1928
Calligaro, Len, B, Wisconsin	1944–45
Campbell, Carter, LB, Weber State	1972–73
Campbell, Glen, E, Kansas Teachers'	1929–33
Cannady, John, B, Indiana	1947–54
Cannella, John, T, Fordham	1933–34
Cantor, Leo, B, UCLA	1942
Capps, Wilbur, B, Oklahoma State Central	1929
Caranci, Roland, T, Colorado	1944
Carney, Art, G, Navy	1925–26
Carr, Henry, DB, Arizona State	1965–67
Carrocio, Russ, G, Virginia	1954–55
Carroll, Jim, LB, Notre Dame	1965–66
Carroll, Vic, T, Nevada	1943–47
Carson, Harry, LB, South Carolina State	1976
Case, Pete, G, Georgia	1965–70
Ceppetelli, Gene, C, Villanova	1969
Chandler, Don, K, Florida	1956–64
Chandler, Karl, C, Princeton	1974–76
Cheverko, George, B, Fordham	1947–48
Chickerneo, John, B, Pittsburgh	1942
Childs, Clarence, DB, Florida A&M	1964–67
Cicolella, Mike, LB, Dayton	1966–68
Clancy, Stuart, B, Holy Cross	1933–35
Clatterbuck, Bob, QB, Houston	1954–57
Clay, Randy, B, Texas	1950, 1953
Clay, Roy, B, Colorado	1944
Clements, Vince, RB, Connecticut	1972–73
Coates, Ray, B, Louisiana State	1948–49
Coffey, Junior, RB, Washington	1969–71
Colbert, Rondy, DB, Lamar	1976
Cole, Pete, G, Trinity, Tex.	1937–40
Colhouer, Jake, G, Oklahoma	1949
Collier, Jim, E, Arkansas	1962–63
Collins, Ray, T, Louisiana State	1954
Colvin, Jim, DT, Houston	1967
Comstock, Rudy, G, Georgetown	1930
Condren, Glen, DE, Oklahoma	1965–67
Conerly, Charlie, QB, Mississippi	1948–61
Contoulis, John, DT, Connecticut	1964
Cope, Frank, T, Santa Clara	1938–47
Cordileone, Lou, G, Clemson	1960
Corgan, Charles, E, Arkansas	1927
Corzine, Lester, B, Davis-Elkins	1934–37
Costello, Tom, LB, Dayton	1964–65
Costello, Vince, LB, Ohio U.	1967
Coulter, Dewitt, T, Army	1946–52
Counts, John, B, Illinois	1962–63
Cousino, Brad, LB, Miami, Ohio	1976
Crane, Dennis, T, USC	1970
Crawford, Bill, G, British Columbia	1960
Crawford, Ed, B, Mississippi	1957
Crespino, Bob, E, Mississippi	1964–68
Crist, Chuck, DB, Penn State	1972–74
Crosby, Steve, RB, Fort Hays State	1976
Crow, Lindon, B, USC	1958–60
Crutcher, Tommy, LB, Texas Christian	1968–69
Csonka, Larry, RB, Syracuse	1976
Cuff, Ward, B, Marquette	1937–45
Culwell, Val, G, Oregon	1942

D

Damiani, Francis, T, Manhattan	1944
Danelo, Joe, K, Washington State	1976
Danowski, Ed, QB, Fordham	1934–41
Davis, Don, DT, Cal. State-L.A.	1966–67
Davis, Gains, G, Texas Tech	1936
Davis, Henry, LB, Grambling	1968–69
Davis, Roger, T, Syracuse	1965–66
Davis, Roosevelt, DE, Tennessee State	1965–67
DeFilippo, Lou, C, Fordham	1941, 1945–48
DelGaizo, Jim, QB, Tampa	1974
Dell Isola, John, C, Fordham	1934–40
Dennerlien, Gerry, T, St. Mary's	1937–40
Dennery, Vince, E, Fordham	1941
DeRogatis, Al, T, Duke	1949–52
Dess, Darrell, G, N. Carolina State	1959–64, 1966–69
Dobelstein, Bob, G, Tennessee	1946–48
Doggert, Keith, T, Wichita	1942
Doolan, John, B, Georgetown	1945–46
Douglas, Everett, T, Florida	1953
Douglas, John, LB, Missouri	1970–73
Douglass, Paul, DB, Illinois	1953
Dove, Eddie, DB, Colorado	1963
Dryer, Fred, DE, San Diego State	1969–72
Dubifsky, Maurice, G, Georgetown	1932
Dublinski, Tom, QB, Utah	1958
Dubzinski, Walt, G, Boston College	1943
Duden, Dick, E, Navy	1949
Dudley, Paul, B, Arkansas	1962
Dugan, Leonard, C, Wichita	1936
Duggan, Gil T, Oklahoma	1940
Duhon, Bobby, B, Tulane	1968–72
Dunaway, Dave, WR, Duke	1969
Duncan, Jim, E, Wake Forest	1950–53
Dunlap, Bob, B, Oklahoma	1936
Dvorak, Rick, LB, Wichita State	1974–76

E

Eakin, Kay, B, Arkansas	1940–41
Eaton, Lou, T, California	1945
Eaton, Scott, DB, Oregon State	1967–71
Echhardt, Oscar, B, Texas	1928
Edwards, Bill, G, Baylor,	1941–42, 1946
Ellenbogen, Bill, T, Virginia Tech	1976
Ellison, Mark, G, Dayton	1972–73
Enderle, Dick, G, Minnesota	1972–74
Epps, Bobby, B, Pittsburgh	1954–55, 1957
Erickson, Bill, G, Mississippi	1948
Eshmont, Len, B, Fordham	1940–41
Ettinger, Don, G, Kansas	1948–50
Evans, Charlie, RB, USC	1971–73

F

Faircloth, Art, B, North Carolina	1947–48
Falaschi, Nello, B, Santa Clara	1938–41
Feather, Elwin, B, Kansas State	1929–30, 1932–33
Fennema, Carl, C, Washington	1948–49
Filchock, Frank, QB, Indiana	1946
Files, Jim, LB, Oklahoma	1970–73
Filipowicz, Steve, B, Fordham	1945–46
Filipski, Gene, B, Villanova	1956–57
Fischer, Cletus, B, Nebraska	1949
Fitzgerald, Mike, DB, Iowa State	1967
Flaherty, Ray, E, Gonzaga	1928–35
Flenniken, Max, B, Geneva	1930–31
Flowers, Richmond, DB, Tennessee	1971–72
Ford, Charlie, DB, Houston	1975
Fox, Samuel, E, Ohio State	1945–46
Franck, George, B, Minnesota	1941, 1945–48
Frankian, Mal, E, St. Mary's	1934–35
Friedman, Bennie, QB, Michigan	1929–31
Frederickson, Tucker, FB, Auburn	1965–71
Frugonne, Jim, B, Syracuse	1925
Fuqua, John, RB, Morgan State	1969

G

Gaiters, Bobby, B, New Mexico State	1961–62
Galazian, Stan, C, Villanova	1937–39
Galiffa, Arnold, QB, Army	1953
Gallagher, Dave, DE, Michigan	1975–76
Gallagher, Ed, T, Washington & Jefferson	1928
Garcia, Jim, DE, Purdue	1966
Garner, Bob, G, None	1945
Garvey, Art, G, Notre Dame	1927–28
Garzoni, Mike, G, USC	1948

Roosevelt Grier

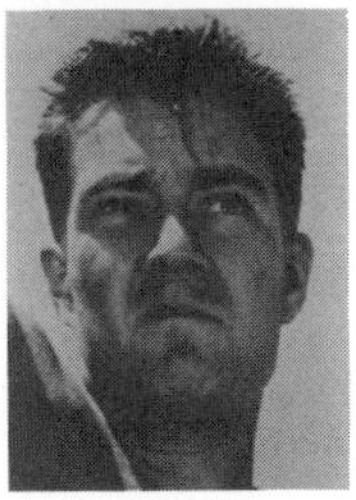
Don Heinrich

John Hicks

Sam Huff

Ron Johnson

Homer Jones

Greg Larsen

Gatewood, Tom, WR, Notre Dame 1972–73
Gehrke, Bruce, E, Columbia 1948
Gehrke, Fred, B, Utah 1948
Gelatka, Charles, E, Mississippi State 1937–40
Gibbons, Mike, T, S.W. Oklahoma State 1976
Giblin, Robert, S, Houston 1975
Gifford, Frank, B-E, USC 1952–60, 1962–64
Gigson, Denver (Butch), G, Grove City 1930–34
Gildea, John, B, St. Bonaventure 1938
Gillette, Walker, WR, Richmond 1974–76
Gladchuk, Chet, C, Boston College 1941, 1946–47
Glass, Chip, TE, Florida 1974
Glover, Rich, DT, Nebraska 1973
Gogolak, Pete, K, Cornell 1966–74
Goich, Dan, DT, California 1972–73
Goodwin, Tod, E, West Virginia 1935–36
Gorgone, Pete, B, Muhlenberg 1946
Gossage, Gene, T, Northwestern 1963
Governali, Paul, QB, Columbia 1947–48
Grandelius, Everett, (Sonny), B, Michigan State 1953
Grant, Len, T, New York U. 1930–37
Grate, Carl, C, Georgia 1945
Green, Joe, DB, Bowling Green 1970–71
Greenhalgh, Bob, B, San Francisco 1949
Gregory, Jack, DE, Delta State 1972–76
Grier, Roosevelt, DT, Penn State 1955–56, 1958–62
Griffing, Glynn, QB, Mississippi 1963
Griffith, Forrest, B, Kansas 1950–51
Grigg, Cecil, B, Stephen F. Austin 1926
Grim, Bob, WR, Oregon State 1972–74
Gross, Andy, G, Auburn 1967–68
Grosscup, Lee, QB, Utah 1960–62
Guglielmi, Ralph, QB, Notre Dame 1962–63
Gunn, Jimmy, LB, USC 1975
Gursky, Al, LB, Penn State 1963
Gutowsky, Leroy (Ace), B, Oklahoma City 1931
Guy, Lou, B, Mississippi 1963
Guy, Melwood, T, Duke 1958
Guyon, Joe, B, Carlisle 1927

H

Hachten, Bill, G, Stanford 1947
Haden, John, T, Arkansas 1936–38
Haggerty, John, B, Georgetown 1926–30
Haines, Henry, B, Penn State 1925–28
Hall, Harold, C, Springfield 1942
Hall, John, E, Iowa 1955
Hall, Pete, E, Marquette 1961–62
Hammond, Bob, RB, Morgan State 1976
Hanken, Ray, E, George Washington 1937–38
Hannah, Herb, T, Alabama 1951
Hanson, Dick, T, N. Dakota State 1971
Hapes, Merle, B, Mississippi 1942–46
Hare, Cecil, B, Gonzaga 1946
Harms, Art, T, Vermont 1927
Harper, Charlie, G, Oklahoma State 1966–72
Harris, Oliver, E, Geneva 1926
Harris, Phil, DB, Texas 1966
Harris, Wendell, DB, Louisiana State 1966–67
Harrison, Ed, E, Boston College 1928
Harrison, Granville, E, Mississippi State 1941
Harrison, Max, E, Auburn 1940
Hathcock, Dave, DB, Memphis State 1967
Hartzog, Howard, T, Baylor 1928
Hasenohrl, George, DT, Ohio State 1974
Hauser, Art, T, Xavier 1959
Hayes, Larry, LB, Vanderbilt 1961
Hazeltine, Matt, LB, California 1970
Heap, Joe, B, Notre Dame 1955
Heck, Ralph, LB, Colorado 1969–71
Hein, Mel, C, Washington State 1931–45
Heinrich, Don, QB, Washington 1954–59
Hendrian, Warren, B, Pittsburgh 1925
Henry, Wilbur, T, Washington & Jefferson 1927
Hensley, Dick E, Kentucky, ... 1949
Herber, Arnie, QB, Regis 1944–45
Hermann, John, B, UCLA 1956
Hernon, Don, B, Ohio State 1960
Herrmann, Don, WR, Waynesburg 1969–74
Hickl, Ray, LB, Texas A&I 1969–70
Hicks, John, G, Ohio State 1974–76
Hienstra, Ed, C, Sterling 1942
Hilert, Hal, B, Oklahoma City 1930
Hill, Charles, B, None 1926
Hill, John, B, Amherst 1926
Hill, John, C, Lehigh 1972–74
Hill, Ralph, C, Florida A&M 1976
Hillebrand, Jerry, LB, Colorado 1963–66
Hilton, Roy, DE, Jackson State 1974
Hinton, Chuck, C, Mississippi 1967–69
Hodel, Merwin, B, Colorado 1953
Hogan, Paul, B, Washington & Jefferson 1926
Holifield, Jimmy, DB, Jackson State 1968–69
Horne, Richard, G, Oregon 1941
Horner, Sam, B, VMI 1962–63
Hornsby, Ron, LB, S.E. Louisiana 1971–74
Houston, Dick, WR, E. Texas State 1969–72
Hovious, John, B, Mississippi 1945
Howard, Bob, G, Marietta 1929–30
Howell, Jim Lee, E, Arkansas 1937–42, 1946–48
Howell, Lane, T, Grambling 1963–64
Hubbard, Cal, T, Geneva 1927–29, 1936
Hudson, Bob, E, Clemson 1951–52
Huff, Sam, LB, West Virginia 1956–63
Hughes, Ed, B, Tulsa 1956–58
Hughes, Pat, C, Boston U. 1970–76
Hunt, George, K, Tennessee 1975
Hutchinson, Ralph, T, Chattanooga 1949
Hutchinson, Bill, B, Dartmouth 1942
Huth, Gerry, G, Wake Forest 1956
Hyland, Bob, G, Boston College 1971–76

I

Imlay, Talma, B, California 1927
Irvin, Cecil, T, Davis-Elkins 1932–35
Iverson, Chris, B, Oregon 1947

J

Jackson, Bob, B, N. Carolina A&T 1950–51
Jackson, Honor, DB, Pacific 1973–74
Jacobs, Allen, FB, Utah 1966–67
Jacobs, Proverb, T, California 1960
Jacobson, Larry, DE, Nebraska 1972–74
James, Dick, B, Oregon 1964
Janarette, Charlie, T, Penn State 1961–62
Jappe, Paul, E, Syracuse 1925, 1927–28
Jelacic, Jon, E, Minnesota 1958
Jenkins, Eddie, RB, Holy Cross 1974
Jennings, Dave, P, St. Lawrence 1974–75
Johnson, Bill, P, Livingston, Ala. 1970
Johnson, Curley, K, Houston 1969
Johnson, Gene, DB, Cincinnati 1961–62
Johnson, Herb, B, None 1954
Johnson, Jon, B, Mississippi 1948
Johnson, Larry, C, Haskell 1936–39
Johnson, Len, G, St. Cloud 1970
Johnson, Randy, QB, Texas A&I 1971–73
Johnson, Ron, RB, Michigan 1970–75
Jones, Homer, E, Texas Southern 1964–69
Jones, Tom, G, Bucknell 1932–36

K

Kanicki, Jim, DT, Michigan State 1970–71
Kaplan, Bernie, G, Western Maryland 1935–36
Kane, Herb, T, Oklahoma Teachers 1944–45
Karcis, John, B, Carnegie Tech 1938–39, 1943
Karilivacz, Carl, DB, Syracuse 1958
Katcavage, Jim, DE, Dayton 1956–68
Keahy, Eulis, G, George Washington 1942
Kearns, Tom, T, Miami 1945
Kelley, Brian, LB, California Lutheran 1973–76
Kelly, John, S., B, Kentucky 1932
Kelly, Ellison, G, Michigan State 1959
Kemp, Jack, QB, Occidental 1958
Kendricks, Jim, T, Texas A&M 1927
Kennard, George, G, Kansas 1952–55
Kennedy, Tom, QB, Cal. State-L.A. 1966–67
Kenyon, Bill, B, Georgetown 1925
Kerrigan, Tom, G, Columbia 1930
Kershaw, George, E, Colgate 1949
Kerzko, Alex, T, Michigan State 1942
Keuper, Ken, B, Georgia 1948
Killett, Charlie, B, Memphis State 1963
Killenger, Glenn, B, Penn State 1926
Kimber, Bill, E, Florida State 1959–60
King, Phil, B, Vanderbilt 1958–63
Kinscherf, Carl, B, Colgate 1943–44
Kitzmiller, John, B, Oregon 1931
Kirby, John, LB, Nebraska 1969–70
Kirouac, Lou, G, Boston College 1963
Klasoskus, Al, T, Holy Cross 1941–42
Kline, Harry, E, Kansas Teachers 1939–41
Klotovich, Mike, B, St. Mary's, Calif. 1945
Knight, Pat, B, Southern Methodist 1952, 1954–55
Kobrosky, Milt, Trinity, Conn. 1937
Kolman, Ed, T, Temple 1949
Koontz, Joe, E, S.F. State 1968
Koppisch, Walter, B, Columbia 1925–26
Kotar, Doug, RB, Kentucky, ... 1974–76
Kotite, Dick, LB, Wagner, ... 1967, 1969–72
Koy, Ernie, B, Texas 1965–70

Andy Robustelli, Roosevelt Grier, and Dick Modzelewski, left to right, vs. Pittsburgh, 1959.

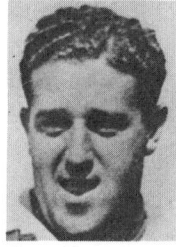

A. (Tuffy) Leemans   *C. (Spider) Lockhart*   *Dick Modzelewski*   *Joe Morrison*   *Harry Newman*   *Bill Paschal*   *Eddie Price*

Krause, Ray, T, Maryland 1951–55

L

Lacey, Bob, E, North Carolina 1965
Lagod, Chester, G, Chattanooga 1953
Lakes, Roland, DT, Wichita 1971
Lalonde, Roger, DT, Muskingum 1965
Landry, Tom, DB, Texas 1950–55
Lane, Gary, QB, Missouri 1968
Lansdell, Grenny, B, USC 1940
Larson, Greg, C, Minnesota 1961–73
Lascari, John, E, Georgetown 1942
Lasky, Frank, T, Florida 1964–65
Lasse, Dick, LB, Syracuse 1962–63
Lechner, Edgar, T, Minnesota 1942
Leemans, Alphonse (Tuffy), B, George Washington . 1936–43
Leo, Jim, LB, Cincinnati 1960
Levitt, Dick, T, Bowdoin 1976
Levy, Harvey, G, Syracuse 1928
Lewis, Art, T, Ohio U. 1936
Lewis, Danny, B, Wisconsin 1966
Lieble, Frank, E, Norwich 1942–44
Lieberum, Don, B, Manchester 1942
Lindahl, Virgil, G, Nebraska State 1945
Little, Jim, T, Kentucky 1945
Livingston, Cliff, LB, UCLA 1954–61
Livingston, Howard, B, None 1944–47
Lloyd, Dan, LB, Washington 1976
Lockhart, Carl (Spider), DB, No. Texas State . 1965–76
Long, Bufford, B, Florida 1953–55
Longo, Tom, DB, Notre Dame 1969–70
Lott, Billy, B, Mississippi 1958
Love, Walter, WR, Westminster, Utah 1973
LoVetere, John, DT, Compton J.C. 1963–65
Lovuolo, Frank, E, St. Bonaventure 1949
Lummus, John, E, Baylor 1941
Lumpkin, Ron, DB, Arizona State 1973
Lunday, Ken, C, Arkansas 1937–41, 1946–47
Lurtsema, Bob, DT, Western Michigan 1967–71
Lynch, Dick, DB, Notre Dame 1959–66
Lyons, George, T, Kansas State 1929

M

MacAfee, Ken, E, Alabama 1954–58
Mackorell, John, B, Davidson 1935
Mackrides, Bill, QB, Nevada 1953
Maher, Burce, DB, Detroit 1968–69
Maikkula, Ken, E, Connecticut 1942
Mallory, Larry, DB, Tennessee State 1976
Mallouf, Ray, QB, Southern Methodist 1949
Mangum, Pete, LB, Mississippi 1954
Manton, Taldon, B, Texas Christian 1936–38
Marefos, Andy, B, St. Mary's 1941–42
Marone, John, G, Manhattan 1943
Maronic, Dusan, G, None 1951
Marker, Cliff, B, Washington State 1927
Marsh, Dick, G, Oklahoma 1933
Marshall, Ed, WR, Cameron State 1976
Martin, Frank, B, Alabama 1945
Martin, George, DE, Oregon 1975–76
Martinkovich, J., E, Xavier 1957
Mastrangelo, John, G, Notre Dame 1950
Matan, Bill, DE, Kansas State 1966
Maynard, Don, B, Texas Western 1958
Mazurek, Ed, B, Xavier 1960
McBride, John, B, Syracuse 1925–28, 1932–33
McCafferty, Don, E, Ohio State 1946
McCann, Jim, P, Arizona State 1973
McCann, Tim, DT, Princeton 1969
McChesney, Bob, E, Hardin-Simmons 1960
McClain, Clint, B, Southern Methodist 1941
McDowell, John, T, St. John's, Minn. 1965
McElhenny, Hugh, B, Washington 1963
McGee, Ed, T, Temple 1940
McGinley, Ed, T, Pennsylvania 1925
McLaughry, John, B, Brown 1940
McMullen, Dan, G, Nebraska 1929
McNeil, Clifton, WR, Grambling 1970–71
McQuay, Leon, RB, Tampa 1974
McRae, Bennie, DB, Michigan 1971
Mead, John, E, Wisconsin 1946–47
Mellus, John, T, Villanova 1938–41
Menasco, Don, B, Texas 1952–53

Mendenhall, John, DT, Grambling 1972–76
Meneffee, Hartwell, E, New Mexico State 1966
Mercer, Jim, QB, Oregon State 1942–43
Mercein, Chuck, FB, Yale 1965–66
Mertes, Bernie, B, Iowa 1949
Messner, Max, LB, Cincinnati 1964
Mielznier, Saul, C, Carnegie Tech 1929–30
Miklich, Bill, B, Idaho 1947–48
Mikolajczyk, Ron, G, Tampa 1976
Miles, Leo, B, Virginia State 1953
Miller, Ed, B, New Mexico 1939–40
Milner, Bill, G, Duke 1950
Milstead, Century, T, Yale 1925, 1927–28
Minisi, Tony, B, Penn 1948
Minniear, Randy, RB, Purdue 1967–69
Mischak, Bob, G, Army 1958
Mitchell, Grandville, E, Davis-Elkins 1935
Mitchell, Harold, T, UCLA 1952
Modzelewski, Dick, DT, Maryland 1956–63
Molden, Frank, DT, Jackson State 1969
Molenda, John, B, Michigan 1932–35
Moore, Henry, B, Arkansas 1956
Moore, Ken, C, West Virginia Wesleyan 1940
Moran, Dale (Hap), B, Carnegie Tech 1928–34
Moran, Jim, T, Idaho 1964–67
Morgan, Bill, T, Oregon 1933–36
Morrall, Earl, QB, Michigan State 1965–67
Morrison, Joe, B-E, Cincinnati 1959–72
Morrow, Bob, B, Illinois Wesleyan 1945
Morton, Craig, QB, California 1974–76
Mote, Kelly, E, Duke 1950–52
Mullen, Tom, G, Southeast Missouri State 1974–76
Mulleneaux, Lee, B, Arizona 1932
Mullins, Noah, B, Kentucky 1949
Munday, George, T, Kansas Teachers 1931–32
Munn, Lyle, E, Kansas State 1929
Murdock, Les, K, Florida State 1967
Murray, Earl, G, Purdue 1951
Murtaugh, George, C, Georgetown 1926–32
Myers, Tom, B, Fordham 1925–26

N

Nash, Bob, T, Rutgers 1925

Neill, Jim, B, Texas Tech 1937
Nelson, Andy, DB, Memphis State 1964
Nesser, Al, E, None 1926–28
Newman, Harry, QB, Michigan 1933–35
Nielsen, Walter, B, Arizona 1940
Niles, Gary, B, Iowa 1946–47
Nix, Emery, QB, Texas Christian 1943–46
Nolan, Dick, DB, Maryland 1954–57, 1959–61
Norby, John, B, Idaho 1934
Nordstrom, Harry, G, Trinity, Conn. 1925
Norton, Jim, DT, Washington 1970
Nutt, Richard, B, Texas State 1949

O

O'Bradovich, Jim, G, Boston College 1965
O'Brien, Dave, G, Boston College 1964
Oldershaw, Doug, G, Santa Barbara 1939–41
Orduna, Joe, RB, Nebraska 1972–73
Ostendarp, Jim, B, Bucknell 1950–51
Owen, Alton, B, Mercer 1939–41
Owen, Steve, T, Phillips 1926–36
Owen, Vilas, QB, Wisconsin Teachers 1942
Owen, William, T, Oklahoma A&M 1929–37
Owens, R.C., E, Idaho 1964

P

Palazzi, Lou, C, Penn State 1946–47
Palm, Mike, B, Penn State 1925–26
Parker, Frank, DT, Oklahoma State 1969
Parker, Ken, DB, Fordham 1970
Parnell, Fred, T, Colgate 1925–27
Parry, Owen, T, Baylor 1937–39
Paschal, Bill, B, George Washington 1943–47
Paschka, Gordon, G, Minnesota 1943
Patton, Jim, DB, Mississippi 1955–66
Patton, Bob, T, Clemson 1952
Peay, Francis, T, Missouri 1966–67
Pederson, Winfield, T, Minnesota 1941–45
Pelfrey, Ray, B, Kentucky State 1953
Perdue, Willard, E, Duke 1944
Pesonen, Dick, QB, Minn.-Duluth 1962–64
Petrilas, William, E, None 1944–45
Pettigrew, Gary, DT, Stanford 1974

Defensive halfback Dick Lynch about to tackle Pittsburgh's Gary Ballman, 1962.

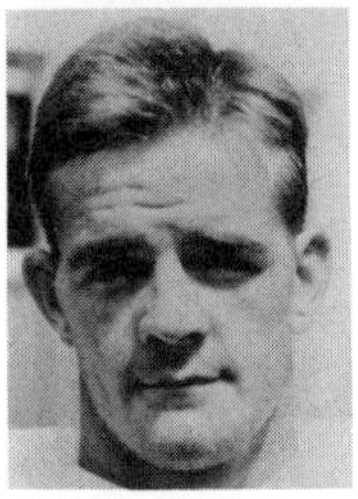

Frances X. Reagan

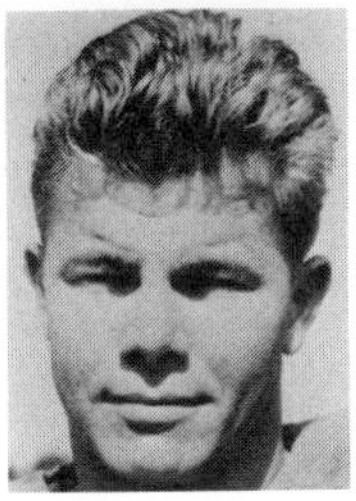

Kyle Rote

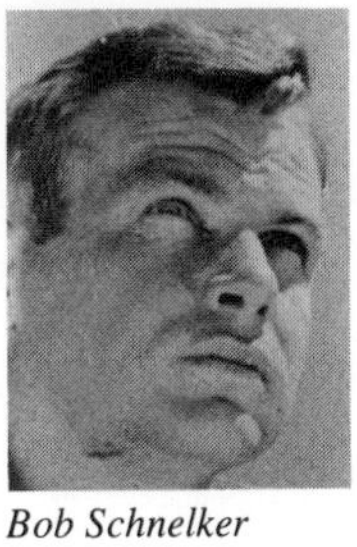

Bob Schnelker

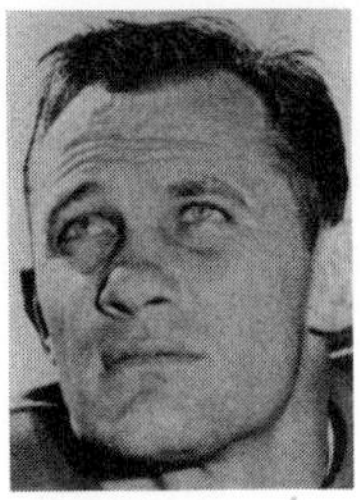

Bill Svoboda

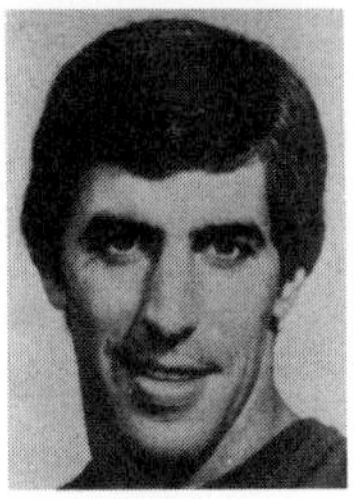

Bob Tucker

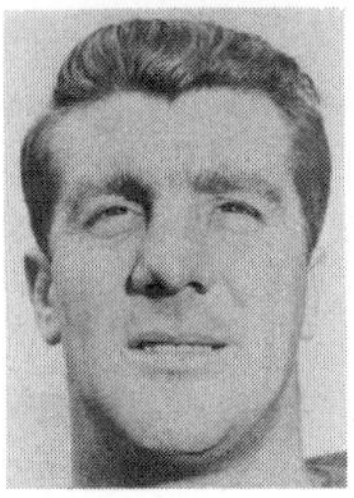

Alex Webster

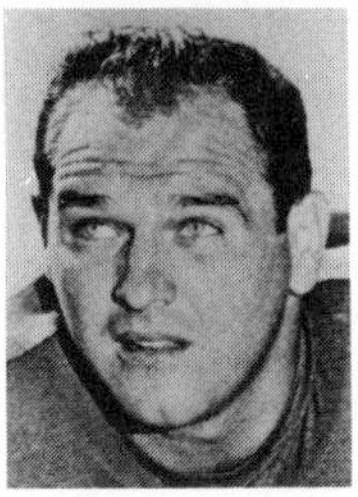

Ray Wietecha

- Peviani, Bob, G, USC ... 1953
- Phillips, Ewell, G, Oklahoma Baptists ... 1936–37
- Piccolo, Bill, C, Canisius ... 1943–45
- Pietrzak, Jim, DT, Eastern Michigan ... 1974–75
- Pipkin, Joyce, E, Arkansas ... 1948
- Plansky, Tony, B, Georgetown ... 1928–29
- Plum, Milt, QB, Penn State ... 1969
- Podoley, Jim, B, Central Michigan ... 1962
- Poole, Barney, E, Mississippi ... 1954–55
- Poole, Jim, E, Mississippi ... 1937–1941, 1946
- Poole, Ray, E, Mississippi ... 1947–52
- Post, Bob, DB, Kings Point ... 1967
- Potteiger, Earl, B, Ursinus ... 1926–28
- Powell, Dick, E, Davis-Elkins ... 1931
- Powers, Clyde, S, Oklahoma ... 1974–76
- Prestel, Jim, DT, Idaho ... 1966
- Price, Eddie, FB, Tulane ... 1950–55
- Principe, Dominic, B, Fordham ... 1940–42
- Pritchard, Bosh, B, VMI ... 1951
- Pritko, Steve, E, Villanova ... 1943
- Pugh, Marion, QB, Texas A&M ... 1941, 1945

Q

- Quatse, Jess, T, Pittsburgh ... 1935

R

- Ragazzo, Phil, T, Western Reserve ... 1945–47
- Ramona, Joe, G, Santa Clara ... 1953
- Rapacz, John, C, Oklahoma ... 1950–54
- Reagan, Frank, B, Pennsylvania ... 1941, 1946–48
- Reed, Henry, DE, Weber State ... 1971–74
- Reed, Mac, C, Bucknell ... 1928
- Reed, Smith, B, Alcorn A&M ... 1965–66
- Reese, Henry, C, Temple ... 1933–34
- Reynolds, Owen, E, Georgia ... 1925
- Rhenquist, Milt, C, Bethany ... 1931
- Rhodes, Ray, WR, Tulsa ... 1974–76
- Rice, Bill, C, None ... 1929
- Rich, Herb, B, Vanderbilt ... 1954–56
- Richards, Elvin, B, Simpson ... 1933–39
- Riley, Lee, DB, Detroit ... 1960
- Rizzo, Jack, RB, Lehigh ... 1974
- Roberts, Gene, B, Chattanooga ... 1947–50
- Roberts, Tom, T, DePaul ... 1943
- Robinson, Jim, WR, Georgia Tech ... 1976
- Robustelli, Andy, DE, Arnold ... 1946–64
- Roland, Johnny, RB, Missouri ... 1973
- Roller, Dave, DT, Kentucky ... 1971
- Roman, George, T, Western Reserve ... 1950
- Rooney, Cobb, B, Colorado ... 1925
- Rosatti, Roman, T, Michigan ... 1928
- Rose, Roy, E, Tennessee ... 1936
- Rote, Kyle, E, Southern Methodist ... 1951–61
- Rovinski, Tony, B, Holy Cross ... 1933
- Rowe, Harmon, B, San Francisco ... 1950–52
- Royston, Ed, G, Wake Forest ... 1948–49
- Rossell, Fay, B, Lafayette ... 1933
- Rucker, Reggie, WR, Boston U. ... 1971

S

- Salschieder, John, B, St. Thomas ... 1949
- Sanchez, John, T, San Francisco ... 1949–50
- Sarausky, Tony, B, Fordham ... 1935–37
- Sark, Harvey, G, Phillips ... 1931
- Satenstein, Bernie, G, New York U. ... 1933
- Schichtle, Henry, QB, Wichita ... 1964
- Schmeelk, Gary, T, Manhattan ... 1942
- Schnelker, Bob, E, Bowling Green ... 1954–60
- Schnellbacher, Otto, B, Kansas ... 1950–51
- Scholtz, Bob, C-T, Notre Dame ... 1965–66
- Schmidt, Bob, T, Minnesota ... 1959–60
- Schmit, Bob, LB, Nebraska ... 1975–76
- Schuette, Paul, G, Wisconsin ... 1928
- Schuler, Bill, T, Yale ... 1947–48
- Schwab, Ray, B, Oklahoma City ... 1931
- Scott, George, B, Miami, Ohio ... 1959
- Scott, Joe, B, San Francisco ... 1948–53
- Scott, Tom, LB, Virginia ... 1959–64
- Sczurek, Stan, LB, Purdue ... 1966
- Sedbrook, Len, B, Oklahoma City ... 1929–31
- Selfridge, Andy, LB, Virginia ... 1974–75
- Seick, Earl, G, Manhattan ... 1942–43
- Shaffer, Leland, QB, Kansas State ... 1935–43, 1945
- Shaw, Dennis, QB, San Diego State ... 1976
- Shaw, George, QB, Oregon ... 1969–60
- Shay, Jerry, DT, Purdue ... 1970–71
- Shediosky, Ed, B, Tulsa ... 1945
- Sherrod, Horace, E, Tennessee ... 1952
- Shiner, Dick, QB, Maryland ... 1970
- Shipp, Bill, T, Alabama ... 1954
- Shirk, Gary, TE, Morehead State ... 1976
- Shofner, Del, E, Baylor ... 1961–67
- Shy, Les, RB, Long Beach State ... 1970
- Siegel, Jules, B, Northwestern ... 1948
- Silas, Sam, DT, Southern Illinois ... 1968
- Simms, Bob, E, Rutgers ... 1960–62
- Simonson, Dave, T, Minnesota ... 1975
- Simpson, Al, T, Colorado State ... 1975–76
- Singer, Walter, E, Syracuse ... 1935–37
- Singletary, Bill, LB, Temple ... 1974
- Sivell, Ralph, G, Auburn ... 1944–45
- Skladany, Leo, E, Pittsburgh ... 1950
- Slaby, Lou, LB, Pittsburgh ... 1964–65
- Small, Eldridge, DB, Texas A&I ... 1972–74
- Smith, Jeff, LB, USC ... 1966–67
- Smith, Richard, G, Notre Dame ... 1930–31
- Smith, Willis, B, Idaho ... 1934–35
- Smith, Zeke, G, Auburn ... 1961–62
- Snead, Norm, QB, Wake Forest ... 1972–76
- Snyder, Gerry, B, Maryland ... 1929
- Soar, Hank, B, Providence ... 1937–44, 1946
- Sohn, Ben, G, USC ... 1941
- Spinks, Jack, G, Alcorn A&M ... 1956–57
- Springer, Harold, E, Oklahoma State ... 1945
- Stafford, Harrison, B, Texas ... 1934
- Stahiman, Dick, E, DePaul ... 1927
- Staten, Randy, DE, Minnesota ... 1967
- Stein, Sam, E, None ... 1931
- Stenn, Paul, T, Villanova ... 1942
- Stevens, Ted, C, Brown ... 1926
- Stienke, Jim, DB, Southwest Texas State ... 1974–76
- Stits, Billy, DB, UCLA ... 1959–61
- Strada, John, TE, William Jewell ... 1974
- Stribling, Bill, E, Mississippi ... 1951–53
- Strong, Ken, B, New York U. ... 1933–35, 1939–47
- Stroud, Jack, G-T, Tennessee ... 1953–64
- Stuckey, Henry, CB, Missouri ... 1974–76
- Stynchula, Andy, D-E, Penn State ... 1964–65
- Sulaitis, Joe, B, None ... 1943–53
- Summerall, Pat, PK, Arkansas ... 1958–61
- Summerell, Carl, QB, East Carolina ... 1974–75
- Sutherin, Don, B, Ohio State ... 1959
- Sutton, Ed, B, North Carolina ... 1960–61
- Svare, Harland, LB, Washington State ... 1955–60
- Svoboda, Bill, LB. Tulane ... 1954–59
- Swein, Bill, LB, Oregon State ... 1965–67
- Swiacki, Bill, E, Columbia ... 1948–50
- Szkzecko, Joe, DT, Northwestern ... 1969

T

- Taffoni, Joe, T, Tennessee-Martin ... 1972–73
- Tarkenton, Fran, QB, Georgia ... 1967–71
- Tarrant, Bob, E, Kansas Teachers ... 1936
- Tate, John, LB, Jackson State ... 1976
- Taylor, Bob, DE, Maryland State ... 1963–64
- Thomas, Aaron, E, Oregon State ... 1962–70
- Thomas, George, B, Oklahoma ... 1952
- Thompson, Rocky, RB, W, Texas State ... 1971–73
- Thorpe, Jim, B, Carlisle ... 1925
- Thurlow, Steve, B, Stanford ... 1964–66
- Tidwell, Travis, QB, Auburn ... 1950–51
- Timberlake, Bob, QB, Michigan ... 1965
- Tipton, Dave, DE, Stanford ... 1971–73
- Tittle, Y.A. QB, Louisiana State ... 1961–64
- Tobin, George, G, Notre Dame ... 1947
- Tomaini, Army, T, Catawba ... 1945
- Tomlin, Tom, G, Syracuse ... 1925
- Toogood, Charlie, DT, Nebraska ... 1958
- Topp, Bob, E, Michigan ... 1954–56
- Treadaway, John, T, Hardin-Simmons ... 1947–48
- Triplett, Bill, HB, Miami, Ohio ... 1967
- Triplett, Mel, FB, Toledo ... 1955–60
- Trocolor, Bob, B, Alabama ... 1942–44
- Tucker, Bob, TE, Bloomsburg State ... 1970–76
- Tunnell, Emlen, DB, Iowa ... 1948–58
- Turbert, Francis, B, Morris Harvey ... 1943
- Tuttle, Orville, G, Oklahoma City ... 1937–41
- Tyler, Pete, B, Hardin-Simmons ... 1938

U

- Umont, Frank, T, None ... 1943–45
- Underwood, Olen, LB, Texas ... 1965

V

- Van Horn, Doug, G, Ohio State ... 1968–76
- Vanoy, Vernon, DT, Kansas ... 1971
- Van Pelt, Brad, LB, Michigan State ... 1973–76
- Vargo, Larry, LB, Detroit ... 1966–67
- Visnic, Larry, G, St. Benedict ... 1943–45
- Vokaty, Otto, B, Heidelberg ... 1932
- Volk, Rick, DB, Michigan ... 1976
- Vosberg, Don, E, Marquette ... 1941
- Voss, Walter, E, Detroit ... 1926

W

- Wafer, Carl, DT, Tennessee State ... 1974
- Walbridge, Lyman, G, Fordham ... 1925
- Walker, Mickey, G, Michigan State ... 1961–65
- Walker, Paul, E, Yale ... 1948
- Wallace, Roger, WR, Bowling Green ... 1976
- Walls, Bill, E, Texas Christian ... 1937–43
- Walton, Joe, E, Pittsburgh ... 1961–63
- Walton, Wayne, G, Abilene Christian ... 1971
- Watkins, Larry, RB, Alcorn A&M ... 1975–76
- Weaver, Larry, B, California State-Fullerton ... 1955
- Webb, Allen, DB, Arnold ... 1961–65
- Webber, Howard, E, Kansas State ... 1926
- Webster, Alex, B, N. Carolina State ... 1955–64
- Weinmeister, Arnie, T, Washington ... 1950–53
- Weisacosky, Ed, LB, Miami ... 1967
- Weiss, John, E, None ... 1944–47
- Wellborn, Joe, C, Texas A&M ... 1966–67
- Wells, Harold, LB, Purdue ... 1969
- Wells, Joel, B, Clemson ... 1961
- Wells, Mike, QB, Illinois ... 1975
- Wesley, Cecil, C, Alabama ... 1928
- West, Stan, G, Oklahoma ... 1955
- Westoupal, Joe, C, Nebraska ... 1929–30
- Wheelwright, Ernie, B, So. Illinois ... 1964–65
- White, Art, G, Alabama ... 1937–39, 1945
- White, Jim, T, Notre Dame ... 1945–50
- White, Freeman, E-LB, Nebraska ... 1966–69
- White, Marsh, RB, Arkansas ... 1975–76
- White, Phil, E, Oklahoma ... 1925–27
- Widseth, Ed, T, Minnesota ... 1937–40
- Wietecha, Ray, C, Northwestern ... 1953–62
- Wilberg, Oscar, B, Nebraska Wesleyan ... 1930
- Wilkins, Dick, E, Oregon, ... 1954
- Wilkinson, Bob, E, UCLA ... 1951–52
- Williams, Ellery, E, Santa Clara ... 1950
- Williams, Frank, B, Utah State ... 1948
- Williams, Joe, G, Lafayette ... 1925–26
- Williams, Willie, DB, Grambling ... 1965, 1967–73
- Williamson, Ernie, T, North Carolina ... 1948
- Wilson, Butch, E, Alabama ... 1968–69
- Wilson, Fay, B, Texas A&M ... 1927–32
- Windauer, Bill, DT, Iowa ... 1975
- Winter, Bill, LB, St. Olaf ... 1962–64
- Wolfe, Hugh, B, Texas ... 1938
- Wood, Gary, QB, Cornell ... 1964–66, 1968–69
- Woodward, Dan, C, Iowa ... 1950–51, 1953
- Word, Roscoe, DB, Jackson State ... 1976
- Wright, Steve, T, Alabama ... 1968–69
- Wycoff, Doug, B, Georgia Tech ... 1927–31
- Wynne, Harry, E, Arkansas ... 1945

Y

- Yeager, Howard, B, Santa Barbara ... 1940–41
- Yelvington, Dick, T, Georgia ... 1952–57
- Younce, Len, G, Oregon State ... 1941–48
- Young, Willie, T, Grambling ... 1966–75
- Youso, Frank, T, Minnesota ... 1958–60
- Yowarsky, Walt, E, Kentucky ... 1955–57

Z

- Zapustas, Joe, E, Fordham ... 1933
- Zeno, Coleman, WR, Grambling ... 1971
- Zofko, Mickey, RB, Auburn ... 1974
- Zyntell, Jim, G, Holy Cross ... 1933

NEW YORK JETS

1959 Harry Wismer and New York were granted a franchise in the American Football League's first organizational meeting in Chicago. The franchise, Wismer announced, was to be called the Titans. George Izo, the Notre Dame quarterback, was the first player selected by New York in the draft. Sammy Baugh was hired as the club's head coach, Dec. 18.

1960 Penn football coach Steve Sebo was hired as the Titans' general manager. Don Maynard, free agent from Canada, became the first to sign a Titans' player contract. Wismer leased the Polo Grounds for his team's home games. The team, whose colors were blue and gold, opened training camp at the University of New Hampshire and more than 100 players reported. In the club's first preseason game, the Titans lost to the Los Angeles Chargers 27–7 before 27,778 at the Los Angeles Coliseum. The Titans finally won for the first time 52–31 over Buffalo in the last preseason game. Wismer's team drew just 9,607—5,727 paid—in the home opener. In 14 games, the second place Titans were 7–7 and attracted 221,285 people for the season, home and away.

1961 Bear Mountain Inn in New York State was chosen as the new headquarters for training camp. The Titans compiled their second consecutive 7–7 record, finishing third. They made Sandy Stephens, Minnesota's All-America quarterback, their top draft choice, December 2.

1962 Steve Sebo quit as general manager to become athletic director at the University of Virginia. Wismer announced Clyde (Bulldog) Turner would succeed Baugh as coach. Wismer settled a dispute when he agreed to pay off Baugh's contract. The club moved to East Stroudsburg, Pennsylvania, State College to open training camp. Just before the opening league game, quarterback Lee Grosscup was signed and he directed a 27–18 victory over Oakland. Wismer could not meet his payroll and the AFL announced it would assume the costs of running the club until the end of the season. In seven home games, the Titans drew just 36,161 people.

1963 A five-man syndicate composed of David (Sonny) Werblin, Townsend B. Martin, Leon Hess, Donald Lillis, and Phil Iselin purchased the franchise for $1 million, March 28. Weeb Ewbank was named the new head coach and the owners changed the name of the team from Titans to "Jets," April 15. The new training camp site was Peekskill, New York. Matt Snell, the Ohio State running back, was drafted number one and became the first top pick to sign with the club. Although finishing only 5–8–1 in the first year under new ownership, the attendance improved to 103,550 in seven games.

1964 The team moved to Shea Stadium and set an AFL record when a crowd of 45,665 watched New York beat Denver 30–6. Two months later, 60,300 showed up to see Buffalo defeat the Jets 20–7. In the most significant trade in the history of the franchise, if not the AFL, the Jets dealt the draft rights to quarterback Jerry Rhome to Houston for a number one draft choice. They used that choice to select quarterback Joe Namath of Alabama.

1965 One day after the Orange Bowl game, Namath signed a Jets' contract reported to be worth $427,000. Heisman trophy winner John Huarte of Notre Dame agreed to a $200,000 contract one week later, giving the Jets over a half-million dollars worth of rookie quarterback talent. Three weeks after signing, Namath underwent surgery for cartilage and ligament damage in his right knee, injured while he was playing for Alabama. Namath recovered in time to throw his first official pass for the Jets against Kansas City, September 18. He started for the first time and passed for 287 yards, but the Jets lost to Buffalo 33–21, September 26. Namath finished the year as the AFL's rookie of the year in both wire service polls, gaining 2,220 yards through the air and throwing 18 touchdown passes.

1966 Namath was named most valuable player in the all-star game. The AFL all-stars defeated Buffalo 30–19. Months later, the Jets opened the first home season after the NFL and AFL agreed to merge by burying Houston 52–13, establishing a club record for points scored. Namath closed the season by beating the Patriots 38–28 to knock them out of the Eastern Division championship. Eleven days later, he reported to the hospital for a tendon transfer and cartilage removal in his right knee.

1967 In the first combined draft, the Jets made Paul Seiler, a tackle from Notre Dame, their top choice. Emerson Boozer, enjoying an outstanding season, went down with torn ligaments in his knee and was lost for the season against Kansas City, November 5. A victory over Boston clinched the Jets' first winning season in history, November 19. But a loss to Oakland in California cost them a chance for the championship. Namath finished the season with 4,007 yards passing, the only pro quarterback ever to throw for that much yardage. The Jets sold out all home games and established an AFL attendance record with 437,036 tickets sold for seven games.

Quarterbacks Joe Namath and Richard Todd, 1976.

1968 Joe Namath entered the hospital and underwent surgery for the repair of a small tear in the tendon of his left knee. Sonny Werblin's partners, Don Lillis, Leon Hess, Townsend Martin, and Phil Iselin, bought him out for a reported $1.6 million. Lillis took over the presidency of the club, May 21. The team relocated its training camp at Hofstra University on Long Island. Don Lillis died, July 23. Phil Iselin was appointed the new club president. In the season opener, Namath controlled the ball the final six minutes as the Jets defeated Kansas City 20–19. "Heidi" became the center of a nationwide controversy, when the decisive final minutes of a game between the Jets and Oakland were interrupted so the children's television special could begin on time. Much of the football audience didn't see the Raiders score twice in the final 42 seconds to win 43–32. A 35–17 victory over Miami was the team's ninth of the year, a club record. In the AFL championship game, Namath and Don Maynard combined on the big plays in the fourth quarter to beat Oakland 27–23.

1969 Namath, in a prediction that would make him a legend, "guaranteed" the Jets would beat Baltimore in Super Bowl III. His shrewd play-calling and sharp passing, combined with a marvelous defensive performance, made the Jets the first AFL team to win a Super Bowl 16–7. It also gave Weeb Ewbank the distinction of becoming the only coach to win the world title in both leagues. Six months later, Namath announced he was retiring as the result of a dispute over his ownership of a Manhattan night spot, Bachelors III. The Jets reported to training camp without Namath, July 8. Ten days later, Namath said he was selling his night club and reporting to work. The Jets beat the College All-Stars 26–24, then blitzed the Giants 37–14 in the first meeting between the two New York teams. Weeb Ewbank celebrated his one-hundredth coaching win in the Jets' first victory at Buffalo. Two months later, another success over the Bills extended the club's record winning streak to six. The Jets defeated Houston 34–26 in Texas to win their second straight Eastern Division title, December 6. But in the playoffs, Kansas City knocked the Jets out of the running 13–6. Weeb Ewbank was named the all-time coach of the AFL and Namath, Maynard, and Gerry Philbin were chosen to the all-time AFL team selected by the Hall of Fame.

1970 In the first Monday night television game, the Jets were beaten by their new AFC rival Cleveland 31–21. Matt Snell was lost for the season with a ruptured Achilles tendon suffered in the Buffalo game, October 4. Namath fractured his right wrist against Baltimore and was out for the year, October 18. In the first regular season game between intracity rivals, the Giants came from behind to beat the Jets 22–10. Behind reserve quarterback Al Woodall, the Jets pulled off two upsets at the end of the year, stunning both Los Angeles and Minnesota.

1971 John Riggins, a running back from Kansas, was the team's number one draft choice. Wide receiver George Sauer announced his retirement from football. Namath, trying to make a tackle after throwing an interception, injured his knee, had to undergo surgery again, and was lost for three and a half months. After spending 19 straight games on the sidelines, Namath returned to throw three touchdown passes and almost beat the 49ers, who barely won 24–21. The Jets set a one-season home attendance record of 441,099.

1972 Namath signed the contract that made him the highest paid player in the game at a reported $250,000 a year. In the best day of his career statistically, Namath passed for 496 yards and six touchdowns to defeat Baltimore and Johnny Unitas 44–34. Riggins ran for 168 yards, Emerson Boozer for 150 in a 41–13 win over New England, marking the second time two backs from the same team ever rushed for

150 yards in a game. Maynard became pro football's all-time receiving leader with his six-hundred thirty-second career catch in the game with Oakland, December 11, Ewbank announced 1973 would be his last as head coach of the Jets.

1973 Charley Winner, the former head coach of the St. Louis Cardinals, was named to succeed Ewbank in 1974 and serve as an assistant coach for one season. Baltimore linebacker Stan White tackled Namath on a blitz, separating the quarterback's shoulder and putting him out for two months. Ewbank closed a 4–10 season, overshadowed on his last day by Buffalo's O.J. Simpson, whose 200-yard afternoon pushed him to an NFL record 2,003 yards rushing for the season.

1974 Winner took over as coach as the NFL Players Association strike began. The Jets moved into a new training center in Hempstead, New York, with facilities for coaches, office personnel, and players, plus a huge practice area. After a 1–7 start, Namath snapped the slump with an emotional 26–20 victory over the Giants in overtime at Yale Bowl. Ewbank announced he would retire as vice president of the club at the end of the season. Six straight late-season victories included surprise victories over two playoff teams, Miami and Buffalo.

1975 The number one pick in the draft was traded to New Orleans for defensive lineman Billy Newsome. Al Ward, a vice president with the Dallas Cowboys, was named general manager to succeed Ewbank. Namath turned down a reported multimillion dollar offer from the World Football League and signed a new two-year agreement with the Jets. The Jets' players walked out of camp the week of the opening game, in support of the New England players' strike. The players returned two days later and the strike was settled. After six losses in a row and a 2–7 record, Winner was fired and Ken Shipp, the offensive coordinator, was named interim head coach. Riggins, one of the few bright spots in a disappointing season, went over 1,000 yards rushing, the first player in the history of the club to reach that figure.

1976 Lou Holtz, coach at North Carolina State, signed a five-year contract to coach the Jets. Richard Todd, another quarterback from Alabama, was the Jets' first choice in the draft. The Jets had another losing season falling 42–3 to Cincinnati in the final game and finishing with a 3–11 record. Holtz resigned to become head coach at the University of Arkansas. President Phil Iselin died in his office, December 28. The board of directors subsequently appointed Leon Hess acting president, and expanded the duties of Al Ward to include complete responsibility of the operation. Longtime assistant Walt Michaels was named head coach.

Halfback Bill Mathis on eight-yard gain, Chicago All-Star Game, 1969.

MEMBERS OF HALL OF FAME:
None

JETS RECORD, 1960–76

Year	Won	Lost	Tied	Pct.	Pts.	OP
New York Titans						
1960	7	7	0	.500	382	399
1961	7	7	0	.500	301	390
1962	5	9	0	.357	278	423
New York Jets						
1963	5	8	1	.385	249	399
1964	5	8	1	.385	278	315
1965	5	8	1	.385	285	303
1966	6	6	2	.500	322	312
1967	8	5	1	.615	371	329
1968**	11	3	0	.786	419	280
1969§	10	4	0	.714	353	269
1970	4	10	0	.286	255	286
1971	6	8	0	.429	212	299
1972	7	7	0	.500	367	324
1973	4	10	0	.286	240	306
1974	7	7	0	.500	279	300
1975	3	11	0	.214	256	433
1976	3	11	0	.214	169	383
17 Years	103	129	6	.445	5,016	5,750

**Super Bowl Champion
§AFL Eastern Division Champion

RECORD HOLDERS

Rushing (Yards)	John Riggins, 1975	1,005
Passing (Pct.)	Joe Namath, 1974	52.9
Passing (Yards)	Joe Namath, 1967	4,007
Passing (TDs)	Al Dorow, 1960, and	
	Joe Namath, 1967	26
Receiving (No.)	George Sauer, 1967	.75
Receiving (Yards)	Don Maynard, 1967	1,434
Interceptions (No.)	Dainard Paulson, 1964	12
Punting (Avg.)	Curley Johnson, 1965	45.3
Punt Ret. (Avg.)	Dick Christy, 1961	21.3
Kickoff Ret. (Avg.)	Leon Burton, 1960	28.7
Touchdowns (Total)	Art Powell, 1960	
	Don Maynard, 1965, and	
	Emerson Boozer, 1972	14
Field Goals Made	Jim Turner, 1968	34
Points (No.)	Jim Turner, 1968	145

COACHING HISTORY

1960–61	Sammy Baugh	14–14–0
1962	Clyde (Bulldog) Turner	5– 9–0
1963–73	Weeb Ewbank	71–77–6
1974–75	Charley Winner*	9–14–0
1975	Ken Shipp	1– 4–0
1976	Lou Holtz	3–11–0

*Replaced after nine games in 1975

FIRST PLAYER SELECTED

1960	George Izo, QB, Notre Dame
1961	Tom Brown, G, Minnesota
1962	Sandy Stephens, QB, Minnesota
1963	Jerry Stovall, S, Louisiana State
1964	Matt Snell, RB, Ohio State
1965	Joe Namath, QB, Alabama
1966	Bill Yearby, DT, Michigan
1967	Paul Seiler, T, Notre Dame
1968	Lee White, RB, Weber State
1969	Dave Foley, T, Ohio State
1970	Steve Tannen, CB, Florida
1971	John Riggins, RB, Kansas
1972	Jerome Barkum, WR, Jackson State
1973	Burgess Owens, DB, Miami
1974	Carl Barzilauskas, DT, Indiana
1975	Anthony Davis, RB (2), USC
1976	Richard Todd, QB, Alabama

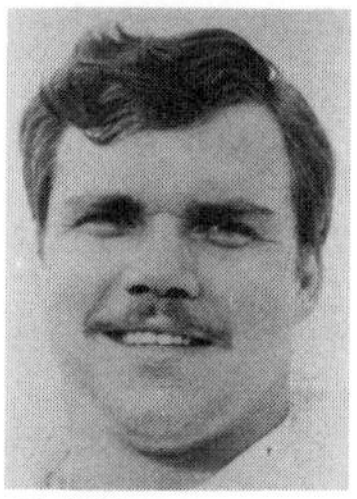

Al Atkinson

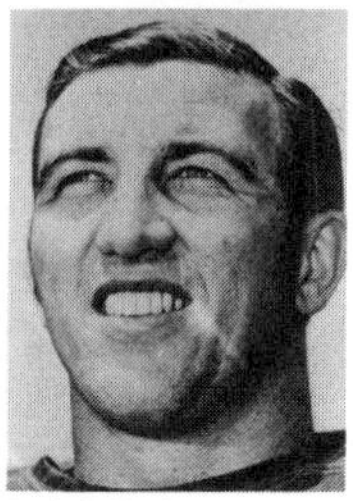

Ralph Baker

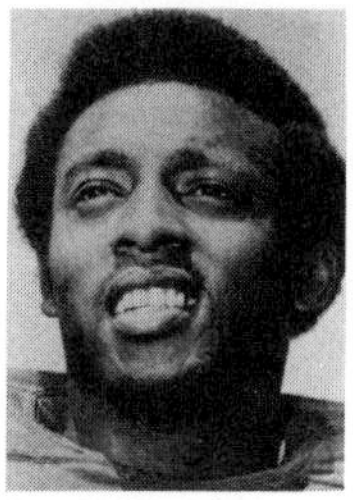

Randy Beverly

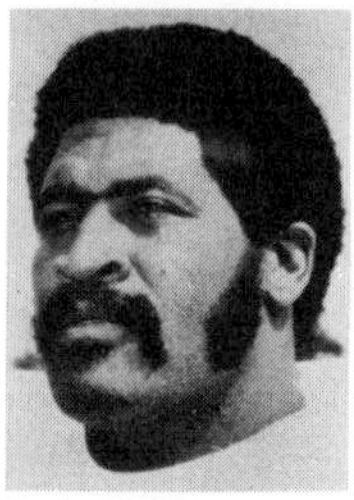

Verlon Biggs

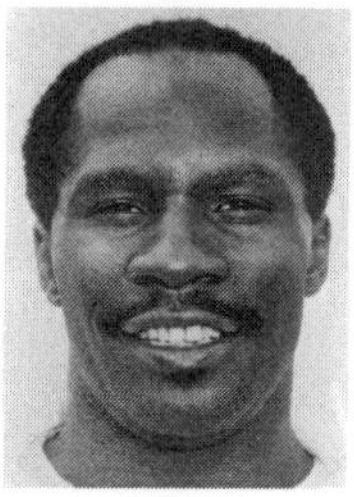

Emerson Boozer

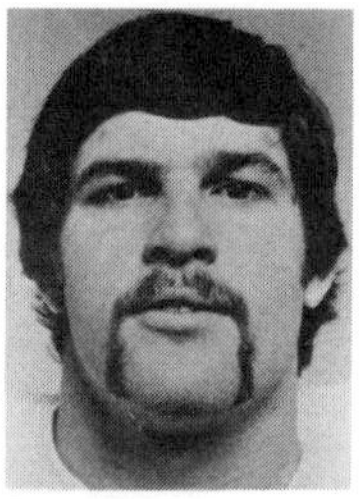

Greg Buttle

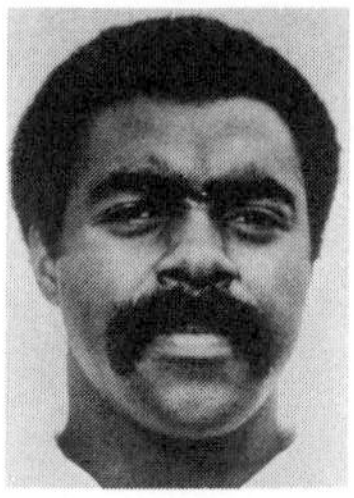

Richard Caster

NEW YORK TITANS, 1960–62;
NEW YORK JETS, 1963–76

Abruzzese, Ray, Alabama 1965–66
Adamle, Mike, RB, Northwestern 1973–74
Adkins, Margene, WR, Hutchinson J.C. 1973
Allard, Don, QB, Boston College 1961
Ames, Dave, HB, Richmond 1961
Apple, Jim, HB, Upsala 1961
Arthur, Gary, TE, Miami, Ohio 1970–71
Atkins, Bill, DB, Auburn 1962–63
Atkinson, Al, LB, Villanova 1965–74
Austin, Darrell, G, South Carolina 1976

B

Baird, Bill, DB, S.F. State 1965–69
Baker, Larry, T, Bowling Green 1960
Baker, Ralph, LB, Penn State 1964–74
Barkum, Jerome, WR, Jackson State 1972–76
Barnes, Ernie, T, N. Carolina College 1960
Barzilauskas, Carl, DT, Indiana 1974–76
Bates, Ted, LB, Oregon State 1963
Battle, Mike, DB, USC 1969–70
Bayless, Tom, G, Purdue 1970
Bell, Ed, DB, Pennsylvania 1960
Bell, Ed, WR, Idaho State 1970–75
Bernhardt, Roger, G, Kansas 1974
Bernich, Ken, LB, Auburn 1975
Beverly, Randy, DB, Colorado State 1967–69
Biggs, Verlon, DE, Jackson State 1965–70
Bjorklund, Hank, RB, Princeton 1972–74
Bobo, Hubert, LB, Ohio State 1961–62
Bohling, Dewey, HB, Hardin-Simmons 1960–61
Bookman, John, DB, Miami 1961
Boozer, Emerson, RB, Maryland State 1966–75
Brannan, Solomon, DB, Morris Brown 1967
Brister, Willie, TE, Southern U. 1974–75
Brooks, Bob, HB, Ohio U. 1961
Brooks, Clifford, CB, Tennessee State 1976
Browne, Gordie, T, Boston College 1974–75
Browning, Charlie, HB, Washington 1965
Buckey, Don, WR, N. Carolina State 1976
Budrewicz, Tom, G, Brown 1961
Burns, Bob, RB, Georgia 1974
Burton, Leon, HB, Arizona State 1960
Buttle, Greg, LB, Penn State 1976
Butler, Bob, G, Kentucky 1963

C

Callahan, Dan, G, Akron 1960
Cambal, Dennis, TE, William & Mary 1973
Campbell, Ken, E, West Chester State 1960
Capria, Carl, S, Purdue 1975
Carrell, Duane, P, Florida State 1976
Carroll, Jim, LB, Notre Dame 1969
Carson, Kern, HB, San Diego State 1965
Carter, Allen, RB, USC 1976
Caster, Richard, WR, Jackson State 1970–76
Chlebek, Ed, QB, Western Michigan 1963
Chomyszak, Steve, DT, Syracuse 1966
Christy, Dick, HB, N. Carolina State 1961–63
Christy, Earl, DB, Maryland State 1966–68
Cockrell, Gene, T, Hardin-Simmons 1960–62
Cooke, Ed, DE, Maryland 1960–63
Cooper, Thurlow, TE, Maine 1960–62
Crane, Paul, LB, Alabama 1966–72
Cummings, Ed, LB, Stanford 1964

D

D'Agostino, Frank, G, Auburn 1960
D'Amato, Mike, DB, Hofstra 1968
Davis, Bob, QB, Virginia 1970–72
Davis, Jerry, DB, Morris Brown 1975
Davis, Steve, RB, Delaware State 1975–76
DeFelice, Nick, T, So. Connecticut State 1965
DeLuca, Sam, G, South Carolina 1964–66
Denson, Keith, WR, San Diego State 1976
Dockery, John, CB, Harvard 1968–71
Dombrowski, Leon, G, Delaware 1960
Donnahoo, Roger, DB, Michigan State 1960
Dorow, Al, B, Michigan State 1960–61
Dudek, Mitch, G, Xavier 1966
Dukes, Mike, LB, Clemson 1965
Dupre, Chuck, DB, Baylor 1960

E

Ebersole, John, LB, Penn State 1970–76
Elliott, John, DT, Texas 1967–73
Ellis, Roger, C, Maine 1960–63
Evans, Jim, E, W. Texas State 1964

F

Fagan, Julian, P, Mississippi 1973
Farasopoulos, Chris, DB, BYU 1971–72
Faulk, Larry, DT, Kent State 1976
Felt, Dick, DB, Brigham Young 1960–61
Ferguson, Bill, LB, San Diego State 1973–74
Ficca, Dan, G, USC 1963–66
Fields, Jerry, LB, Ohio State 1961–62
Fields, Joe, C, Widener 1975–76
Finnie, Roger, T-DT, Florida A&M 1969–72
Flowers, Charlie, FB, Mississippi 1962
Flynn, Don, HB, Houston 1961
Foley, Dave, T, Ohio State 1969–71
Fontes, Wayne, HB, Michigan State 1962
Fournet, Sid, G, Louisiana State 1962–63
Fowler, Bob, FB, Tennessee 1962
Furey, James, DB, Kansas State 1961

G

Gaines, Clark, RB, Wake Forest 1976
Galigher, Ed, DE, UCLA 1972–76
Gantt, Gregg, P, Alabama 1974–75
Garrett, Carl, RB, New Mexico Highlands 1975
Giammona, Louie, RB, Utah State 1976
Glenn, Howard, G, Linfield 1960
Gordon, Cornell, CB, N. Carolina A&T 1965–69
Grantham, James (Larry), LB, Mississippi 1960–72
Gray, Jim, DB, Toledo 1966
Gray, Moses, T, Indiana 1961–62
Green, John, QB, Chattanooga 1962–63
Gregory, Ken, WR, Whittier 1963
Gresham, Bob, RB, West Virginia 1975–76
Grosscup, Lee, QB, Utah 1962
Gucciardo, Pat, DB, Kent State 1966
Guesman, Dick, DT, West Virginia 1960–63

H

Hall, Galen, QB, Penn State 1963
Harkey, Steve, RB, Georgia Tech 1971–72
Harris, Jim, DT, Utah State 1965–67
Hart, Dee, FB, Hardin-Simmons 1960
Haslerig, Clint, RB, Michigan 1976
Hayes, Ray, TD, Toledo 1968
Haynes, Abner, HB, N. Texas State 1967
Heeter, Gene, TE, West Virginia 1963–65
Henke, Karl, DE, Tulsa 1968
Hennigan, Mike, LB, Tennessee State 1976
Herman, Dave, G, Michigan State 1964–73
Herndon, Don, DB, Tampa 1960
Hicks, Wilmer Kenzie (W.K.), S, Texas Southern 1970–72
Hill, Winston, T, Texas Southern 1963–76
Hinton, Chuck, DT, North Carolina 1971
Hoey, George, DB, Michigan 1975
Holloman, Gus, S, Houston 1970–72
Holz, Gordy, DT, Minnesota 1964
Hord, Ambrose (Roy), G, Duke 1963
Howard, Harry, CB, Ohio State 1976
Howell, Delles, CB, Grambling 1973–75
Howfield, Bobby, K, None 1971–73
Hudock, Mike, C, Miami 1960–65
Hudson, Jim, S, Texas 1965–70
Hynes, Paul, DB, Louisiana Tech 1961–62

I

Iacavazzi, Cosmo, FB, Princeton 1965

J

Jackson, Clarence, RB, Western Kentucky 1974–76
Jackson, Joey, DE, New Mexico State 1972–73
Jacobs, Proverb, T, California 1961–62
Jamieson, Dick, QB, Bradley 1960–61
Janerette, Charlie, DT, Penn State 1963
Joachim, Steve, QB, Temple 1976
Jones, Jimmie, DE, Wichita State 1969–70
Jones, John, QB, Fisk 1976
Joe, Billy, RB, Villanova 1967–68
Johnson, John (Curley), HB, Houston 1961–68
Johnston, Mark, DB, Northwestern 1964
Julian, Fred, DB, Michigan 1960

K

Kaimer, Karl, TE, Boston U 1962
Katcik, Joe, T, Notre Dame 1960
Keller, Larry, LB, Houston 1976
Knight, David, WR, William & Mary 1973–76
Krevis, Al, T, Boston College 1976

L

Lamberti, Pasquale, HB, Richmond 1961
Lammons, Pete, TE, Texas 1966–71
Lawson, Alphonzo, WR, Delaware State 1964
Leahy, Patrick, K, St. Louis 1974–76
Lewis, Richard, LB, Portland State 1974–75
Lewis, Sherman, DB, Michigan State 1966
Leonard, Cecil, DB, Tuskegee 1969–70
Liske, Pete, QB-DB, Penn State 1964
Little, John, DT-DE, Oklahoma State 1970–74
Lomas, Mark, DT-DE, No. Arizona 1970–74
Look, Dean, QB, Michigan State 1962
Lusteg, Booth, K, None 1967

M

Mackey, Dee, TE, E. Texas State 1963–65
Marinaro, Ed, RB, Cornell 1976
Marques, Robert, C, Boston U 1960
Marshall, Ed, WR, Cameron State 1976
Martin, Blanche, HB, Michigan State 1960
Martin, Bob, LB, Nebraska 1976
Mathis, Bill, RB, Clemson 1960–69
Matlock, John, C, Miami 1967
Maynard, Don, WR, W. Texas State 1960–72
Marvaso, Tommy, S, Cincinnati 1976
McAdams, Bob, DE, N. Carolina Coll. 1963–64
McAdams, Carl, DT-LB, Oklahoma 1967–69
McCusker, Jim, T, Pittsburgh 1964
McDaniel, Ed (Wahoo), LB, Oklahoma 1964–65
McClain, Clifford, RB, S. Carolina State 1970–73
McMullan, John, G, Notre Dame 1960–62
Mercein, Chuck, RB, Yale 1970
Michaels, Walt, LB, Washington & Lee 1963
Mishak, Bob, G, Army 1960–62
Mooring, John, G, Tampa 1971–73
Morelli, Francis, T, Colgate 1962
Mulligan, Wayne, C, Clemson 1974–75
Mumley, Nick, E, Purdue 1960–62

N

Namath, Joe, QB, Alabama 1965–76
Nance, Jim, RB, Syracuse 1973
Neal, Richard, DT, Southern U 1973–76
Neidert, John, LB, Louisville 1968–69
Newsome, Billy, DE, Grambling 1975–76
Nock, George, RB, Morgan State 1969–71

O

O'Mahoney, Jim, LB, Miami 1965–66
O'Neal, Steve, P, Texas A&M 1969–72
O'Neil, Bob, G, Notre Dame 1961
Onkotz, Dennis, LB, Penn State 1970
Osborne, Richard, TE, Texas A&M 1976
Owens, Burgess, S, Miami 1973–76
Owens, Marv, WR, San Diego State 1974

P

Paglei, Joe, FB, Clemson 1960
Palmer, Scott, DT, Texas 1971
Parilli, Babe, QB, Kentucky 1968–69
Pashe, Bill, DB, George Washington 1964
Paulson, Dainard, DB, Oregon State 1961–66
Perkins, Bill, GB, Iowa 1963
Perreault, Pete, T-G, Boston U 1963–67, 1969–70
Philbin, Gerry, DE, Buffalo 1964–72
Piccone, Lou, WR, West Liberty State 1974–76
Pillers, Lawrence, Alcorn A&M 1976
Plunkett, Sherman, T, Maryland State 1963–67
Powell, Art, WR, San Jose State 1960–62
Poole, Steve, LB, Tennessee 1976
Price, Jim, LB, Auburn 1963
Prout, Bob, S, Knox 1975

Al Dorow

John Elliott

Dave Herman

Pete Lammons

Bill Mathis

Gerry Philbin

John Riggins

Puetz, Garry, G, Valparaiso 1973–76

R

Rademacher, Bill, DB-WR, No. Michigan 1964–68
Randall, Dennis, DT, Oklahoma State 1967
Rasmussen, Randy, G, Kearney State 1967–76
Rechichar, Bert, FB, Tennessee 1961
Reifsnyder, Bob, E, Navy 1960–61
Renn, Bobby, DB, Florida State 1961
Richards, Jim, S, Virginia Tech 1968–69
Richards, Perry, WR, Detroit 1962
Richardson, Jeff, G, Michigan State 1967–68
Riggins, John, RB, Kansas 1971–75
Riley, Leon, DB, Detroit 1961–62
Rivers, Jamie, LB, Bowling Green 1974–75
Roach, Travis, G, Texas 1974

Robinson, Bill, HB, Lincoln 1960
Robinson, Jerry, WR, Grambling 1965
Rochester, Paul, DT, Michigan State 1963–69
Rogers, Steve, RB, Louisiana State 1976
Roman, John, G, Idaho State 1976
Rosecrans, Jim, LB, Penn State 1976
Ross, David, E, Cal. State-L.A. 1960
Rowley, Bob, LB, Virginia 1964
Russ, Carl, LB, Michigan 1976
Ryan, Joe, E, Villanova 1960

S

Saidock, Tom, T, Michigan State 1960–61
Sample, John, CB, Maryland State 1966–68
Sapienza, Americo, HB, Villanova 1960
Satterwhite, Howard, WR, Sam Houston State 1976

Sauer, George Jr., WR, Texas 1965–70
Schmidt, Henry, DT, USC 1966
Schmielsing, Joe, DT, New Mexico State 1974
Schmitt, John, C, Hofstra 1964–73
Schwedes, Gerhard, RB, Syracuse 1960
Schweickert, Bob, WR, Virginia Tech 1965, 1967
Scrabis, Bob, QB, Penn State 1960–62
Seiler, Paul, T-C, Notre Dame 1967, 1969
Shockley, Bill, HB-K, West Chester State .1960, 1962
Simkus, Arnie, DT, Michigan 1965
Smith, Allen, HB, Findlay 1966
Smolinski, Mark, RB-TE, Wyoming 1963–68
Snell, Matt, RB, Ohio State 1964–72
Songin, Ed, (Butch), QB, Boston College 1962
Sowells, Rich, DB, Alcorn A&M 1971–76
Spicer, Rob, LB, Indiana 1973
Starks, Marshall, DB, Illinois 1963–64
Stephens, Harold (Hayseed), QB, Hardin-Simmons 1962
Stewart, Wayne, TE, California 1969–72
Stromberg, Mike, LB, Temple 1968
Stricker, Tony, DB, Colorado 1963
Strugar, George, DT, Washington 1962–63
Studdard, Vern, WR-R, Mississippi 1971
Suggs, Shafer, S, Ball State 1976
Svihus, Bob, T, USC 1971–72
Swinney, Clovis, DT, Arkansas State 1971

T

Talamini, Bob, G, Kentucky 1968
Taliaferro, Mike, QB, Illinois 1964–67
Tannen, Steve, CB, Florida 1970–74
Taylor, Ed, CB, Memphis State 1975–76
Taylor, Mike, LB, Michigan 1972–73
Tharp, Tom, (Corky), DB, Alabama 1960
Thomas, Earlie, CB, Colorado State 1970–74
Thompson, Steve, DT, Washington 1968–73
Tiller, Jim, HB, Purdue 1962
Todd, Richard, QB, Alabama 1976
Torczon, LaVerne, DE, Nebraska 1962–65
Turk, Godwin, LB, Southern U 1974–75
Turner, Jim, K-QB, Utah State 1964–70
Turner, Robert (Bake), WR, Texas Tech 1963–69
Turner, Rocky, WR, Chattanooga 1972–73
Turner, Vince, DB, Missouri 1964

V

Van Galder, Tim, QB, Missouri 1973

W

Walker, Donnie, S, Central State, Ohio 1975
Walsh, Ed, T, Penn Military 1961
Walton, Sam, T, E. Texas State 1968–69
Washington, Clyde, DB, Purdue 1963–65
Waskiewicz, Jim, LB, Wichita State 1966–67
Watters, Bob, De, Lincoln 1962–64
Wegert, Ted, HB, None 1960
Weir, Sammy, WR, Arkansas State 1966
Werl, Bob, DE, Miami 1966
West, David, DB, Central State, Okla. 1963
West, Mel, HB, Missouri 1961–63
West, Willie, DB, Oregon 1964–65
White, Lee, RB, Weber State 1968–70
Whitley, Hall, DB, Texas A&I 1960
Wilder, Bert, DT, N. Carolina State 1964–67
Wise, Phil, S, Nebraska-Omaha 1971–76
Wood, Bill, DB, West Virginia Wesleyan 1963
Wood, Malcolm, (Dick), QB, Auburn 1963–64
Wood, Richard, LB, USC 1975
Woodall, Frank, (Al), QB, Duke 1969–74
Woods, Larry, DT, Tennessee State 1974–75
Woods, Robert, T, Tennessee State 1973–76
Word, Roscoe, CB, Jackson State 1974–76
Wren, Lowe, DB, Missouri 1961
Wright, Gordon, G, Delaware State 1969

Y

Yearby, Bill, DT, Michigan 1966
Yohn, John, (Dave), LB, Gettysburg 1963
Youngelman, Sid, DE, Alabama 1960–61

Z

Zapalac, Bill, DE-LB, Texas 1971–73

Running back John Riggins during his 1,005-yard season, 1975.

OAKLAND RAIDERS

1959 The American Football League was organized, August 14. It held its first player draft, November 22, and another draft, completing 53 rounds in all, December 2.

1960 The Minnesota-St. Paul franchise of the AFL withdrew and elected to play in the National Football League instead. Barron Hilton, owner of the Los Angeles Chargers of the AFL, gave the league an ultimatum that unless it placed another franchise on the West Coast, he would withdraw from the AFL. Oakland became the eighth city to gain an AFL franchise, January 30. The franchise was owned by an eight-man syndicate headed by Y.C. (Chet) Soda and it included Ed McGah, Robert Osborne, and Wayne Valley. The AFL draft was past and the Oakland team got its first players by drafting from the rosters of the seven other clubs. "Dons," then "Senors," then "Raiders" was chosen as the team's name. Eddie Erdelatz of Navy was named the team's head coach. The regents of the University of California would not approve the use of its stadium for the Raiders' games, and they decided to play at Kezar Stadium in San Francisco, which also was the home of the rival 49ers of the NFL. Only 12,703 fans watched the Raiders lose to the Houston Oilers 37–22 in their first game. They had two good quarterbacks, Tom Flores and Babe Parilli, and center Jim Otto and guard Wayne Hawkins were solid players, but the Raiders had little else and finished their first season with a 6–8 record.

1961 The Raiders' home games were moved to Candlestick Park in San Francisco. McGah, Osborne, and Valley bought out their five partners, and McGah was named president of the club. The team lost its first two games to Houston 55–0 and San Diego 44–0. "I don't know what to do about it," Erdelatz said. He was fired as coach. Marty Feldman, one of Erdelatz's assistants, was given the job, but he didn't fare any better. The Raiders scored the fewest points in the league, allowed the most points, played before mostly empty seats, and won only two games. Osborne, discouraged by the turn of events, sold his ownership interest in the club.

1962 Valley told Oakland city officials, "Either build us a stadium or we move." A much-discussed Alameda County-Oakland Coliseum complex was still in the planning stages, so until further action could be taken on it, Frank Youell Field was designated for the Raiders. It was a small high school facility. Temporary stands were built and boosted its seating capacity to 20,000. It was still so small that even if the Raiders sold out every game, they would have lost money had it not been for the league's television contract. The team continued to struggle for victories, as well. Feldman was replaced by Bill (Red) Conkright after two games. On the final day of the season at Frank Youell Field, the Raiders finally won, beating Boston 20–0 for their only victory in 14 games.

1963 After refusing their offers on several occasions, Al Davis, an assistant coach for the San Diego Chargers, accepted a three-year contract as the Raiders' head coach and general manager. "What I want is enough time and money to build the Raiders into a professional football team," Davis told owners Valley and McGah. Davis immediately began reorganizing the entire franchise. He hired a new business manager, director of player personnel, and ticket manager. He signed split end Art Powell, who had played out his option with the New York Titans, got quarterback Tom Flores back from an extended illness, and coaxed several useful players away from other teams. Running back Clemon Daniels, a former tight end, rushed for 1,099 yards, an AFL record. The Oakland

Quarterback Ken Stabler passing in Super Bowl XI; Mark van Eeghen 30, and Art Shell block for him.

defense also prospered under Davis. After a 2–4 start, the Raiders rallied to win their last eight games and finish one game behind San Diego. The last three games, in particular, established Oakland and the AFL in its exciting, wide-open style. Trailing 27–10, the Raiders rallied in the fourth quarter to beat the Chargers 41–27. Then they edged Denver 35–31 and outscored Houston 52–49 in the highest scoring game in AFL history.

1964 Tony Lorick, the number-one draft choice from Arizona State, signed with Oakland. He also signed with Baltimore of the NFL and after a long hassle, wound up playing for the Colts. Davis's team slumped at the start, losing five straight, but came back to score four wins and a tie in the final five games, including victories over Buffalo and San Diego, the teams headed for the AFL title game. Two new acquisitions, 6-foot 7-inch, 265-pound end Ben Davidson and middle linebacker Dan Conners helped fortify Oakland's defense.

1965 Construction officially started on Oakland-Alameda County Coliseum. Davis continued to stockpile talent, acquiring such rookies as receiver Fred Biletnikoff, defensive back Kent McCloughan, linebacker Gus Otto, and tackles Harry Schuh and Bob Svihus. But an inability to beat Buffalo and San Diego—the Raiders lost all four of those games—killed the Raiders' title chances and they finished second to the Chargers in their division again.

1966 Al Davis was named commissioner of the American Football League, succeeding Joe Foss, in April. John Rauch was named Raiders' head coach. The AFL and NFL agreed to a merger, June 8. Davis resigned as AFL commissioner and returned to Oakland as general manager and managing partner. Oakland-Alameda County Coliseum opened; the Kansas City Chiefs defeated the Raiders 32–10 before 50,746, September 18. The Raiders slipped to a 1–3 mark but late season victories over Kansas City, Houston, and San Diego helped produce an 8–5–1 season, for second place in the Western Division.

1967 Davis traded quarterback Tom Flores and wide receiver Art Powell to Buffalo for quarterback Daryle Lamonica and wide receiver Glenn Bass. The Raiders also acquired receiver Bill Miller from Buffalo, cornerback Willie Brown from Denver, and quarterback-kicker George Blanda, who had been released by Houston. Rookie guard Gene Upshaw immediately established himself as one of the league's best blockers. The Raiders smashed Denver 51–0 in the season opener, and, after a 27–14 loss to New York in the fourth week, they won ten straight victories to capture the Western Division title with a 13–1 mark. Blanda won the AFL scoring championship, with 20 field goals and 56 extra points for a total of 116. In the AFL championship game at Oakland, the Raiders stormed Houston 40–7 for the right to meet Green Bay in Super Bowl II. Lamonica was named AFL player of the year, having thrown for 3,228 yards and 30 touchdowns.

1968 The AFL champions met the Green Bay Packers in the second AFL-NFL world championship game. They were no match for the power and efficiency of Vince Lombardi's Packers. Oakland was too young and too inexperienced, and quarterback Bart Starr used up the clock with typical Packers' ball control to win 33-14. As the 1968 season began, the Raiders were hit with an unusual amount of regular season injuries, but found two new stars on offense, wide receiver Warren Wells and running back Charlie Smith. They played the New York Jets at Oakland and were trailing 32-29 with one minute, five seconds to play. The NBC television network switched from the game to begin the movie, "Heidi." The network's switchboard lit up with angry protests; the viewers never saw the Raiders come back with two late touchdowns to win what was later called the "Heidi Game," 43-32. Oakland rolled to a 12-2 record, but it wasn't enough for undisputed first place in the Western Division; they were tied with the Kansas City Chiefs. Oakland crushed the Chiefs 41-6 in a playoff. In the AFL title game in New York, the Raiders and Jets played a dramatic game with Joe Namath finally pulling it out for New York 27-23.

1969 John Rauch became head coach of the Buffalo Bills. John Madden, a 32-year-old Raiders' assistant, replaced him, becoming the youngest head coach in pro football. He emphasized a new, wide-open passing attack. Daryle Lamonica emerged as one of the game's most effective passers. He threw six touchdown passes in the first half on the way to a 50-21 win over Buffalo, October 19. One week later, the Raiders beat San Diego to equal the AFL record for consecutive unbeaten games at 15. The streak ended the following week with a 31-17 loss to Cincinnati, but Oakland won its six remaining games and finished first in the Western Division with a 12-1-1 mark. Lamonica ended the season with 34 touchdown passes. Oakland routed Houston 56-7 in the first round of the playoffs.

1970 Kansas City, the second place team in the division, upset Oakland 17-7 in the AFC championship game at Oakland. The Raiders were placed in the AFC Western Division as realignment of pro football took place. The Raiders' season ticket sales hit a record high of 50,578 September 4. Blanda, 43, produced four victories and a tie in the final seconds of five consecutive games. Blanda threw two touchdown passes in a 31-14 victory over Pittsburgh. The following week he kicked a 48-yard field goal with three seconds remaining to tie Kansas City 17-17. A week later, again with three seconds left, he kicked a 52-yard field goal that gave the Raiders a 23-20 victory over Cleveland. In the next game, with Denver, Blanda came off the bench to ignite a late rally that beat the Broncos 24-19. Then he kicked a field goal with four seconds left to defeat San Diego 20-17. Thanks to Blanda, Oakland became the first AFC team to win four consecutive divisional championships. In the first round of the playoffs, the Raiders beat Miami 21-14 to advance to the championship game against Baltimore.

1971 In the AFC championship game with Baltimore, Blanda completed 17 of 32 passes for 271 yards, but the Colts made three key interceptions. John Unitas staged a Cinderella passing exhibition of his own, and Baltimore advanced to the Super Bowl with a 27-17 victory. The Raiders lost to the New England Patriots 20-6 in the opening game of the regular season but went undefeated for the next nine weeks. The team's two best running backs, Charlie Smith and Hewritt Dixon, both were sidelined with injuries. A 37-14 loss to Baltimore started a three-game losing streak, which included a 16-14 loss to Kansas City in the next to last game. Oakland finished

with an 8-4-2 record. It was the first time in five years the Raiders failed to win the Western Division title.

1972 Marv Hubbard led all rushers in the Pro Bowl game, gaining 57 yards in the AFC's 26-13 win over the NFC. Al Davis and Madden continued to rebuild the Raiders and maintain the same remarkable winning percentage. Youngsters such as Horace Jones, Otis Sistrunk, Art Thoms, and Tony Cline were starting in the defensive line, and Phil Villapiano and Gerald Irons were new linebackers. Offensively, the flashy new addition was Clifford Branch, the world class sprinter from Colorado who was developing into a new deep threat. Branch caught a key 19-yard pass in a last-minute, 21-19 victory over San Diego. The win was the fourth in a six-game streak that closed out the Raiders' 10-3-1 season. After winning the Western Division title, Oakland traveled to Pittsburgh and was defeated 13-7 when Franco Harris scored the winning touchdown on a shoe-top catch of a deflected pass in the final seconds.

1973 The largest Bay Area crowd ever to see a Raiders' game, 74,121 at the University of California, watched Oakland end Miami's winning streak at 18 games with a 12-7 victory. After failing to score a touchdown in the first three games, Lamonica was benched in favor of Ken Stabler at quarterback. A mid-November slump cost the team a 17-9 loss to Pittsburgh and a 7-3 upset at the hands of Cleveland. The Raiders rallied for three consecutive victories, and entered the final game against Denver only a half-game in front of the vastly improved Broncos. The Raiders won 21-17, finishing at 9-4-1 for their sixth division championship in seven years. In the first round of the AFC playoffs, Oakland defeated Pittsburgh 33-14. Miami's defending Super Bowl champions were too strong in the AFC title game, however, and the Raiders fell 27-10.

1974 Madden and his staff coached the AFC to a 15-13 victory over the NFC in the Pro Bowl at Kansas City's Arrowhead stadium. A 27-7 victory over Kansas City began a nine-game winning streak for the Raiders, September 22. The following week, Oakland shut out Pittsburgh 17-0. The streak ended with a 20-17 loss to Denver in the eleventh game, but the Raiders won the next three and finished 12-2 for another Western Division championship. Against Miami in the first round of the AFC playoffs, Stabler took the Raiders on a pressure drive late in the fourth quarter, then threw a clutch touchdown pass to Clarence Davis in the final minutes for a 28-26 victory. Oakland's bid for the Super Bowl was shut off by Pittsburgh, 24-13, in the AFC title game at Oakland, December 29.

1975 Jim Otto, last of the original Raiders, retired after 15 years as the team's starting center. In a nationally televised Monday night game, Oakland opened the season with a 31-21 victory over Miami, ending the Dolphins' 31-game winning streak in the Orange Bowl. The Raiders won their next two games but were jolted 42-10 by Kansas City and lost to Cincinnati 14-10. They rebounded to win seven straight, clinching the division title with a 37-34 overtime victory over Atlanta, November 30. In the first round of the playoffs, the Raiders edged Cincinnati 31-28.

1976 In the AFC title game, Pittsburgh ended the Raiders' hopes again, hanging on for a 16-10 victory at snow-coated Three Rivers Stadium, January 4. Oakland trailed Pittsburgh 16-7 with 1:38 to play and the Steelers in possession on the Raiders' 36-yard line. But a fumble recovery, a 41-yard George Blanda field goal, and a recovered onside kick gave the Raiders a shot at the conference championship with seven seconds left. The game ended as Branch took a pass from Stabler and was tackled at the Pittsburgh 15-yard line. The Raiders opened the regular season with a

turnabout, upending the Steelers 31-28 on Fred Steinfort's field goal with 18 seconds left. The following Monday night, Stabler completed 22 of 28 passing attempts in a 24-21 triumph over Kansas City. The Raiders got to Houston 14-13 on October 3. The following week their injury-riddled defense caved in and allowed New England seven touchdowns in a 48-17 loss. Oakland regrouped to win its last 10 games to finish 13-1 and claim another division championship. Stabler dived in for the winning touchdown with time running out as the Raiders beat New England 24-21 in round one of the playoffs. In the AFC title game, Pittsburgh was weakened by the loss of injured Franco Harris and Rocky Bleier, its two best runners, December 26. Oakland took advantage of the situation, playing a conservative ground game to win 24-7 and earn its first Super Bowl berth in nine years.

1977 Oakland beat Minnesota decisively 32-14 in Super Bowl XI in Pasadena's Rose Bowl, January 9. Fred Biletnikoff, the veteran wide receiver, was named the game's most valuable player after three clutch catches to set up Oakland touchdowns.

MEMBERS OF HALL OF FAME:
None

RAIDERS RECORD, 1960-76

Year	Won	Lost	Tied	Pct.	Pts.	OP
1960	6	8	0	.429	319	388
1961	2	12	0	.143	237	458
1962	1	13	0	.071	213	370
1963	10	4	0	.714	363	288
1964	5	7	2	.417	303	350
1965	8	5	1	.615	298	239
1966	8	5	1	.615	315	288
1967‡	13	1	0	.929	468	233
1968§	12	2	0	.857	453	233
1969§	12	1	1	.923	377	242
1970§	8	4	2	.667	300	293
1971	8	4	2	.667	344	278
1972§	10	3	1	.750	365	248
1973§	9	4	1	.679	292	175
1974§	12	2	0	.857	355	228
1975§	11	3	0	.786	375	255
1976**	13	1	0	.929	350	237
17 Years	148	79	11	.645	5,727	4,803

‡*AFL-AFC Champion*
§*Western Division Champion*
***Super Bowl Champion*

RECORD HOLDERS

Rushing (Yards)	Marv Hubbard, 1972	1,100
Passing (Pct.)	Ken Stabler, 1976	66.7
Passing (Yards)	Daryle Lamonica, 1969	3,302
Passing (TDs)	Daryle Lamonica, 1969	34
Receiving (No.)	Art Powell, 1964	76
Receiving (Yards)	Art Powell, 1964	1,361
Interceptions (No.)	Tom Morrow, 1962, and	
	Dave Grayson, 1968	10
Punting (Avg.)	Ray Guy, 1973	45.3
Punt Ret. (Avg.)	Claude Gibson, 1964	14.4
Kickoff Ret. (Avg.)	Harold Hart, 1975	30.5
Touchdowns (Total)	Art Powell, 1963, and	
	Pete Banaszak, 1975	16
Field Goals Made	George Blanda, 1967, 1969	20
Points (No.)	George Blanda, 1968	117

COACHING HISTORY

1960-61	Eddie Erdelatz*	6-10-0
1961-62	Marty Feldman**	2-15-0
1962	William (Red) Conkright	1-8-0
1963-65	Al Davis	23-16-3
1966-68	John Rauch	33-8-1
1969-76	John Madden	83-22-7

Replaced after two games in 1961
***Replaced after five games in 1962*

FIRST PLAYER SELECTED

1960	Dale Hackbart, CB, Wisconsin
1961	Joe Rutgens, DT, Illinois
1962	Roman Gabriel, QB, North Carolina State
1963	George Wilson, RB (6), Alabama
1964	Tony Lorick, RB, Arizona State
1965	Harry Schuh, T, Memphis State
1966	Rodger Bird, S, Kentucky
1967	Gene Upshaw, G, Texas A&I
1968	Eldridge Dickey, QB, Tennessee State
1969	Art Thoms, DT, Syracuse
1970	Raymond Chester, TE, Morgan State
1971	Jack Tatum, S, Ohio State
1972	Mike Siani, WR, Villanova
1973	Ray Guy, P-K, Southern Mississippi
1974	Henry Lawrence, T, Florida A&M
1975	Neal Colzie, DB, Ohio State
1976	Charles Philyaw, DT (2), Texas Southern

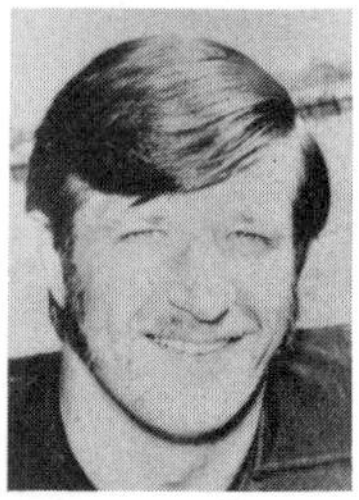
Pete Banaszak

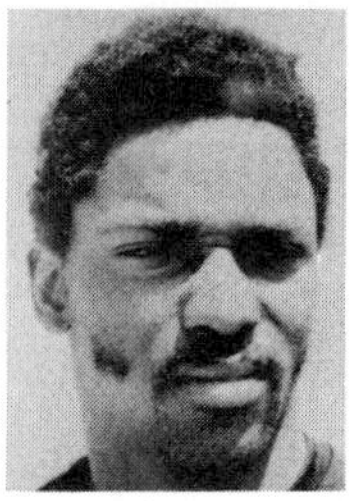
Clifford Branch

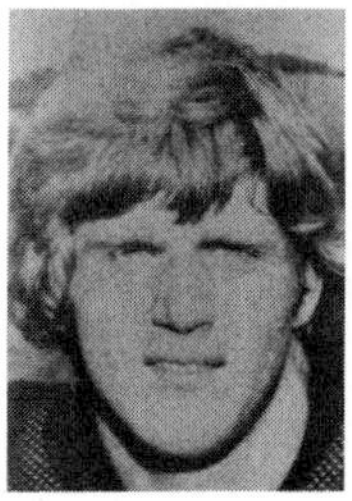
Dave Casper

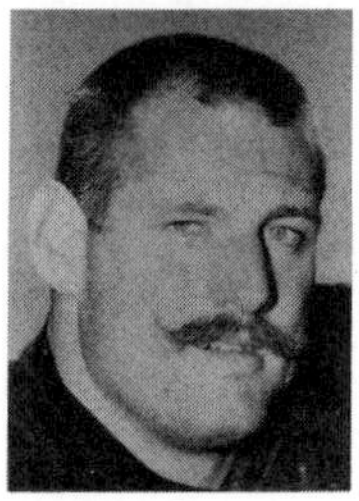
Ben Davidson

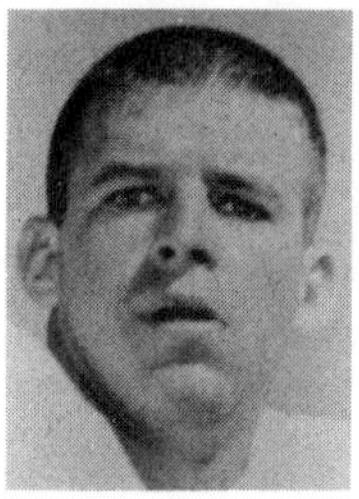
C. (Hoot) Gibson

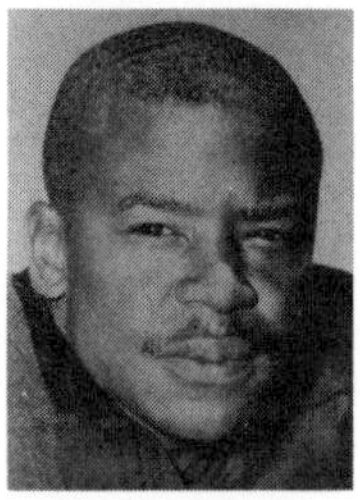
Dave Grayson

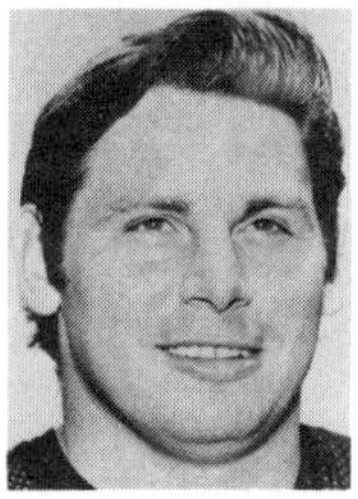
Marv Hubbard

OAKLAND RAIDERS, 1960–76

Agajanian, Ben, K, New Mexico ... 1962
Allen, Dalva, DE, Houston ... 1962–64
Allen, Jackie, DB, Baylor ... 1969
Archer, Dan, T, Oregon ... 1967
Armstrong, Ramon, T, Texas Christian ... 1960
Asad, Doug, E, Northwestern ... 1960–61
Atkins, Pervis, E, New Mexico State ... 1965–66
Atkinson, George, DB, Morris Brown ... 1968–76

B

Banaszak, Pete, RB, Miami ... 1966–76
Banks, Estes, B, Colorado ... 1967
Bankston, Warren, TE, Tulane ... 1973–76
Bansavage, Al, LB, USC ... 1961
Barbee, Joe, T, Kent State ... 1960
Barnes, Larry, LB, Colorado A&M ... 1960
Barnes, Rodrigo, LB, Rice ... 1976
Barrett, Jan, E, Fresno State ... 1963–64
Benson, Duane, LB, Hamline ... 1967–71
Biletnikoff, Fred, WR, Florida State ... 1965–76
Bird, Rodger, DB, Kentucky ... 1967–71
Birdwell, Dan, DT, Houston ... 1962–69
Bishop, Sonny, G, Fresno State ... 1963
Blanda, George, QB, Kentucky ... 1967–75
Blankenship, Greg, LB, Cal State-Hayward ... 1976
Bonness, Rik, LB, Nebraska ... 1976
Boydston, Max, E, Oklahoma ... 1962
Boynton, George, DB, E. Texas State ... 1962
Bradshaw, Morris, WR, Ohio State ... 1974–76
Branch, Cliff, WR, Colorado ... 1972–76
Bravo, Alex, DB, Cal. Poly ... 1960–61
Brewington, Jim, T, N. Carolina College ... 1961
Brown, Bob, T, Nebraska ... 1971–73
Brown, Charles, T, Houston ... 1962
Brown, Doug, DT, Fresno State ... 1964
Brown, Willie, DB, Grambling ... 1967–76
Budness, Bill, LB, Boston U ... 1964–70
Buehler, George, G, Stanford ... 1969–76
Buie, Drew, WR, Catawba ... 1969–71
Burch, Gerald, E, Georgia Tech ... 1961
Butler, Gary, TE, Rice ... 1976

C

Campbell, Stan, G, Iowa State ... 1962
Cannavino, Joe, DB, Ohio State ... 1960–61
Cannon, Billy, TE, Louisiana State ... 1964–69
Carroll, Joe, LB, Pittsburgh ... 1972–73
Carter, Louis, RB, Maryland ... 1976
Casper, Dave, TE, Notre Dame ... 1974–76
Cavalli, Carmen, DE, Richmond ... 1960
Chester, Raymond, TE, Morgan State ... 1970–72
Churchwell, Hansen, DT, Mississippi ... 1960
Cline, Tony, DE Miami ... 1970–75
Colzie, Neal, DB, Ohio State ... 1975–76
Conners, Dan, LB, Miami ... 1964–74
Coolbaugh, Bob, E, Richmond ... 1961
Costa, Dave, DT, Utah ... 1963–65
Craig, Dobie, E, Howard Payne ... 1962–63
Crow, Wayne, RB-DB, California ... 1960–61

D

Dalby, Dave, C UCLA ... 1972–76
Daniels, Clemon, RB, Prairie View ... 1961–67
Daniels, David, DT, Florida A&M ... 1966
Davidson, Ben, DE, Washington ... 1964–71
Davidson, Cotton, QB, Baylor ... 1962–69
Davis, Clarence, RB, USC ... 1971–76
Dennery, Mike, LB, Southern Mississippi ... 1974–75
DePoyster, Jerry, K, Wyoming ... 1971–72
Deskins, Don, G, Michigan ... 1960
Dickey, Eldridge, WR, Tennessee State ... 1968–71
Dickinson, Bo, B, So. Mississippi ... 1964
Diehl, John, DT, Virginia ... 1965
Dittrich, John, G, Wisconsin ... 1960
Dixon, Hewritt, RB, Florida A&M ... 1966–70
Dorsey, Dick, E, USC ... 1962
Dotson, Alphonse, DT, Grambling ... 1968–70
Dougherty, Bob, LB, Kentucky ... 1960–63

E

Eason, John, TE, Florida A&M ... 1968
Edwards, Lloyd, TE, San Diego State ... 1969
Eischeid, Mike, K, Upper Iowa ... 1966–71
Ellison, Glenn, RB, Arkansas ... 1971
Enis, Hunter, QB, Texas Christian ... 1962
Enyart, Bill, LB, Oregon State ... 1971

F

Fairband, Bill, LB, Colorado ... 1967–68
Ficca, Dan, G, USC ... 1962
Fields, George, DT, Bakersfield J.C. ... 1960–61
Finneran, Garry, DT, USC ... 1961
Fleming, George, DB, Washington ... 1961
Flores, Tom, QB, Pacific ... 1960–66
Fuller, Charles, E, S.F. State ... 1961–62

G

Gallegos, Chon, QB, San Jose State ... 1962
Garner, Bob, DB, Fresno State ... 1961–62
Garrett, Carl, RB, New Mexico Highlands ... 1976
Gibson, Claude, DB, N. Carolina State ... 1963–65
Gillett, Fred, E, Louisiana State ... 1964
Ginn, Hubert, RB, Florida A&M ... 1976
Gipson, Tom, DT, N. Texas State ... 1971
Goldstein, Alan, E, North Carolina ... 1960
Grayson, David, DB, Oregon ... 1965–70
Green, Charley, QB, Wittenberg ... 1966
Guy, Louie, DB, Mississippi ... 1964
Guy, Ray, K, Southern Mississippi ... 1973–76

H

Hagberg, Roger, FB, Minnesota ... 1965–69
Hall, Willie, LB, USC ... 1976
Hardy, Charles, E, San Jose State ... 1960–62
Harris, John, DB, Santa Monica ... 1960–61
Hart, Harold, RB, Texas Southern ... 1974–75
Harvey, James, G, Mississippi ... 1966–71
Hawkins, Wayne, G, Pacific ... 1960–70
Heinrich, Don, QB, Washington ... 1962
Hendricks, Ted, LB, Miami ... 1975–76
Hermann, Dick, LB, Florida State ... 1965
Herock, Ken, TE, West Virginia ... 1963–67
Highsmith, Don, RB, Michigan State ... 1970–72
Hoisington, Al, E, Pasadena ... 1960
Hopkins, Jerry, LB, Texas A&M ... 1968
Hubbard, Marv, RB, Colgate ... 1969–75
Hudson, Bob, RB, Northeast Oklahoma ... 1973–74
Humm, David, QB, Nebraska ... 1975–76

I

Irons, Gerald, LB, Maryland State ... 1970–75

J

Jackson, Bobby, B, New Mexico State ... 1964
Jackson, Richard, LB, Southern U. ... 1966
Jacobs, Proverb, T, California ... 1963–64
Jagielski, Harry, DT, Indiana ... 1961
Jakowenko, George, K, Syracuse ... 1974
Jelacic, Jon, DE, Minnesota ... 1961–64
Jennings, Rick, RB, Maryland ... 1976
Johnson, Monte, LB, Nebraska ... 1973–76
Jones, Horace, DE, Louisville ... 1971–75
Jones, Jim, LB, Washington ... 1961
Joyner, L.C., DB, Diablo Valley ... 1960

K

Keating, Tom, DT, Michigan ... 1966–72
Kent, Greg, T, Utah ... 1966
Keyes, Bob, B, San Diego ... 1960
Klein, Dick, T, Iowa ... 1963–64
Kocourek, Dave, TE, Wisconsin ... 1967–68
Koegel, Warren, C, Penn State ... 1971
Korver, Kelvin, DT, Northwestern, Iowa ... 1973–75
Kowalczyk, Walt, B, Michigan State ... 1961
Koy, Ted, TE, Texas ... 1970
Kunz, Terry, RB, Colorado ... 1976
Krakoski, Joe, DB, Illinois ... 1963–65
Kruse, Bob, G, Wayne State ... 1967–68
Kwalick, Ted, TE, Penn State ... 1975–76

L

Lamonica, Daryle, QB, Notre Dame ... 1967–74
Larschied, Jack, RB, Pacific ... 1960–61
Larson, Paul, QB, California ... 1960
Laskey, Bill, LB, Michigan ... 1966–70
Lassiter, Isaac, DE, St. Augustine ... 1965–69
Lawrence, Henry, T, Florida A&M ... 1974–76
Lawrence, Larry, QB, Iowa ... 1974–75
Lewis, Harold, RB, Houston ... 1962
Locklin, Billy Ray, G, New Mexico State ... 1960
Lott, Billy, RB, Mississippi ... 1960
Louderback, Tom LB, San Jose State ... 1960–61

M

Macon, Ed, DB, Pacific ... 1960
MacKinnon, Jacque, TE, Colgate ... 1970
Mann, Errol, K, North Dakota ... 1976
Manoukian, Don, G, Stanford ... 1960
Marinovich, Marv, G, USC ... 1965
Matsos, Arch, LB, Michigan State ... 1963–65
Matuszak, John, DE, Tampa ... 1976
Maxwell, Tom, DB, Texas A&M ... 1971–73
Mayberry, Doug, RB, Utah State ... 1963
McCloughan, Kent, DB, Nebraska ... 1965–70
McFarlan, Nyle, DB, Brigham Young ... 1960
McMath, Herb, DE, Morningside ... 1976
McMillin, Jim, DB, Colorado State ... 1963–64
McMurty, Chuck, DT, Whittier ... 1962–63
Medlin, Dan, G, North Carolina State ... 1974–76
Mendenhall, Terry, LB, San Diego State ... 1971–72
Mercer, Mike, K, Arizona State ... 1963–65
Miller, Alan, FB, Boston College ... 1961–65
Miller, Bill, E, Miami ... 1964–68
Mingo, Gene, K, None ... 1964–65
Mirich, Rex, DT, Arizona State ... 1964–65
Mischak, Bob, G, Army ... 1963–65
Mitchell, Tom, E, Bucknell ... 1966
Mix, Ron, T, USC ... 1971
Montalbo, Mel, DB, Utah State ... 1962
Moore, Bob, TE, Stanford ... 1971–75
Moore, Manfred, RB, USC ... 1976
Morris, Riley, DE, Florida A&M ... 1960–62
Morrison, Dave, DB, S.W. Texas State ... 1968
Morrow, Tom, DB, So. Mississippi ... 1962–64
Mostardi, Rich, DB, Kent State ... 1962
Murdock, Jesse, RB, California Western ... 1963

N

Nicklas, Pete, T, Baylor ... 1962
Norris, Jim, DT, Houston ... 1962–63
Novsek, Joe, DE, Tulsa ... 1962

O

Oats, Carleton, DT, Florida A&M ... 1965–72
Ogas, Dave, LB, San Diego State ... 1968
Oglesby, Paul, T, UCLA ... 1960
Oliver, Ralph, LB, USC ... 1968–69
Osborne, Clancy, LB, Arizona State ... 1963–64
Otto, Gus, LB, Missouri ... 1965–72
Otto, Jim, C, Miami ... 1960–74

P

Papac, Nick, QB, Fresno State ... 1961
Parilli, Babe, QB, Kentucky ... 1960
Peters, Volney, DT, USC ... 1961
Phillips, Charles, DB, USC ... 1975–76
Philyaw, Charles, DE, Texas Southern ... 1976
Pitts, Frank, WR, Southern U. ... 1974
Powell, Art, E, San Jose State ... 1963–66
Powell, Charlie, DE, None ... 1960–61
Powers, Warren, DB, Nebraska ... 1963–68
Prebola, Gene, E, Boston U. ... 1960
Prout, Bob, DB, Knox ... 1974
Pyle, Palmer, G, Michigan State ... 1966

Q

Queen, Jeff, Morgan State ... 1972–73

R

Rae, Mike, QB, USC ... 1976
Reinfeldt, Mike, DB, Wisconsin-Milwaukee ... 1976
Reynolds, Billy, RB, Pittsburgh ... 1960
Reynolds, M.C., QB, Louisiana State ... 1961
Rice, Floyd, LB, Alcorn A&M ... 1976
Rice, Harold, DE, Tennessee State ... 1971
Rice, Ken, T, Auburn ... 1964–65
Ridlehuber, Preston, B, Georgia ... 1968
Rieves, Charles, LB, Houston ... 1962–63

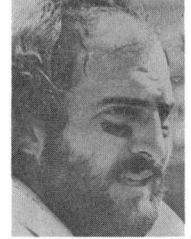      

Monte Johnson *Kent McCloughan* *Bo Roberson* *Art Shell* *Charley Smith* *Phil Villapiano* *Warren Wells*

Rivera, Hank, DB, Oregon State 1962
Roberson, Bo, E, Cornell 1962–65
Roberts, Cliff, DT, Illinois 1961
Roderick, John, E, Southern Methodist 1968
Roedel, Herb, G, Marquette 1961
Rowe, Dave, DT, Penn State 1975–76
Rubke, Karl, DE, USC 1968

S

Sabal, Ron, T, Purdue 1960–61
Schmautz, Ray, LB, San Diego State 1966
Schuh, Harry, T, Memphis State 1965–70
Seiler, Paul, T, Notre Dame 1971–73
Shaw, Glenn, RB, Kentucky 1963–64
Shell, Arthur, T, Maryland State 1968–76
Sherman, Rod, WR, USC 1967–71
Shirkey, George, DT, Stephen F. Austin 1962
Siani, Mike, WR, Villanova 1972–76
Simpson, Jack, LB, Mississippi 1962–64
Simpson, Willie, B, S.F. State 1962
Sistrunk, Otis, DT, None 1972–76
Sligh, Richard, T, N. Carolina College 1967
Slough, Greg, LB, USC 1968–72
Smith, Charles (Bubba), DE, Michigan State 1973–74
Smith Charles, RB, Utah 1968–74
Smith, Hal, DT, UCLA 1961
Smith, James, RB, Compton J.C. 1960
Smith, Ron, DB, Wisconsin 1974

Smith, Willie, G, Michigan 1961
Sommer, Mike, RB, George Washington 1963
Spencer, Ollie, G, Kansas 1963
Stabler, Ken, QB, Alabama 1970–76
Steinfort, Fred, K, Boston College 1976
Stone, Jack, T, Oregon 1961–62
Striegel, Bill, LB, Pacific 1960
Svihus, Bob, T, USC 1965–70
Sweeney, Steve, WR, California 1973
Sylvester, Steve, C-G, Notre Dame 1975–76

T

Tatum, Jack, DB, Ohio State 1971–76
Teresa, Tony, RB, San Jose State 1960
Thomas, Alonzo (Skip), DB, USC 1972–75
Thoms, Art, DT, Syracuse 1969–75
Todd, Larry, E, Arizona State 1965–70
Trask, Orville, DT, Rice 1962
Truax, Dalton, DT, Tulane 1960
Tyson, Richard, G, Tulsa 1966

U

Upshaw, Eugene, G, Texas A&I 1967–76
Urenda, Herman, E, Pacific 1963

V

Valdez, Vernon, DB, San Diego 1962
Van Eeghen, Mark, RB, Colgate 1974–76

Vella, John, T, USC 1972–76
Villapiano, Phil, LB, Bowling Green 1971–76
Voight, Bob, DE, Cal State-L.A. 1961

W

Warren, Jimmy, DB, Illinois 1970–74
Warzeka, Ron, DE, Montana State 1960
Weathers, Carl, LB, San Diego State 1970–71
Weaver, Gary, LB, Fresno State 1973
Wells, Warren, WR, Texas Southern 1967–70
White, Eugene, RB, Florida A&M 1962
Williams, Howie, DB, Howard 1964–69
Williams, Willie, DB, Grambling 1966
Williamson, Fred, DB, Northwestern 1961–64
Williamson, J.R., LB, Louisiana Tech 1964–67
Wilson, Nemiah, DB, Grambling 1968–74
Winans, Jeff, T, USC 1976
Wood, Dick, QB, Auburn 1965
Wyatt, Alvin, DB, Bethune-Cookman 1970

Y

Youso, Frank, T, Minnesota 1963–65

Z

Zecher, Rich, T, Utah State 1965

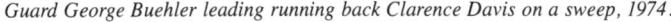

Guard George Buehler leading running back Clarence Davis on a sweep, 1974.

Cornerback Willie Brown intercepts a Kansas City pass and heads upfield, 1974.

PHILADELPHIA EAGLES

1933 Knowing a state law banning sports on Sunday was about to be repealed, Bert Bell and Lud Wray formed a syndicate to purchase the Frankford Yellowjackets' NFL franchise. Bell and Wray bought the team for $2,500, July 9. Bell named the team in honor of the eagle, symbol of the National Recovery Administration of the New Deal. Bell was the team's general manager, Wray the coach. The Eagles opened with a 56–0 loss to the New York Giants. Remarkably, the rookie-laden Eagles regrouped and went four weeks without a loss. They even tied the powerful Chicago Bears 3–3 at Baker Bowl, November 12.

1934 The Eagles became known for their inconsistency in their second season. In one stretch, they lost four straight games while scoring just one touchdown. The following week, they blasted the Cincinnati Reds 64–0 at Baker Bowl. The Eagles' top player was Swede Hanson, a 6-foot 1-inch 190-pound two-way halfback from Temple University. Hanson led the team with 805 yards rushing and was named second-team all-pro. Joe Carter, a receiver from Southern Methodist University, caught 16 passes for 238 yards and four touchdowns to lead the NFL.

1935 Realizing he was losing all the good college players to the top NFL teams, Bell proposed a draft, with the weakest clubs getting first shot at the All-America players. Bell's idea, considered the ideal way of balancing power in the league, was ratified by the owners, May 19. It didn't solve Bell's immediate problems, however. His Eagles continued to lose both games and money. The Eagles scored just two victories despite the addition of halfback Alabama Pitts, who learned to play football while serving time in Sing Sing.

1936 In the first three seasons, the Eagles had lost more than $80,000 and Bell's partners were losing interest in their investment. Bell purchased sole ownership for $4,000, disposed of Wray as head coach, and took the job himself. The first college draft was held and the Eagles, with the first pick, chose Jay Berwanger, the Heisman trophy-winning halfback from the University of Chicago. The Eagles traded the rights for him to the Chicago Bears, however, and he never played pro football. The Eagles' home games were moved from Baker Bowl to Municipal Stadium. They won their opener but then lost 11 straight games. They were shut out six times and their leading scorer was their center, Hank Reese, who made nine points on three field goals.

1937 The Eagles improved but only slightly, winning two games. Bell traded his first draft choice, halfback Sam Francis, to the Chicago Bears for Bill Hewitt, a balding, veteran end with all-pro credentials. Hewitt led the team with 16 pass receptions, five for touchdowns. Bell uncovered an effective backfield pairing, Emmett Mortell of Wisconsin and Dave Smukler of Temple. Mortell led the Eagles with 312 yards rushing.

1938 Bell's blend of youth and experience finally jelled as the Eagles won five games and climbed past Pittsburgh into fourth place in the Eastern Division. The Eagles finished the year with wins over Pittsburgh and Detroit. The offensive star was Smukler, a versatile 6-foot 1-inch, 226-pounder with deceptive speed and agility. Smukler rushed for 313 yards, passed for 524 more, accounted for eight touchdowns and was six-for-six kicking extra points. The receivers, Carter and Hewitt, also had good seasons, catching 45 passes and scoring 11 touchdowns between them.

1939 Bell signed Davey O'Brien, the 5-foot 7-inch, 150-pound quarterback from Texas Christian University. O'Brien signed for $12,000, plus a percentage of

Middle linebacker Bill Bergey in a pileup against Atlanta, 1975.

the gate. Bell had the tiny quarterback insured with Lloyds of London. The policy called for Lloyds to pay the Eagles $1,500 for every game O'Brien missed due to injury. O'Brien not only stayed intact but also set an NFL record for the most passing yardage in one season, 1,324. In a 27–14 loss to the Chicago Bears, O'Brien completed 21 of 36 passes for 247 yards. The Eagles finished with a 1–9–1 record.

1940 O'Brien was brilliant but he could not lift the Eagles out of the Eastern Division cellar. The Eagles switched their home field from Municipal Stadium to Shibe Park in North Philadelphia. The Eagles lost their first nine games before beating Pittsburgh 7–0. The following week, O'Brien and Washington's great Sammy Baugh hooked up in a spectacular passing exhibition. Inspired by playing against his Texas Christian predecessor, O'Brien threw a record 60 passes and completed 33 with no interceptions. He won his personal duel with Baugh, but the Eagles lost 13–6. Following the season, O'Brien retired to join the FBI. Don Looney, a rookie receiver from Texas Christian, led the NFL with 58 catches.

1941 Bell gave up the Eagles in a complicated piece of front-office maneuvering. Bell sold half the fran-

chise to Art Rooney, who had sold his Pittsburgh franchise to Alexis Thompson of New York. Before the teams took the field, Rooney and Bell swapped Thompson their Philadelphia franchise for his Pittsburgh franchise. Thompson hired Earle (Greasy) Neale to coach the Eagles, who were quarterbacked by Tommy Thompson, a Tulsa University graduate who was blind in one eye. Thompson was a deadly long passer and fit easily into Neale's offense. The eagles adopted the T formation.

1942 Most NFL teams lost their quarterbacks to the army as World War II gained force. Not the Eagles, however, since Thompson was passed over due to his bad eye. The military depleted the Eagles in other key areas, however, taking the three top runners—Jim Castiglia, Dan DeSantis, and Terry Fox—as well as Bob Suffridge, Neale's best lineman. The Eagles won their opener over Pittsburgh 24–14, but then lost eight straight.

1943 Faced with financial and manpower problems, the Eagles and Steelers joined forces. The hybrid team was called the "Phil-Pitt Steagles" and was coached jointly by Neale and Pittsburgh's Walt Kiesling. The Steagles uncovered surprising talent in the college ranks as rookie tackles Al Wistert from Michigan and Frank (Bucko) Kilroy from Temple excelled on the line. Free agent Jack Hinkle rushed for 571 yards and scored four touchdowns. Vic Sears, a second-year tackle from Oregon State, won a spot on the United Press all-pro team. Even end Bill Hewitt came out of retirement, wearing a helmet for the first time in his career. The Steagles won five games and finished just one game back in the Eastern Division.

1944 The Eagles and Steelers separated. The Eagles selected halfback Steve Van Buren of Louisiana State University in the first round of the college draft. The Eagles went unbeaten through seven games before losing to the Chicago Bears 28–7 at Shibe Park. Although they finished 7–1–2, their best record ever, the Eagles finished second behind the New York Giants in the Eastern Division. Van Buren, a 6-foot, 220-pound power runner with speed, bowled over the NFL's defenses. Van Buren and Hinkle teamed in a backfield that led the league with 1,661 yards rushing.

1945 The Eagles finished second to Washington with a 7–3 record. Van Buren led the NFL in rushing with 832 yards and scoring with 110 points (18 touchdowns, two extra points). Van Buren was the running game, carrying the ball 143 times. Van Buren scored on a 69-yard run against Detroit and returned a kickoff 98 yards for a touchdown against the New York Giants. The Eagles' top receiver was Jack Ferrante, a product of the Philadelphia sandlots who had never attended college. Ferrante caught 21 passes and scored seven touchdowns. Kilroy, a hard-hitting 6-foot 2-inch, 240-pounder, played middle guard in the defensive line.

1946 Neale added impressive talent to the Eagles' roster, trading for Alex Wojciechowicz, an outstanding center and linebacker, and Joe Muha, a rugged rookie fullback and punter. The Eagles also signed Bosh Pritchard, a quick, breakaway halfback, who was just completing his military duty, and 5-foot 9-inch, 175-pound Russ Craft, a defensive back, from the University of Alabama. An injury to Van Buren slowed the offense, however, and the Eagles' record slipped to 6–5. Van Buren rushed for 529 yards, third in the league.

1947 The last piece fit into Neale's offensive puzzle when the Eagles signed Pete Pihos, a 6-foot 1-inch, 215-pound rookie fullback from Indiana. The Eagles didn't need a fullback, so Neale made Pihos an end. Neale devised the "Pihos screen," a short pass behind the line to Pihos. The threat of Pihos caused defenses to spread out, opening more holes for Van Buren and fullback Pritchard. Van Buren set a league record by rushing for 1,008 yards and 13 touchdowns. Thompson completed 53 percent of his passes. Meanwhile, Neale's Eagle defense caused havoc. He stacked the middle of his line with the likes of Kilroy and Vic Sears and used his linebackers outside to hold up and intimidate the offensive ends. It was a 5–2–4 alignment, extremely physical, with the four deep backs playing up close. It was called the "Eagle" because the Eagles played it. They won their first Eastern Division title, beating Pittsburgh in a playoff 21–0, December 21. The Chicago Cardinals defeated the Eagles in the NFL championship game 28–21 at frozen Comiskey Park, December 28. The Eagles filed their cleats before the game to get better traction, but were discovered doing it and prohibited from wearing the sharpened cleats. Van Buren, slipping on the ice in flat-soled shoes, gained just 26 yards in 18 carries.

1948 The Eagles were winless in their first two games, losing 21–14 to the Chicago Cardinals and tying the Los Angeles Rams 28–28. They caught fire with back-to-back 45–0 victories over the New York Giants and Washington Redskins and Neale's team was unstoppable the rest of the year. Thompson ran the T formation to perfection and completed 57 per-

cent of his passes, and threw for 25 touchdowns. Van Buren led the league's rushers for the third time with 945 yards. Pritchard added seven touchdowns, four on runs, two on passes, and one on a punt return. Pihos caught 46 passes, 11 for touchdowns. Muha led the league with a 47.2-yard punting average. Neale even had the NFL's best kicker, Cliff (Automatic) Patton who converted 50 of 50 extra points and 8 of 12 field goal attempts. Captain Al Wistert, a tenacious 6-foot 1-inch, 215-pounder, was an all-pro tackle. The Eagles won their second Eastern Division title with a 9–2–1 record. They won their first world championship with a 7–0 victory over the Chicago Cardinals at Shibe Park, December 19. The game was played in a blinding snowstorm. Van Buren woke up that morning, saw the snow, and went back to bed, assuming the game was postponed. He was awakened by a phone call from Neale, rode to the stadium in a trolley car, and scored the game's only touchdown on a five-yard run.

1949 Lex Thompson sold the Eagles to a syndicate of 100 local businessmen, organized by James P. Clark, for $250,000, January 15. Vince McNally was named general manager. In the first round of the draft, the Eagles selected Chuck Bednarik, All-America center-linebacker from the University of Pennsylvania. The Eagles rolled through the regular season, winning 11 games and losing only one. The Eagles won the Eastern Division for the third straight year. Van Buren set another league record, rushing for 1,146 yards. The Eagles' most impressive victory was a 38–14 trouncing of the previously unbeaten Los Angeles Rams at Shibe Park. The Rams and Eagles met again in the world championship game in Los Angeles Memorial Coliseum, December 18. A heavy rain turned the field into a quagmire but it didn't slow the Eagles' punishing running attack, which rolled up 274 yards to the Rams' 21. Van Buren carried the ball 31 times for 196 yards to lead the Eagles' 14–0 championship triumph. The Eagles scored on Thompson's 31-yard pass to Pihos and a blocked punt by rookie end Leo Skladany.

1950 In the first week of the season, the defending NFL champion Eagles were matched against the Browns, the upstart newcomers from the All-America Football Conference, before a record 71,237 at Philadelphia's Municipal Stadium. The Browns pulled a stunning 35–10 upset foreshadowing the Eagles' decline. The Eagles won six of their next seven but Van Buren was sidelined with a foot injury and the team lacked the power to handle the top opponents. They lost their last four games to fall to third place in the Eastern Division. A feud between Neale and owner Clark erupted late in the season when the players had to pull Neale off Clark in the Polo Grounds' locker room. Neale was fired following the season.

1951 The Eagles named Alvin (Bo) McMillin head coach in February. McMillin, a successful college coach at Indiana, directed the Eagles to victories in their first two games but illness forced him to resign. Wayne Millner succeeded McMillin and the team sagged to 4–8. Van Buren played on the bad foot and gained just 327 yards on 112 carries. Adrian Burk succeeded the retired Thompson at quarterback and threw a league-high 23 interceptions. One bright note was the addition of Bobby Walston, a 6-foot, 190-pound end and placekicker from the University of Georgia. Walston caught 31 passes, scored eight touchdowns, and added 46 points kicking. He was named NFL rookie of the year.

1952 Former coach Bo McMillin died of stomach cancer. Van Buren suffered a serious knee injury at training camp and retired. The club fired Millner and named Jim Trimble head coach, September 9. Trimble acquired Bobby Thomason from Green Bay and made him the starting quarterback. Trimble also

moved Harry (Bud) Grant, the Eagles' top draft choice from Minnesota in 1951, ahead of Pihos at offensive end. Trimble felt Pihos would be more effective as a defensive end. The moves paid off as the Eagles won seven games and tied the New York Giants for second place. Grant caught 56 passes, seven for touchdowns, to rank second among NFL receivers. With Van Buren gone, most of the ball carrying was done by John Huzvar, a plodding 6-foot 4-inch, 240-pound fullback from North Carolina State.

1953 Clark retired as president and was named chairman of the board. Frank L. McNamee was elected club president. Trimble kept the Eagles in contention despite the loss of Grant, who jumped to the Canadian Football League. Trimble switched Pihos back to offense and he responded by catching 63 passes for 1,049 yards and 10 touchdowns to lead the NFL. Walston caught 41 passes as Thomason and Burk combined to pass for a league-high 3,089 yards. The Eagles had good balance in their running game with three backs—Don Johnson, Jerry Williams, and Frank Ziegler—totaling more than 1,100 yards. Rookie defensive back Tom Brookshier of Colorado led the club with eight interceptions. The highlight of the year came the final week, when the Eagles upset Cleveland 42–27 to spoil the Browns' hopes for a perfect season.

1954 The Eagles beat Cleveland 28–10 in the opener at Shibe Park, stirring hopes of a return to glory. The Eagles won their first four games, including a 49–21 rout of Washington, to take the early lead in the Eastern Division. The Eagles then lost four of five games, including a 6–0 rematch with the Browns. For the third straight year, the Eagles finished second with seven wins. Pihos caught 60 passes to share the NFL receiving title with the 49ers' Billy Wilson. Walston caught 11 touchdown passes and led the league in scoring with 114 points.

1955 The Eagles overcame a 10-point deficit to defeat the New York Giants 27–17 in the league opener at Shibe Park, but the victory was costly. Bucko Kilroy, the all-pro tackle starting his one hundred and first consecutive game, tore ligaments in his knee and never played again. The defense recovered gradually as Norman (Wildman) Willey and Tom Scott developed into a pair of top-flight pass rushing ends. Young Jess Richardson, who played at Alabama, was groomed to replace Kilroy. Bednarik had another great season at linebacker. Pihos continued to show the way on offense, leading the NFL in pass receiving for the third straight year with 62 catches. The Eagles were plagued by an ineffective running game and suffered only their second losing season since 1951.

1956 Trimble was dismissed after four seasons as head coach. Hugh Devore, a Notre Dame graduate, was named to succeed him. The Eagles' veteran nucleus disappeared. Kilroy, Pihos, and defensive tackle Mike Jarmoluk all retired, leaving Devore with the weakest team in the Eastern Division. The Eagles' best runner was Ken Keller, a rookie from North Carolina, who gained 433 yards. The passing attack slipped badly due to the loss of Pihos. The strength of the team was a good defensive secondary, including Brookshier, Ed (Bibbles) Bawel, Jerry Norton, and Eddie Bell.

1957 The Eagles had their best college draft, selecting Michigan State fullback Clarence Peaks, halfbacks Billy Ray Barnes of Wake Forest, and Tommy McDonald of Oklahoma, and quarterback Sonny Jurgensen of Duke. Devore wanted to cut McDonald, claiming he was too small to make it at running back. Assistant coach Charlie Gauer resisted, pleading that McDonald could be a great pass receiver. Devore relented and kept McDonald but refused to play him. Under constant prodding by Gauer, Devore finally used McDonald at flanker against Washington and the

5-foot 10-inch, 180-pound speedster caught two touchdown passes in a 21–12 win. Jurgensen split time with Thomason at quarterback and led the Eagles to a 17–7 upset of Cleveland. Barnes and Peaks combined for more than 1,000 yards rushing. The Eagles won only four games but they had promise for the future.

1958 Devore was fired and Buck Shaw hired as head coach. Shaw saw long-range potential in Jurgensen, but felt the Eagles needed an experienced quarterback to win in the next few years. He traded tackle Buck Lansford, defensive back Jim Harris, and a first-round draft choice to Los Angeles for 32-year-old Norm Van Brocklin. Shaw put together an exciting passing attack, employing McDonald at flanker and moving Pete Retzlaff, a 6-foot 1-inch, 210-pound fullback, to split end. Retzlaff, who was cut by Detroit in 1956, was a duplicate of Pihos with superb hands and an uncanny ability for running patterns. In his first year as a regular, Retzlaff caught 56 passes to tie Baltimore's Raymond Berry for the NFL receiving title. McDonald caught just 29 passes but nine went for touchdowns. Although the Eagles finished the year in last place (2–9–1), Van Brocklin predicted major improvement for next season. The Eagles also moved their home site from Connie Mack Stadium to the University of Pennsylvania's Franklin Field and attendance almost doubled.

1959 Led by Bednarik at center, the Eagles' offensive line gave Van Brocklin time to find his receivers. Given time, the Dutchman could pick apart almost any defense as he proved in a stunning 49–21 upset of the New York Giants, September 22. The win gave the younger Eagles confidence and they swept six of eight games to challenge New York and Cleveland for the Eastern Conference lead. McDonald was virtually unstoppable as he caught 47 passes and scored 11 touchdowns, one on an 81-yard punt return, the longest in Eagles' history. Bert Bell, the one-time Eagles owner and then NFL commissioner, died, October 11. Bell suffered a fatal heart attack while watching the Eagles beat Pittsburgh 28–24 at Franklin Field. The Eagles had a chance to finish alone in second place but they lost to Cleveland 28–21 in the final week. The Eagles and Browns finished tied at 7–5.

1960 The Eagles were jolted by the Cleveland Browns 41–24 in the league opener at Franklin Field. But under the fierce leadership of Van Brocklin and Bednarik, the Eagles regrouped to win their next nine games and clinch their first Eastern Division title in 11 years. The key victory was a 31–29 thriller over Cleveland in which Bobby Walston kicked a 39-yard field goal with two seconds left. The Eagles wrapped up the division with back-to-back wins over the New York Giants, 17–10 and 31–23. Peaks broke his leg at midseason and was replaced by Ted Dean, a rookie from Wichita who also was the club's leading kick returner. A Dean touchdown broke open the second win over New York. When injuries depleted the defense, Bednarik, who was 35, began playing at both center and outside linebacker. The Eagles' running game was weak—only the expansion Dallas Cowboys rushed for fewer yards—but Van Brocklin had a great season, passing for 2,471 yards and 24 touchdowns. Retzlaff, McDonald, and Walston caught a total of 115 passes. The Eagles won their third world championship defeating Green Bay 17–13 before 67,325 fans at Franklin Field, December 26. The Eagles won the title in their typical fashion, coming from behind in the fourth quarter on Dean's five-yard end sweep. After the game, Shaw retired as head coach and Van Brocklin retired as a player. Van Brocklin was the overwhelming choice as the NFL's most valuable player.

1961 The year began with unexpected turmoil as Shaw's top assistant, Nick Skorich, was named head

coach. Van Brocklin was outraged, claiming the Eagles' management had promised he would succeed Shaw. McNally had asked Van Brocklin to stay on as player-coach but he refused, saying "That stuff went out with Johnny Blood." Van Brocklin left to become head coach of the Minnesota Vikings. Few people expected the Eagles to repeat as Eastern Conference champions with the unproved Jurgensen taking over at quarterback. But Jurgensen bombed every secondary he faced, and the Eagles won seven of their first eight games, holding onto first place. The Eagles' title hopes collapsed, however, when Brookshier suffered a broken leg in a 16–14 win over Chicago. Skorich inserted a rookie, Glen Amerson, in Brookshier's spot and New York and Cleveland picked on Amerson to rout the Eagles 38–21 and 45–24. The Eagles still had a chance to catch the Giants late in the season but a controversial roughing-the-kicker penalty against Leo Sugar helped New York beat Philadelphia again, 28–24. The Eagles lost to Detroit in the Playoff Bowl 38–10. But Jurgensen suffered a shoulder separation and tackle J. D. Smith broke his leg. Jurgensen had emerged as the best passer in the NFL, setting two league records—235 completions and 3,723 yards—and tying a third—32 touchdowns.

1962 James P. Clark, former president and chairman of the board of the Eagles, died, April 17. Injuries continued to haunt the Eagles. Jurgensen never fully recovered from his shoulder injury, then went down with a loose knee cartilage. Retzlaff, Walston, and reserve tight end Dick Lucas all suffered broken arms. Peaks and Dean were sidelined with broken bones in their feet. Reserve fullback Theron Sapp was lost with a shoulder separation. Howard (Hopalong) Cassady played only four games before breaking his leg. Don (The Blade) Burroughs, the team's leading pass interceptor, suffered cracked ribs. Only Tommy McDonald, the smallest man on the team, stayed healthy, catching 58 passes and scoring 10 touchdowns. The Eagles struggled through a bleak 3–10–1 season but Jurgensen provided some thrills, completing 33 of 57 passes against New York and throwing for five touchdowns at St. Louis. Timmy Brown amassed 341 yards total offense, in the finale against the Cardinals.

1963 Problems began in training camp as Jurgensen and backup quarterback King Hill left camp to dramatize their demands for more money. Management gave in and the quarterbacks returned. The loss of Bednarik, who retired after 14 brilliant NFL seasons, left a leadership void in the defense. The club also was hit with more injuries as Jurgensen reinjured his arm. McDonald separated his shoulder, Peaks dislocated his elbow, linebacker Maxie Baughan broke his thumb, and tackle Frank Fuller broke his leg. The only bright spot was Brown, who set an NFL record for most total offense in a season, 2,428 yards. Jerry Wolman, an energetic young building tycoon, purchased the sagging franchise for $5.5 million, December 5.

1964 Wolman signed Joe Kuharich, former coach of the Chicago Cardinals and Washington Redskins, to succeed Skorich, February 27. Kuharich quickly dismantled the team, trading McDonald to Dallas, Jurgensen and safety Jim Carr to Washington, Lee Roy Caffey and a first-round draft pick to Green Bay, Dean to Minnesota, and Peaks to Pittsburgh. In return, Kuharich received quarterback Norm Snead, running backs Ollie Matson and Earl Gros, center Jim Ringo, defensive tackle Floyd Peters, and kicker Sam Baker. The Eagles opened with a 38–7 victory over the New York Giants as they successfully employed Burroughs on safety blitzes to harass the immobile Y. A. Tittle. They won four of their first seven games to quiet the grumbling fans, who missed the electrifying Jurgensen-to-McDonald combination. Baker set a

club record of 16 field goals. Kuharich was also named general manager.

1965 The Eagles' record slipped to 5–9 but the team showed encouraging progress, particularly on the offensive line, where Bob Brown, the 6-foot 4-inch, 280-pound former Nebraska All-America, asserted himself at tackle. Ed Blaine, a former Green Bay Packer, matured into a solid guard, as did Jim Skaggs. This youthful group was balanced by Ringo, the 34-year-old former all-pro center. With the line clearing the way, Timmy Brown rushed for 861 yards, third best in the NFL. Retzlaff, switched to tight end at age 34, caught 66 passes for 1,190 yards and 10 touchdowns.

1966 Kuharich traded away two more popular players, shipping Baughan and cornerback Irv Cross to Los Angeles for tackle Frank Molden, linebacker Fred Brown, cornerback Aaron Martin, and flanker Willie Brown. After a sluggish start, the Eagles got their offense going as the line opened big holes for Brown, Gros, and two promising fullbacks, Tom Woodeshick and Izzy Lang. The potent running game offset a dismal season by Snead. With Kuharich rotating his quarterback position among Snead, King Hill, and Jack Concannon, a young scrambler from Boston College, the Eagles won seven of their last nine to tie Cleveland for second place. Typical of the helter-skelter season was a 24–23 upset of division champion Dallas in which Brown returned two kickoffs for touchdowns and Martin scored on a punt return. The Eagles were beaten 20–14 by Baltimore in the Playoff Bowl in Miami.

1967 Inspired by the Eagles' first winning season in five years, Wolman rewarded Kuharich with a 15-year contract as coach and general manager. Kuharich traded Concannon to Chicago for all-pro tight end Mike Ditka and sent Gros to Pittsburgh for split end Gary Ballman. The Eagles' defense collapsed, allowing 409 points. Snead made a strong comeback, climbing to fifth in NFL passing with a club record 3,400 yards and 29 touchdowns. When injuries slowed Ditka and Ballman, Snead turned to Ben Hawkins and the second-year flanker from Arizona State responded, catching 59 passes for 1,265 yards (a club record) and 10 touchdowns.

1968 The tone for the year was established in the preseason opener, when Snead suffered a broken leg on the first play from scrimmage. Running back Timmy Brown was traded to Baltimore for offensive back and kick return specialist Alvin Haymond. After 17 years of training at Hershey, Pennsylvania, the Eagles moved to Albright College, Reading, Pennsylvania. The Eagles lost their first 11 league games, inspiring hope among Eagles' fans that the team would go winless and earn the right to select USC All-America O.J. Simpson in the draft. When the Eagles won two of their last three games, Buffalo (1–12–1) moved past them in the drafting position. Fans organized a "Joe [Kuharich] Must Go" movement, distributing "Joe Must Go" buttons and even paying a skywriter to spread their message above Franklin Field as the Eagles lost to Minnesota 24–17. The season ended with Wolman desperately trying to avoid bankruptcy.

1969 The beleaguered Wolman was forced to sell the franchise to Leonard Tose, a Norristown, Pennsylvania, trucking magnate, for $16.1 million. Tose fired Kuharich, agreeing to pay him for the duration of his contract and hired Retzlaff, the former all-pro receiver, as general manager. Retzlaff hired Jerry Williams, former Eagles halfback and assistant, as head coach. Retzlaff traded Bob Brown and Izzy Lang to Los Angeles for defensive halfback Irv Cross, tackle Joe Carollo, guard Don Chuy, and receiver Harold Jackson. The Eagles drafted Leroy Keyes, the versatile Purdue halfback. Due to a lengthy contract dispute, Keyes did not join the Eagles until September and was slow rounding into shape. Williams used Keyes on offense but he was a disappointment, averaging just three yards per carry. Jackson blossomed with playing time in Philadelphia and caught 65 passes for a league-high 1,116 yards. Jackson and Hawkins combined to give the Eagles scoring punch, catching 17 touchdown passes between them.

1970 Williams planned to switch Keyes to cornerback when a torn Achilles tendon sidelined him. Woodeshick, the leading rusher for three years, injured his knee in preseason training and carried the ball just 52 times. Bill Bradley, heralded as an outstanding safety, suffered torn knee ligaments in the preseason opener and was lost for the year. Tim Rossovich, a defensive end converted to middle linebacker, tore ligaments in his ankle during the preseason but refused to undergo surgery. Rossovich started all 14 league games and led the team with 174 tackles. The Eagles lost their first seven games and spent the season in last place in the Eastern Division. The highlight of the year was a 23–20 upset of the New York Giants in a Monday night television game. Rookie Lee Bouggess caught 50 passes, more than any running back in the NFL.

1971 The Eagles moved to Veterans Stadium with a seating capacity of 66,052. After suffering crushing defeats in the first three league games, Tose fired Williams and promoted defensive line coach Ed Khayat to head coach. Williams called a press conference and bitterly denounced Tose as "a man of little character." The players drafted a statement supporting Williams, and the franchise bordered on anarchy for a week. Khayat, an admirer of General George Patton, ordered all players to cut their hair and shave off their mustaches. Several players, led by Rossovich, resisted before giving in. Quarterback Norm Snead was traded to Minnesota. The Eagles won six and tied one of their final nine games. Bill Bradley set a team record and led the NFL with 11 pass interceptions.

1972 Khayat's stern discipline backfired the second year. Keyes, Bouggess, and linebacker Steve Zabel all suffered serious injuries in a training camp where contact drills were long and punishing. Bradley and Rossovich staged a joint contract holdout which degenerated into a power struggle between Retzlaff and the two players. Retzlaff settled the matter by trading Rossovich to San Diego, and Bradley later signed his contract. Pete Liske played erratically at quarterback and was replaced by John Reaves, the number one draft pick from the University of Florida. Reaves displayed a strong arm and courage working behind the Eagles' blockers but his inexperience led to costly mistakes. The franchise hit an all-time low when the New York Giants buried the Eagles 62–10 at Yankee Stadium. The morning following the season finale, Tose accepted Retzlaff's resignation and fired the entire coaching staff. Bradley became the first player in NFL history to win the interception title two consecutive years; he had nine.

1973 Tose hired Mike McCormack, long-time assistant in Washington, as head coach. An excellent draft yielded Texas tackle Jerry Sisemore, USC tight end Charles Young, Texas Christian center Guy Morriss, Michigan safety Randy Logan, and San Diego cornerback Joe Lavender. McCormack traded a draft choice to Baltimore for fullback Norm Bulaich, then dealt Harold Jackson, plus two number one draft picks, to Los Angeles for Roman Gabriel, a 33-year-old quarterback. Gabriel became the NFL's comeback player of the year as he led the league in four passing categories, including 23 touchdowns. The 6-foot 5-inch Young teamed with 6-foot 8-inch Harold Carmichael and 6-foot 4-inch Don Zimmerman to give the Eagles the tallest receiving corps in football. Carmichael led the NFL with 67 pass receptions. Young led all tight ends with 55. Tom Sullivan emerged as a quality halfback, rushing for 968 yards.

The Eagles won five games, including a 30–16 upset of Dallas.

1974 Hoping to patch up a porous defense, McCormack traded two first-round draft picks and one second to Cincinnati for middle linebacker Bill Bergey. After a disappointing 7–3 loss to St. Louis in the opener, the Eagles won four straight and surged into contention for the first time since 1961. A 31–24 loss in Dallas broke the momentum and the Eagles lost six straight games, forcing McCormack to bench Gabriel and start rookie Mike Boryla at quarterback for the final three weeks. Boryla, a former Stanford star, displayed remarkable poise in his first NFL exposure directing victories over Green Bay, the New York Giants, and Detroit. Young caught 63 passes to lead all NFL receivers. Bergey, an all-pro, made 160 tackles and led the team with five interceptions. After the season, Tose appointed Jim Murray, the team's administrative assistant, as general manager.

1975 The Eagles lost their first two games to opponents they were favored to beat—the New York Giants (23–14) and Chicago (15–13). Following the Chicago loss McCormack remarked that there were two "dogs" on his roster. The statement came to haunt McCormack as the entire squad seethed at the label. With the team floundering at 2–8, McCormack benched Gabriel and went back to Boryla. Boryla won two of his four starts as the Eagles finished 4–10. Three of the losses came on last second field goals. The Eagles defeated Washington twice, their first series sweep of the Redskins since 1961. Following the season, Tose announced he would not renew McCormack's contract.

1976 Tose hired Dick Vermeil to become the Eagles' fifth head coach in nine years, February 8. Vermeil had gained national prominence a month earlier when this underdog UCLA team upset top-ranked Ohio State 23–10 in the Rose Bowl. Gabriel was slow recovering from off-season knee surgery and did not rejoin the team until mid-October. Given the starting spot, Boryla threw eight interceptions in the first three games. Vermeil won his first game as an NFL coach when the Eagles beat the New York Giants 20–7 at Veterans Stadium, September 19. Vermeil uncovered a potential star runner in rookie Mike Hogan, a ninth-round draft pick from Tennessee–Chattanooga. Hogan missed half the season with a dislocated shoulder and still led the team with 561 yards rushing. The Eagles went through a prolonged slump, losing eight of nine games, as the offense scored just two touchdowns in four weeks. The Eagles didn't score more than two touchdowns in the same game until the final week, when they trounced Seattle 27–10.

MEMBERS OF HALL OF FAME:

Chuck Bednarik, Bert Bell, Bill Hewitt, Ollie Matson, Earle (Greasy) Neale, Pete Pihos, Norm Van Brocklin, Steve Van Buren, Alex Wojciechowicz.

EAGLES RECORD, 1933–76

Year	Won	Lost	Tied	Pct.	Pts.	OP
1933	3	5	1	.375	77	158
1934	4	7	0	.364	127	85
1935	2	9	0	.182	60	179
1936	1	11	0	.083	51	206
1937	2	8	1	.200	86	177
1938	5	6	0	.455	154	164
1939	1	9	1	.100	105	200
1940	1	10	0	.091	111	211
1941	2	8	1	.200	119	218
1942	2	9	0	.182	134	239
1943	5	4	1	.556	225	230
1944	7	1	2	.875	267	131
1945	7	3	0	.700	272	133
1946	6	5	0	.545	231	220
1947§	8	4	0	.667	308	242
1948‡	9	2	1	.818	376	156
1949‡	11	1	0	.917	364	134
1950	6	6	0	.500	254	141
1951	4	8	0	.333	234	264
1952	7	5	0	.583	252	271
1953	7	4	1	.636	352	215
1954	7	4	1	.636	284	230
1955	4	7	1	.364	248	231
1956	3	8	1	.273	143	215
1957	4	8	0	.333	173	230
1958	2	9	1	.182	235	306
1959	7	5	0	.583	268	278
1960‡	10	2	0	.833	321	246
1961	10	4	0	.714	361	297
1962	3	10	1	.231	282	356
1963	2	10	2	.167	242	381
1964	6	8	0	.429	312	313
1965	5	9	0	.357	363	359
1966	9	5	0	.643	326	340
1967	6	7	1	.462	351	409
1968	2	12	0	.143	202	351
1969	4	9	1	.308	279	377
1970	3	10	1	.231	241	332
1971	6	7	1	.462	221	302
1972	2	11	1	.179	145	352
1973	5	8	1	.393	310	393
1974	7	7	0	.500	242	217
1975	4	10	0	.286	225	302
1976	4	10	0	.286	165	386
44 Years	215	305	22	.417	10,098	11,177

§NFL Eastern Division Champion
‡NFL Champion

RECORD HOLDERS

Rushing (Yards)	Steve Van Buren, 1949	1,146
Passing (Pct.)	Roman Gabriel, 1973	58.7
Passing (Yards)	Sonny Jurgensen, 1961	3,723
Passing (TDs)	Sonny Jurgensen, 1961	32
Receiving (No.)	Harold Carmichael, 1973	67
Receiving (Yards)	Ben Hawkins, 1967	1,265
Interceptions (No.)	Bill Bradley, 1971	11
Punting (Avg.)	Joe Muha, 1948	47.2
Punt Ret. (Avg.)	Steve Van Buren, 1944	15.3
Kickoff Ret. (Avg.)	Al Nelson, 1972	29.1
Touchdowns (Total)	Steve Van Buren, 1945	18
Field Goals Made	Tom Dempsey, 1973	24
Points (No.)	Bobby Walston, 1954	114

COACHING HISTORY

1933–35	Lud Wray	9–21–1
1936–40	Bert Bell	10–44–2
1941–50	Earle (Greasy) Neale	63–43–5
1951	Alvin (Bo) McMillin*	2– 0–0
1951	Wayne Millner	2– 8–0
1952–55	Jim Trimble	25–20–3
1956–57	Hugh Devore	7–16–1
1958–60	Lawrence (Buck) Shaw	19–16–1
1961–63	Nick Skorich	15–24–3
1964–68	Joe Kuharich	28–41–1
1969–71	Jerry Williams**	7–22–2
1971–72	Ed Khayat	8–15–2
1973–75	Mike McCormack	16–25–1
1976	Dick Vermeil	4–10–0

*Retired after two games in 1951
**Replaced after three games in 1971

FIRST PLAYER SELECTED

1936	Jay Berwanger, B, Chicago	
1937	Sam Francis, B, Nebraska	
1938	Jim McDonald, B, Ohio State	
1939	Davey O'Brien, B, TCU	
1940	George McAfee, B, Duke	
1941	Art Jones, B, Richmond	
1942	Pete Kmetovic, B, Stanford	
1943	Joe Muha, B, VMI	
1944	Steve Van Buren, B, Louisiana State	
1945	John Yonaker, E, Notre Dame	
1946	Leo Riggs, B, USC	
1947	Neill Armstrong, E, Oklahoma A&M	
1948	Clyde (Smackover) Scott, B, Arkansas	
1949	Chuck Bednarik, C, Pennsylvania	
1950	Harry (Bud) Grant, E, Minnesota	
1951	Ebert Van Buren, B, Louisiana State	
1952	Johnny Bright, B, Drake	
1953	Al Conway, B (2), Army	
1954	Neil Worden, B, Notre Dame	
1955	Dick Bielski, B, Maryland	
1956	Bob Pellegrini, C, Maryland	
1957	Clarence Peaks, B, Michigan State	
1958	Walt Kowalczyk, B, Michigan State	
1959	J.D. Smith, T (2), Rice	
1960	Ron Burton, RB, Northwestern	
1961	Art Baker, RB, Syracuse	
1962	Pete Case, G (2), Georgia	
1963	Ed Budde, G, Michigan State	
1964	Bob Brown, T, Nebraska	
1965	Ray Rissmiller, T (2), Georgia	
1966	Randy Beisler, DE, Indiana	
1967	Harry Jones, RB, Arkansas	
1968	Tim Rossovich, DE, USC	
1969	Leroy Keyes, RB, Purdue	
1970	Steve Zabel, TE, Oklahoma	
1971	Richard Harris, DE, Grambling	
1972	John Reaves, QB, Florida	
1973	Jerry Sisemore, T, Texas	
1974	Mitch Sutton, DT (3), Kansas	
1975	Bill Capraun, T (7), Miami	
1976	Mike Smith, DE (4), Florida	

Neill Armstrong *Sam Baker* *Billy Ray Barnes* *Eddie Bell* *Bob Brown* *Don Burroughs* *Marion Campbell*

PHILADELPHIA EAGLES, 1933–76

Absher, Dick, LB, Maryland 1972
Adams, Gary DB, Arkansas 1969
Agajanian, Ben, K, New Mexico 1945
Alexander, Kermit, S, UCLA 1972–73
Allen, Chuck, LB, Washington 1972
Allen, Jackie, DB, Baylor 1972
Allison, Henry, G, San Diego State 1971–72
Amerson, Glen, B, Texas Tech 1961
Amundson, George, RB, Iowa State 1975
Andrews, Leroy, B, Pittsburg State 1934
Antwine, Houston, DT, So. Illinois 1972
Armstrong, Neill, E, Oklahoma A&M 1947–51
Arnold, Jay, B, Texas 1937–40
Arrington, Rick, QB, Tulsa 1970–73
Aschbacher, Darrel, G, Oregon 1959
Auer, Howard, T, Michigan 1933

B

Bailey, Howard, T, Tennessee 1935
Bailey, Tom, B, Florida State 1971–74
Baisi, Albert, G, West Virginia 1947
Baker, John, DE, North Carolina College 1962
Baker, Sam, K, Oregon State 1964–69
Baker, Tony, B, Iowa State 1970–72
Ballman, Gary, E, Michigan State 1967–72
Banas, Stephen, B, Notre Dame 1935
Banducci, Bruno, G, Stanford 1944–45
Banta, Jack, B, USC 1941, 1944–45
Barnes, Bill, B, Wake Forest 1957–61
Barnes, Walter, G, Louisiana State 1948–51
Barnhart, Dan, B, Centenary 1934
Barni, Roy, B, San Francisco 1954–55
Barnum, Leonard, B, West Va. Wesleyan 1940–42
Bartholomew, Sam, B, Tennessee 1941
Basca, Nick, B, Villanova 1941
Bassi, Dick, G, Santa Clara 1940
Bassman, Herman, B, Ursinus 1936
Baughan, Maxie, LB, Georgia Tech 1960–65
Bauman, Alfred, T, Northwestern 1947
Bausch, Frank, C, Kansas 1940–41
Bawel, Ed R., B, Evansville 1952, 1955–56
Baze, Winford, B, Texas Tech 1937
Beaver, Jim, G, Florida 1962
Bednarik, Chuck, C–LB, Pennsylvania 1949–62
Beisler, Randy, DE, Indiana 1966–68
Bell, Eddie, B, Pennsylvania 1955–58
Benson, Harry, G, Western Maryland 1935
Bergey, Bill, LB, Arkansas State 1974–76
Berry, Dan, B, California 1967
Berzinski, Willie, B, Lacrosse, Wisconsin 1956
Bielski, Dick, B, Maryland 1955–59
Binotto, John, B, Duquesne 1942
Bjorklund, Robert, C, Minnesota 1941
Blaine, Ed, G, Missouri 1963–66
Bleamer, Jeff, T, Penn State 1975–76
Bleeker, Mel, B, USC 1944–46
Blye, Ron, RB, Notre Dame 1969
Boedecker, William, B, DePaul 1950
Bogren, Vince, E, New Mexico 1944
Boryla, Mike, QB, Stanford 1974–76
Bouggess, Lee, B, Louisville 1970–73
Bova, Tony, E, St. Francis 1943
Bradley, Bill, DB, Texas 1969–76
Bradley, Harold, G, Iowa 1958
Bredice, John, E, Boston 1956
Brennan, Leo, T, Holy Cross 1942
Brewer, John, B, Louisville 1952–53
Brian, William, T, Gonzaga 1935–36
Brodnicki, Chuck, C, Temple 1934
Brooks, Clifford, DB, Tennessee State 1975–76
Brookshier, Tom, B, Colorado 1953, 1956–61
Brown, Bob, T, Nebraska 1964–68
Brown, Fred, LB, Miami 1967–69
Brown, Timmy, B, Ball State 1960–67
Brown, Willie, FL, USC 1966
Brumm, Don, DE, Purdue 1970
Brunski, Andrew, C, Temple 1943
Budd, Frank, E, Villanova 1962
Bukant, Joe, B, Washington, St. Louis 1938–40
Bulaich, Norm, RB, Texas Christian 1973–74
Bull, Ron, B, Baylor 1971
Bunting, John, LB, North Carolina 1972–76

Burk, Adrian, QB, Baylor 1951–56
Burnette, Tom, B, North Carolina 1938
Burnine, Hank, E, Missouri 1956–57
Burroughs, Don, DB, Colorado State 1960–64
Bushby, Thomas, B, Kansas State 1935
Buss, Art, T, Michigan State 1936–37
Butler, Bob, G, Kentucky 1962
Butler, John, B, Tennessee 1943, 1945
Burke, Mark, DB, West Virginia 1976
Byrne, Bill, G, Boston College 1963

C

Cabrelli, Larry, E, Colgate 1941–47
Caffey, Lee Roy, LB, Texas A&M 1963
Cagle, Jim, DT, Georgia 1974
Cahill, Dave, DT, Arizona State 1966
Calloway, Ernie, DT, Texas Southern 1969–72
Campbell, Glenn, E, Emporia Teachers 1935
Campbell, Marion, T, Georgia 1956–61
Campbell, Stan, G, Iowa State 1959–61
Campbell, Tommy, CB, Iowa State 1976
Campion, Thomas, T, S. E. Louisiana 1947
Canale, Rocco, G, Boston College 1943–45
Carmichael, Harold, E, Southern U. 1971–76
Carollo, Joe, T, Notre Dame 1969–70
Carpe, Joe, T, Millikin 1933
Carr, Jim, B, Morris Harvey 1959–63
Carroccio, Russ, G, Virginia 1955
Carter, Joe, E, Southern Methodist 1933–40
Case, Pete, G, Georgia 1962–64
Cassady, Howard, B, Ohio State 1962
Castiglia, Jim, B, Georgetown 1941, 1945–46
Catlin, Tom, LB, Oklahoma 1959
Cemore, Tony, G, Creighton 1941
Ceppetelli, Gene, C, Villanova 1968–69
Cherundolo, Chuck, C, Penn State 1940

Chesson, Wes, WR, Duke 1973–74
Chuy, Don, G, Clemson 1969
Cifelli, Gus, T, Notre Dame 1954
Clark, Al, CB, Eastern Michigan 1976
Clark, Mike, K–E, Texas A&M 1963
Clark, Myers, B, Ohio State 1934
Clayton, Don, T, None 1936
Cody, Bill, LB, Auburn 1972
Colavito, Rocky, LB, Wake Forest 1975
Cole, J., B, St. Joseph's 1938–40
Coleman, Al, S, Tennessee State 1972
Colman, Wayne, LB, Temple 1968–69
Combs, William, E, Purdue 1942
Concannon, Jack, QB, Boston College 1964–66
Conjar, Larry, B, Notre Dame 1968
Conti, Enio, G, Bucknell 1941–45
Cooke, Ed, E, Maryland 1958
Coston, Fred, C, Texas A&M 1939
Cothren, Paige, K, Mississippi 1959
Cowhig, Gerry, B, Notre Dame 1951
Crabb, Claude, DB, Colorado 1964–65
Craft, Russ, B, Alabama 1946–53
Creech, Bob, LB, Texas Christian 1971–72
Cronin, Bill, E, Boston College 1965
Cross, Irv, DB, Northwestern 1961–65, 1969
Crowe, Larry, EB, Texas Southern 1972
Cuba, Paul, T, Pittsburgh 1933–35
Cullars, Willie, DE, Kansas State 1974
Cunningham, Dick, LB, Arkansas 1973
Cuppoletti, Bree, G, Oregon 1939–40

D

D'Agostino, Frank, G, Auburn 1956
Davis, Al, DB, Tennessee State 1971–72
Davis, Bob, B, Kentucky 1942
Davis, Norm, G, Grambling 1970

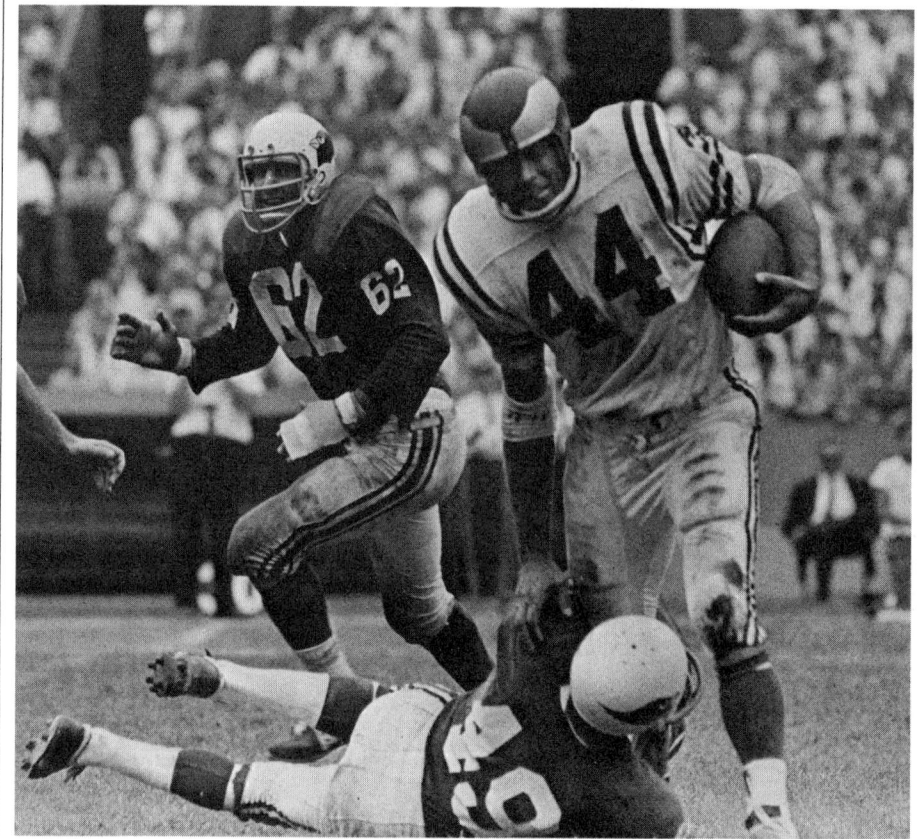

End Pete Retzlaff surrounded by St. Louis Cardinals, 1966.

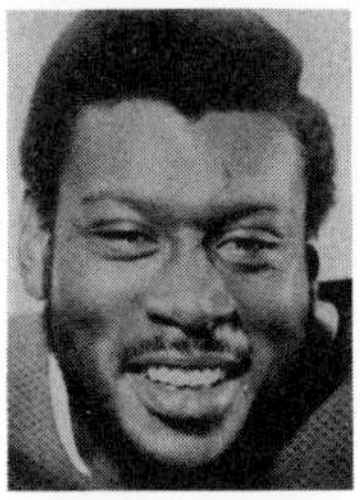
Harold Carmichael

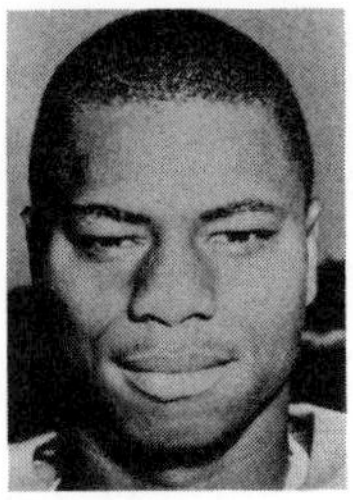
Irv Cross

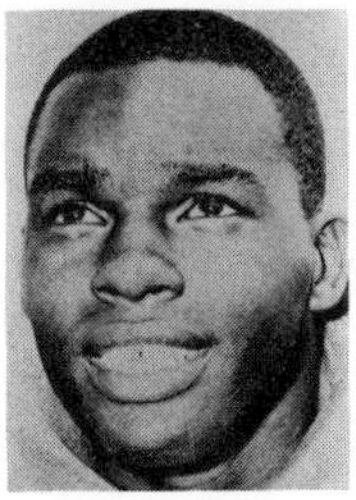
Ted Dean

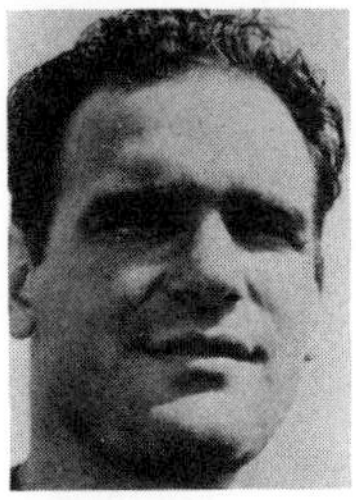
Jack Ferrante

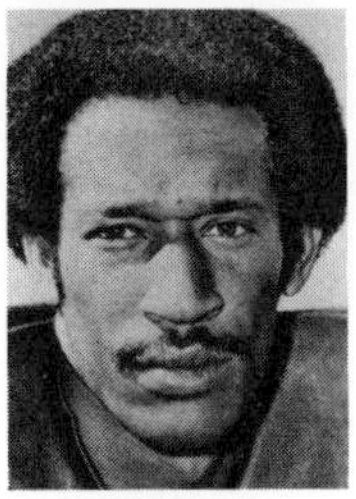
Ben Hawkins

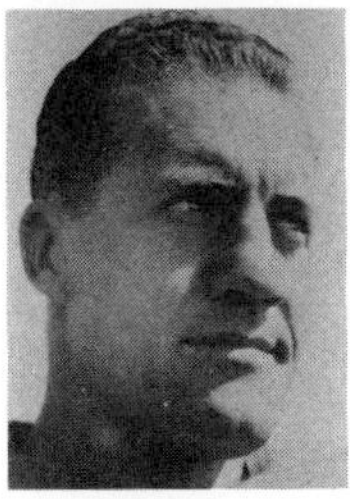
Vic Lindskog

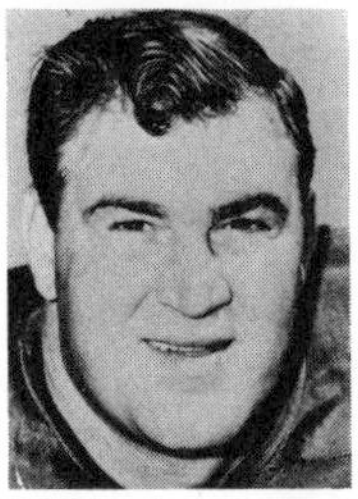
Dave Lloyd

Davis, Stan, WR, Memphis State 1973
Davis, Sylvester, B, Geneva 1933
Davis, Vern, DB, W. Michigan 1971
Dean, Ted, B, Wichita 1960–63
DeLucca, Jerry, T, Mid. Tennessee 1959
Demas, George, G, Washington & Jefferson 1933
Dempsey, Jack, T, Bucknell 1934, 1937
Dempsey, Tom, K, Palomar J.C. 1971–74
DeSantis, Dan, B, Niagara 1941
Dial, Benjy, B, E. New Mexico 1967
DiFilippo, Dave, G, Villanova 1941
Dimmick, Tom, T, Houston 1956
Dirks, Mike, G, Wyoming 1968–72
Disend, Leo, T, Albright 1943
Ditka, Mike, TE, Pittsburgh 1967–68
Dobbins, Herb, T, San Diego State 1974
Dorow, Al, B, Michigan State 1957
Doss, Noble, B, Texas 1947–48
Douglas, Merrill, B, Utah 1962
Douglas, Otis, T, William & Mary 1946–49
Dow, Elwood, B, West Texas State 1938–40
Dowda, Harry, B, Wake Forest 1954–55
Doyle, Ted, T, Nebraska 1943
Dudley, Paul, B, Arkansas 1963
Duncan, Rick, K, E. Montana State 1968
Dunstan, Bill, DT, Utah State 1973–76
Durko, John, E, Albright 1944

E

Ehlers, Tom, LB, Kentucky 1975–76
Elbner, John, T, Kentucky 1941–42, 1946
Elden, Edmund, B, Scranton 1944
Ellis, Drew, T, Texas Christian 1938–40
Ellstrom, Marvin, B, Oklahoma City 1934
Emelianchik, Pete, E, Richmond 1967
Emmons, Franklin, B, Oregon 1940
Enke, Fred, B, Arizona 1952
Erdlitz, Richard, B, Northwestern 1942, 1945
Estes, Larry, DE, Alcorn A&M 1972
Evans, Mike, C, Boston College 1968–73

F

Fagioli, Carl, G, None 1944
Farragut, Ken, C, Mississippi 1951–54
Feather, E. E., B, Kansas State 1933
Felber, Fred, E, North Dakota 1933
Feller, Happy, K, Texas 1971
Fenci, Richard, E, Northwestern 1933
Ferko, John, G, West Chester State 1937–38
Ferrante, Jack, E, None 1941, 1944–50
Ferris, Neil, B, Loyola, L.A. 1952
Fiedler, William, G, Pennsylvania 1938
Field, Richard, G, None 1939–40
Ford, Charles, DB, Houston 1974
Fox, Terry, B, Miami 1941, 1945
Frahm, Herald, B, Nebraska 1935
Frank, Joseph, T, Georgetown 1941, 1943
Franks, Dennis, C, Michigan 1976
Freeman, Bob, B, Auburn 1960–61
Frey, Glenn, B, Temple 1936–37
Friedlund, Bob, E, Michigan State 1946
Friedman, Bob G, Washington 1944
Fritts, George, T, Clemson 1945
Fritz, Ralph, G, Michigan 1941
Fuller, Frank, DT, Kentucky 1963

G

Gabriel, Roman, QB, North Carolina State 1973–76
Gambold, Bob, B, Washington State 1953
Gaona, Bob, T, Wake Forest 1957
Gauer, Charles, E, Colgate 1943–45
Gay, Blenda, DE, Fayetteville State 1975–76
George, Ed, G, Wake Forest 1976
George, Raymond, T, USC 1940
Gerber, Elwood, G, Alabama 1941–42
Gersbach, Carl, LB, West Chester State 1970
Getchell, Gorham, E, Temple 1943
Ghecas, Lou, B, Georgetown 1941
Giancanelli, H., B, Loyola, Calif. 1953–56
Giannelli, Mario, G, Boston College 1948–51
Gibbs, Pat, DB, Lamar 1972
Gibron, Abe, G, Purdue 1956–57
Giddens, Herschel, T, Louisiana Tech 1938
Gill, Roger, B, Texas Tech 1964–65
Ginney, Jerry, G, Santa Clara 1940
Glass, Glenn, B, Tennessee 1964–65
Gloden, Fred, B, Tulane 1941
Glover, Rich, DT, Nebraska 1975
Goldston, Ralph, B, Youngstown 1952, 1954–55
Gollomb, Rudy, G, John Carroll 1936
Gonya, Robert, T, Northwestern 1933–34
Goode, Rob, B, Texas A&M 1955
Goodwin, Ron, E, Baylor 1963–68
Gossage, Gene, E, Northwestern 1960–62
Graham, Dave, T, Virginia 1963–69
Graham, Lyle, C, Richmond 1941
Graham, Tom, G, Temple 1935
Grant, Harry, E, Minnesota 1951–52
Graves, Ray, C, Tennessee 1942–43, 1946
Gray, Jim, B, Toledo 1967
Green, John, E, Tulsa 1947–51
Gregory, Ken, E, Whittier 1962
Gros, Earl, B, Louisiana State 1964–66
Gudd, Leonard, E, Temple 1934
Gude, Henry, G. Vanderbilt 1946
Guglielmi, Ralph, QB, Notre Dame 1963
Guillory, Tony, LB, Lamar Tech 1969
Gunnels, John, T, Georgia 1960–64

H

Hackney, Elmer, B, Kansas State 1940–41
Hairston, Carl, DE, Maryland State 1976
Hajek, Charles, C, Northwestern 1934
Hall, Irving, B, Brown 1942
Halverson, Dean, LB, Washington 1973–75
Halverson, William, T, Oregon State 1942
Hamilton, Ray, E, Arkansas 1940
Hampton, Dave, RB, Wyoming 1976
Hansen, Roscoe, T, North Carolina 1951
Hanson, Thomas (Swede), B, Temple 1933–37
Harding, Roger, C, California 1947
Harper, Maurice, C, Austin 1937–40
Harris, Jim, B, Oklahoma 1957
Harris, Richard, DE, Grambling 1971–73
Harrison, Bob, LB, Oklahoma 1962–63
Harrison, Granville, E, Mississippi State 1941
Hart, Dick, G, None 1967–71
Hartman, Fred, T, Rice 1948
Harvey, Richard, DB, Jackson State 1970
Hawkins, Ben, FL, Arizona State 1966–73
Hayden, Ken, C, Akansas 1942
Hayes, Ed, DB, Morgan State 1970
Haymond, Alvin, DB, Southern U. 1968
Heck, Ralph, LB, Colorado 1963
Henson, Gary, E. Colorado 1963
Hershey, Kirk, E, Cornell 1941
Hewitt, Bill, E, Michigan 1936–39, 1943
Higgin, Tom, T, North Carolina 1954–55
Hill, Fred, E, USC 1965–71
Hill, King, B, Rice 1961–68
Hinkle, Jack, B, Syracuse 1941–47
Hix, Billy, E, Arkansas 1950
Hoague, Joe, B, Colgate 1943
Hobbs, Bill, LB, Texas A&M 1969
Hogan, Mike, RB, Tennessee-Chattanooga 1976
Holcomb, William, T. Texas Tech 1937
Hord, Roy, G, Duke 1962
Horrell, Bill, G, Michigan State 1952
Hoss, Clark, TE, Oregon 1972
Howell, Lane, OT, Grambling 1965–69
Hoyem, Lynn, G, Long Beach State 1964–67
Hrabetin, Frank, T, Loyola 1942
Huarte, John, QB, Notre Dame 1968
Hudson, Bob, B, Clemson, ... 1953–55, 1957–58
Hughes, Chuck, FL, Texas-El Paso 1967–69
Hughes, William, C, Texas 1937–50
Hultz, Don, DT, So. Mississippi 1964–73
Humbert, Dick, E, Richmond 1941, 1945–49
Hunt, Calvin, C, Baylor 1970
Huth, Gerry, G, Wake Forest 1959–60
Huxhold, Ken, G, Wisconsin 1954–58
Huzvar, John, B, N. Carolina State 1952

I

Ignatius, James, G, Holy Cross 1935
Illman, Ed, B, Montana 1933
Irvin, Willie, B, Florida A&M 1953

J

Jackson, Bob, B, Alabama 1960
Jackson, Don, B, North Carolina 1936
Jackson, Harold, WR, Jackson State 1969–72
Jackson, Randy, RB, Wichita State 1974
Jackson, Trenton, FL, Illinois 1966
Jacobs, Proverb, T, California 1958
James, Ron (Po), RB, New Mexico State 1972–75
Janet, Ernie, T, Washington 1975
Jarmoluk, Mike, T, Temple 1949–55
Jarvi, Toimi, B, No. Illinois 1944
Jefferson, William, B, Mississippi State 1942
Johnson, Albert, B, Kentucky 1942
Johnson, Alvin, B, Hardin-Simmons 1948
Johnson, Don, B, California 1953–55
Johnson, Gene, B, Cincinnati 1959–60
Johnson, Jay, LB, E, Texas State 1969
Jonas, Don, B, Penn State 1962
Jones, Don, B, Washington 1940
Jones, Harry, B, Arkansas 1967–71
Jones, Joe, DE, Tennessee State 1974–75
Jones, Ray, DB, Southern U. 1970
Jones, Spike, P, Georgia 1975–76
Jorgenson, Carl, T, St. Mary's 1935
Jurgensen, Sonny, QB, Duke 1957–63

K

Kane, Carl, B, St. Louis 1936
Kapele, John, T, Brigham Young 1962
Kaplan, Bernie, G, Western Maryland 1942
Karnofsky, Sonny, B, Arizona 1945
Kasky, Ed, T, Villanova 1942
Kavel, George, B, Carnegie Tech 1934
Keeling, Ray, T, Texas 1938–39
Keen, Allen, B, Arkansas 1937–38
Kekeris, Jim, T, Missouri 1947
Keller, Ken, B, North Carolina 1956–57
Kelley, Bob, C, W. Texas State 1955–56
Kelley, Dwight, LB, Ohio State 1966–72
Kelly, Jim, E, Notre Dame 1965–67
Kenneally, George, E, St, Bonaventure 1933–35
Kersey, Merritt, P, West Chester State 1974–75
Key, Wade, T, S.W. Texas State 1970–76
Keyes, Leroy, DB, Purdue 1969–72
Keys, Howard, T-C, Oklahoma State 1960–64
Khayat, Ed, T, Tulane 1958–61, 1964–65
Kilroy, Frank, T, Temple 1943–55
King, Don, T, Kentucky 1956
Kirkman, Roger, B, Wash. & Jefferson 1933–35
Kirksey, Roy, G, Maryland State 1973–74
Kish, Ben, B, Pittsburgh 1942–49
Klopenburg, Harry, T, Fordham 1936
Kmetovic, Pete, B, Stanford 1946
Knapper, Joe, B, Ottawa, Ken 1934
Knox, Charles, T, St. Edmonds 1937
Koeninger, Art, C, Chattanooga 1933
Kolberg, Elmer, B, Oregon State 1939–40
Koman, Bill, LB, North Carolina 1957–58
Konopka, John, B, Temple 1936
Kostos, Anthony, E, Bucknell 1933
Kowalczyk, Walt, B, Michigan State 1958–59
Kramer, Kent, TE, Minnesota 1972–74
Krepfle, Keith, TE, Iowa State 1975–76
Kresky, Joseph, G, Wisconsin 1933–35
Krieger, Robert, E, Dartmouth 1941, 1946
Kriel, Emmet, G, Baylor 1939
Kuczynski, Bert, E, Pennsylvania 1946
Kupcinet, Irv, B, North Dakota 1935
Kusko, John, B, Temple 1936–38

L

Laack, Galen, G, Pacific 1958
Lachman, Dick, B, None 1933–35
Lainhart, Porter, B, Washington State 1933
Landsberg, Mort, B, Cornell 1941
Lang, Israel, B, Tennessee State 1964–68
Lankas, James, B, St. Mary's 1942
Lansford, Buck, T, Texas 1955–57
Lapham, Bill, C, Iowa 1960
Laux, Ted, B, St. Joseph's 1942–44
Lavender, Joe, DB, San Diego State 1973–75

Tommy McDonald   *Joe Muha*   *Davey O'Brien*   *Clarence Peaks*   *Gary Pettigrew*   *Bosh Pritchard*   *Pete Retzlaff*

Lawrence, Kent, WR, Georgia	1969
Lazetich, Pete, DT, Stanford	1976
Leathers, Milton, G, Georgia	1933
Ledbetter, Toy, B, Oklahoma A&M	1950, 1953–55
Lechthaler, Roy, G, Lebanon Valley	1933
Lee, Bernie, B, Villanova	1938
LeMaster, Frank, LB, Kentucky	1974–76
Leonard, Jim, B, Notre Dame	1934–37
Levanites, Stepnen, T, Boston College	1942
Lewis, Joe, T, Compton J.C.	1962
Leyendecker, Charles, T, Vanderbilt	1933
Lince, Dave, E, North Dakota	1966–67
Lindskog, Vic, C, Stanford	1944–51
Lio, Augie, C, Georgetown	1946
Lipski, John C, Temple	1933–34
Liske, Pete, QB, Penn State	1971–72
Lloyd, Dave, LB, Georgia	1963–70
Logan, Randy, DB, Michigan	1973–76
Looney, Don, E, Texas Christian	1940
Lou, Ron, C, Arizona State	1975
Louderback, Tom, LB, San Jose State	1958–59
Lucas, Dick, E, Boston College	1960–63
Lueck, Bill, G, Arizona	1975
Luft, Don, E, Indiana	1954
Luken, Tom, G, Purdue	1972–75
Lusk, Herb, RB, Long Beach State	1976

M

Macioszczyk, Art, B, Western Michigan	1944–47
Mack, William, FL, Notre Dame	1964
Mackrides, Bill, B, Nevada	1947–51
Magee, John, G, Rice	1948–55
Mahalic, Drew, LB, Notre Dame	1976
Mallory, John, B, West Virginia	1968
Malone, Art, RB, Arizona State	1975–76
Mandarino, Mike, G, La Salle	1944–45
Manning, Roosevelt, DT, Northeast Oklahoma	1975
Mansfield, Ray, C, Washington	1963
Manske, Edgar (Eggs), E, Northwestern	1935–36
Manton, Taldon, B, Texas Christian	1940
Manzini, Baptiste, C, St. Vincent's	1944–45, 1948
Marchi, Basilio, C, New York U	1941–42
Marcus, Alex, E, Temple	1933
Maronic, Duke, G, None	1944–50
Marshall, Larry, RB, Maryland	1974–76
Martin, Aaron, DB, N. Carolina Coll	1966–67
Mass, Wayne, T, Clemson	1972
Masters, Bob, B, Baylor	1937–38, 1941–43
Masters, Walt, B, Pennsylvania	1936
Matesic, Ed, B, Pittsburgh	1934–35
Matson, Ollie, B, San Francisco	1964–66
Mavraides, Menil, G, Notre Dame	1954, 1957
Maynard, Les, B, Rider	1933
Mazzanti, Jerry, E, Arkansas	1963
MacAfee, Ken, E, Alabama	1959
MacDowell, Jay, E, Washington	1946–51
MacMurdo, Jim, T, Pittsburgh	1934–37
McAfee, Wesley, B, Duke	1941
McAlister, James, RB, UCLA	1975–76
McChesney, Bob, E, Hardin-Simmons	1950
McClellan, Mike, B, Oklahoma	1962–73
McCullough, Hugh, B, Oklahoma	1943
McCusker, Jim, T, Pittsburgh	1959–62
McDonald, Don, E, Oklahoma	1944–45
McDonald, Lester, E, Nebraska	1940
McDonald, Tommy, FL, Oklahoma	1957–63
McDonough, Robert, G, Duke	1942–46
McHugh, Pat, B, Georgia Tech	1947–51
McKeever, Marlin, LB, USC	1973
McNeill, Tom, P, Stephen F, Austin	1971–73
McPherson, Forest, T, Nebraska	1935–37
Meadows, Ed, E, Duke	1958
Medved, Ron, DB, Washington	1966–70
Mellekas, John, T, Arizona	1963
Meyers, John, T, Washington	1964
Meyer, Fred, E, Stanford	1942, 1945
Michaels, Ed, G, Villanova	1943–46
Michels, John, G, Tennessee	1953
Milam, Barnes, G, Austin	1934
Miller, Don, B, Southern Methodist	1954
Miller, Tom, E, Hampden-Sydney	1942–44
Milling, Al, G, Richmond	1942
Mira, George, QB, Miami	1969

Mitcham, Gene, E, Arizona State	1958
Molden, Fran, T, Jackson State	1968
Morgan, Dennis, RB, Western Illinois	1975
Morgan, Mike, LB, Louisiana State	1964–67
Morriss, Guy, C, Texas Christian	1973–76
Mortell, Emmett, B, Wisconsin	1937–39
Moseley, Mark, K, Stephen F, Austin	1970
Moselle, Dom, B, Superior, Wisconsin	1954
Mrkonic, George, T, Kansas	1953
Muha, Joe, B, VMI	1946–50
Muhlmann, Horst, K, None	1975–76
Mulligan, George, E, Catholic U.	1936
Murley, Dick, T, Purdue	1956
Murray, Francis, B, Pennsylvania	1939–40
Myers, Brad, B, Bucknell	1958
Myers, Jack, B, UCLA	1948–50

N

Nacrelli, Andy, E, Fordham	1958
Nelson, Al, DB, Cincinnati	1965–73
Nelson, Dennis, T, Illinois State	1976
Nettles, Jim, DB, Wisconsin	1965–68
Newton, Charles, B, Washington	1939–40
Niland, John, G, Iowa	1975
Nipp, Maurice, G, Loyola, Calif.	1952–53, 1956
Nocera, John, LB, Iowa	1959–62
Norby, Jack, B, Idaho	1934
Nordquist, Mark, G, Pacific	1968–74
Norton, Jerry, B, Southern Methodist	1954–58
Norton, Jim, T, Washington	1968
Nowak, Walt, E, Villanova	1944

O

Oakes, Don, T, Virginia Tech	1961–62
O'Boyle, Harry, B, Notre Dame	1933
O'Brien, Davey, B, Texas Christian	1939–40
Obst, Henry, G, Syracuse	1933
Olds, Bill, RB, Nebraska	1976
Oliver, Greg, RB, Trinity, Texas	1973–74
Opperman, Jim, LB, Colorado State	1975
O'Quinn, John, E, Wake Forest	1951
Ordway, William, B, North Dakota	1939
Oristaglio, Bob, E, Pennsylvania	1952
Ormsbee, Elliott, B, Bradley Tech	1946
Osborne, Richard, TE, Texas A&M	1976
Outlaw, John, DB, Jackson State	1973–76
Overmeyer, Bill, LB, Ashland	1972
Owens, Don, T, So. Mississippi	1958–60

P

Padlow, Max, E, Ohio State	1935
Pagliei, Joe, B, Clemson	1959
Palmer, Leslie, B, N. Carolina State	1948
Papale, Vince, WR, St. Joseph's, Pa.	1976
Pape, Orrin, B, Iowa	1933
Parker, Artimus, DB, USC	1974–76
Parmer, Jim, B, Oklahoma A&M	1948–56
Paschka, Gordon, G, Minnesota	1943
Pate, Rupert, G., Wake Forest	1942
Patton, Cliff, G, Texas Christian	1946–50
Patton, Jerry, DT, Nebraska	1974
Peaks, Clarence, B, Michigan State	1957–63
Pegg, Harold, C, Bucknell	1940
Pellegrini, Bob, LB, Maryland	1956, 1958–61
Peters, Floyd, T, S, F, State	1964–69
Peters, Volney, T, USC	1958
Pettigrew, Gary, DT, Stanford	1966–74
Philbin, Gerry, DE, Buffalo State	1973
Piasecky, Albert, E, Duke	1942
Picard, Bob, WR, Eastern Washington	1973–76
Pihos, Pete, E, Indiana	1947–55
Pilconis, Joe, E, Temple	1934, 1936–37
Pinder, Cyril, B, Illinois	1968–70
Piro, Henry, E, Syracuse	1941
Pitts, Alabama, B, None	1935
Pivarnick, Joe, G, Notre Dame	1936
Poage, Ray, E, Texas	1964–65
Pollard, Al, B, Army	1951–53
Pollock, William, B, Penn Military	1937, 1942–43
Porter, Ron, LB, Idaho	1969–72
Poth, Phil, G, Gonzaga	1934
Powell, Art, B, San Jose State	1959
Preece, Steve, DB, Oregon State	1970–72

Prescott, Harold, E, Hardin-Simmons	1947–49
Priestly, Robert, E, Brown	1942
Prisco, Nick, B, Rutgers	1933
Pritchard, Bosh, B, VMI	1942, 1946–51
Pylman, Bob, T, S. Dakota State	1938–39

Q

Quinlan, Bill, E, Michigan State	1963

R

Rado, George, E, Duquesne	1937–38
Ragazzo, Phil, T, Western Reserve	1940–41
Ramsey, Herschel, E, Texas Tech	1938–40, 1945
Ramsey, Knox, G, William & Mary	1952
Ramsey, Nate, DB, Indiana	1963–72
Raskowski, Leo, T, Ohio State	1935
Ratliff, Don, DE, Maryland	1975
Rauch, John, B, Georgia	1951
Raye, Jim, DB, Michigan State	1969
Reagan, Frank, B, Pennsylvania	1949–51
Reaves, John, QB, Florida	1972–75
Recher, Dave, C, Iowa	1965–68
Reed, Taft, B, Jackson State	1967
Reese, Henry, C, Temple	1935–39
Reeves, Marion, DB, Clemson	1974
Reichow, Jerry, E, Iowa	1960
Reilly, Kevin, LB, Villanova	1973–74
Renfro, Will, E. Memphis State	1961
Restic, Joe, E, Villanova	1952
Retzlaff, Pete, E, S. Dakota State	1956–66
Reutt, Ray, E, VMI	1943
Ricca, Jim, T, Georgetown	1955–56
Richards, Bobby, E, Louisiana State	1962–65
Richardson, Jess, T, Alabama	1953–61
Riffle, Dick, B, Albright	1938–40
Riley, Lee, B, Detroit	1956, 1958–59
Ringo, Jim, C, Syracuse	1964–67
Rissmiller, Ray, T, Georgia	1966
Roberts, John, B, Georgia	1933–34
Robinson, Burle, E, Brigham Young	1935
Robinson, Wayne, LB, Minnesota	1952–56
Robb, Joe, DE, Texas Christian	1959–60
Roffler, William, B, Washington State	1954
Rogala, John, B, Scranton	1945
Rogas, Dan, G, Tulane	1952
Romero, Ray, G, Kansas State	1951
Rossovich, Tim, LB, USC	1968–71
Roton, Herbert, E, Auburn	1937
Roussel, Tom, LB, Southern Mississippi	1973
Rowan, Everitt, E, Ohio State	1933
Rowe, Robert, B, Colgate	1935
Russell, James, T, Temple	1936–37
Russell, Laf, B, Northwestern	1933
Ryan, Rocky, E, Illinois	1956–58

S

Sader, Steve, B, None	1943
Saidock, Tom, T, Michigan State	1957
Sanders, John, G, Southern Methodist	1943, 1945
Sandifer, Dan, B, Louisiana State	1950–51
Sapp, Theron, B, Georgia	1959–63
Savitsky, George, T, Pennsylvania	1948–49
Scarpati, Joe, DB, N. Carolina St.	1964–69, 1971
Schaefer, Don, B, Notre Dame	1956
Schmitt, Ted, C, Pittsburgh	1938–40
Schnelker, Bob, E, Bowling Green	1953
Schneller, Bill, B, Mississippi	1940
Schrader, Jim, C, Notre Dame	1962–64
Schuehle, Jake, B, Rice	1939
Schultz, Eberle, G, Oregon State	1940, 1943
Scott, Clyde, B, Arkansas	1949–52
Scott, Tom, E, Virginia	1953–58
Scotti, Ben, DB, Maryland	1962–63
Sears, Vic, T, Oregon State	1941–53
Sebastian, Mike, B, Pittsburgh	1935
Shann, Bob, B, Boston College	1965, 1967
Sharkey, Ed, T, Duke	1954–55
Shaub, Harry, G, Cornell	1935
Sherman, Allie, B, Brooklyn	1943–47
Shires, Marshall, T, Tennessee	1945
Shonk, John, E, West Virginia	1941
Simerson, John, C, Purdue	1957–58
Sisemore, Jerry, T, Texas	1973–76

Jesse Richardson

Jerry Sisemore

Tom Sullivan

Tommy Thompson

Jerry Williams

Tom Woodeshick

Charles Young

Sistrunk, Manny, DT, Arkansas AM&N 1976
Skaggs, Jim, G, Washington 1963–72
Skladany, Leo, E, Pittsburgh 1949
Smeja, Rudy, E, Michigan 1946
Smith, Charles, WR, Grambling 1974–76
Smith, J.D., T, Rice 1959–63
Smith, Jack, T, Florida 1945
Smith, Jackie, DB, Troy State 1971
Smith, John, E, Stanford 1942
Smith, Milton, E, UCLA 1945
Smith, Ray, C, Missouri 1933
Smith, Ralph, E, Mississippi 1962–64
Smith, Richard, C, Ohio State 1933
Smith, Robert, B, Nebraska 1956
Smith, Steve, T, Michigan 1971–74
Smukler, Dave, B, Temple 1936–39
Snead, Norman, B, Wake Forest 1964–70
Snyder, Lum, T, Georgia Tech 1952–55, 1958
Sodaski, John, LB, Villanova 1972–73
Sokolis, Stan, T, Pennsylvania 1933
Somers, George, T, La Salle 1939–40
Spillers, Ray, T, Arkansas 1937
Stackpool, John, B, Washington 1942
Stafford, Dick, E, Texas Tech 1962–63
Stasica, Leo, B, Colorado 1941
Steele, Ernie, B, Washington 1942–48
Steele, Dick, T, Drake 1951
Steinbock, Laurence, T, St. Thomas 1933
Steinke, Gil, B, Texas A&I 1945–48
Stetz, Bill, G, Boston College 1967
Stevens, Don, B, Illinois 1952, 1954
Stevens, Pete, C, Temple 1936
Stevens, Richard, T, Baylor 1970–74
Steward, Dean, B, Ursinus 1943
Stickel, Walt, T, Pennsylvania 1950–51
Stockton, Herschel, G, McMurry 1937–38
Storm, Edward, B, Santa Clara 1934–35
Stribling, Bill, E, Mississippi 1955–57

Striegel, Bill, G, Pacific 1959
Stringer, Bob, B, Tulsa 1952–53
Stuart, Roy, T, Tulsa 1943
Sturgeon, Cecil, T, N. Dakota State 1941
Sturm, Jerry, C, Illinois 1972
Suffridge, Bob, G, Tennessee 1941–45
Sugar, Leo, E, Purdue 1961
Sullivan, Tom, RB, Miami 1972–76
Supulski, Leonard, E, Dickinson 1942
Sutton, Joe, B, Temple 1950–52
Sutton, Mitch, DT, Kansas 1974–75
Szafaryn, Len, T, North Carolina 1957–58
Szymanski, Frank, C, Notre Dame 1948

T

Talcott, Don, T, Nevada 1947
Taliaferro, George, B, Indiana 1955
Tarasovic, George, E, Louisiana State 1963–65
Tarver, John, RB, Colorado 1975
Tasef, Carl, DB, John Carroll 1961
Tautolo, Terry, LB, UCLA 1976
Thacker, Alvin, B, Morris Harvey 1941
Thomason, Bobby, B, VMI 1952–57
Thomason, Stumpy, B, Georgia Tech 1935–36
Thompson, Don, E, Richmond 1964
Thompson, Russ, T, Nebraska 1940
Thompson, Tommy, B, Tulsa 1941–42, 1945–50
Thornton, Richard, B, Missouri Mines 1933
Thrower, Jim, DB, E, Texas State 1970–72
Thurbon, Robert, B, Pittsburgh 1943
Tom, Mel, DE, San Jose State 1967–73
Tomasetti, Lou, B, Bucknell 1940–42
Tracey, John, E, Texas A&M 1961
Tripucka, Frank, QB, Notre Dame 1949
Trost, Milton, T, Marquette 1940
Troup, Bill, QB, South Carolina 1975
Turnbow, Guy, T, Mississippi 1933–34
Tyrrell, Joe, G, Temple 1952

U

Uperesa, Tuufuli, G, Montana 1971
Urevig, Claude, B, North Dakota 1935

V

Van Brocklin, Norm, QB, Oregon 1958–60
Van Buren, Ebert, B, Louisiana State 1951–53
Van Buren, Steve, B, Louisiana State 1944–51
Van Dyke, Bruce, G, Missouri 1966
Vasys, Arunas, LB, Notre Dame 1966–68

W

Walik, Billy, WR, Villanova 1970–72
Walston, Robert, E, Georgia 1951–62
Walters, Stan, T, Syracuse 1975–76
Walton, John, QB, Elizabeth City State 1976
Ward, Jim, QB, Gettysburg 1971–72
Warren, Buist, B, Tennessee 1945
Watkins, Foster, B, W. Texas State 1940–41
Watkins, Larry, B, Alcorn A&M 1970–72
Wear, Robert, C, Penn State 1942
Weatherall, Jim, T, Oklahoma 1955–57
Weber, Chuck, LB, West Chester State 1959–61
Weedon, Don, G, Texas 1947
Wegert, Ted, B, None 1955–56
Weiner, Albert, B, Muhlenberg 1934
Weinstock, Isadore, B, Pittsburgh 1935
Wells, Billy, B, Michigan State 1958
Wells, Harold, LB, Purdue 1965–68
Wendlick, Joseph, E, Oregon State 1940
West, Hodges, T, Tennessee 1941
Whalen, Bob, E, Boston College 1971
White, John, B, Georgia 1933
White, Allison, T, Texas Christian 1939
Whittingham, Fred, LB, Cal. Poly 1966, 1971
Wiatrak, John, C, Washington 1939
Wilcox, John, T, Oregon 1960
Will, Erwin, DT, Dayton 1965
Willey, Norman, E, Marshall 1950–57
Williams, Boyd, C, Syracuse 1947
Williams, Clyde, T, Georgia Tech 1935
Williams, Jerry, B, Washington State 1953–54
Williams, Roger, QB, Grambling 1973
Williams, Ted, B, Boston College 1942
Williams, Tex, G, Auburn 1942
Wilson, Osborne, G, Pennsylvania 1933–35
Wilson, Bill, E, Gonzaga 1938
Wilson, Harry, B, Nebraska 1967–70
Wilson, Jerry, E, Auburn 1959–60
Winfield, Vern, G, Minnesota 1972
Wink, Dean, DT, Yankton, S.D. 1967–68
Wirgowski, Dennis, DE, Purdue 1973
Wistert, Al, T, Michigan 1943–51
Wittenborn, John, G, S.E. Missouri State 1960–62
Wojciechowicz, Alex, C, Fordham 1946–50
Wolfe, Hugh, B, W. Texas Teachers 1940
Woltman, Clem, T, Purdue 1938–40
Woodeshick, Tom, B, West Virginia 1963–71
Woodruff, Lee, B, Mississippi 1933
Worden, Neil, B, Notre Dame 1954, 1957
Woulfe, Mike, LB, Colorado 1962
Wright, Gordon, G, Delaware State 1967
Wukits, Al, C, Duquesne 1943
Wyhonic, John, G, Alabama 1946–47
Wydo, Frank, T, Cornell 1952–57
Wynn, William, DE, Tennessee State 1973–76

Y

Young, Adrian, LB, USC 1968–72
Young, Charles, TE, USC 1973–76
Youngelman, Sid, T, Alabama 1956–58
Yovicsin, John, E, Gettysburg 1944

Z

Zabel, Steve, E-LB, Oklahoma 1970–74
Ziegler, Frank, B, Georgia Tech 1949–53
Zilly, John, E, Notre Dame 1952
Zimmerman, Don, WR, Northeast Louisiana 1972–76
Zimmerman, Roy, B, San Jose State 1942–46
Zizak, Vince, T, Villanova 1934–37
Zyntell, James, G, Holy Cross 1933–35

Floyd Peters (72), Dave Lloyd (52) stop 49ers' Ken Willard, 1966.

PITTSBURGH STEELERS

1933 Art Rooney, Sr., 32, a former semipro football player and boxer, purchased an NFL franchise for $2,500. Rooney, a highly successful horse handicapper, bought the team with the winnings from a profitable weekend at New York's Saratoga race track. Rooney named the team the "Pirates" after Pittsburgh's National League baseball club. He scheduled home games for Forbes Field but ran into a legal snag when he was informed the state's Blue Law prohibited professional sports on Sunday. Rooney circumvented the problem by giving the superintendent of police free box seats to the games. The Pirates' first coach was Forrest (Jap) Douds. The new team lost its home opener 23–2 to the New York Giants and went on to compile a 3–6–2 record.

1934 Rooney appointed Luby DiMelio head coach and acquired Johnny Blood (McNally), the eccentric but gifted halfback, in a trade with Green Bay. Blood was injured and missed the entire season as the Pirates finished in last place for the second straight year. Their best player was rookie tailback Warren Heller from the University of Pittsburgh who led the team in rushing (528 yards) and passing (112 attempts, 31 completions).

1935 Rooney sent Blood back to Green Bay and tried his third head coach in three years, hiring Joe Bach, the successful Duquesne coach. The Pirates stunned Philadelphia 17–7 in the first game, but lost their next four games. The Pirates had a good defense against the rush but were vulnerable to the pass. Their top lineman was Joe (Tiny) Wiehl, a 5-foot 11-inch, 255-pound tackle from Duquesne.

1936 Bach installed an unbalanced line offense that helped the Pirates win their first three games and take the lead in the Eastern Division. The only games the Pirates lost were to Western Division opponents—Chicago, Green Bay, and Detroit. With one game left in the season, the Pirates (6–5) needed only to beat the Boston Redskins to clinch the division title. However, Rooney had already promised a friend that his team would play an exhibition game on the West Coast. The Pirates were forced to travel by train from Pittsburgh to California and then back to Boston for the big game. Exhausted by the journey, the Pirates lost 30–0 to the Redskins and finished in second place.

1937 Bach returned to his first love, college coaching, and Rooney was forced to look for another head coach. He signed Johnny Blood, 32, as a player-coach and appointed tackle Walt Kiesling as his assistant. The unpredictable Blood ignored curfews and encouraged his players to do the same. "He would vanish for days at a time," Rooney said, "and show up, claiming he had been at the library." In his first game, Blood returned the opening kickoff for a touchdown against the Eagles, turned to his players and said: "Boys, that's the way it should be done." The Pirates, inspired by their extraordinary coach, won their first two games, upset the title-bound Washington Redskins and finished third in the Eastern Division. Blood was the leading receiver with 10 catches, including four for touchdowns.

1938 Rooney signed Byron (Whizzer) White for $15,800, the largest contract in pro football to that date. White, an All-America halfback at Colorado University, agreed to play for the Pirates only after postponing his acceptance of a Rhodes scholarship. White, a 6-foot 1-inch, 195-pound power runner, rushed for a league-leading 567 yards. The Pirates were in contention at midseason, but unknown to Blood, Rooney sold quarterback Frank Filchock to Washington. Without the threat of Filchock's passes, defenses ganged up to stop White and the Pirates lost

Running back Franco Harris against San Francisco, 1973.

their last six games, scoring only two touchdowns.

1939 White left for Oxford University in England and his studies as a Rhodes scholar, suggesting he might never return to pro football. Rooney sold the rights to him to the Detroit Lions. Without White, the Steelers fell on hard times. They won only one game and tied another, losing nine. They were hopelessly outclassed. Blood tried everything but could not lift the team's sagging spirit. When the Bears clobbered the Pirates 32–0, Blood packed his bags and walked out. Kiesling took over as head coach and began enforcing curfew and bedchecks. The Pirates averted a winless season by upsetting Philadelphia 24–12 in their final game.

1940 Kiesling obtained tailback Billy Patterson from Chicago but he was a disappointment, rushing for just 171 yards and throwing 15 interceptions. The Pirates never got their offense untracked but a rugged defense enabled them to go unbeaten through their first three games—one win and two ties. The Pirates managed just one touchdown in the next five weeks, however, and lost all five games. Pittsburgh never scored more

than 10 points in any game and finished with two victories. The showing left Rooney so discouraged he sold the franchise to Alexis Thompson.

1941 Rooney bought into the Philadelphia Eagles with Bert Bell. By April, Thompson was yearning to get back to Philadelphia and Rooney was homesick for Pittsburgh, so they swapped franchises. Back in Pittsburgh, Rooney decided to revamp his team, starting with the nickname. He sponsored a contest for a new name and the winner was "Steelers," suggested by the wife of ticket manager Joe Carr. Bell opened the season as head coach but stepped down after the Steelers lost two games. Rooney hired Buff Donelli, who tried to coach the Steelers and Duquesne at the same time. After five games (all losses), Commissioner Elmer Layden ordered Donelli replaced, declaring his dual coaching interests inappropriate. Kiesling took over for the final four games and the Steelers finished the year with just one victory.

1942 Thanks to a remarkable rookie season by halfback Bill Dudley, the Steelers rocketed to their first winning record (7–4) and second place in the Eastern

Division. Dudley, a 5-foot 10-inch, 175-pound graduate of the University of Virginia, had little speed and a weak arm, but he achieved astonishing success due to his desire. Dudley led the NFL in rushing with 696 yards, scored six touchdowns and passed for two more, returned punts and kickoffs, and led the Steelers in pass interceptions. With Dudley winning rookie of the year honors, Pittsburgh won seven of its last nine games.

1943 World War II depleted the Pittsburgh roster and the Steelers merged with the Philadelphia Eagles to form the "Phil-Pitt Steagles." They lost their top offensive threat when Dudley enlisted in the Army Air Corps and went to the Pacific as a bomber pilot. Kiesling and the Eagles' Earle (Greasy) Neale shared the coaching duties. The Steagles finished a competitive third in the East with a 5–4–1 record, just one game out of first place. Roy Zimmerman, a 35-year-old journeyman, was the starting quarterback, with Allie Sherman in reserve. The club's top rusher was free agent Jack Hinkle, a 6-foot, 215-pounder who gained 571 yards.

1944 The Steelers merged with the weaker Chicago Cardinals, forming Card-Pitt. This hybrid outfit was so bad it became known as the "Carpets," the team everybody walked on. Coached by Kiesling and Phil Handler, Card-Pitt went 0–10 and was outscored 328–108. After the third loss, a 34–7 rout by the Bears, three Card-Pitt players were fined for what management termed "indifferent play." One of those cited was fullback Johnny Grigas, one of the team's few decent players. Grigas rushed for 610 yards to rank second in the NFL, passed for 690 yards, and accounted for nine of the Card-Pitt touchdowns. Grigas became so disgusted with the beating he absorbed each week that he packed his gear and left minutes before the season finale against the Chicago Bears. Without Grigas, the team lost to the Bears 49–7.

1945 The Steelers were once again the exclusive property of Pittsburgh. Jim Leonard took over as head coach. The Steelers won just two games, scored only 79 points, and allowed a division-high 220. The Pittsburgh offense managed eight touchdowns (none by passing) in 10 league games. Dudley returned from the service for the last four games and scored three touchdowns to lead the Steelers.

1946 Rooney hired Dr. John B. (Jock) Sutherland as head coach. In 25 years of coaching, most of them at the University of Pittsburgh, Sutherland never had a losing season. He was a stern disciplinarian and he put the Steelers through a tough training camp. Sutherland and Dudley disliked each other from the start and their hostility was a source of friction on the team. Dudley's differences with the coach did not interfere with his performance. He led the NFL in two big categories, rushing with 604 yards, and pass interceptions with 10. Pittsburgh, behind Dudley, jumped off to a 4–2–1 start. Dudley injured his ribs in a 14–7 win over Washington and Sutherland forced him to play hurt in the remaining four games. Dudley was so enraged he told Rooney he would quit football unless the Steelers traded him after the season. Reluctantly, Rooney dealt Dudley to Detroit for Bob Civers, Paul White, and a number one draft choice.

1947 Sutherland moved Johnny Clement to tailback to replace Dudley and the Steelers' single wing kept rolling. The team started poorly, losing two of the first three games, then won six straight. The key victory was a 35–24 win over the Eagles in which the Steelers overcame a 10-point halftime deficit. Pittsburgh appeared certain to win its first division title, but the team lost 49–7 to the Chicago Bears, then dropped a rematch with the Eagles 21–0. That enabled Philadelphia to tie Pittsburgh for first place and force a playoff for the Eastern Division championship. The week before the playoff game, the Steelers' players

went on strike for a day, insisting they be paid extra for the additional week of practice. Sutherland was outraged and the discontent tore the club apart. In the playoff game, the Eagles dominated Pittsburgh 21–0 at Forbes Field.

1948 Sutherland died in an auto accident in April and Rooney appointed Jock's top assistant, John Michelosen, to succeed him. Michelosen, 32, had quarterbacked Sutherland's Pitt team to a 1936 Rose Bowl victory over Washington. Michelosen, like Sutherland, believed in stern discipline and the single wing. He lacked Sutherland's shrewdness, however, and the Steelers slipped back into their losing ways. They won two of their first three games, then went into a tailspin, losing six of the next seven. Clement, who rushed for 670 years in 1947, slumped to 261 yards. Fullback Jerry Shipkey (eight touchdowns) and halfback–receiver Joe Glamp (56 points) did most of the scoring.

1949 Every other NFL club had adopted the T formation, but Michelosen stayed with the single wing. Rookie Joe Geri of Clemson was Pittsburgh's top offensive player, rushing for 543 yards, passing for 554, accounting for 10 scores, kicking 12 extra points, and averaging over 43 yards per punt. At 5 foot 10 inches and 180 pounds, however, Geri lacked size, and the constant pounding wore him down. Pittsburgh won only two of its last seven games. The top defensive player was Bill McPeak, a 6-foot 1-inch, 200-pound rookie defensive end from Pitt. Another rookie was Jim Finks, a record-setting passer at Tulsa who was switched to defensive back by Michelosen.

1950 Geri had another fine season, rushing for 705 yards, passing for 866, accounting for nine scores, and adding 46 points kicking. However, the Steelers' single wing attack just didn't work anymore. In half their games, the Steelers managed one touchdown or less. They won games on the strength of a stubborn defense led by McPeak and Ernie Stautner, a rookie defensive tackle from Boston College. They upset the New York Giants 17–6 and outlasted the Eagles 9–7 on three Geri field goals. Pittsburgh finished 6–6, tied with Philadelphia for third place.

1951 The offense grew stagnant and Pittsburgh fans became restless in Michelosen's fourth year as head coach. Six times the Steelers' rugged defense held its opponents to two touchdowns or less, yet Pittsburgh was able to win only four games. The Steelers lost their first three games before beating the Chicago Cardinals 28–14. The next day, the local paper ran a banner headline: "Steelers Win, So What?" The fans wanted Michelosen to put Finks on offense and let him throw the ball. Michelosen kept Finks on defense. In the season finale, Michelosen lost both tailbacks, Geri and Chuck Ortman, with injuries and was forced to use Finks. Finks completed 13 of 20 passes to beat Washington 20–10. Michelosen was fired a few days later.

1952 Rooney rehired Joe Bach, the man who coached the Steelers in 1935–36. Rooney was the best man at Bach's wedding and the Steelers' owner regretted ever letting him go. "That bull-headed Irishman was the best organizer I ever had," Rooney said. Bach junked the single wing and installed the T formation. It took the Pittsburgh players time to adjust and they lost their first four league games. As Finks gained confidence at quarterback, the Steelers turned the corner with wins over Washington and the Chicago Cardinals. The highlight of the season was a stunning 63–7 rout of the New York Giants at Forbes Field, November 20. Lynn Chandnois returned the opening kickoff 91 yards for a touchdown and Finks threw four touchdown passes. Finks threw 20 touchdown passes to tie Otto Graham for the NFL lead. Chandnois topped the league in kickoff returns and Elbie Nickel ranked among the leaders with 55 pass receptions, nine for touchdowns.

1953 Finks suffered a preseason knee injury that hampered him. Finks's passing yardage dropped from 2,307 yards to 1,484. His touchdown output dwindled to eight and he began splitting time with Bill Mackrides, a former backup quarterback with the Eagles. With Finks struggling, the Pittsburgh offense slipped badly. The Steelers started the season as dark-horse contenders in the East but needed wins in their last two games to finish 6–6. Nickel's 62 pass receptions ranked second in the NFL. Chandnois had another fine season, accounting for over 1,600 yards in total offense. Pittsburgh's top defender was safety Jack Butler with nine interceptions and three touchdowns.

1954 Illness forced Bach to resign prior to the season and Rooney named Walt Kiesling head coach for the third time. The Steelers started impressively, winning four of their first five games, including their first win ever over the Packers at Green Bay, 21–20. The only defeat in the first month was a 24–22 loss to the Eagles in Philadelphia. Two weeks later, the Steelers gained revenge with a bloody 17–7 win over the Eagles before a standing room only crowd at Forbes Field, October 23. Nickel was the star, scoring on a 53-yard touchdown pass from Finks. Both teams came out of the game so battered they won only four of their remaining 14 games. Pittsburgh's top offensive performer was Ray Mathews, a 6-foot, 185-pound halfback from Clemson who led the club with 44 pass receptions, rushed for 242 yards, and scored eight touchdowns.

1955 Kiesling cut a rookie quarterback named John Unitas in training camp. The Steelers jumped off to another promising start under Kiesling, winning four of their first five. Their only loss was a controversial 27–26 decision to Los Angeles. Pittsburgh's title dreams were crushed when the offense hit a lengthy dry spell starting with a 24–0 loss to the Eagles. Finks drew the fans' ire by throwing a league-high 26 interceptions. The Steelers lost their last seven games and fell to last place for the first time since 1945.

1956 Finks, 28, retired and went to Notre Dame as an assistant coach. Kiesling gave the quarterback job to Ted Marchibroda, a 5-foot 10-inch, 180-pound second-year man from St. Bonaventure. Marchibroda played respectably, completing 45 percent of his passes, 12 for touchdowns. Kiesling made way for several impressive young players—linemen Joe Krupa, Frank Varrichione, and Willie McClung, linebacker John Reger, and safety Gary Glick. The best of the young runners was Lowell Perry of Michigan State, but a fractured pelvis ended his career at midseason. Fran Rogel, a fullback from Penn State, led the Steelers in rushing for the fifth straight year.

1957 In the college draft Kiesling passed over Syracuse fullback Jim Brown in favor of Purdue quarterback Len Dawson. Kiesling called Dawson "my quarterback of the future." Kiesling's future ran out in August when Rooney replaced him with Buddy Parker, who had unexpectedly walked out on his job as head coach in Detroit. Never one to build slowly, Parker made several quick trades for offensive help. He sent two number one draft picks to San Francisco for quarterback Earl Morrall, then acquired halfback Billy Wells from Washington. Morrall passed for 1,900 yards and 11 touchdowns. Wells, a 5-foot 9-inch, 170-pounder from Michigan State, led Pittsburgh in rushing, punt returns, and kickoff returns. Jack (Goose) McClairen, a rangy 6-foot 4-inch, 215-pound receiver, caught 46 passes to rank third in the NFL. Butler tied a team record with 10 pass interceptions.

1958 Parker won three divisional championships in Detroit with Bobby Layne at quarterback, so he jumped at the chance to trade for Layne two weeks into the season. Parker gave up Morrall and two draft choices for the 31-year-old Layne. Layne, a colorful, swashbuckling figure, took over the 0–2 Steelers and pulled off a 24–3 upset of Philadelphia in his debut. After losses to New York and Cleveland, Layne put the Pittsburgh offense in gear, winning six and tying one of the last seven games. The strong finish enabled the Steelers to climb to third place with a 7–4–1 record, their best record since 1947. Parker had assembled a veteran team, led by Layne, ex-Lions halfback Tom Tracy, and ex-Rams fullback Paul (Tank) Younger. Layne ranked second in the NFL in passing with 2,510 yards and 14 touchdowns. Tracy led the team with 714 yards rushing and nine touchdowns. Jimmy Orr was a standout rookie flanker, catching 33 passes for 910 yards and seven touchdowns.

1959 The Steelers opened the season with a 17–7 upset of Cleveland, stretching their unbeaten streak to eight games, but they lacked the consistency to stay with the top Eastern clubs. Parker claimed Buddy Dial, a rookie receiver from Rice who was cut by the New York Giants. Pittsburgh struggled early in the season but finished strong, losing just one of the last six games. Tracy rushed for 794 yards and scored eight touchdowns. Layne was plagued by 21 interceptions and slipped to eighth among NFL quarterbacks.

1960 Veteran safety Jack Butler retired. A series of injuries slowed key members of the offense—Layne (bruised hand), fullback John Henry Johnson (bruised leg), Orr (pulled muscle), and guard Mike Sandusky (bad knee). With an unsettled roster, Parker had difficulty early in the season, winning just two of the first eight games and dropping from contention. The Steelers managed another late rally, winning their final three home games, including a 14–10 upset of Cleveland and a snowy 27–21 win over the NFL title-bound Eagles. Dial, one of the few regulars to stay healthy, had another fine season, catching 40 passes for 972 yards and nine touchdowns. The defense, led by 35-year-old Ernie Stautner and end George Tarasovic, remained formidable.

1961 Another poor start put Pittsburgh out of the race early. The Steelers lost their first four games while Layne was sidelined with an injured shoulder. Rudy Bukich, a 30-year-old journeyman, took over at quarterback and displayed a strong, but erratic, arm. John Henry Johnson, a hard-running veteran of the Canadian Football League, took charge of the Pittsburgh offense, rushing for 787 yards. Dial led the Steelers' receivers for the third straight year, catching 53 passes for 1,047 yards and a club record 12 touchdowns. The defense held up well as Parker acquired Gene (Big Daddy) Lipscomb, a 6-foot 6-inch, 290-pound tackle, and Johnny Sample, a young cornerback, from Baltimore. Sample led the team in interceptions (eight), punt returns, and kickoff returns.

1962 Layne made a stirring comeback and the Steelers had the finest season in their history, winning nine games and finishing second in the Eastern Conference. Parker made several key acquisitions to strengthen the team, adding center Buzz Nutter and defensive end-kicker Lou Michaels from Baltimore and tackles Charlie Bradshaw and Lou Cordileone and safety Clendon Thomas from Los Angeles. Michaels set a Pittsburgh record by scoring 110 points. Thomas led the team with seven interceptions. John Henry Johnson became the first Steeler to rush for over 1,000 yards, gaining 1,141. Layne was injured late in the season and Parker turned the quarterbacking duties over to Ed Brown, a 33-year-old veteran who had just been acquired from the Chicago Bears. Brown led the Steelers to three straight wins and a berth in the Playoff Bowl in Miami, where they lost 17–10 to Detroit.

1963 Layne retired. Lipscomb died of an apparent drug overdose, May 10. Parker installed Brown as the Steelers' number one quarterback and put rookie Frank Atkinson of Stanford in Lipscomb's tackle spot. Pittsburgh displayed surprising early season

strength, routing the New York Giants 31–0 at Pitt Stadium. The Steelers blew a 13-point lead in the final four minutes to lose to St. Louis 24–23 and fell from first place, October 13. Parker was outraged, telling his players: "You disgraced me, you disgraced yourselves." Fearing Parker's wrath, the Steelers regrouped quickly, losing just one of their next eight games to make a serious run at the Eastern Conference crown. Most of their victories were close ones. They beat Washington when safety Dick Haley returned a fourth quarter interception for a touchdown. They beat Dallas when Brown hit flanker Red Mack with an 85-yard touchdown pass in the last three minutes, October 27. They beat Cleveland 9–7 on Brown's late scoring pass to split end Gary Ballman, November 10. They beat Washington 34–28 as Ballman scored two touchdowns and amassed 320 yards on kick returns, November 17. They tied the Eagles 20–20 on Michaels' 24-yard field goal at the gun. They beat Dallas 24–19 on reserve fullback Theron Sapp's 24-yard touchdown run with 1:50 to go. The Steelers had a chance to win the conference title by beating the Giants in the season finale at Yankee Stadium, December 15. On a cold, windy day, the Giants took a 16–0 lead and held on for a 33–17 triumph as Joe Morrison scored three touchdowns. Dial set a Steelers' club record with 1,295 yards on pass receptions. Stautner retired after 14 seasons in Pittsburgh's defensive line.

1964 Parker sent Buddy Dial to Dallas for the NFL draft rights to Scott Appleton, the University of Texas lineman. Appleton signed with the AFL Houston Oilers, leaving the Steelers with nothing to show for the deal. Many of Parker's veteran players faded into mediocrity, particularly Brown, who floundered at quarterback. The only steady performers were John Henry Johnson, who rushed for 1,048 yards, and Ballman, who caught 47 passes. The defense, which allowed 30 points or more in five straight games, was a major factor in the Steelers' fall to sixth place.

1965 Two weeks before the league opener, Parker walked out on the Steelers, informing Art Rooney: "I can't win with this bunch of stiffs." Rooney turned the team over to Mike Nixon, a long-time assistant. The Steelers lost their opener 41–9 to Green Bay and stumbled through a 2–12 season, their poorest in two decades. Ed Brown was traded to Baltimore and Bill Nelsen, in his third season from USC, took over at quarterback. Johnson, 35, carried the ball just three times and retired.

1966 Rooney hired Bill Austin, line coach under Vince Lombardi at Green Bay, to succeed Nixon as head coach. Austin played the Lombardi role, conducting brutal practices and administering frequent verbal lashings, but he lacked Lombardi's magic. The players chafed under Austin's stern methods. Nelsen hurt his knee in the second game and was replaced by Ron Smith, a 22-year-old quarterback waived earlier by the Packers. The club sputtered under Smith and offered no signs of life until Nelsen returned for the final three games. Under Nelsen, Pittsburgh beat the New York Giants 47–28 and Atlanta 57–33 to finish 5–8–1. The Steelers' leading rusher was Willie Asbury, a 6-foot 1-inch, 230-pound fullback from Kent State, who gained 544 yards.

1967 Nelsen's bad knees put him on the bench much of the season and Austin signed Kent Nix, a former Green Bay taxi-squad quarterback to fill in. Nix had his troubles, throwing 19 interceptions. The Steelers won just 2 of their first 11 games and discontent with Austin grew among the players. Two young prospects displayed potential—outside linebacker Andy Russell, who rejoined the team after two seasons in the army, and J. R. Wilburn, a sure-handed wide receiver from the University of South Carolina who led the team with 51 pass receptions.

1968 Austin traded Nelsen (following a dispute with

offensive coach Don Heinrich) to Cleveland for Dick Shiner. The Steelers lost their first six games before winning the infamous "O.J. Bowl" 6–3 over the Eagles on Booth Lusteg's last-second field goal. The two teams were vying with Buffalo for the poorest record and right to draft O.J. Simpson. The only noteworthy performers in the season were halfback Dick Hoak, who rushed for 858 yards, and flanker Roy Jefferson, who caught 58 passes for 1,074 yards and scored 12 touchdowns. Austin was fired after the 2–11–1 year had ended.

1969 Rooney hired Chuck Noll, a 36-year-old assistant with the Baltimore Colts, to replace Austin as head coach. Noll, once a messenger guard under Paul Brown, was considered a defensive genius. In his first season, the Steelers won only one game but they added some promising players. The best of the bunch was Mean Joe Greene, 6-foot 4-inch, 275-pound defensive tackle from North Texas State. Greene started all 14 games and was named NFL defensive rookie of the year. "We're gonna build a championship team in Pittsburgh," Noll promised, "and Joe Greene will be the cornerstone."

1970 The Steelers were one of the three NFL clubs (joining Baltimore and Cleveland) to move to the American Football Conference following the merger. Pittsburgh had first pick in the college draft and selected Terry Bradshaw, a quarterback from Louisiana Tech. Bradshaw's wide-eyed enthusiasm reflected a new spirit on the team, which heightened as the Steelers moved into their new home, Three Rivers Stadium. The Steelers had a young, unpredictable team that was cold (losing three), hot (winning four of five), and cold (losing five of six) during the season. Although the Steelers won just five games, they were clearly on the way up. John (Frenchy) Fuqua set a team rushing record by gaining 218 yards in the finale against Philadelphia, December 20. The rookie crop included Bradshaw, receiver Ron Shanklin, and defensive back Mel Blount.

1971 Another good draft bolstered the Pittsburgh roster with receiver Frank Lewis, linebacker Jack Ham, tight end Larry Brown, guard Gerry Mullins, defensive linemen Dwight White, Ernie Holmes, and Craig Hanneman, and safeties Mike Wagner and Glen Edwards. With those rookies surrounding proven veterans such as Greene, Russell, L.C. Greenwood, Ray Mansfield, and Bruce Van Dyke, the Steelers grew up in a hurry. In their third game, the Steelers beat San Diego 21–17 as the defense twice turned the Chargers back at the goal line. "It's a sign we're coming of age," Russell said. "Two years ago, we would have lost this game." With just four weeks left in the season, Pittsburgh was tied with Cleveland for first place in the Central Division with a 5–5 record. The Browns won their four remaining games, while the Steelers lost three of four. But Noll saw hope for the future. "The experience will prove valuable to our younger players," Noll said. "I expect us to come back stronger than ever next year."

1972 The catalyst for the club's rise was number one draft choice Franco Harris, a 6-foot 2-inch, 230-pound rookie fullback from Penn State. Harris rushed for 1,055 yards, caught 21 passes, scored 11 touchdowns, and was named rookie of the year. With Harris trampling would-be tacklers and Bradshaw maturing rapidly at quarterback, the Pittsburgh offense scored a team record 343 points. With Greene emerging as the NFL's premier lineman, Pittsburgh's defense allowed just 175 points, second only to unbeaten Miami. Two key wins during the regular season were a 40–17 pounding of Cincinnati and a 30–0 shutout of Cleveland, both at Three Rivers Stadium. Against the Browns, Harris rushed for 102 yards. It was the sixth straight 100-yard game for Harris, tying Jim Brown's NFL record. The Steelers clinched their first division title in the 40-year history of the franchise with a 24–2 win over San Diego, December 17. The club's 11–3 record was the best ever. In their first playoff game since 1947, the Steelers edged Oakland 13–7 at Three Rivers Stadium, December 23. The finish was one of the most stunning in NFL history as the Steelers trailed 7–6 with 22 seconds remaining, fourth-and-ten on their own 40-yard line. Bradshaw threw a long pass to Fuqua but Oakland safety Jack Tatum deflected the ball. Harris caught the deflected pass in full stride and carried it in for the winning touchdown. The following week, the Dolphins ended Pittsburgh's miracle season with a 21–17 win in the AFC championship game.

1973 Joe Gilliam, a young black quarterback from Tennessee State, took over when Terry Bradshaw and Terry Hanratty were injured. Gilliam was prone to interceptions. He started a key game against Miami, and threw three interceptions in the first quarter en route to a 30–26 defeat. The Steelers lost three of their last five games and as the "wild card" team had little momentum going into the playoffs. Injuries hampered the Steelers most of the season, sidelining Bradshaw (shoulder separation), Harris (bad knee), Fuqua (broken collarbone) and Hanratty (broken ribs). Considering their medical condition, the Steelers did well to finish 10–4 and make the AFC playoffs. Oakland trounced them 33–14 in the first round.

1974 The season started in turmoil as Noll named Gilliam his starting quarterback prior to the opener. Gilliam led the Steelers to four wins and a tie in six starts but his wide-open, pass-on-every-down style conflicted with Noll's ideas of percentage football. After Gilliam completed 5 of 18 passes against Cleveland, Noll reinstated Bradshaw at quarterback. In Bradshaw's first start, Franco Harris rushed for a career-high 141 yards in a 24–17 win over Atlanta, October 28. The Steelers clinched their second AFC Central Division title December 8 when Harris rushed for 136 yards and rookie Lynn Swann made a spectacular touchdown catch in a 21–17 win over New England. Harris rushed for three touchdowns and the Steelers rolled up 438 yards total offense to crush Buffalo 32–14 in the first round of the AFC playoffs at Three Rivers Stadium, December 22. The Steelers played near-perfect football to upset Oakland 24–13 in the AFC championship game at Oakland, December 29. Harris was the offensive star, rushing for 111 yards and two touchdowns. Pittsburgh's Steel Curtain defense was superb, limiting the Raiders to just 29 yards rushing. Ham's fourth quarter interception ended any Oakland comeback hopes.

1975 Against Minnesota, in Super Bowl IX in New Orleans, Harris rushed for 158 yards (a Super Bowl record) and the Steelers' defense limited the Vikings to just 17 yards on the ground in a 16–6 victory, January 12. After an upset loss to Buffalo the second week, the Steelers won 11 straight in an awesome display of offensive and defensive power. Rocky Bleier, who had recovered from war wounds suffered in Vietnam, emerged as a quality backfield partner for Harris. Bleier rushed for 163 yards in a 16–13 win over Green Bay, October 26. Although Greene was sidelined with a back injury, the Steelers brushed aside Cincinnati (30–24) and Houston (twice) within four weeks to take command in the Central Division. Harris became only the seventh runner in NFL history to surpass 1,000 yards three times in a 31–17 win over Cleveland, December 7. Harris finished with 1,246 yards (a club record) and scored 11 touchdowns. Bradshaw had his best season, completing 58 percent of his passes, 18 for touchdowns. Swann caught more touchdown passes (11) than anyone in the AFC. Mel Blount led the league with 11 interceptions. A ferocious second-year man from Kent State, Jack Lambert, took over at middle linebacker and became the defensive leader. The Steelers won the Central Division

with a 12–2 record, with Cincinnati (11–3) and Houston (10–4) breathing down their necks. The Steelers rolled over Baltimore in their AFC playoff 28–10.

1976 The Steelers nailed down their second straight AFC championship with a 16–10 win over Oakland at Three Rivers Stadium, January 4. The game was played in zero degree temperatures resulting in 13 turnovers. The Steelers upended Dallas 21–17 in Super Bowl X, January 18. Swann won the game's most valuable player award, catching four passes for 161 yards, including the game-winning 64-yard scoring bomb from Bradshaw. A blocked punt by reserve fullback Reggie Harrison turned the game in Pittsburgh's favor in the second half. The Steelers lost four of their first five games in the 1976 season and did not escape last place in the Central Division until the ninth week. After that start, however, Pittsburgh recovered to win 10 straight games and clinch its fourth Central Division crown since 1972. The turnabout began with a 23–6 win over Cincinnati in Three Rivers Stadium, October 17. Rookie quarterback Mike Kruczek subbed for the injured Bradshaw and handed off to Harris 41 times (an NFL record) in the game. With people dismissing their playoff chances as hopeless, the Steelers' defense put together its most astounding display of football ever, not permitting a touchdown for 22 quarters, recording three consecutive shutouts, not allowing a touchdown in eight of the last nine league games and totally blanking five of its final eight opponents. The key game in the comeback was a 7–3 win over Cincinnati that pulled the Steelers within one game of the lead with two to play, November 28. The following week, Pittsburgh moved into a tie for first with a 42–0 win over Tampa Bay as Harris surpassed 1,000 yards for the fourth time, only the fourth NFL back to accomplish the feat. The Steelers clinched the division title with a 21–0 win over Houston in the finale, December 11. In their last nine league games, the Steelers allowed just 28 points. The Steelers hit their peak in a 40–14 rout of Baltimore in the first round of the AFC playoffs in Baltimore, December 19. Harris gained 132 yards on 18 carries (giving him 958 yards in 10 postseason games) and Bradshaw completed 14 of 18 passes for 264 yards and three touchdowns. Without the injured Harris (ribs) and Bleier (foot), the Steelers lost 24–7 to Oakland in the AFC championship game in Oakland, December 26.

MEMBERS OF HALL OF FAME:
Bert Bell, Johnny Blood (McNally), Bill Dudley, Cal Hubbard, Walt Kiesling, Bobby Layne, Marion Motley, Art Rooney, Sr., Ernie Stautner.

STEELERS RECORD, 1933–76

Year	Won	Lost	Tied	Pct.	Pts.	OP
Pittsburgh Pirates						
1933	3	6	2	.333	67	208
1934	2	10	0	.167	51	206
1935	4	8	0	.333	100	209
1936	6	6	0	.500	98	187
1937	4	7	0	.364	122	145
1938	2	9	0	.182	79	169
1939	1	9	1	.100	114	216
1940	2	7	2	.222	60	178
Pittsburgh Steelers						
1941	1	9	1	.100	103	276
1942	7	4	0	.636	167	119
1943	5	4	1	.556	225	230
1944	0	10	0	.000	108	328
1945	2	8	0	.200	79	220
1946	5	5	1	.500	136	117
1947	8	4	0	.667	240	259
1948	4	8	0	.333	200	243
1949	6	5	1	.545	224	214
1950	6	6	0	.500	180	195
1951	4	7	1	.364	183	235
1952	5	7	0	.417	300	273
1953	6	6	0	.500	211	263
1954	5	7	0	.417	219	263
1955	4	8	0	.333	195	285
1956	3	8	1	.273	143	215
1957	6	6	0	.500	161	178
1958	7	4	1	.636	261	230
1959	6	5	1	.545	257	216
1960	5	6	1	.455	240	275

Year	Won	Lost	Tied	Pct.	Pts.	OP
1961	6	8	0	.429	295	287
1962	9	5	0	.643	312	363
1963	7	4	3	.636	321	295
1964	5	9	0	.357	253	315
1965	2	12	0	.143	202	397
1966	5	8	1	.385	316	347
1967	4	9	1	.308	281	320
1968	2	11	1	.154	244	397
1969	1	13	0	.071	218	404
1970	5	9	0	.357	210	272
1971	6	8	0	.429	246	292
1972§	11	3	0	.786	343	175
1973§	10	4	0	.714	347	210
1974**	10	3	1	.750	305	189
1975**	12	2	0	.857	373	162
1976§	10	4	0	.714	342	138
44 Years	**224**	**301**	**20**	**.429**	**9,131**	**10,715**

§*AFC Eastern Division Champion* **Super Bowl Champion

RECORD HOLDERS

Rushing (Yards)	Franco Harris, 1975	1,246
Passing (Pct.)	Terry Bradshaw, 1975	57.7
Passing (Yards)	Ed Brown, 1963	2,982
Passing (TDs)	Ed Brown, 1963	21
Receiving (No.)	Roy Jefferson, 1967	67
Receiving (Yards)	Buddy Dial, 1963	1,295
Interceptions (No.)	Mel Blount, 1975	11
Punting (Avg.)	Bobby Joe Green, 1961	47.0
Punt Ret. (Avg.)	Art Jones, 1941	16.6
Kickoff Ret. (Avg.)	Lynn Chandnois, 1952	35.2
Touchdowns (Total)	Franco Harris, 1976	14
Field Goals Made	Roy Gerela, 1972	28
Points (No.)	Roy Gerela, 1973	123

COACHING HISTORY

1933	Forrest Douds	3– 6–2
1934	Luby DiMelio	2–10–0
1935–36	Joe Bach	10–14–0
1937–39	Johnny Blood (McNally)*	6–19–0
1939–40	Walt Kiesling	3–13–3
1941	Bert Bell**	0– 2–0
1941	Aldo (Buff) Donelli***	0– 5–0
1941–44	Walt Kiesling****	13–20–2
1945	Jim Leonard	2– 8–0
1946–47	Jock Sutherland	13– 9–1
1948–51	John Michelosen	20–26–2
1952–53	Joe Bach	11–13–0
1954–56	Walt Kiesling	12–23–1
1957–64	Raymond (Buddy) Parker	51–47–6
1965	Mike Nixon	2–12–0
1966–68	Bill Austin	11–28–3
1969–76	Chuck Noll	65–46–0

Replaced after three games in 1939
**Resigned after two games in 1941*
***Replaced after five games in 1941*
****Co-coach with Phil Handler of 1944 Chicago Cardinals-Pittsburgh merged team*

FIRST PLAYER SELECTED

1936	Bill Shakespeare, B, Notre Dame
1937	Mike Basrak, C, Duquesne
1938	Byron (Whizzer) White, B, Colorado
1939	Sid Luckman, B, Columbia
1940	Kay Eakin, B, Arkansas
1941	Chet Gladchuk, C, Boston College
1942	Bill Dudley, B, Virginia
1943	Bill Daley, B, Minnesota
1944	Johnny Podesto, B, St. Mary's, California
1945	Paul Duhart, B, Florida
1946	Felix (Doc) Blanchard, B, Army
1947	Hub Bechtol, E, Texas
1948	Dan Edwards, E, Georgia
1949	Bobby Gage, B, Clemson
1950	Lynn Chandnois, B, Michigan State
1951	Butch Avinger, B, Alabama
1952	Ed Modzelewski, B, Maryland
1953	Ted Marchibroda, B, St. Bonaventure
1954	Johnny Lattner, B, Notre Dame
1955	Frank Varrichione, T, Notre Dame
1956	Gary Glick, B, Colorado A&M
1957	Len Dawson, B, Purdue
1958	Larry Krutko, B, West Virginia
1959	Tom Barnett, B, Purdue
1960	Jack Spikes, RB, Texas Christian
1961	Myron Pottios, LB (2), Notre Dame
1962	Bob Ferguson, RB, Ohio State
1963	Frank Atkinson, T, Stanford
1964	Paul Martha, S, Pittsburgh
1965	Roy Jefferson, WR (2), Utah
1966	Dick Leftridge, RB, West Virginia
1967	Don Shy, RB (2), San Diego State
1968	Mike Taylor, T, USC
1969	Joe Greene, DT, North Texas State
1970	Terry Bradshaw, QB, Louisiana Tech
1971	Frank Lewis, WR, Grambling
1972	Franco Harris, RB, Penn State
1973	James Thomas, CB, Florida State
1974	Lynn Swann, WR, USC
1975	Dave Brown, DB, Michigan
1976	Bennie Cunningham, TE, Clemson

Rocky Bleier

Charlie Bradshaw

Terry Bradshaw

Rudy Bukich

Lynn Chandnois

John Fuqua

Joe Geri

PITTSBURGH PIRATES, 1933–40;
PITTSBURGH STEELERS, 1941–76

The Steelers merged with the Philadelphia Eagles in 1943 and with the Chicago Cardinals in 1944.

Adamchik, Ed, T, Pittsburgh 1965
Adams, Bob, TE, Pacific 1969–71
Adams, Paul, C, Morehead Teachers 1947
Agajanian, Ben, K, New Mexico 1945
Alban, Dick, E, Northwestern 1956–59
Alberghini, Tom, G, Holy Cross 1945
Albrecht, Art, C-T, Wisconsin 1942
Alderton, John, E, Maryland 1953
Allen, Charles, LB, Washington 1965
Allen, Chuck, LB, Washington 1970–71
Allen, Jimmy, DB, UCLA 1974–76
Allen, Lou, T, Duke 1950–51
Alley, Don, WR, Adams State 1969
Anadabaker, Rudy, G, Pittsburgh 1952, 1954
Anderson, Art, T, Idaho 1963
Anderson, Chet, E, Minnesota 1967
Anderson, Ralph, DB, W. Texas State 1971–72
Arndt, Al, G, S. Dakota State 1935
Arndt, Dick, T, Idaho 1967–70
Arnold, Jay, QB, Texas 1941
Artman, Corwan, T, Stanford 1933
Asbury, Willie, B, Kent State 1966–68
Askson, Burt, DE, Texas Southern 1971
Atkinson, Frank, T, Stanford 1963
Augusterfer, Gene, B, Catholic U. 1935
Austin, Ocie, DB, Utah State 1970–71

B

Badar, Rich, QB, North Carolina 1967
Baker, Conway, T, Centenary 1944
Baker, John, DE, N. Carolina Coll. 1966–67
Baldacci, Lou, B, Michigan 1956
Ballman, Gary, B, Michigan State 1962–66
Balog, Bob, C, Denver 1949–50
Banaszak, John, DE, Eastern Michigan 1975–76
Bankston, Warren, RB, Tulane 1969–72
Banonis, Vince, C, Detroit 1944
Barbolak, Pete, T, Purdue 1949
Barker, Ed, E, Washington State 1953
Barnett, Tom, B, Purdue 1959–60
Barry, Fred, DB, Boston College 1970
Bartaanen, Jim, C, Michigan 1938
Bartlett, Earl, B, Centre 1939
Basrak, Mike, C, Duquesne 1937–38
Bassi, Dick, G, Santa Clara 1941
Beams, Byron, T, Notre Dame 1959–60
Beatty, Charles, DB, N. Texas State 1969–72
Beatty, Ed, C, Mississippi 1957–61
Becker, Wayland, E, Marquette 1939
Bell, Theo, WR, Arizona 1976
Bernet, Ed, E, Southern Methodist 1955
Bettis, Tom, LB, Purdue 1962
Billock, Frank, G, St. Mary's, Minn. 1937
Binotto, John, B, Duquesne 1942
Bishop, Don, B, Los Angeles Coll. 1958–59
Bivins, Charles, B, Morris Brown 1967
Blankenship, Greg, LB, Cal. State-Hayward 1976
Bleier, Rocky, B, Notre Dame 1968, 1970–76
Blount, Mel, DB, Southern U. 1970–76
Bolkovac, Nick, T, Pittsburgh 1953–54
Bond, Randall, QB, Washington 1939
Bonelli, Ernie, B, Pittsburgh 1946
Booth, Clarence, B, Southern Methodist 1944
Bova, Tony, E, St. Francis 1942–47
Bowman, Bill, B, William & Mary 1957
Boyd, Sam, E, Baylor 1939–40
Boyle, Shorty, E 1934
Bradley, Ed, LB, Wake Forest 1972–75
Bradshaw, Charles, T, Baylor 1961–66
Bradshaw, Jim, B, Chattanooga 1963–67
Bradshaw, Terry, QB, Louisiana Tech 1970–76
Brady, Pat, B, Nevada 1952–54
Brandau, Art, C, Tennessee 1945–46
Brandt, Jim, B, St. Thomas 1952–54
Bray, Maurice, T, Southern Methodist 1935–36
Breedlove, Rod, LB, Maryland 1965–66
Breedon, Bill, B, Oklahoma 1937
Breen, Gene, LB, Virginia Tech 1965–66
Brett, Ed, E, Washington State 1936–37

Brewster, Darrel (Pete), E, Purdue 1959–60
Broussard, Fred, C, Texas A&M 1955
Brovelli, Angelo, QB, St. Mary's, Cal. 1933–34
Brown, Dave, DB, Michigan 1975
Brown, Ed, QB, San Francisco 1962–65
Brown, John, T, Syracuse 1967–72
Brown, Larry, TE, Kansas 1971–76
Brown, Tom, E, William & Mary 1942
Brown, William, QB, Texas Tech 1945
Browning, Gregg, E, Denver 1947
Bruder, Henry, QB, Northwestern 1940
Brumbaugh, Boyd, B, Duquesne 1939–41
Brumfield, Jim, RB, Indiana State 1971
Brundage, Dewey, E, Brigham Young 1954
Bruney, Fred, B, Ohio State 1956–57
Bryant, Hubie, WR, Minnesota 1970
Bucek, Felix, G, Texas A&M 1946
Buda, Carl, G, Tulsa 1945
Bukich, Rudy, QB, USC 1960–61
Bulger, Chester, T, Auburn 1944
Bullocks, Amos, B, So. Illinois 1966
Burleson, John, G, Southern Methodist 1933
Burnett, Len, DB, Oregon 1961
Burnette, Tom, B, North Carolina 1938
Burrell, John, E, Rice 1962–64
Butler, Jack, B, St. Bonaventure 1951–59
Butler, Jim, B, Edward Waters 1965–67
Butler, John, B, Tennessee 1943–44
Bykowski, Frank, G, Purdue 1940

C

Cabrelli, Larry, E, Colgate 1943
Calcagni, Ralph, T, Pennsylvania 1947
Call, John, B, Colgate 1959
Calland, Lee, DB, Louisville 1969–72
Calvin, Tom, B, Alabama 1952–54
Cameron, Paul, B, UCLA 1954
Campbell, Bob, RB, Penn State 1969
Campbell, Don, T, Carnegie Tech 1939–41
Campbell, Glenn, E, Emporia State 1935
Campbell, John, LB, Minnesota 1965–69
Campbell, Leon, B, Arkansas 1955
Campbell, Ray, LB, Marquette 1958–60
Canale, Rocco, G, Boston College 1943

Capp, Dick, E, Boston College 1968
Cara, Dom, E, N. Carolina State 1937–38
Cardwell, Joe, T, Duke 1937–38
Carpenter, Preston, E, Arkansas 1960–63
Casper, Charles, QB, Texas Christian 1935
Cenci, John, C, Pittsburgh 1956
Chamberlain, Garth, G, Brigham Young 1945
Chandnois, Lynn, B, Michigan State 1950–56
Cheatham, Ernest, T, Loyola 1954
Cherry, Edgar, B, Hardin-Simmons 1939
Cherundolo, Chuck, C, Penn State 1941–42, 1945–48
Christy, Dick, B, N. Carolina State 1958
Cibulas, Joe, T, Duquesne 1945
Ciccone, Ben, C, Duquesne 1934–35
Cichowski, Gene, B, Indiana 1957
Cifelli, Gus, T, Notre Dame 1954
Cifers, Bob, QB, Tennessee 1947–48
Clack, Jim, C, Wake Forest 1971–76
Clark, Jim, B, Pittsburgh 1933–34
Clark, Mike, K, Texas A&M 1964–67
Clement, Henry, E, North Carolina 1961
Clement, John, B, Southern Methodist 1946–48
Cole, Terry, B, Indiana 1970
Collier, Mike, RB, Morgan State 1975
Compagno, Tony, B, St. Mary's Cal. 1946–48
Compton, Dick, E, McMurry 1967–68
Condit, Merlyn, B, Carnegie Tech 1940, 1946
Conn, Dick, DB, Georgia 1974
Connelly, Mike, C, Utah State 1968
Conti, Enio, G, Bucknell 1943
Coomer, Joe, T, Austin 1941, 1945–46
Cooper, Sam T, Geneva 1933
Cordileone, Lou, G, Clemson 1962–63
Coronado, Bob, E, Pacific 1961
Cotton, Russell, B, Texas Mines 1942
Craft, Russ, B, Alabama 1954
Cregar, William, G, Holy Cross 1947–48
Crennel, Carl, LB, West Virginia 1970
Critchfield, Larry, G, Grove City 1933
Croft, Winfield, G, Utah 1936
Cropper, Marshall, E, Maryland 1967–69
Cunningham, Bennie, TE, Clemson 1976
Currivan, Don, E, Boston College 1944
Curry, Roy, B, Jackson State 1963

Marv Woodson with interception, John Campbell (53), Clendon Thomas vs. Dallas, 1966.

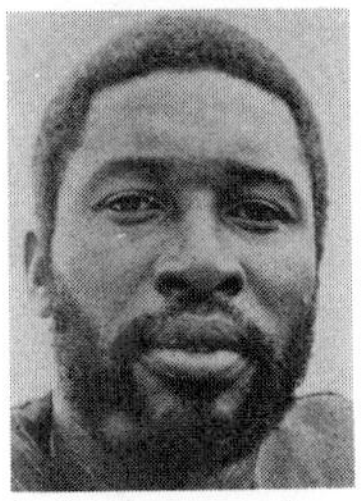

L.C. Greenwood

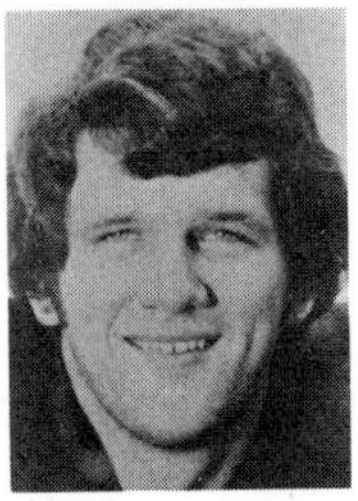

Jack Ham

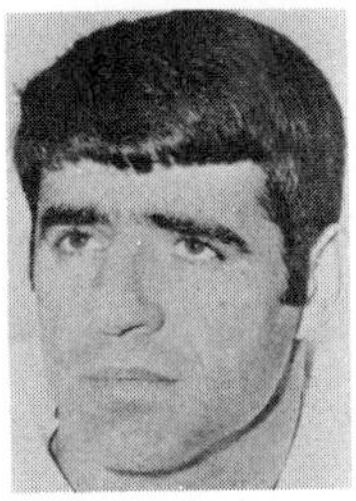

Dick Hoak

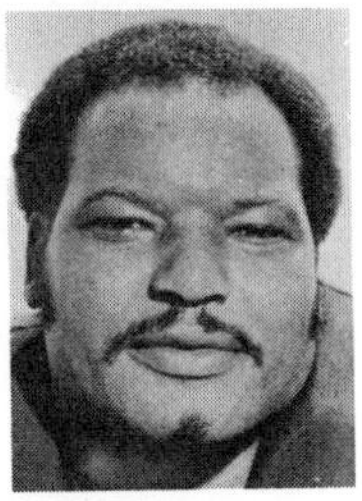

Ernie Holmes

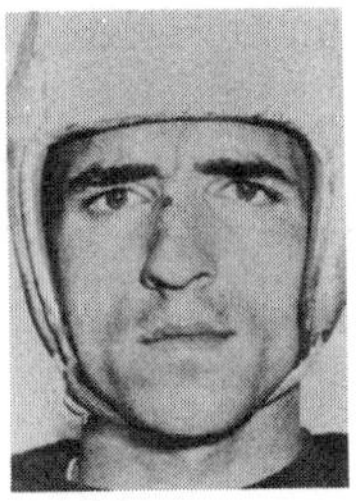

Val Jansante

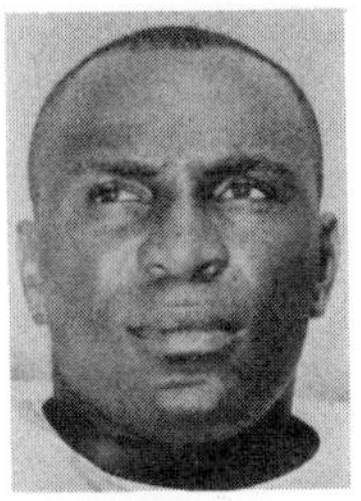

Brady Keys

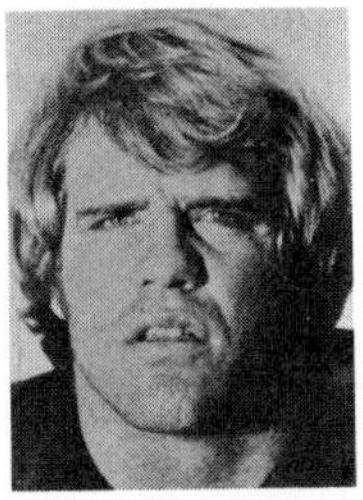

Jon Kolb

D

Dailey, Ted, E, Pittsburgh ... 1933
Daniel, Willie, B, Mississippi State ... 1961–66
Davidson, Bill, B, Temple ... 1937–39
Davis, Art, B, Mississippi State ... 1956
Davis, Charlie, DT, Texas Christian ... 1974
Davis, Dave, WR, Tennessee State ... 1973
Davis, Henry, LB, Grambling ... 1970–73
Davis, Paul, QB, Otterbein ... 1947–48
Davis, Robert, E, Penn State ... 1946–50
Davis, Sam, G, Allen ... 1967–75
Davis, Steve, RB, Delaware State ... 1972–74
Dawson, Len, QB, Purdue ... 1957–59
DeCarbo, Nick, G, Duquesne ... 1933
DeCarlo, Art, B, Georgia ... 1953
Deloplaine, Jack, RB, Salem, W. Va. ... 1976
Demko, George, T, Appalachian State ... 1961
Dempsey, John, T, Bucknell ... 1934
DePascal, Carmine, E, Wichita ... 1945
DePaul, Henry, G, Duquesne ... 1945
Derby, Dean, B, Washington ... 1957–61
Dess, Darrell, G, N. Carolina State ... 1958
Dial, Buddy, E, Rice ... 1959–63
Dicus, Chuck, WR, Arkansas ... 1973
Dockery, John, CB, Harvard ... 1972–73
Dodrill, Dale, G, Colorado A&M ... 1951–59
Dodson, Les, B, Mississippi ... 1941
Doehring, John, B ... 1935
Dolly, Dick, E, West Virginia ... 1941–45
Doloway, Cliff, E, Carnegie Tech ... 1935
Donelli, Allan, B, Duquesne ... 1941–42
Douds, Forrest, T, Wash. & Jefferson ... 1933–35
Dougherty, Bob, LB, Kentucky ... 1958
Douglas, Bob, B, Kansas State ... 1938
Doyle, Dick, B, Ohio State ... 1955
Doyle, Ted, T, Nebraska ... 1938–44
Drulis, Al, B, Temple ... 1947
Druschel, Rick, G, North Carolina State ... 1974
Dudley, Bill, B, Virginia ... 1942, 1945–46
Dugan, Len, C, Wichita ... 1939
Duggan, Gil, T, Oklahoma ... 1944
Duhart, Paul, B, Florida ... 1945
Dunn, Gary, DT, Miami ... 1976
Dutton, Bill, B, Pittsburgh ... 1946

E

Eaton, Vic, QB, Missouri ... 1955
Edwards, Glen, QB, Florida A&M ... 1971–76
Elliott, Jim, K, Presbyterian ... 1967
Ellstrom, Marv, B, Oklahoma ... 1935
Elter, Leo, B, Villanova ... 1953–54, 1958–59
Engebretsen, Paul, G, Northwestern ... 1933
Evans, Jon, E, Oklahoma A&M ... 1958
Evans, Ray, QB, Kansas ... 1948

F

Farrar, Venice, B, N. Carolina State ... 1939
Farrell, Ed, B, Muhlenberg ... 1938
Farroh, Shipley, G, Iowa ... 1938
Feher, Nick, G, Georgia ... 1955
Feniello, Gerry, G, Wake Forest ... 1947
Ferguson, Bob, B, Ohio State ... 1962–63
Ferry, Lou, T, Villanova ... 1952–55
Fife, Ralph, C, Pittsburgh ... 1946
Filchock, Frank, QB, Indiana ... 1938
Finks, Jim, QB, Tulsa ... 1949–55
Fisher, Doug, LB, San Diego State ... 1969–70
Fisher, Everett, B, Santa Clara ... 1940
Fisher, Ray, T, E. Illinois ... 1959
Fiske, Max, B, DePaul ... 1936–39
Flanagan, Dick, G, Ohio State ... 1953–55
Folkins, Lee, E, Washington ... 1965
Folts, Vern, C, St. Vincents ... 1945
Ford, Henry, B, Pittsburgh ... 1956
Foruria, John, B, Idaho ... 1967–68
Fournet, Sid, G, Louisiana State ... 1957
Francis, Sam, B, Nebraska ... 1939
Frank, Joe, T, Georgetown ... 1943
Frketich, Len, T, Penn State ... 1945
Fugler, Dick, T, Tulane ... 1952
Fullerton, Ed, B, Maryland ... 1953
Fuqua, John, B, Morgan State ... 1970–76
Furness, Steve, DT, Rhode Island ... 1972–76

G

Gage, Bob, B, Clemson ... 1949–50
Gagner, Larry, G, Florida ... 1966–69
Gaona, Bob, T, Wake Forest ... 1953–56
Garnaas, Wilford, B, Minnesota ... 1946–48
Garrett, Reggie, WR, Eastern Michigan ... 1974–75
Gasparella, Joe, QB, Notre Dame ... 1948, 1950–51
Gauer, Charles, E, Colgate ... 1943
Gentry, Byron, G, USC ... 1937–39
Gerela, Roy, K, New Mexico State ... 1971–76
Geri, Joe, B, Clemson ... 1949–51
Gildea, John, QB, St. Bonaventure ... 1935–37
Gilliam, Joe, QB, Tennessee State ... 1972–75
Girard, Earl, B, Wisconsin ... 1957
Glamp, Joe, B, Louisiana State ... 1947–49
Glass, Glenn, B, Tennessee ... 1962–63
Glass, Park, C, Westminster ... 1947
Glatz, Fred, E, Pittsburgh ... 1956
Glick, Gary, DB, Colorado A&M ... 1956–59
Goff, Clark, T, Florida ... 1940
Goldsmith, Bill, C, Emporia Teachers ... 1947
Gonda, George, B, Duquesne ... 1942
Gorinski, Walt, B, Louisiana State ... 1946
Grabinski, Thaddeus, C, Duquesne ... 1939–40
Graff, Neil, QB, Wisconsin ... 1976
Graham, Ken, DB, Washington State ... 1970
Gravelle, Gordon, T, Brigham Young ... 1972–76
Graves, Ray, C, Tennessee ... 1943
Gray, Sam, E, Tulsa ... 1946–47
Green, Bob, K, Florida ... 1960–61
Greene, Joe, DT, N. Texas State ... 1969–76
Greenwood, L. C., DE, Arkansas AM&N ... 1969–76
Greeney, Norm, G, Notre Dame ... 1934–35
Grigas, John, B, Holy Cross ... 1944
Gros, Earl, B, Louisiana State ... 1967–69
Grossman, Randy, TE, Temple ... 1974–76
Gunderman, Bob, B, Virginia ... 1957
Gunnels, Riley, T, Georgia ... 1965–66

H

Hackney, Elmer, B, Kansas State ... 1941
Haggerty, Mike, G, Miami ... 1967–70
Haines, Byron, B, Washington ... 1937
Haley, Dick, B, Pittsburgh ... 1961–64
Hall, Ron, B, Missouri Valley ... 1959
Ham, Jack, LB, Penn State ... 1971–76
Hanlon, Bob, B, Loras ... 1949
Hanneman, Craig, DT, Oregon State ... 1972–73
Hanratty, Terry, QB, Notre Dame ... 1969–75
Hanson, Tom, B, Temple ... 1938
Harkey, Lem, B, Emporia State ... 1955
Harper, Maurice, C, Austin ... 1941
Harris, Bill, E, Hardin-Simmons ... 1937
Harris, Franco, RB, Penn State ... 1972–76
Harris, Lou, B, Kent State ... 1968
Harrison, Reggie, RB, Cincinnati ... 1974–76
Harrison, Richard, E, Boston College ... 1964
Harrison, Robert, LB, Oklahoma ... 1964
Hartley, Howard, B, Duke ... 1949–52
Hayduk, Henry, G, Washington State ... 1935
Hayes, Dick, LB, Clemson ... 1959–60, 1962
Hays, George, E, St. Bonaventure ... 1950–52
Hebert, Ken, E, Houston ... 1968
Hegarty, Bill, T, Villanova ... 1953
Held, Paul, QB, San Jose State ... 1954
Heller, Warren, B, Pittsburgh ... 1934–36
Henderson, Jon, B, Colorado State ... 1968–69
Hendley, Dick, QB, Clemson ... 1951
Henry, Mike, LB, USC ... 1959–61
Henry, Urban, DT, Georgia Tech ... 1964
Hensley, Dick, E, Kentucky ... 1952
Henson, Ken, C, Texas Christian ... 1965
Hewitt, Bill, E, Michigan ... 1943
Hickey, Howard, E, Arkansas ... 1941
Hill, Harlon, E, Florence State ... 1962
Hill, Jim, B, Tennessee ... 1955
Hillebrand, Jerry, LB, Colorado ... 1968–70
Hilton, John, E, Richmond ... 1965–69
Hines, Glen Ray, T, Arkansas ... 1973
Hinkle, John, B, Syracuse ... 1943
Hinte, Hale, E, Pittsburgh ... 1942
Hinton, Chuck, T, N. Carolina Coll. ... 1964–71
Hipps, Claude, B, Georgia ... 1952–53
Hoague, Joe, B, Colgate ... 1941–42
Hoak, Dick, B, Penn State ... 1961–70
Hoel, Bob, G, Minnesota ... 1935
Hogan, Darrell, G, Trinity, Tex ... 1949–53
Hohn, Bob, B, Nebraska ... 1965–69
Holcomb, Bill, T, Texas Tech ... 1937
Holler, Ed, LB, South Carolina ... 1964
Hollingsworth, Joe, B, E, Kentucky ... 1949–51
Holm, Bernard, B, Alabama ... 1933
Holmer, Walt, B, Northwestern ... 1933
Holmes, Ernie, DT, Texas Southern ... 1972–76
Holmes, Mel, T, N. Carolina A&T ... 1971–73
Hood, Frank, B, Pittsburgh ... 1933
Hornick, Bill, T, Tulane ... 1947
Hubbard, Cal, T, Centenary ... 1936
Hubka, Gene, B, Bucknell ... 1947
Hughes, Dennis, TE, Georgia ... 1970–71
Hughes, Dick, B, Tulsa ... 1957
Hughes, George, G, William & Mary ... 1950–54
Hunter, Art, C, Notre Dame ... 1965

I

Itzel, John, B, Pittsburgh ... 1945
Ivy, Frank (Pop), E, Oklahoma ... 1940
Izo, George, QB, Notre Dame ... 1966

J

James, Dan, T, Ohio State ... 1960–66
Janecek, Clarence, G, Purdue ... 1933, 1935
Jansante, Val, E, Duquesne ... 1946–51
Jarvi, Toimi, B, No. Illinois ... 1945
Jecha, Ralph, G, Northwestern ... 1956
Jefferson, Roy, E, Utah ... 1965–69
Jelley, Tom, E, Miami ... 1951
Jenkins, Ralph, C, Clemson ... 1947
Jeter, Tony, E, Nebraska ... 1966, 1968
Johnson, John Henry, B, Arizona St. ... 1960–65
Johnston, Chet, B, Marquette ... 1939–40
Johnston, Rex, B, USC ... 1960
Jones, Art, B, Richmond ... 1941, 1945

K

Kahler, Royal, T, Nebraska ... 1941
Kakasic, George, G, Duquesne ... 1936–39
Kalina, Dave, WR, Miami ... 1970
Kapele, John, T, Brigham Young ... 1960–62
Kaplan, Phil, G, Miami ... 1947
Karcis, John, B, Carnegie Tech ... 1936–38
Karpowich, Ed, T, Catholic U. ... 1936–39
Karras, Ted, T, Indiana ... 1958–59
Kase, George, G, Duquesne ... 1939
Kavel, George, B, Carnegie Tech ... 1934
Keating, Tom, DT, Michigan ... 1973
Kellum, Marv, LB, Wichita State ... 1974–76
Kelly, Jim, E, Notre Dame ... 1964
Kelsch, Mose, B, Christian ... 1933–34
Kemp, Jack, QB, Occidental ... 1957
Kemp, Ray, T, Duquesne ... 1933
Kenerson, John, G, Kentucky State ... 1962
Kerkorian, Gary, QB, Stanford ... 1952
Keys, Brady, DB, Colorado State ... 1961–67
Kichefski, Walt, E, Miami ... 1940–42, 1944
Kielbasa, Max, B, Duquesne ... 1946
Kiesling, Walt, G, St. Thomas ... 1937–38
Kiick, George, B, Bucknell ... 1940, 1945
Killorin, Pat, C, Syracuse ... 1966
Kilroy, Frank (Bucko), T, Temple ... 1943
Kimble, Frank, E, West Virginia ... 1945
King, Phil, B, Vanderbilt ... 1964
Kirk, Ken, LB, Mississippi ... 1960
Kish, Ben, B, Pittsburgh ... 1943
Kissell, Ed, B, Wake Forest ... 1952–54
Klapstein, Earl, T, Pacific ... 1946
Klein, Dick, T, Iowa ... 1961
Klumb, John, E, Washington State ... 1940
Kolb, Jon, C, Oklahoma State ... 1969–76
Kolberg, Elmer, E, Oregon State ... 1941
Kondria, John, T, St. Vincent's ... 1945
Kortas, Ken, T, Louisville ... 1965–68
Kosanovich, Bronco, C, Penn State ... 1947
Koshlap, Jules, B, Georgetown ... 1945

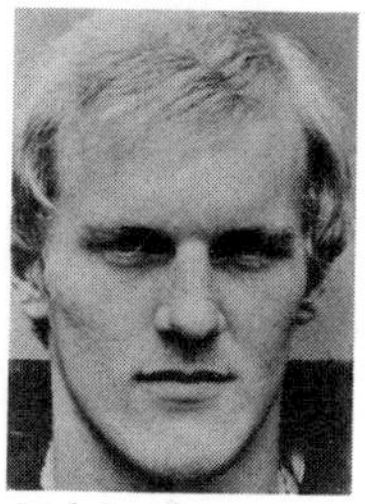

Jack Lambert

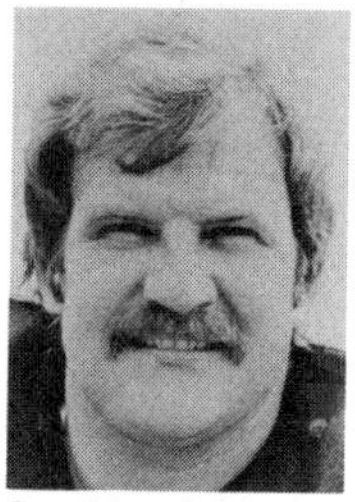

Ray Mansfield

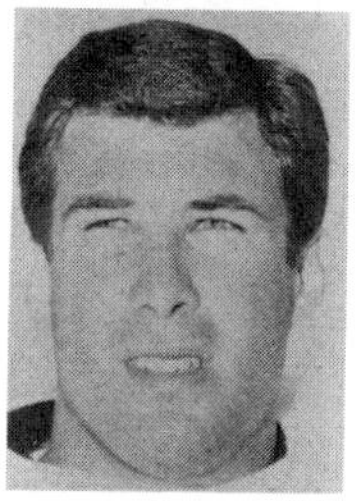

Paul Martha

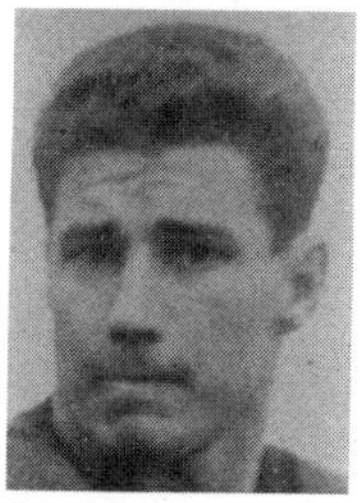

Ray Mathews

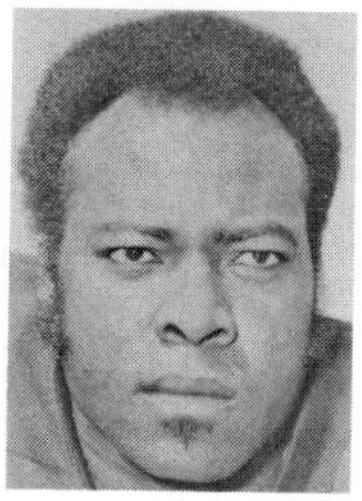

Ben McGee

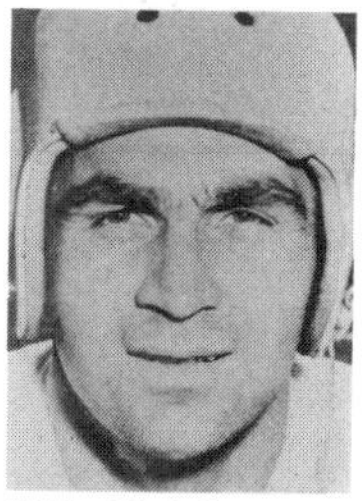

Elbie Nickel

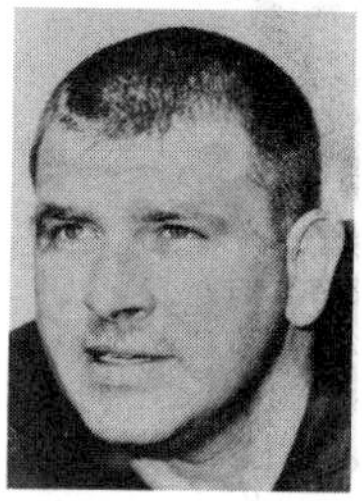

John Reger

Kotite, Dick, TE, Wagner . . . 1968
Kottler, Martin, B, Centre . . . 1933
Kresky, Joe, G, Wisconsin . . . 1935
Krisher, Bill, G, Oklahoma . . . 1958
Kruczek, Mike, QB, Boston College . . . 1976
Krupa, Joe, DT, Purdue . . . 1956–64
Kurrasch, Roy, E, UCLA . . . 1948
Kvaternik, Cvonimir, G, Kansas . . . 1934

L

Lach, Steve, B, Duke . . . 1946–47
Ladygo, Pete, G, Maryland . . . 1952, 1954
Lajousky, Bill, G, Catholic U. . . . 1936
Lamas, Joe, G, Mount St. Mary's . . . 1942
Lambert, Frank, K, Mississippi . . . 1965–66
Lambert, Jack, LB, Kent State . . . 1974–76
Lantz, Montgomery, C, Grove City . . . 1933
LaRose, Dan, T, Missouri . . . 1964
Lassahn, Lou, E, Western Maryland . . . 1938
Lasse, Dick, LB, Syracuse . . . 1958–59
Lattner, John, B, Notre Dame . . . 1954
Laux, Ted, B, St. Joseph's, Pa. . . . 1943
Law, Hubbard, C, Sam Houston . . . 1942, 1945
Layne, Bobby, QB, Texas . . . 1958–62
Lea, Paul, T, Tulane . . . 1951
Leahy, Bob, QB, Emporia State . . . 1971
Leahy, Gerald, T, Colorado . . . 1957
Lee, Bernard, B, Villanova . . . 1938
Lee, Herman, T, Florida A&M . . . 1957
Lee, John, B, Carnegie Tech . . . 1939
Leftridge, Dick, B, West Virginia . . . 1966
Lemek, Ray, G, Notre Dame . . . 1962–65
Letsinger, Jim, G, Purdue . . . 1933
Levanti, Lou, G, Illinois . . . 1951–52
Levey, Jim, B, None . . . 1934–36
Lewis, Frank, WR, Grambling . . . 1971–76
Lewis, Joe, T, Compton J. C. . . . 1958–60
Liddick, Dave, T, George Washington . . . 1957
Lind, Mike, B, Notre Dame . . . 1965–66
Lipscomb, Gene (Big Daddy), T, None . . . 1961–62
Littlefield, Carl, B, Washington State . . . 1939
Logan, Charles, E, Northwestern . . . 1964
Long, Bill, E, Oklahoma A&M . . . 1949–50
Longnecker, Ken, T, Lebanon Valley . . . 1960
Looney, Don, E, Texas Christian . . . 1941–42
Lowther, Russ, B, Detroit . . . 1945
Lucente, John, B, West Virginia . . . 1945
Luna, Bob, B, Alabama . . . 1959
Lusteg, Booth, K, Connecticut . . . 1968

M

Mack, Red, B, Notre Dame . . . 1961–63, 1965
Mackrides, Bill, QB, Nevada . . . 1953
Magac, Mike, G, Missouri . . . 1965–66
Magulick, George, B, St. Francis . . . 1944
Maher, Francis, B, Toledo . . . 1941
Malkovich, Joe, C, Duquesne . . . 1935
Mallick, Francis, T, None . . . 1965
Mansfield, Ray, C, Washington . . . 1964–76
Manske, Edgar (Eggs), E, Northwestern . . . 1938
Maples, Bob, C, Baylor . . . 1971
Maras, Joe, C, Duquesne . . . 1938–40
Marchi, Basilio, C, New York U. . . . 1934
Marchibroda, Ted, QB, Detroit . . . 1953, 1955–56
Marion, Jerry, B, Wyoming . . . 1967
Marker, Henry, B, West Virginia . . . 1934
Marotti, Lou, G, Toledo . . . 1944
Martha, Paul, B, Pittsburgh . . . 1964–69
Martin, John, B, Oklahoma . . . 1944
Martin, Vernon, B, Texas . . . 1944
Masters, Bob, B, Baylor . . . 1939, 1943
Masters, Walt, B, Pennsylvania . . . 1944
Mastrangelo, John, G, Notre Dame . . . 1947–48
Matesic, Ed, B, Pittsburgh . . . 1936
Matesic, Joe, T, Arizona State . . . 1954
Mathews, Ray, B, Clemson . . . 1951–59
Mattioli, Fran, G, Pittsburgh . . . 1946
Matuszak, Marv, LB, Tulsa . . . 1953, 1955–56
May, Ray, LB, USC . . . 1967–69
Mayhew, Hayden, G, Texas Mines . . . 1936–38
Massanti, Jerry, E, Arkansas . . . 1967
McCabe, Richie, B, Pittsburgh . . . 1955, 1957–58
McCaffray, Art, T, Pacific . . . 1946
McCall, Don, RB, USC . . . 1969
McCarthy, John, B, St. Francis . . . 1944
McClairen, Jack, E, Bethune-Cookman . . . 1955–60
McClung, Willie, T, Florida A&M . . . 1955–57
McConnell, Dewey, E, Wyoming . . . 1954
McCullough, Hugh, B, Oklahoma . . . 1939, 1943
McDade, Karl, C, Portland . . . 1938
McDonald, Ed, B, Duquesne . . . 1936
McDonough, Coley, QB, Dayton . . . 1939–41, 1944
McDonough, Paul, E, Utah . . . 1938
McFadden, Marv, G, Michigan St. . . . 1953, 1956
McGee, Ben, DE, Jackson State . . . 1964–72
McMakin, John, TE, Clemson . . . 1972–74
McNally (Blood), Johnny, B, St. John's, Minn. . . 1934, 1937–39
McNamara, Ed, T, Holy Cross . . . 1945
McPeak, Bill, E, Pittsburgh . . . 1949–57
McWilliams, Tom, B, Mississippi State . . . 1950
Meadows, Ed, E, Duke . . . 1955
Meeks, Bryant, C, South Carolina . . . 1947–48
Mehelech, Chuck, E, Duquesne . . . 1946–51
Meilinger, Steve, E, Kentucky . . . 1961
Merkovsky, Elmer, T, Pittsburgh . . . 1944–46
Messner, Max, LB, Cincinnati . . . 1964–65
Meyer, Dennis, S, Arkansas . . . 1973
Meyer, Ron, QB, S. Dakota State . . . 1966
Michael, Bill, G, Ohio State . . . 1957
Michaels, Ed, G, Villanova . . . 1943
Michaels, Lou, DE, Kentucky . . . 1961–63
Michalik, Art, G, St. Ambrose . . . 1955–56
Midler, Lou, G, Minnesota . . . 1939
Miller, Tom, E, Hampden-Sydney . . . 1943
Minarik, Henry, E, Michigan State . . . 1951
Miner, Tom, E, Tulsa . . . 1958
Mingo, Gene, K, None . . . 1969–70
Minini, Frank, B, San Jose State . . . 1949
Modzelewski, Dick, T, Maryland . . . 1955
Modzelewski, Ed, B, Maryland . . . 1952
Moegle, Dick, B, Rice . . . 1960
Momsen, Tony, C, Michigan . . . 1951
Moore, Bill, B, Loyola, La. . . . 1933
Moore, Red, G, Penn State . . . 1947–49
Morales, Gonzales, B, St. Mary's, Cal. . . . 1947–48
Morgan, Bob, B, New Mexico . . . 1967–68
Morrall, Earl, QB, Michigan State . . . 1957–58
Morris, John, B, Oregon . . . 1960
Mosher, Clure, C, Louisville . . . 1942
Mosley, Norm, B, Alabama . . . 1948
Moss, Paul, E, Purdue . . . 1933
Motley, Marion, B, Nevada . . . 1955
Mott, Norm, B, Georgia . . . 1934
Mulleneaux, Lee, C, Utah State . . . 1935–36
Mullins, Gerry, G, USC . . . 1971–76
Murley, Dick, T, Purdue . . . 1956
Murray, Earl, G, Purdue . . . 1952
Musulin, George, Pittsburgh . . . 1938

N

Nagler, Gern, E, Santa Clara . . . 1959
Naiota, John, B, St. Francis . . . 1942, 1945
Nardi, Dick, B, Ohio State . . . 1939
Nelsen, Bill, QB, USC . . . 1963–67
Nery, Carl, G, Duquesne . . . 1940–41
Niccolai, Armand, T, Duquesne . . . 1934–42
Nichols, Allen, B, Temple . . . 1945
Nichols, Bob, T, Stanford . . . 1965
Nickel, Elbie, E, Cincinnati . . . 1947–57
Nicksich, George, G, St. Bonaventure . . . 1950
Nisby, John, G, Pacific . . . 1957–61
Nix, Kent, QB, Texas Christian . . . 1967–69
Nixon, Mike, B, Pittsburgh . . . 1935
Nobile, Leo, G, Penn State . . . 1948–49
Nofsinger, Terry, QB, Utah . . . 1961–64
Noppenberg, John, B, Miami . . . 1940–41
Nosich, John, T, Duquesne . . . 1938
Nutter, Madison (Buzz), C, Virginia Tech . . . 1961–64
Nuzum, Jerry, B, New Mexico A&M . . . 1948–51

O

O'Brien, Fran, T, Michigan State . . . 1966–67
O'Brien, John, E, Florida . . . 1954–56
O'Delli, Mel, B, Duquesne . . . 1944–45
Oehler, John, C, Purdue . . . 1933–34
Oelerich, John, B, St. Ambrose . . . 1938
Olejniczak, Stan, T, Pittsburgh . . . 1935
Oliver, Clarence, DB, San Diego St. . . . 1969–70
Olszewski, Al, Pittsburgh . . . 1945
O'Malley, Joe, E, Georgia . . . 1955–56
O'Neil, Bob, G, Notre Dame . . . 1956–57
Oniskey, Dick, G, Chattanooga . . . 1955
Orr, Jimmy, E, Georgia . . . 1958–60
Ortman, Chuck, QB, Michigan . . . 1951

P

Palmer, Tom, T, Wake Forest . . . 1953–54
Papach, George, B, Purdue . . . 1948–49
Paschell, Bill, B. . . . 1940
Pascka, Gordon, G, Minnesota . . . 1943
Pastin, Frank, G, Waynesburg . . . 1942
Patrick, John, B, Penn State . . . 1941, 1945–46
Patterson, Bill, QB, Baylor . . . 1940
Pavia, Ralph, G, Dayton . . . 1947
Pavkov, Stonko, G, Idaho . . . 1939–40
Peaks, Clarence, B, Michigan State . . . 1964–65
Pearson, Barry, WR, Northwestern . . . 1972–73
Pearson, Preston, B, Illinois . . . 1970–74
Pense, Leon, QB, Arkansas . . . 1945
Perko, John, G, Duquesne . . . 1937–40, 1944–47
Perry, Lowell, B, Michigan . . . 1956
Petchel, John, QB, Duquesne . . . 1945
Petrella, John, B, Penn State . . . 1945
Pierre, John, E, Pittsburgh . . . 1945
Pillath, Roger, T, Wisconsin . . . 1966
Pine, Ed, LB, Utah . . . 1965
Pinney, Ray, C, Washington . . . 1976
Pirro, Rocco, G, Catholic U. . . . 1940–41
Pittman, Mel, C, Hardin-Simmons . . . 1935
Platukas, George, E, Duquesne . . . 1938–41
Popovich, John, B, St. Vincent's . . . 1944–45
Postus, Al, B, Villanova . . . 1945
Pottios, Myron, LB, Notre Dame . . . 1963–65
Potts, Bill, B, Villanova . . . 1934
Pough, Ernest, WR, Texas Southern . . . 1976
Powell, Tim, E, Northwestern . . . 1966
Powers, John, E, Notre Dame . . . 1962–66
Priatko, Bill, LB, Pittsburgh . . . 1957

Q

Quatse, Jesse, T, Pittsburgh . . . 1933–34

R

Raborn, Carroll, C, Southern Methodist . . . 1936–37
Rado, Alex, B, New River State . . . 1934–35
Rado, George, G, Duquesne . . . 1935–37
Radosevich, George, C, Pittsburgh . . . 1953
Ragunas, Vince, B, VMI . . . 1949
Rajkovich, Pete, B, Detroit . . . 1934
Randour, Hub, Pittsburgh . . . 1935
Rankin, Walt, B, Texas Tech . . . 1944
Raskowski, Leo, T, Ohio State . . . 1933
Reavis, Dave, T, Arkansas . . . 1974–75
Rechichar, Bert, B, Tennessee . . . 1960
Recutt, Ray, E, VMI . . . 1943
Reger, John, LB, Pittsburgh . . . 1955–63
Renfro, Will, G, Memphis State . . . 1960
Repko, Joe, T, Boston College . . . 1946–47
Reynolds, Jim, B, Oklahoma A&M . . . 1946
Reynolds, Billy, B, Pittsburgh . . . 1958
Rhodes, Don, T, Washington & Jefferson . . . 1933
Ribble, Loran, G, Hardin-Simmons . . . 1934–35
Richards, Perry, E, Detroit . . . 1957
Riffle, Dick, B, Albright . . . 1941–42
Rizzo, Tony, Duquesne . . . 1938
Roberts, John, B, Georgia . . . 1934
Robinson, Gil, E, Catawba . . . 1933
Robinson, Jack, T, N.E. Missouri State . . . 1938
Robnett, Marshall, C, Texas A&M . . . 1944
Rodak, Mike, B, Western Reserve . . . 1942
Rogel, Fran, B, Penn State . . . 1950–57
Rogers, Cullen, B, Texas A&M . . . 1946
Rorison, Jim, T, USC . . . 1938
Rosepink, Marty, G, Pittsburgh . . . 1947
Rowley, Bob, LB, Virginia . . . 1963
Rowser, John, DB, Michigan . . . 1970–73
Rozelle, Aubrey, LB, Delta State . . . 1957
Rucinski, Ed, E, Indiana . . . 1944
Ruple, Ernie, T, Arkansas . . . 1968–69

Fran Rogel *Mike Sandusky* *Jerry Shipkey* *Frank Sinkovitz* *Lynn Swann* *Tom Tracy* *Mike Wagner*

Russell, Andy, LB, Missouri 1963, 1966–76
Ryan, Ed, E, St. Mary's, Cal. 1948

S

Sader, Steve, B, None 1943
Sample, John, DB, Maryland State 1961–62
Samuel, Don, B, Oregon State 1949–50
Samuelson, Carl, T, Nebraska 1948–51
Sandberg, Sigurd, T, Iowa Wesleyan 1935–37
Sandefur, Wayne, B, Purdue 1936–37
Sanders, John, G, Southern Methodist 1940–42
Sandig, Curt, B, St. Mary's, Texas 1942
Sandusky, Mike, T, Maryland 1957–65
Sapp, Theron, B, Georgia 1963–65
Saul, Bill, LB, Penn State 1964, 1966–68
Saumer, Sylvester, B, St. Olaf 1934
Scales, Charles, B, Indiana 1960–61
Scarbath, Jack, QB, Maryland 1956
Scherer, Bernard, E, Nebraska 1939
Schiechl, John, C, Santa Clara 1941–42
Schmidt, John, C, Carnegie Tech 1940
Schmitz, Bob, LB, Montana State 1961–66
Schnelker, Bob, E, Bowling Green 1961
Schuelke, Karl, B, Wisconsin 1939
Schultz, Eberle, G, Oregon State 1941–42
Schwartz, Elmer, B, Washington State 1933
Schweder, John, G, Pennsylvania 1951–55
Scolnik, Glenn, WR, Indiana 1973
Scot, Wilbert, LB, Indiana 1961
Scudero, Joe, B, San Francisco 1960
Seabright, Charles, QB, West Virginia 1946–50
Sears, Vic, T, Oregon State 1943
Sebastian, Mike, B, Pittsburgh 1935
Semes, Bernard, B, Duquesne 1944
Shaffer, George, B, Washington & Jefferson 1933
Shanklin, Ron, WR, N. Texas State 1970–75
Sharp, Rick, T, Washington 1970–71
Shell, Donnie, DB, South Carolina State 1974–76
Shepard, Charles, B, N. Texas State 1956
Sheriff, Stan, LB, Cal. Poly SLO 1954
Sherman, Allie, QB, Brooklyn 1943
Sherman, Bob, B, Iowa 1964–65
Shields, Burrell, B, John Carroll 1954
Shiner, Dick, QB Maryland 1968–69
Shipkey, Jerry, B, UCLA 1958–52
Shorter, Jim, B, Detroit 1969
Shurtz, Hubert, T, Louisiana State 1948
Shy, Don, B, San Diego State 1967–68
Simerson, John, T, Purdue 1958
Simington, Milt, G, Arkansas 1942
Simmons, Jerry, B, Bethune-Cookman 1965–66
Simms, Bob, E, Rutgers 1962
Simpson, Jack, B, Florida 1961–62
Sinkovitz, Frank, C, Duke 1947–52
Sirochman, George, G, Duquesne 1942
Sites, Vince, E, Pittsburgh 1936–37
Skladany, Joe, E, Pittsburgh 1934

Skorich, Nick, G, Cincinnati 1946–48
Skoronski, Ed, E, Purdue 1935–36
Skulos, Mike, G, Washington & Jefferson 1938
Slater, Walt, B, Tennessee 1947
Smith, Ben, E, Alabama 1934–35
Smith, Billy Ray, T, Arkansas 1958–60
Smith, Bob, B, N. Texas State 1966
Smith, Dave, E, Indiana, Pa. 1970–72
Smith, Ron, QB, Richmond 1966
Smith, Steve, E, Michigan 1966
Smith, Stu, QB, Bucknell 1937–38
Smith, Truett, QB, Mississippi State 1950–51
Smith, Warren, T, Kansas Wesleyan 1948
Snyder, Bill, B, Ohio U. 1934–35
Sodaski, John, DB, Villanova 1970
Soleau, Bob, LB, William & Mary 1964
Somers, George, T, LaSalle 1941–42
Sorce, Ross, T, Georgetown 1945
Sortet, Wilbur, E, West Virginia 1933–40
Souchak, Frank, E, Pittsburgh 1939
Spinks, Jack, G, Alcorn A&M 1952
Spizak, Charley, QB, Carnegie Tech 1938
Staggers, Jon, WR, Missouri 1970–71
Stallworth, John, WR, Alabama A&M 1974–76
Stanton, John, B, N. Carolina State 1961
Starret, Ben, B, St. Mary's, Cal. 1941
Stautner, Ernie, DT, Boston College 1950–63
Steele, Ernie, B, Washington 1943
Stehouwer, Ron, B, Colorado State 1960–64
Stenger, Brian, LB, Notre Dame 1969–72
Stenn, Paul, T, Villanova 1947
Steward, Denn, B, Ursinus 1943
Stock, John, E, Pittsburgh 1956
Stofko, Ed, B, St. Francis 1945
Stough, Glen, T, Duke 1945
Strand, Eli, G, Iowa State 1966
Strugar, George, DT, Washington 1962
Strutt, Art, B, Duquesne 1935–36
Suhey, Steve, G, Penn State 1948–49
Sulima, George, E, Boston U. 1952–54
Sullivan, Frank, C, Loyola, La. 1940
Sullivan, Robert, B, Holy Cross, Iowa 1947
Sutherin, Don, B, Ohio State 1959–60
Swann, Lynn, WR, USC 1974–76
Szot, Walter, T, Bucknell 1949–50

T

Tanguay, Jim, B, New York U 1933
Tarasovic, George, E, Louisiana State ... 1952–53, 1956–63
Tatum, Jess, E, N. Carolina State 1938
Taylor, Mike, T, USC 1968–69
Tepe, Lou, C, Duke 1953–55
Tesser, Ray, E, Carnegie Tech 1933–34
Thomas, Clendon, B, Oklahoma 1962–68
Thomas, J.T., CB, Florida State 1973–76
Thompson, Clarence, B, Minnesota 1937–38
Thompson, Tommy, QB, Tulsa 1940

Thurbon, Bob, B, Pittsburgh 1943–44
Tiller, Morgan, E, Denver 1945
Tinsley, Sid, B, Clemson 1945
Titus, George, C, Holy Cross 1946
Titus, Silas, E, Holy Cross 1945
Toews, Loren, LB, California 1973–76
Tomasetti, Lou, B, Bucknell 1939–40
Tomasic, Andy, B, Temple 1942–46
Tomlinson, Dick, G, Kansas 1950–51
Tommerson, Clarence, B, Wisconsin 1938–39
Tosi, John, G, Niagara 1939
Tracy, Tom, B, Tennessee 1958–63
Tsoutsouvas, Lou, C, Stanford 1938
Turley, John, QB, Ohio Wesleyan 1935–36

V

Van Dyke, Bruce, G, Missouri 1967–73
Varrichione, Frank, T, Notre Dame 1955–60
Vaughan, John, QB, Indiana, Pa. 1933–34
Vidoni, Vic, E, Duquesne 1935–36
Voss, Lloyd, T, Nebraska 1966–71

W

Wade, Bob, DB, Morgan State 1968
Wade, Tom, QB, Texas 1964–65
Wager, Clint, E, St. Mary's, Minn. 1944
Wagner, Mike, S, Western Illinois 1971–76
Walden, Bobby, K, Georgia 1968–76
Walsh, Bill, C, Notre Dame 1949–50
Warren, Buist, B, Tennessee 1945
Washington, Clarence, DT, Arkansas AM&N 1969–70
Watkins, Tom, B, Iowa State 1968
Watson, Allen, K, Newport, Wales 1970
Watson, Sid, B, Northeastern 1955–57
Webster, George, LB, Michigan State 1972–73
Webster, Mike, C, Wisconsin 1974–76
Weed, Thurlow, K, Ohio State 1955
Weinberg, Henry, G, Duquesne 1934
Weinstock, Izzy, B, Pittsburgh 1937–38
Weisenbaugh, Henry, B, Pittsburgh 1935
Wells, Billy, B, Michigan State 1957
Wendlick, Joe, E, Oregon State 1941
Wenzel, Ralph, E, Tulane 1942
Wenzel, Ralph, G, San Diego State 1966–70
Westfall, Ed, B, Ohio Wesleyan 1933
Wetzel, Damon, B, Ohio State 1935
Whalen, Tom, B, Catholic U. 1933
Wheeler, Ernie, B, N. Dakota State 1939
White, Byron (Whizzer), B, Colorado 1938
White, Dwight, DE, E. Texas State 1971–76
White, Paul, B, Michigan 1947
Wiehl, Joe, T, Duquesne 1935
Wilburn, J.R., WR, South Carolina 1966–70
Wiley, Jack, T, Waynesburg 1946–50
Williams, Dave, WR, Washington 1973
Williams, Don, G, Texas 1941
Williams, Erwin, WR, Maryland State 1969
Williams, Joe, B, Lafayette 1939
Williams, Sidney, LB, Southern U. 1969
Williamson, Fred, DB, Northwestern 1960
Wilson, Bill, E, Gonzaga 1938
Winfrey, Carl, LB, Wisconsin 1972
Wistert, Al, T, Michigan 1943
Wolf, Jim, DE, Prairie View 1974
Womack, Joe, B, Cal. State-L.A. 1962
Woodson, Marv, DB, Indiana 1964–69
Woudenberg, John, T, Denver 1940–42
Wren, Lowe, B, Missouri 1960
Wukits, Al, C, Duquesne 1943–45
Wydo, Frank, T, Cornell 1947–51

Y

Young, Al, WR, S. Carolina State 1971–72
Young, Dick, B, Chattanooga 1957
Younger, Paul, B, Grambling 1958
Yurchey, John, B, Duquesne 1940

Z

Zaninelli, Silvio, B, Duquesne 1934–37
Zimmerman, Leroy, QB, San Jose State 1943
Zombek, Joe, E, Pittsburgh 1954
Zopetti, Frank, B, Duquesne 1941

Ray Mathews running, Bob O'Neil (86) and Fran Rogel (33) blocking vs. Detroit, 1956.

ST. LOUIS CARDINALS

1899–1919 The Cardinals were organized in 1899 by a painting and decorating contractor named Chris O'Brien. He formed a neighborhood team in a predominantly Irish area of Chicago's south side, and it played under the name Morgan Athletic Club. The team soon changed its playing site to Normal Field (on the corner of Normal Boulevard and Racine Avenue) and began to call itself the Normals. In 1901, O'Brien found a bargain in second-hand jerseys discarded by the University of Chicago. They were faded maroon in color; O'Brien labeled them "cardinal." The jersey color plus the location of the field led to a new and obvious nickname: the Racine Cardinals. In Chicago at the time, football competition was exclusively amateur, but such opposition became increasingly hard to find, and in 1906 the team had to disband. In 1913 O'Brien reorganized the Cardinals. By 1917 they were able to buy new uniforms and hire a coach, Marston Smith. That year they lost only two games and were champions of the Chicago Football League. The war in Europe and a flu epidemic in this country forced the team to suspend operations once again in 1918. Following Armistice Day, O'Brien organized the Cardinals for a third time. From then on, the Cardinals were a permanent part of the professional football establishment in America.

1920 For a $100 franchise fee, the Racine Cardinals became a charter member of the American Professional Football Association, the forerunner of the NFL. Immediately after joining the league, O'Brien lured a great halfback, John (Paddy) Driscoll, to the Cardinals for a $3,000 a year contract. It was a price considered outlandish for the times, but Driscoll was an authentic superstar, a superior runner, blocker, punter, and maybe the best dropkicker ever to play football. O'Brien then sought to reduce the competition in Chicago. There were two teams in the city, the Cardinals and the Chicago Tigers; the Staleys were in Decatur, Illinois. Two teams competing for the same fan dollar would be ruinous to both. So O'Brien offered—and the Tigers agreed—to play for the right to represent Chicago. The winner would remain as the city's only professional team; the loser would fold its operation. Driscoll scored the game's only touchdown on a 40-yard run and the Cardinals won 6–3. As promised, the Tigers dropped out of competition. That same year, a Cardinals–Staleys rivalry was born. They split two games in 1920. In the Cardinals' 7–6 win, a touchdown was scored behind a blocking wall of partisan fans who had come down from the stands. They were so frenzied that the officials allowed the score. The Cardinals won five games, lost two, and tied one under coach Marshall Smith.

1921 Paddy Driscoll became player-coach of the Racine Cardinals. The Staleys' sponsor agreed to let them move to Chicago if they would keep their Staleys' nickname one more year. Manager George Halas consulted league president Joe Carr, who broached the subject to O'Brien of the Cardinals. With his victory over the Tigers in 1920, O'Brien held the rights to professional football in Chicago; he could block any team from settling there. Inexplicably, he approved Halas's request. The Cardinals finished eighth in the NFL with a 2–3–2 record. In their only encounter with the Staleys, the Cardinals held their rivals, who won the league title with a 10–1–1 record, to a scoreless tie.

1922 A team from Racine, Wisconsin, joined the NFL, making it imperative the Cardinals change their name. The new designation was the Chicago Cardinals. The Cardinals moved their playing site to White Sox Park. The Cardinals had a much better year in the

Quarterback Jim Hart throws a swing pass to running back Terry Metcalf vs. Philadelphia, 1973.

standings. Their 8–3 record was good for third place behind the Canton Bulldogs and the Bears. Included in the Cardinals' eight wins were two over the Bears. The margin of victory in both contests was Paddy Driscoll's dropkicking; he accumulated all 15 points in 6–0 and 9–0 wins. The rival Staleys changed their name too, to Chicago Bears.

1923 Another Cardinals' star, quarterback Arnold Horween, replaced Driscoll as player-coach. Horween was a Harvard man from a wealthy family. He disdained fame and sometimes pay. Professional football was still considered a low occupation; Horween and his brother, Ralph, often played under the alias "McMahon," apparently to protect the social status of their family and the good name of his alma mater. He took money for playing only when O'Brien could reconcile his accounts. In Horween's first year as coach, the Cardinals had an 8–4 record and finished sixth.

1924 With Arnold Horween still the coach, Chicago had an uneventful year, finishing ninth with a 5–4–1 record.

1925 The Cardinals had a new coach, Norman Barry, whose first season was notable for domination over the Bears and a tainted league championship. The Cardinals were still led by the great Paddy Driscoll; his three field goals carried them to a 9–0 early season win over their cross-town rivals. The two teams met on Thanksgiving Day in a rematch. This time, the Bears had a new halfback, Red Grange, who had signed with them right after his last game with the University of Illinois. Grange was making headlines with his spectacular running. But the Cardinals held him and the Bears scoreless; the game ended in 0–0 tie. They stopped Grange by the simple expedient of Driscoll's punting. Paddy kicked out of bounds or away from Grange, and the ploy stifled Grange's

famous runback ability. The Cardinals were one-half game behind the league-leading Pottsville Maroons when the two met on December 6 in the final game of the season. Pottsville won easily 21–7. One week later, Pottsville played an exhibition in Philadelphia against the Notre Dame All-Stars. The coach of the Frankford Yellowjackets, Guy Chamberlin, protested to league president Carr that his territorial boundaries had been violated; Frankford is a Philadelphia suburb. Carr upheld the protest. He instructed the Cardinals to play two more games. They did, defeating Hammond, Indiana and Milwaukee. Hammond had a 1–4 and Milwaukee an 0–6 record. The Cardinals now had a better record than Pottsville and were proclaimed NFL champions.

1926 O'Brien had never been an astute businessman; as owner of the Cardinals, he was in constant distress financially. Even the championship season of 1925 failed to help. Reluctantly, he sold Paddy Driscoll to the Bears. George Halas had wanted Driscoll for years, and he was willing to pay $3,500 for him. The league encouraged the sale. It was in competition with a new group, the American Football League. The AFL had Red Grange, and Carr thought the Bears would have to replace Grange with another big star or cease to be a top NFL draw. Chicago's entry in the AFL, the Bulls, leased Comiskey Park, so the Cardinals had to move back to smaller Normal Field. Without Driscoll, their attendance declined even further. A year after winning a championship, the Cardinals finished in tenth place, with five wins, six losses, and a tie.

1927 O'Brien signed Fred Gillies to replace Norman Barry as coach. But the Cardinals ended the season with a 3–7–1 record.

1928 The Cardinals changed coaches again. Guy Chamberlin, who had won recent championships with Canton, Cleveland, and Frankford, replaced Gillies. Even he could not stop the Cardinals' slide, however, and they finished next to last with a 1–5–0 record.

1929 O'Brien sold the Cardinals to a Chicago doctor named David Jones for $25,000. Jones wasted little time in his attempts to restore the team. He returned them to Comiskey Park. He brought Ernie Nevers out of retirement to be player-coach, replacing Guy Chamberlin. Still in his prime at 26, Nevers lost none of his great skill. On Thanksgiving Day against the Bears, he scored 40 points on six touchdowns and four extra points, all the points in a 40–6 win. As a team, however, the Cardinals improved only slightly, finishing in fourth place with a 6–6–1 record.

1930 In Ernie Nevers's second year as player-coach, the Cardinals finished seventh with a 5–6–2 record. They did their part for depression relief, however, playing an exhibition game against the Bears with the proceeds going to the unemployed. The game was notable because it was played indoors, in Chicago Stadium, and the field was only 80 yards long. Dirt was hauled in to form a six-inch layer covering the marble floor of the stadium.

1931 LeRoy Andrews became the head coach, but he resigned after the Cardinals lost their first two games. Nevers took over once again, and the team responded with a 5–2 record the rest of the way. Nevers played every minute of every game, as well as coaching. Nevers and center Frank McNally were named all-pro.

1932 The twin ravages of aggressive play and 60-minute games finally caught up with Ernie Nevers, and he retired. Jack Chevigny replaced him as coach, but nobody could take Nevers's place on the field. Dr. Jones had seen his team deteriorate in the four years he had owned it. As a result, he was primed for a bash. He got the opportunity while at a dinner party aboard a yacht owned by Chicago tycoon Charles W. Bidwill, Sr., who was a vice-president of the Chicago Bears. In an offhand remark, somebody suggested to Jones that he sell the Cardinals to Bidwill. Jones replied that the team could be had for a price; he named $50,000 as that sum. Bidwill took $2,000 out of his pocket and secured the deal. Bidwill divested himself of his Bears' holdings. Without Nevers, the Cardinals were hapless. They won only two games and finished next to last. The Cardinals' fine tackle, Duke Slater, retired after a 10-year career. Guard Walt Kiesling made all-pro.

1933 Bidwill's regime brought some immediate changes. His business partner, Ray Bennigsen, became chief assistant in football matters. Paul Schissler was appointed coach. The league had changed, too. It was divided into divisions, the Eastern and the Western. The new arrangement did not help the Cardinals. They finished last in the Western division.

1934 The ineptitude of the 1933 team was not lost on Charles Bidwill. Only six veterans were kept, and the 1934 squad contained 17 rookies. The youngsters responded well enough, as the Cardinals won five games, all by shutout. They finished fourth in a five-team divison.

1935 Milan Creighton, a 27-year-old end, took over as player-coach. The young Cardinals started the season with three straight wins but settled into .500 ball after that. Their offense was conspicuously weak, but they still tied the Bears for third place. Led primarily by second-year men, the Cardinals' defense became one of the toughest in the league. Fullback-linebacker Mike Mikulak and two-way end Bill Smith were named to the all-pro team. Quarterback Phil Sarboe and rookie tackle Tony Blazine were selected to the second team.

1936 The Cardinals defeated the Bears for the first time since Ernie Nevers scored 40 points in the Thanksgiving Day game of 1929. Otherwise it was a dismal season. Chicago's offense was not strong to begin with, and its leading runner, Doug Russell, went out for the season with an injury.

1937 The Cardinals made good use of the college draft. They selected an entire passing attack from Lousiana State University in quarterback Pat Coffee and end Gaynell Tinsley. The Cardinals' best players, Russell and Bill Smith, were slowed by injuries for most of the year. Chicago finished fourth with a 5–5–1 record. Rookie Tinsley, with 675 yards in receptions, was the lone Cardinal to make all-pro.

1938 Chicago repeated a pattern of backsliding after a promising season. The Cardinals managed only two wins and finished last once more. Tinsley provided the bulk of excitement. He led the league in receptions with 41 and was named all-pro for the second year in a row.

1939 Owner Bidwill fired Milan Creighton and brought back one-time superstar Ernie Nevers as coach. Any chance for improvement was lost, however, when Tinsley held out for more money than Bidwill was willing to pay. Tinsley retired to coach high school football. Two fine rookies showed promise, 195-pound center Ki Aldrich and All-America fullback Marshall Goldberg. But neither they nor Nevers could revive the Cardinals after Tinsley left. The Cardinals finished in last place.

1940 Bidwill fired Ernie Nevers and replaced him with former Staleys–Bears quarterback Jimmy Conzelman. Conzelman was a fun-loving coach with many avocations. He was acknowledged as an offensive genius, but that was not enough to restore the talent-thin Cardinals. The year's only bright spot was a 21–7 victory over the Bears in the third game of the year. It was one of only two victories that year.

1941 For the first time in four years, the Cardinals did not finish last. They won only three games, but seemed to be making progress.

1942 The war hit the team heavily. The Cardinals' top passer, receiver, and lineman all went into the service. Without Johnny Clement, Bill Dewell, and Joe Kuharich, the team finished next-to-the-last once again. The Cardinals won their first two games of the season but lost eight of their final nine. Jimmy Conzelman quit to work in the front office of the St. Louis Browns' baseball team.

1943 Long-time assistant and former Cardinals' guard Phil Handler was named coach. For the second season in a row, the top passer and receiver went into the service. Handler had rookie Ronnie Cahill to replace Bud Schenk at tailback. But he replaced Frank (Pop) Ivy at end with veteran Eddie Rucinski, and Rucinski went on to be named all-pro. The Cardinals lost all 10 games.

1944 As a wartime emergency measure, the Cardinals combined with the Pittsburgh Steelers to play as one team. It was called Card–Pitt. Former Cardinals' guard Walt Kiesling was Pittsburgh's coach, and he combined with Handler as cocoach. The team split its home games between Comiskey Park and Forbes Field in Pittsburgh and failed to win a game in 10 tries.

1945 The Card-Pitt union dissolved. Although the Cardinals finished last again, they made some major changes. They converted to the T formation when Bidwill and Bennigsen found a quarterback, Paul Christman from the University of Missouri. Christman was an ungainly runner, but was a natural passer and a fine leader. Joe Kuharich and Bill Dewell came back from the service to fortify the line and the passing game. The Cardinals won only one game, but that was against the Bears, 16–7.

1946 The All-America Football Conference began play. Its founder, Arch Ward, sports editor of the *Chicago Tribune*, wanted an AAFC team in his city. The Chicago Rockets became the third team in the city but they faced stern competition. Ward publicly campaigned for the Cardinals to leave town. Incensed at the suggestion, Bidwill grew protective of his team's right to be in Chicago, and he vowed anew to make them a winner. His first gesture was to hire Jimmy Conzelman for a second term as Cardinals coach. Next, he acquired an outstanding set of rookies. Fullback Pat Harder was the number one draft choice. Unheralded halfback Elmer Angsman also showed considerable promise. There were also speedy end Mal Kutner and tough linemen Stan Mauldin and Garrard (Buster) Ramsey. These youngsters combined with veterans Christman, Goldberg, and Dewell to form a solid nucleus. The Cardinals moved out of the cellar with a 6–5–0 record. They beat the Bears 35–28 in the last game of the season.

1947 Bidwill signed Georgia All-America Charlie Trippi to the biggest contract in league history, $100,000 spread over four years, January 16. Trippi turned down an offer from baseball's New York Yankees for twice that much. Halfback Trippi immediately became a member of what Bidwill would call, "my million dollar backfield," which also included Angsman, Harder, and Christman. Those four, plus Conzelman's offensive ingenuity led Chicago to its greatest glory. But Charley Bidwill was not around to see it. He died, April 19. His widow, Violet, authorized Ray Bennigsen to carry on; she took no part in football operations in 1947. The Cardinals opened with three straight wins, including one over the Bears. They lost to the Los Angeles Rams, then ran off four more victories. They won the Western Division title with a 30–21 victory over the Bears in the last game of the regular season. The championship game against the Eagles was played on a frozen field at Comiskey Park. The Cardinals wore tennis shoes, which aided their footing. The Eagles wore them, too, but not until the second quarter, when they trailed 14–0. With Trippi and Angsman running virtually at will, the Cardinals won the championship 28–21.

1948 The Cardinals routed the College All-Stars 28–0, then carried the momentum into the season opener with Philadelphia, which they won 21–14. Cardinals' tackle Stan Mauldin collapsed in the dressing room after the game and died of a brain hemorrhage. The Cardinals lost their only game of the regular season the following week, against the Bears. Then they posted 10 victories in a row to finish first in the Western Division for the second year in a row. Once again, they faced the Eagles for the NFL championship. The game was played in miserable weather. The field was covered with snow, and the yard lines were obliterated. Paul Christman had a fractured finger and couldn't play. Philadelphia's Steve Van Buren broke a scoreless tie with a fourth quarter touchdown, and the Eagles won 7–0. Jimmy Conzelman resigned after the game.

1949 Violet Bidwill married St. Louis businessman Walter Wolfner, and they became involved in team operations together. Ray Bennigsen, still nominally in charge of operations, thought assistant coach Raymond (Buddy) Parker should be elevated to head coach. The Wolfners favored Phil Handler. They compromised by naming the two men cocoaches. Chicago lost four of its first six games before the Wolfners acted. They moved Handler into the front office and made Parker the coach on the field. Under Parker, the team finished respectably, winning or tying five of the last six games. But as a final indignity, the Cardinals lost to the Bears 52–21 in the last game of the season. The All-America Football Conference and its Chicago franchise died.

1950 Buddy Parker quit as coach when Violet Wolfner failed to give him assurance he would be retained as coach. Earl (Curly) Lambeau, the long-time coach of the Green Bay Packers, was hired as coach by Ray Bennigsen. Bennigsen then resigned. The Cardinals were placed in the American Conference of the newly aligned NFL. Christman was 31 years old, and injuries had begun to reduce his ability. Lambeau traded him to Green Bay just before the season and promoted second-string quarterback Jim Hardy. Hardy had talent but he was inconsistent. He made the Cardinals' record book twice—throwing eight interceptions against Philadelphia, September 24, and throwing six touchdown passes against Baltimore, October 2. With many of the players from the glory years injured or retired, the Cardinals finished fifth with a 5–7 record.

1951 The Cardinals' front office was reorganized. Violet Bidwill Wolfner was named chairman of the board; Walter Wolfner was named managing director; and Bidwill's two sons, Charles Jr. (Stormy) and Bill, were named president and vice president, respectively. The control of the team lay with Walter Wolfner. The Cardinals moved their training camp to Lake Forest Academy in Lake Forest, Illinois. Lambeau made Charlie Trippi his new quarterback. Lambeau quarreled with Wolfner all year, and he quit with two games left to play. Assistant coaches Cecil Isbell and Phil Handler ran the team for the rest of the year. The season's only solace was two victories over the Bears, the last of which spoiled that team's chances for a conference title. The Cardinals fell into last place with a 3–9 record.

1952 The Cardinals drafted Ollie Matson in the first round. Matson was an Olympic medalist and a spectacular halfback from the University of San Francisco. Wolfner hired former Cardinals guard Joe Kuharich as coach. Quarterback Frank Tripucka and Matson led the team to three wins in its first four games. But in the fifth game, Tripucka separated his shoulder. After that, the team dropped seven of its remaining eight games, to finish fifth with a 4–8 record. Kuharich quit after the season.

1953 Wolfner hired Joe Stydahar, former star tackle for the rival Bears and coach of the Los Angeles Rams. Ollie Matson went into the army just before the season. The Cardinals won only one game—against the Bears in the season's final game—and finished last.

1954 Quarterback Lamar McHan of Arkansas was the first-round draft choice. Ollie Matson returned from the service. Chicago acquired cornerback Dick (Night Train) Lane from the Rams before the season. The Cardinals 2–10 record was the poorest in the NFL. Joe Stydahar was fired after the season and replaced by assistant coach Ray Richards.

1955 The team had its best record in five years under Richards. The Cardinals went 4–7–1 and finished fourth in the Eastern Conference. Among their wins was a stunning 53–14 victory over the Bears, ruining the Bears' chances for a conference title.

1956 The Cardinals continued to improve under Richards. McHan completed 47 percent of his passes. Matson gained 924 yards to set a Cardinals' rushing record, and fourth-year fullback Johnny Olszewski added 598. Dick Lane got some help in the defensive backfield from second-year man Lindon Crow. Midseason injuries to linemen Chuck Ulrich and Tony Pasquesi slowed the defense. The Cardinals were in contention until the next to the last game of the year against the Bears. Matson had touchdown runs of 83 and 65 yards against the Bears called back because of penalties and the Cardinals lost 10–3. They finished second behind the Giants with a 7–5 record.

1957 The Cardinals dropped to a 3–9 record with virtually the same team that finished second in 1956. Richards was fired as head coach.

1958 Frank (Pop) Ivy, a Cardinals' star of the 1940s, was brought in to coach the team. Ivy had been coaching in Canada, and in the CFL he was known for his complicated offenses. After joining the Cardinals, he installed a double wing formation. The Cardinals

drafted running back John David Crow of Texas A&M and quarterback King Hill of Rice. The Cardinals tied Philadelphia for fifth place with a 2–9–1 record.

1959 The Cardinals rebuilt their offensive and defensive lines through trades. Night Train Lane was sent to Detroit for defensive end Perry Richards. Linebacker Bill Koman was acquired from Philadelphia for Chuck Weber. Then the Cardinals traded Ollie Matson to the Rams for the rights to nine players. The deal gave the Cardinals three players immediately, linemen Frank Fuller, Glen Holtzman, and Ken Panfil. They also got three draft choices. Two players, linemen Art Hauser and John Tracey, were added later, and so was another draft choice. The Cardinals finished last with a 2–10 record. With a losing team, declining attendance, and no television revenue, the team's situation in Chicago was desperate.

1960 Expansion studies done by the league office had found St. Louis to be a desirable city for an NFL franchise. All signs pointed to an expansion team locating there for the 1961 season. But at the same time, the new American Football League was making overtures to St. Louis. The NFL was in an expansion mood and did not want to lose such a promising bit of territory to the new league. The owners voted unanimously to allow the Chicago Cardinals to relocate in St. Louis, March 13. The Cardinals had to share 34,000-seat Busch Stadium with the baseball Cardinals. There was no regular place to practice, so the team worked out in an open field at a city park. Season ticket sales fell well below the 25,000 some city fathers had promised the league. The Cardinals quickly won over the town, however, when they beat the Rams in the season opener 43–21. They had their best year since 1956 and finished fourth with a 6–5–1 record. John David Crow broke Ollie Matson's season team rushing record by gaining 1,071 yards. Included were 203 yards gained in one game, against Pittsburgh the last week of the year.

1961 Ivy signed the Canadian Football League's leading passer for the last decade, Sam Etcheverry. Etcheverry had played college football at the University of Denver, but had been passed over by the NFL teams because of his size (5 foot 11 inches, 186 pounds). Ivy was so convinced of Etcheverry's ability that he traded away his best quarterback of the previous year, John Roach. In return, he got two starters from Cleveland, running back Prentice Gautt and tight end Taz Anderson. Etcheverry hurt his arm in training and never rebounded from the injury. Ivy traded quarterback George Izo, the club's number one draft choice of 1960, to Washington for quarterback Ralph Guglielmi. Etcheverry and Guglielmi shared the position. Offensive lineman Ken Panfil dislocated a kneecap in the first preseason game, and John David Crow broke his ankle in the second one. Ivy resigned with two games left on the schedule. Assistant coaches Chuck Drulis, Ray Prochaska, and Ray Willsey took over for those games, and the Cardinals won them both to finish 7–7.

1962 Violet Bidwill Wolfner died, January 29. Under the terms of Mrs. Wolfner's will, all her property reverted to her sons upon death. She had owned 90 percent of the Cardinals, 10 percent having been bought by St. Louis beer magnate Joseph Griesedieck. Walter Wolfner contested the will, but a probate court in Chicago ruled it valid, March 28. With that, Charles and Bill Bidwill became legal owners of the Cardinals. The two men retained their titles of president (Charles or Stormy) and vice president (Bill), but each took a more active role in operations. Bill became the on-site director of activities. Charles kept his home and offices in Chicago, but planned to spend at least 40 percent of his time in St. Louis. The Bidwills selected Wally Lemm, who had been an assistant under both Ray Richards and Pop

Ivy, as coach. Charley Johnson, who was selected in the tenth round of the 1960 draft as a future, became the starting quarterback in the fourth game. Lemm also switched running back Bobby Joe Conrad to flanker, and Conrad responded by catching 62 passes. Johnson completed 49 percent of his passes for over 2,400 yards.

1963 The Cardinals had an exceptional draft, selecting defensive end Don Brumm, end Billy Gambrell, linebacker Dave Meggyesy, offensive tackle Bob Reynolds, defensive tackle Sam Silas, tight end Jackie Smith, linebacker Larry Stallings, defensive back Jerry Stovall, and running backs Bill Thornton and Bob Paremore. Prentice Gautt was lost for the year with a knee injury in the first game. John David Crow was hobbled most of the year by injuries. Ground was broken for a new all-sports stadium in St. Louis. The Cardinals finished third in the Eastern Conference; the 9–5 record was their best since 1948. Bobby Joe Conrad caught 73 passes for 967 yards. Charley Johnson set four club passing records—attempts (423), completions (222), yardage (3,280), and touchdowns (28). The day after the season ended, Lemm signed a new contract as coach.

1964 The completion date of 1965 for St. Louis's new stadium was obviously not going to be met. In July, a group from Atlanta approached the Bidwills about moving the team to that city. Atlanta was building a new stadium. The stadium authority in St. Louis matched Atlanta's terms; that plus renewed civic support for the team convinced the Bidwills to stay in St. Louis. The Cardinals had another successful year, stumbling only at midseason when they lost to Baltimore, Dallas, and New York. The team's 9–3–2 record was only one-half game behind Cleveland's 10–3–1. In two games against the Browns, the Cardinals got a tie and a victory. The Cardinals defeated Green Bay 24–17 in the Playoff Bowl in Miami.

1965 The Cardinals drafted quarterback Joe Namath of Alabama in the first round but couldn't sign him. John David Crow was traded to the 49ers for kick returner Abe Woodson. The Cardinals won four of their first five games, but Charley Johnson injured his shoulder in the fourth game and was not effective for the rest of the season. Both starting running backs, Prentice Gautt and Joe Childress, missed most of the season with injuries, and defensive backs Larry Wilson and Jerry Stovall were handicapped by injuries. The Cardinals lost eight of their last nine games and tied Philadelphia for fifth place in the Eastern Conference with a 5–9 record. Lemm announced after the last game that he would not return as coach.

1966 Charley Winner was named coach. The Cardinals moved into Busch Memorial Stadium, which had an AstroTurf playing surface and seated 51,392. The Cardinals made their debut in Busch with a 20–10 preseason victory over the Atlanta Falcons, August 6. The team started fast under Winner, going 7–1–1 in its first nine games. Then Charley Johnson was injured and lost for the year. A succession of injuries followed. Such key players as wide receiver Sonny Randle, cornerback Pat Fischer, and offensive linemen Bob DeMarco, Ken Gray, and Irv Goode were lost for varying lengths of time with injuries. The Cardinals scored only 52 points in their last five games. They lost four of them and finished fourth with an 8–5–1 record.

1967 After expanding to 16 teams, the NFL realigned its divisional setup. St. Louis was now in the Century Division of the Eastern Conference, along with Cleveland, New York, and Pittsburgh. Wide receiver Sonny Randle was traded to San Francisco. Charley Johnson and linebacker Larry Stallings were inducted into the army in August. Jim Hart, a free agent from Southern Illinois who had made the taxi squad in 1966, became the starting quarterback. Johnson and Stallings were available on some weekends. The

Cardinals finished third in the four-team division with a 6–7–1 record.

1968 Linebackers Bill Koman and Dale Meinert and running back Prentice Gautt retired. Defensive end Joe Robb, cornerback Pat Fischer, and split end Billy Gambrell were traded. St. Louis beat Cleveland twice during the season, but had trouble with Coastal Division teams, losing to Los Angeles, Baltimore, and San Francisco. Jim Hart passed for over 2,000 yards. The Cardinals accumulated a 9–4–1 record and finished second, one-half game behind the Browns in the Century Division.

1969 Injuries decimated the Cardinals as 11 members of the team underwent surgery. The defense was particularly affected. By mid-year Larry Wilson was the only healthy veteran defensive back. The team became highly vulnerable to the pass, and it gave up an average of 27.7 points a game. Charley Johnson returned from the army and won his quarterback job back in training camp from Jim Hart. The Cardinals dropped to third place in the Century Division with a 4–9–1 record.

1970 The NFL officially merged with the AFL and in the realignment St. Louis was put in the Eastern Division of the NFC with Dallas, New York, Washington, and Philadelphia. Charley Johnson was traded to Houston in a deal that brought quarterback Pete Beathard to St. Louis, January 21. Winner was re-signed to a one-year contract, February 20. The Cardinals lost to the Rams 34–13 in the season opener, but then won eight, lost one, and tied one. They went into the twelfth week of the season in first place with an 8–2–1 record. Then St. Louis collapsed, losing to Detroit, New York, and Washington in succession. That dropped them into third place in the Eastern Division. Winner was dismissed.

1971 The Cardinals drafted defensive back Norm Thompson, offensive lineman Dan Dierdorf, and wide receiver Mel Gray. Bob Hollway, an assistant with the Minnesota Vikings, was named coach, February 14. Jim Hart shared the quarterback job with Pete Beathard. The team dropped to 4–9–1 and finished fourth in the Eastern Division.

1972 Bill Bidwill bought his brother Charles's share of the team, September 12. Assistant coach Chuck Drulis collapsed on the airplane carrying the team home from a preseason game in Houston; by the time the plane made an emergency landing in Little Rock, Arkansas, Drulis was dead of a heart attack. The Cardinals traded wide receiver John Gilliam to Minnesota for quarterback Gary Cuozzo. Tim Van Galder, who had been on the taxi squad since 1967, outplayed both Cuozzo and Hart in the preseason, and became the number one quarterback. Van Galder was injured in the fourth game of the season, and the position became uncertain again. Two weeks before the season ended, Larry Wilson announced the end of his 13-year playing career. For the second year in succession the Cardinals had a 4–9–1 record. After the last game, Bob Hollway was fired as coach.

1973 Bidwill named Don Coryell, formerly of San Diego State, as the twenty-sixth head coach in the Cardinals' history, January 18. Joe Sullivan, assistant general manager under George Allen in Washington, was named the Cardinals' director of operations, February 23. Running back Terry Metcalf of Long Beach State was drafted. Training camp was moved to Illinois State University in Normal, Illinois. Coryell unequivocally named Jim Hart as his starter at quarterback. The Cardinals finished 4–9–1 for the third season in a row.

1974 The Cardinals won their first seven games, then lost the next two before winning three of their last five. They clinched the Eastern Division title with a 26–14 win over the New York Giants in the last game of the season. St. Louis was involved in its first post-season championship competition of any kind since

1948. The Cardinals lost 30–14 to the Minnesota Vikings in a divisional playoff game.

1975 The Cardinals trained at Eastern Illinois University in Charleston, Illinois. They clinched their second consecutive Eastern Division title in the thirteenth week of the season when they beat the Chicago Bears 34–20. They finished with an 11–3 record, their best since the 1948 team went 11–1. Fullback Jim Otis led the NFC in rushing with 1,076 yards. Terry Metcalf set an NFL record for total yardage by gaining 2,462 with his running, receiving, and returning. The Cardinals met the Rams in Los Angeles in the first round of the playoffs. The Rams' Lawrence McCutcheon gained 202 yards on 37 carries and Los Angeles returned two interceptions of Hart passes for touchdowns in the first half. The Cardinals trailed 28–9 at halftime and lost 35–23.

1976 The training camp was moved to Lindenwood College in St. Charles, Missouri. The Cardinals lost 43–24 to San Diego in the third game and they never got above second place after that. After 11 weeks, Dallas was on top with a 9–2 record. St. Louis was second with 8–3, and Washington third at 7–4. However, Washington had beaten the Cardinals twice; in the event of a second-place tie, the Redskins would go to the playoffs as the wild card team. St. Louis lost to Dallas on Thanksgiving Day, and that dropped them into a tie with the Redskins. Both teams went on to win their last two games, but despite a 10–4 record the Cardinals failed to make the playoffs for the first time since Coryell's initial season.

MEMBERS OF THE HALL OF FAME:
Charles Bidwill, Sr., Guy Chamberlin, Jimmy Conzelman, John (Paddy) Driscoll, Walt Kiesling, Earl (Curly) Lambeau, Dick (Night Train) Lane, Ollie Matson, Ernie Nevers, Jim Thorpe, Charlie Trippi.

CARDINALS RECORD, 1920–76

Year	Won	Lost	Tied	Pct.	Pts.	OP
Chicago Cardinals						
1920	5	2	1	.714		
1921	2	3	2	.400		
1922	8	3	0	.727		
1923	8	4	0	.667		
1924	5	4	1	.556		
1925‡	11	2	1	.846		
1926	5	6	1	.455		
1927	3	7	1	.300		
1928	1	5	0	.167		
1929	6	6	1	.500		
1930	5	6	2	.455		
1931	5	4	0	.556		
1932	2	6	2	.250		
1933	1	9	1	.100	52	101
1934	5	6	0	.455	80	84
1935	6	4	2	.600	99	97
1936	3	8	1	.273	74	143
1937	5	5	1	.500	135	165
1938	2	9	0	.182	111	168
1939	1	10	0	.091	84	254
1940	2	7	0	.222	139	222
1941	3	7	1	.300	127	197
1942	3	8	0	.273	98	209
1943	0	10	0	.000	95	238
1944	0	10	0	.000	108	328
1945	1	9	0	.100	98	228
1946	6	5	0	.545	260	198
1947‡	9	3	0	.750	306	231
1948§	11	1	0	.917	395	226
1949	6	5	1	.545	360	301
1950	5	7	0	.417	233	287
1951	3	9	0	.250	210	287
1952	4	8	0	.333	172	221
1953	1	10	1	.091	190	337
1954	2	10	0	.167	183	347
1955	4	7	1	.364	224	252
1956	7	5	0	.583	240	182
1957	3	9	0	.250	200	299
1958	2	9	1	.182	261	356
1959	2	10	0	.167	234	324
St. Louis Cardinals						
1960	6	5	1	.545	288	230
1961	7	7	0	.500	279	267
1962	4	9	1	.308	287	361
1963	9	5	0	.643	341	283
1964	9	3	2	.750	357	331
1965	5	9	0	.357	296	309
1966	8	5	1	.615	264	265
1967	6	7	1	.462	333	356
1968	9	4	1	.692	325	289
1969	4	9	1	.308	314	389
1970	8	5	1	.615	325	228
1971	4	9	1	.308	231	279
1972	4	9	1	.308	193	303
1973	4	9	1	.321	286	365
1974†	10	4	0	.714	285	218
1975†	11	3	0	.786	356	276
1976	10	4	0	.714	309	267
57 Years	**281**	**362**	**36**	**.440**		

‡NFL Champion §NFL Western Division Champion †NFC Eastern Division Champion

RECORD HOLDERS

Rushing (Yards)	Jim Otis, 1975	1,076
Passing (Pct.)	Jim Hart, 1973	55.6
Passing (Yards)	Charley Johnson, 1963	3,280
Passing (TDs)	Charley Johnson, 1963	28
Receiving (No.)	Bobby Joe Conrad, 1963	73
Receiving (Yards)	Jackie Smith, 1967	1,205
Interceptions (No.)	Bob Nussbaumer, 1949	12
Punting (Avg.)	Jerry Norton, 1960	45.6
Punt Ret. (Avg.)	John (Red) Cochran, 1949	20.9
Kickoff Ret. (Avg.)	Ollie Matson, 1958	35.5
Touchdowns (Total)	Sonny Randle, 1960	15
Field Goals Made	Jim Bakken, 1967	27
Points (No.)	Jim Bakken, 1967	117

COACHING HISTORY

1920	Marshall Smith	5– 2–1
1921–22	John (Paddy) Driscoll	10– 6–2
1923–24	Arnold Horween	13– 8–1
1925–26	Norman Barry	16– 8–2
1927	Fred Gillies	3– 7–1
1928	Guy Chamberlin	1– 5–0
1929–30	Ernie Nevers	11–12–3
1931	LeRoy Andrews*	0– 2–0
1931	Ernie Nevers	5– 2–0
1932	Jack Chevigny	2– 6–2
1933–34	Paul Schissler	6–15–1
1935–38	Milan Creighton	16–26–4
1939	Ernie Nevers	1–10–0
1940–42	Jimmy Conzelman	8–22–3
1943–45	Phil Handler**	1–29–0
1946–48	Jimmy Conzelman	26– 9–0
1949	Phil Handler, Raymond (Buddy) Parker	6– 5–1
1950–51	Earl (Curly) Lambeau	8–16–0
1952	Joe Kuharich	4– 8–0
1953–54	Joe Stydahar	3–20–1
1955–57	Ray Richards	14–21–1
1958–61	Frank (Pop) Ivy	17–31–3
1962–65	Wally Lemm	27–26–3
1966–70	Charley Winner	35–30–5
1971–72	Bob Hollway	8–18–2
1973–76	Don Coryell	35–20–1

*Resigned after two games in 1931
**Co-coach with Walt Kiesling of 1944 Chicago Cardinals–Pittsburgh merged team

FIRST PLAYER SELECTED

1936	Jim Lawrence, B, Texas Christian
1937	Ray Buivid, B, Marquette
1938	Jack Robbins, B, Arkansas
1939	Charles (Ki) Aldrich, B, Texas Christian
1940	George Cafego, B, Tennessee
1941	John Kimbrough, B, Texas A&M
1942	Steve Lach, B, Duke
1943	Glenn Dobbs, B, Tulsa
1944	Pat Harder, B, Wisconsin
1945	Charley Trippi, B, Georgia
1946	Dub Jones, B, Louisiana State
1947	DeWitt (Tex) Coulter, T, Army
1948	Jim Spavital, B, Oklahoma A&M
1949	Bill Fischer, G, Notre Dame
1950	Jack Jennings, T (2), Ohio State
1951	Jerry Groom, C, Notre Dame
1952	Ollie Matson, B, San Francisco
1953	Johnny Olszewski, B, California
1954	Lamar McHan, B, Arkansas
1955	Max Boydston, E, Oklahoma
1956	Joe Childress, B, Auburn
1957	Jerry Tubbs, C, Oklahoma
1958	King Hill, B, Rice
1959	Billy Stacy, B, Mississippi State
1960	George Izo, QB, Notre Dame
1961	Ken Rice, T, Auburn
1962	Fate Echols, DT, Northwestern
1963	Jerry Stovall, S, Louisiana State
1964	Ken Kortas, DT, Louisville
1965	Joe Namath, QB, Alabama
1966	Carl McAdams, LB, Oklahoma
1967	Dave Williams, WR, Washington
1968	MacArthur Lane, RB, Utah State
1969	Roger Wehrli, CB, Missouri
1970	Larry Stegent, RB, Texas A&M
1971	Norm Thompson, CB, Utah
1972	Robert Moore, RB-WR, Oregon
1973	Dave Butz, DT, Purdue
1974	J. V. Cain, TE, Colorado
1975	Tim Gray, DB, Texas A&M
1976	Mike Dawson, DT, Arizona

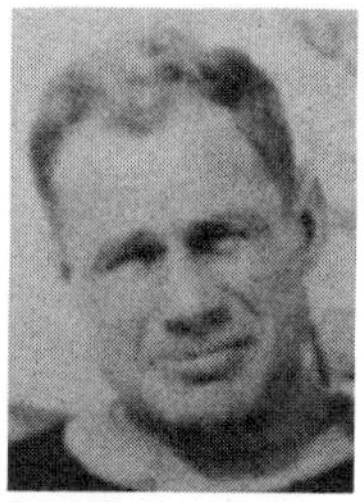
Roy (Bullet) Baker

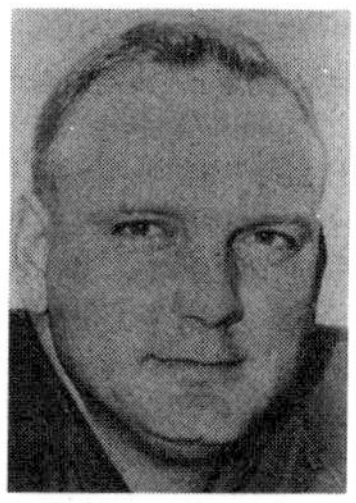
Joe Childress

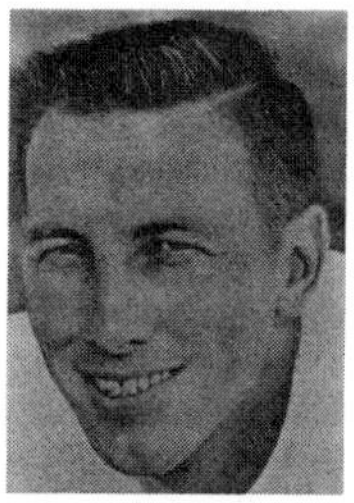
Bobby Joe Conrad

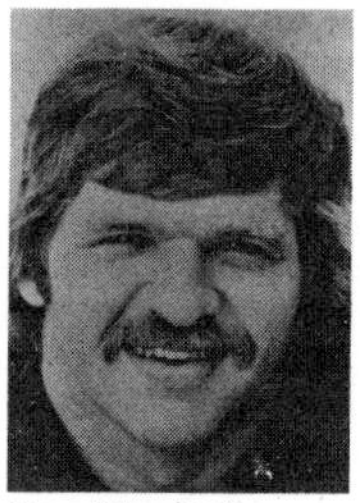
Dan Dierdorf

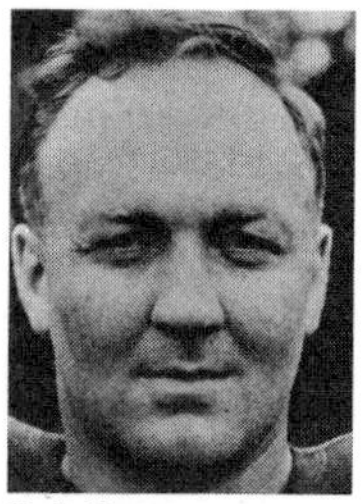
Bob Dove

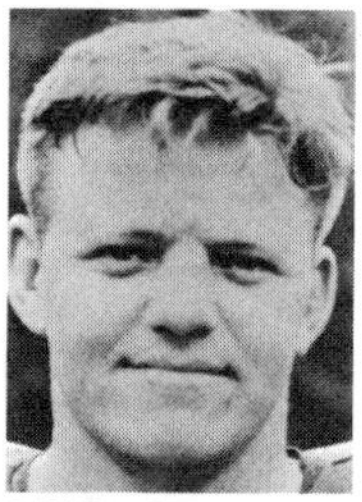
Bill Fischer

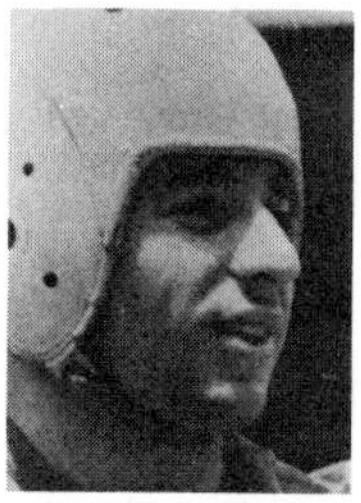
Marshall Goldberg

CHICAGO CARDINALS, 1920–59;
ST. LOUIS CARDINALS, 1960–76

Adams, Henry, C, Pittsburgh 1939
Agee, Sam, B, Vanderbilt 1938–39
Albert, Sergio, K, U.S. International 1974
Albrecht, Art, T, Wisconsin 1943
Aldrich, Ki, C, Texas Christian 1939–40, 1943
Alford, Mike, C, Auburn 1965
Allen, Ed, E, Creighton 1928
Allen, Jeff, DB, Iowa State 1971
Allison, Henry, T, San Diego State 1975–76
Allton, Joe, T, Oklahoma 1942, 1944
Anderson, Charley, E, Louisiana Tech 1956
Anderson, Cliff, E, Indiana 1952–53
Anderson, Donny, RB, Texas Tech 1972–74
Anderson, Ed, E, Notre Dame 1922–25
Anderson, Taz, TE, Georgia Tech 1961–64
Andros, Plato, G, Oklahoma 1947–50
Angle, Bob, B, Iowa State 1950
Angsman, Elmer, B, Notre Dame 1946–52
Apolskis, Ray, T, Marquette 1941–42, 1945–50
Arms, Lloyd, G, Oklahoma A&M 1946–48
Arneson, Mark, LB, Arizona 1972–76
Arterburn, Elmer, B, Texas Tech 1954
Ashton, Josh, RB, Tulsa 1975
Atkins, Robert, DB, Grambling 1968–69
Auer, Howard, T, Michigan 1933

B

Babartsky, Al, T, Fordham 1938–39, 1941–42
Badaczewski, John, G, Western Reserve 1948
Bagdon, Ed, G, Michigan State 1950–51
Bailey, Claron (Monk), DB, Utah 1964–65
Baker, Conway, T, Centenary 1936–43, 1945
Baker, Mel, WR, Texas Southern 1976
Baker, Roy, B, USC 1929–30
Bakken, Jim, K, Wisconsin 1962–76
Balaz, Frank, B, Iowa 1941, 1945
Banks, Tom, C, Auburn 1971–76
Banonis, Vince, C, Detroit 1942, 1946–50
Barnes, Mike, DB, Texas-Arlington 1967–68
Barnes, Pete, LB, Southern U. 1973
Barni, Roy, B, San Francisco 1952–53
Barry, Norm, B, Notre Dame 1921
Barry, Paul, B, Tulsa 1954
Bates, Ted, LB, Oregon State 1959–62
Bausch, Jim, B, Kansas 1934–36
Baynham, Craig, RB, Georgia Tech 1972
Beal, Norm, DB, Missouri 1962
Beathard, Pete, QB, USC 1970–71
Beatty, Chuck, DB, No. Texas State 1972
Beauchamp, Al, LB, Southern U. 1976
Beckman, Tom, DE, Michigan 1972
Beinor, Ed, E, Notre Dame 1940–41
Belden, Charles, B, None 1929–31
Bell, Bob, DE, Cincinnati 1974–76
Belton, Willie, RB, Maryland State 1973–74
Bennett, Charles, B, None 1933
Bergerson, Gil, T, Oregon State 1933
Bernardi, Frank, B, Colorado 1955–57
Berquist, Jay, G, Nebraska 1927
Berry, Gil, B, Illinois 1935
Bertagnolli, Libero, G, Washington, Mo. 1942, 1945
Bienermann, Tom E, Drake 1951–56
Bilbo, Jon, T, Mississippi 1938–39
Birlem, Keith, B, San Jose State 1939
Blackburn, Bill, C, Rice 1946–50
Blackwell, Hal, B, South Carolina 1945
Blazine, Tony, T, Illinois Wesleyan 1935–40
Bliss, Homer, G, Washington & Jefferson 1928
Blumenthal, Morris, B, Northwestern 1925
Blumer, Herb, E, Missouri 1925–30, 1933
Bock, Wayne, T, Illinois 1957
Bogue, George, B, Stanford 1930
Bohlman, Frank, G, Marquette 1942
Bonelli, Ernie, B, Pittsburgh 1945
Booth, Clarence, T, SMU 1943
Bova, Tony, E, St. Francis 1944
Boyd, Bill, B, Westminster, Mo. 1930–31
Boydston, Max, E, Oklahoma 1955–58
Boyette, Garland, LB, Grambling 1962–63
Braden, Dave, G, Marquette 1945
Bradley, Dave, G, Penn State 1972
Bradley, Hal, E, Elon 1938–39
Brahaney, Tom, C, Oklahoma 1973–76
Braidwood, Charles, E, Chattanooga 1932
Bredde, Bill, B, Oklahoma A&M 1954
Brennan, Willis, T, None 1920–27
Brett, Ed, E, Washington State 1936
Brettschneider, Carl, LB, Iowa State 1956–59
Britton, Earl, B, Illinois 1929
Brooks, Leo, DE, Texas 1973–76
Brosky, Al, B, Illinois 1954
Brown, Bob, TE, Alcorn A&M 1969–70
Brown, Hardy, LB, Tulsa 1956
Brown, Terry, DB, Oklahoma State 1969–71
Brubaker, Dick, E, Ohio State 1955, 1957
Bruckner, Les, B, Michigan State 1945
Brumm, Don, DE, Purdue 1963–69, 1972
Bryan, John, B, Chicago 1922
Bryant, Charlie, RB, Allen 1966–67
Bryant, Chuck, E, Ohio State 1962
Buckeye, Garland, T, None 1920–24
Bucklin, Tom, B, Idaho 1927
Bukant, Joe, B, Washington, Mo. 1942–43
Bulger, Chet, T, Auburn 1942–43, 1945–49
Burkett, Jeff, E, Louisiana State 1947
Burl, Alex, B, Colorado A&M 1956
Burnett, Ray, B, None 1938
Burns, Leon, RB, Cal State-Long Beach 1972
Burson, Jimmy, DB, Auburn 1963–67
Busler, Ray, T, Marquette 1940–41, 1945
Busse, Ellis, B, Chicago 1929
Butler, Jim, RB, Edward Waters 1972
Butler, John, B, Tennessee 1944
Butts, Ed, B, Chico State 1929
Butz, Dave, DE, Purdue 1973–74

C

Cahill, Ron, B, Holy Cross 1943
Cain, Jim, E, Alabama 1949
Cain, J.V., WR, Colorado 1974–76
Campana, Al, B, Youngstown 1953
Campbell, Bill, G, Oklahoma 1945–49
Cantor, Leo, B, UCLA 1945
Carey, Joe, G, None 1920
Carlson, Hal, G, DePaul 1937
Carr, Jim, B, Morris Harvey 1955, 1957
Carter, Joe, E, Southern Methodist 1945
Carter, Ross, G, Oregon 1936–39
Carter, Willie, B, Tennessee State 1953
Caywood, Les, G, St. John's 1931
Cheatham, Lloyd, QB, Auburn 1942
Chamberlin, Guy, C, Nebraska 1927
Charpier, Len, B, Illinois 1921
Cherry, Ed, B, Hardin-Simmons 1938–39
Chickillo, Nick, G, Miami 1953
Childress, Joe, RB, Auburn 1956–65
Chisick, Andy, C, Villanova 1940–41
Christenson, Marty, B, Minnesota 1940
Christman, Paul, QB, Missouri 1945–49
Ciccone, Ben, C, Duquesne 1942
Clark, Beryl, B, Oklahoma 1940
Clark, Bill, G, None 1920
Clark, Charles, G, Harvard 1924
Clark, Ernie, LB, Michigan State 1968
Clatt, Corwin, B, Notre Dame 1948–49
Claypool, Ralph, C, Purdue 1925–26, 1928
Clement, John, B, Southern Methodist 1941
Cobb, Tom, T, Arkansas 1931
Cochran, John, B, Wake Forest 1947–50
Coffee, Jim, B, Louisiana State 1937–38
Colhouer, Jake, G, Oklahoma A&M 1946–48
Collins, Paul, B, Missouri 1945
Compton, Ogden, QB, Hardin-Simmons 1955
Conley, Steve, LB, Kansas 1972
Conoly, Bill, G, Texas 1946
Conrad, Bobby Joe, WR, Texas A&M 1958–68
Cook, Dave, B, Illinois 1934–36
Cook, Ed, G, Notre Dame 1958–65
Coomer, Joe, T, Stephen F. Austin 1947–49
Coppage, Al, E, Oklahoma 1940–42
Cosner, Don, B, Montana State 1939
Cowhig, Jerry, B, Notre Dame 1950
Crangle, John, B, Illinois 1923
Crass, Bill, B, Louisiana State 1937
Creighton, Milan, E, Arkansas 1931–37
Crenshaw, Willis, RB, Kansas State 1964–69
Crittendon, John, E, Wayne State 1954
Cross, Bill, B, W. Texas State 1951–53
Cross, Bob, T, Stephen F. Austin 1958–59
Crow, John David, RB, Texas A&M 1958–64
Crow, Lindon, DB, USC 1955–57
Crowder, Earl, B, Oklahoma 1939
Crum, Bob, DE, Arizona 1974
Crump, Dwayne, DB, Fresno State 1973–76
Cuff, Ward, B, Marquette 1946
Culpepper, Ed, G, Alabama 1958–60
Cuozzo, Gary, QB, Virginia 1972
Cuppoletti, Bree, G, Oregon 1934–38
Curcillo, Tony, B, Ohio State 1953
Curran, Harry, B, Boston College 1920–21
Currivan, Don, E, Boston College 1943
Curzon, Harry, B, None 1928

D

Daanen, Jerry, WR, Miami 1968–70
Daddio, Bill, E, Pittsburgh 1941–42
Dahms, Tom T, San Diego State 1956
Davidson, Joe, G, Colgate 1928
Davis, Bill, T, Texas Tech 1940–41
Davis, Charlie, DT, Texas Christian 1975–76
Davis, Jerry, B, S.E. Louisiana 1948–51
Davis, Ray, E, Howard, Ala. 1935
Davis, Ron, DE, Virginia State 1973
Dawson, Mike, DT, Arizona 1976
Day, Tom, G, N. Carolina A&T 1960
DeCorrevant, Bill, B, Northwestern 1947–48
Delevan, Burt, T, Pacific 1955–56
DeMarco, Bob, C, Dayton 1961–69
DesJardien, Paul, G, Chicago 1920
Deskin, Versil, E, Drake 1935–39
DeStefano, Fred, B, Northwestern 1924–25
Detwiler, Chuck, S, Utah State 1973
Dewell, Bill, E, Southern Methodist 1940–41, 1945–49
Dickson, Paul, DT, Baylor 1971
Diehl, Charles, G, Idaho 1930–31
Dierdorf, Dan, G, Michigan 1971–76
Dimancheff, Babe, B, Purdue 1947–50
Dittrich, John, G, Wisconsin 1956
Dobler, Conrad, G, Wyoming 1972–76
Donckers, Bill, QB, San Diego State 1976
Doolan, John, B, Georgetown 1947–48
Dorris, Andy, DE, New Mexico State 1973
Douds Forrest, T, Washington & Jefferson 1932
Dougherty, Phil, C, Santa Clara 1938
Dove, Bob, E, Notre Dame 1948–53
Dowell, Gwyn, B, Texas Tech 1935–36
Dowling, Pat, E, DePaul 1929
Doyle, Ted, E, Nebraska 1944
Driscoll, John (Paddy), B, Northwestern 1920–25
Driskill, Joe, DB, N.E. Louisiana 1960–61
Druis, Al, B, Temple 1945–46
Dugan, Len, C, Wichita 1937–39
Duggan, Gil, T, Oklahoma 1942–43, 1945
Duggins, George, E, Purdue 1934
Duncum, Bobby, T, W. Texas State 1968
Dunn, Joe, B, Marquette 1925–26
Dunstan, Elwyn, T, Portland 1938–39
Duren, Clarence, S, California 1973
Durko, John, E, Albright 1945

E

Ebli, Ray, E, Notre Dame 1942
Echols, Fate, T, Northwestern 1962–63
Eckl, Bob, T, Wisconsin 1945
Edwards, Cid, RB, Tennessee State 1968–71
Egan, Dick, E, Wilmington 1920–23
Eggers, Doug, LB, S. Dakota State 1958
Eikenberg, Charles, QB, Rice 1948
Elkins, Fait, B, Haskell 1929
Ellis, Walt, T, Detroit 1926–27
Ellstrom, Marv, B, Oklahoma 1936
Ellzey, Charles, C, So. Mississippi 1960–61
Elwell, Jack, E, Purdue 1962
Embree, Mel, E, Pepperdine 1954
Emerson, Vernon, T, Minnesota-Duluth 1969–71
Engebretsen, Paul, G, Northwestern 1933
Enich, Steve, G, Marquette 1945

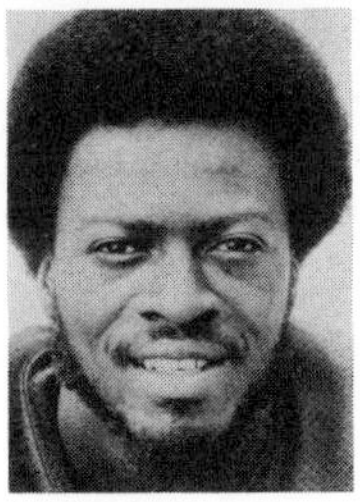
Mel Gray

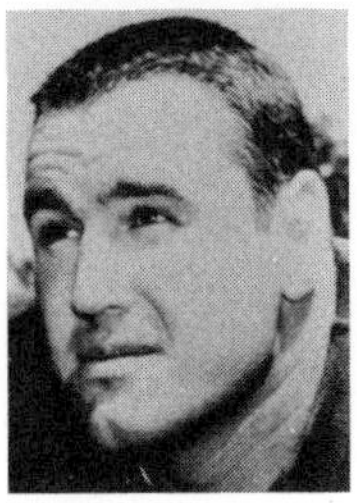
Jerry Groom

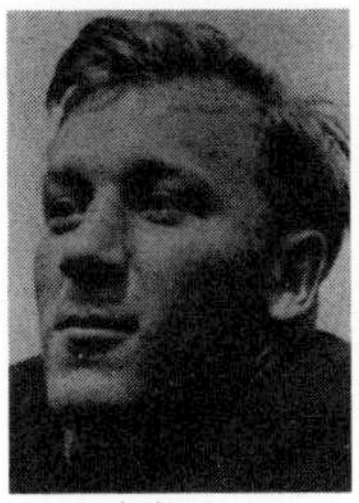
Pat Harder

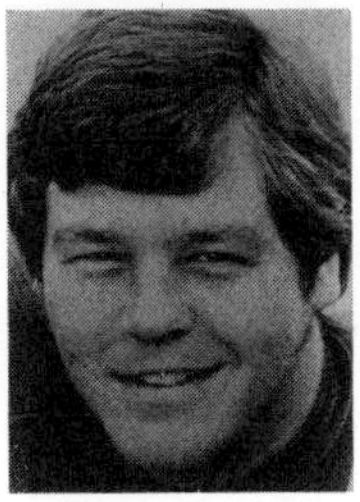
Jim Hart

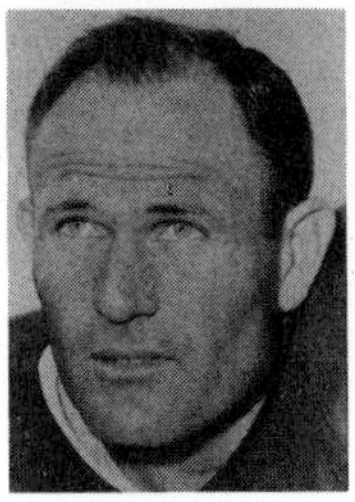
Ed Henke

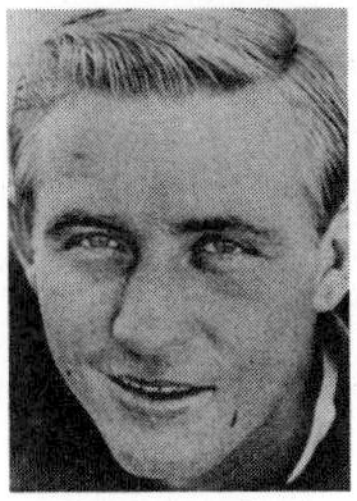
Charley Johnson

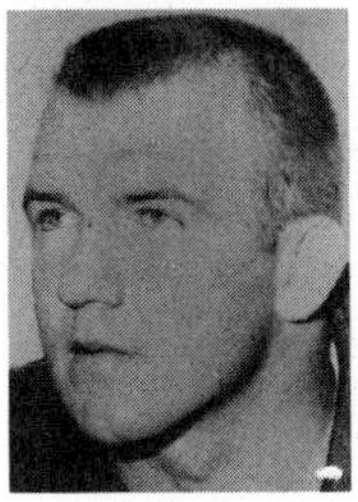
Bill Koman

Erickson, Hal, B, Wash. & Jefferson 1925–28
Erickson, Mickey, C, Northwestern 1930–31
Esser, Clarence, E, Wisconsin 1947
Evans, Dick, E, Iowa 1940, 1943
Evans, Earl, T, Harvard 1925
Etcheverry, Sam, QB, Denver 1961–62

F

Failing, Fred, G, Central J.C., Kansas 1930
Fanucci, Ledio, T, Fresno State 1954
Farr, Miller, CB, Wichita State 1970–72
Faust, George, B, Minnesota 1939
Ferry, Lou, T, Villanova 1951
Field, Harry, T, Oregon State 1934–36
Fife, Ralph, G, Pittsburgh 1942, 1945
Finn, Bernie, B, Holy Cross 1932
Finnie, Roger, T, Florida A&M 1973–76
Finnin, Tom, T, Detroit 1957
Fischer, Bill, T, Notre Dame 1949–53
Fischer, Pat, CB, Nebraska 1961–67
Fisher, Ev, B, Santa Clara 1938–39
Fiske, Max, B, DePaul 1937
Fitzgibbon, Paul, B, Creighton 1928
Flanagan, Latham, E, Carnegie Tech 1931
Flenniken, Max, B., Geneva 1930
Florence, Paul, E, Loyola, Ill. 1920
Folz, Art, B, None 1923–25
Foster, Ralph, T, Oklahoma A&M 1945–46
Francis, Gene, B, Chicago 1926
Fritsch, Ernest, C, Detroit 1960
Fugler, Dick, T, Tulane 1954
Fuller, Frank, T, Kentucky 1959–62

G

Gainor, Charles, E, North Dakota 1939
Gambrell, Billy, WR, South Carolina 1963–67
Gasparella, Joe, B, Notre Dame 1951
Gautt, Prentice, RB, Oklahoma 1961–67
Gay, Bill, B, Notre Dame 1951–52
Gehrke, Fred, B, Utah 1950
George, Steve, DT, Houston 1974
Geri, Joe, B, Georgia 1952
German, Jim, B, Centre 1940
Gersbach, Carl, LB, West Chester State 1976
Ghersanich, Vernon, G, Auburn 1943
Gibbons, Austin, C, DePaul 1929
Gilchrist, George, T, Tennessee State 1953
Gillette, Walker, WR, Richmond 1972–73
Gilliam, John, WR, S. Carolina State 1969–71
Gillies, Fred, T, Cornell 1920–28
Gillis, Don, C, Rice 1958–61
Glasscow, Willis, B, Iowa 1931
Glick, Fred, DB, Colorado State 1959–60
Goble, Les, B, Alfred 1954–55
Goldberg, Biggie, B, Marshall 1939–40, 1946–48
Goldman, Sam, E, Howard 1948
Goldsberry, John, T, Indiana 1949–50
Goode, Irv, C, Kentucky 1962–71
Goodman, Aubrey T, Chicago 1927
Gordon, Bob, B, Tennessee 1958
Gordon, Lou, T, Illinois 1930–35
Graham, Al, G, None 1932–33
Granger, Charles, G, Southern U. 1961
Grant, Hugh, B, St. Mary's, Calif. 1928
Gray, Ken, G, Howard Payne 1958–69
Gray, Mel, WR, Missouri 1971–76
Gray, Tim, DB, Texas A&M 1975
Greene, Ed, E, Loyola, Ill. 1926–27
Greene, Frank, B, Tulsa 1934
Griffin, Bob, C, Arkansas 1961
Griffith, Homer, B, USC 1934
Grigas, John, B, Holy Cross 1943–44
Groome, Jerry, C, Notre Dame 1951–55
Grosvernor, George, B, Colorado 1936–37
Guglielmi, Ralph, QB, Notre Dame 1961

H

Hackbart, Dale, S, Wisconsin 1971–72
Hall, John, B, Texas Christian 1940–41, 1943
Hall, Ken, RB, Texas A&M 1959, 1961
Halstrom, Bernie, B, Illinois 1920–21
Hammack, Mal, RB, Florida 1955, 1957–66
Hammond, Gary, WR, Southern Methodist 1973–76
Handler, Phil, G, Texas Christian 1930–36
Hanke, Carl, E, Minnesota 1924
Hanlon, Bob, B, Loras 1948
Hansen, Cliff, B, Luther 1933
Hanson, Homer, G, Kansas State 1935–36
Harder, Pat, B, Wisconsin 1946–50
Hardy, Jim, B, USC 1949–51
Hargrove, Jim, LB, Howard Payne 1971–72
Harmon, Ham, C, Tulsa 1937
Harris, Ike, WR, Iowa State 1975–76
Harrison, Reggie, RB, Cincinnati 1974
Hart, Jim, QB, So. Illinois 1966–76
Hartle, Greg, LB, Newberry 1974–76
Hartong, George, G, Chicago 1924
Hartshorn, Larry, G, Kansas State 1955
Hatley, John, G, Sul Ross State 1954–55
Hauser, Art, G, Xavier 1959
Hayden, Leo, RB, Ohio State 1972–73
Healy, Chip, LB, Vanderbilt 1959–70
Heater, Don, RB, Montana Tech 1972
Heidel, Jimmy, DB, Mississippi 1966
Henke, Ed, DE, USC 1961–63
Hennessey, Jerry, E, Santa Clara 1950–51
Heron, Fred, DT, San Jose State 1966–72
Hickman, Larry, B, Baylor 1959
Higgins, John, G, Trinity, Tex. 1941
Higgins, Tom, T, North Carolina 1953
Hill, Don, B, Stanford 1929
Hill, Irv, Trinity, Tex. 1931–32
Hill, Jim, DB, Sam Houston 1955–57, 1959–64
Hill, King, QB, Rice 1958–60, 1969
Hillebrand, Jerry, LB, Colorado 1967
Hinchman, Hub, B, Butler 1933–34
Hock, John, T, Santa Clara 1950
Hoel, Bob, G, Pittsburgh 1937–38
Hoey, George, DB, Michigan 1971
Hoffman, John, DE, Hawaii 1972
Hogan, Tom, T, Detroit 1926
Hogland, Doug, G, Oregon State 1956–58
Hogue, Murrell, T, Centenary 1929
Holm, Bernie, B, Alabama 1932
Holmer, Walt, B, Northwestern 1931–32
Horstmann, Roy, B, Purdue 1934
Horween, Arnold, B, Harvard 1921–24
Horween, Ralph, B, Harvard 1921–23
Houghton, Jerry, T, Washington State 1951
Houser, John, G, Redlands 1963
Huffman, Frank, G, Marshall 1939–41
Hughes, Bernie, C, Oregon 1934–36
Hultz, George, DT, So. Mississippi 1962
Hummel, Arnie, B, Lombard 1927
Humphrey, Buddy, QB, Baylor 1963–65
Hurlburt, John, G, Chicago 1924–25
Husmann, Ed, G, Nebraska 1953, 1956–59
Hust, Al, E, Tennessee 1946
Hutchison, Chuck, G, Ohio State 1970–72
Hyatt, Freddie, WR, Auburn 1968–72

I

Illman, Ed, B, Montana 1928
Imhof, Martin, DE, San Diego State 1972
Isaacson, Ted, T, Washington 1934–35
Ivy, Frank (Pop), E, Oklahoma 1940–42, 1945–47
Izo, George, QB, Notre Dame 1960

J

Jackson, Charley, B, Southern Methodist 1958
Jackson, Roland, RB, Rice 1962
Jacobs, Marv, T, None 1948
Jagielski, Harry, T, Indiana 1956
Jankovich, Keever, E, Pacific 1963
Jennings, John, T, Ohio State 1950–57
Johnson, Al, B, Kentucky 1939–41
Johnson, Charley, QB, New Mexico State 1961–69
Johnson, Ray, B, Denver 1940
Johnson, Jim, B, Washington 1946
Jones, Ben, B, Grove City 1927–28
Jones, Steve, RB, Duke 1974–76
Joyce, Don, T, Tulane 1951–53
Joyce, Terry, TE, Missouri Southern St. 1976

K

Karras, John, B, Illinois 1952
Karwales, John, E, Michigan 1947
Kasparek, Dick, C, Iowa State 1966–68
Kassel, Charles, E, Illinois 1929–33
Keane, Tom, B, West Virginia 1955
Kearney, Tim, LB, Northern Michigan 1976
Kearns, Tom, T, Miami 1946
Keithley, Gary, QB, Texas-El Paso 1973–75
Kellogg, Clarence, B, St. Mary's, Calif. 1936
Kellogg, Bill, B, Syracuse 1926
Kenneally, George, G, St. Bonaventure 1930
Keys, Brady, DB, Colorado State 1968
Kichefski, Walt, E, Miami 1944
Kiesling, Walt, G, St. Thomas, Minn. 1929–33
Kiley, Roger, E, Notre Dame 1923
Kindle, Greg, T, Tennessee State 1974
Kinek, George, B, Tulane 1954
King, Andy, B, West Virginia 1923–24
King, Emmett, B, None 1954
Kingery, Ellsworth, B, Tulane 1954
Klimek, Tony, E, Illinois 1951–52
Klumb, John, E, Washington State 1939–40
Knafelc, Gary, E, Colorado 1954
Knight, Charles, C, None 1920–21
Knolla, John, B, Creighton 1942, 1945
Kochel, Mike, G, Fordham 1939
Koegel, Warren, G, Penn State 1973
Koehler, Bob, G, Northwestern 1921–26
Koken, Mike, B, Notre Dame 1933
Koman, Bill, LB, North Carolina 1959–67
Konovsky, Bob, G, Wisconsin 1956–58
Kortas, Ken, DT, Louisville 1964
Krejci, Joe, E, Peru State, Ind. 1934
Krueger, Rolf, DE, Texas A&M 1969–71
Kuharich, Joe, G, Notre Dame 1940–41, 1945
Kutner, Mal, E, Texas 1946–50
Kuzman, John, T, Fordham 1941

L

Lach, Steve, B, Duke 1942
Ladd, Jim, E, Bowling Green 1954
LaHood, Mike, G, Wyoming 1970
Lainhart, Porter, B, Washington State 1933
Lamb, Roy, B, Lombard 1926–27, 1933
Lane, Dick (Night Train), CB, Scottsbluff J.C. 1954–59
Lane, MacArthur, RB, Utah State 1968–71
Lange, Bill, G, Dayton 1954–55
Lange, Jim, E, Montana State 1929
LaRosa, Paul, E, None 1921–21
Larson, Fred, C, Notre Dame 1929
Larson, Lou, B, None 1929
Larson, Paul, QB, California 1957
Latin, Jerry, RB, Northern Illinois 1975–76
Latourette, Chuck, DB-P, Rice 1967–68, 1970–71
Lauro, Lin, B, Pittsburgh 1951
Lawrence, Jim, B, Texas Christian 1936–39
Ledbetter, Homer, B, Arkansas 1932–33
Lee, Bob, E, Minnesota 1968
Lee, Monte, LB, Texas 1961
Leggett, Dave, B, Ohio State 1955
Leonard, John T, Indiana 1922–23
LeVeck, Jack, LB, Ohio 1973–74
Lewis, Charles, T, Iowa 1959
Lewis, Woodley, B, Oregon 1956–59
Liebel, Frank, E, Norwich 1948
Lillard, Joe, B, Oregon State 1932–33
Lind, Al, C, Northwestern 1936
Lindow, Al, B, Washington, Mo. 1945
Lipinski, Jim T, Fairmont State 1950
Lipostad, Ed, G, Wake Forest 1952
Loepfe, Dick, T, Wisconsin 1948–49
Logan, Chuck, E, Northwestern 1965, 1967–68
Lokanc, Joe, G, Northwestern 1941
Long, Dave, DE, Iowa 1966–68
Longo, Tom, DB, Notre Dame 1971
Lunceford, Dave, T, Baylor 1957
Lunz, Gerry, G, Marquette 1925–26
Lyman, Jeff, LB, Brigham Young 1972
Lynch, Lynn, G, Illinois 1951

M

Madden, Lloyd, B, Colorado Mines 1940
Maddock, Bob, G, Notre Dame 1942, 1946
Maeda, Chet, B, Colorado A&M 1946
Magulick, George, B, St. Francis 1944

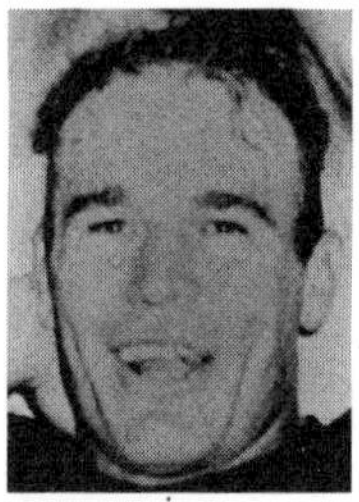
Stan Mauldin

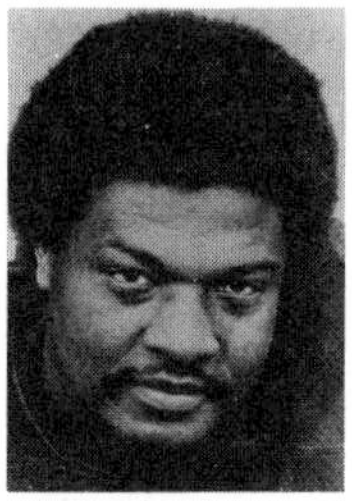
Ernie McMillan

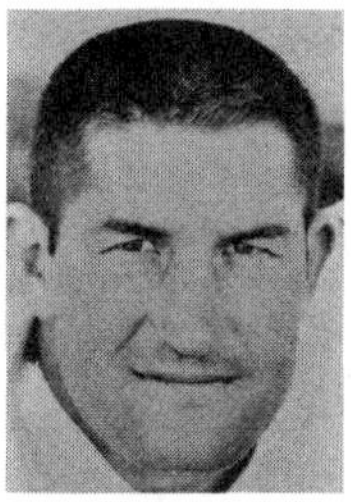
Dale Meinert

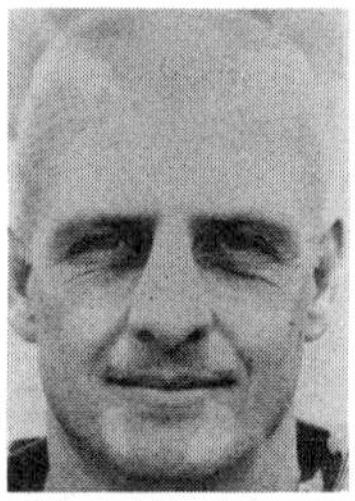
Johnny Olszewski

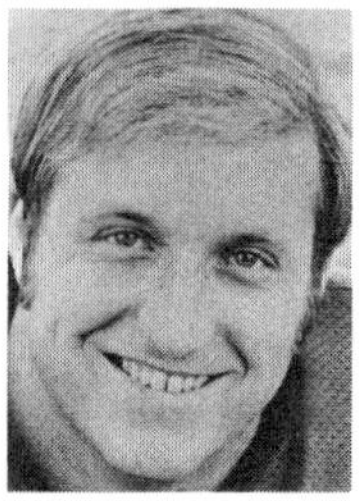
Jim Otis

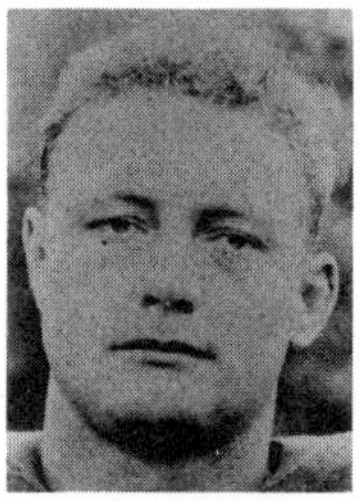
G. (Buster) Ramsay

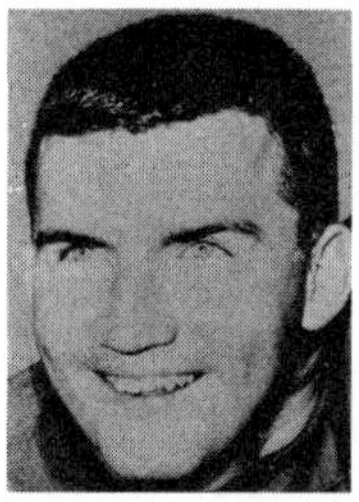
Sonny Randle

Mahoney, Ike, B, Creighton 1925-28, 1931
Mallouf, Ray, B, Southern Methodist 1941, 1946-48
Malloy, Les, B, Loyola, Ill. 1931-33
Mann, Dave, B, Oregon State 1955-57
Maple, Howard, B, Oregon State 1930
Marchibroda, Ted, QB, Detroit 1957
Marcontell, Ed, G, Lamar Tech 1967
Marelli, Ray, G, Notre Dame 1928
Marotti, Lou, G, Toledo 1943-45
Marquardt, John, E, Illinois 1921
Martin, Caleb, T, Louisiana Tech 1947
Martin, Glen, B, So. Illinois 1932
Martin, John, B, Oklahoma 1941-44
Mason, Joel, E, Western Michigan 1939
Masters, Walt, QB, Pennsylvania 1943-44
Matson, Ollie, RB, San Francisco 1952-58
Mauldin, Stan, T, Texas 1946-48
May, Bill, B, Louisiana State 1937-38
Maynard, Don, WR, Texas-El Paso 1973
McBride, Charles, B, Washington State 1936
McCarthy, John, B, St. Francis 1944
McCullough, Hugh, B, Oklahoma 1940-41
McCusker, Jim, T, Pittsburgh 1958
McDermott, Lloyd, T, Kentucky 1950-51
McDole, Roland, DE, Nebraska 1961
McDonald, Mike, LB, Catawba 1976
McDonnell, Mickey, B, None 1925-30
McDonough, Coley, B, Dayton 1939, 1944
McDowell, John, T, St. John's, Minn. 1966
McElwain, Bill, B, Northwestern 1924, 1926
McFarland, Jim, TE, Nebraska 1970-74
McGee, Bob, T, Santa Clara 1938
McGee, Mike, G, Duke 1960-62
McGill, Mike, LB, Notre Dame 1971-72
McGraw, Mike, LB, Wyoming 1976
McHan, Lamar, QB, Arkansas 1954-58
McInerny, Arnie, C, Notre Dame 1920-27
McInnis, Hugh, E, So. Mississippi 1960-62
McMahon, Byron, G, Cornell 1923
McMillan, Ernie, T, Illinois 1961-74
McNally, Frank, C, St. Mary's, Calif. 1931-34
McNulty, Paul, E, Notre Dame 1924-25
McPhee, Frank, E, Princeton 1955
McQuarters, Ed, DT, Oklahoma 1965
Meggyesy, Dave, LB, Syracuse 1963-69
Mehringer, Pete, T, Kansas 1934-36
Meilinger, Steve, E, Kentucky 1961
Meinert, Dale, LB, Oklahoma State 1958-67
Melinkovich, Mike, DE, Gray Harbor J.C., Wash. 1965-66
Memmelaar, Dave, G, Wyoming 1959-61
Mergen, Mike, T, San Francisco 1952
Merkovsky, Elmer, T, Pittsburgh 1944
Mestnik, Frank, RB, Marquette 1960-61
Metcalf, Terry, RB, Long Beach State 1973-76
Method, Russ, B, None 1929
Mikulak, Mike, B, Oregon 1934-36
Miller, Milford, G, Chadron State 1936-37
Miller, Terry, LB, Illinois 1971-74
Moe, Hal, B, Oregon State 1933
Mohardt, John, B, Notre Dame 1922-23
Monahan, Regis, G, Ohio State 1939
Monfort, Avery, B, New Mexico 1941
Montgomery, Bill, B, Louisiana State 1946
Montgomery, Ralph, T, Centre 1923
Mooney, Jim, T, Georgetown 1935
Moore, Bill, B, Loyola, La. 1932
Moran, Francis, B, Grinnell 1927
Morgan, Bob, T, Maryland 1954
Morris, Wayne, RB, Southern Methodist 1976
Morrow, Bob, G, Illinois Wesleyan 1941-43
Morrow, John, G, Kearney State 1937-38
Moss, Eddie, RB, S.E. Missouri State 1973-76
Moynihan, Tim, C, Notre Dame 1932-33
Muellner, Bill, E, De Paul 1937
Mullen, Verne, E, Illinois 1927
Mulleneaux, Lee, C, Arizona 1938
Mulligan, Wayne, C, Clemson 1969-73
Murphy, Bill, G, Washington, Mo. 1940-41
Murphy, Jim, B, St. Thomas, Minn. 1928
Murphy, Tom, B, Arkansas 1934

N

Nagel, Ray, B, UCLA 1953
Nagel, Ross, T, St. Louis 1942
Nagler, Gern, E, Santa Clara 1953, 1955-58
Neacy, Clem, E, Colgate 1928
Neill, Jim, B, Texas Tech 1939
Neils, Steve, LB, Minnesota 1974-76
Nelson, Lee, S, Florida State 1976
Nesbitt, Dick, B, Drake 1933
Nevers, Ernie, B, Stanford 1929-31
Neuman, Bob, E, Illinois Wesleyan 1934-36
Nichelini, Al, B, St. Mary's, Calif. 1935-36
Nichols, Ham, G, Rice 1947-49
Nisbet, Dave, E, Washington 1933
Nofsinger, Terry, QB, Utah 1965-66
Nolan, Dick, B, Maryland 1958
Nolan, Earl, T, Arizona 1937-38
Norman, Bob, C, None 1945
Norton, Jerry, DB, Southern Methodist 1959-61
Nussbaumer, Bob, B, Michigan 1949-50

O

Oates, Brad, T, Brigham Young 1976
O'Brien, Dave, G, Boston College 1966-67
O'Connor, Dan, G, Georgetown 1920-24
Ogden, Ray, TE, Alabama 1965-66
Ogle, Rick, LB, Colorado 1971
Okoniewski, Steve, DT, Montana 1976
Olerich, Dave, LB, San Francisco 1969-70
Oliver, Clancy, CB, San Diego State 1973
Olson, Carl, T, UCLA 1942
Olszewski, Johnny, B, California 1953-57
Otis, Jim, RB, Ohio State 1973-76
Owens, Don, DT, So. Mississippi 1960-63
Owens, Luke, DT, Kent State 1958-65
Owens, Marv, WR, San Diego State 1973

P

Palmer, Scott, DT, Texas 1972
Pancieri, Don, QB, San Francisco 1952
Panfil, Ken, T, Purdue 1960-62
Pangle, Hal, B, Oregon State 1935-38
Pappio, Joe, B, Haskell 1930
Pardonner, Earl, B, Purdue 1934-35
Paremore, Bob, RB, Florida A&M 1963-64
Parish, Don, LB, Stanford 1970-72
Parker, Buddy, B, Centenary 1937-43
Parker, Joe, E, Texas 1946-47
Pasquariello, Ralph, B, Villanova 1951-52
Pasquesi, Tony, T, Notre Dame 1955-57
Pearson, Bert, C, Kansas State 1935-36
Pelfrey, Ray, E, E. Kentucky 1952
Perko, John, G, Minnesota 1944
Person, Ara, TE, Morgan State 1972
Perry, Gerald, K, California 1960-62
Peters, Forest, B, Illinois 1932
Peters, Volney, T, USC 1952-53
Peterson, Ken, B, Gonzaga 1935
Petrovich, George, T, Texas 1949-50
Philpott, Dean, B, Fresno State 1958
Pierce, Don, C, Kansas 1943
Pittman, Charlie, RB, Penn State 1970
Plasman, Dick, E, Vanderbilt 1946-47
Plummer, Tony, DB, Pacific 1970
Polofsky, Gordon, G, Tennessee 1952-54
Polsfoot, Fran, E, Washington State 1950-52
Poole, Jim, E, Mississippi 1945
Popa, Eli, B, Illinois 1952
Popovich, John, B, St. Vincent 1944
Popovich, Milt, B, Montana 1938-42
Potteiger, Earl, B, Ursinus 1921
Provost, Ted, DB, Ohio State 1971
Psaltis, Jim, B, USC 1953, 1955
Puplis, Andy, B, Notre Dame 1943
Purdin, Cal, B, Tulsa 1943
Putman, Earl, C, Arizona State 1957

R

Rabold, Mike, G, Indiana 1960
Ramsey, Garrard (Buster), G, William & Mary 1946-51
Ramsey, Knox, G, William & Mary 1950-51
Ramsey, Ray, B, Bradley 1950-53
Randle, Sonny, WR, Virginia 1959-66
Randolph, Clare, C, Indiana 1930
Rankin, Walt, B, Texas Tech 1941, 1943, 1945-47
Ranspot, Keith, E, Southern Methodist 1940
Rashad, Ahmad, WR, Oregon 1972-73
Ravensburg, Bob, E, Indiana 1948-49
Reaves, Ken, S, Norfolk State 1974-76
Redmond, Tom, DE, Vanderbilt 1960-65
Reed, Joe, B, Louisiana State 1937, 1939
Rexer, Freeman, E, Tulane 1943, 1945
Reynolds, Bill, B, Mississippi 1945
Reynolds, Bob, T, Bowling Green 1963-71, 1973
Reynolds, John, C, Baylor 1937
Reynolds, Mack, QB, Louisiana State 1958-59
Rhea, Floyd, G, Oregon 1943
Ribble, Loran, G, Hardin-Simmons 1933
Richards, Perry, E, Detroit 1959-60
Richardson, John, DT, UCLA 1972-73
Risk, Ed, B, Purdue 1932
Risvold, Ray, B, St. Edwards', Tex. 1927-28
Rivers, Jamie, LB, Bowling Green 1968-73
Roach, John, QB, Southern Methodist 1956, 1959-60
Roach, Rollin, B, Texas Christian 1927
Robb, Joe, DE, Texas Christian 1961-67
Robbins, John, B, Arkansas 1938-39
Roberts, Hal, P, Houston 1974
Robinson, Jack, T, N.E. Missouri 1936-37
Robl, Hal, B, Oshkosh State 1945
Robnett, Marshall, G, Texas A&M 1943, 1945
Rogers, Glenn, G, Texas Christian 1939
Rogge, George, E, Iowa 1931-33
Roland, Johnny, RB, Missouri 1966-72
Romanik, Steve, G, Villanova 1953-54
Rooney, Bill, C, None 1929
Rooney, Cobb, E, None 1929-30
Root, Jim, QB, Miami, Ohio 1953, 1956
Rose, Gene, DB, Wisconsin 1929-32
Rosema, Rocky, LB, Michigan 1968-71
Rowe, Bob, DT, Western Michigan 1967-72
Roy, Frank, G, Utah 1966
Rudolph, Council, DE, Kentucky State 1973-75
Rundquist, Elmer, T, Illinois 1922
Rushing, Marion, LB, So. Illinois 1959, 1962-65
Russell, Doug, B, Kansas State 1934-39
Ryan, Jim, B, Notre Dame 1924
Rydzewski, Frank, T, Notre Dame 1921

S

Sabados, Andy, G, Citadel 1939-40
Sachs, Len, Loyola, Ill. 1920-23, 1925
Sagely, Floyd, E, Arkansas 1957
Sanders, Lonnie, DB, Michigan State 1968-69
Sandifer, Dan, B, Louisiana State 1953
Sanford, Leo, C, Louisiana Tech 1951-57
Sarboe, Phil, B, Washington State 1934-36
Sarringhaus, Paul, B, Ohio State 1946
Sauls, Mac, DB, S.W. Texas State 1968-69
Scales, Hurles, DB, North Texas State 1974
Scanlon, John, B, DePaul 1921
Scardine, Carmen, B, None 1932
Schleicher, Maury, LB, Penn State 1959
Schmeising, Joe, DE, New Mexico State 1968-71
Schmidt, George, E, Lewis 1953
Schneider, Herman, B, Iowa 1940
Schultz, Eberle, G, Oregon State 1944
Schwall, Vic, B, Northwestern 1947-50
Schwartz, Elmer, B, Washington State 1932
Schwenk, Wilson, B, Washington, Mo. 1942
Sears, Jim, DB, USC 1954, 1957-58
Seibold, Champ, T, Wisconsin 1942
Self, Clarence, B, Wisconsin 1949
Semes, Bernes, B, Duquesne 1944
Seno, Frank, B, George Washington 1945-46
Sensibaugh, Mike, S, Ohio State 1976
Severson, Jeff, CB, Long Beach State 1976
Shaw, Bob, E, Ohio State 1950
Shaw, Dennis, QB, San Diego State 1974
Shaw, Jesse, G, USC 1931
Shelley, Dex, B, Texas 1932
Shenefelt, Paul, T, Manchester 1934-35
Shivers, Roy, RB, Utah State 1966-72
Shirk, John, E, Oklahoma 1940
Shook, Fred, C, Texas Christian 1941
Shy, Don, RB, San Diego State 1973
Sikora, Mike, G, Oregon 1952
Silas, Sam, DT, So. Illinois 1963-67

Johnny Roland

Bob Rowe

Duke Slater

Larry Stallings

Don Stonesifer

Jerry Stovall

Roger Wehrli

Silvestri, Carl, DB, Wisconsin 1965
Simas, Bill, B, St. Mary's, Calif. 1932–33
Simmons, Dave, LB, Georgia Tech 1965–66
Simmons, John, C, Detroit 1951–56
Sitko, Emil, B, Notre Dame 1951–52
Siwek, Mike, DT, Western Michigan 1970
Slater, Fred, T, Iowa 1926–31
Sloan, Bonnie, DT, Austin Peay 1973
Sloan, Dwight, QB, Arkansas 1938
Smith, Bill, E, Washington 1934–39
Smith, Charles, B, Georgia 1947
Smith, George, B, Villanova 1943
Smith, Jackie, TE, N.W. Louisiana 1963–76
Smith, Russ, G, 'Illinois 1923
Smith, Wilfred, E, DePaul 1923–25
Snowden, Cal, DE, Indiana 1969–70
Sortun, Rick, G, Washington 1964–69
Speegle, Cliff, C, Oklahoma 1945
Spence, Julian, B, Sam Houston 1956
Spencer, Maurice, DB, N. Carolina Central 1974
Spiller, Phil, DB, Cal.State-L.A. 1967
Spinks, Jack, G, Alcorn A&M 1953
Springsteen, Bill, E, Lehigh 1927–28
Stacy, Billy, DB, Mississippi State 1959–63
Staggs, Jeff, LB, San Diego State 1972–73
Stallings, Larry, LB, Georgia Tech 1963–76
Stegent, Larry, RB, Texas A&M 1971
Steger, Pete, B, None 1921
Stein, Bill, C, Fordham 1927–28
Steinbach, Larry, T, St. Thomas 1931–33
Stennett, Fred, B, St. Mary's, Calif. 1932
Stewart, Vaughan, C, Alabama 1943
Stokes, Lee, Centenary 1943
Stonesifer, Don, E, Northwestern 1951–56
Stovall, Jerry, DB, Louisiana State 1963–71
Strader, Charles, G, Colgate 1928
Strausbaugh, Jim, B, Ohio State 1946

Stringer, Scott, DB, California 1974
Strofolino, Mike, LB, Villanova 1966–68
Stuessy, Mel, T, St. Edward's, Tex. 1926
Sugar, Leo, DE, Purdue 1960
Suminski, Dave, G, Wisconsin 1953
Summerall, Pat, K-E, Arkansas 1953–57
Sutch, George, B, Temple 1946
Svoboda, Bill, LB, Tulane 1950–53
Swanson, Evar, E, Lombard 1925–27
Swistowicz, Mike, B, Notre Dame 1950
Symank, John, DB, Florida 1963
Szot, Walt, T, Bucknell 1946–48

T

Taylor, Mike, T, USC 1973
Trays, Jim, B, Penn State 1925
Teeuws, Len, T, Tulane 1954–57
Thomas, Earl, WR, Houston 1974–75
Thomas, Jim, G, Oklahoma 1931
Thomas, Ralph, E, San Francisco 1952
Thompson, Harry, G, UCLA 1955
Thompson, Norm, DB, Utah 1971–76
Thornton, Bill, RB, Nebraska 1963–65, 1967
Thurbon, Bob, B, Pittsburgh 1944
Tilley, Pat, WR, Louisiana Tech 1976
Tinsley, Gaynell, E, Louisiana State 1937–38, 1940
Tinsley, Jess, T, Louisiana State 1929–33
Tipton, Howard, B, USC 1933–37
Tolbert, Jim, S, Lincoln, Missouri 1973
Tonelli, Mario, B, USC 1939
Toogood, Charley, G, Nebraska 1957
Toscani, Frank, B, St. Mary's, Calif. 1932
Towns, Robert, DB, Georgia 1960
Tracey, John, LB, Texas A&M 1959–60
Trippi, Charley, B, Georgia 1947–55
Triplett, Bill, RB, Miami, Ohio 1962–63, 1965–66
Triplett, Wally, B, Penn State 1952–53

Tripucka, Frank, QB, Notre Dame 1950–52
Tubbs, Jerry, LB, Oklahoma 1957–58
Turner, Herschel, G, Kentucky 1964–65
Tyler, Pete, B, Hardin-Simmons 1937–38

U

Ucovich, Mitch, T, San Jose State 1945
Ulrich, Charles, T, Illinois 1954–58
Underwood, John, G, None 1929
Upshaw, Marvin, DT, Trinity, Texas 1976

V

Van Galder, Tim, QB, Iowa State 1972
Vanzo, Fred, B, Northwestern 1941
Vaughan, Charles, B, Tennessee 1936
Vesser, John, E, Idaho 1927, 1930–31
Vodicka, Joe, B, None 1945
Vokaty, Otto, B, Heidelberg 1933
Volok, Bill, G, Tulsa 1934–39

W

Wager, Clint, E, St. Mary's, Minn. 1943, 1945
Wagstaff, Jim, B, Idaho State 1959
Waldron, Austin, G, Gonzaga 1927
Walker, Chuck, DT, Duke 1964–72
Wallner, Fred, G, Notre Dame 1951–52, 1954–55
Washington, Eric, DB, Texas-El Paso 1972–73
Watford, Gerry, E, Alabama 1953–54
Watkins, Bob, B, Ohio State 1958
Watt, Walt, B, Miami 1945
Weaver, Charles, G, Chicago 1930
Weber, Chuck, LB, West Chester State 1956–58
Wedel, Dick, G, Wake Forest 1948
Wehrli, Roger, CB, Missouri 1969–76
Weller, Ray, T, Nebraska 1926–27
Wendt, Ken, G, Marquette 1932
West, Jeff, P, Cincinnati 1975
West, Stan, G, Oklahoma 1956–57
West, Willie, DB, Oregon 1960–61
Whalen, Bill, T, None 1920–24
Wham, Tom, E, Furman 1949–51
Wheeler, Ernie, B, N. Dakota State 1939, 1942
Wheeler, Ted, G, W. Texas State 1967–68
White, Paul, RB, Texas-El Paso 1970–71
White, Ray, LB, Syracuse 1975–76
Whitman, Laverne, B, Tulsa 1951–53
Wicks, Bob, WR, Utah Stte 1972
Widerquist, Chet, T, Washington & Jefferson 1926–28
Willard, Ken, RB, North Carolina 1974
Williams, Bobby, DB, Central Oklahoma 1966–67
Williams, Clyde, T, Southern U. 1967–71
Williams, Dave, WR, Washington 1967–71
Williams, Jake, T, Texas Christian 1929–33
Williams, Rex, C, Texas Tech 1940
Willingham, Larry, DB, Auburn 1971–72
Wilson, Bill, E, Gonzaga 1935–37
Wilson, Gordon, C, Texas Mines 1942–43, 1945
Wilson, Larry, S, Utah 1960–72
Wilson, Mike, DB, Western Illinois 1969
Withrow, Cal, C, Kentucky 1974
Wood, Bob, T, Alabama 1940
Woodeschick, Tom, RB, West Virginia 1972
Woodruff, Jim, E, Pittsburgh 1926
Woodson, Abe, DB, Illinois 1965–66
Wortman, Keith, G, Nebraska 1976
Wright, Nate, DB, San Diego State 1969–70
Wright, Steve, T, Alabama 1972
Wutkis, Al, C, Duquesne 1944
Wyche, Sam, QB, Furman 1976

Y

Yablonski, Ventan, B, Columbia 1948–51
Yanowski, Ron, DE, Kansas State 1971–76
Yarr, Tom, C, Notre Dame 1933
Yeisley, Don, E, None 1927–28
Young, Bob, G, Howard Payne 1972–76

Z

Zelencik, Frank, T, Oglethorpe 1939
Zimny, Bob, T, Indiana 1945–49
Zoia, Clyde, G, Notre Dame 1920–23
Zontini, Lou, B, Notre Dame 1940–41
Zook, John, DE, Kansas 1976

Safety Larry Wilson returning one of his 52 career interceptions for the Cardinals, 1971.

SAN DIEGO CHARGERS

1959 The Los Angeles Chargers were one of the original six teams as the American Football League was born August 14. Hotel magnate Barron Hilton formed the Chargers. Play was to begin in 1960, with the Chargers to use the Los Angeles Memorial Coliseum. Frank Leahy, legendary former coach of Notre Dame, signed to become general manager. Although Los Angeles already had one pro football team, the National Football League Rams, Hilton and his backers were confident the town could support another. "You've got no worries," George Preston Marshall, the Washington Redskins' owner told Hilton. "Your team will draw in L.A., just like everything else draws. They go for anything out there."

1960 Sid Gillman, who coached the Rams for five years, was signed to a three-year contract as the first coach of the Chargers, January 7. A special tryout camp was conducted in Burbank, and 207 candidates showed up, April 9. General manager Leahy resigned due to ill health, July 1. Gillman took over the additional duties of general manager, July 9. In the team's first preseason game, Paul Lowe, who had called the club and offered his services, took the opening kickoff and returned in 105 yards for a touchdown, August 6. The Chargers won the game 27-7 over the New York Titans, before 27,778 in the Coliseum. A few weeks later, before a considerably smaller crowd, they edged Dallas 21-20 in the first league game, September 10. With Gillman choreographing a flashy, stylish offense, the Chargers won the Western Division championship. But only 9,928 people showed up to watch them defeat Denver 41-33 to clinch the title. Their final regular season record was 10-4.

1961 In the first AFL championship game, the Chargers were beaten 24-16 by the Houston Oilers and George Blanda in Houston, January 1. Those numbers weren't nearly as discouraging to Barron Hilton as the team's financial statement. He found he had lost more than $900,000. At this point the city of San Diego, sensing Hilton's plight, rallied to form committees and sell tickets and boost enthusiasm for the AFL. Hilton was impressed. He applied for and was granted permission to move his team to San Diego, where it would play in an enlarged, 34,000-seat facility, Balboa Stadium, February 10. On a hot August afternoon, the Chargers made their debut in their new home, beating Houston 27-14 before 12,304. The team logo, the lightning bolt seen on players' helmets, seemed to fit this club, with smooth quarterback Jack Kemp, the dangerous breakaway runner Lowe, and a solid collection of talent, particularly at the skilled positions. San Diego began to respond to the show. A crowd of 33,788 turned out to see the Chargers defeat the Dallas Texans 24-14 for their eleventh win of the season and their fifteenth straight overall. They won the Western Division title again, but again couldn't handle Houston in the AFL championship game, losing a tough, defensive struggle 10-3 before 29,556 in Balboa Stadium, December 24.

1962 Coached by Gillman, a West team featuring 11 Chargers, defeated the East 47-27 in the first AFL all-star game before 20,973 in Balboa Stadium. San Diego ends Dave Kocourek and Don Norton each caught touchdown passes. Perhaps the most important draft in the history of the franchise brought in two players who would have a profound effect on this team, wide receiver Lance Alworth from Arkansas and quarterback John Hadl from Kansas. Kemp, nursing an injured throwing hand, was placed on the waiver list and claimed by Buffalo for $100. Groping without an experienced leader and with 23 players who missed two or more games because of injuries,

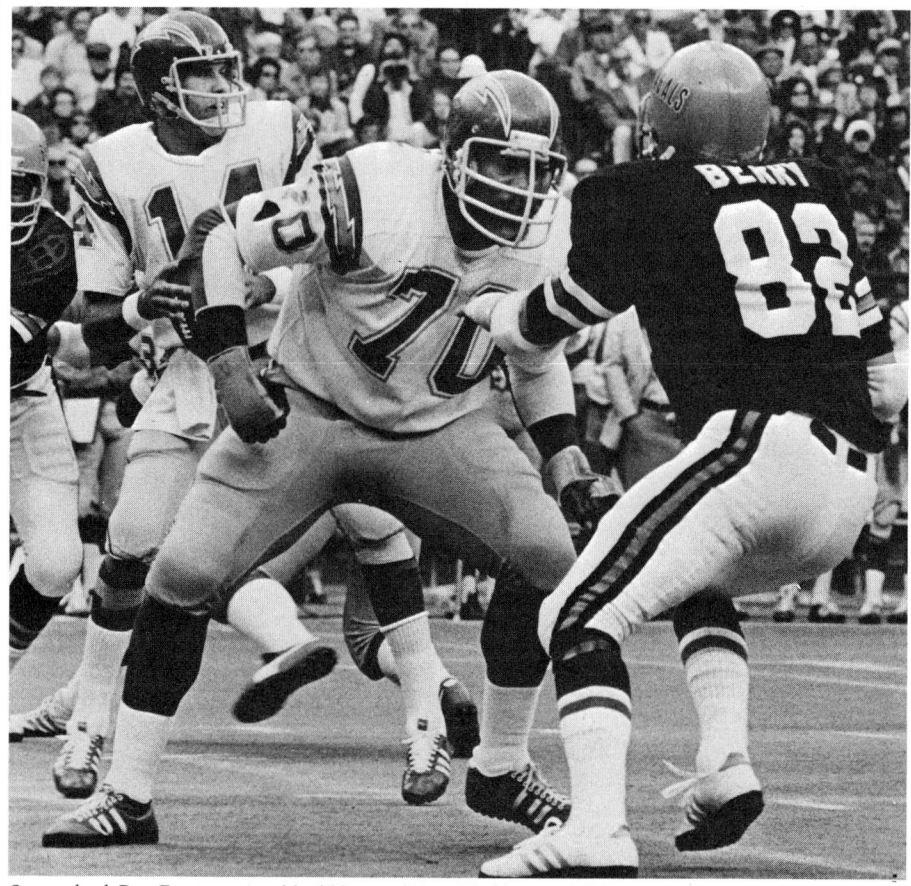

Quarterback Dan Fouts protected by 280-pound Russ Washington, 1974.

the Chargers finished their poorest season at 4-10.

1963 The West defeated the East 21-14 in the second AFL all-star game in Balboa Stadium. Chargers' defensive end Earl Faison was named player of the game. Gillman convinced Tobin Rote, the former National Football League quarterback with Green Bay and Detroit, to sign with the Chargers after he quit Toronto of the Canadian League. Barron Hilton and his father, Conrad, decided to sell one-third interest in the team to San Diego businessmen John Mabee, George Pernicano, Kenneth Swanson, and James Copley, and M.L. Bengston of Los Angeles. Gillman moved the club's training camp to Rough Acres, a desert outpost 40 miles out of town. The Chargers came out of that camp fit and healthy, and, with Alworth and a devastating defensive line led by Faison and 315-pound Ernie Ladd, the team ran up an 11-3 record, topping it off with a 58-20 victory over Denver.

1964 The Chargers climaxed the best season in their history by burying Boston 55-10 before 30,127 in Balboa Stadium to win the AFL championship, January 5. Keith Lincoln, the exceptional all-around back from Washington State, rushed for 206 yards, including touchdown runs of 67 and 56 yards, caught six passes and accounted for 349 yards overall. He was voted the player of the game. Afterward, Otto Graham, the former Cleveland Browns' star and NFL coach, said, "If the Chargers could play the best in the NFL, I'd have to pick the Chargers. They have the linemen and everything to go with them." Lincoln capped his greatest year by winning the honor as the outstanding offensive player as the West defeated the East 27-24 in the AFL all-star game two weeks later. The Chargers opened the 1964 regular season with a win over Houston, then lost three straight. Rote had a sore arm, so Gillman moved Hadl in to start his first game in Boston. Hadl responded by completing 17 of

29 passes for 229 yards and three touchdown's in a 26-17 victory. The club established a San Diego attendance record when 34,865 saw the Chargers lose to Buffalo 27-24, November 26. A 38-3 rout of the New York Jets made it eight wins for the year and clinched a fourth Western Division championship. Alworth, who was considered the best pass receiver in pro football, was injured and missed the AFL title game in Buffalo. And after he sparked the first San Diego scoring drive in that game, Lincoln also went down. Without two of their most prominent weapons, the Chargers were beaten 20-7 by the Bills at War Memorial Stadium, December 26.

1965 Keith Lincoln led the West to a 38-14 victory over the East in the AFL all-star game and again was voted the outstanding offensive player. Gillman suddenly began to have troubles at the bargaining table. Lincoln and linebacker Frank Buncom became stubborn holdouts. Earl Faison and Ernie Ladd both announced their intentions of playing out their options. Ladd was fined, suspended, and finally reinstated. Construction of a $28 million San Diego Stadium in the heart of Mission Valley was authorized by a 73 percent "yes" vote in a special municipal election. Lowe and Alworth both had big years, finishing one-two in the balloting by AFL players for player of the year. The Chargers led the league from opening day, although Oakland and Kansas City made it interesting. A 9-2-3 record was enough, however, although Buffalo was there to spoil things again in the AFL title game, this time 23-0 at Balboa Stadium, December 26.

1966 Linebacker Frank Buncom survived an early injury to become the most valuable defensive player as the AFL all-stars defeated Buffalo 30-19. Alworth scored two touchdowns on Joe Namath passes and Lowe ran for another. In the wake of the new merger agreement between the NFL and AFL, the Chargers and Los Angeles Rams signed a three-year preseason contract for San Diego Stadium. A group of 21 business executives, headed by Eugene Klein and Sam Schulman of Beverly Hills, purchased the Chargers for $10 million. Klein and Schulman became general partners with Klein replacing Hilton as club president and Schulman taking over as chairman of the board. Barron and Conrad Hilton retained a substantial interest in the team. James Copley, San Diego newspaper publisher, and George Pernicano, restaurant owner, retained limited interests. Gillman was signed to a new five-year contract as coach and general manager. Alworth caught eight passes for 156 yards to establish new season and all-time Chargers records of 73 receptions and 1,383 yards. The club finished 7-6-1, however, failing to win the Western Division for the first time since 1962. Official groundbreaking ceremonies were held in Mission Valley to start work on the $28 million, 50,000-seat San Diego Stadium.

1967 San Diego Stadium was dedicated as 45,988 fans looked on, August 20. Playing their first National Football League opponent that night, the Chargers were beaten 38–17 by Detroit in a preseason game. A week later, in their first confrontation with their Southern California rivals, the Los Angeles Rams, the Chargers were whipped 50–7. San Diego opened the regular season with a flourish, however, going 5-0-1 and eventually ran its record to 8-1-1. But four straight losses dropped the Chargers to third place for the second year in a row.

1968 In a memorable preseason game, the Chargers beat the Rams 35–13 behind John Hadl's two touchdown passes and 302 yards, August 24. Getting off to another fast start, San Diego upset Oakland, the defending AFL champion, 23–14. Lance Alworth caught nine passes for 182 yards to hand the Raiders their first loss at home in three years. Once again, an 8-2 start was spoiled by three losses in the final four games. Again, the final record took third place in the AFL Western Division.

1969 The club moved its training camp facilities from Escondido to the University of California at Irvine, 80 miles north of San Diego. The Chargers opened the regular season with two losses on the road, but when they returned home a record crowd of 54,042 was in San Diego Stadium to see them play Joe Namath and the New York Jets. The Chargers won 34–27 as Gary Garrison caught 10 passes for 188 yards and two touchdowns. Sid Gillman announced his retirement from coaching because of a stomach ulcer and chest hernia, November 10. He said he would continue as general manager. Offensive backfield coach Charlie Waller was appointed head coach and the team finished the year 8-6 and in third place for the fourth consecutive year. In the final week against Buffalo, Alworth caught a pass in his ninety-sixth consecutive game to break the pro record of Don Hutson, who was present in San Diego for congratulatory ceremonies. Alworth led the AFL in pass receptions with 68, and running back Dickie Post led the league in rushing with 873 yards.

1970 In the final American Football League all-star game, John Hadl won the most valuable player award, helping the West beat the East 26–3 in Houston. The highlight of the Chargers' season was a 27–10 win over the Browns at Cleveland before 80,047, the largest crowd ever to see San Diego play, November 1. But the team struggled through its first losing season in eight years, although, once again, it finished third in its division. After the 5-6-3 finish, a reorganization was announced, with Gillman coming back as head coach, Charlie Waller staying on as offensive coach, and Irv Kaze promoted to the position of assistant to the president, December 20.

1971 Harland Svare was named general manager. Lance Alworth was traded to Dallas for tight end Pettis Norman, defensive tackle Ron East, and tackle

Tony Liscio. Gene Klein announced Sid Gillman's resignation "by mutual consent," November 22. At one point a couple of years earlier, Klein had said Gillman had a lifetime contract. "Always get your contracts in print," Gillman said, after he was relieved of his duties. General manager Harland Svare, who formerly coached the Rams, was named coach. A record San Diego Stadium crowd of 54,505 saw the Chargers upset Minnesota 30–14, then follow it with a 45–17 rout of Denver. In the season's final game, however, San Diego lost to Houston 49–33.

1972 Harland Svare began a series of major trades by dealing for defensive end David (Deacon) Jones of the Rams, in a transaction that involved three other players and three high draft choices. Svare changed the complexion of the club in a wild 12-hour trading session, acquiring running back Duane Thomas from Dallas, linebacker Tim Rossovich from Philadelphia, and defensive tackle Dave Costa from Denver, July 30. After much controversy, Thomas never played for the Chargers. Following a 2-1-1 start, the Chargers lost 8 of their last 10 games to finish 4-9-1 and in last place in the AFC Western Division. Mike Garrett gained 59 yards in the final game to finish with 1,031 yards and become the only pro player to gain 1,000 with two different teams. He had surpassed 1,000 with Kansas City in 1967.

1973 Heisman Trophy winner Johnny Rodgers was the Chargers' top draft choice, but the Nebraska running back decided to sign with Montreal of the Canadian Football League. Owner Gene Klein, coach Harland Svare, and friends made a tour of Europe, searching for a soccer-style kicker. The placekicker they came up with was Gunther Enz of Vienna, Austria. He kicked six of nine field goals during the preseason but Dennis Partee and Ray Wersching were the Chargers' kickers in 1973. Klein announced the acquisition of all-time great quarterback Johnny Unitas, in a deal that eventually cost the Chargers $650,000. "He's just the guy to run the offense we want here," said Svare. In the second part of that three-team deal, San Diego sent John Hadl to Los Angeles for defensive lineman Coy Bacon and running back Bob Thomas. Unitas completed a 30-yard pass to Mike Garrett to go over 40,000 yards in his career. In Pittsburgh, in the fourth game of the year, a back injury that had plagued Unitas was aggravated and he was rendered almost immobile. The Steelers built a 38–0 halftime lead and rookie Dan Fouts took over at quarterback in the third quarter. Fouts remained there for most of the rest of the season, with Unitas playing in a total of five games and ending his long pro career. Offensive coordinator Bob Schnelker was fired in midseason. Svare announced his resignation as head coach but said he would remain as general manager, November 5. Ron Waller, special teams coach, was appointed interim head coach.

1974 Tommy Prothro, formerly of UCLA and the Los Angeles Rams, was appointed the Chargers' new coach. Prothro immediately began overhauling the team, trading Deacon Jones and Walt Sweeney to Washington to start the changes. The Chargers, Klein, and Svare were implicated in a drug scandal, with NFL Commissioner Pete Rozelle fining the owner, general manager, and several players and placing them on probation. Prothro's first Chargers' training camp at the new United States International University site was interrupted by picketing veterans who were striking as members of the NFL Players Association. Johnny Unitas announced his retirement, July 24. A little known rookie, Don Woods, was picked up on waivers from Green Bay. Before the season was over, Woods established an NFL rookie rushing record, gaining 1,162 yards and winning rookie of the year honors in every poll.

1975 Johnny Sanders, a long-time Los Angeles Rams' executive, was named assistant to the presi-

dent for player personnel, February 21. Paul (Tank) Younger, another ex-Rams player and scout, was appointed assistant general manager, June 17. The team struggled during the season, losing twice in overtime and dropping its first 11 games in a row, before rallying to win two of its final three games. A loss in Cincinnati on the last Sunday made the final record 2-12.

1976 Harland Svare was fired as general manager and replaced by Johnny Sanders, February 16. Joe Washington, the All-America runner from Oklahoma, was the team's top draft choice. The Chargers played the first NFL game outside of North America against the St. Louis Cardinals in Tokyo, August 16; St. Louis won 20–16. Coy Bacon was traded to Cincinnati for wide receiver Charlie Joiner. Washington injured a knee playing a preseason game in his old college stadium at Norman, Oklahoma, and had to undergo surgery. The club opened with its best record in years, 3-0, after beating St. Louis 43–24. But a porous pass defense finally caught up with San Diego and it finished the season 6-8, its best record in six years.

MEMBERS OF HALL OF FAME:
None.

CHARGERS RECORD, 1960-72

Year	Won	Lost	Tied	Pct.	Pts.	OP
Los Angeles Chargers						
1960§	10	4	0	.714	373	336
San Diego Chargers						
1961§	12	2	0	.857	396	219
1962	4	10	0	.286	314	392
1963‡	11	3	0	.786	399	256
1964§	8	5	1	.615	341	300
1965§	9	2	3	.818	340	227
1966	7	6	1	.538	335	284
1967	8	5	1	.615	360	352
1968	9	5	0	.643	382	310
1969	8	6	0	.571	288	276
1970	5	6	3	.455	282	278
1971	6	8	0	.429	311	341
1972	4	9	1	.321	264	344
1973§	2	11	1	.179	188	386
1974	5	9	0	.357	212	285
1975	2	12	0	.143	189	345
1976	6	8	0	.429	248	285
17 Years	116	111	11	.511	5,222	5,216

§AFL Western Division Champion
‡AFL Champion

RECORD HOLDERS

Rushing (Yards)	Don Woods, 1974	1,162
Passing (Pct.)	Tobin Rote, 1963	59.4
Passing (Yards)	John Hadl, 1968	3,473
Passing (TDs)	John Hadl, 1968	27
Receiving (No.)	Lance Alworth, 1966	73
Receiving (Yards)	Lance Alworth, 1965	1,602
Interceptions (No.)	Charlie McNeil, 1961	9
Punting (Avg.)	Dennis Partee, 1969	44.6
Punt Ret. (Avg.)	Keith Lincoln, 1961	21.4
Kickoff Ret. (Avg.)	Leslie (Speedy) Duncan, 1964	34.4
Touchdowns (Total)	Lance Alworth, 1964	15
Field Goals Made	Dennis Partee, 1968	22
Points (No.)	Dennis Partee, 1968	106

COACHING HISTORY

1960-69	Sid Gillman*	82-47-6
1969-70	Charlie Waller	9- 7-3
1971	Sid Gillman**	4- 6-0
1971-73	Harland Svare***	7-17-2
1973	Ron Waller	1- 5-0
1974-76	Tommy Prothro	13-29-0

*Retired after nine games in 1969
**Replaced after 10 games in 1971
***Resigned after eight games in 1973

FIRST PLAYER SELECTED

1960	Monty Stickles, E, Notre Dame
1961	Earl Faison, DE, Indiana
1962	Bob Ferguson, RB, Ohio State
1963	Walt Sweeney, G, Syracuse
1964	Ted Davis, LB, Georgia Tech
1965	Steve DeLong, DE, Tennessee
1966	Don Davis, DT, Cal. State-L.A.
1967	Ron Billingsley, DE, Wyoming
1968	Russ Washington, DT, Missouri
1969	Marty Domres, QB, Columbia
1970	Walker Gillette, WR, Richmond
1971	Leon Burns, RB, Cal. State-Long Beach
1972	Pete Lazetich, DE, Stanford
1973	Johnny Rodgers, RB, Nebraska
1974	Bo Matthews, RB, Colorado
1975	Gary Johnson, DT, Grambling
1976	Joe Washington, RB, Oklahoma

Chuck Allen

Pat Curran

Earl Faison

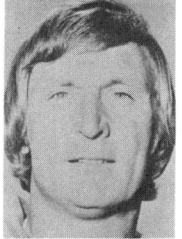
Gary Garrison

Sam Gruneisen

Jim Hill

Emil Karas

LOS ANGELES CHARGERS 1960, SAN DIEGO CHARGERS 1961–76

Agajanian, Ben, K, New Mexico 1960–61, 1964
Aiu, Charles, T, Hawaii 1976
Akin, Harold, T, Oklahoma State 1967–68
Allen, Chuck, LB, Washington 1961–69
Allison, Jim, RB, San Diego State 1965–68
Alworth, Lance, WR, Arkansas 1962–70
Anderson, Ralph, TE, Cal State-L.A. 1960
Andrews, John, TE, Indiana 1972
Appleton, Scott, DT, Texas 1967–68

B

Babich, Bob, LB, Miami, Ohio 1970–72
Baccaglio, Martin, DE, San Jose State 1968
Bacon, Coy, DE, Jackson State 1973–75
Baker, John, LB, Mississippi State 1967
Baker, Mel, WR, Texas Southern 1975
Bansavage, Al, G, USC 1960
Barnes, Ernie, G, N. Carolina College 1960–62
Barnes, Pete, LB, Southern U. 1970–72
Barry, Al, G, USC 1960
Beauchamp, Joe, CB, Iowa State 1966–75
Beirne, Jim, WR, Purdue 1973–74
Bell, Eddie, WR, Idaho State 1976
Belotti, George, G, USC 1961
Berry, Reggie, S, Cal State-Long Beach 1972–74
Bethune, Bob, DB, Mississippi State 1962
Billingsley, Ron, DT, Wyoming 1967–70
Blair, George, DB-K, Mississippi 1961–64
Boatright, Ben, DT, Oklahoma State 1974
Bobo, Hubert, LB, Ohio State 1960
Botchan, Ron, LB, Occidental 1960
Bradley, Chuck, TE, Oregon 1975–76
Braxton, Hezekiah, RB, Virginia Union 1962
Breaux, Don, QB, McNeese State 1964–65
Briggs, Bob, DE, Heidelberg 1968–70
Briscoe, Marlin, WR, Omaha 1975
Brittenum, Jon, QB, Arkansas 1968
Brown, Bob, DT, Arkansas AM&N 1974
Brueckman, Charlie, LB, Pittsburgh 1960
Bruggers, Bob, LB, Minnesota 1968–71
Buncom, Frank, LB, USC 1962–67
Burns, Leon, RB, Cal State-Long Beach 1971

C

Caffey, Lee Roy, LB, Texas A&M 1972
Campbell, Jim, LB, W. Texas State 1969
Carolan, Reg, TE, Idaho 1962–63
Carr, Levert, T, No. Central Illinois 1962–63
Carpenter, Ron, LB, Texas A&M 1964–65
Carter, Mike, WR, Sacramento State 1972
Carter, Virgil, QB, Brigham Young 1975
Chorovich, Dick, DT, Miami 1960–61
Clark, Howard, TE, Chattanooga 1960–61
Clark, Wayne, QB, American Int'l. 1970–72, 1976
Clatterbuck, Bobby, QB, Houston 1960
Cline, Doug, LB, Clemson 1966
Coan, Bert, RB, Kansas 1962
Colbert, Danny, CB, Tulsa 1974–76
Cole, Fred, G, Maryland 1960
Cordill, Olie, WR, Memphis State 1967
Costa, Dave, DT, Utah 1972–73
Cotton, Craig, TE, Youngstown 1975
Curran, Pat, TE, Lakeland 1975–76

D

Davis, Harrison, WR, Virginia 1974
Day, Tom, DE, N. Carolina A&T 1967
Dean, Fred, DE, Louisiana Tech 1975–76
Degan, Dick, LB, Cal. State-Long Beach 1965–66
DeJurnett, Charles, San Jose State 1976
DeLong, Steve, DE, Tennessee 1965–71
DeLuca, Sam, G, South Carolina 1960–61, 1963
Dennis, Al, G, Grambling 1973
Detwiler, Chuck, S, Utah State 1970–72
Dicus, Chuck, WR, Arkansas 1971–72
Domres, Marty, QB, Columbia 1969–71
Donnell, Ben, DE, Vanderbilt 1960
Dorsey, Larry, WR, Tennessee State 1976
Douglas, Jay, T, Memphis State 1973–74
Douglass, Bobby, QB, Kansas 1975

Dragon, Oscar, RB, Arizona State 1972
Duncan, Leslie (Speedy), DB, Jackson State 1964–70
Dunlap, Leonard, CB, N. Texas State 1972–74
Dyer, Ken, DB, Arizona State 1968

E

East, Ron, DT, Montana State 1971–73
Eber, Rick, WR, Tulsa 1969
Edwards, Cid, RB, Tennessee State 1972–74
Enis, Hunter, QB, Texas Christian 1961
Erickson, Bernard, LB, Abilene Christian 1967–68
Erlandson, Tom, LB, Washington State 1968
Estes, Don, G, Louisiana State 1966

F

Faison, Earl, DE, Indiana 1961–66
Fairley, Dick, DB, Boston U. 1968–69
Farr, Miller, DB, Wichita State 1965–66
Farris, John, G, San Diego State 1965–66
Fenner, Lane, WR, Florida State 1968
Ferguson, Gene, T, Norfolk State 1969–70
Ferguson, Howard, RB, None 1960
Ferrante, Orlando, G, USC 1960–61

Fetherston, Jim, LB, California 1968–69
Finneran, Garry, DT, USC 1960
Flanagan, Ed, C, Purdue 1975–76
Fletcher, Chris, S, Temple 1971, 1973
Flowers, Charley, RB, Mississippi 1960–61
Ford, Freddie, G, Cal, Poly-Obispo 1961
Forsberg, Fred, LB, Washington 1974
Foster, Gene, RB, Arizona State 1965–70
Fouts, Dan, QB, Oregon 1973–76
Frazier, Wayne, C, Auburn 1962
Frazier, Willie, TE, Arkansas AM&N 1966–70
Fritsch, Toni, K, Austria Tech 1976
Fuller, Mike, S, Auburn 1975–76

G

Garner, Bob, DB, Fresno State 1960
Garrett, Mike, RB, USC 1970–73
Garrison, Gary, WR, San Diego State 1966–76
Gay, Blenda, DE, Fayetteville State 1974
Gersbach, Carl, LB, West Chester State 1973–74
Gibson, Claude, DB, N. Carolina State 1961–62
Gillett, Fred, LB, Cal. State-L.A. 1962
Gillette, Walker, WR, Richmond 1970–71

Lance Alworth makes a catch in ninety-sixth consecutive game, 1969.

Paul Lowe

Terry Owens

Dickie Post

Walt Sweeney

Dick Westmoreland

Doug Wilkerson

Don Woods

Glick, Gary, DB, Colorado State ... 1963
Gob, Art, LB, Pittsburgh ... 1960
Good, Tom, LB, Marshall ... 1966
Goode, Don, LB, Kansas ... 1974–76
Gordon, Dick, WR, Michigan State ... 1974
Gordon, Ira, T, Kansas State ... 1970–75
Graham, Kenny, DB, Washington State ... 1964–69
Graham, Tom, LB, Oregon ... 1975–76
Grannell, Dave, TE, Arizona State ... 1974
Grant, Wes, DE, UCLA ... 1971
Greene, Tom, QB, Holy Cross ... 1961
Griffin, Jim, DT, Grambling ... 1966–67
Gross, George, DT, Auburn ... 1963–67
Gruneisen, Sam, C, Villanova ... 1962–72

H

Hadl, John, QB, Kansas ... 1961–72
Hardy, Kevin, DT, Notre Dame ... 1971–72
Harris, Dick, DB, McNeese State ... 1960–65
Hayes, Luther, WR, USC ... 1961
Hayes, Tom, CB, San Diego State ... 1976
Henning, Dan, QB, William & Mary ... 1966
Hill, Jim, S, Texas A&I ... 1969–71
Hoey, George, DB, Michigan ... 1974
Holiday, Ron, WR, Pittsburgh ... 1973
Holmes, Robert, RB, Southern U. ... 1973
Hoopes, Mitch, P, Arizona ... 1976
Horn, Bob, LB, Oregon State ... 1976
Horn, Don, QB, San Diego State ... 1974
Horton, Bob, LB, Boston U. ... 1964–65
Howard, Bob, CB, San Diego State ... 1967–74
Hubbert, Brad, RB, Arizona ... 1967–70
Hudson, Bill, DT, Clemson ... 1961–62
Hudson, Richard, T, Memphis State ... 1962
Huey, Gene, WR, Wyoming ... 1969
Hutcherson, Ken, LB, Livingston State ... 1975

J

Jackson, Bob, WR, New Mexico State ... 1962–63
Jeffrey, Neal, QB, Baylor ... 1976
Johnson, Gary, DT, Grambling ... 1975–76
Joiner, Charlie, WR, Grambling ... 1976
Jones, Clint, RB, Michigan State ... 1973
Jones, Curtis, G, Missouri ... 1968
Jones, David (Deacon), DE, S. Carolina State ... 1972–73
Jones, Harris, G, J. C. Smith ... 1971
Jones, Leroy, DE, Norfolk State ... 1976
Jones, Ray, CB, Southern U. ... 1972

K

Karas, Emil, LB, Dayton ... 1960–64, 1966
Kecklin, Val, QB, So. Mississippi ... 1962
Kelcher, Louie, DT, Southern Methodist ... 1975–76
Kemp, Jack, QB, Occidental ... 1960–62
Kempinski, Charles, G, Mississippi ... 1960
Kinderman, Keith, RB, Florida State ... 1963–64
Kindig, Howard, DE, Cal. State-L.A. ... 1965–67
Kirner, Gary, T, USC ... 1964–69
Klotz, Jack, DT, Penn Military ... 1962
Kocourek, Dave, TE, Wisconsin ... 1960–65
Kompara, John, DT, South Carolina ... 1960

L

Ladd, Ernie, DT, Grambling ... 1961–65
Lane, Bobbie, LB, Baylor ... 1963–64
Laraba, Bob, QB-LB, Texas Western ... 1960–61
Latzke, Paul, C, Pacific ... 1966–68
Lazetich, Pete, LB, Stanford ... 1972–74
Lee, John, DT, Nebraska ... 1976
Lee, Mike, LB, Nevada-Las Vegas ... 1974
Lenkaitis, Bill, G, Penn State ... 1968–70
LeVias, Jerry, WR, Southern Methodist ... 1971–74
Lincoln, Keith, RB, Washington State ... 1961–66, 1968
Little, Larry, G, Bethune-Cookman ... 1967–68
London, Mike, LB, Wisconsin ... 1966
Longley, Clint, QB, Abilene Christian ... 1976
Loudd, Rommie, LB, UCLA ... 1960
Lowe, Paul, RB, Oregon State ... 1960–68
Lowe, Woodrow, LB, Alabama ... 1976

M

Macek, Don, G, Boston College ... 1976
Mackey, John, TE, Syracuse ... 1972
MacKinnon, Jacque, TE, Colgate ... 1961–69
Maguire, Paul, LB-K, Citadel ... 1960–63
Marsh, Frank, DB, Oregon State ... 1967
Martin, Blanche, RB, Michigan State ... 1960
Martin, Larry, DT, San Diego State ... 1966
Matsos, Arch, LB, Michigan State ... 1966
Matthews, Bo, RB, Colorado ... 1974–76
Mauck, Carl, C, So. Illinois ... 1971–74
McCall, Ron, LB, Weber State ... 1967–68
McClard, Bill, K, Arkansas ... 1972
McCoy, Lloyd, G, San Diego ... 1966
McDonald, Dwight, WR, San Diego State ... 1975–76
McDougall, Gerry, RB, UCLA ... 1962–64, 1968
McGee, Willie, CB, Alcorn A&M ... 1973
McNeil, Charlie, DB, Compton J.C. ... 1960–64
Mendez, Mario, WR, San Diego State ... 1964
Mercer, Mike, K, No. Arizona ... 1970
Mialik, Larry, TE, Wisconsin ... 1976
Middleton, Rick, LB, Ohio State ... 1976
Mikolajewski, Pete, QB, Kent State ... 1969
Milks, Jack, LB, San Diego State ... 1966
Miller, Paul, DT, Louisiana State ... 1962
Mitchell, Ed, G, Southern U. ... 1965–66
Mitinger, Bob, LB, Penn State ... 1963–66, 1968
Mix, Ron, T, USC ... 1960–69
Montgomery, Mike, RB, Kansas State ... 1971
Moore, Fred, DT, Memphis State ... 1964–66
Morris, Eugene (Mercury), RB, West Texas State ... 1976
Moss, Roland, TE, Toledo ... 1970
Myrtle, Chip, LB, Maryland ... 1974

N

Nery, Ron, DE, Kansas State ... 1960–62
Newell, Steve, WR, Cal State-Long Beach ... 1967
Nix, Doyle, DS, Southern Methodist ... 1960
Norman, Pettis, TE, Johnson C. Smith ... 1971–73
Norris, Trusse, WR, UCLA ... 1960
Norton, Don, WR, Iowa ... 1960–66
Nowak, Gary, T, Michigan State ... 1971

O

Owens, Art, WR, West Virginia ... 1976
Owens, Joe, DE, Alcorn A&M ... 1970
Owens, Terry, T, Jacksonville ... 1972–75

P

Park, Ernest, G, McMurry ... 1963–65
Parks, Billy, WR, Cal State-Long Beach ... 1971
Parris, Gary, TE, Flordia State ... 1973–74
Partee, Dennis, K, Southern Methodist ... 1968–75
Peretta, Ralph, G, Purdue ... 1975–76
Peters, Volney, DT, USC ... 1960
Petrich, Bob, DE, W. Texas State ... 1963–66
Plump, Dave, WR, Fresno State ... 1966
Plunkett, Sherman, T, Maryland State ... 1961–62
Post, Dickie, RB, Houston ... 1967–70
Preston, Ray, LB, Syracuse ... 1976
Print, Bob, LB, Dayton ... 1967–68
Protz, Jack, LB, Syracuse ... 1970

Q

Queen, Jeff, RB, Morgan State ... 1969–71

R

Ray, Eddie, RB, Louisiana State ... 1971
Redman, Rick, LB, Washington ... 1965–73
Rentz, Larry, DB, Florida ... 1969
Rice, Andy, DT, Texas Southern ... 1970–71
Ridge, Houston, DT, San Diego State ... 1966–69
Roberson, Bo, WR, Cornell ... 1961
Robinson, Jerry, WR, Grambling ... 1962–64
Rogers, Don, C, South Carolina ... 1960–64
Rogers, Mel, LB, Florida A&M ... 1971–74
Rossovich, Tim, LB, USC ... 1972–73
Rote, Tobin, QB, Rice ... 1963–64
Rowe, Dave, DT, Penn State ... 1974–75

S

Salter, Bryant, S, Pittsburgh ... 1971–73
Sartin, Dan, C, Mississippi ... 1969
Sayers, Ron, RB, Omaha ... 1969
Scarber, Sam, RB, New Mexico ... 1975–76
Scarpitto, Bob, DB, Notre Dame ... 1961
Schleicher, Maury, LB, Penn State ... 1960–62
Schmedding, Jim, G, Weber State ... 1968–70
Schmidt, Henry, DT, USC ... 1961–64
Sears, Jim, DB, USC ... 1960
Selawski, Gene, T, Purdue ... 1961
Shea, Pat, G, USC ... 1962–65
Shields, Billy T, Georgia Tech ... 1975–76
Singleton, Ron, TE, Grambling ... 1976
Smith, Carlie, RB, Utah State ... 1975
Smith, Dave, RB, Utah ... 1970
Smith, Ron, S, Wisconsin ... 1973
Smith, Russ, RB, Miami ... 1967–70
Snowden, Cal, DE, Indiana ... 1972–73
Speights, Dick, WR, Wyoming ... 1968
Staggs, Jeff, LB, San Diego State ... 1966–71, 1974
Stein, Bob, LB, Minnesota ... 1975
Stephenson, Kay, QB, Florida ... 1967
Stewart, Wayne, TE, California ... 1974
Stratton, Mike, LB, Tennessee ... 1973
Stringert, Harold, CB, Hawaii ... 1975–76
Strozier, Art, TE, Kansas State ... 1970–71
Sweeney, Walt, G, Syracuse ... 1972
Sykes, John, RB, Morgan State ... 1972

T

Tanner, John, LB, Tennessee State ... 1971
Tate, Frank, LB, North Carolina Central ... 1975
Taylor, Jessie, RB, Cincinnati ... 1972
Taylor, Sammie, WR, Grambling ... 1964
Tensi, Steve, QB, Florida State ... 1965–66
Thaxton, James, TE, Tennessee State ... 1973–74
Thomas, Bob, RB, Arizona State ... 1973–74
Thomas, Jesse, DB, Michigan State ... 1960
Thomas, Lee, DE, Jackson State ... 1971–72
Thompson, Tommy, RB, Southern Illinois ... 1974
Tipton, Dave, DE, Stanford ... 1974–75
Tolbert, Jim, DB, Lincoln ... 1966–71, 1976
Trapp, Richard, WR, Florida ... 1969
Travenio, Herb, K, Texas ... 1965
Tuckett, Phil WR, Weber State ... 1968

U

Unitas, John, QB, Louisville ... 1973

V

Van Raaphorst, Dick, R, Ohio State ... 1966–67
Vertefeuille, Brian, G, Idaho State ... 1974

W

Wallace, Henry, DB, Pacific ... 1960
Waller, Ron, RB, Maryland ... 1960
Warren, Jim, DB, Illinois ... 1964–65
Washington, Joe, RB, Oklahoma ... 1976
Washington, Russ, T, Missouri ... 1968–76
Wells, Bob, T, J.C. Smith ... 1968–70
Wenzel, Ralph, G, San Diego State ... 1972
Wersching, Ray, K, California ... 1973–76
West, Jeff, P, Cincinnati ... 1976
Westmoreland, Dick, DB, N. Carolina A&T ... 1963–65
White, Andre, TE, Florida A&M ... 1968
White, Lee, RB, Weber State ... 1972
White, Ray, LB, Syracuse ... 1971–73
Whitehead, Bud, DB, Florida State ... 1961–68
Whitmyer, Nat, DB, Washington ... 1966–67
Wilkerson, Doug, G, N. Carolina Central ... 1972–76
Williams, Dave, WR, Washington ... 1971–72
Williams, Mike, CB, Louisiana State ... 1975–76
Williams, Tom, DT, Cal-Davis ... 1970–71
Williams, Sam, DB, California ... 1974–75
Withrow, Cal, C, Kentucky ... 1970
Wojcik, Greg, DT, USC ... 1972–73
Womble, Royce, WR, No. Texas State ... 1960
Wood, Dick, QB, Auburn ... 1962
Woods, Don, RB, New Mexico ... 1974–76
Wright, Ernie, T, Ohio State ... 1960–67, 1972

Y

Young, Rickey, RB, Jackson State ... 1975–76

Z

Zeman, Bob, DB, Wisconsin ... 1960–61, 1965–66

SAN FRANCISCO 49ERS

1946 Anthony J. (Tony) Morabito, a partner in a San Francisco lumber firm, formed the 49ers as a charter member of the All-America Football Conference. Morabito had tried but failed to get a franchise in the National Football League. One of Morabito's partners in Lumber Terminals of San Francisco, Allen E. Sorrell or E.J. Turre, selected the team's nickname; each has been given credit for it at one time or another. John Blackinger was named general manager of the 49ers. Their original emblem showed a booted prospector in a lumberjack's shirt and checkered pants, his hat blown off and his hair askew, his feet splayed apart and in his hands two six-shooters firing. Morabito raided NFL teams, signing 12 of their players, and signed notable Bay Area college players such as quarterback Frankie Albert and fullback Norm Standlee of Stanford. Lawrence (Buck) Shaw of Santa Clara in the Bay Area was named 49ers' head coach. The team rented Kezar Stadium for its games. It finished second to the Cleveland Browns in the AAFC's Western Division in its first season and won one of its two games against Cleveland, 34–20. Forty-Niners end Alyn Beals led the AAFC in pass receiving with 40 catches for 586 yards.

1947 The 49ers again finished second to the Browns in the Western Division. Morabito borrowed $100,000, bought out his original partners, and divided the ownership of the 49ers on a 75-25 basis with his brother Vic. "There's this nut with a hearing aid in San Francisco who is putting his own money into this damn team," said Harry Wismer, Washington Redskins' broadcaster.

1948 The 49ers had a tremendous season but finished second in the division behind the Browns for the third time in a row. Albert, a 5-foot 9-inch, 175 pound quarterback, completed 29 touchdown passes. He and quarterback Otto Graham of Cleveland were named cowinners of the AAFC most valuable player award.

1949 San Francisco gave Cleveland the worst beating in its history, as Albert threw five touchdown passes in a game at Kezar Stadium, October 9. The Browns, however, finished first in the All-America for the fourth season. There was no division play and there was a playoff of the top four teams for the championship. A merger was arranged between the NFL and AAFC, and, by its terms, Cleveland, San Francisco, and the Baltimore Colts would enter the NFL, December 9. The Browns and 49ers played for the AAFC championship in Cleveland and only 22,550 fans watched as Cleveland won 21–17. Shaw, coach of the 49ers, said, "Four years ago, I'd never even met Paul Brown [the Cleveland coach]. Now I scheme to beat him, dream of beating him, and wind up screaming because I haven't beaten him."

1950 The 49ers struggled through their first season in the NFL, winning only three games. A rival coach said they were "not big enough or tough enough." Tackle Leo Nomellini started his career with San Francisco, playing both offense and defense. Gordy Soltau was another star rookie.

1951 Quarterback Y.A. Tittle was acquired by the 49ers from the extinct 1950 Baltimore Colts franchise to play behind San Francisco quarterback Frankie Albert. Albert, however, suffered a shoulder injury and Tittle was pressed into service immediately. The team became a contender, winning its last three games and finishing third in the NFL's National Conference. End Billy Wilson and linebacker Hardy Brown began their careers with the 49ers.

1952 Lou Spadia was named general manager of the 49ers. Fullback Norm Standlee was stricken with

Charlie Krueger, 14-year defensive tackle, blocks a St. Louis pass by Charley Johnson, 1969.

polio and never played football again. Coowner Tony Morabito suffered a heart attack. Rookie back Hugh McElhenny had a sensational season. Albert and back Johnny (Strike) Strykalski retired.

1953 Bob St. Clair, 6-foot 9-inch, 260-pound tackle, joined the team. The 49ers had their best season to date in the NFL, losing only three games by a total of nine points. Tittle was absent during two of the three defeats with a severe facial injury. Back Joe Perry rushed for 1,018 yards and coowner Tony Morabito gave Perry a bonus check for $5,090—$5 a yard. End Gordy Soltau led the league in scoring for the second straight year.

1954 San Francisco acquired fullback John Henry Johnson from the Pittsburgh Steelers and he joined Tittle, Perry, and McElhenny in one of the best backfields in pro football history. It was broken up, however, when Tittle was sidelined with a broken hand early in the season and McElhenny went out with a shoulder separation in the sixth game; McElhenny had gained 515 yards in only 64 carries before his injury. Perry went on to gain 1,049 yards, becoming the first runner in history to gain 1,000 two years in a row.

1955 Lawrence (Buck) Shaw, the only coach the team had ever had, was fired and replaced by Norman (Red) Strader, a strict disciplinarian who was unpopular with the players. As a result, the team won only four games.

1956 Strader was replaced as coach by former 49ers' quarterback Frankie Albert. The team had a 1-6 record after seven games but righted itself and, with McElhenny and a little-known back named Joe Arenas starring, won four games and tied one for the remainder of the season. The 49ers drew 522,339 fans for 12 games, an NFL record at the time.

1957 Quarterback Tittle and 6-foot 5-inch rookie end R.C. Owens devised the Alley-Oop pass in which Tittle threw the ball in a high arc and Owens ran to the point of reception and outjumped the defensive backs for the ball. The 49ers were an exciting team that great crowds flocked to see wherever they played. Founder Tony Morabito suffered a fatal heart attack during a game against the Chicago Bears at Kezar Stadium. Albert told his players of Morabito's death during halftime, and they made an emotional comeback to beat the Bears 21–17, October 27. Tittle suffered pulled muscles in both his legs in the next-to-last regular season game but rookie quarterback John Brodie came in and threw a touchdown pass to Hugh McElhenny as the 49ers defeated Baltimore 17–13. Tittle limped in the next week and the 49ers came from behind to defeat Green Bay 27–20 and tie the Detroit Lions for the Western Conference championship. The two teams met in a playoff and San Francisco took a 24–7 halftime lead, only to see Detroit come from behind and win 31–27 in one of the greatest comebacks in NFL history, December 22.

1958 Vic Morabito took over the team's operation. It had an up-and-down season and lost twice to Los Angeles by scores of 33–3 and 56–7. Albert resigned as coach.

1959 Assistant coach Howard (Red) Hickey was promoted to head coach. Quarterback John Brodie had a good season and so did back J.D. Smith, who was a converted defensive back. Smith gained over 1,000 yards. Charlie Krueger was a rookie at defensive tackle.

1960 Hickey salvaged a frustrating season when he installed the shotgun formation with the quarterback standing three to five yards back and taking a long snap from center, then passing or handing off. The 49ers won four of their last five games and tied for second place in the Western Conference.

1961 Tittle, who was better suited to the T formation, was traded to the New York Giants for guard Lou Cordileone. There were still three 49ers' quarterbacks to operate the shotgun formation—Brodie, Bobby Waters, and rookie Billy Kilmer, who had played tailback in the single wing formation at UCLA. San Francisco defeated Detroit 49–0 in the third week of the season. After five weeks the 49ers had a 4-1 record. The three quarterbacks alternated running the shotgun. However, the Chicago Bears stopped the 49ers with middle linebacker Bill George playing on the line of scrimmage and often stunting and moving back into the backfield; Chicago won by a shocking 31–0 score. The 49ers went back to the T formation but Hickey said he could have continued to play the shotgun if his players had not lost confidence in it. San Francisco lost to Baltimore 27–24 on the final day of the season and missed a chance to finish in a tie for second place. Brodie had 2,588 yards passing for the season.

1962 The 49ers had their first losing season since 1956—6-8—and lost five out of seven games they played at home at Kezar Stadium.

1963 Hickey resigned as coach and assistant Jack Christiansen was named head coach. The 49ers defeated Chicago 20–14; the Bears went on to win the NFL championship. San Francisco had a disappointing 2-12 record, the poorest in their history. Defensive tackle Leo Nomellini retired from pro football holding the record for consecutive games played, 174.

1964 Owner Vic Morabito died of a heart attack at age 44; his brother, Tony, had been 47 when he died in 1957. Josephine and Jane Morabito, widows of the late brothers, kept control and gave Lou Spadia authority to run the team. End Dave Parks, quarterback George Mira, and linebacker Dave Wilcox had good rookie seasons.

1965 Running back John David Crow was acquired from the St. Louis Cardinals in a trade. San Francisco defeated Chicago 52–24 in the opening game, the most points ever scored against the Bears. Crow and rookie Ken Willard helped the 49ers' running game improve. Brodie had a good season at quarterback and Parks led the NFL with 80 pass receptions.

1966 San Francisco played another respectable but still disappointing season, 6-6-2. Parks had another good season and he and guard John Thomas were named to all-pro teams.

1967 The 49ers got off to a fast start, winning five out of six games. Hit by injuries, however, they then lost

six straight. Mira came off the bench and led them to two victories at the end of the season. Christiansen was relieved as coach.

1968 Spadia took the title of president and Jack White was named general manager. Dallas Cowboys' assistant coach Dick Nolan was named 49ers' head coach. Nolan had a winning season in his first year. Brodie, Willard, and wide receiver Clifton McNeil starred on offense and defensive tackle Krueger, linebacker Wilcox, and cornerback Kermit Alexander on defense.

1969 Injuries hit the defensive line and the 49ers didn't win a game until the sixth week of the season, finishing 4-8-2. Jimmy Johnson emerged as an all-pro cornerback.

1970 The 49ers surged to a 10-3-1 record and the Western Division championship in the first year of realignment after the NFL-AFL merger. San Francisco and AFL rival Oakland were paired in the last game of the season and the 49ers won 38–7 for their tenth victory of the season. They then defeated the Minnesota Vikings 17–14 on two touchdown passes by quarterback Brodie in the fourth quarter, the last to wide receiver Dick Witcher with less than a minute to play in the game. The 49ers advanced to the NFC championship game and Nolan lost to his former teacher, Tom Landry, and the Dallas Cowboys 17–10. Nolan was named NFC coach of the year, Brodie player of the year, and cornerback Bruce Taylor rookie of the year. The NFC Western Division championship was the first title of any kind for the 49ers in their 25-year history.

1971 The 49ers left Kezar Stadium and moved their home games to Candlestick Park. They clinched their second consecutive division championship with a 31–27 victory over the Detroit Lions on the last day of the season. The score was the same as the one by which the Lions had upset the 49ers in their 1957 playoff. San Francisco defeated the Washington Redskins 24–20 but again faced Dallas in the championship game and again lost, this time 14–3. Brodie was intercepted three times in the game but defensive back Cedrick Hardman led a pass rush that sacked Dallas quarterback Roger Staubach six times. Wilcox, Johnson, and center Forrest Blue were named to all-pro teams.

1972 The Minnesota Vikings were the victims of another big San Francisco victory. This time it was the final game of the regular season and the 49ers won 20–17 on two fourth-quarter touchdown passes by Brodie. His final pass again went to Witcher, this time with 19 seconds remaining. The victory gave the 49ers their third Western Division championship in a row, the first time since realignment that any team had won its division three straight seasons. The following week, San Francisco met its nemesis, Dallas, in an NFC first-round divisional playoff and, despite leading 28–13, lost 30–28 as Cowboys' quarterback Roger Staubach led a sensational comeback. Brodie, who shared the quarterback position with Steve Spurrier, retired.

1974 Spurrier was injured the week before the regular season began and was sidelined for most of the season. The 49ers used five different quarterbacks and lost a team record seven games in a row at one point. Dave Wilcox, outstanding linebacker for 11 years, retired.

1975 The 49ers' 24–23 victory at Los Angeles ended a string of 10 straight losses to the Rams in regular season games. The quarterback situation remained uncertain, but ends Cedrick Hardman and Tommy Hart were the leaders of a capable group of defensive players.

1976 Nolan was replaced as head coach by Miami Dolphins' assistant Monte Clark. Quarterback Jim Plunkett was acquired in a trade with the New England Patriots. San Francisco won six of its first

seven games but lost a 23–20 sudden death overtime game at St. Louis, slumped, and finished second in the division behind Los Angeles. Hardman, Hart, Jimmy Webb, and Cleveland Elam became one of the best defensive lines in the league. The team's 8-6 record was its first winning season in four years.

MEMBERS OF HALL OF FAME:
Hugh McElhenny, Leo Nomellini, Joe Perry, Y.A. Tittle

49ERS RECORD, 1946–76

Year	Won	Lost	Tied	Pct.	Pts.	OP
1946	9	5	0	.643	307	189
1947	8	4	2	.667	327	264
1948	12	2	0	.857	495	248
1949	9	3	0	.750	416	227
1950	3	9	0	.250	213	300
1951	7	4	1	.636	255	205
1952	7	5	0	.583	285	221
1953	9	3	0	.750	372	237
1954	7	4	1	.636	313	251
1955	4	8	0	.333	216	298
1956	5	6	1	.455	233	284
1957	8	4	0	.667	260	264
1958	6	6	0	.500	257	324
1959	7	5	0	.583	255	237
1960	7	5	0	.583	208	205
1961	7	6	1	.538	346	272
1962	6	8	0	.429	282	331
1963	2	12	0	.143	198	391
1964	4	10	0	.286	236	330
1965	7	6	1	.538	421	402
1966	6	6	2	.500	320	325
1967	7	7	0	.500	273	337
1968	7	6	1	.538	303	310
1969	4	8	2	.333	277	319
1970§	10	3	1	.769	352	267
1971§	9	5	0	.643	300	216
1972§	8	5	1	.607	353	249
1973	5	9	0	.357	262	319
1974	6	8	0	.429	226	236
1975	5	9	0	.357	255	286
1976	8	6	0	.571	270	190
27 NFL Years	171	173	12	.497	7,541	7,606

§NFC Western Division Champion

RECORD HOLDERS

Rushing (Yards)	Delvin Williams, 1976	1,203
Passing (Pct.)	Y.A. Tittle, 1957	63.1
Passing (Yards)	John Brodie, 1965	3,112
Passing (TDs)	John Brodie, 1965	30
Receiving (No.)	Dave Parks, 1965	80
Receiving (Yards)	Dave Parks, 1965	1,344
Interceptions (No.)	Dave Baker, 1960	10
Punting (Avg.)	Tommy Davis, 1965	45.8
Punt Ret. (Avg.)	Jim Cason, 1950	15.7
Kickoff Ret. (Avg.)	Joe Arenas, 1953	34.4
Touchdowns (Total)	Joe Perry, 1953	13
Field Goals Made	Bruce Gossett, 1973	26
Points (No.)	Gordy Soltau, 1953	114

COACHING HISTORY

1946–54	Lawrence (Buck) Shaw	71–37–6
	NFL only	33–25–2
1955	Norman (Red) Strader	4– 8–0
1956–58	Frankie Albert	19–16–1
1959–63	Howard (Red) Hickey*	27–27–1
1963–67	Jack Christiansen	26–38–3
1968–75	Dick Nolan	54–53–5
1976	Monte Clark	8– 6–0

*Resigned after three games in 1963

FIRST PLAYER SELECTED

1950	Leo Nomellini, T, Minnesota
1951	Y.A. Tittle, B, Louisiana State
1952	Hugh McElhenny, B, Washington
1953	Harry Babcock, E, Georgia
1954	Bernie Faloney, B, Maryland
1955	Dickie Moegle, B, Rice
1956	Earl Morrall, B, Michigan State
1957	John Brodie, B, Stanford
1958	Jim Pace, B, Michigan
1959	Dave Baker, B, Oklahoma
1960	Monty Stickles, E, Notre Dame
1961	Jimmy Johnson, CB, UCLA
1962	Lance Alworth, WR, Arkansas
1963	Kermit Alexander, CB, UCLA
1964	Dave Parks, WR, Texas Tech
1965	Ken Willard, RB, North Carolina
1966	Stan Hindman, DE, Mississippi
1967	Steve Spurrier, QB, Florida
1968	Forrest Blue, C, Auburn
1969	Ted Kwalick, TE, Penn State
1970	Cedrick Hardman, DE, North Texas State
1971	Tim Anderson, DB, Ohio State
1972	Terry Beasley, WR, Auburn
1973	Mike Holmes, DB, Southern U.
1974	Wilbur Jackson, RB, Alabama
1975	Jimmy Webb, DT, Mississippi State
1976	Randy Cross, C (2), UCLA

Kermit Alexander

Frankie Albert

Bruno Banducci

Bruce Bosley

Hardy Brown

Dan Colchico

Cedrick Hardman

SAN FRANCISCO 49ERS, (AAFC), 1946–49
SAN FRANCISCO 49ERS, 1950–76

Abramowicz, Dan, WR, Xavier, Ohio ... 1973–74
Albert, Frankie, QB, Stanford ... 1946–52
Aldridge, Ben, HB, Oklahoma State ... 1952
Alexander, Kermit, DB, UCLA ... 1963–69
Allen, Nate, CB, Texas Southern ... 1975
Anderson, Tim, S, Ohio State ... 1975
Arenas, Joe, HB, Omaha ... 1951–57
Atkins, Bill, HB, Auburn ... 1958–59
Atkins, David, RB, Texas-El Paso ... 1973

B

Babb, Gene, FB, Austin ... 1957–58
Babcock, Harry, E, Georgia ... 1953–55
Bahnsen, Ken, FB, N. Texas State ... 1953
Baker, Dave, HB, Oklahoma ... 1959–61
Baker, Wayne, DT, Brigham Young ... 1975
Balatti, Ed, E, None ... 1946–47
Baldwin, John, C, Centenary ... 1947
Banaszek, Cas, T, Northwestern ... 1968–76
Banducci, Bruno, G, Stanford ... 1946–54
Barnes, Larry, FB, Colorado State ... 1957
Barrett, Jean, T, Tulsa ... 1973–76
Bassi, Dick, G, Santa Clara ... 1946–47
Beals, Alyn, E, Santa Clara ... 1946–51
Beard, Ed, LB, Tennessee ... 1965–72
Beasley, Terry, WR, Auburn ... 1972–75
Beisler, Randy, T, Indiana ... 1969–74
Belk, Bill, DE, Maryland State ... 1968–74
Belser, Ceaser, LB, Arkansas AM&N ... 1974
Bentz, Roman, T, Tulane ... 1948
Berry, Rex, HB, Brigham Young ... 1951–56
Bettiga, Mike, WR, Cal. St.-Humboldt ... 1973
Beverly, Ed, WR, Arizona State ... 1973
Blue, Forrest, C, Auburn ... 1968–74
Boone, J.R., HB, Tulsa ... 1952
Beatty, Ed, C, Mississippi ... 1955–56
Bosley, Bruce, G, West Virginia ... 1956–68
Braggonier, Dennis, DB, Stanford ... 1974
Britt, Charlie, DB, Georgia ... 1964
Brock, Clyde, T, Utah State ... 1963
Brodie, John, QB, Stanford ... 1957–73
Brown, Hardy, LB, Tulsa ... 1951–56
Brown, Pete, C, Georgia Tech ... 1953–54
Bruce, Gail, E, Washington ... 1948–51
Brumfield, Jackson, E, So. Mississippi ... 1954
Bruney, Fred, HB, Ohio State ... 1953, 1956
Bryant, Bob, T, Texas Tech ... 1946–49
Bull, Scott, QB, Arkansas ... 1976
Burke, Don, LB, USC ... 1950–54
Burke, Vern, E, Oregon State ... 1965

C

Campbell, Carter, LB, Weber State ... 1970
Campbell, Marion, T, Georgia ... 1954–55
Campora, Don, T, Pacific ... 1950, 1952
Carapella, Al, T, Miami ... 1951–55
Carpenter, John, T, Michigan ... 1949
Carr, Eddie, HB, None ... 1947–49
Carr, Paul, LB, Houston ... 1955–58
Casanega, Ken, HB, Santa Clara ... 1946, 1948
Casey, Bernie, E, Bowling Green ... 1961–66
Cason, Jim, HB, Louisiana State ... 1948–52, 1954
Cassara, Frank, FB, St. Mary's ... 1954
Cathcart, Royal, HB, Cal-Santa Barbara ... 1950
Cathcart, Sam, HB, Cal-Santa Barbara ... 1949–50, 1952
Cavelli, Tony, C, Stanford ... 1949
Cerne, Joe, C, Northwestern ... 1965–67
Chapple, Jack, LB, Stanford ... 1965
Clark, Don, G, USC ... 1948–49
Clark, Monte, T, USC ... 1959–61
Cline, Tony, DE, Miami ... 1976
Colchico, Dan, E, San Jose State ... 1960–64
Collett, Elmer, G, S.F. State ... 1967–72
Collier, Floyd, T, San Jose State ... 1948
Collins, Greg, LB, Notre Dame ... 1975
Collins, Ray, T, Louisiana State ... 1950–52
Conlee, Gerry, St. Mary's ... 1946–47
Conner, Clyde, E, Pacific ... 1956–63
Connolly, Ted, G, Tulsa ... 1954, 1956–62
Cooper, Bill, FB, Muskingum ... 1961–64
Cooke, Bill, T, Massachusetts ... 1976
Cox, James, G, Stanford ... 1948
Cross, Bob, T, Kilgore Jr. College ... 1956–57
Cross, Randy, C, UCLA ... 1976
Crow, John David, HB, Texas A&M ... 1965–68
Crowe, Paul, HB, St. Mary's ... 1948
Crowell, Otis, T, Hardin-Simmons ... 1947
Cunningham, Doug, RB, Mississippi ... 1967–73

D

Dahms, Tom, T, San Diego State ... 1957
Daniels, Clem, RB, Prairie View ... 1968
Daugherty, Bob, HB, Tulsa ... 1966–67
Davis, Tommy, K, Louisiana State ... 1959–69
Dean, Floyd, LB, Florida ... 1963–64
Domres, Marty, QB, Columbia ... 1976
Donnelly, George, DB, Illinois ... 1965–67
Donohue, Leon, T, San Jose State ... 1962–64
Dove, Eddie, DB, Colorado ... 1959–62
Dow, Harley, G, San Jose State ... 1950
Dowdle, Mike, LB, Texas ... 1963–65
Downs, Bob, G, USC ... 1951
Dugan, Fred, E, Dayton ... 1958–59
Duncan, Maury, QB, S.F. State ... 1954–55
Durdan, Don, HB, Oregon State ... 1946–47

E

Edwards, Earl, DT, Wichita ... 1969–72
Elam, Cleveland, DE, Tennessee State ... 1975–76
Elia, Bruce, LB, Ohio State ... 1975–76
Elliott, Charles, T, Oregon ... 1948
Elston, Art, C, South Carolina ... 1946–48
Enderle, Dick, G, Minnesota ... 1976
Endriss, Al, E, San Francisco St. ... 1952
Eshmont, Len, HB, Fordham ... 1946–49
Evans, Roy, G, Texas Western ... 1950
Evansen, Paul, G, Oregon State ... 1948

F

Fahnhorst, Keith, T, Minnesota ... 1974–76
Feher, Nick, G, Georgia ... 1951–54
Ferrill, Bob, RB, UCLA ... 1976
Fisk, Bill, E, USC ... 1946–47
Forrest, Ed, C, Santa Clara ... 1946–47
Franceschi, Pete, HB, San Francisco ... 1946
Freitas, Jesse, QB, Santa Clara ... 1946–47
Fuller, John, DB, Lamar Tech ... 1968–72

G

Gaiters, Bob, HB, New Mexico State ... 1962–63
Galiffa, Arnie, QB, Army ... 1954
Garlin, Don, HB, USC ... 1949–50
Garrett, Len, TE, New Mexico Highlands ... 1975
Gavric, Momcilo, K, None ... 1969
Gehrke, Fred, HB, Utah ... 1950
Goad, Paul, FB, Abilene Christian ... 1956
Gonsoulin, Austin (Goose), DB, Baylor ... 1967
Gonzaga, John, T, None ... 1956–59
Gossett, Bruce, K, Richmond ... 1970–74
Greenlee, Fritz, LB, Arizona ... 1969
Gregory, Garlin, G, Louisiana Tech ... 1946–47
Grgich, Visco, G, Santa Clara ... 1946–52

H

Hall, Forrest, HB, San Francisco ... 1948
Hall, Parker, HB, Mississippi ... 1946
Hall, Windlan, CB, Arizona State ... 1972–75
Hanley, Dick, C, Fresno State ... 1947
Hantla, Bob, G, Kansas ... 1954–55
Hardman, Cedrick, DE, N. Texas St. ... 1970–76
Hardy, Carroll, HB, Colorado ... 1955
Hardy, Ed, G, Jackson State ... 1973
Hardy, Kevin, DT, Notre Dame ... 1968
Harkey, Lem, HB, Emporia State ... 1955
Harper, Willie, LB, Nebraska ... 1973–76
Harris, Tony, WR, Toledo ... 1971
Harrison, Bob, LB, Oklahoma ... 1959–61, 1965–67
Harrison, Kenny, WR, Southern Methodist ... 1976
Hart, Tom, DE, Morris Brown ... 1968–76
Hart, Jeff, T, Oregon State ... 1975
Hayes, Bob, WR, Florida A&M ... 1975
Hays, Harold, LB, So. Mississippi ... 1968–69
Hazeltine, Matt, LB, California ... 1955–68
Henke, Ed, E, USC ... 1951–52, 1955–60
Herchman, Bill, T, Texas Tech ... 1956–59
Hettema, Dave, T, New Mexico ... 1967
Hindman, Stan, DE, Mississippi ... 1966–71, 1973–74
Hobbs, Homer, G, Georgia ... 1949–50
Hofer, Paul, RB, Mississippi ... 1976
Hogland, Doug, G, Oregon State ... 1953–55
Holladay, Bob, HB, Tulsa ... 1956–57
Hollas, Hugo, DB, Rice ... 1974
Holmes, Mike, DB, Texas Southern ... 1974–75
Holzer, Tom, DE, Louisville ... 1967
Horne, Dick, E, Oregon ... 1947
Hoskins, Bob, G, Wichita ... 1970–75
Howell, Clarence, E, Texas A&M ... 1948
Huff, Marty, LB, Michigan ... 1972
Hull, Tom, LB, Penn State ... 1974
Hunt, Charlie, LB, Florida State ... 1973

I

Isenbarger, John, RB, Indiana ... 1970–73

J

Jackson, Jim, HB, Western Illinois ... 1966–67
Jackson, Randy, RB, Wichita ... 1973
Jackson, Wilbur, RB, Alabama ... 1974–76
Jessup, Bill, E, USC ... 1951–52, 1954–58
Johnson, Bill, C, Tyler J.C. ... 1948–56
Johnson, Charlie, DT, Louisville ... 1966–67
Johnson, Jimmy, DB, UCLA ... 1961–76
Johnson, John Henry, RB, Arizona St. ... 1954–56
Johnson, Kermit, RB, UCLA ... 1975–76
Johnson, Leo, WR, Tennessee State ... 1969–70
Johnson, Rudy, HB, Nebraska ... 1965–65
Johnson, Sammy, RB, North Carolina ... 1974–76

K

Kammerer, Carl, LB, Pacific ... 1961–62
Kelley, Gorden, LB, Georgia ... 1960–61
Kenny, Charles, G, San Francisco ... 1947
Kilgore, Jon, P, Auburn ... 1969
Kilmer, Billy, QB, UCLA ... 1961–66
Kimbrough, Elbert, DB, Northwestern ... 1962–66
Knafelc, Gary, E, Colorado ... 1963
Kopay, Dave, HB, Washington ... 1964–67
Kraemer, Eldred, G, Pittsburgh ... 1955
Kramer, Kent, TE, Minnesota ... 1966
Krueger, Charlie, DT, Texas A&M ... 1959–73
Krueger, Rolf, DE, Texas A&M ... 1972–74
Kuzman, John, T, Fordham ... 1946
Kwalick, Ted, TE, Penn State ... 1969–74

L

Lakes, Roland, T, Wichita ... 1961–70
Land, Fred, T, Louisiana State ... 1948
LaRose, Dan, DE, Missouri ... 1965
Larson, Bill, TE, Colorado State ... 1975
Lash, Jim, WR, Northwestern ... 1976
Laughlin, Bud, FB, Kansas ... 1955
Lawson, Steve, G, Kansas ... 1976
Ledyard, Hal, QB, Chattanooga ... 1953
Lee, Dwight, RB, Michigan State ... 1968
Leonard, Anthony, CB, Virginia Union ... 1976
Lewis, Eddie, CB, Kansas ... 1976
Lewis, Gary, FB, Arizona State ... 1964–69
Lillywhite, Verl, HB, USC ... 1948–51
Lind, Mike, FB, Notre Dame ... 1963–64
Lisbon, Don, HB, Bowling Green ... 1963–64
Livingston, Howie, HB, Fullerton J.C. ... 1950
Lopasky, Bill, G, West Virginia ... 1961
Loyd, Alex, E, Oklahoma State ... 1950
Luna, Bob, HB, Alabama ... 1955
Lyles, Lenny, DB, Louisville ... 1959–60

M

Mackey, Dee, TE, E. Texas State ... 1960
Maderos, George, HB, Chico State ... 1955–56
Magac, Mike, G, Missouri ... 1960–64
Maloney, Norm, E, Purdue ... 1948–49
Manley, Joe, LB, Mississippi State ... 1953
Masini, Leonard, FB, Fresno State ... 1947–48
Matheson, Riley, HB, Texas Western ... 1948
Mathews, Ned, HB, UCLA ... 1946–47
Matthews, Clay, E, Georgia Tech ... 1950, 1953–55
Matuszak, Marv, LB, Tulsa ... 1957–58
Maurer, Andy, G, Oregon ... 1976

Matt Hazeltine

Ted Kwalick

R.C. Owens

Mel Phillips

J. (Strike) Strzykalski

John Thomas

Delvin Williams

McCann, Jim, P, Arizona State 1971–72
McCormick, Dave, T, Louisiana State 1966
McCormick, Tom, HB, Pacific 1956
McCormick, Walt, C, USC 1948
McElhenny, Hugh, HB, Washington 1952–60
McFarland, Jay, HB, Colorado State 1962–68
McGee, Willie, WR, Alcorn A&M 1976
McGill, Ralph, CB, Tulsa 1972–76
McHan, Lamar, QB, Arkansas 1963
McKay, Billy, LB, Purdue 1974
McNeil, Clifton, E, Grambling 1968–69
Mellekas, John, C, Arizona 1962
Mellus, John, T, Villanova 1946
Mertens, Jerry, HB, Drake 1958–65
Messer, Dale, HB, Fresno State 1961–65
Meyers, Bob, FB, Stanford 1952
Michalik, Art, G, St. Ambrose 1953–54
Mike, Bob, T, UCLA 1948–49
Mike-Mayer, Steve, K, Maryland 1975–76
Miller, Clark, DE, Utah State 1962–68
Miller, Hal, T, Georgia Tech 1953
Mira, George, QB, Miami 1964–68
Mitchell, Dale, LB, USC 1976
Mitchell, Tom, TE, Bucknell 1974–76
Mixon, Bill, HB, Georgia 1953–54
Moegle, Dick, HB, Rice 1955–59
Momsen, Bob, G, Ohio State 1952
Monachino, Jim, HB, California 1951
Moore, Eugene, RB, Occidental 1969
Moore, Manfred, RB, USC 1974–75
Morgan, Joe, T, So. Mississippi 1949
Morrall, Earl, QB, Michigan State 1956
Morris, Dennit, LB, Oklahoma 1958
Morris, George, C, Georgia Tech 1956
Morrison, Dennis, QB, Kansas State 1974
Morton, John, LB, Texas Christian 1953
Morze, Frank, C, Boston College 1957–61
Mudd, Howard, G, Hillsdale 1964–69
Myers, Chip, E, N. W. Oklahoma 1967

N

Nix, Jack, E, USC 1950
Nomellini, Leo, DT, Minnesota 1950–63
Norberg, Hank, E, Stanford 1946–47
Nordquist, Mark, G, Pacific 1976
Norton, Jim, T, Washington 1965–66
Norton, Ray, HB, San Jose State 1960–61

Abe Woodson vs. Los Angeles, 1964.

Nunley, Frank, LB, Michigan 1967–76

O

Obradovich, Jim, TE, USC 1976
O'Donahue, Pat, E, Wisconsin 1952
Olerich, Dave, E, San Francisco 1967–68, 1972–73
Olssen, Lance, T, Purdue 1968–69
Osborne, Clancy, LB, Arizona State 1959–60
Owen, Tom, QB, Wichita 1974–75
Owens, R. C., HB, Idaho 1957–61

P

Pace, Jim, HB, Michigan 1958
Palatella, Lou, G, Pittsburgh 1955–58
Parker, Don, G, Virginia 1967
Parks, Dave, E, Texas Tech 1964–67
Parsons, Earle, HB, USC 1946–47
Patera, Dennis, K, Brigham Young 1968
Pavlich, Chuck, G, None 1946
Penchion, Bob, T, Alcorn A&M 1974–75
Peoples, Woody, G, Grambling 1968–75
Perry, Joe, RB, Compton J.C. 1948–60, 1963
Phillips, Mel, DB, North Carolina A&T 1966–76
Pine, Ed, LB, Utah 1962–64
Plunkett, Jim, QB, Stanford 1976
Poole, Bob, E, Clemson 1964–65
Powell, Charley, E, None 1952–53, 1955–57
Powers, Jim, HB, USC 1950–53
Puddy, Harold, T, Oregon 1948

Q

Quilter, Chuck, T, Tyler J.C. 1949

R

Raines, Mike, DT, Alabama 1974
Randle, Sonny, E, Virginia 1967
Randolph, Alvin, DB, Iowa 1966–70
Rasley, Rocky, G, Oregon State 1976
Reed, Joe, QB, Mississippi State 1972–74
Reid, Bill, C, Stanford 1975
Remington, Bill, C, Washington State 1946
Renfro, Dick, FB, Washington State 1946
Rhodes, Bruce, S, San Francisco State 1976
Ridlon, Jim, HB, Syracuse 1957–62
Riley, Preston, WR, Memphis State 1970–72
Rivera, Steve, WR, California 1976
Roberts, C. R., FB, USC 1959–62
Robnett, Ed, HB, Texas Tech 1947
Rock, Walter, T, Maryland 1963–67
Rohde, Len, T, Utah State 1960–73
Roskie, Ken, FB, South Carolina 1946
Rubke, Karl, C, USC 1957–60, 1962–63, 1965
Rucka, Leo, C, Rice 1956

S

Sabucco, Tino, C, San Francisco 1949
Sagely, Floyd, E, Arkansas 1954–56
Salata, Paul, E, USC 1949–50
Sandifer, Bill, DT, UCLA 1974–76
Sandifer, Dan, HB, Louisiana State 1950
Sardisco, Tony, G, Tulane 1956
Satterfield, Alf, T, Vanderbilt 1947
Saunders, Tom, DE, Toledo 1974–75
Schabarum, Pete, HB, California 1951, 1953–54
Schiechl, John, C, Santa Clara 1947
Schmidt, Henry, T, USC 1959–60
Schreiber, Larry, RB, Tennessee Tech 1972–75
Scotti, Ben, DB, Maryland 1964
Sharkey, Ed, G, Nevada 1955–56
Shaw, Charles, G, Oklahoma State 1950
Sheriff, Stan, LB, Cal. Poly 1956–57
Shoener, Hal, E, Iowa 1948–50
Sieminski, Charlie, T, Penn State 1963–65
Silas, Sam, DE, So. Illinois 1969–70
Simpson, Mike, DB, Houston 1970–73
Sitko, Emil, HB, Notre Dame 1950
Smith, Charles, E, Abilene Christian 1956
Smith, Ernie, HB, Compton J.C. 1955–56
Smith, George, C, California 1947
Smith, J. D., HB, North Carolina A&T 1956–64
Smith, Jerry, G, Wisconsin 1952–53
Smith, Noland, RB, Tennessee State 1969
Smith, Steve, E, Michigan 1966–67

Snead, Norm, QB, Wake Forest 1974–75
Sniadecki, Jim, LB, Indiana 1969–73
Soltau, Gordy, E-K, Minnesota 1950–58
Sparks, Dave, G, South Carolina 1951
Spence, Julian, HB, Sam Houston 1957
Spurrier, Steve, QB, Florida 1967–75
Standlee, Norm, FB, Stanford 1946–52
St. Clair, Bob, T, Tulsa 1953–64
Stickles, Monty, TE, Notre Dame 1960–67
Stits, Bill, HB, UCLA 1957–58
Stolhandske, Tom, LB, Texas 1955
Strickland, Bishop, FB, South Carolina 1951
Strong, Jim, RB, Houston 1970
Strzykalski, John (Strike), HB, Marquette 1946–52
Sullivan, Bob, HB, Holy Cross 1948
Susoeff, Nick, E, Washington State 1946–49
Sutro, John, T, San Jose State 1962
Swinford, Wayne, DB, Georgia 1965–67

T

Tanner, Hamp, T, Georgia 1951
Taylor, Bruce, CB, Boston U. 1970–76
Taylor, Roosevelt, S, Grambling 1969–71
Teresa, Tony, HB, San Jose State 1958
Thomas, Aaron, E, Oregon State 1961
Thomas, Jimmy, RB, Texas-Arlington 1969–73
Thomas, John, T, Pacific 1958–67
Thornton, Rupe, G, Santa Clara 1946–47
Tidwell, Bily, HB, Texas A&M 1954
Titchenal, Bob, E, San Jose State 1946
Tittle, Y. A., QB, Louisiana State 1951–60
Toneff, Bob, T, Notre Dame 1952, 1954–59
Trimble, Wayne, DB, Alabama 1967
Tubbs, Jerry, LB, Oklahoma 1958–59
Tucker, Bill, RB, Tennessee State 1967–70

V

Van Doren, Bob, E, USC 1953
Vanderbundt, Skip, LB, Oregon State 1969–76
Vaught, Ted, E, Texas Christian 1953
Vetrano, Joe, HB, So. Mississippi 1946–49
Vollenweider, Jim, FB, Miami 1962–63

W

Wagner, Lowell, HB, USC 1949–53, 1955
Wallace, Bev, QB, Compton J.C. 1947–49
Walker, Val Joe, HB, Southern Methodist 1957
Washington, Dave, LB, Alcorn A&M 1975–76
Washington, Gene, WR, Stanford 1969–76
Washington, Vic, RB, Wyoming 1971–73
Waters, Bob, QB, Presbyterian 1960–64
Watson, John, T, Oklahoma 1971–76
Webb, Jimmy, DT, Mississippi State 1975–76
West, Robert, WR, San Diego State 1974
White, Bob, HB, Stanford 1951–52
Wilcox, Dave, LB, Oregon 1964–74
Willard, Ken, FB, North Carolina 1965–73
Williams, Delvin, RB, Kansas 1974–76
Williams, Howie, HB, Howard 1963
Williams, Joel, C, Texas 1948
Williams, John, HB, USC 1954
Williams, Roy, T, Pacific 1958–64
Wilson, Billy, E, San Jose State 1951–60
Wilson, Jerry, LB, Auburn 1960
Wilson, Jim, G, Georgia 1965–66
Windsor, Bob, E, Kentucky 1967–71
Winston, Lloyd, FB, USC 1962–63
Wismann, Pete, LB, St. Louis 1949–52, 1954
Witcher, Dick, E, UCLA 1966–73
Wittenborn, John, G, S. E. Missouri 1958–60
Wittum, Tom, P, No. Illinois 1973–76
Woitt, John, DB, Mississippi State 1968–69
Wondolowski, Bill, WR, E. Montana 1969
Woodson, Abe, DB, Illinois 1958–64
Woudenberg, John, T, Denver 1946–49

Y

Yonamine, Wally, HB, None 1947
Youngelman, Sid, T, Alabama 1955
Yowarsky, Walt, C, Kentucky 1958

Z

Zamlynsky, Ziggy, HB, Villanova 1946

SEATTLE SEAHAWKS

1972 Seattle Professional Football, Inc., a group of business and community leaders, announced its intention to bid for a National Football League franchise for the city of Seattle, June 15. Herman Sarkowsky, principal owner of the National Basketball Association's Portland Trail Blazers, was spokesman for the group. He was joined by D.E. (Ned) Skinner, Howard S. Wright, M. Lamont Bean, Lynn P. Himmelman, and Lloyd W. Nordstrom. In November, construction began on the $67 million Kingdome with a seating capacity of 65,000 for football.

1974 The National Football League awarded a franchise to Seattle Professional Football, Inc. for $16 million, December 5. The Nordstrom family was the majority owner, with Sarkowski, Skinner, Wright, and Bean partners.

1975 John Thompson, executive director of the NFL Management Council, was named general manager of the Seattle franchise, March 6. In April, Mark Duncan was named assistant general manager and Dick Mansperger, director of player personnel with the Dallas Cowboys, was appointed to a similar post in Seattle. A contest to name the team drew 20,365 entries; "Seahawks" was selected, June 17. Season ticket applications were accepted and 24,168 requests arrived the first day, July 28. The season-ticket sale closed 27 days later with 59,000 purchased. "We anticipated a good sale," Thompson said, "but no one in his right mind would have predicted this." The Seahawks signed their first player, wide receiver Dave Williams. They adopted blue, green, and silver as their official colors. The team signed a 20-year lease to play all home games in the Kingdome.

1976 Jack Patera, assistant coach of the Minnesota Vikings, was named first head coach of the Seahawks, January 3. Lloyd Nordstrom, spokesman for the majority owners, died of a heart attack while vacationing in Mexico, January 20. The Seahawks selected 39 NFL veterans in the allocation draft, March 30. Among the top veterans chosen were tackle Norm Evans of Miami and linebacker Mike Curtis of Baltimore, both former members of Super Bowl champions and all-pro selections. The Seahawks selected 25 rookies in their first college draft, April 8. Steve Niehaus, a 6-foot 4-inch, 270-pound defensive tackle from Notre Dame, was the number one choice. In the second round, Seattle selected linebacker Sammy Green of Florida and receiver Sherman Smith of Miami, Ohio. The Seahawks won two games in their first season. In their league opener, they battled St. Louis furiously before losing 30–24 in the Kingdome, September 12. Jim Zorn, Seattle's left-handed rookie quarterback from California Poly-Pomona, passed for two touchdowns and ran for another. After losing five games, the Seahawks recorded their first victory, beating Tampa Bay 13–10, October 17. Seattle scored its first win over an established team as Sherman Smith, converted to halfback, rushed for 124 yards and two touchdowns in a 30–13 rout of Atlanta, November 7. The following week, Zorn passed for two touchdowns and ran for a third as the Seahawks scared Minnesota before losing 27–21. Smith led Seattle with 537 yards rushing. Steve Largent, a rookie receiver from Tulsa, caught 54 passes to rank third in the NFC. Zorn passed for 2,571 yards, the most ever by a first-year NFL quarterback.

Rookie quarterback Jim Zorn behind Nick Bebout's block vs. Los Angeles, 1976.

The Kingdome during a Seahawks-Cardinals game, 1976.

MEMBERS OF HALL OF FAME:
None

SEAHAWKS' RECORD, 1976

Year	Won	Lost	Tied	Pct.	Pts.	OP
1976	2	12	0	.143	229	429

RECORD HOLDERS

Rushing (Yards)	Sherman Smith, 1976	537
Passing (Pct.)	Jim Zorn, 1976	47.3
Passing (Yards)	Jim Zorn, 1976	2,471
Passing (TDs)	Jim Zorn, 1976	12
Receiving (No.)	Steve Largent, 1976	54
Receiving (Yards)	Steve Largent, 1976	705
Interceptions (No.)	Dave Brown, 1976, and	
	Rolly Woolsey, 1976	4
Punting (Avg.)	Rick Engles, 1976	38.3
Punt Ret. (Avg.)	Lyle Blackwood, 1976	6.9
Kickoff Ret. (Avg.)	Oliver Ross, 1976	21.8
Touchdowns (Total)	Sherman Smith, 1976	5
Field Goals Made	John Leypoldt, 1976	8
Points (No.)	John Leypoldt, 1976	43

COACHING HISTORY

1976	Jack Patera	2–12–0

FIRST PLAYER SELECTED
1976 Steve Niehaus, DT, Notre Dame

Ed Bradley   *Dave Brown*   *Ken Geddes*   *Steve Largent*   *Steve Niehaus*   *Sherman Smith*   *Jim Zorn*

SEATTLE SEAHAWKS, 1976

Bachman, Ted, CB, New Mexico State 1976
Barisich, Carl, DT, Princeton 1976
Bebout, Nick, T, Wyoming 1976
Bitterlich, Don, K, Temple 1976
Blackwood, Lyle, DB, Texas Christian 1976
Bolton, Andrew, RB, Fisk 1976
Bradley, Ed, LB, Wake Forest 1976
Brown, Dave, DB, Michigan 1976

C
Clune, Don, WR, Pennsylvania 1976
Coder, Ron, G, Penn State 1976
Coffield, Randy, LB, Florida State 1976
Collins, Greg, LB, Notre Dame 1976
Cowlings, Al, DE, USC 1976
Curtis, Mike, LB, Duke 1976

D
Darby, Alvis, TE, Florida 1976
Demarie, John, G, Louisiana State 1976
Dufek, Don, DB, Michigan 1976

E
Engles, Rick, P, Tulsa 1976
Evans, Norm, T, Texas Christian 1976

G
Geddes, Ken, LB, Nebraska 1976
Green, Sammy, LB, Florida 1976
Graff, Neil, QB, Wisconsin 1976

H
Hansen, Don, LB, Illinois 1976
Harris, Richard, DE, Grambling 1976
Hoaglin, Fred, C, Pennsylvania 1976
Howard, Ron, TE, Seattle 1976

J
Jolley, Gordon, T, Utah 1976
Jones, Ernie, DB, Miami 1976

K
Kuehn, Art, C, UCLA 1976

L
Largent, Steve, WR, Tulsa 1976
Leypoldt, John, K, None 1976
Lurtsema, Bob, DE, Western Michigan 1976

M
Matthews, Al, DB, Texas A&I 1976
McCullum, Sam, WR, Montana State 1976
McKinnis, Hugh, RB, Arizona State 1976
McMakin, John, TE, Clemson 1976
McMillan, Eddie, DB, Florida State 1976
Munson, Bill, QB, Utah State 1976
Myer, Steve, QB, New Mexico 1976

N
Nelson, Ralph, RB, None 1976
Newton, Bob, G, Nebraska 1976

Niehaus, Steve, DT, Notre Dame 1976

O
Olds, Bill, RB, Nebraska 1976

P
Penchion, Bob, G, Alcorn A&M 1976

R
Raible, Steve, WR, Georgia Tech 1976
Ross, Oliver, RB, Alabama A&M 1976

S
Simonson, Dave, T, Minnesota 1976
Smith, Sherman, RB, Miami, Ohio 1976

T
Testerman, Don, RB, Clemson 1976
Tipton, David L., DE, Stanford 1976

W
White, Jim, DE, Colorado State 1976
Woods, Larry, DT, Tennessee State 1976
Woolsey, Rolly, DB, Boise State 1976

Z
Zorn, Jim, QB, California Poly-Pomona 1976

Linebacker Mike Curtis.

Quarterback Bill Munson.

TAMPA BAY BUCCANEERS

1974 Commissioner Pete Rozelle awarded a National Football League franchise to Tampa Bay in a press conference at New York's Drake Hotel, April 24. Rozelle said the league had long been impressed by Tampa Bay's strong support of NFL preseason games over the years. Overall, 13 preseason contests had been held at Tampa Stadium with an average attendance of 41,000. Philadelphia construction tycoon Tom McCloskey was awarded the franchise, October 30, but he withdrew from the project two weeks later. The franchise was awarded to Hugh F. Culverhouse, a Jacksonville attorney and real estate investor, for $16 million, December 5. Culverhouse had previously attempted to purchase the Los Angeles Rams.

1975 Culverhouse named Bill Marcum the team's director of marketing, January 30. Marcum was the man who had promoted preseason games in Tampa and had organized the movement to bring an NFL franchise to the Tampa Bay area. More than 400 nicknames for the team were submitted to an advisory board and Culverhouse selected "Buccaneers," February 15. The Tampa City Council voted to approve expansion of Tampa Stadium from 46,500 to 72,000 seats, making it the seventh largest stadium in the NFL. Ron Wolf, director of player personnel for the Oakland Raiders, was named vice president of operations, April 30. The Buccaneers adopted the colors of orange and white with red trim and approved the symbol of a swashbuckling buccaneer, June 15. Culverhouse signed John McKay to a five-year contract as head coach, October 31. While at USC, McKay won eight Pacific 8 titles, five Rose Bowls, and four national championships.

1976 Marvin L. Warner, president of a Cincinnati financial services company, purchased a major share of the franchise, February 15. Tampa Bay selected 39 players (20 defensive, 19 offensive) in the veteran allocation draft in New York, March 30. "The quality of players presented on the lists exceeded our expectations," McKay said, citing starters such as tight end Bob Moore of Oakland and defensive end Pat Toomay of Buffalo. The Buccaneers made their first trade, sending two players and a draft choice to San Francisco for quarterback Steve Spurrier, the former Heisman trophy winner from the University of Florida, April 2. A week later, Tampa Bay had the first pick in the college draft and selected Lee Roy Selmon, the All-America defensive tackle from Oklahoma. The Buccaneers drafted his brother, Dewey, a defensive tackle, on the second round. The Buccaneers became the first 0-14 team in NFL history, and the first team to go winless since the 1960 Dallas Cowboys. They failed to score a touchdown in their first three league games and were shut out five times. They opened with a 20-0 loss in Houston, September 12. Their most humiliating defeat was a 42-0 rout in Pittsburgh, December 5. Tampa Bay's leading rusher was Louis Carter, who gained 521 yards. Spurrier, who alternated with rookie quarterback Parnell Dickinson, was the leading passer.

MEMBERS OF HALL OF FAME:
None

BUCCANEERS RECORD, 1976

Year	Won	Lost	Tied	Pct.	Pts.	OP
1976	0	14	0	.000	125	412

RECORD HOLDERS

Rushing (Yards)	Louis Carter, 1976	521
Passing (Pct.)	Steve Spurrier, 1976	50.2
Passing (Yards)	Steve Spurrier, 1976	1,628
Passing (TDs)	Steve Spurrier, 1976	7
Receiving (No.)	Morris Owens, 1976	30
Receiving (Yards)	Morris Owens, 1976	390
Interceptions (No.)	Mark Cotney, 1976	3
Punting (Avg.)	Dave Green, 1976	39.3
Punt Ret. (Avg.)	Manfred Moore, 1976	7.6
Kickoff Ret. (Avg.)	Rod McNeill, 1976	22.6
Touchdowns (Total)	Morris Owens, 1976	6
Field Goals Made	Dave Green, 1976	8
Points (No.)	Morris Owens, 1976	36

COACHING HISTORY

1976	John McKay	0-14-0

FIRST PLAYER SELECTED
1976 Lee Roy Selmon, DE, Oklahoma

Head coach John McKay, 1976.

Wide receiver Morris Owens, 1976.

Louis Carter

Mark Cotney

Bob Moore

Dave Pear

Lee Roy Selmon

Steve Spurrier

Richard Wood

TAMPA BAY BUCCANEERS, 1976

Alward, Tom, G, Nebraska 1976

B

Ball, Larry, LB, Louisville 1976
Blahak, Joe, CB, Nebraska 1976
Brown, Cedric, DB, Kent State 1976

C

Carter, Louis, RB, Maryland 1976
Cooper, Bert, LB, Florida State 1976
Cotney, Mark, DB, Cameron State 1976
Current, Mike, T, Ohio State 1976

D

Davis, Charlie, RB, Colorado 1976
Davis, Ricky, DB, Alabama 1976
Dickinson, Parnell, QB, Mississippi Valley State ... 1976
DuBose, Jimmy, RB, Florida 1976
Douglas, Freddie, WR, Arkansas 1976

F

Fest, Howard, G, Texas 1976

G

Green, Dave, P, Ohio 1976
Gunn, Jimmy, LB, USC 1976

H

Hanratty, Terry, QB, Notre Dame 1976
Hagins, Isaac, WR, Southern 1976
Hunt, Charles, LB, Florida State 1976

J

Jameson, Larry, DT, Indiana 1976
Jennings, Rick, WR, Maryland 1976
Johnson, Essex, RB, Grambling 1976
Jordan, Curtis, DB, Texas Tech 1976

K

Kearney, Tim, LB, Northern Michigan 1976
Kendrick, Vince, RB, Florida 1976

L

Lawrence, Larry, QB, Iowa 1976
Leak, Curtis, WR, Johnson C. Smith 1976
Lemon, Mike, LB, Kansas 1976
Little, Everett, G, Houston 1976

M

Martin, Don, DB, Yale 1976
McAleney, Ed, DE, Massachusetts 1976
McGriff, Lee, WR, Florida 1976
McKay, John, WR, USC 1976
McNeil, Rod, RB, USC 1976
Miller, Johnny, DT, Livingstone 1976
Moore, Bob, TE, Stanford 1976
Moore, Manfred, RB, USC 1976
Moore, Maulty, DT, Bethune-Cookman 1976

N

Novak, Jack, TE, Wisconsin 1976

O

Oliver, Frank, DB, Kentucky State 1976
Owens, Morris, WR, Arizona State 1976

P

Pagac, Ted, TE, Ohio State 1976
Pear, Dave, DT, Washington 1976
Peterson, Calvin, LB, UCLA 1976
Peterson, Jim, LB, San Diego State 1976
Pierson, Reggie, DB, Oklahoma State 1976

R

Reavis, Dave, T, Arkansas 1976
Reece, Danny, CB, USC 1976
Reese, Steve, LB, Louisville 1976
Robinson, Glenn, DE, Oklahoma State 1976
Roder, Mirro, K, None 1976
Rudolph, Council, DE, Kentucky State 1976
Ryczek, Dan, C, Virginia 1976

S

Selmon, Dewey, DT, Oklahoma 1976
Selmon, Lee Roy, DE, Oklahoma 1976
Sims, Jimmy, LB, USC 1976
Smith, Barry, WR, Florida 1976
Spurrier, Steve, QB, Florida 1976
Stone, Ken, DB, Vanderbilt 1976

T

Toomay, Pat, DE, Vanderbilt 1976

W

Ward, John, C, Oklahoma State 1976
Washington, Mike, DB, Alabama 1976
Williams, Ed, RB, Langston 1976
Wilson, Steve, T, Georgia 1976
Wood, Richard, LB, USC 1976
Word, Roscoe, DB, Jackson State 1976

Y

Young, Randy, T, Iowa State 1976
Young, Steve, T, Colorado 1976

Number one draft choice Lee Roy Selmon and owner Hugh Culverhouse, 1976.

WASHINGTON REDSKINS

1932 George Preston Marshall of Washington, D.C. headed a four-man syndicate that included Vincent Bendix, Jay O'Brien, and M. Dorland Doyle that bought the National Football League franchise for Boston. They contracted to play at Braves Field, home of the National League baseball team, and decided to call themselves the Braves, as well. Lud Wray was hired as the first coach. The team finished 4–4–2, lost $46,000 the first season, and all Marshall's partners gave up. Marshall stuck with it.

1933 Marshall moved the club to Fenway Park, home of baseball's American League Red Sox. He changed the name of the team to Redskins. Wray quit to coach Philadelphia. Marshall hired a full-blooded Indian as the team's coach, Will (Lone Star) Dietz. On opening day of practice, the entire club was lined up for the team picture in war paint, feathers and full headdress. Dietz specialized in trick plays, although he had Jim Musick and Cliff Battles, who finished one-two in the league in rushing. The team stayed at .500 with a 5–5–2 record. Money was so tight that when the ball would go into the stands, Marshall would run to the spot and personally ask that it be returned. Glen (Turk) Edwards, a 250-pound tackle from Washington State, missed the first three minutes of the first game of the season and the last seven minutes of the last, but played every minute in between—710 out of a possible 720 minutes.

1934 The Redskins had a good crop of rookies and hoped to win their first championship, but only running backs Battles and Edwards played up to expectations. The team finished second—again at .500 with a 6–6 record. Marshall, however, was encouraged by the improved attendance and felt the franchise would soon turn into a money maker.

1935 In an attempt to draw more fans, Marshall dismissed Dietz and hired hometown hero Eddie Casey, former Harvard player, as his new coach. But Casey didn't make good and neither did Marshall's plan. The Redskins won only 2 of 11 games.

1936 Ray Flaherty was signed as the new head coach, and made his position clear from the outset. He insisted that Marshall stay off the field and in the stands. The team responded to Flaherty's leadership by winning the Eastern Division title with a 14–0 victory over the New York Giants in the final game of the season. When Boston failed to get excited enough for Marshall, he moved the championship game to New York, where nearly 30,000 people watched Green Bay beat the Redskins 21–6.

1937 The National Football League approved the transfer of the Boston Redskins' franchise to Washington, D.C. Marshall's showman instincts seemed to blossom in the nation's capital. He organized the Redskins' band and he produced elaborate halftime shows. The Redskins drafted Sammy Baugh, All-America tailback from Texas Christian University, then signed him for $8,000 a year. Baugh completed 11 of 16 passes his first game. Played in Griffith Stadium on a Thursday night, that first game drew 19,941 to see the Redskins beat the Giants 13–3. New York was the victim again in the game that decided the Eastern Division championship. The Redskins won 49–14 in a game that attracted 10,000 Washington fans to New York. Cliff Battles scored twice on runs of 75 and 76 yards. A week later, Baugh completed 17 of 33 passes for 335 yards and three touchdowns. His favorite receiver, Wayne Millner, caught nine passes for 160 yards, including touchdowns of 77 and 55 yards. And Washington won the world championship 28–21 over George Halas's Chicago Bears. Baugh completed 81 of 171 passes during the season for 1,127 yards and eight touchdowns. Battles gained 874 yards.

Ken Houston intercepts, heads outside; Pat Fischer moves to block vs. New Orleans, 1975.

1938 The Redskins drafted Andy Farkas, a back from Detroit University, number one and also got Wee Willie Wilkin, a tackle from St. Mary's, California. Cliff Battles quit in a salary dispute after gaining more than 3,500 yards rushing in six years. Baugh separated his shoulder in the first game of the season. Baugh came back sooner than expected, but then was injured again. Marshall signed Frank Filchock, a tailback from the University of Indiana, for $1,000—$200 less than Battles had sought. The Redskins used Filchock in a patched-up lineup and finished second to the New York Giants at 6–3–2.

1939 The Redskins trained at Cheyney, Washington. Flaherty, one of the most imaginative coaches in the league, designed a plan to try to keep the sometimes frail Baugh healthy. He alternated Filchock and Baugh at tailback, confusing opposing defenses, which didn't know whether to look for Filchock's runs or Baugh's passes. The Redskins played their first scoreless tie since 1935 against the Giants, October 1. Filchock and Farkas teamed on a record 99-yard touchdown pass play against Pittsburgh, October 15. The Eastern Division title came down to the final game—in fact, the final 45 seconds. But the Redskins' Bo Russell missed a disputed field goal attempt and New York won 9–7. Most of the players thought the kick was good, but the referee ruled the kick had sailed to the right of the goal post. On the train ride home, Marshall called Russell to his compartment and, before newsmen, signed him to a 1940 contract.

1940 The Redskins trained at Gonzaga University in Washington. Farkas was lost with a knee injury that required surgery three weeks before the start of the season. A healthy Baugh led the club to a 9–2 record and the Eastern Division championship, beating the Chicago Bears 7–3 along the way. The Bears complained about the officiating, and Marshall ripped them in the newspapers. "The Bears are front-runners," he said. "Quitters. They're not a second-half team, just a bunch of crybabies." Those remarks may have had something to do with what happened in the rematch with the Bears in the championship game. For the first time, an NFL game was broadcast coast-to-coast. Chicago, using the T formation with man-in-motion, embarrassed the Redskins 73–0. Baugh was asked if an early Washington pass for a touchdown was dropped would have made any difference. "Sure," drawled Baugh, "the game would have wound up 73–7." Baugh had his best season, completing 111 of 177 passes, a 62.7 completion percentage, for 1,367 yards and 12 touchdowns. Dick Todd led the Redskins' rushers with 408 yards.

1941 The draft produced ends Ed Cifers of Tennessee, Joe Aguirre of St. Mary's, California, and Al Krueger of USC, although blocking back Forest Evashevski of Michigan was number one. The Redskins also picked up an all-pro caliber center from the Chicago Cardinals, Charles (Ki) Aldrich. The team trained at San Diego. The Redskins ran up a 5–1 record, then were hit by injuries and finished with only one win in the second half of the season. During a game on December 7, various high ranking government and military personnel were paged over the public address system as the Redskins beat Philadelphia 20–14, but it wasn't until after the game most of the fans learned that World War II had begun for the United States.

1942 Orban (Spec) Sanders, a back from Texas, was the top draft choice. In the second game of the season, the Giants failed to make one first down, gained only one yard rushing, and completed just one pass, but it was good for a touchdown. Another score on an interception gave New York a 14–7 victory, September 27. It was Washington's only loss en route to a 10–1 record. In Flaherty's last year as coach before entering the navy, he was able to avenge that 73–0 defeat to the Bears. To motivate the team, he simply wrote

"73–0" in large figures on the blackboard in the Washington dressing room. That was enough as Baugh threw for one touchdown and Farkas ran for another in a 14–6 triumph that stopped the Bears' undefeated string at 18.

1943 The college draft produced Lou Rymkus, a tackle from Notre Dame, but Jack Jenkins, a back from Missouri, was the first pick. With Flaherty in the service, Arthur (Dutch) Bergman took over as coach. Because of the manpower shortage, Baugh was forced to play both offense and defense. The Redskins were unbeaten, with one tie, in their first seven games, but then lost twice to the New York Giants to finish the season tied with the Giants for the division title. Baugh had 23 touchdown passes and gained 1,754 yards on 133 completions in 239 attempts. In the division playoff, Baugh threw three touchdown passes and Washington defeated New York 28–0. Baugh was injured in the championship game against Chicago and the Bears won 41–21.

1944 Dudley DeGroot was the new head coach, and the new weapon in Washington was the T formation. Marshall hired Clark Shaughnessy, who had been a voluntary assistant coach for the Bears, to teach it to Baugh and company. Baugh, who had always been a tailback, didn't care for it at first, but then slowly made the adjustment. Filchock, just out of the Coast Guard, split the passing with Baugh and led the league with 1,139 yards and 13 touchdowns. The Redskins finished 6–3–1.

1945 USC quarterback Jim Hardy was the number one draft choice. Baugh, who had to do some running while operating the single and double wing, said he could "operate the T in tie and tails." He made it look almost that easy in a 24–14 win over the Giants in which he completed 20 of 24 passes for 265 yards and two touchdowns. The four misses were "throw-aways," Baugh said. Baugh, now settled comfortably into the T, completed a 70.3 percent of his passes to set an NFL record. The Redskins won the Eastern Division title, but lost the NFL championship game to the Cleveland Rams 15–14 in sub-zero weather when Baugh's pass hit the goal post for a safety and Bob Waterfield's try for a Rams' extra point hit the crossbar and bounced over for the margin of victory.

1946 Cal Rossi, a back from UCLA, was the top draftee but was lost when he was declared ineligible for the draft. Marshall refused to compete with the new All-America Football Conference, and lost some key players, such as Willie Wilkin, star end and placekicker Joe Aguirre, and even the coach, De-Groot. A. G. (Turk) Edwards took over as the new coach. Marshall traded Frank Filchock to the New York Giants, a deal that backfired when Baugh was injured. Filchock led the Giants to the Eastern Division championship. The Redskins turned from near-champions to a 5–5–1 team.

1947 Cal Rossi was the number one choice again. Rossi met with Marshall and Edwards, voiced his appreciation of their offer, and then returned to California to become a schoolteacher and small businessman. The Redskins lost 45–42 to Philadelphia on opening day and that set the tone for the season. Baugh had his biggest year, throwing for 11 touchdowns in a two-game stretch but it did little to advance the Redskins' cause in a 4–8 season. Washington scored plenty of points—295—but the opposition scored more—367. Baugh's best season included 210 completions in 354 attempts, for 2,938 yards and 25 touchdowns.

1948 Impressed with Alabama's Harry Gilmer, and worried about grooming a successor to Baugh, Marshall sold the draft rights to Mississippi quarterback Charlie Conerly and signed Gilmer as the top draft choice. Baugh proved there still was some life in his arm, however, as he passed for 446 yards in beating Boston 59–21. The Redskins' erratic defense kept

them away from the championship and in second place with a 7–5 record. It was another big year for Baugh, who completed 185 of 315 passes for 2,599 yards and 22 touchdowns.

1949 Turk Edwards was moved to the front office, and Admiral John (Billick) Whelchel, former Naval Academy coach, was brought in to take over as coach. He signed a five-year contract, but was gone three games before the end of the season and replaced by Herman Ball, a team scout. The team finished 4–7–1. There was considerable discontent in the media over Marshall's failure to sign black players.

1950 The Redskins became one of the first two pro teams to have all of their games televised; the other was Los Angeles in 1950. Young quarterback Gilmer and highly publicized running back Charlie (Choo Choo) Justice of North Carolina were disappointments. Baugh and his aging teammates could not stop the slide that resulted in eight straight losses and a 3–9–0 last-place finish.

1951 Three games into the new season, Ball was fired and Marshall wanted to hire Heartley (Hunk) Anderson, a Bears' assistant coach. But George Halas wouldn't allow it unless the Redskins threw star tackle Paul Lipscomb into the deal. Marshall refused and decided instead to hire former Redskins' star Dick Todd as coach. The team responded by winning its first two games for Todd and finished third at 5–7. Rob Goode from Texas A&M became the closest thing the Redskins ever had to a 1,000-yard runner, when he gained a club record 951 yards.

1952 Larry Isbell, a quarterback from Baylor, was the number one draft pick. Todd signed for another year as coach, but resigned before September. He said he had to have respect to stay as coach, and, although he liked Marshall, he didn't "agree with the way he runs the Redskins." Earl (Curly) Lambeau, the first "name" coach hired by Marshall, took over. Baugh broke his hand in a preseason game and was limited to holding for kicks and teaching rookie Eddie LeBaron from College of the Pacific the nuances of quarterbacking in the pros. Gilmer backed up LeBaron. In the last game of the season, Baugh went in to hold for a placekick against the Philadelphia Eagles but the kick was blocked. Baugh's retirement from pro football after 16 years ended an era in Washington.

1953 The top draftee was quarterback Jack Scarbath of Maryland. LeBaron was the Redskins' starting quarterback. Gilmer was shifted to the defensive backfield, and Choo Choo Justice made a comeback in a year when Lambeau got the team winning again. The defense, featuring end Gene Brito from Loyola of Los Angeles, came on strong down the stretch. A 10–0 shutout of Philadelphia turned out to be Lambeau's 231st—and last—NFL victory.

1954 Lambeau's successor was Joe Kuharich. LeBaron and Brito jumped to the Canadian Football League. The Redskins never recovered in a 3–9–0 season. Tragedy struck near the end of the season when guard Dave Sparks died of a heart attack following a 34–14 loss to Cleveland.

1955 LeBaron and Brito returned from Canada and were joined on the new-look Redskins by Vic Janowicz, the All-America halfback from Ohio State who abandoned a professional baseball career to try the NFL. The Redskins scored 21 points in 137 seconds in a game with Philadelphia, October 1. Trailing 16–0 in the third quarter, Brito recovered a fumble on the Eagles' 32. LeBaron passed to Janowicz for a touchdown. Ralph Thomas recovered the kickoff in the end zone for another touchdown. Lavern Torgeson recovered a fumble on the Eagles' 13. Janowicz scored immediately and the Redskins won 31–30. Janowicz wound up as the second leading scorer in the league, and the rejuvenated Redskins finished second in the Eastern Conference with an 8–4 record.

1956 In a tragic training camp accident a car in which Janowicz was riding left the road. He was thrown from the car and against a tree, suffering brain damage. His football career was over. Sam Baker, a former star fullback at Oregon State, returned from a stint in the Canadian league and assumed Janowicz's punting and placekicking duties. Baker led the league with 17 field goals in 25 attempts and was the Redskins' top scorer with 67 points. But the team, demoralized by Janowicz's tragedy and injuries to quarterbacks LeBaron and Al Dorow, staggered to a 6–6–0 third place finish.

1957 Another training camp tragedy struck when defensive back Roy Barni was shot to death in a barroom brawl. The team struggled through most of the season. With three games left, the defense jelled and held Chicago, Philadelphia, and Pittsburgh to a combined total of 13 points. But the Redskins remained under .500 at 5–6–1.

1958 The club continued to have problems keeping pace with NFL contenders. And the pressure on Marshall to begin signing black players was building again. The Redskins had traded their number one draft choice to Los Angeles for quarterback Rudy Bukich. They chose Mike Sommer, a back from George Washington, on the second round. Of the five previous first round draft picks by Washington, only fullback Don Bosseler of Miami (1956) played regularly. The Redskins struggled through a 4–7–1 season. Kuharich was fired as coach.

1959 Don Allard of Boston College, a back, was the number one draft pick. Assistant coach Mike Nixon was promoted to the top job, but nothing changed. The Redskins still were losing almost all their games—eight of nine at one point. The highlight of the season was Sam Baker's 46-yard field goal that allowed Washington to upset the defending world champion Baltimore Colts 27–24, November 8. The club signed a 30-year lease to play in the proposed D.C. Stadium. Congress gave approval for construction of the stadium.

1960 Still seeking a quarterback after using four number one choices in seven years in an attempt to solve the problem, the Redskins tried again with Richie Lucas of Penn State, who signed with Buffalo and played there. Ralph Guglielmi from Notre Dame kept the quarterback job, but he had to run for his life much of the season. The club scored 16 or fewer points in eight of its nine losses in a 1–9–2 season.

1961 Nixon was replaced by Bill McPeak, a rookie coach who opened with a rookie quarterback, Norm Snead of Wake Forest, the number one draft choice. The pair suffered through a frightful season in their first year in new 55,004-seat D.C. Stadium, which opened October 1. The Redskins lost 12 straight before beating Dallas 34–24 in the final game to avert a winless season. Still, Snead passed for 2,337 yards and 11 touchdowns, the most passing yardage since Baugh's 2,599 in 1948. The running game was pitiful. Dick James led the rushers with just 374 yards.

1962 Marshall made history in Washington by drafting the Redskins' first black player, Heisman trophy winner Ernie Davis from Syracuse. Then he traded Davis to Cleveland for Bobby Mitchell, a black runner-reciever from Illinois. John Nisby of Pacific, Leroy Jackson of Western Illinois, and Ron Hatcher of Michigan State, joined Mitchell as the first blacks on the Redskins' roster. McPeak's team showed immediate improvement. Mitchell became one of the league's most dangerous receivers, and Snead was developing into an effective quarterback, passing for 2,926 yards and 22 touchdowns. The record improved to 5–7–2. Mitchell's 72 receptions were the highest in the league and he gained 1,384 yards while scoring 11 touchdowns. Mitchell also returned a kickoff for one touchdown to lead the club in scoring with 72 points.

Wide receiver Bobby Mitchell getting past Los Angeles's Jack Pardee, 1967.

Tight end Jerry Smith fights into end zone vs. N.Y. Giants, 1972; 42 is Charley Taylor.

1963 The Redskins were exciting on offense, with Snead passing to Mitchell and an assortment of good receivers. Snead threw for a team record 3,043 yards on 175 completions in 363 attempts to top Baugh's 2,938 in 1947. But there was not much running attack. Dick James gained just 384 yards to lead the team. And the defense still needed improvement. Mitchell again led the receivers with 69 catches for 1,436 yards and seven touchdowns.

1964 Snead was traded to Philadelphia for quarterback Sonny Jurgensen. Another controversial deal sent Dick James to the Giants for Sam Huff, the celebrated middle linebacker. Charley Taylor, a wide receiver from Arizona State, was the number one draft choice and he joined with Mitchell to inject speed into the Washington offense. Huff and rookie defensive back Paul Krause from Iowa put some muscle into the defense. The Redskins won five of their last eight games for a 6–8 record. All home games were sellouts. Jurgensen passed for 2,934 yards in his first season in Washington.

1965 Without a running game to balance it, the Washington offense slipped considerably and the team lost its first five games. But then the club played its greatest comeback game in history, rallying from a 21-point deficit for a 34–31 win over Dallas as Jurgensen passed for more than 400 yards and three touchdowns, November 28. The defense was better until cornerback Johnny Sample was suspended late in the season for insubordination.

1966 McPeak was released and Otto Graham, the former Cleveland Browns' all-pro quarterback, was named coach and general manager. Charley Gogolak, a kicker from Princeton, was the number one draft choice. Graham emphasized the passing game even more than McPeak had. The offense improved. But Graham moved seven new players into the lineup on defense, and the best Washington could get was a 7–7 record. Jurgensen had his best season, throwing 436 times and completing 254 for 3,209 yards and 28 touchdowns. Gogolak kicked for 105 points.

1967 Sonny Jurgensen won the league passing title, setting league records for attempts, 508; completions, 288; and yards, 3,747. He also passed for 31 touchdowns, a club record. Three Redskins' receivers were in the top four in NFL receiving, led by Charley Taylor's 70—high in the league—for 990 yards and 9 touchdowns. But, again, the running threat was missing. Team leader A. D. Whitfield gained just 384 yards. The Washington kicking game also deteriorated and the team finished third in the four-team Capitol Division.

1968 Middle linebacker Sam Huff announced his retirement. Graham sent a future first-round draft pick to Los Angeles for Gary Beban, the Heisman trophy winner from UCLA. Beban, after signing a lucrative contract, flopped in training camp, spent most of the year on the taxi squad, and was even tried unsuccessfully as a running back late in the season. Safety Paul Krause was traded to Minnesota. After a disappointing 5–9 season, Graham was fired at the end of the year. Jurgensen's passing yardage dipped to 1,980.

1969 The top draft selection was traded to San Francisco. Vince Lombardi left Green Bay to become part-owner, executive vice-president, and head of the Redskins. Lombardi constructed what the other Washington coaches seemingly had ignored—a strong running game. Rookie halfback Larry Brown of Kansas State (888 yards) and fullback Charley Harraway (428 yards) formed a new backfield combination and the defense tightened considerably on the way to second place in the division. Jurgensen led the NFL in passing with 3,102 yards. Washington had its first winning season since 1955 with a 7–5–2 record.

1970 For the third straight year, the number one draft choice was traded, this time to Los Angeles, but

Running back Larry Brown catching a pass over New York Giants linebacker Pat Hughes, 1973.

Washington picked up defensive end Bill Brundige of Colorado in the second round. Lombardi was missing when training camp opened. He was in the hospital, terminally ill. Two weeks before the start of the season, Lombardi died of cancer, September 3. Assistant coach Bill Austin took over, but the team didn't play with the same precision. Only Larry Brown, coming into his own as an all-pro, had an outstanding year, becoming the first Redskin ever to gain 1,000 yards rushing. He ran for 1,125 on 237 carries, a 4.8 average. Jurgensen threw for 2,354 yards.

1971 Former Los Angeles Rams coach George Allen was named the new head coach and general manager of the Redskins. The top draft choice was traded away again, but Allen got Cotton Speyrer, a wide receiver from Texas, on the second round. Allen immediately implemented the plan he made so successful as Los Angeles coach. He started trading for as many veteran players as possible. They included quarterback Billy Kilmer, who came from New Orleans; wide receiver Roy Jefferson, from Baltimore; defensive tackle Diron Talbert and linebacker Jack Pardee, from Los Angeles; defensive end Ron McDole, from Buffalo; defensive end Verlon Biggs, from the New York Jets; and others, who became known as "The Over-the-Hill-Gang." Construction began on Redskins Park, the team's new practice and training camp facility near Dulles Airport. Washington finished with a 9–4–1 record, the most Redskins' victories in 29 years, and got into its first playoff game in 26 years. Brown just missed 1,000 yards, gaining 948. Kilmer took over from Jurgensen and passed for 2,221 yards. After leading at halftime, the Redskins, who were the NFC "wild card" team, finally lost to San Francisco 24–20 in an NFC divisional playoff. Allen was named NFC coach of the year.

1972 Moses Denson, a running back from Maryland State, was Washington's top draftee after the first choice had been traded again. Led by an outstanding defensive unit, the Redskins beat Dallas out of the division title for the first time since 1965. It was the Redskins' first championship in 30 years. Although Jurgensen was injured much of the time, the Washington offense operated efficiently, with Kilmer (1,648 yards and 19 touchdowns) and Brown maintaining ball control. Washington won a club record 11 games. Although he missed two games with injuries, Brown gained 1,216 yards to lead the conference in rushing and set a Redskins' record. In the first round of the playoffs, the Redskins defeated Green Bay 16–3. Then, in the championship game against their rivals from Dallas, the Redskins defeated the Cowboys 26–3 to gain their first Super Bowl.

1973 The Miami Dolphins, at the peak of their efficiency, downed the Redskins 14–7 in Super Bowl VII in the Los Angeles Coliseum, January 14. The number one draft choice was traded away again and some said Allen's old men couldn't come back. But they did. They were co-champions of the division, finishing with a 10–4 record, and made it as the "wild card" playoff team. Jurgensen and Kilmer shared playing time at quarterback. Kilmer passed for 1,656 yards and Jurgensen for 904. Brown and Harraway provided the running, with Brown gaining 860 yards and Harraway 452. In Minnesota, however, Washington was no match for the Super Bowl-bound Vikings and lost the playoff game 27–20.

1974 The number one draft choice went to Los Angeles. "The Over-the-Hill Gang" proved it wasn't over the hill, again compiling another 10–4 season and making it to the playoffs for the fourth straight season. Jurgensen celebrated his fortieth birthday and

Year	Won	Lost	Tied	Pct.	Pts.	OP
1961	1	12	1	.077	174	392
1962	5	7	2	.417	305	376
1963	3	11	0	.214	279	398
1964	6	8	0	.429	307	305
1965	6	8	0	.429	257	301
1966	7	7	0	.500	351	355
1967	5	6	3	.455	347	353
1968	5	9	0	.357	249	358
1969	7	5	2	.583	307	319
1970	6	8	0	.429	297	314
1971	9	4	1	.692	276	190
1972‡	11	3	0	.786	336	218
1973	10	4	0	.714	325	198
1974	10	4	0	.714	320	196
1975	8	6	0	.571	325	276
1976	10	4	0	.714	291	217
45 Years	268	262	26	.505	10,417	10,837

§NFL Eastern Division Championship
‡NFC Champion

RECORD HOLDERS

Rushing (Yards)	Larry Brown, 1972	1,216
Passing (Pct.)	Sammy Baugh, 1945	70.3
Passing (Yards)	Sonny Jurgensen, 1967	3,747
Passing (TDs)	Sonny Jurgensen, 1967	31
Receiving (No.)	Bobby Mitchell, 1962, and	
	Charley Taylor, 1966	72
Receiving (Yards)	Bobby Mitchell, 1963	1,436
Interceptions (No.)	Don Sandifer, 1948	13
Punting (Avg.)	Sammy Baugh, 1940	51.3
Punt Ret. (Avg.)	Dick Todd, 1941	17.0
Kickoff Ret. (Avg.)	Dick James, 1961	29.4
Touchdowns (Total)	Charley Taylor, 1966	15
Field Goals Made	Curt Knight, 1971	29
Points (No.)	Curt Knight, 1971	114

COACHING HISTORY

1932	Lud Wray	4– 4–2
1933–34	William (Lone Star) Dietz	11–11–2
1935	Eddie Casey	2– 8–1
1936–42	Ray Flaherty	54–21–3
1943	Arthur (Dutch) Bergman	6– 3–1
1944–45	Dudley DeGroot	14– 5–1
1946–48	Glen (Turk) Edwards	16–18–1
1949	John Whelchel*	2– 4–1
1949–51	Herman Ball**	5–15–0
1951	Dick Todd	5– 4–0
1952–53	Earl (Curly) Lambeau	10–13–1
1954–58	Joe Kuharich	26–32–2
1959–60	Mike Nixon	4–18–2
1961–65	Bill McPeak	21–46–3
1966–68	Otto Graham	17–22–3
1969	Vince Lombardi	7– 5–2
1970	Bill Austin	6– 8–0
1971–76	George Allen	58–25–1

*Replaced after seven games in 1949
**Replaced after three games in 1951

FIRST PLAYER SELECTED

1936	Riley Smith, B, Alabama
1937	Sammy Baugh, B, Texas Christian
1938	Andy Farkas, B, Detroit
1939	I.B. Hale, T, Texas Christian
1940	Ed Boell, B, New York U.
1941	Forest Evashevski, B, Michigan
1942	Orban (Spec) Sanders, B, Texas
1943	Jack Jenkins, B, Missouri
1944	Mike Micka, B, Colgate
1945	Jim Hardy, B, USC
1946	Cal Rossi, B, UCLA*
1947	Cal Rossi, B, UCLA
1948	Harry Gilmer, B, Alabama
1949	Rob Goode, B, Texas A&M
1950	George Thomas, B, Oklahoma
1951	Leon Heath, B, Oklahoma
1952	Larry Isbell, B, Baylor
1953	Jack Scarbath, B, Maryland
1954	Steve Meilinger, E, Kentucky
1955	Ralph Guglielmi, B, Notre Dame
1956	Ed Vereb, B, Maryland
1957	Don Bosseler, B, Miami
1958	Mike Sommer, B (2), George Washington
1959	Don Allard, B, Boston College
1960	Richie Lucas, QB, Penn State
1961	Norman Snead, QB, Wake Forest
1962	Leroy Jackson, WR, Illinois Central
1963	Pat Richter, TE, Wisconsin
1964	Charley Taylor, RB-WR, Arizona State
1965	Bob Breitenstein, T (2), Tulsa
1966	Charlie Gogolak, K (2), Princeton
1967	Ray McDonald, RB, Idaho
1968	Jim Smith, DB, Oregon
1969	Eugene Epps, DB, Texas-El Paso
1970	Bill Brundige, DT (2), Colorado
1971	Cotton Speyrer, WR (2), Texas
1972	Moses Denson, RB (8), Maryland State
1973	Charles Cantrell, G (5), Lamar Tech
1974	Jon Keyworth, TE (6), Colorado
1975	Mike Thomas, RB (5), Nevada-Las Vegas
1976	Mike Hughes, G (5), Baylor

*Choice lost due to ineligibility

Cornerback Pat Fischer, 170 pounds, upending MacArthur Lane of Kansas City, 220 pounds, in 1976.

led the NFC in passing. Brown was slowed with knee injuries, gaining only 430 yards. Some signs of age began to show up front in the Redskins' units. In the first round of the playoffs, the Redskins, again the "wild card" team, were beaten by the Los Angeles Rams 19–10.

1975 After 18 seasons in the league, 11 as a Redskin, Jurgensen retired. San Diego got the Redskins' number on draft choice. Allen, who rarely employed first-year players, came up with an outstanding rookie in running back Mike Thomas of Nevada-Las Vegas. Thomas rushed for 919 yards to lead the team. Thomas passed for 2,440 yards, but overall, the Redskins were sluggish on offense and played the poorest defense of the Allen years to miss the playoffs for the first time since he took over as coach. Charley Taylor became the NFL's all-time leading receiver when his career total reached 635. He caught 53 passes.

1976 The number one draft choice was traded to Miami for the rights to Joe Theismann, the eighth straight year the team had gone without a pick in the first round. Allen signed free agent running back John Riggins and Calvin Hill. Again, the reports of the Redskins' collapse proved exaggerated. A new quarterback controversy developed between Kilmer and Theismann. The offense got 1,101 yards from Thomas. Dallas won the Eastern Division title, but Washington's 10–4 record was good for the "wild card" berth again. In the first round of the playoffs, the Redskins were beaten 35–20 by Minnesota.

MEMBERS OF THE HALL OF FAME:
Cliff Battles, Sammy Baugh, Bill Dudley, Glen (Turk) Edwards, Ray Flaherty, Otto Graham, Earl (Curly) Lambeau, Vince Lombardi, George Preston Marshall, Wayne Millner.

REDSKINS' RECORD, 1932–76

Year	Won	Lost	Tied	Pct.	Pts.	OP
Boston Braves						
1932	4	4	2	.500	55	79
Boston Redskins						
1933	5	5	2	.500	103	97
1934	6	6	0	.500	107	94
1935	2	8	1	.200	65	123
1936§	7	5	0	.583	149	110
Washington Redskins						
1937‡	8	3	0	.727	195	120
1938	6	3	2	.667	148	154
1939	8	2	1	.800	242	94
1940§	9	2	0	.818	245	142
1941	6	5	0	.545	176	174
1942‡	10	1	0	.909	227	102
1943§	6	3	1	.667	229	137
1944	6	3	1	.667	169	180
1945§	8	2	0	.800	209	121
1946	5	5	1	.500	171	191
1947	4	8	0	.333	295	367
1948	7	5	0	.583	291	287
1949	4	7	1	.364	268	339
1950	3	9	0	.250	232	326
1951	5	7	0	.417	183	296
1952	4	8	0	.333	240	287
1953	6	5	1	.545	208	215
1954	3	9	0	.250	207	432
1955	8	4	0	.667	246	222
1956	6	6	0	.500	183	225
1957	5	6	1	.455	251	230
1958	4	7	1	.364	214	268
1959	3	9	0	.250	185	350
1960	1	9	2	.100	178	309

Charles (Ki) Aldrich

Steve Bagarus

Don Bosseler

Al DeMao

Harry Gilmer

Rob Goode

Len Hauss

BOSTON BRAVES, 1932;
BOSTON REDSKINS, 1933–36;
WASHINGTON REDSKINS, 1937–76

Absher, Dick, LB, Maryland 1967
Adams, John T, Notre Dame 1945–49
Adams, Willie, LB, New Mexico St. 1965–66
Adducci, Nick, B, Nebraska 1954–55
Aguirre, Joe, E, St. Mary's, Calif. 1941, 1943–45
Akins, Frank, B, Washington State 1943–46
Alban, Dick, B, Northwestern 1952–55
Aldrich, Ki, C, Texas Christian 1941–42, 1945–47
Alford, Bruce, K, Texas Christian 1967
Allen, Gerry, B, Nebraska-Omaha 1967–69
Allen, John, C, Purdue 1955–58
Alston, Mack, TE, Maryland State 1970–72
Ananis, Vito, B, Boston College 1945
Anderson, Bill, E, Tennessee 1958–63
Anderson, Bob, RB, Colorado 1975
Anderson, Bruce, E, Willamette 1970
Andrako, Steve, C, Ohio State 1940
Arenz, Arnold, B, St. Louis 1934
Arneson, Jim, G, Arizona 1975
Artman, Corman, T, Stanford 1932
Atkeson, Dale, B, None 1954–56
Audet, Earl, T, USC 1945
Aveni, John, K, Indiana 1961
Avery, Don, T, USC 1946–47
Avery, Jim, E, No. Illinois 1966

B

Badaczewski, John, G, Western Reserve 1949–51
Bagarus, Steve, B, Notre Dame 1945–46, 1948
Bagdon, Ed, G, Michigan State 1952
Baker, Sam, K, Oregon State 1953, 1956–59
Baltzell, Dick, B, S.W. Kansas 1935
Bandy, Don, G, Tulsa 1967–68
Barber, Ernie, C, San Francisco 1945
Barber, Jim, T, San Francisco 1935–41
Barefoot, Ken, DE, Virginia Tech 1968
Barfield, Ken, T, Mississippi 1954
Barker, Ed, E, Washington State 1954
Barnes, Billy Ray, RB, Wake Forest 1962–63
Barnes, Walt, T, Nebraska 1966–68
Barnett, Steve, T, Oregon 1964
Barni, Roy, B, San Francisco 1955–56
Barrington, Tom, B, Ohio State 1966
Barry, Paul, B, Tulsa 1953
Bartos, Henry, G, North Carolina 1938
Bartos, Joe, B, Navy 1950
Bass, Mike, DB, Michigan 1969–73
Bassi, Dick, G, Santa Clara 1937
Battles, Cliff, B, West Va. Wesleyan 1932–37
Baugh, Sammy, QB, Texas Christian 1937–52
Baughan, Maxie, LB, Georgia Tech 1974
Bausch, Frank, C, Kansas 1934–36
Beatty, Ed, C, Mississippi 1961
Beban, Gary, QB, UCLA 1968–69
Bedore, Tom, G, None 1944
Beinor, Ed, T, Notre Dame 1941–42
Berrang, Ed, E, Villanova 1949–52
Berschet, Merv, G, Illinois 1954–55
Biggs, Verlon, DE, Jackson State 1971–75
Birlem, Keith, B, San Jose State 1939
Boensch, Fred, G, Stanford 1947–48
Boll, Don, T, Nebraska 1953–59
Bond, Chuck, T, Washington 1937–38
Bond, Randall, B, Washington 1938
Bosch, Frank, T, Colorado 1968–69
Bossler, Don, B, Miami 1957–64
Boswell, Ben, T, Texas Christian 1934
Braatz, Tom, DE, Marquette 1957–59
Bradley, Harold, E, Elon 1938–39
Bragg, Mike, K, Richmond 1968–76
Breding, Ed, LB, Texas A&M 1967–68
Breedlove, Rod, LB, Maryland 1960–64
Brewer, Homer, B, Mississippi 1960
Briggs, Bill, DE, Iowa 1966–67
Briggs, Bob, B, Central State, Okla. 1965
Brito, Gene, DE, Loyola, Calif. 1951–53, 1955–58
Britt, Ed, B, Holy Cross 1936–37
Britt, Oscar, G, Mississippi 1946
Brown, Bill, G, Arkansas 1951–52
Brown, Dan, E, Villanova 1950
Brown, Eddie, S, Tennessee 1975–76
Brown, Hardy, LB, Tulsa 1950
Brown, Larry, RB, Kansas State 1969–76
Brown, Tom, DB, Maryland 1969
Brueckman, Charley, C, Pittsburgh 1958
Brundige, Bill, DE, Colorado 1970–76
Brunet, Bob, RB, Louisiana Tech 1968, 1970–76
Budd, Frank, B, Villanova 1963
Buggs, Danny, WR, West Virginia 1976
Bukich, Rudy, QB, USC 1957–58
Buksar, George, B, Purdue 1951–52
Burman, George, G, Northwestern 1971–72
Burrell, John, B, Rice 1966–67
Busick, Sam, E, Ohio State 1936
Butkus, Carl, T, George Washington 1948
Butsko, Harry, LB, Maryland 1963
Butz, Dave, DE, Purdue 1975–76

C

Cafego, George, QB, Tennessee 1943
Campiglio, Bob, QB, West Liberty State 1933
Campora, Don, T, Pacific 1953
Carpe, Joseph, T, Millikin 1929
Carpenter, Preston, E, Arkansas 1964–66
Carr, Jim, LB, Morris Harvey 1964–65
Carroll, Jim, LB, Notre Dame 1966–68
Carroll, Leo, DE, San Diego State 1969–70
Carroll, Vic, T, Nevada 1936–42
Carson, John, E, Georgia 1954–59
Casares, Rick, RB, Florida 1965
Castiglia, Jim, B, Georgetown 1947–48
Cheroke, George, B, Ohio State 1946
Cherne, Hal, T, DePaul 1933
Christensen, Erik, E, Richmond 1956
Churchwell, Don, T, Mississippi 1959
Cichowski, Gene, B, Indiana 1958–59
Cifers, Ed, E, Tennessee 1941–42, 1946
Clair, Frank, E, Ohio State 1941
Clark, Jim, G, Oregon State 1952–53
Clark, Myers, B, Ohio State 1932
Clay, Billie, B, Mississippi 1966
Clay, Ozzie, B, Iowa State 1964
Cloud, John, B, William & Mary 1952–53
Cochran, Tom, B, Auburn 1949
Coia, Angelo, WR, USC 1964–65
Conkright, Bill, C, Oklahoma 1943
Collier, Jim, E, Arkansas 1963
Collins, Paul, E, Pittsburgh 1932–35
Concannon, Ernie, New York U. 1934–36
Condit, Meryln, B, Carnegie Tech 1945
Corbitt, Don, C, Arizona 1948
Couppee, Al, B, Iowa 1946
Cox, Bill, B, Duke 1951–52, 1955
Crabb, Claude, DB, Colorado 1962–63
Crane, Dennis, T, USC 1968–69
Crisler, Harold, E, San Jose State 1948–49
Croftcheck, Don, G, Indiana 1965–66
Cronin, Gene, E, Pacific 1961–62
Crossan, Dave, C, Maryland 1965–69
Crotty, Jim, B, Notre Dame 1960–61
Crow, Orien, C, Haskell 1933–34
Cudzik, Watt, C, Purdue 1954
Cunningham, Doug, RB, Mississippi 1974
Cunningham, Jim, B, Pittsburgh 1961–63
Cvercko, Andy, G, Northwestern 1963

D

Dale, Roland, E, Mississippi 1950
Darre, Bernie, G, Tulane 1961
Davidson, Ben, DT, Washington 1962–63
Davis, Andy, B, George Washington 1952
Davis, Fred, T, Alabama 1941–42, 1945
Davlin, Mike, T, San Francisco 1955
Day, Eagle, QB, Mississippi 1959–60
Deal, Rufus, B, Auburn 1942
DeCarlo, Art, B, Georgia 1956–57
DeCorrevant, Bill, B, Northwestern 1945
Dee, Bob, E, Holy Cross 1957–58
Deeks, Don, T, Washington 1947
DeFruiter, Bob, B, Nebraska 1945–47
Dekker, Al, C, Michigan State 1953
DeMao, Al, C, Duquesne 1945–53
Denson, Moses, RB, Maryland State 1974–75
Dess, Darrell, G, N. Carolina State 1965–66
Didion, John, LB, Oregon State 1969
Doll, Don, DB, USC 1953
Doolan, John, B, Georgetown 1945
Dorow, Al, QB, Michigan State 1954–56
Dow, Ken, B, Oregon State 1941
Dowda, Harry, B, Wake Forest 1949–53
Dowler, Boyd, WR, Colorado 1971
Drazenovich, Chuck, LB, Penn State 1950–59
Duckworth, Joe, E, Colgate 1947
Dudley, Bill, B, Virginia 1950–51, 1953
Dugan, Fred, E, Dayton 1961–63
Duich, Steve, G, San Diego State 1969
Dunn, Coye, B, USC 1943
Duncan, Leslie (Speedy), DB, Jackson State 1971–73
Dusek, Brad, LB, Texas A&M 1974–76
Dwyer, John, B, Loyola, Calif. 1951
Dye, Les, E, Syracuse 1944–45
Dyer, Henry, RB, Grambling 1969–70

E

Ecker, Enrique, T, John Carroll 1952
Edwards, Turk, T, Washington State 1932–40
Edwards, Weldon, T, Texas Christian 1948
Ellstrom, Marv, B, Oklahoma 1943
Elmore, Doug, B, Mississippi 1962
Elter, Leo, B, Duquesne 1955–57
Erickson, Carl C, Washington 1938–39
Erickson, Mike, C, Northwestern 1932
Evans, Charlie, RB, USC 1974

F

Fanucci, Mike, DE, Arizona State 1972
Farkas, Andy, B, Detroit 1938–44
Farman, Dick, G, Washington State 1939–43
Farmer, Tom, B, Iowa 1947–48
Feagin, Tom, G, Houston 1963
Felber, Fred, E, North Dakota 1932
Felton, Ralph, B, Maryland 1954–60
Ferris, Neil, B, Loyola, Calif. 1951–52
Filchock, Frank, QB, Indiana 1938–41, 1944–45
Florentino, Al, G, Boston College 1943–44
Fischer, Pat, CB, Nebraska 1968–76
Fisher, Bob, T, USC 1940
Foltz, Vernon, C, St. Vincent's 1944
Francis, Dave, B, Ohio State 1963
Frankian, Ike, E, St. Mary's, Calif. 1933
Freeman, Bob, B, Auburn 1962
Fritsch, Ted, C, St. Norbert 1976
Fryer, Brian, WR, Alberta 1976
Fugett, Jean, TE, Amherst 1976
Fulcher, Bill, G, Georgia Tech 1956–58
Fuller, Larry, B, None 1944–45

G

Gaffney, Jim, B, Tennessee 1945–46
Garzoni, Mike, B, USC 1947
Gentry, Lee, B, Tulsa 1941
German, Jim, B, Centre 1939
Gibson, Billy Joe, B, Tulsa 1943
Gilmer, Harry, QB, Alabama 1948–52, 1954
Glick, Gary, DB, Colorado A&M 1959–61
Gob, Art, E, Pittsburgh 1959–60
Gogolak, Charlie, K, Princeton 1966–68
Goode, Rob, B, Texas A&M 1949–51, 1954–55
Goodnight, Clyde, E, Tulsa 1949–50
Goodyear, John, B, Marquette 1942
Goosby, Tom, G, Baldwin-Wallace 1966
Grant, Bob, LB, Wake Forest 1971
Grant, Frank, WR, S. Colorado State 1973–76
Gray, Bill, G, Oregon State 1947–48
Grimm, Dan, C, Colorado 1969
Guglielmi, Ralph, QB, Notre Dame 1955, 1958–60

H

Hackbart, Dale, DB, Wisconsin 1961–63
Hageman, Fred, C, Kansas 1961–64
Haley, Dick, B, Pittsburgh 1959–60
Hall, Galen, QB, Penn State 1962
Hamlin, Gene, C, Western Michigan 1970
Hanburger, Chris, LB, North Carolina 1965–76
Hancock, Mike, TE, Idaho State 1973–75
Hanna, Elzaphan, G, South Carolina 1945

Dick James

Vic Janowicz

Bob Masterson

Ron McDole

Brig Owens

John Paluck

Jim Poldoley

Hansen, Ron, G, Minnesota 1954
Hare, Cecil, B, Gonzaga 1941–42, 1945
Hare, Ray, B, Gonzaga 1940–43
Harold, George, B, Allen 1968
Harraway, Charley, RB, San Jose St. 1969–73
Harris, Hank, G, Texas 1947–48
Harris, Jim, B, Howard Payne 1970
Harris, Rickie, DB, Arizona 1962–65, 1970
Hartley, Howard, B, Duke 1948
Hartman, Bill, QB, Georgia 1938
Hatcher, Ron, B, Michigan State 1962
Hauss, Len, C, Georgia 1964–76
Hayden, Ken, C, Arkansas 1943
Haymond, Alvin, S, Southern U. 1972
Haynes, Hall, B, Santa Clara 1950–53
Hazelwood, Ted, T, North Carolina 1953
Heath, Leon, B, Oklahoma 1951–53
Hecker, Norb, DB, Baldwin-Wallace 1955–57
Heenan, Pat, E, Notre Dame 1960
Hegarty, Bill, T, Villanova 1953
Hendershot, Larry, LB, Arizona State 1967
Henderson, Jon, WR, Colorado State 1970
Hendren, Bob, T, USC 1949–51
Hennessey, Jerry, E, Santa Clara 1952–53
Hermeling, Terry, T, Nevada 1970–76
Hernandez, Joe, E, Arizona 1964
Hickman, Dallas, DE, California 1976
Hill, Calvin, RB, Yale 1976
Hodgson, Pat, TE, Georgia 1966
Hoffman, Bob, B, USC 1940–41
Hoffman, John, E, Hawaii 1969–70
Hokuf, Steve, B, Nebraska 1933–35
Hollar, John, B, Appalachian State 1948–49
Holman, Willie, DE, So. Carolina State 1973
Holmer, Walt, B, Northwestern 1933
Horner, Sam, B, VMI 1960–61
Horstmann, Roy, B, Purdue 1933
Houghton, Jerry, T, Washington State 1950
Houston, Ken, S, Prairie View 1973–76
Houston, Walt, G, Purdue 1955
Howell, Millard, B, Alabama 1937
Hudson, Bob, G, Clemson 1959
Huff, Sam, LB, West Virginia 1964–67, 1969
Hughes, Hank, B, Oregon State 1932
Hughley, George, B, Cent. State, Okla. 1965
Hull, Mike, B, USC 1971–74
Hunter, Bill, B, Syracuse 1965
Hurley, George, B, Washington State 1932–33
Hyatt, Fred, WR, Auburn 1973

I

Imhof, Martin, DE, San Jose State 1974
Intriere, Marne, G, Loyola, Md. 1933–34
Irwin, Don, B, Colgate 1936–39
Izo, George, QB, Notre Dame 1961–64

J

Jackson, Leroy, B, Western Illinois 1962–63
Jackson, Steve, LB, Texas-Arlington 1966–67
Jackson, Trenton, B, Illinois 1967
Jacobs, Jack, B, Oklahoma 1946
Jaffurs, John, B, Penn State 1946
Jagielski, Harry, T, Indiana 1956
James, Dick, B, Oregon 1956–63
Janowicz, Vic, B, Ohio State 1954–55
Jaqua, Jon, B, Lewis & Clark 1970–72
Jefferson, Roy, WR, Utah 1971–76
Jencks, Bob, K-E, Miami, Ohio 1965
Jenkins, Jacque, B, Vanderbilt 1943, 1946–47
Johnson, Dennis, DT, Delaware 1976
Johnson, Larry, C, Haskell 1933–35, 1944
Johnson, Mitch, T, UCLA 1966–67, 1972
Johnson, Randy, QB, Texas A&I 1976
Johnston, Jim, B, Washington 1939–40
Jones, Chuck, E, George Washington 1955
Jones, David (Deacon), DE, S. Carolina State 1974
Jones, Harvey, B, Baylor 1947
Jones, Jimmy, DE, Wichita State 1971–73
Jones, Larry, WR, Northeast Missouri State 1974–75
Jones, Stan, T, Maryland 1966
Jordan, Jeff, RB, Washington 1971–72
Justice, Charlie (Choo Choo), B, N. Carolina .. 1950, 1952–54
Justice, Ed, B, Gonzaga 1936–42

Junker, Steve, E, Xavier 1961–62
Jurgensen, Sonny, QB, Duke 1964–74
Juzwik, Steve, B, Notre Dame 1942

K

Kahn, Ed, G, North Carolina 1935–37
Kammerer, Carl, DE, Pacific 1963–69
Kamp, Jim, T, Oklahoma City 1933
Kantor, Joe, B, Notre Dame 1966
Karamatic, George, B, Gonzaga 1938
Karcher, Jim, G, Ohio State 1936–39
Karras, Lou, T, Purdue 1950–51
Katrishen, Mike, T, So. Mississippi 1948–49
Keenan, John, G, South Carolina 1944–45
Kelley, Gordon, LB, Georgia 1962–63
Kelly, John, T, Florida A&M 1966–67
Kenneally, George, E, St. Bonaventure 1929, 1932
Kerr, Jim, B, Penn State 1961–62
Khayat, Bob, K, Mississippi 1960, 1962–63
Khayat, Ed, T, Tulane 1957, 1962–63
Kilmer, Billy, QB, UCLA 1971–76
Kimmel, J.D., T, Houston 1955–56
Kincaid, Jim, B, South Carolina 1954
Knight, Curt, K, Coast Guard 1969–73
Koniszewski, John, T, George Washington 1945–46, 1948
Kopay, Dave, RB, Washington 1969–70
Kovatch, John, E, Notre Dame 1942, 1946
Krakoski, Joe, B, Illinois 1961
Krause, Max, B, Gonzaga 1937–40
Krause, Paul, DB, Iowa 1964–67
Krause, Red, C, St. Louis 1937–40
Kresky, Joe, G, Wisconsin 1932
Krueger, Al, E, USC 1941–42
Kuchta, Frank, C, Notre Dame 1958–59
Kupp, Jake, G, Washington 1966
Kuziel, Bob, C, Pittsburgh 1975–76

L

Laaveg, Paul, T, Iowa 1970–75
Lapka, Ted, E, St. Ambrose 1943–44, 1946
Larson, Pete, B, Cornell 1967–68
Lasse, Dick, T, Syracuse 1960–61
Lavender, Joe, CB, San Diego State 19
Lawrence, Don, T, Notre Dame 1959–61
LeBaron, Eddie, QB, Pacific 1952–53, 1955–59
Lemek, Ray, T, Notre Dame 1957–61
Lennan, Reid, G, None 1945
Leon, Tony, G, Alabama 1943
Lewis, Dan, B, Wisconsin 1965
Lipscomb, Paul, T, Tennessee 1950–54
Livingston, Howie, B, Fullerton J.C. 1948–50
Lockett, J.W., B, Central State, Okla. 1964
Lolotai, Al, G, Weber State 1945
Long, Bob, WR, Wichita 1969
Lookabaugh, John, E, Maryland 1946–47
Looney, Joe Don, RB, Oklahoma 1966–67
Lorch, Karl, DE, USC 1976
Love, John, B, N. Texas State 1967
Lowe, Gary, B, Michigan State 1956–57
Luce, Lew, B, Penn State 1961
Lynch, Dick, DB, Notre Dame 1958

M

MacAfee, Ken, E, Alabama 1959
Macioszczck, Art, B, West. Michigan 1948
MacMurdo, Jim, T, Pittsburgh 1932–33
Madarik, Elmer, B, Detroit 1948
Malinchak, Bill, WR, Indiana 1970–74, 1976
Malone, Charley, E, Texas A&M 1934–40, 1942
Manton, Tillie, B, Texas Christian 1938
Marciniak, Ron, G, Kansas State 1955
Marcus, Peter, E, Kentucky 1944
Marshall, Rich, T, Stephen F. Austin 1966
Martin, Aaron, B, N. Carolina Coll. 1968
Martin, Jim, K, Notre Dame 1964
Mason, Tommy, B, Tulane 1971
Masterson, Bob, E, Miami 1938–43
Mattson, Riley, T, Oregon 1961–64
Mazurek, Fred, B, Pittsburgh 1965–66
McCabe, Dick, B, Pittsburgh 1959
McChesney, Bob, E, UCLA 1936
McDole, Ron, DE, Nebraska 1971–76
McDonald, Ray, RB, Idaho 1967–68

McKee, Paul, E, Syracuse 1947–48
McKeever, Marlin, LB, USC 1968–70
McLinton, Harold, LB, Southern U. 1969–76
McNamara, Bob, E, New York U. 1934
McNeil, Clifton, WR, Grambling 1971–72
McPhail, Harold, B, Xavier 1934–45
McRae, Stan, E, Michigan State 1946
Meade, Jim, B, Maryland 1939–40
Meadows, Ed, T, Duke 1959
Mellinger, Steve, E, Kentucky 1956–57
Merkle, Ed, G, Oklahoma A&M 1944
Menasco, Don, B, Texas 1954
Mercein, Chuck, RB, Yale 1969
Michaels, Ed, G, Villanova 1937
Micka, Mike, B, Colgate 1944–45
Miller, Allen, LB, Ohio U 1962–63
Miller, Clark, E, Utah State 1969
Miller, Fred, DT, Pacific 1955
Miller, John, T, Boston College 1956, 1958–59
Miller, Tom, E, Hampden Sydney 1945
Millner, Wayne, E, Notre Dame 1936–41, 1945
Mingo, Gene, K, None 1967
Mitchell, Bobby, WR-RB, Illinois 1962–68
Modzelewski, Dick, T, Maryland 1953–54
Momsen, Tony, C, Michigan 1952
Monachino, Jim, B, California 1955
Monaco, Ray, G, Holy Cross 1944
Mont, Tommy, B, Maryland 1947–49
Moore, Chuck, G, Arkansas 1962
Moore, Wilbur, B, Minnesota 1939–46
Moran, Jim, G, Holy Cross 1935–36
Morgan, Bob, T, Maryland 1954
Morgan, Boyd, B, USC 1939–40
Morgan, Mike, LB, Louisiana State 1968
Morley, Sam, E, Stanford 1954
Moseley, Mark, K, Stephen F. Austin 1974–76
Moss, Joe, T, Maryland 1952
Mul-Key, Herb, RB, None 1972–74
Musgrove, Spain, DT, Utah State 1967–69
Musick, Jim, B, USC 1932–33, 1935–36

N

Natowich, Andy, B, Holy Cross 1944
Nelson, Ralph, RB, None 1975
Niemi, Laurie, T, Washington State 1949–53
Ninowski, Jim, QB, Michigan State 1967–68
Nisby, John, G, Pacific 1962–64
Nix, Doyle, B, Southern Methodist 1958–59
Nobile, Leo, G, Penn State 1947
Nock, George, RB, Morgan State 1972
Norman, Jim, T, None 1955
Norris, Hal, B, California 1955–56
North, Jim, T, Central Washington 1944
Norton, Jim, T, Washington 1968
Nott, Doug, B, Detroit 1935
Nugent, Dan, G, Auburn 1976
Nussbaumer, Bob, E, Michigan 1947–48

O

O'Brien, Fran, T, Michigan State 1960–66
O'Brien, Gail, T, Nebraska 1934–36
O'Dell, Stu, LB, Indiana 1974–76
Oden, Olaf, B, None 1932
Olsson, Les, G, Mercer 1934–38
Olszewski, John, B, California 1958–60
Osborne, Tom, E, Hastings, Neb. 1960–61
Ostrowski, Chet, E, Notre Dame 1954–59
Owens, Brig, DB, Cincinnati 1966–76
Owens, Don, T, So. Mississippi 1957

P

Paluck, John, E, Pittsburgh 1956, 1959–65
Pape, Oran, B, Iowa 1932
Papit, John, B, Virginia 1951–53
Pardee, Jack, LB, Texas A&M 1971–72
Parks, Ed, C, Oklahoma 1938–40
Pasqua, Joe, T, Southern Methodist 1943
Paternoster, Angelo, G, Georgetown 1943
Peebles, Jim, E, Vanderbilt 1946–49, 1951
Pelligrini, Bob, LB, Maryland 1962–65
Pepper, Gene, G, Missouri 1950–53
Pergine, John, LB, Notre Dame 1973–75
Peters, Floyd, T, S.F. State 1970

Myron Pottios

Vince Promuto

Ray Schoenke

Diron Talbert

Hugh (Bones) Taylor

Mike Thomas

LaVern Torgeson

Peters, Volney, T, USC 1954–57
Peterson, Russ, T, Montana 1932
Petitbon, Richie, S, Tulane 1971–73
Piasecky, Alex, E, Duke 1943–45
Pierce, Dan, RB, Memphis State 1970
Pinckert, Erny, B, USC 1932–40
Plansky, Tony, B, Georgetown 1932
Planutis, Gerry, B, Michigan State 1956
Podoley, Jim, RB, Central Michigan 1957–60
Poillon, Dick, B, Canisius 1942, 1946–49
Polsfoot, Fran, E, Washington State 1953
Pottios, Myron, LB, Notre Dame 1971–73
Pressley, Lee, C, Oklahoma 1945
Prestel, Jim, T, Idaho 1967
Promuto, Vince, G, Holy Cross 1960–70

Q

Quinlan, Bill, E, Michigan 1965
Quirk, Ed, B, Missouri 1948–51

R

Ramsey, Knox, G, William & Mary 1952–53
Rector, Ron, B, Northwestern 1966
Reed, Alvin, TE, Prairie View 1973–75
Reed, Bob, G, Tennessee State 1965
Reger, John, LB, Pittsburgh 1964–66
Rehnquist, Milt, C, Bethany, Kan. 1932
Renfro, Will, T, Memphis State 1957–59
Rentner, Pug, G, Northwestern 1934–36
Reynolds, Mack, QB, Louisiana State 1960
Ribar, Frank, G, Duke 1943
Ricca, Jim, G, Georgetown 1951–54
Richter, Pat, E, Wisconsin 1963–70
Riggins, John, RB, Kansas 1976
Riley, John, T, Northwestern 1933
Roberts, Jack, B, Georgia 1932
Roberts, Walter, WR, San Jose State 1969–70
Robinson, Dave, LB, Penn State 1973–74
Rock, Walter, T, Maryland 1968–73
Rosato, Sal, B, Villanova 1945–47
Rosso, George, B, Ohio State 1954
Roussel, Tom, LB, So. Mississippi 1968–70
Roussos, Mike, T, Pittsburgh 1948–49
Runnels, Tom, B, N. Texas State 1956–57
Russell, Torrance, T, Auburn 1939–40
Rust, Reg, B, Oregon State 1932
Rutgens, Joe, DT, Illinois 1961–69
Ruthstrom, Ralph, B, Southern Methodist 1947
Ryan, Frank, QB, Rice 1969–70
Ryczek, Dan, C, Virginia 1973–75
Rykovich, Julie, B, Notre Dame 1952–53
Rymkus, Lou, T, Notre Dame 1943
Rzempoluch, Ted, T, Virginia 1963

S

Saenz, Ed, B, USC 1946–51
Salem, Ed, B, Alabama 1951
Salter, Bryant, S, Pittsburgh 1974–75
Sample, Johnny, DB, Maryland State 1963–65
Sanchez, John, T, San Francisco 1947–49
Sanders, Lonnie, DB, Michigan State 1963–67
Sandifer, Dan, T, Louisiana State 1948–49
Sanford, Haywood, E, Alabama 1940
Sarboe, Phil, B, Washington State 1934
Sardisco, Tony, G, Tulane 1956
Saul, Ron, G, Michigan State 1976
Scafide, John, T, Tulane 1933
Scarbath, Jack, QB, Maryland 1953–54
Schick, Doyle, LB, Kansas 1961
Schilling, Ralph, E, Oklahoma City 1940
Schmidt, Kermit, E, Cal. Poly 1932
Schoenke, Ray, G, Southern Methodist 1966–75
Schrader, Jim, C, Notre Dame 1954, 1956–61
Schuette, Paul, G, Wisconsin 1932
Scott, Jake, S, Georgia 1976
Scotti, Ben, B, Maryland 1959–61
Scudero, Joe, B, San Francisco 1954–58
Seals, George, G, Missouri 1964
Sebastian, Mike, B, Pittsburgh 1935
Sebek, Nick, B, Indiana 1950
Seedborg, John, K, Arizona State 1965
Seno, Frank, B, George Wash. 1943–44, 1949
Severson, Jeff, DB, Long Beach State 1972
Seymour, Bob, B, Oklahoma 1940–45
Sharp, Ev, T, Cal. Poly 1944–45
Shepherd, Bill, B, Western Maryland 1935
Shiner, Dick, QB, Maryland 1964–66
Shoener, Herb, E, Iowa 1948–49
Shorter, Jim, B, Detroit 1964–67
Shugart, Clyde, G, Iowa State 1939–44
Shula, Don, DB, John Carroll 1957
Siano, Tony, C, Fordham 1932
Siegert, Herb, G, Illinois 1949–51
Siemering, Larry, C, San Francisco 1935–36
Sinko, Steve, T, Duquesne 1934–36
Sistrunk, Manny, DT, Arkansas AM&N 1960–75
Slivinski, Steve, G, Washington 1939–43
Smith, Ben, E, Alabama 1937
Smith, Dick, B, Northwestern 1967–68
Smith, Ed, B, New York U. 1936
Smith, George, C, California 1937, 1941–43
Smith, Hugh, E, Kansas 1962
Smith, Jerry, TE, Arizona State 1966–76
Smith, Jim, B, Oregon 1968
Smith, John, E, Stanford 1943
Smith, Larry, RB, Florida 1974
Smith, Riley, QB, Alabama 1936–38
Snead, Norm, QB, Wake Forest 1961–63
Sneddon, Bob, B, St. Mary's, Calif. 1944
Snidow, Ron, DE, Oregon 1963–67
Snowden, Jim, T, Notre Dame 1965–71
Sobolenski, Joe, G, Michigan 1949
Sommer, Mike, B, George Wash. 1958–59, 1961
Sommers, John, C, UCLA 1947
Spaniel, Frank, B, Notre Dame 1950
Sparks, Dave, G, South Carolina 1954
Spellman, John, E, Brown 1932
Spirida, Jon, E, St. Anselm's 1939
Stacco, Ed, T, Colgate 1948
Stallings, Don, E, North Carolina 1960
Stanfel, Dick, G, San Francisco 1956–58
Starke, George, T, Columbia 1973–76
Stasica, Leo, B, Colorado 1943
Steber, John, G, Georgia Tech 1946–50
Steffen, Jim, B, UCLA 1961–65
Stenn, Paul, T, Villanova 1946
Stephens, Louis, G, San Francisco 1955–60
Steponovich, Mike, G, St. Mary's, Calif. 1933
Stits, Bill, B, UCLA 1959
Stokes, Tim, T, Oregon 1975
Stone, Ken, S, Vanderbilt 1973–75
Stout, Pete, B, Texas Christian 1949–50
Stovall, Dick, C, Abilene Christian 1949
Stralka, Clem, G, Georgetown 1938–42, 1945–46
Stuart, Jim, T, Oregon 1941
Sturt, Fred, G, Bowling Green 1974
Stynchula, Andy, DT, Penn State 1960–63
Suminski, Dave, G, Wisconsin 1953
Sutton, Ed, B, North Carolina 1957–59
Sweeney, Walt, G, Syracuse 1974–76
Sykes, Bob, B, San Jose State 1952
Szafaryn, Len, T, North Carolina 1949

T

Talbert, Diron, DT, Texas 1971–76
Taylor, Charley, WR, Arizona State 1964–75
Taylor, Hugh (Bones), E, Oakland City 1947–54
Taylor, Mike, T, USC 1971
Taylor, Roosevelt, S, Grambling 1972
Temple, Mark, B, Oregon 1936
Tereshinski, Joe, E, Georgia 1947–54
Theismann, Joe, QB, Notre Dame 1974–76
Theofiledes, Harry, QB, Waynesburg 1968
Thomas, Duane, RB, West Texas State 1973
Thomas, George, B, Oklahoma 1950–51
Thomas, Mike, RB, Nevada-Las Vegas 1975–76
Thomas, Ralph, E, San Francisco 1955–56
Thomas, Spencer, S, Washburn 1975
Thurlow, Steve, RB, Stanford 1966–68
Tillman, Russ, LB, No. Arizona 1970–76
Titchenal, Bob, C, San Jose State 1940–42
Todd, Dick, RB, Texas A&M 1939–42, 1945–48
Toneff, Bob, T, Notre Dame 1959–64
Torgeson, LaVern, LB, Wash. State 1955–57
Tosi, Flavio, E, Boston College 1934–36
Tracy, Tom, B, Tennessee 1963–64
Tucker, Dick, B, Manhattan 1938
Turley, Doug, E, Scranton 1944–48
Turner, Jay, B, George Washington 1938–39
Tyrer, Jim, T, Ohio State 1974

U

Ucovich, Mitch, T, San Jose State 1944
Uhrinyak, Steve, G, Marshall 1939
Ulinski, Harry, C, Kentucky 1950–51, 1953–56
Ungerer, Joe, T, Fordham 1944–45

V

Vactor, Ted, DB, Nebraska 1969–74
Varty, Mike, LB, Northwestern 1974
Venuto, Sam, B, Guilford 1952
Vereb, Ed, RB, Maryland 1960
Voytek, Ed, G, Purdue 1957–58

W

Wade, Bob, B, Morgan State 1969
Walters, Tom, B, So. Mississippi 1964–67
Walton, Frank, G, Pittsburgh 1934–35
Walton, Joe, E, Pittsburgh 1957–60
Ward, Bill, G, Washington State 1946–47
Ward, David, G, New Mexico 1933
Washington, Fred, T, N. Texas State 1968
Waters, Dale, E, Florida 1932–33
Watson, Jim, C, Pacific 1945
Watson, Sid, B, Northwestern 1958
Watts, George, B, Appalachian State 1942
Weatherall, Jim, T, Oklahoma 1958
Weisenbaugh, Henry, B, Pittsburgh 1935–36
Weldon, Larry, B, Presbyterian 1944–45
Weller, Lou, B, Haskell 1933
Wells, Billy, B, Michigan State 1954, 1956–57
Westfall, Ed, B, Ohio Wesleyan 1932–33
Whited, Marvin, G, Oklahoma 1942, 1945
Whitfield, A. D., RB, N. Texas State 1966–68
Whitlow, Bob, C, Arizona 1960–61
Wilbur, John, G, Stanford 1971–73
Wilde, George, B, Texas A&M 1947
Wilkin, Willie, T, St. Mary's, Calif. 1938–43
Wilkins, Roy, G, Georgia 1960–61
Williams, Fred, T, Arkansas 1964–65
Williams, Gerard, CB, Langston 1976
Williams, John, B, USC 1952–53
Williams, Sid, LB, Southern U. 1967
Williamson, Ernie, T, North Carolina 1947
Willis, Larry, CB, Texas-El Paso 1973
Wingate, Heath, C, Bowling Green 1967
Winslow, Doug, WR, Drake 1976
Witucki, Casimir, G, Indiana 1950–51, 1953–56
Woodruff, Lee, B, Mississippi 1932
Woodward, Dick, C, Iowa 1952
Wooten, John, G, Colorado 1968
Wright, Steve, T, Alabama 1970
Wright, Ted, B, Denton Teachers, Tex. 1934–35
Wulff, Jim, B, Michigan State 1960–61
Wyant, Fred, QB, West Virginia 1956
Wyche, Sam, QB, Furman 1971–73
Wycoff, Doug, B, Georgia Tech 1934
Wysocki, Pete, LB, Western Michigan 1975–76

Y

Yonaker, John, E, Notre Dame 1952
Youel, Jim, B, Iowa 1946–48
Young, Bill, T, Alabama 1937–42, 1946
Young, Roy, T, Texas A&M 1938
Yowarsky, Walt, E, Kentucky 1951, 1954

Z

Zagers, Bert, B, Michigan St. 1955, 1957–58
Zeno, Joe, G, Holy Cross 1942–44
Zimmerman, Roy, B, San Jose St. 1940–42

Extinct Teams, Extinct Leagues

The Stapleton Stapes, a professional football team on Staten Island in New York's harbor in the twenties, made this announcement to its fans in a game program in 1928:

After many conferences with the officials of this club the National Football League has agreed to sanction the playing of games between our club and the members of that League. It has been our ambition for some time past to be admitted to membership in the National League. Up to this present time our attendance records have not been sufficient to justify league action in granting us a franchise. But we are confident that Staten Island football fans want their team represented in the big League, and no effort or expense on our part will be spared to accomplish this purpose. We therefore make this appeal for increased support. Come and see all of our games and bring a friend.

STAPLETON FOOTBALL CLUB

Stapes fans came to see enough games—and brought their friends often enough—that the team remained in the NFL from 1929 until 1932 when, in the depths of the Great Depression, the franchise joined the many other pro teams and, indeed, entire leagues, that have gone defunct since 1920.

Being in a league is essential for lasting success in pro football; no independent team endures for long. A team in a league can get a schedule. The stars, the big gate attractions of the league, will play at its stadium. Its games will have more meaning because it is playing for a championship. It can attract fans, operate concessions and parking, get a radio contract, sell programs, be guaranteed a share of gate receipts on the road and, in recent years, share in a common network television contract.

A parade of NFL teams failed in the twenties. Canton, hotbed of early pro football a quarter-century before and league champion in 1922 and 1923, dropped out of the league. So did Pottsville, which had disputed the Chicago Cardinals' 1925 championship; the Frankford Yellowjackets, Providence Steamroller, Stapleton Stapes, and many more. The game moved to the cities and every small town team vanished—every one except the indomitable Green Bay Packers.

The NFL had 22 teams in 1926 but by 1932 it had only 8. The next year, 1933, was one of reorganization. The league adopted divisions and an annual championship game. Since then, it has lost only three of its teams—the Cincinnati Reds-St. Louis Gunners in 1934, the Brooklyn Dodgers-Tigers in 1944, and the Boston Yanks-New York Bulldogs-New York Yanks-Dallas Texans, after a long odyssey and no little agony, in 1952.

It was commonplace for football teams of the past to take the names of baseball teams with which they shared stadiums. The new NFL expansion franchise at Crosley Field in Cincinnati in 1933 adopted the nickname of the city's baseball team, "Reds."

It was the year the NFL expanded to 10 teams and split them into divisions. The Philadelphia Eagles and Pittsburgh Pirates, later changed to Steelers, also began that year.

The coaches of the 1933 Reds were named Al Jolley and Mike Palm. The team won three, lost six, and tied one, "better than average for an expansion team," a former player recalls.

Jolley and Palm left the team in 1934. Quarterback Myers (Algy) Clark became the Reds' coach. They began dismally and drew small crowds. A former player told writer Paul Stillwell in 1974 that the Reds' ends and backs ran poor pass patterns, and back Les (Red) Corzine recalled that the team's attack had "no deception whatever."

A Cincinnati paper reported "Weakness continues to brew in the tackle positions, and the ends, but the loudest cry is, 'Our kingdom for a tackle.'"

In August, 1934, an arrangement was made with interests in St. Louis to move the team there. The other NFL owners would not allow it, however, because of the additional travel expenses it would cause. But as attendance and gate receipts in Cincinnati declined further, the NFL relented and approved the transfer to St. Louis.

An independent professional team already existed in St. Louis. It played teams in Memphis, Kansas City, and other nearby cities. It was headquartered at a St. Louis National Guard armory and was called the Gunners. Charles (Chile) Walsh was its coach. (A decade later, Walsh and his brother, Adam, would lead the 1945 Cleveland Rams to the NFL championship as general manager and coach, respectively.)

A merger was arranged. The tattered remains of the Reds arrived in November. Six players made the move. The Gunners were by far the majority party so their name was adopted by the hybrid team. Thus a team that had very likely never received a certificate of membership in the NFL or attended one of its annual meetings as a bona fide member, played three games in the league in November and December, 1934, and won one, lost two.

The Reds-Gunners fell into financial ruin. Their income was attached. A professional soccer league in St. Louis that had been playing pregame matches sought part of the money. There were debts in Cincinnati still remaining to be paid. Creditors and tax collectors kept company with the team. It ceased operations still owing some of the salaries due its players in two cities, money still owed to this day.

But this ill-fated franchise left one record. Gil Lefebvre, a Reds-Gunners back, returned a punt 98 yards for a touchdown December 3, 1933 against Brooklyn. His record has been tied twice but never broken.

CINCINNATI REDS/ST. LOUIS GUNNERS, 1933–34

Abruzzino, Frank, C, Colgate 1933
Alford, Gene, B. Texas Tech 1934
Andrews, Jabby, B. Texas 1934
Arial, Dave (Gump), E. Auburn 1934
Aspatore, Ed, T, Marquette 1934

B

Bausch, Jim, B, Kansas 1933
Berner, Milford, C, Syracuse 1933
Blondin, Tom, G, West Virginia Wesleyan 1933
Braidwood, Chuck, E, Chattanooga 1933
Burdick, Lloyd, T, Illinois 1933
Bushby, Tom, B, Kansas State 1934

C

Casper, Cy, B, TCU 1934
Caywood, Les, G, St. John's 1933–34
Clark, Myers (Algy), B, Ohio State 1933–34
Cole, Pete, G, Trinity (Tex.) 1934
Corzine, Les (Red), B. Davis & Elkins 1933–34
Crakes, Joe, E, South Dakota 1933

D

Diehl, Charlie, G, Idaho 1934
Draveling, Leo, T, Michigan 1933

E

Elkins, Fait (Chief), B, Haskell 1933
Elser, Earl, B, Butler 1934

F

Feather, Elwin (Tiny), B, Kansas State 1934

G

Gladden, Mack, E, Missouri 1934
Grant, Ross, G, NYU 1933–34

H

Hanson, Homer, G, Kansas State 1934
Hilpert, Hal, B, Oklahoma City 1933
Howell, Foster, T, TCU 1934

J

Johnston, Swede, B, Marquette 1934

L

LaPresta, Benny, B, St. Louis 1934
Lay, Russ, G, Michigan State 1934

Lee, Biff, G. Oklahoma 1933–34
Lefebvre, Gil, B, none 1933–34
Lewis, Bill, B, Northwestern 1934
Lyon, George, T, Kansas State 1934

M

Maples, Tal, C, Tennessee 1934
McGirl, Len, G, Missouri 1934
McLaughlin, Jim, B, Villanova 1934
McLeod, Russ, C, St. Louis 1934
Montgomery, Bill, T, St. Louis 1934
Mooney, Jim, E, Georgetown 1933–34
Moore, Cliff, B, Penn State 1934
Moses, Don, E, USC 1933
Moss, Paul E, Purdue 1934
Mott, Norman, B, Georgia 1934
Mulleneaux, Lee, C, Arizona 1934
Munday, George (Sunny), T, Kansas State Teachers . 1934

N

Norby, John, B, Idaho 1934

P

Palm, Mike, B, Penn State 1933
Parriott, Bill, B, West Virginia 1934
Pope, Lew, B, Purdue 1933–34
Powell, Dick, E, Davis & Elkins 1933–34

R

Rapp, Manny, B, St. Louis 1934
Reynolds, Homer, G, Tulsa 1934
Rogers, John, C, Notre Dame 1933–34
Rogge, George, E, Iowa 1934

S

Sandberg, Sandy, T, Iowa Wesleyan 1934
Sark, Harvey, G, Phillips 1934
Saumer, Syl, B, St. Olaf 1934
Schmidt, Kermit, E, Santa Clara 1933
Senn, Bill, B, Knox 1934
Sohn, Ben, B, Washington 1934
Squyres, Seaman, B, Rice 1933
Stevenson, Norris, B, Arizona State 1934

T

Tackwell, Cookie, E, Kansas State 1933–34

V

Vokaty, Otto, B, Heidelberg 1934

W

Weldin, Hal, C, Northwestern 1934
Wiberg, Ossie, B, Nebraska Wesleyan 1933
Wilging, Cole, T, Xavier 1934
Wilkerson, Basil, E, Oklahoma City 1934
Workman, Blake, B, Tulsa 1934

Z

Zunker, Charlie, T, Southwest Texas State 1934

Idle stadiums in winter give birth to pro football teams. Empty seats foster dreams of success in the minds of would-be owners. And none have been more alluring than those in New York City's Ebbets Field and Yankee Stadium, which have given life to more teams—and seen more of them fail—than any other stadiums in the country. During the years that the Giants of the NFL held forth at the Polo Grounds, many other teams, sometimes members of the NFL, sometimes the all-important New York foundations for rival leagues, operated at the other stadiums. As a result, no other city can compare with Gotham for the variety of its experiences in pro football.

The Brooklyn Dodgers of 1930–43 are filed away in history, a curious artifact with the same name as the better-known baseball team that was its landlord at Ebbets Field. But if the football Dodgers became an obscure part of history, it is also true that they were the extinct NFL team that lasted longer than any other. They had colorful owners such as John (Shipwreck) Kelly and Dan Topping. They had two famous coaches, George (Potsy) Clark and Dr. Jock Sutherland. Two of their former players, Frank (Bruiser) Kinard and Clarence (Ace) Parker, are in the Hall of Fame, and no other extinct team since 1933 can make that statement.

The Dodgers never won a championship but they were one of the best teams in the NFL in 1940 and 1941 under Sutherland. They then returned to mediocrity and, in 1944, seeking changes for the

The Cincinnati Reds turn out for passing practice in 1933; number 30 at right is Gil Lefebvre.

better, became the Brooklyn Tigers. The changes did not work and the team lost every game it played. It dropped out of sight but reappeared in 1945 to merge with the Boston Yanks and then, in 1946, jumped to a rival league—the only NFL team since the twenties to do so—and went to its death along with the 1946–49 All-America Football Conference.

"Everything happens to the Dodgers," a popular saying went. The first Brooklyn team in the NFL, called the Lions, was headed by a man named Eddie Butler and entered the league in 1926. There was, however, also an American Football League team playing at Ebbets Field that year, called the Horsemen. That team had two of the former Four Horsemen of Notre Dame, Elmer Layden and Harry Stuhldreher, in its backfield. They failed to become pro football sensations. The two teams in Brooklyn fell on hard times and so they merged and became the Brooklion Horsemen.

When that team folded, it was absorbed by the New York Yankees of AFL founder C.C. Pyle. But his team also lasted only two years in the NFL, 1927–28, and the equipment and some of the manpower of the former Horsemen and Yankees joined the new Stapleton Stapes on Staten Island.

A new and more lasting Brooklyn team began in 1930. Bill Dwyer and John Depler purchased the Dayton, Ohio, Triangles and moved them to Ebbets Field. This was the Dodgers team that would last for 14 years.

It was not particularly successful its first three seasons. Depler and former New York Giants' star tailback Benny Friedman were its coaches. In 1933, however, it began a period in which it was not always a big winner but it was always interesting. Two more former Giants, Chris Cagle and John (Shipwreck) Kelly, joined the team, became its star backfield players, and then, in a move perhaps unprecedented in pro football history, bought it.

Kelly was a dashing and handsome blond-haired figure from the University of Kentucky who had been timed at 9.8 seconds in the 100-yard dash. He was a playboy, a flamboyant and visible item on the New York City social scene when he was not playing football. He was one of many "Shipwreck Kellys." That was the name of a shipwreck victim in maritime lore, and it was also the name of a noted flagpole sitter and daredevil of the twenties.

Kelly and Cagle drew the attention of Dan Topping to the Dodgers. He became their partner and later bought the team outright from them. His ownership of the Dodgers began his involvement in professional sports. A millionaire, perpetually tanned and handsome, he later was the owner—along with Del Webb—of baseball's New York Yankees in their great years after World War II. Topping and Webb sold the Yankees to the Columbia Broadcasting System.

The football Dodgers of the mid-thirties, however, were not as successful for Topping. In 1935, co-owner Kelly set out to land Alabama's star end Don Hutson. He scouted Hutson at the Rose Bowl and so did the Green Bay Packers. This was one year before the institution of the NFL draft, and Huston signed contracts with both teams. A race in the United States mail began. The two contracts reached NFL Commissioner Joe Carr on a Monday morning but Green Bay's arrived at 8:30 A.M. and the Dodgers' contract arrived at 8:47 A.M. Carr awarded Hutson to Green Bay and he went on to become one of the greatest players in NFL history.

A determined Kelly tried still another measure to improve the Dodgers in 1936. A newspaper story of the day was headlined, "Kelly Swears Off Night Life to Aid Dodgers."

"No more night clubs and late hours for John (Shipwreck) Kelly," the story began. "The vice president of the Brooklyn Dodgers has decided to don his old moleskins again in a desperate effort to end the losing streak of his football club.... It will be interesting to see the blond battler from Kentucky running around end again." He apparently had little success,

however, because the Dodgers won only three games.

John (Cap'n Jack) McEwan and Paul Schissler were Brooklyn's head coaches in the mid-thirties. George (Potsy) Clark took over in 1937. He had coached the 1935 NFL champion Detroit Lions, wrote a popular book about football, and tutored the similarly named Earl (Dutch) Clark at Detroit.

Joining Brooklyn in 1937, Potsy Clark acquired another great player, Clarence (Ace) Parker. A former All-America tailback at Duke University, Parker, at 5 foot 11 inches and 168 pounds, became one of the greatest all-round players in NFL history. He ran, passed, caught passes, punted, placekicked, returned punts and kickoffs, and played defense. He also played professional baseball and he twice broke his ankle doing that in the summertime and still reported as usual to play football with the Dodgers.

The Dodgers got another exceptional player when Frank (Bruiser) Kinard joined them in 1938. He was considered a big, bruising tackle even though he weighed only 195 pounds at the start of his career and 218 when it ended. He was a terror in the line on both offense and defense.

Despite having those two players in the lineup and Clark as coach, Brooklyn won only 11 games in the three seasons from 1937–39. Topping then hired Dr. John Bain (Jock) Sutherland, who had developed two national championship teams at the University of Pittsburgh, as Dodgers' coach. Sutherland led Brooklyn to its best seasons ever, 8–3 in 1940 and second place in the Eastern Division, and 7–4 in 1941.

Operating Sutherland's single wing formation, Parker became the outstanding player in the league in 1940. In a game against the Cleveland Rams, he had a hand in every point the Dodgers scored in a come-from-behind 29–14 victory. He intercepted a pass and returned it 68 yards for a touchdown. He threw two touchdown passes. He intercepted another pass and went 43 yards for a touchdown. He ran 19 yards to set up a field goal . . . and then was the holder for the field goal.

Brooklyn held "Ace Parker Day" on a Sunday in November, 1940. Rain fell on the proceedings and, in addition, the Chicago Cardinals took a 9–0 lead over the Dodgers. "The second half opened with a Brooklyn bobble and the Cardinals appeared to be headed for more points," the *New York Daily Mirror* reported. "It looked like a dismal Ace Parker Day. Too bad, everybody said, what with the Ace's family up from Portsmouth, Virginia, the bad weather, and all. . . ." Parker, however, brought the Dodgers from behind, making an interception, running for a touchdown, and scoring another in a 14–9 victory. Parker was named most valuable player in the NFL for 1940.

The Dodgers' systematic decline followed, however. The military draft took many of Sutherland's players and he resigned as coach after the 1941 season. Mike Getto, Pete Cawthon, Ed Kuhale, and Frank Bridges followed him as Dodgers' head coaches. The team sunk to last place in 1943. Colorful new uniforms and a new name, "Tigers," did not help in 1944; they were 0–10.

A period of intrigue followed. Topping learned that Branch Rickey of the baseball Dodgers intended to squeeze the football team out of Ebbets Field. Topping also knew he could not move to Yankee Stadium because the Giants, who played in the Polo Grounds, had "territorial rights" to that side of the city. Topping therefore decided on a spectacular coup.

Several groups were planning rival football leagues to go into operation after the war. Topping intended to be part of one of them, and he needed a bargaining position. He and other members of a syndicate, including Del Webb and Larry McPhail, bought the baseball Yankees. With them came Yankee Stadium.

Players were still scarce because of the war and

Topping merged his team with the Boston Yanks for the 1945 season. That team played one of its 1945 home games at Yankee Stadium.

Then in 1946 Topping obtained a large indemnity payment from each member of the new All-America Football Conference and created the New York Yankees, rivals to the Giants and the All-America's essential Manhattan and Yankee Stadium franchise.

The AAFC also had a team called the Brooklyn Dodgers. It was headed by a different group altogether and bore no relationship to the former team by the same name. "Everything happens to the Dodgers," and in 1949, in the death throes of the AAFC, this team and Topping's Yankees were merged for one season. After that they and their league were buried forever.

BROOKLYN DODGERS/TIGERS, 1930–44

Abruzzino, Frank, C, Colgate ... 1931
Aiello, Tony, B, Youngstown ... 1944
Albanses, Vannie, B, Syracuse ... 1937–38
Alfson, Warren, G, Nebraska ... 1941
Ambrose, John, C, Catholic ... 1932
Andrusking, Sig, G, Detroit ... 1937
Apsit, Marger, B, USC ... 1931
Arial, Dave (Gump), E, Auburn ... 1934
Austin, Jim, E, St. Mary's ... 1937–38

B

Badgro, Morris (Red), E, USC ... 1936
Bailey, Bill, E, Duke ... 1940–41
Bandura, John, E, S.W. Louisiana State ... 1943
Barrett, Jeff, E, LSU ... 1936–38
Barclay, George, G, North Carolina ... 1935
Becker, Wayland, E, Marquette ... 1934–35
Bergerson, Gil, T, Oregon State ... 1935–36
Biacone, John B, Oregon State ... 1936
Bleeker, Mal, C, Columbia ... 1930
Bowdoin, Jim, G, Alabama ... 1932–34
Boyer, Verdi, G, UCLA ... 1936
Britt, Ed, B, Holy Cross ... 1938
Brown, Bill, B, Texas Tech ... 1943–44
Brumbaugh, Boyd, B Duquesne ... 1937–39
Bunyan, John, G NYU ... 1932
Busby, Sherrill, E, Troy State ... 1940
Butcher, Wendell, B, Gustavus-Adolphus ... 1938–42

C

Cafego, George, B, Tennessee ... 1940–43
Cagle, Chris, B, Army ... 1933–34
Cannella, John, T, Fordham ... 1934
Carnelly, Ray, B, Carnegie Tech ... 1939
Carter, Joe, E, SMU ... 1944
Cassiano, Dick, B, Pittsburgh ... 1940
Chalmers, George, C, NYU ... 1933
Clark, Myers (Algy), B, Ohio State ... 1930
Comstock, Ed, G, Washington, St. Louis ... 1930
Condit, Merlyn, B, Carnegie Tech ... 1941–43
Conkright, Bill (Red), C, Oklahoma ... 1943
Cook, Dave, B, Illinois ... 1936
Coon, Ed (Ty), G, North Carolina State ... 1940
Cooper, Norm, C, Howard ... 1937–38
Cotton, Russ, B, Texas Mines ... 1941
Courtney, Gerry, B, Syracuse ... 1942
Crayne, Dick, B, Iowa ... 1936–37
Croft, Win, G, Utah ... 1935
Cronin, Bill, B, Boston College ... 1931
Cronkhite, Henry (Doc), E, Kansas State ... 1934
Crowl, Dick, C, Rutgers ... 1930
Cumisky, Frank, E, Ohio State ... 1937
Cuneo, Ed, G, Columbia ... 1930

D

Daniell, Ave, T, Pittsburgh ... 1937–38
Davis, Gaines, G, Texas Tech ... 1935
Davis, Joe, E, USC ... 1943
Davis, Bill, T, Texas Tech ... 1942–43
Demas, George, G, Washington & Jefferson ... 1934
Deremer, Art, C, Niagara ... 1942
Disend, Leo, T, Albright ... 1938–39
Dixon, Felix, T, Boston U. ... 1938
Dobrus, Pete, T, Carnegie Tech ... 1941
Doherty, George, G, Louisiana Tech ... 1944
Donnell, John, B, Oregon ... 1930
Douglas, Ben, B, Grinnell ... 1933
Dowler, Tom, B, Colgate ... 1931
Druze, Johnny, E, Fordham ... 1938

E

Eagle, Alex, T, Oregon ... 1935
Eberdt, Jess, C, Alabama ... 1932
Edwards, Marshall, B, Wake Forest ... 1943
Eliason, Don, E, Hamline ... 1942
Ellis, John, G, Vanderbilt ... 1944
Ely, Harold, T, Iowa ... 1932–34
Engebretsen, Paul, G, Northwestern ... 1934

F

Falkenstein, Tony, B, St. Mary's ... 1944
Farrell, Ed (Scrapper), B, Muhlenberg ... 1938–39
Fawcett, Jake, T, SMU ... 1943
Feathers, Beattie, B, Tennessee ... 1938–39
Fedora, Walt, B, George Washington ... 1942
Ferguson, J. B., G, none ... 1935
Fishel, Dick, B, Syracuse ... 1933–34
Folk, Dick, G, Arkansas State ... 1939
Francis, Sam, B, Nebraska ... 1939–40
Franklin, Norm (Red), B, Oregon State ... 1935–37
Frick, Ray, C, Pennsylvania ... 1941
Friedman, Benny, B, Michigan ... 1932–34
Fronczek, Andy, T, Richmond ... 1941
Fryer, Kenny, B, West Virginia ... 1944
Fulton, Ted, G, Oglethorpe ... 1931–32
Fuqua, Ray, E, SMU ... 1935–36

G

Garvey, Ed, T, Notre Dame ... 1930
Getz, Fred, E, Chattanooga ... 1930
Gifford, Bob, B, Denver ... 1941–42
Gillson, Bob, G, Colgate ... 1930–31
Goddard, Ed (Rip), B, Washington State ... 1937
Golemgeske, John, T, Wisconsin ... 1937–40
Gordon, Lou, T, Illinois ... 1931
Granato, Samuel, T, none ... 1943
Grandinette, George, G, Fordham ... 1943
Greenberg, Ben, B, Rutgers ... 1930
Greenshields, Donn, T, Penn State ... 1932–33
Grossman, Jack, B, Rutgers ... 1932–36
Grove, Roger, B, Michigan State ... 1937
Gussie, Mike, G, West Virginia ... 1940
Gutknecht, Al, G, Niagara ... 1943
Gutowsky, Leroy (Ace), B, Oklahoma City ... 1939

H

Haak, Bob (Spanky), T, Indiana ... 1939
Hagberg, Rudy, C, West Virginia ... 1930
Hagerty, Loris, B, Iowa State ... 1930
Haines, Harry, T, Colgate ... 1930–31
Halpren, Roy, G, CCNY ... 1932
Hanson, Tom (Swede), B, Temple ... 1931, 37
Hare, Ray, B, Gonzaga ... 1944
Hartman, Jim, B, Colorado St. ... 1936
Hayduk, Henry, G. Washington State ... 1935
Heater, Bill (Red), T, Syracuse ... 1940
Heikkinen, Ralph, G, Michigan ... 1939
Heineman, Ken, B, Texas Mines ... 1943
Heldt, Carl, T, Purdue ... 1935–36
Hickman, Herman, G, Tennessee ... 1932–34
Hill, Harold, E, Howard ... 1938–40
Hodges, Herman, E, Howard ... 1939–42
Hornbeak, Jay, B, Washington ... 1935
Hubbard, Wes (Bud), E, San Jose State ... 1935
Hugret, Joe, E, NYU ... 1933–34
Humphrey, Paul, C, Purdue ... 1939

I

Illowit, Roy, T, CCNY ... 1937

J

Janiak, Len, B, Ohio ... 1939
Jefferson, Billy, C, Mississippi State ... 1942
Jeffries, Bob, G, Missouri ... 1942
Jocher, Art, G, Manhattan ... 1940–42
Johnson, Bert, B, Kentucky ... 1937
Johnson, Cecil, B, East Texas State ... 1943–44
Jonas, Marvin, C, Utah ... 1931
Jones, Bruce, G, Alabama ... 1931–34
Jones, Thurman, B, Abilene Christian ... 1941–43
Jorgenson, Wagner, C, St. Mary's ... 1936–37
Jurich, Mike, T, Denver ... 1941–42

K

Kapitansky, Bernie, G, Long Island U. ... 1942
Kaplanoff, Carl, T, Ohio State ... 1939
Karcis, John (Bull), B, Carnegie Tech ... 1932–35
Kaska, Tony, B, Illinois Wesleyan ... 1936–38
Keahey, Eulis (Duce), G, George Washington ... 1942
Kelly, John (Shipwreck), B, Kentucky ... 1933–34, 37
Kelly, Bill, B, Montana ... 1930
Kelsch, Matt, E, Iowa ... 1930
Kercheval, Ralph, B, Kentucky ... 1934–40
Kinard, Frank (Bruiser), T. Mississippi ... 1938–44
Kirkland, B'ho, G, Alabama ... 1935–36
Kirkleski, Frank, B, Lafayette ... 1931
Kish, Ben, B, Pittsburgh ... 1940
Kloppenberg, Harry, E, Fordham ... 1931, 33–34
Koons, Joe, C, Long Island U. ... 1941
Kosel, Stan, B, Albright ... 1938–39
Kostka, Stan, B, Minnesota ... 1935
Kowalski, Andy, E, Mississippi State ... 1943–44
Kracum, George, B, Pittsburgh ... 1941
Krause, Henry (Red), C, St. Louis ... 1936–37
Kristufek, Frank, T, Pittsburgh ... 1940–41

L

LaFitte, Bill, E, Ouachita ... 1944
Lankas, Jim, B, St. Mary's, Texas ... 1942
Leckonby, Bill, B, St. Lawrence ... 1939–41
Lee, Bill, T, Alabama ... 1935–37
Leisk, Wardell, G, LSU ... 1937
Lenc, George (Chilly), E, Augustana ... 1939
Leon, Tony, G, Alabama ... 1944
Lott, John, T, Bucknell ... 1930
Lubratovich, Milo (Lou), T, Wisconsin ... 1931–35
Lumpkin, Roy (Father), B, Georgia Tech ... 1936–37
Lyons, George, T, Kansas State ... 1932–33

M

McAdams, Dean, B, Washington ... 1941–43
McArthur, Jack, C, St. Mary's ... 1930, 33
McBride, Jack, B, Syracuse ... 1930–32
McCullogh, Harold, B, Cornell ... 1942
McDonald, Walt, C, Utah ... 1935
McFadden, Banks, B, Clemson ... 1940
McGibbony, Charlie, B, Arkansas State ... 1944
McMichaels, John, B, Birmingham ... 1944
McNeil, Frank, E, Washington & Jefferson ... 1932
Mahan, Bob, B, Washington ... 1930
Manders, Clarence (Pug), B, Drake ... 1939–43
Maniaci, Joe, B, Fordham ... 1936–38
Manton, Taldon, (Tilly), B, TCU ... 1943
Marek, Joe, B, Texas Tech ... 1943
Mark, Lou, E, North Carolina ... 1938–40
Marko, Steve, B, none ... 1944
Martin, Frank, B, Alabama ... 1943–44
Masterson, Bob, E, Miami ... 1944
Matisi, John, T, Duquesne ... 1943
Mattison, Ralph, G, Davis & Elkins ... 1930
Mecham, Curt, B, Oregon ... 1942
Merlin, Ed, G, Vanderbilt ... 1938–39
Merrill, Walt, T, Alabama ... 1940–42
Mielziner, Saul, C, Carnegie Tech ... 1931–34
Miller, Jim (Bing), T, NYU ... 1930
Mitchell, Granville (Buster), E, Davis & Elkins ... 1937
Mizell, Warner, B, Georgia Tech ... 1931
Montgomery, Cliff, B, Columbia ... 1934
Mooney, Jim, E, Georgetown ... 1930–31
Mooney, Tex, T, West Texas State ... 1943
Moore, Gene, C, Colorado ... 1938
Morrison, Maynard, C, Michigan ... 1933–34
Myers, Dennis, G, Iowa ... 1930–31

N

Nardi, Dick, B, Ohio State ... 1939
Nash, Tom, E, Georgia ... 1933–34
Nelson, Don, G, Iowa ... 1937
Nemecek, Jerry, E, NYU ... 1931
Nesbitt, Dick, B, Drake ... 1934–35
Nicksick, Mike, B, Pittsburgh ... 1942
Nixon, George, B, Idaho ... 1942
Norby, John, B, Idaho ... 1935
Nori, Reino, B, DeKalb ... 1937–38
Novotny, Ray, B, Ashland ... 1932
Noyes, Len, T, Montana State ... 1938

O

O'Donnell, Dick, E, Minnesota ... 1931
Oehler, John (Cap), C, Purdue ... 1935–36
Owens, Pete, G, Texas Tech ... 1943

P

Parker, Clarence (Ace), B, Duke ... 1937–41
Parker, Dave, E, Hardin-Simmons ... 1941
Peace, Larry, B, Pittsburgh ... 1941
Perry, Claude, T, Alabama ... 1931
Peters, Forest (Frosty), B, Montana ... 1931
Peterson, Les (Tex), E, Texas ... 1933–34
Petro, Steve, G, Pittsburgh ... 1940–41
Pierce, Don, C, Kansas ... 1942
Pivarnik, Joe, G, Notre Dame ... 1942
Plank, Tony, B, Georgetown ... 1930
Plank, Earl, E, Ohio State ... 1930

R

Radick, Ken, E, Marquette ... 1931
Raffel, Bill, E, Pennsylvania ... 1932
Ranspot, Keith, E, SMU ... 1942–43
Raskowski, Leo, T, Ohio State ... 1933
Ratica, Joe, C, St. Vincent's ... 1939
Rayburn, Van, E, Tennessee ... 1933
Reckmack, Ray, B, Syracuse ... 1937
Reissig, Bill, B, Ft. Hays State ... 1938–39
Reynolds, Bill, B, Mississippi ... 1944
Rhea, Floyd, G, Oregon ... 1944
Rhea, Hughie, G, Nebraska ... 1933
Riblett, Paul, E. Pennsylvania ... 1932–36
Richards, Dick, B, Kentucky ... 1933
Robertson, Bob, B, USC ... 1942
Robertson, Thomas, C, Tulsa ... 1940–42
Robinson, Jack, T, Northeast Missouri State ... 1935–36
Rovinski, Tony, B, Holy Cross ... 1934
Rowan, Ev, E, Ohio State ... 1930, 32–33
Rucinski, Ed, E, Indiana ... 1941–42

John (Shipwreck) Kelly (left) and Benny Friedman.

Frank (Bruiser) Kinard.

Clarence (Ace) Parker.

Professional football has reached such levels of popularity and gained so much acceptance in America that only one National Football League team in the second half of the twentieth century has failed completely and passed into utter extinction. That team was the 1952 Dallas Texans. It threw in the towel and vanished completely following a nine-year period in which it played under four different names in three different cities—1944–48 Boston Yanks, 1949 New York Bulldogs, 1950–51 New York Yanks, and 1952 Dallas Texans.

In fact, this team actually had no home at all when it went under for the last time. It had been forsaken in Dallas and it played out its days as a road team, a dismal dinosaur, the last of its breed to go.

Ted Collins was a successful agent in radio broadcasting and the music business. He managed the career of singer Kate Smith. He owned the original Celtics basketball team, the barnstorming team that preceded the Boston Celtics of today, for six years in the thirties. He and Smith traveled with the team and cheered them to baskets. In 1941, Collins owned a football team called the Long Island Indians.

Schedule math often dictates the size of a football league. In 1944, the NFL had only nine teams because the strapped Chicago Cardinals and Pittsburgh Steelers teams had merged themselves for the season. Collins, the radio magnate, had been trying for years to get a team in the NFL and he was now enfranchised to operate a new team.

The same New York Giants' "territorial rights" to upper Manhattan that had frustrated Brooklyn's Dan Topping and kept him out of Yankee Stadium now did the same to Collins. He adopted the nickname he wanted, "Yanks" (part of pro football off and on since 1926 but not in use at the time), and placed his team in Boston at Fenway Park—the Boston Yanks.

Few men in pro football history ever had worse luck or a poorer sense of timing than Collins. His team was one of the NFL's weakest during the last two war years, 1944 and 1945, and throughout the war with the All-America Football Conference, 1946–49. Each war—the world-wide one and the one in pro football—left him unable to find and sign good players for the Yanks.

Quarterback Bobby Layne spent one year with the team. He got very little protection while he was trying to pass and during one season his weight dropped from 200 to 175 pounds. In his year with the team, 1949, it had a 1–10–1 record. Layne was traded to the Detroit Lions.

Collins lost $800,000 operating the Boston Yanks. He longed to move his team to New York and Yankee Stadium. At that point, his sense of timing failed him again and, for readers of the history of his team, tracing New York's teams and their nicknames and stadiums in the late forties becomes a real challenge.

Collins thought the All-America was going to fold before the 1949 season. He arranged a lease on Yankee Stadium for 1949 and also succeeded in getting "territorial rights" granted him by the Giants across the Harlem River in the Polo Grounds. But the AAFC lived to fight another year and Collins was suddenly in a jam; he had no stadium and, in addition, no nickname. There was an AAFC team in the stadium and it was named the Yankees. Collins therefore changed the name of his team to the Bulldogs, in honor, he said, of the the famous Canton Bulldogs in the early years of pro football in Ohio. And Collins found a stadium when Horace Stoneham, owner of the baseball Giants and the Polo Grounds, agreed to allow the new Bulldogs to share that stadium with the football Giants. The 1949 Bulldogs were 1–10–1.

The fifties dawned with great promise for Collins. The AAFC was gone and Collins was given a 10-year lease on Yankee Stadium. He changed the name of his team from Bulldogs back to Yanks. He acquired the popular backfield stars of the former AAFC Yankees, Claude (Buddy) Young and Orban (Spec) Sanders (Sanders had missed the 1949 AAFC season with a knee injury). He got quarterback George Ratterman from the defunct Buffalo Bills and George Taliaferro from the Los Angeles Dons.

It is a little-known fact of history that this team, which would vanish off the face of the pro football map in two years, was on its way to winning the National Conference championship halfway through the 1950 season. It won six of its first seven games. Sanders, who was moved to defense, had a spectacular season in which he made a record 13 interceptions. But the Yanks went into a tailspin in which they lost four straight and finished third in the league.

Collins was ecstatic, however. He had finally had a winning season. The years of frustration seemed to have paid off at last.

The 1951 NFL schedule granted the Yankees four home games. The team started miserably and won only one game. Nothing went right for them and only 31,879 fans attended the entire home schedule. Claiming his eight years as a team owner had cost him $1 million, Collins sold the team to Giles and Connell Miller, heirs to a textile fortune in Dallas, Texas.

The 1952 Dallas Texans hold a place in history as a symbol of pro football futility. There were a number of reasons why they became the last NFL team to go defunct, and the first of them probably was the contract quarterback George Ratterman had signed with the Yanks. It gave him his freedom if the New York franchise was ever moved. When the club went to Dallas, the new Texans were forced to trade Ratterman; he landed in Cleveland with the Browns.

Secondly, the Texans became a team with two excellent runners who happened to be black—George Taliaferro and Claude (Buddy) Young—in a segregated southern city in the fifties.

Thirdly, the Texans were not very good. They had future NFL stars such as defensive linemen Gino Marchetti and Art Donovan, and a spectacular trade that sent rookie linebacker Les Richter to the Los Angeles Rams netted them 11 players, including fullback Dick Hoerner and defensive back Tom Keane. But they lacked a good quarterback. They reeled through eight straight defeats by lopsided scores. Their opening day attendance at Dallas's Cotton Bowl was only 17,000 and they never had another crowd even that large at a home game. When it was clear the team was a failure, Jimmy Phelan, the head coach, broke the news to the players after practice and advised them, "It is my opinion that you should get to the banks with all due haste."

Two final games at the Cotton Bowl were canceled. The team moved to quarters in Hershey, Pennsylvania, and played the Chicago Bears at Akron, Ohio. To the complete surprise of everyone on the two teams and the estimated 3,000 persons in the stands, "Dallas" won 27–23. The NFL's orphan team then lost to the Lions in Detroit and the Eagles at Philadelphia. That was the last game it ever played.

In Baltimore, a former AAFC team named the Colts had lasted only one year in the NFL, 1950. New owners in Baltimore headed by Carroll Rosenbloom bought the defunct Dallas Texans' franchise and created a new team in 1953 called the Baltimore Colts, which by the end of the decade would twice become NFL champions.

But the pages of pro football history books will probably never be without the Yanks-Bulldogs-Yanks-Texans. At least it seems that way. So many spectacular records were set against these teams that they appear to be entrenched in the NFL *Record Manual*. For example, tying a record, the 1944 Boston Yanks made only 36 first downs rushing all season. Showing very little faith at all in their kicker, the 1946 Yanks did not attempt a single field goal. Two different players returned interceptions for touchdowns against Layne and the 1948 Yanks. The 1949 Bulldogs allowed the Chicago Cardinals 65 points in one game, third most ever in a regular season game. Norm Van Brocklin of the Los Angeles Rams set the all-time record with 554 yards passing in a game against the 1951 Yanks. And as the Yanks kept giving up touchdowns and then turning over the ball so the other team could score more touchdowns, Taliaferro returned eight kickoffs in one 1950 game against the New York Giants (the Giants won 51–7) and punted 14 times in one 1951 game against Los Angeles, tying or approaching records.

The coaches of these teams in their nine difficult years were Herb Kopf in 1944–46, Maurice (Clipper) Smith in 1947–48, Charley Ewart in 1949, Norman (Red) Strader in 1950–51, and Phelan in 1952.

BOSTON YANKS/NEW YORK BULLDOGS/NEW YORK YANKS/DALLAS TEXANS, 1944–52

Abbey, Joe, E, North Texas State 1949
Abbruzzi, Lou, B, Rhode Island 1946
Adams, Chet, T, Ohio 1950
Albrecht, Art, T, Wisconsin 1944
Aldridge, Ben, B, Oklahoma A&M 1950–52
Alford, Bruce, E, TCU 1950–51
Anderson, Bill, E, West Virginia 1945
Averno, Sisto, G, Muhlenberg 1951–52

B

Baggett, Billy, B, LSU 1952
Badaczweski, John, G, Western Reserve 1946–48
Bailey, Sam, E, Duke 1946
Barzilauskas, Fritz, G, Yale 1947–49
Batinski, Stan, G, Temple 1948–49
Blake, Tom, T, Cincinnati 1949
Boyda, Mike, B, Washington & Lee 1949
Brown, George G, Texas Christian 1950

C

Cafego, George, B, Tennessee 1944–45
Calcagni, Ralph, T, Pennsylvania 1945–46
Campanela, Joe, T, Ohio State 1952
Campbell, Bill, B, Oklahoma 1949
Canady, Jim, B, Texas 1949
Canale, Rocco, G, Boston College 1946–47
Cannamela, Pat, G, USC 1952
Celeri, Bob, B, California 1951–52
Champion, Jim, G, Mississippi State 1950–51
Chipley, Bill, E, Washington & Lee 1947–49
Clowes, John, T, William & Mary 1950–51
Collins, Bill, G, Texas 1947
Colo, Don, E, Brown 1951–52
Crain, Milt, B, Baylor 1944
Crisler, Hal, E, San Jose State 1946–47
Crowe, Paul, B, St. Mary's, Calif. 1951
Crowley, Joe, E Dartmouth 1944–45
Cullom, Jim, G, California 1951
Currivan, Don, E, Boston College 1945–48

D

Dancewicz, Frank (Boley), B, Notre Dame 1946–48
Davis, Bob, B, Kentucky 1944–46
Davis, Bob, T, Georgia Tech 1948
Davis, Jerome, B, S.E. Louisiana State 1952
Dean, Tom, T, SMU 1946–47
Deeks, Don, T, Washington 1945–47
Dekdebrun, Al, B, Cornell 1948
DeMoss, Bob, B, Purdue 1949
Dimancheff, Boris (Babe), B, Purdue 1945–46
Doherty, George, G, Louisiana Tech 1945
Domnanovich, Joe, C, Alabama 1946–49
Donovan, Art, T, Boston College 1951–52
Dubzinski, Walt, G, Boston College 1944
Duckworth, Joe, E, Colgate 1948
Duhart, Paul, B, Florida 1945

E

Ecklund, Brad, C, Oregon 1950–52
Edwards, Dan, E, Georgia 1950–52
Eliason, Don, E, Hamline 1946
Ellis, Herb, C, Texas A&M 1949

F

Falkenstein, Tony, B, St. Mary's 1944
Famiglietti, Gary, B, Boston U 1946
Felker, Gene, E, Wisconsin 1952
Fiorentino, Al, G, Boston College 1945
Fiorentino, Ed, E, Boston College 1944, 47
Flowers, Keith, G, Texas Christian 1952
Franco, Ed, G, Fordham 1944

G

Gandee, Sherwin (Sonny), E, Ohio State 1952
Garza, Dan, E, Oregon 1951
Gaul, Frank, T, Notre Dame 1949
Gaziano, Frank, G, Holy Cross 1944
Giddens, Hershel (Wimpy), T, Louisiana Tech 1944
Gillette, Jim, B, Virginia 1946
Godwin, Bill, C, Georgia 1947–48
Golding, Joe, B, Oklahoma 1947–49
Goldman, Sam, E, Howard 1944–47
Governali, Paul, B, Columbia 1946–47
Griffin, Bobby, B, Baylor 1951
Grigas, John, B, Holy Cross 1945–47
Grigg, Forrest (Chubby), T, Tulsa 1952
Gudmunson, Scott, B, George Washington 1944–45

H

Harding, Roger, C, California 1949
Hazelhurst, Bob, G, Denver 1948–49
Heywood, Ralph, E, USC 1949
Hoague, Joe, B, Colgate 1946
Hoerner, Dick, B, Iowa 1952
Howard, Sherm, B, Nevada 1950–51
Humble, Weldon, G, Rice 1952

I

Iverson, Chris (Duke), B, Oregon 1950–51

J

Jackson, Ken, T, Texas 1952
Jankovich, Keever, E, College of Pacific 1952
Jarmoluk, Mike, T, Temple 1948–49
Jenkins, Jonathan, T, Dartmouth 1950
Johnson, Harvey, B, William & Mary 1951
Johnson, Nate, T, Illinois 1950
Jones, Ellis, G, Tulsa 1945
Juster, Rube, T, Minnesota 1946

K

Kalmanir, Tom (Cricket), B, Nevada 1952
Karnofsky, Abe (Sonny), B, Arizona 1946
Keane, Tom, B, West Virginia 1952
Kennedy, Bill, E, Michigan State 1947
Kennedy, Bob, B, Washington State 1950
Korisky, Ed, C, Villanova 1944
Kusserow, Lou, B, Columbia 1950

L

Lansford, Jim, T, Texas 1952
Lauricella, Hank, B, Tennessee 1952
Layden, Pete, B, Texas 1950
Layne, Bobby, B, Texas 1949
Lee, Gene, C, Florida 1946
Leon, Tony, G, Alabama 1945–46
Lio, Augie, T, Georgetown 1944–45
Long, Bob, B, Tennessee 1947

M

Magee, Jim, C, Villanova 1944–46
Maley, Howie, B, SMU 1946–47
Malinowski, Gene, B, Detroit 1948
Mancha, Vaughn, C, Alabama 1948
Manders, Clarence (Pug), B, Drake 1945
Marchetti, Gino, E, San Francisco 1952
Mark, Lou, E, North Carolina State 1945
Martin, Frank, B, Alabama 1945
Martin, John, B, Oklahoma 1944–45
Masterson, Bob, E, Miami 1945
Mathews, Ned, B, UCLA 1945
Maznicki, Frank, B, Boston College 1947
McClure, Bob, G, Nevada 1947–48
McCullough, Hugh, B, Oklahoma 1945
McGee, Ed, T, Temple 1944–46
McKissack, Dick, B, Southern Methodist 1952
Meisenheimer, Darrell, B, Oklahoma A&M 1951
Micka, Mike, B, Colgate 1946–48
Mitchell, Paul, T, Minnesota 1950–51
Morelli, John G, Georgetown 1944–45
Muehlheuser, Frank, B, Colgate 1948–49

N

Nagel, Ross T, St. Louis 1951
Nelson, Frank, B, Utah 1948–49
Nolan, John, T, Penn State 1948–50

O

O'Connor, Bill (Zeke), E, Notre Dame 1951
Olsonoski, Larry, G, Minnesota 1949
Ortman, Chuck, B, Michigan 1952
Osmanski, Joe, B, Holy Cross 1949

P

Parker, Clarence (Ace), B, Duke 1945
Paschal, Bill, B, Georgia Tech 1947–48
Pelfrey, Ray, B, Eastern Kentucky 1952
Petitbon, John, B, Notre Dame 1952
Poole, Barney, E, Mississippi 1950–52
Poto, John, B, none 1947–48
Pregulman, Merv, G, Michigan 1949
Prescott, Ace, E, Hardin-Simmons 1949
Pritko, Steve, E, Villanova 1948–49

R

Ransport, Keith, E, SMU 1944–45
Ratterman, George, B, Notre Dame 1950–51
Rauch, Johnny, B, Georgia 1950–51
Reid, Joe, C, Louisiana State 1952
Rhea, Floyd, G, Oregon 1945
Riggs, Thron, T, Washington State 1944
Robison, George, G, VMI 1952
Rodgers, Tom, T, Bucknell 1947
Roman, George, T, Western Reserve 1948–49
Romboli, Rudy, B, none 1946–48
Ruby, Martin, T, Texas A&M 1950
Russell, Jack, E, Baylor 1950
Ryan, Dave, B, Hardin-Simmons 1948

S

Sabasteanski, Joe, C, Fordham 1946–49

Joe Golding (10), Frank Seno (54) of Boston Yanks about to tackle Ralph Ruthstrom of Washington in 1947.

Joe Osmanski of New York Bulldogs against Los Angeles in 1949; no. 26 of Bulldogs is Larry Olsonoski.

Claude (Buddy) Young of the Dallas Texans surrounded by the Packers in a game at Green Bay in 1952.

THE THREE EARLY AFLs

There have been four American Football Leagues— in 1926, 1936–37, 1940–41, and 1960–69. Each entered into competition with the NFL seeking parity with it as an entity of American sport. The fourth succeeded and is now the American Football Conference. The first three failed and are all but forgotten.

Timothy J. Mara purchased an NFL franchise for New York City in 1925. The Giants' games at the Polo Grounds drew small crowds and the team was losing money until the arrival of Red Grange. The great Illinois halfback, "the Galloping Ghost," finished his college career in mid-November, 1925, and within 10 days had signed a contract with the Chicago Bears and played in their then traditional Thanksgiving day game against the Cardinals. A record crowd of 38,000 watched at Wrigley Field. Then the Bears left on a barnstorming tour that would inestimably benefit pro football. When Grange played in the Polo Grounds in New York, 70,000 attended. It made Mara see the potential of pro football.

Grange's personal manager C.C. (Cash and Carry) Pyle, informed the Bears that Grange would not play for them in 1926 unless he was given a five-

Bill Edwards (center), C.C. Pyle (right), 1926 AFL.

Red Grange running for New York Yankees, 1926.

John Kimbrough signs with New York, 1941 AFL.

figure salary and one-third ownership of the team. George Halas and Dutch Sternaman, owners of the team, refused.

So Pyle went to New York, the site of Grange's conquests the year before, and leased Yankee Stadium from the baseball team. He then petitioned the NFL for a franchise.

Mara, whose Giants played just across the Harlem River at the Polo Grounds, would not agree to that. But he and the other NFL owners did agree that a second franchise could be located in New York City provided it was at Ebbets Field in Brooklyn. This compromise was rejected by Pyle, who wanted an NFL team at Yankee Stadium. If he did not get it, he said, he would start his own league, which he did.

The AFL of 1926 was built around Grange and the Yankees. The other teams were the Boston Bulldogs, Brooklyn Horsemen, Chicago Bulls, Cleveland Panthers, Newark Bears, Philadelphia Quakers, and a road team listed as the Los Angeles Wildcats. In addition, the Rock Island, Illinois, Independents left the NFL to join the AFL. Politician and former Princeton athlete Bill Edwards was hired by Pyle to be commissioner of the AFL at a salary of $25,000, 10 times the $2,500 salary paid NFL commissioner Joe Carr. But it is believed that Edwards and AFL coaches and players never received their salaries in full.

New York Giants' coach Bob Folwell left to join the Philadelphia Quakers and so did the Giants' star tackle, Century Milstead. Al Nesser played for a time with the Cleveland Panthers. Mike Michalske played for the Yankees and Ray Flaherty for the Los Angeles Wildcats; both were NFL stars later with the Packers and Giants, respectively. Joey Sternaman, brother of the Bears' co-owner, formed the Chicago Bulls, who leased Comiskey Park, forcing the NFL Cardinals to move to smaller Normal Park.

Support of the AFL was minimal outside New York City. Rock Island dropped out. Newark's team disbanded and its players sued for their salaries. The Brooklyn Horsemen merged with the NFL Brooklyn Lions. Only the Yankees, Quakers, and the traveling Wildcats remained in business at season's end.

Mara of the Giants, who had suffered losses in the war with the AFL, wanted one more crack at it and challenged Pyle's Yankees to a game. Pyle agreed to it at first, then backed down. Mara turned to the Quakers, champions of the AFL. The Quakers, anxious to make a few extra dollars for Christmas, agreed.

The first AFL thus achieved in one year what other challengers to the NFL would not in the years ahead—an interleague playoff. The game the Quakers and Giants played December 12, 1926 has

been called "the first Super Bowl." But the fact remains that the Giants had finished seventh in the NFL that year.

Bad weather engulfed the Polo Grounds on the day of the game and snow obliterated the yard lines. Only 5,000 persons watched as the Quakers managed only one first down and the Giants won 31–0.

As a lone concession to the AFL, the NFL extended membership to the Yankees the following season and they remained in the league for two more years until they went out of business.

1926 AFL STANDINGS	W	L	T	Pct.
Philadelphia Quakers	7	2	0	.778
New York Yankees	9	5	0	.643
Cleveland Panthers	3	2	0	.600
Los Angeles Wildcats	6	6	2	.500
Chicago Bulls	5	6	3	.455
Boston Bulldogs	2	4	0	.333
Rock Island Independents	2	5	1	.283
Brooklyn Horsemen	1	3	0	.250
Newark Bears	0	4	2	.000

Ten years after the demise of the first AFL, another rival league appeared having the same name. It lasted two years and it never had more than six teams as members. The Boston Shamrocks, New York Yankees, Pittsburgh Americans, and Rochester Tigers operated both seasons, 1936 and 1937. The Brooklyn Tigers and Cleveland Rams played only in 1936. And the Cincinnati Bengals and Los Angeles Bulldogs were part of the league only in 1937. Boston won the championship in 1936 and Los Angeles was the undefeated champion in 1937.

The second AFL had a team in Yankee Stadium called the Yankees. This was an obligatory feature of every rival league to operate in the years before the Giants quit the Polo Grounds and moved to Yankee Stadium themselves in 1956.

An AFL team called the Brooklyn Tigers set up shop at Ebbets Field to play home games while the Dodgers were on the road. Dodgers' owner Dan Topping objected strongly to the arrangement. Dr. Harry March, former team physician of the Giants, close friend of Tim Mara's, and author of a 1934 book titled *Pro Football's Ups and Downs,* virtually the only history of the game written before 1940, was the AFL's president. March gave a curious explanation of the Brooklyn arrangement to the newspapers, saying that "continuous football at Ebbets Field . . . would work toward the benefit of both clubs, keeping football interest at a high pitch."

Mike Palm, who may be remembered as co-coach, briefly, of the star-crossed 1934 Cincinnati Reds, became coach of the Brooklyn Tigers. He gathered them in the Catskills for preseason practice. A New York newspaper wrote, "The home opening of the

Brooklyn Tigers, a mysterious group of athletes sequestered, under the wing of Mr. Palm, somewhere around Bear Mountain at the moment, is slated for Oct. 15. It will be a night game against Cleveland."

It was this very league that made the second abortive attempt to establish pro football in Cincinnati. This time the name "Bengals" was adopted, and, while the pros failed again to take hold in the Ohio city, the nickname would reappear with another team—and one that would survive—32 years later.

The second AFL was the first league to have a Los Angeles franchise that did not play every game on the road. The hugely successful 1937 Bulldogs played two of their eight games at home at Gilmore Stadium in Los Angeles.

And in 1936 two teams from this league played the first pro game in a then-insignificant arena in Miami that would grow into the Orange Bowl. Hank Soar scored two touchdowns to lead the Boston Shamrocks to a 14–6 victory over the New York Yankees. The Grange tour had stopped in Miami in 1925 during the Florida land boom, when the Bears and their opponents played in a ramshackle stadium that was thrown up overnight for the occasion and torn down the following day. This AFL game of 1936, then, played an important role in the history of a later and more permanent stadium. As sports editor Dinty Dennis of the *Miami Herald* wrote, "The game was the football 'swan song' for the wooden sports arena, E.E. Seiler, stadium manager [Ernie Seiler, later the empresario of breathtaking Orange Bowl shows], announcing the wrecking crews would go to work early this week to demolish the inadequate stands and make way for the new concrete Orange Bowl stadium."

Notable players were part of the second AFL. There were three well known former New York Giants in the league. Ken Strong played for the Yankees, Harry Newman for Brooklyn and Rochester, and Morris (Red) Badgro was player-coach of Rochester in 1936. Sid Gillman, later a famous coach and general manager, played end for the 1936 Cleveland Rams; he joined them on the weekends, because he was an assistant coach at Denison College in Ohio at the same time.

Difficulty struck the Yankees' franchise when, after an estimated 26,000 fans had already arrived for a game against the Pittsburgh Americans, vandals cut the wires lighting the outside of Yankee Stadium. According to a newspaper report, "With no lights available, ticket sellers could not operate and the drastic act of closing all gates was the only alternative as a milling throng assailed two police emergency squads which were rushed to the gates."

No such problems beset the champion Boston Shamrocks. A Boston paper wrote of "the customary scant crowd at Fenway Park" for a Shamrocks' game. A championship game was scheduled at Cleveland, but the Boston players refused to go because they were owed pay for past games. Boston was the league champion, anyway, because it had the best won-lost record.

1936 AFL STANDINGS	W	L	T	Pct.
Boston Shamrocks	8	3	0	.727
Cleveland Rams	5	2	2	.714
New York Yankees	5	3	2	.625
Pittsburgh Americans	3	2	1	.600
Rochester Tigers	1	6	0	.143
Brooklyn Tigers	0	6	1	.000

The AFL of 1937 had the first genuine Los Angeles franchise, the first to actually operate in that city. It was hoped, as a press release distributed with the schedule explained, that "the powerful Los Angeles club will provide the intersectional tang which has done so much to inspirit collegiate football....

"The Los Angeles club will come East and remain here to complete its away-from-home schedule, then return to its own gridiron to meet successive waves of league invasion."

In another attempt to stimulate public interest, the league announced that "Jack Dempsey, former heavyweight champion; Bing Crosby, screen and radio star; and Abraham Dreier, New York hotel owner, will serve as an advisory board."

The Los Angeles Bulldogs had operated as an independent team the year before they joined the AFL and reportedly defeated three NFL teams in exhibition games. They had a former USC tailback named Bill Howard, another runner of note named Ed (Crazylegs) Stark, and a barefooted punter named Bob Miller. They strengthened themselves with new players for 1937 and even tried unsuccessfully to arrange a film contract for Sammy Baugh of TCU to convince him to sign a contract with them; he signed with the Washington Redskins of the NFL instead.

Gus Henderson was the coach of the Bulldogs. He had been head coach at USC for six years and at the University of Tulsa for 11. He employed spread formations, something he called the "Befuddle Huddle," and details of coaching more often credited to coaches such as Paul Brown. They were described in a Rochester newspaper: "There is a set time for arising in the morning. Only special foods are allowed at the training table—at home and on the road. The players always travel in one group and never are allowed to separate without special permission from Coach Henderson."

The Bulldogs gained the distinction of being the only pro team ever to play out the entire period of its membership in a league without being defeated. They won every game on their eastern swing and then defeated the teams that came to California to play them. The league folded with the Bulldogs as its last champions. (Two years later, Henderson was hired to coach the Detroit Lions. He was fired after only one season but won a settlement from Lions' owner Dick Richards for an estimated $70,000. With that, he retired to Palm Springs, where he died at 76 in 1955.)

Los Angeles was left with a championship in 1937—and no team. But the second American Football League had given birth to a team in Cleveland called the Rams, which under new management applied for and gained NFL membership in 1937. Nine years later, it was this Rams team that left Ohio and moved west to Los Angeles.

1937 AFL STANDINGS	W	L	T	Pct.
Los Angeles Bulldogs	8	0	0	1.000
Rochester Tigers	3	3	1	.500
New York Yankees	2	3	1	.400
Cincinnati Bengals	2	3	2	.400
Boston Shamrocks	2	5	0	.286
Pittsburgh Americans	0	5	0	.000

Of all the rival leagues in history, six have been accorded major league status. Of those six, none was smaller, more poorly timed, or appears to have had less meaning than the third American Football League, which operated in 1940–41.

Organized at a meeting in Buffalo, it immediately faced a challenge over its right to call itself the "American Football League" because there was another group by that name, which had formerly been known as the Mid-West Professional Football League.

That crisis passed and the new AFL set up headquarters in Columbus, Ohio, the same city in which the NFL headquarters had been located since its inception. W.D. Griffith, former publicity director of Ohio State University, became president of the new AFL. And the Columbus Bullies won the league championship in both seasons the league operated.

The Milwaukee Chiefs, who had been denied an NFL franchise because the NFL said the Green Bay Packers had "territorial rights" to Milwaukee, joined the AFL. The league gave birth to another team called the New York Yankees, another called the Cincinnati Bengals, and new teams in Boston, the Bears, and in Buffalo, the Indians.

1940 AFL STANDINGS	W	L	T	Pct.
Columbus Bullies	8	1	1	.888
Milwaukee Chiefs	7	2	0	.777
Boston Bears	5	4	1	.555
New York Yankees	4	5	0	.445
Buffalo Indians	2	8	0	.200
Cincinnati Bengals	1	7	0	.125

The New York Yankees changed their name to the Americans for the 1941 season. The third AFL failed to sign many big-name players but former college stars John Kimbrough of Texas A&M and Tom Harmon of Michigan made their pro football debuts with the Americans October 19, 1941 in a 7–7 tie with the Columbus Bullies. Kimbrough made the all-league team even though he only played half the season.

Center Lee Mulleneaux of the Columbus Bullies had previously played with six different NFL teams and with the Cincinnati Bengals of the second AFL.

A game in Cincinnati was forfeited because the Bengals did not have enough players. The AFL's personnel troubles continued as Harmon and other players enlisted in the armed forces. Kimbrough was in Los Angeles making a movie when the plans were being laid for another season in 1942. As a Hall of Fame press release in later years explained, "World War II was undoubtedly the major reason why AFL number three met with failure, but there was nothing in its two-year existence to indicate any other eventual outcome."

1941 AFL STANDINGS	W	L	T	Pct.
Columbus Bullies	5	1	2	.833
New York Americans	5	2	1	.714
Milwaukee Chiefs	4	3	1	.591
Buffalo Indians	2	6	0	.250
Cincinnati Bengals	1	5	2	.167

THE AAFC

The All-America Football Conference of 1946–49 had a greater influence on professional football, reached more people, and made more inroads on the strength of the National Football League than any other rival league in history now defunct.

The AAFC produced the Baltimore Colts, Cleveland Browns, and San Francisco 49ers. It produced a host of players who went on to star in the NFL such as Otto Graham, Elroy (Crazylegs) Hirsch, Joe Perry, and Y.A. Tittle. It placed the first permanent franchise in California, the 49ers (they and the Los Angeles Dons were in business by those names before the Rams arrived from Cleveland).

The AAFC was the first league to play a 14-game regular season schedule; its teams played that many games in each of its first three years. It was the first to travel by air; it made charter arrangements with airlines while the NFL still rode trains. The AAFC occupied three big stadiums that no NFL team then used—Municipal Stadium in Cleveland, Memorial Coliseum in Los Angeles (which the Dons shared with the new Los Angeles Rams), and Yankee Stadium in New York—and with occasional big crowds in them the AAFC actually had a greater average attendance in the four years of its existence than the NFL—38,319 to 27,602.

Blacks had been part of pro football since the twenties, but they gained increased stature in the game through the play of AAFC stars such as Marion Motley and Bill Willis of Cleveland, Len Ford of Los Angeles, Buddy Young of the New York Yankees, and Joe Perry of San Francisco.

The new league also had a woman executive, vice-president Eleanor Gehrig, wife of the late baseball player Lou Gehrig.

The AAFC probably spawned the widespread use of zone defenses in pro football. It willingly hired college coaches and they had been teaching that kind of pass defense for years while man-for-man was the style in the NFL.

Finally, the AAFC hurt the NFL, signed many of its players, succeeded in getting college stars the NFL wanted, drained away fans and interest, and fought hard for its survival. It gave players an alternative, and NFL teams were forced to pay higher salaries. Those teams that did not became losers. That was how the AAFC, more than anything else, influenced professional football.

World War II weakened the NFL. The Cleveland Rams dropped out of the league one year. Pittsburgh merged its team with Philadelphia one season and with the Chicago Cardinals the next. Players were at such a premium that Bronko Nagurski, who had not worn a football uniform since 1937, rejoined the Chicago Bears and played for them in the 1943 championship game against Washington.

But there was a feeling that there would be prosperity as never before once the war ended. There was so much prosperity, in fact, that a second pro league seemed possible to many visionaries and there were men willing to finance it. Mickey McBride, owner of a taxicab company in Cleveland, had attempted unsuccessfully to buy the Rams. Oilman James F. Brueil, representing Buffalo, had deposited $25,000 with the NFL for a franchise. Anthony Morabito, owner of a lumber business in San Francisco, had been trying to arrange an NFL franchise for that city since 1940. Actor Don Ameche had asked his friend, sports editor Arch Ward of the *Chicago Tribune*, to help him get a team in the NFL.

The climate for sports seemed especially good in Chicago. The major commissioners of sport, Elmer Layden of football and Judge Kenesaw Mountain Landis of baseball, both had their offices there in the early forties. It was in Chicago that the great Bears' teams before the war had first played their T formation with man-in-motion and in 1940 stunned the nation by winning the NFL championship game 73–0. And it was there that Ward, a canny newspaperman, had organized the baseball all-star game and football Chicago All-Star Game and established himself as a man with clout in the world of sport.

Ward's influence at his newspaper was considerable. The promotions he created convinced advertisers of the power of the *Tribune*. This won him the confidence of his publisher, Colonel Robert McCormick, and it was Ward who often represented the paper at *Associated Press* publishers' conventions.

Ward was considered a possibility for the commissionership of the National Football League in 1940. He turned it down. His name came up again in 1941 and he again refused it. But he recommended Elmer Layden, coach and athletic director at Notre Dame, and Layden was hired by the NFL.

Ward still did business with the NFL each year as the director of the Chicago All-Star Game between college players and the NFL champion. He wanted pro football to expand. He wanted to see an annual "world series of football." And he was frustrated that he could not get the NFL to admit his friend, Ameche, as a club owner. For all these reasons, Ward decided to organize a new pro football league that would begin its operations as soon as World War II ended.

Two other groups, the Trans-America League and the United States Football League, also planned to begin play once the war ended. But they faded from view as the AAFC began to gain momentum. The first meeting of the league was held in St. Louis in June, 1944. People representing Buffalo, Chicago, Cleveland, Los Angeles, New York, and San Francisco were present. Miami entered the league a year later. The New York investor withdrew and each AAFC team paid $75,000, and promised $25,000 from its gate receipts, to Dan Topping to move his Brooklyn Dodgers' team from the NFL to the new league. He purchased controlling interest in the baseball Yankees and his football team became the New York Yankees. A new franchise in Brooklyn secured Ebbets Field and took the name Dodgers.

The league chose to name itself "All-America Football Conference" because "All-America" was a popular sports term and it reflected the fact that the league stretched from border to border. Jim Crowley became its commissioner. He had been a member— along with NFL commissioner Layden—of the 1924 Notre Dame backfield that sportswriter Grantland Rice named the "Four Horsemen of Notre Dame."

Layden was present at the *Chicago Tribune's* annual pregame smoker the night before the All-Star Game in August, 1945. He learned that Ward was going to use the occasion to make an announcement about the All-America Football Conference. Layden decided to issue a statement about it through his press agent, George Strickler. Layden recalled later, "I reminded George that over the years there had always been talk about new professional leagues sprouting up and that as far as I was concerned the All-America Conference should 'first get a ball, then make a schedule, and then play a game.'"

The statement would be flung at Layden in print for the next four years. It is the thing that is most remembered from his commissionership, that (as expedient historians have simplified it) he said of the AAFC, "Tell them to get a football first."

Gerald Smith, vice-president of the Street & Smith publishing house that put out a popular annual football magazine, was one of the owners of the Brooklyn team. It hired Dr. Mal Stevens, an orthopedic surgeon, as coach and rented Ebbets Field.

Brueil, the oilman, owned the Buffalo team, called the "Bisons." It hired Sam Cordovano as coach but he was replaced by Lowell (Red) Dawson before the season began. The Bisons rented Memorial Stadium.

John L. Keeshin, owner of a race track, headed the Chicago Rockets. He said their name was "inspired by the new speed age in which rocket travel, even to the moon, is predicted." Dick Hanley was hired as Rockets' coach and Soldier Field was secured for the team's games.

McBride, owner of the Cleveland cab company, became president of the team he later named the Browns. Seeking a coach, he asked John Dietrich of the *Cleveland Press,* "Who is the best football coach in America?"

Dietrich replied, "Paul Brown." McBride hired

the former Ohio high school and Ohio State University coach. And the Browns' owner rented 80,000-seat Municipal Statium although the Cleveland Rams, who had now departed for Los Angeles, had played their regular season games in smaller League Park since 1942.

There were now two pro football teams in Los Angeles, where there had been none. Each scheduled its games at Memorial Coliseum. The AAFC Dons, owned by Ameche, Ben Lindheimer, and others, hired Dudley DeGroot as coach.

Miami Seahawks owner Harvey Hester hired Jack Meagher as coach and secured Orange Bowl Stadium. New York Yankees' owner Topping hired Ray Flaherty to coach his team at Yankee Stadium. And Morabito, founder of the San Francisco 49ers, named Lawrence (Buck) Shaw his coach and rented Kezar Stadium.

The AAFC teams had no trouble finding players. There were scores of them leaving military service or coming out of college football. Brooklyn signed tackle Martin Ruby of Texas A&M, captain of the 1946 College All-Stars, and Glenn Dobbs of Tulsa. Buffalo got Steve Juzwik of Notre Dame. Chicago's coach, Hanley, its most celebrated player, Elroy (Crazylegs) Hirsch, and many of its other players had been together on the team at El Toro Marine Air Base in California and were signed by the Rockets as a group. As a result, it was predicted that the Rockets would be the best team in the league.

One-hundred former NFL players eventually signed with AAFC teams. Cleveland signed Chet Adams of the Rams, saying his contract was with the Cleveland, not the Los Angeles, Rams. A court upheld the Browns' claim to Adams. Cleveland also signed Otto Graham of Northwestern.

Los Angeles lured all-pro tackle Lee Artoe away from the Chicago Bears and won a legal dispute honoring the contract it had signed with Angelo Bertelli of Notre Dame, winner of the Heisman trophy. Miami got Hampton Pool of the Chicago Bears.

Orban (Spec) Sanders had been only a substitute at the University of Texas before World War II, but the New York Yankees, recognizing his potential, signed him to a three-year contract promising him $6,000, $17,000, and $25,000. New York also signed 1944 NFL most valuable player Frank Sinkwich of Detroit. "There is a strong possibility that this may form the basis of a little fight," said coach Gus Dorais of Detroit, but the Yankees kept Sinkwich. The New York team also received one player from each of the other teams in the league, an indemnity in addition to the $75,000 each team paid owner Topping to move to the AAFC.

San Francisco landed Norm Standlee, who had been a star for the Chicago Bears before the war, and Frankie Albert of Stanford.

Forty of the 66 College All-Stars signed with the AAFC. Chicago, Los Angeles, the New York Yankees, and San Francisco were heavily stocked with former service players.

There were enough players, commissioner Crowley said, "for a dozen leagues." The AAFC did not hold a draft its first year and the NFL held its draft in secret to avoid giving the AAFC a ready list of players to seek out and attempt to sign.

The Washington Redskins appeared to be the NFL team hardest hit by the AAFC signings. They lost their pre-war coach, Flaherty, to the New York Yankees; their 1945 coach, DeGroot, to Los Angeles; and a dozen of their players to various teams in the AAFC. They had been Eastern Divisions champions in 1945 but they did not win another championship of any kind for the next quarter of a century.

The AAFC's adoption of air travel was not so much an achievement as it was a necessity. No other league in any sport had ever attempted to play weekly games

Arch Ward, founder, of the AAFC.

Mickey McBride, Cleveland Browns.

Paul Brown, Cleveland Browns.

in cities as far-flung as Los Angeles, San Francisco, and Miami. The charter contract with United Air Lines to carry AAFC clubs in DC-4 planes was called the largest such contract in history. ("The whole league is gonna fly!" said one smiling fan to another in the *Flyin' Dodgers* comic book.) And although there no doubt were suitable training camp sites nearby, the Dodgers trained in Bend, Oregon, the Chicago Rockets in Santa Rosa, California and the Miami Seahawks in North Carolina.

The league schedule was a demanding one not only because of the unprecedented cross-country flights it entailed but also because it was a crazy quilt in which some teams played Sunday, others Friday night, and others at night in the middle of the week.

The Cleveland Browns won their first six games by a total score of 149–20. A crowd of 60,135 watched their regular season opener, when they crushed Miami 44–0. The crowd was a professional football record. It was broken weeks later in Cleveland when 71,134 watched a 31–14 victory over Los Angeles. Graham, the Browns' quarterback, led an attack that featured fullback Marion Motley and ends Dante Lavelli and Mac Speedie. The Browns won 12 of their 14 games and the league championship. Owner McBride promoted the team on his taxicabs, on billboards, and in radio advertising. He formed an all-girl band called the Musical Majorettes, who performed at halftime. The team drew 400,000 fans and made $200,000 in profits. Brown, who had signed as coach for a $25,000 salary and 15 percent of the profits, made $55,000 for the year.

Brooklyn won only three games, but tailback Glenn Dobbs was a sensational performer, leading the league in passing and punting. He was named the AAFC's most valuable player.

In the Dodgers' opening game, Dobbs came out of the game with a chipped bone in his hand. His coach, surgeon Dr. Mal Stevens, applied a flexible splint to the hand. Dobbs then went back in and led the Dodgers to a 28–14 victory.

Troubles struck the Miami Seahawks and Chicago Rockets. The Seahawks played home games on Monday nights. They did not have a very good team, and, although they were in Miami, they became the first pro team to be rained out twice in one season. The largest crowd of the season at their games was 9,700 and the smallest was 2,250. Their coach, Jack Meagher, resigned after six games and Hamp Pool was player-coach for the rest of the season. After the season, the AAFC paid $61,000 in salaries owed to Seahawks players, $19,000 owed to United Air Lines, and expelled the Seahawks from the league. Harvey Hester, the team's portly president, lost his life's savings of $51,000.

Instead of becoming one of the league's best teams as expected, the Chicago Rockets became one of its worst. Hanley, the coach, could not exert the discipline he had practiced as a Marine colonel and coach of many of the same players at El Toro Marine Air Base. Early in the Rockets' season, the players demanded that Hanley be fired and he was replaced by a committee of players—Bob Dove, Ned Matthews, and Willie Wilkin. Hanley's former assistants, Pat Boland and Ernie Nevers, were left in limbo as the players' committee remained in charge for two games and in fact won both of them. The *Chicago Tribune* covered a practice in which Nevers passed the time by stripping to the waist and taking a sun bath. After two games, the team was placed in the hands of Boland and Nevers and it finished in last place.

Stevens, the Brooklyn surgeon and coach, resigned as Dodgers' coach after seven games and was replaced by co-coaches Cliff Battles and Tom Scott.

The all-league team was made up of ends Alyn Beals of San Francisco and Lavelli of Cleveland; tackles Martin Ruby of Brooklyn and Frank (Bruiser)

Orban (Spec) Sanders of the New York Yankees against the Los Angeles Dons in 1946.

Kinard of the New York Yankees; guards Bruno Banducci of San Francisco and Bill Willis of Cleveland; center Bob Nelson of Los Angeles; quarterback Graham of Cleveland; halfbacks Dobbs of Brooklyn and Sanders of the New York Yankees; and fullback Motley of Cleveland.

Noting that costs were high, commissioner Crowley wrote in a magazine article that pro salaries had increased 100 to 200 percent. "Should the two leagues ever agree on a common draft and a hands-off policy, the figures will drop somewhat," he wrote. "But they will never go back to the days when a good lineman played for only $100 to $150 a game."

The minutes of a league meeting in San Francisco said that there was a "resolution of thanks and tribute to Mr. Ward drawn up—it was the first meeting he did not attend."

1946 AAFC STANDINGS

Eastern Division	W	L	T	Pct.	Pts.	OP
New York Yankees	10	3	1	.769	270	192
Brooklyn Dodgers	3	10	1	.231	226	339
Buffalo Bisons	3	10	1	.231	249	370
Miami Seahawks	3	11	0	.154	167	378
Western Division	W	L	T	Pct.	Pts.	OP
Cleveland Browns	12	2	0	.857	423	137
San Francisco 49ers . . .	9	5	0	.643	307	189
Los Angeles Dons	7	5	2	.583	305	290
Chicago Rockets	5	6	3	.455	263	315

AAFC championship: Cleveland 14, N.Y. Yankees 9

LEADING RUSHERS	Att.	Yards	Avg.	TD
Spec Sanders, N.Y. Yankees	140	709	5.0	6
Norm Standlee, San Francisco	134	651	4.8	2
Vic Kulbitski, Buffalo	97	605	6.2	2
Marion Motley, Cleveland	73	601	8.2	5
Edgar Jones, Cleveland	77	539	7.0	4
LEADING PASSERS	Att.	Comp.	Yards	TD
Glenn Dobbs, Brooklyn	269	135	1,886	13
Otto Graham, Cleveland	174	95	1,834	17
Charlie O'Rourke, Los Angeles	182	105	1,250	12
Frankie Albert, San Francisco	197	104	1,404	14
Bob Hoernschemeyer, Chicago	193	95	1,266	14
LEADING RECEIVERS	No.	Yards	Avg.	TD
Dante Lavelli, Cleveland	40	843	21.8	8
Alyn Beals, San Francisco	40	586	14.7	10
Saxon Judd, Brooklyn	34	443	13.0	4
Ed King, Buffalo	30	466	15.5	6
Elroy Hirsch, Chicago	27	347	12.9	3

The failure of the Seahawks and the uncertain launching of the Rockets had embarrassed the All-America Football Conference. In 1947 there were more administrative changes, coaching changes, and symptoms of an illness that could be fatal—

imbalance, a widening gulf between the league's haves and its have-nots.

But 1947 was, nevertheless, the greatest year in the brief history of the AAFC. Cleveland won the championship again and appeared more unbeatable than ever. And the league's teams in New York City and Los Angeles were exciting ones that won more games and attracted more fans than their NFL rivals.

There was no larger manifestation of faith in the league's future than that made by its commissioner, Jim Crowley, who turned his back on the security of his five-year contract, resigned, and headed a group that purchased the struggling Rockets. In addition, Crowley became their coach.

There was another manifestation of faith in the league in New York. Larry MacPhail and Del Webb, co-owners with Dan Topping of the baseball Yankees, bought into his football team.

Crowley was replaced as commissioner by Admiral Jonas J. Ingram, former commander of the Atlantic fleet. He hired as his deputy Admiral O.O. (Scrappy) Kessing. These years were the period of the most intense participation in pro football by admirals; the Washington Redskins of the NFL were coached, with mixed success, by Admiral John (Billich) Whelchel in 1949.

AAFC commissioner Ingram moved the league offices to New York. Its address was: Empire State Building, New York Row 1, New York. The AAFC made a new charter agreement with Howard Hughes's Trans World Airlines and announced a more sensible schedule in which games were confined to Friday nights and Sunday afternoons, except that there would be two Thanksgiving Day games. The New York Yankees got a break in the schedule in that they would play Los Angeles and San Francisco on successive dates whereas all other clubs had to cross the Rockies twice; the Los Angeles Dons would have to fly to the East coast three times.

Representatives seeking a franchise in Baltimore had attended early meetings of the AAFC in 1944 and 1945, but had been unable at first to rent a stadium for their games and missed being charter members of the league. Baltimore now entered the AAFC as its eighth city, replacing Miami. Robert H. Rodenberg was the principal owner of the Baltimore team, the Colts, and he hired Cecil Isbell to coach the team at Municipal Stadium.

George Taliaferro and Art Hodges (75), Los Angeles Dons vs. San Francisco 49ers, 1949.

Dick Barwegan of the Baltimore Colts and a teammate tackle Bill Grimes of Los Angeles, 1949.

Paul Patterson of the Chicago Hornets about to be stopped by Shorty McWilliams of the Dons, 1949.

The Bisons changed their name to the Bills.

National attention was focused on the San Francisco 49ers when owner Tony Morabito drafted Glenn Davis of Army and also traded for the rights to Davis's famous partner in Army's "Mr. Inside and Mr. Outside" backfield, Felix (Doc) Blanchard. Morabito wanted them to delay their 90-day furlough following their graduation from West Point and join the 49ers. There was a great national controversy about whether these men should pursue their army careers or sign professional football contracts. The War Department at last ordered them to abide by existing policy. Davis later played for the Los Angeles Rams, but Blanchard became a career Air Force officer.

Buddy Young of Illinois and George Ratterman of Notre Dame led the College All-Stars to a 16-0 victory over the Chicago Bears and then Young signed a contract with the New York Yankees and Ratterman with the Buffalo Bills.

The powerful Browns were the focus of widespread interest. When they opened their 1947 season by routing Buffalo 30-14, they were watched by the entire coaching staff of the Chicago Bears.

The most sensational AAFC trade occurred when the Dodgers sent most valuable player Glenn Dobbs to Los Angeles, which sent Angelo Bertelli to Chicago, which sent Bob (Hunchy) Hoernschemeyer to Brooklyn. Dodgers' coach Cliff Battles wanted Hoernschemeyer for his quarterback and the Dons wanted an exciting back to compete for attention in Los Angeles with the Rams' Bob Waterfield.

Dobbs made the Dons in Los Angeles an exciting team that played before 304,177 fans, including the professional record crowd of 82,576 that watched the Dons lose to the New York Yankees 30-14 September 12 at the Los Angeles Coliseum.

John Strzykalski of San Francisco gained 906 yards. Otto Graham of Cleveland completed over 60 percent of his passes and teammate Mac Speedie caught 67 passes. But by far the most sensational player of the year was single wing tailback Orban (Spec) Sanders of the New York Yankees. He rushed for 1,432 yards, a figure that would rank as one of the 10 best in history if the AAFC statistics had been accepted for the all-time pro football records. He also passed for 1,442 yards, gained 250 yards rushing in one game against Chicago October 24, had 450 yards of total offense November 9 against San Francisco, punted for a 42.1-yard average, and scored 19 touchdowns.

The AAFC game that is remembered more than any other was played November 23, 1947 at Yankee Stadium. The Yankees (9-2) took the field against the Browns (10-1) before a crowd of 70,060. The Yankees stunned the Browns by going ahead 28-0 in the first half, but Graham brought the Browns from behind in a stirring comeback that was climaxed when Lou Saban, who was playing in place of the injured Lou Groza, kicked the tying extra point and the game ended 28-28. The same two teams played three weeks later for the AAFC championship and Cleveland won again, 14-3.

Cleveland, New York, Buffalo, San Francisco, and Los Angeles all were winners, but Brooklyn, Baltimore, and the Chicago Rockets, who were coached by former Commissioner Crowley, all had dismal records.

Graham was named most valuable player and the all-league team for 1947 was: ends Dante Lavelli and Speedie of Cleveland; tackles Nate Johnson of the New York Yankees and Lou Rymkus of Cleveland; guards Bruno Banducci of San Francisco and Bill Willis of Cleveland; center Bob Nelson of Los Angeles; quarterback Graham; halfbacks Chet Mutryn of Buffalo and Sanders of the New York Yankees; and fullback Marion Motley of Cleveland.

Eastern Division	W	L	T	Pct.	Pts.	OP
New York Yankees	11	2	1	.846	378	239
Buffalo Bills	8	4	2	.667	320	288
Brooklyn Dodgers	3	10	1	.231	181	340
Baltimore Colts	2	11	1	.154	167	377

Western Division	W	L	T	Pct.	Pts.	OP
Cleveland Browns	12	1	1	.923	410	185
San Francisco 49ers ...	8	4	2	.667	327	264
Los Angeles Dons	7	7	0	.500	328	256
Chicago Rockets	1	13	0	.071	263	425

AAFC championship: Cleveland 14, N.Y. Yankees 3.

LEADING RUSHERS	Att.	Yards	Avg.	TD
Spec Sanders, N.Y. Yankees	231	1,432	6.2	19
John Strzykalski, San Francisco	143	906	6.3	5
Marion Motley, Cleveland	146	889	6.0	8
Chet Mutryn, Buffalo	140	868	6.2	9
Buddy Young, N.Y. Yankees	116	712	6.1	3

LEADING PASSERS	Att.	Comp.	Yards	TD
Otto Graham, Cleveland	269	163	2,753	25
Bud Schwenk, Baltimore	327	168	2,236	13
Frankie Albert, San Francisco	242	128	1,692	18
George Ratterman, Buffalo	244	124	1,840	22
Spec Sanders, N.Y. Yankees	171	93	1,442	14

LEADING RECEIVERS	No.	Yards	Avg.	TD
Mac Speedie, Cleveland	67	1,146	17.1	6
Dante Lavelli, Cleveland	49	799	16.3	9
Alyn Beals, San Francisco	47	655	13.9	10
Lamar Davis, Baltimore	46	515	11.2	2
Billy Hillenbrand, Baltimore	39	702	18.0	7

PROFESSIONAL FOOTBALL IN NEW YORK CITY

Team	Stadium/Years
New York Giants, NFL	1925–55 Polo Grnds. 1956–73 Yankee Stad. 1974 Yale Bowl 1975 Shea Stad. 1976–77 Giants Stad.
Brooklyn Horsemen, NFL	1926 Ebbets Field
Brooklyn Lions, first AFL	1926 Ebbets Field
New York Yankees, first AFL	1926 Yankee Stadium
New York Yankees, NFL	1927–28 Yankee Stadium
Stapleton Stapes, NFL	1929–32 Thompson Stadium, Staten Island
Brooklyn Dodgers, NFL	1930–43 Ebbets Field
New York Yankees, second AFL	1936 Yankee Stadium
New York Yankees, third AFL	1940 Yankee Stadium
New York Americans, third AFL	1941 Yankee Stadium
Brooklyn Tigers, NFL	1944 Ebbets Field
Brooklyn Dodgers, AAFC	1946–48 Ebbets Field
New York Yankees, AAFC	1946–48 Yankee Stadium
Brooklyn-N.Y. Yankees, AAFC	1949 Yankee Stadium
New York Bulldogs, NFL	1949 Polo Grounds
New York Yanks, NFL	1950–51 Yankee Stadium
New York Jets (Titans), AFL, AFC	1960–63 Polo Grounds 1964–77 Shea Stadium
New York Stars, WFL	1974 Downing Stadium

The member teams of the AAFC began to see by 1948 that the optimistic predictions they had made earlier for their attendance, income, and success in competing against the National Football League were not being realized. The outlook grew dimmer and dimmer for the league's weak teams. Wholesale ownership and coaching changes began, the commissioner made a novel and unsuccessful attempt to balance competition in the league, and for the first time there were public overtures made to the NFL for a merger.

New ownership headed by Robert C. Embry took over the Baltimore Colts. Branch Rickey, who ran baseball's Brooklyn Dodgers and Ebbets Field, took control of the struggling Dodgers football team. R. Edward Garn headed a Chicago civic group that purchased the Rockets.

The new coaches were Carl Voyles at Brooklyn, Ed McKeever at Chicago, Jimmy Phelan at Los Angeles, and Norman (Red) Strader for the New York Yankees.

AAFC commissioner Ingram ordered the strongest teams in the league to distribute some of their players to weakest clubs in order to create more balance. The Yankees were the only team to abide by both the letter and the spirit of the directive. They apparently were even more generous than they needed to be and, with many of their best players scattered to other cities, dropped to a 6–8 record in 1948. New York never had a strong AAFC team again. The Browns, complying with Ingram's order, gave rookie quarterback Y.A. Tittle outright to the Baltimore Colts.

When committees from the two leagues met in December and issued a joint statement about their willingness to end the war, it was the first time the NFL officially recognized that the AAFC existed. In the talks, the NFL offered to take in Cleveland and San Francisco and let Lindheimer of the Dons' owning group buy into the Los Angeles Rams. An AAFC concession came when Topping of the Yankees offered to cease operations and be satisfied to collect rent from another team for Yankee Stadium. The discussions ended, however, when the NFL adamantly refused to admit any teams other than the Browns and 49ers. The AAFC decided to prolong the struggle another year.

The league's two best teams were together in the same division. Cleveland went through an entire season without losing a game for the first time, and San Francisco was 12–2. When they met in a regular season game at Cleveland, 82,769 were present. Quarterback Otto Graham of Cleveland passed for 25 touchdowns for the season and Frankie Albert of San Francisco had 29. In addition, the 49ers had a team rushing average of 6.1 yards per carry.

The Browns defeated the Yankees in New York on a Sunday, the Rams in Los Angeles the following Thursday (Thanksgiving Day), and the 49ers 31–28 in San Francisco three days later on Sunday—three victories in eight days.

Tailback Glenn Dobbs of Los Angeles passed for 405 yards in a game against the 49ers, but also threw seven interceptions that day and the Dons lost.

Rookie quarterback Y.A. Tittle of the Baltimore Colts had 346 yards passing on just 11 completions, a 31.5 average per completion, in a game against the New York Yankees.

Two teams with .500 records, Baltimore and Buffalo, played off for the Eastern Division championship and the winner, Buffalo, lost the AAFC championship game to Cleveland 49–7.

Graham and Albert were named co-most valuable players. The all-league team was made up of ends Alyn Beals of San Francisco and Mac Speedie of

Glenn Dobbs appearing on KTLA television in Los Angeles in front of a photo of Memorial Coliseum.

Cleveland; tackles Bob Reinhard of Los Angeles and Lou Rymkus of Cleveland; guards Dick Barwegan of Baltimore and Bill Willis of Cleveland; center Bob Nelson of Los Angeles; quarterback Graham; halfbacks Chet Mutryn of Buffalo and John Strzykalski of San Francisco; and fullback Marion Motley of Cleveland.

1948 AAFC STANDINGS

Eastern Division	W	L	T	Pct.	Pts.	OP
Buffalo Bills	7	7	0	.500	360	358
Baltimore Colts	7	7	0	.500	333	327
New York Yankees	6	8	0	.429	265	301
Brooklyn Dodgers	2	12	0	.143	253	387
Western Division	**W**	**L**	**T**	**Pct.**	**Pts.**	**OP**
Cleveland Browns	14	0	0	1.000	389	190
San Francisco 49ers . . .	12	2	0	.857	495	248
Los Angeles Dons	7	7	0	.500	258	305
Chicago Rockets	1	13	0	.071	202	439

Eastern Division playoff: Buffalo 28, Baltimore 17
AAFC championship: Cleveland 49, Buffalo 7

LEADING RUSHERS	Att.	Yards	Avg.	TD
Marion Motley, Cleveland	157	964	6.2	5
John Strzykalski, San Francisco	141	915	6.5	4
Chet Mutryn, Buffalo	147	823	5.6	10
Spec Sanders, N.Y. Yankees	169	759	4.5	9
Lou Tomasetti, Buffalo	134	716	5.3	7

LEADING PASSERS	Att.	Comp.	Yards	TD
Otto Graham, Cleveland	333	173	2,713	25
Glenn Dobbs, Los Angeles	369	185	2,403	21
Y.A. Tittle, Baltimore	289	161	2,522	16
George Ratterman, Buffalo	335	168	2,577	16
Frankie Albert, San Francisco	264	154	1,990	29

LEADING RECEIVERS	No.	Yards	Avg.	TD
Mac Speedie, Cleveland	58	816	14.1	4
Al Baldwin, Buffalo	54	916	17.0	8
Billy Hillenbrand, Baltimore	50	970	19.4	6
Dolly King, Chicago	50	647	12.9	7
Alyn Beals, San Francisco	46	591	12.8	14

The All-America Football Conference was always fully covered in the pages of the *Chicago Tribune.* Arch Ward was the sports editor of the paper and the founder of the league. He was also the director of the Chicago All-Star Game, which matched the NFL champion and the College All-Stars. In 1949 all three came together in a critical issue with Ward at its vortex.

He promised the AAFC he would get its champion into the all-star game. The contract with the NFL was up and Ward told NFL owners he wasn't going to renew. Suddenly, however, Ward reversed himself and signed a new contract with the NFL, shutting out the AAFC.

A gleeful NFL celebrated and some people concluded in print that Ward had lacked faith in the abil-

ity of the AAFC to keep the all-star game alive. But Ward had actually suffered a rare defeat at his newspaper. The NFL owners had gone over his head. Warned by publicity director and former *Tribune* sportswriter George Strickler of Ward's influence with Col. McCormick, the publisher, the NFL went instead to managing editor J. Loy Maloney, who put the question before the paper's board of directors. The board renewed the NFL's contract.

Crushed, the AAFC staggered on. The Brooklyn Dodgers, "Branch Rickey's white elephant," merged with the New York Yankees. The Baltimore Colts acquired their third president in three years, Walter S. Driskill. James C. Thompson and others purchased the struggling Chicago Rockets and renamed them the Hornets.

Lindheimer of the Dons, who apparently aided other clubs as well with outright payments, traded back Herman Wedemeyer to Baltimore and when the Colts said they could not handle his $12,000 contract, Lindheimer agreed to pay half of it.

The league's attendance dropped 30 percent from the previous year. Coaching shuffles were everywhere. Owner Driskill replaced Cecil Isbell as coach at Baltimore after four games; Driskill's record was 1–7. Clem Crowe became coach at Buffalo. Ray Flaherty, former Yankees coach, took over the Chicago Rockets. Of all AAFC coaches, only Paul Brown of Cleveland and Lawrence (Buck) Shaw of San Francisco coached their teams throughout the league's four-year existence.

Admiral Jonas Ingram resigned as commissioner and another nautical commissioner and Ingram's former deputy, O.O. (Scrappy) Kessing, came aboard. He said, "Our league is not dead, not dying, and not going to die."

It died in December, 1949. The merger was instigated by Horace Stoneham, owner of the baseball Giants and the Polo Grounds, where the football Giants played and which was one of the stadiums suffering from the malaise of the pro football war. Stoneham arranged a meeting between George Weiss of the baseball and football Yankees and Bert Bell, commissioner of the NFL, in New York City. Out of this came a meeting between Bell and J. Arthur Friedlund, a lawyer who represented the All-America Football Conference. "They talked for a while there in New York and then came to Philadelphia [to Bell's office] two days ago," the *New York Mirror* reported. "Three days of round-the-clock conferences came to

an end shortly after noon today and the two men, tired but jubilant, summoned reporters to break the news."

The Cleveland Browns, "the one prize the National League wants," Gordon Cobbledick wrote in the *Cleveland Plain-Dealer,* joined the NFL.

So did the San Francisco 49ers, because they were an exciting winning team and because NFL teams on the East Coast could go west and play both Los Angeles and San Francisco for the same amount of plane fare, and receive two cash guarantees from gate receipts.

The Baltimore Colts won only one game in 1949 but they came into the NFL, too. Owner George Preston Marshall of the Washington Redskins, who had been a fiery opponent of the AAFC, became convinced that Baltimore could become a strong rival—and one with little travel costs—for the Redskins. The *New York Times* reported, "It was Marshall's willingness to let the Baltimore Colts into the NFL which reportedly dissolved the four-year feud . . . Marshall revealed he had cleared the way for Baltimore's admission by waiving his territorial rights for a 'nominal fee.' [The 'nominal fee' was $150,000.]

"Puffing on an Indian peace pipe for the benefit of photographers, Marshall called league Commissioner Bert Bell in Philadelphia to try to clear up some points about the armistice.

"'Hello, peace pipe,' he greeted Bell. 'What league am I supposed to be in?'"

The Redskins were placed in the new American Conference of the NFL.

James F. Breuil, owner of the Buffalo Bills, received a 25 percent interest in the Cleveland Browns and the Browns were awarded three Bills' players —Rex Bumgardner, John Kissell, and Abe Gibron.

Six Brooklyn–New York Yankees players were awarded to the New York Giants, including Tom Landry, Otto Schnellbacher, Harmon Rowe, and Arnie Weinmeister. Some called it "the greatest input of talent in the Giants' history."

Ted Collins, owner of the NFL New York Bulldogs, was given a 10-year lease on Yankee Stadium. He had moved his team from Boston to New York, expecting the AAFC to fold earlier, and when it did not he had had to share Horace Stoneham's Polo Grounds with the New York Giants.

Collins's team took the name New York Yanks and acquired the star backs of the old AAFC Yankees, Spec Sanders and Buddy Young. In other notable

Marion Motley.

Dante Lavelli.

Otto Graham playing defense, 1946.

LEADING RECEIVERS	No.	Yards	Avg.	TD
Mac Speedie, Cleveland	62	1,028	16.6	7
Al Baldwin, Buffalo	53	719	13.6	7
Alyn Beals, San Francisco	44	678	15.4	12
Dan Edwards, Chicago	42	573	13.6	3
Lamar Davis, Baltimore	38	548	14.4	1

THE WFL

The overwhelming success of the American Football League of 1960–69 set off an era of expansion in sport. By merging with the NFL, the AFL increased professional football to 26 teams. Baseball grew to 24. Rival basketball and hockey leagues, the American Basketball Association and World Hockey Association, appeared.

The latter creations were the work of Dennis Murphy, a Southern California public relations man, and Gary L. Davidson and Donald J. Regan, lawyers who had an office across the hall from Murphy in a building in Newport Beach. Davidson became the first president of each league, the ABA in 1967 and the WHA in 1971.

He resigned the presidency of the hockey league in October, 1973 and began laying plans for a third creation, the World Football League. He took the title of commissioner and pursued buyers for franchises in the league. It was announced that the league "would eventually encompass the entire world."

Its first meeting took place in Los Angeles in January, 1974. Twelve franchises existed at the time or grew from that meeting. Their locations, their names, and their ownership changed often. Sometimes the owners were from the enfranchised cities and sometimes they were not.

The Birmingham Americans franchise was headed by Bill Putnam, a former Navy underwater demolition expert, vice-president of the J. P. Morgan Company in New York City, executive vice-president of Jack Kent Cooke Enterprises, owner of the Philadelphia Flyers of the National Hockey League, and president of the group controlling the Atlanta Hawks and Atlanta Flames of the NHL. A former secretary named Carol Tygart Stallworth became part-owner and president of the Americans. Jack Gotta was hired as coach and the team arranged to play at Legion Field in Birmingham.

Nick Mileti, part-owner of baseball's Cleveland Indians, basketball's Cleveland Cavaliers, and hockey's Cleveland Crusaders, purchased a franchise he in turn sold to Tom Origer, an owner of apartment buildings in Chicago. This franchise became the Chicago Fire. Origer was the first owner to sign a player, wide receiver Jim Seymour. He named Jim Spavital his coach and secured Soldier Field for the Fire's games.

The Detroit Wheels became the property of a large group of investors headed by Louis R. Lee, a 28-year-old Detroit lawyer and a former University of Michigan football player. The team's identity as a Detroit franchise was strained when it arranged to play at Rynearson Stadium on the campus of Eastern Michigan University, 37 miles away in Ypsilanti. Dan Boisture became the Wheels' coach.

The Florida Blazers had origins elsewhere. E. Joseph Wheeler, owner of a marine biology and engineering company, purchased a franchise he named variously as the Washington Capitals, the Washington–Baltimore Ambassadors, and the Washington Ambassadors. He was unable to lease RFK Stadium in Washington and moved the team to Norfolk, Virginia in April. In May, he sold the team to a group headed by Rommie L. Loudd, which moved it to Orlando and named it the Florida Blazers. Jack Pardee had already been named coach of the team, which rented the Tangerine Bowl Stadium. Loudd

The San Francisco 49ers' Joe Perry, leading AAFC rusher in 1949.

player shifts, end Len Ford of the Dons joined Cleveland and back Bob (Hunchy) Hoernschemeyer of the Yankees joined the Detroit Lions.

The interests of the Chicago Hornets were purchased by the league and the franchise was disbanded.

The merger agreement was announced the day before the Browns and 49ers were to play for the last championship, December 11, 1949. Only 22,000 fans watched as Cleveland won 21–7. The Browns then agreed to play a team of AAFC all-stars in Houston. Only a small crowd attended and the all-stars won 12–7.

The AAFC never named a most valuable player for 1949. The all-star team was made up of ends Alyn Beals of San Francisco and Mac Speedie of Cleveland; tackles Bob Reinhard of Los Angeles and Arnie Weinmeister of Brooklyn–New York; guards Dick Barwegan of Baltimore and Visco Grgich of San Francisco; center (an accommodation because he actually played linebacker) Lou Saban of Cleveland; quarterback Otto Graham of Cleveland; halfbacks Frankie Albert of San Francisco (also an accommodation because he actually played quarterback) and Chet Mutryn of Buffalo; and fullback Joe Perry of San Francisco.

The AAFC's all-time statistical champions were Marion Motley of Cleveland, rushing, 3,024 yards; Graham, passing, 592 completions, 10,085 yards, and 86 touchdowns; Speedie, receiving, 211; and Beals, scoring, 46 touchdowns and two extra points for a total of 278 points.

For a period of about two months after the merger, the NFL in its press releases and in newspaper articles was called the "National-American Football League." That ended in March and the name National Football League was restored.

Many reasons have been given why the AAFC failed. The Cleveland Browns had a 51–4–3 record and were too good for the rest of the league. If Cleveland and New York had been in the same division,

there would have been a tighter race in the East and strong competition in the West between Los Angeles and San Francisco.

The AAFC was in direct competition with the NFL in New York, Chicago, and Los Angeles. During 1946–49, there were three teams in Chicago—the Bears, Cardinals, and Hornets–Rockets.

Former player Buddy Young says, "The weakness of the AAFC was in overall coaching and player depth. Some of the coaches had never been associated with pro football and didn't realize the necessity of having more than eleven or fifteen good players. In college, you could get by that way but in the pros you must have depth."

In a master stroke, NFL Commissioner Bell scheduled the AAFC champion Browns against the NFL champion Philadelphia Eagles on a Saturday night of the 1950 season, before the rest of the league's teams opened the following day. Cleveland won 35–10, lost only two games the entire season, and won the league championship.

1949 AFC STANDINGS	W	L	T	Pct.	Pts.	OP
Cleveland Browns	9	1	2	.900	339	171
San Francisco 49ers ...	9	3	0	.750	416	227
Brooklyn-N.Y. Yankees .	8	4	0	.667	196	206
Buffalo Bills	5	5	2	.500	236	256
Chicago Hornets	4	8	0	.333	179	268
Los Angeles Dons	4	8	0	.333	253	322
Baltimore Colts	1	11	0	.083	172	341

Playoff: Cleveland 31, Buffalo 21
Playoff: San Francisco 17, Brooklyn-New York 7
Championship: Cleveland 21, San Francisco 7

LEADING RUSHERS	Att.	Yards	Avg.	TD
Joe Perry, San Francisco	115	783	6.8	8
Chet Mutryn, Buffalo	131	696	5.3	5
Marion Motley, Cleveland	113	570	5.0	8
Ollie Cline, Buffalo	125	518	4.1	3
Young, Brooklyn-N.Y. Yankees	76	495	6.5	5

LEADING PASSERS	Att.	Comp.	Yards	TD
Otto Graham, Cleveland	285	161	2,785	19
Y.A. Tittle, Baltimore	289	148	2,209	14
George Ratterman, Buffalo	252	146	1,777	14
Frankie Albert, San Francisco	260	129	1,862	27
Hoernschemeyer, Chicago	167	69	1,063	6

had been an All-Pacific Coast end at UCLA in 1954 and 1955 and played with the Los Angeles Chargers and Boston Patriots of the AFL from 1960–62. He also scouted and coached for Boston.

A franchise that became The Hawaiians, in Honolulu, was originally started by Danny Rogers, manager of a sales firm and a former basketball coach. Chris B. Hemmeter, developer of restaurants and building projects in Hawaii, and Sam D. Battistone, the president of Invest West, which owned Sambo's restaurants, became owners of the Hawaiians. Mike Giddings was hired as their coach, and Honolulu Stadium was the site of their home games.

Steve Arnold, a San Franciscan who once was the player agent of Jim Brown of the Cleveland Browns, owned a franchise the WFL first intended for Memphis but which became the Houston Texans. The Astrodome was rented and Jim Garrett became Texans' coach.

Fran Monaco, operator of medical laboratories and co-owner of a restaurant in Deland, Florida with former Chicago Bears middle linebacker Dick Butkus, became the owner of the Jacksonville Sharks. He named his wife, Douglas, as the vice-president and they hired Bud Asher, the coach of New Smyrna Beach, Florida, High School to coach the Sharks. It was to play its games at the Gator Bowl Stadium.

The franchise of John Bassett, Jr., was originally the Toronto, Ontario, Northmen, but it became the Memphis, Tennessee, Southmen. Bassett, a millionaire Canadian, had interests in a television station, a newspaper, a film company, and Toronto's Canadian Football League team and World Hockey Association team. But he had to move his WFL team because of opposition from the CFL, which enlisted the Canadian minister of health and welfare in its cause. Memphis investors joining Bassett in the team's ownership included entertainers Charlie Rich and Isaac Hayes. John McVay was named coach of the Southmen and they rented Memphis Memorial Stadium.

The New York Stars had an active period of development. Howard Baldwin, 31-year-old president of the New England Whalers of the World Hockey Association, originally intended to form a team in Boston that was first called the Bulldogs, then the Bulls. It signed a player, wide receiver George Sauer, and hired a coach, Babe Parilli, while it was still the Bulldogs. Baldwin, however, could not find financial backing. Robert J. Schmertz, land developer and owner of the Boston Celtics of basketball, emerged as the Bulldogs' principal owner and moved them to New York, where they became the Stars. The site they preferred, Yankee Stadium, was undergoing renovation and the Stars found themselves at a serious disadvantage when they had to settle for aging Downing Stadium on Randall's Island.

The city of Philadelphia was represented at the first meeting of the WFL by Ken Bogdanoff, who had once been a lifeguard at an apartment complex in Philadelphia where future Birmingham owner Bill Putnam lived while he was owner of the Flyers hockey team. The two often talked sports at poolside. Bogdanoff later worked as assistant ticket manager of the Flyers, but he was unemployed at the time of the WFL meeting. With money borrowed from relatives, he and a partner raised $50,000 to make a down payment on a WFL franchise priced by Davidson at $400,000. The partner dropped out with his $25,000, however, and so did Bogdanoff on the morning of the organizational meeting. But at the request of the founders, he stayed to answer the roll call for Philadelphia. Control of the team was later passed to John B. Kelly, Jr., wealthy sportsman and Philadelphia city councilman, and then to attorney John Bosacco. The team, which was called the Bell, rented JFK Stadium and named Ron Waller as its coach.

Grant Gelker, an Orange County, California businessman, founder of the Saddleback Inn chain of hotels and motels, and a friend of Davidson, headed a franchise originally intended for New York City but which finally was placed in Portland and became the Storm. Dick Coury became its coach and it leased Civic Stadium.

Larry G. Hatfield was, with Davidson, a member of the Balboa Bay Club at Newport Beach, California. Hatfield had become wealthy operating a computer and graphics company in Jackson, Mississippi, and then a trucking company in Southern California. He formed the Southern California Sun. Al Lapin, head of the parent company of International House of Pancakes and Orange Julius chains, was also a Sun backer. The Southern California team rented Anaheim Stadium and hired Tom Fears as coach.

Franchises in Tokyo and Mexico City were discussed but did not materialize.

The league held a draft of players and arranged a novel schedule in which each team would begin its season in July while the NFL teams were still in training camps, and the majority of the WFL's games would be played Wednesday nights. Each team would play 20 games and there would be no preseason. A contract was made with the independent TVS Television Network for one WFL game a week to be played Thursday night and shown on prime-time television. Never had pro football been played and televised nationally in midweek.

Making a schedule proved a difficult task. Hawaii adamantly insisted on Sunday games, saying midweek football would not go over in Honolulu. Detroit could not play a home game in a week when Eastern Michigan had a home game. Toronto moved to Memphis, and Washington moved to Virginia, then Florida. The problems were overcome, however, and a schedule was announced in May.

The schedule was not the WFL's only novelty. The league's singular instead of plural nicknames began with the Fire in Chicago; the Bell, Storm, and Sun followed. Changes in pro football rules were announced. The WFL voted to kick off from the 30-yard line instead of the 35; to move the goal posts from the goal lines to the end lines; to move in the hashmarks; to ban fair catches of punts; to allow men in motion toward the line of scrimmage before the snap; to play a fifth quarter in the event of a tie; to require receivers to have only one foot inbounds to make a legal catch; to prohibit bump-and-run against receivers once they're three yards past the line of scrimmage; to bring the ball back to the line of scrimmage not the 20-yard line after field goals missed from outside the 20 and fourth down passes incomplete inside the 20; and to count touchdowns as seven instead of six points and have an "action point" counting one point, to be made after a touchdown by either running or passing, not kicking. The WFL decided to use an invention called a "Dickerrod" instead of the orthodox chain unit for measuring down yardage. And the league at first intended to use a football with swirls painted on it, similar to the red, white, and blue basketball used in the American Basketball Association that Davidson once headed. It dropped the colored ball idea, however.

Despite its novelties, skepticism about the WFL prevailed until March 31, 1974 when owner John Bassett, Jr., of the team then known as the Toronto Northmen announced he had signed Larry Csonka, Jim Kiick, and Paul Warfield of the two-time Super Bowl champion Miami Dolphins to three-year contracts starting with the 1975 football season, a year away. What was described as a $3 million package for the three of them had iron-clad guarantees they would get the money whatever happened to the league.

Other signings followed, Bill Bergey of Cincinnati

with the Florida Blazers; John Gilliam of Minnesota, Calvin Hill of Dallas, and Ted Kwalick of San Francisco with the Hawaiians; and Curley Culp of Kansas City and Daryle Lamonica of Oakland with the Southern California Sun. By June 4, WFL teams claimed the signings of 59 NFL players who were playing out their options and would be ready to join the WFL, most of them in 1975. The NFL was stunned and the Dallas Cowboys obtained a restraining order blocking the signing of other Cowboys' players.

Big crowds were reported at opening games of the WFL in mid-July. There was a revelation from Philadelphia, however, that dealt the league a heavy blow. The Bell had announced an attendance of 55,534 for its opening game against Portland and 64,719 for a game 15 days later against the New York Stars. But an official of the team admitted the figures were inflated. He disclosed that for tax purposes the team had actually reported having sold 13,800 tickets for the first game and 6,200 for the second; the rest of the tickets had been given away. Credibility of the league suffered from this news.

Four teams—one-third of the league—fell on hard times two months into the season. The league took over the operations of the Detroit Wheels and Jacksonville Sharks, and then both teams folded. The Houston Texans were moved to Shreveport, Louisiana, and became the Steamer, and the New York Stars moved to Charlotte, North Carolina, and became the Hornets.

Detroit's former general manager had asserted in his team's media book that the Wheels "could make an honest, qualified run at the WFL title in our first year." It did not, losing its first 10 games and drawing no crowd larger than 10,631. The owners of the team reportedly borrowed $265,000 from the league. Troubles continued. According to the *Washington Post*, the Wheels' trainer had to borrow athletic tape from other teams, the players had to bring their own towels, and the coach could not afford to have the games filmed. The team went bankrupt and listed debts of $2.5 million.

In Jacksonville, the owner reportedly borrowed $27,000 from his coach, Asher, and then fired him. Charlie Tate was named the new coach. Players went unpaid for several weeks and Commissioner Davidson visited them when they played in Southern California and handed out an estimated $65,000 in paychecks. The franchise was surrendered to the league October 8.

Difficulty in meeting the Astrodome rent contributed to the relocation of the Texans to Shreveport. In New York, the Stars averaged only 8,000 fans for six home games. On opening night, the keys to the ticket booths at Downing Stadium could not be located and the booths were broken open so tickets could be sold. Traffic in and out of the island stadium jammed often. Relocated in Charlotte, North Carolina, the team was taken over by a group led by Upton Bell, son of former NFL Commissioner Bert Bell and former general manager of the New England Patriots. Difficulties continued and in November the operator of a cleaning service, J. Rodney Ryan, filed suit against the team for money he was owed, and immediately after a game the Hornets had to surrender their jerseys, pants, and other equipment to sheriff's deputies bearing writs impounding the equipment.

Davidson resigned the commissionership October 29. Owners Origer of the Chicago Fire and Bassett of the Memphis Southmen were said to have urged his resignation. Origer, who said he had lost $750,000 to $800,000, apparently threatened to fold his team if Davidson did not quit. A month later, Hemmeter of Hawaii was named the new commissioner.

The WFL playoff structure went through several changes in which the field grew from four teams to six

Anthony Davis of the Southern California Sun runs vs. Memphis, 1975.

Chris Hemmeter, second commissioner of the World Football League.

to eight, the latter only one less than the league membership. The playoff field was then reduced to three, then increased again to six. In the playoffs, Southern California Sun players Booker Brown, Kermit Johnson, and James McAlister did not play following a dispute and the Sun lost in the first round.

The "World Bowl" for the WFL championship December 5 at Birmingham matched two teams that reflected the league's troubles. The Birmingham Americans were supposed to have missed five payrolls in a row, the Florida Blazers fifteen. The Americans were hounded by creditors. Their players threatened to boycott the game and then changed their minds and agreed to play.

Florida was a sentimental favorite, *Sports Illustrated* wrote, "because of its greater deprivation." The team was under the operation of the league. A sale to a new owner had fallen through when, according to newspaper reports, it was learned the buyer was a convicted felon. Coach Jack Pardee and his assistants were providing the team with toilet paper for the locker room.

Alternate quarterbacks George Mira and Matthew Reed led the Americans to a narrow 22–21 victory for the championship. Mira was named the game's most valuable player. When it ended, a Florida player snatched the game ball and dashed away but Birmingham players caught up with him under the stands and, after a tussle, reclaimed the football.

The Americans' uniforms were repossessed after the game by sheriff's deputies. The equipment was later sold as souvenirs by a sporting goods store.

Quarterback Tony Adams of Southern California and running backs J.J. Jennings of Memphis and Tommy Reamon of Florida were named co-most valuable players in the league. Reamon reportedly did not receive any salary from the Sharks all season.

1974 WFL STANDINGS

Eastern Division	W	L	T	Pct.	Pts.	OP
Florida Blazers	14	6	0	.700	419	280
N.Y. Stars–Char. Hornets ..	10	10	0	.500	467	350
Philadelphia Bell	8	11	0	.421	493	413
Jacksonville Sharks	4	10	0	.286	258	358
Central Division	W	L	T	Pct.	Pts.	OP
Memphis Southmen	17	3	0	.850	629	365
Birmingham Americans	15	5	0	.750	503	394
Chicago Fire	7	12	0	.368	446	622
Detroit Wheels	1	13	0	.071	209	358
Western Division	W	L	T	Pct.	Pts.	OP
Southern California Sun	13	7	0	.650	486	441
Hawaiians	9	11	0	.450	413	425
Portland Storm	7	12	1	.375	264	426
Hou. Tex.–Shrev. Steamer ..	7	12	1	.375	240	415

First round playoffs: Florida 18, Philadelphia 3;
Hawaii 34, Southern California 14
Semifinals: Florida, 18, Memphis 15;
Birmingham 22, Hawaii 19
"World Bowl": Birmingham 22, Florida 21

LEADING RUSHERS	Att.	Yards	Avg.	Long	TD
Tommy Reamon, Florida	386	1,576	4.1	55	11
J.J. Jennings, Memphis	300	1,240	4.1	27	8
Jim Nance, Houston-Shreveport	300	1,240	4.1	27	8
John Land, Philadelphia	243	1,136	4.7	46	8
Rufus Ferguson, Portland	260	1,086	4.2	74	6
LEADING PASSERS	Att.	Comp.	Yards	TD	Int.
Tony Adams, So. California	510	276	3,905	23	18
Jim (King) Corcoran, Philadelphia	545	280	3,631	31	24
Bob Davis, Florida	413	232	2,977	21	23
Virg Carter, Chicago	358	195	2,629	27	16
John Huarte, Memphis	296	154	2,416	24	16
LEADING RECEIVERS	No.	Yards	Avg.	Long	TD
Tim Delaney, Hawaii	89	1,232	13.8	42	8
Rick Eber, Houston-Shreveport	66	771	11.7	63	5
James McAlister, So. California	65	772	11.9	70	4
Dennis Homan, Birmingham	61	930	15.3	73	8
Alfred Jenkins, Birmingham	60	1,326	22.1	95	12

The World Football League returned in 1975 saying it was a different organization altogether; it was now the New World Football League. All the debts from the first year would be paid, but no deadline was given. The statistics and records that had been made by the teams the first year appeared in the press manual "as a service to the media who may be interested in the continuity of such records.

"It should be noted, however, that last year's teams played for what is now legally known as the Football Creditor's Payment Plan, Inc., formerly known as the World Football League, and now in Chapter Eleven reorganizational proceedings. This year's World Football League is a completely separate and distinctive league, even though some players and franchise locations are the same as the 'old' World Football League of 1974."

Ten teams were in fact in the same place. Every franchise except the hapless Detroit Wheels was resurrected. Everyone but three had new leadership; John Bassett, Jr., still controlled the Memphis franchise, John Bosacco still owned the Philadelphia Bell, and Upton Bell still led a group controlling the Charlotte team.

The Florida Blazers were moved to Texas to become the San Antonio Wings. Birmingham was now the Vulcans, Chicago the Winds, Jacksonville the Express, and Portland the Thunder. Sometimes Memphis was called the Southmen and sometimes it was called the Grizzlies.

Each ownership group was forbidden to sell for three years, and ordered to escrow $545,000 and make a $75,000 payment to league headquarters, which were relocated in New York. Each team was to adopt an austere budget and face inspection of its books every two weeks. Padding of attendance figures was strictly forbidden.

Hemmeter, the new commissioner, announced a

profit-sharing concept that became known as the Hemmeter Plan. It called for players to share in the net income with their owners; if there was no income, the players would get the minimum salary, $500 a game for 20 games. The Hemmeter Plan did not affect the large contracts such as the ones made between John Bassett, Jr., and Larry Csonka, Jim Kiick, and Paul Warfield.

Two of a team's games would be exhibitions, for which players would get $200 a game. There would be no training camp pay.

The WFL schedule for 1975 called for Saturday night, not Wednesday night games, and had an oddity in that, because of a stadium conflict, there would be a regular season game between Charlotte and San Antonio during the exhibition part of the schedule. TVS did not renew its contract to televise WFL games. An experiment in which linebackers wore red pants, running backs green pants, receivers orange pants, defensive backs yellow pants, offensive linemen white pants, and devensive linemen black pants in exhibition games was roundly criticized and abandoned. The Dickerrod was dropped. And the league decided that for economy reasons only one game official, the referee, would travel; the other officials would be provided locally.

At last the league had well-known players. This was the year for Csonka, Kiick, Warfield, Calvin Hill, John Gilliam, and Ted Kwalick to begin playing in the WFL. Those players appeared with Hemmeter at a press conference at the Waldorf-Astoria Hotel in New York April 17, demonstrating the appeal and solidarity of the "new" WFL. Southern California signed star running back Anthony Davis of USC.

There were troubles elsewhere, however. Bill Bergey, Curley Culp, L.C. Greenwood, and Ken Stabler were star players who broached WFL contracts that had been scheduled to begin in 1975 and returned to the NFL. Joe Namath of the New York Jets spurned a reputed $4 million contract from the Chicago Winds and their representative, Chicago real estate and insurance figure Eugene Pullano.

The "governors" of the team, as the owners were called, were banker Ferd Weil of the Birmingham Vulcans; Bell of the Charlotte Hornets; Pullano of the Chicago Winds; jewelry manufacturer Edward Sultan, Jr., of the Hawaiians; land developer Earl Knabb of the Jacksonville Express; Bassett of the Memphis Southmen or Grizzlies; Bosacco of the Philadelphia Bell; attorney Richard V. Bayless of the Portland Thunder; financial consultant Norm Bevan of the San Antonio Wings; oil and gas executive John B. Atkins, Jr., of the Shreveport Steamer; and former Hawaiians part-owner Sam Battistone, now "gover-

Larry Csonka.

Jim Kiick.

Paul Warfield.

nor" of the Southern California Sun.

Mike Giddings of Hawaii; Babe Parilli, who moved from Charlotte to Chicago; John McVay of Memphis; and Tom Fears of Southern California were the returning coaches. Newcomers were Marvin Bass of Birmingham, Bob Gibson of Charlotte, Charlie Tate of Jacksonville, Willie Wood of Philadelphia, Greg Barton of Portland, Perry Moss of San Antonio, and Marshall Taylor of Shreveport.

The Chicago Winds were the league's first casualty. They failed to sign Namath. Their season ticket sale thereafter did not climb above 2,000. Parilli was hired as their coach and general manager and then fired before the end of July and replaced with two people, Abe Gibron as coach and Leo Cahill as general manager; a furious Parilli said he thought his contract had been "for life." Two of the Winds' investors whom another member of the ownership group, according to a newspaper report, could remember only by their first names, withdrew $175,000 they had on deposit with the league. The WFL responded by booting the team out of the league September 2.

Profiles of the other teams show why they followed the Winds into extinction less than two months later. The Charlotte Hornets were evicted from a baseball park where they practiced because they owed rent on it. The Hawaiians wilted under the expense of flying a 50-man traveling party on a swing that carried them from Honolulu to Jacksonville, Philadelphia, and Portland over 18 days at a cost of $634 per man, $31,700 for the air fare alone on one trip.

The Hawaiians' payroll faltered and alternate quarterbacks Sonny Sixkiller and Rick Cassata quit the team. One of two quarterbacks hurriedly signed to replace them was Jim Fassel, who was reached in California, where he had been employed as the driver of a beer truck. The Hawaiians lost Calvin Hill early in the year with a knee injury.

The blocking dummies and a blocking sled owned by the Jacksonville Express were impounded.

Owner Bosacco of the Philadelphia Bell moved his games from Kennedy Stadium to Franklin Field. The average attendance dipped to 3,222. On the road, the Bell arrived at Anaheim Stadium in Southern California for a practice the day before a game with the Sun. The team drove up in a yellow school bus. The stadium guard did not believe they were a football team until one of the players opened his shirt and revealed a Bell T-shirt.

The next night the Bell and Sun played a wild game that went on for three hours and 32 minutes before Southern California won by the score of 58–39. The game was being televised back to Philadelphia on WTAF, Channel 29. At 1:30 A.M., when there still were 10 minutes left in the game, WTAF played the national anthem and signed off the air.

Portland's franchise encountered hard times and the league assessed the nine other teams more than $300,000 to keep the team going. The San Antonio Wings' players were asked to take pay cuts before a trip to Portland; the Wings' players held a meeting and voted to make the trip. Shreveport struggled to attract enough fans from a city of only 182,000. The Southern California Sun faced financial shortages after the expensive contract they signed with Anthony Davis. The Sun had quarterback troubles as well when Daryle Lamonica was sidelined with an injury and Pat Haden departed in September for his studies in England as a Rhodes scholar.

But two franchises approached being genuinely healthy. Birmingham drew good crowds. It always had; it was over-generous bonuses that had bankrupted the 1974 Americans. Memphis also drew well, but Csonka, its star attraction, went out with a torn tendon in his abdomen in August. Birmingham and Memphis were the only teams to exceed the 20,000 average attendance the WFL had said it needed to

survive the year; Birmingham led the league with 21,524 per game.

The World Football League died October 22, 1975, twelve weeks or a little more than halfway through its second season, and 22 months after its organizational meeting in January, 1974. At the league's offices in New York, Hemmeter read a tatement to the press. He said the league might have made it if it could have held out a couple more years. He said, "In light of an unstable economy, no assurance of national television rights, and a softening market for new sports leagues, we considered this enormous expenditure an unwise investment."

He defended the Hemmeter plan. "The plan worked beautifully," he said. "But it was never intended to develop a market. What we needed was a strong marketing plan. You can have an exciting product, but if it doesn't have customer appeal on the shelf, it's worthless."

Players from folded teams or players released from their contracts were allowed to join NFL teams immediately. Wide receiver John Gilliam played a game with the Minnesota Vikings a week after the demise of the Chicago Winds. Ted Kwalick, former Philadelphia Bell tight end, signed with Oakland and played in six NFL games after 11 in the WFL.

The next season, Csonka signed with the New York Giants, Kiick with Denver, Warfield with Cleveland, and Hill with Washington.

A survey by the *Washington Post* in September, 1976 showed that among players who never played before in the NFL but did in the WFL, three were starting in the NFL. They were wide receiver J.K. McKay of Tampa Bay and punters Danny White of Dallas and Rusty Jackson of Los Angeles.

Six well-known players had jumped from the NFL to the WFL. All played only in 1975. Csonka rushed 99 times for Memphis for 421 yards, a 4.3 average, a long run of 13 yards, and one touchdown. Kiick rushed 121 times for Memphis for 462 yards, a 3.8 average, a long run of 16, and nine touchdowns. Warfield caught 25 passes for Memphis for 422 yards, an average of 16.9 per catch, a long reception of 38 yards, and three touchdowns.

Gilliam caught 20 passes for Chicago for 390 yards, a 19.5 average, a long reception of 49, and two touchdowns. Hill rushed 49 times for Hawaii for 218 yards, a 4.4 average, a long run of 13, and no touchdowns. Kwalick caught 29 passes for Philadelphia for 400 yards, a 13.8 average, a long reception of 46, and four touchdowns.

1975 WFL STANDINGS

Eastern Division	W	L	T	Pct.	Pts.	OP
Birmingham Vulcans	9	3	0	.750	257	186
Memphis Southmen	7	4	0	.636	254	206
Charlotte Hornets	6	5	0	.545	225	199
Jacksonville Express	6	5	0	.545	227	247
Philadelphia Bell	4	7	0	.364	195	237
Western Division	W	L	T	Pct.	Pts.	OP
Southern California Sun . .	7	5	0	.583	354	341
San Antonio Wings	7	6	0	.538	364	268
Shreveport Steamer	5	7	0	.417	276	313
Hawaiians	4	7	0	.364	210	281
Portland Thunder	4	7	0	.364	213	239
Chicago Winds	1	4	0	.200	67	124

LEADING RUSHERS	Att.	Yards	Avg.	Long	TD
Anthony Davis, So. California	239	1,200	5.0	33	16
Art Cantrelle, Birmingham	201	814	4.0	29	10
Rufus Ferguson, Portland	187	768	4.1	61	7
Jim Nance, Shreveport	190	767	4.0	35	7
Al Haywood, Jacksonville	131	687	5.2	25	4

LEADING PASSERS	Att.	Comp.	Yards	TD	Int.
John Walton, San Antonio	338	167	2,405	19	22
Edd Hargett, Shreveport	288	158	2,100	15	11
Pat Haden, So. California	163	98	1,404	11	9
Danny White, Memphis	195	104	1,445	10	8
George Mira, Jacksonville	254	123	1,675	12	12

LEADING RECEIVERS	No.	Yards	Avg.	Long	TD
E. Richardson, San Antonio	46	682	14.8	45	4
Terry Lindsey, So. California	43	669	15.6	76	4
Tim Delaney, Hawaii	44	594	13.5	31	5
Ed Marshall, Memphis	31	582	18.8	58	9
Dennis Hughes, Jacksonville	36	552	15.3	39	4

Team vs. Team Won and Lost

This is the record of games won and lost and points scored by National Football League and 1960–69 American Football League teams since 1933.

The sites of each game are abbreviated and in parentheses. "OT" means overtime game.

Philadelphia and Pittsburgh merged in 1943 and the Chicago Cardinals and Pittsburgh merged in 1944. The scores of Phil-Pitt are under Philadelphia and Pittsburgh, and the scores of Card-Pitt are under the St. Louis Cardinals and Pittsburgh.

Six teams moved from one city to another. Two of the six changed their names. The Portsmouth, Ohio, Spartans became the Detroit Lions in 1934. The Boston Redskins became the Washington Redskins in 1937. The Cleveland Rams became the Los Angeles Rams in 1946. The Chicago Cardinals became the St. Louis Cardinals in 1960. The Los Angeles Chargers became the San Diego Chargers in 1961. The Dallas Texans became the Kansas City Chiefs in 1963. There was another team called the Dallas Texans and it played in the NFL in 1952.

ATLANTA vs. BALTIMORE
Colts lead series, 8–0
1966—Colts, 19–7 (A)
1967—Colts, 38–31 (B)
    Colts, 49–7 (A)
1968—Colts, 28–20 (A)
    Colts, 44–0 (B)
1969—Colts, 21–14 (A)
    Colts, 13–6 (B)
1974—Colts, 17–7 (A)
(Points—Colts 229, Falcons 92)
ATLANTA vs. BUFFALO
Bills lead series, 1–0
1973—Bills, 17–6 (A)
ATLANTA vs. CHICAGO
Falcons lead series, 6–3
1966—Bears, 23–6 (C)
1967—Bears, 23–14 (A)
1968—Falcons, 16–13 (C)
1969—Falcons, 48–31 (A)
1970—Bears, 23–14 (A)
1972—Falcons, 37–21 (C)
1973—Falcons, 46–6 (A)
1974—Falcons, 13–10 (A)
1976—Falcons, 10–0 (C)
(Points—Falcons 204, Bears 150)
ATLANTA vs. CINCINNATI
Series tied, 1–1
1971—Falcons, 9–6 (C)
1975—Bengals, 21–14 (A)
(Points—Bengals 27, Falcons 23)
ATLANTA vs. CLEVELAND
Browns lead series, 3–1
1966—Browns, 49–17 (A)
1968—Browns, 30–7 (C)
1971—Falcons, 31–14 (C)
1976—Browns, 20–17 (A)
(Points—Browns 113, Falcons 72)
ATLANTA vs. DALLAS
Cowboys lead series, 5–1
1966—Cowboys, 47–14 (A)
1967—Cowboys, 37–7 (D)
1969—Cowboys, 24–17 (A)
1970—Cowboys, 13–0 (D)
1974—Cowboys, 24–0 (A)
1976—Falcons, 17–10 (A)
(Points—Cowboys 155, Falcons 55)
ATLANTA vs. DENVER
Falcons lead series, 2–1
1970—Broncos, 24–10 (D)
1972—Falcons, 23–20 (A)
1975—Falcons, 35–21 (A)
(Points—Falcons 68, Broncos 65)
ATLANTA vs. DETROIT
Lions lead series, 9–0
1966—Lions, 28–10 (D)
1967—Lions, 24–3 (D)
1968—Lions, 24–7 (A)
1969—Lions, 27–21 (D)
1971—Lions, 41–38 (D)
1972—Lions, 26–23 (A)
1973—Lions, 31–6 (D)
1975—Lions, 17–14 (A)
1976—Lions, 24–10 (D)
(Points—Lions 242, Falcons 132)
ATLANTA vs. GREEN BAY
Packers lead series, 7–3
1966—Packers, 56–3 (Mil)
1967—Packers, 23–0 (Mil)
1968—Packers, 38–7 (A)
1969—Packers, 28–10 (GB)
1970—Packers, 27–24 (GB)
1971—Falcons, 28–21 (A)
1972—Falcons, 10–9 (Mil)
1974—Falcons, 10–3 (A)
1975—Packers, 22–13 (GB)
1976—Packers, 24–20 (A)
(Points—Packers 251, Falcons 125)
ATLANTA vs. HOUSTON
Series tied, 1–1
1972—Falcons, 20–10 (A)
1976—Oilers, 20–14 (H)
(Points—Falcons 34, Oilers 30)
ATLANTA vs. KANSAS CITY
Chiefs lead series, 1–0
1972—Chiefs, 17–14 (A)
ATLANTA vs. LOS ANGELES
Rams lead series, 17–2–2
1966—Rams, 19–14 (A)
1967—Rams, 31–3 (A)
    Rams, 20–3 (LA)
1968—Rams, 27–14 (LA)
    Rams, 17–10 (A)
1969—Rams, 17–7 (LA)
    Rams, 38–6 (A)
1970—Tie, 10–10 (LA)
    Rams, 17–7 (A)
1971—Tie, 20–20 (LA)
    Rams, 24–16 (A)
1972—Falcons, 31–3 (A)
    Rams, 20–7 (LA)
1973—Rams, 31–0 (LA)
    Falcons, 15–13 (A)
1974—Rams, 21–0 (LA)
    Rams, 30–7 (A)
1975—Rams, 22–7 (LA)
    Rams, 16–7 (A)
1976—Rams, 30–14 (A)
    Rams, 59–0 (LA)
(Points—Rams 485, Falcons 198)
ATLANTA vs. MIAMI
Dolphins lead series, 2–0
1970—Dolphins, 20–7 (A)
1974—Dolphins, 42–7 (M)
(Points—Dolphins 62, Falcons 14)
ATLANTA vs. MINNESOTA
Vikings lead series, 5–4
1966—Falcons, 20–13 (M)
1967—Falcons, 21–20 (M)
1968—Vikings, 47–7 (M)
1969—Falcons, 10–3 (A)
1970—Vikings, 37–7 (A)
1971—Vikings, 24–7 (M)
1973—Falcons, 20–14 (A)
1974—Vikings, 23–10 (M)
1975—Vikings, 38–0 (M)
(Points—Vikings 219, Falcons 102)
ATLANTA vs. NEW ENGLAND
Patriots lead series 1–0
1972—Patriots, 21–20 (NE)
ATLANTA vs. NEW ORLEANS
Falcons lead series, 11–5
1967—Saints, 27–24 (NO)
1969—Falcons, 45–17 (A)
1970—Falcons, 14–3 (NO)
    Falcons, 32–14 (A)
1971—Falcons, 28–6 (A)
    Falcons, 24–20 (NO)
1972—Falcons, 21–14 (NO)
    Falcons, 36–20 (A)
1973—Falcons, 62–7 (NO)
    Falcons, 14–10 (A)
1974—Saints, 14–13 (NO)
    Saints, 13–3 (A)
1975—Falcons, 14–7 (A)
    Saints, 23–7 (NO)
1976—Saints, 30–0 (NO)
    Falcons, 23–20 (A)

(Points—Falcons 360, Saints 245)
ATLANTA vs. N.Y. GIANTS
Falcons lead series, 3–1
1966—Falcons, 27–16 (NY)
1968—Falcons, 24–21 (A)
1971—Giants, 21–17 (A)
1974—Falcons, 14–7 (New Haven)
Points—Falcons 82, Giants 65
ATLANTA vs. N.Y. JETS
Falcons lead series, 1–0
1973—Falcons, 28–20 (NY)
ATLANTA vs. OAKLAND
Series tied, 1–1
1971—Falcons, 24–13 (A)
1975—Raiders, 37–34 (O) OT
(Points—Falcons 58, Raiders 50)
ATLANTA vs. PHILADELPHIA
Eagles lead series, 3–2–1
1966—Eagles, 23–10 (A)
1967—Eagles, 38–7 (A)
1969—Falcons, 27–3 (P)
1970—Tie, 13–13 (P)
1973—Falcons, 44–27 (P)
1976—Eagles, 14–13 (A)
(Points—Eagles 118, Falcons 114)
ATLANTA vs. PITTSBURGH
Steelers lead series, 3–1
1966—Steelers, 57–33 (A)
1968—Steelers, 41–21 (A)
1970—Falcons, 27–16 (A)
1974—Steelers, 24–17 (P)
(Points—Steelers 138, Falcons 98)
ATLANTA vs. ST. LOUIS
Cardinals lead series, 4–1
1966—Falcons, 16–10 (A)
1968—Cardinals, 17–12 (StL)
1971—Cardinals, 26–9 (A)
1973—Cardinals, 32–10 (A)
1975—Cardinals, 23–20 (StL)
(Points—Cardinals 108, Falcons 67)
ATLANTA vs. SAN DIEGO
Falcons lead series, 1–0
1973—Falcons, 41–0 (SD)
ATLANTA vs. SAN FRANCISCO
49ers lead series, 13–8
1966—49ers, 44–7 (A)
1967—49ers, 38–7 (SF)
    49ers, 34–28 (A)
1968—49ers, 28–13 (SF)
    49ers, 14–12 (A)
1969—Falcons, 24–12 (A)
    Falcons, 21–7 (SF)
1970—Falcons, 21–20 (A)
    49ers, 24–20 (SF)
1971—Falcons, 20–17 (A)
    49ers, 24–3 (SF)
1972—Falcons, 49–14 (A)
    49ers, 20–0 (SF)
1973—49ers, 13–9 (A)
    Falcons, 17–3 (SF)
1974—49ers, 16–10 (A)
    49ers, 27–0 (SF)
1975—Falcons, 17–3 (SF)
    Falcons, 31–9 (A)
1976—49ers, 15–0 (SF)
    Falcons, 21–16 (A)
(Points—49ers 433, Falcons 295)
ATLANTA vs. SEATTLE
Seahawks lead series, 1–0
1976—Seahawks, 30–13 (S)
ATLANTA vs. TAMPA BAY
No Games
ATLANTA vs. WASHINGTON
Redskins lead series 4–0–1
1966—Redskins, 33–20 (W)
1967—Tie, 20–20 (A)
1969—Redskins, 27–20 (W)
1972—Redskins, 24–13 (W)
1975—Redskins, 30–27 (A)
(Points—Redskins 134, Falcons 100)

***1950 BALTIMORE vs. **CHI. CARDINALS**
Cardinals won series, 1–0
1950—Cardinals 55–13
*Extinct team
**Franchise moved to St. Louis in 1960
***1950 BALTIMORE vs. CLEVELAND**
Browns won series, 1–0
1950—Browns, 31–0
*Extinct team
***1950 BALTIMORE vs. DETROIT**
Lions won series, 1–0
1950—Lions, 45–21
*Extinct team

***1950 BALTIMORE vs. GREEN BAY**
Colts won series, 1–0
1950—Colts, 41–21
*Extinct team
***1950 BALTIMORE vs. LOS ANGELES**
Rams won series, 1–0
1950—Rams, 70–27
*Extinct team
***1950 BALTIMORE vs. N.Y. GIANTS**
Giants won series, 1–0
1950—Giants, 55–20
*Extinct team
***1950 BALTIMORE vs. *N.Y. YANKS**
Yanks won series, 1–0
1950—Yanks, 51–14
*Both extinct teams
***1950 BALTIMORE vs. PHILADELPHIA**
Eagles won series, 1–0
1950—Eagles, 24–14
*Extinct team
***1950 BALTIMORE vs. PITTSBURGH**
Steelers won series, 1–0
1950—Steelers, 17–7
*Extinct team
***1950 BALTIMORE vs. SAN FRANCISCO**
49ers won series, 1–0
1950—49ers, 17–14
*Extinct team
***1950 BALTIMORE vs. WASHINGTON**
Redskins won series, 2–0
1950—Redskins, 38–14
    Redskins, 38–28
(Points—Redskins 76, Colts 42)
*Extinct team

BALTIMORE vs. ATLANTA
Colts lead series, 8–0
See Atlanta vs. Baltimore
BALTIMORE vs. BUFFALO
Colts lead series, 8–5–1
1970—Tie, 17–17 (Balt)
    Colts, 20–14 (Buff)
1971—Colts, 43–0 (Buff)
    Colts, 24–0 (Balt)
1972—Colts, 17–0 (Buff)
    Colts, 35–7 (Balt)
1973—Bills, 31–13 (Buff)
    Bills, 24–17 (Balt)
1974—Bills, 27–14 (Balt)
    Bills, 6–0 (Buff)
1975—Bills, 38–31 (Balt)
    Colts, 42–35 (Buff)
1976—Colts, 31–13 (Buff)
    Colts, 58–20 (Balt)
(Points—Colts 362, Bills 232)
BALTIMORE vs. CHICAGO
Colts lead series, 20–13
1953—Colts, 13–9 (B)
    Colts, 16–14 (C)
1954—Bears, 28–9 (C)
    Bears, 28–13 (B)
1955—Colts, 23–17 (B)
    Bears, 38–10 (C)
1956—Colts, 28–21 (B)
    Bears, 58–27 (C)
1957—Colts, 21–10 (B)
    Colts, 29–14 (C)
1958—Colts, 51–38 (B)
    Colts, 17–0 (C)
1959—Bears, 26–21 (B)
    Colts, 21–7 (C)
1960—Colts, 42–7 (B)
    Colts, 24–20 (C)
1961—Bears, 24–10 (C)
    Bears, 21–20 (B)
1962—Bears, 35–15 (C)
    Bears, 57–0 (B)
1963—Bears, 10–3 (C)
    Bears, 17–7 (B)
1964—Colts, 52–0 (B)
    Colts, 40–24 (C)
1965—Colts, 26–21 (C)
    Bears, 13–0 (B)
1966—Bears, 27–17 (C)
    Colts, 21–16 (B)
1967—Colts, 24–3 (C)
1968—Colts, 28–7 (B)
1969—Colts, 24–21 (C)
1970—Colts, 21–20 (B)
1975—Colts, 35–7 (C)
(Points—Colts 708, Bears 658)

***1950 BALTIMORE vs. GREEN BAY**
Colts won series, 1–0
1950—Colts, 41–21
*Extinct team

BALTIMORE vs. CINCINNATI
Colts lead series, 3–1
1970—*Colts, 17–0 (B)
1972—Colts, 20–19 (C)
1974—Bengals, 24–14 (B)
1976—Colts 28–27 (B)
(Points—Colts 79, Bengals 70)
*AFC Divisional Playoff
BALTIMORE vs. CLEVELAND
Series tied, 5–5
1956—Colts, 21–7 (C)
1959—Browns, 38–31 (B)
1962—Colts, 36–14 (C)
1964—*Browns, 27–0 (C)
1968—Browns, 30–20 (C)
    * Colts, 34–0 (C)
1971—Browns, 14–13 (B)
    **Colts, 20–3 (C)
1973—Browns, 24–14 (C)
1975—Colts, 21–7 (B)
(Points—Colts 210, Browns 164)
*NFL Championship
**AFC Divisional Playoff
BALTIMORE vs. DALLAS
Colts lead series, 4–3
1960—Colts, 45–7 (D)
1966—*Colts, 35–3 (Miami)
1967—Colts, 23–17 (B)
1969—Cowboys, 27–10 (D)
1971—**Colts, 16–13 (Miami)
1972—Cowboys, 21–0 (B)
1976—Cowboys, 30–27 (D)
(Points—Colts, 156, Cowboys 118)
*Playoff Bowl
**Super Bowl V
BALTIMORE vs. DENVER
Broncos lead series, 1–0
1974—Broncos, 17–6 (B)
BALTIMORE vs. DETROIT
Series tied, 15–15–2
1953—Lions, 27–17 (B)
    Lions, 17–7 (D)
1954—Lions, 35–0 (D)
    Lions, 27–3 (B)
1955—Colts, 28–13 (B)
    Lions, 24–14 (D)
1956—Lions, 31–14 (B)
    Lions 27–3 (D)
1957—Colts, 34–14 (B)
    Lions, 31–27 (D)
1958—Colts, 28–15 (B)
    Colts, 40–14 (D)
1959—Colts, 21–9 (B)
    Colts, 31–24 (D)
1960—Lions, 30–17 (D)
    Lions, 20–15 (B)
1961—Lions, 16–15 (B)
    Colts, 17–14 (D)
1962—Lions, 29–20 (B)
    Lions, 21–14 (D)
1963—Colts, 25–21 (D)
    Colts, 24–21 (B)
1964—Colts, 34–0 (B)
    Lions, 31–14 (B)
1965—Colts, 31–7 (B)
    Tie, 24–24 (D)
1966—Colts, 45–14 (B)
    Lions, 20–14 (D)
1967—Colts, 41–7 (B)
1968—Colts, 27–10 (D)
1969—Tie, 17–17 (B)
1973—Colts, 29–27 (D)
(Points—Colts 690, Lions 637)
BALTIMORE vs. GREEN BAY
Packers lead series, 18–16
1953—Packers, 37–14 (GB)
    Packers, 35–24 (B)
1954—Packers, 7–6 (B)
    Packers, 24–13 (Mil)
1955—Colts, 24–20 (Mil)
    Colts, 14–10 (B)
1956—Packers, 38–33 (Mil)
    Colts, 28–21 (B)
1957—Colts, 45–17 (Mil)
    Packers, 24–21 (B)
1958—Colts, 24–17 (Mil)
    Colts, 56–0 (B)
1959—Packers, 38–21 (B)
    Colts, 28–24 (Mil)
1960—Packers, 35–21 (GB)
    Colts, 38–24 (B)
1961—Packers, 45–7 (GB)
    Colts, 45–21 (B)
1962—Packers, 17–6 (B)
    Packers, 17–13 (GB)
1963—Packers, 31–20 (B)
    Packers, 34–20 (B)
1964—Colts, 21–20 (GB)
    Colts, 24–21 (B)

1965—Packers, 20-17 (Mil)
    Packers, 42-27 (B)
    *Packers, 13-10 (GB) OT
1966—Packers, 24-3 (Mil)
    Packers, 14-10 (B)
1967—Colts, 13-10 (B)
1968—Colts, 16-3 (GB)
1969—Colts, 14-6 (B)
1970—Colts, 13-10 (GB)
(Points—Colts 706, Packers 702)
*Conference Playoff
BALTIMORE vs. HOUSTON
Series tied, 1-1
1970—Colts, 24-20 (H)
1973—Oilers, 31-27 (H)
(Points—Colts 51, Oilers 51)
BALTIMORE vs. KANSAS CITY
Chiefs lead series, 2-1
1970—Chiefs, 44-24 (B)
1972—Chiefs, 24-10 (KC)
1975—Colts, 28-14 (B)
(Points—Chiefs 82, Colts 62)
BALTIMORE vs. LOS ANGELES
Colts lead series, 20-14-2
1953—Rams, 21-13 (B)
    Rams, 45-2 (LA)
1954—Rams, 48-0 (B)
    Colts, 22-21 (LA)
1955—Tie, 17-17 (B)
    Rams, 20-14 (LA)
1956—Colts, 56-21 (B)
    Rams, 31-7 (LA)
1957—Colts, 31-14 (B)
    Rams, 37-21 (LA)
1958—Colts, 34-7 (B)
    Rams, 30-28 (LA)
1959—Colts, 35-21 (B)
    Colts, 45-26 (LA)
1960—Colts, 31-17 (B)
    Rams, 10-3 (LA)
1961—Colts, 27-24 (B)
    Rams, 34-17 (LA)
1962—Colts, 30-27 (B)
    Colts, 14-2 (LA)
1963—Rams, 17-16 (LA)
    Colts, 19-16 (B)
1964—Colts, 35-20 (B)
    Colts, 24-7 (LA)
1965—Colts, 35-20 (B)
    Colts, 20-17 (LA)
1966—Colts, 17-3 (LA)
    Rams, 23-7 (B)
1967—Tie, 24-24 (B)
    Rams, 34-10 (LA)
1968—Colts, 27-10 (B)
    Colts, 28-24 (LA)
1969—Rams, 27-20 (B)
    Colts, 13-7 (LA)
1971—Colts, 24-17 (B)
1975—Rams, 24-13 (LA)
(Points—Colts 779, Rams 763)
BALTIMORE vs. MIAMI
Dolphins lead series, 8-7
1970—Colts, 35-0 (B)
    Dolphins, 34-17 (M)
1971—Dolphins, 17-14 (M)
    Colts, 14-3 (B)
    *Dolphins, 21-0 (M)
1972—Dolphins, 23-0 (B)
    Dolphins, 16-0 (M)
1973—Dolphins, 44-0 (M)
    Colts, 16-3 (B)
1974—Dolphins, 17-7 (M)
    Dolphins, 17-16 (B)
1975—Colts, 33-17 (M)
    Colts, 10-7 (B) OT
1976—Colts, 28-14 (B)
    Colts, 17-16 (M)
(Points—Dolphins 239, Colts 207)
*AFC Championship
BALTIMORE vs. MINNESOTA
Colts lead series, 12-4-1
1961—Colts, 34-33 (B)
    Vikings, 28-20 (M)
1962—Colts, 34-7 (M)
    Colts, 42-17 (B)
1963—Colts, 37-34 (M)
    Colts, 41-10 (B)
1964—Vikings, 34-24 (M)
    Colts, 17-14 (B)
1965—Colts, 35-16 (B)
    Colts, 41-21 (M)
1966—Colts, 38-23 (M)
    Colts, 20-17 (B)
1967—Tie, 20-20 (M)
1968—Colts, 21-9 (B)
    *Colts, 24-14 (B)
1969—Vikings, 52-14 (M)
1971—Vikings, 10-3 (M)

(Points—Colts 465, Vikings 359)
*Conference Championship
BALTIMORE vs. *NEW ENGLAND
Colts lead series, 8-6
1970—Colts, 14-6 (B)
    Colts, 27-3 (Balt)
1971—Colts, 23-3 (NE)
    Patriots, 21-17 (Balt)
1972—Colts, 24-17 (NE)
    Colts, 31-0 (Balt)
1973—Patriots, 24-16 (NE)
    Colts, 18-13 (Balt)
1974—Patriots, 42-3 (NE)
    Patriots, 27-17 (Balt)
1975—Patriots, 21-10 (NE)
    Colts, 34-21 (Balt)
1976—Colts 27-13 (NE)
    Patriots, 21-14 (B)
(Points—Colts 275, Patriots 232)
*Franchise in Boston (B) prior to 1971
BALTIMORE vs. NEW ORLEANS
Colts lead series, 3-0
1967—Colts, 30-10 (B)
1969—Colts, 30-10 (NO)
1973—Colts, 14-10 (B)
(Points—Colts 74, Saints 30)
BALTIMORE vs. N.Y. GIANTS
Colts lead series, 6-3
1954—Colts, 20-14 (B)
1955—Giants, 17-7 (NY)
1958—Giants, 24-21 (NY)
    *Colts, 23-17 (NY) OT
1959—*Colts, 31-16 (B)
1963—Giants, 37-28 (B)
1968—Colts, 26-0 (NY)
1971—Colts, 31-7 (NY)
1975—Colts, 21-0 (NY)
(Points—Colts 208, Giants 132)
*NFL Championship
BALTIMORE vs. N.Y. JETS
Colts lead series, 9-6
1969—*Jets, 16-7 (Miami)
1970—Colts, 29-22 (NY)
    Colts, 35-20 (B)
1971—Colts, 22-0 (B)
    Colts, 14-13 (NY)
1972—Jets, 44-34 (B)
    Jets, 24-20 (NY)
1973—Jets, 34-10 (B)
    Jets, 20-17 (NY)
1974—Colts, 35-20 (NY)
    Jets, 45-38 (B)
1975—Colts, 45-28 (NY)
    Colts, 52-19 (B)
1976—Colts, 20-0 (NY)
    Colts, 33-16 (B)
(Points—Colts 411, Jets 321)
*Super Bowl III
BALTIMORE vs. OAKLAND
Series tied, 2-2
1970—*Colts, 27-17 (B)
1971—Colts, 37-14 (O)
1973—Raiders, 34-21 (B)
1975—Raiders, 31-20 (B)
(Points—Colts 105, Raiders 96)
*AFC Championship
BALTIMORE vs. PHILADELPHIA
Colts lead series 5-2
1953—Eagles, 45-14 (P)
1965—Colts, 34-24 (B)
1967—*Colts, 20-14 (Miami)
    Colts, 38-6 (P)
1969—Colts, 24-20 (B)
1970—Colts, 29-10 (B)
1974—Eagles, 30-10 (P)
(Points—Colts 169, Eagles 149)
*Playoff Bowl
BALTIMORE vs. PITTSBURGH
Steelers lead series 4-2
1957—Steelers, 19-13 (B)
1968—Colts, 41-7 (P)
1971—Colts, 34-21 (B)
1974—Steelers, 30-0 (B)
1975—*Steelers, 28-10 (P)
1976—*Steelers, 40-14 (B)
(Points—Steelers 145, Colts 112)
*AFC Divisional Playoff
BALTIMORE vs. ST. LOUIS
Colts lead series, 3-2
1961—Colts, 16-0 (B)
1964—Colts, 47-27 (B)
1968—Colts, 27-0 (B)
1972—Cardinals, 10-3 (B)
1976—Cardinals, 24-17 (StL)
(Points—Colts 110, Cardinals 61)
BALTIMORE vs. SAN DIEGO
Colts lead series, 2-1
1970—Colts, 16-14 (SD)

1972—Chargers, 23-20 (B)
1976—Colts, 37-21 (SD)
(Points—Colts 74, Chargers 58)
BALTIMORE vs. SAN FRANCISCO
Colts lead series, 21-14
1953—49ers, 38-21 (B)
    49ers, 45-14 (SF)
1954—Colts, 17-13 (B)
    49ers, 10-7 (SF)
1955—Colts, 26-14 (B)
    49ers, 35-24 (SF)
1956—49ers, 20-17 (B)
    49ers, 30-17 (SF)
1957—Colts, 27-21 (B)
    49ers, 17-13 (SF)
1958—Colts, 35-27 (B)
    49ers, 21-12 (SF)
1959—Colts, 45-14 (B)
    Colts, 34-14 (SF)
1960—49ers, 30-22 (B)
    49ers, 34-10 (SF)
1961—Colts, 20-17 (B)
    Colts, 27-24 (SF)
1962—49ers, 21-13 (B)
    Colts, 22-3 (SF)
1963—Colts, 20-14 (SF)
    Colts, 20-3 (B)
1964—Colts, 37-7 (B)
    Colts, 14-3 (SF)
1965—Colts, 27-24 (B)
    Colts, 34-28 (SF)
1966—Colts, 36-14 (B)
    Colts, 30-14 (SF)
1967—Colts, 41-7 (B)
    Colts, 26-9 (SF)
1968—Colts, 27-10 (B)
    49ers, 24-21 (SF)
1969—49ers, 24-21 (B)
    49ers, 20-17 (SF)
1972—49ers, 24-21 (SF)
(Points—Colts 836, 49ers 660)
BALTIMORE vs. SEATTLE
No Games
BALTIMORE vs. TAMPA BAY
Colts lead series, 1-0
1976—Colts, 42-17 (B)
BALTIMORE vs. WASHINGTON
Colts lead series, 13-4
1953—Colts, 27-17 (B)
1954—Redskins, 24-21 (W)
1955—Redskins, 14-13 (B)
1956—Colts, 19-17 (B)
1957—Colts, 21-17 (W)
1958—Colts, 35-10 (B)
1959—Redskins, 27-24 (W)
1960—Colts, 20-0 (B)
1961—Colts, 27-6 (W)
1962—Colts, 34-21 (B)
1963—Colts, 36-20 (W)
1964—Colts, 45-17 (B)
1965—Colts, 38-7 (W)
1966—Colts, 37-10 (B)
1967—Colts, 17-13 (W)
1969—Colts, 41-17 (B)
1973—Redskins, 22-14 (W)
(Points—Colts 469, Redskins 259)

*BOS. YANKS vs. *BROOKLYN DODGERS
Yanks won series, 2-0
1944—Yanks, 17-14
    Yanks 13-6
(Points—Yanks 30, Dodgers 20)
*Extinct team
*BOS. YANKS vs. CHI. BEARS
Bears won series, 3-0
1944—Bears, 21-7
1947—Bears, 28-24
1948—Bears, 51-17
(Points—Bears 100, Yanks 48)
*Extinct team
*BOS. YANKS vs. **CHI. CARDINALS
Cardinals won series, 3-0
1946—Cardinals, 28-14
1947—Cardinals, 27-7
1948—Cardinals, 49-27
(Points—Cardinals 104, Yanks 48)
*Extinct team
**Franchise moved to St. Louis in 1960
*BOS. YANKS vs. DETROIT
Lions won series, 3-2
1944—Lions, 38-7
1945—Lions, 10-9
1946—Yanks, 34-10
1947—Lions, 21-7
1948—Yanks, 17-14

(Points—Lions 93, Yanks 74)
*Extinct team
*BOS. YANKS vs. GREEN BAY
Packers won series, 2-0
1945—Packers, 38-14
    Packers, 28-0
(Points—Packers 66, Yanks 14)
*Extinct team
*BOS. YANKS vs. **LOS ANGELES
Yanks won series, 2-1
1945—Rams, 20-7
1946—Yanks, 40-21
1947—Yanks, 27-16
(Points—Yanks 74, Rams 57)
*Extinct team
**Franchise in Cleveland prior to 1946
*BOS. YANKS vs. N.Y. GIANTS
Giants won series, 5-1-3
1944—Giants, 22-10
    Giants, 31-0
1945—Tie, 13-13
1946—Giants, 17-0
    Tie, 28-28
1947—Tie, 7-7
    Yanks, 14-0
1948—Giants, 27-7
    Giants, 28-14
(Points—Giants 173, Yanks 93)
*Extinct team
*BOS. YANKS vs. PHILADELPHIA
Eagles won series, 7-2
1944—Eagles, 28-7
    Eagles, 38-0
1945—Eagles, 35-7
1946—Eagles, 49-25
    Eagles, 40-14
1947—Eagles, 32-0
    Yanks, 21-14
1948—Eagles, 45-0
    Yanks, 37-14
(Points—Eagles 295, Yanks 111)
*Extinct team
*BOS. YANKS vs. PITTSBURGH
Steelers won series, 5-3
1945—Yanks, 28-7
    Yanks, 10-6
1946—Steelers, 16-7
    Steelers, 33-7
1947—Steelers, 30-14
    Steelers, 17-7
1948—Steelers, 24-14
    Yanks, 13-7
(Points—Steelers 140, Yanks 100)
*Extinct team
*BOS. YANKS vs. WASHINGTON
Redskins won series, 8-2
1944—Redskins, 21-14
    Redskins, 14-7
1945—Yanks, 28-20
    Redskins, 34-7
1946—Redskins, 14-6
    Redskins, 17-14
1947—Yanks, 27-24
    Redskins, 40-13
1948—Redskins, 59-21
    Redskins, 23-7
(Points—Redskins 266, Yanks 144)

*BROOKLYN DODGERS vs. *BOS. YANKS
Yanks won series, 2-0
See *Boston Yanks vs. *Brooklyn Dodgers
*Extinct team
*BROOKLYN DODGERS vs. CHI. BEARS
Bears won series, 11-0
1931—Bears, 26-0
1932—Bears, 13-0
    Bears, 20-0
1933—Bears, 10-0
1934—Bears, 21-7
1935—Bears, 24-14
1937—Bears, 29-7
1938—Bears, 24-6
1940—Bears, 16-7
1942—Bears, 35-0
1943—Bears, 33-21
(Points—Bears 251, Dodgers 62)
*Extinct team
*BROOKLYN DODGERS vs. **CHI. CARDINALS
Dodgers won series, 7-4
1931—Cardinals, 14-7
1932—Cardinals, 27-7
    Dodgers, 3-0
1933—Dodgers, 7-0

    Dodgers, 3-0
1934—Cardinals, 21-0
1936—Dodgers, 9-0
1938—Dodgers, 13-0
1940—Dodgers, 14-9
1941—Dodgers, 20-6
1943—Dodgers, 7-0
(Points—Cardinals 91, Dodgers 76)
*Extinct team
**Franchise moved to St. Louis in 1960
*BROOKLYN DODGERS vs. *CINCINNATI REDS
Series tied, 1-1
1933—Dodgers, 27-0
    Reds, 10-0
(Points—Dodgers 27, Reds 10)
*Extinct team
*BROOKLYN DODGERS vs. **CLEVELAND RAMS
Dodgers won series, 3-1
1937—Dodgers, 9-7
1939—Dodgers, 23-12
1940—Dodgers, 29-14
1942—Rams, 17-0
(Points—Dodgers 61, Rams 50)
*Extinct team
**Franchise moved to Los Angeles in 1946
*BROOKLYN DODGERS vs. **DETROIT
Lions won series, 11-3
1930—Spartans, 14-0
1931—Spartans, 19-0
1932—Spartans, 17-7
1934—Lions, 28-0
1935—Dodgers, 12-10
    Lions, 28-0
1936—Lions, 14-7
    Lions, 14-6
1937—Lions, 30-0
1939—Lions, 27-7
1941—Dodgers, 14-7
1942—Dodgers, 28-7
1943—Lions, 27-0
1944—Lions, 19-14
(Points—Lions 261, Dodgers 95)
*Extinct team
**Franchise in Portsmouth prior to 1934 and known as the Spartans.
*BROOKLYN DODGERS vs. GREEN BAY
Packers won series, 8-0
1931—Packers, 7-0
1932—Packers, 7-0
1936—Packers, 38-7
1938—Packers, 35-7
1939—Packers, 28-0
1941—Packers, 30-7
1943—Packers, 31-7
1944—Packers, 14-7
(Points—Packers 190, Dodgers 35)
*Extinct team
*BROOKLYN DODGERS vs. N.Y. GIANTS
Giants won series, 24-5-3
1926—Giants, 17-0
    Giants, 27-0
1930—Dodgers, 7-6
    Giants, 13-0
1931—Giants, 27-0
    Giants, 19-6
1932—Giants, 20-12
    Giants, 13-7
1933—Giants, 21-7
    Giants, 10-0
1934—Giants, 14-0
    Giants, 27-0
1935—Giants, 10-7
    Giants, 21-0
1936—Tie, 10-10
    Giants, 14-0
1937—Giants, 21-0
    Tie, 13-13
1938—Giants, 28-14
    Tie, 7-7
1939—Giants, 7-6
    Giants, 28-7
1940—Giants, 10-7
    Dodgers, 14-6
1941—Dodgers, 16-13
    Dodgers, 21-7
1942—Dodgers, 17-7
    Giants, 10-0
1943—Giants, 20-0
    Giants, 24-7
1944—Giants, 14-7
    Giants, 7-0
(Points—Giants 491, Dodgers 192)

*Extinct team
*BROOKLYN DODGERS vs. PHILADELPHIA
Dodgers won series, 14–5–1
1934—Dodgers, 10–7
        Eagles, 13–0
1935—Dodgers, 17–6
        Dodgers, 3–0
1936—Dodgers, 18–0
        Dodgers, 13–7
1937—Dodgers, 13–7
        Eagles, 14–10
1938—Dodgers, 10–7
        Dodgers, 32–14
1939—Tie, 0–0
        Dodgers, 23–14
1940—Dodgers, 30–17
        Dodgers, 21–7
1941—Dodgers, 24–13
        Dodgers, 15–6
1942—Dodgers, 35–14
        Eagles, 14–7
1944—Eagles, 21–7
        Eagles, 34–0
(Points—Dodgers 288, Eagles 215)
*Extinct team
*BROOKLYN DODGERS vs. PITTSBURGH
Dodgers won series, 11–8–1
1933—Tie, 3–3
        Dodgers, 32–0
1934—Dodgers, 21–3
        Dodgers, 10–0
1935—Dodgers, 13–7
        Steelers, 16–7
1936—Steelers, 10–6
        Steelers, 10–7
1937—Steelers, 21–0
        Dodgers, 23–0
1938—Steelers, 17–3
        Dodgers, 17–7
1939—Dodgers, 12–7
        Dodgers, 17–13
1940—Dodgers, 10–3
        Dodgers, 21–0
1941—Steelers, 14–7
        Dodgers, 35–7
1942—Steelers, 7–0
        Steelers, 13–0
(Points—Dodgers 244, Steelers 158)
*Extinct team
*BROOKLYN DODGERS vs. **WASHINGTON REDSKINS
Redskins won series, 17–5–3
1932—Dodgers, 14–0
        Redskins, 7–0
1933—Dodgers, 14–0
1934—Dodgers, 10–6
        Redskins, 13–3
1935—Redskins, 7–0
        Tie, 0–0
1936—Redskins, 14–3
        Redskins, 30–3
1937—Redskins, 11–7
        Redskins, 21–0
1938—Tie, 16–16
        Tie, 6–6
1939—Redskins, 41–13
        Redskins, 42–0
1940—Redskins, 24–17
        Dodgers, 16–14
1941—Redskins, 3–0
        Dodgers, 13–7
1942—Redskins, 21–10
        Redskins, 23–3
1943—Redskins, 27–0
        Redskins, 48–10
1944—Redskins, 17–14
        Redskins, 10–0
(Points—Redskins 408, Dodgers 175)
*Extinct team
**Franchise in Boston prior to 1937

BUFFALO vs. ATLANTA
Bills lead series, 1–0;
See Atlanta vs. Buffalo
BUFFALO vs. BALTIMORE
Colts lead series, 8–5–1
See Baltimore vs. Buffalo
BUFFALO vs. CHICAGO
Series tied, 1–1
1970—Bears, 31–13 (C)
1974—Bills, 16–6 (B)
(Points—Bears 37, Bills 29)
BUFFALO vs. CINCINNATI
Bengals lead series, 4–1
1968—Bengals, 34–23 (C)

1969—Bills, 16–13 (B)
1970—Bengals, 43–14 (B)
1973—Bengals, 16–13 (B)
1975—Bengals, 33–24 (C)
(Points—Bengals, 139, Bills 90)
BUFFALO vs. CLEVELAND
Series tied, 1–1
1972—Browns, 27–10 (C)
1974—Bills, 15–10 (C)
(Points—Browns 37, Bills 25)
BUFFALO vs. DALLAS
Cowboys lead series, 1–0
1971—Cowboys, 49–37 (B)
BUFFALO vs. DENVER
Bills lead series, 12–6–1
1960—Broncos, 27–21 (B)
        Tie, 38–38 (D)
1961—Broncos, 22–10 (B)
        Bills, 23–10 (D)
1962—Broncos, 23–20 (B)
        Bills, 45–38 (D)
1963—Bills, 30–28 (B)
        Bills, 27–17 (B)
1964—Bills, 30–13 (B)
        Bills, 30–19 (D)
1965—Bills, 30–15 (D)
        Bills, 31–13 (B)
1966—Bills, 38–21 (B)
1967—Bills, 17–16 (B)
        Broncos, 21–20 (B)
1968—Broncos, 34–32 (D)
1969—Bills, 41–28 (B)
1970—Broncos, 25–10 (B)
1975—Bills, 38–14 (D)
(Points—Bills 531, Broncos 422)
BUFFALO vs. DETROIT
Lions lead series, 1–0–1
1972—Tie, 21–21 (B)
1976—Lions, 27–14 (D)
(Points—Lions 48, Bills 35)
BUFFALO vs. GREEN BAY
Bills lead series, 1–0
1974—Bills, 27–7 (GB)
BUFFALO vs. HOUSTON
Oilers lead series, 16–7
1960—Bills, 25–24 (B)
        Oilers, 31–23 (H)
1961—Bills, 22–12 (H)
        Oilers, 28–16 (B)
1962—Oilers, 28–23 (B)
        Oilers, 17–14 (H)
1963—Bills, 31–20 (B)
        Oilers, 28–14 (H)
1964—Bills, 48–17 (H)
        Bills, 24–10 (B)
1965—Oilers, 19–17 (B)
        Bills, 29–18 (H)
1966—Bills, 27–20 (B)
        Bills, 42–20 (H)
1967—Bills, 20–3 (B)
        Oilers, 10–3 (H)
1968—Bills, 30–7 (B)
        Oilers, 35–6 (H)
1969—Bills, 17–3 (B)
        Oilers, 28–14 (H)
1971—Oilers, 20–14 (B)
1974—Oilers, 21–9 (B)
1976—Oilers, 13–3 (B)
(Points—Oilers 497, Bills 406)
BUFFALO vs. *KANSAS CITY
Series tied, 10–10–1
1960—Texans, 45–28 (B)
        Texans, 24–7 (D)
1961—Bills, 27–24 (B)
        Bills, 30–20 (D)
1962—Texans, 41–21 (D)
        Bills, 23–14 (B)
1963—Tie, 27–27 (B)
        Bills, 35–26 (KC)
1964—Bills, 34–17 (B)
        Bills, 35–22 (KC)
1965—Bills, 23–7 (KC)
        Bills, 34–25 (B)
1966—Chiefs, 42–20 (B)
        Bills, 29–14 (KC)
        **Chiefs, 31–7 (B)
1967—Chiefs, 23–13 (KC)
1968—Chiefs, 18–7 (B)
1969—Chiefs, 29–7 (B)
        Chiefs, 22–19 (KC)
1971—Chiefs, 22–9 (KC)
1973—Bills, 23–14 (B)
(Points—Chiefs 507, Bills 458)
*Franchise in Dallas (D) prior to 1963 and known as Texans
**AFL Championship
BUFFALO vs. LOS ANGELES
Rams lead series, 2–0
1970—Rams, 19–0 (B)

1974—Rams, 19–14 (LA)
(Points—Rams 38, Bills 14)
BUFFALO vs. MIAMI
Dolphins lead series, 17–4–1
1966—Bills, 58–24 (B)
        Bills, 29–0 (M)
1967—Bills, 35–13 (B)
        Dolphins, 17–14 (M)
1968—Tie, 14–14 (M)
        Dolphins, 21–17 (B)
1969—Dolphins, 24–6 (M)
        Bills, 28–3 (B)
1970—Dolphins, 33–14 (B)
        Dolphins, 45–7 (M)
1971—Dolphins, 29–14 (B)
        Dolphins, 34–0 (M)
1972—Dolphins, 24–23 (M)
        Dolphins, 30–16 (B)
1973—Dolphins, 27–6 (M)
        Dolphins, 17–0 (B)
1974—Dolphins, 24–16 (B)
        Dolphins, 35–28 (M)
1975—Dolphins, 35–30 (B)
        Dolphins, 31–21 (M)
1976—Dolphins, 30–21 (B)
        Dolphins, 45–27 (M)
(Points—Dolphins 555, Bills 424)
BUFFALO vs. MINNESOTA
Vikings lead series, 2–0
1971—Vikings, 19–0 (M)
1975—Vikings, 35–13 (B)
(Points—Vikings 54, Bills 13)
BUFFALO vs. **NEW ENGLAND
Bills lead series, 18–16–1
1960—Bills, 13–0 (B)
        Bills, 38–14 (Bu)
1961—Patriots, 23–21 (Bu)
        Patriots, 52–21 (B)
1962—Tie, 28–28 (Bu)
        Patriots, 21–10 (B)
1963—Bills, 28–21 (Bu)
        Patriots, 17–7 (B)
        *Patriots, 26–8 (Bu)
1964—Patriots, 36–28 (Bu)
        Bills, 24–14 (B)
1965—Bills, 24–7 (Bu)
        Bills, 23–7 (B)
1966—Patriots, 20–10 (Bu)
        Patriots, 14–3 (B)
1967—Patriots, 23–0 (Bu)
        Bills, 44–16 (B)
1968—Patriots, 16–7 (Bu)
        Patriots, 23–6 (B)
1969—Bills, 23–16 (Bu)
        Patriots, 35–21 (B)
1970—Bills, 45–10 (B)
        Patriots, 14–10 (Bu)
1971—Patriots, 38–33 (NE)
        Bills, 27–20 (Bu)
1972—Bills, 38–14 (Bu)
        Bills, 27–24 (NE)
1973—Bills, 31–13 (NE)
        Bills, 37–13 (Bu)
1974—Bills, 30–28 (Bu)
        Bills, 29–28 (NE)
1975—Bills, 45–31 (Bu)
        Bills, 34–14 (NE)
1976—Patriots, 26–22 (Bu)
(Points—Bills, 805, Patriots 722)
*Division Playoff
**Franchise in Boston (B) prior to 1971
BUFFALO vs. NEW ORLEANS
Saints lead series, 1–0
1973—Saints, 13–0 (NO)
BUFFALO vs. N.Y. GIANTS
Giants lead series, 2–0
1970—Giants, 20–6 (NY)
1975—Giants, 17–14 (B)
(Points—Giants 37, Bills 20)
BUFFALO vs. *N.Y. JETS
Bills lead series, 18–16
1960—Titans, 27–3 (NY)
        Titans, 17–13 (B)
1961—Bills, 41–31 (B)
        Titans, 21–14 (NY)
1962—Titans, 17–6 (B)
        Bills, 20–3 (NY)
1963—Bills, 45–14 (B)
        Bills, 19–10 (NY)
1964—Bills, 34–24 (B)
        Bills, 20–7 (NY)
1965—Bills, 33–21 (B)
        Jets, 14–12 (NY)
1966—Bills, 33–23 (NY)
        Bills, 14–3 (B)
1967—Bills, 20–17 (B)
        Jets, 20–10 (NY)
1968—Bills, 37–35 (B)

Jets, 25–21 (NY)
1969—Jets, 33–19 (B)
        Jets, 16–6 (NY)
1970—Jets, 34–31 (B)
        Bills, 10–6 (NY)
1971—Jets, 28–17 (NY)
        Jets, 20–7 (B)
1972—Jets, 41–24 (B)
        Jets, 41–3 (NY)
1973—Bills, 9–7 (B)
        Bills, 34–14 (NY)
1974—Bills, 16–12 (B)
        Jets, 20–10 (NY)
1975—Bills, 42–14 (B)
        Bills, 24–23 (NY)
1976—Jets, 17–14 (NY)
        Jets, 19–14 (B)
(Points—Bills 678, Jets 671)
*Jets known as Titans prior to 1963
BUFFALO vs. OAKLAND
Series tied, 10–10
1960—Bills, 38–9 (B)
        Raiders, 20–7 (O)
1961—Raiders, 31–22 (B)
        Bills, 26–21 (O)
1962—Bills, 14–6 (B)
        Bills, 10–6 (O)
1963—Raiders, 35–17 (O)
        Bills, 12–0 (B)
1964—Bills, 23–20 (B)
        Raiders, 16–13 (O)
1965—Bills, 17–12 (B)
        Bills, 17–14 (O)
1966—Bills, 31–10 (O)
1967—Raiders, 24–20 (B)
        Raiders, 28–21 (O)
1968—Raiders, 48–6 (B)
        Raiders, 13–10 (O)
1969—Raiders, 50–21 (O)
1972—Raiders, 28–16 (O)
1974—Bills, 21–20 (B)
(Points—Raiders 411, Bills 362)
BUFFALO vs. PHILADELPHIA
Bills lead series, 1–0
1973—Bills, 27–26 (B)
BUFFALO vs. PITTSBURGH
Steelers lead series, 3–1
1970—Steelers, 23–10 (P)
1972—Steelers, 38–21 (B)
1974—*Steelers, 32–14 (P)
1975—Bills, 30–21 (P)
(Points—Steelers 114, Bills 75)
*AFC Divisional Playoff
BUFFALO vs. ST. LOUIS
Series tied, 1–1
1971—Cardinals, 28–23 (B)
1975—Bills, 32–14 (StL)
(Points—Bills 55, Cardinals 42)
BUFFALO vs. *SAN DIEGO
Chargers lead series, 13–7–2
1960—Chargers, 24–10 (B)
        Bills, 32–3 (LA)
1961—Chargers, 19–11 (B)
        Chargers, 28–10 (SD)
1962—Bills, 35–10 (B)
        Bills, 40–20 (SD)
1963—Chargers, 14–10 (SD)
        Chargers, 23–13 (B)
1964—Bills, 30–3 (B)
        Chargers, 27–24 (SD)
        **Bills, 20–7 (B)
1965—Chargers, 34–3 (B)
        Tie, 20–20 (SD)
        **Bills, 23–0 (SD)
1966—Chargers, 27–7 (SD)
        Tie, 17–17 (B)
1967—Chargers, 37–17 (B)
1968—Chargers, 21–6 (B)
1969—Chargers, 45–6 (SD)
1971—Chargers, 20–3 (SD)
1973—Chargers, 34–7 (SD)
1976—Chargers, 34–13 (B)
(Points—Chargers 464, Bills 360)
*Franchise in Los Angeles (LA) prior to 1961
**AFL Championship
BUFFALO vs. SAN FRANCISCO
Bills lead series, 1–0
1972—Bills, 27–20 (B)
BUFFALO vs. SEATTLE
No games
BUFFALO vs. TAMPA BAY
Bills lead series, 1–0
1976—Bills, 14–9 (TB)
BUFFALO vs. WASHINGTON
Bills lead series, 1–0
1972—Bills, 24–17 (W)

CHICAGO vs. ATLANTA

Falcons lead series, 6–3
See Atlanta vs. Chicago
CHICAGO vs. BALTIMORE
Colts lead series, 20–13;
See Baltimore vs. Chicago
CHICAGO vs. *BOS. YANKS
Bears won series, 3–0
See *Boston Yanks vs. Chicago
*Extinct team
CHICAGO vs. *BROOKLYN DODGERS
Bears won series, 11–0
See *Brooklyn Dodgers vs. Chicago
*Extinct team
CHICAGO vs. BUFFALO
Series tied, 1–1
See Buffalo vs. Chicago
CHICAGO vs. CINCINNATI
Bengals lead series, 1–0
1972—Bengals, 13–3 (Chi)
CHICAGO vs. *CINCINNATI REDS
Bears won series, 2–0
1934—Bears, 21–3
        Bears, 41–7
(Points—Bears 62, Reds 10)
*Extinct team
CHICAGO vs. CLEVELAND
Browns lead series, 5–2
1951—Browns, 42–21 (Cle)
1954—Browns, 39–10 (Chi)
1960—Browns, 42–0 (Cle)
1961—Bears, 17–14 (Chi)
1967—Browns, 24–0 (Cle)
1969—Browns, 28–24 (Chi)
1972—Bears, 17–0 (Cle)
(Points—Browns 189, Bears 89)
CHICAGO vs. *DALLAS TEXANS
Series tied, 1–1
1952—Bears, 38–20
        Texans, 27–23
(Points—Bears 61, Texans 47)
*Extinct team
CHICAGO vs. DALLAS
Cowboys lead series, 4–3
1960—Bears, 17–7 (C)
1962—Bears, 34–33 (D)
1964—Cowboys, 24–10 (C)
1968—Cowboys, 34–3 (C)
1971—Bears, 23–19 (C)
1973—Cowboys, 20–17 (C)
1976—Cowboys, 31–21 (D)
(Points—Cowboys 168, Bears 125)
CHICAGO vs. DENVER
Broncos lead series, 2–1
1971—Broncos, 6–3 (D)
1973—Bears, 33–14 (D)
1976—Broncos, 28–14 (C)
(Points—Bears 50, Broncos 48)
CHICAGO vs. *DETROIT
Bears lead series, 53–37–5
1930—Spartans, 7–6
        Bears, 14–6
1931—Bears, 9–6
        Spartans, 3–0
1932—Tie, 13–13
        Tie, 7–7
        **Bears, 9–0
1933—Bears, 17–14
        Bears, 17–7
1934—Bears, 19–16 (D)
        Bears, 10–7 (C)
1935—Tie, 20–20 (C)
        Lions, 14–2 (D)
1936—Bears, 12–10 (C)
        Lions, 13–7 (D)
1937—Bears, 28–20 (C)
        Bears, 13–0 (D)
1938—Lions, 13–7 (C)
        Lions, 14–7 (D)
1939—Lions, 10–0 (C)
        Bears, 23–13 (D)
1940—Bears, 7–0 (C)
        Lions, 17–14 (D)
1941—Bears, 49–0 (C)
        Bears, 24–7 (D)
1942—Bears, 16–0 (C)
        Bears, 42–0 (D)
1943—Bears, 27–21 (D)
        Bears, 35–14 (C)
1944—Tie, 21–21 (C)
        Lions, 41–21 (D)
1945—Lions, 16–10 (D)
        Lions, 35–28 (C)
1946—Bears, 42–6 (C)
        Bears, 45–24 (D)
1947—Bears, 33–24 (C)
        Bears, 34–14 (D)
1948—Bears, 28–0 (C)
        Bears, 42–14 (D)

1949—Bears, 27–24 (C)
Bears, 28–7 (D)
1950—Bears, 35–21 (D)
Bears, 6–3 (C)
1951—Bears, 28–23 (C)
Lions, 41–28 (C)
1952—Bears, 24–23 (C)
Lions, 45–21 (D)
1953—Lions, 20–16 (C)
Lions, 13–7 (D)
1954—Lions, 48–23 (D)
Bears, 28–24 (C)
1955—Lions, 24–14 (D)
Bears, 21–20 (C)
1956—Lions, 42–10 (D)
Bears, 38–21 (C)
1957—Bears, 27–7 (D)
Lions, 21–13 (C)
1958—Bears, 20–7 (D)
Bears, 21–16 (C)
1959—Bears, 24–14 (D)
Bears, 25–14 (C)
1960—Bears, 28–7 (C)
Lions, 36–0 (D)
1961—Bears, 31–17 (D)
Lions, 16–15 (C)
1962—Lions, 11–3 (D)
Bears, 3–0 (C)
1963—Bears, 37–21 (D)
Bears, 24–14 (C)
1964—Lions, 10–0 (C)
Bears, 27–24 (D)
1965—Bears, 38–10 (C)
Bears, 17–10 (D)
1966—Lions, 14–3 (D)
Tie, 10–10 (C)
1967—Bears, 14–3 (C)
Bears, 27–13 (D)
1968—Lions, 42–0 (D)
Lions, 28–10 (C)
1969—Lions, 13–7 (C)
Lions, 20–3 (D)
1970—Lions, 28–14 (D)
Lions, 16–10 (C)
1971—Bears, 28–23 (D)
Lions, 28–3 (C)
1972—Lions, 38–24 (C)
Lions, 14–0 (D)
1973—Lions, 30–7 (C)
Lions, 40–7 (D)
1974—Bears, 17–9 (C)
Lions, 34–17 (D)
1975—Lions, 27–7 (C)
Bears, 25–21 (C)
1976—Lions, 10–3 (C)
Lions, 14–10 (D)
(Points—Bears 1,728, Lions 1,579)
*Franchise in Portsmouth prior to 1934 and known as the Spartans
**Championship
CHICAGO vs. GREEN BAY
(Bears lead series, 60-50-6)
1921—Staleys, 20–0 (C)
1923—Bears, 3–0 (GB)
1924—Bears, 3–0 (GB)
1925—Packers, 14–10 (GB)
Bears, 21–0 (C)
1926—Tie 6–6 (GB)
Bears, 19–13 (C)
Tie, 3–3 (C)
1927—Bears, 7–6 (GB)
Bears, 14–6 (C)
1928—Tie, 12–12 (GB)
Packers, 16–6 (C)
Packers, 6–0 (C)
1929—Packers, 23–0 (GB)
Packers, 14–0 (C)
Packers, 25–0 (C)
1930—Packers, 7–0 (GB)
Packers, 13–12 (C)
Bears, 21–0 (C)
1931—Packers, 7–0 (GB)
Packers, 6–2 (C)
Bears, 7–6 (C)
1932—Tie, 0–0 (GB)
Packers, 2–0 (C)
Bears, 9–0 (C)
1933—Bears, 14–7 (GB)
Bears, 10–7 (C)
Bears, 7–6 (C)
1934—Bears, 24–10 (GB)
Bears, 27–14 (C)
1935—Packers, 7–0 (GB)
Packers, 17–14 (C)
1936—Bears, 30–3 (GB)
Packers, 21–10 (C)
1937—Bears, 14–2 (GB)
Packers, 24–14 (C)
1938—Bears, 2–0 (GB)

Packers, 24–17 (C)
1939—Packers, 21–16 (GB)
Bears, 30–27 (C)
1940—Bears, 41–10 (GB)
Bears, 14–7 (C)
1941—Bears, 25–17 (GB)
Packers, 16–14 (C)
**Bears, 33–14 (C)
1942—Bears, 44–28 (GB)
Bears, 38–7 (C)
1943—Tie, 21–21 (GB)
Bears, 21–7 (C)
1944—Packers, 42–28 (GB)
Bears, 21–0 (C)
1945—Packers, 31–21 (GB)
Bears, 28–24 (C)
1946—Bears, 30–7 (GB)
Bears, 10–7 (C)
1947—Packers, 29–20 (GB)
Bears, 20–17 (C)
1948—Bears, 45–7 (GB)
Bears, 7–6 (C)
1949—Bears, 17–0 (GB)
Bears, 24–3 (C)
1950—Packers, 31–21 (GB)
Bears, 28–14 (C)
1951—Bears, 31–20 (GB)
Bears, 24–13 (C)
1952—Bears, 24–14 (GB)
Packers, 41–28 (C)
1953—Bears, 17–13 (GB)
Tie, 21–21 (C)
1954—Bears, 10–3 (GB)
Bears, 28–23 (C)
1955—Packers, 24–3 (GB)
Bears, 52–31 (C)
1956—Bears, 37–21 (GB)
Bears, 38–14 (C)
1957—Packers, 21–17 (GB)
Bears, 21–14 (C)
1958—Bears, 34–20 (GB)
Bears, 24–10 (C)
1959—Packers, 9–6 (GB)
Bears, 28–17 (C)
1960—Bears, 17–14 (GB)
Packers, 41–13 (C)
1961—Packers, 24–0 (GB)
Packers, 31–28 (C)
1962—Packers, 49–0 (GB)
Packers, 38–7 (C)
1963—Bears, 10–3 (GB)
Bears, 26–7 (C)
1964—Packers, 23–12 (GB)
Packers, 17–3 (C)
1965—Packers, 23–14 (GB)
Bears, 31–10 (C)
1966—Packers, 17–0 (C)
Packers, 13–6 (GB)
1967—Packers, 13–10 (GB)
Packers, 17–13 (C)
1968—Bears, 13–10 (GB)
Packers, 28–27 (C)
1969—Packers, 17–0 (GB)
Packers, 21–3 (C)
1970—Packers, 20–19 (GB)
Bears, 35–17 (C)
1971—Packers, 17–14 (C)
Packers, 31–10 (GB)
1972—Packers, 20–17 (GB)
Packers, 23–17 (C)
1973—Packers, 31–17 (GB)
Packers, 21–0 (C)
1974—Bears, 10–9 (C)
Packers, 20–3 (Mil)
1975—Bears, 27–14 (C)
Packers, 28–7 (GB)
1976—Bears, 24–13 (C)
Bears, 16–10 (GB)
(Points—Bears 1,881, Packers 1,725)
*Bears known as Staleys prior to 1922
**Conference Playoff
CHICAGO vs. HOUSTON
Bears lead series, 1–0
1973—Bears, 35–14 (C)
CHICAGO vs. KANSAS CITY
Chiefs lead series, 1–0
1973—Chiefs, 19–7 (KC)
CHICAGO vs. **LOS ANGELES
Bears lead series, 39-24-3
1937—Bears, 20–2
Bears, 15–7
1938—Rams, 14–7
Rams, 23–21
1939—Bears, 30–21
Bears, 35–21
1940—Bears, 21–14
Bears, 47–25

1941—Bears, 48–21
Bears, 14–13
1942—Bears, 21–7
Bears, 47–0
1944—Rams, 19–7
Bears, 28–21
1945—Rams, 17–0
Bears, 41–21
1946—Tie, 28–28 (C)
Bears, 27–21 (LA)
1947—Bears, 41–21 (LA)
Rams, 17–14 (C)
1948—Bears, 42–21 (C)
Bears, 21–6 (LA)
1949—Rams, 31–16 (C)
Rams, 27–24 (LA)
1950—Bears, 24–20 (LA)
Bears, 24–14 (C)
*Rams, 24–14 (LA)
1951—Rams, 42–17 (C)
Rams, 7–0 (LA)
1952—Rams, 31–7 (LA)
Rams, 40–24 (C)
1953—Rams, 38–24 (LA)
Bears, 24–21 (C)
1954—Rams, 42–38 (LA)
Bears, 24–13 (C)
1955—Bears, 31–20 (LA)
Bears, 24–3 (C)
1956—Rams, 35–24 (LA)
Bears, 30–21 (C)
1957—Bears, 34–26 (C)
Bears, 16–10 (LA)
1958—Bears, 31–10 (C)
Rams, 41–35 (LA)
1959—Rams, 28–21 (C)
Bears, 26–21 (LA)
1960—Bears, 34–27 (C)
Tie, 24–24 (LA)
1961—Bears, 21–17 (LA)
Bears, 28–24 (C)
1962—Bears, 27–23 (LA)
Bears, 30–14 (C)
1963—Bears, 52–14 (LA)
Bears, 6–0 (C)
1964—Bears, 38–17 (C)
Bears, 34–24 (LA)
1965—Rams, 30–28 (LA)
Bears, 31–6 (C)
1966—Rams, 31–17 (LA)
Bears, 17–10 (C)
1967—Rams, 28–17 (C)
Bears, 17–16 (LA)
1969—Rams, 9–7 (C)
1971—Rams, 17–3 (LA)
1972—Tie, 13–13 (C)
1973—Rams, 26–0 (C)
1975—Rams, 38–10 (LA)
1976—Rams, 20–12 (LA)
(Points—Bears 1,581, Rams 1,355)
*Conference Playoff
**Franchise in Cleveland (CL) prior to 1946
CHICAGO vs. MIAMI
Dolphins lead series, 2–0
1971—Dolphins, 34–3 (M)
1975—Dolphins, 46–13 (C)
(Points—Dolphins 80, Bears 16)
CHICAGO vs. MINNESOTA
Vikings lead series, 16-14-2
1961—Vikings, 37–13 (M)
Bears, 52–35 (C)
1962—Bears, 13–0 (M)
Bears, 31–30 (C)
1963—Bears, 28–7 (M)
Tie, 17–17 (C)
1964—Bears, 34–28 (M)
Vikings, 41–14 (C)
1965—Bears, 45–37 (M)
Vikings, 24–17 (C)
1966—Bears, 13–10 (M)
Bears, 41–28 (C)
1967—Bears, 17–7 (M)
Tie, 10–10 (C)
1968—Bears, 27–17 (M)
Bears, 26–24 (C)
1969—Vikings, 31–0 (C)
Vikings, 31–14 (M)
1970—Vikings, 24–0 (C)
Vikings, 16–13 (M)
1971—Bears, 20–17 (M)
Vikings, 27–10 (C)
1972—Bears, 13–10 (C)
Vikings, 23–10 (M)
1973—Vikings, 22–13 (C)
Vikings, 31–13 (M)
1974—Vikings, 11–7 (M)
Vikings, 17–0 (C)
1975—Vikings, 28–3 (M)
Vikings, 13–9 (C)

1976—Vikings, 20–19 (M)
Bears, 14–13 (C)
(Points—Vikings 686, Bears 556)
CHICAGO vs. NEW ENGLAND
Patriots lead series, 1–0
1973—Patriots, 13–10 (C)
CHICAGO vs. NEW ORLEANS
Bears lead series, 5–1
1968—Bears, 23–17 (NO)
1970—Bears, 24–3 (NO)
1971—Bears, 35–14 (C)
1973—Saints, 21–16 (NO)
1974—Bears, 24–10 (C)
1975—Bears, 42–17 (NO)
(Points—Bears 164, Saints 82)
CHICAGO vs. N.Y. GIANTS
Bears lead series, 25-16-2
1925—Bears, 19–7 (NY)
Giants, 9–0 (C)
1926—Bears, 7–0 (C)
1927—Giants, 13–7 (NY)
1928—Bears, 13–0 (C)
1929—Bears, 26–14 (C)
Giants, 34–0 (NY)
Giants, 14–9 (NY)
1930—Giants, 12–0 (C)
Bears, 12–0 (NY)
1931—Bears, 6–0 (C)
Bears, 12–6 (NY)
Giants, 25–6 (C)
1932—Bears, 28–8 (NY)
Bears, 6–0 (C)
1933—Bears, 14–10 (C)
Giants, 3–0 (NY)
*Bears, 23–21 (C)
1934—Bears, 27–7 (C)
Bears, 10–9 (NY)
*Giants, 30–13 (NY)
1935—Bears, 20–3 (NY)
Giants, 3–0 (C)
1936—Bears, 25–7 (NY)
1937—Tie, 3–3 (NY)
1939—Bears, 16–13 (NY)
1940—Bears, 37–21 (NY)
1941—*Bears, 37–9 (C)
1942—Bears, 26–7 (NY)
1943—Bears, 56–7 (NY)
1946—Giants, 14–0 (NY)
*Bears, 24–14 (NY)
1948—Bears, 35–14 (C)
1949—Giants, 35–28 (NY)
1956—Tie, 17–17 (NY)
*Giants, 47–7 (NY)
1962—Giants, 26–24 (C)
1963—*Bears, 14–10 (C)
1965—Bears, 35–14 (NY)
1967—Bears, 34–7 (C)
1969—Giants, 28–24 (NY)
1970—Bears, 24–16 (NY)
1974—Bears, 16–13 (C)
(Points—Bears 725, Giants 565)
*NFL Championship
CHICAGO vs. N.Y. JETS
Jets lead series, 1–0
1974—Jets, 23–21 (C)
CHICAGO vs. *N.Y. YANKS
Bears won series, 3–1
1950—Yanks, 38–27
Bears, 28–20
1951—Bears, 24–21
Bears, 45–21
(Points—Bears 124, Yanks 100)
*Extinct Team
CHICAGO vs. OAKLAND
Raiders lead series, 2–0
1972—Raiders, 28–24 (O)
1976—Raiders, 28–27 (C)
(Points—Raiders 56, Bears 48)
CHICAGO vs. PHILADELPHIA
Bears lead series, 18-2-1
1933—Tie, 3–3 (P)
1935—Bears, 39–0 (P)
1936—Bears, 17–0 (P)
Bears, 28–7 (P)
1938—Bears, 28–6 (P)
1939—Bears, 27–14 (C)
1941—Bears, 49–14 (P)
1942—Bears, 45–14 (C)
1943—Bears, 48–21 (C)
1944—Bears, 28–7 (P)
1946—Bears, 21–14 (C)
1947—Bears, 40–7 (C)
1948—Eagles, 12–7 (P)
1949—Bears, 38–21 (C)
1955—Bears, 17–10 (C)
1961—Eagles, 16–14 (P)
1963—Bears, 16–7 (C)
1968—Bears, 29–16 (P)
1970—Bears, 20–16 (C)

1972—Bears, 21–12 (P)
(Points—Bears 550, Eagles 230)
CHICAGO vs. PITTSBURGH
Bears lead series, 16-3-1
1934—Bears, 28–0 (P)
1935—Bears, 23–7 (P)
1936—Bears, 27–9 (P)
Bears, 26–6 (C)
1937—Bears, 7–0 (P)
1939—Bears, 32–0 (P)
1941—Bears, 34–7 (C)
1943—Bears, 48–21 (C)
1944—Bears, 34–7 (C)
Bears, 49–7 (P)
1945—Bears, 28–7 (P)
1947—Bears, 49–7 (C)
1949—Bears, 30–21 (C)
1958—Steelers, 24–10 (P)
1959—Bears, 27–21 (C)
1963—Tie, 17–17 (P)
1967—Steelers, 41–13 (P)
1969—Bears, 38–7 (C)
1971—Bears, 17–15 (C)
1975—Steelers, 34–3 (P)
(Points—Bears 540, Steelers 258)
CHICAGO vs. ***ST. LOUIS
Bears lead series, 50-22-6
(Wr denotes Wrigley Field;
Co denotes Comiskey Park;
So denotes Soldier Field
NP denotes Normal Park,
all Chicago)
1920—Cardinals, 7–6 (NP)
Staleys, 10–0 (Wr)
1921—Tie, 0–0 (Wr)
1922—Cardinals, 6–0 (Co)
Cardinals, 9–0 (Co)
1923—Bears, 3–0 (Wr)
1924—Bears, 6–0 (Wr)
Bears, 21–0 (Co)
1925—Cardinals, 9–0 (Co)
Tie, 0–0 (Wr)
1926—Bears, 16–0 (Wr)
Bears, 10–0 (So)
Tie, 0–0 (Wr)
1927—Bears, 9–0 (NP)
Cardinals, 3–0 (Wr)
1928—Bears, 15–0 (NP)
Bears, 34–0 (Wr)
1929—Tie, 0–0 (Wr)
Cardinals, 40–6 (Co)
1930—Bears, 32–6 (Co)
Bears, 6–0 (Wr)
1931—Bears, 26–13 (Wr)
Bears, 18–7 (Wr)
1932—Tie, 0–0 (Wr)
Bears, 34–0 (Wr)
1933—Bears, 12–9 (Wr)
Bears, 22–6 (Wr)
1934—Bears, 20–0 (Wr)
Bears, 17–6 (Wr)
1935—Tie, 7–7 (Wr)
Bears, 13–0 (Wr)
1936—Bears, 7–3 (Wr)
Cardinals, 14–7 (Wr)
1937—Bears, 16–7 (Wr)
Bears, 42–28 (Wr)
1938—Bears, 16–13 (So)
Bears, 34–28 (Wr)
1939—Bears, 44–7 (Wr)
Bears, 48–7 (Co)
1940—Bears, 21–7 (Co)
Bears, 31–23 (Wr)
1941—Bears, 53–7 (Wr)
Bears, 34–24 (Co)
1942—Bears, 41–14 (Co)
Bears, 21–7 (Co)
1943—Bears, 20–0 (Wr)
Bears, 35–24 (Co)
1944—Bears, 34–7 (Wr)
Bears, 49–7 (Pitt)
1945—Cardinals, 16–7 (Wr)
Bears, 28–20 (Co)
1946—Bears, 34–17 (Co)
Cardinals, 35–28 (Wr)
1947—Cardinals, 31–7 (Co)
Cardinals, 30–21 (Wr)
1948—Bears, 28–17 (Co)
Bears, 24–21 (Wr)
1949—Bears, 17–7 (Co)
Bears, 52–21 (Wr)
1950—Bears, 27–6 (Wr)
Cardinals, 20–10 (Co)
1951—Cardinals, 28–14 (Co)
Cardinals, 24–14 (Wr)
1952—Cardinals, 21–10 (Co)
Bears, 10–7 (Co)
1953—Cardinals, 24–17 (Wr)

1954—Bears, 29-7 (CO)
1955—Cardinals, 53-14 (CO)
1956—Bears, 10-3 (Wr)
1957—Bears, 14-6 (CO)
1958—Bears, 30-14 (Wr)
1959—Bears, 31-7 (So)
1965—Bears, 34-13 (Wr)
1966—Cardinals, 24-17 (StL)
1967—Bears, 30-3 (Wr)
1969—Cardinals, 20-17 (StL)
1972—Bears, 27-10 (StL)
1975—Cardinals, 34-20 (So)
(Points—Bears 1,500, Cardinals 911)

*Bears known as Staleys prior to 1922

**Franchise in Chicago prior to 1960

CHICAGO vs. SAN DIEGO
Chargers lead series, 2-0
1970—Chargers, 20-7 (C)
1974—Chargers, 28-21 (SD)
(Points—Chargers 48, Bears 28)

CHICAGO vs. SAN FRANCISCO
49ers lead series, 21-20-1
1950—Bears, 32-20 (SF)
Bears, 17-0 (C)
1951—Bears, 13-7 (C)
1952—49ers, 40-16 (C)
Bears, 20-17 (SF)
1953—49ers, 35-28 (C)
49ers, 24-14 (C)
1954—Bears, 31-24 (C)
Bears, 31-27 (SF)
1955—49ers, 20-19 (C)
Bears, 34-23 (SF)
1956—Bears, 31-7 (C)
Bears, 38-21 (SF)
1957—49ers, 21-17 (C)
49ers, 21-17 (SF)
1958—Bears, 28-6 (C)
Bears, 27-14 (SF)
1959—49ers, 20-17 (SF)
Bears, 14-3 (C)
1960—Bears, 27-10 (C)
49ers, 25-7 (SF)
1961—Bears, 31-0 (C)
49ers, 41-31 (SF)
1962—Bears, 30-14 (SF)
Bears, 34-27 (C)
1963—49ers, 20-14 (SF)
Bears, 27-7 (C)
1964—49ers, 31-21 (C)
Bears, 23-21 (C)
1965—49ers, 52-24 (SF)
Bears, 61-20 (C)
1966—Tie, 30-30 (C)
49ers, 41-14 (SF)
1967—Bears, 28-14 (SF)
1968—Bears, 27-19 (C)
1969—49ers, 42-21 (SF)
1970—49ers, 37-16 (C)
1971—49ers, 13-0 (SF)
1972—49ers, 34-21 (C)
1974—49ers, 34-0 (C)
1975—49ers, 31-3 (SF)
1976—Bears, 19-12 (SF)
(Points—49ers 939, Bears 939)

CHICAGO vs. SEATTLE
Bears lead series, 1-0
1976—Bears, 34-7 (S)

CHICAGO vs. TAMPA BAY
No games

CHICAGO vs. **WASHINGTON
Bears lead series, 16-10-1
1932—Tie, 7-7
1933—Bears, 7-0
Redskins, 10-0
1934—Bears, 21-0
1935—Bears, 30-14
1936—Bears, 26-0
1937—*Redskins, 28-21 (C)
1938—Bears, 31-7 (C)
1940—Redskins, 7-3 (W)
*Bears, 73-0 (W)
1941—Bears, 35-21 (C)
1942—*Redskins, 14-6 (W)
1943—*Bears, 21-7 (W)
*Bears, 41-21 (C)
1945—Redskins, 28-21 (W)
1946—Bears, 24-20 (C)
1947—Bears, 56-20 (W)
1948—Bears, 48-13 (C)
1949—Bears, 31-21 (W)
1951—Bears, 27-0 (W)
1953—Bears, 27-24 (W)
1957—Redskins, 14-3 (C)
1964—Redskins, 27-20 (W)
1968—Redskins, 38-28 (C)
1971—Bears, 16-15 (C)
1974—Redskins, 42-0 (W)
1976—Bears, 33-7 (C)
(Points—Bears 642, Redskins 418)

*NFL Championship

**Franchise in Boston prior to 1937

CINCINNATI vs. ATLANTA
Series tied, 1-1:
See Atlanta vs. Cincinnati

CINCINNATI vs. BALTIMORE
Colts lead series 3-1:
See Baltimore vs. Cincinnati

CINCINNATI vs. BUFFALO
Bengals lead series 4-1:
See Buffalo vs. Cincinnati

CINCINNATI vs. CHICAGO
Bengals lead series 1-0:
See Chicago vs. Cincinnati

CINCINNATI vs. CLEVELAND
Series Tied, 7-7
1970—Browns, 30-27 (Cle)
Bengals, 14-10 (Cin)
1971—Browns, 27-24 (Cin)
Browns, 31-27 (Cle)
1972—Browns, 27-6 (Cle)
Browns, 27-24 (Cin)
1973—Browns, 17-10 (Cin)
Bengals, 34-17 (Cin)
1974—Bengals, 33-7 (Cin)
Bengals, 34-24 (Cle)
1975—Bengals, 24-17 (Cin)
Browns, 35-23 (Cle)
1976—Bengals, 45-24 (Cle)
Bengals, 21-6 (Cin)
(Points—Bengals 346, Browns 299)

CINCINNATI vs. DALLAS
Cowboys lead series, 1-0
1973—Cowboys, 38-10 (D)

CINCINNATI vs. DENVER
Bengals lead series, 5-4
1968—Bengals, 24-10 (C)
Broncos, 10-7 (D)
1969—Bengals, 30-23 (C)
Broncos, 27-16 (D)
1971—Bengals, 24-10 (D)
1972—Bengals, 21-10 (D)
1973—Broncos, 28-10 (D)
1975—Bengals, 17-16 (D)
1976—Bengals, 17-7 (C)
(Points—Bengals 159, Broncos 148)

CINCINNATI vs. DETROIT
Lions lead series, 2-0
1970—Lions, 38-3 (D)
1974—Lions, 23-19 (C)
(Points—Lions 61, Bengals 22)

CINCINNATI vs. GREEN BAY
Series Tied, 1-1
1971—Packers, 20-17 (GB)
1976—Bengals, 28-7 (C)
(Points—Bengals 45, Packers 27)

CINCINNATI vs. HOUSTON
Bengals lead series, 10-5-1
1968—Oilers, 27-17 (C)
1969—Tie, 31-31 (H)
1970—Oilers, 20-13 (C)
Bengals, 30-20 (H)
1971—Oilers, 10-6 (C)
Bengals, 28-13 (C)
1972—Bengals, 30-7 (C)
Bengals, 61-17 (H)
1973—Bengals, 24-10 (C)
Bengals, 27-24 (H)
1974—Oilers, 34-21 (C)
Oilers, 20-3 (H)
1975—Bengals, 21-19 (H)
Bengals, 23-19 (C)
1976—Bengals, 27-7 (H)
Bengals, 31-27 (C)
(Points—Bengals 393, Oilers 305)

CINCINNATI vs. KANSAS CITY
Bengals lead series, 5-4
1968—Chiefs, 13-3 (KC)
Chiefs, 16-9 (C)
1969—Bengals, 24-19 (C)
Chiefs, 42-22 (KC)
1970—Chiefs, 27-19 (C)
1972—Bengals, 23-16 (KC)
1973—Bengals, 14-6 (C)
1974—Bengals, 33-6 (C)
1976—Bengals, 27-24 (KC)
(Points—Bengals 174, Chiefs 169)

CINCINNATI vs. LOS ANGELES
Series Tied, 1-1
1972—Rams 15-12 (LA)
1976—Bengals, 20-12
(Points—Bengals 32, Rams 27)

CINCINNATI vs. MIAMI
Dolphins lead series, 4-2
1968—Dolphins, 24-22 (C)
Bengals, 38-21 (M)
1969—Bengals, 27-21 (C)
1971—Dolphins, 23-13 (C)
1973—*Dolphins, 34-16 (M)
1974—Dolphins, 24-3 (M)
(Points—Dolphins 147, Bengals 119)

*AFC Divisional Playoff

CINCINNATI vs. MINNESOTA
Bengals lead series, 1-0
1973—Bengals, 27-0 (C)

CINCINNATI vs. *NEW ENGLAND
Bengals lead series, 3-2
1968—Patriots, 33-14 (B)
1969—Patriots, 25-14 (C)
1970—Bengals, 45-7 (C)
1972—Bengals, 31-7 (NE)
1975—Bengals, 27-10 (C)
(Points—Bengals 131, Patriots 82)

*Franchise in Boston (B) prior to 1971

CINCINNATI vs. NEW ORLEANS
Bengals lead series, 2-0
1970—Bengals, 26-6 (C)
1975—Bengals, 21-0 (NO)
(Points—Bengals 47, Saints 6)

CINCINNATI vs. N. Y. GIANTS
Bengals lead series, 1-0
1972—Bengals, 13-10 (C)

CINCINNATI vs. N. Y. JETS
Jets lead series, 4-2
1968—Jets, 27-14 (NY)
1969—Jets, 21-7 (C)
Jets, 40-7 (NY)
1971—Jets, 35-21 (NY)
1973—Bengals, 20-14 (C)
1976—Bengals, 42-3 (NY)
(Points—Jets 140, Bengals 111)

CINCINNATI vs. OAKLAND
Raiders lead series, 8-3
1968—Raiders, 31-10 (O)
Raiders, 34-0 (C)
1969—Bengals, 31-17 (C)
Raiders, 37-17 (O)
1970—Bengals, 31-21 (C)
1971—Bengals, 31-27 (O)
1972—Raiders, 20-14 (C)
1974—Raiders, 30-27 (O)
1975—Bengals, 14-10 (C)
*Raiders, 31-28 (O)
1976—Raiders, 35-20 (O)
(Points—Raiders 297, Bengals 219)

*AFC Divisional Playoff

CINCINNATI vs. PHILADELPHIA
Bengals lead series, 2-0
1971—Bengals, 37-14 (C)
1975—Bengals, 31-0 (P)
(Points—Bengals 68, Eagles 14)

CINCINNATI vs. PITTSBURGH
Steelers lead series 10-4
1970—Steelers, 21-10 (P)
Bengals, 34-7 (C)
1971—Steelers, 21-10 (P)
Steelers, 21-13 (C)
1972—Bengals, 15-10 (C)
Steelers, 40-17 (P)
1973—Bengals, 19-7 (C)
Steelers, 20-13 (P)
1974—Bengals, 17-10 (C)
Steelers, 27-3 (P)
1975—Steelers, 30-24 (C)
Steelers, 35-14 (P)
1976—Bengals, 23-6 (P)
Steelers, 7-3 (C)
(Points—Steelers 279, Bengals 198)

CINCINNATI vs. ST. LOUIS
Bengals lead series, 1-0
1973—Bengals, 42-24 (C)

CINCINNATI vs. SAN DIEGO
Bengals lead series, 5-4
1968—Chargers, 29-13 (SD)
Chargers, 31-10 (C)
1969—Bengals, 34-20 (C)
Chargers, 21-14 (SD)
1970—Bengals, 17-14 (SD)
1971—Bengals, 31-0 (C)
1973—Bengals, 20-13 (SD)
1974—Chargers, 20-17 (C)
1975—Bengals, 47-17 (C)
(Points—Bengals 203, Chargers 165)

CINCINNATI vs. SAN FRANCISCO
Bengals lead series, 1-0
1974—Bengals, 21-3 (SF)

CINCINNATI vs. SEATTLE
No Games

CINCINNATI vs. TAMPA BAY
Bengals lead series, 1-0
1976—Bengals, 21-0 (C)

CINCINNATI vs. WASHINGTON
Series tied, 1-1
1970—Redskins, 20-0 (W)
1974—Bengals, 28-17 (C)
(Points—Redskins 37, Bengals 28)

***CINCINNATI REDS vs. *BROOKLYN DODGERS**
Series tied, 1-1; See Brooklyn Dodgers vs. Cincinnati Reds

*Extinct teams

***CINCINNATI REDS vs. CHICAGO**
Bears won series, 2-0
See Chicago vs. *Cincinnati Reds

*Extinct team

***CINCINNATI REDS vs. **CHICAGO CARDINALS**
Cardinals won series, 3-1
1933—Cardinals, 3-0
Reds, 12-9
1934—Cardinals, 9-0
Cardinals, 16-0
(Points—Cardinals 37, Reds 12)

*Extinct team

**Franchise moved to St. Louis in 1960

***CINCINNATI REDS vs. **DETROIT**
Lions won series, 2-1
1933—Spartans, 21-0
Reds, 10-7
1934—Lions, 38-0
(Points—Spartans-Lions 66, Reds 10)

*Extinct team

**Franchise in Portsmouth prior to 1934 and known as the Spartans

***CINCINNATI REDS vs. GREEN BAY**
Packers won series, 1-0
1934—Packers, 41-0

*Extinct team

***CINCINNATI REDS vs. PHILADELPHIA**
Eagles won series, 3-0
1933—Eagles, 6-0
Eagles, 20-3
1934—Eagles, 64-0
(Points—Eagles 26, Reds 3)

*Extinct team

***CINCINNATI REDS vs. PITTSBURGH**
Steelers won series, 2-0-1
1933—Steelers, 17-3
Tie, 0-0
1934—Steelers, 13-0
(Points—Steelers 30, Reds 3)

*Extinct team

CLEVELAND vs. ATLANTA
Browns lead series, 3-1
See Atlanta vs. Cleveland

CLEVELAND vs. *1950 BALTIMORE
Browns won series, 1-0
See *Baltimore vs. Cleveland

*Extinct team

CLEVELAND vs. BALTIMORE
Series tied, 5-5;
See Baltimore vs. Cleveland

CLEVELAND vs. BUFFALO
Series tied, 1-1;
See Buffalo vs. Cleveland

CLEVELAND vs. CHICAGO
Browns lead series, 5-2;
See Chicago vs. Cleveland

CLEVELAND vs. CINCINNATI
Series tied, 7-7;
See Cincinnati vs. Cleveland

CLEVELAND vs. DALLAS
Browns lead series, 14-7
1960—Browns, 48-7 (D)
1961—Browns, 25-7 (C)
Browns, 38-17 (D)
1962—Browns, 19-10 (C)
Cowboys, 45-21 (D)
1963—Browns, 41-24 (C)
Browns, 27-17 (C)
1964—Browns, 27-6 (C)
Browns, 20-16 (D)
1965—Browns, 24-17 (C)
Browns, 24-17 (D)
1966—Browns, 30-21 (C)
Cowboys, 26-14 (D)
1967—Cowboys, 21-14 (C)
*Cowboys, 52-14 (D)
1968—Cowboys, 28-7 (C)
*Browns, 31-20 (C)
1969—Browns, 42-10 (C)
*Browns, 38-14 (C)
1970—Cowboys, 6-2 (C)
1974—Cowboys, 41-17 (D)
(Points—Browns 522, Cowboys 422)

*Conference Championship

CLEVELAND vs. DENVER
Series tied, 3-3
1970—Browns, 27-13 (D)
1971—Broncos, 27-0 (C)
1972—Browns, 27-20 (D)
1974—Browns, 23-21 (C)
1975—Broncos, 16-15 (D)
1976—Broncos, 44-13 (D)
(Points—Broncos 141, Browns 105)

CLEVELAND vs. DETROIT
Lions lead series, 13-2
1952—Lions, 17-6 (D)
*Lions, 17-7 (C)
1953—*Lions, 17-16 (D)
1954—Lions, 14-10 (C)
*Browns, 56-10 (C)
1957—Lions, 20-7 (D)
*Lions, 59-14 (D)
1958—Lions, 30-10 (C)
1961—**Lions, 17-16 (Miami)
1963—Lions, 38-10 (C)
1964—Browns, 37-21 (C)
1967—Lions, 31-14 (D)
1969—Lions, 28-21 (C)
1970—Lions, 41-24 (C)
1975—Lions, 21-10 (D)
(Points—Lions 381, Browns 258)

*NFL Championship

**Playoff Bowl

CLEVELAND vs. GREEN BAY
Packers lead series, 7-4
1953—Browns, 27-0 (Mil)
1955—Browns, 41-10 (Mil)
1956—Browns, 24-7 (Mil)
1961—Packers, 49-17 (C)
1964—*Packers, 40-23 (Miami)
Packers, 28-21 (Mil)
1965—**Packers, 23-12 (GB)
1966—Packers, 21-20 (C)
1967—Packers, 55-7 (Mil)
1969—Browns, 20-7 (C)
1972—Packers, 26-10 (C)
(Points—Packers 266, Browns 222)

*Playoff Bowl

**NFL Championship

CLEVELAND vs. HOUSTON
Browns lead series 11-3
1970—Browns, 28-14 (C)
Browns, 21-10 (H)
1971—Browns, 31-0 (C)
Browns, 37-24 (H)
1972—Browns, 23-17 (H)
Browns, 20-0 (C)
1973—Browns, 42-13 (C)
Browns, 23-13 (H)
1974—Browns, 20-7 (C)
Oilers, 28-24 (H)
1975—Oilers, 40-10 (C)
Oilers, 21-10 (H)
1976—Browns, 21-7 (H)
Browns, 13-10 (C)
(Points—Browns 323, Oilers 204)

CLEVELAND vs. KANSAS CITY
Chiefs lead series, 3-1-1
1971—Chiefs, 13-7 (KC)
1972—Chiefs, 31-7 (C)
1973—Tie, 20-20 (KC)
1975—Browns, 40-14 (C)
1976—Chiefs, 39-14 (KC)
(Points—Chiefs 117, Browns 88)

CLEVELAND vs. LOS ANGELES
Browns lead series, 7-5
1950—*Browns, 30-28 (LA)
1951—Browns, 38-23 (LA)
*Rams, 24-17 (LA)
1952—Browns, 37-7 (C)
1955—*Browns, 38-14 (LA)
1957—Browns, 45-31 (C)
1958—Browns, 30-27 (LA)
1963—Browns, 20-6 (C)
1965—Rams, 42-7 (LA)
1968—**Rams, 30-6 (Miami)
Rams, 24-6 (C)
1973—Rams, 30-17 (LA)
(Points—Browns 291, Rams 286)

*NFL Championship

**Playoff Bowl

CLEVELAND vs. MIAMI
Series tied, 2-2

1970—Browns, 28-0 (M)
1972—*Dolphins, 20-14 (M)
1973—Dolphins, 17-9 (C)
1976—Browns, 17-13
(Points—Browns 68, Dolphins 50)
*AFC Divisional Playoff

CLEVELAND vs. MINNESOTA
Vikings lead series, 5-1
1965—Vikings, 27-17 (C)
1967—Vikings, 14-10 (C)
1969—Vikings, 51-3 (M)
      *Vikings, 27-7 (M)
1973—Vikings, 26-3 (M)
1975—Vikings, 42-10 (M)
(Points—Vikings 183, Browns 54)
*NFL Championship

CLEVELAND vs. NEW ENGLAND
Browns lead series, 2-0
1971—Browns, 27-7 (C)
1974—Browns, 21-14 (NE)
(Points—Browns 48, Patriots 21)

CLEVELAND vs. NEW ORLEANS
Browns lead series, 6-0
1967—Browns, 42-7 (NO)
1968—Browns, 24-10 (NO)
      Browns, 35-17 (C)
1969—Browns, 27-17 (NO)
1971—Browns, 21-17 (NO)
1975—Browns, 17-16 (C)
(Points—Browns 166, Saints 84)

CLEVELAND vs. N. Y. GIANTS
Browns lead series, 24-16-2
1950—Giants, 6-0 (C)
      Giants, 17-13 (N)
      *Browns, 8-3 (C)
1951—Browns, 14-13 (C)
      Browns, 10-0 (NY)
1952—Giants, 17-9 (C)
      Giants, 37-34 (NY)
1953—Browns, 7-0 (NY)
      Browns, 62-14 (C)
1954—Browns, 24-14 (C)
      Browns, 16-7 (NY)
1955—Browns, 24-14 (C)
      Tie, 35-35 (NY)
1956—Giants, 21-9 (C)
      Browns, 24-7 (NY)
1957—Browns, 6-3 (C)
      Browns, 34-28 (NY)
1958—Giants, 21-17 (C)
      Giants, 13-10 (NY)
      *Giants, 10-0 (NY)
1959—Giants, 10-6 (C)
      Giants, 48-7 (NY)
1960—Browns, 17-13 (C)
      Browns, 48-34 (NY)
1961—Giants, 37-21 (C)
      Tie, 7-7 (NY)
1962—Browns, 17-7 (C)
      Giants, 17-13 (NY)
1963—Browns, 35-24 (NY)
      Giants, 33-6 (C)
1964—Browns, 42-20 (C)
      Browns, 52-20 (NY)
1965—Browns, 38-14 (NY)
      Browns, 34-21 (C)
1966—Browns, 28-7 (NY)
      Browns, 49-40 (C)
1967—Giants, 38-34 (NY)
      Browns, 24-14 (C)
1968—Browns, 45-10 (C)
1969—Browns, 28-17 (C)
      Giants, 27-14 (NY)
1973—Browns, 12-10 (C)
(Points—Browns 929, Giants 752)
*Conference Playoff

CLEVELAND vs. N. Y. JETS
Browns lead series, 3-0
1970—Browns, 31-21 (C)
1972—Browns, 26-10 (NY)
1976—Browns, 38-17 (C)
(Points—Browns 95, Jets 48)

CLEVELAND vs. OAKLAND
Raiders lead series, 4-1
1970—Raiders, 23-20 (O)
1971—Raiders, 34-20 (O)
1973—Browns, 7-3 (O)
1974—Raiders, 40-24 (O)
1975—Raiders, 38-17 (O)
(Points—Raiders 138, Browns 88)

CLEVELAND vs. PHILADELPHIA
Browns lead series, 28-10-1
1950—Browns, 35-10 (P)
      Browns, 13-7 (C)
1951—Browns, 20-17 (C)
      Browns, 24-9 (NY)
1952—Browns, 49-7 (P)
      Eagles, 28-20 (C)
1953—Browns, 37-13 (C)
      Eagles, 42-27 (P)
1954—Eagles, 28-10 (P)
      Browns, 6-0 (C)
1955—Browns, 21-17 (C)
      Eagles, 33-17 (P)
1956—Browns, 16-0 (P)
      Browns, 17-14 (C)
1957—Browns, 24-7 (C)
      Eagles, 17-7 (P)
1958—Browns, 28-14 (C)
      Browns, 21-14 (P)
1959—Browns, 28-7 (C)
      Browns, 28-21 (P)
1960—Browns, 41-24 (C)
      Eagles, 31-29 (C)
1961—Eagles, 27-20 (P)
      Browns, 45-24 (C)
1962—Eagles, 35-7 (P)
      Tie, 14-14 (C)
1963—Browns, 37-7 (P)
      Browns, 23-17 (P)
1964—Browns, 28-20 (P)
      Browns, 38-24 (C)
1965—Browns, 35-17 (P)
      Browns, 38-34 (C)
1966—Browns, 27-7 (C)
      Eagles, 33-21 (P)
1967—Eagles, 28-24 (P)
1968—Browns, 47-13 (C)
1969—Browns, 27-20 (P)
1972—Browns, 27-17 (P)
1976—Browns, 24-3 (C)
(Points—Browns 1000, Eagles 700)

CLEVELAND vs. PITTSBURGH
Browns lead series, 36-18
1950—Browns, 30-17 (P)
      Browns, 45-7 (C)
1951—Browns, 17-0 (C)
      Browns, 28-0 (P)
1952—Browns, 21-20 (P)
      Browns, 29-28 (C)
1953—Browns, 34-16 (C)
      Browns, 20-16 (P)
1954—Steelers, 55-27 (P)
      Browns, 42-7 (C)
1955—Browns, 41-14 (C)
      Browns, 30-7 (P)
1956—Browns, 14-10 (P)
      Steelers, 24-16 (C)
1957—Browns, 23-12 (C)
      Browns, 24-0 (C)
1958—Steelers, 45-12 (P)
      Browns, 27-10 (C)
1959—Steelers, 17-7 (P)
      Steelers, 21-20 (C)
1960—Steelers, 28-20 (C)
      Steelers, 14-10 (P)
1961—Browns, 30-28 (P)
      Steelers, 17-13 (C)
1962—Browns, 41-14 (P)
      Browns, 35-14 (C)
1963—Browns, 35-23 (C)
      Steelers, 9-7 (P)
1964—Steelers, 23-7 (C)
      Browns, 30-17 (P)
1965—Browns, 24-19 (C)
      Browns, 42-21 (P)
1966—Browns, 41-10 (C)
      Steelers, 16-6 (P)
1967—Browns, 21-10 (C)
1968—Browns, 31-24 (C)
      Browns, 45-24 (P)
1969—Browns, 42-31 (C)
      Browns, 24-3 (P)
1970—Browns, 15-7 (C)
      Steelers, 28-9 (P)
1971—Browns, 27-17 (C)
      Steelers, 26-9 (P)
1972—Browns, 26-24 (C)
      Steelers, 30-0 (P)
1973—Steelers, 33-6 (P)
      Browns, 21-16 (C)
1974—Steelers, 20-16 (P)
      Steelers, 26-16 (C)
1975—Steelers, 42-6 (C)
      Steelers, 31-17 (P)
1976—Steelers, 31-14 (P)
      Browns, 18-16 (C)
(Points—Browns 1286, Steelers 991)

CLEVELAND vs. *ST. LOUIS
Browns lead series, 29-9-3
1950—Browns, 34-24 (Cle)
      Browns, 10-7 (Chi)
1951—Browns, 34-17 (Chi)
      Browns, 49-28 (Cle)
1952—Browns, 28-13 (Cle)
      Browns, 10-0 (Chi)
1953—Browns, 27-7 (Chi)
      Browns, 27-16 (Cle)
1954—Browns, 31-7 (Cle)
      Browns, 35-3 (Chi)
1955—Browns, 26-20 (Chi)
      Browns, 35-24 (Cle)
1956—Cardinals, 9-7 (Chi)
      Cardinals, 24-7 (Cle)
1957—Browns, 17-7 (Chi)
      Browns, 31-0 (Cle)
1958—Browns, 35-28 (Cle)
      Browns, 38-24 (Chi)
1959—Browns, 34-7 (Cle)
      Browns, 17-7 (Cle)
1960—Browns, 28-27 (C)
      Tie, 17-17 (StL)
1961—Browns, 20-17 (C)
      Browns, 21-10 (StL)
1962—Browns, 34-7 (StL)
      Browns, 38-14 (C)
1963—Cardinals, 20-14 (C)
      Browns, 24-10 (StL)
1964—Tie, 33-33 (C)
      Cardinals, 28-19 (StL)
1965—Cardinals, 49-13 (C)
      Browns, 27-24 (StL)
1966—Cardinals, 34-28 (C)
      Browns, 38-10 (StL)
1967—Browns, 20-16 (C)
      Browns, 20-16 (StL)
1968—Cardinals, 27-21 (C)
      Cardinals, 27-16 (StL)
1969—Tie, 21-21 (C)
      Browns, 27-21 (StL)
1974—Cardinals, 29-7 (StL)
(Points—Browns, 1,018, Cardinals 729)
*Franchise in Chicago (Chi) prior to 1960

CLEVELAND vs. SAN DIEGO
Series tied, 2-2-1
1970—Chargers, 27-10 (C)
1972—Browns, 21-17 (SD)
1973—Tie, 16-16 (C)
1974—Chargers, 36-35 (SD)
1976—Browns, 21-17 (C)
(Points—Chargers 113, Browns 103)

CLEVELAND vs. SAN FRANCISCO
Browns lead series, 6-3
1950—Browns, 34-14 (C)
1951—49ers, 24-10 (SF)
1953—Browns, 23-21 (C)
1955—Browns, 38-3 (SF)
1959—49ers, 21-20 (C)
1962—Browns, 13-10 (SF)
1968—Browns, 33-21 (SF)
1970—49ers, 34-31 (SF)
1974—Browns, 7-0 (C)
(Points—Browns 209, 49ers 148)

CLEVELAND vs. SEATTLE
No games

CLEVELAND vs. TAMPA BAY
Browns lead series, 1-0
1976—Browns, 24-7 (TB)

CLEVELAND vs. WASHINGTON
Browns lead series, 31-6-1
1950—Browns, 20-14 (C)
      Browns, 45-21 (W)
1951—Browns, 45-0 (C)
1952—Browns, 19-15 (C)
      Browns, 48-24 (W)
1953—Browns, 30-14 (W)
      Browns, 27-3 (C)
1954—Browns, 62-3 (C)
      Browns, 34-14 (W)
1955—Redskins, 27-17 (C)
      Browns, 24-14 (W)
1956—Redskins, 20-9 (W)
      Redskins, 20-17 (C)
1957—Browns, 21-17 (W)
      Tie, 30-30 (W)
1958—Browns, 20-10 (W)
      Browns, 21-14 (C)
1959—Browns, 34-7 (C)
      Browns, 31-17 (W)
1960—Browns, 31-10 (W)
      Browns, 27-16 (C)
1961—Browns, 31-7 (C)
      Browns, 17-6 (W)
1962—Redskins, 17-16 (C)
      Redskins, 17-9 (W)
1963—Browns, 37-14 (C)
      Browns, 27-20 (W)
1964—Browns, 27-13 (W)
      Browns, 34-24 (C)
1965—Browns, 17-7 (W)
      Browns, 24-16 (C)
1966—Browns, 38-14 (W)
      Browns, 14-3 (C)
1967—Browns, 42-37 (C)
1968—Browns, 24-21 (W)
1969—Browns, 27-23 (C)
1971—Browns, 20-13 (W)
1975—Redskins, 23-7 (C)
(Points—Browns 1,023, Redskins 585)

DALLAS vs. ATLANTA
Cowboys lead series, 5-1
See Atlanta vs. Dallas

DALLAS vs. BALTIMORE
Colts lead series, 4-3
See Baltimore vs. Dallas

DALLAS vs. BUFFALO
Cowboys lead series, 1-0;
See Buffalo vs. Dallas

DALLAS vs. CHICAGO
Cowboys lead series, 4-3
See Chicago vs. Dallas

DALLAS vs. CINCINNATI
Cowboys lead series, 1-0;
See Cincinnati vs. Dallas

DALLAS vs. CLEVELAND
Browns lead series, 14-7;
See Cleveland vs. Dallas

DALLAS vs. DENVER
Cowboys lead series, 1-0
1973—Cowboys, 22-10 (Den)

DALLAS vs. DETROIT
Cowboys lead series, 5-1
1960—Lions, 23-14 (Det)
1963—Cowboys, 17-14 (Dal)
1968—Cowboys, 59-13 (Dal)
1970—*Cowboys, 5-0 (Dal)
1972—Cowboys, 28-24 (Dal)
1975—Cowboys, 36-10 (Det)
(Points—Cowboys 159, Lions 84)
*NFC Divisional Playoff

DALLAS vs. GREEN BAY
Packers lead series, 8-1
1960—Packers, 41-7 (GB)
1964—Packers, 45-21 (D)
1965—Packers, 13-3 (Mil)
1966—*Packers, 34-27 (D)
1967—*Packers, 21-17 (GB)
1968—Packers, 28-17 (D)
1970—Cowboys, 16-3 (D)
1972—Packers, 16-13 (Mil)
1975—Packers, 19-17 (D)
(Points—Packers 220, Cowboys 138)
*NFL Championship

DALLAS vs. HOUSTON
Cowboys lead series, 2-0
1970—Cowboys, 52-10 (D)
1974—Cowboys, 10-0 (H)
(Points—Cowboys 62, Oilers 10)

DALLAS vs. KANSAS CITY
Series tied, 1-1
1970—Cowboys, 27-16 (KC)
1975—Chiefs, 34-31 (D)
(Points—Cowboys 58, Chiefs 50)

DALLAS vs. LOS ANGELES
Rams lead series, 6-5
1960—Rams, 38-13 (D)
1962—Cowboys, 27-17 (LA)
1967—Rams, 35-13 (D)
1969—Rams, 24-23 (LA)
1970—*Rams, 31-0 (Miami)
1971—Cowboys, 28-21 (D)
1973—Rams, 37-31 (LA)
      **Cowboys, 27-16 (D)
1975—Cowboys, 18-7 (D)
      ***Cowboys, 37-7 (LA)
1976—*Rams, 14-12 (D)
(Points—Rams 247, Cowboys 229)
*Playoff Bowl
**NFC Divisional Playoff
***NFC Championship

DALLAS vs. MIAMI
Series tied, 1-1
1971—*Cowboys, 24-3 (New Orleans)
1973—Dolphins, 14-7 (D)
(Points—Cowboys 31, Dolphins 17)
*Super Bowl VI

DALLAS vs. MINNESOTA
Cowboys lead series, 7-3
1961—Cowboys, 21-7 (D)
      Cowboys, 28-0 (M)
1966—Cowboys, 28-17 (D)
1968—Cowboys, 20-7 (M)
1969—*Cowboys, 17-13 (Miami)
1970—Vikings, 54-13 (M)
1971—**Cowboys, 20-12 (M)
1973—***Vikings, 27-10 (D)

DALLAS vs. NEW ENGLAND
Cowboys lead series, 2-0
1971—Cowboys, 44-21 (D)
1975—Cowboys, 34-31 (NE)
(Points—Cowboys 78, Patriots 52)

DALLAS vs. NEW ORLEANS
Cowboys lead series, 7-1
1967—Cowboys, 14-10 (D)
      Cowboys, 27-10 (NO)
1968—Cowboys, 17-3 (NO)
1969—Cowboys, 21-17 (NO)
      Cowboys, 33-17 (D)
1971—Saints, 24-14 (NO)
1973—Cowboys, 40-3 (D)
1976—Cowboys, 24-6 (NO)
(Points—Cowboys 190, Saints 90)

DALLAS vs. N.Y. GIANTS
Cowboys lead series, 20-9-2
1960—Tie, 31-31 (NY)
1961—Cowboys, 31-10 (D)
      Cowboys, 17-16 (NY)
1962—Cowboys, 41-10 (D)
      Giants, 41-31 (NY)
1963—Cowboys, 37-21 (NY)
      Giants, 34-27 (D)
1964—Tie, 13-13 (D)
      Cowboys, 31-21 (NY)
1965—Cowboys, 31-2 (D)
      Cowboys, 38-20 (NY)
1966—Cowboys, 52-7 (D)
      Cowboys, 17-7 (NY)
1967—Cowboys, 38-24 (D)
1968—Giants, 27-21 (D)
      Cowboys, 28-10 (NY)
1969—Cowboys, 25-3 (D)
1970—Cowboys, 28-10 (D)
      Giants, 23-20 (NY)
1971—Cowboys, 20-13 (D)
      Cowboys, 42-14 (NY)
1972—Cowboys, 23-14 (NY)
      Giants, 23-3 (D)
1973—Cowboys, 45-28 (D)
      Cowboys, 23-10 (New Haven)
1974—Giants, 14-6 (D)
      Cowboys, 21-7 (New Haven)
1975—Cowboys, 13-7 (NY)
      Cowboys, 14-3 (D)
1976—Cowboys, 24-14 (ER)
      Cowboys, 9-3 (D)
(Points—Cowboys 732, Giants 548)

DALLAS vs. N.Y. JETS
Cowboys lead series, 2-0
1971—Cowboys, 52-10 (D)
1975—Cowboys, 31-21 (NY)
(Points—Cowboys 83, Jets 31)

DALLAS vs. OAKLAND
Raiders lead series, 1-0
1974—Raiders, 27-23 (O)

DALLAS vs. PHILADELPHIA
Cowboys lead series, 21-12
1960—Eagles, 27-25 (D)
1961—Eagles, 43-7 (D)
      Eagles, 35-13 (P)
1962—Cowboys, 41-19 (D)
      Eagles, 28-14 (P)
1963—Eagles, 24-21 (P)
      Cowboys, 27-20 (D)
1964—Eagles, 17-14 (D)
      Eagles, 24-14 (P)
1965—Eagles, 35-24 (D)
      Cowboys, 21-19 (P)
1966—Cowboys, 56-7 (D)
      Eagles, 24-23 (P)
1967—Cowboys, 21-14 (P)
      Cowboys, 38-17 (D)
1968—Cowboys, 45-13 (P)
      Cowboys, 34-14 (D)
1969—Cowboys, 38-7 (P)
      Cowboys, 49-14 (D)
1970—Cowboys, 17-7 (D)
      Cowboys, 21-17 (D)
1971—Cowboys, 42-7 (P)
      Cowboys, 20-7 (D)
1972—Cowboys, 28-6 (D)
      Cowboys, 28-7 (P)
1973—Eagles, 30-16 (P)
      Cowboys, 31-10 (D)
1974—Eagles, 13-10 (P)
      Cowboys, 31-24 (D)
1975—Cowboys, 20-17 (P)
      Cowboys, 27-17 (D)

1976—Cowboys, 27–7 (D)
Cowboys, 26–7 (P)
(Points—Cowboys 862, Eagles 584)
DALLAS vs. PITTSBURGH
Cowboys lead series, 10–8
1960—Steelers, 35–28 (D)
1961—Cowboys, 27–24 (D)
Steelers, 37–7 (P)
1962—Steelers, 30–28 (D)
Cowboys, 42–27 (P)
1963—Steelers, 27–21 (P)
Steelers, 24–19 (D)
1964—Steelers, 23–17 (P)
Cowboys, 17–14 (D)
1965—Steelers, 22–13 (P)
Cowboys, 24–17 (D)
1966—Cowboys, 52–21 (D)
Cowboys, 20–7 (P)
1967—Cowboys, 24–21 (P)
1968—Cowboys, 28–7 (D)
1969—Cowboys, 10–7 (P)
1972—Cowboys, 17–13 (D)
1976—*Steelers, 21–17 (Miami)
(Points—Cowboys 411, Steelers 377)
*Super Bowl X
DALLAS vs. ST. LOUIS
Cowboys lead series, 16–13–1
1960—Cardinals, 12–10 (StL)
1961—Cardinals, 31–17 (D)
Cardinals, 31–13 (StL)
1962—Cardinals, 28–24 (D)
Cardinals, 52–20 (StL)
1963—Cardinals, 34–7 (D)
Cowboys, 28–24 (StL)
1964—Cardinals, 16–6 (D)
Cowboys, 31–13 (StL)
1965—Cardinals, 20–13 (StL)
Cowboys, 27–13 (D)
1966—Tie, 10–10 (StL)
Cowboys, 31–17 (D)
1967—Cowboys, 46–21 (D)
1968—Cowboys, 27–10 (StL)
1969—Cowboys, 24–3 (D)
1970—Cardinals, 20–7 (StL)
Cardinals, 38–0 (D)
1971—Cowboys, 16–13 (StL)
Cowboys, 31–12 (D)
1972—Cowboys, 33–24 (D)
Cowboys, 27–6 (StL)
1973—Cowboys, 45–10 (D)
Cowboys, 30–3 (StL)
1974—Cardinals, 31–28 (StL)
Cowboys, 17–14 (D)
1975—Cowboys, 37–31 (D) OT
Cardinals, 31–17 (StL)
1976—Cowboys, 21–17 (StL)
Cowboys, 19–14 (D)
(Points—Cowboys 658, Cardinals 603)
DALLAS vs. SAN DIEGO
Cowboys lead series, 1–0
1972—Cowboys, 34–28 (SD)
DALLAS vs. SAN FRANCISCO
Cowboys lead series, 5–4–1
1960—49ers, 26–14 (D)
1963—49ers, 31–24 (SF)
1965—Cowboys, 39–31 (D)
1967—49ers, 24–16 (SF)
1969—Tie, 24–24 (D)
1970—*Cowboys, 17–10 (SF)
1971—*Cowboys, 14–3 (D)
1972—49ers, 31–10 (D)
**Cowboys, 30–28 (SF)
1974—Cowboys, 20–14 (D)
(Points—49ers 222, Cowboys 208)
*NFC Championship
**NFC Divisional Playoff
DALLAS vs. SEATTLE
Cowboys lead series, 1–0
1976—Cowboys, 28–13 (S)
DALLAS vs. TAMPA BAY
No Games
DALLAS vs. WASHINGTON
Cowboys lead series, 18–14–2
1960—Redskins, 26–14 (W)
1961—Tie, 28–28 (D)
Redskins, 34–24 (W)
1962—Tie, 35–35 (D)
Cowboys, 38–10 (W)
1963—Redskins, 21–17 (W)
Cowboys, 35–20 (D)
1964—Cowboys, 24–18 (D)
Redskins, 28–16 (W)
1965—Cowboys, 27–7 (D)
Redskins, 34–31 (W)
1966—Cowboys, 31–30 (W)
Redskins, 34–31 (D)

1967—Cowboys, 17–14 (W)
Redskins, 27–20 (D)
1968—Cowboys, 44–24 (W)
Cowboys, 29–20 (D)
1969—Cowboys, 41–28 (W)
Cowboys, 20–10 (D)
1970—Cowboys, 45–21 (W)
Cowboys, 34–0 (D)
1971—Redskins, 20–16 (D)
Cowboys, 13–0 (W)
1972—Redskins, 24–20 (W)
Cowboys, 34–24 (D)
*Redskins, 26–3 (W)
1973—Redskins, 14–7 (W)
Cowboys, 27–7 (D)
1974—Redskins, 28–21 (W)
Cowboys, 24–23 (D)
1975—Redskins, 30–24 (W) OT
Cowboys, 31–10 (D)
1976—Cowboys, 20–7 (W)
Redskins, 27–14 (D)
(Points—Cowboys 855, Redskins 709)
*NFC Championship
_____
*DALLAS TEXANS vs. CHICAGO
Series tied, 1–1
See Chicago vs. *Dallas Texans
*Extinct team
*DALLAS TEXANS vs. DETROIT
Lions won series, 2–0
1952—Lions, 43–13
Lions, 41–6
(Points—Lions 84, Texans 19)
*Extinct team
*DALLAS TEXANS vs. GREEN BAY
Packers won series, 2–0
1952—Packers, 24–14
Packers, 42–14
(Points—Packers 66, Texans 28)
*Extinct team
*DALLAS TEXANS vs. LOS ANGELES
Rams won series, 2–0
1952—Rams, 42–20
Rams, 27–6
(Points—Rams 69, Texans 26)
*Extinct team
*DALLAS TEXANS vs. N. Y. GIANTS
Giants won series, 1–0
1952—Giants, 24–6
*Extinct team
*DALLAS TEXANS vs. PHILADELPHIA
Eagles won series, 1–0
1952—Eagles, 38–21
*Extinct team
*DALLAS TEXANS vs. SAN FRANCISCO
49ers won series, 2–0
1952—49ers, 37–14
49ers, 48–21
(Points—49ers 85, Texans 35)
*Extinct team
_____
DENVER vs. ATLANTA
Falcons lead series, 2–1;
See Atlanta vs. Denver
DENVER vs. BALTIMORE
Broncos lead series, 1–0;
See Baltimore vs. Denver
DENVER vs. BUFFALO
Bills lead series, 12–6–1;
See Buffalo vs. Denver
DENVER vs. CHICAGO
Broncos lead series, 1–0;
See Chicago vs. Denver
DENVER vs. CINCINNATI
Bengals lead series, 5–4;
See Cincinnati vs. Denver
DENVER vs. CLEVELAND
Series tied, 3–3;
See Cleveland vs. Denver
DENVER vs. DALLAS
Cowboys lead series, 1–0;
See Dallas vs. Denver
DENVER vs. DETROIT
Series tied, 1–1
1971—Lions, 24–20 (Den)
1974—Broncos, 31–27 (Det)
(Points—Broncos 51, Lions 51)
DENVER vs. GREEN BAY
Series Tied, 1–1
1971—Packers, 34–13 (Mil)
1975—Broncos, 23–13 (D)
(Points—Packers 47, Broncos 36)
DENVER vs. HOUSTON

Oilers lead series, 16–7–1
1960—Oilers, 45–25 (D)
Oilers, 20–10 (H)
1961—Oilers, 55–14 (D)
Oilers, 45–14 (H)
1962—Broncos, 20–10 (D)
Oilers, 34–17 (H)
1963—Oilers, 20–14 (H)
Oilers, 33–24 (D)
1964—Oilers, 38–17 (D)
Oilers, 34–15 (H)
1965—Broncos, 28–17 (D)
Broncos, 31–21 (H)
1966—Oilers, 45–7 (H)
Broncos, 40–38 (D)
1967—Oilers, 10–6 (H)
Oilers, 20–18 (D)
1968—Oilers, 38–17 (H)
Oilers, 24–21 (H)
1969—Broncos, 24–21 (H)
Tie, 20–20 (D)
1970—Oilers, 31–21 (H)
1972—Broncos, 30–17 (D)
1973—Broncos, 48–20 (H)
1974—Broncos, 37–14 (D)
1976—Oilers, 17–3 (H)
(Points—Oilers 666, Broncos 497)
DENVER vs. *KANSAS CITY
Chiefs lead series, 27–7
1960—Texans, 17–14 (D)
Texans, 34–7 (Da)
1961—Texans, 19–12 (D)
Texans, 49–21 (Da)
1962—Texans, 24–3 (D)
Texans, 17–10 (Da)
1963—Chiefs, 59–7 (D)
Chiefs, 52–21 (KC)
1964—Broncos, 33–27 (D)
Chiefs, 49–39 (KC)
1965—Chiefs, 31–23 (D)
Chiefs, 45–35 (KC)
1966—Chiefs, 37–10 (KC)
Chiefs, 56–10 (D)
1967—Chiefs, 52–9 (KC)
Chiefs, 38–24 (D)
1968—Chiefs, 34–2 (KC)
Chiefs, 30–7 (D)
1969—Chiefs, 26–13 (D)
Chiefs, 31–17 (KC)
1970—Broncos, 26–13 (D)
Chiefs, 16–0 (KC)
1971—Chiefs, 16–3 (D)
Chiefs, 28–10 (KC)
1972—Chiefs, 45–24 (D)
Chiefs, 24–21 (KC)
1973—Chiefs, 16–14 (KC)
Broncos, 14–10 (D)
1974—Broncos, 17–14 (KC)
Chief, 42–34 (D)
1975—Broncos, 37–33 (KC)
Chiefs, 26–13 (KC)
1976—Broncos, 35–26 (KC)
Broncos, 17–16 (D)
(Points—Chiefs 1,052, Broncos 582)
*Franchise in Dallas (D) prior to 1963 and known as Texans
DENVER vs. LOS ANGELES
Series tied, 1–1
1972—Broncos, 16–10 (LA)
1974—Rams, 17–10 (D)
(Points—Rams 27, Broncos 26)
DENVER vs. MIAMI
Dolphins lead series, 4–2–1
1966—Dolphins, 24–7 (M)
Broncos, 17–7 (D)
1967—Dolphins, 35–21 (M)
1968—Broncos, 21–14 (D)
1969—Dolphins, 27–24 (M)
1971—Tie, 10–10 (D)
1975—Dolphins, 14–13 (M)
(Points—Dolphins 131, Broncos 113)
DENVER vs. MINNESOTA
Vikings lead series, 1–0
1972—Vikings, 23–20 (D)
DENVER vs. *NEW ENGLAND
Patriots lead series, 11–9
1960—Broncos, 13–10 (B)
Broncos, 31–24 (D)
1961—Patriots, 45–17 (B)
Patriots, 28–24 (D)
1962—Patriots, 41–16 (D)
Patriots, 33–29 (D)
1963—Patriots, 14–10 (D)
Patriots, 40–21 (B)
1964—Patriots, 39–10 (D)
Patriots, 12–7 (B)
1965—Broncos, 27–10 (B)
Patriots, 28–20 (D)

1966—Patriots, 24–10 (D)
Broncos, 17–10 (B)
1967—Broncos, 26–21 (D)
1968—Patriots, 20–17 (D)
Broncos, 35–14 (B)
1969—Broncos, 35–7 (D)
1972—Broncos, 45–21 (D)
1976—Patriots, 38–14 (NE)
(Points—Patriots 475, Broncos 428)
*Franchise in Boston (B) prior to 1971
DENVER vs. NEW ORLEANS
Broncos lead series, 2–0
1970—Broncos, 31–6 (NO)
1974—Broncos, 33–17 (D)
(Points—Broncos 64, Saints 23)
DENVER vs. N. Y. GIANTS
Series tied 1–1
1972—Giants, 29–17 (NY)
1976—Broncos, 14–13 (D)
(Points—Giants 42, Broncos 31)
DENVER vs. *N. Y. JETS
Series tied, 9–9–1
1960—Titans, 28–24 (NY)
Titans, 30–27 (D)
1961—Titans, 35–28 (NY)
Broncos, 27–10 (D)
1962—Broncos, 32–10 (NY)
Titans, 46–45 (D)
1963—Tie, 35–35 (NY)
Jets, 14–9 (D)
1964—Jets, 30–6 (NY)
Broncos, 20–16 (D)
1965—Jets, 45–10 (NY)
Broncos, 16–13 (D)
1966—Jets, 16–7 (D)
1967—Jets, 38–24 (D)
Broncos, 33–24 (NY)
1968—Broncos, 21–13 (NY)
1969—Broncos, 21–19 (D)
1973—Broncos, 40–28 (NY)
1976—Broncos, 46–3 (D)
(Points—Broncos 471, Jets 453)
*Jets known as Titans prior to 1963
DENVER vs. OAKLAND
Raiders lead series 26–6–2
1960—Broncos, 31–14 (D)
Raiders, 48–10 (O)
1961—Raiders, 33–19 (O)
Broncos, 27–24 (D)
1962—Broncos, 44–7 (D)
Broncos, 23–6 (O)
1963—Broncos, 26–10 (O)
Raiders, 35–31 (O)
1964—Raiders, 40–7 (O)
Tie, 20–20 (D)
1965—Raiders, 28–20 (D)
Raiders, 24–13 (O)
1966—Raiders, 17–3 (D)
Raiders, 28–10 (O)
1967—Raiders, 51–0 (O)
Raiders, 21–17 (D)
1968—Raiders, 43–7 (D)
Raiders, 33–27 (O)
1969—Raiders, 24–14 (D)
Raiders, 41–10 (O)
1970—Raiders, 35–23 (O)
Raiders, 24–19 (D)
1971—Raiders, 27–16 (D)
Raiders, 21–13 (O)
1972—Broncos, 30–23 (D)
Raiders, 37–20 (O)
1973—Tie, 23–23 (D)
Raiders, 21–17 (O)
1974—Raiders, 28–17 (O)
Broncos, 20–17 (O)
1975—Raiders, 42–17 (D)
Raiders, 17–10 (O)
1976—Raiders, 17–10 (D)
Raiders, 19–6 (O)
(Points—Raiders 914, Broncos 584)
DENVER vs. PHILADELPHIA
Series tied, 1–1
1971—Eagles, 17–16 (P)
1975—Broncos, 25–10 (D)
(Points—Broncos 41, Eagles 27)
DENVER vs. PITTSBURGH
Broncos lead series, 3–1–1
1970—Broncos, 16–13 (D)
1971—Broncos, 22–10 (P)
1973—Broncos, 23–13 (P)
1974—Tie, 35–35 (D) OT
1975—Steelers, 20–9 (P)
(Points—Broncos 105, Steelers 91)
DENVER vs. ST. LOUIS
Series tied, 0–0–1
1973—Tie, 17–17 (StL)
DENVER vs. *SAN DIEGO
Chargers lead series, 19–14–1

1960—Chargers, 23–19 (D)
Chargers, 41–33 (LA)
1961—Chargers, 37–0 (SD)
Chargers, 19–16 (D)
1962—Broncos, 30–21 (D)
Chargers, 23–20 (SD)
1963—Broncos, 50–34 (D)
Chargers, 58–20 (SD)
1964—Chargers, 42–14 (SD)
Chargers, 31–20 (D)
1965—Chargers, 34–31 (SD)
Chargers, 33–21 (D)
1966—Chargers, 24–17 (SD)
Broncos, 20–17 (D)
1967—Chargers, 38–21 (D)
Chargers, 24–20 (SD)
1968—Chargers, 55–24 (SD)
Chargers, 47–23 (D)
1969—Broncos, 13–0 (D)
Chargers, 45–24 (SD)
1970—Chargers, 24–21 (SD)
Tie, 17–17 (D)
1971—Broncos, 20–16 (D)
Chargers, 45–17 (SD)
1972—Chargers, 37–14 (SD)
Broncos, 38–13 (D)
1973—Broncos, 30–19 (D)
Broncos, 42–28 (SD)
1974—Broncos, 27–7 (D)
Chargers, 17–0 (SD)
1975—Broncos, 27–17 (SD)
Broncos, 13–10 (D) OT
1976—Broncos, 26–0 (D)
Broncos, 17–0 (SD)
(Points—Chargers 893, Broncos 748)
*Franchise in Los Angeles (LA) prior to 1961
DENVER vs. SAN FRANCISCO
49ers lead series, 2–0
1970—49ers, 19–14 (SF)
1973—49ers, 36–34 (D)
(Points—49ers 55, Broncos 48)
DENVER vs. SEATTLE
No Games
DENVER vs. TAMPA BAY
Broncos lead series, 1–0
1976—Broncos, 48–13 (D)
DENVER vs. WASHINGTON
Redskins lead series, 2–0
1970—Redskins, 19–3 (D)
1974—Redskins, 30–3 (W)
(Points—Redskins 49, Broncos 6)
_____
DETROIT vs. ATLANTA
Lions lead series, 9–0;
See Atlanta vs. Detroit
DETROIT vs. *1950 BALTIMORE
Lions won series, 1–0
See *Baltimore vs. Detroit
*Extinct team
DETROIT vs. BALTIMORE
Series tied, 15–15–2;
See Baltimore vs. Detroit
DETROIT vs. *BOSTON YANKS
Lions won series, 3–2
See *Boston Yanks vs. Detroit
*Extinct team
DETROIT vs. *BROOKLYN DODGERS
Lions won series, 11–3
See *Brooklyn Dodgers vs. Detroit
*Extinct team
DETROIT vs. BUFFALO
Lions lead series, 1–0–1
See Buffalo vs. Detroit
DETROIT vs. CHICAGO
Bears lead series, 53–37–5
See Chicago vs. Detroit
DETROIT vs. CINCINNATI
Lions lead series, 2–0;
See Cincinnati vs. Detroit
DETROIT vs. *CINCINNATI REDS
Lions won series, 2–1
See *Cincinnati Reds vs. Detroit
*Extinct team
DETROIT vs. CLEVELAND
Lions lead series, 13–2;
See Cleveland vs. Detroit
DETROIT vs. DALLAS
Cowboys lead series, 5–1;
See Dallas vs. Detroit
DETROIT vs. *DALLAS TEXANS
Lions won series, 2–0;
See *Dallas Texans vs. Detroit
*Extinct team
DETROIT vs. DENVER
Series tied, 1–1;
See Denver vs. Detroit

*DETROIT vs. GREEN BAY
Packers lead series, 48-38-7
1930—Packers, 47-13
  Tie, 6-6
1932—Packers, 15-10
  Spartans, 19-0
1933—Packers, 17-0
  Spartans, 7-0
1934—Lions, 3-0 (GB)
  Packers, 3-0 (D)
1935—Packers, 13-9 (GB)
  Packers, 31-7 (GB)
  Lions, 20-10 (D)
1936—Packers, 20-18 (GB)
  Packers, 26-17 (D)
1937—Packers, 26-6 (GB)
  Packers, 14-13 (D)
1938—Lions, 17-7 (GB)
  Packers, 28-7 (D)
1939—Packers, 26-7 (GB)
  Packers, 12-7 (D)
1940—Lions, 23-14 (GB)
  Packers, 50-7 (D)
1941—Packers, 23-0 (GB)
  Packers, 24-7 (D)
1942—Packers, 38-7 (Mil)
  Packers, 28-7 (D)
1943—Packers, 35-14 (GB)
  Packers, 27-6 (D)
1944—Packers, 27-6 (GB)
  Packers, 14-0 (D)
1945—Packers, 57-21 (Mil)
  Lions, 14-3 (D)
1946—Packers, 10-7 (Mil)
  Packers, 9-0 (D)
1947—Packers, 34-17 (GB)
  Packers, 35-14 (D)
1948—Packers, 33-21 (GB)
  Lions, 24-20 (D)
1949—Packers, 16-14 (GB)
  Lions, 21-7 (D)
1950—Lions, 45-7 (GB)
  Lions, 24-21 (D)
1951—Lions, 24-17 (GB)
  Lions, 52-35 (D)
1952—Lions, 52-17 (GB)
  Lions, 48-24 (D)
1953—Lions, 14-7 (GB)
  Lions, 34-15 (D)
1954—Lions, 21-17 (GB)
  Lions, 28-24 (D)
1955—Packers, 20-17 (GB)
  Lions, 24-10 (D)
1956—Lions, 20-16 (GB)
  Packers, 24-20 (D)
1957—Lions, 24-14 (GB)
  Lions, 18-6 (D)
1958—Tie, 13-13 (GB)
  Lions, 24-14 (D)
1959—Packers, 28-10 (GB)
  Packers, 24-17 (D)
1960—Packers, 28-9 (GB)
  Lions, 23-10 (D)
1961—Lions, 17-13 (Mil)
  Packers, 17-9 (D)
1962—Packers, 9-7 (GB)
  Lions, 26-14 (D)
1963—Packers, 31-10 (Mil)
  Tie, 13-13 (D)
1964—Packers, 14-10 (D)
  Packers, 30-7 (GB)
1965—Packers, 31-21 (D)
  Lions, 12-7 (GB)
1966—Packers, 23-14 (GB)
  Packers, 31-7 (D)
1967—Tie, 17-17 (GB)
  Packers, 27-17 (D)
1968—Packers, 23-17 (GB)
  Tie, 14-14 (D)
1969—Packers, 28-17 (D)
  Lions, 16-10 (GB)
1970—Lions, 40-0 (GB)
  Lions, 20-0 (D)
1971—Lions, 31-14 (D)
  Tie, 14-14 (Mil)
1972—Packers, 24-23 (D)
  Packers, 33-7 (GB)
1973—Tie, 13-13 (GB)
  Lions, 34-0 (D)
1974—Packers, 21-19 (Mil)
  Lions, 19-17 (D)
1975—Lions, 30-16 (Mil)
  Lions, 13-10 (D)
1976—Packers, 24-14 (GB)
  Lions, 27-6 (D)
(Points—Packers 1,748, Lions 1,538)
*Franchise in Portsmouth prior to 1934 and known as the Spartans

DETROIT vs. HOUSTON
Series tied, 1-1
1971—Lions, 31-7 (H)
1975—Oilers, 24-8 (H)
(Points—Lions 39, Oilers 31)

DETROIT vs. KANSAS CITY
Series tied, 1-1
1971—Lions, 32-21 (D)
1975—Chiefs, 34-21 (KC) OT
(Points—Lions 53, Chiefs 45)

DETROIT vs. LOS ANGELES
Rams lead series, 34-32-1
1937—Lions, 28-0
  Lions, 27-7
1938—Rams, 21-17
  Lions, 6-0
1939—Lions, 15-7
  Rams, 14-3
1940—Lions, 6-0
  Rams, 24-0
1941—Lions, 17-7
  Lions, 14-0
1942—Rams, 14-0
  Rams, 27-7
1944—Rams, 20-17
  Lions, 26-14
1945—Rams, 28-21
1946—Rams, 35-14 (LA)
  Rams, 41-20 (D)
1947—Rams, 27-13 (D)
  Rams, 28-17 (LA)
1948—Rams, 44-7 (LA)
  Rams, 34-27 (D)
1949—Rams, 27-24 (LA)
  Rams, 21-10 (D)
1950—Rams, 30-28 (LA)
  Rams, 65-24 (LA)
1951—Rams, 27-31 (D)
  Lions, 24-22 (LA)
1952—Lions, 17-14 (LA)
  Lions, 24-16 (D)
  *Lions, 31-21 (D)
1953—Rams, 31-19 (D)
  Rams, 37-24 (LA)
1954—Lions, 21-3 (D)
  Lions, 27-24 (LA)
1955—Rams, 17-10 (D)
  Lions, 24-13 (LA)
1956—Lions, 24-21 (D)
  Lions, 16-7 (LA)
1957—Lions, 10-7 (D)
  Rams, 35-17 (LA)
1958—Rams, 42-28 (D)
  Lions, 41-24 (LA)
1959—Lions, 17-7 (LA)
  Lions, 23-17 (D)
1960—Rams, 48-35 (LA)
  Lions, 12-10 (D)
1961—Lions, 14-13 (D)
  Lions, 28-10 (LA)
1962—Lions, 13-10 (D)
  Liona, 12-3 (LA)
1963—Lions, 23-2 (LA)
  Rams, 28-21 (D)
1964—Tie, 17-17 (LA)
  Lions, 37-17 (D)
1965—Lions, 20-0 (D)
  Lions, 31-7 (LA)
1966—Rams, 14-7 (D)
  Rams, 23-3 (LA)
1967—Rams, 31-7 (D)
1968—Rams, 10-7 (LA)
1969—Rams, 28-0 (D)
1970—Lions, 28-23 (LA)
1971—Rams, 21-13 (D)
1972—Rams, 34-17 (LA)
1974—Rams, 16-13 (LA)
1975—Lions, 20-0 (D)
1976—Rams, 20-17 (D)
(Points—Rams 1,291, Lions 1,215)
*Conference Playoff
**Franchise in Cleveland prior to 1946

DETROIT vs. MIAMI
Dolphins lead series, 1-0
1973—Dolphins, 34-7 (M)

DETROIT vs. MINNESOTA
Vikings lead series, 19-11-2
1961—Lions, 37-10 (M)
  Lions, 13-7 (D)
1962—Lions, 17-6 (M)
  Lions, 37-23 (D)
1963—Lions, 28-10 (D)
  Vikings, 34-31 (M)
1964—Lions, 24-20 (M)
  Tie, 23-23 (D)
1965—Lions, 31-29 (M)
  Vikings, 29-7 (D)
1966—Lions, 32-31 (M)
  Vikings, 28-16 (D)
1967—Tie, 10-10 (M)
  Lions, 14-3 (D)
1968—Vikings, 24-10 (M)
  Vikings, 13-6 (D)
1969—Vikings, 24-10 (M)
  Vikings, 27-0 (D)
1970—Vikings, 30-17 (D)
  Vikings, 24-20 (M)
1971—Vikings, 16-13 (D)
  Vikings, 29-10 (M)
1972—Vikings, 34-10 (D)
  Vikings, 16-14 (M)
1973—Vikings, 23-9 (D)
  Vikings, 28-7 (M)
1974—Vikings, 7-6 (D)
  Lions, 20-16 (M)
1975—Vikings, 25-19 (M)
  Lions, 17-10 (D)
1976—Vikings, 10-9 (D)
  Vikings, 31-23 (M)
(Points—Vikings 650, Lions 540)

DETROIT vs. NEW ENGLAND
Lions lead series, 2-0
1971—Lions, 34-7 (NE)
1976—Lions, 30-10 (D)
(Points—Lions 64, Patriots 17)

DETROIT vs. NEW ORLEANS
Saints lead series, 3-2-1
1968—Tie, 20-20 (D)
1970—Saints, 19-17 (NO)
1972—Saints, 27-14 (D)
1973—Saints, 20-13 (NO)
1974—Lions, 19-14 (D)
1976—Saints, 17-16 (NO)
(Points—Lions 112, Saints 104)

DETROIT vs. *N. Y. BULLDOGS
Lions won series, 1-0
1949—Lions, 28-27 (D)
*Extinct team

**DETROIT vs. N. Y. GIANTS
ER-East Rutherford, N. J.
Lions lead series, 17-10-1
1930—Giants, 19-6
1931—Spartans, 14-6
  Giants, 14-0
1932—Spartans, 7-0
  Spartans, 6-0
1933—Spartans, 17-7
  Giants, 13-10
1934—Lions, 9-0 (D)
1935—*Lions, 26-7 (D)
1936—Giants, 14-7 (NY)
  Lions, 38-0 (D)
1937—Lions, 17-0 (NY)
1939—Lions, 18-14 (D)
1941—Giants, 20-13 (NY)
1943—Tie, 0-0 (D)
1945—Giants, 35-14 (NY)
1947—Lions, 35-7 (D)
1949—Lions, 45-21 (NY)
1953—Lions, 27-16 (NY)
1955—Giants, 24-19 (D)
1958—Giants, 19-17 (D)
1962—Giants, 17-14 (NY)
1964—Lions, 26-3 (D)
1967—Lions, 30-7 (NY)
1969—Lions, 24-0 (D)
1972—Lions, 30-16 (D)
1974—Lions, 20-19 (D)
1976—Giants, 24-10 (ER)
(Points—Lions 499, Giants 322)
*NFL Championship
**Franchise in Portsmouth prior to 1934 and known as the Spartans

DETROIT vs. N. Y. JETS
Lions lead series, 1-0
1972—Lions, 37-20 (D)

DETROIT vs. *N. Y. YANKS
Lions won series, 2-1-1
1950—Yanks, 44-21
  Lions, 49-14
1951—Lions, 37-10
  Tie, 24-24
(Points—Lions 131, Yanks 92)
*Extinct team

DETROIT vs. OAKLAND
Series tied, 1-1
1970—Lions, 28-14 (D)
1974—Raiders, 35-13 (O)
(Points—Raiders 49, Lions 41)

**DETROIT vs. PHILADELPHIA
Lions lead series, 11-9-1
1933—Spartans, 25-0
1934—Lions, 10-0 (P)
1935—Lions, 35-0 (D)
1936—Lions, 23-0 (P)
1938—Eagles, 21-7 (D)
1940—Lions, 21-0 (P)
1941—Lions, 21-17 (D)
1943—Eagles, 35-34 (Pitt)
1945—Lions, 28-24 (D)
1948—Eagles, 45-21 (P)
1949—Eagles, 22-14 (D)
1951—Lions, 28-10 (P)
1954—Tie, 13-13 (D)
1957—Lions, 27-16 (P)
1960—Eagles, 28-10 (P)
1961—Eagles, 27-24 (D)
1962—*Lions, 38-10 (Miami)
1965—Lions, 35-28 (P)
1968—Eagles, 12-0 (D)
1971—Eagles, 23-20 (D)
1974—Eagles, 28-17 (P)
(Points—Lions 426, Eagles 359)
*Playoff Bowl
**Franchise in Portsmouth prior to 1934 and known as the Spartans

DETROIT vs. PITTSBURGH
Lions lead series, 15-9-1
1934—Lions, 40-7 (D)
1936—Lions, 28-3 (D)
1937—Lions, 7-3 (D)
1938—Lions, 16-7 (D)
1940—Steelers, 10-7 (D)
1942—Steelers, 35-7 (D)
1943—Steelers, 35-34 (P)
1944—Lions, 27-6 (P)
  Lions, 21-7 (D)
1946—Lions, 17-7 (D)
1947—Steelers, 17-10 (P)
1948—Lions, 17-14 (D)
1949—Steelers, 14-7 (P)
1950—Lions, 10-7 (D)
1952—Lions, 31-6 (P)
1953—Lions, 38-21 (D)
1955—Lions, 31-28 (P)
1956—Lions, 45-7 (D)
1959—Tie, 10-10 (D)
1962—Lions, 45-7 (D)
1963—*Lions, 17-10 (Miami)
1966—Steelers, 17-3 (D)
1967—Steelers, 24-14 (D)
1969—Steelers, 16-13 (P)
1973—Steelers, 24-10 (P)
(Points—Lions 505, Steelers 342)
*Playoff Bowl

**DETROIT vs. *ST. LOUIS
Lions lead series, 26-13-5
1930—Tie, 0-0
  Cardinals, 23-0
1931—Cardinals, 20-19
1932—Tie, 7-7
1933—Spartans, 7-6
1934—Lions, 6-0 (D)
  Lions, 17-13 (C)
1935—Tie, 10-10 (D)
  Lions, 7-6 (C)
1936—Lions, 39-0 (D)
  Lions, 14-7 (C)
1937—Lions, 16-7 (C)
  Lions, 16-7 (D)
1938—Lions, 10-0 (C)
  Lions, 7-3 (D)
1939—Lions, 21-13 (D)
  Lions, 17-13 (C)
1940—Tie, 0-0 (Buffalo)
  Lions, 43-14 (C)
1941—Tie, 14-14 (C)
  Lions, 21-3 (D)
1942—Cardinals, 13-0 (C)
  Cardinals, 7-0 (D)
1943—Lions, 35-17 (D)
  Lions, 7-0 (C)
1944—Lions, 27-6 (Pitt)
  Lions, 21-7 (D)
1945—Lions, 10-0 (C)
  Lions, 26-0 (D)
1946—Cardinals, 34-14 (C)
  Cardinals, 36-14 (D)
1947—Cardinals, 45-21 (D)
  Cardinals, 17-7 (D)
1948—Cardinals, 56-20 (C)
  Cardinals, 28-14 (D)
1949—Lions, 24-7 (C)
  Cardinals, 42-19 (D)
1959—Lions, 45-21 (D)
1961—Lions, 45-14 (StL)
1967—Cardinals, 38-28 (StL)
1969—Lions, 20-0 (D)
1970—Lions, 16-3 (D)
1973—Lions, 20-16 (StL)
1975—Cardinals, 24-13 (D)
(Points—Lions 737, Cardinals 587)
*Franchise in Chicago (C) prior to 1960
**Franchise in Portsmouth prior to 1934 and known as the Spartans

DETROIT vs. *ST. LOUIS GUNNERS
Lions won series, 1-0
1934—Lions, 40-7
*Extinct team

DETROIT vs. SAN DIEGO
Lions lead series, 1-0
1972—Lions, 34-20 (D)

DETROIT vs. SAN FRANCISCO
Lions lead series, 22-20-1
1950—Lions, 24-7 (D)
  49ers, 28-27 (SF)
1951—49ers, 20-10 (D)
  49ers, 21-17 (SF)
1952—49ers, 17-3 (SF)
  49ers, 28-0 (D)
1953—Lions, 24-21 (D)
  Lions, 14-10 (SF)
1954—49ers, 37-31 (SF)
  Lions, 48-7 (D)
1955—49ers, 27-24 (D)
  49ers, 38-21 (SF)
1956—Lions, 20-17 (D)
  Lions, 17-13 (SF)
1957—49ers, 35-31 (SF)
  Lions, 31-10 (D)
  *Lions, 31-27 (SF)
1958—49ers, 24-21 (SF)
  Lions, 35-21 (D)
1959—49ers, 34-13 (D)
  49ers, 33-7 (SF)
1960—49ers, 14-10 (D)
  Lions, 24-0 (SF)
1961—49ers, 49-0 (D)
  Tie, 20-20 (SF)
1962—Lions, 45-24 (D)
  Lions, 38-24 (SF)
1963—Lions, 26-3 (D)
  Lions, 45-7 (SF)
1964—Lions, 26-17 (SF)
  Lions, 24-7 (D)
1965—49ers, 27-21 (D)
  49ers, 17-14 (SF)
1966—49ers, 27-24 (SF)
  49ers, 41-14 (D)
1967—Lions, 45-3 (SF)
1968—49ers, 14-7 (D)
1969—Lions, 26-14 (SF)
1970—Lions, 28-7 (D)
1971—49ers, 31-27 (SF)
1973—Lions, 30-20 (D)
1974—Lions, 17-13 (D)
1975—Lions, 28-17 (SF)
(Points—Lions 988, 49ers 871)
*Conference Playoff

DETROIT vs. SEATTLE
Lions lead series, 1-0
1976—Lions, 41-14 (S)

DETROIT vs. TAMPA BAY
No games

**DETROIT vs. *WASHINGTON
Redskins lead series, 12-8
1932—Lions, 10-0
1933—Lions, 13-0
1934—Lions, 24-0
1935—Lions, 17-7
  Lions, 14-0
1938—Redskins, 7-5 (D)
1939—Redskins, 31-7 (W)
1940—Redskins, 20-14 (D)
1942—Redskins, 15-3 (D)
1943—Redskins, 42-20 (W)
1946—Redskins, 17-16 (W)
1947—Lions, 38-21 (D)
1948—Redskins, 46-21 (W)
1951—Lions, 35-17 (D)
1956—Redskins, 18-17 (W)
1965—Lions, 14-10 (D)
1968—Redskins, 14-3 (W)
1970—Redskins, 31-10 (W)
1973—Redskins, 20-0 (D)
1976—Redskins, 20-7 (W)
(Points—Redskins 336, Lions 288)
*Franchise in Boston prior to 1936
**Franchise in Portsmouth prior to 1934

GREEN BAY vs. ATLANTA
Packers lead series, 7-3
See Atlanta vs. Green Bay

GREEN BAY vs. *1950 BALTIMORE
Colts won series, 1-0
See *Baltimore vs. Green Bay
*Extinct team

GREEN BAY vs. BALTIMORE
Packers lead series, 18-16
See Baltimore vs. Green Bay

GREEN BAY vs. *BOSTON YANKS
Packers won series, 2-0
See *Boston Yanks vs. Green Bay
*Extinct team
GREEN BAY vs. *BROOKLYN DODGERS
Packers won series, 8-0
See *Brooklyn Dodgers vs. Green Bay
*Extinct team
GREEN BAY vs. BUFFALO
Bills lead series, 1-0;
See Buffalo vs. Green Bay
GREEN BAY vs. CHICAGO
Bears lead series, 60-50-6
See Chicago vs. Green Bay
GREEN BAY vs. *CINCINNATI REDS
Packers won series, 1-0
See *Cincinnati Reds vs. Green Bay
*Extinct Team
GREEN BAY vs. CINCINNATI
Series tied, 1-1
See Cincinnati vs. Green Bay
GREEN BAY vs. CLEVELAND
Packers lead series, 7-4;
See Cleveland vs. Green Bay
GREEN BAY vs. DALLAS
Packers lead series, 8-1;
See Dallas vs. Green Bay
GREEN BAY vs. *DALLAS TEXANS
Packers won series, 2-0
See *Dallas Texans vs. Green Bay
*Extinct team
GREEN BAY vs. DENVER
Series tied, 1-1;
See Denver vs. Green Bay
GREEN BAY vs. DETROIT
Packers lead series 48-38-7
See Detroit vs. Green Bay
GREEN BAY vs. HOUSTON
Packers lead series, 1-0
1972—Packers, 23-10 (H)
GREEN BAY vs. KANSAS CITY
Packers lead series, 1-0-1
1967—*Packers, 35-10 (Los Angeles)
1973—Tie, 10-10 (Mil)
(Points—Packers 45, Chiefs 20)
*Super Bowl
GREEN BAY vs. LOS ANGELES
Rams lead series, 34-31-2
1937—Packers, 35-10
Packers, 35-7
1938—Packers, 26-17
Packers, 28-7
1939—Rams, 27-24
Packers, 7-6
1940—Packers, 31-14
Tie, 13-13
1941—Packers, 24-7
Packers, 17-14
1942—Packers, 45-28
Packers, 30-12
1944—Packers, 30-21
Packers, 42-7
1945—Rams, 27-14
Rams, 20-7
1946—Rams, 21-17 (Mil)
Rams, 38-17 (LA)
1947—Packers, 17-14 (Mil)
Packers, 30-10 (LA)
1948—Packers, 16-0 (GB)
Rams, 24-10 (LA)
1949—Rams, 48-7 (GB)
Rams, 35-7 (LA)
1950—Rams, 45-14 (Mil)
Rams, 51-14 (LA)
1951—Rams, 28-0 (Mil)
Rams, 42-14 (LA)
1952—Rams, 30-28 (Mil)
Rams, 45-27 (LA)
1953—Rams, 38-20 (Mil)
Rams, 33-17 (LA)
1954—Packers, 35-17 (Mil)
Rams, 35-27 (LA)
1955—Rams, 30-28 (Mil)
Rams, 31-17 (LA)
1956—Packers, 42-17 (Mil)
Rams, 49-21 (LA)
1957—Rams, 31-27 (Mil)
Rams, 42-17 (LA)
1958—Rams, 20-7 (GB)
Rams, 34-20 (LA)
1959—Rams, 45-6 (Mil)
Packers, 38-20 (LA)

1960—Rams, 33-31 (Mil)
Packers, 35-21 (LA)
1961—Packers, 35-17 (GB)
Packers, 24-17 (LA)
1962—Packers, 41-10 (Mil)
Packers, 20-17 (LA)
1963—Packers, 42-10 (GB)
Packers, 31-14 (LA)
1964—Rams, 27-17 (Mil)
Tie, 24-24 (LA)
1965—Packers, 6-3 (Mil)
Rams, 21-10 (LA)
1966—Packers, 24-13 (GB)
Packers, 27-23 (LA)
1967—Rams, 27-24 (LA)
*Packers, 28-7 (Mil)
1968—Rams, 16-14 (Mil)
1969—Rams, 34-21 (LA)
1970—Rams, 31-21 (GB)
1971—Rams, 30-13 (:A)
1973—Rams, 24-7 (LA)
1974—Rams, 17-6 (Mil)
1975—Rams, 22-5 (LA)
(Points—Rams 1555, Packers 1467)
*Conference Playoff.
**Franchise in Cleveland prior to 1946
GREEN BAY vs. MIAMI
Dolphins lead series, 2-0
1971—Dolphins, 27-6 (Mia)
1975—Dolphins, 31-7 (GB)
(Points—Dolphins 58, Packers 13)
GREEN BAY vs. MINNESOTA
Vikings lead series, 18-14
1961—Packers, 33-7 (Minn)
Packers, 28-10 (Mil)
1962—Packers, 34-7 (GB)
Packers, 48-21 (Minn)
1963—Packers, 37-28 (Minn)
Packers, 28-7 (GB)
1964—Vikings, 24-23 (GB)
Packers, 42-13 (Minn)
1965—Packers, 38-13 (Minn)
Packers, 24-19 (GB)
1966—Vikings, 20-17 (GB)
Packers, 28-16 (Minn)
1967—Vikings, 10-7 (Mil)
Packers, 30-27 (Minn)
1968—Vikings, 26-13 (Mil)
Vikings, 14-10 (Minn)
1969—Vikings, 19-7 (Minn)
Vikings, 9-7 (Mil)
1970—Vikings, 13-10 (Mil)
Vikings, 10-3 (Minn)
1971—Vikings, 24-13 (GB)
Vikings, 3-0 (Minn)
1972—Vikings, 27-13 (GB)
Packers, 23-7 (Minn)
1973—Vikings, 11-3 (Minn)
Vikings, 31-7 (GB)
1974—Vikings, 32-17 (GB)
Packers, 19-7 (Minn)
1975—Vikings, 28-17 (GB)
Vikings, 24-3 (Minn)
1976—Vikings, 17-10 (Mil)
Vikings, 20-9 (Minn)
(Points—Packers 604, Vikings 541)
GREEN BAY vs. NEW ENGLAND
Patriots lead series, 1-0
1973—Patriots, 33-24 (NE)
GREEN BAY vs. NEW ORLEANS
Packers lead series, 4-2
1968—Packers, 29-7 (GB)
1971—Saints, 29-21 (NO)
1972—Packers, 30-20 (NO)
1973—Packers, 30-10 (Mil)
1975—Saints, 20-19 (NO)
1976—Packers, 32-27 (Mil)
(Points—Packers 161, Saints 113)
GREEN BAY vs. *N.Y. BULLDOGS
Packers won series, 1-0
1949—Packers, 19-0
*Extinct team
GREEN BAY vs. N.Y. GIANTS
Packers lead series, 21-16-2
1928—Giants, 6-0 (GB)
Packers, 7-0 (NY)
1929—Packers, 20-6 (NY)
1930—Packers, 14-7 (GB)
Giants, 13-6 (NY)
1931—Packers, 27-7 (GB)
Packers, 14-10 (NY)
1932—Packers, 13-0 (GB)
Giants, 6-0 (NY)
1933—Giants, 10-7 (Mil)
Giants, 17-6 (NY)
1934—Packers, 20-6 (Mil)
Giants, 17-3 (NY)
1935—Packers, 16-7 (GB)

1936—Packers, 26-14 (NY)
1937—Giants, 10-0 (NY)
1938—Giants, 15-3 (NY)
*Giants, 23-17 (NY)
1939—*Packers, 27-0 (Mil)
1940—Giants, 7-3 (NY)
1942—Tie, 21-21 (NY)
1943—Packers, 35-21 (NY)
1944—Giants, 24-0 (NY)
*Packers, 14-7 (NY)
1945—Packers, 23-14 (NY)
1947—Tie, 24-24 (NY)
1948—Giants, 49-3 (Mil)
1949—Giants, 30-10 (GB)
1952—Packers, 17-3 (NY)
1957—Giants, 31-17 (GB)
1959—Packers, 20-3 (NY)
1961—Packers, 20-17 (Mil)
*Packers, 37-0 (GB)
1962—*Packers, 16-7 (NY)
1967—Packers, 48-21 (NY)
1969—Packers, 20-10 (Mil)
1971—Giants, 42-40 (GB)
1973—Packers, 16-14 (New Haven)
1975—Packers, 40-14 (Mil)
(Points—Packers 633, Giants 550)
*NFL Championship
GREEN BAY vs. N.Y. JETS
Packers lead series, 1-0
1973—Packers, 23-7 (GB)
GREEN BAY vs. *N.Y. YANKS
Yanks won series, 3-1
1950—Yanks, 44-31
Yanks, 35-17
1951—Packers, 29-27
Yanks, 31-28
(Points—Yanks 137, Packers 105)
*Extinct team
GREEN BAY vs. OAKLAND
Raiders lead series, 2-1
1968—*Packers, 33-14 (Miami)
1972—Raiders, 20-14 (GB)
1976—Raiders, 18-14 (0)
(Points—Packers 61, Raiders 52)
*Super Bowl II
GREEN BAY vs. PHILADELPHIA
Packers lead series, 18-3
1933—Packers, 35-9 (GB)
Packers, 10-0 (P)
1934—Packers, 19-6 (GB)
1935—Packers, 13-6 (P)
1937—Packers, 37-7 (Mil)
1939—Packers, 23-16 (P)
1940—Packers, 27-20 (GB)
1942—Packers, 7-0 (P)
1943—Packers, 38-28 (P)
1946—Packers, 19-7 (P)
1947—Eagles, 28-14 (P)
1951—Packers, 37-24 (GB)
1952—Packers, 12-10 (Mil)
1954—Packers, 37-14 (P)
1958—Packers, 38-35 (GB)
1960—*Eagles, 17-13 (P)
1962—Packers, 49-0 (P)
1968—Packers, 30-13 (GB)
1970—Packers, 30-17 (Mil)
1974—Eagles, 36-14 (P)
1976—Packers, 28-13 (GB)
(Points—Packers 530, Eagles 306)
*NFL Championship
GREEN BAY vs. PITTSBURGH
Packers lead series, 19-8
1933—Packers, 47-0 (GB)
1935—Packers, 27-0 (GB)
Packers, 34-14 (P)
1936—Packers, 42-10 (Mil)
1938—Packers, 20-0 (GB)
1940—Packers, 24-3 (Mil)
1941—Packers, 54-7 (P)
1942—Packers, 24-21 (Mil)
1943—Packers, 38-28 (Phila)
1944—Packers, 34-7 (GB)
Packers, 35-20 (Chi)
1946—Packers, 17-7 (GB)
1947—Steelers, 18-17 (Mil)
1948—Steelers, 38-7 (P)
1949—Steelers, 30-7 (Mil)
1951—Packers, 35-33 (Mil)
Steelers, 28-7 (P)
1953—Steelers, 31-14 (P)
1954—Steelers, 21-20 (GB)
1957—Packers, 27-10 (P)
1960—Packers, 19-13 (P)
1963—Packers, 33-14 (Mil)
1965—Packers, 41-9 (P)
1967—Steelers, 24-17 (GB)
1969—Packers, 38-34 (P)
1970—Packers, 20-12 (P)

1975—Steelers, 16-13 (Mil)
(Points—Packers 711, Steelers 448)
GREEN BAY vs. *ST. LOUIS
Packers lead series, 38-21-4
1921—Tie, 3-3 (C)
1922—Cardinals, 16-3 (C)
1924—Cardinals, 3-0 (C)
1925—Cardinals, 9-6 (C)
1926—Cardinals, 13-7 (GB)
Packers, 3-0 (C)
1927—Packers, 13-0 (GB)
Tie, 6-6 (C)
1928—Packers, 20-0 (GB)
1929—Packers, 9-2 (GB)
Packers, 7-6 (C)
Packers, 12-0 (C)
1930—Packers, 14-0 (GB)
Cardinals, 13-6 (C)
1931—Packers, 26-7 (GB)
Cardinals, 21-13 (C)
1932—Packers, 15-7 (GB)
Packers, 19-9 (C)
1933—Packers, 14-6 (C)
1934—Packers, 15-0 (GB)
Cardinals, 9-0 (Mil)
Cardinals, 6-0 (C)
1935—Cardinals, 7-6 (GB)
Cardinals, 3-0 (Mil)
Cardinals, 9-7 (C)
1936—Packers, 10-7 (GB)
Packers, 24-0 (Mil)
Tie, 0-0 (C)
1937—Cardinals, 14-7 (GB)
Packers, 34-13 (Mil)
1938—Packers, 28-7 (Mil)
Packers, 24-22 (Buffalo)
1939—Packers, 14-10 (GB)
Packers, 27-20 (Mil)
1940—Packers, 31-6 (Mil)
Packers, 28-7 (C)
1941—Packers, 14-13 (Mil)
Packers, 17-9 (GB)
Packers, 17-13 (C)
Packers, 55-24 (GB)
1943—Packers, 28-7 (C)
Packers, 35-14 (Mil)
1944—Packers, 34-7 (GB)
Packers, 35-20 (C)
1945—Packers, 33-14 (GB)
1946—Packers, 19-7 (C)
Cardinals, 24-6 (GB)
1947—Cardinals, 14-10 (GB)
Cardinals, 21-20 (C)
1948—Cardinals, 17-7 (GB)
Cardinals, 42-7 (C)
1949—Cardinals, 39-17 (Mil)
Cardinals, 41-21 (C)
1955—Packers, 31-14 (GB)
1956—Packers, 24-21 (C)
1962—Packers, 17-0 (Mil)
1963—Packers, 30-7 (StL)
1965—**Cardinals, 24-17 (Miami)
1967—Packers, 31-23 (StL)
1969—Packers, 45-28 (GB)
1971—Tie, 16-16 (StL)
1973—Packers, 25-21 (StL)
1976—Cardinals, 29-0 (StL)
(Points—Packers 1,062 Cardinals 770)
*Franchise in Chicago (C) prior to 1960
**Playoff Bowl
GREEN BAY vs. *ST. LOUIS GUNNERS
Packers won series, 1-0
1934—Packers, 21-14
*Extinct team
GREEN BAY vs. SAN DIEGO
Packers lead series, 2-0
1970—Packers, 22-20 (SD)
1974—Packers, 34-0 (GB)
(Points—Packers 56, Chargers 20)
GREEN BAY vs. SAN FRANCISCO
49ers lead series, 21-18-1
1950—Packers, 25-21 (GB)
49ers, 30-14 (SF)
1951—49ers, 31-19 (SF)
1952—49ers, 24-14 (SF)
1953—49ers, 37-7 (Mil)
49ers, 43-14 (SF)
1954—49ers, 23-17 (Mil)
49ers, 35-0 (SF)
1955—Packers, 27-21 (Mil)
Packers, 28-7 (SF)
1956—49ers, 17-16 (GB)
49ers, 38-20 (SF)
1957—49ers, 24-14 (Mil)
49ers, 27-20 (SF)

1958—49ers, 33-12 (Mil)
49ers, 48-21 (SF)
1959—Packers, 21-20 (GB)
Packers, 36-14 (SF)
1960—Packers, 41-14 (GB)
Packers, 13-0 (SF)
1961—Packers, 30-10 (GB)
49ers, 22-21 (SF)
1962—Packers, 31-13 (GB)
Packers, 31-21 (SF)
1963—Packers, 28-10 (GB)
Packers 21-17 (SF)
1964—Packers, 24-14 (Mil)
49ers, 24-14 (SF)
1965—Packers, 27-10 (GB)
Tie, 24-24 (SF)
1966—49ers, 21-20 (GB)
Packers, 20-7 (Mil)
1967—Packers, 13-0 (GB)
1968—49ers, 27-20 (SF)
1969—*Packers, 14-7 (Mil)
1970—49ers, 26-10 (SF)
1972—Packers, 34-24 (Mil)
1973—49ers, 20-6 (SF)
1974—49ers, 7-6 (SF)
1976—49ers, 26-14 (GB)
(Points—49ers 842, Packers 787)
GREEN BAY vs. SEATTLE
Packers lead series, 1-0
1976—Packers, 27-20 (Mil)
GREEN BAY vs. TAMPA BAY
No games
GREEN BAY vs. WASHINGTON
Packers lead series, 13-9-1
1932—Packers, 21-0
1933—Tie, 7-7
Redskins, 20-7
1934—Packers, 10-0
1936—Packers, 31-2
Packers, 7-3
*Packers, 21-6
1937—Redskins, 14-6 (W)
1939—Packers, 24-14 (Mil)
1941—Packers, 22-17 (W)
1943—Packers, 33-7 (Mil)
1946—Packers, 20-7 (W)
1947—Packers, 27-10 (Mil)
1948—Redskins, 23-7 (Mil)
1949—Redskins, 30-0 (W)
1950—Packers, 35-21 (Mil)
1952—Packers, 35-20 (Mil)
1958—Redskins, 37-21 (W)
1959—Packers, 21-0 (GB)
1968—Packers, 27-7 (W)
1972—**Redskins, 16-3 (W)
1974—Redskins, 17-6 (GB)
(Points—Packers 381, Redskins 325)
*Championship playoff
**NFC Divisional playoff
***Franchise in Boston prior to 1937

HOUSTON vs. ATLANTA
Series tied, 1-1
See Atlanta vs. Houston
HOUSTON vs. BALTIMORE
Series tied, 1-1
See Baltimore vs. Houston
HOUSTON vs. BUFFALO
Oilers lead series, 16-7
See Buffalo vs. Houston
HOUSTON vs. CHICAGO
Bears lead series, 1-0
See Chicago vs. Houston
HOUSTON vs. CINCINNATI
Bengals lead series, 10-5-1
See Cincinnati vs. Houston
HOUSTON vs. CLEVELAND
Browns lead series, 11-3
See Cleveland vs. Houston
HOUSTON vs. DALLAS
Cowboys lead series, 2-0
See Dallas vs. Houston
HOUSTON vs. DENVER
Oilers lead series, 16-7-1
See Denver vs. Houston
HOUSTON vs. DETROIT
Series tied, 1-1
See Detroit vs. Houston
HOUSTON vs. GREEN BAY
Packers lead series, 1-0
See Green Bay vs. Houston
HOUSTON vs. *KANSAS CITY
Chiefs lead series, 17-7
1960—Oilers, 20-10 (H)
Texans, 24-0 (D)
1961—Texans, 26-21 (D)
Oilers, 38-7 (H)

1962—Texans, 31-7 (H)
Oilers, 14-6 (D)
**Texans, 20-17 (H) OT
1963—Chiefs, 28-7 (KC)
Oilers, 28-7 (H)
1964—Chiefs, 28-7 (KC)
Chiefs, 28-19 (H)
1965—Chiefs, 52-21 (KC)
Oilers, 38-36 (H)
1966—Chiefs, 48-23 (KC)
1967—Chiefs, 25-20 (H)
Oilers, 24-19 (KC)
1968—Chiefs, 26-21 (H)
Chiefs, 24-10 (KC)
1969—Chiefs, 24-0 (KC)
1970—Chiefs, 24-9 (KC)
1971—Chiefs, 20-16 (H)
1973—Chiefs, 38-14 (KC)
1974—Chiefs, 17-7 (H)
1975—Oilers, 17-13 (KC)
(Points—Chiefs 581, Oilers 398)
Franchise in Dallas (D) prior to 1963 and known as Texans
**AFL Championship*

HOUSTON vs. LOS ANGELES
Rams lead series, 1-0
1973—Rams, 31-26 (H)

HOUSTON vs. MIAMI
Oilers lead series, 6-5
1966—Dolphins, 20-13 (H)
Dolphins, 29-28 (M)
1967—Oilers, 17-14 (H)
Oilers, 41-10 (M)
1968—Oilers, 24-10 (M)
Dolphins, 24-7 (H)
1969—Oilers, 22-10 (H)
Oilers, 32-7 (M)
1970—Dolphins, 20-10 (H)
1972—Dolphins, 34-13 (M)
1975—Oilers, 20-19 (H)
(Points—Oilers 227, Dolphins 197)

HOUSTON vs. MINNESOTA
Vikings lead series, 1-0
1974—Vikings, 51-10 (M)

HOUSTON vs. *NEW ENGLAND
Patriots lead series, 12-10-1
1960—Oilers, 24-10 (B)
Oilers, 37-21 (H)
1961—Tie, 31-31 (B)
Oilers, 27-15 (H)
1962—Patriots, 34-21 (B)
Oilers, 21-17 (H)
1963—Patriots, 45-3 (B)
Patriots, 46-28 (H)
1964—Patriots, 25-24 (B)
Patriots, 34-17 (H)
1965—Oilers, 31-10 (H)
Patriots, 42-14 (B)
1966—Patriots, 27-21 (B)
Patriots, 38-14 (H)
1967—Patriots, 18-7 (B)
Oilers, 27-6 (H)
1968—Oilers, 16-0 (B)
Oilers, 45-17 (H)
1969—Patriots, 24-0 (B)
Oilers, 27-23 (H)
1971—Patriots, 28-20 (NE)
1973—Patriots, 32-0 (H)
1975—Oilers, 7-0 (NE)
(Points—Oilers 470, Patriots 440)
Franchise in Boston (B) prior to 1971

HOUSTON vs. NEW ORLEANS
Oilers lead series, 1-0-1
1971—Tie, 13-13 (H)
1976—Oilers, 31-26 (NO)
(Points—Oilers 44, Saints 39)

HOUSTON vs. N.Y. GIANTS
Giants lead series, 1-0
1973—Giants, 34-14 (NY)

HOUSTON vs. N.Y. JETS
Oilers lead series, 12-8-1
1960—Oilers, 27-21 (H)
Oilers, 42-28 (NY)
1961—Oilers, 49-13 (H)
Oilers, 48-21 (NY)
1962—Oilers, 56-17 (H)
Oilers, 44-10 (NY)
1963—Jets, 24-17 (NY)
Oilers, 31-27 (H)
1964—Jets, 24-21(NY)
Oilers, 33-17 (H)
1965—Oilers, 27-21 (H)
Jets, 41-14 (NY)
1966—Jets, 52-13 (NY)
Oilers, 24-0 (H)
1967—Tie, 28-28 (NY)
1968—Jets, 20-14 (H)
Jets, 26-7 (NY)
1969—Jets, 26-17 (NY)
Jets, 34-26 (H)
1972—Oilers, 26-20 (H)
1974—Oilers, 27-22 (NY)
(Points—Oilers 591, Jets 492)

HOUSTON vs. OAKLAND
Raiders lead series, 16-8
1960—Oilers, 37-22 (O)
Raiders, 14-13 (H)
1961—Oilers, 55-0 (H)
Oilers, 46-16 (O)
1962—Oilers, 28-20 (O)
Oilers, 32-17 (H)
1963—Raiders, 24-13 (H)
Raiders, 52-49 (O)
1964—Oilers, 42-28 (H)
Raiders, 20-10 (O)
1965—Raiders, 21-17 (O)
Raiders, 33-21 (H)
1966—Oilers, 31-0 (H)
Raiders, 38-23 (O)
1967—Raiders, 19-7 (H)
*Raiders, 40-7 (O)
1968—Raiders, 24-15 (H)
1969—Raiders, 21-17 (O)
**Raiders, 56-7 (O)
1971—Raiders, 41-21 (O)
1972—Raiders, 34-0 (H)
1973—Raiders, 17-6 (H)
1975—Oilers, 27-26 (O)
1976—Raiders, 14-13 (H)
(Points—Raiders 583, Oilers 552)
AFL Championship Game
**Inter-Divisional Playoff*

HOUSTON vs. PHILADELPHIA
Eagles lead series, 1-0
1972—Eagles, 18-17 (H)

HOUSTON vs. PITTSBURGH
Steelers lead series, 11-3
1970—Oilers, 19-7 (P)
Steelers, 7-3 (H)
1971—Steelers, 23-16 (P)
Oilers, 29-3 (H)
1972—Steelers, 24-7 (P)
Steelers, 9-3 (H)
1973—Steelers, 36-7 (P)
Steelers, 33-7 (P)
1974—Steelers, 13-7 (H)
Oilers, 13-10 (P)
1975—Steelers, 24-17 (P)
Steelers, 32-9 (H)
1976—Steelers, 32-16 (P)
Steelers, 21-0 (H)
(Points—Steelers 274, Oilers 153)

HOUSTON vs. ST. LOUIS
Cardinals lead series, 2-0
1970—Cardinals, 44-0 (StL)
1974—Cardinals, 31-27 (H)
(Points—Cardinals 75, Oilers 27)

HOUSTON vs. *SAN DIEGO
Chargers lead series, 14-10-1
1960—Oilers, 38-28 (H)
Chargers, 24-21 (LA)
**Oilers, 24-16 (H)
1961—Chargers, 34-24 (SD)
Oilers, 33-13 (H)
**Oilers, 10-3 (SD)
1962—Oilers, 42-17 (SD)
Oilers, 33-27 (H)
1963—Chargers, 27-0 (SD)
Chargers 20-14 (H)
1964—Chargers, 27-21 (SD)
Chargers, 20-17 (H)
1965—Chargers, 31-14 (SD)
Chargers, 37-26 (H)
1966—Chargers, 28-22 (H)
1967—Chargers, 13-3 (SD)
Oilers, 24-17 (H)
1968—Chargers, 30-143 (SD)
1969—Chargers, 21-17 (H)
1970—Tie, 31-31 (SD)
1971—Oilers, 49-33 (H)
1972—Chargers, 34-20 (SD)
1974—Oilers, 21-14 (H)
1975—Oilers, 33-17 (H)
1976—Chargers, 30-27 (SD)
(Points—Chargers 592, Oilers 578)
Franchise in Los Angeles (LA) prior to 1961
**AFL Championship*

HOUSTON vs. SAN FRANCISCO
Series tied, 1-1
1970—49ers, 30-20 (H)
1975—Oilers, 27-13 (SF)
(Points—Oilers 47, 49ers 43)

HOUSTON vs. SEATTLE
No games

HOUSTON vs. TAMPA BAY
Oilers lead series, 1-0
1976—Oilers, 20-0 (H)

HOUSTON vs. WASHINGTON
Series tied, 1-1
1971—Redskins, 22-13 (W)
1975—Oilers, 13-10 (H)
(Points—Redskins 32, Oilers 26)

KANSAS CITY vs. ATLANTA
Chiefs lead series, 1-0;
See Atlanta vs. Kansas City

KANSAS CITY vs. BALTIMORE
Chiefs lead series, 2-1;
See Baltimore vs. Kansas City

KANSAS CITY vs. BUFFALO
Series tied, 10-10-1;
See Buffalo vs. Kansas City

KANSAS CITY vs. CHICAGO
Chiefs lead series, 1-0;
See Chicago vs. Kansas City

KANSAS CITY vs. CINCINNATI
Bengals lead series, 5-4
See Cincinnati vs. Kansas City

KANSAS CITY vs. CLEVELAND
Chiefs lead series, 3-1-1;
See Cleveland vs. Kansas City

KANSAS CITY vs. DALLAS
Series tied, 1-1;
See Dallas vs. Kansas City

KANSAS CITY vs. DENVER
Chiefs lead series, 27-7;
See Denver vs. Kansas City

KANSAS CITY vs. DETROIT
Series tied, 1-1;
See Detroit vs. Kansas City

KANSAS CITY vs. GREEN BAY
Packers lead series, 1-0-1;
See Green Bay vs. Kansas City

KANSAS CITY vs. HOUSTON
Chiefs lead series, 17-7;
See Houston vs. Kansas City

KANSAS CITY vs. LOS ANGELES
Rams lead series, 1-0
1973—Rams, 23-13 (KC)

KANSAS CITY vs. MIAMI
Chiefs lead series, 7-3
1966—Chiefs, 34-16 (KC)
Chiefs, 19-18 (M)
1967—Chiefs, 24-0 (M)
Chiefs, 41-0 (KC)
1968—Chiefs, 48-3 (M)
1969—Chiefs, 17-10 (KC)
1971—*Dolphins, 27-24 (KC) OT
1972—Dolphins, 20-10 (KC)
1974—Dolphins, 9-3 (M)
1976—Chiefs, 20-17 (M) OT
(Points—Chiefs 240, Dolphins 120)
AFC Division Playoff

KANSAS CITY vs. MINNESOTA
Vikings lead series, 2-1
1970—*Chiefs, 23-7 (New Orleans)
Vikings, 27-10 (M)
1974—Vikings, 35-15 (KC)
(Points—Vikings 69, Chiefs 48)
Super Bowl IV

***KANSAS CITY vs. **NEW ENGLAND**
Chiefs lead series, 11-5-3
1960—Patriots, 42-14 (B)
Texans, 34-0 (D)
1961—Patriots, 18-17 (D)
Patriots, 28-21 (B)
1962—Texans, 42-28 (D)
Texans, 27-7 (B)
1963—Tie, 24-24 (B)
Chiefs, 35-3 (KC)
1964—Patriots, 24-7 (B)
Patriots, 31-24 (KC)
1965—Chiefs, 27-17 (KC)
Tie, 10-10 (B)
1966—Chiefs, 43-24 (B)
Tie, 27-27 (KC)
1967—Chiefs, 33-10 (B)
1968—Chiefs, 31-17 (KC)
1969—Chiefs, 31-0 (B)
1970—Chiefs, 23-10 (KC)
1973—Chiefs, 10-7 (NE)
(Points—Chiefs 480, Patriots 327)
Franchise located in Dallas (D) prior to 1963 and known as Texans
**Franchise in Boston (B) prior to 1971*

KANSAS CITY vs. NEW ORLEANS
Series tied, 1-1
1972—Chiefs, 20-17 (NO)
1976—Saints, 27-17 (KC)
(Points—Saints 44, Chiefs 37)

KANSAS CITY vs. N. Y. GIANTS
Giants lead series, 1-0
1974—Giants, 33-27 (KC)

***KANSAS CITY vs. **N. Y. JETS**
Chiefs lead series, 12-9
1960—Titans, 37-35 (D)
Titans, 41-35 (NY)
1961—Titans, 28-7 (NY)
Texans, 35-24 (D)
1962—Texans, 20-17 (D)
Texans, 52-31 (NY)
1963—Jets, 17-0 (NY)
Chiefs, 48-0 (KC)
1964—Jets, 27-14 (NY)
Chiefs, 24-7 (KC)
1965—Chiefs, 15-10 (NY)
Jets, 13-10 (KC)
1966—Chiefs, 32-24 (NY)
1967—Chiefs, 42-18 (NY)
Chiefs, 21-7 (NY)
1968—Jets, 20-19 (KC)
1969—Chiefs, 34-16 (NY)
***Chiefs, 13-6 (NY)
1971—Jets, 13-10 (NY)
1974—Chiefs, 24-16 (KC)
1975—Jets, 30-24 (KC)
(Points—Chiefs 513, Jets 402)
Franchise in Dallas (D) prior to 1963 and known as Texans
**Jets known as Titans prior to 1963*
***Inter-Division Playoff*

***KANSAS CITY vs. OAKLAND**
Raiders lead series, 19-15-2
1960—Texans, 34-16 (O)
Raiders, 20-19 (D)
1961—Texans, 42-35 (O)
Texans, 43-11 (D)
1962—Texans, 26-16 (O)
Texans, 35-7 (D)
1963—Raiders, 10-7 (O)
Raiders, 22-7 (KC)
1964—Chiefs, 21-9 (O)
Chiefs, 42-7 (KC)
1965—Raiders, 37-10 (O)
Chiefs, 14-7 (KC)
1966—Chiefs, 32-10 (O)
Raiders, 34-13 (KC)
1967—Raiders, 23-21 (O)
Raiders, 44-22 (KC)
1968—Chiefs, 24-10 (KC)
Raiders, 38-21 (O)
**Raiders, 41-6 (O)
1969—Raiders, 27-24 (KC)
Raiders, 10-6 (O)
***Chiefs, 17-7 (O)
1970—Tie, 17-17 (KC)
Raiders, 20-6 (O)
1971—Tie, 20-20 (O)
Chiefs, 16-14 (KC)
1972—Chiefs, 27-14 (KC)
Raiders, 26-3 (O)
1973—Chiefs, 16-3 (KC)
Raiders, 37-7 (O)
1974—Raiders, 27-7 (O)
Raiders, 7-6 (KC)
1975—Chiefs, 42-10 (KC)
Raiders, 28-20 (O)
1976—Raiders, 24-21 (KC)
Raiders, 21-10 (O)
(Points—Raiders 709, Chiefs 704)
Franchise in Dallas (D) prior to 1963 and known as Texans
**Division Playoff*
***AFL Championship*

KANSAS CITY vs. PHILADELPHIA
Eagles lead series, 1-0
1972—Eagles, 21-20 (KC)

KANSAS CITY vs. PITTSBURGH
Steelers lead series, 4-2
1970—Chiefs, 31-14 (P)
1971—Chiefs, 38-16 (KC)
1972—Steelers, 16-7 (P)
1974—Steelers, 34-24 (KC)
1975—Steelers, 28-3 (P)
1976—Steelers, 45-0 (KC)
(Points—Steelers 153, Chiefs 103)

KANSAS CITY vs. ST. LOUIS
Chiefs lead series, 1-0-1
1970—Tie, 6-6 (KC)
1974—Chiefs, 17-13 (StL)
(Points—Chiefs 23, Cardinals 19)

***KANSAS CITY vs. **SAN DIEGO**
Chiefs lead series, 18-15-1
1960—Chargers, 21-20 (LA)
Texans, 17-0 (D)
1961—Chargers, 26-10 (D)
Chargers, 24-14 (SD)
1962—Chargers, 32-28 (SD)
Texans, 26-17 (D)
1963—Chargers, 24-10 (SD)
Chargers, 38-17 (KC)
1964—Chargers, 28-14 (KC)
Chiefs, 49-6 (SD)
1965—Tie, 10-10 (SD)
Chiefs, 31-7 (KC)
1966—Chiefs, 24-14 (KC)
Chiefs, 27-17 (SD)
1967—Chargers, 45-31 (SD)
Chargers, 17-16 (KC)
1968—Chiefs, 27-20 (KC)
Chiefs, 40-3 (SD)
1969—Chiefs, 27-9 (SD)
Chiefs, 27-3 (KC)
1970—Chiefs, 26-14 (KC)
Chargers, 31-13 (SD)
1971—Chargers, 21-14 (SD)
Chiefs, 31-10 (KC)
1972—Chiefs, 26-14 (SD)
Chargers, 27-17 (KC)
1973—Chiefs, 19-0 (SD)
Chiefs, 33-6 (KC)
1974—Chiefs, 24-14 (SD)
Chargers, 14-7 (KC)
1975—Chiefs, 12-10 (SD)
Chargers, 28-20 (KC)
1976—Chargers, 30-16 (KC)
Chiefs, 23-20 (SD)
(Points—Chiefs 746, Chargers 600)
Franchise in Dallas (D) prior to 1963 and known as Texans
**Franchise in Los Angeles prior to 1961*

KANSAS CITY vs. SAN FRANCISCO
Series tied, 1-1
1971—Chiefs, 26-17 (SF)
1975—49ers, 20-3 (KC)
(Points—49ers 37, Chiefs 29)

KANSAS CITY vs. SEATTLE
No games

KANSAS CITY vs. TAMPA BAY
Chiefs lead series, 1-0
1976—Chiefs, 28-19 (TB)

KANSAS CITY vs. WASHINGTON
Chiefs lead series, 2-0
1971—Chiefs, 27-20 (KC)
1976—Chiefs, 33-30 (W)
(Points—Chiefs 60, Redskins 50)

LOS ANGELES vs. ATLANTA
Rams lead series, 17-2-2
See Atlanta vs. Los Angeles

LOS ANGELES vs. *1950 BALTIMORE
Rams won series, 1-0
See *Baltimore vs. Los Angeles
Extinct team

LOS ANGELES vs. BALTIMORE
Colts lead series, 20-14-2
See Baltimore vs. Los Angeles

LOS ANGELES vs. *BOSTON YANKS
Yanks won series, 2-1
See *Boston Yanks vs. Los Angeles
Extinct team

LOS ANGELES vs. *BROOKLYN DODGERS
Dodgers won series, 3-1
See *Brooklyn Dodgers vs. Cleveland Rams
Extinct team

LOS ANGELES vs. BUFFALO
Rams lead series, 2-0
See Buffalo vs. Los Angeles

LOS ANGELES vs. CHICAGO
Bears lead series, 39-24-3
See Chicago vs. Los Angeles

LOS ANGELES vs. CINCINNATI
Series tied, 1-1
See Cincinnati vs. Los Angeles

LOS ANGELES vs. CLEVELAND
Browns lead series 7-5
See Cleveland vs. Los Angeles

LOS ANGELES vs. DALLAS
Series tied, 5-5
See Dallas vs. Los Angeles

LOS ANGELES vs. *DALLAS TEXANS
Rams won series, 2-0
See *Dallas Texans vs. Los Angeles
Extinct team

LOS ANGELES vs. DENVER
Series tied, 1-1
See Denver vs. Los Angeles

LOS ANGELES vs. DETROIT
Rams lead series, 34-32-1
See Detroit vs. Los Angeles

LOS ANGELES vs. GREEN BAY
Rams lead series, 34–31–2
See Green Bay vs. Los Angeles
LOS ANGELES vs. HOUSTON
Rams lead series, 1–0
See Houston vs. Los Angeles
LOS ANGELES vs. KANSAS CITY
Rams lead series, 1–0
See Kansas City vs. Los Angeles
LOS ANGELES vs. MIAMI
Series tied, 1–1
1971—Dolphins, 20–14 (LA)
1976—Rams, 31–28 (M)
(Points—Dolphins 48, Rams 44)
LOS ANGELES vs. MINNESOTA
Vikings lead series, 14–7–2
1961—Rams, 31–17 (LA)
    Vikings, 42–21 (M)
1962—Vikings, 38–14 (LA)
    Tie, 24–24 (M)
1963—Rams, 27–24 (LA)
    Vikings, 21–13 (M)
1964—Rams, 22–13 (LA)
    Vikings, 34–13 (M)
1965—Vikings, 38–35 (LA)
    Vikings, 24–13 (M)
1966—Vikings, 35–7 (M)
    Rams, 21–6 (LA)
1967—Rams, 39–3 (LA)
1968—Rams, 31–3 (M)
1969—Vikings, 20–13 (LA)
    *Vikings, 23–20 (M)
1970—Vikings, 13–3 (M)
1972—Vikings, 45–41 (LA)
1973—Vikings, 10–9 (M)
1974—Rams, 20–17 (LA)
    **Vikings, 14–10 (M)
1976—Tie, 10–10 (M) OT
    ***Vikings, 24–13 (M)
(Points—Vikings 498, Rams 450)
  *Conference Championship
  **NFC Championship
  ***NFC Divisional playoff
LOS ANGELES vs. NEW ENGLAND
Patriots lead series, 1–0
1974—Patriots, 20–14 (NE)
LOS ANGELES vs. NEW ORLEANS
Rams lead series, 13–3
1967—Rams 27–13 (NO)
1969—Rams, 36–17 (LA)
1970—Rams, 30–17 (NO)
    Rams, 34–16 (LA)
1971—Saints, 24–20 (NO)
    Rams, 45–28 (LA)
1972—Rams, 34–14 (LA)
    Saints, 19–16 (NO)
1973—Rams, 29–7 (LA)
    Rams, 24–13 (NO)
1974—Rams, 24–0 (LA)
    Saints, 20–7 (NO)
1975—Rams, 38–14 (LA)
    Rams, 14–7 (NO)
1976—Rams, 16–10 (NO)
    Rams, 33–14 (LA)
(Points—Rams 427, Saints 233)
LOS ANGELES vs. *N.Y. BULLDOGS
Rams won series, 1–0
1949—Rams, 42–20
  *Extinct team
*LOS ANGELES vs. N.Y. GIANTS
Rams lead series, 12–4
1938—Giants, 28–0
1940—Rams, 13–0
1941—Giants, 49–14
1945—Rams, 21–17
1946—Rams, 31–21 (NY)
1947—Rams, 34–10 (LA)
1948—Rams, 52–37 (NY)
1953—Rams, 21–7 (LA)
1954—Rams, 17–16 (NY)
1959—Giants, 23–21 (LA)
1961—Rams, 24–14 (NY)
1966—Rams, 55–14 (LA)
1968—Rams, 24–21 (LA)
1970—Rams, 31–3 (NY)
1973—Rams, 40–6 (LA)
1976—Rams, 24–10 (LA)
(Points—Rams 412, Giants 286)
  *Franchise in Cleveland prior to 1946
LOS ANGELES vs. N.Y. JETS
Series tied, 1–1
1970—Jets, 31–20 (LA)
1974—Rams, 20–13 (NY)
(Points—Jets 44, Rams 40)
LOS ANGELES vs. *N.Y. YANKS

Rams won series, 4–0
1950—Rams, 45–28
    Rams, 43–35
1951—Rams, 54–14
    Rams, 48–21
(Points—Rams 190, Yanks 98)
LOS ANGELES vs. OAKLAND
Raiders lead series, 1–0
1972—Raiders, 45–17 (O)
*LOS ANGELES vs. PHILADELPHIA
Rams lead series, 12–8–1
1937—Rams, 21–3
1939—Rams, 35–13
1940—Rams, 21–13
1942—Rams, 24–14
1944—Eagles, 26–13
1945—Eagles, 28–14
1946—Eagles, 25–14 (LA)
1947—Eagles, 14–7 (P)
1948—Tie, 28–28 (LA)
1949—Eagles, 38–14 (P)
    *Eagles, 14–0 (LA)
1950—Eagles, 56–20 (P)
1955—Rams, 23–21 (P)
1956—Rams, 27–7 (LA)
1957—Rams, 17–13 (LA)
1959—Eagles, 23–20 (P)
1964—Rams, 20–10 (LA)
1967—Rams, 33–17 (LA)
1969—Rams, 23–17 (P)
1972—Rams, 34–3 (P)
1975—Rams, 42–3 (P)
(Points—Rams 450, Eagles 386)
  *NFL Championship
  **Franchise in Cleveland prior to 1946
*LOS ANGELES vs. PITTSBURGH
Rams lead series, 11–1–2
1938—Rams, 13–7
1939—Tie, 14–14
1941—Rams, 17–14
1947—Rams, 48–7 (LA)
1948—Rams, 31–14 (LA)
1949—Tie, 7–7 (P)
1952—Rams, 28–14 (LA)
1955—Rams, 27–26 (LA)
1956—Steelers, 30–13 (P)
1961—Rams, 24–14 (LA)
1964—Rams, 26–14 (P)
1968—Rams, 45–10 (LA)
1971—Rams, 23–14 (P)
1975—Rams, 10–3 (LA)
(Points—Rams 326, Steelers 188)
  *Franchise in Cleveland prior to 1946
**LOS ANGELES vs. *ST. LOUIS
Rams lead series, 16–15–2
1937—Cardinals, 6–0
    Cardinals, 13–7
1938—Cardinals, 7–6
    Cardinals, 31–17
1939—Rams, 24–0
    Rams, 14–0
1940—Rams, 26–14
    Cardinals, 17–7
1941—Rams, 10–6
    Cardinals, 7–0
1942—Cardinals, 7–0
    Rams, 7–3
1945—Rams, 21–0
    Rams, 35–21
1946—Cardinals, 34–10 (C)
    Rams, 17–14 (LA)
1947—Rams, 27–7 (LA)
    Cardinals, 17–10 (C)
1948—Cardinals, 27–22 (LA)
    Cardinals, 27–24 (C)
1949—Tie, 28–28 (C)
    Cardinals, 31–27 (LA)
1951—Rams, 45–21 (LA)
1953—Tie, 24–24 (C)
1954—Rams, 28–17 (LA)
1958—Rams, 20–14 (C)
1960—Cardinals, 43–21 (LA)
1965—Rams, 27–3 (StL)
1968—Rams, 24–13 (StL)
1970—Rams, 34–13 (LA)
1972—Cardinals, 24–14 (StL)
1975—***Rams, 35–23 (LA)
1976—Cardinals, 30–28 (LA)
(Points—Rams 639, Cardinals 542)
  *Franchise in Chicago (C) prior to 1960
  **Franchise in Cleveland prior to 1946
  ***NFC Divisional Playoff
LOS ANGELES vs. SAN DIEGO
Rams lead series, 2–0

1970—Rams, 37–10 (LA)
1975—Rams, 13–10 (SD) OT
(Points—Rams 50, Chargers 20)
LOS ANGELES vs. SAN FRANCISCO
Rams lead series, 33–19–2
1950—Rams, 35–14 (SF)
    Rams, 28–21 (LA)
1951—49ers, 44–17 (SF)
    Rams, 23–16 (LA)
1952—Rams, 35–9 (LA)
    Rams, 34–21 (SF)
1953—Rams, 31–30 (SF)
    49ers, 31–27 (LA)
1954—Tie, 24–24 (LA)
    Rams, 42–34 (SF)
1955—Rams, 23–14 (SF)
    Rams, 27–14 (LA)
1956—49ers, 33–30 (SF)
    Rams, 30–6 (LA)
1957—49ers, 23–20 (SF)
    Rams, 37–24 (LA)
1958—Rams, 33–3 (SF)
    Rams, 56–7 (LA)
1959—49ers, 34–0 (SF)
    49ers, 24–16 (LA)
1960—49ers, 13–9 (SF)
    49ers, 23–7 (LA)
1961—49ers, 35–0 (SF)
    Rams, 17–7 (LA)
1962—Rams, 28–14 (SF)
    49ers, 24–17 (LA)
1963—Rams, 28–21 (LA)
    Rams, 21–17 (SF)
1964—Rams, 42–14 (LA)
    49ers, 28–7 (SF)
1965—49ers, 45–21 (LA)
    49ers, 30–27 (SF)
1966—Rams, 34–3 (LA)
    49ers, 21–13 (SF)
1967—49ers, 27–24 (LA)
    Rams, 17–7 (SF)
1968—Rams, 24–10 (LA)
    Tie, 20–20 (SF)
1969—Rams, 27–21 (SF)
    Rams, 41–30 (LA)
1970—49ers, 20–6 (LA)
    Rams, 30–13 (SF)
1971—Rams, 20–13 (SF)
    Rams, 17–6 (LA)
1972—Rams, 31–7 (LA)
    Rams, 26–16 (SF)
1973—Rams, 40–20 (SF)
    Rams, 31–13 (LA)
1974—Rams, 37–14 (LA)
    Rams, 15–13 (SF)
1975—Rams, 23–14 (SF)
    49ers, 24–23 (LA)
1976—49ers, 16–0 (LA)
    Rams, 23–3 (SF)
(Points—Rams 1313, 49ers 1029)
LOS ANGELES vs. SEATTLE
Rams lead series, 1–0
1976—Rams, 45–6 (LA)
LOS ANGELES vs. TAMPA BAY
No games
***LOS ANGELES vs. WASHINGTON
Redskins lead series, 10–5–1
1937—Redskins, 16–7
1938—Redskins, 37–13
1941—Redskins, 17–13
1942—Redskins, 33–14
1944—Redskins, 14–10
1945—*Rams, 15–14
1948—Rams, 41–13 (LA)
1949—Rams, 53–27 (LA)
1951—Redskins, 31–21 (W)
1962—Redskins, 20–14 (W)
1963—Redskins, 37–14 (LA)
1967—Tie, 28–28 (LA)
1969—Rams, 24–13 (W)
1971—Redskins, 38–24 (LA)
1974—Redskins, 23–17 (LA)
    **Rams, 19–10 (LA)
(Points—Redskins 371, Rams 327)
  *Championship Playoff
  **NFC Divisional Playoff
  ***Franchise in Cleveland prior to 1946

MIAMI vs. ATLANTA
Dolphins lead series, 2–0
See Atlanta vs. Miami
MIAMI vs. BALTIMORE
Dolphins lead series, 8–7
See Baltimore vs. Miami
MIAMI vs. BUFFALO
Dolphins lead series, 17–4–1

See Buffalo vs. Miami
MIAMI vs. CHICAGO
Dolphins lead series, 2–0
See Chicago vs. Miami
MIAMI vs. CINCINNATI
Dolphins lead series, 4–2
See Cincinnati vs. Miami
MIAMI vs. CLEVELAND
Series tied, 2–2
See Cleveland vs. Miami
MIAMI vs. DALLAS
Series tied, 1–1
See Dallas vs. Miami
MIAMI vs. DENVER
Dolphins lead series, 4–2–1
See Denver vs. Miami
MIAMI vs. DETROIT
Dolphins lead series, 1–0
See Detroit vs. Miami
MIAMI vs. GREEN BAY
Dolphins lead series, 2–0
See Green Bay vs. Miami
MIAMI vs. HOUSTON
Oilers lead series, 6–5
See Houston vs. Miami
MIAMI vs. KANSAS CITY
Chiefs lead series, 7–3
See Kansas City vs. Miami
MIAMI vs. LOS ANGELES
Series tied, 1–1
See Los Angeles vs. Miami
MIAMI vs. MINNESOTA
Dolphins lead series, 2–1
1972—Dolphins, 16–14 (Minn)
1974—*Dolphins, 24–7 (Houston)
1976—Vikings, 29–7 (Mia)
(Points—Vikings 50, Dolphins 47)
  *Super Bowl VIII
MIAMI vs. *NEW ENGLAND
Dolphins lead series, 14–7
1966—Patriots, 20–14 (M)
1967—Patriots, 41–10 (B)
    Dolphins, 41–32 (M)
1968—Dolphins, 34–10 (B)
    Dolphins, 38–7 (M)
1969—Dolphins, 17–16 (B)
    Patriots, 38–23 (Tampa)
1970—Patriots, 27–14 (B)
    Dolphins, 37–20 (M)
1971—Dolphins, 41–3 (M)
    Patriots, 34–13 (NE)
1972—Dolphins, 52–0 (M)
    Dolphins, 37–21 (NE)
1973—Dolphins, 44–23 (M)
    Dolphins, 30–14 (NE)
1974—Patriots, 34–24 (NE)
    Dolphins, 34–27 (M)
1975—Dolphins, 22–14 (NE)
    Dolphins, 20–7 (M)
1976—Patriots, 30–14 (NE)
    Dolphins, 10–3 (M)
(Points—Dolphins 569, Patriots 421)
  *Franchise in Boston (B) prior to 1971
MIAMI vs. NEW ORLEANS
Dolphins lead series, 2–0
1970—Dolphins, 21–10 (M)
1974—Dolphins, 21–0 (NO)
(Points—Dolphins 42, Saints 10)
MIAMI vs. N.Y. GIANTS
Dolphins lead series, 1–0
1972—Dolphins, 23–13 (NY)
MIAMI vs. N.Y. JETS
Dolphins lead series, 12–10
1966—Jets, 19–14 (M)
    Jets, 30–13 (NY)
1967—Jets, 29–7 (NY)
    Jets, 33–14 (M)
1968—Jets, 35–17 (NY)
    Jets, 31–7 (M)
1969—Jets, 34–31 (NY)
    Jets, 27–9 (M)
1970—Dolphins, 20–6 (NY)
    Dolphins, 16–10 (M)
1971—Jets, 14–10 (M)
    Dolphins, 30–14 (NY)
1972—Dolphins, 27–17 (NY)
    Dolphins, 28–24 (M)
1973—Dolphins, 31–3 (M)
    Dolphins, 24–14 (NY)
1974—Dolphins, 21–17 (M)
    Jets, 17–14 (NY)
1975—Dolphins, 43–0 (NY)
    Dolphins, 27–7 (M)
1976—Dolphins, 16–0 (M)
    Dolphins, 27–7 (NY)
(Points—Dolphins 446, Jets 388)
MIAMI vs. OAKLAND

See Buffalo vs. Miami
MIAMI vs. CHICAGO
Dolphins lead series, 2–0
See Chicago vs. Miami
Raiders lead series, 9–2–1
1966—Raiders, 23–14 (M)
    Raiders, 21–10 (O)
1967—Raiders, 31–17 (O)
1968—Raiders, 47–21 (M)
1969—Raiders, 20–17 (O)
    Tie, 20–20 (M)
1970—Dolphins, 20–13 (M)
    *Raiders, 21–14 (O)
1973—Raiders, 12–7 (O)
    **Dolphins, 27–10 (M)
1974—*Raiders, 28–26 (O)
1975—Raiders, 31–21 (M)
(Points—Raiders 277, Dolphins 214)
  *AFC Divisional Playoff
  **AFC Championship
MIAMI vs. PHILADELPHIA
Series tied, 1–1
1970—Eagles, 24–17 (P)
1975—Dolphins, 24–16 (M)
(Points—Dolphins 41, Eagles 40)
MIAMI vs. PITTSBURGH
Dolphins lead series, 3–1
1971—Dolphins, 24–21 (M)
1972—*Dolphins, 21–17 (P)
1973—Dolphins, 30–26 (M)
1976—Steelers, 14–3 (P)
(Points—Dolphins 78, Steelers 78)
  *AFC Championship
MIAMI vs. ST. LOUIS
Dolphins lead series, 1–0
1972—Dolphins, 31–10 (M)
MIAMI vs. SAN DIEGO
Chargers lead series, 4–3
1966—Chargers, 44–10 (SD)
1967—Chargers, 24–0 (SD)
    Dolphins, 41–24 (M)
1968—Chargers, 34–28 (SD)
1969—Chargers, 21–14 (M)
1972—Dolphins, 24–10 (M)
1974—Dolphins, 28–21 (SD)
(Points—Chargers 178, Dolphins 145)
MIAMI vs. SAN FRANCISCO
Dolphins lead series, 1–0
1973—Dolphins, 21–13 (M)
MIAMI vs. SEATTLE
No games
MIAMI vs. TAMPA BAY
Dolphins lead series, 1–0
1976—Dolphins, 23–20 (TB)
MIAMI vs. WASHINGTON
Series tied, 1–1
1973—*Dolphins, 14–7 (Los Angeles)
1974—Redskins, 20–17 (W)
(Points—Dolphins 31, Redskins 27)
  *Super Bowl VII

MINNESOTA vs. ATLANTA
Vikings lead series, 5–4;
See Atlanta vs. Minnesota
MINNESOTA vs. BALTIMORE
Colts lead series, 12–4–1;
See Baltimore vs. Minnesota
MINNESOTA vs. BUFFALO
Vikings lead series, 2–0;
See Buffalo vs. Minnesota
MINNESOTA vs. CHICAGO
Vikings lead series, 16–14–2
See Chicago vs. Minnesota
MINNESOTA vs. CINCINNATI
Bengals lead series, 1–0;
See Cincinnati vs. Minnesota
MINNESOTA vs. CLEVELAND
Vikings lead series, 5–1;
See Cleveland vs. Minnesota
MINNESOTA vs. DALLAS
Cowboys lead series, 7–3;
See Dallas vs. Minnesota
MINNESOTA vs. DENVER
Vikings lead series, 1–0;
See Denver vs. Minnesota
MINNESOTA vs. DETROIT
Vikings lead series, 19–11–2
See Detroit vs. Minnesota
MINNESOTA vs. GREEN BAY
Vikings lead series, 18–14
See Green Bay vs. Minnesota
MINNESOTA vs. HOUSTON
Vikings lead series, 1–0;
See Houston vs. Minnesota
MINNESOTA vs. KANSAS CITY
Vikings lead series, 2–1;
See Kansas City vs. Minnesota
MINNESOTA vs. LOS ANGELES
Vikings lead series, 13–7–2;
See Los Angeles vs. Minnesota

MINNESOTA vs. MIAMI
Dolphins lead series, 2–1
See Miami vs. Minnesota
MINNESOTA vs. *NEW ENGLAND
Series tied, 1–1
1970—Vikings, 35–14 (B)
1974—Patriots, 17–14 (M)
(Points—Vikings 49, Patriots 31)
*Franchise in Boston (B) prior to 1971
MINNESOTA vs. NEW ORLEANS
Vikings lead series, 6–1
1968—Saints, 20–17 (NO)
1970—Vikings, 26–0 (M)
1971—Vikings, 23–10 (NO)
1972—Vikings, 37–6 (M)
1974—Vikings, 29–9 (M)
1975—Vikings, 20–7 (NO)
1976—Vikings, 40–9 (NO)
(Points—Vikings 192, Saints 61)
MINNESOTA vs. N. Y. GIANTS
Vikings lead series, 6–1
1964—Vikings, 30–21 (NY)
1965—Vikings, 40–14 (M)
1967—Vikings, 27–24 (M)
1969—Giants, 24–23 (NY)
1971—Vikings, 17–10 (NY)
1973—Vikings, 31–7 (New Haven)
1976—Vikings, 24–7 (M)
(Points—Vikings 192, Giants 107)
MINNESOTA vs. N. Y. JETS
Series tied, 1–1
1970—Jets, 20–10 (NY)
1975—Vikings, 29–21 (M)
(Points—Jets 41, Vikings 39)
MINNESOTA vs. OAKLAND
Series tied, 1–1
1973—Vikings, 24–16 (M)
1976—*Raiders 32–14
(Points—Raiders 48, Vikings 38)
*Super Bowl XI
MINNESOTA vs. PHILADELPHIA
Vikings lead series, 6–0
1962—Vikings, 31–21 (M)
1963—Vikings, 34–13 (P)
1968—Vikings, 24–17 (P)
1971—Vikings, 13–0 (P)
1973—Vikings, 28–21 (M)
1976—Vikings, 31–12 (P)
(Points—Vikings 161, Eagles 84)
MINNESOTA vs. PITTSBURGH
Vikings lead series, 4–3
1962—Steelers, 39–31 (P)
1964—Vikings, 30–10 (M)
1967—Vikings, 41–27 (P)
1969—Vikings, 52–14 (M)
1972—Steelers, 23–10 (P)
1975—*Steelers, 16–6 (New Orleans)
1976—Vikings, 17–6 (M)
(Points—Vikings 187, Steelers 135)
*Super Bowl IX
MINNESOTA vs. ST. LOUIS
Series tied, 3–3
1963—Cardinals, 56–14 (M)
1967—Cardinals, 34–24 (M)
1969—Vikings, 27–10 (StL)
1972—Cardinals, 19–17 (M)
1974—Vikings, 28–24 (StL)
      *Vikings, 30–14 (M)
(Points—Cardinals 157, Vikings 140)
*NFC Divisional Playoff
MINNESOTA vs. SAN DIEGO
Series tied, 1–1
1971—Chargers, 30–14 (SD)
1975—Vikings, 28–13 (M)
(Points—Chargers 43, Vikings 42)
MINNESOTA vs. SAN FRANCISCO
Series tied, 10–10–1
1961—49ers, 38–24 (M)
      49ers, 38–28 (SF)
1962—49ers, 21–7 (SF)
      49ers, 35–12 (M)
1963—Vikings, 24–20 (SF)
      Vikings, 45–14 (M)
1964—Vikings, 27–22 (SF)
      Vikings, 24–7 (M)
1965—Vikings, 42–41 (SF)
      49ers, 45–24 (M)
1966—Tie, 20–20 (SF)
      Vikings, 28–3 (SF)
1967—49ers, 27–21 (M)
1968—Vikings, 30–20 (SF)
1969—Vikings, 10–7 (M)
1970—*49ers, 17–14 (M)
1971—49ers, 13–9 (M)

1972—49ers, 20–17 (SF)
1973—Vikings, 17–13 (SF)
1975—Vikings, 27–17 (M)
1976—49ers, 20–16 (SF)
(Points—Vikings 466, 49ers 458)
*NFC Divisional Playoff
MINNESOTA vs. SEATTLE
Vikings lead series, 1–0
1976—Vikings, 27–20 (M)
MINNESOTA vs. TAMPA BAY
No games
MINNESOTA vs. WASHINGTON
Vikings lead series, 4–2
1968—Vikings, 27–14 (M)
1970—Vikings, 19–10 (W)
1972—Redskins, 24–20 (M)
1973—*Vikings, 27–20 (M)
1975—Redskins, 31–30 (W)
1976—*Vikings 35–20 (M)
(Points—Vikings 158, Redskins 119)
*NFC Divisional Playoff

NEW ENGLAND vs. ATLANTA
Patriots lead series, 1–0
See Atlanta vs. New England
NEW ENGLAND vs. BALTIMORE
Colts lead series, 8–6;
See Baltimore vs. New England
NEW ENGLAND vs. BUFFALO
Bills lead series, 18–16–1;
See Buffalo vs. New England
NEW ENGLAND vs. CHICAGO
Patriots lead series, 1–0;
See Chicago vs. New England
NEW ENGLAND vs. CINCINNATI
Bengals lead series, 3–2;
See Cincinnati vs. New England
NEW ENGLAND vs. CLEVELAND
Browns lead series, 2–0;
See Cleveland vs. New England
NEW ENGLAND vs. DALLAS
Cowboys lead series, 2–0;
See Dallas vs. New England
NEW ENGLAND vs. DENVER
Patriots lead series, 11–9;
See Denver vs. New England
NEW ENGLAND vs. DETROIT
Lions lead series, 2–0;
See Detroit vs. New England
NEW ENGLAND vs. GREEN BAY
Patriots lead series, 1–0;
See Green Bay vs. New England
NEW ENGLAND vs. HOUSTON
Patriots lead series, 12–10–1;
See Houston vs. New England
NEW ENGLAND vs. KANSAS CITY
Chiefs lead series, 11–5–3;
See Kansas City vs. New England
NEW ENGLAND vs. LOS ANGELES
Patriots lead series, 1–0;
See Los Angeles vs. New England
NEW ENGLAND vs. MIAMI
Dolphins lead series, 14–7;
See Miami vs. New England
NEW ENGLAND vs. MINNESOTA
Series tied, 1–1;
See Minnesota vs. New England
NEW ENGLAND vs. NEW ORLEANS
Patriots lead series, 2–0
1972—Patriots, 17–10 (NO)
1976—Patriots, 27–6 (NE)
(Points—Patriots 44, Saints 16)
NEW ENGLAND vs. N. Y. GIANTS
Series tied, 1–1
1970—Giants, 16–0 (B)
1974—Patriots, 28–20 (New Haven)
(Points—Giants 36, Patriots 28)
*Franchise in Boston (B) prior to 1971
NEW ENGLAND vs. *N. Y. JETS
Jets lead series, 22–11–1
1960—Patriots, 28–24 (NY)
      Patriots, 38–21 (B)
1961—Titans, 21–20 (B)
      Titans, 37–30 (NY)
1962—Patriots, 43–14 (NY)
      Patriots, 24–17 (B)
1963—Patriots, 38–14 (B)
      Jets, 31–24 (NY)
1964—Patriots, 26–10 (B)
      Jets, 35–14 (NY)
1965—Jets, 30–20 (B)
      Patriots, 27–23 (NY)
1966—Tie, 24–24 (B)

Jets, 38–28 (NY)
1967—Jets, 30–23 (NY)
      Jets, 29–24 (B)
1968—Jets, 47–31 (Birmingham)
      Jets, 48–14 (NY)
1969—Jets, 23–14 (B)
      Jets, 23–17 (NY)
1970—Jets, 31–21 (B)
      Jets, 17–3 (NY)
1971—Patriots, 20–0 (NE)
      Jets, 13–6 (NY)
1972—Patriots, 41–13 (NE)
      Jets, 34–10 (NY)
1973—Jets, 9–7 (NE)
      Jets, 33–13 (NY)
1974—Patriots, 24–0 (NY)
      Jets, 21–16 (NE)
1975—Patriots, 36–7 (NY)
      Jets, 30–28 (NE)
1976—Patriots, 41–7 (NE)
      Jets, 38–24 (NY)
(Points—Jets 835, Patriots 754)
*Known as Titans prior to 1963
**Franchise in Boston (B) prior to 1971
***NEW ENGLAND vs. OAKLAND**
Series tied, 10–10–1
1960—Raiders, 27–14 (O)
      Patriots, 34–28 (B)
1961—Patriots, 20–17 (B)
      Patriots, 35–21 (O)
1962—Patriots, 26–16 (B)
      Raiders, 20–0 (O)
1963—Patriots, 20–14 (O)
      Patriots, 20–14 (B)
1964—Patriots, 17–14 (O)
      Tie, 43–43 (B)
1965—Raiders, 24–10 (B)
      Raiders, 30–21 (O)
1966—Patriots, 24–21 (B)
      Patriots, 35–7 (O)
1967—Raiders, 48–14 (B)
1968—Raiders, 41–10 (O)
1969—Raiders, 38–23 (B)
1971—Patriots, 20–6 (NE)
1974—Raiders, 41–26 (O)
1976—Raiders, 48–17 (NE)
      **Raiders 21–17 (O)
(Points—Raiders 536, Patriots 449)
*Franchise in Boston (B) prior to 1971
**AFC Divisional Playoff
NEW ENGLAND vs. PHILADELPHIA
Eagles lead series, 1–0
1973—Eagles, 24–23 (P)
NEW ENGLAND vs. PITTSBURGH
Steelers lead series, 2–1
1972—Steelers, 33–3 (P)
1974—Steelers, 21–17 (NE)
1976—Patriots, 30–27 (P)
(Points—Steelers 81, Patriots 50)
***NEW ENGLAND vs. ST. LOUIS**
(Cardinals lead series, 2–0
1970—Cardinals, 31–0 (StL)
1975—Cardinals, 24–17 (StL)
(Points—Cardinals 55, Patriots 17)
*Franchise in Boston (B) prior to 1971
***NEW ENGLAND vs. *SAN DIEGO**
Chargers lead series, 12–9–2
1960—Patriots, 35–0 (LA)
      Chargers, 45–16 (B)
1961—Chargers, 38–27 (B)
      Patriots, 41–0 (SD)
1962—Patriots, 24–20 (B)
      Patriots, 20–14 (SD)
1963—Chargers, 17–13 (SD)
      Chargers, 7–6 (B)
      **Chargers, 51–10 (SD)
1964—Patriots, 33–28 (SD)
      Chargers, 26–17 (B)
1965—Tie, 10–10 (B)
      Patriots, 22–6 (SD)
1966—Chargers, 24–0 (SD)
      Patriots, 35–17 (B)
1967—Chargers, 28–14 (SD)
      Tie, 31–31 (SD)
1968—Chargers, 27–17 (B)
1969—Chargers, 13–10 (B)
      Chargers, 28–18 (SD)
1970—Chargers, 16–14 (B)
1973—Patriots, 30–14 (NE)
1975—Chargers, 33–19 (SD)
(Points—Chargers 479, Patriots 476)
*Franchise in Los Angeles (LA) prior to 1961

**AFL Championship
***Franchise in Boston (B) prior to 1971
NEW ENGLAND vs. SEATTLE
No games
NEW ENGLAND vs. TAMPA BAY
Patriots lead series, 1–0
1976—Patriots, 31–14 (TB)
NEW ENGLAND vs. SAN FRANCISCO
Series tied, 1–1
1971—49ers, 27–10 (SF)
1975—Patriots, 24–16 (NE)
(Points—49ers 43, Patriots 34)
NEW ENGLAND vs. WASHINGTON
Patriots lead series, 1–0
1972—Patriots, 24–23 (NE)

NEW ORLEANS vs. ATLANTA
Falcons lead series, 11–5;
Atlanta vs. New Orleans
NEW ORLEANS vs. BALTIMORE
Colts lead series, 3–0;
See Baltimore vs. New Orleans
NEW ORLEANS vs. BUFFALO
Saints lead series, 1–0;
See Buffalo vs. New Orleans
NEW ORLEANS vs. CHICAGO
Bears lead series, 5–1;
See Chicago vs. New Orleans
NEW ORLEANS vs. CINCINNATI
Bengals lead series, 1–0;
See Cincinnati vs. New Orleans
NEW ORLEANS vs. CLEVELAND
Browns lead series, 6–0;
See Cleveland vs. New Orleans
NEW ORLEANS vs. DALLAS
Cowboys lead series, 7–1;
See Dallas vs. New Orleans
NEW ORLEANS vs. DENVER
Broncos lead series, 2–0;
See Denver vs. New Orleans
NEW ORLEANS vs. DETROIT
Saints lead series, 3–2–1;
See Detroit vs. New Orleans
NEW ORLEANS vs. GREEN BAY
Packers lead series, 4–2;
See Green Bay vs. New Orleans
NEW ORLEANS vs. HOUSTON
Oilers lead series, 1–0–1;
See Houston vs. New Orleans
NEW ORLEANS vs. KANSAS CITY
Series tied, 1–1;
See Kansas City vs. New Orleans
NEW ORLEANS vs. LOS ANGELES
Rams lead series, 13–3;
See Los Angeles vs. New Orleans
NEW ORLEANS vs. MIAMI
Dolphins lead series, 2–0;
See Miami vs. New Orleans
NEW ORLEANS vs. MINNESOTA
Vikings lead series, 6–1;
See Minnesota vs. New Orleans
NEW ORLEANS vs. NEW ENGLAND
Patriots lead series, 2–0;
See New England vs. New Orleans
NEW ORLEANS vs. N. Y. GIANTS
Giants lead series, 4–2
1967—Giants, 27–21 (NY)
1968—Giants, 38–21 (NY)
1969—Saints, 25–24 (NY)
1970—Saints, 14–10 (NO)
1972—Giants, 45–21 (NY)
1975—Giants, 28–14 (NY)
(Points—Giants 172, Saints 116)
NEW ORLEANS vs. N. Y. JETS
Jets lead series, 1–0
1972—Jets, 18–17 (NY)
NEW ORLEANS vs. OAKLAND
Raiders lead series, 1–0–1
1971—Tie, 21–21 (NO)
1975—Raiders, 48–10 (O)
(Points—Raiders 69, Saints 31)
NEW ORLEANS vs. PHILADELPHIA
Saints lead series, 4–3
1967—Saints, 31–24 (NO)
      Eagles, 48–21 (P)
1968—Eagles, 29–17 (P)
1969—Eagles, 13–10 (P)
      Saints, 25–17 (NO)
1972—Saints, 21–3 (NO)
1974—Saints, 14–10 (NO)
(Points—Eagles 144, Saints 140)
NEW ORLEANS vs. PITTSBURGH

Saints lead series, 3–2
1967—Steelers, 14–10 (NO)
1968—Steelers, 16–12 (P)
      Saints, 24–14 (NO)
1969—Saints, 27–24 (NO)
1974—Steelers, 28–7 (NO)
(Points—Steelers 92, Saints 84)
NEW ORLEANS vs. ST. LOUIS
Cardinals lead series, 4–2
1967—Cardinals, 31–20 (StL)
1968—Cardinals, 21–20 (NO)
      Cardinals, 31–17 (StL)
1969—Saints, 51–42 (StL)
1970—Cardinals, 24–17 (StL)
1974—Saints, 14–0 (NO)
(Points—Cardinals 149, Saints 139)
NEW ORLEANS vs. SAN DIEGO
Chargers lead series, 1–0
1973—Chargers, 17–14 (SD)
NEW ORLEANS vs. SAN FRANCISCO
49ers lead series, 11–3–2
1967—49ers, 27–13 (SF)
1969—Saints, 43–38 (NO)
1970—Tie, 20–20 (SF)
      49ers, 38–27 (NO)
1971—49ers, 38–20 (NO)
      Saints, 26–20 (SF)
1972—49ers, 37–2 (NO)
      Tie, 20–20 (SF)
1973—49ers, 40–0 (SF)
      Saints, 16–10 (NO)
1974—49ers, 17–13 (NO)
      49ers, 35–21 (SF)
1975—49ers, 35–21 (NO)
      49ers, 16–6 (NO)
1976—49ers, 33–3 (SF)
      49ers, 27–7 (NO)
(Points—49ers 396, Saints 258)
NEW ORLEANS vs. SEATTLE
Saints lead series, 1–0
1976—Saints, 51–27 (S)
NEW ORLEANS vs. TAMPA BAY
No games
NEW ORLEANS vs. WASHINGTON
Redskins lead series, 5–3
1967—Redskins, 30–10 (NO)
      Saints, 30–14 (W)
1968—Saints, 37–17 (NO)
1969—Redskins, 26–20 (NO)
      Redskins, 17–14 (W)
1971—Redskins, 24–14 (W)
1972—Saints, 19–3 (NO)
1975—Redskins, 41–3 (W)
(Points—Redskins 172, Saints 147)

***N. Y. BULLDOGS vs. **CHICAGO CARDINALS**
Cardinals won series, 1–0
1949—Cardinals, 65–20
*Extinct team
**Franchise moved to St. Louis in 1960
***N. Y. BULLDOGS vs. DETROIT**
Lions won series, 1–0
See Detroit vs. N.Y. Bulldogs
*Extinct team
***N. Y. BULLDOGS vs. GREEN BAY**
Packers won series, 1–0
See Green Bay vs. N. Y. Bulldogs
*Extinct team
***N. Y. BULLDOGS vs. LOS ANGELES**
Rams won series, 1–0
See Los Angeles vs. N. Y. Bulldogs
*Extinct team
***N. Y. BULLDOGS vs. N. Y. GIANTS**
Series tied, 1–1
1949—Giants 38–14
      Bulldogs, 31–24
(Points—Giants 62, Bulldogs 45)
*Extinct team
***N. Y. BULLDOGS vs. PHILADELPHIA**
Eagles won series, 2–0
1949—Eagles, 7–0
      Eagles, 42–0
(Points—Eagles 49, Bulldogs 0)
*Extinct team
***N.Y. BULLDOGS vs. PITTSBURGH**
Steelers won series, 2–0
1949—Steelers, 24–13
      Steelers, 27–0
(Points—Steelers 51, Bulldogs 13)
*Extinct team

*N.Y. BULLDOGS vs. WASHINGTON
Redskins won series, 1-0-1
1949—Redskins, 38-14
　　Tie, 14-14
*Extinct team

N.Y. GIANTS vs. ATLANTA
Falcons lead series, 3-1
See Atlanta vs. N.Y. Giants
N.Y. GIANTS vs. *1950 BALTIMORE
Giants won series, 1-0
See *Baltimore vs. N.Y. Giants
*Extinct team
N.Y. GIANTS vs. BALTIMORE
Colts lead series, 6-3
See Baltimore vs. N.Y. Giants
N.Y. GIANTS vs. *BOSTON YANKS
Giants won series, 5-1-3;
See *Boston Yanks vs. N.Y. Giants
*Extinct team
N.Y. GIANTS vs. *BROOKLYN DODGERS
Giant won series, 24-5-3;
See *Brooklyn Dodgers vs. N.Y. Giants
*Extinct team
N.Y. GIANTS vs. BUFFALO
Giants lead series, 2-0;
See Buffalo vs. N.Y. Giants
N.Y. GIANTS vs. CHICAGO
Bears lead series, 25-16-2;
See Chicago vs. N.Y. Giants
N.Y. GIANTS vs. CINCINNATI
Bengals lead series, 1-0;
See Cincinnati vs. N.Y. Giants
N.Y. GIANTS vs. CLEVELAND
Browns lead series, 24-16-2
See Cleveland vs. N.Y. Giants
N.Y. GIANTS vs. DALLAS
Cowboys lead series, 20-9-2;
See Dallas vs. N.Y. Giants
N.Y. GIANTS vs. *DALLAS TEXANS
Giants won series, 1-0;
See *Dallas Texans vs. N.Y. Giants
*Extinct team
N.Y. GIANTS vs. DENVER
Series tied, 1-1;
See Denver vs. N.Y. Giants
N.Y. GIANTS VS. DETROIT
Lion lead series, 17-10-1;
See Detroit vs. N.Y. Giants
N.Y. GIANTS vs. GREEN BAY
Packers lead series, 21-16-2;
See Green Bay vs. N.Y. Giants
N.Y. GIANTS vs. HOUSTON
Giants lead series, 1-0;
See Houston vs. N.Y. Giants
N.Y. GIANTS vs. KANSAS CITY
Giants lead series, 1-0;
See Kansas City vs. N.Y. Giants
N.Y. GIANTS vs. LOS ANGELES
Rams lead series, 10-2
See Los Angeles vs. N.Y. Giants
N.Y. GIANTS vs. MIAMI
Dolphins lead series, 1-0;
See Miami vs. N.Y. Giants
N.Y. GIANTS vs. MINNESOTA
Vikings lead series, 6-1
See Minnesota vs. N.Y. Giants
N.Y. GIANTS vs. NEW ENGLAND
Seried tied 1-1;
See New England vs. N.Y. Giants
N.Y. GIANTS vs. NEW ORLEANS
Giants lead series, 4-2
See New Orleans vs. N.Y. Giants
N.Y. GIANTS vs. N.Y. JETS
Series tied, 1-1
1970—Giants, 22-10 (NYJ)
1974—Jets, 26-20 (New Haven) OT
(Points—Giants 42, Jets 36)
N.Y. GIANTS vs. *N.Y. YANKS
Giants won series, 3-0
1950—Giants, 51-7
1951—Giants, 37-31
　　Giants, 27-17
(Points—Giants 115, Yanks 55)
*Extinct team
N.Y. GIANTS vs. OAKLAND
Raiders lead series, 1-0;
1973—Raiders, 42-0 (O)
N.Y. GIANTS vs. PHILADELPHIA
Giants lead series, 49-35-2
1933—Giants, 56-0 (NY)
　　Giants, 20-14 (P)

1934—Giants, 17-0 (NY)
　　Eagles, 6-0 (P)
1935—Giants, 10-0 (NY)
　　Giants, 21-14 (P)
1936—Eagles, 10-7 (P)
　　Giants, 21-17 (NY)
1937—Giants, 16-7 (P)
　　Giants, 21-0 (NY)
1938—Eagles, 14-10 (P)
　　Giants, 17-7 (NY)
1939—Giants, 13-3 (P)
　　Giants, 27-10 (NY)
1940—Giants, 20-14 (P)
　　Giants, 17-7 (NY)
1941—Giants, 24-0 (P)
　　Giants, 16-0 (NY)
1942—Giants, 35-17 (NY)
　　Giants, 14-0 (P)
1943—Eagles, 28-14 (P)
　　Giants, 42-14 (NY)
1944—Eagles, 24-17 (NY)
　　Tie, 21-21 (P)
1945—Eagles, 38-17 (P)
　　Giants, 28-21 (NY)
1946—Eagles, 24-14 (P)
　　Giants, 45-17 (NY)
1947—Eagles, 23-0 (P)
　　Eagles, 41-24 (NY)
1948—Eagles, 45-0 (P)
　　Eagles, 35-14 (NY)
1949—Eagles, 24-3 (NY)
　　Eagles, 17-3 (P)
1950—Giants, 7-3 (P)
　　Giants, 9-7 (P)
1951—Giants, 26-24 (NY)
　　Giants, 23-7 (P)
1952—Giants, 31-7 (P)
　　Eagles, 14-10 (NY)
1953—Eagles, 30-7 (P)
　　Giants, 37-28 (NY)
1954—Giants, 27-14 (NY)
　　Eagles, 29-14 (P)
1955—Eagles, 27-17 (P)
　　Giants, 31-7 (NY)
1956—Giants, 20-3 (NY)
　　Giants, 21-7 (P)
1957—Giants, 24-20 (P)
　　Giants, 13-0 (NY)
1958—Eagles, 27-24 (P)
　　Giants, 24-10 (NY)
1959—Eagles, 49-21 (P)
　　Giants, 24-7 (NY)
1960—Giants, 17-10 (NY)
　　Eagles, 31-23 (P)
1961—Giants, 38-21 (NY)
　　Giants, 28-24 (P)
1962—Giants, 29-13 (P)
　　Giants, 19-14 (NY)
1963—Giants, 37-14 (P)
　　Giants, 42-14 (NY)
1964—Eagles, 38-7 (P)
　　Eagles, 23-17 (NY)
1965—Giants, 16-14 (P)
　　Giants, 35-27 (NY)
1966—Giants, 35-17 (P)
　　Eagles, 31-3 (NY)
1967—Giants, 44-7 (NY)
1968—Giants, 34-25 (P)
　　Giants, 7-6 (NY)
1969—Eagles, 23-20 (NY)
1970—Giants, 30-23 (NY)
　　Eagles, 23-20 (P)
1971—Eagles, 23-7 (P)
　　Eagles, 41-28 (NY)
1972—Eagles, 27-12 (P)
　　Giants, 62-10 (NY)
1973—Tie, 23-23 (NY)
　　Eagles, 20-16 (P)
1974—Eagles, 36-7 (P)
　　Eagles, 20-7 (New Haven)
1975—Eagles, 23-14 (P)
　　Eagles, 13-10 (NY)
1976—Eagles, 10-0 (ER)
(Points—Giants 1,727, Eagles 1,496)
N.Y. GIANTS vs. PITTSBURGH
ER-East Rutherford, N.J.
Giants lead series, 42-27-3
1933—Giants, 23-2 (P)
　　Giants, 27-3 (NY)
1934—Giants, 14-12 (P)
　　Giants, 17-7 (NY)
1935—Giants, 42-7 (P)
　　Giants, 13-0 (NY)
1936—Steelers, 10-7 (P)
1937—Giants, 10-7 (P)
　　Giants, 17-0 (NY)
1938—Giants, 27-14 (P)

　　Steelers, 13-10 (NY)
1939—Giants, 14-7 (P)
　　Giants, 23-7 (NY)
1940—Tie, 10-10 (P)
　　Giants, 12-0 (NY)
1941—Giants, 37-10 (P)
　　Giants, 28-7 (NY)
1942—Steelers, 13-10 (P)
　　Steelers, 17-9 (NY)
1943—Steelers, 28-14 (NY)
　　Giants, 42-14 (NY)
1944—Giants, 23-0 (NY)
1945—Giants, 34-6 (P)
　　Steelers, 21-7 (NY)
1946—Giants, 17-14 (P)
　　Giants, 7-0 (NY)
1947—Steelers, 38-21 (NY)
　　Steelers, 24-7 (P)
1948—Steelers, 34-27 (NY)
　　Steelers, 38-28 (P)
1949—Giants, 28-7 (P)
　　Steelers, 21-17 (NY)
1950—Giants, 18-7 (P)
　　Steelers, 17-6 (NY)
1951—Tie, 13-13 (NY)
　　Giants, 14-0 (NY)
1952—Steelers, 63-7 (P)
1953—Steelers, 24-14 (P)
　　Steelers, 14-10 (NY)
1954—Giants, 30-6 (P)
　　Giants, 24-3 (NY)
1955—Steelers, 30-23 (P)
　　Steelers, 19-17 (NY)
1956—Giants, 38-10 (NY)
　　Giants, 17-14 (P)
1957—Giants, 35-0 (NY)
　　Steelers, 21-10 (P)
1958—Giants, 17-6 (NY)
　　Steelers, 31-10 (P)
1959—Giants, 21-16 (P)
　　Steelers, 14-9 (NY)
1960—Giants, 19-17 (P)
　　Giants, 27-24 (NY)
1961—Giants, 17-14 (P)
　　Giants, 42-21 (NY)
1962—Giants, 31-27 (P)
　　Steelers, 20-17 (NY)
1963—Steelers, 31-9 (P)
　　Giants, 33-17 (NY)
1964—Steelers, 27-24 (P)
　　Steelers, 44-17 (NY)
1965—Giants, 23-13 (P)
　　Giants, 35-0 (NY)
1966—Tie, 34-34 (P)
　　Steelers, 47-28 (NY)
1967—Giants, 27-24 (P)
　　Giants, 28-20 (NY)
1968—Giants, 34-20 (P)
1969—Giants, 10-7 (NY)
　　Giants, 21-17 (P)
1971—Steelers, 17-13 (P)
1976—Steelers, 27-0 (ER)
(Points—Giants, 1,421, Steelers 1191)
N.Y. GIANTS vs. *ST. LOUIS
ER-East Rutherford, N.J.
Giants lead series, 46-23-1
1926—Giants, 20-0 (NY)
1927—Giants, 28-7 (NY)
1929—Giants, 24-21 (NY)
1930—Giants, 25-12 (NY)
　　Giants, 13-7 (C)
1935—Cardinals, 14-13 (NY)
1936—Giants, 14-6 (NY)
1938—Giants, 6-0 (NY)
1939—Giants, 17-7 (NY)
1941—Cardinals, 10-7 (NY)
1942—Giants, 21-7 (NY)
1943—Giants, 24-13 (NY)
1944—Giants, 23-0 (NY)
1946—Giants, 28-24 (NY)
1947—Giants, 35-31 (NY)
1948—Cardinals, 63-35 (NY)
1949—Giants, 41-38 (C)
1950—Cardinals, 17-3 (C)
　　Giants, 51-21 (NY)
1951—Giants, 28-17 (NY)
　　Giants, 10-0 (C)
1952—Cardinals, 24-23 (NY)
　　Giants, 28-6 (C)
1953—Giants, 21-7 (NY)
　　Giants, 23-20 (C)
1954—Cardinals, 41-10 (C)
　　Giants, 31-17 (NY)
1955—Cardinals, 28-17 (C)
　　Giants, 10-0 (NY)
1956—Cardinals, 35-27 (C)
　　Giants, 23-10 (NY)
1957—Giants, 27-14 (NY)

　　Giants, 28-21 (C)
1958—Giants, 37-7 (Buffalo)
　　Cardinals, 23-6 (NY)
1959—Giants, 9-3 (NY)
　　Giants, 30-20 (Minn)
1960—Giants, 35-14 (StL)
　　Cardinals, 20-13 (NY)
1961—Cardinals, 21-10 (NY)
　　Giants, 24-9 (StL)
1962—Giants, 31-14 (StL)
　　Giants, 31-28 (NY)
1963—Giants, 38-21 (NY)
　　Cardials, 24-17 (NY)
1964—Giants, 34-17 (NY)
　　Tie, 10-10 (StL)
1965—Giants, 14-10 (NY)
　　Giants, 28-15 (StL)
1966—Cardinals, 24-19 (StL)
　　Cardinals, 20-17 (NY)
1967—Giants, 37-20 (StL)
　　Giants, 37-14 (NY)
1968—Cardinals, 28-21 (NY)
1969—Cardinals, 42-17 (StL)
　　Giants, 49-6 (NY)
1970—Giants, 35-17 (NY)
　　Giants, 34-17 (StL)
1971—Giants, 21-20 (StL)
　　Cardinals, 24-7 (NY)
1972—Giants, 27-21 (NY)
　　Giants, 13-7 (StL)
1973—Cardinals, 35-27 (StL)
　　Giants, 24-13 (New Haven)
1974—Cardinals, 23-21 (New Haven)
　　Cardinals, 26-14 (StL)
1975—Cardinals, 26-14 (StL)
　　Cardinals, 20-13 (NY)
1976—Cardinals, 27-21 (StL)
　　Cardinals, 17-14 (ER)
(Points—Giants 1,614, Cardinals 1,210)
*Franchise in Chicago (C) prior to 1960
N. Y. GIANTS vs. SAN DIEGO
Giants lead series, 2-0
1971—Giants, 35-17 (NY)
1975—Giants, 35-24 (NY)
(Points—Giants 70, Chargers 41)
N. Y. GIANTS vs. SAN FRANCISCO
Giants lead series, 6-2
1952—Giants, 23-14 (NY)
1956—Giants, 38-21 (SF)
1957—49ers, 27-17 (NY)
1960—Giants, 21-19 (SF)
1963—Giants, 48-14 (NY)
1968—49ers, 26-10 (NY)
1972—Giants, 23-17 (SF)
1975—Giants, 26-23 (SF)
(Points—Giants 206, 49ers 161)
N. Y. GIANTS vs. SEATTLE
Giants lead series, 1-0
ER—East Rutherford, N. J.
1976—Giants, 28-16 (ER)
N. Y. GIANTS vs. TAMPA BAY
No games
N. Y. GIANTS vs. **WASHINGTON
Giants lead series, 51-35-3
1932—Redskins, 14-6
　　Tie, 0-0
1933—Redskins, 21-20
　　Giants, 7-0
1934—Giants, 16-13
　　Giants, 3-0
1935—Giants, 20-12
　　Giants, 17-6
1936—Giants, 7-0
　　Redskins, 14-0
1937—Redskins, 13-3 (W)
　　Redskins, 49-14 (NY)
1938—Giants, 10-7 (W)
　　Giants, 36-0 (NY)
1939—Tie, 0-0 (W)
　　Giants, 9-7 (NY)
1940—Redskins, 21-7 (W)
　　Giants, 21-7 (NY)
1941—Giants, 17-10 (W)
　　Giants, 20-13 (NY)
1942—Giants, 14-7 (W)
　　Redskins, 14-7 (NY)
1943—Giants, 14-10 (NY)
　　Giants, 31-7 (W)
　　*Redskins, 28-0 (NY)
1944—Giants, 16-13 (NY)
　　Giants, 31-0 (W)
1945—Redskins, 24-14 (NY)
　　Redskins, 17-0 (W)
1946—Redskins, 24-14 (W)
　　Giants, 31-0 (NY)

1947—Redskins, 28-20 (W)
　　Giants, 35-10 (NY)
1948—Redskins, 41-10 (W)
　　Redskins, 28-21 (NY)
1949—Giants, 45-35 (W)
　　Giants, 23-7 (NY)
1950—Giants, 21-17 (W)
　　Giants, 24-21 (NY)
1951—Giants, 35-14 (W)
　　Giants, 28-14 (NY)
1952—Giants, 14-10 (W)
　　Redskins, 27-17 (NY)
1953—Redskins, 13-9 (NY)
　　Redskins, 24-21 (NY)
1954—Giants, 51-21 (W)
　　Giants, 24-7 (NY)
1955—Giants, 35-7 (W)
　　Giants, 27-20 (W)
1956—Redskins, 33-7 (W)
　　Giants, 28-14 (NY)
1957—Giants, 24-20 (W)
　　Redskins, 31-14 (NY)
1958—Giants, 21-14 (W)
　　Giants, 30-0 (NY)
1959—Giants, 45-14 (W)
　　Giants, 24-10 (W)
1960—Tie, 24-24 (NY)
　　Giants, 17-3 (W)
1961—Giants, 24-21 (W)
　　Giants, 53-0 (NY)
1962—Giants, 49-34 (NY)
　　Giants, 42-24 (NY)
1963—Giants, 24-14 (NY)
　　Giants, 44-14 (NY)
1964—Giants, 13-10 (NY)
　　Redskins, 36-21 (NY)
1965—Redskins, 23-7 (NY)
　　Giants, 27-10 (W)
1966—Giants, 13-10 (NY)
　　Redskins, 72-41 (W)
1967—Redskins, 38-34 (NY)
1968—Giants, 48-21 (NY)
　　Giants, 13-10 (W)
1969—Giants, 20-14 (W)
1970—Giants, 35-33 (NY)
　　Giants, 27-24 (NY)
1971—Redskins, 30-3 (NY)
　　Redskins, 23-7 (W)
1972—Redskins, 23-16 (NY)
　　Redskins, 27-13 (W)
1973—Redskins, 21-3 (New Haven)
　　Redskins, 27-24 (W)
1974—Redskins, 13-10 (New Haven)
　　Redskins, 24-3 (W)
1975—Redskins, 49-13 (W)
　　Redskins, 21-13 (NY)
1976—Giants, 12-9 (ER)
(Points—Giants 1,762, Redskins 1,558)
*Conference Playoff
**Franchise in Boston prior to 1937

N. Y. JETS vs. ATLANTA
Falcons lead series, 1-0;
See Atlanta vs. N. Y. Jets
N. Y. JETS vs. BALTIMORE
Colts lead series, 9-6;
See Baltimore vs. N. Y. Jets
N. Y. JETS vs. BUFFALO
Bills lead series, 18-16;
See Buffalo vs. N. Y. Jets
N. Y. JETS vs. CHICAGO
Jets lead series, 1-0;
See Chicago vs. N. Y. Jets
N. Y. JETS vs. CINCINNATI
Jets lead series, 4-2;
See Cincinnati vs. N. Y. Jets
N. Y. JETS vs. CLEVELAND
Browns lead series, 2-0;
See Cleveland vs. N. Y. Jets
N. Y. JETS vs. DALLAS
Cowboys lead series, 2-0;
See Dallas vs. N. Y. Jets
N. Y. JETS vs. DENVER
Series tied, 9-9-1;
See Denver vs. N. Y. Jets
N. Y. JETS vs. DETROIT
Lions lead series, 1-0;
See Detroit vs. N. Y. Jets
N. Y. JETS vs. GREEN BAY
Packers lead series, 1-0;
See Green Bay vs. N. Y. Jets
N. Y. JETS vs. HOUSTON
Oilers lead series, 12-8-1;
See Houston vs. N. Y. Jets
N. Y. JETS vs. KANSAS CITY

Chiefs lead series, 12–9;
See Kansas City vs. N. Y. Jets
N. Y. JETS vs. LOS ANGELES
Series tied, 1–1;
See Los Angeles vs. N. Y. Jets
N. Y. JETS vs. MIAMI
Dolphins lead series, 12–10;
See Miami vs. N. Y. Jets
N. Y. JETS vs. MINNESOTA
Series tied, 1–1;
See Minnesota vs. N. Y. Jets
N. Y. JETS vs. NEW ENGLAND
Jets lead series, 22–11–1
See New England vs. N. Y. Jets
N. Y. JETS vs. NEW ORLEANS
Jets lead series, 1–0;
See New Orleans vs. N. Y. Jets
N. Y. JETS vs. N. Y. GIANTS
Series ties, 1–1;
See N. Y. Giants vs. N. Y. Jets
***N. Y. JETS vs. OAKLAND**
Raiders lead series, 10–9–2
1960—Raiders, 28–27 (NY)
Titans, 31–28 (O)
1961—Titans, 14–6 (O)
Titans, 23–12 (NY)
1962—Titans, 28–17 (O)
Titans, 31–21 (NY)
1963—Jets, 10–7 (NY)
Raiders, 49–26 (O)
1964—Jets, 35–13 (NY)
Raiders, 35–26 (O)
1965—Tie, 24–24 (NY)
Raiders, 24–14 (O)
1966—Raiders, 24–21 (NY)
Tie, 28–28 (O)
1967—Jets, 27–14 (NY)
Raiders, 38–29 (O)
1968—Raiders, 43–32 (O)
**Jets, 27–23 (NY)
1969—Raiders, 27–14 (NY)
1970—Raiders, 14–13 (NY)
1972—Raiders, 24–16 (O)
(Points—Raiders 499, Jets 496)
Jets known as Titans prior to 1963
***AFL Championship*
N. Y. JETS vs. PHILADELPHIA
Eagles lead series, 1–0
1973—Eagles, 24–23 (P)
N. Y. JETS vs. PITTSBURGH
Steelers lead series, 3–0
1970—Steelers, 21–17 (P)
1973—Steelers, 26–14 (P)
1975—Steelers, 20–7 (NY)
(Points—Steelers 67, Jets 38)
N. Y. JETS vs. ST. LOUIS
Cardinals lead series, 2–0
1971—Cardinals, 17–10 (StL)
1975—Cardinals 37–6 (NY)
(Points—Cardinals 54, Jets 16)
***N. Y. JETS vs. **SAN DIEGO**
Chargers lead series, 14–6–1
1960—Chargers, 21–7 (NY)
Chargers, 50–43 (LA)
1961—Chargers, 25–10 (NY)
Chargers, 48–13 (SD)
1962—Chargers, 40–14 (SD)
Titans, 23–3 (NY)
1963—Chargers, 24–20 (SD)
Chargers, 53–7 (NY)
1964—Tie, 17–17 (NY)
Chargers, 38–3 (SD)
1965—Chargers, 34–9 (NY)
Chargers, 38–7 (SD)
1966—Jets, 17–16 (NY)
Chargers, 42–27 (SD)
1967—Jets, 42–31 (SD)
1968—Jets, 23–20 (NY)
Jets, 37–15 (SD)
1969—Chargers, 34–27 (SD)
1971—Chargers, 49–21 (SD)
1974—Jets, 27–14 (NY)
1975—Chargers, 24–16 (SD)
(Points—Chargers 636, Jets 410)
Jets known as Titans prior to 1963
***Franchise in Los Angeles (LA) prior to 1961*
N. Y. JETS vs. SAN FRANCISCO
49ers lead series, 2–0
1971—49ers, 24–21 (NY)
1976—49ers, 17–6 (SF)
(Points—49ers 41, Jets 27)
N. Y. JETS vs. SEATTLE
No games
N. Y. JETS vs. TAMPA BAY
Jets lead series, 1–0
1976—Jets, 34–0 (NY)
N. Y. JETS vs. WASHINGTON
Redskins lead series, 2–0
1972—Redskins, 35–17 (NY)
1976—Redskins, 37–16 (NY)
(Points—Redskins 72, Jets 33)

***N. Y. YANKS vs. *1950 BALTIMORE**
Yanks won series, 1–0;
See *Baltimore vs. *N. Y. Yanks
Extinct team
***N. Y. YANKS vs. CHICAGO**
Bears won series, 3–1;
See Chicago vs. *N. Y. Yanks
Extinct team
***N. Y. YANKS vs. DETROIT**
Lions won series, 2–1–1;
See Detroit vs. *N. Y. Yanks
Extinct team
***N. Y. YANKS vs. GREEN BAY**
Yanks won series, 3–1;
See Green Bay vs. *N. Y. Yanks
Extinct team
***N. Y. YANKS vs. LOS ANGELES**
Rams won series, 4–0;
See Los Angeles vs. *N. Y. Yanks
Extinct team
***N. Y. YANKS vs. N. Y. GIANTS**
Giants won series, 3–0;
See *N. Y. Yanks vs. N. Y. Giants
Extinct team
***N.Y. YANKS vs. SAN FRANCISCO**
Yanks won series, 2–1–1
1950—Yanks, 21–17
Yanks, 29–24
1951—49ers, 19–14
Tie, 10–10
(Points—Yanks 74, 49ers 70)
Extinct team

OAKLAND vs. ATLANTA
Series tied, 1–1;
See Atlanta vs. Oakland
OAKLAND vs. BALTIMORE
Series tied, 2–2;
See Baltimore vs. Oakland
OAKLAND vs. BUFFALO
Series tied, 10–10;
See Buffalo vs. Oakland
OAKLAND vs. CHICAGO
Raiders lead series, 2–0
See Chicago vs. Oakland
OAKLAND vs.CINCINNATI
Raiders lead series, 8–3;
See Cincinnati vs. Oakland
OAKLAND vs. CLEVELAND
Raiders lead series, 4–1;
See Cleveland vs. Oakland
OAKLAND vs. DALLAS
Raiders lead series, 1–0;
See Dallas vs. Oakland
OAKLAND vs. DENVER
Raiders lead series, 26–6–2;
See Denver vs. Oakland
OAKLAND vs. DETROIT
Series tied, 1–1;
See Detroit vs. Oakland
OAKLAND vs. GREEN BAY
Raiders lead series, 2–1;
See Green Bay vs. Oakland
OAKLAND vs. HOUSTON
Raiders lead series, 16–8;
See Houston vs. Oakland
OAKLAND vs. KANSAS CITY
Raiders lead series, 19–15–2;
See Kansas City vs. Oakland
OAKLAND vs. LOS ANGELES
Raiders lead series, 1–0;
See Los Angeles vs. Oakland
OAKLAND vs. MIAMI
Raiders lead series, 9–2–1;
See Miami vs. Oakland
OAKLAND vs. MINNESOTA
Vikings lead series, 1–0;
See Minnesota vs. Oakland
OAKLAND vs. NEW ENGLAND
Patriots lead series, 10–9–1;
See New England vs. Oakland
OAKLAND vs. NEW ORLEANS
Raiders lead series, 1–0–1;
See New Orleans vs. Oakland
OAKLAND vs. N.Y. GIANTS
Raiders lead series, 1–0;
See N.Y. Giants vs. Oakland
OAKLAND vs. N.Y. JETS
Raiders lead series, 10–9–2;
See N.Y. Jets vs. Oakland
OAKLAND vs. PHILADELPHIA
Raiders lead series, 2–0;
1971—Raiders, 34–10 (O)
1976—Raiders, 26–7 (P)
(Points—Raiders 60, Eagles 17)
OAKLAND vs. PITTSBURGH
Series tied, 5–5
1970—Raiders, 31–14 (O)
1972—Steelers, 34–28 (P)
*Steelers, 13–7 (P)
1973—Steelers, 17–9 (O)
*Raiders, 33–14 (O)
1974—Raiders, 17–0 (P)
**Steelers, 24–13 (O)
1975—**Steelers, 16–10 (P)
1976—Raiders, 31–28 (O)
**Raiders, 24–7 (O)
(Points—Raiders 203, Steelers 167)
AFC Divisional Playoff
***AFC Championship*
OAKLAND vs. ST. LOUIS
Raiders lead series, 1–0
1973—Raiders, 17–10 (StL)
OAKLAND vs. *SAN DIEGO
Raiders lead series, 21–11–2
1960—Chargers, 52-28 (LA)
Chargers, 41–17 (O)
1961—Chargers, 44–0 (SD)
Chargers, 41–10 (O)
1962—Chargers, 42–33 (O)
Chargers, 31–21 (SD)
1963—Raiders, 34–33 (SD)
Raiders, 41–27 (O)
1964—Chargers, 31–17 (O)
Raiders, 21–20 (SD)
1965—Chargers, 17–6 (O)
Chargers, 24–14 (SD)
1966—Chargers, 29–20 (O)
Raiders, 41–19 (SD)
1967—Raiders, 51–10 (O)
Raiders, 41–21 (SD)
1968—Chargers, 23–14 (O)
Raiders, 34–27 (SD)
1969—Raiders, 24–12 (SD)
Raiders, 21–16 (O)
1970—Tie, 27–27 (SD)
Raiders, 20–17 (O)
1971—Raiders, 34–0 (SD)
Raiders, 34–33 (O)
1972—Tie, 17–17 (O)
Raiders, 21–19 (SD)
1973—Raiders, 27–17 (O)
Raiders, 31–3 (SD)
1974—Raiders, 14–10 (SD)
Raiders, 17–10 (O)
1975—Raiders, 6–0 (SD)
Raiders, 25-0 (O)
1976—Raiders, 27–17 (SD)
Raiders, 24–0 (O)
(Points—Raiders 812, Chargers 730)
Franchise in Los Angeles (LA) prior to 1961
OAKLAND vs. SAN FRANCISCO
Series tied, 1–1
1970—49ers, 38–7 (O)
1974—Raiders, 35–24 (SF)
(Points—49ers 62, Raiders 42)
OAKLAND vs. SEATTLE
No games
OAKLAND vs. TAMPA BAY
Raiders lead series, 1–0
1976—Raiders, 49–16 (O)
OAKLAND vs. WASHINGTON
Raiders lead series, 2–0
1970—Raiders, 34–20 (O)
1975—Raiders, 26–23 (W) OT
(Points—Raiders 60, Redskins 43)

PHILADELPHIA vs. ATLANTA
Eagles lead series, 3–2–1
See Atlanta vs. Philadelphia
PHILADELPHIA vs. *BALTIMORE
Eagles won series, 1–0
See *Baltimore vs. Philadelphia
Extinct team
PHILADELPHIA vs. BALTIMORE
Colts lead series, 5–2;
See Baltimore vs. Philadelphia
PHILADELPHIA vs. *BOSTON YANKS
Eagles won series, 7–2
See *Boston Yanks vs. Philadelphia
Extinct team
PHILADELPHIA vs. *BROOKLYN DODGERS
Dodgers won series, 14–5–1
See *Brooklyn Dodgers vs. Philadelphia
Extinct team
PHILADELPHIA vs. BUFFALO
Bills lead series, 1–0;
See Buffalo vs. Philadelphia
PHILADELPHIA vs. CHICAGO
Bears lead series, 18–2–1;
See Chicago vs. Philadelphia
PHILADELPHIA vs. CINCINNATI
Bengals lead series, 2–0;
See Cincinnati vs. Philadelphia
PHILADELPHIA vs. *CINCINNATI REDS
Eagles won series, 2–1;
See *Cincinnati Reds vs. Philadelphia
Extinct team
PHILADELPHIA vs. CLEVELAND
Browns lead series, 28–10–1;
See Cleveland vs. Philadelphia
PHILADELPHIA vs. DALLAS
Cowboys lead series, 21–12;
See Dallas vs. Philadelphia
PHILADELPHIA vs. *DALLAS TEXANS
Eagles won series, 1–0;
See *Dallas Texans vs. Philadelphia
Extinct team
PHILADELPHIA vs. DENVER
Series tied, 1–1
See Denver vs. Philadelphia
PHILADELPHIA vs. DETROIT
Lions lead series, 11–9–1
See Detroit vs. Philadelphia
PHILADELPHIA vs. GREEN BAY
Packers lead series, 18–3;
See Green Bay vs. Philadelphia
PHILADELPHIA vs. HOUSTON
Eagles lead series, 1–0;
See Houston vs. Philadelphia
PHILADELPHIA vs. KANSAS CITY
Eagles lead series, 1–0;
See Kansas City vs. Philadelphia
PHILADELPHIA vs. LOS ANGELES
Rams lead series, 12–8–1
See Los Angeles vs. Philadelphia
PHILADELPHIA vs. MIAMI
Series tied, 1–1;
See Miami vs. Philadelphia
PHILADELPHIA vs. MINNESOTA
Vikings lead series, 6–0;
See Minnesota vs. Philadelphia
PHILADELPHIA vs. NEW ENGLAND
Eagles lead series, 1–0;
See New England vs. Philadelphia
PHILADELPHIA vs. NEW ORLEANS
Saints lead series, 4–3;
See New Orleans vs. Philadelphia
PHILADELPHIA vs. *N.Y. BULLDOGS
Eagles won series, 2–0;
See N.Y. Bulldogs vs. Philadelphia
Extinct team
PHILADELPHIA vs. N.Y. GIANTS
Giants lead series, 49–35–2;
See N.Y. Giants vs. Philadelphia
PHILADELPHIA vs. N.Y. JETS
Eagles lead series, 1–0;
See N.Y. Jets vs. Philadelphia
PHILADELPHIA vs. OAKLAND
Raiders lead series, 2–0;
See Oakland vs. Philadelphia
PHILADELPHIA vs. PITTSBURGH
Eagles lead series, 41–25–3
1933—Eagles, 25–6 (Phila)
1934—Eagles, 17–0 (Pitt)
Steelers, 9–7 (Phila)
1935—Steelers, 17–7 (Phila)
Eagles, 17–6 (Pitt)
1936—Steelers, 17–0 (Pitt)
Steelers, 6–0 (Phila)
1937—Steelers, 27–14 (Pitt)
Steelers, 16–7 (Pitt)
1938—Eagles, 27–7 (Buffalo)
Eagles, 14–7 (Charleston, W. Va)
1939—Eagles, 17–14 (Phila)
Steelers, 24–12 (Pitt)
1940—Steelers, 7–3 (Pitt)
Eagles, 7–0 (Phila)
1941—Eagles, 10–7 (Pitt)
Tie, 7–7 (Phila)
1942—Eagles, 24–14 (Pitt)
Steelers, 14–0 (Phila)
1945—Eagles, 45–3 (Pitt)
Eagles, 30–6 (Phila)
1946—Steelers, 10–7 (Pitt)
Eagles, 10–7 (Phila)
1947—Steelers, 35–24 (Pitt)
Eagles, 21–0 (Phila)
*Eagles, 21–0 (Pitt)
1948—Eagles, 34–7 (Pitt)
Eagles, 17–0 (Phila)
1949—Eagles, 38–7 (Pitt)
Eagles, 34–17 (Phila)
1950—Eagles, 17–10 (Pitt)
Steelers, 9–7 (Phila)
1951—Eagles, 34–13 (Pitt)
Steelers, 17–13 (Phila)
1952—Eagles, 31–25 (Pitt)
Eagles, 26–21 (Phila)
1953—Eagles, 23–17 (Phila)
Eagles, 35–7 (Pitt)
1954—Eagles, 24–22 (Phila)
Steelers, 17–7 (Pitt)
1955—Steelers, 13–7 (Pitt)
Eagles, 24–0 (Phila)
1956—Eagles, 35–21 (Pitt)
Eagles, 14–7 (Phila)
1957—Steelers, 6–0 (Pitt)
Eagles, 7–6 (Phila)
1958—Steelers, 24–3 (Pitt)
Steelers, 31–24 (Phila)
1959—Eagles, 28–24 (Phila)
Steelers, 31–0 (Pitt)
1960—Eagles, 34–7 (Phila)
Steelers, 27–21 (Pitt)
1961—Eagles, 21–16 (Phila)
Eagles, 35–24 (Pitt)
1962—Steelers, 13–7 (Pitt)
Steelers, 26–17 (Phila)
1963—Tie, 21–21 (Phila)
Tie, 20–20 (Pitt)
1964—Eagles, 21–7 (Phila)
Eagles, 34–10 (Pitt)
1965—Steelers, 20–14 (Phila)
Eagles, 47–13 (Pitt)
1966—Eagles, 31–14 (Pitt)
Eagles, 27–23 (Phila)
1967—Eagles, 34–24 (Phila)
1968—Steelers, 6–3 (Pitt)
1969—Eagles, 41–27 (Phila)
1970—Eagles, 30–20 (Phila)
1974—Steelers, 27–0 (Pitt)
(Points—Eagles 1,313, Steelers 953)
Conference Playoff
PHILADELPHIA vs. *ST. LOUIS
Cardinals lead series, 31–27–4
1935—Cardinals, 12–3 (C)
1936—Cardinals, 13–0 (C)
1937—Tie, 6–6 (P)
1938—Eagles, 7–0 (C)
1941—Eagles, 21–14 (P)
1943—Eagles, 34–13 (Pitt)
1945—Eagles, 21–6 (P)
1947—Cardinals, 45–21 (P)
**Cardinals, 28–21 (C)
1948—Cardinals, 21–14 (C)
**Eagles, 7–0 (P)
1949—Eagles, 28–3 (P)
1950—Eagles, 45–7 (C)
Cardinals, 14–10 (P)
1951—Eagles, 17–14 (C)
1952—Eagles, 10–7 (P)
Cardinals, 28–22 (C)
1953—Eagles, 56–17 (C)
Eagles, 38–0 (P)
1954—Eagles, 35–16 (C)
Eagles, 30–14 (P)
1955—Tie, 24–24 (C)
Eagles, 27–3 (P)
1956—Cardinals, 20–6 (P)
Cardinals, 28–17 (C)
1957—Eagles, 38–21 (C)
Cardinals, 31–27 (P)
1958—Tie, 21–21 (C)
Eagles, 49–21 (P)
1959—Eagles, 28–24 (Minn)
Eagles, 27–17 (P)
1960—Eagles, 31–27 (P)
Eagles, 20–6 (StL)
1961—Cardinals, 30–27 (P)
Eagles, 20–7 (StL)
1962—Cardinals, 27–21 (P)
Cardinals,. 45–35 (StL)
1963—Cardinals, 28–24 (P)
Cardinals, 38–14 (StL)
1964—Cardinals, 38–13 (P)
Cardinals, 36–34 (StL)
1965—Eagles, 34–27 (P)
Eagles, 28–24 (StL)
1966—Cardinals, 16–13 (StL)
Cardinals, 41–10 (P)
1967—Cardinals, 48–14 (StL)
1968—Cardinals, 45–17 (P)
1969—Eagles, 34–30 (StL)
1970—Cardinals, 35–20 (P)

Cardinals, 23-14 (StL)
1971—Eagles, 37-20 (StL)
Eagles, 19-7 (P)
1972—Tie, 6-6 (P)
Cardinals, 24-23 (StL)
1973—Cardinals, 34-23 (P)
Eagles, 27-24 (StL)
1974—Cardinals, 7-3 (StL)
Cardinals, 13-3 (P)
1975—Cardinals, 31-20 (StL)
Cardinals, 24-23 (P)
1976—Cardinals, 33-14 (P)
Cardinals, 17-14 (StL)
(Points—Eagles 1,345, Cardinals 1,299)
Franchise in Chicago prior 1960
**NFL Championship*

PHILADELPHIA vs. SAN DIEGO
Eagles lead series 1-0
1974—Eagles, 13-7 (SD)

PHILADELPHIA vs. SAN FRANCISCO
49ers lead series, 8-3-1
1951—Eagles, 21-14 (P)
1953—49ers, 31-21 (SF)
1956—Tie, 10-10 (P)
1958—49ers, 30-24 (P)
1959—49ers, 24-14 (SF)
1964—49ers, 28-24 (P)
1966—Eagles, 35-34 (SF)
1967—49ers, 28-27 (P)
1969—49ers, 14-13 (SF)
1971—49ers, 31-3 (P)
1973—49ers, 38-28 (SF)
1975—Eagles, 27-17 (P)
(Points—49ers 299, Eagles 247)

PHILADELPHIA vs. SEATTLE
Eagles lead series, 1-0
1976—Eagles, 27-10 (P)

PHILADELPHIA vs. TAMPA BAY
No games

PHILADELPHIA vs. *WASHINGTON
Redskins lead series, 46-33-6
1937—Eagles, 14-0 (W)
Redskins, 10-7 (P)
1938—Redskins, 26-23 (P)
Redskins, 20-14 (W)
1939—Redskins, 7-0 (P)
Redskins, 7-6 (W)
1940—Redskins, 34-17 (P)
Redskins, 13-6 (W)
1941—Redskins, 21-17 (P)
Redskins, 20-14 (W)
1942—Redskins, 14-10 (P)
Redskins, 30-27 (W)
1943—Tie, 14-14 (P)
Eagles, 27-14 (W)
1944—Tie, 31-31 (P)
Eagles, 37-7 (W)
1945—Redskins, 24-14 (W)
Eagles, 16-0 (P)
1946—Eagles, 28-24 (W)
Redskins, 27-10 (P)
1947—Eagles, 45-42 (P)
Eagles, 38-14 (W)
1948—Eagles, 45-0 (W)
Eagles, 42-21 (P)
1949—Eagles, 49-14 (P)
Eagles, 44-21 (W)
1950—Eagles, 35-3 (P)
Eagles, 33-0 (W)
1951—Redskins, 27-23 (P)
Eagles, 35-21 (W)
1952—Eagles, 38-20 (P)
Redskins, 27-21 (W)
1953—Tie, 21-21 (P)
Redskins, 10-0 (W)
1954—Eagles, 49-21 (W)
Eagles, 41-33 (P)
1955—Redskins, 31-30 (P)
Redskins, 34-21 (W)
1956—Eagles, 13-9 (P)
Redskins, 19-17 (W)
1957—Eagles, 21-12 (P)
Redskins, 42-7 (W)
1958—Redskins, 24-14 (P)
Redskins, 20-0 (W)
1959—Eagles, 30-23 (P)
Eagles, 34-14 (W)
1960—Eagles, 19-13 (P)
Eagles, 38-28 (W)
1961—Eagles, 14-7 (P)
Eagles, 27-24 (W)
1962—Redskins, 27-21 (P)
Eagles, 37-14 (W)
1963—Eagles, 37-24 (W)
Redskins, 13-10 (P)
1964—Redskins, 35-20 (W)
Redskins, 21-10 (P)
1965—Redskins, 23-21 (W)
Eagles, 21-14 (P)
1966—Redskins, 27-13 (p)
Eagles, 37-28 (W)
1967—Eagles, 35-24 (P)
Tie, 35-35 (W)
1968—Redskins, 17-14 (W)
Redskins, 16-10 (P)
1969—Tie, 28-28 (W)
Redskins, 34-29 (P)
1970—Redskins, 33-21 (P)
Redskins, 24-6 (W)
1971—Tie, 7-7 (W)
Redskins, 20-13 (P)
1972—Redskins, 14-0 (W)
Redskins, 23-7 (P)
1973—Redskins, 28-7 (P)
Redskins, 38-20 (W)
1974—Redskins, 27-20 (P)
Redskins, 26-7 (W)
1975—Eagles, 26-10 (P)
Eagles, 26-3 (W)
1976—Redskins, 20-17 (P) OT
Redskins, 24-0 (W)
(Points—Eagles 1,755, Redskins 1,684)
Franchise in Boston prior to 1937

PITTSBURGH vs. ATLANTA
Steelers lead series 3-1;
See Atlanta vs. Pittsburgh

PITTSBURGH vs *1950 BALTIMORE
Steelers won series, 1-0
See *1950 Baltimore vs. Pittsburgh
Extinct team

PITTSBURGH vs. BALTIMORE
Steelers lead series, 3-2;
See Baltimore vs. Pittsburgh

PITTSBURGH vs. *BOSTON YANKS
Steelers won series, 5-3
See *Boston Yanks vs. Pittsburgh
Extinct team

PITTSBURGH vs. *BROOKLYN DODGERS
Dodgers won series, 11-8-1;
See *Brooklyn Dodgers vs. Pittsburgh
Extinct team

PITTSBURGH vs. BUFFALO
Steelers lead series, 3-1;
See Buffalo vs. Pittsburgh

PITTSBURGH vs. CHICAGO
Bears lead series, 16-3-1;
See Chicago vs. Pittsburgh

PITTSBURGH vs. CINCINNATI
Steelers lead series, 10-4;
See Cincinnati vs. Pittsburgh

PITTSBURGH vs. *CINCINNATI REDS
Steelers won series, 2-0-1;
See *Cincinnati Reds vs. Pittsburgh
Extinct team

PITTSBURGH vs. CLEVELAND
Browns lead series 36-18;
See Cleveland vs. Pittsburgh

PITTSBURGH vs. DALLAS
Cowboys lead series, 10-8;
See Dallas vs. Pittsburgh

PITTSBURGH vs. DENVER
Broncos lead series, 3-1-1;
See Denver vs. Pittsburgh

PITTSBURGH vs. DETROIT
Lions lead series, 15-9-1;
See Detroit vs. Pittsburgh

PITTSBURGH vs. GREEN BAY
Packers lead series, 19-8;
See Green Bay vs. Pittsburgh

PITTSBURGH vs. HOUSTON
Steelers lead series 11-3;
See Houston vs. Pittsburgh

PITTSBURGH vs. KANSAS CITY
Steelers lead series, 4-2;
See Kansas City vs. Pittsburgh

PITTSBURGH vs. LOS ANGELES
Rams lead series 11-1-2;
See Los Angeles vs. Pittsburgh

PITTSBURGH vs. MIAMI
Dolphins lead series 3-1;
See Miami vs. Pittsburgh

PITTSBURGH vs. MINNESOTA
Vikings lead series, 4-3;
See Minnesota vs. Pittsburgh

PITTSBURGH vs. NEW ENGLAND
Steelers lead series, 2-1;
See New England vs. Pittsburgh

PITTSBURGH vs. NEW ORLEANS
Saints lead series, 3-2;
See New Orleans vs. Pittsburgh

PITTSBURGH vs. *N.Y. BULLDOGS
Steelers won series, 2-0;
See *N.Y. Bulldogs vs. Pittsburgh
Extinct team

PITTSBURGH vs. N.Y. GIANTS
Giants lead series, 42-27-3;
See N.Y. Giants vs. Pittsburgh

PITTSBURGH vs. N.Y. JETS
Steelers lead series, 3-0;
See N.Y. Jets vs. Pittsburgh

PITTSBURGH vs. OAKLAND
Steelers lead series, 5-4
See Oakland vs. Pittsburgh

PITTSBURGH vs. PHILADELPHIA
Eagles lead series, 41-25-3;
See Philadelphia vs. Pittsburgh

PITTSBURGH vs. *ST. LOUIS
Steelers lead series, 28-20-3
1933—Steelers, 14-13 (C)
1935—Steelers, 17-13 (P)
1936—Cardinals, 14-6 (C)
1937—Cardinals, 13-7 (P)
1939—Cardinals, 10-0 (P)
1940—Tie, 7-7 (P)
1942—Steelers, 19-3 (P)
1943—Steelers, 34-13 (P)
1945—Steelers, 23-0 (P)
1946—Steelers, 14-7 (P)
1948—Cardinals 24-7 (P)
1950—Steelers, 28-17 (C)
Steelers, 28-7 (P)
1951—Steelers, 28-14 (C)
1952—Steelers, 34-28 (C)
Steelers, 17-14 (P)
1953—Steelers, 31-28 (P)
Steelers, 21-17 (C)
1954—Cardinals 17-14 (C)
Steelers, 20-17 (P)
1955—Steelers, 14-7 (P)
Cardinals 27-13 (C)
1956—Steelers, 14-7 (P)
Cardinals, 38-27 (C)
1957—Steelers, 29-20 (P)
Steelers, 27-2 (C)
1958—Steelers, 27-20 (C)
Steelers, 38-21 (P)
1959—Cardinals, 45-24 (C)
Steelers, 35-20 (P)
1960—Steelers, 27-14 (P)
Cardinals, 38-7 (Stl)
1961—Steelers, 30-27 (P)
Cardinals, 20-0 (StL)
1962—Steelers, 26-17 (StL)
Steelers, 19-7 (P)
1963—Steelers, 23-10 (P)
Cardinals, 24-23 (StL)
1964—Cardinals, 34-30 (StL)
Cardinals, 21-20 (P)
1965—Cardinals, 20-7 (P)
Cardinals, 21-17 (P)
1966—Steelers, 30-9 (P)
Cardinals, 6-3 (StL)
1967—Cardinals, 28-14 (P)
Tie, 14-14 (StL)
1968—Tie, 28-28 (StL)
Cardinals, 20-10 (P)
1969—Cardinals, 27-14 (P)
Cardinals, 47-10 (StL)
1972—Steelers, 25-19 (StL)
1976—Steelers, 23-0 (P)
(Points—Steelers 994, Cardinals 934)
Franchise in Chicago (C) prior to 1960

PITTSBURGH vs. *ST. LOUIS GUNNERS
Gunners won series, 1-0
1934—Gunners, 6-0
Extinct team

PITTSBURGH vs. SAN DIEGO
Steelers lead series, 5-0
1991—Steelers, 21-17 (P)
1972—Steelers, 24-2 (SD)
1973—Steelers, 38-21 (P)
1975—Steelers, 37-0 (SD)
1976—Steelers, 23-0 (P)
(Points—Steelers 143, Chargers 40)

PITTSBURGH vs. SAN FRANCISCO
49ers lead series, 5-3
1951—49ers, 28-24 (P)
1952—Steelers, 24-7 (SF)
1954—49ers, 31-3 (SF)
1958—49ers, 23-20 (SF)
1961—Steelers, 20-10 (P)
1965—49ers, 27-17 (SF)
1968—49ers, 45-28 (P)
1973—Steelers, 37-14 (SF)
(Points—49ers 185, Steelers 173)

PITTSBURGH vs. SEATTLE
No games

PITTSBURGH vs. TAMPA BAY
Steelers lead series, 1-0
1976—Steelers, 42-0 (P)

PITTSBURGH vs. *WASHINGTON
Redskins lead series, 40-27-4
1933—Redskins, 21-6
Steelers, 16-14
1934—Redskins, 7-0
Redskins, 39-0
1935—Steelers, 6-0
Redskins, 13-3
1936—Steelers, 10-0
Redskins, 30-0
1937—Redskins, 34-20 (W)
Steelers, 21-13 (P)
1938—Redskins, 7-0 (P)
Redskins, 15-0 (W)
1939—Redskins, 44-14 (W)
Redskins, 21-14 (P)
1940—Redskins, 40-10 (P)
Redskins, 37-10 (W)
1941—Redskins, 24-20 (P)
Redskins, 23-3 (W)
1942—Redskins, 28-14 (W)
Redskins, 14-0 (P)
1943—Tie, 14-14 (P)
Steelers, 27-14 (W)
1944—Redskins, 42-20 (W)
1945—Redskins, 14-0 (P)
Redskins, 24-0 (W)
1946—Tie, 14-14 (W)
Steelers, 14-7 (P)
1947—Redskins, 27-26 (W)
Steelers, 21-14 (P)
1948—Redskins, 17-14 (W)
Steelers, 10-7 (P)
1949—Redskins, 27-14 (P)
Redskins, 27-14 (W)
1950—Steelers, 26-7 (W)
Redskins, 24-7 (P)
Steelers, 20-10 (W)
1952—Redskins, 28-24 (P)
Steelers, 24-23 (W)
1953—Redskins, 17-9 (P)
Steelers, 14-13 (W)
1954—Steelers, 37-7 (P)
Redskins, 37-7 (P)
Redskins, 17-14 (W)
1955—Redskins, 23-14 (P)
Redskins, 28-17 (W)
1956—Steelers, 30-13 (P)
Steelers, 23-0 (W)
1957—Steelers, 28-7 (P)
Redskins, 10-3 (W)
1958—Steelers, 24-16 (P)
Tie, 14-14 (W)
1959—Redskins, 23-17 (P)
Steelers, 27-6 (W)
1960—Tie, 27-27 (W)
Steelers, 22-10 (P)
1961—Steelers, 20-0 (P)
Steelers, 30-14 (P)
1962—Steelers, 23-21 (P)
Steelers, 27-24 (W)
1963—Steelers, 38-27 (P)
Steelers, 34-28 (W)
1964—Redskins, 30-0 (P)
Steelers, 14-7 (W)
1965—Redskins, 31-3 (P)
Redskins, 35-14 (W)
1966—Redskins, 33-27 (P)
Redskins, 24-10 (W)
1967—Redskins, 15-10 (P)
1968—Redskins, 16-13 (W)
1969—Redskins, 14-7 (P)
1973—Steelers, 21-16 (P)
(Points—Redskins 1,352, Steelers 1,074)
Franchise in Boston prior to 1937

ST. LOUIS vs. ATLANTA
Cardinals lead series, 4-1;
See Atlanta vs. St. Louis

ST. LOUIS vs. *BALTIMORE
Cardinals won series, 1-0
See *Baltimore vs. Chicago Cardinals
Extinct team

ST. LOUIS vs. BALTIMORE
Colts lead series, 3-2;
See Baltimore vs. St. Louis

ST. LOUIS vs. *BOSTON YANKS
Cardinals won series, 3-0;
See *Boston Yanks vs. Chicago Cardinals
Extinct team

ST. LOUIS vs. *BROOKLYN DODGERS
Dodgers won series, 7-4;
See *Brooklyn Dodgers vs. Chicago Cardinals
Extinct team

ST. LOUIS vs BUFFALO
Series tied, 1-1;
See Buffalo vs. St. Louis

ST. LOUIS vs. CHICAGO
Bears lead series, 50-22-6;
See Chicago vs. St. Louis

ST. LOUIS vs. CINCINNATI
Bengals lead series, 1-0;
See Cincinnati vs. St. Louis

ST. LOUIS vs. *CINCINNATI REDS
Cardinals won series, 3-1;
See *Cincinnati Reds vs. Chicago Cardinals
Extinct team

ST. LOUIS vs. CLEVELAND
Browns lead series, 29-9-3;
See Cleveland vs. St. Louis

ST. LOUIS vs. DALLAS
Cowboys lead series, 16-13-1;
See Dallas vs. St. Louis

ST. LOUIS vs. DENVER
Series tied, 0-0-1;
See Denver vs. St. Louis

ST. LOUIS vs. DETROIT
Lions lead series, 25-11-3;
See Detroit vs. St. Louis

ST. LOUIS vs. GREEN BAY
Packers lead series 38-21-4
See Green Bay vs. St. Louis

ST. LOUIS vs. HOUSTON
Cardinals lead series, 2-0;
See Houston vs. St. Louis

ST. LOUIS vs. KANSAS CITY
Chief lead series, 1-0-1;
See Kansas City vs. St. Louis

ST. LOUIS vs. LOS ANGELES
Rams lead series, 16-15-2
See Los Angeles vs. St. Louis

ST. LOUIS vs. MIAMI
Dolphins lead series, 1-0;
See Miami vs. St. Louis

ST. LOUIS vs. MINNESOTA
Series tied, 3-3;
See Minnesota vs. St. Louis

ST. LOUIS vs. NEW ENGLAND
Cardinals lead series, 2-0;
See New England vs. St. Louis

ST. LOUIS vs. NEW ORLEANS
Cardinals lead series, 4-2;
See New Orleans vs. St. Louis

ST. LOUIS vs. *N.Y. BULLDOGS
Cardinals won series, 1-0
See *N.Y. Bulldogs vs. St. Louis
Extinct team

ST. LOUIS vs. N.Y. GIANTS
Giants lead series, 46-23-1;
See N.Y. Giants vs. St. Louis

ST. LOUIS vs. N.Y. JETS
Cardinals lead series, 2-0;
See N.Y. Jets vs. St. Louis

ST. LOUIS vs. OAKLAND
Raiders lead series, 1-0;
See Oakland vs. St. Louis

ST. LOUIS vs. PHILADELPHIA
Cardinals lead series, 31-27-4;
See Philadelphia vs. St. Louis

ST. LOUIS vs. PITTSBURGH
Steelers lead series, 28-20-3;
See Pittsburgh vs. St. Louis

ST. LOUIS vs. SAN DIEGO
Chargers lead series, 2-0;
1971—Chargers, 20-17 (SD)
1976—Chargers, 43-24 (SD)
(Points—Chargers 63, Cardinals 41)

***ST. LOUIS vs. SAN FRANCISCO**
Cardinals lead series, 4-3
1951—Cardinals, 27-21 (SF)
1957—Cardinals, 20-10 (SF)
1962—49ers, 24-17 (StL)
1964—Cardinals, 23-13 (SF)
1968—49ers, 35-17 (SF)
1971—49ers, 26-14 (StL)
1974—Cardinals, 34-9 (SF)
(Points—Cardinals 152, 49ers 138)
Team in Chicago prior to 1960

ST. LOUIS vs. SEATTLE
Cardinals lead series, 1-0
1976—Cardinals, 30-24 (S)

ST. LOUIS vs. TAMPA BAY
No games

*ST. LOUIS vs. WASHINGTON
Redskins lead series, 35–29–2
1932—Cardinals, 9–0
　　　Redskins, 8–6
1933—Redskins, 10–0
　　　Tie, 0–0
1934—Redskins, 9–0
1935—Cardinals, 6–0
1936—Redskins, 13–10
1937—Cardinals, 21–14 (W)
1939—Redskins, 28–7 (W)
1940—Redskins, 28–21 (W)
1942—Redskins, 28–0 (W)
1943—Redskins, 13–7 (W)
1944—Redskins, 42–20 (W)
1945—Redskins, 24–21 (W)
1947—Redskins, 45–21 (W)
1949—Cardinals, 38–7 (C)
1950—Cardinals, 38–28 (W)
1951—Redskins, 7–3 (C)
　　　Redskins, 20–17 (W)
1952—Cardinals, 23–7 (C)
　　　Cardinals, 17–6 (W)
1953—Redskins, 24–13 (C)
　　　Redskins, 28–17 (W)
1954—Cardinals, 38–16 (C)
　　　Redskins, 37–20 (W)
1955—Cardinals, 24–10 (W)
　　　Redskins, 31–0 (C)
1956—Cardinals, 31–3 (W)
　　　Redskins, 17–14 (C)
1957—Redskins, 37–14 (C)
　　　Cardinals, 44–14 (W)
1958—Cardinals, 37–10 (C)
　　　Redskins, 45–31 (W)
1959—Cardinals, 49–21 (C)
　　　Redskins, 23–14 (W)
1960—Cardinals, 44–7 (StL)
　　　Cardinals, 26–14 (W)
1961—Cardinals, 24–0 (W)
　　　Cardinals, 38–24 (StL)
1962—Redskins, 24–14 (W)
　　　Tie, 17–17 (StL)
1963—Cardinals, 21–7 (W)
　　　Cardinals, 24–20 (StL)
1964—Cardinals, 23–17 (W)
　　　Cardinals, 38–24 (StL)
1965—Cardinals, 37–16 (W)
　　　Redskins, 24–20 (StL)
1966—Cardinals, 23–7 (StL)
　　　Redskins, 26–20 (W)
1967—Cardinals, 27–21 (W)
1968—Cardinals, 41–14 (StL)
1969—Redskins, 33–17 (W)
1970—Cardinals, 27–17 (StL)
　　　Cardinals, 28–27 (W)
1971—Redskins, 24–17 (StL)
　　　Redskins, 20–0 (W)
1972—Redskins, 24–10 (W)
　　　Redskins, 33–3 (StL)
1973—Cardinals, 34–27 (StL)
　　　Redskins, 31–13 (W)
1974—Cardinals, 17–10 (W)
　　　Cardinals, 23–20 (StL)
1975—Redskins, 27–17 (W)
　　　Cardinals, 20–17 (StL) OT
1976—Redskins, 20–10 (W)
　　　Redskins, 16–10 (StL)
(Points—Cardinals 1,297, Redskins
1,278)
　*Team in Chicago (C) prior to 1960
**Team in Boston prior to 1937

***ST. LOUIS GUNNERS vs.
DETROIT**
Lions won series, 1–0
See Detroit vs. *St. Louis Gunners
*Extinct team
***ST. LOUIS GUNNERS vs. GREEN
BAY**
Packers won series, 1–0;
See Green Bay vs. *St. Louis
Gunners
*Extinct team
***ST. LOUIS GUNNERS vs.
PITTSBURGH**
Gunners won series, 1–0;
See Pittsburgh vs. *St. Louis
Gunners
*Extinct team

SAN DIEGO vs. ATLANTA
Falcons lead series, 1–0;
See Atlanta vs. San Diego
SAN DIEGO vs. BALTIMORE
Colts lead series, 2–1;
See Baltimore vs. San Diego
SAN DIEGO vs. BUFFALO
Chargers lead series, 13–7–2;

See Buffalo vs. San Diego
SAN DIEGO vs. CHICAGO
Chargers lead series, 2–0;
See Chicago vs. San Diego
SAN DIEGO vs. CINCINNATI
Bengals lead series, 5–4;
See Cincinnati vs. San Diego
SAN DIEGO vs. CLEVELAND
Series tied, 2–2–1;
See Cleveland vs. San Diego
SAN DIEGO vs. DALLAS
Cowboys lead series, 1–0;
See Dallas vs. San Diego
SAN DIEGO vs. DENVER
Chargers lead series, 19–14–1;
See Denver vs. San Diego
SAN DIEGO vs. DETROIT
Lions lead series, 1–0;
See Detroit vs. San Diego
SAN DIEGO vs. GREEN BAY
Packers lead series, 2–0;
See Green Bay vs. San Diego
SAN DIEGO vs. HOUSTON
Chargers lead series, 14–10–1;
See Houston vs. San Diego
SAN DIEGO vs. KANSAS CITY
Chiefs lead series, 18–15–1;
See Kansas City vs. San Diego
SAN DIEGO vs. LOS ANGELES
Rams lead series, 2–0;
See Los Angeles vs. San Diego
SAN DIEGO vs. MIAMI
Chargers lead series, 4–3;
See Miami vs. San Diego
SAN DIEGO vs. MINNESOTA
Series tied, 1–1;
See Minnesota vs. San Diego
SAN DIEGO vs. NEW ENGLAND
Chargers lead series, 12–9–2;
See New England vs. San Diego
SAN DIEGO vs. NEW ORLEANS
Chargers lead series, 2–0;
See New Orleans vs. San Diego
SAN DIEGO vs. N.Y. GIANTS
Giants lead series, 2–0;
See N.Y. Giants vs. San Diego
SAN DIEGO vs. N.Y. JETS
Chargers lead series, 14–6–1;
See N.Y. Jets vs. San Diego
SAN DIEGO vs. OAKLAND
Raiders lead series, 21–11–2;
See Oakland vs. San Diego
SAN DIEGO vs. PHILADELPHIA
Eagles lead series, 2–0;
See Philadelphia vs. San Diego
SAN DIEGO vs. PITTSBURGH
Steelers lead series, 5–0;
See Pittsburgh vs. San Diego
SAN DIEGO vs. ST. LOUIS
Chargers lead series, 2–0;
See St. Louis vs. San Diego
SAN DIEGO vs. SAN FRANCISCO
Series tied, 1–1;
1972—49ers, 34–3 (SF)
1976—Chargers, 13–7 (SD) OT
(Points—49ers 41, Chargers 16)
SAN DIEGO vs. SEATTLE
No games
SAN DIEGO vs. TAMPA BAY
Chargers lead series, 1–0;
1976—Chargers, 23–0 (TB)
SAN DIEGO vs. WASHINGTON
Redskins lead series, 1–0;
1973—Redskins, 38–0 (W)

SAN FRANCISCO vs. ATLANTA
49ers lead series, 13–7;
See Atlanta vs. San Francisco
**SAN FRANCISCO vs. *1950
BALTIMORE**
49ers won series, 1–0;
See *Baltimore vs. San Francisco
*Extinct team
**SAN FRANCISCO vs.
BALTIMORE**
Colts lead series, 21–14;
See Baltimore vs. San Francisco
SAN FRANCISCO vs. BUFFALO
Bills lead series, 1–0;
See Buffalo vs. San Francisco
SAN FRANCISCO vs. CHICAGO
49ers lead series, 21–20–1;
See Chicago vs. San Francisco
SAN FRANCISCO vs. CINCINNATI
Bengals lead series, 2–0;
See Cincinnati vs. San Francisco
**SAN FRANCISCO vs.
CLEVELAND**
Browns lead series, 6–3;

See Cleveland vs. San Francisco
SAN FRANCISCO vs. DALLAS
Cowboys lead series, 5–4–1;
See Dallas vs. San Francisco
**SAN FRANCISCO vs. *DALLAS
TEXANS**
49ers won series, 2–0;
See *Dallas Texans vs. San
Francisco
*Extinct team
SAN FRANCISCO vs. DENVER
49ers won series, 2–0;
See Denver vs. San Francisco
SAN FRANCISCO vs. DETROIT
Lions lead series, 22–20–1;
See Detroit vs. San Francisco
**SAN FRANCISCO vs. GREEN
BAY**
49ers lead series, 21–18–1;
See Green Bay vs. San Francisco
SAN FRANCISCO vs. HOUSTON
Series tied, 1–1;
See Houston vs. San Francisco
**SAN FRANCISCO vs. KANSAS
CITY**
Series tied, 1–1;
See Kansas City vs. San Francisco
**SAN FRANCISCO vs. LOS
ANGELES**
Rams lead series, 33–19–2;
See Los Angeles vs. San Francisco
SAN FRANCISCO vs. MIAMI
Dolphins lead series, 1–0;
See Miami vs. San Francisco
**SAN FRANCISCO vs.
MINNESOTA**
Series tied, 10–10–1;
See Minnesota vs. San Francisco
**SAN FRANCISCO vs. NEW
ENGLAND**
Series tied, 1–1;
See New England vs. San
Francisco
**SAN FRANCISCO vs. NEW
ORLEANS**
49ers lead series, 11–3–2;
See New Orleans vs. San Francisco
**SAN FRANCISCO vs. N.Y.
GIANTS**
Giants lead series, 6–2;
See N.Y. Giants vs. San Francisco
SAN FRANCISCO vs. N.Y. JETS
49ers lead series, 2–0;
See N.Y. Jets vs. San Francisco
**SAN FRANCISCO vs. *N.Y.
YANKS**
Yanks won series, 2–1–1;
See *N.Y. Yanks vs. San Francisco
*Extinct team
SAN FRANCISCO vs. OAKLAND
Series tied, 1–1;
See Oakland vs. San Francisco
**SAN FRANCISCO vs.
PHILADELPHIA**
49ers lead series, 8–3–1;
See Philadelphia vs. San Francisco
**SAN FRANCISCO vs.
PITTSBURGH**
49ers lead series, 5–3;
See Pittsburgh vs. San Francisco
SAN FRANCISCO vs. ST. LOUIS
Cardinals lead series, 4–3;
See St. Louis vs. San Francisco
SAN FRANCISCO vs. SAN DIEGO
Series tied, 1–1;
See San Diego vs. San Francisco
SAN FRANCISCO vs. SEATTLE
49ers lead series, 1–0;
1976—49ers, 37–21 (S)
SAN FRANCISCO vs. TAMPA BAY
No games
**SAN FRANCISCO vs.
WASHINGTON**
49ers lead series, 5–4–1;
1952—49ers, 23–17 (W)
1954—49ers, 41–7 (SF)
1955—Redskins, 7–0 (W)
1961—49ers, 35–3 (SF)
1967—Redskins, 31–28 (W)
1969—Tie, 17–17 (SF)
1970—49ers, 26–17 (SF)
1971—*49ers, 24–20 (SF)
1973—Redskins, 33–9 (W)
1976—Redskins, 24–21 (SF)
(Points—49ers 224, Redskins 176)
*NFC Divisional Playoff

SEATTLE vs. ATLANTA
Seahawks lead series, 1–0;

See Atlanta vs. Seattle
SEATTLE vs. BALTIMORE
No games
SEATTLE vs. BUFFALO
No games
SEATTLE vs. CHICAGO
Bears lead series, 1–0;
See Chicago vs. Seattle
SEATTLE vs. CINCINNATI
No games
SEATTLE vs. CLEVELAND
No games
SEATTLE vs. DALLAS
Cowboys lead series, 1–0;
See Dallas vs. Seattle
SEATTLE vs. DENVER
No games
SEATTLE vs. DETROIT
Lions lead series, 1–0;
See Detroit vs. Seattle
SEATTLE vs. GREEN BAY
Packers lead series, 1–0;
See Green Bay vs. Seattle
SEATTLE vs. HOUSTON
No games
SEATTLE vs. KANSAS CITY
No games
SEATTLE vs. LOS ANGELES
Rams lead series, 1–0;
See Los Angeles vs. Seattle
SEATTLE vs. MIAMI
No games
SEATTLE vs. MINNESOTA
Vikings lead series, 1–0;
See Minnesota vs. Seattle
SEATTLE vs. NEW ENGLAND
No games
SEATTLE vs. NEW ORLEANS
Saints lead series, 1–0;
See New Orleans vs. Seattle
SEATTLE vs. N.Y. GIANTS
Giants lead series, 1–0;
See N.Y. Giants vs. Seattle
SEATTLE vs. N.Y. JETS
No games
SEATTLE vs. OAKLAND
Raiders lead series, 1–0;
See Oakland vs. Seattle
SEATTLE vs. PHILADELPHIA
Eagles lead series, 1–0;
See Philadelphia vs. Seattle
SEATTLE vs. PITTSBURGH
No games
SEATTLE vs. ST. LOUIS
Cardinals lead series, 1–0;
See St. Louis vs. Seattle
SEATTLE vs. SAN DIEGO
No games
SEATTLE vs. SAN FRANCISCO
49ers lead series, 1–0;
See San Francisco vs. Seattle
SEATTLE vs. TAMPA BAY
Seahawks lead series, 1–0–1;
1976—Seahawks, 13–10 (T)
SEATTLE vs. WASHINGTON
Redskins lead series, 1–0;
1976—Redskins, 31–7 (W)

TAMPA BAY vs. ATLANTA
No games
TAMPA BAY vs. BALTIMORE
Colts lead series, 1–0;
See Baltimore vs. Tampa Bay
TAMPA BAY vs. BUFFALO
Bills lead series, 1–0;
See Buffalo vs. Tampa Bay
TAMPA BAY vs. CHICAGO
No games
TAMPA BAY vs. CINCINNATI
Bengals lead series, 1–0;
See Cincinnati vs. Tampa Bay
TAMPA BAY vs. CLEVELAND
Browns lead series, 1–0;
See Cleveland vs. Tampa Bay
TAMPA BAY vs. DALLAS
No games
TAMPA BAY vs. DENVER
Broncos lead series, 1–0;
See Denver vs. Tampa Bay
TAMPA BAY vs. DETROIT
No games
TAMPA BAY vs. GREEN BAY
No games
TAMPA BAY vs. HOUSTON
Oilers lead series, 1–0
See Houston vs. Tampa Bay
TAMPA BAY vs. KANSAS CITY
Chiefs lead series, 1–0
See Kansas City vs. Tampa Bay
TAMPA BAY vs. LOS ANGELES

No games
TAMPA BAY vs. MIAMI
Dolphins lead series, 1–0
See Miami vs. Tampa Bay
TAMPA BAY vs. MINNESOTA
No games
TAMPA BAY vs. NEW ENGLAND
Patriots lead series, 1–0;
See New England vs. Tampa Bay
TAMPA BAY vs. NEW ORLEANS
No games
TAMPA BAY vs. N.Y. GIANTS
No games
TAMPA BAY vs. N.Y. JETS
Jets lead series, 1–0;
See N.Y. Jets vs. Tampa Bay
TAMPA BAY vs. OAKLAND
Raiders lead series, 1–0;
See Oakland vs. Tampa Bay
TAMPA BAY vs. PHILADELPHIA
No games
TAMPA BAY vs. PITTSBURGH
Steelers lead series, 1–0;
See Pittsburgh vs. Tampa Bay
TAMPA BAY vs. ST. LOUIS
No games
TAMPA BAY vs. SAN DIEGO
Chargers lead series, 1–0;
See San Diego vs. Tampa Bay
TAMPA BAY vs. SAN FRANCISCO
No games
TAMPA BAY vs. SEATTLE
Seahawks lead series, 1–0–1;
See Seattle vs. Tampa Bay
TAMPA BAY vs. WASHINGTON
No games

WASHINGTON vs. ATLANTA
Redskins lead series, 4–0–1;
See Atlanta vs. Washington
**WASHINGTON vs. *1950
BALTIMORE**
Redskins won series, 2–0;
See *Baltimore vs. Washington
*Extinct team
WASHINGTON vs. BALTIMORE
Colts lead series, 13–4;
See Baltimore vs. Washington
**WASHINGTON vs. *BOSTON
YANKS**
Redskins won series, 8–2;
See *Boston Yanks vs. Washington
*Extinct team
**WASHINGTON vs. *BROOKLYN
DODGERS**
Redskins won series, 17–5–3;
See *Brooklyn Dodgers vs.
Washington
*Extinct team
WASHINGTON vs. BUFFALO
Bills lead series, 1–0;
See Buffalo vs. Washington
WASHINGTON vs. CHICAGO
Bears lead series, 16–10–1;
See Chicago vs. Washington
WASHINGTON vs. CINCINNATI
Series tied, 1–1;
See Cincinnati vs. Washington
WASHINGTON vs. CLEVELAND
Browns lead series, 31–6–1;
See Cleveland vs. Washington
WASHINGTON vs. DALLAS
Cowboys lead series, 18–14–2;
See Dallas vs. Washington
WASHINGTON vs. DENVER
Redskins lead series, 2–0;
See Denver vs. Washington
WASHINGTON vs. DETROIT
Redskins lead series, 12–8;
See Detroit vs. Washington
WASHINGTON vs. GREEN BAY
Packers lead series, 13–9–1;
See Green Bay vs. Washington
WASHINGTON vs. HOUSTON
Series tied, 1–1;
See Houston vs. Washington
WASHINGTON vs. KANSAS CITY
Chiefs lead series, 2–0;
See Kansas City vs. Washington
WASHINGTON vs. LOS ANGELES
Redskins lead seres, 10–5–1;
See Los Angeles vs. Washington
WASHINGTON vs. MIAMI
Series tied, 1–1;
See Miami vs. Washington
WASHINGTON vs. MINNESOTA
Vikings lead series, 3–2;
See Minnesota vs. Washington

WASHINGTON vs. NEW ENGLAND
Patriots lead series, 1–0;
See New England vs. Washington

WASHINGTON vs. NEW ORLEANS
Redskins lead series, 5–3;
See New Orleans vs. Washington

WASHINGTON vs. *N.Y. BULLDOGS
Redskins won series, 1–0–1;
See *N.Y. Bulldogs vs. Washington
*Extinct team

WASHINGTON vs. N.Y. GIANTS
Giants lead series 51–35–3;
See N.Y. Giants vs. Washington

WASHINGTON vs. N.Y. JETS
Redskins lead series, 2–0;
See N.Y. Jets vs. Washington

WASHINGTON vs. OAKLAND
Raiders lead series, 2–0;
See Oakland vs. Washington

WASHINGTON vs. PHILADELPHIA
Redskins lead series, 46–33–6;
See Philadelphia vs. Washington

WASHINGTON vs. PITTSBURGH
Redskins lead series, 35–24–4;
See Pittsburgh vs. Washington

WASHINGTON vs. ST. LOUIS
Redskins lead series, 35–29–2
See St. Louis vs. Washington

WASHINGTON vs. SAN DIEGO
Redskins lead series, 1–0;
See San Diego vs. Washington

WASHINGTON vs. SAN FRANCISCO
49ers lead series, 5–4–1;
See San Francisco vs. Washington

WASHINGTON vs. SEATTLE
Redskins lead series, 1–0;
See Seattle vs. Washington

WASHINGTON vs. TAMPA BAY
No games

ALL-TIME WINNING PERCENTAGE

Team	Years	Won	Lost	Tied	Pctg.
Detroit Wolverines, 1928	1	7	2	1	.750
Cleveland Browns, 1950–1976	27	229	118	9	.656
Canton Bulldogs/Cleveland Bulldogs, 1921–24	6	37	17	10	.656
Los Angeles Buccaneers, 1926	1	6	3	1	.650
Oakland Raiders, 1960–1976	17	148	79	11	.645
Buffalo All-Americans/Buffalo Bisons, 1921–24	4	23	13	6	.619
Decatur Staleys/Chicago Staleys/ Chicago Bears, 1920–1976	57	422	259	41	.613
Dallas Cowboys, 1960–1976	17	137	93	6	.593
Baltimore Colts, 1953–1976	24	186	128	6	.591
Frankford Yellowjackets, 1924–1931	8	69	46	14	.589
Rock Island, Ill., Independents, 1921–25	5	22	14	10	.587
Minnesota Vikings, 1960–1976	16	127	89	8	.585
Dallas Texans/Kansas City Chiefs, 1960–1976	17	134	94	10	.584
Detroit Panthers, 1925–26	2	12	8	4	.583
Green Bay Packers, 1921–1976	56	388	274	33	.582
Miami Dolphins, 1966–1976	11	88	63	3	.581
Pottsville, Pa., Maroons, 1925–28	4	27	20	1	.573
Providence Steamroller, 1925–1931	7	44	32	10	.570
New York Giants, 1925–1976	52	357	271	31	.565
Toledo Maroons, 1922–23	2	7	5	4	.562
Cleveland Rams/Los Angeles Rams, 1937–1942, 1944–1976	39	258	211	20	.548
Portsmouth Spartans/Detroit Lions, 1930–1976	47	293	258	32	.530
Cincinnati Bengals, 1968–1976	9	65	60	1	.520
Cleveland Bulldogs, 1925 and 1927	2	13	12	2	.519
Los Angeles Chargers/San Diego Chargers, 1960–1976	17	116	111	11	.511
Boston Braves/Boston Redskins/ Washington Redskins, 1932–1976	45	268	262	26	.505
Buffalo Rangers, 1926	1	4	4	2	.500
Boston Bulldogs, 1929	1	4	4	0	.500
San Francisco 49ers, 1950–1976	27	171	173	12	.497
Racine, Wis., Legion, 1922–24, 1926	4	14	15	6	.486
Orange, N.J., Tornadoes, 1929	1	3	4	4	.455
Kansas City Cowboys, 1924–26	3	12	15	2	.448
Duluth Kelleys/Duluth Eskimos, 1923–27	5	16	20	2	.447
New York Titans/New York Jets, 1960–1976	17	103	129	6	.445
Buffalo Bills, 1960–1976	17	101	129	8	.441
Chicago Cardinals/St. Louis Cardinals, 1920–1976	57	281	362	36	.440
Boston Patriots/New England Patriots, 1960–1976	17	100	129	9	.439
Houston Oilers, 1960–1976	17	101	131	6	.437
Cleveland Indians, 1921 and 1923	2	5	7	3	.433
Pittsburgh Pirates/Pittsburgh Steelers, 1933–1976	44	224	301	20	.429
Akron Pros/Akron Indians, 1921–26	6	17	24	8	.429
Philadelphia Eagles, 1933–1976	44	215	305	22	.417
New York Yanks, 1927–28	2	11	16	2	.414
Stapleton Stapes, 1929–1932	4	14	22	9	.411
Milwaukee Badgers, 1922–26	5	16	27	6	.388
Brooklyn Dodgers/Brooklyn Tigers, 1930–1944	15	60	100	9	.382
Denver Broncos, 1960–1976	17	82	147	9	.363
Atlanta Falcons, 1966–1976	11	50	100	4	.338
Hartford Blues, 1926	1	3	7	0	.300
St. Louis All-Stars, 1923	1	1	4	2	.286
New Orleans Saints, 1967–1976	10	36	99	5	.275
Brooklyn Lions, 1926	1	3	8	0	.273
Boston Yanks/New York Bulldogs/ New York Yanks/Dallas Texans, 1944–1952	9	24	73	6	.262
Dayton Triangles, 1921–29	9	13	49	6	.235
Columbus Panhandles/Columbus Tigers, 1921–26	6	10	36	1	.223
Hammond, Ind., Pros, 1921–26	5	4	18	3	.220
Cincinnati Reds/St. Louis Gunners, 1933–34	2	4	16	1	.214
Minneapolis Marines, 1922–24	3	3	14	2	.211
Cleveland Indians, 1931	1	2	8	0	.200
Detroit Heralds, 1921	1	1	7	1	.167
Oorang Indians, Marion, Ohio, 1922–23	2	3	16	0	.158
Buffalo Bisons, 1927, 1927, and 1929	3	2	18	3	.152
Seattle Seahawks, 1976	1	2	12	0	.143
Minneapolis Red Jackets, 1929–1930	2	2	16	1	.132
Newark Tornadoes, 1930	1	1	10	1	.125
Rochester Jeffersons, 1921–25	5	2	24	2	.107
Kenosha, Wis., Maroons, 1924	1	0	5	1	.100
Baltimore Colts, 1950	1	1	11	0	.090
Evansville Crimson Giants, 1922	1	0	2	0	.000
Louisville Colonels, 1926	1	0	4	0	.000
Louisville Brecks, 1922–23	2	0	6	0	.000
Cincinnati Celts, 1921	1	0	8	0	.000
Tampa Bay Buccaneers, 1976	14	0	14	0	.000

Chicago All-Star Games

1934

CHI. BEARS 0, ALL-STARS 0

The first Chicago All-Star game ended in a scoreless tie, punctuated by 12 punts by the Chicago Bears and 11 by the College All-Stars. The All-Stars outgained the Bears 143–123 and had six first downs to the Bears' three.

Chicago moved to the collegians' 9-yard line in the second quarter, but end Bill Hewitt fumbled on a reverse and Ed (Moose) Krause of Notre Dame recovered on the 19-yard line. The All-Stars' Bill Smith attempted a 41-yard field goal on the last play of the game, but it was blocked and recovered by Chicago's Carl Brumbaugh. Smith also missed a 32-yard attempt.

The game matched the 1933 champions of the National Football League and graduated college seniors who were selected in a poll conducted by the sponsoring *Chicago Tribune* and 105 associated newspapers throughout the United States. A crowd of 79,432 was in attendance.

August 31, at Soldier Field

Chi. Bears	Starting Lineups	College All-Stars
Bill Hewitt	LE	E. (Eggs) Manske (N'wstn.)
Roy (Link) Lyman	LT	Ed Krause (Notre Dame)
Jules Carlson	LG	Frank Walton (Pittsburgh)
Charles (Ookie) Miller	C	Chuck Bernard (Michigan)
Joe Zeller	RG	Bob Jones (Indiana)
George Musso	RT	A. Schwammel (Oregon St.)
Luke Johnsos	RE	Joe Skladany (Pittsburgh)
Carl Brumbaugh	QB	Homer Griffith (USC)
Gene Ronzani	LH	Beattie Feathers (Tenn.)
George Corbett	RH	Joe Laws (Iowa)
Bronko Nagurski	FB	Mike Mikulak (Oregon)

Head coaches—George Halas, Chi. Bears; Nobel Kizer (Purdue), College All-Stars

| Chi. Bears | 0 | 0 | 0 | 0 | — | 0 |
| College All-Stars | 0 | 0 | 0 | 0 | — | 0 |

Attendance—79,432

1935

CHI. BEARS 5, ALL-STARS 0

The Chicago Bears, runners-up to the New York Giants for the 1934 NFL championship, combined a field goal and a safety to defeat the College All-Stars in a game that was finished in a driving rainstorm.

The Bears' Jack Manders kicked a 27-yard field goal in the first quarter. All-Stars punter Bill Shepherd of Western Maryland fumbled a snap from center in the fourth quarter and recovered in the end zone, where he was downed for a safety.

The All-Stars had a first down on the Bears' 8-yard line in the fourth quarter, but gave up possession on downs without gaining a yard.

Chicago led 168–62 in total yardage and had nine first downs to five. The punting game dominated the contest. Each team punted 14 times, the Bears averaging 43.2 yards a kick, the All-Stars 37.1.

August 29, at Soldier Field

Chi. Bears	Starting Lineups	College All-Stars
Bill Hewitt	LE	Don Hutson (Alabama)
Art Buss	LT	Tony Blazine (Illinois)
Ray Richards	LG	Regis Monahan (Ohio State)
Ed Kawal	C	George Shotwell (Pitt.)
Joe Kopcha	RG	Billy Bevan (Minnesota)
George Musso	RT	Jim Barber (San Francisco)
Bill Karr	RE	Ray Fuqua (SMU)
Bernie Masterson	QB	Miller Munjas (Pittsburgh)
Beattie Feathers	LH	Bill Shepherd (W. Maryland)
John Sisk	RH	Al Nichelini (St. Mary's)
Jack Manders	FB	Stan Kostka (Minnesota)

Head coaches—George Halas, Chi. Bears; Frank Thomas (Alabama), College All-Stars

| Chi. Bears | 3 | 0 | 0 | 2 | — | 5 |
| College All-Stars | 0 | 0 | 0 | 0 | — | 0 |

Chi—FG Manders 27
Chi—Safety, Shepherd downed in end zone after fumbled center snap
Attendance—77,450

1936

DETROIT 7, ALL-STARS 7

Fullback Sheldon Beise and tailback Vernal (Babe) LeVoir, teammates on the University of Minnesota's 1934 national collegiate champion team, combined their efforts to score the first touchdown of the three-year-old series as the All-Stars battled the Detroit Lions, 1935 NFL champions, to a 7–7 tie.

On fourth down and eight yards for a first down on the Lions' 17-yard line in the second quarter, Beise faked a plunge into the line, then pitched the ball back to LeVoir, who cut over tackle behind good blocking and scored, ending a five-play, 61-yard drive.

Detroit's touchdown came with slightly more than two minutes remaining in the game. Ernie Caddel ran eight yards on fourth down and one.

The game was delayed 24 hours because of rain. The All-Stars led in total yardage 184–128 and had nine first downs to the Lions' six.

September 2, at Soldier Field

Detroit	Starting Lineups	All-Stars
Ed Klewicki	LE	Wayne Millner (Notre Dame)
John Johnson	LT	Dick Smith (Minnesota)
Frank Knox	LG	Paul Tangora (N'wstn.)
Clare Randolph	C	Gomer Jones (Ohio State)
Grover (Ox) Emerson	RG	Vernon Oech (Minnesota)
George Christensen	RT	Truman Spain (SMU)
John Schneller	RE	Keith Topping (Stanford)
Earl (Dutch) Clark	QB	Riley Smith (Alabama)
Ernie Caddel	LH	Jay Berwanger (Chicago)
Frank Christensen	RH	B. Shakespeare (N'tre D'me)
Raymond (Buddy) Parker	FB	Sheldon Beise (Minnesota)

Head coaches—George (Potsy) Clark, Detroit; Bernie Bierman (Minnesota), College All-Stars

| Detroit | 0 | 0 | 0 | 7 | — | 7 |
| College All-Stars | 0 | 7 | 0 | 0 | — | 7 |

All-Stars—LeVoir 17 run (Fromhart kick)
Det —Caddel 8 run (Clark dropkick)
Attendance—76,361

1937

ALL-STARS 6, GREEN BAY 0

Quarterback Sammy Baugh of Texas Christian University completed 7 of 13 passes for 115 yards and one touchdown and intercepted two passes as the College All-Stars defeated the Green Bay Packers 6–0.

After replacing Pittsburgh's Bobby LaRue on the second play of the game, Baugh teamed with Gaynell Tinsley on a first-quarter touchdown pass play that covered 47 yards. The All-Stars threatened three other times but two field goal attempts by Nebraska's Sam Francis and one by Minnesota's Bud Wilkinson failed.

Green Bay, which outgained the collegians 298–180 in total offense and led 17–8 in first downs, moved from its 24-yard line to the All-Stars' 3 in the fourth quarter. On fourth down, Arnie Herber passed in the flat to Don Hutson, who was tackled for no gain by Johnny Drake of Purdue. Herber completed 14 of 38 passes for 202 yards.

September 1, at Soldier Field

Green Bay	Starting Lineups	College All-Stars
Don Hutson	LE	Gaynell Tinsley (LSU)
Ernie Smith	LT	Ed Widseth (Minnesota)
Paul Engebretsen	LG	Max Starcevich (Wash.)
George Svendsen	C	Earl Svendsen (Minnesota)
Lon Evans	RG	Steve Reid (Northwestern)
Lou Gordon	RT	Averell Daniell (Pitt.)
Milt Gantenbein	RE	Merle Wendt (Ohio State)
Hank Bruder	QB	Vern Huffman (Indiana)
Paul Miller	LH	Bobby LaRue (Pittsburgh)
Arnie Herber	RH	Johnny Drake (Purdue)
Clarke Hinkle	FB	Sam Francis (Nebraska)

Head coaches—Earl (Curly) Lambeau, Green Bay; Charles (Gus) Dorais (Detroit), College All-Stars

| Green Bay | 0 | 0 | 0 | 0 | — | 0 |
| College All-Stars | 6 | 0 | 0 | 0 | — | 6 |

All-Stars—Tinsley 47 pass from Baugh (kick failed)
Attendance—84,560

1938

ALL-STARS 28, WASHINGTON 16

Cecil Isbell of Purdue threw a 39-yard touchdown pass to Northwestern's John Kovatch and Bill Daugherty of Santa Clara intercepted a pass by George Karamatic and ran 40 yards for a touchdown as the College All-Stars scored four touchdowns in the second half to defeat the Washington Redskins 28–16.

Isbell was named the most valuable player after completing 7 of 14 passes for 159 yards and a touchdown. The All-Stars trailed 10–3 at halftime after a two-yard touchdown run by Washington's Max Krause and a 30-yard field goal by Riley Smith.

August 31, at Soldier Field

Washington	Starting Lineups	College All-Stars
Wayne Millner	LE	Perry Schwartz (California)
Glen (Turk) Edwards	LT	Fred Shirey (Nebraska)
Les Olsson	LG	Joe Routt (Texas A&M)
Vic Carroll	C	Ralph Wolf (Ohio State)
Jim Karcher	RG	Leroy Monsky (Alabama)
Jim Barber	RT	Vic Markov (Washington)
Charley Malone	RE	C. Sweeney (Notre Dame)
Riley Smith	QB	Andy Puplis (Notre Dame)
Sammy Baugh	LH	Cecil Isbell (Purdue)
George Karamatic	RH	Andy Uram (Minnesota)
Max Krause	FB	Frank Patrick (Pittsburgh)

Head coaches—Ray Flaherty, Washington; Alvin (Bo) McMillin (Indiana), College All-Stars

| Washington | 7 | 3 | 0 | 6 | — | 16 |
| College All-Stars | 3 | 0 | 12 | 13 | — | 28 |

All-Stars—FG McDonald 15
Wash —Krause 2 run (Smith kick)
Wash —FG Smith 30
All-Stars—Kovatch 39 pass from Isbell (kick failed)
All-Stars—Daugherty 40 interception return (kick failed)
All-Stars—Davis 1 run (kick blocked)
Wash —Karamatic 2 run (kick blocked)
All-Stars—Uram 35 interception return (Patrick kick)
Attendance—74,250

1939

N.Y. GIANTS 9, ALL-STARS 0

Field goals of 34 yards by Ward Cuff and 22 and 41 yards by Ken Strong elevated the New York Giants to a 9–0 victory over the College All-Stars.

The game marked Strong's first appearance in a Giants' uniform since the 1935 season. He played for the New York Yankees of the American Football League in 1936–37 and for the Jersey City Giants of the American Professional Football Association in 1938. The APFL was a minor professional football league.

The All-Stars advanced to the Giants' 34-yard line in the second quarter and gave up the ball on downs. Len Barnum's intercepted pass stopped a collegiate drive at New York's 31 in the fourth quarter, and John Mellus's interception at the 22 stopped the All-Stars as the game ended.

August 30, at Soldier Field

N.Y. Giants	Starting Lineups	College All-Stars
Jim Poole	LE	Bowden Wyatt (Tennessee)
Frank Cope	LT	Joe Mihal (Purdue)
John Dell Isola	LG	Francis Twedell (Minn.)
Mel Hein	C	Charlie Brock (Nebraska)
Orville Tuttle	RG	Ralph Heikkinen (Michigan)
John Mellus	RT	Bob Haak (Indiana)
Jim Lee Howell	RE	Earl Brown (Notre Dame)
Ed Danowski	QB	Davey O'Brien (TCU)
Ward Cuff	LH	Marshall Goldberg (Pitt.)
Leland Shaffer	RH	Bob MacLeod (Dartmouth)
John Karcis	FB	Howard Weiss (Wisconsin)

Head coaches—Steve Owen, N.Y. Giants; Elmer Layden (Notre Dame), College All-Stars

| N.Y. Giants | 3 | 3 | 0 | 3 | — | 9 |
| College All-Stars | 0 | 0 | 0 | 0 | — | 0 |

NYG—FG Cuff 34
NYG—FG Strong 22
NYG—FG Strong 41
Attendance—81,456

1940

GREEN BAY 45, ALL-STARS 28

Cecil Isbell and Arnie Herber combined to complete 11 of 20 passes for 306 yards and five touchdowns as the Green Bay Packers outscored the All-Stars.

Ambrose Schindler of USC put the All-Stars ahead with a six-yard run in the first quarter. The score was tied 14–14 in the second quarter and the All-Stars still were within reach of the Packers at 35–28 in the fourth. Isbell threw for three touchdowns, 81 and 35 yards to Don Hutson and 26 yards to Carl Mulleneaux.

August 29, at Soldier Field

Green Bay	Starting Lineups	College All-Stars
Don Hutson	LE	Bill Fisk (USC)
Buford (Baby) Ray	LT	Nick Cutlich (Northwestern)
Russ Letlow	LG	Jim Logan (Indiana)
George Svendsen	C	C. Turner (Hardin-Simmons)
C. (Buckets) Goldenberg	RG	Harry Smith (USC)
Bill Lee	RT	Tad Harvey (Notre Dame)
Milt Gantenbein	RE	Esco Sarkinen (Ohio State)
Larry Craig	QB	Ambrose Schindler (USC)
Cecil Isbell	LH	Nile Kinnick (Iowa)
Joe Laws	RH	Lou Brock (Purdue)
Clarke Hinkle	FB	Joe Thesing (Notre Dame)

Head coaches—Earl (Curly) Lambeau, Green Bay; Eddie Anderson (Iowa), College All-Stars.

Green Bay	14	14	7	10	—	45
College All-Stars	7	14	0	7	—	28

All-Stars—Schindler 6 run (Kinnick dropkick)
GB —Hutson 81 pass from Isbell (Smith kick)
GB —Mulleneaux 26 pass from Isbell (Smith kick)
All-Stars—Washington 1 run (Kellogg kick)
GB —Uram 60 pass from Herber (Engebretsen kick)
GB —Hutson 35 pass from Isbell (Smith kick)
All-Stars—McFadden 56 pass from Kinnick (Kinnick dropkick)
GB —Hutson 29 pass from Herber (Smith kick)
All-Stars—Schindler 1 run (Kinnick dropkick)
GB —FG Smith 34
GB —Isbell 4 run (Hutson kick)
Attendance—84,567

1941

CHI. BEARS 37, ALL-STARS 13

The Chicago Bears marched 45, 71, and 82 yards for touchdowns in the final 12 minutes of play to defeat the College All-Stars 37–13.

The All-Stars trailed 16–6 at the end of the third quarter and closed the score to 16–13 early in the fourth quarter when Charlie O'Rourke of Boston College combined with Jackie Robinson of UCLA.

Harry Clark scored from one yard on the Bears' next possession to give Chicago a 23–13 lead. Quarterback Sid Luckman passed to George McAfee in the flat and McAfee scored on a 25-yard play to increase Chicago's advantage to 30–13.

August 28, at Soldier Field

Chi. Bears	Starting Lineups	College All-Stars
Dick Plasman	LE	Dave Rankin (Purdue)
Joe Stydahar	LT	Ernest Plannell (Texas A&M)
Danny Fortmann	LG	Augie Lio (Georgetown)
Clyde (Bulldog) Turner	C	Rudy Mucha (Washington)
George Musso	RG	Tommy O'Boyle (Tulane)
Lee Artoe	RT	Nick Drahos (Cornell)
George Wilson	RE	Ed Rucinski (Indiana)
Sid Luckman	QB	Forrest Evashevski (Mich.)
Ray Nolting	LH	Tom Harmon (Michigan)
George McAfee	RH	G. (Sonny) Franck (Minn.)
Bill Osmanski	FB	G. Paskvan (Wisconsin)

Head coaches—George Halas, Chi. Bears; Carl Snavely (Cornell), College All-Stars.

Chi. Bears	6	7	3	21	—	37
College All-Stars	6	0	0	7	—	13

Chi —Kavanaugh 34 pass from Luckman (kick blocked)
All-Stars—Franck 22 pass from Harmon (kick blocked)
Chi —Clark 1 run (Manders kick)
Chi —FG Artoe 46
All-Stars—Robinson 46 pass from O'Rourke (Lio kick)
Chi —Clark 1 run (Manders kick)
Chi —McAfee 25 pass from Luckman (Manders kick)
Chi —Nowaskey 9 pass from Bussey (Manders kick)
Attendance—98,203

1942

CHI. BEARS 21, ALL-STARS 0

The Chicago Bears' dominance of the College All-Stars was more apparent than the final score of 21–0. The Bears outrushed the collegians 268–36 and outpassed them 203–77 for a total yardage advantage of 471–113.

The Bears' first touchdown was scored by Hugh Gallarneau on a four-yard run on fourth down after 8:40 of the first quarter. In the first quarter, Steve Juzwick of Notre Dame ran 91 yards from the All-Stars' 3-yard line to the Bears' 6. But the All-Stars did not score, giving up the ball on downs.

Juzwik's fumble at the collegians' 23 in the second period set up Chicago's second touchdown, a 21-yard pass, Young Bussey to Hampton Pool. Gallarneau scored Chicago's final touchdown in the third quarter on an eight-yard run.

August 28, at Soldier Field

Chi. Bears	Starting Lineups	College All-Stars
John Siegal	LE	Mal Kutner (Texas)
Ed Kolman	LT	Jim Daniell (Ohio State)
Danny Fortmann	LG	Rob Jeffries (Missouri)
Clyde (Bulldog) Turner	C	Vince Banonis (Detroit)
Ray Bray	RG	B. Crimmins (Notre Dame)
Lee Artoe	RT	Al Blozis (Georgetown)
Hampton Pool	RE	Judd Ringer (Minnesota)
Sid Luckman	QB	Dick Erdlitz (Northwestern)
Ray Nolting	LH	Bruce Smith (Minnesota)
Hugh Gallarneau	RH	Steve Juzwik (Notre Dame)
Bill Osmanski	FB	Jack Graf (Ohio State)

Head coaches—George Halas, Chi. Bears; Bob Zuppke (Illinois), College All-Stars.

Chi. Bears	7	7	7	0	—	21
College All-Stars	0	0	0	0	—	0

Chi—Gallarneau 4 run (Stydahar kick)
Chi—Pool 21 pass from Bussey (Stydahar kick)
Chi—Gallarneau 8 run (Stydahar kick)
Attendance—101,100

1943

ALL-STARS 27, WASHINGTON 7

The College All-Stars defeated the Washington Redskins 27–7 for their first victory in five years over an NFL champion. The All-Stars' roster was selected by team coaches instead of by a nationwide newspaper poll. The site of the game was switched to Dyche Stadium on the Northwestern University campus.

The All-Stars scored first when Missouri's Bob Steuber returned a punt 50 yards down the sideline for a touchdown.

The All-Stars began pulling away on a 37-yard touchdown pass play, Glenn Dobbs to Pat Harder, who ran the final 20 yards. Washington moved from its 43 to the All-Stars' 18 in the third quarter; Otto Graham, intercepted a pass on the 3 and returned the ball 97 yards for a touchdown.

August 25, at Evanston, Illinois

Washington	Starting Lineups	College All-Stars
Bob Masterson	LE	Pete Pihos (Indiana)
Willie Wilkin	LT	Al Wistert (Michigan)
Dick Farman	LG	Felix Bucek (Texas A&M)
George Smith	C	Vic Lindskog (Stanford)
Steve Slivinski	RG	Buster Ramsey (Wm. & M.)
Clyde Shugart	RT	Dick Wildung (Minnesota)
Bob McChesney	RE	Bill Huber (Notre Dame)
Ray Hare	QB	D. Renfro (Washington St.)
Sammy Baugh	LH	Otto Graham (Northwestern)
Wilbur Moore	RH	Bob Steuber (Missouri)
Bob Seymour	FB	Pat Harder (Wisconsin)

Head coaches—Arthur (Dutch) Bergman, Washington; Harry Stuhldreher (Wisconsin), College All-Stars.

Washington	0	7	0	0	—	7
College All-Stars	7	0	6	7	—	27

All-Stars—Steuber 50 punt return (Harder kick)
Wash —Aguirre 6 pass from Baugh (Masterson kick)
All-Stars—Harder 37 pass from Dobbs (Harder kick)
All-Stars—O. Graham 97 interception return (kick blocked)
All-Stars—Harder 33 run (Graham kick)
Attendance—48,471

1944

CHI. BEARS 24, ALL-STARS 21

Pete Gudauskas's 13-yard field goal with 10:42 left in the game gave the Chicago Bears a 24–21 victory.

Tulsa University's Glenn Dobbs, making his second appearance in the game as a collegian under wartime eligibility rules, threw a four-yard pass to Notre Dame's Creighton Miller for the All-Stars' first touchdown. That concluded a 33-yard drive after a short Bears' punt. The All-Stars went ahead 14–0 later in the first quarter when Dobbs, unable to find a pass receiver, scrambled 12 yards to the Bears' 1. Dobbs fumbled at that point and teammate John Tavener of Indiana recovered in the end zone.

August 30, at Evanston, Illinois

Chi. Bears	Starting Lineups	College All-Stars
Jim Benton	LE	John Dugger (Ohio State)
Dominic Sigillo	LT	Bill Willis (Ohio State)
Pete Gudauskas	LG	Dick Barwegan (Purdue)
Clyde (Bulldog) Turner	C	John Tavener (Indiana)
George Zorich	RG	Lin Houston (Ohio State)
Al Hoptowit	RT	Bob Zimny (Indiana)
George Wilson	RE	John Yonakor (Notre Dame)
John Long	QB	Lou Saban (Indiana)
Ray Nolting	LH	Glenn Dobbs (Tulsa)
Doug McEnulty	RH	Charley Trippi (Georgia)
Gary Famiglietti	FB	C. Miller (Notre Dame)

Head coaches—Heartley (Hunk) Anderson and Luke Johnsos, Chi. Bears; Lynn (Pappy) Waldorf (Northwestern), College All-Stars.

Chi. Bears	0	14	7	3	—	24
College All-Stars	14	0	7	0	—	21

All-Stars—Miller 4 pass from Dobbs (Saban kick)
All-Stars—Tavener fumble recovery in end zone (Saban kick)
Chi —Famiglietti 3 run (Gudauskas kick)
Chi —Benton 12 pass from Luckman (Gudauskas kick)
All-Stars—Saban 1 run (Saban kick)
Chi —McLean 19 run (Gudauskas kick)
Chi —FG Gudauskas 13
Attendance—48,769

1945

GREEN BAY 19, ALL-STARS 7

Don Hutson intercepted a pass by Perry Moss of Tulsa in the first minute of the fourth quarter and ran 85 yards for the final touchdown in the Green Bay Packers' 19–7 victory over the College All-Stars. The game was returned to Soldier Field.

Hutson also kicked a 20-yard field goal and two extra points. The All-Stars scored in the second quarter on a 62-yard pass play, Bob Kennedy of Washington State to Nick Scollard of St. Joseph's, Indiana.

The collegians advanced to the Packers' 24-yard line in the second quarter, but Michigan's Tom Harmon fumbled after a 46-yard run. Georgia's Charley Trippi ran to Green Bay's 2-yard line in the fourth quarter, but a penalty set the collegians back to the 7 and they fumbled on the next play.

August 30, at Soldier Field

Green Bay	Starting Lineups	College All-Stars
Don Hutson	LE	Ted Cook (Alabama)
Buford (Baby) Ray	LT	Bob Zimny (Indiana)
Bill Kuusisto	LG	Damon Tassos (Texas A&M)
Charlie Brock	C	Tex Warrington (Auburn)
C. (Buckets) Goldenberg	RG	Glen Burgeis (Tulsa)
Paul Berezney	RT	R. Foster (Oklahoma A&M)
Joel Mason	RE	Bill Huber (Notre Dame)
Larry Craig	QB	Charles Mitchell (Tulsa)
Irv Comp	LH	Charley Trippi (Georgia)
Lou Brock	RH	Don Greenwood (Illinois)
Ted Fritsch	FB	B. Kennedy (Washington St.)

Head coaches—Earl (Curly) Lambeau, Green Bay; Bernie Bierman (Minnesota), College All-Stars.

Green Bay	3	9	0	7	—	19
College All-Stars	0	7	0	0	—	7

GB —FG Hutson 20
GB —Safety, Kennedy stepped into end zone
GB —McKay 20 pass from Rohrig (Hutson kick)
All-Stars—Scollard 68 pass from Kennedy (Harmon kick)
GB —Hutson 85 interception return (Hutson kick)
Attendance—92,753

1946

ALL-STARS 16, LOS ANGELES 0

Elroy (Crazylegs) Hirsch of the University of Wisconsin ran 68 yards for a first-quarter touchdown and turned a 32-yard pass from Northwestern's Otto Graham into a 62-yard touchdown in the third quarter of the College All-Stars' 16-0 victory over the Los Angeles Rams.

The Rams, representing Los Angeles for the first time since moving from Cleveland after the 1945 season, had the ball on the collegians' 19, 29, 18, 10, and 36 in the first half, but could not score. The All-Stars fumbled seven times in the game and the Rams recovered four.

Because they had played as underclassmen during World War II eligibility rules, some of the players on the college roster were making their second and third appearances in the game.

August 23, at Soldier Field

Los Angeles	Starting Lineups	College All-Stars
Howard (Red) Hickey	LE	Jack Russell (Baylor)
Eberle Schultz	LT	Martin Ruby (Texas A&M)
Riley Matheson	LG	Visco Grgich (Santa Clara)
Bob DeLauer	C	Bill Godwin (Georgia)
Milan Lazetich	RG	Buster Ramsey (Wm. & M.)
Gil Bouley	RT	Derrell Palmer (TCU)
Steve Pritko	RE	Ralph Heywood (USC)
Bob Waterfield	QB	Otto Graham (Northwestern)
Fred Gehrke	LH	Billy Hillenbrand (Indiana)
Jim Gillette	RH	Dub Jones (Tulane)
Pat West	FB	Pat Harder (Wisconsin)

Head coaches—Adam Walsh, Los Angeles; Alvin (Bo) McMillin (Indiana), College All-Stars

Los Angeles	0	0	0	0	—	0
College All-Stars	7	0	7	2	—	16

All-Stars—Hirsch 68 run (Harder kick)
All-Stars—Hirsch 62 pass from Graham (Harder kick)
All-Stars—Safety, Walker tackled Washington in end zone
Attendance—97,380

1947

ALL-STARS 16, CHI. BEARS 0

A record crowd of 105,840 persons, attracted partly by the presence of the hometown Bears and an All-Stars team coached by Notre Dame University's Frank Leahy, saw the collegians score a 16-0 victory, their second shutout in a row by that margin.

The All-Stars used a T-formation offense for the first time in the series. It was an offense made famous by the Bears earlier in the decade. The collegians outgained the professionals 340-116 in total yards and outrushed them 189-35.

The All-Stars went 82 yards in 11 plays the first time they had the ball and 89 in two plays on their second series. Illinois's Claude (Buddy) Young set up both touchdowns by running 31 yards on one play in the first drive and moving 41 yards with a flat pass in the second drive.

August 22, at Soldier Field

Chi. Bears	Starting Lineups	College All-Stars
Ken Kavanaugh	LE	Horace Gillom (Nevada)
Fred Davis	LT	Dick Barwegan (Purdue)
Chuck Drulis	LG	Alex Agase (Illinois)
Clyde (Bulldog) Turner	C	Paul Duke (Georgia Tech)
Ray Bray	RG	Weldon Humble (Rice)
Walt Stickel	RT	J. Mastrangelo (Notre Dame)
Ed Sprinkle	RE	Joe Tereschinski (Georgia)
Sid Luckman	QB	G. Ratterman (Notre Dame)
Ray (Scooter) McLean	LH	C. (Buddy) Young (Illinois)
Hugh Gallarneau	RH	Vic Schwall (Northwestern)
Joe Osmanski	FB	Jim Mello (Notre Dame)

Head coaches—George Halas, Chi. Bears; Frank Leahy (Notre Dame), College All-Stars

Chi. Bears	0	0	0	0	—	0
College All-Stars	13	0	3	0	—	16

All-Stars—Mello 6 run (kick blocked)
All-Stars—Zilly 46 pass from Ratterman (Case kick)
All-Stars—FG Case 21
Attendance—105,840

1948

CHI. CARDINALS 28, ALL-STARS 0

The Chicago Cardinals moved 80 yards to a touchdown the second time they had possession of the ball and went on to a 28-0 victory over the College All-Stars. Charley Trippi, who scored the Cardinals' final touchdown on a 13-yard pass from Ray Mallouf, set a record by appearing in his fifth All-Star game, his first as a professional.

The Cardinals outgained the All-Stars 333-235. The All-Stars marched 84 yards and two feet to the Cardinals' 1-foot line in the third quarter, when the score was 14-0, but Floyd Simmons of Notre Dame was stopped by Marshall Goldberg on fourth down.

Vince Banonis intercepted a pass by Perry Moss of Illinois and ran 31 yards for a touchdown to give Chicago a 21-0 lead in the fourth quarter.

August 20, at Soldier Field

Chi. Cardinals	Starting Lineups	College All-Stars
Bill Dewell	LE	Paul Cleary (USC)
Chet Bulger	LT	G. Connor (Notre Dame)
Lloyd Arms	LG	Arnie Weinmeister (Wash.)
Vince Banonis	C	Dick Scott (Navy)
Garrard (Buster) Ramsey	RG	Howard Brown (Indiana)
Stan Mauldin	RT	Z. Czarobski (Notre Dame)
Mal Kutner	RE	Len Ford (Michigan)
Paul Christman	QB	J. Lujack (Notre Dame)
Charley Trippi	LH	Bob Chappuis (Michigan)
Marshall Goldberg	RH	Charlie Conerly (Miss.)
Pat Harder	FB	C. (Bump) Elliott (Michigan)

Head coaches—Jimmy Conzelman, Chi. Cardinals; Frank Leahy (Notre Dame), College All-Stars

Chi. Cardinals	7	7	0	14	—	28
College All-Stars	0	0	0	0	—	0

Chi—Angsman 2 run (Harder kick)
Chi—Schwall 14 run (Harder kick)
Chi—Banonis 31 interception return (Harder kick)
Chi—Trippi 13 pass from Mallouf (Harder kick)
Attendance—101,220

1949

PHILADELPHIA 38, ALL-STARS 0

The day before the game with the Philadelphia Eagles, Bud Wilkinson, coach of the College All-Stars, said, "We haven't got a chance . . . and I'm not kidding." The Eagles shut the All-Stars' passing game for three yards in losses, outrushed the collegians 228-116 for a 358-113 total yardage advantage, and won 38-0.

The Eagles defensed the collegians' split T formation with an eight-man line. Their three-man secondary also was close to the line. The professionals penetrated so quickly the All-Stars were unable to set up a passing attack.

Philadelphia broke a scoreless tie in the second quarter by marching 71 yards to a touchdown.

August 12, at Soldier Field

Philadelphia	Starting Lineups	College All-Stars
Jack Ferrante	LE	Barney Poole (Mississippi)
Vic Sears	LT	George Petrovich (Texas)
Cliff Patton	LG	Marty Wendell (Notre Dame)
Vic Lindskog	C	Chuck Bednarik (Penn.)
Frank (Bucko) Kilroy	RG	Bill Fischer (Notre Dame)
Al Wistert	RT	Al DeRogatis (Duke)
Pete Pihos	RE	Mel Sheehan (Missouri)
Tommy Thompson	QB	Jack Mitchell (Oklahoma)
Steve Van Buren	LH	George Taliaferro (Indiana)
Bosh Pritchard	RH	Jerry Williams (Wash. St.)
Joe Muha	FB	Joe Geri (Georgia)

Head coaches—Earle (Greasy) Neale, Philadelphia; Bud Wilkinson (Oklahoma), College All-Stars

Philadelphia	0	17	7	14	—	38
College All-Stars	0	0	0	0	—	0

Phil—Van Buren 1 run (Patton kick)
Phil—FG Patton 14
Phil—Craft 4 run (Patton kick)
Phil—Pihos 7 pass from Thompson (Patton kick)
Phil—Doss 5 run (Patton kick)
Phil—Armstrong 13 pass from Mackrides (Patton kick)
Attendance—93,780

1950

ALL STARS 17, PHILADELPHIA 7

Halfback Charlie (Choo Choo) Justice of North Carolina gained 133 yards in nine carries and scored on a 35-yard pass from quarterback Eddie LeBaron of College of Pacific as the College All-Stars defeated the Philadelphia Eagles 17-7. The game was televised nationally for the first time on a 29-station network.

Justice gained 31 and 12 yards as the All-Stars marched 54 yards in six plays to a touchdown on their second series. They led 14-0 at the half after Santa Clara's Hall Haynes recovered a fumble by Clyde (Smackover) Scott at the Eagles' 35; LeBaron scrambled away from a strong rush and dumped the ball to Justice, who caught LeBaron's pass at the line of scrimmage and weaved his way to a touchdown.

August 11, at Soldier Field

Philadelphia	Starting Lineups	College All-Stars
Jack Ferrante	LE	Art Weiner (North Carolina)
Vic Sears	LT	D. (Tiny) Campora (Pacific)
Cliff Patton	LG	Porter Payne (Georgia)
Vic Lindskog	C	Clayton Tonnemaker (Minn.)
Frank (Bucko) Kilroy	RG	George Hughes (Wm. & M.)
Al Wistert	RT	Bill Manley (Oklahoma)
Pete Pihos	RE	Jim Martin (Notre Dame)
Tommy Thompson	QB	Travis Tidwell (Auburn)
Clyde (Smackover) Scott	LH	Doak Walker (SMU)
Joe Muha	RH	Hall Haynes (Santa Clara)
	FB	F. (Curly) Morrison (Ohio St.)

Head coaches—Earle (Greasy) Neale, Philadelphia; Eddie Anderson (Holy Cross), College All-Stars

Philadelphia	0	0	0	7	—	7
College All-Stars	7	7	0	3	—	17

All-Stars—Pasquariello 1 run (Soltau kick)
All-Stars—Justice 35 pass from LeBaron (Soltau kick)
Phil—Van Buren 1 run (Soltau kick)
All-Stars—FG Soltau 23
Attendance—88,885

1951

CLEVELAND 33, ALL-STARS 0

Halfback Dub Jones rushed for 105 yards and two touchdowns and quarterback Otto Graham completed 16 of 30 passes for 263 yards and two touchdowns as the Cleveland Browns outgained the College All-Stars 425-126 and posted a 33-0 victory.

The All-Stars made only five first downs; their longest gain was a 23-yard run by Southern Methodist's Kyle Rote, who led the collegians with 45 yards in eight carries.

The Browns took a 2-0 lead in the first quarter when Rote fumbled a handoff from Notre Dame quarterback Bob Williams, who recovered the ball in the end zone but was downed by Len Ford for a safety. The score was 12-0 at halftime.

August 17, at Soldier Field

Cleveland	Starting Lineups	College All-Stars
Mac Speedie	LE	Don Stonesifer (N'wstn.)
Lou Groza	LT	Bob Gain (Kentucky)
Abe Gibron	LG	Bud McFadin (Texas)
Frank Gatski	C	Jerry Groom (Notre Dame)
Lin Houston	RG	Lynn Lynch (Illinois)
Lou Rymkus	RT	Mike McCormack (Kansas)
Dante Lavelli	RE	Bob Wilkinson (UCLA)
Otto Graham	QB	Bob Williams (Notre Dame)
Rex Bumgardner	LH	Wilford White (Arizona St.)
Dub Jones	RH	Kyle Rote (SMU)
Emerson Cole	FB	Dan Dufek (Michigan)

Head coaches—Paul Brown, Cleveland; Herman Hickman (Yale), College All-Stars

Cleveland	2	10	7	14	—	33
College All-Stars	0	0	0	0	—	0

Cle—Safety, Ford downed Williams in end zone
Cle—Jones 2 run (Groza kick)
Cle—FG Groza 17
Cle—Jones 3 run (Groza kick)
Cle—Lavelli 14 pass from Graham (Groza kick)
Cle—Cole 8 pass from Graham (Groza kick)
Attendance—92,180

1952

LOS ANGELES 10, ALL-STARS 7

The Los Angeles Rams drove 51 yards midway in the fourth quarter to position Bob Waterfield for a 24-yard field goal that gave the Rams a 10–7 victory.

The All-Stars led 7–0 going into the final quarter after a 69-yard touchdown drive that ended with Ohio State's Vic Janowicz running three yards in the second quarter. Quarterback Babe Parilli, who gained 68 yards in seven carries, contributed a 41-yard run to the march.

The professionals tied the score in the early minutes of the fourth period on a three-yard pass, Norm Van Brocklin to Paul (Tank) Younger. The score was set up by a penalty against San Francisco's Ollie Matson, who drew pass interference defending a Van Brocklin pass to Volney (Skeet) Quinlan that put the ball on the 7-yard line.

August 15, at Soldier Field

Los Angeles	Starting Lineups	College All-Stars
Tom Fears	LE	Leo Sugar (Purdue)
Don Simensen	LT	Harold Mitchell (UCLA)
Dick Daugherty	LG	Don Coleman (Michigan St.)
Leon McLaughlin	C	Doug Mosley (Kentucky)
Bill Lange	RG	Bob Ward (Maryland)
Tom Dahms	RT	Bill Pearman (Tennessee)
Elroy (Crazylegs) Hirsch	RE	Billy Howton (Rice)
Bob Waterfield	QB	Babe Parilli (Kentucky)
Dan Towler	LH	Vic Janowicz (Ohio State)
Verda (Vitamin T.) Smith	RH	Hugh McElhenny (Wash.)
John Myers	FB	Ed Modzelewski (Maryland)

Head coaches—Joe Stydahar, Los Angeles; Bobby Dodd (Georgia Tech), College All-Stars

Los Angeles	0	0	0	10	—	10
College All-Stars	0	7	0	0	—	7

All-Stars—Janowicz 3 run (Janowicz kick)
LA —Younger 3 pass from Van Brocklin (Waterfield kick)
LA —FG Waterfield 24
Attendance—88,316

1953

DETROIT 24, ALL-STARS 10

Detroit's Bobby Layne set a record by completing 21 of 31 passes for 323 yards and one touchdown as the Lions rolled up a record 21 first downs and outgained the College All-Stars 473–187 in a 24–10 victory.

Layne's primary receivers were ends Leon Hart, who caught seven passes for 106 yards, and Cloyce Box, five for 108, and halfback Doak Walker, eight for 97. Three All-Star quarterbacks completed only 9 of 27 passes for 81 yards.

The Lions' first touchdown was typical of their free-wheeling attack. They drove 80 yards, with the big play a Layne-to-Hart pass with a lateral from Hart to Walker that covered 47 yards, setting up Bob Hoernschemeyer's five-yard scoring run.

August 14, at Soldier Field

Detroit	Starting Lineups	College All-Stars
Cloyce Box	LE	Bernie Flowers (Purdue)
Lou Creekmur	LT	Kline Gilbert (Mississippi)
Jim Martin	LG	Donn Moomaw (UCLA)
Vince Banonis	C	G. Morris (Georgia Tech)
Dick Stanfel	RG	Harley Sewell (Texas)
Gus Cifelli	RT	J.D. Kimmel (Houston)
Leon Hart	RE	Tom Scott (Virginia)
Bobby Layne	QB	Jack Scarbath (Maryland)
Doak Walker	LH	Fred Bruney (Ohio State)
Bob Hoernschemeyer	RH	Jim Sears (USC)
Pat Harder	FB	H. (Buck) McPhail (Okla.)

Head coaches—Raymond (Buddy) Parker, Detroit; Bobby Dodd (Georgia Tech), College All-Stars

Detroit	0	3	7	7	—	24
College All-Stars	0	3	0	7	—	10

Det —Hoernschemeyer 5 run (Harder kick)
Det —FG Walker 10
All-Stars—FG Dawson 23
Det —Box 8 pass from Layne (Harder kick)
Det —Hoernschemeyer 2 run (Harder kick)
All-Stars—Dawson 17 run (Samuels kick)
Attendance—93,818

1954

DETROIT 31, ALL-STARS 6

The Detroit Lions played without starting quarterback Bobby Layne, but reserve quarterback Tom Dublinski completed 10 of 15 passes for 103 yards as the Lions outgained the College All-Stars 361–144 in total yardage and won 31–6.

Layne did not play because the Lions feared he would be injured by also participating on defense. The game was conducted under collegiate rules as stipulated in the contract between the sponsoring *Chicago Tribune* and NFL. Colleges played one-platoon football in 1953. The Lions and other professional teams played with two platoons. It was the first time in 10 years the All-Star game was played with limited substitution.

August 13, at Soldier Field

Detroit	Starting Lineups	College All-Stars
Dorne Dibble	LE	Carlton Massey (Texas)
Lou Creekmur	LT	Bob Morgan (Maryland)
Jim Martin	LG	Jerry Hilgenberg (Iowa)
LaVern Torgeson	C	Ed Beatty (Mississippi)
Harley Sewell	RG	M. Mavraides (Notre Dame)
Charlie Ane	RT	Stan Jones (Maryland)
Leon Hart	RE	Dick Deitrick (Pittsburgh)
Tom Dublinski	QB	Zeke Bratkowski (Georgia)
Doak Walker	LH	Chet Hanulak (Maryland)
Jack Christiansen	RH	Johnny Lattner (Notre Dame)
Lew Carpenter	FB	Neil Worden (Notre Dame)

Head coaches—Raymond (Buddy) Parker, Detroit; Jim Tatum (Maryland), College All-Stars

Detroit	17	0	7	7	—	31
College All-Stars	0	0	6	0	—	6

Det —FG Martin 46
Det —Walker 5 run (Walker kick)
Det —Carpenter 4 run (Girard kick)
All-Stars—Lattner 4 run (kick blocked)
Det —Carpenter 1 run (Martin kick)
Det —Doran 37 fumble return (Walker kick)
Attendance—93,470

1955

ALL-STARS 30, CLEVELAND 27

The College All-Stars broke a string of four straight victories by the NFL champion and improved their record in the series to 8 victories against 13 losses and 1 tie with a 30–27 win over the Cleveland Browns.

Tad Weed, a 5-foot 6-inch, 146-pound kicker from Ohio State, made field goals of 21, 19, and 41 yards, the last giving the Collegians a 30–20 lead with six minutes remaining.

The Browns were ahead for the final time 20–17 with 19 seconds remaining in the half after a 25-yard pass from George Ratterman to Ray Renfro.

August 12, at Soldier Field

Cleveland	Starting Lineups	College All-Stars
Darrell (Pete) Brewster	LE	Max Boydston (Oklahoma)
Lou Groza	LT	Jim Ray Smith (Baylor)
Abe Gibron	LG	H. Bullough (Michigan St.)
Frank Gatski	C	D. Szymanski (Notre Dame)
Harold Bradley	RG	Bud Brooks (Arkansas)
Mike McCormack	RT	F. Varricchione (Notre Dame)
Dante Lavelli	RE	Henry Hair (Georgia Tech)
George Ratterman	QB	R. Guglielmi (Notre Dame)
Ray Renfro	LH	Dickie Moegle (Rice)
Dub Jones	RH	Dave Middleton (Auburn)
Maurice Bassett	FB	Alan Ameche (Wisconsin)

Head coaches—Paul Brown, Cleveland; Earl (Curly) Lambeau, College All-Stars

Cleveland	7	13	0	7	—	27
College All-Stars	3	14	3	10	—	30

All-Stars—FG Weed 21
Cle —Ratterman 1 run (Weed kick)
All-Stars—Eidom 2 run (Weed kick)
Cle —Renfro 18 run (Groza kick)
All-Stars—Hair 5 pass from Guglielmi (Weed kick)
Cle —Renfro 25 pass from Ratterman (kick blocked)
All-Stars—FG Weed 19
All-Stars—Triplett 1 run (Leggett run)
All-Stars—FG Weed 41
Cle —Morrison 5 run (Groza kick)
Attendance—75,000

1956

CLEVELAND 26, ALL-STARS 0

The Cleveland Browns drove 80 yards in 12 plays the first time they had the ball and won 26–0.

On the first series of plays, Michigan State quarterback Earl Morrall passed 11 yards to Navy's Ron Beagle, ran 10 yards himself, and handed off to Ohio State's Howard (Hopalong) Cassady for a nine-yard gain, moving the All-Stars to Cleveland's 34. Morrall was shaken up, however, on the play involving Cassady, and Jerry Reichow of Iowa replaced him. Reichow threw a pass on his first play and the Browns' Warren Lahr intercepted in the end zone. Cleveland took over on its 20 and moved to the first touchdown. Groza kicked field goals of 45, 37, 24, and 27 yards.

August 10, at Soldier Field

Cleveland	Starting Lineups	College All-Stars
Darrel (Pete) Brewster	LE	Ron Beagle (Navy)
Lou Groza	LT	Frank D'Agostino (Auburn)
Abe Gibron	LG	Hugh Pitts (TCU)
Frank Gatski	C	Bob Pellegrini (Maryland)
Herschel Forester	RG	Sam Huff (West Virginia)
Mike McCormack	RT	Bob Skoronski (Indiana)
Dante Lavelli	RE	Don Holleder (Army)
George Ratterman	QB	Earl Morrall (Michigan St.)
Fred (Curly) Morrison	LH	H. (Hopalong) Cassady (O.St.)
Ray Renfro	RH	Ron McIlhenny (SMU)
Ed Modzelewski	FB	Don Schaefer (Notre Dame)

Head coaches—Paul Brown, Cleveland; Earl (Curly) Lambeau, College All-Stars

Cleveland	7	6	6	7	—	26
College All-Stars	0	0	0	0	—	0

Cle—Morrison 13 pass from Ratterman (Groza kick)
Cle—FG 45 Groza
Cle—FG 37 Groza
Cle—FG 24 Groza
Cle—FG 27 Groza
Cle—Filipski 3 run (Groza kick)
Attendance—75,000

1957

N.Y. GIANTS 22, ALL-STARS 12

Quarterback Charlie Conerly and end Ken McAfee combined on touchdown pass plays of 38 and 10 yards as the New York Giants overcame an early lead to score a 22–12 victory.

Wake Forest's Billy Barnes ran two yards for a touchdown to end a 55-yard drive that began when Illinois's Wayne Bock recovered a fumble by Alex Webster on the collegians' 45-yard line.

A fumble by Barnes in the first quarter was recovered by Charlie Toogood and the Giants converted the turnover into a 33-yard field goal by Ben Agajanian.

August 9, at Soldier Field

N.Y. Giants	Starting Lineups	College All-Stars
Kyle Rote	LE	Ron Kramer (Michigan)
Roosevelt Brown	LT	Carl Vereen (Georgia Tech)
Gerald Huth	LG	Dalton Truax (Tulane)
Ray Wietecha	C	Joe Amstutz (Indiana)
Jack Stroud	RG	Mike Sandusky (Maryland)
Dick Yelvington	RT	Earl Leggett (LSU)
Ken McAfee	RE	Tom Maentz (Michigan)
Don Heinrich	QB	John Brodie (Stanford)
Frank Gifford	LH	Jon Arnett (USC)
Alex Webster	RH	Abe Woodson (Illinois)
Mel Triplett	FB	Don Bosseler (Miami)

Head coaches—Jim Lee Howell, N.Y. Giants; Earl (Curly) Lambeau, College All-Stars

N.Y. Giants	3	7	7	5	—	22
College All-Stars	6	3	0	3	—	12

All-Stars—Barnes 2 run (kick failed)
NYG —FG Agajanian 33
NYG —McAfee 38 pass from Conerly (Agajanian kick)
All-Stars—FG Cothren 12
NYG —McAfee 10 pass from Conerly (Agajanian kick)
NYG —FG Agajanian 45
All-Stars—FG Cothren 25
NYG —Safety, Nolan tackled Woodson in end zone
Attendance—75,000

1958

ALL-STARS 35, DETROIT 19

The Detroit Lions outrushed the College All-Stars 179–3 and had 22 first downs to 11, but the collegians struck for 20 points in the second quarter.

The Lions led 7–0 at the end of the first quarter after a 24-yard pass, Tobin Rote to Jim Doran. On second down at the All-Stars' 40 after a Lions' punt, Jim Pace of Michigan caught a pass from King Hill of Rice at the line of scrimmage and ran 57 yards to Detroit's 3, setting up a 19-yard field goal by Texas A&M's Bobby Joe Conrad.

August 15, at Soldier Field

Detroit	Starting Lineups	College All-Stars
Jim Doran	LE	C. Krueger (Texas A&M)
Lou Creekmur	LT	Lou Michaels (Kentucky)
Harley Sewell	LG	Jerry Kramer (Idaho)
Charlie Ane	C	Dan Currie (Michigan State)
Stan Campbell	RG	Bill Krisher (Oklahoma)
Ken Russell	RT	G. Hickerson (Mississippi)
Steve Junker	RE	Jim Gibbons (Iowa)
Tobin Rote	QB	King Hill (Rice)
Gene Gedman	LH	Jim Pace (Michigan)
H. (Hopalong) Cassady	RH	B. Joe Conrad (Texas A&M)
John Henry Johnson	FB	W. Kowalczyk (Michigan St.)

Head coaches—George Wilson, Detroit; Otto Graham, College All-Stars

Detroit	7	0	6	6	—	19
College All-Stars	0	20	2	13	—	35

Det —Doran 24 pass from Rote (Layne kick)
All-Stars—FG Conrad 19
All-Stars—Mitchell 84 pass from Ninowski (Conrad kick)
All-Stars—Mitchell 18 pass from Ninowski (Conrad kick)
All-Stars—FG Conrad 33
All-Stars—Safety, Jobko tackled Rote in end zone
Det —Gedman 9 run (kick blocked)
All-Stars—FG Conrad 24
All-Stars—Howley 29 interception return (Conrad kick)
Det —Pfeifer 1 run (kick blocked)
Attendance—70,000

1959

BALTIMORE 29, ALL-STARS 0

The College All-Stars had a 19–18 edge in first downs, but the Baltimore Colts converted three turnovers into touchdowns and scored all of their points in the first half en route to a 29–0 victory.

Center Dan James of Ohio State snapped the ball over the head of Southern Methodist punter Dave Scherer and the ball went out of the end zone for a safety. The Colts' Carl Taseff returned the ensuing free kick 42 yards. John Unitas passed 33 yards to Jim Mutscheller and three yards to Raymond Berry for a touchdown and an 8–0 lead.

Bill Stacy of Mississippi State fumbled a punt in the second quarter and Baltimore's Tom Addison recovered, setting up a 29-yard pass, Unitas to Mutscheller.

August 14, at Soldier Field

Baltimore	Starting Lineups	College All-Stars
Raymond Berry	LE	Buddy Dial (Rice)
Jim Parker	LT	Gene Selawski (Purdue)
Art Spinney	LG	Mike Rabold (Indiana)
Madison (Buzz) Nutter	C	Dan James (Ohio State)
Alex Sandusky	RG	A. Cvercko (Northwestern)
George Preas	RT	Fran O'Brien (Michigan St.)
Jim Mutscheller	RE	Dave Sherer (SMU)
John Unitas	QB	Lee Grosscup (Utah)
L.G. Dupre	LH	Don Brown (Houston)
Lenny Moore	RH	Dick Haley (Pittsburgh)
Alan Ameche	FB	N. Pietrosante (Notre Dame)

Head coaches—Weeb Ewbank, Baltimore; Otto Graham (Coast Guard), College All-Stars

Baltimore	8	21	0	0	—	29
College All-Stars	0	0	0	0	—	0

Balt—Safety, James centered ball out of end zone
Balt—Berry 3 pass from Unitas (kick failed)
Balt—Mutscheller 29 pass from Unitas (Rechichar kick)
Balt—Dupre 13 pass from Unitas (Rechichar kick)
Balt—Davis 36 interception return (Rechichar kick)
Attendance—70,000

1960

BALTIMORE 32, ALL-STARS 7

Quarterback John Unitas completed 22 of 42 passes for 281 yards and three touchdowns and the Baltimore Colts outgained the College All-Stars 416–120 in total offense and posted a 32–7 victory.

Baltimore moved 69 yards in seven plays and the second time it had the ball to take a 7–0 lead. The All-Stars moved to the Colts' 5-yard line in the second quarter, but quarterback Don Meredith of Southern Methodist fumbled. The Colts' Gino Marchetti recovered, and Baltimore marched 95 yards to a touchdown.

August 12, at Soldier Field

Baltimore	Starting Lineups	College All-Stars
Raymond Berry	LE	Carroll Dale (Virginia Tech)
George Preas	LT	B. Denton (Col. of Pacific)
Art Spinney	LG	C. Janerette (Penn State)
Madison (Buzz) Nutter	C	Bill Lapham (Iowa)
Alex Sandusky	RG	Mike McGee (Duke)
Jim Parker	RT	G. Gossage (Northwestern)
Jim Mutscheller	RE	H. McInnis (So. Mississippi)
Johnny Unitas	QB	George Izo (Notre Dame)
Lenny Moore	LH	Prentice Gautt (Oklahoma)
Alan Ameche	RH	Tom Moore (Vanderbilt)
L.G. Dupre	FB	Frank Mestnik (Marquette)

Head coaches—Weeb Ewbank, Baltimore; Otto Graham (Coast Guard), College All-Stars

Baltimore	7	17	5	3	—	32
College All-Stars	0	0	0	7	—	7

Balt —Moore 4 pass from Unitas (Myhra kick)
Balt —Moore 3 pass from Unitas (Myhra kick)
Balt —FG Myhra 38
Balt —Moore 14 pass from Unitas (Myhra kick)
Balt —Safety, Lipscomb and Joyce tackled Izo in end zone
Balt —FG Myhra 27
All-Stars—Gautt 60 pass from Meredith (Khayat kick)
Balt —FG Myhra 26
Attendance—70,000

1961

PHILADELPHIA 28, ALL-STARS 14

Trapped behind the line of scrimmage, quarterback Sonny Jurgensen improvised with a behind-the-back pass to Pete Retzlaff for a first down that sustained the first of four touchdown drives in the Philadelphia Eagles' 28–14 victory over the College All-Stars.

August 4, at Soldier Field

Philadelphia	Starters, Offense	College All-Stars
Pete Retzlaff	LE	A. Thomas (Oregon State)
Jim McCusker	LT	Roland Lakes (Wichita)
John Wittenborn	LG	Billy Shaw (Georgia Tech)
Chuck Bednarik	C	Greg Larson (Minnesota)
Stan Campbell	RG	H. Antwine (So. Illinois)
J.D. Smith	RT	Jim Tyrer (Ohio State)
Bobby Walston	RE	Mike Ditka (Pittsburgh)
Sonny Jurgensen	QB	Norm Snead (Wake Forest)
Billy Barnes	LHB	P. Atkins (New Mexico St.)
Tommy McDonald	RHB	B. Casey (Bowling Green)
Clarence Peaks	FB	Bill Brown (Illinois)
Starters, Defense		
Leo Sugar	LE	Earl Faison (Indiana)
Jess Richardson	LT	Joe Rutgens (Illinois)
Ed Khayat	RT	Ernie Ladd (Grambling)
Marion Campbell	RE	Bob Lilly (Texas Christian)
John Nocera	LLB	Frank Visted (Navy)
Chuck Weber	MLB	E.J. Holub (Texas Tech)
Maxie Baughan	RLB	Fred Hageman (Kansas)
Jim Carr	LHB	Ed Sharockman (Pittsburgh)
Tom Brookshier	RHB	C. Gibson (No. Caro. St.)
Bob Freeman	LS	Tom Matte (Ohio State)
Don Burroughs	RS	Joe Krakoski (Illinois)

Head coaches—Nick Skorich, Philadelphia; Otto Graham (Coast Guard), College All-Stars

Philadelphia	14	7	0	7	—	28
College All-Stars	0	0	0	14	—	14

Phil —McDonald 27 pass from Jurgensen (Walston kick)
Phil —Retzlaff 25 pass from Jurgensen (Walston kick)
Phil —McDonald 24 pass from Hill (Walston kick)
Phil —McDonald 24 pass from Jurgensen (Walston kick)
All-Stars—Gregory 18 pass from Kilmer (Fleming kick)
All-Stars—Grecni 57 interception return (Fleming kick)
Attendance—66,000

1962

GREEN BAY 42, ALL-STARS 20

Quarterback Bart Starr completed 13 of 22 passes for 255 yards and a record five touchdowns.

August 3, at Soldier Field

Green Bay	Starters, Offense	College All-Stars
Max McGee	LE	Reg Carolan (Idaho)
Bob Skoronski	LT	Fate Echols (Northwestern)
Fred (Fuzzy) Thurston	LG	B. Hudson (Memphis State)
Jim Ringo	C	Wayne Frazier (Auburn)
Jerry Kramer	RG	R. Winston (Louisiana State)
Forrest Gregg	RT	Joe Carollo (Notre Dame)
Ron Kramer	RE	Charles Bryant (Ohio State)
Bart Starr	QB	John Hadl (Kansas)
Paul Hornung	LH	Curtis McClinton (Kansas)
Boyd Dowler	RH	Lance Alworth (Arkansas)
Jim Taylor	FB	Earl Gros (Louisiana State)
Starters, Defense		
Willie Davis	LE	Frank Parker (Okla. State)
Dave Hanner	LT	Merlin Olsen (Utah State)
Henry Jordan	RT	John Meyers (Washington)
Bill Quinlan	RE	Clark Miller (Utah State)
Dan Currie	LLB	Bill Saul (Penn State)
Ray Nitschke	MLB	Larry Onesti (Northwestern)
Bill Forester	RLB	Frank Buncom (USC)
Hank Gremminger	LH	James Saxton (Texas)
Jesse Whittenton	RH	W. Harris (Louisiana State)
John Symank	LS	T. Dellinger (No. Caro. St.)
Willie Wood	RS	A. Dabiero (Notre Dame)

Head coaches–Vince Lombardi, Green Bay; Otto Graham (Coast Guard), College All-Stars

Green Bay	7	7	7	21	—	42
College All-Stars	3	7	10	0	—	20

All-Stars—Gros 1 run (Mather kick)
GB —Dowler 22 pass from Starr (Hornung kick)
All-Stars—FG Mather 26
GB —R. Kramer 4 pass from Starr (Hornung kick)
All-Stars—Bryant 21 pass from Hadl (Mather kick)
GB —Dowler 22 pass from Starr (Hornung kick)
All-Stars—FG Mather 15
GB —McGee 20 pass from Starr (Hornung kick)
GB —McGee 36 pass from Starr (Hornung kick)
GB —Pitts 3 run (Hornung kick)
Attendance—65,000

1963

ALL-STARS 20, GREEN BAY 17

A short third-down pass from quarterback Ron VanderKelen to Pat Richter, VanderKelen's University of Wisconsin teammate, resulted in the All-Stars' first victory in the series since 1958.

August 2, at Soldier Field

Green Bay	Starters, Offense	College All-Stars
Max McGee	LE	Pat Richter (Wisconsin)
Bob Skoronski	LT	Bob Vogel (Ohio State)
Fred (Fuzzy) Thurston	LG	Ed Budde (Michigan State)
Jim Ringo	C	D. Behrman (Michigan State)
Jerry Kramer	RG	Don Chuy (Clemson)
Forrest Gregg	RT	Daryl Sanders (Ohio State)
Ron Kramer	RE	Bob Jencks (Miami, Ohio)
Bart Starr	QB	Ron VanderKelen (Wis.)
Boyd Dowler	FL	Paul Flatley (Northwestern)
Tom Moore	HB	Larry Ferguson (Iowa)
Jim Taylor	FB	Bill Thornton (Nebraska)
Starters, Defense		
Willie Davis	LE	Fred Miller (Louisiana State)
Dave Hanner	LT	Charles Sieminski (Penn St.)
Henry Jordan	RT	Jim Dunaway (Mississippi)
Urban Henry	RE	Don Brumm (Purdue)
Dan Currie	LLB	Dave Robinson (Penn State)
Ken Iman	MLB	Lee Roy Jordan (Alabama)
Bill Forester	RLB	Bobby Bell (Minnesota)
Herb Adderley	LHB	Tom Janik (Texas A&I)
Jesse Whittenton	RHB	Larry Glueck (Villanova)
Hank Gremminger	LS	L. Sanders (Michigan St.)
Willie Wood	RS	Kermit Alexander (UCLA)

Head coaches—Vince Lombardi, Green Bay; Otto Graham (Coast Guard), College All Stars

Green Bay	7	3	0	7	—	17
College All-Stars	3	7	10	0	—	20

GB —Taylor 2 run (J. Kramer kick)
All-Stars—FG Jencks 20
All-Stars—Ferguson 6 run (Jencks kick)
GB —FG Kramer 21
All-Stars—FG Jencks 33
All-Stars—Richter 73 pass from VanderKelen (Jencks kick)
GB —Taylor 1 run (J. Kramer kick)
Attendance—65,000

1964

CHICAGO 28, ALL-STARS 17

The Chicago Bears overcame the College All-Stars' 10-7 halftime lead with three unanswered touchdowns in the third and fourth quarters on their way to a 28-17 victory.

August 7, at Soldier Field

Chicago	Starters, Offense	College All-Stars
Gary Barnes	LE	C. Logan (Northwestern)
Herman Lee	LT	Lloyd Voss (Nebraska)
Ted Karras	LG	Harrison Rosdahl (Penn St.)
Mike Pyle	C	Ray Kubala (Texas A&M)
Jim Cadile	RG	Dick Evey (Tennessee)
Bob Wetoska	RT	Ernie Borghetti (Pittsburgh)
Mike Ditka	RE	Ted Davis (Georgia Tech)
Bill Wade	QB	Pete Beathard (USC)
Johnny Morris	FL	Paul Warfield (Ohio State)
Ron Bull	HB	Tony Lorick (Arizona State)
Joe Marconi	FB	W. Crenshaw (Kansas St.)
	Starters, Defense	
Ed O'Bradovich	LE	George Seals (Missouri)
Stan Jones	LT	Tom Keating (Michigan)
Earl Leggett	RT	Geo. Bednar (Notre Dame)
Doug Atkins	RE	Ed Lothamer (Michigan)
Joe Fortunato	LLB	Wally Hilgenberg (Iowa)
Bill George	MLB	Mike Reilly (Iowa)
Larry Morris	RLB	Dave Wilcox (Oregon)
Bennie McRae	LHB	George Rose (Auburn)
Dave Whitsell	RHB	J. Richardson (W. Texas St.)
Richie Petitbon	LS	Perry Lee Dunn (Miss.)
Roosevelt Taylor	RS	Mel Renfro (Oregon)

Head coaches—George Halas, Chicago; Otto Graham (Coast Guard), College All-Stars

Chicago	0	7	14	7	—	28
College All-Stars	0	10	0	7	—	17

All-Stars—FG Van Raaphorst 14
Chi —Ditka 13 pass from Wade (Jencks kick).
All-Stars—Davis 14 pass from Taylor (Van Raaphorst kick)
Chi —Wade 1 run (Jencks kick)
Chi —Barnes 20 pass from Wade (Jencks kick)
Chi —Bivins 30 pass from Bukich (Jencks kick)
All-Stars—Taylor 5 pass from Mira (Van Raaphorst kick)
Attendance—65,000

1965

CLEVELAND 24, ALL-STARS 16

Cleveland's Jamie Caleb blocked a punt by Mississippi's Frank Lambert when the College All-Stars had 10 men on the field in the second quarter and Stan Sczurek recovered the ball in the end zone.

August 6, at Soldier Field

Cleveland	Starters, Offense	College All-Stars
Paul Warfield	LE	Bob Hayes (Florida, A&M)
Dick Schafrath	LT	Ralph Neely (Oklahoma)
John Wooten	LG	Bob Breitenstein (Tulsa)
John Morrow	C	Bill Curry (Georgia Tech)
Gene Hickerson	RG	Jim Wilson (Georgia)
Monte Clark	RT	Harry Schuh (Memphis St.)
Johnny Brewer	RE	Fred Brown (Miami)
Frank Ryan	QB	Roger Staubach (Navy)
Gary Collins	FL	Fred Biletnikoff (Florida St.)
Ernie Green	HB	Pat Donnelly (Navy)
Jim Brown	FB	Ken Willard (North Carolina)
	Starters, Defense	
Paul Wiggin	LE	Jim Garcia (Purdue)
Dick Modzelewski	LT	J. Szczecko (N'western)
Jim Kanicki	RT	Jim Norton (Washington)
Bill Glass	RE	Verlon Biggs (Jackson St.)
Jim Houston	LLB	Don Croftcheck (Indiana)
Vince Costello	MLB	Dick Butkus (Illinois)
Galen Fiss	RLB	Marty Schottenheimer (Pitt.)
Bernie Parrish	LHB	C. Williams (Washington St.)
Walter Beach	RHB	Roy Jefferson (Utah)
Ross Fichtner	LS	Al Nelson (Cincinnati)
Larry Benz	RS	George Donnelly (Illinois)

Head coaches—Blanton Collier, Cleveland; Otto Graham (Coast Guard), College All-Stars

Cleveland	7	10	7	0	—	24
College All-Stars	0	3	6	7	—	16

Cle —Brown 7 run (Groza kick)
All-Stars—FG Mercein 36
Cle —Sczurek, blocked punt recovery in end zone
Cle —FG Groza 30
Cle —Collins 10 pass from Ryan (Groza kick)
All-Stars—Mercein 5 pass from Huarte (kick failed)
All-Stars—Rentzel 5 pass from Huarte (Mercein kick)
Attendance—68,000

1966

GREEN BAY 38, ALL-STARS 0

Quarterback Steve Sloan of Alabama fumbled on the game's first play from scrimmage, and Green Bay's Lionel Aldridge recovered on the College All-Stars' 33-yard line. Five plays later the Packers scored.

August 5, at Soldier Field

Green Bay	Starters, Offense	College All-Stars
Carroll Dale	LE	G. Garrison (San Diego St.)
Bob Skoronski	LT	D. McCormick (LSU)
Fred (Fuzzy) Thurston	LG	John Niland (Iowa)
Ken Bowman	C	Pat Killorin (Syracuse)
Jerry Kramer	RG	Tom Mack (Michigan)
Forrest Gregg	RT	Francis Peay (Missouri)
Bill Anderson	RE	Milt Morin (Massachusetts)
Bart Starr	QB	Steve Sloan (Alabama)
Boyd Dowler	HB	D. Anderson (Texas Tech)
Paul Hornung	HB	Roy Shivers (Utah State)
Jim Taylor	FB	Johnny Roland (Missouri)
	Starters, Defense	
Willie Davis	LE	Stan Hindman (Mississippi)
Ron Kostelnik	LT	Jerry Shay (Purdue)
Henry Jordan	RT	George Rice (Louisiana St.)
Lionel Aldridge	RE	Aaron Brown (Minnesota)
Dave Robinson	LLB	Doug Buffone (Louisville)
Ray Nitschke	MLB	Tommy Nobis (Texas)
Lee Roy Caffey	RLB	Don Hansen (Illinois)
Herb Adderley	LH	S. Quintana (New Mexico)
Bob Jeter	RH	Charlie King (Purdue)
Willie Wood	LS	Doug McFalls (Georgia)
Tom Brown	RS	Nick Rassas (Notre Dame)

Head coaches—Vince Lombardi, Green Bay; John Sauer, College All-Stars

Green Bay	7	21	10	0	—	38
College All-Stars	0	0	0	0	—	0

GB—Dowler 10 pass from Starr (Chandler kick)
GB—B. Anderson 13 pass from Starr (Chandler kick)
GB—Taylor 1 run (Chandler kick)
GB—Adderley 36 interception return (Chandler kick)
GB—FG Chandler 17
GB—Taylor 13 run (Chandler kick)
Attendance—72,000

1967

GREEN BAY 27, ALL-STARS 0

Quarterback Bart Starr completed 15 of 21 passes for 212 yards and two touchdowns and turned nine third-down situations into six first downs before leaving the game at the end of the half with the Green Bay Packers leading the College All-Stars 20-0.

August 4, at Soldier Field

Green Bay	Starters, Offense	College All-Stars
Boyd Dowler	LE	G. Washington (Michigan St.)
Bob Skoronski	LT	Gene Upshaw (Texas A&I)
Gale Gillingham	LG	Tom Regner (Notre Dame)
Ken Bowman	C	B. Hyland (Boston College)
Jerry Kramer	RG	Norman Davis (Grambling)
Forrest Gregg	RT	Mike Current (Ohio State)
Allen Brown	TE	Tom Beer (Houston)
Bart Starr	QB	Steve Spurrier (Florida)
Carroll Dale	FL	Dave Williams (Wash.)
Elijah Pitts	RB	Floyd Little (Syracuse)
Ben Wilson	RB	Mel Farr (UCLA)
	Starters, Defense	
Willie Davis	LE	Leo Carroll (San Diego St.)
Ron Kostelnik	LT	Bubba Smith (Michigan St.)
Henry Jordan	RT	Dave Rowe (Penn. State)
Lionel Aldridge	RE	Alan Page (Notre Dame)
Dave Robinson	LLB	G. Webster (Michigan St.)
Ray Nitschke	MLB	Jim Lynch (Notre Dame)
Lee Roy Caffey	RLB	Paul Naumoff (Tennessee)
Herb Adderley	LH	Bob Grim (Oregon State)
Bob Jeter	RH	Phil Clark (Northwestern)
Tom Brown	LS	Rick Volk (Michigan)
Willie Wood	RS	Henry King (Utah State)

Head coaches—Vince Lombardi, Green Bay; John Sauer, College All-Stars

Green Bay	6	14	0	7	—	27
College All-Stars	0	0	0	0	—	0

GB—FG Chandler 13
GB—FG Chandler 16
GB—Dowler 11 pass from Starr (Chandler kick)
GB—Long 22 pass from Starr (Chandler kick)
GB—Grabowski 22 run (Chandler kick)
Attendance—70,934

1968

GREEN BAY 34, ALL STARS 17

Quarterback Bart Starr completed 17 of 23 passes for 288 yards and three touchdowns.

August 2, at Soldier Field

Green Bay	Starters, Offense	College All-Stars
Boyd Dowler	LE	B. Wallace (Texas-El Paso)
Bob Skoronski	LT	Mo Moorman (Texas A&M)
Gale Gillingham	LG	Bill Leuck (Arizona)
Ken Bowman	C	Bob Johnson (Tennessee)
Jerry Kramer	RG	John Williams (Minnesota)
Forrest Gregg	RT	Ron Yary (USC)
Marv Fleming	TE	C. Sanders (Minnesota)
Bart Starr	QB	Gary Beban (UCLA)
Carroll Dale	FL	Dennis Homan (Alabama)
Elijah Pitts	RB	MacArthur Lane (Utah St.)
Jim Grabowski	RB	Larry Csonka (Syracuse)
	Starters, Defense	
Willie Davis	LE	C. Humphrey (Tenn. St.)
Ron Kostelnik	LT	Curley Culp (Arizona State)
Henry Jordan	RT	Bill Staley (Utah State)
Lionel Aldridge	RE	M. Upshaw (Trinity, Tex.)
Dave Robinson	LLB	Fred Carr (Texas-El Paso)
Ray Nitschke	MLB	Mike McGill (Notre Dame)
Lee Roy Caffey	RLB	Adrian Young (USC)
Herb Adderley	LHB	J. Henderson (Colorado St.)
Bob Jeter	RHB	Jim Smith (Oregon)
Tom Brown	LS	M. Hazelton (Florida A&M)
Willie Wood	RS	Bob Atkins (Grambling)

Head coaches—Phil Bengtson, Green Bay; Norm Van Brocklin, College All-Stars

Green Bay	7	17	0	10	—	34
College All-Stars	0	3	7	7	—	17

GB —Anderson 1 run (Kramer kick)
GB —Dale 20 pass from Starr (Kramer kick)
GB —Dale 36 pass from Starr (Kramer kick)
All-Stars—FG DePoyster 22
GB —FG Traynham 30
All-Stars—McCullouch 7 pass from Beban (DePoyster kick)
GB —Dale 23 pass from Starr (Kramer kick)
GB —FG Kramer 47
All-Stars—McCullouch 24 pass from Landry (DePoyster kick)
Attendance—69,917

1969

N.Y. JETS 26, ALL-STARS 24

The New York Jets, the first AFL representative in the game, scored a 26-24 victory.

August 1, at Soldier Field

N.Y. Jets	Starters, Offense	College All-Stars
George Sauer	WR	Jim Seymour (Notre Dame)
Winston Hill	LT	Dave Foley (Ohio State)
Randy Rasmussen	LG	Mike Montler (Colorado)
John Schmitt	C	Jon Kolb (Oklahoma State)
Dave Herman	RG	John Shinners (Xavier)
Sam Walton	RT	George Kunz (Notre Dame)
Pete Lammons	TE	Bob Klein (USC)
Don Maynard	WR	Jerry LeVias (SMU)
Joe Namath	QB	Terry Hanratty (Notre Dame)
Emerson Boozer	RB	Altie Taylor (Utah State)
Matt Snell	RB	Paul Gipson (Houston)
	Starters, Defense	
Gerry Philbin	LE	Bill Stanfill (Georgia)
Paul Rochester	LT	Rich Moore (Villanova)
John Elliott	RT	Rolf Krueger (Texas A&M)
Verlon Biggs	RE	Fred Dryer (San Diego St.)
John Neidert	LLB	Ron Pritchard (Arizona St.)
Al Atkinson	MLB	Bill Bergey (Arkansas State)
Ralph Baker	RLB	Bob Babich (Miami, Ohio)
Johnny Sample	LCB	J. Marsalis (Tennessee State)
Randy Beverly	RCB	B. Thompson (Maryland St.)
Bill Baird	LS	Gene Eps (Texas-El Paso)
Jim Hudson	RS	Roger Wehrli (Missouri)

Head coaches—Weeb Ewbank, N.Y. Jets; Otto Graham, College All-Stars

N.Y. Jets	6	7	10	3	—	26
College All-Stars	0	0	17	7	—	24

NYJ —FG J. Turner 43
NYJ —FG Turner 16
NYJ —Snell 3 run (J. Turner kick)
All-Stars—Washington 17 pass from Cook (Gerela kick)
All-Stars—FG Gerela 28
NYJ —Snell 35 run (J. Turner kick)
All-Stars—Klein 12 pass from Cook (Gerela kick)
NYJ —FG J. Turner 18
All-Stars—LeVias 19 pass from Cook (Gerela kick)
Attendance—74,208

1970

KANSAS CITY 24, ALL-STARS 3

Len Dawson was successful on 17 of 21 passes, including 12 of 14 for 117 yards and one touchdown in the first half, as the Kansas City Chiefs defeated the College All-Stars 24–3.

Dawson's 36-yard pass to Frank Pitts put Kansas City ahead 7–0 the first time it had the ball.

July 31, at Soldier Field

Kansas City	Starters, Offense	College All-Stars
Frank Pitts	WR	Jerry Hendren (Idaho)
Jim Tyrer	LT	Bob McKay (Texas)
Ed Budde	LG	D. Wilkerson (No. Car. Cent.)
E. J. Holub	C	Sid Smith (USC)
Mo Moorman	RG	C. Hutchison (Ohio State)
Dave Hill	RT	Bob Asher (Vanderbilt)
Fred Arbanas	TE	R. Caster (Jackson State)
Otis Taylor	WR	Ron Shanklin (No. Texas St.)
Len Dawson	QB	D. Shaw (San Diego State)
Mike Garrett	RB	Bob Anderson (Colorado)
Robert Holmes	RB	Art Malone (Arizona State)
	Starters, Defense	
Jerry Mays	LE	Al Cowlings (USC)
Curley Culp	LT	Mike McCoy (Notre Dame)
Buck Buchanan	RT	Mike Reid (Penn State)
Aaron Brown	RE	C. Hardman (No. Texas St.)
Bobby Bell	LLB	John Small (The Citadel)
Willie Lanier	MLB	Steve Zabel (Oklahoma)
Jim Lynch	RLB	Jim Files (Oklahoma)
Jim Marsalis	LCB	Bruce Taylor (Boston U.)
Emmitt Thomas	RCB	Al Mathews (Texas A&I)
Jim Kearney	LS	Steve Tannen (Florida)
Johnny Robinson	RS	Charlie Waters (Clemson)

Head coaches–Hank Stram, Kansas City; Otto Graham, College All-Stars

Kansas City	10	14	0	0	—	24
College All-Stars	0	0	3	0	—	3

KC —Pitts 36 pass from Dawson (Stenerud kick)
KC —FG Stenerud 43
KC —McVea 3 run (Stenerud kick)
KC —Kearney 65 interception return (Stenerud kick)
All-Stars–FG Delaney 26
Attendance—69,940

1971

BALTIMORE 24, ALL-STARS 17

The Baltimore Colts' 24–17 victory over the College All-Stars was the professionals' eighth in a row and gave them a record of 27 victories, 9 losses, and 2 ties in the series.

July 30, at Soldier Field

Baltimore	Starters, Offense	College All-Stars
Ed Hinton	WR	J. D. Hill (Arizona State)
Bob Vogel	LT	Marv Montgomery (USC)
Glenn Ressler	LG	Steve Lawson (Kansas)
Bill Curry	C	Warren Koegel (Penn State)
John Williams	RG	H. Allison (San Diego St.)
Dan Sullivan	RT	Vern Holland (Tenn. State)
John Mackey	TE	Bob Moore (Stanford)
Ray Perkins	WR	E. Jennings (Air Force)
Earl Morrall	QB	Jim Plunkett (Stanford)
Tom Matte	RB	J. Brockington (Ohio State)
Norm Bulaich	RB	M. Adamle (Northwestern)
	Starters, Defense	
Charles (Bubba) Smith	LE	Jack Youngblood (Florida)
Jim Bailey	LT	J. Adams (Texas Southern)
Billy Newsome	RT	Tony McGee (Bishop)
Roy Hilton	RE	Richard Harris (Grambling)
Ray May	LLB	Ron Hornsby (SE Louisiana)
Mike Curtis	MLB	I. Robertson (Southern U.)
Ted Hendricks	RLB	Jack Ham (Penn State)
Charlie Stukes	LCB	C. Scott (Kansas State)
Jim Duncan	RCB	Ike Thomas (Bishop)
Jerry Logan	LS	Charles Hall (Pittsburgh)
Rick Volk	RS	Jack Tatum (Ohio State)

Head coaches—Don McCafferty, Baltimore; Blanton Collier, College All-Stars

Baltimore	7	7	3	7	—	24
College All-Stars	0	10	0	7	—	17

Balt —Perkins 24 pass from Morrall (O'Brien kick)
All-Stars—Brockington 1 run (Pastorini kick)
Balt —Matte 15 pass from Morrall (O'Brien kick)
All-Stars—FG Jacobs 40
Balt —FB O'Brien 22
Balt —Mitchell 44 pass from Morrall (O'Brien kick)
All-Stars—Ham 47 fumble return (Jacobs kick)
Attendance—52,289

1972

DALLAS 20, ALL-STARS 7

The Dallas Cowboys converted a pass interception and recovered fumble into 10 points.

Mel Renfro intercepted a pass by Jerry Tagge at the All-Stars' 30 in the first quarter; the Cowboys turned the mistake into Mike Clark's 31-yard field goal.

July 28, at Soldier Field

Dallas	Starters, Offense	College All-Stars
Bob Hayes	WR	Mike Siani (Villanova)
Ralph Neely	LT	Lionel Antoine (So. Illinois)
John Niland	LG	R. McKenzie (Michigan)
Dave Manders	C	Bob Kuziel (Pittsburgh)
Blaine Nye	RG	S. Okoniewski (Montana)
Rayfield Wright	RT	Dan Yockum (Syracuse)
Mike Ditka	TE	Riley Odoms (Houston)
Lance Alworth	WR	Glenn Doughty (Michigan)
Roger Staubach	QB	Jerry Tagge (Nebraska)
Duane Thomas	RB	Jeff Kinney (Nebraska)
Walt Garrison	RB	Franco Harris (Penn State)
	Starters, Defense	
Larry Cole	LE	Walt Patulski (Notre Dame)
Jethro Pugh	LT	J. Mendenhall (Grambling)
Bob Lilly	RT	Pete Lazetich (Stanford)
George Andrie	RE	Sherman White (California)
Dave Edwards	LLB	Willie Hall (USC)
Lee Roy Jordan	MLB	Jeff Siemon (Stanford)
Chuck Howley	RLB	Mike Taylor (Michigan)
Herb Adderley	LCB	W. Buchanon (San Diego St.)
Mel Renfro	RCB	Tommy Casanova (L.S.U.)
Cornell Green	LS	Thom Darden (Michigan)
Cliff Harris	RS	Craig Clemons (Iowa)

Head coaches–Tom Landry, Dallas; Bob Devaney (Nebraska), College All-Stars

Dallas	3	7	7	3	—	20
College All-Stars	0	0	0	7	—	7

Dall —FG Clark 31
Dall —Sellers 18 pass from Morton (Clark kick)
Dall —Hayes 24 pass from Morton (Fritsch kick)
Dall —FG Fritsch 33
All-Stars—Newhouse 1 run (Marcol kick)
Attendance—54,162

1973

MIAMI 14, ALL-STARS 3

The Miami Dolphins marched 66 yards to Larry Csonka's three-yard touchdown run the first time they had the ball and went on to defeat the College All-Stars 14–3.

Csonka gained 76 yards in 17 carries as the professionals outgained the collegians 251–143 in total offense.

July 27, at Soldier Field

Miami	Starters, Offense	College All-Stars
Paul Warfield	WR	Barry Smith (Florida State)
Wayne Moore	LT	Paul Seymour (Michigan)
Bob Kuechenberg	LG	Pete Adams (USC)
Jim Langer	C	Dave Brown (USC)
Larry Little	RG	John Hannah (Alabama)
Norm Evans	RT	Jerry Sisemore (Texas)
Marv Fleming	TE	Charles Young (USC)
Howard Twilley	WR	Steve Holden (Arizona St.)
Bob Griese	QB	Bert Jones (Louisiana State)
Jim Kiick	RB	T. Metcalf (Long Beach St.)
Larry Csonka	RB	Chuck Foreman (Miami)
	Starters, Defense	
Vern Den Herder	LE	W. Chambers (E. Kentucky)
Manny Fernandez	LT	John Grant (USC)
Bob Heinz	RT	Richard Glover (Nebraska)
Bill Stanfill	RE	John Matuszak (Tampa)
Doug Swift	LLB	Jim Merlo (Stanford)
Nick Buoniconti	MLB	J. Youngblood (Tenn. Tech)
Bob Matheson	RLB	Gary Weaver (Fresno State)
Tim Foley	LCB	Burgess Owens (Miami)
Curtis Johnson	RCB	M. Holmes (Texas Southern)
Charlie Babb	LS	J. T. Thomas (Florida State)
Dick Anderson	RS	Jackie Wallace (Arizona)

Head coaches–Don Shula (Miami); John McKay (USC), College All-Stars

Miami	7	0	0	7	—	14
College All-Stars	0	3	0	0	—	3

Mia —Csonka 3 run (Yepremian kick)
All-Stars—FG Guy 10
Mia —Csonka 7 run (Yepremian kick)
Attendance—54,103

1974

NO GAME

The forty-first Chicago All-Star game was canceled by the sponsoring *Chicago Tribune* after the NFL Players Association said it would not give full sanction to the game between the College All-Stars and Miami Dolphins.

The Players' Association and NFL owners were involved in a collective bargaining dispute that had resulted in some of the Association's members striking their summer training camps. The All-Stars voted not to continue preparation for the contest unless the players and owners settled their dispute.

1975

PITTSBURGH 21, ALL-STARS 14

Trailing 14–7 at the half, the Pittsburgh Steelers rallied for a 21–14 victory over the College All-Stars behind quarterback Joe Gilliam, who passed for two touchdowns in the fourth quarter.

Gilliam replaced starter Terry Bradshaw.

August 1, at Soldier Field

Pittsburgh	Starters, Offense	College All-Stars
Frank Lewis	WR	Pat McInally (Harvard)
Jon Kolb	LT	Dennis Harrah (Miami)
Jim Clack	LG	Ken Huff (North Carolina)
Ray Mansfield	C	Kyle Davis (Oklahoma)
Gerry Mullins	RG	L. Boden (South Dakota St.)
Gordon Gravelle	RT	Kurt Schumacher (Ohio St.)
Larry Brown	TE	Russ Francis (Oregon)
Ron Shanklin	WR	Emmett Edwards (Kansas)
Terry Bradshaw	QB	S. Bartkowski (California)
Rocky Bleier	RB	Walter Payton (Jackson St.)
Franco Harris	RB	Stan Winfrey (Arkansas St.)
	Starters, Defense	
L. C. Greenwood	LE	Mike Fanning (Notre Dame)
Joe Greene	LT	Mike Hartenstine (Penn St.)
Ernie Holmes	RT	Randy White (Maryland)
Dwight White	RE	Robert Brazile (Jackson St.)
Jack Ham	LLB	Glenn Cameron (Florida)
Jack Lambert	MLB	Ralph Ortega (Florida)
Andy Russell	RLB	Richard Wood (USC)
J. T. Thomas	LCB	Neal Colzie (Ohio State)
Mel Blount	RCB	Louis Wright (San Jose St.)
Mike Wagner	LS	Charles Phillips (USC)
Glen Edwards	RS	Marvin Cobb (USC)

Head coaches—Chuck Noll, Pittsburgh; John McKay (USC), College All-Stars

Pittsburgh	0	7	0	14	—	21
College All-Stars	7	7	0	0	—	14

All-Stars—McInally 26 pass from Bartkowski (Mike-Mayer kick)
Pitt —Grossman 2 pass from Bradshaw (Gerela kick)
All-Stars—Livers 86 punt return (Mike-Mayer kick)
Pitt —Bleier 6 pass from Gilliam (Gerela kick)
Pitt —Lewis 21 pass from Gilliam (Gerela kick)
Attendance—54,103

1976

PITTSBURGH 24, ALL-STARS 0

The Pittsburgh Steelers won 24–0 in the last Chicago All-Star Game. It was called with 1:22 left in the third quarter. A thunderstorm flooded the field and 12 minutes later game officials agreed with NFL Commissioner Pete Rozelle to suspend play.

July 23, at Soldier Field

Pittsburgh	Starters, Offense	College All-Stars
Frank Lewis	WR	D. Harris (New Mexico St.)
Jon Kolb	LT	Mark Koncar (Colorado)
Jim Clack	LG	Tom Glassic (Virginia)
Mike Webster	C	Pete Brock (Colorado)
Gerry Mullins	RG	Jackie Slater (Jackson St.)
Gordon Gravelle	RT	Dennis Lick (Wisconsin)
Larry Brown	TE	B. Cunningham (Clemson)
Lynn Swann	WR	Brian Baschnagel (Ohio St.)
Terry Bradshaw	QB	M. Kruczek (Boston Coll.)
Rocky Bleier	RB	Joe Washington (Oklahoma)
Franco Harris	RB	Tony Galbreath (Missouri)
	Starters, Defense	
L. C. Greenwood	LE	Troy Archer (Colorado)
Joe Greene	LT	L. Roy Selmon (Oklahoma)
Ernie Holmes	RT	Dewey Selmon (Oklahoma)
Dwight White	RE	James White (Oklahoma St.)
Jack Ham	LLB	Kevin McLain (Colorado St.)
Jack Lambert	MLB	Ed Simonini (Texas A&M)
Andy Russell	RLB	Larry Gordon (Arizona St.)
J. T. Thomas	LCB	Aaron Kyle (Wyoming)
Mel Blount	RCB	Mario Clark (Oregon)
Mike Wagner	LS	Shafer Suggs (Ball State)
Glen Edwards	RS	Ed Lewis (Kansas)

Head coaches–Chuck Noll, Pittsburgh; Ara Parseghian, College All-Stars

Pittsburgh	3	6	15	—	24
College All-Stars	0	0	0	—	0

Pitt—FG Gerela 29
Pitt—FG Gerela 32
Pitt—FG Gerela 23
Pitt—Safety, Pinney centered ball out of end zone
Pitt—Harris 21 run (Gerela) kick
Pitt—Reamon 2 run (kick failed)
Attendance—52,895

CHICAGO ALL-STAR GAME HISTORY

Date	Result	Site (attendance)
Aug. 31, 1934	Chi. Bears 0, College All-Stars 0	Soldier Field, Chicago (79,432)
Aug. 29, 1935	Chi. Bears 5, College All-Stars 0	Soldier Field, Chicago (77,450)
Sept. 3, 1936	College All-Stars 7, Detroit Lions 0	Soldier Field, Chicago (76,000)
Sept. 1, 1937	College All-Stars 6, Green Bay Packers 0	Soldier Field, Chicago (84,560)
Aug. 31, 1938	College All-Stars 28, Washington 16	Soldier Field, Chicago (74,250)
Aug. 30, 1939	N.Y. Giants 9, College All-Stars 0	Soldier Field, Chicago (81,456)
Aug. 29, 1940	Green Bay 45, College All-Stars 28	Soldier Field, Chicago (84,567)
Aug. 28, 1941	Chi Bears 37, College All-Stars 13	Soldier Field, Chicago (98,203)
Aug. 28, 1942	Chi. Bears 21, College All-Stars 0	Soldier Field, Chicago (101,100)
Aug. 25, 1943	College All-Stars 27, Washington 7	Dyche Stadium, Evanston (48,471)
Aug. 30, 1944	Chi. Bears 24, College All-Stars 21	Dyche Stadium, Evanston (48,769)
Aug. 30, 1945	Green Bay 19, College All-Stars 7	Soldier Field, Chicago (92,753)
Aug. 23, 1946	College All-Stars 16, Los Angeles 0	Soldier Field, Chicago (97,380)
Aug. 22, 1947	College All-Stars 16, Chi. Bears 0	Soldier Field, Chicago (105,840)
Aug. 20, 1948	Chi. Cardinals 28, College All-Stars 0	Soldier Field, Chicago (101,220)
Aug. 12, 1949	Philadelphia 38, College All-Stars 0	Soldier Field, Chicago (93,780)
Aug. 11, 1950	College All-Stars 17, Philadelphia 7	Soldier Field, Chicago (88,885)
Aug. 17, 1951	Cleveland 33, College All-Stars 0	Soldier Field, Chicago (92,180)
Aug. 15, 1952	Los Angeles 10, College All-Stars 7	Soldier Field, Chicago (88,316)
Aug. 14, 1953	Detroit 24, College All-Stars 10	Soldier Field, Chicago (93,818)
Aug. 13, 1954	Detroit 31, College All-Stars 6	Soldier Field, Chicago (93,470)
Aug. 12, 1955	College All-Stars 30, Cleveland 27	Soldier Field, Chicago (75,000)
Aug. 10, 1956	Cleveland 26, College All-Stars 0	Soldier Field, Chicago (75,000)
Aug. 9, 1957	N.Y. Giants 22, College All-Stars 12	Soldier Field, Chicago (75,000)
Aug. 15, 1958	College All-Stars 35, Detroit 19	Soldier Field, Chicago (70,000)
Aug. 14, 1959	Baltimore 29, College All-Stars 0	Soldier Field, Chicago (70,000)
Aug. 12, 1960	Baltimore 32, College All-Stars 7	Soldier Field, Chicago (70,000)
Aug. 4, 1961	Philadelphia 28, College All-Stars 14	Soldier Field, Chicago (66,000)
Aug. 3, 1962	Green Bay 42, College All-Stars 20	Soldier Field, Chicago (65,000)
Aug. 2, 1963	College All-Stars 20, Green Bay 17	Soldier Field, Chicago (65,000)
Aug. 7, 1964	Chicago 28, College All-Stars 17	Soldier Field, Chicago (65,000)
Aug. 6, 1965	Cleveland 24, College All-Stars 16	Soldier Field, Chicago (68,000)
Aug. 5, 1966	Green Bay 38, College All-Stars 0	Soldier Field, Chicago (72,000)
Aug. 4, 1967	Green Bay 27, College All-Stars 0	Soldier Field, Chicago (70,934)
Aug. 2, 1968	Green Bay 34, College All-Stars 17	Soldier Field, Chicago (69,917)
Aug. 1, 1969	N.Y. Jets 26, College All-Stars 24	Soldier Field, Chicago (74,208)
July 31, 1970	Kansas City 24, College All-Stars 3	Soldier Field, Chicago (69,940)
July 30, 1971	Baltimore 24, College All-Stars 17	Soldier Field, Chicago (52,289)
July 28, 1972	Dallas 20, College All-Stars 7	Soldier Field, Chicago (54,162)
July 27, 1973	Miami 14, College All-Stars 3	Soldier Field, Chicago (54,103)
July 26, 1974	No game was played because of NFL players-owners dispute	
Aug. 1, 1975	Pittsburgh 21, College All-Stars 14	Soldier Field, Chicago (54,103)
July 23, 1976	Pittsburgh 24, College All-Stars 0	Soldier Field, Chicago (52,895)

Professional teams, 31 victories; College All-Stars 10 victories; 1 tie

Divisional Playoff Games

1941

CHI. BEARS 33, GREEN BAY 14

A brilliant sun couldn't melt the snow that framed the playing area on a 16-degree day at Wrigley Field, where Hugh Gallarneau's 81-yard punt return for a touchdown in the first quarter signaled 30 unanswered points for Chicago. Gallarneau had fumbled the opening kickoff, setting up a five-play, 18-yard touchdown drive that put the Packers ahead 7–0.

Green Bay and Chicago tied for first with 10–1 records in the NFL's Western Division, necessitating the playoff, which was conducted with rules allowing for sudden death overtime periods.

Chicago outrushed Green Bay 267–35 as George McAfee ran for 119 yards; Norm Standlee gained 79.

December 14, at Chicago

Green Bay	Starting Lineups	Chi. Bears
Don Hutson	LE	Dick Plasman
Buford (Baby) Ray	LT	Ed Kolman
C. (Buckets) Goldenberg	LG	Danny Fortmann
George Svendsen	C	Clyde (Bulldog) Turner
Lee McLaughlin	RG	Ray Bray
Charlie Schultz	RT	Lee Artoe
Ray Riddick	RE	John Siegal
Larry Craig	QB	Sid Luckman
Cecil Isbell	LH	Ray Nolting
Herman Rohrig	RH	Hugh Gallarneau
Clarke Hinkle	FB	Norm Standlee

Green Bay	7	0	7	0	— 14
Chi. Bears	6	24	0	3	— 33

GB—Hinkle 1 run (Hutson kick)
Chi—Gallarneau 81 punt return (kick blocked)
Chi—FG Snyder 24
Chi—Standlee 3 run (Stydahar kick)
Chi—Standlee 2 run (Stydahar kick)
Chi—Swisher 9 run (Stydahar kick)
GB—Van Every 10 pass from Isbell (Hutson kick)
Chi—FG Snyder 26
Attendance—43,425

1943

WASHINGTON 28, N.Y. GIANTS 0

Washington's Sammy Baugh roamed the Polo Grounds completing 16 of 21 passes for 199 yards and one touchdown and intercepting two passes, returning one 28 yards to set up another score. Baugh also punted four times for a 40-yard average as the Redskins snapped a two-game losing streak to the Giants, who had beaten them 14–0 and 31–7 the previous two Sundays in the final games of the regular season.

Fullback Andy Farkas scored touchdowns on runs of 2, 2, and 1 yard; all of them came behind blocks from right guard Steve Slivinski.

The Redskins outgained the Giants 296–98 in total offense and threw New York's Alphonse (Tuffy) Leemans for 25 yards in rushing losses. The Giants crossed midfield twice. Their deepest penetration was Washington's 32-yard line on a 42-yard pass, Leemans to Ward Cuff.

December 19, at New York

Washington	Starting Lineups	N.Y. Giants
Bob Masterson	LE	Frank Liebel
Lou Rymkus	LT	Frank Cope
Clyde Shugart	LG	Len Younce
George Smith	C	Mel Hein
Steve Slivinski	RG	Vic Carroll
Joe Pasqua	RT	Al Blozis
Joe Aguirre	RE	Steve Pritko
Ray Hare	QB	Leland Shaffer
George Cafego	LH	Ward Cuff
Frank Seno	RH	Dave Brown
Andy Farkas	FB	Hank Soar

Washington	0	14	0	14	— 28
N.Y. Giants	0	0	0	0	— 0

Wash—Farkas 2 run (Masterson kick)
Wash—Farkas 2 run (Masterson kick)
Wash—Farkas 1 run (Masterson kick)
Wash—Lapka 11 pass from Baugh (Masterson kick)
Attendance—42,800

1947

PHILADELPHIA 21, PITTSBURGH 0

End Pete Pihos blocked Bob Cifers's punt in the first quarter, setting up the Philadelphia Eagles' first touchdown in a 21–0 victory over Pittsburgh at Forbes Field. Two plays after the blocked punt, quarterback Tommy Thompson passed 15 yards to Steve Van Buren.

Pittsburgh and Philadelphia had divided their regular season games and tied for first in the Eastern Division with 8–4 records.

Thompson threw for one other touchdown, 28 yards to Jack Ferrante in the second quarter, and completed 11 of 18 passes for 131 yards. Van Buren, who in 1947 became the second man in the NFL's 28-season history to rush for 1,000 yards, gained 47 yards in 18 carries. Ferrante caught 5 passes for 73.

The 1947 Steelers coached by Dr. Jock Sutherland were the last single wing team to reach the NFL playoffs. Sutherland died in an auto crash in 1948.

December 21, at Pittsburgh

Philadelphia	Starting Lineups	Pittsburgh
Jack Ferrante	LE	Charles Mehelich
Jay MacDowell	LT	Jack Wiley
Cliff Patton	LG	Bill Moore
Alex Wojciechowicz	C	Chuck Cherundolo
Frank (Bucko) Kilroy	RG	John Mastrangelo
Al Wistert	RT	Frank Wydo
Pete Pihos	RE	Bob Davis
Tommy Thompson	QB	Charlie Seabright
Steve Van Buren	LH	Walter Slater
Bosh Pritchard	RH	Bob Cifers
Joe Muha	FB	Tony Compagno

Philadelphia	7	7	7	0	— 21
Pittsburgh	0	0	0	0	— 0

Phil—Van Buren 15 pass from Thompson (Patton kick)
Phil—Ferrante 28 pass from Thompson (Patton kick)
Phil—Pritchard 79 punt return (Patton kick)
Attendance—35,729

1950

CLEVELAND 8, N.Y. GIANTS 3

Lou Groza's 28-yard field goal with 58 seconds left in the game broke a 3–3 tie as the Cleveland Browns beat the New York Giants 8–3 in 17-degree weather.

Trailing 3–0 in the fourth quarter, the Giants had a first down on Cleveland's 4-yard line after Gene Roberts ran 32 yards on a reverse. On third down from the 3, Charlie Conerly passed to Bob McChesney in the end zone, but the Giants were penalized for being offside. On fourth down Conerly's pass was intercepted by Tom James, but Cleveland was penalized for holding. The Giants were penalized for being in motion before the snap of the ball on the next play and moved back to the 9. On the sixth play of the sequence, New York's Joe Scott collided with his blocker, Joe Sulaitis, and went down at the 13. Randy Clay then kicked a 20-yard field goal that tied the score.

December 17, at Cleveland

N.Y. Giants	Starting Lineups	Cleveland
Ellery Williams	LE	Mac Speedie
Arnie Weinmeister	LT	Lou Groza
Bill Milner	LG	Weldon Humble
John Rapacz	C	Frank Gatski
Bill Austin	RG	Lin Houston
Al DeRogatis	RT	Lou Rymkus
Bob McChesney	RE	Dante Lavelli
Travis Tidwell	QB	Otto Graham
Charlie Conerly	LH	Rex Bumgardner
Joe Scott	RH	Dub Jones
Eddie Price	FB	Marion Motley

N.Y. Giants	0	0	0	3	— 3
Cleveland	3	0	0	5	— 8

Cle —FG Groza 11
NYG—FG Clay 20
Cle —FG Groza 28
Cle —Safety, Willis tackled Conerly in end zone
Attendance—33,754

1950

LOS ANGELES 24, CHI. BEARS 14

Quarterback Bob Waterfield, unable to practice all week because of an attack of the flu, came off the bench late in the first quarter and threw three touchdown passes to Tom Fears on an 84-degree afternoon the Rams defeated the Chicago Bears 24–14.

Waterfield completed 14 of 21 passes for 280 yards and Fears caught 7 for 198 after Waterfield replaced starter Norm Van Brocklin, who completed 2 of 10 passes for 17 yards. With the Bears leading 7–3 in the second quarter, Waterfield and Fears combined on 43- and 68-yard touchdown plays to put Los Angeles ahead 17–7 at the half. A 27-yard Waterfield-to-Fears pass made the score 24–7 in the third quarter.

The Bears led the Rams 229–74 in rushing yardage and 422–371 in total yardage.

December 17, at Los Angeles

Chi. Bears	Starting Lineups	Los Angeles
Bill Wightkin	LE	Tom Fears
George Connor	LT	Dick Huffman
Dick Barwegan	LG	John Finlay
Clyde (Bulldog) Turner	C	Art Statuto
Ray Bray	RG	Dave Stephenson
Paul Stenn	RT	Bob Reinhard
Ed Sprinkle	RE	Elroy (Crazylegs) Hirsch
Johnny Lujack	QB	Norm Van Brocklin
George Gulyanics	LH	Glenn Davis
Julie Rykovich	RH	Verda (Vitamin T.) Smith
Fred (Curly) Morrison	FB	Dick Hoerner

Chi. Bears	0	7	0	7	— 14
Los Angeles	3	14	7	0	— 24

LA —FG Waterfield 43
Chi—Campana 23 run (Lujack kick)
LA —Fears 43 pass from Waterfield (Waterfield kick)
LA —Fears 68 pass from Waterfield (Waterfield kick)
LA —Fears 27 pass from Waterfield (Waterfield kick)
Chi—Morrison 4 run (Lujack kick)
Attendance—83,501

1952

DETROIT 31, LOS ANGELES 21

Detroit's Pat Harder was an elusive figure in the dense fog and 37-degree weather of Briggs Stadium. He rushed for 72 yards in eight carries, scored two touchdowns and four extra points, and kicked a 43-yard field goal in the Lions' 31–21 victory over Los Angeles.

Harder's third-quarter field goal gave the Lions a 24–7 lead. The Rams rallied for two fourth-quarter touchdowns to close the margin to 24–21. LaVern Torgeson intercepted a pass by the Rams' Bob Waterfield in the final minute of play, setting up Bob Hoernschmeyer's nine-yard touchdown run with 30 seconds left. Detroit's Leon Hart caught 5 passes for 86 yards and one touchdown.

December 21, at Detroit

Los Angeles	Starting Lineups	Detroit
Tom Fears	LE	Cloyce Box
Don Simensen	LT	Lou Creekmur
Dick Daugherty	LG	Jim Martin
Leon McLaughlin	C	Vince Banonis
Harry Thompson	RG	Dick Stanfel
Tom Dahms	RT	Gus Cifelli
Elroy (Crazylegs) Hirsch	RE	Leon Hart
Norm Van Brocklin	QB	Bobby Layne
Dan Towler	LH	Doak Walker
Verda (Vitamin T.) Smith	RH	Byron Bailey
Paul (Tank) Younger	FB	Pat Harder

Los Angeles	0	7	0	14	— 21
Detroit	7	7	10	7	— 31

Det—Harder 12 run (Harder kick)
Det—Harder 4 run (Harder kick)
LA —Fears 14 pass from Van Brocklin (Waterfield kick)
Det—Hart 24 pass from Walker (Harder kick)
Det—FG Harder 43
LA —Towler 5 run (Waterfield kick)
LA —Smith 56 punt return (Harder kick)
Det—Hoernschmeyer 9 run (Harder kick)
Attendance—47,645

1957

DETROIT 31, SAN FRANCISCO 27

Tom Tracy, a seldom-used fullback, replaced the injured John Henry Johnson in the third quarter and scored two touchdowns in the span of 89 seconds as the Detroit Lions overcame a 20-point deficit to defeat the San Francisco 49ers 31–27.

The 49ers led 27–7 when quarterback Y.A. Tittle fumbled and Bob Long recovered on Detroit's 27. The Lions marched 73 yards to Tracy's one-yard touchdown run. After a San Francisco punt, Tracy ran 58 yards on Detroit's first play for a touchdown. Three minutes later Gene Gedman scored to put Detroit in front.

December 22, at San Francisco

Detroit	Starting Lineups	San Francisco
Jim Doran	LE	Clyde Conner
Lou Creekmur	LT	Bob Cross
Harley Sewell	LG	Bruce Bosley
Frank Gatski	C	Frank Morze
Stan Campbell	RG	Lou Palatella
Charlie Ane	RT	Bob St. Clair
Steve Junker	RE	Billy Wilson
Tobin Rote	QB	Y.A. Tittle
Howard (Hopalong) Cassady	LH	Hugh McElhenny
Dave Middleton	RH	R.C. Owens
John Henry Johnson	FB	Joe Perry

Detroit	0	7	14	10	—	31
San Francisco	14	10	3	0	—	27

SF —Owens 34 pass from Tittle (Soltau kick)
SF —McElhenny 47 pass from Tittle (Soltau kick)
Det—Junker 4 pass from Rote (Martin kick)
SF —Wilson 12 pass from Tittle (Soltau kick)
SF —FG Soltau 25
SF —FG Soltau 10
Det—Tracy 1 run (Martin kick)
Det—Tracy 58 run (Martin kick)
Det—Gedman 2 run (Martin kick)
Det—FG Martin 13
Attendance—60,118

1958

N.Y. GIANTS 10, CLEVELAND 0

The New York Giants scored on a play they had first worked on in practice the week of the game to defeat the Cleveland Browns 10–0. Alex Webster took a handoff from quarterback Charlie Conerly, then handed off to Frank Gifford on a double reverse. Gifford ran eight yards to the Browns' 10 and lateraled to Conerly, who was trailing the play. Conerly ran for the touchdown. "The lateral was optional," said Conerly. "I was there if Gifford needed me."

Cleveland's Jim Brown, who set an NFL record with 1,527 yards rushing during the season, was held to 8 yards in 7 carries; the Browns totaled 86 yards, 24 rushing and 62 passing. Cleveland moved to New York's 6-yard line early in the fourth quarter, but Sam Huff intercepted Milt Plum's pass and the Giants controlled the ball for 10 of the last 11 minutes.

Gifford led all rushers with 95 yards in 23 carries.

December 21, at New York

Cleveland	Starting Lineups	N.Y. Giants
Darrell (Pete) Brewster	LE	Kyle Rote
Lou Groza	LT	Roosevelt Brown
Jim Ray Smith	LG	Al Barry
Art Hunter	C	Ray Wietecha
Chuck Noll	RG	Jack Stroud
Willie McClung	RT	Frank Youso
Preston Carpenter	RE	Bob Schnelker
Milt Plum	QB	Don Heinrich
Ray Renfro	LH	Frank Gifford
Bobby Mitchell	RH	Alex Webster
Jim Brown	FB	Mel Triplett

Cleveland	0	0	0	0	—	0
N.Y. Giants	7	3	0	0	—	10

NYG—Conerly 10 lateral from Gifford, who had run 8 (Summerall kick)
NYG—FG Summerall 26
Attendance—61,274

1963 AFL

BOSTON 26, BUFFALO 8

Fullback Larry Garron turned short pass receptions from Babe Parilli into 59- and 17- yard touchdowns as the Boston Patriots beat the Buffalo Bills in 20-degree weather in War Memorial Stadium.

December 28, at Buffalo

Boston	Starters, Offense	Buffalo
Gino Cappelletti	LE	Bill Miller
Don Oakes	LT	Stew Barber
Chuck Long	LG	Tom Day
Walt Cudzik	C	Al Bemiller
Billy Neighbors	RG	Billy Shaw
Milt Graham	RT	Ken Rice
Tony Romeo	RE	Ernie Warlick
Babe Parilli	QB	Jack Kemp
Ron Burton	LH	Elbert Dubenion
Jim Colclough	RH	Glenn Bass
Larry Garron	FB	Cookie Gilchrist
	Starters, Defense	
Bob Dee	LE	Ron McDole
Houston Antwine	LT	Tom Sestak
Jesse Richardson	RT	Jim Dunaway
Jim Hunt	RE	Mack Yoho
Tom Addison	LLB	John Tracey
Nick Buoniconti	MLB	Harry Jacobs
Jack Rudolph	RLB	Mike Stratton
Dick Felt	LCB	Willie West
Bob Suci	RCB	Booker Edgerson
Ron Hall	LS	George Saimes
Ross O'Hanley	RS	Ray Abruzzese

Boston	10	6	0	10	—	26
Buffalo	0	0	8	0	—	8

Bos—FG Cappelletti 28
Bos—Garron 59 pass from Parilli (Cappelletti kick)
Bos—FG Cappelletti 12
Bos—FG Cappelletti 33
Buff—Dubenion 93 pass from Lamonica (Tracey pass from Lamonica)
Bos—Garron 17 pass from Parilli (Cappelletti kick)
Bos—FG Cappelletti 36
Attendance—33,044

1965 NFL

GREEN BAY 13, BALTIMORE 10

Don Chandler's field goal at 13:39 of sudden death overtime won the game. Baltimore led for more than 58 minutes, although quarterbacks John Unitas and Gary Cuozzo were injured and Ed Brown had been acquired too late for postseason play. Halfback Tom Matte taped the game plan to his wrist and played quarterback in 1965 for the first time since 1960.

December 26, at Green Bay

Baltimore	Starters, Offense	Green Bay
Raymond Berry	LE	Boyd Dowler
Bob Vogel	LT	Bob Skoronski
Jim Parker	LT	Fred (Fuzzy) Thurston
Dick Szymanski	C	Ken Bowman
Alex Sandusky	RG	Jerry Kramer
George Preas	RT	Forrest Gregg
John Mackey	RE	Bill Anderson
Tom Matte	QB	Bart Starr
Lenny Moore	LH	Paul Hornung
Jimmy Orr	RH	Carroll Dale
Jerry Hill	FB	Jim Taylor
	Starters, Defense	
Lou Michaels	LE	Willie Davis
Fred Miller	LT	Ron Kostelnik
Billy Ray Smith	RT	Henry Jordan
Ordell Braase	RE	Lionel Aldridge
Steve Stonebreaker	LLB	Dave Robinson
Dennis Gaubatz	MLB	Ray Nitschke
Don Shinnick	RLB	Lee Roy Caffey
Bobby Boyd	LCB	Herb Adderley
Lenny Lyles	RCB	Doug Hart
Jerry Logan	LS	Tom Brown
Wendell Harris	RS	Willie Wood

Baltimore	7	3	0	0	0	—	10
Green Bay	0	0	7	3	3	—	13

Balt—Shinnick 25 fumble return (Michaels kick)
Balt—FG Michaels 15
GB—Hornung 1 run (Chandler kick)
GB—FG Chandler 27
GB—FG Chandler 25
Attendance—50,484

1967 NFL

GREEN BAY 28, LOS ANGELES 7

After losing to Los Angeles 27–24 two weeks before, Green Bay yielded a first-quarter touchdown to the Rams, then went on to win 28–7.

Rookie running back Travis Williams rushed for 88 yards and scored on runs of 46 and 2 yards. Quarterback Bart Starr completed 17 of 23 passes for 222 yards.

December 23, at Milwaukee

Los Angeles	Starters, Offense	Green Bay
Jack Snow	LE	Boyd Dowler
Joe Carollo	LT	Bob Skoronski
Tom Mack	LG	Gale Gillingham
Ken Iman	C	Ken Bowman
Joe Scibelli	RG	Jerry Kramer
Charlie Cowan	RT	Forrest Gregg
Billy Truax	RE	Marv Fleming
Roman Gabriel	QB	Bart Starr
Les Josephson	LH	Donny Anderson
Bernie Casey	RH	Carroll Dale
Dick Bass	FB	Chuck Mercein
	Starters, Defense	
David (Deacon) Jones	LE	Willie Davis
Merlin Olsen	LT	Ron Kostelnik
Roger Brown	RT	Henry Jordan
Lamar Lundy	RE	Lionel Aldridge
Jack Pardee	LLB	Dave Robinson
Myron Pottios	MLB	Ray Nitschke
Maxie Baughan	RLB	Lee Roy Caffey
Clancy Williams	LCB	Herb Adderley
Irv Cross	RCB	Bob Jeter
Chuck Lamson	LS	Tom Brown
Ed Meador	RS	Willie Wood

Los Angeles	7	0	0	0	—	7
Green Bay	0	14	7	7	—	28

LA —Casey 29 pass from Gabriel (Gossett kick)
GB—Williams 46 run (Chandler kick)
GB—Dale 17 pass from Starr (Chandler kick)
GB—Mercein 6 run (Chandler kick)
GB—Williams 2 run (Chandler kick)
Attendance—49,861

1967 NFL

DALLAS 52, CLEVELAND 14

End Bob Hayes teamed with quarterback Don Meredith on an 86-yard touchdown pass play and set up two other scores on punt returns of 68 and 64 yards.

December 24, at Dallas

Cleveland	Starters, Offense	Dallas
Paul Warfield	LE	Bob Hayes
Dick Schafrath	LT	Tony Liscio
John Wooten	LG	John Niland
Fred Hoaglin	C	Mike Connelly
Gene Hickerson	RG	Leon Donohue
Monte Clark	RT	Ralph Neely
Ralph Smith	RE	Pettis Norman
Frank Ryan	QB	Don Meredith
Leroy Kelly	LH	Dan Reeves
Gary Collins	RH	Lance Rentzel
Ernie Green	FB	Don Perkins
	Starters, Defense	
Paul Wiggin	LE	Willie Townes
Walter Johnson	LT	Jethro Pugh
Jim Kanicki	RT	Bob Lilly
Bill Glass	RE	George Andrie
Jim Houston	LLB	Chuck Howley
Dale Lindsey	MLB	Lee Roy Jordan
John Brewer	RLB	Dave Edwards
Erich Barnes	LCB	Cornell Green
Mike Howell	RCB	Mike Johnson
Ernie Kellerman	LS	Mel Renfro
Ross Fichtner	RS	Phil Clark

Cleveland	0	7	0	7	—	14
Dallas	14	10	21	7	—	52

Dall—Baynham 3 pass from Meredith (Villanueva kick)
Dall—Perkins 4 run (Villanueva kick)
Dall—Hayes 86 pass from Meredith (Villanueva kick)
Dall—FG Villanueva 10
Cle—Morin 13 pass from Ryan (Groza kick)
Dall—Baynham 1 run (Villanueva kick)
Dall—Perkins 1 run (Villanueva kick)
Dall—Green 60 interception return (Villanueva kick)
Dall—Baynham 1 run (Villanueva kick)
Cle—Warfield 75 pass from Ryan (Groza kick)
Attendance—70,786

1968 AFL

OAKLAND 41, KANSAS CITY 6

Quarterback Daryle Lamonica threw for 347 yards and five touchdowns and the Kansas City Chiefs went without a touchdown for the first time since 1963 as the Raiders scored a 41–6 victory.

December 22, at Oakland

Kansas City	Starters, Offense	Oakland
Frank Pitts	LE	Warren Wells
Jim Tyrer	LT	Bob Svihus
Ed Budde	LG	Gene Upshaw
E. J. Holub	C	Jim Otto
Mo Moorman	RG	Jim Harvey
Dave Hill	RT	Harry Schuh
Fred Arbanas	TE	Billy Cannon
Len Dawson	QB	Daryle Lamonica
Mike Garrett	LH	Charlie Smith
Otis Taylor	RH	Fred Biletnikoff
Robert Holmes	FB	Hewritt Dixon
	Starters, Defense	
Jerry Mays	LE	Isaac Lassiter
Ed Lothamer	LT	Dan Birdwell
Buck Buchanan	RT	Carleton Oats
Aaron Brown	RE	Ben Davidson
Bobby Bell	LLB	Ralph (Chip) Oliver
Willie Lanier	MLB	Dan Conners
Jim Lynch	RLB	Gus Otto
Goldie Sellers	LCB	George Atkinson
Emmitt Thomas	RCB	Willie Brown
Jim Kearney	LS	Rodger Bird
Johnny Robinson	RS	Dave Grayson

Kansas City	0	6	0	0	—	6
Oakland	21	7	0	13	—	41

Oak—Biletnikoff 24 pass from Lamonica (Blanda kick)
Oak—Wells 23 pass from Lamonica (Blanda kick)
Oak—Biletnikoff 44 pass from Lamonica (Blanda kick)
KC —FG Stenerud 10
KC —FG Stenerud 8
Oak—Biletnikoff 54 pass from Lamonica (Blanda kick)
Oak—Wells 35 pass from Lamonica (Blanda kick)
Oak—FG Blanda 41
Oak—FG Blanda 40
Attendance—53,605

1968 NFL

CLEVELAND 31, DALLAS 20

The Cleveland Browns scored three touchdowns in a three-and-a-half-minute period at the conclusion of the first half and start of the second half and went on to defeat the Dallas Cowboys 31–20.

December 21, at Cleveland

Dallas	Starters, Offense	Cleveland
Bob Hayes	WR	Paul Warfield
Tony Liscio	LT	Dick Schafrath
John Niland	LG	John Demarie
Malcolm Walker	C	Fred Hoaglin
John Wilbur	RG	Gene Hickerson
Ralph Neely	RT	Monte Clark
Pettis Norman	TE	Milt Morin
Don Meredith	QB	Bill Nelsen
Lance Rentzel	WR	Gary Collins
Don Perkins	RB	Leroy Kelly
Craig Baynham	RB	Charley Harraway
	Starters, Defense	
Larry Cole	LE	Ron Snidow
Jethro Pugh	LT	Walter Johnson
Bob Lilly	RT	Jim Kanicki
George Andrie	RE	Jack Gregory
Chuck Howley	LLB	Jim Houston
Lee Roy Jordan	MLB	Bob Matheson
Dave Edwards	RLB	Dale Lindsey
Cornell Green	LCB	Erich Barnes
Mel Renfro	RCB	Ben Davis
Mike Gaechter	LS	Ernie Kellerman
Dick Daniels	RS	Mike Howell

Dallas	7	3	3	7	—	20
Cleveland	3	7	14	7	—	31

Cle—FG Cockroft 38
Dall—Howley 44 fumble return (Clark kick)
Dall—FG Clark 16
Cle—Kelly 45 pass from Nelsen (Cockroft kick)
Cle—Lindsey 27 interception return (Cockroft kick)
Cle—Kelly 35 run (Cockroft kick)
Dall—FG Clark 47
Cle—Green 2 run (Cockroft kick)
Dall—Garrison 2 pass from Morton (Clark kick)
Attendance—81,497

1968 NFL

BALTIMORE 24, MINNESOTA 14

Touchdown passes from Earl Morrall to Tom Mitchell and John Mackey and a 60-yard touchdown run with a fumble by Mike Curtis gave the Baltimore Colts a 21–0 lead through three quarters in a game they went on to win 24–14. The game was played in a steady downpour.

December 22, at Baltimore

Minnesota	Starters, Offense	Baltimore
Gene Washington	WR	Jimmy Orr
Grady Alderman	LT	Bob Vogel
Jim Vellone	LG	Glenn Ressler
Mick Tingelhoff	C	Bill Curry
Milt Sunde	RG	Dan Sullivan
Doug Davis	RT	Sam Ball
John Beasley	TE	John Mackey
Joe Kapp	QB	Earl Morrall
John Henderson	WR	Willie Richardson
Bill Brown	RB	Tom Matte
Dave Osborn	RB	Preston Pearson
	Starters, Defense	
Carl Eller	LE	Charles (Bubba) Smith
Alan Page	LT	Billy Ray Smith
Gary Larsen	RT	Fred Miller
Jim Marshall	RE	Ordell Braase
Roy Winston	LLB	Mike Curtis
Lonnie Warwick	MLB	Dennis Gaubatz
Wally Hilgenberg	RLB	Don Shinnick
Earsell Mackbee	LCB	Bobby Boyd
Ed Sharockman	RCB	Lenny Lyles
Karl Kassulke	LS	Jerry Logan
Paul Krause	RS	Rick Volk

Minnesota	0	0	0	14	—	14
Baltimore	0	7	14	3	—	24

Balt —Mitchell 3 pass from Morrall (Michaels kick)
Balt —Mackey 49 pass from Morrall (Michaels kick)
Balt —Curtis 60 fumble return (Michaels kick)
Minn—Martin 1 pass from Kapp (Cox kick)
Balt —FG Michaels 33
Minn—Brown 7 pass from Kapp (Cox kick)
Attendance—60,238

1969 AFL

KANSAS CITY 13, N.Y. JETS 6

The Kansas City Chiefs moved 80 yards in two plays early in the fourth quarter, scoring on Len Dawson's 19-yard pass to Gloster Richardson, and defeated the New York Jets 13–6.

The Jets had a first down on the Chiefs' 1-yard line late in the third quarter but settled for a field goal by Jim Turner that tied the score 6–6.

December 20, at New York

Kansas City	Starters, Offense	N.Y. Jets
Frank Pitts	WR	George Sauer
Jim Tyrer	LT	Winston Hill
Ed Budde	LG	Randy Rasmussen
E. J. Holub	C	John Schmitt
Mo Moorman	RG	Dave Herman
Dave Hill	RT	Roger Finnie
Fred Arbanas	TE	Pete Lammons
Otis Taylor	WR	Robert (Bake) Turner
Len Dawson	QB	Joe Namath
Mike Garrett	RB	Emerson Boozer
Robert Holmes	RB	Matt Snell
	Starters, Defense	
Jerry Mays	LE	Gerry Philbin
Curley Culp	LT	Steve Thompson
Buck Buchanan	RT	John Elliott
Aaron Brown	RE	Verlon Biggs
Bobby Bell	LLB	Ralph Baker
Willie Lanier	MLB	Al Atkinson
Jim Lynch	RLB	Larry Grantham
Jim Marsalis	LCB	Cornell Gordon
Emmitt Thomas	RCB	Randy Beverly
Johnny Robinson	LS	Bill Baird
Jim Kearney	RS	Jim Richards

Kansas City	0	3	3	7	—	13
N.Y. Jets	3	0	0	3	—	6

NYJ—FG J. Turner 27
KC —FG Stenerud 23
KC —FG Stenerud 25
NYJ—FG J. Turner 7
KC —Richardson 19 pass from Dawson (Stenerud kick)
Attendance—62,977

1969 AFL

OAKLAND 56, HOUSTON 7

The Oakland Raiders scored four touchdowns within a span of 4:22 and led 28–0 after the first eight minutes of play after capitalizing on two fumbles and a pass interception, then coasted to a 56–7 victory.

December 21, at Oakland

Houston	Starters, Offense	Oakland
Jim Beirne	WR	Rod Sherman
Walt Suggs	LT	Bob Svihus
Tom Regner	LG	Gene Upshaw
Bobby Maples	C	Jim Otto
Erwin (Sonny) Bishop	RG	Jim Harvey
Glen Ray Hines	RT	Harry Schuh
Alvin Reed	RE	Billy Cannon
Jerry LeVias	WR	Fred Biletnikoff
Pete Beathard	QB	Daryle Lamonica
Woody Campbell	RB	Charlie Smith
Hoyle Granger	RB	Hewritt Dixon
	Starters, Defense	
Pat Holmes	LE	Isaac Lassiter
Carel Stith	LT	Carleton Oats
Tom Domres	RT	Tom Keating
Elvin Bethea	RE	Ben Davidson
George Webster	LLB	Ralph (Chip) Oliver
Garland Boyette	MLB	Dan Conners
Olen Underwood	RLB	Gus Otto
Miller Farr	LCB	Nemiah Wilson
Zeke Moore	RCB	Willie Brown
Ken Houston	LS	George Atkinson
Johnny Peacock	RS	Dave Grayson

Houston	0	0	0	7	—	7
Oakland	28	7	14	7	—	56

Oak—Biletnikoff 13 pass from Lamonica (Blanda kick)
Oak—Atkinson 57 interception return (Blanda kick)
Oak—Sherman 24 pass from Lamonica (Blanda kick)
Oak—Biletnikoff 31 pass from Lamonica (Blanda kick)
Oak—Smith 60 pass from Lamonica (Blanda kick)
Oak—Sherman 23 pass from Lamonica (Blanda kick)
Oak—Cannon 3 pass from Lamonica (Blanda kick)
Hou—Reed 8 pass from Beathard (Gerela kick)
Oak—Hubbard 4 run (Blanda kick)
Attendance—53,539

1969 NFL

MINNESOTA 23, LOS ANGELES 20

The Minnesota Vikings drove 65 yards to a fourth quarter touchdown and added a safety 35 seconds later. Joe Kapp completed three passes for 40 yards and ran the final two yards in the touchdown march.

December 27, at Bloomington, Minnesota

Los Angeles	Starters, Offense	Minnesota
Jack Snow	WR	Gene Washington
Charlie Cowan	LT	Grady Alderman
Tom Mack	RG	Jim Vellone
Ken Iman	C	Mick Tingelhoff
Mike LaHood	RG	Milt Sunde
Bob Brown	RT	Ron Yary
Billy Truax	TE	John Beasley
Wendell Tucker	WR	John Henderson
Roman Gabriel	QB	Joe Kapp
Larry Smith	RB	Dave Osborn
Les Josephson	RB	Bill Brown
Starters, Defense		
David (Deacon) Jones	LE	Carl Eller
Merlin Olsen	LT	Gary Larsen
Coy Bacon	RT	Alan Page
Diron Talbert	RE	Jim Marshall
Jack Pardee	LLB	Roy Winston
Doug Woodlief	MLB	Lonnie Warwick
Maxie Baughan	RLB	Wally Hilgenberg
Clancy Williams	LCB	Earsell Mackbee
Jim Nettles	RCB	Ed Sharockman
Richie Petitbon	LS	Karl Kassulke
Ed Meador	RS	Paul Krause

Los Angeles	7	10	0	3	—	20
Minnesota	7	0	7	9	—	23

LA —Klein 3 pass from Gabriel (Gossett kick)
Minn—Osborn 1 run (Cox kick)
LA —FG Gossett 20
LA —Truax 2 pass from Gabriel (Gossett kick)
Minn—Osborn 1 run (Cox kick)
LA —FG Gossett 27
Minn—Kapp 2 run (Cox kick)
Minn—Safety, Eller tackled Gabriel in end zone
Attendance—47,900

1969 NFL

CLEVELAND 38, DALLAS 14

Bill Nelsen completed 15 of 22 passes for 184 yards and one touchdown as the Cleveland Browns took a 17-0 halftime lead and went on to a 38-14 victory over the Dallas Cowboys.

December 28, at Dallas

Cleveland	Starters, Offense	Dallas
Paul Warfield	WR	Bob Hayes
Dick Schafrath	LT	Tony Liscio
John Demarie	LG	John Niland
Fred Hoaglin	C	Malcolm Walker
Gene Hickerson	RG	John Wilbur
Monte Clark	RT	Ralph Neely
Milt Morin	TE	Pettis Norman
Gary Collins	WR	Lance Rentzel
Bill Nelsen	QB	Craig Morton
Leroy Kelly	RB	Calvin Hill
Robert (Bo) Scott	RB	Walt Garrison
Starters, Defense		
Ron Snidow	LE	Larry Cole
Walter Johnson	LT	Jethro Pugh
Jim Kanicki	RT	Bob Lilly
Jack Gregory	RE	George Andrie
Jim Houston	LLB	Dave Edwards
Dale Lindsey	MLB	Lee Roy Jordan
John Garlington	RLB	Chuck Howley
Erich Barnes	LCB	Cornell Green
Walt Sumner	RCB	Otto Brown
Ernie Kellerman	LS	Mike Gaechter
Mike Howell	RS	Mel Renfro

Cleveland	7	10	7	14	—	38
Dallas	0	0	7	7	—	14

Cle —Scott 2 run (Cockroft kick)
Cle —Morin 6 pass from Nelsen (Cockroft kick)
Cle —FG Cockroft 29
Cle —Scott 2 run (Cockroft kick)
Dall—Morton 2 run (Clark kick)
Cle —Kelly 1 run (Cockroft kick)
Cle —Sumner 88 interception return (Cockroft kick)
Dall—Rentzel 5 pass from Staubach (Clark kick)
Attendance—69,321

1970 AFC

BALTIMORE 17, CINCINNATI 0

Fifteen-year veteran John Unitas threw touchdown passes of 45 and 53 yards to Roy Jefferson and Eddie Hinton to lead the Baltimore Colts to a 17-0 victory over the Cincinnati Bengals.

The Bengals had won their last seven games to finish the regular season with an 8-6 record and gain the playoffs in their third year. No expansion team had been able to achieve that level in that period.

December 26, at Baltimore

Cincinnati	Starters, Offense	Baltimore
Philip (Chip) Myers	WR	Eddie Hinton
Ernie Wright	LT	Bob Vogel
Rufus Mayes	LG	Glenn Ressler
Bob Johnson	C	Bill Curry
Pat Matson	RG	John Williams
Howard Fest	RT	Dan Sullivan
Bob Trumpy	TE	John Mackey
Louis (Speedy) Thomas	WR	Roy Jefferson
Virgil Carter	QB	John Unitas
Paul Robinson	RB	Norm Bulaich
Jess Phillips	RB	Tom Nowatzke
Starters, Defense		
Royce Berry	LE	Charles (Bubba) Smith
Mike Reid	LT	Billy Ray Smith
Steve Chomyszak	RT	Fred Miller
Ron Carpenter	RE	Roy Hilton
Al Beauchamp	LLB	Ray May
Bill Bergey	MLB	Mike Curtis
Ken Avery	RLB	Ted Hendricks
Lemar Parrish	LCB	Charlie Stukes
Ken Riley	RCB	Jim Duncan
Fletcher Smith	LS	Jerry Logan
Ken Dyer	RS	Rick Volk

Cincinnati	0	0	0	0	—	0
Baltimore	7	3	0	7	—	17

Balt—Jefferson 45 pass from Unitas (O'Brien kick)
Balt—FG O'Brien 44
Balt—Hinton 53 pass from Unitas (O'Brien kick)
Attendance—51,127

1970 AFC

OAKLAND 21, MIAMI 14

An 82-yard pass play from quarterback Daryle Lamonica to wide receiver Rod Sherman with 9:34 remaining was the difference as the Oakland Raiders defeated Miami on a field slowed by heavy rain.

Lamonica threw a 37-yard pass to Sherman, who caught the ball on the side line over Curtis Johnson, trying for an interception.

December 27, at Oakland

Miami	Starters, Offense	Oakland
Paul Warfield	WR	Warren Wells
Doug Crusan	LT	Art Shell
Bob Kuechenberg	LG	Gene Upshaw
Carl Mauck	C	Jim Otto
Larry Little	RG	Jim Harvey
Norm Evans	RT	Harry Schuh
Marv Fleming	TE	Raymond Chester
Howard Twilley	WR	Fred Biletnikoff
Bob Griese	QB	Daryle Lamonica
Jim Kiick	RB	Charlie Smith
Larry Csonka	RB	Hewritt Dixon
Starters, Defense		
Jim Riley	LE	Tony Cline
Frank Cornish	LT	Carleton Oats
John Richardson	RT	Tom Keating
Bill Stanfill	RE	Ben Davidson
Doug Swift	LLB	Bill Laskey
Nick Buoniconti	MLB	Dan Conners
Mike Kolen	RLB	Gus Otto
Curtis Johnson	LCB	Kent McCloughan
Lloyd Mumphord	RCB	Willie Brown
Dick Anderson	LS	George Atkinson
Jake Scott	RS	Dave Grayson

Miami	0	7	0	7	—	14
Oakland	0	7	7	7	—	21

Mia—Warfield 16 pass from Griese (Yepremian kick)
Oak—Biletnikoff 22 pass from Lamonica (Blanda kick)
Oak—Brown 50 interception return (Blanda kick)
Oak—Sherman 82 pass from Lamonica (Blanda kick)
Mia—W. Richardson 7 pass from Griese (Yepremian kick)
Attendance—54,401

1970 NFC

DALLAS 5, DETROIT 0

Rookie running back Duane Thomas gained 135 yards in 30 carries, including 104 in 22 in the second half, but the Dallas Cowboys used a field goal and safety to produce a 5-0 victory.

The Cowboys controlled the ball for seven minutes on a 15-play, 77-yard drive that ended at Detroit's 1-yard line in the fourth quarter. Three plays later, George Andrie trapped Lions quarterback Greg Landry in the end zone for a safety.

December 26, at Dallas

Detroit	Starters, Offense	Dallas
Earl McCullouch	WR	Bob Hayes
Roger Shoals	LT	Ralph Neely
Chuck Walton	LG	John Niland
Ed Flanagan	C	Dave Manders
Frank Gallagher	RG	Blaine Nye
Rockne (Rocky) Freitas	RT	Rayfield Wright
Charlie Sanders	TE	Pettis Norman
Larry Walton	WR	Reggie Rucker
Greg Landry	QB	Craig Morton
Mel Farr	RB	Duane Thomas
Altie Taylor	RB	Walt Garrison
Starters, Defense		
Jim Mitchell	LE	Larry Cole
Alex Karras	LT	Jethro Pugh
Jerry Rush	RT	Bob Lilly
Larry Hand	RE	George Andrie
Paul Naumoff	LLB	Dave Edwards
Mike Lucci	MLB	Lee Roy Jordan
Wayne Walker	RLB	Chuck Howley
Lem Barney	LCB	Herb Adderley
Dick LeBeau	RCB	Mel Renfro
Mike Weger	LS	Cornell Green
Tom Vaughn	RS	Charlie Waters

Detroit	0	0	0	0	—	0
Dallas	3	0	0	2	—	5

Dall—FG Clark 26
Dall—Safety, Andrie tackled Landry in end zone
Attendance—73,167

1970 NFC

SAN FRANCISCO 17, MINNESOTA 14

Quarterback John Brodie scored on a 1-yard run with 1:20 left in the game, giving San Francisco a 17-7 lead en route to a 17-14 victory.

On a day when the temperature fluctuated between 5 and 11 degrees and winds gusted at 15 miles an hour, the 49ers overcame a 7-0 Vikings lead in the first quarter.

December 27, at Bloomington, Minnesota

San Francisco	Starters, Offense	Minnesota
Gene Washington	WR	Gene Washington
Len Rohde	LT	Grady Alderman
Randy Beisler	LG	Jim Vellone
Forrest Blue	C	Mick Tingelhoff
Woody Peoples	RG	Milt Sunde
Cas Banaszek	RT	Ron Yary
Bob Windsor	TE	John Beasley
Dick Witcher	WR	John Henderson
John Brodie	QB	Gary Cuozzo
Ken Willard	RB	Clinton Jones
Bill Tucker	RB	Dave Osborn
Starters, Defense		
Tommy Hart	LE	Carl Eller
Charlie Krueger	LT	Gary Larsen
Roland Lakes	RT	Alan Page
Bill Belk	RE	Jim Marshall
Dave Wilcox	LLB	Roy Winston
Frank Nunley	MLB	Lonnie Warwick
Jim Sniadecki	RLB	Wally Hilgenberg
Jimmy Johnson	LCB	Bobby Bryant
Bruce Taylor	RCB	Ed Sharockman
Roosevelt Taylor	LS	Karl Kassulke
Mel Phillips	RS	Paul Krause

San Francisco	7	3	0	7	—	17
Minnesota	7	0	0	7	—	14

Minn—Krause 22 fumble return (Cox kick)
SF —Witcher 26 pass from Brodie (Gossett kick)
SF —FG Gossett 40
SF —Brodie 1 run (Gossett kick)
Minn—Washington 24 pass from Cuozzo (Cox kick)
Attendance—45,103

1971 AFC

MIAMI 27, KANSAS CITY 24

Garo Yepremian kicked a 37-yard field goal after 7:40 of the sixth quarter to give the Miami Dolphins a 27–24 victory over the Kansas City Chiefs in the longest professional football game in history.

December 25, at Kansas City

Miami	Starters, Offense	Kansas City
Paul Warfield	WR	Elmo Wright
Doug Crusan	LT	Jim Tyrer
Bob Kuechenberg	LG	Ed Budde
Bob DeMarco	C	Jack Rudnay
Larry Little	RG	Mo Moorman
Norm Evans	RT	Dave Hill
Marv Fleming	TE	Morris Stroud
Howard Twilley	WR	Otis Taylor
Bob Griese	QB	Len Dawson
Jim Kiick	RB	Wendell Hayes
Larry Csonka	RB	Ed Podolak
	Starters, Defense	
Jim Riley	LE	Marvin Upshaw
Manny Fernandez	LT	Curley Culp
Bob Heinz	RT	Buck Buchanan
Bill Stanfill	RE	Aaron Brown
Doug Swift	LLB	Bobby Bell
Nick Buoniconti	MLB	Willie Lanier
Bob Matheson	RLB	Jim Lynch
Tim Foley	LCB	Jim Marsalis
Curtis Johnson	RCB	Emmitt Thomas
Jake Scott	LS	Jim Kearney
Dick Anderson	RS	Johnny Robinson

Miami	0	10	7	7	0	3	—	27
Kansas City	10	0	7	7	0	0	—	24

KC —FG Stenerud 24
KC —Podolak 7 pass from Dawson (Stenerud kick)
Mia—Csonka 1 run (Yepremian kick)
Mia—FG Yepremian 14
KC —Otis 1 run (Stenerud kick)
Mia—Kiick 1 run (Yepremian kick)
KC —Podolak 3 run (Stenerud kick)
Mia—Fleming 5 pass from Griese (Yepremian kick)
Mia—FG Yepremian 37
Attendance—50,374

1971 AFC

BALTIMORE 20, CLEVELAND 3

Rookie running back Don Nottingham, a replacement for injured Norm Bulaich rushed for 92 yards and scored Baltimore's first two touchdowns.

Nottingham's runs of one and seven yards gave the Colts a 14–0 halftime lead. Cleveland scored on Don Cockroft's 14-yard field goal. Charles (Bubba) Smith blocked two other field goal attempts.

December 26, at Cleveland

Baltimore	Starters, Offense	Cleveland
Eddie Hinton	WR	Fair Hooker
Bob Vogel	LT	Doug Dieken
Glenn Ressler	LG	John Demarie
Bill Curry	C	Jim Copeland
John Williams	RG	Gene Hickerson
Dan Sullivan	RT	Bob McKay
Tom Mitchell	TE	Milt Morin
Ray Perkins	WR	Frank Pitts
John Unitas	QB	Bill Nelsen
Tom Matte	RB	Leroy Kelly
Don Nottingham	RB	Robert (Bo) Scott
	Starters, Defense	
Charles (Bubba) Smith	LE	Ron Snidow
Billy Newsome	LT	Walter Johnson
Fred Miller	RT	Jerry Sherk
Roy Hilton	RE	Jack Gregory
Ray May	LLB	John Garlington
Mike Curtis	MLB	Jim Houston
Ted Hendricks	LLB	Bill Andrews
Charlie Stukes	LCB	Clarence Scott
Rex Kern	RCB	Ben Davis
Jerry Logan	LS	Walt Sumner
Rick Volk	RS	Mike Howell

Baltimore	0	14	3	3	—	20
Cleveland	0	0	3	0	—	3

Balt—Nottingham 1 run (O'Brien kick)
Balt—Nottingham 7 run (O'Brien kick)
Cle —FG Cockroft 14
Balt—FG O'Brien 42
Balt—FG O'Brien 15
Attendance–74,082

1971 NFC

DALLAS 20, MINNESOTA 12

Safety Cliff Harris intercepted a pass by Bob Lee to set up a 13-yard touchdown by Duane Thomas that gave the Dallas Cowboys a 13–3 lead in the third quarter en route to a 20–12 victory over the Minnesota Vikings.

December 25, at Bloomington, Minnesota

Dallas	Starters, Offense	Minnesota
Bob Hayes	WR	Gene Washington
Tony Liscio	LT	Grady Alderman
John Niland	LG	Ed White
Dave Manders	C	Mick Tingelhoff
Blaine Nye	RG	Milt Sunde
Rayfield Wright	RT	Ron Yary
Mike Ditka	TE	Bob Brown
Lance Alworth	WR	Bob Grim
Roger Staubach	QB	Bob Lee
Calvin Hill	RB	Clinton Jones
Duane Thomas	RB	Dave Osborn
	Starters, Defense	
Larry Cole	LE	Carl Eller
Jethro Pugh	LT	Gary Larsen
Bob Lilly	RT	Alan Page
George Andrie	RE	Jim Marshall
Dave Edwards	LLB	Carl Winfrey
Lee Roy Jordan	MLB	Lonnie Warwick
Chuck Howley	RLB	Wally Hilgenberg
Herb Adderley	LCB	Bobby Bryant
Mel Renfro	RCB	Ed Sharockman
Cornell Green	LS	Charlie West
Cliff Harris	RS	Paul Krause

Dallas	3	3	14	0	—	20
Minnesota	0	3	0	9	—	12

Dall —FG Clark 26
Minn—FG Cox 27
Dall —FG Clark 44
Dall —D. Thomas 13 run (Clark kick)
Dall —Hayes 9 pass from Staubach (Clark kick)
Minn—Safety, Page tackled Staubach in end zone.
Minn—Voight 6 pass from Cuozzo (Cox kick)
Attendance—49,100

1971 NFC

SAN FRANCISCO 24, WASHINGTON 20

With the San Francisco 49ers leading 17–13 early in the fourth quarter, Washington punter Mike Bragg had a poor snap from center roll through his legs. The 49ers' Bob Hoskins recovered in the end zone.

December 26, at San Francisco

Washington	Starters, Offense	San Francisco
Clifton McNeil	WR	Dick Witcher
Jim Snowden	LT	Len Rohde
Ray Schoenke	LG	Randy Beisler
Len Hauss	C	Forrest Blue
John Wilbur	RG	Woody Peoples
Walt Rock	RT	Cas Banaszek
Jerry Smith	TE	Ted Kwalick
Roy Jefferson	WR	Gene Washington
Billy Kilmer	QB	John Brodie
Larry Brown	RB	Vic Washington
Charley Harraway	RB	Ken Willard
	Starters, Defense	
Ron McDole	LE	Tommy Hart
Manny Sistrunk	LT	Charlie Krueger
Diron Talbert	RT	Earl Edwards
Verlon Biggs	RE	Cedrick Hardman
Jack Pardee	LLB	Dave Wilcox
Myron Pottios	MLB	Frank Nunley
Chris Hanburger	RLB	William (Skip) Vanderbundt
Pat Fischer	LCB	Jimmy Johnson
Mike Bass	RCB	Bruce Taylor
Richie Petitbon	LS	Mel Phillips
Brig Owens	RS	Roosevelt Taylor

Washington	7	3	3	7	—	20
San Francisco	0	3	14	7	—	24

Wash—Smith 5 pass from Kilmer (Knight kick)
SF   —FG Gossett 23
Wash—FG Knight 40
SF   —G. Washington 78 pass from Brodie (Gossett kick)
SF   —Windsor 2 pass from Brodie (Gossett kick)
Wash—FG Knight 36
SF   —Hoskins, fumble recovery in end zone (Gossett kick)
Wash—Brown 16 pass from Kilmer (Knight kick)
Attendance—45,364

1972 AFC

PITTSBURGH 13, OAKLAND 7

Pittsburgh came from behind to defeat the Oakland Raiders 13–7 when Terry Bradshaw's fourth down pass in the final 22 seconds ricocheted off Oakland's Jack Tatum and was picked off at the shootops on the Raiders' 42 by Franco Harris, who scored on a 60-yard touchdown play with five seconds left.

Ken Stabler scrambled 30 yards with 1:13 left for Oakland's touchdown and a 7–6 lead.

December 23, at Pittsburgh

Oakland	Starters, Offense	Pittsburgh
Mike Siani	WR	Al Young
Art Shell	LT	Jon Kolb
Gene Upshaw	LG	Sam Davis
Jim Otto	C	Ray Mansfield
George Buehler	RG	Bruce Van Dyke
Bob Brown	RT	Gerry Mullins
Raymond Chester	TE	John McMakin
Fred Biletnikoff	WR	Ron Shanklin
Daryle Lamonica	QB	Terry Bradshaw
Charlie Smith	RB	Franco Harris
Marv Hubbard	RB	John Fuqua
	Starters, Defense	
Tony Cline	LE	L. C. Greenwood
Otis Sistrunk	LT	Joe Greene
Art Thoms	RT	Ben McGee
Horace Jones	RE	Dwight White
Phil Villapiano	LLB	Jack Ham
Dan Conners	MLB	Henry Davis
Gerald Irons	RLB	Andy Russell
Nemiah Wilson	LCB	John Rowser
Willie Brown	RCB	Mel Blount
George Atkinson	LS	Glen Edwards
Jack Tatum	RS	Mike Wagner

Oakland	0	0	0	7	—	7
Pittsburgh	0	0	3	10	—	13

Pitt —FG Gerela 18
Pitt —FG Gerela 29
Oak—Stabler 30 run (Blanda kick)
Pitt —Harris 60 pass from Bradshaw (Gerela kick)
Attendance—50,350

1972 AFC

MIAMI 20, CLEVELAND 14

Miami marched 80 yards to a fourth-quarter touchdown that overcame a 14–13 lead. Bob Griese passed 15 and 35 yards to Paul Warfield. Warfield was fouled by Bill Andrews on a 10-yard pass. That put the ball on the 8; Jim Kiick scored the next play.

December 24, at Miami

Cleveland	Starters, Offense	Miami
Fair Hooker	WR	Paul Warfield
Doug Dieken	LT	Wayne Moore
Gene Hickerson	LG	Bob Kuechenberg
Bob DeMarco	C	Jim Langer
John Demarie	RG	Larry Little
Bob McKay	RT	Norm Evans
Milt Morin	TE	Marv Fleming
Frank Pitts	WR	Howard Twilley
Mike Phipps	QB	Bob Griese
Leroy Kelly	RB	Jim Kiick
Robert (Bo) Scott	RB	Larry Csonka
	Starters, Defense	
Nick Roman	LE	Vern Den Herder
Walter Johnson	LT	Manny Fernandez
Jerry Sherk	RT	Bob Heinz
Bob Briggs	RE	Bill Stanfill
Charlie Hall	LLB	Doug Swift
Dale Lindsey	MLB	Nick Buoniconti
Bill Andrews	RLB	Mike Kolen
Clarence Scott	LCB	Tom Foley
Ben Davis	RCB	Curtis Johnson
Thom Darden	LS	Jake Scott
Walt Sumner	RS	Dick Anderson

Cleveland	0	0	7	7	—	14
Miami	10	0	0	10	—	20

Mia—Babb 5 blocked punt return (Yepremian kick)
Mia—FG Yepremian 40
Cle —Phipps 5 run (Cockroft kick)
Mia—FG Yepremian 46
Cle —Hooker 27 pass from Phipps (Cockroft kick)
Mia—Kiick 8 run (Yepremian kick)
Attendance—80,010

1972 NFC

WASHINGTON 16, GREEN BAY 3

A five-man defensive line helped the Washington Redskins contain the Green Bay Packers' running attack in a 16–3 victory. Rookie John Brockington, who rushed for 1,027 yards for Green Bay during the season, was limited to 13 yards in nine carries.

The Redskins led 10–3 at halftime and held off Green Bay in the second half with two field goals.

December 24, at Washington

Green Bay	Starters, Offense	Washington
Leland Glass	WR	Charley Taylor
Bill Hayhoe	LT	Terry Hermeling
Bill Lueck	LG	Paul Laaveg
Ken Bowman	C	Len Hauss
Malcolm Snider	RG	Ray Schoenke
Dick Himes	RT	Walt Rock
Len Garrett	TE	Mack Alston
Carroll Dale	WR	Roy Jefferson
Scott Hunter	QB	Billy Kilmer
MacArthur Lane	RB	Larry Brown
John Brockington	RB	Charley Harraway
	Starters, Defense	
Clarence Williams	LE	Ron McDole
Mike McCoy	LT	Bill Brundige
Bob Brown	RT	Diron Talbert
Alden Roche	RE	Verlon Biggs
Dave Robinson	LLB	Jack Pardee
Jim Carter	MLB	Myron Pottios
Fred Carr	RLB	Chris Hanburger
Willie Buchanon	LCB	Pat Fischer
Ken Ellis	RCB	Mike Bass
Al Matthews	LS	Brig Owens
Jim Hill	RS	Roosevelt Taylor

Green Bay	0	3	0	0	—	3
Washington	0	10	0	6	—	16

GB —FG Marcol 17
Wash—Jefferson 32 pass from Kilmer (Knight kick)
Wash—FG Knight 42
Wash—FG Knight 35
Wash—FG Knight 46
Attendance—53,140

1972 NFC

DALLAS 30, SAN FRANCISCO 28

Roger Staubach completed 12 of 20 passes for 174 yards and 2 touchdowns in the fourth quarter as Dallas scored 17 points to overcome a 28–13 49ers lead.

December 28, at San Francisco

Dallas	Starters, Offense	San Francisco
Ron Sellers	WR	Gene Washington
Ralph Neely	LT	Len Rohde
John Niland	LG	Randy Beisler
Dave Manders	C	Forrest Blue
Blaine Nye	RG	Woody Peoples
Rayfield Wright	RT	Cas Banaszek
Mike Ditka	TE	Ted Kwalick
Lance Alworth	WR	Preston Riley
Craig Morton	QB	John Brodie
Calvin Hill	RB	Vic Washington
Walt Garrison	RB	Larry Schreiber
	Starters, Defense	
Larry Cole	LE	Tommy Hart
Jethro Pugh	LT	Charlie Krueger
Bob Lilly	RT	Earl Edwards
Pat Toomay	RE	Cedrick Hardman
Dave Edwards	LLB	Dave Wilcox
Lee Roy Jordan	MLB	Ed Beard
D.D. Lewis	RLB	William (Skip) Vanderbundt
Charlie Waters	LCB	Jimmy Johnson
Mel Renfro	RCB	Bruce Taylor
Cornell Green	LS	Windlan Hall
Cliff Harris	RS	Mike Simpson

Dallas	3	10	0	17	—	30
San Francisco	7	14	7	0	—	28

SF —V. Washington 97 kickoff return (Gossett kick)
Dall—FG Fritsch 37
SF —Schreiber 1 run (Gossett kick)
SF —Schreiber 1 run (Gossett kick)
Dall—FG Fritsch 45
Dall—Alworth 28 pass from Morton (Fritsch kick)
SF —Schreiber 1 run (Gossett kick)
Dall—FG Fritsch 27
Dall—Parks 20 pass from Staubach (Fritsch kick)
Dall—Seller 10 pass from Staubach (Fritsch kick)
Attendance—61,214

1973 AFC

OAKLAND 33, PITTSBURGH 14

The Oakland Raiders moved 82 yards in 16 plays after the opening kickoff to score with 4:51 to play in the first quarter on their way to a 33–14 victory over the Pittsburgh Steelers.

December 22, at Oakland

Pittsburgh	Starters, Offense	Oakland
Frank Lewis	WR	Mike Siani
Jon Kolb	LT	Art Shell
Sam Davis	LG	Gene Upshaw
Ray Mansfield	C	Jim Otto
Bruce Van Dyke	RG	George Buehler
Glen Ray Hines	RT	John Vella
John McMakin	TE	Bob Moore
Barry Pearson	WR	Fred Biletnikoff
Terry Bradshaw	QB	Ken Stabler
Preston Pearson	RB	Charlie Smith
Franco Harris	RB	Marv Hubbard
	Starters, Defense	
L. C. Greenwood	LE	Tony Cline
Joe Greene	LT	Otis Sistrunk
Tom Keating	RT	Art Thoms
Dwight White	RE	Horace Jones
Jack Ham	LLB	Phil Villapiano
Henry Davis	MLB	Dan Conners
Andy Russell	RLB	Gerald Irons
John Rowser	LCB	Nemiah Wilson
Mel Blount	RCB	Willie Brown
Mike Wagner	LS	George Atkinson
Glen Edwards	RS	Jack Tatum

Pittsburgh	0	7	0	7	—	14
Oakland	7	3	13	10	—	33

Oak—Hubbard 1 run (Blanda kick)
Oak—FG Blanda 25
Pitt—B. Pearson 4 pass from Bradshaw (Gerela kick)
Oak—FG Blanda 31
Oak—FG Blanda 22
Oak—W. Brown 54 interception return (Blanda kick)
Oak—Blanda 10
Pitt—Lewis 26 pass from Bradshaw (Gerela kick)
Oak—Hubbard 1 run (Blanda kick)
Attendance—51,110

1973 AFC

MIAMI 34, CINCINNATI 16

The Miami Dolphins put together touchdown drives of 80, 80, and 75 yards, rolling up 400 yards offense and setting a playoff record with 27 first downs.

December 23, at Miami

Cincinnati	Starters, Offense	Miami
Charlie Joiner	WR	Paul Warfield
Rufus Mayes	LT	Wayne Moore
Howard Fest	LG	Bob Kuechenberg
Bob Johnson	C	Jim Langer
Pat Matson	RG	Larry Little
Vernon Holland	RT	Norm Evans
Bob Trumpy	TE	Jim Mandich
Isaac Curtis	WR	Marlin Briscoe
Ken Anderson	QB	Bob Griese
Essex Johnson	RB	Eugene (Mercury) Morris
Charles (Boobie) Clark	RB	Larry Csonka
	Starters, Defense	
Royce Berry	LE	Vern Den Herder
Mike Reid	LT	Maulty Moore
Ron Carpenter	RT	Bob Heinz
Sherman White	RE	Bill Stanfill
Al Beauchamp	LLB	Doug Swift
Bill Bergey	MLB	Nick Buoniconti
Ken Avery	RLB	Mike Kolen
Lemar Parrish	LCB	Lloyd Mumphord
Ken Riley	RCB	Curtis Johnson
Neal Craig	LS	Jake Scott
Tommy Casanova	RS	Dick Anderson

Cincinnati	3	13	0	0	—	16
Miami	14	7	10	3	—	34

Mia —Warfield 13 pass from Griese (Yepremian kick)
Cinn—FG Muhlmann 24
Mia —Csonka 1 run (Yepremian kick)
Mia —Morris 4 run (Yepremian kick)
Cinn—Craig 45 interception return (Muhlmann kick)
Cinn—FG Muhlmann 46
Cinn—FG Muhlmann 10
Mia —Mandich 7 pass from Griese (Yepremian kick)
Mia —FG Yepremian 50
Mia —FG Yepremian 46
Attendance—74,770

1973 NFC

MINNESOTA 27, WASHINGTON 20

Quarterback Fran Tarkenton threw touchdown passes of 28 and 8 yards to John Gilliam within a period of 1:05 of the third quarter as the Minnesota Vikings overcame a 13–10 deficit.

December 22, at Bloomington, Minnesota

Washington	Starters, Offense	Minnesota
Charley Taylor	WR	Carroll Dale
Terry Hermeling	LT	Grady Alderman
Paul Laaveg	LG	Ed White
Len Hauss	C	Mick Tingelhoff
John Wilbur	RG	Milt Sunde
George Starke	RT	Ron Yary
Jerry Smith	TE	Stu Voight
Roy Jefferson	WR	John Gilliam
Billy Kilmer	QB	Fran Tarkenton
Larry Brown	RB	Chuck Foreman
Charley Harraway	RB	Oscar Reed
	Starters, Defense	
Ron McDole	LE	Carl Eller
Bill Brundige	LT	Gary Larsen
Diron Talbert	RT	Alan Page
Verlon Biggs	RE	Jim Marshall
Dave Robinson	LLB	Roy Winston
Myron Pottios	MLB	Jeff Siemon
Chris Hanburger	RLB	Wally Hilgenberg
Pat Fischer	LCB	Nate Wright
Mike Bass	RCB	Bobby Bryant
Ken Houston	LS	Jeff Wright
Brig Owens	RS	Paul Krause

Washington	0	7	3	10	—	20
Minnesota	0	3	7	17	—	27

Minn—FG Cox 19
Wash—Brown 2 run (Knight kick)
Minn—B. Brown 2 run (Cox kick)
Wash—FG Knight 52
Wash—FG Knight 42
Minn—Gilliam 28 pass from Tarkenton (Cox kick)
Minn—Gilliam 8 pass from Tarkenton (Cox kick)
Wash—Jefferson 28 pass from Kilmer (Knight kick)
Minn —FG Cox 30
Attendance—45,475

1973 NFC

DALLAS 27, LOS ANGELES 16

Drew Pearson caught a 34-yard pass between Steve Preece and Eddie McMillan and ran 49 yards to an 83-yard touchdown in the Cowboys' victory.

December 23, at Irving, Texas

Los Angeles	Starters, Offense	Dallas
Harold Jackson	WR	Bob Hayes
Charlie Cowan	LT	Ralph Neely
Tom Mack	LG	John Niland
Ken Iman	C	John Fitzgerald
Joe Scibelli	RG	Blaine Nye
John Williams	RT	Rayfield Wright
Bob Klein	TE	Billy Joe DuPree
Jack Snow	WR	Drew Pearson
John Hadl	QB	Roger Staubach
Jim Bertelsen	RB	Calvin Hill
L. McCutcheon	RB	Walt Garrison
	Starters, Defense	
Jack Youngblood	LE	Larry Cole
Merlin Olsen	LT	Jethro Pugh
Larry Brooks	RT	Bob Lilly
Fred Dryer	RE	Pat Toomay
Ken Geddes	LLB	Dave Edwards
Jack Reynolds	MLB	Lee Roy Jordan
Isiah Robertson	RLB	D. D. Lewis
Charlie Stukes	LCB	Charlie Waters
Eddie McMillan	RCB	Mel Renfro
Dave Elmendorf	LS	Cornell Green
Steve Preece	RS	Cliff Harris

Los Angeles	0	6	0	10	—	16
Dallas	14	3	0	10	—	27

Dall—Hill 3 run (Fritsch kick)
Dall—Pearson 4 pass from Staubach (Fritsch kick)
Dall—FG Fritsch 39
LA —FG Ray 33
LA —FG Ray 37
LA —FG Ray 40
LA —Baker 5 run (Ray kick)
Dall—Pearson 83 pass from Staubach (Fritsch kick)
Dall—FG Fritsch 12
Attendance—64,291

1974 AFC

OAKLAND 28, MIAMI 26

After Benny Malone ran 23 yards to put the Miami Dolphins ahead 26–21 with 2:08 remaining in the game, the Oakland Raiders marched 68 yards to the winning touchdown with 26 seconds remaining.

December 21, at Oakland

Miami	Starters, Offense	Oakland
Paul Warfield	WR	Clifford Branch
Wayne Moore	LT	Art Shell
Bob Kuechenberg	LG	Gene Upshaw
Jim Langer	C	Jim Otto
Larry Little	RG	George Buehler
Norm Evans	RT	John Vella
Marv Fleming	TE	Bob Moore
Nat Moore	WR	Fred Biletnikoff
Bob Griese	QB	Ken Stabler
Benny Malone	RB	Clarence Davis
Larry Csonka	RB	Marv Hubbard
	Starters, Defense	
Vern Den Herder	LE	Charles (Bubba) Smith
Manny Fernandez	LT	Otis Sistrunk
Bob Heinz	RT	Art Thoms
Bill Stanfill	RE	Horace Jones
Bob Matheson	LLB	Phil Villapiano
Nick Buoniconti	MLB	Dan Conners
Mike Kolen	RLB	Gerald Irons
Tim Foley	LCB	Alonzo (Skip) Thomas
Curtis Johnson	RCB	Nemiah Wilson
Dick Anderson	LS	George Atkinson
Jake Scott	RS	Jack Tatum

Miami	7	3	6	10	—	26
Oakland	0	7	7	14	—	28

Mia —N. Moore 89 kickoff return (Yepremian kick)
Oak—C. Smith 31 pass from Stabler (Blanda kick)
Mia —FG Yepremian 33
Oak—Biletnikoff 13 pass from Stabler (Blanda kick)
Mia —Warfield 16 pass from Griese (kick failed)
Mia —FG Yepremian 46
Oak—Branch 72 pass from Stabler (Blanda kick)
Mia —Malone 23 run (Yepremian kick)
Oak—Davis 8 pass from Stabler (Blanda kick)
Attendance—52,817

1974 AFC

PITTSBURGH 32, BUFFALO 14

Franco Harris scored three touchdowns within a 4-minute, 52-second stretch of the second quarter as the Pittsburgh Steelers scored a total of 26 points in the quarter and coasted to a 32–14 victory.

December 22, at Pittsburgh

Buffalo	Starters, Offense	Pittsburgh
J. D. Hill	WR	Frank Lewis
Dave Foley	LT	Jon Kolb
Reggie McKenzie	LG	Jim Clack
Mike Montler	C	Ray Mansfield
Joe DeLamielleure	RG	Gerry Mullins
Donnie Green	RT	Gordon Gravelle
Paul Seymour	TE	Larry Brown
Ahmad Rashad	WR	Ron Shanklin
Joe Ferguson	QB	Terry Bradshaw
O.J. Simpson	RB	Rocky Bleier
Jim Braxton	RB	Franco Harris
	Starters, Defense	
Walt Patulski	LE	L. C. Greenwood
Mike Kadish	MG-LT	Joe Greene
Earl Edwards	RE-RT	Ernie Holmes
Dave Washington	OLB-RE	Dwight White
Jim Cheyunski	ILB-LLB	Jack Ham
Doug Allen	ILB-MLB	Jack Lambert
Bo Cornell	OLB-RLB	Andy Russell
Robert James	LCB	J. T. Thomas
Dwight Harrison	RCB	Mel Blount
Neal Craig	LS	Mike Wagner
Rex Kern	RS	Glen Edwards

Buffalo	7	0	7	0	—	14
Pittsburgh	3	26	0	3	—	32

Pitt —FG Gerela 21
Buff—Seymour 22 pass from Ferguson (Leypoldt kick)
Pitt —Bleier 27 pass from Bradshaw (kick blocked)
Pitt —Harris 1 run (Gerela kick)
Pitt —Harris 4 run (kick blocked)
Pitt —Harris 1 run (Gerela kick)
Buff—Simpson 3 pass from Ferguson (Leypoldt kick)
Pitt —FG Gerela 22
Attendance—48,321

1974 NFC

MINNESOTA 30, ST. LOUIS 14

With the score 7–7 in the third quarter, the Minnesota Vikings' Jeff Wright intercepted a pass by Jim Hart to set up a field goal by Fred Cox. One minute later, Nate Wright picked up a fumble by Terry Metcalf and ran 20 yards to give Minnesota a 17–7 lead.

December 21, at Bloomington, Minnesota

St. Louis	Starters, Offense	Minnesota
Earl Thomas	WR	Jim Lash
Roger Finnie	LT	Charles Goodrum
Bob Young	LG	Andy Maurer
Tom Brahaney	C	Mick Tingelhoff
Conrad Dobler	RG	Ed White
Dan Dierdorf	RT	Ron Yary
Jackie Smith	TE	Stu Voigt
Mel Gray	WR	John Gilliam
Jim Hart	QB	Fran Tarkenton
Terry Metcalf	RB	Chuck Foreman
Jim Otis	RB	Dave Osborn
	Starters, Defense	
Council Rudolph	LE	Carl Eller
Leo Brooks	LT	Doug Sutherland
Bob Rowe	RT	Alan Page
Ron Yankowski	RE	Jim Marshall
Larry Stallings	LLB	Roy Winston
Mark Arneson	MLB	Jeff Siemon
Pete Barnes	RLB	Wally Hilgenberg
Norm Thompson	LCB	Nate Wright
Roger Wehrli	RCB	Jackie Wallace
Jim Tolbert	LS	Jeff Wright
Clarence Duren	RS	Paul Krause

St. Louis	0	7	0	7	—	14
Minnesota	0	7	16	7	—	30

StL —Thomas 13 pass from Hart (Bakken kick)
Minn—Gilliam 16 pass from Tarkenton (Cox kick)
Minn—FG Cox 37
Minn—N. Wright 20 fumble return (Cox kick)
Minn—Gilliam 38 pass from Tarkenton (kick failed)
Minn—Foreman 4 run (Cox kick)
StL —Metcalf 11 run (Bakken kick)
Attendance—44,626

1974 NFC

LOS ANGELES 19, WASHINGTON 10

The temperature was 61 degrees with the wind blowing at 25 miles per hour in Los Angeles as the Rams turned two fumble recoveries into field goals to take a 13–10 lead at the beginning of the fourth quarter and go on to a 19–10 victory over the Washington Redskins.

December 22, at Los Angeles

Washington	Offense	Los Angeles
Charley Taylor	WR	Harold Jackson
Ray Schoenke	LT	Charlie Cowan
Paul Laaveg	LG	Tom Mack
Len Hauss	C	Ken Iman
Walt Sweeney	RG	Joe Scibelli
George Starke	RT	John Williams
Jerry Smith	TE	Bob Klein
Roy Jefferson	WR	Jack Snow
Billy Kilmer	QB	James Harris
Larry Brown	RB	Jim Bertelsen
Moses Denson	RB	Lawrence McCutcheon
	Starters, Defense	
Ron McDole	LE	Jack Youngblood
Bill Brundige	LT	Merlin Olsen
Diron Talbert	RT	Larry Brooks
Verlon Biggs	RE	Fred Dryer
Dave Robinson	LLB	Ken Geddes
Rusty Tillman	MLB	Jack Reynolds
Chris Hanburger	RLB	Isiah Robertson
Pat Fischer	LCB	Charlie Stukes
Mike Bass	RCB	Al Clark
Ken Houston	LS	Dave Elmendorf
Brig Owens	RS	Bill Simpson

Washington	3	7	0	0	—	10
Los Angeles	7	0	3	9	—	19

LA —Klein 10 pass from Harris (Ray kick)
Wash—FG Bragg 35
Wash—Denson 1 run (Bragg kick)
LA —FG Ray 37.
LA —FG Ray 26
LA —Robertson 59 interception return (pass failed)
Attendance—80,118

1975 AFC

PITTSBURGH 28, BALTIMORE 10

The Pittsburgh Steelers' Franco Harris set a divisional playoff record by rushing for 153 yards in 27 carries, scoring one touchdown in a 28–10 victory.

The Steelers scored three second-half touchdowns to overcome a 10–7 lead by the Colts, who were limited to 154 yards—82 rushing, 72 passing.

December 27, at Pittsburgh

Baltimore	Starters, Offense	Pittsburgh
Roger Carr	WR	Frank Lewis
David Taylor	LT	Jon Kolb
Robert Pratt	LG	Jim Clack
Ken Mendenhall	C	Ray Mansfield
Elmer Collett	RG	Gerry Mullins
George Kunz	RT	Gordon Gravelle
Raymond Chester	TE	Larry Brown
Glenn Doughty	WR	Lynn Swann
Bert Jones	QB	Terry Bradshaw
Lydell Mitchell	RB	Rocky Bleier
Bill Olds	RB	Franco Harris
	Starters, Defense	
Fred Cook	LE	L. C. Greenwood
Mike Barnes	LT	Steve Furness
Joe Erhmann	RT	Ernie Holmes
John Dutton	RE	Dwight White
Tom MacLeod	LLB	Jack Ham
Jim Cheyunski	MLB	Jack Lambert
Stan White	RLB	Andy Russell
Lloyd Mumphord	LCB	J.T. Thomas
Nelson Munsey	RCB	Mel Blount
Bruce Laird	LS	Mike Wagner
Jackie Wallace	RS	Glen Edwards

Baltimore	0	7	3	0	—	10
Pittsburgh	7	0	7	14	—	28

Pitt —Harris 8 run (Gerela kick)
Balt—Doughty 5 pass from Domres (Linhart kick)
Balt—FG Linhart 21
Pitt —Bleier 7 run (Gerela kick)
Pitt —Bradshaw 2 run (Gerela kick)
Pitt —Russell 93 fumble return (Gerela kick)
Attendance—49,053

1975 AFC

OAKLAND 31, CINCINNATI 28

Quarterback Ken Stabler completed 17 of 23 passes for 199 yards and three touchdowns as the Oakland Raiders built a 31–14 lead early in the fourth quarter, then held off the Cincinnati Bengals 31–28.

December 28, at Oakland

Cincinnati	Starters, Offense	Oakland
Isaac Curtis	WR	Clifford Branch
Rufus Mayes	LT	Art Shell
Howard Fest	LG	Gene Upshaw
Bob Johnson	C	Dave Dalby
John Shinners	RG	George Buehler
Vernon Holland	RT	John Vella
Bob Trumpy	TE	Bob Moore
Charlie Joiner	WR	Mike Siani
Ken Anderson	QB	Ken Stabler
Stan Fritts	RB	Clarence Davis
Charles (Boobie) Clark	RB	Marv Hubbard
	Starters, Defense	
Ken Johnson	LE	Otis Sistrunk
Bob Brown	LT-MG	Art Thoms
Ron Carpenter	RT-RE	Horace Jones
Sherman White	RE-OLB	Ted Hendricks
Al Beauchamp	LLB-ILB	Phil Villapiano
Jim LeClair	MLB-ILB	Monte Johnson
Ron Pritchard	RLB-OLB	Gerald Irons
Lemar Parrish	LCB	Alonzo (Skip) Thomas
Ken Riley	RCB	Neal Colzie
Tommy Casanova	LS	George Atkinson
Bernard Jackson	RS	Jack Tatum

Cincinnati	0	7	7	14	—	28
Oakland	3	14	7	7	—	31

Oak—FG Blanda 27
Oak—Siani 9 pass from Stabler (Blanda kick)
Cin —Fritts 1 run (Green kick)
Oak—Moore 8 pass from Stabler (Blanda kick)
Oak—Banaszak 6 run (Blanda kick)
Cin —Elliott 6 run (Green kick)
Oak—Casper 2 pass from Stabler (Blanda kick)
Cin —Joiner 25 pass from Anderson (Green kick)
Cin —Curtis 14 pass from Anderson (Green kick)
Attendance—53,039

1975 NFC

LOS ANGELES 35, ST. LOUIS 23

Los Angeles and St. Louis accounted for 803 yards offense—440 for Los Angeles, 363 for St. Louis. The Rams' Lawrence McCutcheon set an NFC post-season record, 202 yards rushing and 37 carries.

December 27, at Los Angeles

St. Louis	Starters, Offense	Los Angeles
Mel Gray	WR	Harold Jackson
Roger Finnie	LT	Doug France
Bob Young	LG	Tom Mack
Tom Banks	C	Rich Saul
Conrad Dobler	RG	Joe Scibelli
Dan Dierdorf	RT	John Williams
Jackie Smith	TE	Terry Nelson
J.V. Cain	WR	Ron Jessie
Jim Hart	QB	Ron Jaworski
Terry Metcalf	RB	Cullen Bryant
Jim Otis	RB	Lawrence McCutcheon
	Starters, Defense	
Bob Bell	LE	Jack Youngblood
Charlie Davis	LT	Merlin Olsen
Bob Rowe	RT	Cody Jones
Ron Yankowski	RE	Fred Dryer
Larry Stallings	LLB	Ken Geddes
Greg Hartle	MLB	Jack Reynolds
Pete Barnes	RLB	Isiah Robertson
Norm Thompson	LCB	Eddie McMillan
Roger Wehrli	RCB	Monte Jackson
Ken Reaves	LS	Dave Elmendorf
Clarence Duren	RS	Bill Simpson

St. Louis	0	9	7	7	—	23
Los Angeles	14	14	0	7	—	35

LA—Jaworski 5 run (Dempsey kick)
LA—Jack Youngblood 47 interception return (Dempsey kick)
LA—Simpson 65 interception return (Dempsey kick)
StL—Otis 3 run (kick blocked)
LA—H. Jackson 66 pass from Jaworski (Dempsey kick)
StL—FG Bakken 39
StL—Gray 11 pass from Hart (Bakken kick)
LA—Jessie 2 fumble return (Dempsey kick)
StL—Jones 3 run (Bakken kick)
Attendance—72,650

1975 NFC

DALLAS 17, MINNESOTA 14

The Dallas Cowboys marched 85 yards in the game's last two minutes to upend the Minnesota Vikings 17–14. The winning touchdown came on Roger Staubach's pass to Drew Pearson, who ran the final 5 yards to complete a 50-yard play with 24 seconds left.

Staubach completed other passes of 9, 7, and 25 yards to Pearson during the eight-play drive.

December 28, at Bloomington, Minnesota

Dallas	Starters, Offense	Minnesota
Golden Richards	WR	Jim Lash
Ralph Neely	LT	Steve Riley
Burton Lawless	LG	Andy Maurer
John Fitzgerald	C	Mick Tingelhoff
Blaine Nye	RG	Ed White
Rayfield Wright	RT	Ron Yary
Jean Fugett	TE	Stu Voigt
Drew Pearson	WR	John Gilliam
Roger Staubach	QB	Fran Tarkenton
Preston Pearson	RB	Ed Marinaro
Robert Newhouse	RB	Chuck Foreman
	Starters, Defense	
Ed (Too Tall) Jones	LE	Carl Eller
Jethro Pugh	LT	Doug Sutherland
Larry Cole	RT	Alan Page
Harvey Martin	RE	Jim Marshall
Dave Edwards	LLB	Fred McNeill
Lee Roy Jordan	MLB	Jeff Siemon
D.D. Lewis	RLB	Wally Hilgenberg
Mark Washington	LCB	Nate Wright
Mel Renfro	RCB	Bobby Bryant
Charlie Waters	LS	Terry Brown
Cliff Harris	RS	Paul Krause

Dallas	0	0	7	10	—	17
Minnesota	0.	7	0	7	—	14

Minn—Foreman 1 run (Cox kick)
Dall—Dennison 4 run (Fritsch kick)
Dall—FG Fritsch 24
Minn—McClanahan 1 run (Cox kick)
Dall—D. Pearson 50 pass from Staubach (Fritsch kick)
Attendance—46,425

1976 AFC

OAKLAND 24, NEW ENGLAND 21

Ken Stabler's one-yard run with 10 seconds left gave Oakland a 24–21 victory. The Raiders marched 73 yards after New England's John Smith was short on a 50-yard field goal with 4:30 remaining. A penalty stalled the Patriots on Oakland's 27-yard line.

December 18, at Oakland

New England	Starters, Offense	Oakland
Randy Vataha	WR	Clifford Branch
Leon Gray	LT	Art Shell
John Hannah	LG	Gene Upshaw
Bill Lenkaitis	C	Dave Dalby
Sam Adams	RG	George Buehler
Bob McKay	RT	John Vella
Russ Francis	TE	Dave Casper
Darryl Stingley	WR	Fred Biletnikoff
Steve Grogan	QB	Ken Stabler
Andy Johnson	RB	Clarence Davis
Sam Cunningham	RB	Mark van Eeghen
	Starters, Defense	
Mel Lunsford	LE	John Matuszak
Ray Hamilton	MG	Dave Rowe
Julius Adams	RE	Otis Sistrunk
Steve Zabel	OLB	Phil Villapiano
Sam Hunt	ILB	Monte Johnson
Steve Nelson	ILB	Willie Hall
Pete Barnes	OLB	Ted Hendricks
Bob Howard	LCB	Alonzo (Skip) Thomas
Mike Haynes	RCB	Willie Brown
Prentice McCray	LS	George Atkinson
Tim Fox	RS	Jack Tatum

New England	7	0	14	0	—	21
Oakland	3	7	0	14	—	24

NE—Johnson 1 run (Smith kick)
Oak—FG Mann 40
Oak—Biletnikoff 31 pass from Stabler (Mann kick)
NE—Francis 26 pass from Grogan (Smith kick)
NE—Phillips 3 run (Smith kick)
Oak—van Eeghen 1 run (Mann kick)
Oak—Stabler 1 run (Mann kick)
Attendance—53,045

1976 AFC

PITTSBURGH 40, BALTIMORE 14

Terry Bradshaw, who had missed six starting assignments because of injuries, completed 14 of 18 passes for 264 yards and three touchdowns as Pittsburgh, favored by three points, beat Baltimore by 26.

December 19, at Baltimore

Pittsburgh	Starters, Offense	Baltimore
Lynn Swann	WR	Roger Carr
Jon Kolb	LT	David Taylor
Sam Davis	LG	Robert Pratt
Mike Webster	C	Ken Mendenhall
Jim Clack	RG	Elmer Collett
Gerry Mullins	RT	George Kunz
Larry Brown	TE	Raymond Chester
Frank Lewis	WR	Glenn Doughty
Terry Bradshaw	QB	Bert Jones
Franco Harris	RB	Lydell Mitchell
Rocky Bleier	RB	Roosevelt Leaks
	Starters, Defense	
L.C. Greenwood	LE	Fred Cook
Joe Greene	LT	Mike Barnes
Ernie Holmes	RT	Joe Ehrmann
Dwight White	RE	John Dutton
Jack Ham	LLB	Derrel Luce
Jack Lambert	MLB	Jim Cheyunski
Andy Russell	RLB	Stan White
J.T. Thomas	LCB	Lloyd Mumphord
Mel Blount	RCB	Ray Oldham
Mike Wagner	LS	Bruce Laird
Glen Edwards	RS	Jackie Wallace

Pittsburgh	9	17	0	14	—	40
Baltimore	7	0	0	7	—	14

Pitt—Lewis 76 pass from Bradshaw (kick failed)
Pitt—FG Gerela 45
Balt—Carr 17 pass from Jones (Linhart kick)
Pitt—Harrison 1 run (Gerela kick)
Pitt—Swann 29 pass from Bradshaw (Gerela kick)
Pitt—FG Gerela 25
Pitt—Swann 11 pass from Bradshaw (Gerela kick)
Balt—Leaks 1 run (Linhart kick)
Pitt—Harrison 9 run (Mansfield kick)
Attendance—60,020

1976 NFC

MINNESOTA 35, WASHINGTON 20

Tight end Stu Voigt, left guard Charles Goodrum, and running back Chuck Foreman blocked right on Minnesota's first play and Brent McClanahan ran left 41 yards to set up the Vikings' first touchdown.

December 18, at Bloomington, Minnesota

Washington	Starters, Offense	Minnesota
Frank Grant	WR	Ahmad Rashad
Tim Stokes	LT	Steve Riley
Ron Saul	LG	Charles Goodrum
Len Hauss	C	Mick Tingelhoff
Terry Hermeling	RG	Ed White
George Starke	RT	Ron Yary
Jean Fugett	TE	Stu Voigt
Roy Jefferson	WR	Sammy White
Billy Kilmer	QB	Fran Tarkenton
John Riggins	RB	Brent McClanahan
Mike Thomas	RB	Chuck Foreman
	Starters, Defense	
Ron McDole	LE	Carl Eller
Dave Butz	LT	Doug Sutherland
Diron Talbert	RT	Alan Page
Dennis Johnson	RE	Jim Marshall
Brad Dusek	LLB	Matt Blair
Harold McLinton	MLB	Jeff Siemon
Chris Hanburger	RLB	Wally Hilgenberg
Pat Fischer	LCB	Nate Wright
Joe Lavender	RCB	Bobby Bryant
Ken Houston	LS	Jeff Wright
Jake Scott	RS	Paul Krause

Washington	3	0	3	14	—	20
Minnesota	14	7	14	0	—	35

Minn—Voigt 18 pass from Tarkenton (Cox kick)
Wash—FG Moseley 47
Minn—White 27 pass from Tarkenton (Cox kick)
Minn—Foreman 2 run (Cox kick)
Minn—Foreman 30 run (Cox kick)
Wash—FG Moseley 35
Minn—White 9 pass from Tarkenton (Cox kick)
Wash—Grant 12 pass from Kilmer (Moseley kick)
Wash—Jefferson 3 pass from Kilmer (Moseley kick)
Attendance—47,221

1976 NFC

LOS ANGELES 14, DALLAS 12

With four seconds left in the game, Los Angeles punter Rusty Jackson took the snap from center in his end zone and ran out of the end zone as the game ended, giving Dallas a two-point safety but clinching the Rams' 14–12 victory. Dallas's Charlie Waters had blocked two of Jackson's punts earlier in the game, one setting up a Cowboys field goal.

December 19, Irving, Texas

Los Angeles	Starters, Offense	Dallas
Harold Jackson	WR	Golden Richards
Doug France	LT	Ralph Neely
Tom Mack	LG	Herbert Scott
Rich Saul	C	John Fitzgerald
Dennis Harrah	RG	Blaine Nye
John Williams	RT	Rayfield Wright
Bob Klein	TE	Billy Joe DuPree
Ron Jessie	WR	Drew Pearson
Pat Haden	QB	Roger Staubach
Lawrence McCutcheon	RB	Preston Pearson
John Cappelletti	RB	Robert Newhouse
	Starters, Defense	
Jack Youngblood	LE	Ed (Too Tall) Jones
Merlin Olsen	LT	Jethro Pugh
Larry Brooks	RT	Larry Cole
Fred Dryer	RE	Harvey Martin
Jim Youngblood	LLB	Bob Breunig
Jack Reynolds	MLB	Lee Roy Jordan
Isiah Robertson	RLB	D.D. Lewis
Rod Perry	LCB	Benny Barnes
Monte Jackson	RCB	Mark Washington
Dave Elmendorf	LS	Charlie Waters
Bill Simpson	RS	Cliff Harris

Los Angeles	0	7	0	7	—	14
Dallas	3	7	0	2	—	12

Dall—FG Herrera 44
LA—Haden 4 run (Dempsey kick)
Dall—Laidlaw 1 run (Herrera kick)
LA—McCutcheon 1 run (Dempsey kick)
Dall—Safety, R. Jackson ran out of end zone
Attendance—62,436

L. McCutcheon	*Andy Farkas*	*Daryle Lamonica*	*Willie Wood*	*Preston Pearson*	*Vic Washington*	*Andy Russell*

POSTSEASON RECORDS

Legend
SB   Super Bowl
AFC   AFL or AFC championship game
NFC   NFL or NFC championship game
P   Divisional playoff game

RUSHING
Most Attempts, Game
37   Lawrence McCutcheon, P, Los Angeles vs. St. Louis, 1975
Most Yards, Game
206   Keith Lincoln, AFC: San Diego vs. Boston, 1963
Longest Gain
71   Hugh McElhenny, P, San Francisco vs. Detroit, 1957
Most Touchdowns, Game
3   Andy Farkas, P, Washington vs. N.Y. Giants, 1943
Otto Graham, NFC, Cleveland vs. Detroit, 1954
Tom Matte, NFC, Baltimore vs. Cleveland, 1968
Larry Schrieber, P, San Francisco vs. Dallas, 1972
Larry Csonka, AFC, Miami vs. Oakland, 1973
Franco Harris, P, Pittsburgh vs. Buffalo, 1974

PASSING
Most Attempts, Game
49   Joe Namath, AFC, N.Y. Jets vs. Oakland, 1968
Billy Kilmer, P, Washington vs. Minnesota, 1976
Most Completions, Game
27   Tommy Thompson, NFC, Philadelphia vs. Chi. Cardinals, 1947
Most Yards, Game
401   Daryle Lamonica, AFC, Oakland vs. N.Y. Jets, 1968
Longest Gain
93   Daryle Lamonica, P, Buffalo vs. Boston, 1963 (TD)
Most Touchdowns, Game
6   Daryle Lamonica, P, Oakland vs. Houston, 1969
Most Had Intercepted, Game
6   Frank Filchock, NFC, N.Y. Giants vs. Chi. Bears, 1946
Bobby Layne, NFC, Detroit vs. Cleveland, 1954
Norm Van Brocklin, NFC, Los Angeles vs. Cleveland, 1955

RECEIVING
Most Receptions, Game
12   Raymond Berry, NFC, Baltimore vs. N.Y. Giants, 1958
Most Yards, Game
198   Tom Fears, P, Los Angeles vs. Chi. Bears, 1950
Longest Gain
93   Elbert Dubenion, P, Buffalo vs. Boston, 1963 (TD)
Most Touchdowns, Game
3   Tom Fears, P; Los Angeles vs. Chi. Bears, 1950
Gary Collins, NFC: Cleveland vs. Baltimore, 1964
Fred Biletnikoff, P: Oakland vs. Kansas City, 1968
Preston Pearson, NFC, Dallas vs. Los Angeles, 1975

INTERCEPTIONS BY
Most Interceptions, Game
3   Joe Laws, NFC, Green Bay vs. N.Y. Giants, 1944
Most Yards, Game
88   Walt Sumner, NFC, Cleveland vs. Dallas, 1969
Longest Return
88   Walt Sumner, NFC, Cleveland vs. Dallas, 1969 (TD)
Most Touchdowns, Game
1   By 19 players

PUNTING
Most Punts, Game
11   Ken Strong, NFC, N.Y. Giants vs. Chi. Bears, 1933
Jim Norton, AFC, Houston vs. Oakland, 1967
Ode Burrell, P, Houston vs. Oakland, 1969
Longest
76   Ed Danowski, NFC, N.Y. Giants vs. Detroit, 1935
Highest Average, Game (4 punts)
52.5   Sammy Baugh, NFC, Washington vs. Chi. Bears, 1942 (6)

PUNT RETURNS
Most Punt Returns, Game
7   Ron Gardin, P, Baltimore vs. Cincinnati, 1970
Most Yards, Game
141   Bob Hayes, P, Dallas vs. Cleveland, 1967
Longest Return
81   Hugh Gallarneau, P, Chi. Bears vs. Green Bay, 1941 (TD)
Most Touchdowns
1   Hugh Gallarneau, P, Chi. Bears vs. Green Bay, 1941
Bosh Pritchard, P, Philadelphia vs. Pittsburgh, 1947
Charley Trippi, NFC; Chi. Cardinals vs. Philadelphia, 1947
Verda (Vitamin T.) Smith, P, Los Angeles vs. Detroit, 1952
George (Butch) Byrd, AFC, Buffalo vs. San Diego, 1965
Golden Richards, NFC, Dallas vs. Minn., 1973

KICKOFF RETURNS
Most Kickoff Returns, Game
7   Don Bingham, NFC, Chi. Bears vs. N.Y. Giants, 1956
Most Yards, Game
170   Leslie (Speedy) Duncan, P, Washington vs. San Francisco, 1971
Longest Return
97   Vic Washington, P, San Francisco vs. Dallas, 1972 (TD)
Most Touchdowns
1   Vic Washington, P, San Francisco vs. Dallas, 1972
Nat Moore, P, Miami vs. Oakland, 1974

SCORING
Most Points, Game
19   Pat Harder, P, Detroit vs. Los Angeles, 1952 (2 TD, 1 FG, 4 PAT)
Paul Hornung, NFC; Green Bay vs. N.Y. Giants, 1961 (1 TD, 3 FG, 4 PAT)
Most Touchdowns, Game
3   By 11 players
Most Points After Touchdown, Game
8   Lou Groza, NFC, Cleveland vs. Detroit, 1954 (8 att)
Jim Martin, NFC, Detroit vs. Cleveland, 1957 (8 att)
George Blanda, P, Oakland vs. Houston, 1969 (8 att)
Most Field Goals Attempted, Game
6   George Blanda, AFC, Oakland vs. Houston, 1967 (4 made)
David Ray, P, Los Angeles vs. Dallas, 1973 (3 made)
Most Field Goals, Game
4   Gino Cappelletti, AFC, Boston vs. Buffalo, 1963 (5 att)
George Blanda, AFC, Oakland vs. Houston, 1967 (6 att)
Don Chandler, SB, Green Bay vs. Oakland, 1968 (4 att)
Curt Knight, NFC, Washington vs. Dallas, 1972 (4 att)
George Blanda, P, Oakland vs. Pittsburgh, 1973 (5 att)
Longest Field Goal
52   Lou Groza, NFC, Cleveland vs. Los Angeles, 1951
Curt Knight, P, Washington vs. Minnesota, 1973

DIVISIONAL PLAYOFF HISTORY

Date	Playoff	Result	Site (Attendance)
Dec. 14, 1941	NFL Western Division	Chi. Bears 33, Green Bay 14	Wrigley Field, Chicago (43,425)
Dec. 19, 1943	NFL Eastern Division	Washington 28, N.Y. Giants 0	Polo Grounds, New York (42,800)
Dec. 21, 1947	NFL Eastern Division	Philadelphia 21, Pittsburgh 0	Forbes Field, Pittsburgh (35,729)
Dec. 17, 1950	NFL American Conference	Cleveland 8, N.Y. Giants 3	Memorial Stadium, Cleveland (33,754)
Dec. 17, 1950	NFL National Conference	Los Angeles 24, Chi. Bears 14	Los Angeles Memorial Coliseum (83,501)
Dec. 21, 1952	NFL National Conference	Detroit 31, Los Angeles 21	Briggs Stadium, Detroit (47,645)
Dec. 22, 1957	NFL Western Division	Detroit 31, San Francisco 27	Kezar Stadium, San Francisco (60,118)
Dec. 21, 1958	NFL Eastern Conference	N.Y. Giants 10, Cleveland 0	Yankee Stadium, New York (61,274)
Dec. 28, 1963	AFL Eastern Division	Boston 26, Buffalo 8	War Memorial Stadium, Buffalo (33,044)
Dec. 26, 1965	NFL Western Conference	Green Bay, 13, Baltimore 10	Lambeau Field, Green Bay (50,484)
Dec. 23, 1967	NFL Western Conference	Green Bay 28, Los Angeles 7	Milwaukee County Stadium (49,861)
Dec. 24, 1967	NFL Eastern Conference	Dallas 52, Cleveland 14	Cotton Bowl, Dallas (70,786)
Dec. 21, 1968	NFL Eastern Conference	Cleveland 31, Dallas 20	Memorial Stadium, Cleveland (81,497)
Dec. 22, 1968	AFL Western Division	Oakland 41, Kansas City 6	Oakland Coliseum (53,605)
Dec. 22, 1968	NFL Western Conference	Baltimore 24, Minnesota 14	Memorial Stadium, Baltimore (60,238)
Dec. 20, 1969	AFL Inter-Divisional	Kansas City 13, N.Y. Jets 6	Shea Stadium, New York (62,977)
Dec. 21, 1969	AFL Inter-Divisional	Oakland 56, Houston 7	Oakland Coliseum (53,539)
Dec. 27, 1969	NFL Western Conference	Minnesota 23, Los Angeles 20	Metropolitan Stadium, Bloomington (47,900)
Dec. 28, 1969	NFL Eastern Conference	Cleveland 38, Dallas 14	Cotton Bowl, Dallas (69,321)
Dec. 26, 1970	AFC First Round	Baltimore 17, Cincinnati 0	Memorial Stadium, Baltimore (51,127)
Dec. 27, 1970	AFC First Round	Oakland 21, Miami 14	Oakland Coliseum (54,401)
Dec. 26, 1970	NFC First Round	Dallas 5, Detroit 0	Cotton Bowl, Dallas (73,167)
Dec. 27, 1970	NFC First Round	San Francisco 17, Minnesota 14	Metropolitan Stadium, Bloomington (45,103)
Dec. 25, 1971	AFC First Round	Miami 27, Kansas City 24	Memorial Stadium, Kansas City (50,374)
Dec. 26, 1971	AFC First Round	Baltimore 20, Cleveland 3	Memorial Stadium, Cleveland (74,082)
Dec. 25, 1971	NFC First Round	Dallas 20, Minnesota 12	Metropolitan Stadium, Bloomington (49,100)
Dec. 26, 1971	NFC First Round	San Francisco 24, Washington 20	Candlestick Park, San Francisco (45,364)
Dec. 23, 1972	AFC First Round	Pittsburgh 13, Oakland 7	Three Rivers Stadium, Pittsburgh (50,350)
Dec. 24, 1972	AFC First Round	Miami 20, Cleveland 14	Orange Bowl, Miami (80,010)
Dec. 23, 1972	NFC First Round	Dallas 30, San Francisco 28	Candlestick Park, San Francisco (61,214)
Dec. 24, 1972	NFC First Round	Washington 16, Green Bay 3	RFK Stadium, Washington (53,140)
Dec. 22, 1973	AFC First Round	Oakland 33, Pittsburgh 14	Oakland Coliseum (51,110)
Dec. 23, 1973	AFC First Round	Miami 34, Cincinnati 16	Orange Bowl, Miami (74,770)
Dec. 22, 1973	NFC First Round	Minnesota 27, Washington 20	Metropolitan Stadium, Bloomington (45,475)
Dec. 23, 1973	NFC First Round	Dallas 27, Los Angeles 16	Texas Stadium, Irving (64,291)
Dec. 21, 1974	AFC First Round	Oakland 28, Miami 26	Oakland Coliseum (52,817)
Dec. 22, 1974	AFC First Round	Pittsburgh 32, Buffalo 14	Three Rivers Stadium, Pittsburgh (48,321)
Dec. 21, 1974	NFC First Round	Minnesota 30, St. Louis 14	Metropolitan Stadium, Bloomington (44,626)
Dec. 22, 1974	NFC First Round	Los Angeles 19, Washington 10	Los Angeles Memorial Coliseum (80,118)
Dec. 27, 1975	AFC First Round	Pittsburgh 28, Baltimore 10	Three Rivers Stadium, Pittsburgh (49,053)
Dec. 27, 1975	AFC First Round	Oakland 31, Cincinnati 28	Oakland Coliseum (53,039)
Dec. 27, 1975	NFC First Round	Los Angeles 35, St. Louis 23	Los Angeles Memorial Coliseum (72,650)
Dec. 28, 1975	NFC First Round	Dallas 17, Minnesota 14	Metropolitan Stadium, Bloomington (46,425)
Dec. 18, 1976	AFC First Round	Oakland 24, New England 21	Oakland Coliseum (53,045)
Dec. 19, 1976	AFC First Round	Pittsburgh 40, Baltimore 14	Memorial Stadium, Baltimore (60,020)
Dec. 18, 1976	NFC First Round	Minnesota 35, Washington 20	Metropolitan Stadium, Bloomington (47,221)
Dec. 19, 1976	NFC First Round	Los Angeles 14, Dallas 12	Texas Stadium, Irving (62,436)

Championship Games

1933

CHI. BEARS 23, N.Y. GIANTS 21

Karr (22) caught Hewitt lateral, scored winning TD.

The Chicago Bears came from behind in the final three minutes to defeat the New York Giants 23–21.

The Bears, trailing 7–6 at the half, 14–9 in the third quarter, and 21–16 in the fourth quarter, went ahead for the last time after the Giants' Ken Strong punted eight yards and Chicago took over on New York's 46-yard line. Keith Molesworth passed nine yards to Carl Brumbaugh. Bronko Nagurski, the Bears' leading rusher with 65 yards in 14 carries, gained four yards to the 33. On the next play, Nagurski threw a jump pass to Bill Hewitt. Hewitt gained 14 yards and lateraled to Bill Karr. Karr covered the remaining 19 yards for the winning score.

Fog hung over Wrigley Field and it was misting in the first half, when the Giants took a 7–6 lead on Harry Newman's 29-yard pass to Morris (Red) Badgro.

Newman, who completed 12 of 17 passes for 201 yards and two touchdowns, figured in the game's most exciting play on the first play of the fourth quarter. After the Bears went in front 16–14, Newman began moving the Giants from their 26-yard line. Five successive pass completions put the ball on the Bears' 8. Strong took a handoff on the next play but became trapped near the sideline. He lateraled to the surprised Newman, who scrambled until he was trapped at the 15. Newman then threw a desperation pass to Strong, who had slipped free in the corner of the end zone and caught the ball for a touchdown.

December 17, at Chicago

N.Y. Giants	Starting Lineups	Chi. Bears
Morris (Red) Badgro	LE	Bill Hewitt
Len Grant	LT	Roy (Link) Lyman
Denver (Butch) Gibson	LG	Jules Carlson
Mel Hein	C	Charles (Ookie) Miller
Tom (Pottsville) Jones	RG	Joe Kopcha
Steve Owen	RT	George Musso
Ray Flaherty	RE	Bill Karr
Harry Newman	QB	Carl Brumbaugh
Ken Strong	LH	Keith Molesworth
Dale Burnett	RH	Gene Ronzani
John (Bo) Molenda	FB	Bronko Nagurski

N.Y. Giants	0	7	7	7	—	21
Chi. Bears	3	3	10	7	—	23

Chi —FG Manders 16
Chi —FG Manders 40
NYG—Badgro 29 pass from Newman (Strong kick)
Chi —FG Manders 28
NYG—Krause 1 run (Strong kick)
Chi —Karr 8 pass from Nagurski (Manders kick)
NYG—Strong 8 pass from Newman (Strong kick)
Chi —Karr 19 lateral from Hewitt, who caught 14 pass from Nagurski (Brumbaugh kick)
Attendance—26,000

TEAM STATISTICS	NYG	Chi.
First downs	13	12
Rushing	4	9
Passing	8	3
By penalty	1	0
Total yardage	307	311
Net rushing yardage	99	161
Net passing yardage	208	150
Passes att.-comp.-had int.	20-14-1	16-7-1

1934

N.Y. GIANTS 30, CHI. BEARS 13

Strong's 38-yard field goal gave Giants a 3–0 lead.

The New York Giants rallied for 27 points to overcome a 13–3 Chicago lead and score a 30–13 victory in the "sneakers game." The Giants switched from football shoes to basketball shoes on a frozen field in the Polo Grounds.

Giants' president John V. Mara inspected the playing field the morning of the game and reported the condition to head coach Steve Owen. The temperature was nine degrees. Owen and team captain Ray Flaherty discussed the idea of wearing basketball shoes. Some of the Giants' players were asked to bring their own sneakers to the game. Abe Cohen, a clubhouse equipment aide, made a trip to Manhattan College for additional pairs. There were no sporting goods stores open.

The Giants did not put on the rubber-soled shoes until the start of the third quarter. They trailed 10–3 at the half and fell behind 13–3 in the third quarter. The comeback did not begin until well into the final period. Rookie Ed Danowski, who replaced the injured Harry Newman at tailback in the Giants' single-wing formation in midseason, threw a 28-yard touchdown pass to Malcolm (Ike) Frankian to make the score 13–10. The Bears did not advance on their next possession and, after a 20-yard punt, the Giants took over on Chicago's 42. Ken Strong, behind blocking from tackle Bill Morgan, fullback John (Bo) Molenda, and Danowski ran straight up the field for a touchdown to give New York a 17–13 lead.

December 9, at New York

Chi. Bears	Starting Lineups	N.Y. Giants
Bill Hewitt	LE	Malcolm (Ike) Frankian
Roy (Link) Lyman	LT	Bill Morgan
Bert Pearson	LG	Denver (Butch) Gibson
Ed Kawal	C	Mel Hein
Jules Carlson	RG	Tom (Pottsville) Jones
George Musso	RT	Cecil (Tex) Irvin
Bill Karr	RE	Ray Flaherty
Carl Brumbaugh	QB	Ed Danowski
Gene Ronzani	LH	Dale Burnett
Keith Molesworth	RH	Ken Strong
Bronko Nagurski	FB	John (Bo) Molenda

Chi. Bears	0	10	3	0	—	13
N.Y. Giants	3	0	0	27	—	30

NYG—FG Strong 38
Chi—Nagurski 1 run (Manders kick)
Chi —FG Manders 17
Chi —FG Manders 24
NYG—Frankian 28 pass from Danowski (Strong kick)
NYG—Strong 42 run (Strong kick)
NYG—Strong 11 run (kick failed)
NYG—Danowski 9 run (Molenda kick)
Attendance—35,059

TEAM STATISTICS	Chi.	NYG
First downs	10	12
Rushing	7	7
Passing	3	5
By penalty	0	0
Total yardage	165	276
Net rushing yardage	89	173
Net passing yardage	76	103
Passes att.-comp.-had int.	15-6-3	12-7-2

1935

DETROIT 26, N.Y. GIANTS 7

Gutowsky's two-yard run put Lions ahead 6–0.

The Detroit Lions took the opening kickoff and marched 61 yards to a touchdown and never trailed the New York Giants on a day when wind, rain, sleet, and snow turned the University of Detroit field into a swamp. The Lions' 26–7 victory marked their first NFL championship and it came two months after the baseball Tigers had won their first World Series.

Ace Gutowsky ran two yards for Detroit's first score. Earl (Dutch) Clark increased the Lions' lead to 13–0 in the first period with a twisting run of 40 yards. The Giants did not score until midway in the third quarter, when Ed Danowski threw a pass to Ken Strong. Gutowsky, who was defending on the play, deflected the pass with his fingertips but Strong gained control of the ball and ran 31 yards to complete a 42-yard play.

With three minutes left in the game Danowski tried a quick-kick, but the kick was low and hit the back of one of the Giants' blockers. Detroit's George Christiansen recovered on New York's 26-yard line. The Lions ran five plays into the line. On the sixth, from the 4-yard line, Clark faked into the middle and Ernie Caddel swept around the drawn-in defense for a touchdown.

Harry Newman returned the kickoff to the Giants' 32-yard line, then replaced Danowski as New York lined up in a T formation. Raymond (Buddy) Parker intercepted Newman's flat pass on first down and ran 22 yards to the 10. Caddel ran four yards and Parker two before Parker scored from the 4-yard line in the final seconds.

December 15, at Detroit

N.Y. Giants	Starting Lineups	Detroit
Malcolm (Ike) Frankian	LE	Ed Klewicki
Bill Morgan	LT	John Johnson
Tom (Pottsville) Jones	LG	Regis Monahan
Mel Hein	C	Clare Randolph
Bill Owen	RG	Grover (Ox) Emerson
Len Grant	RT	George Christiansen
Charles (Tod) Goodwin	RE	John Schneller
Ed Danowski	QB	Glenn Presnell
Elvin (Kink) Richards	LH	Frank Christiansen
Ken Strong	RH	Ernie Caddel
Les (Red) Corzine	FB	Leroy (Ace) Gutowsky

N.Y. Giants	0	7	0	0	—	7
Detroit	13	0	0	13	—	26

Det —Gutowsky 2 run (Presnell kick)
Det —Clark 40 run (kick failed)
NYG—Strong 42 pass from Danowski (Strong kick)
Det —Caddel 4 run (kick failed)
Det —Parker 4 run (Clark kick)
Attendance—15,000

TEAM STATISTICS	NYG	Det
First downs	9	16
Rushing	4	14
Passing	3	2
By penalty	2	0
Total yardage	194	298
Net rushing yardage	106	246
Net passing yardage	88	52
Passes att.-comp.-had int.	13-4-2	5-2-0

1936

GREEN BAY 21, BOSTON REDSKINS 6

Hinkle (41) gained 10 yards for Packers.

The Polo Grounds was the site of the championship game, although the participating teams were Western champion Green Bay and Eastern champion Boston. George Preston Marshall, owner of the Redskins, moved the game from Boston to New York, because the Redskins were going to transfer to another city, most likely Washington. Green Bay won 21–6.

For the first time in the four-year history of the championship game, the weather was not severe. The temperature was 36 degrees and the sun was shining.

Boston's all-league halfback Cliff Battles, who gained 18 yards in his first two carries, was injured on the tenth play of the game. On that play, teammate Riley Smith fumbled Battles's lateral and Lou Gordon recovered for Green Bay on the Packers' 46-yard line. Three plays later Arnie Herber completed a touchdown pass to Don Hutson on a long side line pattern. The play covered 50 yards and put Green Bay ahead 7–0 after Ernie Smith's conversion kick.

Ernest (Pug) Rentner, Battles's replacement, scored Boston's only touchdown in the second quarter. Rentner gained 13 yards in five carries and completed two passes for 41 yards in a 10-play, 78-yard drive that ended with Rentner's scoring from the 2.

Green Bay increased its lead to 14–6 in the third quarter on Herber's five-yard pass to Milt Gantenbein. A 55-yard pass play—Herber to Johnny Blood (McNally)—set up the score. Boston's Riley Smith was in punt formation from the Redskins' 22-yard line in the fourth quarter when his kick was blocked by Lon Evans and recovered on the 3-yard line by Clarke Hinkle. Bob Monnett, who was in the game for Herber, scored on the second play from the 3.

Dec. 13, at New York

Green Bay	Starting Lineups	Boston
Milt Gantenbein	LE	Wayne Millner
Ernie Smith	LT	Glen (Turk) Edwards
Paul Engebretsen	LG	Les Olsson
George Svendsen	C	Frank Bausch
Lon Evans	RG	Jim Karcher
Lou Gordon	RT	Jim Barber
Don Hutson	RE	Charley Malone
Hank Bruder	QB	Riley Smith
George Sauer	LH	Cliff Battles
Arnie Herber	RH	Ed Justice
Clarke Hinkle	FB	Don Irwin

Green Bay	7	0	7	7	— 21
Boston	0	6	0	0	— 6

GB —Hutson 50 pass from Herber (E. Smith kick)
Bos—Rentner 2 run (kick failed)
GB —Gantenbein 5 pass from Herber (E. Smith kick)
GB —Monnett 3 run (Engebretsen kick)
Attendance—29,545

TEAM STATISTICS	GB	Bos.
First downs	7	8
Rushing	2	4
Passing	4	3
By penalty	1	1
Total yardage	220	130
Net rushing yardage	67	39
Net passing yardage	153	91
Passes att.-comp.-had int.	23-9-2	26-7-1

1937

WASHINGTON 28, CHI. BEARS 21

Baugh (eluding Dick Plasman) threw for three TDs.

Sammy Baugh completed 18 of 33 passes for 335 yards and three touchdowns, including scoring passes of 78 and 35 yards in the fourth quarter as the Washington Redskins came from behind to defeat the Chicago Bears 28–21. Baugh's performance was achieved on an icy field in 15-degree weather.

Baugh, a rookie from Texas Christian University, established the Redskins' intentions on their first play from scrimmage. Passing from his own end zone, Baugh hit fullback Cliff Battles, who advanced the ball to Washington's 49, a gain of 42 yards. The Redskins were forced to punt, but the next time they had possession Baugh moved them 53 yards in 10 plays to a touchdown.

The Bears contained the Redskins for the remainder of the half and led 14–7 in the third quarter. Washington tied the score when Baugh passed to Wayne Millner, who ran a crossing pattern, caught the ball at Chicago's 35-yard line, and outran Bernie Masterson to complete a 55-yard play.

After Chicago went back in front 21–14 with a touchdown that concluded a 13-play, 73-yard advance, the Redskins struck for their two last-quarter touchdowns. They took the kickoff on their 22-yard line with 9:04 remaining in the game. On the first play, Baugh threw a 28-yard pass to Millner, who ran 50 yards, with Jack Manders and Bronko Nagurski in pursuit, to score on a 78-yard play. After the Bears punted following the next kickoff, Washington went 80 yards in 11 plays, Baugh combining with Ed Justice on a 35-yard scoring pass.

December 12, at Chicago

Washington	Starting Lineups	Chi. Bears
Wayne Millner	LE	Edgar (Eggs) Manske
Glen (Turk) Edwards	LT	Joe Stydahar
Les Olsson	LG	Danny Fortmann
Frank Bausch	C	Ed Kawal
Jim Karcher	RG	George Musso
Jim Barber	RT	Del Bjork
Charley Malone	RE	George Wilson
Riley Smith	QB	Bernie Masterson
Sammy Baugh	LH	Ray Nolting
Erny Pinckert	RH	Jack Manders
Cliff Battles	FB	Bronko Nagurski

Washington	7	0	7	14	— 28
Chi. Bears	7	7	7	0	— 21

Wash—Battles 7 run (R. Smith kick)
Chi —Manders 10 run (Manders kick)
Chi —Manders 37 pass from Masterson (Manders kick)
Wash—Millner 55 pass from Baugh (R. Smith kick)
Chi —Manske 3 pass from Masterson (Manders kick)
Wash—Millner 78 pass from Baugh (R. Smith kick)
Wash—Justice 35 pass from Baugh (R. Smith kick)
Attendance—15,870

TEAM STATISTICS	Wash.	Chi.
First downs	18	11
Rushing	8	7
Passing	10	4
By penalty	0	0
Total yardage	441	335
Net rushing yardage	70	128
Net passing yardage	371	207
Passes att.-comp.-had int.	40-22-3	31-8-3

1938

N.Y. GIANTS 23, GREEN BAY 17

Giants' blockers cleared Leemans for 14-yard gain.

The Green Bay Packers outgained the New York Giants 379–208 in total yardage, but the Giants' defense blocked two punts that led to nine points and a 23–17 victory. The crowd of 48,120 on a 31-degree afternoon in the Polo Grounds set a record.

Clarke Hinkle was in punt formation on his goal line with third down and 11 yards for a first down during the Packers' second possession in the first quarter. The Giants' Jim Lee Howell blocked Hinkle's kick and Leland Shaffer recovered for New York on the 7-yard line. Ward Cuff kicked a 14-yard field goal on fourth down for a 3–0 lead.

Cecil Isbell's punt was blocked by Jim Poole with Howell recovering on Green Bay's 28 during the Packers' next possession. Alphonse (Tuffy) Leemans ran six yards for a touchdown four plays later. After John Gildea missed the extra point, the Packers replaced their entire team except for guard Charles (Buckets) Goldenberg.

Green Bay took a 17–16 lead in the third quarter when it marched 53 yards to Paul Engebretsen's 15-yard field goal. The Giants began the following series on their 39-yard line. Halfback Hank Soar carried the ball on five of the next six plays. He threw an incomplete pass on the seventh, then caught a pass for nine yards from quarterback Ed Danowski, and ran three yards to put the ball on Green Bay's 23-yard line. Danowski lofted a 17-yard pass. Soar and Poole leaped for the ball with two defenders. Soar made the catch and dragged a Packers defensive back the last six yards for the winning touchdown.

December 11, at New York

Green Bay	Starting Lineups	N.Y. Giants
Wayland Becker	LE	Jim Poole
Champ Seibold	LT	Ed Widseth
Russ Letlow	LG	John Dell Isola
Lee Mulleneaux	C	Mel Hein
Charles Goldenberg	RG	Orville Tuttle
Bill Lee	RT	Owen (Ox) Parry
Milt Gantenbein	RE	Jim Lee Howell
Herman Schneidman	QB	Ed Danowski
Cecil Isbell	LH	Hank Soar
Joe Laws	RH	Ward Cuff
Clarke Hinkle	FB	Leland Shaffer

Green Bay	0	14	3	0	— 17
N.Y. Giants	9	7	7	0	— 23

NYG—FG Cuff 14
NYG—Leemans 6 run (kick failed)
GB —C. Mulleneaux 40 pass from Herber (Engebretsen kick)
NYG—Barnard 21 pass from Danowski (Cuff kick)
GB —Hinkle 1 run (Engebretsen kick)
GB —FG Engebretsen 15
NYG—Soar 23 pass from Danowski (Cuff kick)
Attendance—48,120

TEAM STATISTICS	GB	NYG
First downs	14	10
Rushing	9	6
Passing	4	2
By penalty	1	2
Total yardage	378	212
Net rushing yardage	164	118
Net passing yardage	214	94
Passes att.-comp.-had int.	19-8-1	15-8-1

1939

GREEN BAY 27, N.Y. GIANTS 0

Giants' Falaschi (left) recovered blocked punt.

Winds blowing across the Wisconsin flatlands through the open ends of Milwaukee's State Fair Park were measured in gusts up to 35 miles per hour. The Green Bay Packers' passers, Arnie Herber and Cecil Isbell, were intercepted three times, but they completed 7 of 10 attempts for 96 yards and two touchdowns. Giants passers completed 9 of 26 passes for 98 yards and had 6 intercepted as the Packers scored a 27–0 victory.

The Packers scored on a 54-yard drive in the first quarter when Herber passed seven yards to Milt Gantenbein, who was open between the goal posts in the end zone after the Giants assigned double coverage to Don Hutson. The score was 7–0 at the half. New York had three scoring opportunities, but Ward Cuff missed field goal attempts of 42 and 41 yards, and Lem Barnum missed from 47.

Paul Engebretsen put the Packers in front 10–0 with a 23-yard field goal in the third quarter. Joe Laws returned a punt 30 yards to his 45 and the Packers moved 32 yards in seven plays to position Engebretsen. The score became 17–0 in the third quarter after Gantenbein intercepted a pass by Ed Danowski at the Giants' 33. Cecil Isbell threw a 25-yard pass on second down to Laws, who caught the ball on the 6-yard line and scored to complete a 31-yard play.

Ernie Smith's 42-yard field goal and Ed Jankowski's one-yard run finished the scoring in the fourth quarter. The Giants were on the 3-yard line when the game ended. Their deepest penetration had been the 16 in the third quarter, when the score was 17–0.

Dec. 10, at Milwaukee

N.Y. Giants	Starting Lineups	Green Bay
Jim Poole	LE	Don Hutson
Frank Cope	LT	Buford (Baby) Ray
John Dell Isola	LG	Russ Letlow
Mel Hein	C	Earl Svendsen
Orville Tuttle	RG	Charles Goldenberg
John Mellus	RT	Bill Lee
Jim Lee Howell	RE	Milt Gantenbein
Ed Danowski	QB	Larry Craig
Elvin (Kink) Richards	LH	Cecil Isbell
Ward Cuff	RH	Joe Laws
Nello Falaschi	FB	Clarke Hinkle

N.Y. Giants	0	0	0	0	—	0
Green Bay	7	0	10	10	—	27

GB—Gantenbein 7 pass from Herber (Engebretsen kick)
GB—FB Engebretsen 23
GB—Laws 31 pass from Isbell (Engebretsen kick)
GB—FG E. Smith 42
GB—Jankowski 1 run (E. Smith kick)
Attendance—32,279

TEAM STATISTICS	NYG	GB
First downs	9	10
Rushing	5	6
Passing	3	2
By penalty	1	2
Total yardage	168	230
Net rushing yardage	70	131
Net passing yardage	98	99
Passes att.-comp.-had int.	26-9-6	10-7-3

1940

CHI. BEARS 73, WASHINGTON 0

Osmanski turned corner on 68-yard run for score.

Fullback Bill Osmanski of the Chicago Bears ran around left end for 68 yards and a touchdown on the second play of the game. The next time the Bears were on offense they held possession of the ball for 17 plays, marching 79 yards and two feet before scoring on quarterback Sid Luckman's one-foot plunge. The third time Chicago had the ball, fullback Joe Maniaci swept end for 42 yards and a touchdown on the first play. The Bears scored three touchdowns in the first 12 minutes, 40 seconds of the game; they rushed for 382 yards overall, amassed 501 total yards, intercepted eight passes, and won their second NFL championship, 73–0 over the Washington Redskins, the team that had beaten them 7–3 three weeks before in the ninth game of the season.

The Bears led 28–0 at the half after Luckman's 30-yard touchdown pass to Ken Kavanaugh. Luckman did not play the second half; quarterbacks Bernie Masterson, Bob Snyder, and Saul Sherman directed the team on four more scoring drives. The defense returned three passes for touchdowns. Redskins fans in Griffith Stadium began hooting in derision whenever the home team did something positive.

The Bears' T formation with man-in-motion was awesome. Stanford University also had the T in 1940. It became the most popular formation.

Dec. 8, at Washington

Chi. Bears	Starting Lineups	Washington
Bob Nowaskey	LE	Bob Masterson
Joe Stydahar	LT	Willie Wilkin
Danny Fortmann	LG	Dick Farman
Clyde (Bulldog) Turner	C	Bob Titchenal
George Musso	RG	Steve Slivinski
Lee Artoe	RT	Jim Barber
George Wilson	RE	Charley Malone
Sid Luckman	QB	Max Krause
Ray Nolting	LH	Sammy Baugh
George McAfee	RH	Ed Justice
Bill Osmanski	FB	Jim Johnston

Chi. Bears	21	7	26	19	—	73
Washington	0	0	0	0	—	0

Chi—Osmanski 68 run (Manders kick)
Chi—Luckman 1 run (Snyder kick)
Chi—Maniaci 42 run (Martinovich kick)
Chi—Kavanaugh 30 pass from Luckman (Snyder kick)
Chi—Pool 15 interception return (Plasman kick)
Chi—Nolting 23 run (kick failed)
Chi—McAfee 34 interception return (Stydahar kick)
Chi—Turner 24 interception return (kick failed)
Chi—Clark 44 run (kick failed)
Chi—Famiglietti 2 run (Maniaci, pass from Sherman)
Chi—Clark 1 run (pass failed)
Attendance—36,034

TEAM STATISTICS	Chi.	Wash.
First downs	17	17
Rushing	13	4
Passing	3	10
By penalty	1	3
Total yardage	501	245
Net rushing yardage	382	22
Net passing yardage	119	223
Passes att.-comp.-had int.	10-7-0	51-20-8

1941

CHI. BEARS 37, N.Y. GIANTS 9

Bears' Norm Standlee (22) stopped Leemans.

The Chicago Bears won their third championship and became the first team to win two in a row when they broke a 9–9 tie in the third quarter and defeated the New York Giants 37–9. The Wrigley Field crowd of 13,341 persons was the smallest in playoff history, coming one week after the Bears defeated Green Bay 33–14 for the Western Conference championship in a divisional playoff before 43,425.

The Bears trailed 6–3 at the end of the first quarter. They led 9–6 at the half after having possession of the ball 53 plays to the Giants' 10. Chicago controlled the ball for the first 10:34 of the first quarter, scoring on Bob Snyder's 14-yard field goal. This followed a series of penalties against Chicago and a blocked field goal that hit New York's Ken (Kayo) Lunday in the face but was recovered by the Bears. New York scored its only touchdown after the field goal. It marched 59 yards in four plays, scoring on Alphonse (Tuffy) Leemans's 31-yard pass to George Franck.

The Bears, who had a total yardage edge of 389–157, began pulling away from the Giants after Ward Cuff's 16-yard field goal tied the score in the first three minutes of the third quarter. The Bears went 71, 66, and 54 yards for touchdowns. Their last score came in the final nine seconds of the game. The Giants' Hank Soar lateraled to Andy Marefos, who attempted to throw a pass on a halfback option. Marefos was hit by several Bears defenders and fumbled. Ken Kavanaugh picked up the ball and ran 42 yards.

December 21, at Chicago

N.Y. Giants	Starting Lineups	Chicago Bears
Jim Poole	LE	Dick Plasman
John Mellus	LT	Ed Kolman
Ken (Kayo) Lunday	LG	Danny Fortmann
Mel Hein	C	Clyde (Bulldog) Turner
Len Younce	RG	Ray Bray
Bill Edwards	RT	Lee Artoe
Jim Lee Howell	RE	John Siegal
Nello Falaschi	QB	Sid Luckman
George Franck	LH	Ray Nolting
Ward Cuff	RH	Hugh Gallarneau
Alphonse (Tuffy) Leemans	FB	Norm Standlee

N.Y. Giants	6	0	3	0	—	9
Chi. Bears	3	6	14	14	—	37

Chi —FG Snyder 14
NYG—Franck 31 pass from Leemans (kick failed)
Chi —FG Snyder 39
Chi —FG Snyder 37
NYG—FG Cuff 16
Chi —Standlee 2 run (Snyder kick)
Chi —Standlee 7 run (Maniaci kick)
Chi —McAfee 5 run (Artoe kick)
Chi —Kavanaugh 42 fumble return (McLean kick)
Attendance—13,341

TEAM STATISTICS	NYG	Chi.
First downs	8	20
Rushing	4	14
Passing	2	5
By penalty	2	1
Total yardage	157	389
Net rushing yardage	84	207
Net passing yardage	73	182
Passes att.-comp.-had int.	15-3-3	19-11-0

1942

WASHINGTON 14, CHI. BEARS 6

Bears (striped jerseys) surrounded Farkas.

The Washington Redskins defeated the Chicago Bears 14–6 in a game in which the Bears were favored by 22 points. Chicago had won 24 games in a row, including postseason and exhibition contests, and 39 of its previous 40 games. The Bears had not been beaten since a 16–14 loss to Green Bay November 2, 1941.

Chicago took a 6–0 lead in the second quarter when Lee Artoe, a 230-pound tackle, ran 50 yards for a touchdown with a recovered fumble. The fumble resulted when Chicago's George Wilson tackled Dick Todd. The Redskins returned the following kickoff to the Bears' 42-yard line and scored in three plays, Sammy Baugh passing 38 yards to Wilbur Moore for the touchdown. Andy Farkas's one-yard run in the third quarter completed the scoring.

Baugh, who completed 5 of 13 passes for 66 yards, made one of the game's biggest defensive plays when he stopped a Bears' drive that had reached Washington's 12-yard line by intercepting a pass in the end zone. The Bears marched to the Redskins' 27- and 28-yard lines in the first period but came up empty when Artoe missed a 46-yard field goal the first time and they fumbled the second time. Chicago went 79 yards from its 20 to Washington's 1 in the fourth quarter. Halfback Hugh Gallarneau scored on the next play, but the Bears were penalized for backfield in motion. They surrendered the ball on downs and the Redskins controlled possession the last three minutes.

Washington and Chicago each finished the season with 11–1 records, including the championship playoff. The Redskins' loss was 14–7 to New York, which was beaten 26–7 by Chicago.

December 13, at Washington

Chi. Bears	Starting Lineups	Washington
Bob Nowaskey	LE	Bob Masterson
Ed Kolman	LT	Willie Wilkin
Danny Fortmann	LG	Dick Farman
Clyde (Bulldog) Turner	C	Charles (Ki) Aldrich
Ray Bray	RG	Steve Slivinski
Lee Artoe	RT	Bill Young
George Wilson	RE	Ed Cifers
Sid Luckman	QB	Ray Hare
Ray Nolting	LH	Sammy Baugh
Hugh Gallarneau	RH	Ed Justice
Gary Famiglietti	FB	Andy Farkas

Chi. Bears	0	6	0	0	—	6
Washington	0	7	7	0	—	14

Chi—Artoe 50 fumble return (kick failed)
Wash—Moore 38 pass from Baugh (Masterson kick)
Wash—Farkas 1 run (Masterson kick)
Attendance—36,006

TEAM STATISTICS	Chi.	Wash.
First downs	10	9
Rushing	4	5
Passing	5	2
By penalty	1	2
Total yardage	199	166
Net rushing yardage	69	101
Net passing yardage	130	65
Passes att.-comp.-had int.	20-10-3	13-5-2

1943

CHI. BEARS 41, WASHINGTON 21

Moore skirted Bears' defense.

Quarterback Sid Luckman completed 14 of 26 passes for 276 yards and five touchdowns and rushed for 64 yards in eight carries as the Chicago Bears defeated Washington 41–21.

The Bears, who were idle for 29 days after clinching the NFL West championship with a victory over the Chicago Cardinals, gained a total of 455 yards to the Redskins' 249 but trailed 7–0 after Andy Farkas concluded a 60-yard Redskins drive with a one-yard run in the second quarter. The Bears went 67 and 55 yards for touchdowns after the Washington score to take a 14–7 lead.

Redskins quarterback Sammy Baugh left the game after one play of the first quarter and sat on the bench weeping for the remainder of the half as physicians tried to determine the severity of a concussion he sustained on the opening kickoff. Baugh returned in the second half and completed 7 of 11 passes for 106 yards and two touchdowns. His replacement, George Cafego, completed 3 of 11 for 76 yards.

The championship game was the third in four years between the Bears and Washington. Typical of the rivalry between them was an incident in the first half when Redskins owner George Preston Marshall was ejected from the playing field after attempting to gain access to the Redskins' bench. Bears general manager Ralph Brizzolara ordered police to remove Marshall, who returned later and termed the Bears' action "a first-class bush league trick."

December 26, at Chicago

Washington	Starting Lineups	Chicago Bears
Bob Masterson	LE	Jim Benton
Lou Rymkus	LT	Dominic Sigillo
Clyde Shugart	LG	Danny Fortmann
George Smith	C	Clyde (Bulldog) Turner
Steve Slivinski	RG	George Musso
Joe Pasqua	RT	Al Hoptowit
Joe Aguirre	RE	George Wilson
Ray Hare	QB	Bob Snyder
Frank Seno	LH	Harry Clark
George Cafego	RH	Dante Magnani
Andy Farkas	FB	Bob Masters

Washington	0	7	7	7	—	21
Chi. Bears	0	14	13	14	—	41

Wash—Farkas 1 run (Masterson kick)
Chi—Nagurski 3 run (Snyder kick)
Chi—Clark 31 pass from Luckman (Snyder kick)
Chi—Magnani 36 pass from Luckman (Snyder kick)
Chi—Magnani 66 pass from Luckman (kick failed)
Wash—Farkas 17 pass from Baugh (Masterson kick)
Chi—Benton 26 pass from Luckman (Snyder kick)
Chi—Clark 16 pass from Luckman (Snyder kick)
Wash—Aguirre 25 pass from Baugh (Aguirre kick)
Attendance—34,320

TEAM STATISTICS	Wash.	Chi.
First downs	11	14
Rushing	4	8
Passing	6	6
By penalty	1	0
Total yardage	249	455
Net rushing yardage	50	169
Net passing yardage	199	286
Passes att.-comp.-had int.	24-11-4	27-15-0

1944

GREEN BAY 14, N.Y. GIANTS 7

Laws gained 72 yards in 13 carries for the Packers.

The Green Bay Packers won their third NFL championship and first in five years when they scored a 14–7 victory over the New York Giants, who were losers for the fifth time in seven championship games. The Packers, who outgained the Giants 235–187 in total yards, scored all of their points in the second quarter on touchdowns by fullback Ted Fritsch.

Fritsch scored on a one-yard run early in the quarter, following a block by left guard Charles (Buckets) Goldenberg, the Packers' 33-year-old, 12-year veteran. The touchdown came on fourth down after the Giants had held the Packers without a gain for three downs.

Fritsch scored again on a 26-yard pass from Irv Comp. Don Hutson, the Packers' all-league end, figured prominently in the play. After Hutson gained 24 yards on a pass from Comp that put the ball on the 30, Hutson served as a decoy on the next play. Hutson ran a crossing pattern from his left end position, drawing the Giants' secondary with him. Fritsch looped out of the backfield and caught Comp's pass on the 5. There wasn't a defender within 10 yards.

New York, which did not advance beyond its 35-yard line in the first half, scored on Ward Cuff's one-yard run in the fourth quarter. Cuff, who had played wingback in the Giants' single wing formation for his entire eight-season career, scored from the tailback position. The touchdown was set up by a 41-yard pass from Arnie Herber to Frank Liebel. Herber, who had been out of pro football four years before joining the Giants in 1944, played with the Packers from 1930 through 1940.

December 17, at New York

Green Bay	Starting Lineups	N.Y. Giants
Don Hutson	LE	O'Neal Adams
Buford (Baby) Ray	LT	Frank Cope
Bill Kuusisto	LG	Len Younce
Charles Brock	C	Mel Hein
Charles Goldenberg	RG	Jim Sivell
Paul Berezney	RT	Vic Carroll
Harry Jacunski	RE	Frank Liebel
Larry Craig	QB	Len Calligaro
Irv Comp	LH	Arnie Herber
Joe Laws	RH	Ward Cuff
Ted Fritsch	FB	Howie Livingston

Green Bay	0	14	0	0	—	14
N.Y. Giants	0	0	0	7	—	7

GB—Fritsch 1 run (Hutson kick)
GB—Fritsch 26 pass from Comp (Hutson kick)
NYG—Cuff 1 run (Strong kick)
Attendance—46,016

TEAM STATISTICS	GB	NYG
First downs	11	10
Rushing	9	5
Passing	2	4
By penalty	0	1
Total yardage	235	187
Net rushing yardage	162	70
Net passing yardage	73	117
Passes att.-comp.-had int.	11-3-3	22-8-4

1945

CLEVELAND 15, WASHINGTON 14

When Baugh passed, ball hit goal post for safety.

Rookie quarterback Bob Waterfield completed 14 of 27 passes for 192 yards and two touchdowns; halfback Jim Gillette gained 101 yards in 17 carries and scored once, and end Jim Benton caught nine passes for 125 yards and a touchdown as the Cleveland Rams defeated the Washington Redskins 15–14. The difference between a victory and a defeat for Cleveland was a hurriedly thrown pass by Redskins quarterback Sammy Baugh in the first quarter. Baugh's pass from Washington's end zone struck the goal post and fell into the end zone for a safety.

Baugh, who had been injured in the Redskins' victory over the New York Giants the week before, was taken out of the game in the first quarter and returned only to hold the ball on extra points. Frank Filchock, Baugh's replacement, completed 8 of 14 passes for 178 yards and two touchdowns. Filchock helped put the Redskins ahead 7–2 with 9:09 left in the first half when he combined with halfback Steve Bagarus on a 38-yard pass play.

Waterfield's 38-yard pass to Benton put Cleveland back in front with three minutes remaining in the half. Waterfield's extra point was partially blocked and struck the goal post crossbar, teetered for a moment, and dropped into the end zone, giving Cleveland a 9–7 lead. The Rams increased their advantage to 15–7 in the third quarter, when Waterfield threw a 35-yard pass to Gillette, who caught the ball and ran nine yards to complete a 44-yard play.

The game was played in six-degree weather. The Memorial Stadium side line was piled with snow after workers arrived early to clear the playing area.

December 16, at Cleveland

Washington	Starting Lineups	Cleveland
Wayne Millner	LE	Floyd Konetsky
Fred Davis	LT	Eberle Schultz
Al Lolotai	LG	Riley Matheson
Charles (Ki) Aldrich	C	Mike Scarry
Marvin Whited	RG	Milan Lazetich
Earl Audet	RT	Gil Bouley
Doug Turley	RE	Steve Pritko
Sammy Baugh	QB	Steve Nemeth
Dick Todd	LH	Fred Gehrke
Merlyn Condit	RH	Jim Gillette
Frank Akins	FB	Pat West

Washington	0	7	7	0	— 14
Cleveland	2	7	6	0	— 15

Cle —Safety, Baugh's pass hit goal post
Wash—Bagarus 38 pass from Filchock (Aguirre kick)
Cle —Benton 38 pass from Waterfield (Waterfield kick)
Cle —Gillette 44 pass from Waterfield (kick failed)
Wash—Seymour 8 pass from Filchock (Aguirre kick)
Attendance—32,178

TEAM STATISTICS	Wash	Cle
First downs	8	14
Rushing	3	9
Passing	4	4
By penalty	0	1
Total yardage	214	372
Net rushing yardage	35	180
Net passing yardage	179	192
Passes att.-comp.-had int.	20-9-2	27-14-2

1946

CHI. BEARS 24, N.Y. GIANTS 14

Luckman surprised the Giants with 19-yard TD run.

The Chicago Bears won their fifth NFL championship playoff in 14 years when they scored a 24–14 victory over the New York Giants. A crowd of 58,346 persons in the Polo Grounds set a playoff record. The Giants overcame a 14–0 Bears lead, but with the score tied 14–14 early in the fourth quarter, Bears quarterback Sid Luckman crossed up the Giants' defense and scored the winning touchdown. The play was called "ninety-seven bingo, keep it" in the Bears' nomenclature. From the Giants' 19-yard line, Luckman looked over the defense and then called time out for a conference with coach George Halas. "Now?" Luckman inquired of the coach about a specially designed trap play. "Now," said Halas. Luckman faked a handoff to halfback George McAfee, hid the ball on his hip and ran to his right while the Giants' defense followed the Bears' line, which pulled to the left. Luckman scored his only touchdown of 1946 after shaking off a tackler at the 10-yard line and picking up blocks from center Clyde (Bulldog) Turner and guard Ray Bray.

Luckman's run made the score 21–14. He contributed to one other touchdown, throwing a 21-yard pass to Ken Kavanaugh that gave the Bears a 7–0 lead. Luckman completed 9 of 22 passes for 144 yards and a touchdown.

The Giants tied the score in the third quarter. End Jim Lee Howell recovered Joe Osmanski's fumble on Chicago's 20. A roughing penalty put the ball on the 10. Three plays later Filchock passed five yards to Steve Filipowicz.

December 15, at New York

Chi. Bears	Starting Lineups	N.Y. Giants
Ken Kavanaugh	LE	Jim Poole
Fred Davis	LT	DeWitt (Tex) Coulter
Rudy Mucha	LG	Bob Dobelstein
Clyde (Bulldog) Turner	C	Chet Gladchuk
Ray Bray	RG	Len Younce
Mike Jarmoluk	RT	Jim White
George Wilson	RE	Jim Lee Howell
Joe Osmanski	QB	Steve Filipowicz
Dante Magnani	LH	Dave Brown
Hugh Gallarneau	RH	Howie Livingston
Bill Osmanski	FB	Ken Strong

Chi. Bears	14	0	0	10	— 24
N.Y. Giants	7	0	7	0	— 14

Chi —Kavanaugh 21 pass from Luckman (Maznicki kick)
Chi —Magnani 19 pass interception (Maznicki kick)
NYG—Liebel 38 pass from Filchock (Strong kick)
NYG—Filipowicz 5 pass from Filchock (Strong kick)
Chi —Luckman 19 run (Maznicki kick)
Chi —FG Maznicki 26
Attendance—58,346

TEAM STATISTICS	Chi.	NYG
First downs	10	13
Rushing	5	6
Passing	4	4
By penalty	1	3
Total yardage	245	248
Net rushing yardage	101	120
Net passing yardage	144	128
Passes att.-comp.-had int.	23-9-2	26-9-5

1947

CHI. CARDINALS 28, PHILADELPHIA 21

Charley Trippi (62) was one of Cardinals' heroes.

A frozen field in Comiskey Park did not prevent an offensive game as the Chicago Cardinals defeated the Philadelphia Eagles 28–21 in their first NFL championship playoff. The Cardinals' Elmer Angsman set a record by rushing for 159 yards in 10 carries, scoring twice on 70-yard runs. Philadelphia's Tommy Thompson set a record with 27 pass completions in 44 attempts. Thompson accounted for 297 yards and one touchdown. The Cardinals' Charley Trippi ran 44 yards from scrimmage for one touchdown and returned a kickoff 75 yards for another. Chicago held Steve Van Buren, the NFL's leading ground gainer with 945 yards, to 26 yards in 18 carries.

The Cardinals started the game wearing basketball shoes. The Eagles followed suit a few minutes later but Philadelphia was penalized for wearing illegal equipment. Some of the Eagles' players had wrapped tape around their shoes. At this point, the Cardinals held a 7–0 lead after Trippi's 44-yard touchdown run with 8:38 left in the first quarter. It was 14–0 before the Eagles scored on Thompson's pass to William (Pat) McHugh, who caught a 36-yard pass on Chicago's 17 and completed a 53-yard play.

Philadelphia never got closer than one touchdown as the Cardinals held leads of 21–7 and 28–14 in the second half. Philadelphia led 357–336 in total offense, partly because Paul Christman of the Cardinals completed 3 of 14 passes for 54 yards. The Eagles' eight-man defensive line succeeded in pressuring Christman into hurried passes but it could not stop the Cardinals' running attack.

December 28, at Chicago

Philadelphia	Starting Lineups	Chi. Cardinals
Jack Ferrante	LE	Bill Blackburn
Vic Sears	LT	Dick Plasman
Cliff Patton	LG	Lloyd Arms
Alex Wojiechowicz	C	Vince Banonis
Frank (Bucko) Kilroy	RG	Hamilton Nichols
Al Wistert	RT	Stan Mauldin
Pete Pihos	RE	John Doolan
William (Pat) McHugh	QB	Bill Campbell
Steve Van Buren	LH	John (Red) Cochran
Bosh Pritchard	RH	Marshall Goldberg
Joe Muha	FB	Walt Rankin

Philadelphia	0	7	7	7	— 21
Chi. Cardinals	7	7	7	7	— 28

Chi—Trippi 44 run (Harder kick)
Chi—Angsman 70 run (Harder kick)
Phil—McHugh 53 pass from Thompson (Patton kick)
Chi—Trippi 75 punt return (Harder kick)
Phil—Van Buren 1 run (Patton kick)
Chi—Angsman 70 run (Harder kick)
Phil—Craft 1 run (Patton kick)
Attendance—30,759

TEAM STATISTICS	Phil	Chi
First downs	22	11
Rushing	10	8
Passing	11	2
By penalty	1	1
Total yardage	357	336
Net rushing yardage	60	282
Net passing yardage	297	54
Passes att.-comp.-had int.	44-27-3	14-3-2

1948

PHILADELPHIA 7, CHI. CARDINALS 0

The Eagles on offense in seven inches of snow.

A protective tarpaulin was not removed from the playing field in Shibe Park until 30 minutes before the kickoff, but snow blanketed the entire field by game time. Of the 36,309 persons who bought tickets and assured a sellout, a total of 28,664 were on hand as the Philadelphia Eagles defeated the Chicago Cardinals 7–0 in a rematch of the teams that played for the NFL championship in 1947.

The Eagles scored the only touchdown at the end of a sequence that began near the conclusion of the third quarter. The Cardinals' Elmer Angsman fumbled a handoff on his 17-yard line and Philadelphia's Frank (Bucko) Kilroy recovered. Three plays into the fourth quarter, Steve Van Buren scored on a five-yard run.

Conditions were so adverse that the stadium lights cast eerie shadows on the piles of snow along the side and on the field. NFL commissioner Bert Bell decreed that while the 10-yard first-down chain would be used there would be no measuring; the referee would be the final judge of all first downs. The sidelines were marked by ropes tied to stakes carried by officials. Each time a field goal was tried, players from the kicking team would kneel and clear the snow with their hands to get a firmer footing.

The first time the Eagles had possession of the ball quarterback Tommy Thompson combined with end Jack Ferrante on a 65-yard pass play for a "touchdown." An official's white penalty flag was thrown but it was invisible in the snow. When the Eagles realized the play would be called back because of an offside violation, Ferrante asked the official who had moved across the line of scrimmage before the snap of the ball. "You," said the official.

December 19, at Philadelphia

Chi. Cardinals	Starting Lineups	Philadelphia
John (Red) Cochran	LE	John Green
Bob Zimny	LT	Jay MacDowell
Garrard (Buster) Ramsey	LG	Duke Maronic
Vince Banonis	C	Vic Lindskog
Plato Andros	RG	Frank (Bucko) Kilroy
Chet Bulger	RT	Al Wistert
Corwin Clatt	RE	Neil Armstrong
Jerry Davis	QB	Tommy Thompson
Charley Trippi	LH	Ernie Steele
Elmer Angsman	RH	Russ Craft
Pat Harder	FB	Joe Muha

Chi. Cardinals	0	0	0	0	—	0
Philadelphia	0	0	0	7	—	7

Phil—Van Buren 5 run (Patton kick)
Attendance—28,864

TEAM STATISTICS	Chi.	Phil
First downs	6	16
Rushing	3	15
Passing	3	0
By penalty	0	1
Total yardage	131	232
Net rushing yardage	96	225
Net passing yardage	35	7
Passes att.-comp.-had int.	11–3–1	12–2–2

1949

PHILADELPHIA 14, LOS ANGELES 0

Van Buren set records for yards, number of carries.

The NFL was finishing its thirtieth season and the Philadelphia Eagles defeated the Los Angeles Rams 14–0 in the seventeenth championship playoff as fullback Steve Van Buren set records with 31 carries and 196 yards gained. Van Buren achieved the record after a storm that began 24 hours before kickoff dropped almost two inches of rain in Los Angeles. A crowd of more than 60,000, which would have set a playoff record, was expected before the storm. A total of 22,245 of the 27,980 persons who purchased tickets attended the game, which was played on a muddy field.

With Van Buren carrying the ball, the Eagles were able to control possession for 70 plays, compared to the Rams' 51. Philadelphia rushed for 274 yards, compared to 21 for Los Angeles. The Rams did not advance the ball further than the Eagles' 26-yard line. Philadelphia scored one of its touchdowns, the first of the game in the second quarter, on a 31-yard pass, quarterback Tommy Thompson to end Pete Pihos. It was Pihos's seventh touchdown in five games against Los Angeles.

The Eagles' other score came in the third quarter. Defensive end Len Skladany blocked Bob Waterfield's punt from the 5-yard line. The snap of the ball from center Don Paul was high and Waterfield had no chance to get the kick away. Skladany picked up the bouncing ball on the 2-yard line and scored.

The victory was Philadelphia's second in a row and it marked the Eagles' third straight appearance in the championship playoff, climaxing the rise that began when Earle (Greasy) Neale was hired as coach in 1941.

December 18, at Los Angeles

Philadelphia	Starting Lineups	Los Angeles
Jack Ferrante	LE	Tom Fears
Vic Sears	LT	Dick Huffman
Cliff Patton	LG	Hal Dean
Vic Lindskog	C	John Martin
Frank (Bucko) Kilroy	RG	Ray Yagiello
Al Wistert	RT	Gil Bouley
Pete Pihos	RE	Bill Smyth
Tommy Thompson	QB	Bob Waterfield
Steve Van Buren	LH	Tom Kalmanir
Clyde (Smackover) Scott	RH	Verda (Vitamin T.) Smith
John Myers	FB	Dick Hoerner

Philadelphia	0	7	7	0	—	14
Los Angeles	0	0	0	0	—	0

Phil—Pihos 31 pass from Thompson (Patton kick)
Phil—Skladany 2 blocked punt return (Patton kick)
Attendance—22,245

TEAM STATISTICS	Phil	LA
First downs	17	7
Rushing	12	0
Passing	4	6
By penalty	1	1
Total yardage	342	119
Net rushing yardage	274	21
Net passing yardage	68	98
Passes att.-comp.-had int.	9–5–1	27–10–2

1950

CLEVELAND 30, LOS ANGELES 28

All eyes were on Groza's winning field goal.

The Cleveland Browns, who joined the NFL in 1950 after winning four consecutive All-America Football Conference championships, defeated the Los Angeles Rams 30–28 on Lou Groza's 16-yard field goal with 20 seconds left in the game. Although the game was played on a frozen field amid snow flurries in 27-degree weather, Groza's kick was the final offensive thrust on an afternoon in which 832 yards were amassed, 418 by the Rams, 414 by Cleveland. Los Angeles quarterback Bob Waterfield threw for 312 yards and one touchdown but had four passes intercepted. Cleveland's Otto Graham threw for 298 yards and four touchdowns and had one interception.

The Rams led 14–13 at halftime but the Browns took a 20–14 lead on a 39-yard pass play involving Graham and Dante Lavelli, who caught 11 passes for 128 yards and two touchdowns. The Rams went back in front 28–20 at the end of the third quarter. Cleveland closed to 28–27 with 4:35 left in the game after a 65-yard, 14-play drive. Graham completed nine passes during the march, including five in a row to Lavelli. Two minutes remained when the Browns took a Rams punt on their 32. They moved to the 11 to position Groza's field goal.

The Rams succeeded in stopping Marion Motley, the Browns fullback who led the NFL with 810 yards rushing. Motley gained nine yards in six attempts, but Graham gained 99 in 12 carries when he was unable to find open receivers.

December 24, at Cleveland

Los Angeles	Starting Lineups	Cleveland
Tom Fears	LE	Mac Speedie
Dick Huffman	LT	Lou Groza
John Finlay	LG	Weldon Humble
Fred Naumetz	C	Frank Gatski
Harry Thompson	RG	Lin Houston
Bob Reinhard	RT	Lou Rymkus
Jack Zilly	RE	Dante Lavelli
Bob Waterfield	QB	Otto Graham
Glenn Davis	LH	Rex Bumgardner
Verda (Vitamin T.) Smith	RH	Dub Jones
Dick Hoerner	FB	Marion Motley

Los Angeles	14	0	14	0	—	28
Cleveland	7	6	7	10	—	30

LA —Davis 82 pass from Waterfield (Waterfield kick)
Cle—Jones 32 pass from Graham (Groza kick)
LA —Hoerner 3 run (Waterfield kick)
Cle—Lavelli 35 pass from Graham (kick failed)
Cle—Lavelli 39 pass from Graham (Groza kick)
LA —Hoerner 1 run (Waterfield kick)
LA —Brink 6 fumble return (Waterfield kick)
Cle—Bumgardner 14 pass from Graham (Groza kick)
LA —FG Groza 16
Attendance—29,751

TEAM STATISTICS	L.A.	Cle.
First downs	22	22
Rushing	9	8
Passing	12	13
By penalty	1	1
Total yardage	418	414
Net rushing yardage	106	116
Net passing yardage	312	298
Passes att.-comp.-had int.	32–18–5	33–22–1

1951

LOS ANGELES 24, CLEVELAND 17

Hoerner (31) scored the Rams' first touchdown.

The Los Angeles Rams won their first NFL championship since moving from Cleveland in 1946. The Rams defeated the Cleveland Browns 24–17 with the winning play a 73-yard pass and run involving quarterback Norm Van Brocklin and end Tom Fears. On third down and three yards for a first down from the 27-yard line, Van Brocklin threw a 23-yard pass to Fears. Fears ran between defenders Cliff Lewis and Tom James, caught the ball at the 50-yard line, and ran to the end zone with 7:25 remaining in the game.

The Rams took a 7–0 lead in the second quarter on Dick Hoerner's one-yard run but they trailed 10–7 at the half after Lou Groza set a playoff record with a 52-yard field goal and Otto Graham threw a 17-yard touchdown pass to Dub Jones. The Rams assumed a 17–10 lead early in the fourth quarter after a one-yard run by Dan Towler and a 17-yard field goal by Bob Waterfield. The Browns tied the score on a 70-yard, eight-play drive that featured a 52-yard pass gain, Graham to Mac Speedie.

Fears described Van Brocklin's effort as "the best thrown pass I've ever caught. He laid it right in there full stride." Browns coach Paul Brown thought the play would not have worked if Lewis and James had not collided trying to cover Fears.

The Browns had a 372–334 edge in total offense, outpassing the Rams 280–253 and outrushing them 92–81. Fears caught four passes for 146 yards in his best game of the season; he had been troubled with a sore knee.

December 23, at Los Angeles

Cleveland	Starting Lineups	Los Angeles
Mac Speedie	LE	Tom Fears
Lou Groza	LT	Don Simensen
Abe Gibron	LG	Dick Daugherty
Frank Gatski	C	Leon McLaughlin
Bob Gaudio	RG	Bill Lange
Lou Rymkus	RT	Tom Dahms
Dante Lavelli	RE	Elroy (Crazylegs) Hirsch
Otto Graham	QB	Bob Waterfield
Ken Carpenter	LH	Dan Towler
Dub Jones	RH	Paul (Tank) Younger
Marion Motley	FB	Dick Hoerner

Cleveland	0	10	0	7	— 17
Los Angeles	0	7	7	10	— 24

LA—Hoerner 1 run (Waterfield kick)
Cle—FG Groza 52
Cle—Jones 17 pass from Graham (Groza kick)
LA—Towler 1 run (Waterfield kick)
LA—FG Waterfield 17
Cle—Carpenter 2 run (Groza kick)
LA—Fears 73 pass from Van Brocklin (Waterfield kick)
Attendance—57,522

TEAM STATISTICS	Cle	LA
First downs	22	20
Rushing	6	9
Passing	16	9
By penalty	0	2
Total yardage	372	334
Net rushing yardage	92	81
Net passing yardage	280	253
Passes att.-comp.-had int.	41-19-3	30-13-2

1952

DETROIT 17, CLEVELAND 7

The Lions opened big hole, Layne scored.

The Cleveland Browns outgained the Detroit Lions 384–258 and had 22 first downs to 10, but the Lions stopped Cleveland on their 21-, 21-, 24-, 5-, and 8-yard lines and scored a 17–7 victory for their first NFL championship since 1935. The Lions' most important defensive stand came in the fourth quarter when the score was 14–7. Cleveland fullback Marion Motley ran 43 yards to the Lions' 5. Motley was thrown for a five-yard loss on the next play. Quarterback Otto Graham was thrown for a 12-yard loss attempting to pass on the next play. The Browns gained a yard on third down and Graham threw an incomplete pass to Motley on fourth down.

Detroit went ahead early in the second quarter when quarterback Bobby Layne scored on a two-yard run at the end of a 50-yard drive. The score became 14–0 in the third quarter when halfback Doak Walker ran 67 yards for a touchdown. Walker, who had been injured most of the season, had not scored a touchdown coming into the game. The Browns scored their touchdown on the following series, marching 67 yards in 11 plays. Fullback Harry (Chick) Jagade scored on a seven-yard run.

Pat Harder's 36-yard field goal in the fourth quarter clinched the victory for Detroit. The Lions had been forced to punt but the Browns' Ken Carpenter fumbled Bob Smith's kick and Jim Martin recovered for Detroit on the 23. Following Harder's placement, the Browns moved from their 15-yard line to Detroit's 8 in the final minutes. Graham passed to Ray Renfro in the end zone but Renfro deflected the ball to Darrell (Pete) Brewster. It was an illegal catch—two offensive players made contact before a defensive player.

December 28, at Cleveland

Detroit	Starting Lineups	Cleveland
Cloyce Box	LE	Darrell (Pete) Brewster
Bob Miller	LT	Lou Groza
Lou Creekmur	LG	Abe Gibron
Vince Banonis	C	Frank Gatski
Jim Martin	RG	Joe Skibinski
Gus Cifelli	RT	John Sandusky
Leon Hart	RE	Dante Lavelli
Bobby Layne	QB	Otto Graham
Doak Walker	LH	Ken Carpenter
Bob Hoernschemeyer	RH	Rex Bumgardner
Pat Harder	FB	Harry (Chick) Jagade

Detroit	0	7	7	3	— 17
Cleveland	0	0	7	0	— 7

Det—Layne 2 run (Harder kick)
Det—Walker 67 run (Harder kick)
Cle—Jagade 7 run (Groza kick)
Det—FG Harder 36
Attendance—50,934

TEAM STATISTICS	Det	Cle
First downs	10	22
Rushing	8	15
Passing	2	7
By penalty	0	0
Total yardage	258	384
Net rushing yardage	199	227
Net passing yardage	59	157
Passes att.-comp.-had int.	10-7-0	36-20-1

1953

DETROIT 17, CLEVELAND 16

Layne scrambled around Browns' Bill Willis.

The Detroit Lions marched 80 yards to a touchdown late in the game to defeat the Cleveland Browns 17–16 in Briggs Stadium for their second straight NFL championship.

After Lou Groza kicked a 43-yard field goal to put the Browns ahead 16–10, the Lions took the kickoff on their 20-yard line with 4:10 remaining. Quarterback Bobby Layne passed 18 yards to Jim Doran on the first play. Two more passes were incomplete, but on third down Layne passed 18 yards to Doran for a first down on Cleveland's 44. Layne then passed nine yards to Cloyce Box, but Bob Hoernschemeyer was stopped for no gain. On third down and one, Layne dived over center for a first down at Cleveland's 33. Layne then called a time out and discussed strategy with Lions coach Raymond (Buddy) Parker, who had been informed by coaches in the press box that the rush of Cleveland defensive end Len Ford created the possibility of the Lions succeeding on a screen pass to one of their running backs.

When Layne returned to the huddle he decided on another play. "Doran had been begging me to throw deep all day," said Layne. "Doran said he could get a step on Warren Lahr. The Lions' receiver was behind Lahr when he caught the ball on the 10-yard line. Doran, who was in the game because of an injury to starter Leon Hart, scored with 2:08 remaining; Doak Walker's extra point provided the final score.

The Lions led 10–3 at the half, but the Browns went ahead on a touchdown by Harry (Chick) Jagade and two field goals by Groza.

December 27, at Detroit

Detroit	Starting Lineups	Cleveland
Dorne Dibble	LE	Darrell (Pete) Brewster
Lou Creekmur	LT	Lou Groza
Harley Sewell	LG	Abe Gibron
Vince Banonis	C	Frank Gatski
Dick Stanfel	RG	Chuck Noll
Ollie Spencer	RT	John Sandusky
Leon Hart	RE	Dante Lavelli
Bobby Layne	QB	Otto Graham
Doak Walker	LH	Ken Carpenter
Gene Gedman	RH	Billy Reynolds
Bob Hoernschemeyer	FB	Harry (Chick) Jagade

Cleveland	0	3	7	6	— 16
Detroit	7	3	0	7	— 17

Det—Walker 1 run (Walker kick)
Cle—FG Groza 13
Det—FG Walker 23
Cle—Jagade 9 run (Groza kick)
Cle—FG Groza 15
Cle—FG Groza 43
Det—Doran 33 pass from Layne (Walker kick)
Attendance—54,577

TEAM STATISTICS	Cle	Det
First downs	11	18
Rushing	9	10
Passing	1	7
By penalty	1	1
Total yardage	191	293
Net rushing yardage	182	129
Net passing yardage	9	164
Passes att.-comp.-had int.	16-3-2	25-12-2

1954

CLEVELAND 56, DETROIT 10

Renfro beat Lions for 2 TD passes from Graham.

Otto Graham completed 9 of 12 passes for 163 yards and three touchdowns and scored on runs of one, five, and one yard as the Cleveland Browns defeated the Detroit Lions 56–10.

The Browns had lost seven games in a row to the Lions, including a 14–10 defeat in the final minute of the last regular season game the week before. Cleveland had lost its league opener 28–10 to Philadelphia and had been beaten 55–27 by Pittsburgh in the third game. Although they had appeared in championship games every year since 1946, when they were members of the All-America Football Conference, the Browns had not won an NFL title since 1950, their first year in the league.

The Browns converted six Detroit fumbles and interceptions into touchdowns. A penalty on Gil Mains for roughing kicker Horace Gillom set up another. That came on a 35-yard pass, Graham to Ray Renfro, that gave Cleveland a 7–3 lead.

Renfro caught two passes and scored two touchdowns. The Browns had noticed that Bill Stits played close to the line when Cleveland was in a straight T formation with no pass receiving flanker in the loss to Detroit the previous week. The Browns decided to send Renfro out of the backfield on passes and they engaged the Lions' safeties by sending their ends on crossing patterns. Stits did not have support and was unable to cover Renfro himself.

December 26, at Cleveland

Detroit	Starting Lineups	Cleveland
Dorne Dibble	LE	Darrell (Pete) Brewster
Lou Creekmur	LT	Lou Groza
Harley Sewell	LG	Abe Gibron
Andy Miketa	C	Frank Gatski
Jim Martin	RG	Chuck Noll
Charlie Ane	RT	John Sandusky
Earl (Jug) Girard	RE	Dante Lavelli
Bobby Layne	QB	Otto Graham
Doak Walker	LH	Ray Renfro
Lew Carpenter	RH	Billy Reynolds
Bill Bowman	FB	Maurice Bassett

Detroit	3	7	0	0	—	10
Cleveland	14	21	14	7	—	56

Det—FG Walker 36
Cle—Renfro 35 pass from Graham (Groza kick)
Cle—Brewster 10 pass from Graham (Groza kick)
Cle—Graham 1 run (Groza kick)
Det—Bowman 5 run (Walker kick)
Cle—Graham 5 run (Groza kick)
Cle—Renfro 31 pass from Graham (Groza kick)
Cle—Graham 1 run (Groza kick)
Cle—Morrison 12 run (Groza kick)
Cle—Hanulak 10 run (Groza kick)
Attendance—43,827

TEAM STATISTICS	Det	Cle
First downs	16	17
Rushing	5	8
Passing	9	6
By penalty	2	2
Total yardage	331	303
Net rushing yardage	136	140
Net passing yardage	195	163
Passes att.-comp.-had int.	44–19–6	12–9–2

1955

CLEVELAND 38, LOS ANGELES 14

Cleveland's Paul (right) raced 65 yards.

Quarterback Otto Graham ended a 10-year professional football career by completing 14 of 25 passes for 209 yards and two touchdowns and scoring on runs of 1 and 15 yards as the Cleveland Browns defeated the Los Angeles Rams 38–14 before a record championship playoff crowd of 85,693 persons. Graham announced his retirement after the game. In 10 seasons with the Browns, Graham was the quarterback in 10 championship games.

Graham had three passes intercepted, but the Rams were unable to convert. The Browns intercepted six of Los Angeles quarterback Norm Van Brocklin's passes. They converted four of the interceptions into a total of 24 points—the margin of difference.

The Rams moved from their 20 to Cleveland's 24 in the first quarter. Ken Konz intercepted Van Brocklin on first down and the Browns marched to Lou Groza's 26-yard field goal. In the second quarter, Van Brocklin was intercepted by Don Paul, who set a playoff record with a 65-yard return for a touchdown. After another interception by Tom James, Graham passed 50 yards to Dante Lavelli for a touchdown that made the score 17–7 at the half. An interception by Sam Palumbo set in motion a drive that ended with Graham's one-yard touchdown and a 31–7 Browns' lead in the third quarter.

The Rams scored on a 67-yard pass play, Van Brocklin to Volney (Skeet) Quinlan, in the second quarter and on a four-yard run by Ron Waller in the fourth quarter.

December 26, at Los Angeles

Cleveland	Starting Lineups	Los Angeles
Darrell (Pete) Brewster	LE	Tom Fears
Lou Groza	LT	Bob Cross
Abe Gibron	LG	Duane Putnam
Frank Gatski	C	Leon McLaughlin
Harold Bradley	RG	John Hock
Mike McCormack	RT	Charley Toogood
Dante Lavelli	RE	Elroy (Crazylegs) Hirsch
Otto Graham	QB	Norm Van Brocklin
Ray Renfro	LH	Ron Waller
Fred (Curly) Morrison	RH	Volney (Skeet) Quinlan
Ed Modzelewski	FB	Dan Towler

Cleveland	3	14	14	7	—	38
Los Angeles	0	7	0	7	—	14

Cle—FG Groza 26
Cle—Paul 65 interception return (Groza kick)
LA—Quinlan 67 pass from Van Brocklin (Richter kick)
Cle—Lavelli 50 pass from Graham (Groza kick)
Cle—Graham 15 run (Groza kick)
Cle—Graham 1 run (Groza kick)
Cle—Renfro 35 pass from Graham (Groza kick)
LA—Waller 4 run (Richter kick)
Attendance—85,693

TEAM STATISTICS	Cle	LA
First downs	17	17
Rushing	7	8
Passing	10	8
By penalty	0	1
Total yardage	371	259
Net rushing yardage	202	143
Net passing yardage	169	116
Passes att.-comp.-had int.	25–14–3	28–11–7

1956

N.Y. GIANTS 47, CHI. BEARS 7

Webster scored to give the Giants a 27–7 lead.

Gene Filipski returned George Blanda's opening kickoff 53 yards to the Chicago Bears' 39-yard line. The New York Giants scored four plays later on Mel Triplett's 17-yard run, signaling a 34-point first half en route to a 47–7 victory. The championship was the Giants' first since 1938 and was reminiscent of their victory over the Bears in the 1934 title game.

In 1934, the Giants beat the Bears 30–13 in the Polo Grounds in 9-degree weather on a frozen field after they switched from football cleats to basketball shoes in the second half. Before the 1956 game, which was played in 20-degree weather in Yankee Stadium, Giants' coach Jim Lee Howell sent Filipski and defensive back Ed Hughes to test the field. Hughes, who was wearing football shoes, slipped and fell after taking a few steps. Filipski maneuvered without trouble in basketball shoes. "Everyone wear sneakers," Howell announced to the team.

The Bears also wore rubber-soled shoes but they fell behind 20–0 before scoring a touchdown and trailed 34–7 at the half. It was 13–0 at the end of the first quarter, when Charlie Conerly replaced Don Heinrich at quarterback for New York. Conerly directed three second-period touchdown drives and threw two touchdown passes in the second half. Conerly completed 7 of 10 passes for 195 yards. Frank Gifford caught four for 131 and one touchdown and Alex Webster five for 76.

December 30, at New York

N.Y. Giants	Starting Lineups	Chi. Bears
Kyle Rote	LE	Harlon Hill
Roosevelt Brown	LT	Bill Wightkin
Bill Austin	LG	Herman Clark
Ray Wietecha	C	Larry Strickland
Jack Stroud	RG	Stan Jones
Dick Yelvington	RT	Kline Gilbert
Ken MacAfee	RE	Bill McColl
Don Heinrich	QB	George Blanda
Frank Gifford	LH	Bob Watkins
Alex Webster	RH	John Hoffman
Mel Triplett	FB	Rick Casares

Chi. Bears	0	7	0	0	—	7
N.Y. Giants	13	21	6	7	—	47

NYG—Triplett 17 run (Agajanian kick)
NYG—FG Agajanian 17
NYG—FG Agajanian 43
NYG—Webster 3 run (Agajanian kick)
Chi—Casares 9 run (Blanda kick)
NYG—Webster 1 run (Agajanian kick)
NYG—Moore blocked punt recovery in end zone (Agajanian kick)
NYG—Rote 9 pass from Conerly (kick failed)
NYG—Gifford 14 pass from Conerly (Agajanian kick)
Attendance—56,836

TEAM STATISTICS	Chi	NYG
First downs	19	16
Rushing	8	8
Passing	10	8
By penalty	1	0
Total yardage	280	348
Net rushing yardage	67	126
Net passing yardage	213	222
Passes att.-comp.-had int.	47–20–2	20–11–0

1957

DETROIT 59, CLEVELAND 14

Gedman (fourth from left) scored for Lions.

The Detroit Lions defeated the Cleveland Browns 59–14 for their third NFL championship in six seasons, and four months and 19 days after coach Raymond (Buddy) Parker resigned at a "Meet the Lions" banquet at which Parker said, "This team is dead." After winning three of their first six games, the Lions captured five of their last six to tie for the NFL West championship, then defeated San Francisco in a playoff for the right to meet Cleveland.

Quarterback Tobin Rote, acquired from Green Bay at the start of training camp and the Lions' regular since Bobby Layne was hurt late in the season's eleventh game against Cleveland, completed 12 of 19 passes for 280 yards and four touchdowns. One of Rote's most important passes came in the second quarter. Fullback Jim Brown had run 29 yards for a touchdown to end a Browns drive of 78 yards that made the score 17–7 in favor of Detroit. The Lions moved to Cleveland's 26 on their next possession and apparently were going to attempt a field goal on fourth down. Rote kneeled to accept the snap from center and place the ball for kicker Jim Martin. But instead of acting as Martin's holder, Rote straightened up, moved to his right, and threw a 26-yard pass to Steve Junker that made the score 24–7.

The Browns never got closer than 31–14, which was the score after Lew Carpenter ran five yards in the third quarter.

December 29, at Detroit

Cleveland	Starting Lineups	Detroit
Darrel (Pete) Brewster	LE	Jim Doran
Lou Groza	LT	Lou Creekmur
Herschel Forester	LG	Harley Sewell
Art Hunter	C	Frank Gatski
Fred Robinson	RG	Stan Campbell
Mike McCormack	RT	Ken Russell
Preston Carpenter	RE	Steve Junker
Tommy O'Connell	QB	Tobin Rote
Ray Renfro	LH	Gene Gedman
Lew Carpenter	RH	Howard (Hopalong) Cassady
Jim Brown	FB	John Henry Johnson

Cleveland	0	7	7	0	— 14
Detroit	17	14	14	14	— 59

Det—FG Martin 31
Det—Rote 1 run (Martin kick)
Det—Gedman 1 run (Martin kick)
Cle—Brown 29 run (Groza kick)
Det—Junker 26 pass from Rote (Martin kick)
Det—Barr 19 interception return (Martin kick)
Cle—Carpenter 5 run (Groza kick)
Det—Doran 78 pass from Rote (Martin kick)
Det—Junker 23 pass from Rote (Martin kick)
Det—Middleton 32 pass from Rote (Martin kick)
Det—Cassady 16 pass from Reichow (Martin kick)
Attendance—55,263

TEAM STATISTICS	Cle	Det
First downs	17	22
Rushing	11	9
Passing	5	10
By penalty	1	3
Total yardage	313	433
Net rushing yardage	218	137
Net passing yardage	95	296
Passes att.-comp.-had int.	21–9–4	21–13–0

1958

BALTIMORE 23, N.Y. GIANTS 17

Unitas threw for 349 yards.

The Baltimore Colts, who tied the game 17–17 on Steve Myhra's 20-yard field goal with seven seconds to play, defeated the New York Giants 23–17 in the first championship playoff to be decided in sudden death overtime. The Colts marched 80 yards in 13 plays after taking a Giants punt in the extra period and scored on Alan Ameche's one-yard run with 8:15 elapsed. Quarterback John Unitas completed four passes during the drive, including two for 33 yards to end Raymond Berry. The key play in the march was a 23-yard run by Ameche that put the ball on the Giants' 20. Ameche profited from guard Art Spinney's trap block on tackle Dick Modzelewski. Tackle George Preas of the Colts then cut off Giants middle linebacker Sam Huff.

Unitas completed 26 of 40 passes for 349 yards and one touchdown. Berry set playoff records with 12 catches for 178 yards. Unitas's 15-yard pass to Berry gave Baltimore a 14–3 lead at halftime. After the Giants stopped a 58-yard Colts drive on the 5-yard line in the third quarter, they marched 95 yards to a touchdown. The big play was a pass play involving Charlie Conerly and Kyle Rote that covered 62 yards. When Rote fumbled at Baltimore's 24, Alex Webster picked up the ball and ran to the 1.

The Giants took a 17–14 lead in the first minute of the fourth quarter after an 81-yard drive. Conerly threw to end Bob Schnelker for gains of 17 and 46 yards, then connected with halfback Frank Gifford from the 15-yard line for the touchdown.

December 28, at New York

Baltimore	Starting Lineups	N.Y. Giants
Raymond Berry	LE	Kyle Rote
Jim Parker	LT	Roosevelt Brown
Art Spinney	LG	Al Barry
Madison (Buzz) Nutter	C	Ray Wietecha
Alex Sandusky	RG	Bob Mischak
George Preas	RT	Frank Youso
Jim Mutscheller	RE	Bob Schnelker
John Unitas	QB	Don Heinrich
L. G. Dupre	LH	Frank Gifford
Lenny Moore	RH	Alex Webster
Alan Ameche	FB	Mel Triplett

Baltimore	0	14	0	3	6	— 23
N.Y. Giants	3	0	7	7	0	— 17

NYG—FG Summerall 36
Balt—Ameche 2 run (Myhra kick)
Balt—Berry 15 pass from Unitas (Myhra kick)
NYG—Triplett 1 run (Summerall kick)
NYG—Gifford 15 pass from Conerly (Summerall kick)
Balt—FG Myhra 20
Balt—Ameche 1 run (no extra point attempted)
Attendance—64,185

TEAM STATISTICS	Balt.	N.Y.
First downs	27	10
Rushing	9	3
Passing	17	7
By penalty	1	0
Total yardage	460	266
Net rushing yardage	138	88
Net passing yardage	322	178
Passes att.-comp.-had int.	40–26–1	18–12–0

1959

BALTIMORE 31, N.Y. GIANTS 16

Colts fans tore down goal posts after victory.

Trailing 9–7 as the third quarter was coming to an end, the Baltimore Colts began a 55-yard drive that concluded with a touchdown and was the start of 24 straight points that buried the New York Giants and gave the Colts a 31–16 victory.

Field goals of 23, 37, and 22 yards by the Giants' Pat Summerall had overcome an early Baltimore lead of 7–0 that had materialized the first time the Colts had the ball. Baltimore moved in six plays, scoring on a 59-yard pass play, John Unitas to Lenny Moore. After Summerall's third kick, which concluded a 71-yard advance, the Colts moved back in front on Unitas's four-yard run, which came on the heels of a 36-yard Unitas-to-Moore pass that moved the ball to New York's 13.

Andy Nelson intercepted a pass by Charlie Conerly and returned the ball 17 yards to New York's 14 to set up Baltimore's next touchdown, a 12-yard pass from Unitas to Gerry Richardson. The Colts moved in front 28–9 when Johnny Sample intercepted a Conerly pass, ran 42 yards for a score. Sample intercepted another Conerly pass and his 24-yard return set up a 25-yard field goal by Steve Myhra.

Trailing 31–9, the Giants moved 70 yards, scoring with 32 seconds left in the game on Conerly's 32-yard pass to Bob Schnelker. The pass gave New York a final total yardage advantage of 323–280 over the Colts, who were outrushed 118–73 and led only 207–205 in passing yardage.

December 27, at Baltimore

N.Y. Giants	Starting Lineups	Baltimore
Kyle Rote	LE	Raymond Berry
Roosevelt Brown	LT	Jim Parker
Darrell Dess	LG	Art Spinney
Ray Wietecha	C	Madison (Buzz) Nutter
Jack Stroud	RG	Alex Sandusky
Frank Youso	RT	George Preas
Bob Schnelker	RE	Jim Mutscheller
Charlie Conerly	QB	John Unitas
Frank Gifford	LH	Mike Sommer
Alex Webster	RH	Lenny Moore
Mel Triplett	FB	Alan Ameche

N.Y. Giants	3	3	3	7	— 16
Baltimore	7	0	0	24	— 31

Balt—Moore 59 pass from Unitas (Myrha kick)
NYG—FG Summerall 23
NYG—FG Summerall 37
NYG—FG Summerall 22
Balt—Unitas 4 run (Myrha kick)
Balt—Richardson 12 pass from Unitas (Myrha kick)
Balt—Sample 42 interception return (Myrha kick)
Balt—FG Myrha 25
NYG—Schnelker 32 pass from Conerly (Summerall kick)
Attendance—57,545

TEAM STATISTICS	NYG	Balt
First downs	16	13
Rushing	4	3
Passing	11	10
By penalty	1	0
Total yardage	323	280
Net rushing yardage	118	73
Net passing yardage	205	207
Passes att.-comp.-had int.	38–17–3	29–18–0

1960 NFL

PHILADELPHIA 17, GREEN BAY 13

Packers held Dean until key kickoff return.

The Philadelphia Eagles overcame leads of 6–0 and 13–10 by the Green Bay Packers to score a 17–13 victory for their first NFL championship in 11 years and in the final game for head coach Lawrence (Buck) Shaw and quarterback Norm Van Brocklin, who announced their retirements. Concluding a 12-year career, Van Brocklin passed for 197 years and one touchdown. Rookie halfback Ted Dean rushed for 54 yards in 13 carries and scored once.

Bill Quinlan intercepted Van Brocklin's first pass on the second play of the game. The Packers gave up the ball on downs at the 5, but they regained possession when Dean fumbled on the 22. Five plays later Paul Hornung kicked a 20-yard field goal. Hornung's 22-yard field goal increased Green Bay's lead to 6–0 in the second quarter. Philadelphia got on the scoreboard with a two-play, 57-yard drive. Van Brocklin passed 22 yards to Tommy McDonald, then teamed with McDonald on a 35-yard TD pass.

It was 10–6 at the half after Bobby Walston's 15-yard field goal for Philadelphia, but Green Bay took a 13–10 lead in the first two minutes of the fourth quarter. Bart Starr's seven-yard pass to Max McGee marked the Packers' only touchdown. Dean returned Hornung's ensuing kickoff 58 yards to the Packers' 39. A holding penalty moved the Eagles to the 32. Dean made six yards and Billy Barnes followed with six for a first down on the 20. Van Brocklin was thrown for a loss of seven, but he recovered with a 13-yard pass to Barnes. Dean and Barnes carried the ball in for the score from there.

December 26, at Philadelphia

Green Bay	Starting Lineups	Philadephia
Max McGee	LE	Pete Retzlaff
Bob Skoronski	LT	Jim McCusker
Fred (Fuzzy) Thurston	LG	Gerry Huth
Jim Ringo	C	Chuck Bednarik
Jerry Kramer	RG	Stan Campbell
Forrest Gregg	RT	J.D. Smith
Gary Knafelc	RE	Bobby Walston
Bart Starr	QB	Norm Van Brocklin
Paul Hornung	LH	Billy Barnes
Boyd Dowler	RH	Tommy McDonald
Jim Taylor	FB	Ted Dean

Green Bay	3	3	0	7	—	13
Philadelphia	0	10	0	7	—	17

GB —FG Hornung 20
GB —FG Hornung 22
Phil—McDonald 35 pass from Van Brocklin (Walston kick)
Phil—FG Walston 15
GB —McGee 7 pass from Starr (Hornung kick)
Phil—Dean 5 run (Walston kick)
Attendance—67,325

TEAM STATISTICS	G.B.	Phil.
First downs	22	13
Rushing	14	5
Passing	8	6
By penalty	0	2
Total yardage	401	296
Net rushing yardage	223	99
Net passing yardage	178	197
Passes att.-comp.-had int.	35-21-0	20-9-0

1960 AFL

HOUSTON 24, LOS ANGELES 16

Houston's Smith scored on pass from Blanda.

The Houston Oilers defeated the Los Angeles Chargers 24–16 in the American Football League's first championship game, which was played in 50-degree weather on New Year's Day, 1961, in Jeppesen Stadium on the University of Houston campus. The rivalry between the teams, who divided two hotly contested regular season games, was so intense that Los Angeles's Maury Schleicher and Houston's Julian Spence and Hogan Wharton were thrown out of the game for fighting.

Houston led 17–16 in the fourth quarter but won on its 12-yard line. Quarterback George Blanda then threw a medium-deep side line pass to Billy Cannon, who caught the ball, broke a tackle, and outran the Chargers' secondary to complete an 88-yard touchdown. Los Angeles moved to Houston's 22 in the final minute but was stopped on fourth down. Had Los Angeles scored a touchdown it would have tried for a two-point conversion that could have tied the game and created a sudden death overtime.

January 1, at Houston

Los Angeles	Starters, Offense	Houston
Don Norton	LE	Bill Groman
Ernie Wright	LT	Al Jamison
Orlando Ferrante	LG	Bob Talamini
Don Rogers	C	George Belotti
Fred Cole	RG	Hogan Wharton
Ron Mix	RT	John Simerson
Dave Kocourek	RE	John Carson
Jack Kemp	QB	George Blanda
Paul Lowe	LH	Billy Cannon
Royce Womble	RH	Charley Hennigan
Howie Ferguson	FB	Dave Smith
	Starters, Defense	
Maury Schleicher	LE	Dalva Allen
Volney Peters	LT	Orville Trask
Garry Finneran	RT	George Shirkey
Ron Nery	RE	Dan Lanphear
Ron Botchan	LLB	Al Witcher
Emil Karas	MLB	Dennit Morris
Rommie Loudd	RLB	Mike Dukes
Charlie McNeil	LCB	Jim Norton
Dick Harris	RCB	Mark Johnston
Jim Sears	LS	Julian Spence
Bob Zeman	RS	Bobby Gordon

Los Angeles	6	3	7	0	—	16
Houston	0	10	7	7	—	24

LA —FG Agajanian 38
LA —FG Agajanian 22
Hou—Smith 17 pass from Blanda (Blanda kick)
Hou—FG Blanda 18
LA —FG Agajanian 27
Hou—Groman 7 pass from Blanda (Blanda kick)
LA —Lowe 2 run (Agajanian kick)
Hou—Cannon 88 pass from Blanda (Blanda kick)
Attendance—32,183

TEAM STATISTICS	LA	Hou
First downs	21	17
Rushing	11	4
Passing	9	13
By penalty	1	0
Total yardage	333	401
Net rushing yardage	162	100
Net passing yardage	171	301
Passes att.-comp.-had int.	41-21-2	32-16-0

1961 AFL

HOUSTON 10, SAN DIEGO 3

Tolar led rushers with 52 yards in 16 carries.

The Houston Oilers defeated the San Diego Chargers 10-3 for the AFL championship in the fifth game between the teams that season. The two teams also played for the 1960 title, when the Chargers were representing Los Angeles. The Chargers defeated the Oilers twice in the 1961 preseason and the teams divided two regular season games, the Oilers winning the last meeting 33-13 to snap the Chargers' 11-game winning streak.

Houston led 3-0 after a 46-yard field goal by George Blanda in the second quarter. On third and five yards at San Diego's 35 in the third quarter, Blanda was forced to leave the passing pocket when his receivers were covered. Running to his right, Blanda threw an 18-yard pass to Billy Cannon, who was running to his left and jumped to catch the ball. As Cannon came down, he shook off a tackler at the 17 and ran for a touchdown and 10-0 lead. The Chargers' only score came with 12 seconds elapsed in the fourth quarter when George Blair kicked a 12-yard field goal. There were 10 interceptions in the game, six by San Diego.

December 24, at San Diego

Houston	Starters, Offense	San Diego
Bill Groman	LE	Don Norton
Al Jamison	LT	Ernie Wright
Bob Talamini	LG	Ernie Barnes
Bob Schmidt	C	Don Rogers
Hogan Wharton	RG	Ron Mix
Rich Michael	RT	Sherman Plunkett
Willard Dewveall	RE	Dave Kocourek
George Blanda	QB	Jack Kemp
Billy Cannon	LH	Paul Lowe
Charley Hennigan	RH	Bob Scarpitto
Charlie Tolar	FB	Keith Lincoln
	Starters, Defense	
Dalva Allen	LE	Earl Faison
George Shirkey	LT	Henry Schmidt
Ed Husmann	RT	Bill Hudson
Don Floyd	RE	Ron Nery
Doug Cline	LLB	Maury Schleicher
Dennit Morris	MLB	Emil Karas
Mike Dukes	RLB	Bob Laraba
Tony Banfield	LCB	Claude Gibson
Mark Johnston	RCB	Dick Harris
Jim Norton	LS	Charlie McNeil
Fred Glick	RS	Bob Zeman

Houston	0	3	7	0	—	10
San Diego	0	0	0	3	—	3

Hou—FG Blanda 46
Hou—Cannon 35 pass from Blanda (Blanda kick)
SD —FG Blair 12
Attendance—29,556

TEAM STATISTICS	Hou	SD
First downs	18	15
Rushing	6	6
Passing	8	8
By penalty	4	1
Total yardage	256	256
Net rushing yardage	96	79
Net passing yardage	160	177
Passes att.-comp.-had int.	41-18-6	32-17-4

1961 NFL

GREEN BAY 37, N.Y. GIANTS 0

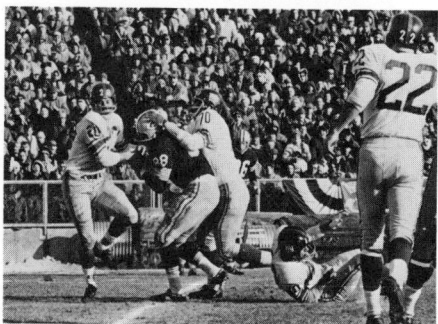

Kramer (88) scored to give Green Bay a 21–0 lead.

Pvt. Paul Hornung, on leave from the U.S. Army, rushed for 89 yards in 20 carries and scored a record total of 19 points as the Green Bay Packers won their first championship in 17 years, defeating the New York Giants 37–0 in 21-degree weather at Lambeau Field. In their last appearance in a championship game, the Packers scored a 14–7 victory over the Giants in 1944.

Despite the cold, the field was in good condition. Fifty stadium workers had begun removing 14 inches of snow that covered 20 tons of hay at 6 A.M. the morning of the game. The bench areas of both teams were warmed by large infra-red heating units.

The Packers, who outgained New York 345-130 in total yardage, scored 24 points to break open the game in the second quarter following a scoreless first period. Hornung's six-yard run four seconds into the second quarter was followed by touchdown passes of 13 and 14 yards from Bart Starr to Boyd Dowler and Ron Kramer and a 17-yard field goal by Hornung just before halftime.

December 31, at Green Bay

N.Y. Giants	Starters, Offense	Green Bay
Del Shofner	LE	Max McGee
Roosevelt Brown	LT	Bob Skoronski
Darrell Dess	LG	Fred (Fuzzy) Thurston
Ray Wietecha	C	Jim Ringo
Jack Stroud	RG	Forrest Gregg
Greg Larson	RT	Norm Masters
Joe Walton	RE	Ron Kramer
Y.A. Tittle	QB	Bart Starr
Joel Wells	LH	Paul Hornung
Kyle Rote	RH	Boyd Dowler
Alex Webster	FB	Jim Taylor
	Starters, Defense	
Jim Katcavage	LE	Willie Davis
Dick Modzelewski	LT	Dave Hanner
Roosevelt Grier	RT	Henry Jordan
Andy Robustelli	RE	Bill Quinlan
Cliff Livingston	LLB	Dan Currie
Sam Huff	MLB	Ray Nitschke
Tom Scott	RLB	Bill Forester
Erich Barnes	LHB	Hank Gremminger
Dick Lynch	RHB	Jesse Whittenton
Joe Morrison	LS	John Symank
Jim Patton	RS	Willie Wood

N.Y. Giants	0	0	0	0	—	0
Green Bay	0	24	10	3	—	37

GB—Hornung 6 run (Hornung kick)
GB—Dowler 13 pass from Starr (Hornung kick)
GB—R. Kramer 14 pass from Starr (Hornung kick)
GB—FG Hornung 17
GB—FG Hornung 22
GB—R. Kramer 13 pass from Starr (Hornung kick)
GB—FG Hornung 19
Attendance—39,029

TEAM STATISTICS	NYG	GB
First downs	6	19
Rushing	1	10
Passing	4	8
By penalty	1	1
Total yardage	130	345
Net rushing yardage	31	181
Net passing yardage	99	164
Passes att.-comp.-had int.	29-10-4	19-10-0

1962 AFL

DALLAS 20, HOUSTON 17

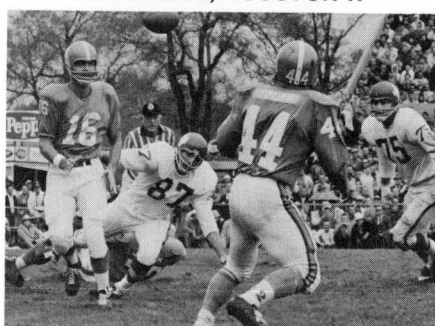

Blanda (16) passed to Tolar for eight-yard gain.

The Dallas Texans won the longest game in the history of professional football (to that point) on Tommy Brooker's 25-yard field goal at 2:54 of the sixth quarter—after 17:54 of sudden death overtime. Brooker's kick gave the Texans a 20–17 victory over the Houston Oilers before a record AFL championship crowd of 37,981 in Jeppesen Stadium.

The kick also saved Abner Haynes, Dallas's all-league halfback and captain, from being an embarrassing footnote to history. When Haynes went to the center of the field to participate in the coin toss at the start of the fifth quarter, he put the Texans in jeopardy. Haynes won the toss and inadvertently said the Texans "would kick to the clock," not only giving the Oilers possession of the ball, but with the wind at their backs. Houston was not able to capitalize on either advantage, although the Oilers got to Dallas's 35-yard line. On second down, a George Blanda pass was intercepted by Texans defensive end Bill Hull, who ran 23 yards to midfield. Dallas then started its winning drive.

December 23, at Houston

Dallas	Starters, Offense	Houston
Tommy Brooker	LE	Willard Dewveall
Jim Tyrer	LT	Al Jamison
Marvin Terrell	LG	Bob Talamini
Jon Gilliam	C	Bob Schmidt
Al Reynolds	RG	Hogan Wharton
Jerry Cornelison	RT	Rich Michael
Fred Arbanas	RE	Bob McLeod
Len Dawson	QB	George Blanda
Abner Haynes	LH	Billy Cannon
Frank Jackson	RH	Charley Hennigan
Curtis McClinton	FB	Charlie Tolar
	Starters, Defense	
Curt Merz	LE	Gary Cutsinger
Paul Rochester	LT	Ed Culpepper
Jerry Mays	RT	Ed Husmann
Mel Branch	RE	Don Floyd
E.J. Holub	LLB	Doug Cline
Sherrill Headrick	MLB	Gene Babb
Walt Corey	RLB	Mike Dukes
Duane Wood	LCB	Tony Banfield
Dave Grayson	RCB	Bobby Jancik
Bobby Hunt	LS	Jim Norton
Bobby Ply	RS	Fred Glick

Dallas Texans	3	14	0	0	0	3	—	20
Houston	0	0	7	10	0	0	—	17

Dall —FG Brooker 16
Dall —Haynes 28 pass from Dawson (Brooker kick)
Dall —Haynes 2 run (Brooker kick)
Hous —Dewveall 15 pass from Blanda (Blanda kick)
Hous —FG Blanda 31
Hous —Tolar 1 run (Blanda kick)
Dall —FG Brooker 25
Attendance—37,981

TEAM STATISTICS	Dall	Hou
First downs	19	21
Rushing	10	6
Passing	5	15
By penalty	4	0
Total yardage	237	359
Net rushing yardage	199	98
Net passing yardage	38	261
Passes att.-comp.-had int.	14-9-0	46-23-5

1962 NFL

GREEN BAY 16, N.Y. GIANTS 7

Green Bay's Nitschke (66) was defensive star.

The Green Bay Packers fought off the New York Giants in 13-degree cold and winds that gusted up to 40 miles per hour in Yankee Stadium to score a 16–7 victory for their fifth NFL championship and second in a row. The Giants lost in the championship playoff for the fourth time in five years and the tenth time in thirteen appearances. Offensive backfield coach Kyle Rote, who retired as a Giants player after the 1961 season, remarked, "I never before saw a team that tried so hard and lost."

The Giants concentrated most of their efforts on fullback Jim Taylor, who tied a record with 31 carries. Taylor gained 85 yards, scored on a seven-yard touchdown run in the second quarter, and maintained a constant exchange with Giants defenders, challenging them to "hit me harder."

Although they outgained Green Bay 291–244 in total yards, the Giants never led. Their only touchdown came when the score was 13–0 in the third quarter. Erich Barnes blocked Max McGee's punt and Jim Collier recovered in the end zone for a touchdown.

December 30, at New York

Green Bay	Starters, Offense	N.Y. Giants
Max McGee	LE	Del Shofner
Norm Masters	LT	Roosevelt Brown
Fred (Fuzzy) Thurston	LG	Darrell Dess
Jim Ringo	C	Ray Wietecha
Jerry Kramer	RG	Greg Larson
Forrest Gregg	RT	Jack Stroud
Ron Kramer	RE	Joe Walton
Bart Starr	QB	Y.A. Tittle
Paul Hornung	LH	Phil King
Boyd Dowler	RH	Frank Gifford
Jim Taylor	FB	Alex Webster
	Starters, Defense	
Willie Davis	LE	Jim Katcavage
Dave Hanner	LT	Dick Modzelewski
Henry Jordan	RT	Roosevelt Grier
Bill Quinlan	RE	Andy Robustelli
Dan Currie	LLB	Bill Winter
Ray Nitschke	MLB	Sam Huff
Bill Forester	RLB	Tom Scott
Herb Adderley	LHB	Erich Barnes
Jesse Whittenton	RHB	Dick Lynch
Hank Gremminger	LS	Alan Webb
Willie Wood	RS	Jim Patton

Green Bay	3	7	3	3	—	16
N.Y. Giants	0	0	7	0	—	7

GB —FG J. Kramer 26
GB —Taylor 7 run (J. Kramer kick)
NYG—Collier blocked punt recovery in end zone (Chandler kick)
GB —FG J. Kramer 29
GB —FG J. Kramer 30
Attendance—64,892

TEAM STATISTICS	GB	NYG
First downs	18	18
Rushing	11	5
Passing	6	11
By penalty	1	2
Total yardage	244	291
Net rushing yardage	148	94
Net passing yardage	96	197
Passes att.-comp.-had int.	22-10-0	41-18-1

1963 NFL

CHICAGO 14, N.Y. GIANTS 10

Tittle was injured when tackled by Larry Morris.

The sun was shining but the temperature was 11 degrees in Wrigley Field, where the Chicago Bears intercepted five passes by New York Giants quarterback Y.A. Tittle, two of them setting up touchdowns in a 14–10 victory. Tittle played the second half with a severely strained knee, the result of a second-quarter tackle by Larry Morris.

The Bears scored their first touchdown after linebacker Morris intercepted a screen pass intended for Phil King and returned the ball 61 yards to New York's 5-yard line. Quarterback Bill Wade scored on a two-yard run. The second touchdown followed an interception of another screen pass, this by defensive end Ed O'Bradovich, who returned the ball 10 yards to the Giants' 14. Wade scored five plays later from the 1.

The Giants led 7–0 after Tittle's 14-yard pass to Frank Gifford in the first quarter and 10–7 after Don Chandler's 13-yard field goal in the second quarter. The Giants' defeat was their fifth in a row in the championship playoff. Their overall record was 3-11 since they lost to the Bears 23–21 in Wrigley Field in the NFL's first playoff game in 1933.

December 29, at Chicago

N.Y. Giants	Starters, Offense	Chicago
Del Shofner	LE	John Farrington
Roosevelt Brown	LT	Herman Lee
Darrell Dess	LG	Ted Karras
Greg Larson	C	Mike Pyle
Treva (Bookie) Bolin	RG	Roger Davis
Jack Stroud	RT	Bob Wetoska
Joe Walton	RE	Mike Ditka
Y.A. Tittle	QB	Bill Wade
Frank Gifford	FL	Johnny Morris
Phil King	HB	Willie Galimore
Joe Morrison	FB	Joe Marconi
	Starters, Defense	
Jim Katcavage	LE	Ed O'Bradovich
Dick Modzelewski	LT	Stan Jones
John LoVetere	RT	Fred Williams
Andy Robustelli	RE	Doug Atkins
Jerry Hillebrand	LLB	Joe Fortunato
Sam Huff	MLB	Bill George
Tom Scott	RLB	Larry Morris
Erich Barnes	LHB	Bennie McRae
Dick Lynch	RHB	Dave Whitsell
Dick Pesonen	LS	Richie Petitbon
Jim Patton	RS	Roosevelt Taylor

N.Y. Giants	7	3	0	0	—	10
Chicago	7	0	7	0	—	14

NYG—Gifford 14 pass from Tittle (Chandler kick)
Chi —Wade 2 run (Jencks kick)
NYG—FG Chandler 13
Chi —Wade 1 run (Jencks kick)
Attendance—45,801

TEAM STATISTICS	NYG	Chi
First downs	18	14
Rushing	8	6
Passing	9	7
By penalty	1	1
Total yardage	268	222
Net rushing yardage	128	93
Net passing yardage	140	129
Passes att.-comp.-had int.	30-11-5	28-10-0

1963 AFL

SAN DIEGO 51, BOSTON 10

Boston couldn't defense the Chargers' Lincoln.

Fullback Keith Lincoln of San Diego outgained the Boston Patriots 334-261 in total offense and led the Chargers to a 51–10 victory. Chargers coach Sid Gillman, pointing to the rival NFL, said after the game, "We're the champions of the world. If anyone wants to debate it, let them play us."

Lincoln gained 206 yards in 13 carries and scored on a 67-yard run. He caught seven passes for 128 yards and scored on a 25-yard pass from John Hadl. The Chargers, who led 21–7 at the end of the first quarter and 31–10 at halftime, rushed for 318 yards and passed for 292—a total offense of 610 yards. The Chargers' running attack averaged almost 10 yards for each attempt. Halfback Paul Lowe backed up Lincoln with 94 yards in 12 carries and scored on a 58-yard run. Flanker Lance Alworth caught four passes for 77 yards.

"I didn't think it would ever go like this . . . not like this," said Patriots coach Mike Holovak.

January 5, at San Diego

Boston	Starters, Offense	San Diego
Gino Cappelletti	LE	Don Norton
Don Oakes	LT	Ernie Wright
Charlie Long	LG	Sam DeLuca
Walt Cudzik	C	Don Rogers
Billy Neighbors	RG	Pat Shea
Milt Graham	RT	Ron Mix
Tony Romeo	RE	Dave Kocourek
Babe Parilli	QB	Tobin Rote
Ron Burton	LH	Paul Lowe
Jim Colclough	RH	Lance Alworth
Larry Garron	FB	Keith Lincoln
	Starters, Defense	
Larry Eisenhauer	LE	Earl Faison
Jesse Richardson	LT	Henry Schmidt
Houston Antwine	RT	George Gross
Bob Dee	RE	Bob Petrich
Tom Addison	LLB	Emil Karas
Nick Buoniconti	MLB	Chuck Allen
Jack Rudolph	RLB	Paul Maguire
Dick Felt	LCB	Bud Whitehead
Bob Suci	RCB	Dick Harris
Ron Hall	LS	George Blair
Ross O'Hanley	RS	Gary Glick

Boston	7	3	0	0	—	10
San Diego	21	10	7	13	—	51

SD —Rote 2 run (Blair kick)
SD —Lincoln 67 run (Blair kick)
Bos—Garron 7 run (Cappelletti kick)
SD —Lowe 58 run (Blair kick)
SD —FG Blair 11
Bos—FG Cappelletti 15
SD —Norton 14 pass from Rote (Blair kick)
SD —Alworth 48 pass from Rote (Blair kick)
SD —Lincoln 25 pass from Hadl (pass failed)
SD —Hadl 1 run (Blair kick)
Attendance—30,127

TEAM STATISTICS	Bos	SD
First downs	14	21
Rushing	6	11
Passing	8	9
By penalty	0	1
Total yardage	261	610
Net rushing yardage	75	318
Net passing yardage	186	292
Passes att.-comp.-had int.	37-17-2	26-17-0

1964 AFL

BUFFALO 20, SAN DIEGO 7

Gilchrist, 240-pounds, shredded San Diego defense.

The San Diego Chargers scored on a 26-yard pass from quarterback Tobin Rote to end Dave Kocourek and were driving again in the first quarter when Rote threw an 11-yard pass to fullback Keith Lincoln, who had swung out of the backfield. Bills linebacker Mike Stratton came up to make the tackle and hit Lincoln with such force that the San Diego star suffered a broken rib and had to be carried off the field. Lincoln, who also had rushed for 47 yards in three carries, did not return. The Chargers struggled without him and dropped a 20–7 decision to the Buffalo Bills.

An AFL championship game record crowd of 40,242 persons in War Memorial Stadium saw the Bills take a 13–7 halftime lead on field goals of 12 and 17 yards by Pete Gogolak, sandwiched around a four-yard run by Wray Carlton. Quarterback Jack Kemp and end Glenn Bass combined on a 48-yard pass play in the fourth quarter to set up the Bills' final score. Kemp went over from the 1-yard line two plays later.

Kemp completed 10 of 20 passes for 188 yards. Fullback Cookie Gilchrist gained 122 yards in 16 carries and Carlton added 70 in 18.

December 26, at Buffalo

San Diego	Starters, Offense	Buffalo
Don Norton	LE	Glenn Bass
Ernie Wright	LT	Stew Barber
Pat Shea	LG	Billy Shaw
Don Rogers	C	Walt Cudzik
Walt Sweeney	RG	Al Bemiller
Ron Mix	RT	Dick Hudson
Dave Kocourek	RE	Ernie Warlick
Tobin Rote	QB	Jack Kemp
Paul Lowe	LHB	Wray Carlton
Jerry Robinson	RHB	Elbert Dubenion
Keith Lincoln	FB	Cookie Gilchrist
	Starters, Defense	
Earl Faison	LE	Ron McDole
George Gross	LT	Jim Dunaway
Ernie Ladd	RT	Tom Sestak
Bob Petrich	RE	Tom Day
Ron Carpenter	LLB	John Tracey
Chuck Allen	MLB	Harry Jacobs
Frank Buncom	RLB	Mike Stratton
Jim Warren	LCB	Charlie Warner
Dick Westmoreland	RCB	George (Butch) Byrd
Kenny Graham	LS	Gene Sykes
Bud Whitehead	RS	George Saimes

San Diego	7	0	0	0	—	7
Buffalo	3	10	0	7	—	20

SD—Kocourek 26 pass from Rote (Lincoln kick)
Buff—FG Gogolak 12
Buff—Carlton 4 run (Gogolak kick)
Buff—FG Gogolak 17
Buff—Kemp 1 run (Gogolak kick)
Attendance—40,242

TEAM STATISTICS	SD	Buff
First downs	15	21
Rushing	7	12
Passing	7	8
By penalty	1	1
Total yardage	259	387
Net rushing yardage	124	219
Net passing yardage	135	168
Passes att.-comp.-had int.	36-13-3	20-10-0

1964 NFL	1965 AFL	1965 NFL

1964 NFL

CLEVELAND 27, BALTIMORE 0

Ryan threw for three touchdowns to Gary Collins.

Forty-year-old Lou Groza, playing in the twelfth championship game of his 18-year career in professional football, kicked two field goals, including a 43-yard attempt that began the Cleveland Browns' 27–0 victory over the Baltimore Colts. Browns quarterback Frank Ryan completed 11 of 18 passes for 197 yards and three touchdowns to Gary Collins; fullback Jim Brown rushed for 114 yards in 27 carries, and the Browns' defense restricted the Colts to 92 yards passing and 89 yards rushing. The Colts gained only 54 yards in 22 offensive plays in the second half.

After a scoreless first half, the Browns scored 17 points in the third quarter, benefitting partly from a blustery wind at their backs. Groza's first field goal was followed by an 18-yard touchdown pass from Ryan to flanker Collins. The play was set up by a 46-yard run by Jim Brown. Collins, who caught five passes for 130 yards, scored again on a 42-yard pass play in the third quarter and on a 51-yard pass play in the fourth quarter.

Ryan's performance climaxed a strong personal finish to the season. He threw five touchdown passes the week before in the last regular season game.

December 27, at Cleveland

Baltimore	Starters, Offense	Cleveland
Raymond Berry	LE	Paul Warfield
Bob Vogel	LT	Dick Schafrath
Jim Parker	LG	John Wooten
Dick Szymanski	C	John Morrow
Alex Sandusky	RG	Gene Hickerson
George Preas	RT	Monte Clark
John Mackey	RE	John Brewer
John Unitas	QB	Frank Ryan
Jimmy Orr	FL	Gary Collins
Lenny Moore	HB	Ernie Green
Jerry Hill	FB	Jim Brown
	Starters, Defense	
Gino Marchetti	LE	Paul Wiggin
Guy Reese	LT	Dick Modzelewski
Fred Miller	RT	Jim Kanicki
Ordell Braase	RE	Bill Glass
Steve Stonebreaker	LLB	Jim Houston
Bill Pellington	MLB	Vince Costello
Don Shinnick	RLB	Galen Fiss
Bobby Boyd	LHB	Bernie Parrish
Lenny Lyles	RHB	Walter Beach
Jerry Logan	LS	Larry Benz
Jim Welch	RS	Ross Fichter

Baltimore	0	0	0	0	—	0
Cleveland	0	0	17	10	—	27

Cle—FG Groza 43
Cle—Collins 18 pass from Ryan (Groza kick)
Cle—Collins 42 pass from Ryan (Groza kick)
Cle—FG Groza 10
Cle—Collins 51 pass from Ryan (Groza kick)
Attendance—79,544

TEAM STATISTICS	Balt	Cle
First downs	11	20
Rushing	5	8
Passing	4	9
By penalty	2	3
Total yardage	181	339
Net rushing yardage	92	142
Net passing yardage	89	197
Passes att.-comp.-had int.	20-12-2	18-11-1

1965 AFL

BUFFALO 23, SAN DIEGO 0

Clarke blocked Harris, freed Byrd on return.

Mixing their defensive alignments, the Buffalo Bills used a three-man line with an end dropping off to cover passes and a safety blitz to confuse the San Diego Chargers' offense. They also assigned double coverage to pass receiver Lance Alworth, in addition to using two tight ends on offense. The result was a 23–0 victory over a team that had outgained them 816-381 in total offense in two regular season games. San Diego had won one of those games 34–3; the other was a 20–20 tie.

The Chargers never penetrated beyond Buffalo's 24-yard line. Buffalo scored first-half touchdowns on an 18-yard pass from quarterback Jack Kemp to tight end Ernie Warlick and on a 74-yard punt return by George (Butch) Byrd. Pete Gogolak kicked field goals of 11 and 39 yards in the third quarter and 32 yards in the fourth quarter.

Paul Lowe, whose 1,121 yards rushing during the regular season had set an AFL record and was 28 yards more than nine Bills runners netted all year, gained 57 yards in 12 carries. Forty-seven of Lowe's yards came on one carry.

December 26, at San Diego

Buffalo	Starters, Offense	San Diego
Charlie Ferguson	LE	Don Norton
Stew Barber	LT	Ernie Wright
George Flint	LG	Ernest Park
Al Bemiller	C	Sam Gruneisen
Joe O'Donnell	RG	Walt Sweeney
Dick Hudson	RT	Ron Mix
Paul Costa	RE	Dave Kocourek
Jack Kemp	QB	John Hadl
Billy Joe	LH	Paul Lowe
Irwin (Bo) Roberson	FL	Lance Alworth
Wray Carlton	FB	Gene Foster
	Starters, Defense	
Ron McDole	LE	Earl Faison
Jim Dunaway	LT	George Gross
Tom Sestak	RT	Ernie Ladd
Tom Day	RE	Bob Petrich
John Tracey	LLB	Dick Degen
Harry Jacobs	MLB	Chuck Allen
Mike Stratton	RLB	Frank Buncom
Booker Edgerson	LCB	Jim Warren
George (Butch) Byrd	RCB	Leslie (Speedy) Duncan
Hagood Clarke	LS	Kenny Graham
George Saimes	RS	Bud Whitehead

Buffalo	0	14	6	3	—	23
San Diego	0	0	0	0	—	0

Buff—Warlick 18 pass from Kemp (Gogolak kick)
Buff—Byrd 74 interception return (Gogolak kick)
Buff—FG Gogolak 11
Buff—FG Gogolak 39
Buff—FG Gogolak 32
Attendance—30,361

TEAM STATISTICS	Buff	SD
First downs	23	12
Rushing	13	5
Passing	9	7
By penalty	1	0
Total yardage	260	229
Net rushing yardage	108	119
Net passing yardage	152	110
Passes att.-comp.-had int.	20-9-1	25-12-2

1965 NFL

GREEN BAY 23, CLEVELAND 12

Taylor (31) battled Browns with tough running.

Lambeau Field was cleared of four inches of snow but a freezing rain turned the field into mud as the Green Bay Packers defeated the Cleveland Browns 23–12 and held fullback Jim Brown to 50 yards in 12 carries. Brown had led the NFL with 1,544 yards rushing during the season. Packers runners Paul Hornung and Jim Taylor met with more success.

Taylor never gained more than eight yards on a single attempt, but when the Packers controlled the ball for almost 14 minutes during two second-half drives to a touchdown and field goal, he was given the ball 12 times in 24 plays.

The Packers led 13–12 at the half; they pulled away in the third quarter on a 13-yard run by Hornung and on Don Chandler's 29-yard field goal in the fourth quarter.

"The snow and mud were our allies," said Packers coach Vince Lombardi. "When you have conditions like these, it's best to be basic, not fancy. And we're the most basic offensive team there is."

January 2, at Green Bay

Cleveland	Starters, Offense	Green Bay
Paul Warfield	LE	Boyd Dowler
John Brown	LT	Bob Skoronski
John Wooten	LG	Fred (Fuzzy) Thurston
John Morrow	C	Ken Bowman
Gene Hickerson	RG	Jerry Kramer
Monte Clark	RT	Forrest Gregg
John Brewer	RE	Bill Anderson
Frank Ryan	QB	Bart Starr
Gary Collins	FL	Carroll Dale
Ernie Green	HB	Paul Hornung
Jim Brown	FB	Jim Taylor
	Starters, Defense	
Paul Wiggin	LE	Willie Davis
Dick Modzelewski	LT	Ron Kostelnik
Jim Kanicki	RT	Henry Jordan
Bill Glass	RE	Lionel Aldridge
Jim Houston	LLB	Dave Robinson
Vince Costello	MLB	Ray Nitschke
Galen Fiss	RLB	Lee Roy Caffey
Bernie Parrish	LHB	Herb Adderley
Walter Beach	RHB	Doug Hart
Ross Fichtner	LS	Tom Brown
Larry Benz	RS	Willie Wood

Cleveland	9	3	0	0	—	12
Green Bay	7	6	7	3	—	23

GB—Dale 47 pass from Starr (Chandler kick)
Cle—Collins 17 pass from Ryan (kick failed)
Cle—FG Groza 24
GB—FG Chandler 15
GB—FG Chandler 23
Cle—FG Groza 28
GB—Hornung 13 run (Chandler kick)
GB—FG Chandler 29
Attendance—50,777

TEAM STATISTICS	Cle	GB
First downs	8	21
Rushing	2	10
Passing	5	9
By penalty	1	2
Total yardage	161	332
Net rushing yardage	64	204
Net passing yardage	97	128
Passes att.-comp.-had int.	18-8-2	19-10-1

1966 AFL

KANSAS CITY 31, BUFFALO 7

Buffalo had no solution for Dawson's passing.

The Kansas City Chiefs qualified as the AFL's first representative in the Super Bowl when they defeated the Buffalo Bills 31–7. The Chiefs, who won the 1962 AFL title as the Dallas Texans, had a total yardage advantage of 277-255; their defense was responsible for the game's s biggest play.

Trailing 14–7 near the end of the first half, Buffalo had the ball on the Chiefs' 10 yard line. Quarterback Jack Kemp passed to Bobby Crockett, but Chiefs safety Johnny Robinson intercepted the ball and ran 72 yards. The Chiefs converted the interception into Mike Mercer's 32-yard field goal and led 17–7 at halftime. Instead of a possible tie with Kansas City, the Bills trailed by 10 points at the start of the second half.

The Chiefs' Mike Garrett scored on runs of 1 and 18 yards in the fourth quarter. Quarterback Len Dawson, who completed 16 of 24 passes for 227 yards, passed 29 yards each to tight end Fred Arbanas and flanker Otis Taylor to produce touchdowns in the first half. Buffalo scored on a 69-yard pass play, Kemp to Elbert Dubenion.

January 1, at Buffalo

Kansas City	Starters, Offense	Buffalo
Chris Burford	LE	Bobby Crockett
Jim Tyrer	LT	Stew Barber
Ed Budde	LG	Billy Shaw
Wayne Frazier	C	Al Bemiller
Curt Merz	RG	Joe O'Donnell
Dave Hill	RT	Dick Hudson
Fred Arbanas	RE	Paul Costa
Len Dawson	QB	Jack Kemp
Mike Garrett	LH	Bob Burnett
Otis Taylor	FL	Elbert Dubenion
Curtis McClinton	FB	Wray Carlton
	Starters, Defense	
Jerry Mays	LE	Ron McDole
Ed Lothamer	LT	Jim Dunaway
Buck Buchanan	RT	Tom Sestak
Chuck Hurston	RE	Tom Day
Bobby Bell	LLB	John Tracey
Sherrill Headrick	MLB	Harry Jacobs
E.J. Holub	RLB	Mike Stratton
Fred Williamson	LCB	Tom Janik
Willie Mitchell	RCB	George (Butch) Byrd
Bobby Hunt	LS	Hagood Clarke
Johnny Robinson	RS	George Saimes

Kansas City	7	10	0	14	—	31
Buffalo	7	0	0	0	—	7

KC —Arbanas 29 pass from Dawson (Mercer kick)
Buff—Dubenion 69 pass from Kemp (Lusteg kick)
KC —Taylor 29 pass from Dawson (Mercer kick)
KC —FG Mercer 32
KC —Garrett 1 run (Mercer kick)
KC —Garrett 18 run (Mercer kick)
Attendance—42,080

TEAM STATISTICS	KC	Buff
First downs	14	9
Rushing	6	2
Passing	8	7
By penalty	0	0
Total yardage	277	255
Net rushing yardage	113	40
Net passing yardage	164	215
Passes att.-comp.-had int.	24-16-0	27-12-2

1966 NFL

GREEN BAY 34, DALLAS 27

Packers' Dale beat Green on a 51-yard pass play.

With less than two minutes remaining in the game, the Dallas Cowboys had a first down on the Green Bay Packers' 2-yard line, but they failed to score and the Packers won 34–27 in the Cotton Bowl.

Packers quarterback Bart Starr, who completed 19 of 28 passes for 304 yards and four touchdowns, passed 28 yards to end Max McGee to put Green Bay ahead 34–20 with 5:20 left in the game. Don Chandler's extra-point attempt was blocked by Bob Lilly. Dallas scored on a 68-yard pass play, Don Meredith to Frank Clarke. With 4:09 left the score was 34–27. The Packers' next possession ended with a 16-yard punt by Chandler. Dallas took over on Green Bay's 47. On second down from the 22, Green Bay's Tom Brown was called for pass interference on Clarke in the end zone. That put the ball on the 2-yard line with 1:52 left. On fourth down, Meredith threw a pass that was intercepted by Brown in the end zone with 28 seconds remaining.

January 1, at Dallas

Green Bay	Starters, Offense	Dallas
Carroll Dale	LE	Bob Hayes
Bob Skoronski	LT	Jim Boeke
Fred (Fuzzy) Thurston	LG	Tony Liscio
Bill Curry	C	Dave Manders
Jerry Kramer	RG	Leon Donohue
Forrest Gregg	RT	Ralph Neely
Marv Fleming	RE	Pettis Norman
Bart Starr	QB	Don Meredith
Boyd Dowler	FL	Pete Gent
Elijah Pitts	HB	Dan Reeves
Jim Taylor	FB	Don Perkins
	Starters, Defense	
Willie Davis	LE	Willie Townes
Ron Kostelnik	LT	Jim Colvin
Henry Jordan	RT	Bob Lilly
Lionel Aldridge	RE	George Andrie
Dave Robinson	LLB	Chuck Howley
Ray Nitschke	MLB	Lee Roy Jordan
Lee Roy Caffey	RLB	Dave Edwards
Herb Adderley	LHB	Cornell Green
Bob Jeter	RHB	Warren Livingston
Tom Brown	LS	Mike Gaechter
Willie Wood	RS	Mel Renfro

Green Bay	14	7	7	6	—	34
Dallas	14	3	3	7	—	27

GB —Pitts 17 pass from Starr (Chandler kick)
GB —Grabowski 18 fumble return (Chandler kick)
Dall—Reeves 3 run (Villanueva kick)
Dall—Perkins 23 run (Villanueva kick)
GB —Dale 51 pass from Starr (Chandler kick)
Dall—FG Villanueva 11
Dall—FG Villanueva 32
GB —Dowler 16 pass from Starr (Chandler kick)
GB —McGee 28 pass from Starr (kick blocked)
Dall—Clarke 68 pass from Meredith (Villanueva kick)
Attendance—74,152

TEAM STATISTICS	GB	Dall
First downs	19	23
Rushing	3	12
Passing	14	10
By penalty	2	1
Total yardage	367	418
Net rushing yardage	102	187
Net passing yardage	265	231
Passes att.-comp.-had int.	28-19-0	31-15-1

1967 AFL

OAKLAND 40, HOUSTON 7

Lamonica passed for two touchdowns.

The Oakland Raiders scored a touchdown on a fake field goal with 18 seconds remaining in the half and went on to defeat the Houston Oilers 40–7 for their first AFL championship. With the score 10–0, Oakland quarterback Daryle Lamonica took the snap from center for an apparent field goal attempt by George Blanda from the Oilers' 17-yard line. Instead, Lamonica ran to his right and passed to end Dave Kocourek, who was open at the 10-yard line and scored to give Oakland a 17–0 lead at the half.

The Raiders had built a 10–0 lead on a 37-yard field goal by Blanda and a 69-yard run by fullback Hewritt Dixon. They increased their advantage to 30–0 in the fourth quarter before Houston scored on Pete Beathard's five-yard pass to Charlie Frazier.

Dixon carried the ball 21 times for 144 yards, two yards less than the Oilers' total offense. Pete Banaszak rushed for 116 yards in 15 carries. Lamonica completed 10 of 24 passes for 111 yards and two touchdowns.

December 31, at Oakland

Houston	Starters, Offense	Oakland
Lionel Taylor	LE	Bill Miller
Walt Suggs	LT	Bob Svihus
Bob Talamini	LG	Gene Upshaw
Bobby Maples	C	Jim Otto
Erwin (Sonny) Bishop	RG	Wayne Hawkins
Glen Ray Hines	RT	Harry Schuh
Alvin Reed	TE	Billy Cannon
Pete Beathard	QB	Daryle Lamonica
Ode Burrell	FL	Fred Biletnikoff
Woody Campbell	RB	Pete Banaszak
Hoyle Granger	RB	Hewritt Dixon
	Starters, Defense	
Pat Holmes	LE	Isaac Lassiter
Willie Parker	LT	Dan Birdwell
George Rice	RT	Tom Keating
Richard Marshall	RE	Ben Davidson
George Webster	LLB	Bill Laskey
Garland Boyette	MLB	Dan Conners
Olen Underwood	RLB	Gus Otto
Miller Farr	LCB	Kent McCloughan
W. K. Hicks	RCB	Willie Brown
Ken Houston	LS	Warren Powers
Jim Norton	RS	Dave Grayson

Houston	0	0	0	7	—	7
Oakland	3	14	10	13	—	40

Oak —FG Blanda 37
Oak —Dixon 69 run (Blanda kick)
Oak —Kocourek 17 pass from Lamonica (Blanda kick)
Oak —Lamonica 1 run (Blanda kick)
Oak —FG Blanda 40
Oak —FG Blanda 42
Hous—Frazier 5 pass from Beathard (Wittenborn kick)
Oak —FG Blanda 36
Oak —Miller 12 pass from Lamonica (Blanda kick)
Attendance—53,330

TEAM STATISTICS	Hou	Oak
First downs	11	18
Rushing	4	11
Passing	6	6
By penalty	1	1
Total yardage	146	364
Net rushing yardage	38	263
Net passing yardage	108	101
Passes att.-comp.-had int.	35-15-1	26-10-0

1967 NFL

GREEN BAY 21, DALLAS 17

Starr (15) scored, climaxing winning drive.

No professional football playoff ever took place in conditions to match the 13-below temperature and 15-miles-per-hour winds that enveloped Lambeau Field. Breathing steam and spitting ice, the Green Bay Packers and Dallas Cowboys came to the final 13 seconds, when Packers quarterback Bart Starr scored a touchdown and gave Green Bay a 21–17 victory—their third consecutive NFL championship, a record, and fifth title in seven years.

Starr slid across the goal line between blocks by center Ken Bowman and right guard Jerry Kramer on third down after Green Bay had taken its final time out. The score climaxed a 12-play, 68-yard drive that began after Dallas had gone ahead 17–14 on a 50-yard pass play, halfback Dan Reeves to flanker Lance Rentzel, eight seconds into the final quarter. The big play in the winning drive for the Packers, who led 14–0 in the first half, came with two minutes left. Starr threw a short pass to halfback Chuck Mercein, who ran 19 yards to the Dallas 11. Mercein then gained eight yards to the 3. Starr scored three plays later.

December 31, at Green Bay

Dallas	Starters, Offense	Green Bay
Bob Hayes	LE	Boyd Dowler
Tony Liscio	LT	Bob Skoronski
John Niland	LG	Gale Gillingham
Mike Connelly	C	Ken Bowman
Leon Donohue	RG	Jerry Kramer
Ralph Neely	RT	Forrest Gregg
Pettis Norman	TE	Marv Fleming
Don Meredith	QB	Bart Starr
Lance Rentzel	FL	Carroll Dale
Dan Reeves	RB	Donny Anderson
Don Perkins	RB	Chuck Mercein
	Starters, Defense	
Willie Townes	LE	Willie Davis
Jethro Pugh	LT	Ron Kostelnik
Bob Lilly	RT	Henry Jordan
George Andrie	RE	Lionel Aldridge
Chuck Howley	LLB	Dave Robinson
Lee Roy Jordan	MLB	Ray Nitschke
Dave Edwards	RLB	Lee Roy Caffey
Cornell Green	LHB	Herb Adderley
Mike Johnson	RHB	Bob Jeter
Mike Gaechter	LS	Tom Brown
Mel Renfro	RS	Willie Wood

Dallas	0	10	0	7	—	17
Green Bay	7	7	0	7	—	21

GB —Dowler 8 pass from Starr (Chandler kick)
GB —Dowler 46 pass from Starr (Chandler kick)
Dall—Andrie 7 fumble return (Villanueva kick)
Dall—FG Villanueva 21
Dall—Rentzel 50 pass from Reeves (Villanueva kick)
GB —Starr 1 run (Chandler kick)
Attendance—50,861

TEAM STATISTICS	Dall	GB
First downs	11	18
Rushing	4	5
Passing	6	10
By penalty	1	3
Total yardage	192	195
Net rushing yardage	92	80
Net passing yardage	100	115
Passes att.-comp.-had int.	26-11-1	24-14-1

1968 AFL

N.Y. JETS 27, OAKLAND 23

Jets' Snell led rushers with 71 yards in 19 carries.

The Oakland Raiders had the ball on the New York Jets' 24-yard line in the final two minutes of the game; rookie halfback Charlie Smith fumbled a lateral from quarterback Daryle Lamonica and linebacker Ralph Baker of the Jets picked up the free ball to save a 27–23 victory for New York and its first AFL championship before a record AFL playoff crowd of 62,627 persons.

Despite icy winds and a hard playing surface in Shea Stadium, the Jets and Raiders raced up and down the field, piling up a combined total of 843 yards offense. Namath and Lamonica filled the air with 96 passes. Lamonica completed 20 of 47 for 401 yards and one touchdown. Namath completed 19 of 49 for 266 yards and three touchdowns.

The Jets led 10–0 at the end of the first quarter; the Raiders caught them at 13–13 in the third period, fell behind 20–13, then went ahead 23–20. The Jets moved back in front 27–23 in the final period.

December 29, at New York

Oakland	Starters, Offense	N.Y. Jets
Warren Wells	LE	George Sauer
Bob Svihus	LT	Winston Hill
Gene Upshaw	LG	Bob Talamini
Jim Otto	C	John Schmitt
Jim Harvey	RG	Randy Rasmussen
Harry Schuh	RT	Dave Herman
Billy Cannon	TE	Pete Lammons
Daryle Lamonica	QB	Joe Namath
Fred Biletnikoff	FL	Don Maynard
Charlie Smith	RB	Emerson Boozer
Hewritt Dixon	RB	Matt Snell
	Starters, Defense	
Isaac Lassiter	LE	Gerry Philbin
Dan Birdwell	LT	Paul Rochester
Carleton Oats	RT	John Elliott
Ben Davidson	RE	Verlon Biggs
Ralph (Chip) Oliver	LLB	Ralph Baker
Dan Conners	MLB	Al Atkinson
Gus Otto	RLB	Larry Grantham
George Atkinson	LCB	Johnny Sample
Willie Brown	RCB	Randy Beverly
Rodger Bird	LS	Jim Hudson
Dave Grayson	RS	Bill Baird

Oakland	0	10	3	10	—	23
N.Y. Jets	10	3	7	7	—	27

NYJ—Maynard 14 pass from Namath (J. Turner kick)
NYJ—FG J. Turner 33
Oak—Biletnikoff 29 pass from Lamonica (Blanda kick)
NYJ—FG J. Turner 36
Oak—FG Blanda 26
Oak—FG Blanda 9
NYJ—Lammons 20 pass from Namath (J. Turner kick)
Oak—FG Blanda 20
Oak—Banaszak 5 run (Blanda kick)
NYJ—Maynard 6 pass from Namath (J. Turner kick)
Attendance—62,627

TEAM STATISTICS	Oak	NYJ
First downs	18	25
Rushing	3	9
Passing	14	15
By penalty	1	1
Total yardage	443	400
Net rushing yardage	50	144
Net passing yardage	393	256
Passes att.-comp.-had int.	47-20-0	49-19-1

1968 NFL

BALTIMORE 34, CLEVELAND 0

Browns' Ryan (13) watched ball bounce away.

The Baltimore Colts were hailed as one of the greatest teams in NFL history after winning their fifteenth game against one loss by blanking the Cleveland Browns 34–0 for their first championship since 1959. The shutout was only the second in the Browns' 24-year history.

The Colts broke the game open with 17 points in the second quarter, beginning with a 28-yard field goal by Lou Michaels. Halfback Tom Matte scored touchdowns on runs of 1 and 12 yards, then tied a record with his third touchdown, on a two-yard run, in the third quarter.

Baltimore finished the Browns in the fourth quarter on Michaels's 10-yard field goal and Timmy Brown's four-yard run.

The Colts outgained the Browns 353-173 in total offense and had 22 first downs to 12. Baltimore held a 184-56 rushing advantage as Matte gained 88 yards in 17 carries and fullback Jerry Hill 60 in 11. Cleveland's Leroy Kelly, who led professional football in 1968 with 1,239 yards rushing, was held to 28 yards in 13 carries.

December 29, at Cleveland

Baltimore	Starters, Offense	Cleveland
Jimmy Orr	LE	Paul Warfield
Bob Vogel	LT	Dick Schafrath
Glenn Ressler	LG	John Demarie
Bill Curry	C	Fred Hoaglin
Dan Sullivan	RG	Gene Hickerson
Sam Ball	RT	Monte Clark
John Mackey	TE	Milt Morin
Earl Morrall	QB	Bill Nelsen
Willie Richardson	FL	Gary Collins
Tom Matte	RB	Leroy Kelly
Jerry Hill	RB	Charley Harraway
	Starters, Defense	
Charles (Bubba) Smith	LE	Ron Snidow
Billy Ray Smith	LT	Jim Kanicki
Fred Miller	RT	Walter Johnson
Ordell Braase	RE	Jack Gregory
Mike Curtis	LLB	Jim Houston
Dennis Gaubatz	MLB	Bob Matheson
Don Shinnick	RLB	Dale Lindsey
Bobby Boyd	LHB	Erich Barnes
Lenny Lyles	RHB	Ben Davis
Jerry Logan	LS	Ernie Kellermann
Rick Volk	RS	Mike Howell

Baltimore	0	17	7	10	—	34
Cleveland	0	0	0	0	—	0

Balt—FG Michaels 28
Balt—Matte 1 run (Michaels kick)
Balt—Matte 12 run (Michaels kick)
Balt—Matte 2 run (Michaels kick)
Balt—FG Michaels 10
Balt—Brown 4 run (Michaels kick)
Attendance—78,410

TEAM STATISTICS	Balt	Cle
First downs	22	12
Rushing	13	2
Passing	8	8
By penalty	1	2
Total yardage	353	173
Net rushing yardage	184	56
Net passing yardage	169	117
Passes att.-comp.-had int.	25-11-1	32-13-2

1969 AFL

KANSAS CITY 17, OAKLAND 7

Chiefs' Arbanas blocked for Garrett.

The Kansas City Chiefs won the last championship of the AFL when they defeated the Oakland Raiders 17–7 after losing to that team twice in the regular season. The Chiefs turned the ball over three times inside their 30-yard line in the fourth quarter, but they intercepted three of Raiders quarterback Daryle Lamonica's passes during that time. Kansas City won two other titles in 1962 as the Dallas Texans and 1966, during the 10-year history of the AFL.

The Chiefs broke a 7–7 tie midway in the third quarter. Faced with a third-and-14 situation on his 2-yard line, quarterback Len Dawson scrambled out of trouble in his end zone and completed a 35-yard pass to Otis Taylor. That play began a 98-yard march to the touchdown that made the score 14–7. The Raiders' first opportunity to tie came with Lamonica, who had returned to the game after jamming his throwing hand against the helmet of Kansas City's Aaron Brown early in the quarter, moved Oakland from its 6-yard line to Kansas City's 39. Jim Kearney intercepted for Kansas City at the 24. Two series later Emmitt Thomas intercepted Lamonica and the Chiefs went 62 yards to Jan Stenerud's 22-yard field goal.

January 4, at Oakland

Kansas City	Starters, Offense	Oakland
Frank Pitts	WR	Rod Sherman
Jim Tyrer	LT	Bob Svihus
Ed Budde	LG	Gene Upshaw
E.J. Holub	C	Jim Otto
Mo Moorman	RG	Jim Harvey
Dave Hill	RT	Harry Schuh
Fred Arbanas	TE	Billy Cannon
Otis Taylor	WR	Fred Biletnikoff
Len Dawson	QB	Daryle Lamonica
Mike Garrett	RB	Charlie Smith
Robert Holmes	RB	Hewritt Dixon
	Starters, Defense	
Jerry Mays	LE	Isaac Lassiter
Curley Culp	LT	Carleton Oats
Buck Buchanan	RT	Tom Keating
Aaron Brown	RE	Ben Davidson
Bobby Bell	LLB	Ralph (Chip) Oliver
Willie Lanier	MLB	Dan Conners
Jim Lynch	RLB	Gus Otto
Jim Marsalis	LCB	Nemiah Wilson
Emmitt Thomas	RCB	Willie Brown
Jim Kearney	LS	George Atkinson
Johnny Robinson	RS	Dave Grayson

Kansas City	0	7	7	3	— 17
Oakland	7	0	0	0	— 7

Oak—Smith 3 run (Blanda kick)
KC —Hayes 1 run (Stenerud kick)
KC —Holmes 5 run (Stenerud kick)
KC —FG Stenerud 22
Attendance—53,564

TEAM STATISTICS	KC	Oak
First downs	13	18
Rushing	5	6
Passing	6	10
By penalty	2	2
Total yardage	207	233
Net rushing yardage	86	79
Net passing yardage	121	154
Passes att.-comp.-had int.	17-7-0	45-17-4

1969 NFL

MINNESOTA 27, CLEVELAND 7

Three Browns couldn't stop Kapp.

Snow was stacked along the side lines and the temperature was eight degrees in Metropolitan Stadium as the Minnesota Vikings became the first expansion team to win the NFL championship when they defeated the Cleveland Browns 27–7. The 50-year-old NFL, led by a team that was completing its ninth season of play, was scheduled to merge with the 10-year-old AFL the following year.

The Vikings scored the first two times they had the ball. Quarterback Joe Kapp, who joined them in 1967 after playing eight seasons in the Canadian Football League, scored on a seven-yard run and teamed with Gene Washington on a 75-yard touchdown pass. Washington caught three passes for 120 yards and a touchdown and Kapp completed 7 of 13 passes for 169 yards and a touchdown.

Fred Cox kicked a 30-yard field goal for a 17–0 lead in the second quarter and Dave Osborn, who led all rushers with 108 yards in 18 carries, made the score 24–0 at halftime with a 20-yard run. It was 27–0 in the third quarter after Cox's 32-yard field goal.

January 4, at Bloomington, Minnesota

Cleveland	Starters, Offense	Minnesota
Paul Warfield	WR	Gene Washington
Dick Schafrath	LT	Grady Alderman
John Demarie	LG	Jim Vellone
Fred Hoaglin	C	Mick Tingelhoff
Gene Hickerson	RG	Milt Sunde
Monte Clark	RT	Ron Yary
Milt Morin	TE	John Beasley
Gary Collins	WR	John Henderson
Bill Nelsen	QB	Joe Kapp
Leroy Kelly	RB	Dave Osborn
Robert (Bo) Scott	RB	Bill Brown
	Starters, Defense	
Ron Snidow	LE	Carl Eller
Walter Johnson	LT	Gary Larsen
Jim Kanicki	RT	Alan Page
Jack Gregory	RE	Jim Marshall
Jim Houston	LLB	Roy Winston
Dale Lindsey	MLB	Lonnie Warwick
John Garlington	RLB	Wally Hillgenberg
Erich Barnes	LCB	Earsell Mackbee
Walt Sumner	RCB	Ed Sharockman
Ernie Kellermann	LS	Karl Kassulke
Mike Howell	RS	Paul Krause

Cleveland	0	0	0	7	— 7
Minnesota	14	10	3	0	— 27

Minn—Kapp 7 run (Cox kick)
Minn—Washington 75 pass from Kapp (Cox kick)
Minn—FG Cox 30
Minn—Osborn 20 run (Cox kick)
Minn—FG Cox 32
Cle —Collins 3 pass from Nelsen (Cockroft kick)
Attendance—46,503

TEAM STATISTICS	Cle	Minn
First downs	14	18
Rushing	4	13
Passing	10	5
By penalty	0	0
Total yardage	268	383
Net rushing yardage	97	222
Net passing yardage	171	161
Passes att.-comp.-had int.	33-17-2	13-7-0

1970 AFC

BALTIMORE 27, OAKLAND 17

Colts' Charles (Bubba) Smith harrassed Blanda.

The Baltimore Colts became the first champion of the American Football Conference when they defeated the Oakland Raiders 27–17. The Raiders were an original AFL squad but the Colts joined the AFC with Pittsburgh and Cleveland from the NFL after the two leagues merged in 1970.

Running back Norm Bulaich and quarterback John Unitas provided the offensive impetus for the Colts. George Blanda, who replaced Daryle Lamonica in the second quarter for Oakland, set a record for being the oldest quarterback to perform in a championship game. The 42-year-old Blanda threw for two touchdowns and completed 17 of 32 passes for 217 yards.

Bulaich gained 71 yards in 22 carries and scored twice. His 11-yard run in the third quarter gave the Colts a 20–10 lead. After Oakland closed to 20–17 on a 15-yard, Blanda-to-Warren Wells pass, the Colts put the game away on a 68-yard pass play, Unitas to Ray Perkins. Perkins got behind Oakland's Nemiah Wilson, who fell trying to cover Perkins.

January 3, at Baltimore

Oakland	Offense	Baltimore
Warren Wells	WR	Eddie Hinton
Art Shell	LT	Bob Vogel
Gene Upshaw	LG	Glenn Ressler
Jim Otto	C	Dan Curry
Jim Harvey	RG	John Williams
Harry Schuh	RT	Dan Sullivan
Raymond Chester	TE	John Mackey
Fred Biletnikoff	WR	Roy Jefferson
Daryle Lamonica	QB	John Unitas
Charlie Smith	RB	Norm Bulaich
Hewritt Dixon	RB	Tom Nowatzke
	Defense	
Tony Cline	LE	Charles (Bubba) Smith
Carleton Oats	LT	Billy Ray Smith
Tom Keating	RT	Fred Miller
Ben Davidson	RE	Roy Hilton
Bill Laskey	LLB	Ray May
Dan Conners	MLB	Mike Curtis
Gus Otto	RLB	Ted Hendricks
Kent McCloughan	LCB	Charlie Stukes
Willie Brown	RCB	Jim Duncan
George Atkinson	LS	Jerry Logan
Dave Grayson	RS	Rick Volk

Oakland	0	3	7	7	— 17
Baltimore	3	7	10	7	— 27

Balt—FG O'Brien 16
Balt—Bulaich 2 run (O'Brien kick)
Oak—FG Blanda 48
Oak—Biletnikoff 38 pass from Blanda (Blanda kick)
Balt—FG O'Brien 23
Balt—Bulaich 11 run (O'Brien kick)
Oak—Wells 15 pass from Blanda (Blanda kick)
Balt—Perkins 68 pass from Unitas (O'Brien kick)
Attendance—54,799

TEAM STATISTICS	Oak	Balt
First downs	16	18
Rushing	5	7
Passing	10	11
By penalty	1	0
Total yardage	336	363
Net rushing yardage	107	126
Net passing yardage	229	237
Passes att.-comp.-had int.	36-18-3	30-11-0

1970 NFC

DALLAS 17, SAN FRANCISCO 10

Victorious Cowboys surrounded coach Landry.

Rookie running back Duane Thomas rushed for 143 yards in 27 carries and scored on a 13-yard run as the Dallas Cowboys defeated the San Francisco 49ers 17–10 and won their first conference championship after losses in the playoffs four consecutive years.

Middle linebacker Lee Roy Jordan of the Cowboys intercepted a pass by John Brodie to set up Thomas's touchdown run that broke a 3–3 tie in the third quarter. Another interception by cornerback Mel Renfro paved the way for the clinching touchdown, a five-yard pass from quarterback Craig Morton to running back Walt Garrison in the third quarter.

Trailing 17–3, the 49ers scored in the fourth quarter on a 26-yard pass from Brodie to wide receiver Dick Witcher. Brodie completed 19 of 40 passes for 262 yards and a touchdown with two interceptions. The game marked the 49ers' final appearance in Kezar Stadium, their home since they began play in the All-America Football Conference in 1946. They were scheduled to move into Candlestick Park in 1971.

January 3, at San Francisco

Dallas	Starters, Offense	San Francisco
Bob Hayes	WR	Dick Witcher
Ralph Neely	LT	Len Rohde
John Niland	LG	Randy Beisler
Dave Manders	C	Forrest Blue
Blaine Nye	RG	Woody Peoples
Rayfield Wright	RT	Cas Banaszek
Pettis Norman	TE	Bob Windsor
Reggie Rucker	WR	Gene Washington
Craig Morton	QB	John Brodie
Duane Thomas	RB	Ken Willard
Walt Garrison	RB	Doug Cunningham
	Starters, Defense	
Larry Cole	LE	Tom Hart
Jethro Pugh	LT	Charlie Krueger
Bob Lilly	RT	Roland Lakes
George Andrie	RE	Bill Belk
Dave Edwards	LLB	Dave Wilcox
Lee Roy Jordan	MLB	Frank Nunley
Chuck Howley	RLB	Jim Sniadecki
Herb Adderley	LCB	Jimmy Johnson
Mel Renfro	RCB	Bruce Taylor
Cornell Green	LS	Mel Phillips
Charlie Waters	RS	Roosevelt Taylor

Dallas	0	3	14	0	—	17
San Francisco	3	0	7	0	—	10

SF —FG Gossett 16
Dall—FG Clark 21
Dall—Thomas 13 run (Clark kick)
Dall—Garrison 5 pass from Morton (Clark kick)
SF —Witcher 26 pass from Brodie (Gossett kick)
Attendance—59,364

TEAM STATISTICS	Dall	SF
First downs	22	15
Rushing	16	2
Passing	5	12
By penalty	1	1
Total yardage	319	307
Net rushing yardage	229	61
Net passing yardage	90	246
Passes att.-comp.-had int.	22–7–0	40–19–2

1971 AFC

MIAMI 21, BALTIMORE 0

Anderson cut to side line on touchdown return.

The Miami Dolphins led the Baltimore Colts 7–0 in the third quarter at the Orange Bowl. After repeatedly throwing hook passes to wide receiver Eddie Hinton, Baltimore quarterback John Unitas had Hinton open deep. But the ball was thrown short, and Hinton tipped it away from Miami's Curtis Johnson. The Dolphins' Dick Anderson intercepted, setting off a chain reaction. One by one, six Baltimore players were knocked down in the open field by Miami blockers as Anderson weaved 62 yards to a touchdown. The Dolphins went on to win 21–0.

Anderson's convoy included safety Jake Scott, cornerback Tim Foley, linebackers Doug Swift and Mike Kolen, defensive end Bill Stanfill, and defensive tackle Bob Heinz, who flattened Unitas, the last Colt in Anderson's way. Miami scored again in the fourth quarter on Larry Csonka's five-yard run.

Miami had taken the lead in the first quarter. Dolphins quarterback Bob Griese faked Csonka into the line; the fake froze Baltimore safety Rick Volk. When Volk retreated to cover wide received Paul Warfield, he was too late to stop Griese's perfect pass—one that resulted in a 75-yard touchdown.

January 2, at Miami

Baltimore	Starters, Offense	Miami
Eddie Hinton	WR	Paul Warfield
Bob Vogel	LT	Doug Crusan
Glenn Ressler	LG	Bob Kuechenberg
Bill Curry	C	Bob DeMarco
John Williams	RG	Larry Little
Dan Sullivan	RT	Norm Evans
Tom Mitchell	TE	Marv Fleming
Ray Perkins	WR	Howard Twilley
John Unitas	QB	Bob Griese
Don McCauley	RB	Jim Kiick
Don Nottingham	RB	Larry Csonka
	Starters, Defense	
Charles (Bubba) Smith	LE	Jim Riley
Billy Newsome	LT	Manny Fernandez
Fred Miller	RT	Bob Heinz
Roy Hilton	RE	Bill Stanfill
Ray May	LLB	Doug Swift
Mike Curtis	MLB	Nick Buoniconti
Ted Hendricks	RLB	Mike Kolen
Charlie Stukes	LCB	Tim Foley
Rex Kern	RCB	Curtis Johnson
Jerry Logan	LS	Dick Anderson
Rick Volk	RS	Jake Scott

Baltimore	0	0	0	0	—	0
Miami	7	0	7	7	—	21

Mia—Warfield 75 pass from Griese (Yepremian kick)
Mia—Anderson 62 interception return (Yepremian kick)
Mia—Csonka 5 run (Yepremian kick)
Attendance—76,622

TEAM STATISTICS	Balt	Mia
First downs	16	13
Rushing	6	8
Passing	10	4
By penalty	0	1
Total yardage	302	286
Net rushing yardage	93	144
Net passing yardage	209	142
Passes att.-comp.-had int.	36–20–3	8–4–1

1971 NFC

DALLAS 14, SAN FRANCISCO 3

Touchdown by Thomas (33) wrapped up victory.

The Dallas Cowboys broke a scoreless tie in the second quarter when defensive end George Andrie, hidden by San Francisco tackle Len Rohde, emerged to intercept John Brodie's screen pass to running back Ken Willard and run the ball eight yards to the 49ers' 2-yard line. Calvin Hill scored from the one and the touchdown was sufficient as Dallas won its second straight NFC championship over San Francisco, 14–3.

Dallas led 7–3 in the fourth quarter when strong safety Mel Phillips of San Francisco went out with an ankle injury. Reacting immediately on third and two at the 49ers' 12, Dallas coach Tom Landry sent in a pass play to tight end Mike Ditka. Ditka caught a five-yard pass that set up a two-yard touchdown run by Duane Thomas two plays later.

Dallas converted 8 of 14 third downs into first downs, including 4 on the 80-yard, 14-play drive that led to the final score. San Francisco converted 1 of 11 third down situations.

January 2, at Irving, Texas

San Francisco	Starters, Offense	Dallas
Dick Witcher	WR	Bob Hayes
Len Rohde	LT	Tony Liscio
Randy Beisler	LG	John Niland
Forrest Blue	C	Dave Manders
Woody Peoples	RG	Blaine Nye
Cas Banaszek	RT	Rayfield Wright
Ted Kwalick	TE	Mike Ditka
Gene Washington	WR	Lance Alworth
John Brodie	QB	Roger Staubach
Ken Willard	RB	Calvin Hill
Vic Washington	RB	Duane Thomas
	Starters, Defense	
Tommy Hart	LE	Larry Cole
Charlie Krueger	LT	Jethro Pugh
Earl Edwards	RT	Bob Lilly
Cedrick Hardman	RE	George Andrie
Dave Wilcox	LLB	Dave Edwards
Frank Nunley	MLB	Lee Roy Jordan
William (Skip) Vanderbundt	RLB	Chuck Howley
Jimmy Johnson	LCB	Herb Adderley
Bruce Taylor	RCB	Mel Renfro
Mel Phillips	LS	Cornell Green
Roosevelt Taylor	RS	Cliff Harris

San Francisco	0	0	3	0	—	3
Dallas	0	7	0	7	—	14

Dall—Hill 1 run (Clark kick)
SF —FG Gossett 28
Dall—Thomas 2 run (Clark kick)
Attendance—63,409

TEAM STATISTICS	SF	Dall
First downs	9	16
Rushing	2	9
Passing	7	7
By penalty	0	0
Total yardage	239	244
Net rushing yardage	61	172
Net passing yardage	178	72
Passes att.-comp.-had int.	30–14–3	18–9–0

1972 AFC
MIAMI 21, PITTSBURGH 17

Seiple fooled Steelers with run from punt formation.

Quarterback Bob Griese, sidelined since the fifth game of the season with a broken ankle, came off the bench at the start of the second half and directed touchdown marches of 80 and 49 yards that broke a 7–7 tie and led the Miami Dolphins to a 21–17 victory over the Pittsburgh Steelers. The victory was Miami's second in a row in the AFC championship and their sixteenth of the season without defeat.

Pittsburgh took a 7–0 lead in the first quarter after quarterback Terry Bradshaw fumbled in the Miami end zone and the fumble was recovered by teammate Gerry Mullins. In the second quarter, Miami's Larry Seiple was in punt formation at Pittsburgh's 49 when he noticed that the defense had retreated to set up a punt return. Seiple ran instead of punting, gaining 37 yards to the 12 and set up Miami's first touchdown. That came on a nine-yard pass from quarterback Earl Morrall to running back Larry Csonka.

The running of Csonka (68 yards in 24 carries) and Mercury Morris (76 in 16) helped Miami control the ball. The Dolphins had 65 plays to Pittsburgh's 48 and led in total offense 314–250.

December 31, at Pittsburgh

Miami	Starters, Offense	Pittsburgh
Paul Warfield	WR	Al Young
Wayne Moore	LT	Jon Kolb
Bob Kuechenberg	LG	Sam Davis
Jim Langer	C	Ray Mansfield
Larry Little	RG	Bruce Van Dyke
Norm Evans	RT	Gerry Mullins
Marv Fleming	TE	John McMakin
Howard Twilley	WR	Ron Shanklin
Earl Morrall	QB	Terry Bradshaw
Eugene (Mercury) Morris	RB	Franco Harris
Larry Csonka	RB	John Fuqua
	Starters, Defense	
Vern Den Herder	LE	L. C. Greenwood
Manny Fernandez	LT	Joe Greene
Bob Heinz	RT	Ben McGee
Bill Stanfill	RE	Dwight White
Doug Swift	LLB	Jack Ham
Nick Buoniconti	MLB	Henry Davis
Mike Kolen	RLB	Andy Russell
Tim Foley	LCB	John Rowser
Curtis Johnson	RCB	Mel Blount
Jake Scott	LS	Glen Edwards
Dick Anderson	RS	Mike Wagner

Miami	0	7	7	7	—	21
Pittsburgh	7	0	3	7	—	17

Pitt —Mullins fumble recovery in end zone (Gerela kick)
Mia —Csonka 9 pass from Griese (Yepremian kick)
Pitt —FG Gerela 14
Mia —Kiick 2 run (Yepremian kick)
Mia —Kiick 3 run (Yepremian kick)
Pitt —Young 12 pass from Bradshaw (Gerela kick)
Attendance—50,845

TEAM STATISTICS	Mia	Pitt
First downs	19	13
Rushing	11	6
Passing	6	6
By penalty	2	1
Total yardage	314	250
Net rushing yardage	193	128
Net passing yardage	121	122
Passes att.-comp.-had int.	16–10–1	20–10–2

1972 NFC
WASHINGTON 26, DALLAS 3

Taylor scored on 45-yard pass for 16–3 lead.

Quarterback Billy Kilmer threw touchdown passes of 15 and 45 yards to wide receiver Charley Taylor and the Washington Redskins did not allow Dallas to move beyond its 30-yard line in the third quarter and not beyond midfield in the second half. The Redskins scored a 26–3 victory for their first championship since 1942. Kilmer completed 14 of 18 passes for 194 yards and two touchdowns and Taylor caught 7 passes for 146 yards and two touchdowns.

Taylor's first scoring catch gave Washington a 10–0 lead in the second quarter. His second provided a 17–3 advantage in the fourth quarter. The Redskins scored first on Curt Knight's 18-yard field goal, which came at the end of a 16-play, 62-yard drive that consumed nine and one-half minutes of the first quarter.

Knight kicked four field goals without a miss, giving him seven in a row in the playoffs. The Redskins controlled the ball for 62 plays to Dallas's 45. They outgained the Cowboys 316-169.

December 31, at Washington

Dallas	Starters, Offense	Washington
Ron Sellers	WR	Charley Taylor
Ralph Neely	LT	Terry Hermeling
John Niland	LG	Paul Laaveg
Dave Manders	C	Len Hauss
Blaine Nye	RG	John Wilbur
Rayfield Wright	RT	Walter Rock
Mike Ditka	TE	Jerry Smith
Lance Alworth	WR	Roy Jefferson
Roger Staubach	QB	Billy Kilmer
Calvin Hill	RB	Larry Brown
Walt Garrison	RB	Charley Harraway
	Starters, Defense	
Larry Cole	LE	Ron McDole
Jethro Pugh	LT	Manny Sistrunk
Bob Lilly	RT	Diron Talbert
Pat Toomay	RE	Verlon Biggs
Dave Edwards	LLB	Jack Pardee
Lee Roy Jordan	MLB	Myron Pottios
D.D. Lewis	RLB	Chris Hanburger
Charlie Waters	LCB	Pat Fischer
Mel Renfro	RCB	Mike Bass
Cornell Green	LS	Brig Owens
Cliff Harris	RS	Roosevelt Taylor

Dallas	0	3	0	0	—	3
Washington	0	10	0	16	—	26

Wash—FG Knight 18
Wash—Taylor 15 pass from Kilmer (Knight kick)
Dall —FG Fritsch 35
Wash—Taylor 45 pass from Kilmer (Knight kick)
Wash—FG Knight 39
Wash—FG Knight 46
Wash—FG Knight 45
Attendance—53,129

TEAM STATISTICS	Dall	Wash
First downs	8	16
Rushing	3	4
Passing	3	11
By penalty	2	1
Total yardage	169	316
Net rushing yardage	96	122
Net passing yardage	73	194
Passes att.-comp.-had int.	21-9-0	18-14-0

1973 AFC
MIAMI 27, OAKLAND 10

Miami defense caused fourth quarter fumble.

The Miami Dolphins scored a touchdown the first time they had the ball, marched 63 yards to another score in the closing seconds of the first half, and went on to a 27–10 victory over the Oakland Raiders for their third straight AFC championship. Dolphins quarterback Bob Griese, who scrambled 27 yards to the Raiders' 11 on the play before running back Larry Csonka scored Miami's first touchdown, threw six passes as the Dolphins rushed for 266 yards.

The Raiders scored on George Blanda's 21-yard field goal that cut the score to 14–3 in the third quarter, but that was balanced on the next series by a 42-yard field goal by Garo Yepremian after Miami's Charlie Leigh returned the kickoff 52 yards. The Raiders made it 17–10 near the end of the quarter on a 25-yard pass from quarterback Ken Stabler to wide receiver Mike Siani, but the Dolphins put it away on Yepremian's second field goal and Csonka's third touchdown.

December 30, at Miami

Oakland	Starters, Offense	Miami
Mike Siani	WR	Paul Warfield
Art Shell	LT	Wayne Moore
Gene Upshaw	LG	Bob Kuechenberg
Jim Otto	C	Jim Langer
George Buehler	RG	Larry Little
John Vella	RT	Norm Evans
Bob Moore	TE	Jim Mandich
Fred Biletnikoff	WR	Marlin Briscoe
Ken Stabler	QB	Bob Griese
Charlie Smith	RB	Eugene (Mercury) Morris
Marv Hubbard	RB	Larry Csonka
	Starters, Defense	
Tony Cline	LE	Vern Den Herder
Otis Sistrunk	LT	Manny Fernandez
Art Thoms	RT	Bob Heinz
Horace Jones	RE	Bill Stanfill
Phil Villapiano	LLB	Doug Swift
Dan Conners	MLB	Nick Buoniconti
Gerald Irons	RLB	Mike Kolen
Nemiah Wilson	LCB	Lloyd Mumphord
Willie Brown	RCB	Curtis Johnson
George Atkinson	LS	Jake Scott
Jack Tatum	RS	Dick Anderson

Oakland	0	0	10	0	—	10
Miami	7	7	3	10	—	27

Mia —Csonka 11 run (Yepremian kick)
Mia —Csonka 2 run (Yepremian kick)
Oak—FG Blanda 21
Mia —FG Yepremian 42
Oak—Siani 25 pass from Stabler (Blanda kick)
Mia —FG Ypremian 26
Mia —Csonka 2 run (Yepremian kick)
Attendance—74,384

TEAM STATISTICS	Oak	Mia
First downs	15	21
Rushing	4	18
Passing	9	2
By penalty	2	1
Total yardage	236	292
Net rushing yardage	107	266
Net passing yardage	129	26
Passes att.-comp.-had int.	23-15-1	6-3-1

1973 NFC

MINNESOTA 27, DALLAS 10

Foreman gained 76 yards, scored once for Vikings.

The Minnesota Vikings outgained the Dallas Cowboys 306-153 in total yardage, had 20 first downs to 9, and ran 72 plays to the Cowboys' 49 to score a 27-10 victory in Texas Stadium for the NFC championship.

The Vikings led 10-0 at the end of the first half after a 55-yard field goal by Fred Cox and a five-yard run by Chuck Foreman that concluded an 86-yard drive. Dallas, which did not score an offensive touchdown, cut the lead to 10-7 in the third quarter on a 63-yard punt return by Golden Richards. But three plays later Vikings quarterback Fran Tarkenton combined with wide receiver John Gilliam, who had gotten a step behind cornerback Mel Renfro, on a 54-yard pass that restored Minnesota's 10-point lead.

When Dallas was behind 24-10 in the fourth quarter, Cowboys quarterback Roger Staubach threw to wide receiver Drew Pearson. Cornerback Nate Wright of Minnesota deflected the ball to free safety Jeff Wright, whose interception set up another Cox field goal.

December 30, At Irving, Texas

Minnesota	Starters, Offense	Dallas
Carroll Dale	WR	Bob Hayes
Grady Alderman	LT	Ralph Neely
Ed White	LG	John Niland
Mick Tingelhoff	C	John Fitzgerald
Milt Sunde	RG	Blaine Nye
Ron Yary	RT	Rayfield Wright
Stu Voigt	TE	Billy Joe DuPree
John Gilliam	WR	Drew Pearson
Fran Tarkenton	QB	Roger Staubach
Chuck Foreman	RB	Robert Newhouse
Oscar Reed	RB	Walt Garrison
	Starters, Defense	
Carl Eller	LE	Larry Cole
Gary Larsen	LT	Jethro Pugh
Alan Page	RT	Bill Gregory
Jim Marshall	RE	Pat Toomay
Roy Winston	LLB	Dave Edwards
Jeff Siemon	MLB	Lee Roy Jordan
Wally Hilgenberg	RLB	D.D. Lewis
Nate Wright	LCB	Charlie Waters
Bobby Bryant	RCB	Mel Renfro
Jeff Wright	LS	Cornell Green
Paul Krause	RS	Cliff Harris

Minnesota	3	7	7	10	—	27
Dallas	0	0	10	0	—	10

Minn—FG Cox 44
Minn—Foreman 5 run (Cox kick)
Dall —Richards 63 punt return (Fritsch kick)
Minn—Gilliam 54 pass from Tarkenton (Cox kick)
Dall —FG Fritsch 17
Minn—Bryant 63 interception return (Cox kick)
Minn—FG Cox 34
Attendance—59,688

TEAM STATISTICS	Minn	Dall
First downs	20	9
Rushing	14	3
Passing	6	5
By penalty	0	1
Total yardage	306	153
Net rushing yardage	203	90
Net passing yardage	103	63
Passes att.-comp.-had int.	21-10-1	21-10-4

1974 AFC

PITTSBURGH 24, OAKLAND 13

Swann beat Thomas; Bradshaw (12) watched.

A 21-point final quarter gave the Pittsburgh Steelers a 24-13 victory over the Oakland Raiders.

The Steelers trailed 10-3 at the end of the third quarter, but tied the score on Franco Harris's eight-yard run. Steelers linebacker Jack Ham intercepted a pass by Oakland quarterback Ken Stabler on the next series and Pittsburgh converted Ham's play into a six-yard touchdown pass from quarterback Terry Bradshaw to wide receiver Lynn Swann.

Oakland had an opportunity to tie the score, but on third down and six yards for a first down at the Steelers' 12, Stabler had to throw the ball away under a heavy pass rush. The Raiders settled for a 24-yard field goal by George Blanda.

Pittsburgh controlled the ball and the scoreboard clock late in the game when Bradshaw fumbled at Oakland's 46. Raiders linebacker Gerald Irons could not get to the ball, and Rocky Bleier recovered for Pittsburgh, which gained a first down on the next play. The Steelers then drove to the clinching touchdown, a 21-yard run by Harris.

December 29, at Oakland

Pittsburgh	Starters, Offense	Oakland
Frank Lewis	WR	Clifford Branch
Jon Kolb	LT	Art Shell
Jim Clack	LG	Gene Upshaw
Ray Mansfield	C	Jim Otto
Gerry Mullins	RG	George Buehler
Gordon Gravelle	RT	John Vella
Larry Brown	TE	Bob Moore
Ron Shanklin	WR	Fred Biletnikoff
Terry Bradshaw	QB	Ken Stabler
Rocky Bleier	RB	Clarence Davis
Franco Harris	RB	Marv Hubbard
	Starters, Defense	
L.C. Greenwood	LE	Charles (Bubba) Smith
Joe Greene	LT	Otis Sistrunk
Ernie Holmes	RT	Art Thoms
Dwight White	RE	Horace Jones
Jack Ham	LLB	Phil Villapiano
Jack Lambert	MLB	Dan Conners
Andy Russell	RLB	Gerald Irons
J.T. Thomas	LCB	Alonzo (Skip) Thomas
Mel Blount	RCB	Nemiah Wilson
Mike Wagner	LS	George Atkinson
Glen Edwards	RS	Jack Tatum

Pittsburgh	0	3	0	21	—	24
Oakland	3	0	7	3	—	13

Oak—FG Blanda 40
Pitt —FG Gerela 23
Oak—Branch 38 pass from Stabler (Blanda kick)
Pitt —Harris 8 run (Gerela kick)
Pitt —Swann 6 pass from Bradshaw (Gerela kick)
Oak—FG Blanda 24
Pitt —Harris 21 run (Gerela kick)
Attendance—53,023

TEAM STATISTICS	Pitt	Oak
First downs	20	15
Rushing	11	0
Passing	7	13
By penalty	2	2
Total yardage	305	278
Net rushing yardage	210	29
Net passing yardage	95	249
Passes att.-comp.-had int.	17-8-1	36-19-3

1974 NFC

MINNESOTA 14, LOS ANGELES 10

Hilgenberg's interception in end zone hurt Rams.

Minnesota was in the midst of a winter heat wave. It was 31 degrees and the sun was blinding as the Minnesota Vikings defeated the Los Angeles Rams 14-10 in the Rams' first appearance in a championship game since 1955 and the Vikings' third appearance in six years.

The Rams outgained the Vikings 340-269, a total that included a 98-yard drive in the third quarter in which Los Angeles did not score. The big play was a 73-yard pass and run involving quarterback James Harris and wide receiver Harold Jackson. Safety Jeff Wright knocked Jackson out of bounds on the 2. On second down at the 1, Rams guard Tom Mack was called for illegal motion, moving the ball back to the 6. Harris ran for four yards on third down, but his fourth-down pass to tight end Pat Curran was deflected by cornerback Jackie Wallace and caught in the end zone for a touchback by linebacker Wally Hilgenberg. Minnesota still led 7-3.

The Vikings increased their lead to 14-3 on Dave Osborn's one-yard run in the fourth quarter.

December 29, at Bloomington, Minnesota

Los Angeles	Starters, Offense	Minnesota
Harold Jackson	WR	Jim Lash
Charlie Cowan	LT	Charles Goodrum
Tom Mack	LG	Andy Maurer
Ken Iman	C	Mick Tingelhoff
Joe Scibelli	RG	Ed White
John Williams	RT	Ron Yary
Bob Klein	TE	Stu Voigt
Jack Snow	WR	John Gilliam
James Harris	QB	Fran Tarkenton
Jim Bertelsen	RB	Chuck Foreman
Lawrence McCutcheon	RB	Dave Osborn
	Starters, Defense	
Jack Youngblood	LE	Carl Eller
Merlin Olsen	LT	Doug Sutherland
Larry Brooks	RT	Alan Page
Fred Dryer	RE	Jim Marshall
Ken Geddes	LLB	Roy Winston
Jack Reynolds	MLB	Jeff Siemon
Isiah Robertson	RLB	Wally Hilgenberg
Charlie Stukes	LCB	Nate Wright
Al Clark	RCB	Jackie Wallace
Dave Elmendorf	LS	Jeff Wright
Bill Simpson	RS	Paul Krause

Los Angeles	0	3	0	7	—	10
Minnesota	0	7	0	7	—	14

Minn—Lash 29 pass from Tarkenton (Cox kick)
LA —FG Ray 27
Minn—Osborn 4 run (Cox kick)
LA —Jackson 44 pass from Harris (Ray kick)
Attendance—48,444

TEAM STATISTICS	LA	Minn
First downs	15	18
Rushing	5	9
Passing	10	7
By penalty	0	2
Total yardage	340	269
Net rushing yardage	121	164
Net passing yardage	219	105
Passes att.-comp.-had int.	23-13-2	20-10-1

1975 AFC

PITTSBURGH 16, OAKLAND 10

Harris shook off Colzie on icy touchdown run.

With snow in the 18-degree air and ice on the Three Rivers Stadium playing field, the Pittsburgh Steelers held off a late charge by the Oakland Raiders to win 16–10 for their second straight AFC championship.

With 17 seconds left in the game, Oakland trailed 16–7. On third down and two yards at Pittsburgh's 24-yard line, Oakland's 48-year-old George Blanda kicked his longest field goal of the year, 41 yards. The Raiders attempted an onside kick on the ensuing kickoff. Marv Hubbard recovered the ball when Pittsburgh's Reggie Garrett fumbled. Seven seconds remained in the game. Quarterback Ken Stabler of Oakland threw a 37-yard pass to Cliff Branch, who caught the ball on the Steelers' 15. Time ran out before Branch could get out of bounds.

There were eight fumbles and five pass interceptions. Jack Lambert's recovery of Clarence Davis's fumble at Pittsburgh's 30 late in the third quarter started the Steelers on a 70-yard drive to their first touchdown. Franco Harris, running brilliantly on the icy turf, scored the touchdown on a 25-yard end sweep to give the Steelers a 10–0 lead.

January 4, at Pittsburgh

Oakland	Starters, Offense	Pittsburgh
Clifford Branch	WR	Frank Lewis
Art Shell	LT	Jon Kolb
Gene Upshaw	LG	Jim Clack
Dave Dalby	C	Ray Mansfield
George Buehler	RG	Gerry Mullins
John Vella	RT	Gordon Gravelle
Bob Moore	TE	Larry Brown
Mike Siani	WR	Lynn Swann
Ken Stabler	QB	Terry Bradshaw
Clarence Davis	RB	Rocky Bleier
Marv Hubbard	RB	Franco Harris
	Starters, Defense	
Otis Sistrunk	LE	L.C. Greenwood
Art Thoms	MG-LT	Joe Greene
Horace Jones	RE-RT	Ernie Holmes
Phil Villapiano	OLB-RE	Dwight White
Monte Johnson	ILB-LLB	Jack Ham
Gerald Irons	ILB-MLB	Jack Lambert
Ted Hendricks	OLB-RLB	Andy Russell
Alonzo (Skip) Thomas	LCB	J. T. Thomas
Neal Colzie	RCB	Mel Blount
George Atkinson	LS	Mike Wagner
Jack Tatum	RS	Glen Edwards

Oakland	0	0	0	10	—	10
Pittsburgh	0	3	0	13	—	16

Pitt —FG Gerela 36
Pitt —Harris 25 run (Gerela kick)
Oak—Siani 14 pass from Stabler (Blanda kick)
Pitt —Stallworth 20 pass from Bradshaw (no kick; bad snap)
Oak—FG Blanda 41
Attendance—50,609

TEAM STATISTICS	Oak	Pitt
First downs	18	16
Rushing	3	5
Passing	13	10
By penalty	2	1
Total yardage	321	332
Net rushing yardage	93	117
Net passing yardage	228	215
Passes att.-comp.-had int.	42-18-2	25-15-3

1975 NFC

DALLAS 37, LOS ANGELES 7

P. Pearson's first score put Dallas in front.

Running back Preston Pearson, waived by Pittsburgh at the end of the preseason and signed as a free agent by Dallas, caught seven passes for 123 yards and three touchdowns as the Cowboys defeated the Los Angeles Rams 37–7.

Pearson took a short pass from quarterback Roger Staubach and scissored through the Rams' defense for 18 yards and Dallas' first touchdown after linebacker D.D. Lewis intercepted Rams quarterback James Harris's first pass of the game. Staubach, who threw four touchdown passes, kept the Rams' defense off balance by leaving his passing pocket and scrambling seven times for 54 yards. The Cowboys averaged a gain of 5.7 yards for each of their 78 offensive plays; the Rams averaged 2.6 for each of their 45 plays.

Los Angeles trailed 7–0 in the first quarter when Tom Dempsey lined up for a 34-yard field goal. Rookie linebacker Thomas Henderson blocked the kick.

January 4, at Los Angeles

Dallas	Offense	Los Angeles
Golden Richards	WR	Harold Jackson
Ralph Neely	LT	Charlie Cowan
Burton Lawless	LG	Tom Mack
John Fitzgerald	C	Rich Saul
Blaine Nye	RG	Joe Scibelli
Rayfield Wright	RT	John Williams
Jean Fugett	TE	Terry Nelson
Drew Pearson	WR	Ron Jessie
Roger Staubach	QB	James Harris
Preston Pearson	RB	Lawrence McCutcheon
Robert Newhouse	RB	Cullen Bryant
	Defense	
Ed (Too Tall) Jones	LE	Jack Youngblood
Jethro Pugh	LT	Merlin Olsen
Larry Cole	RT	Cody Jones
Harvey Martin	RE	Fred Dryer
Dave Edwards	LLB	Ken Geddes
Lee Roy Jordan	MLB	Jack Reynolds
D. D. Lewis	RLB	Isiah Robertson
Mark Washington	LCB	Eddie McMillan
Mel Renfro	RCB	Monte Jackson
Charlie Waters	LS	Bill Simpson
Cliff Harris	RS	Dave Elmendorf

Dallas	7	14	13	3	—	37
Los Angeles	0	0	0	7	—	7

Dall—P. Pearson 18 pass from Staubach (Fritsch kick)
Dall—Richards 4 pass from Staubach (Fritsch kick)
Dall—P. Pearson 15 pass from Staubach (Fritsch kick)
Dall—P. Pearson 19 pass from Staubach (Fritsch kick)
Dall—FG Fritsch 40
Dall—FG Fritsch 26
LA —Cappelletti 1 run (Dempsey kick)
Dall—FG Fritsch 26
Attendance—88,919

TEAM STATISTICS	Dall	LA
First downs	24	9
Rushing	8	1
Passing	15	7
By penalty	1	1
Total yardage	441	118
Net rushing yardage	195	22
Net passing yardage	246	96
Passes att.-comp.-had int.	28-18-1	24-11-3

1976 AFC

OAKLAND 24, PITTSBURGH 7

Bankston was alone, caught pass in end zone.

After losses in the playoffs in seven of the eight previous years, the Oakland Raiders defeated the Pittsburgh Steelers 24–7 for their first conference championship since 1967.

Quarterback Ken Stabler completed 10 of 16 passes for 88 yards and two touchdowns as the Raiders broke to a 10–0 lead and put an important touchdown on the scoreboard in the last 19 seconds of the first half. With a first down on the Steelers' 4-yard line, the Raiders lined up with three tight ends as if to run. Pittsburgh braced with an eight-man line. Oakland quarterback Ken Stabler called for a fake run to the right side as tight end Warren Bankston slipped free to the left side and caught Stabler's pass for a 17–7 halftime lead.

Pittsburgh played without running backs Franco Harris and Rocky Bleier and started the game using a three-tight-end offense. Harris, who gained 1,128 yards during the regular season, had sore ribs. Bleier, who gained 1,036 yards, had a bruised big toe. Their replacements for most of the game were John (Frenchy) Fuqua and Reggie Harrison.

December 26, at Oakland

Pittsburgh	Starters, Offense	Oakland
Larry Brown	WR	Fred Biletnikoff
Jon Kolb	LT	Art Shell
Sam Davis	LG	Gene Upshaw
Mike Webster	C	Dave Dalby
Jim Clack	RG	George Buehler
Gerry Mullins	RT	John Vella
Bennie Cunnigham	TE	Dave Casper
Lynn Swann	WR	Clifford Branch
Terry Bradshaw	QB	Ken Stabler
Randy Grossman	RB	Clarence Davis
Reggie Harrison	RB	Mark van Eeghen
	Starters, Defense	
L.C. Greenwood	LE	John Matuszak
Joe Greene	LT-MG	Dave Rowe
Ernie Holmes	RT-RE	Otis Sistrunk
Dwight White	RE-OLB	Phil Villapiano
Jack Ham	LLB-ILB	Monte Jackson
Jack Lambert	MLB-ILB	Willie Hall
Andy Russell	RLB-OLB	Ted Hendricks
J.T. Thomas	LCB	Alonzo (Skip) Thomas
Mel Blount	RCB	Willie Brown
Glen Edwards	LS	George Atkinson
Mike Wagner	RS	Jack Tatum

Pittsburgh	0	7	0	0	—	7
Oakland	3	14	7	0	—	24

Oak—FG Mann 39
Oak—Davis 1 run (Mann kick)
Pitt —Harrison 3 run (Mansfield kick)
Oak—Bankston 4 pass from Stabler (Mann kick)
Oak—Banaszak 5 pass from Stabler (Mann kick)
Attendance—53,739

TEAM STATISTICS	Pitt	Oak
First downs	13	15
Rushing	3	7
Passing	8	7
By penalty	2	1
Total yardage	237	228
Net rushing yardage	72	157
Net passing yardage	165	71
Passes att.-comp.-had int.	34-14-1	16-10-0

1976 NFC

MINNESOTA 24, LOS ANGELES 13

Foreman dodged three Rams for 57-yard gain.

The Minnesota Vikings became the first team to qualify for four Super Bowl appearances when they defeated the Los Angeles Rams 24–13 on a day when the temperature was 12 degrees under a bright sun and the windchill factor was 12 below.

Running back Chuck Foreman gained 118 yards in 15 carries and caught five passes for 81 yards. With the Vikings leading 10–0 and in possession of the ball on the first series of the third quarter, Foreman broke through the Rams' right side, faked safety Bill Simpson, and ran 62 yards to the 2-yard line. Foreman scored two plays later.

The Vikings led 17–13 in the fourth quarter when Foreman turned a short pass from quarterback Fran Tarkenton into a 57-yard gain that put the ball on the Rams' 12 with 1:57 remaining. Sammy Johnson scored to put the game out of reach.

Los Angeles's Lawrence McCutcheon was the game's leading ground gainer with 128 yards in 26 carries and one touchdown. The Rams outgained the Vikings 336–267 in total offense and had 21 first downs to 13.

December 26, at Bloomington Minnesota

Los Angeles	Starters, Offense	Minnesota
Harold Jackson	WR	Ahmad Rashad
Doug France	LT	Steve Riley
Tom Mack	LG	Charles Goodrum
Rich Saul	C	Mick Tingelhoff
Dennis Harrah	RG	Ed White
John Williams	RT	Ron Yary
Bob Klein	TE	Stu Voigt
Ron Jessie	WR	Sammy White
Pat Haden	QB	Fran Tarkenton
John Cappelletti	RB	Brent McClanahan
Lawrence McCutcheon	RB	Chuck Foreman
	Starters, Defense	
Jack Youngblood	LE	Carl Eller
Merlin Olsen	LT	Doug Sutherland
Larry Brooks	RT	Alan Page
Fred Dryer	RE	Jim Marshall
Jim Youngblood	LLB	Matt Blair
Jack Reynolds	MLB	Amos Martin
Isiah Robertson	RLB	Wally Hilgenberg
Rod Perry	LCB	Nate Wright
Monte Jackson	RCB	Bobby Bryant
Dave Elmendorf	LS	Jeff Wright
Bill Simpson	RS	Paul Krause

Los Angeles	0	0	13	0	— 13
Minnesota	7	3	7	7	— 24

Minn—Bryant 90 blocked field goal return (Cox kick)
Minn—FG Cox 25
Minn—Foreman 2 run (Cox kick)
LA   —McCutcheon 10 run (kick failed)
LA   —H. Jackson 5 pass from Haden (Dempsey kick)
Minn—Johnson 12 run (Cox kick)
Attendance—47,191

TEAM STATISTICS	LA	Minn
First downs	21	13
Rushing	14	6
Passing	7	7
By penalty	0	0
Total yardage	336	267
Net rushing yardage	193	158
Net passing yardage	143	109
Passes att.-comp.-had int.	22-9-2	27-12-1

CHAMPIONSHIP INDIVIDUAL RECORDS

RUSHING

Most Attempts, Career
NFC   106   Jim Taylor, Green Bay, 5 games
AFC   68   Larry Csonka, Miami, 3 games

Most Attempts, Game
NFC   31   Steve Van Buren, Philadelphia vs. Los Angeles, 1949
            Jim Taylor, Green Bay vs. N.Y. Giants, 1962
AFC   29   Larry Csonka, Miami vs. Oakland, 1973
            Franco Harris, Pittsburgh vs. Oakland, 1974

YARDS GAINED

Most Yards Gained, Career
NFC   392   Jim Taylor, Green Bay, 5 games
AFC   380   Paul Lowe, Los Angeles/San Diego, 5 games

Most Yards Gained, Game
AFC   206   Keith Lincoln, San Diego vs. Boston, 1963
NFC   196   Steve Van Buren, Philadelphia vs. Los Angeles, 1949

Longest Run From Scrimmage
NFC   70   Elmer Angsman, Chi. Cardinals vs. Philadelphia, 1947 (twice, 2 TDs)
AFC   69   Hewritt Dixon, Oakland vs. Houston, 1967 (TD)

Highest Average Gain, Career, 20 or more atts.
AFC   12.0   Keith Lincoln, San Diego, 4 games (23-276)
NFC   9.6   Elmer Angsman, Chi. Cardinals, 2 games (20–192)

Highest Average Gain, Game, 10 or more atts.
NFC   15.9   Elmer Angsman, Chi. Cardinals vs. Philadelphia, 1947 (10–159)
AFC   15.8   Keith Lincoln, San Diego vs. Boston, 1963 (13–206)

Most Touchdowns, Career
NFC   5   Otto Graham, Cleveland, 6 games
AFC   4   Larry Csonka, Miami, 3 games

Most Touchdowns, Game
NFC   3   Otto Graham, Cleveland vs. Detroit, 1954
            Tom Matte, Baltimore vs. Cleveland, 1968
AFC   3   Larry Csonka, Miami vs. Oakland, 1973

PASSING

Most Passes Attempted, Career
NFL   184   George Blanda, Chi. Bears NFL, 1 game, Houston-Oakland AFC, 10 games
NFC   159   Otto Graham, Cleveland, 6 games
AFC   157   George Blanda, Houston-Oakland 10 games

Most Passes Attempted, Game
AFC   49   Joe Namath, N.Y. Jets vs. Oakland, 1968
NFC   44   Tommy Thompson, Philadelphia vs. Chi. Cardinals, 1947

Most Passes Completed, Career
NFL   88   George Blanda, Chi. Bears, NFC 1 game, Houston-Oakland AFC, 10 games
NFC   86   Otto Graham, Cleveland, 6 games
AFC   76   George Blanda, Houston-Oakland, 10 games

Most Passes Completed, Game
NFC   27   Tommy Thompson, Philadelphia vs. Chi. Cardinals, 1947
AFC   23   George Blanda, Houston vs. Dallas, 1962.

Highest Completion Percentage, Career, 40 or more atts.
NFC   62.9   John Unitas, Baltimore, 3 games (89–56)
AFC   58.2   Len Dawson, Dallas/Kansas City, 3 games (55–32)

Highest Completion Percentage, Game, 20 or more atts.
NFC   68.8   Otto Graham, Cleveland vs. Los Angeles, 1950 (32–22)
AFC   66.7   Len Dawson, Kansas City vs. Buffalo, 1966 (24–16)

YARDS GAINED

Most Yards Gained, Career
NFL   1,177   John Unitas, Baltimore NFC, 3 games (708), Baltimore AFC, 2 games (469)
NFC   1,161   Otto Graham, Cleveland, 6 games
AFC   1,017   George Blanda, Houston-Oakland, 10 games

Most Yards Gained, Game
AFC   401   Daryle Lamonica, Oakland vs. N.Y. Jets, 1968
NFC   349   John Unitas, Baltimore vs. N.Y. Giants, 1958

Longest Pass Completion
AFC   88   George Blanda, Houston vs. Los Angeles, 1960 (Cannon, TD)
NFC   82   Bob Waterfield, Los Angeles vs. Cleveland, 1950 (Davis, TD)

TOUCHDOWNS

Most Touchdown Passes, Career
NFC   11   Bart Starr, Green Bay, 6 games
AFC   7   George Blanda, Houston-Oakland, 10 games

Most Touchdown Passes, Game
NFC   5   Sid Luckman, Chi. Bears vs. Washington, 1943
AFC   3   George Blanda, Houston vs. Los Angeles, 1960
            Joe Namath, N.Y. Jets vs. Oakland, 1968

HAD INTERCEPTED

Lowest Percentage, Passes Had Intercepted, Career (40 or more attempts)
AFC   0.00   Len Dawson, Dallas/Kansas City, 3 games (55–0)
NFC   0.70   Bart Starr, Green Bay, 6 games (142–1)

Most Attempts, Consecutive, Without Interception, Game
AFC   47   Daryle Lamonica, Oakland vs. N.Y. Jets, 1968
NFC   34   Bart Starr, Green Bay vs. Philadelphia, 1960

Most Passes Had Intercepted, Career
NFL   15   George Blanda, Chi. Bears NFL, 1 game (27 atts.), Houston-Oakland, AFC, 10 games
AFC   14   George Blanda, Houston-Oakland, 10 games (157 atts.)
NFC   13   Frank Filchock, Washington-N.Y. Giants, 3 games (63 atts)

Most Passes Had Intercepted, Game
NFC   6   Frank Filchock, N.Y. Giants vs. Chi. Bears, 1946 (26 atts.)
            Bobby Layne, Detroit vs. Cleveland, 1954 (42 atts.)
            Norm Van Brocklin, Los Angeles vs. Cleveland, 1955 (25 atts.)
AFC   5   George Blanda, Houston vs. San Diego, 1961 (40 atts).; vs. Dallas, 1962 (46 atts.)

    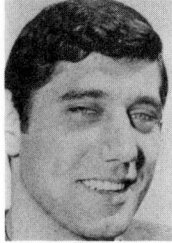  

Elmer Angsman *Keith Lincoln* *Hewritt Dixon* *Larry Csonka* *Joe Namath* *Billy Cannon* *Glenn Davis*

RECEIVING
Most Receptions, Career
NFC	24	Dante Lavelli, Cleveland, 6 games
AFC	22	Billy Cannon, Houston-Oakland, 6 games

Most Receptions, Game
NFC	12	Raymond Berry, Baltimore vs. N.Y. Giants, 1958
AFC	9	Cliff Branch, Oakland vs. Pittsburgh, 1974

YARDS GAINED
Most Yards Gained, Career
AFC	361	Fred Biletnikoff, Oakland, 7 games
NFC	340	Dante Lavelli, Cleveland, 6 games

Most Yards Gained, Game
AFC	190	Fred Biletnikoff, Oakland vs. N.Y. Jets, 1968 (7)
NFC	178	Raymond Berry, Baltimore vs. N.Y. Giants, 1958 (12)

Longest Reception
AFC	88	Billy Cannon, Houston vs. Los Angeles, 1960 (Blanda, TD)
NFC	82	Glenn Davis, Los Angeles vs. Cleveland, 1950 (Waterfield, TD)

Most Touchdowns, Career
NFC	5	Gary Collins, Cleveland, 4 games
AFC	2	Billy Cannon, Houston-Oakland, 6 games
		Dave Kocourek, Los Angeles/San Diego-Oakland, 6 games
		Don Maynard, N.Y. Jets, 1 game
		Fred Biletnikoff, Oakland, 6 games
		Mike Siani, Oakland, 2 games

Most Touchdowns, Game
NFC	3	Gary Collins, Cleveland vs. Baltimore, 1964
		Preston Pearson, Dallas vs. Los Angeles, 1975
AFC	2	Don Maynard, N.Y. Jets vs. Oakland, 1968

INTERCEPTIONS BY
Most Interceptions By, Career
NFC	4	Ken Konz, Cleveland, 4 games
		Joe Laws, Green Bay, 4 games
		Clyde (Bulldog) Turner, Chi. Bears, 5 games
		Bobby Bryant, Minnesota, 2 games
AFC	3	Johnny Robinson, Dallas/Kansas City, 3 games
		Emmitt Thomas, Kansas City, 2 games

Most Interceptions By, Game
NFC	3	Joe Laws, Green Bay vs. N.Y. Giants, 1944
AFC	2	Charles McNeil, San Diego vs. Houston, 1961
		Bud Whitehead, San Diego vs. Houston, 1961
		Bob Zeman, San Diego vs. Houston, 1961
		Johnny Robinson, Dallas vs. Houston, 1962
		Emmitt Thomas, Kansas City vs. Oakland, 1969
		Jack Ham, Pittsburgh vs. Oakland, 1974
		Jack Tatum, Oakland vs. Pittsburgh, 1975
		Mike Wagner, Pittsburgh vs. Oakland, 1975

YARDS GAINED
Most Yards Gained, Career
AFC	122	Johnny Robinson, Dallas/Kansas City, 3 games (3)
NFC	97	Don Paul, Cleveland, 3 games (2)

Most Yards Gained, Game
AFC	72	Johnny Robinson, Kansas City vs. Buffalo, 1966 (1)
NFC	66	John Sample, Baltimore vs. N.Y. Giants, 1959 (2)

Longest Return
AFC	72	Johnny Robinson, Kansas City vs. Buffalo, 1966
NFC	65	Don Paul, Cleveland vs. Los Angeles, 1955 (TD)

TOUCHDOWNS
Most Touchdowns, Game
NFC	1	Hampton Pool, Chi. Bears vs. Washington, 1940
		George McAfee, Chi. Bears vs. Washington, 1940
		Clyde (Bulldog) Turner, Chi. Bears vs. Washington, 1940
		Dante Magnani, Chi. Bears vs. N.Y. Giants, 1946
		Don Paul, Cleveland vs. Los Angeles, 1955
		Terry Barr, Detroit vs. Cleveland, 1957
		John Sample, Baltimore vs. N.Y. Giants, 1959
		Bobby Bryant, Minnesota vs. Dallas, 1973
AFC	1	Dick Anderson, Miami vs. Baltimore, 1971

PUNTING
Most Punts, Career
NFC	38	Don Chandler, N.Y. Giants–Green Bay, 9 games
AFC	25	Paul Maguire, San Diego–Buffalo, 5 games

Most Punts, Game
NFC	11	Ken Strong, N.Y. Giants vs. Chi. Bears, 1933
AFC	11	Jim Norton, Houston vs. Oakland, 1967

Longest Punt
NFC	76	Ed Danowski, N.Y. Giants vs. Detroit, 1935
AFC	68	Tom Yewcic, Boston vs. San Diego, 1963

AVERAGE YARDAGE
Highest Punting Average, Career (10 or more punts)
AFC	44.0	Mike Eischeid, Oakland, 4 games (22)
NFC	42.6	Ron Widby, Dallas, 2 games (12)

Highest Punting Average, Game (4 or more punts)
NFC	52.5	Sammy Baugh, Washington vs. Chi. Bears, 1942 (6)
AFC	51.4	John Hadl, San Diego vs. Buffalo, 1965 (5)

HAD BLOCKED
Most Punts Had Blocked, Career
NFC	2	Ed Danowski, N.Y. Giants, 1 game (4)
		Riley Smith, Boston/Washington, 2 games (11)
		Clarke Hinkle, Green Bay, 3 games (5)
AFC	0	

Most Punts Had Blocked, Game
NFC	2	Ed Danowski, N.Y. Giants vs. Detroit, 1935
		Riley Smith, Boston vs. Green Bay, 1936
AFC	0	

PUNT RETURNS
Most Punt Returns, Career
NFC	8	Keith Molesworth, Chi. Bears, 3 games
		Willie Wood, Green Bay, 5 games
AFC	7	Rodger Bird, Oakland, 2 games
		Mike Garrett, Kansas City, 2 games
		George Atkinson, Oakland, 6 games

Most Punt Returns, Game
AFC	5	Rodger Bird, Oakland vs. Houston, 1967
		Rick Volk, Baltimore vs. Miami, 1971
NFC	4	Keith Molesworth, Chi. Bears vs. N.Y. Giants, 1934
		Irv Comp, Green Bay vs. N.Y. Giants, 1944
		Steve Bagarus, Washington vs. Cleveland, 1945
		Ray Renfro, Cleveland vs. Detroit, 1952
		Carl Taseff, Baltimore vs. N.Y. Giants, 1958
		Willie Wood, Green Bay vs. Dallas, 1967
		Alvin Haymond, Washington vs. Dallas, 1972

FAIR CATCHES
Most Fair Catches, Career
NFC	5	Bob Hayes, Dallas, 7 games (10)
AFC	4	Rodger Bird, Oakland, 2 games (11)

Most Fair Catches, Game
AFC	4	Rodger Bird, Oakland vs. Houston, 1967 (9)
NFC	3	Mel Renfro, Dallas vs. Green Bay, 1967 (3)
		Timmy Brown, Baltimore vs. Cleveland, 1968 (4)
		Bobby Bryant, Minnesota vs. Dallas, 1973 (4)

YARDAGE
Most Yards Gained, Career
NFC	113	Charley Trippi, Chi. Cardinals, 4 games (4)
AFC	87	George (Butch) Byrd, Buffalo, 3 games (6)

Most Yards Gained, Game
NFC	102	Charley Trippi, Chi. Cardinals vs. Philadelphia, 1947 (2)
AFC	87	George (Butch) Byrd, Buffalo vs. San Diego, 1965 (3)

Longest Return
NFC	75	Charley Trippi, Chi. Cardinals vs. Philadelphia, 1947 (TD)
AFC	74	George (Butch) Byrd, Buffalo vs. San Diego, 1965 (TD)

AVERAGE RETURN
Highest Average Gain, Career (4 or more returns)
NFC	28.3	Charley Trippi, Chi. Cardinals, 2 games (4)
AFC	14.5	George (Butch) Byrd, Buffalo, 3 games (6)

Highest Average Gain, Game (3 or more returns)
AFC	29.0	George (Butch) Byrd, Buffalo vs. San Diego, 1965 (3)
NFC	22.0	Ken Strong, N.Y. Giants vs. Chi. Bears, 1934 (3)

TOUCHDOWNS
NFC	1	Charley Trippi, Chi. Cardinals vs. Philadelphia, 1947
		Golden Richards, Dallas vs. Minnesota, 1973
AFC	1	George (Butch) Byrd, Buffalo vs. San Diego, 1965

KICKOFF RETURNS
Most Kickoff Returns, Career
NFC	9	Ken Carpenter, Cleveland, 4 games
AFC	9	Bobby Jancik, Houston, 2 games
		George Atkinson, Oakland, 7 games

Most Kickoff Returns, Game
NFC	7	Don Bingham, Chi. Bears vs. N.Y. Giants, 1956
AFC	5	Bobby Jancik, Houston vs. Dallas, 1962
		Charley Warner, Buffalo vs. Kansas City, 1966

Gary Collins

Rodger Bird

Ken Carpenter

Jim Martin

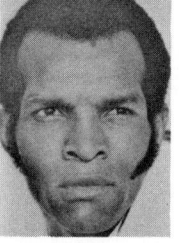
Herb Adderley

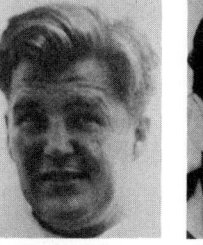
F. (Bucko) Kilroy

Ken Kavanaugh

YARDAGE

Most Yards Gained, Career
AFC	244	George Atkinson, Oakland, 7 games
NFC	208	Ken Carpenter, Cleveland, 4 games

Most Yards Gained, Game
AFC	147	Leslie (Speedy) Duncan, San Diego vs. Buffalo, 1964 (3)
NFC	132	Ken Carpenter, Cleveland vs. Los Angeles, 1951 (5)

Longest Return
AFC	72	Leslie (Speedy) Duncan, San Diego vs. Buffalo, 1964
NFC	62	Max Krause, Washington vs. Chi. Bears, 1940

AVERAGE RETURN

Highest Average Gain, Career (4 or more returns)
AFC	41.8	Leslie (Speedy) Duncan, San Diego, 2 games (5)
NFC	31.8	Woodley Lewis, Los Angeles, 1 game (4)

Highest Average Gain, Game (3 or more returns)
AFC	49.0	Leslie (Speedy) Duncan, San Diego vs. Buffalo, 1964 (3)
NFC	31.8	Woodley Lewis, Los Angeles vs. Cleveland, 1955 (4)

TOUCHDOWNS

Most Touchdowns, Game
None

SCORING

POINTS

Most Points, Career
NFL	64	George Blanda, Chi. Bears NFC 1 game (1 PAT), Houston-Oakland AFC, 10 games (18 PAT, 15 FG)
AFC	63	George Blanda, Houston-Oakland, 10 games (18 PAT, 15 FG)
NFC	55	Lou Groza, Cleveland, 9 games (25 PAT, 10 FG)

Most Points, Game
NFC	19	Paul Hornung, Green Bay vs. N.Y. Giants, 1961 (1 TD, 4 PAT, 3 FG)
AFC	18	Larry Csonka, Miami vs. Oakland, 1973 (3 TD)

TOUCHDOWNS

Most Touchdowns, Career
NFC	5	Otto Graham, Cleveland, 6 games (5 R)
		Gary Collins, Cleveland, 4 games (5 P)
AFC	5	Larry Csonka, Miami, 3 games (4 R, 1 P)

Most Touchdowns, Game
NFC	3	Otto Graham, Cleveland vs. Detroit, 1954 (3 R)
		Gary Collins, Cleveland vs. Baltimore, 1964 (3 P)
		Tom Matte, Baltimore vs. Cleveland, 1968 (3 R)
		Preston Pearson, Dallas vs. Los Angeles, 1975 (3 P)
AFC	3	Larry Csonka, Miami vs. Oakland, 1973 (3 R)

POINTS AFTER TOUCHDOWN

Most Points After Touchdown, Career
NFC	25	Lou Groza, Cleveland, 9 games (25 atts.)
AFC	18	George Blanda, Houston-Oakland, 10 games (18 atts.)

Most Points After Touchdown, Game
NFC	8	Lou Groza, Cleveland vs. Detroit, 1954 (8 atts.)
		Jim Martin, Detroit vs. Cleveland, 1957 (8 atts.)
AFC	6	George Blair, San Diego vs Boston, 1963 (6 atts.)

FIELD GOALS

Most Field Goals Attempted, Career
AFC	27	George Blanda, Houston-Oakland, 10 games
NFC	17	Lou Groza, Cleveland, 9 games

Most Field Goals Attempted, Game
AFC	6	George Blanda, Oakland vs. Houston, 1967
NFC	5	Jerry Kramer, Green Bay vs. N.Y. Giants, 1962

Most Field Goals, Career
AFC	15	George Blanda, Houston-Oakland, 10 games
NFC	10	Lou Groza, Cleveland, 9 games

Most Field Goals, Game
AFC	4	George Blanda, Oakland vs. Houston, 1967
NFC	4	Curt Knight, Washington vs. Dallas, 1972

Longest Field Goal
NFC	52	Lou Groza, Cleveland vs. Los Angeles, 1951
AFC	48	George Blanda, Oakland vs. Baltimore , 1970

SERVICE

Most Games, Player
NFL	11	George Blanda, Chi. Bears NFC, 1956; Houston AFC, 1960–62; Oakland AFC, 1967–70, 1973–75
AFC	10	George Blanda, Houston, 1960–62, Oakland, 1967–70, 1973–75
NFC	9	Lou Groza, Cleveland, 1950–55, 1957, 1964–65

Most Games, Winning Team, Player
NFC	7	Herb Adderley, Green Bay, 1961–62, 1965–67; Dallas, 1970–71
AFC	3	By many players

Most Games, Coach
NFC	8	Steve Owen, N.Y. Giants, 1933–35, 1938–39, 1941, 1944, 1946 (won 2, lost 6)
AFC	6	John Madden, Oakland, 1969–70, 1973–76 (won 1, lost 5)

Most Games, Winning Team, Coach
NFC	5	George Halas, Chi. Bears, 1933, 1940–41, 1946, 1963
		Vince Lombardi, Green Bay, 1961–62, 1965–67
AFC	3	Hank Stram, Dallas Texans, 1962; Kansas City 1966, 1969
		Don Shula, Miami, 1971–73

COMBINED NET YARDS

ATTEMPTS

Most Attempts, Career
NFC	122	Jim Taylor, Green Bay, 5 games
AFC	79	Franco Harris, Pittsburgh, 3 games

Most Attempts, Game
NFC	34	Jim Taylor, Green Bay vs. N.Y. Giants, 1962
AFC	32	Franco Harris, Pittsburgh vs. Oakland, 1975

YARDAGE

Most Yards Gained, Career
AFC	573	Billy Cannon, Houston-Oakland, 6 games
NFC	501	Jim Taylor, Green Bay, 5 games

Most Yards Gained, Game
AFC	329	Keith Lincoln, San Diego vs. Boston, 1963
NFC	241	Ken Strong, N.Y. Giants vs. Chi. Bears, 1934

FUMBLES

Most Fumbles, Career
NFC	4	Chuck Foreman, Minnesota, 3 games
AFC	2	Jack Kemp, Los Angeles/San Diego-Buffalo, 5 games
		Len Dawson, Dallas/Kansas City, 3 games
		Mike Garrett, Kansas City, 2 games
		Robert Holmes, Kansas City, 1 game
		Terry Bradshaw, Pittsburgh, 4 games
		Marv Hubbard, Oakland, 4 games
		Rocky Bleier, Pittsburgh, 4 games
		Lynn Swann, Pittsburgh, 3 games

Most Fumbles, Game
NFC	3	Chuck Foreman, Minnesota vs. Los Angeles, 1974
AFC	2	Jack Kemp, San Diego vs. Houston, 1961
		Mike Garrett, Kansas City vs. Oakland, 1969
		Robert Holmes, Kansas City vs. Oakland, 1969

RECOVERIES

Most Total Fumbles, Recovered, Career
NFC	3	Frank (Bucko) Kilroy, Philadelphia, 2 games (2-own, 1-opp)
		Alex Webster, N.Y. Giants, 6 games (3-own)
AFC	3	Jack Lambert, Pittsburgh, 3 games (3-opp)

Most Own Fumbles Recovered, Career
NFC	3	Alex Webster, N.Y. Giants, 3 games
AFC	2	Dave Casper, Oakland, 2 games

Most Opponents' Fumbles Recovered, Career
AFC	3	Jack Lambert, Pittsburgh, 3 games
NFC	2	Andy Robustelli, Los Angeles-N.Y. Giants, 8 games
		Gerry Perry, Detroit, 2 games
		Ray Krouse, Detroit-Baltimore, 3 games
		Ray Nitschke, Green Bay, 5 games
		Erich Barnes, N.Y. Giants-Cleveland, 2 games
		Cliff Harris, Dallas, 5 games
		Gary Larsen, Minnesota, 3 games
		Dave Elmendorf, Los Angeles, 3 games
		Matt Blair, Minnesota, 2 games

Most Total Fumbles Recovered, Career
AFC	3	Jack Lambert, Pittsburgh vs. Oakland, 1975 (3-opp)
NFC	2	Nate Wright, Minnesota vs. Los Angeles, 1974 (1-own, 1-opp)

Most Own Fumbles Recovered, Game
NFC	2	Frank (Bucko) Kilroy, Philadelphia vs. Los Angeles, 1949
		Dub Jones, Cleveland vs. Los Angeles, 1951
AFC	2	Dave Casper, Oakland vs. Pittsburgh, 1976

Most Opponents' Fumbles Recovered, Game
AFC	3	Jack Lambert, Pittsburgh vs. Oakland, 1975
NFC	2	Ray Krouse, Baltimore vs. N.Y. Giants, 1958
		Ray Nitschke, Green Bay vs. N.Y. Giants, 1962
		Gary Larsen, Minnesota vs. Dallas, 1973
		Dave Elmendorf, Los Angeles vs. Minnesota, 1974
		Matt Blair, Minnesota vs. Los Angeles, 1976

YARDAGE

Most Yards Gained, Career
NFC	24	Alex Webster, N.Y. Giants vs. Baltimore, 1958
AFC	0	By many players

Most Yards Gained, Game
NFC	24	Alex Webster, N.Y. Giants vs. Baltimore, 1958
AFC	0	By many players

Longest Return, Own Team's Fumbles
NFC	24	Alex Webster, N.Y. Giants vs. Baltimore, 1958
AFC	0	By many players

Longest Return, Opponents' Fumbles
NFC	50	Lee Artoe, Chi. Bears vs. Washington, 1942 (TD)
AFC	21	Bobby Hunt, Kansas City vs. Buffalo, 1966

TOUCHDOWNS
Most Touchdowns, Own Fumbles, Game
AFC	1	Gerry Mullins, Pittsburgh vs. Miami, 1972 (0 yds)
NFC	0	

Most Touchdowns, Opponents' Fumbles, Game
NFC	1	Ken Kavanaugh, Chi. Bears vs. N.Y. Giants, 1941 (42 yds)
		Lee Artoe, Chi. Bears vs. Washington, 1942 (50 yds)
		Larry Brink, Los Angeles vs. Cleveland, 1950 (6 yds)
		Jim Grabowski, Green Bay vs. Dallas, 1966 (18 yds)
		George Andrie, Dallas vs. Green Bay, 1967 (7 yds)
AFC	0	

CHAMPIONSHIP TEAM RECORDS

GAMES, VICTORIES, DEFEATS
Most Games
NFC	14	N.Y. Giants, 1933–35, 1938–39, 1941, 1944, 1946, 1956, 1958–59, 1961–63
AFC	8	Oakland, 1967–70, 1973–76

Most Consecutive Games
NFC	6	Cleveland, 1950–55
AFC	4	Oakland, 1967–70, 1973–76

Most Games Won
NFC	8	Green Bay, 1936, 1939, 1944, 1961–62, 1965–67
AFC	3	Dallas/Kansas City, 1962, 1966, 1969
		Miami, 1971–73

Most Consecutive Games Won
NFC	3	Green Bay, 1965–67
AFC	3	Miami, 1971–73

Most Games Lost
NFC	11	N.Y. Giants, 1933, 1935, 1939, 1941, 1944, 1946, 1958–59, 1961–63
AFC	6	Oakland, 1968–70, 1973–75

Most Consecutive Games Lost
NFC	3	Cleveland, 1951–53
		N.Y. Giants, 1961–63
AFC	3	Oakland, 1968–70, 1973–75

RUSHING
Most Attempts, Game
NFC	65	Detroit vs. N.Y. Giants, 1935
AFC	54	Dallas vs. Houston, 1962

Fewest Attempts, Game
AFC	13	Buffalo vs. Kansas City, 1966
NFC	14	Washington vs. Chi. Bears, 1940
		N.Y. Giants vs. Green Bay, 1961

Most Attempts, Both Teams, Game
NFC	109	Detroit (65) vs. N.Y. Giants (44), 1935
AFC	84	Dallas (54) vs. Houston (30), 1962

Fewest Attempts, Both Teams, Game
AFC	46	Buffalo (13) vs. Kansas City (33), 1966
NFC	49	N.Y. Giants (24) vs. Baltimore (25), 1959

Most Yards Gained, Game
NFC	382	Chi. Bears vs. Washington, 1940
AFC	318	San Diego vs. Boston, 1963

Fewest Yards Gained, Game
NFC	21	Los Angeles vs. Philadelphia, 1949
AFC	29	Oakland vs. Pittsburgh, 1974

Most Yards Gained, Both Teams, Game
NFC	426	Cleveland (227) vs. Detroit (199), 1952
AFC	393	San Diego (318) vs. Boston (75), 1963

Fewest Yards Gained, Both Teams, Game
NFC	106	Boston (39) vs. Green Bay (67), 1936
AFC	153	Buffalo (40) vs. Kansas City (113), 1966

Longest Run From Scrimmage
NFC	70	Chi. Cardinals vs. Philadelphia, 1947 (twice, 2 TDs)
AFC	67	Oakland vs. Houston, 1967 (TD)

AVERAGE YARDAGE
Highest Average Gain, Game
AFC	9.94	San Diego vs. Boston, 1963 (32-318)
NFC	7.23	Chi. Cardinals vs. Philadelphia, 1947 (39-282)

Lowest Average Gain, Game
NFC	0.88	Los Angeles vs. Philadelphia, 1949, (24-21)
AFC	1.38	Oakland vs. Pittsburgh, 1974, (21-29)

Highest Average Gain, Both Teams, Game
AFC	8.19	San Diego (9.94) vs. Boston (4.69), 1963
NFC	6.26	Cleveland (6.68) vs. Detroit (5.85), 1952

Lowest Average Gain, Both Teams, Game
NFC	1.54	Boston (1.22) vs. Green Bay (1.81), 1936
AFC	2.46	Kansas City (2.21) vs. Oakland (2.82), 1969

TOUCHDOWNS
Most Touchdowns, Game
NFC	7	Chi. Bears vs. Washington, 1940
AFC	4	San Diego vs. Boston, 1963

Most Touchdowns, Both Teams, Game
NFC	7	Chi. Bears (7) vs. Washington (0), 1940
AFC	5	San Diego (4) vs. Boston (1), 1963

Fewest Touchdowns, Both Teams, Game
NFC	0	Washington vs. Cleveland, 1945; vs. Dallas, 1972
		Los Angeles vs. Philadelphia, 1949
		Baltimore vs. Cleveland, 1964
AFC	0	San Diego vs. Houston, 1961; vs. Buffalo, 1965

PASSING
Most Attempts, Game
NFC	51	Washington vs. Chi. Bears, 1940
AFC	49	N.Y. Jets vs. Oakland, 1968

Fewest Attempts, Game
NFC	5	Detroit vs. N.Y. Giants, 1935
AFC	6	Miami vs. Oakland, 1973

Most Attempts, Both Teams, Game
AFC	96	N.Y. Jets (49) vs. Oakland (47), 1968
NFC	71	Washington (40) vs. Chi. Bears (31), 1937
		Cleveland (41) vs. Los Angeles (30), 1951

Fewest Attempts, Both Teams, Game
NFC	18	Detroit (5) vs. N.Y. Giants (13), 1935
AFC	29	Miami (6) vs. Oakland (23), 1973

COMPLETIONS
Most Completions, Game
NFC	27	Philadelphia vs. Chi. Cardinals, 1947
AFC	23	Houston vs. Dallas, 1962

Fewest Completions, Game
NFC	2	Detroit vs. N.Y. Giants, 1935
		Philadelphia vs. Chi. Cardinals, 1948
AFC	3	Miami vs. Oakland, 1973

Most Completions, Both Teams, Game
NFC	40	Cleveland (22) vs. Los Angeles (18), 1950
AFC	39	Oakland (20) vs. N.Y. Jets (19), 1968

Fewest Completions, Both Teams, Game
NFC	5	Philadelphia (2) vs. Chi. Cardinals (3), 1948
AFC	18	Miami (3) vs. Oakland (15), 1973

COMPLETION PERCENTAGE
Highest Completion Percentage, Game (10 or more atts)
NFC	77.8	Washington vs. Dallas, 1972 (18-14)
AFC	66.7	Kansas City vs. Buffalo, 1966 (24-16)

Lowest Completion Percentage, Game (10 or more atts)
NFC	16.7	Philadelphia vs. Chi. Cardinals, 1948 (12-2)
AFC	36.1	San Diego vs. Buffalo, 1964 (36-13)

Highest Completion Percentage, Both Teams, Game
NFC	65.5	N.Y. Giants (66.7) vs. Baltimore (65.0), 1958 (58-38)
AFC	62.1	Oakland (65.2) vs. Miami (50.0), 1973 (29-18)

Lowest Completion Percentage, Both Teams, Game
NFC	21.7	Philadelphia (16.7) vs. Chi. Cardinals (27.3), 1948 (23-5)
AFC	38.7	Oakland (37.8) vs. K.C. (41.2), 1969 (62-24)

NET YARDAGE
Most Yards Gained, Game
AFC	393	Oakland vs. N.Y. Jets, 1968
NFC	371	Washington vs. Chi. Bears, 1937

Fewest Yards Gained, Game
NFC	3	Chi. Cardinals vs. Philadelphia, 1948
AFC	26	Miami vs. Oakland, 1973

Most Yards Gained, Both Teams, Game
AFC	649	Oakland (393) vs. N.Y. Jets (256), 1968
NFC	578	Washington (371) vs. Chi. Bears (207), 1937

Fewest Yards Gained, Both Teams, Game
NFC	10	Chi. Cardinals (3) vs. Philadelphia (7), 1948
AFC	155	Miami (26) vs. Oakland (129), 1973

Longest Gain
AFC	88	Houston vs. Los Angeles, 1960 (TD)
NFC	82	Los Angeles vs. Cleveland, 1950 (TD)

TOUCHDOWNS
Most Touchdowns, Game
NFC	5	Chi. Bears vs. Washington, 1943
		Detroit vs. Cleveland, 1957
AFC	3	Houston vs. Los Angeles, 1960
		San Diego vs. Boston, 1963
		N. Y. Jets vs. Oakland, 1968

Most Touchdowns, Both Teams, Game
NFC	7	Chi. Bears (5) vs. Washington (2), 1943
AFC	4	N.Y. Jets (3) vs. Oakland (1), 1968

Fewest Touchdowns, Both Teams, Game
NFC	0	Philadelphia vs. Chi. Cardinals, 1948
		Cleveland vs. Detroit, 1952; vs. Baltimore, 1968
		Green Bay vs. N.Y. Giants, 1962
		San Francisco vs. Dallas, 1971
AFC	0	Kansas City vs. Oakland, 1969

INTERCEPTIONS BY
Most Interceptions By, Game
NFC	8	Chi. Bears vs. Washington, 1940 (51 atts)
AFC	6	San Diego vs. Houston, 1961 (41 atts)

Most Interceptions By, Both Teams, Game
NFC	10	Cleveland (7) vs. Los Angeles (3), 1955 (53 atts)
AFC	10	San Diego (6) vs. Houston (4), 1961 (73 atts)

YARDAGE
Most Yards Gained, Game
AFC	136	Dallas vs. Houston, 1962 (5)
NFC	123	Green Bay vs. N.Y. Giants, 1939 (6)

Most Yards Gained, Both Teams, Game
NFC	156	Green Bay (123) vs. N.Y. Giants (33), 1939 (9)
AFC	136	Dallas (136) vs. Houston, 1962 (5)

Longest Return
AFC	72	Kansas City vs. Buffalo, 1966
NFC	65	Cleveland vs. Los Angeles, 1955 (TD)

TOUCHDOWNS
Most Touchdowns, Game
NFC	3	Chi. Bears vs. Washington, 1940
AFC	1	Miami vs. Baltimore, 1971

PUNTING
Most Punts, Game
NFC	13	N.Y. Giants vs. Chi. Bears, 1933
AFC	11	Houston vs. Oakland, 1967

Fewest Punts, Game
AFC	1	Miami vs. Oakland, 1973
NFC	2	Chi. Bears vs. Washington, 1940; vs. N.Y. Giants, 1941
		Baltimore vs. Cleveland, 1968

Most Punts, Both Teams, Game
NFC	23	N.Y. Giants (13) vs. Chi. Bears (10), 1933
AFC	17	N.Y. Jets (10) vs. Oakland (7), 1968

Fewest Punts, Both Teams, Game
AFC	3	Miami (1) vs. Oakland (2), 1973
NFC	5	Chi. Bears (2) vs. Washington (3), 1940

AVERAGE YARDAGE
Highest Punting Average, Game (3 or more punts)
NFC	52.5	Washington vs. Chi. Bears, 1942 (6)
AFC	51.3	Pittsburgh vs. Miami, 1972 (4)

Lowest Punting Average, Game (3 or more punts)
NFC	22.5	Detroit vs. N.Y. Giants, 1935 (4)
AFC	31.3	Dallas vs. Houston, 1962 (8)

Highest Punting Average, Both Teams, Game
NFC	47.7	Baltimore (50.8) vs. N.Y. Giants (45.7), 1958 (10)
AFC	47.0	Oakland (51.0) vs. Miami (39.0), 1973 (3)

Lowest Punting Average, Both Teams, Game
NFC	32.5	Los Angeles (29.4) vs. Minnesota (35.1), 1976
AFC	33.5	Dallas (31.3) vs. Houston (39.3), 1962 (11)

PUNT RETURNS
Most Punt Returns, Game
NFC	8	Green Bay vs. N.Y. Giants, 1944 (10)
AFC	6	Oakland vs. Houston, 1967 (11)

Fewest Punt Returns, Game
NFC	0	Chi. Bears vs. Washington, 1937 (7); vs. N.Y. Giants, 1941 (5)
		N.Y. Giants vs. Chi. Bears, 1941 (2)
		Green Bay vs. Dallas, 1966 (4)
		Dallas vs. Green Bay, 1967 (8)
AFC	0	Houston vs. Los Angeles, 1960 (4); vs. Oakland, 1967 (4)
		Boston vs. San Diego, 1963 (2)
		San Diego vs. Boston, 1963 (7)
		Miami vs. Pittsburgh, 1972 (4)
		Oakland vs. Pittsburgh, 1974 (4)

Most Punt Returns, Both Teams, Game
NFC	11	Green Bay (8) vs. N.Y. Giants (3), 1944 (20)
AFC	8	Buffalo (5) vs. Kansas City (3), 1966 (14)

Fewest Punt Returns, Both Teams, Game
AFC	0	Boston vs. San Diego, 1963 (9)
NFC	0	Chi. Bears vs. N.Y. Giants, 1941 (7)

FAIR CATCHES
Most Fair Catches, Game
NFC	5	Dallas vs. Green Bay, 1967 (8)
AFC	5	Oakland vs. Houston, 1967 (11)

Most Fair Catches, Both Teams, Game
NFC	7	Dallas (5) vs. Green Bay (2), 1967 (16)
AFC	6	Oakland (5) vs. Houston (1), 1967 (15)

YARDAGE
Most Yards Gained, Game
NFC	150	Chi. Cardinals vs. Philadelphia, 1947 (4)
AFC	87	Buffalo vs. San Diego, 1965 (3)

Fewest Yards Gained, Game
NFC	−10	Green Bay vs. Cleveland, 1965 (2)
AFC	−1	Oakland vs. Kansas City, 1969 (2)

Most Yards Gained, Both Teams, Game
NFC	160	Chi. Cardinals (150) vs. Philadelphia (10), 1947 (7)
AFC	99	Buffalo (87) vs. San Diego (12), 1965 (4)

Fewest Yards Gained, Both Teams, Game
NFC	−9	Dallas (−9) vs. Green Bay (0), 1966 (3)
AFC	0	Dallas (0) vs. Houston (0), 1962 (2)
		Boston vs. San Diego, 1963 (0)

Longest Return
NFC	75	Chi. Cardinals vs. Philadelphia, 1947 (TD)
AFC	74	Buffalo vs. San Diego, 1965 (TD)

AVERAGE RETURN
Highest Average Gain, Game (3 or more returns)
NFC	37.5	Chi. Cardinals vs. Philadelphia, 1947 (4)
AFC	29.0	Buffalo vs. San Diego, 1965 (3)

Highest Average Gain, Both Teams, Game
AFC	24.8	Buffalo (29.0) vs. San Diego (12.0), 1965 (4)
NFC	22.9	Chi. Cardinals (37.5) vs. Philadelphia (3.3), 1947 (7)

TOUCHDOWNS
Most Touchdowns, Game
NFC	1	Chi. Cardinals vs. Philadelphia, 1947
		Dallas vs. Minnesota, 1973
AFC	1	Buffalo vs. San Diego, 1965

KICKOFF RETURNS
Most Kickoff Returns, Game
NFC	9	Chi. Bears vs. N.Y. Giants, 1956 (9)
AFC	9	Boston vs. San Diego, 1963 (10)
		Houston vs. Oakland, 1967 (9)

Fewest Kickoff Returns, Game
NFC	0	Green Bay vs. Boston, 1936 (2); vs. N.Y. Giants, 1939 (1)
		Washington vs. Dallas, 1972 (2)
AFC	0	Houston vs. San Diego, 1961 (2)

Most Kickoff Returns, Both Teams, Game
AFC	12	Boston (9) vs. San Diego (3), 1963 (13)
NFC	12	Dallas (6), vs. Green Bay (6), 1966 (12)

Fewest Kickoff Returns, Both Teams, Game
NFC	1	Green Bay vs. Boston (1), 1936 (6)
AFC	2	Houston vs. San Diego (2), 1961 (5)

CHAMPIONSHIP HISTORY

Date	Lg or Conf	Result	Site (Attendance)
Dec. 17, 1933	NFL	Chi. Bears 23, N.Y. Giants 21	Wrigley Field, Chicago (26,000)
Dec. 9, 1934	NFL	N.Y. Giants 30, Chi. Bears 13	Polo Grounds, New York (35,059)
Dec. 15, 1935	NFL	Detroit 26, N.Y. Giants 7	University of Detroit Stadium (15,000)
Dec. 13, 1936	NFL	Green Bay 21, Boston Redskins 6	Polo Grounds, New York (29,545)
Dec. 12, 1937	NFL	Washington 28, Chi. Bears 21	Wrigley Field, Chicago (15,870)
Dec. 11, 1938	NFL	N.Y. Giants 23, Green Bay 17	Polo Grounds, New York (48,120)
Dec. 10, 1939	NFL	Green Bay 27, N.Y. Giants 0	State Fair Park, Milwaukee (32,279)
Dec. 8, 1940	NFL	Chi. Bears 73, Washington 0	Griffith Stadium, Washington (36,034)
Dec. 21, 1941	NFL	Chi. Bears 37, N.Y. Giants 9	Wrigley Field, Chicago (13,341)
Dec. 13, 1942	NFL	Washington 14, Chi. Bears 6	Griffith Stadium, Washington (36,006)
Dec. 26, 1943	NFL	Chi. Bears 41, Washington 21	Wrigley Field, Chicago (34,320)
Dec. 17, 1944	NFL	Green Bay 14, N.Y. Giants 7	Polo Grounds, New York (46,016)
Dec. 16, 1945	NFL	Cleveland Rams 15, Washington 14	Municipal Stadium, Cleveland (32,178)
Dec. 15, 1946	NFL	Chi. Bears 24, N.Y. Giants 14	Polo Grounds, New York (58,346)
Dec. 28, 1947	NFL	Chi. Cardinals 28, Philadelphia 21	Comiskey Park, Chicago (30,759)
Dec. 19, 1948	NFL	Philadelphia 7, Chi. Cardinals 0	Shibe Park, Philadelphia (28,664)
Dec. 18, 1949	NFL	Philadelphia 14, Los Angeles 0	Los Angeles Memorial Coliseum (22,245)
Dec. 24, 1950	NFL	Cleveland 30, Los Angeles 28	Municipal Stadium, Cleveland (29,751)
Dec. 23, 1951	NFL	Los Angeles 24, Cleveland 17	Los Angeles Memorial Coliseum (57,522)
Dec. 28, 1952	NFL	Detroit 17, Cleveland 7	Memorial Stadium, Cleveland (50,934)
Dec. 27, 1953	NFL	Detroit 17, Cleveland 16	Briggs Stadium, Detroit (54,577)
Dec. 26, 1954	NFL	Cleveland 56, Detroit 10	Municipal Stadium, Cleveland (43,827)
Dec. 26, 1955	NFL	Cleveland 38, Los Angeles 14	Los Angeles Memorial Coliseum (85,693)
Dec. 30, 1956	NFL	N.Y. Giants 47, Chi. Bears 7	Yankee Stadium, New York (56,836)
Dec. 29, 1957	NFL	Detroit 59, Cleveland 14	Briggs Stadium, Detroit (55,263)
Dec. 28, 1958	NFL	Baltimore 23, N.Y. Giants 17	Yankee Stadium, New York (64,185)
Dec. 27, 1959	NFL	Baltimore 31, N.Y. Giants 16	Memorial Stadium, Baltimore (57,545)
Dec. 26, 1960	NFL	Philadelphia 17, Green Bay 13	Franklin Field, Philadelphia (67,235)
Jan. 1, 1961	AFL	Houston 24, Los Angeles Chargers 16	Jeppesen Stadium, Houston (32,183)
Dec. 24, 1961	AFL	Houston 10, San Diego 3	Balboa Stadium, San Diego (29,556)
Dec. 31, 1961	NFL	Green Bay 37, N.Y. Giants 0	Lambeau Field, Green Bay (39,029)
Dec. 23, 1962	AFL	Dallas Texans 20, Houston 17	Jeppesen Stadium, Houston (37,981)
Dec. 30, 1962	NFL	Green Bay 16, N.Y. Giants 7	Yankee Stadium, New York (64,892)
Dec. 29, 1963	NFL	Chicago 14, N.Y. Giants 10	Wrigley Field, Chicago (45,801)
Jan. 5, 1964	AFL	San Diego 51, Boston 10	Balboa Stadium, San Diego (30,127)
Dec. 26, 1964	AFL	Buffalo 20, San Diego 7	War Memorial Stadium, Buffalo (40,242)
Dec. 27, 1964	NFL	Cleveland 27, Baltimore 0	Municipal Stadium, Cleveland (79,544)
Dec. 26, 1965	AFL	Buffalo 23, San Diego 0	Balboa Stadium, San Diego (30,361)
Jan. 2, 1966	NFL	Green Bay 23, Cleveland 12	Lambeau Field, Green Bay (50,777)
Jan. 1, 1967	AFL	Kansas City 31, Buffalo 7	War Memorial Stadium, Buffalo (42,080)
Jan. 1, 1967	NFL	Green Bay 34, Dallas 27	Cotton Bowl, Dallas (74,152)
Dec. 31, 1967	AFL	Oakland 40, Houston 7	Oakland (53,330)
Dec. 31, 1967	NFL	Green Bay 21, Dallas 17	Lambeau Field, Green Bay (50,861)
Dec. 29, 1968	AFL	N.Y. Jets 27, Oakland 23	Shea Stadium, New York (62,627)
Dec. 29, 1968	NFL	Baltimore 34, Cleveland 0	Memorial Stadium, Cleveland (78,410)
Jan. 4, 1969	AFL	Kansas City 17, Oakland 7	Oakland Coliseum (53,564)
Jan. 4, 1969	NFL	Minnesota 27, Cleveland 7	Metropolitan Stadium, Bloomington (46,503)
Jan. 3, 1970	AFC	Baltimore 27, Oakland 17	Memorial Stadium, Baltimore (54,799)
Jan. 3, 1970	NFC	Dallas 17, San Francisco 10	Candlestick Park, San Francisco (59,364)
Jan. 2, 1971	AFC	Miami 21, Baltimore 0	Orange Bowl, Miami (76,622)
Jan. 2, 1971	NFC	Dallas 14, San Francisco 3	Texas Stadium, Irving (63,409)
Dec. 31, 1972	AFC	Miami 21, Pittsburgh 17	Three Rivers Stadium, Pittsburgh (50,845)
Dec. 31, 1972	NFC	Washington 26, Dallas 3	RFK Stadium, Washington (53,129)
Dec. 30, 1973	AFC	Miami 27, Oakland 10	Orange Bowl, Miami (79,325)
Dec. 30, 1973	NFC	Minnesota 27, Dallas 10	Texas Stadium, Irving (64,222)
Dec. 29, 1974	AFC	Pittsburgh 24, Oakland 13	Oakland Coliseum (53,800)
Dec. 29, 1974	NFC	Minnesota 14, Los Angeles 10	Metropolitan Stadium, Bloomington (48,444)
Jan. 4, 1976	AFC	Pittsburgh 16, Oakland 10	Three Rivers Stadium, Pittsburgh (50,609)
Jan. 4, 1976	NFC	Dallas 37, Los Angeles 7	Los Angeles Memorial Coliseum (88,919)
Dec. 26, 1976	AFC	Oakland 24, Pittsburgh 7	Oakland Coliseum (53,739)
Dec. 26, 1976	NFC	Minnesota 24, Los Angeles 13	Metropolitan Stadium, Bloomington (47,191)

The
Super Bowl

SUPER BOWL I

GREEN BAY 35, KANSAS CITY 10

The Green Bay Packers, leading 14–10 at halftime, scored two third-quarter touchdowns and advanced to a 35–10 victory over the Kansas City Chiefs in the first Super Bowl, officially designated as the AFL-NFL World Championship Game.

The Super Bowl was the result of a 1966 merger between the American Football League and National Football League. The game matched champions from each league in the Los Angeles Memorial Coliseum. Green Bay of the NFL was a 13½-point favorite but the game was in doubt after Kansas City of the AFL outgained the Packers 181–164 and led 11–9 in first downs in the first half.

Green Bay was the first team to score after nine minutes of the first quarter. The Packers marched 43 yards in five plays to the Chiefs' 37-yard line after an exchange of punts. On the sixth play, quarterback Bart Starr froze the Chiefs' secondary with a play-action fake at the line of scrimmage, then passed to end Max McGee. The ball was thrown slightly behind McGee, who caught the pass with one hand, balanced the ball on his hip, and outran the Chiefs the remaining 19 yards to the end zone.

The 34-year old McGee, who caught four passes for 91 yards and one touchdown during the regular season, replaced Boyd Dowler on the second play of the game. Dowler reinjured a shoulder blocking linebacker E.J. Holub on a sweep to the left side of the field by Elijah Pitts.

Kansas City tied the score 7–7 in the second quarter with a six-play, 66-yard drive. Quarterback Len Dawson threw a lead pass from the 7-yard line to fullback Curtis McClinton, who caught the ball in the end zone. The Packers went ahead 14–7 on their next possession. A 64-yard pass play, Starr to Carroll Dale, that went for a touchdown was called back because left tackle Bob Skoronski was in motion before the snap of the ball. The Packers recovered from the setback to score 11 plays later. Fullback Jim Taylor, behind blocks from guards Fred (Fuzzy) Thurston and Jerry Kramer, swept left end for 14 yards, concluding a 73-yard drive that took 14 plays. The Packers kept the drive going by converting four third downs into first downs.

The Chiefs started from their 26 on the next series. After Dawson was dropped for an eight-yard loss on first down, Kansas City moved 50 yards in five plays. On third and 10 from Green Bay's 32, Dawson connected with running back Mike Garrett for an eight-yard gain. Mike Mercer then kicked a 31-yard field goal with 54 seconds remaining in the half, cutting the Packers' lead to 14–10.

The Chiefs marched 20 yards in three plays after taking the kickoff for the third quarter. On third down and five yards from Kansas City's 49, Dawson received a heavy rush from tackle Henry Jordan and end Willie Davis. Jordan hit Dawson's arm as he followed through on a pass and Willie Wood intercepted. Wood returned the ball 50 yards to the Chiefs' 5-yard line. Elijah Pitts went through left tackle on the next play for a touchdown that made it 21–10.

The Chiefs did not threaten again. They had the ball for six more series and punted each time—from the 50-yard line and their 18, 2, 39, 40, and 16.

Packers coach Vince Lombardi, whose team converted 10 of 14 third-down situations into first downs, was asked to compare the Chiefs with teams of the NFL, a question many sports fans had been asking.

"In my opinion, the Chiefs don't rate with the top names in the NFL," he said. "They are a good football team with fine speed, but I'd have to say NFL football is better. Dallas is a better team and so are several others. That's what you wanted me to say, wasn't it?"

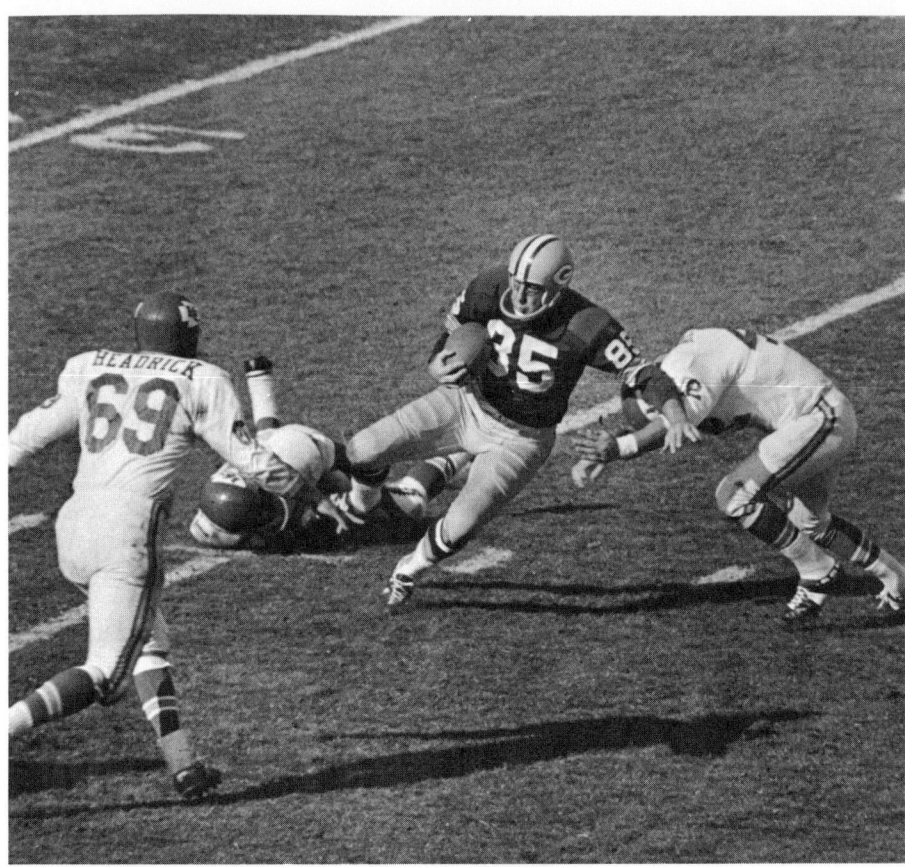

Green Bay's McGee makes one of his seven catches between Kansas City's Headrick (69) and Robinson.

Participants—Green Bay Packers, champions of the National Football League, and Kansas City Chiefs, champions of the American Football League
Date—January 15, 1967
Site—Los Angeles Memorial Coliseum
Time—1:05 P.M. PST
Conditions—72 degrees, sunny
Playing Surface—Grass
Television and Radio—National Broadcasting Company (NBC) and Columbia Broadcasting System (CBS)
Regular Season Records—Green Bay, 12-2; Kansas City, 11-2-1
League Championships—Green Bay defeated the Dallas Cowboys 34-27 for the NFL title; Kansas City defeated the Buffalo Bills 31-7 for the AFL title
Players' Shares—$15,000 to each member of the winning team; $7,500 to each member of the losing team
Attendance—61,946
Gross Receipts—$2,768,259.64
Officials—Referee, Norm Schacter, NFL; umpire, George Young, AFL; line judge, Al Sabato, AFL; head linesman, Bernie Ulman, NFL; back judge, Jack Reader, AFL; field judge, Mike Lisetski, NFL
Coaches—Vince Lombardi, Green Bay; Hank Stram, Kansas City

Kansas City	Starters, Offense	Green Bay
Chris Burford	LE	Carroll Dale
Jim Tyrer	LT	Bob Skoronski
Ed Budde	LG	Fred (Fuzzy) Thurston
Wayne Frazier	C	Bill Curry
Curt Merz	RG	Jerry Kramer
Dave Hill	RT	Forrest Gregg
Fred Arbanas	RE	Marv Fleming
Len Dawson	QB	Bart Starr
Otis Taylor	FL	Boyd Dowler
Mike Garrett	RB	Elijah Pitts
Curtis McClinton	RB	Jim Taylor
	Starters, Defense	
Jerry Mays	LE	Willie Davis
Andy Rice	LT	Ron Kostelnik
Buck Buchanan	RT	Henry Jordan
Chuck Hurston	RE	Lionel Aldridge
Bobby Bell	LLB	Dave Robinson
Sherrill Headrick	MLB	Ray Nitschke
E. J. Holub	RLB	Lee Roy Caffey
Fred Williamson	LHB	Herb Adderley
Willie Mitchell	RHB	Bob Jeter
Bobby Hunt	LS	Tom Brown
Johnny Robinson	RS	Willie Wood

Kansas City	0	10	0	0	—	10
Green Bay	7	7	14	7	—	35

GB—McGee 37 pass from Starr (Chandler kick)
KC—McClinton 7 pass from Dawson (Mercer kick)
GB—Taylor 14 run (Chandler kick)
KC—FG Mercer 31
GB—Pitts 5 run (Chandler kick)
GB—McGee 13 pass from Starr (Chandler kick)
GB—Pitts 1 run (Chandler kick)

TEAM STATISTICS	KC	GB
First downs	17	21
Rushing	4	10
Passing	12	11
By penalty	1	0
Total yardage	239	358
Net rushing yardage	72	130
Net passing yardage	167	228
Passes att.-comp.-had int.	32-17-1	24-16-1

RUSHING

Kansas City—Dawson, 3 for 24; Garrett, 6 for 17; McClinton, 6 for 16; Beathard, 1 for 14; Coan, 3 for 1.
Green Bay—J. Taylor, 16 for 53; 1 TD; Pitts, 11 for 45, 2 TDs; D. Anderson, 4 for 30; Grabowski, 2 for 2.

PASSING

Kansas City—Dawson, 16 of 27 for 211, 1 TD, 1 int.; Beathard, 1 of 5 for 17.
Green Bay—Starr, 16 of 23 for 250, 2 TDs, 1 int.; Bratkowski, 0 of 1.

RECEIVING

Kansas City—Burford, 4 for 67; O. Taylor, 4 for 57; Garrett, 3 for 28; McClinton, 2 for 34, 1 TD; Arbanas, 2 for 30; Carolan, 1 for 7; Coan, 1 for 5.
Green Bay—McGee, 7 for 138, 2 TDs; Dale, 4 for 59; Pitts, 2 for 32; Fleming, 2 for 22; J. Taylor, 1 for −1.

PUNTING

Kansas City—Wilson, 7 for 317, 45.3 average.
Green Bay—Chandler, 3 for 130, 43.3 average; D. Anderson, 1 for 43.

PUNT RETURNS

Kansas City—Garrett, 2 for 17; E. Thomas, 1 for 2.
Green Bay—D. Anderson, 3 for 25; Wood, 1 for −2, 1 fair catch.

KICKOFF RETURNS

Kansas City—Coan, 4 for 87; Garrett, 2 for 23.
Green Bay—Adderley, 2 for 40; D. Anderson, 1 for 25.

INTERCEPTIONS

Kansas City—Mitchell, 1 for 0.
Green Bay—Wood, 1 for 50.

Dawson looks for a receiver as Green Bay's Davis closes in.

Kansas City's Mitchell is too late as Pitts scores the Packers' final touchdown.

GREEN BAY PACKERS

No.	Name	Pos.	Ht.	Wt.	Age	Year	College
26	Adderley, Herb	DB	6-0	210	27	6	Michigan State
82	Aldridge, Lionel	DE	6-4	245	25	4	Utah State
88	Anderson, Bill	E	6-3	216	30	8	Tennessee
44	Anderson, Donny	RB	6-2	210	22	1	Texas Tech
57	Bowman, Ken	C	6-3	230	23	3	Wisconsin
12	Bratkowski, Zeke	QB	6-3	200	34	11	Georgia
78	Brown, Bob	DE	6-5	270	25	1	Arkansas AM&N
40	Brown, Tom	DB	6-1	190	25	3	Maryland
60	Caffey, Lee Roy	LB	6-3	250	25	4	Texas A&M
34	Chandler, Don	PK	6-2	210	32	11	Florida
56	Crutcher, Tommy	LB	6-3	230	24	3	Texas Christian
50	Curry, Bill	C	6-2	235	24	2	Georgia Tech
84	Dale, Carroll	FL	6-2	200	28	7	Virginia Tech
87	Davis, Willie	DE	6-3	245	32	9	Grambling
86	Dowler, Boyd	E	6-5	225	28	8	Colorado
81	Fleming, Marv	TE	6-4	235	24	4	Utah
68	Gillingham, Gale	G	6-3	250	22	1	Minnesota
33	Grabowski, Jim	RB	6-2	215	21	1	Illinois
75	Gregg, Forrest	T	6-4	250	32	10	Southern Methodist
43	Hart, Doug	DB	6-0	190	27	3	Texas-Arlington
45	Hathcock, Dave	DB	6-0	190	23	1	Memphis State
5	Hornung, Paul	RB	6-2	215	30	9	Notre Dame
21	Jeter, Bob	DB	6-1	205	29	4	Iowa
74	Jordan, Henry	DT	6-3	250	31	10	Virginia
77	Kostelnik, Ron	DT	6-4	260	26	6	Cincinnati
64	Kramer, Jerry	G	6-3	245	30	9	Idaho
80	Long, Bob	FL	6-3	190	24	3	Wichita
27	Mack, Bill (Red)	FL	5-10	185	29	6	Notre Dame
85	McGee, Max	E	6-3	205	34	11	Tulane
66	Nitschke, Ray	LB	6-3	240	29	9	Illinois
22	Pitts, Elijah	RB	6-1	205	27	6	Philander Smith
89	Robinson, Dave	LB	6-3	245	25	4	Penn State
76	Skoronski, Bob	DT	6-3	250	32	9	Indiana
15	Starr, Bart	QB	6-1	200	32	11	Alabama
31	Taylor, Jim	RB	6-0	215	30	9	Louisiana State
63	Thurston, Fred (Fuzzy)	G	6-1	245	32	9	Valparaiso
37	Vandersea, Phil	RB	6-3	225	23	1	Massachusetts
73	Weatherwax, Jim	DT	6-7	275	23	1	Cal. State-L.A.
24	Wood, Willie	DB	5-10	190	29	7	USC
72	Wright, Steve	T	6-6	250	24	3	Alabama

Head coach—Vince Lombardi. **Assistants**—Phil Bengtson, Jerry Burns, John (Red) Cochran, Dave Hanner, Bob Schnelker, Ray Witecha.

KANSAS CITY CHIEFS

No.	Name	Pos.	Ht.	Wt.	Age	Year	College
52	Abell, Bud	LB	6-3	220	25	1	Missouri
84	Arbanas, Fred	TE	6-3	240	27	5	Michigan State
10	Beathard, Pete	QB	6-2	210	24	3	USC
78	Bell, Bobby	LB	6-4	228	26	4	Minnesota
61	Biodrowski, Denny	G	6-1	225	26	4	Memphis State
87	Brown, Aaron	DE	6-5	265	22	1	Minnesota
86	Buchanan, Buck	DT	6-7	287	26	4	Grambling
71	Budde, Ed	G	6-5	260	65	4	Michigan State
88	Burford, Chris	E	6-3	220	28	7	Stanford
80	Carolan, Reg	TE	6-6	238	25	5	Idaho
23	Coan, Bert	RB	6-4	220	26	5	Kansas
56	Corey, Walt	LB	6-1	233	28	6	Miami
16	Dawson, Len	QB	6-0	190	31	10	Purdue
72	DiMidio, Tony	T	6-3	250	25	1	West Chester State
66	Frazier, Wayne	C	6-3	245	25	3	Auburn
21	Garrett, Mike	RB	5-9	195	22	1	USC
69	Headrick, Sherrill	LB	6-2	240	29	8	Texas Christian
73	Hill, Dave	T	6-5	264	25	4	Auburn
55	Holub, E. J.	LB	6-4	236	28	6	Texas Tech
20	Hunt, Bobby	DB	6-1	193	24	5	Auburn
85	Hurston, Chuck	DE	6-6	240	24	2	Auburn
75	Mays, Jerry	DE	6-4	252	26	6	Southern Methodist
32	McClinton, Curtis	RB	6-3	227	27	5	Kansas
15	Mercer, Mike	K	6-0	210	28	6	Arizona State
64	Merz, Curt	G	6-4	267	27	7	Iowa
22	Mitchell, Willie	DB	6-1	185	24	3	Tennessee State
25	Pitts, Frank	FL	6-2	190	22	2	Southern U.
14	Ply, Bobby	DB	6-1	196	25	5	Baylor
60	Reynolds, Al	G	6-3	250	28	7	Tarkio, Mo.
58	Rice, Andy	DT	6-2	260	24	1	Texas Southern
42	Robinson, Johnny	DB	6-1	205	27	7	Louisiana State
17	Smith, Fletcher	DB	6-2	188	22	1	Tennessee State
35	Stover, Stewart (Smokey)	LB	6-0	227	27	7	N.E. Louisiana
89	Taylor, Otis	FL	6-2	211	23	2	Prairie View
18	Thomas, Emmitt	DB	6-2	189	22	1	Bishop
45	Thomas, Gene	RB	6-1	210	23	1	Florida A&M
77	Tyrer, Jim	T	6-6	292	27	6	Ohio State
24	Williamson, Fred	DB	6-3	209	28	7	Northwestern
44	Wilson, Jerrel	P	6-4	222	24	4	Southern Mississippi

Head coach—Hank Stram. **Assistants**—Tom Bettis, Darrell (Pete) Brewster, Chuck Mills, Tom Pratt, Bill Walsh.

SUPER BOWL II

GREEN BAY 33, OAKLAND 14

The Green Bay Packers, 14-point favorites at the start of the game, defeated the Oakland Raiders 33–14 for their second straight Super Bowl victory. Packers quarterback Bart Starr completed 13 of 24 passes for 202 yards and one touchdown and helped the Packers convert 6 of 11 third-down situations into first downs.

The Packers moved 34 yards in 10 plays the first time they had the ball. On fourth down and 11 yards for a first down at Oakland's 32, Don Chandler kicked a 39-yard field goal, his first of four. The Packers held the ball for 8:40 during their second possession, moving 84 yards, from their 3 to the Raiders' 13, in 17 plays. Chandler kicked a 20-yard field goal on fourth down for a 6–0 lead.

Green Bay increased its lead to 13–0 in the second quarter. On the first play from the Packers' 38-yard line after a punt, Starr passed to Boyd Dowler, a 6-foot 5-inch end who ran inside of cornerback Kent McCloughan and was beyond the last defender when he caught the ball and completed a 62-yard touchdown. "I just bulled by McCloughan," Dowler explained. "He was playing me tight and bumped me and I ran through him. There was no one left to stop me." Carroll Dale had been the primary receiver, but when the Raiders blitzed, Starr sensed that Dowler would be open and changed direction.

Oakland closed to 13–7 on the following series. The Raiders moved 78 yards in nine plays, scoring on Daryle Lamonica's 23-yard pass to end Bill Miller. The drive took 1:54 as Lamonica completed four of five passes for 58 yards. Miller got behind defensive backs Herb Adderley and Tom Brown in the end zone. "I was supposed to take Miller deep, but I played him too 'soft,'" said Brown. "Linebacker Dave Robinson dropped back with him as far as he could and I should have taken him, but I didn't."

Green Bay led 16–7 at halftime after Oakland's Rodger Bird fumbled a fair catch on a punt at the Raiders' 45-yard line. Dick Capp, who had been activated by Green Bay the day before, made the recovery. Starr completed a pass to Dowler for a nine-yard gain to the 36 with six seconds left in the half. Chandler then kicked a 43-yard field goal.

The Packers broke open the game in the third quarter, just as they had done in defeating the Kansas City Chiefs 35–10 in Super Bowl I. They went 82 yards in 11 plays on their second possession. Donny Anderson scored a touchdown from the 2-yard line to make the score 23–7. Starr converted two third-down situations during that drive, once passing to Max McGee for a 25-yard gain on third and one and passing 11 yards to Dale on third and nine.

Chandler's 31-yard field goal gave Green Bay a 26–7 lead at the end of the quarter. Early in the fourth period, defensive back Herb Adderley intercepted a pass by Lamonica and ran 60 yards for Green Bay's final touchdown. "Lamonica was trying to hit Fred Biletnikoff on a slant-in," said Adderley. "I played the ball and cut in front of him. It was no gamble."

Oakland scored the final touchdown with 9:13 remaining in the game. The Raiders went 74 yards in four plays, Lamonica throwing to Miller again for 23 yards and the touchdown. Miller beat Brown once more after a pass play from Lamonica to Pete Banaszak covered 41 yards and set up the play.

"It wasn't our best," said Packers coach Vince Lombardi of his team's effort. "All year it seemed like as soon as we got a couple touchdowns ahead we let up. Maybe that's the sign of a veteran team, such as ours. I don't know."

Several days after the game Lombardi announced that he was retiring as the Packers' coach to devote full time to his job as general manager.

Green Bay's Brown watches as Miller pulls in his second touchdown pass for Oakland.

Participants—Green Bay Packers, champions of the National Football League, and Oakland Raiders, champions of the American Football League

Date—January 14, 1968

Site—Orange Bowl, Miami

Time—3:05 P.M. EST

Conditions—86 degrees, partly cloudy

Playing Surface—Grass

Television and Radio—Columbia Broadcasting System (CBS)

Regular Season Records—Green Bay, 9-4-1, Oakland, 13-1

League Championships—Green Bay defeated the Dallas Cowboys 21-17 for the NFL title; Oakland defeated the Houston Oilers 40-7 for the AFL title

Players' Shares—$15,000 to each member of the winning team; $7,500 to each member of the losing team

Attendance—75,546

Gross Receipts—$3,349,106.89

Officials—Referee, Jack Vest, AFL; umpire, Ralph Morcroft, NFL; line judge, Bruce Alford, NFL; head linesman, Tony Veteri, AFL; back judge, Stan Javie, NFL; field judge, Bob Bauer, AFL judge

Coaches—Vince Lombardi, Green Bay; John Rauch, Oakland

Green Bay	Starters, Offense	Oakland
Boyd Dowler	LE	Bill Miller
Bob Skoronski	LT	Bob Svihus
Gale Gillingham	LG	Gene Upshaw
Ken Bowman	C	Jim Otto
Jerry Kramer	RG	Wayne Hawkins
Forrest Gregg	RT	Harry Schuh
Marv Fleming	RE	Billy Cannon
Bart Starr	QB	Daryle Lamonica
Carroll Dale	FL	Fred Biletnikoff
Donny Anderson	RB	Pete Banaszak
Ben Wilson	RB	Hewritt Dixon
	Starters, Defense	
Willie Davis	LE	Isaac Lassiter
Ron Kostelnik	LT	Dan Birdwell
Henry Jordan	RT	Tom Keating
Lionel Aldridge	RE	Ben Davidson
Dave Robinson	LLB	Bill Laskey
Ray Nitschke	MLB	Dan Conners
Lee Roy Caffey	RLB	Gus Otto
Herb Adderley	LHB	Kent McCloughan
Bob Jeter	RHB	Willie Brown
Tom Brown	LS	Warren Powers
Willie Wood	RS	Howie Williams

Green Bay	3	13	10	7	— 33
Oakland	0	7	0	7	— 14

GB —FG Chandler 39
GB —FG Chandler 20
GB —Dowler 62 pass from Starr (Chandler kick)
Oak—Miller 23 pass from Lamonica (Blanda kick)
GB —FG Chandler 43
GB —Anderson 2 run (Chandler kick)
GB —FG Chandler 31
GB —Adderley 60 interception (Chandler kick)
Oak—Miller 23 pass from Lamonica (Blanda kick)

TEAM STATISTICS

	GB	Oak
First downs	19	16
Rushing	11	5
Passing	7	10
By penalty	1	1
Total yardage	322	293
Net rushing yardage	160	107
Net passing yardage	162	186
Passes att.-comp.-had int.	24-13-0	34-15-1

RUSHING

Green Bay—Wilson, 17 for 62; Anderson, 14 for 48, 1 TD; Williams, 8 for 36; Starr, 1 for 14; Mercein, 1 for 0.

Oakland—Dixon, 12 for 54; Todd, 2 for 37; Banaszak, 6 for 16.

PASSING

Green Bay—Starr, 13 of 24 for 202, 1 TD.

Oakland—Lamonica, 15 of 34 for 208, 2 TDs, 1 int.

RECEIVING

Green Bay—Dale, 4 for 43; Fleming, 4 for 35; Anderson, 2 for 18; Dowler, 2 for 71, 1 TD; McGee, 1 for 35.

Oakland—Miller, 5 for 84, 2 TDs; Banaszak, 4 for 69; Biletnikoff, 2 for 10; Cannon, 2 for 25; Dixon, 1 for 3; Wells, 1 for 17.

PUNTING

Green Bay—Anderson, 6 for 234, 39.0 average.

Oakland—Eischeid, 6 for 264, 44.0 average.

PUNT RETURNS

Green Bay—Wood, 5 for 35.

Oakland—Bird, 2 for 12, 1 fair catch.

KICKOFF RETURNS

Green Bay—Adderley, 1 for 24; Williams, 1 for 18; Crutcher, 1 for 7.

Oakland—Todd, 3 for 63; Grayson, 2 for 61; Hawkins, 1 for 3; Kocourek, 1 for 0, Kocourek lateraled to Grayson, who returned 11 yards.

INTERCEPTIONS

Green Bay—Adderley, 1 for 60, 1 TD.

Oakland—None.

Adderley steps in front of Biletnikoff to intercept; he went 60 yards to score.

Starr lofts a pass for Green Bay over the onrushing Birdwell.

GREEN BAY PACKERS

No.	Name	Pos.	Ht.	Wt.	Age	Year	College
26	Adderley, Herb	DB	6-0	200	28	7	Michigan State
82	Aldridge, Lionel	DE	6-4	245	26	5	Utah State
44	Anderson, Donny	RB	6-3	210	24	2	Texas Tech
57	Bowman, Ken	C	6-3	230	24	4	Wisconsin
12	Bratkowski, Zeke	QB	6-3	210	34	12	Georgia
83	Brown, Allen	TE	6-5	235	24	2	Mississippi
78	Brown, Bob	DE	6-5	260	26	2	Arkansas AM&N
40	Brown, Tom	DB	6-1	195	26	4	Maryland
60	Caffey, Lee Roy	LB	6-3	250	26	5	Texas A&M
88	Capp, Dick	TE	6-3	235	23	1	Boston College
34	Chandler, Don	K	6-2	210	33	12	Florida
56	Crutcher, Tommy	LB	6-3	230	25	4	Texas Christian
84	Dale, Carroll	E	6-2	200	28	8	Virginia Tech
87	Davis, Willie	DE	6-3	245	32	10	Grambling
86	Dowler, Boyd	E	6-5	225	29	9	Colorado
55	Flanigan, Jim	LB	6-3	240	21	1	Pittsburgh
81	Fleming, Marv	TE	6-4	235	25	5	Utah
68	Gillingham, Gale	G	6-3	255	23	2	Minnesota
33	Grabowski, Jim	RB	6-2	220	23	2	Illinois
75	Gregg, Forrest	T	6-4	250	33	11	Southern Methodist
43	Hart, Doug	DB	6-0	190	28	4	Texas-Arlington
13	Horn, Don	QB	6-2	195	22	1	San Diego State
50	Hyland, Bob	C-G	6-5	250	21	1	Boston College
21	Jeter, Bob	DB	6-1	205	30	5	Iowa
74	Jordan, Henry	DT	6-3	250	32	11	Virginia
77	Kostelnik, Ron	DT	6-4	260	27	7	Cincinnati
64	Kramer, Jerry	G	6-3	245	31	10	Idaho
80	Long, Bob	FL	6-3	205	24	4	Wichita
85	McGee, Max	E	6-3	210	35	12	Tulane
30	Mercein, Chuck	FB	6-2	225	24	4	Yale
66	Nitschke, Ray	LB	6-3	235	30	10	Illinois
89	Robinson, Dave	LB	6-3	240	26	5	Penn State
45	Rowser, John	DB	6-1	180	21	1	Michigan
76	Skoronski, Bob	T	6-3	245	33	10	Indiana
15	Starr, Bart	QB	6-1	190	33	12	Alabama
63	Thurston, Fred (Fuzzy)	G	6-1	245	33	10	Valparaiso
73	Weatherwax, Jim	DL	6-7	260	24	2	Cal. State-L.A.
23	Williams, Travis	HB	6-1	210	21	1	Arizona State
36	Wilson, Ben	FB	6-1	230	27	4	USC
24	Wood, Willie	DB	5-10	190	30	8	USC
72	Wright, Steve	T	6-6	250	25	4	Alabama

Head coach—Vince Lombardi. **Assistants**—Phil Bengtson, Jerry Burns, Dave Hanner, Tom McCormick, Bob Schnelker, Ray Witecha.

OAKLAND RAIDERS

No.	Name	Pos.	Ht.	Wt.	Age	Year	College
78	Archer, Dan	G-T	6-5	245	22	1	Oregon
40	Banaszak, Pete	RB	5-11	200	23	2	Miami
50	Benson, Duane	LB	6-2	215	21	1	Hamline
25	Biletnikoff, Fred	FL	6-1	190	24	3	Florida State
21	Bird, Rodger	DB	5-11	195	23	2	Kentucky
53	Birdwell, Dan	DT	6-4	250	29	6	Houston
16	Blanda, George	K-QB	6-3	215	40	18	Kentucky
24	Brown, Willie	DB	6-1	190	27	5	Grambling
48	Budness, Bill	LB	6-2	215	24	4	Boston U.
33	Cannon, Billy	TE	6-1	215	30	8	Louisiana State
55	Conners, Dan	LB	6-1	230	25	4	Miami
83	Davidson, Ben	DE	6-7	265	28	7	Washington
35	Dixon, Hewritt	RB	6-1	220	26	5	Florida A&M
11	Eischeid, Mike	K	6-0	190	26	2	Upper Iowa
45	Grayson, Dave	DB	5-10	185	28	7	Oregon
30	Hagberg, Roger	RB	6-1	215	28	6	Minnesota
70	Harvey, Jim	G	6-5	245	23	2	Mississippi
65	Hawkins, Wayne	G	6-0	240	29	8	Pacific
84	Herock, Ken	E	6-2	230	26	4	West Virginia
74	Keating, Tom	DT	6-2	247	25	4	Michigan
88	Kocourek, Dave	TE	6-5	240	29	9	Wisconsin
62	Kruse, Bob	G	6-2	250	22	5	Wayne State
3	Lamonica, Daryle	QB	6-3	215	25	5	Notre Dame
42	Laskey, Bill	LB	6-3	235	25	3	Michigan
77	Lassiter, Isaac	DE	6-5	270	26	6	St. Augustine, N.C.
47	McCloughan, Kent	DB	6-1	190	23	3	Nebraska
89	Miller, Bill	E	6-0	190	28	6	Miami
85	Oats, Carleton	DE	6-2	235	24	3	Florida A&M
34	Otto, Gus	LB	6-2	220	24	3	Missouri
00	Otto, Jim	C	6-2	240	28	8	Miami
20	Powers, Warren	DB	6-0	190	26	5	Nebraska
79	Schuh, Harry	T	6-2	260	24	3	Memphis State
23	Sherman, Rod	FL	6-0	190	21	1	USC
73	Sligh, Richard	DT-DE	7-0	300	22	1	North Carolina College
76	Svihus, Bob	T	6-4	245	24	3	USC
22	Todd, Larry	RB	6-1	185	24	3	Arizona State
63	Upshaw, Gene	G	6-5	255	22	1	Texas A&I
81	Wells, Warren	E	6-1	190	24	2	Texas Southern
29	Williams, Howie	DB	6-1	186	28	6	Howard
52	Williamson, John	LB	6-2	220	25	4	Louisiana Tech

Head coach—John Rauch. **Assistants**—Tom Dahms, John Madden, John Polonchek, Ollie Spencer, Charlie Sumner.

SUPER BOWL III

N.Y. JETS 16, BALTIMORE 7

The New York Jets defeated the Baltimore Colts 16–7 to become the first American Football League team to defeat a National Football League team in the Super Bowl. Quarterback Joe Namath "guaranteed" a victory by the Jets, although the Colts were favored by three touchdowns and were considered one of the greatest teams in the 49-year history of the NFL.

Namath appeared at the Miami Touchdown Club dinner at Miami Springs Villa to receive an award three days before the game. "This isn't an award for me," he said of a player-of-the-year honor presented by AFL commissioner Milt Woodard. "Had it not been for my high school coach, Larry Bruno, and my college coach at Alabama, Paul Bryant, and many other people—including all my teammates—I wouldn't be here. This should be a most valuable player award for the entire team. You can be the greatest athlete in the entire world, but if you don't win those football games, it doesn't mean anything.

"And we're going to win Sunday, I'll guarantee you."

Namath's remarks made national headlines and caused widespread comment among other Jets and Colts. It created more interest in a game that many thought would be more one-sided than the Green Bay Packers' 35-10 and 33–14 victories over AFL champion teams in Super Bowls I and II. One sportswriter predicted the Colts would win 55–0; another forecast a Baltimore victory by 48–0.

The Jets took the opening kickoff. On the first play fullback Matt Snell gained three yards at left tackle. On the second play, Snell gained nine yards before he was tackled by safety Rick Volk. When the players unpiled after the tackle Snell returned to the Jets' huddle. But Volk remained on the ground. Volk had been knocked momentarily unconscious by the impact of the collision. The Jets had established a running game in which Snell would set Super Bowl records with 30 carries for 121 yards.

The Jets took a 7–0 lead in the second quarter when Snell ran four yards off left tackle, ending an 80-yard, 12-play drive. Snell gained 35 yards in six carries during the drive and Namath completed four of five passes for 43 yards, including one pass of 12 yards to Snell.

Field goals of 32, 30, and 9 yards by Jim Turner gave the Jets a 16–0 lead in the fourth quarter.

Baltimore marched 80 yards in 15 plays to score its touchdown, a one-yard run by fullback Jerry Hill with 3:19 left in the game. The Colts' Tom Mitchell recovered Lou Michaels's onside kick after the touchdown and Baltimore moved to New York's 19, but John Unitas's fourth-down pass to Jimmy Orr was overthrown and New York took over with 2:21 remaining.

Unitas, who missed most of the season with an injury, replaced Earl Morrall in the third quarter as Baltimore's quarterback. Morrall, the NFL's most valuable player in 1968, missed an open receiver, Orr, in the end zone near the end of the half; a Morrall pass to Jerry Hill was intercepted by Jim Hudson on a play which began with Morrall's handing off to Tom Matte, who passed back to Morrall. The quarterback did not see Orr.

"We didn't make the big plays we have all season," said Baltimore coach Don Shula. "We just didn't do it . . . they deserved the victory."

Namath at first refused to talk to writers from cities with teams in the NFL when the Jets opened their dressing room to the media. "If you had seen us all year, you wouldn't have been surprised," he said.

"Hello, world, welcome to the American Football League," said Turner, the Jets' kicker.

Curtis (32) blitzes for Baltimore but Namath gets the pass away on time to Mathis (31).

Participants—New York Jets, champions of the American Football League, and Baltimore Colts, champions of the National Football League

Date—January 12, 1969

Site—Orange Bowl, Miami

Time—3:05 P.M. EST

Conditions—73 degrees, overcast, threat of rain

Playing Surface—Grass

Television and Radio—National Broadcasting Company (NBC)

Regular Season Records—New York, 11-3; Baltimore, 13-1

League Championships—New York defeated Oakland Raiders 27-23 for the AFL title; Baltimore defeated Cleveland Browns 34-0 for the NFL title

Players' Shares—$15,000 to each member of the winning team; $7,500 to each member of the losing team

Attendance—75,389

Gross Receipts—$3,349,106.89

Officials—Referee, Tommy Bell, NFL; umpire, Walt Parker, AFL; line judge, Cal LePore, AFL; head linesman, George Murphy, NFL; back judge, Jack Reader, AFL; field judge, Joe Gonzales, NFL

Coaches—Weeb Ewbank, New York; Don Shula, Baltimore .

N.Y. Jets	Starters, Offense	Baltimore
George Sauer	LE	Jimmy Orr
Winston Hill	LT	Bob Vogel
Bob Talamini	LG	Glenn Ressler
John Schmitt	C	Bill Curry
Randy Rasmussen	RG	Dan Sullivan
Dave Herman	RT	Sam Ball
Pete Lammons	RE	John Mackey
Joe Namath	QB	Earl Morrall
Don Maynard	FL	Willie Richardson
Emerson Boozer	RB	Tom Matte
Matt Snell	RB	Jerry Hill
	Starters, Defense	
Gerry Philbin	LE	Charles (Bubba) Smith
Paul Rochester	LT	Billy Ray Smith
John Elliott	RT	Fred Miller
Verlon Biggs	RE	Ordell Braase
Ralph Baker	LLB	Mike Curtis
Al Atkinson	MLB	Dennis Gaubatz
Larry Grantham	RLB	Don Shinnick
Johnny Sample	LHB	Bobby Boyd
Randy Beverly	RHB	Lenny Lyles
Jim Hudson	LS	Jerry Logan
Bill Baird	RS	Rick Volk

New York Jets	0	7	6	3	— 16
Baltimore	0	0	0	7	— 7

NYJ—Snell 4 run (Turner kick)
NYJ—FG Turner 32
NYJ—FG Turner 30
NYJ—FG Turner 9
Balt—Hill 1 run (Michaels kick)

TEAM STATISTICS	NYJ	Balt
First downs	21	18
Rushing	10	7
Passing	10	9
By penalty	1	2
Total yardage	337	324
Net rushing yardage	142	143
Net passing yardage	195	181
Passes att.-comp.-had int.	29-17-0	41-17-4

RUSHING

New York Jets—Snell, 30 for 121, 1 TD; Boozer, 10 for 19; Mathis, 3 for 2.

Baltimore—Matte, 11 for 116; Hill, 9 for 29, 1 TD; Unitas, 1 for 0; Morrall, 2 for −2.

PASSING

New York Jets—Namath, 17 of 28 for 206; Parilli, 0 of 1.

Baltimore—Morrall, 6 of 17 for 71, 3 int.; Unitas, 11 of 24 for 110, 1 int.

RECEIVING

New York Jets—Sauer, 8 for 133; Snell, 4 for 40; Mathis, 3 for 20; Lammons, 2 for 13.

Baltimore—Richardson, 6 for 58; Orr, 3 for 42; Mackey, 3 for 35; Matte, 2 for 30; Hill, 2 for 1; Mitchell, 1 for 15.

PUNTING

New York Jets—C. Johnson, 4 for 155, 38.8 average.

Baltimore—Lee, 3 for 144, 44.3 average.

PUNT RETURNS

New York Jets—Baird, 1 for 0, 1 fair catch.

Baltimore—Brown, 4 for 34.

KICKOFF RETURNS

New York Jets—Christy, 1 for 25.

Baltimore—Pearson, 2 for 59; Brown, 2 for 46.

INTERCEPTIONS

New York Jets—Beverly, 2 for 0; Hudson, 1 for 9; Sample, 1 for 0.

Baltimore—None

Snell starts one of the weakside slants he ran the entire game for 121 yards.

Matte goes 58 yards in the second quarter; an interception ended the drive.

NEW YORK JETS

No.	Name	Pos.	Ht.	Wt.	Age	Year	College
62	Atkinson, Al	LB	6-2	230	25	4	Villanova
46	Baird, Bill	DB	5-10	180	29	6	San Francisco State
51	Baker, Ralph	LB	6-3	235	26	5	Penn State
42	Beverly, Randy	DB	5-11	198	24	2	Colorado State
86	Biggs, Verlon	DE	6-4	268	25	4	Jackson State
32	Boozer, Emerson	HB	5-11	202	25	3	Maryland State
45	Christy, Earl	DB	5-11	195	25	3	Maryland State
56	Crane, Paul	LB-C	6-2	205	24	3	Alabama
47	D'Amato, Mike	DB	6-2	204	25	1	Hofstra
43	Dockery, John	DB	6-0	186	23	1	Harvard
80	Elliott, John	DT	6-4	249	23	2	Texas
48	Gordon, Cornell	DB	6-0	187	27	4	North Carolina A&T
60	Grantham, Larry	LB	6-0	212	30	9	Mississippi
67	Herman, Dave	G	6-1	255	27	5	Michigan State
75	Hill, Winston	T	6-4	280	26	6	Texas Southern
22	Hudson, Jim	DB	6-2	210	25	4	Texas
33	Johnson, Curley	P-TE	6-0	215	33	11	Houston
87	Lammons, Pete	TE	6-3	233	24	3	Texas
31	Mathis, Bill	HB	6-1	220	29	9	Clemson
13	Maynard, Don	FL	6-1	179	31	11	Texas-El Paso
50	McAdams, Carl	DT-LB	6-3	245	24	2	Oklahoma
12	Namath, Joe	QB	6-2	195	25	4	Alabama
63	Neidert, John	LB	6-2	230	23	1	Louisville
15	Parilli, Babe	QB	6-0	190	38	15	Kentucky
81	Philbin, Gerry	DE	6-2	245	27	5	Buffalo
23	Rademacher, Bill	SE	6-1	190	26	5	Northern Michigan
66	Rasmussen, Randy	G	6-2	255	23	2	Kearney State
26	Richards, Jim	DB	6-1	180	21	1	Virginia Tech
74	Richardson, Jeff	T-C	6-3	250	23	2	Michigan State
72	Rochester, Paul	DT	6-2	250	30	9	Michigan State
24	Sample, John	DB	6-1	204	31	11	Maryland State
83	Sauer, George	SE	6-2	195	24	4	Texas
52	Schmitt, John	C	6-4	245	24	5	Hofstra
30	Smolinski, Mark	FB	6-1	215	29	8	Wyoming
41	Snell, Matt	FB	6-2	219	27	5	Ohio State
61	Talamini, Bob	G	6-1	255	29	9	Kentucky
85	Thompson, Steve	DE	6-5	240	23	1	Washington
29	Turner, Robert (Bake)		6-1	179	28	7	Texas Tech
11	Turner, Jim	K-QB	6-2	205	27	5	Utah State
71	Walton, Sam	T	6-5	276	25	1	East Texas State

Head coach—Weeb Ewbank. **Assistants**—Walt Michaels, Clive Rush, Buddy Ryan, Jose Spencer.

BALTIMORE COLTS

No.	Name	Pos.	Ht.	Wt.	Age	Year	College
37	Austin, Ocie	DB	6-3	200	21	1	Utah State
73	Ball, Sam	T	6-4	240	24	3	Kentucky
40	Boyd, Bobby	DB	5-10	192	30	9	Oklahoma
81	Braase, Ordell	DE	6-4	245	36	12	South Dakota
2	Brown, Timmy	RB	5-11	200	31	10	Ball State
34	Cole, Terry	RB	6-1	220	22	1	Indiana
50	Curry, Bill	C	6-2	235	26	4	Georgia Tech
32	Curtis, Mike	LB	6-2	232	24	4	Duke
53	Gaubatz, Dennis	LB	6-2	232	28	6	Lousiana State
25	Hawkins, Alex	FL	6-1	186	31	10	South Carolina
45	Hill, Jerry	RB	5-11	215	28	7	Wyoming
85	Hilton, Roy	DE	6-6	240	25	4	Jackson State
61	Johnson, Cornelius	G	6-2	245	24	1	Virginia Union
49	Lee, David	K	6-4	215	24	3	Louisiana Tech
20	Logan, Jerry	DB	6-1	190	27	6	West Texas State
43	Lyles, Lenny	DB	6-2	204	32	11	Louisville
88	Mackey, John	TE	6-2	224	26	6	Syracuse
41	Matte, Tom	RB	6-0	214	29	8	Ohio State
79	Michaels, Lou	DE-K	6-2	250	31	11	Kentucky
76	Miller, Fred	DT	6-3	250	28	6	Louisiana State
84	Mitchell, Tom	TE	6-2	235	23	1	Bucknell
15	Morrall, Earl	QB	6-2	206	34	13	Michigan State
28	Orr, Jimmy	FL	5-11	185	32	11	Georgia
26	Pearson, Preston	RB	6-1	190	23	2	Illinois
27	Perkins, Ray	E	6-0	183	26	2	Alabama
55	Porter, Ron	LB	6-2	232	23	2	Idaho
62	Ressler, Glenn	G	6-3	250	25	4	Penn State
87	Richardson, Willie	FL	6-2	198	28	6	Jackson State
66	Shinnick, Don	LB	6-0	228	33	12	UCLA
74	Smith, Billy Ray	DT	6-4	250	33	10	Arkansas
78	Smith, Charles (Bubba)	DE	6-7	295	23	2	Michigan State
47	Stukes, Charlie	DB	6-3	212	24	2	Maryland State
71	Sullivan, Dan	G	6-3	250	29	7	Boston College
52	Szymanski, Dick	C	6-3	235	35	13	Notre Dame
19	Unitas, John	QB	6-1	196	35	13	Louisville
72	Vogel, Bob	T	6-5	250	26	6	Ohio State
21	Volk, Rick	DB	6-3	195	23	2	Michigan
16	Ward, Jim	QB	6-2	195	24	2	Gettysburg
75	Williams, John	G	6-3	256	22	1	Minnesota
64	Williams, Sidney	LB	6-2	235	26	5	Southern U.

Head coach—Don Shula. **Assistants**—Bill Arnsparger, Dick Bielski, Don McCafferty, Chuck Noll, John Sandusky.

SUPER BOWL IV

KANSAS CITY 23, MINNESOTA 7

Quarterback Len Dawson, who missed six regular season games because of a knee injury and whose name had been linked to a federal gambling investigation in Detroit five days before the Super Bowl, completed 12 of 17 passes for 142 yards and one touchdown as the Kansas City Chiefs defeated the Minnesota Vikings 23–7.

The Chiefs' victory was the second in a row by an AFL team over a heavily favored NFL team. The New York Jets were three-touchdown underdogs before they defeated Baltimore in Super Bowl III; the Chiefs were two-touchdown underdogs before the fourth Super Bowl.

Dawson was eventually cleared of impropriety in the gambling investigation. The attention made him the focal point in the game; an added burden was what many considered a poor performance by Dawson in Super Bowl I, when the Chiefs were beaten by Green Bay 35–10.

Whereas the Chiefs never led in Super Bowl I, they never trailed in Super Bowl IV. They marched 42 yards to Jan Stenerud's 48-yard field goal the first time they had the ball. They moved 55 yards to Stenerud's 32-yard field goal on their second possession, and they went 27 yards to Stenerud's 25-yard field goal the third time.

This gave Kansas City a 9–0 lead with 6:52 left in the half. Charlie West fumbled Stenerud's kickoff after the third field goal and Remi Prudhomme recovered for the Chiefs at Minnesota's 19-yard line. Dawson was tackled for a loss of eight yards by Jim Marshall on the first play. Fullback Wendell Hayes ran 13 yards on the second play and Dawson passed 10 yards to Otis Taylor on the third play. Halfback Mike Garrett lost a yard to the 5 on the following play. Dawson kept the ball for no gain and it was third down. On the next play, the Chiefs' line pulled in one direction; the Vikings gave pursuit, and Garrett went back against the grain and scored a five-yard touchdown for a 16–0 lead with 5:34 remaining in the half.

The Vikings forced the Chiefs to punt on the first series of the third quarter and took possession on their 31-yard line. They moved 69 yards in 10 plays, scoring on Dave Osborn's four-yard run with 4:32 left in the quarter. The touchdown made the score 16–7. "Let's put out that fire, Lenny," Chiefs coach Hank Stram said to Dawson. "Let's make sure they don't get any closer." The Chiefs started from their 18-yard line. In five plays they had reached their 32; it was third down and seven yards for a first down.

Dawson had handed the ball to receiver Frank Pitts on reverses twice in the first half. Pitts had gained 19 yards the first time as the Chiefs marched to their third field goal. He had gained 11 yards the second time. Dawson called for the reverse a third time and Pitts gained seven yards, enough for another first down.

From the Minnesota 46, Dawson threw a short pass to Taylor, who caught the ball on the 41 in front of Earsell Mackbee. Taylor ran through Mackbee, who had suffered a pinched nerve in his neck earlier and whose arm was numb. The last person with a chance to catch Taylor was Vikings' safety Karl Kassulke. Taylor faked Kassulke, who fell down at the 10-yard line.

The touchdown gave Kansas City a 23–7 lead with 1:22 remaining in the third quarter. The Vikings had the ball three times in the fourth quarter, giving it up at Kansas City's 46 and their 38 and 48.

"The best thing about this game is that we don't have to answer for it next three years, like we did last time," said Dawson after the victory. Then Dawson went to answer a telephone call. It was President Richard Nixon, offering his congratulations.

Garrett scores a five-yard touchdown, giving Kansas City a 16–0 lead at halftime.

Participants—Kansas City Chiefs, champions of the American Football League, and Minnesota Vikings, champions of the National Football League
Date—January 11, 1970
Site—Tulane Stadium, New Orleans
Time—2:35 P.M. CST
Conditions—61 degrees, heavy overcast, wet field
Playing Surface—Grass
Television and Radio—Columbia Broadcasting System (CBS)
Regular Season Records—Kansas City, 11-3; Minnesota, 12-2
League Championships—Kansas City defeated the Oakland Raiders 17-7 for the AFL title; Minnesota defeated the Cleveland Browns 27-7 for the NFL title
Players' Shares—$15,000 to each member of the winning team; $7,500 to each member of the losing team
Attendance—80,562
Gross Receipts—$3,817,872.69
Officials—Referee, John McDonough, NFL; umpire, Lou Palazzi, AFL; line judge, Bill Schleibaum, NFL; head linesman, Harry Kessel, NFL; back judge, Tom Kelleher, NFL; field judge, Charlie Musser, AFL
Coaches—Hank Stram, Kansas City; Bud Grant, Minnesota

Minnesota	0	0	7	0	—	7
Kansas City	3	13	7	0	—	23

KC —FG Stenerud 32
KC —FG Stenerud 25
KC —Garrett 5 run (Stenerud kick)
Minn—Osborn 4 run (Cox kick)
KC —Taylor 46 pass from Dawson (Stenerud kick)

TEAM STATISTICS	Minn	KC
First downs	13	18
Rushing	2	8
Passing	10	7
By penalty	1	3
Total yardage	239	279
Net rushing yardage	67	157
Net passing yardage	172	122
Passes att.-comp.-had int.	28-17-3	17-12-0

RUSHING
Minnesota—Brown, 6 for 26; Reed, 4 for 17; Osborn, 7 for 15, 1 TD; Kapp, 2 for 9.
Kansas City—Garrett, 11 for 39, 1 TD; Pitts, 3 for 37; Hayes, 8 for 31; McVea, 12 for 26; Dawson, 3 for 11; Holmes, 5 for 7.
PASSING
Minnesota—Kapp, 16 of 25 for 183, 2 int.; Cuozzo, 1 of 3 for 16, 1 int.
Kansas City—Dawson, 12 of 17 for 142, 1 TD, 1 int.
RECEIVING
Minnesota—Henderson, 7 for 111; Brown, 3 for 11; Beasley, 2 for 41; Reed, 2 for 16; Osborn, 2 for 11; Washington, 1 for 9.
Kansas City—Taylor, 6 for 81, 1 TD; Pitts, 3 for 33; Garrett, 2 for 25; Hayes, 1 for 3.
PUNTING
Minnesota—Lee, 3 for 111, 37.0 average.
Kansas City—Wilson, 4 for 194, 48.5 average.
PUNT RETURNS
Minnesota—West, 2 for 18
Kansas City—Garrett, 1 for 0.
KICKOFF RETURNS
Minnesota—West, 3 for 46; Jones, 1 for 33.
Kansas City—Hayes, 2 for 36.
INTERCEPTIONS
Minnesota—Krause, 1 for 0.
Kansas City—Lanier, 1 for 9; Robinson, 1 for 9; Thomas, 1 for 6.

Minnesota	Starters, Offense	Kansas City
Gene Washington	WR	Frank Pitts
Grady Alderman	LT	Jim Tyrer
Jim Vellone	LG	Ed Budde
Mick Tingelhoff	C	E. J. Holub
Milt Sunde	RG	Mo Moorman
Ron Yary	RT	Dave Hill
John Beasley	RE	Fred Arbanas
John Henderson	WR	Otis Taylor
Joe Kapp	QB	Len Dawson
Dave Osborn	RB	Mike Garrett
Bill Brown	RB	Robert Holmes
	Starters, Defense	
Carl Eller	LE	Jerry Mays
Gary Larsen	LT	Curley Culp
Alan Page	RT	Buck Buchanan
Jim Marshall	RE	Aaron Brown
Roy Winston	LLB	Bobby Bell
Lonnie Warwick	MLB	Willie Lanier
Wally Hilgenberg	RLB	Jim Lynch
Earsell Mackbee	LCB	Jim Marsalis
Ed Sharockman	RCB	Emmitt Thomas
Karl Kassulke	LS	Jim Kearney
Paul Krause	RS	Johnny Robinson

Minnesota's Brown tries to struggle out of grasp of Chiefs' Buchanan.

KANSAS CITY CHIEFS

No.	Name	Pos.	Ht.	Wt.	Age	Year	College
84	Arbanas, Fred	TE	6-3	240	30	8	Michigan State
78	Bell, Bobby	LB	6-4	228	29	7	Minnesota
24	Belser, Ceaser	S	6-0	212	24	2	Arkansas AM&N
87	Brown, Aaron	DE	6-5	265	25	3	Minnesota
86	Buchanan, Buck	DT	6-7	287	29	7	Grambling
71	Budde, Ed	G	6-5	260	28	7	Michigan State
61	Culp, Curley	DT	6-1	265	23	2	Arizona State
60	Daney, George	G	6-4	240	22	2	Texas-El Paso
16	Dawson, Len	QB	6-0	190	34	13	Purdue
12	Flores, Tom	QB	6-1	202	31	9	Pacific
21	Garrett, Mike	RB	5-9	190	25	4	USC
38	Hayes, Wendell	RB	6-1	220	27	5	Humboldt State
73	Hill, Dave	T	6-5	260	28	7	Auburn
45	Holmes, Robert	RB	5-9	220	23	2	Southern U.
55	Holub, E. J.	C	6-4	236	31	9	Texas Tech
85	Hurston, Chuck	LB	6-6	240	26	5	Auburn
46	Kearney, Jim	S	6-2	206	26	5	Prairie View
63	Lanier, Willie	LB	6-1	245	24	3	Morgan State
10	Livingston, Mike	QB	6-3	205	23	2	Southern Methodist
82	Lothamer, Ed	DT	6-5	270	26	6	Michigan State
51	Lynch, Jim	LB	6-1	235	24	3	Notre Dame
40	Marsalis, Jim	DB	5-11	194	24	1	Tennessee State
75	Mays, Jerry	DE	6-4	252	29	9	Southern Methodist
32	McClinton, Curtis	TE	6-3	227	29	8	Kansas
6	McVea, Warren	RB	5-10	182	23	2	Houston
22	Mitchell, Willie	CB	6-0	185	29	6	Tennessee State
76	Moorman, Mo	G	6-5	252	24	2	Texas A&M
25	Pitts, Frank	WR	6-2	199	25	5	Southern U.
14	Podolak, Ed	RB	6-1	204	22	1	Iowa
65	Prudhomme, Remi	C	6-4	250	27	4	Louisiana State
30	Richardson, Gloster	WR	6-0	200	26	3	Jackson State
42	Robinson, Johnny	S	6-1	205	31	10	Louisiana State
20	Sellers, Goldie	CB	6-2	198	27	4	Grambling
66	Stein, Bob	LB	6-3	235	21	1	Minnesota
3	Stenerud, Jan	K	6-2	187	26	3	Montana State
89	Taylor, Otis	WR	6-3	215	27	5	Prairie View
18	Thomas, Emmitt	CB	6-2	192	26	4	Bishop
74	Trosch, Gene	DE	6-7	277	24	2	Miami
77	Tyrer, Jim	T	6-6	275	30	9	Ohio State
44	Wilson, Jerrel	P	6-4	222	26	7	Southern Mississippi

Head coach—Hank Stram. **Assistants**—Tom Bettis, Darrell (Pete) Brewster, Tommy O'Boyle, Tom Pratt, Alvin Roy, Bill Walsh.

MINNESOTA VIKINGS

No.	Name	Pos.	Ht.	Wt.	Age	Year	College
67	Alderman, Grady	T	6-2	245	30	10	Detroit
87	Beasley, John	TE	6-3	230	24	3	California
30	Brown, Bill	RB	5-11	230	31	9	Illinois
14	Cox, Fred	K	5-10	200	30	7	Pittsburgh
15	Cuozzo, Gary	QB	6-1	195	28	7	Virginia
71	Davis, Doug	T	6-4	255	25	4	Kentucky
76	Dickson, Paul	DT	6-5	250	32	11	Baylor
81	Eller, Carl	DE	6-6	250	27	6	Minnesota
27	Grim, Bob	WR	6-0	195	24	3	Oregon State
49	Hackbart, Dale	S	6-3	205	31	8	Wisconsin
50	Hargrove, Jim	LB	6-3	233	24	2	Howard Payne
35	Harris, Bill	RB	6-2	204	23	2	Colorado
80	Henderson, John	WR	6-3	190	26	5	Michigan
58	Hilgenberg, Wally	LB	6-3	231	27	5	Iowa
26	Jones, Clinton	RB	6-0	200	24	3	Michigan State
11	Kapp, Joe	QB	6-3	208	31	3	California
29	Kassulke, Karl	S	6-0	195	28	7	Drake
89	Kramer, Kent	TE	6-4	235	25	3	Minnesota
22	Krause, Paul	S	6-3	188	27	6	Iowa
77	Larsen, Gary	DT	6-5	255	29	6	Concordia, Minn.
19	Lee, Bob	QB-P	6-3	195	24	1	Pacific
21	Lindsey, Jim	RB	6-2	210	24	4	Arkansas
46	Mackbee, Earsell	CB	6-0	195	28	5	Utah State
70	Marshall, Jim	DE	6-3	247	31	10	Ohio State
55	McGill, Mike	LB	6-2	235	22	2	Notre Dame
41	Osborn, Dave	RB	6-0	205	26	5	North Dakota
88	Page, Alan	DT	6-4	245	24	3	Notre Dame
32	Reed, Oscar	RB	6-0	220	25	2	Colorado State
57	Reilly, Mike	LB	6-2	240	27	6	Iowa
45	Sharockman, Ed	CB	6-0	200	29	8	Pittsburgh
74	Smith, Steve	DE	6-5	250	25	3	Michigan
64	Sunde, Milt	G	6-2	250	27	6	Minnesota
53	Tingelhoff, Mick	C	6-2	237	29	8	Nebraska
63	Vellone, Jim	G	6-3	255	25	4	USC
59	Warwick, Lonnie	LB	6-2	235	27	5	Tennessee Tech
84	Washington, Gene	WR	6-3	208	25	3	Michigan State
40	West, Charlie	S	6-1	190	23	2	Texas-El Paso
62	White, Ed	G	6-3	260	21	1	California
60	Winston, Roy	LB	5-11	226	29	8	Louisiana State
73	Yary, Ron	T	6-5	265	23	2	USC

Head coach—Bud Grant. **Assistants**—Jerry Burns, Bob Hollway, Bus Mertes, John Michels, Jack Patera, Jerry Reichow.

The Chiefs' Pitts on one of the three reverses he ran for 19, 11, and 7 yards.

SUPER BOWL V

BALTIMORE 16, DALLAS 13

Jim O'Brien's 32-yard field goal with five seconds remaining in the game gave Baltimore a 16–13 victory over the Dallas Cowboys in Super Bowl V, a game marked by 11 fumbles and interceptions and 14 penalties. The Colts led in interceptions and fumbles 7–4; Dallas led in penalties 9–4. "Super Bowl" now was the game's *official* designation after four years as "AFL-NFL World Championship Game."

Dallas moved 47 yards in eight plays to score on Mike Clark's 14-yard field goal for a 3–0 lead with 5:32 left in the first quarter. The Cowboys went 57 yards in eight plays to Clark's 30-yard field goal and a 6–0 advantage eight seconds into the second quarter.

Baltimore tied the score 42 seconds later. On the third play after the kickoff, quarterback John Unitas threw a medium-deep pass to Eddie Hinton. Hinton tipped the ball; Cowboys defensive back Mel Renfro also tipped the ball. Colts tight end John Mackey, who was running free behind the defense, finally caught the pass at Dallas's 45-yard line. Mackey ran untouched to the end zone, completing a 75-yard touchdown play. O'Brien's point after touchdown was blocked by Mark Washington when fullback Tom Nowatzke failed to pick up the defender.

The Cowboys moved in front 13–6 with 6:53 remaining in the half. Unitas, back to pass, scrambled under pressure and fumbled when he was hit by middle linebacker Lee Roy Jordan. Tackle Jethro Pugh recovered at Baltimore's 28-yard line. Three plays later quarterback Craig Morton threw a seven-yard scoring pass to rookie running back Duane Thomas.

Dallas had a chance to score another touchdown early in the third quarter, but Thomas fumbled on the 1-yard line when he was hit by safety Jerry Logan; Jim Duncan recovered for the Colts. A pass from Morton to running back Walt Garrison in the fourth quarter was intercepted by Colts safety Rick Volk, who returned the ball 30 yards to the Cowboys' 3. Nowatzke scored on the second play and O'Brien's point after touchdown made the score 13–13 with 6:35 left in the game.

Dallas took over on Baltimore's 48-yard line with 1:52 remaining after a punt. Thomas lost a yard on the first play and Fred Miller sacked Morton for a loss of nine on the second play. Dallas was penalized for holding on the same play and was pushed back on its 27-yard line with 1:09 remaining. Morton's high pass to running back Dan Reeves bounced off Reeves's hands and was intercepted by middle linebacker Mike Curtis, who ran 13 yards to Dallas's 28.

Two running plays gained three yards and used 50 of the remaining 59 seconds. The ball was on the Cowboy's 25-yard line when O'Brien entered the field of play for his field goal attempt. The Cowboys called time.

When play resumed, the Cowboys attempted to take time again but were informed by referee Norm Schachter that they could not call successive time outs without a play being run. The Cowboys were trying to unnerve O'Brien. When Morrall kneeled to take the snap from center Tom Goode, O'Brien whispered, "The wind . . . the wind?" "There is no wind," said Morrall. "Just kick the ball straight."

O'Brien's kick went end over end, curved toward the right goal post, then veered back to the middle and through the uprights.

When it was suggested the Colts were lucky to have won, guard Bob Vogel said, "So what? I've had luck decide against us so many times I'm sick of it. I quit being proud years ago when we lost games we should have won. The way I look at it, we're going to get the Super Bowl ring because we won the games that counted this year. We deserve it."

Dallas misses a chance to score in the third quarter as Thomas is hit and fumbles at the goal line.

Participants—Baltimore Colts, champions of the American Football Conference, and Dallas Cowboys, champions of the National Football Conference

Date—January 17, 1971

Site—Orange Bowl, Miami

Time—2:00 P.M. EST

Conditions—70 degrees, clear skies

Playing Surface—Poly-Turf

Television and Radio—National Broadcasting Company (NBC)

Regular Season Records—Baltimore, 11-2-1; Dallas, 10-4

Conference Championships—Baltimore defeated the Oakland Raiders 27-17 for the AFC title; Dallas defeated the San Francisco 49ers 17-10 for the NFC title

Players' Shares—$15,000 to each member of the winning team; $7,500 to each member of the losing team

Attendance—79,204

Gross Receipts—$3,991,820.01

Officials—Referee, Norm Schacter, umpire, Paul Trepinski; line judge, Jack Fette; head linesman, Ed Marion; back judge, Hugh Gamber; field judge, Fritz Graf

Coaches—Tom Landry, Dallas; Don McCafferty, Baltimore

Baltimore	Starters, Offense	Dallas
Eddie Hinton	WR	Bob Hayes
Bob Vogel	LT	Ralph Neely
Glenn Ressler	LG	John Niland
Bill Curry	C	Dave Manders
John Williams	RG	Blaine Nye
Dan Sullivan	RT	Rayfield Wright
John Mackey	TE	Pettis Norman
Roy Jefferson	WR	Reggie Rucker
John Unitas	QB	Craig Morton
Norm Bulaich	RB	Duane Thomas
Tom Nowatzke	RB	Walt Garrison
	Starters, Defense	
Charles (Bubba) Smith	LE	Larry Cole
Billy Ray Smith	LT	Jethro Pugh
Fred Miller	RT	Bob Lilly
Roy Hilton	RE	George Andrie
Ray May	LLB	Dave Edwards
Mike Curtis	MLB	Lee Roy Jordan
Ted Hendricks	RLB	Chuck Howley
Charlie Stukes	LC	Herb Adderley
Jim Duncan	RC	Mel Renfro
Jerry Logan	LS	Cornell Green
Rick Volk	RS	Charlie Waters

Baltimore	0	6	0	10	— 16
Dallas	3	10	0	0	— 13

Dall—FG Clark 14
Dall—FG Clark 30
Balt—Mackey 75 pass from Unitas (kick blocked)
Dall—Thomas 7 pass from Morton (Clark kick)
Balt—Nowatzke 2 run (O'Brien kick)
Balt—FG O'Brien 32

TEAM STATISTICS	Balt	Dall
First downs	14	10
Rushing	4	4
Passing	6	5
By penalty	4	1
Total yardage	329	215
Net rushing yardage	69	102
Net passing yardage	260	113
Passes att.-comp.-had int.	25-11-3	26-12-3

RUSHING

Baltimore—Nowatzke, 10 for 33, 1 TD; Bulaich, 18 for 28; Unitas, 1 for 4; Havrilak, 1 for 3; Morrall, 1 for 1.

Dallas—Garrison, 12 for 65; Thomas, 18 for 35; Morton, 1 for 2.

PASSING

Baltimore—Unitas, 3 of 9 for 88, 1 TD, 2 int.; Morrall, 7 for 15 for 147, 1 int.; Havrilak, 1 of 1 for 25.

Dallas—Morton, 12 of 26 for 127, 1 TD, 3 int.

RECEIVING

Baltimore—Jefferson, 3 for 52; Mackey, 2 for 80, 1 TD; Hinton, 2 for 51; Havrilak, 2 for 27; Nowatzke, 1 for 45; Bulaich, 1 for 5.

Dallas—Reeves, 5 for 46; Thomas, 4 for 21, 1 TD; Garrison, 2 for 19; Hayes, 1 for 41.

PUNTING

Baltimore—Lee, 4 for 168, 41.5 average.

Dallas—Widby, 9 for 377, 41.9 average.

PUNT RETURNS

Baltimore—Logan, 1 for 8; Gardin, 4 for 4, 3 fair catches.

Dallas—Hayes, 3 for 9.

KICKOFF RETURNS

Baltimore—Duncan, 4 for 90.

Dallas—Harris, 1 for 18; Hill, 1 for 14; Kiner, 1 for 2.

INTERCEPTIONS

Baltimore—Volk, 1 for 30; Logan, 1 for 14; Curtis, 1 for 13.

Dallas—Howley, 2 for 22; Renfro, 1 for 0.

Curtis intercepts for Baltimore with the score tied and one minute left to play.

Vogel (72), kicker O'Brien (80), Smith (78) after game-winning kick.

BALTIMORE COLTS

No.	Name	Pos.	Ht.	Wt.	Age	Year	College
73	Ball, Sam	T	6-4	240	26	5	Kentucky
36	Bulaich, Norm	RB	6-1	218	24	1	Texas Christian
50	Curry, Bill	C	6-2	235	28	6	Georgia Tech
32	Curtis, Mike	LB	6-2	232	26	6	Duke
35	Duncan, Jim	CB	6-2	200	24	2	Maryland State
30	Gardin, Ron	CB	5-11	180	26	1	Arizona
53	Goode, Tom	C	6-3	245	31	9	Mississippi State
51	Grant, Bob	LB	6-2	225	24	3	Wake Forest
17	Havrilak, Sam	RB	6-2	195	23	2	Bucknell
83	Hendricks, Ted	LB	6-7	215	23	2	Miami
45	Hill, Jerry	RB	5-11	217	31	10	Wyoming
85	Hilton, Roy	DE	6-6	240	27	6	Jackson State
33	Hinton, Ed	WR	6-0	200	23	2	Oklahoma
87	Jefferson, Roy	WR	6-2	195	26	6	Utah
61	Johnson, Cornelius	G	6-2	245	27	3	Virginia Union
49	Lee, David	P	6-4	230	27	5	Louisiana Tech
20	Logan, Jerry	S	6-1	190	29	8	West Texas State
88	Mackey, John	TE	6-2	224	29	8	Syracuse
40	Maitland, Jack	RB	6-1	210	22	1	Williams
42	Maxwell, Tom	CB	6-2	195	23	2	Texas A&M
56	May, Ray	LB	6-1	230	25	4	USC
76	Miller, Fred	DT	6-3	250	30	8	Louisiana State
84	Mitchell, Tom	TE	6-2	215	26	4	Bucknell
15	Morrall, Earl	QB	6-2	206	36	15	Michigan State
81	Newsome, Billy	DE	6-4	240	22	1	Grambling
52	Nichols, Robbie	LB	6-3	220	24	1	Tulsa
34	Nowatzke, Tom	RB	6-3	230	27	6	Indiana
80	O'Brien, Jim	K-WR	6-0	195	23	1	Cincinnati
28	Orr, Jimmy	WR	5-11	185	35	13	Georgia
27	Perkins, Ray	WR	6-0	183	29	4	Alabama
62	Ressler, Glenn	G	6-3	250	27	6	Penn State
74	Smith, Billy Ray	DT	6-4	250	35	12	Arkansas
78	Smith, Charles (Bubba)	DE	6-7	295	25	4	Michigan State
47	Stukes, Charlie	CB	6-3	212	27	4	Maryland State
71	Sullivan, Dan	G	6-3	250	31	9	Boston College
19	Unitas, John	QB	6-1	196	37	15	Louisville
72	Vogel, Bob	T	6-5	250	29	8	Ohio State
21	Volk, Rick	S	6-3	195	25	4	Michigan
75	Williams, John	G	6-3	256	25	3	Minnesota
60	Wright, George	DT	6-3	260	23	1	Sam Houston

Head coach—Don McCafferty. **Assistants**—Dick Bielski, Bobby Boyd, Hank Bullough, John Idzik, Lou Rymkus, John Sandusky.

DALLAS COWBOYS

No.	Name	Pos.	Ht.	Wt.	Age	Year	College
26	Adderley, Herb	CB	6-1	200	31	10	Michigan State
66	Andrie, George	DE	6-6	250	30	9	Marquette
78	Asher, Bob	T	6-5	250	22	1	Vanderbilt
83	Clark, Mike	K	6-1	205	30	8	Texas A&M
63	Cole, Larry	DE	6-4	225	24	3	Hawaii
89	Ditka, Mike	TE	6-3	225	31	10	Pittsburgh
77	East, Ron	DT	6-4	242	27	4	Montana State
52	Edwards, Dave	LB	6-1	225	31	8	Auburn
45	Flowers, Richmond	S	6-0	180	23	2	Tennessee
32	Garrison, Walt	RB	6-0	205	26	5	Oklahoma State
34	Green, Cornell	S	6-3	208	30	9	Utah State
43	Harris, Cliff	S	6-0	184	22	1	Ouachita
22	Hayes, Bob	WR	5-11	185	27	6	Florida A&M
35	Hill, Calvin	RB	6-4	227	23	2	Yale
24	Homan, Dennis	WR	6-1	181	24	3	Alabama
54	Howley, Chuck	LB	6-2	225	34	12	West Virginia
55	Jordan, Lee Roy	LB	6-1	221	29	8	Alabama
60	Kiner, Steve	LB	6-0	218	23	1	Tennessee
50	Lewis, D. D.	LB	6-1	225	25	2	Mississippi State
74	Lilly, Bob	DT	6-5	260	31	10	Texas Christian
72	Liscio, Tony	T	6-5	255	30	7	Tulsa
51	Manders, Dave	C	6-2	250	29	6	Michigan State
14	Morton, Craig	QB	6-4	214	27	6	California
73	Neely, Ralph	G	6-6	255	27	6	Oklahoma
76	Niland, John	G	6-3	245	26	5	Iowa
84	Norman, Pettis	TE	6-3	220	31	9	Johnson C. Smith
61	Nye, Blaine	G	6-4	251	24	3	Stanford
75	Pugh, Jethro	DT	6-6	260	26	6	Elizabeth City State
30	Reeves, Dan	RB	6-1	220	26	6	South Carolina
20	Renfro, Mel	S	6-0	190	29	7	Oregon
88	Rucker, Reggie	WR	6-2	190	23	1	Boston U.
12	Staubach, Roger	QB	6-3	197	28	2	Navy
56	Stincic, Tom	LB	6-4	230	24	2	Michigan
33	Thomas, Duane	RB	6-1	220	23	1	West Texas State
67	Toomay, Pat	DE	6-5	244	22	1	Vanderbilt
46	Washington, Mark	CB	5-10	188	23	1	Morgan State
41	Waters, Charlie	S	6-1	193	22	1	Clemson
42	Welch, Claxton	RB	5-11	203	23	2	Oregon
10	Widby, Ron	P	6-4	210	25	3	Tennessee
70	Wright, Rayfield	T	6-6	255	25	4	Ft. Valley State

Head coach—Tom Landry. **Assistants**—Ermal Allen, Bobby Franklin, Jim Myers, Dan Reeves, Ray Renfro, Ernie Stautner, Jerry Tubbs.

SUPER BOWL VI

DALLAS 24, MIAMI 3

The Dallas Cowboys defeated the Miami Dolphins 24–3 in Super Bowl VI, setting a Super Bowl team rushing record of 252 yards and controlling the ball for 69 plays to Miami's 44.

Mike Clark kicked a nine-yard field goal with 1:23 left in the first quarter to give Dallas a 3–0 lead. The Cowboys had moved 50 yards in 11 plays after linebacker Chuck Howley recovered a fumble by Larry Csonka on Dallas's 48-yard line. It was Csonka's first fumble of the season.

The Cowboys defense was evident on the next series. On third down and nine yards for a first down at Miami's 38, Dolphins' quarterback Bob Griese went back to pass; with no receivers open, Griese scrambled, trying to avoid tackle Bob Lilly, who finally ran down the quarterback and tackled him for a 29-yard loss as the quarter ended.

Dallas moved ahead 10–0 with a 76-yard, 11-play drive that culminated with seven-yard touchdown pass from Roger Staubach to Lance Alworth with 1:15 remaining in the half. Alworth caught the ball in the corner of the end zone.

Miami drove 44 yards in five plays to position Garo Yepremian for a 31-yard field goal with four seconds left in the quarter that made the score 10–3 at halftime. Griese completed three of five passes during the march.

The Cowboys took the second half kickoff and went 71 yards in eight plays, scoring a touchdown on Duane Thomas's three-yard run that raised their lead to 17–3. Calvin Hill, playing in relief of Thomas, caught one pass for 12 yards, but the other seven plays on the drive were runs. Walt Garrison ran wide for three, Thomas wide for four and seven, then through the right side for 23. Wide receiver Bob Hayes ran a reverse for 16 and Garrison set up the touchdown by going three yards around the left side.

After the touchdown, Dallas gained 11 yards in 10 offensive plays for the remainder of the third quarter. Miami had the ball for 11 plays during the quarter and gained 13 yards. The Dolphins had the ball on their 49-yard line on the fourth play of the fourth quarter. Griese's pass intended for running back Jim Kiick was intercepted by Howley, who ran 41 yards to the Dolphins' 9. Three plays later Staubach passed seven yards to Mike Ditka for a touchdown.

Leading 24–3, Dallas moved 79 yards from its 20 to Miami's 1 in seven plays, controlling the ball for six minutes and 40 seconds (his Baltimore team was beaten by the New York Jets in Super Bowl fumbled and Manny Fernandez recovered on the 4 for Miami. The Dolphins advanced to their 24 when the game ended.

"My biggest disappointment was that we never challenged," said Miami coach Don Shula, a loser in the Super Bowl for the second time (his Baltimore team was beaten by the New York Jets in Super Bowl III). "They completely dominated."

The Cowboys also shut off a play that had been suggested to Shula by President Richard Nixon. Shula had received a telephone call from the President after the Dolphins defeated Baltimore and qualified for the Super Bowl. "The Cowboys are a good defensive team," Shula said Nixon told him, "but I think you can hit Paul Warfield on that down-and-in pattern."

Paul Warfield, a Dolphins' wide receiver, had raced downfield and veered toward the middle of the field to catch a pass that went for a 50-yard gain against Baltimore. But the Cowboys double-teamed Warfield and he was unsuccessful running the pattern.

"We made sure they didn't complete that pass on us," said Cowboys coach Tom Landry.

Alworth catches Staubach's pass and just makes it into the corner of the end zone for a touchdown.

Participants—Dallas Cowboys, champions of the National Football Conference, and Miami Dolphins, champions of the American Football Conference
Date—January 16, 1972
Site—Tulane Stadium, New Orleans
Time—1:35 P.M. CST
Conditions—39 degrees, sunny
Playing Surface—Poly-Turf
Television and Radio—Columbia Broadcasting System (CBS)
Regular Season Records—Dallas, 11-3; Miami, 10-3-1
Conference Championships—Dallas defeated the San Francisco 49ers 14-3 for the NFC title; Miami defeated the Baltimore Colts 21-0 for the AFC title
Players' Shares—$15,000 to each member of the winning team; $7,500 to each member of the losing team
Attendance—81,023
Gross Receipts—$4,041,527.89
Officials—Referee, Jim Tunney; umpire, Joe Connell; line judge, Art Holst; head linesman, Al Sabato; back judge, Ralph Vandenberg; field judge, Bob Wortman
Coaches—Tom Landry, Dallas; Don Shula, Miami

Dallas	Starters, Offense	Miami
Bob Hayes	WR	Paul Warfield
Tony Liscio	LT	Doug Crusan
John Niland	LG	Bob Kuechenberg
Dave Manders	C	Bob DeMarco
Blaine Nye	RG	Larry Little
Rayfield Wright	RT	Norm Evans
Mike Ditka	TE	Marv Fleming
Lance Alworth	WR	Howard Twilley
Roger Staubach	QB	Bob Griese
Duane Thomas	RB	Jim Kiick
Walt Garrison	RB	Larry Csonka
	Starters, Defense	
Larry Cole	LE	Jim Riley
Jethro Pugh	LT	Manny Fernandez
Bob Lilly	RT	Bob Heinz
George Andrie	RE	Bill Stanfill
Dave Edwards	LLB	Doug Swift
Lee Roy Jordan	MLB	Nick Buoniconti
Chuck Howley	RLB	Mike Kolen
Herb Adderley	LC	Tim Foley
Mel Renfro	RC	Curtis Johnson
Cornell Green	LS	Dick Anderson
Cliff Harris	RS	Jake Scott

Dallas	3	7	7	7	— 24
Miami	0	3	0	0	— 3

Dall—FG Clark 9
Dall—Alworth 7 pass from Staubach (Clark kick)
Mia—FG Yepremian 31
Dall—D. Thomas 3 run (Clark kick)
Dall—Ditka 7 pass from Staubach (Clark kick)

TEAM STATISTICS	Dall	Mia
First downs	23	10
Rushing	15	3
Passing	8	7
By penalty	0	0
Total yardage	352	185
Net rushing yardage	252	80
Net passing yardage	100	105
Passes att.-comp.-had int.	19-12-0	23-12-1

RUSHING
Dallas—D. Thomas, 19 for 95, 1 TD; Garrison, 14 for 74; Hill, 7 for 25; Staubach, 5 for 18; Ditka, 1 for 17; Hayes, 1 for 16; Reeves, 1 for 7.
Miami—Csonka, 9 for 40; Kiick, 10 for 40; Griese, 1 for 0.

PASSING
Dallas—Staubach, 12 of 19 for 119, 2 TDs.
Miami—Griese, 12 of 23 for 134, 1 int.

RECEIVING
Dallas—D. Thomas, 3 for 17; Alworth, 2 for 28, 1 TD; Ditka, 2 for 28, 1 TD; Hayes, 2 for 23; Garrison, 2 for 11; Hill, 1 for 12.
Miami—Warfield, 4 for 39; Kiick, 3 for 21; Csonka, 2 for 18; Fleming, 1 for 27; Twilley, 1 for 20; Mandick, 1 for 9.

PUNTING
Dallas—Widby, 5 for 166, 37.2 average.
Miami—Seiple, 5 for 200, 40.0 average.

PUNT RETURNS
Dallas—Hayes, 1 for -1, 1 fair catch; Harris, 2 fair catches.
Miami—Scott, 1 for 21.

KICKOFF RETURNS
Dallas—I. Thomas, 1 for 23; Waters, 1 for 11.
Miami—Morris, 4 for 90; Ginn, 1 for 32.

INTERCEPTIONS
Dallas—Howley, 1 for 41.
Miami—None.

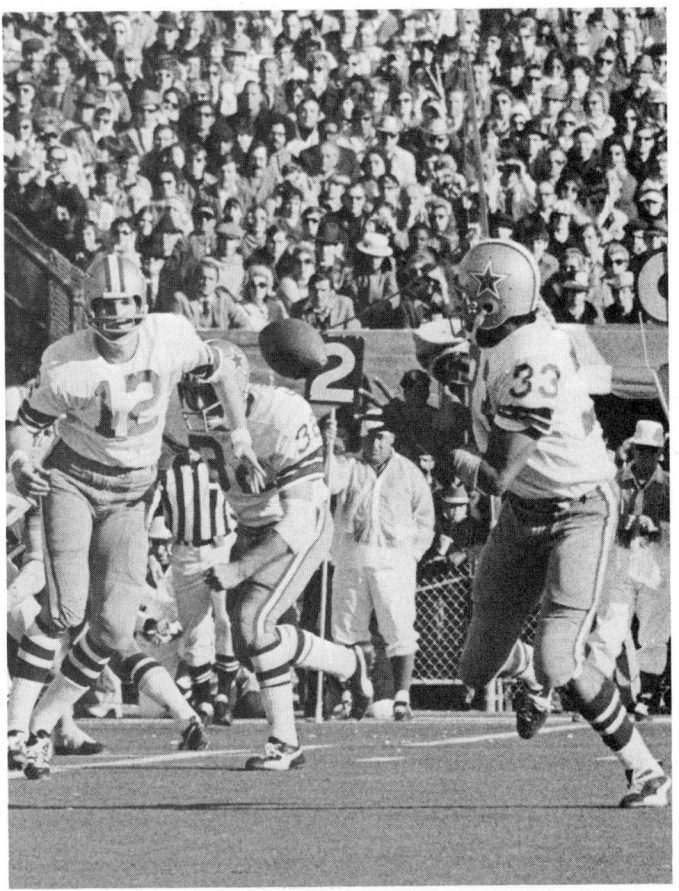

Cowboys' Thomas takes pitchout from Staubach on way to touchdown.

Howley runs 41 yards to the Miami 9-yard line after intercepting Griese's pass.

DALLAS COWBOYS

No.	Name	Pos.	Ht.	Wt.	Age	Year	College
26	Adderley, Herb	CB	6-1	200	32	11	Michigan State
19	Alworth, Lance	WR	6-0	180	31	10	Arkansas
66	Andrie, George	DE	6-6	250	31	10	Marquette
60	Caffey, Lee Roy	LB	6-3	240	30	9	Texas A&M
83	Clark, Mike	K	6-1	205	30	9	Texas A&M
63	Cole, Larry	DE	6-4	250	25	4	Hawaii
89	Ditka, Mike	TE	6-3	213	31	11	Pittsburgh
52	Edwards, Dave	LB	6-1	225	31	9	Auburn
62	Fitzgerald, John	C	6-5	250	23	1	Boston U.
32	Garrison, Walt	RB	6-0	205	27	6	Oklahoma State
34	Green, Cornell	S	6-3	208	31	10	Utah State
79	Gregg, Forrest	G	6-4	250	37	15	Southern Methodist
77	Gregory, Bill	DT	6-5	255	21	1	Wisconsin
43	Harris, Cliff	S	6-0	184	22	2	Ouachita
22	Hayes, Bob	WR	5-11	185	28	7	Florida A&M
35	Hill, Calvin	RB	6-4	227	24	3	Yale
54	Howley, Chuck	LB	6-2	225	35	13	West Virginia
55	Jordan, Lee Roy	LB	6-1	221	30	9	Alabama
50	Lewis, D. D.	LB	6-1	225	25	3	Mississippi State
74	Lilly, Bob	DT	6-5	260	32	11	Texas Christian
64	Liscio, Tony	T	6-5	255	31	8	Tulsa
51	Manders, Dave	C	6-2	250	30	7	Michigan State
14	Morton, Craig	QB	6-4	214	28	7	California
76	Niland, John	G	6-3	245	27	6	Iowa
61	Nye, Blaine	G	6-4	251	25	4	Stanford
75	Pugh, Jethro	DT	6-6	260	27	7	Elizabeth City State
30	Reeves, Dan	RB	6-1	200	27	7	South Carolina
20	Renfro, Mel	CB	6-0	190	29	8	Oregon
31	Richardson, Gloster	WR	6-2	200	29	5	Jackson State
85	Smith, Tody	DE	6-5	245	22	1	USC
12	Staubach, Roger	QB	6-3	197	29	3	Navy
33	Thomas, Duane	RB	6-1	205	24	2	West Texas State
37	Thomas, Ike	CB	6-2	193	23	1	Bishop
67	Toomay, Pat	DE	6-5	244	23	2	Vanderbilt
87	Truax, Billy	TE	6-5	240	28	8	Louisiana State
71	Wallace, Rodney	G	6-5	255	22	1	New Mexico
41	Waters, Charlie	S	6-1	193	22	2	Clemson
42	Welch, Claxton	RB	5-11	203	24	3	Oregon
10	Widby, Ron	P	6-4	210	26	4	Tennessee
70	Wright, Rayfield	T	6-6	255	26	5	Ft. Valley State

Head coach—Tom Landry. **Assistants**—Ermal Allen, Bobby Franklin, Jim Myers, Dan Reeves, Ray Renfro, Ernie Stautner, Jerry Tubbs.

MIAMI DOLPHINS

No.	Name	Pos.	Ht.	Wt.	Age	Year	College
40	Anderson, Dick	S	6-2	196	25	4	Colorado
85	Buoniconti, Nick	LB	5-11	220	30	10	Notre Dame
31	Cole, Terry	RB	6-1	220	26	4	Indiana
77	Crusan, Doug	T	6-4	250	25	4	Indiana
39	Csonka, Larry	RB	6-2	237	24	4	Syracuse
61	DeMarco, Bob	C	6-2	250	31	11	Dayton
86	Den Herder, Vern	DE	6-6	250	22	1	Central Iowa
73	Evans, Norm	T	6-5	252	28	7	Texas Christian
75	Fernandez, Manny	DT	6-2	248	25	4	Utah
80	Fleming, Marv	TE	6-4	235	29	9	Utah
25	Foley, Tim	CB	6-0	194	22	2	Purdue
32	Ginn, Hubert	RB	5-10	188	24	2	Florida A&M
12	Griese, Bob	QB	6-1	190	26	5	Purdue
72	Heinz, Bob	DT	6-6	280	24	3	Pacific
45	Johnson, Curtis	CB	6-1	196	23	2	Toledo
71	Cornish, Frank	DT	6-3	285	27	6	Grambling
21	Kiick, Jim	RB	5-11	215	25	4	Wyoming
57	Kolen, Mike	LB	6-2	220	23	2	Auburn
67	Kuechenberg, Bob	G	6-2	247	23	2	Notre Dame
62	Langer, Jim	G	6-2	250	23	2	South Dakota
15	Leigh, Charles	RB	5-11	205	25	3	None
66	Little, Larry	G	6-1	265	25	5	Bethune-Cookman
88	Mandich, Jim	TE	6-2	224	23	2	Michigan
53	Matheson, Bob	LB	6-4	240	26	5	Duke
10	Mira, George	QB	5-11	192	29	7	Miami
79	Moore, Wayne	T	6-6	265	25	2	Lamar Tech
22	Morris, Eugene (Mercury)	RB	5-10	190	24	3	West Texas State
26	Mumphord, Lloyd	CB	6-0	180	24	3	Texas Southern
89	Noonan, Karl	WR	6-2	198	27	6	Iowa
48	Petrella, Bob	S	5-11	190	26	6	Tennessee
56	Powell, Jesse	LB	6-2	215	24	3	West Texas State
70	Riley, Jim	DE	6-4	250	26	5	Oklahoma
13	Scott, Jake	S	6-0	188	26	2	Georgia
20	Seiple, Larry	P	6-0	215	26	5	Kentucky
84	Stanfill, Bill	DE	6-5	250	24	3	Georgia
82	Stowe, Otto	WR	6-2	188	2!	1	Iowa State
59	Swift, Doug	LB	6-3	228	23	2	Amherst
81	Twilley, Howard	WR	5-10	185	28	6	Tulsa
42	Warfield, Paul	WR	6-0	185	28	8	Ohio State
1	Yepremian, Garo	K	5-8	172	27	4	None

Head coach—Don Shula. **Assistants**—Bill Arnsparger, Monte Clark, Tom Keane, Mike Scarry, Howard Schnellenberger, Carl Taseff.

SUPER BOWL VII

MIAMI 14, WASHINGTON 7

The Miami Dolphins defeated the Washington Redskins 14–7 in Super Bowl VII and completed a season in which they won all of their 17 games, a professional football record.

The Dolphins, who entered the game as two-point underdogs, were outgained 253-228 in total yardage but never trailed and never were seriously threatened.

The Dolphins took a 7–0 lead the third time they had the ball, marching 63 yards in six plays and scoring on a 28-yard pass play—quarterback Bob Griese to wide receiver Howard Twilley—on the next to last play of the first quarter. Twilley ran inside then outside on his pattern, turning Redskins cornerback Pat Fischer completely around.

The Dolphins scored again when Griese passed 37 yards to Paul Warfield, who caught the ball on the Redskins' 10 and completed a 47-yard play, but Marlin Briscoe, the wide receiver opposite Warfield moved forward before the snap of the ball and the touchdown was nullified.

Washington forced the Dolphins to punt and began a drive from its own 17-yard line. On third down from the Dolphins' 48-yard line, the Redskins quarterback Billy Kilmer threw a pass that was intercepted by middle linebacker Nick Buoniconti, who returned the ball 32 yards to Washington's 27.

The Dolphins scored with 18 seconds left in the half on the fifth play after the interception. Jim Kiick went across from the 1-yard line behind right guard Larry Little.

Miami missed an opportunity to go ahead 21–0 in the third quarter. The Dolphins moved 78 yards from their 17 to the Redskins' 5, but on the eighth play of the drive Griese's pass for tight end Marv Fleming was intercepted in the end zone by Brig Owens.

Washington moved from its 11-yard line to the Dolphins' 10 in the fourth quarter, a 79-yard advance that took 14 plays and consumed more than seven minutes of play. Quarterback Billy Kilmer's pass to Charley Taylor was intercepted in the end zone by Jake Scott, who returned the ball 55 yards to the Redskins' 48.

Miami advanced 17 yards in five plays to position Garo Yepremian for a 42-yard field goal attempt. The snap from center Howard Kindig was low. Holder Earl Morrall had to place the ball quickly. Yepremian's kick was low and Bill Brundige blocked the attempt. Yepremian picked up the ball and attempted to pass. The ball fell out of his hand and went into the air. Washington's Mike Bass caught the ball and ran 49 yards for a touchdown with 2:07 remaining in the game.

Leading 14–7, Miami controlled the ball for six plays, punting to Washington, which took over on its 30-yard line with 1:14 left. Kilmer's first two passes were incomplete. His third, to running back Larry Brown, resulted in a four-yard loss. Kilmer was thrown for a loss of nine yards on fourth down. There were 33 seconds remaining in the game. Game officials stopped the clock to clear the field of fans; the clock started again and time ran out before Miami could launch a play.

"This is the first time the goat of the game is in the winners' locker room," Yepremian said. "I should have fallen on the ball, but my mind went blank."

"We were never really in the game . . . and we were never really out of it," said Jack Pardee, linebacker and co-captain of the Redskins.

"The pressure's off," said Miami coach Don Shula, whose teams had been beaten in two previous Super Bowls. "I was aware of the reputation I had gotten . . . the losses were there; you couldn't hide them. But that's all in the past."

Brown, the NFC's leading rusher, is collared by Miami's Fernandez; Brown was held to 72 yards.

Participants—Miami Dolphins, champions of the American Football Conference, and Washington Redskins, champions of the National Football Conference
Date—January 14, 1973
Site—Los Angeles Memorial Coliseum
Time—12:30 P.M. PST
Conditions—84 degrees, sunny, hazy
Playing Surface—Grass
Television and Radio—National Broadcasting Company (NBC)
Regular Season Records—Miami, 14-0; Washington, 11-3
Conference Championships—Miami defeated the Pittsburgh Steelers 21-17 for the AFC title; Washington defeated the Dallas Cowboys 26-3 for the NFC title
Players' Shares—$15,000 to each member of the winning team; $7,500 to each member of the losing team
Attendance—90,182
Gross Receipts—$4,125,695.00
Officials—Referee, Tom Bell; umpire, Lou Palazzi; line judge, Bruce Alford; head linesman, Tony Veteri; back judge, Tom Kelleher; field judge, Tony Skover
Coaches—Don Shula, Miami; George Allen, Washington

Miami	Starters, Offense	Washington
Paul Warfield	WR	Charley Taylor
Wayne Moore	LT	Terry Hermeling
Bob Kuechenberg	LG	Paul Laaveg
Jim Langer	C	Len Hauss
Larry Little	RG	John Wilbur
Norm Evans	RT	Walter Rock
Marv Fleming	TE	Jerry Smith
Howard Twilley	WR	Roy Jefferson
Bob Greise	QB	Billy Kilmer
Jim Kiick	RB	Larry Brown
Larry Csonka	RB	Charley Harraway
	Starters, Defense	
Vern Den Herder	LE	Ron McDole
Manny Fernandez	LT	Bill Brundige
Bob Heinz	RT	Diron Talbert
Bill Stanfill	RE	Verlon Biggs
Doug Swift	LLB	Jack Pardee
Nick Buoniconti	MLB	Myron Pottios
Mike Kolen	RLB	Chris Hanburger
Lloyd Mumphord	LC	Pat Fischer
Curtis Johnson	RC	Mike Bass
Dick Anderson	LS	Brig Owens
Jake Scott	RS	Roosevelt Taylor

Miami	7	7	0	0	—	14
Washington	0	0	0	7	—	7

Mia —Twilley 28 pass from Griese (Yepremian kick)
Mia —Kiick 1 run (Yepremian kick)
Wash—Bass 49 fumble return (Knight kick)

TEAM STATISTICS	Mia	Wash
First downs	12	16
Rushing	7	9
Passing	5	7
By penalty	0	0
Total yardage	253	228
Net rushing yardage	184	141
Net passing yardage	69	87
Passes att.-comp.-had int.	11-8-1	28-14-3

RUSHING
Miami—Csonka, 15 for 112; Kiick, 12 for 38, 1 TD; Morris, 10 for 34. Washington—Brown, 22 for 72; Harraway, 10 for 37; Kilmer, 2 for 18; C. Taylor, 1 for 8; Smith, 1 for 6.
PASSING
Miami—Griese, 8 of 11 for 88, 1 TD, 1 int. Washington—Kilmer, 14 of 28 for 104, 3 int.
RECEIVING
Miami—Warfield, 3 for 36; Kiick, 2 for 6; Twilley, 1 for 28, 1 TD; Mandich, 1 for 19; Csonka, 1 for -1. Washington—Jefferson, 5 for 50; Brown, 5 for 26; C. Taylor, 2 for 20; Smith, 1 for 11; Harraway, 1 for -3.
PUNTING
Miami—Seiple, 7 for 301, 43.0 average. Washington—Bragg, 5 for 156, 31.2 average.
PUNT RETURNS
Miami—Scott, 2 for 4, 2 fair catches; Anderson, 2 fair catches. Washington—Haymond, 4 for 9; Vactor, 2 fair catches.
KICKOFF RETURNS
Miami—Morris, 2 for 33. Washington—Haymond, 2 for 30; Mul-Key, 1 for 15.
INTERCEPTIONS
Miami—Scott, 2 for 63; Buoniconti, 1 for 32. Washington—Owens, 1 for 0.

Scott makes his key interception in the end zone for the Dolphins.

Csonka, symbol of Dolphins' power, on the way to part of his total of 112 yards.

MIAMI DOLPHINS

No.	Name	Pos.	Ht.	Wt.	Age	Year	College
40	Anderson, Dick	S	6-2	196	26	5	Colorado
49	Babb, Charlie	S	6-0	190	22	1	Memphis State
51	Ball, Larry	LB	6-6	225	23	1	Louisville
86	Briscoe, Marlin	WR	5-11	178	26	4	Omaha
85	Buoniconti, Nick	LB	5-11	220	31	11	Notre Dame
77	Crusan, Doug	T	6-4	250	26	5	Indiana
39	Csonka, Larry	RB	6-2	237	25	5	Syracuse
11	Del Gaizo, Jim	QB	6-1	198	25	1	Tampa
83	Den Herder, Vern	DE	6-6	250	23	2	Central Iowa
78	Dunaway, Jim	DT	6-4	277	31	10	Mississippi
73	Evans, Norm	T	6-5	250	29	8	Texas Christian
75	Fernandez, Manny	DT	6-2	250	26	5	Utah
80	Fleming, Marv	TE	6-4	232	30	10	Utah
25	Foley, Tim	CB	6-0	194	23	3	Purdue
32	Ginn, Hubert	RB	5-10	185	25	3	Florida A&M
12	Griese, Bob	QB	6-1	190	27	6	Purdue
72	Heinz, Bob	DT	6-6	265	25	4	Pacific
60	Jenkins, Al	G-T	6-2	245	26	3	Tulsa
28	Jenkins, Ed	RB	6-2	210	22	1	Holy Cross
45	Johnson, Curtis	CB	6-1	196	24	3	Toledo
68	Kadish, Mike	DT	6-5	265	22	1	Notre Dame
21	Kiick, Jim	RB	5-11	214	26	5	Wyoming
54	Kindig, Howard	T-C	6-6	260	31	6	Cal. State-L.A.
57	Kolen, Mike	LB	6-2	220	24	3	Auburn
67	Kuechenberg, Bob	G	6-2	248	24	3	Notre Dame
62	Langer, Jim	C	6-2	250	24	3	South Dakota State
23	Leigh, Charles	RB	5-11	206	26	4	None
66	Little, Larry	G	6-1	265	26	6	Bethune Cookman
7	Lothridge, Billy	P	6-1	200	30	9	Georgia
88	Mandich, Jim	TE	6-2	224	24	3	Michigan
53	Matheson, Bob	LB	6-4	235	27	6	Duke
65	Moore, Maulty	DT	6-5	265	26	1	Bethune-Cookman
79	Moore, Wayne	T	6-6	265	26	3	Lamar Tech
15	Morrall, Earl	QB	6-2	210	38	17	Michigan State
22	Morris, Eugene (Mercury)	RB	5-10	190	25	4	West Texas State
26	Mumphord, Lloyd	CB	5-10	176	25	4	Texas Southern
89	Noonan, Karl	WR	6-2	198	28	7	Iowa
56	Powell, Jesse	LB	6-2	220	25	4	West Texas State
13	Scott, Jake	S	6-0	188	27	3	Georgia
20	Seiple, Larry	P	6-0	214	27	6	Kentucky
84	Stanfill, Bill	DE	6-5	250	25	4	Georgia
82	Stowe, Otto	WR	6-2	188	23	2	Iowa State
47	Stuckey, Henry	DB	6-0	180	22	1	Missouri
59	Swift, Doug	LB	6-3	226	24	3	Amherst
81	Twilley, Howard	WR	5-10	185	28	7	Tulsa
42	Warfield, Paul	WR	6-0	188	29	9	Ohio State
1	Yepremian, Garo	K	5-8	175	28	5	None

Head coach—Don Shula. **Assistants**—Bill Arnsparger, Monte Clark, Tom Keane, Mike Scarry, Howard Schnellenberger, Carl Taseff.

WASHINGTON REDSKINS

No.	Name	Pos.	Ht.	Wt.	Age	Year	College
81	Alston, Mack	TE	6-2	230	25	3	Maryland State
41	Bass, Mike	CB	6-0	190	27	5	Michigan
89	Biggs, Verlon	DE	6-4	275	29	8	Jackson State
4	Bragg, Mike	P	5-11	186	25	5	Richmond
43	Brown, Larry	RB	5-11	195	25	4	Kansas State
77	Brundige, Bill	DT	6-5	270	23	3	Colorado
26	Brunet, Bob	RB	6-1	205	26	4	Louisiana Tech
58	Burman, George	C-G	6-3	255	29	7	Northwestern
45	Duncan, Leslie (Speedy)	S	5-10	180	30	9	Jackson State
68	Fanucci, Mike	DE	6-4	225	22	1	Arizona State
37	Fischer, Pat	CB	5-9	170	32	12	Nebraska
55	Hanburger, Chris	LB	6-2	218	31	8	North Carolina
31	Harraway, Charley	RB	6-2	215	27	7	San Jose State
56	Hauss, Len	C	6-2	235	30	9	Georgia
13	Haymond, Alvin	S	6-0	194	30	9	Southern U.
75	Hermeling, Terry	T	6-5	255	26	3	Nevada-Reno
25	Hull, Mike	RB	6-3	220	27	5	USC
48	Jaqua, Jon	S	6-0	190	24	3	Lewis & Clark
80	Jefferson, Roy	WR	6-2	195	28	8	Utah
63	Johnson, Mitch	T	6-4	250	30	7	UCLA
82	Jones, Jimmie	DE	6-5	215	25	4	Wichita State
17	Kilmer, Billy	QB	6-0	204	32	11	UCLA
50	Kiner, Steve	LB	6-1	220	25	3	Tennessee
5	Knight, Curt	K	6-2	190	29	4	Coast Guard
73	Laaveg, Paul	G	6-4	250	23	3	Iowa
79	McDole, Ron	DE	6-4	265	32	12	Nebraska
53	McLinton, Harold	LB	6-2	235	25	4	Southern U.
85	McNeil, Clifton	WR	6-2	187	31	9	None
28	Mul-Key, Herb	RB	6-0	190	22	1	None
40	Nock, George	RB	5-10	205	26	4	Morgan State
23	Owens, Brig	S	5-11	190	29	7	Cincinnati
32	Pardee, Jack	LB	6-2	225	36	15	Texas A&M
16	Petitbon, Richie	S	6-3	208	34	14	Tulane
66	Pottios, Myron	LB	6-2	232	33	12	Notre Dame
76	Rock, Walter	T	6-5	255	30	10	Maryland
62	Schoenke, Ray	T	6-4	250	31	9	Southern Methodist
44	Severson, Jeff	DB	6-1	180	22	1	Cal. State-Long Beach
64	Sistrunk, Manny	DT	6-5	265	25	3	Arkansas AM&N
87	Smith, Jerry	TE	6-3	208	29	8	Arizona State
72	Talbert, Diron	DT	6-5	255	28	6	Texas
19	Taliaferro, Mike	QB	6-2	202	31	9	Illinois
42	Taylor, Charley	WR	6-2	210	30	9	Arizona State
22	Taylor, Roosevelt	S	5-11	186	34	12	Grambling
67	Tillman, Rusty	LB	6-2	230	26	3	Northern Arizona
29	Vactor, Ted	CB	6-0	185	28	4	Nebraska
60	Wilbur, John	G	6-3	251	29	7	Stanford
18	Wyche, Sam	QB	6-4	218	27	5	Furman

Head coach—George Allen, **Assistant**—Boyd Dowler, Ralph Hawkins, Marv Levy, Ted Marchibroda, Mike McCormack, LaVern Torgeson, Charlie Waller, Charley Winner.

SUPER BOWL VIII

MIAMI 24, MINNESOTA 7

The Miami Dolphins defeated the Minnesota Vikings 24–7 in Super Bowl VIII, a game in which the Dolphins took control on the first series of offensive plays.

Miami moved 62 yards in 10 plays, scoring on Larry Csonka's five yard run after accepting the opening kickoff. After Minnesota ran three plays and punted, Miami marched 56 yards in 10 plays, scoring on Jim Kiick's one-yard run.

At the end of the first quarter, Miami had run 20 plays and gained 118 yards. Minnesota had run six plays and gained 16 yards. The Dolphins had eight first downs, the Vikings none.

The Dolphins marched 44 yards in seven plays to Yepremian's 28-yard field goal that made the score 17–0 with 6:02 left in the half. The Vikings had run 12 plays and gained 27 yards at this point. Miami had run 31 plays that had gained 153 yards. Minnesota took the following kickoff and drove 74 yards to the Dolphins' 6-yard line. On fourth down and one yard for a first down, Oscar Reed fumbled when hit by Nick Buoniconti and Miami's Jake Scott recovered on the 6.

Minnesota lost a chance to get back into the game at the beginning of the third quarter. John Gilliam returned Garo Yepremian's kickoff 65 yards to Miami's 34-yard line, but Minnesota's Stu Voigt was penalized for clipping and the ball was returned to the Vikings' 11-yard line. The Vikings punted four plays later and Miami began from Minnesota's 43. In eight plays the Dolphins scored on Larry Csonka's two-yard run.

Csonka was confused on the play on which he scored his second touchdown, which punctuated a performance in which he set Super Bowl records with 33 carries and 145 yards rushing. Quarterback Bob Griese forgot the number on which the ball was supposed to be snapped by center Jim Langer. "What's the count?" Griese asked Csonka. The running back thought for a moment. "What's the count?" Griese demanded. "It's on two, isn't it?" said Csonka. "No, no...it's on one," said Jim Kiick, the other running back. Griese finally agreed with Csonka. But Langer snapped the ball to the startled quarterback on one; Griese juggled the ball and handed off to Csonka, who followed Kiick, Langer, guard Larry Little, and tackle Norm Evans into the end zone.

"Bob had that wide-eyed look when he gave me the ball," said Csonka. "I'm just happy I didn't cause him to drop the ball."

Minnesota scored its touchdown after a drive that began on the Vikings' 43-yard line with 1:34 left in the third quarter and concluded with quarterback Fran Tarkenton's four-yard touchdown run 1:35 into the final quarter.

The Vikings moved from their 3-yard line to Miami's 32 later in the quarter but Tarkenton's pass to Jim Lash was intercepted on the goal line by Curtis Johnson. Miami took possession with 6:24 remaining in the game and moved 61 yards in 13 plays before the clock ran out and the game ended.

The victory was Miami's second in a row in the Super Bowl, equalling Green Bay's achievement in Super Bowls I and II. Csonka was asked if he thought Miami was stronger than the Packers' teams.

"I don't know about legends or statistics," said Csonka. "Football is a 'now' game; that's all that matters."

Miami also set a record by making its third appearance in the game. Minnesota set a record by losing for the second time.

The Dolphins take control and Csonka scores the first touchdown 10 plays after the opening kickoff.

Participants—Miami Dolphins, champions of the American Football Conference, and Minnesota Vikings, champions of the National Football Conference
Date—January 13, 1974
Site—Rice Stadium, Houston
Time—2:30 P.M. CST
Conditions—50 degrees, overcast
Playing Surface—AstroTurf
Television and Radio—Columbia Broadcasting System (CBS)
Regular Season Records—Miami, 12-2; Minnesota, 12-2
Conference Championships—Miami defeated the Oakland Raiders 27-10 for the AFC title; Minnesota defeated the Dallas Cowboys 27-10 for the NFC title
Players' Shares—$15,000 to each member of the winning team; $7,500 to each member of the losing team
Attendance—71,882
Gross Receipts—$3,854,311.00
Officials—Referee, Ben Dreith; umpire, Ralph Morcroft; line judge, Jack Fette; head linesman, Leo Miles; back judge, Stan Javie; field judge, Fritz Graf
Coaches—Don Shula, Miami; Bud Grant, Minnesota

Minnesota	0	0	0	7	—	7
Miami	14	3	7	0	—	24

Mia —Csonka 5 run (Yepremian kick)
Mia —Kiick 1 run (Yepremian kick)
Mia —FG Yepremian 28
Mia —Csonka 2 run (Yepremian kick)
Minn—Tarkenton 4 run (Cox kick)

TEAM STATISTICS

	Minn	Mia
First downs	14	21
Rushing	5	13
Passing	8	4
By penalty	1	4
Total yardage	238	259
Net rushing yardage	72	196
Net passing yardage	166	63
Passes att.-comp.-had int.	28-18-1	7-6-0

RUSHING
Minnesota—Reed, 11 for 32; Foreman, 7 for 18; Tarkenton, 4 for 17, 1 TD; Marinaro, 1 for 3; B. Brown, 1 for 2.
Miami—Csonka, 33 for 145, 2 TDs; Morris, 11 for 34; Kiick, 7 for 10, 1 TD; Griese, 2 for 7.
PASSING
Minnesota—Tarkenton, 18 of 28 for 182, 1 int.
Miami—Griese, 6 of 7 for 73.
RECEIVING
Minnesota—Foreman, 5 for 27; Gilliam, 4 for 44; Voigt, 3 for 46; Marinaro, 2 for 39; B. Brown, 1 for 9; Kingsriter, 1 for 9; Lash, 1 for 9; Reed, 1 for -1.
Miami—Warfield, 2 for 33; Mandich, 2 for 21; Briscoe, 2 for 19.
PUNTING
Minnesota—Eischeid, 5 for 42.2 average.
Miami—Seiple, 3 for 39.6 average.
PUNT RETURNS
Minnesota—Brown, 1 fair catch.
Miami—Scott, 3 for 20, 1 fair catch.
KICKOFF RETURNS
Minnesota—Gilliam, 2 for 41; West, 2 for 28.
Miami—Scott, 2 for 47.
INTERCEPTIONS
Minnesota—None.
Miami—Johnson, 1 for 10.

Minnesota	Starters, Offense	Miami
Carroll Dale	WR	Paul Warfield
Grady Alderman	LT	Wayne Moore
Ed White	LG	Bob Kuechenberg
Mick Tingelhoff	C	Jim Langer
Frank Gallagher	RG	Larry Little
Ron Yary	RT	Norm Evans
Stu Voigt	TE	Jim Mandich
John Gilliam	WR	Marlin Briscoe
Fran Tarkenton	QB	Bob Griese
Chuck Foreman	RB	Eugene (Mercury) Morris
Oscar Reed	RB	Larry Csonka
	Starters, Defense	
Carl Eller	LE	Vern Den Herder
Gary Larsen	LT	Manny Fernandez
Alan Page	RT	Bob Heinz
Jim Marshall	RE	Bill Stanfill
Roy Winston	LLB	Doug Swift
Jeff Siemon	MLB	Nick Buoniconti
Wally Hilgenberg	RLB	Mike Kolen
Nate Wright	LC	Lloyd Mumphord
Bob Bryant	RC	Curtis Johnson
Jeff Wright	LS	Dick Anderson
Paul Krause	RS	Jake Scott

Tarkenton sneaks over for a Vikings' touchdown in the fourth quarter.

Defenders Stanfill (84), Kolen (57), and Matheson (53) stop the Vikings' Reed.

MINNESOTA VIKINGS

No.	Name	Pos.	Ht.	Wt.	Age	Year	College
67	Alderman, Grady	T	6-2	247	34	14	Detroit
85	Ballman, Gary	TE	6-1	215	33	12	Michigan State
17	Berry, Bob	QB	5-11	185	31	9	Oregon
30	Brown, Bill	RB	5-11	222	35	13	Illinois
24	Brown, Terry	S	6-2	205	26	4	Oklahoma State
20	Bryant, Bob	CB	6-1	170	29	6	South Carolina
14	Cox, Fred	K	5-10	200	34	11	Pittsburgh
84	Dale, Carroll	WR	6-2	200	35	14	Virginia Tech
86	Dawson, Rhett	WR	6-1	182	24	2	Florida State
11	Eischeid, Mike	P	6-0	190	31	7	Upper Iowa
81	Eller, Carl	DE	6-6	247	31	10	Minnesota
44	Foreman, Chuck	RB	6-2	216	23	1	Miami
66	Gallagher, Frank	G	6-2	245	30	7	North Carolina
42	Gilliam, John	WR	6-1	195	28	7	South Carolina State
68	Goodrum, Charles	T-G	6-3	256	23	1	Florida A&M
58	Hilgenberg, Wally	LB	6-3	229	31	10	Iowa
89	Kingsriter, Doug	TE	6-2	222	23	1	Minnesota
22	Krause, Paul	S	6-3	200	31	10	Iowa
77	Larsen, Gary	DT	6-5	255	33	10	Concordia, Minn.
82	Lash, Jim	WR	6-2	199	22	1	Northwestern
65	Lawson, Steve	G	6-3	265	24	3	Kansas
75	Lurtsema, Bob	DT-DE	6-6	250	31	7	Western Michigan
49	Marinaro, Ed	RB	6-2	212	23	2	Cornell
70	Marshall, Jim	DE	6-4	240	35	14	Ohio State
55	Martin, Amos	LB	6-3	228	24	2	Louisville
33	McClanahan, Brent	RB	5-10	202	22	1	Arizona State
41	Osborn, Dave	RB	6-0	208	30	9	North Dakota
88	Page, Alan	DT	6-4	245	28	7	Notre Dame
52	Porter, Ron	LB	6-3	232	28	7	Idaho
34	Randolph, Al	S	6-2	205	29	7	Iowa
32	Reed, Oscar	RB	6-0	222	29	6	Colorado State
50	Siemon, Jeff	LB	6-2	230	23	2	Stanford
74	Smiley, Larry	DT	6-5	248	23	1	Texas Southern
64	Sunde, Milt	G	6-2	250	31	10	Minnesota
69	Sutherland, Doug	DT	6-3	250	25	4	Wisconsin State-Superior
10	Tarkenton, Fran	QB	6-0	190	33	13	Georgia
53	Tingelhoff, Mick	C	6-2	237	33	12	Nebraska
83	Voigt, Stu	TE	6-1	225	25	4	Wisconsin
25	Wallace, Jackie	CB	6-2	203	22	1	Arizona
15	Wells, Mike	QB	6-5	229	22	1	Illinois
40	West, Charlie	CB	6-1	197	26	6	Texas-El Paso
62	White, Ed	G	6-3	262	25	5	California
60	Winston, Roy	LB	5-11	222	33	12	Louisiana State
23	Wright, Jeff	S	5-11	190	24	3	Minnesota
43	Wright, Nate	CB	5-11	180	26	5	San Diego State
73	Yary, Ron	T	6-6	255	27	6	USC
51	Zaunbrecher, Godfrey	C	6-2	240	25	3	Louisiana State

Head coach—Bud Grant. **Assistants**—Neill Armstrong, Jerry Burns, Bus Mertes, John Michels, Jocko Nelson, Jack Patera.

MIAMI DOLPHINS

No.	Name	Pos.	Ht.	Wt.	Age	Year	College
40	Anderson, Dick	S	6-2	196	27	6	Colorado
49	Babb, Charles	S	6-0	190	23	2	Memphis State
51	Ball, Larry	LB	6-6	235	24	2	Louisville
58	Bannon, Bruce	LB	6-3	225	22	1	Penn State
86	Briscoe, Marlin	WR	5-11	175	27	6	Omaha
85	Buoniconti, Nick	LB	5-11	220	32	12	Notre Dame
77	Crusan, Doug	T	6-4	250	27	6	Indiana
39	Csonka, Larry	RB	6-2	237	26	6	Syracuse
83	Den Herder, Vern	DE	6-6	252	24	3	Central Iowa
73	Evans, Norm	T	6-5	250	30	9	Texas Christian
75	Fernandez, Manny	DT	6-2	250	27	6	Utah
80	Fleming, Marv	TE	6-4	230	31	11	Utah
25	Foley, Tim	CB	6-0	194	24	4	Purdue
55	Goode, Irv	C-G	6-5	262	32	11	Kentucky
12	Griese, Bob	QB	6-1	190	28	7	Purdue
72	Heinz, Bob	DT-DE	6-6	265	26	5	Pacific
45	Johnson, Curtis	CB	6-1	196	25	4	Toledo
21	Kiick, Jim	RB	5-11	214	27	6	Wyoming
57	Kolen, Mike	LB	6-2	222	25	4	Auburn
67	Kuechenberg, Bob	G	6-2	252	25	4	Notre Dame
62	Langer, Jim	C	6-2	253	25	4	South Dakota State
23	Leigh, Charles	RB	5-11	206	27	5	None
66	Little, Larry	G	6-1	265	27	7	Bethune-Cookman
88	Mandich, Jim	TE	6-2	224	25	4	Michigan
53	Matheson, Bob	LB	6-4	235	28	7	Duke
65	Moore, Maulty	DT	6-5	265	27	2	Bethune-Cookman
79	Moore, Wayne	T	6-6	265	27	4	Lamar Tech
15	Morrall, Earl	QB	6-2	210	39	18	Michigan State
22	Morris, Eugene (Mercury)	RB	5-10	192	26	5	West Texas State
26	Mumphord, Lloyd	CB	5-10	176	26	5	Texas Southern
64	Newman, Ed	G	6-2	245	22	1	Duke
36	Nottingham, Don	RB	5-10	210	24	3	Kent State
82	Rather, David (Bo)	WR	6-1	182	22	1	Michigan
13	Scott, Jake	S	6-0	188	28	4	Georgia
20	Seiple, Larry	P-TE	6-0	214	28	7	Kentucky
34	Sellers, Ron	WR	6-4	204	26	5	Florida State
29	Smith, Tom	RB	6-1	218	23	1	Miami
84	Stanfill, Bill	DE	6-5	252	26	5	Georgia
10	Strock, Don	QB	6-5	216	22	1	Virginia Tech
48	Stuckey, Henry	CB	6-1	180	24	1	Missouri
59	Swift, Doug	LB	6-3	226	25	4	Amherst
81	Twilley, Howard	WR	5-10	185	29	8	Tulsa
89	Wade, Charley	WR	5-10	170	23	1	Tennessee State
42	Warfield, Paul	WR	6-0	188	30	10	Ohio State
70	Woods, Larry	DT	6-6	260	25	3	Tennessee State
1	Yepremian, Garo	K	5-8	175	29	7	None
76	Young, Willie	T	6-5	262	26	4	Alcorn A&M

Head coach—Don Shula. **Assistants**—Bill Arnsparger, Monte Clark, Tom Keane, Bill McPeak, Mike Scarry, Carl Taseff.

SUPER BOWL IX

PITTSBURGH 16, MINNESOTA 6

Fullback Franco Harris set Super Bowl records by rushing 34 times for 158 yards and the Pittsburgh Steelers outrushed the Minnesota Vikings 249-17 and won Super Bowl IX 16–6, the club's first championship in its 42-year history. The loss was the Vikings' third without a victory in the Super Bowl.

The Steelers led 2–0 at halftime. With 6:11 left in the second quarter Minnesota quarterback Fran Tarkenton fumbled a pitchout to running back Dave Osborn. Attempting to regain possession of the ball, Tarkenton slid into the end zone where he was downed by Dwight White for a safety.

Harris, who gained 97 yards in 22 carries in the second half, scored on a nine-yard run to increase Pittsburgh's lead to 9–0 after just 1:35 of the third quarter. The Steelers moved 30 yards in four plays to the score after Marv Kellum recovered a fumble on the kickoff by Minnesota's Bill Brown.

The score remained 9–0 until early in the fourth quarter. Bobby Walden was in punt formation for the Steelers on fourth down at Pittsburgh's 15-yard line. Linebacker Matt Blair blocked the punt and the ball was recovered in the end zone by the Vikings' Terry Brown for a touchdown with 10:33 remaining in the game. Fred Cox's extra point hit the left upright and the score was 9–6.

The Steelers began their next series on the 34-yard line. At the 42, quarterback Terry Bradshaw faced third down and two yards for a first down. Disdaining the run and a short pass, Bradshaw threw a 30-yard completion to tight end Larry Brown. After Harris and Rocky Bleier carried the ball from the Vikings' 28 to the 5, Bradshaw faced another third down situation. He rolled to his right, searched for a receiver, and found Brown for a touchdown that resulted in a 16–6 lead.

"I looked first to pass to the halfback [Rocky Bleier]," said Bradshaw. "It depended on what their cornerbacks did. If they had come up, I would have passed; if they had laid back I would have run. They laid back, so I started to run, but I knew I couldn't run the ball in for a touchdown."

Bradshaw said Brown made a smart move. "He stopped after running toward the corner of the end zone, then started again. That made the middle linebacker [Jeff Siemon] commit himself, and I drilled the ball to Larry." The Steelers had driven 66 yards in 12 plays and controlled the ball for seven minutes and two seconds.

Minnesota took over on its 9-yard line with 3:20 remaining. Tarkenton threw a 29-yard pass to John Gilliam, who was running down the middle of the field on first down. Free safety Mike Wagner intercepted the pass on Pittsburgh's 33 and returned the ball 26 yards to Minnesota's 41. Pittsburgh held possession for seven more plays, surrendering the ball on downs to the Vikings' at their 23 with 41 seconds left.

The Steelers appeared to confuse the Vikings with misdirection running plays as they outgained Minnesota 333-119 in total offense. Harris and Bleier repeatedly found holes in the defense that were opened when Vikings linemen followed the flow of pulling Steelers linemen. On defense, the Steelers put a man directly over center Mick Tingelhoff. Tackle Ernie Holmes sometimes would attack Tingelhoff directly after the snap of the ball; sometimes Holmes would loop around Joe Greene to the outside and participate in double-teaming action with Greene. Tarkenton was the objective. He completed just 11 of 26 passes for 102 yards with three interceptions. Four attempts were deflected and many others were thrown under severe pressure.

Bleier cuts down the Vikings' Marshall as Harris sweeps left end behind tackle Kolb.

Participants—Pittsburgh Steelers, champions of the American Football Conference, and Minnesota Vikings, champions of the National Football Conference
Date—January 12, 1975
Site—Tulane Stadium, New Orleans
Time—2:00 P.M. CST
Conditions—46 degrees, cloudy
Playing Surface—Poly-Turf
Television and Radio—National Broadcasting Company (NBC)
Regular Season Records—Pittsburgh, 10-3-1; Minnesota, 10-4
Conference Championships—Pittsburgh defeated the Oakland Raiders 24-13 for the AFC title; Minnesota defeated the Los Angeles Rams 14-10 for the NFC title
Players' Shares—$15,000 to each member of the winning team; $7,500 to each member of the losing team
Attendance—80,997
Gross Receipts—$5,126,000.00
Officials—Referee, Bernie Ulman; umpire, Al Conway; line judge, Bruce Alford; head linesman, Ed Marion; back judge, Ray Douglas; field judge, Dick Dolack
Coaches—Chuck Noll, Pittsburgh; Bud Grant, Minnesota

Pittsburgh	Starters, Offense	Minnesota
Frank Lewis	WR	Jim Lash
Jon Kolb	LT	Charles Goodrum
Jim Clack	LG	Andy Maurer
Ray Mansfield	C	Mick Tingelhoff
Gerry Mullins	RG	Ed White
Gordon Gravelle	RT	Ron Yary
Larry Brown	TE	Stu Voigt
Ron Shanklin	WR	John Gilliam
Terry Bradshaw	QB	Fran Tarkenton
Rocky Bleier	RB	Chuck Foreman
Franco Harris	RB	Dave Osborn
	Starters, Defense	
L. C. Greenwood	LE	Carl Eller
Joe Greene	LT	Doug Sutherland
Ernie Holmes	RT	Alan Page
Dwight White	RE	Jim Marshall
Jack Ham	LLB	Roy Winston
Jack Lambert	MLB	Jeff Siemon
Andy Russell	RLB	Wally Hilgenberg
J. T. Thomas	LC	Nate Wright
Mel Blount	RC	Jackie Wallace
Mike Wagner	LS	Jeff Wright
Glen Edwards	RS	Paul Krause

Pittsburgh	0	2	7	7	— 16
Minnesota	0	0	0	6	— 6

Pitt —Safety, White downed Tarkenton in end zone
Pitt —Harris 12 run (Gerela kick)
Minn—T. Brown recovered blocked punt in end zone (kick failed)
Pitt —L. Brown 4 pass from Bradshaw (Gerela kick)

TEAM STATISTICS	Pitt	Minn
First downs	17	9
Rushing	11	2
Passing	5	5
By penalty	1	2
Total yardage	333	119
Net rushing yardage	249	17
Net passing yardage	84	102
Passes att.-comp.-had int.	14-9-0	26-11-3

RUSHING
Pittsburgh—Harris, 34 for 158, 1 TD; Bleier, 17 for 65; Bradshaw, 5 for 33; Swann, 1 for -7.
Minnesota—Foreman, 12 for 18; Tarkenton, 1 for 0; Osborn, 8 for -1.

PASSING
Pittsburgh—Bradshaw, 9 of 14 for 97, 1 TD.
Minnesota—Tarkenton, 11 of 26 for 102, 3 int.

RECEIVING
Pittsburgh—Brown, 3 for 49, 1 TD; Stallworth, 3 for 24; Bleier, 2 for 11; Lewis, 1 for 12.
Minnesota—Foreman, 5 for 50; Voigt, 2 for 31; Osborn, 2 for 7; Gilliam, 1 for 16; Reed, 1 for -2.

PUNTING
Pittsburgh—Walden, 7 for 34.7 average.
Minnesota—Eischeid, 6 for 37.2 average.

PUNT RETURNS
Pittsburgh—Swann, 3 for 34; Edwards, 2 for 2.
Minnesota—McCullum, 3 for 11; N. Wright, 1 for 1; Wallace, 1 fair catch.

KICKOFF RETURNS
Pittsburgh—Harrison, 2 for 17; Pearson, 1 for 15.
Minnesota—McCullum, 1 for 26; McClanahan, 1 for 22; B. Brown, 1 for 2.

INTERCEPTIONS
Pittsburgh—Wagner, 1 for 26; Blount, 1 for 10; Greene, 1 for 10.
Minnesota—None.

White (78), Holmes (63), and Lambert (58) rack up Osborn of the Vikings.

Blair blocks Walden's punt; Terry Brown recovered in end zone for touchdown.

PITTSBURGH STEELERS

No.	Name	Pos.	Ht.	Wt.	Age	Year	College
45	Allen, Jim	CB	6-2	194	22	R	UCLA
20	Bleier, Rocky	RB	5-11	210	28	6	Notre Dame
47	Blount, Mel	CB	6-3	205	26	5	Southern U.
38	Bradley, Ed	LB	6-2	239	24	3	Wake Forest
12	Bradshaw, Terry	QB	6-3	218	26	5	Louisiana Tech
87	Brown, Larry	TE	6-4	229	25	4	Kansas
50	Clack, Jim	G-C	6-3	250	27	4	Wake Forest
22	Conn, Richard	S	6-0	185	23	R	Georgia
77	Davis, Charlie	DT	6-1	265	23	R	Texas Christian
57	Davis, Sam	G	6-1	255	30	8	Allen
35	Davis, Steve	RB	6-1	218	25	3	Delaware State
73	Druschel, Rick	G-T	6-2	248	22	R	North Carolina State
27	Edwards, Glen	S	6-0	185	27	4	Florida A&M
64	Furness, Steve	DT-DE	6-4	255	24	3	Rhode Island
86	Garrett, Reggie	WR	6-1	172	23	R	Eastern Michigan
10	Gerela, Roy	K	5-10	185	26	6	New Mexico State
17	Gilliam, Joe	QB	6-2	187	23	3	Tennessee State
71	Gravelle, Gordon	G-T	6-5	250	25	3	Brigham Young
75	Greene, Joe	DT	6-4	275	28	6	North Texas State
68	Greenwood, L. C.	DE	6-6	245	28	6	Arkansas AM&N
84	Grossman, Randy	TE	6-1	215	21	R	Temple
59	Ham, Jack	LB	6-1	225	25	4	Penn State
5	Hanratty, Terry	QB	6-1	210	26	6	Notre Dame
32	Harris, Franco	RB	6-2	230	24	3	Penn State
46	Harrison, Reggie	RB	5-11	215	24	R	Cincinnati
63	Holmes, Ernie	DT	6-3	260	26	3	Texas Southern
54	Kellum, Marv	LB	6-2	225	22	R	Wichita State
55	Kolb, Jon	T	6-3	262	27	6	Oklahoma State
58	Lambert, Jack	LB	6-4	215	22	R	Kent State
43	Lewis, Frank	WR	6-1	196	27	4	Grambling
56	Mansfield, Ray	C	6-3	260	33	12	Washington
89	McMakin, John	TE	6-3	232	24	3	Clemson
72	Mullins, Gerry	G-T	6-3	244	25	4	USC
26	Pearson, Preston	RB	6-1	205	29	8	Illinois
74	Reavis, Dave	T	6-5	250	24	1	Arkansas
34	Russell, Andy	LB	6-2	225	33	10	Missouri
25	Shanklin, Ron	WR	6-1	190	26	5	North Texas State
31	Shell, Donnie	S-CB	5-11	190	22	R	South Carolina State
82	Stallworth, John	WR	6-2	183	22	R	Alabama A&M
88	Swann, Lynn	WR	5-10	178	22	R	USC
24	Thomas, J. T.	CB	6-2	196	23	2	Florida State
51	Toews, Loren	LB	6-3	212	23	2	California
23	Wagner, Mike	S	6-1	210	25	4	Western Illinois
39	Walden, Bobby	P	6-0	190	36	11	Georgia
52	Webster, Mike	C-G	6-1	232	22	R	Wisconsin
78	White, Dwight	DE	6-4	255	25	4	East Texas State
62	Wolf, Jim	DE	6-2	230	22	R	Prairie View

Head coach—Chuck Noll. **Assistants**—Bud Carson, Dick Hoak, George Perles, Dan Radakovich, Lionel Taylor, Woody Widenhofer.

MINNESOTA VIKINGS

No.	Name	Pos.	Ht.	Wt.	Age	Year	College
67	Alderman, Grady	T	6-2	247	36	15	Detroit
56	Anderson, Scott	C	6-4	234	23	R	Missouri
17	Berry, Bob	QB	5-11	185	32	10	Oregon
21	Blahak, Joe	CB-S	5-10	188	24	2	Nebraska
59	Blair, Matt	LB	6-5	229	23	R	Iowa State
71	Boone, Dave	DE	6-3	248	23	R	Eastern Michigan
30	Brown, Bill	RB	5-11	222	36	14	Illinois
24	Brown, Terry	S	6-2	205	27	5	Oklahoma State
14	Cox, Fred	K	5-10	200	36	12	Pittsburgh
84	Craig, Steve	TE	6-3	231	23	R	Northwestern
11	Eischeid, Mike	P	6-0	190	34	8	Upper Iowa
81	Eller, Carl	DE	6-6	247	32	11	Minnesota
44	Foreman, Chuck	RB	6-2	207	24	2	Miami
42	Gilliam, John	WR	6-1	195	29	8	South Carolina State
68	Goodrum, Charles	T-G	6-3	256	25	2	Florida A&M
58	Hilgenberg, Wally	LB	6-3	229	32	11	Iowa
85	Holland, John	WR	6-0	190	24	R	Tennessee State
89	Kingsriter, Doug	TE	6-2	222	24	2	Minnesota
22	Krause, Paul	S	6-3	200	34	11	Iowa
77	Larsen, Gary	DT	6-5	255	34	11	Concordia, Minn.
82	Lash, Jim	WR	6-2	199	23	2	Northwestern
65	Lawson, Steve	G	6-3	265	26	4	Kansas
75	Lurtsema, Bob	DE-DT	6-6	250	32	8	Western Michigan
49	Marinaro, Ed	RB	6-2	212	24	3	Cornell
70	Marshall, Jim	DE	6-4	240	37	15	Ohio State
55	Martin, Amos	LB	6-3	228	25	3	Louisville
66	Maurer, Andy	G	6-3	247	26	5	Oregon
33	McClanahan, Brent	RB	5-10	202	24	2	Arizona State
80	McCullum, Sam	WR	6-2	203	22	R	Montana State
54	McNeill, Fred	LB	6-2	229	24	R	UCLA
41	Osborn, Dave	RB	6-0	208	31	10	North Dakota
88	Page, Alan	DT	6-4	245	29	8	Notre Dame
29	Poltl, Randy	CB	6-3	190	24	R	Stanford
32	Reed, Oscar	RB	6-0	222	30	7	Colorado State
78	Riley, Steve	T	6-6	258	22	R	USC
50	Siemon, Jeff	LB	6-2	230	24	3	Stanford
64	Sunde, Milt	G	6-2	250	32	11	Minnesota
69	Sutherland, Doug	DT	6-3	250	26	5	Wisconsin State-Superior
10	Tarkenton, Fran	QB	6-0	190	34	14	Georgia
53	Tingelhoff, Mick	C	6-2	240	34	13	Nebraska
83	Voigt, Stu	TE	6-1	225	26	5	Wisconsin
25	Wallace, Jackie	CB	6-3	197	23	1	Arizona
62	White, Ed	G	6-3	268	27	6	California
60	Winston, Roy	LB	5-11	222	34	13	Louisiana State
23	Wright, Jeff	S	5-11	190	25	4	Minnesota
43	Wright, Nate	CB	5-11	180	27	6	San Diego State
73	Yary, Ron	T	6-6	255	28	7	USC

Head coach—Bud Grant. **Assistants**—Neill Armstrong, Jerry Burns, Bus Mertes, John Michels, Jocko Nelson, Jack Patera.

SUPER BOWL X

PITTSBURGH 21, DALLAS 17

Quarterback Terry Bradshaw threw a pass that covered 59 yards to wide receiver Lynn Swann, who carried the ball the final five yards for a 64-yard touchdown that proved to be the crucial points in the Steelers' 21–17 victory over the Dallas Cowboys in Super Bowl X. Bradshaw was knocked unconscious when he was hit by safety Cliff Harris and did not see Swann make the catch.

The touchdown gave Pittsburgh a 21–10 lead with 3:02 remaining in the game. Dallas took over on its 20-yard line with 2:54 remaining and went 80 yards in five plays, scoring with 1:48 remaining on Roger Staubach's 34-yard pass to tight end Percy Howard.

Pittsburgh began the next series of plays on Dallas's 42 after tackle Gerry Mullins of Pittsburgh recovered Toni Fritsch's onside kick. On fourth down and nine at the Cowboys' 41, the Steelers did not punt and running back Rocky Bleier was stopped after a two-yard gain. Dallas moved to the Steelers' 38-yard line before Staubach's pass to Drew Pearson was intercepted by Glen Edwards in the end zone. Edwards returned the ball 30 yards as the game came to an end.

In a game that generally was acclaimed the best and most exciting of the Super Bowl series, the Steelers outgained Dallas 339-270 but did not take the lead until the fourth quarter.

Pittsburgh's Bobby Walden was in punt formation at the end of the Steelers' first offensive series. Walden bobbled the snap from center and recovered at his 29-yard line, where he was tackled by Billy Joe DuPree.

Staubach then threw a pass to Drew Pearson, who was alone on a crossing pattern in the middle of the field at the 15-yard line; Pearson scored the game's first touchdown after 4:36 of play.

The Steelers answered on the next series, moving 67 yards in eight plays and scoring on a seven-yard pass from Bradshaw to tight end Randy Grossman. Dallas went ahead 10–7 on the next series by marching 46 yards in 11 plays to Fritsch's 36-yard field goal.

Dallas held its three-point lead for the rest of the second quarter, all of the third quarter, and for the first 3:32 of the fourth quarter, a total of 33 minutes, 17 seconds. At that point, Pittsburgh's Reggie Harrison blocked a punt by Mitch Hoopes and the ball rolled out of the end zone for a safety and two points for the Steelers.

After Hoopes punted on the ensuing free kick, the Steelers moved 25 yards in six plays to position Roy Gerela for a 36-yard field goal. Pittsburgh led 12–10 with 8:14 left. Mike Wagner of the Steelers intercepted a pass from Staubach that was intended for Drew Pearson who ran the same pattern on which he scored in the first quarter. Wagner's 19-yard return set up an 18-yard field goal by Gerela that came on fourth down and goal to go at the Cowboys' 1. Pittsburgh led 15–10 with 6:37 remaining.

Pittsburgh took over again with 4:25 left in the game. On third down and four yards at the Steelers' 36, Bradshaw called for a play that is known as "60 Flanker Post" in the Steelers' nomenclature. The flanker, Swann, is supposed to run a diagonal pattern to the goal posts. Bradshaw took the snap from center and backpedaled. Swann headed toward the goal posts, cornerback Mark Washington matching him stride for stride. Harris blitzed and arrived at Bradshaw at about the same time as tackle Larry Cole. Bradshaw unloaded his pass and immediately was hit by Harris. Swann got a step on Washington as the pass hurtled out of the late-afternoon sky.

Bradshaw was helped to the dressing room a few moments later. It was there that someone told him that his pass to Swann had gone for a touchdown.

Wagner (23) can't close in fast enough to stop Drew Pearson on Dallas's first touchdown of the game.

Participants—Pittsburgh Steelers, champions of the American Football Conference, and Dallas Cowboys, champions of the National Football Conference
Date—January 18, 1976
Site—Orange Bowl, Miami
Time—2:00 P.M. EST
Conditions—57 degrees, clear
Playing Surface—Poly-Turf
Television and Radio—Columbia Broadcasting System (CBS)
Regular Season Records—Pittsburgh, 12-2; Dallas, 10-4
Conference Championships—Pittsburgh defeated the Oakland Raiders 16-10 for the AFC title; Dallas defeated the Los Angeles Rams 37-7 for the NFC title
Players' Shares—$15,000 to each member of the winning team; $7,500 to each member of the losing team
Attendance—80,187
Gross Receipts—$5,242,641.00
Officials—Referee, Norm Schachter; umpire, Joe Connell; line judge, Jack Fette; head linesman, Leo Miles; back judge, Stan Javie; field judge, Bill O'Brien
Coaches—Chuck Noll, Pittsburgh; Tom Landry, Dallas

Dallas	7	3	0	7	— 17
Pittsburgh	7	0	0	14	— 21

Dall—D. Pearson 29 pass from Staubach (Fritsch kick)
Pitt—Grossman 7 pass from Bradshaw (Gerela kick)
Dall—FG Fritsch 36
Pitt—Safety, Harrison blocked Hoopes' punt through end zone
Pitt—FG Gerela 36
Pitt—FG Gerela 18
Pitt—Swann 64 pass from Bradshaw (kick failed)
Dall—P. Howard 34 pass from Staubach (Fritsch kick)

TEAM STATISTICS	Dall	Pitt
First downs	14	13
Rushing	6	7
Passing	8	6
By penalty	0	0
Total yardage	270	339
Net rushing yardage	108	149
Net passing yardage	162	190
Passes att.-comp.-had int.	24-15-3	19-9-0

RUSHING
Dallas—Newhouse, 16 for 56; Staubach, 5 for 22; Dennison, 5 for 16; P. Pearson, 5 for 14.
Pittsburgh—Harris, 27 for 82; Bleier, 15 for 51; Bradshaw, 4 for 16.
PASSING
Dallas—Staubach, 15 of 24 for 204, 2 TDs, 3 int.
Pittsburgh—Bradshaw, 9 for 19 for 209, 2 TDs.
RECEIVING
Dallas—P. Pearson, 5 for 53; Young, 3 for 31; D. Pearson, 2 for 59, 1 TD; Newhouse, 2 for 12; P. Howard, 1 for 34, 1 TD; Fugett, 1 for 9; Dennison, 1 for 6.
Pittsburgh—Swann, 4 for 161, 1 TD; Stallworth, 2 for 8; Harris, 1 for 26; Grossman, 1 for 7; L. Brown, 1 for 7.
PUNTING
Dallas—Hoopes, 7 for 35.0 average.
Pittsburgh—Walden, 4 for 39.8 average.
PUNT RETURNS
Dallas—Richards, 1 for 5, 3 fair catches.
Pittsburgh—D. Brown, 3 for 14; Edwards, 2 for 17.
KICKOFF RETURNS
Dallas—T. Henderson, 48 after a lateral; P. Pearson, 4 for 48.
Pittsburgh—Blount, 3 for 64; Collier, 1 for 25.
INTERCEPTIONS
Dallas—None.
Pittsburgh—Edwards, 1 for 35; Thomas, 1 for 35; Wagner, 1 for 19.

Dallas	Starters, Offense	Pittsburgh
Golden Richards	WR	John Stallworth
Ralph Neely	LT	Jon Kolb
Burton Lawless	LG	Jim Clack
John Fitzgerald	C	Ray Mansfield
Blaine Nye	RG	Gerry Mullins
Rayfield Wright	RT	Gordon Gravelle
Jean Fugett	TE	Larry Brown
Drew Pearson	WR	Lynn Swann
Roger Staubach	QB	Terry Bradshaw
Preston Pearson	RB	Rocky Bleier
Robert Newhouse	RB	Franco Harris
	Starters, Defense	
Ed Jones	LE	L. C. Greenwood
Jethro Pugh	LT	Joe Greene
Larry Cole	RT	Ernie Holmes
Harvey Martin	RE	Dwight White
Dave Edwards	LLB	Jack Ham
Lee Roy Jordan	MLB	Jack Lambert
D. D. Lewis	RLB	Andy Russell
Mark Washington	LC	J. T. Thomas
Mel Renfro	RC	Mel Blount
Charlie Waters	LS	Mike Wagner
Cliff Harris	RS	Glen Edwards

Harrison blocks Hoopes's punt; the ball rolled out of the end zone for a safety.

Far downfield at 10-yard line, Swann takes Bradshaw's long bomb and scores.

DALLAS COWBOYS

No.	Name	Pos.	Ht.	Wt.	Age	Year	College
31	Barnes, Benny	CB	6-1	185	24	4	Stanford
53	Breunig, Bob	LB	6-2	227	22	R	Arizona State
59	Capone, Warren	LB	6-1	218	24	1	Louisiana State
63	Cole, Larry	DT	6-5	250	29	8	Hawaii
57	Davis, Kyle	C	6-4	240	23	R	Oklahoma
21	Dennison, Doug	RB	6-0	195	24	2	Kutztown State
67	Donovan, Pat	T	6-4	250	22	R	Stanford
89	DuPree, Billy Joe	TE	6-4	228	25	3	Michigan State
52	Edwards, Dave	LB	6-1	225	36	13	Auburn
62	Fitzgerald, John	C	6-5	255	27	5	Boston College
15	Fritsch, Toni	K	5-7	195	30	4	None
84	Fugett, Jean	TE-WR	6-3	226	24	4	Amherst
77	Gregory, Bill	DT	6-5	252	26	5	Wisconsin
43	Harris, Cliff	S	6-1	190	27	6	Ouachita
56	Henderson, Thomas	LB	6-2	220	22	R	Langston, Okla.
9	Hoopes, Mitch	P	6-1	210	22	R	Arizona
81	Howard, Percy	WR	6-4	210	23	R	Austin Peay
87	Howard, Ron	TE	6-4	225	24	2	Seattle
42	Hughes, Randy	S	6-4	200	22	R	Oklahoma
72	Jones, Ed	DE	6-9	260	24	2	Tennessee State
55	Jordan, Lee Roy	LB	6-1	221	34	13	Alabama
66	Lawless, Burton	G	6-4	250	22	R	Florida
50	Lewis, D.D.	LB	6-1	218	30	7	Mississippi
19	Longley, Clint	QB	6-1	193	23	2	Abilene Christian
79	Martin, Harvey	DE	6-5	250	25	3	East Texas State
73	Neely, Ralph	T	6-6	260	32	11	Oklahoma
44	Newhouse, Robert	RB	5-10	200	26	4	Houston
61	Nye, Blaine	G	6-4	255	29	8	Stanford
88	Pearson, Drew	WR	6-0	180	25	3	Tulsa
26	Pearson, Preston	RB	6-1	205	31	9	Illinois
58	Peterson, Calvin	LB	6-3	220	23	2	UCLA
75	Pugh, Jethro	DT	6-6	250	31	11	Elizabeth City State
20	Renfro, Mel	CB	6-0	190	34	12	Oregon
83	Richards, Golden	WR	6-0	183	25	3	Hawaii
68	Scott, Herbert	G	6-2	250	23	R	Virginia Union
12	Staubach, Roger	QB	6-3	197	33	7	Navy
78	Walton, Bruce	T	6-6	252	24	3	UCLA
46	Washington, Mark	CB	5-11	186	28	6	Morgan State
41	Waters, Charlie	S	6-2	193	27	6	Clemson
54	White, Randy	LB	6-4	245	23	R	Maryland
45	Woolsey, Roland	DB	6-1	182	22	R	Boise State
70	Wright, Rayfield	T	6-6	260	30	9	Ft. Valley State
30	Young, Charles	RB	6-1	210	23	2	North Carolina State

Head coach—Tom Landry. **Assistants**—Ermal Allen, Mike Ditka, Ed Hughes, Jim Myers, Dan Reeves, Gene Stallings, Ernie Stautner, Jerry Tubbs.

PITTSBURGH STEELERS

No.	Name	Pos.	Ht.	Wt.	Age	Year	College
45	Allen, Jim	DB	6-2	194	23	2	UCLA
76	Banaszak, John	DE	6-3	232	25	R	Eastern Michigan
20	Bleier, Rocky	RB	5-11	210	29	7	Notre Dame
47	Blount, Mel	CB	6-3	200	27	6	Southern U.
38	Bradley, Ed	LB	6-2	232	25	4	Wake Forest
12	Bradshaw, Terry	QB	6-3	210	27	6	Louisiana Tech
36	Brown, Dave	DB	6-1	200	23	R	Michigan
87	Brown, Larry	TE	6-4	230	26	5	Kansas
50	Clack, Jim	G	6-3	250	28	5	Wake Forest
44	Collier, Mike	RB	5-11	200	22	R	Morgan State
57	Davis, Sam	G	6-1	250	31	9	Allen
27	Edwards, Glen	S	6-0	185	28	5	Florida A&M
33	Fuqua, John	RB	5-11	200	29	7	Morgan State
64	Furness, Steve	DT	6-4	255	25	4	Rhode Island
86	Garrett, Reggie	WR	6-1	175	24	2	Eastern Michigan
10	Gerela, Roy	K	5-10	190	27	7	New Mexico State
17	Gilliam, Joe	QB	6-2	187	25	4	Tennessee State
71	Gravelle, Gordon	T	6-5	255	26	4	Brigham Young
75	Greene, Joe	DT	6-4	275	29	7	North Texas State
68	Greenwood, L.C.	DE	6-6	245	29	7	Arkansas AM&N
84	Grossman, Randy	TE	6-1	215	22	2	Temple
59	Ham, Jack	LB	6-1	225	27	5	Penn State
5	Hanratty, Terry	QB	6-1	205	27	7	Notre Dame
32	Harris, Franco	RB	6-2	230	25	4	Penn State
46	Harrison, Reggie	RB	5-11	215	26	2	Cincinnati
63	Holmes, Ernie	DT	6-3	260	27	4	Texas Southern
54	Kellum, Marv	LB	6-2	225	23	2	Wichita State
55	Kolb, Jon	T	6-3	262	28	7	Oklahoma State
58	Lambert, Jack	LB	6-4	220	23	2	Kent State
43	Lewis, Frank	WR	6-1	196	28	5	Grambling
56	Mansfield, Ray	C	6-3	260	34	13	Washington
72	Mullins, Gerry	G-T	6-3	240	26	5	USC
74	Reavis, Dave	T	6-5	254	25	2	Arkansas
34	Russell, Andy	LB	6-2	220	34	11	Missouri
31	Shell, Donnie	DB	5-11	195	23	2	South Carolina State
82	Stallworth, John	WR	6-2	185	23	2	Alabama A&M
88	Swann, Lynn	WR	6-0	180	23	2	USC
24	Thomas, J.T.	CB	6-2	196	24	3	Florida State
51	Toews, Loren	LB	6-3	222	24	3	California
23	Wagner, Mike	S	6-1	210	26	5	Western Illinois
39	Walden, Bobby	P	6-0	197	37	12	Georgia
52	Webster, Mike	C	6-1	245	23	2	Wisconsin
78	White, Dwight	DE	6-4	255	26	5	East Texas State

Head coach—Chuck Noll. **Assistants**—Bud Carson, Dick Hoak, George Perles, Dan Radakovich, Lionel Taylor, Woody Widenhofer.

SUPER BOWL XI

OAKLAND 32, MINNESOTA 14

The Oakland Raiders, making their first appearance in the Super Bowl in nine years, defeated the Minnesota Vikings 32–14 to score the most decisive victory in the series since Dallas beat Miami by 21 points in Super Bowl VI. Minnesota lost in the Super Bowl for the fourth time in four appearances.

Oakland took the ball after the opening kickoff and went from its 34 to the Vikings' 11 in eight plays. On fourth down, Errol Mann attempted a 29-yard field goal but the ball hit the left upright. Raiders quarterback Ken Stabler summed up the confidence of his team when he conferred with head coach John Madden after the missed field goal. "Don't worry," said Stabler. "There's more where that came from."

Oakland's Ray Guy sustained the first blocked punt of his four-season NFL career late in the first quarter. Minnesota's Fred McNeill blocked the ball at Oakland's 28. Guy finally tackled McNeill at the 3 after a wild scramble for the ball. But the Vikings' Brent McClanahan fumbled on the second play after the recovery and Oakland's Willie Hall recovered. Using the last 4:35 of the first quarter and the first 48 seconds of the second quarter, the Raiders then drove 90 yards in 12 plays. Mann's 24-yard field goal put Oakland on top 3–0.

Minnesota gave up the ball without gaining a first down on its next possession. Beginning at its 36, Oakland moved 64 yards in 10 plays, scoring on Stabler's one-yard pass to Dave Casper, who was alone in the end zone. The Vikings could not gain a first down on their next series and, after a 25-yard punt return by Neal Colzie, Oakland went 35 yards in five plays, Pete Banaszak getting the touchdown that supplied a 16–0 halftime lead.

After 30 minutes of play, Oakland had gained 288 yards, Minnesota 86. Oakland had 16 first downs, Minnesota 4. Clarence Davis of Oakland had gained 86 yards in 11 carries (his game total 137 yards, in 16 carries, represented a high for his six-year pro career).

The Raiders, who were directing most of their attack over the left side of their line—behind tackle Art Shell and guard Gene Upshaw—moved 31 yards in five plays to Mann's 40-yard field goal from the 23-yard line and a 19–0 lead with 5:16 left in the third quarter.

Minnesota scored on the next series. Fran Tarkenton's eight-yard pass to Sammy White with 47 seconds remaining in the quarter concluded a 12-play, 68-yard advance.

Tarkenton had the Vikings on the move in the fourth period. They went from their 22 to Oakland's 37, but Tarkenton's pass intended for Chuck Foreman at the 30 was intercepted by Hall, who brought the ball back 16 yards. That served as the catalyst for a 54-yard march that ended with Banaszak scoring from the 2. The big play of the series was a 48-yard pass from Stabler to Fred Biletnikoff. Oakland led 26–7 with 7:21 remaining.

The Vikings' next thrust reached the Minnesota 47. On first down, Tarkenton threw a side line pass to White. Willie Brown intercepted at the 25 and outraced Tarkenton, the final defender, on a 75-yard touchdown return that made it 32–7.

Minnesota scored the final touchdown on a nine-play, 86-yard drive that culminated with an eight-yard pass from Bob Lee, who had replaced Tarkenton, to Stu Voigt. Twenty-five seconds remained in the game.

"When you've got the horses, you ride them," said Stabler, referring to Shell and Upshaw. "We're not a fancy team. We just line up and try to knock you out of there. Nobody's better at it than those two guys."

Tight end Casper of the Raiders is all alone in the end zone, scoring the first touchdown.

Participants—Oakland Raiders, champions of the American Football Conference, and Minnesota Vikings, champions of the National Football Conference.
Date—January 9, 1977
Site—Rose Bowl, Pasadena
Time—12:30 P.M. PST
Conditions—58 degrees, clear and sunny
Playing Surface—Grass
Television and Radio—National Broadcasting Company (NBC)
Regular Season Records—Oakland, 13–1; Minnesota, 11–2–1
Conference Championships—Oakland defeated the Pittsburgh Steelers 24–7 for the AFC title; Minnesota defeated the Los Angeles Rams 24–13 for the NFC title.
Players' Shares—$15,000 to each member of the winning team; $7,500 to each member of the losing team
Attendance—100,421
Gross Receipts—$5,618,480.00
Officials—Referee, Jim Tunney; umpire, Lou Palazzi; line judge, Bill Swanson; head linesman, Ed Marion; back judge, Tom Kelleher; field judge, Armen Terzian
Coaches—John Madden, Oakland; Bud Grant, Minnesota

Oakland	Starters, Offense	Minnesota
Clifford Branch	WR	Ahmad Rashad
Art Shell	LT	Steve Riley
Gene Upshaw	LG	Charles Goodrum
Dave Dalby	C	Mick Tingelhoff
George Buehler	RG	Ed White
John Vella	RT	Ron Yary
Dave Casper	TE	Stu Voigt
Fred Biletnikoff	WR	Sammy White
Ken Stabler	QB	Fran Tarkenton
Mark van Eeghen	RB	Chuck Foreman
Clarence Davis	RB	Brent McClanahan
	Starters, Defense	
John Matuszak	LE	Carl Eller
Dave Rowe	MG-LT	Doug Sutherland
Otis Sistrunk	RE-RT	Alan Page
Phil Villapiano	OLB-RE	Jim Marshall
Monte Johnson	ILB-LLB	Matt Blair
Willie Hall	ILB-MLB	Jeff Siemon
Ted Hendricks	OLB-RLB	Wally Hilgenberg
Alonzo (Skip) Thomas	LCB	Nate Wright
Willie Brown	LCB	Bobby Bryant
George Atkinson	LS	Jeff Wright
Jack Tatum	RS	Paul Krause

Oakland	0	16	3	13	—	32
Minnesota	0	0	7	7	—	14

Oak —FG Mann 24
Oak —Casper 1 pass from Stabler (Mann kick)
Oak —Banaszak 1 run (kick failed)
Oak —FG Mann 40
Minn—White 8 pass from Tarkenton (Cox kick)
Oak —Banaszak 2 run (Mann kick)
Oak —Brown 75 interception return (kick failed)
Minn—Voigt 13 pass from Lee (Cox kick)

TEAM STATISTICS	Oak	Minn
First downs	21	20
Rushing	13	2
Passing	8	15
By penalty	0	3
Total yardage	429	353
Net rushing yardage	266	71
Net passing yardage	163	282
Passes att.-comp.-had int.	19-12-0	44-24-2

RUSHING
Oakland—Davis, 16, for 137; van Eeghen, 18 for 73; Garrett, 4 for 19; Banaszak, 10 for 19, 2 TDs; Ginn, 2 for 9; Rae, 2 for 9.
Minnesota—Foreman, 17 for 44; McClanahan, 3 for 3; Miller, 2 for 4; Lee, 1 for 4; S. White, 1 for 7; Johnson, 2 for 9.
PASSING
Oakland—Stabler, 12 of 19 for 180, 1 TD.
Minnesota—Tarkenton, 17 of 35 for 205, 1 TD, 2 int.; Lee, 7 of 9 for 81, 1 TD.
RECEIVING
Oakland—Biletnikoff, 4 for 79; Casper, 4 for 70, 1 TD; Garrett, 1 for 11; Branch, 3 for 20.
Minnesota—S. White, 5 for 77, 1 TD; Foreman, 5 for 62; Voigt, 4 for 49, 1 TD; Miller, 4 for 19; Rashad, 3 for 53; Johnson, 3 for 26.
PUNTING
Oakland—Guy, 4 for 162, 40.5 average.
Minnesota—Clabo, 7 for 265, 37.9 average.
PUNT RETURNS
Oakland—Colzie, 4 for 43.
Minnesota—Willis, 3 for 57.
KICKOFF RETURNS
Oakland—Garrett, 2 for 47; Siani, 1 for 0.
Minnesota—Willis, 3 for 57; S. White, 4 for 79.
INTERCEPTIONS
Oakland—1 for 75; Hall, for 16.
Minnesota—None.

Biletnikoff rambles 48 yards to set up Oakland's first fourth-period touchdown.

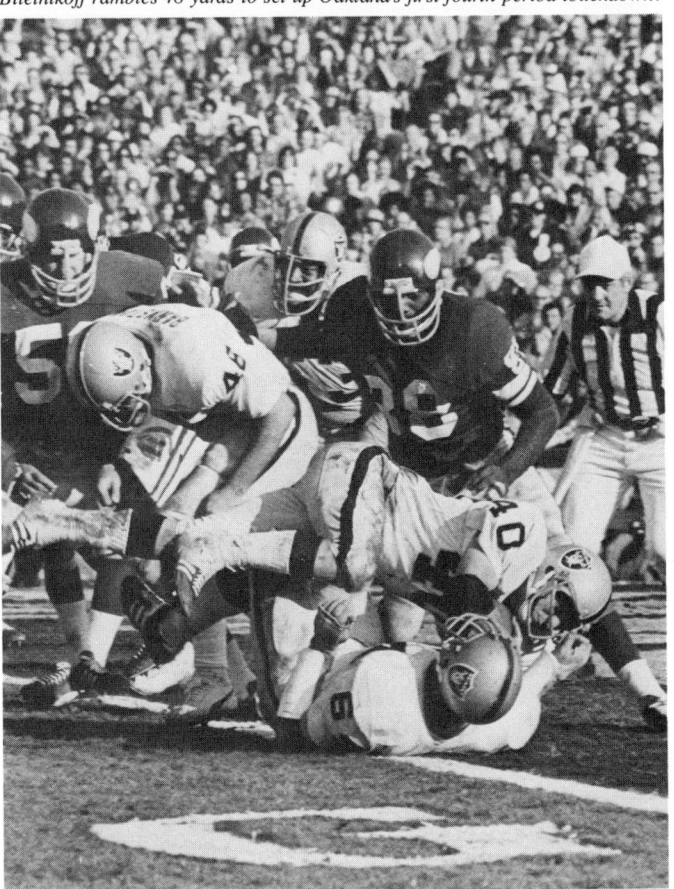

Bankston (46), Buehler (on ground) block as Banaszak scores second time.

OAKLAND RAIDERS

No.	Name	Pos.	Ht.	Wt.	Age	Year	College
43	Atkinson, George	S	6-0	185	30	9	Morris Brown
40	Banaszak, Pete	RB	6-0	210	32	11	Miami
46	Bankston, Warren	RB-TE	6-4	235	29	8	Tulane
51	Barnes, Rodrigo	LB	6-1	215	26	4	Rice
25	Biletnikoff, Fred	WR	6-1	190	33	12	Florida State
54	Bonness, Rik	LB	6-3	220	22	R	Nebraska
81	Bradshaw, Morris	WR	6-1	195	24	3	Ohio State
21	Branch, Clifford	WR	5-11	170	28	5	Colorado
24	Brown, Willie	CB	6-1	210	36	14	Grambling
64	Buehler, George	G	6-2	270	29	8	Stanford
87	Casper, Dave	TE	6-4	228	25	3	Notre Dame
20	Colzie, Neal	CB	6-2	205	23	2	Ohio State
50	Dalby, Dave	C	6-3	250	26	5	UCLA
28	Davis, Clarence	RB	5-10	195	27	6	USC
31	Garrett, Carl	RB	5-10	205	29	8	New Mexico Highlands
29	Ginn, Hubert	RB	5-9	185	30	7	Florida A&M
8	Guy, Ray	K	6-3	195	27	4	Southern Mississippi
39	Hall, Willie	LB	6-2	225	27	4	USC
83	Hendricks, Ted	LB	6-7	220	29	8	Miami
11	Humm, David	QB	6-2	184	24	2	Nebraska
58	Johnson, Monte	LB	6-5	240	25	4	Nebraska
70	Lawrence, Henry	T	6-4	273	25	3	Florida A&M
14	Mann, Errol	K	6-0	205	35	9	North Dakota
72	Matuszak, John	DE	6-7	270	26	4	Tampa
61	McMath, Herb	DE	6-4	245	22	R	Morningside
79	Medlin, Dan	G	6-4	252	27	3	North Carolina State
36	Moore, Manfred	RB	6-0	200	26	3	USC
47	Phillips, Charles	S	6-2	215	24	2	USC
77	Philyaw, Charles	DE	6-9	270	22	R	Texas Southern
15	Rae, Mike	QB	6-1	190	25	R	USC
52	Rice, Floyd	LB	6-3	225	27	6	Alcorn A&M
74	Rowe, Dave	DT	6-7	271	31	10	Penn State
78	Shell, Art	T	6-5	265	30	9	Maryland-E.S.
49	Siani, Mike	WR	6-2	195	26	5	Villanova
60	Sistrunk, Otis	DE	6-3	273	29	5	None
12	Stabler, Ken	QB	6-3	215	31	7	Alabama
66	Sylvester, Steve	C	6-4	262	23	2	Notre Dame
32	Tatum, Jack	S	5-11	206	28	5	Ohio State
26	Thomas, Alonzo (Skip)	CB	6-1	205	26	5	USC
63	Upshaw, Gene	G	6-5	255	31	10	Texas A&I
30	van Eeghen, Mark	RB	6-2	225	24	3	Colgate
75	Vella, John	T	6-4	260	26	5	USC
41	Villapiano, Phil	LB	6-2	225	27	6	Bowling Green

Head coach—John Madden. **Assistants**—Tom Dahms, Lew Erber, Tom Flores, Joe Scannella, Don Shinnick, Ollie Spencer, Bob Zeman.

MINNESOTA VIKINGS

No.	Name	Pos.	Ht.	Wt.	Age	Year	College
20	Allen, Nate	CB	5-11	174	26	6	Texas Southern
27	Beamon, Autry	S	6-1	190	23	2	East Texas State
17	Berry, Bob	QB	5-11	185	34	12	Oregon
59	Blair, Matt	LB	6-5	229	25	3	Iowa State
20	Bryant, Bobby	CB	6-1	170	32	8	South Carolina
74	Buetow, Bart	T	6-5	250	26	3	Minnesota
12	Clabo, Neil	P	6-2	200	24	2	Tennessee
14	Cox, Fred	K	5-10	200	38	14	Pittsburgh
84	Craig, Steve	TE	6-3	231	25	3	Northwestern
57	Dumler, Doug	C	6-3	245	26	4	Nebraska
81	Eller, Carl	DE	6-6	247	34	13	Minnesota
44	Foreman, Chuck	RB	6-2	207	26	4	Miami
68	Goodrum, Charles	T	6-3	256	27	4	Florida A&M
26	Grim, Bob	WR	6-0	188	31	10	Oregon State
47	Groce, Ron	RB	6-2	211	22	R	Macalester
40	Hall, Windlan	S	5-11	175	26	5	Arizona State
61	Hamilton, Wes	G	6-3	255	23	R	Tulsa
58	Wally Hilgenberg	LB	6-3	229	34	13	Iowa
48	Johnson, Sammy	RB	6-1	226	24	3	North Carolina
22	Krause, Paul	S	6-3	200	34	13	Iowa
19	Lee, Bob	QB	6-2	195	31	8	Pacific
70	Marshall, Jim	DE	6-4	240	39	17	Ohio State
55	Martin, Amos	LB	6-2	228	27	5	Louisville
33	McClanahan, Brent	RB	5-10	202	26	4	Arizona State
54	McNeill, Fred	LB	6-2	229	24	3	UCLA
35	Miller, Robert	RB	5-11	204	24	2	Kansas
77	Mullaney, Mark	DE	6-6	242	23	2	Colorado State
88	Page, Alan	DT	6-4	245	31	10	Notre Dame
28	Rashad, Ahmad	WR	6-2	200	27	4	Oregon
78	Riley, Steve	T	6-5	258	24	3	USC
50	Siemon, Jeff	LB	6-3	237	26	5	Stanford
69	Sutherland, Doug	DT	6-3	250	28	7	Superior State, Wisconsin
10	Tarkenton, Fran	QB	6-0	190	36	16	Georgia
53	Tingelhoff, Mick	C	6-2	240	36	15	Nebraska
83	Voigt, Stu	TE	6-1	225	28	7	Wisconsin
62	White, Ed	G	6-2	270	29	8	California
72	White, James	DT	6-3	263	23	R	Oklahoma State
85	White, Sammy	WR	5-11	189	22	R	Grambling
80	Willis, Leonard	WR	5-10	180	23	R	Ohio State
60	Winston, Roy	LB	5-11	222	36	15	Louisiana State
23	Wright, Jeff	S	5-11	190	27	6	Minnesota
42	Wright, Nate	CB	5-11	180	29	8	San Diego State
73	Yary, Ron	T	6-5	255	30	9	USC

Head coach—Bud Grant. **Assistants**—Neill Armstrong, Jerry Burns, Bus Mertes, John Michels, Jocko Nelson, Buddy Ryan.

Tom Matte

Elijah Pitts

Fran Tarkenton

Otis Taylor

Max McGee

George Sauer

John Mackey

SUPER BOWL INDIVIDUAL RECORDS

RUSHING

ATTEMPTS
Most Attempts, Lifetime
61 Franco Harris, Pittsburgh, 2 games
57 Larry Csonka, Miami, 3 games
Most Attempts, Game
34 Franco Harris, Pittsburgh IX

YARDS GAINED
Most Yards Gained, Lifetime
297 Larry Csonka, Miami, 3 games
240 Franco Harris, Pittsburgh, 2 games
Most Yards Gained, Game
158 Franco Harris, Pittsburgh, IX
Longest Gain
58 Tom Matte, Baltimore, III

TOUCHDOWNS
Most Touchdowns, Lifetime
2 Elijah Pitts, Green Bay, 1 game
Jim Kiick, Miami, 3 games
Larry Csonka, Miami, 3 games
Pete Banaszak, Oakland, 2 games
Most Touchdowns, Game
2 Elijah Pitts, Green Bay, I
Larry Csonka, Miami, VIII
Pete Banaszak, Oakland, XI

PASSING

ATTEMPTS
Most Attempts, Lifetime
89 Fran Tarkenton, Minnesota, 3 games (46 comp)
47 Bart Starr, Green Bay, 2 games (29 comp)
Most Attempts, Game
35 Fran Tarkenton, Minnesota, XI (17 comp)

COMPLETIONS
Most Completions, Lifetime
46 Fran Tarkenton, Minnesota, 3 games (89 att)
Most Completions, Game
18 Fran Tarkenton, Minnesota, VIII (28 att)

PASSING EFFICIENCY
Highest Efficiency, Lifetime, 30 or more attempts
63.6 Len Dawson, Kansas City, 2 games (28-44)
63.4 Bob Griese, Miami, 3 games (26-41)
Highest efficiency, Game, 10 or more attempts
72.7 Bob Griese, Miami, VII (8-11)

YARDS GAINED
Most Yards Gained, Lifetime
489 Fran Tarkenton, Minnesota, 3 games
452 Bart Starr, Green Bay, 2 games
Most Yards Gained, Game
250 Bart Starr, Green Bay, I
Longest Completion
75 John Unitas (to Mackey), Baltimore, V (TD)

TOUCHDOWNS
Most Touchdowns, Lifetime
4 Roger Staubach, Dallas, 2 games
3 Bart Starr, Green Bay, 2 games
Terry Bradshaw, Pittsburgh, 2 games
Most Touchdowns, Game
2 Bart Starr, Green Bay, I
Daryle Lamonica, Oakland, II
Roger Staubach, Dallas, VI
Terry Bradshaw, Pittsburgh, X

HAD INTERCEPTED
Fewest Had Intercepted, Most Attempts, Game
0 Joe Namath, N.Y. Jets, III (28 att)
Most Had Intercepted, Lifetime
6 Fran Tarkenton, Minnesota, 3 games (89 att)
4 Earl Morrall, Baltimore and Miami, 4 games (32 att)

Most Had Intercepted, Game
3 Earl Morrall, Baltimore, III (17 att)
Craig Morton, Dallas, V (26 att)
Billy Kilmer, Washington, VII (28 att)
Fran Tarkenton, Minnesota, IX (26 att)
Roger Staubach, Dallas, X (24 att)

RECEIVING

Most Receptions, Lifetime
15 Chuck Foreman, Minnesota, 3 games
10 Otis Taylor, Kansas City, 2 games
Most Receptions, Game
8 George Sauer, N.Y. Jets, III (133 yards)

YARDS GAINED
Most Yards Gained, Lifetime
173 Max McGee, Green Bay, 2 games
161 Lynn Swann, Pittsburgh, 2 games
Most Yards Gained, Game
161 Lynn Swann, Pittsburgh, X
Longest Reception
75 John Mackey (from Unitas), Baltimore, V (TD)

TOUCHDOWNS
Most Touchdowns, Lifetime
2 Max McGee, Green Bay, 2 games
Bill Miller, Oakland, 1 game
Most Touchdowns, Game
2 Max McGee, Green Bay, I
Bill Miller, Oakland, II

INTERCEPTIONS BY

Most Interceptions By, Lifetime
3 Chuck Howley, Dallas, 2 games
2 Randy Beverly, N.Y. Jets, 1 game
Jake Scott, Miami, 3 games
Mike Wagner, Pittsburgh, 2 games
Most Interceptions By, Game
2 Randy Beverly, N.Y. Jets, III
Chuck Howley, Dallas, V
Jake Scott, Miami, VII

YARDS GAINED
Most Yards Gained, Lifetime
75 Willie Brown, Oakland, 2 games
63 Chuck Howley, Dallas, 2 games
Jake Scott, Miami, 3 games
Most Yards Gained, Game
75 Willie Brown, Oakland, XI

TOUCHDOWNS
Most Touchdowns, Game
1 Herb Adderley, Green Bay, II
Willie Brown, Oakland, XI

PUNTING
Most Punts, Lifetime
17 Mike Eischeid, Oakland and Minnesota, 3 games
15 Larry Seiple, Miami, 3 games
Most Punts, Game
9 Ron Widby, Dallas, V
Longest Punt
61 Jerrel Wilson, Kansas City, I
Highest Punting Average, Game, 3 minimum
48.5 Jerrel Wilson, Kansas City IV (4 punts)

PUNT RETURNS
Most Punt Returns, Lifetime
6 Willie Wood, Green Bay, 2 games
Jake Scott, Miami, 3 games
Most Punt Returns, Game
5 Willie Wood, Green Bay, II
Most Fair Catches, Game
3 Ron Gardin, Baltimore, V
Golden Richards, Dallas, X

YARDS GAINED
Most Yards Gained, Lifetime
45 Jake Scott, Miami, 3 games
43 Neal Colzie, Oakland, 1 game
Most Yards Gained, Game
43 Neal Colzie, Oakland, XI

Bill Miller

Chuck Howley

Jake Scott

Willie Brown

E. (Mercury) Morris

Thomas Henderson

Jim Duncan

Longest Punt Return
  31 Willie Wood, Green Bay, II
Highest Average, Game, 3 minimum
  11.3 Lynn Swann, Pittsburgh, IX (3)
Most Touchdowns, Game
  None

KICKOFF RETURNS
Most Kickoff Returns, Lifetime
  7 Preston Pearson, Baltimore, Pittsburgh, and Dallas, 3 games
  6 Eugene (Mercury) Morris, Miami, 3 games
Most Kickoff Returns, Game
  4 Bert Coan, Kansas City, I
    Jim Duncan, Baltimore, V
    Eugene (Mercury) Morris, Miami, VI
    Preston Pearson, Dallas, X
    Sammy White, Minnesota, XI

YARDS GAINED
Most Yards Gained, Lifetime
  123 Eugene (Mercury) Morris, Miami, 3 games
  122 Preston Pearson, Baltimore, Pittsburgh, and Dallas, 3 games
Most Yards Gained, Game
  90 Jim Duncan, Baltimore, V (4 ret)
    Eugene (Mercury) Morris, Miami, VI (4 ret)
Longest Kickoff Return
  48 Thomas Henderson, Dallas, X (received lateral pass after 5-yard return by Preston Pearson)
Highest Average, Game, 3 minimum
  22.5 Jim Duncan, Baltimore, V (4 ret)
    Eugene (Mercury) Morris, Miami, VI (4 ret)
Most Touchdowns, Game
  None

SCORING
Most Points, Lifetime
  20 Don Chandler, Green Bay, 2 games
  13 Mike Clark, Dallas, 2 games
Most Points, Game
  15 Don Chandler, Green Bay, II (4 FG, 3 PAT)

TOUCHDOWNS
Most Touchdowns, Lifetime
  2 Max McGee, Green Bay, 2 games (2 p)
    Elijah Pitts, Green Bay, 1 game (2 r)
    Bill Miller, Oakland, 1 game (2 p)
    Duane Thomas, Dallas, 2 games (1 r, 1 p)
    Jim Kiick, Miami, 3 games (2 r)
    Larry Csonka, Miami, 3 games (2 r)
    Pete Banaszak, Oakland, 2 games (2 r)
Most Touchdowns, Game
  2 Max McGee, Green Bay, I (2 p)
    Elijah Pitts, Green Bay, I (2 r)
    Bill Miller, Oakland, II (2 p)
    Larry Csonka, Miami, VIII (2 r)
    Pete Banaszak, Oakland, XI (2 r)

POINTS AFTER TOUCHDOWN
Most Points After Touchdown, Lifetime
  8 Don Chandler, Green Bay, 2 games (8 att)
  5 Garo Yepremian, Miami, 2 games (5 att)
Most Points After Touchdown, Game
  5 Don Chandler, Green Bay, I (5 att)

FIELD GOALS
Field Goals Attempted, Lifetime
  6 Roy Gerela, Pittsburgh, 2 games
  5 Jim Turner, N.Y. Jets, 1 game
Most Field Goals Attempted, Game
  5 Jim Turner, N.Y. Jets, III
Most Field Goals, Lifetime
  4 Don Chandler, Green Bay, 2 games (4 att)
  3 Mike Clark, Dallas, 2 games (3 att)
    Jan Stenerud, Kansas City, 1 game (3 att)
    Jim Turner, N.Y. Jets, 1 game (5 att)
Most Field Goals, Game
  4 Don Chandler, Green Bay, II
Longest Field Goal
  48 Jan Stenerud, Kansas City, IV
Most Safeties, Game
  1 Dwight White, Pittsburgh, IX
    Reggie Harrison, Pittsburgh, X

SERVICE
Most games
  5 Marv Fleming, Green Bay, I and II; Miami, VI, VII, and VIII
  4 Herb Adderley, Green Bay, I and II; Dallas, V and VI
    Earl Morrall, Baltimore, III and V; Miami VII and VIII
Most Games, Coach
  4 Don Shula, Baltimore, III; Miami, VI, VII, VIII
    Harry (Bud) Grant, Minnesota, IV, VII, IX, XI

FUMBLES
Most Fumbles, Lifetime
  3 Franco Harris, Pittsburgh, 2 games
    Roger Staubach, Dallas, 2 games
  2 Jake Scott, Miami, 3 games
    Franco Harris, Pittsburgh, 1 game
    Fran Tarkenton, Minnesota, 2 games
    Bobby Walden, Pittsburgh, 2 games
Most Fumbles, Game
  3 Roger Staubach, Dallas, X
Most Fumbles Recovered, Lifetime
  2 Jake Scott, Miami, 3 games (1 own, 1 opp)
    Fran Tarkenton, Minnesota, 3 games (2 own)
    Franco Harris, Pittsburgh, 2 games (2 own)
    Roger Staubach, Dallas, 2 games (2 own)
    Bobby Walden, Pittsburgh, 2 games (2 own)
Most Fumbles Recovered, Game
  2 Jake Scott, Miami, VIII (1 own, 1 opp)
    Roger Staubach, Dallas, X (2 own)
Most Yards Gained, Game
  49 Mike Bass, Washington, VII (opp)
Most Touchdowns, Game
  1 Mike Bass, Washington, VII

SUPER BOWL TEAM RECORDS

RUSHING
ATTEMPTS
Most Attempts, Game
  57 Pittsburgh, IX
Fewest Attempts, Game
  19 Kansas City, I
    Minnesota, IV
Most Attempts, Both Teams, Game
  78 Pittsburgh (57) vs. Minnesota (21), IX
    Oakland (52) vs. Minnesota (26), XI
Fewest Attempts, Both Teams, Game
  52 Kansas City (19) vs. Green Bay (33)

YARDS GAINED
Most Yards Gained, Game
  266 Oakland, XI
Fewest Yards Gained, Game
  17 Minnesota, IX
Most Yards Gained, Both Teams, Game
  337 Oakland (266) vs. Minnesota (71), XI
Fewest Yards Gained, Both Teams, Game
  171 Baltimore (69) vs. Dallas (102), V

TOUCHDOWNS
Most Touchdowns, Game
  3 Green Bay, I
    Miami, VIII
Most Touchdowns, Both Teams, Game
  4 Miami (3) vs. Minnesota (1), VIII
Fewest Touchdowns, Both Teams, Game
  0 Pittsburgh vs. Dallas, X

PASSING
ATTEMPTS
Most Passes Attempted, Game
  44 Minnesota, XI
Fewest Passes Attempted, Game
  7 Miami, VIII
Most Passes Attempted, Both Teams, Game
  70 Baltimore (41) vs. N.Y. Jets (29), III
Fewest Passes Attempted, Both Teams, Game
  35 Miami (7) vs. Minnesota (28), VIII

Don Chandler   *Duane Thomas*   *Jim Kiick*   *Roy Gerela*   *Dwight White*   *Reggie Harrison*   *Marv Fleming*

COMPLETIONS
Most Passes Completed, Game
24   Minnesota, XI
Fewest Passes Completed, Game
6   Miami, VIII
Most Passes Completed, Both Teams, Game
36   Minnesota (24) vs. Oakland (12), XI
Fewest Passes Completed, Both Teams, Game
20   Pittsburgh (9) vs. Minnesota (11), IX

YARDS GAINED
Most Yards Gained, Game
282   Minnesota, XII
Fewest Yards Gained, Game
63   Miami, VIII
Most Yards Gained, Both Teams, Game
445   Minnesota (282) vs. Oakland (163), XI
Fewest Yards Gained, Both Teams, Game
156   Miami (69) vs. Washington (87), VII

TACKLED ATTEMPTING PASSES
Most Times Tackled Attempting Passes, Game
7   Dallas, X
Fewest Times Tackled Attempting Passes, Both Teams, Game
0   Baltimore, III and V
Minnesota, IX
Most Times Tackled Attempting Passes, Both Teams, Game
9   Kansas City (6) vs. Green Bay (3), I
Dallas (7) vs. Pittsburgh (2), X
Fewest Times Tackled Attempting Passes, Both Teams, Game
2   Baltimore (0) vs. N.Y. Jets (2), III
Baltimore (0) vs. Dallas (2), V
Minnesota (0) vs. Pittsburgh (2), IX

TOUCHDOWNS
Most Touchdowns, Game
2   Green Bay, I
Oakland, II
Dallas, VI
Pittsburgh, X
Minnesota, XI
Fewest Touchdowns, Game
0   Baltimore, III
N.Y. Jets, III
Minnesota, IV, VIII and IX
Miami VI and VIII
Washington, VII
Most Touchdowns, Both Teams, Game
4   Pittsburgh (2) vs. Dallas (2), X

INTERCEPTIONS BY
Most Interceptions by, Game
4   N.Y. Jets, III
Most Yards Gained, Game
95   Miami, VII
Most Interceptions by, Both Teams, Game
6   Baltimore (3) vs. Dallas (3), V
Most Touchdowns, Game
1   Green Bay, II
Oakland, XI

PUNTING
Most Punts, Game
9   Dallas, V
Fewest Punts, Game
3   Baltimore, III
Minnesota, IV
Miami, VIII
Most Punts, Both Teams, Game
13   Dallas (9) vs. Baltimore (4), V
Pittsburgh (7) vs. Minnesota (6), IX
Fewest Punts, Both Teams, Game
7   Baltimore (3) vs. N.Y. Jets (4), III
Minnesota (3) vs. Kansas City (4), IV

PUNTING AVERAGE
Highest Average, Game
48.5   Kansas City (4 punts)
Lowest Average, Game
31.2   Washington, VII (5 punts)

PUNT RETURNS
Most Punt Returns, Game
5   Green Bay, II
Baltimore, V
Pittsburgh, IX
Fewest Punt Returns, Game
0   Minnesota, VIII
Most Punt Returns, Both Teams, Game
9   Pittsburgh (5) vs. Minnesota (4), IX
Fewest Punt Returns, Both Teams, Game
2   Dallas (1) vs. Miami (1), VI

YARDS GAINED
Most Yards Gained, Game
43   Oakland, XI
Fewest Yards Gained, Game
−1   Dallas, VI (1)
Most Yards Gained, Both Teams, Game
57   Oakland (43) vs. Minnesota (14), XI
Fewest Yards Gained, Both Teams, Game
13   Miami (4) vs. Washington (9), VII
Highest Average Gain, Game
9.0   Minnesota, IV (2 ret)
Most Touchdowns, Game
None

KICKOFF RETURNS
Most Kickoff Returns, Game
7   Oakland, II
Minnesota, XI
Fewest Kickoff Returns, Game
1   N.Y. Jets, III
Most Kickoff Returns, Both Teams, Game
10   Oakland (7) vs. Green Bay (3), II
Fewest Kickoff Returns, Both Teams, Game
5   N.Y. Jets (1) vs. Baltimore (4), III
Miami (2) vs. Washington (3), VII

YARDS GAINED
Most Yards Gained, Game
136   Minnesota, XI
Fewest Yards Gained, Game
25   N.Y. Jets, III (1 ret)
Most Yards Gained, Both Teams, Game
195   Kansas City (130) vs. Green Bay (65), I
Fewest Yards Gained, Both Teams, Game
78   Miami (33) vs. Washington (45), VII

AVERAGE GAIN
Highest Average Gain, Game
26.3   Baltimore, II (4)
Most Touchdowns, Game
None

SCORING
Most Points, Game
35   Green Bay, I
Fewest Points, Game
3   Miami, VI
Most Points, Both Teams, Game
47   Green Bay (33) vs. Oakland (14), II
Fewest Points, Both Teams, Game
21   Washington (7), vs. Miami (14), VII

SUPER BOWL HISTORY

Date	Game	Result	Win Lg or Conf	Site (attendance)
Jan. 15, 1967	I	Green Bay 35, Kansas City 10	NFL	Los Angeles Memorial Coliseum (61,946)
Jan. 14, 1968	II	Green Bay 33, Oakland 14	NFL	Orange Bowl, Miami (75,546)
Jan. 12, 1969	III	N.Y. Jets 16, Baltimore 7	AFL	Orange Bowl, Miami (75,389)
Jan. 11, 1970	IV	Kansas City 23, Minnesota 7	AFL	Tulane Stadium, New Orleans (80,562)
Jan. 17, 1971	V	Baltimore 16, Dallas 13	AFC	Orange Bowl, Miami (79,204)
Jan. 16, 1972	VI	Dallas 24, Miami 3	NFC	Tulane Stadium, New Orleans (81,023)
Jan. 14, 1973	VII	Miami 14, Washington 7	AFC	Los Angeles Memorial Coliseum (90,182)
Jan. 13, 1974	VIII	Miami 24, Minnesota 7	AFC	Rice Stadium, Houston (71,882)
Jan. 12, 1975	IX	Pittsburgh 16, Minnesota 6	AFC	Tulane Stadium, New Orleans (80,997)
Jan. 18, 1976	X	Pittsburgh 21, Dallas 17	AFC	Orange Bowl, Miami (80,187)
Jan. 9, 1977	XI	Oakland 32, Minnesota 14	AFC	Rose Bowl, Pasadena (100,421)

Pro Bowl
Games

1939

N.Y. GIANTS 13, PRO ALL-STARS 10

Ward Cuff's 18-yard field goal with five minutes remaining in the game provided the New York Giants, 1938 NFL champions, with a 13–10 victory over the Pro All-Stars, comprised of players from other NFL teams and members of the Los Angeles Bulldogs, an independent professional team.

A crowd estimated at 20,000 persons watched in Wrigley Field, a baseball stadium in Los Angeles. Game officials predicted that 30,000 persons would attend and said the lower turnout was the result of a heavy fog that covered the Los Angeles basin.

The Giants trailed 10–3 entering the fourth quarter and tied the score on a 22-yard touchdown pass from Ed Danowski to Chuck Gelatka.

January 15, at Los Angeles

N.Y. Giants	Starting Lineups	Pro All-Stars
Jim Lee Howell	LE	G. Tinsley (Chi. Cardinals)
Ed Widseth	LT	Joe Stydahar (Chi. Bears)
Orville Tuttle	LG	Byron Gentry (Pittsburgh)
Mel Hein	C	John Wiatrak (Detroit)
Ken (Kayo) Lunday	RG	P. Mehringer (L.A. Bulldogs)
Owen (Ox) Parry	RT	F. (Bruiser) Kinard (Bkn)
Jim Poole	RE	Perry Schwartz (Brooklyn)
Nello Falaschi	QB	Erny Pinckert (Washington)
Hank Soar	LH	Lloyd Cardwell (Detroit)
Ward Cuff	RH	S. Baugh (Washington)
Ed Danowski	FB	Clarke Hinkle (Green Bay)

Head coaches—Steve Owen, N.Y. Giants; Ray Flaherty (Washington), and Elmer (Gus) Henderson (Detroit), Pro All-Stars

N.Y. Giants	0	3	0	10	—	13
Pro All-Stars	0	3	7	0	—	10

NYG —FG Barnum 18
All-Americans—FG E. Smith 25
All-Americans—Cardwell 71 pass from Baugh (Stydahar kick)
NYG —Gelatka 22 pass from Danowski (Cuff kick)
NYG —FG Cuff 18
Attendance—20,000

JANUARY, 1940

GREEN BAY 16, PRO ALL-STARS 7

Cecil Isbell and Don Hutson combined to produce a 92-yard touchdown as the Green Bay Packers, winners of the 1939 NFL championship, defeated selected players from other NFL teams 16–7.

The Packers were leading 6–0 in the second quarter and had the ball on their 8-yard line. Isbell took the snap from center, faked a running play, and hurled a 61-yard pass to Hutson, sprinting free at the All-Stars' 31-yard line.

The game had been postponed a week because of threatening weather and rains that soaked the playing field in Gilmore Stadium, home field for the Hollywood Bears of the Pacific Coast League and a stadium built for football.

January 14, at Los Angeles

Green Bay	Starting Lineups	Pro All-Stars
Don Hutson	LE	Jim Poole (N.Y. Giants)
Buford (Baby) Ray	LT	Joe Stydahar (Chi. Bears)
Paul Engebretsen	LG	Byron Gentry (Pittsburgh)
Tom Greenfield	C	Mel Hein (N.Y. Giants)
C. (Buckets) Goldenberg	RG	F. (Bruiser) Kinard (Bkn)
Bill Lee	RT	Ray George (Detroit)
Milt Gantenbein	RE	Perry Schwartz (Brooklyn)
Larry Craig	QB	Fred Vanzo (Detroit)
Cecil Isbell	LH	Parker Hall (Cleveland)
Arnie Herber	RH	Erny Pinckert (Washington)
Clarke Hinkle	FB	Johnny Drake (Cleveland)

Head coaches—Earl (Curly) Lambeau, Green Bay; Steve Owen (N.Y. Giants), Pro All-Stars

Green Bay	3	10	0	3	—	16
Pro All-Stars	0	0	7	0	—	7

GB —FG Hinkle 45
GB —FG Smith 15
GB —Hutson 92 pass from Isbell (Smith kick)
All-Americans—Carter 4 pass from O'Brien (Cuff kick)
GB —FG Smith 7
Attendance—18,000

DECEMBER, 1940

CHI. BEARS 28, PRO ALL-STARS 14

Dick Plasman intercepted a pass by Sammy Baugh and ran 26 yards to the 5-yard line, setting up the touchdown that broke a 14–14 tie and helped the Chicago Bears to a 28–14 victory over the Pro All-Stars before an overflow crowd of 21,624 persons in Gilmore Stadium.

Bears quarterback Sid Luckman scored from the 1-yard line three plays after Plasman's interception to give Chicago a 21–14 lead. Plasman also figured in the Bears' first touchdown. He caught a short pass from Luckman at midfield, advanced two yards, then lateraled to Hampton Pool, who ran 48 yards to a touchdown.

December 29, at Los Angeles

Chi. Bears	Starting Lineups	Pro All-Stars
Dick Plasman	LE	C. Mulleneaux (Green Bay)
Joe Stydahar	LT	Jim Barber (Washington)
Danny Fortmann	LG	D. Oldershaw (N.Y. Giants)
Clyde (Bulldog) Turner	C	Mel Hein (N.Y. Giants)
George Musso	RG	Dick Bassi (Philadelphia)
Lee Artoe	RT	F. (Bruiser) Kinard (Bkn)
Hampton Pool	RE	Jim Poole (N.Y. Giants)
Sid Luckman	QB	C. (Pug) Manders (Bkn)
Ray Nolting	LH	Merlyn Condit (Pittsburgh)
Gary Famiglietti	RH	Sammy Baugh (Wash.)
Bill Osmanski	FB	Johnny Drake (Cleveland)

Head coaches—George Halas, Chi. Bears; Ray Flaherty (Washington), Pro All-Stars

Chi. Bears	7	7	7	7	—	28
Pro All-Stars	0	14	0	0	—	14

Chi —Pool 48 lateral from Plasman, who caught 9 pass from Luckman (Martinovich kick)
All-Stars—Livingston 10 interception return (Hinkle kick)
Chi —Clark 65 pass from Luckman (Martinovich kick)
All-Stars—Looney 3 pass from Baugh (Hutson kick)
Chi —Luckman 1 run (Snyder kick)
Chi —Maniachi 3 run (Maniachi kick)
Attendance—21,624

JANUARY, 1942

CHI. BEARS 35, PRO ALL-STARS 24

The Chicago Bears scored three touchdowns in the second quarter and turned back an All-Stars threat in the third quarter to score a 35–24 victory. The game was moved to the Polo Grounds in New York because of the danger inherent in large gatherings in cities on the West Coast, which was protecting against the possibility of a Japanese attack not long after the bombing of Pearl Harbor in Hawaii.

The Bears drove 53 yards to George McAfee's one-yard touchdown run for their first score. McAfee gave them a 14–3 lead with a 68-yard punt return.

January 4, at New York

Chi. Bears	Starting Lineups	Pro All-Stars
Dick Plasman	LE	Perry Schwartz (Brooklyn)
Ed Kolman	LT	Willie Wilkin (Washington)
Danny Fortmann	LG	Jim Sivell (Brooklyn)
Clyde (Bulldog) Turner	C	Mel Hein (N.Y. Giants)
Ray Bray	RG	J. Kuharich (Chi. Cardinals)
Lee Artoe	RT	F. (Bruiser) Kinard (Bkn)
John Siegal	RE	B. Dewell (Chi. Cardinals)
Sid Luckman	QB	N. Falaschi (N.Y. Giants)
Ray Nolting	LH	F. Filchock (Washington)
Hugh Gallarneau	RH	Ward Cuff (N.Y. Giants)
Norm Standlee	FB	C. (Pug) Manders (Bkn)

Head coaches—George Halas, Chi. Bears; Steve Owen (N.Y. Giants), Pro All-Stars

Chi. Bears	0	21	7	7	—	35
Pro All-Stars	3	0	14	7	—	24

All-Stars—FG Cuff 19
Chi —McAfee 1 run (Snyder kick)
Chi —McAfee 68 punt return (Artoe kick)
Chi —Swisher 6 run (Stydahar kick)
All-Stars—Schwartz 15 pass from Baugh (Cuff kick)
All-Stars—Dewell 24 pass from Baugh (Cuff kick)
Chi —McLean 50 pass from Luckman (Stydahar kick)
Chi —Kavanaugh 7 pass from Bussey (Stydahar kick)
All-Stars—Schwartz 26 pass from Baugh (Cuff kick)
Attendance—17,725

DECEMBER, 1942

PRO ALL-STARS 17, WASHINGTON 14

The Washington Redskins lost to the All-Stars in Philadelphia without star player Sammy Baugh.

Baugh explained that an automobile was supposed to have been provided by Redskins management to take him from Sweetwater, Texas (30 miles from his ranch in Rotan), to the airport in Dallas for an 11:50 P.M. flight the Friday before the Sunday game. Baugh said the car was not there, so he had the Sweetwater police call the airport in nearby Abilene. The police were told the last flight already had left Abilene at 6 P.M. Baugh said he then tried to get a taxi from Sweetwater to Dallas (230 miles away), "but the taxi driver was in a movie and when he got out it was too late. So I came home."

December 27, at Philadelphia

Washington	Starting Lineups	Pro All-Stars
Bob Masterson	LE	Perry Schwartz (Brooklyn)
Fred Davis	LT	Chet Adams (Cleveland)
Dick Farman	LG	Augie Lio (Detroit)
Charles (Ki) Aldrich	C	C. Cherundolo (Pittsburgh)
Steve Slivinski	RG	Enio Conti (Philadelphia)
Bill Young	RT	J. Woudenberg (Pittsburgh)
Ed Cifers	RE	Eddie Rucinski (Brooklyn)
Ray Hare	QB	T. Thompson (Philadelphia)
Roy Zimmerman	LH	Bill Dudley (Pittsburgh)
Ed Justice	RH	Merlyn Condit (Brooklyn)
Andy Farkas	FB	Harry Hopp (Detroit)

Head coaches—Ray Flaherty, Washington; Heartley (Hunk) Anderson (Chi. Bears), Pro All-Stars

Washington	7	0	7	0	—	14
Pro All-Stars	0	0	14	3	—	17

Wash —Aldrich 30 punt return (Masterson kick)
All-Stars—Dudley 97 interception return (Maznicki kick)
All-Stars—Petty 2 run (Maznicki kick)
Wash —Seymour 14 pass from Zimmerman (Masterson kick)
All-Stars—FG Artoe 43
Attendance—18,671

1951

AMERICAN 28, NATIONAL 27

Quarterback Otto Graham of the Cleveland Browns was named player of the game after scoring touchdowns on runs of 6 and 10 yards in the third quarter as the American Conference All-Stars overcame a 27–14 National Conference lead to win the first Pro Bowl in the game's revival in Memorial Coliseum, Los Angeles. Graham also completed 19 of 27 passes.

Quarterbacks Bob Waterfield and Norm Van Brocklin of the Los Angeles Rams combined to complete 21 of 44 passes for 294 yards and three touchdowns for the National Conference.

January 14, at Los Angeles

American Conf.	Starting Lineups	National Conf.
Pete Pihos (Philadelphia)	LE	Tom Fears (Los Angeles)
Lou Groza (Cleveland)	LT	Dick Huffman (Los Angeles)
Weldon Humble (Cleveland)	LG	Dick Barwegan (Chicago)
Bill Walsh (Pittsburgh)	C	Brad Ecklund (N.Y. Yanks)
Bill Willis (Cleveland)	RG	Lou Creekmur (Detroit)
Al Wistert (Philadelphia)	RT	Thurman McGraw (Detroit)
Bob Shaw (Chi. Cardinals)	RE	Dan Edwards (N.Y. Yanks)
Otto Graham (Cleveland)	QB	B. Waterfield (Los Angeles)
Gene Roberts (N.Y. Giants)	LH	Glenn Davis (Los Angeles)
E. Angsman (Chi. Card.)	RH	Billy Grimes (Green Bay)
Marion Motley (Cleveland)	FB	Dick Hoerner (Los Angeles)

Head coaches—Paul Brown (Cleveland), American Conference; Joe Stydahar (Los Angeles), National Conference

American Conf.	7	7	14	0	—	28
National Conf.	7	13	7	0	—	27

National —Fears 22 pass from Waterfield (Waterfield kick)
American—Dudley 47 punt return (Groza kick)
National —FG Waterfield 30
American—Shaw 47 pass from Graham (Groza kick)
National —FG Waterfield 27
National —Fears 5 pass from Van Brocklin (Waterfield kick)
National —Edwards 65 pass from Waterfield (Waterfield kick)
American—Graham 6 run (Harder kick)
American—Graham 10 run (Harder kick)
Attendance—53,678

1952

NATIONAL 30, AMERICAN 13

The National Conference All-Stars capitalized on two fourth-quarter fumbles by American Conference quarterback Sammy Baugh to score two touchdowns in a 20-point period in which they overcame a 13–10 American Conference lead to win 30–13. Baugh, playing in the fourth quarter, fumbled four times in a driving rain and had his only pass intercepted.

With the Nationals leading 16–13, Baugh fumbled on the Americans' 24. Defensive tackle Leo Nomellini picked up the ball on the 20 and ran for a touchdown that put the National team ahead 23–13.

January 12, at Los Angeles

National Conf.	Starting Lineups	American Conf.
G. Soltau (San Francisco)	LE	F. Polsfoot (Chi. Cardinals)
George Connor (Chi Bears)	LT	Lou Groza (Cleveland)
Lou Creekmur (Detroit)	LG	B. Fischer (Chi. Cardinals)
Brad Ecklund (N.Y. Yanks)	C	Bill Walsh (Pittsburgh)
Dick Barwegan (Chi. Bears)	RG	George Hughes (Pittsburgh)
M. McCormack (N.Y. Yanks)	RT	D. (Tex) Coulter (N.Y.G.)
E. (Crazylegs) Hirsch (L.A.)	RE	Dante Lavelli (Cleveland)
B. Waterfield (Los Angeles)	QB	Otto Graham (Cleveland)
Dan Towler (Los Angeles)	LH	Ken Carpenter (Cleveland)
P. (Tank) Younger (L.A.)	RH	Dub Jones (Cleveland)
John Dottley (Chi. Bears)	FB	Eddie Price (N.Y. Giants)

Head coaches—Paul Brown (Cleveland), American Conference; Raymond (Buddy) Parker (Detroit), National Conference

National Conf.	3	7	0	20	—	30
American Conf.	7	6	0	0	—	13

American—Jones 44 pass from Graham (Graham kick)
National—FG Waterfield 30
American—FG Groza 45
American—FG Groza 11
National—Soltau 1 pass from Van Brocklin (Waterfield kick)
National—Dottley 2 run (kick failed)
National—Nomellini 20 fumble return (Waterfield kick)
National—Hirsch 7 pass from Walker (Lujack kick)
Attendance—19,400

1953

NATIONAL 27, AMERICAN 7

Fullback Dan Towler took a handoff from quarterback Bobby Layne and threw a 13-yard pass to Hugh McElhenny for the game's first score in a 27–7 National Conference victory. The pass was the first Towler had thrown in three seasons as a professional.

Towler's Los Angeles Rams teammate, Norm Van Brocklin, replaced Layne at quarterback on the next offensive series. On Van Brocklin's first play, he threw a 39-yard pass to Green Bay's Bill Howton, who caught the ball on the American Conference's 35-yard line and ran for a touchdown that completed a 74-yard play.

Van Brocklin completed 5 of 15 passes.

January 10, at Los Angeles

National Conf.	Starting Lineups	American Conf.
Cloyce Box (Detroit)	LE	H. (Bones) Taylor (Wash.)
Lou Creekmur (Detroit)	LT	Lou Groza (Cleveland)
Dick Barwegan (Chi. Bears)	LG	Abe Gibron (Cleveland)
B. Johnson (San Francisco)	C	D. (Tex) Coulter (N.Y.G.)
John Wozniak (Dallas)	RG	B. Fischer (Chi. Cardinals)
Fred Williams (Chi. Bears)	RT	F. (Bucko) Kilroy (Phil.)
E. (Crazylegs) Hirsch (L.A.)	RE	Elbie Nickel (Pittsburgh)
Bobby Layne (Detroit)	QB	Otto Graham (Cleveland)
B. Hoernschmeyer (Detroit)	LH	Ray Mathews (Pittsburgh)
Billy Howton (Green Bay)	RH	L. Chandnois (Pittsburgh)
Dan Towler (Los Angeles)	FB	O. Matson (Chi. Cardinals)

Head coaches—Paul Brown (Cleveland), American Conference; Raymond (Buddy) Parker (Detroit), National Conference

National Conf.	14	0	3	10	—	27
American Conf.	0	0	0	7	—	7

National—McElhenny 13 pass from Towler (Harder kick)
National—Howton 74 pass from Van Brocklin (Harder kick)
National—FG Harder 23
American—Graham 1 run (Groza kick)
National—FG Harder 33
National—McElhenny 7 pass from Van Brocklin (Harder kick)
Attendance—34,208

1954

EAST 20, WEST 9

Linebacker Chuck Bednarik of the Philadelphia Eagles returned an intercepted pass for a touchdown, recovered a fumble that led to a field goal, punted five times for a 43-yard average, and was named player of the game as the East scored a 20–9 victory.

The East took a 3–0 lead in the first quarter on an 11-yard field goal by Groza that followed a fumble by Perry which was recovered by Emlen Tunnell. Don Kindt tackled East quarterback Otto Graham in the end zone for a safety that made the score 3–2 at halftime.

West halfback Hugh McElhenny had 74 yards in 10 carries. Perry had 60 yards in 12 carries.

January 17, at Los Angeles

East	Starting Lineups	West
Pete Pihos (Philadelphia)	LE	G. Soltau (San Francisco)
Lou Groza (Cleveland)	LT	Lou Creekmur (Detroit)
Abe Gibron (Cleveland)	LG	Dick Barwegan (Baltimore)
K. Farragut (Philadelphia)	C	B. Johnson (San Francisco)
George Hughes (Pittsburgh)	RG	Dick Stanfel (Detroit)
Ken Snyder (Philadelphia)	RT	L. Nomellini (San Francisco)
Dante Lavelli (Cleveland)	RE	E. (Crazylegs) Hirsch (L.A.)
Otto Graham (Cleveland)	QB	Bobby Layne (Detroit)
Ray Renfro (Cleveland)	LH	Doak Walker (Detroit)
L. Chandnois (Pittsburgh)	RH	P. (Tank) Younger (L.A.)
H. (Chick) Jagade (Cle.)	FB	Joe Perry (San Francisco)

Head coaches—Paul Brown (Cleveland), East; Raymond (Buddy) Parker (Detroit), West

East	3	0	10	7	—	20
West	0	2	0	7	—	9

East—FG Groza 11
West—Safety, Kindt tackled Graham in end zone
East—FG Groza 25
East—Bednarik 24 interception return (Groza kick)
West—Perry 16 run (Walker kick)
East—Renfro 25 run (Groza kick)
Attendance—44,214

1955

WEST 26, EAST 19

Player-of-the-game Billy Wilson caught 11 passes for 157 yards and one touchdown as the West overcame a 19–3 East lead in the second quarter to score a 26–19 victory.

Doak Walker's 30-yard field goal tied the game 19–19 with 11:31 remaining in the fourth quarter. On the East's next possession, quarterback Adrian Burk's pass was intercepted by LaVern Torgeson, who returned the ball 37 yards to the East's 4-yard line. Fullback Joe Perry gained three yards on the first play and scored from the 1 on the next play.

Y. A. Tittle completed 16 of 26 passes for the West.

January 16, at Los Angeles

West	Starting Lineups	East
Harlon Hill (Chi. Bears)	LE	Pete Pihos (Philadelphia)
Lou Creekmur (Detroit)	LT	Lou Groza (Cleveland)
B. Banducci (S. F.)	LG	Bill Austin (N.Y. Giants)
L. McLaughlin (L.A.)	C	Frank Gatski (Cleveland)
D. Putnam (Los Angeles)	RG	Abe Gibron (Cleveland)
Bill Bishop (Chi. Bears)	RT	K. Snyder (Philadelphia)
Billy Wilson (S.F.)	RE	Dante Lavelli (Cleveland)
Y.A. Tittle (S.F.)	QB	Otto Graham (Cleveland)
J.H. Johnson (S.F.)	LH	O. Matson (Chi. Cardinals)
Doak Walker (Detroit)	RH	Kyle Rote (N.Y. Giants)
Joe Perry (San Francisco)	FB	Eddie Price (N.Y. Giants)

Head coaches—Joe Kuharich (Washington), East; Lawrence (Buck) Shaw (San Francisco), West

West	3	6	7	10	—	26
East	13	6	0	0	—	19

East—Matson 6 pass from Graham (Groza kick)
East—Willey 5 fumble return (kick failed)
West—FG Walker 35
East—Taylor 33 pass from Burk (kick failed)
West—Wilson 14 pass from Tittle (kick failed)
West—Hill 42 pass from Tittle (Walker kick)
West—FG Walker 30
West—Perry 1 run (Walker kick)
Attendance—43,972

1956

EAST 31, WEST 30

The West's Jack Christensen returned the opening kickoff 103 yards for a touchdown. The East's Ollie Matson returned the second half kickoff 91 yards.

After moving from its 24 to the West's 44 in nine plays, the East came to fourth down and three yards for a first down. Lou Groza put the East ahead 24–23 with a 50-yard field goal.

Matson was named player of the game. He gained 83 yards in 11 carries and scored one touchdown, caught three passes for 9 yards, returned two punts 57 yards, and two kickoffs 137 yards, scoring once.

January 15, at Los Angeles

West	Starting Lineups	East
Harlon Hill (Chi. Bears)	LE	C. Massey (Cleveland)
Lou Creekmur (Detroit)	LT	Lou Groza (Cleveland)
Duane Putnam (L.A.)	LG	Abe Gibron (Cleveland)
D. Szymanski (Baltimore)	C	H. Ulinski (Washington)
Stan Jones (Chi. Bears)	RG	Jack Stroud (N.Y. Giants)
Bill Wightkin (Chi. Bears)	RT	F. Varrichone (Pittsburgh)
Billy Wilson (S.F.)	RE	Pete Pihos (Philadelphia)
Norm Van Brocklin (L.A.)	QB	Adrian Burk (Philadelphia)
Ron Waller (Los Angeles)	LH	F. Gifford (N.Y. Giants)
Doak Walker (Detroit)	RH	Ray Mathews (Pittsburgh)
H. Ferguson (Green Bay)	FB	F. (Curly) Morrison (Cle.)

Head coaches—Joe Kuharich (Washington), East; Sid Gillman (Los Angeles), West

West	7	7	9	7	—	30
East	7	0	14	10	—	31

West—Christensen 103 kickoff return (Richter kick)
East—Pihos 12 pass from LeBaron (Groza kick)
West—Howton 73 pass from Brown (Richter kick)
East—Matson 91 kickoff return (Groza kick)
West—Ferguson 1 run (kick blocked)
East—Matson 15 run (Groza kick)
West—FG Rechichar 46
East—FG Groza 50
East—Mathews 20 pass from LeBaron
West—Waller 3 run (Richter kick)
Attendance—37,867

1957

WEST 19, EAST 10

In a game in which the total offense of both teams was 229 yards, the West's Bert Rechichar provided the difference with field goals of 41, 44, 44, and 52 yards in a 19–10 victory by the West.

Pittsburgh's Ernie Stautner blocked Rechichar's first field goal attempt, from 47 yards in the first quarter. The East then marched 40 yards in 10 plays to score its only touchdown. Frank Gifford ran three yards to the 1-yard line and fumbled. Kyle Rote recovered in the end zone for the touchdown.

The West scored its touchdown after Joe Schmidt recovered Ollie Matson's fumble on the East's 12-yard line.

January 13, at Los Angeles

West	Starting Lineups	East
Harlon Hill (Chi. Bears)	LE	D. Brewster (Cleveland)
Lou Creekmur (Detroit)	LT	R. Brown (N.Y. Giants)
Stan Jones (Chi. Bears)	LG	B. Lansford (Philadelphia)
Charlie Ane (Detroit)	C	J. Simmons (Chi. Cardinals)
Bill George (Chi. Bears)	RG	Dick Stanfel (Washington)
B. St. Clair (San Francisco)	RT	M. McCormack (Cleveland)
Billy Howton (Green Bay)	RE	Elbie Nickel (Pittsburgh)
Ed Brown (Chi. Bears)	QB	C. Conerly (N.Y. Giants)
H. McElhenny (S.F.)	LH	F. Gifford (N.Y. Giants)
B. Wilson (San Francisco)	RH	O. Matson (Chi. Cardinals)
Rick Casares (Chi. Bears)	FB	Fran Rogel (Pittsburgh)

Head coaches—Jim Lee Howell (N.Y. Giants), East; John (Paddy) Driscoll (Chi. Bears), West

West	7	3	3	6	—	19
East	0	7	3	0	—	10

West—Brown 1 run (Layne kick)
East—Rote, end zone fumble recovery (Baker kick)
West—FG Rechichar 41
East—FG Baker 52
West—FG Rechichar 44
West—FG Rechichar 44
West—FG Rechichar 52
Attendance—44,177

1958

WEST 26, EAST 7

The West trailed 7–6 after Earl Morrall's 39-yard touchdown pass to Ray Renfro in the second quarter. Bert Rechichar's nine-yard field goal with 38 seconds left in the half put the West back in front 9–7 and it never trailed again, scoring a 26–7 victory before a record crowd of 66,634 persons.

West quarterbacks Y.A. Tittle and John Unitas completed 15 of 25 passes for 159 yards and one touchdown. East quarterbacks Morrall and Eddie LeBaron completed 5 of 20 for 75 yards.

The West had a 17–7 advantage in first downs and outgained the East 340-149. Alan Ameche was the West's leading ground gainer with 85 yards in nine carries.

January 12, at Los Angeles

West	Starting Lineups		East
Billy Howton (Green Bay)	LE	L. Sanford (Chi. Cardinals)
Lou Creekmur (Detroit)	LT	M. McCormack (Cleveland)
D. Putnam (Los Angeles)	LG	Bob Gain (Cleveland)
Jim Ringo (Green Bay)	C	C. Bednarik (Philadelphia)
Harley Sewell (Detroit)	RG	E. Stautner (Pittsburgh)
Kline Gilbert (Chi. Bears)	RT	R. Brown (N.Y. Giants)
B. Wilson (San Francisco)	RE	Walt Michaels (Cleveland)
Y.A. Tittle (San Francisco)	QB	E. LeBaron (Washington)
Jon Arnett (Los Angeles)	LH	E. Tunnell (N.Y. Giants)
H. McElhenny (S.F.)	RH	J. Norton (Philadelphia)
Alan Ameche (Baltimore)	FB	B.R. Barnes (Philadelphia)

Head coaches—Raymond (Buddy) Parker (Pittsburgh), East; George Wilson (Detroit), West

West	6	3	10	7	—	26
East	0	7	0	0	—	7

West—Dillon 39 interception return (kick blocked)
East—Renfro 39 pass from Morrall (Groza kick)
West—FG Rechichar 9
West—FG Rechichar 23
West—T. Wilson 10 run (Rechichar kick)
West—Ameche 8 pass from Tittle (Rechichar kick)
Attendance—66,634

1959

EAST 28, WEST 21

Frank Gifford, voted the game's outstanding back, gained 12 yards in six carries, caught three passes for 54 yards, and completed three of four passes for 75 yards and a touchdown.

Trailing 21–16 at the end of three quarters, the East scored a touchdown, field goal, and a safety in the fourth quarter to win 28–21 before a record crowd of 72,250 persons.

Each of the East's passers—Gifford, Eddie LeBaron, and Van Brocklin—threw for a touchdown. They completed 16 of 34 passes for 214 yards.

January 11, at Los Angeles

East	Starting Lineups		West
P. Retzlaff (Philadelphia)	LE	Raymond Berry (Baltimore)
R. Brown (N.Y. Giants)	LT	Jim Parker (Baltimore)
Jim Ray Smith (Cleveland)	LG	D. Putnam (Los Angeles)
Jim Schrader (Washington)	C	Jim Ringo (Green Bay)
Dick Stanfel (Washington)	RG	Harley Sewell (Detroit)
F. Varrichione (Pittsburgh)	RT	B. St. Clair (San Francisco)
Bob Schnelker (N.Y. Giants)	RE	B. Wilson (San Francisco)
N. Van Brocklin (Phil.)	QB	John Unitas (Baltimore)
F. Gifford (N.Y. Giants)	LH	Jon Arnett (Los Angeles)
Alex Webster (N.Y. Giants)	RH	Lenny Moore (Baltimore)
Jim Brown (Cleveland)	FB	Alan Ameche (Baltimore)

Head coaches—Jim Lee Howell (N.Y. Giants), East; Weeb Ewbank (Baltimore), West

East	9	7	0	12	—	28
West	7	7	7	0	—	21

West—Ameche 1 run (Richter kick)
East—FG Groza 25
East—Webster 40 pass from Gifford (kick blocked)
West—McElhenny 20 pass from Wade (Richter kick)
East—Nagler 7 pass from LeBaron (Groza kick)
West—Wade 10 run (Richter kick)
East—FG Groza 25
East—Retzlaff 15 pass from Van Brocklin (Groza kick)
East—Safety, Scott tackled McElhenny in end zone
Attendance—72,250

1960

WEST 38, EAST 21

John Unitas and Y.A. Tittle combined to complete 27 of 40 passes for 365 yards and four touchdowns for the West, which led 31–14 at the half enroute to a 38–21 victory. Unitas completed 14 of 22 passes for 187 yards and three touchdowns, ran for 43 yards in six carries, and was selected the outstanding back.

Unitas and Tittle threw to eight different receivers. Unitas's Baltimore Colts teammate, Lenny Moore, caught five for 103 yards and two touchdowns, and Del Shofner of the Los Angeles Rams caught six for 88. The West's Jon Arnett led rushers with 61 yards in 11 carries.

January 17, at Los Angeles

East	Starting Lineups		West
B. Anderson (Washington)	LE	Del Shofner (Los Angeles)
R. Brown (N.Y. Giants)	LT	Jim Parker (Baltimore)
E. Stautner (Pittsburgh)	LG	Art Spinney (Baltimore)
Jim Schrader (Washington)	C	Jim Ringo (Green Bay)
John Nisby (Pittsburgh)	RG	Stan Jones (Chi. Bears)
K. Panfil (Chi. Cardinals)	RT	B. St. Clair (San Francisco)
B. Schnelker (N.Y. Giants)	RE	Raymond Berry (Baltimore)
Bobby Layne (Pittsburgh)	QB	John Unitas (Baltimore)
F. Gifford (N.Y. Giants)	LH	Jon Arnett (Los Angeles)
T. McDonald (Philadelphia)	RH	Lenny Moore (Baltimore)
Jim Brown (Cleveland)	FB	J.D. Smith (San Francisco)

Head coaches—Lawrence (Buck) Shaw (Philadelphia), East; Howard (Red) Hickey (San Francisco), West

East	7	7	0	7	—	21
West	10	21	0	7	—	38

East—Patton 23 interception return (Groza kick)
West—Berry 22 pass from Unitas (Hornung kick)
West—FG Hornung 16
East—McDonald 63 pass from Layne (Groza kick)
West—Moore 13 pass from Tittle (Hornung kick)
West—Moore 65 pass from Unitas (Hornung kick)
West—Smith 6 pass from Unitas (Hornung kick)
East—J. Brown 2 pass from Layne (Groza kick)
West—Hornung 2 run (Hornung kick)
Attendance—56,876

1961

WEST 35, EAST 31

The West and East divided eight touchdowns in the last three quarters, with the difference in the West's 35–31 victory coming in the first quarter, when it scored a touchdown on Jim Taylor's two-yard run and the East's Bobby Walston kicked a field goal

Taylor scored three touchdowns and Sonny Randle scored two touchdowns for the East. West quarterback John Unitas was voted the outstanding back after completing 10 of 18 passes for 218 yards and a touchdown and directing each of his team's five touchdown drives.

January 15, at Los Angeles

East	Starting Lineups		West
Bill Anderson (Washington)	LE	Gail Cogdill (Detroit)
R. Brown (N.Y. Giants)	LT	Jim Parker (Baltimore)
Jim Ray Smith (Cleveland)	LG	B. Bosley (San Francisco)
Ray Wietecha (N.Y. Giants)	C	Jim Ringo (Green Bay)
Jack Stroud (N.Y. Giants)	RG	Stan Jones (Chicago)
Mike McCormack (Cleve.)	RT	B. St. Clair (S.F.)
Sonny Randle (St. Louis)	RE	Jim (Red) Phillips (L.A.)
N. Van Brocklin (Phil.)	QB	John Unitas (Baltimore)
J. David Crow (St. Louis)	LH	Paul Hornung (Green Bay)
T. McDonald (Philadelphia)	RH	Lenny Moore (Baltimore)
Jim Brown (Cleveland)	FB	Jim Taylor (Green Bay)

Head coaches—Lawrence (Buck) Shaw (Philadelphia), East; Vince Lombardi (Green Bay), West

East	3	14	7	7	—	31
West	7	14	7	7	—	35

West—Taylor 2 run (Hornung kick)
East—FG Walston 22
West—Taylor 1 run (Hornung kick)
East—Randle 51 pass from Plum (Waltson kick)
East—McDonald 46 pass from Van Brocklin (Walston kick)
West—Moore 44 pass from Unitas (Hornung kick)
West—Taylor 1 run (Hornung kick)
East—Retzlaff 43 pass from Van Brocklin (Walston kick)
West—Arnett 20 run (Hornung kick)
East—Randle 36 pass from Van Brocklin (Walston kick)
Attendance—62,971

1962 AFL

WEST 47, EAST 27

January 7, at San Diego

East		West	
Gino Cappelletti (Boston)	LE	Don Norton (San Diego)
Al Jamison (Houston)	LT	Ernie Wright (San Diego)
Chuck Leo (Boston)	RT	Ken Adamson (Denver)
Bob Schmidt (Houston)	C	Jim Otto (Oakland)
Bob Mischak (N.Y. Titans)	RG	Bill Krisher (Dallas)
Ken Rice (Buffalo)	RT	Ron Mix (San Diego)
Bob McLeod (Houston)	RE	Dave Kocourek (San Diego)
George Blanda (Houston)	QB	Jack Kemp (San Diego)
Billy Cannon (Houston)	LH	Abner Haynes (Dallas)
C. Hennigan (Houston)	RH	Lionel Taylor (Denver)
Bill Mathis (N.Y. Titans)	FB	Alan Miller (Oakland)

Starters, Defense

LaVerne Torczon (Buffalo)	LE	Earl Faison (San Diego)
Chuck McMurtry (Buffalo)	LT	Bud McFadin (Denver)
Jim Hunt (Boston)	RT	Paul Rochester (Dallas)
Don Floyd (Houston)	RE	Mel Branch (Dallas)
Tom Addison (Boston)	LLB	Emil Karas (San Diego)
Archie Matsos (Buffalo)	MLB	Sherrill Headrick (Dallas)
Dennit Morris (Houston)	RLB	E.J. Holub (Dallas)
Tony Banfield (Houston)	LCB	Fred Williamson (Oakland)
Dick Felt (N.Y. Titans)	RCB	Dave Webster (Dallas)
Bill Atkins (Buffalo)	LS	Austin Gonsoulin (Denver)
Fred Bruney (Boston)	RS	Charlie McNeil (San Diego)

Head coaches—Wally Lemm (Houston), East; Sid Gillman (San Diego), West

East	5	7	7	8	—	27
West	0	21	14	12	—	47

East—FG Blanda 32
East—Safety, Haynes tackled in end zone
West—Stone 45 pass from Davidson (Blair kick)
East—Cannon 34 pass from Blanda (Blanda kick)
West—Haynes 12 run (Blair kick)
West—Kocourek 24 pass from Davidson (Blair kick)
West—Haynes 66 punt return (Blair kick)
West—Norton 10 pass from Davidson (Blair kick)
East—Cappelletti 5 pass from Blanda (Blanda kick)
West—Williamson 53 interception return (kick failed)
East—Hennigan 2 pass from Dorow (Dorow run)
West—Stone 15 run (pass failed)
Attendance—20,973

1962 NFL

WEST 31, EAST 30

Jon Arnett scored and the West won a narrow 31–30 victory.

January 14, at Los Angeles

East	Starters, Offense		West
Del Shofner (N.Y. Giants)	LE	Raymond Berry (Baltimore)
Ray Lemek (Washington)	LT	Jim Parker (Baltimore)
John Nisby (Pittsburgh)	LG	Stan Jones (Chicago)
John Morrow (Cleveland)	C	Jim Ringo (Green Bay)
Jim Ray Smith (Cleveland)	RG	T. Connolly (San Francisco)
M. McCormack (Cleveland)	RT	B. St. Clair (San Francisco)
B. Walston (Philadelphia)	RE	J. (Red) Phillips (L.A.)
Y. A. Tittle (N.Y. Giants)	QB	Bart Starr (Green Bay)
Don Perkins (Dallas)	LHB	Jon Arnett (Los Angeles)
T. McDonald (Philadelphia)	RHB	Lenny Moore (Baltimore)
Jim Brown (Cleveland)	FB	Jim Taylor (Green Bay)

Starters, Defense

Jim Katcavage (N.Y. Giants)	LE	Doug Atkins (Chicago)
Bob Gain (Cleveland)	LT	Henry Jordan (Green Bay)
Bob Toneff (Washington)	RT	Alex Karras (Detroit)
Ernie Stautner (Pittsburgh)	RE	Gino Marchetti (Baltimore)
John Reger (Pittsburgh)	LLB	Bill Forester (Green Bay)
Sam Huff (N.Y. Giants)	MLB	Joe Schmidt (Detroit)
M. Baughan (Philadelphia)	RLB	Bill George (Chicago)
Erich Barnes (N.Y. Giants)	LHB	D. (Night Train) Lane (Det.)
Jimmy Hill (St. Louis)	RHB	J. Whitenton (San Francisco)
Jerry Norton (St. Louis)	LS	A. Woodson (S.F.)
Jim Patton (N.Y. Giants)	RS	Eddie Dove (San Francisco)

Head coaches—Allie Sherman (N.Y. Giants), East; Norm Van Brocklin (Minnesota), West

East	3	7	6	14	—	30
West	14	3	7	7	—	31

East—FG Walston 33
West—Berry 16 pass from Unitas (Martin kick)
West—Lane 42 pass interception (Martin kick)
East—Bielski 10 pass from Tittle (Walston kick)
West—FG Martin 27
West—McElhenny 10 pass from Starr (Martin kick)
East—Walston 12 pass from Plum (kick blocked)
East—Webster 2 pass from Tittle (Walston kick)
East—Brown 70 run (Walston kick)
West—Arnett 12 pass from Unitas (Martin kick)
Attendance—57,409

1963 AFL

WEST 21, EAST 14

Denver Broncos teammates Frank Tripucka and Lionel Taylor combined on a 20-yard pass with 8:56 remaining in the game for the touchdown that provided the West a 21–14 victory.

Tripucka replaced Kansas City's Len Dawson.

January 13, at San Diego

West	Starters, Offense	East
Reg Carolan (San Diego)	LE	Ernie Warlick (Buffalo)
Jim Tyrer (Dallas)	LT	Al Jamison (Houston)
Marvin Terrell (Dallas)	LG	Bob Talamini (Houston)
Jim Otto (Oakland)	C	Bob Schmidt (Houston)
Ron Mix (San Diego)	RG	Bob Mischak (N.Y. Titans)
Jerry Cornelison (Dallas)	RT	Rich Michael (Houston)
Dave Kocourek (San Diego)	RE	Willard Dewveal (Houston)
Len Dawson (Dallas)	QB	George Blanda (Houston)
Abner Haynes (Dallas)	LH	Dick Christy (N.Y. Titans)
Lionel Taylor (Denver)	RH	C. Hennigan (Houston)
Curtis McClinton (Dallas)	FB	Cookie Gilchrist (Buffalo)
	Starters, Defense	
Earl Faison (San Diego)	LE	Don Floyd (Houston)
Bud McFadin (Denver)	LT	Ed Husmann (Houston)
Ernie Ladd (San Diego)	RT	Tom Sestak (Buffalo)
Mel Branch (Dallas)	RE	Dick Klein (Boston)
Emil Karas (San Diego)	LLB	Tom Addison (Boston)
Sherrill Headrick (Dallas)	MLB	Arche Matsos (Buffalo)
Jim Fraser (Denver)	RLB	Marv Matuszak (Buffalo)
Fred Williamson (Oakland)	LCB	Tony Banfield (Houston)
Bob Zeman (Denver)	RCB	Fred Bruney (Boston)
A. Gonsoulin (Denver)	LS	Jim Norton (Houston)
Dave Grayson (Dallas)	RS	Fred Glick (Houston)

Head coaches—Frank (Pop) Ivy (Houston), East; Hank Stram (Dallas), West

West	7	7	0	7	—	21
East	0	0	14	0	—	14

West—McClinton 64 run (Mingo kick)
West—Kocourek 11 pass from Dawson (Mingo kick)
East—Hennigan 8 pass from Blanda (Blanda kick)
East—Grantham 32 interception return (Blanda kick)
West—Taylor 20 pass from Tripucka (Mingo kick)
Attendance—27,641

1963 NFL

EAST 30, WEST 20

Jim Brown gained 144 yards and scored twice and John Unitas passed for 210 yards to give the East a 30–20 victory.

January 13, at Los Angeles

East	Starters, Offense	West
Del Shofner (N.Y. Giants)	LE	Gail Cogdill (Detroit)
R. Brown, (N.Y. Giants)	LT	Jim Parker (Baltimore)
Jim Ray Smith (Cleveland)	LG	Harley Sewell (Detroit)
Ray Wietecha (N.Y. Giants)	C	Jim Ringo (Green Bay)
John Nisby (Washington)	RG	Jerry Kramer (Green Bay)
M. McCormack (Cleveland)	RT	Forrest Gregg (Green Bay)
P. Carpenter (Pittsburgh)	RE	Mike Ditka (Chicago)
Y. A. Tittle (N.Y. Giants)	QB	John Unitas (Baltimore)
J. David Crow (St. Louis)	LHB	Dick Bass (Los Angeles)
T. McDonald (Philadelphia)	RHB	Lenny Moore (Baltimore)
Jim Brown (Cleveland)	FB	J.D. Smith (San Francisco)
	Starters, Defense	
Lou Michaels (Pittsburgh)	LE	Doug Atkins (Chicago)
Bob Gain (Cleveland)	LT	Alex Karras (Detroit)
Big Daddy Lipscomb (Pitt.)	RT	Roger Brown (Detroit)
J. Katcavage (N.Y. Giants)	RE	Gino Marchetti (Baltimore)
Galen Fiss (Cleveland)	LLB	Joe Fortunato (Chicago)
Jerry Tubbs (Dallas)	MLB	Joe Schmidt (Detroit)
R. Breedlove (Washington)	RLB	Bill Forester (Green Bay)
Erich Barnes (N.Y. Giants)	LHB	D. (Night Train) Lane (Det.)
Jimmy Hill (St. Louis)	RHB	Abe Woodson (S.F.)
Jimmy Patton (N.Y. Giants)	LS	W. Wood (Green Bay)
Larry Wilson (St. Louis)	RS	Yale Lary (Detroit)

Head coaches—Allie Sherman (N.Y. Giants), East; Vince Lombardi (Green Bay), West

East	13	0	0	17	—	30
West	0	3	17	0	—	20

East—J. Brown 1 run (Michaels kick)
East—J. Brown 50 run (kick failed)
West—FG Davis 49
West—Bass 1 run (Davis kick)
West—FG Davis 32
West—Ditka 6 pass from Unitas (Davis kick)
East—Carpenter 19 pass from Tittle (Gain kick)
East—FG Michaels 27
East—Bishop 20 fumble return (Michaels kick)
Attendance—61,374

1964 NFL

WEST 31, EAST 17

The West broke open the game with two quick touchdowns in the third quarter and won 31–17 over the East.

January 12, at Los Angeles

East	Starters, Offense	West
Del Shofner (N.Y. Giants)	LE	Raymond Berry (Baltimore)
Dick Schafrath (Cleveland)	LT	G. Alderman (Minnesota)
Darrell Dess (N.Y. Giants)	LG	John Gordy (Detroit)
Bob DeMarco (St. Louis)	C	Jim Ringo (Green Bay)
Ken Gray (St. Louis)	RG	Jerry Kramer (Green Bay)
C. Bradshaw (Pittsburgh)	RT	Forrest Gregg (Green Bay)
Pete Retzlaff (Philadelphia)	RE	Mike Ditka (Chicago)
C. Johnson (St. Louis)	QB	John Unitas (Baltimore)
B. Mitchell (Washington)	FL	Terry Barr (Detroit)
Timmy Brown (Philadelphia)	HB	Tommy Mason (Minnesota)
Jim Brown (Cleveland)	FB	Jim Taylor (Green Bay)
	Starters, Defense	
Bill Glass (Cleveland)	LE	Doug Atkins (Chicago)
J. LoVetere (N.Y. Giants)	LT	Merlin Olsen (Los Angeles)
Joe Krupa (Pittsburgh)	RT	Roger Brown (Detroit)
J. Katcavage (N.Y. Giants)	RE	Gino Marchetti (Baltimore)
Myron Pottios (Pittsburgh)	LLB	Wayne Walker (Detroit)
Galen Fiss (Cleveland)	MLB	Joe Fortunato (Chicago)
Dale Meinert (St. Louis)	RLB	Rip Hawkins (Minnesota)
Erich Barnes (N.Y. Giants)	LHB	Herb Adderley (Green Bay)
Dick Lynch (N.Y. Giants)	RHB	J. Whittenton (Green Bay)
C. Thomas (Pittsburgh)	LS	Richie Petitbon (Chicago)
Larry Wilson (St. Louis)	RS	Roosevelt Taylor (Chicago)

Head coaches—Allie Sherman (N.Y. Giants), East; George Halas (Chicago), West

East	3	0	0	14	—	17
West	7	7	14	3	—	31

East—FG Baker 30
West—Taylor 37 run (T. Davis kick)
West—Berry 4 pass from Unitas (T. Davis kick)
West—Whittenton 26 interception return (T. Davis kick)
West—Cogdill 5 pass from Unitas (T. Davis kick)
East—J. Brown 8 run (Baker kick)
West—FG T. Davis 38
East—J. Brown 3 run (Baker kick)
Attendance—67,242

1964 AFL

WEST 27, EAST 24

Cotton Davidson threw a 25-yard pass to Oakland teammate Art Powell in the final 43 seconds for a 27–24 West victory.

January 19, at San Diego

West	Starters, Offense	East
Art Powell (Oakland)	LE	Gino Cappelletti (Boston)
Jim Tyrer (Kansas City)	LT	Stew Barber (Buffalo)
Wayne Hawkins (Oakland)	LG	Billy Shaw (Buffalo)
Jim Otto (Oakland)	C	Bob Schmidt (Houston)
Ed Budde (Kansas City)	RG	Chuck Long (Boston)
Ron Mix (San Diego)	RT	Rich Micheal (Houston)
Dave Kocourek (San Diego)	RE	Ernie Warlick (Buffalo)
Tobin Rote (San Diego)	QB	Babe Parilli (Boston)
Clemon Daniels (Oakland)	LH	Larry Garron (Boston)
Lance Alworth (San Diego)	RH	C. Hennigan (Houston)
Keith Lincoln (San Diego)	FB	Cookie Gilchrist (Buffalo)
	Starters, Defense	
Earl Faison (San Diego)	LE	Bob Dee (Boston)
Dave Costa (Oakland)	LT	Ed Husmann (Houston)
Ernie Ladd (San Diego)	RT	Tom Sestak (Buffalo)
Mel Branch (Kansas City)	RE	Larry Eisenhauer (Boston)
Emil Karas (San Diego)	LLB	Nick Buoniconti (Boston)
Archie Matsos (Buffalo)	MLB	Tom Addison (Boston)
Jim Fraser (Denver)	RLB	Larry Grantham (N.Y. Jets)
Fred Williamson (Oakland)	LCB	Galen Hall (N.Y. Jets)
A. Gonsoulin (Denver)	RCB	Tony Banfield (Houston)
J. Robinson (Kansas City)	LS	Jim Norton (Houston)
Dave Grayson (Kansas City)	RS	Fred Glick (Houston)

Head coaches—Mike Holovak (Boston), East; Sid Gillman (San Diego), West

West	0	3	14	10	—	27
East	10	14	0	0	—	24

East—Gilchrist 1 run (Cappelletti kick)
East—FG Cappelletti 35
West—FG Fraser 19
East—Garron 12 pass from Parilli (Cappelletti kick)
East—Mathis 3 pass from Parilli (Cappelletti kick)
West—Lincoln 64 run (Fraser kick)
West—Lowe 5 run (Fraser kick)
West—FG Fraser 7
West—Powell 25 pass from Davidson (Fraser kick)
Attendance—20,016

1965 NFL

WEST 34, EAST 14

The West outgained the East 300–47 in the first half and led 17–7 on a 15-yard field goal by Wayne Walker and touchdowns of two yards each by Bill Brown.

January 10, at Los Angeles

East	Starters, Offense	West
Raymond Berry (Baltimore)	LE	Paul Warfield (Cleveland)
Bob Vogel (Baltimore)	LT	Dick Schafrath (Cleveland)
John Gordy (Detroit)	LG	Vince Promuto (Washington)
Dick Szymanski (Baltimore)	C	Jim Ringo (Philadelphia)
Jim Parker (Baltimore)	RG	Ken Gray (St. Louis)
Forrest Gregg (Green Bay)	RT	C. Bradshaw (Pittsburgh)
Mike Ditka (Chicago)	RE	P. Retzlaff (Philadelphia)
John Unitas (Baltimore)	QB	Frank Ryan (Cleveland)
Terry Barr (Detroit)	FL	Bobby Mitchell (Cleveland)
Lenny Moore (Baltimore)	HB	C. Taylor (Washington)
Jim Taylor (Green Bay)	FB	Jim Brown (Cleveland)
	Starters, Defense	
Willie Davis (Green Bay)	LE	Bill Glass (Cleveland)
Merlin Olsen (Los Angeles)	LT	Bob Lilly (Dallas)
Roger Brown (Detroit)	RT	F. Peters (Philadelphia)
Gino Marchetti (Baltimore)	RE	John Paluck (Washington)
Wayne Walker (Detroit)	LLB	M. Baughan (Philadelphia)
Ray Nitschke (Green Bay)	MLB	Myron Pottios (Pittsburgh)
Joe Fortunato (Chicago)	RLB	Jim Houston (Cleveland)
Bobby Boyd (Baltimore)	LHB	Pat Fischer (St. Louis)
Dick LeBeau (Detroit)	RHB	Irv Cross (Philadelphia)
Willie Wood (Green Bay)	LS	Mel Renfro (Dallas)
Ed Meador (Los Angeles)	RS	Paul Krause (Washington)

Head coaches—Blanton Collier (Cleveland), East; Don Shula (Baltimore), West

West	3	14	10	7	—	34
East	0	7	0	7	—	14

West—FG Walker 15
West—B. Brown 2 run (Walker kick)
East—Renfro 47 interception return (Baker kick)
West—B. Brown 2 pass from Tarkenton (Walker kick)
West—Nitschke 42 interception return (Walker kick)
West—FG Walker 28
West—Moore 2 run (Walker kick)
East—J. Brown 27 pass from Jurgensen (Baker kick)
Attendance—60,598

1965 AFL

WEST 38, EAST 14

The All-Star game was moved from San Diego's Balboa Stadium to Houston's Jeppesen Stadium. The West won its fourth consecutive game over the East 38–14.

January 16, at Houston

West	Starters, Offense	East
Art Powell (Oakland)	LE	G. Cappeletti (Boston)
Jim Tyrer (Kansas City)	LT	Stew Barber (Buffalo)
Wayne Hawkins (Oakland)	LG	Billy Shaw (Buffalo)
Jim Otto (Oakland)	C	Jon Morris (Boston)
W. Sweeney (San Diego)	RG	Bob Talamini (Houston)
Ron Mix (San Diego)	RT	S. Plunkett (N.Y. Jets)
D. Kocourek (San Diego)	RE	E. Warlick (Buffalo)
Len Dawson (Kansas City)	QB	Babe Parilli (Boston)
C. Daniels (Oakland)	LH	Larry Garron (Boston)
Lance Alworth (San Diego)	RH	C. Hennigan (Houston)
K. Lincoln (San Diego)	FB	Sid Blanks (Houston)
	Starters, Defense	
B. Bell (Kansas City)	LE	Bob Dee (Boston)
J. Mays (Kansas City)	LT	Tom Sestak (Buffalo)
Ernie Ladd (San Diego)	RT	H. Antwine (Boston)
E. Faison (San Diego)	RE	L. Eisehauer (Boston)
Jim Fraser (Denver)	LLB	Tom Addison (Boston)
C. Allen (San Diego)	MLB	N. Buoniconti (Boston)
F. Buncom (San Diego)	RLB	L. Grantham (N.Y. Jets)
D. Grayson (Kansas City)	LCB	Pete Jaquess (Houston)
W. Brown (Denver)	RCB	G. (Butch) Byrd (Buff.)
A. Gonsoulin (Denver)	LS	Fred Glick (Houston)
B. Hunt (Kansas City)	RS	G. Saimes (Buffalo)

Head coaches—Lou Saban (Buffalo), East; Sid Gillman (San Diego), West

West	7	10	14	7	—	38
East	0	14	0	0	—	14

West—Lincoln 73 pass from Dawson (Brooker kick)
West—Daniels 5 pass from Hadl (Brooker kick)
East—Blanks 5 run (Cappelletti kick)
West—FG Brooker 46
East—Buoniconti 17 fumble return (Cappelletti kick)
West—Lincoln 80 run (Brooker kick)
West—Alworth 7 pass from Hadl (Brooker kick)
West—Powell 17 pass from Hadl (Brooker kick)
Attendance—15,446

1966

AFL ALL-STARS 30, BUFFALO 19

A team of AFL All-Stars defeated the champion Bills.

January 15, at Houston

Buffalo	Starters, Offense	All-Stars
Paul Costa	LE	Art Powell (Oakland)
Stew Barber	LT	E. Danenhauer (Denver)
Billy Shaw	LG	B. Talamini (Houston)
Al Bemiller	C	Jim Otto (Oakland)
George Flint	RG	W. Hawkins (Oakland)
Dick Hudson	RT	J. Tyrer (Kansas City)
Ernie Warlick	RE	W. Frazier (Houston)
Jack Kemp	QB	John Hadl (San Diego)
Bob Smith	LH	Paul Lowe (S.D.)
Ed Rutowski	RH	C. Hennigan (Houston)
Billy Joe	FB	C. Gilchrist (Buffalo)
	Starters, Defense	
Tom Day	LE	J. Mays (Kansas City)
Cecil (Dud) Meredith	LT	E. Ladd (San Diego)
Jim Dunaway	RT	H. Antwine (Boston)
Ron McDole	RE	Earl Faison (San Diego)
Mike Stratton	LLB	S. Headrick (Kansas City)
Harry Jacobs	MLB	N. Buoniconti (Boston)
John Tracey	RLB	Bobby Bell (Kansas City)
Booker Edgerson	LCB	W. Brown (Denver)
George (Butch) Byrd	RCB	Dave Grayson (Oakland)
Hagood Clark	LS	K. Graham (San Diego)
George Saimes	RS	J. Robinson (Kansas City)

Head coaches—Sid Gillman (San Diego), AFL All-Stars; Lou Saban, Buffalo

Buffalo	10	3	0	6	—	19
AFL All-Stars	0	6	17	7	—	30

Buff —FG Gogolak 20
Buff —Saimes 61 fumble return (Gogolak kick)
All-Stars—FG Cappelletti 46
Buff —FG Gogolak 11
All-Stars—FG Cappelletti 14
All-Stars—FG Cappelletti 32
All-Stars—Lowe 1 run (Cappelletti kick)
All-Stars—Alworth 43 pass from Namath (Cappelletti kick)
All-Stars—Alworth 10 pass from Namath (Cappelletti kick)
Buff —Carlton 34 pass from Lamonica (run failed)
Attendance—35,572

1966 NFL

EAST 36, WEST 7

Fullback Jim Brown scored on three short runs in the first half as the East built a 23–0 lead. Brown was in his ninth Pro Bowl and his final.

January 16, at Los Angeles

East	Starters, Offense	West
S. Randle (St. Louis)	LE	D. Parks (San Francisco)
R. Brown (N.Y. Giants)	LT	Bob Vogel (Baltimore)
J. Wooten (Cleveland)	LG	Jim Parker (Baltimore)
Jim Ringo (Philadelphia)	C	B. Bosley (San Francisco)
G. Hickerson (Cle.)	RG	John Gordy (Detroit)
B. Brown (Philadelphia)	RT	W. Rock (San Francisco)
P. Retzlaff (Philadelphia)	RE	J. Mackey (Baltimore)
Frank Ryan (Cleveland)	QB	J. Brodie (San Francisco)
G. Collins (Cleveland)	FL	T. McDonald (Los Angeles)
T. Brown (Philadelphia)	HB	Gale Sayers (Chicago)
Jim Brown (Cleveland)	FB	K. Willard (San Francisco)
	Starters, Defense	
P. Wiggin (Cleveland)	LE	W. Davis (Green Bay)
S. Silas (St. Louis)	LT	M. Olsen (Los Angeles)
Bob Lilly (Dallas)	RT	Roger Brown (Detroit)
G. Andrie (Dallas)	RE	Doug Atkins (Chicago)
Jim Houston (Cleveland)	LLB	Joe Fortunato (Chicago)
D. Meinert (St. Louis)	MLB	Dick Butkus (Chicago)
M. Baughan (Phil.)	RLB	L. Roy Coffey (Green Bay)
P. Fischer (St. Louis)	LHB	H. Adderley (Green Bay)
I. Cross (Philadelphia)	RHB	Dick LeBeau (Detroit)
Mel Renfro (Dallas)	LS	E. Meador (Los Angeles)
P. Krause (Washington)	RS	W. Wood (Green Bay)

Head coaches—Blanton Collier (Cleveland), East; Vince Lombardi (Green Bay), West

East	10	13	3	10	—	36
West	0	0	0	7	—	7

East —FG Bakken 41
East —J. Brown 2 run (Bakken kick)
East —J. Brown 2 run (Bakken kick)
East —J. Brown 1 run (kick failed)
East —FG Bakken 36
East —FG Bakken 42
East —Renfro 20 interception return (Bakken kick)
West—McDonald 31 pass from Brodie (Walker kick)
Attendance — 60,124

1967 AFL

EAST 30, WEST 23

The East-West format was restored. Torrential rains flooded Oakland as the East rallied for a 30–23 win.

January 21, at Oakland

East	Starters, Offense	West
George Sauer (N.Y. Jets)	SE	Art Powell (Oakland)
Stew Barber (Buffalo)	LT	Jim Tyrer (Kansas City)
Billy Shaw (Buffalo)	LG	Wayne Hawkins (Oakland)
Jon Morris (Boston)	C	Jim Otto (Oakland)
Bob Talamini (Houston)	RG	Ed Budde (Kansas City)
S. Plunkett (N.Y. Jets)	RT	Ron Mix (San Diego)
Paul Costa (Buffalo)	TE	J. MacKinnon (San Diego)
Jack Kemp (Buffalo)	QB	Len Dawson (Kansas City)
Charley Frazier (Houston)	FL	Lance Alworth (San Diego)
Bobby Burnett (Buffalo)	HB	Clemon Daniels (Oakland)
Matt Snell (N.Y. Jets)	FB	C. McClinton (Kansas City)
	Starters, Defense	
Larry Eisenhauer (Boston)	LE	Jerry Mays (Kansas City)
Jim Dunaway (Buffalo)	LT	Tom Keating (Oakland)
Houston Antwine (Boston)	RT	B. Buchanan (Kansas City)
Verlon Biggs (N.Y. Jets)	RE	Ben Davidson (Oakland)
Mike Stratton (Buffalo)	LLB	Bobby Bell (Kansas City)
Nick Buoniconti (Boston)	MLB	S. Headrick (Kansas City)
Larry Grantham (N.Y. Jets)	RLB	E.J. Holub (Kansas City)
W. K. Hicks (Houston)	LCB	K. McCloughan (Oakland)
G. (Butch) Byrd (Buffalo)	RCB	Dave Grayson (Oakland)
Willie West (Miami)	LS	A. Gonsoulin (Denver)
George Saimes (Buffalo)	RS	J. Robinson (Kansas City)

Head coaches—Mike Holovak (Boston), East; John Rauch (Oakland), West

East	0	0	16	14	—	30
West	9	7	7	0	—	23

West—McClinton 31 pass from Dawson (Van Raaphorst kick)
West—Safety, center snap out of end zone
West—Dixon 17 pass from Flores (Van Raaphorst kick)
East —Safety, Dawson tackled in end zone
West—Buchanan 39 fumble return (Van Raaphorst kick)
East —Biggs 50 interception return (Cappelletti kick)
East —Carlton 3 pass from Parilli (Cappelletti kick)
East —Burnett 12 run (Cappelletti kick)
East —Frazier 17 pass from Parilli (Cappelletti kick)
Attendance—18,876

1967 NFL

EAST 20, WEST 10

The East scored a 20–10 victory, although Gale Sayers of the West was named outstanding back after gaining 110 yards in 11 carries, breaking runs of 52 and 42 yards on a muddy field slowed by heavy rains.

Penalties spoiled 80- and 55-yard plays by Sayers.

January 22, at Los Angeles

West	Starters, Offense	East
Dave Parks (S.F.)	LE	Bob Hayes (Dallas)
G. Alderman (Minnesota)	LT	Dick Schafrath (Cleveland)
Howard Mudd (S.F.)	LG	John Wooten (Cleveland)
M. Tingelhoff (Minnesota)	C	Dave Manders (Dallas)
Milt Sunde (Minnesota)	RG	G. Hickerson (Cleveland)
Forrest Gregg (Green Bay)	RT	Bob Brown (Philadelphia)
John Mackey (Baltimore)	RE	Jackie Smith (St. Louis)
John Unitas (Baltimore)	QB	Don Meredith (Dallas)
Pat Studstill (Detroit)	FL	Gary Collins (Cleveland)
Gale Sayers (Chicago)	HB	Leroy Kelly (Cleveland)
Dick Bass (Los Angeles)	FB	Don Perkins (Dallas)
	Starters, Defense	
D. (Deacon) Jones (L.A.)	LE	Joe Robb (St. Louis)
Merlin Olsen (Los Angeles)	LT	F. Peters (Philadelphia)
Roger Brown (Detroit)	RT	Bob Lilly (Dallas)
Willie Davis (Green Bay)	RE	George Andrie (Dallas)
Dave Robinson (Green Bay)	LLB	Chuck Howley (Dallas)
Dick Butkus (Chicago)	MLB	Tommy Nobis (Atlanta)
M. Baughan (Los Angeles)	RLB	John Brewer (Cleveland)
Herb Adderley (Green Bay)	LH	Cornell Green (Dallas)
Dick LeBreau (Detroit)	RH	Brady Keys (Pittsburgh)
Willie Wood (Green Bay)	LS	Mel Renfro (Dallas)
Richie Petitbon (Chicago)	RS	Larry Wilson (St. Louis)

Head coaches—Tom Landry (Dallas), East; George Allen (Los Angeles), West

West	0	0	3	7	—	10
East	6	14	0	0	—	20

East —FG Clark 18
East —FG Clark 17
East —Roland 1 run (Clark kick)
East —Collins 18 pass from Ryan (Clark kick)
West—FG Gossett 27
West—Willard 51 pass from Starr (Gossett kick)
Attendance—15,062

1968 AFL

EAST 25, WEST 24

A record AFL All-Star game crowd of 40,103 in the Gator Bowl in Jacksonville, Florida, saw the East win 25–24.

January 21, at Jacksonville, Florida

East	Starters, Offense	West
George Sauer (N.Y. Jets)	LE	Lance Alworth (San Diego)
Walt Suggs (Houston)	LT	Ron Mix (San Diego)
Bob Talamini (Houston)	LG	Walt Sweeney (San Diego)
Jon Morris (Boston)	C	Jim Otto (Oakland)
Billy Shaw (Buffalo)	RG	Wayne Hawkins (Oakland)
Don Oakes (Boston)	RT	Harry Schuh (Oakland)
Pete Lammons (N.Y. Jets)	TE	Fred Arbanas (Kansas City)
Joe Namath (N.Y. Jets)	QB	Daryle Lamonica (Oakland)
Don Maynard (N.Y. Jets)	FL	Al Denson (Denver)
Keith Lincoln (Buffalo)	RB	Mike Garrett (Kansas City)
Jim Nance (Boston)	RB	Hewritt Dixon (Oakland)
	Starters, Defense	
Ron McDole (Buffalo)	LE	Jerry Mays (Kansas City)
Jim Hunt (Boston)	LT	Tom Keating (Oakland)
Jim Dunaway (Buffalo)	RT	B. Buchanan (Kansas City)
Verlon Biggs (N.Y. Jets)	RE	Ben Davidson (Oakland)
Larry Grantham (N.Y. Jets)	LLB	Bobby Bell (Kansas City)
Nick Buoniconti (Boston)	MLB	Dan Conners (Oakland)
Mike Stratton (Buffalo)	RLB	Frank Buncom (San Diego)
Miller Farr (Houston)	LCB	Willie Brown (Oakland)
Dick Westmoreland (Miami)	RCB	L. (Speedy) Duncan (S.D.)
George Saimes (Buffalo)	LS	Kenny Graham (San Diego)
Jim Norton (Houston)	RS	J. Robinson (Kansas City)

Head coaches—Joe Collier (Buffalo), East; Lou Saban (Denver), West

East	3	10	0	12	—	25
West	7	14	0	3	—	24

East —FG Mercer 10
West—Duncan 90 punt return (Blanda kick)
West—Frazier 3 pass from Lamonica (Blanda kick)
East —Lammons 35 pass from Namath (Mercer kick)
West—Alworth 9 pass from Lamonica (Blanda kick)
East —FG Mercer 33
West—FG Blanda 28
East —Maynard 24 pass from Namath (pass failed)
East —Namath 1 run (run failed)
Attendance—40,103

1968 NFL

WEST 38, EAST 20

The West rallied for 21 points and beat the East 38–20.

January 21, at Los Angeles

East	Starters, Offense	West
Bob Hayes (Dallas)	LE	B. Dowler (Green Bay)
D. Schafrath (Clev.)	LT	B. Vogel (Baltimore)
Ken Gray (St. Louis)	LG	J. Kramer (Green Bay)
Jim Ringo (Philadelphia)	C	M. Tingelhoff (Minn.)
G. Hickerson (Clev.)	RG	Tom Mack (Los Angeles)
R. Neely (Dallas)	RT	F. Gregg (Green Bay)
J. Smith (Washington)	TE	John Mackey (Baltimore)
Don Meredith (Dallas)	QB	John Unitas (Baltimore)
H. Jones (N.Y. Giants)	FL	W. Richardson (Balt.)
Leroy Kelly (Cleveland)	RB	Gale Sayers (Chicago)
Don Perkins (Dallas)	RB	Bill Brown (Minnesota)
	Starters, Defense	
Paul Wiggin (Cleveland)	LE	D. (Deacon) Jones (L.A.)
F. Peters (Philadelphia)	LT	M. Olsen (Los Angeles)
Bob Lilly (Dallas)	RT	Roger Brown (Los Angeles)
G. Andrie (Dallas)	RE	W. Davis, (Green Bay)
Chuck Howley (Dallas)	LLB	D. Robinson (Green Bay)
D. Meinert (St. Louis)	MLB	Dick Butkus (Chicago)
C. Hanburger (Washington)	RLB	M. Baughan (Los Angeles)
Cornell Green (Dallas)	LHB	H. Adderley (Green Bay)
D. Whitsell (New Orleans)	RHB	Bob Jeter (Green Bay)
J. Stovall (St. Louis)	LS	R. Petitbon (Chicago)
L. Wilson (St. Louis)	RS	Willie Wood (Green Bay)

Head coaches—Otto Graham (Washington), East; Don Shula (Baltimore), West

East	0	13	7	0	—	20
West	10	7	0	21	—	38

West—FG Chandler 26
West—Josephson 4 run (Chandler kick)
East —FG Bakken 45
East —FG Bakken 25
West—Farr 39 pass from Gabriel (Chandler kick)
East —Kelly 1 run (Bakken kick)
East —Taylor 9 pass from Meredith (Bakken kick)
West—Sayers 3 run (Chandler kick)
West—Petitbon 70 interception return (Chandler kick)
West—B. Brown 19 run (Chandler kick)
Attendance—53,289

1969 AFL

WEST 38, EAST 25

January 19, at Jacksonville, Florida

East	Starters, Offense	West
G. Sauer, N.Y. Jets	LE	W. Wells (Oakland)
W. Hill (N.Y. Jets)	LT	Jim Tyrer (K.C.)
Billy Shaw (Buffalo)	LG	Ed Budde (Kansas City)
Jon Morris (Boston)	C	Jim Otto (Oakland)
D. Herman (N.Y. Jets)	RG	W. Sweeney (San Diego)
G.R. Hines (Houston)	RT	Ron Mix (San Diego)
Alvin Reed (Houston)	TE	J. MacKinnon (San Diego)
Joe Namath (N.Y. Jets)	QB	John Hadl (San Diego)
D. Maynard (N.Y. Jets)	FL	Lance Alworth (San Diego)
Jim Kiick (Miami)	RB	Paul Robinson (Cin.)
H. Granger (Houston)	RB	H. Dixon (Oakland)
	Starters, Defense	
G. Philbin (N.Y. Jets)	LE	J. Mays (Kansas City)
J. Dunaway (Buffalo)	LT	Dan Birdwell (Oakland)
H. Antwine (Boston)	RT	B. Buchanan (Kansas City)
V. Biggs (N.Y. Jets)	RE	Ben Davidson (Oakland)
G. Webster (Houston)	LLB	Bobby Bell (K.C.)
G. Boyette (Houston)	MLB	D. Conners (Oakland)
M. Stratton (Buffalo)	RLB	Jim Lynch (Kansas City)
M. Farr (Houston)	LCB	G. Atkinson (Oakland)
G. (Butch) Byrd (Buffalo)	RCB	W. Brown (Oakland)
Ken Houston (Houston)	LS	K. Graham (San Diego)
G. Saimes (Buffalo)	RS	J. Robinson (Kansas City)

Head coaches—George Wilson (Miami), East; Lou Saban (Denver), West

West	3	0	10	25	—	38
East	3	16	3	3	—	25

East—FG Turner 27
West—FG Stenerud 51
East—Kiick 2 run (Turner kick)
East—FG Turner 16
East—FG Turner 19
East—FG Turner 13
West—Trumpy 6 pass from Dawson (Stenerud kick)
East—FG Turner 18
West—FG Stenerud 30
East—FG Turner 21
West—Dixon 1 run (Stenerud kick)
West—Robinson 1 run (Robinson run)
West—Robinson 1 run (Stenerud kick)
West—FG Stenerud 32
Attendance—41,058

1969 NFL

WEST 10, EAST 7

The Los Angeles Rams' delegation played the major role in the West's 10–7 victory. George Allen was head coach, quarterback Roman Gabriel the outstanding back, and defensive tackle Merlin Olsen the outstanding lineman.

With 3:52 remaining in the game, Gabriel started the West on a march to the winning touchdown.

January 19, at Los Angeles

East	Starters, Offense	West
H. Jones (N.Y. Giants)	LE	C. McNeil (San Francisco)
Bob Reynolds (St. Louis)	LT	C. Cowan (Los Angeles)
John Niland (Dallas)	LG	Tom Mack (Los Angeles)
Len Hauss (Washington)	C	M. Tingelhoff (Minn.)
G. Hickerson (Cleveland)	RG	H. Mudd (San Francisco)
Bob Brown (Philadelphia)	RT	F. Gregg (Green Bay)
J. Smith (St. Louis)	TE	J. Mackey (Baltimore)
Don Meredith (Dallas)	QB	E. Morrall (Baltimore)
P. Warfield (Cleveland)	FL	W. Richardson (Baltimore)
Leroy Kelly (Cleveland)	RB	Tom Matte (Baltimore)
Don Perkins (Dallas)	RB	Ken Willard (San Francisco)
	Starters, Defense	
Don Brumm (St. Louis)	LE	D. (Deacon) Jones (L.A.)
W. Johnson (Cleveland)	LT	M. Olsen (Los Angeles)
Bob Lilly (Dallas)	RT	Alan Page (Minnesota)
George Andrie (Dallas)	RE	Jim Marshall (Minnesota)
C. Howley (Dallas)	LLB	Mike Curtis (Baltimore)
L.R. Jordan (Dallas)	MLB	Dick Butkus (Chicago)
C. Hanburger (Washington)	RLB	M. Baughan (Los Angeles)
E. Barnes (Cleveland)	LHB	Lem Barney (Detroit)
Mel Renfro (Dallas)	RHB	K. Alexander (San Fran.)
E. Kellerman (Cleveland)	LS	W. Wood (Green Bay)
L. Wilson (St. Louis)	RS	R. Taylor (Chicago)

Head coaches—Tom Landry (Dallas), East; George Allen (Los Angeles), West

East	0	0	7	0	—	7
West	0	3	0	7	—	10

West—FG Gossett 20
East—Warfield 3 pass from Meredith (Baker kick)
West—Brown 1 run (Gossett kick)
Attendance—32,050

1970 AFL

WEST 26, EAST 3

The Houston Astrodome was the site of the final AFL All-Star game. John Hadl completed 18 of 26 passes for 224 yards and one touchdown in the West's 26–3 victory.

January 17, at Houston

East	Starters, Offense	West
G. Sauer (N.Y. Jets)	WR	F. Biletnikoff (Oakland)
W. Hill (N.Y. Jets)	LT	J. Tyrer (Kansas City)
Billy Shaw (Buffalo)	LG	Ed Budde (Kansas City)
Jon Morris (Boston)	C	Jim Otto (Oakland)
Dave Herman (N.Y. Jets)	RG	Walt Sweeney (San Diego)
G.R. Hines (Houston)	RT	Harry Schuh (Oakland)
Alvin Reed (Houston)	TE	Billy Cannon (Oakland)
Ron Sellers (Boston)	WR	Lance Alworth (San Diego)
M. Talliaferro (Boston)	QB	John Hadl (San Diego)
Carl Garrett (Boston)	RB	Dickie Post (San Diego)
Matt Snell (N.Y. Jets)	RB	R. Holmes (Kansas City)
	Starters, Defense	
G. Philbin (N.Y. Jets)	LE	Rich Jackson (Denver)
Jim Hunt (Boston)	LT	Curley Culp (Kansas City)
J. Elliott (N.Y. Jets)	RT	B. Buchanan (Kansas City)
Elvin Bethea (Houston)	RE	Steve DeLong (San Diego)
G. Boyette (Houston)	LLB	Bobby Bell (Kansas City)
N. Buoniconti (Miami)	MLB	W. Lanier (Kansas City)
L. Grantham (N.Y. Jets)	RLB	Gus Otto (Oakland)
Miller Farr (Houston)	LCB	J. Marsalis (Kansas City)
G. (Butch) Byrd (Buffalo)	RCB	Willie Brown (Oakland)
Ken Houston (Houston)	LS	Kenny Graham (San Diego)
Don Webb (Boston)	RS	Dave Grayson (Oakland)

Head coaches—George Wilson (Miami), East; Lou Saban (Denver), West

East	0	0	3	0	—	3
West	13	0	3	10	—	26

West—Post 1 run (kick failed)
West—Alworth 21 pass from Hadl (Stenerud kick)
West—FG Stenerud 38
East—FG Turner 44
West—FG Stenerud 30
West—Livingston 11 run (Stenerud kick)
Attendance—30,170

1970 NFL

WEST 16, EAST 13

Almost replaying the final minutes of the 1969 game, Los Angeles Rams quarterback Roman Gabriel marched the West 55 yards to the winning touchdown, overcoming a 13–9 East lead.

January 18, at Los Angeles

East	Starters, Offense	West
P. Warfield (Cleveland)	WR	G. Washington (Minn.)
Bob Reynolds (St. Louis)	LT	G. Alderman (Minnesota)
John Niland (Dallas)	LG	Tom Mack (Los Angeles)
Len Hauss (Washington)	C	M. Tingelhoff (Minnesota)
G. Hickerson (Cleveland)	RG	G. Gillingham (Green Bay)
Ralph Neely (Dallas)	RT	C. Cowan (Los Angeles)
R. Jefferson (Pitt.)	TE	C. Sanders (Detroit)
J. Smith (Washington)	WR	C. Dale (Green Bay)
Bill Nelsen (Cleveland)	QB	R. Gabriel (Los Angeles)
L. Brown (Washington)	RB	Gale Sayers (Chicago)
Leroy Kelly (Cleveland)	RB	Tom Matte (Baltimore)
	Starters, Defense	
T. Rossovich (Phil.)	LE	Carl Eller (Minnesota)
W. Johnson (Cleveland)	LT	M. Olsen (Los Angeles)
Bob Lilly (Dallas)	RT	Alan Page (Minnesota)
G. Andrie (Dallas)	RE	J. Marshall (Minnesota)
C. Hanburger (Washington)	LLB	D. Robinson (Green Bay)
Dave Lloyd (Philadelphia)	MLB	Dick Butkus (Chicago)
Chuck Howley (Dallas)	RLB	D. Wilcox (S.F.)
Pat Fischer (Wash.)	LCB	Lem Barney (Detroit)
Mel Renfro (Dallas)	RCB	Bob Jeter (Green Bay)
J. Stovall (St. Louis)	LS	Rick Volk (Baltimore)
L. Wilson (St. Louis)	RS	P. Krause (Minnesota)

Head coaches—Tom Fears (New Orleans), East; Norm Van Brocklin (Atlanta), West

East	7	6	0	0	—	13
West	0	7	0	9	—	16

East—Kelly 10 run (Dempsey kick)
East—FG Dempsey 46
West—Gabriel 1 run (Etter kick)
East—FG Dempsey 27
West—Safety, Brezina tackled Walden in end zone
West—Dale 28 pass from Gabriel (Etter kick)
Attendance—57,786

1971

NFC 27, AFC 6

Dallas's Mel Renfro broke open the first game between the all-stars of the American Football Conference and National Football Conference when he returned punts 82 and 56 yards for touchdowns.

January 24, at Los Angeles

AFC	Starters, Offense	NFC
Warren Wells (Oakland)	WR	G. Washington (S.F.)
Jim Tyrer (Kansas City)	LT	C. Cowan (Los Angeles)
Ed Budde (Kansas City)	LG	Tom Mack (Los Angeles)
Jim Otto (Oakland)	C	Ed Flanagan (Detroit)
Walt Sweeney (San Diego)	RG	G. Gillingham (Green Bay)
Harry Schuh (Oakland)	RT	Ernie McMillan (St. Louis)
R. Chester (Oakland)	TE	Charlie Sanders (Detroit)
Marlin Briscoe (Buffalo)	WR	G. Washington (Minnesota)
Daryle Lamonica (Oakland)	QB	J. Brodie (San Francisco)
Leroy Kelly (Cleveland)	RB	Larry Brown (Washington)
Hewritt Dixon (Oakland)	RB	MacArthur Lane (St. Louis)
	Starters, Defense	
C. (Bubba) Smith (Balt.)	LE	D. (Deacon) Jones (L.A.)
Joe Greene (Pittsburgh)	LT	Alan Page (Minnesota)
B. Buchanan (Kansas City)	RT	Bob Lilly (Dallas)
Rich Jackson (Denver)	RE	Carl Eller (Minnesota)
Bobby Bell (Kansas City)	LLB	L. Stallings (St. Louis)
W. Lanier (Kansas City)	MLB	Dick Butkus (Chicago)
Andy Russell (Pittsburgh)	RLB	Fred Carr (Green Bay)
Jim Marsalis (Kansas City)	LC	J. Johnson (San Francisco)
Willie Brown (Oakland)	RC	Mel Renfro (Dallas)
Ken Houston (Houston)	LS	Willie Wood (Green Bay)
J. Robinson (Kansas City)	RS	Larry Wilson (St. Louis)

Head coaches—John Madden (Oakland), AFC; Dick Nolan (San Francisco), NFC

AFC	0	3	3	0	—	6
NFC	0	3	10	14	—	27

AFC—FG Stenerud 37
NFC—FG Cox 13
NFC—Osborn 23 pass from Brodie (Cox kick)
NFC—FG Cox 35
AFC—FG Stenerud 16
NFC—Renfro 82 punt return (Cox kick)
NFC—Renfro 56 punt return (Cox kick)
Attendance—48,222

1972

AFC 26, NFC 13

Len Dawson entered the game as quarterback in the third quarter and directed the AFC to two touchdowns and three field goals for a 26–13 victory.

January 23, at Los Angeles

NFC	Starters, Offense	AFC
G. Washington (S.F.)	WR	Fred Biletnikoff (Oakland)
Ron Yary (Minnesota)	LT	Jim Tyrer (Kansas City)
John Niland (Dallas)	LG	Ed Budde (Kansas City)
F. Blue (San Francisco)	C	Bill Curry (Baltimore)
G. Gillingham (Green Bay)	RG	Walt Sweeney (San Diego)
George Kunz (Atlanta)	RT	Winston Hill (N.Y. Jets)
T. Kwalick (San Francisco)	TE	R. Chester (Oakland)
Dick Gordon (Chicago)	WR	Paul Warfield (Miami)
Roger Staubach (Dallas)	QB	Bob Griese (Miami)
Larry Brown (Washington)	RB	Larry Csonka (Miami)
Steve Owens (Detroit)	RB	Floyd Little (Denver)
	Starters, Defense	
Claude Humphrey (Atlanta)	LE	C. (Bubba) Smith (Balt.)
Alan Page (Minnesota)	LT	Joe Greene (Pittsburgh)
Bob Lilly (Dallas)	RT	B. Buchanan (Kansas City)
C. Hardman (S. F.)	RE	Elvin Bethea (Houston)
D. Wilcox (San Francisco)	LLB	Ted Hendricks (Baltimore)
Dick Butkus (Chicago)	MLB	Mike Curtis (Baltimore)
Chuck Howley (Dallas)	RLB	Bobby Bell (Kansas City)
J. Johnson (San Francisco)	LC	E. Thomas (Kansas City)
Roger Wehrli (St. Louis)	RC	Willie Brown (Oakland)
Cornell Green (Dallas)	RS	Ken Houston (Houston)
Mel Renfro (Dallas)	LS	Rick Volk (Baltimore)

Head coaches—Don McCafferty (Baltimore), AFC; Dick Nolan (San Francisco), NFC

NFC	0	6	0	7	—	13
AFC	0	3	13	10	—	26

NFC—Grim 50 pass from Landry (kick failed)
AFC—FG Stenerud 25
AFC—FG Stenerud 23
AFC—FG Stenerud 48
AFC—Morin 5 pass from Dawson (Stenerud kick)
AFC—FG Stenerud 42
NFC—V. Washington 2 run (Knight kick)
AFC—F. Little 6 run (Stenerud kick)
Attendance—53,647

1973

AFC 33, NFC 28

The NFL Pro Bowl left Los Angeles after 22 years.

January 21, at Irving, Texas

AFC	Starters, Offense	NFC
Otis Taylor (Kansas City)	WR	G. Washington (San Fran.)
Art Shell (Oakland)	LT	Ron Yary (Minnesota)
Gene Upshaw (Oakland)	LG	John Niland (Dallas)
Jim Otto (Oakland)	C	F. Blue (San Francisco)
Larry Little (Miami)	RG	Tom Mack (Los Angeles)
Winston Hill (New York)	RT	Rayfield Wright (Dallas)
R. Chester (Oakland)	TE	T. Kwalick (San Francisco)
Gary Garrison (San Diego)	WR	John Gilliam (Minnesota)
D. Lamonica (Oakland)	QB	Bill Kilmer (Washington)
O. J. Simpson (Buffalo)	RB	Ron Johnson (New York)
Franco Harris (Pittsburgh)	RB	J. Brockington (Green Bay)
	Starters, Defense	
Deacon Jones (San Diego)	LE	Claude Humphrey (Atlanta)
Joe Greene (Pittsburgh)	LT	Merlin Olsen (Los Angeles)
Mike Reid (Cincinnati)	RT	Bob Brown (Green Bay)
Elvin Bethea (Houston)	RE	Coy Bacon (San Diego)
Ted Hendricks (Baltimore)	LLB	D. Wilcox (San Francisco)
Willie Lanier (Kansas City)	MLB	Tommy Nobis (Atlanta)
Andy Russell (Pittsburgh)	RLB	C. Hanburger (Washington)
Robert James (Buffalo)	LC	J. Johnson (San Francisco)
Willie Brown (Oakland)	RC	Lem Barney (Detroit)
Ken Houston (Houston)	RS	Cornell Green (Dallas)
Jake Scott (Miami)	LS	Bill Bradley (Philadelphia)

Head coaches—Chuck Noll (Pittsburgh), AFC; Tom Landry (Dallas), NFC.

AFC	0	10	10	13	— 33
NFC	14	0	0	14	— 28

NFC—Brockington 1 run (Marcol kick)
NFC—Brockington 3 pass from Kilmer (Marcol kick)
AFC—Simpson 7 run (Gerela kick)
AFC—FG Gerela 18
AFC—FG Gerela 22
AFC—Hubbard 11 run (Gerela kick)
AFC—Taylor 5 pass from Lamonica (no kick; bad snap)
AFC—Bell 12 interception return (Gerela kick)
NFC—Brockington 1 run (Marcol kick)
NFC—Kwalick 12 pass from Snead (Marcol kick)
Attendance—47,879

1974

AFC 15, NFC 13

Garo Yepremian kicked five field goals in five attempts, the last with 21 seconds remaining, for all of the AFC's points in a 15–13 victory.

January 20, at Kansas City

NFC	Starters, Offense	AFC
C. Taylor (Washington)	WR	Isaac Curtis (Cincinnati)
Ron Yary (Minnesota)	LT	Art Shell (Oakland)
Tom Mack (Los Angeles)	LG	Gene Upshaw (Oakland)
F. Blue (San Francisco)	C	Jim Langer (Miami)
John Niland (Dallas)	RG	Larry Little (Miami)
Rayfield Wright (Dallas)	RT	Winston Hill (New York)
T. Kwalick (San Francisco)	TE	Riley Odoms (Denver)
H. Jackson (Los Angeles)	WR	F. Biletnikoff (Oakland)
John Hadl (Los Angeles)	QB	Ken Stabler (Oakland)
C. Foreman (Minnesota)	RB	O. J. Simpson (Buffalo)
J. Brockington (Green Bay)	RB	M. Hubbard (Oakland)
	Starters, Defense	
John Zook (Atlanta)	LE	L. C. Greenwood (Pitt.)
Merlin Olsen (Los Angeles)	LT	Joe Greene (Pittsburgh)
Alan Page (Minnesota)	RT	Paul Smith (Denver)
Claude Humphrey (Atlanta)	RE	Elvin Bethea (Houston)
D. Wilcox (San Francisco)	LLB	T. Hendricks (Baltimore)
Jeff Siemon (Minnesota)	MLB	Willie Lanier (Kansas City)
C. Hanburger (Washington)	RLB	Andy Russell (Pittsburgh)
Lem Barney (Detroit)	LCB	C. Scott (Cleveland)
Mel Renfro (Dallas)	RCB	Willie Brown (Oakland)
Ken Houston (Washington)	RS	Dick Anderson (Miami)
Paul Krause (Minnesota)	LS	Jake Scott (Miami)

Head coach—John Madden (Oakland), AFC; Tom Landry (Dallas), NFC.

NFC	0	10	0	3	— 13
AFC	3	3	3	6	— 15

AFC—FG Yepremian 16
NFC—FG Mike-Mayer 27
NFC—McCutcheon 14 pass from Gabriel (Mike-Mayer kick)
AFC—FG Yepremian 37
AFC—FG Yepremian 27
AFC—FG Yepremian 41
NFC—FG Mike-Mayer 21
AFC—FG Yepremian 42
Attendance—51,482

1975

NFC 17, AFC 10

James Harris, a pregame roster replacement for the injured Fran Tarkenton, and a second-quarter quarterback substitute for the injured Jim Hart, threw two eight-yard touchdown passes in the fourth quarter and the NFC won the first nighttime Pro Bowl game.

January 20, at Miami

NFC	Starters, Offense	AFC
C. Taylor (Washington)	WR	Cliff Branch (Oakland)
Ron Yary (Minnesota)	LT	Art Shell (Oakland)
Tom Mack (Los Angeles)	LG	Gene Upshaw (Oakland)
Jeff Van Note (Atlanta)	C	Jim Langer (Miami)
G. Gillingham (Green Bay)	RG	Larry Little (Miami)
Rayfield Wright (Dallas)	RT	R. Washington (S.D.)
C. Young (Philadelphia)	TE	Riley Odoms (Denver)
Drew Pearson (Dallas)	WR	Isaac Curtis (Cincinnati)
Jim Hart (St. Louis)	QB	Ken Stabler (Oakland)
Chuck Foreman (Minnesota)	RB	O. J. Simpson (Buffalo)
L. McCutcheon (L.A.)	RB	Otis Armstrong (Denver)
	Starters, Defense	
Carl Eller (Minnesota)	LE	L. C. Greenwood (Pitt.)
Merlin Olsen (Los Angeles)	LT	Joe Greene (Pittsburgh)
Alan Page (Minnesota)	RT	Jerry Sherk (Cleveland)
Claude Humphrey (Atlanta)	RE	Bill Stanfill (Miami)
Ted Hendricks (Green Bay)	LLB	Jack Ham (Pittsburgh)
Bill Bergey (Philadelphia)	MLB	Mike Curtis (Baltimore)
C. Hanburger (Washington)	RLB	Andy Russell (Pittsburgh)
W. Buchanon (Green Bay)	LCB	Robert James (Buffalo)
Roger Wehrli (St. Louis)	RCB	E. Thomas (Kansas City)
Ken Houston (Washington)	LS	Dick Anderson (Miami)
Paul Krause (Minnesota)	RS	Jack Tatum (Oakland)

Head coaches—John Madden (Oakland), AFC; Chuck Knox (Los Angeles), NFC.

NFC	0	3	0	14	— 17
AFC	0	0	10	0	— 10

NFC—FG Marcol 33
AFC—Warfield 32 pass from Griese (Gerela kick)
AFC—FG Gerela 33
NFC—Gray 8 pass from J. Harris (Marcol kick)
NFC—Taylor 8 pass from J. Harris (Marcol kick)
Attendance—26,484

1976

NFC 23, AFC 20

Quarterback replacement Mike Boryla threw two touchdown passes for a 23–20 NFC victory. Billy Johnson had 233 yards in kick returns for the AFC.

January 26, at New Orleans

AFC	Starters, Offense	NFC
Isaac Curtis (Cincinnati)	WR	Mel Gray (St. Louis)
Art Shell (Oakland)	LT	Ron Yary (Minnesota)
Gene Upshaw (Oakland)	LG	Ed White (Minnesota)
Jim Langer (Miami)	C	Tom Banks (St. Louis)
Bob Kuechenberg (Miami)	RG	Conrad Dobler (St. Louis)
George Kunz (Baltimore)	RT	Dan Dierdorf (St. Louis)
Riley Odoms (Denver)	TE	C. Young (Philadelphia)
Lynn Swann (Pittsburgh)	WR	John Gilliam (Minnesota)
Ken Anderson (Cincinnati)	QB	Jim Hart (St. Louis)
O.J. Simpson (Buffalo)	RB	Terry Metcalf (St. Louis)
Franco Harris (Pittsburgh)	RB	C. Foreman (Minnesota)
	Starters, Defense	
L.C. Greenwood (Pitt.)	LE	J. Youngblood (L.A.)
Joe Greene (Pittsburgh)	LT	Merlin Olsen (Los Angeles)
Jerry Sherk (Cleveland)	RT	Alan Page (Minnesota)
John Dutton (Baltimore)	RE	C. Hardman (San Fran.)
Jack Ham (Pittsburgh)	LLB	I. Robertson (Los Angeles)
Jack Lambert (Pittsburgh)	MLB	Jeff Siemon (Minnesota)
Andy Russell (Pittsburgh)	RLB	C. Hanburger (Washington)
Lemar Parrish (Cincinnati)	LCB	Lem Barney (Detroit)
Mel Blount (Pittsburgh)	RCB	Roger Wehrli (St. Louis)
Mike Wagner (Pittsburgh)	LS	Ken Houston (Washington)
Jake Scott (Miami)	RS	Cliff Harris (Dallas)

Head coaches—John Madden (Oakland), AFC; Chuck Knox (Los Angeles), NFC.

AFC	0	13	0	7	— 20
NFC	0	0	9	14	— 23

AFC—FG Stenerud 20
AFC—FG Stenerud 35
AFC—Burrough 64 pass from Pastorini (Stenerud kick)
NFC—FG Bakken 42
NFC—Foreman 4 pass from Hart (kick blocked)
AFC—Johnson 90 punt return (Stenerud kick)
NFC—Metcalf 14 pass from Boryla (Bakken kick)
NFC—Gray 8 pass from Boryla (Bakken kick)
Attendance—32,108

1977

AFC 24, NFC 14

The AFC intercepted six passes—five by members of the Pittsburgh Steelers, including two by cornerback Mel Blount—in a 24–14 victory. The crowd of 63,214 was the largest since 1964.

January 17, at Seattle

NFC	Starters, Offense	AFC
Mel Gray (St. Louis)	WR	Cliff Branch (Oakland)
Ron Yary (Minnesota)	LT	Art Shell (Oakland)
Ed White (Minnesota)	LG	J. Hannah (New England)
Tom Banks (St. Louis)	C	Jim Langer (Miami)
Conrad Dobler (St. Louis)	RG	J. DeLamielleure (Buffalo)
Dan Dierdorf (St. Louis)	RT	George Kunz (Baltimore)
Billy Joe Dupree (Dallas)	TE	Dave Casper (Oakland)
Drew Pearson (Dallas)	WR	Isaac Curtis (Cincinnati)
Roger Staubach (Dallas)	QB	Bert Jones (Baltimore)
Walter Payton (Chicago)	RB	O.J. Simpson (Buffalo)
D. Williams (San Francisco)	RB	L. Mitchell (Baltimore)
	Starters, Defense	
Tommy Hart (San Francisco)	LE	Coy Bacon (Cincinnati)
C. Elam (San Francisco)	LT	Curley Culp (Houston)
Wally Chambers (Chicago)	RT	Jerry Sherk (Cleveland)
J. Youngblood (L.A.)	RE	John Dutton (Baltimore)
I. Robertson (Los Angeles)	LLB	Jack Ham (Pittsburgh)
Bill Bergey (Philadelphia)	MLB	Jack Lambert (Pittsburgh)
Brad Van Pelt (N.Y. Giants)	RLB	Robert Brazile (Houston)
M. Jackson (Los Angeles)	LCB	Lemar Parrish (Cincinnati)
Roger Wehrli (St. Louis)	RCB	Mel Blount (Pittsburgh)
Ken Houston (Washington)	LS	T. Casanova (Cincinnati)
Cliff Harris (Dallas)	RS	Glen Edwards (Pittsburgh)

Coaches—John Madden (Oakland), AFC; Chuck Knox (Los Angeles), NFC.

NFC	0	14	0	0	— 14
AFC	10	7	0	7	— 24

AFC—Simpson 3 run (Linhart kick)
AFC—FG Linhart 31
NFC—Thomas 15 run (Bakken kick)
AFC—Joiner 12 pass from Anderson (Linhart kick)
NFC—McCutcheon 1 run (Bakken kick)
AFC—Branch 27 pass from Anderson (Linhart kick)
Attendance—63,214

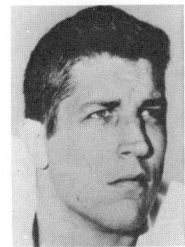      

George Andrie   *Fred Arbanas*   *Jon Arnett*   *Maxie Baughan*   *Elvin Bethea*   *Mel Blount*   *Ordell Braase*

PRO BOWL SELECTIONS

The year shown refers to the year in which the game was played, not the season it followed.

Adamle, Tony, RB, Cleveland (2) 1951–52
Adams, Chet, T, Cleveland Rams (2) Jan. 1942, Dec. 1942
Adamson, Ken, G, Denver (1) 1962
Adderley, Herb, DB, Green Bay (5) 1964–68
Addison, Tom, LB, Boston (4) 1962–65
Alban, Dick, RB, Washington (1) 1955
Albert, Frankie, QB, San Francisco (1) 1951
Alderman, Grady, T, Minnesota (6) 1964–68, 1970
Aldrich, Charles (Ki), C (2) Chi. Cardinals, 1940; Wash., 1942
Alexander, Kermit, S, San Francisco (1) 1969
Allen, Chuck, LB, San Diego (2) 1964–65
Alworth, Lance, WR, San Diego (7) 1964–70
Ameche, Alan, RB, Baltimore (4) 1956–59
Anderson, Bill, E, Washington (2) 1960–61
Anderson, Dick, S, Miami (3) 1973–75
Anderson, Ken, QB, Cincinnati (1) 1976–77
Andrie, George, DE, Dallas (5) 1966–70
Ane, Charley, T, Detroit (2) 1957, 1959
Angsman, Elmer, RB, Chi. Cardinals (1) 1951
Antwine, Houston, DT, Boston Patriots (6) 1964*, 1965–69
Apolskis, Ray, C, Chi. Cardinals (1) Jan. 1942
Arbanas, Fred, TE (5) Dallas Texans, 1963; Kansas City, 1964*, 1965*, 1966, 1968
Armstrong, Otis, RB, Denver (1) 1975
Arnett, Jon, RB, Los Angeles (5) 1958–62
Artoe, Lee, T, Chi. Bears (3) 1940, Jan. 1942, Dec. 1942
Atkins, Bill, DB, Buffalo (1) 1962
Atkins, Doug, DE, Chi. Bears (8) 1958–64, 1966
Atkinson, Al, LB, N.Y. Jets (1) 1969
Atkinson, George, S, Oakland (2) 1969–70
Austin, Bill, G, N.Y. Giants (1) 1955

B

Bacon, Coy, DE (2) Los Angeles, 1973; Cincinnati, 1977
Baisi, Al, G, Chi. Bears (2) Dec. 1940, Jan. 1942
Baker, Dave, S, San Francisco (1) 1960
Baker, Jon, G, N.Y. Giants (2) 1952–53
Baker, Sam, K (4) Washington, 1957; Dallas, 1964; Philadelphia, 1965, 1969
Baker, Tony, RB, New Orleans (1) 1970*
Bakken, Jim, K, St. Louis (3) 1966, 1968, 1977
Balaz, Frank, G, Green Bay (1) Jan. 1940
Ballman, Gary, WR, Pittsburgh (2) 1965–66
Banducci, Bruno, G, San Francisco (1) 1955
Banfield, Tony, DB, Houston (3) 1962–64
Banks, Tom, C, St. Louis (1) 1977
Barber, Stew, T, Buffalo (5) 1964–68
Barkum, Jerome, WR, N.Y. Jets (1) 1974
Barnard, Hap, E, N.Y. Giants (1) 1939
Barnes, Billy Ray, RB, Philadelphia (3) 1958–60
Barnes, Erich, DB (6) Chicago, 1960; N.Y. Giants, 1962–65; Cleveland, 1969
Barnes, Walt, G, Philadelphia (1) 1951
Barney, Lem, CB, Detroit (6) 1968–70, 1973–74, 1977
Barnum, Len (Feets), B, N.Y. Giants (1) 1939
Barr, Terry, WR, Detroit (2) 1964–65
Barwegan, Dick, G (4) Chi. Bears, 1951–53; Baltimore, 1954
Bass, Dick, RB, Los Angeles (3) 1963–64, 1967
Bassi, Dick, G, Philadelphia (1) 1940
Baugh, Sammy, QB, Washington (5) 1939, Dec. 1940, Jan. 1942, Dec. 1942*, 1952
Baughan, Maxie, LB (9) Philadelphia, 1961–62, 1964–66; Los Angeles, 1967–69, 1970*
Bausch, Frank, C, Chi. Bears (1) Dec. 1940
Bednarik, Chuck, LB, Philadelphia (8) 1951–55, 1957–58, 1961
Behrman, Dave, LB, Buffalo (1) 1966
Beinor, Ed, T, Washington (1) Dec. 1942
Bell, Bobby, LB, Kansas City (7) 1965–68, 1971–73
Bemiller, Al, G, Buffalo (1) 1966
Benton, Jim, E, Cleveland Rams (1) Jan. 1940
Bergey, Bill, LB (3) Cincinnati, 1970; Philadelphia, 1975–76
Berry, Bob, QB, Atlanta (1) 1970
Berry, Raymond, WR, Baltimore (5) 1959–60, 1962, 1964–65
Bertelsen, Jim, RB, Los Angeles (1) 1974
Bethea, Elvin, DE (6) Buffalo, 1970; Houston, 1972–76
Bielski, Dick, E, Dallas (1) 1962

Biggs, Verlon, DE, N.Y. Jets (3) 1967–69
Biletnikoff, Fred, WR, Oakland (6) 1968, 1970–72, 1974–75
Bingaman, Les, G, Detroit (2) 1952, 1954
Birdwell, Dan, DE, Oakland (1) 1969
Bishop, Bill, T, Chicago (1) 1955
Bishop, Don, DB, Dallas (1) 1963
Bishop, Sonny, G, Houston (1) 1969
Bjork, Del, T, Chicago (1) 1939
Blair, George, DB, San Diego (1) 1962
Blanda, George, QB-K (4) Houston, 1962–64; Oakland, 1968
Blanks, Sid, RB, Houston (1) 1965
Blazine, Tony, T, Chi. Cardinals (1) Jan. 1940
Blount, Mel, CB, Pittsburgh (2) 1976–77
Blozis, Al, T, N.Y. Giants (1) Dec. 1942
Blue, Forrest, C, San Francisco (4) 1972–75
Boozer, Emerson, RB, N.Y. Jets (2) 1967, 1969
Boryla, Mike, QB, Philadelphia (1) 1976
Bosley, Bruce, C, San Francisco (4) 1961, 1966–68
Bosseler, Don, RB, Washington (1) 1960
Boyd, Bob, E, Los Angeles (1) 1955
Boyd, Bobby, DB, Baltimore (2) 1965, 1969
Boyette, Garland, LB, Houston (2) 1969–70
Box, Cloyce, E, Detroit (2) 1951, 1953
Braase, Ordell, DE, Baltimore (2) 1967–68
Bradley, Bill, S, Philadelphia (2) 1972–73
Bradshaw, Charlie, T, Pittsburgh (2) 1964–65
Bradshaw, Terry, QB, Pittsburgh (1) 1976
Bramlett, John, LB (2) Denver, 1967; Miami, 1968
Branch, Cliff, WR, Oakland (3) 1975–77
Branch, Mel, DE (3) Dallas Texans, 1962–63; Kansas City, 1964
Bray, Ray, G, Chi. Bears (4) 1940, Jan. 1942, 1951–52
Brazile, Robert, LB, Houston (1) 1977
Breedlove, Rod, LB, Washington (1) 1963
Brewer, John, LB, Cleveland (1) 1967
Brewster, Darrell (Pete), E, Cleveland (2) 1956–57
Brezina, Greg, LB, Atlanta (1) 1970
Brink, Larry, DE, Los Angeles (2) 1951–52
Briscoe, Marlin, WR, Buffalo (1) 1971
Brito, Gene, DE, Washington (5) 1954, 1956–59
Brock, Charles, C, Green Bay (3) 1940, Dec. 1940, Dec. 1942
Brockington, John, RB, Green Bay (3) 1972–74
Brodie, John, QB, San Francisco (2) 1966, 1971
Brooker, Tommy, K, Kansas City (1) 1965
Brookshier, Tom, DB, Philadelphia (2) 1960–61
Brown, Bill, RB, Minnesota (4) 1965–66, 1968–69
Brown, Bob, T (6) Philadelphia, 1966–67, 1969; Los Angeles, 1970*, 1971*; Oakland, 1972*
Brown, Bob, DT, Green Bay (2) 1971, 1973
Brown, Ed, QB, Chicago (2) 1956–57
Brown, Eddie, KR, Washington (1) 1977
Brown, Hardy, LB, San Francisco (1) 1953
Brown, Jim, RB, Cleveland (9) 1958–66
Brown, Larry, RB, Washington (4) 1970–72, 1973*
Brown, Roger, DT (6) Detroit, 1963–66; Los Angeles, 1967–68
Brown, Roosevelt, T, N.Y. Giants (9) 1956–61, 1963, 1965–66
Brown, Timmy, RB, Philadelphia (3) 1963–64, 1966
Brown, Willie, CB (9) Denver, 1965–66; Oakland, 1968–74
Bruder, Henry, B, Green Bay (1) Jan. 1940
Brumm, Don, DE, St. Louis (1) 1969
Bruney, Fred, DB, Boston (2) 1962–63
Bryant, Bobby, CB, Minnesota (1) 1977
Buchanan, Buck, DT, Kansas City (8)1965–72
Buchanon, Willie, CB, Green Bay (2) 1974–75
Budde, Ed, G, Kansas City (7) 1964, 1967–72
Buhler, Larry, B, Green Bay (1) Jan. 1940
Bulaich, Norm, RB, Baltimore (1) 1972*
Buncom, Frank, LB, San Diego (3) 1965, 1966, 1968
Buoniconti, Nick, LB (8) Boston Patriots, 1964–68; Miami, 1970, 1973*, 1974
Burford, Chris, E, Dallas Texans (1) 1962
Burk, Adrian, QB, Philadelphia (2) 1955–56
Burnett, Bob, RB, Buffalo (1) 1967
Burnett, Dale, B, N.Y. Giants (1) 1939
Burrell, Ode, WR, Houston (1) 1966
Bussey, Young, B, Chi. Bears (1) Jan. 1942
Butkus, Dick, LB, Chicago (8) 1966–73
Butler, Jack, DB, Pittsburgh (4) 1956–59
Butler, Jim, RB, Atlanta (1) 1970
Byrd, George (Butch), CB, Buffalo (5) 1965–67, 1969–70

C

Caffey, Lee Roy, LB, Green Bay (1) 1966
Campbell, Marion, DT, Philadelphia (2) 1960–61

Campbell, Woodie, RB, Houston (1) 1968*
Cannady, John, C, N.Y. Giants (2) 1951, 1953
Cannon, Billy, RB-TE (2) Houston, 1962; Oakland, 1970
Cappelletti, Gino, WR-K, Boston (5) 1962, 1964–67
Carapella, Al, T, San Francisco (1) 1955
Carlton, Wray, RB, Buffalo (2) 1966–67
Cardwell, Lloyd, B, Detroit (1) 1939
Carmichael, Harold, WR, Philadelphia (1) 1974
Carolan, Reg, E, Dallas Texans (1) 1963
Caroline, J.C., B, Chi. Bears (1) 1957
Carpenter, Ken, B, Cleveland (1) 1952
Carpenter, Preston, E, Pittsburgh (1) 1963
Carr, Fred, LB, Green Bay (3) 1971, 1973, 1976
Carr, Roger, WR, Baltimore (1) 1977
Carroll, Vic, G, Washington (1) Dec. 1942
Carson, John, E, Washington (1) 1958
Carter, Jim, LB, Green Bay (1) 1974
Carter, Joe, E, Philadelphia (2) 1939, Jan. 1940
Casanova, Tommy, S, Cincinnati (2) 1975, 1977
Casares, Rick, RB, Chicago (5) 1956–60
Casey, Bernie, WR, Los Angeles (1) 1968
Cason, Jim, B, San Francisco (2) 1952, 1955
Casper, Dave, TE, Oakland (1) 1977
Caster, Rich, TE, N.Y. Jets (3) 1973, 1975–76
Chambers, Wally, DT, Chicago (3) 1974, 1976–77
Chandler, Don, K, Green Bay (1) 1968
Chandnois, Lynn, B, Pittsburgh (2) 1953–54
Chapple, Dave, P, Los Angeles (1) 1973
Cherundolo, Chuck, C, Pittsburgh (2) Jan. 1942, Dec. 1942
Chesney, Chester, C, Chi. Bears (1) Dec. 1940
Chester, Raymond, TE, Oakland (3) 1971–73
Christiansen, Jack, S, Detroit (5) 1954–58
Christy, Dick, RB, N.Y. Jets (1) 1963
Cifers, Ed, E, Washington (1) Dec. 1942
Clancy, Jack, WR, Miami (1) 1968
Clark, Harry, B, Chicago (2) Dec. 1940, Jan. 1942
Clark, Mike, T, Pittsburgh (1) 1967
Clarke, Hagood, DB, Buffalo (1) 1966
Clarke, Leon, E, Los Angeles (2) 1956–57
Cogdill, Gail, WR, Detroit (3) 1961, 1963–64
Colclough, Jim, E, Boston Patriots (1) 1963*
Cole, Pete, G, N.Y. Giants (1) 1939
Collett, Elmer, G, San Francisco (1) 1970
Collins, Gary, WR, Cleveland (2) 1966–67
Colo, Don, T, Cleveland (5) 1955–56, 1958, 1959
Condit, Merlyn, B (2) Pittsburgh, Dec. 1940; Brooklyn Dodgers, Dec. 1942
Conerly, Charlie, QB, N.Y. Giants (2) 1951, 1957
Conners, Dan, LB, Oakland (3) 1967–69
Connolly, Ted, G, San Francisco (1) 1962
Connor, George, T, Chi. Bears (4) 1951–54
Conrad, Bobby Joe, WR, St. Louis (1) 1965
Conti, Enio, G, Philadelphia (1) Dec. 1942
Cooke, Ed, DE, Miami (1) 1967
Coomer, Joe, T, Pittsburgh (1) Jan. 1942
Cope, Frank, T, N.Y. Giants (2) 1939, Dec. 1940
Cordell, Ollie, B, Cleveland Rams (1) Dec. 1940
Corey, Walt, LB, Kansas City (1) 1964
Cornelison, Jerry, T, Dallas Texans (1) 1963
Costa, Dave, DT (5) Oakland, 1964; Buffalo, 1967; Denver, 1968–70
Costa, Paul, TE, Buffalo (1) 1966
Coulter, DeWitt (Tex), T, N.Y. Giants (2) 1952–53
Cowan, Charlie, T, Los Angeles (3) 1969–71
Cox, Fred, K, Minnesota (1) 1971
Craft, Russ, B, Philadelphia (2) 1952–53
Craig, Larry, QB, Green Bay (3) Jan. 1940, Jan. 1942, Dec. 1942
Creekmur, Lou, T, Detroit (8) 1951–58
Cross, Irv, DB, Philadelphia (2) 1965–66
Crow, John David, RB (4) St. Louis, 1960–61, 1963; S.F., 1966
Crow, Lindon, DB (3) St. Louis, 1957–58; N.Y. Giants, 1960
Csonka, Larry, RB, Miami (3) 1971–72, 1973*, 1974* 1975
Cuff, Ward, B, N.Y. Giants (3) 1939, Jan. 1940, Dec. 1942
Culp, Curley, DT (4) Kansas City, 1970, 1972; Houston, 1976–77
Current, Mike, T, Denver (1) 1970
Currie, Dan, LB, Green Bay (1) 1961
Curry, Bill, C, Baltimore (2) 1972–73
Curtis, Isaac, WR, Cincinnati (4) 1974–77
Curtis, Mike, LB, Baltimore (4) 1969, 1971–72, 1975

---

*Selected but did not play

Nick Buoniconti *Fred Carr* *John David Crow* *Isaac Curtis* *Carroll Dale* *Conrad Dobler* *Norm Evans*

D

Dale, Carroll, WR, Green Bay (3) 1969–71
Danenhauer, Eldon, T, Denver (2) 1963, 1966
Daniels, Clemon, RB, Oakland (4) 1964–67
Danowski, Ed, B, N.Y. Giants (1) 1939
Daugherty, Dick, LB, Los Angeles (1) 1958
David, Jim, DB, Detroit (6) 1955–60
Davidson, Ben, DE, Oakland (3) 1967–69
Davidson, Cotton, QB (2) Dallas Texans, 1962; Oakland, 1964
Davis, Ben, CB, Cleveland (1) 1973
Davis, Fred, T (2) Washington, Dec. 1942; Chi. Bears, 1951
Davis, Glenn, B, Los Angeles (1) 1951
Davis, Tommy, K, San Francisco (2) 1963–64
Davis, Willie, DE, Green Bay (5) 1964–68
Day, Tom, DE, Buffalo (1) 1966
Deal, Rufus, B, Washington (1) Dec. 1942
Dean, Ted, RB, Philadelphia (1) 1962
Dee, Bob, DE, Boston Patriots (4) 1962, 1964–66
DeLamielleure, Joe, G, Buffalo (2) 1976–77
DeLong, Steve, DE, San Diego (1) 1966
DeMarco, Bob, C, St. Louis (3) 1964, 1966, 1968*
Dempsey, Tom, K, New Orleans (1) 1970
Denson, Al, WR, Denver (2) 1968, 1970
Derby, Dean, B, Pittsburgh (1) 1960
DeRogatis, Al, T, N.Y. Giants (2) 1951–52
Dess, Darrell, G, N.Y. Giants (2) 1963–64
Dewell, Bill, E, Chi. Cardinals (1) Jan. 1942
Dewveall, Willard, E, Houston (1) 1963
Dial, Buddy, WR, Pittsburgh (1) 1962
Dierdorf, Dan, T, St. Louis (3) 1975–77
Dillon, Bobby, B, Green Bay (4) 1956–59
Ditka, Mike, TE, Chicago (5) 1962–66
Dixon, Hewritt, RB, Oakland (4) 1967–69, 1971
Dobler, Conrad, G, St. Louis (2) 1976–77
Dodrill, Dale, G, Pittsburgh (4) 1954–56, 1958
Doll, Don, DB (4) Detroit 1951–53; Washington, 1954
Donovan, Art, T, Baltimore (5) 1954–58
Doran, Jim, E, Dallas (1) 1961
Dorow, Al, QB (2) Washington, 1957; N.Y. Titans, 1962
Dottley, John, B, Chi. Bears (1) 1952
Dougherty, Phil, C, Chi. Cardinals (1) 1939
Dove, Bob, E, Chi. Cardinals (1) 1951
Dove, Eddie, DB, San Francisco (1) 1962
Dowler, Boyd, WR, Green Bay (2) 1966, 1968
Drake, Johnny, B, Clev. Rams (3) 1939, Jan. 1940, Dec. 1940
Drazenovich, Chuck, LB, Washington (4) 1956–59
Drulis, Chuck, G, Chi. Bears (1) Dec. 1942
Dubenion, Elbert, WR, Buffalo (1) 1965
Dudley, Bill, B (3) Pittsburgh, Dec. 1942; Washington, 1951–52
Dunaway, Jim, DT, Buffalo (4) 1966–69
Duncan, Leslie (Speedy), DB (4) San Diego, 1966–68; Washington, 1972
DuPree, Billy Joe, TE, Dallas (1) 1977
Dutton, John, DE, Balitmore (2) 1976–77

E

Ecklund, Brad, C, N.Y. Yanks (2) 1951–52
Edgerson, Booker, DB, Buffalo (1) 1966
Edwards, Dan, E, N.Y. Giants (1) 1951
Edwards, Glen (Turk), T, Washington (1) Jan. 1940
Edwards, Glen, S, Pittsburgh (2) 1976–77
Eisenhauer, Larry, DE, Boston (4) 1963–65, 1967
Elam, Cleveland, DT, San Francisco (1) 1977
Eller, Carl, DE, Minnesota (6) 1969–72, 1974*, 1975
Elliott, John, DT, N.Y. Jets (3) 1969–71
Ellis, Ken, CB, Green Bay (2) 1974–75
Ellison, Willie, RB, Los Angeles (1) 1972*
Elter, Leo, B, Washington (1) 1957
Engebretsen, Paul, G, Green Bay (1) Jan. 1940
Erlandson, Tom, LB, Miami (1) 1967
Etter, Bob, K, Atlanta (1) 1970
Evans, Norm, T, Miami (2) 1973, 1975

F

Faison, Earl, DE, San Diego (5) 1962–66
Falaschi, Nello, B, N.Y. Giants (2) 1939, Jan. 1942
Famiglietti, Gary, B, Chi. Bears (3) Dec. 1940, Jan. 1942, Dec. 1942
Farkas, Andy, B, Washington (2) Jan. 1940, Dec. 1942
Farman, Dick, G, Washington (1) Dec. 1942

Farr, Mel, RB, Detroit (2) 1968, 1971
Farr, Miller, DB, Houston (3) 1968–69, 1970
Farragut, Ken, C, Philadelphia (1) 1954
Fears, Tom, E, Los Angeles (1) 1951
Federovich, John, T, Chi. Bears (1) Jan. 1942
Felt, Dick, DB (2) N.Y. Titans, 1962; Boston, 1963
Ferguson, Charley, E, Buffalo (1) 1966
Ferguson, Howie, RB, Green Bay (1) 1956
Filchock, Frank, B, Washington (2) Jan. 1940, Jan. 1942
Finks, Jim, QB, Pittsburgh (1) 1953
Fischer, Bill, G, Chi. Cardinals (3) 1951–53
Fischer, Pat, CB (3) St. Louis, 1965–66; Washington, 1970
Fiss, Galen, LB, Cleveland (2) 1963–64
Flanagan, Ed, C, Detroit (4) 1970–72, 1974
Flatley, Paul, WR, Minnesota (1) 1967
Flint, George, G, Buffalo (1) 1966
Flores, Tom, QB, Oakland (1) 1967
Floyd, Don, DE, Houston (2) 1962–63
Foley, Dave, T, Buffalo (1) 1974
Folkins, Lee, TE, Dallas (1) 1964
Ford, Len, DE, Cleveland (4) 1952–55
Foreman, Chuck, RB, Minnesota (4) 1974–76, 1977*
Forester, Bill, LB, Green Bay (4) 1960–63
Forte, Aldo, G, Chi. Bears (2) Dec. 1940, Jan. 1942
Fortmann, Danny, G, Chi. Bears (3) Dec. 1940, Jan. 1942, Dec. 1942
Fortunato, Joe, LB, Chi. Bears (5) 1959, 1963–66
Francis, Russ, TE, New England (1) 1977
Fraser, Jim, LB (3) Denver, 1963; Kansas City, 1964–65
Frazier, Charlie, TE, Houston (1) 1967
Frazier, Willie, TE, San Diego (3) 1966, 1968, 1970
Frederickson, Tucker, RB, N.Y. Giants (1) 1966
Freitas, Rockne (Rocky), T, Detroit (1) 1973*
Fuller, Frank, T, St. Louis (1) 1960

G

Gabriel, Roman, QB (4) L. A., 1968–70; Philadelphia, 1974
Gain, Bob, DT, Cleveland (5) 1958–60, 1962–63
Galazin, Stan, C, N.Y. Giants (1) 1939
Galimore, Willie, RB, Chi. Bears (1) 1959
Gallarneau, Hugh, B, Chi. Bears (1) Jan. 1942
Gantenbein, Milt, E, Green Bay (1) Jan. 1942
Garrett, Carl, RB, Boston Patriots (1) 1970
Garrett, Mike, RB, Kansas City (2) 1967–68
Garrison, Gary, WR, San Diego (4) 1969, 1971*, 1972–73
Garrison, Walt, RB, Dallas (1) 1973
Garron, Larry, RB, Boston (3) 1962, 1964–65
Gatski, Frank, C, Cleveland (1) 1955
Gelatka, Chuck, E, N.Y. Giants (1) 1939
Gentry, Byron, G, Pittsburgh (2) 1939, Jan. 1940
George, Bill, LB, Chicago (8) 1955–62
George, Ray, T, Detroit (1) Jan. 1940
Gerela, Roy, K, Pittsburgh (2) 1973, 1975
Geri, Joe, B, Pittsburgh (2) 1951–52
Gibbons, Jim, TE, Detroit (3) 1961–62, 1965
Gibron, Abe, G, Cleveland (4) 1953–56
Gifford, Frank, RB, N.Y. Giants (7) 1954–57, 1959–60, 1964
Gilbert, Kline, T, Chi. Bears (1) 1958
Gilchrist, Cookie, RB (4) Buffalo 1963–65; Denver, 1966
Gildea, John, B, N.Y. Giants (1) 1939
Gilliam, John, WR, Minnesota (4) 1973–76
Gilliam, Jon, C, Dallas Texans (1) 1962
Gillingham, Gale, G, Green Bay (5) 1970–72, 1974*, 1975
Gillom, Horace, E-P, Cleveland (1) 1953
Gilmer, Harry, QB, Washington (2) 1951, 1953
Glass, Bill, DE, Cleveland (4) 1963–65, 1968
Glick, Fred, DB, Houston (3) 1963–65
Goddard, Ed, B, Cleveland Rams (1) 1939
Goeddeke, George, G, Denver (1) 1970
Gogolak, Pete, K, Buffalo (1) 1966
Goldenberg, Charles (Buckets), G, Green Bay (1) Jan. 1940
Gonsoulin, Austin (Goose), DB, Denver (5) 1962–65, 1967
Goode, Rob, RB, Washington (2) 1952, 1955
Goode, Irv, G, St. Louis (2) 1965, 1968
Goode, Tom, C, Miami (1) 1970
Gordon, Dick, WR, Chicago (2) 1971–72
Gordy, John, G, Detroit (3) 1964–66
Gossett, Bruce, K, Los Angeles (2) 1967, 1969
Gradishar, Randy, LB, Denver (1) 1976
Graham, Kenny, DB, San Diego (4) 1966, 1968–70
Graham, Otto, QB, Cleveland (5) 1951–55
Granger, Hoyle, RB, Houston (2) 1968–69

Grantham, Larry, LB, N.Y. Jets (5) 1963–65, 1967, 1970
Gray, Ken, G, St. Louis (6) 1962, 1964–65, 1967–69
Gray, Leon, T, New England (1) 1977
Gray, Mel, WR, St. Louis (3) 1975–77
Grayson, Dave, DB (6) Dallas Texans, 1963; Kansas City, 1964–65; Oakland, 1966–67, 1970
Green, Bobby Joe, P, Chicago (1) 1971
Green, Cornell, DB, Dallas (5) 1966–68, 1972–73
Green, Ernie, RB, Cleveland (2) 1967–68
Green, John, E, Philadelphia (1) 1951
Greene, Joe, DT, Pittsburgh (8) 1970–77
Greenfield, Tom, C, Green Bay (1) Jan. 1940
Greenwood, L.C., DE, Pittsburgh (4) 1974–77
Gregg, Forrest, T, Green Bay (9) 1960–65, 1967–69
Gregory, Jack, DE (2) Cleveland, 1970; N.Y. Giants, 1973
Grgich, Visco, G, San Francisco (1) 1951
Grier, Roosevelt, DT, N.Y. Giants (3) 1954, 1957, 1961
Griese, Bob, QB, Miami (6) 1968–69, 1971–72, 1974–75
Grimes, Billy, B, Green Bay (2) 1951–52
Groom, Jerry, T, Chi. Cardinals (1) 1955
Groza, Lou, T-K, Cleveland (9) 1951–56, 1958–60
Guy, Ray, P, Oakland (4) 1974–77

H

Haden, Jack, T, N.Y. Giants (1) 1939
Hadl, John, QB (6) San Diego, 1965–66, 1969–70, 1973; Los Angeles, 1974
Hall, Parker, B, Cleveland Rams (1) Jan. 1940
Hall, Ron, DB, Boston (1) 1964
Ham, Jack, LB, Pittsburgh (4) 1974*, 1975–77
Hanburger, Chris, LB, Washington (9) 1967–70, 1973–76, 1977*
Hanken, Ray, E, N.Y. Giants (1) 1939
Hannah, John, G, New England (1) 1977
Hanner, Dave, DT, Green Bay (2) 1954–55
Harder, Pat, RB, Chi. Cardinals (2) 1951, 1953
Hardman, Cedrick, DE, San Francisco (2) 1972, 1976
Hardy, Jim, QB, Chi. Cardinals (1) 1951
Hare, Cecil, B, Washington (2) Jan. 1942, Dec. 1942
Hare, Ray, B, Washington (1) Dec. 1942
Harris, Cliff, S, Dallas (2) 1975–76
Harris, Dick, DB, San Diego (1) 1962
Harris, Franco, RB, Pittsburgh (5) 1973–76, 1977*
Harris, James, QB, Los Angeles (1) 1975
Hart, Jim, QB, St. Louis (2) 1975–76
Hart, Leon, E, Detroit (1) 1952
Hart, Tommy, DE, San Francisco (1) 1977
Hauss, Len, C, Washington (5) 1967, 1969–71, 1973
Hawkins, Rip, LB, Minnesota (1) 1964
Hawkins, Wayne, G, Oakland (3) 1964–68
Hayes, Bob, WR, Dallas (3) 1966–68
Haynes, Abner, RB (3) Dallas Texans, 1962–63; K. C., 1965
Haynes, Mike, CB, New England (1) 1977*
Hazeltine, Matt, LB, San Francisco (2) 1963, 1965
Headrick, Sherrill, LB (4) Dal. Texans, 1962–63; K. C., 1966–67
Hein, Mel, C, N.Y. Giants (4) 1939, Jan. 1940, Dec. 1940, Jan. 1942
Hendricks, Ted, LB (4) Baltimore, 1972–74; Green Bay, 1975
Henke, Ed, E, San Francisco (1) 1953
Hennigan, Charley, WR, Houston (5) 1962–66
Herber, Arnie, B, Green Bay (1) Jan. 1940
Herman, Dave, G, N.Y. Jets (2) 1969–70
Hickerson, Gene, G, Cleveland (6) 1966–71
Hicks, W.K., DB, Houston (1) 1967
Hill, Calvin, RB, Dallas (4) 1970*, 1973, 1974*, 1975
Hill, Harlon, E, Chi. Bears (3) 1955–57
Hill, J.D., WR, Buffalo (1) 1973
Hill, Jimmy, DB, St. Louis (3) 1961–63
Hill, Mack Lee, RB, Kansas City (1) 1965
Hill, Winston, T, N.Y. Jets (8) 1965, 1968–74
Hines, Glen Ray, T, Houston (2) 1969–70
Hinkle, Clarke, B, Green Bay (3) 1939, Jan. 1940, Dec. 1940
Hirsch, Elroy, E, Los Angeles (3) 1952–54
Hoaglin, Fred, C, Cleveland (1) 1970
Hoak, Dick, RB, Pittsburgh (1) 1969
Hock, John, G, Los Angeles (1) 1957
Hoerner, Dick, RB, Los Angeles (1) 1951
Hoernschemeyer, Bob (Hunchy), B, Detroit (2) 1952–53
Hoffman, John, B-E, Chi. Bears (2) 1954, 1956
Holmes, Robert, RB, Kansas City (1) 1970
Holmes, Pat, DE, Houston (2) 1968–69
Holub, E.J., LB (5) Dallas Texans, 1962, 1963*; Kansas City, 1965*, 1966–67

Tucker Frederickson   *John Gilliam*   **Ken Gray**   *John Hadl*   *Winston Hill*   *George Kunz*   *Ernie Ladd*

Hopp, Harry, B, Detroit (1) Dec. 1942
Hornung, Paul, RB, Green Bay (2) 1960–61
Houston, Jim, LB, Cleveland (4) 1965–66, 1970–71
Houston, Ken, S (9) Houston, 1969–73; Washington, 1974–77
Howell, Jim Lee, E, N.Y. Giants (1) 1939
Howley, Chuck, LB, Dallas (6) 1966–72
Howton, Bill, E, Green Bay (4) 1953, 1956–58
Hubbard, Marv, RB, Oakland (3) 1972–74
Hubbert, Brad, RB, San Diego (1) 1968
Hudson, Bill, DT, San Diego (1) 1962
Hudson, Dick, T, Buffalo (1) 1964
Huff, Sam, LB (5) N.Y. Giants, 1959–62; Washington, 1965
Huffman, Dick, T, Los Angeles (1) 1951
Hughes, Bill, C, Chi. Bears (1) Jan. 1942
Hughes, George, G, Pittsburgh (2) 1952, 1954
Humbert, Dick, E, Philadelphia (1) Jan. 1942
Humble, Weldon, G, Cleveland (1) 1951
Humphrey, Claude, DE, Atlanta (5) 1971–75
Hunt, Bobby, DB, Kansas City (1) 1965
Hunt, Jim, DT, Boston Patriots (3) 1967–68, 1970
Hunter, Art, C, Cleveland (1) 1960
Husmann, Ed, DT, Houston (3) 1962–64
Hutson, Don, E, Green Bay (4) Jan. 1940, Dec. 1940, Jan. 1942, Dec. 1942

I

Isbell, Cecil, B, Green Bay (4) 1939, Jan. 1940, Jan. 1942, Dec. 1942
Ivy, Frank (Pop), E, Chi. Cardinals (1) Dec. 1942

J

Jackson, Frank, WR, Kansas City (1) 1966
Jackson, Harold, WR (4) Philadelphia, 1970, 1973; Los Angeles, 1974, 1976
Jackson, Monte, CB, Los Angeles (1) 1977
Jackson, Rich, DE, Denver (3) 1969–71
Jacobs, Harry, LB, Buffalo (2) 1966, 1970
Jacunski, Harry, E, Green Bay (1) Jan. 1940
Jagade, Harry (Chick), B, Cleveland (1) 1954
James, Dick, RB, Washington (1) 1962
James, John, P, Atlanta (2) 1976–77
James, Robert, CB, Buffalo (3) 1973–75
James, Tommy, B, Cleveland (1) 1954
Jamison, Al, T, Houston (2) 1962–63
Janik, Tom, DB, Buffalo (2) 1966, 1968
Jankowski, Ed, B, Green Bay (1) Jan. 1940
Jaquess, Lindel (Pete), DB, Houston (1) 1965
Jarmoluk, Mike, T, Philadelphia (1) 1952
Jauron, Dick, KR, Detroit (1) 1975
Jefferson, Roy, WR (3) Pittsburgh, 1969–70; Washington, 1972
Jessie, Ron, WR, Los Angeles (1) 1977
Jeter, Bob, DB, Green Bay (2) 1968, 1970
Joe, Billy, RB, Buffalo (1) 1966
Johnson, Bill, C, San Francisco (2) 1953–54
Johnson, Billy, WR, Houston (1) 1976
Johnson, Bob, C, Cincinnati (1) 1969
Johnson, Charley, QB, St. Louis (1) 1964
Johnson, Curley, P, N.Y. Jets (1) 1966
Johnson, Jimmy, CB, San Francisco (5) 1970*, 1971–73, 1975
Johnson, John, T, Detroit (1) Jan. 1940
Johnson, John Henry, RB (4) S. F., 1955; Pittsburgh, 1963–65
Johnson, Larry, C, N.Y. Giants (1) 1939
Johnson, Ron, RB, N.Y. Giants (2) 1971, 1973
Johnson, Walter, DT, Cleveland (3) 1968–70
Johnston, Mark, DB, Houston (1) 1962
Joiner, Charlie, WR, San Diego (1) 1977
Jones, Art, B, Pittsburgh (1) Jan. 1942
Jones, Bert, QB, Baltimore (1) 1977
Jones, David (Deacon), DE (8) Los Angeles, 1965–71; San Diego, 1973
Jones, Dub, B, Cleveland (1) 1952
Jones, Homer, WR, N.Y. Giants (2) 1968–69
Jones, Stan, G, Chi. Bears (7) 1956–62
Jordan, Henry, DT, Green Bay (4) 1961–62, 1964, 1967
Jordan, Lee Roy, LB, Dallas (5) 1968–69, 1970*, 1974*, 1975
Josephson, Les, RB, Los Angeles (1) 1968
Joyce, Don, DE, Baltimore (1) 1959
Jurgensen, Sonny, QB (5) Philadelphia, 1962*; Washington, 1965, 1967*, 1968*, 1970*
Justice, Ed, B, Washington (1) Dec. 1942

K

Kaminski, Larry, C, Denver (1) 1968

Kapp, Joe, QB, Minnesota (1) 1970*
Karas, Emil, LB, San Diego (3) 1962–64
Karcis, John, B, N.Y. Giants (1) 1939
Karras, Alex, DT, Detroit (4) 1961–63, 1966
Kassulke, Karl, S, Minnesota (1) 1971
Katcavage, Jim, DE, N.Y. Giants (3) 1962–64
Kavanaugh, Ken, E, Chi. Bears (2) Dec. 1940, Jan. 1942
Keane, Tom, DB, Baltimore (1) 1954
Keating, Tom, DT, Oakland (2) 1967–68
Kell, Paul, T, Green Bay (1) Jan. 1940
Kellerman, Ernie, DB, Cleveland (1) 1969
Kelly, Leroy, RB, Cleveland (6) 1967–72
Kemp, Jack, QB (7) San Diego, 1962; Buffalo, 1963, 1964*, 1965–67, 1970
Keys, Brady, DB, Pittsburgh (1) 1967
Khayat, Bobby, G, Washington (1) 1961
Kiick, Jim, RB, Miami (2) 1969–70
Kilmer, Billy, QB, Washington (1) 1973
Kilroy, Frank (Bucko), G, Philadelphia (3) 1953–55
Kinard, Frank (Bruiser), T, Brooklyn Dodgers (5) 1939, Jan. 1940, Dec. 1940, Jan. 1942, Dec. 1942
Kindt, Don, B, Chi. Bears (1) 1954
Klein, Dick, T, Boston Patriots (1) 1963
Knight, Curt, K, Washington (1) 1972
Kocourek, Dave, TE, San Diego (4) 1962–65
Kolman, Ed, T, Chi. Bears (3) Dec. 1940, Jan. 1942, Dec. 1942
Koman, Bill, DE, St. Louis (2) 1963, 1965
Konz, Ken, DB, Cleveland (1) 1956
Koy, Ernie, RB, N.Y. Giants (1) 1968
Kramer, Jerry, G, Green Bay (3) 1963–64, 1968
Kramer, Ron, TE, Green Bay (1) 1963
Krause, Paul, S (8) Washington, 1965–66; Minnesota, 1970, 1972–76
Krisher, Bill, G, Dallas Texans (1) 1962
Krouse, Ray, T, N.Y. Giants (1) 1955
Krueger, Al, E, Washington (1) Dec. 1942
Krueger, Charlie, DT, San Francisco (2), 1961, 1965
Kuechenberg, Bob, G, Miami (2) 1975–76
Kuharich, Joe, G, Chi. Cardinals (1) Jan. 1942
Kunz, George, T (5) Atlanta, 1970, 1972, 1974; Baltimore, 1976–77
Kupp, Jake, G, New Orleans (1) 1970
Kwalick, Ted, TE, San Francisco (3) 1972–74

L

Ladd, Ernie, DT, San Diego (4) 1963–66
Lahar, Harold, G, Chi. Bears (1) Jan. 1942
Laird, Bruce, KR, Baltimore (1) 1973
Lambert, Jack, LB, Pittsburgh (2) 1976–77
Lammons, Pete, TE, N.Y. Jets (1) 1968
Lamonica, Daryle, QB (4) Buffalo, 1966; Oakland, 1968, 1971, 1973
Landry, Greg, QB, Detroit (1) 1972
Landry, Tom, DB, N.Y. Giants (1) 1955
Lane, Dick (Night Train), DB (7) Chi. Cardinals, 1955–57, 1959; Detroit, 1961–63
Lane, MacArthur, RB, St. Louis (1) 1971
Langer, Jim, C, Miami (4) 1974–77
Lanier, Willie, LB, Kansas City (8) 1969–76
Lansford, Buck, G, Philadelphia (1) 1957
Larsen, Gary, DT, Minnesota (2) 1970–71
Larson, Greg, C, N.Y. Giants (1) 1969
Lary, Yale, S, Detroit (9) 1954, 1957–63, 1965
Laskey, Bill, LB, Buffalo (1) 1966
Lassiter, Isaac, DE, Oakland (1) 1967
Lattner, Johnny, B, Pittsburgh (1) 1955
Lavelli, Dante, E, Cleveland (3) 1951, 1954–55
Lawrence, James, B, Green Bay (1) Jan. 1940
Laws, Joe, B, Green Bay (1) Jan. 1940
Layne, Bobby, QB (5) Detroit, 1952–54, 1957; Pittsburgh, 1960
LeBaron, Eddie, QB (4) Washington, 1956, 1958–59; Dallas, 1963
LeBeau, Dick, DB, Detroit (3) 1965–67
LeClair, Jim, LB, Cincinnati (1) 1977
Lee, Bill, T, Green Bay (1) Jan. 1940
Leemans, Alphonse (Tuffy), B, N.Y. Giants (2) 1939, Jan. 1942
Lemek, Ray, T, Washington (1) 1962
Leo, Charles, G, Boston (1) 1962
Letlow, Russ, G, Green Bay (2) 1939, Jan. 1940
LeVias, Jerry, WR, Houston (1) 1970*
Lewis, Woodley, DB, Los Angeles (1) 1951
Lilly, Bob, DT, Dallas (10) 1963, 1965–72, 1974
Lincoln, Keith, RB (5) San Diego, 1963–66; Buffalo, 1968

Linhart, Toni, K, Baltimore (1) 1977
Lio, Augie, G, Detroit (2) Jan. 1942, Dec. 1942
Lipscomb, Gene (Big Daddy), DT (3) Baltimore, 1959–60; Pittsburgh, 1963
Lipscomb, Paul, T, Washington (4) 1951–54
Little, Floyd, RB, Denver (5) 1969–72, 1974
Little, Larry, G, Miami (5) 1970, 1972–75
Livingston, Andy, RB, New Orleans (1) 1970
Livingston, Mike, QB, Kansas City (1) 1970
Livingston, Ted, G, Cleveland Rams (1) Dec. 1940
Lloyd, Dave, LB, Philadelphia (1) 1970
Lockhart, Carl (Spider), DB, N.Y. Giants (2) 1967, 1969
Logan, Jerry, S, Baltimore (3) 1966, 1971–72
Long, Charley, G, Boston Patriots (2) 1963–64
Looney, Don, E, Philadelphia (1) Dec. 1940
LoVetere, John, DT, N.Y. Giants (1) 1964
Lowe, Paul, RB, San Diego (2) 1964, 1966
Lucci, Mike, LB, Detroit (1) 1972
Luckman, Sid, QB, Chi. Bears (3) Dec. 1940, Jan. 1942, Dec. 1942
Lujack, Johnny, QB, Chi. Bears (2) 1951–52
Lunday, Ken (Kayo), G, N.Y. Giants (1) 1939
Lundy, Lamar, DE, Los Angeles (1) 1960
Lyles, Lenny, DB, Baltimore (1) 1967
Lynch, Dick, DB, N.Y. Giants (1) 1964
Lynch, Jim,,LB, Kansas City (1) 1969

M

Mack, Tom, G, Los Angeles (9) 1968–76
Mackey, John, TE, Baltimore (5) 1964, 1966–69
MacKinnon, Jacques, TE, San Diego (2) 1967, 1969
Magnani, Dante, B, Cleveland Rams (1) Dec. 1942
Maguire, Paul, LB (2) San Diego, 1963; Buffalo, 1966
Malone, Charley, E, Washington (1) Dec. 1942
Manders, Dave, C, Dallas (1) 1967
Manders, Clarence (Pug), B, Brooklyn Dodgers (3) Jan. 1940, Dec. 1940, Jan. 1942
Maniaci, Joe, B, Chi. Bears (2) Dec. 1940, Jan. 1942
Manske, Edgar (Eggs), E, Chi. Bears (1) Dec. 1940
Maples, Bobby, C, Houston (1) 1969
Marchetti, Gino, DE, Baltimore (10) 1955–58, 1960–65
Marcol, Chester, K, Green Bay (2) 1973, 1975
Marconi, Joe, RB, Chicago (1) 1964
Marsalis, Jim, CB, Kansas City (2) 1970–71
Marshall, Jim, DE, Minnesota (2) 1969–70
Martin, Harvey, DE, Dallas (1) 1977
Martin, Jim, K, Detroit (1) 1962
Martinkovic, John, E, Green Bay (2) 1954, 1956
Martinovich, Phil, G, Chi. Bears (1) Dec. 1940
Mason, Tommy, RB, Minnesota (3) 1963–65
Massey, Carlton, E, Cleveland (1) 1956
Masterson, Bernie, QB, Chi. Bears (1) Dec. 1940
Masterson, Bob, E, Washington (1) Dec. 1942
Mathews, Ray, B, Pittsburgh (2) 1953, 1956
Mathis, Bill, RB (2) N.Y. Titans, 1962; N.Y. Jets, 1964
Matson, Ollie, RB, Chi. Cardinals (5) 1953, 1955–58
Matsos, Archie, LB (3) Buffalo, 1962–63; Oakland, 1964
Matte, Tom, RB, Baltimore (2) 1969–70
Matuszak, Marv, LB (3) Pittsburgh, 1954; San Francisco, 1958; Buffalo, 1963
Matuza, Al, C, Chi. Bears (1) Jan. 1942
Maynard, Don, WR, N.Y. Jets (3) 1966, 1968, 1970*
Mays, Jerry, DE (7) Dallas Texans, 1963; Kansas City, 1965–69, 1971
Maznicki, Frank, B, Chi. Bears (1) Dec. 1942
McAfee, George, B, Chi. Bears (1) Jan. 1942
McChesney, Bob, E, Washington (2) 1939, Dec. 1942
McClairen, Jack, E, Pittsburgh (1) 1958
McClinton, Curtis, RB (3) Dallas Texans, 1963; Kansas City, 1967–68
McCloughan, Kent, CB, Oakland (2) 1967,1968*
McCord, Darris, DE, Detroit (1) 1958
McCormack, Mike, T (6) N.Y. Yanks, 1951; Cleveland, 1957–58, 1961–63
McCutcheon, Lawrence, RB, Los Angeles (4) 1974–77
McDole, Ron, DE, Buffalo (2) 1965, 1967
McDonald, Tommy, WR (6) Philadelphia, 1959–63; Los Angeles, 1966
McElhenny, Hugh, RB (6) San Francisco, 1953–54, 1957–59; Minnesota, 1962
McFadin, Bud, T (5) Los Angeles, 1956–57; Denver, 1962–64

*Selected but did not play

Eddie LeBaron

Chester Marcol

Dave Parks

Floyd Peters

Jack Rudnay

Bob St. Clair

Jerry Sherk

McGee, Ben, DE, Pittsburgh (2) 1967, 1969
McGee, Max, E, Green Bay (1) 1962
McGraw, Thurman, T, Detroit (1) 1951
McKeever, Marlin, DE, Los Angeles (1) 1967
McLaughlin, Leon, C, Los Angeles (1) 1955
McLean, Ray (Scooter), B, Chi. Bears (2) Dec. 1940, Jan. 1942
McLeod, Bob, E, Houston (1) 1962
McMillan, Ernie, T, St. Louis (4) 1966, 1968, 1970–71
McMurtry, Chuck, DT, Buffalo (1) 1962
McNeil, Charles, DB, San Diego (1) 1962
McNeil, Clifton, WR, San Francisco (1) 1969
McPeak, Bill, E, Pittsburgh (3) 1953–54, 1957
Meador, Eddie, DB, Los Angeles (5) 1961, 1965–67, 1969
Meinert, Dale, LB, St. Louis (3) 1964, 1966, 1968
Mellus, John, T, N.Y. Giants (2) 1939, Jan. 1942
Mercer, Mike, K, Buffalo (1) 1968
Meredith, Don, QB, Dallas (3) 1967–69
Meredith, Dudley, DT, Buffalo (1) 1966
Mertens, Jerry, B, San Francisco (1) 1959
Metcalf, Terry, RB, St. Louis (2) 1975–76
Michael, Rich, T, Houston (2) 1963–64
Michaels, Lou, K–DE, Pittsburgh (2) 1963–64
Michaels, Walt, LB, Cleveland (5) 1956–60
Michalik, Art, G, San Francisco (1) 1954
Mihal, Joe, T, Chi. Bears (2) Dec. 1940, Jan. 1942
Mike-Mayer, Nick, K, Atlanta (1) 1974
Miller, Alan, RB, Oakland (1) 1962
Miller, Fred, DT, Baltimore (3) 1968–69, 1970*
Miller, Paul, DE, Los Angeles (2) 1956–57
Mills, Pete, DE, Buffalo (1) 1966
Mingo, Gene, K–RB, Denver (1) 1963
Mischak, Bob, G (2) N.Y. Titans 1962; N.Y. Jets, 1963
Mitchell, Bobby, RB (4) Cleveland, 1961; Washington 1963–65
Mitchell, Jim, TE, Atlanta (2) 1970, 1973
Mitchell, Leroy, DB, Boston Patriots (1) 1968
Mitchell, Lydell, RB, Baltimore (2) 1976–77
Mix, Ron, T, San Diego (8) 1962–69
Modzelewski, Dick, DT, Cleveland (1) 1965
Moegle, Dickie, RB, San Francisco (1) 1956
Moore, Al, E, Green Bay (1) Jan. 1940
Moore, Lenny, RB, Baltimore (7) 1957, 1959–63, 1965
Moore, Tom, RB, Green Bay (1) 1963
Moore, Wayne, T, Miami (1) 1974*
Moore, Wilbur, B, Washington (1) Dec. 1942
Moore, Zeke, CB, Houston (2) 1970–71
Morin, Milt, TE, Cleveland (2) 1969, 1972
Morrall, Earl, QB (2) Pittsburgh, 1958; Baltimore, 1969
Morris, Dennit, LB, Houston (1) 1962
Morris, Johnny, B, Chicago (1) 1961
Morris, Jon, C, Boston (7) 1965–71
Morris, Eugene (Mercury), RB, Miami (3) 1972–73, 1974*
Morrison, Fred (Curley), B, Cleveland (1) 1956
Morrow, John, C, Cleveland (2) 1962, 1964
Moses, Haven, WR, Denver (1) 1974
Motley, Marion, B, Cleveland (1) 1951
Mudd, Howard, G, San Francisco (3) 1967–69
Mul-Key, Herb, KR, Washington (1) 1974
Mulleneaux, Carl, E, Green Bay (2) Jan. 1940, Dec. 1940
Musso, George, G, Chi. Bears (3) Jan. 1940, Dec. 1940, Jan. 1942
Mutscheller, Jim, E, Baltimore (1) 1958
Myers, Philip (Chip), WR, Cincinnati (1) 1973

N

Nagler, Gern, E, Chi. Cardinals (1) 1959
Namath, Joe, QB, N.Y. Jets (4) 1966, 1968–69, 1970*
Nance, Jim, RB, Boston (2) 1967*, 1968
Naumoff, Paul, LB, Detroit (1) 1971
Neal, Ed, C, Green Bay (1) 1951
Neely, Ralph, T, Dallas (2) 1968, 1970
Neighbors, Billy, G, Boston (1) 1964
Nelsen, Bill, QB, Cleveland (1) 1970
Nelson, Andy, S, Baltimore (1) 1961
Neville, Tom, T, Boston (1) 1967
Nickel, Elbie, E, Pittsburgh (3) 1953–54, 1957
Niemi, Laurie, T, Washington (1) 1952–53
Niland, John, G, Dallas (6) 1969–74
Nisby, John, G, Pittsburgh (3) 1960, 1962–63
Nitschke, Ray, LB, Green Bay (1) 1965
Nobis, Tommy, LB, Atlanta (5) 1967–69, 1971, 1973
Nolting, Ray, B, Chi. Bears (2) Dec. 1940, Jan. 1942
Nomellini, Leo, DT, San Francisco (10) 1951–54, 1957–62
Noonan, Karl, WR, Miami (1) 1969

Norton, Don, E, San Diego (2) 1962, 1963*
Norton, Jerry, S (5) Philadelphia, 1958–59; St. Louis, 1960–62
Norton, Jim, DB, Houston (3) 1963–64, 1968
Nowaskey, Bob, E, Chi. Bears (2) Dec. 1940, Jan. 1942
Nutter, Madison (Buzz), C, Pittsburgh (1) 1963
Nye, Blaine, G, Dallas (2) 1975, 1977

O

Oakes, Don, T, Boston (1) 1968
O'Brien, Davey, B, Philadelphia (1) Jan. 1940
Odoms, Riley, TE, Denver (3) 1974–76
O'Donnell, Joe, T, Buffalo (1) 1966
Oldershaw, Doug, G, N.Y. Giants (1) Dec. 1940
Olsen, Merlin, DT, Los Angeles (14) 1963–70, 1971*, 1972–76
Olson, Harold, T, Buffalo (1) 1962
Olszewski, Johnny, B, Chi. Cardinals (2) 1954, 1956
Orr, Jimmy, WR (2) Pittsburgh, 1960; Baltimore, 1966
Osborn Dave, RB, Minnesota (1) 1971
Osmanski, Bill, B, Chi. Bears (2) Dec. 1940, Jan. 1942
Otis, Jim, RB, St. Louis (1) 1976
Otto, Gus, LB, Oakland (1) 1970
Otto, Jim, C, Oakland (12) 1962–73
Owens, Steve, RB, Detroit (1) 1972

P

Page, Alan, DT, Minnesota (9) 1969–76, 1977*
Paluck, John, DE, Washington (1) 1965
Panfil, Ken, T, St. Louis (1) 1960
Pardee, Jack, LB, Los Angeles (1) 1964
Parilli, Babe, QB, Boston Patriots (2) 1964–65
Parker, Jim, T, Baltimore (8) 1959–66
Parks, Dave, WR, San Francisco (2) 1965, 1967
Parrish, Bernie, DB, Cleveland (2) 1961, 1964
Parrish, Lemar, CB–KR, Cincinnati (5) 1971–72, 1975–77
Parry, Owen (Ox), T, N.Y. Giants (1) 1939
Pastorini, Dan, QB, Houston (1) 1976
Patton, Jim, S, N.Y. Giants (5) 1959, 1960–63
Paul, Don S (4) Chi. Cardinals, 1954; Cleveland, 1957–59
Paul, Don, LB, Los Angeles (3) 1952–54
Paulson, Dainard, DB, N.Y. Jets (2) 1965–66
Payton, Walter, RB, Chicago (1) 1977
Pearson, Drew, WR, Dallas (2) 1975, 1977
Peoples, Woody, G, San Francisco (2) 1973–74
Perkins, Don, RB, Dallas (6) 1962–64, 1967–69
Perry, Joe, RB, San Francisco (3) 1953–55
Peters, Floyd, DT, Philadelphia (3) 1965, 1967–68
Peters, Volney, T, Washington (1) 1956
Petitbon, Richie, DB, Chicago (4) 1963–64, 1967–68
Petty, John, B, Chi. Bears (1) Dec. 1942
Philbin, Gerry, DE, N.Y. Jets (2) 1969–70
Phillips, Jim, WR, Los Angeles (3) 1961–63
Pietrosante, Nick, RB, Detroit (2) 1961–62
Pihos, Pete, E, Philadelphia (6) 1951–56
Pinckert, Erny, B, Washington (2) 1939, Jan. 1940
Plasman, Dick, E, Chi. Bears (2) Dec. 1940, Jan. 1942
Plum, Milt, QB, Cleveland (2) 1961–62
Plunkett, Sherman, T, N.Y. Jets (2) 1965, 1967
Podoley, Jim, B, Washington (1) 1958
Poillon, Dick, B, Washington (1) Dec. 1942
Polsfoot, Fran, E, Chi. Cardinals (1) 1952
Pool, Hampton, E, Chi. Bears (2) Dec. 1940, Jan. 1942
Poole, Jim, E, N.Y. Giants (3) 1939, Jan. 1940, Dec. 1940
Post, Dickie, RB, San Diego (2) 1968*, 1970
Pottios, Myron, LB, Pittsburgh (3) 1962, 1964–65
Powell, Art, E, Oakland (4) 1964–67
Price, Cotton, B, Detroit (1) Dec. 1940
Price, Eddie, RB, N.Y. Giants (3) 1952–53, 1955
Pritchard, Bosh, B, Philadelphia (1) Dec. 1942
Promuto, Vince, G, Washington (2) 1964–65
Pruitt, Greg, KR–RB, Cleveland (3) 1974–75, 1977
Putnam, Duane, G, Los Angeles (4) 1955–56, 1958–59
Pyle, Mike, C, Chicago (1) 1964

Q

Quinlan, Volney (Skeet), B, Los Angeles (1) 1955

R

Radovich, Bill, G, Detroit (1) 1939
Randle, Sonny, WR, St. Louis (4) 1961–63, 1966
Ray, Buford (Baby), T, Green Bay (1) Jan. 1940
Reaves, Ken, CB, Atlanta (1) 1970
Rechichar, Bert, B–K, Baltimore (3) 1956–58
Redman, Rick, LB, San Diego (1) 1968

Reed, Alvin, TE, Houston (2) 1969–70
Reger, John, LB, Pittsburgh (3) 1960–62
Reichow, Jerry, E, Minnesota (1) 1962
Reid, Mike, DT, Cincinnati (2) 1973, 1974*
Renfro, Mel, DB, Dallas (10) 1965–72, 1973*, 1974*
Renfro, Ray, B, Cleveland (3) 1954, 1958, 1961
Retzlaff, Pete, E, Philadelphia (5) 1959, 1961, 1964–66
Reynolds, Bob, T, St. Louis (3) 1967, 1969, 1970
Reynolds, Jack, LB, Los Angeles (1) 1976
Rice, Ken, T, Buffalo (1) 1962
Richards, Elvin, B, N.Y. Giants (2) 1939, Dec. 1940
Richardson, Jesse, T, Philadelphia (1) 1960
Richardson, Willie, WR, Baltimore (2) 1968–69
Richter, Les, LB, Los Angeles (8) 1955–62
Riffle, Dick, B, Pittsburgh (1) Jan. 1942
Riggins, John, RB, N.Y. Jets (1) 1976
Ringo, Jim, C (10) Green Bay, 1958–64; Phil., 1965–66, 1968
Robb, Joe, DE, St. Louis (1) 1967
Roberson, Irwin (Bo), WR, Buffalo (1) 1966
Roberts, Gene, B, N.Y. Giants (1) 1951
Robertson, Isiah, LB, Los Angeles (5) 1972, 1974–77
Robinson, Dave, LB, Green Bay (3) 1967–68, 1970
Robinson, Johnny, S, K.C. (4) 1964, 1965*, 1966–69, 1971
Robinson, Paul, RB, Cincinnati (2) 1969–70
Robinson, Wayne, LB, Philadelphia (2) 1955–56
Robustelli, Andy, DE (7) Los Angeles, 1954, 1956; N.Y. Giants, 1957–58, 1960–62
Rochester, Paul, DT, Dallas Texans (1) 1962
Rock, Walter, T, San Francisco (1) 1966
Rogel, Fran, B, Pittsburgh (1) 1957
Rohde, Len T, San Francisco (1) 1971
Roland, Johnny, RB, St. Louis (2) 1967, 1968*
Rossovich, Tim, LB, Philadelphia (1) 1970
Rote, Kyle, E, N.Y. Giants (4) 1954*, 1955–57
Rote, Tobin, QB (2) Green Bay, 1957; San Diego, 1964
Rowe, Bob, DE, St. Louis (1) 1969
Rucinski, Eddie, S, Brooklyn Dodgers (1) Dec. 1942
Rudnay, Jack, C, Kansas City (4) 1974–77
Russell, Andy, LB, Pittsburgh (7) 1969, 1971–76
Rutgens, Joe, DT, Washington (2) 1964, 1966
Rutkowski, Ed, WR, Buffalo (1) 1966
Ryan, Frank, QB, Cleveland (2) 1965–67

S

Saimes, George, CB, Buffalo (5) 1965–69
Sanders, Charlie, TE, Detroit (7) 1969–72, 1975–77
Sanders, Orban (Spec), B, N.Y. Yanks (1) 1951
Sandusky, Mike, G, Pittsburgh (1) 1961
Sanford, Leo, C, Chi. Cardinals (2) 1957–58
Sauer, George, WR, N.Y. Jets (4) 1967–70
Saul, Rich, C, Los Angeles (1) 1977
Sayers, Gale, RB, Chicago (4) 1966–68, 1970
Scarpitto, Bob, WR, Denver (1) 1967
Schafrath, Dick, T, Cleveland (6) 1964–69
Schmidt, Bob, C, Houston (3) 1962–64
Schmidt, Henry, DT, Buffalo (1) 1966
Schmidt, Joe, LB, Detroit (9) 1955–63
Schnelker, Bob, E, N.Y. Giants (2) 1959–60
Schnellbacher, Otto, DB, N.Y. Giants (2) 1951–52
Schottenheimer, Marty, LB, Buffalo (1) 1966
Schrader, Jim, C, Washington (3) 1959–60, 1962
Schroeder, Gene, E, Chi. Bears (1) 1953
Schuh, Harry, T, Oakland (3) 1968, 1970–71
Schultz, Charles, T, Green Bay (1) Jan. 1940
Schwartz, Perry, E, Brooklyn Dodgers (4) 1939, Jan. 1940, Jan. 1942, Dec. 1942
Scott, Clarence, CB, Cleveland (1) 1974
Scott, Jake, S, Miami (5) 1972*, 1973–74, 1975*, 1976
Scott, Tom, E, Philadelphia (2) 1958–59
Scudero, Joe, B, Washington (1) 1956
Sellers, Ron, WR, Boston Patriots (1) 1970
Sestak, Tom, T, Buffalo (4) 1963–65, 1966*
Sewell, Harley, G, Detroit (4) 1958–60, 1963
Seymour, Bob, B, Washington (1) Dec. 1942
Shaffer, Leland, B, N.Y. Giants 1939
Shanklin, Ron, WR, Pittsburgh (1) 1974
Shaw, Billy, G, Buffalo (8) 1963–70
Shaw, Bob, E, Chi. Cardinals (1) 1951
Shell, Art, T, Oakland (5) 1973–77
Sherman, Saul, QB, Chi. Bears (1) Dec. 1940
Sherman, Will, S, Los Angeles (2) 1956, 1959
Shipkey, Jerry, B, Pittsburgh (3) 1951–53
Sherk, Jerry, DT, Cleveland (4) 1974–77

Jerry Smith

Matt Snell
Gordy Soltau

Gene Upshaw

Gene Washington

Russ Washington

Jack Youngblood

Shirk, John, E. Chi. Cardinals (1) Dec. 1940
Shofner, Del, WR (5) L.A., 1959–60; N.Y. Giants, 1962–64
Shonta, Chuck, DB, Boston (1) 1967
Shugart, Clyde, G, Washington (2) Jan. 1942, Dec. 1942
Siegal, John, E, Chi. Bears (3) Dec. 1940, Jan. 1942, Dec. 1942
Siemon, Jeff, LB, Minnesota (3) 1974, 1976–77
Silas, Sam, DT, St. Louis (1) 1966
Simington, Milt, G, Pittsburgh (1) Dec. 1942
Simmons, Jack, C, Chi. Cardinals (1) 1956
Simpson, O.J., RB, Buffalo (6) 1970, 1973–77
Sistrunk, Otis, DT, Oakland (1) 1975
Sivell, Jim, G, Brooklyn Dodgers (1) Jan. 1942
Skoronski, Bob, T, Green Bay (1) 1967
Slivinski, Steve, G, Washington (1) Jan. 1942
Smith, Bill, E, Chi. Cardinals (1) Jan. 1940
Smith, Bob, RB, Buffalo (1) 1966
Smith, Bob, B, Detroit (1) 1953
Smith, Charles (Bubba), DE, Baltimore (2) 1971–72
Smith, Ernie, T, Green Bay (1) Jan. 1940
Smith, George, C, Washington (1) Dec. 1942
Smith, Harry, G, Detroit (1) Dec. 1940
Smith, Jackie, TE, St. Louis (5) 1967–71
Smith, J.D., T, Philadelphia (1) 1962*
Smith, J.D., RB, San Francisco (2) 1960, 1963
Smith, Jerry, TE, Washington (2) 1968, 1970
Smith, Jim Ray, G, Cleveland (5) 1959–63
Smith, Paul, DT, Denver (2) 1973–74
Smith, Ron, KR, Chicago (1) 1973
Smith, Stu, B, Pittsburgh (1) 1939
Snead, Norm, QB (3) Wash., 1964; Phil., 1966; N.Y. Giants, 1973
Snell, Matt, RB, N.Y. Jets (3) 1965*, 1967, 1970
Snow, Jack, WR, Los Angeles (1) 1968*
Snyder, Bob, B, Chi. Bears (2) Dec. 1940, Jan. 1942
Snyder, Ken, T, Philadelphia (2) 1954–55
Soar, Hank, B, N.Y. Giants (1) 1939
Soltau, Gordy, E, San Francisco (3) 1952–54
Spadaccini, Vic, QB, Cleveland Rams (1) Dec. 1940
Speedie, Mac, E, Cleveland (1) 1951
Spinney, Art, G, Baltimore (2) 1960–61
Sprinkle, Ed, DE, Chi. Bears (4) 1951–53, 1955
Stabler, Ken, QB, Oakland (3) 1974–75, 1977
Stacy, Bill, DB, St. Louis (1) 1962
Stallings, Larry, LB, St. Louis (1) 1971
Standlee, Norm, B, (2) Chi. Bears, Jan. 1942; S.F., 1951
Stanfel, Dick, G (5) Detroit, 1954; Washington, 1956–59
Stanfill, Bill, DE, Miami (5) 1970, 1972, 1973*, 1974*, 1975
Starr, Bart, QB, Green Bay (4) 1961–63, 1967
Staubach, Roger, QB, Dallas (4) 1972*, 1975*
Stautner, Ernie, DE, Pittsburgh (9) 1953–54, 1956–62
St. Clair, Bob, T, San Francisco (5) 1957, 1959–62
Stenerud, Jan, K, Kansas City (5) 1969–72, 1976
Stits, Bill, B, Detroit (1) 1955
St. Jean, Len, G, Boston Patriots (1) 1967
Stone, Donnie, RB, Denver (1) 1962
Stovall, Jerry, DB, St. Louis (3) 1967–68, 1970
Stralka, Clem, G, Washington (1) Dec. 1942
Stratton, Mike, LB, Buffalo (6) 1964–69
Strickland, Larry, C, Chi. Bears (1) 1957
Stroud, Jack, G, N.Y. Giants (3) 1956, 1958, 1961
Stryzkalski, John (Strike), B, San Francisco (1) 1951
Studstill, Pat, WR, Detroit (2) 1966–67
Sturm, Jerry, C, Denver (2) 1965, 1967
Stydahar, Joe, T, Chi. Bears (4) 1939, Jan. 1940, Dec. 1940, Jan. 1942
Sugar, Leo, DE, St. Louis (2) 1959, 1961
Suggs, Walt, T, Houston (2) 1968–69
Sunde, Milt, G, Minnesota (1) 1967
Svendsen, Bud, C, Green Bay (1) Jan. 1940
Svoboda, Bill, B, Chi. Cardinals (1) 1954
Swann, Lynn, WR, Pittsburgh (1) 1976
Sweeney, Walt, G, San Diego (9) 1965–73
Swisher, Bob, B, Chi. Bears (2) Dec. 1940, Jan. 1942
Szymanski, Dick, C, Baltimore (3) 1956, 1963, 1965

T

Talamini, Bob, G, Houston (6) 1963–68
Talbert, Diron, DT, Washington (1) 1975
Taliaferro, George, B (3) N.Y. Yanks, 1952; Dallas Texans, 1953; Baltimore 1954
Taliaferro, Mike, QB, Boston (1) 1970
Tarkenton, Fran, QB (9) Minnesota, 1965–66; N.Y. Giants, 1968–71; Minnesota, 1975*, 1976*, 1977*
Tatum, Jack, S, Oakland (3) 1974–76

Taylor, Bruce, CB, San Francisco (1) 1972*
Taylor, Charley, WR, Washington (8) 1965–68, 1973–76
Taylor, Hugh (Bones), E, Washington (2) 1953, 1955
Taylor, Jim, RB, Green Bay (4) 1961–62, 1964–65
Taylor, Lionel, E, Denver (3) 1962–63, 1966*
Taylor, Otis, WR, Kansas City (2) 1972–73
Taylor, Roosevelt, DB, Chicago (2) 1964, 1969
Terrell, Marvin, G, Dallas Texans (1) 1963
Teteak, Deral, G, Green Bay (1) 1953
Thomas, Aaron, WR, N.Y. Giants (1) 1965
Thomas, Clendon, DB, Pittsburgh (1) 1964
Thomas, Emmitt, CB, Kansas City (5) 1969, 1972–73, 1975–76
Thomas, John, G, San Francisco (1) 1967
Thomason, Bobby, QB, Philadelphia (3) 1954, 1956–57
Thompson, Tommy, QB, Philadelphia (1) Dec. 1942
Tingelhoff, Mick, C, Minnesota (6) 1965–70
Tinsley, Gaynell, E, Chi. Cardinals (1) 1939
Tinsley, Pete, G, Green Bay (1) Jan. 1940
Titchenal, Bob, C, Washington (1) Dec. 1942
Tittle, Y.A., QB (6) San Francisco, 1954–55, 1958, 1960; N.Y. Giants, 1962–63
Todd, Dick, B, Washington (2) Dec. 1940, Dec. 1942
Tolar, Charlie, RB, Houston (2) 1962–63
Toneff, Bob, DT (4) San Francisco, 1956; Washington, 1960–62
Tonnemaker, Clayton, LB, Green Bay (1) 1954
Torczon, LaVerne, DE, Buffalo (1) 1962
Torgeson, LaVern, LB (3) Detroit, 1955; Washington, 1956–57
Torrance, Jack, T, Chi. Bears (1) Dec. 1940
Toth, Zollie, B, N.Y. Yanks (1) 1951
Towler, Dan, RB, Los Angeles (4) 1952–55
Tracey, John, LB, Buffalo (2) 1966–67
Tracy, Tom, RB, Pittsburgh (2) 1959, 1961
Trippi, Charley, B, Chi. Cardinals (2) 1953–54
Tripson, John, T, Detroit (1) Jan. 1942
Tripucka, Frank, QB, Denver (1) 1963
Trumpy, Bob, TE, Cincinnati (4) 1969, 1970*, 1971, 1974
Tubbs, Jerry, LB, Dallas (1) 1963
Tunnell, Emlen, S (9) N.Y. Giants, 1951–58; Green Bay, 1960
Turner, Robert (Bake), WR, N.Y. Jets (1) 1964
Turner, Cecil, KR, Chicago (1) 1971
Turner, Clyde (Bulldog), C, Chi. Bears (4) Dec. 1941, Jan. 1942, 1951–52
Turner, Jim, K, N.Y. Jets (2) 1969–1970
Tuttle, Orville, G, N.Y. Giants (2) 1939, Jan. 1940
Tyrer, Jim, T (9) Dallas Texans, 1963; K. C., 1964–67, 1969–72

U

Ulinski, Harry, C, Washington (1) 1956
Unitas, John, QB, Baltimore (10) 1958–65, 1967–68
Upchurch, Rick, KR, Denver (1) 1977
Upshaw, Gene, G, Oakland (6) 1969, 1973–77
Uram, Andy, B, Green Bay (1) Jan. 1940

V

Van Brocklin, Norm, QB (9) Los Angeles, 1951–56; Philadelphia, 1959–61
Van Dyke, Bruce, G, Pittsburgh (1) 1974
Van Note, Jeff, C, Atlanta (3) 1975–77
Van Pelt, Brad, LB, N.Y. Giants (1) 1977
Van Raaphorst, Dick, K, San Diego (1) 1967
Vanzo, Fred, B, Detroit (1) Jan. 1940
Varrichione, Frank, T (5) Pitt., 1956, 1958–59, 1961; L. A., 1963
Vogel, Bob, T, Baltimore (4) 1965–66, 1968, 1972
Volk, Rick, DB, Baltimore (3) 1968, 1970, 1972

W

Wade, Bill, QB (2) Los Angeles, 1959; Chicago, 1964
Wagner, Mike, S, Pittsburgh (2) 1976–77
Walden, Bobby, P, Pittsburgh (1) 1970
Walker, Chuck, DT, St. Louis (1) 1967
Walker, Doak, B, Detroit (5) 1951–52, 1954–56
Walker, Wayne, LB-K, Detroit (3) 1964–66
Waller, Ron, B, Los Angeles (1) 1956
Wallner, Fred, G, Chi. Cardinals (1) 1956
Walsh, Bill, C, Pittsburgh (2) 1951–52
Walston, Bobby, E-K, Philadelphia (2) 1961–62
Warfield, Paul, WR (8) Cleveland, 1965, 1969–70; Miami, 1971–72, 1973*, 1974*, 1975
Warlick, Ernie, E, Buffalo (4) 1963–66
Warner, Charles, DB, Buffalo (1) 1966
Warren, Jim, DB, Miami (1) 1967
Washington, Gene, WR, Minnesota (2) 1970–71
Washington, Gene, WR, San Francisco (4) 1970–73

Washington, Russ, T, San Diego (2) 1975–76
Washington, Vic, RB, San Francisco (1) 1972
Waterfield, Bob, QB, Los Angeles (2) 1951–52
Waters, Charlie, S, Dallas (1) 1977
Watts, George, T, Washington (1) Dec. 1942
Weatherall, Jim, T, Philadelphia (2) 1956–57
Webb, Don, CB, Boston Patriots (1) 1970
Webster, Alex, RB, N.Y. Giants (2) 1959, 1962
Webster, David, DB, Dallas Texans (1) 1968
Webster, George, LB, Houston (3) 1968*, 1969, 1970*
Wehrli, Roger, CB, St. Louis (4) 1971*, 1975–77
Weinmeister, Arnie, T, N.Y. Giants (4) 1951–54
Weisgerber, Dick, B, Green Bay (1) Jan. 1940
Wells, Billy, B, Washington (1) 1955
Wells, Warren, WR, Oakland (2) 1969, 1971
West, Stan, G, Los Angeles (2) 1952–53
West, Willie, DB (2) Buffalo, 1964; Miami, 1967
Westmoreland, Dick, DB, Miami (1) 1968
Wham, Tom, E, Chi. Cardinals (1) 1952
White, Arthur (Tarzan), G, N.Y. Giants (1) 1939
White, Dwight, DE, Pittsburgh (2) 1973–74
White, Ed, G, Minnesota (2) 1976–77
White, Sammy, WR, Minnesota (1) 1977
Whited, Marvin, B, Washington (1) Dec. 1942
Whitsell, David, DB, New Orleans (1) 1968
Whittenton, Jesse, DB, Green Bay (2) 1962, 1964
Wiatrak, John, C, Cleveland Rams (1) 1939
Widby, Ron, P, Dallas (1) 1972
Widseth, Ed, T, N.Y. Giants (1) 1939
Wietecha, Ray, C, N.Y. Giants (4) 1958–59, 1961, 1963
Wiggin, Paul, DE, Cleveland (2) 1966, 1968
Wightkin, Bill, T, Chi. Bears (1) 1956
Wilcox, Dave, LB, S. F. (7) 1967, 1969–70, 1971*, 1972–74
Wildung, Dick, T, Green Bay (1) 1952
Wilkin, Willie, T, Wash. (3) Dec. 1940, Jan. 1942, Dec. 1942
Willard, Ken, RB, San Francisco (4) 1966–67, 1969–70
Willey, Norm, E, Philadelphia (2) 1955–56
Williams, Delvin, RB, San Francisco (1) 1977
Williams, Fred, T, Chi. Bears (4) 1953–54, 1959–60
Williams, Johnny, B, Washington (1) 1953
Williams, Willie, DB, N.Y. Giants (1) 1970
Williamson, Fred, DB, Oakland (3) 1962–64
Willis, Bill, G, Cleveland (3) 1951–53
Wilson, Billy, E, San Francisco (6) 1955–60
Wilson, George, E, Chi. Bears (3) Dec. 1940, Jan. 1942, Dec. 1942
Wilson, Jerrel, P, Kansas City (3) 1971–73
Wilson, Larry, S, St. Louis (8) 1963–64, 1966–71
Wilson, Nemiah, DB, Oakland (1) 1968
Wilson, Tom, B, Los Angeles (1) 1958
Wimberly, Abner, E, Green Bay (1) 1953
Winkler, Jim, T, Los Angeles (1) 1953
Wistert, Al, T, Philadelphia (1) 1951
Wittum, Tom, P, San Francisco (2) 1974–75
Wood, Duane, DB, Kansas City (1) 1964
Wood, Willie, S, Green Bay (8) 1963, 1965–71
Woodeshick, Tom, RB, Philadelphia (1) 1969
Woodson, Abe, B, San Francisco (5) 1960–64
Woodson, Marv, DB, Pittsburgh (1) 1968
Wooten, John, G, Cleveland (2) 1966–67
Woudenberg, John, T, Pittsburgh (1) Dec. 1942
Wozniak, John, G, Dallas Texans (1) 1953
Wright, Ernie, T, San Diego (3) 1962, 1964, 1966
Wright, Rayfield, T, Dallas (6) 1972–77

Y

Yary, Ron, T, Minnesota (6) 1972–77
Yepremian, Garo, K, Miami (1) 1974
Young, Bill, T, Washington (1) Dec. 1942
Young, Buddy, B, Baltimore (1) 1955
Young, Charles, TE, Philadelphia (3) 1974–76
Youngblood, Jack, DE, Los Angeles (3) 1974–76
Younger, Paul (Tank), RB, Los Angeles (4) 1952–54, 1956*

Z

Zarnas, Gus, G, Green Bay (1) Jan. 1940
Zatkoff, Roger, LB, Green Bay (3) 1955–57
Zeman, Bob, DB, Denver (1) 1963
Zeno, Joe, G, Washington (1) Dec. 1942
Zimmerman, Roy, B, Washington (1) Dec. 1942
Zook, John, DE, Atlanta (1) 1974

*Selected but did not play

PRO BOWL INDIVIDUAL RECORDS

RUSHING

Most Attempts, Game
20 Hoyle Granger, Houston, AFL East, 1969
Most Yards Gained, Game
141 Jim Brown, Cleveland, NFL East, 1963
Longest Run From Scrimmage
80 Keith Lincoln, San Diego, AFL West, 1965

PASSING

Most Passes Attempted, Game
37 Norm Van Brocklin, Philadelphia, NFL East, 1961
Joe Namath, N.Y. Jets, AFL East, 1968
Most Passes Completed, Game
19 Otto Graham, Cleveland, NFL American Conference, 1951
Most Yards Gained, Game
288 Norm Van Brocklin, Phliadelphia, NFL East, 1961
Longest Pass Completion
92 Cecil Isbell, Green Bay, Jan. 1940 (Hutson, TD)
Highest Completion Percentage, Game
72.2 Y.A. Tittle, San Francisco, NFL West, 1960 (18-13)
Most Touchdown Passes, Game
3 Sammy Baugh, Washington, Pro All-Stars, Jan. 1942
John Unitas, Baltimore, NFL West, 1960
Norm Van Brocklin, Philadelphia, NFL East, 1961
Cotton Davidson, Dallas Texans, AFL West, 1962
John Hadl, San Diego, AFL West, 1965
Most Passes Had Intercepted, Game
6 John Brodie, San Francisco, NFL West, 1966

RECEIVING

Most Receptions, Game
11 Billy Wilson, San Francisco, NFL West, 1955
Most Yards Gained, Game
157 Billy Wilson, San Francisco, NFL West, 1955
Lenny Moore, Baltimore, NFL West, 1961
Longest Reception
92 Don Hutson, Green Bay, Jan. 1940 (Isbell, TD)
Most Touchdowns, Game
2 Perry Schwartz, Brooklyn Dodgers, Pro All-Stars, Jan. 1942
Tom Fears, Los Angeles, NFL National Conference, 1951
Hugh McElhenny, San Francisco, NFL National Conference, 1953
Lenny Moore, Baltimore, NFL West, 1960
Sonny Randle, St. Louis, NFL East, 1961
Lance Alworth, San Diego, AFL All-Stars, 1966

INTERCEPTIONS BY

Most Interceptions By, Game
2 Emlen Tunnell, N.Y. Giants, NFL East, 1954
Dick (Night Train) Lane, Chi. Cardinals, NFL East, 1955
Joe Schmidt, Detroit, NFL West, 1956
Jack Christiansen, Detroit, NFL West, 1957
Yale Lary, Detroit, NFL West, twice, 1958 and 1959
Fred Williamson, Oakland, AFL West, twice, 1962 and 1963
Paul Krause, Washington, NFL East, 1966
George Saimes, Buffalo, AFL East, 1967
Jimmy Warren, Miami, AFL East, 1967
Leslie (Speedy) Duncan, San Diego, AFL West, 1968
Jim Lynch, Kansas City, AFL West, 1969
George Webster, Houston, AFL West, 1969
Mel Blount, Pittsburgh, AFC, 1977
Most Yards Gained, Game
97 Bill Dudley, Pittsburgh, Pro All-Stars, Dec. 1942
Longest Return
97 Bill Dudley, Pittsburgh, Pro All-Stars, Dec. 1942
Most Touchdowns, Game
1 By nine players

PUNTING

Most Punts, Game
10 Babe Parilli, Boston Patriots, AFL East, 1967
Longest Punt
65 Jerry Norton, Philadelphia, NFL East, 1958
Highest Punting Average, Game (3 or more punts)
52.2 Sam Baker, Philadelphia, NFL East, 1965 (4)

PUNT RETURNS

Most Punt Returns, Game
4 Emlen Tunnel, N.Y. Giants, NFL East, 1953
Yale Lary, Detroit, NFL West, 1954
George Atkinson, Oakland, AFL West, 1970
Cecil Turner, Chicago, NFC, 1971
Greg Pruitt, Cleveland, AFC, 1974
Billy Johnson, Houston, AFC, 1976
Most Fair Catches, Game
2 Yale Lary, Detroit, NFL West, 1958
Jerry Logan, Baltimore, AFC, 1971
Dick Anderson, Miami, AFC, 1974
Most Yards Gained, Game
159 Billy Johnson, Houston, AFC, 1976 (4)
Longest Return
90 Billy Johnson, Houston, AFC, 1976 (TD)
Most Touchdowns, Game
2 Mel Renfro, Dallas, NFC, 1971

KICKOFF RETURNS

Most Kickoff Returns Game
6 Charley Warner, Buffalo, 1966
Most Yards Gained, Game
175 Leslie (Speedy) Duncan, Washington, NFC, 1972
Longest Return
103 Jack Christiansen, Detroit, NFL West, 1956
Most Touchdowns, Game
1 Jack Christiansen, Detroit, NFL West, 1956
Ollie Matson, Chi. Cardinals, NFL East, 1956
Leslie (Speedy) Duncan, San Diego, AFL West, 1968

SCORING

Most Points, Game
19 Jim Turner, N.Y. Jets, AFL East, 1969 (6 FG, 1 PAT)
Most Touchdowns, Game
3 Jim Taylor, Green Bay, NFL West, 1961 (3 R)
John Brockington, Green Bay, NFC, 1973 (2 R, 1 P)
Most Points After Touchdown, Game
5 Paul Hornung, Green Bay, West, twice, 1960 and 1961
George Blair, San Diego, AFL West, 1962
Tommy Brooker, Kansas City, AFL West, 1965
Don Chandler, Green Bay, NFL West, 1968
Most Field Goals, Game
6 Jim Turner, N.Y. Jets, AFL East, 1969
Longest Field Goal
52 Sam Baker, Washington, NFL East, 1957
Bert Rechichar, Baltimore, NFL West, 1957
Jan Stenerud, Kansas City, AFL West, 1969

SERVICE

Most Selections
14 Merlin Olsen, Los Angeles, 1963–1970, 1971*, 1972–76
12 Jim Otto, Oakland, 1962–1973
10 Leo Nomellini, San Francisco, 1951–54, 1957–1962
Gino Marchetti, Baltimore, 1955–58, 1960–65
Jim Ringo, Green Bay, 1958–1964; Philadelphia, 1965–66, 1968
John Unitas, Baltimore, 1958–1965, 1967–68
Bob Lilly, Dallas, 1963, 1965–1972, 1974
Mel Renfro, Dallas, 1965–1972, 1973*, 1974*

Selected but did not play

Most Consecutive Selections
14 Merlin Olsen, Los Angeles, 1963–1970, 1971*, 1972–76
12 Jim Otto, Oakland, 1962–1973
10 Mel Renfro, Dallas, 1965–1972, 1973*, 1974*

Selected but did not play

Most Consecutive Appearances, No Misses
12 Jim Otto, Oakland, 1962–1973
9 Joe Schmidt, Detroit, 1955–1963
Jim Brown, Cleveland, 1958–1966
Jim Ringo, Green Bay, 1958–1964; Philadelphia, 1965–66
Walt Sweeney, San Diego, 1965–1973
Tom Mack, Los Angeles, 1968–1976
Ken Houston, Houston, 1969–1973; Washington, 1974–77
Alan Page, Minnesota, 1969–1977

Merlin Olsen, Los Angeles, selected for the Pro Bowl 14 times.

PRO BOWL TEAM RECORDS

RUSHING
Most Attempts, Game
50 AFC, 1974
Fewest Attempts, Game
17 AFL West, 1967
Most Attempts, Both Teams, Game
80 AFC (50) vs. NFC (30), 1974
Fewest Attempts, Both Teams, Game
44 AFL East (19) vs. AFL West (25), 1965
AFL West (17) vs. AFL East (27), 1967
Most Yards Gained, Game
224 NFC, 1976
Fewest Yards Gained, Game
13 NFL East, 1955
Most Yards Gained, Both Teams, Game
425 NFC (224) vs. AFC (201), 1976
Fewest Yards Gained, Both Teams, Game
47 NFL American Conference (23) vs. NFL National Conference (24), 1951
Most Touchdowns, Game
4 NFL West, 1961

PASSING
Most Passes Attempted, Game
50 NFL East, 1968
Fewest Passes Attempted, Game
17 NFC, 1972
Most Attempts, Both Teams, Game
82 AFL East (45) vs. AFL West (37), 1962
Fewest Attempts, Both Teams, Game
42 NFC (17) vs. AFC (25), 1972
Most Passes Completed, Game
27 NFL West, 1960
Fewest Passes Completed, Game
7 NFC, 1972
Most Passes Completed, Both Teams, Game
40 NFL American Conference (19) vs. NFL National Conference (21), 1951
Fewest Passes Completed, Both Teams, Game
18 NFC (7) vs. AFC (11), 1972
Most Yards Gained, Game
362 NFL West, 1960
Fewest Yards Gained, Game
80 AFC, 1971
Most Yards Gained, Both Teams, Game
574 NFL West (362) vs. NFL East (212), 1960
Fewest Yards Gained, Both Teams, Game
215 AFC (126) vs. NFC (89), 1972
Most Times Tackled Attempting Passes, Game
8 NFL West, 1970
Fewest Times Tackled Attempting Passes, Game
0 By many teams
Most Touchdowns, Game
4 NFL East, 1961
Fewest Touchdowns, Game
0 AFC, three times, 1971, 1974, and 1977
Most Touchdowns, Both Teams, Game
6 NFL East (3) vs. NFL West (3), 1962
AFL East (3) vs. AFL West (3), 1962
Fewest Touchdowns, Both Teams, Game
1 NFC (1) vs. AFC (0), 1971
NFC (1) vs. AFC (0), 1974

INTERCEPTIONS BY
Most Interceptions By, Game
8 NFL East, 1966
Most Interceptions By, Both teams, Game
10 Chi. Bears (5) vs. Pro All-Stars (5), Jan. 1942
Most Yards Gained, Game
144 NFL East, 1966
Most Yards Gained, Both Teams, Game
180 Pro All-Stars (128) vs. Washington (52), Dec. 1942
Most Touchdowns, Game
1 By 10 teams

SCORING
Most Points, Game
47 AFL West, 1962
Fewest Points, Game
3 AFL East, 1970
Most Points, Both Teams, Game
74 AFL West (47) vs. AFL East (27), 1962
Fewest Points, Both Teams, Game
17 NFL West (10) vs. NFL East (7), 1969
Most Touchdowns, Game
7 AFL West, 1962
Fewest Touchdowns, Game
0 AFL East, 1970
AFC, 1971, 1974
Most Touchdowns, Both Teams, Game
10 AFL West (7) vs. AFL East (3), 1962
Fewest Touchdowns, Both Teams, Game
1 NFC (1) vs. AFC (0), 1974

Most Points After Touchdown, Game
5 NFL West, twice, 1960 and 1961
AFL West, twice, 1962 and 1965
NFL West, 1968
Most Points After Touchdown, Both Teams, Game
9 NFL West (5) vs. NFL East (4), 1961
Most Field Goals Attempted, Game
6 AFC, 1972
Most Field Goals Attempted, Both Teams, Game
9 AFL East (6) vs. AFL West (3), 1969
Most Field Goals, Game
6 AFL East, 1969
Most Field Goals, Both Teams, Game
9 AFL East (6) vs. AFL West (3), 1969

NET YARDS GAINED RUSHING AND PASSING
Most Net Yards Gained, Game
411 NFL West, 1965
Fewest Net Yards Gained, Game
112 NFL American Conference, 1952
Most Net Yards Gained, Both Teams, Game
715 NFC (381) vs. AFC (334), 1976
Fewest Net Yards Gained, Both Teams, Game
369 AFL East (189) vs. AFL West (180), 1966

Norm Van Brocklin of Philadelphia and the East, 1961, his last game in the NFL.

PRO BOWL HISTORY

Date	Result	Site (attendance)	Honored players
Jan. 15, 1939	N.Y. Giants 13, Pro All-Stars 10	Wrigley Field, Los Angeles (20,000)	
Jan. 14, 1940	Green Bay 16, Pro All-Stars 7	Gilmore Stadium, Los Angeles (18,000)	
Dec. 29, 1940	Chi. Bears 28, Pro All-Stars 14	Gilmore Stadium, Los Angeles (21,624)	
Jan. 4, 1942	Chi. Bears 35, Pro All-Stars 24	Polo Grounds, New York (17,725)	
Dec. 27, 1942	Pro All-Stars 17, Washington 14	Shibe Park, Philadelphia (18,671)	
Jan. 14, 1951	American Conf. 28, National Conf. 27	Los Angeles Memorial Coliseum (53,676)	Otto Graham, Cleveland, player of the game
Jan. 12, 1952	National Conf. 30, American Conf. 13	Los Angeles Memorial Coliseum (19,400)	Dan Towler, Los Angeles, player of the game
Jan. 10, 1953	National Conf. 27, American Conf. 7	Los Angeles Memorial Coliseum (34,208)	Don Doll, Detroit, player of the game
Jan. 17, 1954	East 20, West 9	Los Angeles Memorial Coliseum (44,214)	Chuck Bednarik, Philadelphia, player of the game
Jan. 1, 1955	West 26, East 19	Los Angeles Memorial Coliseum (43,972)	Billy Wilson, San Francisco, player of the game
Jan. 15, 1956	East 31, West 30	Los Angeles Memorial Coliseum (37,867)	Ollie Matson, Chi. Cardinals, player of the game
Jan. 13, 1957	West 19, East 10	Los Angeles Memorial Coliseum (44,177)	Bert Rechichar, Baltimore, outstanding back Ernie Stautner, Pittsburgh, outstanding lineman
Jan. 12, 1958	West 26, East 7	Los Angeles Memorial Coliseum (66,634)	Hugh McElhenny, San Francisco, outstanding back Gene Brito, Washington, outstanding lineman
Jan. 11, 1959	East 28, West 21	Los Angeles Memorial Coliseum (72,250)	Frank Gifford, N.Y. Giants, outstanding back Doug Atkins, Chi. Bears, outstanding lineman
Jan. 17, 1960	West 38, East 21	Los Angeles Memorial Coliseum (56,876)	John Unitas, Baltimore, outstanding back Gene (Big Daddy) Lipscomb, Baltimore, outstanding lineman
Jan. 15, 1961	West 35, East 31	Los Angeles Memorial Coliseum (62,971)	John Unitas, Baltimore, outstanding back Sam Huff, N.Y. Giants, outstanding lineman
Jan. 7, 1962	AFL West 47, East 27	Balboa Stadium, San Diego (20,973)	Cotton Davidson, Dallas Texans, player of the game
Jan. 14, 1962	NFL West 31, East 30	Los Angeles Memorial Coliseum (57,409)	Jim Brown, Cleveland, outstanding back Henry Jordan, Green Bay, outstanding lineman
Jan. 13, 1963	AFL West 21, East 14	Balboa Stadium, San Diego (27,641)	Curtis McClinton, Dallas Texans, outstanding offensive player Earl Faison, San Diego, outstanding defensive player
Jan. 13, 1963	NFL East 30, West 20	Los Angeles Memorial Coliseum (61,374)	Jim Brown, Cleveland, player of the game Gene (Big Daddy) Lipscomb, Pittsburgh, outstanding lineman
Jan. 12, 1964	NFL West 31, East 17	Los Angeles Memorial Coliseum (67,242)	John Unitas, Baltimore, player of the game Gino Marchetti, Baltimore, outstanding lineman
Jan. 19, 1964	AFL West 27, East 24	Balboa Stadium, San Diego (20,016)	Keith Lincoln, San Diego, outstanding offensive player Archie Matsos, Oakland, outstanding defensive player
Jan. 10, 1965	NFL West 34, East 14	Los Angeles Memorial Coliseum (60,598)	Fran Tarkenton, Minnesota, outstanding back Terry Barr, Detroit, outstanding lineman
Jan. 16, 1965	AFL West 38, East 14	Jeppesen Stadium, Houston (15,446)	Keith Lincoln, San Diego, outstanding offensive player Willie Brown, Denver, outstanding defensive player
Jan. 15, 1966	AFL All-Stars 30, Buffalo 19	Rice Stadium, Houston (35,572)	Joe Namath, N.Y. Jets, most valuable player, offense Frank Buncom, San Diego, most valuable player, defense
Jan. 15, 1966	NFL East 36, West 7	Los Angeles Memorial Coliseum (60,124)	Jim Brown, Cleveland, outstanding back Dale Meinert, St. Louis, outstanding lineman
Jan. 21, 1967	AFL East 30, West 23	Oakland Coliseum (18,876)	Babe Parilli, Boston, outstanding offensive player Verlon Biggs, N.Y. Jets, outstanding defensive player
Jan. 22, 1967	NFL East 20, West 10	Los Angeles Memorial Coliseum (15,062)	Gale Sayers, Chicago, outstanding back Floyd Peters, Philadelphia, outstanding lineman
Jan. 21, 1968	AFL East 25, West 24	Gator Bowl, Jacksonville, Fla. (40,103)	Joe Namath & Don Maynard, N.Y. Jets, out. off. players Leslie (Speedy) Duncan, San Diego, out. def. player
Jan. 21, 1968	NFL West 38, East 20	Los Angeles Memorial Coliseum (53,289)	Gale Sayers, Chicago, outstanding back Dave Robinson, Green Bay, outstanding lineman
Jan. 19, 1969	AFL West 38, East 25	Gator Bowl, Jacksonville, Fla. (41,058)	Len Dawson, Kansas City, outstanding offensive player George Webster, Houston, outstanding defensive player
Jan. 19, 1969	NFL West 10, East 7	Los Angeles Memorial Coliseum (32,050)	Roman Gabriel, Los Angeles, outstanding back Merlin Olsen, Los Angeles, outstanding lineman
Jan. 17, 1970	AFL West 26, East 3	Astrodome, Houston (30,170)	John Hadl, San Diego, player of the game
Jan. 18, 1970	NFL West 16, East 13	Los Angeles Memorial Coliseum (57,486)	Gale Sayers, Chicago, outstanding back George Andrie, Dallas, outstanding lineman
Jan. 24, 1971	NFC 27, AFC 6	Los Angeles Memorial Coliseum (48,222)	Mel Renfro, Dallas, outstanding back Fred Carr, Green Bay, outstanding lineman
Jan. 23, 1972	AFC 26, NFC 13	Los Angeles Memorial Coliseum (53,647)	Jan Stenerud, Kansas City, outstanding offensive player Willie Lanier, Kansas City, outstanding defensive player
Jan. 21, 1973	AFC 33, NFC 28	Texas Stadium, Irving (47,879)	O.J. Simpson, Buffalo, player of the game
Jan. 20, 1974	AFC 15, NFC 13	Arrowhead, Kansas City (51,484)	Garo Yepremian, Miami, player of the game
Jan. 20, 1975	NFC 17, AFC 10	Orange Bowl, Miami (26,484)	James Harris, Los Angeles, player of the game
Jan. 26, 1976	NFC 23, AFC 20	Louisiana Superdome, New Orleans (32,108)	Billy Johnson, Houston, player of the game
Jan. 17, 1977	AFC 24, NFC 14	Kingdome, Seattle (63,214)	Mel Blount, Pittsburgh, player of the game

A Diagram History of Football

Legend
■ the center
● other offensive players
▼ defensive linemen
■ linebackers and defensive backs

Football diagrams are little utopias. Any play can appear devastating in a diagram. The following plays and formations and strategies were successful often enough that they have survived where perhaps several hundred thousand others over the last 100 years have not.

1 Wedge

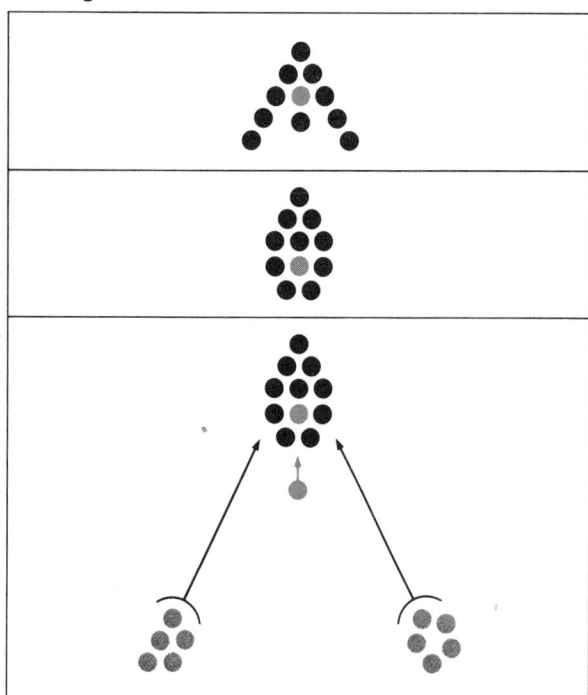

Historian Alexander Weyand wrote that the Princeton wedge of 1884 (top) was "the first great tactical weapon to make its appearance in American football." The ball wasn't kicked off or centered; rather, play began when the wedge moved forward. The person behind the ball carrier pushed him. The wedge was fearsome but Walter (Pudge) Heffelfinger found a solution to it. According to one historian, Heffelfinger "rushed at the mighty engine, leaped high in the air, completely cleared its forward ramparts, and came down on top of the men on the inside of the wedge, whom he flattened to the ground, and among whom was the carrier of the ball." Walter Camp of Yale adopted the wedge for scrimmage play and modified it, making the "shoving wedge" (center). Harvard then contributed the most frightening formation of all in the "mass play" era, the "flying wedge" (below). Two groups of five players each started from 25 yards back, converged around the ball carrier at full speed, and they smashed into the opposition.

2 T Formation

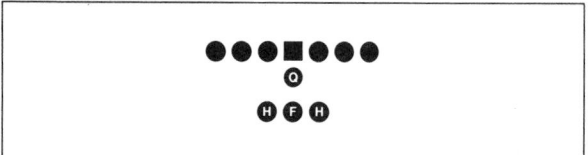

Football players who took the brunt of the wedges actually died on the playing field. "Mass play" led to the reforms requiring seven men on the line of scrimmage when the ball was centered—another innovation. The first T formation resulted.

3 Tackles Back

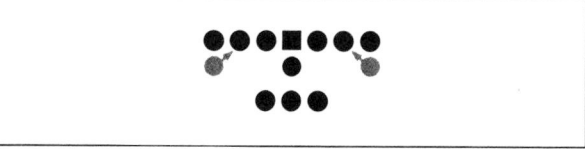

Tackles back, ends back, and guards back conformed to the regulation but tried to restore the momentum of the wedge by shifting linemen up to the line on the snap. This strategy led to the multiple shifts that followed. The tackles back formation shown here was copied from the 1920 book of plays of the Decatur Staleys coached by George Halas.

4 Minnesota Shift

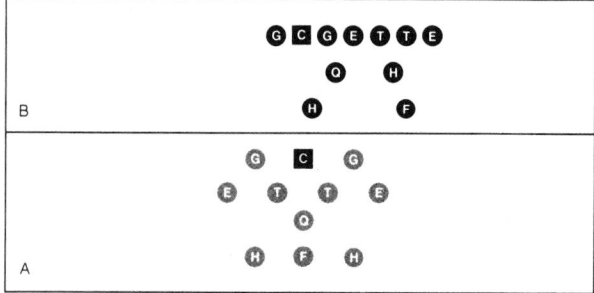

A brilliant coach at the University of Minnesota named Dr. Henry Williams introduced this shift in 1910, according to Alexander Weyand. The original position of the players is shown in diagram A, their eventual position in B.

5 Heisman Shift

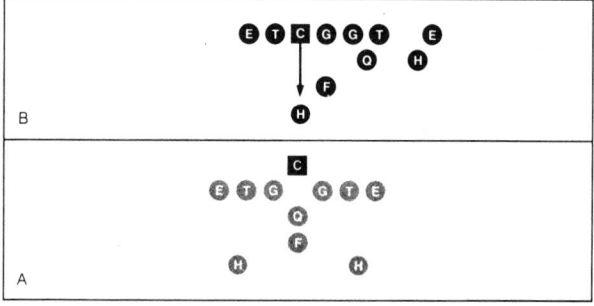

Another popular shift was this one invented by John Heisman, coach of Georgia Tech. He was later the person for whom the Heisman trophy, given each year to the outstanding college player, was named.

6 Single Wing

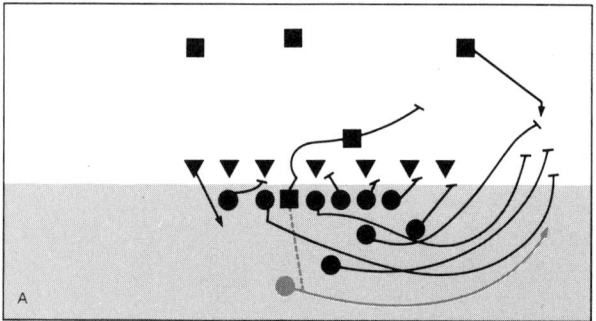

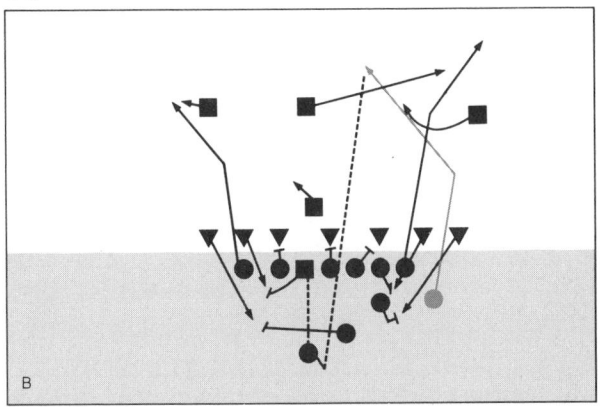

Invented by Glenn (Pop) Warner about 1906, it was one of the most successful formations ever and the typical running play (A) was, as Warner himself said, "one of the strongest plays ever developed." It still is today—The Green Bay sweep. A Princeton single wing tailback, Dick Kazmaier, won the Heisman trophy in 1951 and the formation was still being played in 1954 by UCLA, Arkansas, and the Pittsburgh Steelers. A typical single wing pass is shown above.

7 Short Punt

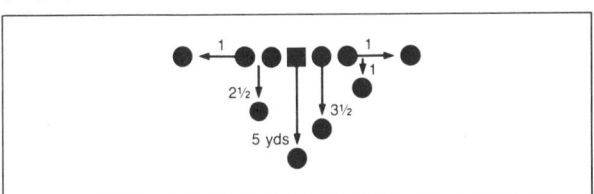

Punting played so large a part in strategy that it was not uncommon for teams to line up in punt formation all the time, hence this popular alignment of the twenties and thirties.

8 Rockne Shift

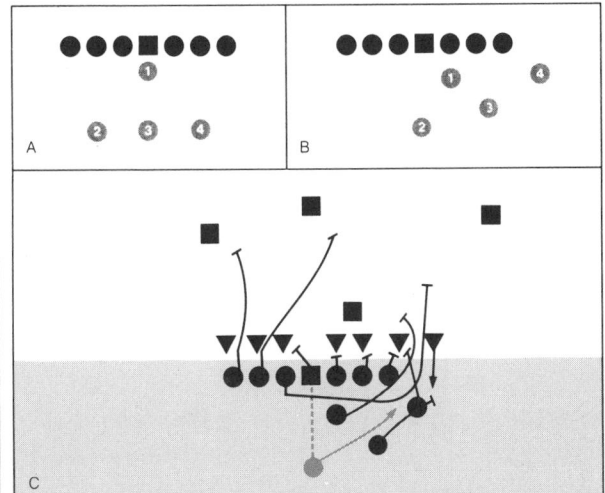

In the Notre Dame system devised by coach Knute Rockne about 1920, the Fighting Irish shifted from the T formation (A) into their "box"

GLENN (POP) WARNER

Warner was the second most innovative coach after Stagg and he was also second to Stagg in most victories in college football, 313 to 314. Warner pioneered the single wing formation that Jim Thorpe brought into pro football with Canton in 1916, and the double wing that Sammy Baugh played with the Washington Redskins.

(B) and were then off on a devastating end run, practically all in one motion. The rules were eventually changed to require that all players be still a full second before the snap. Rockne's annual games against Howard Jones of USC displayed the best football to be seen anywhere and coaches flocked to the games, Braven Dyer of the *Los Angeles Times* wrote, "as young doctors would to the Mayo Clinic, to see the masters at work."

9 Double Wing

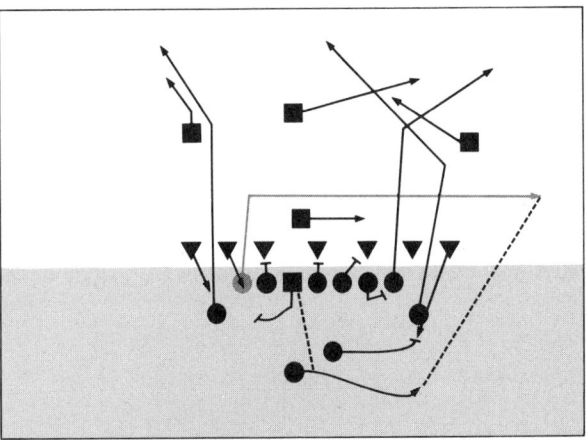

While Rockne was having a poor season in 1928, Glenn (Pop) Warner brought his Stanford University team to New York City to play Army. Warner had had the double wingback formation in his system perhaps as early as 1911, when he was at Carlisle, but did not play it on a regular basis until he moved to Stanford in the twenties. His team beat Army easily and the system was widely adopted while imitation of Rockne waned. Double wing laid the foundation for spread formations such as shotguns that would still be firing in the seventies.

10 Early Man-in-Motion

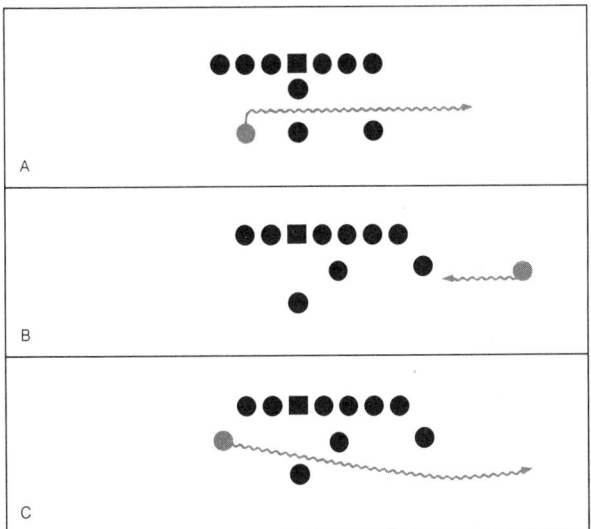

The element that the Chicago Bears would add to the ancient T formation in 1930 had actually been around a long time (A) in the turn-of-the-century T of Amos Alonzo Stagg at the University of Chicago, (B) in the single wing, and (C) in the double wing.

GEORGE HALAS

Halas won more games, 321, than any other professional or college coach. With associates such as Ralph Jones and Clark Shaughnessy, he popularized the T formation with man-in-motion. He immensely influenced the style of play in the NFL, the mechanics of its officials, and the equipment worn by players.

11   Bears' T with Man-in-Motion

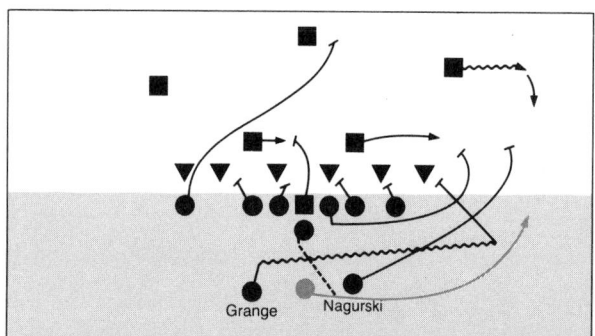

Grange   Nagurski

In 1932, two years after the Bears first used this formation, they played six ties, three of them scoreless, and Ralph Jones, the T-with-motion father, quit as coach. But this formation spread the defense, then light years behind in development; put little, fast men out wide where they could get running room or get downfield for passes; and reinstated a quarterback under the center. The play shown is a lateral to Bronko Nagurski with Red Grange, the man-in-motion, making a crackback block on the defensive end.

12   Invention of Inbounds Lines

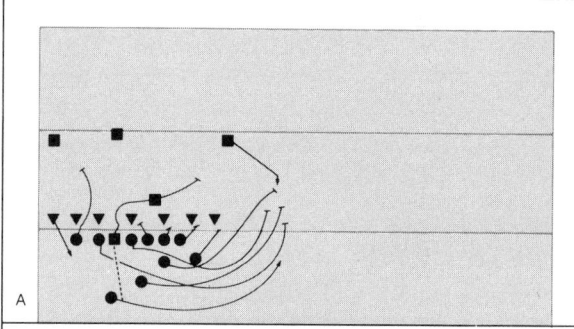

A

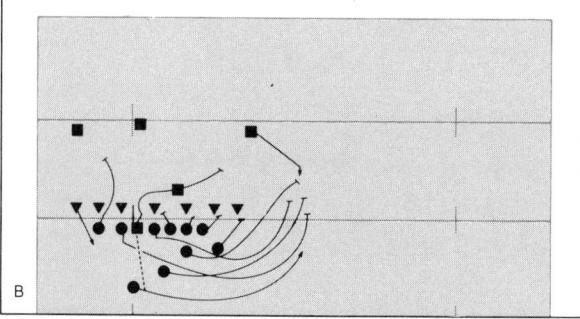

B

The Inbounds lines, or hashmarks, limed onto the dirt floor of the Chicago Stadium in 1932 for the Bears-Spartans playoff, turned coaches into strategists who studied not only power, speed, and deception, but also geography. Plays that ended near the sideline or with the runner going out of bounds had started at the sideline (A); they now began 10 yards in from the sideline (B). Also, the field now had a "short" side and "wide" side of predictable breadth; the side most favored by a team in its running game could be studied by scouts. And hashmarks set up points of reference for players taking their stances or running pass routes, and defenders mapping out the territorial zones they would cover.

13   The Five-Three Defense

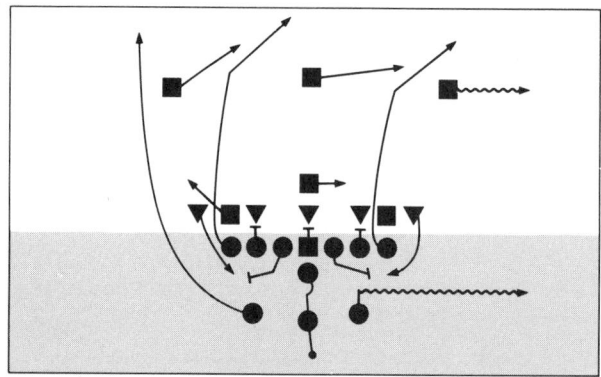

Defenses had previously placed nine, eight, seven, or six men on the line of scrimmage. To reduce that number to five, in order to get more men back in pass protection, was a brazen step. It was probably first taken at Temple in 1930 by a line coach named John (Ox) DaGrosa. The New York Giants copied it in 1934. This became the standard NFL defense for a decade. The five-three had a middle linebacker—30 years before Bill George, Sam Huff, Les Richter, and Joe Schmidt.

14   Don Hutson's First Play in the NFL

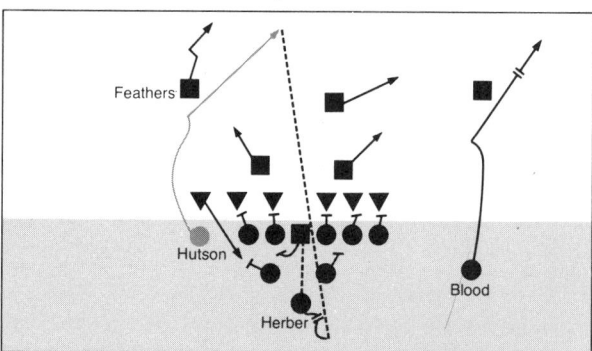

Feathers   Hutson   Herber   Blood

Don Hutson, the Green Bay Packers' great end, scored an 83-yard touchdown on his first play from scrimmage in the NFL. Chicago Bears safety Beattie Feathers stole a look at Arnie Herber's fake to Johnny Blood, and at that moment Hutson, who had been loping along, went into high gear and left Feathers far behind. *True Sport* said, "Herber's pass, counting his retreat, as checked on motion pictures, went 66 yards in the air."

15   Dutch Meyer Spreads

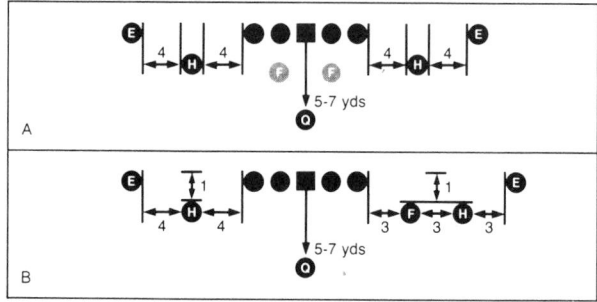

A

B

It is wrong to say that Clark Shaughnessy or anyone else in pro football invented the "three-end offense." Three represented a modest number

EARLE (GREASY) NEALE

Neale was the second NFL coach after George Halas to adopt the T formation. Neale built a power offense around Steve Van Buren that grew stronger each year in the forties and eventually won NFL championships in 1948 and 1949. He also devised the Eagle defense, which was one of the forerunners of the four-three.

15 continued

of ends in the spread formations played by Dutch Meyer at Texas Christian University in the thirties. These were the formations played by TCU quarterbacks, or tailbacks, Sammy Baugh and Davey O'Brien.

16 A Typical Sammy Baugh Pass

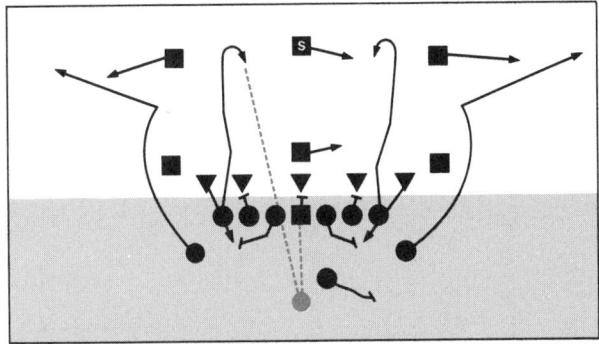

Baugh picked apart the five-three defenses of the NFL as a rookie with the Washington Redskins in 1937. He passed for 335 yards in the championship game against the Bears.

17 Steve Owen's A Formation

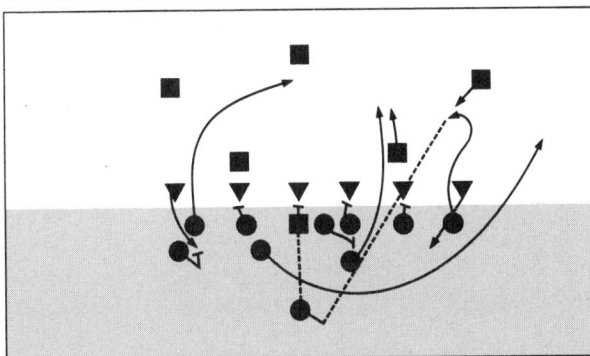

The A formation of coach Steve Owen of the New York Giants had unusual line splits, a line strong to one side and a backfield strong to the other, and a direct snap to the left halfback instead of a T-quarterback. Owen played it and other formations from 1937 to 1952. As a stunt, he once had his team run three plays from three different formations.

18 Oklahoma Defense

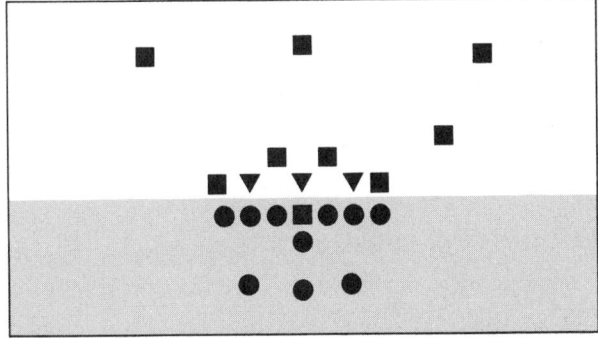

Begun at the University of Oklahoma by coach Bud Wilkinson, probably in 1947, it strongly influenced the new pro defenses that sprouted

immediately afterward. It became the dominant defense in college football for the next 20 years but was scoffed at by the pros until Miami adopted it in 1972 and had a 17-0 season. It is alternately dismissed as weak against the run or weak against the pass. The pros have refined it immensely, and it might become the next standard defense in pro football.

19 Eagle Defense

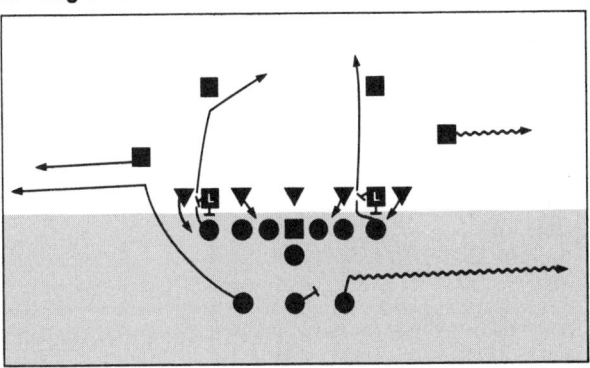

It was first played by the Philadelphia Eagles and coach Greasy Neale about 1948. It evolved out of the five-three and it had the first four-deep secondary, but no middle linebacker. The outside linebackers no longer had to try to cover deep passes but instead harassed and delayed receivers and covered short passes.

20 Steps Taken Against the Eagle

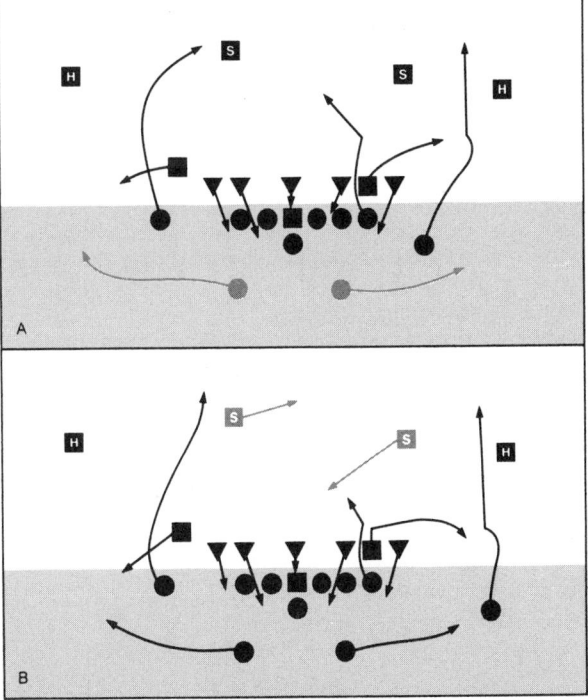

It was woefully weak over the middle. The offenses simply sent their backs to the flat areas to lure the linebackers away, and get an end free in the middle (A). The defense reacted by having one safety fill that area; the other covered behind him if the end went deep, perhaps the start of "combination" pass defense in the NFL (B).

STEVE OWEN

The development of the Eagle defense of Neale and the "umbrella" defense of Owen coincided with the advent of unlimited free substitution in pro football. These three factors combined to bring about the style of defense in the NFL in the 1950s and 1960s. Owen coached the New York Giants from 1931 until 1953.

21 Otto Graham Passes

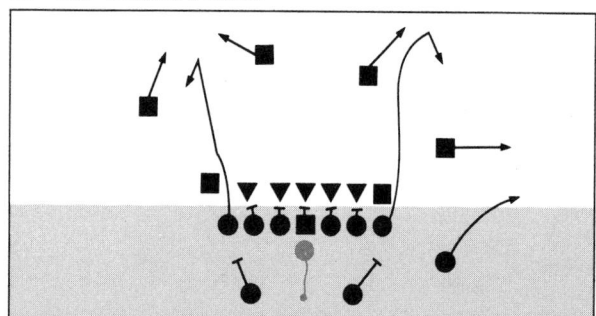

The Eagle was very important as a defense that offenses exploited and out of which much of modern football evolved. Its next challenge was quarterback Otto Graham and the Cleveland Browns, who met Philadelphia for the first time in 1950. Cleveland won 35-10 and its ends, Mac Speedie and Dante Lavelli, were the first to run "comeback" patterns—17 yards downfield, then turning back for the ball at 15 yards. The Eagles had not seen such pass routes before.

22 Umbrella Defense

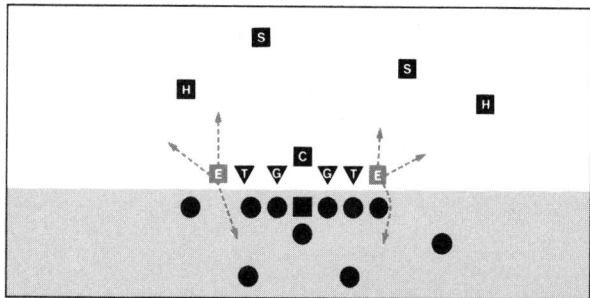

Steve Owen of the New York Giants devised it for the Browns in 1950 and shut them out once and also won a second game. The Giants' deep backs threw a figurative "umbrella" over the passing game, and their ends sometimes rushed and sometimes dropped off to cover passes, in the manner of later outside linebackers.

23 A Rams' Bomb to Hirsch

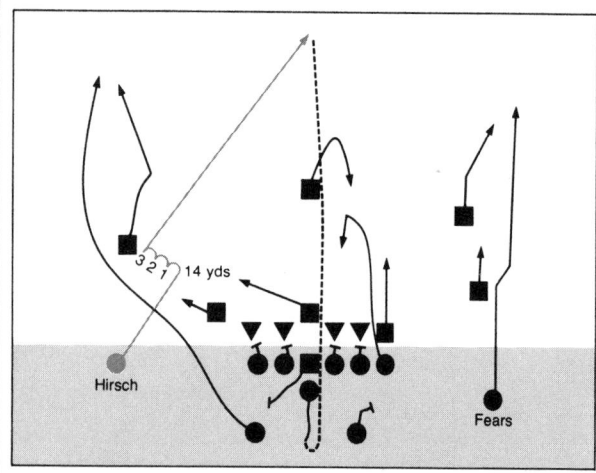

For all its offensive brilliance, Cleveland still played the outdated five-

three defense in the early fifties. Its three-deep secondary was no match for Los Angeles's great end Elroy Hirsch. He scored 17 touchowns during the 1951 season and Los Angeles won the championship from Cleveland. This pass route was Hirsch's favorite during his career.

24 Split T and the Belly Series

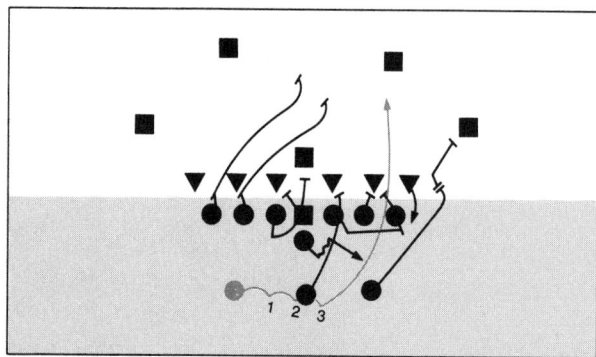

Innovative changes in the T formation had taken place at Missouri, Oklahoma, Maryland, College of the Pacific, and other institutions where football teams were using the split T formation and belly series. The quarterback slid down the line of scrimmage riding the ball in the belly of a back and left it there, kept it, handed off again, pitched, or ran with it. The collegiate triple option, wishbone, and veer systems of later years evolved out of the split T.

25 Continuing Changes in the Eagle

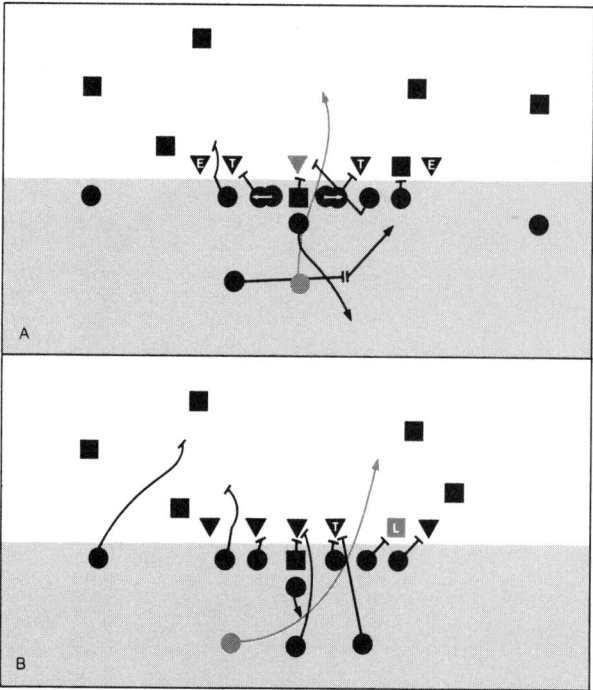

It was put to rest at last by the big line splits that the pros adopted as a result of the popularity of split T. These splits moved the offensive tackles out so far that the defensive middle guard found himself isolated, forced to try to stop the inside running plays alone (A). If his defensive tackles closed in to help, that isolated the outside linebacker (B).

PAUL BROWN
Brown is the professional coach most responsible for an important attitude of coaches of the 1960s and 1970s: that no aspect of organization can be ignored if the coach is to be successful. The careful filming and grading of plays and players and the dominance of the game from the side line are the results of Brown's influence.

26 Four-Three Defense

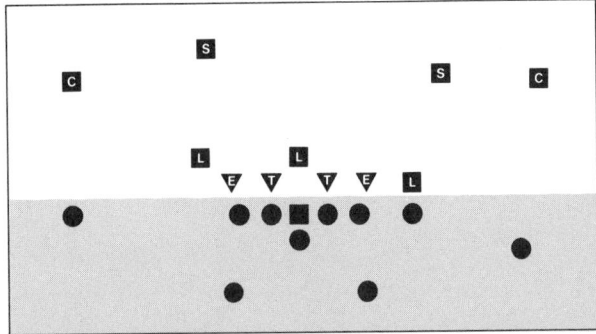

Teams playing the Eagle in the mid-fifties decided to drop their middle guard off and make him a middle linebacker. If their middle guard was unsuited for the new position, they found a player who was. This evolution in the Eagle was as much responsible for the adoption of the modern four-three defense as was the New York umbrella. The distinctive identity of each position in the four-three also crystallized as the result of free substitution, since it was now possible to send an entirely different team into the game to play defense.

27 Slot-T

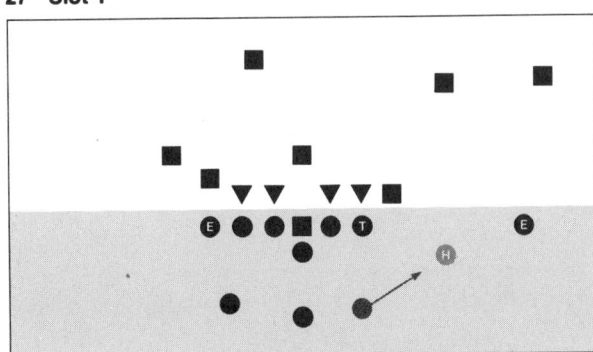

Two decades before, the Chicago Bears had removed one man from the offensive formation by putting him in motion. By the late forties, that player was being permanently stationed out wide, rather than going in motion into that position. He was the "flanker." An alignment placing him in a slot between the spread end and tackle was popular in the NFL throughout the fifties.

28 Three-End Offense

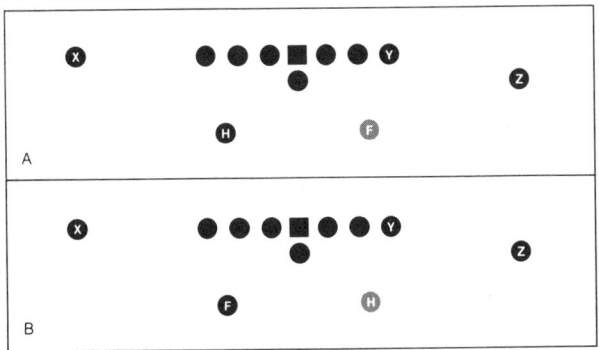

28 continued

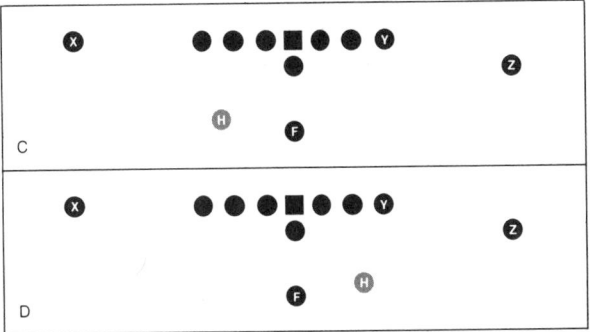

The "flanker" gradually came to be seen not as a halfback removed from the backfield but instead as a third end. Later, the terms "wide receiver" and "tight end" were adopted to name the three ends. Here are four of the most important three-end formations and the names given them in the various systems of language spoken by pro teams: (A) full, split right, or red; (B) half, split left, or green; (C) far, opposite, or brown; and (D) near, wing, or blue.

29 Pass Rush and Linebacker Blitz

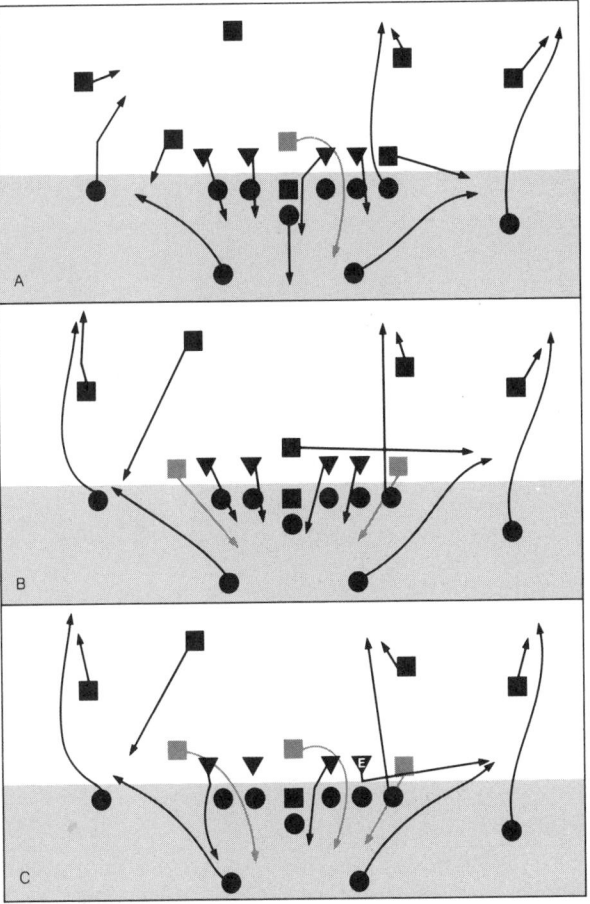

The offense had spread itself wider than ever and was increasingly

CLARK SHAUGHNESSY

He was the most enigmatic and yet the most imaginative of all pro coaches. He conceived the language that grew up around the Chicago Bears' T formation with man-in-motion in the forties and later the equally unusual language surrounding the reckless Bears' defense of the fifties. Jargon became inherent in pro football.

dependent on the pass. The defense now mounted such methods of rushing the passer as these: (A) the four linemen and the middle linebacker; (B) the line and the outside linebackers; and (C) actual "blitz," the line and all three linebackers.

30 Man-for-Man Coverage

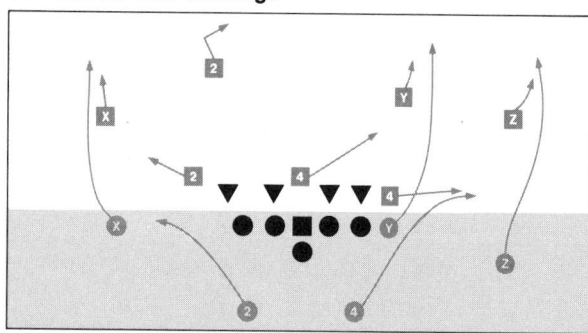

This is man-for-man defense at its simplest and in a form played widely in the fifties in the NFL. The numerals 2 and 4 are the offensive backs and the coaching symbols X, Y, and Z stand for the wide receivers and tight end. Corresponding symbols on defensive players name who is responsible for each.

31 Zone Defense

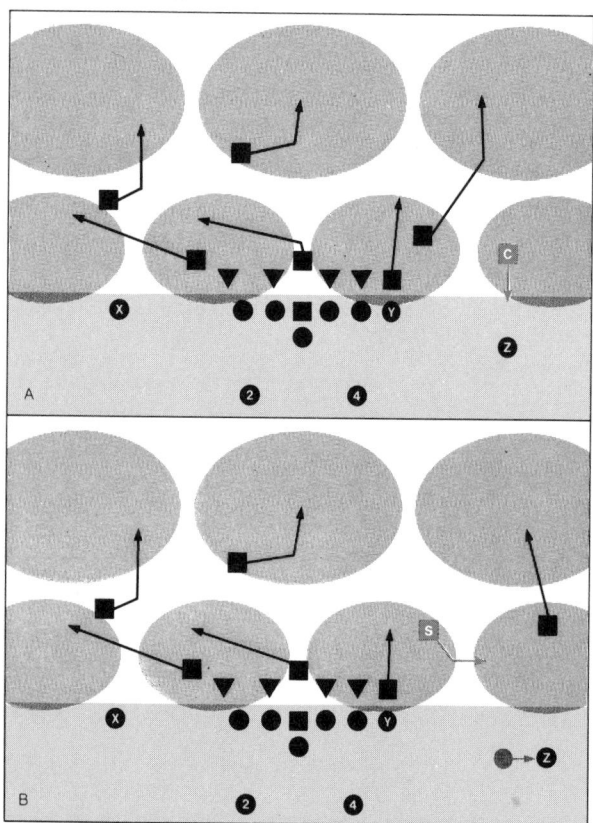

The most basic type of zone defense is "rotation," and was played expertly by the Detroit Lions in the fifties. The defense has "rotated" to the side of the tight end and flanker and there are four zones (oval areas) up

close and three deep. In diagram B, the flanker has taken a position so wide that if it were a running play he could crack back on the cornerback. Seeing this, the defense has changed its zone so the safety not the cornerback is up close. It is this swapping of coverage areas among cornerbacks, safeties, and linebackers that has made zones grow in complexity and produce great problems for young quarterbacks.

32 Green Bay Sweep

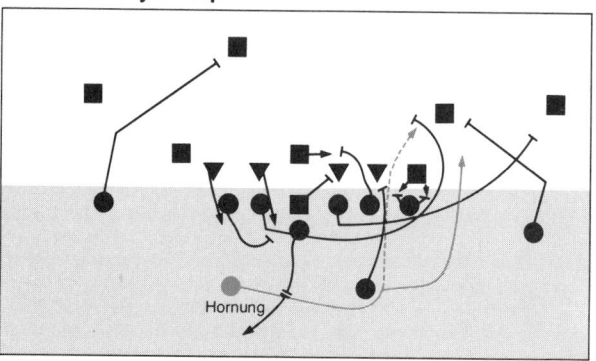

When Vince Lombardi became coach of the Green Bay Packers in 1959, he was convinced that defenses had become so sophisticated that it was time for the offense to go back to the basics—to avoid frills and to carry out fundamentals well. These principles were borne out in his Green Bay sweep, with Paul Hornung carrying the ball. Hornung followed pulling guards Fuzzy Thurston and Jerry Kramer and fullback Jim Taylor in a devastating end run. It is interesting to compare the play with those of Warner and Rockne in diagrams 6A and 8C.

33 Weakside Slant and its Companion Play

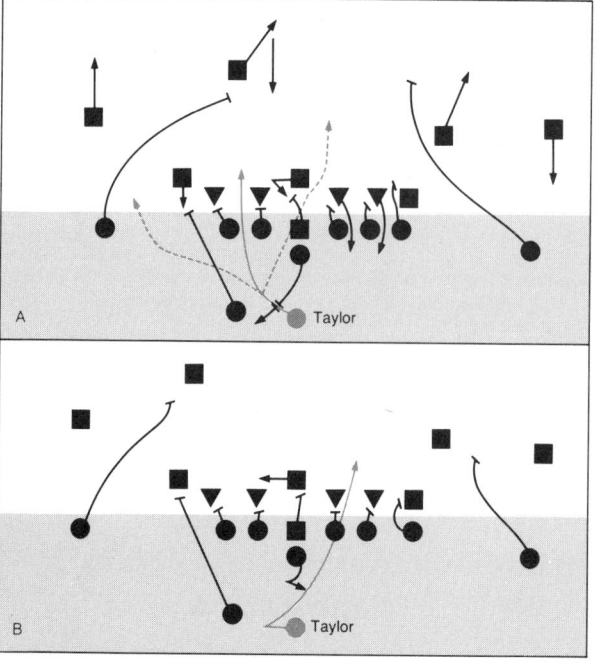

The weakside slant (A) and the companion play it set up (B) became the heart of the Packers' offense after defenses found ways to stop the sweep. Jim Taylor "ran to daylight" where he found it. Jim Brown of Cleve-

VINCE LOMBARDI

*Lombardi reinstated the simple
verities of football in the NFL and
reversed the trend to a more and
more complicated sport. He took
the Green Bay Packers and the entire game back to the basics and
won by running the same plays
over and over—strongside sweeps
with Paul Hornung and weakside
slants with Jim Taylor.*

33 continued

land, Taylor's contemporary, also ran the weakside slant among other
plays, and the play is the most basic one in pro football today.

34 Shotgun

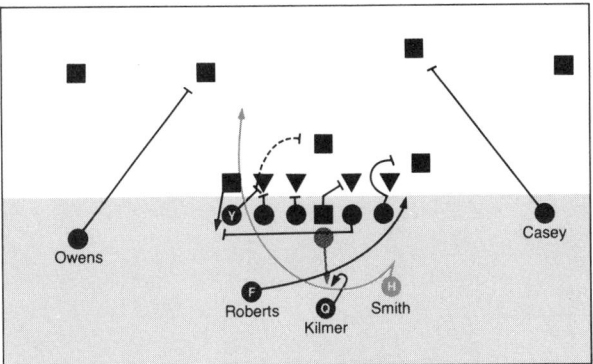

The patterns of play in the four-three defense and three-end offense
had grown rather stereotyped by 1960. That was one reason why coach
Red Hickey of San Francisco created what he called the shotgun formation. The quarterback stood back from the center as in the formations
of old. San Francisco played it with success for part of 1960 and 1961,
until it was stopped by Chicago and Pittsburgh and 49ers' players lost
confidence in it. Bill Kilmer, John Brodie, and Bobby Waters alternated
at quarterback in the system. The play shown here is a shovel pass to
halfback J. D. Smith, a play that was also a favorite of the Dallas Cowboys
when they revived the shotgun in 1975 and played it part of the time while
winning the NFC Championship.

35 Shotgun-inspired Spreads

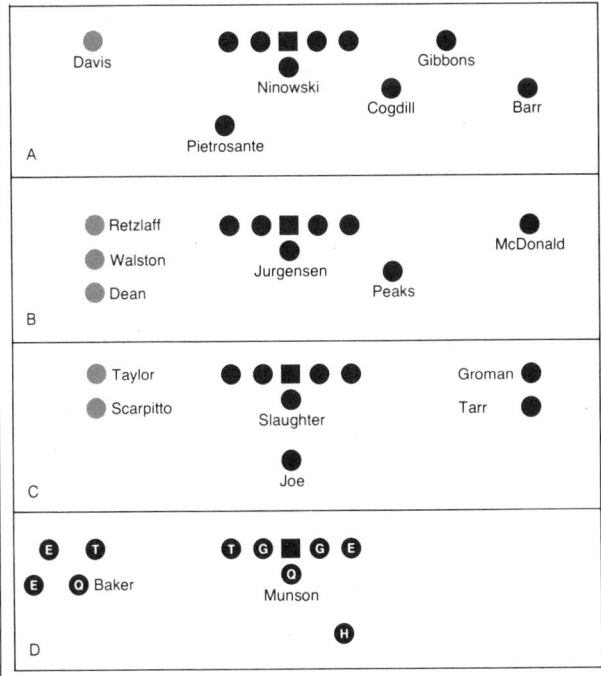

A variety of formations that, like the shotgun, spread receivers and running
backs across the field but unlike the shotgun kept the quarterback under

center, sprang up around the league. Examples shown here are (A) Detroit's "Zephyr" formation of 1961, an attempt to exploit the speed of
former Olympic sprinter Glenn Davis, "the Zephyr"; (B) Philadelphia's
"stacked deck" of the same season, designed for the Eagles' young quarterback Sonny Jurgensen; (C) Denver's "double stack" in the American
Football League; and (D) Los Angeles's "outpost and settlement" of
1964. In the latter, the group of players around the ball and quarterback
Bill Munson was the "settlement" and the group around a second quarterback, Terry Baker, was the "outpost."

36 Two That Endured—T Double Wing and Triple Wing

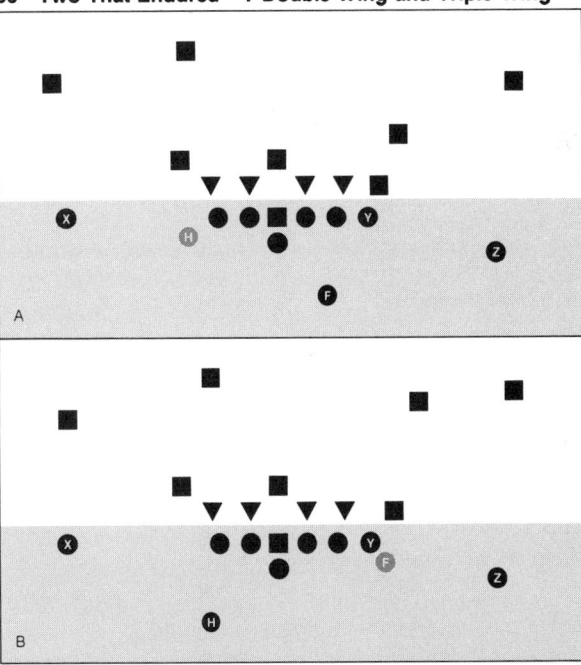

The double wing and triple wing survive today from the era of the original
shotgun and its imitations. Triple wing is also called "trips." In double
wing (A), the halfback is up close to the line, and in triple wing (B) it is the
fullback who is up close to release quickly for a pass. The names for each
of them lack real literal meaning, having been plagiarized from the past
and Pop Warner.

37 I and its Varieties

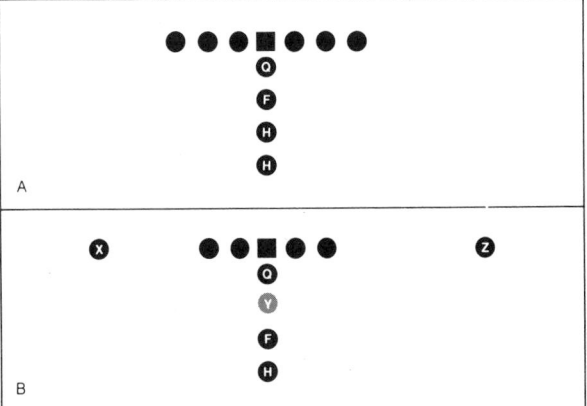

37 continued

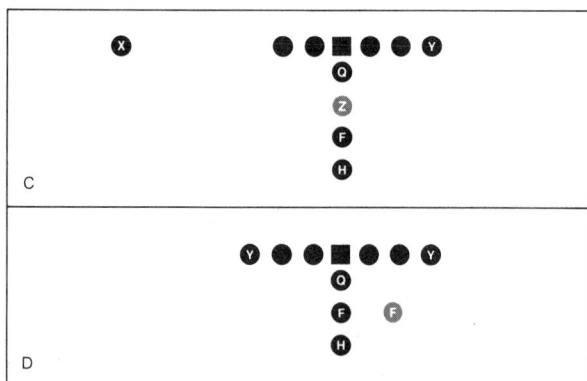

The I formation popular in the NFL today was invented by an obscure college coach named Tom Nugent in the fifties. Hank Stram of the Kansas City Chiefs was the first to place his tight end in the I (B). The Dallas Cowboys frequently have lined up their flanker in the I (C) before shifting. The power I (D) that John McKay perfected at USC is seen in the NFL in short-yardage situations.

38 Wishbone

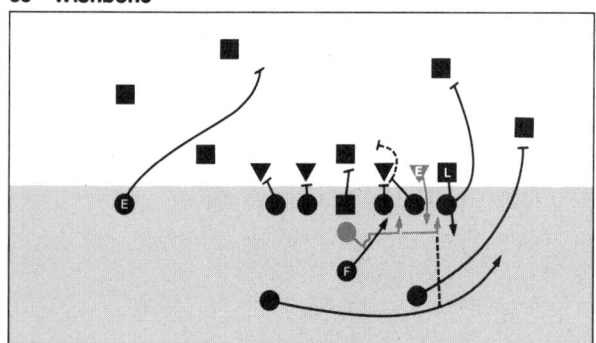

The wishbone reinstated balance in college football and made it more exciting after introduction of the offense by the University of Texas in 1968. But it is a grind-it-out, ball-control offense with only one spread end compared to at least two, and often more, in professional formations.

39 Relocated Hashmarks

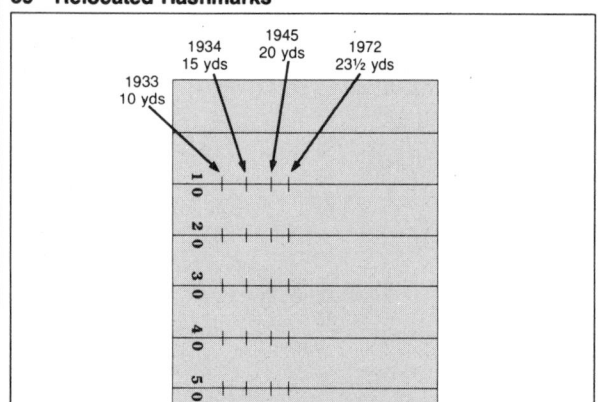

Moving NFL hashmarks in 1972 helped the offense. The defense previously had an advantage on any run or pass to the narrow side of the field.

The 1972 move was actually the third by the NFL since 1933. Hashmarks on college fields remain at a point about 17½ yards from the sideline.

40 Evolution of a Cowboys' Play

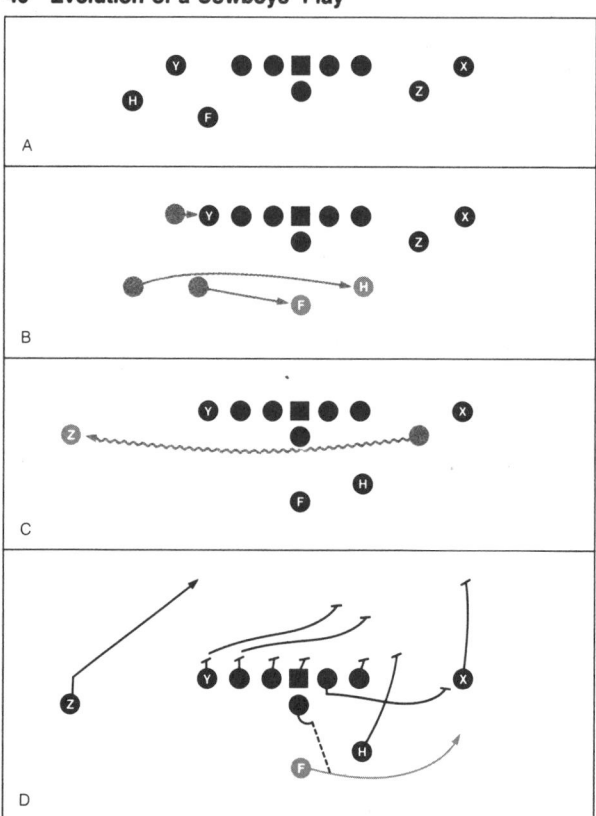

Man-in-motion, which A. A. Stagg used, and shifts, which Dr. Henry Williams popularized, are part of the "preshift" used today by the Dallas Cowboys. It is one of the most unique strategies now being played. Here is an example of how it works: (A) the backs and receivers leave the huddle and line up this way; (B) the backs shift as shown (C) The flanker goes in motion; and (D) the Cowboys are now in their brown left formation, ready to run their play.

Pro Football Language

Pro football teams have their own language. It is different from the language of the sports page or the television booth. It is strange, even bizarre. And it may be the single most complex aspect of the sport.

The following terms are authentic. Coaches and players actually speak them to each other. Terms such as these and others that teams adopt for a season make up the jargon they speak—the secret language of their meetings, practices, and games. But if coaches and players can understand pro football language, others can, too. In doing so, it is possible to gain greater insight into the true nature of the game and how its people think.

A 1. The halfback on the left side. 2. The onside guard pulling and blocking a cornerback or safety.

ace A formation with two wide receivers on one side, a third wide receiver or back on the other side out wide, and one back in the backfield.

alley The area between the hashmarks and the field numbers, from the line of scrimmage to 15 yards downfield.

audible A call changing the offensive and defensive plan at the line of scrimmage.

away The remaining back going away from the point of attack.

ax Knocking down a receiver.

B The back on the right side.

back A call by Mac to change the defense from a called front to a four-three front.

backer A linebacker.

Ben A block by a back on a defensive end.

blast Pass rush by defensive tackles.

blitz Jill or Sam dogging.

blue A formation with the fullback behind the quarterback and the halfback on the strongside; same as near, strong, two left, and wing.

Bob A block by a back on a backer.

bomb A long pass intended to be a touchdown.

bomber Force by a backer; same as bronco.

bootleg The quarterback moving with the ball away from the flow.

boss A block by the near back on the first defensive back to show.

both near A formation with both X and Z one to three yards from the offensive tackles.

bronco Force by a backer; same as bomber.

brown A formation with the fullback behind the quarterback and the halfback on the weakside; same as far, four right, and opposite.

Buck The backside or weakside linebacker; same as Wanda and Willie.

Buck ax Buck knocking down a receiver.

Buck I Buck dogging.

buzz A linebacker covering passes; same as drop.

call A command.

check with me A call by the quarterback in the huddle telling the team he will audible a play at the line of scrimmage.

Cleo 1. Force by a cornerback; same as cloud and crash. 2. A block by a wide receiver on a cornerback.

close The alignment of a slot receiver in tight less than three yards from the tackle.

cloud Force by a cornerback; same as Cleo and crash.

club A block by a tackle on a middle linebacker.

combo Combination pass coverage by Jill and Sam on Y and the strongside back.

corner The deep outside zone of the field.

counter A play in which one or more backs move away from the point of attack.

crackback A block by a wide receiver on a linebacker; same as slash.

crash Force by a cornerback; same as Cleo and cloud.

cross A call alerting the defense that a receiver is crossing shallow.

cutback Maintaining inside position on a running back and tackling him when he turns inside; same as fill.

deep middle The middle one-third of the field from 15 yards from the line of scrimmage to the goal line; same as post.

delayed sweep A sweep with backfield deception and which develops late.

dog Pass rush by defensive players other than linemen.

double wing A formation with two wide receivers on each side and only the halfback in the backfield behind the quarterback; same as dual, deuce, and duce.

down A block by the tight end and tackle one man farther in than usual, the tight end now blocking the defensive end and the tackle blocking the defensive tackle.

draw A running play with a delayed handoff and delayed blocking off an initial action that shows pass.

drop A linebacker covering passes; same as buzz.

dual Same as double wing.

duce Same as double wing and dual.

eat A double team block by a tight end and tackle on a defensive end.

even 1. A defensive front with tackles head on the offensive guards and ends head on the offensive tackles. 2. Ordinary run blocking with each lineman responsible for the defender in front of him. 3. A block by the onside guard pulling and blocking a cornerback or safety, with the tackle going through on the middle linebacker and the center cut-blocks.

F 1. A series or family of running plays in which the fullback hits over the onside guard as a blocker, faker, or ball carrier. 2. A replacement block by a back on a defensive tackle.

fan The areas of the field between the flats and the corners.

far 1. A formation with the fullback behind the quarterback and the halfback on the weakside; same as brown, four right, and opposite. 2. A position of the weakside back more than three yards from the tackle.

fill Maintaining inside position on a running back and tackling him when he turns inside; same as cutback.

fire A call by a defensive player as soon as he has made an interception; same as oskie.

five-three A defense with five linemen and three linebackers.

flanker Z.

flare action The coordinated movement of running backs to block dogging linebackers, or if there are none, to go out for passes.

flat The area of the field from the line of scrimmage to a point eight yards downfield and, horizontally, from two yards outside the field numbers on each side of the side lines.

flex 1. A defense with the linemen staggered on and off the line of scrimmage. 2. The alignment of X only three to six yards from the tackle.

flip 1. A quick lateral pass to a back in the two or four position. 2. A series or family of plays built around that play. 3. A block by the onside tackle on the cornerback or safety.

float Alignment of Z three to six yards from Y; same as X in flex.

flood Putting more than one receiver in a zone so the defender playing that zone can't cover them all.

flop Change sides.

flow 1. The direction of play. 2. Movement of the remaining back or backs to the side of the point of attack. 3. A series or family of plays with the backs moving toward the same side.

flux A formation with X flexed and Z floating.

fly A back in motion to the weakside.

fold A combination block by the center and a guard against an even front, the center blocking on the de-

fensive tackle and the guard pulling through and blocking the middle linebacker.

force Turning a running play inside; same as support.

four position Behind the right offensive tackle.

four I A formation with the tight end and the two running backs in a line behind the quarterback.

four right Early name for formation in which the back in the four position moves out to become the flanker; same as brown, far, and opposite.

four-three A defense with four linemen and three linebackers.

front The defensive line and linebackers.

full 1. A formation with the running backs behind the tackles and the fullback in the four position; same as red and split right. 2. A series or family of plays in which attack as a blocker, faker, or ball carrier. 3. A block by a back or a defensive tackle or linebacker after the guard has pulled.

G A block by the onside guard, pulling and blocking the outside man on the line of scrimmage, usually the outside linebacker.

gadget A trick play.

gap 1. The space between two offensive linemen. 2. A defense with a man in every gap.

gap over A defense with the weakside defensive tackle moving into the weakside guard-center gap.

gap under A defense with the strongside defensive tackle moving into the strongside guard-center gap.

gas A double-team block by the center and a guard on a defensive tackle.

go A back in motion to the strongside.

gob A block by a guard on a backer; same as G.

gone A defense without a middle linebacker.

green A formation with the running backs behind the tackles and the halfback in the four position; same as half and split left.

gut A cross block by the onside guard and tackle, the guard going first.

half A formation with the running backs behind the tackles and the halfback in the four position; same as green and split left.

half zoom Z in motion toward the ball and the ball snapped before he reaches the tight end.

hole The area of the field between the hooks.

hook 1. A block by a tight end on a linebacker, preventing him from going outside. 2. The area of the field extending from the Y position to points 15 to 18 yards upfield.

I 1. A formation with two running backs in a line behind the quarterback. 2. A series or family of plays from the I formation.

I man A defensive tackle.

influence Deception by the offensive line, denying keys to the defense and leading it away from the play.

isolation block A block by a back on a defensive lineman who has been influenced.

Jack A combination block with the guard blocking the middle linebacker

Jerry A charge by a defensive tackle to the inside gap.

Jill The weakside or free safety.

jumbo A defense with six or more linemen.

key An alignment or movement telling a defensive player where the ball is going or what blocks to expect.

lead A block by a running back, preceding the other running back into the line and blocking the first defender in his path.

Les The left safety, who could be Jill or Sam.

Lex A stunt by Lon and Lin, crossing at the snap of the ball.

Lin The left I man or defensive tackle.

Linda Zone rotation left.

Link The left linebacker, who might be Stub or Buck.

Linki Link inside his normal position.

Numbering Positions and Plays

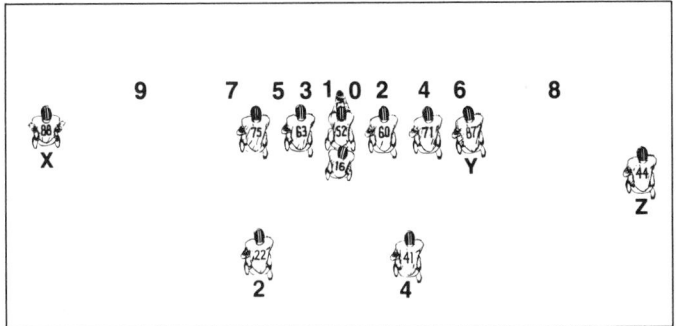

The play is the back plus the hole; 26 is the 2 back in the 6 hole.

Formations

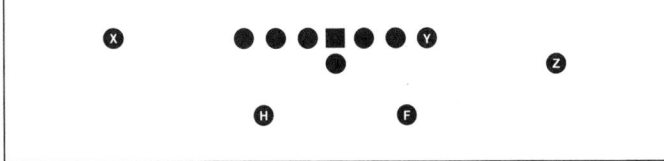

Full, red, or split right.

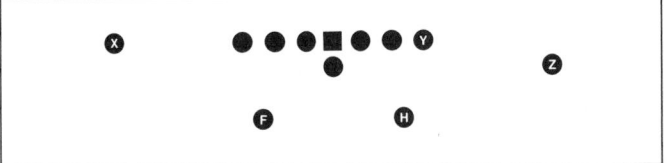

Half, green, or split left.

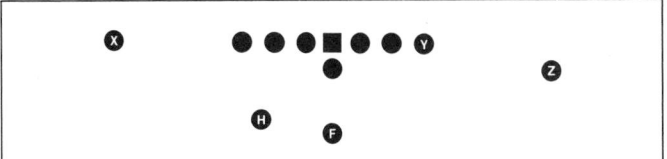

Brown, far, four right, or opposite.

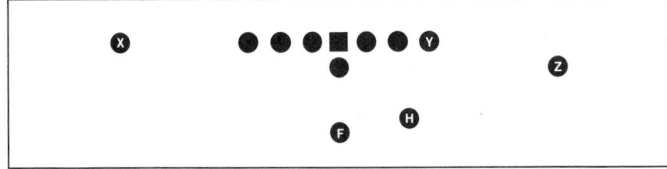

Blue, near, strong, two left, or wing.

Types of Back Action

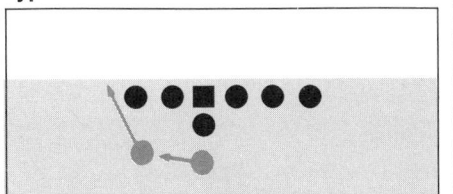

Flow action: both backs to the same side.

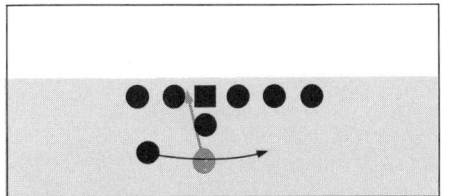

Full action: fullback over guard away from p.o.a.

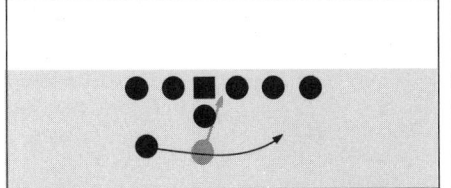

F action: fullback over guard on side of p.o.a.

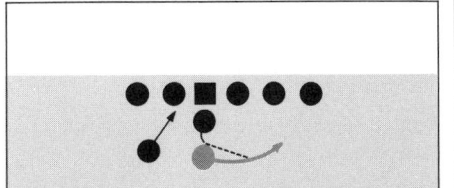

Toss action: toss to one back, other hits into line.

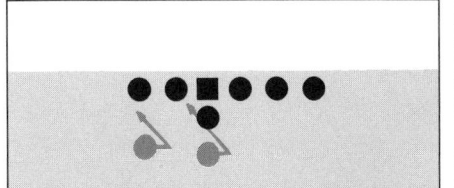

Counter action: one or more backs step away from point of attack, then counter.

Blocks

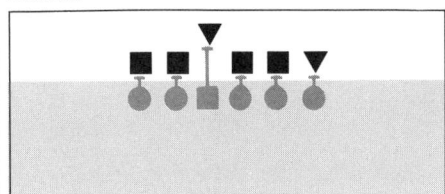

Man: ordinary man-for-man blocking.

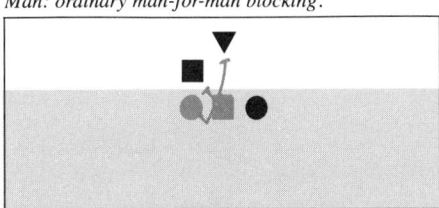

Scissors: cross-blocking.

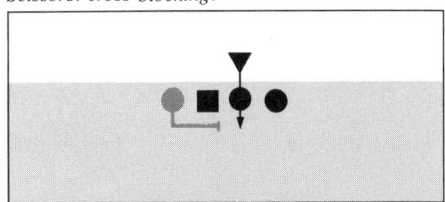

Trap: the off guard to the onside.

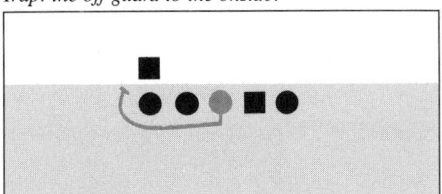

Gob: A guard on a backer.

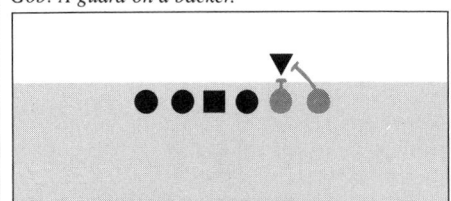

Double team: two men block one.

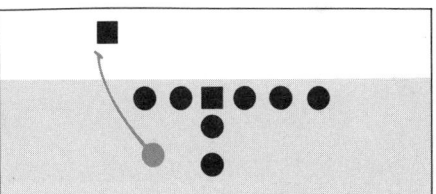

Bob: a back on a backer.

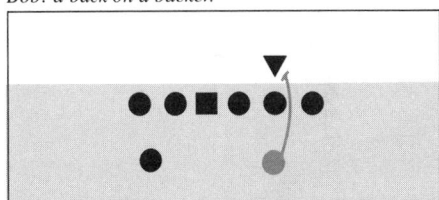

Ben: a back on an end.

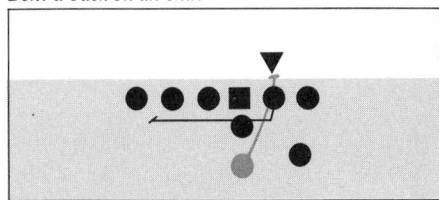

Replacement: a back on a tackle.

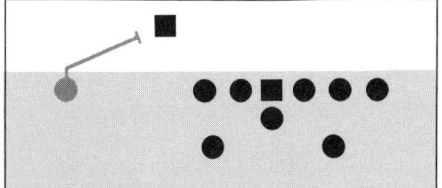

Slash: a wide receiver on a linebacker.

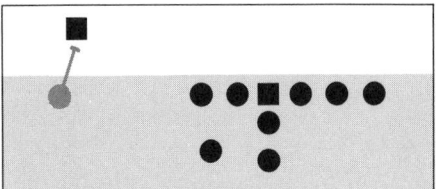

Shield: a wide receiver on a cornerback.

Pass Patterns

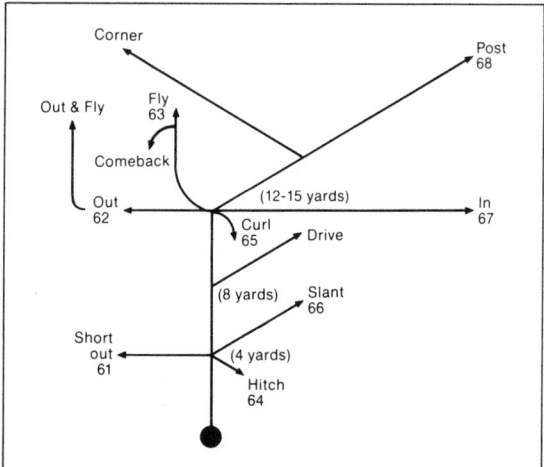

The "tree" of possible pass routes by a wide receiver.

Back Routes

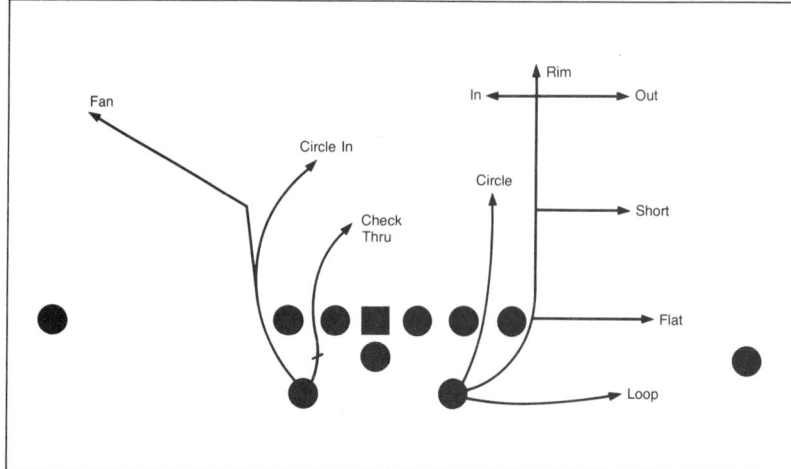

The "tree" of possible routes by a running back.

Types of Flare Action

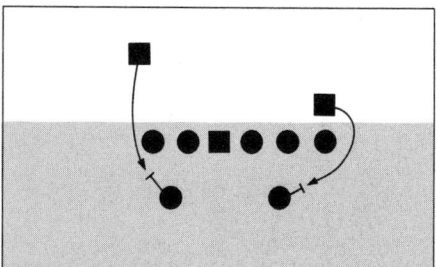

Both backs stay in to block.

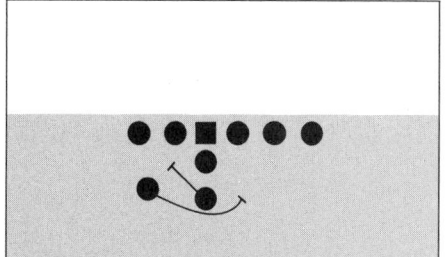

They cross, then block.

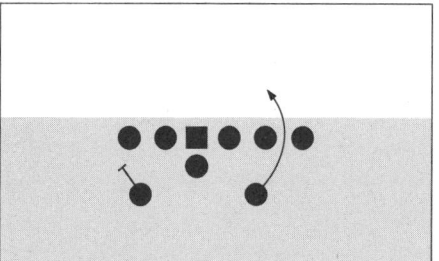

One blocks, the other runs a circle.

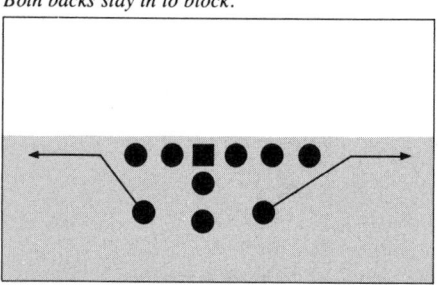

Both run to the flats.

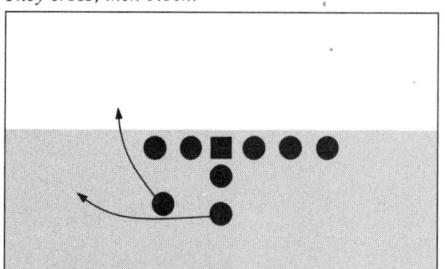

Both run to the weakside.

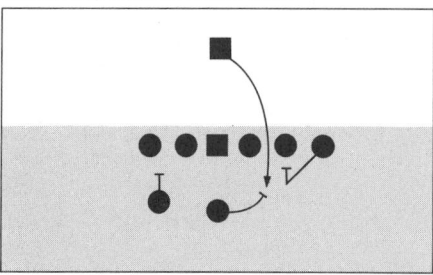

Seeing a dog coming, backs and Y stay home.

Linko Link outside his normal position.

lion A slant by both defensive tackles to the left.

log A block by a pulling lineman hooking the defender to the inside.

Lon the left O man or defensive end.

Lou The left cornerback.

Mac The middle linebacker.

Mac I Mac dogging.

mad dog Mac, Stub, and Buck dogging.

man-for-man Pass coverage in which each defender is assigned to a specific receiver for the entire play.

Mike A middle guard.

misdirection Deception by the offensive backfield, denying keys to the defense and leading it away from the play.

mix A stunt by Mac and a defensive tackle.

mombo Combination pass coverage by Mac and the outside linebacker on Y and the first back out of the backfield.

near 1. A formation with the fullback behind the quarterback and the halfback on the strongside; same as blue, strong, two left, and wing. 2. Alignment of X one to three yards from the tackle.

nickel A defense with five defensive backs.

nose man A defensive lineman head on the center.

O A block by the offside guard, pulling to the onside and leading the back through the hole.

odd A defense that is not even, i.e., an over or under.

offside The side away from the play.

Okie A three-four defense.

O man A defensive end.

onside The side to which the play goes.

opposite A formation with the fullback behind the quarterback and the halfback on the weakside; same as brown, far, and four right.

option 1. Running without predetermining the hole in the line where the ball carrier must go, allowing him to run wherever he sees open space; same as running to daylight. 2. A running play in which the quarterback moves down the line and has the option to hand off, pitch, or run. 3. A play in which the runner has the option to run or pass. 4. Blocking in which the lineman carries the defender in the direction his own momentum is taking him rather than in a predetermined direction.

oskie A call by a defensive player as soon as he has made an interception; same as fire.

over A defense with the weakside defensive tackle head on the center and Mac head on the weakside guard.

peel A dogging linebacker or defensive back stopping his rush and covering an offensive back who releases for a pass.

pick A screen by a receiver on a defensive back to take him out of coverage.

pinch A charge by the defensive linemen to the inside.

pix Y when he is the only receiver on his side.

play action Plays in which the quarterback fakes a handoff and passes; same as play pass.

play pass Same as play action.

poc Alignment of Y one to three yards from the tackle.

port Early name for left defensive halfback.

post 1. The middle one-third of the field from a point 15 yards from the line of scrimmage to the goal line; same as deep middle. 2. The outside receiver on the two-receiver side of a slot formation. 3. A call by defenders to teammates that a receiver has broken for the deep middle.

power 1. Any formation with three running backs in the backfield. 2. Double-team blocking at the point of attack.

prevent Any defense designed specifically to stop long passes.

pro A four-three defense.

queen A combination block with the tackle blocking the middle linebacker.

Rat A right linebacker farther in than Ripi.

read See a key and interpret it.

red A formation with the running backs behind the tackles and the fullback in the four position; same as full and split right.

red dog Stub and Buck dogging.

replacement block A back filling the space left when a lineman pulls, blocking the defender in that gap.

Rex A stunt by Ric and Roy, crossing at the snap of the ball.

Ric The right I man or defensive tackle.

Rip 1. The right linebacker, who could be Stub or Buck. 2. A charge by Mike to the right.

Ripi Rip inside his normal position.

Ripo Rip outside his normal position.

Roger Zone rotation right.

Rose The right cornerback.

rotation Shifting zone coverage left or right.

Roy The right O man or defensive end.

rule blocking The coordinated action by which offensive linemen know substitute blocking assignments if the defense changes its alignment.

run to daylight Running without predetermining the hole in the line where the ball carrier must go, allowing him to run wherever he sees open space; same as option running.

Russ The right safety, who could be Jill or Sam.

Sam The strongside safety.

Sara The strongside linebacker; same as Stub.

scissors Cross-blocking.

scoop A block by an offside lineman toward the onside, usually against an odd front.

scramble screen A screen pass in which the tackles pass protect and the guards and center fake a roll or cut-block and scramble to set up a blocking wall left or right.

scrape Charge by a linebacker off the position of a defensive lineman.

screen A pass that develops behind the line of scrimmage, in which the rushers are allowed to penetrate while the offensive linemen fake blocks and then set up a wall for the receiver.

shield A block by a wide receiver or a cornerback.

shotgun A red formation with the quarterback seven to nine yards behind and taking a long snap from center.

shovel pass A pass behind the line of scrimmage to a receiver who then runs in a designated hole.

Sid The middle safety of a three-deep defense.

sky 1. Force by a safety; same as stone. 2. A block by a wide receiver on a safety.

slam The strongside defensive end charging to the inside.

slant 1. A planned charge by a defensive lineman to the left or right instead of straight ahead. 2. A running play hitting sharply off guard or tackle. 3. A series or family of plays built around that play.

slash A block by a wide receiver on a linebacker; same as crackback.

slot 1. A formation with both wide receivers on the same side; same as twin. 2. The inside receiver on that side. 3. The area between X and his tackle and, on the other side, between Z and Y, to points eight yards downfield.

split left A formation with the running backs behind the tackles and the halfback in the four position; same as green and half.

split right A formation with the running backs behind the tackles and the fullback in the four position; same as full and red.

split end X.

spread A formation with no running backs at all in the backfield with the quarterback.

Defensive Positions

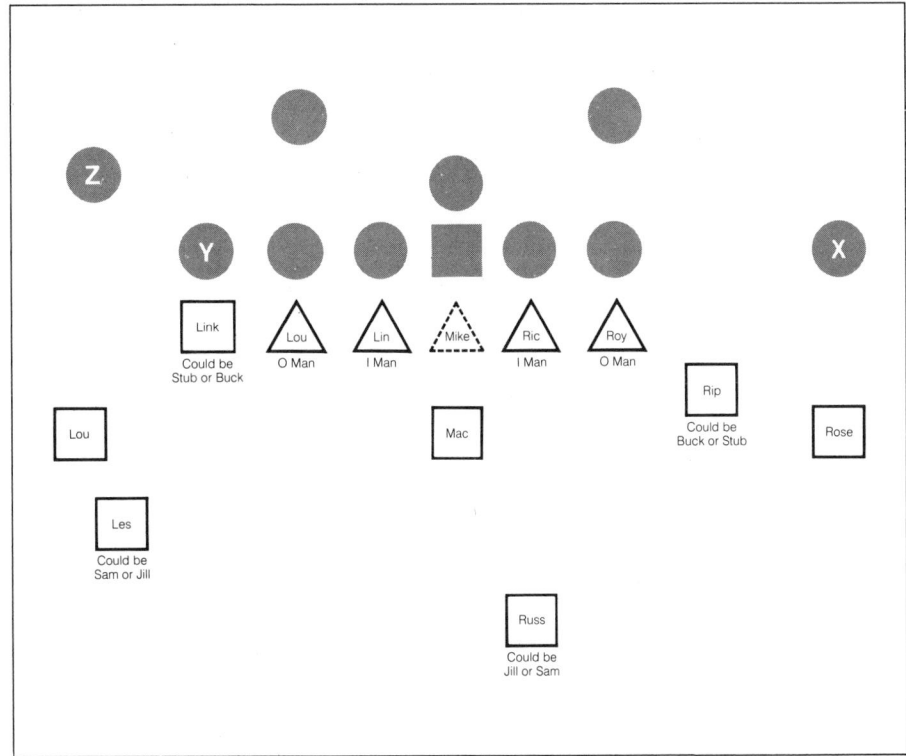

An example of pro football jargon for the 11 defensive positions.

Stunts

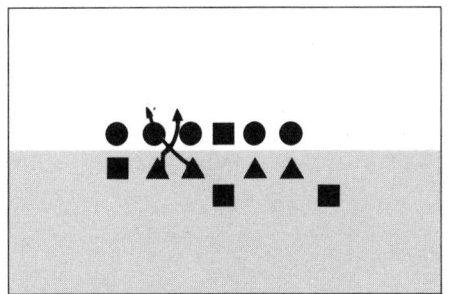

Lex: a stunt on the left side.

Rex: a stunt on the right side.

Tex: Lex and Rex at the same time.

Types of Forces

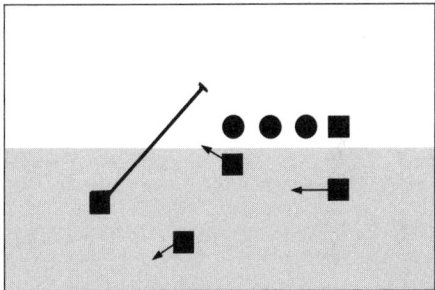

Crash: by the cornerback.

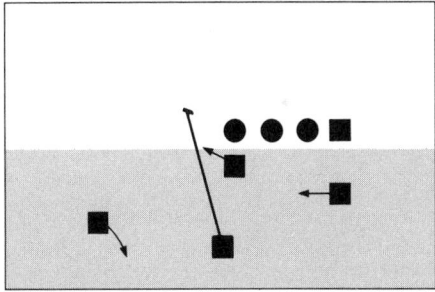

Sky: by the safety.

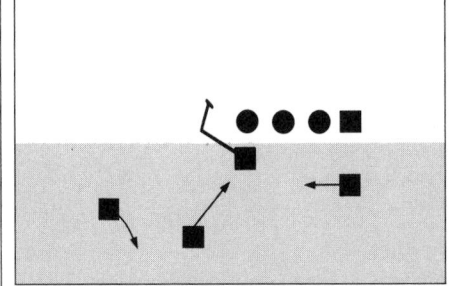

Bomber: by the backer.

Zones of the Field

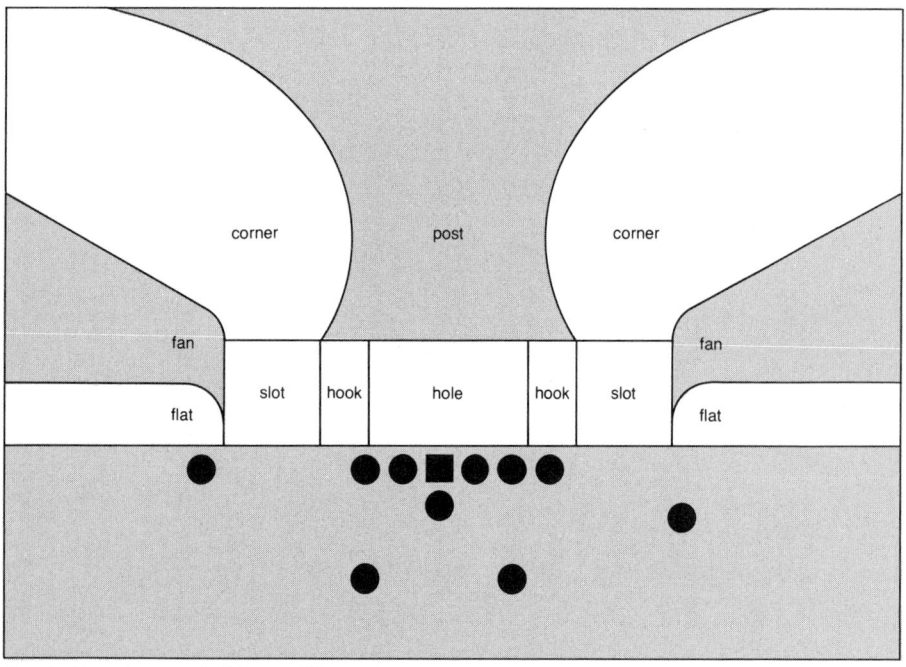

A typical team's concept of the possible passing zones.

spy Restrained pass rush by a defensive lineman as he watches for draw plays or screens.

stack 1. A linebacker behind the linemen. 2. A defense with the line shifting to the tight end and the linebackers behind the linemen.

starboard Early name for the right defensive halfback.

stone Force by a safety; same as sky.

strong A formation with the fullback behind the quarterback and the halfback on the strongside; same as blue, near, and wing.

strong dog and cat Mac and Stub dogging.

strongside The side of the offensive formation with Y and Z, the tight end or flanker, or if slot formation, the side with the two wide receivers.

strong zone Zone rotated to the strongside.

Stub The strongside linebacker; same as Sara.

Stub ax Stub knocking down a receiver.

stunt An unusual charge by linebackers and linemen, or by linemen alone, in which they loop around each other instead of charging straight ahead.

sucker play A play in which the back runs into the hole left when the defensive lineman is lured away chasing a pulling guard.

support Force.

tag A double team block by a tackle and a guard on a defensive tackle.

Tex Lex and Rex at the same time.

three I A formation with a wide receiver and the two running backs in a line behind the quarterback.

three position In the backfield directly behind the quarterback.

tight end. Y.

toss A pitchout.

trap A block by an offside guard pulling to the onside and driving the defender out.

trey A formation with three receivers on one side and only the fullback behind the quarterback.

triple Same as trey.

trips Same as trey and triple.

twin A formation with both wide receivers on the same side; same as slot.

two position Behind the left offensive tackle.

two left Early name for formation in which the back in the two position moves out to become the flanker; same as blue, near, strong and wing.

two Y A formation with two tight ends.

unbalanced A line with both tackles lined up beside each other, creating four linemen on one side and two on the other.

under A defense with the strongside defensive tackle head on the center and Mac head on the strongside guard.

Viking A charge by a nose man straight into the center and controlling both gaps to the left and right of him.

waggle The quarterback moving with the ball away from the flow with protection.

Wanda The weakside linebacker; same as Buck or Willie.

weakside The side of the offensive formation with only one receiver.

weak dog and cat Mac and Buck dogging.

weak zone Zone rotated to the weakside.

wedge Double-team blocking; shoulder-to-shoulder, straight ahead.

wham The weakside defensive end charging to the inside.

Willie The weakside linebacker; same as Buck or Wanda.

wing 1. A formation with the fullback behind the quarterback and the halfback on the strongside; same as blue, near, strong, and two left. 2. Z aligned one to three yards from Y.

X The split end.

Y The tight end.

yoyo Double coverage on the tight end.

Z The flanker.

zone Pass coverage in which defenders are assigned specific areas to cover, not specific receivers.

zoom Z going in motion.

The
Hall of Fame

Cliff Battles

Cliff Battles

Halfback. 6-1, 201. Born in Akron, Ohio, May 1, 1910. West Virginia Wesleyan. Inducted in 1968. 1932 Boston Braves, 1933–36 Boston Redskins, 1937 Washington Redskins.

Cliff Battles played only six seasons in the NFL but he gained 3,542 yards for the Braves and Redskins. Big and fast, he was the first NFL runner to gain more than 200 yards in a game. Battles scored three touchdowns and had runs of 74, 75, 76, and 78 yards. A Phi Beta Kappa scholar, he was one of the first professional stars to come from a small college, West Virginia Wesleyan. His final season, 1937, was a memorable one in which he gained 874 yards, won his second rushing title, and earned all-NFL honors for the third time in six years.

RUSHING

Year	Team	Att.	Yards	Avg.	TD
1932	Boston Braves	148	576	3.9	3
1933	Boston Redskins	136	737	5.0	3
1934	Boston Redskins	96	511	5.0	6
1935	Boston Redskins	67	230	3.4	1
1936	Boston Redskins	176	614	3.5	5
1937	Washington	216	874	4.0	5
Totals		839	3,542	4.2	23

SCORING
31 TD, 1 FG, 1 PAT, 190 Points

Sammy Baugh

Quarterback. 6-2, 180. Born in Temple, Texas, March 17, 1914. Texas Christian. Inducted in 1963. 1937–52 Washington Redskins.

In his 16-year career in the pros, Sammy Baugh led the league in passing six times. His passing efficiency percentage of 70.33 in 1945 is an NFL record. He held virtually every passing record when he retired. All of that is even more remarkable when you consider that he came to pro football from Texas Christian as a single wing tailback and had to make a transition to T formation quarterback halfway through his career; he was a tailback for eight years and a quarterback for another eight years. He set the NFL record for career punting average, 45.1, made 28 interceptions while playing safety in the one-platoon era, and in one season, 1943, led the league in passing, punting, and interceptions.

PASSING

Year	Team	Att.	Comp.	Yards	TD	Int.
1937	Washington	171	81	1,127	8	14
1938	Washington	128	63	853	5	11
1939	Washington	96	53	518	6	9
1940	Washington	177	111	1,367	12	10
1941	Washington	193	106	1,236	10	19
1942	Washington	225	132	1,524	16	11
1943	Washington	239	133	1,754	23	19
1944	Washington	146	82	849	4	8
1945	Washington	182	128	1,669	11	4
1946	Washington	161	87	1,163	8	17
1947	Washington	354	210	2,938	25	15
1948	Washington	315	185	2,599	22	23
1949	Washington	255	145	1,903	18	14
1950	Washington	166	90	1,130	10	11
1951	Washington	154	67	1,104	7	17
1952	Washington	33	20	152	2	1
Totals		2,995	1,693	21,886	187	203

PUNTING

Year	Team	No.	Yards	Avg.	Long	Blk.
1937	Washington					
1938	Washington					
1939	Washington	26		38.0	69	
1940	Washington	35		51.3	85	
1941	Washington	30		48.7	75	0
1942	Washington	37		46.6	74	0
1943	Washington	50		45.9	81	3
1944	Washington	44		40.6	76	1
1945	Washington	33		43.3	57	0
1946	Washington	33		45.1	60	0
1947	Washington	35		43.7	67	2
1948	Washington	0	0	0.0	0	0
1949	Washington	1	53	53.0	53	0
1950	Washington	9		39.1	58	1
1951	Washington	4		55.3	58	0
1952	Washington	1	48	48.0	48	0

INTERCEPTIONS

Year	Team	No.	Yards	Avg.	Long	TD
1937	Washington					
1938	Washington					
1939	Washington					
1940	Washington					
1941	Washington	4	83	20.8	35	0
1942	Washington	5	77	15.4	29	0
1943	Washington	11	112	10.2	23	0
1944	Washington	4	21	5.2	18	0
1945	Washington	4	114	28.5	74	0
1946	Washington	0	0	0.0	0	0
1947	Washington	0	0	0.0	0	0
1948	Washington	0	0	0.0	0	0
1949	Washington	0	0	0.0	0	0
1950	Washington	0	0	0.0	0	0
1951	Washington	0	0	0.0	0	0
1952	Washington	0	0	0.0	0	0

RUSHING
324 Att., 325 Yards, 1.0 Avg., 41 Long, 9 TD

Sammy Baugh

Bert Bell

Chuck Bednarik

Raymond Berry

Charles W. Bidwill, Sr.

Chuck Bednarik

Center-linebacker. 6-3, 230. Born in Bethlehem, Pennsylvania, May 1, 1925. Pennsylvania. Inducted in 1967. 1949–1962 Philadelphia Eagles.

Pro football was a highly specialized game by 1960 but Chuck Bednarik, at 35, played both offensively and defensively in a string of key games that helped the Eagles into the NFL title game, where he played over 50 minutes. His tackle of Jim Taylor, nine yards short of the goal line, preserved Philadelphia's win over Green Bay, on the game's final play. In 14 seasons, the durable Bednarik missed only three games. He won all-pro honors both as a center and a linebacker. A three-time All-America at Pennsylvania, Bednarik was the NFL's "bonus" draft choice in 1949. He played in eight Pro Bowls, and was honored as player of the game in the 1954 game.

Bert Bell

Commissioner. Team owner. Born in Philadelphia, Pennsylvania, February 25, 1895. Died October 11, 1959. Pennsylvania. Inducted in 1963. 1933–1940 Philadelphia Eagles, 1941–46 Pittsburgh Steelers.

Bert Bell, who was elected commissioner in 1946, saw the NFL through a bitter and costly power struggle with the rival All-America Football Conference. Bell provided strong leadership until his death in the grandstand at an Eagles–Steelers game in 1959. He was a football man most of his life, having played at Pennsylvania and later coaching there and at other schools. Bell, who took charge of the newly formed Philadelphia Eagles in 1933, sought to increase competitive balance in the NFL by proposing the college player draft in 1935. After serving the Eagles as general manager, ticket manager, publicity director, and head coach. he joined the Steelers as coowner and head coach in 1941. In later work as commissioner he laid down strong anti-gambling policies and instituted the home television "blackout" of NFL games.

Raymond Berry

End. 6-2. 187. Born in Corpus Christi, Texas, February 27, 1933. Southern Methodist. Inducted in 1973. 1955–1967 Baltimore Colts.

Raymond Berry proved that dedication, concentration, and long hours of practice can compensate for limited physical skills. Berry worked with quarterback John Unitas at Baltimore to form a remarkable passing combination. When he retired he was the leading receiver in NFL history. His 12 receptions in the memorable 1958 "sudden death" championship game are still a record. He used gadgets such as tinted goggles to gain an advantage over his opponents and he practiced long after regular sessions were over; he had average size and speed. His play was much more than average, however. He and Unitas perfected the sideline pass. In 13 seasons he fumbled only once. A twentieth round draft choice, he was on all-pro teams three times and played in five Pro Bowls.

RECEIVING

Year	Team	No.	Yards	Avg.	Long	TD
1955	Baltimore	13	205	15.8	45	0
1956	Baltimore	37	601	16.2	54	2
1957	Baltimore	47	800	17.0	67t	6
1958	Baltimore	56	794	14.2	54	9
1959	Baltimore	66	959	14.5	55t	14
1960	Baltimore	74	1,298	17.5	70t	10
1961	Baltimore	75	873	11.6	44	0
1962	Baltimore	51	687	13.5	37	3
1963	Baltimore	44	703	16.0	64t	3
1964	Baltimore	43	663	15.4	46	6
1965	Baltimore	58	739	12.7	40	7
1966	Baltimore	56	786	14.0	40t	7
1967	Baltimore	11	167	15.2	40	1
Totals		631	9,275	14.7	70t	68

SCORING
68 TD, 408 Points

Charles W. Bidwill, Sr.

Team owner. Born in Chicago, Illinois, September 16, 1895. Died April 19, 1947. Loyola of Chicago. Inducted in 1967. 1933–1947 Chicago Cardinals.

Charles Bidwill's interest in pro football preceded his ownership of the Chicago Cardinals by some years. His financial support enabled George Halas to retain ownership of the Chicago Bears during the early days of the Depression. Bidwill took over the Cardinals in 1933. The team lost games but he kept his faith in the sport. After World War II, Bidwill signed Charley Trippi to a $100,000 contract to complete a "dream backfield" that also included Paul Christman, Elmer Angsman, and Pat Harder. But Bidwill wasn't around to see his team win the NFL championship in 1947. He died in April of that year. The ownership of the team passed to his wife, Violet, and eventually to his sons, Charles, Jr., and Bill. A non-conformist, Bidwill was often called "Blue Shirt" Bidwill because he spurned traditional white shirts and businessmen's shoes in favor of blue shirt and high boots.

Jim Brown

Paul Brown

Jim Brown

Fullback. 6-2, 232. Born in St. Simons, Georgia, February 17, 1936. Syracuse. Inducted in 1971. 1957–1965 Cleveland Browns.

The amazingly durable Jim Brown never missed a game in nine years of NFL play, during which he gained a record 12,312 yards. A player who was the perfect combination of size, speed, and power, Brown is considered by many the finest runner ever in football. He led the NFL in rushing in eight of his nine seasons, made an all-pro team eight times, in addition to playing in nine straight Pro Bowls. He scored 756 points, the highest NFL total by a non-kicker. And only twice did he fail to go over the 1,000-yard rushing mark, his first season and 1962, when he played with a severely sprained wrist. The former Syracuse fullback rushed for more than 100 yards a game 58 times, almost half his pro starts. He retired at the top of his game, prior to the 1966 season, to pursue an acting career.

RUSHING

Year	Team	Att.	Yards	Avg.	Long	TD
1957	Cleveland	202	942	4.7	69t	9
1958	Cleveland	257	1,527	5.9	65t	17
1959	Cleveland	290	1,329	4.6	70t	14
1960	Cleveland	215	1,257	5.8	71t	9
1961	Cleveland	305	1,408	4.6	38	8
1962	Cleveland	230	996	4.3	31	13
1963	Cleveland	291	1,863	6.4	80t	12
1964	Cleveland	280	1,446	5.2	71	7
1965	Cleveland	289	1,544	5.3	67	17
Totals		2,359	12,312	5.2	80t	106

RECEIVING

Year	Team	No.	Yards	Avg.	Long	TD
1957	Cleveland	16	55	3.4	12	1
1958	Cleveland	16	138	8.6	46	1
1959	Cleveland	24	190	7.9	25	0
1960	Cleveland	19	204	10.7	37t	2
1961	Cleveland	46	459	10.0	77t	2
1962	Cleveland	47	517	11.0	53t	5
1963	Cleveland	24	268	11.2	83t	3
1964	Cleveland	36	340	9.4	40t	2
1965	Cleveland	34	328	9.6	32t	4
Totals		262	2,499	9.5	83t	20

SCORING

126 TD, 756 Points

Paul Brown

Coach. Born in Norwalk, Ohio, September 7, 1908. Miami, Ohio. Inducted in 1967. 1946–49 Cleveland Browns (AAFC), 1950–1962 Cleveland Browns, 1968–1975 Cincinnati Bengals.

Many of the things that are part of pro football today—full-time coaching staffs, calling plays via "messengers," precise pass routes—were either Paul Brown innovations or were raised to a higher level of efficiency by him. Brown was hired by the Cleveland Browns of the newly organized All-America Football Conference in 1945, when he was still coaching at Great Lakes Naval Training Station. He took over in Cleveland in 1946 and the Browns won league championships all four seasons of the AAFC's existence. In 1950, after the AAFC merged with the NFL, Brown and the Browns again won the championship, and they were in the title game the next five seasons. Brown's Cleveland teams won three NFL titles and seven divisional championships in 13 seasons. Only once—the year after Otto Graham retired—did a Paul Brown Cleveland team finish below .500. Brown began a second successful coaching career with the Cincinnati Bengals in 1968, a year after his induction into the Hall of Fame, and retired as a coach after the 1975 season.

Roosevelt Brown

Offensive tackle. 6-3, 255. Born in Charlottesville, Virginia, October 20, 1932. Morgan State. Inducted in 1975. 1953–1965 New York Giants.

Almost any biography of Roosevelt Brown mentions him as one of the NFL's most notable "sleeper" draft choices. He was picked on the twenty-seventh round in 1953. He became a starter his first season and stayed there for 13. From 1956 through 1963, Brown was an all-pro tackle and played in nine Pro Bowl games. The Giants made excellent use of Brown's outstanding speed by designing special plays that used him as a pulling blocker from his tackle position. Prior to this, pulling was done mainly by offensive guards. Brown was also used defensively on goal-line stands. Phlebitis forced his retirement in 1966.

Tony Canadeo

Joe Carr

Roosevelt Brown

Tony Canadeo

Halfback. 5-11, 195. Born in Chicago, Illinois, May 5, 1919. Gonzaga. Inducted in 1974. 1941–44 Green Bay Packers, 1946–1952 Green Bay Packers

Tony Canadeo was a versatile, two-way performer. He ran, passed, punted, returned punts and kickoffs, caught passes, and played defense. He was adept at all of them. Taking all categories into account, Canadeo averaged 75 yards a game over his 11 seasons. Before World War II, he was the Packers' leading passer. Upon his return from the service, he was their heavy-duty runner. In 1949, he became only the third man in NFL history to rush for more that 1,000 yards in a season; he rushed for 4,197 yards in his career. A fiery competitor, Canadeo refused to let tacklers help him to his feet. Art Daley, a Green Bay writer, said Canadeo even thumbed his nose at opponents.

RUSHING

Year	Team	Att.	Yards	Avg.	Long	TD
1941	Green Bay	43	137	3.2	16	3
1942	Green Bay	89	272	3.1	50	3
1943	Green Bay	94	489	5.2	35	3
1944	Green Bay	31	149	4.8	34	0
1945	Military Service					
1946	Green Bay	122	476	3.9	27	0
1947	Green Bay	103	464	4.5	35	2
1948	Green Bay	123	589	4.8	49	4
1949	Green Bay	208	1,052	5.1	54	4
1950	Green Bay	93	247	2.6	15	4
1951	Green Bay	54	131	2.4	15	1
1952	Green Bay	65	191	2.9	35	2
	Totals	1,025	4,197	4.1	54	26

PASSING
268 Att., 108 Comp., 1,642 Yards, 16 TD, 20 Int.
RECEIVING
69, 579 Yards, 8.4 Avg., 46 Long, 5 TD
INTERCEPTIONS
9, 129 Yards, 14.3 Avg., 35 Long, 0 TD
PUNTING
45, 1,669 Yards, 37.1 Avg., 62 Long, 0 Blk.
PUNT RETURNS
46, 513 Yards, 11.2 Avg., 26 Long, 0 TD
KICKOFF RETURNS
75, 1,736 Yards, 23.1 Avg., 55 Long, 0 TD
SCORING
31 TD, 186 Points

Joe Carr

NFL president. Born in Columbus, Ohio, October 22, 1880. Died May 20, 1939. Did not attend college. Inducted in 1963. President, 1921–1939 National Football League.

A sports promoter and sportswriter, Joe Carr was involved in pro football long before there was an NFL. He founded the Columbus, Ohio, Panhandles in 1904. The Panhandles later featured the six legendary Nesser brothers. Carr was also a pro basketball and minor league baseball executive. In 1921 he became president of the American Professional Football Association, which changed its name to the National Football League in 1922. During his tenure, the league moved from sandlots and rickety ballparks to the nation's largest stadiums. Carr was a pioneer in other areas, too. He introduced the standard player contract and barred collegiate players from signing with NFL teams until their class was graduated. As president, he set down guidelines followed in later years by other NFL leaders. His administration, regarded as strict but fair, ended with his death in 1939.

Guy Chamberlin

End. Coach. 6-2, 210. Born in Blue Springs, Nebraska, January 16, 1894. Died April 4, 1967. Nebraska. Inducted in 1965. 1920 Decatur Staleys, 1921 Chicago Staleys, 1922–23 Canton Bulldogs,1924 Cleveland Bulldogs,1925–26 Frankford Yellowjackets, 1927–28 Chicago Cardinals.

Wherever Guy Chamberlin went, victories seemed to follow. He established a reputation as a fine pass-catcher at a time when passing wasn't commonplace. And he also turned end-around plays into long gainers. It was said he was never hurt, as a collegian or pro. In 1920 and 1921 Chamberlin was paired with another of football's biggest names—George Halas—at end for the Decatur and Chicago Staleys. The ex-Nebraska All-America served as a part-time player as well as a coach from 1922–26, when he helped win four NFL championships with three different teams—Canton, Cleveland, and Frankford. At Cleveland in 1924, Chamberlin was one of the first coaches to institute planned, daily practices. His coaching record was 56-14-5. Chamberlin was named as an end on the all-time team of the 1920s.

Guy Chamberlin

Jack Christiansen

George Connor

Jack Christiansen

Defensive Back. 6-1, 185. Born in Sublette, Kansas, December 20, 1928. Colorado State. Inducted in 1970. 1951–58 Detroit Lions.

As a rookie in 1951, Jack Christiansen set an NFL record by returning four punts for touchdowns. The record stood alone until Denver's Rick Upchurch tied it in 1976. Christiansen's two touchdowns in a single game on punt returns in 1951 set another record that has since been tied. In eight years, Christiansen scored a record eight times on punt returns. He led the NFL in interceptions in 1953 and 1957 on the way to a career total of 46. The Lions' secondary was named "Chris's Crew" after him. He was one of the first defensive specialists to become a dangerous weapon. Opponents passed and punted the ball away from him.

INTERCEPTIONS

Year	Team	No.	Yards	Avg.	Long	TD
1951	Detroit	2	53	26.5	53	0
1952	Detroit	2	47	23.5	32	0
1953	Detroit	12	238	19.8	92t	1
1954	Detroit	8	84	10.5	30t	1
1955	Detroit	3	49	16.3	29	0
1956	Detroit	8	109	13.6	33	0
1957	Detroit	10	137	13.7	52	1
1958	Detroit	1	0	0.0	0	0
Totals		46	717	15.6	92t	3

PUNT RETURNS

Year	Team	No.	Yards	Avg.	Long	TD
1951	Detroit	18	343	19.1	89t	4
1952	Detroit	15	322	21.5	79t	2
1953	Detroit	8	22	2.8	10	0
1954	Detroit	23	225	9.8	61t	1
1955	Detroit	12	87	7.3	42	0
1956	Detroit	6	73	12.2	66t	1
1957	Detroit	3	12	4.0	8	0
1958	Detroit	0	0	0.0	0	0
Totals		85	1,084	12.8	89t	8

KICKOFF RETURNS
59, 1,329 Yards, 22.5 Avg., 46 Long, 0 TD

Earl (Dutch) Clark

Quarterback. 6-0, 185. Born in Fowler, Colorado, October 11, 1906. Colorado College. Inducted in 1963. 1931–32 Portsmouth Spartans, 1934–38 Detroit Lions.

Earl (Dutch) Clark was a scoring threat from anywhere, in any manner. As a tailback in the single wing, he was a legitimate triple-threat. He scored by running, passing, and kicking. He was the last of the NFL's dropkickers. He was the Lions' player-coach in 1937 and 1938. Clark, the only All-America ever produced at tiny Colorado College, made an all-pro team in six of his seven playing seasons. He led NFL scorers three times—in 1932, 1935, and 1936.

RUSHING

Year	Team	Att.	Yards	Avg.	TD
1931	Portsmouth Spartans				
1932	Portsmouth Spartans	111	461	4.2	2
1933	Did not play football				
1934	Detroit	123	763	6.2	6
1935	Detroit	120	412	3.4	4
1936	Detroit	123	628	5.1	6
1937	Detroit	96	468	4.9	5
1938	Detroit	7	25	3.6	0

PASSING
197 Att., 97 Comp., 1,235 Yards, 8 TD, 14 Int.

SCORING
42 TD, 15 FG, 72 PAT, 369 Points

George Connor

Tackle-linebacker. 6-3, 240. Born in Chicago, Illinois, January 1, 1925. Holy Cross, Notre Dame. Inducted in 1975. 1948–1955 Chicago Bears.

George Connor was an All-America at Holy Cross and Notre Dame. He was all-pro at three positions: offensive tackle, defensive tackle, and linebacker. Connor, a native Chicagoan, played for Holy Cross in 1942–43 and for Notre Dame in 1946–47. He was drafted by the New York Giants in 1946, when his original Holy Cross class graduated. The rights to him were traded by the Giants in 1948 to the Boston Yanks for quarterback Paul Governali, and the Yanks in turn traded the rights to Connor to the Bears for end-tackle Mike Jarmaluk. Connor joined the Bears as a two-way tackle. But in 1949 the Bears moved him to linebacker, where he became one of the prototypes for the big, fast, agile, and aggressive men who play that position in today's NFL. He was strong enough to meet and stop the power plays smaller linebackers couldn't handle, and he also was an intelligent player who was good at reading plays. In two years, he made all-pro teams on both offense and defense, and he played in four Pro Bowls. A leg injury ended his career at 30.

Jimmy Conzelman

Quarterback. Coach. Team owner. 6-0, 180. Born in St. Louis, Missouri, March 6, 1898. Died July 31, 1970. Washington, Mo. Inducted in 1964. 1920 Decatur Staleys, 1921–22 Rock Island, Ill., Independents, 1923–24 Milwaukee Badgers; owner-coach, 1925–26 Detroit Panthers, 1927–28, coach, 1929–1930 Providence Steamroller; coach. 1940–42 Chicago Cardinals, 1946–48 Chicago Cardinals.

As a collegian Jimmy Conzelman played in the 1919 Rose Bowl. He then was a teammate of George Halas at Great Lakes Naval Training Station. As a two-way professional player, he starred with five teams, including Halas's 1920 Decatur Staleys, before a knee injury ended his playing career in 1928. That season, as player-coach, he led Providence to an NFL championship. He owned and coached the Detroit Panthers in the mid-1920s. As a non-playing coach, he took a floundering Chicago Cardinals team and won two divisional titles and in 1947, an NFL championship. He was also an actor, author, executive, songwriter, and orator.

Art Donovan

Earl (Dutch) Clark

Jimmy Conzelman

Paddy Driscoll

Bill Dudley

Art Donovan

Defensive tackle. 6-3, 265. Born in Bronx, New York, June 5, 1925. Boston College. Inducted in 1968. 1950 Baltimore Colts, 1951 New York Yanks, 1952 Dallas Texans, 1953–1961 Baltimore Colts.

Art Donovan didn't come into the NFL until he was 25, because of Marine Corps service. After playing on mediocre teams his first three seasons he became a star on Colts' championship teams. He was a complete defensive lineman, outstanding against both the run and the pass. Donovan was on all-pro teams four times and appeared in five Pro Bowls. His father was a boxing referee and his grandfather was a middleweight boxing champion.

John (Paddy) Driscoll

Quarterback. 5-11, 160. Born in Evanston, Illinois, January 11, 1896. Died June 29, 1968. Northwestern. Inducted in 1965. 1920 Decatur Staleys, 1920–25 Chicago Cardinals, 1926–29 Chicago Bears. Head coach, 1956–57 Chicago Bears.

Paddy Driscoll was a teammate of George Halas at Great Lakes Naval Training Station during World War I and joined Halas on the Decatur Staleys in 1920. Driscoll then switched to the Chicago Cardinals, where he became a fine all-around player, particularly adept at kicking. He was an accurate dropkicker and placekicker, who was booed for punting away from Red Grange in Grange's first appearance as a pro. He also was a slick broken-field runner and an accurate passer throwing the large football of his day. Driscoll's contract was sold to the Bears in 1926. He took over as coach in 1956 and 1957, winning a divisional championship his first year. He stayed with the team in various jobs until his death in 1968.

Bill Dudley

Halfback. 5-10, 176. Born in Bluefield, Virginia, December 24, 1921. Virginia. Inducted in 1966. 1942, 1945–46 Pittsburgh Steelers, 1947–49 Detroit Lions, 1950–51, 1953 Washington Redskins.

"Bullet Bill" Dudley threw sidearm passes. He got most of his rushing yardage through effective use of blockers rather than his own speed. He didn't use any approach steps as a placekicker. He simply stood where the ball was to be placed down, swung his right leg back, and then forward as he kicked. Dudley led the NFL in rushing, interceptions, and punt returns in 1946. Dudley was the NFL's first draft choice in 1942 after an All-America career at Virginia, and he rushed for a league-leading 696 yards his first season. Dudley divided his nine-year pro career in three segments with the Steelers, Lions, and Redskins, and he remains among the most popular players ever to perform in those cities. His combined yardage on rushing, receiving, and returns was 8,147.

RUSHING

Year	Team	Att.	Yards	Avg.	Long	TD
1942	Pittsburgh	162	696	4.3	66	5
1943	Military service					
1944	Military service					
1945	Pittsburgh	57	204	3.5	32	3
1946	Pittsburgh	146	604	4.1	41	3
1947	Detroit	80	302	3.8	28	2
1948	Detroit	33	97	2.9	11	0
1949	Detroit	125	402	3.2	26	3
1950	Washington	66	339	5.1	27	1
1951	Washington	91	398	4.4	40	2
1952	Did not play football					
1953	Washington	5	15	3.0	7	0
Totals		765	3,057	4.0	66	19

INTERCEPTIONS

Year	Team	No.	Yards	Avg.	Long	TD
1942	Pittsburgh	3	60	20.0	25	0
1943	Military service					
1944	Military service					
1945	Pittsburgh	2	47	23.5	25	0
1946	Pittsburgh	10	242	24.2	80t	1
1947	Detroit	5	104	20.8	41t	1
1948	Detroit	1	3	3.0	3	0
1949	Detroit	0	0	0.0	0	0
1950	Washington	2	3	1.5	3	0
1951	Washington	0	0	0.0	0	0
1952	Did not play football					
1953	Washington	0	0	0.0	0	0
Totals		23	459	20.0	80t	2

PUNT RETURNS

Year	Team	No.	Yards	Avg.	Long	TD
1942	Pittsburgh	20	271	13.5	47	0
1943	Military service					
1944	Military service					
1945	Pittsburgh	5	20	4.0	6	0
1946	Pittsburgh	27	385	14.2	52	0
1947	Detroit	11	182	16.5	84t	1
1948	Detroit	8	67	8.4	18	0
1949	Detroit	11	199	18.1	67t	1
1950	Washington	12	185	15.4	96t	1
1951	Washington	22	172	7.8	27	0
1952	Did not play football					
1953	Washington	8	34	4.3	16	0
Totals		124	1,515	12.2	96t	3

PASSING
222 Att., 81 Comp., 985 Yards, 6 TD, 17 Int.
RECEIVING
123, 1,383 Yards, 11.2 Avg., 18 TD
PUNTING
191, 38.2 Avg., 4 Blk.
KICKOFF RETURNS
78, 1,743 Yards, 22.3 Avg., 1 TD
SCORING
44 TD, 33 FG, 121 PAT, 484 Points

Glen (Turk) Edwards   *Ray Flaherty*

Danny Fortmann

Len Ford

Bill George

Glen (Turk) Edwards

Tackle, 6-2, 260. Born in Mold, Washington, September 28, 1907. Died January 10, 1973. Washington State. Inducted in 1969. 1932 Boston Braves, 1933–36 Boston Redskins, 1937–1940 Washington Redskins.

At 260 pounds Glen (Turk) Edwards was bigger than most linemen of his time. He made all-pro teams in 1932, 1933, 1936, and 1937. Edwards was outstanding both as an offensive blocker and as a defender, largely because of his unusual quickness and agility. An All-America and Rose Bowl star at Washington State, Edwards played for $150 a game when he joined the Boston Braves in 1932. His career ended in a strange way. After meeting Mel Hein—his former Washington State teammate and New York Giants' center and captain—at the center of the field for a pre-game coin toss, Edwards turned to go back to the bench. But his knee collapsed and he never played again.

Tom Fears

End. 6-2, 215. Born in Los Angeles, California, December 3, 1923. Santa Clara, UCLA. Inducted in 1970. 1948–1956 Los Angeles Rams.

Tom Fears came into pro football projected as a defensive specialist, but in each of his first three seasons, he led the NFL in pass receiving. In 1950, Fears caught 84 passes, a record that stood for a decade. His 18 catches in one game against the Packers that season is still a record. In his career, Fears, who was not only big and fast but ran precise patterns, caught 400 passes for 5,397 yards and 38 touchdowns. He made three touchdown catches as the Rams won a divisional championship in 1950, and in 1951 he scored on a 73-yard pass-and-run play as Los Angeles beat the Cleveland Browns and won its only NFL title.

RECEIVING

Year	Team	No.	Yards	Avg.	Long	TD
1948	Los Angeles	51	698	13.7	80t	4
1949	Los Angeles	77	1,013	13.2	51t	9
1950	Los Angeles	84	1,116	13.3	53t	7
1951	Los Angeles	32	528	16.5	54	3
1952	Los Angeles	48	600	12.5	36	6
1953	Los Angeles	23	278	12.1	31	4
1954	Los Angeles	36	546	15.2	43	3
1955	Los Angeles	44	569	12.9	31	2
1956	Los Angeles	5	49	9.8	18	0
Totals		400	5,397	13.5	80t	38

SCORING
39 TD, 1 FG, 12 PAT, 249 Points

Ray Flaherty

Coach. Born in Spokane, Washington, September 1, 1904. Gonzaga. Inducted in 1976. 1926 Los Angeles Wildcats (AFL), 1927 New York Yankees, 1928–29, 1931–35 New York Giants. Coach, 1936 Boston Redskins, 1937–1942 Washington Redskins, 1946–1948 New York Yankess (AAFC), 1949 Chicago Hornets (AAFC).

Ray Flaherty was an all-pro end with the New York Giants in 1928 and 1932, leading the NFL in pass receptions in 1932, the first season official statistics were kept. He was captain of the Giants and later an assistant coach with New York before taking over the Redskins as head coach in 1936. Flaherty won four Eastern Division titles and two world championships with the Redskins and his record overall was 80-37-5. His All-America Football Conference New York Yankees won divisional titles in 1946 and 1947 but lost the title game to the Cleveland Browns in both years. It was Flaherty who suggested the use of sneakers in the 1934 NFL championship won by the Giants over the Bears. In college at Gonzaga a heel bruise forced him to wear tennis shoes in practice one day and he found they gave him excellent traction on frozen fields.

Len Ford

End. 6-5, 260. Born in Washington, D.C., February 18, 1926. Died March 14, 1972. Michigan. Inducted in 1976. 1948–49 Los Angeles Dons (AAFC), 1950–57 Cleveland Browns, 1958 Green Bay Packers.

Len Ford entered professional football as a two-way end and caught 67 passes for the Los Angeles Dons of the All-America Football Conference in 1948 and 1949. But when the Dons and their league folded, Ford was acquired by Cleveland and used exclusively as a defensive end. He made all-pro teams five consecutive years, 1951–55. Ford was one of the first defensive ends to be known for his all-out pass rush. He often leaped over blockers to get to the quarterback. Ford recovered 20 fumbles during his career, and played in the Pro Bowl four times. After missing much of the 1950 season because of severe facial injuries, he wore a special mask and played an outstanding game in the Browns' 1950 championship victory over the Rams.

Danny Fortmann

Guard. 6-0, 207. Born in Pearl River, New York, April 11, 1916. Colgate. Inducted in 1965. 1936–1943 Chicago Bears.

George Halas of the Chicago Bears reportedly chose Danny Fortmann of Colgate as he was making the last selection of the 1936 college player draft because he liked the sound of his name. Fortmann was small for a lineman even for that day, and his football career also appeared unpromising because he wanted to be a doctor. But he played eight years. He became one of the best linemen of all time, making all-pro six consecutive years, 1938–1943, playing offensively and defensively. A Phi Beta Kappa student in college, Fortmann was one of a group whose members attended medical or dental school while playing for Chicago. Fortmann was a practicing physician before he retired as a Bears' player in 1943. He later served the Los Angeles Rams as team doctor.

Bill George

Linebacker. 6-2, 230. Born in Waynesburg, Pennsylvania, October 27, 1930. Wake Forest. Inducted in 1974. 1952–1965 Chicago Bears, 1966 Los Angeles Rams.

The Chicago Bears thought so highly of Bill George they selected him on the second round of the 1951 draft, when he still had a year of eligibility left. He reported in 1952. He went on to play 14 years, longer than any other Bears' player. He played middle linebacker and called defensive signals. He recovered 16 fumbles and had 18 interceptions. George played in eight Pro Bowl games and made all-pro as many times. Early in his career he placekicked, scoring 26 points on four field goals and 14 extra points.

Tom Fears

Frank Gifford

Otto Graham

Red Grange

Frank Gifford

Halfback. 6-1, 195. Born in Santa Monica, California, August 16, 1930. USC. Inducted in 1977. 1952–1960, 1962–64 New York Giants.

The New York Giants made the NFL title game five times with Frank Gifford on the team. In 1956, the season they won the NFL championship 47–7 over the Bears, Gifford was one of the top players in the league. Gifford, who had been a college star at USC, played running back, flanker, and—early in his career—defensive back for the Giants. He was all-pro in 1955, 1956, 1957, and 1959. He had a spectacular year in 1956, rushing for 819 yards and catching 51 passes for 603 yards, including one for a touchdown from Charlie Conerly in the championship game.

RUSHING

Year	Team	Att.	Yards	Avg.	Long	TD
1952	N.Y. Giants	38	116	3.1	15	0
1953	N.Y. Giants	50	157	3.1	15	2
1954	N.Y. Giants	66	368	5.6	30	2
1955	N.Y. Giants	86	351	4.1	49	3
1956	N.Y. Giants	159	819	5.2	69	5
1957	N.Y. Giants	136	528	3.9	41	5
1958	N.Y. Giants	115	468	4.1	33	8
1959	N.Y. Giants	106	540	5.1	79	3
1960	N.Y. Giants	77	232	3.0	13	4
1961	Did not play football					
1962	N.Y. Giants	2	18	9.0	12	1
1963	N.Y. Giants	4	10	2.5	12	0
1964	N.Y. Giants	1	2	2.0	2t	1
	Totals	840	3,609	4.3	79	34

RECEIVING

Year	Team	No.	Yards	Avg.	Long	TD
1952	N.Y. Giants	5	36	7.2	11	0
1953	N.Y. Giants	18	292	16.2	49t	4
1954	N.Y. Giants	14	154	11.0	35t	4
1955	N.Y. Giants	33	437	13.2	54	4
1956	N.Y. Giants	51	603	11.8	48	4
1957	N.Y. Giants	41	588	14.3	63	4
1958	N.Y. Giants	29	330	11.4	41	2
1959	N.Y. Giants	42	768	18.3	77t	4
1960	N.Y. Giants	24	344	14.3	44t	3
1961	Did not play football					
1962	N.Y. Giants	39	796	20.4	63t	7
1963	N.Y. Giants	42	657	15.6	64	7
1964	N.Y. Giants	29	429	14.8	40t	3
	Totals	367	5,434	14.8	77t	43

PASSING
63 Att., 29 Comp. 823 Yards, 14 TD, 6 Int.

INTERCEPTIONS BY
2, 112 Yards, 56.0 Avg., 1 TD

PUNT RETURNS
24, 118 Yards, 4.9 Avg., 0 TD

KICKOFF RETURNS
18, 480 Yards, 26.7 Avg., 0 TD

SCORING
78 TD, 2 FG, 10 PAT, 484 Points

Otto Graham

Quarterback. 6-1, 195. Born in Waukegan, Illinois, December 6, 1921. Northwestern. Inducted in 1965. 1946–49 Cleveland Browns (AAFC), 1950–55 Cleveland Browns.

Otto Graham was converted from a college single wing tailback to a T formation quarterback in pro football. Graham became the top-ranked passer of his time. In 10 seasons with the Browns, he led them into 10 championship games. He led the All-America Football Conference in passing each of his four years in that league, and the NFL twice. In the 1950 NFL championship game, Graham threw for four touchdowns. In the 1954 title game, he threw for three and ran for three. In addition to becoming a star football player at Northwestern, Graham was a basketball All-America.

PASSING

Year	Team	Att.	Comp.	Yards	TD	Int.
1946	Cleveland (AAFC)	174	95	1,834	17	5
1947	Cleveland (AAFC)	269	163	2,753	25	11
1948	Cleveland (AAFC)	333	173	2,713	25	15
1949	Cleveland (AAFC)	285	161	2,785	19	10
1950	Cleveland	253	137	1,943	14	20
1951	Cleveland	265	147	2,205	17	16
1952	Cleveland	364	181	2,816	20	24
1953	Cleveland	258	167	2,722	11	9
1954	Cleveland	240	142	2,092	11	17
1955	Cleveland	185	98	1,721	15	8
	NFL Totals	1,565	872	13,499	88	94

RUSHING
306 Att., 682 Yards, 2.2 Avg., 36 Long, 33 TD

Red Grange

Halfback. 6-0, 185. Born in Forksville, Pennsylvania, June 13, 1903. Illinois. Inducted in 1963. 1925 Chicago Bears, 1926 New York Yankees (AFL), 1927 New York Yankees, 1929–1934 Chicago Bears.

Red Grange's reputation as a runner was already established when he joined the Chicago Bears on Thanksgiving Day in 1925. The man nicknamed "the Galloping Ghost" had been one of the most famous college players ever, and his name brought the first huge crowds to pro football, perhaps assuring a successful future for the sport. Grange and the Bears went on an 18-game coast-to-coast tour after the 1925 season, giving the game a display it had never had. Grange and his personal manager, C.C. (Cash and Carry) Pyle, established the first American Football League in 1926. It folded after one season and Grange and other players joined the NFL. A knee injury caused Grange to miss all of the 1928 season and robbed him of much elusiveness, but he remained a fine defensive player and a big box-office attraction.

Forrest Gregg

Tackle. 6-4, 250. Born in Sulphur Springs, Texas, October 18, 1933. Southern Methodist. Inducted in 1977. 1956, 1958–1970 Green Bay Packers, 1971 Dallas Cowboys.

Forrest Gregg joined Green Bay in 1956, and his career was interrupted by 21 months of military service. Gregg came back in 1958, Vince Lombardi became Packers' coach in 1959, and they made one of the most dramatic turnarounds in NFL history. Gregg was a key player at tackle and guard, and was named to the Pro Bowl seven out of eight years, nine times in all. He played on three Super Bowl-winning teams, two in Green Bay and one in Dallas, his last season as an active player.

Lou Groza

Tackle-Kicker. 6-3, 250. Born in Martin's Ferry, Ohio, January 25, 1924. Ohio State. Inducted in 1974. 1946–49 Cleveland Browns (AAFC), 1950–59 Cleveland Browns, 1961–67 Cleveland Browns.

Lou (the Toe) Groza was one of the greatest kickers in NFL history. He scored 1,349 points in the NFL. His last-seconds field goal won the 1950 NFL championship game 30–28 for the Browns over the Rams. Altogether, he played in 13 championship games, four in the All-America Football Conference, nine in the NFL. He played in nine Pro Bowls. And he was more than just a kicker. He was also an excellent tackle, six times all-pro, pass blocking for Otto Graham and opening holes for Marion Motley, Dub Jones, Bobby Mitchell, and Jim Brown. A back injury forced him to retire in 1960 but he came back in 1961 and played strictly as a kicker for seven more years.

SCORING

Year	Team	FG	PAT	Points
1946	Cleveland (AAFC)	13-29	45-47	84
1947	Cleveland (AAFC)	7-21	39-42	60
1948	Cleveland (AAFC)	8-19	51-52	75
1949	Cleveland (AAFC)	2- 7	34-35	40
1950	Cleveland	13-19	29-29	*74
1951	Cleveland	10-23	43-43	73
1952	Cleveland	19-33	32-32	89
1953	Cleveland	23-26	39-40	108
1954	Cleveland	16-24	37-38	85
1955	Cleveland	11-22	44-45	77
1956	Cleveland	11-20	18-18	51
1957	Cleveland	15-22	32-32	77
1958	Cleveland	8-19	36-38	60
1959	Cleveland	5-16	33-37	48
1960	Retired from football			
1961	Cleveland	16-23	37-38	85
1962	Cleveland	14-31	33-35	75
1963	Cleveland	15-23	40-43	85
1964	Cleveland	22-33	49-49	115
1965	Cleveland	16-25	45-45	93
1966	Cleveland	9-23	51-52	78
1967	Cleveland	11-23	43-43	76
NFL Totals		234-405	641-657	1,349

* Includes a touchdown.

Joe Guyon

Halfback. 6-1, 180. Born in Mahnomen, Minnesota, November 26, 1892. Died November 27, 1971. Carlisle, Georgia Tech. Inducted in 1966. 1920 Canton Bulldogs, 1921 Cleveland Indians, 1922–23 Oorang Indians, 1924 Rock Island, Ill., Independents, 1924–25 Kansas City Cowboys, 1927 New York Giants.

The career of Joe Guyon, a Chippewa Indian from Minnesota, roughly paralleled that of Jim Thorpe. Guyon played with Thorpe at Carlisle Indian School. Then Guyon was an All-America tackle at Georgia Tech. He was a triple-threat halfback in the pros. He played on four different teams with Thorpe. In 1927, a touchdown pass by Guyon gave the New York Giants a victory over the Chicago Bears and won the NFL championship for the Giants. Guyon didn't confine his athletic activity to football. He played minor league baseball in the summers—when football started later and the baseball season was shorter. A baseball injury in 1928 ended Guyon's pro football career.

George Halas

End. Coach. Team Owner. Born in Chicago, Illinois, February 2, 1895. Illinois. Inducted in 1963. 1920 Decatur Staleys, 1921 Chicago Staleys, 1922–29 Chicago Bears; coach 1933–1942, 1946–1955, 1958–67 Chicago Bears. Chairman of the board of the Bears.

George Halas's career parallels the history of the National Football League. Just out of college at Illinois, Halas was in Canton, Ohio, on September 17, 1920 when the NFL's organizational meeting was held. He remained active in the administration of the Chicago Bears—the only man in the NFL in 1977 to have been associated with it since its inception. Halas, known as "Papa Bear," coached the Chicago team for 40 seasons and his 325 NFL victories are the most by any coach. Before settling into coaching and administration, Halas was a top two-way end for 11 seasons. In 1923, he picked up a Jim Thorpe fumble and ran it back 98 yards for a touchdown, an NFL record for a fumble return until it was broken in 1972. He coached the Bears to eight divisional titles and six NFL championships.

Ed Healey

Tackle. 6-3, 220. Born in Indian Orchard, Massachusetts, December 28, 1894. Dartmouth. Inducted in 1964. 1920–22 Rock Island, Ill., Independents, 1922–27 Chicago Bears.

After playing at Dartmouth, Ed Healey went into coaching—until he decided to try out in the new professional league at Rock Island, Illinois in 1920 and made the team. While playing for the Rock Island Independents in 1922, Healey impressed George Halas and the Chicago coach made one of the first player deals to get him. Healey's contract was transferred to the Bears for $100. Halas later called Healey "the most versatile tackle ever." Healey's teammate, Red Grange, said, "He loved to come downfield under a punt. He was an absolutely vicious player." Healey was outstanding in the Bears' long barnstorming tour after the 1925 season. The tour was set up to showcase Grange, but it turned Healey into a star, too.

Forrest Gregg

Lou Groza

Joe Guyon

George Halas

Ed Healey

W. (Pete) Henry

Mel Hein

Arnie Herber

Bill Hewitt

Mel Hein

Center. 6-2, 225. Born in Redding, California, August 22, 1909. Washington State. Inducted in 1963. 1931–1945 New York Giants.

Mel Hein was outstanding as a center, guard, and tackle at Washington State, but he had to write to three NFL teams offering his services before he was signed by the New York Giants for $150 a game. He became the Giants' regular center and started there and at linebacker for 15 seasons. He never missed a game and he rarely played less than the full 60 minutes. He was a strong blocker despite having to deliver accurate long snaps before blocking opposing linemen. On defense, he covered passes and tackled as well as any player in the league. He was all-pro for eight consecutive seasons, 1933–1940.

Wilbur (Pete) Henry

Tackle. 6-0, 250. Born in Mansfield, Ohio, October 31, 1897. Died February 7, 1952. Washington & Jefferson. Inducted in 1963. 1920–23, 1925–26 Canton Bulldogs, 1927 New York Giants, 1927–28 Pottsville Maroons.

Wilbur Henry was a hefty player nicknamed "Fats." But he was a quick and powerful man who did many things well. He played tackle, but sometimes he was used as a power ball carrier, or as the receiver on a tackle-eligible pass play. He was called the best kick-blocker of his time. He also kicked, sharing the record for the longest dropkick field goal (50 yards) with fellow Hall of Famer Paddy Driscoll. His 94-yard punt was an unofficial NFL record for nearly half a century. A three-time college All-America at Washington & Jefferson, Henry signed with the Canton Bulldogs the day the NFL was organized in that Ohio town, and he was an offensive and defensive standout as the team won consecutive NFL titles in 1922 and 1923.

Arnie Herber

Quarterback. 6-1, 200. Born in Green Bay, Wisconsin, April 2, 1910. Died October 14, 1969. Wisconsin, Regis College. Inducted in 1966. 1930–1940 Green Bay Packers, 1944–45 New York Giants.

Pro football's first heralded passing combination was quarterback Arnie Herber of the Green Bay Packers to receiver Don Hutson in the 1930s. Herber pre-dated Hutson by five seasons, and had built a reputation as a star by the time Hutson arrived. In the days when the forward pass was mostly a desperation play, Herber and the Green Bay Packers used it anytime and anywhere with great success. He was especially effective throwing long. Herber led the Packers to four NFL championships, and was the league's top passer three seasons—1932, 1934, and 1936. He retired in 1940, but came back in 1944 with the New York Giants and led them to the Eastern Division title. His lifetime statistics show 8,033 yards passing and 66 touchdown passes, despite the fact he had small fingers and had to pass the melon-shaped ball the first three seasons of his career.

PASSING

Year	Team	Att.	Comp.	Yards	TD	Int.
1930	Green Bay					
1931	Green Bay					
1932	Green Bay	101	37	639	9	9
1933	Green Bay	126	56	656	4	12
1934	Green Bay	115	42	799	8	12
1935	Green Bay	106	40	729	8	6
1936	Green Bay	173	77	1,239	11	13
1937	Green Bay	104	47	676	7	10
1938	Green Bay	55	22	336	4	4
1939	Green Bay	139	57	1,107	8	9
1940	Green Bay	89	38	560	5	7
1941	Retired from football					
1942	Retired from football					
1943	Retired from football					
1944	N.Y. Giants	86	36	651	6	8
1945	N.Y. Giants	80	35	641	9	8

Bill Hewitt

End. 5-11, 191. Born in Bay City, Michigan, October 8, 1909. Died January 14, 1947. Michigan. Inducted in 1971. 1932–36 Chicago Bears, 1937–39 Philadelphia Eagles, 1943 Phil-Pitt Steagles.

Bill Hewitt was not especially big but he was an intense player. His initial charge was so quick opponents often claimed he was offside. Hewitt played without a helmet from 1932–39 and his return to the league from retirement in 1943 may have prompted the rules change making the wearing of helmets mandatory. He was one of the first linemen to pursue all over the field. He made an all-pro team with two different clubs, the Chicago Bears in 1933 and 1934 and the Philadelphia Eagles in 1936 and 1937. He had perhaps his finest game in the NFL when he led the Bears to victory in the 1933 championship game against the New York Giants. He was killed in an automobile accident in Pennsylvania in January, 1947.

RECEIVING

Year	Team	No.	Yards	Avg.	TD
1932	Chi. Bears				
1933	Chi. Bears	16	274	17.1	2
1934	Chi. Bears	10	151	15.1	5
1935	Chi. Bears	5	80	16.0	0
1936	Chi. Bears	15	358	23.9	6
1937	Philadelphia	16	197	12.3	5
1938	Philadelphia	18	237	13.2	4
1939	Philadelphia	15	243	16.2	1
1940	Retired from football				
1941	Retired from football				
1942	Retired from football				
1943	Phil-Pitt	2	22	11.0	0

Clarke Hinkle

Fullback. 5-11, 201. Born in Toronto, Ohio, April 10, 1912. Bucknell. Inducted in 1964. 1932–1941 Green Bay Packers.

Hinkle has been called the fiercest competitor ever in his sport. He had stirring personal duels with Bronko Nagurski of the Bears. Hinkle was a battering-ram runner and a hard-tackling linebacker but he also passed, punted, placekicked, and caught passes and defended against them. An all-pro choice four times, he was the NFL's all-time leading ground gainer when he retired, with 3,860 yards. He had a 43.4-yard punting average. Hinkle also led the NFL in scoring in 1938 and in field goals in 1940 and 1941.

RUSHING

Year	Team	Att.	Yards	Avg.	Long	TD
1932	Green Bay	95	331	3.4	27	3
1933	Green Bay	139	413	2.9	33	4
1934	Green Bay	144	359	2.4	32	1
1935	Green Bay	77	273	3.5	17	2
1936	Green Bay	100	476	4.7	57	5
1937	Green Bay	129	552	4.2	41	5
1938	Green Bay	114	299	2.6	46	3
1939	Green Bay	135	381	2.7	29	5
1940	Green Bay	109	383	3.5	31	2
1941	Green Bay	129	393	3.0	20	5
Totals		1,171	3,860	3.2	57	35

RECEIVING
49, 537 Yards, 11.0 Avg., 9 TD
SCORING
42 TD, 26 FG, 28 PAT, 358 Points

Elroy (Crazylegs) Hirsch

Halfback-End. 6-2, 190. Born in Wausau, Wisconsin, June 17, 1923. Wisconsin, Michigan. Inducted in 1968. 1946–48 Chicago Rockets (AAFC), 1949–1957 Los Angeles Rams.

Elroy Hirsch is remembered mostly as one of the most spectacular pass receivers ever to play in the NFL but he got his nickname—"Crazylegs"— because of his unusual running style. He was one of the first backs to be moved out wide and made a flanker, with the Los Angeles Rams in 1950. A star with the Chicago Rockets of the All-America Football Conference before coming to the NFL, Hirsch teamed with fellow Hall of Famers Tom Fears, Bob Waterfield, and Norm Van Brocklin to set scoring records that still stand. In 1951, Hirsch caught 66 passes for 1,495 yards and 17 touchdowns. He was honored as the flanker on the all-time NFL team for the first 50 years in 1969. He ended his career in 1957 with 387 catches for 7,209 yards and 60 touchdowns. He played the title role in his film biography and starred in two other movies.

RECEIVING

Year	Team	No.	Yards	Avg.	Long	TD
1946	Chicago Rockets (AAFC)	27	347	12.9		3
1947	Chicago Rockets (AAFC)	10	282	28.2		3
1948	Chicago Rockets (AAFC)	7	101	14.4		1
1949	Los Angeles	22	326	14.8	48t	4
1950	Los Angeles	42	687	16.4	58t	7
1951	Los Angeles	66	1,495	22.7	91t	17
1952	Los Angeles	25	590	23.6	84t	4
1953	Los Angeles	61	941	15.4	70	4
1954	Los Angeles	35	720	20.6	66	3
1955	Los Angeles	25	460	18.4	72t	2
1956	Los Angeles	35	603	17.2	76t	6
1957	Los Angeles	32	477	14.9	45	6
NFL Totals		343	6,299	18.4	91t	53

RUSHING
74 Att., 317 Yards, 4.3 Avg., 51 Long, 2 TD

Cal Hubbard

Tackle. 6-5, 250. Born in Keytesville, Missouri, October 11, 1900. Centenary, Geneva. Inducted in 1963. 1927–28 New York Giants, 1929–1933, 1935 Green Bay Packers, 1936 New York Giants, 1936 Pittsburgh Pirates.

Cal Hubbard is the only man to be enshrined in both the Pro Football Hall of Fame and the Baseball Hall of Fame. He was the most feared lineman of his era and one of the few early pros who was as large as today's players. As a rookie in 1927, he was a keystone in the New York Giants' championship defense, which limited opponents to 20 points for the season. A powerful blocker, he stood out on defense, too, being one of the first players to pull out of the line and pursue. He was selected as a tackle on the NFL's all-time team, chosen in 1969. After retiring from football, Hubbard was a respected American League baseball umpire and became umpire-in-chief.

Lamar Hunt

Team Owner. Born in El Dorado, Arkansas, August 2, 1932. Southern Methodist. Inducted in 1972. 1960–62 Dallas Texans, 1963–1977 Kansas City Chiefs.

Lamar Hunt failed several times in a bid to gain an NFL franchise for his home state of Texas in the 1950s. He formed the American Football League in 1959, and it began play in 1960. Hunt was owner and founder of the Dallas Texans. After a difficult struggle the league merged with the NFL in 1966. Hunt moved the Dallas franchise to Kansas City in 1963, and it became one of football's strongest organizations, winning the Super Bowl IV championship in 1970. Hunt once played football behind Raymond Berry at Southern Methodist. When he was elected to the Hall of Fame, he said it was a triumph symbolic of all the officials, coaches, and players of the AFL.

E. (Crazylegs) Hirsch

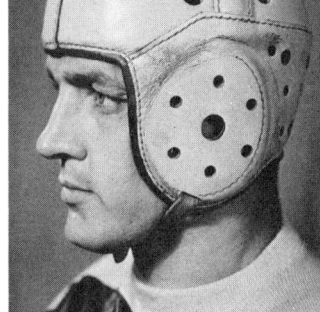

Cal Hubbard　　　　*Clarke Hinkle*

Don Hutson

F. (Bruiser) Kinard

Lamar Hunt

Walt Kiesling

Earl (Curly) Lambeau

Don Hutson

End. 6-1, 180. Born in Pine Bluff, Arkansas, January 31, 1913. Alabama. Inducted in 1963. 1935–1945 Green Bay Packers.

Don Hutson entered the NFL in the mid-1930s but he was similar to today's receivers in his style of play. He dominated the NFL. He was an all-pro nine times and he led the NFL in receptions eight times. Five times he topped the NFL's scorers. He caught at least one pass in 95 straight games from 1937 through 1945, a record that lasted almost a quarter century. During his 11-year career. Hutson caught 488 passes, 99 of them for touchdowns. He was also an accomplished kicker. He played in the one-platoon era and his defensive position was end for awhile, but he switched to safety so he would risk injury less often, and to use his ball-hawking ability there.

RECEIVING

Year	Team	No.	Yards	Avg.	Long	TD
1935	Green Bay	18	420	23.3	83	6
1936	Green Bay	34	536	15.8	87	8
1937	Green Bay	41	552	13.5	78	7
1938	Green Bay	32	548	17.1	54	9
1939	Green Bay	34	846	24.9	92	6
1940	Green Bay	45	664	14.8	36	7
1941	Green Bay	58	738	12.7	45	10
1942	Green Bay	74	1,211	16.4	73	17
1943	Green Bay	47	776	16.5	79	11
1944	Green Bay	58	866	14.9	55t	9
1945	Green Bay	47	834	17.7	75t	9
Totals		488	7.991	16.4	92	99

SCORING

Year	Team	TD	FG	PAT	Points
1935	Green Bay	7	0-	1-	43
1936	Green Bay	9	0-	0-	54
1937	Green Bay	7	0-	0-	42
1938	Green Bay	9	0-	3-	57
1939	Green Bay	6	0-0	2-	38
1940	Green Bay	7	0-0	15-	57
1941	Green Bay	12	1-2	20-24	95
1942	Green Bay	17	1-4	33-34	138
1943	Green Bay	12	3-5	36-36	117
1944	Green Bay	9	0-3	31-33	85
1945	Green Bay	10	2-4	31-35	97
Totals		105	7-	172-	823

RUSHING
62 Att., 284 Yards, 4.6 Avg., 27 Long, 3 TD

INTERCEPTIONS
30, 389 Yards, 13.0 Avg., 84 Long, 1 TD

Walt Kiesling

Guard. Coach. 6-2, 245. Born in St. Paul, Minnesota, March 27, 1903. Died March 2, 1962. St. Thomas (Minnesota). Inducted in 1966. 1926–27 Duluth Eskimos, 1928 Pottsville Maroons, 1929-1933 Chicago Cardinals, 1934 Chicago Bears, 1935–36 Green Bay Packers, 1937–38 Pittsburgh Pirates; coach, 1939–1942 Pittsburgh Steelers; Cocoach 1943 Phil-Pitt, 1944 Card-Pitt.; 1954–56 Pittsburgh Steelers.

As a player and coach, Walt Kiesling was in the NFL 34 years. He spent 13 of those years as a guard for six different teams. As a coach, he spent most of his time as a Steelers' assistant, but also was head coach of the team twice, a dozen years apart. And during World War II, he was co-head coach of the 1943 Phil-Pitt and 1944 Card-Pitt merged teams. Kiesling helped give perennial loser Pittsburgh its first winning season in 1942. As a player he had a tackle's size but was used at guard offensively because of his quickness in pulling to lead plays. Defensively, he was one of the league's best. His finest playing years were with the Cardinals in 1929–1933 when he made all-pro teams almost every season, and 1934, when he starred for an unbeaten Chicago Bears' team.

Frank (Bruiser) Kinard

Tackle. 6-1, 210. Born in Pelahatchie, Mississippi, October 23, 1914. Mississippi. Inducted in 1971. 1938–1944 Brooklyn Dodgers-Tigers, 1946–47 New York Yankees (AAFC).

A two-time All America at Mississippi, Frank (Bruiser) Kinard was the second-round draft choice of the Brooklyn Dodgers in 1938. At 6 foot 1 inch and 210 pounds, he was small for the tackle position, but he also was tough, aggressive, fast, and durable. A 60-minute performer, he was outstanding as a blocker and smothering as a tackler, and was out of a game with injuries only once in his nine-year career. He was the first man to be an all-pro in both the NFL (1940, 1941, 1943, and 1944) and the All-America Football Conference (1946). In 1945, he was named all-Armed Services. Kinard came from a football family. His brother, George, was a teammate on the Dodgers. And a younger brother, Billy, also played pro ball.

Earl (Curly) Lambeau

Coach. Born in Green Bay, Wisconsin, April 9, 1898. Died June 1, 1965. Notre Dame. Inducted in 1963. 1919–1949 Green Bay Packers, 1950–51 Chicago Cardinals, 1952–53 Washington Redskins.

Earl (Curly) Lambeau and the Green Bay Packers joined the NFL in 1921. Lambeau, who had played at Notre Dame under Knute Rockne, was a fine passer, and is credited with having been the first coach to exploit the forward pass as an important part of a professional team's offense. Later, he had players such as Arnie Herber and Cecil Isbell throwing to receivers such as Don Hutson and Johnny Blood (McNally). The Packers won six NFL championships under Lambeau, and his 231 career victories are second only to George Halas. In addition to having been a successful coach, Lambeau was a star player for nearly a dozen years. The support of the citizens and Lambeau's commitment to the team helped it survive as the NFL's only "town team."

Dante Lavelli

D. (Night Train) Lane

Dick (Night Train) Lane

Defensive Back. 6-2. 210. Born in Austin, Texas, April 16, 1928. Scottsbluff Junior College. Inducted in 1974. 1952–53 Los Angeles Rams, 1954–59 Chicago Cardinals, 1960–65 Detroit Lions.

Dick (Night Train) Lane tried out for the Los Angeles Rams' team in 1952. He had only one season of junior college football and some service ball as experience. But the Rams took a chance, signing him to a free-agent contract. Lane became a great player. As a rookie, he set an NFL record of 14 interceptions in one season. The Rams traded him to the Chicago Cardinals, where he continued to play all-pro caliber defensive back and saw occasional activity as a receiver. One of those appearances got him into the NFL record book again. He was on the receiving end in a 98-yard pass play. Lane was traded again to Detroit. Lane was all-pro five times and played in six Pro Bowls. He retired in 1965 with a total of 68 interceptions. He was voted to the all-time NFL team in 1969.

INTERCEPTIONS

Year	Team	No.	Yards	Avg.	Long	TD
1952	Los Angeles	14	298	21.3	80	2
1953	Los Angeles	3	9	3.0	8	0
1954	Chi. Cardinals	10	181	18.1	64	0
1955	Chi. Cardinals	6	69	11.5	26	0
1956	Chi. Cardinals	7	206	29.4	66t	1
1957	Chi. Cardinals	2	47	23.5	33	0
1958	Chi. Cardinals	2	0	0.0	0	0
1959	Chi. Cardinals	3	125	41.7	69	1
1960	Detroit	5	102	20.4	80t	1
1961	Detroit	6	73	12.2	32	0
1962	Detroit	4	16	4.0	13	0
1963	Detroit	5	70	14.0	33	0
1964	Detroit	1	11	11.0	11	0
1965	Detroit	0	0	0.0	0	0
Totals		68	1,207	17.8	80t	5

Dante Lavelli

End. 6-0, 199. Born in Hudson, Ohio, February 23, 1923. Ohio State. Inducted in 1975. 1946–49 Cleveland Browns (AAFC), 1950–56 Cleveland Browns.

Dante Lavelli was another player who didn't figure to star in the National Football League. When he reported to the Cleveland Browns' camp in 1946 (when the team was in the All-America Football Conference) he had played in only three varsity games at Ohio State, then served with the U.S. Infantry for several years. But he became a starter his first season, and led the AAFC in receptions. Early in his career he teamed with Mac Speedie to give the Browns a set of great pass catching ends. Lavelli had unusually large hands, and rarely dropped a ball. In the Browns' first NFL championship game, in 1950, he caught all 11 passes Otto Graham threw him. And he has a record 24 receptions in championship play. His last year, 1956, was the only one in which Lavelli didn't play in a championship game. He made all-pro teams four times, twice each in the AAFC and NFL.

INTERCEPTIONS

Year	Team	No.	Yards	Avg.	Long	TD
1946	Cleveland (AAFC)	40	843	21.8		8
1947	Cleveland (AAFC)	49	799	16.3		9
1948	Cleveland (AAFC)	25	463	18.5		5
1949	Cleveland (AAFC)	28	475	17.0		7
1950	Cleveland	37	565	15.3	43	5
1951	Cleveland	43	586	13.6	47	6
1952	Cleveland	21	336	16.0	41	4
1953	Cleveland	45	783	17.4	55t	6
1954	Cleveland	47	802	17.1	64	7
1955	Cleveland	31	492	15.9	49	4
1956	Cleveland	20	344	17.2	68t	1
NFL Totals		244	3,908	16.0	68t	33

Bobby Layne

Bobby Layne

Quarterback. 6-2, 190. Born in Santa Anna, Texas, December 19, 1926. Texas. Inducted in 1967. 1948 Chicago Bears, 1949 New York Bulldogs, 1950–58 Detroit Lions, 1958–1962 Pittsburgh Steelers.

Bobby Layne was as good a clutch player as any who ever played the game. He was a master of the two-minute offense at the end of a half or a game. After spending a year each with the Chicago Bears and the New York Bulldogs, the fun-loving Texan came into his own in Detroit, where he led the Lions to four divisional and three NFL championships in the 1950s. After being traded to Pittsburgh, Layne gave that long-struggling franchise its most potent offense until the Steelers' recent championships. He completed 1,814 passes in 3,700 attempts for 26,768 yards and 196 touchdowns but his greatest skills were in more intangible areas—play-calling and leadership.

PASSING

Year	Team	Att.	Comp.	Yards	TD	Int.
1948	Chi. Bears	52	16	232	3	2
1949	N.Y. Bulldogs	299	155	1,796	9	18
1950	Detroit	336	152	2,323	16	18
1951	Detroit	332	152	2,403	26	23
1952	Detroit	287	139	1,999	19	20
1953	Detroit	273	125	2,088	16	21
1954	Detroit	246	135	1,818	14	12
1955	Detroit	270	143	1,830	11	17
1956	Detroit	244	129	1,909	9	17
1957	Detroit	179	87	1,169	6	12
1958	Detroit	26	12	171	0	2
	Pittsburgh	268	133	2,339	14	10
1959	Pittsburgh	297	142	1,986	20	21
1960	Pittsburgh	209	103	1,814	13	17
1961	Pittsburgh	149	75	1,205	11	16
1962	Pittsburgh	233	116	1,686	9	17
Totals		3,700	1,814	26,768	196	243

RUSHING
611 Att., 2,451 Yards, 4.0 Avg., 36 Long, 25 TD

SCORING
25 TD, 34 FG, 124 PAT, 372 Points

Sid Luckman

Roy (Link) Lyman

Vince Lombardi

Tim Mara

Gino Marchetti

G. Preston Marshall

Vince Lombardi

Coach. Born in Brooklyn, New York, June 11, 1913. Died: September 3, 1970. Fordham. Inducted in 1971. 1959–1967 Green Bay Packers, 1969 Washington Redskins.

Vince Lombardi didn't get his first head coaching job above the high school level until he was 45. But he turned the Green Bay Packers into league champions within two years and built one of the dynasties of sports. In nine seasons he compiled an 89–29–4 record, as his Packers won five NFL titles. In addition, his club won the first two Super Bowls. Lombardi was a strict coach who thought execution, rather than razzle-dazzle, was the way to win. He retired as Green Bay coach after Super Bowl II. After sitting out the 1968 season, Lombardi returned to coach the Washington Redskins in 1969 and gave them their first winning season, 7–5–2, since 1953. Lombardi died of cancer in 1970.

Sid Luckman

Quarterback. 6-0, 195. Born in Brooklyn, New York, November 21, 1916. Columbia. Inducted in 1965. 1939–1950 Chicago Bears.

After an All-America career as a tailback at Columbia, Sid Luckman became the first of pro football's great T formation quarterbacks. He was a rare combination of mental and athletic brilliance. He mastered the Bears' highly-complex offense and executed it flawlessly. The near-perfect performance of Luckman and the Bears in a 73–0 win over Washington in the 1940 title game caused a sudden switch to the T formation with man-in-motion at all levels of football. Luckman was all-pro five times. He was a superb ball-handler and play-caller and also excelled on defense and as a punter.

PASSING

Year	Team	Att.	Comp.	Yards	TD	Int.
1939	Chi. Bears	51	23	636	5	4
1940	Chi. Bears	105	48	941	4	9
1941	Chi. Bears	119	68	1,181	9	6
1942	Chi. Bears	105	57	1,024	10	13
1943	Chi. Bears	202	110	2,194	28	12
1944	Chi. Bears	143	71	1,018	11	12
1945	Chi. Bears	217	117	1,727	14	10
1946	Chi. Bears	229	110	1,826	17	16
1947	Chi. Bears	323	176	2,712	24	31
1948	Chi. Bears	163	89	1,047	13	14
1949	Chi. Bears	50	22	200	1	3
1950	Chi. Bears	37	13	180	1	2
Totals		1,744	904	14,686	137	132

RUSHING
204 Att., −239 Yards, −1.2 Avg., 40 Long, 4 TD
INTERCEPTIONS
17, 310 Yards, 18.2 Avg., 54 Long, 2 TD
PUNTING
230, 8,842 Yards, 38.4 Avg., 78 Long, 1 Blk.

Roy (Link) Lyman

Tackle. 6-2, 252. Born in Table Rock, Nebraska, November 30, 1898. Died December 28, 1972. Nebraska. Inducted in 1964. 1922–23 Canton Bulldogs, 1924 Cleveland Bulldogs, 1925 Canton Bulldogs, 1925 Frankford Yellowjackets, 1926–28, 1930–31, 1933–34 Chicago Bears.

Roy (Link) Lyman is credited with pioneering the "stunting and gambling" style of tackle play. At times, he would change positions as the ball was about to be snapped, a maneuver unheard of at the time. Lyman was a standout on four NFL championship teams, the 1922 and 1923 Canton Bulldogs, 1924 Cleveland Bulldogs, and 1933 Chicago Bears. He joined the Bears for Red Grange's barnstorming tour in 1925, and remained with them the rest of his career. In 16 seasons of college and pro ball, he was on only one losing team. He retired at 36, when he was still an effective player.

Tim Mara

Owner, Born in New York, New York, July 29, 1887. Died February 17, 1959. Did not attend college. Inducted in 1963. 1925–1959 New York Giants.

Reasoning that "a New York franchise for anything ought to be worth $2,500," Tim Mara paid that price to buy a team in the NFL in 1925. The move gave the league the major status it sought and needed; it had been centered in the small cities of the Midwest. Mara, hampered by bad weather, suffered heavy financial losses in 1925 but when Red Grange and the Bears appeared at the Polo Grounds that December, the Giants' fortunes improved. Mara still faced a struggle, however. He had to fight the first American Football League in 1926 and in 1946, the All-America Football Conference. Mara's Giants survived the confrontations as one of the NFL's most stable franchises. Under Mara, the team won three NFL and eight divisional titles.

Gino Marchetti

Defensive end. 6-4, 245. Born in Antioch, California, January 2, 1927. San Francisco. Inducted in 1972. 1952 Dallas Texans, 1953–1964, 1966 Baltimore Colts.

Gino Marchetti was selected the best defensive end in the NFL's first 50 years in 1969. He played his position as few have, and was especially adept at rushing the passer. Marchetti played in 10 Pro Bowls. He made all-pro teams for seven years, 1956–1962. Marchetti was first tried as an offensive tackle in the pros but he quickly found a place at defensive end. More than anyone, he proved that speed could be coupled with size at that position. As a collegian, Marchetti played on the great University of San Francisco teams that sent nearly a dozen players to the pros, including fellow Hall of Famer Ollie Matson.

George Preston Marshall

Team Owner. Born in Grafton, West Virginia, October 11, 1897. Died August 9, 1969. Randolph-Macon. Inducted in 1963. 1932 Boston Braves, 1933–36 Boston Redskins, 1937–1969 Washington Redskins.

George Preston Marshall brought showmanship to the NFL. He popularized the marching band and the spectacular halftime show. He was an early exponent of publicity and public relations. He conceived a far-flung radio network that carried Redskins' games throughout the South, and later covered the same area with televised games. But Marshall was more than just a showman. It was at his suggestion—despite the fact he'd been in the league just one season—that most of the sweeping rules changes of 1933 and 1934 took place. The changes, which opened up the game, included a set schedule, two divisions with a championship playoff, moving the goal posts to the goal line, and a slimmed-down football for more passing.

Ollie Matson

Ollie Matson

Halfback. 6-2, 220. Born in Trinity, Texas, May 1, 1930. San Francisco. Inducted in 1972. 1952 Chicago Cardinals, 1954–58 Chicago Cardinals, 1959–1962 Los Angeles Rams, 1963 Detroit Lions, 1964–66 Philadelphia Eagles.

While others were preparing for their rookie seasons in the NFL, Ollie Matson was competing in the 1952 Olympics, where he won a bronze medal in the 400-meter run. Playing for the Chicago Cardinals that fall, he made more than 1,000 yards in total offense—rushing, receiving, and returning punts and kickoffs. He went on to become one of the most versatile and productive backs in pro history. The Los Angeles Rams so coveted him that in 1959 they traded nine players to get him. During his career he was constantly shifted from position to position and platoon to platoon, and he never played on a championship team. But he retired with 12,844 combined net yards—3,746 of them on kickoff returns, on which he was very dangerous. He was an all-pro four consecutive years, 1954–57.

RUSHING

Year	Team	Att.	Yards	Avg.	Long	TD
1952	Chi. Cardinals	96	344	3.6	25	3
1953	Military service					
1954	Chi. Cardinals	101	506	5.0	79t	4
1955	Chi. Cardinals	109	475	4.4	54	1
1956	Chi. Cardinals	192	924	4.8	79t	5
1957	Chi. Cardinals	134	577	4.3	56t	6
1958	Chi. Cardinals	129	505	3.9	55t	5
1959	Los Angeles	161	863	5.4	50	6
1960	Los Angeles	61	170	2.9	27	1
1961	Los Angeles	24	181	7.5	69t	2
1962	Los Angeles	3	0	0.0	2	0
1963	Detroit	13	20	1.5	9	0
1964	Philadelphia	96	404	4.2	63	4
1965	Philadelphia	22	103	4.7	22	2
1966	Philadelphia	29	101	3.5	28	1
Totals		1,170	5,173	4.4	79t	40

RECEIVING

Year	Team	No.	Yards	Avg.	Long	TD
1952	Chi. Cardinals	11	187	17.0	47t	3
1953	Military service					
1954	Chi. Cardinals	34	611	18.0	70	3
1955	Chi. Cardinals	17	237	13.9	70t	2
1956	Chi. Cardinals	15	199	13.3	45t	2
1957	Chi. Cardinals	20	451	22.6	75t	3
1958	Chi. Cardinals	33	465	14.1	59	3
1959	Los Angeles	18	130	7.2	49	0
1960	Los Angeles	15	98	6.5	24	0
1961	Los Angeles	29	537	18.5	96t	3
1962	Los Angeles	3	49	16.3	20t	1
1963	Detroit	2	20	10.0	17	0
1964	Philadelphia	17	242	14.2	32	1
1965	Philadelphia	2	29	14.5	20	1
1966	Philadelphia	6	30	5.0	11	1
Totals		222	3,285	14.8	96t	23

PUNT RETURNS

Year	Team	No.	Yards	Avg.	Long	TD
1952	Chi. Cardinals	9	86	9.6	23	0
1953	Military service					
1954	Chi. Cardinals	11	100	9.1	59t	1
1955	Chi. Cardinals	13	245	18.8	78t	2
1956	Chi. Cardinals	5	39	7.8	16	0
1957	Chi. Cardinals	10	54	5.4	28	0
1958	Chi. Cardinals	0	0	0.0	0	0
1959	Los Angeles	14	61	4.4	20	0
1960	Los Angeles	1	0	0.0	0	0
1961	Los Angeles	0	0	0.0	0	0
1962	Los Angeles	0	0	0.0	0	0
1963	Detroit	0	0	0.0	0	0
1964	Philadelphia	2	10	5.0	9	0
1965	Philadelphia	0	0	0.0	0	0
1966	Philadelphia	0	0	0.0	0	0
Totals		65	595	9.2	78t	3

KICKOFF RETURNS

Year	Team	No.	Yards	Avg.	Long	TD
1952	Chi. Cardinals	20	624	31.2	100t	2
1953	Military service					
1954	Chi. Cardinals	17	449	26.4	91t	1
1955	Chi. Cardinals	15	368	24.5	37	0
1956	Chi. Cardinals	13	362	27.8	105t	1
1957	Chi. Cardinals	7	154	22.0	32	0
1958	Chi. Cardinals	14	497	35.5	101t	2
1959	Los Angeles	16	367	22.9	48	0
1960	Los Angeles	9	216	24.0	42	0
1961	Los Angeles	0	0	0.0	0	0
1962	Los Angeles	0	0	0.0	0	0
1963	Detroit	3	61	20.3	30	0
1964	Philadelphia	3	104	34.7	43	0
1965	Philadelphia	0	0	0.0	0	0
1966	Philadelphia	26	544	20.9	31	0
Totals		143	3,746	26.2	105t	6

SCORING
73 TD, 438 Points

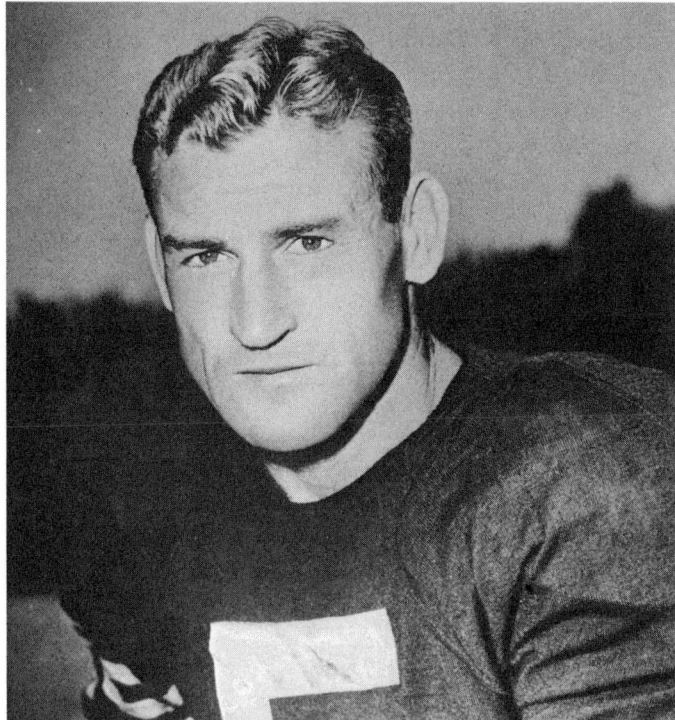

George McAfee

Halfback. 6-0, 177. Born in Ironton, Ohio, March 13, 1918. Duke. Inducted in 1966. 1940–41, 1945–1950 Chicago Bears.

Military service caused him to miss three seasons at his peak, but George McAfee was still a great NFL breakaway runner. He was sometimes called "One-Play McAfee." Most of his 39 touchdowns in the NFL were on long, spectacular plays. Lean and lightning fast, McAfee was at his best running the ball, but he also was an accomplished left-footed punter and left-handed passer. He popularized the wearing of low-cut shoes in his rookie season. He also holds the record for the highest career average on punt returns, 12.78 yards. McAfee was used primarily as a defensive back after his return from World War II, and intercepted 21 passes.

RUSHING

Year	Team	Att.	Yards	Avg.	Long	TD
1940	Chi. Bears	47	253	5.4		2
1941	Chi. Bears	65	474	7.3	70	6
1942	Military service					
1943	Military service					
1944	Military service					
1945	Chi. Bears	16	139	8.6	38	3
1946	Chi. Bears	14	53	3.8	14	0
1947	Chi. Bears	63	209	3.3	39	3
1948	Chi. Bears	92	392	4.3	23	5
1949	Chi. Bears	42	161	3.8	23	3
1950	Chi. Bears	2	4	2.0	4	0
Totals		341	1,685	4.9	70	22

PUNT RETURNS

Year	Team	No.	Yards	Avg.	Long	TD
1940	Chi. Bears					
1941	Chi. Bears	5	158	31.6	74t	1
1942	Military service					
1943	Military service					
1944	Military service					
1945	Chi. Bears	1	8	8.0	8	0
1946	Chi. Bears	1	24	24.0	24	0
1947	Chi. Bears	18	261	14.5	35	0
1948	Chi. Bears	30	417	13.9	60t	1
1949	Chi. Bears	24	279	11.6	33	0
1950	Chi. Bears	33	284	8.6	25	0

RECEIVING
85, 1,539 Yards, 16.0 Avg., 65 Long, 11 TD

INTERCEPTIONS
21, 294 Yards, 14.0 Avg., 1 TD

SCORING
34 TD, 234 Points

Hugh McElhenny

Halfback. 6-1, 198. Born in Los Angeles, California, December 31, 1928. Washington. Inducted in 1970. 1952–1960 San Francisco 49ers, 1961–62 Minnesota Vikings, 1963 New York Giants, 1964 Detroit Lions.

Few NFL players ever have enjoyed a finer season than Hugh McElhenny did as a rookie in 1952. The first time he carried the ball for the San Francisco 49ers he scored a 40-yard touchdown. He led the league in rushing, averaging seven yards a carry, scored 60 points, and was named rookie of the year. There have been runners who gained more yards, and who were faster, but likely none who ever ran in a more exciting manner than McElhenny, who was nicknamed "the King." He made instinctive moves no one duplicated, sometimes going 40 yards criss-crossing the field, to get a five-yard gain. He was an all-pro in 1952 and 1953, and played in six Pro Bowls. Thought to be over the hill by the 49ers because his knees had worn down after so much cutting, dodging, twisting, and turning, McElhenny was drafted by the expansion Vikings in 1961, and contributed over 1,000 total yards. He had 11,369 in his career.

RUSHING

Year	Team	Att.	Yards	Avg.	Long	TD
1952	San Francisco	98	684	7.0	89t	6
1953	San Francisco	112	503	4.5	33	3
1954	San Francisco	64	515	8.0	60t	6
1955	San Francisco	90	327	3.6	44	4
1956	San Francisco	185	916	5.0	86t	8
1957	San Francisco	102	478	4.7	61	1
1958	San Francisco	113	451	4.0	34	6
1959	San Francisco	18	67	3.7	19	1
1960	San Francisco	95	347	3.7	38	0
1961	Minnesota	120	570	4.8	41	3
1962	Minnesota	50	200	4.0	27	0
1963	N.Y. Giants	55	175	3.2	23	0
1964	Detroit	22	48	2.2	14	0
Totals		1,124	5,281	4.7	89t	38

RECEIVING

Year	Team	No.	Yards	Avg.	Long	TD
1952	San Francisco	26	367	14.1	77	3
1953	San Francisco	30	474	15.8	71	2
1954	San Francisco	8	162	20.3	53	0
1955	San Francisco	11	203	18.5	55t	2
1956	San Francisco	16	193	12.1	22	0
1957	San Francisco	37	458	12.4	43	2
1958	San Francisco	31	366	11.8	59t	2
1959	San Francisco	22	329	15.0	62t	3
1960	San Francisco	14	114	8.1	45	1
1961	Minnesota	37	283	7.6	26	3
1962	Minnesota	16	191	11.9	41	0
1963	N.Y. Giants	11	91	8.3	24	2
1964	Detroit	5	16	3.2	27	0
Totals		264	3.247	12.3	77	20

PUNT RETURNS
126, 920 Yards, 7.3 Avg. 94 Long, 2 TD

KICKOFF RETURNS
83, 1,921 Yards, 23.1 Avg., 55 Long, 0 TD

SCORING
60 TD, 360 Points

George McAfee

Hugh McElhenny

J. Blood (McNally)

Johnny Blood (McNally)

Halfback. 6-0, 185. Born in New Richmond, Wisconsin, November 27, 1904. St. John's of Minnesota. Inducted in 1963. 1925–26 Milwaukee Badgers, 1926–27 Duluth Eskimos, 1928 Pottsville Maroons, 1929–1933 Green Bay Packers, 1934 Pittsburgh Pirates, 1935–36 Green Bay Packers, Player-coach, 1937–38 Pittsburgh Pirates, 1939 Pittsburgh Steelers.

Johnny Blood took his name from a movie marquee for the Rudolph Valentino film, *Blood and Sand*. A free spirit, Blood was also a superbly gifted athlete. He made a reputation as a pass receiver and a breakaway runner when straight-ahead power football was still the accepted method of attack. Despite his eccentric behavior, he was a vital part of four Green Bay Packers' championship teams. He scored 37 touchdowns and 224 points in his 15 seasons, a record NFL tenure at the time he retired. He was also player-coach with Pittsburgh three years.

Mike Michalske

Guard. 6-0, 209. Born in Cleveland, Ohio, April 24, 1903. Penn State. Inducted in 1964. 1926 New York Yankees (AFL), 1927–28 New York Yankees, 1929–1935 Green Bay Packers, 1937 Green Bay Packers.

After making All-America at Penn State, Mike Michalske joined the New York Yankees of the American Football League in 1926. He and the Yankees moved to the NFL in 1927 and he was traded to Green Bay in 1929. The Packers were NFL champions in 1929–1931 and Michalske had his greatest years. Offensively, Michalske led interference on most plays, regardless of which direction they went. Defensively, he had a style like today's blitzing linebackers and was adept at stopping power thrusts. Michalske was the first guard inducted into the Hall of Fame.

Wayne Millner

End. 6-0, 191. Born in Roxbury, Massachusetts, January 31, 1913. Died November 19, 1976. Notre Dame. Inducted in 1968. 1936 Boston Redskins, 1937–1941 Washington Redskins, 1945 Washington Redskins.

Wayne Millner was one of the main reasons the Washington Redskins won NFL championships under Ray Flaherty. He had excellent statistics as a pass receiver but his value to the team was enhanced by his aggressive line and downfield blocking and his defensive play. ''I always knew if I got open,'' Hall of Fame running back Cliff Battles said, ''Millner would be there to throw a block for me.'' In the 1937 championship game, Millner caught two touchdown passes—for 78 and 55 yards—as the Redskins won 28–21. A two-time All-America at Notre Dame, Millner caught 124 passes. He missed three years of football because of military service.

RECEIVING

Year	Team	No.	Yards	Avg.	Long	TD
1936	Boston	18	211	11.7		0
1937	Washington	14	216	15.4		2
1938	Washington	18	232	12.9		1
1939	Washington	19	294	15.5		4
1940	Washington	22	233	10.6		3
1941	Washington	20	262	13.1	55	0
1942	Military service					
1943	Military service					
1944	Military service					
1945	Washington	13	130	10.0	11	2
Totals		124	1,578	12.7		12

Lenny Moore

Back. 6-1, 198. Born in Reading, Pennsylvania, November 25, 1933. Penn State. Inducted in 1975. 1956–1967 Baltimore Colts.

Opponents often knew if Lenny Moore was flanked wide, he was going to get a pass; if he was in the backfield, he was going to run the ball. Knowing this, they still had trouble stopping him. In 12 NFL seasons, he made more than 11,000 yards in total offense. He made all-pro teams for five years, and played in seven Pro Bowls. Only Jim Brown, with 126 touchdowns, scored more than Moore's 113. Moore put together a string of 18 consecutive games in which he scored at least one touchdown. After missing most of the 1963 season he earned comeback player of the year honors in 1964, gaining more than 1,000 yards rushing and receiving, and scoring 20 touchdowns.

RUSHING

Year	Team	Att.	Yards	Avg.	Long	TD
1956	Baltimore	86	649	7.5	79t	8
1957	Baltimore	98	488	5.0	55t	3
1958	Baltimore	82	598	7.3	73t	7
1959	Baltimore	92	422	4.6	31t	2
1960	Baltimore	91	374	4.1	57t	4
1961	Baltimore	92	648	7.0	54t	7
1962	Baltimore	106	470	4.4	25	2
1963	Baltimore	27	136	5.0	25t	2
1964	Baltimore	157	584	3.7	32t	16
1965	Baltimore	133	464	3.5	28t	5
1966	Baltimore	63	209	3.3	18	3
1967	Baltimore	42	132	3.1	21	4
Totals		1,069	5,174	4.8	79t	63

RECEIVING

Year	Team	No.	Yards	Avg.	Long	TD
1956	Baltimore	11	102	9.3	27	1
1957	Baltimore	40	687	17.2	82t	7
1958	Baltimore	50	938	18.5	77t	7
1959	Baltimore	47	846	18.0	71	6
1960	Baltimore	45	936	20.8	80t	9
1961	Baltimore	49	728	14.9	72t	8
1962	Baltimore	18	215	11.9	80t	2
1963	Baltimore	21	288	13.7	34	2
1964	Baltimore	21	472	22.5	74t	3
1965	Baltimore	27	414	15.3	52t	3
1966	Baltimore	21	260	12.4	36	0
1967	Baltimore	13	153	11.8	37	0
Totals		363	6,039	16.6	82t	48

KICKOFF RETURNS
49, 1,180 Yards, 24.1 Avg., 92 Long, 1 TD
SCORING
113 TD, 678 Points

Mike Michalske

Wayne Millner

Lenny Moore

Marion Motley

Marion Motley

Fullback. 6-1, 238. Born in Leesburg, Georgia, June 5, 1920. South Carolina State, Nevada. Inducted in 1968. 1946–49 Cleveland Browns (AAFC), 1950–53 Cleveland Browns, 1955 Pittsburgh Steelers.

Marion Motley was inducted into the Hall of Fame in 1968. He grew up in Canton, site of the Hall of Fame, and starred for McKinley High. A devastating power runner of the post-World War II years, Motley contributed to the Browns in many ways. He protected for Otto Graham on pass plays—and he ran devastating draw plays. He was a top linebacker early in his career, too, and was used often on Cleveland's goal line defense. Motley gained more yards than any back in the All-America Football Conference, and led the NFL in his first season in the league in 1950. His rushing total in the NFL was 1,696 yards.

RUSHING

Year	Team	Att.	Yards	Avg.	Long	TD
1946	Cleveland (AAFC)	73	601	8.2		5
1947	Cleveland (AAFC)	146	889	6.0		8
1948	Cleveland (AAFC)	157	964	6.1		5
1949	Cleveland (AAFC)	113	570	5.0		8
1950	Cleveland	140	810	5.8	69t	3
1951	Cleveland	61	273	4.5	26	1
1952	Cleveland	104	444	4.3	59	1
1953	Cleveland	32	161	5.0	34	0
1954	Did not play football					
1955	Pittsburgh	2	8	4.0	8	0
NFL Totals		339	1,696	5.0	69t	5

RECEIVING
40, 463 Yards, 11.6 Avg. 68 Long, 3 TD

Bronko Nagurski

Fullback. 6-2, 225. Born in Rainy River, Ontario, Canada, November 3, 1908. Minnesota. Inducted in 1963. 1930–37 Chicago Bears, 1943 Chicago Bears.

Bronko Nagurski is still the standard by which power runners are measured. He came out of Minnesota after having made All-America teams as both a tackle and a fullback. He teamed with Red Grange in his early pro years to give Chicago an awesome running game, and Nagurski's blocking enabled Beattie Feathers to rush for 1,004 yards in 1934, the first NFL runner to top 1,000. He retired in 1937 to become a professional wrestler but he came back to the Bears for the 1943 season. He was used mostly at tackle but he played fullback in the key final game win over the Chicago Cardinals that clinched the divisional championship. The Bears won the NFL title the following week. He also was a remarkable linebacker.

RUSHING

Year	Team	Att.	Yards	Avg.	Long	TD
1930	Chi. Bears					
1931	Chi. Bears					
1932	Chi. Bears	111	496	4.5		4
1933	Chi. Bears	128	533	4.2		1
1934	Chi. Bears	123	586	4.8		7
1935	Chi. Bears	37	137	3.7		1
1936	Chi. Bears	122	529	4.3		3
1937	Chi. Bears	73	343	4.7		1
1938	Retired from football					
1939	Retired from football					
1940	Retired from football					
1941	Retired from football					
1942	Retired from football					
1943	Chi. Bears	16	84	5.3	11	1

Bronko Nagurski

Earle (Greasy) Neale　　　　*Ernie Nevers*

Earle (Greasy) Neale

Coach. Born in Parkersburg, West Virginia, November 5, 1891. Died November 2, 1973. West Virginia Wesleyan. Inducted in 1969. 1941–1950 Philadelphia Eagles.

Earle (Greasy) Neal played major league baseball (he was the Cincinnati Reds' leading hitter in the 1919 World Series) at about the same time he was starting his pro football career with the pre-NFL Canton Bulldogs of 1917, under an assumed name. Later he was to have an extensive college coaching career before he finally entered the NFL as coach of the Philadelphia Eagles in 1941. The Eagles had been a perennial second-division club since they were founded in 1933 but Neale built them into a power. They were runners-up in 1944, 1945, and 1946, then won the Eastern Division championship in 1947 and were NFL champions in 1948 and 1949. His 1948 and 1949 clubs won the titles with back-to-back shutouts in the championship games. He devised the Eagle defense, one of the forerunners of the four-three.

Ernie Nevers

Fullback. 6-1, 205. Born in Willow River, Minnesota, June 11, 1903. Died May 3, 1976. Stanford. Inducted in 1963. 1926–27 Duluth Eskimos, 1929–1931 Chicago Cardinals.

Off all the men in the Hall of Fame, Ernie Nevers's career was the most brief—just five NFL seasons. But he was a brilliant player. He was an iron man who missed only 26 minutes of play in a 29-game season in 1926. The 40 points he scored—six touchdowns and four extra points—for the Cardinals against the Chicago Bears in 1929 is still an NFL record. Glenn (Pop) Warner, who had coached Jim Thorpe earlier, said Nevers was "the greatest player I ever coached." Warner had Nevers at Stanford, where Nevers was an All-America. Nevers's signing as Duluth's player-coach in 1926 had almost as much of an impact as Red Grange's had the year before. Nevers was player-coach with the Chicago Cardinals. In addition to football, he also was a pitcher for the St. Louis Browns and he played professional basketball.

Leo Nomellini

Defensive tackle. 6-3, 264. Born in Lucca, Italy, June 19, 1924. Minnesota. Inducted in 1969. 1950–1963 San Francisco 49ers.

Military service delayed Leo Nomellini's debut until he was 26, but he made up for the late start, playing until he was 39. Nomellini, who was nicknamed "the Lion," didn't miss a game during his entire 14-year tenure in San Francisco. His 174 consecutive games were a record when he retired. Counting preseason, regular season, playoff, and Pro Bowl games, Nomellini's string was 266 games. He cleared the way for Hugh McElhenny, Joe Perry, J.D. Smith, and John Henry Johnson on offense but it was on defense where he earned his most recognition. He was named a defensive tackle on the NFL's all-time team in 1969.

Leo Nomellini

Steve Owen

Clarence (Ace) Parker

Jim Parker

Steve Owen

Tackle. Coach. 6-0, 235. Born in Cleo Springs, Oklahoma, April 21, 1898. Died May 17, 1964. Phillips. Inducted in 1966. 1924–25 Kansas City Cowboys, 1926–1930 New York Giants. Coach, 1931–1953 New York Giants.

Steve Owen was called a defensive coaching genius, and he devised the so-called "Umbrella" defense. He also played what he called the A formation. He was one of the first coaches to exploit the field goal as a scoring weapon. Owen learned football through his line play in the early NFL. He was big and rough, the equal of any tackle in the game. Starting in 1931, he coached the New York Giants for 23 years "on a handshake" each season with owner Tim Mara; Owen never signed a formal contract. His record was 151–100–7 and his teams won eight divisional and two NFL championships.

Clarence (Ace) Parker

Quarterback. 5-11, 168. Born in Portsmouth, Virginia, May 17, 1912. Duke. Inducted in 1972. 1937–1941 Brooklyn Dodgers, 1945 Boston Yanks, 1946 New York Yankees (AAFC).

Clarence (Ace) Parker was a celebrated All-America tailback at Duke who joined the Brooklyn football Dodgers in 1937. He signed with them but expected to play pro football only briefly because he'd also signed a major league baseball contract with the Philadelphia Athletics. He stayed with the Dodgers, however, and won all-pro honors in 1938 and 1940. Parker, a triple-threat, two-way back despite the fact that he wasn't very big or very fast, led the Dodgers to their finest seasons in 1940 and 1941. After his return from World War II service, he led the New York Yankees to the All-America Football Conference Eastern Division title in 1946.

RUSHING

Year	Team	Att.	Yards	Avg.	Long	TD
1937	Brooklyn Dodgers	34	26	0.8		1
1938	Brooklyn Dodgers	93	253	2.7		2
1939	Brooklyn Dodgers	104	271	2.6		5
1940	Brooklyn Dodgers	89	306	3.4		2
1941	Brooklyn Dodgers	85	301	3.5	60	0
1942	Military service					
1943	Military service					
1944	Military service					
1945	Boston Yanks	18	–49	–2.7	7	0
1946	N.Y. Yankees (AAFC)	75	184	2.5		3
NFL Totals		423	1,108	2.6		10

PASSING

Year	Team	Att.	Comp.	Yards	TD	Int.
1937	Brooklyn Dodgers	61	28	514	1	7
1938	Brooklyn Dodgers	148	63	865	5	7
1939	Brooklyn Dodgers	157	72	977	4	13
1940	Brooklyn Dodgers	111	49	817	10	7
1941	Brooklyn Dodgers	102	51	639	2	8
1942	Military service					
1943	Military service					
1944	Military service					
1945	Boston Yanks	24	10	123	0	5
1946	N.Y. Yankees (AAFC)	115	62	763	8	3
NFL Totals		603	273	3,935	22	47

Jim Parker

Guard-tackle. 6-3, 273. Born in Macon, Georgia, April 3, 1934. Ohio State. Inducted in 1973. 1957–1967 Baltimore Colts.

Jim Parker, a two-time All-America at Ohio State and winner of the 1956 Outland trophy as the nation's top college lineman, was the first lineman elected to the Hall of Fame exclusively as an offensive performer. Noted for his defensive skills at Ohio State, Parker was thought by many to be destined for pro duty on defense, too, but from his first day of pro practice he was at left tackle on offense. That's where he stayed until midway through his sixth season, when he was moved to left guard, despite the great difference in requirements at the positions. He was outstanding as a blocker both on passing and running plays. His special assignment was to protect quarterback Johnny Unitas, which he did superbly. Parker played in eight Pro Bowls.

Joe Perry

Hugh (Shorty) Ray

Pete Pihos

Joe Perry

Fullback. 6-0, 200. Born in Stevens, Arkansas, January 27, 1927. Compton Junior College. Inducted in 1969. 1948–49 San Francisco 49ers (AAFC), 1950–1960 San Francisco 49ers, 1961-62 Baltimore Colts, 1963 San Francisco 49ers.

Joe Perry, nicknamed "the Jet" by 49ers quarterback Frankie Albert because of his quick starts, came into the pros without having played college football, only junior college and the navy football. In 16 seasons, a large number for a running back, Perry became one of the leading ground gainers in pro football history. He was the first NFL runner to put together back-to-back 1,000-yard seasons, in 1953 and 1954. In the early 1950s, Perry was a member of the 49ers' "Million Dollar Backfield," which also included Joe Arenas, Hugh McElhenny, and Y.A. Tittle. Perry was all-AAFC in 1949 and all-NFL in 1953 and 1954. He played in three Pro Bowls.

RUSHING

Year	Team	Att.	Yards	Avg.	Long	TD
1948	San Francisco (AAFC)	77	562	7.3		10
1949	San Francisco (AAFC)	115	783	6.8		8
1950	San Francisco	124	647	5.2	78t	5
1951	San Francisco	136	677	5.0	58t	3
1952	San Francisco	158	725	4.6	78t	8
1953	San Francisco	192	1,018	5.3	51t	10
1954	San Francisco	173	1,049	6.1	58	8
1955	San Francisco	156	701	4.5	42	2
1956	San Francisco	115	520	4.5	39	3
1957	San Francisco	97	454	4.7	34	3
1958	San Francisco	125	758	6.1	73t	4
1959	San Francisco	139	602	4.4	40	3
1960	San Francisco	36	95	2.6	21	1
1961	Baltimore	168	675	4.0	27	3
1962	Baltimore	94	359	3.8	21	0
1963	San Francisco	24	98	4.1	16	0
NFL Totals		1,737	8,378	4.8	78t	53

RECEIVING

Year	Team	No.	Yards	Avg.	Long	TD
1948	San Francisco (AAFC)	8	79	9.9		1
1949	San Francisco (AAFC)	11	146	13.3		3
1950	San Francisco	13	69	5.3	16	1
1951	San Francisco	18	167	9.3	35	1
1952	San Francisco	15	81	5.4	17	0
1953	San Francisco	19	191	10.1	60t	3
1954	San Francisco	26	203	7.8	70	0
1955	San Francisco	19	55	2.9	19	1
1956	San Francisco	18	104	5.8	20	0
1957	San Francisco	15	130	8.7	17	0
1958	San Francisco	23	218	9.5	64t	1
1959	San Francisco	12	53	4.4	15	0
1960	San Francisco	3	–3	–1.0	3	0
1961	Baltimore	34	322	9.5	27	1
1962	Baltimore	22	194	8.8	32	0
1963	San Francisco	4	12	3.0	8	0
NFL Totals		241	1,796	7.4	70	8

Pete Pihos

End. 6-1, 210 Born in Orlando, Florida, October 22, 1923. Indiana. Inducted in 1970. 1947–1955 Philadelphia Eagles.

Throughout his nine-year career with the Philadelphia Eagles, Pete Pihos was moved from platoon to platoon, and even played the full 60 minutes at times. Playing primarily on offense, he was an all-pro in 1948 and 1949. In 1952, he made it on defense. Back on offense, he was all-pro in 1953, 1954, and 1955; he was also the NFL's leading pass catcher in each of those years. Pihos was chosen to play in five Pro Bowl games in a row. Pihos had been drafted by the Eagles in 1945 but military service delayed the completion of his education at Indiana and he didn't report to the pros until 1947. Despite his long service on defense, Pihos had 373 receptions, good for 5,619 years and 378 points.

RECEIVING

Year	Team	No.	Yards	Avg.	Long	TD
1947	Philadelphia	23	382	16.6	66t	7
1948	Philadelphia	46	766	16.7	48	11
1949	Philadelphia	34	484	14.2	49	4
1950	Philadelphia	38	447	11.8	43	6
1951	Philadelphia	35	536	15.3	38t	5
1952	Philadelphia	12	219	18.3	47	1
1953	Philadelphia	63	1,049	16.7	59	10
1954	Philadelphia	60	872	14.5	34	10
1955	Philadelphia	62	864	13.9	40t	7
Totals		373	5,619	15.1	66t	61

Hugh (Shorty) Ray

Supervisor of officials. Born in Highland Park, Illinois, September 21, 1884. Died Septebmer 16, 1956. Illinois. Inducted in 1966.

"Hugh (Shorty) Ray" is not an instantly-recognizable pro football name, but his contributions to the game were great. As technical advisor to and supervisor of officials for the NFL from 1938 to 1956, Ray was responsible for much of the streamlining that made pro football the fast-moving, exciting game it has become. Armed with a stopwatch, pencils, charts, and field glasses, Ray observed hundreds of games and thousands of plays, making countless notations. All of them were designed to make the game faster and safer. Ray toured the league's training camps annually to clarify and explain the game's rules to players and coaches. He also worked tirelessly to improve the techniques and quality of officiating.

Andy Robustelli   *Daniel F. Reeves*

Bart Starr

Art Rooney

Dan Reeves

Team owner. Born in New York, New York, June 30, 1912. Died April 15, 1971. Georgetown. Inducted in 1967. 1941–45 Cleveland Rams, 1946–1971 Los Angeles Rams.

Dan Reeves's interest in professional football stemmed from his friendship with Jack Mara, son of Giants' owner Tim Mara, who was a schoolmate. Reeves purchased the Cleveland Rams in 1941 and, when he moved the title-winning club of 1945 to Los Angeles for the 1946 season, he was responsibile for making the NFL a coast-to-coast league. Many NFL owners were reluctant to approve the move but Reeves persuaded them to go along with him. He was also the first owner after World War II to sign black players, the first of which were Kenny Washington and Woody Strode, and the Rams signed the first player from a predominantly black college, Paul (Tank) Younger of Grambling in 1949. The Rams won the NFL title in 1951.

Andy Robustelli

Defensive end. 6-0, 230. Born in Stamford, Connecticut, December 6, 1925. Arnold College. Inducted in 1971. 1951–55 Los Angeles Rams, 1956–1964 New York Giants.

Arnold College (onetime enrollment 350) doesn't even exist anymore but it sent Andy Robustelli to pro football and the Hall of Fame. He was chosen by the Rams on the nineteenth round of the 1951 draft. Used as both an offensive and defensive end early in his career, he settled into the defensive end position. He was a two-time all-pro with the Rams and, after being traded to the Giants, he was all-pro five more times. He was an important part of the Giants' heralded defensive unit during the mid and late 1950s and the early 1960s. Robustelli was intelligent, quick, strong, and durable. He missed only one game in 14 years. He played in eight NFL championship games, and in seven Pro Bowls.

Art Rooney

Team owner. Born in Coulterville, Pennsylvania, January 27, 1901. Georgetown, Duquesne. Inducted in 1964. 1933–1940 Pittsburgh Pirates, 1941–42 Pittsburgh Steelers; 1943 Phil-Pitt Steagles; 1944 Card-Pitt, 1949–1977 Pittsburgh Steelers.

When Pennsylvania blue laws were repealed in 1933, Art Rooney purchased an NFL franchise for Pittsburgh for $2,500. His teams always seemed to be luckless, ill-fated, and, in some cases, just plain bad. He survived the Depression days and the talent-thin times of World War II. When the man who had supported pro, semipro, and amateur sports of all types in Western Pennsylvania even before he bought the Steelers, finally realized his first championships—victories in Super Bowls IX and X—the sports world gave him the acclaim he had never enjoyed before.

Gale Sayers

Running back. 6-0, 200. Born in Wichita, Kansas, May 30, 1943. Kansas. Inducted in 1977. 1965–1971 Chicago Bears.

A pair of injured knees stopped Gale Sayers, after just seven pro seasons, and only five of them had been healthy ones for him. But they were among the most brilliant any running back has had. Sayers gained 4,956 total yards on 991 carries, and twice went over 1,000 yards, 1966 and 1969. When Sayers did it the second time, he had just had knee surgery. In his last two seasons, Sayers played in only four games. In the five seasons preceding 1970, however, he set half a dozen NFL records and 16 Bears' team records. At the end of his career, he led active NFL players in punt returns, and was second in kickoff returns. Sayers, who had almost incredible quickness and balance when he was sound, was named all-NFL five times.

RUSHING

Year	Team	Att.	Yards	Avg.	Long	TD
1965	Chicago	166	867	5.2	61t	14
1966	Chicago	229	1,231	5.4	58t	8
1967	Chicago	186	880	4.7	70	7
1968	Chicago	138	856	6.2	63	2
1969	Chicago	236	1,032	4.4	28	8
1970	Chicago	23	52	2.3	15	0
1971	Chicago	13	38	2.9	9	0
Totals		991	4,956	5.0	70	39

RECEIVING

Year	Team	No.	Yards	Avg.	Long	TD
1965	Chicago	29	507	17.5	80t	6
1966	Chicago	34	447	13.1	80t	2
1967	Chicago	16	126	7.9	32	1
1968	Chicago	15	117	7.8	21	0
1969	Chicago	17	116	6.8	25	0
1970	Chicago	1	-6	-6.0	-6	0
1971	Chicago	0	0	0.0	0	0
Totals		112	1,307	11.6	80t	9

PUNT RETURNS

Year	Team	No.	Yards	Avg.	Long	TD
1965	Chicago	16	238	14.9	85t	1
1966	Chicago	6	44	7.3	27	0
1967	Chicago	3	80	26.7	58	1
1968	Chicago	2	29	14.5	18	0
1969	Chicago	0	0	0.0	0	0
1970	Chicago	0	0	0.0	0	0
1971	Chicago	0	0	0.0	0	0
Totals		27	391	14.5	85t	2

KICKOFF RETURNS

Year	Team	No.	Yards	Avg.	Long	TD
1965	Chicago	21	66	33.0	42	1
1966	Chicago	23	718	31.2	93t	2
1967	Chicago	16	603	37.7	103t	3
1968	Chicago	17	461	27.1	46	0
1969	Chicago	14	339	24.2	52	0
1970	Chicago	0	0	0.0	0	0
1971	Chicago	0	0	0.0	0	0
Totals		91	2,187	24.0	103t	6

SCORING
56 TD, 336 Points

Joe Schmidt

Ernie Stautner

Gale Sayers

Ken Strong

Joe Schmidt

Linebacker. 6-0, 222. Born in Pittsburgh, Pennsylvania, January 19, 1932. Pittsburgh. Inducted in 1973. 1953–1965 Detroit Lions, Coach, 1967–1972 Detroit Lions.

Injuries in college kept Joe Schmidt from being a high pro draft choice. He wasn't selected until the seventh round in 1953. But he moved into the then-evolving middle linebacker position almost immediately, and became an NFL institution. He was chosen all-pro eight times, and played in nine consecutive Pro Bowls. He was the Lions' team leader, and was named the team's most valuable player four times. Schmidt led by example. Not especially big or fast, he had an exceptional knack for diagnosing a play, moving to the point of attack, and making the tackle. Very strong against running plays, he also made 24 career interceptions.

Bart Starr

Quarterback. 6-1, 200. Born in Montgomery, Alabama, January 9, 1934. Alabama. Inducted in 1977. 1956–1971 Green Bay Packers. Coach, 1975–77 Green Bay Packers.

Bart Starr had a back injury at the University of Alabama, and he wasn't drafted by Green Bay until the seventeenth round in 1956. For four seasons, he had to share quarterbacking duties with several other Packers' quarterbacks. But he gained regular status late in 1959 under coach Vince Lombardi and helped Green Bay to its first winning season in 12 years. Together, Lombardi and Starr—along with many talented compatriots—made history. Starr led the NFL's passers three times—in 1963, 1964, and 1966. It was his brilliance in postseason play that set Starr apart. In six NFL title games, he completed 84 of 145 passes for 1,090 yards and 11 touchdowns, and he was intercepted only once. He was even more deadly in Green Bay's two Super Bowl wins.

PASSING

Year	Team	Att.	Comp.	Yards	TD	Int.
1956	Green Bay	44	24	325	2	3
1957	Green Bay	215	117	1,489	8	10
1958	Green Bay	157	78	875	3	12
1959	Green Bay	134	70	972	6	7
1960	Green Bay	172	98	1,358	4	8
1961	Green Bay	295	172	2,418	16	16
1962	Green Bay	285	178	2,438	12	9
1963	Green Bay	244	132	1,855	15	10
1964	Green Bay	272	163	2,144	15	4
1965	Green Bay	251	140	2,055	16	9
1966	Green Bay	251	156	2,257	14	3
1967	Green Bay	210	115	1,823	9	17
1968	Green Bay	171	109	1,617	15	8
1969	Green Bay	148	92	1,161	9	6
1970	Green Bay	255	140	1,645	8	13
1971	Green Bay	45	24	286	0	3
Totals		3,149	1,808	24,718	152	138

RUSHING
247 Att., 1,308 Yards, 5.3 Avg., 39 Long, 15 TDs

Ernie Stautner

Defensive tackle. 6-2, 235. Born in Calm, Bavaria, Germany, April 20, 1925. Boston College. Inducted in 1969. 1950–1963 Pittsburgh Steelers.

Ernie Stautner was small by later standards for NFL defensive tackles but the Pittsburgh Steelers chose him on the second round of the 1950 draft and he responded with 14 starring seasons in the NFL. As much as anyone, it was Stautner who gave the Steelers of the 1950s a reputation as a team that could not be beaten physically, even though it was losing on the scoreboard. Stautner played in nine Pro Bowls. He recovered 21 opponents' fumbles, a total among the best in NFL history, and no player has topped his three lifetime safeties. When he retired, the Steelers retired his jersey.

Ken Strong

Halfback. 5-11, 210. Born in New Haven, Connecticut. August 6, 1906. New York University. Inducted in 1967. 1929–1932 Stapleton Stapes, 1933–35 New York Giants, 1936–37 New York Yanks (AFL), 1939 New York Giants, 1944–47 New York Giants.

Ken Strong, ex-New York University All-America, was an efficient kicker for a long time. He also was one of the most versatile backs ever to play in the NFL. He ran, passed, punted, placekicked, and played defense. He was the man Steve Owen chose to kick when he decided to turn the field goal into a more frequently used weapon. In the 1934 title game against the Chicago Bears, Strong scored 17 points on two touchdowns, two extra points, and a field goal as New York came from behind to win with a 27-point rally in the fourth quarter.

SCORING

Year	Team	TD	FG	PAT	Points
1929	Stapleton Stapes	4	0-	9-13	33
1930	Stapleton Stapes	7	1-	8-11	53
1931	Stapleton Stapes	7	2-	5- 8	53
1932	Stapleton Stapes	4	1-	6-	33
1933	N.Y. Giants	6	5-	13-	64
1934	N.Y. Giants	6	4-	8-	56
1935	N.Y. Giants	1	4-	11-	29
1936	N.Y. Yanks AFL				
1937	N.Y. Yanks AFL				
1938	Did not play football				
1939	N.Y. Giants	0	4-	7-	19
1940	Military service				
1941	Military service				
1942	Military service				
1943	Military service				
1944	N.Y. Giants	0	6-12	23-24	41
1945	N.Y. Giants	0	6-13	23-23	41
1946	N.Y. Giants	0	4- 9	32-32	44
1947	N.Y. Giants	0	2- 5	24-25	30
NFL Totals		35	39-	169-	496

RUSHING
379 Att., 1,228 Yards, 3.2 Avg., 12 TD

PASS RECEIVING
22, 254 Yards, 11.5 Avg., 2 TD

Joe Stydahar

Jim Thorpe

Joe Stydahar

Tackle. 6-4, 230. Born in Kaylor, Pennsylvania, March 3, 1912. West Virginia. Inducted in 1967. 1936–1942, 1945–46 Chicago Bears.

The college player draft was held for the first time in 1936 and on his first pick, George Halas of the Chicago Bears chose Joe Stydahar, tackle from West Virginia. Starting as a rookie, the man nicknamed "Jumbo Joe" went on to become all-pro four straight seasons, and was an integral part of a Bears' team that appeared in five NFL title games and won three of them. A two-way tackle, Stydahar was especially effective on defense, where he was both extremely powerful and very agile. Like other pros of his era, Stydahar spurned helmets until rules required them. Stydahar was away from the Bears two seasons because of military service, then came back to the team for two more years.

Jim Taylor

Fullback. 6-0, 216. Born in Baton Rouge, Louisiana, September 20, 1935. Louisiana State. Inducted in 1976. 1958–1966 Green Bay Packers, 1967 New Orleans Saints.

Jim Taylor was overshadowed by Jim Brown during their playing careers but Taylor accomplished something neither Brown nor anyone else ever did—he gained more than 1,000 yards in five consecutive seasons. Taylor was called "the most determined runner I've ever seen" by his coach, Vince Lombardi. Taylor typified the rugged power of the Packers' championship teams. His personal duels with the Giants' Sam Huff were sensational. In addition to providing the Packers with ball control during the 1962 championship game, Taylor led the NFL in rushing and scoring that season. His 19 touchdowns rushing set a record. Teammate Paul Hornung made yardage on the Packers' sweeps and Taylor on their weakside slants, each running to daylight. He played his final season in New Orleans in 1967 in his native Louisiana.

RUSHING

Year	Team	Att.	Yards	Avg.	Long	TD
1958	Green Bay	52	247	4.8	25	1
1959	Green Bay	120	452	3.8	21	6
1960	Green Bay	230	1,101	4.8	32	11
1961	Green Bay	243	1,307	5.4	53	15
1962	Green Bay	272	1,474	5.4	51	19
1963	Green Bay	248	1,018	5.1	40t	9
1964	Green Bay	235	1,169	5.0	84t	12
1965	Green Bay	207	734	3.5	35	4
1966	Green Bay	204	705	3.5	19	4
1967	New Orleans	130	390	3.0	16	2
Totals		1,941	8,597	4.4	84t	83

RECEIVING

Year	Team	No.	Yards	Avg.	Long	TD
1958	Green Bay	4	72	18.0	31t	1
1959	Green Bay	9	71	7.9	20t	2
1960	Green Bay	15	121	8.1	27	0
1961	Green Bay	25	175	7.0	18	1
1962	Green Bay	22	106	4.8	25	0
1963	Green Bay	13	68	5.2	27t	1
1964	Green Bay	38	354	9.3	35t	3
1965	Green Bay	20	207	10.4	41	0
1966	Green Bay	41	331	8.1	21	2
1967	New Orleans	38	251	6.6	27	0
Totals		225	1,756	7.8	41t	10

SCORING

93 TD, 558 Points

Jim Thorpe

Halfback. 6-1, 190. Born in Prague, Oklahoma, May 28, 1888. Died March 28, 1953. Carlisle. Inducted in 1963. 1920 Canton Bulldogs, 1921 Cleveland Indians, 1922–23 Oorang Indians, 1923 Toledo Maroons, 1924 Rock Island Independents, 1925 New York Giants, 1926 Canton Bulldogs, 1928 Chicago Cardinals.

Jim Thorpe's success in the 1912 Olympics made him the nation's number one sports figure. Myth and legend surround the Sac and Fox Indian's career but he is regarded by many as America's greatest all-around athlete. Before there was a National Football League, Thorpe did much to give pro football acceptance by signing with the Canton Bulldogs in 1915. He also played major league baseball. By the time the NFL was organized, Thorpe was past his peak as a player but the newly formed league unanimously named him its charter president. After leaving Canton in 1921, Thorpe played with numerous NFL teams until he was almost 40 years old. His salary was $250 a game, in a time when the average player was paid almost nothing. In 1950 Thorpe was voted America's male athlete of the first half century.

Y.A. Tittle

Jim Taylor

Charley Trippi

Y.A. Tittle

Quarterback. 6-0, 200. Born in Marshall, Texas, October 24, 1926. Louisiana State. Inducted in 1971. 1948–49 Baltimore Colts (AAFC), 1950 Baltimore Colts, 1951–1960 San Francisco 49ers, 1961–64 New York Giants.

The San Francisco 49ers, for whom Tittle threw the "Alley-Oop" passes to R.C. Owens, traded him to the New York Giants for a rookie tackle in 1961 after Tittle had played for them 10 years. The bald, ungainly-looking quarterback had great seasons in 1961–63 with the Giants, and he led the team into the title game in three of his four years in New York. When Tittle retired, no one had passed for more yards in the NFL than he had, 28,339. He also had 212 touchdown passes and went over 300 yards passing in 13 games. In 1962, he threw a record 33 touchdown passes, then broke the record the next season with 36. He played in six Pro Bowls.

PASSING

Year	Team	Att.	Comp.	Yards	TD	Int.
1948	Baltimore (AAFC)	289	161	2,522	16	9
1949	Baltimore (AAFC)	289	148	2,209	14	18
1950	Baltimore	315	161	1,884	8	19
1951	San Francisco	114	63	808	8	9
1952	San Francisco	208	106	1,407	11	12
1953	San Francisco	259	149	2,121	20	16
1954	San Francisco	295	170	2,205	9	9
1955	San Francisco	287	147	2,185	17	28
1956	San Francisco	218	124	1,641	7	12
1957	San Francisco	279	176	2,157	13	15
1958	San Francisco	208	120	1,467	9	15
1959	San Francisco	199	102	1,331	10	15
1960	San Francisco	127	69	694	4	3
1961	N.Y. Giants	285	163	2,272	17	12
1962	N.Y. Giants	375	200	3,224	33	20
1963	N.Y. Giants	367	221	3,145	36	14
1964	N.Y. Giants	281	147	1,798	10	22
	NFL Totals	3,817	2,118	28,339	212	221

RUSHING
291 Att., 999 Yards, 3.4 Avg., 45 Long, 33 TD

George Trafton

Center. 6-2, 235. Born in Chicago, Illinois, December 6, 1896. Died September 5, 1971. Notre Dame. Inducted in 1964. 1920 Decatur Staleys, 1921 Chicago Staleys, 1922–1932 Chicago Bears.

George Trafton became a charter player in the NFL with the Decatur Staleys in 1920, after only one season of football at Notre Dame, and he stayed on to become a fixture in each of the league's first 13 seasons. Rugged and aggressive, Trafton defied fate by wearing jersey number 13. He was a man fans loved to hate, especially in Green Bay, because of his flamboyant, even roughhouse, play. Trafton was the first center to make a one-handed snap, in the days when the center had to snap the ball long to a tailback. He also excelled on defense, where he was an innovator in the "roving" style of play, from side line to side line.

Charley Trippi

Halfback. 6-0, 185. Born in Pittston, Pennsylvania, December 14, 1922. Georgia. Inducted in 1968. 1947–1955 Chicago Cardinals.

Charley Trippi of Georgia was a single-wing tailback when he came to the Chicago Cardinals but he played many positions in nine pro seasons. He was primarily a halfback for five, a quarterback for two, and a defensive back for two. He excelled at each position. Drafted as a "future" on the first round in 1945, Trippi found himself in the middle of a bidding war between the NFL and the All-America Football Conference. He signed a multi-year contract in 1947 for $100,000 despite rumors he was offered more by the AAFC. Trippi became the catalyst for the Cardinals' "Dream Backfield," and in the championship game of 1947 he scored two touchdowns—one on a 44-yard run, the other on a 75-yard punt return. In 1948, his average of 5.4 yards a carry topped the NFL. Because of unique wartime rules, he played four Chicago All-Star games as a collegian.

RUSHING

Year	Team	Att.	Yards	Avg.	Long	TD
1947	Chi. Cardinals	83	401	4.8	41	2
1948	Chi. Cardinals	128	690	5.4	50t	6
1949	Chi. Cardinals	112	553	4.9	55	3
1950	Chi. Cardinals	99	426	4.3	22	3
1951	Chi. Cardinals	78	501	6.4	32	4
1952	Chi. Cardinals	72	350	4.9	59t	4
1953	Chi. Cardinals	97	433	4.5	21	0
1954	Chi. Cardinals	18	152	8.4	57t	1
1955	Chi. Cardinals	0	0	0.0	0	0
	Totals	687	3,506	5.1	59t	23

PASSING
434 Att., 205 Comp., 2,547 Yards, 16 TD, 31 Int.

RECEIVING
130, 1,321 Yards, 10.2 Avg., 11 TD

SCORING
37 TD, 222 Points

PUNT RETURNS
63, 864 Yards, 13.7 Avg., 67 Long, 2 TD

KICKOFF RETURNS
66, 1,457 Yards, 22.1 Avg., 50 Long, 0 TD

George Trafton

Emlen Tunnell

Emlen Tunnell

Safety. 6-1, 200. Born in Bryn Mawr, Pennsylvania, March 29, 1925. Died July 23, 1975. Toledo, Iowa. Inducted in 1967. 1948–1958 New York Giants, 1959–1961 Green Bay Packers.

Like another Hall of Fame defensive back, Dick (Night Train) Lane, Emlen Tunnell walked into a team office and asked for a pro tryout. Tunnell, a free agent who played collegiately at Toledo and Iowa, became a key in the New York Giants "Umbrella" defense. He was the team's "offense on defense" because of his yardage totals on punt returns and interceptions. In 1952, for example, he gained 924 yards on returns. That was more yards than NFL rushing leader Dan Towler had that season. His lifetime interceptions (79 for 1,282 yards) and punt return yards (2,209) set NFL records. Tunnell played in nine Pro Bowl games and was all-pro four times. During much of his time with the Giants, Vince Lombardi was one of the Giants' assistant coaches, and Lombardi took Tunnell with him to Green Bay. There Tunnell lent stability to the Packers' young defense.

INTERCEPTIONS

Year	Team	No.	Yards	Avg.	Long	TD
1948	N.Y. Giants	7	116	16.6	43t	1
1949	N.Y. Giants	10	251	25.1	55t	2
1950	N.Y. Giants	7	167	23.9	35	0
1951	N.Y. Giants	9	74	8.2	30	0
1952	N.Y. Giants	7	149	21.3	40	0
1953	N.Y. Giants	6	117	19.5	44	0
1954	N.Y. Giants	8	108	13.5	43	0
1955	N.Y. Giants	7	76	10.9	26	0
1956	N.Y. Giants	6	87	14.5	23	0
1957	N.Y. Giants	6	87	14.5	52t	1
1958	N.Y. Giants	1	8	8.0	8	0
1959	Green Bay	2	20	10.0	18	0
1960	Green Bay	3	22	7.3	22	0
1961	Green Bay	0	0	0.0	0	0
Totals		79	1,282	16.2	55t	4

PUNT RETURNS

Year	Team	No.	Yards	Avg.	Long	TD
1948	N.Y. Giants	12	115	9.6	25	0
1949	N.Y. Giants	26	315	12.1	67t	1
1950	N.Y. Giants	31	305	9.8	43	0
1951	N.Y. Giants	34	489	14.4	81t	3
1952	N.Y. Giants	30	411	13.7	60	0
1953	N.Y. Giants	38	223	5.9	37	0
1954	N.Y. Giants	21	70	3.3	12	0
1955	N.Y. Giants	25	98	3.9	66t	1
1956	N.Y. Giants	22	120	5.5	14	0
1957	N.Y. Giants	12	60	5.0	23	0
1958	N.Y. Giants	6	0	0.0	0	0
1959	Green Bay	1	3	3.0	3	0
1960	Green Bay	0	0	0.0	0	0
1961	Green Bay	0	0	0.0	0	0
Totals		258	2,209	8.6	81t	5

KICKOFF RETURNS

46, 1,265 Yards, 27.5 Avg., 100 Long, 1 TD

Clyde (Bulldog) Turner

Center. 6-2, 235. Born in Sweetwater, Texas, November 10, 1919. Hardin-Simmons. Inducted in 1966. 1940–1952 Chicago Bears.

Long before other teams in the NFL began doing it, the Chicago Bears picked players from obscure colleges and developed them into all-stars. Clyde (Bulldog) Turner was one of the best examples. His college was Hardin-Simmons, and Turner was a first-round choice by the Bears. He became an all-pro six times. Turner was big, fast, tough, and a student of football; his grasp of the Bears' complicated T formation was on a par with that of quarterback Sid Luckman. He was effective both as an offensive blocker and as a linebacker. In 1942, he led the league in interceptions. Turner played on four NFL championship teams, and in the five title games in which he participated, he made four interceptions.

C. (Bulldog) Turner

Norm Van Brocklin

Steve Van Buren

Norm Van Brocklin

Quarterback. 6-1, 190. Born in Eagle Butte, South Dakota, March 15, 1926. Oregon. Inducted in 1971. 1949–1957 Los Angeles Rams, 1958–1960 Philadelphia Eagles.

Norm Van Brocklin divided playing time during most of his career with two other Los Angeles Rams quarterbacks—first Hall of Famer Bob Waterfield, then Bill Wade. It wasn't until he joined the Philadelphia Eagles in 1958 that he had the position to himself. But he always starred. In the 1951 title game, his pass to Tom Fears helped win the NFL championship for the Rams. In the 1960 title game, his passing was the key as the Eagles beat the Green Bay Packers in Vince Lombardi's only defeat in a championship game. Van Brocklin led the NFL's passers three different years; he also led the league in punting twice. His mark of 554 yards passing in a game in 1951 set a record. He had 23,611 yards passing and 173 touchdowns. He played in eight Pro Bowls.

PASSING

Year	Team	Att.	Comp.	Yards	TD	Int.
1949	Los Angeles	58	32	601	6	2
1950	Los Angeles	233	127	2,061	18	14
1951	Los Angeles	194	100	1,725	13	11
1952	Los Angeles	205	113	1,736	14	17
1953	Los Angeles	286	156	2,393	19	14
1954	Los Angeles	260	139	2,637	13	21
1955	Los Angeles	272	144	1,890	8	15
1956	Los Angeles	124	68	966	7	12
1957	Los Angeles	265	132	1,105	20	21
1958	Philadelphia	374	198	2,409	15	20
1959	Philadelphia	340	191	2,617	16	14
1960	Philadelphia	284	153	2,471	24	17
Totals		2,895	1,553	23,611	173	178

PUNTING

Year	Team	No.	Avg.	Long	Blk.
1949	Los Angeles	2	45.5	46	0
1950	Los Angeles	11	42.4	51	0
1951	Los Angeles	48	41.5	62	1
1952	Los Angeles	29	43.1	66	0
1953	Los Angeles	60	42.2	57	0
1954	Los Angeles	44	42.6	61	0
1955	Los Angeles	60	44.6	61	0
1956	Los Angeles	48	43.1	72	0
1957	Los Angeles	54	44.3	71	0
1958	Philadelphia	54	41.2	58	1
1959	Philadelphia	53	42.7	59	1
1960	Philadelphia	60	43.1	70	0
Totals		523	42.9	72	3

RUSHING
102 Att., 40 Yards, 0.4 Avg., 16 Long, 11 TD

Steve Van Buren

Halfback. 6-1, 200. Born in La Ceiba, Honduras, December 28, 1920. Louisiana State. Inducted in 1965. 1944–1951 Philadelphia Eagles.

Steve Van Buren was a runner who combined speed, power, and elusiveness. He had halfback speed and fullback size. In 1947, he became only the second man in NFL history to gain more than 1,000 yards. He led the NFL's rushers four times in his eight-year pro career. Three were consecutive, (1947–49) and he went over 1,000 yards twice. He led the NFL in touchdowns those seasons. He finished his career with 5,860 yards. As a rookie in 1944, Van Buren led the league in punt returns; he set the pace in kickoff returns the following year. He was a blocking back in college for baseball star Alvin Dark. As a professional, he doubled as a defensive back much of his career.

RUSHING

Year	Team	Att.	Yards	Avg.	Long	TD
1944	Philadelphia	80	444	5.5	70t	5
1945	Philadelphia	143	832	5.8	69t	15
1946	Philadelphia	116	529	4.6	58	5
1947	Philadelphia	217	1,008	4.6	45	13
1948	Philadelphia	201	945	4.7	29	10
1949	Philadelphia	263	1,146	4.4	41	11
1950	Philadelphia	188	629	3.3	41	4
1951	Philadelphia	112	327	2.9	17	6
Totals		1,320	5,860	4.4	70t	69

RECEIVING
45, 523 Yards, 11.6 Avg., 50 Long, 3 TD

PUNT RETURNS
34, 473 Yards, 13.9 Avg., 55 Long, 2 TD

KICKOFF RETURNS
76, 2,030 Yards, 26.7 Avg., 98 Long, 3 TD

SCORING
77 TD, 2 PAT, 464 Points

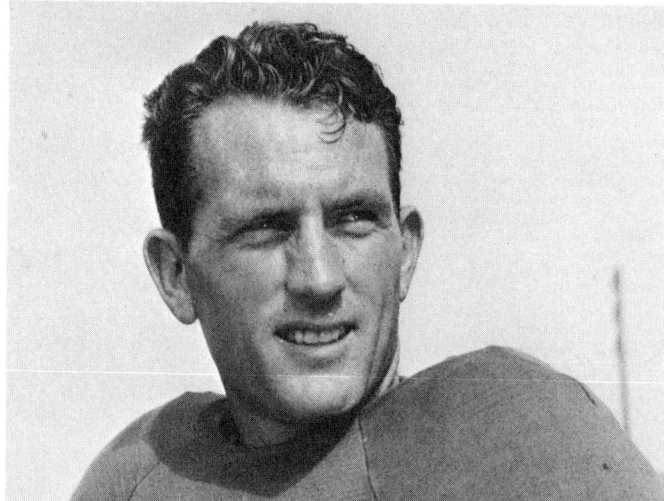

Bob Waterfield

Bill Willis

Alex Wojciechowicz

Bob Waterfield

Quarterback. 6-2, 200. Born in Elmira, New York, July 26, 1920. UCLA. Inducted in 1965. 1945 Cleveland Rams, 1946–1952 Los Angeles Rams.

Bob Waterfield led his team to an NFL championship in his first pro season. His two touchdown passes provided the victory in the 1945 title game. A cool, gifted performer in all phases of athletics, Waterfield passed well enough to lead the league in 1946 and 1951. He made 315 extra points and 60 field goals. His punting average was 42.4 yards. On defense, he made 20 interceptions. He was one of the first quarterbacks to throw the long pass consistently on third down.

PASSING

Year	Team	Att.	Comp.	Yards	TD	Int.
1945	Cleveland Rams	171	89	1,609	14	17
1946	Los Angeles	251	127	1,747	17	17
1947	Los Angeles	221	96	1,210	8	18
1948	Los Angeles	180	87	1,354	14	18
1949	Los Angeles	296	154	2,168	17	24
1950	Los Angeles	213	122	1,540	11	13
1951	Los Angeles	176	88	1,566	13	10
1952	Los Angeles	109	51	655	3	11
Totals		1,617	814	11,849	97	128

PUNTING

Year	Team	No.	Yards	Avg.	Long	Blk.
1945	Cleveland Rams	39	1,588	40.7	68	1
1946	Los Angeles	39	1,745	44.6	65	0
1947	Los Angeles	59	2,500	42.4	86	1
1948	Los Angeles	43	1,843	42.6	88	0
1949	Los Angeles	49	2,177	44.4	61	1
1950	Los Angeles	52	2,087	40.1	61	2
1951	Los Angeles	4	166	41.5	52	0
1952	Los Angeles	30	1,276	42.5	88	0
Totals		315	13,382	42.4	88	5

RUSHING
75 Att., 21 Yards, 0.3 Avg., 25 Long, 13 TD
INTERCEPTIONS
20, 228 Yards, 11.4 Avg., 35 Long, 0 TD
SCORING
13 TD, 60 FG, 315 PAT, 573 Points

Bill Willis

Guard. 6-2, 215. Born in Columbus, Ohio, October 5, 1921. Ohio State. Inducted in 1977. 1946–49 Cleveland Browns (AAFC), 1950–53 Cleveland Browns.

Bill Willis was one of the two black players signed by Paul Brown of the Cleveland Browns in 1946 (Marion Motley was the other) when the color line was broken in the All-America Football Conference. The Los Angeles Rams were doing the same thing in the NFL with the signing of Kenny Washington and Woody Strode. Willis, a smallish lineman out of Ohio State, excelled for four seasons as the Browns won four straight AAFC titles, and was with them four more years when they moved to the NFL. An all-star in the AAFC, Willis was all-pro all four of his years in the NFL. He was a middle guard, not a middle linebacker.

Alex Wojciechowicz

Center. 6-0, 235. Born in South River, New Jersey, August 12, 1915. Fordham. Inducted in 1968. 1938–1946 Detroit Lions, 1946–1950 Philadelphia Eagles.

His name was hard to pronounce, and equally hard to spell but he was a great player. He came into pro football with much expected of him. He was a two-time All-America at Fordham, and with Vince Lombardi, one of the "Seven Blocks of Granite" in that school's line. The Detroit Lions made him their number one draft pick. Even though the team was not a contender in his era, he was a top-flight, two-way center. Midway through his eighth season in the league, he was acquired by the Eagles and Earle (Greasy) Neale made him a fulltime linebacker: Wojciechowicz excelled at the role. He was solid against running plays, but he was also noted for his play against the pass. He was the NFL's best at chucking receivers. As a center, he was known for his unusually wide stance over the ball.

The Pro Football Hall of Fame in Canton, Ohio.

The rotunda and its seven-foot statue of Jim Thorpe.

A view of the twin enshrinement galleries.

HALL OF FAME CLASSES

1963
Charter members
September 7, 1963 at Canton, Ohio
Sammy Baugh
Bert Bell
Joe Carr
Earl (Dutch) Clark
Red Grange
George Halas
Mel Hein
Wilbur (Pete) Henry
Cal Hubbard
Don Hutson
Earl (Curly) Lambeau
Tim Mara
George Preston Marshall
Johnny Blood (McNally)
Bronko Nagurski
Ernie Nevers
Jim Thorpe

1964
September 6, 1964 at Canton, Ohio
Jimmy Conzelman
Ed Healey
Clarke Hinkle
Roy (Link) Lyman
August (Mike) Michalske
Art Rooney
George Trafton

1965
September 12, 1965 at Canton, Ohio
Guy Chamberlin
John (Paddy) Driscoll
Danny Fortmann
Otto Graham
Sid Luckman
Steve Van Buren
Bob Waterfield

1966
September 17, 1966 at Canton, Ohio
Bill Dudley
Joe Guyon
Arnie Herber
Walt Kiesling
George McAfee
Steve Owen
Hugh (Shorty) Ray
Clyde (Bulldog) Turner

1967
August 5, 1967 at Canton, Ohio
Chuck Bednarik
Charles W. Bidwill
Paul Brown
Bobby Layne
Daniel F. Reeves
Ken Strong
Joe Stydahar
Emlen Tunnell

1968
August 3, 1968 at Canton, Ohio
Cliff Battles
Art Donovan
Elroy (Crazylegs) Hirsch
Wayne Millner
Marion Motley
Charley Trippi
Alex Wojciechowicz

1969
September 13, 1969 at Canton, Ohio
Glen (Turk) Edwards
Earle (Greasy) Neale
Leo Nomellini
Joe Perry
Ernie Stautner

1970
August 8, 1970 at Canton, Ohio
Jack Christiansen
Tom Fears
Hugh McElhenny
Pete Pihos

1971
July 31, 1971 at Canton, Ohio
Jim Brown
Bill Hewitt
Frank (Bruiser) Kinard
Vince Lombardi
Andy Robustelli
Y. A. Tittle
Norm Van Brocklin

1972
July 29, 1972 at Canton, Ohio
Lamar Hunt
Gino Marchetti
Ollie Matson
Clarence (Ace) Parker

1973
July 28, 1973 at Canton, Ohio
Raymond Berry
Jim Parker
Joe Schmidt

1974
July 27, 1974 at Canton, Ohio
Tony Canadeo
Bill George
Lou Groza
Dick (Night Train) Lane

1975
August 2, 1975 at Canton, Ohio
Roosevelt Brown
George Connor
Dante Lavelli
Lenny Moore

1976
July 24, 1976 at Canton, Ohio
Ray Flaherty
Len Ford
Jim Taylor

1977
July 30, 1977 at Canton, Ohio
Frank Gifford
Forrest Gregg
Gale Sayers
Bart Starr
Bill Willis

PRESENTERS
Presenters make the speeches of presentation for inductees at the annual ceremonies at the Hall of Fame during "Football's Greatest Weekend" in Canton, Ohio. At first presenters were appointed by the Hall of Fame but later the policy was changed allowing each Hall of Fame nominee to choose the person who would present him for induction.

Inductee	Presenter
Cliff Battles	Edward Bennett Williams
Sammy Baugh	Harry Stuhldreher
Chuck Bednarik	Earle (Greasy) Neale
Bert Bell	David McDonald
Art Rooney accepted for the late Bell	
Raymond Berry	Weeb Ewbank
Charles W. Bidwill	Art Rooney
Charles W. (Stormy) Bidwill, Jr. accepted for his late father	
Jim Brown	Ken Malloy
Paul Brown	Otto Graham
Roosevelt Brown	Talmadge Hill
Tony Canadeo	Dick Bourguignon
Joe Carr	Earl Schreiber
Dan Tehan accepted for the late Carr	
Guy Chamberlin	Wallace (Doc) Elliott
Jack Christiansen	Raymond (Buddy) Parker
Earl (Dutch) Clark	Senator Philip A. Hart
George Connor	George S. Halas
Jimmy Conzelman	Justice William O. Douglas
Art Donovan	Jim Mutscheller
John (Paddy) Driscoll	Jimmy Conzelman
Bill Dudley	Bob Waterfield
Glen (Turk) Edwards	Mel Hein
Tom Fears	Hal Dean
Ray Flaherty	Jim Barber
Len Ford	Ted McIntyre
Debbie Ford accepted for her late father	
Danny Fortmann	Andy Kerr
Bill George	Ed McCaskey
Frank Gifford	
Otto Graham	Paul Brown
Red Grange	Jimmy Conzelman
Forrest Gregg	
Lou Groza	Paul Brown
Joe Guyon	Jimmy Conzelman
George Halas	David L. Lawrence
Ed Healey	Harry Stuhldreher
Mel Hein	Frank T. Bow
Wilbur (Pete) Henry	E.E. (Rip) Miller
Harry Robb accepted for the late Henry	

Inductee	Presenter
Arnie Herber	Clarke Hinkle
Bill Hewitt	Upton Bell
Mrs. Mary Ellen Cocozza, daughter of the late Mr. Hewitt, accepted for him	
Clarke Hinkle	Bronko Nagurski
Elroy (Crazylegs) Hirsch	Hampton Pool
Cal Hubbard	Paul Kerr
Lamar Hunt	William H. Sullivan, Jr.
Don Hutson	Dante Lavelli
Walt Kiesling	Justice Byron R. White
Johnny Blood (McNally) accepted for the late Kiesling	
Frank (Bruiser) Kinard	Jack White
Earl (Curly) Lambeau	Jim Crowley
Dick (Night Train) Lane	W.E. Pigford
Dante Lavelli	Paul Brown
Bobby Layne	Raymond (Buddy) Parker
Vince Lombardi	Wellington Mara
Vince Lombardi, Jr., accepted for his late father	
Sid Luckman	Lou Little
Roy (Link) Lyman	William E. Umstattd
Tim Mara	Arthur Daley
Jack Mara accepted for his late father	
Gino Marchetti	Carroll Rosenbloom
George Preston Marshall	Maj. Gen. Harry W. Abendroth
Milton King accepted for Marshall, who was ill	
Ollie Matson	Joe Kuharich
George McAfee	Dick Gallagher
Hugh McElhenny	Lou Spadia
Johnny Blood (McNally)	Justice Byron R. White
August (Mike) Michalske	L.C. Timm
Wayne Millner	Ray Flaherty
Lenny Moore	Andy Stopper
Marion Motley	Bill Willis
Bronko Nagurski	Don Miller
Earle (Greasy) Neale	Chuck Bednarik
Ernie Nevers	Elmer Layden
Leo Nomellini	Mrs. Victor Morabito
Steve Owen	Mel Hein
Jim Lee Howell accepted for the late Owen	
Clarence (Ace) Parker	Jack White
Jim Parker	Woody Hayes
Joe Perry	Mrs. Tony Morabito
Pete Pihos	Howard Brown
Hugh (Shorty) Ray	Dan Tehan
Hugh L. Ray, Jr., accepted for his late father	
Daniel F. Reeves	Bob Waterfield
Andy Robustelli	J. Walter Kennedy
Art Rooney	David L. Lawrence
Gale Sayers	
Joe Schmidt	William Clay Ford
Bart Starr	
Ernie Stautner	Art Rooney
Ken Strong	Chick Meehan
Joe Stydahar	Dr. Danny Fortmann
Jim Taylor	Marie Lombardi
Jim Thorpe	Henry A. Roemer
Pete Calac accepted for the late Thorpe	
Y.A. Tittle	Wellington Mara
George Trafton	Ernie Nevers
Charley Trippi	Paul Shebby
Emlen Tunnell	Father Benedict Dudley, O.F.M.
Clyde (Bulldog) Turner	Ed Healey
Norm Van Brocklin	Rankin Smith
Steve Van Buren	Clarke Hinkle
Bob Waterfield	Pat O'Brien
Bill Willis	
Alex Wojciechowicz	Earle (Greasy) Neale

All-Pros

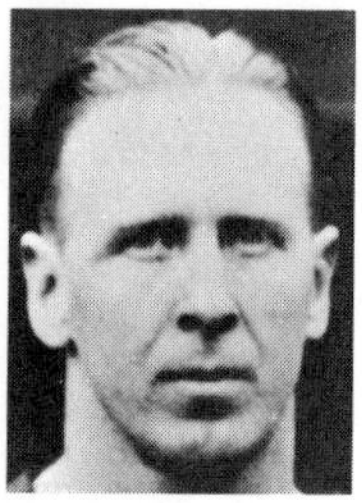
M. (Red) Badgro

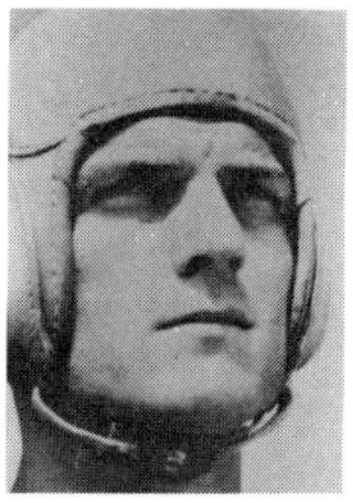
Ernie Caddel

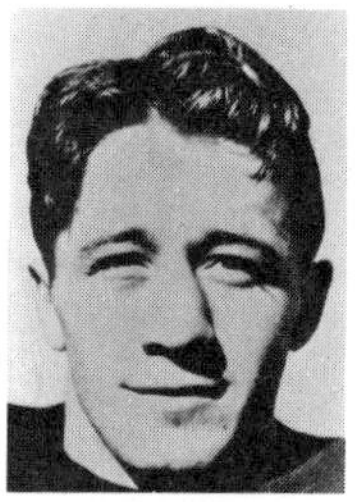
Gaynell Tinsley

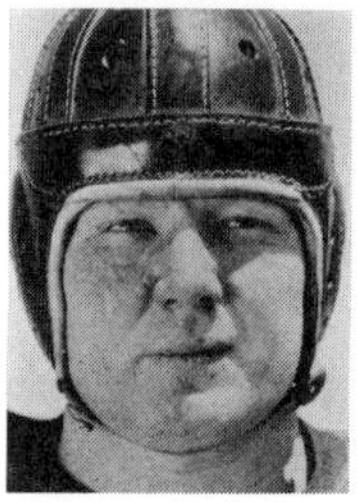
Willie Wilkin

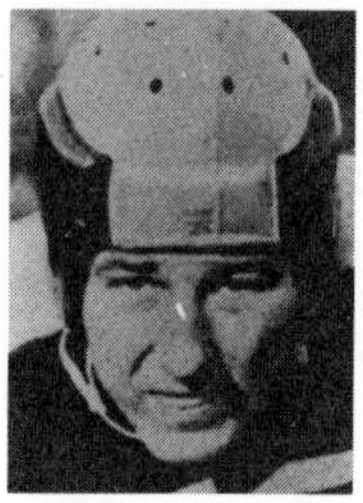
Al Wistert

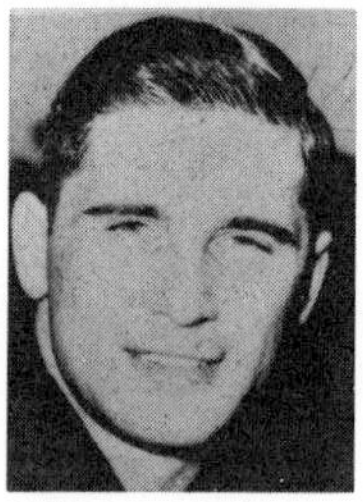
Johnny Lujack

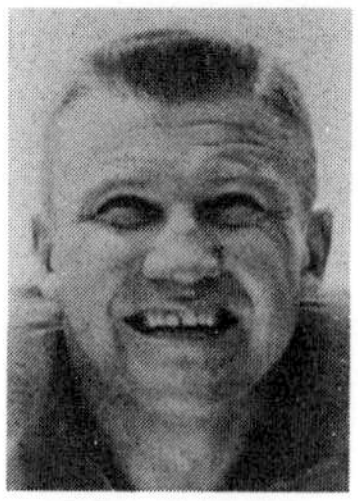
Lou Creekmur

1931
Lavern Dilweg, Green Bay . . . E
Morris (Red) Badgro, N.Y. Giants . . . E
Cal Hubbard, Green Bay . . . T
George Christensen, Portsmouth . . . T
Mike Michalske, Green Bay . . . G
Denver (Butch) Gibson, N.Y. Giants . . . G
Frank McNally, Chicago Cardinals . . . C
Earl (Dutch) Clark, Portsmouth . . . QB
Harold (Red) Grange, Chicago Bears . . . HB
Johnny Blood, (McNally), Green Bay . . . HB
Ernie Nevers, Chicago Cardinals . . . FB
1932
Ray Flaherty, N.Y. Giants . . . E
Luke Johnsos, Chicago Bears . . . E
Cal Hubbard, Green Bay . . . T
Glen (Turk) Edwards, Boston . . . T
Jules Carlson, Chicago Bears . . . G
Walt Kiesling, Chicago Cardinals . . . G
Nate Barrager, Green Bay . . . C
Earl (Dutch) Clark, Portsmouth . . . QB
Arnie Herber, Green Bay . . . HB
Roy Lumpkin, Portsmouth . . . HB
Bronko Nagurski, Chicago Bears . . . FB
1933
Bill Hewitt, Chicago Bears . . . E
Morris (Red) Badgro, N.Y. Giants . . . E
Cal Hubbard, Green Bay . . . T
Glen (Turk) Edwards, Boston Redskins . . . T
Herman Hickman, Brooklyn Dodgers . . . G
Joe Kopcha, Chicago Bears . . . G
Mel Hein, N.Y. Giants . . . C
Harry Newman, N.Y. Giants . . . QB
Glenn Presnell, Portsmouth . . . HB
Cliff Battles, Boston . . . HB
Bronko Nagurski, Chicago Bears . . . FB
1934
Bill Hewitt, Chicago Bears . . . E
Morris (Red) Badgro, N.Y. Giants . . . E
George Christensen, Detroit . . . T
Bill Morgan, N.Y. Giants . . . T
Denver (Butch) Gibson, N.Y. Giants . . . G
Joe Kopcha, Chicago Bears . . . G
Mel Hein, N.Y. Giants . . . C
Earl (Dutch) Clark, Detroit . . . QB
Beattie Feathers, Chicago Bears . . . HB
Ken Strong, N.Y. Giants . . . HB
Bronko Nagurski, Chicago Bears . . . FB
1935
Bill Smith, Chicago Cardinals . . . E
Bill Karr, Chicago Bears . . . E
Bill Morgan, N.Y. Giants . . . T
George Musso, Chicago Bears . . . T
Joe Kopcha, Chicago Bears . . . G
Mike Michalske, Green Bay . . . G
Mel Hein, N.Y. Giants . . . C
Earl (Dutch) Clark, Detroit . . . QB
Ed Danowski, N.Y. Giants . . . HB
Ernie Caddel, Detroit . . . HB
Mike Mikulak, Chicago Cardinals . . . FB
1936
Bill Hewitt, Philadelphia . . . E
Don Hutson, Green Bay . . . E
Glen (Turk) Edwards, Boston Redskins . . . T
Ernie Smith, Green Bay . . . T
Lon Evans, Green Bay . . . G
Grover (Ox) Emerson, Detroit . . . G
Mel Hein, N.Y. Giants . . . C
Earl (Dutch) Clark, Detroit . . . QB
Cliff Battles, Boston Redskins . . . HB
Alphonse (Tuffy) Leemans, N.Y. Giants . . . HB
Clarke Hinkle, Green Bay . . . FB
1937
Bill Hewitt, Philadelphia . . . E
Gaynell Tinsley, Chicago Cardinals . . . E
Joe Stydahar, Chicago Bears . . . T
Glen (Turk) Edwards, Washington . . . T
Lon Evans, Green Bay . . . G
George Musso, Chicago Bears . . . G
Mel Hein, N.Y. Giants . . . C
Earl (Dutch) Clark, Detroit . . . QB
Cliff Battles, Washington . . . HB
Sammy Baugh, Washington . . . HB
Clarke Hinkle, Green Bay . . . FB
1938
Don Hutson, Green Bay . . . E
Gaynell Tinsley, Chicago Cardinals . . . E
Ed Widseth, N.Y. Giants . . . T
Joe Stydahar, Chicago Bears . . . T
Danny Fortmann, Chicago Bears . . . G
Russ Letlow, Green Bay . . . G
Mel Hein, N.Y. Giants . . . C
Clarence (Ace) Parker, Brooklyn . . . QB
Ed Danowski, N.Y. Giants . . . HB
Lloyd Cardwell, Detroit . . . HB
Clarke Hinkle, Green Bay . . . FB
1939
Don Hutson, Green Bay . . . E
Jim Poole, N.Y. Giants . . . E
Joe Stydahar, Chicago Bears . . . T
Jim Barber, Washington . . . T
Danny Fortmann, Chicago Bears . . . G
John Dell Isola, N.Y. Giants . . . G
Mel Hein, N.Y. Giants . . . C
Davey O'Brien, Philadelphia . . . QB
Alphonse (Tuffy) Leemans, N.Y. Giants . . . HB
Andy Farkas, Washington . . . HB
Bill Osmanski, Chicago Bears . . . FB
1940
Don Hutson, Green Bay . . . E
Perry Schwartz, Brooklyn Dodgers . . . E
Joe Stydahar, Chicago Bears . . . T
Frank (Bruiser) Kinard, Brooklyn Dodgers . . . T
Danny Fortmann, Chicago Bears . . . G
John Wiethe, Detroit . . . G
Mel Hein, N.Y. Giants . . . C
Clarence (Ace) Parker, Brooklyn Dodgers . . . QB
Sammy Baugh, Washington . . . HB
Byron (Whizzer) White, Detroit . . . HB
Johnny Drake, Cleveland Rams . . . FB
1941
Don Hutson, Green Bay . . . E
Perry Schwartz, Brooklyn Dodgers . . . E
Frank (Bruiser) Kinard, Brooklyn Dodgers . . . T
Willie Wilkin, Washington . . . T
Danny Fortmann, Chicago Bears . . . G
Joe Kuharich, Chicago Cardinals . . . G
Clyde (Bulldog) Turner, Chicago Bears . . . C
Sid Luckman, Chicago Bears . . . QB
Cecil Isbell, Green Bay . . . HB
George McAfee, Chicago Bears . . . HB
Clarke Hinkle, Green Bay . . . FB
1942
Don Hutson, Green Bay . . . E
Bob Masterson, Washington . . . E
Willie Wilkin, Washington . . . T
Lee Artoe, Chicago Bears . . . T
Danny Fortmann, Chicago Bears . . . G
Bill Edwards, N.Y. Giants . . . G
Clyde (Bulldog) Turner, Chicago Bears . . . C
Sid Luckman, Chicago Bears . . . QB
Cecil Isbell, Green Bay . . . HB
Bill Dudley, Pittsburgh . . . HB
Gary Famiglietti, Chicago Bears . . . FB
1946
Jim Benton, Los Angeles . . . E
Ken Kavanaugh, Chicago Bears . . . E
Al Wistert, Philadelphia . . . T
Jim White, N.Y. Giants . . . T
Augie Lio, Philadelphia . . . G
Riley Matheson, Los Angeles . . . G
Clyde (Bulldog) Turner, Chicago Bears . . . C
Bob Waterfield, Los Angeles . . . QB
Bill Dudley, Pittsburgh . . . HB
Frank Filchock, N.Y. Giants . . . HB
Ted Fritsch, Green Bay . . . FB
1947
Ken Kavanaugh, Chicago Bears . . . E
Mal Kutner, Chicago Cardinals . . . E
Al Wistert, Philadelphia . . . T
Fred Davis, Chicago Bears . . . T
Len Younce, N.Y. Giants . . . G
Bill Moore, Pittsburgh . . . G
Vince Banonis, Chicago Cardinals . . . C
Sid Luckman, Chicago Bears . . . QB
Steve Van Buren, Philadelphia . . . HB
Sammy Baugh, Washington . . . HB
Pat Harder, Chicago Cardinals . . . FB
1948
Pete Pihos, Philadelphia . . . E
Mal Kutner, Chicago Cardinals . . . E
Al Wistert, Philadelphia . . . T
Dick Huffman, Los Angeles . . . T
Ray Bray, Chicago Bears . . . G
Buster Ramsey, Chicago Cardinals . . . G
Clyde (Bulldog) Turner, Chicago Bears . . . C
Sammy Baugh, Washington . . . QB
Steve Van Buren, Philadelphia . . . HB
Charley Trippi, Chicago Cardinals . . . HB
Pat Harder, Chicago Cardinals . . . FB
1949
Pete Pihos, Philadelphia . . . E
Tom Fears, Los Angeles . . . E
Vic Sears, Philadelphia . . . T
Dick Huffman, Los Angeles . . . T
Ray Bray, Chicago Bears . . . G
Garrard (Buster) Ramsey, Chicago Cardinals . . . G
Fred Naumetz, Los Angeles . . . C
Bob Waterfield, Los Angeles . . . QB
Steve Van Buren, Philadelphia . . . HB
Tony Canadeo, Green Bay . . . HB
Pat Harder, Chicago Cardinals . . . FB
1950
Tom Fears, Los Angeles . . . E
Dan Edwards, N.Y. Yanks . . . E
Mac Speedie, Cleveland . . . E
George Connor, Chicago Bears . . . T
Arnie Weinmeister, N.Y. Giants . . . T
Dick Barwegan, Chicago Bears . . . G
Joe Signaigo, N.Y. Yanks . . . G
Bill Willis, Cleveland . . . G
Chuck Bednarik, Philadelphia . . . C
Clayton Tonnemaker, Green Bay . . . C
Johnny Lujack, Chicago Bears . . . QB
Doak Walker, Detroit . . . HB
Joe Geri, Pittsburgh . . . HB
Marion Motley, Cleveland . . . FB
1951
Offense
Elroy (Crazylegs) Hirsch, Los Angeles . . . E
Leon Hart, Detroit . . . E
Dante Lavelli, Cleveland . . . E
George Connor, Chicago Bears . . . T
Lou Groza, Cleveland . . . T
Leo Nomellini, San Francisco . . . T
DeWitt (Tex) Coulter, N.Y. Giants . . . T
Lou Creekmur, Detroit . . . G
Dick Barwegan, Chicago Bears . . . G
Vic Lindskog, Philadelphia . . . C
Frank Gatski, Cleveland . . . C
Otto Graham, Cleveland . . . QB
Doak Walker, Detroit . . . HB
Dub Jones, Cleveland . . . HB
Eddie Price, N.Y. Giants . . . FB
Dan Towler, Los Angeles . . . FB
Defense
Larry Brink, Los Angeles . . . DE
Leon Hart, Detroit . . . DE
Len Ford, Cleveland . . . DE
Arnie Weinmeister, N.Y. Giants . . . DT
Al DeRogatis, N.Y. Giants . . . DT
George Connor, Chicago Bears . . . DT
Bill Willis, Cleveland . . . G
Les Bingaman, Detroit . . . G
Jon Baker, N.Y. Giants . . . G
Chuck Bednarik, Philadelphia . . . LB
Paul (Tank) Younger, Los Angeles . . . LB
Tony Adamle, Cleveland . . . LB
Otto Schnellbacher, N.Y. Giants . . . DB
Jerry Shipkey, Pittsburgh . . . DB
Warren Lahr, Cleveland . . . DB
Emlen Tunnell, N.Y. Giants . . . DB
1952
Offense
Cloyce Box, Detroit . . . E
Mac Speedie, Cleveland . . . E
Gordy Soltau, San Francisco . . . E
George Connor, Chicago Bears . . . T
Lou Groza, Cleveland . . . T

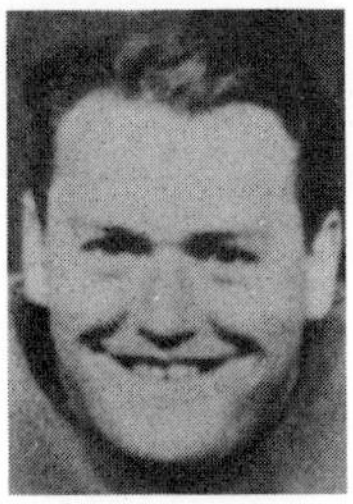

Arnie Weinmeister

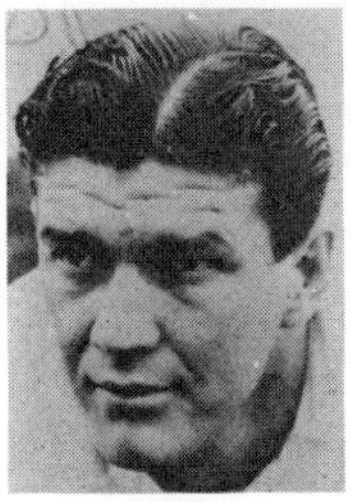

Mac Speedie

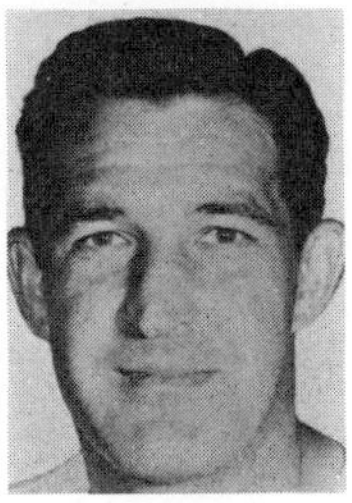

Dale Dodrill

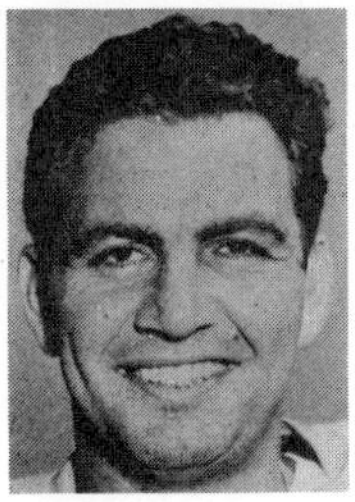

Don Paul

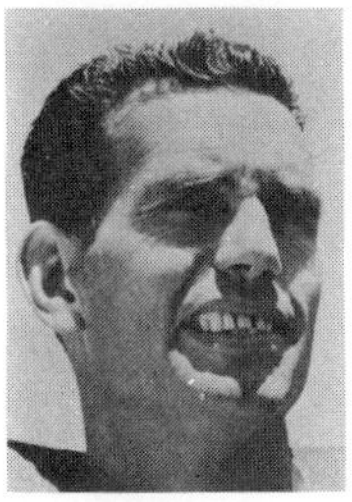

Billy Wilson

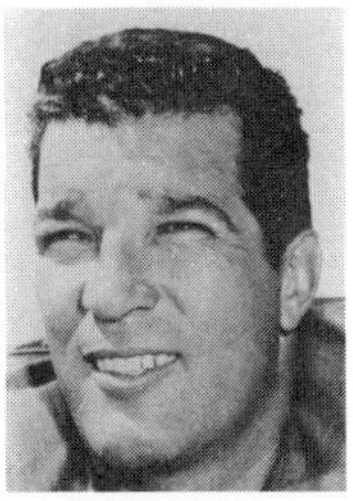

Gene Brito

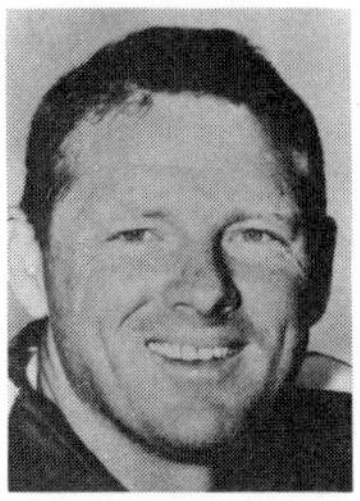

Billy Howton

Leo Nomellini, San Francisco ... T
Lou Creekmur, Detroit ... G
Bill Fischer, Chicago Cardinals ... G
Frank Gatski, Cleveland ... C
Bill Walsh, Pittsburgh ... C
Bobby Layne, Detroit ... QB
Otto Graham, Cleveland ... QB
Hugh McElhenny, San Francisco ... HB
Dan Towler, Los Angeles ... HB
Eddie Price, N.Y. Giants ... FB

Defense

Larry Brink, Los Angeles ... DE
Len Ford, Cleveland ... DE
Pete Pihos, Philadelphia ... DE
Arnie Weinmeister, N.Y. Giants ... DT
Thurman McGraw, Detroit ... DT
Stan West, Los Angeles ... G
Bill Willis, Cleveland ... G
Les Bingaman, Detroit ... G
Chuck Bednarik, Philadelphia ... LB
Jerry Shipkey, Pittsburgh ... LB
George Connor, Chicago Bears ... LB
Jack Christiansen, Detroit ... DB
Ollie Matson, Chicago Cardinals ... DB
Bob Smith, Detroit ... DB
Herb Rich, Los Angeles ... DB
Emlen Tunnell, N.Y. Giants ... DB

1953

Offense

Pete Pihos, Philadelphia ... E
Dante Lavelli, Cleveland ... E
Elroy (Crazylegs) Hirsch, Los Angeles ... E
George Connor, Chicago Bears ... T
Lou Groza, Cleveland ... T
Lou Creekmur, Detroit ... T
Dick Stanfel, Detroit ... G
Bruno Banducci, San Francisco ... G
Frank Gatski, Cleveland ... C
Otto Graham, Cleveland ... QB
Hugh McElhenny, San Francisco ... HB
Doak Walker, Detroit ... HB
Dan Towler, Los Angeles ... HB
Joe Perry, San Francisco ... FB

Defense

Len Ford, Cleveland ... DE
Andy Robustelli, Los Angeles ... DE
Norm Willey, Philadelphia ... DE
Arnie Weinmeister, N.Y. Giants ... DT
Leo Nomellini, San Francisco ... DT
Les Bingaman, Detroit ... G
Bill Willis, Cleveland ... G
Dale Dodrill, Pittsburgh ... G
Chuck Bednarik, Philadelphia ... LB
Don Paul, Los Angeles ... LB
George Connor, Chicago Bears ... LB
Tommy Thompson, Cleveland ... DB
Tom Keane, Baltimore ... DB
Jack Christiansen, Detroit ... DB
Ken Gorgal, Cleveland ... DB

1954

Offense

Pete Pihos, Philadelphia ... E
Bob Boyd, Los Angeles ... E
Harlon Hill, Chicago Bears ... E
Lou Creekmur, Detroit ... T
Lou Groza, Cleveland ... T
Dick Stanfel, Detroit ... G
Bruno Banducci, San Francisco ... G
Bill Walsh, Pittsburgh ... C
Otto Graham, Cleveland ... QB
Doak Walker, Detroit ... HB
Ollie Matson, Chicago Cardinals ... HB
Joe Perry, San Francisco ... FB

Defense

Len Ford, Cleveland ... DE
Norm Willey, Philadelphia ... DE
Leo Nomellini, San Francisco ... DT
Art Donovan, Baltimore ... DT
Les Bingaman, Detroit ... G
Dale Dodrill, Pittsburgh ... G
Frank (Bucko) Kilroy, Philadelphia ... G
Chuck Bednarik, Philadelphia ... LB
Joe Schmidt, Detroit ... LB
Roger Zatkoff, Green Bay ... LB
Tom Landry, N.Y. Giants ... DB
Bobby Dillon, Green Bay ... DB
Jim David, Detroit ... DB
Jack Christiansen, Detroit ... DB

1955

Offense

Harlon Hill, Chicago Bears ... E
Billy Wilson, San Francisco ... E
Pete Pihos, Philadelphia ... E
Lou Groza, Cleveland ... T
Bill Wightkin, Chicago Bears ... T
Bob St. Clair, San Francisco ... T
Stan Jones, Chicago Bears ... G
Duane Putnam, Los Angeles ... G
Abe Gibron, Cleveland ... G
Bill Austin, N.Y. Giants ... G
Frank Gatski, Cleveland ... C
Otto Graham, Cleveland ... QB
Ollie Matson, Chicago Cardinals ... HB
Frank Gifford, N.Y. Giants ... HB
Ron Waller, Los Angeles ... HB
Alan Ameche, Baltimore ... FB

Defense

Gene Brito, Washington ... DE
Len Ford, Cleveland ... DE
Andy Robustelli, Los Angeles ... DE
Art Donovan, Baltimore ... DT
Bob Toneff, San Francisco ... DT
Don Colo, Cleveland ... DT
Bill George, Chicago Bears ... MG
Dale Dodrill, Pittsburgh ... MG
Chuck Bednarik, Philadelphia ... LB
George Connor, Chicago Bears ... LB
Roger Zatkoff, Green Bay ... LB
Joe Schmidt, Detroit ... LB
Bobby Dillon, Green Bay ... DB
Will Sherman, Los Angeles ... DB
Don Paul, Cleveland ... DB
Jack Christiansen, Detroit ... DB
Emlen Tunnell, N.Y. Giants ... DB

1956

Offense

Harlon Hill, Chicago Bears ... E
Billy Howton, Green Bay ... E
Lou Creekmur, Detroit ... T
Roosevelt Brown, N.Y. Giants ... T
Stan Jones, Chicago Bears ... G
Dick Stanfel, Washington ... G
Larry Strickland, Chicago Bears ... C
Charlie Ane, Detroit ... C
Bobby Layne, Detroit ... QB
Frank Gifford, N.Y. Giants ... HB
Ollie Matson, Chicago Cardinals ... HB
Rick Casares, Chicago Bears ... FB

Defense

Andy Robustelli, N.Y. Giants ... DE
Gene Brito, Washington ... DE
Roosevelt Grier, N.Y. Giants ... DT
Art Donovan, Baltimore ... DT
Ernie Stautner, Pittsburgh ... DT
Bill George, Chicago Bears ... MG
Joe Schmidt, Detroit ... LB
Chuck Bednarik, Philadelphia ... LB
Les Richter, Los Angeles ... LB
Dick (Night Train) Lane, Chicago Cardinals ... DB
Emlen Tunnell, N.Y. Giants ... DB
Jack Christiansen, Detroit ... DB
Yale Lary, Detroit ... DB
Bobby Dillon, Green Bay ... DB

1957

Offense

Billy Wilson, San Francisco ... E
Billy Howton, Green Bay ... E
Roosevelt Brown, N.Y. Giants ... T
Lou Creekmur, Detroit ... T
Lou Groza, Cleveland ... T
Duane Putnam, Los Angeles ... G
Dick Stanfel, Washington ... G
Jim Ringo, Green Bay ... C
Larry Strickland, Chicago Bears ... C
Y. A. Tittle, San Francisco ... QB
Frank Gifford, New York ... HB
Ollie Matson, Chicago Cardinals ... HB
Jim Brown, Cleveland ... FB

Defense

Gino Marchetti, Baltimore ... DE
Andy Robustelli, N.Y. Giants ... DE
Gene Brito, Washington ... DE
Leo Nomellini, San Francisco ... DT
Art Donovan, Baltimore ... DT
Joe Schmidt, Detroit ... LB
Marv Matuszak, San Francisco ... LB
Bill George, Chicago Bears ... LB
Jack Christiansen, Detroit ... DB
Bobby Dillon, Green Bay ... DB
Jack Butler, Pittsburgh ... DB
Yale Lary, Detroit ... DB
Milt Davis, Baltimore ... DB

1958

Offense

Raymond Berry, Baltimore ... E
Del Shofner, Los Angeles ... E
Roosevelt Brown, New York ... T
Jim Parker, Baltimore ... T
Dick Stanfel, Washington ... G
Duane Putnam, Los Angeles ... G
Ray Wietecha, New York ... C
John Unitas, Baltimore ... QB
Lenny Moore, Baltimore ... HB
Jon Arnett, Los Angeles ... HB
Jim Brown, Cleveland ... FB

Defense

Gino Marchetti, Baltimore ... DE
Andy Robustelli, N.Y. Giants ... DE
Gene Brito, Washington ... DE
Gene (Big Daddy) Lipscomb, Baltimore ... DT
Ernie Stautner, Pittsburgh ... DT
Joe Schmidt, Detroit ... LB
Sam Huff, N.Y. Giants ... LB
Bill George, Chicago Bears ... LB
Jack Butler, Pittsburgh ... DB
Yale Lary, Detroit ... DB
Jim Patton, N.Y. Giants ... DB
Bobby Dillon, Green Bay ... DB

1959

Offense

Raymond Berry, Baltimore ... E
Del Shofner, Los Angeles ... E
Roosevelt Brown, N.Y. Giants ... T
Jim Parker, Baltimore ... T
Jim Ray Smith, Cleveland ... G
Stan Jones, Chicago Bears ... G
Art Spinney, Baltimore ... G
Jim Ringo, Green Bay ... C
John Unitas, Baltimore ... QB
Frank Gifford, N.Y. Giants ... HB
Lenny Moore, Baltimore ... HB
J. D. Smith, San Francisco ... HB
Jim Brown, Cleveland ... FB

Defense

Gino Marchetti, Baltimore ... DE
Andy Robustelli, N.Y. Giants ... DE
Gene (Big Daddy) Lipscomb, Baltimore ... DT
Leo Nomellini, San Francisco ... DT
Joe Schmidt, Detroit ... LB
Sam Huff, N.Y. Giants ... LB
Bill George, Chicago Bears ... LB
Abe Woodson, San Francisco ... DB
Jack Butler, Pittsburgh ... DB
Dean Derby, Pittsburgh ... DB
Jim Patton, N.Y. Giants ... DB
Andy Nelson, Baltimore ... DB

1960 NFL

Offense

Raymond Berry, Baltimore ... E
Sonny Randle, St. Louis ... E
Jim Parker, Baltimore ... T
Forrest Gregg, Green Bay ... T
Roosevelt Brown, N.Y. Giants ... T
Jim Ray Smith, Cleveland ... G
Stan Jones, Chicago ... G
Jerry Kramer, Green Bay ... G
Jim Ringo, Green Bay ... C
Norm Van Brocklin, Philadelphia ... QB

Del Shofner *Jim Ringo* *Jim Otto* *Abner Haynes* *Ron Mix* *Cookie Gilchrist* *Larry Wilson*

Paul Hornung, Green Bay	HB
Lenny Moore, Baltimore	HB
Jim Brown, Cleveland	FB

Defense

Gino Marchetti, Baltimore	DE
Andy Robustelli, N.Y. Giants	DE
Doug Atkins, Chicago	DE
Henry Jordan, Green Bay	DT
Alex Karras, Detroit	DT
Chuck Bednarik, Philadelphia	LB
Bill Forester, Green Bay	LB
Bill George, Chicago	LB
Tom Brookshier, Philadelphia	DB
Abe Woodson, San Francisco	DB
Dick (Night Train) Lane, Detroit	DB
Jerry Norton, St. Louis	DB
Jim Patton, N.Y. Giants	DB

1960 AFL

Offense

Bill Groman, Houston	E
Lionel Taylor, Denver	E
Rich Michael, Houston	T
Ron Mix, Los Angeles	T
Bill Krisher, Dallas	G
Bob Mischak, N.Y. Titans	G
Jim Otto, Oakland	C
Jack Kemp, Los Angeles	QB
Abner Haynes, Dallas	HB
Paul Lowe, Los Angeles	HB
Dave Smith, Houston	FB

Defense

LaVerne Torczon, Buffalo	DE
Mel Branch, Dallas	DE
Bud McFadin, Denver	DT
Volney Peters, Los Angeles	DT
Archie Matsos, Buffalo	LB
Sherrill Headrick, Dallas	LB
Tom Addison, Boston	LB
Richie McCabe, Buffalo	DB
Dick Harris, Los Angeles	DB
Ross O'Hanley, Boston	DB
Austin (Goose) Gonsoulin, Denver	DB

1961 NFL

Offense

Del Shofner, N.Y. Giants	E
Jim (Red) Phillips, Los Angeles	E
Mike Ditka, Chicago	E
Roosevelt Brown, N.Y. Giants	T
Jim Parker, Baltimore	T
Forrest Gregg, Green Bay	T
Jim Ray Smith, Cleveland	G
Fred (Fuzzy) Thurston, Green Bay	G
Jim Ringo, Green Bay	C
Sonny Jurgensen, Philadelphia	QB
Y. A. Tittle, N.Y. Giants	QB
Lenny Moore, Baltimore	HB
Paul Hornung, Green Bay	HB
Jim Taylor, Green Bay	HB
Jim Brown, Cleveland	FB

Defense

Gino Marchetti, Baltimore	DE
Jim Katcavage, N.Y. Giants	DE
Doug Atkins, Chicago	DE
Henry Jordan, Green Bay	DT
Alex Karras, Detroit	DT
Gene (Big Daddy) Lipscomb, Pittsburgh	DT
Joe Schmidt, Detroit	LB
Dan Currie, Green Bay	LB
Bill George, Chicago	LB
Bill Forester, Green Bay	LB
Dick (Night Train) Lane, Detroit	DB
Jesse Whittenton, Green Bay	DB
Erich Barnes, N.Y. Giants	DB
Jimmy Hill, St. Louis	DB
Jim Patton, N.Y., Giants	DB
Johnny Sample, Pittsburgh	DB
Jerry Norton, St. Louis	DB

1961 AFL

Offense

Lionel Taylor, Denver	E
Charley Hennigan, Houston	E
Ron Mix, San Diego	T
Al Jamison, Houston	T

Bob Mischak, N.Y. Titans	G
Chuck Leo, Boston	G
Jim Otto, Oakland	C
George Blanda, Houston	QB
Abner Haynes, Dallas	HB
Billy Cannon, Houston	HB
Billy Mathis, N.Y. Titans	FB

Defense

Earl Faison, San Deigo	DE
Don Floyd, Houston	DE
Bud McFadin, Denver	DT
Chuck McMurtry, Buffalo	DT
Sherrill Headrick, Dallas	LB
Archie Matsos, Buffalo	LB
Chuck Allen, San Deigo	LB
Tony Banfield, Houston	DB
Dick Harris, San Diego	DB
Dave Webster, Dallas	DB
Charlie McNeil, San Deigo	DB

1962 NFL

Offense

Del Shofner, N.Y. Giants	SE
Mike Ditka, Chicago	TE
Ron Kramer, Green Bay	TE
Bobby Mitchell, Washington	FL
Forrest Gregg, Green Bay	T
Roosevelt Brown, N.Y. Giants	T
Jim Parker, Baltimore	T
Jerry Kramer, Green Bay	G
Jim Parker, Baltimore	G
Jim Ray Smith, Cleveland	G
Fred (Fuzzy) Thurston, Green Bay	G
Jim Ringo, Green Bay	C
Y. A. Tittle, N.Y. Giants	QB
Jim Taylor, Green Bay	RB
Don Perkins, Dallas	RB
Dick Bass, Los Angeles	RB

Defense

Gino Marchetti, Baltimore	DE
Jim Katcavage, N.Y. Giants	DE
Willie Davis, Green Bay	DE
Roger Brown, Detroit	DT
Alex Karras, Detroit	DT
Henry Jordan, Green Bay	DT
Joe Schmidt, Detroit	MLB
Dan Currie, Green Bay	LB
Bill Forester, Green Bay	LB
Dick (Night Train) Lane, Detroit	CB
Herb Adderley, Green Bay	CB
Abe Woodson, San Francisco	CB
Yale Lary, Detroit	S
Jim Patton, N.Y. Giants	S

1962 AFL

Offense

Charley Hennigan, Houston	SE
Dave Kocourek, San Diego	TE
Chris Burford, Dallas	FL
Eldon Danenhauer, Denver	T
Jim Tyrer, Dallas	T
Bob Talamini, Houston	G
Ron Mix, San Diego	G
Jim Otto, Oakland	C
Len Dawson, Dallas	QB
Abner Haynes, Dallas	HB
Cookie Gilchrist, Buffalo	FB

Defense

Don Floyd, Houston	DE
Mel Branch, Dallas	DE
Bud McFadin, Denver	DT
Jerry Mays, Dallas	DT
Larry Grantham, N.Y. Titans	LB
E. J. Holub, Dallas	LB
Sherrill Headrick, Dallas	MLB
Tony Banfield, Houston	CB
Fred Williamson, Oakland	CB
Austin (Goose) Gonsoulin, Denver	S
Bob Zeman, Denver	S

1963 NFL

Offense

Del Shofner, N.Y. Giants	SE
Mike Ditka, Chicago	TE
Bobby Joe Conrad, St. Louis	FL
Bobby Mitchell, Washington	FL

Forrest Gregg, Green Bay	T
Roosevelt Brown, N.Y. Giants	T
Dick Schafrath, Cleveland	T
Jerry Kramer, Green Bay	G
Jim Parker, Baltimore	G
Ken Gray, St. Louis	G
Jim Ringo, Green Bay	C
Y. A. Tittle, N.Y. Giants	QB
Tommy Mason, Minnesota	RB
Jim Brown, Cleveland	RB

Defense

Doug Atkins, Chicago	DE
Jim Katcavage, N.Y. Giants	DE
Gino Marchetti, Baltimore	DE
Henry Jordan, Green Bay	DT
Roger Brown, Detroit	DT
Bill George, Chicago	MLB
Joe Schmidt, Detroit	MLB
Joe Fortunato, Chicago	LB
Jack Pardee, Los Angeles	LB
Myron Pottios, Pittsburgh	LB
Bill Forester, Green Bay	LB
Dick Lynch, N.Y. Giants	CB
Herb Adderley, Green Bay	CB
Abe Woodson, San Francisco	CB
Dick (Night Train) Lane, Detroit	CB
Roosevelt Taylor, Chicago	S
Richie Petitbon, Chicago	S
Willie Wood, Green Bay	S
Larry Wilson, St. Louis	S

1963 AFL

Offense

Art Powell, Oakland	SE
Fred Arbanas, Kansas City	TE
Lance Alworth, San Diego	FL
Ron Mix, San Diego	T
Jim Tyrer, Kansas City	T
Billy Shaw, Buffalo	G
Bob Talamini, Houston	G
Jim Otto, Oakland	C
Tobin Rote, San Diego	QB
Clemon Daniels, Oakland	HB
Keith Lincoln, San Diego	FB

Defense

Larry Eisenhauer, Boston	DE
Earl Faison, San Diego	DE
Tom Sestak, Buffalo	DT
Houston Antwine, Boston	DT
Archie Matsos, Oakland	MLB
E. J. Holub, Kansas City	LB
Tom Addison, Boston	LB
Dave Grayson, Kansas City	CB
Fred Williamson, Oakland	CB
Fred Glick, Houston	S
Austin (Goose) Gonsoulin, Denver	S

1964 NFL

Offense

Frank Clarke, Dallas	SE
Paul Warfield, Cleveland	SE
Bobby Mitchell, Washington	SE
Mike Ditka, Chicago	TE
Johnny Morris, Chicago	FL
Forrest Gregg, Green Bay	T
Dick Schafrath, Cleveland	T
Bob Vogel, Baltimore	T
Jim Parker, Baltimore	G
Ken Gray, St. Louis	G
John Gordy, Detroit	G
Mick Tingelhoff, Minnesota	C
Bob DeMarco, St. Louis	C
John Unitas, Baltimore	QB
Lenny Moore, Baltimore	RB
Jim Brown, Cleveland	RB

Defense

Willie Davis, Green Bay	DE
Gino Marchetti, Baltimore	DE
Bob Lilly, Dallas	DT
Henry Jordan, Green Bay	DT
Merlin Olsen, Los Angeles	DT
Ray Nitschke, Green Bay	MLB
Dale Meinert, St. Louis	MLB
Joe Fortunato, Chicago	LB
Maxie Baughan, Philadelphia	LB

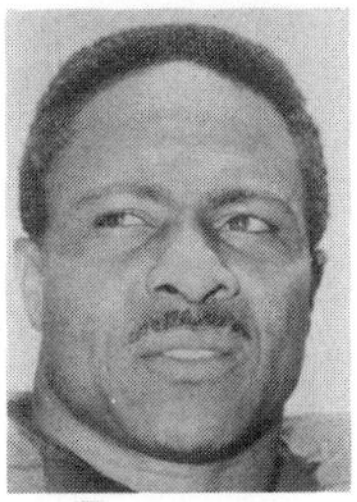
Clemon Daniels

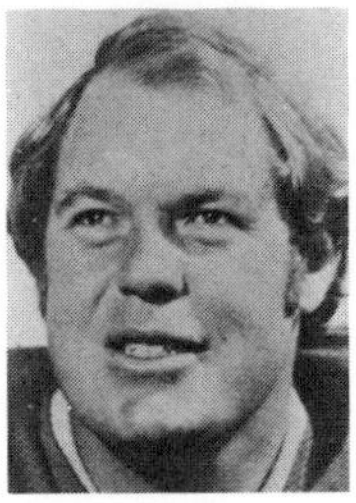
Merlin Olsen

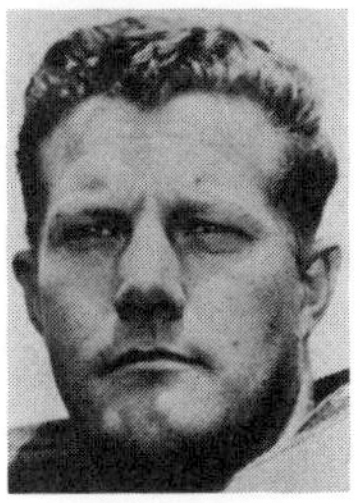
Larry Grantham

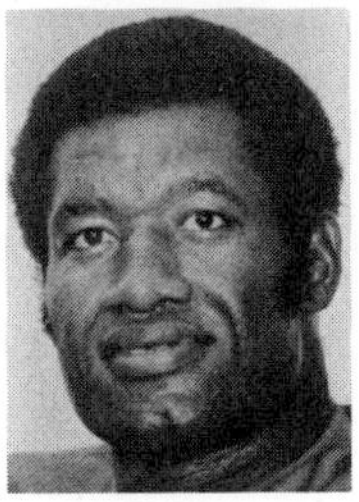
Bobby Bell

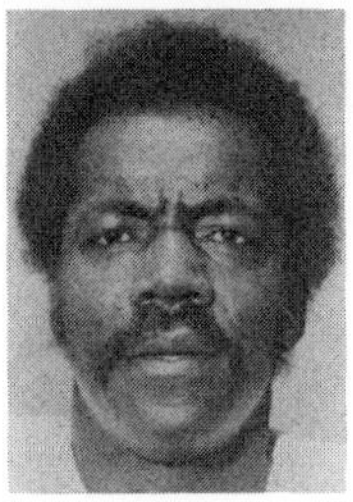
Cornell Green

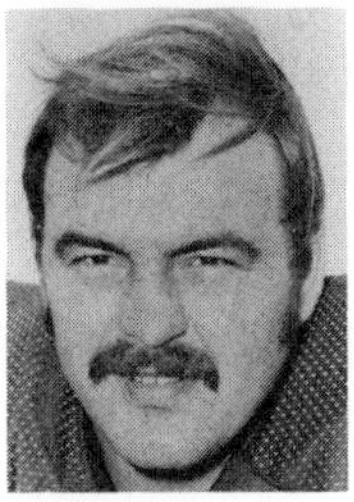
Dick Butkus

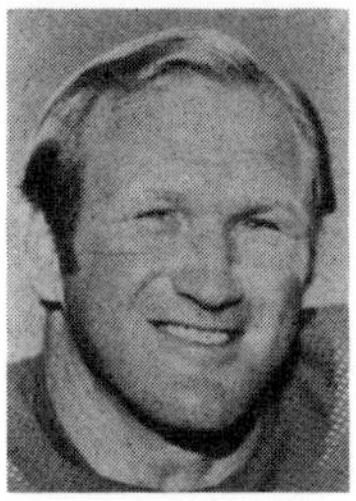
Tommy Nobis

Jim Houston, Cleveland ... LB
Wayne Walker, Detroit ... LB
Pat Fischer, St. Louis ... HB
Bobby Boyd, Baltimore ... HB
Erich Barnes, N.Y. Giants ... HB
Paul Krause, Washington ... S
Willie Wood, Green Bay ... S

1964 AFL

Offense

Art Powell, Oakland ... SE
Charley Hennigan, Houston ... SE
Fred Arbanas, Kansas City ... TE
Ron Mix, San Diego ... FL
Lance Alworth, San Diego ... T
Jim Tyrer, Kansas City ... T
Billy Shaw, Buffalo ... G
Bob Talamini, Houston ... G
Jim Otto, Oakland ... C
Babe Parilli, Boston ... QB
Keith Lincoln, San Diego ... HB
Cookie Gilchrist, Buffalo ... FB

Defense

Earl Faison, San Diego ... DE
Larry Eisenhauer, Boston ... DE
Tom Sestak, Buffalo ... DT
Jerry Mays, Kansas City ... DT
Nick Buoniconti, Boston ... MLB
Tom Addison, Boston ... LB
Larry Grantham, N.Y. Jets ... LB
Willie Brown, Denver ... CB
Dave Grayson, Kansas City ... CB
Fred Glick, Houston ... S
Dainard Paulson, N.Y. Jets ... S

1965 NFL

Offense

Dave Parks, San Francisco ... SE
Pete Retzlaff, Philadelphia ... TE
Jimmy Orr, Baltimore ... FL
Gary Collins, Cleveland ... FL
Bob Brown, Philadelphia ... T
Dick Schafrath, Cleveland ... T
Forrest Gregg, Green Bay ... T
Bob Vogel, Baltimore ... T
Jim Parker, Baltimore ... G
John Gordy, Detroit ... G
Ken Gray, St. Louis ... G
Forrest Gregg, Green Bay ... G
Mick Tingelhoff, Minnesota ... C
John Unitas, Baltimore ... QB
Gale Sayers, Chicago ... RB
Jim Brown, Cleveland ... RB

Defense

Willie Davis, Green Bay ... DE
David (Deacon) Jones, Los Angeles ... DE
Alex Karras, Detroit ... DT
Bob Lilly, Dallas ... DT
Dick Butkus, Chicago ... MLB
Ray Nitschke, Green Bay ... MLB
Wayne Walker, Detroit ... LB
Joe Fortunato, Chicago ... LB
Jim Houston, Cleveland ... LB
Bobby Boyd, Baltimore ... CB
Herb Adderley, Green Bay ... CB
Willie Wood, Green Bay ... S
Paul Krause, Washington ... S
Mel Renfro, Dallas ... S

1965 AFL

Offense

Art Powell, Oakland ... SE
Lionel Taylor, Denver ... SE
Willie Frazier, Houston ... TE
Lance Alworth, San Diego ... FL
Jim Tyrer, Kansas City ... T
Eldon Danenhauer, Denver ... T
Billy Shaw, Buffalo ... G
Bob Talamini, Houston ... G
Jim Otto, Oakland ... C
Jack Kemp, Buffalo ... QB
Paul Lowe, San Diego ... HB
Cookie Gilchrist, Denver ... FB
Pete Gogolak, Buffalo ... K
Curley Johnson, N.Y. Jets ... P

Defense

Earl Faison, San Diego ... DE
Jerry Mays, Kansas City ... DE
Tom Sestak, Buffalo ... DT
Ernie Ladd, San Diego ... DT
Nick Buoniconti, Boston ... MLB
Mike Stratton, Buffalo ... LB
Bobby Bell, Kansas City ... LB
Dave Grayson, Oakland ... CB
George (Butch) Byrd, Buffalo ... CB
George Saimes, Buffalo ... S
Johnny Robinson, Kansas City ... S

1966 NFL

Offense

Bob Hayes, Dallas ... SE
Dave Parks, San Francisco ... SE
John Mackey, Baltimore ... TE
Pat Studstill, Detroit ... FL
Bob Brown, Philadelphia ... T
Forrest Gregg, Green Gay ... T
Jerry Kramer, Green Bay ... G
John Thomas, San Francisco ... G
John Gordy, Detroit ... G
Gene Hickerson, Cleveland ... G
Mick Tingelhoff, Minnesota ... C
Bart Starr, Green Bay ... QB
Leroy Kelly, Cleveland ... RB
Gale Sayers, Chicago ... RB

Defense

Willie Davis, Green Bay ... DE
David (Deacon) Jones, Los Angeles ... DE
Bob Lilly, Dallas ... DT
Merlin Olsen, Los Angeles ... DT
Ray Nitschke, Green Bay ... MLB
Chuck Howley, Dallas ... LB
Lee Roy Caffey, Green Bay ... LB
Maxie Baughan, Los Angeles ... LB
Herb Adderley, Green Bay ... CB
Cornell Green, Dallas ... CB
Bobby Boyd, Baltimore ... CB
Larry Wilson, St. Louis ... S
Willie Wood, Green Bay ... S

1966 AFL

Offense

Art Powell, Oakland ... SE
Fred Arbanas, Kansas City ... TE
Lance Alworth, San Diego ... FL
Jim Tyrer, Kansas City ... T
Sherman Plunkett, N.Y. Jets ... T
Billy Shaw, Buffalo ... G
Bob Talamini, Houston ... G
Jim Otto, Oakland ... C
Len Dawson, Kansas City ... QB
Clemon Daniels, Oakland ... HB
Jim Nance, Boston ... FB
Gino Cappelletti, Boston ... K
Bob Scarpitto, Denver ... P

Defense

Jerry Mays, Kansas City ... DE
Larry Eisenhauer, Boston ... DE
Houston Antwine, Boston ... DT
Buck Buchanan, Kansas City ... DT
Nick Buoniconti, Boston ... MLB
Mike Stratton, Buffalo ... LB
Bobby Bell, Kansas City ... LB
Dave Grayson, Oakland ... CB
George (Butch) Byrd, Buffalo ... CB
Johnny Robinson, Kansas City ... S
George Saimes, Buffalo ... S

1967 NFL

Offense

Charley Taylor, Washington ... WR
Homer Jones, N.Y. Giants ... WR
Willie Richardson, Baltimore ... WR
John Mackey, Baltimore ... TE
Jackie Smith, St. Louis ... TE
Ralph Neely, Dallas ... T
Forrest Gregg, Green Bay ... T
Ernie McMillan, St. Louis ... T
Bob Vogel, Baltimore ... T
Gene Hickerson, Cleveland ... G
Jerry Kramer, Green Bay ... G
Howard Mudd, San Francisco ... G
Mick Tingelhoff, Minnesota ... C
Bob DeMarco, St. Louis ... C
John Unitas, Baltimore ... QB
Leroy Kelly, Cleveland ... RB
Gale Sayers, Chicago ... RB

Defense

Willie Davis, Green Bay ... DE
David (Deacon) Jones, Los Angeles ... DE
Bob Lilly, Dallas ... DT
Merlin Olsen, Los Angeles ... DT
Dick Butkus, Chicago ... MLB
Tommy Nobis, Atlanta ... MLB
Dave Robinson, Green Bay ... LB
Chuck Howley, Dallas ... LB
Dave Wilcox, San Francisco ... LB
Bob Jeter, Green Bay ... CB
Cornell Green, Dallas ... CB
Willie Wood, Green Bay ... S
Eddie Meador, Los Angeles ... S
Larry Wilson, St. Louis ... S

1967 AFL

Offense

George Sauer, N.Y. Jets ... SE
Billy Cannon, Oakland ... TE
Lance Alworth, San Diego ... FL
Ron Mix, San Diego ... T
Jim Tyrer, Kansas City ... T
Bob Talamini, Houston ... G
Walt Sweeney, San Diego ... G
Jim Otto, Oakland ... C
Daryle Lamonica, Oakland ... QB
Mike Garrett, Kansas City ... RB
Jim Nance, Boston ... RB

Defense

Ben Davidson, Oakland ... DE
Pat Holmes, Houston ... DE
Buck Buchanan, Kansas City ... DT
Tom Keating, Oakland ... DT
Nick Buoniconti, Boston ... MLB
George Webster, Houston ... LB
Bobby Bell, Kansas City ... LB
Miller Farr, Houston ... CB
Kent McCloughan, Oakland ... CB
George Saimes, Buffalo ... S
Johnny Robinson, Kansas City ... S

1968 NFL

Offense

Clifton McNeil, San Francisco ... WR
Paul Warfield, Cleveland ... WR
Bob Hayes, Dallas ... WR
John Mackey, Baltimore ... TE
Ralph Neely, Dallas ... T
Bob Brown, Philadelphia ... T
Bob Vogel, Baltimore ... T
Gene Hickerson, Cleveland ... G
Howard Mudd, San Francisco ... G
Mick Tingelhoff, Minnesota ... C
Earl Morrall, Baltimore ... QB
Leroy Kelly, Cleveland ... RB
Gale Sayers, Chicago ... RB

Defense

David (Deacon) Jones, Los Angeles ... DE
Carl Eller, Minnesota ... DE
Merlin Olsen, Los Angeles ... DT
Bob Lilly, Dallas ... DT
Dick Butkus, Chicago ... LB
Mike Curtis, Baltimore ... LB
Chuck Howley, Dallas ... LB
Dave Robinson, Green Bay ... LB
Lem Barney, Detroit ... CB
Bobby Boyd, Baltimore ... CB
Cornell Green, Dallas ... CB
Larry Wilson, St. Louis ... S
Eddie Meador, Los Angeles ... S
Willie Wood, Green Bay ... S
Rick Volk, Baltimore ... S

1968 AFL

Offense

Lance Alworth, San Diego ... WR
George Sauer, N.Y. Jets ... WR
Jim Whalen, Boston ... TE
Ron Mix, San Diego ... T
Jim Tyrer, Kansas City ... T
Walt Sweeney, San Diego ... G

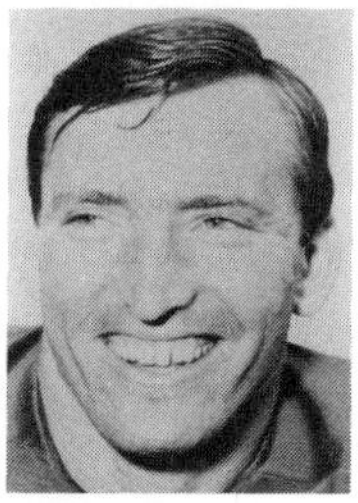
Dave Wilcox

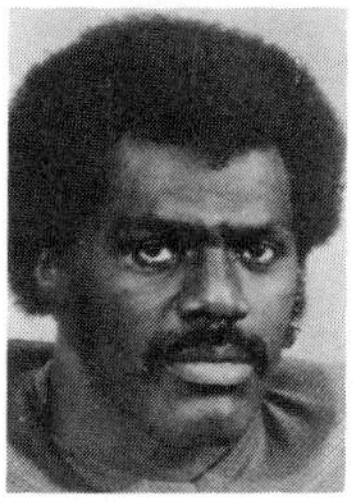
Alan Page

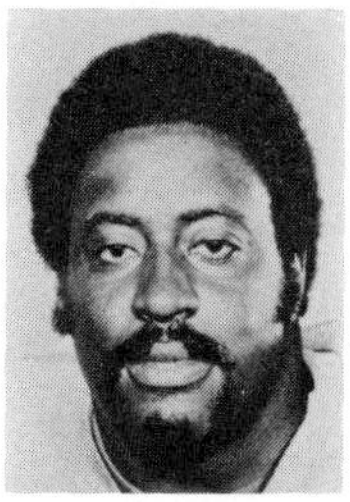
Larry Little

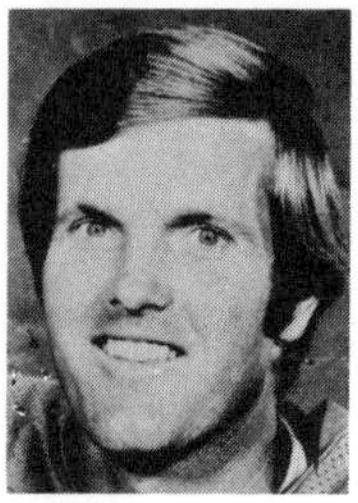
Bob Griese

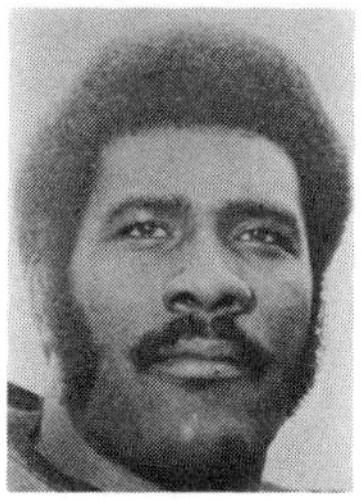
Joe Greene

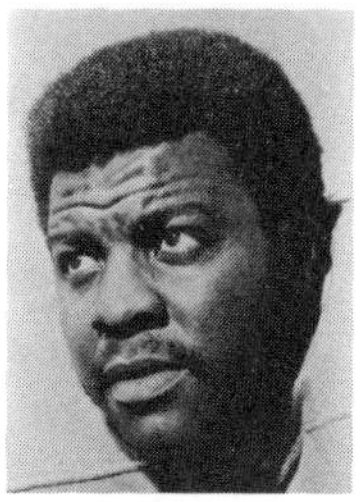
Riley Odoms

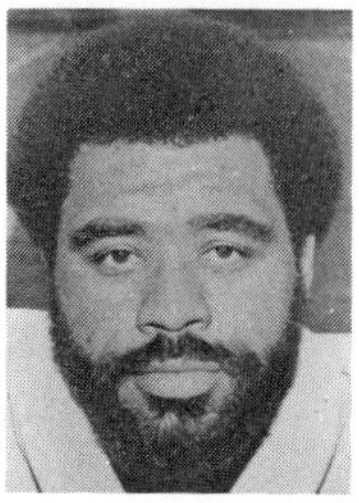
Curley Culp

Gene Upshaw, Oakland ... G
Jim Otto, Oakland ... C
Joe Namath, N.Y. Jets ... QB
Paul Robinson, Cincinnati ... RB
Hewritt Dixon, Oakland ... RB
Defense
Gerry Philbin, Y.Y. Jets ... DE
Rich Jackson, Denver ... DE
Buck Buchanan, Kansas City ... DT
Dan Birdwell, Oakland ... DT
Willie Lanier, Kansas City ... MLB
George Webster, Houston ... LB
Bobby Bell, Kansas City ... LB
Miller Farr, Houston ... CB
Willie Brown, Oakland ... CB
Dave Grayson, Oakland ... S
Johnny Robinson, Kansas City ... S
1969
Offense
Lance Alworth, San Diego ... WR
Paul Warfield, Cleveland ... WR
Bob Trumpy, Cincinnati ... TE
Bob Brown, Los Angeles ... T
Jim Tyrer, Kansas City ... T
Tom Mack, Los Angeles ... G
Gene Hickerson, Cleveland ... G
Mick Tingelhoff,Minnesota ... C
Roman Gabriel, Los Angeles ... QB
Gale Sayers, Chicago ... RB
Calvin Hill, Dallas ... RB
Jan Stenerud, Kansas City ... K
David Lee, Baltimore ... P
Defense
David (Deacon) Jones, Los Angeles ... DE
Carl Eller, Minnesota ... DE
Merlin Olsen, Los Angeles ... DT
Bob Lilly, Dallas ... DT
Dick Butkus, Chicago ... MLB
Bobby Bell, Kansas City ... LB
Chuck Howley, Dallas ... LB
Lem Barney, Detroit ... CB
Willie Brown, Oakland ... CB
Larry Wilson, St. Louis ... S
Johnny Robinson, Kansas City ... S
1970
Offense
Gene Washington, San Francisco ... WR
Dick Gordon, Chicago ... WR
Charlie Sanders, Detroit ... TE
Jim Tyrer, Kansas City ... T
Bob Brown, Los Angeles ... T
Gene Upshaw, Oakland ... G
Gene Hickerson, Cleveland ... G
Mick Tingelhoff, Minnesota ... C
John Brodie, San Francisco ... QB
Larry Brown, Washington ... RB
Ron Johnson, N.Y. Giants ... RB
Jan Stenerud, Kansas City ... K
Dave Lewis, Cincinnati ... P
Defense
Carl Eller, Minnesota ... DE
Rich Jackson, Denver ... DE
Alan Page, Minnesota ... DT
Merlin Olsen, Los Angeles ... DT
Bobby Bell, Kansas City ... LB
Chuck Howley, Dallas ... LB
Dick Butkus, Chicago ... MLB
Willie Brown, Oakland ... CB
Jimmy Johnson, San Francisco ... CB
Johnny Robinson, Kansas City ... S
Larry Wilson, St. Louis ... S
1971
Offense
Otis Taylor, Kansas City ... WR
Paul Warfield, Miami ... WR
Charlie Sanders, Detroit ... TE
Ron Yary, Minnesota ... T
Rayfield Wright, Dallas ... T
Larry Little, Miami ... G
John Niland, Dallas ... G
Forrest Blue, San Francisco ... C
Bob Griese, Miami ... QB
John Brockington, Green Bay ... RB
Larry Csonka, Miami ... RB
Garo Yepremian, Miami ... K
Jan Stenerud, Kansas City ... K
Jerrel Wilson, Kansas City ... P
Defense
Carl Eller, Minnesota ... DE
Bubba Smith, Baltimore ... DE
Bob Lilly, Dallas ... DT
Alan Page, Minnesota ... DT
Jimmy Johnson, San Francisco ... CB
Ted Hendricks, Baltimore ... LB
Dave Wilcox, San Francisco ... LB
Willie Lanier, Kansas City ... MLB
Willie Brown, Oakland ... CB
Rick Volk, Baltimore ... S
Bill Bradley, Philadelphia ... S
1972
Offense
Gene Washington, San Francisco ... WR
Otis Taylor, Kansas City ... WR
Bob Tucker, N.Y. Giants ... TE
Rayfield Wright, Dallas ... T
Bob Brown, Oakland ... T
Larry Little, Miami ... G
Gene Upshaw, Oakland ... G
Forrest Blue, San Francisco ... C
Joe Namath, N.Y. Jets ... QB
Larry Brown, Washington ... RB
O. J. Simpson, Buffalo ... RB
Chester Marcol, Green Bay ... K
Jerrel Wilson, Kansas City ... P
Defense
Claude Humphrey, Atlanta ... DE
Jack Gregory, N.Y. Giants ... DE
Joe Greene, Pittsburgh ... DT
Mike Reid, Cincinnati ... DT
Dick Butkus, Chicago ... MLB
Chris Hanburger, Washington ... LB
Dave Wilcox, San Francisco ... LB
Jimmy Johnson, San Francisco ... CB
Willie Brown, Oakland ... CB
Dick Anderson, Miami ... S
Bill Bradley, Philadelphia ... S
1973
Offense
Harold Jackson, Los Angeles ... WR
Harold Carmichael, Philadelphia ... WR
Charles Young, Philadelphia ... TE
Ron Yary, Minnesota ... T
Rayfield Wright, Dallas ... T
Larry Little, Miami ... G
Reggie McKenzie, Buffalo ... G
Forrest Blue, San Francisco ... C
John Hadl, Los Angeles ... QB
O.J. Simpson, Buffalo ... RB
Calvin Hill, Dallas ... RB
Defense
Claude Humphrey, Atlanta ... DE
Bill Stanfill, Miami ... DE
Joe Greene, Pittsburgh ... DT
Alan Page, Minnesota ... DT
Lee Roy Jordan, Dallas ... MLB
Dave Wilcox, San Francisco ... LB
Isiah Robertson, Los Angeles ... LB
Willie Brown, Oakland ... CB
Mel Renfro, Dallas ... CB
Jake Scott, Miami ... S
Dick Anderson, Miami ... S
Garo Yepremian, Miami ... K
Ray Guy, Oakland ... P
1974
Offense
Cliff Branch, Oakland ... WR
Drew Pearson, Dallas ... WR
Riley Odoms, Denver ... TE
Ron Yary, Minnesota ... T
Art Shell, Oakland ... T
Tom Mack, Los Angeles ... G
Larry Little, Miami ... G
Jim Langer, Miami ... C
Ken Stabler, Oakland ... QB
Otis Armstrong, Denver ... RB
O.J. Simpson, Buffalo ... RB
Defense
L.C. Greenwood, Pittsburgh ... DE
Jack Youngblood, Los Angeles ... DE
Joe Greene, Pittsburgh ... DT
Alan Page, Minnesota ... DT
Bill Bergey, Philadelphia ... MLB
Jack Ham, Pittsburgh ... LB
Ted Hendricks, Green Bay ... LB
Emmitt Thomas, Kansas City ... CB
Robert James, Buffalo ... CB
Tony Greene, Buffalo ... S
Ken Houston, Washington ... S
Chester Marcol, Green Bay ... K
Ray Guy, Oakland ... P
1975
Offense
Mel Gray, St. Louis ... WR
Lynn Swann, Pittsburgh ... WR
Charles Young, Philadelphia ... TE
Ron Yary, Minnesota ... T
Dan Dierdorf, St. Louis ... T
Larry Little, Miami ... G
Joe DeLamielleure, Buffalo ... G
Jim Langer, Miami ... C
Fran Tarkenton, Minnesota ... QB
O.J. Simpson, Buffalo ... RB
Chuck Foreman, Minnesota ... RB
Defense
Jack Youngblood, Los Angeles ... DE
L.C. Greenwood, Pittsburgh ... DE
Alan Page, Minnesota ... DT
Curley Culp, Houston ... DT
Jack Lambert, Pittsburgh ... MLB
Andy Russell, Pittsburgh ... LB
Jack Ham, Pittsburgh ... LB
Mel Blount, Pittsburgh ... CB
Roger Wehrli, St. Louis ... CB
Paul Krause, Minnesota ... S
Ken Houston, Washington ... S
Jim Bakken, St. Louis ... K
Ray Guy, Oakland ... P
1976
Offense
Clifford Branch, Oakland ... WR
Drew Pearson, Dallas ... WR
Dave Casper, Oakland ... TE
Dan Dierdorf, St. Louis ... T
Ron Yary, Minnesota ... T
Joe DeLamielleure, Buffalo ... G
John Hannah, New England ... G
Jim Langer, Miami ... C
Bert Jones, Baltimore ... QB
O.J. Simpson, Buffalo ... RB
Walter Payton, Chicago ... RB
Defense
Jack Youngblood, Los Angeles ... DE
Tommy Hart, San Francisco ... DE
Wally Chambers, Chicago ... DT
Jerry Sherk, Cleveland ... DT
Jack Lambert, Pittsburgh ... MLB
Jack Ham, Pittsburgh ... LB
Robert Brazile, Houston ... LB
Monte Johnson, Los Angeles ... CB
Roger Wehrli, St. Louis ... CB
Ken Houston, Washington ... S
Cliff Harris, Dallas ... S
Jim Bakken, St. Louis ... K
Ray Guy, Oakland ... P

ALL-PRO SQUAD OF THE 1920s

The New York Giants with ball vs. Chicago Bears and Red Grange, 1925.

The roster chosen by the Hall of Fame Selection Committee

Name	Pos.	Ht.	Wt.	Teams
Guy Chamberlin	End	6-2	210	1920 Decatur Staleys, 1921 Chicago Staleys, 1922-23 Canton Bulldogs, 1924 Cleveland Bulldogs, 1925-26 Frankford Yellowjackets, 1927 Chicago Cardinals
Lavern Dilweg	End	6-3	203	1926 Milwaukee Badgers, 1927-34 Green Bay Packers
George Halas	End	6-1	180	1920 Decatur Staleys, 1921 Chicago Staleys, 1922-29 Chicago Bears
Ed Healey	Tackle	6-3	220	1920-22 Rock Island Independents, 1922-27 Chicago Bears
Wilbur (Pete) Henry	Tackle	6-0	250	1920-23, 1925-26 Canton Bulldogs, 1927 New York Giants, 1927-28 Pottsville Maroons
Cal Hubbard	Tackle	6-5	250	1927-28 New York Giants, 1929-1933, 1935 Green Bay Packers, 1936 New York Giants, 1936 Pittsburgh Pirates
Steve Owen	Tackle	6-2	235	1924-25 Kansas City Cowboys, 1926-1931, 1933 New York Giants
Heartley (Hunk) Anderson	Guard	5-11	195	1922-25 Chicago Bears
Walt Kiesling	Guard	6-2	245	1926-27 Duluth Eskimos, 1928 Pottsville Maroons, 1929-1933 Chicago Cardinals, 1934 Chicago Bears, 1935-36 Green Bay Packers, 1937-38 Pittsburgh Pirates
Mike Michalske	Guard	6-0	209	1926 New York Yankees (AFL), 1927-28 New York Yankees (NFL), 1929-1935, 1937 Green Bay Packers
George Trafton	Center	6-2	235	1920 Decatur Staleys, 1921 Chicago Staleys, 1922-1932 Chicago Bears
Jimmy Conzelman	Quarterback	6-0	180	1920 Decatur Staleys, 1921-22 Rock Island Independents, 1923-24 Milwaukee Badgers, 1925-26 Detroit Panthers, 1927-29 Providence Steamrollers
John (Paddy) Driscoll	Quarterback	5-11	160	1920 Decatur Staleys, 1920-25 Chicago Cardinals, 1926-29 Chicago Bears
Harold (Red) Grange	Halfback	6-0	185	1925 Chicago Bears, 1926 New York Yankees (AFL), 1927 New York Yankees, 1929-1934 Chicago Bears
Joe Guyon	Halfback	6-1	180	1920 Canton Bulldogs, 1921 Cleveland Indians, 1922-23 Oorang Indians, 1924 Rock Island Independents, 1924-25 Kansas City Cowboys, 1927 New York Giants
Earl (Curly) Lambeau	Halfback	6-0	195	1921-29 Green Bay Packers
Jim Thorpe	Halfback	6-1	190	1920 Canton Bulldogs, 1921 Cleveland Indians, 1922-23 Oorang Indians, 1923 Toledo Maroons, 1924 Rock Island Independents, 1925 New York Giants, 1926 Canton Bulldogs, 1928 Chicago Cardinals
Ernie Nevers	Fullback	6-1	205	1926-27 Duluth Eskimos, 1929-1931 Chicago Cardinals

ALL-PRO SQUAD OF THE 1930s

Bill Hewitt (56, with no helmet) and the Bears vs. Green Bay Packers, 1937.

The roster chosen by the Hall of Fame Selection Committee

Name	Pos.	Ht.	Wt.	Teams
Bill Hewitt	End	5-11	191	1932-36 Chicago Bears, 1937-39 Philadelphia Eagles, 1943 Phil-Pitt
Don Hutson	End	6-1	180	1935-1945 Green Bay Packers
Wayne Millner	End	6-0	191	1936 Boston Redskins, 1937-1941, 1945 Washington Redskins
Gaynell Tinsley	End	6-1	200	1937-38, 1940 Chicago Cardinals
George Christensen	Tackle	6-2	238	1931-33 Portsmouth Spartans, 1934-38 Detroit Lions
Frank Cope	Tackle	6-3	234	1938-1947 New York Giants
Glen (Turk) Edwards	Tackle	6-2	260	1932 Boston Braves, 1933-36 Boston Redskins, 1937-1940 Washington Redskins
Bill Lee	Tackle	6-2	235	1935-37 Brooklyn Dodgers, 1937-1942, 1946 Green Bay Packers
Joe Stydahar	Tackle	6-4	230	1936-1942, 1945-46 Chicago Bears
Grover (Ox) Emerson	Guard	6-0	190	1931-33 Portsmouth Spartans, 1934-37 Detroit Lions, 1938 Brooklyn Dodgers
Danny Fortmann	Guard	6-0	207	1936-1943 Chicago Bears
Charles (Buckets) Goldenberg	Guard	5-10	222	1933-1945 Green Bay Packers
Ross Letlow	Guard	6-0	212	1936-1942, 1946 Green Bay Packers
Mel Hein	Center	6-2	225	1931-1945 New York Giants
George Svendsen	Center	6-4	240	1935-37, 1940-41 Green Bay Packers
Cliff Battles	Halfback	6-1	201	1932 Boston Braves, 1933-36 Boston Redskins, 1937 Washington Redskins
Earl (Dutch) Clark	Quarterback	6-0	185	1931-32 Portsmouth Spartans, 1934-38 Detroit Lions
Arnie Herber	Quarterback	6-1	200	1930-1940 Green Bay Packers, 1944-45 New York Giants
Cecil Isbell	Quarterback	6-0	190	1938-1942 Green Bay Packers
Beattie Feathers	Halfback	5-11	177	1934-37 Chicago Bears, 1938-39 Brooklyn Dodgers, 1940 Green Bay Packers
Alphonse (Tuffy) Leemans	Halfback	6-0	200	1936-1943 New York Giants
Johnny Blood (McNally)	Halfback	6-0	185	1925-26 Milwaukee Badgers, 1926-27 Duluth Eskimos, 1928 Pottsville Maroons, 1929-1933 Green Bay Packers, 1934 Pittsburgh Pirates, 1935-36 Green Bay Packers, 1937-38 Pittsburgh Pirates, 1939 Pittsburgh Steelers
Ken Strong	Halfback	5-11	210	1929-1932 Stapleton Stapes, 1933-35 New York Giants, 1936-37 New York Yanks (AFL), 1939, 1944-47 New York Giants
Clarke Hinkle	Fullback	5-11	191	1932-1941 Green Bay Packers
Bronko Nagurski	Fullback	6-2	225	1930-37, 1943 Chicago Bears

ALL-PRO SQUAD OF THE 1940s

Steve Van Buren of Philadelphia running against Washington, late 1940s.

The roster chosen by the Hall of Fame Selection Committee

Name	Pos.	Ht.	Wt.	Teams
Jim Benton	End	6-3	210	1938-1940, 1942, 1944-45 Cleveland Rams, 1943 Chicago Bears, 1946-47 Los Angeles Rams
Jack Ferrante	End	6-1	205	1941, 1944-50 Philadelphia Eagles
Ken Kavanaugh	End	6-3	205	1940-41, 1945-50 Chicago Bears
Dante Lavelli	End	6-0	192	1946-49 Cleveland Browns (AAFC), 1950-56 Cleveland Browns
Pete Pihos	End	6-1	210	1947-1955 Philadelphia Eagles
Mac Speedie	End	6-3	205	1946-49 Cleveland Browns (AAFC), 1950-52 Cleveland Browns
Ed Sprinkle	End	6-1	207	1944-1955 Chicago Bears
Al Blozis	Tackle	6-7	250	1942-44 New York Giants
George Connor	Tackle	6-3	240	1948-1955 Chicago Bears
Frank (Bucko) Kilroy	Tackle	6-2	244	1943 Phil-Pitt, 1944-1955 Philadelphia Eagles
Buford (Baby) Ray	Tackle	6-6	250	1938-1948 Green Bay Packers
Vic Sears	Tackle	6-3	236	1941-42 Philadelphia Eagles, 1943 Phil-Pitt, 1945-1953 Philadelphia Eagles
Al Wistert	Tackle	6-1	214	1943 Phil-Pitt, 1944-1951 Philadelphia Eagles
Bruno Banducci	Guard	5-11	220	1944-45 Philadelphia Eagles, 1946-49 San Francisco 49ers (AAFC), 1950-54 San Francisco 49ers
Bill Edwards	Guard	6-3	218	1940-42, 1946 New York Giants
Garrard (Buster) Ramsey	Guard	6-1	220	1946-1951 Chicago Cardinals
Bill Willis	Guard	6-2	215	1946-49 Cleveland Browns (AAFC), 1950-53 Cleveland Browns
Len Younce	Guard	6-1	210	1941, 1943-44, 1946-48 New York Giants
Charles Brock	Center	6-2	210	1939-1947 Green Bay Packers
Clyde (Bulldog) Turner	Center	6-2	235	1940-1952 Chicago Bears
Alex Wojciechowicz	Center	6-0	235	1938-1946 Detroit Lions, 1946-1950 Philadelphia Eagles
Sammy Baugh	Quarterback	6-2	180	1937-1952 Washington Redskins
Sid Luckman	Quarterback	6-0	195	1939-1950 Chicago Bears
Bob Waterfield	Quarterback	6-2	200	1945 Cleveland Rams, 1946-1952 Los Angeles Rams
Tony Canadeo	Halfback	5-11	195	1941-44, 1946-1952 Green Bay Packers
Bill Dudley	Halfback	5-10	176	1942,1945-46 Pittsburgh Steelers, 1947-49 Detroit Lions, 1950-51, 1953 Washington Redskins
George McAfee	Halfback	6-0	177	1940-41, 1945-1950 Chicago Bears
Charley Trippi	Halfback	6-0	185	1947-1955 Chicago Cardinals
Steve Van Buren	Halfback	6-1	200	1944-1951 Philadelphia Eagles
Byron (Whizzer) White	Halfback	6-1	188	1938 Pittsburgh Pirates, 1940-41 Detroit Lions
Pat Harder	Fullback	5-11	205	1946-1950 Chicago Cardinals, 1951-53 Detroit Lions
Marion Motley	Fullback	6-1	238	1946-49 Cleveland Browns (AAFC), 1950-53 Cleveland Browns, 1955 Pittsburgh Steelers
Bill Osmanski	Fullback	5-11	200	1939-1943, 1946-47 Chicago Bears

ALL-PRO SQUAD OF THE 1950s

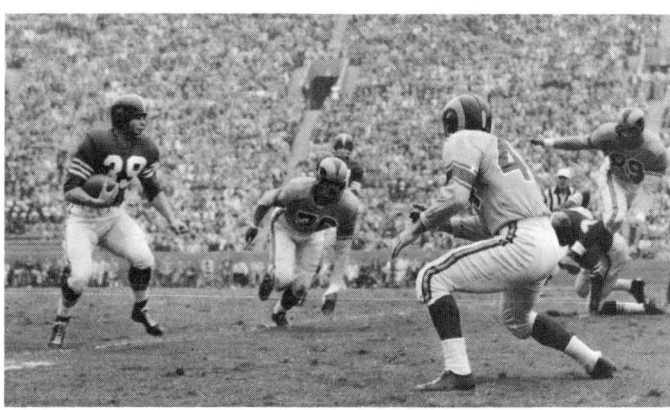

Hugh McElhenny of San Francisco looking for opening against Rams, 1954.

The roster chosen by the Hall of Fame Selection Committee

OFFENSE

Name	Pos.	Ht.	Wt.	Teams
Raymond Berry	End	6-2	187	1955-1967 Baltimore Colts
Tom Fears	End	6-2	215	1948-1956 Los Angeles Rams
Bobby Walston	End	6-0	195	1951-1962 Philadelphia Eagles
Elroy (Crazylegs) Hirsch	Halfback-End	6-2	190	1946-48 Chicago Rockets (AAFC), 1949-1957 Los Angeles Rams
Lenny Moore	Back	6-1	190	1956-1967 Baltimore Colts
Roosevelt Brown	Tackle	6-3	255	1953-1965 New York Giants
Bob St. Clair	Tackle	6-9	265	1953-1963 San Francisco 49ers
Dick Barwegan	Guard	6-1	228	1947 New York Yankees (AAFC), 1948-49 Baltimore Colts (AAFC), 1950-52 Chicago Bears, 1953-54 Baltimore Colts
Jim Parker	Guard	6-3	273	1957-1967 Baltimore Colts
Dick Stanfel	Guard	6-3	240	1952-55 Detroit Lions, 1956-58 Washington Redskins
Chuck Bednarik	Center	6-3	230	1949-1962 Philadelphia Eagles
Otto Graham	Quarterback	6-1	195	1946-49 Cleveland Browns (AAFC), 1950-55 Cleveland Browns
Bobby Layne	Quarterback	6-2	190	1948 Chicago Bears, 1949 New York Bulldogs, 1950-58 Detroit Lions, 1958-1962 Pitt. Steelers
Norm Van Brocklin	Quarterback	6-1	190	1949-1957 Los Angeles Rams, 1958-1960 Philadelphia Eagles
Frank Gifford	Halfback	6-1	200	1952-1960, 1962-64 New York Giants
Ollie Matson	Halfback	6-2	220	1952, 1954-58 Chicago Cardinals, 1959-1962 Los Angeles Rams, 1963 Detroit Lions, 1964-66 Philadelphia Eagles
Hugh McElhenny	Halfback	6-1	198	1952-1960 San Francisco 49ers, 1961-62 Minnesota Vikings, 1963 New York Giants, 1964 Detroit Lions
Alan Ameche	Fullback	6-1	220	1955-1960 Baltimore Colts
Joe Perry	Fullback	6-0	200	1948-49 San Francisco 49ers (AAFC), 1950-1960 San Francisco 49ers, 1961-62 Baltimore Colts, 1963 San Francisco 49ers
Lou Groza	Kicker	6-3	250	1946-49 Cleveland Browns (AAFC), 1950-59, 1961-67 Cleveland Browns

DEFENSE

Name	Pos.	Ht.	Wt.	Teams
Len Ford	End	6-5	248	1948-49 Los Angeles Dons (AAFC), 1950-57 Cleveland Browns, 1958 Green Bay Packers
Gino Marchetti	End	6-4	245	1952 Dallas Texans, 1953-1964, 1966 Baltimore Colts
Art Donovan	Tackle	6-3	265	1950 Baltimore Colts, 1951 New York Yanks, 1952 Dallas Texans, 1953-1961 Baltimore Colts
Leo Nomellini	Tackle	6-3	264	1950-1963 San Francisco 49ers
Ernie Stautner	Tackle	6-2	235	1950-1963 Pittsburgh Steelers
Joe Fortunato	Linebacker	6-1	225	1955-1966 Chicago Bears
Bill George	Linebacker	6-2	230	1952-1965 Chicago Bears, 1966 Los Angeles Rams
Sam Huff	Linebacker	6-1	230	1956-1963 New York Giants, 1964-67, 1969 Washington Redskins
Joe Schmidt	Linebacker	6-0	222	1953-1965 Detroit Lions
Jack Butler	Halfback	6-1	193	1951-59 Pittsburgh Steelers
Dick (Night Train) Lane	Halfback	6-2	210	1952-53 Los Angeles Rams, 1954-59 Chicago Cardinals, 1960-65 Detroit Lions
Jack Christiansen	Safety	6-1	185	1951-58 Detroit Lions
Yale Lary	Safety	5-11	190	1952-53, 1956-1964 Detroit Lions
Emlen Tunnell	Safety	6-1	200	1948-1958 New York Giants, 1959-1961 Green Bay Packers

ALL-PRO SQUAD OF THE 1960s

Jim Brown of Cleveland after taking a handoff from Frank Ryan, 1964.

The roster chosen by the Hall of Fame Selection Committee

OFFENSE

Name	Pos.	Ht.	Wt.	Teams
Del Shofner	Split End	6-3	190	1957-1960 Los Angeles Rams, 1961-67 New York Giants
Charley Taylor	Split End	6-3	210	1964- Washington Redskins
Gary Collins	Flanker	6-4	215	1962-1967 Cleveland Browns
Boyd Dowler	Flanker	6-5	225	1959-1969 Green Bay Packers, 1971 Washington Redskins
John Mackey	Tight End	6-2	224	1963-1961 Baltimore Colts, 1972 San Diego Chargers
Bob Brown	Tackle	6-4	295	1964-68 Philadelphia Eagles, 1969–1970 Los Angeles Rams, 1971-73 Oakland Raiders
Forrest Gregg	Tackle	6-4	250	1956, 1958-1970 Green Bay Packers, 1971 Dallas Cowboys
Ralph Neely	Tackle	6-6	265	1965- Dallas Cowboys
Gene Hickerson	Guard	6-3	260	1958-1960, 1962-1973 Cleveland Browns
Jerry Kramer	Guard	6-3	254	1958-1968 Green Bay Packers
Howard Mudd	Guard	6-2	254	1964-69 San Francisco 49ers, 1969-1970 Chicago Bears
Jim Ringo	Center	6-2	230	1953-1963 Green Bay Packers, 1964-67 Philadelphia Eagles
Sonny Jurgensen	Quarterback	6-0	203	1957-1963 Philadelphia Eagles, 1964-1974 Washington Redskins
Bart Starr	Quarterback	6-1	190	1956-1971 Green Bay Packers
John Unitas	Quarterback	6-1	196	1956-1972 Baltimore Colts, 1973 San Diego Chargers
John David Crow	Halfback	6-2	224	1958-59 Chicago Cardinals, 1960-64 St. Louis Cardinals, 1965-68 San Francisco 49ers
Paul Hornung	Halfback	6-2	215	1957-1962, 1964-66 Green Bay Packers
Leroy Kelly	Halfback	6-0	200	1964-1973 Cleveland Browns
Gale Sayers	Halfback	6-0	198	1965-1971 Chicago Bears
Jim Brown	Fullback	6-2	232	1957-1965 Cleveland Browns
Jim Taylor	Fullback	6-0	215	1958-1966 Green Bay Packers, 1967 New Orleans Saints
Jim Bakken	Kicker	6-0	200	1962- St. Louis Cardinals
Don Chandler	Punter	6-2	210	1956-1964 New York Giants, 1965-67 Green Bay Packers

DEFENSE

Name	Pos.	Ht.	Wt.	Teams
Doug Atkins	End	6-8	270	1953-54 Cleveland Browns, 1955-1966 Chicago Bears, 1967-69 New Orleans Saints
Willie Davis	End	6-3	245	1958-59 Cleveland Browns, 1960-69 Green Bay Packers
David (Deacon) Jones	End	6-5	260	1961-71 Los Angeles Rams, 1972-73 San Diego Chargers, 1974 Washington Redskins
Alex Karras	Tackle	6-2	245	1958-62, 1964-1970 Detroit Lions
Bob Lilly	Tackle	6-5	260	1961-1974 Dallas Cowboys
Merlin Olsen	Tackle	6-5	270	1962-1976 Los Angeles Rams
Dick Butkus	Linebacker	6-3	245	1965-1973 Chicago Bears
Larry Morris	Linebacker	6-2	220	1955-57 Los Angeles Rams, 1959-1965 Chicago Bears, 1966 Atlanta Falcons
Ray Nitschke	Linebacker	6-3	240	1958-1972 Green Bay Packers
Tommy Nobis	Linebacker	6-2	235	1966- Atlanta Falcons
Dave Robinson	Linebacker	6-3	240	1963-1972 Green Bay Packers, 1973-74 Washington Redskins
Herb Adderley	Cornerback	6-0	200	1961-69 Green Bay Packers, 1970-72 Dallas Cowboys
Lem Barney	Cornerback	6-0	202	1967- Detroit Lions
Bobby Boyd	Cornerback	5-10	192	1960-68 Baltimore Colts
Eddie Meador	Safety	5-11	199	1959-1970 Los Angeles Rams
Larry Wilson	Safety	6-0	190	1960-1972 St. Louis Cardinals
Willie Wood	Safety	5-10	160	1960-1971 Green Bay Packers

ALL-TIME AFL TEAM

Joe Namath of the New York Jets throws a jump pass to Matt Snell, 1965.

Chosen by AFL members of the Hall of Fame Selection Committee

OFFENSE

Name	Pos.	Ht.	Wt.	Teams
Lance Alworth	Flanker	6-0	180	1962-1970 San Diego Chargers, 1971-72 Dallas Cowboys
Don Maynard	End	6-1	179	1958 New York Giants, 1960-62 New York Titans, 1963-1972 New York Jets
Fred Arbanas	Tight End	6-3	240	1962 Dallas Texans, 1963-1970 Kansas City Chiefs
Ron Mix	Tackle	6-4	250	1960 Los Angeles Chargers, 1961-69 San Diego Chargers, 1971 Oakland Raiders
Jim Tyrer	Tackle	6-6	274	1961-62 Dallas Texans, 1963-1973 Kansas City Chiefs, 1974 Washington Redskins
Ed Budde	Guard	6-5	265	1963-1976 Kansas City Chiefs
Billy Shaw	Guard	6-2	258	1961-69 Buffalo Bills
Jim Otto	Center	6-2	248	1960-1974 Oakland Raiders
Joe Namath	Quarterback	6-2	195	1965- New York Jets
Clemon Daniels	Running Back	6-1	220	1960 Dallas Texans, 1961-67 Oakland Raiders, 1968 San Francisco 49ers
Paul Lowe	Running Back	6-0	205	1960 Los Angeles Chargers, 1961, 1963-68 San Diego Chargers, 1968-69 Kansas City Chiefs
George Blanda	Kicker	6-2	215	1949-1958 Chicago Bears, 1960-66 Houston Oilers, 1967-1975 Oakland Raiders
Jerrel Wilson	Punter	6-2	222	1963- Kansas City Chiefs

DEFENSE

Name	Pos.	Ht.	Wt.	Teams
Jerry Mays	End	6-4	252	1961-62 Dallas Texans, 1963-1970 Kansas City Chiefs
Gerry Philbin	End	6-2	245	1964-1972 New York Jets, 1973 Philadelphia Eagles
Houston Antwine	Tackle	6-1	270	1961-1970 Boston Patriots, 1971 New England Patriots
Tom Sestak	Tackle	6-4	260	1962-68 Buffalo Bills
Bobby Bell	Linebacker	6-4	228	1963-1974 Kansas City Chiefs
George Webster	Linebacker	6-4	223	1967-1972 Houston Oilers, 1972-73 Pittsburgh Steelers, 1974- New England Patriots
Nick Buoniconti	Linebacker	5-11	220	1962-68 Boston Patriots, 1969- Miami Dolphins
Willie Brown	Cornerback	6-1	190	1963-66 Denver Broncos, 1967- Oakland Raiders
Dave Grayson	Cornerback	5-10	187	1961-62 Dallas Texans, 1963-64 Kansas City Chiefs, 1965-1970 Oakland Raiders
Johnny Robinson	Safety	6-1	205	1960-62 Dallas Texans, 1963-1971 Kansas City Chiefs
George Saimes	Safety	5-11	186	1963-69 Buffalo Bills, 1970-72 Denver Broncos

ALL-PRO SQUAD OF THE 1970s

O.J. Simpson of Buffalo on his way through the Detroit Lions, 1976.

The roster chosen by the Hall of Fame Selection Committee

OFFENSE

Name	Pos.	Ht.	Wt.	Teams
Fred Biletnikoff	Wide Receiver	6-1	190	1965–1976 Oakland Raiders
Cliff Branch	Wide Receiver	5-11	170	1972–1976 Oakland Raiders
Otis Taylor	Wide Receiver	6-3	215	1965–1975 Kansas City Chiefs
Paul Warfield	Wide Receiver	6-0	188	1964–69, 1976 Cleveland Browns, 1970–74 Miami Dolphins, 1975 Memphis WFL
Charlie Sanders	Tight End	6-4	230	1968–1976 Detroit Lions
Bob Trumpy	Tight End	6-6	228	1968–1976 Cincinnati Bengals
Ron Yary	Tackle	6-6	255	1968–1976 Minnesota Vikings
Ernie McMillan	Tackle	6-6	255	1961–1974 St. Louis Cardinals
Rayfield Wright	Tackle	6-6	260	1967–1976 Dallas Cowboys
Larry Little	Guard	6-1	265	1967–68 San Diego Chargers, 1969–1976 Miami Dolphins
Gene Upshaw	Guard	6-5	255	1967–1976 Oakland Raiders
Ed White	Guard	6-3	270	1969–1976 Minnesota Vikings
Jim Otto	Center	6-2	255	1960–1974 Oakland Raiders
Mick Tingelhoff	Center	6-2	240	1962–1976 Minnesota Vikings
Ken Stabler	Quarterback	6-3	215	1970–76 Oakland Raiders
Roger Staubach	Quarterback	6-3	197	1969–1976 Dallas Cowboys
Fran Tarkenton	Quarterback	6-0	190	1961–66, 1970–76 Minnesota Vikings, 1967–69 New York Giants
Larry Brown	Running Back	5-11	195	1969–1976 Washington Redskins
Larry Csonka	Running Back	6-3	235	1968–1974 Miami Dolphins, 1975 Memphis WFL, 1976 New York Giants
Chuck Foreman	Running Back	6-2	215	1973–76 Minnesota Vikings
Franco Harris	Running Back	6-3	230	1972–76 Pittsburgh Steelers
Floyd Little	Running Back	5-10	195	1967–1975 Denver Broncos
O.J. Simpson	Running Back	6-1	216	1969–1976 Buffalo Bills
George Blanda	Kicker	6-2	215	1949 Chicago Bears, 1950 Baltimore Colts, 1950–58 Chicago Bears, 1960–66 Houston Oilers, 1967–1975 Oakland Raiders
Ray Guy	Punter	6-3	195	1973–1976 Oakland Raiders

DEFENSE

Name	Pos.	Ht.	Wt.	Teams
Carl Eller	End	6-6	247	1964–1976 Minnesota Vikings
L. C. Greenwood	End	6-6	245	1969–1976 Pittsburgh Steelers
Claude Humphrey	End	6-6	265	1968–1974, 1976 Atlanta Falcons
Buck Buchanan	Tackle	6-7	270	1963–1975 Kansas City Chiefs
Joe Greene	Tackle	6-4	275	1969–1976 Pittsburgh Steelers
Alan Page	Tackle	6-4	245	1967–1976 Minnesota Vikings
Nick Buoniconti	Linebacker	5-11	220	1962–68 Boston Patriots, 1969–1974, 1976 Miami Dolphins
Chris Hanburger	Linebacker	6-2	218	1965–1976 Washington Redskins
Lee Roy Jordan	Linebacker	6-1	221	1963–1976 Dallas Cowboys
Willie Lanier	Linebacker	6-1	245	1967–1976 Kansas City Chiefs
Andy Russell	Linebacker	6-2	220	1963, 1966–76 Pittsburgh Steelers
Pat Fischer	Cornerback	5-9	170	1961–67 St. Louis Cardinals, 1968–1976 Washington Redskins
Jim Johnson	Cornerback	6-2	185	1961–1976 San Francisco 49ers
Roger Wehrli	Cornerback	6-0	190	1969–1976 St. Louis Cardinals
Ken Houston	Safety	6-3	198	1967–1972 Houston Oilers, 1973–76 Washington Redskins
Paul Krause	Safety	6-3	200	1964–67 Washington Redskins, 1968–1976 Minnesota Vikings
Jake Scott	Safety	6-0	188	1970–75 Miami Dolphins, 1976 Washington Redskins

The Draft

The advent of a draft of college football players by teams of the National Football League, beginning in 1936, brought needed order to the process of acquiring new players and helped the league achieve more competitive balance by allowing the team with the poorest won-lost record each year to make the first draft choice.

The National and American Football Leagues held separate drafts from 1960 through 1966. Their first joint action after their agreement to merge was the combined draft of college players March 14 and 15, 1967. Defensive tackle Bubba Smith of Michigan State was the number one selection, by Baltimore.

Another interesting era in the history of the draft was the 12-year period of the bonus choice, from 1947 to 1958. The first selection each year was awarded to each team on a rotating basis. The bonus choices were Bob Fenimore, Harry Gilmer, Chuck Bednarik, Leon Hart, Kyle Rote, Billy Wade, Harry Babcock, Bobby Garrett, George Shaw, Gary Glick, Paul Hornung, and King Hill.

The table lists only the first players selected by each team. If the player was not a first round choice, his team having traded a choice or choices, the player's actual round is in parentheses. Bold face indicates the first draft choice of the entire league for the year.

1936
Boston Redskins, Riley Smith, B ... Alabama
Brooklyn Dodgers, Dick Crayne, B ... Iowa
Chi. Bears, Joe Stydahar, T ... West Virginia
Chi. Cardinals, Jim Lawrence, B ... TCU
Detroit, Sid Wagner, G ... Michigan State
Green Bay, Russ Letlow, G ... San Francisco
N.Y. Giants, Art Lewis, T ... Ohio U.
Philadelphia, Jay Berwanger, B ... Chicago
Pittsburgh, Bill Shakespeare, B ... Notre Dame

1937
Boston Redskins, Sammy Baugh, B ... TCU
Brooklyn Dodgers, Ed Goddard, B ... Washington State
Chi. Bears, Les McDonald, E ... Nebraska
Chi. Cardinals, Ray Buivid, B ... Marquette
Detroit, Lloyd Cardwell, B ... Nebraska
Green Bay, Ed Jankowski, B ... Wisconsin
N.Y. Giants, Ed Widseth, T ... Minnesota
Philadelphia, Sam Francis, B ... Nebraska
Pittsburgh, Mike Basrak, C ... Duquesne
John Drake, B* ... Purdue
*Awarded to the league's new franchise, which became the Cleveland Rams.

1938
Brooklyn Dodgers, Boyd Brumbaugh, B ... Duquesne
Chi. Bears, Joe Gray, B ... Oregon State
Chi. Cardinals, Jack Robbins, B ... Arkansas
Cleveland Rams, Corby Davis, B ... Indiana
Detroit, Alex Wojciechowicz, C ... Fordham
Green Bay, Cecil Isbell, B ... Purdue
N.Y. Giants, George Karamatic, B ... Gonzaga
Philadelphia, Jim McDonald, B ... Ohio State
Pittsburgh, Byron (Whizzer) White, B ... Colorado
Washington, Andy Farkas, B ... Detroit

1939
Brooklyn Dodgers, Bob MacLeod, B ... Dartmouth
Chi. Bears, Bill Osmanski, B ... Holy Cross
Chi. Cardinals, Charles (Ki) Aldrich, C ... TCU
Cleveland Rams, Parker Hall, B ... Mississippi
Detroit, John Pingel, B ... Michigan State
Green Bay, Larry Buhler, B ... Minnesota
N.Y. Giants, Walt Nielson, B ... Arizona
Philadelphia, Davey O'Brien, B ... TCU
Pittsburgh, Sid Luckman, B ... Columbia
Washington, I.B. Hale, T ... TCU

1940
Brooklyn Dodgers, Banks McFadden, B ... Clemson
Chi. Bears, Clyde (Bulldog) Turner, C ... Hardin-Simmons
Chi. Cardinals, George Cafego, B ... Tennessee
Cleveland Rams, Ollie Cordill, B ... Rice
Detroit, Doyle Nave, B ... USC
Green Bay, Hal VanEvery, B ... Marquette
N.Y. Giants, Grenny Lansdell, B ... USC
Philadelphia, George McAfee, B ... Duke
Pittsburgh, Kay Eakin, B ... Arkansas
Washington, Ed Boell, B ... New York U.

1941
Brooklyn Dodgers, Dean McAdams, B ... Washington
Chi. Bears, Tom Harmon, B ... Michigan
Chi. Cardinals, John Kimbrough, B ... Texas A&M
Cleveland Rams, Rudy Mucha, C ... Washington
Detroit, Jim Thomason, B ... Texas A&M
Green Bay, George Paskvan, B ... Wisconsin
N.Y. Giants, George Franck, B ... Minnesota
Philadelphia, Art Jones, B ... Richmond
Pittsburgh, Chet Gladchuk, C ... Boston College
Washington, Forest Evashevski, B ... Michigan

1942
Brooklyn Dodgers, Bob Robertson, B ... USC
Chi. Bears, Frankie Albert, B ... Stanford
Chi. Cardinals, Steve Lach, B ... Duke
Cleveland Rams, Jack Wilson, B ... Baylor
Detroit, Bob Westfall, B ... Michigan
Green Bay, Urban Odson, T ... Minnesota
N.Y. Giants, Merle Hapes, B ... Mississippi
Philadelphia, Pete Kmetovic, B ... Stanford
Pittsburgh, Bill Dudley, B ... Virginia
Washington, Orban (Spec) Sanders, B ... Texas

1943
Brooklyn Dodgers, Paul Governali, B ... Columbia
Chi. Bears, Bob Steuber, B ... Missouri
Chi. Cardinals, Glenn Dobbs, B ... Tulsa
Cleveland Rams, Mike Holovak, B ... Boston College
Detroit, Frank Sinkwich, B ... Georgia
Green Bay, Dick Wildung, T ... Minnesota
N.Y. Giants, Steve Filipowicz, B ... Fordham
Philadelphia, Joe Muha, B ... VMI
Pittsburgh, Bill Daley, B ... Minnesota
Washington, Jack Jenkins, B ... Missouri

1944
Boston Yanks, Angelo Bertelli, B ... Notre Dame
Brooklyn Dodgers, Creigton Miller, B ... Notre Dame
Chi. Bears, Ray Evans, B ... Kansas
Chi. Cardinals, Pat Harder, B ... Wisconsin
Cleveland, Tony Butkovich, B ... Illinois
Detroit, Otto Graham, B ... Northwestern
Green Bay, Merv Pregulman, G ... Michigan
N.Y. Giants, Billy Hillenbrand, B ... Indiana
Philadelphia, Steve Van Buren, B ... LSU
Pittsburgh, Johnny Podesto, B ... St. Mary's, Calif.
Washington, Mike Micka, B ... Colgate

1945
Boston Yanks, Eddie Prokop, B ... Georgia Tech
Brooklyn Dodgers, Joe Renfroe, B ... Tulane
Chi. Bears, Don Lund, B ... Michigan
Chi. Cardinals, Charley Trippi, B ... Georgia
Cleveland Rams, Elroy (Crazylegs) Hirsch, B ... Wisconsin
Detroit, Frank Szymanski, C ... Notre Dame
Green Bay, Walt Schlinkman, B ... Texas Tech
N.Y. Giants, Elmer Barbour, B ... Wake Forest
Philadelphia, John Yonakor, E ... Notre Dame
Pittsburgh, Paul Duhart, B* ... Florida
Washington, Jim Hardy, B ... USC
*Duhart played for Green Bay in 1944. Under wartime eligibility rules, he was subject to the 1945 NFL draft and was selected by Pittsburgh.

1946
Boston Yanks, Frank Dancewicz, B ... Notre Dame
Chi. Bears, Johnny Lujack, B ... Notre Dame
Chi. Cardinals, Dub Jones, B ... LSU
Detroit, Bill Dellastatious, B ... Missouri
Green Bay, Johnny Strzykalski, B ... Marquette
Los Angeles, Emil Sitko, B ... Notre Dame
N.Y. Giants, George Connor, T ... Notre Dame
Philadelphia, Leo Riggs, B ... USC
Pittsburgh, Felix (Doc) Blanchard, B ... Army
Washington, Cal Rossi, B* ... UCLA
*Choice lost due to ineligibility.

1947
Boston Yanks, Fritz Barzilauskas, G ... Yale
Chi. Bears, Bob Fenimore, B* ... Oklahoma A&M
Chi. Cardinals, DeWitt (Tex) Coulter, T** ... Army
Detroit, Glenn Davis, B ... Army
Green Bay, Ernie Case, B ... UCLA
Los Angeles, Herman Wedemeyer, B ... St. Mary's, Calif.
N.Y. Giants, Vic Schwall, B ... Northwestern
Philadelphia, Neill Armstrong, E ... Oklahoma A&M
Pittsburgh, Hub Bechtol, E ... Texas
Washington, Cal Rossi, B ... UCLA
*Bonus choice
**Coulter was eligible for the 1947 draft although he played for New York in 1946.

1948
Boston Yanks, Vaughan Mancha, C ... Alabama
Chi. Bears, Bobby Layne, B* ... Texas
Chi. Cardinals, Jim Spavital, B ... Oklahoma A&M
Detroit, Y. A. Tittle, B ... LSU
Green Bay, Earl (Jug) Girard, B ... Wisconsin
Los Angeles, Tom Keane, B(2) ... West Virginia
N.Y. Giants, Tony Minisi, B ... Pennsylvania
Philadelphia, Clyde (Smackover) Scott, B ... Arkansas
Pittsburgh, Dan Edwards, E ... Georgia
Washington, Harry Gilmer, B** ... Alabama
*The choice used to select Layne was traded by Pittsburgh through Detroit to the Chicago Bears—the first record of a traded draft choice.
**Bonus choice

1949
Boston Yanks, Doak Walker, B ... Southern Methodist
Chi. Bears, Dick Harris, C ... Texas
Chi. Cardinals, Bill Fischer, G ... Notre Dame
Detroit, John Rauch, B ... Georgia
Green Bay, Stan Heath, B ... Nevada
Los Angeles, Bobby Thomason, B ... VMI
N.Y. Giants, Paul Page, B ... SMU
Philadelphia, Chuck Bednarik, C* ... Pennsylvania
Pittsburgh, Bobby Gage, B ... Clemson
Washington, Rob Goode, B ... Texas A&M
*Bonus choice

1950
Baltimore, Adrian Burk, B ... Baylor
Chi. Bears, Chuck Hunsinger, B ... Florida
Chi. Cardinals, Jack Jennings, T (2) ... Ohio State
Cleveland, Ken Carpenter, B ... Oregon State
Detroit, Leon Hart, E* ... Notre Dame
Green Bay, Clayton Tonnemaker, C ... Minnesota
Los Angeles, Ralph Pasquariello, B ... Villanova
N.Y. Yanks, Art Weiner, E (2) ... North Carolina
N.Y. Giants, Travis Tidwell, B ... Auburn
Philadelphia, Harry (Bud) Grant, E ... Minnesota
Pittsburgh, Lynn Chandnois, B ... Michigan State
San Francisco, Leo Nomellini, T ... Minnesota
Washington, George Thomas, B ... Oklahoma
*Bonus choice.

1951
Chi. Bears, Billy Stone, B* ... Bradley
Chi. Cardinals, Jerry Groom, C ... Notre Dame
Cleveland, Ken Konz, B ... LSU
Detroit, Dick Stanfel, G (2) ... San Francisco
Green Bay, Bob Gain, T ... Kentucky
Los Angeles, Bud McFadin, G ... Texas
N.Y. Giants, Kyle Rote, B** ... SMU
N.Y. Yanks, Ken Jackson, T ... Texas
Philadelphia, Ebert Van Buren, B ... LSU
Pittsburgh, Butch Avinger, B ... Alabama
San Francisco, Y. A. Tittle, B* ... LSU
Washington, Leon Heath, B ... Oklahoma
*Players of the extinct Baltimore team were eligible for the draft.
**Bonus choice.

1952
Chi. Bears, Jim Dooley, B ... Miami
Chi. Cardinals, Ollie Matson, B ... San Francisco
Cleveland, Bert Rechichar, B ... Tennessee
Detroit, Yale Lary, B (3) ... Texas A&M
Green Bay, Babe Parilli, B ... Kentucky
Los Angeles, Bill Wade, QB* ... Vanderbilt
N.Y. Giants, Frank Gifford, B ... USC
Philadelphia. Johnny Bright, B ... Drake
Pittsburgh, Ed Modzelewski, B ... Maryland
San Francisco, Hugh McElhenny, B ... Washington
Dallas Texans, Les Richter, G ... California
Washington, Larry Isbell, B ... Baylor
*Bonus choice.

1953
Baltimore. Billy Vessels, B ... Oklahoma
Chi. Bears, Billy Anderson, B ... Compton J.C.
Chi. Cardinals, Johnny Olszewski, B ... California
Cleveland, Doug Atkins, T ... Tennessee
Detroit, Harley Sewell, G ... Texas
Green Bay, Al Carmichael, B ... USC
Los Angeles, Donn Moomaw, C ... UCLA
N.Y. Giants, Bobby Marlow, B ... Alabama
Philadelphia, Al Conway, B(2) ... Army
Pittsburgh, Ted Marchibroda, B ... St. Bonaventure
San Francisco, Harry Babcock, E* ... Georgia
Washington, Jack Scarbath, B ... Maryland
*Bonus choice.

1954
Baltimore, Cotton Davidson, B ... Baylor
Chi. Bears, Stan Wallace, B ... Illinois
Chi. Cardinals, Lamar McHan, B ... Arkansas
Cleveland, Bobby Garrett, QB* ... Stanford
Detroit, Dick Chapman, T ... Rice
Green Bay, Art Hunter, T ... Notre Dame
Los Angeles, Ed Beatty, C ... Mississippi
N.Y. Giants, Ken Buck, E ... Pacific
Philadelphia, Neil Worden, B ... Notre Dame
Pittsburgh, Johnny Lattner, B ... Notre Dame
San Francisco, Bernie Faloney, B ... Maryland
Washington, Steve Meilinger, E ... Kentucky
*Bonus choice.

1955
Baltimore, George Shaw, QB* ... Oregon
Chi. Bears, Ron Drzewiecki, B ... Marquette
Chi. Cardinals, Max Boydston, E ... Oklahoma
Cleveland, Kurt Burris, C ... Oklahoma
Detroit, Dave Middleton, B ... Auburn
Green Bay, Tom Bettis, G ... Purdue
Los Angeles, Larry Morris, C ... Georgia Tech
N.Y. Giants, Joe Heap, B ... Notre Dame
Philadelphia, Dick Bielski, B ... Maryland
Pittsburgh, Frank Varrichione, T ... Notre Dame
San Francisco, Dickie Moegle, B ... Rice
Washington, Ralph Guglielmi, B ... Notre Dame
*Bonus choice.

1956
Baltimore, Lenny Moore, B ... Penn State
Chi. Bears, Menan (Tex) Schriewer, E ... Texas
Chi. Cardinals, Joe Childress, B ... Auburn
Cleveland, Preston Carpenter, B ... Arkansas

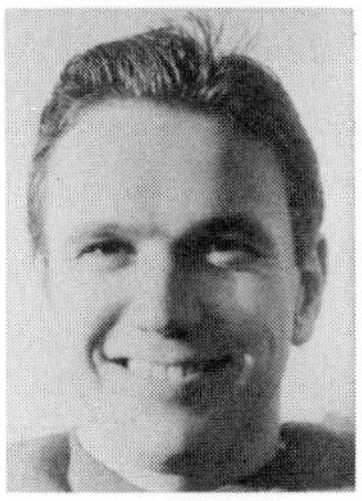
Frankie Albert

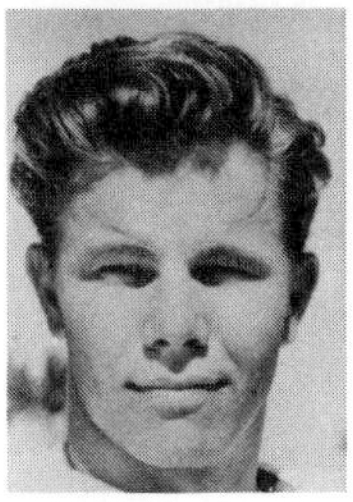
Kyle Rote

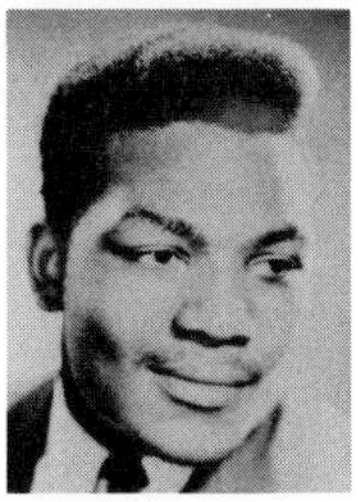
Jim Brown

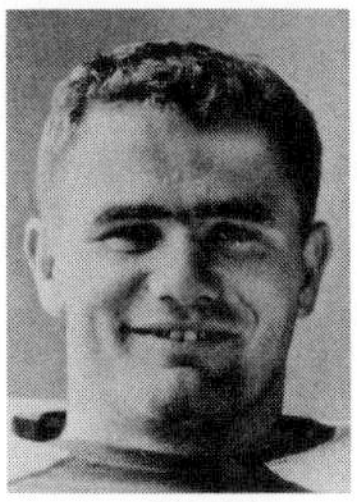
Marlin McKeever

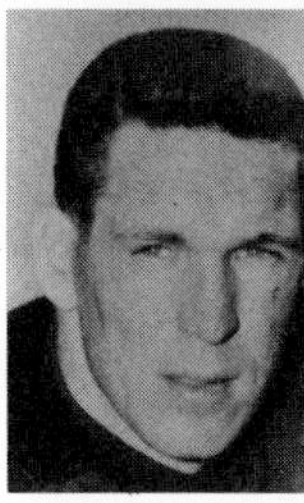
Lee Roy Jordan

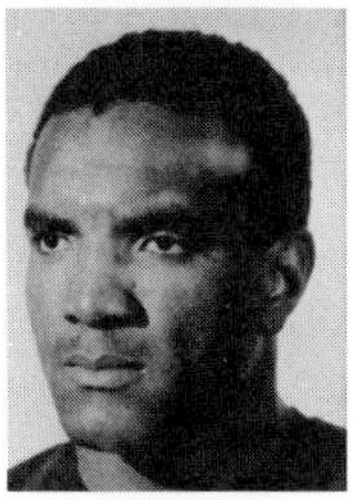
Calvin Hill

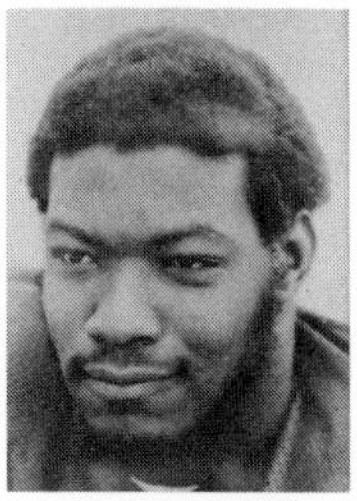
Lee Roy Selmon

Detroit, Howard (Hopalong) Cassady, B .... Ohio State
Green Bay, Jack Losch, B .... Miami
Los Angeles, Joe Marconi, B .... West Virginia
N.Y. Giants, Henry Moore, B .... Arkansas
Philadelphia, Bob Pellegrini, C .... Maryland
Pittsburgh, Gary Glick, B* .... Colorado A&M
San Francisco, Earl Morrall, B .... Michigan State
Washington, Ed Vereb, B .... Maryland
*Bonus choice.

1957

Baltimore, Jim Parker, G .... Ohio State
Chi. Bears, Earl Leggett, T .... LSU
Chi. Cardinals, Jerry Tubbs, C .... Oklahoma
Cleveland, Jim Brown, B .... Syracuse
Detroit, Bill Glass, G .... Baylor
Green Bay, Paul Hornung, B* .... Notre Dame
Los Angeles, Jon Arnett, B .... USC
N.Y. Giants, Sam DeLuca, T(2) .... South Carolina
Philadelphia, Clarence Peaks, B .... Michigan State
Pittsburgh, Len Dawson, B .... Purdue
San Francisco, John Brodie, B .... Stanford
Washington, Don Bosseler, B .... Miami
*Bonus choice.

1958

Baltimore, Lenny Lyles, B .... Louisville
Chi. Bears, Chuck Howley, G .... West Virginia
Chi. Cardinals, King Hill, B* .... Rice
Cleveland, Jim Shofner, B .... TCU
Detroit, Alex Karras, T .... Iowa
Green Bay, Dan Currie, C .... Michigan State
Los Angeles, Lou Michaels, T .... Kentucky
N.Y. Giants, Phil King, B .... Vanderbilt
Philadelphia, Walt Kowalczyk, B .... Michigan State
Pittsburgh, Larry Krutko, B .... West Virginia
San Francisco, Jim Pace, B .... Michigan
Washington, Mike Sommer, B .... George Washington
*Bonus choice.

1959

Baltimore, Jackie Burkett, C .... Auburn
Chi. Bears, Don Clark, B .... Ohio State
Chi. Cardinals, Billy Stacy, B .... Mississippi State
Cleveland, Rich Kreitling, E .... Illinois
Detroit, Nick Pietrosante, B .... Notre Dame
Green Bay, Randy Duncan, B .... Iowa
Los Angeles, Dick Bass, B .... Pacific
N.Y. Giants, Lee Grosscup, B .... Utah
Philadelphia, J. D. Smith, T(2) .... Rice
Pittsburgh, Tom Barnett, B(8) .... Purdue
San Francisco, Dave Baker, B .... Oklahoma
Washington, Don Allard, B .... Boston College

1960 NFL

Baltimore, Ron Mix, T .... USC
Chicago, Roger Davis, G .... Syracuse
Cleveland, Jim Houston, E .... Ohio State
Detroit, Johnny Robinson, B .... LSU
Green Bay, Tom Moore, B .... Vanderbilt
Los Angeles, Billy Cannon, B .... LSU
N.Y. Giants, Lou Cordileone, T .... Clemson
Philadelphia, Ron Burton, B .... Northwestern
Pittsburgh, Jack Spikes, B .... TCU
San Francisco, Monty Stickles, E .... Notre Dame
St. Louis, George Izo, B .... Notre Dame
Washington, Richie Lucas, B .... Penn State

1960 AFL

Boston Patriots, Gerhard Schwedes, B .... Syracuse
Buffalo, Richie Lucas, QB .... Penn State
Dallas Texans, Don Meredith, QB .... Southern Methodist
Denver, Roger Leclerc, C .... Trinity, Conn.
Houston, Billy Cannon, B .... LSU
Los Angeles Chargers, Monty Stickles, E .... Notre Dame
Minneapolis, Dale Hackbart, B* .... Wisconsin
N.Y. Titans, George Izo, B .... Notre Dame
*Minneapolis became the Minnesota NFL franchise. The Minneapolis AFL draft list was turned over to Oakland.

1961 NFL

Baltimore, Tom Matte, B .... Ohio State
Chicago, Mike Ditka, E .... Pittsburgh
Cleveland, Bobby Crespino, B .... Mississippi
Dallas, Bob Lilly, T .... TCU
Detroit, Danny LaRose, T(2) .... Missouri
Green Bay, Herb Adderley, B .... Michigan State
Los Angeles, Marlin McKeever, E .... USC
Minnesota, Tommy Mason, B .... Tulane
N.Y. Giants, Bruce Tarbox, G(2) .... Syracuse
Philadelphia, Art Baker, B .... Syracuse
Pittsburgh, Myron Pottios, G(2) .... Notre Dame
St. Louis, Ken Rice, T .... Auburn
San Francisco, Jimmy Johnson, B .... UCLA
Washington, Norman Snead, B .... Wake Forest

1961 AFL

Boston Patriots, Tommy Mason, B .... Tulane
Buffalo, Ken Rice, T .... Auburn
Dallas Texans, E.J. Holub, LB .... Texas Tech
Denver, Bob Gaiters, B .... New Mexico State
Houston, Mike Ditka, E. .... Pittsburgh
N.Y. Titans, Tom Brown, G .... Minnesota
Oakland, Joe Rutgens, T .... Illinois
San Diego, Earl Faison, E .... Indiana

1962 NFL

Baltimore, Wendell Harris, B .... LSU
Chicago, Ronnie Bull, B .... Baylor
Cleveland, Gary Collins, E .... Maryland
Dallas, Sonny Gibbs, B(2) .... TCU
Detroit, John Hadl, B .... Kansas
Green Bay, Earl Gros, B .... LSU
Los Angeles, Roman Gabriel, B .... N. Carolina State
Minnesota, Bill Miller, E(2) .... Miami
N.Y. Giants, Jerry Hillebrand, E .... Colorado
Philadelphia, Pete Case, T(2) .... Georgia
Pittsburgh, Bob Ferguson, B .... Ohio State
St. Louis, Fate Echols, T .... Northwestern
San Francisco, Lance Alworth, B .... Arkansas
Washington, Ernie Davis, B .... Syracuse

1962 AFL

Boston Patriots, Gary Collins, E .... Maryland
Buffalo, Ernie Davis, B .... Syracuse
Dallas Texans, Ronnie Bull, B .... Baylor
Denver, Merlin Olsen, T .... Utah State
Houston, Ray Jacobs, T .... Howard Payne
N.Y. Titans, Sandy Stephens, B .... Minnesota
Oakland, Roman Gabriel, QB .... N. Carolina State
San Diego, Bob Ferguson, B .... Ohio State

1963 NFL

Baltimore, Bob Vogel, T .... Ohio State
Chicago, Dave Behrman, C .... Michigan State
Cleveland, Tom Hutchinson, E .... Kentucky
Dallas, Lee Roy Jordan, C .... Alabama
Detroit, Daryl Sanders, T .... Ohio State
Green Bay, Dave Robinson, E .... Penn State
Los Angeles, Terry Baker, B .... Oregon State
Minnesota, Jim Dunaway, T .... Mississippi
N.Y. Giants, Frank Lasky, T(2) .... Florida
Philadelphia, Ed Budde, T .... Michigan State
Pittsburgh, Frank Atkinson, T(8) .... Stanford
St. Louis, Jerry Stovall, B .... LSU
San Francisco, Kermit Alexander, B .... UCLA
Washington, Pat Richter, E .... Wisconsin

1963 AFL

Boston Patriots, Art Graham, E .... Boston College
Buffalo, Dave Behrman, C .... Michigan State
Denver, Kermit Alexander, B .... UCLA
Houston, Danny Brabham, B .... Arkansas
Kansas City, Buck Buchanan, T .... Grambling
N.Y. Jets, Jerry Stovall, B .... LSU
Oakland, Butch Wilson, B(6) .... Alabama
San Diego, Walt Sweeney, E .... Syracuse

1964 NFL

Baltimore, Marv Woodson, B .... Indiana
Chicago, Dick Evey, T .... Tennessee
Cleveland, Paul Warfield, B .... Ohio State
Dallas, Scott Appleton, T .... Texas
Detroit, Pete Beathard, B .... USC
Green Bay, Lloyd Voss, T .... Nebraska
Los Angeles, Bill Munson, B .... Utah State
Minnesota, Carl Eller, T .... Minnesota
N.Y. Giants, Joe Don Looney, B. .... Oklahoma
Philadelphia, Bob Brown, G .... Nebraska
Pittsburgh, Paul Martha, B .... Pittsburgh
St. Louis, Ken Kortas, T .... Louisville
San Francisco, Dave Parks, E .... Texas Tech
Washington, Charley Taylor, B .... Arizona State

1964 AFL

Boston Patriots, Jack Concannon, QB .... Boston College
Buffalo, Carl Eller, T .... Minnesota
Denver, Bob Brown, G .... Nebraska
Houston, Scott Appleton, T .... Texas
Kansas City, Pete Beathard, B .... USC
N.Y. Jets, Matt Snell, B .... Ohio State
Oakland, Tony Lorick, B .... Arizona State
San Diego, Ted Davis, E .... Georgia Tech

1965 NFL

Baltimore, Mike Curtis, B .... Duke
Chicago, Dick Butkus, C .... Illinois
Cleveland, Jim Garcia, T(2) .... Purdue
Dallas, Craig Morton, B .... California
Detroit, Tom Nowatzke, B .... Indiana
Green Bay, Donny Anderson, B .... Texas Tech
Los Angeles, Clancy Williams, B .... Washington State
Minnesota, Jack Snow, E .... Notre Dame
N.Y. Giants, Tucker Frederickson, B .... Auburn
Philadelphia, Ray Rissmiller, T(2) .... Georgia
Pittsburgh, Roy Jefferson, B(2) .... Utah
St. Louis, Joe Namath, B .... Alabama
San Francisco, Ken Willard, B .... North Carolina
Washington, Bob Breitenstein, T(2) .... Tulsa

1965 AFL

Boston Patriots, Jerry Rush, T .... Michigan State
Buffalo, Jim Davidson, T .... Ohio State
Denver, Dick Butkus, C(2) .... Illinois
Houston, Lawrence Elkins, E .... Baylor
Kansas City, Gale Sayers, B .... Kansas
N.Y. Jets, Joe Namath, QB .... Alabama
Oakland, Harry Schuh, T .... Memphis State
San Diego, Steve DeLong, G .... Tennessee

1966 NFL

Atlanta, Tommy Nobis, LB .... Texas
Baltimore, Sam Ball, T .... Kentucky
Chicago, George Rice, T .... LSU
Cleveland, Milt Morin, E .... Massachusetts
Dallas, John Niland G .... Iowa
Detroit, Nick Eddy, B(2) .... Notre Dame
Green Bay, Jim Grabowski, B .... Illinois
Los Angeles, Tom Mack, T .... Michigan
Minnesota, Jerry Shay, T .... Purdue
N.Y. Giants, Francis Peay, T .... Missouri
Philadelphia, Randy Beisler, E .... Indiana
Pittsburgh, Dick Leftridge, B .... West Virginia
St. Louis, Carl McAdams, C .... Oklahoma
San Francisco, Stan Hindman, T .... Mississippi
Washington, Charley Gogolak, K .... Princeton

1966 AFL

Boston Patriots, Karl Singer, T .... Purdue
Buffalo, Mike Dennis, B .... Mississippi
Denver, Jerry Shay, T .... Purdue
Houston, Tommy Nobis, G .... Texas
Kansas City, Aaron Brown, E .... Minnesota
Miami, Jim Grabowski, B .... Illinois
N.Y. Jets, Bill Yearby, T .... Michigan
Oakland, Rodger Bird, B .... Kentucky
San Diego, Don Davis, T .... Cal. State-L.A.

1967

Combined Draft

Atlanta, Leo Carroll, DE(2) .... San Diego State
Baltimore, Charles (Bubba) Smith, DT ...... Michigan State
Boston Patriots, John Charles, DB .... Purdue
Buffalo, John Pitts, WR .... Arizona State
Chicago, Lloyd Phillips, DE .... Arkansas
Cleveland, Bob Matheson, LB .... Duke
Dallas, Phil Clark, DB(3) .... Northwestern
Denver, Floyd Little, RB .... Syracuse
Detroit, Mel Farr, RB .... UCLA
Green Bay, Bob Hyland, G .... Boston College
Houston, George Webster, LB .... Michigan State
Kansas City, Gene Trosch, DT .... Miami
Los Angeles, Willie Ellison, RB(2) .... Texas Southern
Miami, Bob Griese, QB .... Purdue
Minnesota, Clinton Jones, RB .... Michigan State
N.Y. Giants, Lou Thompson, DT(2) .... Alabama
N.Y. Jets, Paul Seiler, G .... Notre Dame
New Orleans, Les Kelley, RB .... Alabama
Oakland, Gene Upshaw, G .... Texas A&I
Philadelphia, Harry Jones, RB .... Arkansas
Pittsburgh, Don Shy, RB(2) .... San Diego State
St. Louis, Dave Williams, WR .... Washington
San Diego, Ron Billingsley, DT .... Wyoming
San Francisco, Steve Spurrier, QB .... Florida
Washington, Ray McDonald, RB .... Idaho

1968

Atlanta, Claude Humphrey, DE .... Tennessee State

Baltimore, John Williams, T ... Minnesota
Boston Patriots, Dennis Byrd, T ... N. Carolina State
Buffalo, Haven Moses, WR ... San Diego State
Chicago, Mike Hull, RB ... USC
Cleveland, Marvin Upshaw, DE ... Trinity, Tex.
Cincinnati, Bob Johnson, C ... Tennessee
Dallas, Dennis Homan, WR ... Alabama
Denver, Curley Culp, DE(2) ... Arizona State
Detroit, Greg Landry, QB ... Massachusetts
Green Bay, Fred Carr, LB ... Texas-El Paso
Houston, Mac Haik, WR(2) ... Mississippi
Kansas City, Mo Moorman, G ... Texas A&M
Los Angeles, Gary Beban, QB(2) ... UCLA
Miami, Larry Csonka, RB ... Syracuse
Minnesota, Ron Yary, T ... USC
New Orleans, Kevin Hardy, DE ... Notre Dame
N.Y. Giants, Rich Buzin, T(2) ... Penn State
N.Y. Jets, Lee White, RB ... Weber State
Oakland, Eldridge Dickey, QB ... Tennessee State
Philadelphia, Tim Rossovich, DE ... USC
Pittsburgh, Mike Taylor, T ... USC
St. Louis, MacArthur Lane, RB ... Utah State
San Diego, Russ Washington, T ... Missouri
San Francisco, Forrest Blue, C ... Auburn
Washington, Jim Smith, DB ... Oregon

1969

Atlanta, George Kunz, T ... Notre Dame
Baltimore, Eddie Hinton, WR ... Oklahoma
Boston Patriots, Ron Sellers, WR ... Florida State
Buffalo, O.J. Simpson, RB ... USC
Chicago, Rufus Mayes, T ... Ohio State
Cincinnati, Greg Cook, QB ... Cincinnati
Cleveland, Ron Johnson, RB ... Michigan
Dallas, Calvin Hill, RB ... Yale
Denver, Grady Cavness, DB(2) ... Texas-El Paso
Detroit, Altie Taylor, RB(2) ... Utah State
Green Bay, Rich Moore, DT ... Villanova
Houston, Ron Pritchard, LB ... Arizona State
Kansas City, Jim Marsalis, DB ... Tennessee State
Los Angeles, Larry Smith, RB ... Florida
Miami, Bill Stanfill, DE ... Georgia
Minnesota, Ed White, G(2) ... California
N.Y. Giants, Fred Dryer, DE ... San Diego State
N.Y. Jets, Dave Foley, T ... Ohio State
New Orleans, John Shinners, G ... Xavier
Oakland, Art Thoms, DT ... Syracuse
Philadelphia, Leroy Keyes, RB ... Purdue
Pittsburgh, Joe Greene, DT ... N. Texas State
St. Louis, Roger Wehrli, DB ... Missouri
San Diego, Marty Domres, QB ... Columbia
San Francisco, Ted Kwalick, TE ... Penn State
Washington, Eugene Epps, DB(2) ... Texas-El Paso

1970

Atlanta, John Small, LB ... The Citadel
Baltimore, Norm Bulaich, RB ... TCU
Boston Patriots, Phil Olsen, DT ... Utah State
Buffalo, Al Cowlings, DE ... USC
Chicago, George Farmer, WR(3) ... UCLA
Cincinnati, Mike Reid, DT ... Penn State
Cleveland, Mike Phipps, QB ... Purdue
Dallas, Duane Thomas, RB ... W. Texas State
Denver, Bobby Anderson, RB ... Colorado
Detroit, Steve Owens, RB ... Oklahoma
Green Bay, Mike McCoy, DT ... Notre Dame
Houston, Doug Wilkerson, G ... N. Carolina Central
Kansas City, Sid Smith, T ... USC
Los Angeles, Jack Reynolds, LB ... Tennessee
Miami, Jim Mandich, TE(2) ... Michigan
Minnesota, John Ward, T ... Oklahoma
New Orleans, Ken Burrough, WR ... Texas Southern
N.Y. Giants, Jim Files, LB ... Oklahoma
N.Y. Jets, Steve Tannen, DB ... Florida
Oakland, Raymond Chester, TE ... Morgan State
Philadelphia, Steve Zabel, TE ... Oklahoma
Pittsburgh, Terry Bradshaw, QB ... Louisiana Tech
St. Louis, Larry Stegent, RB ... Texas A&M
San Diego, Walker Gillette, WR ... Richmond
San Francisco, Cedrick Hardman, DE ... N. Texas State
Washington, Bill Brundige, DE(2) ... Colorado

1971

Atlanta, Joe Profit, RB ... N.E. Louisiana
Baltimore, Don McCauley, RB ... North Carolina
Buffalo, J. D. Hill, WR ... Arizona State
Chicago, Joe Moore, RB ... Missouri
Cincinnati, Vernon Holland, T ... Tennessee State
Cleveland, Clarence Scott, DB ... Kansas State
Dallas, Tody Smith, DE ... USC
Denver, Marv Montgomery, T ... USC
Detroit, Bob Bell, DT ... Cincinnati
Green Bay, John Brockington, RB ... Ohio State
Houston, Dan Pastorini, QB ... Santa Clara
Kansas City, Elmo Wright, WR ... Houston
Los Angeles, Isiah Robertson, LB ... Southern U.
Miami, Otto Stowe, WR(2) ... Iowa State
Minnesota, Leo Hayden, RB ... Ohio State
New England, Jim Plunkett, QB ... Stanford
New Orleans, Archie Manning, QB ... Mississippi
N.Y. Giants, Rocky Thompson, WR ... W. Texas State
N.Y. Jets, John Riggins, RB ... Kansas
Oakland, Jack Tatum, DB ... Ohio State
Philadelphia, Richard Harris, DE ... Grambling
Pittsburgh, Frank Lewis, WR ... Grambling
St. Louis, Norm Thompson, DB ... Utah
San Diego, Leon Burns, RB ... Cal. State-Long Beach
San Francisco, Tim Anderson, DB ... Ohio State
Washington, Cotton Speyrer, WR(2) ... Texas

1972

Atlanta, Clarence Ellis, DB ... Notre Dame
Baltimore, Tom Drougas, T ... Oregon
Buffalo, Walt Patulski, DE ... Notre Dame
Chicago, Lionel Antoine, T ... Southern Illinois
Cincinnati, Sherman White, DE ... California
Cleveland, Thom Darden, DB ... Michigan
Dallas, Bill Thomas, RB ... Boston College
Denver, Riley Odoms, TE ... Houston
Detroit, Herb Orvis, DE ... Colorado
Green Bay, Willie Buchanon, DB ... San Diego State
Houston, Greg Sampson, DE ... Stanford
Kansas City, Jeff Kinney, RB ... Nebraska
Los Angeles, Jim Bertelsen, RB(2) ... Texas
Miami, Mike Kadish, DT ... Notre Dame
Minnesota, Jeff Siemon, LB ... Stanford
New England, Tom Reynolds, WR(2) ... San Diego State
New Orleans, Royce Smith, G ... Georgia
N.Y. Giants, Eldridge Small, DB ... Texas A&I
N.Y. Jets, Jerome Barkum, WR ... Jackson State
Oakland, Mike Siani, WR ... Villanova
Philadelphia, John Reaves, QB ... Florida
Pittsburgh, Franco Harris, RB ... Penn State
St. Louis, Bobby Moore, WR ... Oregon
San Diego, Pete Lazetich, DE(2) ... Stanford
San Francisco, Terry Beasley, WR ... Auburn
Washington, Moses Denson, RB(8) ... Maryland State

1973

Atlanta, Greg Marx, DT(2) ... Notre Dame
Baltimore, Bert Jones, QB ... LSU
Buffalo, Paul Seymour, T ... Michigan
Chicago, Wally Chambers, DE ... Eastern Kentucky
Cincinnati, Isaac Curtis, WR ... San Diego State
Cleveland, Pete Adams, T ... USC
Dallas, Billy Joe Dupree, TE ... Michigan State
Denver, Otis Armstrong, RB ... Purdue
Detroit, Ernie Price, DE ... Texas A&I
Green Bay, Barry Smith, WR ... Florida State
Houston, John Matuszak, DE ... Tampa
Kansas City, Gary Butler, TE(2) ... Rice
Los Angeles, Cullen Bryant, DB(2) ... Colorado
Miami, Chuck Bradley, T(2) ... Oregon
Minnesota, Chuck Foreman, RB ... Miami
New England, John Hannah, G ... Alabama
N.Y. Giants, Brad Van Pelt, LB ... Michigan State
N.Y. Jets, Burgess Owens, DB ... Miami
Oakland, Ray Guy, P-K ... So. Mississippi
Philadelphia, Jerry Sisemore, T ... Texas
Pittsburgh, James Thomas, CB ... Florida State
St. Louis, Dave Butz, DT ... Purdue
San Diego, Johnny Rodgers, RB ... Nebraska
San Francisco, Mike Holmes, DB ... Southern U.
Washington, Charles Cantrell, G(5) ... Lamar Tech

1974

Atlanta, Gerald Tinker, WR(2) ... Kent State
Baltimore, John Dutton, DE ... Nebraska
Buffalo, Reuben Gant, TE ... Oklahoma State
Chicago, Waymond Bryant, LB ... Tennessee State
Cincinnati, Bill Kollar, DT ... Montana State
Cleveland, Billy Corbett, T(2) ... Johnson C. Smith
Dallas, Ed Jones, DE ... Tennessee State
Denver, Randy Gradishar, LB ... Ohio State
Detroit, Ed O'Neil, LB ... Penn State
Green Bay, Barty Smith, RB ... Richmond
Houston, Steve Manstedt, LB(4) ... Nebraska
Kansas City, Woody Green, RB ... Arizona State
Los Angeles, John Cappelletti, RB ... Penn State
Miami, Don Reese, DE ... Jackson State
Minnesota, Fred McNeill, LB ... UCLA
New England, Steve Corbett, G(2) ... Boston College
New Orleans, Rick Middleton, LB ... Ohio State
N.Y. Giants, John Hicks, G ... Ohio State
N.Y. Jets, Carl Barzilauskas, DT ... Indiana
Oakland, Henry Lawrence, T ... Florida A&M
Philadelphia, Mitch Sutton, DT(3) ... Kansas
Pittsburgh, Lynn Swann, WR ... USC
St. Louis, J. V. Cain, TE ... Colorado
San Diego, Bo Matthews, RB ... Colorado
San Francisco, Wilbur Jackson, RB ... Alabama
Washington, Jon Keyworth, TE(6) ... Colorado

1975

Atlanta, Steve Bartkowski, QB ... California
Baltimore, Ken Huff, G ... North Carolina
Buffalo, Tom Ruud, LB ... Nebraska
Chicago, Walter Payton, RB ... Jackson State
Cincinnati, Glenn Cameron, LB ... Florida
Cleveland, Mack Mitchell, DE ... Houston
Dallas, Randy White, LB ... Maryland
Denver, Louie Wright, DB ... San Jose State
Detroit, Lynn Boden, G ... S. Dakota State
Green Bay, Bill Bain, G(2) ... USC
Houston, Robert Brazile, LB ... Jackson State
Kansas City, Elmore Stephens, TE(2) ... Kentucky
Los Angeles, Mike Fanning, DT ... Notre Dame
Miami, Darryl Carlton, T ... Tampa
Minnesota, Mark Mullaney, DE ... Colorado State
New England, Russ Francis, TE ... Oregon
New Orleans, Larry Burton, WR ... Purdue
N.Y. Giants, Al Simpson, T(2) ... Colorado State
N.Y. Jets, Anthony Davis, RB(2) ... USC
Oakland, Neal Colzie, DB ... Ohio State
Philadelphia, Bill Capraun, T(7) ... Miami
Pittsburgh, Dave Brown, DB ... Michigan
St. Louis, Tim Gray, DB ... Texas A&M
San Diego, Gary Johnson, DT ... Grambling
San Francisco, Jimmy Webb, DT ... Mississippi State
Washington, Mike Thomas, RB(5) ... Nevada-Las Vegas

1976

Atlanta, Bubba Bean, RB ... Texas A&M
Baltimore, Ken Novak, DT ... Purdue
Buffalo, Mario Clark, DB ... Oregon
Chicago, Dennis Lick, T ... Wisconsin
Cincinnati, William Brooks, WR ... Oklahoma
Cleveland, Mike Pruitt, RB ... Purdue
Dallas, Aaron Kyle, DB ... Wyoming
Denver, Tom Glassic, G ... Virginia
Detroit, James Hunter, DB ... Grambling
Green Bay, Mark Koncar, T ... Colorado
Houston, Mike Barber, TE(2) ... Louisiana Tech
Kansas City, Rod Walters, G ... Iowa
Los Angeles, Kevin McLain, LB ... Colorado State
Miami, Larry Gordon, LB ... Arizona State
Minnesota, James White, DT ... Oklahoma State
New England, Mike Haynes, DB ... Arizona State
New Orleans, Chuck Muncie, RB ... California
N.Y. Giants, Troy Archer, DE ... Colorado
N.Y. Jets, Richard Todd, QB ... Alabama
Oakland, Charles Philyaw, DT(2) ... Texas Southern
Philadelphia, Mike Smith, DE(4) ... Florida
Pittsburgh, Bennie Cunningham, TE ... Clemson
St. Louis, Mike Dawson, DT ... Arizona
San Diego, Joe Washington, RB ... Oklahoma
San Francisco, Randy Cross, C(2) ... UCLA
Seattle, Steve Niehaus, DT ... Notre Dame
Tampa Bay, Lee Roy Selmon, DE ... Oklahoma
Washington, Mike Hughes, G(5) ... Baylor

All-Time
Records

O.J. Simpson

Lydell Mitchell

Andy Uram

Bob Gage

Beattie Feathers

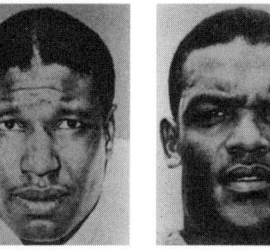
Marion Motley   *Lenny Moore*

INDIVIDUAL RECORDS

RUSHING

Most Seasons Leading League
8 Jim Brown, Cleveland, 1957–61, 1963–65
4 Steve Van Buren, Philadelphia, 1945, 1947–49
   O.J. Simpson, Buffalo, 1972–73, 1975–76
2 By many players

Most Consecutive Seasons Leading League
5 Jim Brown, Cleveland, 1957–61
3 Steve Van Buren, Philadelphia, 1947–49
   Jim Brown, Cleveland, 1963–65
2 Bill Paschal, N.Y. Giants, 1943–44
   Joe Perry, San Francisco, 1953–54
   Jim Nance, Boston, 1966–67
   Leroy Kelly, Cleveland, 1967–68
   O.J. Simpson, Buffalo, 1972–73, 1975–76

RUSHING ATTEMPTS

Most Attempts, Lifetime
2,359 Jim Brown, Cleveland, 1957–65
1,997 O.J. Simpson, Buffalo, 1969–76
1,941 Jim Taylor, Green Bay, 1958–66; New Orleans, 1967

Most Attempts, Season
332 O.J. Simpson, Buffalo, 1973
329 O.J. Simpson, Buffalo, 1975
311 Walter Payton, Chicago, 1976

Most Attempts, Game
41 Franco Harris, Pittsburgh vs. Cincinnati, Oct. 17, 1976
40 Lydell Mitchell, Baltimore vs. N.Y. Jets, Oct. 20, 1974
39 O.J. Simpson, Buffalo vs. Kansas City, Oct. 29, 1973

RUSHING YARDAGE

Most Yards Gained, Lifetime
12,312 Jim Brown, Cleveland, 1957–65
9,626 O.J. Simpson, Buffalo, 1969–76
8,597 Jim Taylor, Green Bay, 1958–66; New Orleans, 1967

Most Seasons 1,000 or More Yards Rushing
7 Jim Brown, Cleveland, 1958–61, 1963–65
5 Jim Taylor, Green Bay, 1960–64
   O.J. Simpson, Buffalo, 1972–76
4 Franco Harris, Pittsburgh, 1972, 1974–76

Most Yards Gained, Season
2,003 O.J. Simpson, Buffalo, 1973
1,863 Jim Brown, Cleveland, 1963
1,817 O.J. Simpson, Buffalo, 1975

Most Yards Gained, Game
273 O.J. Simpson, Buffalo vs. Detroit, Nov. 25, 1976
250 O.J. Simpson, Buffalo vs. New England, Sept. 16, 1973
247 Willie Ellison, Los Angeles vs. New Orleans, Dec. 5, 1971

Most Games, 100 or More Yards Rushing, Lifetime
58 Jim Brown, Cleveland, 1957–65
39 O.J. Simpson, Buffalo, 1969–76
27 Leroy Kelly, Cleveland, 1964–73

Most Games, 100 or More Yards Rushing, Season
11 O.J. Simpson, Buffalo, 1973
9 Jim Brown, Cleveland, 1958, 1963
8 Jim Brown, Cleveland, 1959, 1965
   Jim Nance, Boston, 1966
   O.J. Simpson, Buffalo, 1975

Most Consecutive Games, 100 or More Yards Rushing
7 O.J. Simpson, Buffalo, 1972–73
6 Jim Brown, Cleveland, 1958
   Franco Harris, Pittsburgh, 1972
5 Rob Goode, Washington, 1951
   Jim Brown, Cleveland, 1961
   Jim Nance, Boston, 1966
   O.J. Simpson, Buffalo, 1973, 1975

Longest Run From Scrimmage
97 Andy Uram, Green Bay vs. Chi. Cardinals, Oct. 8, 1939 (TD)
   Bob Gage, Pittsburgh vs. Chi. Bears, Dec. 4, 1949 (TD)
96 Jim Spavital, Baltimore vs. Green Bay, Nov. 5, 1950 (TD)
   Bob Hoernschemeyer, Detroit vs. N.Y. Yanks, Nov. 23, 1950 (TD)
94 O.J. Simpson, Buffalo vs. Pittsburgh, Oct. 29, 1972 (TD)

AVERAGE GAIN RUSHING

Highest Average Gain, Lifetime (700 attempts)
5.22 Jim Brown, Cleveland, 1957–65 (2,359–12,312)
5.14 Eugene (Mercury) Morris, Miami, 1969–75; San Diego, 1976 (804–4,133)
5.00 Gale Sayers, Chicago, 1965–71 (991–4,956)

Highest Average Gain, Season (Qualifiers)
9.94 Beattie Feathers, Chi. Bears, 1934 (101–1,004)
6.87 Bobby Douglass, Chicago, 1972 (141–968)
6.78 Dan Towler, Los Angeles, 1951 (126–854)

Highest Average Gain, Game (10 attempts)
17.09 Marion Motley, Cleveland vs. Pittsburgh, Oct. 29, 1950 (11–188)
16.70 Bill Grimes, Green Bay vs. N.Y. Yanks, Oct. 8, 1950 (10–167)
16.57 Bobby Mitchell, Cleveland vs. Washington, Nov. 15, 1959 (14–232)

TOUCHDOWNS RUSHING

Most Touchdowns Rushing, Lifetime
106 Jim Brown, Cleveland, 1957–65
83 Jim Taylor, Green Bay, 1958–66; New Orleans, 1967
74 Leroy Kelly, Cleveland, 1964–73

Most Touchdowns Rushing, Season
19 Jim Taylor, Green Bay, 1962
17 Jim Brown, Cleveland, 1958, 1965
16 Lenny Moore, Baltimore, 1964
   Leroy Kelly, Cleveland, 1968
   Pete Banaszak, Oakland, 1975
   O.J. Simpson, Buffalo, 1975

Most Touchdowns Rushing, Game
6 Ernie Nevers, Chi. Cardinals vs. Chi. Bears, Nov. 28, 1929
5 Jim Brown, Cleveland vs. Baltimore, Nov. 1, 1959
   Cookie Gilchrist, Buffalo vs. N.Y. Jets, Dec. 8, 1963
4 By many players. Last time Bobby Douglass, Chicago vs. Green Bay, Nov. 4, 1973

Most Consecutive Games Rushing For Touchdowns
11 Lenny Moore, Baltimore, 1963–64
9 Leroy Kelly, Cleveland, 1968
8 Steve Van Buren, Philadelphia, 1947

PASSING

Most Seasons Leading League
6 Sammy Baugh, Washington, 1937, 1940, 1943, 1945, 1947, 1949
4 Len Dawson, Dallas Texans,1962; Kansas City, 1964, 1966, 1968
3 Arnie Herber, Green Bay, 1932, 1934, 1936
   Norm Van Brocklin, Los Angeles, 1950, 1952, 1954
   Bart Starr, Green Bay, 1962, 1964, 1966

Most Consecutive Seasons Leading League
2 Cecil Isbell, Green Bay, 1941–42
   Milt Plum, Cleveland, 1960–61
   Ken Anderson, Cincinnati, 1974–75

PASSING ATTEMPTS

Most Passes Attempted, Lifetime
5,637 Fran Tarkenton, Minnesota, 1961–66, 1972–76; N.Y. Giants, 1967–71
5,186 John Unitas, Baltimore, 1956–72; San Diego, 1973
4,610 John Hadl, San Diego, 1962–72; Los Angeles, 1973–74; Green Bay, 1974–75; Houston, 1976

Most Passes Attempted, Season
508 Sonny Jurgensen, Washington, 1967
505 George Blanda, Houston, 1964
491 Joe Namath, N.Y. Jets, 1967

Most Passes Attempted, Game
68 George Blanda, Houston vs. Buffalo, Nov. 1, 1964
62 Joe Namath, N.Y. Jets vs. Baltimore, Oct. 18, 1970
60 Davey O'Brien, Philadelphia vs. Washington, Dec. 1, 1940
   George Blanda, Houston vs. Oakland, Nov. 7, 1965
   Joe Namath, N.Y. Jets vs. Denver, Dec. 3, 1967

PASSING COMPLETIONS

Most Passes Completed, Lifetime
3,186 Fran Tarkenton, Minnesota, 1961–66, 1972–76; N.Y. Giants, 1967–71
2,830 John Unitas, Baltimore, 1956–72; San Diego, 1973
2,469 John Brodie, San Francisco, 1957–73

Most Passes Completed, Season
288 Sonny Jurgensen, Washington, 1967
274 Sonny Jurgensen, Washington, 1969
273 Fran Tarkenton, Minnesota, 1975

Most Passes Completed, Game
37 George Blanda, Houston vs. Buffalo, Nov. 1, 1964 (68 atts)
36 Charlie Conerly, N.Y. Giants vs. Pittsburgh, Dec. 5, 1948 (53 atts)
   Bert Jones, Baltimore vs. N.Y. Jets, Dec. 15, 1974 (53 atts)
34 Mickey Slaughter, Denver vs. Houston, Dec. 20, 1964 (53 atts)
   Joe Namath, N.Y. Jets vs. Baltimore, Oct. 18, 1970 62 atts)

Most Consecutive Passes Completed
17 Bert Jones, Baltimore vs. N.Y. Jets, Dec. 15, 1974
16 Ken Anderson, Cincinnati vs. Baltimore (8) Nov. 3 and vs. Pittsburgh (8) Nov. 10, 1974
15 Len Dawson, Kansas City vs. Houston, Sept. 9, 1967
   Joe Namath, N.Y. Jets vs. Miami (12) Oct. 22 and vs. Boston (3) Oct. 29, 1967

Cecil Isbell   *Adrian Burk*   *Joe Kapp*   *Art Powell*   *Charley Hennigan*   *Dan Abramowicz*   *Jim Benton*

COMPLETION PERCENTAGE
Highest Completion Percentage, Lifetime (1,500 attempts)
- 57.76 Ken Anderson, Cincinnati, 1971–76 (1,804–1,042)
- 57.42 Bart Starr, Green Bay, 1956–71 (3,149–1,808)
- 57.10 Len Dawson, Pittsburgh, 1957–59; Cleveland, 1960–61; Dallas Texans, 1962; Kansas City, 1963–75 (3,741–2,136)

Highest Completion Percentage, Season (Qualifiers)
- 70.33 Sammy Baugh, Washington, 1945 (182–128)
- 66.67 Ken Stabler, Oakland, 1976 (291–194)
- 66.43 Len Dawson, Kansas City, 1975 (140–93)

Highest Completion Percentage, Game (20 attempts)
- 90.91 Ken Anderson, Cincinnati vs. Pittsburgh, Nov. 10, 1974 (22–20)
- 86.21 Ken Stabler, Oakland vs. Baltimore, Oct. 28, 1973 (29–25)
- 85.71 Sammy Baugh, Washington vs. Pittsburgh, Oct. 14, 1945 (21–18)

PASSING YARDAGE
Most Yards Gained, Lifetime
- 41,801 Fran Tarkenton, Minnesota, 1961–66, 1972–76; N.Y. Giants, 1967–71
- 40,239 John Unitas, Baltimore, 1956–72; San Diego, 1973
- 33,427 John Hadl, San Diego, 1962–72; Los Angeles, 1973–74; Green Bay, 1974–75; Houston, 1976

Most Seasons, 3,000 or More Yards Passing
- 5 Sonny Jurgensen, Philadelphia, 1961–62; Washington, 1966–67, 1969
- 3 George Blanda, Houston, 1961, 1963–64
  - John Unitas, Baltimore, 1960, 1963, 1967
  - Joe Namath, N.Y. Jets, 1966–68
  - Daryle Lamonica, Oakland, 1967–69
  - John Hadl, San Diego, 1967–68, 1971
- 2 Y.A. Tittle, N.Y. Giants, 1962–63
  - John Brodie, San Francisco, 1965, 1968

Most Yards Gained, Season
- 4,007 Joe Namath, N.Y. Jets, 1967
- 3,747 Sonny Jurgensen, Washington, 1967
- 3,723 Sonny Jurgensen, Philadelphia, 1961

Most Yards Gained, Game
- 554 Norm Van Brocklin, Los Angeles vs. N.Y. Yanks, Sept. 28, 1951
- 505 Y.A. Tittle, N.Y. Giants vs. Washington, Oct. 28, 1962
- 496 Joe Namath, N.Y. Jets vs. Baltimore, Sept. 24, 1972

Most Games, 300 or More Yards Passing
- 26 John Unitas, Baltimore, 1956–72; San Diego, 1973
- 25 Sonny Jurgensen, Philadephia, 1957–63; Washington, 1964–74
- 21 Joe Namath, N.Y. Jets, 1965–76

Longest Pass Completion (all TDs except as noted)
- 99 Frank Filchock (to Farkas) Washington vs. Pittsburgh, Oct. 15, 1939
  - George Izo (to Mitchell) Washington vs. Cleveland, Sept. 15, 1963
  - Karl Sweetan (to Studstill) Detroit vs. Baltimore, Oct. 16, 1966
  - Sonny Jurgensen (to Allen) Washington vs. Chicago, Sept. 15, 1968
- 98 Doug Russell (to Tinsley) Chi. Cardinals vs. Cleveland Rams, Nov. 27, 1938
  - Ogden Compton (to Lane) Chi. Cardinals vs. Green Bay, Nov. 13, 1955
  - Bill Wade (to Farrington) Chi. Bears vs. Detroit, Oct. 8, 1961
  - Jacky Lee (to Dewveall) Houston vs. San Diego, Nov. 25, 1962
  - Earl Morrall (to Jones) N.Y. Giants vs. Pittsburgh, Sept. 11, 1966
  - Jim Hart (to Moore) St. Louis vs. Los Angeles, Dec. 10, 1972 (no TD)
- 97 Pat Coffee (to Tinsley) Chi. Cardinals vs. Chi. Bears, Dec. 5, 1937
  - Bobby Layne (to Box) Detroit vs. Green Bay, Nov. 26, 1953
  - George Shaw (to Tarr) Denver vs. Boston, Sept. 21, 1962

TOUCHDOWN PASSES
Most Seasons Leading League
- 4 John Unitas, Baltimore, 1957–60
  - Len Dawson, Dallas Texans, 1962; Kansas City, 1963, 1965–66
- 3 Arnie Herber, Green Bay, 1932, 1934, 1936
  - Sid Luckman, Chi. Bears, 1943, 1945–46
  - Y.A. Tittle, San Francisco, 1955; N.Y. Giants, 1962–63
- 2 By many players

Most Touchdown Passes, Lifetime
- 308 Fran Tarkenton, Minnesota, 1961–66, 1972–76; N.Y. Giants, 1967–71
- 290 John Unitas, Baltimore, 1956–72; San Diego, 1973
- 255 Sonny Jurgensen, Philadelphia, 1957–63; Washington, 1964–74

Most Touchdown Passes, Season
- 36 George Blanda, Houston, 1961
  - Y.A. Tittle, N.Y. Giants, 1963
- 34 Daryle Lamonica, Oakland, 1969
- 33 Y.A. Tittle, N.Y. Giants, 1962

Most Touchdown Passes, Game
- 7 Sid Luckman, Chi. Bears vs. N.Y. Giants, Nov. 14, 1943
  - Adrian Burk, Philadelphia vs. Washington, Oct. 17, 1954
  - George Blanda, Houston vs. N.Y. Titans, Nov. 19, 1961
  - Y.A. Tittle, N.Y. Giants vs. Washington, Oct. 28, 1962
  - Joe Kapp, Minnesota vs. Baltimore, Sept. 28, 1969
- 6 By many players. Last time Joe Namath, N.Y. Jets vs. Baltimore, Sept. 24, 1972

Most Consecutive Games, Touchdown Passes
- 47 John Unitas, Baltimore, 1956–60
- 25 Daryle Lamonica, Oakland, 1968–70
- 23 Frank Ryan, Cleveland, 1965–67
  - Sonny Jurgensen, Washington, 1966–68

PASSES HAD INTERCEPTED
Fewest Passes Had Intercepted, Season (Qualifiers)
- 1 Joe Ferguson, Buffalo, 1976
- 3 Gary Wood, N.Y. Giants, 1964
  - Bart Starr, Green Bay, 1966
- 4 Sammy Baugh, Washington, 1945
  - Harry Gilmer, Detroit, 1955
  - Charlie Conerly, N.Y. Giants, 1959
  - Bart Starr, Green Bay, 1964
  - Roger Staubach, Dallas, 1971
  - Len Dawson, Kansas City, 1975
- 5 By eight players

Most Consecutive Passes Attempted, None Intercepted
- 294 Bart Starr, Green Bay, 1964–65
- 208 Milt Plum, Cleveland, 1959–60
- 206 Roman Gabriel, Los Angeles, 1968–69

Most Passes Had Intercepted, Lifetime
- 277 George Blanda, Chi. Bears, 1949–58; Baltimore, 1950; Houston, 1960–66; Oakland, 1967–75
- 265 John Hadl, San Diego, 1962–72; Los Angeles, 1973–74; Green Bay, 1974–75; Houston, 1976
- 257 Norm Snead, Washington, 1961–63; Philadelphia, 1964–70; Minnesota, 1971; N.Y. Giants, 1972–74; San Francisco, 1974–75; N.Y. Giants, 1976

Most Passes Had Intercepted, Season
- 42 George Blanda, Houston, 1962
- 34 Frank Tripucka, Denver, 1960
- 32 John Hadl, San Diego, 1968

Most Passes Had Intercepted, Game
- 8 Jim Hardy, Chi. Cardinals vs. Philadelphia, Sept. 24, 1950
- 7 Parker Hall, Cleveland Rams vs. Green Bay, Nov. 8, 1942
  - Frank Sinkwich, Detroit vs. Green Bay, Oct. 24, 1943
  - Bob Waterfield, Los Angeles vs. Green Bay, Oct. 17, 1948
  - Zeke Bratkowski, Chi. Bears vs. Baltimore, Oct. 2, 1960
  - Tommy Wade, Pittsburgh vs. Philadelphia, Dec. 12, 1965
- 6 By many players

Lowest Percentage Passes Had Intercepted, Lifetime (1,500 attempts)
- 3.15 Ken Anderson, Cincinnati, 1971–76 (1,804–58)
- 3.34 Roman Gabriel, Los Angeles, 1962–72; Philadelphia, 1973 (4,403–147)

Lowest Percentage Passes Had Intercepted, Season (Qualifiers)
- 0.07 Joe Ferguson, Buffalo, 1976 (151–1)
- 1.20 Bart Starr, Green Bay, 1966 (251–3)
- 1.47 Bart Starr, Green Bay, 1964 (272–4)

RECEIVING
Most Seasons Leading League
- 8 Don Hutson, Green Bay, 1936–37, 1939, 1941–45
- 5 Lionel Taylor, Denver, 1960–63, 1965
- 3 Tom Fears, Los Angeles, 1948–50
  - Pete Pihos, Philadelphia, 1953–55
  - Billy Wilson, San Francisco, 1954, 1956–57
  - Raymond Berry, Baltimore, 1958–60
  - Lance Alworth, San Diego, 1966, 1968–69

Most Consecutive Seasons Leading League
- 5 Don Hutson, Green Bay, 1941–45
- 4 Lionel Taylor, Denver, 1960–63
- 3 Tom Fears, Los Angeles, 1948–50
  - Pete Pihos, Philadelphia, 1953–55
  - Raymond Berry, Baltimore, 1958–60

Most Pass Receptions, Lifetime
- 635 Charley Taylor, Washington, 1964–75
- 633 Don Maynard, N.Y. Giants, 1958; N.Y. Jets, 1960–72; St. Louis, 1973
- 631 Raymond Berry, Baltimore, 1955–67

Most Seasons, 50 or More Pass Receptions
- 7 Raymond Berry, Baltimore, 1958–62, 1965–66
  - Art Powell, N.Y. Titans, 1960–62; Oakland, 1963–66
  - Lance Alworth, San Diego, 1963–69
  - Charley Taylor, Washington, 1964, 1966–67, 1969, 1973–75
- 6 Lionel Taylor, Denver, 1960–65
  - Bobby Mitchell, 1962–67
- 5 Billy Wilson, San Francisco, 1953–57
  - Pete Retzlaff, Philadelphia, 1958, 1961, 1963–65
  - Bernie Casey, San Francisco, 1962, 1964–66; Los Angeles, 1967
  - Don Maynard, N.Y. Titans, 1960, 1962; N.Y. Jets, 1965, 1967–68

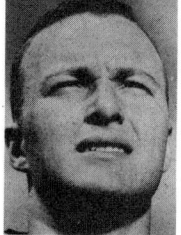

Johnny Robinson *Bill Bradley* *Bobby Dillon* *Jack Butler* *Dave Baker* *Dick Anderson* *Charlie McNeil*

RECEIVING (Continued)

Most Pass Receptions, Season
- 101 Charley Hennigan, Houston, 1964
- 100 Lionel Taylor, Denver, 1961
- 93 Johnny Morris, Chicago, 1964

Most Pass Receptions, Game
- 18 Tom Fears, Los Angeles vs. Green Bay, Dec. 3, 1950
- 16 Sonny Randle, St. Louis vs. N.Y. Giants, Nov. 4, 1962
- 14 Don Looney, Philadelphia vs. Washington, Dec. 1, 1940
     Don Hutson, Green Bay vs. N.Y. Giants, Nov. 22, 1942
     Jim Keane, Chi. Bears vs. N.Y. Giants, Oct. 23, 1949
     Ralph Heywood, N.Y. Bulldogs vs. Detroit, Dec. 4, 1949

Most Consecutive Games, Pass Receptions
- 105 Dan Abramowicz, New Orleans, 1967–73; San Francisco, 1973–74
- 96 Lance Alworth, San Diego, 1962–69
- 95 Don Hutson, Green Bay, 1937–45

YARDAGE RECEIVING

Most Yards Gained, Pass Receiving, Lifetime
- 11,834 Don Maynard, N.Y. Giants, 1958; N.Y. Jets, 1960–72; St. Louis, 1973
- 10,266 Lance Alworth, San Diego, 1962–70; Dallas, 1971–72
- 9,275 Raymond Berry, Baltimore, 1955–67

Most Seasons 1,000 or More Yards, Pass Receiving
- 7 Lance Alworth, San Diego, 1963–69
- 5 Art Powell, N.Y. Titans, 1960, 1962; Oakland, 1963–64, 1966
    Don Maynard, N.Y. Jets, 1960, 1962, 1965, 1967–68
- 4 Del Shofner, Los Angeles, 1958; N.Y. Giants, 1961–63
    Lionel Taylor, Denver, 1960–61, 1963, 1965

Most Yards Gained, Pass Receiving, Season
- 1,746 Charley Hennigan, Houston, 1961
- 1,602 Lance Alworth, San Diego, 1965
- 1,546 Charley Hennigan, Houston, 1964

Most Yards Gained, Pass Receiving, Game
- 303 Jim Benton, Cleveland Rams vs. Detroit, Nov. 22, 1945
- 302 Cloyce Box, Detroit vs. Baltimore, Dec. 3, 1950
- 272 Charley Hennigan, Houston vs. Boston, Oct. 13, 1961

Longest Pass Reception (all TDs except as noted)
- 99 Andy Farkas (from Filchock) Washington vs. Pittsburgh, Oct. 15, 1939
    Bobby Mitchell (from Izo) Washington vs. Cleveland, Sept. 15, 1963
    Pat Studstill (from Sweetan) Detroit vs. Baltimore, Oct. 16, 1966
    Gerry Allen (from Jurgensen) Washington vs. Chicago, Sept. 15, 1968
- 98 Gaynell Tinsley (from Russell) Chi. Cardinals vs. Cleveland Rams, Nov. 17, 1938
    Dick (Night Train) Lane (from Compton) Chi. Cardinals vs. Green Bay, Nov.13, 1955
    John Farrington (from Wade) Chicago vs. Detroit, Oct. 8, 1961
    Willard Dewveall (from Lee) Houston vs. San Diego, Nov. 25, 1962
    Homer Jones (from Morrall) N.Y. Giants vs. Pittsburgh, Sept. 11, 1966
    Bobby Moore (from Hart) St. Louis vs. Los Angeles, Dec. 10, 1972 (no TD)
- 97 Gaynell Tinsley (from Coffee) Chi. Cardinals vs. Chi. Bears, Dec. 5, 1937
    Cloyce Box (from Layne) Detroit vs. Green Bay, Nov. 26, 1953
    Jerry Tarr (from Shaw) Denver vs. Boston, Sept. 21, 1962

TOUCHDOWNS RECEIVING

Most Seasons Leading League
- 9 Don Hutson, Green Bay, 1935–38, 1940–44
- 3 Lance Alworth, San Diego, 1964–66
- 2 By many players

Most Touchdown Passes, Lifetime
- 99 Don Hutson, Green Bay, 1935–45
- 88 Don Maynard, N.Y. Giants, 1958; N.Y. Jets, 1960–72; St. Louis, 1973
- 85 Lance Alworth, San Diego, 1962–70; Dallas, 1971–72

Most Touchdown Passes, Season
- 17 Don Hutson, Green Bay, 1942
     Elroy (Crazylegs) Hirsch, Los Angeles, 1951
     Bill Groman, Houston, 1961
- 16 Art Powell, Oakland, 1963
- 15 Cloyce Box, Detroit, 1952
     Sonny Randle, St. Louis, 1960

Most Touchdown Passes, Game
- 5 Bob Shaw, Chi. Cardinals vs. Baltimore, Oct. 2, 1950
- 4 By many players. Last time Paul Warfield, Miami vs. Detroit, Dec. 15, 1973

Most Consecutive Games, Touchdown Passes
- 11 Elroy (Crazylegs) Hirsch, Los Angeles, 1950–51
     Buddy Dial, Pittsburgh, 1959–60
- 9 Lance Alworth, San Diego, 1963
- 8 Bill Groman, Houston, 1961
    Dave Parks, San Francisco, 1965

INTERCEPTIONS BY

Most Seasons Leading League
- 2 Dick (Night Train) Lane, Los Angeles, 1952; Chi. Cardinals, 1954
    Jack Christiansen, Detroit, 1953, 1957
    Milt Davis, Baltimore, 1957, 1959
    Dick Lynch, N.Y. Giants, 1961, 1963
    Johnny Robinson, Kansas City, 1966, 1970
    Bill Bradley, Philadelphia, 1971–72
    Emmitt Thomas, Kansas City, 1969, 1974

Most Interceptions By, Lifetime
- 79 Emlen Tunnell, N.Y. Giants, 1948–58; Green Bay, 1959–61
- 74 Paul Krause, Washington, 1964–67; Minnesota, 1968–76
- 68 Dick (Night Train) Lane, Los Angeles, 1952–53; Chi. Cardinals, 1954–59; Detroit, 1960–65

Most Interceptions By, Season
- 14 Dick (Night Train) Lane, Los Angeles, 1952
- 13 Dan Sandifer, Washington, 1948
     Orban (Spec) Sanders, N.Y. Yanks, 1950
- 12 By eight players

Most Interceptions By, Game
- 4 Sammy Baugh, Washington vs. Detroit, Nov. 14, 1943
    Dan Sandifer, Washington vs. Boston Yanks, Oct. 31, 1948
    Don Doll, Detroit vs. Chi. Cardinals, Oct. 23, 1949
    Bob Nussbaumer, Chi. Cardinals vs. N.Y. Bulldogs, Nov. 13, 1949
    Russ Craft, Philadelphia vs. Chi. Cardinals, Sept. 24, 1950
    Bobby Dillon, Green Bay vs. Detroit, Nov. 26, 1953
    Jack Butler, Pittsburgh vs. Washington, Dec. 13, 1953
    Austin (Goose) Gonsoulin, Denver vs. Buffalo, Sept. 18, 1960
    Jerry Norton, St. Louis vs. Washington, Nov. 20, 1960; vs. Pittsburgh, Nov. 26, 1961
    Dave Baker, San Francisco vs. Los Angeles, Dec. 4, 1960
    Bobby Ply, Dallas Texans vs. San Diego, Dec. 16, 1962
    Bobby Hunt, Kansas City vs. Houston, Oct. 4, 1964
    Willie Brown, Denver vs. N.Y. Jets, Nov. 15, 1964
    Dick Anderson, Miami vs. Pittsburgh, Dec. 3, 1973

Most Consecutive Games, Passes Intercepted By
- 8 Tom Morrow, Oakland, 1962–63
- 7 Paul Krause, Washington, 1964
    Larry Wilson, St. Louis, 1966
    Ben Davis, Cleveland, 1968
- 6 By six players

INTERCEPTION YARDAGE

Most Yards Returned, Lifetime
- 1,282 Emlen Tunnell, N.Y. Giants, 1948–58; Green Bay, 1959–61
- 1,207 Dick (Night Train) Lane, Los Angeles, 1952–53; Chi. Cardinals, 1954–59; Detroit, 1960–65
- 1,090 Paul Krause, Washington, 1964–67; Minnesota, 1968–76

Most Yards Returned, Season
- 349 Charley McNeil, San Diego, 1961
- 301 Don Doll, Detroit, 1949
- 298 Dick (Night Train) Lane, Los Angeles, 1952

Most Yards Returned, Game
- 177 Charley McNeil, San Diego vs. Houston, Sept. 24, 1961
- 167 Dick Jauron, Detroit vs. Chicago, Nov. 18, 1973
- 137 Tom Janik, Buffalo vs. N.Y. Jets, Sept. 29, 1968

Longest Return (all TDs)
- 102 Bob Smith, Detroit vs. Chi. Bears, Nov. 24, 1949
     Erich Barnes, N.Y. Giants vs. Dallas, Oct. 22, 1961
- 101 Richie Petitbon, Chicago vs. Los Angeles, Dec. 9, 1962
     Henry Carr, N.Y. Giants vs. Los Angeles, Nov. 13, 1966
     Tony Greene, Buffalo vs. Kansas City, Oct. 3, 1976
- 100 Vern Huffman, Detroit vs. Brooklyn, Oct. 17, 1937
     Mike Gaechter, Dallas vs. Philadelphia, Oct. 14, 1962
     Leslie (Speedy) Duncan, San Diego vs. Kansas City, Oct. 15, 1967
     Tom Janik, Buffalo vs. N.Y. Jets, Sept. 29, 1968

TOUCHDOWNS ON INTERCEPTIONS

Most Touchdowns, Lifetime
- 9 Ken Houston, Houston, 1967–72; Washington, 1973–76
- 7 Herb Adderley, Green Bay, 1961–69; Dallas, 1970–72
    Erich Barnes, Chi. Bears, 1958–60; N.Y. Giants, 1961–64; Cleveland, 1965–70
    Lem Barney, Detroit, 1967–76
- 6 Tom Janik, Denver, 1963–64; Buffalo, 1965–68; Boston, 1969–70; New England, 1971
    Miller Farr, Denver, 1965; San Diego, 1965–66; Houston, 1967–69; St. Louis, 1970–72; Detroit, 1973
    Lem Barney, Detroit, 1967–75
    Bobby Bell, Kansas City, 1963–74

Most Touchdowns, Season
- 4 Ken Houston, Houston, 1971
    Jim Kearney, Kansas City, 1972
- 3 Dick Harris, San Diego, 1961

Bob Smith

Erich Barnes

Ken Houston

Jerrel Wilson

Steve O'Neal

Bob Cifers

L. (Speedy) Duncan

Most Touchdowns, Season (Continued)
    Dick Lynch, N.Y. Giants, 1963
    Herb Adderley, Green Bay, 1965
    Lem Barney, Detroit, 1967
    Miller Farr, Houston, 1967
    Monte Jackson, Los Angeles, 1976
  2 By many players

Most Touchdowns, Game
  2 Bill Blackburn, Chi. Cardinals vs. Boston Yanks, Oct. 24, 1948
    Dan Sandifer, Washington vs. Boston Yanks, Oct. 31, 1948
    Bob Franklin, Cleveland vs. Chicago, Dec. 11, 1960
    Bill Stacy, St. Louis vs. Dallas, Nov. 5, 1961
    Jerry Norton, St. Louis vs. Pittsburgh, Nov. 26, 1961
    Miller Farr, Houston vs. Buffalo, Dec. 7, 1968
    Ken Houston, Houston vs. San Diego, Dec. 19, 1971
    Jim Kearney, Kansas City vs. Denver, Oct. 1, 1972
    Lemar Parrish, Cincinnati vs. Houston, Dec. 17, 1972
    Dick Anderson, Miami vs. Pittsburgh, Dec. 3, 1973
    Prentice McCray, New England vs. N.Y. Jets, Nov. 21, 1976

PUNTING

Most Seasons Leading League
  4 Sammy Baugh, Washington, 1940–43
    Jerrel Wilson, Kansas City, 1965, 1968, 1972–73
  3 Yale Lary, Detroit, 1959, 1961, 1963
    Jim Fraser, Denver, 1962–64
  2 By many players

Most Punts, Lifetime
  970 Bobby Joe Green, Pittsburgh, 1960–61; Chicago, 1962–73
  865 Jerrel Wilson, Kansas City, 1963–75
  831 Bobby Walden, Minnesota, 1964–67; Pittsburgh, 1968–75

Most Punts, Season
  105 Bob Scarpitto, Denver, 1967
  101 Tom Blanchard, New Orleans, 1976
    John James, Atlanta, 1976
  100 Paul Maguire, Buffalo, 1968
  96 John James, Atlanta, 1974

Most Punts, Game
  14 Dick Nesbitt, Chi. Cardinals vs. Chi. Bears, Nov. 30, 1933
    Keith Molesworth, Chi. Bears vs. Green Bay, Dec. 10, 1933
    Sammy Baugh, Washington vs. Philadelphia, Nov. 5, 1939
    John Kinscherf, N.Y. Giants vs. Detroit, Nov. 7, 1943
    George Taliaferro, N.Y. Yanks vs. Los Angeles, Sept. 28, 1951
  12 Parker Hall, Cleveland vs. Green Bay, Nov. 26, 1939
    Beryl Clark, Chi. Cardinals vs. Detroit, Sept. 15, 1940
    Len Barnum, Philadelphia vs. Washington, Oct. 4, 1942
    Horace Gillom, Cleveland vs. Philadelphia, Dec. 3, 1950
    Adrian Burk, Philadelphia vs. Green Bay, Nov. 2, 1952; vs. N.Y. Giants, Dec. 12, 1954
    Bob Scarpitto, Denver vs. Oakland, Sept. 10, 1967
    Bill Van Heusen, Denver vs. Cincinnati, Oct. 6, 1968
    Tom Blanchard, New Orleans vs. Minnesota, Nov. 16, 1975
  11 By many players

Longest Punt
  98 Steve O'Neal, N.Y. Jets vs. Denver, Sept. 21, 1969
  94 Joe Lintzenich, Chi. Bears vs. N.Y. Giants, Nov. 16, 1931
  90 Don Chandler, Green Bay vs. San Francisco, Oct. 10, 1965

AVERAGE YARDS PUNTING
Highest Average, Punting, Lifetime (300 punts)
  45.10 Sammy Baugh, Washington, 1937–52
  44.68 Tommy Davis, San Francisco, 1959–69
  44.29 Yale Lary, Detroit, 1952–53, 1956–64

Highest Average, Punting, Season (Qualifiers)
  51.40 Sammy Baugh, Washington, 1940
  48.94 Yale Lary, Detroit, 1963
  48.73 Sammy Baugh, Washington, 1941

Highest Average, Punting, Game (4 punts)
  61.75 Bob Cifers, Detroit vs. Chi. Bears, Nov. 24, 1946
  61.60 Roy McKay, Green Bay vs. Chi. Cardinals, Oct. 28, 1945
  59.40 Sammy Baugh, Washington vs. Detroit, Oct. 27, 1940

PUNT RETURNS

Most Seasons Leading League
  3 Leslie (Speedy) Duncan, San Diego, 1965–66; Washington, 1971
  2 Dick Christy, N.Y. Titans, 1961–62
    Claude Gibson, Oakland, 1963–64

Most Punt Returns, Lifetime
  258 Emlen Tunnell, N.Y. Giants, 1948–58; Green Bay, 1959–61
  253 Alvin Haymond, Baltimore, 1964–67; Philadelphia, 1968; Los Angeles, 1969–71; Washington, 1972; Houston, 1973
  235 Ron Smith, Chicago, 1965, 1970–72; Atlanta, 1966–67; Los Angeles, 1968–69; San Diego, 1973; Oakland, 1974

Most Punt Returns, Season
  54 Rolland Lawrence, Atlanta, 1970
  53 Alvin Haymond, Los Angeles, 1970
    Larry Jones, Washington, 1975
  48 Neal Colzie, Oakland, 1975
    Eddie Brown, Washington, 1976

Most Punt Returns, Games
  9 Rodger Bird, Oakland vs. Denver, Sept. 10, 1967
    Ralph McGill, San Francisco vs. Atlanta, Oct. 29, 1972
    Ed Podolak, Kansas City vs. San Diego, Nov. 10, 1974
  9 Anthony Leonard, San Francisco vs. New Orleans, Oct. 17, 1976
  9 Butch Johnson, Dallas vs. Buffalo, Nov. 15, 1976
  8 Emlen Tunnell, N.Y. Giants vs. N.Y. Yanks, Dec. 3, 1950
    Joe Arenas, San Francisco vs. Detroit, Oct. 16, 1955
    Hugh McElhenny, San Francisco vs. Detroit, Nov. 2, 1958
    Tommy Pharr, Buffalo vs. N.Y. Jets, Oct. 25, 1970
    Neal Colzie, Oakland vs. San Diego, Oct. 5, 1975
  7 By many players

Most Fair Catches, Season
  24 Ken Graham, San Diego, 1969
  21 Ed Podolak, Kansas City, 1970
  20 Ron Gardin, Baltimore, 1970
    Rick Volk, Baltimore, 1971
    Jon Staggers, Green Bay, 1972

Most Fair Catches, Game
  7 Len Barney, Detroit vs. Chicago, Nov. 21, 1976
  6 Jake Scott, Miami vs. Buffalo, Dec. 20, 1970
  5 Bill Butler, Minnesota vs. Baltimore, Nov. 17, 1963
    Wayne Swinford, San Francisco vs. Chicago, Sept. 19, 1965
    Tom Watkins, Detroit vs. Los Angeles, Sept. 19, 1965
    Johnny Roland, St. Louis vs. Green Bay, Oct. 30, 1967
    Ken Graham, San Diego vs. Cincinnati, Oct. 4, 1969
    Walt Sumner, Cleveland vs. Miami, Oct. 25, 1970
    Willie Wood, Green Bay vs. Chicago, Nov. 15, 1970
    Howard Stevens, New Orleans vs. Chicago, Oct. 7, 1973
    Jake Scott, Miami vs. New England, Oct. 28, 1973

YARDS RETURNING PUNTS
Most Yards Returned, Lifetime
  2,209 Emlen Tunnell, N.Y. Giants, 1948–58; Green Bay, 1959–61
  2,201 Leslie (Speedy) Duncan, San Diego, 1964–70; Washington, 1971–74
  2,148 Alvin Haymond, Baltimore, 1964–67; Philadelphia, 1968; Los Angeles, 1969–71; Washington, 1972; Houston, 1973

Most Yards Returned, Season
  655 Neal Colzie, Oakland, 1975
  646 Eddie Brown, Washington, 1976
  612 Rodger Bird, Oakland, 1967
    Billy Johnson, Houston, 1975
  577 Lynn Swann, Pittsburgh, 1974

Most Yards Returned, Game
  205 George Atkinson, Oakland vs. Buffalo, Sept. 15, 1968
  184 Tom Watkins, Detroit vs. San Francisco, Oct. 6, 1963
  175 Jack Christiansen, Detroit vs. Green Bay, Nov. 22, 1951

Longest Punt Return (all TDs)
  98 Gil LeFebvre, Cincinnati Reds vs. Brooklyn, Dec. 3, 1933
    Charlie West, Minnesota vs. Washington, Nov. 3, 1968
    Dennis Morgan, Dallas vs. St. Louis, Oct. 13, 1974
  96 Bill Dudley, Washington vs. Pittsburgh, Dec. 3, 1950
  95 Frank Bernardi, Chi. Cardinals vs. Washington, Oct. 14, 1956
    Leslie (Speedy) Duncan, San Diego vs. N.Y. Jets, Nov. 24, 1968
    Steve Odom, Green Bay vs. Chicago, Nov. 10, 1974

AVERAGE YARDS RETURNING PUNTS
Highest Average, Lifetime (75 returns)
  13.19 Billy Johnson, Houston, 1974–76
  12.78 George McAfee, Chi. Bears, 1940–41, 1945–50
  12.75 Jack Christiansen, Detroit, 1951–58

Highest Average, Season (Qualifiers)
  23.00 Herb Rich, Baltimore, 1950
  21.47 Jack Christiansen, Detroit, 1952
  21.28 Dick Christy, N.Y. Titans, 1961

Highest Average, Game (3 returns)
  47.67 Chuck Latourette, St. Louis vs. New Orleans, Sept. 29, 1968
  47.33 Johnny Roland, St. Louis vs. Philadelphia, Oct. 2, 1966
  45.67 Dick Christy, N.Y. Titans vs. Denver, Sept. 24, 1961

TOUCHDOWNS RETURNING PUNTS
Most Touchdowns, Lifetime
  8 Jack Christiansen, Detroit, 1951 (4), 1952 (2), 1954, 1956
  5 Emlen Tunnell, N.Y. Giants, 1949, 1951 (3), 1955
  4 Dick Christy, N.Y. Titans, 1961 (2), 1962 (2)
    Leslie (Speedy) Duncan, San Diego, 1965 (2), 1966, 1968
    Lemar Parrish, Cincinnati, 1970, 1972, 1974 (2)
    Rick Upchurch, Denver, 1975–76

Billy Johnson　　*Chuck Latourette*　　*Rick Upchurch*　　*Bobby Jancik*　　*Al Carmichael*　　*Travis Williams*　　*Timmy Brown*

PUNT RETURNS (Continued)
Most Touchdowns, Season
4	Jack Christiansen, Detroit, 1951	
4	Rick Upchurch, Denver, 1976	
3	Emlen Tunnell, N.Y. Giants, 1951	
	Billy Johnson, Houston, 1975	
2	By many players	

Most Touchdowns, Game
- 2 Jack Christiansen, Detroit vs. Los Angeles, Oct. 14, 1951; vs. Green Bay, Nov. 22, 1951
- Dick Christy, N.Y. Titans vs. Denver, Sept. 24, 1961
- Rick Upchurch, Denver vs. Cleveland, Sept. 26, 1976

KICKOFF RETURNS
Most Seasons Leading League
- 3 Abe Woodson, San Francisco, 1959, 1962–63
- 2 Lynn Chandnois, Pittsburgh, 1951–52
- Bobby Jancik, Houston, 1962–63
- Travis Williams, Green Bay, 1967; Los Angeles, 1971

Most Kickoff Returns, Lifetime
- 275 Ron Smith, Chicago, 1965, 1970–72; Atlanta, 1966–67; Los Angeles, 1968–69; San Diego, 1973; Oakland, 1974
- 193 Abe Woodson, San Francisco, 1958–64; St. Louis, 1965–66
- 191 Al Carmichael, Green Bay, 1953–58; Denver, 1960–61

Most Kickoff Returns, Season
- 47 Odell Barry, Denver, 1964
- Larry Jones, Washington, 1975
- 46 Chuck Latourette, St. Louis, 1968
- Dave Hampton, Green Bay, 1971
- 45 Bobby Jancik, Houston, 1963

Most Kickoff Returns, Game
- 9 Noland Smith, Kansas City vs. Oakland, Nov. 23, 1967
- 8 George Taliaferro, N.Y. Yanks vs. N.Y. Giants, Dec. 3, 1950
- Bobby Jancik, Houston vs. Boston Patriots, Dec. 8 and vs. Oakland, Dec. 22, 1963
- Mel Renfro, Dallas vs. Green Bay, Nov. 29, 1964
- Willie Porter, Boston Patriots vs. N.Y. Jets, Sept. 22, 1968
- 7 By many players

YARDS RETURNING KICKOFFS
Most Yards Returned, Lifetime
- 6,922 Ron Smith, Chicago, 1965, 1970–72; Atlanta, 1966–67; Los Angeles, 1968–69; San Diego, 1973; Oakland, 1974
- 5,538 Abe Woodson, San Francisco, 1958–64; St. Louis, 1965–66
- 4,798 Al Carmichael, Green Bay, 1953–58; Denver, 1960–61

Most Yards Returned, Season
- 1,317 Bobby Jancik, Houston, 1963
- 1,314 Dave Hampton, Green Bay, 1971
- 1,245 Odell Barry, Denver, 1964

Most Yards Returned, Game
- 294 Wally Triplett, Detroit vs. Los Angeles, Oct. 29, 1950
- 247 Timmy Brown, Philadelphia vs. Dallas, Nov. 6, 1966
- 244 Noland Smith, Kansas City vs. San Diego, Oct. 15, 1967

Longest Kickoff Return (all TDs)
- 106 Al Carmichael, Green Bay vs. Chi. Bears, Oct. 7, 1956
- Noland Smith, Kansas City vs. Denver, Dec. 17, 1967
- 105 Frank Seno, Chi. Cardinals vs. N.Y. Giants, Oct. 20, 1946
- Ollie Matson, Chi. Cardinals vs. Washington, Oct. 14, 1956
- Abe Woodson, San Francisco vs. Los Angeles, Nov. 8, 1959
- Timmy Brown, Philadelphia vs. Cleveland, Sept. 17, 1961
- Jon Arnett, Los Angeles vs. Detroit, Oct. 29, 1961
- Eugene (Mercury) Morris, Miami vs. Cincinnati, Sept. 14, 1969
- Travis Williams, Los Angeles vs. New Orleans, Dec. 5, 1971
- 104 By many players

AVERAGE YARDS RETURNING KICKOFFS
Highest Average, Lifetime (75 returns)
- 30.56 Gale Sayers, Chicago, 1965–71
- 29.57 Lynn Chandnois, Pittsburgh, 1950–56
- 28.69 Abe Woodson, San Francisco, 1958–64; St. Louis, 1965–66

Highest Average, Season (Qualifiers)
- 41.06 Travis Williams, Green Bay, 1967
- 37.69 Gale Sayers, Chicago, 1967
- 35.50 Ollie Matson, Chi. Cardinals, 1958

Highest Average, Game (3 returns)
- 73.50 Wally Triplett, Detroit vs. Los Angeles, Oct. 29, 1950
- 67.33 Lenny Lyles, San Francisco vs. Baltimore, Dec. 18, 1960
- 65.33 Ken Hall, Houston vs. N.Y. Titans, Oct. 23, 1960

TOUCHDOWNS RETURNING KICKOFFS
Most Touchdowns, Lifetime
- 6 Ollie Matson, Chi. Cardinals, 1952 (2), 1954, 1956, 1958 (2)
- Gale Sayers, Chicago, 1965, 1966 (2), 1967 (3)
- Travis Williams, Green Bay, 1967 (4), 1969; Los Angeles, 1971
- 5 Bobby Mitchell, Cleveland, 1958, 1960, 1961; Washington, 1962, 1963
- Abe Woodson, San Francisco, 1959, 1961, 1963 (3)
- Timmy Brown, Philadelphia, 1961, 1962, 1963, 1966 (2)
- 4 Cecil Turner, Chicago, 1970 (4)

Most Touchdowns, Season
- 4 Travis Williams, Green Bay, 1967
- Cecil Turner, Chicago, 1970
- 3 Verda (Vitamin T) Smith, Los Angeles, 1950
- Abe Woodson, San Francisco, 1963
- Gale Sayers, Chicago, 1967
- 2 By many players

Most Touchdowns, Game
- 2 Timmy Brown, Philadelphia vs. Dallas, Nov. 6, 1966
- Travis Williams, Green Bay vs. Cleveland, Nov. 12, 1967

SCORING
Most Seasons Leading League
- 5 Don Hutson, Green Bay, 1940–44
- Gino Cappelletti, Boston Patriots, 1961, 1963–66
- 3 Earl (Dutch) Clark, Portsmouth Spartans, 1932; Detroit, 1935–36
- Pat Harder, Chi. Cardinals, 1947–49
- Paul Hornung, Green Bay, 1959–61
- 2 By seven players

POINTS
Most Points, Lifetime
- 2,002 George Blanda, Chi. Bears, 1949–58; Baltimore, 1950; Houston, 1960–66; Oakland, 1967–75 (9 TD, 943 PAT, 335 FG)
- 1,349 Lou Groza, Cleveland, 1950–59, 1961–67 (1 TD, 641 PAT, 234 FG)
- 1,316 Fred Cox, Minnesota, 1963–76 (494 PAT, 274 FG)

Most Points, Season
- 176 Paul Hornung, Green Bay, 1960 (15 TD, 41 PAT, 15 FG)
- 155 Gino Cappelletti, Boston, 1964 (7 TD, 38 PAT, 25 FG)
- 147 Gino Cappelletti, Boston, 1961 (8 TD, 48 PAT, 17 FG)

Most Seasons, 100 or More Points
- 6 Gino Cappelletti, Boston Patriots, 1961–66
- George Blanda, Houston, 1960–61; Oakland, 1967–69, 1973
- Bruce Gossett, Los Angeles, 1966–67, 1969; San Francisco, 1970–71, 1973
- 5 Lou Michaels, Pittsburgh, 1962; Baltimore, 1964–65, 1967–68
- Jan Stenerud, Kansas City, 1967–71
- 4 Fred Cox, Minnesota, 1964–65, 1969–70

Most Points, Rookie, Season
- 132 Gale Sayers, Chicago, 1965 (22 TD)
- 128 Doak Walker, Detroit, 1950 (11 TD, 38 PAT, 8 FG)
- Cookie Gilchrist, Buffalo, 1962 (15 TD, 14 PAT, 8 FG)
- Chester Marcol, Green Bay, 1972 (29 PAT, 33 FG)
- 123 Gene Mingo, Denver, 1960 (6 TD, 33 PAT, 18 FG)

Most Points, Game
- 40 Ernie Nevers, Chi. Cardinals vs. Chi. Bears, Nov. 28, 1929 (6 TD, 4 PAT)
- 36 Dub Jones, Cleveland vs. Chi. Bears, Nov. 25, 1951 (6 TD)
- Gale Sayers, Chicago vs. San Francisco, Dec. 12, 1965 (6 TD)
- 33 Paul Hornung, Green Bay vs. Baltimore, Oct. 8, 1961 (4 TD, 6 PAT, 1 FG)

Most Consecutive Games Scoring
- 151 Fred Cox, Minnesota, 1963–73
- 118 Jim Turner, N.Y. Jets, 1966–70; Denver, 1971–74
- 110 Sam Baker, Dallas, 1962–63; Philadelphia, 1964–69

TOUCHDOWNS
Most Seasons Leading League
- 8 Don Hutson, Green Bay, 1935–38, 1941–44
- 3 Jim Brown, Cleveland, 1958–59, 1963
- Lance Alworth, San Diego, 1964–66
- 2 By many players

Most Touchdowns, Lifetime
- 126 Jim Brown, Cleveland, 1957–65 (106 R, 20 P)
- 113 Lenny Moore, Baltimore, 1956–67 (63 R, 48 P, 2 RB)
- 105 Don Hutson, Green Bay, 1935–45 (3 R, 99 P, 3 RB)

Most Touchdowns, Season
- 23 O.J. Simpson, Buffalo, 1975 (16 R, 7 P)
- 22 Gale Sayers, Chicago, 1965 (14 R, 6 P, 1 PRB, 1 KRB)
- Chuck Foreman, Minnesota, 1975 (13 R, 9 P)
- 21 Jim Brown, Cleveland, 1965 (17 R, 4 P)

Most Touchdowns, Rookie, Season
- 22 Gale Sayers, Chicago, 1965 (14 R, 6 P, 1 PRB, 1 KRB)
- 15 Cookie Gilchrist, Buffalo, 1962 (13 R, 2 P)
- 13 Billy Howton, Green Bay, 1952 (13 P)
- Bob Hayes, Dallas, 1965 (1 R, 12 P)

 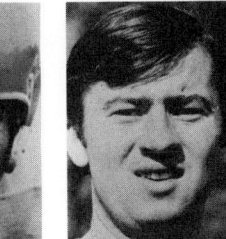   

Gino Cappelletti   *Dub Jones*   *Charlie Gogolak*   *Tommy Davis*   *Curt Knight*   *Roger LeClerc*   *Lou Michaels*

Most Touchdowns, Game
- 6   Ernie Nevers, Chi. Cardinals vs. Chi. Bears, Nov. 28, 1929 (6 R)
  - Dub Jones, Cleveland vs. Chi. Bears, Nov. 25, 1951 (4 R, 2 P)
  - Gale Sayers, Chicago vs. San Francisco, Dec. 12, 1965 (4 R, 1 P, 1 PRB)
- 5   Bob Shaw, Chi. Cardinals vs. Baltimore, Oct. 2, 1950 (5 P)
  - Jim Brown, Cleveland vs. Baltimore, Nov. 1, 1959 (5 R)
  - Abner Haynes, Dallas Texans vs. Oakland, Nov. 26, 1961 (4 R, 1 P)
  - Billy Cannon, Houston vs. N.Y. Titans, Dec. 10, 1961 (3 R, 2 P)
  - Cookie Gilchrist, Buffalo vs. N.Y. Jets, Dec. 8, 1963 (5 R)
  - Paul Hornung, Green Bay vs. Baltimore, Dec. 12, 1965 (3 R, 2 P)
- 4   By many players. Last time Chuck Foreman, Minnesota vs. Buffalo, Dec. 20, 1975 (2 R, 2 P)

Most Consecutive Games Scoring Touchdowns
- 18   Lenny Moore, Baltimore, 1963–65
- 14   O.J. Simpson, Buffalo, 1975
- 11   Elroy (Crazylegs) Hirsch, Los Angeles, 1950–51
  - Buddy Dial, Pittsburgh, 1959–60

POINTS AFTER TOUCHDOWN
Most Seasons Leading League
- 8   George Blanda, Chi. Bears, 1956; Houston, 1961–62; Oakland, 1967–69, 1972, 1974
- 4   Bob Waterfield, Cleveland, 1945; Los Angeles, 1946, 1950, 1952
- 3   Earl (Dutch) Clark, Portsmouth Spartans, 1932; Detroit, 1935–36
  - Jack Manders, Chi. Bears, 1933–35
  - Don Hutson, Green Bay, 1941–42, 1945

Most Points After Touchdown Attempted, Lifetime
- 959   George Blanda, Chi. Bears, 1949–58; Baltimore, 1950; Houston, 1960–66; Oakland, 1967–75
- 657   Lou Groza, Cleveland, 1950–59, 1961–67
- 510   Fred Cox, Minnesota, 1963–76

Most Points After Touchdown Attempted, Season
- 65   George Blanda, Houston, 1961
- 58   Bob Waterfield, Los Angeles, 1950
- 57   George Blanda, Oakland, 1967
  - John Leypoldt, Buffalo, 1975

Most Points After Touchdown Attempted, Game
- 10   Charlie Gogolak, Washington vs. N.Y. Giants, Nov. 27, 1966
- 9   Pat Harder, Chi. Cardinals vs. N.Y. Giants, Oct. 17, 1948; vs. N.Y. Bulldogs, Nov. 13, 1949
  - Bob Waterfield, Los Angeles vs. Baltimore, Oct. 22, 1950
- 8   By many players

Most Points After Touchdown, Lifetime
- 943   George Blanda, Chi. Bears, 1949–58; Baltimore, 1950; Houston, 1960–66; Oakland, 1967–75
- 641   Lou Groza, Cleveland, 1950–59, 1961–67
- 494   Fred Cox, Minnesota, 1963–76

Most Points After Touchdown, Season
- 64   George Blanda, Houston, 1961
- 56   Danny Villaneuva, Dallas, 1966
  - George Blanda, Oakland, 1967
- 54   Bob Waterfield, Los Angeles, 1950
  - Mike Clark, Dallas, 1968
  - George Blanda, Oakland, 1968

Most Points After Touchdown, Game
- 9   Pat Harder, Chi. Cardinals vs. N.Y. Giants, Oct. 17, 1948
  - Bob Waterfield, Los Angeles vs. Baltimore, Oct. 22, 1950
  - Charlie Gogolak, Washington vs. N.Y. Giants, Nov. 27, 1966
- 8   By many players

Most Consecutive Points After Touchdown
- 234   Tommy Davis, San Francisco, 1959–65
- 221   Jim Turner, N.Y. Jets, 1967–70; Denver, 1971–74
- 201   George Blanda, Oakland, 1967–71

Highest Point After Touchdown Percentage, Lifetime (200 PATs)
- 99.4   Tommy Davis, San Francisco, 1959–69 (350–348)
- 98.3   George Blanda, Chi. Bears, 1949–58; Baltimore, 1950; Houston, 1960–66; Oakland, 1967–75 (959–943)
- 96.3   Jan Stenerud, Kansas City, 1967–76 (326–314)

Most Points After Touchdown No Misses, Season
- 56   Danny Villaneuva, Dallas, 1966
- 54   Mike Clark, Dallas, 1968
  - George Blanda, Oakland, 1968
- 53   Pat Harder, Chi. Cardinals, 1948

Most Points After Touchdown No Misses, Game
- 9   Pat Harder, Chi. Cardinals vs. N.Y. Giants, Oct. 17, 1948
  - Bob Waterfield, Los Angeles vs. Baltimore, Oct. 22, 1950
- 8   By many players

FIELD GOALS
Most Seasons Leading League
- 5   Lou Groza, Cleveland, 1950, 1952–54, 1957
- 4   Jack Manders, Chi. Bears, 1933–34, 1936–37
  - Ward Cuff, N.Y. Giants, 1938–39, 1943; Green Bay, 1947
- 3   Bob Waterfield, Los Angeles, 1947, 1949, 1951
  - Gino Cappelletti, Boston Patriots, 1961, 1963–64
  - Fred Cox, Minnesota, 1965, 1969–70
  - Jan Stenerud, Kansas City, 1967, 1970, 1975

Most Field Goals Attempted, Lifetime
- 638   George Blanda, Chi. Bears, 1949–58; Baltimore, 1950; Houston, 1960–66; Oakland, 1967–75
- 438   Fred Cox, Minnesota, 1963–76
- 426   Jim Turner, N.Y. Jets, 1964–70, Denver, 1971–76

Most Field Goals Attempted, Season
- 49   Bruce Gossett, Los Angeles, 1966
  - Curt Knight, Washington, 1971
- 48   Chester Marcol, Green Bay, 1972
- 47   Jim Turner, N.Y. Jets, 1969
  - David Ray, Los Angeles, 1973

Most Field Goals Attempted, Game
- 9   Jim Bakken, St. Louis vs. Pittsburgh, Sept. 24, 1967
- 8   Lou Michaels, Pittsburgh vs. St. Louis, Dec. 2, 1962
  - Garo Yepremian, Detroit vs. Minnesota, Nov. 13, 1966
  - Jim Turner, N.Y. Jets vs. Buffalo, Nov. 3, 1968
- 7   By many players

Most Field Goals, Lifetime
- 335   George Blanda, Chi. Bears, 1949–58; Baltimore, 1950; Houston, 1960–66; Oakland, 1967–75
- 274   Fred Cox, Minnesota, 1963–76
- 267   Jim Turner, N.Y. Jets, 1964–70; Denver, 1971–76

Most Field Goals, Season
- 34   Jim Turner, N.Y. Jets, 1968
- 33   Chester Marcol, Green Bay, 1972
- 32   Jim Turner, N.Y. Jets, 1969

Most Field Goals, Game
- 7   Jim Bakken, St. Louis vs. Pittsburgh, Sept. 24, 1967
- 6   Gino Cappelletti, Boston Patriots vs. Denver, Oct. 4, 1964
  - Garo Yepremian, Detroit vs. Minnesota, Nov. 13, 1966
  - Jim Turner, N.Y. Jets vs. Buffalo, Nov. 3, 1968
  - Tom Dempsey, Philadelphia vs. Houston, Nov. 12, 1972
  - Bobby Howfield, N.Y. Jets vs. New Orleans, Dec. 3, 1972
  - Jim Bakken, St. Louis vs. Atlanta, Dec. 9, 1973
- 5   By many players

Most Field Goals, One Quarter
- 4   Garo Yepremian, Detroit vs. Minnesota, Nov. 13, 1966 (second quarter)
  - Curt Knight, Washington vs. N.Y. Giants, Nov. 15, 1970 (second quarter)
- 3   By many players

Most Consecutive Games Scoring Field Goals
- 31   Fred Cox, Minnesota, 1968–70
- 28   Jim Turner, N.Y. Jets (13) 1970 and Denver (15) 1971–72
- 21   Bruce Gossett, San Francisco, 1970–72

Most Consecutive Field Goals
- 16   Jan Stenerud, Kansas City, 1969
  - Don Cockroft, Cleveland, 1974–75
- 13   Bruce Gossett, San Francisco, 1973
  - Garo Yepremian, Miami, 1974–75
- 12   Lou Groza, Cleveland, 1953
  - Bobby Layne, Detroit, 1956–57

Longest Field Goal
- 63   Tom Dempsey, New Orleans vs. Detroit, Nov. 8, 1970
- 57   Don Cockroft, Cleveland vs. Denver, Oct. 29, 1972
- 56   Bert Rechichar, Baltimore vs. Chi. Bears, Sept. 27, 1953

Highest Field Goal Percentage, Lifetime (100 Field Goals)
- 67.1   Garo Yepremian, Detroit, 1966–67; Miami, 1970–76 (225–151)
- 66.2   Don Cockroft, Cleveland, 1968–76 (222–147)
- 65.5   Jan Stenerud, Kansas City, 1967–76 (365–239)

Highest Field Goal Percentage, Season (14 attempts)
- 88.5   Lou Groza, Cleveland, 1953 (26–23)
- 87.5   Don Cockroft, Cleveland, 1974 (16–14)
- 85.0   George Blair, San Diego, 1962 (20–17)

Highest Field Goal Percentage, Game (5 attempts)
- 100.0   Gino Cappalletti, Boston Patriots vs. Denver, Oct. 4, 1964 (6–6)
  - Roger LeClerc, Chicago vs. Detroit, Dec. 3, 1961 (5–5)
  - Lou Michaels, Baltimore vs. San Francisco, Sept. 25, 1966 (5–5)
  - Mac Percival, Chicago vs. Philadelphia, Oct. 20, 1968 (5–5)
  - Roy Gerela, Houston vs. Miami, Sept. 28, 1969 (5–5)
  - Jan Stenerud, Kansas City vs. Buffalo, Nov. 2 and Dec. 7, 1969 (5–5)
  - Horst Muhlmann, Cincinnati vs. Buffalo, Nov. 8, 1970; vs. Pittsburgh, Sept. 24, 1972 (5–5)
  - Bruce Gossett, San Francisco vs. Denver, Sept. 23, 1973 (5–5)
  - Nick Mike-Mayer, Atlanta vs. Los Angeles, Nov. 4, 1973 (5–5)
  - Curt Knight, Washington vs. Baltimore, Nov. 18, 1973 (5–5)

George Blanda   *Jim Turner*   *Fred Cox*   *Danny Villanueva*   *Bruce Gossett*   *Jim Bakken*   *Garo Yepremian*

SAFETIES

Most Safeties, Lifetime

3 Bill McPeak, Pittsburgh, 1954, 1956, 1957
  Charlie Krueger, San Francisco, 1959, 1960, 1961
  Ernie Stautner, Pittsburgh, 1950, 1958, 1962
  Jim Katcavage, N.Y. Giants, 1958, 1961, 1965
  Roger Brown, Detroit, 1962 (2), 1965
  Bruce Maher, Detroit, 1960, 1963, 1967
  Ron McDole, Buffalo, 1964 (2); Washington, 1976
  Ted Hendricks, Green Bay, 1974; Oakland, 1975, 1976
2 Tom Nash, Green Bay, 1932 (2)
  Leo Nomellini, San Francisco, 1957, 1960
  Dick Modzelewski, Washington, 1954; N.Y. Giants, 1961
  Darris McCord, Detroit, 1957, 1962
  Roosevelt Grier, N.Y. Giants, 1960; Los Angeles, 1966
  Jethro Pugh, Dallas, 1967, 1968
  Alan Page, Minnesota, 1971
  Fred Dryer, Los Angeles, 1973 (2)
  Benny Barnes, Dallas, 1973 (2)
  Elvin Bethea, Houston, 1969, 1975
  Dwight White, Pittsburgh, 1973, 1975
  Claude Humphrey, Atlanta, 1968–74, 1976

Most Safeties, Season

2 Tom Nash, Green Bay, 1932
  Roger Brown, Detroit, 1962
  Ron McDole, Buffalo, 1964
  Alan Page, Minnesota, 1971
  Fred Dryer, Los Angeles, 1973
  Benny Barnes, Dallas, 1973

Most Safeties, Game

2 Fred Dryer, Los Angeles vs. Green Bay, Oct. 21, 1973

SERVICE

Most Seasons, Player

26 George Blanda, Chi. Bears, 1949–58; Baltimore, 1950; Houston, 1960–66; Oakland, 1967–75
21 Earl Morrall, San Francisco, 1956; Pittsburgh, 1957–58; Detroit, 1958–64; N.Y. Giants, 1965–67; Baltimore, 1968–71; Miami, 1972–76
19 Len Dawson, Pittsburgh, 1957–59; Cleveland, 1960–61; Dallas Texans, 1962; Kansas City, 1963–75

Most Games Played, Lifetime

340 George Blanda, Chi. Bears, 1949–58; Baltimore, 1960–66; Oakland, 1967–75
255 Earl Morrall, San Francisco, 1965–67; Baltimore, 1968–71; Miami, 1972–76
236 Jim Marshall, Cleveland, 1960; Minnesota, 1961–76

Most Consecutive Games Played, Lifetime

236 Jim Marshall, Cleveland, 1960; Minnesota, 1961–76 (current)
224 George Blanda, Houston, 1960–66; Oakland, 1967–75
210 Jim Otto, Oakland, 1960–74
  Mick Tingelhoff, Minnesota, 1962–76 (current)

Most Seasons, Head Coach

40 George Halas, Chi. Bears, 1920–29, 1933–42, 1946–55, 1958–67
33 Earl (Curly) Lambeau, Green Bay, 1921–49; Chi. Cardinals, 1950–51; Washington, 1952–53
23 Steve Owen, N.Y. Giants, 1931–53

COMBINED NET YARDS

Rushing, receiving, interception returns, punt returns, kickoff returns, and fumble returns.

Most Attempts, Lifetime

2,658 Jim Brown, Cleveland, 1957–65
2,196 O.J. Simpson, Buffalo, 1969–76
2,180 Jim Taylor, Green Bay, 1958–66; New Orleans, 1967

Most Attempts, Season

358 O.J. Simpson, Buffalo, 1975
356 Chuck Foreman, Minnesota, 1975
354 Jim Brown, Cleveland, 1961

Most Attempts, Game

43 Lydell Mitchell, Baltimore vs. N.Y. Jets, Oct. 20, 1974
41 Ron Johnson, N.Y. Giants vs. Philadelphia, Oct. 2, 1972
  Franco Harris, Pittsburgh vs. Cincinnati, Oct. 17, 1976
39 Jim Brown, Cleveland vs. Chi. Cardinals, Oct. 4, 1959
  O.J. Simpson, Buffalo vs. Kansas City, Oct. 29, 1973

YARDS

Most Yards Gained, Lifetime

15,459 Jim Brown, Cleveland, 1957–65
14,078 Bobby Mitchell, Cleveland, 1958–61; Washington, 1962–68
12,884 Ollie Matson, Chi. Cardinals, 1952, 1954–58; Los Angeles, 1959–62; Detroit, 1963; Philadelphia, 1964–66

Most Yards Gained, Season

2,462 Terry Metcalf, St. Louis, 1975
2,444 Mack Herron, New England, 1974
2,440 Gale Sayers, Chicago, 1966

Most Yards Gained, Game

373 Billy Cannon, Houston vs. N.Y. Titans, Dec. 10, 1961
341 Timmy Brown, Philadelphia vs. St. Louis, Dec. 16, 1962
339 Gale Sayers, Chicago vs. Minnesota, Dec. 18, 1966

COMBINED KICK RETURNS

Most Combined Kick Returns, Lifetime

510 Ron Smith, Chicago, 1965, 1970–72; Atlanta, 1966–67; Los Angeles, 1968–69; San Diego, 1973; Oakland, 1974 (P 235, K 275)
423 Alvin Haymond, Baltimore, 1964–67; Philadelphia, 1968; Los Angeles, 1969–71; Washington, 1972; Houston, 1973 (P 253, K 170)
382 Leslie (Speedy) Duncan, San Diego, 1964–70; Washington, 1971–74 (P 202, K 180)

Most Combined Kick Returns, Season

100 Larry Jones, Washington, 1975 (P 53, K 47)
88 Alvin Haymond, Los Angeles, 1970 (P 53, K 35)
74 Chuck Latourette, St. Louis, 1968 (P 28, K 46)

Most Combined Kick Returns, Game

12 Mel Renfro, Dallas vs. Green Bay, Nov. 29, 1964 (P 4, K 8)
  Larry Jones, Washington vs. Dallas, Dec. 13, 1975 (P 6, K 6)
11 Noland Smith, Kansas City vs. Oakland, Nov. 23, 1967 (P 2, K 9)
  Larry Jones, Washington vs. Oakland, Nov. 23, 1975 (P 6, K 5)
10 By many players

YARDAGE

Most Yards Returned, Lifetime

8,710 Ron Smith, Chicago, 1965, 1970–72; Atlanta, 1966–67; Los Angeles, 1968–69; San Diego, 1973; Oakland, 1974 (P 1,788, K 6,922)
6,740 Leslie (Speedy) Duncan, San Diego, 1964–70; Washington, 1971–74 (P 2,201, K 4,539)
6,586 Alvin Haymond, Baltimore, 1964–67; Philadelphia, 1968; Los Angeles, 1969–71, Washington, 1972; Houston, 1973 (P 2,148, K 4,438)

Most Yards Returned, Season

1,582 Chuck Latourette, St. Louis, 1968 (P 345, K 1,237)
1,493 Larry Jones, Washington, 1975, (P 407, K 1,086)
1,462 Bobby Jancik, Houston, 1963 (P 145, K 1,317)

Most Yards Returned, Game

294 Wally Triplett, Detroit vs. Los Angeles, Oct. 29, 1950 (K 294)
  Woodley Lewis, Los Angeles vs. Detroit, Oct. 18, 1953 (P 120, K 174)
282 Leslie (Speedy) Duncan, San Diego vs. N.Y. Jets, Nov. 24, 1968 (P 102, K 180)
273 Mel Renfro, Dallas vs. Green Bay, Nov. 29, 1964 (P 117, K 156)

TOUCHDOWNS

Most Touchdowns, Lifetime

9 Ollie Matson, Chi. Cardinals, 1952 (2), 1954 (2), 1955 (2), 1956, 1958 (2) (P 3, K 6)
8 Jack Christiansen, Detroit, 1951 (4), 1952 (2), 1954, 1956 (P 8)
  Bobby Mitchell, Cleveland, 1958 (2), 1959, 1960, 1961 (2); Washington, 1962, 1963 (P 3, K 5)
  Gale Sayers, Chicago, 1965 (2), 1966 (2), 1967 (4) (P 2, K 6)
7 Abe Woodson, San Francisco, 1959, 1961 (2), 1962, 1963 (3) (P2, K 5)

Most Touchdowns, Season

4 Jack Christiansen, Detroit, 1951 (P 4)
  Emlen Tunnell, N.Y. Giants, 1951 (P 3, K 1)
  Gale Sayers, Chicago, 1967 (P 1, K 3)
  Travis Williams, Green Bay, 1967 (K 4)
  Cecil Turner, Chicago, 1970 (K 4)
  Billy Johnson, Houston, 1975 (P 3, K1)
  Rick Upchurch, Denver, 1976 (P 4)
3 Verda (Vitamin T) Smith, Los Angeles, 1950 (K 3)
  Abe Woodson, San Francisco, 1963 (K 3)
2 By many players

Most Touchdowns, Game

2 Jack Christiansen, Detroit vs. Los Angeles, Oct. 14, 1951 (P 2); vs. Green Bay, Nov. 22, 1951 (P 2)
  Jim Patton, N.Y. Giants vs. Washington, Oct. 30, 1955 (P 1, K 1)
  Bobby Mitchell, Cleveland vs. Philadelphia, Nov. 23, 1958 (P 1, K 1)
  Dick Christy, N.Y. Titans vs. Denver, Sept. 24, 1961 (P 2)
  Al Frazier, Denver vs. Boston, Dec. 3, 1961 (P 1, K 1)
  Timmy Brown, Philadelphia vs. Dallas, Nov. 6, 1966 (K 2)
  Travis Williams, Green Bay vs. Cleveland, Nov. 12, 1967 (K 2); vs. Pittsburgh, Nov. 2, 1969 (P 1, K 1)
  Gale Sayers, Chicago vs. San Francisco, Dec. 3, 1967 (P 1, K 1)
  Rick Upchurch, Denver vs. Cleveland, Sept. 26, 1976 (P 2)

FUMBLES

Most Fumbles, Lifetime

105 Roman Gabriel, Los Angeles, 1962–72; Philadelphia, 1973–76
95 John Unitas, Baltimore, 1956–72; San Diego, 1973
84 Len Dawson, Pittsburgh, 1957–59; Cleveland, 1960–61; Dallas Texans 1962; Kansas City, 1963–75

Ron Smith *Don Hultz* *Jack Tatum* *Bob Lilly* *Chris Hanburger* *Mike Ditka* *Al Nelson*

Most Fumbles, Season
    17 Dan Pastorini, Houston, 1973
    16 Don Meredith, Dallas, 1964
    15 Paul Christman, Chi. Cardinals, 1946
        Sammy Baugh, Washington, 1947
        Sam Etcheverry, St. Louis, 1961
        Len Dawson, Kansas City, 1964
Most Fumbles, Game
    7   Len Dawson, Kansas City vs. San Diego, Nov. 15, 1964
    6   Sam Etcheverry, St. Louis vs. N. Y. Giants, Sept, 17, 1961
    5   Paul Christman, Chi. Cardinals vs. Green Bay, Nov. 10, 1946
        Charlie Conerly, N.Y. Giants vs San Francisco, Dec. 1, 1957
        Jack Kemp, Buffalo vs. Houston, Oct. 29, 1967

FUMBLES RECOVERED
Most Fumbles Recovered, Lifetime, Own and Opponents'
    38 Jack Kemp, Pittsburgh, 1957; Los Angeles Chargers, 1960; San Diego, 1961–62; Buffalo, 1962–67, 1969 (38 own)
    37 Roman Gabriel, Los Angeles, 1962–72; Philadelphia, 1973–76 (37 own)
    34 Fran Tarkenton, Minnesota, 1961–66; 1972–76; N.Y. Giants, 1967–76 (34 own)
Most Fumbles Recovered, Season, Own and Opponents'
    9   Don Hultz, Minnesota, 1963 (9 opp)
    8   Paul Christman, Chi. Cardinals, 1945 (8 own)
        Joe Schmidt, Detroit, 1955 (8 opp)
        Bill Butler, Minnesota, 1963 (8 own)
        Kermit Alexander, San Francisco, 1965 (4 own, 4 opp)
        Jack Lambert, Pittsburgh, 1976 (1 own, 7 opp)
    7   Sammy Baugh, Washington, 1947 (7 own)
        Tommy Thompson, Philadelphia, 1947 (7 own)
        Jack Larscheid, Oakland, 1960 (7 own)
        John Roach, St. Louis, 1960 (7 own)
        Dick Butkus, Chicago, 1965 (1 own, 6 opp)
        Alan Page, Minnesota, 1970 (7 opp)
        Gary Huff, Chicago, 1974 (7 own)
        Terry Metcalf, St. Louis, 1974 (7 own)
Most Fumbles Recovered, Game, Own and Opponents'
    4   Otto Graham, Cleveland vs. N.Y. Giants, Oct. 25, 1953 (4 own)
        Sam Etcheverry, St. Louis vs. N.Y. Giants, Sept. 17, 1961 (4 own)
        Roman Gabriel, Los Angeles vs San Francisco, Oct. 12, 1969 (4 own)
    3   By many players

OWN FUMBLES RECOVERED
Most Own Fumbles Recovered, Lifetime
    38 Jack Kemp, Pittsburgh, 1957; Los Angeles Chargers, 1960; San Diego, 1961–62; Buffalo, 1962–67, 1969
    37 Roman Gabriel, Los Angeles, 1962–72; Philadelphia, 1973–76
    34 Fran Tarkenton, Minnesota, 1961–66, 1972–76; N.Y. Giants, 1967–71
Most Own Fumbles Recovered, Season
    8   Paul Christman, Chi. Cardinals, 1945
        Bill Butler, Minnesota, 1963
    7   Sammy Baugh, Washington, 1947
        Tommy Thompson, Philadelphia, 1947
        John Roach, St. Louis, 1960
        Jack Larscheid, Oakland, 1960
        Gary Huff, Chicago, 1974
        Terry Metcalf, St. Louis, 1974
    6   By Many players
Most Own Fumbles Recovered, Game
    4   Otto Graham, Cleveland vs. N.Y. Giants, Oct. 25, 1953
        Sam Etcheverry, St. Louis vs. N.Y. Giants, Sept. 17, 1961
        Roman Gabriel, Los Angeles vs. San Francisco, Oct. 12, 1969
    3   By many players

OPPONENTS' FUMBLES RECOVERED
Most Opponents' Fumbles Recovered, Lifetime
    26 Jim Marshall, Cleveland, 1960; Minnesota, 1961–76
    25 Dick Butkus, Chicago, 1965–73
    22 Andy Robustelli, Los Angeles, 1951–55; N.Y. Giants, 1956–64
        Joe Fortunato, Chi. Bears, 1955–66
Most Opponents' Fumbles Recovered, Season
    9   Don Hultz, Minnesota, 1963
    8   Joe Schmidt, Detroit, 1955
    7   Alan Page, Minnesota, 1970
        Jack Lambert, Pittsburgh, 1976
Most Opponents' Fumbles Recovered, Game
    3   Corwin Clatt, Chi. Cardinals vs. Detroit, Nov. 6, 1949
        Vic Sears, Philadelphia vs. Green Bay, Nov. 2, 1952
        Ed Beatty, San Francisco vs. Los Angeles, Oct. 7, 1956
        Ron Carroll, Houston vs. Cincinnati, Oct. 27, 1974
        Maurice Spencer, New Orleans vs. Atlanta, Oct. 10, 1976
    2   By many players

YARDS RETURNING FUMBLES
Longest Fumble Run (all TDs)
    104 Jack Tatum, Oakland vs. Green Bay, Sept. 24, 1972 (opp)
    98   George Halas, Chi. Bears vs. Oorang Indians, Marion, Ohio, Nov. 4, 1923 (opp)
    97   Chuck Howley, Dallas vs. Atlanta, Oct. 2, 1966 (opp)

TOUCHDOWNS
Most Touchdowns, Lifetime (Total)
    3   Ralph Heywood, Boston Yanks, 1948 (2); New York Bulldogs, 1949
        Leo Sugar, Chi. Cardinals, 1954, 57 (2)
        Bud McFadin, Los Angeles, 1956; Denver, 1962, 1963
        Doug Cline, Houston, 1961 (2); 1966
        Bob Lilly, Dallas, 1963, 1969, 1971
        Chris Hanburger, Washington, 1969, 1971, 1974
        Lemar Parrish, Cincinnati, 1971, 1973, 1974
        Paul Krause, Washington, 1965; Minnesota, 1972, 1975
    2   By many players
Most Touchdowns, Season (Total)
    2   Harold McPhail, Boston Redskins, 1934
        Harry Ebding, Detroit, 1937
        John Morelli, Boston Yanks, 1944
        Frank Maznicki, Boston Yanks, 1947
        Fred Evans, Chicago Bears, 1948
        Ralph Heywood, Boston Yanks, 1948
        Art Tait, N.Y. Yanks, 1951
        John Dwyer, Los Angeles, 1952
        Leo Sugar, Chi. Cardinals, 1957
        Doug Cline, Houston, 1961
        Jim Bradshaw, Pittsburgh, 1964
        Royce Berry, Cincinnati, 1970
        Ahmad Rashad, Buffalo, 1974
Most Touchdowns, Lifetime (Own Recovered)
    2   Ken Kavanaugh, Chi. Bears, 1948, 1950
        Mike Ditka, Chicago, 1962, 1964
        Gail Cogdill, Detroit, 1962, 1964
        Ahmad Rashad, Buffalo, 1974 (2)
        Jim Mitchell, Atlanta, 1971, 1975
Most Touchdowns, Season (Own Recovered)
    2   Ahmad Rashad, Buffalo, 1974
    1   By many players
Most Touchdowns, Lifetime (Opponents' Recovered)
    3   Leo Sugar, Chi. Cardinals, 1954, 1957 (2)
        Bud McFadin, Los Angeles, 1956; Denver, 1962, 1963
        Doug Cline, Houston, 1961 (2)
        Bob Lilly, Dallas, 1963, 1969, 1971
        Chris Hanburger, Washington, 1969, 1971, 1974
        Lemar Parrish, Cincinnati, 1971, 1973, 1974
        Paul Krause, Washington, 1965; Minnesota, 1972, 1975
    2   By many players
Most Touchdowns, Season (Opponents' Recovered)
    2   Harold McPhail, Boston Redskins, 1934
        Harry Ebding, Detroit, 1937
        John Morelli, Boston Yanks, 1944
        Frank Maznicki, Boston Yanks, 1947
        Fred Evans, Chicago Bears, 1948
        Ralph Heywood, Boston Yanks, 1948
        Art Tait, N.Y. Yanks, 1951
        John Dwyer, Los Angeles, 1952
        Leo Sugar, Chi. Cardinals, 1957
        Doug Cline, Houston, 1961
        Jim Bradshaw, Pittsburgh, 1964
        Royce Berry, Cincinnati, 1970
Most Touchdowns, Game (Opponents' Recovered)
    2   Fred Evans, Chi. Bears vs. Washington, Nov. 28, 1948

MISSED FIELD GOAL RETURNS
Longest Return of Missed Field Goal (all TDs)
    101 Al Nelson, Philadelphia vs. Dallas, Sept. 26, 1971
    100 Al Nelson, Philadelphia vs. Cleveland, Dec. 11, 1966
         Ken Ellis, Green Bay vs. N.Y. Giants, Sept. 19, 1971
    99   Jerry Williams, Los Angeles vs. Green Bay, Dec. 16, 1951
         Carl Taseff, Baltimore vs. Los Angeles, Dec. 12, 1959
         Timmy Brown, Philadelphia vs. St. Louis, Sept. 16, 1962

TEAM RECORDS

CHAMPIONSHIPS
Most Seasons League Champion
- 11   Green Bay, 1929–31, 1936, 1939, 1944, 1961–62, 1965–67
- 8   Chi. Bears, 1921, 1932–33, 1940–41, 1943, 1946, 1963
- 4   N.Y. Giants, 1927, 1934, 1938, 1956
  - Detroit, 1935, 1952–53, 1957
  - Cleveland, 1950, 1954–55, 1964
  - Baltimore, 1958–59, 1968, 1970

Most Consecutive Seasons League Champion
- 3   Green Bay, 1929–31; 1965–67
- 2   Canton, Ohio, Bulldogs, 1922–23
  - Chi. Bears, 1932–33; 1940–41
  - Philadelphia, 1948–49
  - Detroit, 1952–53
  - Cleveland, 1954–55
  - Baltimore, 1958–59
  - Houston, 1960–61
  - Green Bay, 1961–62
  - Buffalo, 1964–65
  - Miami, 1972–73
  - Pittsburgh, 1974–75

Most Times Finishing First, Regular Season (Since 1933)
- 14   N.Y. Giants, 1933–35, 1938–39, 1941, 1944, 1946, 1956, 1958–59, 1961–63
- 13   Cleveland, 1950–55, 1957, 1964–65, 1967–69, 1971
- 11   Green Bay, 1936, 1938–39, 1944, 1960–62, 1965–67, 1972

Most Consecutive Times Finishing First, Regular Season (Since 1933)
- 6   Cleveland, 1950–55
  - Dallas, 1966–71
- 4   Chi. Bears, 1940–43
  - Oakland, 1967–70; 1972–75
  - Minnesota, 1968–71
  - Miami, 1971–74
- 3   N.Y. Giants, 1933–35; 1961–63
  - Philadelphia, 1947–49
  - Los Angeles, 1949–51; 1973–75
  - Detroit, 1952–54
  - Green Bay, 1960–62; 1965–67
  - Houston, 1960–62
  - San Diego, 1963–65
  - Buffalo, 1964–66
  - Cleveland, 1967–69
  - San Francisco, 1970–72
  - Minnesota, 1973–75

VICTORIES
Most Consecutive Victories (All Games)
- 18   Chi. Bears, 1933–34; 1941–42
  - Miami, 1972–73

Most Consecutive Victories (Regular Season)
- 17   Chi. Bears, 1933–34
- 16   Chi. Bears, 1941–42
  - Miami, 1971–73
- 15   Los Angeles Chargers, 1960; San Diego, 1961

Most Games, Consecutive, Without Defeat (Incl. Postseason Games)
- 24   Canton, Ohio, Bulldogs, 1922–23 (won 21, tied 3)
- 23   Green Bay, 1928–30 (won 21, tied 2)
- 18   Miami, 1972–73 (won 18)

Most Games, Consecutive, Without Defeat (Regular Season)
- 24   Canton, Ohio, Bulldogs, 1922–23 (won 21, tied 3)
  - Chi. Bears, 1941–43 (won 23, tied 1)
- 23   Green Bay, 1928–30 (won 21, tied 2)
- 17   Chi. Bears, 1933–34 (won 17)

Most Victories, One Season (Incl. Postseason Games)
- 17   Miami, 1972
- 15   Miami, 1973
  - Baltimore, 1968
  - Pittsburgh, 1975
- 14   By many teams

Most Victories, Season (Since 1932)
- 14   Miami, 1972
- 13   Chi. Bears, 1934
  - Green Bay, 1962
  - Oakland, 1967
  - Baltimore, 1968
- 12   By many teams

Most Victories, Consecutive, One Season (Incl. Postseason Games)
- 17   Miami, 1972
- 13   Chi. Bears, 1934
- 12   Minnesota, 1969

Most Victories, Consecutive, One Season
- 14   Miami, 1972
- 13   Chi. Bears, 1934
- 12   Minnesota, 1969

Most Victories, Consecutive, Start of Season
- 14   Miami, 1972, (entire season)
- 13   Chi. Bears, 1934, entire season
- 11   Chi. Bears, 1942, entire season
  - Cleveland, 1953
  - San Diego, 1961
  - Los Angeles, 1969

Most Victories, Consecutive, End of Season
- 14   Miami, 1972, entire season
- 13   Chi. Bears, 1934, entire season
- 11   Chi. Bears, 1942, entire season
  - Cleveland, 1951

Most Games, Consecutive, Without Defeat, One Season (Incl. Postseason Games)
- 17   Miami, 1972
- 13   Chi. Bears, 1926, 1934
  - Green Bay, 1929
  - Baltimore, 1967
- 12   Canton, Ohio, Bulldogs, 1922, 1923
  - Minnesota, 1969

Most Games, Consecutive, Without Defeat, One Season
- 14   Miami, 1972
- 13   Chi. Bears, 1926, 1934
  - Green Bay, 1929
  - Baltimore, 1967
- 12   Canton, Ohio, Bulldogs, 1922, 1923
  - Minnesota, 1969

Most Games, Consecutive, Without Defeat, Beginning of Season
- 14   Miami, 1972, entire season
- 13   Chi. Bears, 1926, 1934 (entire season)
  - Green Bay, 1929, (entire season)
  - Baltimore, 1967
- 12   Canton, Ohio, Bulldogs, 1922, 1923 (entire seasons)

Most Games, Consecutive, Without Defeat, End of Season
- 14   Miami, 1972, entire season
- 13   Green Bay, 1929, entire season
  - Chi. Bears, 1934, entire season
- 12   Canton, Ohio, Bulldogs 1922, 1923, entire seasons

Most Consecutive Shutout Victories (Regular Season)
- 7   Detroit, 1934
- 3   N.Y. Giants, 1935
  - St. Louis, 1970

DEFEATS
Most Losses, Season (Since 1932)
- 14   Tampa Bay, 1976
- 13   Oakland, 1962
  - Chi. Bears, 1969
  - Pittsburgh, 1969
  - Buffalo, 1971
  - Houston, 1972, 1973

Most Consecutive Losses (Regular Season)
- 29   Chi. Cardinals, 1942–45
- 19   Oakland, 1961–62
- 18   Houston, 1972–73

Most Consecutive Shutout Losses (Regular Season)
- 6   Brooklyn, 1942–43
- 4   Philadelphia, 1936

TIES
Most Tie Games, Season
- 6   Chicago Bears, 1932
- 5   Frankford Yellowjackets, 1929
- 4   Chi. Bears, 1924
  - Orange, New Jersey, Tornadoes, 1929
  - Portsmouth Spartans, 1929

Most Consecutive Tie Games
- 3   Chi. Bears, 1932
- 2   By many teams

Scoreless Tie Games
- 16   Last time N.Y. Giants at Detroit, Nov. 7, 1943

TEAM RECORDS, OFFENSE

RUSHING

Most Seasons Leading League
- 11 Chi. Bears, 1932, 1934–35, 1939–42, 1951, 1955–56, 1968
- 6 Cleveland, 1958–59, 1963, 1965–67
- 4 Green Bay, 1946, 1961–62, 1964
- Dallas Texans/Kansas City, 1961, 1966, 1968–69
- Buffalo, 1962, 1964, 1973, 1975

RUSHING ATTEMPTS
Most Rushing Attempts, Season
- 659 Los Angeles, 1973
- 643 Oakland, 1975
- 632 Detroit, 1934
- Philadelphia, 1949

Fewest Rushing Attempts, Season
- 274 Detroit, 1946
- 285 Philadelphia, 1937
- 294 Detroit, 1943

Most Rushing Attempts, Game
- 72 Chi. Bears vs. Brooklyn Dodgers, Oct. 20, 1935
- 70 Chi. Cardinals vs. Green Bay, Nov. 25, 1951
- 69 Chi. Cardinals vs. Green Bay, Dec. 6, 1936

Fewest Rushing Attempts, Game
- 6 Chi. Cardinals vs. Boston Redskins, Oct. 29, 1933
- 7 Oakland vs. Buffalo, Oct. 15, 1963
- 8 Denver vs. Oakland, Dec. 17, 1960

Most Rushing Attempts, Both Teams, Game
- 108 Chi. Cardinals (70) vs. Green Bay (38), Dec. 5, 1948
- 105 Oakland (62) vs. Atlanta (43), Nov. 30, 1975 (ot)
- 102 Green Bay (51) vs. Pittsburgh (51), Nov. 20, 1949

Fewest Rushing Attempts, Both Teams, Game
- 36 Cincinnati (16) vs. Chi. Bears (20), Sept. 30, 1934
- 38 N.Y. Jets (13) vs. Buffalo (25), Nov 8, 1964
- 39 Denver (16) vs. N.Y. Titans (23), Sept. 24, 1961
- Denver (14) vs. Boston Patriots (25), Sept. 21, 1962
- Denver (14) vs. Houston (25), Dec. 2, 1962

RUSHING YARDAGE
Most Yards Gained Rushing, Season
- 3,088 Buffalo, 1973
- 2,974 Buffalo, 1975
- 2,960 Miami, 1972

Fewest Yards Gained Rushing, Season
- 298 Philadelphia, 1940
- 467 Detroit, 1946
- 471 Boston Yanks, 1944

Most Yards Gained Rushing, Game
- 426 Detroit vs. Pittsburgh, Nov. 4, 1934
- 423 N.Y. Giants vs. Baltimore, Nov. 19, 1950
- 420 Boston Redskins vs. N.Y. Giants, Oct. 8, 1933

Fewest Yards Gained Rushing, Game
- −53 Detroit vs. Chi. Cardinals, Oct. 17, 1943
- −36 Philadelphia vs. Chi. Bears, Nov. 19, 1939
- −33 Phil–Pitt vs. Brooklyn, Oct. 2, 1943

Most Yards Gained Rushing, Both Teams, Game
- 595 Los Angeles (371) vs. N.Y. Yanks (224), Nov. 18, 1951
- 574 Chicago Bears (396) vs. Pittsburgh (178), Oct. 10, 1934
- 557 Chicago Bears (406) vs. Green Bay (151), Nov. 6, 1955

Fewest Yards Gained Rushing, Both Teams, Game
- −15 Detroit (−53) vs. Chi. Cardinals (38), Oct. 17, 1943
- 4 Detroit (−10) vs. Chi. Cardinals (14), Sept. 15, 1940
- 63 Chi. Cardinals (−1) vs. N.Y. Giants (64), Oct. 18, 1953

AVERAGE GAIN RUSHING
Highest Average Gain, Rushing, Season
- 5.74 Cleveland, 1963
- 5.65 San Francisco, 1954
- 5.56 San Diego, 1963

Lowest Average Gain, Rushing, Season
- 0.94 Philadelphia, 1940
- 1.45 Boston Yanks, 1944
- 1.55 Pittsburgh, 1935

TOUCHDOWNS RUSHING
Most Touchdowns, Rushing, Season
- 36 Green Bay, 1962
- 30 Chi. Bears, 1941
- 29 Green Bay, 1960
- Baltimore, 1964

Fewest Touchdowns, Rushing, Season
- 1 Brooklyn Dodgers, 1934
- 2 Chi. Cardinals, 1933
- Cincinnati Reds, 1933
- Pittsburgh, 1934, 1940
- Philadelphia, 1935–38, 1972
- 3 By seven teams

Most Touchdowns, Rushing, Game
- 7 Los Angeles vs. Atlanta, Dec. 4, 1976
- 6 By many teams. Last time N.Y. Jets vs. Boston, Oct. 27, 1968

Most Touchdowns, Rushing, Both Teams, Game
- 8 Los Angeles (6) vs. N.Y. Yanks (2), Nov. 18, 1951
- Cleveland (6) vs. Los Angeles (2), Nov. 24, 1957
- 7 In many games

PASSING

Most Seasons Leading League
- 10 Washington, 1937, 1939–40, 1942–45, 1947, 1967, 1974
- 9 N.Y. Giants, 1932, 1934–35, 1938, 1948, 1959, 1962–63, 1972
- 6 Los Angeles, 1946, 1949–51, 1954, 1973

PASSING ATTEMPTS
Most Passes Attempted, Season
- 592 Houston, 1964
- 568 Denver, 1961
- 559 Denver, 1962

Fewest Passes Attempted, Season
- 102 Cincinnati Reds, 1933
- 106 Boston Redskins, 1933
- 120 Detroit, 1937

Most Passes Attempted, Game
- 68 Houston vs. Buffalo, Nov 1, 1964
- 62 N.Y. Jets vs. Denver, Dec. 3, 1967; vs Baltimore, Oct. 18, 1970
- 61 Houston vs. Oakland, Nov. 7, 1965

Fewest Passes Attempted, Game
- 0 Green Bay vs. Portsmouth, Ohio, Spartans, Oct. 8, 1933; vs. Chi. Bears, Sept. 25, 1949
- Detroit vs. Cleveland Rams, Sept. 10, 1937
- Pittsburgh vs. Brooklyn Dodgers, Nov. 16, 1941; vs. Los Angeles, Nov. 13, 1949
- Cleveland vs. Philadelphia, Dec. 3, 1950

Most Passes Attempted, Both Teams, Game
- 98 Minnesota (56) vs. Baltimore (42), Sept. 28, 1969
- 97 Denver (53) vs. Houston (44), Dec. 2, 1962
- 95 Los Angeles (48) vs. Chicago (47), Oct. 11, 1964

Fewest Passes Attempted, Both Teams, Game
- 4 Chi. Cardinals (1) vs. Detroit (3), Nov. 3, 1935
- Detroit (0) vs. Cleveland Rams (4), Sept. 10, 1937
- 6 Chi. Cardinals (2) vs. Detroit (4), Sept 15, 1940
- 8 Brooklyn Dodgers (2) vs. Philadelphia (6), Oct. 1, 1939

PASSING COMPLETIONS
Most Passes Completed, Season
- 301 Washington, 1967
- 299 Houston, 1964
- 292 Denver, 1962

Fewest Passes Completed, Season
- 25 Cincinnati Reds, 1933
- 33 Boston Redskins, 1933
- 34 Chi. Cardinals, 1934
- Detroit, 1934

Most Passes Completed, Game
- 37 Houston vs. Buffalo, Nov. 1, 1964
- 36 N.Y. Giants vs. Pittsburgh, Dec. 5, 1948
- Minnesota vs. Baltimore, Sept. 28, 1969
- Baltimore vs. N.Y. Jets, Dec. 15, 1974
- 35 Denver vs. Houston, Dec. 20, 1964

Most Passes Completed, Both Teams, Game
- 56 Minnesota (36) vs. Baltimore (20), Sept. 28, 1969
- 55 Chi. Bears (30) vs. San Francisco (25), Nov. 1, 1953
- Philadelphia (29) vs. St. Louis (26), Oct. 14, 1973
- Baltimore (36) vs. N.Y. Jets (19), Dec. 15, 1974
- 53 Denver (35) vs. Houston (18), Dec. 20, 1964

Fewest Passes Completed, Both Teams, Game
- 1 Chi. Cardinals (0) vs. Philadelphia (1), Nov. 8, 1936
- Detroit (0) vs. Cleveland Rams (1), Sept. 10, 1937
- Chi. Cardinals (0) vs. Detroit (1), Sept. 15, 1940
- Brooklyn Dodgers (0) vs. Pittsburgh (1), Nov. 29, 1942
- 2 Chi. Cardinals (0) vs. Detroit (2), Nov. 3, 1935
- Buffalo (0) vs. N.Y. Jets (2), Sept. 29, 1974
- 3 Brooklyn Dodgers (1) vs. Philadelphia (2), Oct. 1, 1939

PASSING YARDAGE
Most Seasons Leading League, Passing Yardage
- 8 Chi. Bears, 1932, 1939, 1941, 1943, 1945, 1949, 1954, 1964
- 7 Washington, 1938, 1940, 1944, 1947–48, 1967, 1974
- 5 Green Bay, 1934–37, 1942
- Philadelphia, 1953, 1955, 1961–62, 1973

Most Yards Gained, Passing, Season
- 4,392 Houston, 1961
- 3,845 N.Y. Jets, 1967
- 3,730 Washington, 1967

Fewest Yards Gained, Passing, Season
- 302 Chi. Cardinals, 1934
- 357 Cincinnati Reds, 1933
- 459 Boston Redskins, 1934

Most Yards Gained, Passing, Game
- 554 Los Angeles vs. N.Y. Yanks, Sept. 28, 1951
- 530 Minnesota vs. Baltimore, Sept. 28, 1969
- 505 N.Y. Giants vs. Washington, Oct. 28, 1962

Fewest Yards Gained, Passing, Game
- −53 Denver vs. Oakland, Sept. 10, 1967
- −52 Cincinnati vs. Houston, Oct. 31, 1971
- −32 Washington vs. Pittsburgh, Nov. 27, 1955

Most Yards Gained, Passing, Both Teams, Game
- 834 Philadelphia (419) vs. St. Louis (415), Dec. 16, 1962
- 822 N.Y. Jets (490) vs. Baltimore (332), Sept. 24, 1972
- 821 N.Y. Giants (505) vs. Washington (316), Oct. 28, 1962

Fewest Yards Gained, Passing, Both Teams, Game
- −11 Green Bay (−10) vs. Dallas (−1), Oct. 24, 1965
- 1 Chi. Cardinals (0) vs. Philadelphia (1), Nov. 8, 1936
- 7 Brooklyn Dodgers (0) vs. Pittsburgh (7), Nov. 29, 1942

TACKLED ATTEMPTING PASSES
Most Times Tackled, Attempting Passes, Season
- 70 Atlanta, 1968
- 68 Dallas, 1964
- 66 Pittsburgh, 1966

Fewest Times Tackled, Attempting Passes, Season
- 8 San Francisco, 1970
  - St. Louis, 1975
- 9 N.Y. Jets, 1966
- 10 N.Y. Giants, 1972

Most Times Tackled, Attempting Passes, Game
- 12 Pittsburgh vs. Dallas, Nov. 20, 1966
- 11 St. Louis vs. N.Y. Giants, Nov. 1, 1964
  - Los Angeles vs. Baltimore, Nov. 22, 1964
  - Denver vs. Buffalo, Dec. 13, 1964; vs. Oakland, Nov. 5, 1967
  - Buffalo vs. Oakland, Oct. 15, 1967
  - Green Bay vs. Detroit, Nov. 5, 1967
  - Atlanta vs. St. Louis, Nov. 24, 1968
  - Detroit vs. Dallas, Oct. 6, 1975
- 10 By many teams

Most Times Tackled, Attempting Passes, Both Teams, Game
- 17 Buffalo (10) vs. N.Y. Titans (7), Nov. 23, 1961
  - Pittsburgh (12) vs. Dallas (5), Nov. 20, 1966
- 16 Los Angeles (11) vs. Baltimore (5), Nov. 22, 1964
  - Buffalo (11) vs. Oakland (5), Oct. 15, 1967
- 15 Denver (11) vs. Buffalo (4), Dec. 13, 1964

COMPLETION PERCENTAGE
Most Seasons Leading League, Completion Percentage
- 11 Washington, 1937, 1939-40, 1942-45, 1947-48, 1969-70
- 7 Green Bay, 1936, 1941, 1961-62, 1964, 1966, 1968
- 6 Cleveland, 1951, 1953-55, 1959-60
  - Dallas Texans/Kansas City, 1962, 1964, 1966-69

Highest Completion Percentage, Season
- 64.3 Oakland, 1976
- 64.0 Washington, 1945
- 63.5 Cincinnati, 1974

Lowest Completion Percentage, Season
- 22.9 Philadelphia, 1936
- 24.5 Cincinnati, 1933
- 25.0 Pittsburgh, 1941

TOUCHDOWNS
Most Touchdowns, Passing, Season
- 48 Houston, 1961
- 39 N.Y. Giants, 1963
- 36 Oakland, 1969

Fewest Touchdowns, Passing, Season
- 0 Cincinnati Reds, 1933
  - Pittsburgh 1945
- 1 Boston Braves, 1932
  - Boston Redskins, 1933
  - Chi. Cardinals, 1934
  - Cincinnati Reds/St. Louis Gunners, 1934
  - Detroit, 1942
- 2 Chi. Cardinals, 1932, 35
  - Stapleton Stapes, 1932
  - Brooklyn Dodgers, 1936
  - Pittsburgh, 1942

Most Touchdowns, Passing, Game
- 7 Chi. Bears vs. N.Y. Giants, Nov. 14, 1943
  - Philadelphia vs. Washington, Oct. 17, 1954
  - Houston vs. N.Y. Titans, Nov. 19, 1961 and Oct. 14, 1962
  - N.Y. Giants vs. Washington, Oct. 28, 1962
  - Minnesota vs. Baltimore, Sept. 28, 1969
- 6 By many teams

Most Touchdowns, Passing, Both Teams, Game
- 12 New Orleans (6) vs. St. Louis (6), Nov. 2, 1969
- 11 N.Y. Giants (7) vs. Washington (4), Oct. 28, 1962
  - Oakland (6) vs. Houston (5), Dec. 22, 1963
- 9 In many games

PASSES HAD INTERCEPTED SEASON
Most Passes Had Intercepted, Season
- 48 Houston, 1962
- 45 Denver, 1961
- 41 Card-Pitt, 1944

Fewest Passes Had Intercepted, Season
- 5 Cleveland, 1960
  - Green Bay, 1966
- 6 Green Bay, 1964
- 7 Los Angeles, 1969

Most Passes Had Intercepted, Game
- 9 Detroit vs. Green Bay, Oct. 24, 1943
  - Pittsburgh vs. Philadelphia, Dec. 12, 1965
- 8 Green Bay vs. N.Y. Giants, Nov. 21, 1948
  - Chi. Cardinals vs. Philadelphia, Sept. 24, 1950
  - N.Y. Yanks vs. N.Y. Giants, Dec. 16, 1951
  - Denver vs. Houston, Dec. 2, 1962
  - Chi. Bears vs. Detroit, Sept. 22, 1968
  - Baltimore vs. N.Y. Jets, Sept. 23, 1973
- 7 By many teams

Most Passes Had Intercepted, Both Teams, Game
- 13 Denver (8) vs. Houston (5), Dec. 2, 1962
- 11 Philadelphia (7) vs. Boston Redskins (4), Nov. 3, 1935
  - Boston Redskins (6) vs. Pittsburgh (5), Dec. 1, 1935
  - Cleveland Rams (7) vs. Green Bay (4), Oct. 30, 1938
  - Green Bay (7) vs. Detroit (4), Oct. 20, 1940
  - Detroit (7) vs. Chi. Bears (4), Nov. 22, 1942
  - Detroit (7) vs. Cleveland Rams (4), Nov. 26, 1944
  - Chi. Cardinals (8) vs. Philadelphia (3), Sept. 24, 1950
  - Washington (7) vs. N.Y. Giants (4), Dec. 8, 1963
  - Pittsburgh (9) vs. Philadelphia (2), Dec 12, 1965
- 10 In many games

PUNTING
Most Seasons Leading League (Average Distance)
- 6 Washington, 1940-43, 1945, 1958
- 5 Denver, 1962-64, 1966-67
- 4 Los Angeles, 1946, 1949, 1955-56
  - Kansas City, 1968, 1971-73

Most Punts, Season
- 113 Boston Redskins, 1934
  - Brooklyn Dodgers, 1934
- 112 Boston Redskins, 1935

Fewest Punts, Season
- 32 Chi. Bears, 1941
- 33 Washington, 1945
- 38 Chi. Bears, 1947

Most Punts, Game
- 17 Chi. Bears vs. Green Bay, Oct. 22, 1933
  - Cincinnati vs. Pittsburgh, Oct. 22, 1933
- 16 Cincinnati vs. Portsmouth Ohio, Spartans, Sept. 17, 1933
  - Chi. Cardinals vs. Chi. Bears, Nov. 30, 1933; vs. Detroit, Sept. 15, 1940

Fewest Punts, Game
- 0 By many teams. Last time, Cincinnati vs. Buffalo, Nov. 17, 1975

Most Punts, Both Teams, Game
- 31 Cincinnati Reds, (17) vs. Pittsburgh (14), Oct. 22, 1933
  - Chi. Bears (17) vs. Green Bay (14), Oct. 22, 1933
- 29 Chi. Cardinals (15), vs. Cincinnati Reds, (14), Nov. 12, 1933
  - Chi. Cardinals (16) vs. Chi. Bears (13), Nov. 30, 1933
  - Chi. Cardinals (16) vs. Detroit (13), Sept. 15, 1940

Fewest Punts, Both Teams, Game
- 1 Dallas (0) vs. Cleveland (1), Dec. 3, 1961
  - Chicago (0) vs. Detroit (1), Oct. 1, 1972
  - San Francisco (0) vs. N.Y. Giants (1), Oct. 15, 1972
- 2 Philadelphia (0) vs. Cleveland (2), Sept. 25, 1960
  - Philadelphia (0) vs. Dallas (2), Oct. 22, 1961
  - Detroit (0) vs. Kansas City (2), Nov. 25, 1971
  - N.Y. Giants (1) vs. Philadelphia (1), Nov. 25, 1973
  - Buffalo (0) vs. New England (2), Nov. 3, 1974
- 3 In many games

Highest Average Distance, Punting, Season
- 47.6 Detroit, 1961
- 47.0 Pittsburgh, 1961
- 46.9 Pittsburgh, 1953

Lowest Average Distance, Punting, Season
- 32.7 Card-Pitt, 1944
- 33.9 Detroit, 1969
- 34.4 Phil-Pitt, 1943

PUNT RETURNS
Most Seasons Leading League
- 8 Detroit, 1943-45, 1951-52, 1962, 1966, 1969
- 5 Chi. Cardinals, 1948-49, 1955-56, 1959
  - Cleveland, 1958, 1960, 1964-65, 1967
  - Green Bay, 1950, 1953-54, 1961, 1972
- 3 Denver, 1963, 1967, 1969
  - Dallas Texans/Kansas City, 1960, 1968, 1970
  - San Diego, 1965-66, 1973

Most Punt Returns, Season
- 71 Pittsburgh, 1976
- 67 Pittsburgh, 1974
- 63 Denver, 1970
  - San Francisco, 1975

Fewest Punt Returns, Season
- 14 Los Angeles, 1961
  - Philadelphia, 1962
- 15 Houston, 1960
  - Washington, 1960
  - Oakland, 1961
  - N.Y. Giants, 1969
  - Philadelphia, 1973
- 16 Chi. Cardinals, 1943
  - N.Y. Titans, 1960
  - Atlanta, 1968
  - New Orleans, 1971, 1972
  - St. Louis, 1972

Most Punt Returns, Game
- 12 Philadelphia vs. Cleveland, Dec. 3, 1950
- 11 Chi. Bears vs. Chi. Cardinals, Oct. 8, 1950
- 10 Philadelphia vs. N.Y. Giants, Nov. 26, 1950

Most Punt Returns, Both Teams, Game
- 17 Philadelphia (12) vs. Cleveland (5), Dec. 3, 1950
- 16 N.Y. Giants (9) vs. Philadelphia (7), Dec. 12, 1954
- 15 Detroit (8) vs. Cleveland Rams (7), Sept. 27, 1942
  - Los Angeles (8) vs. Baltimore (7), Nov. 27, 1966
  - Pittsburgh (8) vs. Houston (7), Dec. 1, 1974

Most Fair Catches, Season
- 34 Baltimore, 1971
- 32 San Diego, 1969
- 30 St. Louis, 1967

Fewest Fair Catches, Season
- 0 San Diego, 1975
  - New England, 1976
  - Tampa Bay, 1976
- 1 Cleveland, 1974
  - San Francisco, 1975
- 2 N.Y. Giants, 1974
  - N.Y. Jets, 1974
  - Houston, 1975
  - Los Angeles, 1975

Most Fair Catches, Game
- 7 Minnesota vs. Dallas, Sept. 25, 1966
  - Detroit vs. Chicago, Nov. 21, 1976
- 6 Minnesota vs. Baltimore, Nov. 17, 1963; vs. Atlanta, Nov. 28, 1971
  - Chi. Bears vs. St. Louis, Oct. 31, 1966; vs. Minnesota, Dec. 10, 1967
  - Cleveland vs. St. Louis, Dec. 17, 1966
  - San Francisco vs. Baltimore, Oct. 13, 1968
  - Miami vs. Buffalo, Dec. 20, 1970
  - Cincinnati vs. Pittsburgh, Sept. 26, 1971
  - N.Y. Giants vs. Minnesota, Oct. 31, 1971
  - Baltimore vs. N.Y. Jets, Nov. 14, 1971
  - Green Bay vs. Chicago, Dec. 16, 1973
- 5 By many teams

YARDS RETURNING PUNTS
Most Yards, Punt Returns, Season
- 781 Chi. Bears, 1948
- 774 Pittsburgh, 1974
- 729 Green Bay, 1950

Fewest Yards, Punt Returns, Season
- 27 St. Louis, 1965
- 35 N.Y. Giants, 1965
- 37 New England, 1972

Most Yards, Punt Returns, Game
- 231 Detroit vs. San Francisco, Oct. 6, 1963
- 225 Oakland vs. Buffalo, Sept. 15, 1968
- 178 Pittsburgh vs. Brooklyn Dodgers, Nov. 29, 1942

Most Yards, Punt Returns, Both Teams, Game
- 245 Detroit (231) vs. San Francisco (14), Oct. 6, 1963
- 244 Oakland (225) vs. Buffalo (19), Sept. 15, 1968
- 226 Pittsburgh (178) vs. Brooklyn Dodgers (48), Nov. 29, 1942

AVERAGE YARDS RETURNING PUNTS
Highest Average, Punt Returns, Season
- 20.2 Chi. Bears, 1941
- 19.1 Chi. Cardinals, 1948
- 18.2 Chi. Cardinals, 1949

Lowest Average, Punt Returns, Season
- 1.2 St. Louis, 1965
- 1.5 N.Y. Giants, 1965
- 1.7 Washington, 1970

TOUCHDOWNS RETURNING PUNTS
Most Touchdowns, Punt Returns, Season
- 5 Chi. Cardinals, 1959
- 4 Chi. Cardinals, 1948
  - Detroit, 1951
  - N.Y. Giants, 1951
- 3 Washington, 1941
  - Detroit, 1952
  - Pittsburgh, 1952
  - Houston, 1975

Most Touchdowns, Punt Returns, Game
- 2 Detroit vs. Los Angeles, Oct. 14 and vs. Green Bay, Nov. 22, 1951
  - Chi. Cardinals vs. Pittsburgh, Nov. 1, 1959; vs. N.Y. Giants, Nov. 22, 1959
  - N.Y. Titans vs. Denver, Sept. 24, 1961
  - Denver vs. Cleveland, Sept. 26, 1976

Most Touchdowns, Punt Returns, Both Teams, Game
- 2 Philadelphia (1) vs. Washington (1), Nov. 9, 1952
  - Kansas City (1) vs. Buffalo (1), Sept. 11, 1966
  - Denver (2) vs. Cleveland (0), Sept. 26, 1976

KICKOFF RETURNS
Most Seasons Leading League
- 6 Washington, 1942, 1947, 1962–63, 1973–74
- 5 N.Y. Giants, 1944, 1946, 1949, 1951, 1953
  - Chi. Bears, 1943, 1948, 1958, 1966, 1972
- 4 Houston, 1960, 1962–63, 1968

Most Kickoff Returns, Season
- 82 Atlanta, 1966
- 80 N.Y. Giants, 1966
- 78 Denver, 1963

Fewest Kickoff Returns, Season
- 17 N.Y. Giants, 1944
- 20 N.Y. Giants, 1941
  - Chicago Bears, 1942
  - N.Y. Giants, 1943
- 23 Washington, 1942

Most Kickoff Returns, Game
- 12 N.Y. Giants vs. Washington, Nov. 27, 1966
- 10 By many teams

Most Kickoff Returns, Both Teams, Game
- 19 N.Y. Giants (12) vs. Washington (7), Nov. 27, 1966
- 18 Houston (10) vs. Oakland (8), Dec. 22, 1963
- 16 N.Y. Giants (10) vs. Chi. Cardinals (6), Oct. 17, 1948
  - N.Y. Titans (10) vs. Los Angeles Chargers (6), Dec. 18, 1960
  - Cleveland (8) vs. St. Louis (8), Sept. 20, 1964
  - Cleveland (8) vs. N.Y. Giants (8), Dec. 4, 1966

YARDS RETURNING KICKOFFS
Most Yards, Kickoff Returns, Season
- 1,824 Houston, 1963
- 1,801 Denver, 1963
- 1,799 Houston, 1973

Fewest Yards, Kickoff Returns, Season
- 282 N.Y. Giants, 1940
- 381 Green Bay, 1940
- 424 Chicago, 1963

Most Yards, Kickoff Returns, Game
- 362 Detroit vs. Los Angeles, Oct. 29, 1950
- 304 Chi. Bears vs. Green Bay, Nov. 9 1952
- 295 Denver vs. Boston, Oct. 4, 1964

Most Yards, Kickoff Returns, Both Teams, Game
- 560 Detroit (362) vs. Los Angeles (198), Oct. 29, 1950
- 453 Washington (236) vs. Philadelphia (217), Sept. 28, 1947
- 447 N.Y. Giants (236) vs. Cleveland (211), Dec. 4, 1966

AVERAGE YARDS RETURNING KICKOFFS
Highest Average, Kickoff Returns, Season
- 29.4 Chicago, 1972
- 28.9 Pittsburgh, 1952
- 28.2 Washington, 1962

Lowest Average, Kickoff Returns, Season
- 16.3 Chicago, 1963
- 16.5 San Diego, 1961
- 16.7 Chi. Cardinals, 1947

TOUCHDOWNS RETURNING KICKOFFS
Most Touchdowns, Kickoff Returns, Season
- 4 Green Bay, 1967
  - Chicago, 1970
- 3 Los Angeles, 1950
  - Chi. Cardinals, 1954
  - San Francisco, 1963
  - Denver, 1966
  - Chicago, 1967
- 2 By many teams

Most Touchdowns, Kickoff Returns, Game
- 2 Chi. Bears vs. Green Bay, Sept. 22, 1940 and Nov. 9, 1952
  - Philadelphia vs. Dallas, Nov. 6, 1966
  - Green Bay vs. Cleveland, Nov. 12, 1967

Most Touchdowns, Kickoff Returns, Both Teams, Game
- 2 Washington (1) vs. Philadelphia (1), Nov. 1, 1942
  - Washington (1) vs. Philadelphia (1), Sept. 28, 1947
  - Los Angeles (1) vs. Detroit (1), Oct. 29, 1950
  - N.Y. Yanks (1) vs. N.Y. Giants (1), Nov. 4, 1951 (consecutive)
  - Baltimore (1) vs. Chi. Bears (1), Oct. 4, 1958
  - Buffalo (1) vs. Boston Patriots (1), Nov. 3, 1962
  - Pittsburgh (1) vs. Dallas (1), Oct. 30, 1966
  - St. Louis (1) vs. Washington (1), Sept. 23, 1973 (consecutive)

SCORING
Most Seasons Leading League
- 9 Chi. Bears, 1934–35, 1939, 1941–43, 1946–47, 1956
- 6 Green Bay, 1932, 1936–38, 1961–62
  - Los Angeles, 1950–52, 1957, 1967, 1973
- 4 Oakland, 1967–69, 1974

POINTS
Most Points, Season
- 513 Houston, 1961
- 468 Oakland, 1967
- 466 Los Angeles, 1950

Fewest Points, Season (Since 1932)
- 37 Cincinnati Reds/St. Louis Gunners, 1934
- 38 Cincinnati Reds, 1933
  - Detroit, 1942
- 51 Pittsburgh, 1934
  - Philadelphia, 1936

Most Points, Game
- 72 Washington vs. N.Y. Giants, Nov. 27, 1966
- 70 Los Angeles vs. Baltimore, Oct. 22, 1950
- 65 Chi. Cardinals vs. N.Y. Bulldogs, Nov. 13, 1949
  - Los Angeles vs. Detroit, Oct. 29, 1950

Most Points, Both Teams, Game
- 113 Washington (72) vs. N.Y. Giants (41), Nov. 27, 1966
- 101 Oakland (52) vs. Houston (49), Dec. 22, 1963
- 98 Chi. Cardinals (63) vs. N.Y. Giants (35), Oct. 17, 1948

Most Points, One Quarter
- 41 Green Bay vs. Detroit, Oct. 7, 1945 (second quarter)
  - Los Angeles vs. Detroit, Oct. 29, 1940 (third quarter)
- 35 Chi. Cardinals vs. Boston Yanks, Oct. 24, 1948 (third quarter)
  - Green Bay vs. Cleveland, Nov. 12, 1967 (first quarter)
- 31 Chi. Cardinals vs. N.Y. Bulldogs, Nov. 13, 1949 (second quarter)
  - Oakland vs. Denver, Dec. 17, 1960 (fourth quarter); vs. San Diego, Dec. 8, 1963 (fourth quarter)
  - Buffalo vs. Kansas City, Sept. 13, 1964 (first quarter)

SCORING (Continued)

Most Points, Both Teams, One Quarter
49 Oakland (28) vs. Houston (21), Dec. 22, 1963 (second quarter)
48 Green Bay (41) vs. Detroit (7), Oct. 7, 1945 (second quarter)
     Los Angeles (41) vs. Detroit (7), Oct. 29, 1950 (third quarter)
47 St. Louis (27) vs. Philadelphia (20), Dec. 13, 1964 (second quarter)

Most Points, Each Quarter
35 Green Bay vs. Cleveland, Nov. 12, 1967 (first quarter)
41 Green Bay vs. Detroit, Oct. 7, 1945 (second quarter)
     Los Angeles vs. Detroit, Oct. 29, 1950 (third quarter)
31 Oakland vs. Denver, Dec. 17, 1960; vs. San Diego, Dec. 8, 1963 (fourth quarter)

Most Points, Both Teams, Each Quarter
42 Green Bay (35) vs. Cleveland (7), Nov. 12, 1967 (first quarter)
49 Oakland (28) vs. Houston (21), Dec. 22, 1963 (second quarter)
48 Los Angeles (41) vs. Detroit (7), Oct. 29, 1950 (third quarter)
42 Chi. Cardinals (28) vs. Philadelphia (14), Dec. 7, 1947 (fourth quarter)
     Green Bay (28) vs. Chi. Bears (14), Nov. 6, 1955
     N.Y. Jets (28) vs. Boston (14), Oct. 27, 1968
     Pittsburgh (21), vs. Cleveland (21), Oct. 18, 1969

GAMES

Most Consecutive Games Scoring
274 Cleveland, 1950–71
179 Kansas City, 1963–76
161 Minnesota, 1962–73

TOUCHDOWNS

Most Touchdowns, Season
66 Houston, 1961
64 Los Angeles, 1950
58 Oakland, 1967

Fewest Touchdowns, Season (Since 1932)
3 Cincinnati, 1933
4 Cincinnati Reds/St. Louis Gunners, 1934
5 Detroit, 1942

Most Touchdowns, Game
10 Philadelphia vs. Cincinnati, Nov. 6, 1934
     Los Angeles vs. Baltimore, Oct. 22, 1950
     Washington vs. N.Y. Giants, Nov. 27, 1966
9 Chi. Cardinals vs. Rochester Jeffersons, Oct. 7, 1923; vs. N.Y. Giants, Oct. 17, 1948; vs. N.Y. Bulldogs, Nov. 13, 1949
     Los Angeles vs. Detroit, Oct. 29, 1950
     Pittsburgh vs. N.Y. Giants, Nov. 30, 1952
     Chi. Bears vs. San Francisco, Dec. 12, 1965
8 By many teams. Last time Atlanta vs. New Orleans, Sept. 16, 1973

Most Touchdowns, Both Teams, Game
16 Washington (10) vs. N.Y. Giants (6), Nov. 27, 1966
14 Chi. Cardinals (9) vs. N.Y. Giants (5), Oct. 17, 1948
     Los Angeles (10) vs. Baltimore (4), Oct. 22, 1950
     Houston (7) vs. Oakland (7), Dec. 22, 1963
13 New Orleans (7) vs. St. Louis (6), Nov. 2, 1969

POINTS AFTER TOUCHDOWNS

Most Points After Touchdown, Season (Kicking)
65 Houston, 1961
59 Los Angeles, 1950
56 Dallas, 1966
     Oakland, 1967

Fewest Points After Touchdown, Season (Kicking)
2 Chi. Cardinals, 1933
3 Cincinnati Reds, 1933
     Pittsburgh, 1934
4 Cincinnati Reds/St. Louis Gunners, 1934

Most Points After Touchdown, Game (Kicking)
10 Los Angeles vs. Baltimore, Oct. 22, 1950
9 Chi. Cardinals vs. N.Y. Giants, Oct. 17, 1948
     Pittsburgh vs. N.Y. Giants, Nov. 30, 1952
     Washington vs. N.Y. Giants, Nov. 27, 1966
8 By many teams

Most Points After Touchdown, Both Teams, Game (Kicking)
14 Chi. Cardinals (9) vs. N.Y. Giants (5), Oct. 17, 1948
     Houston (7) vs. Oakland (7), Dec. 22, 1963
     Washington (9) vs. N.Y. Giants (5), Nov. 27, 1966
13 Los Angeles (10) vs. Baltimore (3), Oct. 22, 1950
12 In many games

FIELD GOALS

Most Field Goals Attempted, Season
49 Los Angeles, 1966
     Washington, 1971
48 Green Bay, 1972
47 N.Y. Jets, 1969
     Los Angeles, 1973

Fewest Field Goals Attempted, Season (Since 1938)
0 Chi. Bears, 1944
2 Cleveland Rams, 1939
     Card-Pitt, 1944
     Boston Yanks, 1946
     Chi. Bears, 1947
3 Chi. Bears, 1945
     Cleveland Rams, 1945

Fewest Field Goals Attempted, Game
9 St. Louis vs. Pittsburgh, Sept. 24, 1967
8 Pittsburgh vs. St. Louis, Dec. 2, 1962
     Detroit vs. Minnesota, Nov. 13, 1966
     N.Y. Jets vs. Buffalo, Nov. 3, 1968
7 By many teams

Most Field Goals Attempted, Both Teams, Game
11 St. Louis (6) vs. Pittsburgh (5), Nov. 13, 1966
     Washington (6) vs. Chicago (5), Nov. 14, 1971
     Green Bay (6) vs. Detroit (5), Sept. 29, 1974
     Washington (6) vs. N.Y. Giants (5), Nov. 14, 1976
10 Denver (5) vs. Boston Patriots (5), Nov. 11, 1962
     Boston Patriots (7) vs. San Diego (3), Sept. 20, 1964
     Buffalo (7) vs. Houston (3), Dec.5, 1965
     St. Louis (7) vs. Atlanta (3), Dec. 11, 1966
     Boston (7) vs. Buffalo (3), Sept. 24, 1967
     Detroit (7) vs. Minnesota (3), Sept. 20, 1971
     Washington (7) vs. Houston (3), Oct. 10, 1971
     Green Bay (5) vs. St. Louis (5), Dec. 5, 1971
     Kansas City (7) vs. Buffalo (3), Dec. 19, 1971
     Kansas City (5) vs. San Diego (5), Oct. 29, 1972
     Minnesota (6) vs. Chicago (4), Sept. 23, 1973
     Cleveland (7) vs. Denver (3), Oct. 19, 1975
9 In many games

Most Field Goals, Season
34 N.Y. Jets, 1968
33 Green Bay, 1972
32 N.Y. Jets, 1969

Fewest Field Goals, Season (Since 1932)
0 Boston Braves, 1932
     Chi. Cardinals, 1932, 1945
     Green Bay, 1932, 1944
     N.Y. Giants, 1932
     Boston Redskins, 1935
     Brooklyn Dodgers, 1944
     Card-Pitt, 1944
     Chi. Bears, 1944, 1947
     Boston Yanks, 1946
     Baltimore, 1950
     Dallas Texans, 1952

Most Field Goals, Game
7 St. Louis vs. Pittsburgh, Sept. 24, 1967
6 Boston vs. Denver, Oct. 4, 1964
     Detroit vs. Minnesota, Nov. 13, 1966
     N.Y. Jets vs. Buffalo, Nov. 3, 1968; vs. New Orleans, Dec. 3, 1972
     Philadelphia vs. Houston, Nov. 12, 1972
     St. Louis vs. Atlanta, Dec. 9, 1973
5 By many teams

Most Field Goals, Both Teams, Game
8 Cleveland (4) vs. St. Louis (4), Sept. 20, 1964
     Chicago Bears (5) vs. Philadelphia (3), Oct. 20, 1968
     Washington (5) vs. Chicago (3), Nov. 14, 1971
     Kansas City (5) vs. Buffalo (3), Dec. 19, 1971
     Detroit (4) vs. Green Bay (4), Sept. 29, 1974
     Cleveland (5) vs. Denver (3), Oct. 19, 1975
     New England (4) vs. San Diego (4), Nov. 9, 1975
7 Denver (4) vs. Los Angeles Chargers (3), Oct. 16, 1960
     Boston Patriots (4) vs. Denver (3), Nov. 11, 1962
     Boston Patriots (6) vs. Denver (1), Oct. 4, 1964
     Detroit (6) vs. Minnesota (1), Nov. 13, 1966
     St. Louis (7) vs. Pittsburgh (0), Sept. 24, 1967
     Baltimore (4) vs. San Francisco (3), Nov. 26, 1967
     Kansas City (5) vs. Buffalo (2), Dec. 7, 1969
     Washington (5) vs. Houston (2), Oct. 10, 1971
     Philadelphia (6) vs. Houston (1), Nov. 12, 1972
     N.Y. Jets (6) vs. New Orleans (1), Dec. 3, 1972
     Minnesota (5) vs. Chicago (2), Sept. 23, 1973
     San Francisco (5) vs. Denver (2), Sept. 23, 1973
     Atlanta (5) vs. Los Angeles (2), Nov. 4, 1973
     St. Louis (6) vs. Atlanta (1), Dec. 9, 1973
     Pittsburgh (4) vs. Cleveland (3), Nov. 17, 1974
6 In many games

Most Consecutive Games Scoring Field Goals
31 Minnesota, 1968–70
21 San Francisco, 1970–72
20 Los Angeles, 1970–71
     Miami, 1970–72

SAFETIES

Most Safeties, Season
4 Detroit, 1962
3 Green Bay, 1932, 1975
     Pittsburgh, 1947
     N.Y. Yanks, 1950
     Detroit, 1960
     St. Louis, 1960
     Buffalo, 1964
     Minnesota, 1965
     Cleveland, 1970
     Los Angeles, 1973
2 By many teams

Most Safeties, Game
2 Cincinnati vs. Chi. Cardinals, Nov. 19, 1933
     Detroit vs. Brooklyn Dodgers, Dec. 1, 1935
     N.Y. Giants vs. Pittsburgh, Sept. 17, 1950; vs. Washington, Nov. 5, 1961
     Chicago Bears vs. Pittsburgh, Nov. 9, 1969
     Dallas vs. Philadelphia, Nov. 19, 1972
     Los Angeles vs. Green Bay, Oct. 21, 1973
     Oakland vs. San Diego, Oct. 26, 1975

FIRST DOWNS

Most Seasons Leading League
- 9 Chi. Bears, 1935, 1939, 1941, 1943, 1945, 1947–49, 1955
- 6 Los Angeles, 1946, 1950–51, 1954, 1957, 1973
- 5 Green Bay, 1940, 1942, 1944, 1960, 1962

Most First Downs, Season
- 318 Buffalo, 1975
- 315 Oakland, 1975
- 314 Minnesota, 1975

Fewest First Downs, Season
- 51 Cincinnati, 1933
- 64 Pittsburgh, 1935
- 67 Philadelphia, 1937

Most First Downs, Game
- 38 Los Angeles vs. N.Y. Giants, Nov. 13, 1966
- 37 Green Bay vs. Philadelphia, Nov. 11, 1962
- 35 Pittsburgh vs. Chi. Cardinals, Dec. 13, 1958

Fewest First Downs, Game
- 0 N.Y. Giants vs. Green Bay, Oct. 1, 1933; vs. Washington, Sept. 27, 1942
  Pittsburgh vs. Boston Redskins, Oct. 29, 1933
  Philadelphia vs. Detroit, Sept. 20, 1935
  Denver vs. Houston, Sept. 3, 1966

Most First Downs, Both Teams, Game
- 58 Los Angeles (30) vs. Chi. Bears (28), Oct. 24, 1954
  Denver (34) vs. Kansas City (24), Nov. 18, 1974
- 57 Los Angeles (32) vs. N.Y. Yanks (25), Nov. 19, 1950
  Baltimore (33) vs. N.Y. Jets (24), Dec. 15, 1974
- 54 New York Giants (31) vs. Pittsburgh (23), Dec. 5, 1948
  Dallas (31) vs. San Francisco (23), Nov. 10, 1963
  Washington (30) vs. San Francisco (24), Nov. 12, 1967
  Cincinnati (34) vs. Buffalo (20), Nov. 17, 1975

Fewest First Downs, Both Teams, Game
- 5 N.Y. Giants (0) vs. Green Bay (5), Oct. 1, 1933

Most First Downs, Rushing, Season
- 177 Los Angeles, 1973
- 170 Miami, 1972
- 162 Buffalo, 1975

Fewest First Downs, Rushing, Season
- 36 Cleveland Rams, 1942
  Boston Yanks, 1944
- 39 Brooklyn Dodgers, 1943
- 40 Philadelphia, 1940
  Detroit, 1945

Most First Downs, Rushing, Game
- 25 Philadelphia vs. Washington, Dec. 2, 1951
- 21 Cleveland vs. Philadelphia, Dec. 13, 1959
  Los Angeles vs. New Orleans, Nov. 25, 1973
- 20 By seven teams

Fewest First Downs, Rushing, Game
- 0 By many teams

Most First Downs, Passing, Season
- 186 Houston, 1964
  Oakland, 1964
- 182 Houston, 1961
- 180 N.Y. Jets, 1967

Fewest First Downs, Passing, Season
- 18 Pittsburgh, 1941
- 23 Brooklyn Dodgers, 1942
  N.Y. Giants, 1944
- 24 N.Y. Giants, 1943

Most First Downs, Passing, Game
- 25 Denver vs. Kansas City, Nov. 18, 1974
- 24 Houston vs. Buffalo, Nov. 1, 1964
  Minnesota vs. Baltimore, Sept. 28, 1969
- 23 Dallas vs. San Francisco, Nov. 10, 1963
  Denver vs. Houston, Dec. 20, 1964

Fewest First Downs, Passing, Game
- 0 By many teams

Most First Downs, Penalty, Season
- 34 Detroit, 1971
- 32 Chicago Bears, 1963
- 31 New Orleans, 1969, 1971
  San Diego, 1971
  St. Louis, 1973

Fewest First Downs, Penalty, Season
- 2 Brooklyn Dodgers, 1940
- 4 Chi. Cardinals, 1940
  N.Y. Giants, 1942, 1944
  Washington, 1944
  Cleveland, 1952
  Kansas City, 1969
- 5 Brooklyn Dodgers, 1939
  Chi. Bears, 1939
  Detroit, 1953
  Los Angeles, 1953

Most First Downs, Penalty, Game
- 9 Chi. Bears vs. Cleveland, Nov. 25, 1951
- 7 Boston vs. Houston, Sept. 19,, 1965
  Baltimore vs. Detroit, Nov. 19, 1967
  Oakland vs. Boston, Oct. 6, 1968
- 6 By many teams

Fewest First Downs, Penalty, Game
- 0 By many teams

NET YARDS GAINED RUSHING AND PASSING

Most Seasons Leading League
- 12 Chi. Bears, 1932, 1934–35, 1939, 1941–44, 1947, 1949, 1955–56
- 6 Los Angeles, 1946, 1950–51, 1954, 1957, 1973
- 5 Baltimore, 1958–60, 1964, 1967
  Dallas, 1966, 1968–69, 1971, 1974

Most Yards Gained, Season
- 6,288 Houston, 1961
- 5,696 Oakland, 1968
- 5,506 Los Angeles, 1951

Fewest Yards Gained, Season
- 1,150 Cincinnati Reds, 1933
- 1,443 Chi. Cardinals, 1934
- 1,486 Chi. Cardinals, 1933

Most Yards Gained, Game
- 735 Los Angeles vs. N.Y. Yanks, Sept. 28, 1951
- 683 Pittsburgh vs. Chi. Cardinals, Dec. 13, 1958
- 682 Chi. Bears vs. N.Y. Giants, Nov. 14, 1943

Fewest Yards Gained, Game
- −5 Denver vs. Oakland, Sept. 10, 1967
- 14 Chi. Cardinals vs. Detroit, Sept. 15, 1940
- 16 Detroit vs. Chi. Cardinals, Sept. 15, 1940

Most Yards Gained, Both Teams, Game
- 1,133 Los Angeles (636) vs. N.Y. Yanks (497), Nov. 19, 1950
- 1,087 St. Louis (589) vs. Philadelphia (498), Dec. 16, 1962
- 1,057 San Diego (581) vs. Denver (476), Oct. 20, 1968

Fewest Yards Gained, Both Teams, Game
- 30 Chi. Cardinals (14) vs. Detroit (16), Sept. 15, 1940

FUMBLES

Most Fumbles, Season
- 56 Chi. Bears, 1938
- 54 Philadelphia, 1946
- 51 New England, 1973

Fewest Fumbles, Season
- 8 Cleveland, 1959
- 11 Green Bay, 1944
- 12 Brooklyn Dodgers, 1934
  Detroit, 1943

Most Fumbles, Game
- 10 Phil-Pitt vs. N.Y. Giants, Oct. 9, 1943
  Detroit vs. Minnesota, Nov. 12, 1967
  Kansas City vs. Houston, Oct. 12, 1969
- 9 Philadelphia vs. Green Bay, Oct. 13, 1946
  Kansas City vs. San Diego, Nov. 15, 1964
  N.Y. Giants vs. Buffalo, Oct. 20, 1975
- 8 By many teams

Most Fumbles, Both Teams, Game
- 14 Chi. Bears (7) vs. Cleveland Rams (7), Nov. 24, 1940
  St. Louis (8) vs. N.Y. Giants (6), Sept. 17, 1961
  Kansas City (10) vs. Houston (4), Oct. 12, 1969
- 13 Washington (8) vs. Pittsburgh (5), Nov. 14, 1937
  Philadelphia (7) vs. Boston Yanks (6), Dec. 8, 1946
  N.Y. Giants (7) vs. Washington (6), Nov. 5, 1950
  Kansas City (9) vs. San Diego (4), Nov. 15, 1964
  Buffalo (7) vs. Denver (6), Dec. 13, 1964
  N.Y. Jets (7) vs. Houston (6), Sept. 12, 1965
  Houston (8) vs. Pittsburgh (5), Dec. 9, 1973
- 12 In many games

FUMBLES RECOVERED

Most Fumbles Recovered, Season (Own and Opponents')
- 58 Minnesota, 1963 (27 own, 31 opp)
- 51 Chi. Bears, 1938 (37 own, 14 opp)
- 46 N.Y. Giants, 1946 (20 own, 26 opp)

Fewest Fumbles Recovered, Season (Own and Opponents')
- 13 Baltimore, 1967 (5 own, 8 opp)
  N.Y. Jets, 1967 (7 own, 6 opp)
  Philadelphia, 1968 (6 own, 7 opp)
  Miami, 1973 (5 own, 8 opp)
- 14 Cleveland, 1956 (6 own, 8 opp)
  Kansas City, 1966 (5 own, 9 opp)
- 15 Chi. Bears, 1943 (9 own, 6 opp)
  San Francisco, 1951 (6 own, 9 opp)
  Cleveland, 1959 (3 own, 12 opp)
  Kansas City, 1971 (9 own, 6 opp)

Most Fumbles Recovered, Game (Own and Opponents')
- 10 Denver vs. Buffalo, Dec. 13, 1964 (5 own, 5 opp)
  Pittsburgh vs. Houston, Dec. 9, 1973 (5 own, 5 opp)
  Washington vs. St. Louis, Oct. 25, 1976 (2 own, 8 opp)
- 9 St. Louis vs. N.Y. Giants, Sept. 17, 1961 (6 own, 3 opp)
  Houston vs. Cincinnati, Oct. 27, 1974 (4 own, 5 opp)
  Kansas City vs. Dallas, Nov. 10, 1975 (4 own, 5 opp)
- 8 By many teams

Most Own Fumbles Recovered, Season
- 37 Chi. Bears, 1938
- 27 Philadelphia, 1946
  Minnesota, 1963
- 26 Washington, 1940
  Pittsburgh, 1948

Fewest Own Fumbles Recovered, Season
- 2 Washington, 1958
- 3 Detroit, 1956
  Cleveland, 1959
- 4 By many teams

FUMBLES (Continued)

Most Opponents' Fumbles Recovered, Season
- 31 Minnesota, 1963
- 29 Cleveland, 1951
- 28 Green Bay, 1946

Fewest Opponents' Fumbles Recovered, Season
- 3 Los Angeles, 1974
- 4 Philadelphia, 1944
- 6 Brooklyn, 1939
  - Chi. Bears, 1943, 1945
  - Washington, 1945
  - N.Y. Jets, 1967
  - San Diego, 1969
  - Kansas City, 1971
  - Oakland, 1975

Most Opponents' Fumbles Recovered, Game
- 8 Washington vs. St. Louis, Oct. 25, 1976
- 7 Buffalo vs. Cincinnati, Nov. 30, 1969
- 6 By many teams

Most Touchdowns, Fumbles Recovered, Season (Own and Opponents')
- 5 Chi. Bears, 1942 (1 own, 4 opp)
  - Los Angeles, 1952 (1 own, 4 opp)
  - San Francisco, 1965 (1 own, 4 opp)
- 4 Chi. Bears, 1948 (1 own, 3 opp)
  - Boston Yanks, 1948 (4 opp)
- 3 By many teams

Most Touchdowns, Own Fumbles Recovered, Season
- 2 Chi. Bears, 1953
  - New England, 1973
  - Buffalo, 1974
  - Denver, 1975

Most Touchdowns, Opponents' Fumbles Recovered, Season
- 4 Detroit, 1937
  - Chi. Bears, 1942
  - Boston Yanks, 1948
  - Los Angeles, 1952
  - San Francisco, 1965
- 3 Philadelphia, 1938, 1952, 1974
  - Los Angeles, 1947
  - Chi. Bears, 1948
  - N.Y. Giants, 1950
  - Buffalo, 1961
  - Cleveland, 1964
  - Pittsburgh, 1965
  - Washington, 1965
  - Cincinnati, 1970
  - Minnesota, 1970
- 2 By many teams

TOUCHDOWNS

Most Touchdowns, Fumbles Recovered, Game (Own and Opponents)
- 2 Detroit vs. Cleveland, Nov. 7, 1937, (2 opp); vs. Los Angeles, Sept. 17, 1950 (1 own, 1 opp); vs. Chi. Cardinals, Dec. 6, 1959 (1 own, 1 opp); vs. Minnesota, Dec. 9, 1962 (1 own, 1 opp)
  - Philadelphia vs. N.Y. Giants, Sept. 25, 1938 (2 opp); St. Louis, Nov. 21, 1971 (1 own, 1 opp)
  - Chi. Bears vs. Washington, Nov. 28, 1948 (2 opp)
  - N.Y. Giants vs. Pittsburgh, Sept. 17, 1950 (2 opp); vs. Green Bay, Sept. 19, 1971 (2 opp)
  - Cleveland vs. Dallas, Dec. 3, 1961 (2 opp); vs. N.Y. Giants, Oct 25, 1964 (2 opp)
  - Green Bay vs. Dallas, Nov. 26, 1964 (2 opp)
  - San Francisco vs. Detroit, Nov. 14, 1965 (2 opp)
  - Oakland vs. Buffalo, Dec. 24, 1967 (2 opp)
  - Washington vs. San Diego, Sept. 16, 1973 (2 opp)
  - New Orleans vs. San Francisco, Oct 19, 1975 (2 opp)

Most Touchdowns, Own Fumbles Recovered, Game
- 1 By many teams

Most Touchdowns, Opponents' Fumbles Recovered, Game
- 2 Detroit vs. Cleveland, Nov. 7, 1937
  - Philadelphia vs. N.Y. Giants, Sept. 25, 1938
  - Chi. Bears vs. Washington, Nov. 28, 1948
  - N.Y. Giants vs. Pittsburgh, Sept. 17, 1950; vs. Green Bay, Sept. 19, 1971
  - Cleveland vs. Dallas, Dec. 3, 1961; vs. N.Y. Giants, Oct. 25, 1964
  - Green Bay vs. Dallas, Nov. 26, 1964
  - San Francisco vs. Detroit, Nov. 14, 1965
  - Oakland vs. Buffalo, Dec. 24, 1967
  - Washington vs. San Diego, Sept. 16, 1973
  - New Orleans vs. San Francisco, Oct. 19, 1975

PENALTIES

Most Seasons Leading League, Fewest Penalties
- 9 Pittsburgh, 1946–47, 1950–52, 1954, 1963, 1965, 1968
- 5 Green Bay, 1955–56, 1966–67, 1974
- 4 Boston Patriots/New England, 1962, 1964–65, 1973

Most Seasons Leading League, Most Penalties
- 16 Chi. Bears, 1941–44, 1946–49, 1951, 1959–61, 1963, 1965, 1968, 1976
- 5 Oakland, 1963, 1966, 1968–69, 1975
- 4 Los Angeles, 1950, 1952, 1962, 1969

Fewest Penalties, Season
- 19 Detroit, 1937
- 21 Boston Redskins, 1935
- 24 Philadelphia, 1936

Most Penalties, Season
- 122 Washington, 1948
  - Chi. Bears, 1948
- 121 Chi. Bears, 1944
- 118 Chi. Bears, 1951

Fewest Penalties, Game
- 0 By many teams

Most Penalties, Game
- 22 Brooklyn Dodgers vs. Green Bay, Sept. 17, 1944
  - Chi. Bears vs. Philadelphia, Nov. 26, 1944
- 21 Cleveland vs. Chi. Bears, Nov. 25, 1951
- 20 Tampa Bay vs. Seattle, Oct. 17, 1976

Fewest Penalties, Both Teams, Game
- 0 Brooklyn Dodgers vs. Pittsburgh, Oct. 28, 1934
  - Brooklyn Dodgers vs. Boston Redskins, Sept. 28, 1936
  - Cleveland Rams vs. Chi. Bears, Oct. 9, 1938
  - Pittsburgh vs. Philadelphia, Nov. 10, 1940

Most Penalties, Both Teams, Game
- 37 Cleveland (21) vs. Chi. Bears (16), Nov. 25, 1951
- 35 Tampa Bay (20) vs. Seattle (15), Oct, 17, 1976
- 33 Brooklyn (22) vs. Green Bay (11), Sept. 17, 1944

Most Seasons Leading League, Fewest Yards Penalized
- 7 Pittsburgh, 1946–47, 1950, 1952, 1962, 1965, 1968
  - Boston Redskins/Washington, 1935, 1953–54, 1956–58, 1970
- 4 Philadelphia, 1936, 1940, 1951, 1964
  - Boston Patriots, 1962, 1964–66
- 3 Brooklyn Dodgers, 1939, 1942–43
  - Baltimore, 1967, 1969, 1971
  - Detroit, 1937, 1948, 1972
  - Miami, 1967–68, 1973

Most Seasons Leading League, Most Yards Penalized
- 15 Chi. Bears, 1935, 1937, 1939–44, 1946–47, 1949, 1951, 1961–62, 1968
- 5 Oakland, 1963–64, 1968–69, 1975
- 4 Buffalo, 1962, 1967, 1970, 1972

Fewest Yards Penalized, Season
- 139 Detroit, 1937
- 146 Philadelphia, 1937
- 159 Philadelphia, 1936

Most Yards Penalized, Season
- 1,274 Oakland, 1969
- 1,194 Chicago, 1968
- 1,108 Buffalo, 1970

Fewest Yards Penalized, Game
- 0 By many teams

Most Yards Penalized, Game
- 209 Cleveland vs. Chi. Bears, Nov. 25, 1951
- 189 Houston vs. Buffalo, Oct. 31, 1965
- 184 Green Bay vs. Boston Yanks, Oct. 21, 1945

Fewest Yards Penalized, Both Teams, Game
- 0 Brooklyn Dodgers vs. Pittsburgh, Oct. 28, 1934
  - Brooklyn Dodgers vs. Boston Redskins, Sept. 28, 1936
  - Cleveland Rams vs. Chi. Bears, Oct. 9, 1938
  - Pittsburgh vs. Philadelphia, Nov. 10, 1940

Most Yards Penalized, Both Teams, Game
- 374 Cleveland (209) vs. Chi. Bears (165), Nov. 25, 1951
- 309 Green Bay (184) vs. Boston Yanks (125), Oct. 21, 1945
- 281 Oakland (176) vs. Boston Patriots (105), Sept. 28, 1969

TEAM RECORDS, DEFENSE

RUSHING

Fewest Yards Allowed, Rushing, Season
- 519 Chi. Bears, 1942
- 558 Philadelphia, 1944
- 793 Phil-Pitt, 1943

Most Yards Allowed, Rushing, Season
- 2,876 Seattle, 1976
- 2,857 Baltimore, 1950
- 2,850 New England, 1973

Fewest Touchdowns Allowed, Rushing, Season
- 2 Detroit, 1934
    - Dallas, 1968
    - Minnesota, 1971
- 3 By many teams

Most Touchdowns Allowed, Rushing, Season
- 36 Oakland, 1961
- 29 Baltimore, 1950
    - N.Y. Yanks, 1950
    - Minnesota, 1961
- 27 Detroit, 1948
    - New England, 1972

PASSING

Fewest Yards Allowed, Passing, Season
- 545 Philadelphia, 1934
- 558 Portsmouth, Ohio, Spartans 1933
- 585 Chi. Cardinals, 1934

Most Yards Allowed, Passing, Season
- 3,674 Dallas, 1962
- 3,602 Washington, 1962
- 3,532 St. Louis, 1969

Most Opponents Tackled Attempting Passes, Season
- 67 Oakland, 1967
- 60 Dallas, 1966
- 59 Baltimore, 1975

Fewest Opponents Tackled Attempting Passes, Season
- 15 New England, 1972
- 16 Miami, 1966
    - Cincinnati, 1969
- 17 New Orleans, 1970
    - Philadelphia, 1972, 1975

Most Opponents Tackled Attempting Passes, Game
- 12 Dallas vs. Pittsburgh, Nov. 20, 1966
- 11 N.Y. Giants vs. St. Louis, Nov. 1, 1964
    - Baltimore vs. Los Angeles, Nov. 22, 1964
    - Buffalo vs. Denver, Dec. 13, 1964
    - Oakland vs. Buffalo, Oct. 15, 1967; vs. Denver, Nov. 5, 1967
    - Detroit vs. Green Bay, Nov. 5, 1967
    - St. Louis vs. Atlanta, Nov. 24, 1968
    - Dallas vs. Detroit, Oct. 6, 1975
- 10 By many teams

Most Opponents Yards Lost Attempting to Pass, Season
- 666 Oakland, 1967
- 526 Boston Patriots, 1963
- 499 N.Y. Giants, 1963

Fewest Opponents Yards Lost Attempting to Pass, Season
- 75 Green Bay, 1956
- 77 N.Y. Bulldogs, 1949
- 78 Green Bay, 1958

Fewest Touchdowns Allowed, Passing, Season
- 1 Portsmouth, Ohio, Spartans, 1932
    - Philadelphia, 1934
- 2 Brooklyn Dodgers, 1933
    - Chi. Bears, 1934
- 3 Chi. Bears, 1932, 1936
    - Green Bay, 1932, 1934
    - N.Y. Giants, 1939, 1944

Most Touchdowns Allowed, Passing, Season
- 40 Denver, 1963
- 38 St. Louis, 1969
- 37 Washington, 1961

INTERCEPTIONS BY

Most Seasons Leading League
- 9 N.Y. Giants, 1933, 1937–39, 1944, 1948, 1951, 1954, 1961
- 8 Green Bay, 1940, 1942–43, 1947, 1955, 1957, 1962, 1965
- 6 Chi. Bears, 1935–36, 1941–42, 1946, 1963
    - Kansas City, 1966–70, 1974

Most Passes Intercepted By, Season
- 49 San Diego, 1961
- 42 Green Bay, 1943
- 41 N.Y. Giants, 1951

Fewest Passes Intercepted By, Season
- 6 Houston, 1972
- 7 Los Angeles, 1959
- 8 Pittsburgh, 1940
    - Boston Patriots, 1970

Most Passes Intercepted By, Game
- 9 Green Bay vs. Detroit, Oct. 24, 1943
    - Philadelphia vs. Pittsburgh, Dec. 12, 1965
- 8 N.Y. Giants vs. Green Bay, Nov. 21, 1948; vs. N.Y. Yanks, Dec. 16, 1951
    - Philadelphia vs. Chi. Cardinals, Sept. 24, 1950
    - Houston vs. Denver, Dec. 2, 1962
    - Detroit vs. Chicago Bears, Sept. 22, 1968
    - N.Y. Jets vs. Baltimore, Sept. 23, 1973
- 7 By many teams

Most Consecutive Games, One or More Interceptions By
- 46 Los Angeles Chargers/San Diego, 1960–63
- 37 Detroit, 1960–63
- 36 Boston Yanks, 1944–47
    - Washington, 1962–65

Most Yards Returning Interceptions, Season
- 929 San Diego, 1961
- 712 Los Angeles, 1952
- 676 Houston, 1967

Fewest Yards Returning Interceptions, Season
- 5 Los Angeles, 1959
- 51 Philadelphia, 1968
- 62 Pittsburgh, 1940

Most Yards Returning Interceptions, Game
- 314 Los Angeles vs. San Francisco, Oct. 18, 1964
- 245 Houston vs. N.Y. Jets, Oct. 15, 1967
- 235 Buffalo vs. N.Y. Jets, Sept. 29, 1968

Most Touchdowns, Returning Interceptions, Season
- 9 San Diego, 1961
- 6 Cleveland, 1960
    - Green Bay, 1966
    - Detroit, 1967
    - Houston, 1967
- 5 By 10 teams

PAID ATTENDANCE

Year	League	Reg. Season Games	Reg. Season Attendance	Average	Post-season Games	Postseason Attendance	Super Bowl	
1934	NFL	60	492,684	8,211	1	35,059		
1935	NFL	53	638,178	12,041	1	15,000		
1936	NFL	54	816,007	15,111	1	29,545		
1937	NFL	55	963,039	17,510	1	15,878		
1938	NFL	55	937,197	17,040	1	48,120		
1939	NFL	55	1,071,200	19,476	1	32,279		
1940	NFL	55	1,063,025	19,328	1	36,034		
1941	NFL	55	1,108,615	20,157	2	55,870		
1942	NFL	55	887,920	16,144	1	36,006		
1943	NFL	50	969,128	19,383	2	71,315		
1944	NFL	50	1,019,649	20,393	1	46,016		
1945	NFL	50	1,270,401	25,408	1	32,178		
1946	NFL	55	1,732,135	31,493	1	58,346		
1947	NFL	60	1,837,437	30,624	2	66,268		
1948	NFL	60	1,525,243	25,421	1	36,309		
1949	NFL	60	1,391,735	23,196	1	27,980		
1950	NFL	78	1,977,753	25,356	3	136,647		
1951	NFL	72	1,913,019	26,570	1	57,522		
1952	NFL	72	2,052,126	28,502	2	97,507		
1953	NFL	72	2,164,585	30,064	1	54,577		
1954	NFL	72	2,190,571	30,425	1	43,827		
1955	NFL	72	2,521,836	35,026	1	85,693		
1956	NFL	72	2,551,263	35,434	1	56,836		
1957	NFL	72	2,836,318	39,393	2	119,579		
1958	NFL	72	3,006,124	41,752	2	123,659		
1959	NFL	72	3,140,000	43,617	1	57,545		
1960	AFL	56	926,156	16,538	1	32,183		
	NFL	78	3,128,296	40,106	1	67,325		
1961	AFL	56	1,002,657	17,904	1	29,556		
	NFL	98	3,986,159	40,675	1	39,029		
1962	AFL	56	1,147,302	20,487	1	37,981		
	NFL	98	4,003,421	40,851	1	64,892		
1963	AFL	56	1,208,697	21,584	2	63,171		
	NFL	98	4,163,643	42,486	1	45,801		
1964	AFL	56	1,447,875	25,855	1	40,242		
	NFL	98	4,563,049	46,562	1	79,544		
1965	AFL	56	1,782,384	31,828	1	30,361		
	NFL	98	4,634,021	47,286	2	100,304		
1966	AFL	63	2,160,369	34,291	1	42,080		
	NFL	105	5,337,044	50,829	1	74,152	I	61,946
1967	AFL	63	2,295,697	36,439	1	53,330		
	NFL	112	5,938,924	53,026	3	166,208	II	75,546
1968	AFL	70	2,635,004	37,634	2	114,438		
	NFL	112	5,882,313	52,521	3	215,902	III	75,377
1969	AFL	70	2,843,373	40,620	3	167,088		
	NFL	112	6,096,127	54,430	3	162,279	IV	80,562
1970	NFL	182	9,533,333	52,381	8	458,593	V	79,204
1971	NFL	182	10,076,035	55,363	8	485,891	VI	81,023
1972	NFL	182	10,445,827	57,395	8	483,345	VII	90,182
1973	NFL	182	10,730,933	58,961	8	525,433	VIII	71,882
1974	NFL	182	10,236,322	56,244	8	438,664	IX	80,997
1975	NFL	182	10,213,193	56,116	8	475,919	X	80,187
1976	NFL	196	11,044,018	56,347	8	386,866	XI	100,421

SPECIAL ACHIEVEMENTS

1922
Wilbur (Pete) Henry, Canton Bulldogs, drop-kicked a 50-yard field goal vs. Toledo Maroons, November 13.
John (Paddy) Driscoll, Chicago Cardinals, drop-kicked three field goals (30, 23, and 12 yards) vs. Chicago Bears, December 10.

1923
John (Paddy) Driscoll, Chicago Cardinals, scored 27 points (four touchdowns, three extra points) vs. Rochester Jeffersons, October 7.
George Halas, Chicago Bears, recovered a fumble and returned it 98 yards for a touchdown vs. Oorang Indians, Marion, Ohio, November 4.

1924
John (Paddy) Driscoll, Chicago Cardinals, drop-kicked a 50-yard field goal vs. Milwaukee Badgers, September 28.
John (Paddy) Driscoll, Chicago Cardinals, drop-kicked four field goals (23, 18, 50, and 35 yards) vs. Columbus Tigers, October 11.
John (Paddy) Driscoll, Chicago Cardinals, drop-kicked 11 field goals in a season (14 games).

1929
Ernie Nevers, Chicago Cardinals, scored 40 points (six touchdowns rushing, four extra points) vs. Chicago Bears, November 28.

1933
Frank McNally, Chicago Cardinals, intercepted a lateral and returned it 51 yards vs. Pittsburgh Pirates, September 27.
Martin Kottler, Pittsburgh Pirates, intercepted a pass and returned it 99 yards vs. Chicago Cardinals, September 27.
Cliff Battles, Boston Redskins, gained 215 yards rushing (16 attempts) vs. New York Giants, October 8.
Jack McBride, New York Giants, kicked five extra points vs. Philadelphia Eagles, October 15.
Gil Lefebvre, Cincinnati Reds, returned a punt 98 yards vs. Brooklyn Dodgers, December 3.
Harry Newman, New York Giants, attempted 136 passes, completed 53 for 973 yards passing in a season.

1934
Doug Russell, Chicago Cardinals, returned a kickoff 102 yards vs. Cincinnati Reds, September 24.
Glenn Presnell, Detroit Lions, kicked a 54-yard field goal vs. Green Bay Packers, October 7.
Harry Newman, New York Giants, carried the ball 39 times vs. Green Bay Packers, November 11.
Beattie Feathers, Chicago Bears, gained 1,004 yards rushing (101 attempts) in a season and averaged 9.94 yards per carry (11 games; he missed two games of a 13-game season because of a shoulder injury).
Jack Manders, Chicago Bears, scored 76 points (three touchdowns, 10 field goals, 28 extra points) in a season.

1936
Alphonse (Tuffy) Leemans, New York Giants, carried the ball 206 times in a season (12 games).
Arnie Herber, Green Bay Packers, attempted 173 passes, completed 77 for 1,239 yards passing in a season (12 games).
Don Hutson, Green Bay Packers, caught 34 passes for 536 yards and eight touchdowns in a season (12 games).

1937
Vern Huffman, Detroit Lions, intercepted a pass and returned it 100 yards vs. Brooklyn Dodgers, October 17.
Ray Buivid, Chicago Bears, threw five touchdown passes vs. Chicago Cardinals, December 5.
Pat Coffee and Gaynell Tinsley, Chicago Cardinals, combined for a 97-yard touchdown pass vs. Chicago Bears, December 5.
Riley Smith, Washington Redskins, kicked seven extra points vs. New York Giants, December 5.
Cliff Battles, Washington Redskins, carried the ball 216 times in a season (11 games).
Sammy Baugh, Washington Redskins, attempted 171 passes, completed 81 for 1,127 yards passing in a season (11 games).
Don Hutson, Green Bay Packers, caught 41 passes in a season (11 games).

1938
Doug Russell and Gaynell Tinsley, Chicago Cardinals, combined for a 98-yard touchdown pass vs. Cleveland Rams, November 27.

1939
Andy Uram, Green Bay Packers, had a 97-yard run from scrimmage vs. Chicago Cardinals, October 8.
Frank Filchock and Andy Farkas, Washington Redskins, combined for a 99-yard touchdown pass vs. Pittsburgh Pirates, October 15.
Parker Hall, Cleveland Rams, completed 106 passes (208 attempts) in a season (11 games).
Don Hutson, Green Bay Packers, had 846 yards (34 receptions) pass receiving in a season (11 games).

1940
Lee Artoe, Chicago Bears, kicked a 52-yard field goal vs. New York Giants, October 27.
Sammy Baugh, Washington Redskins, had a 59.4 punting average (five punts) vs. Detroit Lions, October 27.
Davey O'Brien, Philadelphia Eagles, completed 33 of 60 passes for 316 yards vs. Washington Redskins, December 1.
Don Looney, Philadelphia Eagles, caught 14 passes for 180 yards vs. Washington Redskins, December 1.
Sammy Baugh, Washington Redskins, completed 111 passes (177 attempts) for 1,367 yards passing in a season and a 62.7 completion percentage (11 games).
Davey O'Brien, Philadelphia Eagles, attempted 277 passes (124 completions) in a season (11 games).
Don Looney, Philadelphia Eagles, caught 58 passes in a season (11 games).

1941
Cecil Isbell, Green Bay Packers, completed 117 passes (206 attempts) for 1,479 yards passing and 15 touchdowns in a season (11 games).
Don Hutson, Green Bay Packers, scored 95 points (12 touchdowns, one field goal, 20 extra points) in a season (11 games).

1942
Don Hutson, Green Bay Packers, caught 13 passes for 209 yards pass receiving vs. Cleveland Rams, October 18.
Cecil Isbell, Green Bay Packers, had 333 yards passing (10 completions) vs. Chicago Cardinals, November 1.
Cecil Isbell, Green Bay Packers, completed 146 of 268 passes for 2,021 yards passing and 24 touchdowns in a season (11 games).
Cecil Isbell, Green Bay Packers, completed a string in which he threw at least one touchdown pass in 23 consecutive games in 1941 and 1942.
Wilson Schwenk, Chicago Cardinals, attempted 295 passes (126 completions) in a season (11 games).
Don Hutson, Green Bay Packers, caught 74 passes for 1,211 yards pass receiving and 17 touchdowns in a season (11 games).
Clyde (Bulldog) Turner, Chicago Bears, intercepted eight passes in a season (11 games).
Don Hutson, Green Bay Packers, scored 138 points (17 touchdowns, one field goal, 33 extra points) in a season (11 games).

1943
Sammy Baugh, Washington Redskins, had 376 yards passing (28 attempts, 16 completions) for six touchdowns vs. Brooklyn Dodgers, October 31.
Wilbur Moore, Washington Redskins, had 213 yards pass receiving (seven receptions) vs. Brooklyn Dodgers, October 31.
Sid Luckman, Chicago Bears, completed 21 of 32 passes for 433 yards passing and seven touchdowns vs. New York Giants, November 14.
Bob Snyder, Chicago Bears, kicked eight extra points vs. New York Giants, November 14.
Don Hutson, Green Bay Packers, had 237 yards pass receiving (eight receptions) vs. Brooklyn Dodgers, November 21.
Sid Luckman, Chicago Bears, attempted 202 passes, completed 110 for 2,194 yards passing and 28 touchdowns in a season (10 games).
Sammy Baugh, Washington Redskins, intercepted 11 passes in a season (10 games).
Bob Snyder, Chicago Bears, kicked 39 extra points in a season (10 games).

1944
Don Hutson, Green Bay Packers, completed a string in which he scored one or more points in 41 consecutive games.

1945
Don Hutson, Green Bay Packers, caught four touchdown passes and scored 29 points in one quarter (the second), 31 in the game (four touchdowns, seven extra points) vs. Detroit Lions, October 7.
Jim Benton, Cleveland Rams, had 303 yards pass receiving (10 receptions) vs. Detroit Lions, November 22.
Sammy Baugh, Washington Redskins, had a 70.3 completion percentage in passing (182 attempts, 128 completions) for a season and only four of his passes were intercepted (10 games).
Don Hutson, Green Bay Packers, retired from football with a string of 95 consecutive games in which he caught at least one pass.
Steve Van Buren, Philadelphia Eagles, scored 18 touchdowns, 15 of them rushing, in a season (10 games).

1946
Frank Seno, Chicago Cardinals, returned a kickoff 105 yards vs. New York Giants, October 20.

1947
Steve Van Buren, Philadelphia Eagles, gained 1,008 yards rushing (217 attempts) in a season (12 games).
Sammy Baugh, Washington Redskins, attempted 354 passes, completed 210 for 2,938 yards passing in a season (12 games).

1948
Pat Harder, Chicago Cardinals, kicked nine extra points vs. New York Giants, October 17.
Bob Waterfield, Los Angeles Rams, made an 88-yard punt vs. Green Bay Packers, October 17.
Sammy Baugh, Washington Redskins, had 446 yards passing (17 completions) vs. Boston Yanks, October 31.
Dick Poillon, Washington Redskins, kicked eight extra points vs. Boston Yanks, October 31.
Dick Poillon, Washington Redskins, intercepted a lateral and returned it 93 yards for a touchdown vs. Philadelphia Eagles, November 21.
Fred (Dippy) Evans, Chicago Bears, scored two touchdowns on fumble recoveries vs. Washington Redskins, November 28.
Charlie Conerly, New York Giants, completed 36 passes (53 attempts) vs. Pittsburgh Steelers, December 5.
Dan Sandifer, Washington Redskins, intercepted 13 passes and had 258 yards in interception returns in a season.
Pat Harder, Chicago Cardinals, kicked 53 extra points without a miss.
Jim Hardy, Los Angeles Rams, threw 114 passes without an interception.

1949
Jim Keane, Chicago Bears, caught 14 passes (193 yards) vs. New York Giants, October 23.
Bob Smith, Detroit Lions, intercepted a pass and returned it 102 yards for a touchdown vs. Chicago Bears, November 24.
Ralph Heywood, New York Bulldogs, caught 14 passes (151 yards) vs. Detroit Lions, December 4.
Bob Gage, Pittsburgh Steelers, ran 97 yards from scrimmage vs. Chicago Bears, December 4.
Johnny Lujack, Chicago Bears, had 468 yards passing (24 completions) vs. Chicago Cardinals, December 11.
Bob Shaw, Los Angeles Rams, caught four touchdown passes vs. Washington Redskins, December 11.
Tom Fears, Los Angeles Rams, caught 77 passes in a season (12 games).
Cliff Patton, Philadelphia Eagles, completed a string in which he made 84 consecutive extra points between 1947 and 1949.

1950
Bob Shaw, Chicago Cardinals, caught five touchdown passes vs. Baltimore Colts, October 2.
Norm Van Brocklin, Los Angeles Rams, completed 11 consecutive passes vs. Detroit Lions (10), October 15, and Baltimore Colts (1), October 22.
Marion Motley, Cleveland Browns, averaged 17.09 yards per rushing attempt (11 for 188 yards) vs. Pittsburgh Steelers, October 29.
Wally Triplett, Detroit Lions, returned four kickoffs for 294 yards, a 73.5-yard average, vs. Los Angeles Rams, October 29.
Gene Roberts, New York Giants, gained 218 yards rushing (26 attempts) vs. Chicago Cardinals, November 12.
George Buksar and Ernie Zalejski, Baltimore Colts, combined for a 99-yard return of an intercepted lateral (18 yards by Buksar, 81 by Zalejski) vs. Washington Redskins, November 26.
Tom Fears, Los Angeles Rams, caught 18 passes (189 yards) vs. Green Bay, December 3.
Cloyce Box, Detroit Lions, had 302 yards in pass receiving (12 receptions) vs. Baltimore Colts, December 3.
Doak Walker, Detroit Lions, scored 128 points in his rookie season (11 touchdowns, eight field goals, 38 extra points).
Orban (Spec) Sanders, New York Yanks, intercepted 13 passes in a season (12 games).
Tom Fears, Los Angeles Rams, caught 84 passes (1,116 yards) in a season (12 games).

1951
Norm Van Brocklin, Los Angeles Rams, had 554 yards passing (41 attempts, 27 completions) vs. N. Y. Yanks, September 28.
Jack Christiansen, Detroit Lions, returned punts twice for touchdowns, in two different games, vs. Los Angeles Rams, October 14, and vs. Green Bay Packers, November 22. He had 175 yards in punt returns (four returns, 43.8 average) vs. Green Bay.
Dub Jones, Cleveland Browns, scored six touchdowns (four rushing, two pass receiving) vs. Chicago Bears, November 25.
Bob Waterfield, Los Angeles Rams, kicked five field goals (17, 40, 25, 20, and 39 yards) vs. Detroit Lions, December 9.
Jerry Williams, Los Angeles Rams, returned a missed field goal 99 yards for a touchdown vs. Green Bay Packers, December 16.
Eddie Price, New York Giants, carried the ball 271 times (971 yards) in a season (12 games).
Elroy (Crazylegs) Hirsch, Los Angeles Rams, had 1,495 yards in pass receiving (66 receptions) and scored 17 touchdowns pass receiving in a season (12 games).

1952
Otto Graham, Cleveland Browns, attempted 364 passes (181 completions) in a season (12 games).
Dick (Night Train) Lane, Los Angeles Rams, intercepted 14 passes (298 yards) in a season (12 games).
Lou Groza, Cleveland Browns, kicked 19 field goals (33 attempts) in a season (12 games).

1953
Bert Rechichar, Baltimore Colts, kicked a 56-yard field goal vs. Chicago Bears, September 27.
Lou Groza, Cleveland Browns, kicked 23 field goals (26 attempts) in a season (12 games).
Lou Groza, Cleveland Browns, completed a string of 109 consecutive extra points and another of scoring in 45 consecutive regular season games between 1950 and 1953.

1954
Adrian Burk, Philadelphia Eagles, threw seven touchdown passes vs. Washington Redskins, October 17.
Tobin Rote, Green Bay Packers, attempted 382 passes (180 completions) in a season.

1956
George Ratterman, Cleveland Browns, completed 11 consecutive passes vs. Pittsburgh Steelers, October 6.
Al Carmichael, Green Bay Packers, returned a kickoff 106 yards for a touchdown vs. Chicago Bears, October 7.
Tommy Wilson, Los Angeles Rams, gained 223 yards rushing (23 attempts) vs. Green Bay Packers, December 16.
George Blanda, Chicago Bears, completed a string in which he made 156 consecutive extra points between 1951 and 1956.

1957
Jim Brown, Cleveland Browns, gained 237 yards rushing (31 attempts) vs. Los Angeles Rams, November 24.

1958
Jim Brown, Cleveland Browns, gained 1,527 yards rushing (257 attempts) in a season (12 games), and had 100 yards or more in a game nine times.
Jim Brown, Cleveland Browns, scored 18 touchdowns (17 rushing, 1 pass receiving) in a season (12 games).
1959
Carl Taseff, Baltimore Colts, returned a missed field goal 99 yards for a touchdown vs. Los Angeles Rams, December 12.
John Unitas, Baltimore Colts, threw 32 touchdown passes in a season (12 games).
Jim Brown, Cleveland Browns, carried the ball 290 times (1,329 yards) in a season (12 games).
1960
Milt Plum, Cleveland Browns, completed 11 consecutive passes vs. Washington Redskins, October 30.
Frank Tripucka, Denver Broncos, attempted 52 passes (30 completions) vs. Houston Oilers, November 6.
George Blanda, Houston Oilers, attempted 55 passes (31 completions) vs. Los Angeles Chargers, November 13.
Frank Tripucka, Denver Broncos, attempted 478 passes in a season (12 games).
Milt Plum, Cleveland Browns, completed a string in which he threw 208 consecutive passes without an interception in 1959 and 1960.
John Unitas, Baltimore Colts, had 3,099 yards passing (190 completions) and threw 25 touchdown passes.
John Unitas, Baltimore Colts, completed a string in which he threw a touchdown pass in 47 consecutive regular season games between 1956 and 1960, plus three in two championship games during that period.
Lionel Taylor, Denver Broncos, caught 92 passes (1,235 yards) in a season (14 games).
Paul Hornung, Green Bay Packers, scored 176 points (13 touchdowns, 13 rushing, 2 pass receiving, 15 field goals, and 41 extra points) in a season (14 games).
1961
Paul Hornung, Green Bay Packers, scored 33 points (four touchdowns, one field goal, six extra points) vs. Baltimore Colts, October 8.
Erich Barnes, New York Giants, intercepted a pass and returned it 102 yards for a touchdown vs. Dallas Cowboys, October 22.
George Blanda, Houston Oilers, threw seven touchdown passes vs. New York Titans, November 19.
Jim Brown, Cleveland Browns, gained 237 yards rushing (34 attempts) vs. Philadelphia Eagles, November 19.
Roger Leclerc, Chicago Bears, kicked five field goals (12, 30, 12, 32, and 15 yards) vs. Detroit Lions, December 3.
Fran Tarkenton, Minnesota Vikings, completed 13 consecutive passes vs. Los Angeles Rams, December 3.
Jim Brown, Cleveland Browns, carried the ball 305 times (1,408 yards) in a season (14 games).
John Unitas, Baltimore Colts, attempted 420 passes (229 completions) in a season (14 games).
George Blanda, Houston Oilers, threw 36 touchdown passes in a season (14 games).
Sonny Jurgensen, Philadelphia Eagles, completed 235 passes (416 attempts) for 3,723 yards and 32 touchdowns in a season (14 games).
Al Dorow, New York Titans, completed a string in which he threw touchdown passes in 19 straight games in 1960 and 1961.
Lionel Taylor, Denver Broncos, caught 100 passes (1,176 yards) in a season (14 games).
Charley Hennigan, Houston Oilers, had 1,746 yards pass receiving (82 receptions) in a season (14 games).
Bill Groman, Houston Oilers, caught 17 touchdown passes in a season (14 games).
George Blanda, Houston Oilers, kicked 64 out of 65 extra point attempts in a season (14 games).
1962
Timmy Brown, Philadelphia Eagles, returned a missed field goal 99 yards for a touchdown vs. St. Louis Cardinals, September 15.
Frank Tripucka, Denver Broncos, attempted 56 passes (29 completions) vs. Buffalo Bills, September 15.
Y. A. Tittle, New York Giants, threw seven touchdown passes and had 505 yards passing (39 attempts, 27 completions) vs. Washington Redskins, October 28.
Sonny Randle, St. Louis Cardinals, caught 16 passes and had 256 yards pass receiving vs. New York Giants, November 4.
Y. A. Tittle, New York Giants, threw 33 touchdown passes in a season (14 games).
Abner Haynes, Dallas Texans, scored 19 touchdowns (13 rushing, 6 pass receiving) in a season (14 games).
Jim Taylor, Green Bay Packers, scored 19 touchdowns (all rushing) in a season (14 games).
Cookie Gilchrist, Buffalo Bills, scored touchdowns rushing in seven consecutive games.
Lou Michaels, Pittsburgh Steelers, made 26 field goals (42 attempts) in a season (14 games).
Roger Brown, Detroit Lions, scored two safeties in a season (14 games).
1963
George Izo and Bobby Mitchell, Washington Redskins, combined for a 99-yard touchdown pass vs. Cleveland Browns, September 15.
Tom Watkins, Detroit Lions, gained 184 yards on punt returns (5 returns) vs. San Francisco 49ers, October 6.
Cookie Gilchrist, Buffalo Bills, gained 243 yards rushing (36 attempts) vs. New York Jets, December 8.
Jim Brown, Cleveland Browns, gained 1,863 yards rushing (291 attempts), had 200 or more in a game two times. Altogether he gained 100 or more yards in a game nine times.
Charley Johnson, St. Louis Cardinals, attempted 423 passes (222 completions) in a season (14 games).
John Unitas, Baltimore Colts, completed 237 passes (410 attempts) in a season (14 games).
Y. A. Tittle, New York Giants, threw 36 touchdown passes in a season (14 games).
Tommy Morrow, Oakland Raiders, completed a string in which he intercepted passes in eight consecutive games in 1962 and 1963.
1964
Gino Cappelletti, Boston Patriots, kicked six field goals in six attempts vs. Denver Broncos, October 4.
George Blanda, Houston Oilers, attempted 68 passes (37 completions) vs. Buffalo Bills, November 1.
Rudy Bukich, Chicago Bears, completed 13 consecutive passes vs. San Francisco 49ers (6), November 22, and Detroit Lions (7), November 26.
Jim Bakken, St. Louis Cardinals, kicked five field goals vs. Philadelphia Eagles, December 13.
George Blanda, Houston Oilers, attempted 505 passes and completed 262 in a season (14 games).
Charley Hennigan, Houston Oilers, caught 101 passes in a season (14 games).
Johnny Morris, Chicago Bears, caught 93 passes in a season (14 games).
Paul Krause, Washington Redskins, intercepted passes in seven consecutive games.
Lenny Moore, Baltimore Colts, scored 20 touchdowns (16 rushing, 3 pass receiving, 1 fumble return) in a season (14 games).
Lance Alworth, San Diego Chargers, scored touchdowns in nine consecutive games.
1965
Gale Sayers, Chicago Bears, scored six touchdowns (four rushing, 1 pass receiving, 1 punt return) vs. San Francisco 49ers, December 12.
John Brodie, San Francisco 49ers, completed 242 passes (391 attempts) in a season (14 games).
Bart Starr, Green Bay Packers, completed a string in which he threw 294 consecutive passes without an interception between 1964 and 1965.
Gale Sayers, Chicago Bears, scored a record 22 touchdowns in his rookie season (14 rushing, 6 pass receiving, 1 punt return, 1 kickoff return for 132 points).
Lenny Moore, Baltimore Colts, completed a string in which he scored touchdowns in 18 consecutive games between 1963 and 1965.
Tommy Davis, San Francisco 49ers, completed a string in which he kicked 234 consecutive extra points between 1959 and 1965.
1966
Karl Sweetan and Pat Studstill, Detroit Lions, combined for a 99-yard touchdown pass vs. Baltimore Colts, October 16.
Garo Yepremian, Detroit Lions, kicked four field goals in one quarter (the second) and six in the game vs. Minnesota Vikings, November 13.
Charlie Gogolak, Washington Redskins, kicked nine extra points in 10 attempts vs. New York Giants, November 27.
Timmy Brown, Philadelphia Eagles, returned two kickoffs for touchdowns vs. Dallas Cowboys, November 6.
Al Nelson, Philadelphia Eagles, returned a missed field goal 100 yards for a touchdown vs. Cleveland Browns, December 11.
Larry Wilson, St. Louis Cardinals, intercepted passes in seven consecutive games.
Bruce Gossett, Los Angeles Rams, kicked 28 field goals (49 attempts) in a season (14 games).
Tommy Brooker, Kansas City Chiefs, completed a string in which he scored in 45 consecutive games and another in which he kicked 149 consecutive extra points between 1962 and 1966.
Danny Villaneuva, Dallas Cowboys, kicked 56 extra points without a miss.
1967
Len Dawson, Kansas City Chiefs, completed 15 consecutive passes vs. Houston Oilers, September 9.
Bill Nelsen, Pittsburgh Steelers, completed a string in which he completed 13 consecutive passes vs. Atlanta Falcons (11), December 18, 1966, and Chi. Bears (2), September 17, 1967.
Jim Bakken, St. Louis Cardinals, kicked seven field goals (nine attempts) vs. Pittsburgh Steelers, September 24.
Joe Namath, New York Jets, completed 15 consecutive passes vs. Miami Dolphins (12), October 22, and Boston Patriots (3), October 29.
Travis Williams, Green Bay Packers, returned two kickoffs for touchdowns vs. Cleveland Browns, November 12.
Billy Kilmer and Walter Roberts, New Orleans Saints, combined for a 96-yard pass, not a touchdown, vs. Philadelphia Eagles, November 19.
Noland Smith, Kansas City Chiefs, returned a kickoff 106 yards for a touchdown vs. Denver Broncos, December 17.
Joe Namath, New York Jets, had 4,007 yards passing in a season (14 games).
Sonny Jurgensen, Washington Redskins, completed 288 of 508 passes for 3,747 yards passing in a season (14 games).
Travis Williams, Green Bay Packers, had 739 yards in kickoff returns (18 returns) and a 41.1 average, and four kickoff returns for touchdowns in a season (14 games).
Jim Turner, New York Jets, completed a string in which he kicked field goals in 18 consecutive games in 1966 and 1967.
1968
George Atkinson, Oakland Raiders, had 205 yards in punt returns (five returns) vs. Buffalo Bills, September 15.
Sonny Jurgensen and Gerry Allen, Washington Redskins, combined for a 99-yard touchdown pass vs. Chicago Bears, September 15.
Charley West, Minnesota Vikings, returned a punt 98 yards for a touchdown vs. Washington Redskins, November 3.
Jim Turner, New York Jets, kicked 34 field goals in a season (14 games).
Dennis Partee, San Diego Chargers, kicked 10 consecutive field goals, November 3 through December 15.
1969
Steve O'Neal, New York Jets, made a 98-yard punt vs. Denver Broncos, September 21.
Joe Kapp, Minnesota Vikings, threw seven touchdown passes vs. Baltimore Colts, September 28.
Lance Alworth, San Diego Chargers, completed a string in which he caught at least one pass in 96 consecutive games between 1962 and 1969.
Jan Stenerud, K. C. Chiefs, kicked 16 consecutive field goals.
1970
Tom Dempsey, New Orleans Saints, kicked a 63-yard field goal vs. Detroit Lions, November 8.
Curt Knight, Washington Redskins, kicked four field goals in one quarter (the second) vs. New York Giants, November 15.
Ken Houston, Houston Oilers, returned two interceptions for touchdowns vs. San Diego Chargers, December 19.
John Brockington, Green Bay Packers, gained 1,105 yards rushing (216 attempts) in his rookie season.
Bob Tucker, a tight end for the New York Giants, caught 59 passes.
Ken Houston, Houston Oilers, returned four interceptions for touchdowns in a season (14 games).
Cecil Turner, Chicago Bears, returned four kickoffs for touchdowns in a season (14 games).
Fred Cox, Minnesota Vikings, completed a string in which he made at least one field goal in 31 consecutive games between 1968 and 1970.
1971
Ken Ellis, Green Bay Packers, returned a missed field goal 100 yards vs. New York Giants, September 19.
Al Nelson, Philadelphia Eagles, returned a missed field goal 101 yards vs. Dallas Cowboys, September 26.
Willie Ellison, Los Angeles Rams, gained 247 yards rushing (26 attempts) vs. New Orleans Saints, December 5.
Curt Knight, Washington Redskins, attempted 49 field goals and made 29 in a season (14 games).
1972
Jack Tatum, Oakland Raiders, recovered a fumble and returned it 104 yards vs. Green Bay Packers, September 24.
Jim Hart and Bobby Moore (later named Ahmad Rashad), St. Louis Cardinals, combined for a 98-yard pass, not a touchdown, vs. Los Angeles Rams, December 10.
Bobby Douglass, quarterback for the Chicago Bears, gained 968 yards rushing (141 attempts) in a season (14 games).
Jim Kearney, Kansas City Chiefs, returned four interceptions for touchdowns in a season (14 games).
1973
O.J. Simpson, Buffalo Bills, gained 250 yards rushing and carried the ball 29 times vs. N. E. Patriots, September 16.
Fred Dryer, Los Angeles Rams, made two safeties vs. Green Bay Packers, October 21.
O.J. Simpson, Buffalo Bills, gained 2,003 yards rushing (332 attempts) had 200 or more in a game three times, and 100 or more in a game 11 times.
1974
Dennis Morgan, Dallas Cowboys, returned a punt 98 yards for a touchdown vs. St. Louis Cardinals, October 13.
Lydell Mitchell, Baltimore Colts, made 40 rushing attempts vs. New York Jets, October 20.
Ken Anderson, Cincinnati Bengals, completed 16 consecutive passes vs. Baltimore Colts (8), November 3, and Pittsburgh Steelers (8), November 10.
Bert Jones, Baltimore Colts, completed 17 consecutive passes vs. New York Jets, December 15.
Dan Abramowicz, San Francisco 49ers, completed a string in which he caught at least one pass in 105 consecutive games between 1967 and 1973 for the New Orleans Saints (1967–1973) and 49ers (1973–74).
1975
O.J. Simpson, Buffalo Bills, scored 23 touchdowns (16 rushing, 7 pass receiving) in a season (14 games).
Don Cockroft, Cleveland Browns, completed a string in which he kicked 16 consecutive field goals in 1974 and 1975.
1976
Rick Upchurch, Denver Broncos, returned two punts for touchdowns vs. Cleveland Browns, September 26.
Franco Harris, Pittsburgh Steelers, made 41 rushing attempts vs. Cincinnati Bengals, October 17.
O.J. Simpson, Buffalo Bills, gained 273 yards rushing (29 attempts) vs. Detroit Lions, November 25.
Rick Upchurch, Denver Broncos, returned four punts for touchdowns in a season (14 games).

1,000 YARDS RUSHING IN A SEASON

Year	Player, Team	Att.	Yards	Avg.	Long	TD
1934	**Beattie Feathers, Chi. Bears**	101	1,004	9.9	82	8
1947	Steve Van Buren, Philadelphia	217	1,008	4.6	45	13
1949	Steve Van Buren, Philadelphia2	263	1,146	4.4	41	11
	Tony Canadeo, Green Bay	208	1,052	5.1	54	4
1953	Joe Perry, San Francisco	192	1,018	5.3	51	10
1954	Joe Perry, San Francisco2	173	1,049	6.1	58	8
1956	Rick Casares, Chi. Bears	234	1,126	4.8	68	12
1958	Jim Brown, Cleveland	257	1,527	5.9	65	17
1959	Jim Brown, Cleveland2	290	1,329	4.6	70	14
	J. D. Smith, San Francisco	207	1,036	5.0	73	10
1960	Jim Brown, Cleveland3	215	1,257	5.8	71	9
	Jim Taylor, Green Bay	230	1,101	4.8	32	11
	John David Crow, St. Louis	183	1,071	5.9	57	6
1961	Jim Brown, Cleveland4	305	1,408	4.6	38	8
	Jim Taylor, Green Bay2	243	1,307	5.4	53	15
1962	Jim Taylor, Green Bay3	272	1,474	5.4	51	19
	John Henry Johnson, Pittsburgh	251	1,141	4.5	40	7
	Cookie Gilchrist, Buffalo	214	1,096	5.1	44	13
	Abner Haynes, Dallas Texans	221	1,049	4.7	71	13
	Dick Bass, Los Angeles	196	1,033	5.3	57	6
	Charlie Tolar, Houston	244	1,012	4.1	25	7
1963	Jim Brown, Cleveland5	291	1,863	6.4	80	12
	Clemon Daniels, Oakland	215	1,099	5.1	74	3
	Jim Taylor, Green Bay4	248	1,018	4.1	40	9
	Paul Lowe, San Diego	177	1,010	5.7	66	8
1964	Jim Brown, Cleveland6	280	1,446	5.2	71	7
	Jim Taylor, Green Bay5	235	1,169	5.0	84	12
	John Henry Johnson, Pittsburgh2	235	1,048	4.5	45	7
1965	Jim Brown, Cleveland7	289	1,544	5.3	67	17
	Paul Lowe, San Diego2	222	1,121	5.0	59	7
1966	Jim Nance, Boston	299	1,458	4.9	65	11
	Gale Sayers, Chicago	229	1,231	5.4	58	8
	Leroy Kelly, Cleveland	209	1,141	5.5	70	15
	Dick Bass, Los Angeles2	248	1,090	4.4	50	8
1967	Jim Nance, Boston2	269	1,216	4.5	53	7
	Leroy Kelly, Cleveland2	235	1,205	5.1	42	11
	Hoyle Granger, Houston	236	1,194	5.1	67	6
	Mike Garrett, Kansas City	236	1,087	4.6	58	9
1968	Leroy Kelly, Cleveland3	248	1,239	5.0	65	16
	Paul Robinson, Cincinnati	238	1,023	4.3	87	8
1969	Gale Sayers, Chicago2	236	1,032	4.4	28	8
1970	Larry Brown, Washington	237	1,125	4.7	75	5
	Ron Johnson, N.Y. Giants	263	1,027	3.9	68	8
1971	Floyd Little, Denver	284	1,133	4.0	40	6
	John Brockington, Green Bay	216	1,105	5.1	52	4
	Larry Csonka, Miami	195	1,051	5.4	28	7
	Steve Owens, Detroit	246	1,035	4.2	23	8
	Willie Ellison, Los Angeles	211	1,000	4.7	80	4
1972	O. J. Simpson, Buffalo	292	1,251	4.3	94	6
	Larry Brown, Washington2	285	1,216	4.3	38	8
	Ron Johnson, N.Y. Giants2	298	1,182	4.0	35	9
	Larry Csonka, Miami2	213	1,117	5.2	45	6
	Marv Hubbard, Oakland	219	1,100	5.0	39	4
	Franco Harris, Pittsburgh	188	1,055	5.6	75	10
	Calvin Hill, Dallas	245	1,036	4.2	26	6
	Mike Garrett, San Diego2	272	1,031	3.8	41	6
	John Brockington, Green Bay2	274	1,027	3.7	30	8
	Eugene (Mercury) Morris, Miami	190	1,000	5.3	33	12
1973	O. J. Simpson, Buffalo2	332	2,003	6.0	80	12
	John Brockington, Green Bay3	265	1,144	4.3	53	3
	Calvin Hill, Dallas2	273	1,142	4.2	21	6
	Lawrence McCutcheon, Los Angeles	210	1,097	5.2	37	2
	Larry Csonka, Miami3	219	1,003	4.6	25	5
1974	Otis Armstrong, Denver	263	1,407	5.3	43	9
	Don Woods, San Diego	227	1,162	5.1	56	7
	O. J. Simpson, Buffalo3	270	1,125	4.2	41	3
	Lawrence McCutcheon, Los Angeles2	236	1,109	4.7	23	3
	Franco Harris, Pittsburgh2	208	1,006	4.8	54	5
1975	O. J. Simpson, Buffalo4	329	1,817	5.5	88	16
	Franco Harris, Pittsburgh3	262	1,246	4.8	36	10
	Lydell Mitchell, Baltimore	289	1,193	4.1	70	11
	Jim Otis, St. Louis	269	1,076	4.0	30	5
	Chuck Foreman, Minnesota	280	1,070	3.8	31	13
	Greg Pruitt, Cleveland	217	1,067	4.9	50	8
	John Riggins, N.Y. Jets	238	1,005	4.2	42	8
	Dave Hampton, Atlanta	250	1,002	4.0	22	5
1976	O. J. Simpson, Buffalo5	290	1,503	5.2	75	8
	Walter Payton, Chicago	311	1,390	4.5	60	13
	Delvin Williams, San Francisco	248	1,203	4.9	80	7
	Lydell Mitchell, Baltimore2	289	1,200	4.2	43	5
	Lawrence McCutcheon, Los Angeles3	291	1,168	4.0	40	9
	Chuck Foreman, Minnesota2	278	1,155	4.2	46	13
	Franco Harris, Pittsburgh4	289	1,128	3.9	30	14
	Mike Thomas, Washington	254	1,101	4.3	28	5
	Rocky Bleier, Pittsburgh	220	1,036	4.7	28	5
	Mark van Eeghen, Oakland	233	1,012	4.3	21	3
	Otis Armstrong, Denver2	247	1,008	4.1	31	5
	Greg Pruitt, Cleveland2	209	1,000	4.8	64	4

Bold face—first year in the league.

Joe Perry, San Francisco 49ers

Dick Bass, Los Angeles Rams

Walter Payton, Chicago Bears

200 YARDS RUSHING IN A GAME

Date	Player, Team, Opponent	Att.	Yards	TD
Oct. 8, 1933	Cliff Battles, Bos. Redskins vs. N.Y. Giants	16	215	1
Nov. 27, 1949	Steve Van Buren, Philadelphia vs. Pittsburgh	27	205	0
Nov. 12, 1950	Gene Roberts, N.Y. Giants vs. Chi. Cardinals	26	218	2
Nov. 22, 1953	Dan Towler, Los Angeles vs. Baltimore	14	205	1
Dec. 16, 1956	Tom Wilson, Los Angeles vs. Green Bay	23	223	0
Nov. 24, 1957	Jim Brown, Cleveland vs. Los Angeles	31	237	4
Nov. 15, 1959	Bobby Mitchell, Cleveland vs. Washington	14	232	3
Dec. 18, 1960	John David Crow, St. Louis vs. Pittsburgh	24	203	0
Nov. 19, 1961	Jim Brown, Cleveland vs. Philadelphia	34	237	4
Dec. 10, 1961	Billy Cannon, Houston vs. N.Y. Titans	25	216	3
Sept. 22, 1963	Jim Brown, Cleveland vs. Dallas	20	232	2
Oct. 20, 1963	Clemon Daniels, Oakland vs. N.Y. Jets	27	200	2
Nov. 3, 1963	Jim Brown, Cleveland vs. Philadelphia	28	223	1
Dec. 8, 1963	Cookie Gilchrist, Buffalo vs. N.Y. Jets	36	243	5
Oct. 10, 1964	John Henry Johnson, Pittsburgh vs. Cleveland	30	200	3
Oct. 30, 1966	Jim Nance, Boston vs. Oakland	38	208	2
Nov. 3, 1968	Gale Sayers, Chicago vs. Green Bay	24	205	0
Dec. 20, 1970	John (Frenchy) Fuqua, Pittsburgh vs. Philadelphia	20	218	2
Dec. 5, 1971	Willie Ellison, Los Angeles vs. New Orleans	26	247	1
Sept. 16, 1973	O.J. Simpson, Buffalo vs. New England	29	250	2
Dec. 9, 1973	O.J. Simpson, Buffalo vs. New England	22	219	1
Dec. 16, 1973	O.J. Simpson, Buffalo vs. N.Y. Jets	34	200	1
Sept. 28, 1975	O.J. Simpson, Buffalo vs. Pittsburgh	28	227	1
Dec. 14, 1975	Greg Pruitt, Cleveland vs. Kansas City	26	214	3
Oct. 24, 1976	Chuck Foreman, Minnesota vs. Philadelphia	28	200	2
Nov. 25, 1976	O.J. Simpson, Buffalo vs. Detroit	29	273	2
Dec. 5, 1976	O.J. Simpson, Buffalo vs. Miami	24	203	1

400 YARDS PASSING IN A GAME

Date	Player, Team, Opponent	Att.	Comp.	Yards	TD
Nov. 14, 1943	Sid Luckman, Chi. Bears vs. N.Y. Giants	32	21	433	7
Oct. 31, 1948	Sammy Baugh, Washington vs. Boston Yanks	24	17	446	4
Oct. 31, 1948	Jim Hardy, Los Angeles vs. Chi. Cardinals	53	28	406	3
Dec. 11, 1949	Johnny Lujack, Chi. Bears vs. Chi. Cardinals	39	24	468	6
Sept. 28, 1951	Norm Van Brocklin, Los Angeles vs. N.Y. Yanks	41	27	554	5
Oct. 4, 1952	Otto Graham, Cleveland vs. Pittsburgh	49	21	401	3
Nov. 8, 1953	Bobby Thomason, Philadelphia vs. N.Y. Giants	44	22	437	4
Dec. 13, 1958	Bobby Layne, Pittsburgh vs. Chi. Cardinals	49	23	409	2
Oct. 13, 1961	Jacky Lee, Houston vs. Boston	41	27	457	2
Oct. 29, 1961	George Blanda, Houston vs. Buffalo	32	18	464	4
Oct. 29, 1961	Sonny Jurgensen, Philadelphia vs. Washington	41	27	436	3
Nov. 19, 1961	George Blanda, Houston vs. N.Y. Titans	32	20	418	7
Dec. 17, 1961	Sonny Jurgensen, Philadelphia vs. Detroit	42	27	403	3
Sept. 15, 1962	Frank Tripucka, Denver vs. Buffalo	56	29	447	2
Oct. 28, 1962	Y.A. Tittle, N.Y. Giants vs. Washington	39	27	505	7
Nov. 18, 1962	Billy Wade, Chicago vs. Dallas	46	28	466	2
Dec. 16, 1962	Sonny Jurgensen, Philadelphia vs. St. Louis	34	15	419	5
Oct. 13, 1963	Charley Johnson, St. Louis vs. Pittsburgh	41	20	428	2
Nov. 10, 1963	Don Meredith, Dallas vs. San Francisco	48	30	460	3
Nov. 17, 1963	Norm Snead, Washington vs. Pittsburgh	40	23	424	2
Dec. 22, 1963	Tom Flores, Oakland vs. Houston	29	17	407	6
Oct. 16, 1964	Babe Parilli, Boston vs. Oakland	47	25	422	4
Oct. 25, 1964	Cotton Davidson, Oakland vs. Denver	36	23	427	5
Nov. 1, 1964	Len Dawson, Kansas City vs. Denver	38	23	435	6
Oct. 24, 1965	Fran Tarkenton, Minnesota vs. San Francisco	35	21	407	3
Nov. 28, 1965	Sonny Jurgensen, Washington vs. Dallas	43	26	411	3
Nov. 13, 1966	Don Meredith, Dallas vs. Washington	29	21	406	2
Sept. 17, 1967	John Unitas, Baltimore vs. Atlanta	32	22	401	2
Oct. 1, 1967	Joe Namath, N.Y. Jets vs. Miami	39	23	415	3
Nov. 26, 1967	Sonny Jurgensen, Washington vs. Cleveland	50	32	418	3
Sept. 9, 1968	Pete Beathard, Houston vs. Kansas City	48	23	413	2
Sept. 28, 1969	Joe Kapp, Minnesota vs. Baltimore	43	28	449	7
Dec. 21, 1969	Don Horn, Green Bay vs. St. Louis	31	22	410	5
Sept. 24, 1972	Joe Namath, N.Y. Jets vs. Baltimore	28	15	496	6
Dec. 11, 1972	Joe Namath, N.Y. Jets vs. Oakland	46	25	403	1
Nov. 18, 1974	Charley Johnson, Denver vs. Kansas City	42	28	445	2
Nov. 17, 1975	Ken Anderson, Cincinnati vs. Buffalo	46	30	447	2
Oct. 3, 1976	James Harris, Los Angeles vs. Miami	29	17	436	2

O.J. Simpson, Buffalo Bills

Sonny Jurgensen, Washington Redskins

Charley Johnson, Denver Broncos

Joe Namath, New York Jets

1,200 YARDS RECEIVING IN A SEASON

Year	Player, Team	No.	Yards	Avg.	Long	TD
1942	Don Hutson, Green Bay	74	1,211	16.4	73	17
1951	Elroy (Crazylegs) Hirsch, Los Angeles	66	1,495	22.7	91	17
1952	**Billy Howton, Green Bay**	53	1,231	23.2	90	13
1954	Bob Boyd, Los Angeles	53	1,212	22.9	80	6
1960	**Bill Groman, Houston**	72	1,473	20.5	92	12
	Raymond Berry, Baltimore	74	1,298	17.5	70	10
	Don Maynard, N.Y. Titans	72	1,265	17.6	65	6
	Lionel Taylor, Denver	92	1,235	13.4	80	12
1961	Charley Hennigan, Houston	82	1,746	21.3	80	12
1962	Bobby Mitchell, Washington	72	1,384	19.2	81	11
1963	Bobby Mitchell, Washington	69	1,436	20.8	99	7
	Art Powell, Oakland	73	1,304	17.9	85	16
	Buddy Dial, Pittsburgh	60	1,295	21.6	83	9
1963	Lance Alworth, San Diego	61	1,205	19.8	85	11
1964	Charley Hennigan, Houston	101	1,546	15.3	53	8
	Art Powell, Oakland	76	1,361	17.9	77	11
	Lance Alworth, San Diego	61	1,235	20.2	82	13
	Johnny Morris, Chicago	93	1,200	12.9	63	10
1965	Lance Alworth, San Diego	69	1,602	23.2	85	14
	Dave Parks, San Francisco	80	1,344	16.8	53	12
	Don Maynard, N.Y. Jets	68	1,218	17.9	56	14
1966	Lance Alworth, San Diego	73	1,383	18.9	78	13
	Otis Taylor, Kansas City	58	1,297	22.4	89	8
	Pat Studstill, Detroit	67	1,266	18.9	99	5
	Bob Hayes, Dallas	64	1,232	19.3	95	13
1967	Don Maynard, N.Y. Jets	71	1,434	20.2	75	10
	Ben Hawkins, Philadelphia	59	1,265	21.4	87	10
	Homer Jones, N.Y. Giants	49	1,209	24.7	70	13
	Jackie Smith, St. Louis	56	1,205	21.5	76	9
1968	Lance Alworth, San Diego	68	1,312	19.3	80	10
	Don Maynard, N.Y. Jets	57	1,297	22.8	87	10
1969	Warren Wells, Oakland	47	1,260	26.8	80	14

Bob Boyd, Los Angeles Rams

250 YARDS RECEIVING IN A GAME

Date	Player, Team, Opponent	No.	Yards	TD
Nov. 22, 1945	Jim Benton, Cleveland vs. Detroit	10	303	1
Dec. 3, 1950	Cloyce Box, Detroit vs. Baltimore	12	302	4
Oct. 21, 1956	Billy Howton, Green Bay vs. Los Angeles	7	257	2
Oct. 13, 1961	Charley Hennigan, Houston vs. Boston	13	272	1
Oct. 28, 1962	Del Shofner, N.Y. Giants vs. Washington	11	269	1
Nov. 4, 1962	Sonny Randle, St. Louis vs. N.Y. Giants	16	256	1

2,000 COMBINED NET YARDS IN A SEASON

Year	Player, Team	Rushing Att-Yards	Pass Receptions	Punt Returns	Kickoff Returns	Fumble Runs	Total Yards
1960	**Abner Haynes, Dallas Texans**	156-875	55-576	14-215	19-434	4-0	248-2,100
1961	Billy Cannon, Houston	200-948	43-586	9-70	18-439	2-0	272-2,043
1962	Tim Brown, Philadelphia	137-545	52-849	6-81	30-831	4-0	229-2,306
	Dick Christy, N.Y. Titans	114-535	62-538	15-250	38-824	2-0	231-2,147
1963	Timmy Brown, Philadelphia	192-841	36-487	16-152	33-945	2-3	279-2,428
	Jim Brown, Cleveland	291-1,863	24-268	0-0	0-0	0-0	315-2,131
1965	**Gale Sayers, Chicago**	166-867	29-507	16-238	21-660	4-0	236-2,272
1966	Gale Sayers, Chicago	229-1,231	34-447	6-44	23-718	3-0	295-2,440
	Leroy Kelly, Cleveland	209-1,141	32-366	13-104	19-403	0-0	273-2,014
1973	O.J. Simpson, Buffalo	332-2,003	6-70	0-0	0-0	0-0	338-2,073
1974	Mack Herron, New England	231-824	38-474	35-517	28-629	3-0	335-2,444
	Otis Armstrong, Denver	263-1,407	38-405	0-0	16-386	1-0	318-2,198
	Terry Metcalf, St. Louis	152-718	50-377	26-340	20-623	7-0	255-2,058
1975	Terry Metcalf, St. Louis	165-816	43-378	23-285	35-960	2-23	268-2,462
	O.J. Simpson, Buffalo	329-1,817	28-426	0-0	0-0	1-0	358-2,243

Cloyce Box, Detroit Lions

300 COMBINED NET YARDS IN A GAME

Date	Player, Team, Opponent	No.	Yards	TD
Nov. 22, 1945	Jim Benton, Cleveland vs. Detroit	10	303	1
Oct. 29, 1950	Wally Triplett, Detroit vs. Los Angeles	11	331	1
Dec. 3, 1950	Cloyce Box, Detroit vs. Baltimore	13	302	4
Nov 19, 1961	Jim Brown, Cleveland vs. Philadelphia	38	313	4
Dec. 10, 1961	Billy Cannon, Houston vs. N.Y. Titans	32	373	5
Dec. 16, 1962	Timmy Brown, Philadelphia vs. St. Louis	19	341	2
Nov. 17, 1963	Gary Ballman, Pittsburgh vs. Washington	12	320	2
Dec. 12, 1965	Gale Sayers, Chicago vs. San Francisco	17	336	6
Dec. 18, 1966	Gale Sayers, Chicago vs. Minnesota	20	339	2
Nov. 2, 1969	Travis Williams, Green Bay vs. Pittsburgh	11	314	3
Dec. 6, 1969	Jerry LeVias, Houston vs. N.Y. Jets	18	329	1
Oct. 4, 1970	O.J. Simpson, Buffalo vs. N.Y. Jets	26	303	2
Nov. 1, 1970	Eugene (Mercury) Morris, Miami vs. Baltimore	17	302	0
Nov. 23, 1975	Greg Pruitt, Cleveland vs. Cincinnati	28	304	2
Dec. 21, 1975	Walter Payton, Chicago vs. New Orleans	32	300	1

TOP 10 RUSHERS

Player	Years	Att.	Yards	Avg.	Long	TD
Jim Brown	9	2,359	12,312	5.2	80	106
O.J. Simpson	8	1,997	9,626	4.8	94	57
Jim Taylor	10	1,941	8,597	4.4	84	83
Joe Perry	14	1,737	8,378	4.8	78	53
Leroy Kelly	10	1,727	7,274	4.2	70	74
John Henry Johnson	13	1,571	6,803	4.3	87	48
Larry Csonka	8	1,446	6,469	4.5	54	45
Floyd Little	9	1,641	6,323	3.9	80	43
Don Perkins	8	1,500	6,217	4.1	59	42
Ken Willard	10	1,622	6,105	3.8	69	45

Billy Cannon, Houston Oilers

Bold face—first year in the league.

TOP 20 PASSERS

Player	Years	Games	Att.	Comp.	Pct. Comp.	Yards	TD	Pct. TD	Int.	Pct. Int.	Avg. Gain	Rating
Ken Anderson	6	78	1,804	1,042	57.8	13,326	88	4.9	58	3.2	7.39	84.1
Sonny Jurgensen	18	218	4,262	2,433	57.1	32,224	255	6.0	189	4.4	7.56	82.8
Len Dawson	20	211	3,741	2,136	57.1	28,711	239	6.4	183	4.9	7.67	82.6
Fran Tarkenton	16	221	5,637	3,186	56.5	41,801	308	5.5	220	3.9	7.42	82.2
Bart Starr	16	196	3,149	1,808	57.4	24,718	152	4.8	138	4.4	7.85	80.3
Roger Staubach	8	86	1,723	977	56.7	13,304	83	4.8	73	4.2	7.72	80.0
John Unitas	18	211	5,186	2,830	54.6	40,239	290	5.6	253	4.9	7.76	78.2
Otto Graham	6	72	1,565	872	55.7	13,499	88	5.6	94	6.0	8.63	78.1
Frank Ryan	13	126	2,133	1,090	51.1	16,042	149	7.0	111	5.2	7.52	77.7
Bob Griese	10	117	2,477	1,361	54.9	18,099	139	5.6	128	5.2	7.31	75.3
Norm Van Brocklin	12	140	2,895	1,553	53.6	23,611	173	6.0	178	6.1	8.16	75.3
Sid Luckman	12	128	1,744	904	51.8	14,686	137	7.9	132	7.6	8.42	75.0
Don Meredith	9	104	2,308	1,170	50.7	17,199	135	5.8	111	4.8	7.45	74.7
Roman Gabriel	15	170	4,495	2,365	52.6	29,429	201	4.5	149	3.3	6.55	74.5
Earl Morrall	21	255	2,689	1,379	51.3	20,809	161	6.0	148	5.5	7.74	74.2
Y.A. Tittle	15	178	3,817	2,118	55.5	28,339	212	5.6	221	5.8	7.42	73.8
Daryle Lamonica	12	150	2,601	1,288	49.5	19,154	164	6.3	138	5.3	7.36	72.9
John Brodie	17	200	4,491	2,469	55.0	31,548	214	4.8	224	5.0	7.02	72.3
Bill Wade	13	128	2,523	1,370	54.3	18,530	124	4.9	134	5.3	7.34	72.2
Sammy Baugh	16	165	2,995	1,693	56.5	21,886	187	6.2	203	6.8	7.31	72.0

1,500 or more attempts. The passing ratings are based on performance standards established for completion percentage, interception percentage, touchdown percentage, and average gain. Passers are allocated points according to how their marks compare with those standards.

TOP 10 RECEIVERS

Player	Years	No.	Yards	Avg.	Long	TD
Charley Taylor	12	635	8,952	14.1	88	79
Don Maynard	15	633	11,834	18.7	87	88
Raymond Berry	13	631	9,275	14.7	70	68
Lionel Taylor	10	567	7,195	12.7	80	45
Lance Alworth	11	542	10,266	18.9	85	85
Fred Biletnikoff	12	536	8,243	15.4	82	69
Bobby Mitchell	11	521	7,954	15.3	99	65
Billy Howton	12	503	8,459	16.8	90	61
Tommy McDonald	12	495	8,410	17.0	91	84
Don Hutson	11	488	7,991	16.4	92	99

TOP 10 INTERCEPTORS

Player	Years	No.	Yards	Avg.	Long	TD
Emlen Tunnell	14	79	1,282	16.2	55	4
Paul Krause	13	76	1,111	14.6	81	3
Dick (Night Train) Lane	14	68	1,207	17.8	80	5
Dick LeBeau	13	62	762	12.3	70	3
Bobby Boyd	9	57	994	17.4	74	4
Johnny Robinson	12	57	741	13.0	57	1
Pat Fischer	16	56	941	16.8	69	4
Emmitt Thomas	11	55	937	17.0	73	5
Lem Barney	10	53	1,050	19.8	71	7
Bob Dillon	8	52	976	18.8	61	5
Jack Butler	9	52	826	15.9	52	4
Larry Wilson	13	52	800	15.4	96	5
Jim Patton	12	52	712	13.7	51	2

TOP 10 PUNTERS

Player	Years	No.	Yards	Avg.	Long	Blk.
Sammy Baugh	16	338	15,245	45.1	85	9
Tommy Davis	11	511	22,833	44.7	82	2
Yale Lary	11	503	22,279	44.3	74	4
Horace Gillom	7	385	16,872	43.8	80	5
Jerry Norton	11	358	15,671	43.8	78	2
Jerrel Wilson	14	930	40,708	43.8	72	11
Don Chandler	12	660	28,678	43.5	90	4
Norm Van Brocklin	12	523	22,413	42.9	72	3
Danny Villanueva	8	488	20,862	42.8	68	2
Bobby Joe Green	14	970	41,317	42.6	75	3

300 or more punts.

TOP 10 PUNT RETURNERS

Player	Years	No.	Yards	Avg.	Long	TD
Billy Johnson	3	108	1,424	13.2	83	3
George McAfee	8	112	1,431	12.8	74	2
Jack Christiansen	8	85	1,084	12.8	89	8
Claude Gibson	5	110	1,381	12.6	85	3
Neal Colzie	2	89	1,103	12.4	64	0
Bill Dudley	9	124	1,515	12.2	96	3
Mack Herron	3	84	982	11.7	66	0
Bill Thompson	8	156	1,811	11.6	60	0
Rodger Bird	3	94	1,063	11.3	78	0
Bosh Pritchard	6	95	1,072	11.3	81	2

75 or more returns.

TOP 10 KICKOFF RETURNERS

Player	Years	No.	Yards	Avg.	Long	TD
Gale Sayers	7	91	2,781	30.6	103	6
Lynn Chandnois	7	92	2,720	29.6	93	3
Abe Woodson	9	193	5,538	28.7	105	5
Claude (Buddy) Young	6	90	2,514	27.9	104	2
Travis Williams	5	102	2,801	27.5	105	6
Clarence Davis	6	76	2,077	27.3	76	0
Joe Arenas	7	139	3,798	27.3	96	1
Terry Metcalf	4	75	2,032	27.1	94	2
Steve Van Buren	8	76	2,030	26.7	98	3
Lenny Lyles	12	81	2,161	26.7	103	3

75 or more returns.

Larry Wilson, St. Louis Cardinals

Bill Thompson, Denver Broncos

Abe Woodson, San Francisco 49ers

TOP 10 SCORERS

Player	Years	TD	FG	PAT	TP
George Blanda	26	9	335	943	2.002
Lou Groza	17	1	234	641	1,349
Fred Cox	14	0	274	494	1,316
Jim Bakken	15	0	264	472	1,264
Jim Turner	13	0	267	427	1,228
Gino Cappelletti	11	42	176	350	1,130
Bruce Gossett	11	0	219	374	1,031
Jan Stenerud	10	0	239	314	1,031
Sam Baker	15	2	179	428	977
Lou Michaels	13	1	187	386	955

Cappelletti's total includes four two-point conversions; Michaels's includes a safety.

TOP 10 TOUCHDOWN SCORERS

Player	Years	Rush.	Pass Rec.	Returns	Total TD
Jim Brown	9	106	20	0	126
Lenny Moore	12	63	48	2	113
Don Hutson	11	3	99	3	105
Jim Taylor	10	83	10	0	93
Bobby Mitchell	11	18	65	8	91
Leroy Kelly	10	74	13	3	90
Charley Taylor	12	11	79	0	90
Don Maynard	15	0	88	0	88
Lance Alworth	11	2	85	0	87
Tommy McDonald	12	0	84	1	85

George Blanda, Oakland Raiders

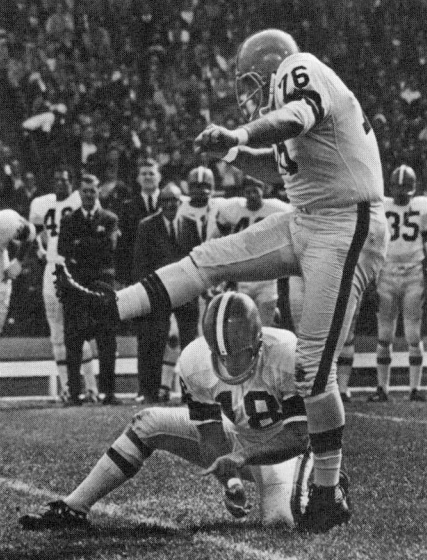

Lou Groza, Cleveland Browns

Lenny Moore, Baltimore Colts

Jim Brown, Cleveland Browns

Rick Casares, Chicago Bears

Len Dawson, Kansas City Chiefs

ANNUAL RUSHING LEADERS

Year	Player, Team	Att.	Yards	Avg.	TD
1932	**Cliff Battles, Boston Braves**	148	576	3.9	3
1933	Jim Musick, Boston Redskins	173	809	4.7	5
1934	**Beattie Feathers, Chi. Bears**	101	1,004	9.9	8
1935	Doug Russell, Chi. Cardinals	140	499	3.6	0
1936	**Alphonse (Tuffy) Leemans, N.Y. Giants**	206	830	4.0	2
1937	Cliff Battles, Washington	216	874	4.0	5
1938	**Byron (Whizzer) White, Pittsburgh**	152	567	3.7	4
1939	**Bill Osmanski, Chi. Bears**	121	699	5.8	7
1940	Byron (Whizzer) White, Detroit	146	514	3.5	5
1941	Clarence (Pug) Manders, Brooklyn	111	486	4.4	5
1942	**Bill Dudley, Pittsburgh**	162	696	4.3	5
1943	**Bill Paschal, N.Y. Giants**	147	572	3.9	10
1944	Bill Paschal, N.Y. Giants	196	737	3.8	9
1945	Steve Van Buren, Philadelphia	143	832	5.8	15
1946	Bill Dudley, Pittsburgh	146	604	4.1	3
1947	Steve Van Buren, Philadelphia	217	1,008	4.6	13
1948	Steve Van Buren, Philadelphia	201	945	4.7	10
1949	Steve Van Buren, Philadelphia	263	1,146	4.4	11
1950	**Marion Motley, Cleveland**	140	810	5.8	3
1951	Eddie Price, N.Y. Giants	271	971	3.6	7
1952	Dan Towler, Los Angeles	156	894	5.7	10
1953	Joe Perry, San Francisco	192	1,018	5.3	10
1954	Joe Perry, San Francisco	173	1,049	6.1	8
1955	**Alan Ameche, Baltimore**	213	961	4.5	9
1956	Rick Casares, Chi. Bears	234	1,126	4.8	12
1957	**Jim Brown, Cleveland**	202	942	4.7	9
1958	Jim Brown, Cleveland	257	1,527	5.9	17
1959	Jim Brown, Cleveland	290	1,329	4.6	14
1960	Jim Brown, Cleveland, NFL	215	1,257	5.8	9
	Abner Haynes, Dallas Texans, AFL	156	875	5.6	9
1961	Jim Brown, Cleveland, NFL	305	1,408	4.6	8
	Billy Cannon, Houston, AFL	200	948	4.7	6
1962	Jim Taylor, Green Bay, NFL	272	1,474	5.4	19
	Cookie Gilchrist, Buffalo, AFL	214	1,096	5.1	13
1963	Jim Brown, Cleveland, NFL	291	1,863	6.4	12
	Clemon Daniels, Oakland, AFL	215	1,099	5.1	3
1964	Jim Brown, Cleveland, NFL	280	1,446	5.1	7
	Cookie Gilchrist, Buffalo, AFL	230	981	4.3	6
1965	Jim Brown, Cleveland, NFL	289	1,544	5.3	17
	Paul Lowe, San Diego, AFL	222	1,121	5.0	7
1966	Jim Nance, Boston, AFL	299	1,458	4.9	11
	Gale Sayers, Chicago, NFL	229	1,231	5.4	8
1967	Jim Nance, Boston, AFL	269	1,216	4.5	7
	Leroy Kelly, Cleveland, NFL	235	1,205	5.1	11
1968	Leroy Kelly, Cleveland, NFL	248	1,239	5.0	16
	Paul Robinson, Cincinnati, AFL	238	1,023	4.3	8
1969	Gale Sayers, Chicago, NFL	236	1,032	4.4	8
	Dickie Post, San Diego, AFL	182	873	4.8	6
1970	Larry Brown, Washington, NFC	237	1,125	4.7	5
	Floyd Little, Denver, AFC	209	901	4.3	3
1971	Floyd Little, Denver, AFC	284	1,133	4.0	6
	John Brockington, Green Bay, NFC	216	1,105	5.1	4
1972	O.J. Simpson, Buffalo, AFC	292	1,251	4.3	6
	Larry Brown, Washington, NFC	285	1,216	4.3	8
1973	O.J. Simpson, Buffalo, AFC	332	2,003	6.0	12
	John Brockington, Green Bay, NFC	265	1,144	4.3	3
1974	Otis Armstrong, Denver, AFC	263	1,407	5.3	9
	Lawrence McCutcheon, Los Angeles, NFC	236	1,109	4.7	3
1975	O.J. Simpson, Buffalo, AFC	329	1,817	5.5	16
	Jim Otis, St. Louis, NFC	269	1,076	4.0	5
1976	O.J. Simpson, Buffalo, AFC	290	1,503	5.2	8
	Walter Payton, Chicago, NFC	311	1,390	4.5	13

Bold face—first year in the league.

PASSING

Year	Player, Team	Att.	Comp.	Yards	TD	Int.
1932	Arnie Herber, Green Bay	101	37	639	9	9
1933	**Harry Newman, N.Y. Giants**	136	53	973	11	17
1934	Arnie Herber, Green Bay	115	42	799	8	12
1935	Ed Danowski, N.Y. Giants	113	57	794	10	9
1936	Arnie Herber, Green Bay	173	77	1,239	11	13
1937	**Sammy Baugh, Washington**	171	81	1,127	8	14
1938	Ed Danowski, N.Y. Giants	129	70	848	7	8
1939	**Parker Hall, Cleveland Rams**	208	106	1,227	9	13
1940	Sammy Baugh, Washington	177	111	1,367	12	10
1941	Cecil Isbell, Green Bay	206	117	1,479	15	11
1942	Cecil Isbell, Green Bay	268	146	2,021	24	14
1943	Sammy Baugh, Washington	239	133	1,754	23	19
1944	Frank Filchock, Washington	147	84	1,139	13	9
1945	Sammy Baugh, Washington	182	128	1,669	11	4
	Sid Luckman, Chi. Bears	217	117	1,725	14	10
1946	Bob Waterfield, Los Angeles	251	127	1,747	18	17
1947	Sammy Baugh, Washington	354	210	2,938	25	15
1948	Tommy Thompson, Philadelphia	246	141	1,965	25	11
1949	Sammy Baugh, Washington	255	145	1,903	18	14
1950	Norm Van Brocklin, Los Angeles	233	127	2,061	18	14
1951	Bob Waterfield, Los Angeles	176	88	1,566	13	10
1952	Norm Van Brocklin, Los Angeles	205	113	1,736	14	17
1953	Otto Graham, Cleveland	258	167	2,722	11	9
1954	Norm Van Brocklin, Los Angeles	260	139	2,637	13	21
1955	Otto Graham, Cleveland	185	98	1,721	15	8
1956	Ed Brown, Chi. Bears	168	96	1,667	11	12
1957	Tommy O'Connell, Cleveland	110	63	1,229	9	8
1958	Eddie LeBaron, Washington	145	79	1,365	11	10
1959	Charlie Conerly, N.Y. Giants	194	113	1,706	14	4
1960	Milt Plum, Cleveland, NFL	250	151	2,297	21	5
	Jack Kemp, L.A. Chargers, AFL	406	211	3,018	20	25
1961	George Blanda, Houston, AFL	362	187	3,330	36	22
	Milt Plum, Cleveland, NFL	302	177	2,416	18	10
1962	Len Dawson, Dallas, AFL	310	189	2,759	29	17
	Bart Starr, Green Bay, NFL	285	178	2,438	12	9
1963	Y.A. Tittle, N.Y. Giants, NFL	367	221	3,145	36	14
	Tobin Rote, San Diego, AFL	286	170	2,510	20	17
1964	Len Dawson, Kansas City, AFL	354	199	2,879	30	18
	Bart Starr, Green Bay, NFL	272	163	2,144	15	4
1965	Rudy Bukich, Chicago, NFL	312	176	2,641	20	9
	John Hadl, San Diego, AFL	348	174	2,798	20	21
1966	Bart Starr, Green Bay, NFL	251	156	2,257	14	3
	Len Dawson, Kansas City, AFL	284	159	2,527	26	10
1967	Sonny Jurgensen, Washington, NFL	508	288	3,747	31	16
	Daryle Lamonica, Oakland, AFL	425	220	3,228	30	20
1968	Len Dawson, Kansas City, AFL	224	131	2,109	17	9
	Earl Morrall, Baltimore, NFL	317	182	2,909	26	17
1969	Sonny Jurgensen, Washington, NFL	442	274	3,102	22	15
	Greg Cook, Cincinnati, AFL	197	106	1,854	15	11
1970	John Brodie, San Francisco, NFC	378	223	2,941	24	10
	Daryle Lamonica, Oakland, AFC	356	179	2,516	22	15
1971	Roger Staubach, Dallas, NFC	211	126	1,882	15	4
	Bob Griese, Miami, AFC	263	145	2,089	19	9
1972	Norm Snead, N.Y. Giants, NFC	325	196	2,307	17	12
	Earl Morrall, Miami, AFC	150	83	1,360	11	7
1973	Roger Staubach, Dallas, NFC	286	179	2,428	23	15
	Ken Stabler, Oakland, AFC	260	163	1,997	14	10
1974	Ken Anderson, Cincinnati, AFC	328	213	2,667	18	10
	Sonny Jurgensen, Washington, NFC	167	107	1,185	11	5
1975	Ken Anderson, Cincinnati, AFC	377	228	3,169	21	11
	Fran Tarkenton, Minnesota, NFC	425	273	2,994	25	13
1976	Ken Stabler, Oakland, AFC	291	194	2,737	27	17
	James Harris, Los Angeles, NFC	158	91	1,460	8	6

Charley Taylor, Washington Redskins

Bill Bradley, Philadelphia Eagles

PASS RECEIVING

Year	Player, Team	No.	Yards	Avg.	TD
1932	Ray Flaherty, N.Y. Giants	21	350	16.7	3
1933	John (Shipwreck) Kelly, Brooklyn	22	246	11.2	3
1934	Joe Carter, Philadelphia	16	238	14.9	4
	Morris (Red) Badgro, N.Y. Giants	16	206	12.9	1
1935	**Tod Goodwin, N.Y. Giants**	26	432	16.6	4
1936	Don Hutson, Green Bay	34	536	15.8	8
1937	Don Hutson, Green Bay	41	552	13.5	7
1938	Gaynell Tinsley, Chi. Cardinals	41	516	12.6	1
1939	Don Hutson, Green Bay	34	846	24.9	6
1940	**Don Looney, Philadelphia**	58	707	12.2	4
1941	Don Hutson, Green Bay	58	738	12.7	10
1942	Don Hutson, Green Bay	74	1,211	16.4	17
1943	Don Hutson, Green Bay	47	776	16.5	11
1944	Don Hutson, Green Bay	58	866	14.9	9
1945	Don Hutson, Green Bay	47	834	17.7	9
1946	Jim Benton, Los Angeles	63	981	15.6	6
1947	Jim Keane, Chi. Bears	64	910	14.2	10
1948	**Tom Fears, Los Angeles**	51	698	13.7	4
1949	Tom Fears, Los Angeles	77	1,013	13.2	9
1950	Tom Fears, Los Angeles	84	1,116	13.3	7
1951	Elroy (Crazylegs) Hirsch, Los Angeles	66	1,495	22.7	17
1952	Mac Speedie, Cleveland	62	911	14.7	5
1953	Pete Pihos, Philadelphia	63	1,049	16.7	10
1954	Pete Pihos, Philadelphia	60	872	14.5	10
	Billy Wilson, San Francisco	60	830	13.8	5
1955	Pete Pihos, Philadelphia	62	864	13.9	7
1956	Billy Wilson, San Francisco	60	889	14.8	5
1957	Billy Wilson, San Francisco	52	757	14.6	6
1958	Raymond Berry, Baltimore	56	794	14.2	9
	Pete Retzlaff, Philadelphia	56	766	13.7	2
1959	Raymond Berry, Baltimore	66	959	14.5	14
1960	Lionel Taylor, Denver, AFL	92	1,235	13.4	12
	Raymond Berry, Baltimore, NFL	74	1,298	17.5	10
1961	Lionel Taylor, Denver, AFL	100	1,176	11.8	4
	Jim (Red) Phillips, Los Angeles, NFL	78	1,092	14.0	5
1962	Lionel Taylor, Denver, AFL	77	908	11.8	4
	Bobby Mitchell, Washington, NFL	72	1,384	19.2	11
1963	Lionel Taylor, Denver, AFL	78	1,101	14.1	10
	Bobby Joe Conrad, St. Louis, NFL	73	967	13.2	10
1964	Charley Hennigan, Houston, AFL	101	1,546	15.3	8
	Johnny Morris, Chicago, NFL	93	1,200	12.9	10
1965	Lionel Taylor, Denver, AFL	85	1,131	13.3	6
	Dave Parks, San Francisco, NFL	80	1,344	16.8	12
1966	Lance Alworth, San Diego, AFL	73	1,383	18.9	13
	Charley Taylor, Washington, NFL	72	1,119	15.5	12
1967	George Sauer, N.Y. Jets, AFL	75	1,189	15.9	6
	Charley Taylor, Washington, NFL	70	990	14.1	9
1968	Clifton McNeil, San Francisco, NFL	71	994	14.0	7
	Lance Alworth, San Diego, AFL	68	1,312	19.3	10
1969	Dan Abramowicz, New Orleans, NFL	73	1,015	13.9	7
	Lance Alworth, San Diego, AFL	64	1,003	15.7	4
1970	Dick Gordon, Chicago, NFC	71	1,026	14.5	13
	Marlin Briscoe, Buffalo, AFC	57	1,036	18.2	8
1971	Fred Biletnikoff, Oakland, AFC	61	929	15.2	9
	Bob Tucker, N.Y. Giants, NFC	59	791	13.4	4
1972	Harold Jackson, Philadelphia, NFC	62	1,048	16.9	4
	Fred Biletnikoff, Oakland, AFC	58	802	13.8	7
1973	Harold Carmichael, Philadelphia, NFC	67	1,116	16.7	9
	Fred Willis, Houston, AFC	57	371	6.5	1
1974	Lydell Mitchell, Baltimore, AFC	72	544	7.6	2
	Charles Young, Philadelphia, NFC	63	696	11.0	3
1975	Chuck Foreman, Minnesota, NFC	73	691	9.5	9
	Reggie Rucker, Cleveland, AFC	60	770	12.8	3
	Lydell Mitchell, Baltimore, AFC	60	544	9.1	4
1976	MacArthur Lane, Kansas City, AFC	66	686	10.4	1
	Drew Pearson, Dallas, NFC	58	806	13.9	6

Bold face—first year in the league.

INTERCEPTIONS

Year	Player, Team	No.	Yards	TD
1940	Clarence (Ace) Parker, Brooklyn	6	146	1
	Kent Ryan, Detroit	6	65	0
	Don Hutson, Green Bay	6	24	0
1941	Marshall Goldberg, Chi. Cardinals	7	54	0
	Art Jones, Pittsburgh	7	35	0
1942	**Clyde (Bulldog) Turner, Chi. Bears**	8	96	1
1943	Sammy Baugh, Washington	11	112	0
1944	**Howard Livingston, N.Y. Giants**	9	172	1
1945	Roy Zimmerman, Philadelphia	7	90	0
1946	Bill Dudley, Pittsburgh	10	242	1
1947	Frank Reagan, N.Y. Giants	10	203	0
	Frank Seno, Boston Yanks	10	100	0
1948	**Dan Sandifer, Washington**	13	258	2
1949	Bob Nussbaumer, Chi. Cardinals	12	157	0
1950	**Orban (Spec) Sanders, N.Y. Yanks**	13	199	0
1951	Otto Schnellbacher, N.Y. Giants	11	194	2
1952	**Dick (Night Train) Lane, Los Angeles**	14	298	2
1953	Jack Christiansen, Detroit	12	238	1
1954	Dick (Night Train) Lane, Chi. Cardinals	10	181	0
1955	Will Sherman, Los Angeles	11	101	0
1956	Lindon Crow, Chi. Cardinals	11	170	0
1957	**Milt Davis, Baltimore**	10	219	2
	Jack Christiansen, Detroit	10	137	1
	Jack Butler, Pittsburgh	10	85	0
1958	Jim Patton, N.Y. Giants	11	183	0
1959	Dean Derby, Pittsburgh	7	127	0
	Milt Davis, Baltimore	7	119	1
	Don Shinnick, Baltimore	7	70	0
1960	**Austin (Goose) Gonsoulin, Denver, AFL**	11	98	0
	Dave Baker, San Francisco, NFL	10	96	0
	Jerry Norton, St. Louis, NFL	10	96	0
1961	Billy Atkins, Buffalo, AFL	10	158	0
	Dick Lynch, N.Y. Giants, NFL	9	60	0
1962	Lee Riley, N.Y. Titans, AFL	11	122	0
	Willie Wood, Green Bay, NFL	9	132	0
1963	Fred Glick, Houston, AFL	12	180	1
	Dick Lynch, N.Y. Giants, NFL	9	251	3
	Roosevelt Taylor, Chicago, NFL	9	172	1
1964	Dainard Paulson, N.Y. Jets, AFL	12	157	1
	Paul Krause, Washington, NFL	12	140	1
1965	W.K. Hicks, Houston, AFL	9	156	0
	Bob Boyd, Baltimore, NFL	9	78	1
1966	Larry Wilson, St. Louis, NFL	10	180	2
	Johnny Robinson, Kansas City, AFL	10	136	1
	Bobby Hunt, Kansas City, AFL	10	113	0
1967	Miller Farr, Houston, AFL	10	264	3
	Lem Barney, Detroit, NFL	10	232	3
	Tom Janik, Buffalo, AFL	10	222	2
	Dave Whitsell, New Orleans, NFL	10	178	2
	Dick Westmoreland, Miami, AFL	10	127	1
1968	Dave Grayson, Oakland, AFL	10	195	1
	Willie Williams, N.Y. Giants, NFL	10	103	0
1969	Mel Renfro, Dallas, NFL	10	118	0
	Emmitt Thomas, Kansas City, AFL	9	146	1
1970	Johnny Robinson, Kansas City, AFC	10	155	0
	Dick LeBeau, Detroit, NFC	9	96	0
1971	Bill Bradley, Philadelphia, NFC	11	248	0
	Ken Houston, Houston, AFC	9	220	4
1972	Bill Bradley, Philadelphia, NFC	9	73	0
	Mike Sensibaugh, Kansas City, AFC	8	65	0
1973	Dick Anderson, Miami, AFC	8	163	2
	Mike Wagner, Pittsburgh, AFC	8	134	0
	Bobby Bryant, Minnesota, NFC	7	105	1
1974	Emmitt Thomas, Kansas City, AFC	12	214	2
	Ray Brown, Atlanta, NFC	8	164	1
1975	Mel Blount, Pittsburgh, AFC	11	121	0
	Paul Krause, Minnesota, NFC	10	201	0
1976	Monte Jackson, Los Angeles, NFC	10	173	3
	Ken Riley, Cincinnati, AFC	9	141	1

PUNTING

Year	Player, Team	No.	Avg.	Long
1939	**Parker Hall, Cleveland Rams**	58	40.8	80
1940	Sammy Baugh, Washington	35	51.4	85
1941	Sammy Baugh, Washington	30	48.7	75
1942	Sammy Baugh, Washington	37	48.2	74
1943	Sammy Baugh, Washington	50	45.9	81
1944	Frank Sinkwich, Detroit	45	41.0*	73
1945	Roy McKay, Green Bay	44	41.2	73
1946	Roy McKay, Green Bay	64	42.7	64
1947	Jack Jacobs, Green Bay	57	43.5	74
1948	Joe Muha, Philadelphia	57	47.3	82
1949	**Mike Boyda, N.Y. Bulldogs**	56	44.2	61
1950	**Fred (Curly) Morrison, Chi. Bears**	57	43.3	65
1951	Horace Gillom, Cleveland	73	45.5	66
1952	Horace Gillom, Cleveland	61	45.7	73
1953	Pat Brady, Pittsburgh	80	46.9	64
1954	Pat Brady, Pittsburgh	66	43.2	72
1955	Norm Van Brocklin, Los Angeles	60	44.6	61
1956	Norm Van Brocklin, Los Angeles	48	43.1	72
1957	Don Chandler, N.Y. Giants	60	44.6	61
1958	Sam Baker, Washington	48	45.4	64
1959	Yale Lary, Detroit	45	47.1	67
1960	Jerry Norton, St. Louis, NFL	39	45.6	62
	Paul Maguire, Los Angeles, AFL	43	40.5	61
1961	Yale Lary, Detroit, NFL	52	48.4	71
	Billy Atkins, Buffalo, AFL	85	44.5	70
1962	Tommy Davis, San Francisco, NFL	48	45.6	82
	Jim Fraser, Denver, AFL	55	43.6	75
1963	Yale Lary, Detroit, NFL	35	48.9	73
	Jim Fraser, Denver, AFL	81	44.4	66
1964	**Bobby Walden, Minnesota, NFL**	72	46.4	73
	Jim Fraser, Denver, AFL	73	44.2	67
1965	Gary Collins, Cleveland, NFL	65	46.7	71
	Jerrel Wilson, Kansas City, AFL	69	45.4	64
1966	Bob Scarpitto, Denver, AFL	76	45.8	70
	David Lee, Baltimore, NFL	49	45.6	64
1967	Bob Scarpitto, Denver, AFL	105	44.9	73
	Billy Lothridge, Atlanta, NFL	87	43.7	62
1968	Jerrel Wilson, Kansas City, AFL	63	45.1	70
	Billy Lothridge, Atlanta, NFL	75	44.3	70
1969	David Lee, Baltimore, NFL	57	45.3	66
	Dennis Partee, San Diego, AFL	71	44.6	62
1970	**Dave Lewis, Cincinnati, AFC**	79	46.2	63
	Julian Fagan, New Orleans, NFC	77	42.5	64
1971	Dave Lewis, Cincinnati, AFC	72	44.8	56
	Tom McNeill, Philadelphia, NFC	73	42.0	64
1972	Jerrel Wilson, Kansas City, AFC	66	44.8	69
	Dave Chapple, Los Angeles, NFC	53	44.2	70
1973	Jerrel Wilson, Kansas City, AFC	80	45.5	68
	Tom Wittum, San Francisco, NFC	79	43.7	62
1974	Ray Guy, Oakland, AFC	74	42.2	66
	Tom Blanchard, New Orleans, NFC	88	42.1	71
1975	Ray Guy, Oakland, AFC	68	43.8	64
	Herman Weaver, Detroit, NFC	80	42.0	61
1976	Marv Bateman, Buffalo, AFC	86	42.8	78
	John James, Atlanta, NFC	101	42.1	67

PUNT RETURNS

Year	Player, Team	No.	Yards	Avg.	Long	TD
1941	Byron (Whizzer) White, Detroit	19	262	13.8	64	0
1942	Merlyn Condit, Brooklyn	21	210	10.0	23	0
1943	Andy Farkas, Washington	15	168	11.2	33	0
1944	**Steve Van Buren, Philadelphia**	15	230	15.3	55	1
1945	**Dave Ryan, Detroit**	15	220	14.7	56	0
1946	Bill Dudley, Pittsburgh	27	385	14.3	52	0
1947	Walt Slater, Pittsburgh	28	435	15.5	33	0
1948	George McAfee, Chi. Bears	30	417	13.9	60	1
1949	Verda (Vitamin T) Smith, Los Angeles	27	427	15.8	85	1
1950	**Herb Rich, Baltimore**	12	276	23.0	86	1
1951	Claude (Buddy) Young, N.Y. Yanks	12	231	19.3	79	1
1952	Jack Christiansen, Detroit	15	322	21.5	79	2
1953	Charley Trippi, Chi. Cardinals	21	239	11.4	38	0
1954	**Veryl Switzer, Green Bay**	24	306	12.8	93	1
1955	Ollie Matson, Chi. Cardinals	13	245	18.8	78	2
1956	Ken Konz, Cleveland	13	187	14.4	65	1
1957	Bert Zagers, Washington	14	217	15.5	76	2
1958	Jon Arnett, Los Angeles	18	223	12.4	58	0
1959	Johnny Morris, Chi. Bears	14	171	12.2	78	1
1960	**Abner Haynes, Dallas Texans, AFL**	14	215	15.4	46	0
	Abe Woodson, San Francisco, NFL	13	174	13.4	48	0
1961	Dick Christy, N.Y. Titans, AFL	18	383	21.3	70	2
	Willie Wood, Green Bay, NFL	14	225	16.1	72	2
1962	Dick Christy, N.Y. Titans, AFL	15	250	16.7	73	2
	Pat Studstill, Detroit, NFL	29	457	15.8	44	0
1963	Dick James, Washington, NFL	16	214	13.4	39	0
	Claude Gibson, Oakland, AFL	26	307	11.8	85	2
1964	Bobby Jancik, Houston, AFL	12	220	18.3	82	1
	Tommy Watkins, Detroit, NFL	16	238	14.9	68	2
1965	Leroy Kelly, Cleveland, NFL	17	265	15.6	67	2
	Leslie (Speedy) Duncan, San Diego, AFL	30	464	15.5	66	2
1966	Leslie (Speedy) Duncan, San Diego, AFL	18	238	13.2	81	1
	Johnny Roland, St. Louis, NFL	20	221	11.1	86	1
1967	Floyd Little, Denver, AFL	16	270	16.9	72	1
	Ben Davis, Cleveland, NFL	18	229	12.7	52	1
1968	Bob Hayes, Dallas, NFL	15	312	20.8	90	2
	Noland Smith, Kansas City, AFL	18	270	15.0	80	1
1969	Alvin Haymond, Los Angeles, NFL	33	435	13.2	52	0
	Bill Thompson, Denver, AFL	25	288	11.5	40	0
1970	Ed Podolak, Kansas City, AFC	23	311	13.5	60	0
	Bruce Taylor, San Francisco, NFC	43	516	12.0	76	0
1971	Leslie (Speedy) Duncan, Washington, NFC	22	233	10.6	33	0
	Leroy Kelly, Cleveland, AFC	30	292	9.7	74	0
1972	**Ken Ellis, Green Bay, NFC**	14	215	15.4	80	1
	Chris Farasopoulos, N.Y. Jets, AFC	17	179	10.5	65	1
1973	Bruce Taylor, San Francisco, NFC	15	207	13.8	61	0
	Ron Smith, San Diego, AFC	27	352	13.0	84	2
1974	Lemar Parrish, Cincinnati, AFC	18	338	18.8	90	2
	Dick Jauron, Detroit, NFC	17	286	16.8	58	0
1975	Billy Johnson, Houston, AFC	40	612	15.3	83	3
	Terry Metcalf, St. Louis, NFC	23	285	12.4	69	1
1976	Rick Upchurch, Denver, AFC	39	536	13.7	92	4
	Eddie Brown, Washington, NFC	48	646	13.5	71	1

Jerrel Wilson, Kansas City Chiefs

Leslie (Speedy) Duncan, San Diego Chargers

Al Carmichael, Green Bay Packers

Travis Williams, Green Bay Packers

KICKOFF RETURNS

Year	Player, Team	No.	Yards	Avg.	Long	TD
1941	Marshall Goldberg, Chi. Cardinals	12	290	24.2	41	0
1942	Marshall Goldberg, Chi. Cardinals	15	393	26.2	95	1
1943	Ken Heineman, Brooklyn	16	444	27.8	69	0
1944	Bob Thurbon, Card–Pitt	12	291	24.3	55	0
1945	Steve Van Buren, Philadelphia	13	373	28.7	98	1
1946	Abe Karnofsky, Boston Yanks	21	599	28.5	97	1
1947	Ed Saenz, Washington	29	797	27.4	94	2
1948	**Joe Scott, N.Y. Giants**	20	569	28.5	99	1
1949	**Don Doll, Detroit**	21	536	25.5	56	0
1950	Verda (Vitamin T) Smith, Los Angeles	22	742	33.7	97	3
1951	Lynn Chandois, Pittsburgh	12	390	32.5	55	0
1952	Lynn Chandois, Pittsburgh	17	599	35.2	93	2
1953	Joe Arenas, San Francisco	16	551	34.4	82	0
1954	Billy Reynolds, Cleveland	14	413	29.5	51	0
1955	Al Carmichael, Green Bay	14	418	29.9	100	1
1956	Tom Wilson, Los Angeles	15	477	31.8	103	1
1957	**Jon Arnett, Los Angeles**	18	504	28.0	98	1
1958	Ollie Matson, Chi. Cardinals	14	497	35.5	101	2
1959	Abe Woodson, San Francisco	13	382	29.4	105	1
1960	**Tom Moore, Green Bay, NFL**	12	397	33.1	84	0
	Ken Hall, Houston, AFL	19	594	31.3	104	1
1961	Dick Bass, Los Angeles, NFL	23	698	30.3	64	0
	Dave Grayson, Dallas Texans, AFL	16	453	28.3	73	0
1962	Abe Woodson, San Francisco, NFL	37	1,157	31.3	79	0
	Bobby Jancik, Houston, AFL	24	726	30.3	61	0
1963	Abe Woodson, San Francisco, NFL	29	935	32.2	103	3
	Bobby Jancik, Houston, AFL	45	1,317	29.3	53	0
1964	**Clarence Childs, N.Y. Giants, NFL**	34	987	29.0	100	1
	Erwin (Bo) Roberson, Oakland, AFL	36	975	27.1	59	0
1965	Tommy Watkins, Detroit, NFL	17	584	34.4	94	0
	Abner Haynes, Denver, AFL	34	901	26.5	60	0
1966	Gale Sayers, Chicago, NFL	23	718	31.2	93	2
	Goldie Sellers, Denver, AFL	19	541	28.5	100	2
1967	**Travis Williams, Green Bay, NFL**	18	739	41.1	104	4
	Zeke Moore, Houston, AFL	14	405	28.9	92	1
1968	Preston Pearson, Baltimore, NFL	15	527	35.1	102	2
	George Atkinson, Oakland, AFL	32	802	25.1	60	0
1969	Bobby Williams, Detroit, NFL	17	563	33.1	96	1
	Bill Thompson, Denver, AFL	18	513	28.5	63	0
1970	Jim Duncan, Baltimore, AFC	20	707	35.4	99	1
	Cecil Turner, Chicago, NFC	23	752	32.7	96	4
1971	Travis Williams, Los Angeles, NFC	25	743	29.7	105	1
	Eugene (Mercury) Morris, Miami, AFC	15	423	28.2	94	1
1972	Ron Smith, Chicago, NFC	30	924	30.8	94	1
	Bruce Laird, Baltimore, AFC	29	843	29.1	73	0
1973	Carl Garrett, Chicago, NFC	16	486	30.4	67	0
	Wallace Francis, Buffalo, AFC	23	687	29.9	101	2
1974	Terry Metcalf, St. Louis, NFC	20	623	31.2	94	1
	Greg Pruitt, Cleveland, AFC	22	606	27.5	88	1
1975	**Walter Payton, Chicago, NFC**	14	444	31.7	70	0
	Harold Hart, Oakland, AFC	17	518	30.5	102	1
1976	**Duriel Harris, Miami, AFC**	17	559	32.9	69	0
	Cullen Bryant, Los Angeles, NFC	16	459	28.7	90	1

Bold face—first year in the league.

Terry Metcalf, St. Louis Cardinals

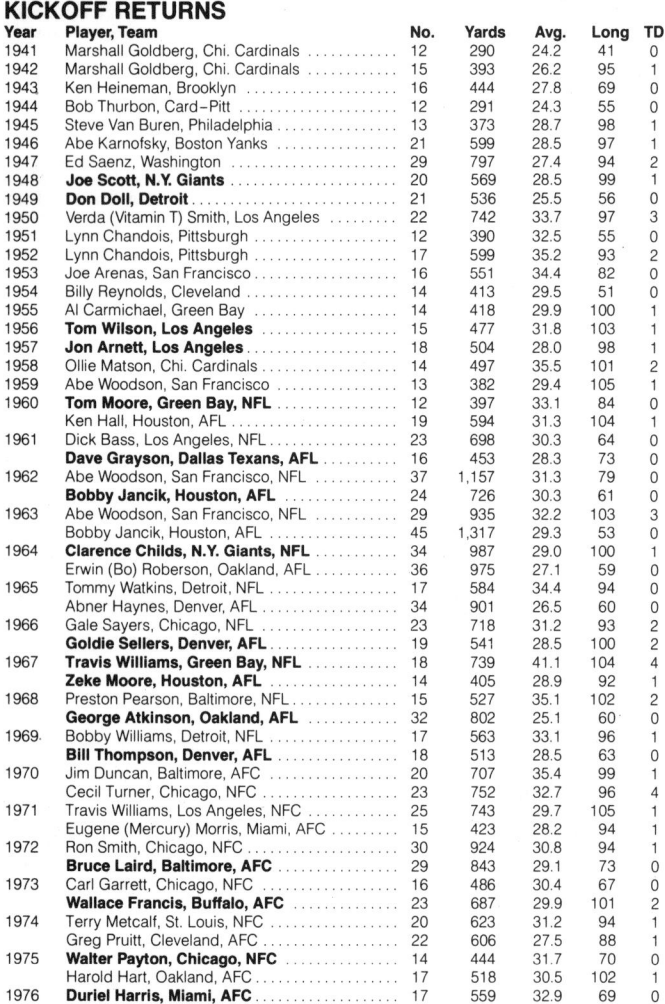

Doak Walker, Detroit Lions

Fred Cox, Minnesota Vikings

SCORING

Year	Player, Team	TD	FG	PAT	TP
1932	Earl (Dutch) Clark, Portsmouth	6	3	10	55
1933	Ken Strong, N.Y. Giants	6	5	13	64
	Glenn Presnell, Portsmouth	6	6	10	64
1934	Jack Manders, Chi. Bears	3	10	28	76
1935	Earl (Dutch) Clark, Detroit	6	1	16	55
1936	Earl (Dutch) Clark, Detroit	7	4	19	73
1937	Jack Manders, Chi. Bears	5	8	15	69
1938	Clarke Hinkle, Green Bay	7	3	7	58
1939	Andy Farkas, Washington	11	0	2	68
1940	Don Hutson, Green Bay	7	0	15	57
1941	Don Hutson, Green Bay	12	1	20	95
1942	Don Hutson, Green Bay	17	1	33	138
1943	Don Hutson, Green Bay	12	3	36	117
1944	Don Hutson, Green Bay	9	0	31	85
1945	Steve Van Buren, Philadelphia	18	0	2	110
1946	Ted Fritsch, Green Bay	10	9	13	100
1947	Pat Harder, Chi. Cardinals	7	7	39	102
1948	Pat Harder, Chi. Cardinals	6	7	53	110
1949	Pat Harder, Chi. Cardinals	8	3	45	102
	Gene Roberts, N.Y. Giants	17	0	0	102
1950	**Doak Walker, Detroit**	11	8	38	128
1951	Elroy (Crazylegs) Hirsch, Los Angeles	17	0	0	102
1952	Gordy Soltau, San Francisco	7	6	34	94
1953	Gordy Soltau, San Francisco	6	10	48	114
1954	Bobby Walston, Philadelphia	11	4	36	114
1955	Doak Walker, Detroit	7	9	27	96
1956	Bobby Layne, Detroit	5	12	33	99
1957	Sam Baker, Washington	1	14	29	77
	Lou Groza, Cleveland	0	15	32	77
1958	Jim Brown, Cleveland	18	0	0	108
1959	Paul Hornung, Green Bay	7	7	31	94
1960	Paul Hornung, Green Bay, NFL	15	15	41	176
	Gene Mingo, Denver, AFL	6	18	33	123
1961	Gino Cappelletti, Boston, AFL	8	17	48	147
	Paul Hornung, Green Bay, NFL	10	15	41	146
1962	Gene Mingo, Denver, AFL	4	27	32	137
	Jim Taylor, Green Bay, NFL	19	0	0	114
1963	Gino Cappelletti, Boston, AFL	2	22	35	113
	Don Chandler, N.Y. Giants, NFL	0	18	52	106
1964	Gino Cappelletti, Boston, AFL	7	25	36	155
	Lenny Moore, Baltimore, NFL	20	0	0	120
1965	**Gale Sayers, Chicago, NFL**	22	0	0	132
	Gino Cappelletti, Boston, AFL	9	17	27	132
1966	Gino Cappelletti, Boston, AFL	6	16	35	119
	Bruce Gossett, Los Angeles, NFL	0	28	29	113
1967	Jim Bakken St. Louis, NFL	0	27	36	117
	George Blanda, Oakland, AFL	0	20	56	116
1968	Jim Turner, N.Y. Jets, AFL	0	34	43	145
	Leroy Kelly, Cleveland, NFL	20	0	0	120
1969	Jim Turner, N.Y. Jets	0	32	33	129
	Fred Cox, Minnesota, NFL	0	26	43	121
1970	Fred Cox, Minnesota, NFC	0	30	35	125
	Jan Stenerud, Kansas City, AFC	0	30	26	116
1971	Garo Yepremian, Miami, AFC	0	28	33	117
	Curt Knight, Washington, NFC	0	29	27	114
1972	**Chester Marcol, Green Bay, NFC**	0	33	29	128
	Bobby Howfield, N.Y. Jets, AFC	0	27	40	121
1973	David Ray, Los Angeles, NFC	0	30	40	130
	Roy Gerela, Pittsburgh, AFC	0	29	36	123
1974	Chester Marcol, Green Bay, NFC	0	25	19	94
	Roy Gerela, Pittsburgh, AFC	0	20	33	93
1975	O.J. Simpson, Buffalo, AFC	23	0	0	138
	Chuck Foreman, Minnesota, NFC	22	0	0	132
1976	Chuck Foreman, Minnesota, NFC	22	0	0	132
	Franco Harris, Pittsburgh, AFC	14	0	0	84

FIELD GOALS

Year	Player, Team	Attempts	Made	Pct.
1932	Earl (Dutch) Clark, Portsmouth		3	
1933	**Jack Manders, Chi. Bears**		6	
	Glenn Presnell, Portsmouth		6	
1934	Jack Manders, Chi. Bears		10	
1935	Armand Niccolai, Pittsburgh		6	
	Bill Smith, Chi. Cardinals		6	
1936	Jack Manders, Chi. Bears		7	
	Armand Niccolai, Pittsburgh		7	
1937	Jack Manders, Chi. Bears		8	
1938	Ward Cuff, N.Y. Giants	9	5	55.6
	Ralph Kercheval, Brooklyn	13	5	38.5
1939	Ward Cuff, N.Y. Giants	16	7	43.8
1940	Clarke Hinkle, Green Bay	14	9	64.3
1941	Clarke Hinkle, Green Bay	14	6	42.9
1942	Bill Daddio, Chi. Cardinals	10	5	50.0
1943	Ward Cuff, N.Y. Giants	9	3	33.3
	Don Hutson, Green Bay	5	3	60.0
1944	Ken Strong, N.Y. Giants	12	6	50.0
1945	Joe Aguirre, Washington	13	7	53.8
1946	Ted Fritsch, Green Bay	17	9	52.9
1947	Ward Cuff, Green Bay	16	7	43.8
	Pat Harder, Chi. Cardinals	10	7	70.0
	Bob Waterfield, Los Angeles	16	7	43.8
1948	Cliff Patton, Philadelphia	12	8	66.7
1949	Cliff Patton, Philadelphia	18	9	50.0
	Bob Waterfield, Los Angeles	16	9	56.3
1950	**Lou Groza, Cleveland**	19	13	68.4
1951	Bob Waterfield, Los Angeles	23	13	56.5
1952	Lou Groza, Cleveland	33	19	57.6
1953	Lou Groza, Cleveland	26	23	88.5
1954	Lou Groza, Cleveland	24	16	66.7
1955	Fred Cone, Green Bay	24	16	66.7
1956	Sam Baker, Washington	25	17	68.0
1957	Lou Groza, Cleveland	22	15	68.2
1958	Paige Cothren, Los Angeles	25	14	56.0
	Tom Miner, Pittsburgh	28	14	50.0
1959	Pat Summerall, N.Y. Giants	29	20	69.0
1960	Tommy Davis, San Francisco, NFL	32	19	59.4
	Gene Mingo, Denver, AFL	28	18	64.3
1961	Steve Myhra, Baltimore, NFL	39	21	53.8
	Gino Cappelletti, Boston, AFL	32	17	53.1
1962	Gene Mingo, Denver, AFL	39	27	69.2
	Lou Michaels, Pittsburgh, NFL	42	26	61.9
1963	Jim Martin, Baltimore, NFL	39	24	61.5
	Gino Cappelletti, Boston, AFL	38	22	57.9
1964	Jim Bakken, St. Louis, NFL	38	25	65.8
	Gino Cappelletti, Boston, AFL	39	25	64.1
1965	Pete Gogolak, Buffalo, AFL	46	28	60.9
	Fred Cox, Minnesota, NFL	35	23	65.7
1966	Bruce Gossett, Los Angeles, NFL	49	28	57.1
	Mike Mercer, Oakland-Kansas City, AFL	30	21	70.0
1967	Jim Bakken, St. Louis, NFL	39	27	69.2
	Jan Stenerud, Kansas City, AFL	36	21	58.3
1968	Jim Turner, N.Y. Jets, AFL	46	34	73.9
	Mac Percival, Chicago, NFL	36	25	69.4
1969	Jim Turner, N.Y. Jets, AFL	47	32	68.1
	Fred Cox, Minnesota, NFL	37	26	70.3
1970	Fred Cox, Minnesota, NFL	46	30	65.2
	Jan Stenerud, Kansas City, AFC	42	30	71.4
1971	Curt Knight, Washington, NFC	49	29	59.2
	Garo Yepremian, Miami, AFC	40	28	70.0
1972	**Chester Marcol, Green Bay, NFC**	48	33	68.8
	Roy Gerela, Pittsburgh, AFC	41	28	68.3
1973	David Ray, Los Angeles, NFC	47	30	63.8
	Roy Gerela, Pittsburgh, AFC	43	29	67.4
1974	Chester Marcol, Green Bay, NFC	39	25	64.1
	Roy Gerela, Pittsburgh, AFC	29	20	69.0
1975	Jan Stenerud, Kansas City, AFC	32	22	68.8
	Toni Fritsch, Dallas, NFC	35	22	62.9
1976	Mark Moseley, Washington, NFC	34	22	64.7
	Jan Stenerud, Kansas City, AFC	38	21	55.3

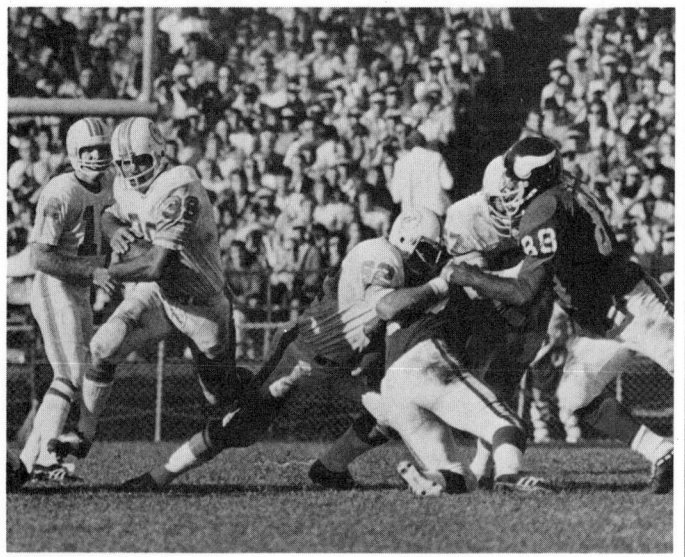

Larry Csonka, Miami Dolphins' 2,960-yard rushing attack, 1972.

Glenn Davis, Los Angeles Rams, 1950.

TEAM RUSHING

Year	Team	Yards
1932	Chi. Bears	1,770
1933	Boston Redskins	2,260
1934	Chi. Bears	2,847
1935	Chi. Bears	2,096
1936	Detroit	2,885
1937	Detroit	2,074
1938	Detroit	1,893
1939	Chi. Bears	2,043
1940	Chi. Bears	1,818
1941	Chi. Bears	2,263
1942	Chi. Bears	1,881
1943	Phil-Pitt	1,730
1944	Philadelphia	1,661
1945	Cleveland Rams	1,714
1946	Green Bay	1,765
1947	Los Angeles	2,171
1948	Chi. Cardinals	2,560
1949	Philadelphia	2,607
1950	N.Y. Giants	2,336
1951	Chi. Bears	2,408
1952	San Francisco	1,905
1953	San Francisco	2,230
1954	San Francisco	2,498
1955	Chi. Bears	2,388
1956	Chi. Bears	2,468
1957	Los Angeles	2,142
1958	Cleveland	2,526
1959	Cleveland	2,149
1960	St. Louis, NFL	2,356
	Oakland, AFL	2,056
1961	Green Bay, NFL	2,350
	Dallas Texans, AFL	2,189
1962	Buffalo, AFL	2,480
	Green Bay, NFL	2,460
1963	Cleveland, NFL	2,639
	San Diego, AFL	2,203
1964	Green Bay, NFL	2,276
	Buffalo, AFL	2,040
1965	Cleveland, NFL	2,331
	San Diego, AFL	2,085
1966	Kansas City, AFL	2,274
	Cleveland, NFL	2,166
1967	Cleveland, NFL	2,139
	Houston, AFL	2,122
1968	Chicago, NFL	2,377
	Kansas City, AFL	2,227
1969	Dallas, NFL	2,276
	Kansas City, AFL	2,220
1970	Dallas, NFC	2,300
	Miami, AFC	2,082
1971	Miami, AFC	2,429
	Detroit, NFC	2,376
1972	Miami, AFC	2,960
	Chicago, NFC	2,360
1973	Buffalo, AFC	3,088
	Los Angeles, NFC	2,925
1974	Dallas, NFC	2,454
	Pittsburgh, AFC	2,417
1975	Buffalo, AFC	2,974
	Dallas, NFC	2,432
1976	Pittsburgh, AFC	2,971
	Los Angeles, NFC	2,528

PASSING YARDAGE

Year	Team	Yards
1932	Chi. Bears	1,013
1933	N.Y. Giants	1,348
1934	Green Bay	1,165
1935	Green Bay	1,449
1936	Green Bay	1,629
1937	Green Bay	1,398
1938	Washington	1,536
1939	Chi. Bears	1,965
1940	Washington	1,887
1941	Chi. Bears	2,002
1942	Green Bay	2,407
1943	Chi. Bears	2,310
1944	Washington	2,021
1945	Chi. Bears	1,857
1946	Los Angeles	2,080
1947	Washington	3,336
1948	Washington	2,861
1949	Chi. Bears	3,055
1950	Los Angeles	3,709
1951	Los Angeles	3,296
1952	Cleveland	2,566
1953	Philadelphia	3,089
1954	Chi. Bears	3,104
1955	Philadelphia	2,472
1956	Los Angeles	2,419
1957	Baltimore	2,388
1958	Pittsburgh	2,752
1959	Baltimore	2,753
1960	Houston, AFL	3,203
	Baltimore, NFL	2,956
1961	Houston, AFL	4,392
	Philadelphia, NFL	3,605
1962	Denver, AFL	3,404
	Philadelphia, NFL	3,385
1963	Baltimore, NFL	3,296
	Houston, AFL	3,222
1964	Houston, AFL	3,527
	Chicago, NFL	2,841
1965	San Francisco, NFL	3,487
	San Diego, AFL	3,103
1966	N.Y. Jets, AFL	3,464
	Dallas, NFL	3,023
1967	N.Y. Jets, AFL	3,845
	Washington, NFL	3,730
1968	San Diego, AFL	3,623
	Dallas, NFL	3,026
1969	Oakland, AFL	3,271
	San Francisco, NFL	3,158
1970	San Francisco, NFC	2,923
	Oakland, AFC	2,865
1971	San Diego, AFC	3,134
	Dallas, NFC	2,786
1972	N.Y. Jets, AFC	2,777
	San Francisco, NFC	2,735
1973	Philadelphia, NFC	2,998
	Denver, AFC	2,519
1974	Washington, NFC	2,978
	Cincinnati, AFC	2,804
1975	Cincinnati, AFC	3,241
	Washington, NFC	2,917
1976	Baltimore, AFC	2,933
	Minnesota, NFC	2,855

Leadership in this statistic has been based on net yards since 1952.

TOTAL YARDS GAINED

Year	Team	Yards
1932	Chi. Bears	2,755
1933	N.Y. Giants	2,973
1934	Chi. Bears	3,900
1935	Chi. Bears	3,454
1936	Detroit	3,703
1937	Green Bay	3,201
1938	Green Bay	3,037
1939	Chi. Bears	3,988
1940	Green Bay	3,400
1941	Chi. Bears	4,265
1942	Chi. Bears	3,900
1943	Chi. Bears	4,045
1944	Chi. Bears	3,239
1945	Washington	3,549
1946	Los Angeles	3,793
1947	Chi. Bears	5,053
1948	Chi. Cardinals	4,705
1949	Chi. Bears	4,873
1950	Los Angeles	5,420
1951	Los Angeles	5,506
1952	Cleveland	4,352
1953	Philadelphia	4,811
1954	Los Angeles	5,187
1955	Chi. Bears	4,316
1956	Chi. Bears	4,537
1957	Los Angeles	4,143
1958	Baltimore	4,539
1959	Baltimore	4,458
1960	Houston, AFL	4,936
	Baltimore, NFL	4,245
1961	Houston, AFL	6,288
	Philadelphia, NFL	5,112
1962	N.Y. Giants, NFL	5,005
	Houston, AFL	4,971
1963	San Diego, AFL	5,153
	N.Y. Giants, NFL	5,024
1964	Buffalo, AFL	5,206
	Baltimore, NFL	4,779
1965	San Francisco, NFL	5,270
	San Diego, AFL	5,188
1966	Dallas, NFL	5,145
	Kansas City, AFL	5,114
1967	N.Y. Jets, AFL	5,152
	Baltimore, NFL	5,008
1968	Oakland, AFL	5,696
	Dallas, NFL	5,117
1969	Dallas, NFL	5,122
	Oakland, AFL	5,036
1970	Oakland, AFC	4,829
	San Francisco, NFC	4,503
1971	Dallas, NFC	5,035
	San Diego, AFC	4,738
1972	Miami, AFC	5,036
	N.Y. Giants, NFC	4,483
1973	Los Angeles, NFC	4,906
	Oakland, AFC	4,773
1974	Dallas, NFC	4,983
	Oakland, AFC	4,718
1975	Buffalo, AFC	5,467
	Dallas, NFC	5,025
1976	Baltimore, AFC	5,236
	St. Louis, NFC	5,136

Al DeRogatis (78), Arnie Weinmeister (73), N.Y. Giants' defense, 1951.

Glen Edwards (27), Pittsburgh Steelers' defense, 1974.

POINTS SCORED

Year	Team	Points
1932	Green Bay	152
1933	N.Y. Giants	244
1934	Chi. Bears	286
1935	Chi. Bears	192
1936	Green Bay	248
1937	Green Bay	220
1938	Green Bay	223
1939	Chi. Bears	298
1940	Washington	245
1941	Chi. Bears	396
1942	Chi. Bears	376
1943	Chi. Bears	303
1944	Philadelphia	267
1945	Philadelphia	272
1946	Chi. Bears	289
1947	Chi. Bears	363
1948	Chi. Cardinals	395
1949	Philadelphia	364
1950	Los Angeles	466
1951	Los Angeles	392
1952	Los Angeles	349
1953	San Francisco	372
1954	Detroit	337
1955	Cleveland	349
1956	Chi. Bears	363
1957	Los Angeles	307
1958	Baltimore	381
1959	Baltimore	374
1960	N.Y. Titans, AFL	382
	Cleveland, NFL	362
1961	Houston, AFL	513
	Green Bay, NFL	391
1962	Green Bay, NFL	415
	Dallas Texans, AFL	389
1963	N.Y. Giants, NFL	448
	San Diego, AFL	399
1964	Baltimore, NFL	428
	Buffalo, AFL	400
1965	San Francisco, NFL	421
	San Diego, AFL	340
1966	Kansas City, AFL	448
	Dallas, NFL	445
1967	Oakland, AFL	468
	Los Angeles, NFL	398
1968	Oakland, AFL	453
	Dallas, NFL	431
1969	Minnesota, NFL	379
	Oakland, AFL	377
1970	San Francisco, NFC	352
	Baltimore, AFC	321
1971	Dallas, NFC	406
	Oakland, AFC	344
1972	Miami, AFC	385
	San Francisco, NFC	353
1973	Los Angeles, NFC	388
	Denver, AFC	354
1974	Oakland, AFC	355
	Washington, NFC	320
1975	Buffalo, AFC	420
	Minnesota, NFC	377
1976	Baltimore, AFC	417
	Los Angeles, NFC	351

FEWEST YARDS RUSHING ALLOWED

Year	Team	Yards
1933	Brooklyn	964
1934	Chi. Cardinals	954
1935	Boston Redskins	998
1936	Boston Bears	1,148
1937	Chi. Bears	933
1938	Detroit	1,081
1939	Chi. Bears	812
1940	N.Y. Giants	977
1941	Washington	1,042
1942	Chi. Bears	519
1943	Phil–Pitt	793
1944	Philadelphia	558
1945	Philadelphia	817
1946	Chi. Bears	1,060
1947	Philadelphia	1,329
1948	Philadelphia	1,209
1949	Chi. Bears	1,196
1950	Detroit	1,367
1951	N.Y. Giants	913
1952	Detroit	1,145
1953	Philadelphia	1,117
1954	Cleveland	1,050
1955	Cleveland	1,189
1956	N.Y. Giants	1,443
1957	Baltimore	1,174
1958	Baltimore	1,291
1959	N.Y. Giants	1,261
1960	St. Louis, NFL	1,212
	Dallas Texans, AFL	1,338
1961	Boston, AFL	1,041
	Pittsburgh, NFL	1,463
1962	Detroit, NFL	1,231
	Dallas Texans, AFL	1,250
1963	Boston, AFL	1,107
	Chicago, NFL	1,442
1964	Buffalo, AFL	913
	Los Angeles, NFL	1,501
1965	San Diego, AFL	1,094
	Los Angeles, NFL	1,409
1966	Buffalo, AFL	1,051
	Dallas, NFL	1,176
1967	Dallas, NFL	1,081
	Oakland, AFL	1,129
1968	Dallas, NFL	1,195
	N.Y. Jets, AFL	1,195
1969	Dallas, NFL	1,050
	Kansas City, AFL	1,091
1970	Detroit, NFC	1,152
	N.Y. Jets, AFC	1,283
1971	Baltimore, AFC	1,113
	Dallas, NFC	1,144
1972	Dallas, NFC	1,515
	Miami, AFC	1,548
1973	Los Angeles, NFC	1,270
	Oakland, AFC	1,470
1974	Los Angeles, NFC	1,302
	New England, AFC	1,587
1975	Minnesota, NFC	1,532
	Houston, AFC	1,680
1976	Pittsburgh, AFC	1,457
	Los Angeles, NFC	1,564

FEWEST YARDS PASSING ALLOWED

Year	Team	Yards
1933	Portsmouth	558
1934	Philadelphia	545
1935	Chi. Cardinals	793
1936	Philadelphia	853
1937	Detroit	804
1938	Chi. Bears	897
1939	Washington	1,116
1940	Philadelphia	1,012
1941	Pittsburgh	1,168
1942	Washington	1,093
1943	Chi. Bears	980
1944	Chi. Bears	1,052
1945	Washington	1,121
1946	Pittsburgh	939
1947	Green Bay	1,790
1948	Green Bay	1,626
1949	Philadelphia	1,607
1950	Cleveland	1,581
1951	Pittsburgh	1,687
1952	Washington	1,580
1953	Washington	1,751
1954	Cleveland	1,608
1955	Pittsburgh	1,295
1956	Cleveland	1,103
1957	Cleveland	1,300
1958	Chi. Bears	1,769
1959	N.Y. Giants	1,582
1960	Chicago, NFL	1,388
	Buffalo, AFL	2,124
1961	Baltimore, NFL	1,913
	San Diego, AFL	2,363
1962	Green Bay, NFL	1,746
	Oakland, AFL	2,306
1963	Chicago, NFL	1,734
	Oakland, AFL	2,589
1964	Green Bay, NFL	1,647
	San Diego, AFL	2,518
1965	Green Bay, NFL	1,981
	San Diego, AFL	2,168
1966	Green Bay, NFL	1,959
	Oakland, AFL	2,118
1967	Green Bay, NFL	1,377
	Buffalo, AFL	1,825
1968	Houston, AFL	1,671
	Green Bay, NFL	1,796
1969	Minnesota, NFL	1,631
	Kansas City, AFL	2,072
1970	Minnesota, NFC	1,438
	Kansas City, AFC	2,010
1971	Atlanta, NFC	1,638
	Baltimore, AFC	1,739
1972	Minnesota, NFC	1,699
	Cleveland, AFC	1,736
1973	Miami, AFC	1,290
	Atlanta, NFC	1,430
1974	Pittsburgh, AFC	1,466
	Atlanta, NFC	1,572
1975	Minnesota, NFC	1,621
	Cincinnati, AFC	1,729
1976	Minnesota, NFC	1,575
	Cincinnati, AFC	1,758

Leadership in this statistic has been based on net yards since 1952.

Jim Marshall tackling Travis Williams, Minnesota Vikings defense, 1969.

WINNINGEST COACHES

Coaches with 60 or more National Football League and 1960–69 American Football League regular season victories.

Rank	Yrs.	W	L	T
1. George Halas, 1920–29 Chicago Bears (85-31-18); 1933–1942 Chicago Bears (85-22-4); 1946–1955 Chicago Bears (75-42-2); 1958–1967 Chicago Bears (75-53-6)	40	320	148	30
2. Earl (Curly) Lambeau, 1921–1949 Green Bay Packers (213-104-22); 1950–51 Chicago Cardinals (8-16-0); 1952–53 Washington Redskins (10-13-1)	33	231	133	23
3. Paul Brown, 1950–1962 Cleveland Browns (111-44-5); 1968–1975 Cincinnati Bengals (55-56-1)	21	166	100	6
4. Steve Owen, 1931–1953 New York Giants (151-100-17)	23	151	100	17
5. Don Shula, 1963–69 Baltimore Colts (71-23-4); 1970–76 Miami Dolphins (73-24-1)	14	144	47	5
6. Tom Landry, 1960–1976 Dallas Cowboys (137-93-6)	17	137	93	6
7. Weeb Ewbank, 1954–1962 Baltimore Colts (59-52-1); 1963–1973 New York Jets (71-77-6)	20	130	129	7
8. Hank Stram, 1960–62 Dallas Texans (25-17-0); 1963–1974 Kansas City Chiefs (99–49–10); 1976 New Orleans Saints (4-10-0)	16	128	86	10
9. Sid Gillman, 1955–59 Los Angeles Rams (28-31-1); 1960 Los Angeles Chargers (10-4-0); 1961–69 San Diego Chargers (72-43-6); 1971 San Diego Chargers (4-6-0); 1973–74 Houston Oilers (8-15-0)	18	122	99	7
10. George Allen, 1966–1970 Los Angeles Rams (49-17-4); 1971–76 Washington Redskins (58-25-1)	11	107	42	5
11. Raymond (Buddy) Parker, 1949 Chicago Cardinals (6-5-1); 1951–56 Detroit Lions (47-23-2); 1957–1964 Pittsburgh Steelers (51-47-6)	15	104	75	9
12. Bud Grant, 1967–1976 Minnesota Vikings (98-38-4)	10	98	38	4
13. Vince Lombardi, 1959–1967 Green Bay Packers (89-29-4); 1969 Washington Redskins (7-5-2)	10	96	34	6
14. Lou Saban, 1960–61 Boston Patriots (7-12-0); 1962–65 Buffalo Bills (36-17-3); 1967–1971 Denver Broncos (20-42-3); 1972–76 Buffalo Bills (32-28-1)	16	95	99	7
15. Jimmy Conzelman, 1922 Rock Island Independents (4-2-1); 1923–24 Milwaukee Badgers (12-10-3); 1925–26 Detroit Panthers (12-8-4); 1927–30 Providence Steamroller (26-16-6); 1940–42 Chicago Cardinals (8-22-3); 1946–48 Chicago Cardinals (26-9-0)	15	88	67	17
16. John Madden, 1969–1976 Oakland Raiders (85-22-7)	8	85	22	7
17. Blanton Collier, 1963–1970 Cleveland Browns (76-34-2)	8	76	34	2
18. George (Potsy) Clark, 1930–33 Portsmouth Spartans (28-16-7); 1934–36 Detroit Lions (25-10-2); 1937–39 Brooklyn Dodgers (11-17-5); 1940 Detroit Lions (5-5-1)	11	69	48	15
19. George Wilson, 1957–1964 Detroit Lions (53-45-6); 1966–69 Miami Dolphins (15-39-2)	12	68	84	8
20. Norm Van Brocklin, 1961–66 Minnesota Vikings (29-51-4); 1968–1974 Atlanta Falcons (37-49-3)	13	66	100	7
21. Chuck Noll, 1969–1976 Pittsburgh Steelers (65-46-1)	8	65	46	1
22. Wally Lemm, 1961 Houston Oilers (9-0-0); 1962–65 St. Louis Cardinals (27-26-3); 1966–1970 Houston Oilers (28-38-4)	11	64	64	7
23. Earle (Greasy) Neale, 1941–1950 Philadelphia Eagles (63-43-5)	10	63	43	5

Highest percentage—John Madden, .776; Don Shula, .747; Vince Lombardi, .728; Bud Grant, .714; George Allen, .711; Blanton Collier, .688; George Halas, .673; Earl (Curly) Lambeau, .627; Paul Brown, .621; Steve Owen, .595.

FEWEST TOTAL YARDS ALLOWED

Year	Team	Yards
1933	Brooklyn	1,789
1934	Chi. Cardinals	1,539
1935	Boston Redskins	1,996
1936	Boston Redskins	2,181
1937	Washington	2,123
1938	N.Y. Giants	2,029
1939	Washington	2,116
1940	N.Y. Giants	2,219
1941	N.Y. Giants	2,368
1942	Chi. Bears	1,703
1943	Chi. Bears	2,262
1944	Philadelphia	1,943
1945	Philadelphia	2,073
1946	Washington	2,451
1947	Green Bay	3,396
1948	Chi. Bears	2,931
1949	Philadelphia	2,831
1950	Cleveland	3,154
1951	N.Y. Giants	3,250
1952	Cleveland	3,075
1953	Philadelphia	2,998
1954	Cleveland	2,658
1955	Cleveland	2,841
1956	N.Y. Giants	3,081
1957	Pittsburgh	2,791
1958	Chi. Bears	3,066
1959	N.Y. Giants	2,843
1960	St. Louis, NFL	3,029
	Buffalo, AFL	3,866
1961	San Diego, AFL	3,726
	Baltimore, NFL	3,782
1962	Detroit, NFL	3,217
	Dallas Texans, AFL	3,951
1963	Chicago, NFL	3,176
	Boston, AFL	3,834
1964	Green Bay, NFL	3,179
	Buffalo, AFL	3,878
1965	San Diego, AFL	3,262
	Detroit, NFL	3,557
1966	St. Louis, NFL	3,492
	Oakland, AFL	3,910
1967	Oakland, AFL	3,294
	Green Bay, NFL	3,300
1968	Los Angeles, NFL	3,118
	N.Y. Jets, AFL	3,363
1969	Minnesota, NFL	2,720
	Kansas City, AFL	3,163
1970	Minnesota, NFC	2,803
	N.Y. Jets, AFC	3,655
1971	Baltimore, AFC	2,852
	Minnesota, NFC	3,406
1972	Miami, AFC	3,297
	Green Bay, NFC	3,474
1973	Los Angeles, NFC	2,951
	Oakland, AFC	3,160
1974	Pittsburgh, AFC	3,074
	Washington, NFC	3,285
1975	Minnesota, NFC	3,153
	Oakland, AFC	3,629
1976	Pittsburgh, AFC	3,323
	San Francisco, NFC	3,562

FEWEST POINTS ALLOWED

Year	Team	Points
1932	Chi. Bears	44
1933	Brooklyn	54
1934	Detroit	59
1935	Green Bay	96
	N.Y. Giants	96
1936	Chi. Bears	94
1937	Chi. Bears	100
1938	N.Y. Giants	79
1939	N.Y. Giants	85
1940	Brooklyn	120
1941	N.Y. Giants	114
1942	Chi. Bears	84
1943	Washington	137
1944	N.Y. Giants	75
1945	Washington	121
1946	Pittsburgh	117
1947	Green Bay	210
1948	Chi. Bears	151
1949	Philadelphia	134
1950	Philadelphia	141
1951	Cleveland	152
1952	Detroit	192
1953	Cleveland	162
1954	Cleveland	162
1955	Cleveland	218
1956	Cleveland	177
1957	Cleveland	172
1958	N.Y. Giants	183
1959	N.Y. Giants	170
1960	San Francisco, NFL	205
	Dallas Texans, AFL	253
1961	San Diego, AFL	219
	N.Y. Giants, NFL	220
1962	Green Bay, NFL	148
	Dallas Texans, AFL	233
1963	Chicago, NFL	144
	San Diego, AFL	255
1964	Baltimore, NFL	225
	Buffalo, AFL	242
1965	Green Bay, NFL	224
	Buffalo, AFL	226
1966	Green Bay, NFL	163
	Buffalo, AFL	255
1967	Los Angeles, NFL	196
	Houston, AFL	199
1968	Baltimore, NFL	144
	Kansas City, AFL	170
1969	Minnesota, NFL	133
	Kansas City, AFL	177
1970	Minnesota, NFC	143
	Miami, AFC	228
1971	Minnesota, NFC	139
	Baltimore, AFC	140
1972	Miami, AFC	171
	Washington, NFC	218
1973	Miami, AFC	150
	Minnesota, NFC	168
1974	Los Angeles, NFC	181
	Pittsburgh, AFC	189
1975	Los Angeles, NFC	135
	Pittsburgh, AFC	162
1976	Pittsburgh, AFC	138
	Minnesota, NFC	176

Stadiums of Pro Football

ATLANTA FALCONS

Atlanta-Fulton County Stadium

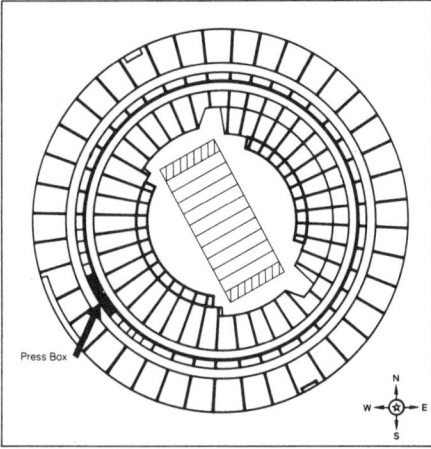

Address: 521 Capitol Avenue, S.W., Atlanta, Georgia 30312.

Architects: Finch-Heery, Architects and Engineers.

Contractors: Thompson and Street, Inc.

Cost: $18 million.

Year Opened: 1965.

Origin of Stadium Name: For the city and county.

Owner: Atlanta and Fulton County.

Manager: Fulton County Recreation Authority

Recent Improvements: Over 7,000 moveable seats were installed in 1976.

Planned Improvements: None.

Special Seating Facilities: Five private suites.

Miscellaneous Facts: None.

Playing Surface: Grass

Scoreboard Manufacturer: General Indicator Corporation.

Scoreboard Features: Scores, messages.

Parking Lot Capacity: 4,000.

Tenants: Falcons and Atlanta Braves baseball team.

Football Seating Capacity: 60,489.

Falcons' Attendance Record: 58,860, December 17, 1972 vs. Kansas City Chiefs

BALTIMORE COLTS

Memorial Stadium

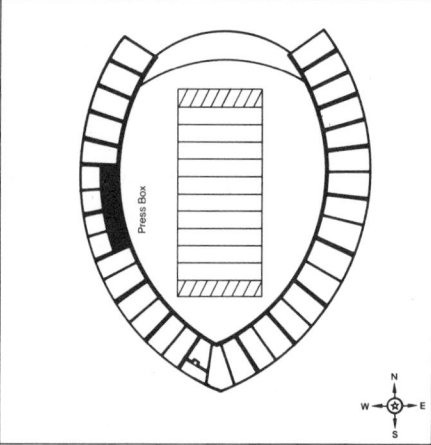

Address: 1000 East 33rd Street, Baltimore, Maryland 21218

Architects: Hall, Border, Donaldson-Architects

Contractors: Joseph F. Hughes and Company, Inc.

Cost: $6 million.

Year Opened: 1954.

Origin of Stadium Name: In honor of the men and women who served in American wars.

Owner: Baltimore

Manager: Baltimore Division of Recreation and Parks Department.

Recent Improvements: Fixed seats were replaced with new aluminum benches beginning in 1975.

Planned Improvements: Installation of moveable stands in right and left field.

Special Seating Facilities: None.

Miscellaneous Facts: None.

Playing Surface: Grass.

Scoreboard Manufacturer: General Indicator Corporation.

Scoreboard Features: Scores, messages.

Parking Lot Capacity: 5,400.

Tenants: Colts and Baltimore Orioles baseball team.

Football Seating Capacity: 60,020.

Colts' Attendance Record: 60,240, six times in 1970.

BUFFALO BILLS

Rich Stadium

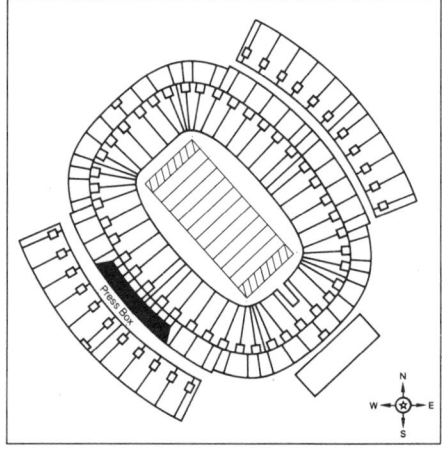

Address: One Bills Drive, Orchard Park, New York 14127.

Architects: Finch-Heery, Architects and Engineers.

Contractors: Cowper Construction Company.

Cost: $22 million.

Year Opened: 1973.

Origin of Stadium Name: The stadium name was purchased by Rich Products Corporation at the time the stadium was built.

Owner: Erie County.

Manager: The Bills have an exclusive 25-year tenancy and are responsible for maintenance and operation costs.

Recent Improvements: The Bills spent $3 million on private suites, the scoreboard, landscaping, and office improvements.

Planned Improvements: None.

Special Seating Facilities: 34 private suites, each seating 25, leased on an annual basis.

Miscellaneous Facts: The playing field is 50 feet below ground level.

Playing Surface: AstroTurf.

Scoreboard Manufacturer: Conrac Corporation.

Scoreboard Features: Scores, messages; the scoreboard is 30 feet high and 105 feet wide and has message and instant replay capabilities.

Parking Lot Capacity: 16,000

Tenants: Bills.

Football Seating Capacity: 80,020.

Bills' Attendance Record: 80,020, many times.

CHICAGO BEARS

Soldier Field

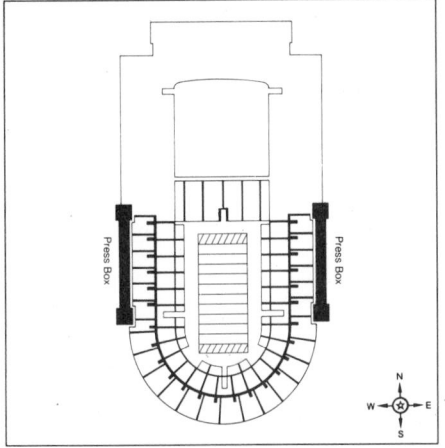

Address: 425 McFetridge Place, Chicago, Illinois 60605.

Architects: Holabird and Roche-Architects.

Contractors: Many during three periods of construction—1922, 1929, and 1940.

Cost: Approximately $10 million.

Year Opened: 1926.

Origin of Stadium Name: In honor of men and women who served in American wars.

Owner: Chicago.

Manager: Chicago Park District.

Recent Improvements: The Bears renovated the facility in 1971 by repositioning the field for better viewing and adding special bleachers at one end.

Planned Improvements: A major renovation is under consideration.

Special Seating Facilities: None.

Playing Surface: AstroTurf.

Scoreboard Manufacturer: General Indicator Corporation.

Scoreboard features: Scores.

Parking Lot Capacity: 8,000.

Tenants: Bears and Chicago Sting soccer team.

Football Seating Capacity: 57,351.

Bears' Attendance Record: 67,343, September 9, 1951 vs. Cleveland Browns; Soldier Field's football attendance record of 111,000 was set at its dedication date, November 27, 1926 at the twenty-ninth Army-Navy game.

CINCINNATI BENGALS

Taft Riverfront Stadium

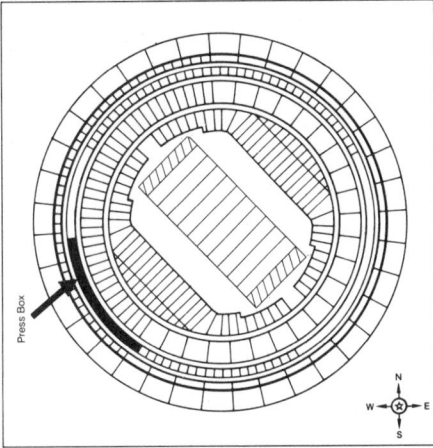

Address: 200 East Second Street, Cincinnati, Ohio 45202.

Architects: Heery and Heery-Architects.

Contractors: Huber, Hunt, and Nichols, Inc.

Cost: $45 million.

Year Opened: 1970.

Origin of Stadium Name: The stadium was renamed Charles P. Taft Riverfront Stadium in January, 1977 in honor of a former member of the city council for 30 years, and for its location on the Ohio River.

Owner: Hamilton County.

Manager: City of Cincinnati.

Recent Improvements: None.

Planned Improvements: None.

Special Seating Facilities: 20 private boxes.

Miscellaneous Facts: It encompasses more than eight acres; one section of the grandstand has moveable stands.

Playing Surface: AstroTurf.

Scoreboard Manufacturer: American Sign Indicator Corporation.

Scoreboard Features: Scores, messages, and animation through a computer; the scoreboard is 20 feet high and 180 feet wide.

Parking Lot Capacity: 4,500; 20,000 cars can be parked within a 12-block radius of the stadium.

Tenants: Bengals and Cincinnati Reds baseball team.

Football Seating Capacity: 56,200.

Bengals' Attendance Record: 60,284, October 17, 1971 vs. Cleveland Browns.

CLEVELAND BROWNS

Cleveland Stadium

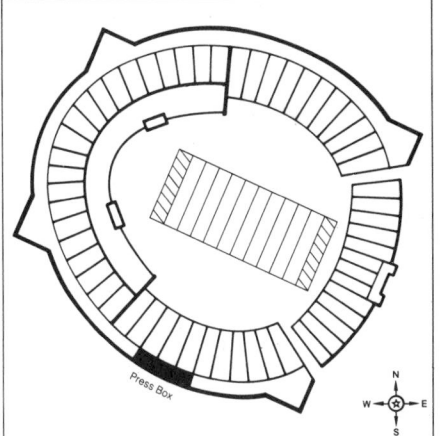

Address: West Third Street, Cleveland, Ohio 44114.

Architects: Osborn Engineering Company.

Contractors: Osborn Engineering Company.

Cost: Original construction, $3.5 million; 1973–77 renovation; $7 million.

Year Opened: 1932.

Origin of Stadium Name: For the city.

Owner: Cleveland.

Manager: Cleveland Stadium Corporation.

Recent Improvements: A new scoreboard was installed in 1977.

Planned Improvements: None.

Special Seating Facilities: 108 private loges, each with a suite, seating 8 to 10 people.

Miscellaneous Facts: None.

Playing Surface: Grass.

Scoreboard Manufacturer: Cleveland Stadium Corporation, formed by the Browns to gather the component parts and construct a new scoreboard in 1977.

Scoreboard Features: Scores, messages, and a computerized game-in-progress capacity.

Parking Lot Capacity: 4,000.

Tenants: Browns and Cleveland Indians baseball team.

Football Seating Capacity: 80,165.

Browns' Attendance Record: 85,703, September 21, 1971 vs. New York Jets.

DALLAS COWBOYS

Texas Stadium

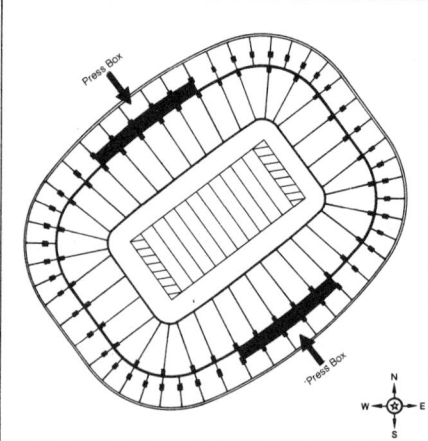

Address: Irving, Texas 75062.
Architect: A. Warren Morey and Associates.
Contractors: J.W. Bateson and Co., Inc.
Cost: $29.5 million.
Year Opened: 1971.
Origin of Stadium Name: For the state.
Owner: City of Irving.
Manager: Texas Stadium Corporation.
Recent Improvements: None.
Planned Improvements: None.
Special Seating Facilities: 178 private suites, each seating 12; each suite investment $50,000, with payment covering all years until 2008. Purchaser receives $60,000 return for $50,000 investment no later than 2008.
Miscellaneous Facts: A seven-and-three-quarter-acre roof covers all seats. There is a two and one-quarter acre opening in the middle of the roof.
Playing Surface: Tartan Turf.
Scoreboard Manufacturer: Conrac Corporation.
Scoreboard Features: Computer operated: matrix message portion measures 18 feet by 70 feet.
Parking Lot Capacity: 15,000.
Tenants: Cowboys.
Football Seating Capacity: 65,101.
Cowboys' Attendance Record: 65,101, many times.

DENVER BRONCOS

Denver Mile High Stadium

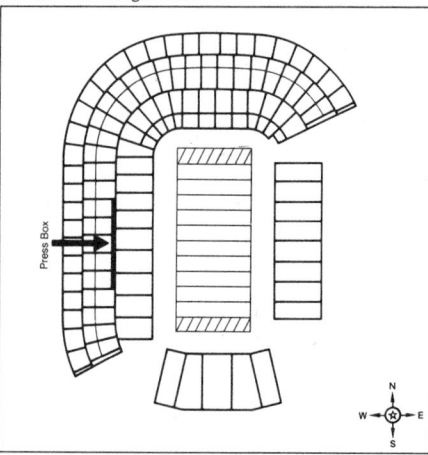

Address: 1900 West Eliot, Denver, Colorado 80204.
Architects: 1976–77 expansion, DMJM Phillips-Reister.
Contractors: Gerald H. Phipps Construction Co.; 1971 and 1976–77 expansion, Nick Petry Construction Co.
Cost: 1976–77 expansion, $25 million.
Year Opened: 1948.
Origin of Stadium Name: Indicative of the city and its elevation, it was adopted in 1967; the earlier name was "Bears Stadium," for its baseball team.
Owners: Denver and Denver County.
Manager: Denver and Denver County.
Recent Improvements: Expansion in 1976–77 increased the stadium's capacity by 12,500 and added a new scoreboard and other features.
Planned Improvements: None.
Special Seating Facilities: 54 private suites.
Miscellaneous Facts: None.
Playing Surface: Prescription Athletic Turf.
Scoreboard Manufacturer: Electric Division, Stewart-Warner Corporation.
Scoreboard Features: Scores, messages, instant replays, photograph reproductions.
Parking Lot Capacity: 7,000.
Tenants: Broncos and Denver Bears minor league baseball team.
Football Seating Capacity: 75,000.
Broncos' Attendance Record: 63,431, October 17, 1976 vs. Oakland Raiders.

DETROIT LIONS

Pontiac Silverdome

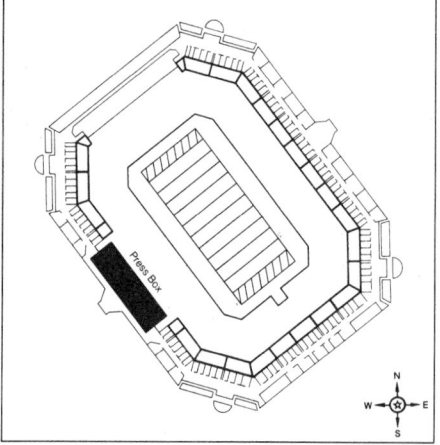

Address: 1200 Featherstone Road Box 4200, Pontiac, Michigan 48057.
Architects: O'Dell/Hewlett and Luckenbach, Inc.
Contractors: Barton-Malow Company.
Cost: $55 million.
Year Opened: 1975.
Origin of Stadium Name: Inspired by the stadium's unique appearance, it was adopted in 1976; it was originally called Pontiac Metropolitan Stadium, or Ponmet.
Owner: The city of Pontiac.
Manager: Pontiac Stadium Building Authority.
Recent Improvements: None.
Planned Improvements: None.
Special Seating Facilities: 102 private suites, each featuring closed-circuit color television.
Miscellaneous Facts: It is the only domed stadium that has a Fiberglas roof, which is kept inflated by 25 blowers during events; two blowers do the job at other times. The roof cost $4.5 million.
Playing Surface: AstroTurf.
Scoreboard Manufacturer: American Sign Company.
Scoreboard Features: Scores, messages, instant replays.
Parking Lot Capacity: 9,900.
Tenants: Lions.
Football Seating Capacity: 80,638.
Lions' Attendance Record: 79,784, October 6, 1975 vs. Dallas Cowboys.

GREEN BAY PACKERS

Lambeau Field

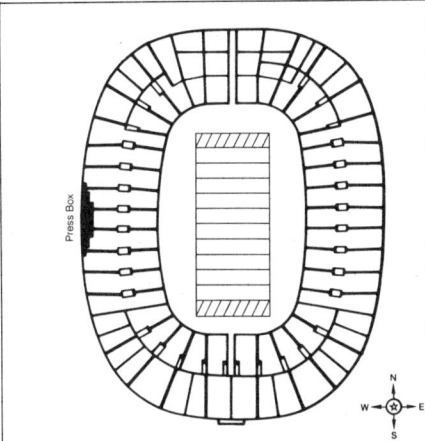

Address: 1265 Lombardi Avenue, Green Bay, Wisconsin 54303.
Architects: John E. Somerville Associates, Inc.
Contractors: George M. Hougard and Sons.
Cost: Renovations between 1961 and 1970, $3,778,000.
Year Opened: 1957.
Origin of Stadium Name: For the late Earl (Curly) Lambeau, founder, player, and coach of the team.
Owner: Green Bay
Manager: Stadium Commission.
Recent Improvements: Renovations between 1961 and 1970 have increased the stadium to its present seating capacity.
Planned Improvements: None.
Special Seating Facilities: None.
Miscellaneous Facts: The field has electric heating coils, which are installed to provide proper footing despite the elements. No seat in the oval bowl is more than 250 feet from the playing surface.
Playing Surface: Grass.
Scoreboard Manufacturer: American Sign Company.
Scoreboard Features: Scores, messages.
Parking Lot Capacity: 7,000.
Tenants: Packers and Green Bay high school teams.
Football Seating Capacity: 56,267.
Packers' Attendance Record: 56,267. All league games sold out since 1959.

GREEN BAY PACKERS

Milwaukee County Stadium

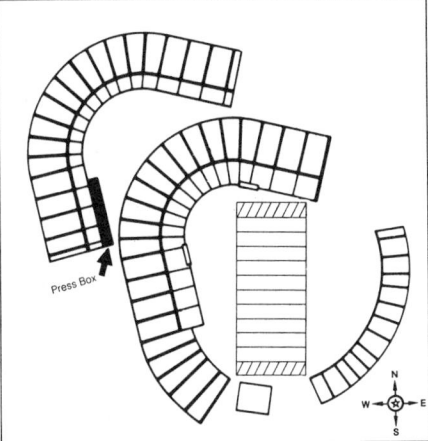

Address: 201 South 46th Street, Milwaukee, Wisconsin 53214
Architects: Osborn Engineering Company.
Contractors: Huntzinger Construction Company—General Contractors.
Cost: $6 million.
Year Opened: 1953.
Origin of Stadium Name: For the county.
Owner: Milwaukee County.
Manager: County of Milwaukee Park Commission.
Recent Improvements: The capacity was increased from 47,823 to its present amount.
Planned Improvements: None.
Special Seating Facilities: None.
Miscellaneous Facts: None.
Playing Surface: Grass.
Scoreboard Manufacturer: General Indicator Corporation.
Scoreboard Features: Scores, messages.
Parking Lot Capacity: 11,500.
Tenants: Packers and Milwaukee Brewers baseball team.
Football Seating Capacity: 55,896.
Packers' Attendance Record in Milwaukee: 55,896 three times in 1976.

HOUSTON OILERS

Astrodome

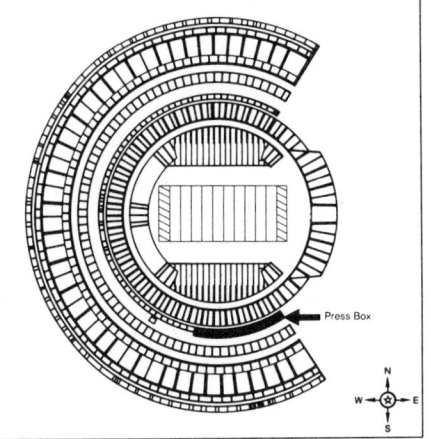

Address: Loop 610 South at Kirby Drive, Houston, Texas 77202.
Architects: Lloyd and Morgan, and Wilson, Morris, Crain and Anderson.
Contractors: H. A. Lott, Inc.
Cost: $38 million.
Year Opened: 1965.
Origin of Stadium Name: In recognition of Houston's NASA space center; the stadium's status as the first domed stadium, and for the Houston Astros baseball team.
Owner: Harris County.
Manager: Astrodome-Astroball Stadium Corp.
Recent Improvements: The original roof was replaced with an all-aluminum one in 1975.
Planned Improvements: None.
Special Seating Facilities: 52 private suites and two private clubs.
Miscellaneous Facts: The Astrodome was the first domed stadium. Some of the stands are moveable. There are 1,906 floodlights around the perimeter of the stadium.
Playing Surface: AstroTurf.
Scoreboard Manufacturers: Fair Play Scoreboard Company and Federal Sign and Signal Corp.
Scoreboard Features: Scores, messages, animated sequences; the scoreboard is four stories high and 474 feet wide.
Parking Lot Capacity: 30,000.
Tenants: Oilers, Houston Astros baseball team, and Astro-Bluebonnet Bowl.
Football Seating Capacity: 50,000.
Oilers' Attendance Record: 55,310, August 28, 1969 vs. Dallas Cowboys.

KANSAS CITY CHIEFS

Arrowhead

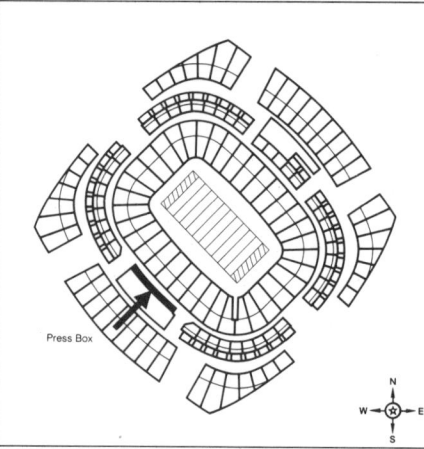

Address: One Arrowhead Drive, Kansas City, Missouri 64129.

Architects: Kivett-Myers and Associates.

Contractors: Sharp-Kidde-Webb.

Cost: Dual stadium complex, which includes the adjacent Royals Stadium, $73 million.

Year Opened: 1972.

Origin of Stadium Name: In recognition of the arrowhead emblem worn on the Chiefs' helmet.

Owner: Jackson County Sports Authority.

Manager: Kansas City Chiefs.

Recent Improvements: None.

Planned Improvements: None.

Special Seating Facilities: 83 private suites.

Miscellaneous Facts: Arrowhead is a complete bowl, with all seats facing toward the center of the field. It is exclusively designed for football.

Playing Surface: Tartan Turf.

Scoreboard Manufacturer: Stewart-Warner Company.

Scoreboard Features: Scores, messages, instant replays, and animation.

Parking Lot Capacity: 20,000.

Tenants: Chiefs.

Football Seating Capacity: 78,198.

Chiefs' Attendance Record: 82,094, November 5, 1972 vs. Oakland Raiders.

LOS ANGELES RAMS

Memorial Coliseum

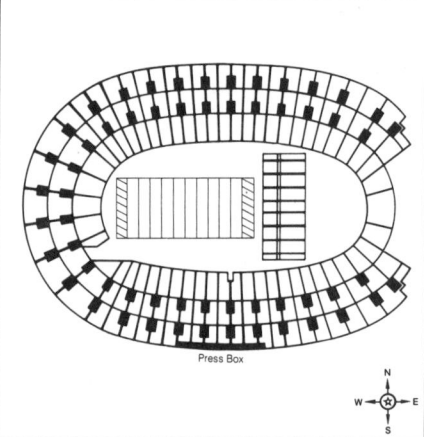

Address: 3911 South Figueroa Street, Los Angeles, California 90037.

Architects: John and Donald B. Parkinson.

Contractors: Edwards, Wildey, and Dixon Company.

Cost: Original construction, $954,872.98; 1931 enlargement, $950,293.88.

Year Opened: 1923.

Origin of Stadium Name: In honor of those who died in World War I.

Owner: City and County of Los Angeles, State of California.

Manager: Coliseum Commission.

Recent Improvements: The field was repositioned and bleachers added in the east end zone for 1977.

Planned Improvements: None.

Special Seating Facilities: None.

Miscellaneous Facts: The stadium was the site of the 1932 Olympic Games.

Playing Surface: Grass.

Scoreboard Manufacturer: Joint venture, Federal Sign Company and Stewart-Warner Company.

Scoreboard Features: Scores, messages, instant replays, animation.

Parking Lot Capacity: 6,500.

Tenants: Rams and USC and UCLA college football teams.

Football Seating Capacity: 92,604; compact capacity 71,432.

Rams' Attendance Record: 102,368, November 10, 1957 vs. San Francisco 49ers; the Coliseum's football attendance record of 105,236 was set December 6, 1947 when USC played Notre Dame.

MIAMI DOLPHINS

Orange Bowl

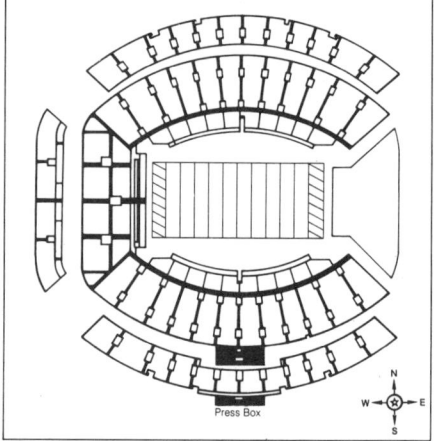

Address: 1500 Northwest Third Street, Miami, Florida 33125.

Architects: 1938-1959, City of Miami public works engineers; 1960-1970, Kunde & Associates.

Contractors: Original construction, Works Progress Administration.

Cost: Original construction, $325,000; 1945 addition, $88,500; 1947, $300,000; 1949-1950, $196,000; 1950-51, $21,000; 1954, $13,250; 1955-56, $532,737; 1959-59, $350,000; total of $8.5 million.

Year Opened: 1938.

Origin of Stadium Name: For the college bowl classic.

Owner: Miami.

Manager: Miami.

Recent Improvements: Renovations increased the stadium's capacity from its original figure of 22,000 in 1938 to its present amount.

Planned Improvements: A new scoreboard.

Special Seating Facilities: None.

Miscellaneous Facts: None.

Playing Surface: Prescription Athletic Turf.

Scoreboard Manufacturer: Fair Play Scoreboard Company.

Scoreboard Features: Game in progress information.

Parking Lot Capacity: 3,600.

Tenants: Dolphins, Univ. of Miami, Orange Bowl.

Football Seating Capacity: 75,449.

Dolphins' Attendance Record: 78,914, November 19, 1972 vs. New York Jets. The Orange Bowl's football attendance record of 80,699 was set in the 1971 Orange Bowl when Nebraska played Louisiana State University.

MINNESOTA VIKINGS

Metropolitan Stadium

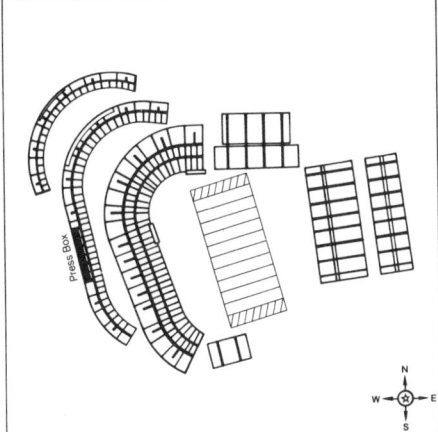

Address: 8001 Cedar Avenue South, Bloomington, Minnesota 55420.

Architects: Cerny and Associates, Inc.

Contractors: Johnson, Drake & Piper, Inc., General Contractors.

Cost: $8.5 million.

Year Opened: 1956.

Origin of Stadium Name: For the metropolitan area of Minneapolis-St. Paul.

Owner: The original 2,400 bond holders who financed the construction.

Manager: Metropolitan Sports Area Commission.

Recent Improvements: The first major expansion came in 1961, increasing the capacity from 24,000 to 40,800; Permanent east side bleachers were added in 1964, adding nearly 9,000 seats.

Planned Improvements: None.

Special Seating Facilities: 20 private boxes.

Miscellaneous Facts: None.

Playing Surface: Grass.

Scoreboard Manufacturer: General Indicator Corporation.

Scoreboard Features: Scores, messages.

Parking Lot Capacity: 14,000.

Tenants: Vikings, Minnesota Twins baseball team, and Minnesota Kicks soccer team.

Football Seating Capacity: 48,446.

Vikings' Attendance Record: 49,784, many times.

NEW ENGLAND PATRIOTS

Schaefer Stadium

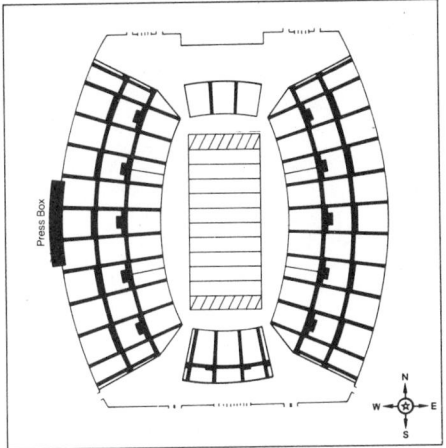

Address: Route One, Foxboro, Massachusetts 02035.

Architects: David M. Berg Incorporated, structural engineer; Finch-Heery-Architects and Engineers, consulting architects.

Contractors: J.F. White Construction Company.

Cost: $6.7 million.

Year Opened: 1971.

Origin of Stadium Name: For Schaefer Brewing Company, which purchased $1,000,000 worth of stock.

Owner: Privately owned; more than 400,000 shares of Stadium Realty Trust stock were sold.

Manager: Stadium Realty Trust.

Recent Improvements: New scoreboard.

Planned Improvements: Installation of a new artificial playing surface.

Special Seating Facilities: None.

Miscellaneous Facts: The stadium is part of a sports complex in suburban Boston that includes the adjoining New England Harness Raceway.

Playing Surface: Artificial turf.

Scoreboard Manufacturer: Donnelly Manufacturing Company, scoreboard; Conrac Corporation, message board.

Scoreboard Features: Scores, messages.

Parking Lot Capacity: 16,000.

Tenants: Patriots.

Football Seating Capacity: 61,279.

Patriots' Attendance Record: 61,457, December 5, 1971 vs. Miami Dolphins.

NEW ORLEANS SAINTS

Louisiana Superdome

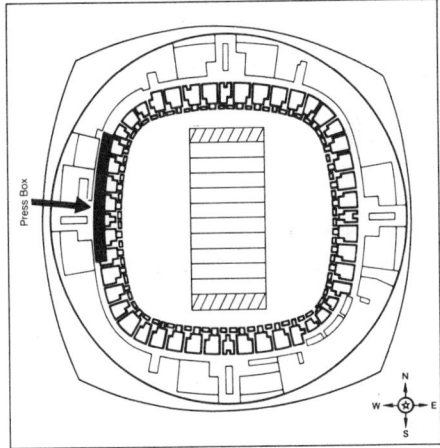

Address: 1500 Poydras Street, New Orleans, Louisiana 70112.

Prime Architects: Curtis & Davis-Architects & Planners, Inc.

Contractors: Huber, Hunt, and Nichols, Inc., and Blount Brothers, Inc.

Cost: $163 million.

Year Opened: 1975.

Origin of Stadium Name: For the state and the size and the type of building.

Owner: State of Louisiana.

Manager: Louisiana Department of Administration.

Recent Improvements: The addition of a wall on fifth level service concourse in 1977 to discourage patrons from throwing articles onto lower seats.

Planned Improvements: None.

Special Seating Facilities: 64 private suites, seating up to 29.

Miscellaneous Facts: The dome rises 273 feet, more than twice as high as the U.S. Capitol in Washington.

Playing Surface: AstroTurf (Mardi Grass).

Scoreboard Manufacturer: Ad Art Incorporated of California.

Scoreboard Features: Four scoreboards feature scores, messages; six giant television screens show instant replays and advertising.

Parking Lot Capacity: 5,000.

Tenants: Saints, New Orleans Jazz basketball team, Tulane University, and Sugar Bowl.

Football Seating Capacity: 72,675. Expanded Football Capacity, 76,791.

Saints' Attendance Record: 72,434, August 9, 1975 vs. Houston Oilers.

NEW YORK GIANTS

Giants Stadium

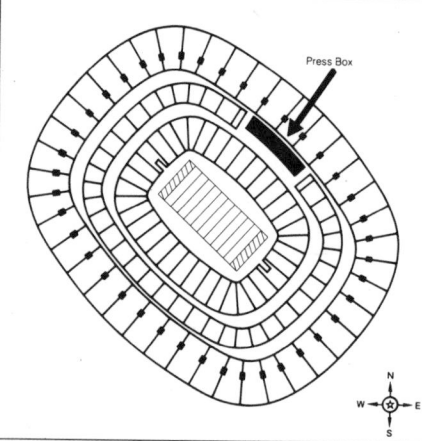

Address: East Rutherford, New Jersey 07073.
Architects: Ewing, Cole, Erdman, Ewbank, Clauss and Nolan-Architects, Engineers, and Planners.
Contractors: George A. Fuller Company, Frank Briscoe Company.
Cost: $71,071,000.
Year Opened: 1976.
Origin of Stadium Name: For the team.
Owner: Privately financed.
Manager: New Jersey Sports and Exposition Authority.
Recent Improvements: None.
Planned Improvements: Additional office and locker room space.
Special Seating Facilities: 72 private suites, each seating 16, and a private stadium club seating 1,400.
Miscellaneous Facts: Giants Stadium is part of the New Jersey Sports & Exposition Complex that includes the adjacent Meadowlands Racetrack.
Playing Surface: AstroTurf.
Scoreboard Manufacturer: Stewart-Warner Company.
Scoreboard Features: Scores, messages, full-color instant replays.
Parking Lot Capacity: 20,000.
Tenants: Giants and New York Cosmos soccer team.
Football Seating Capacity: 76,000.
Giants' Attendance Record: 78,000, October 10, 1976 vs. Dallas Cowboys.

NEW YORK JETS

Shea Stadium

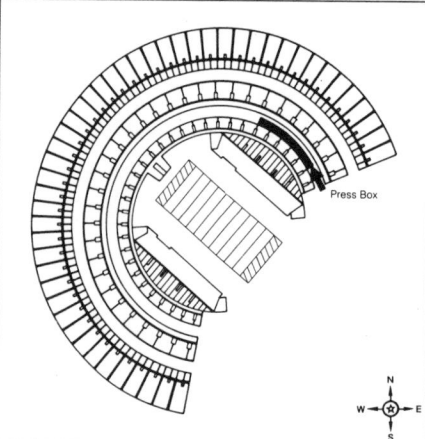

Address: Flushing, New York 11368.
Architects: Praeger-Kavanagh-Waterbury, Engineers-Architects.
Contractors: P.J. Carlin Construction Co., Thomas Crimmins Contracting Co.
Cost: $26 million.
Year Opened: 1964.
Origin of Stadium Name: For William Shea, attorney and a member of the Mayor's Commission for Sports.
Owner: City of New York.
Manager: New York Department of Parks.
Recent Improvements: None.
Planned Improvements: None.
Special Seating Facilities: None.
Miscellaneous Facts: When the stadium is converted to football, two blocks containing over 10,000 seats are electrically powered on tracks to parallel the side lines of the field.
Playing Surface: Grass.
Scoreboard Manufacturer: General Indicator Corporation.
Scoreboard Features: Scores, messages.
Parking Lot Capacity: 7,500.
Tenants: Jets and New York Mets baseball team.
Football Seating Capacity: 60,000.
Jets' Attendance Record: 63,962, November 5, 1972 vs. Washington Redskins.

OAKLAND RAIDERS

Oakland-Alameda County Coliseum

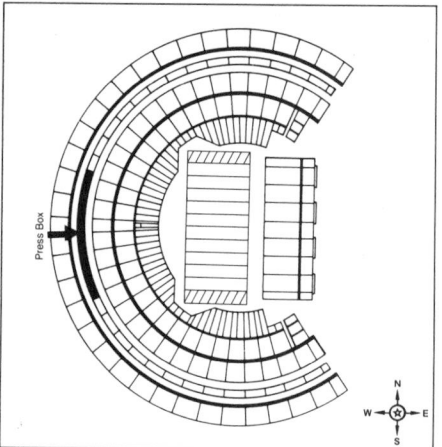

Address: Hegenberger Road and Nimitz Freeway, Oakland, California 94621.
Architects: Skidmore, Owings and Merrill-Architects.
Contractors: Guy F. Atkinson Company.
Cost: $30 million.
Year Opened: 1966.
Origin of Stadium Name: For the city and county.
Owners: Oakland and Alameda County.
Manager: Oakland-Alameda County Coliseum, Inc.
Recent Improvements: The seating capacity was increased by 550 in 1977.
Planned Improvements: None.
Special Seating Facilities: None.
Miscellaneous Facts: The Coliseum is part of a complex that also includes an adjacent arena, which is the home of the Golden State Warriors basketball team.
Playing Surface: Grass.
Scoreboard Manufacturer: Conrac Corporation.
Scoreboard Features: Scores, messages.
Parking Lot Capacity: 10,000.
Tenants: Raiders, Oakland Athletics baseball team, and Golden Gaters WTT tennis team.
Football Seating Capacity: 54,587.
Raiders' Attendance Record: 54,843, December 11, 1972 vs. New York Jets.

PHILADELPHIA EAGLES

Philadelphia Veterans Stadium

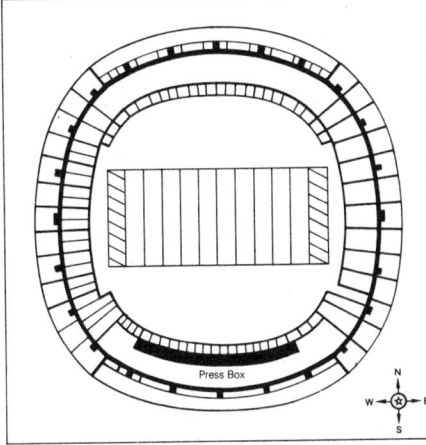

Address: Broad Street and Pattison Avenue, Philadelphia, Pennsylvania 19148.

Architects: Ewing, Stonorov and Haws, General Contractors.

Contractors: McCloskey and Company.

Cost: $48 million.

Year Opened: 1971.

Origin of Stadium Name: In honor of veterans of American wars.

Owner: Philadelphia.

Manager: Philadelphia.

Recent Improvements: Replacement of the AstroTurf and installation of a new warning track.

Planned Improvements: Replacement of the AstroTurf.

Special Seating Facilities: 23 suites; a stadium restaurant seats 500.

Miscellaneous Facts: None.

Playing Surface: AstroTurf.

Scoreboard Manufacturer: Artkraft Strauss Sign Corporation.

Scoreboard Features: Scores, messages, animation.

Parking Lot Capacity: 6,000 and another 6,000 in surrounding lots.

Tenants: Eagles and Philadelphia Phillies baseball team.

Football Seating Capacity: 66,052.

Eagles' Attendance Record: 65,947, November 10, 1974 vs. Washington Redskins.

PITTSBURGH STEELERS

Three Rivers Stadium

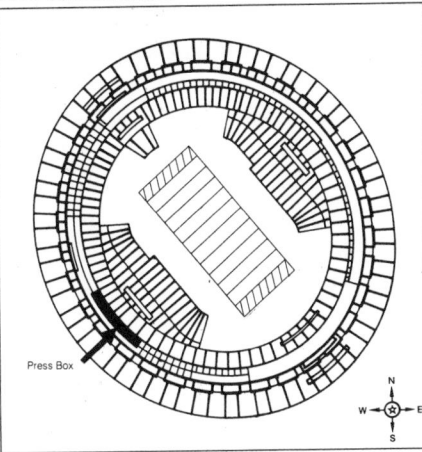

Address: 300 Stadium Circle, Pittsburgh, Pennsylvania 15212.

Architects: Deeter, Richey, Sipple, Architects.

Contractors: Hubert, Hunt and Nichols-Architects.

Cost: $45 million.

Year Opened: 1970.

Origin of Stadium Name: Because of its location, the point at which the Allegheny and Monongahela Rivers join to form the Ohio River.

Owner: Stadium Authority, City of Pittsburgh.

Manager: Three Rivers Management Corporation.

Recent Improvements: None.

Planned Improvements: None.

Special Seating Facilities: 41 private suites; a private stadium club has 1,200 members.

Miscellaneous Facts: Moveable stands are used to convert the stadium from baseball configuration to football.

Playing Surface: Tartan Turf.

Scoreboard Manufacturer: Stewart-Warner Corporation.

Scoreboard Features: Scores, messages, animation; the scoreboard is 30 feet high and 274 feet wide.

Parking Lot Capacity: 8,000 within a 12-block radius.

Tenants: Steelers and Pittsburgh Pirates baseball team.

Football Seating Capacity: 50,350.

Steelers' Attendance Record: 50,350, many times.

ST. LOUIS CARDINALS

Busch Memorial Stadium

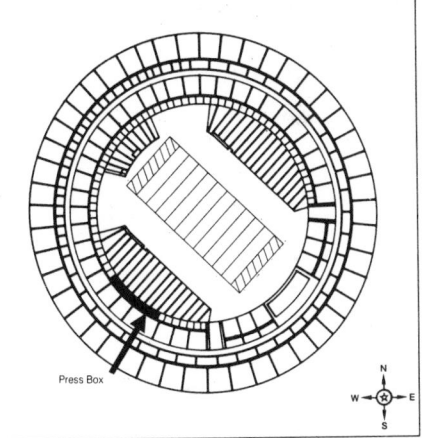

Address: 300 Stadium Plaza, St. Louis, Missouri 63102.

Architects: Sverdrup and Parcel and Associates, Inc.; Schwarz and Van Hofen; and design collaborator Edward Durrell Stone.

Contractors: Fruin-Colnon, Millstone-General Contractors.

Cost: $27 million.

Year Opened: 1966.

Origin of Stadium Name: As a memorial to the family of August A. Busch, Jr., retired chairman of the board of Anheuser-Busch.

Owner: Privately financed.

Manager: Civic Center Redevelopment Corporation.

Recent Improvements: A new sound system was installed in 1972.

Planned Improvements: None.

Special Seating Facilities: 39 suites; a stadium restaurant overlooks the field.

Miscellaneous Facts: Moveable stands in right and left field convert the stadium from baseball configuration to football or soccer in less than two hours.

Playing Surface: AstroTurf.

Scoreboard Manufacturer: Fair Play Scoreboard Company.

Scoreboard Features: Scores, messages.

Parking Lot Capacity: 6,982.

Tenants: Cardinals and St. Louis Cardinals baseball team.

Football Seating Capacity: 51,392.

Cardinals' Football Attendance Record: 50,365, October 31, 1976 vs. San Francisco 49ers.

SAN DIEGO CHARGERS

San Diego Stadium

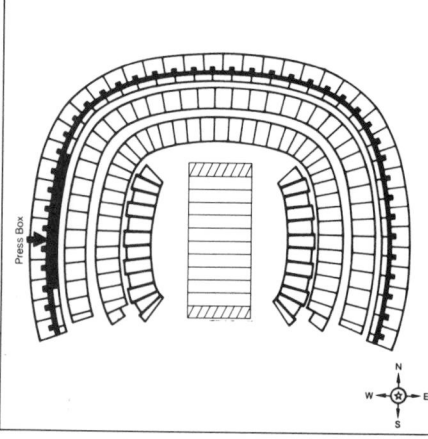

Address: 9449 Friars Road, San Diego, California 92120.

Architects: Frank L. Hope, principal in charge of design; Charles B. Hope, principal in charge of engineering. Hope-Hope and Associated-Gary Allen, Ernest R. Lord.

Contractors: Robertson-Larsen-Donovan-Contractors.

Cost: $28 million.

Year Opened: 1967.

Origin of Stadium Name: For the city.

Owner: City of San Diego and San Diego County.

Manager: City of San Diego.

Recent Improvements: The infield was renovated in 1974.

Planned Improvements: None.

Special Seating Facilities: None.

Miscellaneous Facts: Moveable stands convert the stadium from baseball configuration to football.

Playing Surface: Grass.

Scoreboard Manufacturer: Cubic and Associates.

Scoreboard Features: Scores and messages.

Parking Lot Capacity: 17,000.

Tenants: Chargers, San Diego Padres baseball team, and San Diego State.

Football Seating Capacity: 54,000.

Chargers' Attendance Record: 54,611, December 3, 1972 vs. Oakland Raiders.

SAN FRANCISCO 49ERS

Candlestick Park

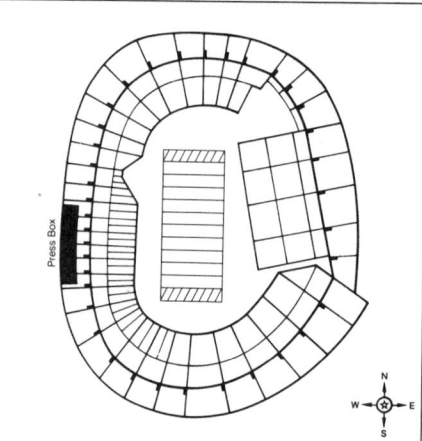

Address: San Francisco, California 94124.

Architect: John Bolles.

Contractors: Original construction, Charles Harney, General Contractors; 1971 improvements, Williams and Burrough, General Contractors.

Cost: Original construction, $11 million; 1971 improvements, $15 million.

Year Opened: 1958.

Origin of Stadium Name: For its location on Candlestick Point on San Francisco Bay.

Owner: San Francisco.

Manager: City Parks & Recreation Department.

Recent Improvements: A major renovation in 1971 added more than 16,000 seats to the original 45,000 capacity. The renovation also enclosed the stadium, cutting off the winds off San Francisco Bay, and included the construction of a football press box.

Planned Improvements: None.

Special Seating Facilities: None.

Miscellaneous Facts: Moveable stands convert the stadium from baseball configuration to football.

Playing Surface: AstroTurf.

Scoreboard Manufacturer: Conrac Corporation.

Scoreboard Features: Scores, messages.

Parking Lot Capacity: 14,400.

Tenants: 49ers and San Francisco Giants baseball team.

Football Seating Capacity: 61,246.

49ers' Attendance Record: 61,214, four times in 1972.

SEATTLE SEAHAWKS

Kingdome

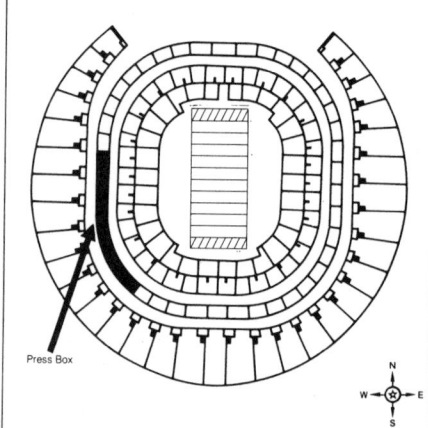

Address: 201 South King Street, Seattle, Washington 98104.

Architect: Naramore, Skilling and Praeger, Architects.

Contractors: Donald M. Drake Company; Peter Kiewit and Sons.

Cost: $67 million.

Year Opened: 1976.

Origin of Stadium Name: For the county and the kind of building.

Owner: King County.

Manager: King County Corporation.

Recent Improvements: None.

Planned Improvements: None.

Special Seating Facilities: None.

Miscellaneous Facts: Retractable and removeable stands permit the conversion of the field for various sports and functions; the walls of the dome anchor the world's largest self-supporting concrete roof.

Playing Surface: AstroTurf.

Scoreboard Manufacturer: Conrac Corporation.

Scoreboard Features: Scores, messages, instant replays.

Parking Lot Capacity: 17,000 within a nine-block radius.

Tenants: Seahawks, Seattle Mariners baseball team, and Seattle Sounders soccer team.

Football Seating Capacity: 65,000.

Seahawks' Attendance Record: 62,532, August 14, 1976 vs. Los Angeles Rams, a preseason game.

TAMPA BAY BUCCANEERS

Tampa Stadium

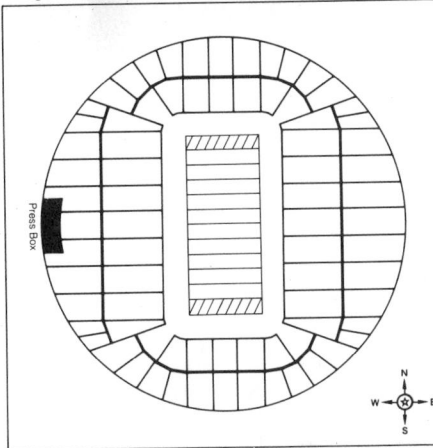

Address: 4201 North Dale Mabry Highway, Tampa, Florida 33607.
Architect: Watson and Company.
Contractors: Original construction, Jones-Mahoney Corporation; 1976 expansion, J. A. Jones Company.
Cost: Original construction, $4.6 million; 1976 expansion, $10.5 million.
Year Opened: 1967.
Origin of Stadium Name: For the city.
Owner: Tampa Sports Authority.
Manager: Tampa Sports Authority.
Recent Improvements: Expansion in 1976 added nearly 25,000 seats to the stadium's original 46,500 capacity.
Planned Improvements: None.
Special Seating Facilities: 22 private lounge boxes, each featuring closed-circuit television.
Miscellaneous Facts: None.
Playing Surface: Grass.
Scoreboard Manufacturer: American Sign and Indicator Corporation.
Scoreboard Features: Scores, messages, animation.
Parking Lot Capacity: 10,000.
Tenants: Buccaneers and Tampa Bay Rowdies soccer team.
Football Seating Capacity: 71,000.
Buccaneers' Attendance Record: 67,466, August 21, 1976 vs. Miami Dolphins, a preseason game.

WASHINGTON REDSKINS

RFK Memorial Stadium

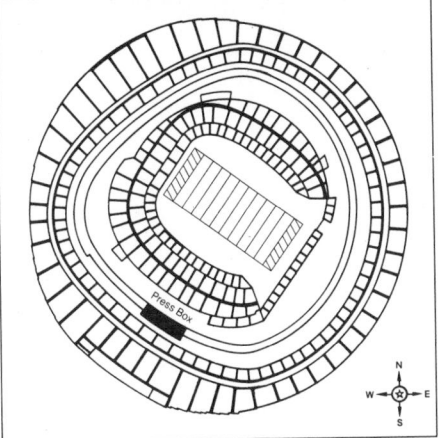

Address: 22nd and East Capitol Streets N.W., Washington, D.C. 20003.
Architects: George L. Dahl; Osborn Company.
Contractors: McCloskey and Company.
Cost: $22 million.
Year Opened: 1961.
Origin of Stadium Name: For the late Robert F. Kennedy in 1968; the original name was District of Columbia Stadium.
Owner: D.C. Armory Board.
Manager: District of Columbia Armory Board.
Recent Improvements: A new playing surface was installed in 1975.
Planned Improvements: None.
Special Seating Facilities: None.
Miscellaneous Facts: Moveable stands permit the conversion of the field for various sports and functions.
Playing Surface: Prescription Athletic Turf.
Scoreboard Manufacturer: Spencer Sign Company.
Scoreboard Features: Scores, messages.
Parking Lot Capacity: 10,000.
Tenants: Redskins and Washington Diplomats soccer team.
Football Seating Capacity: 54,398.
Redskins' Attendance Record: 61,214, four times in 1972.

Rules of
the Game

DIGEST OF NFL RULES

RULE 1   THE FIELD

It is 360 feet long and 160 feet wide. The end zones are 30 feet or 10 yards deep. The hashmarks or inbounds lines are 70 feet 9 inches from each side line. The lines used for tries-for-point are two yards from each goal line.

Side lines and end lines are out of bounds. The goal line is in the end zone. A player with the ball in his possession scores when the ball is on, above, or over the goal line.

Goal posts must be the single standard type, offset from the end line and painted bright gold. The actual goal is the plane extending indefinitely above the crossbar between the outer edges of the posts. Goal posts must be 18 feet 6 inches wide and the top face of the crossbar 10 feet above the ground. The post must extend at least 30 feet above the crossbar.

Decorations in the end zone and at the 50-yard line must be approved by the commissioner to avoid confusing where the goal lines, side lines, and end lines are.

RULE 2   THE BALL

The ball must be a Wilson ball bearing the signature of Commissioner Pete Rozelle.

It shall be made of an inflated rubber bladder enclosed in a pebble-grained leather case of natural tan color without corrugations of any kind. It shall have the form of a prolate spheroid. It shall be inflated to from 12½ to 13½ pounds.

The home team must have 24 balls available for testing by the referee one hour before each game.

RULE 3   DEFINITIONS

Chucking is warding off an opponent who is in front of a defender by contacting him with a quick extension of the arm or arms, followed by the return of the arm or arms to a flexed position, thereby breaking the original contact.

Clipping is throwing the body across the back of an opponent's leg or hitting him from the back while moving up from behind unless the opponent is a runner or the action is in close line play.

Close line play is the the area between the positions normally occupied by the offensive tackles, extending three yards on each side of the line of scrimmage.

A dead ball is a ball not in play.

A double foul is a foul by each team during the same down.

A down is the period of action that starts when the ball is put in play and ends when it is dead.

Encroachment occurs when a player moves across the neutral zone and makes contact with an opponent before the ball is snapped.

A fair catch is an unhindered catch of a kick by a member of the receiving team who must raise one arm at full length above his head while the kick is in flight.

A foul is any violation of a playing rule.

A free kick is a kickoff, a kick after safety, or a kick after a fair catch. It may be a placekick, a dropkick, or punt, except a punt may not be used on a kickoff.

A fumble is the loss of possession of the ball.

Impetus is the action of a player that gives momentum to the ball.

A live ball is a ball legally free kicked or snapped and it continues in play until the down ends.

A loose ball is a live ball not in the possession of any player.

A muff is the touching of a loose ball by a player in an unsuccessful attempt to obtain possession.

The neutral zone is the space the length of the ball between the two scrimmage lines.

Offside means a player has any part of his body beyond his scrimmage or free-kick line when the ball is snapped.

Possession is when a player holds the ball long enough to give him control to perform any act common to the game.

A punt is a kick made when a player drops the ball and kicks it while it is in flight.

A safety is when the ball is dead on or behind a team's own goal if the impetus comes from a player of that team.

A shift is the movement of two or more offensive players at the same time before the snap.

Sudden death is the continuation of a tied game into sudden death overtime in which the team scoring first by safety, field goal, or touchdown wins.

A touchback is when a ball is dead on or behind a team's own goal line and the impetus came from a player on the opposing team and the play was not a touchdown or missed field goal.

A touchdown is when any part of the ball, legally in possession of a player inbounds, is on, above, or over the opponent's goal line, provided it is not a touchback.

Unsportsmanlike conduct is any act contrary to the generally understood principles of sportsmanship.

RULE 4   HOW THE GAME IS STARTED, CONDUCTED, AND TIMED

A game is 60 minutes long, divided into four periods of 15 minutes each. Halftime is 20 minutes long.

The stadium electric clock keeps the official time. The line judge supervises the timing. The clock operator starts and stops the clock upon the signal of any official.

The toss of the coin takes place three minutes before the kickoff. The visiting captain calls the toss. The winner of the toss makes one of two choices, whether his team will receive or kick or secondly, the goal his team will defend. The loser of the toss gets the other choice. For the second half, the loser of the toss has the first choice of the two privileges.

The teams change goals at the end of the first and third periods.

The clock operator starts the clock when the ball is kicked off to start the game and thereafter following any time out the clock starts when the ball is snapped or free kicked.

Three charged team time outs are allowed each team during each half.

Time outs last one minute 30 seconds.

The referee may allow two minutes for an injured player and three minutes for repair of equipment.

The offense has 30 seconds to put the ball in play.

The clock starts when the ball is snapped following a change of possession.

In the last two minutes of each half the clock does not start on a kickoff until the ball has been legally touched by a player of either team in the field of play.

A team cannot get an extra time out and take a penalty in the last two minutes of each half. But a fourth time out is allowed without a penalty for an injured player who must be removed immediately. A fifth time out or more is allowed for an injury and a five-yard penalty is assessed if the clock was running. In addition, if the clock is running and the score is tied or the team in possession is losing, the ball cannot be put in play for at least 10 seconds on the fourth or more time out. The half or game can end while those 10 seconds are being run off the clock.

The down is replayed on a foul by the defense on the last play of the half or game if the penalty is accepted by the offense.

The down is not replayed on a foul by the offense on the last play of the half or game, and the play in which the foul was committed is nullified. Excep-

tions are fair catch interference, a foul following a change of possession, and illegal touching. No score by the offense counts.

The down is replayed when a double foul occurs on the last play of the half or game.

RULE 5   THE PLAYERS, SUBSTITUTES, AND THEIR EQUIPMENT

Each team is permitted 11 men on the field at the snap.

All players are to be numbered according to their positions: quarterbacks and kickers, 1 to 19; running backs and defensive backs, 20 to 49; centers and linebackers, 50 to 59; interior offensive linemen, except centers, and defensive linemen, 60 to 79; and wide receivers and tight ends, 80 to 89. Numbers in the 90s are reserved for preseason games, when rosters are large. Veterans who had numbers not conforming to these rules before they went into effect may keep those numbers.

Substitutes may not enter the field while the ball is in play. They may enter at any time while the ball is dead, provided the players they replace have cleared the field on their own side between the end lines prior to the snap or free kick. Players who have been substituted for may not linger on the field. If they do it is unsportsmanlike conduct.

A substitute is not to report to any official. He becomes a player when he informs a teammate he is replacing him; a teammate voluntarily withdraws upon his entering; he participates in at least one play after communicating with a teammate; or, in the absence of any of these, he is on the field at the time of the snap or free kick.

No player can wear equipment that, in the opinion of the officials, endangers other players.

RULE 6   THE FREE KICK

A free kick called a kickoff puts the ball in play at the start of each half, after a try for point, and after a successful field goal.

The free-kick line is the 35.

The kicker may use a tee up to three inches high on a kickoff.

A kickoff is illegal unless it travels 10 yards or is touched by the receiving team. It is a free ball once it is touched by the receiving team. The receiving team may recover and advance it. The kicking team may recover but not advance it unless it was first possessed and lost by the receiving team. If it recovers it in the end zone it is a touchdown.

If a kickoff goes through the opponent's goal posts it is not a field goal.

When a kickoff goes out of bounds between the goal lines without being touched by the receiving team it must be kicked again and there is a five-yard penalty against the kicking team.

A kick after a safety and a kick after a fair catch are also free kicks. In each case a dropkick, placekick, or punt may be used. A punt may not be used on a kickoff.

On a kick after a fair catch the receiving team has the option to put the ball in play by a punt, dropkick, or placekick without a tee, or by a snap. If the team dropkicks or placekicks and the ball goes between the uprights of the opponent's goal it is a field goal.

RULE 7   THE SCRIMMAGE

The offensive team must have at least seven players on the line of scrimmage at the snap.

Offensive players not on the line of scrimmage, except for the player who takes the snap, must be at least one yard back.

No player of either team may enter the neutral zone before the snap.

All offensive players must be stationary at the snap, except that one back may be in motion parallel to the line of scrimmage or backward from it. No interior linemen may move after taking or simulating a three-point stance. No offensive player may charge or move after assuming a set position in such a manner as to lead the defense to believe that the play has started when it has not.

A quarterback can be called for a false start penalty if his action is judged to be an obvious attempt to draw an opponent offside.

Linemen may lock legs only with the snapper.

After a shift all offensive players must come to an absolute stop for at least one second before the snap.

A double shift is legal if it has been shown three times before in the game outside the opponent's 20-yard line.

RULE 8 FORWARD AND BACKWARD PASS AND FUMBLE

The offense may make only one forward pass each play.

The passer must be behind his line of scrimmage.

A forward pass may be touched or caught only by an eligible player—an offensive player on either end of the line or at least one yard behind the line at the snap, except for the quarterback, or any defensive player.

If a forward pass is touched by a defensive player before, at the same time as, or after touching by an eligible offensive player, all offensive players then become eligible.

If a forward pass is caught simultaneously by eligible players of both teams it goes to the passing team.

A pass is incomplete and the ball is dead if the pass hits the ground, goes out of bounds, hits the goal posts, is caught by an offensive player after it touches an ineligible offensive player, is caught by a second eligible offensive player after first being touched by an eligible offensive player and then a defensive player, or is caught by the passer.

A forward pass is complete when a receiver has possession of the ball and touches the ground with both feet inbounds. If he is carried out of bounds by an opponent while in possession in the air, the pass is complete where he went out of bounds.

If a pass is incomplete on fourth down on a play that starts inside the opponent's 20-yard line, the defense gets the ball at the line of scrimmage, not the 20-yard line.

It is intentional grounding when the ball strikes the ground after the passer throws, tosses, or lobs it to prevent loss of yards by his team.

No defensive player may run into a passer of a legal forward pass after the ball has left the passer's hands. The referee must determine whether the opponent had a reasonable chance to stop his momentum during an attempt to block the pass or tackle the passer while he still had the ball.

A pass begins when the passer starts to bring his hand forward. If the ball then hits the ground it is an incomplete pass. If the passer loses control of it before he brings his hand forward it is a fumble.

The restriction against pass interference begins for the passing team at the snap. The restriction begins for the defensive team when the ball leaves the passer's hand. The restrictions end for both when the ball is touched by anyone.

If there is defensive pass interference in the end zone, it is first down for the offense on the defense's 1-yard line.

It is not intereference when two or more eligible players make a simultaneous and bona fide attempt to catch or bat the ball, each playing the ball and making contact unavoidable and incidental to the act of trying to catch or bat the ball. Defensive players have as much right to the path of the ball as eligible receivers.

Any pass that is not a forward pass is a backward pass, or lateral.

A runner may pass backward at any time.

Any player on either team may catch the pass or recover the ball after it touches the ground. The offense can recover and advance it but the defense can only recover it, unless it is in the air, and in that case the defense can both recover and advance it.

A fumble may be advanced by any player on either team regardless of whether it is recovered before or after the ball hits the ground.

Only the offensive player fumbling the ball may advance it on an intentional fourth down fumble inside the opponent's 10-yard line during a play from scrimmage and when the ball has not been touched by any defensive player. If it is touched by any other offensive player, it is dead at the spot of the fumble unless it is recovered behind the spot of the fumble. In that case, the ball is dead at the spot of the recovery.

RULE 9 THE SCRIMMAGE KICK

Scrimmage kicks are punts, dropkicks, and placekicks.

During a scrimmage kick only the end men on the line of scrimmage at the snap may go beyond the line before the ball is kicked. If there is an eligible receiver aligned or in motion behind the line and more than one yard outside the end man on his side, clearly making him the outside receiver, he may replace the end man as the player eligible to go downfield before the snap.

Any punt that is blocked and does not cross the line of scrimmage may be recovered and advanced by either team. If the offensive team recovers after the ball has been touched by the defensive team, the offensive team must make the yardage necessary for its first down, if it is fourth down, to retain possession of the ball.

The kicking team may never advance its own kick beyond the line of scrimmage.

No player on the receiving team may run into or rough the kicker.

The penalty for running into the kicker is 5 yards and for roughing the kicker it is 15. If the roughing the kicker is flagrant it is disqualification.

It is legal for a player on the receiving team to run into or rough the kicker if the contact is incidental to and after the receiving team player has touched the ball in flight; the contact is caused by the kicker's own motions; or, the contact occurs during a quick kick or a kick made after a run or when the kicker recovers a loose ball. It is a loose ball when the kicker muffs the snap or the snap hits the ground.

If a member of the kicking team who is attempting to down the ball on or inside the opponent's 5-yard line carries it into the end zone, it is a touchback.

Any member of the punting team may down the ball anywhere in the field of play.

If the receiving team commits a foul before gaining possession and the ball is still in the air or rolling on the ground after a punt or field goal attempt, the receiving team will retain possession of the ball and be penalized for its foul.

The defensive team may advance all kicks from scrimmage, including missed field goals, whether the ball crosses the defensive team's goal line or not.

It is illegal for a defensive player to stand on, jump on, or be picked up by a teammate or use a hand or hands on a teammate to gain additional height in an attempt to block a kick.

When a field goal is missed and the line of scrimmage is beyond the 20, the defensive team gets the ball at the line of scrimmage. When a field goal is missed inside the 20, the ball reverts to the 20.

RULE 10 THE FAIR CATCH

It is a legal fair catch signal when one arm is raised at full length above the head while the ball is in flight.

No opponent may interfere with the fair catcher, the ball, or his path to the ball.

The fair catcher is not required to catch the ball.

After signaling he cannot block or initiate contact with any opponent until the ball touches someone.

The fair catch signal is off if the ball is touched by a member of the kicking team while it is in flight, or it hits the ground.

It is delay of game and a five-yard penalty if the fair catcher unduly advances the ball. The ball is dead at the spot of the catch.

If time expires while the ball is in play and a fair catch is awarded, the receiving team may choose to extend the period with one free-kick down.

RULE 11 SCORING

The team that scores the most points in the game is the winner.

A touchdown counts six points, a field goal three, a safety two, and a successful try for point one.

The ball is automatically dead at the instant of legal player possession on, above, or behind the opponent's goal line.

The referee may award a touchdown when the offended team is deprived of one by a palpably unfair act, such as the act of a player coming off the bench and tackling a runner apparently en route to a touchdown.

The ball may be spotted for a try for point anywhere between the inbounds lines, two or more yards from the goal line.

A successful conversion counts one point whether it is by run, pass, or kick.

The defensive team can never score on a try for point.

RULE 12 CONDUCT OF PLAYERS

A runner may ward off opponents with his hands and arms but no other player on offense may use his hands or arms to obstruct an opponent by grasping with the hands or pushing or encircling any part of his body during a block.

No offensive player may assist the runner except by blocking for him. There can be no interlocking interference.

Any offensive player who pretends to possess the ball or to whom a teammate pretends to give the ball may be tackled provided he is crossing his scrimmage line between the ends of a normal tight offensive line.

An offensive player who lines up more than two yards outside his own tackle and who moves toward the ball in an area within three yards on either side of the line may not contact an opponent below the waist—a crackback block.

Pass blocking is the obstructing of an opponent by the use of the blocker's body above the knee. The hands must be cupped or closed and remain inside the blocker's elbows and inside the frame of his and the opponent's bodies. The arms may be in a flexed position but not fully extended to create a push. The blocker may ward off an opponent's attempt to grasp his jersey or arms and prevent contact to his head by up and down action of his flexed arms.

A defensive player may not tackle or hold an opponent other than the runner.

A defensive player may use his hands and arms only to ward off an obstructing opponent, to push or pull an opponent out of the way on the line of scrimmage, in an actual attempt to get at or tackle the runner, to push or pull an opponent out of the way in a legal attempt to recover a loose ball, during a legal block on an opponent who is not an eligible pass receiver; and when legally blocking an eligible pass receiver above the waist.

A defensive player may not contact an opponent above the shoulders with the palm of his hand—head slap—except during his initial charge or to ward him off the line. It cannot be a repeated act against the same opponent during any one contact.

A defensive player may use his hands or arms to contact or chuck an eligible receiver legally as many times as he can within three yards of the line of scrimmage. Beyond that point he can chuck him only once.

A defensive player may block an eligible receiver below the waist—roll block him—provided the receiver is within three yards of the line of scrimmage and lined up within two yards of the tackle.

A player may bat or punch a loose ball in the field of play but not toward the opponent's goal line. In either end zone, he may not bat or punch a loose ball in any direction.

A player may not bat or punch a ball while it is in player possession.

A player may not kick at a ball except as a punt, dropkick, or placekick.

A player may not strike with the fists, kick, knee, or strike on the head, neck or face with the heel, back, or side of the hand, wrist, forearm, elbow, or clasped hands.

A player may not grasp the face mask of an opponent.

There shall be no piling on, unnecessary roughness, clipping, crawling, or unsportsmanlike conduct.

Clipping is legal in close line play, in an area extending laterally to the positions originally occupied by the offensive tackles and longitudinally three yards on either side of the line of scrimmage.

RULE 13 CONDUCT OF NON-PLAYERS

There shall be no unsportsmanlike conduct by a substitute, coach, attendants, or any other non-player.

Loudspeaker coaching from the sideline is not permitted.

Coaches may move in an area extending 10 yards in both directions from the middle of the team's bench.

Each team may have no more than 15 non-players in its bench area.

RULE 14 ENFORCEMENT PENALTIES

Penalties are enforced from four spots: (1) the previous spot is where the ball was put in play; (2) the spot of the foul is where it occurred; (3) the spot of the snap, pass, fumble, return kick, or free kick is where one of those things occurred; (4) the succeeding spot is where the ball would be put in play if no distance penalty were to be enforced.

Fouls by the offense behind the line of scrimmage and on the field of play are penalized from the previous spot.

If there is a double foul during a down in which there is a change of possession, the team last gaining possession may keep the ball unless its foul was committed prior to the change of possession.

If there is a double foul after a change of possession the defensive team retains the ball at the spot it gained possession.

If one of the fouls of a double foul involves disqualification the player must be removed but no penalty yardage is assessed.

The penalty is assessed on the following kickoff when a team scores and either team commits a personal foul, unsportsmanlike conduct, or any obviously unfair act.

RULE 15 OFFICIALS DUTIES

They are the referee, umpire, head linesman, line judge, back judge, and field judge.

If one of them is absent, the crew is to be arranged on the most feasible basis.

All officials are to wear the uniform prescribed by the league.

Officials have concurrent jurisdiction over fouls.

The referee has general oversight and control of the game. He is the final authority for the score and number of the down. He sees that the ball is properly put in play. He notifies the coach and captain when a team has used its three time outs and he notifies both coaches when two minutes remain in a half.

The umpire has primary jurisdiction over the equipment of the players and the conduct and action of the players on the line of scrimmage.

The head linesman is primarily responsible for offside, encroaching, any actions pertaining to scrimmage line prior to the snap, and the work of the chain crew.

The line judge times the game and in case the stadium clock becomes inoperative takes over the timing on the field. He works on the side of the field opposite the head linesman and is primarily responsible for watching illegal motion behind the line at the snap and illegal shifts. He fires a pistol signaling that time has expired at the end of a period.

The back judge works on the same side of the field as the line judge, 17 yards deep. He is responsible for watching all eligible receivers on his side of the field. After receivers have cleared the line of scrimmage, he concentrates on action in the area between the umpire and the field judge.

The field judge is in the defensive secondary 22 yards deep and watches forward passes, kicks from scrimmage, loose balls out of the range of the umpire, back judge, or head linesman, times the 30 seconds the offensive team has to put the ball in play, and checks for illegal substitutions.

RULE 16 SUDDEN DEATH

Sudden death prevails for all games, but preseason and regular season games have a maximum of one 15-minute period of overtime.

The team scoring first during overtime play is the winner of the game.

RULE 17 HANDLING AN EMERGENCY

If any non-player enters the field or end zones and in the judgment of an official interferes with play, the referee, after consulting with the crew, shall enforce any such penalty or score as the interference warrants.

If in the opinion of the referee the game cannot continue, he shall declare a time out, note the down, distance to be gained, position of the ball on the field, and time remaining, and then instruct the home team to clear the field and restore order. When that is done, the game is to continue. It must be completed.

An NFL official retrieves his penalty flag.

MAJOR RULES CHANGES

The rules of football had already gone through a half-century of development before the league that became the NFL arrived in 1920.

College football was by then a major part of American life. And just as millions followed the sport in the huge arenas where it was played or through newspaper accounts of the game's heroes, the way it was played and governed was also of great interest. The decisions reached at the annual meeting of the rules committee were reported and studied and argued over.

By the time of the NFL, this annual process had been going on for a long time. The colleges had already established the major rules that laid the foundation for the game: the field 100 by 53 yards (1876); 11 players on a side (1880); three downs to make five yards (1881), later settling at four downs to make 10 yards (1912); seven men required on the offensive line at the snap (1895); the ball a prolate spheroid (1897); a neutral zone between the lines (1906); three points for a field goal (1909) and six for a touchdown (1912); and a four-man officials' crew of referee, umpire, field judge, and head linesman (1907).

The rule books used today in professional, college, and high school football resemble very much the single rule book used in the nineteenth century in its headings and the way it was organized. A chapter in a rule book is a "rule." The headings in today's books resemble those in the book of 1900—"Rule 1, The Field; Rule 2, The Ball; Rule 3, Players and Substitutes, etc."

The subdivisions of today's rule books are the same as those in the book used at the turn of the century by men of property such as Walter Camp and Walter Okeson who also dabbled in football and set up the rules in the language of a legal covenant—rule, section, article. Just as any legal document has a chapter on the definitions of the agreement, so does a football rule book, only in this case what it defines are fair catches, field goals, huddles, and the line of scrimmage.

No one in pro football "wrote the rule book." Building on the original book of Camp and others, the governing bodies of professional, college, and high school football made committees that wrote changes to meet their needs. The NFL made no major changes in the rules for 13 years—until the league meetings of 1933 and 1934, when it invented hashmarks or inbounds lines, moved the goal posts to the goal line (a rules change it would find necessary to undo in the seventies), and allowed forward passes from anywhere behind the line of scrimmage.

The payment of adults to play football was once considered heresy. "Professionalism" was a tainted word. How could a game played by pros be anything more than tedium? How could there be any real incentive for football players away from pennant-waving crowds, raccoon coats, coeds, and Saturday's Big Game?

The NFL was compelled, therefore, to open up its game and make it exciting and irresistible. Its decision to do so underlies the whole history of its rules changes. It got the game off the sideline through its invention of hashmarks and ended wasted downs that were necessary to move the ball to the middle of the field for genuine attempts to make yardage. It passed rules favoring forward passes at a time when many dismissed them as the lazy man's way to touchdowns. The NFL more readily accepted free substitution, opening the way to specialization. And it consistently moved against tied races and tied games, finally adopting sudden death for all games (preseason and regular season games were given a maximum of one 15-minute overtime period).

One of the persons who had the greatest influence on the NFL rules and how they are enforced was Hugh (Shorty) Ray, the league's "technical advisor" from 1938 until 1956. So great were Ray's contributions that he was elected to the Hall of Fame in 1966.

Ray advised the NFL owners on rules changes to be considered each year. Ray selected, tested, graded, and supervised the work of NFL officials. He improved the way officials work, made the game safer, and made it move faster.

A small (5 feet 6 inches), squeaky-voiced mechanical drawing instructor at Harrison High School in Chicago, Ray was one of the best game officials in the Big Ten Conference when George Halas of the Chicago Bears recommended that the NFL hire him. Ray became technical advisor and rule book associate editor for the National Federation of State High School Associations at the same time he was also employed by the NFL. For that reason, the rules of high school and professional football were similar in Ray's years and immediately thereafter.

Ray constantly pushed NFL officials to be the best in the sport. He held clinics for them, made them take tests, mailed them open-book examinations to take and return to him for grading, and mailed them a steady stream of announcements, approved rules, and the annual "play situation book," forerunner of the present-day "case books."

"He pounded the rules into his officials so they could average ninety-five percent on a test on even the most difficult problems," George Halas recalled.

During games, Ray and his part-time assistants watched officials from the press box or grandstands with watches, clipboards, and pencils at the ready, timing every move. If Ray did not get an eyewitness report on a game, he studied movies of the game with his time and motion movie projector. When the season ended, he presented his conclusions to league meetings in voluminous ring binders packed with data on every NFL game played, every down, every play situation.

As a result, NFL officials learned to work efficiently and at high speed because they knew they were being watched and graded every play. The pros began to run off more plays and their games ended sooner.

In addition, Ray changed officials mechanics on long incomplete passes and out-of-bounds plays. Previously, the receiver or the field judge ran back to the line of scrimmage returning the football or, after a play went out-of-bounds, an official ran back with the ball. That took too much time, Ray reasoned. He ordered that in those instances a second football be passed to the referee at the previous spot or at the hashmark, to be spotted there immediately by the referee and play resumed.

A summary of the important year-by-year changes in the NFL rules follows.

1929 A fourth official, the line judge, is added.

1933 The ball will be moved in 10 yards to the hashmarks or inbounds lines whenever it is in play within five yards of the side lines.

The clipping penalty is increased to 25 yards. The goal posts are moved to the goal lines.

1934 A player entering the game may communicate with his teammates immediately instead of waiting until one play is completed.

Officials must notify the coach when a team has exhausted its three legal time outs in each half.

A forward pass made hand-to-hand behind the line of scrimmage that becomes incomplete is a fumble and may be advanced by either team.

Within 10 yards of the goal, a defensive team can be penalized only half the distance for offside violations.

The second incomplete pass over the goal line in the same series or a fourth down incompletion in the

end zone results in a touchback.

Forward passing is legalized from any spot behind the line of scrimmage.

A runner who falls to the ground, or who is tackled, may advance unless a defender continues to hold him on the ground.

Flying blocks and flying tackles are permitted.

Players of the receiving team may be stationed at any place on the field, so long as they do not advance within 10 yards of the ball before it is kicked.

The ball may be kicked off from a dirt tee.

A fumbled ball, except fumbles resulting from lateral passes, may be advanced by either team, no matter whether the ball strikes the ground or not. If the defense recovers a fumbled lateral, the ball is dead; if the offense recovers a fumbled lateral, it may advance.

When a team completes a legal forward pass, which is in turn followed by a second forward pass, the penalty will be loss of five yards from the point of the second and illegal forward pass.

1935 All penalties will be enforced from the point where the ball was put in play and not from the point where the foul occurred.

A pass thrown beyond the line of scrimmage intended as a lateral but going forward will be declared downed at the point of throwing.

The ball, when fumbled, is free except when kicked or thrown.

A fourth down incomplete pass, or a second incomplete pass in the same series that goes into the end zone, is returned to the point where the ball was put in play, except when the previous play originated inside the 20 yard line.

The hashmarks or inbounds lines are moved for the second time: a ball out of bounds will be brought in 15 yards.

1936 When the goal posts interfere with the play of the team that is in possession of the ball, it will have the privilege of moving the ball five yards to either side of the goal posts without penalty.

1937 No changes.

1938 After a kickoff goes out of bounds, the ball will be put in play on the receiving team's 45 yard line.

Any two players withdrawn from a game during fourth quarter may re-enter once.

All penalties against the defense within the 10 yard line will be half the distance to the goal line.

The referee may penalize 15 yards for deliberate roughing of a passer after the ball has left his hand.

The penalty for a second forward pass behind the line of scrimmage is loss of down instead of loss of down and five yards.

If a kickoff goes out of bounds between the goal lines, the opponents will have the option of putting it in play by a scrimmage anywhere on their 45 yard line or at a point 15 yards in from where the ball crossed the side line. If the ball is last touched by the receivers, the ball will be put in play at the inbounds spot.

1939 During the last two minutes of the second half, additional time outs by the offense after its third legal one are not allowed unless it is for a designated injured player who is to be removed. A fourth time out under these conditions is not penalized, but additional time outs are treated as excess time outs.

During a kickoff, the kicking team may use only a natural tee made of the soil in the immediate vicinity of the kick and it must not be more than three inches in height.

The penalty for a forward pass touching an ineligible player on or behind his line of scrimmage is loss of down and 15 yards from the previous spot, and this penalty may not be declined.

The penalty for a forward pass striking an ineligible player beyond the line of scrimmage will be loss of the ball at the previous spot.

Before a forward pass is thrown from behind the

line of scrimmage, ineligible players may not legally cross that line except in an initial line charge while blocking an opponent. The penalty is loss of down and 15 yards.

1940 The clipping penalty is reduced to 15 yards.

The defense has the choice of loss of down and 15 yards from the previous spot or a touchback for pass interference by the offense behind the defense's goal line.

The penalty for a forward pass not from scrimmage is five yards.

A penalty enforced in the field of play cannot carry the ball more than one half the distance to the offenders' goal line.

The penalty for a foul prior to a kick or pass from behind the line is enforced from the previous spot or behind that spot if the offensive team commits a foul behind the previous spot.

1941 The penalty for an illegal shift is five yards.

A kick from scrimmage or a return kick crossing the receivers' goal line from the impetus of the kick is a touchback.

The penalty for a personal foul by the opponents of the scoring team is enforced on the kickoff.

Illegal touching of a kicked ball is not an offset foul and the ball is dead when illegally recovered.

The penalty for a disqualifying foul is 15 yards.

The penalty for an illegal bat or kick is 15 yards.

The umpire is to time the game and the head linesman and field judge are to supervise substitutions.

1942 The snapper is not offside unless some portion of his body is ahead of the defense's line.

A free kick cannot be made in a side zone.

A detachable kicking toe is illegal.

Pass interference by the offense in the defense's end zone is a touchback during any down.

A forward pass that has touched a second eligible or an ineligible player may be intercepted.

The coach's area is to extend 10 yards in both directions from the center of his team's bench.

1943 Free substitution is permitted.

The time out rule applies at the end of both halves.

Players must wear helmets.

The offense may intercept and advance the defense's illegal pass from end zone.

1944 A substitute is not required to report to an official and he becomes a player when he informs a teammate that he is replacing him or when he communicates with any teammate.

All enforcements for fouls during a free kick, except fair catch interference, are from the previous spot.

Communication between players and their coach is legal provided the coach is in his prescribed area and it does not cause delay.

Offensive pass interference in the end zone is not a touchback.

A designated center, guard, or tackle or one shifted to an end or back position may return to any position if he is withdrawn for one play.

1945 The hashmarks or inbounds lines are moved a third time, to a point 20 yards from the side line.

It is mandatory to enforce a penalty for encroachment if the defensive signal caller is beyond his line after the neutral zone is established.

A player under the center who extends his hands must receive the snap.

When the snap in flight is muffed by the receiver and then touches the ground, the defense may recover and advance.

The ball is dead when any receiver catches after a fair catch signal unless the kick is touched in flight by the members of the kicking team.

It is first and 10 for the offense when it recovers a kick from scrimmage anywhere in the field of play after it has first been touched by the defense beyond the line.

A player in blocking may not strike an opponent below the shoulders with elbows by pivoting or turning his trunk at the waist.

Players must wear long stockings in league games.

During a try, the snap may be made two or more yards from the goal line.

The referee is to designate an offending player when known.

A rule regarding attempts to consume or conserve time at the end of the second and fourth periods is extended to also include the first and third periods.

On a personal foul prior to a completion or an interception of a legal pass by the offended team, it will have the choice of the usual penalty or 15 yards from the spot of the dead ball.

1946 An offensive player is on his line provided one hand is touching the ground and it is on or within one foot of his line.

When a forward pass from behind the line touches either team's goal post or crossbar it is incomplete.

The toss of the coin must be held before the teams leave the field at the conclusion of pregame warm-ups.

The captains are to meet at the center of the field at the usual three minutes before game time, but only the receivers and their goal are to be indicated.

The penalty for an invalid fair catch signal is five yards from the spot of the signal.

The penalty for illegal equipment is five yards for delay and suspension for at least one down.

Substitution is limited to no more than three men at one time.

The receiving team is permitted to run punts and unsuccessful field goal attempts out from behind the goal line.

1947 The officials automatically will re-spot the ball on the nearest inbounds line when the spot of the snap is between the inbounds lines and inside the offense's 10 yard line.

When a team has less than 11 players on the field prior to the snap or free kick, officials are not to inform them.

During a try, if the kick is not successful, the ball becomes dead as soon as the failure is evident.

When a scrimmage or return kick crosses the receivers' goal line from the impetus of the kick, it is a touchback.

The kicker loses his usual protection if he kicks after recovering a loose ball on the ground.

A fifth official, the back judge, is added.

During a forward pass if the spot of a pass violation is behind the offense's goal line, the penalty is enforced from previous spot.

The field judge may use his whistle to assist the referee or other officials in declaring the ball dead.

Sudden death is adopted for divisional playoffs and championship games.

1948 Officials notifying each team that there are five minutes before the start of the second half must notify the head coach personally.

If an intended pass is downed behind the line, it is a referee's time out until any players who have gone downfield for a pass have had a reasonable time to return.

Plastic helmets are prohibited and coaches are to assume primary responsibility for the use of equipment that endangers their own or opponents' players.

A flexible artificial tee may be used at the kickoff.

If a foul occurs beyond the line during a backward pass or a fumble from scrimmage, the basic spot of enforcement is the spot of the pass or fumble.

It is illegal to bat or punch a ball in any direction while it is in player's possession.

When a player is disqualified, the referee must notify his coach.

1949 Any number of substitutes may enter while the ball is dead during time in.

EVOLUTION of NFL OFFICIALS

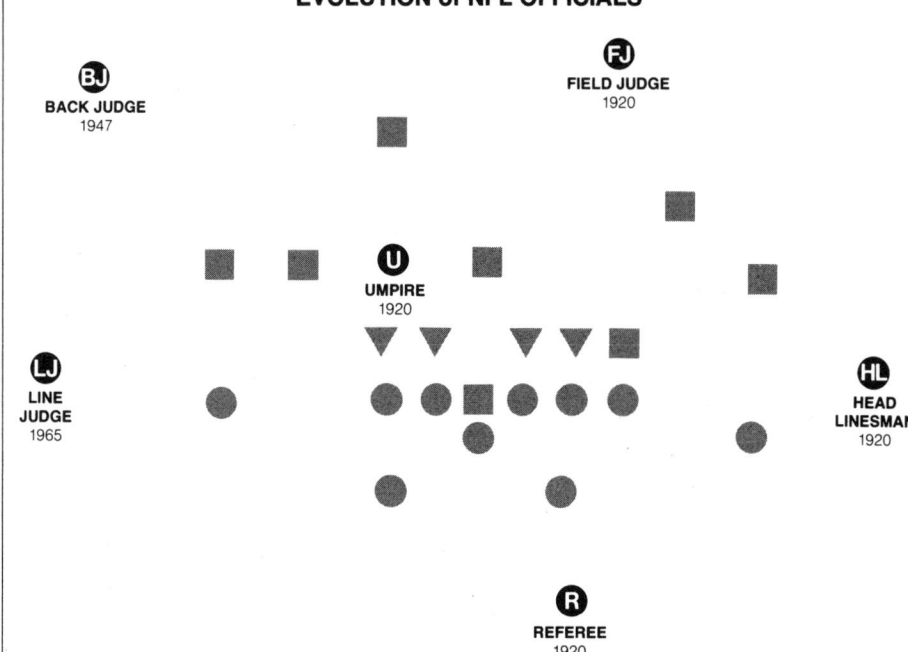

BACK JUDGE 1947

FIELD JUDGE 1920

UMPIRE 1920

LINE JUDGE 1965

HEAD LINESMAN 1920

REFEREE 1920

Eligible pass receivers of a given team may wear different color helmets than their teammates. All the receivers must wear the same color.

Both the players' benches may be located on the same side of the field.

Plastic helmets are permitted.

1950 Free substitution is readopted.

A backward pass going out of bounds between the goal lines belongs to the team last in possession.

1951 Aluminum shoe cleats are illegal.

A center, guard, or tackle is not eligible to touch a forward pass from scrimmage even when he is on the end of the line.

An illegal-touching violation by a member of the kicking team does not offset a foul by the receivers.

1952 All players must be numbered according to their position "except as provided for nationally known players."

A player is not considered to be illegally in motion provided he is not going forward at the snap.

The penalty for offensive pass interference is 15 yards from the previous spot and not loss of down.

1953 Withdrawn players and substitutes do not have to participate for at least one play or down.

A foul between downs must occur after the play has definitely ended.

Rules regarding hurdling cover only the act of a runner.

Players must be moving forward to be considered illegally in motion.

1954 The referee is the sole judge of and must pressure gauge all game balls on the field prior to the start of a game.

In case of rain or a wet or slippery field, playable balls can be requested at any time by the offensive team, and are to be furnished by the home team attendant from the side lines.

There will be a referee's time out for at least 10 seconds during change of possession, longer when required.

The use of a tee for a free kick after a fair catch is prohibited.

Illegal "kicking" of ball must be with the foot to be considered a foul.

1955 The ball is put in play at the spot of the interception when intercepting momentum causes the ball to be declared dead in the end zone possession.

Ten seconds may be run off the clock for the team in possession during the last two minutes of a half if it is behind in the score or the game is tied.

If a player touches the ground with any part of his body, except his hands or feet, while in the grasp of an opponent and irrespective of the grasp being broken, the ball is declared dead immediately.

A player on the kicking team who has been out of bounds may not touch, recover, or advance a scrimmage kick beyond the line.

1956 When a runner is contacted by a defensive player and he touches the ground with any part of his body except his hands or feet, the ball shall be declared dead immediately.

A brown ball with white stripes will be used for night games.

No artificial material shall be permitted to assist in the execution of a field goal or try-for-point.

Halftime will be 20 minutes long.

It is illegal to grab or grasp face guards, except the ball carrier's.

Loudspeaker coaching from sidelines is not permitted.

When an interior lineman takes a three-point stance and moves after taking that stance, he must be ruled offside or illegally in motion.

1957 On all requested time outs the referee will not sound his whistle for play to start until 60 seconds have elapsed.

Head linesmen will use a clamp on the chains when measuring for a first down.

1958 The back judge will be the official timer of the game.

On all requested time outs, the referee will not signify that the ball will be put in play prior to one minute and 30 seconds of elapsed time.

1959 No changes.

1960 American Football League permits one- or two-point conversion.

The official time is kept on the scoreboard clock in the AFL.

1961 No changes.

1962 No player shall grasp the face mask of an opponent. A flagrant offender will be disqualified.

The sudden death rule applies to the Pro Bowl game.

1963 When the spot of the snap is inside the offense's

15 yard line and between the inbounds lines, the ball is spotted at the nearest inbound line.

1964 No changes.

1965 The color of the officials' flags will be bright gold.

A sixth official, the line judge, is added.

A shift will begin after players assume a set position instead of when they come out of the huddle.

1966 Goal posts will be offset from the goal line and the uprights will extend a minimum of 20 feet above the crossbar and will be painted bright gold in color.

1967 A player who signals for a fair catch may not block or initiate contact with one of the kickers until the ball touches a player.

Goal posts will be single standard.

Fields will be rimmed by a white border, six feet wide.

1968 No changes.

1969 Kicking shoes will be of standard production and not subsequently modified in any manner.

The referee can charge a team time out when it is apparent an injured player cannot leave the field under his own power. The referee does not have to wait until the captain requests the team time out.

The kicker as well as the holder may be beyond the line when a placekick is made.

1970 The official time will be kept on the scoreboard clock.

1971 A team will not be charged a time out for an injured player unless the injury occurs in the last two minutes of either half.

The defense may advance on unsuccessful field goal attempt after it crosses the defense's goal line.

Holding, illegal use of hands, and clipping fouls committed by the offensive team behind the line of scrimmage during forward passes will be penalized from the previous spot.

If there is a double foul during a down in which there is a change of possession, the team last gaining possession may keep the ball after enforcement for its foul, provided its foul was not prior to the final change of possession—the "clean hands" rule.

A new pass blocking definition is added. Pass blocking is the obstruction of an opponent by the use of that part of the blocker's body above his knees. During a legal block, the hands must be cupped or closed and remain inside the blocker's elbows and must remain inside the frame of the opponent as well as the blocker's body. The arms must be in a flexed position, but cannot be fully extended to create a push. By use of up and down action of flexed arms, the blocker is permitted to ward off the opponent's attempt to grasp his jersey or arms and prevent legal contact to his head. The blocker is not permitted to push, clamp down on, hang on to, or encircle the opponent.

A passer can be penalized when he throws, tosses, or lobs the ball away with a deliberate attempt to prevent a loss of yardage by his team.

1972 The inbounds lines or hashmarks are moved to 70 feet, 9 inches from the side lines.

When it is fourth down for the offense at or inside its 15 yard line, the ball will be spotted 20 yards from the side line.

The penalty for an illegal receiver accidentally going out of bounds and returning to touch a pass is reduced from 15 yards and loss of down to loss of down.

The penalty for grasping a face mask, unless flagrantly, is reduced to five yards.

The commissioner will notify teams when a brown ball with white stripes will be used for a late-starting game.

A kick from scrimmage that crosses the goal line may be advanced by the defensive team into the field of play.

All fouls by the offense behind the line of scrimmage in the field of play will be penalized from the previous spot.

Disqualified players may not re-enter during overtime periods.

1973 The clock will start on the snap following all changes of team possession.

Periods can be extended if there is a change of team possession after there is a foul by the offense.

All players are to be numbered according to their positions.

Close line play is defined as the area ordinarily occupied by offensive tackles and longitudinally three yards on either side of the line of scrimmage.

A defensive player who jumps or stands on a teammate or who is picked up by a teammate cannot attempt to block a kick.

If the receiving team commits a foul during a kick from scrimmage after the ball is kicked, it will not lose the ball as part of its penalty.

1974 The goal posts are moved from the goal line to the end line.

Kickoffs will be made from the 35 not the 40 yard line.

During a kick from scrimmage, only the end men are permitted to go beyond the line of scrimmage before the ball is kicked.

Field goals attempted and missed from scrimmage line beyond the 20 yard line will result in the defensive team taking possession of the ball at the line of scrimmage. Field goals attempted and missed from the line of scrimmage inside the 20 yard line will result in the defensive team taking possession at the 20 yard line.

When the spot of enforcement for holding, illegal use of hands, arms, or body on offense as well as tripping fouls is not in the field of play at or behind the line of scrimmage or no deeper than three yards beyond the line of scrimmage, the penalty will be 10 yards.

Eligible pass receivers can only be chucked once by any defender after the receiver has gone three yards beyond the line of scrimmage.

Eligible receivers who line up in a position within two yards of a tackle may be legally blocked below the waist at the line of scrimmage.

Eligible receivers who line up more than two yards from a tackle may not be blocked below the waist at or behind the line of scrimmage.

It is illegal for an offensive player to block an opponent below the waist within an area three yards on either side of the line of scrimmage if the blocker is aligned in a position more than two yards outside his tackle and is moving in toward the position of the ball, either at the snap or after it is made—an illegal crackback.

The sudden death system of determining the winner when the score is tied at end of regulation playing time is in effect for preseason and regular season games except that the playing time will be limited to a maximum of one 15-minute period.

A broken limit line is to encompass the entire field two feet outside the white border except in the coaching areas.

1975 End zone markings and club identification at the 50 yard line must be approved by the commissioner.

Pylons not flags will be used for goal line and end line markings.

There will be standard side line markers and chain crews will be uniformly attired.

Ball boys will be clearly identifiable.

Unsportsmanlike conduct includes lingering on the field when being substituted for.

A team may use a double shift on or inside the opponent's 20 yard line after showing it at least three times previously in the game.

A fourth down pass that is incomplete in or through the end zone when the line of scrimmage is inside the 20 will result in the opponent taking possession at the previous line of scrimmage.

If there are penalties on each team on the same play and one results in disqualification, the penalties will be offsetting, but the disqualification will stand.

The penalty for an ineligible player downfield on a forward pass is reduced from 15 to 10 yards.

The penalty for offensive pass interference is reduced from 15 to 10 yards.

Penalties for defensive holding or illegal use of hands will be assessed from the previous line of scrimmage rather than from the spot where the ball is blown dead if that spot is behind the line of scrimmage.

1976 There will be 24 not 12 footballs available each game.

Footballs with stripes will no longer be used.

The toss of the coin will be held three minutes before the kickoff, not 30 minutes before.

A delay of game penalty will no longer be enforced when a runner carries the ball in a manner clearly designed to consume playing time.

Any foul committed by the defense which prevents the try-for-point from being attempted will result in the down being replayed and the kicking team having the option as to when the yardage penalty will be assessed—on the next try or on the ensuing kickoff. Any foul committed by the defense on a successful try will result in a distance penalty being assessed on the following kickoff.

It is illegal for a defender to use a hand or hands on a teammate to gain additional height in an attempt to block a kick.

Each team may not have more than 15 persons in addition to its uniformed players on each side line.

When spectators enter the playing field before the game is over, the field must be cleared in order to allow completion of the game.

Two 30-second clocks visible to players, officials, and fans will be displayed, noting the official time between the ready-for-play signal and the snap of the ball.

A ribbon 2 inches by 36 inches long will be attached to the top of each goal post to assist in determining wind direction.

A player who reports a change in his eligibility, prior to a touchdown, can legally return to his original position for a try-for-point attempt without having to leave the field for one play.

A defender is not permitted to rough a ball carrier who falls to the ground untouched by running or diving into him.

Whenever a disqualified player is banished from a game, he must leave the entire playing field area.

WHERE OFFICIALS STAND

DURING A KICKOFF

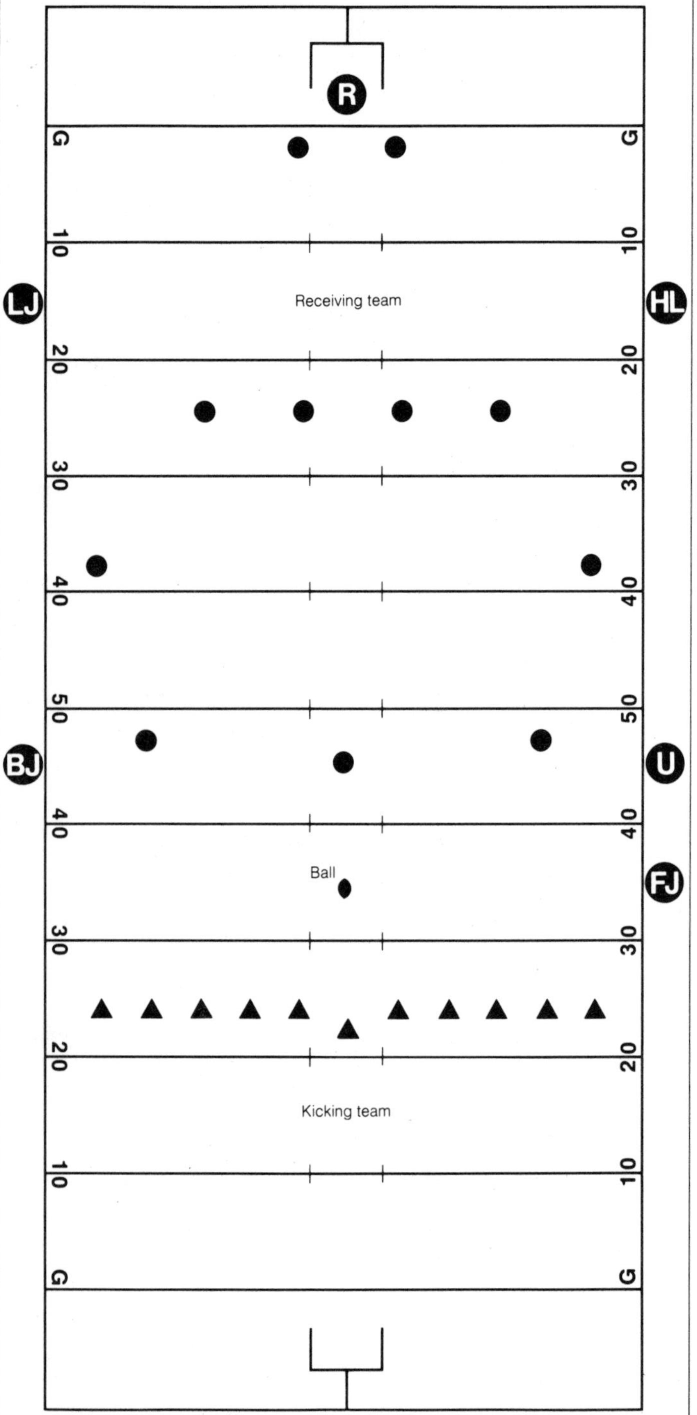

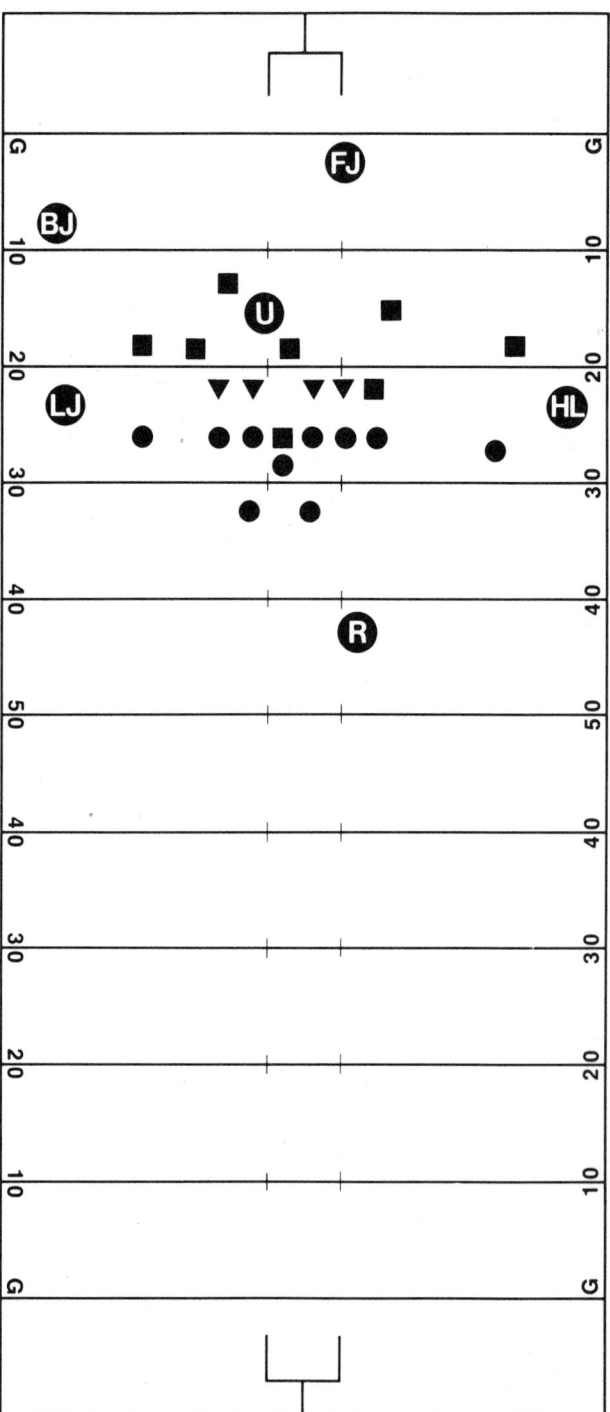

Receiving team

Ball

Kicking team

DURING A PLAY FROM SCRIMMAGE

Legend
R Referee
U Umpire
LJ Line Judge
HL Head Linesman
BJ Back Judge
FJ Field Judge

AFTER A PASS IS THROWN

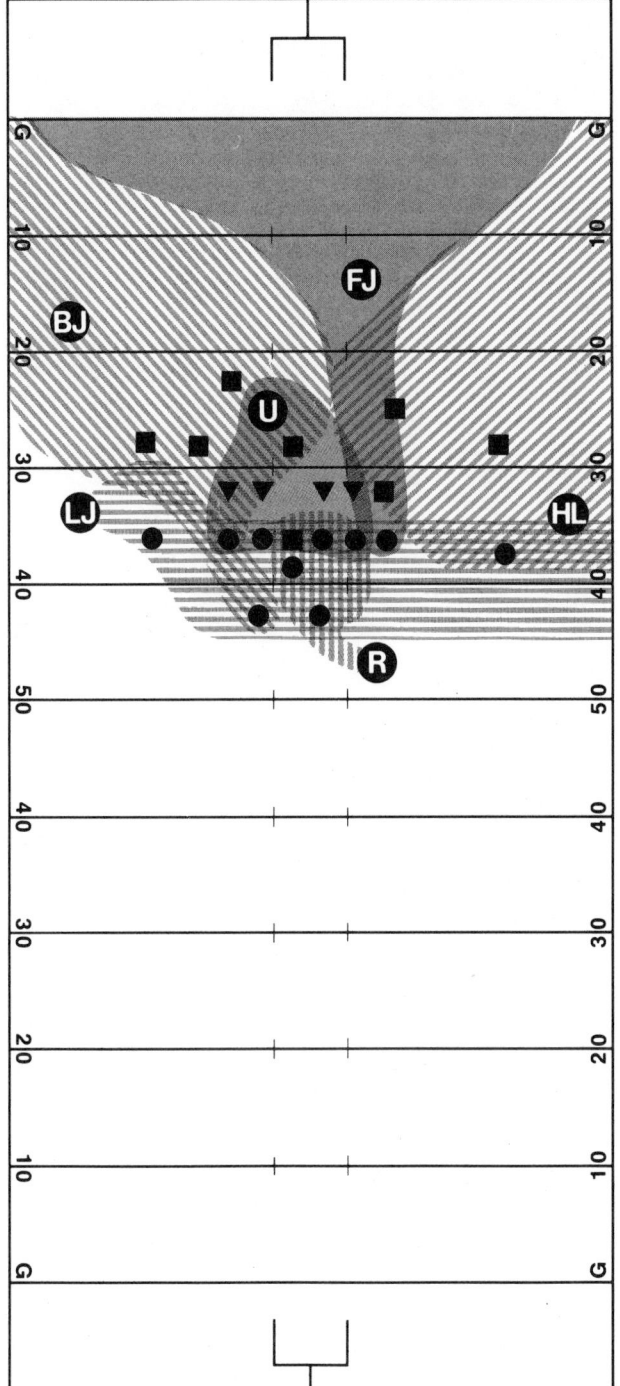

DURING A FIELD GOAL ATTEMPT

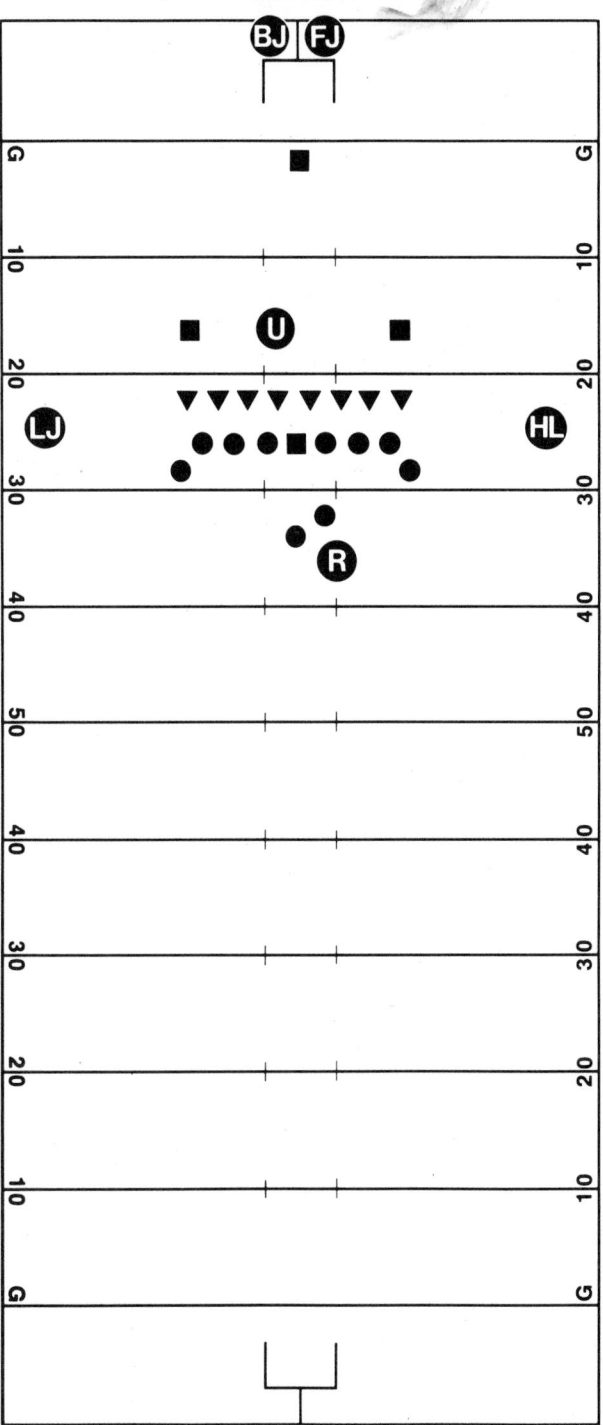

DURING A PUNT

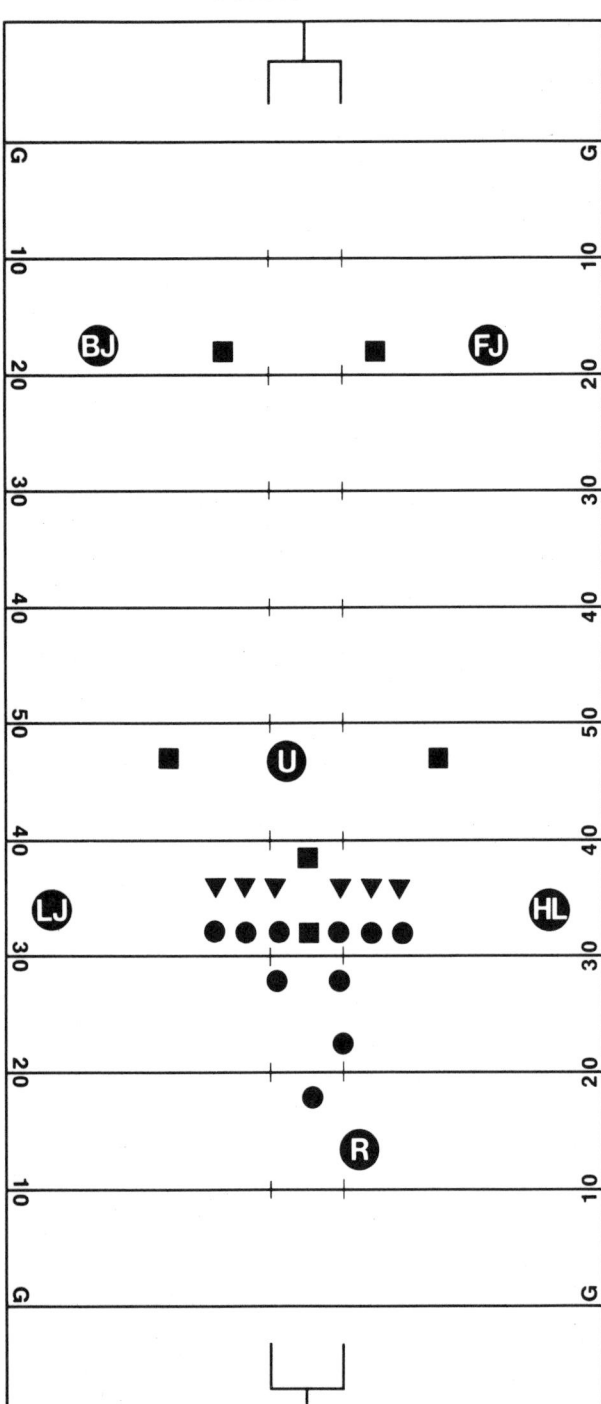

TOOLS OF NFL OFFICIALS

UNIFORM Uniforms—especially striped shirts—are the trademarks of officials. The distinctive long-sleeved shirts worn in the NFL, with two-inch vertical stripes throughout and the official's number on the back, are made for the league by the Wilson Sporting Goods Company; no other model is allowed. A new official hired by the NFL gets two Wilson shirts, one of which he pays for; the other is free. He also is issued a new pair of knickers, or pants, standard black stockings with horizontal white stripes, and two penalty flags. He provides his own cap (white for all six officials, there is no second color for the referee in the NFL), belt, shoes, and other items. Measures are taken to insure standard appearance. There is no rule for how and where the knickers are tucked under at the knee, but the black stockings must be worn on the outside, with cotton socks and sanitary hose underneath. Longtime umpire Lou Palazzi was the last official to wear cotton socks outside his stockings. Furthermore, officials are forbidden to cut the stirrups; thus, their uniform height on the calf is maintained. Belts must be solid black and so must shoes; they cannot have stripes, swirls, stars, or any of the other treatments that adorn most athletic shoes. In inclement weather, officials wear solid white plastic rain jackets with vertical stripes. When it is very cold they may wear thermal underwear or rubberized sweatwear under their uniforms. They are encouraged not to put on pair after pair of extra socks that may make them slow afoot; instead, ordinary grocery store Baggies on each foot have been found to serve extremely well as an insulator. A ski headband and gloves are acceptable, too, in cold weather, but they must be black or white in color. The late Jack Vest once wore blue gloves during a chilly Monday night television game and the letters received later at NFL headquarters making light of Vest's blue gloves have never been forgotten.

BALL It is manufactured by the Wilson Sporting Goods Company in Ada, Ohio and sold at a retail price of $35.00. The home team in every game must provide 24 of them to the referee and it is his responsibility before the game to make sure they are properly inflated and, using a wet towel or a special cloth provided by Wilson, to wipe away the gloss that may still be on the ball from the factory.

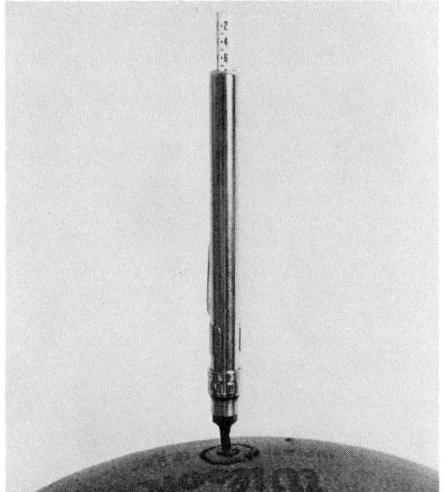

PRESSURE GAUGE It is provided by the league to all its referees and it is the tool they use to insure that the 24 balls used in each game are properly inflated to 12½ to 13½ pounds of air.

COIN The referee tosses it to determine which team wins the right to choose whether to receive or kick off. It is not league issue; referees provide it from their own pockets. Silver dollars are used more than any other coins and referees like to use a coin with sentimental value, for example one that has been in their family for a long time. Now that regular and postseason games may go into sudden death and another coin toss is necessary to start it, the coin must be carried in the pocket for the entire game instead of being stored in a bag.

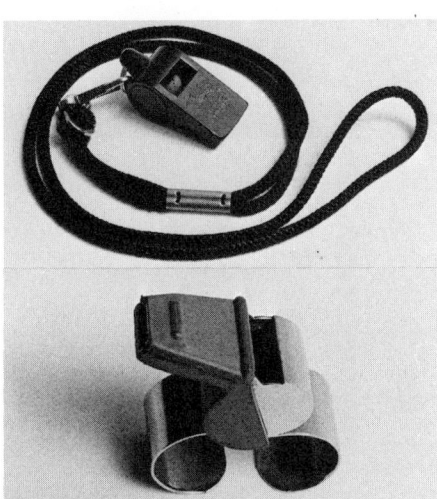

WHISTLES Officials signal to start and end plays hundreds of times during a game. They need a strong pair of lungs and a good whistle. It is estimated that 60 percent of the NFL officials prefer to wear their whistles around their necks, on a necklace of cord, leather, or ordinary hobby shop lanyard. The whistle rests on the end of the necklace or is carried in the lips and blown at the proper time. The other 40 percent of the officials favor the finger whistle; they argue that, carried on the finger, the whistle must be brought to the lips before it can be blown and therefore there is no chance for a "quick whistle."

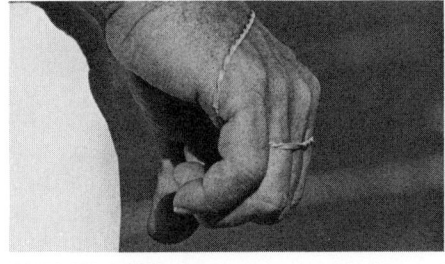

RUBBER BAND Improvisation is the hallmark of any good official and ordinary office supply rubber bands serve an important function. Two of them are knotted together and, worn round a wrist and the correct fingers, keep the official informed of the down in progress. One finger, first down; two fingers, second down; and so on.

PENALTY FLAG It is the instrument with which NFL games are policed. Flying through the air, it is the sight coaches and players like to see least. It can end drives, break hearts, and shorten careers . . . and there would be no league without it. The league issues it to the official but he must sew some object into a corner of it—a fishing lead or a nut, bolt, or washer—that will weight it and make it land accurately near the point of the infraction. When not in use it is tucked away in the official's back pocket.

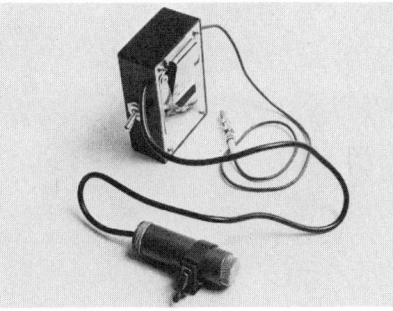

MICROPHONE The referee is the only official equipped with a microphone and he uses it to announce penalties. He wears a Vega transmitter with a four-inch antenna on his belt behind him. The transmitter has a nine-volt battery, a frequency of 150 megacycles, and a power output of 20 milowatts. A cord connects the transmitter to a microphone worn clipped to the official's striped shirt at the chest. Only announcements are heard because he has an on-and-off switch on his transmitter. The radio unit, which is built exclusively for stadium use to prevent receiving other signals on the business band, is connected to the public address system.

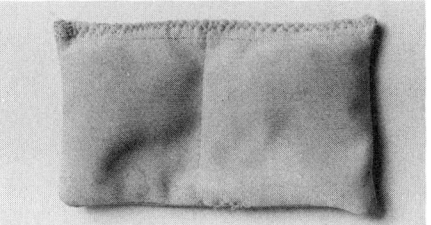

BEANBAG Rarely used, it marks the spot of the change of possession—where the interception was made, where the fumble was picked up. Its role can be vital when a foul occurs after such a change of possession. The deep officials on kicks—head linesmen and line judge on kickoffs, back and field judge on punts—also assist statisticians by marking the spot where the kickoff or punt was caught. The statistician in the press box can then determine the length of the kick and return, especially if the kickoff is fielded in the end zone, where there are no yard lines. Beanbags once were yellow but everyone kept confusing them with penalty flags. They changed to green but then no one could see them. They then changed to blue.

HEAD LINESMAN'S CLIP This important tool is used when first down measurements are made. The chain unit must be moved from the side line to the hashmarks and so its location must be carefully noted before it is moved. The head linesman marks it with this clip at the nearest major yard line and adjusts the disc attached to the clip to indicate the yard line. Moved to the hashmarks for the measurement, the chain is then put down and stretched from the identical forward edge of the same yard line for the measurement.

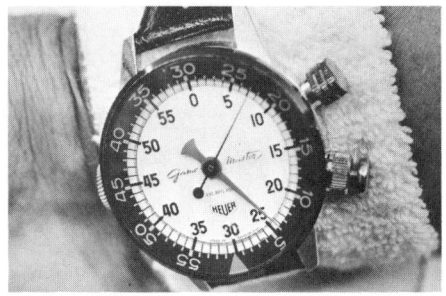

STOPWATCH Electronics has taken over the job of timing pro football games but there are still two officials equipped with stopwatches in case the machines fail. Backing up the clock operator who is on the side line or in the press box, the back judge times the game with a Swiss Heuer Game Master stopwatch, worth approximately $90, worn on his wrist. The reset button on the base of the watch can be screwed tight so the field judge can continue to start and stop the watch using the other buttons, free of worry about hitting the reset button and losing track of time. The field judge also is equipped with a stopwatch. He backs up the 30-second clock operator in timing the offense putting the ball in play. He wears a $185 Longines Chronograph for this job.

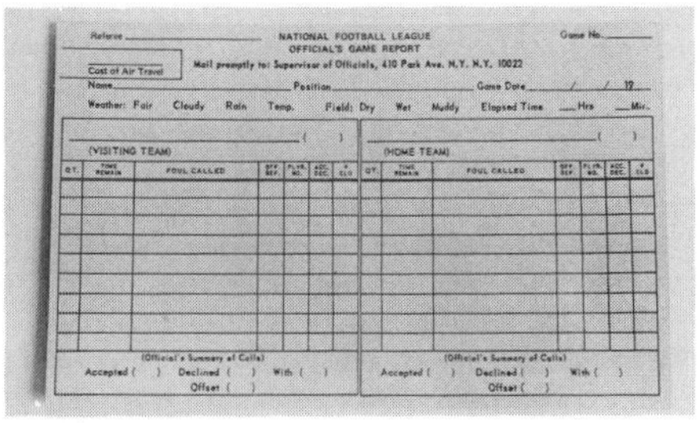

Referee ______ NATIONAL FOOTBALL LEAGUE Game No. ______

OFFICIAL'S GAME REPORT

Cost of Air Travel

Mail promptly to: Supervisor of Officials, 410 Park Ave. N.Y. N.Y. 10022

Name ______ Position ______ Game Date __/__/19__

Weather: Fair Cloudy Rain Temp. Field: Dry Wet Muddy Elapsed Time __Hrs __Min.

(VISITING TEAM) ______ ( )

(HOME TEAM) ______ ( )

(Official's Summary of Calls) Accepted ( ) Declined ( ) With ( ) Offset ( )

(Official's Summary of Calls) Accepted ( ) Declined ( ) With ( ) Offset ( )

GAME DATA CARD It is the referee's report to the league of every call made by his crew during the game. Each crew member charts his calls and other important information during the game and it is then placed on a single card by the referee and mailed to the NFL headquarters immediately after the game.

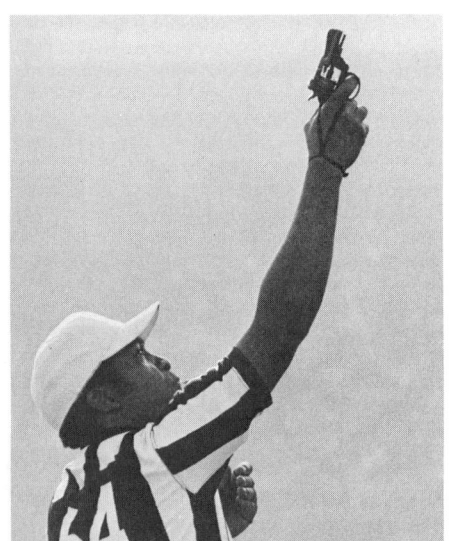

PISTOL The field judge carries a .22 caliber pistol and fires it to signal the end of each quarter. The pistol fires blanks. It was once carried from game to game by the field judge but the era of hijackings of airplanes, and the resultant tightened security measures, ended that. Now each team's equipment manager stores a pistol in the locker room and turns it over to the field judge before each game.

FIELD AND STADIUM HARDWARE

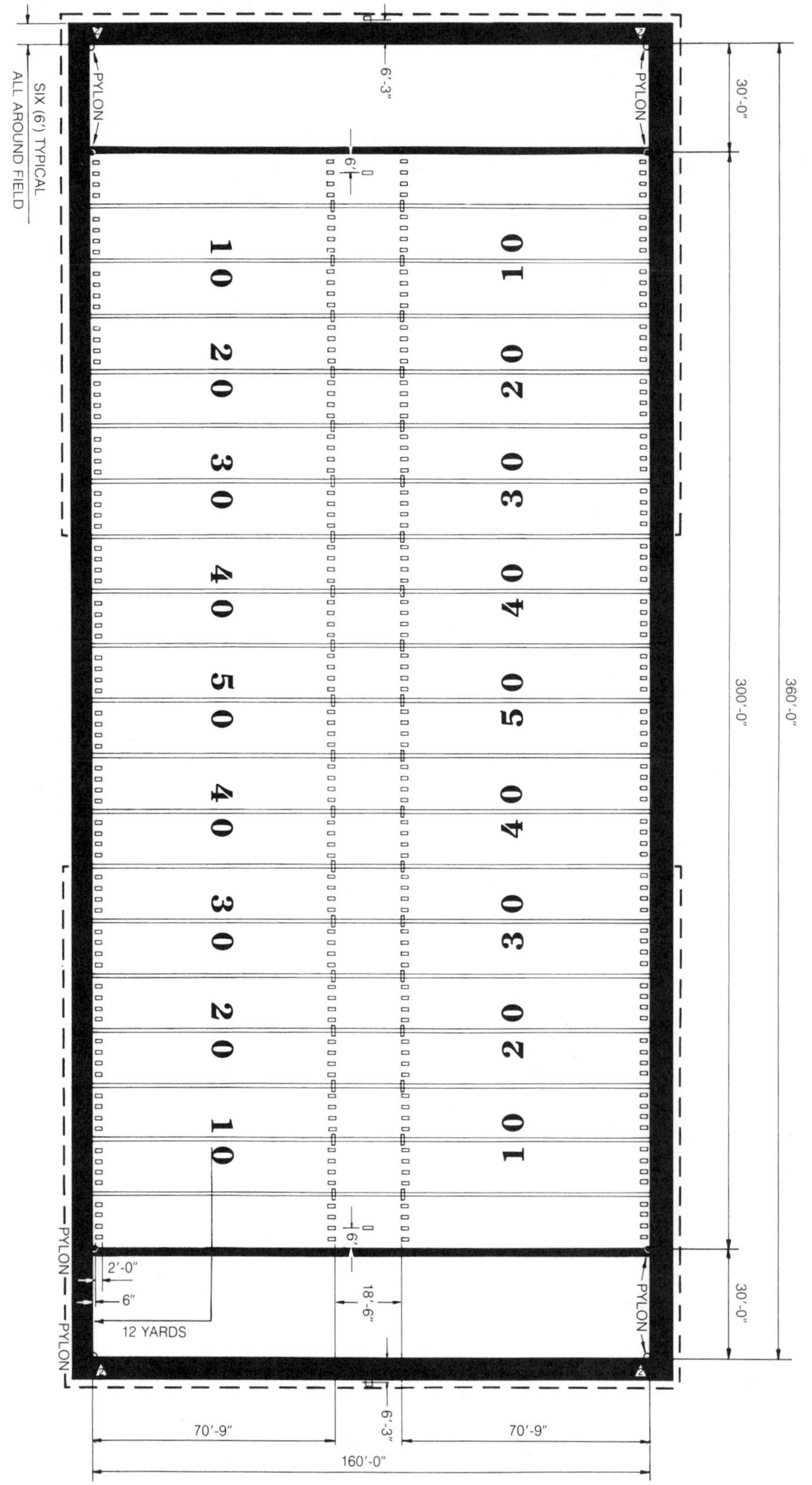

FIELD This is the official NFL diagram for a football field. It is distributed to each team and must be followed explicitly. The field is 160 feet wide and, including the end zones, 360 feet long. It is surrounded by a six-foot wide white border that appears in black on the diagram;this border assists officials in making sideline calls, improves fan vantage, and restrains and protects photographers. The numbers are 36 feet, or 12 yards, from each sideline; the hashmarks 70 feet 9 inches, or about 23 yards from each sideline.

STADIUM CLOCK It is the official timekeeper for the game and is operated by an experienced and knowledgeable football official who is appointed by the commissioner. That is his only job. The additional functions of electronic message and scoreboards are done by other people. Their jobs are unrelated to the all-important timing of the game.

30-SECOND CLOCK Another official appointed by the commissioner operates the 30-second clock. It was used for the first time in 1976 and is manufactured by the General Indicator Company. It is four feet high and six feet wide and is raised at least five feet off the ground so it can be seen clearly by fans, quarterback, the referee, and the field judge. There is a 30-second clock at each end of the field. The offense has 30 seconds to put the ball in play from the time the referee signals ready for play. If it does not, it incurs a five-yard delay of game penalty.

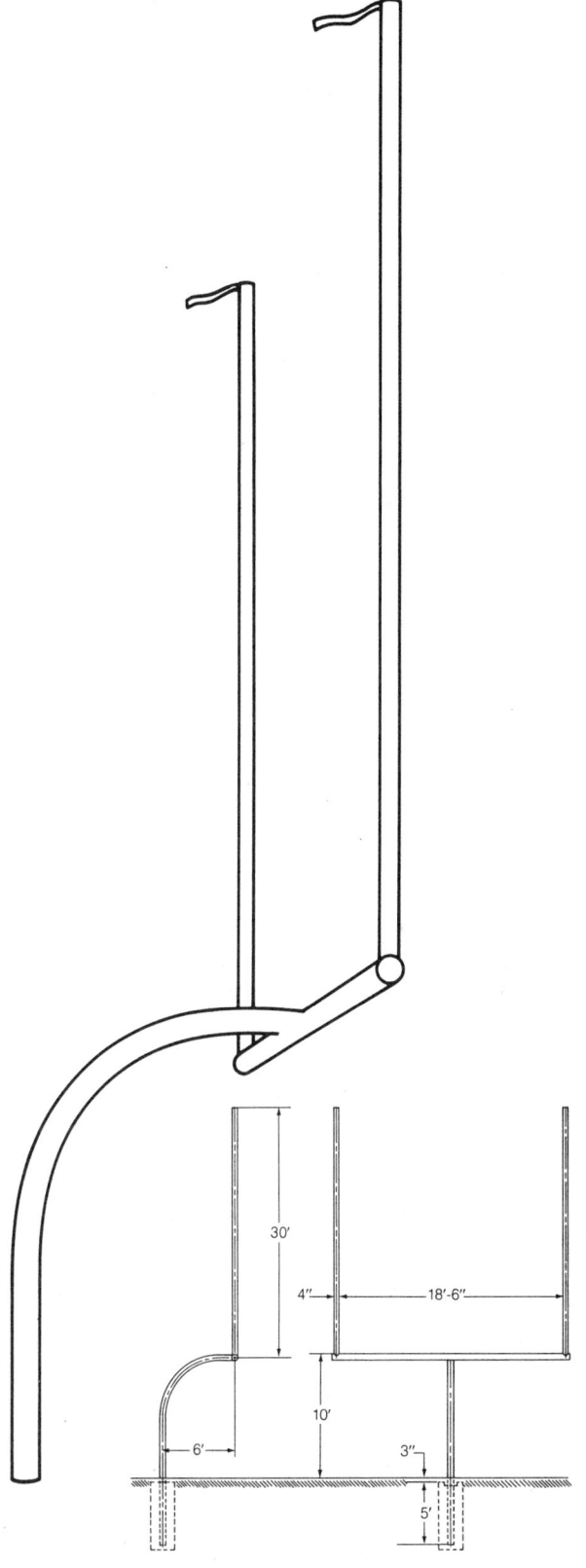

GOAL POSTS The bright gold single standard offset Triman Tele-Goal is used in every NFL stadium. It was invented by Jim Trimble, who is now director of pro personnel for the New York Giants and at the time was a Canadian Football League coach, and Joel Rottman, a Canadian engineer and football fan. It weighs 240 pounds. The crossbar is 10 feet above the end line and the uprights soar 30 feet above the crossbar, a full 20 feet higher than those in high school and college. This eliminates a large share of the arguments that occur when placekicks go above not between the uprights. Ribbons 2″ by 36″ were added in 1976 to assist kickers in determining wind direction.

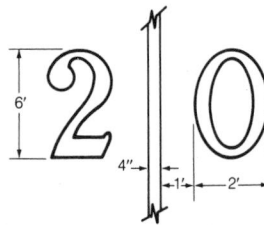

NUMBERS It would be aggravating to watch a game—and impossible to broadcast it or study a game film of it—without field numbers. They are six feet high, large enough so that they can be seen from the farthest seat in the largest NFL stadiums. This is the official detail specification given NFL teams for making their field numbers. The type face, roughly approximating a face called Caslon, is old-fashioned but highly readable.

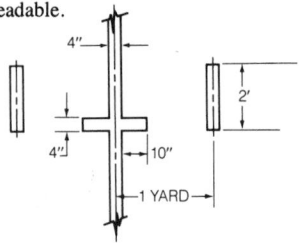

HASHMARKS This is the official detail specification given NFL teams for making their field hashmarks. When the ball is carried outside the hashmarks, it is returned to them for the start of the next play. Since there are yard lines only every five yards, hashmarks themselves are yard lines.

SIDE LINE YARD LINE MARKER Each side line yard line marker used in NFL games is an A-frame fabric cover over a polyfoam pad, for safety in case players or others strike it, and it has lead imbedded in the corners to keep it from being carried away if the wind is blowing. This and all the following products are made for the NFL by the 5-K Products Company of El Reno, Oklahoma.

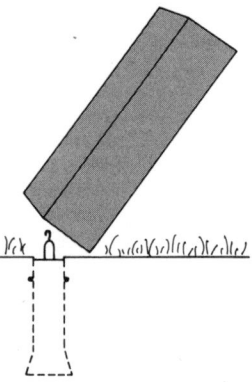

PYLON A pylon marks the corner of each end zone. It is a 4″ × 4″ × 18″ polyfoam pad anchored in the ground. It will bend on contact and snap back to an upright position after it has been struck. It is much safer than the flag and metal flagstaff that was used in each corner of the end zone before 1975. When pass receivers cut toward the flag they ran "flag patterns." This should be changed in NFL playbooks to "pylon patterns," but it is highly unlikely that will ever happen.

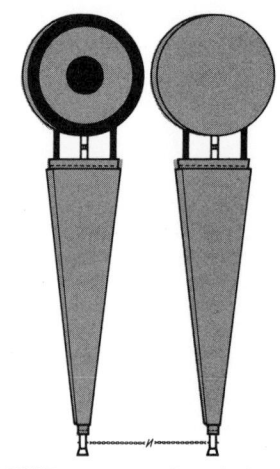

CHAIN UNIT In an age of synthetics the simple metal chain remains the best way to measure the 10 yards of a football field the offense must cover to make a first down. Chain is still best because it does not stretch or tear. The shafts or poles at each end are bright orange for visibility and padded for safety.

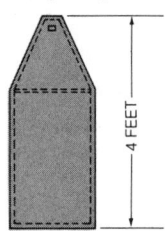

FIRST DOWN GROUND SPOTTER A furious sweep or off-tackle play coming hard for the side line can send even the most well-meaning chain crew member scrambling for safety. When that happens, the sticks are left unattended and their place may be lost, and, in addition, the ball carrier who is driving earnestly for the forward stick to make a first down has lost his target when the stick is thrown to the ground and the chain crew dashes away. In such a situation the first down ground spotter saves the day. Four feet long and bright red in color, it remains in place on the ground even when the sticks are taken away.

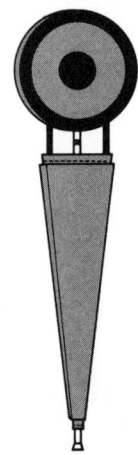

OPPOSITE SIDE BULLSEYE The chain unit is used on one side of the field for the first half and on the other half of the field for the second half. Therefore, on any plays going in the direction away from the chain unit it would be impossible for the runner, receiver, and quarterback to determine the point they must reach to make a first down without the opposite side bullseye. The "bullseye" name and design correctly reflect the exclamation of these players—and their coach—when they reach it.

INDICATOR It indicates the down. The carrier flips over a new card to indicate a new down.

DRIVE START MARKER This is the only tool of NFL officials that has virtually nothing to do with the policing of the game and instead is there entirely for the benefit of the fans and press. It marks the start of a drive made by the offense and is not moved until a score is made or the ball changes hands. It resembles a railroad crossing traffic sign and, at the end of a long drive, the lonely member of the chain crew standing at the far end of the field with the drive start marker shows everyone in the stadium just how far the offense traveled.

The field crew at Oakland-Alameda County Stadium, Raiders vs. New England Patriots, AFC divisional playoff, 1976.

OFFICIAL SIGNALS

TOUCHDOWN, FIELD GOAL, or SUCCESSFUL TRY
Both arms extended above head.

ILLEGAL FORWARD PASS
One hand waved behind back. Same signal followed by raised hand flung downward: **Intentional Grounding of Pass.**

FIRST DOWN
Arm pointed toward defensive team's goal.

DEAD BALL or NEUTRAL ZONE ESTABLISHED
One arm above head with an open hand. With fist closed: **Fourth Down.**

LOSS OF DOWN
Fingertips tap both shoulders (following signal for foul).

ILLEGAL CHUCKING
One open hand extended forward.

NO TIME OUT or TIME IN WITH WHISTLE
Full arm circled to simulate winding clock.

DELAY OF GAME or EXCESS TIME OUT
Folded arms. Same signal followed by forearms rotated over and over in front of body: **Illegal Formation.**

PERSONAL FOUL
One wrist striking the other above head.

HOLDING
Grasping one wrist, the fist clenched, in front of chest.

ILLEGAL USE OF HANDS
Grasping one wrist, the hand open and facing forward, in front of chest.

PENALTY REFUSED, INCOMPLETE PASS, PLAY OVER, or MISSED GOAL
Hands shifted in horizontal plane.

DOUBLE TOUCH
Fingertips of one hand brush fingers of other hand above head (following incomplete pass signal).

PASS JUGGLED INBOUNDS AND CAUGHT OUT OF BOUNDS
Hands up and down in front of chest (following incomplete pass signal).

SAFETY
Palms together above head.

INTERFERENCE WITH FORWARD PASS OR FAIR CATCH
Hands open and extended forward from shoulders with hands vertical.

INVALID FAIR CATCH SIGNAL
One hand waved above head (following Interference with fair catch signal).

INELIGIBLE RECEIVER or INELIGIBLE MEMBER OF KICKING TEAM DOWNFIELD
Both hands placed on cap.

TIME OUT
Hands crisscrossed above head. Same signal followed by placing one hand on top of cap: **Referee's Time Out:** Same signal followed by arm swung at side: **Touchback.**

OFFSIDE, ENCROACHING, or FREE KICK VIOLATION
Hands on hips.

ILLEGAL MOTION AT SNAP
Horizontal arc with one hand.

CRAWLING, PUSHING, or HELPING RUNNER
Pushing movement of hands to front with arms downward.

UNSPORTSMANLIKE CONDUCT
Arms outstretched, palms down. (Same signal means continuous action fouls are disregarded.)

ILLEGAL CUT
Bent at waist with both hands at knees.

PENALTIES

5 YARDS

1. Crawling.
2. Defensive holding or illegal use of the hands, including chucking an eligible receiver more than once after he is more than three yards downfield (an automatic first down).
3. Delay of game (15 yards if at the start of the half).
4. Encroachment.
5. Too many time outs.
6. False start.
7. Illegal formation.
8. Illegal shift.
9. Illegal motion.
10. Illegal substitution.
11. Kickoff out of bounds between the goal lines and not touched.
12. Invalid fair catch signal.
13. More than 11 players on the field for either team.
14. Less than seven men on the offensive line at the snap.
15. Offside.
16. Failure to pause one second after a shift or huddle.
17. Running into the kicker (an automatic first down).
18. More than one man in motion at the snap.
19. Grasping the face mask of opponent (an automatic first down if by the defense).
20. Player out of bounds at the snap.
21. Ineligible member(s) of the kicking team going beyond the line of scrimmage before the ball is kicked.

5 YARDS AND LOSS OF DOWN

1. Forward pass thrown from beyond the line of scrimmage.

5 YARDS AND SUSPENSION FROM GAME

1. Illegal equipment; the player may return after one down when he is legally equipped.

10 YARDS

1. Offensive pass interference.
2. Ineligible player downfield during a passing down.

10 YARDS AND LOSS OF DOWN

1. Forward pass intentionally touched by an ineligible receiver on or behind the line of scrimmage.
2. Forward pass intentionally or accidentally touched by an ineligible receiver beyond the line of scrimmage.

15 YARDS

1. Clipping.
2. Fair catch interference.
3. Illegal batting, kicking, or punching a loose ball.
4. Illegal crackback block by the offense.
5. Piling on—an automatic first down.
6. Roughing the kicker—an automatic first down.
7. Roughing the passer—an automatic first down.
8. Twisting, turning, or pulling an opponent by the face mask.
9. Unnecessary roughness.
10. Unsportsmanlike conduct.
11. Delay of the game at the start of either half.
12. Helping the runner.
13. Holding, illegal use of hands, or tripping on offense (10 yards if enforced from a spot at or behind the line of scrimmage or no deeper than three yards downfield).

15 YARDS AND LOSS OF DOWN

1. Intentional grounding of a forward pass.

15 YARDS AND DISQ. IF FLAGRANT

1. Striking an opponent with a fist.
2. Kicking or kneeing an opponent.
3. Striking an opponent on the head or neck with a forearm, elbow, or hands.
4. Roughing the kicker.
5. Roughing the passer.
6. Malicious unnecessary roughness.
7. Unsportsmanlike conduct.

LOSS OF DOWN—NO YARDAGE

1. Second forward pass behind the line.
2. Forward pass striking the ground, goal post, or crossbar.
3. Forward pass going out of bounds.
4. Forward pass first touched by an eligible receiver who has gone out of bounds and returned.
5. Forward pass touched or caught by a second eligible receiver before it is touched by the defense.
6. Forward pass accidentally touching an ineligible receiver on or behind the line of scrimmage.

AUTOMATIC FIRST DOWN

1. All defensive fouls except offside, encroachment, delay of game, illegal substitution, and excessive time outs.

A TOUCHDOWN AWARDED

1. When the referee determines that a palpably unfair act deprives a team of a touchdown, such as the act of a player coming off the bench and tackling a runner apparently en route to a touchdown.

TRY-FOR-POINT AWARDED

1. The defense committing a foul during a try-for-point which would ordinarily result in a safety.

SCORE AWARDED

1. Repeated fouling by the defense near its goal line to prevent a score by halving the distance.

LOSS OF HALF DISTANCE TO GOAL

1. Incurring a distance penalty moving the ball more than half the distance to the goal line.
2. Defensive pass interference in its end zone on a play in which the previous spot was inside the defense's 1-yard line.

BALL PLACED ON THE 1-YARD LINE

1. Defensive pass interference in its end zone on a play in which the previous spot was outside the defense's 1-yard line.

A History of Football Equipment

There is an old saying that, "Clothes make the man." And there is an enduring conviction in the sport of football that new equipment—a change of uniforms—can help transform a losing team into a winner. It is the first impulse of any new coach, about to embark on a campaign to build a juggernaut upon the rubble of long years of poor won-and-lost records, to march earnestly to the office of the general manager or athletic director and persuade him that, hang the expense, the team must order new uniforms right away.

George (Potsy) Clark left the Detroit Lions in 1937 to become the coach of the Brooklyn Dodgers. An enterprising and imaginative man, he had steered the Lions to the NFL championship in 1934 and, in 1935, authored *Football by Potsy Clark,* one of the first magazines about professional football. He now planned to stand the league on its ear by dressing the Dodgers in scintillating new uniforms. They were going to be so grand, the *Brooklyn Eagle* said, "that Solomon in all his glory would look like Mahatma Gandhi.

"One of the things that may have been the matter with the Dodgers last year was their drab and lifeless uniform," the newspaper continued. "No athlete with any aesthetic sensibility could be expected to gain ground wearing the hideous green and white combination in which they were clothed.

"It has been proven time and again that gorgeous uniforms make soldiers brave. A man might be able to fight just as well in a two-pants suit or a pair of overalls, but he wouldn't have the inspiration that makes heroes."

To tackle the problem, Clark called in Wilford A. Lindberg, color engineer of the Chrysler Corporation. "He has a laboratory that the late Thomas A. Edison would have envied," the *Eagle* wrote. "He polished up his instruments, whirled his discs, started his machines, and got down his big black books. When everything had been added up and measured and divided up and so on, the answer was 'Toreador Red.'

"That would be the dominant motif for Brooklyn's football team. It will be the color of their jerseys. Their trousers, helmets, and even their shoelaces, meanwhile, will be silver. These colors suggest action and energy. The red falls between the Lithum lines of 6708 and 6104 Angstrom units and is very high intensity, calculated to create interest on the part of the spectators.

"It is easy to see what the psychological effect of these costumes will be. Potsy likes for his players to come out of the huddle as if shot from guns. In these new suits they will look like a burst of flame as they jump to their positions."

The other teams in the NFL, unfortunately, kept from being charred by the Dodgers. In fact, Brooklyn won only 11 games and lost 17 during the next three years with Clark as their coach and Toreador red as their motif. Wilford A. Lindberg was never consulted again by any football team but he continued to design the color combinations for Chrysler automobiles until 1945. The Dodgers became a winning team for a time under another coach, Dr. John B. (Jock) Sutherland, but went out of business in 1945.

Equipment may or may not be able to turn losers into winners, but it definitely performs a larger function: It protects players and prevents injuries. It is an obvious fact, however, that football players still get injured. That is why manufacturers keep devising better equipment and teams and leagues keep insisting that they do so.

The soccer game Princeton and Rutgers played in 1869, called the first college football game in America, involved no equipment at all other than the ball. The players merely "laid aside their hats, coats, and vests," according to Allison Danzig. "Neither

team was in uniform, although some Rutgers players wore scarlet stocking-caps."

When Harvard played McGill University of Montreal in 1874, the Harvard players wore sweaters and handkerchiefs around their heads, and the McGill players wore white trousers, striped jerseys, and turbans, according to Rawlings Sporting Goods. Princeton or Yale in 1876 may have been the first to wear a complete uniform in its games. Football gradually became an overwhelmingly popular college sport. Its rules were still rather amorphous and the combatants played the Princeton wedge, shoving wedge, and flying wedge with great gusto. There were 18 deaths from playing football in 1905, according to Amos Alonzo Stagg. Public outcries about football violence almost brought about its extinction. It was saved when reforms were made in its rules in 1906, 1907, and 1909. There remained a great demand for enough equipment to supply all the teams playing football, and for quality equipment that would make the game safer.

A. G. Spalding & Company Sporting Goods was the first manufacturer of athletic equipment. Others sprang up rapidly and played an important role in the growth of the game of football. Spalding was notable not only as a manufacturer but as a publisher as well. It published the *Official Football Guide,* for college football, from 1895 until 1940, when it was taken over by the National Collegiate Athletic Association. The book was edited by Walter Camp each year until his death in 1925. Spalding also issued the *Official National Football League Guide* from 1935 until 1940, when it was taken over by the NFL. These pocket books were only part of *Spalding's Athletic Library* of record books and instructional manuals.

A man named Ed Thorp had a great influence on the sport. Thorp was the referee of the 1925 Rose Bowl game between the Notre Dame team that had the "Four Horsemen" in the backfield and the Stanford team that had Ernie Nevers at fullback. Thorp refereed other important games, became well known in college and pro football, and formed Thorp Sporting Goods. It is not clear how it happened, but the trademark for a football called "The Duke" was sold by Thorp to Wilson Sporting Goods and became the trademark on the official ball of the NFL. Wilson was the manufacturer but it was stamped "Thorp Sporting Goods," and elsewhere, "The Duke." After his death, sometime in the 1930s, the NFL began awarding the Ed Thorp Memorial Trophy to the winner of the title game, and it was called not the "NFL championship" but the "Ed Thorp Memorial Championship Game."

There was a time when it appeared that manufacturers of football equipment would become extinct, and equipment would become unnecessary. "The roughness of the game has been practically eliminated by the new rules," the 1909 *Spalding Guide* said. "Still, shin guards and shoulder pads are sometimes needed."

That report proved optimistic. Football players did not begin to wear fewer pads but in fact became covered with them. And the rules organizations for high school, college, and—after 1920—professional football went right on changing the game and writing strict rules about equipment.

The first major rules change the NFL made having to do with equipment was the seemingly long-overdue requirement in 1943 that players wear helmets; "head protectors" was the language used. Elmer Layden, commissioner of the NFL in 1941–46, believed genuinely that many of the players in the league had rather bad-looking legs and he considered it one of the momentous acts of his administration that he pushed through a rule in 1945 requiring them to wear long stockings.

Plastic helmets were banned in 1948 and permitted in 1949; they went on to become standard throughout

the sport. It was all right to grab a face mask in 1956 provided it was the ball carrier's; the grabbing of any face mask was prohibited in 1962.

White footballs with black stripes were made illegal in 1956, in favor of a brown ball with white stripes. In 1972, the commissioner was made the judge of when teams could use a brown ball with white stripes for late-starting games. In 1976, they were outlawed altogether.

Beginning in 1970, the members of the league required themselves—not in their rules, but in their by-laws—to give the commissioner a year's notice before changing their uniform.

Injuries are a regrettable by-product of football. They have concerned football leagues and teams as long as the game has existed. In 1974, the NFL commissioned a study of injuries by the Stanford Research Institute in Menlo Park, California. It was actually the third such report prepared by that organization for the NFL. Its findings were exhaustive, covering every facet of football injuries. Among them: There were 1,169 injuries in the NFL in 1974; 1,044 in 1973; and 1,157 in 1972. There are more knee injuries than any other. A kickoff is the most dangerous play. Running back and cornerback are the most hazardous positions. Offensive players get more injuries than defensive players, but neither are injured as often as special teams players. And shoulder pads cause more injuries than helmets.

Teams understandably spare no expense to get the best equipment possible. The Los Angeles Rams said in 1976 they spend an estimated $40,000 a year on equipment. They own enough of it to completely outfit 100 football players, which they must do every year because that is the average number of players reporting at the start of training camp. When they take a trip, the Rams said, they load 4,000 pounds of equipment on the airplane; if they expect foul weather, more gear such as heavy parkas swells the load to 5,500 pounds. Thus, the equipment taken on one road trip by an NFL team in the seventies probably equals the combined weight of all the players who took part in that famous game between Princeton and Rutgers back in 1869.

I. THE BALL

Dr. Glenn Seaborg, Nobel Prize winner and former chairman of the Atomic Energy Commission, was seen crossing the campus of the University of California carrying an official NFL football. Since he was not a member of Cal's football team, there had to be another reason why this eminent physicist was carrying a football across the campus. There was. He was on his way to teach the university's large freshman chemistry class, College Chemistry I, and was going to use a football to demonstrate the shape of the nucleus of the uranium atom—a prolate spheroid.

The unusual shape of a football, which Dr. Seaborg used to advantage, contributes immeasurably to the variety of the sport played with it and the fascination others have for it. Not being round, it bounces oddly. Being elliptical, it is aerodynamically superior to a round ball, so it passes better. It can be handed off and carried more easily than a round ball of the same size.

The word prolate is from the latin, *prolatus,* meaning stretched out. The polar axis of a prolate spheroid is longer than its equatorial diameter. Most of the sports balls in the world are round or oblate, not prolate. Of all the sports shown in a 1974 book, *Rules of the Game,* only four used prolate balls. They were rugby and American, Australian, and Canadian football.

Rugby began in England in 1823. Players could run with or lateral the ball as well as kick it; rugby balls became prolate. Soccer frowned on all that and remained a kicking game; soccer balls stayed round.

The game between Princeton and Rutgers in 1869

Peck & Snyder "Foot Ball Inflator," 1886.

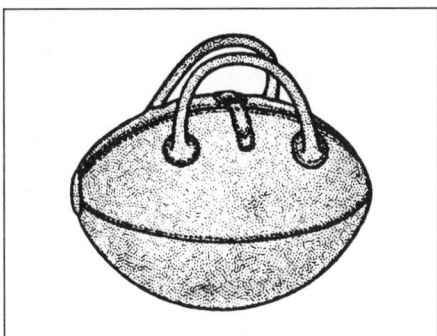

For team that has everything, "Football Carrier," 1925.

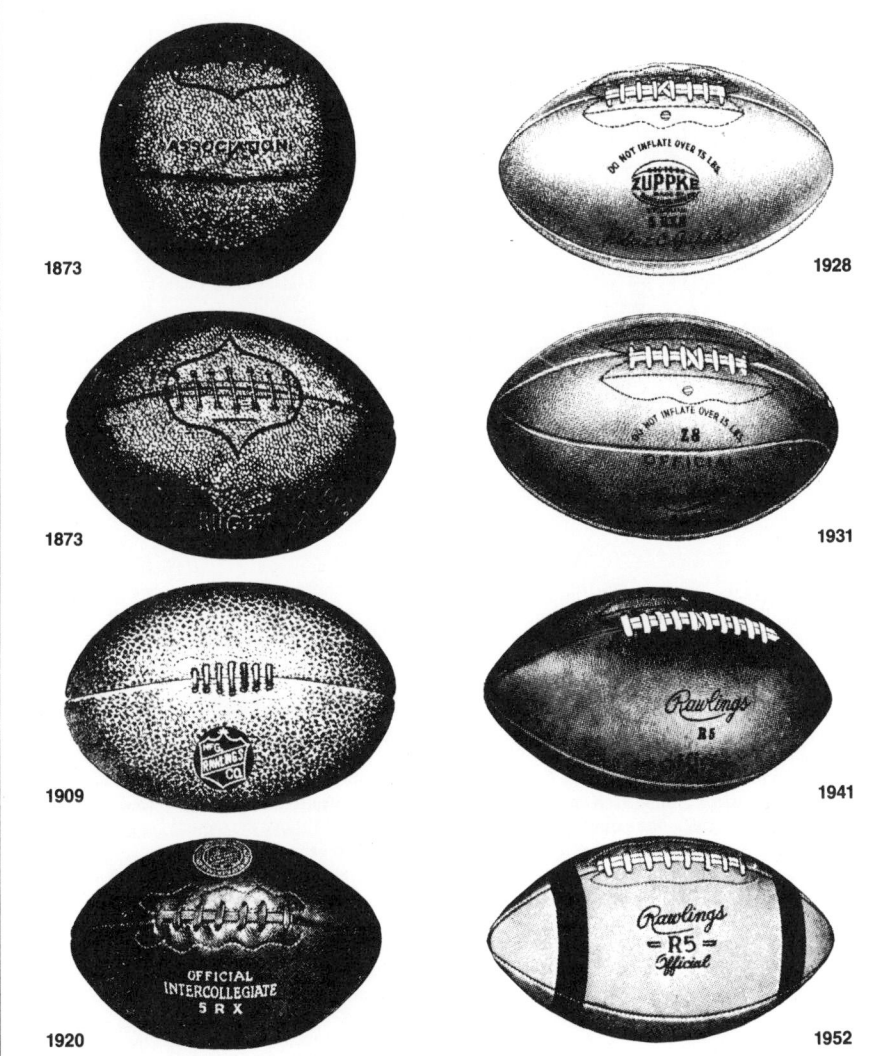

1873

1873

1909

1920

1928

1931

1941

1952

Footballs made by Rawlings Sporting Goods through the years.

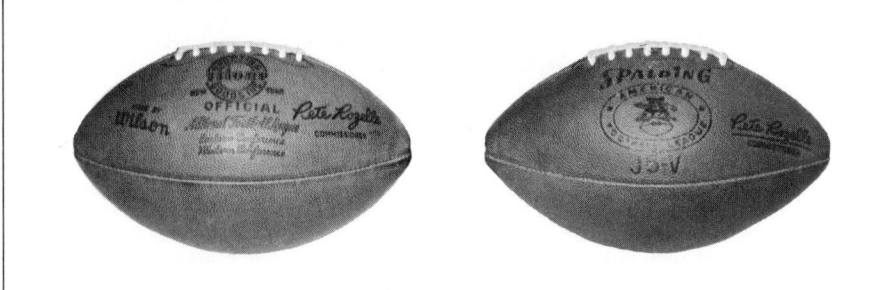

The 1960s Wilson ball for the NFL, left, and Spalding's for the AFL.

was played with a round English soccer ball. Rugby gained the upper hand, however, when McGill University of Montreal put it on display in games against Harvard in 1874. Rugby football went on to become, simply, football. The hopes of the exponents of a round ball for the sport went flat, and prolate spheroids became the rule.

As its name implies, football was originally played only with the feet. Everything man had learned to do with his hands since the thumb became independent of the four fingers was left out of the game. Rugby brought the hands into play in 1823. The ball could be picked up and passed. Nearly another century went by, however, before it could be passed *forward*.

Traditions die hard. The rule permitting the forward pass in 1906 was virtually ignored until well-known teams—for example, the 1913 Notre Dame team with Gus Dorais at tailback and Knute Rockne at end—began using the forward pass. Changes in the ball's specifications were ordered. It became slimmer, lighter, and easier to pass. It changed dramatically; pumpkins, watermelons, and other fruits suffered in the public eye as writers used them for comparisons to describe what the football had been, in contrast to its new, sleek shape.

Five rules were made—all by college and not professional football—affecting the football's shape. Its weight was set at 14 to 15 ounces in 1912. Its long axis became 28″ to 28½″ the same year. Its short axis—around the middle—went from 22½″ to 23″ in 1912, to 22″ to 22½″ in 1929, to 21¼″ to 21½″ in 1934. Its length became 11 to 11¼″ in 1931. And the amount of air that can be pumped into it was set at 12½ to 13½ pounds in 1934.

Manufacturers met those specifications in varying degrees. The Pro Football Hall of Fame has on display a half-moon templet used before games in the early days of football. The ball was lowered into it to determine whether it had the proper shape and amount of inflation. A similar operation is performed before games today; the referee personally checks every football, 24 in all, to make sure each has 12½ to 13½ pounds of air pressure in it.

The rules changes affecting the shape of the football ended in 1934. That roughly coincided with the NFL's rules changes of 1933 and 1934, the first significant ones it ever made, creating inbounds lines or hashmarks to which the ball had to be returned for the start of a new play whenever it was carried near or over the sideline, and allowing forward passes from anywhere behind the line of scrimmage. The colleges had been responsible for slimming the football. The pros were responsible for removing puritanical strictures limiting the amount of passing in a game, and moving the ball nearer the center of the field, opening the way for rollout, bootleg, and sprint-out passing.

Footballs are not "pigskins." Yet that term persisted for years. Why? This explanation is usually offered: "The earliest footballs generally were inflated animal bladders, often those of pigs, which led to the term 'pigskin.'"

But do sports terms endure so long as that? Surely it has been centuries since any civilized person actually ripped the bladder from some poor slain hog—and it would have had to have been a large one to have a bladder big enough to become part of a game of football—and gone off kicking it around. Furthermore, a pig's skin and the membrane covering one of its internal organs, it bladder, are two different things; are we to believe the person who supposedly coined the phrase confused the two? A more likely explanation is that he was woefully uninformed, and his error was repeated by others who were equally uninformed, of the simple fact that footballs are made of steerhide.

Rubber gained a foothold in 1951. "There was wild rejoicing among the bovine population throughout

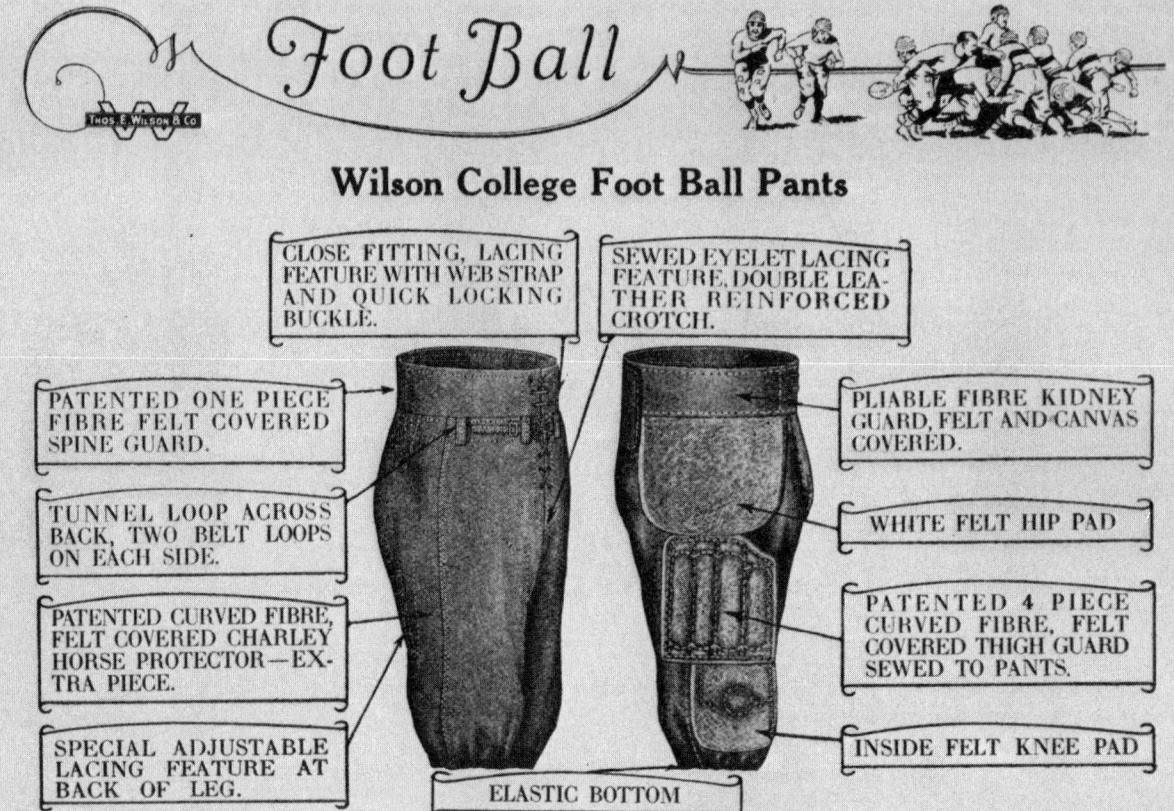

Foot Ball

Wilson College Foot Ball Pants

CLOSE FITTING, LACING FEATURE WITH WEB STRAP AND QUICK LOCKING BUCKLE.

SEWED EYELET LACING FEATURE, DOUBLE LEATHER REINFORCED CROTCH.

PATENTED ONE PIECE FIBRE FELT COVERED SPINE GUARD.

PLIABLE FIBRE KIDNEY GUARD, FELT AND CANVAS COVERED.

TUNNEL LOOP ACROSS BACK, TWO BELT LOOPS ON EACH SIDE.

WHITE FELT HIP PAD

PATENTED CURVED FIBRE, FELT COVERED CHARLEY HORSE PROTECTOR—EXTRA PIECE.

PATENTED 4 PIECE CURVED FIBRE, FELT COVERED THIGH GUARD SEWED TO PANTS.

SPECIAL ADJUSTABLE LACING FEATURE AT BACK OF LEG.

INSIDE FELT KNEE PAD

ELASTIC BOTTOM

B905. Wilson Football Pants made of khaki colored 8 oz. duck; double stitched, reinforced crotch; tunnel loops; flexible hip pad of heavy white felt; pliable fibre kidney guard protected by felt and covered with canvas; one piece fibre spine guard, patented curved fibre thigh guards and Charley Horse pad covered with white felt. Special adjustable lacing feature at back of leg. Inside white felt knee pad; elastic bottoms..............Per Pair, $10.00

There were even "Charley Horse pads" in these "College Foot Ball Pants" offered by Wilson Sporting Goods, 1925.

the land," *Pro Football Illustrated* wrote. The victory was short-lived. Steerhide remained the preferred material for quality footballs. Cowhide is second best. The next alternative is bullhide but it is never used; bulls escape the auctioneer's gavel and remain in the pasture to father new offspring.

The bladder in a football has nothing to do with pigs and it is made of rubber. Inflating it and keeping it inflated was a problem that plagued the sport for 50 years. The ball in the second game in 1869 between Rutgers and Princeton, according to Allison Danzig, kept losing its shape and "several times during the game play had to be stopped, and a little key was brought out from the side line to unlock the small nozzle tucked into the ball. The players took turns blowing the ball up."

In 1886, the Peck & Snyder Sporting Goods catalog advertised a device resembling a syringe called "The New Patent Foot Ball Inflator." It was "far superior, in every respect, to the old style large brass pumps. With it the largest ball can be inflated to its fullest capacity in five minutes time while the old way took half an hour.

"It is not advisable to inflate Foot Balls with the breath, as the moisture that collects in them soon rots the bladder."

Stem valves that protruded from the ball and had to be tucked in during play gave way to metal valves such as those on automobile tires. They were considered unsafe and so rubber valves were developed for footballs. The final step in making an efficient ball was prelacing; it developed about 1920 and after that

the ball no longer had to unlaced to be inflated.

White footballs were used for a time, too. In 1956, the NFL okayed the use of white footballs in night games. For the next 20 years, there were "night footballs" with white stripes around each end. They were prohibited in 1976 because the paint made the balls slick. The rules continued to call for a ball that is "...a pebble grained, leather case of natural tan color."

The Spalding J5-V was the official NFL ball from 1920 until 1940, and it was used in the AFL between 1960 and 1969. Spalding named the ball "The Duke" apparently during the 1930s. "The Duke" was the boyhood nickname of Wellington Mara of the New York Giants. Thorp Sporting Goods began making a ball called "The Duke," and sold the registered name to Spalding. Wilson Sporting Goods took it over when it became the manufacturer of official NFL footballs in 1941. "The Duke" was retired in 1969 and Wilson's ball renamed, simply, "NFL."

The leather Wilson uses comes primarily from the Horween Leather Company, which is owned and operated by Arnold Horween, Sr., who was the coach at Harvard University in 1926-30. He tans hides and sells them to Wilson. It uses only full grain steerhide, the full thickness of the hide, in NFL footballs. The four panels for the ball are cut in such a way that any blemishes on the hide are avoided. The panels are skived to a specified thickness and then weighed to make sure they meet specifications, and checked to make sure their appearance is uniform.

Linings for each panel and reinforcements for the

bladder opening and the valve ring are added. The panels are sewn together inside out. The ball is then turned through the lace opening using an iron post, in an operation that requires strength and dexterity. The bladder is inserted and the ball is laced. It is inflated to 80 pounds, 65 above the required amount of pressure, so it can be examined for appearance, stitching, and shape. If it meets every requirement, it is stamped "NFL," deflated, and delivered. It is then used in an NFL game—preseason, regular season, and post-season. It becomes the object of all the blocking and tackling, blitzing and cracking back, bombs and bumps-and-runs, the only truly essential piece of equipment in the game.

II. PANTS AND JERSEYS

The first football pants and jerseys, in the 1870s, were made of canvas. They were knee-length togs or breeches and long- or short-sleeved jackets that laced in the front. Canvas is sturdy and durable; it is good for making tents. After a long, hot game in which the players had perspired freely, football uniforms made of canvas must not have needed folding; they probably would have stood up by themselves.

Moleskin, "a heavy-napped cotton twill fabric," replaced canvas in football pants. The tolerance for canvas jerseys must have waned, too; in the 1890s, according to a Rawlings Sporting Goods publication, "No player was seen without his turtle neck sweater."

The most significant thing that happened to pants and jerseys, however, was that they were sewn together to make one unit, an all-purpose football-playing suit of canvas, moleskin, or leather into which a player gradually inserted himself, laced it up all around, and went out to scrimmage. The Smock football suit, the varsity union suit, and "Whitley's Football Armor" were examples of this medieval contraption. It became a museum piece about the turn of the century, and pants and jerseys went back to being worn separately.

The wedge play and the flying tackle were the rule in football. It was a furious sport and manufacturers took steps to make equipment safer. New types of pads appeared to protect the knees, thighs, hips, kidneys, and ribs. The best way to hold them in place, it seemed, was to lace them to or hang them from the player's pants. Experiments began to find the right way to connect pads and pants, and went on for the next 25 years.

Strips of cane sewn into the lining for thigh pads appeared in the advertisements in the *Spalding Guide* in 1906; these hard strips must have been a bell-ringer for a head-on tackler. The next step was laces around each leg, permitting the thigh pads to be raised and lowered. Tunnel belt-loops and a reinforced crotch arrived. There was a period of time in which manufacturers came to see the pants as merely a "shell" on which all manner of pads were to be hung. In 1915, Spalding offered a "complete padded harness with heavy felt hip pad connected with wide elastic belt at back, fiber thigh guards laced in special canvas and webbing reinforced pockets all securely mounted on simple but strong skeleton pants form." It must have taken a long time to dress for football in those days.

At last, a simpler pair of pants emerged. They had pockets on the inside for the player to insert his thigh and knee pads; all other pads were strapped on independent of the pants.

Beginning with canvas, moleskin, and leather, a great variety of fabrics have been used in football pants. Khaki cloth or drill, fustian cloth, and duckcloth were first used about 1910. According to Rawling Sporting Goods, "Duck became the primary pants material for over 30 years."

Spalding's "Intercollegiate" pants in 1931 were made of Army duck. But in 1933 its "College Speed Pants," the top of the Spalding line, were made of "Skookum Cloth, the strongest, lighest fabric suitable for football pants."

There was, however, a family of new synthetic fibers that would make Skookum Cloth, whatever it may have been, obsolete for football pants. Knits first appeared in 1934, according to Rawlings Sporting Goods. "The first all-knit shell was introduced in 1936 and the first half-fabric, half-knit model made its bow in 1937. Many different combinations of knit materials have been developed through the years, with the latest knit incorporating the highly-popular Spandex, a stretch polyurethane material."

Spandex was the principal fiber in the most expensive model pants displayed in the 1976 catalog of Rawlings and two other major manufacturers. It actually is the general term for all fibers that resemble rubber in that they have a high extensibility and highly retractive forces that derive from their chemical nature, according to chemist R. W. Moncrieff. Its special properties make it very good for football pants and a far cry from the canvas, moleskin, and leather of the 1900s.

One final characteristic of football pants remains to be explored. A coach talks about it often with his players, especially when they're going up against a really tough opponent. It appears they don't have a prayer. But, as the coach points out, trying to encourage them, "The other team puts its pants on one leg at a time."

Jerseys had a somewhat more limited history. Canvas was the first fabric used in them; before the turn of the century, players were sometimes called "canvas-

A canvas football jacket, 1886.

Sleeveless vest of a "canvasback," 1906.

Jersey with "grip-sure cloth," 1928.

Full-block lettering, left, and "NCAA."

backs" because of the sleeveless canvas vests they wore over their turtlenecks.

The first real football jerseys were made of cotton and wool and those fabrics prevailed for 40 years, until the arrival of synthetics in jerseys in about 1950. They were, according to Rawlings Sporting Goods, rayon-durene, nylon-durene, rayon-cotton, and nylon-cotton. Nylon-mesh jerseys arrived and were even lighter and more comfortable that the rest; even the NFL teams in the coolest climates favored them, wearing them on cold days over thermal underwear.

Among the innovations in jerseys that did not succeed were Rawlings's 1928–29 model, which featured "grip-sure cloth, sewn to the jersey front to aid in holding onto the ball," and "tear-away jerseys," which allowed a runner to rip free from the grasp of a tackler holding onto his shirt, but which threatened to bankrupt the teams that used them as they struggled to keep their running backs in jerseys game after game.

Decorations on jerseys go back at least as far as 1876, when each Princeton player wore a "P" on his sweater in a game against Pennsylvania. Either Amos Alonzo Stagg or Glenn (Pop) Warner invented jersey numbers about 1905. Manufacturers arrayed the numbers and stripes on jerseys on a great variety that knew little restraint. The Canton Bulldogs of 1921 wore horizontal stripes around their middles, which only accentuated the considerable girth of their star tackle, Fats Henry. The St. Louis Gunners of 1934 wore jerseys with a cannon superimposed on a patriotic shield. They left history a photograph of one of their players wearing this creation; the player was Homer Reynolds, "The Human Cannon." His uniform and those of countless other football players over the last 100 years have at times reflected the willingness of manufacturers to offer any fashion or style, no matter how unorthodox and even silly, as long as there were coaches who would buy them.

Numbers are the focal points of jerseys. Old-fashioned "NCAA"-style numbers were in vogue for a time but were replaced by the "full block" style; the Washington Redskins were the last NFL team to wear NCAA-style letters.

The NFL established a system for numbering players in 1952, with a vague exemption for "nationally known players." A year later, such players as Otto Graham and Marion Motley changed their jersey numbers to conform to the system, Graham switching from 60 to 14 and Motley from 76 to 36. According to the system, quarterbacks and kickers are numbered 1 to 19; running and defensive backs, 20 to 49; centers and linebackers, 50 to 59; defensive linemen and interior offensive linemen, except for centers, 60 to 79; and wide receivers and tight ends, 80 to 89.

Football pants and jerseys are the largest parts of the uniform; they cover the player from his knees to his neck. They are very important to the game and sometimes they can be a very personal thing, as they were for star tackle George Christiansen of the 1932 Portsmouth Spartans. As the local newspaper reported, "The Spartans were stumped about an easy way to inform Chris that his last year's pants had seen plenty service and would not harmonize with the new ones the team will use. Before anyone could say a word, Chris began bemoaning the fact that he lost his pants and would have to buy a new pair. 'What a break!' his buddies chorused gleefully."

III. THE HELMET

Jerseys and pants identify players. Helmets and pads protect them. The one event that more than any other was responsible for making these articles of protection necessary took place in 1888. The annual rules convention for the emerging sport of college football passed a rule permitting tackling below the waist. Football changed dramatically. Teams no longer arrayed themselves across the entire breadth of the field (such "spread" formations a half-century later would be termed radical breakthroughs in strategy, and coaches who used them great innovators). Teams bunched themselves around the runner to block for him. The wedge and "mass play" arrived. Football became, for a time, a savage sport full of fights, brawling, even fatalities.

Grudgingly, football players accepted the wearing of protective equipment. Step-by-step, courageous figures whose names are lost to history braved being called sissies to wear pads of various types that in just a few years would be considered essential.

The article they accepted last of all was the helmet. The banal head harnesses and then the leather helmets that emerged were always disdained by a macho few. Even Glenn (Pop) Warner, the famous coach, counseled his Carlisle players against them in 1912. "Playing without helmets gives players more confidence, saves their heads from many hard jolts, and keeps their ears from becoming torn or sore," he said. "I do not encourage their use . . . I have never seen an accident to the head which was serious, but I have many times seen cases when hard bumps on the head so dazed the player receiving them that he lost his memory for a time and had to be removed from the game."

Gerald Ford, who later became president of the United States, played center for the University of Michigan in 1932–34 without a helmet. It was not a required article of equipment in college football until 1939.

The National Football League did not require the wearing of helmets until 1943, although the great majority of professional players had long since taken to wearing them. Through the imperfect method of examining all the available photographs, it has been determined that the last NFL player to play in a game without a helmet was probably end Dick Plasman of the Chicago Bears in 1940. There is a photo of him without one, taken during the 1940 championship game in which Chicago crushed the Washington Redskins 73–0.

End Bill Hewitt of the Bears and Philadelphia Eagles was another player who took the field without anything covering his head, and he was eventually elected to the Hall of Fame, making him far better known than Plasman. Hewitt, however, retired in 1939. He came back for one season during World War II, 1943, but by then the rules required him to put on a helmet.

Ivy League teams played in the first games, wrote the first rules, and formed the first college football association. In 1889, Princeton players adopted the practice of growing their hair long to protect themselves against head injuries. According to researcher Paul Quam, "this fad swept the country, and football players with their unsightly mops of hair became the delight of cartoonists."

Yale's powerful team, led by Camp, took up the practice. Their flowing locks became their trademark for a time, and they dominated their rivals. "Interlopers invited to play in the sacrosanct New Haven precincts were supposed to succumb with grace and speed to the horrendous longhairs who wore the Blue," wrote Stanley Woodward.

Wearing long hair while playing football went out of fashion, according to Quam, "when a championship Yale team appeared with close-cropped heads in 1895." (The crew-cut became *de rigueur* and remained in fashion for nearly 70 years.) The next phase in the development of the head harness began with the appearance of the head harness. Its name had a little of the livery stable in it, and that is not surprising since the age of the automobile in America was just beginning.

Quam found a reference to a head harness being used in 1893. In *Gang Way for Navy* in 1951, Admiral

Joseph Mason Reeves explained how he had invented a football headgear and wore it for the first time in the 1893 Army game. The young cadet had had it made, he said, "after a Navy doctor warned him that another kick in the head most likely would mean insanity."

A somewhat less colorful claim is made for halfback George Barclay of Lafayette College in 1896. He "designed a headgear which had three thick leather straps forming a tight fit around his head, and had it made by a harness maker. It was only logical that it became known as a head harness."

Contraptions made of an assortment of straps and pads turned into leather caps. They acquired ear flaps and then the flaps acquired ear holes, which must have improved communication greatly. There is no way these things could have provided anything more than rudimentary protection to the portion of the football-playing population (the percentage of which is uncertain) that wore them.

"Nose protectors" were an interesting by-product of the head harness era. Edgar Allen Poe was one of six sons of a nephew of the famous poet who played football for Princeton. He used a nose guard against Yale in 1890. Other players started using it. A hard leather proboscis hung from a strap around the forehead, fit over the nose, and had an extension at

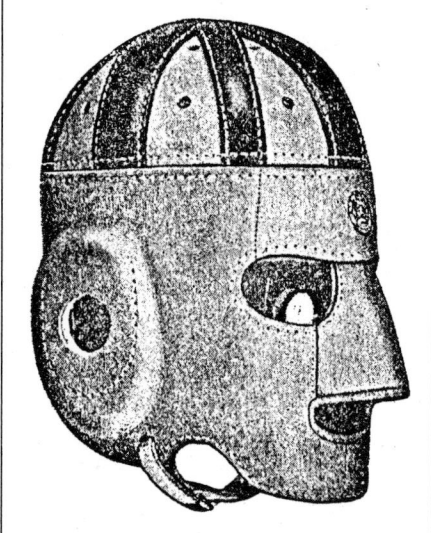

A "nose protector helmet," 1931.

the bottom which the wearer clenched in his teeth to hold the device in place. They interfered with good vision and that even more important requisite of a person going through strenuous activity—the ability to breathe easily. "No player should wear a nose protector unless he has a sore nose," said Pop Warner in 1912. One of the oddest creations in the history of football equipment soon went out of style.

The head harness began to take the shape and appearance we would recognize today as a football helmet. That became its name, instead of "head harness." But it still had a serious deficiency. As long as it sat right down on the skull, it was only pretending to protect the wearer. Then suspension appeared, probably in 1917, to cradle the skull away from the leather shell. Straps of fabric formed a pattern inside the helmet. They absorbed and distributed the impact better, and they allowed for ventilation. It was a tremendous breakthrough in helmet-making. Rawlings introduced the Zuppke helmet, designed by the Illinois coach, and Spalding introduced the first of what would become a well-known line, its "ZH" helmets, in 1925.

An innovation 14 years later, however, dwarfed all that had gone before. Gerry E. Morgan and other

employees of the John T. Riddell Company in Chicago, manufacturers of sporting goods, invented and patented a plastic football helmet in 1939. It was a single molded shell. It was a stronger, more durable, and lighter than leather helmets, and it wouldn't rot or mildew the way they did if it became damp. It had a revolutionary web suspension inside it.

In 1940, Riddell devised the first chinstrap worn on the chin and not the Adam's apple, and the first plastic face mask.

A Concise Guide to Plastics defines them as materials "that contain as an essential ingredient an organic substance or large molecular weight, is solid in its finished state, and at some stage in its manufacture or in its processing into finished articles, can be shaped by flow." Most plastics are synthetic. They are derived from petroleum, coal, salt, air, and water. They are light in weight, "but for their weight they are prodigiously strong." Thermoplastics are one type; the name means they are remeltable. Among the 15 or more types of thermoplastics are acrylonitrile-butadiene-styrene (ABS) and polycarbonate. Their features are "excellent toughness" and "high impact strength." They are the plastics used in football helmets.

From 1939 through 1940, Chicago was a sports hotbed and a sports laboratory. The All-Star Game, which was founded by *Chicago Tribune* sports editor Arch Ward, was drawing crowds of 80,000 or more annually. Clark Shaughnessy was advising the Chicago Bears' coaches and they were creating the blocking and ball-handling wizardry and original play-calling language of their T formation with man-in-motion, which would alter the course of football.

Riddell made its plastic helmets and they were worn for the first time in a game by some of the players on the College All-Star team of 1939. The company also had another first. Founder John T. Riddell, Sr. and owner-coach George Halas of the Bears devised low-cut football shoes and the 1940 Bears became the first team ever to wear such shoes. National attention was focused on the Bears when they smashed the Washington Redskins 73–0 in the NFL championship game.

Riddell's plastic helmet emerged in such an atmosphere. It was "a little flat on top" at first but it gradually changed to its characteristic teardrop shape, which allowed the impact of a blow to slide to one side or the other rather than be met head-on. Its web suspension could be raised or lowered to fit the head of whatever person pulled it on proudly, expanding the frontiers of football science.

The eve of a world war, however, is not the best time to come up with a new sports invention. Football is not exactly an essential industry and Riddell could not get plastic. The full-fledged assault on the leather helmet would have to wait until the war ended.

That does not mean Riddell did not turn a profit immediately as a result of its invention. It did. Inventing the plastic helmet at the start of World War II proved one of the master strokes of timing in the history of American business. The army had a problem in that it was impractical to manufacture steel helmets in sizes; it was both too expensive and impractical. The army purchased Riddell's patent rights and ordered the manufacturing of millions of M-1 helmet liners in sizes, to be worn by soldiers under what they called their "steel pots." G.I.s at Corregidor, Anzio, and Omaha Beach went ashore wearing on their heads the practical wartime application of an invention created for the sport of football.

Military use of first the plastic and later the fiberglass helmet expanded with the arrival of jet airplanes, and the extra protection required in high-speed escape, after World War II. Pilots of fighters, bombers, and helicopters adopted such helmets. Civi-

Continued on page 492

TRIAL BALLOONS

Americans love to invent, and they love football. They have combined the two many times. A host of inventions have been offered to improve the football, the field, players' equipment, and training apparatus. Some have been enormously successful. Rae Crowther, an end for the 1925–26 Frankford Yellowjackets of the NFL, invented a two-man blocking sled in 1933 and it was patented the next year. It became one of the most popular of all practice field apparatus; there is virtually no high school, college, or professional football coach who is not familiar with it, and such men as Paul Brown and Vince Lombardi have used and endorsed it. Over 16,000 Crowther two-man sleds have been sold since 1934.

Glenn (Pop) Warner's tackling dummy, Jim Trimble's and Joel Rottman's single standard goal post, and Gerry Morgan's energy-absorbing and sizing means for helmets are other notable inventions. They were practical and useful and gained widespread acceptance in the sport of football.

A far greater number of inventions for the sport, however, met none of those criteria. They weren't particularly practical or useful, and hardly anyone took them seriously. That didn't bother the inventors, however, or spoil the fun they had creating the invention out of their imagination and seeing it actually patented by the United States Government.

Football inventions great and small are stored, along with the inventions Americans have made for countless other pursuits, in the U.S. Department of Commerce Patent and Trademark Office, the "Inventor's Hall of Fame" in Arlington, Virginia. The walls of the outer lobby are filled with plaques honoring such men as Fulton, Morse, McCormick, and the Wright Brothers. Inside, patents are stored in dizzying profusion in row after row of shelves spilling over into room after room, other floors, and even other buildings nearby.

Football patents are difficult to find in this maze. It is necessary to search through categories, classes, and sub-classes. Seeking football shoes, one may instead stumble into disposable leggings for dogs and electrically heated boots. In search of shoulder pads, one gets caught in halters. Wanting football one finds space helmets.

The sub-class of Games Apparatus proved fruitful, however. It yielded an array of football patents registered with the government over the last 75–80 years. Some of them were worthwhile and others were almost completely useless. All were interesting. A sampling of them appear on the following pages. They are genuine and they are published with the permission of the Patent and Trademark Office.

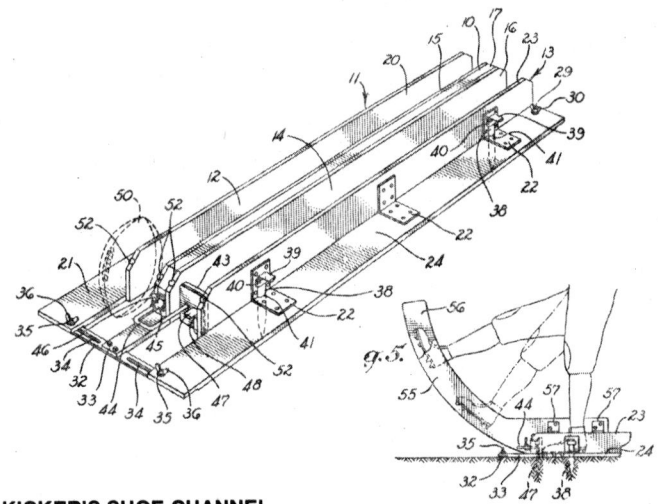

KICKER'S SHOE CHANNEL
Millard W. Peterson, Westwood, California, 1941

Millard W. Peterson's creation was "a straight guide channel wide enough to permit the forward movement therethrough of a player's foot in approaching and kicking the ball, but narrow enough to restrict such forward path of the foot substantially to a straight line." Many years have passed since the invention first appeared, and the inability of anyone to recall ever having seen one on or near a football field is a testimony to its marked lack of success. It appears a player might have benefited from practicing his kicking with this apparatus, but he would have come away from the experience with a rather bruised and battered kicking foot. It also seems to have been completely unfit for a bowlegged person.

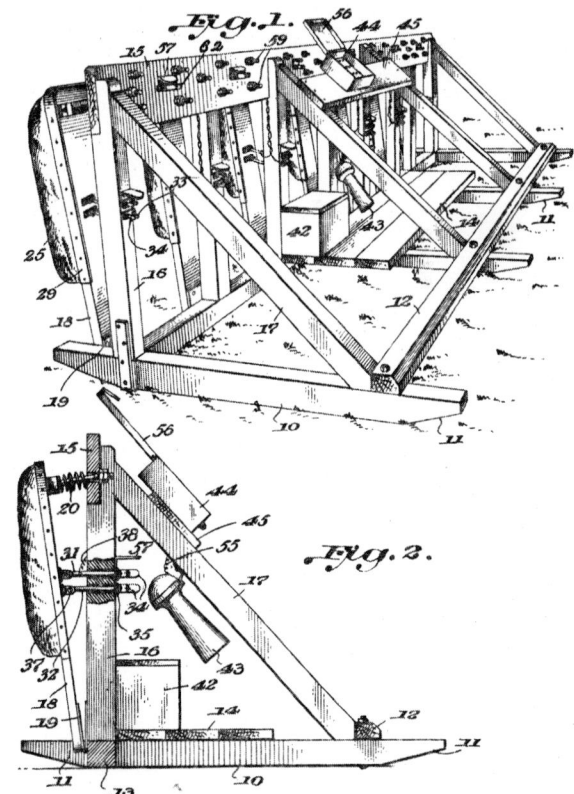

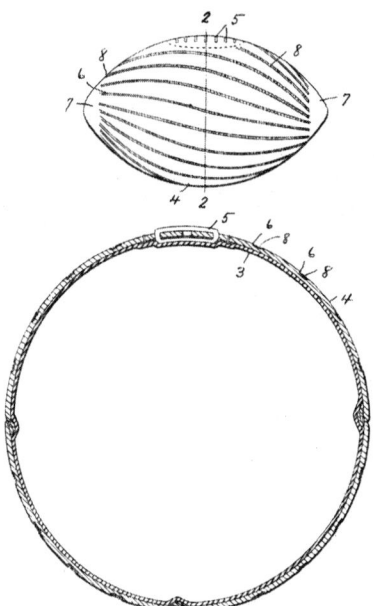

ANTI-FUMBLE FOOTBALL
John L. Buckner and James C. Ward, Paris, Kentucky, 1933

Ah, the cursed fumble. It has stopped numerous drives, lost an untold number of big games, and sent many an inventor scurrying home from the stadium to find an antidote. The anti-fumble football devised by John L. Buckner and James C. Ward gained as much acceptance as many of them, namely, very little at all. Buckner and Ward proposed longitudinal grooves filled with sand and held in place by waterproof glue. They demonstrated a certain fuzziness about how players catch and punt when they specified that the pointed ends of their ball would not be corrugated "so as not to injure the hand of a potential receiver or interfere with kicking."

NO-LOAFING BLOCKING SLED
Allen J. Gardenhour, Waynesboro, Pennsylvania, 1951

"When the going gets tough, the tough get going." But as for everyone on the team who isn't so tough, there's always seven-man sled practice. There, if a player can land one of the inside positions, he can take a breather and pretend to be working hard, while actually letting the others do the work. Allen J. Gardenhour tried to put an end to such malingering. He wired horns behind each dummy on his sled so any coach using it could immediately tell who was goofing off; they would have failed to hit their dummies hard enough to blow their horns. That would have provoked the coach—if Allen J. Gardenhour's invention had ever gone any farther than the drawing board—to call sharply to the guilty player, "Take a lap, Smith!"

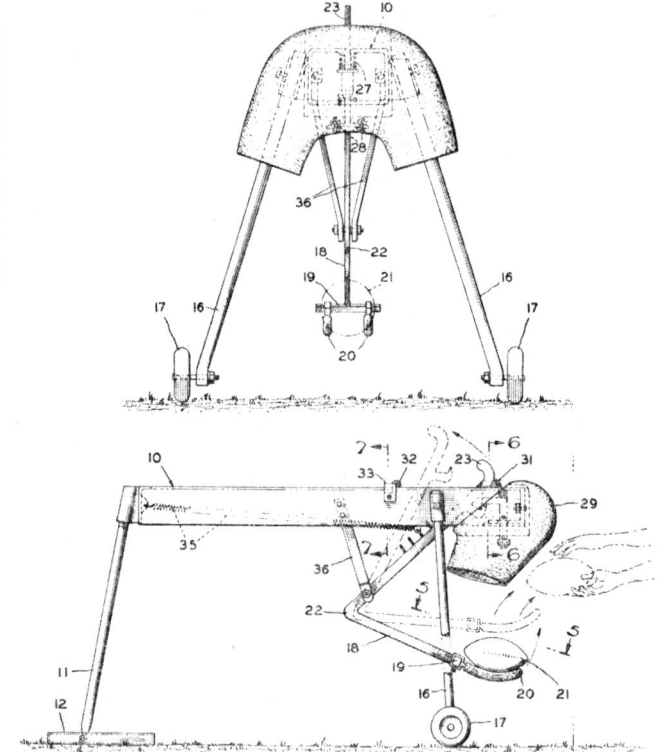

MECHANICAL CENTER

Hervy R. Maxcey, Jr., and Felton T. Wright, Brownwood, Texas, 1956

Pity the poor center. Year after year, practice after practice, game after game, he must get down into the most awkward of positions, view the world upside down, and center the ball over and over to the quarterback, carrying out the same dull, repetitive act thousands upon thousands of times. Well, in 1956, centers found two sympathetic friends—Hervy R. Maxcey, Jr. and Felton T. Wright. They trundled out their mechanical center, operated by the quarterback triggering a hook between the automatic center's legs. This device weighed "about 25 pounds" and at first was rather noisy and not very sturdy but, Maxcey said, they went back to the drawing board and eventually sold "400 or 500" of them to high schools and colleges around the country and made "about $10,000" profit. The Garry Moore television show wanted them but, "I was sick and Felton was busy, and we never made it." Enthusiasm waned and the mechanical centers rolled off America's football fields, never to be seen again.

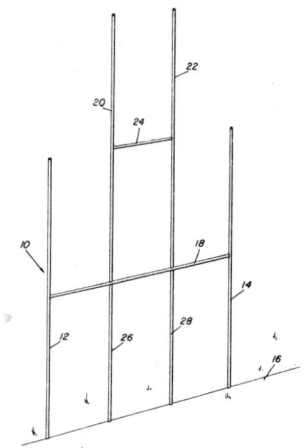

GRADED-SCORING GOAL POSTS

Charles Simmons, Elkins, West Virginia, 1958

"The kicking of field goals has become quite prevalent in obtaining scores," Charles Simmons's patent complained, "and the extra point...has become almost automatic." He proposed adding a second pair of goal posts between the ones already there. A graded scoring system was to have been set up, with a larger number of points being awarded to the kicks that were the most difficult. Since kicks pass through the uprights in an instant, and it is sometimes no small problem to even determine whether they have passed through the 18 feet 6 inches of the existing uprights, Charles Simmons could have given NFL teams and officials some interesting afternoons if his invention had been accepted.

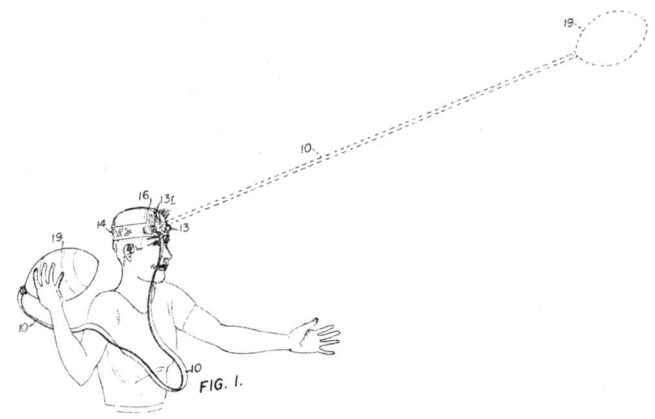

HEAD-MOUNTED SNAP-BACK FOOTBALL

George R. Masters, Fort Worth, Texas, 1962

If Gus Dorais had had this invention during his epic summer vacation in 1913, when he perfected his forward passes, he would never have needed Knute Rockne to catch them. Of course, he would also have needed a particularly strong neck to absorb the considerable shock of the ball reaching its farthest point at the end of the elastic tether. George R. Masters, the inventor, foresaw no such problem. He pointed out in his patent, which is as far as this invention ever got, that the player could "turn and run away from his throw and receive the ball over his shoulder while running."

KICKER'S ANKLE-LOCK

Ryals E. Lee, James E. Houston, and
George M. Norman, Tallahassee, Florida, 1967

The Kicker's Shoe Channel had tried unsuccessfully to solve the critical problem of shanked placekicks in 1941. Another valiant effort was made by Ryals E. Lee and two other football fans in Tallahassee, Florida in 1967. They proposed to lash a rigid shaft to the kicker's ankle and calf. Metal "didn't pan out," however, and plastic bent. Further, they discovered that the rules of football expressly prohibit such devices. And, Lee said, "I admit the invention did restrict the player from running very well after he kicked off." But if the practicality of the invention was poor, its timing was worse. It was introduced to help kick the ball straight-on exactly at the time when NFL teams were filling up with soccer players who kicked sideways.

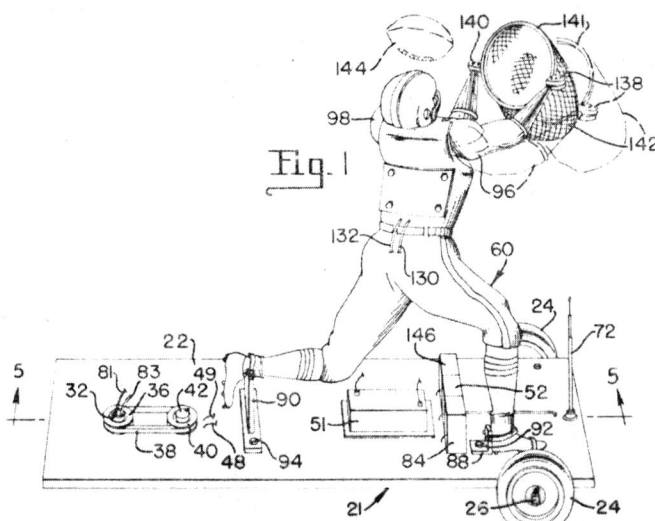

RADIO-CONTROLLED PASS CATCHER
Willie H. Grimes, Stamford, Texas, 1968

Willie H. Grimes's radio-controlled pass catcher presumably could have been programmed for all the patterns—hitch, short out, slant, curl, comeback, post, and fly. It was designed to move "at speeds up to the maximum at which a player is expected to run." Controlled by radio impulses, it was to have been mounted on a wheeled frame with a motorized mechanism inside, for the operation of the arms, which would move the pass-receiving basket from side to side to make the catch.

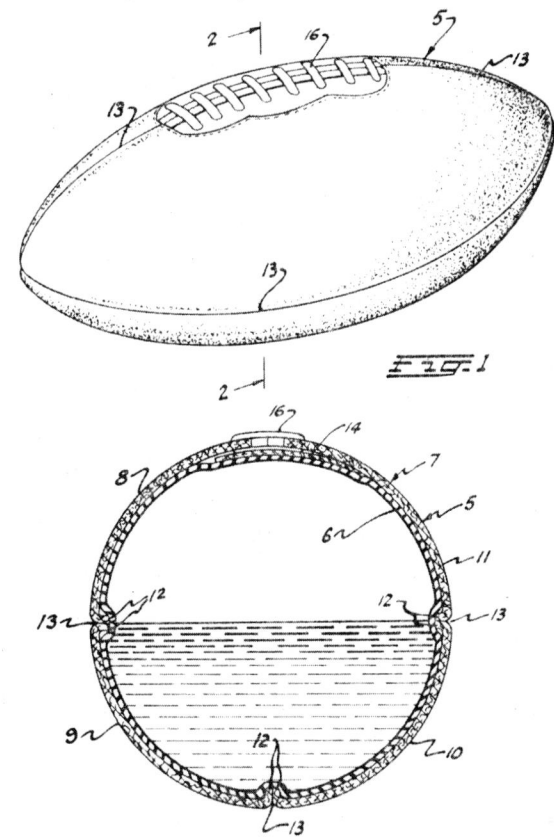

WATER-HOLDING ANTI-FUMBLE FOOTBALL
Albert J. Russo, Salem, Virginia, 1969

Water makes footballs slippery and must be dried from them in order to prevent fumbles. But Albert J. Russo suggested another way to achieve the same results, namely, to pour water—a couple of quarts, in fact—into the football. Ball carriers would carry it in practice and learn to hold on as the water sloshed around inside. In a regular game, "the player fumbles less because he has learned to grip the ball more firmly, using a ball that is heavier and which has a variable, gravitational pull according to the second-to-second location of the shifting fluid." Russo's invention found its way into several training camps. There, veterans used it to play practical jokes on unwitting rookie placekickers.

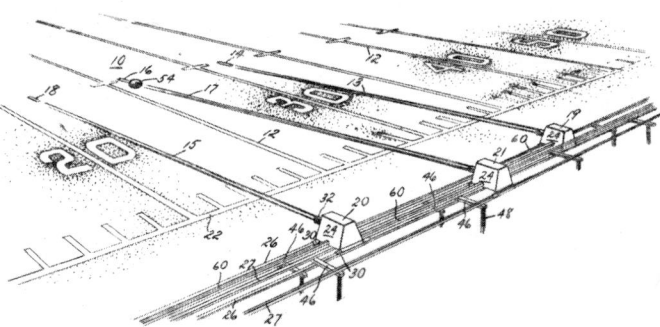

LASER BEAM FIRST DOWN DEVICE
Willis C. Pioch, East Paterson, New Jersey, 1973

The laser beam device of Willis C. Pioch would make the chain unit extinct. There would never be any doubt about the placement of the ball on the hashmarks. The laser would put down a ray of light across the field that would be visible to everyone in the stadium. It could also catch offside violations in the act. If it were adopted for the goalposts, it could help on kicks, sending an infinite beam of light into the sky straight up from the uprights (laser beams have been bounced off the moon). The only problem for Pioch was to convince teams and stadium managers to go to the great expense in money and manpower to install the laser hardware.

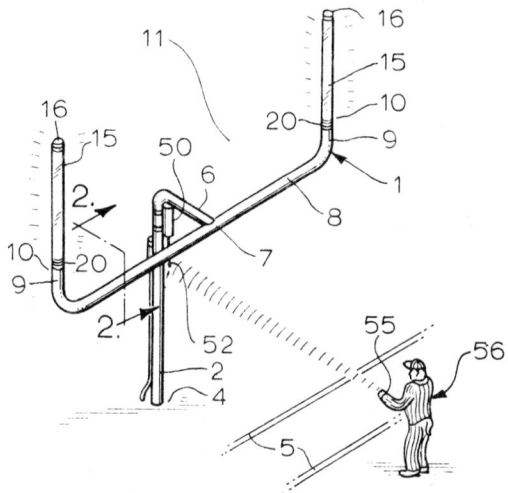

LIGHT-UP GOAL POSTS
Nick G. Zapos, Chicago, Illinois, 1974

Nick G. Zapos complained that when he was seated on the far end of the football field during a night game, he couldn't always see the referee raise his hands signaling a touchdown. So Zapos invented goal posts that lit up, activated by a remote transmitter operated by the referee. The goal posts were actually to be translucent tubes connected to a radio receiver and timer. Teams often "shock" each other, according to sports page headlines; if Zapos's invention had ever been put into service but somehow had gone haywire, the headlines could have become reality.

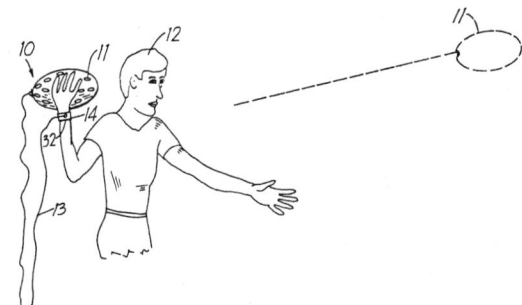

WRIST-MOUNTED SNAP-BACK FOOTBALL
Benny I. Civita, Forest Hills, New York, 1976

Idle hands are the devil's workshop, and Benny I. Civita invented this gadget "for independently practicing the art of tossing a ball." He improved on the head-mounted football of George R. Masters, mercifully relocating the tether on the wrist. His invention was intended for the practice field, but if it ever found its way into an NFL game it would certainly be one way for the passer to fake out the defense.

Continued from page 488

lian use of them was made by cyclists, race drivers, and speedboat racers.

The fact that the United States Military Academy football team of 1944 became the first to ever wear plastic helmets may have resulted from the army being privy to Riddell's research, or it may have been because Army was coached by a bright, innovative, and far-thinking man, Earl (Red) Blaik. He won national collegiate championships in 1944, 1945, and 1946, and he had Felix (Doc) Blanchard, "Mr. Inside," at fullback and Glenn Davis, "Mr. Outside", in his backfield in 1944–47. Blanchard and Davis wore the new Riddell plastic helmets.

There were problems, however. The plastic in the helmets of Riddell and those of competitors who entered the market was sometimes brittle; a drill boring a hole to attach a face mask would pop right through. The plastic's resistance to blows was in doubt after linebacker Fred Naumetz of the Los Angeles Rams, according to *The Pros*, split nine plastic helmets in one season. They were banned from use in the NFL in 1948. Riddell's future was in doubt. It was apparently saved by the intercession in its behalf by Halas of the Bears. The plastic helmet was restored for 1949 and with that the leather helmet became extinct.

Paint on football helmets goes back almost as far as helmets themselves. Rawlings introduced a white one in 1920 that it said "may be kept white with gasoline or painted in college colors if desired." The Brooklyn Dodgers had silver helmets in 1937. Halfback Fred Gehrke of the Los Angeles Rams painted a horn design on the Los Angeles Rams' helmets in 1948, the first helmet emblem. Distinctive designs became the trademarks of pro football teams.

Gehrke's paint kept chipping off every game, however, and he and his teammates had to paint the emblems back on the helmets constantly. The legalization of plastic helmets in 1949 made it possible to bake color into helmets and greatly expand its use on them. As a result, football became far more colorful. Helmets became coordinated with jerseys and pants.

There was a short-lived experiment on the part of some teams to employ a different colored helmet for X, the split end; Y, the tight end; and Z, the flanker. The rules at first insisted the receivers all wear the same color even though it was different from their teammates, and then changed that to require the color be the same as their teammates'. (There was a similar experiment at about the same time, which was equally short-lived, to dress each member of the officiating crew in a different-colored shirt. Retired referee Bud Brubaker recalls that period and a fan who shouted to his crew, "Hey you jockeys, where's your horses?" Later, in 1974, the World Football League introduced, and quickly withdrew after it was repudiated, a plan to dress players at each position on the team in different-colored pants.)

It would probably be too difficult to get into one locker room all the retired football players who believe they invented the face mask. This merciful innovation protects the face and eyes.

The "nose protector" was the forerunner of the face mask. "Nose protector helmets" were the transition from one to the other. The manufacturers began making them as early as 1927; that was the first year one appeared in the *Spalding Guide*. A molded piece of leather with holes for the eyes and mouth covered the entire face. It looked like a ski mask or the visor of a knight errant. Without a doubt, it was the most bizarre-looking piece of football apparel ever made.

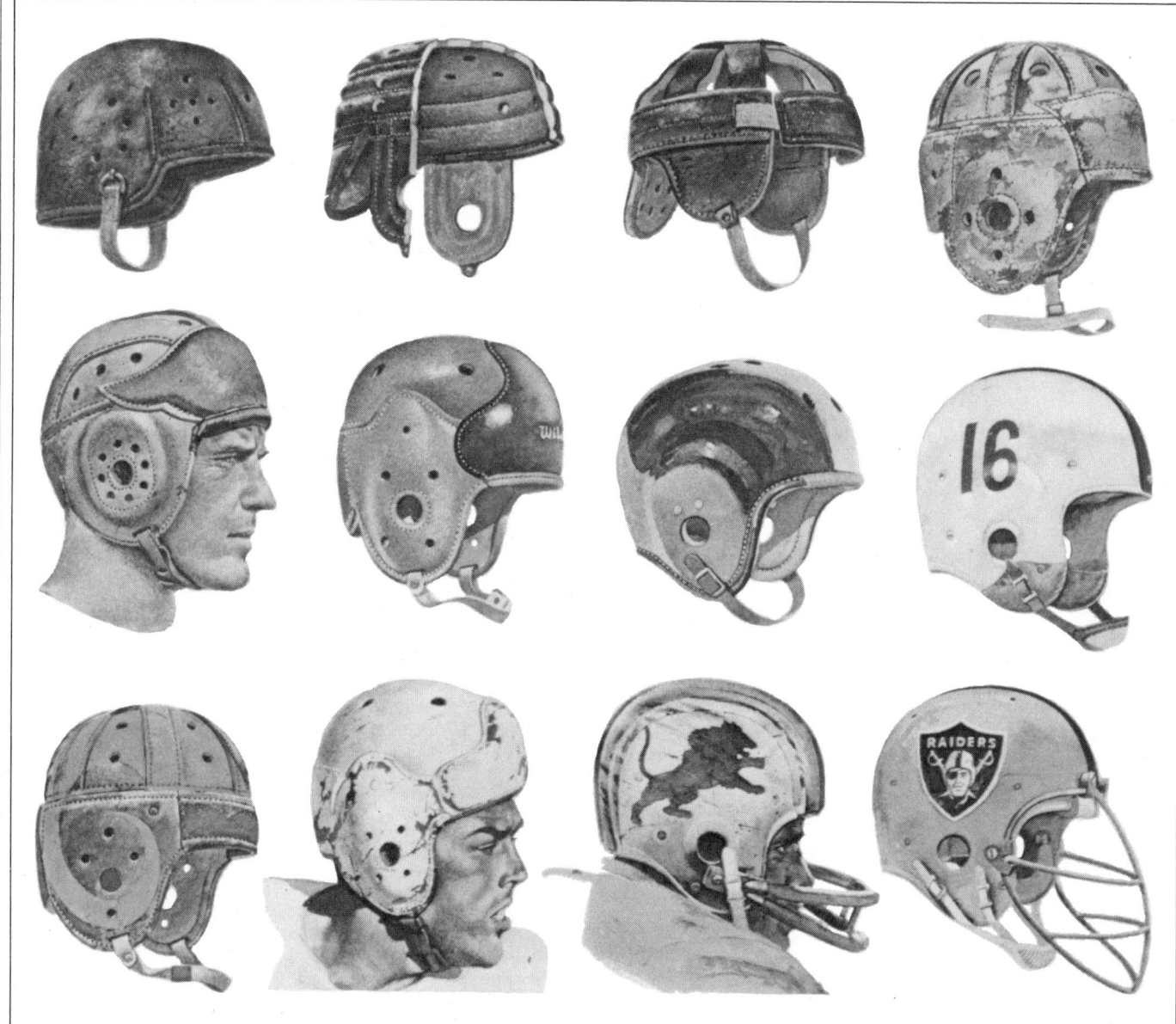

From head harnesses to micro-fit helmets; the players shown are, in order, Earl (Dutch) Clark, Otto Graham, and John Gordy.

The dearth of photographs of anyone wearing one of them bears out their confirmed lack of acceptance, probably because they were unbearably hot. It is a good thing. One manufacturer offered a nose protector helmet with this chilling feature: "It is reinforced with soft steel that may be bent to the individual's profile." It is hoped that all the bending was done by him and not his opponent.

The first person to devise a bar face mask on a football helmet, according to G.E. Morgan, was Vern McMillan, the owner of a sporting goods store in Terre Haute, Indiana. It was a rubber-covered wire mask on a leather helmet. Morgan can't recall when this happened. But he was in high school in Chicago in 1932–36 and he recalls such masks being used then. There is a face mask on the helmet of a New York Giants' player in a photo in a 1937 issue of *SPORT*.

The superior rigidity of the plastic helmet made the universality of the face mask possible. The hole drilled for the bolt holding the mask would not expand the way it would if it was drilled through leather. And the sides of the plastic helmet would not collapse, driving the nut into the wearer's face.

As use of the plastic helmet spread, so did makeshift face masks. Linemen needed them more than backs, and began crafting odd cages of leather- and tape-covered wire. When Joe Perry of the San Francisco 49ers suffered a broken jaw in 1954, he wore a face mask manufactured of clear lucite plastic. Lucite, however, frequently shattered and it was banned. The breakthrough in face masks came in 1955. Morgan and Paul Brown, coach of the Cleveland Browns and a consultant to Riddell, invented the BT-5 face mask for quarterback Otto Graham, who was dominating pro football and against whom pass rushers sometimes led with the elbow. The "BT" in the invention's name was for bar tubular; it was a single tubular bar that was a combination of rubber and plastic. Graham wore it one year and retired from pro football.

From the BT-5 came a variety of single bars, double bars, triple bars, masks, cages, and "birdcages." Plastic and rubber tubing or welded steel or aluminum with a vinyl plastisol coating were used in their construction. Cages once reserved only for linemen came to be adopted by backs as well. Bobby Layne of the Pittsburgh Steelers, who retired in 1962, was one of the last players to play without a face mask. Years later, Billy Kilmer of the Washington Redskins was one of the few men still playing with only a single bar.

Morgan and Brown came up with another invention the year after their BT-5 face mask. They put a Citizen's Band radio in quarterback George Ratterman's helmet. Brown, who was on the side line, had a transmitter and Ratterman had a receiver. The quarterback couldn't talk back to the coach. The experiment with this device in a game was brief. There was interference on the frequency (a malady common to CB'ers years later when it became a national mania). Expecting to hear Brown call the next play, Ratterman instead heard two women talking incoherently. The experiment ended and the next year the NFL banned radio-equipped football helmets.

Chin straps were improved by the addition of ribbed vinyl-coated chin cups. College football, intent on preventing injuries by keeping the helmet securely on the head, began requiring four-point chin straps in 1976; they snapped onto the helmet at four places instead of two.

Raymond Berry, an end for the Baltimore Colts from 1955–67, once experimented with shatterproof goggles during sunny games against the Rams at the Los Angeles Memorial Coliseum. Alex Karras, defensive tackle for the Detroit Lions in 1958–70, had poor vision and played largely, he said, "by feel." Karras refused to wear contact lenses but they became

popular among other players and, according to a *New York Times* survey in 1976, there were about 50 users of them in the NFL. The Washington Redskins had one cornerback, Pat Fischer, who wore contact lenses and another, Joe Lavender, who wore tinted sunglasses while he played. Running back Chuck Muncie of New Orleans wore eyeglasses while he played, despite the fact that he broke three pairs during the preseason of his rookie year, 1976.

Mouthpieces became a requisite in college football and some players continued to wear them as they entered pro football. Others complained that the rubber mouthpieces made it difficult to speak or even breathe at times and could even induce gagging and nausea.

Energy-absorbing helmets of the space age entered pro football in 1971. G.E. Morgan, by then chairman of the board of Riddell, was granted United States Patent 3,609,764, "Energy Absorbing and Sizing Means for Helmets." The result was the company's new HA-91 and HA-92 energy-absorbing, "micro-fit" helmets. They had valves on their crown to allow air to be pumped into vinyl cushions that were crammed into every available space inside the helmet. The player put it on and then had it pumped up by the equipment manager to fit firmly around the player's head. Fluid could be pumped in, too. These were the so-called "water helmets." Actually, an anti-freeze solvent was used, to prevent a helmet from freezing atop a player's head in the middle of a cold day at Green Bay or Bloomington.

Riddell's older TK-2 web suspension helmet, however, refused to give way to the micro-fits. Veterans everywhere in the NFL who had worn Riddell's and other suspension helmets stayed with them. Among other things, they said, suspension provided better ventilation. Players at the speed positions such as running back, wide receiver, and cornerback preferred suspension helmets because they were lighter.

Riddell's PAC-3, a "padded aero cell," made its debut in 1974. This time the vinyl cushions did not have to be pumped up; maintenance was reduced and players did not have to stand in line at the equipment manager's desk to have their helmets blown up. The PAC-3 had "32 individual vinyl air cushions with layers of energy-absorbing foam." Small holes in the crown allowed the cushions inside to dissipate the force of the impact and carry it away through the orifices in the surface. According to Riddell, this helmet immediately began to outsell all its competitors.

Linemen have the most collisions and so they need the best padding and the largest cages or face masks. With all this hardware on and in the helmet, it can get rather heavy. Norm Evans, a tackle for the Seattle Seahawks who was formerly with the Miami Dolphins, said in *On the Line*, "Until I learned to do exercises to strengthen my neck, the hardest part of every training camp for me was starting to wear a helmet again. The first time I'd put the helmet on, my head would go *clunk*! over to one side. You know those things weigh about two-and-a-half pounds . . . After a few days I'd get to where I could draw my head down into my neck. Then there's a way I could tilt the face mask at a certain angle. Between the two positions, I could keep my helmet upright."

The testing of helmets for athletes, pilots, motorcycle riders, and all others who wear them, is one of the leading activities in American consumerism. Joseph A. Mulvey invented a pneumatic helmet with an inflatable bladder in its crown in 1938 and tested it at Harvard, according to *Scholastic Coach*, "by having players run against the goal posts wearing it." *Flight* published a photo of early testing of pilots' helmets; a gentleman wearing one was running full speed into the side of a hangar. According to *Plastics World*, Riddell conducted tests on helmets for seven

years and puts each shell it receives from its molder through a process in which it drops a 20-pound weight on it from 13 feet up; if it shows any cracking or crazing, it is rejected. Wayne State University conducts tests on helmets for the National Operating Committee on Standards for Athletic Equipment (NOCSAE). The Snell Memorial Foundation conducted tests for motorcycle helmets, according to *Cycle Guide*, by using cadavers "to determine accurately how much force is required to injure the human head. The cadavers were dropped, with the head striking hard, unyielding surfaces."

The Stanford Research Institute noted in its 1974 study that helmets "have gradually become thicker and more rigid." The National Collegiate Athletic Association and National Federation of State High School Associations made it mandatory that beginning in 1978 all players would wear helmets that met NOCSAE test standards.

One of the reasons given for the absence of a soft football helmet is that coaches appreciate hearing the crack of the plastic helmet as a tackle or block is made. NOCSAE, however, is experimenting with soft helmets and the Stanford study urged NFL teams to try them in practice. Arguments against them are diverse. A coach using them would be doing the same as a nuclear power disarming unilaterally. The expense of constantly reconditioning the outer padding would be too great. The helmet emblem wouldn't stay on. The extra weight of the padding would increase the pressure a helmet places on the neck. All of those reasons seem too vague to prevent the inevitable arrival of reforms sorely needed in the helmet.

IV. PADS

"Football isn't a contact sport," the saying goes. "Dancing is a contact sport; football is a *collision* sport." People who play it are therefore required to wear pads. Of all the ones they wear, the most obvious are the shoulder pads. They make massive NFL linemen appear even more massive. They are elaborate apparatus of straps, foam, and plastic. Their mission is to protect the clavicle.

At one time, shoulder pads were flimsy contraptions that slumped weakly over the crown of each shoulder. The principle of cantilevering appeared in them apparently about 1935; that is the first year Spalding displayed such pads in its guide and the first year Rawlings refers to them in its history of equipment. Straps held the epaulets of the pads away from the shoulder, high above it, to absorb shock. Cantilever shoulder pads transformed many skinny high school youngsters into fearsome-looking football players.

Elastic underarm straps, deeper chest plates, "snubbers" to hold the flap in place under the epaulet, and nylon covering and stitching were further breakthroughs in shoulder pads. Varying sizes were developed—massive engineering marvels for big linemen, smaller models for linebackers and running backs, and an even smaller size for quarterbacks, wide receivers, defensive backs, and kickers.

Thigh and knee pads are molded foam rubber parts that are inserted in pockets inside football players' pants. Shin, elbow, and forearm pads, and padded, fingerless gloves, are articles of padding that players may tape onto themselves. Shin guards protect against leg-whipping. Elbow pads prevent artificial turf burns. Forearm pads and gloves aid defensive linemen who hand-slap and offensive linemen who use the permissible technique of cupped hands in blocking. The use of elbow pads depends on whether the field is artificial, and the other incidental pads are almost exclusively reserved for linemen.

No player wants to play without protection. All are concerned about their safety and having a long, profitable career. The cutaway photos of players cov-

Shoulder pads for linemen, upper left; linebackers, right; and running backs.

Shoes with cleats for grass.

Shoes with cleats for artificial turf.

ered from head to toe in padding, which appear in sporting goods catalogs and in sports magazines, are a sales manager's fondest dream and not a reality. Few players, if any, wear every possible pad. Gerald (Dad) Braiser, equipment manager of the Green Bay Packers, says rib pads are worn by players only when they're hurt, and Don Hewitt of the Los Angeles Rams says, "There is hardly a player in the NFL wearing hip pads."

Players walk a fine line between being fast enough to do their job and being underequipped. Cornerbacks and safeties slice padding, trimming it down for added quickness. At the same time that manufacturers offer elaborate girdle and snap-on hip pads, players in the NFL are fashioning makeshift

substitutes—odd cuts of foam stuck inside the strap of their supporters.

V. SHOES

There had been football for a number of years. Players had tried a variety of footwear. Then a breakthrough occurred—white football shoes! A sporting goods company advertised them as its number one model. You can plainly see it right there in the Peck & Snyder catalog. The year? 1886.

The idea, however, did not catch on and another 80 years went by before quarterback Joe Namath of the New York Jets popularized white football shoes once more.

Shoes show off players' individualism. They are

compelled to wear jerseys, pants, helmets, and stockings the same as everyone else. In their shoes, however, they express themselves. Because of this, and because of the advent of artificial turf and the many models made especially for it, an almost endless variety of football shoes is available.

Baseball shoes were the first football shoes. They looked like the shoes of Whistler's mother. Cleat history began when leather was laid over the sharp baseball cleats. Kangaroo leather instead of cowhide arrived not in some postwar "modern" era but as early in 1906; in fact, Spalding said then that it had been making kangaroo leather shoes for Yale, Princeton, Penn and other college teams for years. The farmer's brogan style gave way to low-cut oxfords in 1940. A roof was built over a stadium, the Houston Astrodome, in 1965, and a carpet floor called "artificial turf" was laid in it. Other fields, indoors and out, took on artificial turf. The existing manufacturers and others that sprang up seemingly overnight raced to make the best shoe for it.

Inverted truncated pyramid football cleats appeared in the 1890s, according to Rawlings Sporting Goods. They were made of pieces of leather glued together and nailed to the shoe. One-piece fiber cleats, once again nailed to the shoe, appeared in 1915, according to the same source. Interchangeable cleats arrived in 1921; they screwed on and off a metal post jutting from the sole of the shoe.

It is not hard to imagine what a threat to safety these metal posts posed if a cleat came off during the course of a game. In 1939, the college football rules committee ordered a change. "Female" football cleats were outlawed; that is, the cleat had to become the "male" part with the metal post, the shoe the "female" part into which the post was inserted.

Fiber gave way to rubber and rubber gave way to aluminum and nylon, steel-tipped cleats. Aluminum, however, was banned from use in cleats by the NFL in 1951.

Cleats lock in the ground and that can be a major cause of knee injuries. Of all the countless inventions that have been offered to prevent "cleat-lock" in football shoes, perhaps none was more interesting and compelling than Dr. Bruce Cameron's swivel shoe, which he called the "Wolverine Swivler." An orthopedic surgeon in Houston, he offered the product for the first time in about 1970. It had a swivel cleat on the front of the sole that turned 360 degrees, but, he said, "It is not free-swinging; the wedge joint sets with the body weight. It takes about a week for a player to get used to it."

The Stanford Research Institute study of 1974 for the NFL offered more orthodox solutions for the problems cleats cause. It recommended more and shorter cleats, and the manufacturers of soccer-style football shoes for artificial surfaces have begun to make them. The SRI study called for an end to the use of the "traditional long conical cleat" on natural turf and said the more cleats, the better, to keep them from "locking into the turf."

All football equipment has gradually become lighter in weight and the game has become faster and more exciting as a result. One of the most important steps in this process was the popularization of low-cut shoes by the Chicago Bears, starting in 1940. The Riddell company has a photograph of George Halas in mackinaw and galoshes inspecting the brand new cut-down shoes of George McAfee, Bobby Swisher, Hampton Pool, Harry Clark, Ken Kavanaugh, Ray Nolting, and Ray (Scooter) McLean at the Bears' practice field in 1940. The backs and ends on other college and pro teams adopted low-cuts and, finally, linemen started wearing them, too. The age-old process of football equipment was repeated once more as something went from being "sissy-looking" to being a characteristic element of the game.

Topics of Conversation

Lance Alworth   Ken Anderson

Jim Bakken

Lance Alworth

Wide Receiver. 6-0, 180. Born in Houston, Texas, August 3, 1940. Arkansas.

RECEIVING

Year	Team	No.	Yards	Avg.	Long	TD
1962	San Diego	10	226	22.6	67	3
1963	San Diego	61	1,205	19.8	85	11
1964	San Diego	61	1,235	20.2	82	13
1965	San Diego	69	1,602	23.2	85	14
1966	San Diego	73	1,383	18.9	78	13
1967	San Diego	52	1,010	19.4	71t	9
1968	San Diego	68	1,312	19.3	80t	10
1969	San Diego	64	1,003	15.7	76t	4
1970	San Diego	35	608	17.4	80t	4
1971	Dallas	34	487	14.3	26	2
1972	Dallas	15	195	13.0	30	2
Totals		542	10,266	18.9	85	85

Ken Anderson

Quarterback. 6-2, 210. Born in Batavia, Illinois, February 15, 1949. Augustana.

PASSING

Year	Team	Att.	Comp.	Yards	TD	Int.
1971	Cincinnati	131	72	777	5	4
1972	Cincinnati	301	171	1,918	7	7
1973	Cincinnati	329	179	2,428	18	12
1974	Cincinnati	328	213	2,667	18	10
1975	Cincinnati	377	228	3,169	21	11
1976	Cincinnati	338	179	2,367	19	14
Totals		1,804	1,042	13,326	88	58

Jim Bakken

Kicker. 6-0, 200. Born in Madison, Wisconsin, November 2, 1940. Wisconsin.

SCORING

Year	Team	FG	PAT	Points
1962	St. Louis	0-1	0-0	0
1963	St. Louis	11-21	44-44	77
1964	St. Louis	25-38	40-40	115
1965	St. Louis	21-31	33-33	96
1966	St. Louis	23-40	27-28	96
1967	St. Louis	27-39	36-36	117
1968	St. Louis	15-24	40-40	85
1969	St. Louis	12-24	38-40	74
1970	St. Louis	20-32	37-38	97
1971	St. Louis	21-32	24-24	87
1972	St. Louis	14-22	19-21	61
1973	St. Louis	23-32	31-31	100
1974	St. Louis	13-22	30-36	69
1975	St. Louis	19-24	40-41	97
1976	St. Louis	20-27	33-35	93
Totals		264-409	472-487	1,264

Lem Barney

Cornerback. 6-0, 190. Born in Gulfport, Mississippi, September 8, 1945. Jackson State.

INTERCEPTIONS

Year	Team	No.	Yards	Avg.	Long	TD
1967	Detroit	10	232	23.2	71t	3
1968	Detroit	7	82	11.7	62	0
1969	Detroit	8	126	15.8	32	0
1970	Detroit	7	168	24.0	49t	2
1971	Detroit	3	78	26.0	28t	1
1972	Detroit	3	88	29.3	64	0
1973	Detroit	4	130	32.5	38	0
1974	Detroit	4	61	15.3	39	0
1975	Detroit	5	23	4.6	13	0
1976	Detroit	2	36	18.0	26	1
Totals		53	1,024	19.8	71t	7

PUNT RETURNS

Year	Team	No.	FC	Yards	Avg.	Long	TD
1967	Detroit	4	8	14	3.5	6	0
1968	Detroit	13	14	79	6.1	18	0
1969	Detroit	9	5	191	21.2	74t	1
1970	Detroit	25	3	259	10.4	65	1
1971	Detroit	14	2	122	8.7	38	0
1972	Detroit	15	8	108	7.2	26	0
1973	Detroit	27	7	231	8.6	42	0
1974	Detroit	5	1	37	7.4	11	0
1975	Detroit	8	3	80	10.0	30	0
1976	Detroit	23	22	191	8.3	30	0
Totals		143	73	1,312	9.2	74t	2

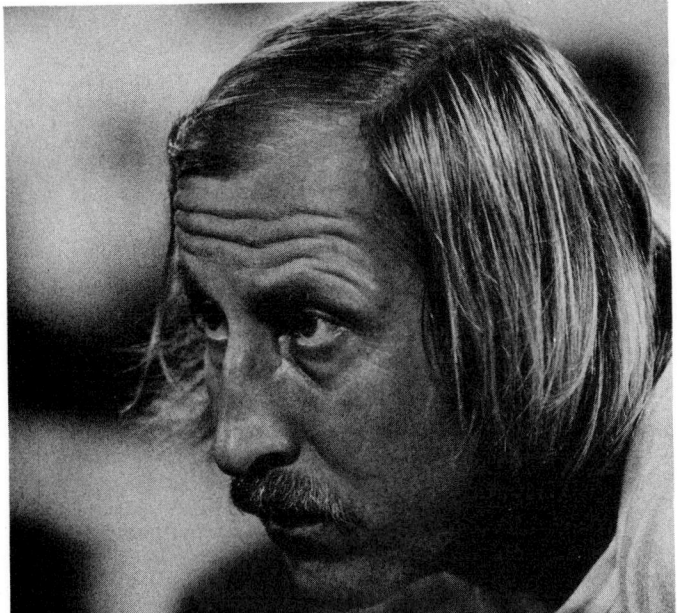

Fred Biletnikoff

George Blanda

Lem Barney

Fred Biletnikoff

Wide Receiver. 6-1, 190. Born in Erie, Pennsylvania, February 23, 1943. Florida State.

RECEIVING

Year	Team	No.	Yards	Avg.	Long	TD
1965	Oakland	24	331	13.8	53	0
1966	Oakland	17	272	16.0	78	3
1967	Oakland	40	876	21.9	72	5
1968	Oakland	61	1,037	17.0	82	6
1969	Oakland	54	837	15.5	53t	12
1970	Oakland	45	768	17.1	51	7
1971	Oakland	61	929	15.2	49	9
1972	Oakland	58	802	13.8	39t	7
1973	Oakland	48	660	13.8	32	4
1974	Oakland	42	593	14.1	46	7
1975	Oakland	43	587	13.7	26	2
1976	Oakland	43	551	12.8	32	7
Totals		536	8,243	15.4	82	69

George Blanda

Quarterback-Kicker. 6-2, 215. Born in Youngwood, Pennsylvania, September 17, 1927. Kentucky.

SCORING

Year	Team	TD	FG	PAT	Points
1949	Chi. Bears	1	7-15	0-0	27
1950	Baltimore	0	0-0	0-0	0
	Chi. Bears	0	6-15	0-0	18
1951	Chi. Bears	0	6-17	26-26	44
1952	Chi. Bears	1	6-25	30-30	54
1953	Chi. Bears	0	7-20	27-27	48
1954	Chi. Bears	0	8-16	23-23	47
1955	Chi. Bears	2	11-16	37-37	82
1956	Chi. Bears	0	12-28	45-47	81
1957	Chi. Bears	1	14-26	23-23	71
1958	Chi. Bears	0	11-23	36-37	69
1959	Did not play pro football				
1960	Houston	4	15-34	46-47	115
1961	Houston	0	16-26	64-65	112
1962	Houston	0	11-26	48-49	81
1963	Houston	0	9-22	39-39	66
1964	Houston	0	13-29	37-38	76
1965	Houston	0	11-21	28-28	61
1966	Houston	0	16-30	39-40	87
1967	Oakland	0	20-30	56-57	116
1968	Oakland	0	21-34	54-54	117
1969	Oakland	0	20-37	45-45	105
1970	Oakland	0	16-29	36-36	84
1971	Oakland	0	15-22	41-42	86
1972	Oakland	0	17-26	44-44	95
1973	Oakland	0	23-33	31-31	100
1974	Oakland	0	11-17	44-46	77
1975	Oakland	0	13-21	44-48	83
Totals		9	335-638	943-959	2,002

PASSING

Year	Team	Att.	Comp.	Yards	TD	Int.
1949	Chi. Bears	21	9	197	0	5
1950	Baltimore	0	0	0	0	0
	Chi. Bears	0	0	0	0	0
1951	Chi. Bears	0	0	0	0	0
1952	Chi. Bears	131	47	664	8	11
1953	Chi. Bears	362	169	2,164	14	23
1954	Chi. Bears	281	131	1,929	15	17
1955	Chi. Bears	97	42	459	4	7
1956	Chi. Bears	69	37	439	7	4
1957	Chi. Bears	19	8	65	0	3
1958	Chi. Bears	7	2	19	0	0
1959	Did not play pro football					
1960	Houston	363	169	2,413	24	22
1961	Houston	362	187	3,330	36	22
1962	Houston	418	197	2,810	27	42
1963	Houston	423	224	3,003	24	25
1964	Houston	505	262	3,287	17	27
1965	Houston	442	186	2,542	20	30
1966	Houston	271	122	1,764	17	21
1967	Oakland	38	15	285	3	3
1968	Oakland	49	30	522	6	2
1969	Oakland	13	6	73	2	1
1970	Oakland	55	29	461	6	5
1971	Oakland	58	32	378	4	6
1972	Oakland	15	5	77	1	0
1973	Oakland	0	0	0	0	0
1974	Oakland	4	1	28	1	0
1975	Oakland	3	1	11	0	1
Totals		4,007	1,911	26,920	236	277

John Brodie

Tom Brookshier

John Brodie

Quarterback. 6-1, 210. Born in San Francisco, California, August 14, 1935. Stanford.
PASSING

Year	Team	Att.	Comp.	Yards	TD	Int.
1957	San Francisco	21	11	160	2	3
1958	San Francisco	172	103	1,224	6	13
1959	San Francisco	64	30	354	2	7
1960	San Francisco	207	103	1,111	6	9
1961	San Francisco	283	155	2,588	14	12
1962	San Francisco	304	175	2,272	18	16
1963	San Francisco	61	30	367	3	4
1964	San Francisco	392	193	2,498	14	16
1965	San Francisco	391	242	3,112	30	16
1966	San Francisco	427	232	2,810	16	22
1967	San Francisco	349	168	2,013	11	16
1968	San Francisco	404	234	3,020	22	21
1969	San Francisco	347	194	2,405	16	15
1970	San Francisco	378	223	2,941	24	10
1971	San Francisco	387	208	2,642	18	24
1972	San Francisco	110	70	905	9	8
1973	San Francisco	194	98	1,126	3	12
Totals		4,491	2,469	31,548	214	224

Tom Brookshier

Defensive Halfback. 6-1, 198. Born in Roswell, New Mexico, December 16, 1931. Colorado.
INTERCEPTIONS

Year	Team	No.	Yards	Avg.	Long	TD
1953	Philadelphia	8	41	5.1	22	0
1954	Military service					
1955	Military service					
1956	Philadelphia	1	31	31.0	31	0
1957	Philadelphia	4	74	18.5	40	0
1958	Philadelphia	1	0	0.0	0	0
1959	Philadelphia	3	13	4.3	8	0
1960	Philadelphia	1	14	14.0	14	0
1961	Philadelphia	2	20	10.0	20	0
Totals		20	193	9.7	40	0

Larry Brown

Larry Brown

Running Back, 5-11, 195, Born in Clairton, Pennsylvania, September 19, 1947. Kansas State.
RUSHING

Year	Team	Att.	Yards	Avg.	Long	TD
1969	Washington	202	888	4.4	57	4
1970	Washington	237	1,125	4.7	75t	5
1971	Washington	253	948	3.7	34	4
1972	Washington	285	1,216	4.3	38t	8
1973	Washington	273	860	3.2	27	8
1974	Washington	163	430	2.6	16	3
1975	Washington	97	352	3.6	43	3
1976	Washington	20	56	2.8	11	0
Totals		1,530	5,875	3.8	75t	35

Fred Cox

Kicker, 5-10, 205. Born in Monongahela, Pennsylvania, December 11, 1938. Pittsburgh.
SCORING

Year	Team	FG	PAT	Points
1963	Minnesota	12-24	39-39	75
1964	Minnesota	21-33	40-42	103
1965	Minnesota	23-35	44-44	113
1966	Minnesota	18-33	34-34	88
1967	Minnesota	17-33	26-26	77
1968	Minnesota	19-29	31-32	88
1969	Minnesota	26-37	43-43	121
1970	Minnesota	30-46	35-35	125
1971	Minnesota	22-32	25-25	91
1972	Minnesota	21-33	34-34	97
1973	Minnesota	21-35	33-33	96
1974	Minnesota	12-20	32-39	68
1975	Minnesota	13-17	46-48	85
1976	Minnesota	19-31	32-36	89
Totals		274-438	494-510	1,316

Fred Cox

Larry Csonka

Larry Csonka

Running Back, 6-3, 235. Born in Stowe, Ohio, December 25, 1946. Syracuse.
RUSHING

Year	Team	Att.	Yards	Avg.	Long	TD
1968	Miami	138	540	3.9	40	6
1969	Miami	131	566	4.3	54t	2
1970	Miami	193	874	4.5	53	6
1971	Miami	195	1,051	5.4	28	7
1972	Miami	213	1,117	5.2	45	6
1973	Miami	219	1,003	4.6	25	5
1974	Miami	197	749	3.8	24	9
1975	Memphis WFL	99	421	4.3	13	1
1976	N.Y. Giants	160	569	3.6	13	4
AFL and NFL Totals		1,446	6.469	4.5	54t	45

Len Dawson

Len Dawson

Quarterback. 6-0, 190, Born in Alliance, Ohio, June 20, 1935. Purdue

PASSING

Year	Team	Att.	Comp.	Yards	TD	Int.
1957	Pittsburgh	4	2	25	0	0
1958	Pittsburgh	6	1	11	0	2
1959	Pittsburgh	7	3	60	1	0
1960	Cleveland	13	8	23	0	0
1961	Cleveland	15	7	85	1	3
1962	Dallas Texans	310	189	2,759	29	17
1963	Kansas City	352	190	2,389	26	19
1964	Kansas City	354	199	2,879	30	18
1965	Kansas City	305	163	2,262	21	14
1966	Kansas City	284	159	2,527	26	10
1967	Kansas City	357	206	2,651	24	17
1968	Kansas City	224	131	2,109	17	9
1969	Kansas City	166	98	1,323	9	13
1970	Kansas City	262	141	1,876	13	14
1971	Kansas City	301	167	2,504	15	13
1972	Kansas City	305	175	1,835	13	12
1973	Kansas City	101	66	725	2	5
1974	Kansas City	235	138	1,573	7	13
1975	Kansas City	140	93	1,095	5	4
	Totals	3,741	2,136	28,711	239	183

Tom Dempsey

Kicker. 6-1, 260, Born in Milwaukee, Wisconsin, January 12, 1947. Palomar Junior College.

SCORING

Year	Team	FG	PAT	Points
1969	New Orleans	22-41	33-35	99
1970	New Orleans	18-34	16-17	70
1971	Philadelphia	12-17	13-14	49
1972	Philadelphia	20-35	11-12	71
1973	Philadelphia	24-40	34-34	106
1974	Philadelphia	10-16	26-30	56
1975	Los Angeles	21-26	31-36	94
1976	Los Angeles	17-26	36-44	87
	Totals	144-235	200-222	632

Pat Fischer

Cornerback. 5-9, 170, Born in Omaha, Nebraska, January 2, 1940. Nebraska.

INTERCEPTIONS

Year	Team	No.	Yards	Avg.	Long	TD
1961	St. Louis	0	0	0.0	0	0
1962	St. Louis	3	41	13.7	25	0
1963	St. Louis	8	169	21.1	55	0
1964	St. Louis	10	164	16.4	39t	2
1965	St. Louis	3	30	10.0	16	0
1966	St. Louis	1	40	40.0	40	0
1967	St. Louis	4	85	21.3	69t	1
1968	Washington	2	14	7.0	13	0
1969	Washington	2	28	14.0	27	0
1970	Washington	2	13	6.5	10	0
1971	Washington	3	103	34.3	53t	1
1972	Washington	4	61	15.3	35	0
1973	Washington	3	99	33.0	67	0
1974	Washington	3	52	17.3	30	0
1975	Washington	3	4	1.3	4	0
1976	Washington	5	38	7.6	32	0
	Totals	56	941	16.8	69t	4

Chuck Foreman

Running Back. 6-2, 215. Born In Frederick, Maryland, October 26, 1950. Miami.

RUSHING

Year	Team	Att.	Yards	Avg.	Long	TD
1973	Minnesota	182	801	4.4	50t	4
1974	Minnesota	199	777	3.9	32	9
1975	Minnesota	280	1,070	3.8	31t	13
1976	Minnesota	278	1,155	4.2	46	13
	Totals	939	3,803	4.1	50t	39

RECEIVING

Year	Team	No.	Yards	Avg.	Long	TD
1973	Minnesota	37	362	9.8	46	2
1974	Minnesota	53	586	11.1	66t	6
1975	Minnesota	73	691	9.5	33	9
1976	Minnesota	55	567	10.3	41t	1
	Totals	218	2,206	10.1	66t	18

Tom Dempsey

Pat Fischer

Chuck Foreman

Roman Gabriel

Roman Gabriel

Quarterback. 6-4, 220, Born in Wilmington, North Carolina, August 5, 1940. North Carolina State.
PASSING

Year	Team	Att.	Comp.	Yards	TD	Int.
1962	Los Angeles	101	57	670	3	2
1963	Los Angeles	281	130	1,947	8	11
1964	Los Angeles	143	65	1,236	9	5
1965	Los Angeles	173	83	1,321	11	5
1966	Los Angeles	397	217	2,540	10	16
1967	Los Angeles	371	196	2,779	25	13
1968	Los Angeles	366	184	2,364	19	16
1969	Los Angeles	399	217	2,549	24	7
1970	Los Angeles	407	211	2,552	16	12
1971	Los Angeles	352	180	2,238	17	10
1972	Los Angeles	323	165	2,027	12	15
1973	Philadelphia	460	270	3,219	23	12
1974	Philadelphia	338	193	1,867	9	12
1975	Philadelphia	292	151	1,644	13	11
1976	Philadelphia	92	46	476	2	2
Totals		4,495	2,365	29,429	201	149

Mike Garrett

Running Back. 5-9, 195. Born in Los Angeles, California, April 12, 1944. USC.
RUSHING

Year	Team	No.	Yards	Avg.	Long	TD
1966	Kansas City	147	801	5.5	77	6
1967	Kansas City	236	1,087	4.6	58	9
1968	Kansas City	164	564	3.4	37	3
1969	Kansas City	168	732	4.4	34t	6
1970	Kansas City	21	62	3.0	18	0
	San Diego	46	146	3.2	22	1
1971	San Diego	140	591	4.2	36	4
1972	San Diego	272	1,031	3.8	41t	6
1973	San Diego	114	467	4.1	68	0
Totals		1,308	5,481	4.2	77	35

Bob Griese

Quarterback. 6-1, 190. Born in Evansville, Indiana, February 3, 1945. Purdue.
PASSING

Year	Team	Att.	Comp.	Yards	TD	Int.
1967	Miami	331	166	2,005	15	18
1968	Miami	355	186	2,473	21	16
1969	Miami	252	121	1,695	10	16
1970	Miami	245	142	2,019	12	17
1971	Miami	263	145	2,089	19	9
1972	Miami	97	53	638	4	4
1973	Miami	218	116	1,422	17	8
1974	Miami	253	152	1,968	16	15
1975	Miami	191	118	1,693	14	13
1976	Miami	272	162	2,097	11	12
Totals		2,477	1,361	18,099	139	128

Ray Guy

Punter. 6-3, 195. Born in Swainsboro, Georgia, December 22, 1949. Southern Mississippi.
PUNTING

Year	Team	No.	Yards	Avg.	Long	Blk.
1973	Oakland	69	3,127	45.3	72	0
1974	Oakland	74	3,124	42.2	66	0
1975	Oakland	68	2,979	43.8	64	0
1976	Oakland	67	2,785	41.6	66	0
Totals		278	12,015	43.2	72	0

Franco Harris

Running Back. 6-3, 230. Born in Fort Dix, New Jersey, March 7, 1950. Penn State.
RUSHING

Year	Team	Att.	Yards	Avg.	Long	TD
1972	Pittsburgh	188	1,055	5.6	75t	10
1973	Pittsburgh	188	698	3.7	35	3
1974	Pittsburgh	208	1,006	4.8	54	5
1975	Pittsburgh	262	1,246	4.8	36	10
1976	Pittsburgh	289	1,128	3.9	30	14
Totals		1,135	5,133	4.5	75t	42

Mike Garrett

Bob Griese

Ray Guy

Franco Harris

Bob Hayes

Bob Hayes

Wide Receiver. 5-11, 185. Born in Jacksonville, Florida, December 20, 1942. Florida A&M.

RECEIVING

Year	Team	No.	Yards	Avg.	Long	TD
1965	Dallas	46	1,003	21.8	82	12
1966	Dallas	64	1,232	19.3	95t	13
1967	Dallas	49	998	20.4	64	10
1968	Dallas	53	909	17.2	54	10
1969	Dallas	40	746	18.7	67	4
1970	Dallas	34	889	26.1	89	10
1971	Dallas	35	840	24.0	85	8
1972	Dallas	15	200	13.3	29	0
1973	Dallas	22	360	16.4	47	3
1974	Dallas	7	118	16.9	35t	1
1975	San Francisco	6	119	19.8	36	0
Totals		371	7,414	20.0	95t	71

Paul Hornung

Running Back. 6-2, 220. Born in Louisville, Kentucky, December 23, 1935. Notre Dame.

RUSHING

Year	Team	Att.	Yards	Avg.	Long	TD
1957	Green Bay	60	319	5.3	72	3
1958	Green Bay	69	310	4.5	55	2
1959	Green Bay	152	681	4.5	63	7
1960	Green Bay	160	671	4.2	37	13
1961	Green Bay	127	597	4.7	54t	8
1962	Green Bay	57	219	3.8	37	5
1963	Suspended					
1964	Green Bay	103	415	4.0	40	5
1965	Green Bay	89	299	3.4	17	5
1966	Green Bay	76	200	2.6	9	2
Totals		893	3,711	4.2	72	50

SCORING

Year	Team	TD	FG	PAT	Points
1957	Green Bay	3	0-4	0-0	18
1958	Green Bay	2	11-21	22-23	67
1959	Green Bay	7	7-17	31-32	94
1960	Green Bay	15	15-28	41-41	176
1961	Green Bay	10	15-22	41-41	146
1962	Green Bay	7	6-10	14-14	74
1963	Suspended				
1964	Green Bay	5	12-38	41-43	107
1965	Green Bay	8	0-0	0-0	48
1966	Green Bay	5	0-0	0-0	30
Totals		62	66-140	190-194	760

Paul Hornung

Ken Houston

Defensive Back. 6-3, 195. Born in Lufkin, Texas, November 12, 1944. Prairie View A&M.

INTERCEPTIONS

Year	Team	No.	Yards	Avg.	Long	TD
1967	Houston	4	151	37.8	78	2
1968	Houston	5	160	32.0	66t	2
1969	Houston	4	87	21.8	51t	1
1970	Houston	3	32	10.7	9	0
1971	Houston	9	220	24.4	48t	4
1972	Houston	0	0	0.0	0	0
1973	Washington	6	32	5.3	22	0
1974	Washington	2	40	20.0	37	0
1975	Washington	4	33	8.3	19	0
1976	Washington	4	25	6.3	12	0
Totals		41	780	19.0	78	9

Jimmy Johnson

Defensive Back. 6-2, 187. Born in Dallas, Texas, March 31, 1938. UCLA.

INTERCEPTIONS

Year	Team	No.	Yards	Avg.	Long	TD
1961	San Francisco	5	116	23.2	63	0
1962	San Francisco	0	0	0.0	0	0
1963	San Francisco	2	36	18.0	36	0
1964	San Francisco	3	65	21.7	43	0
1965	San Francisco	6	47	7.8	26	0
1966	San Francisco	4	57	14.3	35t	1
1967	San Francisco	2	68	34.0	38	0
1968	San Francisco	1	25	25.0	25	0
1969	San Francisco	5	18	3.6	18	0
1970	San Francisco	2	36	18.0	36t	1
1971	San Francisco	3	16	5.3	10	0
1972	San Francisco	4	18	4.5	15	0
1973	San Francisco	4	46	11.5	30	0
1974	San Francisco	3	50	16.7	37	0
1975	San Francisco	2	0	0.0	0	0
1976	San Francisco	1	17	17.0	17	0
Totals		47	615	13.1	63	2

Ken Houston

Jimmy Johnson

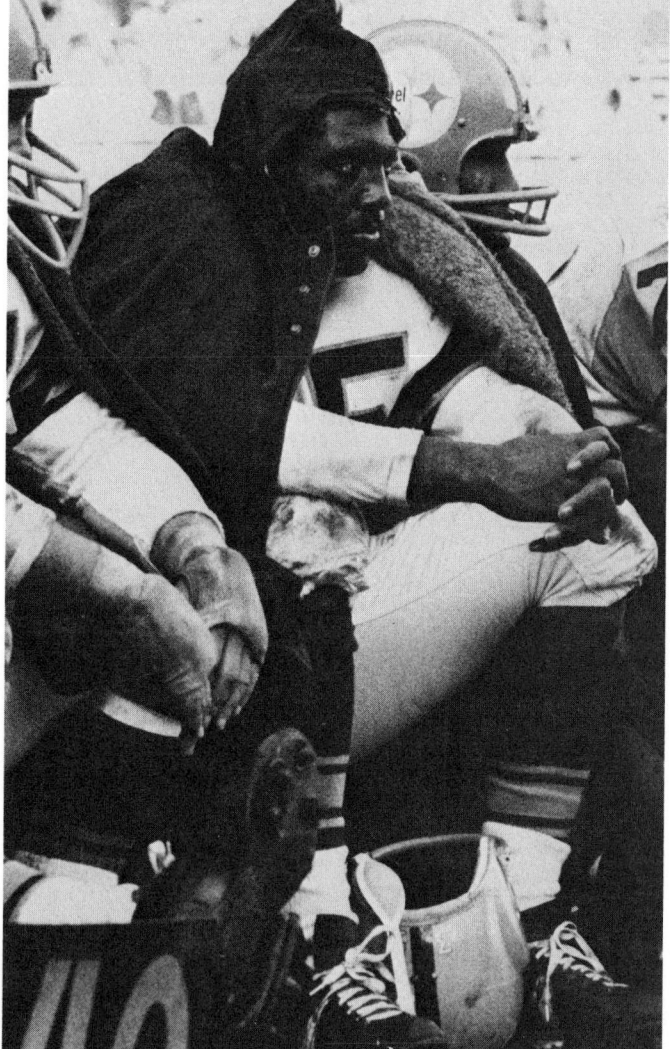

John Henry Johnson

Leroy Kelly

John Henry Johnson

Running Back. 6-2, 215. Born in Pittsburgh, California, November 24, 1929. Arizona State.
RUSHING

Year	Team	Att.	Yards	Avg.	Long	TD
1954	San Francisco	129	681	5.3	38t	9
1955	San Francisco	19	69	3.6	12	1
1956	San Francisco	80	301	3.8	54	2
1957	Detroit	129	621	4.8	62	5
1958	Detroit	56	254	4.5	19	0
1959	Detroit	82	270	3.3	39	2
1960	Pittsburgh	118	621	5.3	87t	2
1961	Pittsburgh	213	787	3.7	44	6
1962	Pittsburgh	251	1,141	4.5	40	7
1963	Pittsburgh	186	773	4.2	48	4
1964	Pittsburgh	235	1,048	4.5	45t	7
1965	Pittsburgh	3	11	3.7	7	0
1966	Houston	70	226	3.2	28	3
Totals		1,571	6,803	4.3	87t	48

Bert Jones

Quarterback. 6-2, 215. Born in Ruston, Louisiana, October 23, 1951. Louisiana State.
PASSING

Year	Team	Att.	Comp.	Yards	TD	Int.
1973	Baltimore	108	43	539	4	12
1974	Baltimore	270	143	1,610	8	12
1975	Baltimore	344	203	2,483	18	8
1976	Baltimore	343	207	3,104	24	9
Totals		1,065	596	7,736	54	41

Sonny Jurgensen

Quarterback. 6-0, 203. Born in Wilmington, North Carolina, August 23, 1934. Duke.
PASSING

Year	Team	Att.	Comp.	Yards	TD	Int.
1957	Philadelphia	70	33	470	5	8
1958	Philadelphia	22	12	259	0	1
1959	Philadelphia	5	3	27	1	0
1960	Philadelphia	44	24	486	5	1
1961	Philadelphia	416	235	3,723	32	24
1962	Philadelphia	366	196	3,261	22	26
1963	Philadelphia	184	99	1,413	11	13
1964	Washington	385	207	2,934	24	13
1965	Washington	356	190	2,367	15	16
1966	Washington	436	254	3,209	28	19
1967	Washington	508	288	3,747	31	16
1968	Washington	292	167	1,980	17	11
1969	Washington	442	274	3,102	22	15
1970	Washington	337	202	2,354	23	10
1971	Washington	28	16	170	0	2
1972	Washington	59	39	633	2	4
1973	Washington	145	87	904	6	5
1974	Washington	167	107	1,185	11	5
Totals		4,262	2,433	32,224	255	189

Leroy Kelly

Running Back. 6-0, 205. Born in Philadelphia, Pennsylvania, May 20, 1942. Morgan State.
RUSHING

Year	Team	Att.	Yards	Avg.	Long	TD
1964	Cleveland	6	12	2.0	5	0
1965	Cleveland	37	139	3.8	16	0
1966	Cleveland	209	1,141	5.5	70t	15
1967	Cleveland	235	1,205	5.1	42t	11
1968	Cleveland	248	1,239	5.0	65	16
1969	Cleveland	196	817	4.2	31	9
1970	Cleveland	206	656	3.2	33t	6
1971	Cleveland	234	865	3.7	35	10
1972	Cleveland	224	811	3.6	18	4
1973	Cleveland	132	389	2.9	19	3
1974	Chicago WFL	77	315	4.1	24	1
NFL Totals		1,727	7,274	4.2	70t	74

Bert Jones

Sonny Jurgensen

Billy Kilmer

Paul Krause

Yale Lary

Billy Kilmer

Quarterback. 6-0, 204. Born in Topeka, Kansas, September 5, 1939. UCLA.

PASSING

Year	Team	Att.	Comp.	Yards	TD	Int.
1961	San Francisco	34	19	286	0	4
1962	San Francisco	13	8	191	1	3
1963	Injured, did not play					
1964	San Francisco	14	8	92	1	1
1965	Injured, did not play					
1966	San Francisco	16	5	84	0	1
1967	New Orleans	204	97	1,341	6	11
1968	New Orleans	315	167	2,060	15	17
1969	New Orleans	360	193	2,532	20	17
1970	New Orleans	237	135	1,557	6	17
1971	Washington	306	166	2,221	13	13
1972	Washington	225	120	1,648	19	11
1973	Washington	227	122	1,656	14	9
1974	Washington	234	137	1,632	10	6
1975	Washington	346	178	2,440	23	16
1976	Washington	206	108	1,252	12	10
Totals		2,737	1,463	18,992	140	136

Paul Krause

Safety. 6-3, 200. Born in Flint, Michigan, February 19, 1942. Iowa.

INTERCEPTIONS

Year	Team	No.	Yards	Avg.	Long	TD
1964	Washington	12	140	11.7	35t	1
1965	Washington	6	118	19.7	43	0
1966	Washington	2	0	0.0	0	0
1967	Washington	8	75	9.4	32	0
1968	Minnesota	7	82	11.7	29	0
1969	Minnesota	5	82	16.4	77t	1
1970	Minnesota	6	90	15.0	40	0
1971	Minnesota	6	112	18.7	31	0
1972	Minnesota	6	109	18.2	35	1
1973	Minnesota	4	28	7.0	24	0
1974	Minnesota	2	53	26.5	45	0
1975	Minnesota	10	201	20.1	81	0
1976	Minnesota	2	21	10.1	19	0
Totals		76	1,111	14.6	81	3

Yale Lary

Defensive Back. 5-11, 189. Born in Fort Worth, Texas, November 24, 1930. Texas A&M.

INTERCEPTIONS

Year	Team	No.	Yards	Avg.	Long	TD
1952	Detroit	4	61	15.3	53	0
1953	Detroit	5	98	19.6	32	0
1954	Military service					
1955	Military service					
1956	Detroit	8	182	22.8	73t	1
1957	Detroit	2	64	32.0	63	0
1958	Detroit	3	70	23.3	31	0
1959	Detroit	3	0	0.0	0	0
1960	Detroit	3	44	14.7	22	0
1961	Detroit	6	95	15.8	42	0
1962	Detroit	8	51	6.4	32	0
1963	Detroit	2	21	10.5	21t	1
1964	Detroit	6	101	16.8	30	0
Totals		50	787	15.7	73t	2

PUNTING

Year	Team	No.	Yards	Avg.	Long	Blk.
1952	Detroit	5		36.2	43	0
1953	Detroit	28		39.7	61	0
1954	Military service					
1955	Military service					
1956	Detroit	42		40.4	61	0
1957	Detroit	54		39.9	66	0
1958	Detroit	59		42.8	62	1
1959	Detroit	45	2,118	47.1	67	0
1960	Detroit	64	2,802	43.8	63	2
1961	Detroit	52		48.4	71	0
1962	Detroit	52	2,402	45.3	68	1
1963	Detroit	35	1,713	48.9	73	0
1964	Detroit	67		46.3	74	0
Totals		503		44.3	74	4

Don Maynard

Floyd Little

Terry Metcalf

Floyd Little

Running Back. 5-10, 195. Born in New Haven, Connecticut, July 4, 1942. Syracuse.

RUSHING

Year	Team	Att.	Yards	Avg.	Long	TD
1967	Denver	130	381	2.9	14	1
1968	Denver	158	584	3.7	55t	3
1969	Denver	146	729	5.0	48t	6
1970	Denver	209	901	4.3	80t	3
1971	Denver	284	1,139	4.0	40	6
1972	Denver	216	859	4.0	55t	9
1973	Denver	256	979	3.8	47	12
1974	Denver	117	312	2.7	22	1
1975	Denver	125	445	3.6	19	2
Totals		1,641	6,323	3.9	80t	43

Don Maynard

Wide Receiver. 6-1, 185. Born in Crosbyton, Texas, January 25, 1937. Texas-El Paso.

RECEIVING

Year	Team	No.	Yards	Avg.	Long	TD
1958	N.Y. Giants	5	84	16.8	31	0
1959	Did not play					
1960	N.Y. Titans	72	1,265	17.6		6
1961	N.Y. Titans	43	629	14.6	45	8
1962	N.Y. Titans	56	1,041	18.6	86	8
1963	N.Y. Jets	38	780	20.5	73	9
1964	N.Y. Jets	46	847	18.4	68	8
1965	N.Y. Jets	68	1,218	17.9	56	14
1966	N.Y. Jets	48	840	17.8	55	5
1967	N.Y. Jets	71	1,434	20.2	75t	10
1968	N.Y. Jets	57	1,297	22.8	87t	10
1969	N.Y. Jets	47	938	20.0	60t	6
1970	N.Y. Jets	31	525	16.9	47	0
1971	N.Y. Jets	21	408	19.4	74t	2
1972	N.Y. Jets	29	510	17.6	41	2
1973	St. Louis	1	18	18.0	18	0
Totals		633	11,834	18.7	87t	88

Don Meredith

Quarterback. 6-2, 205. Born in Mount Vernon, Texas, April 10, 1938. Southern Methodist.

PASSING

Year	Team	Att.	Comp.	Yards	TD	Int.
1960	Dallas	68	29	281	2	5
1961	Dallas	182	94	1,161	9	11
1962	Dallas	212	105	1,679	15	8
1963	Dallas	310	167	2,381	17	18
1964	Dallas	323	158	2,143	9	16
1965	Dallas	305	141	2,415	22	13
1966	Dallas	344	177	2,805	24	12
1967	Dallas	255	128	1,834	16	16
1968	Dallas	309	171	2,500	21	12
Totals		2,308	1,170	17,199	135	111

Terry Metcalf

Running Back. 5-10, 190. Born in Seattle, Washington, September 24, 1951. Cal State-Long Beach.

RUSHING

Year	Team	Att.	Yards	Avg.	Long	TD
1973	St. Louis	148	628	4.2	50	2
1974	St. Louis	152	718	4.7	75t	6
1975	St. Louis	165	816	4.9	52t	9
1976	St. Louis	134	537	4.0	36	3
Totals		599	2,699	4.5	75t	20

PUNT RETURNS

Year	Team	No.	FC	Yards	Avg.	Long	TD
1973	St. Louis	0	0	0	0.0	0	0
1974	St. Louis	26	3	340	13.1	43	0
1975	St. Louis	23	3	285	12.4	69t	1
1976	St. Louis	17	1	188	11.1	39	0
Totals		66	7	813	12.3	69t	1

Kickoff Returns

Year	Team	No.	Yards	Avg.	Long	TD
1973	St. Louis	4	124	31.0	48	0
1974	St. Louis	20	623	31.2	94t	1
1975	St. Louis	35	960	27.4	93t	1
1976	St. Louis	16	325	20.3	33	0
Totals		75	2,032	27.1	94t	2

Don Meredith

Earl Morrall　　　　　　*Don Perkins*

Joe Namath

Jim Nance

Earl Morrall

Quarterback. 6-2, 210. Born in Muskegon, Michigan, May 17, 1934. Michigan State.

PASSING

Year	Team	Att.	Comp.	Yards	TD	Int.
1956	San Francisco	78	38	621	1	6
1957	Pittsburgh	289	139	1,900	11	12
1958	Pittsburgh	46	16	275	1	7
	Detroit	32	9	188	5	9
1959	Detroit	137	65	1,102	5	6
1960	Detroit	49	32	423	4	3
1961	Detroit	150	69	909	7	9
1962	Detroit	52	32	449	4	4
1963	Detroit	328	174	2,621	24	14
1964	Detroit	91	50	588	4	3
1965	N.Y. Giants	302	155	2,446	22	12
1966	N.Y. Giants	151	71	1,105	7	12
1967	N.Y. Giants	24	13	181	3	1
1968	Baltimore	317	182	2,909	26	17
1969	Baltimore	99	46	755	5	7
1970	Baltimore	93	51	792	9	4
1971	Baltimore	167	84	1,210	7	12
1972	Miami	150	83	1,360	11	7
1973	Miami	38	17	253	0	4
1974	Miami	27	17	301	2	3
1975	Miami	43	26	273	3	2
1976	Miami	26	10	148	1	1
Totals		2,689	1,379	20,809	161	148

Joe Namath

Quarterback. 6-2, 200. Born in Beaver Falls, Pennsylvania, May 31, 1943. Alabama.

PASSING

Year	Team	Att.	Comp.	Yards	TD	Int.
1965	N.Y. Jets	340	164	2,220	18	15
1966	N.Y. Jets	471	232	3,379	19	27
1967	N.Y. Jets	491	258	4,007	26	28
1968	N.Y. Jets	380	187	3,147	15	17
1969	N.Y. Jets	361	185	2,734	19	17
1970	N.Y. Jets	179	90	1,259	5	12
1971	N.Y. Jets	59	28	537	5	6
1972	N.Y. Jets	324	162	2,816	19	21
1973	N.Y. Jets	133	68	966	5	6
1974	N.Y. Jets	361	191	2,616	20	22
1975	N.Y. Jets	326	157	2,286	15	28
1976	N.Y. Jets	230	114	1,090	4	16
Totals		3,655	1,836	27,057	170	215

Jim Nance

Running Back. 6-1, 240. Born in Indiana, Pennsylvania, December 30, 1942. Syracuse

RUSHING

Year	Team	Att.	Yards	Avg.	Long	TD
1965	Boston	111	321	2.9	20	5
1966	Boston	299	1,458	4.9	11t	11
1967	Boston	269	1,216	4.5	53	7
1968	Boston	177	593	3.4	30t	4
1969	Boston	193	750	3.9	43	6
1970	Boston	145	522	3.6	21	5
1971	New England	129	463	3.6	50t	5
1972	Did not play football					
1973	N.Y. Jets	18	78	4.3	18	0
1974	Houston-Shreveport WFL	300	1,240	4.1	25	8
1975	Shreveport WFL	190	767	4.0	35	7
AFL and NFL Totals		1,341	5,401	4.0	53	45

Don Perkins

Running Back. 5-10, 205. Born in Waterloo, Iowa, March 4, 1938. New Mexico.

RUSHING

Year	Team	Att.	Yards	Avg.	Long	TD
1961	Dallas	200	815	4.1	47	4
1962	Dallas	222	945	4.3	35	7
1963	Dallas	149	614	4.1	19t	7
1964	Dallas	174	768	4.4	59	6
1965	Dallas	177	690	3.9	43	0
1966	Dallas	186	726	3.9	24	8
1967	Dallas	201	823	4.1	30	6
1968	Dallas	191	836	4.4	28t	4
Totals		1,500	6,217	4.1	59	42

Mel Renfro

Jake Scott

Frank Ryan

Charlie Sanders

Mel Renfro

Defensive Back-Running Back. 6-0, 190. Born in Houston, Texas, December 30, 1941. Oregon.

INTERCEPTIONS

Year	Team		No.	Yards	Avg.	Long	TD
1964	Dallas		7	110	15.7	39t	1
1965	Dallas		2	92	46.2	90t	1
1966	Dallas		2	57	28.5	33	0
1967	Dallas		7	38	5.4	30	0
1968	Dallas		3	5	1.7	5	0
1969	Dallas		10	118	11.8	41	0
1970	Dallas		4	3	0.8	3	0
1971	Dallas		4	11	2.8	7	0
1972	Dallas		1	0	0.0	0	0
1973	Dallas		2	65	32.5	35	1
1974	Dallas		1	6	6.0	6	0
1975	Dallas		4	70	17.5	22	0
1976	Dallas		3	23	7.7	23	0
Totals			50	598	12.0	90t	3

RUSHING

Year	Team	Att.	Yards	Avg.	Long	TD
1966	Dallas	8	52	6.5	27	0

RECEIVING

Year	Team	No.	Yards	Avg.	Long	TD
1966	Dallas	4	65	16.3	42	0

PUNT RETURNS

Year	Team	No.	FC	Yards	Avg.	Long	TD
1964	Dallas	32	9	418	13.1	69t	1
1965	Dallas	24	4	145	6.0	35	0
1966	Dallas	21	6	123	5.9	38	0
1967	Dallas	3	4	−1	−0.3	7	0
1968	Dallas	0	2	0	0.0	0	0
1969	Dallas	15	7	80	5.3	34	0
1970	Dallas	13	6	77	5.9	29	0
1971	Dallas	0	1	0	0.0	0	0
1974	Dallas	1	1	0	0.0	0	0
Totals		109	40	842	7.7	69t	1

KICKOFF RETURNS

Year	Team	No.	Yards	Avg.	Long	TD
1964	Dallas	40	1,017	25.4	65	0
1965	Dallas	21	630	30.0	100t	1
1966	Dallas	19	487	25.6	87t	1
1967	Dallas	5	112	22.4	30	0
Totals		85	2,246	26.4	100t	2

Frank Ryan

Quarterback. 6-3, 200. Born in Fort Worth, Texas, July 12, 1936. Rice.

PASSING

Year	Team	Att.	Comp.	Yards	TD	Int.
1958	Los Angeles	14	5	34	1	3
1959	Los Angeles	89	42	709	2	4
1960	Los Angeles	128	62	816	7	9
1961	Los Angeles	142	72	1,115	5	7
1962	Cleveland	194	112	1,541	10	7
1963	Cleveland	256	135	2,026	25	13
1964	Cleveland	334	174	2,404	25	19
1965	Cleveland	243	119	1,751	18	13
1966	Cleveland	382	200	2,974	29	14
1967	Cleveland	280	136	2,026	20	16
1968	Cleveland	66	31	639	7	6
1969	Washington	1	1	4	0	0
1970	Washington	4	1	3	0	0
Totals		2,133	1,090	16,042	149	111

Charlie Sanders

Tight end. 6-4, 230. Born in Greensboro, North Carolina, August 25, 1946. Minnesota.

RECEIVING

Year	Team	No.	Yards	Avg.	Long	TD
1968	Detroit	40	533	13.3	25	1
1969	Detroit	42	656	15.6	47	3
1970	Detroit	40	544	13.6	34	6
1971	Detroit	31	502	16.2	49t	5
1972	Detroit	27	416	15.4	38	2
1973	Detroit	28	433	15.5	54	2
1974	Detroit	42	532	12.7	47	3
1975	Detroit	37	486	13.1	32	3
1976	Detroit	35	545	15.6	34	5
Totals		322	4,647	14.4	54	30

O.J. Simpson

Jackie Smith

Ken Stabler

Roger Staubach

Jake Scott

Safety. 6-0, 188. Born in Greenwood, South Carolina, July 20, 1945. Georgia.

INTERCEPTIONS

Year	Team	No.	Yards	Avg.	Long	TD
1970	Miami	5	112	22.4	47	0
1971	Miami	7	34	4.9	21	0
1972	Miami	5	73	14.6	31	0
1973	Miami	4	71	17.8	29	0
1974	Miami	8	75	9.4	30	0
1975	Miami	6	60	10.0	38	0
1976	Washington	4	12	3.0	6	0
Totals		34	437	12.9	47	0

O.J. Simpson

Running Back. 6-1, 216. Born in San Francisco, California, July 9, 1947. USC.

RUSHING

Year	Team	Att.	Yards	Avg.	Long	TD
1969	Buffalo	181	697	3.9	32t	2
1970	Buffalo	120	488	4.1	56t	5
1971	Buffalo	183	742	4.1	46t	5
1972	Buffalo	292	1,251	4.3	94t	6
1973	Buffalo	332	2,003	6.0	80t	12
1974	Buffalo	270	1,125	4.2	41t	3
1975	Buffalo	329	1,817	5.5	88t	16
1976	Buffalo	290	1,503	5.2	75	8
Totals		1,997	9,626	4.8	94t	57

RECEIVING

Year	Team	No.	Yards	Avg.	Long	TD
1969	Buffalo	30	343	11.4	55t	3
1970	Buffalo	10	139	13.9	36	0
1971	Buffalo	21	162	7.7	38	0
1972	Buffalo	27	193	11.7	25	0
1973	Buffalo	6	70	11.7	24	0
1974	Buffalo	15	189	12.6	29t	1
1975	Buffalo	28	426	15.2	64t	7
1976	Buffalo	22	264	12.0	75	1
Totals		159	1,786	11.2	75	12

Jackie Smith

Tight End. 6-3, 208. Born in Columbia, Mississippi, July 19, 1944. Arizona State.

RECEIVING

Year	Team	No.	Yards	Avg.	Long	TD
1963	St. Louis	28	445	15.9	55t	2
1964	St. Louis	47	657	14.0	78t	4
1965	St. Louis	41	648	15.8	70t	2
1966	St. Louis	45	810	18.0	69t	3
1967	St. Louis	56	1,205	21.5	76t	9
1968	St. Louis	49	789	16.1	65t	2
1969	St. Louis	43	561	13.0	34	1
1970	St. Louis	37	687	18.6	59t	4
1971	St. Louis	21	379	18.0	61t	4
1972	St. Louis	26	407	15.7	71	2
1973	St. Louis	41	600	14.6	42	1
1974	St. Louis	25	413	16.5	81	3
1975	St. Louis	13	246	18.9	45	2
1976	St. Louis	3	22	7.3	16	0
Totals		475	7,869	16.6	81	39

Ken Stabler

Quarterback. 6-3, 215. Born in Foley, Alabama, December 25, 1945. Alabama.

PASSING

Year	Team	Att.	Comp.	Yards	TD	Int.
1970	Oakland	7	2	52	0	1
1971	Oakland	48	24	268	1	4
1972	Oakland	74	44	524	4	3
1973	Oakland	260	163	1,997	14	10
1974	Oakland	310	178	2,469	26	12
1975	Oakland	293	171	2,296	16	24
1976	Oakland	291	194	2,737	27	17
Totals		1,283	776	10,343	88	71

Roger Staubach

Quarterback. 6-3, 197. Born in Cincinnati, Ohio, February 5, 1942. Navy.

PASSING

Year	Team	Att.	Comp.	Yards	TD	Int.
1969	Dallas	47	23	421	1	2
1970	Dallas	82	44	542	2	8
1971	Dallas	211	126	1,882	15	4
1972	Dallas	20	9	98	0	2
1973	Dallas	286	179	2,428	23	15
1974	Dallas	360	190	2,552	11	15
1975	Dallas	348	198	2,666	17	16
1976	Dallas	369	208	2,715	14	11
Totals		1,723	977	13,304	83	73

Jan Stenerud

Fran Tarkenton

Jan Stenerud

Kicker. 6-2, 187. Born in Fetsend, Norway, November 26, 1942. Montana State.

SCORING

Year	Team	FG	PAT	Points
1967	Kansas City	21-36	45-45	108
1968	Kansas City	30-40	39-40	129
1969	Kansas City	27-35	38-38	119
1970	Kansas City	30-42	26-26	116
1971	Kansas City	26-44	32-32	110
1972	Kansas City	21-36	32-32	95
1973	Kansas City	24-38	21-23	93
1974	Kansas City	17-24	24-26	75
1975	Kansas City	22-32	30-31	96
1976	Kansas City	21-38	27-33	90
Totals		239-365	314-326	1,031

Pat Summerall

End-Kicker. 6-4, 220. Born in Lake City, Florida, May 10, 1930. Arkansas.

SCORING

Year	Team	FG	PAT	Points
1952	Detroit	0-0	0-0	0
1953	Chi. Cardinals	9-24	23-23	50
1954	Chi. Cardinals	8-18	21-23	45
1955	Chi. Cardinals	8-19	23-25	*53
1956	Chi. Cardinals	10-22	30-30	60
1957	Chi. Cardinals	6-17	24-26	42
1958	N.Y. Giants	12-23	28-30	64
1959	N.Y. Giants	20-29	30-30	90
1960	N.Y. Giants	13-26	32-32	71
1961	N.Y. Giants	14-34	46-46	88
Totals		100-212	257-265	563

*Includes one touchdown.

Fran Tarkenton

Quarterback. 6-0, 190. Born in Richmond, Virginia, February 3, 1940. Georgia.

PASSING

Year	Team	Att.	Comp.	Yards	TD	Int.
1961	Minnesota	280	157	1,997	18	17
1962	Minnesota	329	163	2,595	22	25
1963	Minnesota	297	170	2,311	15	15
1964	Minnesota	306	171	2,506	22	11
1965	Minnesota	329	171	2,609	19	11
1966	Minnesota	358	192	2,561	17	16
1967	N.Y. Giants	377	204	3,088	29	19
1968	N.Y. Giants	337	182	2,555	21	12
1969	N.Y. Giants	409	220	2,918	23	8
1970	N.Y. Giants	389	219	2,777	19	12
1971	N.Y. Giants	386	226	2,567	11	21
1972	Minnesota	378	215	2,651	18	13
1973	Minnesota	274	169	2,113	15	7
1974	Minnesota	351	199	2,598	17	12
1975	Minnesota	425	273	2,994	25	13
1976	Minnesota	412	255	2,961	17	8
Totals		5,637	3,186	41,801	308	220

RUSHING

Year	Team	Att.	Yards	Avg.	Long	TD
1961	Minnesota	56	308	5.5	52t	5
1962	Minnesota	41	361	8.8	31	2
1963	Minnesota	28	162	5.8	24	1
1964	Minnesota	50	330	6.6	31	2
1965	Minnesota	56	356	6.4	36	1
1966	Minnesota	62	376	6.1	28	4
1967	N.Y. Giants	44	306	7.0	22	2
1968	N.Y. Giants	67	301	5.3	22	3
1969	N.Y. Giants	37	172	4.6	21	0
1970	N.Y. Giants	43	236	5.5	20	2
1971	N.Y. Giants	30	111	3.7	16	3
1972	Minnesota	27	180	6.7	21	0
1973	Minnesota	41	202	4.9	16	1
1974	Minnesota	21	120	5.7	15	2
1975	Minnesota	16	108	6.8	21t	2
1976	Minnesota	27	45	1.7	20	1
Totals		636	3,674	5.8	52t	31

Pat Summerall

Lionel Taylor

Jim Turner

Charley Taylor

Wide Receiver-Running Back. 6-3, 210. Born in Grand Prairie, Texas, September 28, 1941. Arizona State.

RECEIVING

Year	Team	No.	Yards	Avg.	Long	TD
1964	Washington	53	814	15.4	80t	5
1965	Washington	40	577	14.4	69	3
1966	Washington	72	1,119	15.5	86t	12
1967	Washington	70	990	14.1	86t	9
1968	Washington	48	650	13.5	47	5
1969	Washington	71	883	12.4	88t	8
1970	Washington	42	593	14.1	41	8
1971	Washington	24	370	15.4	71t	4
1972	Washington	49	673	13.7	70t	7
1973	Washington	59	801	13.6	53	7
1974	Washington	54	738	13.7	51	5
1975	Washington	53	774	14.0	64	6
1976	Injured, did not play					
Totals		635	8,982	14.1	88t	79

RUSHING

Year	Team	Att.	Yards	Avg.	Long	TD
1964	Washington	199	755	3.8	50	5
1965	Washington	145	402	2.8	39	3
1966	Washington	87	262	3.0	24	3
1967	Washington	0	0	0.0	0	0
1968	Washington	2	—3	—1.5	4	0
1969	Washington	3	24	8.0	18	0
1970	Washington	1	17	17.0	17	0
1971	Washington	0	0	0.0	0	0
1972	Washington	3	39	13.0	17	0
1973	Washington	1	—7	—7.0	—7	0
1974	Washington	1	—1	—1.0	—1	0
1975	Washington	0	0	0.0	0	0
1976	Injured, did not play					
Totals		442	1,488	3.4	50	11

Lionel Taylor

End. 6-2, 215. Born in Kansas City, Missouri, August 15, 1936. New Mexico Highlands.

RECEIVING

Year	Team	No.	Yards	Avg.	Long	TD
1959	Chi. Bears	0	0	0.0	0	0
1960	Denver	92	1,235	13.4		12
1961	Denver	100	1,176	11.8	52	4
1962	Denver	77	908	11.8	45	4
1963	Denver	78	1,101	14.1	72	10
1964	Denver	76	873	11.5	57	7
1965	Denver	85	1,131	13.3	63	6
1966	Denver	35	448	12.8	29	1
1967	Houston	18	233	12.9	23	1
1968	Houston	6	90	15.0	35	0
Totals		567	7,195	12.7		45

Jim Turner

Kicker. 6-2, 205. Born in Martinez, California, March 28, 1941. Utah State.

SCORING

Year	Team	FG	PAT	Points
1964	N.Y. Jets	13-27	33-33	72
1965	N.Y. Jets	20-34	31-31	91
1966	N.Y. Jets	18-35	34-35	88
1967	N.Y. Jets	17-32	36-39	87
1968	N.Y. Jets	34-46	43-43	145
1969	N.Y. Jets	32-47	33-33	129
1970	N.Y. Jets	19-35	28-28	85
1971	Denver	25-38	18-18	93
1972	Denver	20-29	37-37	97
1973	Denver	22-33	40-40	106
1974	Denver	11-21	35-38	68
1975	Denver	21-28	23-26	86
1976	Denver	15-21	36-39	81
Totals		267-426	427-440	1,228

Charley Taylor

John Unitas

Jerrel Wilson

Garo Yepremian

John Unitas

Quarterback. 6-1, 195. Born in Pittsburgh, Pennsylvania, May 7, 1933. Louisville.

PASSING

Year	Team	Att.	Comp.	Yards	TD	Int.
1956	Baltimore	198	110	1,498	9	10
1957	Baltimore	301	172	2,550	24	17
1958	Baltimore	263	136	2,007	19	7
1959	Baltimore	367	193	2,899	32	14
1960	Baltimore	378	190	3,099	25	24
1961	Baltimore	420	229	2,990	16	24
1962	Baltimore	389	222	2,967	23	23
1963	Baltimore	410	237	3,481	20	12
1964	Baltimore	305	158	2,824	19	6
1965	Baltimore	282	164	2,530	23	12
1966	Baltimore	348	195	2,748	22	24
1967	Baltimore	436	255	3,428	20	16
1968	Baltimore	32	11	139	2	4
1969	Baltimore	327	178	2,342	12	20
1970	Baltimore	321	166	2,213	14	18
1971	Baltimore	176	92	942	3	9
1972	Baltimore	157	88	1,111	4	6
1973	San Diego	76	34	471	3	7
Totals		5,186	2,830	40,239	290	253

Paul Warfield

Wide Receiver. 6-0, 188. Born in Warren, Ohio, November 28, 1942. Ohio State.

RECEIVING

Year	Team	No.	Yards	Avg.	Long	TD
1964	Cleveland	52	920	17.7	62t	9
1965	Cleveland	3	30	10.0	13	0
1966	Cleveland	36	741	20.6	51	5
1967	Cleveland	32	702	21.9	49t	8
1968	Cleveland	50	1,067	21.3	65t	12
1969	Cleveland	42	886	21.1	82t	10
1970	Miami	28	703	25.1	54	6
1971	Miami	43	996	23.2	86t	11
1972	Miami	29	606	20.9	47	3
1973	Miami	29	514	17.7	45t	11
1974	Miami	27	536	19.9	54	2
1975	Memphis WFL	25	422	16.9	38	3
1976	Cleveland	38	613	16.1	37	6
NFL Totals		409	8,314	20.3	86t	83

Ken Willard

Running Back. 6-1, 219. Born in Richmond, Virginia, July 14, 1943. North Carolina.

RUSHING

Year	Team	Att.	Yards	Avg.	Long	TD
1965	San Francisco	189	778	4.1	32	5
1966	San Francisco	191	763	4.0	49	5
1967	San Francisco	169	510	3.0	20	5
1968	San Francisco	227	967	4.3	69t	7
1969	San Francisco	171	557	3.3	18	7
1970	San Francisco	236	789	3.3	20	7
1971	San Francisco	216	855	4.0	49	4
1972	San Francisco	100	345	3.5	23	4
1973	San Francisco	83	366	4.4	33	1
1974	St. Louis	40	175	4.4	12	0
Totals		1,622	6,105	3.8	69t	45

Jerrel Wilson

Punter. 6-2, 222. Born in New Orleans, Louisiana, October 4, 1941. Southern Mississippi.

PUNTING

Year	Team	No.	Yards	Avg.	Long	Blk.
1963	Kansas City	60	2,628	43.8	72	0
1964	Kansas City	77	3,292	42.8	70	0
1965	Kansas City	68	3,132	46.1	64	0
1966	Kansas City	61	2,715	44.5	69	0
1967	Kansas City	41	1,739	42.4	59	1
1968	Kansas City	63	2,841	45.1	70	0
1969	Kansas City	68	3,022	44.4	62	0
1970	Kansas City	76	3,415	44.9	68	0
1971	Kansas City	64	2,865	44.8	68	1
1972	Kansas City	66	2,960	44.8	69	1
1973	Kansas City	80	3,642	45.5	68	1
1974	Kansas City	83	3,462	41.7	64	2
1975	Kansas City	54	2,233	41.4	64	1
1976	Kansas City	65	2,729	42.0	62	1
Totals		926	40,675	43.9	72	8

Paul Warfield

Ken Willard

Garo Yepremian

Kicker. 5-8, 175. Born in Cyprus, June 2, 1944. No college.

SCORING

Year	Team	FG	PAT	Points
1966	Detroit	13-22	11-11	50
1967	Detroit	2-6	22-23	28
1968	Did not play football			
1969	Did not play football			
1970	Miami	22-29	31-31	97
1971	Miami	28-40	33-33	117
1972	Miami	24-37	43-45	115
1973	Miami	25-37	38-38	113
1974	Miami	8-15	43-43	67
1975	Miami	13-16	40-46	79
1976	Miami	16-23	29-31	77
Totals		151-225	290-301	743

ACKNOWLEDGMENTS

A project the size of *The NFL's Official Encyclopedic History of Professional Football* could not have been realized without the contributions of many people.

We enlisted a literal team of researchers, writers, editors, proof-readers, fact-checkers, typists, designers, and production people to accomplish the ambitious task.

Three of the six men listed on the title page as writers and editors of this book are members of the staff of the Creative Services Division of NFL Properties, Inc. They are David Boss, publisher; John Wiebusch, editor, and Tom Bennett, managing editor. A fourth man on that list, Rick Smith, was an associate editor at Creative Services until he left to become director of public relations for the San Diego Chargers in February, 1977.

The other two men on the list are Jim Campbell, librarian for the Pro Football Hall of Fame in Canton, Ohio, and Seymour Siwoff, head of the Elias Sports Bureau, official statistician for the NFL as well as many other sports organizations.

Other researchers, writers, and editors, who participated in the project included Steve Bisheff, San Diego; Steve Cassady, San Francisco; Dwight Chapin, Los Angeles; Ray Didinger, Philadelphia; Duane Esper, Los Angeles; Jack Faulkner, Los Angeles; Chuck Garrity, Sr., Los Angeles; Bud Goode, Los Angeles; Jack Hand, New York; and Don Smith, Canton, Ohio.

Proof-readers, fact-checkers, and typists included Bill Barron, Dan Berger, Ted Brock, Patricia Cross, Earlene Doran, Esper, Chuck Garrity, Jr., Faye Howe, Harlan Patterson, Tom Patty, and Lynn Schnider, all of Los Angeles, and Hand of New York.

David Johnston of Los Angeles was the designer of the book. Patrick McKee and his assistant, Jere Wright, both of Los Angeles, managed the production. Other production people included Hope Barlow, Jim Chaffin, Alan Deakins, Felice Mataré, Rob Meneilly, Kathleen Oldenburg, Carole Thomas, and Tina Thomas, all of Los Angeles.

Special contributions to the section entitled "A History of Football Equipment" came from Oscar Mastin of the United States Department of Commerce, Patent and Trademark Office, Washington; Ken Hubble of 5-K Products, El Reno, Oklahoma; the Stanford Research Institute, Menlo Park, California; and Wright-Patterson Air Force Base, Dayton, Ohio.

NFL officials who provided assistance included Joe Browne, Joel Bussert, Jan Van Duser, Bill Granholm, Jim Heffernan, Jim Kensil, Stu Kirkpatrick, Art McNally, Jim Rooney, Bill Stewart, Don Weiss, and Claude (Buddy) Young, all of New York.

Jack Wrobbel, vice-president of operations for Creative Services, and his assistant, Muriel Lorenz, both of Los Angeles, kept their eyes on the overall project, making sure schedules and budgets were met and quality control was maintained.

Jeremy Friedlander, editor at Rutledge Books, gave the book a final examination. Lori Stein, production manager at Rutledge, handled the production coordination with the printer, R. R. Donnelley & Sons. The book was printed at Donnelley's Willard, Ohio, plant, and the type set by CAPCO of Los Angeles.

We are grateful to all of the people listed above. *The NFL's Official Encyclopedic History of Professional Football* could not have happened without their assistance.

THE EDITORS

PHOTOGRAPHY CREDITS

All of the head shots in the book were provided by the Professional Football Hall of Fame and selected, identified, and catalogued by Jim Campbell and Anne Monnot of the Hall of Fame staff.

Bob and Sylvia Allen 160a, 225a, 226a, 334a, 335ab, 337b
Arthur Anderson 82a, 114b, 171a, 416c, 477ab, 479a, 500d
Fred Anderson 314a
Associated Press 244c, 302a
Atlanta Falcons 454a
Charles Aqua Viva 68a, 102a, 218a, 303c, 305bc, 306b, 418c, 423b
Lee Balterman (for Sports Illustrated) 58a
Baltimore Colts 50c, 66b, 454b, 503a
John Biever 6a, 73d, 83b, 308, 329b, 339a
Vernon Biever 45a, 47c, 49d, 55a, 61c, 63d, 65a, 70a, 74b, 113a, 164a, 243c, 304ac, 306c, 311a, 312ac, 321a, 324a, 325b, 328a, 369a, 386a, 424ab, 425ab, 428a, 501b
David Boss 52a, 60a, 63ac, 67b, 72a, 79a, 97a, 98a, 224a, 225b, 226b, 313b, 322a, 323b, 331ab, 332a, 333b, 336a, 338a, 340a, 341ab, 358a, 359a, 384d, 391c, 393b, 395d, 399b, 417c, 420b, 423a, 497b, 502a
Clifton Boutelle 97b, 367a, 417a, 503c, 509d, 511a
Chance Brockway 117a, 216a
Frank Bryan 500a
Buffalo Bills 454c
Dick Burnell 64a, 76b, 95a
Stan Caplan 480–481 all
Chicago Bears 8b, 455a
Chicago Tribune 246a
Cincinnati Bengals 66a, 455b, 496b
Rich Clarkson 309a
Cleveland Browns 51b, 54c
Cleveland Press 250c, 383b, 455c
Otto Collier 172a
Tim Culek 7b, 300b
Culver Pictures, Inc. 385d
Dallas Cowboys 204a, 456a, 496a, 505b, 506a
Denver Broncos 456b, 504b, 509bc
Detroit Lions 49c, 456c, 497c
Dan Dmitruk 74c, 508b
Malcolm Emmons 56a, 68b, 69b, 115a, 153a, 308c, 309b, 310a, 323a, 326a, 327a, 333a, 399c, 417d, 420a, 498c, 499b, 500c, 502b, 504d
Nate Fine 37ab, 39b, 40b, 44b, 47a, 243a, 391d, 414a, 503d
Paul Fine 228a, 230ab, 231a, 232a, 422a
James Flores 500b
Football Illustrated 299c
George Gellatly 207a, 300c, 382a, 390c, 503e, 504d, 506d
George Gojkovich 114a, 184a
Green Bay Packers 457a
Green Bay Press Gazette 36b, 388c
Hall of Fame 18a, 19abc, 20ab, 21abc, 23abc, 24a, 25ab, 26abc, 27a, 29ab, 30b, 31abc, 32abc, 33a, 35a, 36a, 38ac, 39a, 44c, 52b, 54b, 59b, 239a, 241abc, 244a, 246b, 253b, 254abc, 294a, 296c, 298c, 299a, 302c, 263a, 365a, 366a, 378 all, 379ad, 380a, 381bcd, 382b, 383de, 384abc, 385ac, 386cd, 387abc, 388ab, 389acd, 390abe, 391b, 392 all, 393a, 394 all, 395abc, 396ab, 397 all, 398d, 399d, 400 all, 401 all, 402, 403b, 404 all, 405 all, 413, 498b, 500e, 503b
Ron Hanna 71a, 150a, 153b, 398d, 415b, 421b, 508a
H. Lee Hansen 247a, 248abc, 249a, 250a
Ken Hardin 125a, 307b
Jocelyn Hinsen 71b
Houston Oilers 457c
Kansas City Chiefs 8a, 51c, 458a, 510b
Fred Kaplan 386b
Laughead Photographers 147a
Hank Lefevre 387d, 388b
Ross Lewis 76a, 501c
Life 384d
Los Angeles Rams 73c, 458b, 499b
Los Angeles Times 43a
Tak Makita 187a
Jack Martin 427b
Rob Meneilly 475 all, 476ab
Miami Dolphins 458c, 505a, 506b, 510c
Miami Herald 162a
Peter Read Miller 200a, 253a, 424c
Milwaukee County Stadium 457b
Minnesota Vikings 64c, 459a, 498d
Moffett Studio 368a
National Football League Properties 166a, 167a, 185a, 227a, 302b, 305a, 310c, 311b
New England Patriots 459b
New Orleans Saints 64b, 459c
New York Daily News 41b
New York Giants 49a, 460a
New York Jets 60b, 74a, 460b, 405a, 504a, 505d
Darryl Norenberg 379c, 383a, 396c, 398c, 399a
Oakland Raiders 64d, 307c, 460c
Ohio State University 246c
Evan Peskin (for Sports Illustrated) 46a
Philadelphia Eagles 47b, 50b, 199a, 379b, 461a
Photo Associates 417b
Pittsburgh Steelers 461b

Pro Football Illustrated 296c, 297abc, 298b
Pro Football Weekly 298a
Dick Raphael 61b, 73a, 83a, 163a, 168a, 169a, 307a, 308b, 309c, 310b, 313a, 325a
Russ Reed 50a, 66c, 80c, 313c, 419b
Frank Rippon 45b, 46b, 48a, 81a, 126a, 174b, 220a, 250b, 251a, 416a, 421a, 468a, 476c
Don Robbins 162b
Fred Roe 53a, 57b, 110a
Ron Ross 77a, 498e
Abbie Rowe 427a
Dan Rubin 179a, 181a, 182a, 385b, 398a, 509a
M.V. Rubio 94b, 192a, 337a, 380b, 497a, 507cd
Russ Russell 71c, 122a, 125b, 370a, 510a
St. Louis Cardinals 461c, 504c, 511b
St. Louis Post-Dispatch 383c
San Diego Chargers 54a, 59a, 462a
San Francisco 49ers 49b, 462b, 498a, 501d
Jules Shick 303a
Seattle Seahawks 462c
Carl Skalak, Jr. 116b
Robert L. Smith 75a, 80d, 103a, 105a, 416a, 507a
Southern Methodist University 419b
Jay Spencer 311c, 426a
Sport 390d
Sports Illustrated 301a, 301c, 306a
Sports Productions, Inc. 420c
R. H. Stagg 499a
Stanford University 363a, 419a
Staver/Scott 127a, 128a
Vic Stein 38b, 40a, 41a, 42a, 44a, 48b, 52c, 94a, 223a, 243b, 299b, 300a, 320a, 321b, 364a, 381a, 398b, 403a, 414b, 416b, 418ab, 419c, 426b
Syracuse University 419c
Tampa Bay Buccaneers 463a
George Tiedemann 78b
Tony Tomsic 62a, 504a, 506c
Tony Triolo 84a
University of Alabama 419e
University of Oklahoma 419g
University of Southern California 419d
United Press International 22a, 24b, 28a, 30a, 33b, 34a, 244b, 294bc, 295abc, 296a, 301b, 303b, 413a
Washington Redskins 463b, 499c
Herb Weitman 61a, 69a, 70c, 73b, 106a, 173a, 174a, 196a, 208a, 215a, 224b, 330a, 339b, 391a, 415a, 419a, 420c, 422b, 496c, 501a, 505c
Wide World Photos 329a
Lou Witt 57a, 63b, 146a, 304b, 327b
Yale University 415f
Michael Zagaris 78a, 116a, 149a, 312b, 507b
Jack Zehrt cover